A TOPICAL APPROACH TO LIFE-SPAN DEVELOPMENT

Tenth Edition

JOHN W. SANTROCK

University of Texas at Dallas

Mc
Graw
Hill

A TOPICAL APPROACH TO LIFE-SPAN DEVELOPMENT, TENTH EDITION

Published by McGraw-Hill Education, 2 Penn Plaza, New York, NY 10121. Copyright ©2020 by McGraw-Hill Education. All rights reserved. Printed in the United States of America. Previous editions ©2018, 2016, and 2014. No part of this publication may be reproduced or distributed in any form or by any means, or stored in a database or retrieval system, without the prior written consent of McGraw-Hill Education, including, but not limited to, in any network or other electronic storage or transmission, or broadcast for distance learning.

Some ancillaries, including electronic and print components, may not be available to customers outside the United States.

This book is printed on acid-free paper.

1 2 3 4 5 6 7 8 9 LWI 24 23 22 21 20 19

ISBN   978-1-260-06092-8
MHID   1-260-06092-6

Senior Portfolio Manager: *Ryan Treat*
Product Development Manager: *Dawn Groundwater*
Marketing Managers: *Olivia Kaiser, AJ Laferrera*
Content Project Managers: *Mary E. Powers (Core), Jodi Banowetz (Assessment)*
Buyer: *Sandy Ludovissy*
Design: *David W. Hash*
Content Licensing Specialist: *Carrie Burger*
Cover Image: *©onebluelight/Getty Images*
Compositor: *Aptara®, Inc.*

All credits appearing on page or at the end of the book are considered to be an extension of the copyright page.

Library of Congress Cataloging-in-Publication Data

Names: Santrock, John W., author.
Title: A topical approach to life-span development / John W. Santrock,
   University of Texas at Dallas.
Description: Tenth Edition. | Dubuque : McGraw-Hill Education, [2019] |
   Revised edition of the author's A topical approach to life-span
   development, [2018]
Identifiers: LCCN 2019017651| ISBN 9781260060928 (alk. paper) | ISBN
   1260060926 (alk. paper)
Subjects: LCSH: Developmental psychology.
Classification: LCC BF713 .S257 2019 | DDC 305.2–dc23 LC record available at https://lccn.loc.gov/2019017651

The Internet addresses listed in the text were accurate at the time of publication. The inclusion of a website does not indicate an endorsement by the authors or McGraw-Hill Education, and McGraw-Hill Education does not guarantee the accuracy of the information presented at these sites.

brief contents

McGraw-Hill Education Psychology APA Documentation Style Guide

contents

SECTION 1   THE LIFE-SPAN PERSPECTIVE   1

FatCamera/E+/Getty Images

SECTION 2   BIOLOGICAL PROCESSES, PHYSICAL DEVELOPMENT, AND HEALTH   45

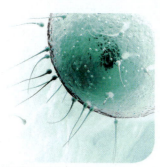

MedicalRF.com/Getty Images

JGI/Jamie Grill/Getty Images

SECTION 5   SOCIAL CONTEXTS OF DEVELOPMENT   463

ImageDJ/age fotostock

about the author

John W. Santrock

John Santrock received his Ph.D. from the University of Minnesota in 1973. He taught at the University of Charleston and the University of Georgia before joining the program in Psychology in the School of Behavioral and Brain Sciences at the University of Texas at Dallas, where he currently teaches a number of undergraduate courses and has received the University's Effective Teaching Award.

John has been a member of the editorial boards of *Child Development* and *Developmental Psychology.* His research on father custody is widely cited and used in expert witness testimony to promote flexibility and alternative considerations in custody disputes. He also has conducted research on children's self-control. John has authored these exceptional McGraw-Hill texts: *Psychology* (7th edition), *Children* (14th edition), *Child Development* (14th edition), *Adolescence* (17th edition), *Life-Span Development* (17th edition), and *Educational Psychology* (6th edition).

John Santrock (back row middle) with the 2015 recipients of the Santrock Travel Scholarship Award in developmental psychology. Created by Dr. Santrock, this annual award provides undergraduate students with the opportunity to attend a professional meeting. A number of the students shown here attended the meeting of the Society for Research in Child Development.
Courtesy of Jessica Serna

For many years, John was involved in tennis as a player, teaching professional, and a coach of professional tennis players. As an undergraduate, he was a member of the University of Miami (FL) tennis team that still holds the record for most consecutive wins (137) in any NCAA Division I sport. John has been married for four decades to his wife, Mary Jo, who created and directed the first middle school program for children with learning disabilities and behavioral disorders in the Clarke County Schools in Athens, Georgia, when she was a professor at the University of Georgia. More recently, Mary Jo has worked as a Realtor. He has two daughters—Tracy and Jennifer—both of whom are Realtors after long careers in technology marketing and medical sales, respectively. In 2016, Jennifer became only the fifth female to have been inducted into the SMU Sports Hall of Fame. He has one granddaughter, Jordan, age 25, who completed her master's degree from the Cox School of Business at SMU and currently works for Ernst & Young, and two grandsons—the Belluci brothers: Alex, age 14, and Luke, age 13. In the last decade, John also has spent time painting expressionist art.

With special appreciation to my mother, Ruth Santrock, and my father, John Santrock.

expert consultants

Life-span development has become an enormous, complex field, and no single author, or even several authors, can possibly keep up with all of the rapidly changing content in the many periods and different areas in this field. To solve this problem, author John Santrock has sought the input of leading experts about content in a number of areas of life-span development. These experts have provided detailed evaluations and recommendations in their area(s) of expertise.

The following individuals were among those who served as expert consultants for one or more of the previous editions of this text:

Karen Adolph	Elena Grigorenko	Charles Nelson
David Almeida	Scott Hofer	Crystal Park
Karlene Ball	William Hoyer	Denise Park
John Bates	Janet Shibley Hyde	Ross Parke
Martha Ann Bell	Rachel Keen	Glenn Roisman
Jay Belsky	Jennifer Lansford	Carolyn Saarni
James Birren	James Marcia	Robert J. Sternberg
Kirby Deater-Deckard	Linda Mayes	Elizabeth Stine-Morrow
Susanne Denham	Patricia Miller	Ross Thompson
James Garbarino	David Moore	Doug Wahlsten
Linda George	Daniel Mroczek	Allan Wigfield
Gilbert Gottlieb	Darcia Narváez	

Following are the expert consultants for the tenth edition, who (like those of previous editions) literally represent a *Who's Who* in the field of life-span development.

K. Warner Schaie K. Warner Schaie is widely recognized as one of the main pioneers who created the field of life-span development and continues to be one of its leading experts. He currently is the Evan Pugh Professor Emeritus of Human Development and Psychology at Pennsylvania State University. Dr. Schaie also holds an appointment as an Affiliate Professor of Psychiatry and Behavioral Sciences at the University of Washington. He obtained his Ph.D. from the Friedrich-Schiller University of Jena, Germany, and an honorary ScD degree from West Virginia University. He has been given the Kleemeier Award for Distinguished Research Contributions in Gerontology from the Gerontological Society of American, the MENSA lifetime career award, and the Distinguished Scientific Contributions award from the American Psychological Association. Dr. Schaie is the author of 60 books, including the textbook *Adult Development and Aging* (5th Ed., with S.L. Willis) and the *Handbook of the Psychology of Aging* (8th Ed., with S.L. Willis). He has directed the Seattle Longitudinal Study of cognitive aging since 1956 and is the author of more than 300 journal articles and chapters on the psychology of aging.

"This is an excellent chapter ('Intelligence') bringing up-to-date discussions of both present status and long-term changes in topics covered by experts in the field. . . . This is thorough, yet easily understood discussions of a set of very complex issues." **–K. Warner Schaie**

Courtesy Dr. K. Warner Schaie

Julia Mendez Julia Mendez is an expert on ethnic minority children's development and resilience, with a focus on African American and Latino children from low-income backgrounds. She received her Ph.D. in Clinical-Community Psychology with a concentration in early childhood development from the University of Pennsylvania and is a Professor of Psychology at the University of North Carolina at Greensboro. Dr. Mendez examines how programs and policies support child development and learning opportunities within the family, school, and community settings. She has developed and tested interventions for engaging families in Head Start programs and other community settings. Dr. Mendez has partnered with local schools to develop Parent Academy programs to provide information and resources for school-aged children and their families to facilitate academic success and social development. Currently, she is a co-investigator with the National Research Center on Hispanic Children and Families, leading the research agenda on early care and education (ECE) opportunities for Hispanic children and families in the United States. Dr. Mendez has served on the editorial boards of *Journal of Applied Developmental Psychology* and *Journal of School Psychology*. Her research has been published in *Child Development*, *Early Childhood Research Quarterly*, *Cultural Diversity and Ethnic Minority Psychology*, *Early Education and Development*, and *Journal of Community Psychology*.

"Students who use this text will develop an appreciation for the multiple domains of development, transactions over time, and how children, youth, and adults develop across the life span within particular ecological contexts. The consideration of contextual influences including family, school, peers, and the larger multicultural society are woven into many of the chapters using contemporary and seminal research studies." **–Julia Mendez**

Courtesy of Julia Smith

Dante Cicchetti Dante Cicchetti is the world's foremost expert on child maltreatment as well as a leading expert on many aspects of developmental psychopathology. He currently has a joint appointment at the University of Minnesota's Institute of Child Development and Medical School's Department of Psychiatry. He holds the McKnight Presidential Endowed Chair and the William Harris Endowed Chair, as well as the research director in the area of children's mental health at the University's Institute for Translational Research. Previously, he was the Shirley Cox Kearns Professor of Psychology, Psychiatry, and Pediatrics at the

University of Rochester. Prior to that appointment, Dr. Cicchetti was a professor at Harvard University. Dr. Cicchetti received a doctorate from the University of Minnesota's Institute of Child Development and a doctorate in clinical psychology from the University's Department of Psychology. While at the University of Rochester, he was Director of the Mt. Hope Family Center. Dr. Cicchetti has been the editor of the international journal *Development and Psychopathology* for more than 30 years and has been given numerous awards by the American Psychological Association, including the Boyd McCandless Award for early distinctions for contributions to developmental psychology and the APA Distinguished Contributions in Research in Clinical Child Psychology Award. His current major research interests focus on formulating an integrative theory than can account for both normal and abnormal aspects of an individual's developmental history. Dr. Cicchetti's research has investigated such topics as multiple levels of developmental psychopathology, developmental consequences of children's maltreatment, neural plasticity and sensitive periods, traumatic experiences and brain development, attachment, resilience, and epigenetics.

"I think the narrative and perspective provided reflect the latest and most important research extant in the field. . . . He develops ideas clearly and in a concise and understandable fashion. I have read other works by Dr. Santrock and he has a knack for presenting complex material in ways that grab the attention of readers. This is not common in most academics. . . . The book can motivate undergraduate students to pursue further study in developmental psychology. . . . I think Professor Santrock has written an excellent text and it will be a successful one." —**Dante Cicchetti**

Courtesy of Dante Cicchetti

 Darcia Narváez Darcia Narváez is one of the world's leading experts on moral development. She received her Ph.D. from the University of Minnesota and currently is a professor of psychology at the University of Notre Dame. Her current research and theoretical interests focus on moral development and flourishing from an interdisciplinary perspective. Along these lines, she is exploring how early life experiences and culture interact to influence character development in children and adults. Dr. Narváez integrates neurobiological, developmental, clinical, and educational influences in her theoretical views and research studies. She publishes extensively on parenting and moral development. Dr. Narváez is a fellow in the American Psychological Association and the American Educational Research Association. Her publications appear in leading journals, such as *Developmental Psychology, Journal of Educational Psychology,* and *Early Childhood Research Quarterly.* She has written a number of books, including *Neurobiology and the Development of Morality,* which recently won the William James Book Award from the American Psychological Association.

". . . I think Chapter 13 ('Moral Development, Values, and Religion') does a good job of reviewing important current research and theories. . . It is written in an easy-to-read engaging manner." —**Darcia Narváez**

Courtesy of Matthew Cashore

 Philip David Zelazo Philip David Zelazo is one of the world's leading experts on brain development in children, as well as the development of executive function. He is currently the Nancy M. and John E. Lindahl Professor at the Institute of Child Development, University of Minnesota. Previously,

Dr. Zelazo taught at the University of Toronto, where he held the Canada Research Chair in Developmental Neuroscience. He obtained his Ph.D. from Yale University. Professor Zelazo's research on the development and neural bases of executive function (the control of thought, action, and emotion) has been honored by numerous awards, including a Boyd McCandless Young Scientist Award from the American Psychological Association (APA) and Canada's Top 40 Under 40 Award. Dr. Zelazo is a Fellow of the American Psychological Association, the American Psychological Society, and the Mind and Life Institute. He also is President of the Jean Piaget Society and he is a member of a number of editorial boards, including *Child Development, Emotion, Frontiers in Human Neuroscience, Development and Psychopathology, Monographs of the SRCD,* and *Developmental Cognitive Neuroscience.* In addition, Dr. Zelazo is the co-editor of *The Cambridge Handbook of Consciousness* and the editor of the two-volume *Oxford Handbook of Developmental Psychology.*

"Overall, the narrative structure and choice of topics seem excellent. I think John Santrock does a great job of reflecting recent research." —**Philip David Zelazo**

Courtesy of Philip David Zelazo

 Pamela Cole Pamela Cole is one of the world's leading experts in the development of emotion regulation. She obtained her Ph.D. in clinical and developmental psychology from The Pennsylvania State University and currently is Liberal Arts Professor of Psychology and Human Development and Family Studies at The Pennsylvania State University, having previously worked at the National Institute of Mental Health and at the University of Houston. Her research focuses on young children's development of emotion regulation, especially regulation of frustration and disappointment. Topics of Dr. Cole's current research projects include the role of early childhood language development in the development of emotion regulation, the development of strategy effectiveness, and innovative methods for studying emotion regulation as a dynamic process that changes with age. Dr. Cole is a Fellow in Division 7 (Developmental Psychology) of the American Psychological Association and is an Associate Editor of *Developmental Psychology,* also having served on the editorial boards of several other major developmental journals. Her book, co-edited with Tom Hollenstein, *Emotion Regulation: A Matter of Time,* was published in 2018 and presents conceptual and empirical papers on developmental aspects of emotion regulation. Dr. Cole's work has been published in leading research journals such as *Child Development, Developmental Psychology, Emotion,* and *Development and Psychopathology.*

"The coverage of John Santrock's chapter, "Emotional Development and Attachment," is impressive. It provides a great deal of information about emotion and emotion-related phenomena. . . . There is a strong framework for the chapter, ideas are fully developed, and students will come away from the chapter with a clear understanding of the chapter." —**Pamela Cole**

Courtesy of Pamela Cole

 Priscilla Lui Priscilla Lui is a leading expert on multicultural research, including research on ethnicity. She received her Ph.D. in clinical psychology from Purdue University and completed a clinical psychology internship at the Northwestern University Feinberg School of Medicine. Dr. Lui currently is a professor of psychology at Southern Methodist University. Her research program has focused on parenting and intergenerational conflict in Asian and Latinx American immigrant families and the impact of sociocultural factors, including acculturation and racial discrimination, on individuals' psychological adjustment and alcohol use. She also has designed and evaluated self-report survey measures that are culturally appropriate and responsive to diverse ethnic groups. Dr. Lui has authored numerous research articles in leading journals, including *Psychological Bulletin*, *Assessment*, *Psychology of Addictive Behaviors*, *Cultural Diversity and Ethnic Minority Psychology*, *Alcoholism: Clinical and Experimental Research*, and *American Journal of Orthopsychiatry*. As an early career psychologist, she has received awards and recognitions from national professional organizations, including being named a Rising Star by the Association for Psychological Science.

"The chapters I reviewed reflect some of the latest and most pertinent information concerning life-span development. . . . I really appreciate the consideration of life-span development and the use of a continuity perspective to frame various developmental tasks and content areas."
–Priscilla Lui

Connecting *Research* and *Results*

As a master teacher, John Santrock connects current research and real-world applications. Through an integrated, personalized digital learning program, students gain the insight they need to study smarter and improve performance.

McGraw-Hill Education's **Connect** is a digital assignment and assessment platform that strengthens the link between faculty, students, and course work, helping everyone accomplish more in less time. *Connect for Life-Span Development* includes assignable and assessable videos, quizzes, exercises, and interactivities, all associated with learning objectives. Interactive assignments and videos allow students to experience and apply their understanding of psychology to the world with fun and stimulating activities.

Apply Concepts and Theory in an Experiential Learning Environment

An engaging and innovative learning game, **Quest: Journey through the Lifespan** provides students with opportunities to apply content from their human development curriculum to real-life scenarios. Students play unique characters who range in age and make decisions that apply key concepts and theories for each age as they negotiate events in an array of authentic environments. Additionally, as students analyze real-world behaviors and contexts, they are exposed to different cultures and intersecting biological, cognitive, and socioemotional processes. Each quest has layered replayability, allowing students to make new choices each time they play–or offering different students in the same class different experiences. Fresh possibilities and outcomes shine light on the complexity of and variations in real human development. This new experiential learning game includes follow-up questions, assignable in Connect and auto-graded, to reach a higher level of critical thinking.

Real People, Real World, Real Life

At the higher end of Bloom's taxonomy (analyze, evaluate, create), the McGraw-Hill Education **Milestones** video series is an observational tool that allows students to experience life as it unfolds, from infancy to late adulthood. This ground-breaking, longitudinal video series tracks the development of real children as they progress through the early stages of physical, social, and emotional development in their first few weeks, months, and years of life. Assignable and assessable within Connect for Life-Span Development, Milestones also includes interviews with adolescents and adults to reflect development throughout the entire life span.

Prepare Students for Higher-Level Thinking

Also at the higher end of Bloom's taxonomy, **Power of Process** for Psychology helps students improve critical thinking skills and allows instructors to assess these skills efficiently and effectively in an online environment. Available through Connect, pre-loaded journal articles are available for instructors to assign. Using a scaffolded framework such as understanding, synthesizing, and analyzing, Power of Process moves students toward higher-level thinking and analysis.

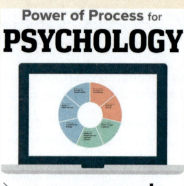

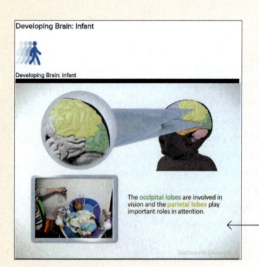

Inform and Engage on Psychological Concepts

At the lower end of Bloom's taxonomy, students are introduced to **Concept Clips**—the dynamic, colorful graphics and stimulating animations that break down some of psychology's most difficult concepts in a step-by-step manner, engaging students and aiding in retention. They are assignable and assessable in Connect or can be used as a jumping-off point in class. Accompanied by audio narration, Concept Clips cover topics such as object permanence and conservation, as well as theories and theorists like Bandura's social cognitive theory, Vygotsky's sociocultural theory, Buss's evolutionary theory, and Kuhl's language development theory.

Powerful Reporting

Whether a class is face-to-face, hybrid, or entirely online, Connect for Life-Span Development provides tools and analytics to reduce the amount of time instructors need to administer their courses. Easy-to-use course management tools allow instructors to spend less time administering and more time teaching, while easy-to-use reporting features allow students to monitor their progress and optimize their study time.

- **Connect Insight** is a one-of-a-kind visual analytics dashboard—available for both instructors and students—that provides at-a-glance information regarding student performance.

- The **At-Risk Student Report** provides instructors with one-click access to a dashboard that identifies students who are at risk of dropping out of the course due to low engagement levels.

- The **Category Analysis Report** details student performance relative to specific learning objectives and goals, including APA outcomes and levels of Bloom's taxonomy.

Better Data, Smarter Revision, Improved Results

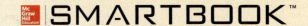

Content revisions for *A Topical Approach to Life-Span Development* were informed by data collected anonymously through McGraw-Hill's SmartBook.

McGraw-Hill Education's **SmartBook** helps students distinguish the concepts they know from the concepts they don't, while pinpointing the concepts they are about to forget. SmartBook's real-time reports help both students and instructors identify the concepts that require more attention, making study sessions and class time more efficient.

Here's how the SmartBook student data was used:

STEP 1. Over the course of three years, data points showing concepts that caused students the most difficulty were anonymously collected from Connect for Life-Span Development's SmartBook®.

STEP 2. The data from SmartBook was provided to the author in the form of a *Heat Map*, which graphically illustrates "hot spots" in the text that affect student learning (see image at right).

STEP 3. The author used the *Heat Map* data to refine the content and reinforce student comprehension in the new edition. Additional quiz questions and assignable activities were created for use in Connect to further support student success.

RESULT: Because the *Heat Map* gave the author empirically based feedback at the paragraph and even sentence level, he was able to develop the new edition using precise student data that pinpointed concepts that gave students the most difficulty.

New to this edition, SmartBook is now optimized for mobile and tablet use and is accessible for students with disabilities. Content-wise, it has been enhanced with improved learning objectives that are measurable and observable to improve student outcomes. SmartBook personalizes learning to individual student needs, continually adapting to pinpoint knowledge gaps and focus learning on topics that need the most attention. Study time is more productive and, as a result, students are better prepared for class and coursework. For instructors, SmartBook tracks student progress and provides insights that can help guide teaching strategies.

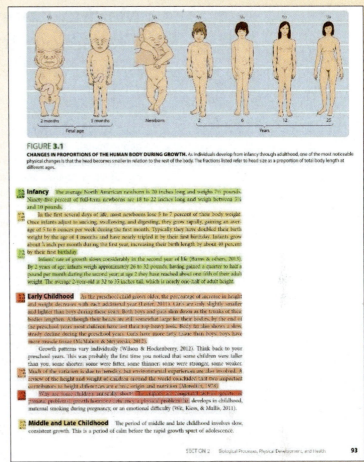

FIGURE 3.1

CHANGES IN PROPORTIONS OF THE HUMAN BODY DURING GROWTH. As individuals develop from infancy through adulthood, one of the most noticeable physical changes is that the head becomes smaller in relation to the rest of the body. The fractions listed refer to head size as a proportion of total body length at different ages.

Online Instructor Resources

The resources listed here accompany *A Topical Approach to Life-Span Development,* Tenth Edition. Please contact your McGraw-Hill representative for details concerning the availability of these and other valuable materials that can help you design and enhance your course.

Instructor's Manual   Broken down by chapter, this resource provides chapter outlines, suggested lecture topics, classroom activities and demonstrations, suggested student research projects, essay questions, and critical thinking questions.

Test Bank and Computerized Test Bank   This comprehensive Test Bank includes more than 1,500 multiple-choice and approximately 75 essay questions. Organized by chapter, the questions are designed to test factual, applied, and conceptual understanding.

PowerPoint Slides   The PowerPoint presentations, now WCAG compliant, highlight the key points of the chapter and include supporting visuals. All of the slides can be modified to meet individual needs.

preface

Making Connections . . . From My Classroom to *A Topical Approach to Life-Span Development* to You

Having taught life-span development every semester for three decades now, I'm always looking for ways to improve my course and *A Topical Approach to Life-Span Development*. Just as McGraw-Hill looks to those who teach the life-span development course for input, each year I ask the approximately 200 students in my life-span development course to tell me what they like about the course and the text, and what they think could be improved. What have my students told me about my course and text? Students said that highlighting connections among the different aspects of life-span development would help them to better understand the concepts. As I thought about this, it became clear that a *connections* theme would provide a systematic, integrative approach to the course material. I used this theme to shape my goals for my life-span development course, which, in turn, I incorporated into *A Topical Approach to Life-Span Development*:

1. **Connecting with today's students** To help students learn about life-span development more effectively.

2. **Connecting research to what we know about development** To provide students with the best and most recent theory and research in the world today about each of the periods of the human life span.

3. **Connecting topical processes in development** To guide students in making *topical connections* across different aspects of development through the life span.

4. **Connecting development to the real world** To help students understand ways to *apply* content about the human life span to the real world and improve people's lives; and to motivate them to think deeply about *their own personal journey through life* and better understand who they were, are, and will be.

Connecting with Today's Students

In *A Topical Approach to Life-Span Development,* I recognize that today's students are as different in some ways from the learners of the last generation as today's discipline of life-span development is different from the field 30 years ago. Students now learn in multiple modalities; rather than sitting down and reading traditional printed chapters in linear fashion from beginning to end, their work preferences tend to be more visual and more interactive, and their reading and study often occur in short bursts. For many students, a traditionally formatted printed textbook is no longer enough when they have instant, 24/7 access to news and information from around the globe. Two features that specifically support today's students are the adaptive ebook, Smartbook (see page xvi), and the learning goals system.

The Learning Goals System

My students often report that the life-span development course is challenging because of the amount of material covered. To help today's students focus on the key ideas, the Learning Goals System I developed for *A Topical Approach to Life-Span Development* provides extensive learning connections throughout the

| 1 Body Growth and Change | LG1 | Discuss major changes in the body through the life span. |

| Patterns of Growth | Height and Weight in Infancy and Childhood | Puberty | Early Adulthood | Middle Adulthood | Late Adulthood |

chapters. The learning system connects the chapter opening outline, learning goals for the chapter, mini-chapter maps that open each main section of the chapter, *Review, Connect, Reflect* questions at the end of each main section, and the chapter summary at the end of each chapter.

The learning system keeps the key ideas in front of the student from the beginning to the end of the chapter. The main headings of each chapter correspond to the learning goals that are presented in the chapter-opening spread. Mini-chapter maps that link up with the learning goals are presented at the beginning of each major section in the chapter.

Then, at the end of each main section of a chapter, the learning goal is repeated in *Review, Connect, Reflect,* which prompts students to review the key topics in the section, connect to existing knowledge, and relate what they learned to their own personal journey through life. *Reach Your Learning Goals,* at the end of the chapter, guides students through the bulleted chapter review, connecting with the chapter outline/learning goals at the beginning of the chapter and the *Review, Connect, Reflect* questions at the end of major chapter sections.

<h3>reach your learning goals</h3>

Physical Development and Biological Aging

1 Body Growth and Change — LG1 Discuss major changes in the body through the life span.

- Patterns of Growth
- Height and Weight in Infancy and Childhood
- Puberty

- Human growth follows cephalocaudal (fastest growth occurs at the top) and proximodistal patterns (growth starts at the center of the body and moves toward the extremities).
- Height and weight increase rapidly in infancy and then take a slower course during childhood.
- Puberty is a brain-neuroendocrine process occurring primarily in early adolescence that provides stimulation for the rapid physical changes that accompany this period of development.
- A number of changes occur in sexual maturation. The growth spurt involves rapid increases in height and weight and occurs about two years earlier for girls than for boys.
- Extensive hormonal changes characterize puberty. Puberty began occurring much earlier in the twentieth century mainly because of improved health and nutrition. The basic genetic program for puberty is wired into the nature of the species, but nutrition, health, and other environmental factors affect the timing of puberty.
- Adolescents show heightened interest in their bodies and body images. Younger adolescents are more preoccupied with these images than older adolescents. Adolescent girls often have a more negative body image than do adolescent boys.

Connecting Research to What We Know about Development

Over the years, it has been important for me to include the most up-to-date research available. I continue that tradition in this edition by looking closely at specific areas of research, involving experts in related fields, and updating research throughout. ***Connecting with Research*** describes a study or program to illustrate how research in life-span development is conducted and how it influences our understanding of the discipline. Topics range from *How Are Preterm Infants Affected by Touch?* to *Does Intervention Reduce Juvenile Delinquency?* to *Parenting and Children's Achievement: My Child Is My Report Card, Tiger Moms, and Tiger Babies Strike Back.*

The tradition of obtaining detailed, extensive input from a number of leading experts in different areas of life-span development also continues in this edition. Biographies and photographs of the leading experts in the field of life-span development appear on pages xii to xiv, and the chapter-by-chapter highlights of new research content are listed on pages xxii to xli. Finally, the research discussions have been updated in every area and topic. I expended every effort to make this edition of *A Topical Approach to Life-Span Development* as contemporary and up-to-date as possible. To that end, there are more than 1,500 citations from 2017, 2018, and 2019.

connecting with research

How Stressful Is Caring for an Alzheimer Patient at Home?

Researchers have found that the stress of caring for an Alzheimer patient at home can prematurely age the immune system, putting caregivers at risk for developing age-related diseases (Chiu, Wesson, & Sadavoy, 2014; Glaser & Kiecolt-Glaser, 2005; Kiecolt-Glaser & Wilson, 2017; Wilson & others, 2019). In one study, 119 older adults who were caring for a spouse with Alzheimer disease or another form of dementia (which can require up to 100 hours a week) were compared with 106 older adults who did not have to care for a chronically ill spouse (Kiecolt-Glazer & others, 2003). The age of the older adults upon entry into the study ranged from 55 to 89, with an average age of 70.

Periodically during the six-year study, blood samples were taken and the levels of a naturally produced immune chemical called interleukin-6, or IL-6, were measured. IL-6 increases with age and can place people at risk for a number of illnesses, including cardiovascular disease, type 2 diabetes, frailty, and certain cancers. The researchers found that the levels of IL-6 increased much faster in the Alzheimer caregivers than in the older adults who did not have to care for a critically ill spouse (see Figure 5).

Each time IL-6 was assessed by drawing blood, the participants also completed a 10-item perceived stress scale to assess the extent to which they perceived their daily life during the prior week as being "unpredictable, uncontrollable, and overloading" (Kiecolt-Glazer & others, 2003, p. 9091). Participants rated each item from 0 (never) to 4 (very often). Alzheimer caregivers reported greater stress than the noncaregiver controls across each of the six annual assessments.

Since family members are especially important in helping Alzheimer patients cope, an important research agenda is to assess the benefits of respite care and to find additional ways to relieve the stress the disease can impose on others.

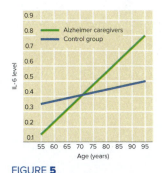

FIGURE 5

COMPARISON OF IL-6 LEVELS IN ALZHEIMER CAREGIVERS AND A CONTROL GROUP OF NONCAREGIVERS. Notice that IL-6 (an immune chemical that places individuals at risk for a number of diseases) increased for both the Alzheimer caregivers and a control group of noncaregivers. However, also note that IL-6 increased significantly more in the Alzheimer caregivers. A higher score for IL-6 reflects a higher level of the immune chemical.

What kinds of studies might help provide some answers? What challenges will researchers face in collecting data?

developmental connection

Peers

How does adult friendship differ among female friends, male friends, and cross-gender friends? Connect to "Peers and the Sociocultural World."

Connecting Developmental Processes

Too often we forget or fail to notice the many connections from one point or topic in development to another. *Developmental Connections,* which appear multiple times in each chapter, point readers to where the topic is discussed in a previous or subsequent chapter. *Developmental Connections* highlight links across topics and age periods of development *and* connections between biological, cognitive, and socioemotional processes. These key developmental processes are typically discussed in isolation from each other, and students often fail to see their connections. Included in the *Developmental Connections* is a brief description of the backward or forward connection.

Also, a *Connect* question appears in the section self-reviews—*Review, Connect, Reflect*—so students can practice making connections between topics. For example, students are asked to connect a chapter's discussion of the gender-intensification hypothesis to what they have already read about identity development in adolescence.

Connecting Development to the Real World

In addition to helping students make research and developmental connections, *A Topical Approach to Life-Span Development* shows the important connections between the concepts discussed and the real world. In recent years, students in my life-span development course have increasingly told me that they want more of this type of information. In this edition, real-life connections are explicitly made through *Connecting Development to Life,* the *Milestones* program that helps students watch life as it unfolds, and *Connecting with Careers.*

Connecting Development to Life, along with a variety of life-span connecting boxed features, describes the influence of development in a real-world context on topics including *Helping Overweight Children Lose Weight, Working During College,* and *Communicating with a Dying Person.*

The *Milestones* program, described on page xv, shows students what developmental concepts look like by letting them watch actual humans develop. Starting from infancy, students track several individuals, seeing them achieve major developmental milestones, both physically and cognitively. Clips continue through adolescence and adulthood, capturing attitudes toward issues such as family, sexuality, and death and dying.

Connecting with Careers profiles careers ranging from an educational psychologist to a toy designer to a marriage and family therapist to a teacher of English language learners to a home

connecting development to life

Are Social Media an Amplification Tool for Adolescent Egocentrism?

Earlier generations of adolescents did not have social media to connect with large numbers of people; instead, they connected with fewer people, either in person or via telephone. Might today's teens be drawn to social media and its virtually unlimited friend base to express their imaginary audience and sense of uniqueness? A research analysis concluded that amassing a large number of friends (audience) may help to validate adolescents' perception that their life is on stage and everyone is watching them (Psychster Inc, 2010). A look at a teen's home Twitter® comments may suggest to many adults that what teens are reporting is often rather mundane and uninteresting as they update to the world at large what they are doing and having, such as: "Studying heavy. Not happy tonight." or "At Starbucks with Jesse. Lattes are great." Possibly for adolescents, though, such tweets are not trivial but rather an expression of the personal fable's sense of uniqueness (Psychster Inc, 2010).

One study of social networking sites found that the indiscriminate monologue communication from one to many, in which the diverse interests of others are not considered, that often occurs on such sites as Facebook® may produce an egocentric tendency that undermines prosocial behavior (Chiou, Chen, & Liao, 2014). A recent meta-analysis concluded that a greater use of social networking sites was linked to a higher level of narcissism (Gnambs & Appel, 2018).

What do you think? Are social media, such as Facebook® and Twitter®, amplifying the expression of adolescents' imaginary audience, personal fable sense of uniqueness, and narcissistic tendencies?

In what ways might frequent use of social media, such as Facebook®, influence adolescents' cognitive development?
Andrey_Popov/Shutterstock

hospice nurse, each of which requires knowledge about human development.

A number of new profiles appear in this edition. These include Gustavo Medrano, a clinical psychologist who works at the Family Institute at Northwestern University, especially providing therapy for Latino children; Dr. Faize Mustaf-Infante, a pediatrician who is passionate about preventing obesity in children; Dr. Melissa Jackson, a child and adolescent psychiatrist who provides therapy for children with a number of psychological disorders, including ADHD, anxiety, depression, and post-traumatic stress disorder; Carissa Barnes, a special education teacher; and Ahou Vaziri, a Teach for America instructor and curriculum designer.

connecting with careers

Ahou Vaziri, Teach for America Instructor

Ahou Vaziri was a top student in author John Santrock's educational psychology course at the University of Texas at Dallas where she majored in Psychology and Child Development. The following year she served as a teaching intern for the educational psychology course, then submitted an application to join Teach for America and was accepted. Ahou was assigned to work in a low-income area of Tulsa, Oklahoma, where she taught English to seventh- and eighth-graders. In her words, "The years I spent in the classroom for Teach for America were among the most rewarding experiences I have had thus far in my career. I was able to go home every night after work knowing that I truly made a difference in the lives of my students."

After her two-year teaching experience with Teach for America, Ahou continued to work for the organization in their recruitment of college students to become Teach for America instructors. Subsequently, she moved into a role that involved developing curricula for Teach for America. Recently she earned a graduate degree in counseling from Southern Methodist University, and she is continuing her work in improving children's lives.

Ahou Vaziri with her students in the Teach for America program. *What is Teach for America?*
Courtesy of Ahou Vaziri

The careers highlighted extend from the Careers Appendix that provides a comprehensive overview of careers in life-span development to show students where knowledge of human development could lead them.

Part of applying development to the real world is understanding its impact on oneself. An important goal I have established for my life-span development course and this text is to motivate students to think deeply about their own journey of life. To further encourage students to make personal connections to content in the text, *Reflect: Your Own Personal Journey of Life* appears in the end-of-section review in each chapter. This feature involves a question that asks students to reflect on some aspect of the discussion in the section they have just read and connect it to their own life. For example, students are asked:

Imagine what your development would have been like in a culture that offered fewer or distinctly different choices. How might your development have been different if your family had been significantly richer or poorer than it was when you were growing up?

In addition, students are asked a number of personal connections questions in the photograph captions.

Content Revisions

A significant reason why *A Topical Approach to Life-Span Development* has been successfully used by instructors for edition after edition is the painstaking effort and review that goes into making sure the text provides the latest research on all topic areas discussed in the classroom. This new edition is no exception, with more than 1,500 citations from 2017, 2018, and 2019.

New research and content that has especially been updated and expanded in this new edition focuses on the following topics: diversity and culture; genetics and epigenetics; neuroscience and the brain; identity issues, especially gender and transgender; health; technology; and successful aging. Following is a sample of the many chapter-by-chapter changes that were made in this new edition of *A Topical Approach to Life-Span Development*. Although every chapter has been extensively updated, two chapters ("Cognitive Developmental Approaches" and "The Self, Identity, and Personality") were especially targeted for revisions based on the results of the Heat Map data discussed on page xvii.

Chapter 1: Introduction

- Update on life expectancy in the United States (U.S. Census Bureau, 2018)

- New commentary indicating that for the first time in U.S. history, in 2019 there were more individuals over the age of 60 than under the age of 18

- New *Connecting with Careers* on Gustavo Medrano, a clinical psychologist who works at the Family Institute at Northwestern University and specializes in working with Latina(o) clients

- Updated data on the percentage of U.S. children and adolescents 17 years and younger from different ethnic groups in 2017 and projected to 2050, with dramatic increases in Latino and Asian American children (ChildStats.gov, 2018)

- Updated data on the percentage of U.S. children and adolescents under 18 years of age living in poverty, including data reported separately for African American and Latino families, which has declined since 2015 (Fontenot, Semega, & Kollar, 2018)

- In the coverage of cross-cultural studies, coverage of a recent study in 26 countries indicating that individuals in Chile had the highest life satisfaction; those in Bulgaria and Spain had the lowest (Jang & others, 2017)

- New description of the positive outcomes when individuals have pride in their ethnic group, including recent research (Umana-Taylor, 2019; Umana-Taylor & others, 2018)

- In the discussion of gender, new content on the gender category of transgender (Bradford & Syed, 2019; Budge & Orovecz, 2018)

- New projections on the significant increase in older adults in the world with estimates of a doubling of the population of individuals 60 and over and a tripling or quadrupling of those 80 and over by 2050 (United Nations, 2017)

- New commentary about how significant projected increases in the older population in countries around the world make it necessary for countries to develop innovative policies and expanded services that include housing, employment, health care, and transportation.

- In the section on contemporary topics, a new topic—technology—was added and discussed, including an emphasis on how pervasive it has become in people's lives and how it might influence their development

- Coverage of a recent study of cohort effects in which older adults report fewer constraints nowadays than their counterparts 18 years ago while younger adults report more constraints now than those 18 years ago (Drewelies & others, 2018)

- Inclusion of recent research across 150 countries that found that health was a better predictor of life satisfaction in individuals 58 years and older than in younger age groups (Joshanloo & Jovanovic, 2019)

- Updated content on Bandura's (2018) social cognitive theory, in which he now emphasizes *forethought* as a key cognitive factor in the theory

- Updated content on cohort effects involving increased interest in a new generation that is labeled generation Z and/or post-millennial, characterized by even greater technological immersion and sophistication, greater ethnic diversity, and being better educated than the millennial generation (Dimock, 2019; Fry & Parker, 2018)

Chapter 2: Biological Beginnings

- Editing and updating of chapter based on comments by Janet DiPietro, a leading expert on prenatal development and birth

- Updated and expanded discussion of genome-wide association studies, including research on autism (Ramswami & Geschwind, 2018), attention deficit hyperactivity disorder (Verhoef & others, 2019), cancer (Chen & others, 2019), obesity (Riveros-McKay & others, 2019), and Alzheimer disease (Hao & others, 2019)

- Updated and expanded coverage of linkage analysis studies, including those focused on cardiovascular disease (Hedberg-Oldfors & others, 2019) and posttraumatic stress disorder (van der Merwe & others, 2019)

- Updated data on the number of genes that humans have, now raised to 21,306 (Salzberg & others, 2018)

- Updated and expanded research on how diet, tobacco use, and sleep can modify the expression of genes through the process of methylation (Lahtinen & others, 2019)

- Inclusion of recent research indicating that methylation may be involved in depression (Li & others, 2019), breast cancer (Parashar & others, 2018), leukemia (Bewersdorf & others, 2019), obesity (Caballero, 2019), and attention deficit hyperactivity disorder (Kim & others, 2018)

- Updated and expanded coverage of susceptibility genes, including those involved in cancer (Liu & Tan, 2019) and cardiovascular disease (Taylor & others, 2019)

- Updated and expanded research on gene-gene interaction to include immune system functioning (Pazmondi & others, 2019), alcoholism (Chen & others, 2017), cancer (Lee & others, 2019), obesity (Wang & others, 2019), type 2 diabetes (Saxena, Srivastaya, & Banergee, 2018), arthritis (Fathollahi & others, 2019), cardiovascular disease (Drone & Hegele, 2019), and Alzheimer disease (Nazarian, Yashin, & Kulminski, 2019)

- New content on the number of children born worldwide with sickle-cell anemia and how stem cell transplantation is being explored in the treatment of infants with sickle-cell anemia (Azar & Wong, 2017)

- New *Connecting with Careers* on Jennifer Leonhard, genetic counselor

- New commentary about neurogenesis being largely complete by about the end of the fifth month of prenatal development (Borsani & others, 2019)

- New coverage of cell-free fetal DNA in maternal blood and its testing as early as 10 weeks into the first trimester of pregnancy to test for such disorders as Down syndrome (Hui, 2019)

- Coverage of a recent study using non-invasive fetal diagnosis that determined fetal sex at 4.5 weeks (D'Aversa & others, 2018)

- Coverage of a recent study that confirmed a significant risk for suicidal behavior in adolescents with FASD (O'Connor & others, 2019)

- New content about a recent large scale U.S. study in which 11.5 percent of adolescent and 8.7 percent of adult pregnant women reported using alcohol in the previous month (Oh & others, 2017)

- Discussion of a recent meta-analysis of 15 studies that concluded smoking during pregnancy increases the risk of children having ADHD and that the risk is greater if their mother is a heavy smoker (Huang & others, 2019)

- New commentary that cessation of smoking by pregnant women by the third trimester is linked to improved birth outcomes (Crume, 2019)

- Coverage of a recent study in which chronic exposure to e-cigarette aerosols was linked to low birth weight in offspring (Orzabal & others, 2019)

- Inclusion of a longitudinal study in which prenatal cocaine exposure was linked to early use of marijuana, arrest history, conduct disorder, and emotion regulation problems at 21 years of age (Richardson & others, 2019)

- Discussion of a recent study that found newborns born to mothers who used marijuana during pregnancy were more likely to be born preterm or low birth weight (Petrangelo & others, 2019)

- New section, Synthetic Opioids and Opiate-Related Pain Killers, that discusses the increasing use of these substances by pregnant women and their possible harmful outcomes for pregnant women and their offspring (Brimdyr & Cadwell, 2019; Clemens-Cope & others, 2019)

- Description of a recent research review that concluded tobacco smoking is linked to impaired male fertility and increases in DNA damage, aneuploidy (abnormal number of chromosomes in a cell), and mutations in sperm (Beal, Yauk, & Marchetti, 2017)

- Coverage of a recent study in which yoga was effective in reducing depressive symptoms in pregnant women (Ng & others, 2019)

- Description of a recent study that found pregnant women 43 years and older were more likely to have infants who were stillborn (Wu & others, 2019)

- Inclusion of recent research indicating that pregnant women who exercised regularly in the second and third trimesters rated their quality of life higher (Krzepota, Sadowska, & Biernat, 2019)

- Discussion of a recent large-scale study that found women who participated in CenteringPregnancy had offspring that were less likely to be born preterm or low birth weight (Cunningham & others, 2019)

- Inclusion of recent research that indicated women who participated in CenteringPregnancy used pain relief less during labor and were more likely to breast feed their infants (Rijnders & others, 2019)

- New coverage of the positive influence of exercise on pregnancy and offspring (Newton & May, 2019), including a recent study that revealed regular exercise by pregnant women was linked to more advanced development in the neonatal brain (Laborte-Lemoyne, Currier, & Ellenberg, 2017)

- Inclusion of recent research in which two weekly 70-minute yoga sessions reduced pregnant women's stress and enhanced their immune system functioning (Chen & others, 2017)

- Coverage of a recent Swedish study that found women who gave birth in water had fewer vaginal tears, shorter labor, needed fewer drugs for pain relief and interventions by medical personnel, and rated their birth experience more positive than women who had conventional spontaneous vaginal births (Ulfsdottir, Saltvedt, & Gerogesson, 2018)

- Inclusion of recent studies in which massage reduced women's pain during labor (Gallo & others, 2018; Unalmis Erdogan, Yanikkerem, & Goker, 2017)

- New description of global cesarean delivery rates with the Dominican Republic and Brazil having the highest rates (56 percent) and New Zealand and the Czech Republic the lowest (26 percent) (McCullough, 2016). The World Health Organization recommends a cesarean rate of 10 percent or less.

- Revised and updated content on cesarean delivery to include the two most common reasons why it is carried out: failure to progress through labor and fetal distress

- Updated data on the percentage of U.S. infants who are born preterm, including ethnic variations (March of Dimes, 2018)

- Updated weights for classification as a low birth weight baby, a very low birth weight baby, and an extremely low birth weight baby

- Updated data on the percentage of U.S. babies born with low birth weight, including ethnic variations (United Health Foundation, 2018)

- Description of recent research indicating that extremely preterm and low birth weight infants have lower executive function, especially in working memory and planning (Burnett & others, 2019)

- Discussion of a longitudinal study in which the nurturing positive effects of kangaroo care with preterm and low birth weight infants at one year of age were still present 20 years later in a number of positive developmental outcomes (Charpak & others, 2019)

- Coverage of a recent study that revealed worsening or minimal improvement in sleep problems from 6 weeks to 7 months postpartum were associated with increased depressive symptoms (Lewis & others, 2018)

- Inclusion of recent research in Japan indicating that 11.2 percent of fathers had postpartum depression one month following delivery (Nishigori & others, 2019)
- Description of a recent study that found fathers with postpartum depression had lower levels of responsiveness, mood, and sensitivity when interacting with their infants (Koch & others, 2019)

Chapter 3: Physical Development and Biological Aging

- New discussion of how infant growth is often not smooth and continuous but rather is episodic, occurring in spurts (Adolph, 2018; Lampl, 2018)
- Coverage of a recent Chinese study that found a higher body mass index (BMI) was associated with earlier pubertal onset (Deng & others, 2018)
- New research that revealed young adolescent boys had a more positive body image than their female counterparts (Morin & others, 2017)
- New study of 12- to 14-year-olds indicating that heavier social media use was associated with body dissatisfaction (Burnette, Kwitowski, & Mazzeo, 2017)
- New discussion of research with seventh to twelfth graders in Thailand that revealed increasing time spent on the Internet, especially when engaging in activities related to self-image and eating attitudes/behavior, was linked to increasing body dissatisfaction (Kaewpradub & others, 2017)
- Inclusion of a recent study of U.S. college women that found more time on Facebook was related to more frequent body and weight concern comparison with other women, more attention to the physical appearance of others, and more negative feelings about their own bodies (Eckler, Kalyango, Paasch, 2017)
- Coverage of a recent studying that found early-maturing girls had higher rates of depression and antisocial age as middle-aged adults mainly because their difficulties began in adolescence and did not lessen over time (Mendle. Ryan, & McKone, 2019)
- New research indicating that early-maturing girls are at risk for physical and verbal abuse in dating (Chen, Rothman, & Jaffee, 2019)
- Expanded and updated content on weight gain and obesity in middle age (Jia, Hill, & Sowers, 2018; Petrie & others, 2018)
- Updated data on the percentage of middle-aged adults who are obese compared to their younger adult counterparts (National Center for Health Statistics, 2018)
- Description of a recent study that revealed a healthy diet in adolescence was linked to a lower risk of cardiovascular disease in middle-aged women (Dahm & others, 2019)
- Coverage of the American Heart Association's seven simple factors that best help individuals improve their cardiovascular health (Mok & others, 2019)
- Recent data on the percentage of women and men 65 to 74 years of age who have hypertension (Centers for Disease Control and Prevention, 2018)
- Inclusion of recent research on 65+-year-olds indicating that a Mediterranean diet lowered their risk of cardiovascular problems (Nowson & others, 2018)

- Coverage of recent research documenting that attention (Bartolomeo & Seidel Malkinson, 2019) and emotion (Gainotti, 2019) are predominantly right hemisphere activities
- New description of some of the aspects of brain activity that the brain imaging technique fNIRS can assess in infancy, including face processing, perception, attention, and memory (Emberson & others, 2019; Zhang & Roeyers, 2019)
- Inclusion of a longitudinal study in which maltreatment risk and home adversity in infancy were linked to cortical delays and brain immaturity at 8 years of age (Bick & others, 2019). However, children in the study who were assigned to an attachment and biobehavioral catch-up intervention showed better brain functioning.
- Inclusion of a recent study documenting that the density of fibers increases in the corpus callosum during adolescence (Genc & others, 2018)
- Coverage of a recent study of older adults in which declines in memory functioning were linked to lower gray matter volume (which contains most of the brain's neuronal cell bodies) in the temporal lobe and hippocampus (Schneider & others, 2019)
- Description of research in which analysis of essays written when nuns were 18 to 32 years of age found that those whose essays were more self-reflective and indicated a higher level of parental autonomy support lived longer (Weinstein & others, 2019)
- Discussion of a study of 732 cases of SIDS that found bed-sharing occurred in 53 percent of the deaths (Drake & others, 2019)
- Coverage of a recent study in which shorter sleep duration in infancy was linked to lower cognitive and language development at two years of age (Smithson & others, 2018)
- Description of a recent Chinese study that revealed sleep deprivation in early childhood was associated with ADHD in middle and late childhood (Tso & others, 2019)
- Discussion of a recent study of 13- to 19-year-olds in Singapore indicating that short sleep duration of less than seven hours on school nights was associated with being overweight, having depression symptoms, being less motivated, not being able to concentrate adequately, having a higher level of anxiety, and engaging in self-harm/suicidal thoughts (Yeo & others, 2019)
- Coverage of a recent study in which spending multiple hours with portable electronic devices was linked to shorter sleep duration in adolescence while time spent with non-portable electronic devices was not related to shorter sleep duration (Twenge, Hisler, & Rizan, 2019)
- Inclusion of a recent national study of high schools that found using electronic devices 5 hours a day or more was linked to getting inadequate sleep (Kenney & Gortmaker, 2017)
- Description of recent research in which the Seattle School District delayed the school start time for secondary school students by nearly one hour and it improved student sleep duration by an average of 34 minutes, resulted in a 4.5 percent increase in grade point average, and improved school attendance (Dunster & others, 2018)
- Coverage of a recent study of college students in which shorter sleep duration was associated with increased suicide risk (Becker & others, 2018a)
- Inclusion of a recent study of college students that found 27 percent described their sleep as poor and 36 percent

reported getting 7 hours or less of sleep on weeknights (Becker & others, 2018b)

- Description of a recent experimental study in which emerging adults who were given a brief sleep quality intervention reported improved sleep, stopped using electronic devices earlier, kept a more regular sleep schedule, and had earlier weekday rise times than a control group who did not get the intervention (Hershner & O'Brien, 2018)

- Discussion of a recent study of college students indicating that a higher level of text messaging activity during the day and at night was related to a lower level of sleep quality (Murdock, Horissian, & Crichlow-Ball, 2017)

- In recent experimental study, emerging adults (mean age = 21.9 years), who were given a brief sleep quality intervention reported improved sleep, stopped using electronic devices earlier, kept a more regular sleep schedule, and had an earlier weekday rise time than a control group who did not get the intervention (Hershner & O'Brien, 2018)

- Coverage of a recent Chinese study in which older adults who engaged in a higher overall level of physical activity, leisure-time exercise, and household activity were less likely to have sleep problems (Li & others, 2018)

- Updated data on U.S. life expectancy for 65-year-olds, including gender differences (U.S. Census Bureau, 2018)

- Updated data on life expectancy in different countries in 2018 with Monaco having the highest (89.6 years), the United States in fifty-third place (79.2 years), and South Africa the lowest (50.6 years) (Geoba.se, 2019)

- Discussion of recent projections for life expectancy in 2030 in 35 developed countries with the United States increasing in life expectancy but having one of the lowest projected increases of all countries in the study (Kontis & others, 2017). In this study, South Korea is expected to have the highest life expectancy of the 35 countries in 2030 with South Korean women the first group to break the 90-year barrier with a projected life expectancy of 90.8 in 2030.

- New description of a study using the Chinese Longitudinal Healthy Longevity study indicating that severe loneliness at prior assessment points predicted poorer cognitive function at subsequent assessment points (Zhong & others, 2017)

- Update on the oldest living person in the world and in the United States in 2019, Maggie Kidd, age 114, who lives in Georgia

- New content indicating that of the 36 oldest centenarians in the world in 2018, 34 of them were women

- Inclusion of a recent study that revealed shorter telomere length was linked to a greater risk of Alzheimer disease (Scarabino & others, 2017)

- Updated and expanded coverage of the diseases that are linked to mitochondrial dysfunction to include cardiovascular disease (Roushandeh, Kuwahara, & Roudkenar, 2019), Parkinson disease (Zhi & others, 2019), diabetic kidney disease (Forbes & Thorburn, 2018), and impaired liver functioning (Borrelli, 2018)

Chapter 4: Health

- New discussion of a longitudinal study that revealed when young children were exposed to environmental tobacco smoke,

they were more likely to engage in antisocial behavior at 12 years of age (Pagani & others, 2017)

- Description of recent data from the Youth Risk Behavior System documenting a continued linear decline through 2017, indicating that 59.2 percent of U.S. high school students did not eat one or more vegetables in the last 7 days (Kann & others, 2018)

- Inclusion of recent research indicating that a higher level of parental monitoring was linked to adolescents' healthier diet intake and lower weight status (Kim & others, 2019)

- Expanded discussion of the factors likely involved in the greater incidence of health problems in emerging adulthood than in adolescence (Hill, 2019)

- Coverage of a recent study of 65+-year-olds that found a Mediterranean diet lowered their risk of cardiovascular problems (Nowson & others, 2018)

- Update on the leading causes of death in older adults with recent data indicating that beginning in the 65–74 year age range, cancer has replaced cardiovascular disease as the leading cause of death in the U.S. (Centers for Disease Control and Prevention, 2018)

- Updated data on the percentage of older adults with Alzheimer disease and updates on the significant increase in Alzheimer's disease in individuals 85 and older (Alzheimer's Association, 2018)

- New content on women being more likely to have the ApoE4 gene than men (Dubol & others, 2017)

- New content on APP, PSEN1, and PSEN2 gene mutations being linked to the early onset of Alzheimer disease (Carmona, Hardy, & Guerreiro, 2018)

- New discussion of the epigenetics of Alzheimer disease, including the role of DNA methylation (Lindahl-Jacobsen & Christensen, 2019; Smith & others, 2019)

- Update on drugs that have been approved by the U.S. Food and Drug Administration to treat Alzheimer disease that now totals five drugs (Almeida, 2018)

- Inclusion of a recent research review that concluded deep brain stimulation (DBS) improves motor function in Parkinson patients for up to 10 years, but improvement tends to decline over time (Limousin & Foltynie, 2019)

- Changes based on feedback from leading children's nutrition expert, Maureen Black

- Updated support for the role of breastfeeding in reducing a number of disease risks for children and their mothers (Bartick & others, 2019)

- Inclusion of a recent research review indicating that breastfeeding is not associated with a reduced risk of allergies in young children (Heinrich, 2017)

- Description of recent research indicating a reduction in hospitalization for breastfed infants and breastfeeding mothers for a number of conditions (Bartick & others, 2018)

- New *Connecting with Careers* on Dr. Faize Mustafa-Infante, a pediatrician who is especially passionate about preventing obesity in infants and children

- Updated data on the percentage of children who are obese with continuing increases through 2015–2016 (Hales & others, 2017)

- New description of the recently devised 5-2-1-0 obesity prevention guidelines for young children: 5 or more servings of fruits and vegetables, no more than 2 hours of screen time,

- minimum of 1 hour of physical activity, and 0 sugar-sweetened beverages daily (Khalsa & others, 2017)
- Coverage of a recent research review that concluded obesity is linked with low self-esteem in children (Moharei & others, 2018)
- Discussion of a recent study of Latino families in which parents who had a healthy weight were 3.7 times more likely to have a child who had a healthy weight (Coto & others, 2019)
- Inclusion of a recent cross-cultural study of adolescent 15-year-olds in 35 countries that found U.S. adolescents had the highest rate of obesity (31 percent) and Danish adolescents the lowest (10 percent) (OECD, 2017)
- Discussion of a recent Chinese study in which children and adolescents who were obese were more likely to have depression and anxiety symptoms than their non-obese counterparts (Wang & others, 2019)
- New content indicating that adolescents who engage in higher levels of screen time are more likely to be overweight or obese (Furthner & others, 2018)
- Coverage of a recent meta-analysis that concluded supervised exercise, especially aerobic exercise, was linked to a reduction of abdominal fat in adolescents (Gonzalez-Ruis & others, 2017)
- Inclusion of research in which an after-school athletics program reduced the obesity risk of adolescents after one year of intervention (Glabaska & others, 2019)
- Description of a recent study that indicated a combination of regular exercise and a diet plan resulted in weight loss and enhanced executive function (Xie & others, 2017)
- Update and revised definitions of anorexia nervosa and bulimia nervosa based on the DSM-V classification system
- New research indicating that having an increase in Facebook friends across two years in adolescence was linked to an enhanced motivation to be thin (Tiggemann & Slater, 2017)
- Coverage of a recent meta-analysis that concluded both anorexics and bulimics engage in maladaptive perfectionism (Norris, Gleaves, & Hutchinson, 2019)
- Description of a recent national study of three disorders—anorexia, bulimia, and binge eating disorder—that found all three disorders were associated with a higher incidence of major depressive disorder than any other disorder, followed by alcohol use disorder (Udo & Grilo, 2019)
- Inclusion of recent national U.S. data on the prevalence of obesity in adults overall and in early, middle, and late adulthood age groups, as well as gender and ethnic differences (Haynes & others, 2017)
- New data indicating that the adult obesity rate in 2016 in the U.S. went up 9.1 percent since 2000 and 4.7 percent since 2012 (Haynes & others, 2017)
- Discussion of a Chinese study that found men and women who gained an average of 22 pounds or more from 20 to 45-60 years of age had an increased risk of hypertension and cholesterol, as well as elevated triglyceride levels in middle age (Zhou & others, 2018)
- Description of a recent large-scale study in which obesity was associated with shorter longevity and increased risk of death due to cardiovascular disease compared with normal weight individuals (Khan & others, 2018)
- New research that indicated obese middle-aged and older adults were more likely to have chronic diseases and earlier death than their normal weight counterparts (Stenholm & others, 2017)
- Coverage of a recent research review that revealed depression was linked to abdominal obesity in older adults (Repousi & others, 2018)
- Discussion of recent international comparisons of 33 countries in which the United States had the highest percentage of obese adults (38.2 percent) and Japan the lowest percentage (3.7); the average of the countries was 23.2 percent of the population being obese (OECD, 2017)
- New commentary that researchers have found higher levels of physical activity, especially endurance training, are linked to weight loss maintenance (Petridou, Sippi, & Mouglos, 2019)
- Description of a recent analysis in which it was concluded that antioxidant vitamins do not increase the life span and can even increase the incidence of diseases (Millsav, Ribaric, & Poljsak, 2019)
- Discussion of a recent study that examined children's physical activity in the transition from elementary to middle school (Pate & others, 2019). In this study, the following activities were associated with children's greater physical activity: Parents' encouragement of physical activity, parents' support of physical activity, time children spent outdoors, children's sports participation, and number of activity facilities near their home.
- Description of a meta-analysis that concluded prolonged exercise interventions with 6- to 12-year-olds were effective in improving the children's executive function in general and inhibitory control in particular (Xue, Yang, & Huang, 2019)
- Updated data on adolescent exercise rates by gender and ethnicity (Kann & others, 2018)
- Inclusion of a recent large-scale study of Dutch adolescents that revealed physically active adolescents had fewer emotional and peer problems (Kuiper & others, 2018)
- Coverage of a recent research review that concluded school and community-based physical activity interventions improve overweight and obese adolescents' executive function (Martin & others, 2018)
- Inclusion of recent research indicating that a school-based exercise program of 20 minutes each day over the course of 8 weeks improved students' working memory (Ludyga & others, 2018)
- New content on research with ADHD adolescents that revealed regular exercise was linked with lower ADHD symptoms (Jeyanthi, Arumugam, & Parasher, 2019; Rassovsky & Alfassi, 2019)
- Coverage of a recent national U.S. study that found only 22.9 percent of adults 18 to 64 years of age met government guidelines for aerobic and muscle-strengthening exercise (Blackwell & Clarke, 2018). In this poll, 27.2 percent of men and 18.7 percent of women met these guidelines.
- Inclusion of a study of middle-aged adults indicating that their estimated age based on exercise stress testing was a better predictor of how long they would live than their chronological age (Herb & others, 2019)
- Description of a recent research review that concluded regular exercise reduces depression in older adults (Seo & Caho, 2018)

- Updated national data on the extent of illicit drug use by U.S. eighth, tenth, and twelfth graders (Johnston & others, 2019)
- Inclusion of new content indicating increasing concern about the increase in adolescents who mix alcohol and energy drinks, which is linked to a higher rate of risky driving (Wilson & others, 2018)
- Updated national data on the dramatic increase in U.S. adolescents who are vaping nicotine, which now far surpasses their cigarette smoking, which continues to decline (Johnston & others, 2019)
- Coverage of a recent meta-analysis of longitudinal studies that found when adolescents use e-cigarettes they are at risk for subsequent cigarette smoking (Soneji & others, 2018)
- Description of a recent intervention study that revealed Latino parents who had participated in a program that emphasized the importance of parental monitoring had adolescents who had a lower level of drug use than a control group of adolescents who did not receive the program (Estrada & others, 2017)
- Coverage of a recent meta-analysis of parenting factors involved in adolescents' alcohol use that indicated higher levels of parental monitoring, support, and involvement were associated with a lower risk of adolescent alcohol misuse (Yap & others, 2017)
- Inclusion of a recent study that revealed adolescent dishonesty increased future alcohol use by reducing parental monitoring knowledge (Lushin, Jaccard, & Kaploun, 2017)
- Description of a recent study of 14- and 15-year-olds that found heavy episodic drinking by parents was a risk factor for adolescent drinking, with girls being especially vulnerable to their parents' episodic drinking (Homel & Warren, 2019)
- Discussion of a recent large scale national study in which friends' use was a stronger influence on adolescents' alcohol use than parental use (Deutsch, Wood, & Shutske, 2018)
- Updated data on binge drinking in college and through early adulthood (Schulenberg & others, 2017)
- Inclusion of a longitudinal study that revealed frequent binge drinking and marijuana use in the freshman year of college predicted delayed college graduation (White & others, 2018)
- Updated data on the percentage of individuals in emerging adulthood and early adulthood who are using electronic vaporizers (which include e-cigarettes) (Schulenberg & others, 2017)
- New content on the importance of optimizing drug use in late adulthood to improve successful aging (Petrovic & others, 2019)
- Inclusion of a recent study that revealed moderate drinkers were more likely to be alive and not have a cognitive impairment at 85 years of age (Richard & others, 2018)

Chapter 5: Motor, Sensory, and Perceptual Development

- Revisions based on feedback from leading children's motor development expert, Karen Adolph
- Much expanded content on the latest dynamic systems theory's model of motor development that emphasizes how motor development has four key characteristics: 1) embodied, 2) embedded, 3) enculturated, and 4) enabling (Adolph & Hoch, 2019)
- New summary content on a key aspect of motor development that involves behavioral flexibility to do what is necessary to accomplish life's everyday goals (Adolph & Hoch, 2019). For example, an infant's movements cannot be repeated in the same way across time and situations because bodies, environments, and tasks are changing and require infants to engage in adaptive behavior.
- Description of recent research indicating that higher motor skill proficiency in preschool was linked to engaging in a higher level of physical activity in adolescence (Venetsanou & Kambas, 2017)
- Inclusion of recent research that found children with a low level of motor competence had a lower motivation for sports participation and lower global self-worth than their counterparts who had a high level of motor competence (Bardid & others, 2019)
- Coverage of recent research indicating that adolescents who participate in sports have a lower risk profile for cardiovascular disease (Herbert & others, 2017)
- Inclusion of a recent study of out-of-school time that revealed time spent in organized sports was associated with increased positive self-identity (Lee & others, 2018)
- New research content on middle-aged and older adults in which those who had limited mobility had lower cognitive functioning (Demnitz & others, 2018)
- Discussion of a recent large-scale study that indicated a 554-step-per-day increase in mobility would reduce physical function limitations by 3.9 percent and improve quality of life by 3.2 percent (Kahiri & others, 2018)
- New coverage of links between a slowing of walking speed in older adults is associated with limited mobility, less community participation, greater cognitive decline, and increased risk of falls
- Inclusion of a recent study of older adult women that revealed a slowing of walking speed occurred on average at about 71 years of age (Noce Kirkwood & others, 2018)
- Inclusion of a recent study that found older adults who walk slowly are at risk for developing mild cognitive impairment (Rajtar-Zembaty & others, 2019)
- Updated and expanded content on eye-tracking to include research on intermodal perception (Gergely & others, 2019), language (Comishen, Bialystok, & Adler, 2019), object categorization (LaTourrette & Waxman, 2019), and understanding of others' needs (Koster & others, 2019)
- New description of the concept of *perceptual narrowing,* in which infants are more likely to distinguish between faces in which they have been exposed to than faces they have never seen before (Kobayashi & others, 2018; Minor & Lewkowicz, 2018)
- Revision of the nature/nurture section in the content on perceptual development to better reflect the Gibsons' view
- Coverage of a longitudinal study of individuals 60 years and older in which visual and hearing difficulties predicted cognitive difficulties 8 years later, with the greatest cognitive decline occurring in individuals who had both a visual and a hearing problem (de la Fuente & others, 2019)
- New discussion of a recent Japanese study of older adults (mean age: 76 years) in which having had cataract surgery reduced their risk of developing mild cognitive impairment (Miyata & others, 2018)
- New description of a large-scale study of Korean adolescents that revealed 17 percent had at least a slight hearing loss and

this loss was associated with cumulative hours spent in gaming centers (Rhee & others, 2019). The adolescents' hearing loss also was related to lower academic performance.

- Inclusion of a recent study in which hearing impairment was associated with accelerated cognitive decline in older adults (Alattar & others, 2019)
- New discussion of a recent study of 65- to 85-year-olds that dual sensory loss in vision and hearing was linked to reduced social participation and less social support, as well as increased loneliness (Mick & others, 2018)
- Coverage of a recent study of elderly adults that found those who had a dual sensory impairment involving vision and hearing had functional limitations, experienced cognitive decline, were lonely, and had communication problems (Davidson & Gutherie, 2018)
- In another recent study, older adults with a dual sensory impairment involving vision and hearing had more depressive symptoms (Han & others, 2019)
- Inclusion of a recent study of older adults in which high levels of pain were associated with memory impairment (van der Leeuw & others, 2018)

Chapter 6: Cognitive Developmental Approaches

- Improved clarity in the section "Evaluation of the Sensorimotor Stage"
- Inclusion of recent research showing the effectiveness of the Tools of the Mind approach in improving a number of cognitive processes and academic skills in young children (Blair & Raver, 2014)
- Coverage of a recent study in which greater use of social networking sites was linked to being more narcissistic (Grambs & Appel, 2018)

Chapter 7: Information Processing

- Coverage of a recent study of older adults with a cognitive impairment that found slower processing speed was associated with an increase in unsafe driving acts that became worse with advancing age (Hotta & others, 2018)
- Expanded content on why habituation is an important aspect of infant cognitive and perceptual development
- New and updated research on the expansiveness of joint attention's influence that includes sustained attention, self-regulation, and executive function (Gueron-Sela & others, 2018)
- Coverage of a recent study in which both joint attention and sustained attention at 9 months of age predicted vocabulary size at 12 and 15 months, but sustained attention was a better predictor of vocabulary size (Yu, Suanda, & Smith, 2019)
- Description of a recent research view that concluded media multitasking is associated with poorer memory, increased impulsivity, and less effective functioning in the brain's cerebral cortex (Uncapher & others, 2017)
- Discussion of a recent study in which heavy media multitaskers were less likely to delay gratification and more likely to endorse intuitive, but wrong, answers on a cognitive reflection task (Schutten, Stokes, & Arnell, 2017)

- Inclusion of recent research on 3- to 6-year-olds that found the volume of their autographical memories was linked to the volume of their self-knowledge (Ross, Hutchison, & Cunningham, 2019)
- Description of a recent research review that concluded interviewer support is linked to children's memory accuracy (Saywitz & others, 2019)
- New content indicating that attention and processing speed likely play a role in declining working memory in older adults (Jariat, Portrat, & Hot, 2018)
- Inclusion of recent research in which aerobic endurance was linked to better working memory in older adults (Zettel-Watson & others, 2017)
- Coverage of a recent study revealed that imagery strategy training improved the working memory of older adults (Borella & others, 2017)
- Description of a recent study that found a mindfulness training program improved older adults' explicit memory (Banducci & others, 2017)
- Inclusion of a recent study that found support for the reminiscent bump in public events, but only for the most frequently mentioned and highly impactful ones (Tekcan & others, 2018)
- Coverage of a recent study in which a cognitive training program that increased frontal and parietal lobe brain activity improved older adults' working memory (Gajewski & Falkenstein, 2018)
- Description of a recent study that found longer encoding time improved older adults' working memory (Bartsch, Loaiza, & Oberauer, 2019)
- Discussion of a recent study of older adults' source memory that found older adults with better source memory were characterized by healthy cardiovascular markers and psychological traits (higher achievement, less depression, for example) while lower source memory was predicted by relevant life experiences such as being retired and heavy drinking (Cansino & others, 2019)
- Inclusion of recent research indicating that prospective memory is impaired in individuals with mild Alzheimer disease (Lecouvey & others, 2019)
- New section, Conclusions about Memory and Aging, to improve student learning due to the many different types of memory and their developmental trajectories
- Discussion of a recent study that found strategies involving elaboration and self-referential processing were effective in older adults' memory, actually helping older adults' memory more than younger adults' memory (Trelle, Henson, & Simons, 2015)
- Inclusion of a recent study of older adults in which using compensation strategies was associated with higher levels of independence in everyday living in both cognitively normal and mild cognitively impaired older adults (Tomaszewski & others, 2018)
- Description of a recent study that found when older adults engaged in higher physical activity levels their memory improved (de Lima & others, 2019)
- Coverage of a recent cohort study that revealed young children in the 2000s are delaying gratification longer than their counterparts in the 1960s and 1980s, including content about why this might be happening (Carlson & others, 2018)
- Inclusion of a recent study of children in low-income families in the African country of Ghana that indicated executive

function assessed at five years of age predicted higher subsequent literacy and math skills across the next two years (Wolf & McCoy, 2019)

- Coverage of a recent study in which higher parent education predicted children's superior executive function whereas harsh parenting forecasted children's lower executive function (Halse & others, 2019)

- Coverage of a recent study in which a lower level of executive function in preschool children was linked to the new onset and worsening of attention deficit hyperactivity disorder and depression at 6 to 12 years of age (Hawkey & others, 2019)

- Description of a recent study that found fathers' autonomy support improved young children's executive function (Meuwissen & Carlson, 2018)

- Discussion of a recent study that indicated teachers who conducted a 6-week small group training program that focused on mindfulness and reflective thinking improved young children's executive function better than a business as usual condition, but a literacy training program was as effective in improving their executive function as the mindfulness and reflective thinking condition (Zelazo & others, 2018)

- Inclusion of recent research that found mindfulness-based intervention improved attention self-regulation (Felver & others, 2017)

- New section, "Executive Function," in the adolescence section of higher level thinking

- New coverage of the distinction between "hot" executive function and "cool" executive function (Koukari, Tsermentseli, & Monks, 2018; Semenov & Zelazo, 2018)

- Description of a recent study of 12- to 17-year-olds in which cool executive function increased with age while hot executive function peaked at 14 to 15 years of age and then declined (Poon, 2018)

- Description of a recent study in which young adolescents showed a better understanding of metaphors than children and this increased understanding was linked to increased cognitive flexibility (Willinger & others, 2019)

- Description of a recent study that revealed across a 10-year period, physically active women experienced less decline in executive function (Hamer, Munoz Terrera, & Demakokos, 2018)

- New section, "Executive Function in Adolescents and Emerging Adults," that especially highlights improving in these time frames in cognitive control (Chevalier, Dauvier, & Blaye, 2018)

- New section, "Executive Function and Aging," that describes the decline in executive function in late adulthood, which is especially influenced by a decline in prefrontal cortex functioning

- New content on the decline in older adults' cognitive flexibility (Chiu & others, 2018)

- Inclusion of a recent study in which aerobic exercise improved older adults' executive function (McSween & others, 2019)

- New section, "Mindfulness," reflecting the increased interest in mindfulness training in improving older adults' cognitive functioning (Kovach & others, 2018; Oken & others, 2018)

- Discussion of a recent study of older adults in 10 European countries that revealed improved memory between 2004 and 2013 with the changes more positive for those who had decreases in cardiovascular diseases and increases in exercise and educational achievement (Hessel & others, 2018)

- New coverage of a recent Australian study that found older adults retired from occupations that involved higher complexity maintained their cognitive advantage over their counterparts who worked in less complex occupations (Lane & others, 2017)

- Inclusion of recent research revealed that older adults with type 2 diabetes had greater cognitive impairment than their counterparts who did not have the disease (Riederer & others, 2017)

- Coverage of a recent study of the oldest-old Chinese that revealed early-stage kidney disease was associated with cognitive decline (Bai & others, 2017)

- Description of a recent study of older adults in which moderate to intense physical activity modified the depression-cognition connection and preserved cognitive function (Hu & others, 2019)

- New content on links between nutrition and cognitive aging, including a recent research review that concluded multinutrient approaches using the Mediterranean diet are linked to a lower risk of cognitive impairment (Abbatecola, Ruso, & Barbieri, 2018)

- New content on the concept of terminal decline and cognition, including recent research (Wilson & others, 2018)

- Discussion of a recent study that revealed time to death in terms of terminal decline was a good predictor of cognitive decline over time (Bendayan & others, 2017)

- Updated story of Helen Small's remarkable life and longevity

- Coverage of a recent meta-analysis that concluded meditation, tai chi, and yoga interventions are effective in improving older adults' cognitive functioning (Chan & others, 2019)

- Description of a recent meta-analysis that indicated video games can have a small positive effect on older adults' memory but have no effect on other cognitive functions (Mansor, Chow, & Halaki, 2019)

- Inclusion of a recent study of 3- to 5-year-old children that revealed earlier development of executive function predicted theory of mind performance, especially for false-belief tasks (Doenyas, Yavuz, & Selcuk, 2018)

- New section, "Developmental Changes in Theory of Mind in Adolescence and Adulthood"

Chapter 8: Intelligence

- Description of the most recent revision of the Wechsler Intelligence Scale for Children–V, and its increase in the number of subtests and composite scores (Canivez, Watkins, & Dombrowski, 2017)

- Discussion of a recent study of older adults in which emotional intelligence was positively linked to their cognitive functioning (Saad & others, 2019)

- Inclusion of a recent study that revealed higher-IQ adolescents engaged in a range of healthier behviors, such as exercise, better diet, and not smoking in middle adulthood (Wraw & others, 2018)

- Coverage of a recent study in which higher IQ in adolescence was associated with having a younger subjective age 50 years later in late adulthood (Stephan & others, 2018)

- Discussion of a recent study in which longitudinal changes in general intelligence were linked to developmental changes that occurred in the increasing thickness and surface area of the frontal and parietal lobes of the brain (Roman & others, 2018)

- Description of a recent study that found genes were much more strongly linked to a person's scientific achievement than to his/or artistic achievement (de Manzano & Ullen, 2018)
- Inclusion of a recent study of 22 countries in which intelligence varied across the countries with the variation linked to income, educational attainment, health, and socioeconomic status (Lynn, Fuerst, & Kirkegaard, 2018)
- New content indicating that intelligence has decreased in several Scandinavian countries and the possible reasons for this (Dutton & Lynn, 2013; Ronnlund & others, 2013)
- New coverage of content on how IQ gains continue to occur in the United States and developing countries (Flynn & Shaver, 2018), including a study that found IQ increased by 10 points from 2004 to 2016 in Khartoum, the capital of the African country of Sudan
- Inclusion of a recent study that indicated intelligence showed considerable stability across four developmental periods—infancy, early childhood, middle and late childhood, and adolescence (Yu & others, 2018)
- Coverage of a recent study in which fluid intelligence decreased in individuals 65 years and older but not in individuals 45 to 60 years of age (Cornelis & others, 2019)
- New discussion of the role of personality traits in creativity (Feist, 2019)
- Inclusion of a recent study in which the personality trait of openness to experience was linked to a higher level of creativity in the arts while intellect was associated with creativity in the sciences (Kaufman & others, 2016)
- Coverage of recent research on 24- to 93-year-olds that found everyday problem solving performance increased from early to middle adulthood but began to show a decline at about 50 years of age (Chen, Hertzog, & Park, 2017). In this study, fluid intelligence predicted everyday problem solving performance in young adults but with increasing age, crystallized intelligence became a better predictor.
- Coverage of a number of recent studies focused on the developmental aspects of wisdom at different points in life (Ardelt & Jeste, 2018; Igareshi, Levenson, & Aldwin, 2018)
- New discussion of a study that found the search for and presence of meaning was linked to wisdom in emerging adults (Webster & others, 2018)
- Description of a recent study in which self-reflective exploratory processing of difficult life circumstances was linked to a higher level of wisdom (Westrate & Gluck, 2017)
- Inclusion of a recent study that found the personality trait of openness to experience in early adulthood predicted wisdom 60 years later (Ardelt, Gerlach, & Vaillant, 2018). Also in this study, wisdom in later adulthood could be traced back to experiences and characteristics at different points in development: A supportive childhood, adolescent competence, emotional stability in young adults, and generativity in middle adulthood.
- Coverage of a recent study that indicated wisdom peaked in midlife with education especially linked to a higher level of wisdom (Ardelt, Pridgen, & Nutter-Pridgen, 2018)

Chapter 9: Language Development

- Inclusion of revisions and updates based on feedback from leading experts Roberta Golinkoff and Virginia Marchman
- Coverage of a recent study in which a lack of babbling in infants was linked to having future speech and language problems (Lohmander & others, 2017)
- New commentary on how infants' babbling influences the behavior of their caregivers, creating social interaction that facilitates their own communicative development (Albert, Schwade, & Goldstein, 2019)
- New research on babbling onset predicting when infants would say their first words (McGillion & others, 2017a)
- New commentary on why gestures such as pointing promote further advances in language development
- Coverage of a recent study in which infants at high risk for autism spectrum disorder used fewer gestures than their low risk autism counterparts (Choi & others, 2019)
- Expanded discussion of statistical learning, including how infants soak up statistical regularities around them merely through exposure to them (Aslin, 2017)
- New discussion of English-speaking preschool children that revealed those from lower income families had less advanced language-processing skills, as well as a smaller vocabulary and syntax deficiencies (Levine & others, 2019b)
- Description of recent research that indicated 3-year-old bilingual children adapted to the needs of their communication partners better than their monolingual counterparts (Gampe, Wermelinger, & Daum, 2019)
- Inclusion of a recent study that found parent coaching of 6- and 10-month-old infants that involved the amount of child-directed speech, back and forth interactions, and parentese speech style improved the infants' language outcomes (more advanced babbling and greater word production) at 14 months of age (Ferjan Ramirez & others, 2019)
- New discussion of how adolescents are better than children at persuasive writing
- Coverage of recent research in which child-directed speech in a one-to-one social context for 11- to 14-month-olds was related to productive vocabulary at 2 years of age for Spanish-English bilingual infants for both languages and each language independently (Ramirez-Esparza, Garcia-Sierra, & Kuhl, 2017)
- Inclusion of a recent met-analysis that concluded shared picture book reading was linked to children having better expressive and receptive language (Dowdall & others, 2019)
- New discussion of recent research in several North American urban areas and the small island of Tanna in the South Pacific Ocean that found that fathers in both types of contexts engaged in child-directed speech with their infants (Broesch & Bryant, 2018)
- Expanded emphasis on the importance of social cues in infant language learning (Akun & others, 2018; McGillion & others, 2017b)
- Coverage of a recent study in which both full term and preterm infants who heard more caregiver talk based on all day recordings at 16 months of age had better language skills at 18 months of age (Adams & others, 2018)

- New content on the American Association of Pediatrics (2016) recent position statement on co-viewing of videos indicating that infants can benefit when parents watch videos with them and communicate with them about the videos
- Expanded coverage of how parents can facilitate infants' and toddlers' language development

Chapter 10: Emotional Development and Attachment

- Edits based on feedback from leading experts Pamela Cole and Joan Grusec
- New transition paragraph from the description of emotion in general to content on emotion regulation that emphasizes the positive, adaptive nature of emotion, which is reflected in our ability to regulate our emotions
- Coverage of a recent study that found emotion-dismissing mothers' parenting was linked to toddlers' lower emotional competence while mothers' emotion-coaching parenting was associated with their toddlers' higher emotional competence (Ornaghi & others, 2019)
- Discussion of a recent study in which maternal sensitivity was linked to lower levels of infant fear (Gartstein, Hancock, & Iverson, 2018)
- Description of a recent study that revealed excessive crying in 3-month-olds doubled the risk of behavioral, hyperactive, and mood problems at 5 to 6 years of age (Smarius & others, 2017)
- New discussion of a study in which young children with a negative temperament used fewer attention regulation strategies while maternal sensitivity to infants was linked to more adaptive emotion regulation (Thomas & others, 2017)
- Inclusion of a recent study in which maternal sensitivity was linked to better emotional self-regulation in 10-month-old infants (Frick & others, 2018)
- Coverage of a recent intervention study that involved training mothers to effectively use soothing techniques in the fourth week after birth, which resulted in infants waking up less each night and crying less when assessed at 7, 11, and 23 weeks after birth (Ozturk Donmez & Temel, 2019)
- Description of a recent study in which young children with higher emotion regulation were more popular with their peers (Nakamichi, 2019)
- New discussion of a longitudinal study in which a higher level of emotion regulation in early childhood was linked to a higher level of externalizing problems in adolescence (Perry & others, 2017)
- New *Connecting with Careers* insert on Dr. Melissa Jackson, child and adolescent psychiatrist
- New discussion of emotion regulation in adolescence and how lower levels of emotion regulation are linked to a number of problems in adolescence (Hollenstein & Lanteigne, 2018)
- Discussion of a recent study in which older men showed greater engagement with highly positive contexts than younger men did (Martins & others, 2018)
- Inclusion of a recent meta-analysis that concluded emotional experiences in older adults are more positive than for younger adults (Laureiro-Martinez, Trujillo, & Unda, 2017). Also, in

this review, it was concluded that older adults focus less on negative events in the past than younger adults.
- New commentary about the fact that since older adults have a decreasing number of years to live, this influences them to place more emphasis on prioritizing meaningful relationships (Moss & Wilson, 2019)
- New research that found positive affectivity, surgency, and self-regulation capacity assessed at 4 months of age was linked to school readiness at 4 years of age (Gartstein, Putnam, & Kliewer, 2016)
- Inclusion of two new research studies that linked a lower level of effortful control at 3 years of age with ADHD symptoms in the first grade (Willoughby, Gottfredson, & Stifter, 2017) and at 13 years of age (Einziger & others, 2018)
- Description of a recent study that revealed if parents had a childhood history of behavioral inhibition, their children who also had a high level of behavioral inhibition were at risk for developing anxiety disorders (Stumper & others, 2017)
- New coverage of recent research in which having a difficult temperament at 5 years of age was linked to delinquency at 15 years of age (DiLalla & DiLalla, 2018)
- Inclusion of a recent meta-analysis that concluded secure attachment is linked to being more resilient (Darling Rasmussen & others, 2018)
- Discussion of a recent study that found an infant's secure attachment to its father was not enough to reduce the infant's stress reactivity when the mother-infant attachment was insecure (Kuo & others, 2019)
- Description of recent research that revealed providing parents who engage in inadequate or problematic caregiving with practice and feedback focused on interacting sensitively enhances parent-infant attachment security (Dozier, Bernard, & Roben, 2019; Woodhouse, 2018 & others, 2019)
- New content about mothers playing 3 times more often with children than fathers do (Cabrera & Rossman, 2017)
- Inclusion of recent research with low-income families indicating that fathers' playfulness at 2 years of age was associated with more advanced vocabulary skills at 4 years of age while mothers' playfulness at 2 years of age was linked to a higher level of emotion regulation at 4 years of age (Cabrera & others, 2017)
- Discussion of a recent study that found negative outcomes on cognitive development in infancy when fathers were more withdrawn and depressed and positive outcomes on cognitive development when they were more engaged and sensitive, as well as less controlling (Sethna & others, 2018)
- Description of recent research on 5- to 18-year-olds involving a series of meta-analyses revealed distinctive patterns between secure attachment and parenting behaviors as well as between avoidant attachment and parenting behaviors, but not between ambivalent attachment and parenting behaviors (Koehn & Kerns, 2018)
- Coverage of recent research indicating that most adolescents have a fairly stable attachment style but that attachment stability increased in adulthood (Jones & others, 2018). Also in this study, family conflict and parental separation/divorce were likely candidates for undermining attachment stability.

- New research of a longitudinal study that found a secure base of attachment knowledge in adolescence and emerging adulthood was predicted by observations of maternal sensitivity across childhood and adolescence (Waters, Ruiz, & Roisman, 2017)
- Coverage of a recent study that revealed when they had grown up in poverty, adolescents engaged in less risk-taking if they had a history of secure attachments to caregivers (Delker, Bernstein, & Laurent, 2018)
- Inclusion of a recent analysis that found secure attachment to the mother and to the father was associated with fewer depressive symptoms in adolescents (Kerstis, Aslund, & Sonnby, 2018)
- Coverage of a recent research review that concluded insecure attachment was linked to a higher level of social anxiety in adults (Manning & others, 2017)
- Description of recent research indicating that insecure anxious and insecure avoidant individuals were more likely than securely attached individuals to engage in risky health behaviors, be more susceptible to physical illness, and have poorer disease outcomes (Pietromonaco & Beck, 2018)
- Inclusion of a longitudinal study from 13 to 72 years of age in which avoidant attachment declined across the life span and being in a relationship predicted lower levels of anxious and avoidant attachment across adulthood (Chopik, Edelstein, & Grimm, 2019)
- Coverage of a recent study of older adult women that found avoidant attachment was linked to higher levels of social isolation (Spence, Jacobs, & Bifulco, 2019)
- Updated data on the number of Americans who have tried Internet matchmaking and gender differences in the categories males and females lie about in Internet matchmaking (statisticbrain.com, 2017)
- Description of recent research on how romantic relationships change in emerging adulthood, including different characteristics of adolescent and emerging adult romantic relationships (Lantagne & Furman, 2017)
- New section on cross-cultural variations in romantic relationships
- New coverage of recent comparisons of romantic relationships in Japan, France, Argentina, and Qatar (Ansari, 2015)

Chapter 11: The Self, Identity, and Personality

- Coverage of a recent study that found an instrumental reminiscence intervention improved the coping skills of older adults (Satorres & others, 2017)
- New discussion of a recent book—*Challenging the Cult of Self-Esteem in Education* (Bergeron, 2018)—that criticizes education for promising high self-esteem for students, especially those who are impoverished or marginalized
- Coverage of a longitudinal study that found a higher level of self-control in childhood was linked to a slower pace of aging at 26, 32, and 38 years of age (Belsky & others, 2017)
- New discussion of a longitudinal study in which a lower level of emotion regulation in early childhood was linked to a higher level of externalizing problems in adolescence (Perry & others, 2018a)

- Inclusion of recent research that revealed overcontrolling parenting at age 2 was related to lower emotion regulation at age 5, which in turn were associated with more emotional and school problems at age 10 (Perry & others, 2018b)
- Expanded and updated coverage of the importance of self-regulation in adolescence (Casey & others, 2019; Van Maderen & others, 2019)
- New discussion of recent research on more than 5,000 individuals from 10 to 30 years of age from around the world that revealed sensation seeking steadily increased from 11 years of age through late adolescence, peaking at 19 years of age and declining through the 20s (Steinberg & others, 2019)
- New description of a recent study in which a reciprocal relation between school engagement and self-regulation in adolescence was found (Stefansson & others, 2018)
- Coverage of a recent study of middle school students that revealed self-control was a key factor in developing good health habits (Kang & You, 2018)
- Inclusion of a recent study of Mexican American adolescents that indicated effortful control was linked to coping with stress more effectively (Taylor, Widman, & Robins, 2017)
- Discussion of a recent study of fifth to eleventh graders that found a bidirectional pattern between effortful control and school behavior problems (Atherton & others, 2019)
- New description of a recent meta-analysis of children up to 18 years of age that indicated those who were securely attached engaged in better effortful control (Pallini & others, 2018)
- Inclusion of a recent study in which older adults who had a higher daily level of self-control perceived themselves to be younger (Bellingtier & Neurpert, 2019)
- New commentary that too little research attention has been given to the domains of identity (Galliher, McLean, & Syed, 2017)
- New inclusion of Luc Goosen's and Koen Luyckx's criticisms of Marcia's identity statuses report (Luyckx & others, 2017, 2018)
- New content on the newer *dual cycle identity model* that separates out identity development into two processes: 1) A formation cycle, and 2) a maintenance cycle (Luyckx & others, 2014, 2017, 2018)
- New section, "Identity Development and the Digital Environment," that explores the widening audience adolescents and emerging adults have to express their identity and get feedback about it in their daily connections on social media such as Instagram, Snapchat, and Facebook (Davis & Weinstein, 2017)
- Coverage of a recent study of Mexican-origin adolescents in the United States in which a positive ethnic identity, social support, and anger suppression helped them with racial discrimination whereas anger expression reduced their ability to cope with the discrimination (Park & others, 2018)
- Coverage of a recent study in which openness to experience declined in advance of death in older adults (Sharp & others, 2019)
- Discussion of a recent study that revealed older adults characterized by high conscientiousness were experiencing optimal aging (Melendez & others, 2019) and less likely to develop dementia (Kaup, Hammell, & Yaffe, 2019)
- Inclusion of recent research that found conscientiousness was linked to being more academically successful in medical

school (Sobowale & others, 2018) and not being as addicted to Instagram (Kircaburun & Griffiths, 2018)

- Description of recent research indicating that obese adults were characterized by low conscientiousness (Cheng & others, 2019)
- Discussion of research in which nursing professionals who were high in conscientiousness and low in neuroticism were characterized by lower work burnout rates (Perez-Fuentes & others, 2019)
- Inclusion of recent research in which more pessimistic college students had more anxious mood and stress symptoms (Lau & others, 2017)
- Discussion of a recent study of married couples that revealed the worst health outcomes occurred when both spouses decreased their optimism across a four-year period (Chopik, Kim, & Smith, 2018)
- Description of a recent study in which lonely individuals who were optimistic had a lower suicide risk (Chang & others, 2018)
- Coverage of a recent study that found older adults engaged in more proactive coping when experiencing minor daily hassles in their lives than younger adults did (Neubauer, Smyth, & Sliwinski, 2019)
- Discussion of a recent study in which participating in an intergenerational civic engagement program enhanced older adults' self-perceptions of generativity (Grunewald & others, 2016)
- Inclusion of recent research that found a higher level of generativity in middle age was linked to greater wisdom in late adulthood (Ardelt, Gerlach, & Vaillant, 2018)
- Inclusion of a recent study of middle-aged adults that revealed intrinsically-rewarding work was associated with feelings of generativity (Chen & other, 2019)

Chapter 12: Gender and Sexuality

- Clearer definition of congenital adrenal hyperphasia (CAH)
- Inclusion of two recent studies of CAH girls who engaged in more problematic behaviors in childhood (Kung & others, 2018; Spencer & others, 2018)
- Coverage of a recent study in which 3-year-old boys with higher prenatal testosterone levels had shorter delay of gratification and more attention problems (Korner & others, 2019)
- Inclusion of Janet Shibley Hyde and her colleagues' (Hyde & others, 2019) recent conclusion that because the distributions for males and females on different brain features are so overlapping, in most instances is more accurate to characterize human brains as a mosaic of these features rather than as male-typical and female-typical brains
- Updated data on math and reading scores at the fourth and eighth grade levels in the National Assessment of Educational Progress (2017)
- Coverage of a recent large scale study of seventh grade girls that found girls' perceptions of teachers' gendered math expectations and how relevant and meaningful the math curriculum was for them were linked to their math beliefs and math achievement (McKellar & others, 2019)
- Update on Urban Prep Academy, the first all-male African American charter school, indicating that from 2010, its first year as a school, through 2018, 100 percent of the students in each graduating class went on to college

- Inclusion of a recent study that revealed females are better than males at facial emotion perception across the life span (Olderbak & others, 2019)
- Coverage of a recent study of adolescents that revealed those who observed relational aggression on television were more likely to engage in relational aggression when they were texting one year later (Coyne & others, 2019)
- Description of a recent study in which androgynous boys and girls had high self-esteem and few internalizing problems (Pauletti & others, 2017)
- A number of changes made based on feedback from leading experts Bonnie Halpern-Felsher and Ritch Savin-Williams
- New emphasis on the similarities in sexual timing and developmental sequences in heterosexual and sexual minority adolescents except that sexual minority adolescents have to cope with the more stressful aspects of their sexual identity and disclosing this identity (Savin-Williams, 2019)
- Significant updating of the percentage of individuals 18 to 44 years of age in the United States who report they are heterosexual, gay, lesbian, or bisexual, as well as the percentages of these men and women who report about various feelings involving sexual orientation (Copen, Chandra, & Febo-Vazquez, 2016)
- Inclusion of recent research in which sexual activity in adults on day 1 was linked to greater well-being the next day (Kashdan & others, 2018). In this study, higher reported sexual pleasure and intimacy predicted more positive affect and less negative affect the next day.
- New commentary that whether an individual is heterosexual, gay, lesbian, or bisexual, the person cannot be talked out of his or her sexual orientation (King, 2017, 2019)
- Coverage of the recent significant increase in gonorrhea, syphilis, and chlamydia rates in the United States (Centers for Disease Control and Prevention, 2019; Feltman, 2018)
- Updated data on the number of HIV cases in the United States
- New content on the high percentage of college men who admit that they fondle women against their will and force them to have sex with them (Wiersma-Mosley, Jozkowski, & Martinez, 2017)
- Updated data on the percentage of high school students, including female vs. male students, who have been forced to have sexual intercourse against their will (Kann & others, 2018)
- New description of the No Means No worldwide program that is being widely implemented with adolescents in Kenya and Malawi and has been effective in reducing sexual assaults in adolescence
- New coverage of the Me Too movement and how awareness of the widespread sexual harassment of women quickly spread beginning in 2017
- Inclusion of a recent study of prime-time television shows that U.S. adolescents and emerging adults watched found that sexual violence and abuse, casual sex, lack of contraception use, and no coverage of the negative consequences of risky sexual behavior were common (Kinsler & others, 2019)
- Description of a recent study of television shows revealed that sexual behavior with casual acquaintances was almost as common as sexual behavior in committed relationships (Timmermans & Van den Bulck, 2018)

- Inclusion of a recent study of emerging adults in which receiving unwanted sexts and sexting under coercion were linked to higher levels of depression, anxiety, and stress, and lower self-esteem (Klettke & others, 2019)

- Updated data on the percentage of U.S. high school students who have ever had sexual intercourse, are currently sexually active, had sexual intercourse before 13 years of age, and engaged in sexual intercourse with 4 or more persons (Kann & others, 2018)

- Updated data on ethnic variations in adolescents who have ever had sexual intercourse (Kann & others, 2018)

- Coverage of a recent national study of 7,000 15- to 24-year-olds' engagement in oral sex, including the low percentage of youth who use a condom when having oral sex (Holway & Hernandez, 2018)

- Description of a recent study of South African youth that found that early sexual debut predicted a lower probability of graduating from high school (Bengesai, Khan, & Dube, 2018)

- Inclusion of a recent Australian study in which sex at age 15 or younger predicted higher rates of emerging adult pregnancy, lifetime sexual partners, and sex without using a condom (Prendergrast & others, 2019)

- Coverage of a recent study of Korean adolescent girls in which early menarche was linked to earlier initiation of sexual intercourse (Kim & others, 2019)

- New discussion of links between substance abuse and sexual risk practices, including a recent study in which the likelihood of initiating sexual intercourse before age 13 increased in those engaged in substance abuse and having mental health problems (Okumu & others, 2019)

- Coverage of a recent study in which talk about sexual protection with extended family members was linked to adolescents having fewer sexual partners while such talk about sexual risks was associated with adolescents having more sexual partners (Grossman & others, 2019)

- Description of a recent study of African American girls that revealed those for whom religion was very or extremely important were much more likely to have a later sexual debut (George Dalmida & others, 2018)

- Updated data on the percentage of U.S. adolescents who used a contraceptive the last time they had sexual intercourse (Kann & others, 2018)

- Important new section on the increasing number of medical organizations and experts who have recently recommended that adolescents use long-acting reversible contraception (LARC), which consists of intrauterine devices (IUDs) and contraceptive implants (Apter, 2018; Deidrich, Klein, & Peipert, 2017; Fridy & others, 2018; Society for Adolescent Medicine, 2017a; Summit & others, 2019; Turner, 2019; World Health Organization, 2018)

- Updated data on STIs in young people with those 15 to 24 years of age accounting for 50 percent of the new STIs in the United States (Kann & others, 2018)

- Updated data on HIV in the United States with individuals 13 to 24 years of age having 21 percent of all HIV diagnoses and, of these individuals, 81 percent were gay or bisexual males (Kann & others, 2018)

- Updated data on births to U.S. 15- to 19-year-olds, which in 2017 reached its lowest rate in history (Centers for Disease Control and Prevention, 2019). Especially noteworthy was the substantial decline in births to Latina and African American adolescent girls.

- New research on pregnancy in adolescence and factors that are linked to it (Dee & others, 2017; Maravilla & others, 2017)

- New position of the Adolescent Society of Health and Medicine (2017b) that states research clearly indicates that comprehensive sex education programs and policies are effective in delaying sexual intercourse and reducing other sexual risk behaviors

- Coverage of a recent study in which emerging adults reported that on days they had vaginal sex they said they experience more positive affect; however, they reported that higher levels of negative affect occurred on days they had sex with a non-dating partner or had more negative experiences in the sexual encounter (Vasilenko & Lefkotwitz, 2018)

- Discussion of a recent study that revealed the more minutes per week that women exercised during the menopausal transition, the lower their stress level was (Guerin & others, 2019)

- Description of a recent analysis of research that concluded mindfulness training is linked to improved psychological adjustment during the menopausal transition (Molefi-Youri, 2019)

- Coverage of a recent cross-cultural study in China that found Mosuo women had fewer negative menopausal symptoms and higher self-esteem than Han Chinese women (Zhang & others, 2019)

- Inclusion of a consensus that there is a slight increase in breast cancer for women taking hormone replacement therapy (American Cancer Society, 2019; www.breastcancer.org, 2019)

- Discussion of recent studies and research reviews that indicate testosterone replacement therapy does not increase the risk of prostate cancer (Debruyne & others, 2017; Yassin & others, 2017)

- Description of a recent study in which TRT-related benefits in quality of life and sexual function were maintained for 36 months after initial treatment (Rosen & others, 2017)

- Revised conclusions about TRT and cardiovascular disease with recent research being inconclusive about this association (Fode & others, 2019)

- Discussion of a recent study that found the more frequently middle-aged and older adults had sex, the better their overall cognitive functioning was, and especially so in working memory and executive function (Wright, Jenks, & Demeyere, 2018)

- Inclusion of recent research on healthy middle-aged women indicating that interpersonal factors such as emotional support and relationship satisfaction, as well as the personality traits of optimism and self-esteem, were key predictors of the quality of sexual functioning (Memone, Fiacco, & Ehlert, 2019)

- Coverage of recent research in which older adults who engaged in sexual activity was linked to greater enjoyment in life (Smith & others, 2019)

- Description of a recent study in which older adults were asked about their motivation for having sex (Gewirtz-Meydan & Avalon, 2019). In this study, five main reasons for having sex were: 1) to maintain overall functioning; 2) to feel young again; 3) to feel attractive and desirable; 4) to go from lust to love; and 5) to change from "getting sex" to "giving sex."

Chapter 13: Moral Development, Values, and Religion

- Based on feedback from instructors and students, content on Kohlberg's theory was reduced and made easier for students to understand

- Extensive revisions and updated based on feedback from leading expert consultant, Darcia Narváez

- Inclusion of Albert Bandura's (2015) most recent social cognitive views on morality in which he describes how people can morally disengage themselves yet still feel good about themselves

- New discussion of how recent research has documented the role of guilt in young children's cooperation (Vaish, 2018; Vaish, Carpenter, & Tomasello, 2016)

- Coverage of a recent study that found a higher degree of empathy was linked to greater civic engagement by adolescents (Metzger & others, 2018)

- Description of a recent meta-analysis that concluded better quality parent-child and peer relationships were linked to higher levels of adolescents' empathy (Boele & others, 2019)

- Inclusion of a recent study of individuals from adolescence through middle adulthood that revealed as they got older their external moral identity motivation decreased while their internal moral identity motivation increased (Krettenaur & Victor, 2017)

- Coverage of a recent study that found maternal supportive (emotion-focused and problem-focused) behavior was linked to an increase in young children's prosocial behavior (Eisenberg & others, 2018)

- New Figure 2 that gives students an opportunity to evaluate the extent to which they have a moral identity

- Updated content on the number of states in 2018 that legislatively mandated character education in schools (18), had legislation that encouraged character education (18), supported character education but without legislation (7), and no legislation that specifies character education (8)

- Discussion of a recent study of links between purpose and character, with three components of character (gratitude, compassion, and grit) linked to character in young adolescents (Malin, Liauw, & Damon, 2017)

- Deletion of the section, "Cognitive Moral Education," as less attention is being given to it than in the past

- Coverage of two recent studies in which forgiveness of others was associated with a lower risk of suicidal behavior in adolescence (Dangel, Webb, & Hirsch, 2018; Quintana-Orts & Rey, 2018)

- Inclusion of recent research on middle school students in which a higher level of gratitude was linked to having a higher level of purpose (Malin, Liauw, & Damon, 2017)

- Updated data on the percentage of older adults who engage in volunteering (U.S. Bureau of Labor Statistics, 2016)

- Inclusion of recent research on links between volunteering by older adults and improved health (Burr & others, 2018; Carr, Kail, & Rowe, 2018), better cognitive functioning (Prouix & others, 2018), and less loneliness (Carr & others, 2018)

- Expanded and updated discussion of why volunteering by older adults has positive outcomes for them (Carr, 2018)

- Updated statistics on gender differences in juvenile delinquency in the United States (Hockenberry & Puzzanchera, 2017)

- Coverage of a recent study that found delinquency in adolescence was linked to a greater likelihood of being unemployed in adulthood (Carter, 2019)

- Description of a recent study of middle school adolescents that found peer pressure for fighting and friends' delinquent behavior were linked to adolescents' aggression and delinquent behavior (Farrell, Thompson, & Mehari, 2017)

- Inclusion of a recent study of more than 10,000 children and adolescents that revealed a family environment characterized by poverty and child maltreatment was linked to entering the juvenile justice system in adolescence (Vidal & others, 2017)

- Discussion of a recent study that revealed an increase in the proportion of classmates who engage in delinquent behavior increased the likelihood that other classmates would become delinquents (Kim & Fletcher, 2018)

- Inclusion of a recent study that indicated adolescent delinquents were high on affiliating with deviant peers and engaging in pseudomature behavior and low on peer popularity and school achievement (Gordon Simons & others, 2018)

- Description of a recent study that revealed having a best friend who was delinquent increased the probability that adolescents themselves would become delinquent (Levey & others, 2019)

- Coverage of a recent study in which low self-control was linked to a higher incidence of delinquent behavior (Fine & others, 2016)

- Inclusion of recent research in which having callous-unemotional traits predicts an increased risk of engaging in delinquency for adolescent males (Ray & others, 2017)

- Discussion of recent research indicating for populations with high risk profiles, as little as one teacher screening taken during kindergarten or the first grade predicted which males would have adult criminal convictions by age 25 (Kassing & others, 2019)

- Updated data on the goals of first-year college students in relation to the relative importance they assign to developing a meaningful philosophy of life versus becoming well-off financially (Stolzenberg & others, 2019)

- Updated data on the continuing decrease in college freshmen who say they attended a religious service occasionally or frequently in the past year (Stolzenberg & others, 2017)

- Description of a recent study that revealed high school students who reported turning to spiritual beliefs when they were experiencing problems were less likely to engage in substance use (Debnam & others, 2018)

- Discussion of a recent study across three countries (England, Scotland, and Canada) found that adolescents who reported having a higher level of spirituality were more likely to have positive health outcomes (Brooks & others, 2018)

- Inclusion of a recent Slovakian study of adolescents in which spirituality but not religiosity was linked to better self-rated health, fewer health complaints, and higher life satisfaction (Dankulincova Veselska & others, 2019)

- New research that indicated adults who volunteered had lower resting pulse rates and their resting pulse rate improved when they were deeply committed to religion (Krause, Ironson, & Hill, 2017)

- Inclusion of a national poll of people in the United States that found they are increasingly spiritual but not religious (Lipka & Gecewicz, 2017)

Chapter 14: Families

- Description of a recent study in which inadequate dyadic synchrony was found in the preterm infant-mother relationship compared with more positive dyadic synchrony in the full term infant-mother relationship (Spairani & others, 2018)
- Coverage of a recent study that revealed improvement in a couples' relationship coping decreased their coparenting conflict (Zemp & others, 2018)
- Discussion of recent research with adolescents in which light use of digital media was associated with much higher psychological well-being than heavy use of digital media (Twenge & Campbell, 2019)
- Description of a recent study that found that social media use of more than 2 hours a day was linked to lower academic achievement in both middle and high school students (Sampas-Kanyinga, Chaput, & Hamilton, 2019)
- Updated data on the percentage of U.S. individuals 18 and older who are single (U.S. Census Bureau, 2018)
- Inclusion of data from the Match.com Singles in America 2017 national poll that describes Millenials' interest in having sex before a first date, interest in marrying but taking considerable time to get to know someone before committing to a serious relationship, and males interest in having females initiate the first kiss and asking a guy for his phone number (Fisher, 2017; Match.com, 2017)
- Updated data on the continuing increase in cohabitation in U.S. adults (Brown & Wright, 2017)
- Inclusion of recent research that confirms cohabitation is a risk factor for intimate partner violence in emerging adults (Manning, Longmore, & Giordano, 2018)
- Updated data on the increasing percentage of emerging and young adults who are cohabiting (U.S. Census Bureau, 2018)
- Discussion of a recent study in which cohabiting individuals were more likely to engage in risky sexual relationships and more likely to have an unintended birth (Nugent & Daugherty, 2018)
- Description of a recent study that indicated cohabitation was associated with a risk for increased marijuana use among women but not men (Hoffman, 2018)
- Coverage of a recent study in which cohabiting individuals were not as mentally healthy as their counterparts in committed marital relationships (Braithwaite & Holt-Lunstad, 2017)
- Description of a recent study of long-term cohabitation (more than 3 years) in emerging adulthood that found emotional distress was higher in long-term cohabitation than in time spent single, with men especially driving the effect (Memitz, 2019). However, heavy drinking was more common in time spent single than in long-term cohabitation.
- Inclusion of recent research indicating that women who cohabited within the first year of a sexual relationship were less likely to get married than women who waited more than one year before cohabiting (Sassler, Michelmore, & Qian, 2018)

- Updated data on the increasing number of middle-aged and older adult men and women who are cohabiting (Brown & Wright, 2017)
- Updated data on the percentage of U.S. adults who are married (U.S. Census Bureau, 2018)
- New comparison of age at first marriage in a number of developed countries with individuals in Sweden getting married latest and those in Turkey earliest
- Updated data on the continuing increase in being older before getting married in the U.S. with the age for men now at 29.5 years and for women 27.4 years (Livingston, 2017)
- Coverage of a recent study of recently married low income adults that revealed those who received premarital education were more likely to seek therapy when the marriage became distressed than those who had not received premarital therapy (Williamson & others, 2018)
- New Figure 3: Trends and Proposal for Improving Premarital Education in the Next Generation (Clyde, Hawkins, & Willoughby, 2019)
- Inclusion of a longitudinal study of middle-aged married adults that found negative behavior in their marriage decreased and positive behavior increased across 13 years in middle age (Verstaen & others, 2019)
- Update on the countries in which the divorce rate is the highest (Russia) and the lowest (Chile)
- New discussion of the increasing divorce rate in middle-aged adults and the reasons for the increase (Stepler, 2017), as well as the recent labeling of divorce in 50+-year-old adults as "gray divorce" (Crowley, 2018)
- Coverage of a recent study that found the greatest risks for getting divorce in middle adulthood were a shorter duration of marriage, lower marital quality, having financial problems, and not owning a home (Lin & others, 2018). Also in this study, onset of an empty nest, the wife's or husband's retirement, and the wife or husband having a chronic health condition were not related to risk for divorce in middle adulthood.
- Inclusion of a recent Korean study in which middle-aged individuals who were divorced were more likely to smoke, binge drink, get inadequate sleep, and be depressed than their married counterparts (Kim, Lee, & Park, 2018)
- Updated data on the percentage of older adults who are divorced (U.S. Census Bureau, 2016)
- New research on the factors that are associated with having a longer marriage as older adults (Lin & others, 2018)
- Inclusion of a recent study of older adults in Great Britain that revealed those who were divorced were more likely to die earlier and have lower life satisfaction than their married counterparts (Bourassa, Ruiz, & Sbarra, 2019)
- Description of a recent study in which partnered older adults were more likely to receive social security benefits and less likely to live in poverty (Lin, Brown, & Hammersmith, 2017)
- New discussion of why remarried adults often find it difficult to stay married and their divorce rate is increasing (Ganong & Coleman, 2018)
- Coverage of a recent study involving the Bringing Home Baby project found that fathers who participated in the program

- felt more appreciated by their wives and also wives were more satisfied with the division of labor when fathers were more involved in parenting (Shapiro, Gottman, & Fink, 2019)
- Inclusion of a recent study that found better parental monitoring was linked to lower marijuana use by adolescents (Haas & others, 2018) and another study that revealed lower parental monitoring was associated with earlier initiation of alcohol use, binge drinking, and marijuana use in 13- to 14-year-olds (Rusby & others, 2018)
- Description of a recent study that indicated parental media monitoring was linked to lower media use by adolescents (Padilla-Walker & others, 2018)
- Discussion of a recent study that discovered a higher level of general parental monitoring of adolescents' money spending, friends, and whereabouts was linked to the adolescents having a lower weight status, better dietary habits, more physical exercise, and less screen time (Kim & others, 2019)
- Coverage of a recent study of young adolescents that revealed they got more sleep when their parents engaged in more monitoring of their waking activities (Gunn & others, 2019)
- Inclusion of recent research that found adolescents who engaged in problem behavior were more secretive and disclosed less information to parents (Darling & Tilton-Weaver, 2019)
- Coverage of a recent study in which an authoritarian style, as well as pressure to eat, were associated with a higher risk for being overweight or obese in young children (Melis Yavuz & Selkuk, 2018)
- Description of a recent study that revealed authoritarian parenting was associated with being a bully perpetrator in adolescence (Krisnana & others, 2019)
- Discussion of a recent study that found authoritarian parenting was linked to all forms of child maltreatment while authoritative parenting was associated with a lower risk for all types of child maltreatment (Lo & others, 2019)
- Inclusion of a recent review that concluded there is widespread approval of corporal punishment by U.S. parents (Ciocca, 2017)
- Description of a recent study in which daughters reported being less likely to experience physical punishment and the daughters also indicated they were less likely to be physically punished by both parents (Mehlhasen-Hassoen, 2019)
- Discussion of recent research that revealed coparenting when children were 3- to 5-years-of-age was linked less to externalizing problems 8 to 10 years later (Parkes, Green, & Mitchell, 2019)
- Updated data on the extent of child maltreatment in the United States, including new data on specific types of abuse
- Coverage of a recent study that found physical abuse was linked to lower levels of cognitive performance and school engagement in children (Font & Cage, 2018)
- Discussion of a longitudinal study in which experiencing early abuse and neglect in the first five years of life was linked to having more interpersonal problems and lower academic achievement from childhood through their 30s (Raby & others, 2019)
- Description of a recent study of Chinese American families that found parent-adolescent conflict increased in early adolescence, peaked at about 16 years of age, and then declined through late adolescence and emerging adulthood (Juang & others, 2018)
- Coverage of a recent study that revealed when they had grown up in poverty, adolescents engaged in less risk-taking if they had a history of secure attachments to caregivers (Delker, Bernstein, & Laurent, 2018)
- Inclusion of a recent analysis that found secure attachment to the mother and to the father was associated with fewer depressive symptoms in adolescents (Kerstis, Aslund, & Sonnby, 2018)
- Coverage of recent research indicating the continued importance of parenting through the fourth year of college as low parental permissiveness was associated with reducing risk for drinking even as their offspring turned 21 (Mallett & others, 2019)
- Inclusion of a recent cross-cultural study that found college students in four countries (United States, Germany, Hong Kong, and Korea) experienced frequent contact with and support from their parents (Fingerman & others, 2017). In this study, Asian students were given more frequent support than U.S. or German students but were less satisfied with it.
- Description of two recent national surveys on working parents focusing on various issues in working parent families (Career Builder, 2018; Livingston & Bialik, 2018)
- Discussion of a recent study in which experiencing parents' divorce, as well as child maltreatment, in childhood was linked to midlife suicide ideation (Stansfield & others, 2017)
- Inclusion of a recent meta-analysis that revealed when their parents had become divorced, as adults they were more likely to have depression (Sands, Thompson, & Gavsina, 2017)
- Description of a recent study in which stepfathers' affinity-seeking (developing a friendship relation with his stepchildren) was linked to less conflict with stepchildren, a better couple relationship, and closer stepfamily ties (Ganong & others, 2019)
- Inclusion of recent research indicating that positive adolescent-stepfather relationship quality was associated with a higher level of physical health and a lower level of mental health problems for adolescents (Jensen & Harris, 2017; Jensen & others, 2018)
- Coverage of a large-scale study that found a birth order effect for intelligence, with older siblings having slightly higher intelligence, but no birth order effects for life satisfaction, internal/external control, trust, risk taking, patience, and impulsivity (Rohrer, Egloff, & Schukle, 2017)
- Description of a recent cross-cultural study in which U.S. grandparents were characterized by higher parental efficacy, more role satisfaction, better well-being, and more attachment than Chinese grandparents, who were characterized by more resilience and a higher level of authoritative parenting (Wang & others, 2019)
- Discussion of a recent study in which high levels of parental control and helicopter parenting were detrimental to emerging adults' vocational identity development and perceived competence in transitioning to adulthood (Lindell, Campione-Barr, & Killoren, 2017)
- Coverage of a recent study that revealed helicopter parenting was related to more negative emotional functioning, less competent decision making, and lower grades/poorer adjustment in college students (Luebbe & others, 2018)
- New content on "lawnmower parents" who "mow down" obstacles, stressors, and potential failure for children rather than let them learn how to make decisions and develop coping strategies on their own

Chapter 15: Peers and the Sociocultural World

- Description of a recent study of adolescents in which peer rejection increased the likelihood that both victims and bullies would engage in increased non-suicidal self-injury (Esposito, Bacchini, & Affuso, 2019)

- Inclusion of recent research indicating that mothers with a permissive parenting style have adolescents who are negatively attached to their peers (Llorca, Richaud, & Malonda, 2017)

- Coverage of a recent study of 12- to 15-year-olds in 48 countries worldwide that found being the victim of bullying was linked to an increased risk of suicide in 47 of the 48 countries (Koyanagi & others, 2019)

- New commentary about overweight and obese children being at risk for being bullied (Bacchini & others, 2017)

- Description of a recent study of 10- to 14-year-olds in which being a victim of a bully often led to a cascading effect of bullying perpetration that eventually produced disordered eating behavior (Lee & Vaillancourt, 2019)

- Coverage of a recent study that revealed the most common behavioral reactions to cyberbullying were informing a friend, counterattacking, and ignoring the cyber incident (Heiman, Olenik-Shemesh, & Frank, 2019)

- New discussion of five ways that social media have transformed the way that peer and friendship interactions and relationships take place in adolescence (Nesi, Choukas-Bradley, & Prinstein, 2018)

- Description of a recent study of 2- to 5-year-olds in which television/DVD/video viewing was negatively linked to young children's social skills, while outdoor play was positively associated with their social skills (Hinkley & others, 2018)

- Coverage of a Danish study across 33 years of individuals 20 to 93 years of age found that those who engaged in a light level of leisure time physical activity lived 2.8 years longer, those who engaged in a moderate level of leisure time physical activity lived 4.5 years longer, and those who engaged in a high level of leisure time physical activity lived 5.5 years longer (Schnohr & others, 2017)

- Inclusion of a recent study of more than 300,000 individuals 50 to 71 years of age in which those who engaged in the most leisure-time physical activity were at lower risk for all cause, cardiovascular-related disease related, and cancer-related mortality (Saint-Maurice & others, 2019)

- Discussion of a recent study of 29 European countries that examined age discrimination in individuals aged 15 to 115 years of age (Bratt & others, 2018). In this study, younger individuals displayed more age discrimination than did older individuals.

- Coverage of a recent research review that concluded Japan is becoming more individualistic in a number of areas of people's lives (Ogihara, 2017)

- Description of a recent study of preschool children in which those who used screen time two or more hours a day were much more likely to have inattention problems compared with children who used screen time less than 30 minutes a day, including a higher risk of developing ADHD symptoms and externalizing problems (Tamana & others, 2019)

- Discussion of a recent study of 13- to 16-year-olds that found increased night-time mobile phone use was linked to increased externalizing problems and decreased self-esteem (Vernon, Modecki, & Barber, 2018)

- Inclusion of information about adolescents' engaging in media multitasking while they are doing homework and almost two-thirds don't think it interferes with the quality of their homework (Common Sense Media, 2015)

- Coverage of a recent study of 11- to 18-year-olds in Spain in which media multitasking during homework was linked to lower executive function, a lower level of working memory, and worse academic performance in language and math (Martin-Perona, Vinas Poch, & Malo Cerrato, 2019)

- Description of a recent meta-analysis that found children's exposure to prosocial media is linked to higher levels of prosocial behavior and empathetic concern (Coyne & others, 2018)

- Coverage of two recent research views indicating that violent videogame exposure is linked to increased aggression and decreased empathy and prosocial behavior in children and adolescents (Anderson & others, 2017; Calvert & others, 2017)

- Inclusion of a recent study in which African American and Latino adolescents who have lived 10 to 15 years in a high poverty neighborhood improved their physical fitness by playing Wii Fit games for 6 weeks (Flynn & others, 2018)

- Discussion of recent research indicating that parental monitoring of media violence exposure was liked to lower levels of aggression in adolescents (Khurana & others, 2018)

- Description of two recent studies of adolescents that found higher levels of screen time were linked to lower academic achievement (Hunter & others, 2018; Poulan & others, 2018)

- Coverage of recent research that found less screen time was linked to adolescents' better health-related quality of life (Yan & others, 2017) and that a higher level of social media use was associated with a higher level of heavy drinking by adolescents (Brunborg, Andreas, & Kvaavik, 2017)

- Coverage of a recent national study of social media indicating how extensively 18- to 24-year-olds are using various sites such as Snapchat, Instagram, twitter, and YouTube (Smith & Anderson, 2018)

- Updated data on the significant increase in Internet, smartphone, and social networking use by U.S. older adults (Anderson, 2017)

- Coverage of a recent Hong Kong study that found adults 75 years and older who used smartphones and the Internet to connect with family, friends, and neighbors had a higher level of psychological well-being than their counterparts who did not use this information and communicative technology (Fang & others, 2018)

- Inclusion of a recent survey that revealed older adults continue to watch extensive amounts of television (51+ hours per week), far more than any age group (Recode, 2016)

- Description of a recent study that found of 13 risk factors, low SES was the most likely to be associated with smoking initiation in fifth graders (Wellman & others, 2017)

- Discussion of a recent Chinese study in which adolescents were more likely to have depressive symptoms in low SES families (Zhou, Fan, & Zin, 2017)

- Coverage of a U.S. longitudinal study that revealed low SES in adolescence was linked to having a higher level of depressive symptoms at age 54 for females (Pino & others, 2018). In this study, low SES females who completed college were less likely to have depressive symptoms than low SES females who did not complete college.
- Inclusion of a U.S. longitudinal study that found low SES in adolescence was a risk factor for cardiovascular disease 30 years later (Doom & others, 2017)
- Coverage of a longitudinal study that indicated low child SES was associated with lower cognitive function and more cognitive decline in middle and late adulthood (Liu & Lachman, 2019)
- Description of a recent Australian study in which children and adolescents from lower SES backgrounds were less likely to achieve a healthy level of physical fitness than their higher SES counterparts (Peralta & others, 2019)
- Inclusion of a recent study of more than 13,000 high school students that found those who attended more affluent schools had a greater likelihood of drug use, being intoxicated, and engaging in property crime while those who attended poorer schools were more likely to have a higher level of depressive and anxiety symptoms, as well as engaging in more violent behavior (Coley & others, 2018)
- Updated poverty rates for African American, Latino, and non-Latino White children under 18 years of age (U.S. Census Bureau, 2018)
- Updated poverty rates for single parent mothers (U.S. Census Bureau, 2018)
- Updated poverty data for older adults, including gender and ethnic variations (U.S. Census Bureau, 2018)
- New opening commentary in the section on Ethnicity focused on the importance of not using a deficit model in studying ethnic minority adolescents and to recognize not just stressors in their lives but also the positive aspects of their lives (Bornstein & Cote, 2019; Helegunseth, 2019; Perreria & others, 2019)
- Updated data on the percentage of 18-year-old and younger children from different ethnic groups as well as predictions on when ethnic minority children will begin to outnumber non-Latino White children in the U.S. (U.S. Census Bureau, 2018)
- Coverage of a recent study in which immigrant children who were once separated from their parents had a lower level of literacy and a higher level of psychological problems than those who migrated with parents (Lu, He, & Brooks-Gunn, 2019). Also in this study, a protracted period of separation and prior undocumented status of parents further increased the children's disadvantages.
- Inclusion of a recent study that found a higher level of family obligation was associated with higher academic achievement (Anguiano, 2018)

Chapter 16: Schools, Achievement, and Work

- Update on the implementation of ESSA into the American education system (Ujifusa & Klein, 2019; Ujifusa, 2019)
- New description of leading American businessman, Jeff Bezos, the CEO of Amazon who became the world's richest person in 2018, who recently provided 2 billion dollars to fund a new network of preschools in underserved communities that he says will be Montessori inspired (Guernsey, 2019)
- Coverage of a recent multigenerational study that found when both Head Start children and their mothers had participated in Head Start, positive cognitive and socioemotional outcomes occurred for the children (Chor, 2018)
- Description of two recent studies that confirmed the importance of improved parenting engagement and skills in the success of Head Start programs (Ansari & Gershoff, 2016; Roggman & others, 2016)
- Discussion of an early childhood intervention designed to improve preschool children's developmental outcomes and the Head Start programs they attended in a high violence, high crime area of Chicago (Watts & others, 2018). The program was effective in improving the children's executive function and academic achievement, but not their behavioral outcomes, 10 to 11 years after the intervention.
- Inclusion of a recent Spanish study that documented middle school students had a lower self-concept in a number of areas (academic, social, family, and physical) than elementary school students (Onetti, Fernandez-Garcia, & Castillo-Rodriquez, 2019)
- Coverage of a recent study in which teacher warmth was higher in the last 4 years of elementary school then dropped in the middle school years (Hughes & Cao, 2018). The drop in teacher warmth was associated with lower student math scores.
- Description of a longitudinal study that found both breadth and intensity of extracurricular activities in the tenth grade were associated with higher educational attainment 8 years later (Haghighat & Knifsend, 2019)
- Inclusion of new information on the Bill and Melinda Gates Foundation (2017, 2019) indicating that many adolescents graduate from high school without the necessary academic skills to succeed in college or to meet the demands of the modern workplace
- Updated data on school dropout rates, which have dropped considerably in recent years with the biggest percentage decline occurring for Latino adolescents (National Center for Education Statistics, 2018)
- Updated data on lifetime and annual earnings of college graduates versus high school graduates (Georgetown University Center on Education, 2016)
- Updated data on the percentage of first-year college students who feel overwhelmed with what they have to, which has increased to almost 40 percent (Stolzenberg & others, 2019)
- Updated data on the percentage of children with a disability receiving special education services in different disability categories (National Center for Education Statistics, 2017)
- New content on links between ADHD and increased risk of school dropout, adolescent pregnancy, substance abuse, and antisocial behavior (Machado & others, 2019; Regnart, Truter, & Meyer, 2017)
- Discussion of a recent study that found childhood ADHD was associated with long-term underachievement in math and reading (Voight & others, 2017)
- Inclusion of a recent study that revealed children with ADHD were more likely to become parents at 12 to 16 years of age (Ostergaard & others, 2017)

- Coverage of a recent meta-analysis that found neurofeedback had medium effects on improving children's attention and reducing their hyperactivity/impulsivity (Van Doren & others, 2019)

- Discussion of a research review that indicated physical exercise was effective in improving the attention of children with ADHD (Jeyanthi, Arumugam, & Parasher, 2019)

- Description of a recent review that concluded there are approximately 800 genes linked to autism (Gabrielli, Manzardo, & Butler, 2019)

- Inclusion of a longitudinal study that involved implementation of the Child-Parent Center Program in high-poverty neighborhoods of Chicago that provided school-based educational enrichment and comprehensive family services from 3 to 9 years of age (Reynolds, Ou, & Temple, 2018). Children who participated in the program had higher rates of postsecondary completion, including more years of education, an associate's degree or higher, and a master's degree.

- New content on Teach for America (2019) and its efforts to place college graduates in teaching positions in schools located in low-income areas and a new *Connecting with Careers* feature on a Teach for America instructor

- Inclusion of a recent meta-analysis that concluded self-determination plays a central role in human motivation (Howard, Gagne, & Bureau, 2018)

- Description of a recent Chinese study in which autonomy-supportive parenting was asscociated with adolescents' adaptive school adjustment, while a higher level of parental psychological control was linked to their maladaptive school adjustment (Xiang, Liu, & Bai, 2017)

- Discussion of a recent study that revealed having a growth mindset protected women's and minorities' outlook when they chose to confront expressions of bias toward them in the workplace (Rattan & Dweck, 2018)

- New main section, "Grit"

- Inclusion of recent research linking grit to academic engagement and success, including students' grade point average (Muenks, 2018; Steinmayr, Weidinger, & Wigfield, 2018)

- Updated information about the fastest growing jobs anticipated through 2026 in the 2018–2019 *Occupational Outlook Handbook*

- Updated data on the percentage of full-time and part-time college students who work, which has slightly decreased in recent years (National Center for Education Statistics, 2017)

- Updated data from a recent survey that revealed that employers say that 2017 is the best year for recent college graduates to be on the job market since 2007 (CareerBuilder, 2017)

- Inclusion of recent research in which an increase in job strain increased workers' insomnia while a decrease in job strain reduced their insomnia (Halonen & others, 2018)

- Description of a recent study that found depression following job loss predicted increased risk of continued unemployment (Stolove & others, 2017)

- Discussion of a recent study in which following a period of unemployment, recovery of a sense of well-being upon reemployment was fast and enduring even when individuals took less favorable jobs upon returning to work (Zhou & othes, 2019)

- Coverage of a study that revealed heavy drinking from 16 to 30 years of age was linked to higher unemployment in middle age (Berg & others, 2018)

- Update on job outlook for U.S. college graduates in 2018, which is the best it has been in more than a decade (careerbuilder.com)

- Inclusion of a recent study in which heavy drinking from 16 to 30 years of age was linked to a greater risk of being unemployed in middle adulthood (Berg & others, 2018)

- Discussion of a recent study that indicated the following were among the most important motives and preconditions involved when older adults worked beyond retirement age: financial, health, knowledge, and purpose in life (Swedas & others, 2017)

- Inclusion of a recent study that revealed older adults who continued to work in paid jobs had better physical and cognitive functioning than retirees (Tan & others, 2017)

- Coverage of recent cross-cultural comparisons of retirement age, with France having the earliest age and South Korea the oldest (OECD, 2017)

- Description of a recent study that revealed workplace organizational pressures, financial security, and poor physical and mental health were the main antecedents of retirement (Topa, Depolo, & Alcover, 2018)

Chapter 17: Death, Dying, and Grieving

- Inclusion of a recent study in which completion of an advanced directive was associated with a lower probability of receiving life-sustaining treatment (Yen & others, 2018)

- New separate descriptions and recent updates of countries that allow euthanasia (Belgium, Colombia, Luxembourg, and the Netherlands) and assisted suicide (Belgium, Canada, Finland, Luxembourg, the Netherlands, and Switzerland)

- Update on the increasing number of states that allow assisted suicide—California, Colorado, Montana, Oregon, Vermont, and Washington, as well as Washington, DC

- New definition of assisted suicide as a key term and clearer distinctions made between euthanasia, in which the patient self-administers the lethal medication and is allowed to decide when and where to do this (assisted suicide), and euthanasia, in which the physician or a third party administers the lethal medication

- Inclusion of a recent Gallup poll in which 69 percent of U.S. adults said that euthanasia should be legal, 51 percent said that they would consider ending their own lives if faced with a terminal illness, and 50 percent reported that physician-assisted suicide is morally acceptable (Swift, 2016)

- New content on recent criticisms of the "good death" concept to move away from focusing on a single event in time to improving people's last years and decades of life (Pollock & Seymour; Smith & Periyakoil, 2018)

- New coverage of the shortage of trained individuals to work in hospices and as home health aides for dying individuals (Landes & Weng, 2019)

- Significantly revised content in the section on children's conceptions of death to include recent research indicating that young children have a better understanding of death than previously thought, as well as developmental changes that occur (Panagiotaki & others, 2018; Rosengren, Guitierrez, & Schein, 2014a,b)

- Coverage of a recent research review that concluded relatively brief interventions with bereaved children after the death of a parent can prevent children from developing severe problems, such as traumatic grief and mental disorders (Bergman, Axberg, & Hanson, 2017)

- Description of recent experimental studies that found the Family Bereavement Program, a 12-session program designed to promote effective parenting and teach coping skills following the death of a parent or caregiver, was effective in improving children's and adolescents' adjustment 6 years after the program (Sandler & others, 2017)

- Discussion of a recent study in which the Family Bereavement Program resulted in fewer mental health problems and less service use by bereaved young adults and their parents (Sandler & others, 2018)

- Inclusion of a study of young and middle-aged adults in which women had more difficulty than men in adjusting to the death of a parent and also women had a more intense grief response to a parent's death (Hayslip, Purett, & Caballero, 2015)

- New coverage of suicide rates for individuals of all ages, with Lithuania having the highest rate, followed by South Korea, and South Africa having the lowest rate (OECD, 2017)

- New discussion of cross-cultural suicide rates for 15- to 19-year-olds, with New Zealand, followed by Iceland, having the highest rates, and Greece and Israel the lowest rates (OECD, 2017)

- Updated data on the percentage of U.S. adolescents who seriously consider suicide each year and attempt suicide each year, including gender and ethnicity figures (Kann & others, 2018)

- New coverage of the influence of genes on adolescent suicide (Jokinen & others, 2018)

- Description of a recent study that confirmed childhood sexual abuse was linked to later suicide attempts (Ng & others, 2018)

- Coverage of a recent study in which a sense of hopelessness predicted an increase in suicide ideation in depressed adolescents (Wolfe & others, 2019)

- Discussion of a recent cross-cultural study of more than 130,000 12-to 15-year-olds that indicated that in 47 of 48 countries being a victim of bullying was associated with a higher probability of attempting suicide (Kovangi & others, 2019)

- Inclusion of a recent research review that revealed half of the studies involving heart failure patient interventions emphasizing meaning-making coping substantially improved the quality of life of the patients compared to less than one-third of the interventions not focusing on meaning-making coping (self-care or medical adherence, for example) (Sacco, Leahey, & Park, 2019)

- Coverage of a recent study in which meaning was negatively associated with depression but positively linked to grief in suicide survivors (Scharer & Hibberd, 2019)

- New research on the percentage of adult bereavement cases that involve prolonged grief disorder and ages at which this disorder is more likely to occur (Lundorff & others, 2017)

- Inclusion of a 7-year longitudinal study of older adults in which those experiencing prolonged grief had greater cognitive decline than those with normal grief (Perez & others, 2018)

- Discussion of a recent study that found individuals with complicated grief had a higher level of the personality trait neuroticism (Goetter & others, 2019)

- In recent research, cognitive behavior therapy reduced prolonged grief symptoms (Bartl & others, 2018; Lichtenthal & others, 2019)

- Updated content about a recent extension of the dual-process model of bereavement, which focused mainly on an individual's bereavement, toward an integrative intrapersonal/interpersonal model that includes bereaved immediate family members and relatives who also have experienced the loss (Stroebe & others, 2017; Stroebe & Schutt, 2017)

- Inclusion of recent research using the dual-process model as a conceptual framework, including studies on parents' use of oscillating coping strategies following their infant's death (Currie & others, 2019) and the importance of restoration-rather than loss-oriented coping both early and late in the bereavement process following a spouse's death (Lundorff & others, 2019)

- Description of a recent meta-analysis of mental disorders in widows with depressive disorders being the most prevalent followed by anxiety disorders (Balnner Kristiansen & others, 2019)

- Coverage of a recent study of widows' and widowers' mental health coping strategies in which widows were more likely to use positive reframing, active distraction, help-seeking, and turning to God for strength, while widowers were more likely to use avoidant strategies and seek connection with their late spouse (Carr, 2019)

- In a recent study, volunteering reduced widowed older adults' loneliness (Carr & others, 2018)

- Updated data on cremation with continuing increases in cremation in the United States and Canada (Cremation Association of North America, 2018)

- Updated data on the percentage of widowed women and men 65 years and older in the United States (Administration on Aging, 2018)

acknowledgments

I very much appreciate the support and guidance provided to me by many people at McGraw-Hill. Ryan Treat, Senior Portfolio Manager for Psychology, has provided excellent guidance, vision, and direction for this edition. Vicki Malinee provided considerable expertise in coordinating many aspects of the editorial process. Janet Tilden again did an outstanding job as the text's copy editor. Mary Powers did a terrific job in coordinating the text's production. Dawn Groundwater, Product Development Manager, did excellent work on various aspects of the development, technology, and learning systems. Thanks also to A.J. Laferrera and Olivia Kaiser for their extensive and outstanding work in marketing *A Topical Approach to Life-Span Development*. And Jennifer Blankenship again has provided me with excellent choices of new photographs.

I also want to thank my parents, John and Ruth Santrock, my wife, Mary Jo, our children, Tracy and Jennifer, and our grandchildren, Jordan, Alex, and Luke, for their wonderful contributions to my life and for helping me to better understand the marvels and mysteries of life-span development.

QUEST: JOURNEY THROUGH THE LIFESPAN BOARD OF ADVISORS AND SUBJECT MATTER EXPERTS

Admiration and appreciation to the following experts who have devoted a significant portion of their time and expertise to creating the first of its kind learning game for Developmental Psychology: Cheri Kittrell, *State College of Florida*; Brandy Young, *Cypress College*; Becky Howell, *Forsyth Technical College*; Gabby Principe, *College of Charleston*; Karen Schrier Shaenfield, *Marist College*; Steven Prunier, *Ivy Tech*; Amy Kolak, *College of Charleston*; Kathleen Hughes Stellmach, *Pasco-Hernando State College*; Lisa Fozio-Thielk, *Waubonsee Community College*; Tricia Wessel-Blaski, *University of Wisconsin-Milwaukee, Washington County*; Margot Underwood, *Joliet Junior College*; Claire Rubman, *Suffolk County Community College*; Alissa Knowles, *University of California- Irvine*; Cortney Simmons, *University of California-Irvine*; Kelli Dunlap; Level Access-WCAG Accessibility Partners.

EXPERT CONSULTANTS

As I develop a new edition, I consult with leading experts in their respective areas of life-span development. Their invaluable feedback ensures that the latest research, knowledge, and perspectives are presented. Their willingness to devote their time and expertise to this endeavor is greatly appreciated. The Expert Consultants who contributed to this edition can be found on pages xii-xiv.

REVIEWERS

I owe a special debt of gratitude to the reviewers who have provided detailed feedback on *A Topical Approach to Life-Span Development* over the years.

Anora Ackerson, *Kalamazoo Community College*; **Katherine Adams,** *Valdosta State University*; **Randy Allen,** *Barton Community College*; **Denise M. Arehart,** *University of Colorado–Denver*; **Harriet Bachner,** *Northeastern State University*; **Andrea Backschneider,** *University of Houston*; **Catherine E. Barnard,** *Kalamazoo Valley Community College*; **Terra Bartee,** *Cisco Community College*; **Sheri Bauman,** *University of Arizona*; **Jay Belsky,** *Birkbeck College, University of London*; **James E. Birren,** *University of California–Los Angeles*; **Tracie L. Blumentritt,** *University of Wisconsin–La Crosse*; **John Bonvillian,** *University of Virginia*; **Janet Boseovski,** *University of North Carolina–Greensboro*; **Brenda Butterfield,** *University of Minnesota–Duluth*; **Ann Calhoun-Sauls,** *Belmont Abbey College*; **Silvia Canetto,** *Colorado State University*; **Rick Chandler,** *Itawamba Community College*; **Andrea D. Clements,** *East Tennessee State University*; **Sunshine Corwan,** *University of Central Oklahoma*; **Gregory Cutler,** *Bay de Noc Community College*; **Scott Delys,** *North Central Texas College*; **Susanne Denham,** *George Mason University*; **Kimberly DuVall,** *James Madison University*; **Jerri Edwards,** *University of South Florida–Tampa*; **Marion A. Eppler,** *East Carolina University*; **Carolyn Fallahi,** *Central Connecticut State University*; **Dan P. Fawaz,** *Georgia Perimeter College*; **E. Richard Ferraro,** *University of North Dakota*; **Fan Flovell,** *Eastern Kentucky University*; **James Forbes,** *Angelo State University*; **Tom Frangicetto,** *Northampton Community College*; **James Garbarino,** *Cornell University*; **Janet Gebelt,** *University of Portland*; **Suzanne Gibson,** *Meridian Community College*; **Gilbert Gottlieb,** *University of North Carolina-Chapel Hill*; **Trione Grayson,** *Florida Community College at Jacksonville, South Campus*; **Elena Grigorenko,** *Yale University*; **James Guinee,** *University of Central Arkansas*; **Jim Hanson,** *Grand View University*; **Yvette Harris,** *Miami (Ohio) University*; **Carol H. Hoare,** *George Washington University*; **Scott Hofer,** *Pennsylvania State University*; **La Tishia Horrell,** *Ivy Tech Community College*; **William Hoyer,** *Syracuse University*; **Fergus Hughes,** *University of Wisconsin*; **Mary P. Hughes Stone,** *San Francisco State University*; **Janet Shibley Hyde,** *University of Wisconsin–Madison*; **Alisah Janowsky,** *University of Central Florida*; **Emily J. Johnson,** *University of Wisconsin–La Crosse*; **Seth Kalichman,** *University of Connecticut*; **Robert Kastenbaum,** *Emeritus, Arizona State University*; **Kevin Keating,** *Broward Community College*; **Rachel Keen,** *University of Virginia*; **Sue Kelley,** *Lycoming College*; **Melanie Killian,** *University of Maryland*; **Larry Kollman,** *North Area Iowa Community College–Mason City*; **Suzanne G. Krinsky,** *University of Southern Colorado*; **Richard P. Lanthier,** *George Washington University*; **Kathleen Lawler,** *University of Tennessee*; **Gary Leka,** *University of Texas–Pan American*; **Gloria Lopez,** *Sacramento City College*; **Salvador Macias III,** *University of South Carolina*; **James Marcia,** *Simon Fraser University*; **Carole Martin,** *Colorado College*; **Gabriela Martorell,** *Portland State University*; **Linda Mayes,** *Yale University*; **Lara Mayeux,** *University of Oklahoma–Norman*; **Monica McCoy,** *Converse College*; **Katrina McDaniel,** *Barton College*; **Sharon McNeely,** *Northeastern Illinois University*; **Gigliana Meltzi,** *New York University*; **Patricia A. Mills,** *Miami University*; **Daniel K. Mroczek,** *Fordham University*; **Winnie Mucherah,** *Ball State University*; **Bridget Murphy-Kelsey,** *University of Oklahoma*; **Charles Nelson,** *Harvard University*; **Margaret M. Norwood,** *Thomas Nelson Community College*; **Lois Oestreich,** *Salt Lake Community College*; **Pamela Balls Organista,** *University of San Francisco*; **Rob Palkovitz,** *University of Delaware*; **Debbie Palmer,** *University of Wisconsin–Stevens Point*; **Laura Pannell,** *Itawamba Community College*; **Crystal Park,** *University of Connecticut*; **Denise Park,** *University of Texas at Dallas*; **Ross Parke,** *University of California–Riverside*; **Scott Peterson,** *Cameron University*; **Warren Phillips,** *Iowa State University*; **Peter Phipps,** *Dutchess Community College*; **Janet Polivy,** *University of Toronto*; **James S. Previte,** *Victor Valley College*; **Mary Kay Reed,** *York College of Pennsylvania*; **Janet Reis,** *University of Illinois–Champaign*; **Madeline Rex-Lear,** *University of Texas–Arlington*; **Elizabeth Rodriguez,** *Salt Lake City Community College*; **Theresa Sawyer,** *Carroll Community College*; **Kim Schrenk,** *Montana State University*; **Pamela Schuetze,** *Buffalo State College*; **Matthew Scullin,** *West Virginia University*; **Rebecca Shiner,** *Colgate University*; **Jerry Snead,** *Coastal Carolina Community College*; **Karina Sokol,** *Glendale Community College*; **Thomas D. Spencer,** *San Francisco State University*; **Robert J. Sternberg,** *University of Colorado*; **Robert B. Stewart, Jr.,** *Oakland University*; **Pam Terry,** *Gordon College*; **Ross Thompson,** *University of California–Davis*; **Jonathan Tudge,** *University of North Carolina–Greensboro*; **Robin Valeri,** *St. Bonaventure University*; **Kay Walsh,** *James Madison University*; **Allan Wigfield,** *University of Maryland*; **Clarissa Willis,** *Arkansas Technical University*; **Linda M. Woolf,** *Webster University*; **Dawn Young,** *Boissier Parish Community College*.

All the world's a stage,
And all the men and women merely players;
They have their exits and their entrances,
And one man in his time plays many parts.

—WILLIAM SHAKESPEARE
English Playwright, 17th Century.

The Life-Span Perspective

Our focus in this course is on human development—its universal features, its individual variations, its nature. Every life is distinct, a new biography in the world. Examining the shape of life-span development allows us to understand it better. *A Topical Approach to Life-Span Development* is about the rhythm and meaning of people's lives, about turning mystery into under-standing, and about weaving a portrait of who each of us was, is, and will be. In Section 1, you will read the chapter titled "Introduction."

chapter 1

INTRODUCTION

chapter outline

① The Life-Span Perspective

Learning Goal 1 Discuss the distinctive features of a life-span perspective on development.

The Importance of Studying Life-Span Development
Characteristics of the Life-Span Perspective
Some Contemporary Concerns

② The Nature of Development

Learning Goal 2 Identify the most important processes, periods, and issues in development.

Biological, Cognitive, and Socioemotional Processes
Periods of Development
The Significance of Age
Developmental Issues

③ Theories of Development

Learning Goal 3 Describe the main theories of human development.

Psychoanalytic Theories
Cognitive Theories
Behavioral and Social Cognitive Theories
Ethological Theory
Ecological Theory
An Eclectic Theoretical Orientation

④ Research on Life-Span Development

Learning Goal 4 Explain how research on life-span development is conducted.

Methods for Collecting Data
Research Designs
Time Span of Research
Conducting Ethical Research
Minimizing Bias

Ariel Skelley/Blend Images/Getty Images

preview

A Topical Approach to Life-Span Development is a window into the journey of human development—your own and that of every other member of the human species. Every life is distinct, a new biography in the world. Examining the shape of life-span development helps us to understand it better. In this chapter, we explore what it means to take a life-span perspective on development, examine the nature of development, discuss theories of development, and outline how science helps us to understand it.

1 The Life-Span Perspective

 LG1 Discuss the distinctive features of a life-span perspective on development.

| The Importance of Studying Life-Span Development | Characteristics of the Life-Span Perspective | Some Contemporary Concerns |

Each of us develops partly like all other individuals, partly like some other individuals, and partly like no other individuals. Most of the time, our attention is directed to an individual's uniqueness. But as humans, we have all traveled some common paths. Each of us—Leonardo da Vinci, Joan of Arc, George Washington, Martin Luther King, Jr., and you—walked at about 1 year, engaged in fantasy play as a young child, and became more independent as a youth. Each of us, if we live long enough, will experience hearing problems and the death of family members and friends. This is the general course of our **development**—the pattern of movement or change that begins at conception and continues through the human life span.

In this section, we explore what is meant by the concept of development and why the study of life-span development is important. We outline the main characteristics of the life-span perspective and discuss various sources of contextual influences. In addition, we examine some contemporary concerns in life-span development.

THE IMPORTANCE OF STUDYING LIFE-SPAN DEVELOPMENT

How might people benefit from examining life-span development? Perhaps you are, or will be, a parent or a teacher. If so, responsibility for children is, or will be, a part of your everyday life. The more you learn about them, the better you can deal with them. Perhaps you hope to gain some insight about your own history—as an infant, a child, an adolescent, or an adult. Perhaps you want to know more about what your life will be like as you move through the adult years—as a middle-aged adult or as an adult in old age, for example. Or perhaps you have just stumbled upon this course, thinking that it sounded intriguing and that the study of the human life span might raise some provocative issues. Whatever your reasons, you will discover that the study of life-span development is filled with intriguing information about who we are, how we came to be this way, and where our future will take us.

Most development involves growth, but it also includes decline and dying. In exploring development, we examine the life span from the point of conception until the time when life—at least, life as we know it—ends. You will see yourself as an infant, as a child, and as an adolescent, and be stimulated to think about how those years influenced the kind of individual you are today. And you will see yourself as a young adult, as a middle-aged adult, and as an adult in old age, and be motivated to think about how your experiences today will influence your development through the remainder of your adult years.

CHARACTERISTICS OF THE LIFE-SPAN PERSPECTIVE

Although growth and development are dramatic during the first two decades of life, development is not something that happens only to children and adolescents (Benetos, 2019; Park & Festini, 2018). The traditional approach to the study of development emphasizes

development The pattern of movement or change that begins at conception and continues through the human life span.

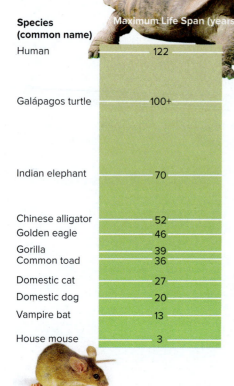

Species (common name)	Maximum Life Span (years)
Human	122
Galápagos turtle	100+
Indian elephant	70
Chinese alligator	52
Golden eagle	46
Gorilla	39
Common toad	36
Domestic cat	27
Domestic dog	20
Vampire bat	13
House mouse	3

FIGURE 1

MAXIMUM RECORDED LIFE SPAN FOR DIFFERENT SPECIES. Our only competitor for the maximum recorded life span is the Galápagos turtle.
(tortoise): MedioImages/SuperStock;
(mouse): Redmond Durrell/Alamy Stock Photo

extensive change from birth to adolescence (especially during infancy), little or no change during adulthood, and decline in old age. But a great deal of change does occur in the five or six decades after adolescence. The life-span perspective emphasizes developmental change throughout adulthood as well as during childhood.

The recent increase in human life expectancy has contributed to the popularity of the life-span approach to development. The upper boundary of the human life span (based on the oldest age documented) is 122 years, as indicated in Figure 1; this maximum life span of humans has not changed since the beginning of recorded history. What has changed is *life expectancy:* the average number of years that a person born in a particular year can expect to live. During the twentieth century alone, life expectancy in the United States increased by 30 years, thanks to improvements in sanitation, nutrition, and medicine (see Figure 2). For individuals born in 2017 in the United States, their life expectancy is 79 years of age (U.S. Census Bureau, 2018).

For the first time in U.S. history, in 2019 there were more people over 60 years of age than under 18 years of age. In less than a century, more years were added to human life expectancy than in all of the prior millennia.

Laura Carstensen (2015, 2016) recently described the challenges and opportunities involved in this dramatic increase in life expectancy. In her view, the remarkable increase in the number of people living into old age has happened in such a short time that science, technology, and social expectations have not kept pace. She proposes that the challenge is to change from a world constructed mainly for young people to a world that is more compatible and supportive for the increasing number of people living to age 100 and beyond.

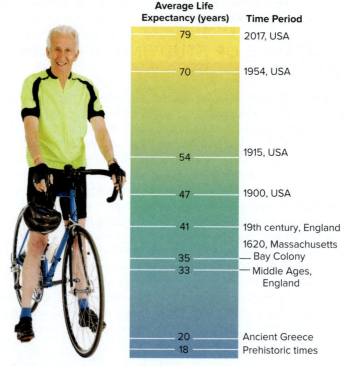

Average Life Expectancy (years)	Time Period
79	2017, USA
70	1954, USA
54	1915, USA
47	1900, USA
41	19th century, England
35	1620, Massachusetts Bay Colony
33	Middle Ages, England
20	Ancient Greece
18	Prehistoric times

FIGURE 2

HUMAN LIFE EXPECTANCY AT BIRTH FROM PREHISTORIC TO CONTEMPORARY TIMES. It took 5,000 years to extend human life expectancy from 18 to 41 years of age.
leezsnow/iStock.com

In further commentary, Carstensen (2015, p. 70) remarked that making this transformation would be no small feat:

> . . . parks, transportation systems, staircases, and even hospitals presume that the users have both strength and stamina; suburbs across the country are built for two parents and their young children, not single people, multiple generations or elderly people who are not able to drive. Our education system serves the needs of young children and young adults and offers little more than recreation for experienced people.
>
> Indeed, the very conception of work as a full-time endeavor ending in the early sixties is ill suited for long lives. Arguably the most troubling is that we fret about ways the older people lack the qualities of younger people rather than exploit a growing new resource right before our eyes: citizens who have deep expertise, emotional balance, and the motivation to make a difference.

What characterizes the life-span perspective on development?
Hill Street Studios/DigitalVision/Getty Images

Certainly, some progress has been made recently in improving the lives of older adults (Fernandez-Ballesteros, 2019; Marquez-Gonzalez, Cheng, & Losada, 2019). In our discussion of late adulthood, you will read about progress in understanding topics related to aging such as modifying the activity of genes related to aging, improving brain function in the elderly, and slowing or even reversing the effects of various chronic diseases. You'll also learn about ways to help people plan for a better life when they get old, become more cognitively sharp as they age, improve their physical fitness, and feel more satisfied with their lives as older adults. But much more remains to be accomplished, as described earlier by Laura Carstensen.

The belief that development occurs throughout life is central to the **life-span perspective** on human development, but this perspective has other characteristics as well. According to life-span development expert Paul Baltes (1939–2006), the life-span perspective views development as lifelong, multidimensional, multidirectional, plastic, multidisciplinary, and contextual, and as a process that involves growth, maintenance, and regulation of loss (Baltes, 1987, 2003; Baltes, Lindenberger, & Staudinger, 2006). In Baltes' view, it is important to understand that development is constructed through biological, sociocultural, and individual factors working together. Let's look at each of these characteristics.

Development Is Lifelong

In the life-span perspective, early adulthood is not the endpoint of development; rather, no age period dominates development. Researchers increasingly study the experiences and psychological orientations of adults at different points in their lives. Later in this chapter, we consider the age periods of development and their characteristics.

Development Is Multidimensional

At every age, your body, your mind, your emotions, and your relationships change and affect each other. Development has biological, cognitive, and socioemotional dimensions (Dale & others, 2018; Moss & Wilson, 2018; Zammit & others, 2018). Within each of these dimensions are many components—for example, attention, memory, abstract thinking, speed of processing information, and social intelligence are just a few of the components of the cognitive dimension.

Development Is Multidirectional

Throughout life, some dimensions or components of a dimension expand and others shrink (Kuntzmann, 2019; Sternberg & Hagen, 2018; Strandberg, 2019). For example, when one language (such as English) is acquired early in development, the capacity for acquiring second and third languages (such as Spanish and Chinese) decreases later in development, especially after early childhood (Levelt, 1989). During adolescence, as individuals establish romantic relationships, their time spent with friends may decrease. During late adulthood, older adults might become wiser by calling on past experience to guide their intellectual decision making (Kuntzmann, 2019; Rakoczy & others, 2018), but they perform more poorly on tasks that require speed in processing information (Karlamangla & others, 2017; Salthouse, 2017).

Development Has Plasticity

Developmentalists debate how much *plasticity* people have in various dimensions at different points in their development (Kinugawa, 2019; Park & Festini, 2018). Plasticity means the capacity for change. For example, can you still improve your intellectual skills when you are in your seventies or eighties? Or might these intellectual skills be fixed by the time you are in your thirties, so that further improvement is impossible? Researchers have found that the cognitive skills of older adults can be improved through training and development of better strategies (Calero, 2019). However, possibly we possess less

One's children's children's children: Look back to us as we look to you; we are related by our imaginations. If we are able to touch, it is because we have imagined each other's existence, our dreams running back and forth along a cable from age to age.

—ROGER ROSENBLATT
American Writer, 20th Century

life-span perspective View of development as being lifelong, multidimensional, multidirectional, plastic, multidisciplinary, and contextual; involving growth, maintenance, and regulation of loss; and constructed through biological, sociocultural, and individual factors working together.

Paul Baltes, a leading architect of the life-span perspective of development, converses with one of the long-time research participants in the Berlin Aging Study that he directs. She joined the study in the early 1990s and has participated six times in extensive physical, medical, psychological, and social assessments. In her professional life, she was a practicing physician.
Margaret M. and Paul B. Baltes Foundation

capacity for change when we become old (Salthouse, 2014, 2017; Shivarama Shetty & Sajikumar, 2017). The search for plasticity and its constraints is a key element on the contemporary agenda for developmental research (Kinugawa, 2019; Walker, 2019).

Developmental Science Is Multidisciplinary Psychologists, sociologists, anthropologists, neuroscientists, and medical researchers all share an interest in unlocking the mysteries of development through the life span. How do your heredity and health limit your intelligence? Do intelligence and social relationships change with age in the same way around the world? How do families and schools influence intellectual development? These are examples of research questions that cut across disciplines.

Development Is Contextual All development occurs within a context, or setting. Contexts include families, neighborhoods, schools, peer groups, work settings, churches, university laboratories, cities, countries, and so on. Each of these settings is influenced by historical, economic, social, and cultural factors (Lowenstein, Katz, & Tur-Sinai, 2019; Wahl & Gitlin, 2019).

Contexts, like individuals, change (Huang & others, 2019; Nair, Roche, & White, 2018). Thus, individuals are changing beings in a changing world. As a result of these changes, contexts exert three types of influences (Baltes, 2003): (1) normative age-graded influences, (2) normative history-graded influences, and (3) nonnormative or highly individualized life events. Each type of influence can have a biological or an environmental impact on development (Lindahl-Jacobsen & Christensen, 2019).

Normative age-graded influences are similar for individuals in a particular age group. These influences include biological processes such as puberty and menopause. They also include sociocultural or environmental processes such as beginning formal education (usually at about age 6 in most cultures) and retirement (which takes place during the fifties and sixties in most cultures).

Normative history-graded influences are common to people of a particular generation because of historical circumstances (Atkins & others, 2019; Jeuring & others, 2019). For example, in their youth, American baby boomers shared experiences that included the Cuban missile crisis, the assassination of John F. Kennedy, and the Beatles invasion. Other examples of normative history-graded influences include economic, political, and social upheavals such as the Great Depression of the 1930s, World War II during the 1940s, the civil rights and women's rights movements of the 1960s and 1970s, the terrorist attacks of 9/11/2001, as well as the integration of computers, smart phones, the Internet, and social media into everyday life in recent decades (Dimock, 2019; Smith & Anderson, 2018). Long-term changes in the genetic and cultural makeup of a population (due to immigration or changes in fertility rates) are also part of normative historical change.

Nonnormative life events are unusual occurrences that have a major impact on an individual's life. These events do not happen to all people, and when they do occur they can influence people in different ways (Kurita, 2019; Shah & others, 2018). Examples include experiencing the death of a parent when one is still a child, becoming pregnant in early adolescence, surviving a fire that destroys one's home, winning the lottery, or getting an unexpected career opportunity.

Nonnormative life events, such as Hurricane Sandy in October 2012, are unusual circumstances that have a major impact on a person's life.
Adam Hunger/Reuters/Landov Images

normative age-graded influences Influences that are similar for individuals in a particular age group.

normative history-graded influences Influences that are common to people of a particular generation because of historical circumstances.

nonnormative life events Unusual occurrences that have a major impact on an individual's life.

Development Involves Growth, Maintenance, and Regulation of Loss

Baltes and his colleagues (2006) assert that achieving mastery of life often involves conflicts and competition among three goals of human development: growth, maintenance, and regulation of loss. As individuals age into middle and late adulthood, the maintenance and regulation of loss in their capacities shift their attention away from growth. Thus, a 75-year-old man might aim not to improve his memory or his golf swing but to maintain his independence and merely to continue playing golf.

Development Is a Co-construction of Biology, Culture, and the Individual

Development is a co-construction of biological, cultural, and individual factors working together (Baltes, Reuter-Lorenz, & Rosler, 2012; De La Fuente, 2019). For example, the brain shapes culture, but it is also shaped by culture and the experiences that individuals have or pursue.

In terms of individual factors, we can go beyond what our genetic inheritance and environment have given us. We can author a unique developmental path by actively choosing from the environment the things that optimize our lives (Rathunde & Csikszentmihalyi, 2006).

SOME CONTEMPORARY CONCERNS

Pick up a newspaper or magazine and you might see headlines like these: "Technology Threatens Communication Skills," "Political Leanings May Be Written in the Genes," "Mother Accused of Tossing Children into Bay," "Gender Gap Widens," "FDA Warns About Side Effects of ADHD Drug," "Religious Group Protests Transgender Bathrooms," "Heart Attack Death Rates Higher in African American Patients," "Test May Predict Alzheimer Disease." Researchers using the life-span perspective are examining these and many other topics of contemporary concern. The roles that health and well-being, parenting, education, and sociocultural contexts play in life-span development, as well as how social policy is related to these issues, are a particular focus of *A Topical Approach to Life-Span Development*.

Health and Well-Being Health professionals today recognize the power of lifestyles and psychological states in health and well-being (Donatelle, 2019; Teague, Mackenzie, & Rosenthal, 2020). Does a pregnant woman endanger her fetus if she drinks a few beers per week? How does a poor diet affect a child's ability to learn? Are children getting less exercise today than in the past? What roles do parents and peers play in whether adolescents abuse drugs? What health-enhancing and health-compromising behaviors do college students engage in? What factors are causing the obesity epidemic in the United States and around the world? How can older adults cope with declining health? We will discuss many questions like these regarding health and well-being (Goode, 2020; Telljohann & others, 2020). In every chapter, issues of health and well-being are integrated into our discussion.

Clinical psychologists are among the health professionals who help people improve their well-being. Read about one clinical psychologist who helps adolescents and adults improve their developmental outcomes in the *Connecting with Careers* profile.

connecting with careers

Gustavo Medrano, Clinical Psychologist

Gustavo Medrano specializes in helping children, adolescents, and adults of all ages improve their lives when they have problems involving depression, anxiety, emotion regulation, chronic health conditions, and life transitions. He works individually with clients and provides therapy for couples and families. As a native Spanish speaker, he also provides bicultural and bilingual therapy for clients.

Dr. Medrano is a faculty member at the Family Institute at Northwestern University. He obtained his undergraduate degree in psychology at Northwestern and then became a teacher for Teach for America, which involves a minimum of two years spent teaching in a high-poverty area. He received his master's and doctoral degrees in clinical psychology at the University of Wisconsin—Milwaukee. As a faculty member at Northwestern, in addition to doing clinical therapy with clients, he also conducts research with a focus on how family experiences, especially parenting, influence children's and adolescents' coping and pain.

Gustavo Medrano, clinical psychologist, who does therapy with children, adolescents, and adults, especially using his bilingual background and skills to work with Latino clients.
©Avis Mandel Pictures

Children learn to love when they are loved

Robert Maust/Photo Agora

developmental **connection**

Parenting

Which parenting style is most often associated with positive child outcomes? Connect to "Families, Lifestyles, and Parenting."

culture The behavior, patterns, beliefs, and all other products of a group of people that are passed on from generation to generation.

cross-cultural studies Comparisons of one culture with one or more other cultures. These provide information about the degree to which development is similar, or universal, across cultures, and the degree to which it is culture-specific.

ethnicity Categorization of an individual based on cultural heritage, nationality characteristics, race, religion, and language.

socioeconomic status (SES) Classification of a person's position in society based on occupational, educational, and economic characteristics.

gender The characteristics of people as females or males.

Parenting and Education   Can two gay men raise a healthy family? Are children harmed if both parents work outside the home? Are U.S. schools failing to teach children how to read and write and calculate adequately? We hear many questions like these related to pressures on the contemporary family and the problems of U.S. schools (Bornstein & Lansford, 2019; Fiese, 2019; Goldberg & Romero, 2019). In other chapters, we analyze child care, the effects of divorce, parenting styles, intergenerational relationships, early childhood education, relationships between childhood poverty and education, dual-language learning, children with disabilities, new educational efforts to improve lifelong learning, and many other issues related to parenting and education (Hallahan, Kauffman, & Pullen, 2019; Morrison, 2018; Powell, 2019).

Sociocultural Contexts and Diversity   Health, parenting, and education—like development itself—are shaped by their sociocultural context (Bornstein & Lansford, 2019; Lansford & Banati, 2018). In analyzing this context, four concepts are especially useful: culture, ethnicity, socioeconomic status, and gender.

Culture encompasses the behavior patterns, beliefs, and all other products of a particular group of people that are passed on from generation to generation. Culture results from the interaction of people over many years (Nascimento & Little, 2019). A cultural group can be as large as the United States or as small as an isolated Appalachian town. Whatever its size, the group's culture influences the behavior of its members (Li & Hein, 2019). **Cross-cultural studies** compare aspects of two or more cultures. The comparison provides information about the degree to which development is similar, or universal, across cultures, or instead is culture-specific (Rescorla & others, 2019; Wagner, 2018). For example, in a recent study of 26 countries, individuals in Chile had the highest life satisfaction, those in Bulgaria and Spain the lowest (Jang & others, 2017).

Ethnicity (the word *ethnic* comes from the Greek word for "nation") is rooted in cultural heritage, nationality, race, religion, and language. African Americans, Latinos, Asian Americans, Native Americans, European Americans, and Arab Americans are examples of broad ethnic groups in the United States. Diversity exists within each ethnic group (Hou & Kim, 2018). A special concern is the discrimination and prejudice experienced by ethnic minority children and youth (Varner & others, 2018; Zeiders & others, 2019). Recent research indicates that pride in one's ethnic identity group has positive outcomes (Umana-Taylor, 2019; Umana-Taylor & others, 2018).

The sociocultural context of the United States has become increasingly diverse in recent years. Its population includes a greater variety of cultures and ethnic groups than ever before. Relatively high rates of minority immigration have contributed significantly to the growth in the proportion of ethnic minorities in the U.S. population (Nieto & Bode, 2018; Perreira & Pedroza, 2019). In 2017, 50.5 percent of children 17 years and younger were non-Latino White; by 2050, this figure is projected to decrease to 38.8 percent (ChildStats.gov, 2018). In 2017 in the United States, 25.2 percent of children were Latino, but in 2050 that figure is projected to increase to 31.9 percent. Asian Americans are expected to be the fastest-growing ethnic group of children percentage-wise: In 2017, 5.1 percent were Asian American, and that figure is expected to grow to 7.4 percent in 2050. The percentage of African American children is anticipated to decrease from 2017 to 2050 (13.6 to 13.1 percent). This changing demographic tapestry promises not only the richness that diversity produces but also difficult challenges in extending the American dream to all individuals (Mendoza-Denton & Worrell, 2019; Parke & Elder, 2020).

Socioeconomic status (SES) refers to a person's position within society based on occupational, educational, and economic characteristics. Socioeconomic status implies certain inequalities. Differences in the ability to control resources and to participate in society's rewards produce unequal opportunities (Justice & others, 2019; Koller, Santana, & Raffaelli, 2018).

Gender refers to the characteristics of people as males and females. Few aspects of our development are more central to our identity and social relationships than gender (Best & Puzio, 2019; Dettori & Gupta, 2018; Xiao & others, 2019).

Recently, considerable attention has focused on a category of gender classification, *transgender,* a broad term that refers to individuals who adopt a gender identity that differs from the one assigned to them at birth (Bradford & Syed, 2019; Budge & Orovecz, 2018). For example, individuals may have a female body but identify more strongly with being masculine

Two Korean-born children on the day they became United States citizens. Asian American and Latino children are the fastest-growing immigrant groups in the United States. *How diverse are the students in your life-span development class? How are their experiences in growing up likely similar to or different from yours?*
Skip O'Rourke/Zuma Press Inc./Alamy Stock Photo

Around the world women too often are treated as burdens rather than assets in the political process. *What can be done to strengthen women's roles in the political process?*
Andy Nelson/The Christian Science Monitor/Getty Images

Doly Akter, pictured here at age 17, grew up in a slum in Dhaka, Bangladesh, where sewers overflowed, garbage rotted in the streets, and children were undernourished. Nearly two-thirds of young women in Bangladesh marry before they are 18. Doly organized a club supported by UNICEF in which girls go door-to-door monitoring the hygiene habits of households in their neighborhood, leading to improved hygiene and health in the families. Also, her group has stopped several child marriages by meeting with parents and convincing them that it is not in their daughter's best interests. When talking with parents, the girls in the club emphasize the importance of staying in school and how this will improve their daughters' future. Doly says that the girls in her UNICEF group are far more aware of their rights than their mothers ever were (UNICEF, 2007).
Naser Siddique/UNICEF Bangladesh

than feminine, or have a male body but identify more strongly with being feminine than masculine. A transgender identity of being born male but identifying with being a female is much more common than the reverse (Zucker, Lawrence, & Kreukels, 2016). We will have much more to say about gender and transgender later in the text.

Social Policy **Social policy** is a government's course of action designed to promote the welfare of its citizens. Values, economics, and politics all shape a nation's social policy (Akinsola & Petersen, 2018; Garbarino, Governale, & Kostelny, 2019). Out of concern that policy makers are doing too little to protect the well-being of children and older adults, life-span researchers are increasingly undertaking studies that they hope will lead to the enactment of effective social policy (Bornstein & Lansford, 2019; Lerner & others, 2018).

Statistics such as infant mortality rates, mortality among children under age 5, and the percentage of children who are malnourished or living in poverty provide benchmarks for evaluating how well children are doing in a particular society (UNICEF, 2019). For many years, Marian Wright Edelman, a tireless advocate of children's rights, has pointed out that indicators like these place the United States at or near the lowest rank among industrialized nations in the treatment of children.

developmental connection
Environment
An increasing number of studies are showing that positive outcomes can be achieved through intervention in the lives of children living in poverty. Connect to "Peers and the Sociocultural World."

Marian Wright Edelman, president of the Children's Defense Fund (shown here advocating for health care), has been a tireless advocate of children's rights and instrumental in calling attention to the needs of children. *What are some of these needs?*
Courtesy of the Children's Defense Fund and Marian Wright Edelman

social policy A government's course of action designed to promote the welfare of its citizens.

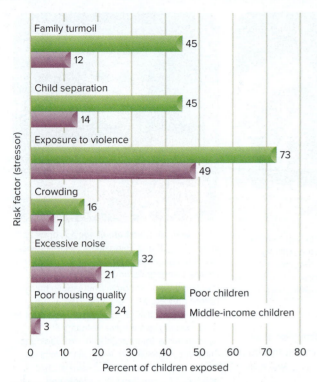

Family turmoil
45
12

Child separation
45
14

Exposure to violence
73
49

Crowding
16
7

Excessive noise
32
21

Poor housing quality
24
3

Poor children
Middle-income children

Risk factor (stressor)

0   10   20   30   40   50   60   70   80
Percent of children exposed

FIGURE 3

EXPOSURE TO SIX STRESSORS AMONG POOR AND MIDDLE-INCOME CHILDREN. One study analyzed the exposure to six stressors among poor children and middle-income children (Evans & English, 2002). Poor children were much more likely to face each of these stressors.

Source	Characteristic
Individual	Good intellectual functioning
	Appealing, sociable, easygoing disposition
	Self-confidence, high self-esteem
	Talents
	Faith
Family	Close relationship to caring parent figure
	Authoritative parenting: warmth, structure, high expectations
	Socioeconomic advantages
	Connections to extended supportive family networks
Extrafamilial Context	Bonds to caring adults outside the family
	Connections to positive organizations
	Attending effective schools

FIGURE 4

CHARACTERISTICS OF RESILIENT CHILDREN: INDIVIDUAL FACTORS AND SOCIAL CONTEXTS

Children who grow up in poverty represent a special concern (Barry & Overland, 2019; Koller, Santana, & Raffaelli, 2018). In 2017, 17.5 percent of U.S. children under 18 years of age were living in families with incomes below the poverty line, with African American (33 percent, down from 36 percent in 2015) and Latino (26 percent, down from 30 percent in 2015) families with children having especially high rates of poverty (Jiang, Granja, & Koball, 2017). This is an increase from 2001 (16 percent) but a decrease from a peak of 23 percent in 1993 and also down from 19.7 percent in 2015 (Fontenot, Semega, & Kollar, 2018).

As indicated in Figure 3, one study found that a higher percentage of U.S. children in poor families than in middle-income families were exposed to family turmoil, separation from a parent, violence, crowding, excessive noise, and poor housing (Evans & English, 2002). Another study revealed that the more years children spent living in poverty, the higher were their physiological indices of stress (Evans & Kim, 2007).

The U.S. figure of 17.5 percent of children living in poverty is much higher than child poverty rates in other industrialized nations. For example, Canada has a child poverty rate of 9 percent and Sweden has a rate of 2 percent.

Edelman says that parenting and nurturing the next generation of children are our society's most important functions and that we need to take them more seriously than we have in the past. To read about efforts to improve the lives of children through social policies, see *Connecting Development to Life*.

Some children triumph over poverty or other adversities. They show resilience. Are there certain characteristics that make children resilient? Ann Masten (2001, 2006, 2009, 2011, 2013, 2015, 2017, 2019; Masten & Kalstabakken, 2018; Masten & Palmer, 2019) concludes that individual factors, especially good intellectual functioning, and social contexts, especially positive parenting, are key attributes of children who show resilience in the face of adversity. Figure 4 shows the individual factors and social contexts that tend to characterize resilient children.

At the other end of the life span, efforts to promote the well-being of older adults also create policy issues (Jennifer, 2018; Vaughn & others, 2019; Willink & others, 2019). Key concerns are controlling health-care costs and ensuring that older adults have access to adequate health care (Andrew & Meeks, 2018; Boulton & others, 2019). One study found that the health-care system fails older adults in many ways (Wenger & others, 2003). For example, older adults received the recommended care for general medical conditions such as heart disease only 52 percent of the time; they received appropriate care for undernourishment and Alzheimer disease only 31 percent of the time.

These concerns about the well-being of older adults are heightened by two facts. First, the number of older adults in the United States is growing dramatically, as Figure 5 shows. Second, many of these older Americans are likely to need society's help (Mendoza-Nunez & de la Luz Martinez-Maldonado, 2019). Compared with earlier decades, U.S. adults today are less likely to be married, more likely to be childless, and more likely to live alone (Machielse, 2015). As the older population continues to expand, an increasing number of older adults will be without either a spouse or children—traditionally the main sources of support for older adults. These individuals will need social relationships, networks, and supports (Andrew & Meeks, 2018; Antonnuci & Webster, 2019).

Not only is the population of older adults growing in the United States, but also the world's population of people 60 years and older is projected to increase from 962 million in 2017 to 2.1 billion in 2050 (United Nations, 2017). The world's population 80 years of age and older is expected to triple or quadruple in this time frame. These significant increases in the world's older population have important implications for many sectors of society. As the percentage of a country's older population grows, governments must develop innovative policies and services that include improved housing, employment, health care, and transportation for older adults.

Improving Family Policy

In the United States, the national government, state governments, and city governments all have the capacity to improve the well-being of children (Bojorquez & Fry-Bowers, 2019; Lerner & others, 2018). When families neglect or seriously endanger a child's well-being, governments often step in to help. At the national and state levels, policy makers have debated for decades whether helping poor parents will benefit their children. Researchers are providing some answers by examining the effects of specific policies (Lansford & Banati, 2018; Rose-Clarke & others, 2019).

For example, the **Minnesota Family Investment Program (MFIP)** was designed in the 1990s primarily to influence the behavior of adults—specifically, to move adults off the welfare rolls and into paid employment. A key element of the program was its guarantee that adults participating in the program would receive more income if they worked than if they did not. When the adults' income rose, how did that affect their children? A study of the effects of **MFIP** found that increases in the incomes of working poor parents were linked with benefits for their children (Gennetian & Miller, 2002). The children's achievement in school improved, and their behavior problems decreased. A current **MFIP** study is examining the influence of providing specific services to low-income families at risk for child maltreatment and other negative outcomes for children (Minnesota Family Investment Program, 2009).

Increasing interest has been directed toward developing two-generation educational interventions to improve the academic success of children living in poverty (Gardner, Brooks-Gunn, & Chase-Lansdale, 2016; Sommer & others, 2016). For example, a recent large-scale effort to help children escape from poverty is the *Ascend* two-generation educational intervention being conducted by the Aspen Institute (2013, 2018). The intervention emphasizes education (increasing postsecondary education for mothers and improving the quality of their children's early childhood education), economic

What are some ways that researchers are attempting to improve the lives of children living in poverty?
Scott Keeler/Tampa Bay Times/Zuma Wire/Alamy Stock Photo

support (housing, transportation, financial education, health insurance, and food assistance), and social capital (peer support including friends and neighbors; participation in community and faith-based organizations; school and work contacts).

Developmental psychologists and other researchers have examined the effects of many other government policies. They are seeking ways to help families living in poverty improve their well-being, and they have offered many suggestions for improving government policies (Crosnoe & Ressler, 2019; McManus & others, 2019; Parke & Elder, 2020).

How does the life-span perspective support this and other research on the role government should play in improving the well-being of children?

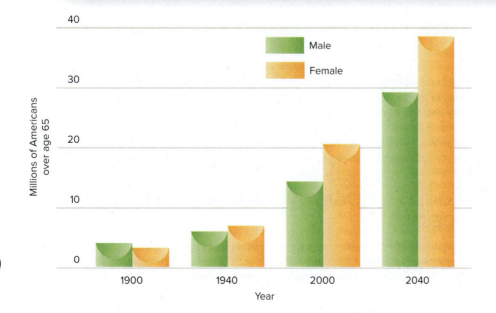

FIGURE 5

THE AGING OF AMERICA. The number of Americans over 65 has grown dramatically since 1900 and is projected to continue increasing until 2040. A significant increase will also occur in the number of individuals in the 85-and-over age group.

Technology A final discussion in our exploration of contemporary topics is the recent dramatic, almost overwhelming increase in the use of technology at all points in human development (Gillain & others, 2019; Lever-Duffy & McDonald, 2018). From the introduction of television in the mid '50s, to the replacement of typewriters with computers that can do far more than just print words, and later to the remarkable invention of the Internet and the proliferation of smartphones, followed by the pervasiveness of social media and the development of robots that can do some jobs better than humans can, our way of life has been changed permanently by technological advances.

We will explore many technology topics in this edition. In chapter 7, "Information Processing", you will read about the emerging field of developmental robotics in our discussion of information processing, and you will ponder the influence of technology on generations such as the millennials. Other topics we will examine include whether babies should watch television and videos, with special attention to potential effects of audiovisual media on language development; indications that too much screen time reduces children's engagement in physical activities and increases their risk for obesity and cardiovascular disease; the effects on learning when many adolescents spend more time using various media than they do in school; the question of whether multitasking with various electronic devices while doing homework is harmful or beneficial; as well as the degree to which older adults are adapting to the extensive role of technology in their lives, especially since they grew up without so much technology.

Review Connect Reflect

LG1 Discuss the distinctive features of a life-span perspective on development.

Review
- What is meant by the concept of development? Why is the study of life-span development important?
- What are eight main characteristics of the life-span perspective? What are three sources of contextual influences on development?
- What are some contemporary concerns in life-span development?

Connect
- In other courses and throughout your life you have learned that no two people are exactly alike. How might the life-span perspective explain this observation?

Reflect *Your Own Personal Journey of Life*
- Imagine what your development would have been like in a culture that offered fewer or distinctly different choices. How might your development have been different if your family had been significantly richer or poorer than it was when you were growing up?

2 The Nature of Development

 LG2 Identify the most important processes, periods, and issues in development.

Biological, Cognitive, and Socioemotional Processes	Periods of Development	The Significance of Age	Developmental Issues

In this section, we explore what is meant by developmental processes and periods, as well as variations in the way age is conceptualized. We examine key developmental concepts, explore how they describe development, and discuss strategies we can use to evaluate them.

A chronicle of the events in any person's life can quickly become a confusing and tedious array of details. Two concepts help provide a framework for describing and understanding an individual's development: developmental processes and periods of development.

BIOLOGICAL, COGNITIVE, AND SOCIOEMOTIONAL PROCESSES

At the beginning of this chapter, we defined development as the pattern of change that begins at conception and continues throughout the life span. The pattern is complex because it is the product of biological, cognitive, and socioemotional processes.

Biological Processes   **Biological processes** produce changes in an individual's physical nature. Genes inherited from parents, the development of the brain, height and weight gains, changes in motor skills, nutrition, exercise, the hormonal changes of puberty, and cardiovascular decline are all examples of biological processes that affect development.

Cognitive Processes   **Cognitive processes** refer to changes in the individual's thought process, intelligence, and language. Watching a colorful mobile swinging above the crib, putting together a two-word sentence, memorizing a poem, imagining what it would be like to be a movie star, and solving a crossword puzzle all involve cognitive processes.

Socioemotional Processes   **Socioemotional processes** involve changes in the individual's relationships with other people, changes in emotions, and changes in personality. An infant's smile in response to a parent's touch, a toddler's aggressive attack on a playmate, a school-age child's development of assertiveness, an adolescent's joy at the senior prom, and the affection of an elderly couple all reflect the influence of socioemotional processes on development.

Connecting Biological, Cognitive, and Socioemotional Processes   Biological, cognitive, and socioemotional processes are inextricably intertwined (Diamond, 2013). Consider a baby smiling in response to a parent's touch. This response depends on biological processes (the physical nature of touch and responsiveness to it), cognitive processes (the ability to understand intentional acts), and socioemotional processes (the act of smiling often reflects a positive emotional feeling, and smiling helps to connect us in positive ways with other human beings). Nowhere is the connection across biological, cognitive, and socioemotional processes more obvious than in two rapidly emerging fields:

- *Developmental cognitive neuroscience,* which explores links between development, cognitive processes, and the brain (Bell & others, 2018; Kinugawa, 2019)
- *Developmental social neuroscience,* which examines connections between socioemotional processes, development, and the brain (Gutchess, 2019; Sullivan & Wilson, 2018)

In many instances, biological, cognitive, and socioemotional processes are bidirectional. For example, biological processes can influence cognitive processes and vice versa. Thus, although usually we study the different processes of development (biological, cognitive, and socioemotional) in separate locations, keep in mind that we are talking about the development of an integrated individual with a mind and body that are interdependent.

biological processes Processes that produce changes in an individual's physical nature.

cognitive processes Processes that involve changes in an individual's thought, intelligence, and language.

socioemotional processes Processes that involve changes in an individual's relationships with other people, emotions, and personality.

PERIODS OF DEVELOPMENT

The interplay of biological, cognitive, and socioemotional processes produces the periods of the human life span (see Figure 6). *A developmental period* refers to a time frame in a person's life that is characterized by certain features. For the purposes of organization and understanding, we commonly describe development in terms of these periods. The most widely used classification of developmental periods involves the eight-period sequence shown in Figure 7. Approximate age ranges are listed for the periods to provide a general idea of when each period begins and ends.

The prenatal period is the time from conception to birth. It involves tremendous growth—from a single cell to an organism complete with brain and behavioral capabilities—and takes place within approximately a nine-month period.

Infancy is the developmental period from birth to 18 or 24 months. Infancy is a time of extreme dependence upon adults. During this period, many psychological activities—language, symbolic thought, sensorimotor coordination, and social learning, for example—are just beginning.

Early childhood is the developmental period from the end of infancy to age 5 or 6. This period is sometimes called the "preschool years." During this time, young children learn to become more self-sufficient and to care for themselves, develop school readiness skills (following instructions, identifying letters), and spend many hours in play with peers. First grade typically marks the end of early childhood.

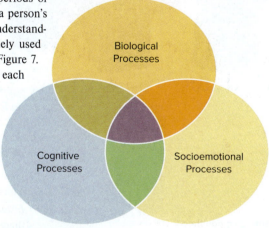

FIGURE **6**

PROCESSES INVOLVED IN DEVELOPMENTAL CHANGES. Biological, cognitive, and socioemotional processes interact as individuals develop.

Periods of Development

| Prenatal period (conception to birth) | Infancy (birth to 18–24 months) | Early childhood (3–5 years) | Middle and late childhood (6–10/11 years) | Adolescence (10–12 to 18–21 years) | Early adulthood (20s and 30s) | Middle adulthood (40s and 50s) | Late adulthood (60s–70s to death) |

Biological Processes

Cognitive Processes

Socioemotional Processes

Processes of Development

(Left to right): Steve Allen/Brand X Pictures/Getty Images; Courtesy of Dr. John Santrock; Laurence Mouton/Photoalto/PictureQuest; Digital Vision/Getty Images; SW Productions/Getty Images; Blue Moon Stock/Alamy Stock Photo; Sam Edwards/Caiaimage/Getty Images; Ronnie Kaufman/Blend Images LLC

FIGURE 7

PROCESSES AND PERIODS OF DEVELOPMENT. The unfolding of life's periods of development is influenced by the interaction of biological, cognitive, and socioemotional processes.

Middle and late childhood is the developmental period from about 6 to 11 years of age, approximately corresponding to the elementary school years. During this period, the fundamental skills of reading, writing, and arithmetic are mastered. The child is formally exposed to the larger world and its culture. Achievement becomes a more central theme of the child's world, and self-control increases.

Adolescence is the developmental period of transition from childhood to early adulthood, entered at approximately 10 to 12 years of age and ending at 18 to 21 years of age. Adolescence begins with rapid physical changes—dramatic gains in height and weight, changes in body contour, and the development of sexual characteristics such as enlargement of the breasts, growth of pubic and facial hair, and deepening of the voice. At this point in development, the pursuit of independence and an identity are prominent. Thought is more logical, abstract, and idealistic. More time is spent outside the family.

Recently, considerable interest has been directed toward the period of transition from adolescence to adulthood, now referred to as **emerging adulthood,** which lasts from approximately 18 to 25 years of age. Experimentation and exploration characterize the emerging adult (Arnett, 2006, 2012, 2014, 2015a, b, 2016a, b). At this point in their development, many individuals are still exploring which career path they want to follow, what they want their identity to be, and which lifestyle they want to adopt (for example, single, cohabiting, or married) (Padilla-Walker, Memmott-Elison, & Nelson, 2017; Schwartz & Petrova, 2019).

Jeffrey Arnett (2006) described five key features that characterize emerging adulthood:

Ieva/iStockPhoto.com

- *Identity exploration,* especially in love and work. Emerging adulthood is the time during which key changes in identity take place for many individuals.
- *Instability.* Residential changes peak during emerging adulthood, a time during which there also is often instability in love, work, and education.
- *Self-focused.* According to Arnett (2006, p. 10), emerging adults "are self-focused in the sense that they have little in the way of social obligations, little in the way of duties and commitments to others, which leaves them with a great deal of autonomy in running their own lives."

emerging adulthood The developmental time frame occurring from approximately 18 to 25 years of age; this transitional period between adolescence and adulthood is characterized by experimentation and exploration.

- *Feeling in-between.* Many emerging adults don't consider themselves adolescents or full-fledged adults.
- *The age of possibilities, a time when individuals have an opportunity to transform their lives.* Arnett (2006) describes two ways in which emerging adulthood is the age of possibilities: (1) many emerging adults are optimistic about their future; and (2) for emerging adults who have experienced difficult times while growing up, emerging adulthood presents an opportunity to direct their lives in a more positive way.

Recent research indicates that these five aspects characterize not only individuals in the United States as they make the transition from adolescence to early adulthood, but also their counterparts in European countries and Australia (Arnett, 2015 a, b; Sirsch & others, 2009). Although emerging adulthood does not characterize a specific period of development in all cultures, it does appear to occur in those where assuming adult roles and responsibilities is postponed (Kins & Beyers, 2010).

Early adulthood is the developmental period that begins in the twenties and lasts through the thirties. It is a time of establishing personal and economic independence, pursuing career development, and, for many, selecting a mate, learning to live with someone in an intimate way, starting a family, and rearing children.

Middle adulthood is the developmental period from approximately 40 years of age to about 60. It is a time of expanding personal and social involvement and responsibility; of assisting the next generation in becoming competent, mature individuals; and of reaching and maintaining satisfaction in a career.

Late adulthood is the developmental period that begins during the sixties or seventies and lasts until death. It is a time of life review, retirement from paid employment, and adjustment to new social roles involving decreasing strength and health. Late adulthood is the longest period of development, and—as noted earlier—the number of people in this age group has been increasing dramatically. As a result, life-span developmentalists have been paying more attention to differences within late adulthood. Paul Baltes and Jacqui Smith (2003) argue that a major change takes place in older adults' lives as they become the "oldest old," on average at about 85 years of age. For example, the "young old" (classified as 65 through 84 in this analysis) have substantial potential for physical and cognitive fitness, retain much of their cognitive capacity, and can develop strategies to cope with the gains and losses of aging. In contrast, the oldest old (85 and older) show considerable loss in cognitive skills, experience an increase in chronic stress, and are more frail (Baltes & Smith, 2003). Nonetheless, as we see in other chapters, considerable variation exists in the degree to which the oldest old retain their capabilities (Park & Festini, 2018; Ribeiro & Araujo, 2019; Robine, 2019). As described in the *Connecting with Research* interlude, situational contexts, including time of day, play an important role in how well older adults perform in cognitive and physical activities.

> We reach backward to our parents and forward to our children, and through their children to a future we will never see, but about which we need to care.
>
> —CARL JUNG
> *Swiss Psychiatrist, 20th Century*

THE SIGNIFICANCE OF AGE

In the earlier description of developmental periods, an approximate age range was linked with each period. But there are also variations in the capabilities of individuals who are the same age, and we have seen how changes with age can be exaggerated. How important is age when we try to understand an individual?

Age and Happiness   Is one age in life better than another? An increasing number of studies indicate that at least in the United States adults are happier as they age. For example, a study of more than 300,000 U.S. adults revealed that psychological well-being increased after the age of 50 years (Stone & others, 2010). In a recent study of individuals from 22 to 93 years of age, older adults reported having more positive emotional experiences than younger adults did (English & Carstensen, 2014).

Consider also a U.S. study of approximately 28,000 individuals from age 18 to 88 that revealed happiness increased with age (Yang, 2008). For example, about 33 percent were very happy at 88 years of age compared with only about 24 percent in their late teens and early twenties. Why might older people report being happier and more satisfied with their lives than younger people? Despite the increase in physical problems and losses older adults experience, they are more content with their lives, have better relationships with the people who matter to them, are less pressured to achieve, have more time for leisurely pursuits, and have many

Is There a Best Time of Day to Conduct Research?

Laura Helmuth (2003) described how researchers are finding that certain testing conditions exaggerate the severity of age-related declines in older adults' performance. Optimum testing conditions are not the same for young adults as they are for older adults. Most researchers conduct their studies in the afternoon, a convenient time for researchers and undergraduate participants. Traditional-aged college students in their late teens and early twenties are often more alert and function optimally in the afternoon, but about 75 percent of older adults are "morning people" who perform at their best early in the day (Helmuth, 2003).

Lynn Hasher and her colleagues (2001) tested the memory of college students 18 to 32 years of age and community volunteers 58 to 78 years of age in the late afternoon (about 4 to 5 p.m.) and in the morning (about 8 to 9 a.m.). Regardless of the time of day, the younger college students performed better than the older adults on the memory tests, which involved recognizing sentences from a story and memorizing a list of words. However, when the participants took the memory tests in the morning rather than in the late afternoon, the age difference in performance decreased considerably (see Figure 8).

The relevance of information also affects memory. Thomas Hess and his colleagues (2003) asked younger adults (18 to 30 years of age) and older adults (62 to 84 years of age) to listen to a drawn-out description that was identified as either someone's experiences on a first job or their experiences while searching for a retirement home. The younger adults remembered the details of both circumstances. However, the older adults showed a keen memory for the retirement-home search but not for the first-job experience.

In short, researchers have found that age differences in memory are robust when researchers ask for information that doesn't matter much, but when older adults are asked about information that is rel-

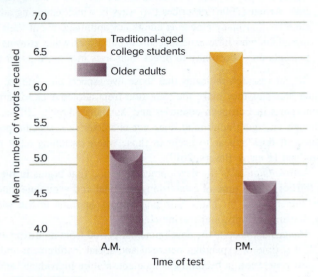

FIGURE 8

MEMORY, AGE, AND TIME OF DAY TESTED (A.M. or P.M.). In one study, traditional-aged college students performed better than older adults in both the morning and the afternoon. Note, however, that the memory of the older adults was better when they were tested in the morning than in the afternoon, whereas the memory of the traditional-aged college students was not as good in the morning as it was in the afternoon (Hasher & others, 2001).

evant to their lives, differences in the memory capacity of younger and older adults tend to be much smaller (Hasher, 2003). Thus, the type of information selected by researchers may produce an exaggerated view of age-related declines in memory.

What other factors besides time of day or types of information retained do you think might affect research results in a study of cognitive differences between two age groups?

years of experience that may help them use their accrued wisdom to adapt better to their circumstances than younger adults do (Antonucci & Webster, 2019; Kuntzmann, 2019; Paul, 2019). Also in the study, baby boomers (those born between 1946 and 1964) reported being less happy than individuals born earlier—possibly because they are not lowering their aspirations and idealistic hopes as they age as did earlier generations. Because growing older is a certain outcome of living, it is good to know that we are likely to be happier as older adults than we were during earlier periods of our lives.

However, not all research indicates that increased life satisfaction accompanies increased age (Steptoe, Deaton, & Stone, 2015). Some studies indicate that the lowest levels of life satisfaction occur in middle age, especially from 45 to 54 years of age (OECD, 2014). Other studies have found that life satisfaction varies across some countries. For example, respondents in research studies conducted in the former Soviet Union and Eastern Europe, as well as in South American countries, reported decreased life satisfaction with advancing age (Deaton, 2008). Further, older adults in poor health, such as those with cardiovascular disease, chronic lung disease, and depression, tend to be less satisfied with their lives than their healthier older adult counterparts are (Lamont & others, 2017). A recent study across 150 countries found that health was a better predictor of life satisfaction in individuals 58 years and older than in younger age groups (Joshanloo & Joyanovic, 2019).

Now that you have read about age variations in life satisfaction, think about how satisfied you are with your life. To help you answer this question, complete the items in Figure 9, which presents the most widely used measure in research on life satisfaction (Diener, 2019).

Conceptions of Age *Chronological age*–the number of years that have elapsed since birth–is not the only way of measuring age. Age has been conceptualized not just as chronological age but also as biological age, psychological age, and social age (Hoyer & Roodin, 2009).

Biological age is a person's age in terms of biological health. Determining biological age involves knowing the functional capacities of a person's vital organs. One person's vital capacities may be better or worse than those of others of comparable age (Benetos, 2019). A recent study of 17-year survival rates in Korean adults 20 to 93 years of age found that mortality rates were higher for individuals whose biological age was greater than their chronological age (Yoo & others, 2017). The younger the person's biological age, the longer the person is expected to live, regardless of chronological age.

Psychological age reflects an individual's adaptive capacities compared with those of other individuals of the same chronological age. Thus, older adults who continue to learn, are flexible, cope effectively with stress, think clearly, and are conscientious are engaging in more adaptive behaviors than their chronological age-mates who don't engage in these behaviors (Bercovitz, Ngnoumen, & Langer, 2019; Rakoczy & others, 2018). Reflecting the importance of psychological age, a longitudinal study of more than 1,200 individuals across seven decades revealed that the personality trait of conscientiousness (being organized, careful, and disciplined, for example) predicted lower mortality risk from childhood through late adulthood (Martin, Friedman, & Schwartz, 2007). Another study found that a higher level of conscientiousness was protective of cognitive functioning in older adults (Wilson & others, 2015).

Social age refers to connectedness with others and the social roles individuals adopt. Individuals who have better social relationships with others are happier with their lives and are likely to live longer than those who are lonely (Antonucci & Webster, 2019).

Below are five statements that you may agree or disagree with. Using the 1–7 scale below, indicate your agreement with each item by placing the appropriate number on the line preceding that item. Please be open and honest in your responding.

Scale

7 Strongly agree
6 Agree
5 Slightly agree
4 Neither agree nor disagree
3 Slightly disagree
2 Disagree
1 Strongly disagree

Response	Statement
_____	In most ways my life is close to my ideal.
_____	The conditions of my life are excellent.
_____	I am satisfied with my life.
_____	So far I have gotten the important things I want in life.
_____	If I could live my life over, I would change almost nothing.
_____	Total score

Scoring

31–35 Extremely satisfied
26–30 Satisfied
21–25 Slightly satisfied
   20 Neutral
15–19 Slightly dissatisfied
10–14 Dissatisfied
  5–9 Extremely dissatisfied

FIGURE 9

HOW SATISFIED AM I WITH MY LIFE?
Source: Diener, E., Emmons, R. A., Larson, R. J., & Griffin, S. (1985). The Satisfaction with Life Scale, *Journal of Personality Assessment*, 49, 71–75.

(*Left*) Pam McSwain, competing in the high jump in the Senior Olympics in Memphis; (*right*) a sedentary, overweight middle-aged man. *Even though Pam McSwain's chronological age is older, might her biological age be younger than the middle-aged man's?*
(*Left*): Karen Pulfer Focht/The Commercial Appeal/Landov Images; (*Right*): Firehorse/E+/Getty Images

From a life-span perspective, an overall age profile of an individual involves not just chronological age but also biological age, psychological age, and social age. For example, a 70-year-old man (chronological age) might be in good physical health (biological age), be experiencing memory problems and not be coping well with the demands placed on him by his wife's recent hospitalization (psychological age), and have a number of friends with whom he regularly plays golf (social age).

Three Developmental Patterns of Aging   K. Warner Schaie (2016) described three different developmental patterns that provide a portrait of how aging can involve individual variations:

- *Normal aging* characterizes most individuals; in this pattern psychological functioning often peaks in early middle age, remains relatively stable until the late fifties to early sixties, and then shows a modest decline through the early eighties. However, marked decline can occur as individuals near death.
- *Pathological aging* characterizes individuals who show greater than average declines as they age through the adult years. For example, they may have mild cognitive impairment in early old age, develop Alzheimer disease later on, or have a chronic disease that impairs their daily functioning.
- *Successful aging* characterizes individuals whose positive physical, cognitive, and socioemotional development is maintained longer, declining later in old age than is the case for most people. For too long, only the declines that occur in late adulthood were highlighted, but recently there has been increased interest in the concept of successful aging (Benetos, 2019; Fernandez-Ballesteros & others, 2019; Robine, 2019).

DEVELOPMENTAL ISSUES

Is your own journey through life marked out ahead of time, or can your life experiences change your path? Are the experiences that take place early in your journey more important than later ones? Is your journey more like taking an elevator up a skyscraper with distinct stops along the way, or more like cruising down a river with smoother ebbs and flows? These questions point to three issues about the nature of development: the roles played by nature and nurture, by stability and change, and by continuity and discontinuity.

Nature and Nurture   The **nature-nurture issue** involves the extent to which development is influenced by nature and by nurture. Nature refers to an organism's biological inheritance, nurture to its environmental experiences.

According to those who emphasize the role of nature, just as a sunflower grows in an orderly way—unless flattened by an unfriendly environment—so too a human grows in an orderly way. An evolutionary and genetic foundation produces commonalities in growth and development (Buss & Schmitt, 2019; Mader & Windelspecht, 2020). We walk before we talk, speak one word before two words, grow rapidly in infancy and less so in early childhood, experience a rush of sex hormones in puberty, reach the peak of our physical strength in late adolescence and early adulthood, and then decline physically. Proponents of the developmental influence of nature acknowledge that extreme environments—those that are psychologically barren or hostile—can depress development. However, they believe that basic growth tendencies are genetically programmed into humans (Hoefnagels, 2019; Willey, Sandman, & Wood, 2020).

By contrast, others emphasize the impact of nurture, or environmental experiences, on development (Bornstein, 2019; Parke & Elder, 2020; Wahl & Gitlin, 2019). Experiences run the gamut from the individual's biological environment (nutrition, medical care, drugs, and physical accidents) to the social environment (family, peers, schools, community, media, and culture).

Stability and Change   Is the shy child who hides behind the sofa when visitors arrive destined to become a wallflower at college dances, or might the child become a sociable, talkative individual? Is a fun-loving, carefree adolescent bound to have difficulty

developmental **connection**

Nature Versus Nurture

Can specific genes be linked to specific environmental experiences? Connect to "Biological Beginnings."

developmental **connection**

Personality

Is personality more stable at some points in adult development than at others? Connect to "The Self, Identity, and Personality."

nature-nurture issue Debate about whether development is primarily influenced by nature or nurture. Nature refers to an organism's biological inheritance, nurture to its environmental experiences. The "nature proponents" claim biological inheritance is the more important influence on development; the "nurture proponents" claim that environmental experiences are more important.

stability-change issue Debate as to whether and to what degree we become older renditions of our earlier selves (stability) or whether we develop into someone different from who we were at an earlier point in development (change).

holding down a 9-to-5 job as an adult? These questions reflect the **stability-change issue,** which involves the degree to which early traits and characteristics persist or change as a person matures.

Many developmentalists who emphasize stability in development argue that stability is the result of heredity and possibly early experiences in life. Developmentalists who emphasize change take the more optimistic view that later experiences can produce change. Recall that in the life-span perspective, plasticity—the potential for change—exists throughout the life span.

The roles of early and later experience are an aspect of the stability-change issue that has long been hotly debated (Almy & Cicchetti, 2018; Farrell & others, 2019). Some argue that unless infants experience warm, nurturant caregiving in the first year or so of life, their development will never be optimal (Cassidy, 2016). The later-experience advocates see children as malleable throughout development, with sensitive caregiving and positive close relationships playing important roles later in child development, adolescence, and adulthood just as they do in infancy (Antonucci & Webster, 2019; De La Fuente, 2019; Fraley, 2019; Joling & others, 2018).

Continuity and Discontinuity When developmental change occurs, is it gradual or abrupt? Think about your own development for a moment. Did you gradually become the person you are? Or did you experience sudden, distinct changes as you matured? For the most part, developmentalists who emphasize nurture describe development as a gradual, continuous process. Those who emphasize nature often describe development as a series of distinct stages.

The **continuity-discontinuity issue** focuses on the degree to which development involves either gradual, cumulative change (continuity) or distinct stages (discontinuity). In terms of continuity, as the oak grows from seedling to giant tree, it becomes more and more an oak—its development is continuous (see Figure 10). Similarly, a child's first word, though seemingly an abrupt, discontinuous event, is actually the result of weeks and months of growth and practice. Puberty might seem abrupt, but it is a gradual process that occurs over several years.

In terms of discontinuity, as an insect grows from a caterpillar to a chrysalis to a butterfly, it passes through a sequence of stages in which change differs qualitatively rather than quantitatively. Similarly, at some point a child moves from not being able to think abstractly about the world to being able to do so. This is a qualitative, discontinuous change in development rather than a quantitative, continuous change.

Evaluating the Developmental Issues Most life-span developmentalists acknowledge that development is not all nature or all nurture, not all stability or all change, and not all continuity or all discontinuity. Nature and nurture, stability and change, continuity and discontinuity characterize development throughout the human life span (Kinugawa, 2019; Lindahl-Jacobsen & Christensen, 2019).

Although most developmentalists do not take extreme positions on these three important issues, there is spirited debate regarding how strongly development is influenced by each of them (Antonucci & Webster, 2019; Ellis & Del Giudice, 2019; Johnson & Losos, 2020).

Continuity

Discontinuity

FIGURE **10**

CONTINUITY AND DISCONTINUITY IN DEVELOPMENT. *Is our development like that of a seedling gradually growing into a giant oak tree? Or is it more like that of a caterpillar suddenly becoming a butterfly?*

continuity-discontinuity issue Debate that focuses on the extent to which development involves gradual, cumulative change (continuity) or distinct stages (discontinuity).

Review **Connect** Reflect

LG2 Identify the most important processes, periods, and issues in development.

Review
- What are three key developmental processes?
- What are eight main developmental periods?
- How is age related to development?
- What are three main developmental issues?

Connect
- In this chapter, you learned about the importance of the life-span perspective on development. Do you think this view provides more support for a focus on nature, on nurture, or on both? Why?

Reflect *Your Own Personal Journey of Life*
- Think about your own development in adolescence, early adulthood, middle adulthood, and late adulthood. During which age period do you think you are likely to be happiest? Why?

| Psychoanalytic Theories | Cognitive Theories | Behavioral and Social Cognitive Theories | Ethological Theory | Ecological Theory | An Eclectic Theoretical Orientation |

Science refines everyday thinking.

—ALBERT EINSTEIN

German-born American Physicist, 20th Century

Sigmund Freud, the pioneering architect of psychoanalytic theory. *How did Freud portray the organization of an individual's personality?*
Bettmann/Getty Images

theory An interrelated, coherent set of ideas that helps to explain phenomena and make predictions.

hypotheses Specific assumptions and predictions that can be tested to determine their accuracy.

psychoanalytic theories Theories that describe development as primarily unconscious and heavily colored by emotion. Behavior is merely a surface characteristic, and the symbolic workings of the mind must be analyzed to understand behavior. Early experiences with parents are emphasized.

How can we answer questions about the roles of nature and nurture, stability and change, and continuity and discontinuity in development? How can we determine, for example, whether special care can repair the harm inflicted by child neglect or whether memory loss in older adults can be prevented? The scientific method is the best tool we have to answer such questions (Smith & Davis, 2016).

The *scientific method* is essentially a four-step process: (1) conceptualize a process or problem to be studied; (2) collect research information (data); (3) analyze data; and (4) draw conclusions.

In step 1, when researchers are formulating a problem to study, they often draw on theories and develop hypotheses. A **theory** is an interrelated, coherent set of ideas that helps to explain phenomena and make predictions. It may suggest **hypotheses,** which are specific assertions and predictions that can be tested. For example, a theory on mentoring might state that sustained support and guidance from an adult improve the lives of children from impoverished backgrounds because the mentor gives the children opportunities to observe and imitate the behavior and strategies of the mentor.

This section outlines key aspects of five theoretical orientations to development: psychoanalytic, cognitive, behavioral and social cognitive, ethological, and ecological. Each contributes an important piece to the life-span development puzzle. Although the theories disagree about certain aspects of development, many of their ideas are complementary rather than contradictory. Together they let us see the total landscape of life-span development in all its richness.

PSYCHOANALYTIC THEORIES

Psychoanalytic theories describe development as primarily unconscious (beyond awareness) and heavily colored by emotion. Psychoanalytic theorists emphasize that behavior is merely a surface characteristic and that a true understanding of development requires analyzing the symbolic meanings of behavior and the deep inner workings of the mind. Psychoanalytic theorists also stress that early experiences with parents extensively shape development. These characteristics are highlighted in the main psychoanalytic theory, that of Sigmund Freud (1856–1939).

Freud's Theory As Freud listened to, probed, and analyzed his patients, he became convinced that their problems were the result of experiences early in life. He thought that as children grow up, their focus of pleasure and sexual impulses shifts from the mouth to the anus and eventually to the genitals. As a result, we go through five stages of psychosexual development: oral, anal, phallic, latency, and genital (see Figure 11). Our adult personality,

Oral Stage	**Anal Stage**	**Phallic Stage**	**Latency Stage**	**Genital Stage**
Infant's pleasure centers on the mouth.	Child's pleasure focuses on the anus.	Child's pleasure focuses on the genitals.	Child represses sexual interest and develops social and intellectual skills.	A time of sexual reawakening; source of sexual pleasure becomes someone outside the family.
Birth to 1½ Years	**1½ to 3 Years**	**3 to 6 Years**	**6 Years to Puberty**	**Puberty Onward**

FIGURE 11

FREUDIAN STAGES. Because Freud emphasized sexual motivation, his stages of development are known as psychosexual stages. In his view, if the need for pleasure at any stage is either undergratified or overgratified, an individual may become fixated, or locked in, at that stage of development.

Freud (1917) claimed, is determined by the way we resolve conflicts between sources of pleasure at each stage and the demands of reality.

Freud's theory has been significantly revised by a number of psychoanalytic theorists. Many of today's psychoanalytic theorists argue that Freud overemphasized sexual instincts; they place more emphasis on cultural experiences as determinants of an individual's development. Unconscious thought remains a central theme, but thought plays a greater role than Freud envisioned. Next, you will read about the ideas of an important revisionist of Freud's ideas—Erik Erikson.

Erikson's Psychosocial Theory Erik Erikson recognized Freud's contributions but stressed that Freud misjudged some important dimensions of human development. For one thing, Erikson (1950, 1968) said we develop in psychosocial stages, rather than in psychosexual stages as Freud maintained. According to Freud, the primary motivation for human behavior is sexual in nature; according to Erikson, it is social and reflects a desire to affiliate with other people. According to Freud, our basic personality is shaped in the first five years of life; according to Erikson, developmental change occurs throughout the life span. Thus, in terms of the early-versus-later-experience issue described earlier in the chapter, Freud viewed early experiences as far more important than later experiences, whereas Erikson emphasized the importance of both early and later experiences.

In **Erikson's theory,** eight stages of development unfold as we go through life (see Figure 12). At each stage, a unique developmental task confronts individuals with a crisis that must be resolved. According to Erikson, this crisis is not a catastrophe but a turning point marked by both increased vulnerability and enhanced potential. The more successfully individuals resolve these crises, the healthier their development will be.

Trust versus mistrust is Erikson's first psychosocial stage, which is experienced in the first year of life. Trust in infancy sets the stage for a lifelong expectation that the world will be a good and pleasant place to live.

Autonomy versus shame and doubt is Erikson's second stage. This stage occurs in late infancy and toddlerhood (1 to 3 years). After gaining trust in their caregivers, infants begin to discover that their behavior is their own. They start to assert their sense of independence or autonomy. They realize their will. If infants and toddlers are restrained too much or punished too harshly, they are likely to develop a sense of shame and doubt.

Initiative versus guilt, Erikson's third stage of development, occurs during the preschool years. As preschool children encounter a widening social world, they face new challenges that require active, purposeful, responsible behavior. Feelings of guilt may arise, though, if the child is irresponsible and is made to feel too anxious.

Industry versus inferiority is Erikson's fourth developmental stage, occurring approximately in the elementary school years. Children now need to direct their energy toward mastering knowledge and intellectual skills. The negative outcome is that the child may develop a sense of inferiority—feeling incompetent and unproductive.

During the adolescent years individuals face finding out who they are, what they are all about, and where they are going in life. This is Erikson's fifth developmental stage, *identity versus identity confusion.* If adolescents explore roles in a healthy manner and arrive at a positive path to follow in life, they achieve a positive identity; if they do not, identity confusion reigns.

Intimacy versus isolation is Erikson's sixth developmental stage, which individuals experience during early adulthood. At this time, individuals face the developmental task of forming intimate relationships. If young adults form healthy friendships and an intimate relationship with another, intimacy will be achieved; if not, isolation will result.

Generativity versus stagnation, Erikson's seventh developmental stage, occurs during middle adulthood. By generativity Erikson means primarily a concern for helping the younger generation to develop and lead useful lives. The feeling of having done nothing to help the next generation is stagnation.

Integrity versus despair is Erikson's eighth and final stage of development, which individuals experience in late adulthood. During this stage, a person reflects on the past. If the person's life review reveals a life well spent, integrity will be achieved; if not, the retrospective glances likely will yield doubt or gloom—the despair Erikson described.

We examine Erikson's theory in more detail in the chapter on "The Self, Identity, and Personality."

Erikson's Stages	Developmental Period
Integrity versus despair	Late adulthood (60s onward)
Generativity versus stagnation	Middle adulthood (40s, 50s)
Intimacy versus isolation	Early adulthood (20s, 30s)
Identity versus identity confusion	Adolescence (10 to 20 years)
Industry versus inferiority	Middle and late childhood (elementary school years, 6 years to puberty)
Initiative versus guilt	Early childhood (preschool years, 3 to 5 years)
Autonomy versus shame and doubt	Infancy (1 to 3 years)
Trust versus mistrust	Infancy (first year)

FIGURE 12

ERIKSON'S EIGHT LIFE-SPAN STAGES. Like Freud, Erikson proposed that individuals go through distinct, universal stages of development. Thus, in terms of the continuity-discontinuity issue discussed in this chapter, both favor the discontinuity side of the debate. Notice that the timing of Erikson's first four stages is similar to that of Freud's stages. *What are the implications of saying that people go through stages of development?*

Erikson's theory Theory that proposes eight stages of human development. Each stage consists of a unique developmental task that confronts individuals with a crisis that must be resolved.

Evaluating Psychoanalytic Theories Contributions of psychoanalytic theories include an emphasis on a developmental framework, family relationships, and unconscious aspects of the mind. These theories have been criticized, however, for a lack of scientific support, too much emphasis on sexual underpinnings, and an image of people that is viewed as too negative.

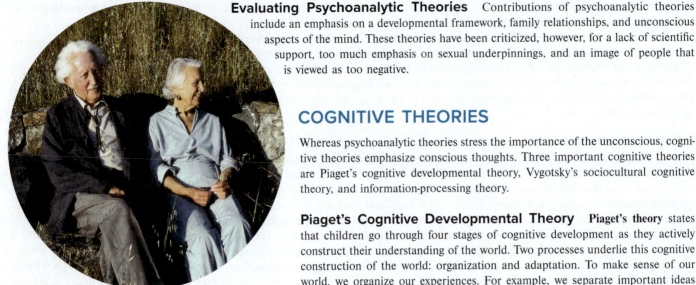

Erik Erikson with his wife, Joan, an artist. Erikson generated one of the most important developmental theories of the twentieth century. *Which stage of Erikson's theory are you in? Does Erikson's description of this stage characterize you?*
Jon Erikson/The Image Works

COGNITIVE THEORIES

Whereas psychoanalytic theories stress the importance of the unconscious, cognitive theories emphasize conscious thoughts. Three important cognitive theories are Piaget's cognitive developmental theory, Vygotsky's sociocultural cognitive theory, and information-processing theory.

Piaget's Cognitive Developmental Theory **Piaget's theory** states that children go through four stages of cognitive development as they actively construct their understanding of the world. Two processes underlie this cognitive construction of the world: organization and adaptation. To make sense of our world, we organize our experiences. For example, we separate important ideas from less important ideas, and we connect one idea to another. In addition to organizing our observations and experiences, we adapt in response to new environmental demands (Miller, 2015; Nikitin & Freund, 2019).

Jean Piaget (1954) also proposed that we go through four stages in understanding the world (see Figure 13). Each age-related stage consists of a distinct way of thinking, a *different way* of understanding the world. Thus, according to Piaget, the child's cognition is *qualitatively different* in one stage compared with another. What are Piaget's four stages of cognitive development?

The *sensorimotor stage,* which lasts from birth to about 2 years of age, is the first Piagetian stage. In this stage, infants construct an understanding of the world by coordinating sensory experiences (such as seeing and hearing) with physical, motoric actions—hence the term *sensorimotor.*

The *preoperational stage,* which lasts from approximately 2 to 7 years of age, is Piaget's second stage. In this stage, children begin to go beyond simply connecting sensory information with physical action and represent the world with words, images, and drawings. However, according to Piaget, preschool children still lack the ability to perform what he calls operations, which are internalized mental actions that allow children to do mentally what they previously could only do physically. For example, if you imagine putting two sticks together to see whether they would be as long as another stick, without actually moving the sticks, you are performing a concrete operation.

The *concrete operational stage,* which lasts from approximately 7 to 11 years of age, is the third Piagetian stage. In this stage, children can perform operations that involve objects, and they can reason logically when the reasoning can be applied to specific or concrete examples. For instance, concrete operational thinkers cannot imagine the steps necessary to complete an algebraic equation, which is too abstract for thinking at this stage of development.

The *formal operational stage,* which appears between the ages of 11 and 15 and continues through adulthood, is Piaget's fourth and final stage. In this stage, individuals move beyond concrete experiences and think in abstract and more logical terms. As part of thinking more abstractly, adolescents develop images of ideal circumstances. They might think about what an ideal parent is like and compare their parents to this ideal standard. They begin to entertain

Piaget's theory Theory stating that children actively construct their understanding of the world and go through four stages of cognitive development.

Vygotsky's theory Sociocultural cognitive theory that emphasizes how culture and social interaction guide cognitive development.

Information-processing theory Theory emphasizing that individuals manipulate information, monitor it, and strategize about it. Central to this theory are the processes of memory and thinking.

Jean Piaget, the famous Swiss developmental psychologist, changed the way we think about the development of children's minds. *What are some key ideas in Piaget's theory?*
Yves de Braine/Black Star/Stock Photo

Sensorimotor Stage	Preoperational Stage	Concrete Operational Stage	Formal Operational Stage
The infant constructs an understanding of the world by coordinating sensory experiences with physical actions. An infant progresses from reflexive, instinctual action at birth to the beginning of symbolic thought toward the end of the stage.	The child begins to represent the world with words and images. These words and images reflect increased symbolic thinking and go beyond the connection of sensory information and physical action.	The child can now reason logically about concrete events and classify objects into different sets.	The adolescent reasons in more abstract, idealistic, and logical ways.
Birth to 2 Years of Age	**2 to 7 Years of Age**	**7 to 11 Years of Age**	**11 Years of Age Through Adulthood**

FIGURE 13

PIAGET'S FOUR STAGES OF COGNITIVE DEVELOPMENT. According to Piaget, how a child thinks—not how much the child knows—determines the child's stage of cognitive development.
(*Left to right*): Stockbyte/Getty Images; Jacobs Stock Photography/BananaStock/Getty Images; image100/Corbis; Purestock/Getty Images

possibilities for the future and are fascinated with what they can become. In solving problems, they become more systematic, developing hypotheses about why something is happening the way it is and then testing these hypotheses. We examine Piaget's cognitive developmental theory in more detail in the chapter on "Cognitive Developmental Approaches."

Vygotsky's Sociocultural Cognitive Theory

Like Piaget, the Russian developmentalist Lev Vygotsky (1896–1934) maintained that children actively construct their knowledge. However, Vygotsky (1962) gave social interaction and culture far more important roles in cognitive development than Piaget did. **Vygotsky's theory** is a sociocultural cognitive theory that emphasizes how culture and social interaction guide cognitive development.

Vygotsky portrayed the child's development as inseparable from social and cultural activities (Daniels, 2017). He argued that cognitive development involves learning to use the inventions of society, such as language, mathematical systems, and memory strategies. Thus, in one culture, children might learn to count with the help of a computer; in another, they might learn by using beads. According to Vygotsky, children's social interaction with more-skilled adults and peers is indispensable to their cognitive development (Holzman, 2017). Through this interaction, they learn to use the tools that will help them adapt and be successful in their culture (Daniels, 2017). In the chapter on "Cognitive Developmental Approaches," we examine ideas about learning and teaching that are based on Vygotsky's theory.

The Information-Processing Theory

Information-processing theory emphasizes that individuals manipulate information, monitor it, and strategize about it. Unlike Piaget's theory, but like Vygotsky's theory, information-processing theory does not describe development as stage-like. Instead, according to this theory, individuals develop a gradually increasing capacity

Lev Vygotsky was born the same year as Piaget, but he died much earlier, at the age of 37. There is considerable interest today in Vygotsky's sociocultural cognitive theory of child development. *What are some key characteristics of Vygotsky's theory?*
A.R. Lauria/Dr. Michael Cole, Laboratory of Human Cognition, University of California, San Diego

David Cook/www.blueshiftstudios.co.uk/Alamy Stock Photo

for processing information, which allows them to acquire increasingly complex knowledge and skills (Chevalier, Dauvier, & Blaye, 2018; Goldstein, 2019).

Robert Siegler (2006, 2013), a leading expert on children's information processing, states that thinking is information processing. In other words, when individuals perceive, encode, represent, store, and retrieve information, they are thinking. Siegler (2017) emphasizes that an important aspect of development is learning good strategies for processing information. For example, becoming a better reader might involve learning to monitor the key themes of the material being read. In the chapter on "Information Processing," we explore the information-processing approach in greater depth.

Siegler (2006) also argues that the best way to understand how children learn is to observe them while they are learning. He emphasizes the importance of using the *microgenetic method* to obtain detailed information about processing mechanisms as they are occurring moment to moment. Siegler concludes that most research methods indirectly assess cognitive change, being more like snapshots than movies. The microgenetic method seeks to discover not just what children know but the cognitive processes involved in how they acquired the knowledge (Miller, 2015). A number of microgenetic studies have focused on a specific aspect of academic learning, such as how children learn whole number arithmetic, fractions, and other math skills (Braithwaite & Siegler 2018a, b; Fazio, DeWolf, & Siegler, 2016).

Evaluating Cognitive Theories   Contributions of cognitive theories include a positive view of development and an emphasis on the active construction of understanding. Criticisms include skepticism about the pureness of Piaget's stages and insufficient attention given to individual variations.

BEHAVIORAL AND SOCIAL COGNITIVE THEORIES

Behaviorism essentially holds that we can study scientifically only what we can directly observe and measure. Out of the behavioral tradition grew the belief that development is observable behavior that we can learn through experience with the environment (Maag, 2018). In terms of the continuity-discontinuity issue discussed earlier in this chapter, the behavioral and social cognitive theories emphasize continuity in development and argue that development does not occur in stage-like fashion. Let's explore two versions of behaviorism: Skinner's operant conditioning and Bandura's social cognitive theory.

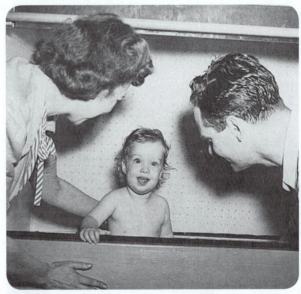

B. F. Skinner was a tinkerer who liked to make new gadgets. The younger of his two daughters, Deborah, spent much of her infancy in Skinner's enclosed Air-Crib, which he invented because he wanted to control her environment completely. The Air-Crib was sound-proofed and temperature controlled. Debbie, shown here as a child with her parents, is currently a successful artist, married and living in London. *What do you think about Skinner's Air-Crib?*
AP Images

Skinner's Operant Conditioning   According to B. F. Skinner (1904–1990), through *operant conditioning* the consequences of a behavior produce changes in the probability of the behavior's occurrence. A behavior followed by a rewarding stimulus is more likely to recur, whereas a behavior followed by a punishing stimulus is less likely to recur. For example, when an adult smiles at a child after the child has done something, the child is more likely to engage in that behavior again than if the adult gives the child a disapproving look.

In Skinner's (1938) view, such rewards and punishments shape development. For Skinner the key aspect of development is behavior, not thoughts and feelings. He emphasized that development consists of the pattern of behavioral changes that are brought about by rewards and punishments. For example, Skinner would say that shy people learned to be shy as a result of experiences they had while growing up. It follows that modifications in an environment can help a shy person become more socially oriented.

social cognitive theory Theoretical view that behavior, environment, and cognition are the key factors in development.

Bandura's Social Cognitive Theory   Some psychologists agree with the behaviorists' notion that development is learned and is influenced strongly by environmental interactions. However, unlike Skinner, they also see cognition as important in understanding development (Mischel, 2014). **Social cognitive theory** holds that behavior, environment, and cognition are the key factors in development.

American psychologist Albert Bandura (1925–) is the leading architect of social cognitive theory. Bandura (2001, 2010a, b, 2012, 2015, 2018) emphasizes that cognitive processes have important links with the environment and behavior. His early research program focused heavily on *observational learning* (also called *imitation,* or *modeling*), which is learning that occurs through observing what others do. For example, a young boy might observe his father yelling in anger and treating other people with hostility; with his peers, the young boy later acts very aggressively, showing the same characteristics as his father's behavior. Social cognitive theorists stress that people acquire a wide range of behaviors, thoughts, and feelings through observing others' behavior and that these observations form an important part of life-span development.

What is *cognitive* about observational learning in Bandura's view? He proposes that people cognitively represent the behavior of others and then sometimes adopt this behavior themselves.

Bandura's (2001, 2010a, b, 2012, 2015, 2018) model of learning and development includes three elements: behavior, the person/cognition, and the environment. An individual's sense of being in control of his or her success is an example of a person factor; strategies are an example of a cognitive factor. Recently, Bandura (2018) described *forethought* as a key cognitive factor in his social cognitive theory. When engaging in forethought, individuals guide and motivate themselves by creating action plans, formulating goals, and visualizing positive outcomes of their actions. As shown in Figure 14, behavior, person/cognition, and environmental factors operate interactively.

Further discussion of Bandura's social cognitive theory appears in the chapter on "Schools, Achievement, and Work."

Evaluating Behavioral and Social Cognitive Theories Contributions of the behavioral and social cognitive theories include an emphasis on scientific research and environmental determinants of behavior. These theories have been criticized for deemphasizing the role of cognition (Skinner) and giving inadequate attention to developmental changes.

ETHOLOGICAL THEORY

Ethology stresses that behavior is strongly influenced by biology, is tied to evolution, and is characterized by critical or sensitive periods. These are specific time frames during which, according to ethologists, the presence or absence of certain experiences has a long-lasting influence on individuals.

European zoologist Konrad Lorenz (1903–1989) helped bring ethology to prominence. In his best-known research, Lorenz (1965) studied the behavior of greylag geese, which will follow their mothers as soon as they hatch. Lorenz separated the eggs laid by one goose into two groups. One group he returned to the goose to be hatched by her. The other group was hatched in an incubator. The goslings in the first group performed as predicted. They followed their mother as soon as they hatched. However, those in the second group, which saw Lorenz when they first hatched, followed him everywhere as though he were their mother. Lorenz marked the goslings and then placed both groups under a box. Mother goose and "mother" Lorenz stood aside as the box was lifted. Each group of goslings went directly to its "mother." Lorenz called this process *imprinting:* the rapid, innate learning that involves attachment to the first moving object that is seen.

John Bowlby (1969, 1989) illustrated an important application of ethological theory to human development. Bowlby stressed that attachment to a caregiver over the first year of life has important consequences throughout the life span. In his view, if this attachment is positive and secure, the individual will likely develop positively in childhood and adulthood. If the attachment is negative and insecure, life-span development will likely not be optimal. In the chapter on "Emotional Development," we explore the concept of infant attachment in much greater detail.

In Lorenz's view, imprinting needs to take place at a certain, very early time in the life of the animal, or else it will not take place. This point in time is called a *critical period.* A related concept involves the existence of a *sensitive period,* and an example of this is the time during infancy when, according to Bowlby, attachment should occur in order to promote optimal development of social relationships.

Albert Bandura has been one of the leading architects of social cognitive theory. *How does Bandura's theory differ from Skinner's?*
Courtesy of Dr. Albert Bandura

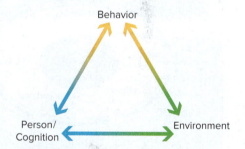

FIGURE 14

BANDURA'S SOCIAL COGNITIVE MODEL. The arrows illustrate how relations between behavior, person/cognition, and environment are reciprocal rather than one-way. Person/cognition refers to cognitive processes (for example, thinking and planning) and personal characteristics (for example, believing that you can control your experiences).

developmental **connection**

Achievement

Bandura emphasizes that self-efficacy is a key person/cognitive factor in achievement. Connect to "Schools, Achievement, and Work."

ethology Theory stressing that behavior is strongly influenced by biology, is tied to evolution, and is characterized by critical or sensitive periods.

Konrad Lorenz, a pioneering student of animal behavior, is followed through the water by three imprinted greylag geese. Describe Lorenz's experiment with the geese. *Do you think his experiment would have the same results with human babies? Explain.*
Nina Leen/Time Life Pictures/Getty Images

Another theory that emphasizes biological foundations of development—evolutionary psychology (Bjorklund, 2018; Buss & Schmidt, 2019)—is presented in the chapter on "Biological Beginnings," along with views on the role of heredity in development (Toupance & Benetos, 2019). In addition, we examine a number of biological theories of aging in the chapter on "Physical Development and Biological Aging" (Falandry, 2019).

Contributions of ethological theory include its focus on the biological and evolutionary basis of development and its use of careful observations in naturalistic settings. Ethological theory has been criticized for its overemphasis on biological foundations and lack of flexibility regarding the concepts of critical and sensitive periods.

ECOLOGICAL THEORY

While ethological theory stresses biological factors, ecological theory emphasizes environmental factors. One ecological theory that has important implications for understanding life-span development was created by Urie Bronfenbrenner (1917–2005).

Bronfenbrenner's ecological theory (1986, 2004; Bronfenbrenner & Morris, 1998, 2006) holds that development reflects the influence of several environmental systems. The theory identifies five environmental systems: microsystem, mesosystem, exosystem, macrosystem, and chronosystem (see Figure 15).

The *microsystem* is the setting in which the individual lives. Contexts within it include the person's family, peers, school, and neighborhood. It is in the microsystem that the most direct interactions with social agents take place—with parents, friends, and teachers, for example. The individual is not a passive recipient of experiences in these settings, but someone who helps to construct the settings.

The *mesosystem* involves relations between microsystems or connections between contexts. Examples are the relationship of family experiences to school experiences, school experiences to church experiences, and family experiences to peer experiences. For example, children whose parents have rejected them may have difficulty developing positive relations with teachers.

The *exosystem* consists of links between the individual's immediate context and a social setting in which the individual does not play an active role. For example, a father's or child's experience at home may be influenced by a mother's experiences at work. The mother might receive a promotion that requires more travel, which might increase conflict with her husband and change patterns of interaction with their child.

The *macrosystem* involves the culture in which individuals live. Remember from earlier in the chapter that culture refers to the behavior patterns, beliefs, and all other products of a group of people that are passed on from generation to generation. Remember also that

FIGURE 15

BRONFENBRENNER'S ECOLOGICAL THEORY OF DEVELOPMENT. Bronfenbrenner's ecological theory consists of five environmental systems: microsystem, mesosystem, exosystem, macrosystem, and chronosystem.

Bronfenbrenner's ecological theory Bronfenbrenner's environmental systems theory that focuses on five environmental systems: microsystem, mesosystem, exosystem, macrosystem, and chronosystem.

cross-cultural studies—the comparison of one culture with one or more other cultures—provide information about the generality of development.

The *chronosystem* consists of the patterning of environmental events and transitions over the life course, as well as sociohistorical circumstances. For example, divorce is one transition. Researchers have found that the negative effects of divorce on children often peak during the first year after the divorce (Hetherington, 1993, 2006). By two years after the divorce, family interaction is more stable. As an example of sociohistorical circumstances, consider how the opportunities for women to pursue a career have increased since the 1960s.

Bronfenbrenner (2004; Bronfenbrenner & Morris, 2006) subsequently added biological influences to his theory, describing it as a bioecological theory. Nonetheless, it is still dominated by ecological, environmental contexts.

Contributions of the theory include its systematic examination of micro and macro dimensions of environmental systems, and its attention to connections between environmental systems. A further contribution of Bronfenbrenner's theory is an emphasis on a range of social contexts beyond the family, such as neighborhood, religious community, school, and workplace, as influential in children's development (Gauvain, 2016). The theory has been criticized for giving inadequate attention to the influence of biological and cognitive factors.

AN ECLECTIC THEORETICAL ORIENTATION

No single theory described in this chapter can explain entirely the rich complexity of life-span development, but each has contributed to our understanding of development. Psychoanalytic theory best explains the workings of the unconscious mind. Erikson's theory best describes the changes that occur in adult development. Piaget's, Vygotsky's, and the information-processing views provide the most complete description of cognitive development. The behavioral and social cognitive and ecological theories have been the most adept at examining the environmental determinants of development. The ethological theories have highlighted biology's role and the importance of sensitive periods in development.

In short, although theories can be helpful guides, relying on a single theory to explain development probably would be a mistake. Our solution to this dilemma is to take an **eclectic theoretical orientation**—rather than following a single theoretical approach, an eclectic approach selects from each theory whatever is considered its best features. Figure 16 compares the main theoretical perspectives in terms of how they view important issues in human development.

Urie Bronfenbrenner developed ecological theory, a perspective that is receiving increased attention today. His theory emphasizes the importance of both micro and macro dimensions of the environment in which the child lives.
Courtesy of Cornell University Photography

eclectic theoretical orientation An orientation that does not follow any one theoretical approach but rather selects from each theory whatever is considered best in it.

THEORY	ISSUES	
	Continuity/discontinuity, early versus later experiences	**Biological and environmental factors**
Psychoanalytic	Discontinuity between stages—continuity between early experiences and later development; early experiences very important; later changes in development emphasized in Erikson's theory	Freud's biological determination interacting with early family experiences; Erikson's more balanced biological-cultural interaction perspective
Cognitive	Discontinuity between stages in Piaget's theory; continuity between early experiences and later development in Piaget's and Vygotsky's theories; no stages in Vygotsky's theory or information-processing theory	Piaget's emphasis on interaction and adaptation; environment provides the setting for cognitive structures to develop; information-processing view has not addressed this issue extensively but mainly emphasizes biological-environmental interaction
Behavioral and social cognitive	Continuity (no stages); experience at all points of development important	Environment viewed as the cause of behavior in both views
Ethological	Discontinuity but no stages; critical or sensitive periods emphasized; early experiences very important	Strong biological view
Ecological	Little attention to continuity/discontinuity; change emphasized more than stability	Strong environmental view

FIGURE 16

A COMPARISON OF THEORIES AND ISSUES IN LIFE-SPAN DEVELOPMENT.

4 Research on Life-Span Development

LG4 Explain how research on life-span development is conducted.

| Methods for Collecting Data | Research Designs | Time Span of Research | Conducting Ethical Research | Minimizing Bias |

If they follow an eclectic orientation, how do scholars and researchers determine that one feature of a theory is somehow better than another? The scientific method discussed earlier in this chapter provides the guide. Through scientific research, they can test and refine the features of theories (Gravetter & Forzano, 2019; Stanovich, 2019).

Generally, research in life-span development is designed to test hypotheses, which in some cases are derived from the theories just described. Through research, theories are modified to reflect new data, and occasionally new theories arise.

METHODS FOR COLLECTING DATA

Whether we are interested in studying attachment in infants, the cognitive skills of children, or social relationships in older adults, we can choose from several ways of collecting data. Here we consider the measures most often used, beginning with observation.

Observation   Scientific observation requires an important set of skills (Stanovich, 2019). For observations to be effective, they have to be systematic. We need to have some idea of what we are looking for. We have to know whom we are observing, when and where we will observe, how we will make our observations, and how we will record them.

Where should we make our observations? We have two choices: the laboratory and the everyday world.

When we observe scientifically, we often need to control certain factors that determine behavior but are not the focus of our inquiry (Graziano & Raulin, 2020). For this reason, some research in life-span development is conducted in a **laboratory,** a controlled setting where many of the complex factors of the "real world" are absent. For example, suppose you want to observe how children react when they see other people act aggressively. If you observe children in their homes or schools, you have no control over how much aggression the children observe, what

laboratory A controlled setting from which many of the complex factors of the "real world" have been removed.

What are some important strategies in conducting observational research with children?
Charles Fox/Philadelphia Inquirer/MCT/Landov Images

kind of aggression they see, which people they see acting aggressively, or how other people treat the children. In contrast, if you observe the children in a laboratory, you can control these and other factors and therefore have more confidence about how to interpret your observations.

Laboratory research does have some drawbacks, however, including the following:

· It is almost impossible to conduct research without the participants knowing they are being studied.

· The laboratory setting is unnatural and therefore can cause the participants to behave unnaturally.

· People who are willing to come to a university laboratory may not fairly represent groups from diverse cultural backgrounds.

· People who are unfamiliar with university settings may be intimidated by the laboratory atmosphere.

Naturalistic observation provides insights that sometimes cannot be obtained in the laboratory (Neuman, 2020). **Naturalistic observation** means observing behavior in real-world settings, making no effort to manipulate or control the situation. Life-span researchers conduct naturalistic observations at sporting events, child-care centers, schools, work settings, malls, and other places people live in and frequent.

Naturalistic observation was used in one study that focused on conversations in a children's science museum (Crowley & others, 2001). When visiting exhibits at the science museum, parents were three times as likely to engage boys as girls in explanatory talk. This finding suggests a gender bias that encourages boys more than girls to be interested in science (see Figure 17).

Survey and Interview   Sometimes the best and quickest way to get information about people is to ask them for it. One technique is to *interview* them directly. A related method is the survey—sometimes referred to as a *questionnaire*—which is especially useful when information from many people is needed (Ary & others, 2019; Neuman, 2020). A standard set of questions is used to obtain people's self-reported attitudes or beliefs about a particular topic. In a good survey, the questions are clear and unbiased, allowing respondents to answer unambiguously.

Surveys and interviews can be used to study a wide range of topics, from religious beliefs to sexual habits to attitudes about gun control to beliefs about how to improve schools. Surveys and interviews may be conducted in person, over the telephone, and over the Internet.

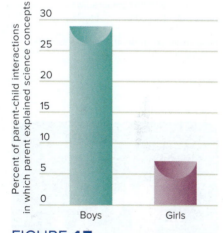

FIGURE 17

PARENTS' EXPLANATIONS OF SCIENCE TO SONS AND DAUGHTERS AT A SCIENCE MUSEUM. In a naturalistic observation study at a children's science museum, parents were three times more likely to explain science to boys than to girls (Crowley & others, 2001). The gender difference occurred regardless of whether the father, the mother, or both parents were with the child, although the gender difference was greatest for fathers' science explanations to sons and daughters.

naturalistic observation Observing behavior in real-world settings.

One problem with surveys and interviews is the tendency of participants to answer questions in a way that they think is socially acceptable or desirable rather than to say what they truly think or feel. For example, on a survey or in an interview some individuals might say that they do not take drugs even though they do.

Standardized Test A **standardized test** has uniform procedures for administration and scoring. Many standardized tests allow a person's performance to be compared with that of other individuals; thus, they provide information about individual differences among people (Kaplan & Saccuzzo, 2018). One example is the Stanford-Binet intelligence test, which is described in the chapter on "Intelligence." Your score on the Stanford-Binet test tells you how your performance compares with that of thousands of other people who have taken the test.

One criticism of standardized tests is that they assume a person's behavior is consistent and stable, although personality and intelligence—two primary targets of standardized testing—can vary with the situation. For example, a person may perform poorly on a standardized intelligence test in an office setting but score much higher at home, where he or she is less anxious.

Mahatma Gandhi was the spiritual leader of India in the middle of the 20th century. Erik Erikson conducted an extensive case study of Gandhi's life to determine what contributed to his identity development. *What are some limitations of the case study approach?*
Bettmann/Getty Images

standardized test A test with uniform procedures for administration and scoring. Many standardized tests allow a person's performance to be compared with the performance of other individuals.

case study An in-depth look at a single individual.

Case Study A **case study** is an in-depth look at a single individual. Case studies are performed mainly by mental health professionals when, for either practical or ethical reasons, the unique aspects of an individual's life cannot be duplicated and tested in other individuals. A case study provides information about one person's experiences; it may focus on nearly any aspect of the subject's life that helps the researcher understand the person's mind, behavior, or other attributes. In other chapters, we discuss vivid case studies, such as that of Michael Rehbein, who had much of the left side of his brain removed at 7 years of age to end severe epileptic seizures.

A case study can provide a dramatic, in-depth portrayal of an individual's life, but we must be cautious when generalizing from this information. The subject of a case study is unique, with a genetic makeup and personal history that no one else shares. In addition, case studies involve judgments of unknown reliability. Researchers who conduct case studies rarely check to see if other professionals agree with their observations or findings.

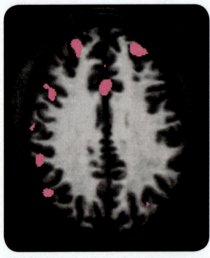

Physiological Measures Researchers are increasingly using physiological measures when they study development at different points in the life span. Hormone levels are increasingly examined in developmental research. Cortisol is a hormone produced by the adrenal gland that is linked to the body's stress level and has been measured in studies of temperament, emotional reactivity, mood, and peer relations (Bell & others, 2018; Freberg, 2019). Also, as puberty unfolds, the blood levels of certain hormones increase. To determine the nature of these hormonal changes, researchers analyze blood samples from adolescent volunteers (Li & others, 2019).

Another physiological measure that is increasingly being used is neuroimaging, especially *functional magnetic resonance imaging* (fMRI), in which electromagnetic waves are used to construct images of a person's brain tissue and biochemical activity (Kinugawa, 2019; Park & Festini, 2018). Figure 18 compares the brain images of two adolescents—one a nondrinker and the other a heavy drinker—while they are engaged in a memory task.

FIGURE 18

BRAIN IMAGING OF 15-YEAR-OLD ADOLESCENTS. These two brain images indicate how alcohol can influence the functioning of an adolescent's brain. Notice the pink and red coloring (which indicates effective brain functioning involving memory) in the brain of a 15-year-old nondrinker (*left*) while engaging in a memory task, and compare it with the lack of those colors in the brain of a 15-year-old heavy drinker (*right*) under the influence of alcohol.
Dr. Susan F. Tapert, University of California, San Diego

Electroencephalography (EEG) is a physiological measure that has been used for many decades to monitor overall electrical charges in the brain (Feinberg & Campbell, 2019; Sheinkopf & others, 2019). Recent electroencephalography research includes studies of infants' attention and memory (Bell & others, 2018).

Heart rate has been used as an indicator of infants' and children's development of perception, attention, and memory (Billeci & others, 2018). Further, heart rate has been used as an index of different aspects of emotional development, such as inhibition, stress, and anxiety (Amole & others, 2017; Cheetham-Blake & others, 2019).

Eye movement also is increasingly being assessed to learn more about perceptual development and other developmental topics. Sophisticated eye-tracking equipment is used to provide more detailed information about infants' perception (van Renswoude & others, 2018), attention (Mastorakos & Scott, 2019), face processing (Chhaya & others, 2018), and the development of autism (Traynor & others, 2019).

Yet another dramatic change in physiological methods is the advancement in methods to assess the actual units of hereditary information—genes—in studies of biological influences on development (Falandry, 2019; Toupance & Benetos, 2019). For example, recent advances in gene assessment have identified several specific genes that are linked to childhood obesity (Wang & others, 2019; Zandona & others, 2017). And in a later chapter you will read about the role of the ApoE4 gene in Alzheimer disease (Park & Festini, 2018).

RESEARCH DESIGNS

In conducting research on life-span development, in addition to having a method for collecting data, you also need a research design. There are three main types of research designs: descriptive, correlational, and experimental.

Descriptive Research All of the data-collection methods that we have discussed can be used in **descriptive research,** which aims to observe and record behavior. For example, a researcher might observe the extent to which people are altruistic or aggressive toward each other. By itself, descriptive research cannot prove what causes some phenomenon, but it can reveal important information about people's behavior (Ary & others, 2019; Neuman, 2020).

Correlational Research In contrast with descriptive research, correlational research goes beyond describing phenomena to provide information that will help us to predict how people will behave (Gravetter & Forzano, 2019). In **correlational research,** the goal is to describe the strength of the relationship between two or more events or characteristics. The more strongly the two events are correlated (or related or associated), the more effectively we can predict one event from the other (Aron, Coups, & Aron, 2019).

For example, to find out whether children of permissive parents have less self-control than other children, you would need to carefully record observations of parents' permissiveness and their children's self-control. You might observe that the higher a parent was in permissiveness, the lower the child was in self-control. You would then analyze these data statistically to yield a numerical measure, called a **correlation coefficient,** a number based on a statistical analysis that is used to describe the degree of association between two variables. The correlation coefficient ranges from −1.00 to +1.00. A negative number means an inverse (reversed) relation. In the example just given, you might find an inverse correlation between permissive parenting and children's self-control, with a coefficient of, say, −.30. By contrast, you might find a positive correlation of +.30 between parental monitoring of children and children's self-control.

The higher the correlation coefficient (whether positive or negative), the stronger the association between the two factors. A correlation of 0 means that there is no association between the factors. A correlation of −.40 is stronger than a correlation of +.20 because we disregard whether the correlation is positive or negative in determining the strength of the correlation.

A caution is in order, however. Correlation does not equal causation (Aron, Coups, & Aron, 2019; Howell, 2017). The correlational finding just mentioned does not mean that permissive parenting necessarily causes low self-control in children. It could have that meaning, but it also could mean that a child's lack of self-control caused the parents to throw up their arms in despair and give up trying to control the child. It also could mean that other factors, such as heredity or poverty, caused the correlation between permissive parenting and low self-control in children. Figure 19 illustrates these possible interpretations of correlational data.

descriptive research A type of research that aims to observe and record behavior.

correlational research A type of research that strives to describe the strength of the relationship between two or more events or characteristics.

correlation coefficient A number based on a statistical analysis that is used to describe the degree of association between two variables.

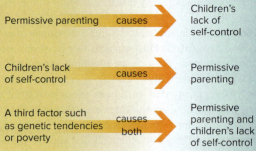

Observed Correlation: As permissive parenting increases, children's self-control decreases.

Possible explanations for this observed correlation

Permissive parenting → causes → Children's lack of self-control

Children's lack of self-control → causes → Permissive parenting

A third factor such as genetic tendencies or poverty → causes both → Permissive parenting and children's lack of self-control

An observed correlation between two events cannot be used to conclude that one event causes the second event. Other possibilities are that the second event causes the first event or that a third event causes the correlation between the first two events.

FIGURE 19

POSSIBLE EXPLANATIONS OF CORRELATIONAL DATA.
JupiterImages/Getty Images

experiment Carefully regulated procedure in which one or more factors believed to influence the behavior being studied are manipulated while all other factors are held constant.

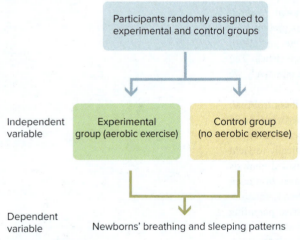

Participants randomly assigned to experimental and control groups

Independent variable → Experimental group (aerobic exercise) | Control group (no aerobic exercise)

Dependent variable → Newborns' breathing and sleeping patterns

FIGURE 20

PRINCIPLES OF EXPERIMENTAL RESEARCH. Imagine that you decide to conduct an experimental study of the effects of aerobic exercise by pregnant women on their newborns' breathing and sleeping patterns. You would randomly assign pregnant women to experimental and control groups. The experimental-group women would engage in aerobic exercise over a specified number of sessions and weeks. The control group would not. Then, when the infants are born, you would assess their breathing and sleeping patterns. If the breathing and sleeping patterns of newborns whose mothers were in the experimental group are more positive than those of the control group, you would conclude that aerobic exercise caused the positive effects.

Experimental Research To study causality, researchers turn to experimental research. An **experiment** is a carefully regulated procedure in which one or more factors believed to influence the behavior being studied are manipulated while all other factors are held constant. If the behavior under study changes when a factor is manipulated, the manipulated factor has caused the behavior to change (Christensen, Johnson, & Turner, 2020). In other words, the experiment has demonstrated cause and effect. The cause is the factor that was manipulated. The effect is the behavior that changed because of the manipulation. Nonexperimental research methods (descriptive and correlational research) cannot establish cause and effect because they do not involve manipulating factors in a controlled way (Gravetter & Forzano, 2019).

Independent and Dependent Variables Experiments include two types of changeable factors, or variables: independent and dependent. An *independent variable* is a manipulated, influential, experimental factor. It is a potential cause. The label "independent" is used because this variable can be manipulated independently of other factors to determine its effect. An experiment may include one independent variable or several of them.

A *dependent variable* is a factor that can change in an experiment, in response to changes in the independent variable. As researchers manipulate the independent variable, they measure the dependent variable for any resulting effect.

For example, suppose that you are conducting a study to determine whether pregnant women could change the breathing and sleeping patterns of their newborn babies by engaging in aerobic exercise during pregnancy. You might require one group of pregnant women to engage in a certain amount and type of aerobic exercise each day while another group would not exercise; the aerobic exercise is thus the independent variable. When the infants are born, you would observe and measure their breathing and sleeping patterns. These patterns are the dependent variable, the factor that changes as the result of your manipulation.

Experimental and Control Groups Experiments can involve one or more experimental groups and one or more control groups (Graziano & Raulin, 2020). An experimental group is a group whose experience is manipulated. A *control group* is a comparison group that resembles the experimental group as closely as possible and is treated in every way like the experimental group except for the manipulated factor (independent variable). The control group serves as a baseline against which the effects of the manipulated condition can be compared.

Random assignment is an important principle for deciding whether each participant will be placed in the experimental group or in the control group. Random assignment means that researchers assign participants to experimental and control groups by chance. It reduces the likelihood that the experiment's results will be due to any preexisting differences between groups (Gravetter & Forzano, 2019). In the example of the effects of aerobic exercise by pregnant women on the breathing and sleeping patterns of their newborns, you would randomly assign half of the pregnant women to engage in aerobic exercise over a period of weeks (the experimental group) and the other half not to exercise during the same number of weeks (the control group). Figure 20 illustrates the nature of experimental research.

TIME SPAN OF RESEARCH

Researchers in life-span development have a special concern with studies that focus on the relation of age to some other variable. They have several options: Researchers can study different individuals of varying ages and compare them, or they can study the same individuals as they age over time.

Cross-Sectional Approach   The **cross-sectional approach** is a research strategy that simultaneously compares individuals of different ages. A typical cross-sectional study might include three groups of children: 5-year-olds, 8-year-olds, and 11-year-olds. Another study might include groups of 15-year-olds, 25-year-olds, and 45-year-olds. The groups can be compared with respect to a variety of dependent variables: IQ, memory, peer relations, attachment to parents, hormonal changes, and so on. All of these comparisons can be accomplished in a short time. In some studies, data are collected in a single day. Even in large-scale cross-sectional studies with hundreds of subjects, data collection does not usually take longer than several months to complete.

The main advantage of the cross-sectional study is that the researcher does not have to wait for the individuals to grow up or become older. Despite its efficiency, though, the cross-sectional approach has its drawbacks. It gives no information about how individuals change or about the stability of their characteristics. It can obscure the increases and decreases of development—the hills and valleys of growth and development. For example, a cross-sectional study of life satisfaction might reveal average increases and decreases, but it would not show how the life satisfaction of individual adults waxed and waned over the years. It also would not tell us whether the same adults who had positive or negative perceptions of life satisfaction in early adulthood maintained their relative degree of life satisfaction as they became middle-aged or older adults.

Longitudinal Approach   The **longitudinal approach** is a research strategy in which the same individuals are studied over a period of time, usually several years or more. For example, in a longitudinal study of life satisfaction, the same adults might be assessed periodically over a 70-year time span—at the ages of 20, 35, 45, 65, and 90, for example.

Longitudinal studies provide a wealth of information about vital issues such as stability and change in development and the importance of early experience for later development, but they do have drawbacks (Almy & Cicchetti, 2018; Evans & others, 2019). They are expensive and time consuming. The longer the study lasts, the more participants drop out—they move, get sick, lose interest, and so forth. The participants who remain may be dissimilar to those who drop out, biasing the outcome of the study. Those individuals who remain in a longitudinal study over a number of years may be more responsible and conformity-oriented, for example, or they might lead more stable lives.

Cohort Effects   Earlier in our focus on characteristics of the life-span perspective on development, we described the importance of considering historical effects. An important term that is used in studying historical effects is *cohort*, a group of people who are born at a similar point in history and share similar experiences as a result, such as living through the Vietnam War or growing up in the same city around the same time. These shared experiences may produce a range of differences among cohorts (Hohls & others, 2019; Messerlian & Basso, 2018). For example, people who were teenagers during World War II are likely to differ from people who were teenagers during the booming 1990s in their educational opportunities and economic status, in how they were raised, and in their attitudes toward sex and religion. In life-span development research, **cohort effects** are due to a person's time of birth, era, or generation but not to actual age.

Cohort effects are important because they can powerfully affect the dependent measures in a study ostensibly concerned with age (Atkins & others, 2019; Ishtiak-Ahmed & others, 2018). Researchers have shown it is especially important to be aware of cohort effects when assessing adult intelligence (Schaie, 2013, 2016). Individuals born at different points in time—such as 1930, 1960, and 1990—have had varying opportunities for education. Individuals born in earlier years had less access to education, and this fact may have a significant effect on how this cohort performs on intelligence tests. Some researchers have found that cross-sectional studies indicate more than 90 percent of cognitive decline in aging is due to a slowing of processing speed, whereas longitudinal studies reveal that 20 percent or less of cognitive decline is due to processing speed (MacDonald & Stawski, 2016). Further, in a recent study, older adults nowadays report fewer constraints than their counterparts 18 years ago, but younger adults report more constraints and lower mastery beliefs today than those 18 years ago (Drewelies & others, 2018).

Cross-sectional studies can show how different cohorts respond, but they can confuse age changes and cohort effects. Longitudinal studies are effective in studying age changes but only within one cohort.

cross-sectional approach A research strategy in which individuals of different ages are compared at one time.

longitudinal approach A research strategy in which the same individuals are studied over a period of time, usually several years or more.

cohort effects Characteristics attributable to a person's time of birth, era, or generation but not to actual age.

Cohort effects are due to time of birth or generation but not a person's specific age. Think for a moment about growing up in (a) the Great Depression and (b) today. *How might your development be different depending on which of these time frames has dominated your life? your parents' lives? your grandparents' lives?*
(*Left*) Ariel Skelley/Blend Images/Getty Images; (*right*) Jamie Grill/Blend Images/Corbis

How are today's generation Z/post-millennials experiencing youth differently from earlier generations?
Hero Images/Alamy Stock Photo

Various generations have been given labels by the popular culture. Figure 21 describes the labels of various generations, their historical periods, and the reasons for their labels.

Until recently, the youngest generation was labeled *millennials,* and this group was recognized as being more technologically sophisticated and more ethnically diverse than earlier generations. However, the Pew Research Center, which has periodically assessed generational trends in recent decades, recently decided to describe millennials as anyone born between 1981 and 1996, with anyone born in 1997 or later as part of a new generation (Dimock, 2019). The name of this new generation has not yet been selected, but two potential names are *generation Z* and *post-millennial.* The oldest members of this new generation turn 23 in 2020, while the oldest millennials turn 40 in 2020. What characterizes this new Z/post-millennial generation? They are even more technologically sophisticated and ethnically diverse than millennials. These young people have technological devices that are always available and always on; they are immersed in social media; and they tend to communicate with others online and through

FIGURE 21
GENERATIONS, THEIR HISTORICAL PERIODS, AND CHARACTERISTICS

Generation	Historical Period	Reasons for Label
Generation Z/Post-Millennials	Individuals born in 1997 and later	More immersed in a technological world, more ethnically diverse, and better educated than millennials.
Millennials	Individuals born between 1981 and 1996	First generation to come of age and enter emerging adulthood (18 to 25 years of age) in the twenty-first century (the new millennium). Two main characteristics: (1) connection to technology, and (2) ethnic diversity.
Generation X	Individuals born between 1965 and 1980	Described as lacking an identity and savvy loners.
Baby Boomers	Individuals born between 1946 and 1964	Label used because this generation represents the spike in the number of babies born after World War II; the largest generation ever to enter late adulthood in the United States.
Silent Generation	Individuals born between 1928 and 1945	Children of the Great Depression and World War II; described as conformists and civic minded.

mobile devices far more than in person. Also, generation Z/post-millennials are the best-educated generation yet: they are more likely to go to college and to have a college-educated parent than millennials are (Fry & Parker, 2018).

CONDUCTING ETHICAL RESEARCH

Ethics in research may affect you personally if you ever serve as a participant in a study. In that event, you need to know your rights as a participant and the responsibilities of researchers to assure that these rights are safeguarded.

If you ever become a researcher in life-span development yourself, you will need an even deeper understanding of ethics. Even if you only carry out experimental projects in psychology courses, you must consider the rights of the participants in those projects. A student might think, "I volunteer in a home for individuals with intellectual disabilities several hours per week. I can use the residents of the home in my study to see if a particular treatment helps improve their memory for everyday tasks." But without proper permissions, the most well-meaning and considerate studies still violate the rights of the participants (Ary & others, 2019; Neuman, 2020).

Today, proposed research at colleges and universities must pass the scrutiny of a research ethics committee before the research can begin. In addition, the American Psychological Association (APA) has developed ethics guidelines for its members. The code of ethics instructs psychologists to protect their participants from mental and physical harm. The participants' best interests need to be kept foremost in the researcher's mind. APA's guidelines address four important issues:

1. *Informed consent*. All participants must know what their research participation will involve and what risks might develop. Even after informed consent is given, participants must retain the right to withdraw from the study at any time and for any reason.

2. *Confidentiality*. Researchers are responsible for keeping all of the data they gather on individuals completely confidential and, when possible, completely anonymous.

3. *Debriefing*. After the study has been completed, participants should be informed of its purpose and the methods that were used. In most cases, the experimenter also can inform participants in a general manner beforehand about the purpose of the research without leading participants to behave in a way they think the experimenter is expecting.

4. *Deception*. In some circumstances, telling the participants beforehand what the research study is about substantially alters the participants' behavior and invalidates the researcher's data. Thus, researchers may deceive the participants about the details of the study. In all cases of deception, however, the psychologist must ensure that the deception will not harm the participants and that the participants will be *debriefed* (told the actual nature of the study) as soon as possible after the study is completed.

MINIMIZING BIAS

Studies of life-span development are most useful when they are conducted without bias or prejudice toward any group of people. Of special concern is bias based on gender and bias based on culture or ethnicity.

Gender Bias   For most of its existence, our society has had a strong gender bias, a preconceived notion about the abilities of women and men that prevented individuals from pursuing their own interests and achieving their potential. Gender bias also has had a less obvious effect within the field of life-span development. For example, it is not unusual for conclusions to be drawn about females' attitudes and behaviors from research conducted with males as the only participants (Best & Puzio, 2019; Helgeson, 2017).

Furthermore, when researchers find gender differences, their reports sometimes magnify those differences (Denmark & others, 1988). For example, a researcher might report that 74 percent of the men in a study had high achievement expectations versus only 67 percent of the women and go on to talk about the differences in some detail. In reality, this might be a rather small difference. It also might disappear if the study were repeated, or the study might have methodological problems that don't allow such strong interpretations.

Pam Reid is a leading researcher who studies gender and ethnic bias in development. To read about Pam's interests, see the *Connecting with Careers* profile.

Pam Reid, Educational and Development Psychologist

When she was a child, Pam Reid liked to play with chemistry sets. Reid majored in chemistry during college and wanted to become a doctor. However, when some of her friends signed up for a psychology class as an elective she also decided to take the course. She was intrigued by learning about how people think, behave, and develop—so much so that she changed her major to psychology. Reid went on to obtain her Ph.D. in psychology (American Psychological Association, 2003, p. 16).

For a number of years, Reid was professor of education and psychology at the University of Michigan, where she also was a research scientist at the Institute for Research on Women and Gender. Her main focus has been on how children and adolescents develop social skills, with a special interest in the development of African American girls (Reid & Zalk, 2001). In 2004, Reid became Provost and Executive Vice-President at Roosevelt University in Chicago, and in 2007 she became president of Saint Joseph College in Hartford, Connecticut.

Pam Reid (*center*), with students at Saint Joseph College in Hartford, Connecticut.
Courtesy of Dr. Pam Reid.

For more information about what educational psychologists do, see the Careers in Life-Span Development appendix.

Cultural and Ethnic Bias   There is a growing awareness that research on life-span development needs to include more people from diverse ethnic groups. Historically, people from ethnic minority groups (African American, Latino, Asian American, and Native American) were excluded from most research in the United States and simply thought of as variations from the norm or average. If minority individuals were included in samples and their scores didn't fit the norm, they were viewed as confounds or "noise" in data and discounted (Nieto & Bode, 2018). Given the fact that individuals from diverse ethnic groups were excluded from research on life-span development for so long, we might reasonably conclude that people's real lives are perhaps more varied than research data have indicated in the past.

Researchers also have tended to overgeneralize about ethnic groups. **Ethnic gloss** involves using an ethnic label such as African American or Latino in a superficial way that portrays an ethnic group as being more homogeneous than it really is (Trimble, 1988). For example, a researcher might describe a research sample like this: "The participants were 60 Latinos."

ethnic gloss Use of an ethnic label such as African American or Latino in a superficial way that portrays an ethnic group as being more homogeneous than it really is.

Look at these two photographs, one of all non-Latino White males, the other of a diverse group of females and males from different ethnic groups, including some non-Latino White males. Consider a topic in life-span development, such as parenting, love, or cultural values. *If you were conducting research on this topic, might the results of the study be different depending on whether the participants in your study were the individuals in the photograph on the left or the right?*
(*Left*): Anthony Cassidy/The Image Bank/Getty Images; (*right*): Punchstock/Digital Vision

A more complete description of the Latino group might be something like this: "The 60 Latino participants were Mexican Americans from low-income neighborhoods in the southwestern area of Los Angeles. Thirty-six were from homes in which Spanish is the dominant spoken language, 24 from homes in which English is the main spoken language. Thirty were born in the United States, 30 in Mexico. Twenty-eight described themselves as Mexican American, 14 as Mexican, 9 as American, 6 as Chicano, and 3 as Latino." Ethnic gloss can cause researchers to obtain samples of ethnic groups that are not representative of the group's diversity, which can lead to overgeneralization and stereotyping.

The growing proportion of minority families in the U.S. population in approaching decades will mainly be due to the immigration of Latino and Asian families. Researchers need "to take into account their acculturation level and generational status of parents and children" and consider how these factors influence family processes and child outcomes (Parke & Buriel, 2006, p. 487). More attention also needs to be given to biculturalism, because the complexity of diversity means that some children of color identify with two or more ethnic groups (Safa & others, 2019; Syed, Juang, & Svensson, 2018). And language development research needs to focus more on dual-language acquisition and how it is linked to school achievement (Diaz-Rico, 2018).

Review *Connect* Reflect

 LG4 Explain how research on life-span development is conducted.

Review

- What methods do researchers use to collect data on life-span development?
- What research designs are used to study human development?
- How are cross-sectional and longitudinal research designs different?
- What are researchers' ethical responsibilities to the people they study?
- How can gender, cultural, and ethnic bias affect the outcome of a research study?

Connect

- Earlier in this chapter you read about research on age-related memory decline that revealed some potential biases based on the type of information involved and the time of day when the testing was done. How might researchers study memory decline while accounting for such possible biases?

Reflect *Your Own Personal Journey of Life*

- Imagine that you are conducting a research study on the sexual attitudes and behaviors of adolescents. What ethical safeguards should you use in conducting the study?

reach your **learning goals**

Introduction

1 The Life-Span Perspective

The Importance of Studying Life-Span Development

Characteristics of the Life-Span Perspective

LG1 Discuss the distinctive features of a life-span perspective on development.

- Development is the pattern of change that begins at conception and continues through the life span. It includes both growth and decline.

- Studying life-span development helps prepare us to take responsibility for children, gives us insight about our own lives, and gives us knowledge about what our lives will be like as we age.

- The life-span perspective includes the following basic concepts: development is lifelong, multi-dimensional, multidirectional, and plastic; its study is multidisciplinary; it is embedded in contexts; it involves growth, maintenance, and regulation; and it is a co-construction of biological, sociocultural, and individual factors.

Some Contemporary Concerns

- Three important sources of contextual influences are (1) normative age-graded influences, (2) normative history-graded influences, and (3) nonnormative life events.

- Health and well-being, parenting, education, sociocultural contexts and diversity, and social policy are all areas of contemporary concern that are closely tied to life-span development.

- Important dimensions of the sociocultural context include culture, ethnicity, socioeconomic status, and gender.

- There is increasing interest in social policy issues related to children and to older adults, as well as the importance of resiliency in development.

- Recently there has been a dramatic infusion of technology in the lives of people of all ages, and the influence of technology on development is an important contemporary issue.

2 The Nature of Development

LG2 Identify the most important processes, periods, and issues in development.

Biological, Cognitive, and Socioemotional Processes

- Three key categories of developmental processes are biological, cognitive, and socioemotional. Development is influenced by an interplay of these processes.

Periods of Development

- The life span is commonly divided into the following periods of development: prenatal, infancy, early childhood, middle and late childhood, adolescence, early adulthood, middle adulthood, and late adulthood.

- Attention is increasingly being directed to age differences in functioning within the late adulthood period, especially between the young old (65 through 84) and oldest old (85 and older).

- An increasing number of studies have found that as adults get older they are happier.

The Significance of Age

- We often think of age only in terms of chronological age, but a full evaluation of age requires consideration of chronological, biological, psychological, and social age.

- The nature-nurture issue focuses on the extent to which development is mainly influenced by nature (biological inheritance) or nurture (experience).

Developmental Issues

- The stability-change issue focuses on the degree to which we become older renditions of our early experience or develop into someone different from who we were earlier in development. A special aspect of the stability-change issue is the extent to which development is determined by early versus later experiences.

- Developmentalists describe development as continuous (gradual, a cumulative change) or as discontinuous (abrupt, a sequence of stages).

- Most developmentalists recognize that extreme positions on the nature-nurture, stability-change, and continuity-discontinuity issues are unwise. Despite this consensus, there is still spirited debate on these issues.

3 Theories of Development

LG3 Describe the main theories of human development.

Psychoanalytic Theories

- The scientific method involves four main steps: (1) conceptualize a problem, (2) collect data, (3) analyze data, and (4) draw conclusions. Theory is often involved in conceptualizing a problem. A theory is an interrelated, coherent set of ideas that helps to explain phenomena and to make predictions. Hypotheses are specific assertions and predictions, often derived from theory, that can be tested.

- According to psychoanalytic theories, development primarily depends on the unconscious mind and is heavily couched in emotion. Freud also argued that individuals go through five psychosexual stages.

- Erikson's theory emphasizes eight psychosocial stages of development: trust versus mistrust, autonomy versus shame and doubt, initiative versus guilt, industry versus inferiority, identity versus identity confusion, intimacy versus isolation, generativity versus stagnation, and integrity versus despair.

- Contributions of psychoanalytic theories include an emphasis on a developmental framework, family relationships, and unconscious aspects of the mind. Criticisms include a lack of scientific support for psychoanalytic theories, too much emphasis on sexual underpinnings, and an image of people that is too negative.

Cognitive Theories

- Three main cognitive theories are Piaget's, Vygotsky's, and information processing. Cognitive theories emphasize thinking, reasoning, language, and other cognitive processes.

- Piaget proposed a cognitive developmental theory in which children use their cognition to adapt to their world. In Piaget's theory, children go through four cognitive stages: sensorimotor, preoperational, concrete operational, and formal operational.

- Vygotsky's sociocultural cognitive theory emphasizes how culture and social interaction guide cognitive development.

- The information-processing approach emphasizes that individuals manipulate information, monitor it, and strategize about it.

- Contributions of cognitive theories include an emphasis on the active construction of understanding and developmental changes in thinking. Criticisms include giving too little attention to individual variations and underrating the unconscious aspects of thought.

Behavioral and Social Cognitive Theories

- Two main behavioral and social cognitive theories are Skinner's operant conditioning and social cognitive theory.

- In Skinner's operant conditioning, the consequences of a behavior produce changes in the probability of the behavior's occurrence.

- In social cognitive theory, observational learning is a key aspect of life-span development. Bandura emphasizes reciprocal interactions among person/cognition, behavior, and environment.

- Contributions of the behavioral and social cognitive theories include an emphasis on scientific research, a focus on environmental factors, and recognition of the importance of person and cognitive factors in social cognitive theory. Criticisms include inadequate attention to developmental changes, too much emphasis on environmental determinants, and (in Skinner's behaviorism) too little attention to cognition.

Ethological Theory

- Ethology stresses that behavior is strongly influenced by biology, is tied to evolution, and is characterized by critical or sensitive periods.

- Contributions of ethological theory include its focus on the biological and evolutionary basis of development. Criticisms include inflexibility regarding the concepts of critical and sensitive periods.

Ecological Theory

- Ecological theory emphasizes environmental contexts. Bronfenbrenner's environmental systems view of development proposes five environmental systems: microsystem, mesosystem, exosystem, macrosystem, and chronosystem.

- Contributions of the theory include a systematic examination of micro and macro dimensions of environmental systems and consideration of sociohistorical influences. Criticisms include inadequate attention to biological factors, as well as a lack of emphasis on cognitive factors.

An Eclectic Theoretical Orientation

- An eclectic theoretical orientation does not follow any one theoretical approach but rather selects from each theory whatever is considered the best in it.

4 Research on Life-Span Development

 LG4 Explain how research on life-span development is conducted.

Methods for Collecting Data

- Methods for collecting data about life-span development include observation (in a laboratory or a naturalistic setting), survey (questionnaire) or interview, standardized test, case study, and physiological measures.

Research Designs

- Three main research designs are descriptive, correlational, and experimental. Descriptive research aims to observe and record behavior. The goal of correlational research is to describe the strength of the relationship between two or more events or characteristics. Experimental research involves conducting an experiment, which can determine cause and effect. An independent variable is the manipulated, influential, experimental factor. A dependent variable is a factor that can change in an experiment, in response to changes in the independent variable. Experiments can involve one or more experimental groups and control groups. In random assignment, researchers assign participants to experimental and control groups by chance.

- When researchers decide about the time span of their research, they can conduct cross-sectional or longitudinal studies. Life-span researchers are especially concerned about cohort effects.

- Researchers' ethical responsibilities include seeking participants' informed consent, ensuring their confidentiality, debriefing them about the purpose and potential personal consequences of participating, and avoiding unnecessary deception of participants.

- Researchers need to guard against gender, cultural, and ethnic bias in research. Every effort should be made to make research equitable for both females and males.

- Individuals from varied ethnic backgrounds need to be included as participants in life-span research, and overgeneralization about diverse members within a group must be avoided.

key **terms**

biological processes	culture	hypotheses	Piaget's theory
Bronfenbrenner's ecological theory	descriptive research	information-processing theory	psychoanalytic theories
	development	laboratory	social cognitive theory
case study	eclectic theoretical orientation	life-span perspective	social policy
cognitive processes	emerging adulthood	longitudinal approach	socioeconomic status (SES)
cohort effects	Erikson's theory	naturalistic observation	socioemotional processes
continuity-discontinuity issue	ethnic gloss	nature-nurture issue	stability-change issue
correlation coefficient	ethnicity	nonnormative life events	standardized test
correlational research	ethology	normative age-graded influences	theory
cross-cultural studies	experiment	normative history-graded influences	Vygotsky's theory
cross-sectional approach	gender		

key **people**

Jeffrey Arnett	Laura Carstensen	Konrad Lorenz	B. F. Skinner
Paul Baltes	Marian Wright Edelman	Ann Masten	Lev Vygotsky
Albert Bandura	Erik Erikson	Jean Piaget	
Urie Bronfenbrenner	Sigmund Freud	Robert Siegler	

appendix

Careers in Life-Span Development

The field of life-span development offers an amazing breadth of careers that can provide extremely satisfying work. College and university professors teach courses in many areas of life-span development. Teachers impart knowledge, understanding, and skills to children and adolescents. Counselors, clinical psychologists, nurses, and physicians help people of different ages to cope more effectively with their lives and improve their well-being.

These and many other careers related to life-span development offer many rewards. By working in the field of life-span development, you can help people to improve their lives, understand yourself and others better, possibly advance the state of knowledge in the field, and have an enjoyable time while you are doing these things. Many careers in life-span development pay reasonably well. For example, psychologists earn well above the median salary in the United States.

If you are considering a career in life-span development, would you prefer to work with infants? children? adolescents? older adults? As you go through this term, try to spend some time with people of different ages. Observe their behavior. Talk with them about their lives. Think about whether you would like to work with people of this age on a daily basis.

In addition, to find out about careers in life-span development you might talk with people who work in various jobs. For example, if you have some interest in becoming a school counselor, call a school, ask to speak with a counselor, and set up an appointment to discuss the counselor's career and work. If you have an interest in becoming a nurse, call the nursing department at a hospital and set up an appointment to speak with the nursing coordinator about a nursing career.

Another way to explore careers in life-span development is to work in a related job while you are in college. Many colleges and universities offer internships or other work experiences for students who major in specific fields. Course credit or pay is given for some of these jobs. Take advantage of these opportunities. They can help you decide if this is the right career for you, and they can help you get into graduate school if you choose to acquire additional education after earning your undergraduate degree.

An advanced degree is not absolutely necessary for some careers in life-span development, but usually you can considerably expand your opportunities (and income) by obtaining a graduate degree. If you think you might want to go to graduate school, talk with one or more professors about your interests, maintain a high grade-point average, take appropriate courses, and realize that you likely will need to take the Graduate Record Examination at some point.

We will profile a number of careers in four areas: education/research; clinical/counseling; medical/nursing/physical development; and families/relationships. These are not the only career options in life-span development, but the profiles should give you an idea of the range of opportunities available. For each career, we describe the work and address the amount of education required and the nature of the training. We have provided chapter titles after some entries telling you where to find *Connecting with Careers*, the career profiles of people who hold some of these positions.

Education/Research

Numerous careers in life-span development involve education or research. The opportunities range from college professor to preschool teacher to school psychologist.

College/University Professor

Professors teach courses in life-span development at many types of institutions, including research universities with master's or Ph.D. programs in life-span development, four-year colleges with no graduate programs, and community colleges. The courses in life-span development are offered in many different programs and schools, including psychology, education, nursing, child and family studies, social work, and medicine. In addition to teaching at the undergraduate or graduate level (or both), professors may conduct research, advise students or direct their research, and serve on college or university committees. Research is part of a professor's job description at most universities with master's and Ph.D. programs, but some college professors do not conduct research and focus instead on teaching.

Teaching life-span development at a college or university almost always requires a Ph.D. or master's degree. Obtaining a Ph.D. usually takes four to six years of graduate work; a master's degree requires approximately two years. The training involves taking graduate courses, learning to conduct research, and attending and presenting papers at professional meetings. Many graduate students work as teaching or research assistants for professors in an apprenticeship relationship that helps them to become competent teachers and researchers. **Read the profiles of professors in "Gender and Sexuality" and "Peers and the Sociocultural World."**

Researcher

Some individuals in the field of life-span development work in research positions. They might work for a university, a government agency such as the National Institute of Mental Health, or private industry. They generate research ideas, plan studies, carry out the research, and usually attempt to publish the research results in a scientific journal. A researcher often works in collaboration with other researchers. One researcher might spend much of his or her time in a laboratory; another researcher might work in the field, such as in schools, hospitals, and so on. Most researchers in life-span development have either a master's degree or a Ph.D.

Elementary or Secondary School Teacher

Elementary and secondary school teachers teach one or more subject areas, preparing the curriculum, giving tests, assigning grades, monitoring students' progress, conducting parent-teacher conferences, and attending workshops. Becoming an elementary or secondary school teacher requires a minimum of an undergraduate degree. The training involves taking a wide range of courses with a major or concentration in education as well as completing supervised practice teaching.

Exceptional Children (Special Education) Teacher

Teachers of exceptional children spend concentrated time with children who have a disability such as ADHD, mental retardation, or cerebral palsy, or with children who are gifted. Usually some of their work occurs outside of the students' regular classroom and some of it inside the students' regular classroom. A teacher of exceptional children works closely with the student's regular classroom teacher and parents to create the best educational program for the student. Teachers of exceptional children often continue their education after obtaining their undergraduate degree and attain a master's degree.

Early Childhood Educator

Early childhood educators work on college faculties and usually teach in community colleges that award an associate degree in early childhood education. They have a minimum of a master's degree in their field. In graduate school, they take courses in early childhood education and receive supervisory training in child-care or early childhood programs.

Preschool/Kindergarten Teacher

Preschool teachers teach mainly 4-year-old children, and kindergarten teachers primarily teach 5-year-old children. They usually have an undergraduate degree in education, specializing in early childhood education. State certification to become a preschool or kindergarten teacher usually is required.

Family and Consumer Science Educator

Family and consumer science educators may specialize in early childhood education or instruct middle and high school students about such matters as nutrition, interpersonal relationships, human sexuality, parenting, and human development. Hundreds of colleges and universities throughout the United States offer two- and four-year degree programs in family and consumer science. These programs usually require an internship. Additional education courses may be needed to obtain a teaching certificate. Some family and consumer educators go on to graduate school for further training, which provides a background for possible jobs in college teaching or research. **Read a profile of a family and consumer science educator in "Gender and Sexuality."**

Educational Psychologist

Educational psychologists most often teach in a college or university and conduct research in various areas of educational psychology such as learning, motivation, classroom management, and assessment. They help train students for positions in educational psychology, school psychology, and teaching. Most educational psychologists have a doctorate in education, which takes four to six years of graduate work. **Read a profile of an educational psychologist in "Introduction."**

School Psychologist

School psychologists focus on improving the psychological and intellectual well-being of elementary, middle/junior, and high school students. They give psychological tests, interview students and their parents, consult with teachers, and may provide counseling to students and their families. They may work in a centralized office in a school district or in one or more schools.

School psychologists usually have a master's or doctoral degree in school psychology. In graduate school, they take courses in counseling, assessment, learning, and other areas of education and psychology.

Gerontologist

Gerontologists usually work in research in some branch of the federal or state government. They specialize in the study of aging with a particular focus on government programs for older adults, social policy, and delivery of services to older adults. In their research, gerontologists define problems to be studied, collect data, interpret the results, and make recommendations for social policy. Most gerontologists have a master's or doctoral degree and have taken a concentration of coursework in adult development and aging.

Clinical/Counseling

A wide variety of clinical and counseling jobs are linked with life-span development. These range from child clinical psychologist to adolescent drug counselor to geriatric psychiatrist.

Clinical Psychologist

Clinical psychologists seek to help people with psychological problems. They work in a variety of settings, including colleges and universities, clinics, medical schools, and private practice. Some clinical psychologists only conduct psychotherapy; others do psychological assessment and psychotherapy; some also do research. Clinical psychologists may specialize in a particular age group, such as children (child clinical psychologist) or older adults (geropsychologist).

Clinical psychologists have either a Ph.D. (which involves clinical and research training) or a Psy.D. degree (which only involves clinical training). This graduate training usually takes five to seven years and includes courses in clinical psychology and a one-year supervised internship in an accredited setting toward the end of the training. Many geropsychologists pursue a year or two of postdoctoral training. Most states require clinical psychologists to pass a test in order to become licensed in the state and to call themselves clinical psychologists.

Psychiatrist

Psychiatrists obtain a medical degree and then do a residency in psychiatry. Medical school takes approximately four years and the psychiatry residency another three to four years. Unlike most psychologists (who do not go to medical school), psychiatrists can administer drugs to clients. (Recently, several states gave clinical psychologists the right to prescribe drugs.)

Like clinical psychologists, psychiatrists might specialize in working with children (child psychiatry) or with older adults (geriatric psychiatry). Psychiatrists might work in medical schools in teaching and research roles, in a medical clinic or hospital, or in private practice. In addition to administering drugs to help improve the lives of people with psychological problems, psychiatrists also may conduct psychotherapy. **Read a profile of a child psychiatrist in "Schools, Achievement, and Work."**

Counseling Psychologist

Counseling psychologists work in the same settings as clinical psychologists and may do psychotherapy, teach, or conduct research. Many counseling psychologists do not do therapy with individuals who have severe mental disorders, such as schizophrenia.

Counseling psychologists go through much the same training as clinical psychologists, although in a graduate program in counseling rather than clinical psychology. Counseling psychologists have either a master's degree or a doctoral degree. They also must go through a licensing procedure. One type of master's degree in counseling leads to the designation of licensed professional counselor.

School Counselor

School counselors help students cope with adjustment problems, identify their abilities and interests, develop academic plans, and explore career options. The focus of the job depends on the age of the children. High school counselors advise students about vocational and technical training and admissions requirements for college, as well as about taking entrance exams, applying for financial aid, and choosing a major. Elementary school counselors mainly counsel students about social and personal problems. They may observe children in the classroom and at play as part of their work. School counselors may work with students individually, in small groups, or even in a classroom. They often consult with parents, teachers, and school administrators when trying to help students. School counselors usually have a master's degree in counseling. **Read a profile of a high school counselor in "The Self, Identity, and Personality."**

Career Counselor

Career counselors help individuals to identify their best career options and guide them in applying for jobs. They may work in private industry or at a college or university. They usually interview individuals and give them vocational and/or psychological tests to identify appropriate careers that fit their interests and abilities. Sometimes they help individuals to create résumés or conduct mock interviews to help them feel comfortable in a job interview. They might arrange and promote job fairs or other recruiting events to help individuals obtain jobs.

Rehabilitation Counselor

Rehabilitation counselors work with individuals to identify career options, develop adjustment and coping skills to maximize independence, and resolve problems created by a disability. A master's degree in rehabilitation counseling or guidance or counseling psychology is generally considered the minimum educational requirement.

Social Worker

Many social workers are involved in helping people with social or economic problems. They may investigate, evaluate, and attempt to rectify reported cases of abuse, neglect, endangerment, or domestic disputes. They may intervene in families and provide counseling and referral services to individuals and families. Some social workers specialize in a certain area. For example, a medical social worker might coordinate support services to people with a long-term disability; family-care social workers often work with families with children or an older adult who needs support services. Social workers often work for publicly funded agencies at the city, state, or national level, although increasingly they work in the private sector in areas such as drug rehabilitation and family counseling.

Social workers have a minimum of an undergraduate degree from a school of social work that includes coursework in sociology and psychology. Some social workers also have a master's or doctoral degree. For example, medical social workers have a master's degree in social work (M.S.W.) and complete graduate coursework and supervised clinical experiences in medical settings.

Drug Counselor

Drug counselors provide counseling to individuals with drug-abuse problems. Some drug counselors specialize in working with adolescents or older adults. They may work on an individual basis with a substance abuser or conduct group therapy. They may work in private practice, with a state or federal government agency, for a company, or in a hospital.

At a minimum, drug counselors complete an associate's or certificate program. Many have an undergraduate degree in substance-abuse counseling, and some have master's and doctoral degrees. Most states provide a certification procedure for obtaining a license to practice drug counseling.

Medical/Nursing/Physical Development

This third main area of careers in life-span development includes a wide range of choices in the medical and nursing areas, as well as jobs pertaining to improving some aspect of a person's physical development.

Obstetrician/Gynecologist

An obstetrician/gynecologist prescribes prenatal and postnatal care, performs deliveries in maternity cases, and treats diseases and injuries of the female reproductive system. Becoming an obstetrician/gynecologist requires a medical degree plus three to five years of residency in obstetrics/gynecology. Obstetricians may work in private practice, a medical clinic, a hospital, or a medical school.

Pediatrician

A pediatrician monitors infants' and children's health, works to prevent disease or injury, helps children attain optimal health, and treats children with health problems. Pediatricians have earned a medical degree and completed a three- to five-year residency in pediatrics.

Pediatricians may work in private practice or at a medical clinic, a hospital, or a medical school.

Many pediatricians on the faculty of medical schools also teach and conduct research on children's health and diseases.

Geriatric Physician

Geriatric physicians diagnose medical problems of older adults, evaluate treatment options, and make recommendations for nursing care or other arrangements. They have a medical degree and specialize in geriatric medicine by doing a three- to five-year residency. Like other doctors, geriatric physicians may work in private practice or at a medical clinic, a hospital, or a medical school. Those in medical school settings may not only treat older adults but also teach future physicians and conduct research.

Neonatal Nurse

Neonatal nurses deliver care to newborn infants. They may work with infants born under normal circumstances or premature and critically ill neonates. A minimum of an undergraduate degree in nursing with a specialization in the newborn is required. This training involves coursework in nursing and the biological sciences, as well as supervised clinical experiences.

Nurse-Midwife

A nurse-midwife formulates and provides comprehensive care to expectant mothers as they prepare to give birth, guides them through the birth process, and cares for them after the birth. The nurse-midwife also may provide care to the newborn, counsel parents on the infant's development and parenting, and provide guidance about health practices. Becoming a nurse-midwife generally requires an undergraduate degree from a school of nursing. A nurse-midwife most often works in a hospital setting. **Read a profile of a perinatal nurse in "Biological Beginnings."**

Pediatric Nurse

Pediatric nurses monitor infants' and children's health, work to prevent disease or injury, and help children attain optimal health. They may work in hospitals, schools of nursing, or with pediatricians in private practice or at a medical clinic.

Pediatric nurses have a degree in nursing that takes two to five years to complete. They take courses in biological sciences, nursing care, and pediatrics, usually in a school of nursing. They also undergo supervised clinical experiences in medical settings. Some pediatric nurses go on to earn a master's or doctoral degree in pediatric nursing. **Read a profile of a pediatric nurse in "Health."**

Geriatric Nurse

Geriatric nurses seek to prevent or intervene in the chronic or acute health problems of older adults. They may work in hospitals, nursing homes, schools of nursing, or with geriatric medical specialists or psychiatrists in a medical clinic or in

private practice. Like pediatric nurses, geriatric nurses take courses in a school of nursing and obtain a degree in nursing, which takes from two to five years. They complete courses in biological sciences, nursing care, and mental health as well as supervised clinical training in geriatric settings. They also may obtain a master's or doctoral degree in their specialty. **Read a profile of a geriatric nurse in "Physical Development and Biological Aging."**

Physical Therapist

Physical therapists work with individuals who have a physical problem due to disease or injury to help them function as competently as possible. They may consult with other professionals and coordinate services for the individual. Many physical therapists work with people of all ages, although some specialize in working with a specific age group, such as children or older adults.

Physical therapists usually have an undergraduate degree in physical therapy and are licensed by a state. They take courses and undergo supervised training in physical therapy.

Occupational Therapist

Occupational therapists initiate the evaluation of clients with various impairments and manage their treatment. They help people regain, develop, and build skills that are important for independent functioning, health, well-being, security, and happiness. An "Occupational Therapist Registered" (OTR) must have a master's and/or doctoral degree with education ranging from two to six years. Training includes occupational therapy courses in a specialized program. National certification is required and licensing/registration is required in some states.

Therapeutic/Recreation Therapist

Therapeutic/recreation therapists maintain or improve the quality of life for people with special needs through intervention, leisure education, and recreation. They work in hospitals, rehabilitation centers, local government agencies, at-risk youth programs, and other settings. Becoming a therapeutic/recreation therapist requires an undergraduate degree with coursework in leisure studies and a concentration in therapeutic recreation. National certification is usually required. Coursework in anatomy, special education, and psychology is beneficial.

Audiologist

Audiologists assess and identify the presence and severity of hearing loss, as well as problems in balance. They may work in a medical clinic, with a physician in private practice, in a hospital, or in a medical school.

An audiologist completes coursework and supervised training to earn a minimum of an undergraduate degree in hearing science. Some audiologists also go on to obtain a master's or doctoral degree.

Speech Therapist

Speech therapists identify, assess, and treat speech and language problems. They may work with physicians, psychologists, social workers, and other health care professionals in a team approach to help individuals with physical or psychological problems that involve speech and language. Some speech therapists specialize in working with individuals of a particular age or people with a particular type of speech disorder. Speech therapists have a minimum of an undergraduate degree in speech and hearing science or in a type of communication disorder. They may work in private practice, hospitals and medical schools, and government agencies. **Read a profile of a speech therapist in "Language Development."**

Genetic Counselor

Genetic counselors identify and counsel families at risk for genetic disorders. They work as members of a health care team, providing information and support to families who have members who have genetic defects or disorders or are at risk for a variety of inherited conditions. They also serve as educators and resource people for other health care professionals and the public. Almost half of genetic counselors work in university medical centers; one-fourth work in private hospital settings.

Genetic counselors have specialized graduate degrees and experience in medical genetics and counseling. Most enter the field after majoring in undergraduate school in such disciplines as biology, genetics, psychology, nursing, public health, or social work. **Read a profile of a genetic counselor in "Biological Beginnings."**

Families/Relationships

A number of careers and jobs related to life-span development focus on working with families and addressing relationship problems. These range from home health aide to marriage and family therapist.

Home Health Aide

A home health aide provides services to older adults in the older adults' homes, helping them with basic self-care tasks. No higher education is required for this position. There is brief training by an agency.

Child Welfare Worker

Child protective services in each state employ child welfare workers. They protect children's rights, evaluate any maltreatment, and may have children removed from their homes if necessary. A child social worker has a minimum of an undergraduate degree in social work.

Child Life Specialist

Child life specialists work with children and their families when the child needs to be hospitalized. They monitor the child's activities, seek to reduce the child's stress, and help the child to cope and to enjoy the hospital experience as much as possible. Child life specialists may provide parent education and develop individualized treatment plans based on an assessment of the child's development, temperament, medical plan, and available social supports. Child life specialists have an undergraduate degree. They have taken courses in child development and education and usually completed additional courses in a child life program.

Marriage and Family Therapist

Marriage and family therapists work on the principle that many individuals who have psychological problems benefit when psychotherapy is provided in the context of a marital or family relationship. Marriage and family therapists may provide marital therapy, couple therapy to individuals in a relationship who are not married, and family therapy to two or more members of a family.

Marriage and family therapists have a master's or a doctoral degree. They complete a training program in graduate school similar to a clinical psychologist's but with a focus on marital and family relationships. In most states, it is necessary to go through a licensing procedure to practice marital and family therapy. **Read a profile of a marriage and family therapist in "Families, Lifestyles, and Parenting."**

Further Careers

Knowledge of developmental psychology can prepare you for these careers and many others. The *Connecting with Careers* profiles highlight additional careers, including an infant assessment specialist, child care director, toy designer, health psychologist, teacher of English language learners, college/career counselor, parent educator, pastoral counselor, and home hospice nurse. *What other careers can you think of that require knowledge of human development?*

section two

> *Babies are such a nice way to start people.*
>
> **—Don Herold**
> *American Writer, 20th Century*

Biological Processes, Physical Development, and Health

The rhythm and meaning of life involve biological foundations. How, from so simple a beginning, can endless forms develop and grow and mature? What was this organism, what is it, and what will it be? In Section 2, you will read and study four chapters: "Biological Beginnings," "Physical Development and Biological Aging," "Health," and "Motor, Sensory, and Perceptual Development."

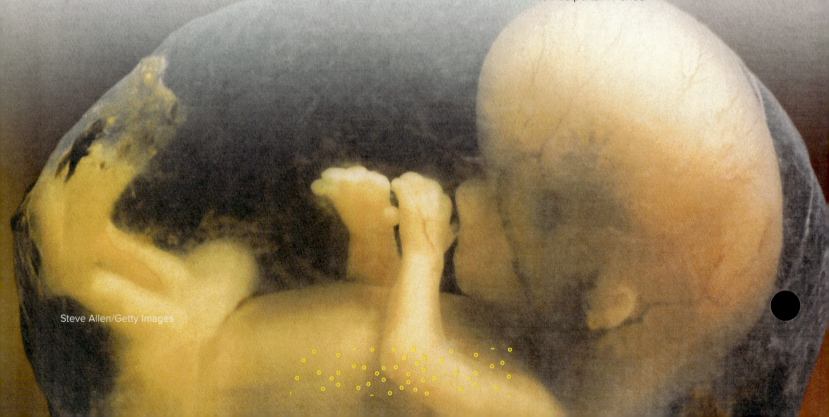

chapter 2

BIOLOGICAL BEGINNINGS

chapter **outline**

① The Evolutionary Perspective

Learning Goal 1 Discuss the evolutionary perspective on life-span development.

Natural Selection and Adaptive Behavior
Evolutionary Psychology

② Genetic Foundations of Development

Learning Goal 2 Describe what genes are and how they influence human development.

The Collaborative Gene
Genes and Chromosomes
Genetic Principles
Chromosomal and Gene-Linked Abnormalities

③ Heredity and Environment Interaction: The Nature-Nurture Debate

Learning Goal 3 Explain some of the ways that heredity and environment interact to produce individual differences in development.

Behavior Genetics
Heredity-Environment Correlations
The Epigenetic View and Gene × Environment (G × E) Interaction
Conclusions About Heredity-Environment Interaction

④ Prenatal Development

Learning Goal 4 Characterize the course of prenatal development and its hazards.

The Course of Prenatal Development
Prenatal Diagnostic Tests
Hazards to Prenatal Development
Prenatal Care

⑤ Birth and the Postpartum Period

Learning Goal 5 Summarize how birth takes place and describe the nature of the postpartum period.

The Birth Process
The Transition from Fetus to Newborn
Low Birth Weight and Preterm Infants
Bonding
The Postpartum Period

Steve Allen/Getty Images

preview

Organisms are not like billiard balls, moved by simple external forces to predictable positions on life's table. Environmental experiences and biological foundations work together to make us who we are. In this chapter, we explore life's biological beginnings and experiences, charting growth from conception through the prenatal period and examining the birth process itself. We will begin our exploration of biological foundations by considering possible evolutionary influences.

1 The Evolutionary Perspective

LG1 Discuss the evolutionary perspective on life-span development.

Natural Selection and Adaptive Behavior

Evolutionary Psychology

From the perspective of evolutionary time, humans are relative newcomers to Earth. As our earliest ancestors left the forest to feed on the savannahs and then to form hunting societies on the open plains, their minds and behaviors changed, and humans eventually became the dominant species on Earth. How did this evolution come about?

NATURAL SELECTION AND ADAPTIVE BEHAVIOR

Charles Darwin (1859) described *natural selection* as the evolutionary process by which those individuals of a species that are best adapted to their environment are the ones that are most likely to survive and reproduce. He reasoned that an intense, constant struggle for food, water, and resources must occur among the young of each generation, because many of them do not survive. Those that do survive and reproduce pass on their characteristics to the next generation (Mader & Windelspecht, 2020). Darwin concluded that these survivors are better adapted to their world than are the nonsurvivors. The best-adapted individuals survive and leave the most offspring. Over the course of many generations, organisms with the characteristics needed for survival make up an increased percentage of the population (Hoefnagels, 2019; Willey, Sandman, & Wood, 2020).

EVOLUTIONARY PSYCHOLOGY

Although Darwin introduced the theory of evolution by natural selection in 1859, his ideas have only recently become a popular framework for explaining behavior (Buss & Schmitt, 2019; Freeman & others, 2020; Mogliski & others, 2019). Psychology's newest approach, **evolutionary psychology,** emphasizes the importance of adaptation, reproduction, and "survival of the fittest" in shaping behavior. ("Fit" in this sense refers to the ability to bear offspring that survive long enough to bear offspring of their own.) In this view, natural selection favors behaviors that increase reproductive success—that is, the ability to pass genes to the next generation (Bjorklund, 2018; McDowell, 2019).

David Buss (2008, 2012, 2015, 2018) argues that just as evolution shapes our physical features, such as body shape and height, it also pervasively influences how we make decisions, how aggressive we are, our fears, and our mating patterns. For example, assume that our ancestors were hunters and gatherers on the plains and that men did most of the hunting and women stayed close to home, gathering seeds and plants for food. If you had to walk some distance from your home in an effort to track and slay a fleeing animal, you would need not only certain physical traits but also the ability to perform certain types of spatial thinking. Men with these traits would be more likely than men without them to survive, to bring home lots of food, and to be considered attractive mates—and thus to reproduce and potentially pass on these characteristics to their children. In other words, if these assumptions were correct, these traits would provide a reproductive advantage for

How does the attachment of this Vietnamese baby to its mother reflect the evolutionary process of adaptive behavior?
frans lemmens/age fotostock

evolutionary psychology A branch of psychology that emphasizes the importance of adaptation, reproduction, and "survival of the fittest" in shaping behavior.

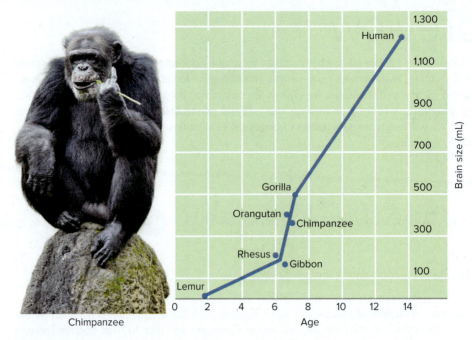

Chimpanzee

FIGURE 1

THE BRAIN SIZES OF VARIOUS PRIMATES AND HUMANS IN RELATION TO THE LENGTH OF THE CHILDHOOD PERIOD. Compared with other primates, humans have both a larger brain and a longer childhood period. *What conclusions can you draw from the relationship indicated by this graph?*
Tier Und Naturfotografie J und C Sohns/Getty Images

Children in all cultures are interested in the tools that adults in their cultures use. Shown here is a young child using a machete to cut wood near the Ankgor temples in Cambodia. *Might the child's behavior be evolutionary-based or be due to both biological and environmental conditions?*
Carol Adam/Getty Images

developmental **connection**

Life-Span Perspective

Baltes described eight main characteristics of the life-span perspective. Connect to "Introduction".

males, and over many generations, men with good spatial thinking skills might become more numerous in the population. Critics point out that this scenario might or might not have actually happened.

Evolutionary Developmental Psychology   There is growing interest in using the concepts of evolutionary psychology to understand human development (Bjorklund, 2018; Ellis & Del Guidice, 2019; Sneve & others, 2019). Following are some ideas proposed by evolutionary developmental psychologists (Bjorklund & Pellegrini, 2002).

One important concept is that an extended childhood period might have evolved because humans require time to develop a large brain and learn the complexity of human societies. Humans take longer to become reproductively mature than any other mammal (see Figure 1). During this extended childhood period, they develop a large brain and have the experiences needed to become competent adults in a complex society.

Evolved characteristics are not always adaptive in contemporary society. Some behaviors that were adaptive for our prehistoric ancestors may not serve us well today. For example, the food-scarce environment of our ancestors likely led to humans' propensity to gorge when food is available and to crave high-caloric foods, a trait that might lead to an epidemic of obesity when food is plentiful.

Evolution and Life-Span Development   In evolutionary theory, what matters is that individuals live long enough to reproduce and pass on their characteristics (Urry & others, 2020). So why do humans live so long after their reproductive capacity has ended? Perhaps evolution favored longevity because having older people around improves the survival rates of babies. Possibly an evolutionary advantage came from having grandparents alive to care for the young while parents were out hunting and gathering food.

According to life-span developmentalist Paul Baltes (2003), the benefits conferred by evolutionary selection decrease with age. Natural selection has not weeded out many harmful conditions and nonadaptive characteristics that appear among older adults. Why? Natural selection operates primarily on characteristics that are tied to reproductive fitness, which extends through the earlier part of adulthood. Thus, says Baltes, selection primarily operates during the first half of life.

As an example, consider Alzheimer disease, an irreversible brain disorder characterized by gradual deterioration. This disease typically does not appear until age 70 or later. If it were a disease that struck 20-year-olds, perhaps natural selection would have eliminated it eons ago.

Thus, unaided by evolutionary pressures against nonadaptive conditions, we suffer the aches, pains, and infirmities of aging. And, as the benefits of evolutionary selection decrease with age, argues Baltes, the need for culture increases (see Figure 2). That is, as older adults weaken biologically, they need culture-based resources such as cognitive skills, literacy, medical technology, and social support. For example, older adults may need help and training from other people to maintain their cognitive skills (Calero, 2019; Kinugawa, 2019).

Evaluating Evolutionary Psychology Evolutionary psychology has its critics (Hyde & DeLamater, 2017). Common criticisms are that much of evolutionary psychology cannot be tested scientifically and that it relies mainly on *post hoc* (after the fact) explanations. Another criticism was offered by Albert Bandura (1998), the leading architect of social cognitive theory. He acknowledges the influence of evolution on human adaptation but rejects what he calls "one-sided evolutionism," which views social behavior as strictly the product of evolved biology. An alternative is a bidirectional view, in which environmental and biological conditions influence each other. In this view, evolutionary pressures created changes in biological structures that allowed the use of tools, which enabled our ancestors to manipulate the environment, constructing new environmental conditions. In turn, environmental innovations produced new selection pressures that led to the evolution of specialized biological systems for consciousness, thought, and language.

In other words, evolution has given us body structures and biological potentialities, but it does not dictate behavior. People have used their biological capacities to produce diverse cultures—aggressive and peaceful; egalitarian and autocratic.

The "big picture" idea of natural selection leading to the development of human traits and behaviors is difficult to refute or test because evolution occurs on a time scale that does not lend itself to empirical study. Thus, studying specific genes in humans and other species—and their links to traits and behaviors—may be the best approach for testing ideas coming out of the evolutionary psychology perspective.

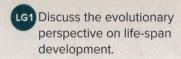

FIGURE 2

BALTES' VIEW OF EVOLUTION AND CULTURE ACROSS THE LIFE SPAN. Benefits derived from evolutionary selection decrease as we age, whereas the need for culture increases with age.

Review Connect Reflect

LG1 Discuss the evolutionary perspective on life-span development.

Review

- How can natural selection and adaptive behavior be defined?
- What is evolutionary psychology? What basic ideas about human development are proposed by evolutionary psychologists? How might evolutionary influences have different effects at different points in the life span? How can evolutionary psychology be evaluated?

Connect

- In the section on ethological theory in the "Introduction," the concept of a critical time period is explored. How does this concept relate to what you learned about older adults and aging in this section?

Reflect *Your Own Personal Journey of Life*

- Which is more persuasive to you as an explanation of your development: the views of evolutionary psychologists or those of their critics? Why?

2 Genetic Foundations of Development

LG2 Describe what genes are and how they influence human development.

The Collaborative Gene

Genes and Chromosomes

Genetic Principles

Chromosomal and Gene-Linked Abnormalities

Genetic influences on behavior evolved over time and across many species. Our many traits and characteristics that are genetically influenced have a long evolutionary history that is retained in our DNA (Johnson & Losos, 2020; Hoefnagels, 2019). In other words, our DNA is not just inherited from our parents; it's also what we've inherited as a species from the species that were our ancestors. Let's take a closer look at DNA and its role in human development.

How are characteristics that suit a species for survival transmitted from one generation to the next? Darwin could not answer this question because genes and the principles of genetics had not yet been discovered. Each of us carries a "genetic code" that we inherited from our parents. Because a fertilized egg carries this human code, a fertilized human egg cannot grow into an egret, eagle, or elephant.

THE COLLABORATIVE GENE

Each of us began life as a single cell weighing about one twenty-millionth of an ounce! This tiny piece of matter housed our entire genetic code—information that helps us grow from that single cell to a person made of trillions of cells, each containing a replica of the original code. That code is carried by our genes. What are genes and what do they do? For the answer, we need to look into our cells.

The nucleus of each human cell contains **chromosomes,** which are threadlike structures made up of deoxyribonucleic acid, or DNA. **DNA** is a complex molecule that has a double helix shape, like a spiral staircase, and it contains genetic information. **Genes,** the units of hereditary information, are short segments of DNA, as you can see in Figure 3. They help cells to reproduce themselves and to assemble proteins. Proteins, in turn, are the building blocks of cells as well as the regulators that direct the body's processes (Belk & Maier, 2019; Klug & others, 2020).

Each gene has its own location, its own designated place on a particular chromosome. Today, there is a great deal of enthusiasm about efforts to discover the specific locations of genes that are linked to certain functions and developmental outcomes (Simon, 2020; Tortora & others, 2019). An important step in this direction was accomplished in 2003 when the Human Genome Project completed a preliminary map of the human *genome*—the complete set of developmental information for creating proteins that initiate the making of a human organism (Norman-McKay, 2019).

chromosomes Threadlike structures made up of deoxyribonucleic acid, or DNA.

DNA A complex molecule that has a double helix shape and contains genetic information.

genes Units of hereditary information composed of DNA. Genes help cells to reproduce themselves and assemble proteins that direct body processes.

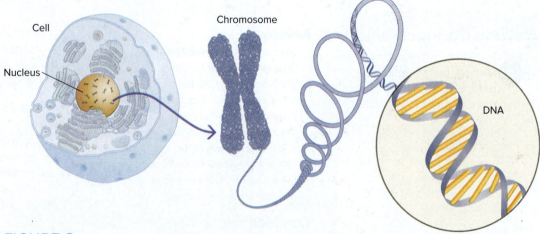

FIGURE 3

CELLS, CHROMOSOMES, DNA, AND GENES. (*Left*) The body contains trillions of cells. Each cell contains a central structure, the nucleus. (*Middle*) Chromosomes are threadlike structures located in the nucleus of the cell. Chromosomes are composed of DNA. (*Right*) DNA has the structure of a spiral staircase. A gene is a segment of DNA.

Among the major approaches to gene identification and discovery that are being used today are the genome-wide association method, linkage analysis, next-generation sequencing, and the Thousand Genomes Project:

- Completion of the Human Genome Project has led to use of the *genome-wide association method* to identify genetic variations linked to a particular disorder (Pei & others, 2019; Schurz & others, 2019a; Yasukochi & others, 2018). To conduct a genome-wide association study, researchers obtain DNA from individuals who have the disease and those who don't have it. Then, each participant's complete set of DNA, or genome, is purified from the blood or cells and scanned on machines to determine markers of genetic variation. If the genetic variations occur more frequently in people who have the disease, the variations point to the region in the human genome where the disease-causing problem exists. Genome-wide association studies have recently been conducted for cancer (Chen & others, 2019), obesity (Riveros-McKay & others, 2019), cardiovascular disease (Taylor & others, 2019), depression (Amare & others, 2019), suicide (Levey & others, 2019), autism (Schork & others, 2019), attention deficit hyperactivity disorder (Verhoef & others, 2019), glaucoma (MacGregor & others, 2018), and Alzheimer disease (Hao & others, 2019).

- *Linkage analysis*, in which the goal is to discover the location of one or more genes in relation to a marker gene (whose position is already known), is often used in the search for disease genes (Burrello & others, 2017). Genes transmitted to offspring tend to be in close proximity to each other so that the gene(s) involved in the disease are usually located near the marker gene. Gene linkage studies are now being conducted on a wide variety of disorders, including cardiovascular disease (Hedberg-Oldfors & others, 2019), attention deficit hyperactivity disorder (Lacosta & others, 2019), autism (Ramaswami & Geschwind, 2018), depression (Vereczkei & others, 2019), posttraumatic stress disorder (van der Merwe & others, 2019), and Alzheimer disease (D.F. Zhang & others, 2019).

- *Next-generation sequencing* is a term used to describe the vast increase in genetic data generated at a much reduced cost and in a much shorter period of time. Using recently developed next-generation sequencing, an entire human genome can be sequenced in one day. Prior to recent improvements, deciphering the human genome took longer than an entire decade! The new technology sequences millions of small DNA fragments. Next-generation sequencing has considerably increased knowledge about genetic influences on development in recent years (Mei & others, 2019; Singer & Anderson, 2019; Sulovari & Li, 2019; Xu, Zheng, & Li, 2019).

- The human genome varies between individuals in small but very important ways. Understanding these variations will require examination of the whole genomes of many individuals. A current project that began in 2008, the Thousand Genomes Project, is the most detailed study of human genetic variation to date. This project has the goal of determining the genomic sequences of at least 1,000 individuals from different ethnic groups around the world (Li & others, 2017). By compiling complete descriptions of the genetic variations of many people, the project will make it possible for genetic variations in disease to be studied in greater detail.

One of the big surprises of the Human Genome Project was a report indicating that humans have only about 30,000 genes (U.S. Department of Energy, 2001). In subsequent analyses, the number of human genes was revised downward to approximately 20,500 (Ensembl Human, 2008; Flicek & others, 2013). However, recently the humane gene figure was raised to 21,306 (Salzberg & others, 2018). Scientists had thought that humans had as many as 100,000 or more genes. They had also maintained that each gene programmed just one protein. In fact, because humans appear to have far more proteins than they have genes, there cannot be a one-to-one correspondence between genes and proteins (Commoner, 2002). Each gene is not translated, in automaton-like fashion, into one and only one protein. A gene does not act independently, as developmental psychologist David Moore (2001) emphasized by titling his book *The Dependent Gene*.

Rather than being a group of independent genes, the human genome consists of many genes that collaborate both with each other and with nongenetic factors inside and outside the body. The collaboration operates at many points. For example, the cellular machinery mixes, matches, and links small pieces of DNA to reproduce the genes, and that machinery is influenced by what is going on around it (Moore, 2013, 2015, 2017).

Whether a gene is turned "on," working to assemble proteins, is also a matter of collaboration. The activity of genes (*genetic expression*) is affected by their environment (Gottlieb, 2007; Moore, 2017). For example, hormones that circulate in the blood make their way into the cell where they can turn genes "on" and "off." And the flow of hormones can be affected by environmental conditions such as light, day length, nutrition, and behavior. Numerous studies have shown that external events outside of the original cell and the person, as well as events inside the cell, can excite or inhibit gene expression (Gottlieb, 2007; Moore, 2017). Recent research has documented that factors such as stress, exercise, nutrition, respiration, radiation, temperature, and sleep can influence gene expression (Cuevas-Sierra & others, 2019; Kesaniemi & others, 2019; Stephens & Tsintzas, 2018; Wang, Lee, & Tian, 2019; Zimmerman & others, 2019). For example, one study revealed that an increase in the concentration of stress hormones such as cortisol produced a fivefold increase in DNA damage (Flint & others, 2007). Another study found that exposure to radiation changed the rate of DNA synthesis in cells (Lee & others, 2011). And research indicates that sleep deprivation can affect gene expression in negative ways, causing increased inflammation, expression of stress-related genes, and impairment of protein functioning (Gaine, Chatterjee, & Abel, 2018).

Scientists have found that certain genes are turned on or off as a result of exercise, mainly through a process called *methylation*, in which tiny atoms attach themselves to the outside of a gene (Marioni & others, 2018; Schenk & others, 2019). This process makes the gene more or less capable of receiving and responding to biochemical signals from the body. In this way the behavior of the gene, but not its structure, is changed. Researchers also have found that diet, tobacco use, and sleep may also affect gene behavior through the process of methylation (Chatterton & others, 2017; Lahtinen & others, 2019; Zaghlool & others, 2018). Also, recent research indicates that methylation may be involved in depression (Li & others, 2019), breast cancer (Parashar & others, 2018), leukemia (Bewersdorf & others, 2019), obesity (Caballero, 2019), and attention deficit hyperactivity disorder (Kim & others, 2019).

GENES AND CHROMOSOMES

Genes are not only collaborative, they are enduring. How do genes manage to get passed from generation to generation and end up in all of the trillion cells in the body? The answer lies in three processes that happen at the cellular level: mitosis, meiosis, and fertilization.

Mitosis, Meiosis, and Fertilization   All of the cells in your body, except your sperm or eggs, have 46 chromosomes arranged in 23 pairs. These cells reproduce by a process called **mitosis.** During mitosis, the cell's nucleus—including the chromosomes—duplicates itself and the cell divides. Two new cells are formed, each containing the same DNA as the original cell, arranged in the same 23 pairs of chromosomes (Mader & Windelspecht, 2020).

However, a different type of cell division—**meiosis**—forms eggs and sperm (which also are called *gametes*). During meiosis, a cell of the testes (in men) or ovaries (in women) duplicates its chromosomes but then divides twice, thus forming four cells, each of which has only half of the genetic material of the parent cell (Belk & Maier, 2019). By the end of meiosis, each egg or sperm has 23 *unpaired* chromosomes.

During **fertilization,** an egg and a sperm fuse to create a single cell, called a **zygote** (see Figure 4). In the zygote, the 23 unpaired chromosomes from the egg and the 23 unpaired chromosomes from the sperm combine to form one set of 23 paired chromosomes—one chromosome of each pair from the mother's egg and the other from the father's sperm. In this manner, each parent contributes half of the offspring's genetic material.

Figure 5 shows 23 paired chromosomes of a male and a female. The members of each pair of chromosomes are both similar and different: Each chromosome in the pair contains varying forms of the same genes, at the same location on the chromosome. A gene that influences hair color, for example, is located on both members of one pair of chromosomes, in the same location on each. However, one of those chromosomes might carry a gene associated with blond hair, and the other chromosome in the pair might carry a gene associated with brown hair.

Do you notice any obvious differences between the chromosomes of the male and the chromosomes of the female in Figure 5? The difference lies in the 23rd pair. Ordinarily, in females this pair consists of two chromosomes called X chromosomes; in males the 23rd pair consists of an X and a Y chromosome. The presence of a Y chromosome is one factor that makes a person male rather than female.

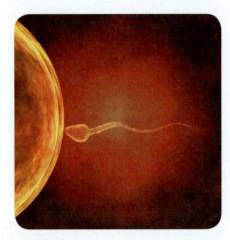

FIGURE 4

A SINGLE SPERM PENETRATING AN EGG AT THE POINT OF FERTILIZATION
3Dalia/Shutterstock

mitosis Cellular reproduction in which the cell's nucleus duplicates itself; two new cells are formed, each containing the same DNA as the original cell, arranged in the same 23 pairs of chromosomes.

meiosis A specialized form of cell division that occurs to form eggs and sperm (or gametes).

fertilization A stage in reproduction when an egg and a sperm fuse to create a single cell, called a zygote.

zygote A single cell formed through fertilization.

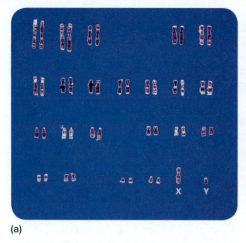

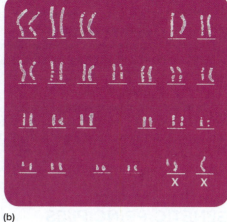

(a)   (b)

Sources of Variability   Combining the genes of two parents in offspring increases genetic variability in the population, which is valuable for a species because it provides more characteristics on which natural selection can operate (Norman-MacKay, 2019). In fact, the human genetic process includes several important sources of variability (Klug & others, 2020; Tortora & others, 2019).

First, the chromosomes in the zygote are not exact copies of those in the mother's ovaries or the father's testes. During the formation of the sperm and egg in meiosis, the members of each pair of chromosomes are separated, but which chromosome in the pair goes to the gamete is a matter of chance. In addition, before the pairs separate, pieces of the two chromosomes in each pair are exchanged, creating a new combination of genes on each chromosome (Belk & Maier, 2019). Thus, when chromosomes from the mother's egg and the father's sperm are brought together in the zygote, the result is a truly unique combination of genes.

Another source of variability comes from DNA. Chance, a mistake by cellular machinery, or damage from an environmental agent such as radiation may produce a *mutated gene*, which is a permanently altered segment of DNA.

Even when their genes are identical, however, people vary. The difference between genotypes and phenotypes helps us to understand this source of variability. All of a person's genetic material makes up his or her **genotype.**

There is increasing interest in studying *susceptibility genes*, those that make an individual more vulnerable to specific diseases such as cancer (Liu & Tan, 2019) and cardiovascular disease (Taylor & others, 2019), or acceleration of aging (Patel & others, 2018), and *longevity genes*, those that make an individual less vulnerable to certain diseases and more likely to live to an older age (Castillo-Morales & others, 2019; Pignolo, 2019). These are aspects of the individual's genotype.

In the search for longevity genes, Cynthia Kenyon (2010) has extensively studied *C. elegans,* a roundworm, the first animal to have its entire genome sequenced. In early research, Kenyon found that modifying a single gene, *daf-2,* which is linked to hormones, slows aging in the roundworm. She also discovered that another gene, *daf-16,* is necessary for the roundworm to live longer. *Daf-16* encodes a gene switch that turns on a number of genes related to stress resistance, immunity, and metabolism (McLaughlin & Broihier, 2018). These genes possibly may extend life by protecting and repairing body tissues (Xu & others, 2019). Other researchers have found that genetic variants in a human *daf-16* version labeled *FOXO3A* are linked to increased longevity in a wide range of people, including Americans, Europeans, and Chinese (Pradhan & others, 2017; Wang, Hu, & Liu, 2017). Further, *daf-2*-type mutations extend life and slow aging not only in roundworms but also in flies and mice, suggesting that in humans these mutations might contribute to delayed onset and severity of many diseases related to aging, including cancer, cardiovascular disease, and Alzheimer disease (Kenyon, 2010). Recently, Cynthia Kenyon joined a think tank of scientists at Google's Calico (short for California Life Company) division, which seeks to understand the aging process and discover how to modify it. Kenyon believes that interventions to extend the human life span might be possible through the development of drugs that mimic the action of gene mutations that are linked to greater longevity.

genotype All of a person's actual genetic material.

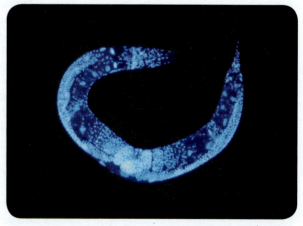

Researcher Cynthia Kenyon found that modifying a gene called *daf-16* slows aging in *C. elegans* (shown above). This type of roundworm was the first animal to have its entire genome sequenced.
Washington University, St. Louis/KRT/Newscom

However, not all of the genetic material is apparent in an individual's observed and measurable characteristics. A **phenotype** consists of observable characteristics, including physical characteristics (such as height, weight, and hair color) and psychological characteristics (such as personality and intelligence). For each genotype, a range of phenotypes can be expressed, providing another source of variability (Hoefnagels, 2019). An individual can inherit the genetic potential to grow very large, for example, but good nutrition, among other things, will be essential for achieving that potential.

How does the process from genotype to phenotype work? It's highly complex, but at a very basic level DNA information in a cell is transcribed to RNA (ribonucleic acid), which in turn is translated into amino acids that will become proteins (Klug & others, 2020). Once proteins have been assembled, they become capable of producing phenotype traits and characteristics. Also, environments interact with genotypes to produce phenotypes.

GENETIC PRINCIPLES

What determines how a genotype is expressed to create a particular phenotype? Much is still unknown about the answer to this question. However, a number of genetic principles have been discovered, such as those involving dominant-recessive genes, sex-linked genes, genetic imprinting, and polygenically determined characteristics.

Dominant-Recessive Genes   In some cases, one gene of a pair always exerts its effects; it is *dominant*, overriding the potential influence of the other gene, called the *recessive* gene. This is the principle of *dominant-recessive* genes. A recessive gene exerts its influence only if the two genes of a pair are both recessive. If you inherit a recessive gene for a trait from each of your parents, you will show the trait. If you inherit a recessive gene from only one parent, you may never know you carry the gene. Brown hair, farsightedness, and dimples rule over blond hair, nearsightedness, and freckles in the world of dominant-recessive genes.

Can two brown-haired parents have a blond-haired child? Yes, they can. Suppose that each parent has a dominant gene for brown hair and a recessive gene for blond hair. Since dominant genes override recessive genes, the parents have brown hair, but both are *carriers* of blondness and pass on their recessive genes for blond hair. With no dominant gene to override them, the recessive genes can make the child's hair blond.

Sex-Linked Genes   Most mutated genes are recessive. When a mutated gene is carried on the X chromosome, the result is called *X-linked inheritance*. It may have very different implications for males and females (Schurz & others, 2019b; Yang & Chen, 2019). Remember that males have only one X chromosome. Thus, if there is an absent or altered disease-relevant gene on the X chromosome, males have no "backup" copy to counter the harmful gene and therefore may develop an X-linked disease. However, females have a second X chromosome, which is likely to be unchanged. As a result, they are not likely to have the X-linked disease. Thus, most individuals who have X-linked diseases are males. Females who have one abnormal copy of the gene on the X chromosome are known as "carriers," and they usually do not show any signs of the X-linked disease. Hemophilia and fragile X syndrome, which we discuss later in this chapter, are examples of X-linked inheritance diseases (Hampson, Hooper, & Niibori, 2019).

Genetic Imprinting   *Genetic imprinting* occurs when genes have differing effects depending on whether they are inherited from the mother or the father (Singh, Shioma, & Belyakin, 2019). A chemical process "silences" one member of the gene pair. For example, as a result of imprinting, only the maternally derived copy of a gene might be active, while the paternally derived copy of the same gene is silenced—or vice versa (Lorgen-Ritchie & others, 2019; Malnou & others, 2019). Only a small percentage of human genes appear to undergo imprinting, but it is a normal and important aspect of development. When imprinting goes awry, development is disturbed, as in the case of Beckwith-Wiedemann syndrome (Bachmann & others, 2019), a growth disorder, and Wilms tumor (Trager & others, 2019), a type of cancer.

phenotype Observable and measurable characteristics of an individual, such as height, hair color, and intelligence.

Polygenic Inheritance   Genetic transmission is usually more complex than the simple examples we have examined thus far (Oreland & others, 2018). Few characteristics reflect the influence of only a single gene or pair of genes. Most are determined by the interaction of many different genes; they are said to be *polygenically determined* (Hill & others, 2019). Even a simple characteristic such as height, for example, reflects the interaction of many genes as well as the influence of the environment.

The term *gene-gene interaction* is increasingly used to describe studies that focus on the interdependence of two or more genes in influencing characteristics, behavior, diseases, and development (Yip & others, 2018). For example, recent studies have documented gene-gene interaction in immune system functioning (Pazmandi & others, 2019); asthma (Hua & others, 2016); obesity (Wang & others, 2019); type 2 diabetes (Saxena, Srivastava, & Banerjee, 2018); cancer (A. Lee & others, 2019); cardiovascular disease (Dron & Hegele, 2019); arthritis (Fathollahi & others, 2019); alcoholism (G. Chen & others, 2017); and Alzheimer disease (Nazarian, Yashin, & Kulminski, 2019).

CHROMOSOMAL AND GENE-LINKED ABNORMALITIES

Sometimes abnormalities characterize the genetic process. Some of these abnormalities involve whole chromosomes that do not separate properly during meiosis. Other abnormalities are produced by harmful genes.

Chromosomal Abnormalities   When a gamete is formed, sometimes the sperm or ovum does not have its normal set of 23 chromosomes. The most notable examples involve Down syndrome and abnormalities of the sex chromosomes (see Figure 6).

Down Syndrome   An individual with **Down syndrome** has a round face, a flattened skull, an extra fold of skin over the eyelids, a protruding tongue, short limbs, and intellectual and motor disabilities (Popadin & others, 2019). It is not known why the extra chromosome is present, but the health of the male sperm or the female ovum may be involved.

Down syndrome appears approximately once in every 700 live births. Women between the ages of 16 and 34 are less likely to give birth to a child with Down syndrome than are younger or older women. African American children have a lower rate of Down syndrome than non-Latino White or Latino children.

Sex-Linked Chromosomal Abnormalities   Recall that a newborn normally has either an X and a Y chromosome or two X chromosomes. Human embryos must possess at least one X chromosome to be viable. The most common sex-linked chromosomal abnormalities involve the presence of an extra chromosome (either an X or Y) or the absence of one X chromosome in females.

Down syndrome A chromosomally transmitted form of intellectual disability caused by the presence of an extra copy of chromosome 21.

Name	Description	Treatment	Incidence
Down syndrome	An extra chromosome causes mild to severe intellectual disability and physical abnormalities.	Surgery, early intervention, infant stimulation, and special learning programs	1 in 1,900 births at age 20 1 in 300 births at age 35 1 in 30 births at age 45
Klinefelter syndrome (XXY)	An extra X chromosome causes physical abnormalities.	Hormone therapy can be effective	1 in 1,000 male births
Fragile X syndrome	An abnormality in the X chromosome can cause intellectual disability, learning disabilities, or short attention span.	Special education, speech and language therapy	More common in males than in females
Turner syndrome (XO)	A missing X chromosome in females can cause intellectual disability and sexual underdevelopment.	Hormone therapy in childhood and puberty	1 in 2,500 female births
XYY syndrome	An extra Y chromosome can cause above-average height.	No special treatment required	1 in 1,000 male births

FIGURE 6

SOME CHROMOSOMAL ABNORMALITIES. The treatments for these abnormalities do not necessarily erase the problem but may improve the individual's adaptive behavior and quality of life.

These athletes, several of whom have Down syndrome, are participating in a Special Olympics competition. Notice the distinctive facial features of the individuals with Down syndrome, such as a round face and a flattened skull. *What causes Down syndrome?*
James Shaffer/PhotoEdit

Klinefelter syndrome is a chromosomal disorder in which males have an extra X chromosome, making them XXY instead of XY. Males with this disorder have undeveloped testes, and they usually have enlarged breasts and become tall. Klinefelter syndrome occurs approximately once in every 1,000 live male births. Only 10 percent of individuals with Klinefelter syndrome are diagnosed before puberty, with the majority not identified until adulthood (Aksglaede & others, 2013).

Fragile X syndrome (FXS) is a chromosomal disorder that results from an abnormality in the X chromosome, which becomes constricted and often breaks (Hall & Berry-Kravis, 2018). Mental deficiency frequently is an outcome, but it may take the form of an intellectual disability, autism, a learning disability, or a short attention span (Hampson, Hooper, & Niibori, 2019). This disorder occurs more frequently in males than in females, possibly because the second X chromosome in females negates the effects of the abnormal X chromosome (Rocca & others, 2016). A recent study found that a higher level of maternal responsivity to the adaptive behavior of children with FXS had a positive effect on the children's communication skills (Warren & others, 2017).

Turner syndrome is a chromosomal disorder in females in which either an X chromosome is missing, making the person XO instead of XX, or part of one X chromosome is deleted (Bianchi, 2019). Females with Turner syndrome are short in stature and have a webbed neck (Skuse, Printzlau, & Wolstencroft, 2018). They might be infertile and have difficulty in mathematics, but their verbal ability is often quite good. Turner syndrome occurs in approximately 1 of every 2,500 live female births (Pinsker, 2012).

The **XYY syndrome** is a chromosomal disorder in which the male has an extra Y chromosome (Berglund & others, 2019). Early interest in this syndrome focused on the belief that the extra Y chromosome found in some males contributed to aggression and violence. However, researchers subsequently found that XYY males are no more likely to commit crimes than are XY males (Witkin & others, 1976).

Gene-Linked Abnormalities   Abnormalities can be produced not only by an abnormal number of chromosomes but also by harmful genes. More than 7,000 such genetic disorders have been identified, although most of them are rare.

Phenylketonuria (PKU) is a genetic disorder in which the individual cannot properly metabolize phenylalanine, an amino acid. It results from a recessive gene and occurs about once in every 10,000 to 20,000 live births. Today, phenylketonuria is easily detected, and it is treated by a diet that prevents an excess accumulation of phenylalanine (Medford & others, 2018; McBride & others, 2019). If phenylketonuria is left untreated, however, excess phenylalanine builds up in the child, producing intellectual disability and hyperactivity. Phenylketonuria accounts for approximately 1 percent of institutionalized individuals who have an intellectual disability, and it occurs primarily in non-Latino Whites.

Sickle-cell anemia, which occurs most often in African Americans, is a genetic disorder that impairs the body's red blood cells (Moerdler & Manwani, 2018). Red blood cells carry oxygen to the body's other cells and are usually shaped like a disk. In sickle-cell anemia, a recessive gene causes the red blood cell to become a hook-shaped "sickle" that cannot carry oxygen properly and dies quickly. As a result, the body's cells do not receive adequate oxygen, causing anemia and often early death (Patterson & others, 2018). About 1 in 400 African American babies is affected by sickle-cell anemia. One in 10 African Americans is a carrier, as is 1 in 20 Latin Americans. Recent research strongly supports the use of hydroxyurea therapy for infants with sickle cell anemia beginning at 9 months of age (Luzzatto & Makani, 2019). Stem cell transplantation also is being explored as a potential treatment for infants with sickle-cell anemia (Azar & Wong, 2017).

Other diseases that result from genetic abnormalities include cystic fibrosis, some forms of diabetes, hemophilia, Alzheimer disease, Huntington disease, spina bifida, and Tay-Sachs disease (Anderson & others, 2019; Iacono & Feltis, 2019; J. Zhang & others, 2019). Figure 7 provides further information about these diseases. Someday, scientists may identify the origins of these and other genetic abnormalities and discover how to cure them.

Klinefelter syndrome A chromosomal disorder in which males have an extra X chromosome, making them XXY instead of XY.

fragile X syndrome (FXS) A chromosomal disorder involving an abnormality in the X chromosome, which becomes constricted and often breaks.

Turner syndrome A chromosomal disorder in females in which either an X chromosome is missing, making the person XO instead of XX, or part of one X chromosome is deleted.

XYY syndrome A chromosomal disorder in which males have an extra Y chromosome.

Name	Description	Treatment	Incidence
Cystic fibrosis	Glandular dysfunction that interferes with mucus production; breathing and digestion are hampered, resulting in a shortened life span.	Physical and oxygen therapy, synthetic enzymes, and antibiotics; most individuals live to middle age.	1 in 2,000 births
Diabetes	Body does not produce enough insulin, which causes abnormal metabolism of sugar.	Early onset can be fatal unless treated with insulin.	1 in 2,500 births
Hemophilia	Delayed blood clotting causes internal and external bleeding.	Blood transfusions/injections can reduce or prevent damage due to internal bleeding.	1 in 10,000 males
Huntington's disease	Central nervous system deteriorates, producing problems in muscle coordination and mental deterioration.	Does not usually appear until age 35 or older; death likely 10 to 20 years after symptoms appear.	1 in 20,000 births
Phenylketonuria (PKU)	Metabolic disorder that, left untreated, causes intellectual disability.	Special diet can result in average intelligence and normal life span.	1 in 10,000 to 1 in 20,000 births
Sickle-cell anemia	Blood disorder that limits the body's oxygen supply; it can cause joint swelling, as well as heart and kidney failure.	Penicillin, medication for pain, antibiotics, and blood transfusions.	1 in 400 African American children (lower among other groups)
Spina bifida	Neural tube disorder that causes brain and spine abnormalities.	Corrective surgery at birth, orthopedic devices, and physical/medical therapy.	2 in 1,000 births
Tay-Sachs disease	Deceleration of mental and physical development caused by an accumulation of lipids in the nervous system.	Medication and special diet are used, but death is likely by 5 years of age.	1 in 30 American Jews is a carrier.

Genetic counselors, usually physicians or biologists who are well versed in the field of medical genetics, provide their clients with information regarding the kinds of problems just described. In working with couples who would like to have children, they can evaluate the likelihood of giving birth to a child with a genetic disorder and offer helpful strategies for offsetting some of the effects of these diseases (Haverbusch & others, 2019; Seiffert & others, 2019; Sharony & others, 2018). To read about the career and work of a genetic counselor, see the *Connecting with Careers* profile.

FIGURE 7
SOME GENE-LINKED ABNORMALITIES

phenylketonuria (PKU) A genetic disorder in which an individual cannot properly metabolize phenylalanine, an amino acid; PKU is now easily detected—but, if left untreated, results in intellectual disability and hyperactivity.

sickle-cell anemia A genetic disorder that affects the red blood cells and occurs most often in African Americans.

connecting with careers

Jennifer Leonhard, Genetic Counselor

Jennifer Leonhard is a genetic counselor at Sanford Bemidji Health Clinic in Bemidji, Minnesota. She obtained an undergraduate degree from Western Illinois University and a master's degree in genetic counseling from the University of Arkansas for Medical Sciences.

Genetic counselors like Leonhard work as members of a health care team, providing information and support to families with birth defects or genetic disorders. They identify families at risk by analyzing inheritance patterns and then explore options with the family. Some genetic counselors, like Leonhard, specialize in prenatal and pediatric genetics, while others focus on cancer genetics or psychiatric genetic disorders.

Genetic counselors hold specialized graduate degrees in medical genetics and counseling. They enter graduate school with undergraduate backgrounds from a variety of disciplines, including biology, genetics, psychology, public health, and social work. There are approximately 30 graduate genetic counseling programs in the United States. If you are interested in this profession, you can obtain further information from the National Society of Genetic Counselors at www.nsgc.org.

Jennifer Leonhard (*right*) is a genetic counselor at Sanford Health in Bemidji, Minnesota.
Courtesy of Jennifer Leonhard

Review Connect Reflect

LG2 Describe what genes are and how they influence human development.

Review
- What are genes?
- How are genes passed on?
- What basic principles describe how genes interact?
- What are some chromosomal and gene-linked abnormalities?

Connect
- Would you want to be able to access a full genome analysis of your offspring? Why or why not?

Reflect *Your Own Personal Journey of Life*
- Imagine that you are considering having a child. Would you want to see a genetic counselor to find out about possible genetic risks that might be transmitted to your offspring? Explain.

3 Heredity and Environment Interaction: The Nature-Nurture Debate

LG3 Explain some of the ways that heredity and environment interact to produce individual differences in development.

| Behavior Genetics | Heredity-Environment Correlations | The Epigenetic View and Gene × Environment (G × E) Interaction | Conclusions About Heredity-Environment Interaction |

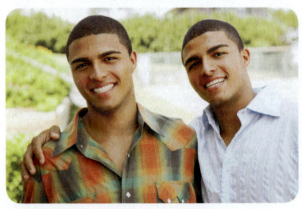

Twin studies compare identical twins with fraternal twins. Identical twins develop from a single fertilized egg that splits into two genetically identical organisms. Fraternal twins develop from separate eggs, making them genetically no more similar than nontwin siblings. *What is the nature of the twin study method?*
Jack Hollingsworth/Getty Images

behavior genetics The field that seeks to discover the influence of heredity and environment on individual differences in human traits and development.

twin study A study in which the behavioral similarity of identical twins is compared with the behavioral similarity of fraternal twins.

adoption study A study in which investigators seek to discover whether, in behavior and psychological characteristics, adopted children are more like their adoptive parents, who provided a home environment, or more like their biological parents, who contributed their heredity. Another form of the adoption study compares adoptive and biological siblings.

Is it possible to untangle the influence of heredity from that of environment and discover the role of each in producing individual differences in development? When heredity and environment interact, how does heredity influence the environment and vice versa?

BEHAVIOR GENETICS

Behavior genetics is the field that seeks to discover the influence of heredity and environment on individual differences in human traits and development. To study the influence of heredity on behavior, behavior geneticists often use either twins or adoption situations (Pinheiro & others, 2018; Rana & others, 2018).

In the most common **twin study,** the behavioral similarity of identical twins (who are genetically identical) is compared with the behavioral similarity of fraternal twins. Recall that although fraternal twins share the same womb, they are no more genetically alike than nontwin siblings. Thus, by comparing groups of identical and fraternal twins, behavior geneticists capitalize on the basic knowledge that identical twins are more similar genetically than are fraternal twins (Fasbender, Wiebe, & Bates, 2019; Inderkum & Tarokh, 2019). For example, one study found that conduct problems were more prevalent in identical twins than in fraternal twins; the researchers concluded that the study demonstrated an important role for heredity in conduct problems (Scourfield & others, 2004).

However, several issues complicate interpretation of twin studies. For example, perhaps the environments of identical twins are more similar than the environments of fraternal twins. Parents and other caregivers might stress the similarities of identical twins more than those of fraternal twins, and identical twins might perceive themselves as a "set" and play together more than fraternal twins do. If so, the influence of the environment on the observed similarities between identical and fraternal twins might be highly significant. To read more about identical twins, see *Connecting Development to Life.*

In an **adoption study,** investigators seek to discover whether the behavioral and psychological characteristics of adopted children are more like those of their adoptive parents, who have provided a home environment, or more like those of their biological parents, who have contributed their heredity (Salvatore & others, 2018). Another form of the adoption study compares adoptive and biological siblings.

Am I an "I" or "We"?

College freshman Colin Kunzweiler (2007) wrote about his thoughts and experiences related to being an identical twin:

> As a monozygotic individual, I am used to certain things. "Which one are you?" happens to be the most popular question I'm asked, which is almost always followed by "You're Colin. No, wait, you're Andy!"
>
> I have two names: one was given to me at birth, the other thrust on me in a random, haphazard way. . . . My twin brother and I are as different from each other as caramel sauce is from gravy. We have different personalities, we enjoy different kinds of music, and I am even taller than he is (by a quarter of an inch). We are different, separate, and individual. I have always been taught that I should maintain my own individuality; that I should be my own person. But if people keep constantly mistaking me for my twin, how can I be my own person with my own identity?

"Am I an 'I' or 'We'?" was the title of an article written by Lynn Perlman (2008) about the struggle twins have in developing a sense of being an individual. Of course, triplets have the same issue, possibly even more strongly so. One set of triplets entered a beauty contest as one person and won the contest!

Perlman, an identical twin herself, is a psychologist who works with twins (her identical twin also is a psychologist). She says that how twins move from a sense of "we" to "I" is a critical task for them as children and sometimes even as adults. For non-twins, separating oneself from a primary caregiver—mother and/or father—is an important developmental task in childhood, adolescence, and emerging adulthood. When a child has a twin, the separation process is likely to be more difficult because of the constant comparison with a twin. Since they are virtually identical in their physical appearance, identical twins are likely to have more problems in distinguishing themselves from their twin than are fraternal twins.

The twin separation process often accelerates in adolescence when one twin is likely to mature earlier than the other (Perlman, 2013). However, for some twins it may not occur until emerging adulthood when they may go to different colleges and/or live apart for the first time. And for some twins, even in adulthood twin separation can be emotionally painful. One 28-year-old identical twin female got a new boyfriend but the relationship caused a great deal of stress and conflict with her twin sister (Friedman, 2013).

In Lynn Perlman's (2008) view, helping twins develop their own identities needs to be done on a child-by-child basis, taking into account their preferences and what is in their best interests. She commented that most of the twins she has counseled consider having a twin a positive experience, and while they also are usually strongly attached to each other they are intensely motivated to be considered unique persons.

HEREDITY-ENVIRONMENT CORRELATIONS

The difficulties that researchers encounter when they interpret the results of twin studies and adoption studies reflect the complexities of heredity-environment interaction. Some of these interactions are *heredity-environment correlations*, which means that individuals' genes may be systematically related to the types of environments to which they are exposed (Klahr & Burt, 2014). In a sense, individuals "inherit," seek out, or "construct" environments that may be related or linked to genetic "propensities." Behavior geneticist Sandra Scarr (1993) described three ways that heredity and environment can be correlated (see Figure 8):

Heredity-Environment Correlation	Description	Examples
Passive	Children inherit genetic tendencies from their parents, and parents also provide an environment that matches their own genetic tendencies.	Musically inclined parents usually have musically inclined children and they are likely to provide an environment rich in music for their children.
Evocative	The child's genetic tendencies elicit stimulation from the environment that supports a particular trait. Thus genes evoke environmental support.	A happy, outgoing child elicits smiles and friendly responses from others.
Active (niche-picking)	Children actively seek out "niches" in their environment that reflect their own interests and talents and are thus in accord with their genotype.	Libraries, sports fields, and a store with musical instruments are examples of environmental niches children might seek out if they have intellectual interests in books, talent in sports, or musical talents, respectively.

FIGURE 8

EXPLORING HEREDITY-ENVIRONMENT CORRELATIONS

- **Passive genotype-environment correlations** occur because biological parents, who are genetically related to the child, provide a rearing environment for the child. For example, the parents might have a genetic predisposition to be intelligent and read skillfully. Because they read well and enjoy reading, they provide their children with books to read. The likely outcome is that their children, because of both their own inherited predispositions and their book-filled environment, will become skilled readers.

- **Evocative genotype-environment correlations** occur because a child's genetically influenced characteristics elicit certain types of environments. For example, active, smiling children receive more social stimulation than passive, quiet children do. Cooperative, attentive children evoke more pleasant and instructional responses from the adults around them than uncooperative, distractible children do.

- **Active (niche-picking) genotype-environment correlations** occur when children seek out environments that they find compatible and stimulating. *Niche-picking* refers to finding a setting that is suited to one's genetically influenced abilities. Children select from their surrounding environment some aspects that they respond to, learn about, or ignore. Their active selections of environments are related to their particular genotype. For example, outgoing children tend to seek out social contexts in which to interact with people, whereas shy children don't. Children who are musically inclined are likely to select musical environments in which they can successfully perform their skills. How these "tendencies" come about will be discussed shortly under the topic of the epigenetic view.

Scarr notes that the relative importance of the three genotype-environment correlations changes as children develop from infancy through adolescence. In infancy, much of the environment that children experience is provided by adults. Thus, passive genotype-environment correlations are more common in the lives of infants and young children than they are for older children and adolescents who can extend their experiences beyond the family's influence and create and select their environments to a greater degree.

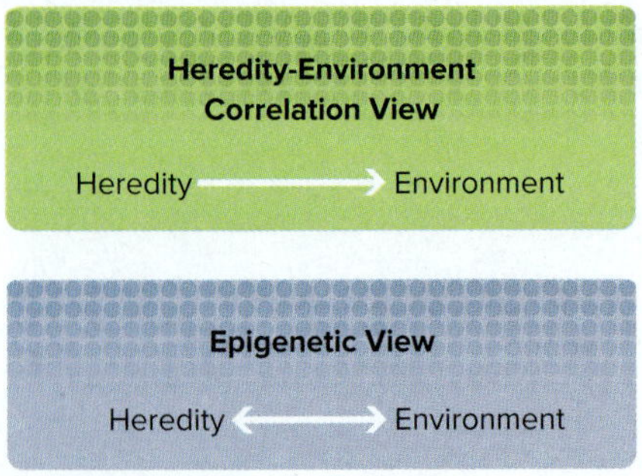

THE EPIGENETIC VIEW AND GENE × ENVIRONMENT (G × E) INTERACTION

In line with the concept of a collaborative gene, Gilbert Gottlieb (2007) proposed an **epigenetic view** which states that development is the result of an ongoing, bidirectional interchange between heredity and the environment. Figure 9 compares the heredity-environment correlation and epigenetic views of development.

Let's look at an example that reflects the epigenetic view. A baby inherits genes from both parents at conception. During prenatal development, toxins, nutrition, and stress can influence some genes to stop functioning while others become more active or less active. During infancy, environmental experiences, such as exposure to toxins, nutrition, stress, learning, and encouragement, continue to modify genetic activity and the activity of the nervous system that directly underlies behavior. Heredity and environment thus operate together—or collaborate—to produce a person's well-being, intelligence, temperament, health, ability to pitch a baseball, ability to read, cope with stress, and so on (Bleker & others, 2019; Quereshi & Mehler, 2018; Schwartz, Wright, & Valgardson, 2019).

An increasing number of studies are exploring how the interaction between heredity and environment influences development, including interactions that involve specific DNA sequences (Gentner & Leppert, 2019; Grunblatt & others, 2018; Lindahl-Jacobsen & Christensen, 2019). The epigenetic mechanisms involve the actual molecular modification of the DNA strand as a result of environmental inputs in ways that alter gene functioning (Byrne & Drake, 2019; Szutorisz & Hurd, 2018).

One study found that individuals who have a short version of a gene labeled 5-HTTLPR (a gene involving the neurotransmitter serotonin) have an elevated risk of developing depression only if they *also* lead stressful lives (Caspi & others, 2003). Thus, the specific gene did not directly cause the development of depression; rather the gene interacted with a stressful environment in a way that allowed the researchers to predict whether individuals would develop depression. A research meta-analysis indicated that the short version of 5-HTTLPR

Heredity-Environment Correlation View

Heredity ——————⟶ Environment

Epigenetic View

Heredity ⟵——————⟶ Environment

FIGURE 9

COMPARISON OF THE HEREDITY-ENVIRONMENT CORRELATION AND EPIGENETIC VIEWS

passive genotype-environment correlations Correlations that exist when the biological parents, who are genetically related to the child, provide a rearing environment for the child.

evocative genotype-environment correlations Correlations that exist when the child's characteristics elicit certain types of environments.

active (niche-picking) genotype-environment correlations Correlations that exist when children seek out environments they find compatible and stimulating.

epigenetic view Perspective emphasizing that development is the result of an ongoing, bidirectional interchange between heredity and environment.

was linked with higher cortisol stress reactivity (Miller & others, 2013). Research studies also have found support for the interaction between the 5-HTTLPR gene and stress levels in predicting depression in adolescents and older adults (Petersen & others, 2012; Zannas & others, 2012).

The type of research just described is referred to as studies of **gene × environment (G × E) interaction**—the interaction of a specific measured variation in DNA and a specific measured aspect of the environment (Ein-Dor & others, 2018; Hein & others, 2019). Although there is considerable enthusiasm about the concept of gene × environment (G × E) interaction, a research review concluded that this topic of study is plagued by difficulties in replicating results, inflated claims, and other weaknesses (Manuck & McCaffery, 2014). The science of G × E interaction is very young and in the next several decades it will likely produce more precise findings (Ecker & Beck, 2019; Fumagalli & others, 2018; Jylhava & others, 2019).

gene × environment (G × E) interaction The interaction of a specific measured variation in the DNA and a specific measured aspect of the environment.

CONCLUSIONS ABOUT HEREDITY-ENVIRONMENT INTERACTION

If an attractive, popular, intelligent girl is elected president of her high school senior class, is her success due to heredity or to environment? Of course, the answer is "both."

The relative contributions of heredity and environment are not additive. That is, we can't say that such-and-such a percentage of nature and such-and-such a percentage of experience make us who we are. Nor is it accurate to say that full genetic expression happens once, at the time of conception or birth, after which we carry our genetic legacy into the world to see how far it takes us. Genes produce proteins throughout the life span, in many different environments. Or they don't produce these proteins, depending in part on how harsh or nourishing those environments are.

The emerging view is that complex behaviors are influenced by genes in ways that give people a propensity for a particular developmental trajectory (Kalashnikova, Goswami, & Burnham, 2019; Ramos & others, 2019). However, the individual's actual development also involves a specific environment. And that environment is complex, just like the mixture of genes we inherit (Almy & Cicchetti, 2018; Antonucci & Webster, 2019; Calero, 2019). Environmental influences range from the things we lump together under "nurture" (such as parenting, family dynamics, schooling, and neighborhood quality) to biological encounters (such as viruses, birth complications, and even biological events in cells).

In developmental psychologist David Moore's (2013, 2015, 2017) view, the biological systems that generate behaviors are extremely complex but too often these systems have been described in overly simplified ways that can be misleading. Thus, although genetic factors clearly contribute to behavior and psychological processes, they don't determine these phenotypes independently from the contexts in which they develop. From Moore's (2017) perspective, it is misleading to talk about "genes for" eye color, intelligence, personality, or other characteristics. Moore commented that in retrospect we should not have expected to be able to make the giant leap from analyzing the molecules in DNA to achieving a complete understanding of human behavior, any more than we should anticipate being able to make the leap from understanding how sound waves move molecules in a concert hall to attaining a full-blown appreciation of a symphony's wondrous experience.

Imagine for a moment that there is a cluster of genes that are somehow associated with youth violence. (This example is hypothetical because we don't know of any such combination.) The adolescent who carries this genetic mixture might experience a world of loving parents, regular nutritious meals, lots of books, and a series of competent teachers. Or the adolescent's world might include parental neglect, a neighborhood in which gunshots and crime are everyday occurrences, and inadequate schooling. In which of these environments are the adolescent's genes likely to manufacture the biological underpinnings of criminality?

If heredity and environment interact to determine the course of development, is that all there is to answering the question of what causes development? Are humans completely at the mercy of their genes and their environment as they develop through the life span? Genetic heritage and environmental experiences are pervasive influences on development. But in thinking about what causes development, consider that development is the co-construction of

To what extent are this young girl's piano skills likely due to heredity, environment, or both?
Francisco Romero/Getty Images

developmental **connection**

Life-Span Perspective

An important aspect of the life-span perspective is the co-construction of biology, culture, and the individual. Connect to "Introduction."

The interaction of heredity and environment is so extensive that to ask which is more important, nature or nurture, is like asking which is more important to a rectangle, height or width.

—WILLIAM GREENOUGH

Developmental psychologist, University of Illinois at Urbana

biology, culture, and the individual. Not only are we the outcomes of our heredity and the environment we experience, but we also can author a unique developmental path by changing our environment. As one psychologist concluded:

> In reality, we are both the creatures and creators of our worlds. We are . . . the products of our genes and environments. Nevertheless, . . . the stream of causation that shapes the future runs through our present choices. . . . Mind matters. . . . Our hopes, goals, and expectations influence our future. (Myers, 2010, p. 168)

Review *Connect* Reflect

 LG3 Explain some of the ways that heredity and environment interact to produce individual differences in development.

Review

- What is behavior genetics?
- What are three types of heredity-environment correlations?
- What is the epigenetic view of development?
- What conclusions can be reached about heredity-environment interaction?

Connect

- Of passive, evocative, and active genotype-environment correlations, which is the best explanation for the similarities discovered between the many sets of adult twins who share characteristics and experiences despite being raised apart?

Reflect *Your Own Personal Journey of Life*

- A friend tells you that she has analyzed her genetic background and environmental experiences and reached the conclusion that environment definitely has had little influence on her intelligence. What would you say to this person about her ability to make this self-diagnosis?

4 Prenatal Development

 LG4 Characterize the course of prenatal development and its hazards.

| The Course of Prenatal Development | Prenatal Diagnostic Tests | Hazards to Prenatal Development | Prenatal Care |

The history of man for nine months preceding his birth would, probably, be far more interesting, and contain events of greater moment, than all three score and ten years that follow it.

—SAMUEL TAYLOR COLERIDGE
English Poet, Essayist, 19th Century

germinal period The period of prenatal development that takes place during the first two weeks after conception; it includes the creation of the zygote, continued cell division, and the attachment of the zygote to the wall of the uterus.

We turn now to a description of how the process of development unfolds from its earliest moment—the moment of *conception*—when two parental cells, with their unique genetic contributions, join to create a new individual.

Conception occurs when a single sperm cell from a male unites with an ovum (egg) in a female's fallopian tube in a process called fertilization. Over the next few months the genetic code discussed earlier directs a series of changes in the fertilized egg, but many events and hazards will influence how that egg develops and becomes a person.

THE COURSE OF PRENATAL DEVELOPMENT

Prenatal development lasts approximately 266 days, beginning with fertilization and ending with birth. It can be divided into three periods: germinal, embryonic, and fetal.

The Germinal Period The **germinal period** is the period of prenatal development that takes place in the first two weeks after conception. It includes the creation of the fertilized egg (the *zygote*), cell division, and the attachment of the zygote to the uterine wall.

Rapid cell division by the zygote begins the germinal period. (Recall from earlier in the chapter that this cell division occurs through a process called *mitosis.*) By approximately one week after conception, the differentiation of these cells—their specialization for different tasks—has already begun. At this stage the group of cells, now called the *blastocyst*, consists of an inner mass of cells that will eventually develop into the embryo, and the *trophoblast*, an outer layer of cells that later provides nutrition and support for the embryo. *Implantation*, the attachment of the zygote to the uterine wall, takes place about 10 to 14 days after conception.

The Embryonic Period The **embryonic period** is the period of prenatal development that occurs from two to eight weeks after conception. During the embryonic period, the rate of cell differentiation intensifies, support systems for cells form, and organs appear.

This period begins as the blastocyst attaches to the uterine wall. The mass of cells is now called an *embryo*, and three layers of cells form. The embryo's *endoderm* is the inner layer of cells, which will develop into the digestive and respiratory systems. The *ectoderm* is the outermost layer, which will become the nervous system, sensory receptors (ears, nose, and eyes, for example), and skin parts (hair and nails, for example). The *mesoderm* is the middle layer, which will become the circulatory system, bones, muscles, excretory system, and reproductive system. Every body part eventually develops from these three layers. The endoderm primarily produces internal body parts, the mesoderm primarily produces parts that surround the internal areas, and the ectoderm primarily produces surface parts. **Organogenesis** is the name given to the process of organ formation during the first two months of prenatal development. While they are being formed, the organs are especially vulnerable to environmental influences (Manning & Peifer, 2019; Rios & Clevers, 2018; Zou, Ding, & Huang, 2019).

As the embryo's three layers form, life-support systems for the embryo develop rapidly. These systems include the amnion, the umbilical cord (both of which develop from the fertilized egg, not the mother's body), and the placenta. The amnion is like a bag or an envelope; it contains a clear fluid in which the developing embryo floats. The amniotic fluid provides an environment that is temperature- and humidity-controlled, as well as shockproof. The *umbilical cord*, which contains two arteries and one vein, connects the baby to the placenta. The *placenta* consists of a disk-shaped group of tissues in which small blood vessels from the mother and the offspring intertwine but do not join.

Very small molecules—oxygen, water, salt, and nutrients from the mother's blood, as well as carbon dioxide and digestive wastes from the baby's blood—pass back and forth between the mother and the embryo or fetus. Virtually any drug or chemical substance the pregnant woman ingests can cross the placenta to some degree, unless it is metabolized or altered during passage, or is too large (Gomez & others, 2019; Koren & Ornoy, 2018). One study confirmed that ethanol crosses the human placenta and primarily reflects maternal alcohol use (Matlow & others, 2013). Another study revealed that cigarette smoke weakens and increases the oxidative stress of fetal membranes from which the placenta develops (Menon & others, 2011). The stress hormone cortisol also can cross the placenta (Mateos & others, 2018). Large molecules that cannot pass through the placental wall include red blood cells and harmful substances such as most bacteria, maternal wastes, and hormones. The complex mechanisms that govern the transfer of substances across the placental barrier are still not entirely understood (Jeong & others, 2018; Malnou & others, 2019).

The Fetal Period The **fetal period,** which lasts about seven months, is the prenatal period that extends from two months after conception until birth in typical pregnancies. Growth and development continue their dramatic course during this time.

Three months after conception, the fetus is about 3 inches long and weighs about 0.8 ounce. It has become active, moving its arms and legs, opening and closing its mouth, and moving its head. The face, forehead, eyelids, nose, and chin are distinguishable, as are the upper arms, lower arms, hands, and lower limbs. In most cases, the genitals can be identified as male or female. By the end of the fourth month of pregnancy, the fetus has grown to about 5 inches in length and weighs about 3.5 ounces. At this time, a growth spurt occurs in the body's lower parts. For the first time, the mother can feel arm and leg movements.

By the end of the fifth month, the fetus is about 11 inches long and weighs close to a pound. Structures of the skin have formed—toenails and fingernails, for example. The fetus is more active, showing a preference for a particular position in the womb. By the end of the sixth month, the fetus is about 14 inches long and has gained another 6 to 12 ounces. The eyes and eyelids are completely formed, and a fine layer of hair covers the head. A grasping reflex is present and irregular breathing movements occur.

As early as six months of pregnancy (about 24 to 25 weeks after conception), the fetus for the first time has a chance of surviving outside the womb—that is, it is *viable*. Infants that

embryonic period The period of prenatal development that occurs from two to eight weeks after conception. During the embryonic period, the rate of cell differentiation intensifies, support systems for the cells form, and organs appear.

organogenesis Process of organ formation that takes place during the first two months of prenatal development.

fetal period The prenatal period of development that begins two months after conception and lasts for seven months, on average.

are born early, or between 24 and 37 weeks of pregnancy, usually need help breathing because their lungs are not yet fully mature. By the end of the seventh month, the fetus is about 16 inches long and weighs about 3 pounds.

During the last two months of prenatal development, fatty tissues develop and the functioning of various organ systems—heart and kidneys, for example—steps up. During the eighth and ninth months, the fetus grows longer and gains substantial weight—about 4 more pounds. At birth, the average American baby weighs 8 pounds and is about 20 inches long.

In addition to describing prenatal development in terms of germinal, embryonic, and fetal periods, prenatal development also can be divided into equal three-month periods, called *trimesters* (see Figure 10). Remember that the three trimesters are not the same as the three prenatal periods we have discussed. The germinal and embryonic periods occur in the first trimester. The fetal period begins toward the end of the first trimester and continues through the second and third trimesters.

Prenatal Growth

First trimester (first 3 months)

Conception to 4 weeks
- Is less than $1/10$ inch long
- Beginning development of spinal cord, nervous system, gastrointestinal system, heart, and lungs
- Amniotic sac envelops the preliminary tissues of entire body
- Is called a "zygote"

8 weeks
- Is about 0.6 inch long
- Face is forming with rudimentary eyes, ears, mouth, and tooth buds
- Arms and legs are moving
- Brain is forming
- Fetal heartbeat is detectable with ultrasound
- Is called an "embryo"

12 weeks
- Is about 2 inches long and weighs about 0.5 ounce
- Can move arms, legs, fingers, and toes
- Fingerprints are present
- Can smile, frown, suck, and swallow
- Sex is distinguishable
- Can urinate
- Is called a "fetus"

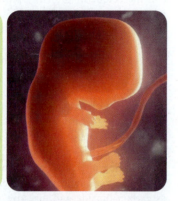

Second trimester (middle 3 months)

16 weeks
- Is about 5 inches long and weighs about 3.5 ounces
- Heartbeat is strong
- Skin is thin, transparent
- Downy hair (lanugo) covers body
- Fingernails and toenails are forming
- Has coordinated movements; is able to roll over in amniotic fluid

20 weeks
- Is about 6.5 inches long and weighs about 11 ounces
- Heartbeat is audible with ordinary stethoscope
- Sucks thumb
- Hiccups
- Hair, eyelashes, eyebrows are present

24 weeks
- Is about 12 inches long and weighs about 1.3 pounds
- Skin is wrinkled and covered with protective coating (vernix caseosa)
- Eyes are open
- Waste matter is collected in bowel
- Has strong grip

Third trimester (last 3 months)

28 weeks
- Is about 15 inches long and weighs about 2.3 pounds
- Is adding body fat
- Is very active
- Rudimentary breathing movements are present

32 weeks
- Is about 17 inches long and weighs about 4 pounds
- Has periods of sleep and wakefulness
- Responds to sounds
- May assume the birth position
- Bones of head are soft and flexible
- Iron is being stored in liver

36 to 38 weeks
- Is 19 to 20 inches long and weighs 6 to $7\frac{1}{2}$ pounds
- Skin is less wrinkled
- Vernix caseosa is thick
- Lanugo is mostly gone
- Is less active
- Is gaining immunities from mother

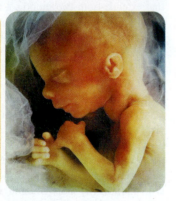

FIGURE 10

THE THREE TRIMESTERS OF PRENATAL DEVELOPMENT. Both the germinal and embryonic periods occur during the first trimester. The end of the first trimester as well as the second and third trimesters are part of the fetal period.
(*Top to bottom*): unlim3d/123RF; SCIEPRO/Science Photo Library/Getty Images; Steve Allen/Brand X Pictures/Getty Images

The Brain   One of the most remarkable aspects of the prenatal period is the development of the brain (Andescavage & others, 2017; Ferrazzi & others, 2018). By the time babies are born, they have approximately 100 billion **neurons,** or nerve cells, which handle information processing at the cellular level in the brain. During prenatal development, neurons move to specific locations and start to become connected. The basic architecture of the human brain is assembled during the first two trimesters of prenatal development. Typically, the third trimester of prenatal development and the first two years of postnatal life are characterized by connectivity and functioning of neurons (van den Heuvel & others, 2018; Vasung & others, 2019).

Four important phases of the brain's development during the prenatal period involve (1) the neural tube, (2) neurogenesis, (3) neural migration, and (4) neural connectivity.

Neural Tube   As the human embryo develops inside its mother's womb, the nervous system begins forming as a long, hollow tube located on the embryo's back. This pear-shaped *neural tube,* which forms at about 21 days after conception, develops out of the ectoderm. The tube closes at the top and bottom by about 27 days after conception (Keunen, Counsell, & Benders, 2017). Figure 11 shows that the nervous system still has a tubular appearance six weeks after conception.

Two birth defects related to a failure of the neural tube to close are anencephaly and spina bifida. When fetuses have *anencephaly* (that is, when the head end of the neural tube fails to close), the highest regions of the brain fail to develop and death occurs in the womb, during childbirth, or shortly after birth (Steric & others, 2015). *Spina bifida*, an incomplete development of the spinal cord, results in varying degrees of paralysis of the lower limbs (Miller, 2019; Savvidou & Jauniaux, 2019). Individuals with spina bifida usually need assistive devices such as crutches, braces, or wheelchairs. A strategy that can help to prevent neural tube defects is for women to consume adequate amounts of the B vitamin folic acid (American Society for Reproductive Medicine & others, 2019). A recent large-scale study in Brazil found that when flour was fortified with folic acid it produced a significant reduction in neural tube defects (Santos & others, 2016).

Both maternal diabetes and obesity place the fetus at risk for developing neural tube defects (O'Malley & others, 2018; Valentin & others, 2018). Researchers also have found that a high level of maternal stress is linked to neural tube defects (Li & others, 2013).

Neurogenesis   In a normal pregnancy, once the neural tube has closed, a massive proliferation of new immature neurons begins to take place at about the fifth prenatal week (Zhu & others, 2018). The generation of new neurons is called *neurogenesis*, which continues through the remainder of the prenatal period although it is largely complete by the end of the fifth month after conception (Borsani & others, 2019). At the peak of neurogenesis, it is estimated that as many as 200,000 neurons are being generated every minute!

Yelyi Nordone, 12, of New York City, casts her line out into the pond during Camp Spifida at Camp Victory, near Millville, Pa., in July 2008. Camp Spifida is a weeklong residential camp for children with spina bifida.
Bill Hughes/Bloomsburg Press Enterprise/AP Images

Neural Migration   At approximately 15 weeks after conception, *neuronal migration* occurs (Keunen, Counsell, & Benders, 2017). Cells begin moving outward from their point of origin to their appropriate locations and creating the different levels, structures, and regions of the brain (Miyazaki, Song, & Takahashi, 2016). Once a cell has migrated to its target destination, it must mature and develop a more complex structure.

Neural Connectivity   At about the 23rd prenatal week, connections between neurons begin to form, a process that continues postnatally (Borsani & others, 2019; van den Heuvel & others, 2018). We will have much more to say about the structure of neurons, their connectivity, and the development of the infant brain in the chapter on "Physical Development and Biological Aging."

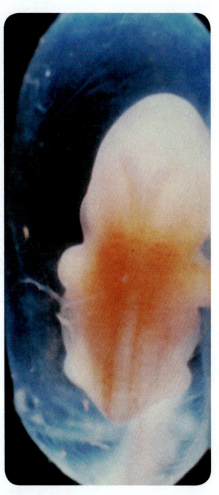

FIGURE 11

EARLY FORMATION OF THE NERVOUS SYSTEM. The photograph shows the primitive, tubular appearance of the nervous system at six weeks in the human embryo.
Claude Edelmann/Science Source

---

developmental **connection**

Brain Development

At birth, infants' brains weigh approximately 25 percent of what they will weigh in adulthood. Connect to "Physical Development and Biological Aging."

---

neurons Nerve cells that handle information processing at the cellular level.

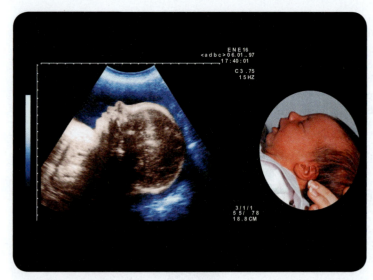

A 6-month-old poses with the ultrasound image take four months into the baby's prenatal development. *What is ultrasound sonography and what can it detect?*
AJ Photo/BSIP/age fotostock

PRENATAL DIAGNOSTIC TESTS

Together with her doctor, a pregnant woman will decide the extent to which she should undergo prenatal testing. A number of tests can indicate whether a fetus is developing normally; these include ultrasound sonography, fetal MRI, chorionic villus sampling, amniocentesis, and maternal blood screening. The decision to have a given test depends on several criteria, such as the mother's age, medical history, and genetic risk factors.

Ultrasound Sonography   An ultrasound test is generally performed 7 weeks into a pregnancy and at various times later in pregnancy. *Ultrasound sonography* is a noninvasive prenatal medical procedure in which high-frequency sound waves are directed into the pregnant woman's abdomen (Majeed & others, 2019; Tamai & others 2018). The echo from the sounds is transformed into a visual representation of the fetus's inner structures. This technique can detect many structural abnormalities in the fetus, including microcephaly, a form of intellectual disability involving an abnormally small brain; it can also give clues to the baby's sex and indicate whether there is more than one fetus (Calvo-Garcia, 2016). A recent research review concluded that many aspects of the developing prenatal brain can be detected by ultrasound in the first trimester and that about 50 percent of spina bifida cases can be identified at this time, most of these being severe cases (Engels & others, 2016). There is virtually no risk to the woman or fetus in using ultrasound. Ultrasound results are available as soon as the images are read by a radiologist.

Fetal MRI   The development of brain-imaging techniques has led to increasing use of *fetal MRI* to diagnose fetal malformations (Cheong & Miller, 2018; Mervak & others, 2019) (see Figure 12). MRI (magnetic resonance imaging) uses a powerful magnet and radio waves to generate detailed images of the body's organs and structures. Currently, ultrasound is still the first choice in fetal screening, but fetal MRI can provide more detailed images than ultrasound

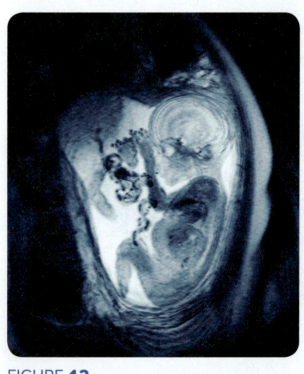

FIGURE 12

A FETAL MRI, WHICH IS INCREASINGLY BEING USED IN PRENATAL DIAGNOSIS OF FETAL MALFORMATIONS.
Du Cane Medical Imaging Ltd/Science Source

(Griffiths & others, 2018). In many instances, ultrasound will indicate a possible abnormality and fetal MRI will then be used to obtain a clearer, more detailed image (Tee & others, 2016). Among the fetal malformations that fetal MRI may be able to detect better than ultrasound sonography are certain abnormalities of the central nervous system, chest, gastrointestinal tract, genital/urinary tract, and placenta (Manganaro & others, 2018; Pfeifer, 2019). In a recent review, it was concluded that fetal MRI often does not provide good results in the first trimester of pregnancy because of small fetal structures and movement artifacts (Wataganara & others, 2016). Also, in this review, it was argued that fetal MRI can be especially beneficial in assessing central nervous system abnormalities in the third trimester of pregnancy.

Chorionic Villus Sampling   At some point between the 10th and 12th weeks of pregnancy, chorionic villus sampling may be used to screen for genetic defects and chromosomal abnormalities. *Chorionic villus sampling (CVS)* is a prenatal medical procedure in which a tiny tissue sample from the placenta is removed and analyzed (Gimovsky & others, 2019). The results are available in about 10 days.

Amniocentesis   Between the 15th and 18th weeks of pregnancy, *amniocentesis* may be performed. In this procedure, a sample of amniotic fluid is withdrawn by syringe and tested for chromosomal or metabolic disorders (Levy & Stosic, 2019). The later in the pregnancy amniocentesis is performed, the better its diagnostic potential. However, the earlier it is performed, the more useful it is in deciding how to handle a pregnancy when the fetus is found to have a disorder. It may take two weeks for enough cells to grow so that amniocentesis test results can be obtained. Amniocentesis brings a small risk of miscarriage: about 1 woman in every 200 to 300 miscarries after amniocentesis.

Maternal Blood Screening and Cell-Free Fetal DNA During the 16th to 18th weeks of pregnancy, maternal blood screening may be performed. *Maternal blood screening* identifies pregnancies that have an elevated risk for birth defects such as spina bifida and Down syndrome, as well as congenital heart disease risk for children (Novak & Graham, 2019). A current blood test, the *triple screen*, measures three substances in the mother's blood in the second trimester of pregnancy. After an abnormal triple screen result, the next step is usually an ultrasound examination. If an ultrasound does not explain the abnormal triple screen results, amniocentesis typically is used.

Recent advances in molecular genetics and DNA sequencing have improved the effectiveness of noninvasive testing to detect genetic abnormalities using cell-free fetal DNA in the mother's blood (Hui, 2019). The cell-free fetal DNA testing has especially improved the accuracy of prenatal testing for fetal abnormalities such as Down syndrome as early as 10 weeks into the first trimester.

Fetal Sex Determination Chorionic villus sampling has often been used to determine the sex of the fetus at some point between 11 and 13 weeks of gestation. Recently, though, some noninvasive techniques have been able to detect the sex of the fetus at an earlier point (Degrelle & Fournier, 2018; Skrzypek & Hui, 2017). Recently, non-invasive diagnosis of plasma was able to accurately determine fetal sex at 4.5 weeks (D'Aversa & others, 2019). Being able to detect an offspring's sex as well as the presence of various diseases and defects at such an early stage raises ethical concerns about couples' motivation to terminate a pregnancy (Breveglieri & others, 2019).

HAZARDS TO PRENATAL DEVELOPMENT

For most babies, the course of prenatal development goes smoothly. Their mother's womb protects them as they develop. Despite this protection, however, the environment can affect the embryo or fetus in many well-documented ways.

General Principles A **teratogen** is any agent that can potentially cause a birth defect or negatively alter cognitive and behavioral outcomes. The field of study that investigates the causes of birth defects is called *teratology* (Boschen & others, 2018; DeSesso, 2019; Kancherla & others, 2019). Teratogens include drugs, incompatible blood types, environmental pollutants, infectious diseases, nutritional deficiencies, maternal stress, advanced maternal and paternal age, and environmental pollutants.

The dose, the genetic susceptibility, and the time of exposure to a particular teratogen influence both the severity of the damage to an embryo or fetus and the type of defect:

- *Dose* The dose effect is obvious—the greater the dose of an agent, such as a drug, the greater the effect.
- *Genetic Susceptibility* The type or severity of abnormalities caused by a teratogen is linked to the genotype of the pregnant woman and the genotype of the embryo or fetus. For example, how a mother metabolizes a particular drug can influence the degree to which the drug effects are transmitted to the embryo or fetus. Differences in placental membranes and placental transport also affect exposure. The extent to which an embryo or fetus is vulnerable to a teratogen may also depend on its genotype (Bianchi, 2019). Also, for unknown reasons, male fetuses are far more likely to be affected by teratogens than female fetuses are.
- *Time of Exposure* Teratogens do more damage at some points in development than at others. Damage during the germinal period may even prevent implantation. In general, the embryonic period is more vulnerable than the fetal period (Feldkamp & others, 2017).

Figure 13 summarizes additional information about the effects of time of exposure to a teratogen. The probability of a structural defect is greatest early in the embryonic period, when organs are being formed. Each body structure has its own critical period of formation (a fixed time period very early in development during which certain experiences or events can have a long-lasting effect on development). The critical period for the nervous system (week 3) is earlier than that for arms and legs (weeks 4 and 5).

After organogenesis is complete, teratogens are less likely to cause anatomical defects. Instead, exposure during the fetal period is more likely to stunt growth or to create problems in the way organs function. To examine some key teratogens and their effects, let's begin with drugs.

teratogen Any agent that can potentially cause a birth defect or negatively alter cognitive and behavioral outcomes.

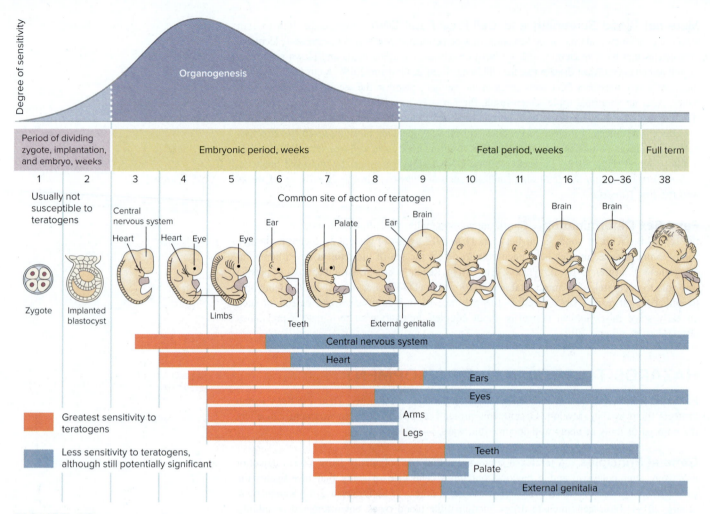

FIGURE 13

TERATOGENS AND THE TIMING OF THEIR EFFECTS ON PRENATAL DEVELOPMENT. The danger of structural defects caused by teratogens is greatest early in embryonic development. The period of organogenesis (red color in the bar graph) lasts for about six weeks. Later assaults by teratogens (blue color in the bar graph) mainly occur in the fetal period and instead of causing structural damage are more likely to stunt growth or cause problems with organ function.

Prescription and Nonprescription Drugs   Prescription drugs that can function as teratogens include antibiotics, such as streptomycin and tetracycline; some antidepressants; certain hormones, such as progestin and synthetic estrogen; and isotretinoin (Accutane®, often prescribed for acne) (Dathe & Schaefer, 2018). Among the birth defects caused by Accutane are heart defects, eye and ear abnormalities, and brain malformation. In a recent study, isotretinoin was the fourth most common drug given to female adolescents who were seeking contraception advice from a physician (Stancil & others, 2019). However, physicians did not give the adolescent girls adequate information about the negative effects of isotretinoin on offspring if the girls were to become pregnant. In a recent review of teratogens that should never be taken during the first trimester of pregnancy, isotreninoin was on the prohibited list (Eltonsy & others, 2016). Nonprescription drugs that can be harmful include diet pills and high doses of aspirin.

Psychoactive Drugs   *Psychoactive drugs* are drugs that act on the nervous system to alter states of consciousness, modify perceptions, and change moods. Examples include caffeine, alcohol, and nicotine, as well as illegal drugs such as cocaine and marijuana.

Caffeine   People often consume caffeine by drinking coffee, tea, colas, or energy drinks, or by eating chocolate. Somewhat mixed results have been found for the extent to which maternal caffeine intake influences an offspring's development (Chen & others, 2016; De Medeiros & others, 2017). However, a large-scale study of almost 60,000 women revealed that maternal caffeine intake was linked to lower birth weight and babies being born small for gestational age (Sengpiel & others, 2013). The effects of maternal consumption of energy drinks that typically have extremely high levels of caffeine have not yet been studied. The U.S. Food and Drug Administration recommends that pregnant women either not consume caffeine or consume it only sparingly.

Alcohol   Heavy drinking by pregnant women can be devastating to offspring. **Fetal alcohol spectrum disorders (FASD)** are a cluster of abnormalities and problems that appear in the offspring of mothers who drink alcohol heavily during pregnancy (Helgesson & others, 2018; McQuire & others, 2019; Mukherjee, 2019). The abnormalities include facial deformities and defective limbs, face, and heart (Del Campo & Jones, 2017). Most children with FASD have learning problems, and many are below average in intelligence; some have an intellectual disability (Khoury & Milligan, 2019). A recent research review concluded that FASD is linked to a lower level of executive function in children, especially in planning (Kingdon, Cardoso, & McGrath, 2016). And in a recent study, FASD was associated with both externalized and internalized behavior problems in childhood (Tsang & others, 2016). Further, in a recent study in the United Kingdom, the life expectancy of individuals with FASD was only 34 years of age, about 42 percent of the life span of members of the general population (Thanh & Jonsson, 2016). In this study, the most common causes of death among individuals with FASD were suicide (15 percent), accidents (14 percent), and poisoning by illegal drugs or alcohol (7 percent). A recent study confirmed the significant risk of suicidal behavior in adolescents with FASD (O'Connor & others, 2019). Although mothers of FASD infants are heavy drinkers, many mothers who are heavy drinkers may not have children with FASD or may have one child with FASD and other children who do not have it.

What are some guidelines for alcohol use during pregnancy? Even drinking just one or two servings of beer or wine or one serving of hard liquor a few days a week can have negative effects on the fetus, although it is generally agreed that this level of alcohol use will not cause fetal alcohol spectrum disorders (American Society for Reproductive Medicine & others, 2019; Sarman, 2018). The U.S. Surgeon General recommends that no alcohol be consumed during pregnancy, as does the French Alcohol Society (Rolland & others, 2016). Despite such recommendations, a recent large-scale U.S. study found that 11.5 percent of adolescent and 8.7 percent of adult pregnant women reported using alcohol in the previous month (Oh & others, 2017).

However, in Great Britain, the National Institutes of Care and Health Excellence have concluded that consuming one to two alcoholic drinks not more than twice a week is safe during pregnancy (O'Keeffe, Greene, & Kearney, 2014). A study of more than 7,000 7-year-olds found that children born to mothers who were light drinkers during pregnancy (up to two drinks per week) did not show more developmental problems than children born to non-drinking mothers (Kelly & others, 2013).

Nicotine   Cigarette smoking by pregnant women can adversely influence prenatal development, birth, and postnatal development (Barboza, 2019; Ostfeld & others, 2019). Preterm births and low birth weights, fetal and neonatal deaths, respiratory problems, sudden infant death syndrome (SIDS, also known as crib death), and cardiovascular problems are all more common among the offspring of mothers who smoked during pregnancy (Zhang & others, 2017). Prenatal smoking has been implicated in as many as 25 percent of infants with low birth weight (Brown & Graves, 2013). And in a recent study, maternal cigarette smoking during pregnancy was linked to higher rates of cigarette smoking among offspring at 16 years of age (De Genna & others, 2016). Researchers also have found that maternal smoking during pregnancy is a risk factor for the development of attention deficit hyperactivity disorder (ADHD) in offspring (Pohlabein & others, 2017). A recent meta-analysis of 15 studies concluded that smoking during pregnancy increased the risk of children having ADHD, and the risk of ADHD was greater if mothers were heavy smokers (Huang & others, 2019). Further, a recent study revealed that daughters whose mothers had smoked during their pregnancy were more likely to subsequently smoke during their own pregnancy (Ncube & Mueller, 2017). Also, a study found that maternal smoking during pregnancy was associated with increased risk of asthma and wheezing in adolescence (Hollams & others, 2014). Despite the plethora of negative outcomes for maternal smoking during pregnancy, a recent large-scale U.S. study revealed that 23 percent of adolescent and 15 percent of adult pregnant women reported using tobacco in the previous month (Oh & others, 2017). Cessation of smoking by pregnant women by the third trimester is linked to improved birth outcomes (Crume, 2019).

Researchers have documented that environmental tobacco smoke is associated with negative outcomes for offspring (Patel & others, 2017). Maternal exposure to environmental tobacco smoke,

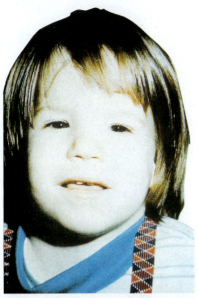

Fetal alcohol spectrum disorders (FASD) are characterized by a number of physical abnormalities and learning problems. Notice the wide-set eyes, flat cheekbones, and thin upper lip in this child with FASD.
Source: Streissguth, AP, Landesman-Dwyer S, Martin, JC, & Smith, DW (1980). Teratogenic effects of alcohol in humans and laboratory animals. *Science, 209,* 353–361.

fetal alcohol spectrum disorders (FASD) A cluster of abnormalities that may appear in the offspring of mothers who drink alcohol heavily during pregnancy.

In what ways are expectant mothers' alcohol and nicotine intake linked to outcomes for their offspring?
Altafulla/Shutterstock

or secondhand smoke, has been linked to an increased risk of low birth weight in offspring (Salama & others, 2013) and to diminished ovarian functioning in female offspring (Kilic & others, 2012). And one study revealed that environmental tobacco smoke was associated with 114 deregulations of gene expression, especially those involving immune functioning, in the fetal cells of offspring (Votavova & others, 2012). Another study found that maternal exposure to environmental tobacco smoke during prenatal development increased the risk of stillbirth (Varner & others, 2014).

A final point about nicotine use during pregnancy involves the recent dramatic increase in the use of e-cigarettes (Cooper & others, 2019; Tegin & others, 2018). In a recent study, chronic exposure to e-cigarette aerosols was linked to low birth weight in offspring (Orzabal & others, 2019). One study found that misconceptions about e-cigarettes were common among pregnant women (Mark & others, 2015). The most common reason pregnant women gave for using e-cigarettes was a perception that they are less harmful than regular cigarettes (74 percent) and that they promote smoking cessation (72 percent).

Cocaine   Does cocaine use during pregnancy harm the developing embryo and fetus? One research study found that cocaine quickly crossed the placenta to reach the fetus (De Giovanni & Marchetti, 2012). The most consistent finding is that cocaine exposure during prenatal development is associated with reduced birth weight, length, and head circumference (Gouin & others, 2011). In other studies, prenatal cocaine exposure has been linked to impaired connectivity of the thalamus and prefrontal cortex in newborns (Salzwedel & others, 2016); lower arousal, less effective self-regulation, higher excitability, and lower quality of reflexes at 1 month of age (Ackerman, Riggins, & Black, 2010; Lester & others, 2002); self-regulation problems at age 12 (Minnes & others, 2016); impaired motor development at 2 years of age and a slower rate of growth through 10 years of age (Richardson, Goldschmidt, & Williford, 2008); elevated blood pressure at 9 years of age (Shankaran & others, 2010); impaired language development and information processing (Beeghly & others, 2006); attention deficit hyperactivity disorder (Richardson & others, 2016); increased likelihood of being in a special education program that offers support services (Levine & others, 2008); increased behavioral problems, especially externalizing problems such as high rates of aggression and delinquency (Minnes & others, 2010; Richardson & others, 2011, 2016); and posttraumatic stress disorder (PTSD) (Richardson & others, 2016). Further, in a longitudinal study prenatal cocaine exposure was linked to early use of marijuana, arrest history, conduct disorder, and emotion regulation problems at 21 years of age (Richardson & others, 2019).

Some researchers argue that these findings should be interpreted cautiously (Accornero & others, 2007). Why? Because other factors in the lives of pregnant women who use cocaine (such as poverty, malnutrition, and other substance abuse) often cannot be ruled out as possible contributors to the problems found in their children (Hurt & others, 2005; Messiah & others, 2011). For example, cocaine users are more likely than nonusers to smoke cigarettes, use marijuana, drink alcohol, and take amphetamines.

Despite these cautions, the weight of research evidence indicates that children born to mothers who use cocaine are likely to have neurological, medical, and cognitive deficits (Baer & others, 2019; Martin & others, 2016; Richardson & others, 2011, 2016, 2018). Cocaine use by pregnant women is never recommended.

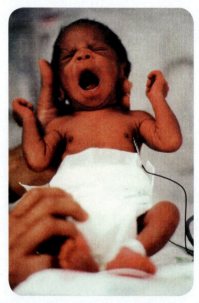

This baby was exposed to cocaine prenatally. *What are some of the possible effects on development of being exposed to cocaine prenatally?*
Chuck Nacke/Alamy Stock Photo

Marijuana   An increasing number of studies find that marijuana use by pregnant women also has negative outcomes for their offspring (Ruisch & others, 2018; Volkow, Compton, & Wargo, 2017). In a recent meta-analysis, marijuana use during pregnancy was linked to offsprings' low birth weight and a greater likelihood of being placed in a neonatal intensive care unit (NICU) (Gunn & others, 2016). In another recent study, newborns born to mothers who had used marijuana during pregnancy were more likely to be born preterm or low birth weight (Petrangelo & others, 2019). One study also found that prenatal marijuana exposure was related to lower intelligence in children (Goldschmidt & others, 2008). Researchers also have found that marijuana use during pregnancy is associated with lower levels of attention, memory, and impulse control in offspring (Wu, Jew, & Lu, 2011). Another study indicated that prenatal exposure to marijuana was linked to marijuana use at 14 years of age (Day, Goldschmidt, & Thomas, 2006). In sum, marijuana use is not recommended for pregnant women.

Despite increasing evidence of negative outcomes, a recent survey found that marijuana use by pregnant women increased from 2.4 percent in 2002 to 3.85 percent in 2014 (Brown & others, 2016). And there is concern that marijuana use by pregnant women may increase further given the increasing number of states that have legalized marijuana (Chasnoff, 2017; Hennessy, 2018).

Synthetic Opioids and Opiate-Related Pain Killers   An increasing number of women are using synthetic opioids, such as fentanyl, and opiate-related pain relievers obtained legally by prescription (such as OxyContin and Vicodin) during their pregnancy (Brimdyr & Caldwell, 2018; Clemens-Cope & others, 2019). Infants born to women using these substances during pregnancy are at risk for experiencing opioid withdrawal (Lacaze-Masmonteil & O'Flaherty, 2018). Other possible outcomes for children exposed to these substances are just beginning to be studied (National Institute of Drug Abuse, 2018). Any prolonged use of synthetic opioids and opiate-related pain relievers is not recommended (Federal Drug Administration, 2018a).

Maternal Diseases   Maternal diseases and infections can produce defects in offspring by crossing the placental barrier, or they can cause damage during birth (Koren & Ornoy, 2018). Rubella (German measles) is one disease that can cause prenatal defects. A recent study found that cardiac defects, pulmonary problems, and microcephaly (a condition in which the baby's head is significantly smaller and less developed than average) were among the most common fetal and neonatal outcomes when women had rubella during pregnancy (Yazigi & others, 2017). Women who plan to have children should have a blood test before they become pregnant to determine whether they are immune to the disease.

Syphilis (a sexually transmitted infection) is more damaging later in prenatal development— four months or more after conception. When syphilis is present at birth, problems can develop in the central nervous system and gastrointestinal tract (Braccio, Sharland, & Ladhani, 2016). Penicillin is the only known treatment for syphilis during pregnancy (Moline & Smith, 2016).

Another infection that has received widespread attention recently is genital herpes. Newborns contract this virus when they are delivered through the birth canal of a mother with genital herpes (Sampath, Maduro, & Schillinger, 2019). If an active case of genital herpes is detected in a pregnant woman close to her delivery date, a cesarean section (in which the infant is delivered through an incision in the mother's abdomen) can be performed to keep the virus from infecting the newborn.

AIDS is a sexually transmitted infection that is caused by the human immunodeficiency virus (HIV), which destroys the body's immune system. A mother can infect her offspring with HIV/AIDS in three ways: (1) across the placenta during gestation, (2) through contact with maternal blood or fluids during delivery, and (3) through breast feeding. The transmission of AIDS through breast feeding is a particular problem in many developing countries (UNICEF, 2018). Babies born to HIV-infected mothers can be (1) infected and symptomatic (show HIV symptoms), (2) infected but asymptomatic (show no HIV symptoms), or (3) not infected at all. An infant who is infected and asymptomatic may still develop HIV symptoms up to 15 months of age.

Maternal Diet and Nutrition   A developing embryo or fetus depends completely on its mother for nutrition, which comes from the mother's blood. The nutritional status of the embryo or fetus is determined by the mother's total caloric intake as well as her intake of proteins, vitamins, and minerals. Children born to malnourished mothers are more likely than other children to be malformed.

Being overweight before and during pregnancy can also put the embryo or fetus at risk, and an increasing number of pregnant women in the United States are overweight (Anderson-Hall & others, 2019; Hu & others, 2019). Maternal obesity adversely affects pregnancy outcomes through elevated rates of hypertension, diabetes, respiratory complications, infections in the mother, and depression (McDowell, Cain, & Brumley, 2019; Preston, Reynolds, & Pearson, 2018). Research studies have found that maternal obesity is linked to an increase in stillbirth (Gardosi & others, 2013) and an increased likelihood that the newborn will be placed in a neonatal intensive care unit (Minsart & others, 2013). Further, two recent research reviews concluded that maternal obesity during pregnancy is associated with an increased likelihood of offspring being obese in childhood and adulthood (Pinto Pereira & others, 2016). Management of obesity that includes weight loss and increased exercise prior to pregnancy is likely to benefit the mother and the baby (Aubuchon-Endsley & others, 2019; Dutton & others, 2018).

developmental connection

Conditions, Diseases, Disorders

The greatest incidence of HIV/AIDS occurs in sub-Saharan Africa, where in some areas as many as 30 percent of mothers have HIV; many are unaware that they are infected with the virus. Connect to "Gender and Sexuality."

developmental connection

Health

What are some key factors that influence whether individuals will become obese? Connect to "Health."

Because the fetus depends entirely on its mother for nutrition, it is important for pregnant women to have good nutritional habits. In Kenya, this government clinic provides pregnant women with information about how their diet can influence the health of their fetus and offspring. *What might the information about diet be like?*
Delphine Bousquet/AFP/Getty Images

How do pregnant women's emotional states and stress levels affect prenatal development and birth?
Skynesher/E+/Getty Images

developmental **connection**

Sexuality

Adolescent pregnancy creates negative developmental trajectories for mothers and their offspring. Connect to "Gender and Sexuality."

What are some of the risks for infants born to adolescent mothers?
Barbara Penoyar/Getty Images

One aspect of maternal nutrition that is important for normal prenatal development is folic acid, a B-complex vitamin. As indicated earlier in the chapter, lack of folic acid is related to neural tube defects in offspring (American Society for Reproductive Medicine & others, 2019; Kancherla & Oakley, 2018). The U.S. Department of Health and Human Services (2019) recommends that pregnant women consume a minimum of 400 micrograms of folic acid per day (about twice the amount the average woman gets in one day). Orange juice and spinach are examples of foods that are rich in folic acid.

Emotional States and Stress   When a pregnant woman experiences intense fears, anxieties, and other emotions or negative mood states, physiological changes occur that may affect her fetus. A mother's stress may also influence the fetus indirectly by increasing the likelihood that the mother will engage in unhealthy behaviors such as taking drugs and receiving poor prenatal care.

High maternal anxiety and stress during pregnancy can have long-term consequences for the offspring (Murray & others, 2019; Shallie & Naicker, 2019). One study found that high levels of depression, anxiety, and stress during pregnancy were linked to internalizing problems in adolescence (Betts & others, 2014). A research review indicated that pregnant women with high levels of stress are at increased risk for having a child with emotional or cognitive problems, attention deficit hyperactivity disorder (ADHD), and language delay (Taige & others, 2007). Further, a recent research review concluded that regardless of the form of maternal prenatal stress or anxiety and the prenatal trimester in which the stress or anxiety occurred, during the first two years of life the offspring displayed lower levels of self-regulation (Korja & others, 2017). Another study revealed that maternal stressful life events prior to conception increased the risk of having a very low birth weight infant (Witt & others, 2014).

Maternal depression also can have an adverse effect on birth outcomes and children's development (Park & others, 2018). Research indicates that maternal depression during pregnancy is linked to preterm birth and low birth weight (Mparmpakas & others, 2013). One study found that maternal depression during pregnancy was associated with low birth weight in full-term offspring (Chang & others, 2014). Another study found that taking antidepressants early in pregnancy was linked to an increased risk of miscarriage (Almeida & others, 2016). Researchers have also found that when fetuses were exposed to serotonin-based antidepressants, they were more likely to be born preterm (Podrebarac & others, 2017). Further, a recent study revealed that taking antidepressants in the second or third trimester of pregnancy was linked to an increased risk of autism spectrum disorders in children (Boukhris & others, 2016). Also, a recent meta-analysis indicated that yoga was effective in reducing depressive symptoms in pregnant women (Ng & others, 2019).

Maternal Age   When possible harmful effects on the fetus and infant are considered, two maternal age groups are of special interest: adolescents and women 35 years of age and older (Kawakita & others, 2016; Kingsbury, Plotnikova, & Najman, 2018). The mortality rate of infants born to adolescent mothers is double that of infants born to mothers in their twenties. Adequate prenatal care decreases the probability that a child born to an adolescent girl will have physical problems. However, adolescents are the least likely age group to obtain prenatal assistance from clinics and health services.

Maternal age is also linked to the risk that a child will have Down syndrome (Jaruratanasirikul & others, 2017). A baby with Down syndrome rarely is born to a mother 16 to 34 years of age. However, when the mother reaches 40 years of age, the probability is slightly over 1 in 100 that a baby born to her will have Down syndrome, and by age 50 it is almost 1 in 10. When mothers are 35 years and older, risks also increase for low birth weight, preterm delivery, and fetal death (Koo & others, 2012). Also, in a recent study, pregnant women aged 43 years and older were more likely to have infants who were stillborn (Wu & others, 2019). A Norwegian study found that maternal age of 30 years or older was linked to the same level of increased risk for fetal deaths as that of 25- to 29-year-old pregnant women who were overweight/obese or were smokers (Waldenstrom & others, 2014).

We still have much to learn about the effects of the mother's age on pregnancy and childbirth. As women remain active, exercise regularly, and are careful about their nutrition, their reproductive systems may remain healthier at older ages than was thought possible in the past.

Environmental Hazards Many aspects of our modern industrial world can endanger the embryo or fetus. Some specific hazards to the embryo or fetus include radiation, toxic wastes, and other chemical pollutants.

Women and their physicians should weigh the risk of undergoing an X-ray when the woman is or might be pregnant (Baysinger, 2010). However, a routine diagnostic X-ray of a body area other than the abdomen, with the woman's abdomen protected by a lead apron, is generally considered safe (Brent, 2009, 2011).

Paternal Factors So far, we have discussed how characteristics of the mother—such as drug use, disease, diet and nutrition, age, and emotional states—can influence prenatal development and the development of the child. Might there also be some paternal risk factors? Indeed, there are several (Mayo & others, 2019; Pedersen & others, 2014). Men's exposure to lead, radiation, certain pesticides, and petrochemicals may cause abnormalities in sperm that lead to miscarriage or diseases such as childhood cancer (Cordier, 2008). The father's smoking during the mother's pregnancy also can cause problems for the offspring (Agricola & others, 2016). A recent research review concluded that tobacco smoking is linked to impaired male fertility, as well as increased DNA damage, aneuploidy (abnormal number of chromosomes in a cell), and mutations in sperm (Beal, Yauk, & Marchetti, 2017). Also, in one study, heavy paternal smoking was associated with increased risk of early miscarriage (Venners & others, 2004). This negative outcome may be related to maternal exposure to secondhand smoke. And in another study, paternal smoking around the time of the child's conception was linked to an increased risk of the child developing leukemia (Milne & others, 2012). Also, a research review concluded that there is an increased risk of spontaneous abortion (miscarriage), autism, and schizophrenic disorders when the father is 40 years of age or older (Liu & others, 2012). And a research study revealed that children born to fathers who were 40 years of age or older had increased risk of developing autism because of an increase in random gene mutations in older fathers (Kong & others, 2012). However, the age of the offspring's mother was not linked to development of autism in children.

The father may contribute to positive outcomes for the fetus by providing support and having a positive attitude toward the pregnancy (Molgora & others, 2019). Earlier you read about how maternal stress and depression have negative developmental outcomes for offspring. Fathers can play an important role in helping mothers keep their stress and depression levels lower by contributing to a positive marital relationship, not engaging in spousal abuse, sharing more in household tasks, and participating in childbirth classes. One study found that intimate partner violence increased the mother's stress level (Fonseca-Machado Mde & others, 2015).

An explosion at the Chernobyl nuclear power plant in the Ukraine produced radioactive contamination that spread to surrounding areas. Thousands of infants were born with health problems and deformities as a result of the nuclear contamination, including this boy whose arm did not form. *In addition to radioactive contamination, what are some other types of environmental hazards to prenatal development?*
Sergey Guneev/RIA Novosti

PRENATAL CARE

Although prenatal care varies enormously from one woman to another, it usually involves a defined schedule of visits for medical care, which typically includes screening for manageable conditions and treatable diseases that can affect the baby or the mother. In addition to medical care, prenatal programs often include comprehensive educational, social, and nutritional services (Marshall & others, 2019). Information about pregnancy, labor, delivery, and caring for the newborn can be especially valuable for first-time mothers. Prenatal care is also very important for women in poverty and immigrant women because it links them with other social services (Fabi, 2019). A recent study found that inadequate prenatal care was associated with very low birth weight (Xaverius & others, 2016).

An innovative program that is rapidly expanding in the United States is CenteringPregnancy (Heredia-Pi & others, 2019). This program is relationship-centered and provides complete prenatal care in a group setting (Hetherington & others, 2018). It replaces traditional 15-minute physician visits with 90-minute peer group support sessions and self-examination led by a physician or certified nurse-midwife. Groups of up to 10 women (and often their partners) meet regularly beginning at 12 to 16 weeks of pregnancy. The sessions emphasize empowering women to play an active role in experiencing a positive pregnancy. Research increasingly shows

In one study in China, the longer fathers smoked, the greater the risk that their children would develop cancer (Ji and others, 1997). *What are some other paternal factors that can influence the development of the fetus and the child?*
David Butow/Corbis/Getty Images

The increasingly widespread CenteringPregnancy program alters routine prenatal care by bringing women out of exam rooms and into relationship-oriented groups.
MBI/Alamy Stock Photo

positive outcomes of CenteringPregnancy for the fetus and child, as well as the mother (Darby-Stewart & Strickland, 2019; Tubay & others, 2019). A recent large-scale study compared women who had received CenteringPregnancy or individual prenatal care at a university medical center (Cunningham & others, 2019). Women who participated in CenteringPregnancy had offspring who were less likely to be born preterm or low birth weight. In another recent study, women who participated in CenteringPregnancy used pain relief less during labor and were more likely to breast feed their infants (Rijnders & others, 2019).

Exercise increasingly is recommended as part of a comprehensive prenatal care program. Exercise during pregnancy helps prevent constipation, conditions the body, reduces excessive weight gain, lowers the risk of developing hypertension, and is associated with a more positive mental state, including a reduced level of depression (Bacchi & others, 2018; Magro-Malosso & others, 2017). Further, a recent study indicated that pregnant women who did not exercise three or more times a week were more likely to develop hypertension (Barakat & others, 2017). Another recent study indicated that two weekly 70-minute yoga sessions reduced pregnant women's stress and enhanced their immune system functioning (Chen & others, 2017). Also, a recent study indicated that pregnant women who exercised regularly in the second and third trimesters rated their quality of life higher (Krzepota, Sadowska, & Biernat, 2019). And regular exercise during pregnancy has benefits for the fetus and infant (Newton & May, 2019). For example, a recent study found that women's regular exercise during pregnancy was linked to more advanced development of the neonatal brain (Laborte-Lemoyne, Currier, & Ellenberg, 2017).

Review Connect Reflect

 LG4 Characterize the course of prenatal development and its hazards.

Review

- What is the course of prenatal development? How does the brain develop during the prenatal period?
- What are some prenatal diagnostic tests?
- What are some of the main hazards to prenatal development?
- What types of resources do prenatal care programs provide?

Connect

- In a previous section of this chapter we discussed chromosomal and gene-linked abnormalities that can affect prenatal development. How are the symptoms of the related conditions or risks similar to or different from those caused by prenatal exposure to teratogens or other hazards?

Reflect Your Own Personal Journey of Life

- If you are a woman, imagine that you have just found out that you are pregnant. What health-enhancing strategies will you follow during the prenatal period? For others, imagine that you are the partner of a woman who has just found out she is pregnant. What will be your role in increasing the likelihood that the prenatal period will go smoothly?

5 Birth and the Postpartum Period

 LG5 Summarize how birth takes place and describe the nature of the postpartum period.

| The Birth Process | The Transition from Fetus to Newborn | Low Birth Weight and Preterm Infants | Bonding | The Postpartum Period |

There was a star danced, and under that I was born.

—**WILLIAM SHAKESPEARE**
English Playwright, 17th Century

The long wait for the moment of birth is over, and the infant is about to appear. What happens during childbirth, and what can be done to make the experience a positive one? Nature writes the basic script for how birth occurs, but parents make important choices about the conditions surrounding birth. We will look first at the sequence of physical steps through which a child is born.

THE BIRTH PROCESS

The birth process occurs in three stages. It may take place in different contexts and in most cases involves one or more attendants.

Stages of Birth   The first stage of the birth process is the longest. Uterine contractions are 15 to 20 minutes apart at the beginning and last up to a minute each. These contractions cause the woman's cervix to stretch and open. As the first stage progresses, the contractions come closer together, occurring every two to five minutes. Their intensity increases. By the end of the first stage, contractions dilate the cervix to an opening of about 10 centimeters (4 inches), so that the baby can move from the uterus to the birth canal. For a woman having her first child, the first stage lasts an average of 6 to 12 hours; for subsequent children, this stage typically is much shorter.

The second birth stage begins when the baby's head starts to move through the cervix and the birth canal. It terminates when the baby emerges completely from the mother's body. With each contraction, the mother bears down hard to push the baby out of her body. By the time the baby's head is out of the mother's body, the contractions come almost every minute and last for about a minute each. This stage typically lasts approximately 45 minutes to an hour.

Afterbirth is the third stage, during which the placenta, umbilical cord, and other membranes are detached and expelled from the uterus. This final stage is the shortest of the three birth stages, lasting only a few minutes.

Childbirth Setting and Attendants   In 2015 in the United States, 98.5 percent of births took place in hospitals (Martin & others, 2017). Of the 1.5 percent of births occurring outside a hospital, 63 percent took place in homes and almost 31 percent in free-standing birthing centers. The percentage of U.S. births at home is the highest since reporting of this context began in 1989. An increase in home births has occurred mainly among non-Latino White women, especially those who were older and married. For these non-Latino White women, two-thirds of their home births are attended by a midwife.

In U.S. hospitals, it has become the norm for the baby's father or a birth coach to be with the mother throughout labor and delivery. In the East African Nigoni culture, by contrast, men are completely excluded from the childbirth process. When a woman is ready to give birth, female relatives move into the woman's hut and the husband leaves, taking his belongings (clothes, tools, weapons, and so on) with him. He is not permitted to return until after the baby is born. In some cultures, childbirth is an open, community affair. For example, in the Pukapukan culture in the Pacific Islands, women give birth in a shelter that is open to villagers, who may observe the birth.

Midwives   A *midwife* is a trained health practitioner who helps women during labor, delivery, and afterbirth (Barger, 2019; Faucher, 2018). Midwifery is practiced in most countries throughout the world (Arabi & others, 2018). In Holland, more than 40 percent of babies are delivered by midwives rather than by doctors. However, in the United States, recently only 8 percent of all hospital births were attended by a midwife (Martin & others, 2017). Nonetheless, the 8 percent figure represents a substantial increase from less than 1 percent in 1975.

Doulas   In some countries, a doula attends a childbearing woman. *Doula* is a Greek word that means "a woman who helps." A **doula** is a caregiver who provides continuous physical, emotional, and educational support for the mother before, during, and after childbirth. Doulas remain with the parents throughout labor, assessing and responding to their needs. Researchers have found positive effects when a doula is present at the birth of a child (Lanning & others, 2019; McLeish & Redshaw, 2018). One study found that doula-assisted mothers were four times less likely to have a low birth weight baby and two times less likely to experience a birth complication involving themselves or their baby (Gruber, Cupito, & Dobson, 2013).

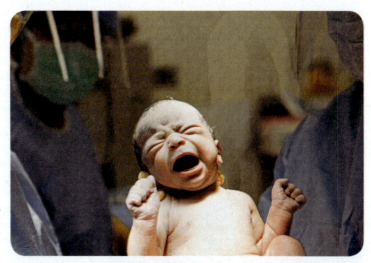

After the long journey of prenatal development, birth takes place. During birth the baby is on a threshold between two worlds. *What are the characteristics of the three stages of birth?*
ERproductions Ltd/Getty Images

In India, a midwife checks on the size, position, and heartbeat of a fetus. Midwives deliver babies in many cultures around the world. *What are some cultural variations in prenatal care?*
Viviane Moos/Corbis/Getty Images

doula A caregiver who provides continuous physical, emotional, and educational support for the mother before, during, and after childbirth.

In the United States, most doulas work as independent service providers hired by the expectant parents. Doulas typically function as part of a "birthing team," serving as an adjunct to the midwife or the hospital's obstetric staff (Kozhimanni & Hardeman, 2016).

Methods of Childbirth   U.S. hospitals often allow the mother and her obstetrician a range of options regarding the method of delivery. Key choices involve the use of medication, whether to use any of a number of nonmedicated techniques to reduce pain, and when to have a cesarean delivery.

Medication   Three basic kinds of drugs that are used for labor are analgesia, anesthesia, and oxytocin/Pitocin. *Analgesia* is used to relieve pain (Wilson & others, 2018). Analgesics include tranquilizers, barbiturates, and narcotics such as Demerol.

Predicting how a drug will affect an individual woman and her fetus is difficult (Kobayashi & others, 2017). A particular drug might have only a minimal effect on one fetus yet have a much stronger effect on another. The drug's dosage is also a factor. Higher doses of tranquilizers and narcotics given to decrease the mother's pain potentially have a more negative effect on the fetus than do lower doses. It is important for the mother to assess her level of pain and have a voice in deciding whether or not she should receive medication.

Natural and Prepared Childbirth   For a brief time not long ago, the idea of avoiding all medication during childbirth gained favor in the United States. Instead, many women chose to reduce the pain of childbirth through techniques known as natural childbirth and prepared childbirth. Today, at least some medication is used in the typical childbirth, but elements of natural childbirth and prepared childbirth remain popular (Bacon & Tomich, 2017).

Natural childbirth is a childbirth method in which no drugs are given to relieve pain or assist in the birth process. The mother and her partner are taught to use breathing methods and relaxation techniques during delivery. French obstetrician Ferdinand Lamaze developed a method similar to natural childbirth that is known as **prepared childbirth,** or the Lamaze method. It includes a special breathing technique to control pushing in the final stages of labor, as well as detailed education about anatomy and physiology. The Lamaze method has become very popular in the United States. The pregnant woman's partner usually serves as her labor coach; he attends childbirth classes with her and guides her breathing and relaxation during labor and delivery. In sum, proponents of current prepared childbirth methods conclude that when information and support are provided, women know how to give birth.

Other Nonmedicated Techniques to Reduce Pain   The effort to reduce stress and control pain during labor has recently led to an increase in the use of some older and some newer nonmedicated techniques (Cooper, Warland, & McCutcheon, 2018; Lewis & others, 2018a, b). These include waterbirth, massage, and acupuncture.

Waterbirth involves giving birth in a tub of warm water. Some women go through labor in the water and get out for delivery; others remain in the water for delivery. The rationale for waterbirth is that the baby has been in an amniotic sac for many months and therefore delivery in a similar environment is likely to be less stressful for the baby and the mother (Taylor & others, 2016). Mothers get into the warm water when contractions become closer together and more intense. Getting into the water too

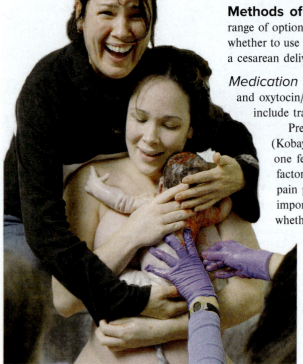

A doula assisting a birth. *What types of support do doulas provide?*
Andersen Ross/Getty Images

natural childbirth A childbirth method that attempts to reduce the mother's pain by decreasing her fear through education about childbirth stages and relaxation techniques during delivery.

An instructor conducts a Lamaze class. *What characterizes the Lamaze method of prepared childbirth?*
Stockbroker/MBI/Alamy Stock Photo

soon can cause labor to slow or stop. An increasing number of studies are either showing no differences in neonatal and maternal outcomes for waterbirth and non-waterbirth deliveries or showing positive outcomes (Davies & others, 2015; Taylor & others, 2016). For example, in a recent Swedish study, women who gave birth in water had a lower risk of vaginal tears, shorter labor, needed fewer drugs for pain relief and interventions for medical problems, and rated their birth experience more positively than women who had conventional spontaneous vaginal births (Ulfsdottir, Saltvedt, & Georgsson, 2018). Also, a recent large-scale study of more than 16,000 waterbirth and non-waterbirth deliveries found fewer negative outcomes for the waterbirth newborns (Bovbjerg, Cheyney, & Everson, 2016). Waterbirth has been practiced more often in European countries such as Switzerland and Sweden than in the United States in recent decades, but it is increasingly being included in U.S. birth plans.

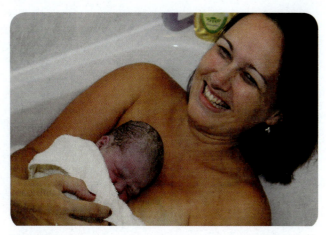

What characterizes the use of waterbirth in delivering a baby?
Judy Lawrance/Alamy Stock Photo

Massage is increasingly used prior to and during delivery (Withers, Kharazmi, & Lim, 2018). Researchers have found that massage therapy reduces pain during labor (Gallo & others, 2018; Shahoei & others, 2017). For example, a recent study found that lower back massage reduced women's labor pain and increased their satisfaction with the birth experience (Unalmis Erdogan, Yanikkerem, & Goker, 2017).

Acupuncture, the insertion of very fine needles into specific locations in the body, is used as a standard procedure to reduce the pain of childbirth in China, although it only recently has begun to be used for this purpose in the United States and Europe (Jo & Lee, 2018; Mollart & others, 2019). Research indicates that acupuncture can have positive effects on labor and delivery (Citkovitz, Schnyer, & Hoskins, 2011).

Cesarean Delivery   Normally, the baby's head comes through the vagina first. But if the baby is in a *breech position,* its buttocks are the first part to emerge from the vagina. In 1 of every 25 deliveries, the baby's head is still in the uterus when the rest of the body is out. Because breech births can cause respiratory problems, if the baby is in a breech position a surgical procedure known as a cesarean delivery is usually performed. In a *cesarean* delivery (or cesarean section), the baby is removed from the uterus through an incision made in the mother's abdomen. The most common causes of cesarean delivery are failure to progress through labor (which can be slowed by epidural anesthesia, for example) and fetal distress.

More cesarean deliveries are performed in the United States than in any other country in the world. However, the U.S. cesarean birth rate in 2015 was 32 percent, the lowest rate since 2007 (Martin & others, 2017). The highest cesarean rates are in the Dominican Republic and Brazil (56 percent); the lowest in New Zealand and the Czech Republic (26 percent) (McCullogh, 2016). The benefits and risks of cesarean deliveries continue to be debated in the United States and around the world (Kupari & others, 2016).

prepared childbirth Developed by French obstetrician Ferdinand Lamaze, a childbirth strategy similar to natural childbirth but one that teaches a special breathing technique to control pushing in the final stages of labor and provides details about anatomy and physiology.

Apgar Scale A widely used method to assess the health of newborns at one and five minutes after birth; it evaluates an infant's heart rate, respiratory effort, muscle tone, body color, and reflex irritability.

THE TRANSITION FROM FETUS TO NEWBORN

Much of our discussion of birth so far has focused on the mother. However, birth also involves considerable stress for the baby. If the delivery takes too long, the baby can develop *anoxia,* a condition in which the fetus or newborn receives insufficient oxygen. Anoxia can cause brain damage.

The baby has considerable capacity to withstand the stress of birth. Large quantities of adrenaline and noradrenaline, hormones that protect the fetus in the event of oxygen deficiency, are secreted in the newborn's body during the birth process (Van Beveren, 2011).

Immediately after birth, the umbilical cord is cut and the baby begins to breathe on its own. Before birth, oxygen came from the mother via the umbilical cord, but a full-term baby's lungs are sufficiently developed to support independent breathing.

Almost immediately after birth, a newborn is weighed, cleaned up, and tested for signs of developmental problems that might require urgent attention. The **Apgar Scale** is widely used to assess the health of newborns at one and five minutes after birth. The Apgar Scale evaluates infants' heart rate, respiratory effort, muscle tone, body color, and reflex

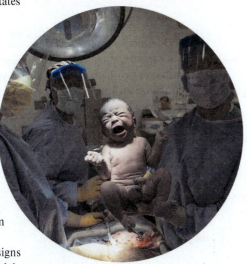

What characterizes the transition from fetus to newborn?
ERproductions Ltd/Blend Images LLC

Score	0	1	2
Heart rate	Absent	Slow—less than 100 beats per minute	Fast—100–140 beats per minute
Respiratory effort	No breathing for more than one minute	Irregular and slow	Good breathing with normal crying
Muscle tone	Limp and flaccid	Weak, inactive, but some flexion of extremities	Strong, active motion
Body color	Blue and pale	Body pink, but extremities blue	Entire body pink
Reflex irritability	No response	Grimace	Coughing, sneezing and crying

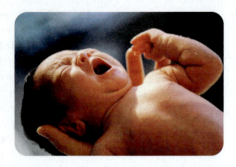

FIGURE 14

THE APGAR SCALE. A newborn's score on the Apgar Scale indicates whether the baby has urgent medical problems.
(*Photo*): Francisco Cruz/Purestock/SuperStock

irritability (see Figure 14). An obstetrician or nurse does the evaluation and gives the newborn a score, or reading, of 0, 1, or 2 on each of these five health signs. A total score of 7 to 10 indicates that the newborn's condition is good. A score of 5 indicates that there may be developmental difficulties. A score of 3 or below signals an emergency and warns that the baby might not survive. The Apgar Scale is especially good at assessing the newborn's ability to respond to the stress of delivery and to adapt to its new environment (Park & others, 2017). It also identifies high-risk infants who need resuscitation. Recent studies have found that low Apgar scores are associated with long-term additional support needs in education and reductions in educational attainment (Tweed & others, 2016), risk of developmental vulnerability at 5 years of age (Razaz & others, 2016), and risk of developing ADHD (Hanc & others, 2018).

Nurses often play important roles in the birth of a baby. To read about the work of a nurse who specializes in caring for women during labor and delivery, see *Connecting with Careers*.

connecting with careers

Linda Pugh, Perinatal Nurse

Perinatal nurses work with childbearing women to support health and growth during the childbearing experience. Linda Pugh, Ph.D., R.N.C., is a perinatal nurse on the faculty at The Johns Hopkins University School of Nursing. She is certified as an inpatient obstetric nurse and specializes in the care of women during labor and delivery. She teaches undergraduate and graduate students, educates professional nurses, and conducts research. In addition, Pugh consults with hospitals and organizations about women's health issues and many of the topics we discuss in this chapter. Her research interests include implementing nursing interventions with low-income breast-feeding women, discovering ways to prevent and ameliorate fatigue during childbearing, and using breathing exercises during labor.

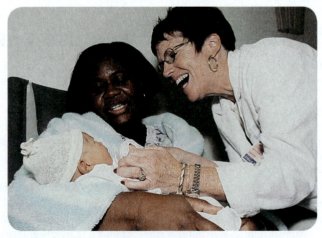

Linda Pugh (*right*) assists a mother and her newborn infant.
Courtesy Dr. Linda Pugh

LOW BIRTH WEIGHT AND PRETERM INFANTS

Three related conditions pose threats to many newborns: low birth weight, preterm birth, and being small for date. **Low birth weight infants** weigh less than 5 pounds and 8 ounces at birth. *Very low birth weight* newborns weigh less than 3 pounds and 4 ounces, and *extremely low birth weight* newborns weigh less than 2 pounds and 3 ounces. **Preterm infants** are born three weeks or more before the pregnancy has reached its full term—in other words, 35 or fewer weeks after conception. **Small for date infants** (also called *small for gestational age infants*) have a birth weight that is below normal when the length of the pregnancy is considered. They weigh less than 90 percent of all babies of the same gestational age. Small for date infants may be preterm or full term. One study found that small for date infants have a 400 percent greater risk of death (Regev & others, 2003).

In 2017, 9.9 percent of U.S. infants were born preterm—a significant increase since the 1980s (March of Dimes, 2018). The increase in preterm births is likely due to such factors as the increasing number of births to women 35 years of age or older, increasing rates of multiple births, increased management of maternal and fetal conditions (for example, inducing labor preterm if medical technology indicates that it will increase the likelihood of survival), increased rates of substance abuse (including tobacco and alcohol), and increased stress. Ethnic variations characterize preterm birth. In 2016, the likelihood of being born preterm in the United States was 8.9 percent for non-Latino White infants, but the rate was 13.4 percent for African American infants and 9.2 percent for Latino infants (March of Dimes, 2018).

Most, but not all, preterm babies are also low birth weight babies. The incidence of low birth weight varies considerably from country to country. In some countries, such as India and Sudan, where poverty is rampant and the health and nutrition of mothers are poor, the rate of low birth weight babies is as high as 31 percent (see Figure 15). In the United States, there has been an increase in low birth weight infants in the last two decades, and the U.S. low birth weight rate of 8.2 percent in 2018 is considerably higher than that of many other developed countries (United Health Foundation, 2018). For example, only 4 percent of the infants born in Sweden, Finland, Norway, and Korea are low birth weight, and only 5 percent of those born in New Zealand, Australia, and France are low birth weight. As with preterm birth, ethnic variations characterize low birth weight, with 13.5 percent of African American babies born low birth weight compared to 7.3 percent of Latino and 7.0 percent of non-Latino White infants (United Health Foundation, 2018).

Consequences of Being Born Preterm and Low Birth Weight   Although most preterm and low birth weight infants are healthy, as a group they have more health and developmental problems than do infants of normal birth weight (Marchman & others, 2019). For preterm birth, the terms *extremely preterm* and *very preterm* are increasingly used (Webb & others, 2014). *Extremely preterm infants* are those born at less than 28 weeks gestation, and *very preterm infants* are those born between 28 and 33 weeks of gestational age.

The number and severity of health problems increase when infants are born very early and very small (Lee & others, 2019; Pascal & others, 2018). Survival rates for infants who are born very early and very small have risen, but with this improved survival rate have come an increased rate of severe brain damage (Rogers & Hintz, 2016), lower level of executive function, especially in working memory and planning (Burnett & others, 2019), and intelligence (Jaekel & others, 2019).

One study revealed that very preterm, low birth weight infants had abnormal axon development in their brains and impaired cognitive development at 9 years of age (Iwata & others, 2012). Low birth weight children are more likely than their normal birth weight counterparts to develop a learning disability, attention deficit hyperactivity disorder, autism spectrum disorder, or breathing problem such as asthma (Brinksma & others, 2017; Ng & others, 2017). Approximately 50 percent of all low birth weight children are enrolled in special education programs. And a study in four Asian countries revealed that very low birth weight infants had a much higher mortality rate than other neonates (Wariki & others, 2013).

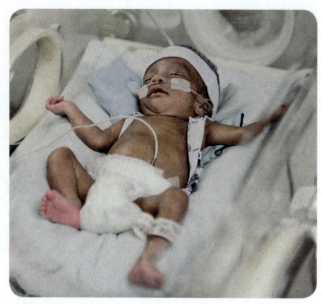

A "kilogram kid," weighing less than 2.3 pounds at birth. *What are some long-term outcomes for infants who weigh so little at birth?*
Andresr/E+/Getty Images

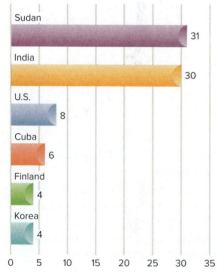

Percentage of infants born with low birth weight

FIGURE 15

PERCENTAGE OF INFANTS BORN WITH LOW BIRTH WEIGHT IN SELECTED COUNTRIES

low birth weight infants Infants who weigh less than 5½ pounds at birth.

preterm infants Infants born three weeks or more before the pregnancy has reached its full term.

small for date infants Infants whose birth weights are below normal when the length of pregnancy is considered; also called small for gestational age infants. Small for date infants may be preterm or full-term.

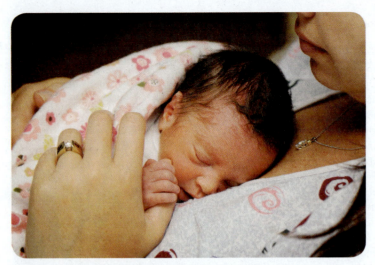

A new mother practicing kangaroo care. *What is kangaroo care?*
casenbina/iStockphoto.com

Nurturing Low Birth Weight and Preterm Infants

Two increasingly used interventions in the neonatal intensive care unit (NICU) are kangaroo care and massage therapy. **Kangaroo care** involves skin-to-skin contact in which the baby, wearing only a diaper, is held upright against the parent's bare chest, much as a baby kangaroo is carried by its mother (Raajashri & others, 2018). Kangaroo care is typically practiced for two to three hours per day over an extended time in early infancy.

Why use kangaroo care with preterm infants? Preterm infants often have difficulty coordinating their breathing and heart rate, and the close physical contact with the parent provided by kangaroo care can help stabilize the preterm infant's heartbeat, temperature, and breathing (Furman, 2019). Preterm infants who experience kangaroo care also gain more weight than their counterparts who are not given this care (Faye & others, 2016; Sharma, Murki, & Oleti, 2018). Recent research also revealed that kangaroo care decreased pain responses in preterm infants (Mooney-Leber & Brummelte, 2017). One study revealed that kangaroo care led to better physical development in low birth weight infants (Bera & others, 2014), and a research review concluded that kangaroo mother care with low birth weight babies was associated with a reduced risk of infant mortality (Conde-Agudelo & Diaz-Rossello, 2014). Further, a recent study found that kangaroo care significantly reduced crying and promoted heart rate stability in preterm infants (Choudhary & others, 2016). And in a longitudinal study, the nurturing positive effects of kangaroo care with preterm and low birth weight infants that were initially found for intelligence and home environment at 1 year of age were still positive 20 years later in emerging adults' reduced school absenteeism, reduced hyperactivity, lower aggressiveness, and better social skills (Charpak & others, 2019).

One U.S. survey found that mothers had a much more positive view of kangaroo care than did neonatal intensive care nurses and that the mothers were more likely to think it should be provided daily (Hendricks-Munoz & others, 2013). There is concern that kangaroo care is not used as often as it could be used in neonatal intensive care units (Davanzo & others, 2013; Kymre, 2014; Smith & others, 2017). Increasingly, kangaroo care is recommended as standard practice for all newborns (Rodgers, 2013).

In addition to kangaroo care, another technique to improve the development of preterm infants is massage therapy. To read about research on massage therapy, see the *Connecting with Research* interlude.

---

developmental **connection**

Attachment

A classic study with surrogate cloth and wire monkeys demonstrates the important role that touch plays in infant attachment. Connect to "Emotional Development and Attachment."

---

developmental **connection**

Attachment

Lorenz demonstrated the importance of early bonding in greylag geese, but the first few days of life are unlikely to be a critical period for bonding in human infants. Connect to "Introduction."

---

kangaroo care A way of holding a preterm infant so that there is skin-to-skin contact.

bonding The formation of a close connection, especially a physical bond between parents and their newborn in the period shortly after birth.

BONDING

A special component of the parent-infant relationship is **bonding,** the formation of a connection, especially a physical bond, between parents and their newborn infant during the period shortly after birth. In the mid-twentieth century, U.S. hospitals seemed almost determined to deter bonding. Anesthesia given to the mother during delivery would make the mother drowsy, interfering with her ability to respond to and stimulate the newborn. Mothers and newborns were often separated shortly after delivery, and preterm infants were isolated from their mothers even more than full-term infants were. In recent decades these practices have changed, but to some extent they are still followed in many hospitals.

Do these practices do any harm? Some physicians believe that during the "critical period" shortly after birth the parents and newborn need to form an emotional attachment as a foundation for optimal development in the years to come (Kennell, 2006; Kennell & McGrath, 1999). Although some research supports this bonding hypothesis (Klaus & Kennell, 1976), a body of research challenges the significance of the first few days of life as a critical period (Bakeman & Brown, 1980; Rode & others, 1981). Indeed, the extreme form of the bonding hypothesis—the insistence that the newborn *must* have close contact with the mother in the first few days of life to develop optimally—simply is not true.

connecting with research

How Are Preterm Infants Affected by Touch?

Many preterm infants experience less touch than full-term infants do because they are isolated in temperature-controlled incubators. Research by Tiffany Field and her colleagues (2001, 2007, 2016, 2017; Diego, Field, & Hernandez-Reif, 2008, 2014; Field, Diego, & Hernandez-Reif, 2008, 2011) has led to a surge of interest in the role that massage might play in improving developmental outcomes for preterm infants. In Field's first study in this area, massage therapy that consisted of firm stroking with the palms of the hands was given three times per day for 15-minute periods to preterm infants (Field & others, 1986). Infants who received massage therapy had 47 percent greater weight gain than infants who received standard medical treatment. The massaged infants also were more active and alert than preterm infants who were not massaged, and they performed better on developmental tests.

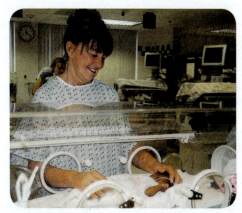

Tiffany Field massages a newborn infant. *What types of infants has massage therapy been shown to help?*
Courtesy of Dr. Tiffany Field

In later studies, Field (2016) demonstrated the benefits of massage therapy for infants who faced a variety of problems. For example, preterm infants exposed to cocaine in utero who received massage therapy gained weight and had higher scores on developmental tests than did their counterparts who had not received massage therapy (Field, 2001). In one study, preterm infants in a neonatal intensive care unit (NICU) were randomly assigned to a massage therapy group or a control group (Hernandez-Reif, Diego, & Field, 2007). For five consecutive days, the preterm infants in the massage group were

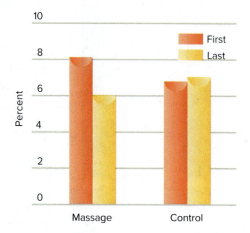

FIGURE 16

PRETERM INFANTS SHOW REDUCED STRESS BEHAVIORS AND ACTIVITY AFTER FIVE DAYS OF MASSAGE THERAPY

given three 15-minute moderate-pressure massages. Behavioral observations of the following stress behaviors were made on the first and last days of the study: crying, grimacing, yawning, sneezing, jerky arm and leg movements, startles, and finger flaring. The various stress behaviors were summarized in a composite stress behavior index. As indicated in Figure 16, massage had a stress-reducing effect on the preterm infants, which is especially important because they encounter numerous stressors while they are hospitalized.

In a review of the use of massage therapy with preterm infants, Field and her colleagues (Field, 2010) concluded that the most consistent findings were two positive results: (1) increased weight gain and (2) discharge from the hospital three to six days earlier. One research study revealed that the mechanisms responsible for increased weight gain as a result of massage therapy were stimulation of the vagus nerve (one of 12 cranial nerves leading to the brain) and in turn the release of insulin (a food absorption hormone) (Field, Diego, & Hernandez-Reif, 2011). Another study found that both massage therapy (moderate-pressure stroking) and exercise (flexion and extension of the limbs) led to weight gain in preterm infants (Diego, Field, & Hernandez-Reif, 2014). In this study, massage was linked to increased vagal activity while exercise was associated with increased calorie consumption.

What results do you think researchers might expect to find if they investigate the effects of massage on full-term infants?

Nevertheless, the weakness of the bonding hypothesis should not be used as an excuse to keep motivated mothers from interacting with their newborns. Such contact brings pleasure to many mothers and may dispel maternal anxiety about the baby's health and safety. In some cases—including preterm infants, adolescent mothers, and mothers from disadvantaged circumstances—early close contact is key to establishing a climate for improved interaction after the mother and infant leave the hospital.

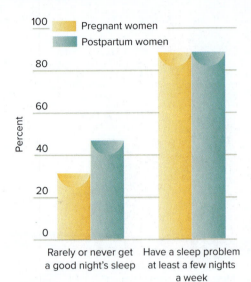

FIGURE 17

SLEEP DEPRIVATION IN PREGNANT AND POSTPARTUM WOMEN

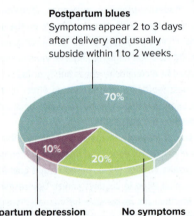

Postpartum blues
Symptoms appear 2 to 3 days after delivery and usually subside within 1 to 2 weeks.

70%

10%   20%

Postpartum depression
Symptoms linger for weeks or months and interfere with daily functioning.

No symptoms

FIGURE 18

POSTPARTUM BLUES AND POSTPARTUM DEPRESSION AMONG U.S. WOMEN. Some health professionals refer to the postpartum period as the "fourth trimester." Though the time span of the postpartum period does not necessarily cover three months, the term "fourth trimester" suggests continuity and the importance of the first several months after birth for the mother.

postpartum period The period after childbirth when the mother adjusts, both physically and psychologically, to the process of childbirth. This period lasts for about six weeks or until her body has completed its adjustment and returned to a near prepregnant state.

Many hospitals now offer a *rooming-in* arrangement, in which the baby remains in the mother's room most of the time during its hospital stay. However, if parents choose not to use this rooming-in arrangement, the weight of the research suggests that this decision will not harm the infant emotionally (Lamb, 1994).

THE POSTPARTUM PERIOD

The weeks after childbirth present challenges for many new parents and their offspring. This is the **postpartum period,** the period after childbirth or delivery that lasts for about six weeks or until the mother's body has completed its adjustment and has returned to a nearly prepregnant state. It is a time when the woman adjusts, both physically and psychologically, to the process of childbearing.

Physical Adjustments   A woman's body makes numerous physical adjustments in the first days and weeks after childbirth (Neiterman & Fox, 2017). She may have a great deal of energy or feel exhausted and let down. Though these changes are normal, the fatigue can undermine the new mother's sense of well-being and confidence in her ability to cope with a new baby and a new family life (Mori & others, 2019).

A concern is the loss of sleep that the primary caregiver experiences during the postpartum period (Paul & Corwin, 2019). In the 2007 Sleep in America survey, a substantial percentage of women reported loss of sleep during pregnancy and in the postpartum period (National Sleep Foundation, 2007) (see Figure 17). The loss of sleep can contribute to stress, marital conflict, and impaired decision making (Thomas & Spieker, 2016). In a recent study, worsening or minimal improvement in sleep problems from 6 weeks to 7 months postpartum were associated with an increase in depressive symptoms (Lewis & others, 2018; Paulson & Miller-Graff, 2019).

After delivery, the mother's body undergoes sudden and dramatic changes in hormone production. When the placenta is delivered, estrogen and progesterone levels drop steeply and remain low until the ovaries start producing hormones again.

Involution is the process by which the uterus returns to its prepregnant size five or six weeks after birth. Immediately following birth, the uterus weighs 2 to 3 pounds. By the end of five or six weeks, the uterus weighs 2 to 3 ounces. Nursing the baby helps contract the uterus at a rapid rate.

Emotional and Psychological Adjustments   Emotional fluctuations are common for mothers in the postpartum period. For some women, emotional fluctuations decrease within several weeks after the delivery, but other women experience more long-lasting emotional swings (O'Hara & Engeldinger, 2018; Pawluski, Lonstein, & Fleming, 2017).

As shown in Figure 18, about 70 percent of new mothers in the United States have what are called the *postpartum blues*. About two to three days after birth, they begin to feel depressed, anxious, and upset. These feelings may come and go for several months after the birth, often peaking about three to five days after birth. Even without treatment, these feelings usually go away after one or two weeks.

However, some women develop **postpartum depression,** which involves a major depressive episode that typically occurs about four weeks after delivery. Women with postpartum depression have such strong feelings of sadness, anxiety, or despair that for at least a two-week period they have trouble coping with their daily tasks. Without treatment, postpartum depression may become worse and last for many months (Di Florio & others, 2014). And many women with postpartum depression don't seek help. For example, one study found that 15 percent of the women surveyed had experienced postpartum depression symptoms but less than half had sought help (McGarry & others, 2009). Estimates indicate that 10 to 14 percent of new mothers experience postpartum depression. Also, researchers found that depression during pregnancy, a history of physical abuse, migrant status, and postpartum physical complications were major risk factors for postpartum depression (Gaillard & others, 2014). And another recent study revealed that women who had a history of depression were 20 times more likely to develop postpartum depression than were women who had no history of depression (Silverman & others, 2017).

Several antidepressant drugs are effective in treating postpartum depression and appear to be safe for breast-feeding women and their infants (O'Hara & McCabe, 2013). Psychotherapy, especially cognitive therapy, also is an effective treatment of postpartum depression for many women (Stamou, Garcia-Palacios, & Botella, 2018; Stewart & Vigod, 2019). Also, engaging in regular exercise may help to relieve postpartum depression (Gobinath & others, 2018).

A mother's postpartum depression affects the way she interacts with her infant (Kleinman & Reizer, 2018). A research review concluded that the interaction difficulties of depressed mothers and their infants occur across cultures and socioeconomic status groups, comprising reduced sensitivity of the mothers and decreased responsiveness on the part of infants (Field, 2010). In a one study, postpartum depression was associated with an increase in 4-month-old infants' injuries caused by neglect (Yamaoka, Fujiwara, & Tamiya, 2016). In another study, depressive symptoms in both the mother and father were linked to impaired bonding with their infant in the postpartum period (Kerstis & others, 2016). Further, a recent study revealed that mothers' postpartum depression, but not generalized anxiety, were linked to their children's emotional negativity and behavior problems at 2 years of age (Prenoveau & others, 2017). Several caregiving activities also are compromised, including feeding, sleep routines, and safety practices.

Fathers also undergo considerable adjustment during the postpartum period, even when they work away from home all day (Paulson & others, 2016). When the mother develops postpartum depression, many fathers also experience depressed feelings (Sundstrom Poromaa & others, 2017). Many fathers feel that the baby comes first and gets all of the mother's attention; some feel that they have been replaced by the baby. A recent Japanese study found that 11.2 percent of fathers had depressive symptoms at one month following delivery (Nishigori & others, 2019). In another recent study, fathers with postpartum depression had lower levels of responsiveness, mood, and sensitivity when interacting with their infants (Koch & others, 2019).

The father's support and caring can influence whether the mother develops postpartum depression (Kumar, Oliffe, & Kelly, 2018). One study revealed that higher support by fathers was related to a lower incidence of postpartum depression in women (Smith & Howard, 2008).

The postpartum period is a time of considerable adjustment and adaptation for both the mother and the father. Fathers can provide an important support system for mothers, especially in helping mothers care for young infants. *What kinds of tasks might the father of a newborn do to support the mother?*
Howard Grey/Getty Images

postpartum depression A major depressive episode that typically occurs about four weeks after delivery; women with this condition have such strong feelings of sadness, anxiety, or despair that they have trouble coping with daily tasks during the postpartum period.

Review *Connect* Reflect

LG5 Summarize how birth takes place and describe the nature of the postpartum period.

Review

- What are the three main stages of birth? What are some different birth strategies?
- What is the transition from fetus to newborn like?
- What are the outcomes for children if they are born preterm or with a low birth weight?
- What is bonding? How is it linked to child outcomes?
- What are some characteristics of the postpartum period?

Connect

- Compare and contrast what you learned about kangaroo care and breast feeding of preterm infants with what you learned about bonding and breast feeding when the mother is suffering from postpartum depression.

Reflect *Your Own Personal Journey of Life*

- If you are a female, which birth strategy would you prefer? Why? If you are a male, how involved would you want to be in helping your partner through pregnancy and the birth of your baby?

Biological Beginnings

1 The Evolutionary Perspective

 LG1 Discuss the evolutionary perspective on life-span development.

Natural Selection and Adaptive Behavior

• Natural selection is the process by which those individuals of a species that are best adapted to their environment are more likely to survive and reproduce.

• Darwin proposed that natural selection fuels evolution. In evolutionary theory, adaptive behavior is behavior that promotes the organism's survival in a natural habitat.

Evolutionary Psychology

• Evolutionary psychology holds that adaptation, reproduction, and "survival of the fittest" are important in shaping behavior. Ideas proposed by evolutionary developmental psychologists include the view that an extended childhood period is needed for humans to develop a large brain and learn the complexity of social communities.

• According to Baltes, the benefits resulting from evolutionary selection decrease with age, mainly because of a decline in reproductive fitness. At the same time, cultural needs increase. Like other theoretical approaches to development, evolutionary psychology has limitations. Bandura rejects "one-sided evolutionism" and argues for a bidirectional link between biology and environment.

2 Genetic Foundations of Development

 LG2 Describe what genes are and how they influence human development.

The Collaborative Gene

• Short segments of DNA constitute genes, the units of hereditary information that help cells to reproduce and manufacture proteins. Genes act collaboratively, not independently.

Genes and Chromosomes

• Genes are passed on to new cells when chromosomes are duplicated during the processes of mitosis and meiosis, which are two ways in which new cells are formed.

• When an egg and a sperm unite in the fertilization process, the resulting zygote contains the genes from the chromosomes in the father's sperm and the mother's egg. Despite this transmission of genes from generation to generation, variability is created in several ways, including the exchange of chromosomal segments during meiosis, mutations, and the distinction between a genotype and a phenotype.

Genetic Principles

• Genetic principles include those involving dominant-recessive genes, sex-linked genes, genetic imprinting, and polygenic inheritance.

Chromosomal and Gene-Linked Abnormalities

• Chromosomal abnormalities produce Down syndrome, which is caused by the presence of an extra copy of chromosome 21. Other sex-linked chromosomal abnormalities include Klinefelter syndrome, fragile X syndrome, Turner syndrome, and XYY syndrome.

• Gene-linked abnormalities involve absent or harmful genes. Gene-linked disorders include phenylketonuria (PKU) and sickle-cell anemia.

3 Heredity and Environment Interaction: The Nature-Nurture Debate

 LG3 Explain some of the ways that heredity and environment interact to produce individual differences in development.

Behavior Genetics

• Behavior genetics is the field that seeks to discover the influence of heredity and environment on individual differences in human traits and development.

• Methods used by behavior geneticists include twin studies and adoption studies.

Heredity-Environment Correlations	• In Scarr's heredity-environment correlations view, heredity may influence the types of environments that children experience. She describes three genotype-environment correlations: passive, evocative, and active (niche-picking). Scarr notes that the relative importance of these three genotype-environment correlations changes as children develop.
The Epigenetic View and Gene × Environment (G × E) Interaction	• The epigenetic view emphasizes that development is the result of an ongoing, bidirectional interchange between heredity and environment.
	• Gene × environment (G × E) interaction involves the interaction of a specific measured variation in DNA and a specific measured aspect of the environment.
Conclusions About Heredity-Environment Interaction	• Complex behaviors have some genetic loading that gives people a propensity for a particular developmental trajectory. However, actual development also requires an environment, and that environment is complex.
	• The interaction of heredity and environment is extensive. Much remains to be discovered about the specific ways that heredity and environment interact to influence development.

4 Prenatal Development

 LG4 Characterize the course of prenatal development and its hazards.

The Course of Prenatal Development	• Prenatal development is divided into three periods: germinal (conception until 10 to 14 days later), which ends when the zygote (a fertilized egg) attaches to the uterine wall; embryonic (two to eight weeks after conception), during which the embryo differentiates into three layers, life-support systems develop, and organ systems begin to form (organogenesis); and fetal (lasting from two months after conception until about nine months, or when the infant is born), a period during which organ systems mature to the point at which life can be sustained outside of the womb.
	• By the time babies are born they have approximately 100 billion neurons, or nerve cells. The nervous system begins with the formation of a neural tube at 18 to 24 days after conception.
	• Neurogenesis, proliferation, and migration are three processes that characterize brain development in the prenatal period. The basic architecture of the brain is formed in the first two trimesters of prenatal development.
Prenatal Diagnostic Tests	• Amniocentesis, ultrasound sonography, fetal MRI, chorionic villus sampling, maternal blood screening, and cell-free fetal DNA in maternal blood are used to determine whether a fetus is developing normally. The sex of the fetus can be determined as early as seven weeks into pregnancy.
Hazards to Prenatal Development	• A teratogen is any agent that can potentially cause a birth defect or negatively alter cognitive and behavioral outcomes. The dose, time of exposure, and genetic susceptibility influence the severity of the damage to an unborn child and the type of defect that occurs.
	• Prescription drugs that can be harmful include antibiotics, some depressants, certain hormones, and acne medication (isotretinoin); nonprescription drugs that can be harmful include diet pills and aspirin. The psychoactive drugs caffeine, alcohol, nicotine, cocaine, marijuana, and synthetic opioids as well as opiate-related pain killers are potentially harmful to offspring. Cigarette smoking by pregnant women also has serious adverse effects on prenatal and child development (such as low birth weight).
	• Problems may also result if a pregnant woman has rubella (German measles), syphilis, genital herpes, or AIDS. A developing fetus depends entirely on its mother for nutrition, and it may be harmed if the mother is malnourished, is overweight, or has a diet deficient in folic acid.
	• High anxiety and stress in the mother are linked with less than optimal prenatal and birth outcomes.
	• Maternal age can negatively affect the offspring's development if the mother is an adolescent or if she is 35 years of age or older.
	• Radiation is a potential environmental hazard. Paternal factors also can affect the developing fetus.
Prenatal Care	• Prenatal care programs provide information about teratogens and other prenatal hazards. In addition, various medical conditions are screened for and medical care is given in a defined schedule of visits. Prenatal classes often give information on nutrition, sexuality during pregnancy, and types of birth.

5 Birth and the Postpartum Period

 LG5 Summarize how birth takes place and describe the nature of the postpartum period.

The Birth Process	• Childbirth occurs in three stages. Childbirth strategies involve the childbirth setting and attendants. Methods of delivery include medicated, natural and prepared, and cesarean. An increasing number of nonmedicated techniques, such as waterbirth, are being used to reduce childbirth pain.
The Transition from Fetus to Newborn	• Being born involves considerable stress for the baby, but the baby is well prepared and adapted to handle the stress. For many years, the Apgar Scale has been used to assess the newborn's health.
Low Birth Weight and Preterm Infants	• Low birth weight infants weigh less than 5 pounds, and they may be preterm or small for date.
	• Although most low birth weight infants are normal and healthy, as a group they have more health and developmental problems than infants of normal birth weight.
	• Kangaroo care and massage therapy have been shown to provide benefits to preterm infants.
Bonding	• Bonding is the formation of a close connection, especially a physical bond between parents and the newborn shortly after birth. Early bonding has not been found to be critical in the development of a competent infant.
The Postpartum Period	• The postpartum period lasts from childbirth until about six weeks after the delivery or until the mother's body has completed its adjustment to a nonpregnant state. The development of postpartum depression is a concern during this period.

---

key **terms**

active (niche-picking) genotype-
    environment correlations
adoption study
Apgar Scale
behavior genetics
bonding
chromosomes
DNA
doula
Down syndrome
embryonic period
epigenetic view

evocative genotype-environment
    correlations
evolutionary psychology
fertilization
fetal alcohol spectrum disorders
    (FASD)
fetal period
fragile X syndrome (FXS)
gene × environment (G × E)
    interaction
genes
genotype

germinal period
kangaroo care
Klinefelter syndrome
low birth weight infants
meiosis
mitosis
natural childbirth
neurons
organogenesis
passive genotype-environment
    correlations
phenotype

phenylketonuria (PKU)
postpartum depression
postpartum period
prepared childbirth
preterm infants
sickle-cell anemia
small for date infants
teratogen
Turner syndrome
twin study
XYY syndrome
zygote

---

key **people**

Paul Baltes
Albert Bandura
David Buss

Charles Darwin
Tiffany Field
Gilbert Gottlieb

Ferdinand Lamaze
David Moore
Sandra Scarr

chapter 3

PHYSICAL DEVELOPMENT AND BIOLOGICAL AGING

chapter outline

1 Body Growth and Change

Learning Goal 1 Discuss major changes in the body through the life span.

Patterns of Growth
Height and Weight in Infancy and Childhood
Puberty
Early Adulthood
Middle Adulthood
Late Adulthood

2 The Brain

Learning Goal 2 Describe how the brain changes through the life span.

The Neuroconstructivist View
Brain Physiology
Infancy
Childhood
Adolescence
Adulthood and Aging

3 Sleep

Learning Goal 3 Summarize how sleep patterns change as people develop.

Why Do We Sleep?
Infancy
Childhood
Adolescence and Emerging Adulthood
Adulthood and Aging

4 Longevity and Biological Aging

Learning Goal 4 Explain longevity and the biological aspects of aging.

Life Expectancy and Life Span
Centenarians
Biological Theories of Aging

Imazins/Getty Images

preview

Think about how much you have changed physically and will continue to change as you age. We come into this life as small beings. But we grow very rapidly in infancy, more slowly in childhood, and once again more rapidly during puberty, and then experience another slowdown. Eventually we decline, but many older adults are still physically robust. In this chapter, we explore changes in body growth, the brain, and sleep across the life span. We also examine longevity and evaluate some fascinating theories about why we age, and we explore both physical and physiological aspects of development.

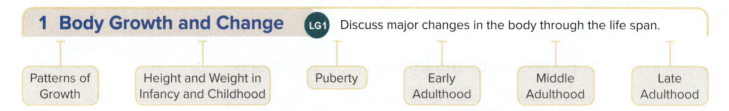

1 Body Growth and Change **LG1** Discuss major changes in the body through the life span.

| Patterns of Growth | Height and Weight in Infancy and Childhood | Puberty | Early Adulthood | Middle Adulthood | Late Adulthood |

In life's long journey, we go through many bodily changes. We grow up, we grow out, we shrink. The very visible changes in height and weight are accompanied by less visible ones in bones, lungs, and every other organ of the body. These changes will help shape how we think about ourselves, how other people think about us, and what we are capable of thinking, doing, and feeling. Are there strict timelines for these changes? Are they set in our genes? Let's begin by studying some basic patterns of growth and then trace bodily changes from the time we are infants through the time we are older adults.

PATTERNS OF GROWTH

Two key patterns of growth are the cephalocaudal and proximodistal patterns. The **cephalocaudal pattern** is the sequence in which the fastest growth in the human body occurs at the top, with the head. Physical growth in size, weight, and feature differentiation gradually works its way down from the top to the bottom (for example, neck, shoulders, middle trunk, and so on). This same pattern occurs in the head area, because the top parts of the head—the eyes and brain—grow faster than the lower parts, such as the jaw. During prenatal development and early infancy, the head constitutes an extraordinarily large proportion of the total body (see Figure 1).

In most cases, sensory and motor development proceeds according to the cephalocaudal pattern. For example, infants see objects before they can control their torso, and they can use their hands long before they can crawl or walk. However, one study contradicted the cephalocaudal pattern by finding that infants reached for toys with their feet before using their hands (Galloway & Thelen, 2004). In this study, infants on average first contacted the toy with their feet when they were 12 weeks old and with their hands when they were 16 weeks old. Thus, contrary to long-standing beliefs, early leg movements can be precisely controlled, some aspects of development that involve reaching do not involve lengthy practice, and early motor behaviors don't always develop in a strict cephalocaudal pattern.

The **proximodistal pattern** is the growth sequence that starts at the center of the body and moves toward the extremities. An example is the early maturation of muscular control of the trunk and arms, compared with that of the hands and fingers. Further, infants use the whole hand as a unit before they can control several fingers.

An important point about growth is that it often is not smooth and continuous but rather is *episodic*, occurring in spurts (Adolph, 2018). In infancy, growth spurts may occur in a single day and alternate with long time frames characterized by little or no growth for days and weeks (Lampl & Johnson, 2011; Lampl, 2018). In two analyses, infants grew seven-tenths of an inch in length in a single day (Lampl, 1993) and their head circumference increased by three-tenths of an inch (Caino & others, 2010).

cephalocaudal pattern The sequence in which the fastest growth occurs at the top of the body—the head—with physical growth in size, weight, and feature differentiation gradually working from top to bottom.

proximodistal pattern The sequence in which growth starts at the center of the body and moves toward the extremities.

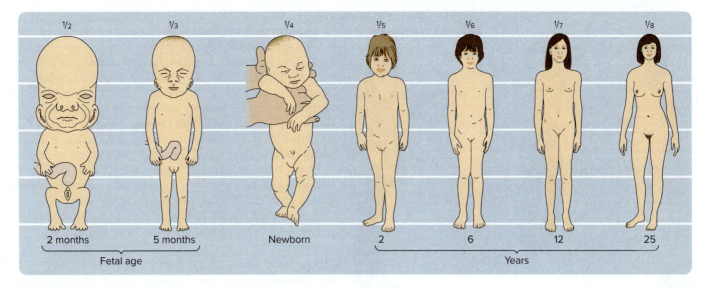

| 1/2 | 1/3 | 1/4 | 1/5 | 1/6 | 1/7 | 1/8 |

| 2 months | 5 months | Newborn | 2 | 6 | 12 | 25 |
| Fetal age | | | Years | | | |

FIGURE 1

CHANGES IN PROPORTIONS OF THE HUMAN BODY DURING GROWTH. As individuals develop from infancy through adulthood, one of the most noticeable physical changes is that the head becomes smaller in relation to the rest of the body. The fractions listed refer to head size as a proportion of total body length at different ages.

HEIGHT AND WEIGHT IN INFANCY AND CHILDHOOD

Height and weight increase rapidly in infancy, then take a slower course during the childhood years.

Infancy   The average North American newborn is 20 inches long and weighs 7½ pounds. Ninety-five percent of full-term newborns are 18 to 22 inches long and weigh between 5½ and 10 pounds.

In the first several days of life, most newborns lose 5 to 7 percent of their body weight. Once infants adjust to sucking, swallowing, and digesting, they grow rapidly, gaining an average of 5 to 6 ounces per week during the first month. Typically, they have doubled their birth weight by the age of 4 months and have nearly tripled it by their first birthday. Infants grow about ¾ inch per month during the first year, increasing their birth length by about 40 percent by their first birthday.

Infants' rate of growth slows considerably in the second year of life (Hockenberry, Wilson, & Rodgers, 2019). By 2 years of age, infants weigh approximately 26 to 32 pounds, having gained a quarter to half a pound per month during the second year; at age 2 they have reached about one-fifth of their adult weight. The average 2-year-old is 32 to 35 inches tall, which is nearly one-half of adult height.

Early Childhood   What is the overall growth rate like in early childhood? As the preschool child grows older, the percentage of increase in height and weight decreases with each additional year (Marcdante & Kliegman, 2018). Girls are only slightly smaller and lighter than boys during these years. Both boys and girls slim down as the trunks of their bodies lengthen. Although their heads are still somewhat large for their bodies, by the end of the preschool years most children have lost their top-heavy look. Body fat also shows a slow, steady decline during the preschool years. Girls have more fatty tissue than boys; boys have more muscle tissue (McMahon & Stryjewski, 2012).

Growth patterns vary individually (Hockenberry, Wilson, & Rodgers, 2019). Think back to your preschool years. This was probably the first time you noticed that some children were taller than you, some shorter; some were fatter, some thinner; some were stronger, some weaker. Much of the variation is due to heredity, but environmental experiences are also involved. A review of the height and

The bodies of 5-year-olds and 2-year-olds are different from one another. The 5-year-old not only is taller and heavier, but also has a longer trunk and legs than the 2-year-old. *What might be some other physical differences between 2- and 5-year-olds?*
Michael Hitoshi/Getty Images

weight of children around the world concluded that two important contributors to height differences are ethnic origin and nutrition (Meredith, 1978).

Why are some children unusually short? The culprits are congenital factors (genetic or prenatal problems), growth hormone deficiency, a physical problem that develops in childhood, maternal smoking during pregnancy, or an emotional difficulty (Hay & others, 2017). A study of children born small for gestational age or short in stature revealed that five years of growth hormone treatment in childhood was linked to an increase to near-average height (Ross & others, 2015). Also, a recent review concluded that accurate assessment of growth hormone deficiency is difficult and that many children who are diagnosed with growth hormone deficiency re-test normal later in childhood (Murray, Dattani, & Clayton, 2016).

In sum, the main factors that contribute to children's height are genetic influences, ethnic origin, and nutrition.

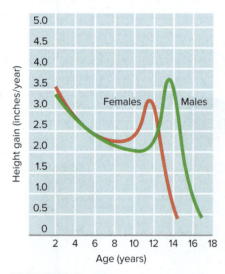

What characterizes children's physical growth in middle and late childhood?
RubberBall Productions/Getty Images

Middle and Late Childhood The period of middle and late childhood involves slow, consistent growth (Perry & others, 2018). This is a period of calm before the rapid growth spurt of adolescence.

During the elementary school years, children grow an average of 2 to 3 inches a year. At the age of 8, the average girl and the average boy are 4 feet 2 inches tall. During the middle and late childhood years, children gain about 5 to 7 pounds a year. The average 8-year-old girl and the average 8-year-old boy weigh 56 pounds. The weight increase is due mainly to increases in the size of the skeletal and muscular systems, as well as the size of some body organs. Muscle mass and strength gradually increase as "baby fat" decreases in middle and late childhood (Marcdante & Kliegman, 2018).

Changes in proportions are among the most pronounced physical changes in middle and late childhood. Head circumference, waist circumference, and leg length decrease in relation to body height (Hockenberry, Wilson, & Rodgers, 2019).

PUBERTY

Puberty is a brain-neuroendocrine process occurring primarily in early adolescence that provides stimulation for the rapid physical changes that take place during this period of development (Nguyen, 2019). In this section, we explore a number of puberty's physical changes and its psychological accompaniments.

Sexual Maturation, Height, and Weight Think back to the onset of your puberty. Of the striking changes that were taking place in your body, what was the first to occur? Researchers have found that male pubertal characteristics typically develop in this order: increase in penis and testicle size, appearance of straight pubic hair, minor voice change, first ejaculation (which usually occurs through masturbation or a wet dream), appearance of curly pubic hair, onset of maximum growth in height and weight, growth of hair in armpits, more detectable voice changes, and, finally, growth of facial hair.

What is the order of appearance of physical changes in females? First, for most girls, their breasts enlarge or pubic hair appears. Later, hair appears in the armpits. As these changes occur, the female grows in height and her hips become wider than her shoulders.

Menarche—a girl's first menstruation—comes rather late in the pubertal cycle. Initially, her menstrual cycles may be highly irregular. For the first several years, she may not ovulate every menstrual cycle; some girls do not ovulate at all until a year or two after menstruation begins.

Marked weight gains coincide with the onset of puberty. During early adolescence, girls tend to outweigh boys, but by about age 14 boys begin to surpass girls. Similarly, at the beginning of the adolescent period, girls tend to be as tall as or taller than boys of their age, but by the end of the middle school years most boys have caught up or, in many cases, surpassed girls in height.

As indicated in Figure 2, the growth spurt occurs approximately two years earlier for girls than for boys. The mean age at the beginning of the growth spurt in girls is 9; for boys, it is 11.

FIGURE 2

PUBERTAL GROWTH SPURT. On average, the peak of the growth spurt during puberty occurs two years earlier for girls (11½) than for boys (13½). *How are hormones related to the growth spurt and to the difference between the average height of adolescent boys and that of girls?*
Source: J. M. Tanner et al., "Standards from Birth to Maturity for Height, Weight, Height Velocity: British Children in 1965" in *Archives of Diseases in Childhood*, 41(219), pp. 454–471, 1966.

puberty A brain-neuroendocrine process occurring primarily in early adolescence that provides stimulation for the rapid physical changes that occur in this period of development.

menarche A girl's first menstrual period.

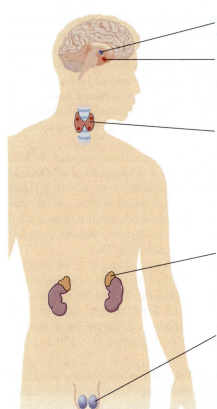

Hypothalamus: A structure in the brain that interacts with the pituitary gland to monitor the bodily regulation of hormones.

Pituitary: This master gland produces hormones that stimulate other glands. It also influences growth by producing growth hormones; it sends gonadotropins to the testes and ovaries and a thyroid-stimulating hormone to the thyroid gland. It sends a hormone to the adrenal gland as well.

Thyroid gland: It interacts with the pituitary gland to influence growth.

Adrenal gland: It interacts with the pituitary gland and likely plays a role in pubertal development, but less is known about its function than about sex glands. Recent research, however, suggests it may be involved in adolescent behavior, particularly for boys.

The gonads, or sex glands: These consist of the testes in males and the ovaries in females. The sex glands are strongly involved in the appearance of secondary sex characteristics, such as facial hair in males and breast development in females. The general class of hormones called estrogens is dominant in females, while androgens are dominant in males. More specifically, testosterone in males and estradiol in females are key hormones in pubertal development.

FIGURE **3**

THE MAJOR ENDOCRINE GLANDS INVOLVED IN PUBERTAL CHANGE

The peak rate of pubertal change occurs at 11½ years for girls and 13½ years for boys. During their growth spurt, girls increase in height about 3½ inches per year, boys about 4 inches.

Hormonal Changes   Behind the first whisker in boys and the widening of hips in girls is a flood of **hormones,** powerful chemical substances secreted by the endocrine glands and carried through the body by the bloodstream (Hsueh & He, 2018). The endocrine system's role in puberty involves the interaction of the hypothalamus, the pituitary gland, and the gonads (see Figure 3). The **hypothalamus,** a structure in the brain, is involved with eating and sexual behavior. The **pituitary gland,** an important endocrine gland, controls growth and regulates other glands; among these, the **gonads**—the testes in males, the ovaries in females—are particularly important in giving rise to pubertal changes in the body.

How do the gonads, or sex glands, work? The pituitary gland sends a signal via **gonadotropins** (hormones that stimulate the testes or ovaries) to the appropriate gland to manufacture hormones. These hormones give rise to such changes as the production of sperm in males and menstruation and the release of eggs from the ovaries in females. The pituitary gland, through interaction with the hypothalamus, detects when the optimal level of hormones is reached and maintains it with additional gonadotropin secretion (Susman & Dorn, 2013). Not only does the pituitary gland release gonadotropins that stimulate the testes and ovaries, but through interaction with the hypothalamus the pituitary gland also secretes hormones that either directly lead to growth and skeletal maturation or produce growth effects through interaction with the thyroid gland, located at the base of the throat.

The concentrations of certain hormones increase dramatically during adolescence (Bhattacharya & others, 2019; Uchida & Kagitani, 2019; Royner & others, 2018). The concentrations of two key hormones increase in puberty and the changes are very different in boys and girls:

- **Testosterone** is a hormone associated in boys with the development of genitals, increased height, and deepening of the voice.
- **Estradiol** is a type of estrogen associated in girls with breast, uterine, and skeletal development.

hormones Powerful chemical substances secreted by the endocrine glands and carried through the body by the bloodstream.

hypothalamus A structure in the brain that is involved with eating and sexual behavior.

pituitary gland An important endocrine gland that controls growth and regulates the activity of other glands.

gonads The sex glands, which are the testes in males and the ovaries in females.

gonadotropins Hormones that stimulate the testes or ovaries.

testosterone A hormone associated in boys with the development of the genitals, increased height, and voice changes.

estradiol A hormone associated in girls with breast, uterine, and skeletal development.

A study documented the growth of the pituitary gland in adolescence and found that its volume was linked to circulating blood levels of estradiol and testosterone (Wong & others, 2014). In another study, testosterone levels increased eighteenfold in boys but only twofold in girls during puberty; estradiol increased eightfold in girls but only twofold in boys (Nottelmann & others, 1987). Thus, both testosterone and estradiol are present in the hormonal makeup of both boys and girls, but testosterone dominates in male pubertal development, estradiol in female pubertal development (Ding & others, 2018; Handelsman, Hirschberg, & Bermon, 2018). A study of 9- to 17-year-old boys found that testosterone levels peaked at 17 years of age (Khairullah & others, 2014).

The same influx of hormones that grows hair on a male's chest and increases the fatty tissue in a female's breasts may also contribute to psychological development in adolescence (Wang & others, 2016). In one study of boys and girls ranging in age from 9 to 14, a higher concentration of testosterone was present in boys who rated themselves as more socially competent (Nottelmann & others, 1987). However, a research review concluded that there is insufficient quality research to confirm that changing testosterone levels during puberty are linked to mood and behavior in adolescent males (Duke, Balzer, & Steinbeck, 2014).

Hormonal effects by themselves do not account for adolescent psychological development (Cicek & others, 2018). For example, in one study, social factors were much better predictors of young adolescent girls' depression and anger than hormonal factors (Brooks-Gunn & Warren, 1989). Behavior and moods also can affect hormones. Stress, eating patterns, exercise, sexual activity, tension, and depression can activate or suppress various aspects of the hormonal system. In sum, the hormone-behavior link is complex (Susman & Dorn, 2013).

Timing and Variations in Puberty   In the United States—where children mature up to a year earlier than children in European countries—the average age of menarche has declined significantly since the mid-nineteenth century. Fortunately, however, we are unlikely to see pubescent toddlers, since what has happened in the past century is likely the result of improved nutrition and health, and the rate of decline in age of onset of puberty has slowed considerably in the last several decades. However, some researchers have found that the onset of puberty is still occurring earlier than in previous generations (Herman-Giddens & others, 2012; McBride, 2013).

Is age of pubertal onset linked to how tall boys and girls will be toward the end of adolescence? A study found that for girls, earlier onset of menarche, breast development, and growth spurt were linked to shorter height at 18 years of age; however, for boys, earlier age of growth spurt and slower progression through puberty were associated with being taller at 18 years of age (Yousefi & others, 2013).

Why do the changes of puberty occur when they do, and how can variations in their timing be explained? The basic genetic program for puberty is wired into the species (Howard & others, 2018; Toro, Aylwin, & Lomniczi, 2019). However, nutrition, health, family stress, and other environmental factors also affect puberty's timing (Black & Rofey, 2018). A recent Chinese study also revealed that a higher BMI was associated with earlier pubertal onset (Deng & others, 2018). Also, a recent study found that child sexual abuse was linked to earlier pubertal onset (Noll & others, 2017).

For most boys, the pubertal sequence may begin as early as age 10 or as late as 13½, and it may end as early as age 13 or as late as 17. Thus, the normal range is wide enough that, given two boys of the same chronological age, one might complete the pubertal sequence before the other one has begun it. For girls, menarche is considered within the normal range if it appears between the ages of 9 and 15.

Psychological Accompaniments of Puberty   What are some links between puberty and psychological characteristics? How do early and late maturation influence adolescents' psychological development?

Body Image   One psychological aspect of puberty is certain for both boys and girls: Adolescents are preoccupied with their bodies (Hoffman & Warschburger, 2017, 2018; Senin-Calderon & others, 2017). At this age you may have looked in the mirror on a daily, and sometimes even hourly, basis to see if you could detect anything different about your changing body. Preoccupation with one's body image is strong throughout adolescence but it is especially acute during puberty, a time when adolescents are more dissatisfied with their bodies than in late adolescence. A recent study found that an increase in Facebook friends across two years in adolescence was linked to an enhanced motivation to be thin (Tiggemann & Slater, 2017).

Gender Differences   Gender differences characterize adolescents' perceptions of their bodies (Hoffman & Warschburger, 2017, 2018). In a recent U.S. study of young adolescents, boys had a more positive body image than girls (Morin & others, 2017). Girls tend to have more negative body images, which to some extent may be due to media portrayals of the attractiveness of being thin while the percentage of girls' body fat is increasing during puberty (Benowitz-Fredericks & others, 2012; Calugi & Dalle Grave, 2019). One study found that both boys' and girls' body images became more positive as they moved from the beginning to the end of adolescence (Holsen, Carlson Jones, & Skogbrott Birkeland, 2012).

Recent dramatic increases in adolescents' use of the Internet and social media have been accompanied by concerns about negative body images (Dumas & Desroches, 2019; Saul & Rodgers, 2018). A recent study of U.S. 12- to 14-year-olds found that heavier use of social media was associated with body dissatisfaction (Burnette, Kwitowski, & Mazzeo, 2017). Also, a recent study of seventh- to twelfth-graders in Thailand found that increased time spent on the Internet, especially in activities related to self-image and eating attitudes and behavior, was linked to increases in body dissatisfaction (Kaewpradub & others, 2017). And in a recent study of U.S. college women, more time spent on Facebook was related to more frequent body and weight comparisons with other women, more attention to the physical appearance of others, and more negative feelings about their own bodies (Eckler, Kalyango, & Paasch, 2017).

Adolescents show a strong preoccupation with their changing bodies and develop images of what their bodies are like. *Why might adolescent males have more positive body images than adolescent females?*
Ali Johnson Photography/Getty Images

Early and Late Maturation   Did you enter puberty early, late, or on time? When adolescents mature earlier or later than their peers, they may have different experiences and perceive themselves differently (Lee & others, 2017; Selkie, 2019). One study found that in the early high school years, late-maturing boys had a more negative body image than early-maturing boys (de Guzman & Nishina, 2014). Similarly, in the Berkeley Longitudinal Study conducted half a century ago, early-maturing boys perceived themselves more positively and had more successful peer relations than did late-maturing boys (Jones, 1965). The findings for early-maturing girls were similar but not as strong as for boys. When the late-maturing boys were in their thirties, however, they had developed a more positive identity than the early-maturing boys had (Peskin, 1967). Perhaps the late-maturing boys had had more time to explore life's options, or perhaps the early-maturing boys continued to focus on their physical status instead of paying attention to career development and achievement.

An increasing number of researchers have found that early maturation increases girls' vulnerability to a number of problems (Black & Rofey, 2018; Hamilton & others, 2014; Selkie, 2018). Early-maturing girls are more likely to smoke, drink, be depressed, have an eating disorder, struggle for earlier independence from their parents, and have older friends. Their bodies are likely to elicit responses from males that lead to earlier dating and earlier sexual experiences (Pomerantz & others, 2017; Wang & others, 2016). One study found that early maturation predicted a stable higher level of depression for adolescent girls (Rudolph & others, 2014). Further, researchers have found that early-maturing girls tend to have sexual intercourse earlier and have more unstable sexual relationships (Moore, Harden, & Mendle, 2014), and are at increased risk for physical and verbal abuse in dating (Chen, Rothman, & Jaffee, 2019). Also, early-maturing girls are more likely to drop out of high school and to cohabit and marry at younger ages (Cavanagh, 2009). And researchers recently found that early-maturing girls had higher rates of depression and antisocial behavior as middle-aged adults mainly because their difficulties began in adolescence and did not lessen over time (Mendle, Ryan, & McKone, 2019).

Apparently as a result of their social and cognitive immaturity, combined with early physical development, early-maturing girls are easily lured into problem behaviors, not recognizing how these behaviors might affect their development. Thus, early-maturing adolescents, especially girls, require earlier risk education efforts related to sexual development, risky behaviors, relationships, and Internet safety than their on-time peers (Susman & Dorn, 2013).

What are some outcomes of early and late maturation in adolescence?
Fuse/Getty Images

developmental **connection**

Sexuality

Early sexual experience is one of a number of risk factors in adolescent development. Connect to "Gender and Sexuality."

In sum, early maturation often has more favorable outcomes for boys than for girls, especially in early adolescence. However, late maturation may be more favorable for boys, especially in terms of identity and career development. Research increasingly has found that early-maturing girls are vulnerable to a number of problems.

EARLY ADULTHOOD

After the dramatic physical changes of puberty, the years of early adulthood might seem to be an uneventful time in the body's history. Physical changes during these years may be subtle, but they do continue.

Height remains rather constant during early adulthood. Peak functioning of the body's joints usually occurs in the twenties. Many individuals also reach a peak of muscle tone and strength in their late teens and twenties (Candow & Chilibeck, 2005). However, these attributes may begin to decline in the thirties. Sagging chins and protruding abdomens may also appear for the first time. Muscles start to have less elasticity, and aches may appear in places not felt before.

Most of us reach our peak levels of physical performance before the age of 30, often between the ages of 19 and 26. This peak of physical performance occurs not only for the average young adult, but for outstanding athletes as well. Different types of athletes, however, reach their peak performances at different ages. Most swimmers and gymnasts peak in their late teens. Golfers and marathon runners tend to peak in their late twenties. In other areas of athletics, peak performance often occurs in the early to mid-twenties. However, in recent years, some highly conditioned athletes—such as Serena Williams (tennis) and Tom Brady (football)—have stretched the upper age limits of award-winning performances.

MIDDLE ADULTHOOD

Like the changes of early adulthood, midlife physical changes are usually gradual. Although everyone experiences some physical change due to aging in middle adulthood, the rates of aging vary considerably from one individual to another. Genetic makeup and lifestyle factors play important roles in whether and when chronic diseases will appear (Koenig, Lincoln, & Garg, 2019; Santacreu, Rodriguez, & Molina, 2019). Middle age is a window through which we can glimpse later life while there is still time to engage in preventive behaviors and influence the course of aging (Agrigoraaei & others, 2019).

Physical Appearance   Individuals lose height in middle age, and many gain weight (Lebenbaum & others, 2018). On average, from 30 to 50 years of age, men lose about half an inch in height, then lose another half-inch from 50 to 70 years of age (Hoyer & Roodin, 2009). The height loss for women can be as much as 2 inches from 25 to 75 years of age. Note that there are large variations in the extent to which individuals become shorter with aging. The decrease in height is due to bone loss in the vertebrae. On average, body fat accounts for about 10 percent of body weight in adolescence; it makes up 20 percent or more in middle age.

Noticeable signs of aging usually are apparent by the forties or fifties. The skin begins to wrinkle and sag because of a loss of fat and collagen in underlying tissues (Cole & others, 2018). Small, localized areas of pigmentation in the skin produce aging spots, especially in areas that are exposed to sunlight, such as the hands and face. A twin study found that twins who had been smoking longer were more likely to have sagging facial skin and wrinkles, especially in the middle and lower portion of the face (Okada & others, 2013). The hair thins and grays because of a lower replacement rate and a decline in melanin production.

Since a youthful appearance is valued in many cultures, many Americans strive to make themselves look younger. Undergoing cosmetic surgery, dyeing hair, purchasing wigs, enrolling in weight reduction programs, participating in exercise regimens, and taking heavy doses of vitamins are common in middle age. Baby boomers have shown a strong interest in plastic surgery and Botox, which may reflect their desire to take control of the aging process (Casabona & others, 2019; Lim & others, 2018).

Regarding weight gain in middle age, in a national U.S. survey, 42.8 percent of adults 40 to 59 years of age were classified as obese in 2016 compared to 35.7 percent of those 20 to 39 years of age (National Center for Health Statistics, 2018). Being overweight is a critical

Famous actor Sean Connery as a young adult in his twenties (*top*) and as a middle-aged adult in his fifties (*bottom*). *What are some of the most outwardly noticeable signs of aging in middle adulthood?*
(*Top*): Bettmann/Getty; (*bottom*): Life Picture Collection/ Getty Images

health problem for middle-aged adults and increases their risk of developing a number of other health problems, including hypertension and diabetes (Jia, Hill, & Sowers, 2018; Petrie, Guzik, & Tonyz, 2018).

Strength, Joints, and Bones   The term *sarcopenia* refers to age-related loss of lean muscle mass and strength (Clark, 2019; Landi & others, 2018). After age 50, muscle loss occurs at a rate of approximately 1 to 2 percent per year. A loss of strength especially occurs in the back and legs. Obesity is a risk factor for sarcopenia (Rubio-Ruiz & others, 2019). Recently, researchers began using the term *sarcopenic obesity* in reference to individuals who have sarcopenia and are obese (Nascimento & others, 2018; Xiao & others, 2018). One study linked sarcopenic obesity to hypertension (Park & others, 2013). Also, in a recent study sarcopenic obesity was associated with a 24 percent increase in risk for all-cause mortality, with a higher risk for men than women (Tian & Xu, 2016). A research review concluded that weight management and resistance training were the best strategies for slowing down sarcopenia (Rolland & others, 2011).

Maximum bone density occurs by the mid- to late thirties. From that point on, there is a progressive loss of bone. The rate of bone loss begins slowly but accelerates during the fifties (Locquet & others, 2018). Women's rate of bone loss is about twice that of men. By the end of midlife, bones break more easily and heal more slowly (de Villiers, 2018). A recent study found that greater intake of fruits and vegetables was linked to increased bone density in middle-aged and older adults (Qiu & others, 2017).

Cardiovascular System   Cardiovascular disease increases considerably in middle age (Mok & others, 2019). The level of cholesterol in the blood increases through the adult years (Mok & others, 2019). Cholesterol comes in two forms: LDL (low-density lipoprotein) and HDL (high-density lipoprotein). LDL is often referred to as "bad" cholesterol because when the level of LDL is too high, it sticks to the lining of blood vessels, a condition that can lead to arteriosclerosis (hardening of the arteries). HDL is often referred to as "good" cholesterol because when it is high and LDL is low, the risk of cardiovascular disease decreases. One study revealed that a higher level of HDL was linked to a higher probability of being alive at 85 years of age (Rahilly-Tierney & others, 2011). In middle age, cholesterol begins to accumulate on the artery walls, thickening them. The result is an increased risk of cardiovascular disease.

Blood pressure, too, usually rises in the forties and fifties, and high blood pressure (hypertension) is linked with an increased rate of mortality as well as lower cognitive functioning (Mrowka, 2017). For example, one study revealed that hypertension in middle age was linked to an increased risk of cognitive impairment in late adulthood (23 years later) (Virta & others, 2013). At menopause, a woman's blood pressure rises sharply and usually remains above that of a man through life's later years (Taler, 2009). The health benefits of cholesterol-lowering and hypertension-lowering drugs are a major factor in improving the health of many middle-aged adults and increasing their life expectancy (Rosenson, Hegele, & Koenig, 2019). Regular exercise and healthy eating habits also have considerable benefits in preventing cardiovascular disease (de Gregorio, 2018; Quindry & others, 2019). In a recent study, a high level of physical activity was associated with a lower risk of cardiovascular disease in the three weight categories studied (normal, overweight, and obese) (Carlsson & others, 2016). Also, risk factors for cardiovascular disease in middle adulthood can show up even earlier in development. A recent study indicated that a healthy diet in adolescence was linked to a lower risk of cardiovascular disease in middle-aged women (Dahm & others, 2019).

As reflected in the research we have just described, the American Heart Association has proposed Life's Simple 7—a list of actions people can take to improve their cardiovascular health. The seven factors are: (1) manage blood pressure, (2) control cholesterol, (3) reduce blood sugar, (4) get active, (5) eat better, (6) lose weight, and (7) quit smoking. In a recent study, optimal Life's Simple 7 at middle age was linked to better cardiovascular health recovery following a heart attack in later in life (Mok & others, 2019).

Lungs   There is little change in lung capacity through most of middle adulthood. However, at about the age of 55, the proteins in lung tissue

> Middle age is when your age starts to show around your middle.
>
> —BOB HOPE
> *20th Century Comedian*

developmental connection
Cardiovascular Disease and Alzheimer Disease
Cardiovascular disease is increasingly recognized as a risk factor in Alzheimer disease. Connect to "Health."

Members of the Masai tribe in Kenya, Africa, can stay on a treadmill for a long time because of their active lives. Incidence of heart disease is extremely low in the Masai tribe, which also can be attributed to their energetic lifestyle.
The Family of Dr. George V. Mann

Researchers have found that almost 50 percent of Canadian and American menopausal women have occasional hot flashes, but only one in seven Japanese women do (Lock, 1998). *What factors might account for these variations?*
BLOOMimage/Getty Images

climacteric The midlife transition during which fertility declines.

menopause The time in middle age, usually in the late forties or early fifties, when a woman's menstrual periods have ceased for one year.

become less elastic. This change, combined with a gradual stiffening of the chest wall, decreases the lungs' capacity to shuttle oxygen from the air people breathe to the blood in their veins.

For smokers, however, the picture is different and bleaker (Kraen & others, 2017). The lung capacity of smokers drops precipitously in middle age. When people quit smoking their lung capacity improves, although not to the level of individuals who have never smoked (Williams, 1995). Physical activity promotes lung health. One study found that lung cancer diagnoses were 68 percent lower among men who were the most physically fit compared with those who were the least physically fit (Lakoski & others, 2013).

Sexuality   **Climacteric** is the midlife transition when fertility declines. **Menopause** is the time in middle age, usually in the late forties or early fifties, when a woman has not had a menstrual period for a full year. The average age at which women have their last period is 52. A small percentage of women—10 percent—go through menopause before age 40. Just as puberty has been coming earlier, however, menopause has been coming later (Birren, 2002). Specific causes of the later incidence of menopause have not been documented, but improved nutrition and lower incidence of infectious diseases may be the reasons.

In menopause, production of estrogen by the ovaries declines dramatically, and this decline produces uncomfortable symptoms in some women—"hot flashes," nausea, fatigue, and rapid heartbeat, for example (Rees & others, 2019; Xi & others, 2017). However, cross-cultural studies reveal wide variations in the menopause experience (Sievert & Obermeyer, 2012). For example, hot flashes are uncommon in Mayan women (Beyene, 1986), and Asian women report fewer hot flashes than women in Western societies (Payer, 1991). It is difficult to determine the extent to which these cross-cultural variations are due to genetic, dietary, reproductive, or cultural factors.

Menopause is not the negative experience for most women that it was once thought to be. One study in Taiwan found no significant effect of menopausal transition on women's quality of life (Cheng & others, 2007). However, the loss of fertility is an important marker for women (Lumsden & Sassarini, 2019).

Do men go through anything like the menopause that women experience? In other words, is there a male menopause? During middle adulthood, most men do not lose their capacity to father children, although there usually is a modest decline in their sexual hormone level and their frequency of sexual activity (Afsharnia & others, 2019; Blumel & others, 2014). Testosterone production begins to decline about 1 percent a year during middle adulthood, and this decline can reduce sexual drive (Hyde & others, 2012). Sperm count usually shows a slow decline, but men do not lose their fertility altogether.

We will have more to say about the climacteric and the sexual attitudes and behaviors of middle-aged women and men in the chapter on "Gender and Sexuality."

LATE ADULTHOOD

Late adulthood brings an increased risk of physical disability, but there is considerable variability in rates of decline in functioning. Let's explore changes in physical appearance and the cardiovascular system in older adults.

Physical Appearance   The changes in physical appearance that take place in middle adulthood become more pronounced in late adulthood. Most noticeable are facial wrinkles and age spots. Our weight usually drops after we reach 60 years of age, likely because we lose muscle, which also gives our bodies a more "sagging" look. Recent research indicates that obesity is linked to mobility limitation in older adults (Adair, Duazo, & Borja, 2019; Anson & others, 2018). The good news is that exercise and weight lifting can help slow the decrease in muscle mass and improve the older adult's body appearance, increase mobility, and reduce frailty (Aoki, Sakuma, & Endo, 2018; Fougiere & Cesari, 2019). One study found that long-term aerobic exercise was linked with greater muscle strength in 65- to 86-year-olds (Crane, Macneil, & Tarnopolsky, 2013). In another study, at-risk overweight and obese older adults lost significant weight and improved their mobility considerably by participating in a community-based weight reduction program (Rejeski & others, 2017).

Circulatory System   Significant changes also take place in the circulatory system of older adults (Benetos & others, 2019; Fajemirove & others, 2018). In older adults, 64 percent of

Sarah Kagan, Geriatric Nurse

Sarah Kagan is a professor of nursing at the University of Pennsylvania School of Nursing. She provides nursing consultation to patients, their families, nurses, and physicians regarding the complex needs of older adults related to their hospitalization. She also consults on research and the management of patients who have head and neck cancers. Kagan teaches in the undergraduate nursing program, where she directs a course on "Nursing Care in the Older Adult." In 2003, she was awarded a MacArthur Fellowship for her work in the field of nursing.

In Kagan's own words:

I'm lucky to be doing what I love—caring for older adults and families—and learning from them so that I can share this knowledge and develop or investigate better ways of caring. My special interests in the care of older adults who have cancer allow me the intimate privilege of being with patients at the best and worst times of their lives. That intimacy acts as a beacon—it reminds me of the value I and nursing as a profession contribute to society and the rewards offered in return (Kagan, 2008, p. 1).

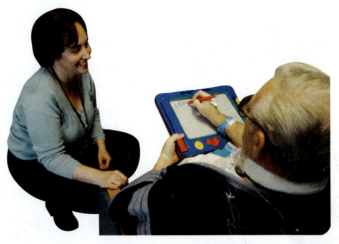

Sarah Kagan with a patient.
Jacqueline Larma/AP Images

For more information about what geriatric nurses do, see the Careers in Life-Span Development appendix.

men and 69 percent of women 65 to 74 years of age have hypertension (high blood pressure) (Centers for Disease Control and Prevention, 2018). Today, most experts on aging recommend that consistent blood pressure above 120/80 should be treated to reduce the risk of heart attack, stroke, or kidney disease. A rise in blood pressure with age can be linked to illness, obesity, stiffening of blood vessels, stress, or lack of exercise (Cheng & others, 2017; Vara-Garcia & others, 2019). The longer any of these factors persist, the higher the individual's blood pressure gets. Various drugs, a healthy diet, and exercise can reduce the risk of cardiovascular disease in older adults (Kantoch & others, 2018; Thompson & others, 2019). In a recent study of adults age 65 and older, a Mediterranean diet lowered their risk of cardiovascular problems (Nowson & others, 2018).

Geriatric nurses can be especially helpful to older adults who experience acute or chronic illness. To read about the work of one geriatric nurse, see the *Connecting with Careers* profile.

Review *Connect* Reflect

 LG1 Discuss major changes in the body through the life span.

Review

- What are cephalocaudal and proximodistal patterns of development?
- How do height and weight change in infancy and childhood?
- What changes characterize puberty?
- What physical changes occur in early adulthood?
- How do people develop physically during middle adulthood?
- What is the nature of physical changes in late adulthood?

Connect

- In this section, you learned that growth spurts in puberty differ for boys and girls. What research methods probably were used to collect such data?

Reflect *Your Own Personal Journey of Life*

- How old were you when you started puberty? How do you think this timing affected your social relationships and development?

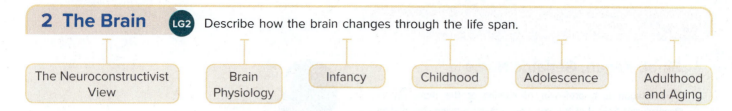

2 The Brain **LG2** Describe how the brain changes through the life span.

| The Neuroconstructivist View | Brain Physiology | Infancy | Childhood | Adolescence | Adulthood and Aging |

Until recently, little was known for certain about how the brain changes as we grow and age. Today, dramatic progress is being made in understanding these changes (Kinugawa, 2019). The study of age-related changes in the brain is one of the most exciting frontiers in science (Topiwala & others, 2019; Vinke, Ikram, & Vernooij, 2019). As we saw in "Biological Beginnings," remarkable changes occur in the brain during prenatal development. Here we consider the changes in the brain from infancy through late adulthood. Before exploring these developmental changes, let's first explore what is meant by the neuroconstructivist view and examine some key structures of the brain and see how they function.

THE NEUROCONSTRUCTIVIST VIEW

Not long ago, scientists thought that our genes exclusively determine how our brains are "wired" and that the cells in the brain responsible for processing information just maturationally unfold with little or no input from environmental experiences. In that view, your genes provide the blueprint for your brain and you are essentially stuck with it. This view, however, has turned out to be wrong. Instead, researchers have found that the brain has plasticity and its development depends on context (Kinugawa, 2019; Pi & others, 2019).

The brain depends on experiences to determine how connections are made (de la Fuente, 2019). Before birth, it appears that genes mainly direct basic wiring patterns. Neurons grow and travel to distant places awaiting further instructions (Borsani, 2019; Shenoda, 2017). After birth, the inflowing stream of sights, sounds, smells, touches, language, and eye contact help shape the brain's neural connections.

Thus, the dogma of the unchanging brain has been discarded and researchers are mainly focused on context-induced plasticity of the brain over time (Hanley, Burianova, & Tommerdahl, 2019; McLaughlin & Broihier, 2018). The development of the brain mainly changes in a bottom-to-top sequence with sensory, appetitive (eating, drinking), sexual, sensation-seeking, and risk-taking brain linkages maturing first and higher-level brain linkages such as self-control, planning, and reasoning maturing later (Zelazo, 2013).

In the increasingly popular **neuroconstructivist view,** (a) biological processes (genes, for example) and environmental experiences (enriched or impoverished, for example) influence the brain's development; (b) the brain has plasticity and is context dependent; and (c) development of the brain is closely linked with cognitive development. These factors constrain or advance the construction of cognitive skills (Mucke & others, 2018; Schreuders & others, 2018). The neuroconstructivist view emphasizes the importance of interactions between experiences and gene expression in the brain's development, much as the epigenetic view proposes (Lindahl-Jacobsen & Christensen, 2019).

BRAIN PHYSIOLOGY

The brain includes a number of major structures. The key components of these structures are *neurons*—nerve cells that handle information processing.

Structure and Function   Looked at from above, the brain has two halves, or hemispheres—left and right (see Figure 4). The top portion of the brain, farthest from the spinal cord, is known as the forebrain. Its outer layer of cells, the cerebral cortex, covers it like a thin cap. The cerebral cortex is responsible for about 80 percent of the brain's volume and is critical in perception, thinking, language, and other important functions.

Each hemisphere of the cortex has four major areas, called lobes. Although the lobes usually work together, each has somewhat different primary functions (see Figure 5):

· *Frontal lobes* are involved in voluntary movement, thinking, personality, emotion, memory, sustained attention, and intentionality or purpose.

· *Occipital lobes* function in vision.

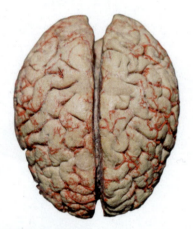

FIGURE 4

THE HUMAN BRAIN'S HEMISPHERES.
The two hemispheres of the human brain are clearly seen in this photograph. It is a myth that the left hemisphere is the exclusive location of language and logical thinking or that the right hemisphere is the exclusive location of emotion and creative thinking.
IgorZD/Shutterstock

neuroconstructivist view Developmental perspective in which biological processes and environmental conditions influence the brain's development; the brain has plasticity and is context dependent; and cognitive development is closely linked with brain development.

- *Temporal lobes* have an active role in hearing, language processing, and memory.
- *Parietal lobes* play important roles in registering spatial location, focusing attention, and maintaining motor control.

Deeper in the brain, beneath the cortex, lie other key structures. These include the hypothalamus and the pituitary gland as well as the amygdala, which plays an important role in emotions, and the hippocampus, which is especially important in memory and emotion.

Neurons As we discussed earlier, neurons process information. Figure 6 shows some important parts of the neuron, including the axon and dendrites. Basically, an axon sends electrical signals away from the central part of the neuron. At tiny gaps called synapses, the axon communicates with the dendrites of other neurons, which then pass the signals on. The communication in the synapse occurs through the release of chemical substances known as *neurotransmitters* (Ostlund, 2019; Zhou & others, 2018).

How complex are these neural connections? In a research analysis, it was estimated that each of the billions of neurons is connected to as many as 1,000 other neurons, producing neural networks with trillions of connections (de Haan, 2015).

As Figure 6 shows, most axons are covered by a myelin sheath, which is a layer of fat cells. Development of this sheath through a process called **myelination** helps impulses travel faster along the axon, increasing the speed and efficiency with which information travels from neuron to neuron (McDougall & others, 2019; van Tilborg & others, 2018). Myelination also is involved in providing energy to neurons and in facilitating communication (Saab & Nave, 2017).

To some extent, the type of information handled by neurons depends on whether they are in the left or the right hemisphere of the cortex (Sidtis & others, 2018). Speech and grammar, for example, depend on activity in the left hemisphere in most people; humor and the use of metaphors depend on activity in the right hemisphere (Holler-Wallscheid & others, 2017). Recent research also indicates that attention (Bartolomeo & Seidel Malkinson, 2019) and emotion (Gainotti, 2019) are predominantly right-hemisphere activities. This specialization of function in one hemisphere of the cerebral cortex or the other is called **lateralization.** However, most neuroscientists agree that complex functions such as reading or performing music involve both hemispheres. Labeling people as "left-brained" because they are logical thinkers or "right-brained" because they are creative thinkers does not reflect the way the brain's hemispheres work. For the most part, complex thinking is the outcome of communication between the hemispheres of the brain (Raemaekers & others, 2018; Wang & others, 2019).

The degree of lateralization may change as people develop through the life span. Let's now explore a number of age-related changes in the brain.

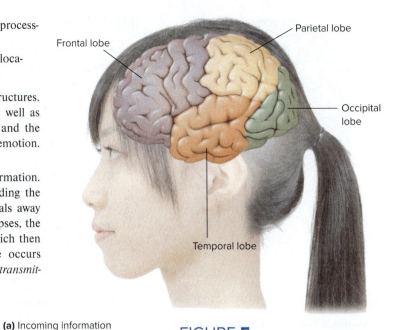

FIGURE 5

THE BRAIN'S FOUR LOBES. Shown here are the locations of the brain's four lobes: frontal, occipital, temporal, and parietal.
Photo: takayuki/Shutterstock

> developmental **connection**
>
> **Brain Development**
> Might some regions of the brain be more closely linked with children's intelligence than others? Connect to "Intelligence."

(a) Incoming information

Cell body

Nucleus

Axon

Dendrites

(b) Outgoing information

(c) Myelin sheath

(d) Terminal button

To next neuron

FIGURE 6

THE NEURON. (*a*) The dendrites of the cell body receive information from other neurons, muscles, or glands through the axon. (*b*) Axons transmit information away from the cell body. (*c*) A myelin sheath covers most axons and speeds information transmission. (*d*) As the axon ends, it branches out into terminal buttons.

myelination The process of encasing axons with a myelin sheath, thereby improving the speed and efficiency of information processing.

lateralization Specialization of function in one hemisphere or the other of the cerebral cortex.

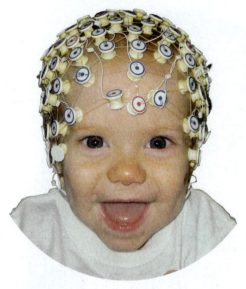

FIGURE 7

MEASURING THE ACTIVITY IN AN INFANT'S BRAIN WITH AN ELECTROENCEPHALOGRAM (EEG). By attaching up to 128 electrodes to a baby's scalp to measure the brain's activity, researchers have found that newborns produce distinctive brain waves that reveal they can distinguish their mother's voice from another woman's, even while they are asleep.
Courtesy of Vanessa Vogel Farley

INFANCY

Brain development occurs extensively during the prenatal period. The brain's development is also substantial during infancy and later (Crone, 2017; Sullivan & Wilson, 2018).

Conducting Research and Measuring the Infant's Brain Activity   Among the researchers who are making strides in finding out more about the brain's development in infancy are the following individuals:

- Martha Ann Bell and her colleagues (Bell, 2015; Bell & Broomell, 2019; Bell, Diaz, & Liu, 2019; Bell, Kraybill, & Diaz, 2014; Bell, Ross, & Patton, 2018; Bell & others, 2018; Blankenship, Broomell, & Bell, 2019; Liu & others, 2018; MacNeil & others, 2019), who are studying brain-behavior links, emotion regulation, temperament, inhibitory control, and the integration of cognition and emotion;

- Charles Nelson and his colleagues (Bick & Nelson, 2016, 2017; Finch & others, 2017; Guyon-Harris & others, 2019; Lamm & others, 2018; Leppanen & others, 2018; Nelson, 2007, 2013; Nelson, Fox, & Zeanah, 2014; Sheridan & others, 2018; Wade & others, 2019; Xie & others, 2019), who are exploring various aspects of memory development, face recognition and facial emotion, and the role of early experience in influencing the course of brain development;

- Mark Johnson and his colleagues (Bussu & others, 2018; Ganea & others, 2018; Gliga & others, 2018; Johnson, Senju, & Tomalski, 2015; Johnson & others, 2015; Kolesnik & others, 2019; Mares & others, 2018; Nystrom & others, 2018; Pijl & others, 2019; Salomone & others, 2018), who are examining neuroconstructivist links between the brain, cognitive and perceptual processes, and environmental influences; studying the development of the prefrontal cortex and its function; and exploring early identification of autism, face processing, and the effects of early social experiences;

- John Richards and his colleagues (Brito & others, 2019; Emberson & others, 2017a; Gao & others, 2019; Lunghi & others, 2019; Reynolds & Richards, 2019; Richards, 2009, 2010, 2013; Richards, Reynolds, & Courage, 2010; Richards & others, 2015; Tonnsen, Richards, & Roberts, 2018; Xie, Mallin, & Richards, 2019; Xie & Richards, 2016, 2017), who are examining sustained attention, perception of TV programs, and eye movements.

Researchers have been successful in using the electroencephalogram (EEG), a measure of the brain's electrical activity, to learn about the brain's development in infancy (Endendijk & others, 2018; Xie, Mallin, & Richards, 2019) (see Figure 7). For example, a recent study found that higher-quality mother-infant interaction early in infancy predicted higher-quality frontal lobe functioning that was assessed with EEG later in infancy (Bernier, Calkins, & Bell, 2016).

Researchers are continuing to explore the use of other techniques to assess infants' brain functioning. Recently Patricia Kuhl and her colleagues at the Institute for Learning and Brain Sciences at the University of Washington have been using magnetoencephalography, or MEG, brain-imaging machines to assess infants' brain activity. MEG maps brain activity by recording magnetic fields produced by electrical currents and is being used with infants to assess perceptual and cognitive activities such as vision, hearing, and language (Ahlfors & Mody, 2019; Chen & others, 2019; Vasung & others, 2019) (see Figure 8). And researchers also are increasingly using functional near-infrared spectroscopy (fNIRS), which uses very low levels of near-infrared light to monitor changes in blood oxygen, to study infants' brain activity in many areas, such as face processing, perception, attention, and memory (de Klerk, Hamilton, & Southgate, 2018; Emberson & others, 2017a, b, 2019; Zhang & Roeyers, 2019). (See Figure 9.) Unlike

FIGURE 8

MEASURING THE ACTIVITY OF AN INFANT'S BRAIN WITH MAGNETOENCEPHALOGRAPHY (MEG). This baby's brain activity is being assessed with a MEG brain-imaging device while the baby is listening to spoken words in a study at the Institute of Learning and Brain Sciences at the University of Washington. The infant sits under the machine and when he or she experiences a word, touch, sight, or emotion, the neurons working together in the infant's brain generate magnetic fields and MEG pinpoints the location of the fields in the brain.
Dr. Patricia Kuhl, Institute for Learning and Brain Sciences, University of Washington

FIGURE 9

FUNCTIONAL NEAR-INFRARED SPECTROSCOPY (FNRIS). This brain-imaging technique is increasingly being used to assess infants' brain activity as they move about their environment.
Oli Scarff/Getty Images

fMRI, which uses magnetic fields or electrical activity, fNIRS is portable and allows the infants to be assessed as they explore the world around them (McDonald & Perdue, 2018).

Changing Neurons At birth, the newborn's brain is about 25 percent of its adult weight. By the second birthday, the brain is about 75 percent of its adult weight. Two key developments during these first two years involve the myelin sheath (the layer of fat cells that speeds up movement of electrical impulses along the axons) and connections between dendrites.

Myelination, the process of encasing axons with a myelin sheath, begins prenatally and continues after birth (see Figure 10). As indicated earlier, myelination plays an especially important role in increasing the speed and efficiency of information traveling from neuron to neuron (McDougall & others, 2019). Myelination for visual pathways occurs rapidly after birth, reaching completion in the first six months. Auditory myelination is not completed until 4 or 5 years of age. Some aspects of myelination continue into adolescence and even into emerging adulthood and possibly beyond (Dahl & others, 2018; Kwon & other, 2019; Sousa & others, 2018). Indeed, the most extensive changes in myelination in the frontal lobes occur during adolescence (Monahan & others, 2016).

Dramatic increases in dendrites and synapses (the tiny gaps between neurons across which neurotransmitters carry information) also characterize the development of the brain in the first two years of life (see Figure 11). Nearly twice as many of these connections are made as will ever be used (Huttenlocher & Dabholkar, 1997). The connections that are used become stronger and survive, while the unused ones are replaced by other pathways or disappear. In the language of neuroscience, these connections are "pruned" (Campbell & others, 2012). Figure 12 vividly illustrates the growth and later pruning of synapses in the visual, auditory, and prefrontal cortex areas of the brain (Huttenlocher & Dabholkar, 1997). As shown in Figure 12, "blooming and pruning" vary considerably by brain region in humans (Gogtay & Thompson, 2010).

Changing Structures The areas of the brain do not mature uniformly (de Haan & Johnson, 2016). The frontal lobe is immature in the newborn. As neurons in the frontal lobe become myelinated and interconnected during the first year of life, infants develop an ability to regulate their physiological states (such as sleep) and gain more control over their reflexes. Cognitive skills that require deliberate thinking do not emerge until later (Bell & others, 2018). At about 2 months of age, the motor control centers of the brain develop to the point at which infants can suddenly reach out and grab a nearby object. At about 4 months, the neural connections necessary for depth perception begin to form. And at about 12 months, the brain's speech centers are poised to produce one of infancy's magical moments: when the infant utters its first word.

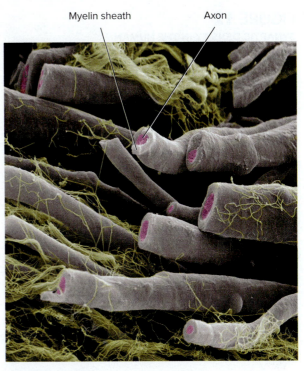

FIGURE 10

MYELINATED NERVE FIBERS. A myelin sheath, shown in gray, encases the axons (shown in pink). *What roles does myelination play in the brain's development and children's cognition?*
Science Photo Library/Getty Images

Myelin sheath   Axon

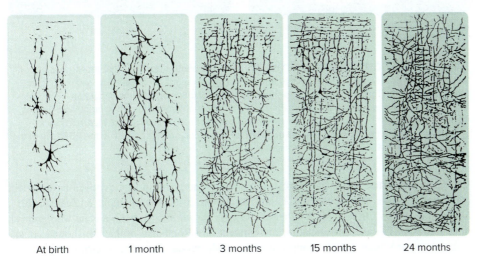

At birth   1 month   3 months   15 months   24 months

FIGURE 11

THE DEVELOPMENT OF DENDRITIC SPREADING. Note the increase in connectedness between neurons over the course of the first two years of life. Leisman, Gerry, "Intentionality and 'free-will' from a neurodevelopmental perspective." *Frontiers in Integrative Science*, June 27, 2012, Figure 4. Copyright ©2012 by Gerry Leisman. All rights reserved. Used with permission.

FIGURE 12

SYNAPTIC DENSITY IN THE HUMAN BRAIN FROM INFANCY TO ADULTHOOD. The graph shows the dramatic increase followed by pruning in synaptic density for three regions of the brain: visual cortex, auditory cortex, and prefrontal cortex. Synaptic density is believed to be an important indication of the extent of connectivity between neurons.

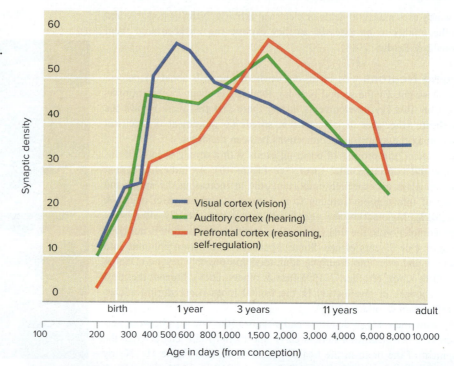

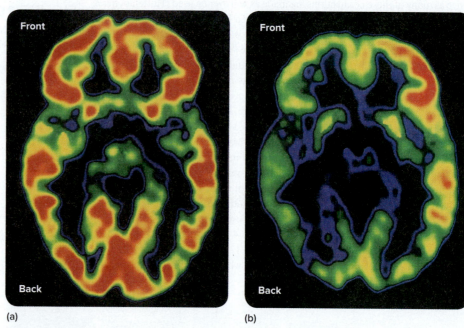

(a)　　　　　　　　　　　　　(b)

FIGURE 13

EARLY DEPRIVATION AND BRAIN ACTIVITY. These two photographs are PET (positron emission tomography) scans—which use radioactive tracers to image and analyze blood flow and metabolic activity in the body's organs. These scans show the brains of (a) a normal child and (b) an institutionalized Romanian orphan who experienced substantial deprivation since birth. In PET scans, the highest to lowest brain activity is reflected in the colors of red, yellow, green, blue, and black, respectively. As can be seen, red and yellow show up to a much greater degree in the PET scan of the normal child than that of the deprived Romanian orphan.
Courtesy of Dr. Harry T. Chugani, Children's Hospital of Michigan

Early Experience and the Brain

Children who grow up in a deprived environment may have depressed brain activity (Lamm & others, 2018; Nelson, Fox, & Zeanah, 2014; Sheridan & others, 2018; Wade & others, 2019). As shown in Figure 13, a child who grew up in the unresponsive and unstimulating environment of a Romanian orphanage showed considerably depressed brain activity compared with a child raised in a normal environment.

Are the effects of deprived environments reversible? There is reason to think that at least to some degree and for some individuals the answer is yes (Dennis & others, 2014). The brain demonstrates both flexibility and resilience (Guyer, Perez-Edgar, & Crone, 2018; Popova & Naumenko, 2019). Consider 14-year-old Michael Rehbein. At age 7, he began to experience uncontrollable seizures—as many as 400 a day. Doctors said the only solution was to remove the left hemisphere of his brain where the seizures were occurring. Recovery was slow, but his right hemisphere began to reorganize and take over functions that normally occur in the brain's left hemisphere, including speech (see Figure 14).

Neuroscientists note that what wires the brain—or rewires it, in the case of Michael Rehbein—is repeated experience (Nash, 1997). Each time a baby tries to touch an attractive object or gazes intently at a face, tiny bursts of electricity shoot through the brain, knitting together neurons into circuits. The results are some of the behavioral milestones we discuss in this and other chapters.

CHILDHOOD

The brain and other parts of the nervous system continue developing through childhood (Bell & others, 2018; Schneider & Ornstein, 2019). These changes enable children to plan their actions, to attend to stimuli more effectively, and to make considerable strides in language development.

During early childhood, the brain and head grow more rapidly than any other part of the body. Figure 15 shows how the growth curve for the head and brain advances more rapidly than the growth curve for height and weight. Some of the brain's increase in size is due to myelination and some is due to an increase in the number and size of dendrites. Some developmentalists conclude that myelination is important in the maturation of a number of abilities in children (Dahl & others, 2018; Kwon & others, 2019). For example, myelination in the areas of the brain related to hand-eye coordination is not complete until about 4 years of age. Myelination in the areas of the brain related to focusing attention is not complete until the end of middle or late childhood.

The brain in early childhood is not growing as rapidly as it did in infancy, yet the anatomical changes in the child's brain between the ages of 3 and 15 are dramatic. By repeatedly obtaining brain scans of the same children for up to four years, scientists have found that children's brains experience rapid, distinct growth spurts (Gogtay & Thompson, 2010). The amount of brain material in some areas can nearly double in as little as one year, followed by a drastic loss of tissue as unneeded cells are purged and the brain continues to reorganize itself.

The substantial increases in memory and rapid learning that characterize infants and young children are related to myelination and synaptic growth. In a recent study, young children with higher cognitive ability showed increased myelination by 3 years of age (Deoni & others, 2016).

These aspects of the brain's maturation, combined with opportunities to experience a widening world, contribute to children's emerging cognitive abilities. Consider a child who is learning to read and is asked by a teacher to read aloud to the class. Input from the child's eyes is transmitted to the child's brain, then passed through many brain systems, which translate (process) the patterns of black and white into codes for letters, words, and associations. The output occurs in the form of messages to the child's lips and tongue. The child's own gift of speech is possible because brain systems are organized in ways that permit language processing.

Recently, researchers have found that contextual factors such as poverty and parenting quality are linked to the development of the brain during childhood (Bick & others, 2019; Black & others, 2017; Kim & others, 2019; Lomanowska & others, 2017; Marshall & others, 2018). In one study, children from the poorest homes had significant maturational lags in their frontal and temporal lobes at 4 years of age, and these lags were associated with lower school readiness skills (Hair & others, 2015). In another study, higher levels of maternal sensitivity in early childhood were associated with higher total brain volume (Kok & others, 2015). Further, a recent study indicated that maltreatment risk and home adversity in infancy were linked to cortical delays and brain immaturity at 8 years of age (Bick & others, 2019). However, children assigned to an attachment and biobehavioral catchup intervention showed improved brain functioning. And in a longitudinal study, 11- to 18-year-olds who lived in poverty conditions had diminished brain functioning at 25 years of age (Brody & others, 2017). However, the adolescents from poverty backgrounds whose families participated in a supportive parenting intervention did not show this diminished brain functioning in adulthood.

FIGURE 14

PLASTICITY IN THE BRAIN'S HEMISPHERES. Michael Rehbein at 14 years of age. Following removal of the left hemisphere of Michael's brain because of uncontrollable seizures, his right hemisphere reorganized to take over the language functions normally carried out by corresponding areas in the left hemisphere of an intact brain.
Courtesy of The Rehbein Family

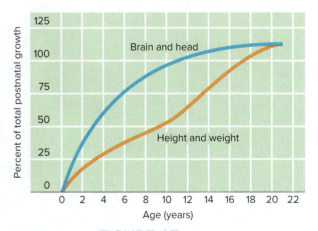

FIGURE 15

GROWTH CURVES FOR THE HEAD AND BRAIN AND FOR HEIGHT AND WEIGHT. The more rapid growth of the brain and head can easily be seen. Height and weight advance more gradually over the first two decades of life.

prefrontal cortex The highest level of the frontal lobes that is involved in reasoning, decision making, and self-control.

corpus callosum A large bundle of axon fibers that connects the brain's left and right hemispheres.

limbic system The region of the brain where emotions and rewards are experienced.

amygdala A part of the brain's limbic system that is the seat of emotions such as anger.

Significant changes in various structures and regions of the brain continue to occur during middle and late childhood (de Haan & Johnson, 2016; Price & others, 2018). In particular, the brain pathways and circuitry involving the **prefrontal cortex,** the highest level in the brain, continue to increase in middle and late childhood (Johnson, Riis, & Noble, 2016). The brain is hierarchically organized and mainly develops from the bottom up, with sensory areas reaching maturity before the higher-level association areas such as the prefrontal cortex.

In one study, researchers found less diffusion and more focal activation in the prefrontal cortex from 7 to 30 years of age (Durston & others, 2006). The activation change was accompanied by increased efficiency in cognitive performance, especially in *cognitive control,* which involves flexible and effective control in a number of areas. These areas include controlling attention, reducing interfering thoughts, inhibiting motor actions, and being cognitively flexible in switching between competing choices (Aben & others, 2019; Diamond, 2013).

Developmental neuroscientist Mark Johnson and his colleagues (Johnson, Grossmann, & Cohen-Kadosh, 2009; Johnson, Jones, & Gliga, 2015) have proposed that the prefrontal cortex likely orchestrates the functions of many other brain regions during development. As part of this neural leadership and organizational role, the prefrontal cortex may provide an advantage to neural connections and networks that include the prefrontal cortex. In their view, the prefrontal cortex likely coordinates the best neural connections for solving a problem.

ADOLESCENCE

Until recently, little research has been conducted on developmental changes in the brain during adolescence. Although research in this area is still in its infancy, an increasing number of studies are under way (Casey & others, 2019; Jadhav & Boutrel, 2019; Reyna, 2018; Sherman, Steinberg, & Chein, 2018). Scientists now note that the adolescent's brain is different from the child's brain, and that in adolescence the brain is still growing (Ladouceur & others, 2019; Lebel & Deoni, 2018; Vijayakumar & others, 2018).

Earlier we indicated that connections between neurons become "pruned" as children and adolescents develop. Because of this pruning, by the end of adolescence individuals have "fewer, more selective, more effective neuronal connections than they did as children" (Kuhn, 2009, p. 153). And this pruning indicates that the activities adolescents choose to engage in or not to engage in influence which neural connections will be strengthened and which will disappear.

Using fMRI brain scans, scientists have discovered that adolescents' brains undergo significant structural changes (Dahl & others, 2018; Fuhrmann & others, 2019; Hinnant & others, 2019; Zanolie & Crone, 2018). These structural changes occur in the corpus callosum, the prefrontal cortex, and the limbic system. The **corpus callosum,** where fibers connect the brain's left and right hemispheres, thickens in adolescence, which improves adolescents' ability to process information (Chavarria & others, 2014). For example, a recent study found that the density of fibers in the corpus callosum increased in adolescence (Genc & others, 2018). We described advances in the development of the prefrontal cortex—the highest level of the frontal lobes involved in reasoning, decision making, and self-control—earlier in this chapter. The prefrontal cortex doesn't finish maturing until the emerging adult years (18 to 25 years old) or later (Casey & others, 2019).

At a lower, subcortical level, the **limbic system,** which is the seat of emotions and where rewards are experienced, matures much earlier than the prefrontal cortex and is almost completely developed by early adolescence (Casey & others, 2019). The limbic system structure that is especially involved in emotion is the **amygdala.** Figure 16 shows the locations of the corpus callosum, prefrontal cortex, and the limbic system.

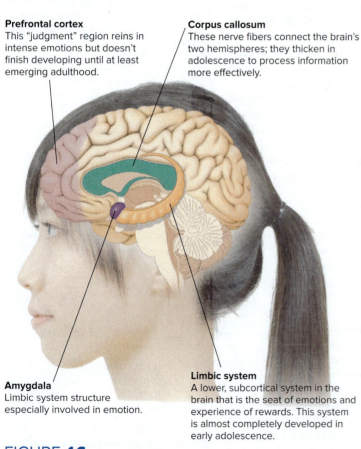

Prefrontal cortex
This "judgment" region reins in intense emotions but doesn't finish developing until at least emerging adulthood.

Corpus callosum
These nerve fibers connect the brain's two hemispheres; they thicken in adolescence to process information more effectively.

Amygdala
Limbic system structure especially involved in emotion.

Limbic system
A lower, subcortical system in the brain that is the seat of emotions and experience of rewards. This system is almost completely developed in early adolescence.

FIGURE 16

THE CHANGING ADOLESCENT BRAIN: PREFRONTAL CORTEX, LIMBIC SYSTEM, AND CORPUS CALLOSUM

Photo: takayuki/Shutterstock

Strategies for Helping Adolescents Reduce Their Risk-Taking Behavior

Beginning in early adolescence, individuals seek experiences that create high-intensity feelings (Dahl & others, 2018). Adolescents like intensity, excitement, and arousal. They are drawn to music videos that shock and bombard the senses. Teenagers flock to horror and slasher movies. They dominate queues waiting to ride high-adrenaline rides at amusement parks. Adolescence is a time when sex, drugs, very loud music, and other high-stimulation experiences take on great appeal. It is a developmental period when an appetite for adventure, a predilection for risks, and desire for novelty and thrills seem to reach naturally high levels. While these patterns of emotional changes are present to some degree in most adolescents, it is important to recognize the wide range of individual differences during this period of development (Dahl, 2004, p. 6).

The self-regulatory skills necessary to inhibit risk taking often don't develop fully until later in adolescence or emerging adulthood (Casey & others, 2019; Steinberg & others, 2018). And, as we just saw, this gap between the increase in risk-taking behavior and the delay in self-regulation is linked to brain development in the limbic system (involved in pleasure seeking and emotion) taking place earlier than development of the frontal lobes (involved in self-regulation) (Monahan & others, 2016).

It is important for parents, teachers, mentors, and other responsible adults to effectively monitor adolescents' behavior. In many cases, adults decrease their monitoring of adolescents too early, leaving them to cope with tempting situations alone or with friends

How might developmental changes in the brain be involved in adolescent risk taking? What are some strategies for reducing adolescent risk taking?
Image Source/Getty Images

and peers. When adolescents are in tempting and dangerous situations with minimal adult supervision, their inclination to engage in risk-taking behavior combined with their immature self-regulatory skills can make them vulnerable to a host of negative outcomes (Casey & others, 2019; Sherman, Steinberg, & Chein, 2018).

What does the nature-nurture debate suggest about the influence of adults who monitor adolescents' lives?

With the onset of puberty, the levels of neurotransmitters change. For example, an increase in the neurotransmitter dopamine occurs in both the prefrontal cortex and the limbic system during adolescence (Dahl & others, 2018; Ladouceur & others, 2019). Increases in dopamine have been linked to increased risk taking and the use of addictive drugs (Gulick & Gamsby, 2018). Researchers have found that dopamine plays an important role in reward seeking during adolescence (Dubol & others, 2018).

Let's further consider the developmental disjunction between the early development of the limbic system and the later development of the prefrontal cortex. This disjunction may account for increased risk taking and other problem behaviors in adolescence. To read further about risk-taking behavior in adolescence, see the *Connecting Development to Life* interlude.

Many of the changes in the adolescent brain that have been described involve the rapidly emerging field of *developmental social neuroscience* (which involves connections between development, the brain, and socioemotional processes) and *developmental cognitive neuroscience* (which involves links between development, cognition, and neuroscience) (Burani & others, 2019; Maatta & others, 2019; Zanolie & Crone, 2018). For example, consider leading researcher Charles Nelson's (2003) view that, although adolescents are capable of very strong emotions, their prefrontal cortex hasn't adequately developed to the point at which they can control these

developmental connection

Brain Development

Developmental social neuroscience and developmental cognitive neuroscience are recently developed fields of study. Connect to "Introduction."

passions. It is as if their brain doesn't have the brakes to slow down their emotions. Or consider this interpretation of the development of emotion and cognition in adolescents: "early activation of strong 'turbo-charged' feelings with a relatively un-skilled set of 'driving skills' or cognitive abilities to modulate strong emotions and motivations" (Dahl, 2004, p. 18). And in the view of leading expert Jay Giedd (2007), biology doesn't make teens rebellious or have purple hair and it does not mean that they are going to do drugs, but it increases their chances of doing such things.

Of course, a major issue is which comes first, biological changes in the brain or experiences that stimulate these changes (Lerner, Boyd, & Du, 2008). Consider a study in which the prefrontal cortex thickened and more brain connections formed when adolescents resisted peer pressure (Paus & others, 2008). Scientists have yet to determine whether the brain changes come first or whether the brain changes are the result of experiences with peers, parents, and others. Once again, we encounter the nature/nurture issue that is so prominent in an examination of development through the life span. Nonetheless, there is adequate evidence that environmental experiences make important contributions to the brain's development (Casey & others, 2019; Dahl & others, 2018).

In closing this section on the development of the brain in adolescence, a further caution is in order. Much of the research on neuroscience and the development of the brain in adolescence is correlational in nature, and thus causal statements need to be scrutinized. This caution, of course, applies to any period in the human life span.

ADULTHOOD AND AGING

Changes in the brain continue during adulthood. Most of the research on the brains of adults, however, has focused on the aging brains of older adults. What are some of the general findings about the aging brain? How much plasticity and adaptability does it retain?

The Shrinking, Slowing Brain   On average, the brain loses 5 to 10 percent of its weight between the ages of 20 and 90. Brain volume also decreases (Ramonoel & others, 2019). A study found a decrease in total brain volume and volume in key brain structures such as the frontal lobes and hippocampus from 22 to 88 years of age (Sherwood & others, 2011). Another study found that the volume of the brain was 15 percent less in older adults than younger adults (Shan & others, 2005). Further, a recent study of older adults revealed that declines in memory functioning were inked to lower gray matter volume (which contains most of the brain's neuronal cell bodies) in the temporal lobe and hippocampus (Schneider & others, 2019). Also, recent analyses concluded that in healthy aging the decrease in brain volume is due mainly to shrinkage of neurons, lower numbers of synapses, reduced length and complexity of axons, and reduced tree-like branching in dendrites, but only to a minor extent attributable to neuron loss (Fjell & Walhovd, 2010; Penazzi, Bakota, & Brandt, 2016; Skaper & others, 2017). In addition, in one study, higher global brain volume predicted lower mortality risk in a large population of stroke-free community-dwelling adults (Van Elderen & others, 2016). Of course, for individuals with disorders such as Alzheimer disease, neuron loss occurs (Poulakis & others, 2018).

Some areas of the brain shrink more than others (Squarzoni & others, 2018). The prefrontal cortex is one area that shrinks with aging, and research has linked this shrinkage with a decrease in working memory and other cognitive activities in older adults (Hoyer, 2015). The sensory regions of the brain—such as the primary visual cortex, primary motor cortex, and somatosensory cortex—are less vulnerable to the aging process (Rodrique & Kennedy, 2011).

A general slowing of function in the brain and spinal cord begins in middle adulthood and accelerates in late adulthood (Salthouse, 2017). Both physical coordination and intellectual performance are affected. For example, after age 70, many adults no longer show a knee jerk reflex and by age 90 most reflexes are much slower (Spence, 1989). The slowing of the brain can impair the performance of older adults on intelligence tests and various cognitive tasks, especially those that are timed (Lu & others, 2011).

Aging also has been linked to a decline in the production of some neurotransmitters. Reduction in acetylcholine is linked to memory loss, especially in people with Alzheimer disease (Kamal & others, 2017). Severe reductions in dopamine are involved in a reduction in motor control in Parkinson disease (da Silva & others, 2017).

Historically, as in the research just discussed, much of the focus on links between brain functioning and aging has been on volume of brain structures and regions. Recently, increased emphasis is being given to changes in myelination and neural networks (Chen & others, 2019; Vuksanovic & others, 2019). Research indicates that demyelination (a deterioration in the myelin sheath that encases axons, which is associated with information processing) of the brain occurs with aging in older adults (Cercignani & others, 2017).

The Adapting Brain The human brain has remarkable repair capability (Kinugawa, 2019; Park & Festini, 2018). Even in late adulthood, the brain loses only a portion of its ability to function, and the activities older adults engage in can influence the brain's development (Ji & others, 2019; Zhu, Bao, & Swaab, 2019). For example, an fMRI study found that higher levels of aerobic fitness were linked with greater volume in the hippocampus, which translates into better memory (Erickson & others, 2011).

Three areas reflect the adaptiveness of the brain in older adults: (1) the capacity to generate new neurons, (2) dendritic growth, and (3) delateralization. Researchers have found that **neurogenesis,** the generation of new neurons, does occur in lower mammalian species such as mice (Jain & others, 2019). Also, research indicates that exercise and an enriched, complex environment can generate new brain cells in mice and that stress reduces the cells' survival rate (Kempermann, 2019; Park & others, 2018) (see Figure 17). For example, in a recent study, mice in an enriched environment learned more flexibly because of adult hippocampal neurogenesis (Garthe, Roeder, & Kempermann, 2016). And one study revealed that coping with stress stimulated hippocampal neurogenesis in adult monkeys (Lyons & others, 2010). Researchers also have discovered that if rats are cognitively challenged to learn something, new brain cells survive longer (Shors, 2009).

It also is now accepted by most researchers that neurogenesis can occur in humans (Shohayeb & others, 2018; Snyder, 2019). However, neurogenesis has been found in only two brain regions: the hippocampus (Koyanagi & others, 2019), which is involved in memory, and the olfactory bulb (Bonzano & De Marchis, 2017), which is involved in smell. It also is not known what functions these new brain cells perform, and at this point researchers have documented that they last only a few weeks (Nelson, 2006).

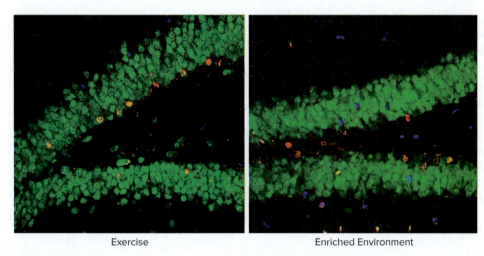

Exercise   Enriched Environment

FIGURE 17

GENERATING NEW NERVE CELLS IN ADULT MICE. Researchers have found that exercise (running) and an enriched environment (a larger cage and many toys) can cause brain cells to divide and form new brain cells (Kempermann, van Praag, & Gage, 2000). Cells were labeled with a chemical marker that becomes integrated into the DNA of dividing cells (red). Four weeks later, they were also labeled to mark neurons (nerve cells). As shown here, both the running mice and the mice in an enriched environment had many cells that were still dividing (red) and others that had differentiated into new nerve cells (orange).
Courtesy of Dr. Fred Gage, The Salk Institute for Biological Studies

neurogenesis The generation of new neurons.

connecting with research

The Nun Study

The Nun Study, directed by David Snowdon, is an intriguing, ongoing investigation of aging in 678 nuns, many of whom have lived in a convent in Mankato, Minnesota (Pakhomov & Hemmy, 2014; Snowdon, 1997, 2002, 2003; Tyas & others, 2007; White & others, 2016). Each of the 678 nuns agreed to participate in annual assessments of her cognitive and physical functioning. The nuns also agreed to donate their brains for scientific research when they die, and they are the largest group of brain donors in the world. Examination of the nuns' donated brains, as well as those donated by others, has led neuroscientists to believe that the brain has a remarkable capacity to change and grow, even in old age. The Sisters of Notre Dame in Mankato lead an intellectually challenging life, and brain researchers believe this contributes to their quality of life as older adults and possibly to their longevity.

Findings from the Nun Study so far include the following:

- Positive emotions early in adulthood were linked to longevity (Danner, Snowdon, & Friesen, 2001). Handwritten autobiographies from 180 nuns, composed when they were 22 years of age, were scored for emotional content. The nuns whose early writings had higher scores for positive emotional content were more likely to still be alive at 75 to 95 years of age than their counterparts whose early writings were characterized by negative emotional content.

- Sisters who had taught for most of their lives showed more moderate declines in intellectual skills than those who had spent most of their lives in service-based tasks, a finding supporting the notion that stimulating the brain with intellectual activity keeps neurons healthy and alive (Snowdon, 2002).

- An analysis of essays written when the nuns were 18 to 32 years of age found that those whose essays reflected a higher level of self-reflection and independence in decision making lived longer (Weinstein & others, 2019)

This study and other research provide hope that scientists will discover ways to tap into the brain's capacity to adapt in order to prevent and treat brain diseases (Alexopoulos & Kelly, 2017; Liu & others, 2017). For example, scientists might learn more effective ways to improve older adults' cognitive functioning, reduce Alzheimer disease, and help older adults recover from strokes (Lovden, Backman, & Lindenberger, 2017; Sperling, 2017). Even when areas of the brain are permanently damaged by stroke, new message routes can be created to get around the blockage or to resume the function of the damaged area, indicating that the brain does have the capacity to adapt.

(a)

(b)

(*a*) Sister Marcella Zachman (*left*) finally stopped teaching at age 97. Now, at 99, she helps ailing nuns exercise their brains by quizzing them on vocabulary or playing a card game called Skip-Bo, at which she deliberately loses. Sister Mary Esther Boor (*right*), also 99 years of age, is a former teacher who stays alert by doing puzzles and volunteering to work the front desk. (*b*) A technician holds the brain of a deceased Mankato nun. The nuns donate their brains for research that explores the effects of stimulation on brain growth.
(Both): ©James Balog

Although the Nun Study's results are intriguing, an order of nuns is in some ways a self-selected group whose members may come to share many social and environmental characteristics through long years of living together. How might future researchers account for any potential biases in such studies?

Researchers currently are studying factors that might inhibit and promote neurogenesis, including various drugs, stress, and exercise (Kempermann, 2019; Liu & Nusslock, 2018). They also are examining how the grafting of neural stem cells to various regions of the brain, such as the hippocampus, might increase neurogenesis (Akers & others, 2018; Takei, 2019). And increasing attention is being given to the possible role neurogenesis might play in reversing the course of neurodegenerative diseases such as Alzheimer disease, Parkinson disease, and Huntington disease (Isaev, Stelmashook, & Genrikhs, 2019; Shohayeb & others, 2018).

Dendritic growth can occur in human adults, possibly even in older adults (Eliasieh, Liets, & Chalupa, 2007). One study compared the brains of adults at various ages (Coleman, 1986). From the forties through the seventies, the growth of dendrites increased. However, in people in their nineties, dendritic growth no longer occurred. This dendritic growth might compensate for the possible loss of neurons through the seventies but not in the nineties. Lack of dendritic growth in older adults could be due to a lack of environmental stimulation and activity.

Changes in lateralization may provide one type of adaptation in aging adults (Hong & others, 2015). Recall that lateralization is the specialization of function in one hemisphere of the brain or the other. Using neuroimaging techniques, researchers have found that brain activity in the prefrontal cortex is lateralized less in older adults than in younger adults when they are engaging in cognitive tasks (Cabeza, 2002; Cabeza & Dennis, 2013; Rossi & others, 2005; Sugiura, 2016). For example, Figure 18 shows that when younger adults are given the task of recognizing words they have previously seen, they process the information primarily in the right hemisphere, while older adults doing the same task are more likely to use both hemispheres (Madden & others, 1999).

The decrease in lateralization in older adults might play a compensatory role in the aging brain (Hong & others, 2015). That is, using both hemispheres may improve the cognitive functioning of older adults. Support for this view comes from another study in which older adults who used both brain hemispheres were faster at completing a working memory task than their counterparts who primarily used only one hemisphere (Reuter-Lorenz & others, 2000). However, the decrease in lateralization may be a mere by-product of aging; it may reflect an age-related decline in the brain's ability to specialize functions. In this view, during childhood the brain becomes increasingly differentiated in terms of its functions; as adults become older, this process may reverse. Support for the dedifferentiation view is found in the higher intercorrelations of performance on cognitive tasks in older adults than in younger adults (Baltes & Lindenberger, 1997).

What kinds of mental activities can slow the changes in the brain that occur with age? To read about how one group of researchers is seeking to answer this question, see the *Connecting with Research* interlude on page 108.

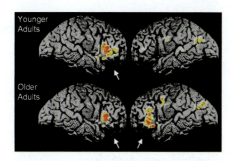

FIGURE 18

THE DECREASE IN BRAIN LATERALIZATION IN OLDER ADULTS. Younger adults primarily used the right prefrontal region of the brain (*top left photo*) during a recall memory task, whereas older adults used both the left and right prefrontal regions (*bottom two photos*). Courtesy of Dr. Roberto Cabeza

Review Connect Reflect

 LG2 Describe how the brain changes through the life span.

Review
- What are the major areas of the brain, and how does it process information?
- How does the brain change during infancy?
- What characterizes the development of the brain in childhood?
- How can the changes in the brain during adolescence be summarized?
- What is the aging brain like?

Connect
- What types of brain research technology can be used to study infants that cannot be used to study them before they are born? Which types can be used on adults but not infants? How might these differences in research tools affect our understanding of how the human brain functions across the life span?

Reflect *Your Own Personal Journey of Life*
- If you could interview the Mankato nuns, what questions would you want to ask them?

3 Sleep **LG3** Summarize how sleep patterns change as people develop.

| Why Do We Sleep? | Infancy | Childhood | Adolescence and Emerging Adulthood | Adulthood and Aging |

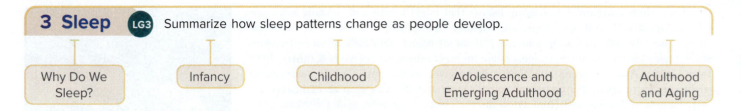

Sleep that knits up the ravelled sleave of care . . . Balm of hurt minds, nature's second course. Chief nourisher in life's feast.

—**WILLIAM SHAKESPEARE**

English Playwright, Late 16th and Early 17th Century

Sleep restores, replenishes, and rebuilds our brains and bodies. What purposes does sleep serve in people's lives? How do sleep patterns change across the life span?

WHY DO WE SLEEP?

A number of theories have been proposed about why we sleep. From an evolutionary perspective, all animals sleep, and this sleep likely is necessary for survival. Thus, sleep may have developed because animals needed to protect themselves at night. A second perspective is that sleep is restorative, with sleep replenishing and rebuilding the brain and body after the day's activities. In support of this restorative function, many of the body's cells show increased production and reduced breakdowns of proteins during sleep (Brinkman & Sharma, 2018; Ferrarelli & others, 2019). Further, a current hypothesis is that sleep is essential to clearing out waste in neural tissues, such as metabolites and cerebrospinal fluid (Dai & others, 2018). A third perspective is that sleep is critical for brain plasticity (Maier & others, 2019). For example, neuroscientists recently have argued that sleep increases synaptic connections between neurons (Tononi & Cirelli, 2019; Belal & others, 2018). These increased synaptic connections during sleep have been linked to improved consolidation of memories (Almeida-Filho, Queiroz, & Ribeiro, 2018). Further, a research review concluded that not only can sleep improve memory, but also losing just a few hours of sleep a night has negative effects on attention, reasoning, and decision making (Diekelmann, 2014; Spruyt & others, 2019).

In sum, sleep likely serves a number of important functions, with no one theory accounting for all of these functions. Let's now turn our attention to how sleep functions at different points in the human life span.

INFANCY

How much do infants sleep? Can any special problems develop regarding infants' sleep?

The Sleep/Wake Cycle   When we were infants, sleep consumed more of our time than it does now. Newborns sleep 16 to 17 hours a day, although some sleep more and others less—the range is from a low of about 10 hours to a high of about 21 hours per day. A research review concluded that infants 0 to 2 years of age slept an average of 12.8 hours out of the 24, within a range of 9.7 to 15.9 hours (Galland & others, 2012). A study also revealed that by 6 months of age the majority of infants slept through the night, awakening their parents only one or two nights per week (Weinraub & others, 2012).

Although total sleep remains somewhat consistent for young infants, their sleep during the day does not always follow a rhythmic pattern. An infant might change from sleeping several long stretches of 7 or 8 hours to three or four shorter sessions only several hours in duration. By about 1 month of age, most infants have begun to sleep longer at night. By 6 months of age, they usually have moved closer to adult-like sleep patterns, spending their longest span of sleep at night and their longest span of waking during the day (Sadeh, 2008).

The most common infant sleep-related problem reported by parents is nighttime waking (Dias & others, 2018). Surveys indicate that 20 to 30 percent of infants have difficulty going to sleep and staying asleep at night (Sadeh, 2008). One study revealed that maternal depression during pregnancy, early introduction of solid foods, infant TV viewing, and child-care attendance were related to shorter duration of infant sleep (Nevarez & others, 2010). Another study found that nighttime wakings at 1 year of age predicted lower sleep efficiency at 4 years of age (Tikotzky & Shaashua, 2012).

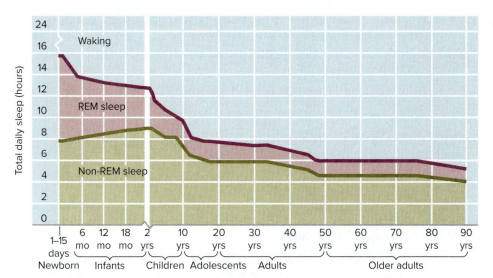

FIGURE **19**

SLEEP ACROSS THE HUMAN LIFE SPAN

REM Sleep A much greater amount of time is taken up by *REM (rapid eye movement)* sleep in infancy than at any other point in the life span (Funk & others, 2016). Figure 19 shows developmental changes in the average number of total hours spent in REM and non-REM sleep. Unlike adults, who spend about one-fifth of their night in REM sleep, infants spend about half of their sleep time in REM sleep, and they often begin their sleep cycle with REM sleep rather than non-REM sleep. By the time infants reach 3 months of age, the percentage of time they spend in REM sleep decreases to about 40 percent, and REM sleep no longer begins their sleep cycle.

Why do infants spend so much time in REM sleep? Researchers are not certain. The large amount of REM sleep may provide infants with added self-stimulation, since they spend less time awake than do older children. REM sleep also might promote the brain's development in infancy (Del Rio-Bermudez & Blumberg, 2018).

When adults are awakened during REM sleep, they frequently report that they have been dreaming, but when they are awakened during non-REM sleep they are much less likely to report having been dreaming (Cartwright & others, 2006). Since infants spend more time than adults in REM sleep, can we conclude that they dream a lot? We don't know whether infants dream or not, because they don't have any way of reporting dreams.

sudden infant death syndrome (SIDS) Condition in which an infant stops breathing, usually during the night, and suddenly dies without an apparent cause.

SIDS **Sudden infant death syndrome (SIDS)** is a condition that occurs when infants stop breathing, usually during the night, and die suddenly without an apparent cause. SIDS remains the highest cause of infant death in the United States, with nearly 3,000 infant deaths attributed to it annually (Heron, 2016). Risk of SIDS is highest at 2 to 4 months of age (Duncan & Byard, 2019; NICHD, 2019).

Since 1992, the American Academy of Pediatrics (AAP) has recommended that infants be placed to sleep on their backs to reduce the risk of SIDS, and the frequency of prone (stomach) sleeping among U.S. infants and infants in many other countries has dropped dramatically (Elder, 2015). Researchers have found that the rate of SIDS does indeed decrease when infants sleep on their backs rather than their stomachs or sides (Bombard & others, 2018; Newberry, 2019). Why? Because sleeping on their backs increases their access to fresh air and reduces their chances of getting overheated.

In addition to sleeping in a prone position (stomach down), researchers have found that the following are risk factors for SIDS:

- Heart arrhythmias are estimated to occur in as many as 15 percent of SIDS cases, and two recent studies found that gene mutations were linked to the occurrence of these arrhythmias (Horne, 2018; Sarquella-Brugada & others, 2016).
- SIDS occurs more often in infants with abnormal brain stem functioning involving the neurotransmitter serotonin (Rognum & others, 2014).
- Six percent of infants with sleep apnea, a temporary cessation of breathing in which the airway is completely blocked (usually for 10 seconds or longer), die of SIDS (Ednick & others, 2010).

Is this a good sleep position for this 3-month-old infant? Why or why not?
Maria Teijeiro/Cultura/Getty Images

- Low birth weight infants are 5 to 10 times more likely to die of SIDS than are their normal-weight counterparts (Horne & others, 2002).
- Infants whose siblings have died of SIDS are two to four times as likely to die of it (Lenoir, Mallet, & Calenda, 2000).
- African American and Eskimo infants are two to six times as likely as all others to die of SIDS (Moon & others, 2017).
- Breast feeding is linked to a lower incidence of SIDS (Carlin & Moon, 2017).
- SIDS is more common in lower socioeconomic groups, especially those living in areas with high poverty rates (Drake & others, 2019).
- SIDS occurs more often in infants who are passively exposed to cigarette smoke (Lavezzi, 2019; Moon & Hauck, 2018).
- SIDS is more common when infants and parents share the same bed (Brownstein & others, 2018). In a study of 732 cases of SIDS, bed-sharing occurred in 53 percent of the deaths (Drake & others, 2019).
- SIDS is more common if infants sleep in soft bedding (Haynes, 2018).
- SIDS is less common when infants sleep in a bedroom with a fan. One study revealed that sleeping in a bedroom with a fan lowers the risk of SIDS by 70 percent (Coleman-Phox, Odouli, & Li, 2008).

It is generally now accepted that the most critical factor in predicting whether an infant will develop SIDS is prone sleeping. In a research review, it was concluded that the two other factors that place infants at the highest risk for SIDS are (1) maternal smoking, and (2) bed sharing (Mitchell & Krous, 2015).

Sleep and Cognitive Development   Infant sleep is being studied for its possible role in children's cognitive development (Franco & others, 2019; Pisch, Wiesemann, & Karmiloff-Smith, 2019). A recent study found that infants with shorter sleep duration were characterized by a lower level of cognitive and language development at 2 years of age (Smithson & others, 2018). Another study revealed that 4-year-olds who had slept longer at night as infants engaged in a higher level of executive function (Bernier & others, 2013). Another study revealed that a lower quality of sleep at 1 year of age was linked to lower attention regulation and more behavior problems at 3 to 4 years of age (Sadeh & others, 2015). The links between infant sleep and children's cognitive functioning likely occur because of sleep's role in brain maturation and memory consolidation, which may improve daytime alertness and learning.

CHILDHOOD

A good night's sleep is an important aspect of a child's development (Mi & others, 2019). Experts recommend that young children get 11 to 13 hours of sleep each night and that first- to fifth-graders get 10 to 11 hours of sleep each night (National Sleep Foundation, 2019). Most young children sleep through the night and have one daytime nap (Moore, 2012).

Following is a sampling of recent research on factors linked to children's sleep problems:

- In a Chinese study, preschool children who slept seven hours per night or less had a worse school readiness profile (including language/cognitive deficits and emotional immaturity) (Tso & others, 2016). Also in this study, preschool children who used electronic devices three or more hours per day had shortened sleep duration.
- Preschool children who had a longer sleep duration were more likely to have better peer acceptance, social skills, and vocabulary (Vaughn & others, 2015).
- In 2- to 5-year-old children, each additional hour of daily screen time was associated with a decrease in sleep time, less likelihood of sleeping 10 hours or more per night, and later bedtime (Xu & others, 2016).
- Recent research indicates that sleep deprivation in childhood is linked to attention deficit hyperactivity disorder (ADHD) (Arns & Vollebreght, 2019; Becker & others, 2019). For example, in a recent Chinese study, sleep deprivation in early childhood was associated with a higher incidence of ADHD in middle and late childhood (Tso & others, 2019).

Children can experience a number of sleep problems (Huhdanpaa & others, 2018; McDonagh, Holmes, & Hsu, 2019). It has been estimated that more than 40 percent of children experience a sleep problem at some point in their development (Boyle & Cropley, 2004). One analysis concluded that chronic sleep disorders that deprive children of adequate sleep may result in impaired brain development (Jan & others, 2010).

Child sleep expert Mona El-Sheikh (2013) recommends controlling the following aspects of the child's environment to improve the child's sleep: making sure the bedroom is cool, dark, and comfortable; maintaining consistent bedtimes and wake times; and creating positive family relationships. Also, helping the child slow down before bedtime often reduces resistance in going to bed. Reading the child a story, playing quietly with the child in the bath, and letting the child sit on the caregiver's lap while listening to music are calming activities.

What characterizes children's sleep?
S. Olsson/PhotoAlto

ADOLESCENCE AND EMERGING ADULTHOOD

Might changing sleep patterns in adolescence contribute to adolescents' health-compromising behaviors? Recently there has been a surge of interest in adolescent sleep patterns (Hoyt & others, 2018a, b; Palmer & others, 2018; Wheaton & others, 2018).

In a national survey of youth, only 32 percent of U.S. adolescents got eight or more hours of sleep on an average school night (Kann & others, 2016a). In this study, the percentage of adolescents getting this much sleep on an average school night decreased as they got older (see Figure 20). Adolescents who got inadequate sleep (eight hours or less) on school nights were more likely to feel tired or sleepy, act cranky and irritable, fall asleep in school, be in a depressed mood, and drink caffeinated beverages than their counterparts who got optimal sleep (nine or more hours). Also, one study of more than 270,000 U.S. adolescents from 1991–2012 found that their average amount of sleep had decreased in recent years (Keyes & others, 2015).

Studies have confirmed that adolescents in other countries also are not getting adequate sleep (Leger & others, 2012; Short & others, 2012). In one study, Asian adolescents had later bedtimes and were getting less sleep than U.S. adolescents (Gradisar, Gardner, & Dohnt, 2011).

Getting too little sleep in adolescence is linked to a number of problems, as indicated in the following recent studies:

- In a study of 13- to 19-year-olds in Singapore, short sleep duration (less than 7 hours) on school nights was associated with an increased risk of being overweight, having depression symptoms, being less motivated, not being able to concentrate adequately, having a high level of anxiety, and engaging in self-harm/suicidal thoughts (Yeo & others, 2019).
- In a longitudinal study in which adolescents completed an activity diary every 14 days in ninth, tenth, and twelfth grades, regardless of how much time students spent studying each day, when the students sacrificed sleep time to study more than usual, they had difficulty understanding what was taught in class and were more likely to struggle with class assignments the next day (Gillen-O'Neel, Huynh, & Fuligni, 2013).
- Swedish studies of 16- to 19-year-olds revealed short sleep duration was linked to a higher incidence of school absence and lower grades (Hysing & others, 2015, 2016).
- An experimental study indicated that when adolescents' sleep was restricted to 5 hours nightly for five nights, then returned to 10 hours nightly for two nights, their sustained attention was negatively affected (especially in the early morning) and did not return to baseline levels during recovery (Agostini & others, 2017).

Why are adolescents getting too little sleep? Among the explanations offered are the use of electronic media, increased caffeine intake, and changes in the brain coupled with early school start times (Hoyt & others, 2018a, b; Kim & others, 2018; Mireku & others, 2019). In

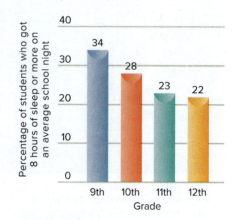

FIGURE **20**

DEVELOPMENTAL CHANGES IN U.S. ADOLESCENTS' SLEEP PATTERNS ON AN AVERAGE SCHOOL NIGHT

What are some developmental changes in sleep patterns during adolescence? How might these changes influence alertness at school?
FatCamera/E+/Getty Images

one study, adolescents engaged in an average of four electronic activities (in some cases, using different devices simultaneously) after 9 p.m. (Calamaro, Mason, & Ratcliffe, 2009). Also, in a recent national study of high school students, using electronic devices other than television 5 or more hours a day was linked to getting inadequate sleep (Kenney & Gortmaker, 2017). Further, in a recent study, spending multiple hours on portable electronic devices was linked to shorter sleep duration in adolescence while time spent on non-portable electronic devices was not related to sleep duration in adolescence (Twenge, Hisler, & Krizan, 2019). And a study of fourth- and seventh-graders found that those sleeping near small screens (smartphones, for example), sleeping with a TV in their room, and engaging in more screen time had shorter sleep duration (Falbe & others, 2015).

Caffeine intake by adolescents also is likely to be associated with insufficient sleep (Ruiz & Scherr, 2018). Greater caffeine intake as early as 12 years of age is linked to later sleep onset, shorter sleep duration, and increased daytime sleepiness (Bryant Ludden & Wolfson, 2010; Carskadon & Tarokh, 2014; Orbeta & others, 2006). The association of caffeine consumption and daytime sleepiness is also related to lower academic achievement (James, Kristjansson, & Sigfusdottir, 2011). Further, researchers have yet to study the effects on adolescent sleep patterns of very high levels of caffeine intake involving energy drinks.

Mary Carskadon (2002, 2004, 2005, 2006, 2011a, b) has conducted a number of research studies on adolescent sleep patterns. She has found that adolescents sleep an average of 9 hours and 25 minutes when given the opportunity to sleep as long as they like. Most adolescents get considerably less sleep than this, especially during the week. This creates a sleep debt, which adolescents often try to make up on the weekend. Carskadon also has found that older adolescents are often more sleepy during the day than are younger adolescents. She concludes that this is not because of factors such as academic work and social pressures. Rather, her research suggests that adolescents' biological clocks undergo a hormonal phase shift as they get older. This pushes the time of wakefulness to an hour later than when they were young adolescents. Carskadon has found that the shift was caused by a delay in the nightly presence of the hormone melatonin, which is produced by the brain's pineal gland in preparing the body for sleep. Melatonin is secreted at about 9:30 p.m. in younger adolescents but is produced approximately an hour later in older adolescents, which delays the onset of sleep.

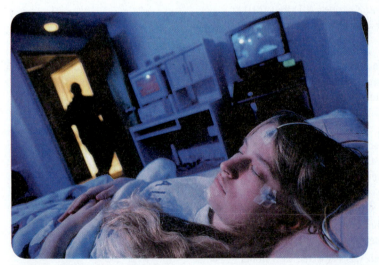

In Mary Carskadon's sleep laboratory at Brown University, an adolescent girl's brain activity is being monitored. Carskadon (2005) says that in the morning, sleep-deprived adolescents' "brains are telling them it's nighttime . . . and the rest of the world is saying it's time to go to school" (p. 19).
Courtesy of Jim LoScalzo

Carskadon determined that early school starting times can result in grogginess and lack of attention in class and poor performance on tests. Based on this research, some schools are now starting later (Gariepy & others, 2017). For example, school officials in Edina, Minnesota, made the decision to start classes at 8:30 a.m. instead of 7:25 a.m. Discipline problems dropped, and so did the number of students reporting illness or depression. Test scores in Edina improved for high school students but not for middle school students—results that support Carskadon's theory that older adolescents are affected more by early school start times than younger adolescents are. Also, a study found that just a 30-minute delay in school start time was linked to improvements in adolescents' sleep, alertness, mood, and health (Owens, Belon, & Moss, 2010). Further, in a recent study, when the Seattle School District delayed the school start time for secondary school students, it resulted in a 34-minute average increase in sleep duration, a 4.5 percent increase in grades, and an improvement in school attendance (Dunster & others, 2019). In another study, early school start times were linked to a higher vehicle crash rate in adolescent drivers (Vorona & others, 2014). The American Academy of Pediatrics has recommended that schools institute start times from 8:30 to 9:30 a.m. to improve adolescents' academic performance and quality of life (Adolescent Sleep Working Group, AAP, 2014).

Do sleep patterns change in emerging adulthood? Research indicates that they do (Galambos, Howard, & Maggs, 2011). A research review concluded that approximately 70 percent of college students do not get adequate sleep and 50 percent report daytime sleepiness (Hershner & Chervin, 2015). Also, in one study, the weekday bedtimes and rise times of first-year college students were approximately 1 hour and 15 minutes later than those of seniors in high school (Lund & others, 2010). However, the first-year college students had later bedtimes and rise times than third- and fourth-year college students, indicating that at about 20 to 22 years of age, a reversal in the timing of bedtimes and rise times occurs. In this study, poor-quality sleep was linked to worse physical and mental health, and the students reported that emotional and academic stress negatively affected their sleep.

Other recent research provides further insight into emerging adult sleep problems. A recent study of college students indicated that shorter sleep duration was associated with increased suicide risk (Becker & others, 2018a). In another recent study of college students, 27 percent described their sleep as poor and 36 percent reported getting 7 hours or less of sleep per night (Becker & others, 2018b). Further, in yet another recent study of college students, a higher level of text messaging (greater number of daily texts, awareness of nighttime cell phone notifications, and compulsion to check nighttime notifications) was linked to a lower level of sleep quality (Murdock, Horissian, & Crichlow-Ball, 2017). And in a recent experimental study, emerging adults (mean age: 21.9 years) who were given a brief sleep quality intervention reported improved sleep, stopped using electronic devices earlier, kept a more regular sleep schedule, and had an earlier weekday rise time than a control group who did not receive the intervention (Hershner & O'Brien, 2018).

ADULTHOOD AND AGING

Young people are not the only ones who are getting inadequate sleep. Many adults don't get enough either. A statement by the American Academy of Sleep Medicine and Sleep Research Society (Luyster & others, 2012) emphasized that chronic sleep deprivation may contribute to cardiovascular disease and a shortened life span, and also result in impaired cognitive and motor skills that increase the risk of motor vehicle crashes and work-related accidents. A study found that chronic sleep deprivation (regularly getting less than 7 hours of sleep in a 24-hour period) was linked to slow reactions to stimuli and increased vehicle crash risk (AAA Foundation, 2016). Drivers reporting 4 to 5 hours of sleep in a 24-hour period were 5.4 times more likely to have a vehicle crash.

The average American adult gets just under seven hours of sleep a night. How much sleep do adults need to function optimally the next day? Research indicates that when older adults sleep less than 7 hours or more than 9 hours a night, their cognitive functioning is harmed (DeVore, Grodstein, & Schemhammer, 2016; Lo & others, 2016). In another study, older adults who slept 9 hours or more a day had lower cognitive functioning (Malek-Ahmadi & others, 2016). In an analysis of sleep patterns from 20 to 90 years of age, total sleep for males decreased about 8 minutes per decade for males and about 10 minutes per decade for females as they got older (Dorffner, Vitr, & Anderer, 2015). Also in this study, as individuals aged, they engaged in more light sleep and less deep sleep. Beginning in the forties, wakeful periods are more frequent and there is less of the deepest type of sleep. The amount of time spent lying awake in bed at night begins to increase in middle age, which can produce a feeling of being less rested in the mornings (Abbott, 2003). Sleep problems in middle-aged adults are more common among individuals who take a higher number of prescription drugs, are obese, have cardiovascular disease, or are depressed (Miner & Kryger, 2017).

Beginning in middle adulthood and continuing through late adulthood, the timing of sleep also changes. Many older adults go to bed earlier at night and wake up earlier in the morning (Liu & Liu, 2005). Many older adults also take a nap in the afternoon.

Approximately 50 percent of older adults complain of having difficulty sleeping (Neikrug & Ancoli-Israel, 2010). Poor sleep can result in falls, obesity, earlier death, and a lower level of cognitive functioning (Miner & Kryger, 2017; Onen & Onen, 2018). For example, a study of healthy older adults revealed that daytime napping and getting 6½ hours of sleep or more were associated with a lower risk of cognitive decline over a 10-year period (Keage & others, 2012).

Many of the sleep problems of older adults are associated with health problems (Brewster, Riegel, & Gehrman, 2018; Li, Vitiello, & Gooneratne, 2018; Miner & Kryger, 2017). For example, one study found that middle-aged adults who sleep less than six hours a night on average had an increased risk of developing stroke symptoms (Ruiter & others, 2012).

The following strategies can help older adults sleep better at night: avoid caffeine, avoid over-the-counter sleep remedies, stay physically active during the day, stay mentally active, and limit naps. Supporting the benefits of physical activity, one study of older adults indicated that walking at or above the internationally recommended level of 150 minutes per week predicted a lower likelihood of sleep onset or sleep maintenance problems four years later (Hartescu, Morgan, & Stevinson, 2016). And a recent Chinese study revealed that older adults who engaged in a higher level of overall physical activity, leisure-time exercise, and household activity were less likely to have sleep problems (Li & others, 2018).

Review Connect Reflect

 LG3 Summarize how sleep patterns change as people develop.

Review

- Why do people sleep?
- How can sleep be characterized in infancy?
- What changes occur in sleep during childhood?
- How does sleep change in adolescence and emerging adulthood?
- What changes in sleep take place during adulthood and aging?

Connect

- How might behavioral theory be applied to help older adults avoid difficulty in sleeping?

Reflect *Your Own Personal Journey of Life*

- How much sleep do you get on a typical night? Do you get enough sleep to function optimally the next day? Explain.

4 Longevity and Biological Aging

 LG4 Explain longevity and the biological aspects of aging.

Life Expectancy and Life Span | Centenarians | Biological Theories of Aging

How long do most people live, and what distinguishes people who live a very long time? What is it like to live to a very ripe old age, and why do we age in the first place?

LIFE EXPECTANCY AND LIFE SPAN

We are no longer a youthful society. As more individuals live to older ages, the proportion of individuals at different ages has become increasingly similar. Indeed, the concept of a period called "late adulthood" is a recent one—until the twentieth century, most individuals died before they reached 65. A much greater percentage of persons live to older ages today. However, the life span has remained virtually unchanged since the beginning of recorded history. **Life span** is the upper boundary of life, the maximum number of years an individual can live. The maximum life span of humans is approximately 120 to 125 years of age.

Life expectancy is the number of years that the average person born in a particular year will probably live. The average life expectancy of individuals born today in the United States is 79 years (U.S. Census Bureau, 2018). Sixty-five-year-olds in the United States today can expect to live an average of 19.5 more years (20.6 for females, 18.4 for males) (U.S. Department of Health and Human Services, 2017). Older adults who are 100 years of age can only expect to live an average of 2.3 years longer (U.S. Census Bureau, 2011). Keep in mind that it is not just improvements in the health and well-being of adults that have contributed to increased longevity but also the substantial reduction in infant deaths in recent decades.

To me old age is always fifteen years older than I am.

—BERNARD BARUCH
American Statesman, 20th Century

life span The upper boundary of life, which is the maximum number of years an individual can live. The maximum life span of humans is about 120 years of age.

How does the United States fare in life expectancy, compared with other countries around the world? We do considerably better than some and somewhat worse than others. In 2018, Monaco had the highest estimated life expectancy at birth (89.4 years), followed by Japan, Singapore, and Macau (a region of China near Hong Kong) (85 years) (Geoba, 2019). Of 224 countries, the United States ranked 53rd at 79.2 years. The lowest estimated life expectancy in 2018 occurred in the African countries of South Africa (50.6), Chad (51), and Namibia (51). Differences in life expectancies across countries are due to factors such as health conditions and medical care throughout the life span.

In a recent analysis, projections of life expectancy in 2030 were made for 35 developed countries (Kontis & others, 2017). It was predicted that life expectancy in the United States would increase to 83.3 years for women and 79.5 years for men by 2030. However, although the United States is expected to increase in life expectancy, it had one of the lowest growth rates in life expectancy for all the countries in the study. South Korea is projected to have the highest life expectancy in 2030 with South Korean women predicted to have an average life expectancy of 90.8, the first nation to break the 90-year life expectancy barrier. What explains the lower growth in life expectancy for the United States and the very high growth for South Korea? The United States has the highest child and maternal mortality rates, homicide rate, and body-mass index of high-income countries in the world. In South Korea, delayed onset of chronic diseases is occurring and children's nutrition is improving. South Korea also has a low rate of obesity, and blood pressure is not as high as it is in most countries.

Life expectancy also differs for various ethnic groups within the United States and for men and women. For example, in 2014 the life expectancy of African Americans (73.1 years) in the United States was 7.2 years lower than the life expectancy for Latinos (80.3 years) and 5.7 years lower than for non-Latino Whites (78.8 years) (U.S. Department of Health and Human Services, 2017). The ethnicity difference in life expectancy has been widening in recent years, likely because of the powerful influence of education. Some experts argue that catch-up may not be possible (Olshansky & others, 2012).

In 2017, the overall life expectancy for women was 81 years of age, and for men it was 77 years of age (U.S. Census Bureau, 2018). Beginning in the mid-thirties, females outnumber males; this gap widens during the remainder of the adult years. By the time adults are 75 years of age, more than 61 percent of the population is female; for those 85 and over, the figure is almost 70 percent female. Why can women expect to live longer than men? Social factors such as health attitudes, habits, lifestyles, and occupations are probably important (Saint Onge, 2009). For example, men are more likely than women to die from the leading causes of death in the United States, such as cancer of the respiratory system, motor vehicle accidents, cirrhosis of the liver, emphysema, and coronary heart disease (especially stroke) (Alfredsson & others, 2018). These causes of death are associated with lifestyle. For example, the sex difference in deaths due to lung cancer and emphysema occur because men tend to be heavier smokers than women. However, women are more likely than men to die from Alzheimer disease and some aspects of cardiovascular disease, such as hypertension-related problems (Ostan & others, 2016).

The sex difference in longevity also is influenced by biological factors (Alfredsson & others, 2018). In virtually all species, females outlive males. Women have more resistance to infections and degenerative diseases (Pan & Chang, 2012). For example, the female's estrogen production helps to protect her from hardening of the arteries. And the additional X chromosome that women carry in comparison with men may be associated with the production of more antibodies to fight off disease. In 1979, the sex difference in longevity favored women by 7.8 years, but in 2013 the difference was down to 4.8 years (U.S. Department of Health and Human Services, 2015).

Comstock/PunchStock

To be seventy years young is sometimes far more cheerful and hopeful than to be forty years old.

—OLIVER WENDELL HOLMES, SR.
American Physician, 19th Century

CENTENARIANS

In industrialized countries, the number of centenarians (individuals 100 years and older) is increasing at a rate of approximately 7 percent each year (Perls, 2007). In the United States, there were only 15,000 centenarians in 1980, but that number rose to 50,000 in 2000 and to 72,000 in 2014 (Xu, 2016). The number of U.S. centenarians is projected to reach 600,000 by 2050 (U.S. Census Bureau, 2011). The United States has the most centenarians, followed by Japan, China, and England/Wales (Goodman, 2019). It is estimated that there are 75 to 100 supercentenarians (individuals 110 years or older) in the United States and about 300 to 450 worldwide (Perls, 2007).

Three participants in the New England Centenarian Study: *(Left)* At 107 years of age, Agnes Fenton of Englewood, New Jersey, said she didn't feel any older than when she was 15. She still cooked her own meals and her only health complaint was arthritis in her hand. *(Center)* Louis Carpenter, age 99, lived in the Boston area and every day carved wooden figures in his basement shop. Louis said his memory was still terrific. *(Right)* Edythe Kirchmaier of the New York City area was Facebook's oldest user at 105 years of age. As of July 2014, Edythe had more than 51,000 Facebook followers! She volunteered every week at her favorite charity, still drove her car, and frequently used the Internet to look up information.
(Left): Carmine Galasso/The Record/MCT/Newscom; *(center):* Courtesy of the New England Centenarian Study, Boston University; *(right):* Isaac Hernandez

Many people expect that "the older you get, the sicker you get." However, researchers are finding that this is not true for some centenarians (Anderson & others, 2019; Revelas & others, 2018; Robine, 2019; Willcox, Scapagnini, & Willcox, 2014). The researchers have found that chronic high-mortality diseases are markedly delayed for many years in centenarians, with many not experiencing disability until near the end of their lives (Ismail & others, 2016; Sebastiani & Perls, 2012). And a study of centenarians from 100 to 119 years of age found that the older the age group (110 to 119 compared with 100 to 104, for example), the later the onset of diseases such as cancer and cardiovascular disease, as well as functional decline (Andersen & others, 2012). The research just described was conducted as part of the ongoing New England Centenarian Study.

In addition to the New England Centenarian study, another major ongoing study is the Georgia Centenarian study conducted by Leonard Poon and his colleagues (Cho & others, 2019; Lee, Martin, & Poon, 2017; Lee & others, 2018; Lockhart & others, 2017; Nakagawa & others, 2019; Poon & others, 2010, 2012; Toyoshima & others, 2018). In a research review, Poon and his colleagues (2010) concluded that social dynamics involving life events (experiencing a higher number of negative life events is linked to lower self-rated health), personality (conscientiousness is positively associated with higher levels of physical and mental health), cognition (cognitive measures are better predictors of mental health than physical health), and socioeconomic resources and support systems (social, economic, and personal resources are related to mental and physical health) contribute to the health and quality of life of older adults, including centenarians. The Georgia Centenarian Study found that physical health impairment and fewer social resources were linked to lower subjective well-being (Cho & others, 2015). In another study, U.S. centenarians were more likely to talk about events related to marriage and children, while Japanese centenarians were more likely to describe historical events, death/grief, and work/retirement events (da Rosa & others, 2014). In a recent study of U.S. and Japanese centenarians, in both countries, health resources (better cognitive function, fewer hearing problems, and positive activities in daily living) were linked to a higher level of well-being (Nakagawa & others, 2018).

Yet another major study is the Chinese Longitudinal Healthy Longevity Survey, which includes older adults, some of whom are centenarians (An & others, 2019; Fong & Feng, 2018; Hu & others, 2019; Liu & others, 2018; Wang & others, 2018; Zhou, Wang, & Fang, 2018; Xiao, Wu, & Zeng, 2019; Xu & others, 2019). In one investigation involving this sample, Chinese centenarians showed better coping and adjustment (greater personal tenacity, optimism, coping with negative moods, secure relationships, and personal control) than their Chinese counterparts in their nineties, eighties, or seventies (Zeng & Shen, 2010). In this study, 94- to 98-year-olds with better resilience had a 43 percent higher likelihood of becoming a centenarian than their same-aged counterparts who were less resilient. In a Chinese Longitudinal Healthy Longevity study, a higher level of education was linked to greater longevity (Luo, Zhang, & Gu, 2015). And in another recent study with this sample, severe loneliness at prior assessment points predicted poorer cognitive function in subsequent assessments (Zhong & others, 2017).

How do centenarians view their lives? What are their explanations for being able to live so long?

- Elza Winn concludes that he has been able to live so long because he made up his mind to do so. He says he was thinking about dying when he was 77 but decided to wait awhile (Segerberg, 1982).

- Ruth Climer was a physical education teacher for many years and later competed in the Senior Olympics. To live to be 100, she says it is important to stay focused on what is good now and not give in to negative thoughts. Ruth also thinks staying busy and continually moving forward are keys to longevity (O'Dell, 2013).

- Misao Okawo, at 117 years of age, was the oldest person in the world in 2016, then died later that year. A resident of Osaka, Japan, she attributed her longevity to eating sushi, getting eight hours of sleep per night, and being able to relax.

- Gertrude Weaver, who at 116 years of age was the oldest person in the United States in 2016, lived in Arkansas and said her faith was what kept her alive. She was a wheelchair-dancing enthusiast for many years. (She died later in 2016.)

- Simo Radulovich thinks living to an old age requires having a sense of humor, living moderately, and sleeping well. He still engages in exercise games with his friends every day and says he never has been afraid of anything, always having the confidence to get through the tough times (O'Dell, 2013).

- Mary Butler says that finding something to laugh about every day helps you live longer. She thinks a good laugh is better than a dose of medicine anytime (Segerberg, 1982).

- Duran Baez remarried at 50 and went on to have 15 more children. At 100 years of age, he was asked if he had any ambitions he had not yet realized. Duran replied, "No" (Segerberg, 1982).

- Jeanne Louise Calment, a Frenchwoman, was the world's longest-living person. She died at 122 years of age in 1997 and attributed her longevity to a number of things. Among her comments as to why she was able to live so long are the following:

  – Don't worry about things you can't do anything about.
  – Have an occasional glass of Port wine and a diet rich in olive oil.
  – Keep a sense of humor.

Regarding her ability to live so long, she once said that God must have forgotten about her. On her 120th birthday, an interviewer asked her what kind of future she anticipated. She replied, "A very short one." Becoming accustomed to the media attention she got, at 117 she stated, "I wait for death . . . and journalists." She walked, biked, and exercised a lot. Jeanne Louise began taking fencing lessons at 85 and rode a bicycle until she was 100.

In 2019, the oldest living person in the world was 116-year-old Kane Tanaka of Japan. The oldest living person in the United States is 114-year-old Maggie Kidd, who lives in Georgia. Of the 36 oldest living centenarians in the world, 34 of them are women.

What chance do you have of living to be 100? Genes play an important role in surviving to an extreme old age (Toupance & Benetos, 2019). There is increasing interest in studying *susceptibility genes* (Patel & others, 2018; Park & others, 2018), which make an individual more vulnerable to specific diseases or acceleration of aging, and *longevity genes* (Blankenburg, Pramstaller, & Domingues, 2018), which make an individual less vulnerable to certain diseases and more likely to live to an older age. But as indicated in Figure 21, there are also other factors at work, such as family history, health (weight, diet, smoking, and exercise), education, personality, and lifestyle (Divo & others, 2018; Scott & others, 2018). The epigenetic approach focuses increasing interest on determining gene × environment (G × E) interactions that influence development (Hein & others, 2019; Kirkland & Meyer-Ficca, 2018). A Chinese study found that a combination of particular FOXO genotypes and drinking tea was associated with the prevention of cognitive decline in the oldest-old, aged 92+ (Zeng & others, 2016).

Nonetheless, most people are not biologically capable of living to be 100 (Bozek & others, 2017; Chapman & others, 2019).

Frenchwoman Jeanne Louise Calment, shown here celebrating her 117th birthday. Calment was the oldest documented living person. She lived to be 122 years of age.
Jean-Pierre Fizet/Sygma/Getty Images

Life Expectancy

This test gives you a rough guide for predicting your longevity. The basic life expectancy for men is age 75, and for women it is 81. Write down your basic life expectancy. If you are in your fifties or sixties, you should add ten years to the basic figure because you have already proved yourself to be a durable individual. If you are over age 60 and active, you can even add another two years.

Decide how each item applies to you and add or subtract the appropriate number of years from your basic life expectancy.

1. Family history
____ Add five years if two or more of your grandparents lived to 80 or beyond.
____ Subtract four years if any parent, grandparent, sister, or brother died of a heart attack or stroke before 50.
____ Subtract two years if anyone died from these diseases before 60.
____ Subtract three years for each case of diabetes, thyroid disorder, breast cancer, cancer of the digestive system, asthma, or chronic bronchitis among parents or grandparents.

2. Marital status
____ If you are married, add four years.
____ If you are over 25 and not married, subtract one year for every unmarried decade.

3. Economic status
____ Add two years if your family income is over $60,000 per year.
____ Subtract three years if you have been poor for the greater part of your life.

4. Physique
____ Subtract one year for every 10 pounds you are overweight.
____ For each inch your girth measurement exceeds your chest measurement deduct two years.
____ Add three years if you are over 40 and not overweight.

5. Exercise
____ Add three years if you exercise regularly and moderately (jogging three times a week).
____ Add five years if you exercise regularly and vigorously (long-distance running three times a week).
____ Subtract three years if your job is sedentary.
____ Add three years if your job is active.

6. Alcohol
____ Add two years if you are a light drinker (one to three drinks a day).
____ Subtract five to ten years if you are a heavy drinker (more than four drinks per day).
____ Subtract one year if you are a teetotaler.

7. Smoking
____ Subtract eight years if you smoke two or more packs of cigarettes per day.
____ Subtract two years if you smoke one to two packs per day.
____ Subtract two years if you smoke less than one pack.
____ Subtract two years if you regularly smoke a pipe or cigars.

8. Disposition
____ Add two years if you are a reasoned, practical person.
____ Subtract two years if you are aggressive, intense, and competitive.
____ Add one to five years if you are basically happy and content with life.
____ Subtract one to five years if you are often unhappy, worried, and often feel guilty.

9. Education
____ Subtract two years if you have less than a high school education.
____ Add one year if you attended four years of school beyond high school.
____ Add three years if you attended five or more years beyond high school.

10. Environment
____ Add four years if you have lived most of your life in a rural environment.
____ Subtract two years if you have lived most of your life in an urban environment.

11. Sleep
____ Subtract five years if you sleep more than nine hours a day.

12. Temperature
____ Add two years if your home's thermostat is set at no more than 68° F.

13. Health care
____ Add three years if you have regular medical checkups and regular dental care.
____ Subtract two years if you are frequently ill.

____ **Your Life Expectancy Total**

FIGURE **21**

CAN YOU LIVE TO BE 100?

BIOLOGICAL THEORIES OF AGING

Even if we stay remarkably healthy, we begin to age at some point. In fact, life-span experts argue that biological aging begins at birth (Schaie, 2000). What are the biological explanations of aging? Intriguing explanations of why we age are provided by these biological theories: evolutionary theory, genetic/cellular process theories, and hormonal stress theory.

Evolutionary Theory   In the evolutionary theory of aging, natural selection has not eliminated many harmful conditions and nonadaptive characteristics in older adults (Brooks & Garratt, 2017). Why? Because natural selection is linked to reproductive fitness, which is present only in the earlier part of adulthood (Laisk & others, 2019). For example, consider Alzheimer disease, an irreversible brain disorder that does not appear until late middle adulthood or beyond. In evolutionary theory, if Alzheimer disease had occurred earlier in development, it might have been eliminated many centuries ago. One criticism is that the "big picture" idea of natural selection leading to the development of human traits and behaviors is difficult to refute or test because evolution occurs on a time scale that does not lend itself to empirical study. Another criticism is the failure of evolutionary theory to account for cultural influences (Singer, 2016).

> ### developmental **connection**
> **Culture**
>
> In Baltes' view, the benefits of evolutionary selection decrease with age and the need for culture increases with age. Connect to "Biological Beginnings."

Genetic/Cellular Process Theories   Recent explanations of aging include cellular maintenance requirements and evolutionary constraints (Brunet & Rando, 2017). In recent decades, there has been a significant increase in research on genetic and cellular processes involved in aging (Falandry, 2019; Toupance & Benetos, 2019). Five such advances involve telomeres, free radicals, mitochondria, sirtuins, and the mTOR pathway.

Cellular Clock Theory   **Cellular clock theory** is Leonard Hayflick's (1977) theory that cells can divide a maximum of about 75 to 80 times and that over time our cells become less capable of dividing. Hayflick found that cells extracted from adults in their fifties to seventies divided fewer than 75 to 80 times. Based on the ways cells divide, Hayflick places the upper limit of the human life span at about 120 to 125 years of age.

In the last decade, scientists have tried to bridge a gap in cellular clock theory (Nene & others, 2018; Toupance & Benetos, 2019). Hayflick did not know why cells die. The answer may lie at the tips of chromosomes, at telomeres, which are DNA sequences that cap chromosomes (Gorenjak & others, 2018; Shay & Wright, 2019).

Each time a cell divides, the telomeres become shorter and shorter (Chang & Blau, 2018; Zhan & Hagg, 2019) (see Figure 22). After about 70 or 80 replications, the telomeres are dramatically reduced and the cell no longer can reproduce. One study revealed that healthy centenarians had longer telomeres than unhealthy centenarians (Terry & others, 2008). Further, a recent study confirmed that shorter telomere length was linked to Alzheimer disease (Scarabino & others, 2017). And researchers even have found that shorter telomere length is linked to having worse social relationships, being less optimistic, and showing greater hostility (Uchino & others, 2012; Zalli & others, 2015).

Injecting the enzyme *telomerase* into human cells grown in the laboratory can substantially extend the life of the cells beyond the approximately 70 to 80 normal cell divisions. However, telomerase is present in approximately 85 percent of cancerous cells and thus may not produce healthy life extension of cells (Cleal, Norris, & Baird, 2019). To capitalize on the high presence of telomerase in cancerous cells, researchers currently are investigating gene therapies that inhibit telomerase and lead to the death of cancerous cells while keeping healthy cells alive (de Vitis, Berardinelli, & Sgura, 2019; Shay & Wright, 2019). A recent focus of these gene therapies is on stem cells and their renewal (Li & Denchi, 2018; Ye, Yang, & Lei, 2019). Telomeres and telomerase are increasingly thought to be key components of the stem cell regeneration process, providing a possible avenue to restrain cancer and delay aging (Gunes, Avila, & Rudolph, 2018; Ullah & Sun, 2019).

Free-Radical Theory   A second genetic/cellular process theory of aging is **free-radical theory,** which states that people age because when cells metabolize energy, the by-products include unstable oxygen molecules known as free radicals. The free radicals ricochet around the cells, damaging DNA and other cellular structures (Jabeen & others, 2018; Vina, 2019). The damage can lead to a range of disorders, including cancer and arthritis (Phull & others, 2018). Overeating is linked with an increase in free radicals, and researchers recently have found that calorie restriction—a diet restricted in calories although adequate in proteins, vitamins, and minerals—reduces the oxidative damage created by free radicals (Wei & Ji, 2018). In addition to diet, researchers also are exploring the role that exercise might play in reducing oxidative damage in cells (Robinson & others, 2017).

Mitochondrial Theory   There is increasing interest in the role that mitochondria—tiny bodies within cells that supply energy for function, growth, and repair—might play in aging (Ahmadi, Golalipour, & Samaei, 2019) (See Figure 23.) **Mitochondrial theory** states that aging is due to the decay of mitochondria. It appears that this decay is primarily due to oxidative damage and loss of critical micronutrients supplied by the cell (Son & Lee, 2019).

How do oxidative damage and loss of nutrients occur? Among the by-products of mitochondrial energy production are the free radicals just described. According to the mitochondrial theory, the damage caused by free radicals initiates a self-perpetuating cycle in which oxidative damage causes impairment of mitochondrial function, which results in the generation of even greater amounts of free radicals (Panel, Ghaleh, & Morin, 2019). The mitochondrial damage may lead to a range of disorders, including cardiovascular disease (Roushandeh, Kuwahara, & Roudkenar, 2019), neurodegenerative diseases such as Alzheimer disease (Birnbaum & others, 2018), Parkinson disease (Zhi & others, 2019), diabetic kidney disease (Forbes & Thorburn, 2018), and impaired liver functioning (Borrelli & others, 2018).

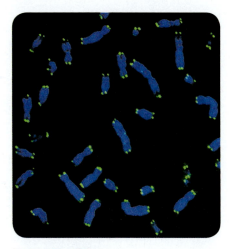

FIGURE 22

TELOMERES AND AGING. The photograph shows actual telomeres lighting up the tips of chromosomes.
Courtesy of Dr. Jerry Shay

FIGURE 23

MITOCHONDRIA. This color-coded illustration of a typical cell shows mitochondria in green. The illustration also includes the nucleus (pink) with its DNA (brown). *How might changes in mitochondria be involved in aging?*
J. Bavosi/Science Source

cellular clock theory Leonard Hayflick's theory that the number of times human cells can divide is about 75 to 80. As we age, our cells become less able to divide.

free-radical theory A microbiological theory of aging stating that people age because when their cells metabolize energy, they generate waste that includes unstable oxygen molecules, known as free radicals, that damage DNA and other structures.

mitochondrial theory The theory that aging is caused by the decay of the mitochondria, which are tiny cellular bodies that supply energy for cell function, growth, and repair.

Sirtuin Theory   **Sirtuins** are a family of proteins that have been linked to longevity, regulation of mitochondria functioning in energy, possible benefits of calorie restriction, stress resistance, and a lower incidence of cardiovascular disease and cancer (Fang, Tang, & Li, 2019; Min, Gao, & Yu, 2019). In another chapter, "Health," we will discuss one of the sirtuins, SIRT 1, that has been connected to DNA repair and aging.

mTOR Pathway Theory   The **mTOR pathway** is a cellular pathway that involves the regulation of growth and metabolism. TOR stands for "target of rapamycin," and in mammals it is called mTOR. Rapamycin is a naturally derived antibiotic and immune system suppressant/modulator, first discovered in the 1960s on Easter Island. It has been commonly used and is FDA approved for preventing rejection of transplanted organs and bone marrow. Recently, proposals have been made that the mTOR pathway plays a central role in the life of cells, acting as a cellular router for growth, protein production/metabolism, and stem cell functioning (Jin & others, 2019; Kraig & others, 2018). Some scientists also argue that the pathway is linked to longevity, the successful outcomes of calorie restriction, and reducing cognitive decline, and that it plays a role in a number of diseases, including cancer, cardiovascular disease, and Alzheimer disease (Maid & Power, 2018; Rostamzadeh & others, 2019). Rapamycin has not been approved as an anti-aging drug and has some serious side effects, including increased risk of infection and lymphoma, a deadly cancer. Some critics argue that scientific support for sirtuins and the mTOR pathway as key causes of aging in humans has not been found and that research has not adequately documented the use of drugs such as rapamycin to slow the aging process or extend the human life span (Ehninger, Neff, & Xie, 2014; Park, Mori, & Shimokawa, 2013).

Hormonal Stress Theory   The theories of aging that we have discussed so far attempt to explain aging at the evolutionary and genetic/cellular process levels. In contrast, **hormonal stress theory** argues that aging in the body's hormonal system can lower resistance to stress and increase the likelihood of disease.

When faced with external challenges such as stressful situations, the human body adapts by altering internal physiological processes (Steptoe & others, 2017; van Deurzen & Vanhoutte, 2019). This process of adaptation and adjustment is referred to as *allostasis*. Allostasis is adaptive in the short term; however, continuous accommodation of physiological systems in response to stressors may result in *allostatic load*, a wearing down of body systems due to constant activity (Piazza, Stawski, & Sheffler, 2019).

Normally, when people experience stressors, the body responds by releasing certain hormones. As people age, the hormones stimulated by stress remain at elevated levels longer than when they were younger (Finch, 2011; Gekle, 2017). These prolonged, elevated levels of stress-related hormones are associated with increased risks for many diseases, including cardiovascular disease, cancer, diabetes, and hypertension (Steptoe & others, 2017).

A variation of hormonal stress theory has emphasized the contribution of a decline in immune system functioning with aging (de la Fuente, 2019; Fulop & others, 2019). In a recent study, the percentage of T cells (a type of white blood cell essential for immunity) decreased in older adults in their seventies, eighties, and nineties (Song & others, 2018). Aging contributes to immune system deficits that give rise to infectious diseases in older adults (Le Page & others, 2018; Moura & others, 2019). The extended duration of stress and diminished restorative processes in older adults may accelerate the effects of aging on immunity. Researchers are exploring stress buffering strategies, including exercise, in an effort to find ways to attenuate some of the negative effects of stress on the aging process (Marquez-Gonzalez, Cheng, & Losada, 2019; Santacreu, Rodriguez & Molina, 2019).

Conclusions   Which of these biological theories best explains aging? That question has not yet been answered. It likely will turn out that more than one—or perhaps all—of these biological processes contribute to aging. In a research analysis, it was concluded that aging is a very complex process involving multiple degenerative factors, including interacting evolutionary, genetic/cellular, and organ/hormonal level communications (de Magalhaes & Tacutu, 2016). Although there are some individual aging triggers such as telomere shortening, a full understanding of biological aging involves multiple processes operating at different biological levels.

sirtuins A family of proteins that have been proposed as having important influences on longevity, mitochondrial functioning in energy, calorie restriction benefits, stress resistance, and cardiovascular functioning

mTOR pathway A cellular pathway that involves the regulation of growth and metabolism and has been proposed as a key aspect of longevity

hormonal stress theory The theory that aging in the body's hormonal system can lower resistance to stress and increase the likelihood of disease.

reach your **learning goals**

Physical Development and Biological Aging

1 Body Growth and Change

LG1 Discuss major changes in the body through the life span.

Patterns of Growth

Height and Weight in Infancy and Childhood

Puberty

Early Adulthood

Middle Adulthood

- Human growth follows cephalocaudal (fastest growth occurs at the top) and proximodistal patterns (growth starts at the center of the body and moves toward the extremities).

- Height and weight increase rapidly in infancy and then take a slower course during childhood.

- Puberty is a brain-neuroendocrine process occurring primarily in early adolescence that provides stimulation for the rapid physical changes that accompany this period of development.

- A number of changes occur in sexual maturation. The growth spurt involves rapid increases in height and weight and occurs about two years earlier for girls than for boys.

- Extensive hormonal changes characterize puberty. Puberty began occurring much earlier in the twentieth century mainly because of improved health and nutrition. The basic genetic program for puberty is wired into the nature of the species, but nutrition, health, and other environmental factors affect the timing of puberty.

- Adolescents show heightened interest in their bodies and body images. Younger adolescents are more preoccupied with these images than older adolescents. Adolescent girls often have a more negative body image than do adolescent boys.

- Early maturation often favors boys, at least during early adolescence, but as adults, late-maturing boys have a more positive identity than do early-maturing boys. Early-maturing girls are at risk for a number of developmental problems.

- In early adulthood, height remains rather constant. Many individuals reach their peak of muscle tone and strength in their late teens and twenties; however, their physical capacity may decline during their thirties.

- In middle adulthood, changes usually are gradual. Visible signs of aging, such as the wrinkling of skin, appear in the forties and fifties. Middle-aged individuals also tend to lose height and gain weight. Strength, joints, and bones show declines in middle age. The cardiovascular system declines in functioning, and lung capacity begins to decline, more so in smokers than nonsmokers.

- The climacteric is the midlife transition in which fertility declines. Menopause is the time in middle age, usually in the late forties or early fifties, when a woman has not had a menstrual period for a year. Men do not experience an inability to father children in middle age, although their testosterone level declines.

Late Adulthood

- In late adulthood, outwardly noticeable physical changes become more prominent, individuals get shorter, and weight often decreases because of muscle loss. The circulatory system declines further.

2 The Brain

LG2 Describe how the brain changes through the life span.

The Neuroconstructivist View

- This increasingly popular view of brain development states that biological processes and environmental conditions influence the brain's development; the brain has plasticity; and cognitive development is closely linked with brain development.

Brain Psychology

- The brain has two hemispheres, each of which has four lobes (frontal, occipital, temporal, and parietal).

- Throughout the brain, nerve cells called neurons process information. Communication among neurons involves the axon, dendrites, synapses, neurotransmitters, and the myelin sheath. Clusters of neurons, known as neural circuits, work together to handle specific types of information.

Infancy

- Researchers have found that early experience influences the brain's development. Myelination begins prenatally and continues after birth. In infancy, one of the most impressive changes in the brain is the enormous increase in dendrites and synapses. These connections between neurons are overproduced and then pruned. Specialization of functioning does occur in the brain's hemispheres, as in language, but for the most part both hemispheres are at work in most complex functions.

Childhood

- During early childhood, the brain and head grow more rapidly than any other part of the body. Researchers have found that dramatic anatomical changes in brain patterns occur from 3 to 15 years of age, often involving spurts of brain activity and growth.

Adolescence

- The corpus callosum, a large bundle of axon fibers that connects the brain's left and right hemispheres, thickens in adolescence, and this thickening improves the adolescent's ability to process information.

- The prefrontal cortex, the highest level of the frontal lobes that are involved in reasoning, decision making, and self-control, continues to mature through emerging adulthood or later.

- The amygdala, the part of the limbic system that is the seat of emotions such as anger, matures earlier than the prefrontal cortex. The later development of the prefrontal cortex combined with the earlier maturity of the amygdala may explain the difficulty adolescents have in putting the brakes on their emotional intensity.

Adulthood and Aging

- On average, the brain loses 5 to 10 percent of its weight between the ages of 20 and 90. Brain volume also decreases with aging. Shrinking occurs in some areas of the brain, such as the prefrontal cortex, more than in other areas.

- A general slowing of function of the central nervous system begins in middle adulthood and increases in late adulthood. A decline in the production of some neurotransmitters is related to aging.

- Neurogenesis has been demonstrated in lower mammals, but whether it occurs in human adults is still controversial. It appears that dendritic growth can occur in adults. The brain has the capacity to virtually rewire itself to compensate for loss in late adulthood. Brain lateralization usually decreases in older adults.

3 Sleep

LG3 Summarize how sleep patterns change as people develop.

Why Do We Sleep?

- A number of theories have been proposed about the functions of sleep, including evolutionary theory and sleep's role in survival; the role of sleep as a restorative function involving protein production and neural waste removal; and the role of sleep in brain plasticity. Sleep likely serves a number of important functions.

Infancy	• Newborns sleep about 16 to 17 hours a day. By about 4 months of age, most infants have sleep patterns similar to those of adults. REM sleep occurs more in infancy than in childhood and adulthood. A special concern is sudden infant death syndrome.
Childhood	• Most experts recommend that young children get 11 to 13 hours of sleep each night. Most young children sleep through the night and have one daytime nap. Inadequate sleep is linked to children's depression and attention problems. Children can experience a number of sleep problems.
Adolescence and Emerging Adulthood	• Many adolescents stay up later and sleep longer in the morning than they did when they were children. Recent interest focuses on biological explanations of these developmental changes in sleep during adolescence and their link to school success. Recent research indicates that a majority of first-year college students have sleep difficulties and that they go to bed even later and get up later than adolescents do. However, by the end of college they have begun to reverse this trend.
Adulthood and Aging	• An increasing concern is that adults do not get enough sleep. In middle age, wakeful periods may interrupt nightly sleep more often. Many older adults go to bed earlier and wake up earlier. Almost half of older adults report having some insomnia.

4 Longevity and Biological Aging Explain longevity and the biological aspects of aging.

Life Expectancy and Life Span	• Life expectancy is the number of years an individual is expected to live when he or she is born. Life span is the maximum number of years any member of a species has been known to live. On average, females live about five years longer than males do. The sex difference is likely due to biological and social factors. An increasing number of individuals live to be 100 or older.
Centenarians	• Heredity, family history, health, education, personality, and lifestyle are important factors in living to be a centenarian. The ability to cope with stress also is important.
Biological Theories of Aging	• The evolutionary theory of aging proposes that natural selection has not eliminated many harmful conditions and nonadaptive characteristics in older adults; thus, the benefits conferred by evolution decline with age because natural selection is linked to reproductive fitness.
	• One recent view is that aging is caused by a combination of cellular maintenance requirements and evolutionary constraints. Among the key genetic and cellular processes that have been proposed to explain aging are those involving telomeres, free radicals, mitochondria, sirtuins, and the mTOR pathway.
	• According to hormonal stress theory, aging in the body's hormonal system can lower resilience and increase the likelihood of disease.

key terms

amygdala	gonads	menarche	prefrontal cortex
cellular clock theory	hormonal stress	menopause	proximodistal
cephalocaudal pattern	theory	mitochondrial theory	pattern
climacteric	hormones	mTor pathway	puberty
corpus callosum	hypothalamus	myelination	sirtuins
estradiol	lateralization	neuroconstructivist view	sudden infant death
free-radical theory	life span	neurogenesis	syndrome (SIDS)
gonadotropins	limbic system	pituitary gland	testosterone

key people

Martha Ann Bell	Mona El-Sheikh	Mark Johnson	John Richards
Mary Carskadon	Leonard Hayflick	Charles Nelson	

chapter 4

HEALTH

chapter outline

① Health, Illness, and Disease

Learning Goal 1 Describe developmental changes in health.

Children's Health
Adolescents' Health
Emerging and Young Adults' Health
Health and Aging

② Nutrition and Eating Behavior

Learning Goal 2 Characterize developmental changes in nutrition and eating behavior.

Infancy
Childhood
Adolescence
Adult Development and Aging

③ Exercise

Learning Goal 3 Summarize the roles of exercise in child and adult health.

Childhood and Adolescence
Adulthood
Aging and Longevity

④ Substance Use

Learning Goal 4 Evaluate substance use in adolescence and adulthood.

Adolescence and Emerging Adulthood
Substance Use in Older Adults

Ariel Skelley/Getty Images

preview

Life is more than just existing. It is important to lead a healthy life. As we grow and develop through the life span, we have many opportunities to engage in health-enhancing or health-compromising behaviors, either by our choosing or because of the contexts provided by our caregivers. In this chapter, we will explore many aspects of health, including illness and disease, nutrition and eating behavior, exercise, and substance use.

Changing patterns of illness have fueled an interest in searching not just for biological causes of health, illness, and disease, but for psychological and sociocultural causes as well. With these multiple causes in mind, let's now examine changes in health throughout the life span.

CHILDREN'S HEALTH

Many factors affect children's health. In this chapter, we focus on two of the most important influences: prevention and poverty. We will also consider the health impact of immunization, accidents, and access to health care.

Prevention Although the dangers of many diseases for children have greatly diminished, it is still important for parents to keep their children on a timely immunization schedule (Fisker & Thysen, 2018; Robinson & others, 2019). The recommended ages for various immunizations are shown in Figure 1.

In addition to immunization, another important way to prevent health problems in children is to avoid accidents, which are the leading cause of death during childhood (Puodziuviene & others, 2018). Infants need close monitoring as they gain locomotor and manipulative skills along with a strong curiosity to explore their environment. Aspiration of foreign objects, suffocation, falls, poisoning, burns, and motor vehicle accidents are among the most common accidents in infancy (Moehrlen & others, 2018).

The status of children's motor, cognitive, and socioemotional development makes their health-care needs unique (Conover & Romero, 2018; Telljohann & others, 2020). For example, think about how the motor skills of infants and young children are inadequate to ensure their personal safety while riding in an automobile. Adults must take preventive measures to restrain infants and young children in car seats (Giannakakos, Vladescu, & Simon, 2018). Young children also lack the cognitive skills, including reading ability, to discriminate between safe and unsafe household substances. And they may lack the impulse control to stop themselves from running out into a busy street while chasing a ball or toy.

Caregivers play an important role in promoting children's health (Bauer & others, 2019; Onders & others, 2019). An increasing number of studies reach the conclusion that children are at risk for health problems when they live in homes where a parent smokes (Gatzke-Kopp & others, 2019; Neophytou & others, 2018). For example, children exposed to tobacco smoke in the home are more likely to develop wheezing symptoms and asthma than are children in homes where nobody smokes (Hatoun & others, 2018; Rosen & others, 2018). And a recent study found that young children who were exposed to environmental tobacco smoke were more likely to engage in antisocial behavior when they were 12 years old (Pagani & others, 2017). By driving at safe speeds, decreasing or eliminating drinking—especially before driving—and not smoking around children, caregivers can enhance their children's health and safety (Lepore & others, 2018; Wu & others, 2019).

Poverty Of special concern in the United States is the poor health of many young children from low-income families. An estimated 7 percent of U.S. children have no usual source of

Age	Immunization
Birth	Hepatitis B
2 months	Diphtheria Polio Influenza
4 months	Diphtheria Polio Influenza
6 months	Diphtheria Influenza
1 year	TB test
15 months	Measles Mumps Rubella Influenza
18 months	Diphtheria Polio
4 to 6 years	Diphtheria Polio
11 to 12 years	Measles Mumps Rubella
14 to 16 years	Tetanus-diphtheria

FIGURE 1

RECOMMENDED IMMUNIZATION SCHEDULE FOR INFANTS AND CHILDREN.

Many children in impoverished countries die before reaching the age of 5 from dehydration and malnutrition brought about by diarrhea. *What are some of the other main causes of death in young children around the world?*
Bojstudios/Shutterstock

developmental **connection**

Environment

Poverty is linked to many environmental inequities in childhood. Connect to "Peers and the Sociocultural World."

health care. Approximately 11 million preschool children in the United States are malnourished. Their malnutrition places their health at risk. Many have poor resistance to diseases—including minor ones, such as colds, and major ones, such as influenza.

What is the best way to improve the health of children who live in poverty? Some experts argue that offering medical care is not enough. If you give an antibiotic to a child with a sore throat who then returns to a home where she will be cold and hungry, have you provided good health care? One approach to children's health aims to treat not only medical problems of the individual child but also the conditions of the entire family. In fact, some programs seek to identify children who are at risk for problems and then try to alter the risk factors in an effort to prevent illness and disease (Kelleher, Reece, & Sandel, 2019; Meeks, Heit, & Page, 2020).

State of the World's Children Each year UNICEF produces a report titled *The State of the World's Children.* In recent reports, UNICEF (2018, 2019) emphasized the importance of information about the under-5 mortality rate of a nation. UNICEF concluded that the under-5 mortality rate is the result of a wide range of factors, including the nutritional health and health knowledge of mothers, the level of immunization, dehydration, availability of maternal and child health services, income and food availability in the family, availability of clean water and safe sanitation, and the overall safety of the child's environment.

In countries where poverty rates are high, the effects on children's health are devastating (UNICEF, 2018, 2019). The poor are the majority in nearly one of every five nations in the world. They often experience lives of hunger, malnutrition, illness, inadequate access to health care, unsafe water, and a lack of protection from harm (UNICEF, 2018, 2019; Zamora-Sarabia & others, 2019).

In recent decades, there has been a dramatic increase in the number of young children who have died because of HIV/AIDS transmitted to them by their parents (UNICEF, 2018, 2019). Deaths of young children due to HIV/AIDS especially occur in countries with high rates of poverty and low levels of education (Boyes & others, 2019). Many of the deaths of young children around the world could be prevented by reducing poverty and improving nutrition, sanitation, education, and health services (UNICEF, 2018, 2019).

ADOLESCENTS' HEALTH

Adolescence is a critical juncture for adopting behaviors that affect health (Akinsola & Petersen, 2018). Many of the factors linked to poor health habits and early death in the adult years begin during adolescence (Donatelle, 2019; Insel & Roth, 2020).

Social contexts, including families, peers, schools, neighborhoods, and culture, influence adolescent health (Epperson & others, 2019; James & others, 2018). Parents and older siblings can serve as important models of health-enhancing behaviors (Baker & others, 2019; Miller, Baptist, & Johannes, 2018). In the National Longitudinal Study of Health, which was based on data collected from more than 12,000 seventh- through twelfth-graders, youth who did not eat dinner with a parent five or more days a week had dramatically higher rates of smoking cigarettes, using marijuana, getting into fights, and initiating sexual activity (Council of Economic Advisors, 2000). Parental caring and monitoring often combine to improve health-enhancing behavior and reduce risk taking in youth (Bendezu & others, 2018; Lindsay & others, 2018). For example, a recent study found that a higher level of parental monitoring was linked to adolescents' healthier diet intake and lower weight status (Kim & others, 2019).

What are some influences on adolescents' health?
FatCamera/Getty Images

Peers also can influence adolescents' health (Vitaro, Boivin, & Poulin, 2018). Adolescents who have a limited capacity to resist dares often engage in risk taking at the urging of their peers. Peer pressure can instigate health-compromising behaviors such as cigarette smoking, substance abuse, early sexual activity, and violence (Prinstein & others, 2018). One study found that adolescents whose friends drank alcohol were more likely to binge drink in adolescence and early adulthood (Soloski, Kale Monk, & Durtschi, 2016).

Because adolescents spend so much time in school, it is not surprising that what goes on there can influence their health behavior. Teachers, like parents, can serve as important health role models.

Health experts increasingly recognize that whether adolescents will develop a health problem or be healthy depends primarily on their own behavior (Graham, Holt/Hale, & Parker, 2020; Hales, 2019). Improving adolescent health involves (1) reducing adolescents' health-compromising behaviors, such as drug abuse, violence, unprotected sexual intercourse, and dangerous driving; and (2) increasing health-enhancing behaviors, such as eating nutritious foods, exercising, and wearing seat belts.

developmental **connection**

Brain Development

Developmental changes in the adolescent's brain may be related to increased risk taking. Connect to "Physical Development and Biological Aging."

EMERGING AND YOUNG ADULTS' HEALTH

Emerging adults have more than twice the mortality rate of adolescents (Park & others, 2008) (see Figure 2). As indicated in Figure 2, males are mainly responsible for the higher mortality rate of emerging adults. Also, compared with adolescents, emerging adults engage in more health-compromising behaviors, have higher rates of chronic health problems, are more likely to be obese, and are more likely to have a mental health disorder (Hill, 2019; Irwin, 2010).

Why might emerging adults have higher levels of such health problems? The likely causes include increased independence, decreased parental monitoring, changing peer/friendship networks and living conditions that provide less support, and increased academic/financial pressures (Hill, 2019; Schulenberg & others, 2004).

Although emerging adults may know what it takes to be healthy, they often don't apply this information to their own behavior. In many cases, emerging adults are not as healthy as they seem.

In emerging and early adulthood, few individuals stop to think about how their personal lifestyles will affect their health later in their adult lives. As young adults, many of us develop a pattern of not eating breakfast, not eating regular meals and relying on snacks as our main food source during the day, eating excessively to the point where we exceed the normal weight for our height, smoking moderately or excessively, drinking moderately or excessively, failing to exercise, and getting by with only a few hours of sleep at night (Fahey, Insel, & Roth, 2019; Schiff, 2019). These lifestyles are associated with poor health, which in turn impairs life satisfaction (Donatelle & Ketcham, 2020). In some cases, unhealthy behavior increases as individuals go

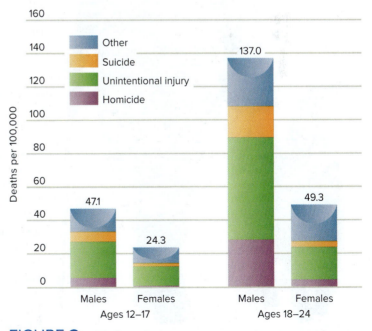

FIGURE **2**

MORTALITY RATES OF U.S. ADOLESCENTS AND EMERGING ADULTS

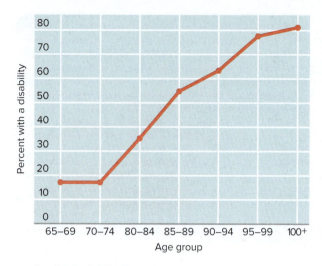

Note: Data for the 75 to 79 age group were unavailable.

FIGURE 3

PERCENTAGE OF U.S. OLDER ADULTS OF DIFFERENT AGES WHO HAVE A DISABILITY

What characterizes osteoporosis? What are some strategies for reducing the severity of osteoporosis?
Apple Tree House/Photodisc/Getty Images

through college. For example, a study found that rates of being overweight or obese increased from 25.6 percent for college freshmen to 32 percent for college seniors (Nicoteri & Miskovsky, 2014). Also, in the Berkeley Longitudinal Study—in which individuals were evaluated over a period of 40 years—physical health at age 30 predicted life satisfaction at age 70, more so for men than for women (Mussen, Honzik, & Eichorn, 1982).

HEALTH AND AGING

Aging can bring new health problems, such as Alzheimer disease. Keep in mind, though, that many older adults are healthy (Fernandez-Ballesteros, Benetos, & Robine, 2019). For example, only 17 percent of U.S. adults from 65 to 74 years of age have a disability. As shown in Figure 3, the percentage of Americans without a disability remains above 50 percent until they reach 85 years and older.

Chronic Disorders   **Chronic disorders** are characterized by a slow onset and long duration. Chronic disorders are rare in early adulthood, increase in middle adulthood, and become common in late adulthood.

The most common chronic disorders in middle age differ for females and males (Shlyakhto, 2018). The most common chronic disorders in middle adulthood for U.S. women, in order of prevalence, are arthritis, hypertension, and sinus problems; the most common ones for U.S. men are hypertension, arthritis, hearing impairments, and heart disease. Men have a higher incidence of fatal chronic conditions (such as coronary heart disease, cancer, and stroke); women have a higher incidence of nonfatal ones (such as sinus problems, varicose veins, and bursitis). Older women have higher incidences of arthritis and hypertension and are more likely to have visual problems, but they are less likely to have hearing problems than older men are.

Nearly 60 percent of U.S. adults 65 to 74 years of age die of cancer or cardiovascular disease (Center for Health Statistics, 2018). Cancer has replaced cardiovascular disease as the leading cause of death in U.S. middle-aged adults (Heron, 2013). The same realignment of causes of death has also occurred in 65- to 74-year-olds, with cancer now the leading cause of death in this age group (Center for Health Statistics, 2018). The decline in cardiovascular disease in middle-aged and older adults has been attributed to improved drugs, decreased rates of smoking, improved diets, and increased exercise (Benetos & others, 2019; Nowson & others, 2018).

However, in the 75-to-84 and 85-and-over age groups, cardiovascular disease still is the leading cause of death (Center for Health Statistics, 2018). As individuals age through the late adult years, the older they are the more likely it becomes that they will die of cardiovascular disease rather than cancer.

Even when adults over the age of 65 have a physical impairment, many of them can still carry on their everyday activities or work. Chronic conditions associated with the greatest limitation on work are heart conditions (52 percent), diabetes (34 percent), asthma (27 percent), and arthritis (27 percent).

Arthritis—an inflammation of the joints accompanied by pain, stiffness, and movement problems—is the most common chronic disorder in older adults (Paterson & Gates, 2019; Senthelal & Thomas, 2018). There is no known cure for arthritis, but the symptoms can be treated with drugs such as aspirin, range-of-motion exercises, weight reduction, and in extreme cases, replacement of the crippled joint with a prosthesis (Messier & others, 2018; Szekanecz & others, 2019). Recent research has documented the benefits of exercise for older adults with arthritis (Allen & others, 2018; Tan & others, 2019).

Normal aging involves some loss of bone tissue from the skeleton. However, in some instances loss of bone tissue can become severe. **Osteoporosis** involves an extensive loss of bone tissue. Osteoporosis is the main reason many older adults walk with a marked stoop (Fougere & Cesari, 2019). Women are especially vulnerable to osteoporosis, which is the leading cause of broken bones in women (Madrasi & others, 2018). Approximately 80 percent of osteoporosis cases in the United States occur in females, 20 percent in males. Almost two-thirds of all women over the age of

60 are affected by osteoporosis. This aging disorder is most common in non-Latina White, thin, and small-framed women.

Osteoporosis is related to deficiencies in calcium, vitamin D, and estrogen, as well as lack of exercise (Lewiecki, Binkley, & Bilezikian, 2019). To prevent osteoporosis, young and middle-aged women should eat foods rich in calcium, exercise regularly, and avoid smoking (Varahra & others, 2018).

Health problems that accompany aging also can involve neurological disorders. Next, we examine a neurological disorder in aging that has dramatically increased in recent decades—Alzheimer disease.

Alzheimer Disease **Dementia** is a global term for any neurological disorder in which the primary symptoms involve a deterioration of mental functioning. Individuals with dementia often lose the ability to care for themselves and can become unable to recognize familiar surroundings and people, including family members (Brown & Wolf, 2018; Serrano-Pozo & Growdon, 2019). Dementia is a broad category, and it is important to identify the specific cause of a person's deteriorating mental functioning (Dooley, Bass, & McCabe, 2018).

One form of dementia is **Alzheimer disease**—a progressive, irreversible brain disorder that is characterized by a gradual deterioration of memory, reasoning, language, and eventually, physical function. In 2018, an estimated 5.7 million adults in the United States had Alzheimer disease, and it has been projected that 10 million baby boomers will develop Alzheimer disease in their lifetime (Alzheimer's Association, 2018). Ten percent of individuals 65 and older have Alzheimer disease. The percentage of individuals with Alzheimer disease increases dramatically with age: 3 percent aged 65 to 74, 17 percent aged 75 to 84, and 32 percent aged 85 and older (Alzheimer's Association, 2018).

Women are more likely than men to develop Alzheimer disease because they live longer than men and their longer life expectancy increases the number of years during which they can develop it. It is estimated that Alzheimer disease triples the health-care costs of Americans 65 years of age and older (Alzheimer's Association, 2018). Because of the increasing prevalence of Alzheimer disease, researchers have stepped up their efforts to discover the causes of the disease and to find more effective ways to treat it (Di Domenico & others, 2018; Falandry, 2019).

Causes Alzheimer disease involves a deficiency in the brain messenger chemical acetylcholine, which plays an important role in memory (Guest, 2019; Kumar & others, 2018). Also, as Alzheimer disease progresses, the brain shrinks and deteriorates (see Figure 4). This deterioration is characterized by the formation of *amyloid plaques* (dense deposits of

chronic disorders Disorders characterized by slow onset and long duration.

osteoporosis A disorder that involves an extensive loss of bone tissue and is the main reason many older adults walk with a marked stoop. Women are especially vulnerable to osteoporosis.

dementia A global term for any neurological disorder in which the primary symptom is deterioration of mental functioning.

Alzheimer disease A progressive, irreversible brain disorder characterized by a gradual deterioration of memory, reasoning, language, and eventually, physical function.

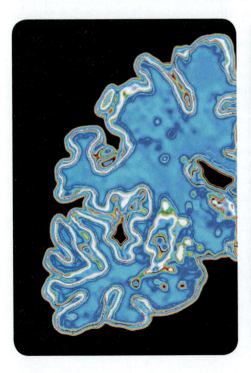
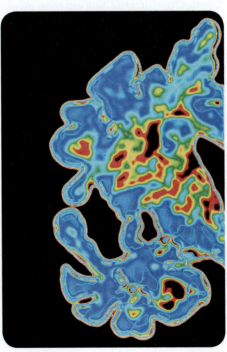

FIGURE 4

TWO BRAINS: NORMAL AGING AND ALZHEIMER DISEASE. The computer graphic on the left shows a slice of a normal aging brain, while the photograph on the right shows a slice of a brain ravaged by Alzheimer disease. Notice the deterioration and shrinking in the diseased brain.
Alfred Pasieka/Science Source

protein that accumulate in the blood vessels) (Gong & others, 2019; Morbelli & Baucknecht, 2018) and *neurofibrillary tangles* (twisted fibers that build up in neurons) (Santos & others, 2019; Villemagne & others, 2018). Neurofibrillary tangles consist mainly of a protein called *tau* (Franzmeier & others, 2019; Kuznetsov & Kuznetsov, 2018). Currently, there is considerable research interest in the roles that amyloid and tau play in Alzheimer disease (Rabinovici, 2019).

There is increasing interest in the role that oxidative stress might play in the development of Alzheimer disease (Butterfield, 2018; Yeung & others, 2019). Oxidative stress occurs when the body's antioxidant defenses are unable to cope with free-radical attacks and oxidation in the body (Feltosa, 2018). Recall from the chapter on "Physical Development and Aging" that free-radical theory is one of the major explanations of the aging process.

Although scientists have not identified the specific causes of Alzheimer disease, age is an important risk factor and genes also are likely to play an important role (Onojighofia Tobore, 2019; Park & Festini, 2018). The number of individuals with Alzheimer disease doubles every five years after the age of 65. A gene called *apolipoprotein E (ApoE)* is linked to an increasing presence of plaques and tangles in the brain. Special attention has focused on the presence of an allele (an alternative form of a gene) labeled ApoE4 that has been identified as a strong risk factor for Alzheimer disease (Akhter & Bekris, 2019; Chen & others, 2018; Roda, Montoliu-Gaya, & Villegas, 2019). More than 60 percent of individuals with Alzheimer disease have at least one ApoE4 allele (Dubal & Rogine, 2017). Also, women are more likely than men to have the ApoE4 gene (Dubal & Rogine, 2017).

Despite links between the presence of the ApoE4 allele and Alzheimer disease, less than 50 percent of the individuals who are carriers of the ApoE4 allele develop dementia in old age. Knowledge gained from the Human Genome Project has recently resulted in identification of additional genes that are risk factors for Alzheimer disease, although they are not as strongly linked to the disease as the ApoE4 allele (Shi & others, 2017). APP, PSEN1, and PSEN2 also are gene mutations that are linked to early-onset Alzheimer disease (Carmona, Hardy, & Guerreiro, 2018).

Although individuals with a family history of Alzheimer disease are at greater risk than the general population, the disease is complex and likely to be caused by a number of factors, including lifestyle choices (Lindahl-Jacobsen & Christensen, 2019). Recently there has been increasing interest in how epigenetics may improve understanding of Alzheimer disease (Gangisetty, Cabrera, & Murugan, 2018; Smith & others, 2019). This interest especially has focused on DNA methylation, which we discussed in "Biological Beginnings." Recall that DNA methylation involves tiny atoms attaching themselves to the outside of a gene, a process that is increased through exercise and healthy diet but reduced by tobacco use (Bihagi, 2019). Thus, lifestyles likely interact with genes to influence Alzheimer disease (Kader, Ghai, & Maharaj, 2018; Lindahl-Jacobsen & Christensen, 2019).

Researchers are finding that healthy lifestyle factors may lower the risk of Alzheimer disease or delay the onset of the disease. For example, older adults with Alzheimer disease are more likely to have cardiovascular disease than are individuals who do not have Alzheimer disease (Silva & others, 2019; Wen & Wong, 2019). Recently, many cardiac risk factors have been implicated in Alzheimer disease—obesity, smoking, atherosclerosis, high cholesterol, and lipids (Falsetti & others, 2018; Sweeney & others, 2019). One of the best strategies for preventing or delaying the onset of Alzheimer disease in people who are at risk is to improve their cardiac functioning through diet, drugs, and exercise (Pedrinolla, Schena, & Venturelli, 2018; Serrano-Pozo & Growdon, 2019).

Early Detection Mild cognitive impairment *(MCI)* represents a transitional state between the cognitive changes of normal aging and very early Alzheimer disease and other dementias (Gasquoine, 2018; Venneri & others, 2019). MCI is increasingly recognized as a risk factor for Alzheimer disease. It is estimated that as many as 10 to 20 percent of individuals 65 years of age and older have MCI (Alzheimer's Association, 2018). Some individuals with MCI do not go on to develop Alzheimer disease, but MCI is a risk factor for Alzheimer disease (Cui & others, 2019).

Memory loss is a common characteristic of Alzheimer disease. Written reminders can help individuals with Alzheimer disease remember daily tasks.
Ingram Publishing

Distinguishing between individuals who merely have age-associated declines in memory and those with MCI is difficult, as is predicting which individuals with MCI will subsequently develop Alzheimer disease (G. Lee & others, 2019; Mendoza Laiz & others, 2018). One study revealed that individuals with mild cognitive impairment who developed Alzheimer disease had at least one copy of the ApoE4 allele (Alegret & others, 2014). In this study, the extent of memory impairment was the key factor linked to the speed of decline from mild cognitive impairment to Alzheimer disease.

Drug Treatment of Alzheimer Disease Five drugs have been approved by the U.S. Food and Drug Administration (FDA) for the treatment of Alzheimer disease (Almeida, 2018). Three of the medications, Aricept (donepezil), Razadyne (galantamine), and Exelon (rivastigmine), are cholinesterase inhibitors designed to improve memory and other cognitive functions by increasing levels of acetylcholine in the brain (Gareri & others, 2017). A fourth drug, Namenda (memantine), regulates the activity of glutamate, which is involved in processing information. Namzatric, a combination of memantine and donepezil, is the fifth approved medicine to treat Alzheimer disease; this medicine is designed to improve cognition and overall mental ability (Almeida, 2018). A research review concluded that cholinesterase inhibitors do not reduce progression to dementia from mild cognitive impairment (Masoodi, 2013). Also, keep in mind that the current drugs used to treat Alzheimer disease only slow the downward progression of the disease; they do not address its cause (Rajeshwari & others, 2019). Also, no drugs have yet been approved by the Food and Drug Administration (FDA) for the treatment of MCI (Alzheimer's Association, 2018).

Caring for Individuals with Alzheimer Disease A special concern is the stress involved in caring for Alzheimer patients (Alzheimer's Association, 2019; Wolff & others, 2018). Health-care professionals emphasize that the family can be an important support system for the Alzheimer patient, but this support can have costs for family members who become emotionally and physically drained from providing the extensive care required for a person with Alzheimer disease (C. L. White & others, 2018). One study compared family members' perceptions of caring for someone with Alzheimer disease, cancer, or schizophrenia (Papastavrou & others, 2012). In this study, the highest perceived burden was reported for Alzheimer disease.

Respite care (services that provide temporary relief for those who are caring for individuals with disabilities or illnesses) can ease the stress experienced by people who have to meet the day-to-day needs of Alzheimer patients. This type of care provides an important break from the burden of providing chronic care (Riekkola & others, 2019; Wolff & others, 2018). One study confirmed that family caregivers' health-related quality of life in the first three years after they began caring for a family member with Alzheimer disease deteriorated more than their same-age and same-gender counterparts who were not caring for an Alzheimer patient

developmental **connection**

Memory

A number of changes in memory occur in late adulthood. Connect to "Information Processing."

A wife feeding her husband who has Alzheimer disease. *What are some concerns about the family caregivers of individuals with Alzheimer disease?*
©Ray Chavez/MCT/Landov

How Stressful Is Caring for an Alzheimer Patient at Home?

Researchers have found that the stress of caring for an Alzheimer patient at home can prematurely age the immune system, putting caregivers at risk for developing age-related diseases (Chiu, Wesson, & Sadavoy, 2014; Glaser & Kiecolt-Glaser, 2005; Kiecolt-Glaser & Wilson, 2017; Wilson & others, 2019). In one study, 119 older adults who were caring for a spouse with Alzheimer disease or another form of dementia (which can require up to 100 hours a week) were compared with 106 older adults who did not have to care for a chronically ill spouse (Kiecolt-Glazer & others, 2003). The age of the older adults upon entry into the study ranged from 55 to 89, with an average age of 70.

Periodically during the six-year study, blood samples were taken and the levels of a naturally produced immune chemical called interleukin-6, or IL-6, were measured. IL-6 increases with age and can place people at risk for a number of illnesses, including cardiovascular disease, type 2 diabetes, frailty, and certain cancers. The researchers found that the levels of IL-6 increased much faster in the Alzheimer caregivers than in the older adults who did not have to care for a critically ill spouse (see Figure 5).

Each time IL-6 was assessed by drawing blood, the participants also completed a 10-item perceived stress scale to assess the extent to which they perceived their daily life during the prior week as being "unpredictable, uncontrollable, and overloading" (Kiecolt-Glazer & others, 2003, p. 9091). Participants rated each item from 0 (never) to 4 (very often). Alzheimer caregivers reported greater stress than the noncaregiver controls across each of the six annual assessments.

Since family members are especially important in helping Alzheimer patients cope, an important research agenda is to assess the benefits of respite care and to find additional ways to relieve the stress the disease can impose on others.

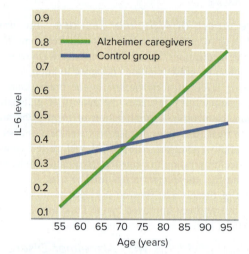

FIGURE 5

COMPARISON OF IL-6 LEVELS IN ALZHEIMER CAREGIVERS AND A CONTROL GROUP OF NONCAREGIVERS. Notice that IL-6 (an immune chemical that places individuals at risk for a number of diseases) increased for both the Alzheimer caregivers and a control group of noncaregivers. However, also note that IL-6 increased significantly more in the Alzheimer caregivers. A higher score for IL-6 reflects a higher level of the immune chemical.

What kinds of studies might help provide some answers? What challenges will researchers face in collecting data?

(Valimaki & others, 2016). To read further about individuals who care for Alzheimer patients, see the *Connecting with Research* interlude.

Parkinson Disease   Another type of dementia is **Parkinson disease,** a chronic, progressive disorder characterized by muscle tremors, slowing of movement, and partial facial paralysis. Parkinson disease is triggered by degeneration of dopamine-producing neurons in the brain (Foley, 2019; Goldstein & others, 2018). Dopamine is a neurotransmitter that is necessary for normal brain functioning. Why these neurons degenerate is not known.

The main treatment for Parkinson disease involves administering drugs that enhance the effect of dopamine (dopamine agonists) in the disease's earlier stages and later administering the drug L-dopa, which is converted by the brain into dopamine (Radhakrishnan & Goval, 2018; Trujillo & others, 2019). However, it is difficult to determine the correct dosage of L-dopa, and it loses its efficacy over time. Another treatment for advanced Parkinson disease is deep brain stimulation (DBS), which involves implanting electrodes in the brain (Krishnan & others, 2018). The electrodes are then stimulated by a pacemaker-like device. A recent research

Parkinson disease A chronic, progressive disease characterized by muscle tremors, slowing of movement, and partial facial paralysis.

review concluded that DBS improves motor function for up to 10 years in Parkinson patients, but improvement tends to decline over time (Limousin & Foltynie, 2019). Stem cell transplantation and gene therapy offer hope for the future in treating Parkinson disease (Mohamed & others, 2019; Parmar, 2019).

Stress and Disease   Stress is increasingly being identified as a factor in many diseases (Fulop & others, 2019; Yu & others, 2018). The cumulative effect of chronic stress often takes a toll on the health of individuals by the time they reach middle age (Dixon & Lachman, 2019; Leonard, 2018). One study of middle-aged adults found that when they had a high level of allostatic load (wearing down of the body's systems in response to high stress levels), their episodic memory and executive function were harmed (Karlamangla & others, 2013). And a study of occupationally active 44- to 58-year-olds revealed that perceived stress symptoms in midlife were linked to self-care disability and mobility limitations 28 years later (Kulmala & others, 2013). Margie Lachman and her colleagues (Agrigoroaei & others, 2019; Lachman, Agrigoroaei, & Hahn, 2016; Lachman, Neupert, & Agrigoroaei, 2011) argue that having a sense of control is one of the most important modifiable factors in reducing stress and delaying the onset of diseases in middle adulthood and reducing the frequency of diseases in late adulthood.

Chronic stressors have been linked to a downturn in immune system functioning in a number of contexts, including worries about living next to a damaged nuclear reactor, failures in close relationships (divorce, separation, and marital distress), depression, loneliness, and burdensome caregiving for a family member with progressive illness (Bennett, Fagundes, & Kiecolt-Glaser, 2016; Fagundes & others, 2016; Jaremka, Derry, & Kiecolt-Glaser, 2016; Kiecolt-Glazer, 2018; Kiecolt-Glazer, Wilson, & Madison, 2019; Wilson & others, 2019). One study discovered that chronic stress accelerated pancreatic cancer growth (Kim-Fuchs & others, 2014). Recent research indicates that stress-reducing activities such as yoga, relaxation, and hypnosis have positive influences on immune system functioning (Lurie, 2019).

How individuals react to stressors is linked to health outcomes. In one study, how people reacted to daily stressors in their lives was linked to future chronic health problems (Piazza & others, 2013). In another study, adults who did not maintain positive affect when confronted with minor stressors in everyday life had elevated levels of IL-6, an inflammation marker (Sin & others, 2016). And in yet another study, a greater decrease in positive affect in response to daily stressors was associated with earlier death (Mroczek & others, 2015).

Health Treatment for Older Adults   The development of alternative forms of home and community-based care has decreased the percentage of older adults who are living in nursing homes (Gardner & others, 2017). Still, as older adults age, their probability of being in a nursing home increases (see Figure 6). What is the quality of nursing homes and extended-care facilities for older adults? What is the relationship between older adults and health-care providers?

The quality of nursing homes and other extended-care facilities for older adults varies enormously and is a source of ongoing concern (Marshall & Hale, 2018; Ryskina, Lam, & Jung, 2019). More than one-third of these facilities are seriously deficient. They fail federally mandated inspections because they do not meet the minimum standards for physicians, pharmacists, and various rehabilitation specialists (occupational and physical therapists). Further concerns focus on protecting the patient's right to privacy, providing access to medical information, preventing inappropriate prescriptions, ensuring safety, and preserving lifestyle freedom within the individual's range of mental and physical capabilities (Stafford, Alswayan, & Tenni, 2010; Weech-Maldonado & others, 2019).

Because of the inadequate quality of many nursing homes and the escalating costs for nursing home care, many specialists in the health problems of the aged stress that home health care, elder-care centers, and preventive

Muhammad Ali, who was one of the world's leading sports figures, had Parkinson disease.
AP Images

developmental connection

Stress

A variation of hormonal stress theory identifies a decline in immune system functioning as an important contributor to lower resistance to stress in older adults. Connect to "Physical Development and Biological Aging."

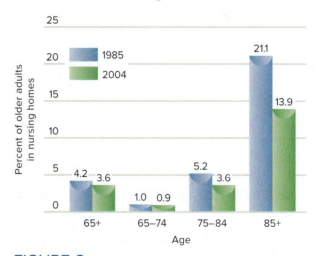

FIGURE 6

PERCENT OF U.S. OLDER ADULTS LIVING IN NURSING HOMES: 1985 TO 2004. *Note:* The calculations are based on the 1985 and 2004 National Nursing Home Survey (NNHS), National Center for Health Statistics.

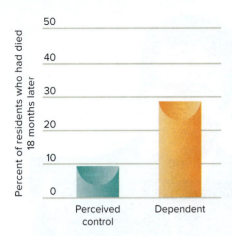

FIGURE 7

PERCEIVED CONTROL AND MORTALITY.
In the study by Rodin and Langer (1977), nursing home residents who were encouraged to feel more in control of their lives were more likely to be alive 18 months later than those who were treated as being more dependent on the nursing home staff.

medicine clinics are good alternatives (Rotenberg & others, 2018). They are potentially less expensive than hospitals and nursing homes. They also are less likely to engender the feelings of depersonalization and dependency that occur so often in residents of institutions. Currently, there is an increased demand for home-care workers because of the expanding population of older adults and their preference to stay in their own homes (Barooah & others, 2019l; Franzosa, Tsui, & Baron, 2018). In a study of elderly adults with cognitive impairment, those being cared for at home were less depressed, had better cognitive functioning, and reported a higher level of social connectedness than their counterparts experiencing formal institutional care (Nikmat, Al-Mashoor, & Hashim, 2015).

In a classic study that focused on the way older adults are cared for in nursing homes, Judith Rodin and Ellen Langer (1977) found that an important factor related to health, and even survival, in a nursing home is the patient's feelings of control and self-determination. A group of elderly nursing home residents were encouraged to make more day-to-day choices and thus feel they had greater control over their lives. They began to decide such matters as what they ate, when their visitors could come, what movies they saw, and who could come to their rooms. A similar group in the same nursing home was told by the administrator how caring the nursing home was and how much the staff wanted to help, but these elderly nursing home residents were given no opportunities to take more control over their lives. Eighteen months later, the residents who had been given responsibility and control were more alert and active, and said they were happier, than the residents who had been encouraged only to feel that the staff would try to satisfy their needs. And the "responsible" or "self-control" group had significantly better improvement in their health than did the "dependent" group. Even more important was the finding that after 18 months only half as many nursing home residents in the "responsibility" group had died as in the "dependent" group (see Figure 7). Perceived control over one's environment, then, can literally be a matter of life or death.

Review *Connect* Reflect

LG1 Describe developmental changes in health.

Review
- How can children's health be characterized?
- What is the nature of adolescents' health?
- What characterizes the health of emerging and young adults?
- How extensively does health decline in old age?

Connect
- What have you learned in earlier chapters about risk-taking behavior

that might help explain the attitudes that many young adults have toward their own health?

Reflect *Your Own Personal Journey of Life*
- What changes in your lifestyle right now might help you to age more successfully when you get older?

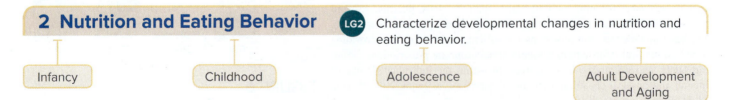

2 Nutrition and Eating Behavior

LG2 Characterize developmental changes in nutrition and eating behavior.

Infancy | Childhood | Adolescence | Adult Development and Aging

Nutritional needs, eating behavior, and related issues vary to some extent across the life span. Let's begin by exploring what takes place with infants.

INFANCY

For infants, the importance of receiving adequate energy intake and nutrients in a loving and supportive environment cannot be overstated (Rolfes, Pinna, & Whitney, 2018; Schiff, 2019). From birth to 1 year of age, human infants triple their weight and increase their length by 50 percent. Because infants vary in their nutrient reserves, body composition, growth rates, and activity patterns, their nutrient needs vary as well. However, because parents need guidelines, nutritionists recommend that infants consume approximately 50 calories per day for each pound they weigh—more than twice an adult's requirement per pound.

Caregivers play very important roles in infants' and young children's development of eating patterns (Baye, Tariku, & Mouquet-Rivier, 2019; Feldman-Winter & others, 2018; MacMillan Uribe, Woelky, & Olson, 2019). Caregivers who are not sensitive to developmental changes in infants' nutritional needs, neglectful caregivers, and conditions of poverty can contribute to the development of eating problems in infants (Kayle & others, 2019; Perez-Escamilla & Moran, 2017). One study found that low maternal sensitivity when infants were 15 and 24 months of age was linked to a higher risk of obesity in adolescence (Anderson & others, 2012).

Too many young children also already have developed a pattern of not eating enough fruits and vegetables, a pattern that can have negative consequences later in development. For example, a recent study revealed that 2½-year-old children's liking for fruits and vegetables was related to their eating more fruits and vegetables at 7 years of age (Fletcher & others, 2019).

Breast Versus Bottle Feeding   For the first four to six months of life, human milk or an alternative formula is the baby's source of nutrients and energy. For years, debate has focused on whether breast feeding is better for the infant than bottle feeding. The growing consensus is that breast feeding is better for the baby's health (Blake, Munoz, & Volpe, 2019; Schiff, 2019; Vieira & others, 2019). Since the 1970s, breast feeding by U.S. mothers has soared (see Figure 8). In 2016, 81 percent of U.S. mothers breast fed their newborns, and 52 percent breast fed their 6-month-olds (Centers for Disease Control and Prevention, 2016). The American Academy of Pediatrics Section on Breastfeeding (2012) reconfirmed its recommendation of exclusive breast feeding in the first six months followed by continued breast feeding as complementary foods are introduced, with further breast feeding for one year or longer as mutually desired by the mother and infant.

Outcomes of Breast Feeding for Children   What are some of the benefits of breast feeding for children, based on research?

- *Gastrointestinal infections.* Breast fed infants have fewer gastrointestinal infections (Bartick & others, 2017, 2019).
- *Lower respiratory tract infections.* Breast fed infants have fewer infections of the lower respiratory tract (Bartick & others, 2019).
- *Allergies.* A recent research review found no evidence that breastfeeding reduces the risk of allergies in young children (Heinrich, 2017).
- *Asthma.* Exclusive breast feeding for three months protects against wheezing in babies, but whether it prevents asthma in older children is unclear (Greer & others, 2008; J. Wang & others, 2019).
- *Otitis media.* Breast-fed infants are less likely to develop this middle ear infection (Pelton & Leibovitz, 2009).
- *Overweight and obesity.* Consistent evidence indicates that breast-fed infants are less likely to become overweight or obese in childhood, adolescence, and adulthood (Uwaezuoke, Eneh, & Ndu, 2019).
- *Diabetes.* Breast-fed infants are less likely to develop type 1 diabetes in childhood (Ping & Hagopian, 2006) and type 2 diabetes in adulthood (Villegas & others, 2008).
- *SIDS.* Breast-fed infants are less likely to experience SIDS (Wennergren & others, 2015).
- *Hospitalization.* Recent research found that breastfed infants had lower rates of hospitalization for a number of conditions, including gastrointestinal problems and lower respiratory tract infections (Bartick & others, 2019).

developmental **connection**

Conditions, Diseases, and Disorders
What characterizes SIDS? Connect to "Physical Development and Biological Aging."

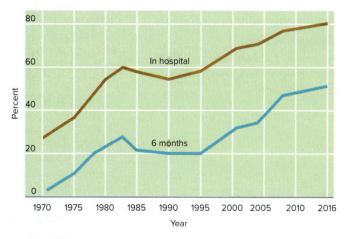

FIGURE 8

TRENDS IN BREAST FEEDING IN THE UNITED STATES: 1970–2016

Human milk or an alternative formula is a baby's source of nutrients for the first four to six months. The growing consensus is that breast feeding is better than bottle feeding for the baby's health, although controversy still surrounds the issue of breast feeding versus bottle feeding. *Why is breast feeding strongly recommended by pediatricians?*
Blend Images/Getty Images

A large-scale research review found no conclusive evidence that breast feeding improves children's cognitive development and cardiovascular functioning (Agency for Healthcare Research and Quality, 2007; Ip & others, 2009).

Outcomes of Breast Feeding for the Mother What are the outcomes of breast feeding for the mother, based on research?

- *Breast cancer.* Consistent evidence indicates a lower incidence of breast cancer in women who breast feed their infants (Bartick, 2017).
- *Ovarian cancer.* Evidence also reveals a reduction in ovarian cancer in women who breast feed their infants (Stuebe & Schwarz, 2010).
- *Type 2 diabetes.* Some evidence suggests a small reduction in type 2 diabetes in women who breast feed their infants (Bartick, 2017).
- *Hospitalization.* Recent research found that mothers who breast fed their babies had lower rates of hospitalization for cardiovascular problems and diabetes (Bartick & others, 2019).

Large-scale research reviews found no conclusive evidence that breast feeding accelerates the mother's return to prepregnancy weight, prevents osteoporosis, or prevents postpartum depression (Agency for Healthcare Research and Quality, 2007; Ip & others, 2009).

As mentioned previously, the American Academy of Pediatrics Section on Breastfeeding (2012) strongly endorses exclusive breast feeding through six months and further recommends breast feeding for another year. Are there circumstances when mothers should not breast feed? Yes, a mother should not breast feed (1) if she has HIV or some other infectious disease that can be transmitted through her milk; (2) if she has active tuberculosis; or (3) if she is taking any drug that may not be safe for the infant (Schultz, Kostic, & Kharasch, 2018).

Some women cannot breast feed their infants because of physical difficulties; others feel guilty if they terminate breast feeding early. Mothers may also worry that they are depriving their infants of important emotional and psychological benefits if they bottle feed rather than breast feed. Some researchers have found, however, that there are no psychological differences between breast-fed and bottle-fed infants (Fergusson, Horwood, & Shannon, 1987; Young, 1990).

A further issue in interpreting the benefits of breast feeding was underscored in a large-scale research review (Ip & others, 2009). While highlighting a number of breast feeding benefits for children and mothers, the report issued a caution about breast feeding research: None of the findings implies causality. Breast versus bottle feeding studies are correlational, not experimental, and women who breast feed tend to be wealthier, older, more educated, and likely more health-conscious than their bottle feeding counterparts—characteristics that could explain why breast-fed children are healthier.

Adequate early nutrition is an important aspect of healthy development (Perez-Escamilla & Engmann, 2019; Rolfes, Pinna, & Whitney, 2018). In addition to sound nutrition, children need a nurturing, supportive environment (Black & Hurley, 2017; Schiff, 2019). One individual who has stood out as an advocate of caring for children and who has been especially passionate about preventing child obesity is pediatrician Faize Mustafa-Infante, who is featured in *Connecting with Careers*.

developmental connection

Research Methods

How does a correlational study differ from an experimental study? Connect to "Introduction."

CHILDHOOD

Malnutrition continues to be a major threat to millions during the childhood years (Blake, Munoz, & Volpe, 2019). Malnutrition and starvation are a daily fact of life for children in many developing countries (UNICEF, 2018, 2019). One study revealed that two food-assisted maternal and child health programs (both of which emphasized food provision, communication about behavior change, and preventive health services) helped to reduce the impact of economic hardship on stunting of children's growth in Haiti (Donegan & others, 2010).

Poor nutrition also is a special concern in the lives of infants from low-income families in the United States (Donatelle & Ketcham, 2020). To address this problem, the WIC (Women, Infants, and Children) program provides federal grants to states for healthy supplemental foods, health-care referrals, and nutrition education for women from low-income families

Dr. Faize Mustafa-Infante, Pediatrician

Dr. Mustafa-Infante grew up in Colombia, South America. After completing her undergraduate education she taught elementary school students in Colombia for several years and then returned to college to obtain her medical degree with a specialty in pediatrics. Once she finished her medical training, she moved to San Bernardino, California, where she worked as a health educator with a focus on preventing and treating childhood obesity in low-income communities.

Dr. Mustafa-Infante currently works at Mission Pediatrics in Riverside, California, where she mainly treats infants. She has continued striving to prevent obesity in children and also serves as a volunteer for Ayacucho Mission, a nonprofit organization that provides culturally sensitive medical care for people living in poverty in Ayacucho, Peru.

In regard to her cultural background, Dr. Mustafa-Infante describes herself as a Latino doctor with a Middle-Eastern name that reflects her strong family commitments to both heritages. Dr. Mustafa-Infante says that hard work and education have been the keys to her success and personal satisfaction.

beginning in pregnancy, and to infants and young children up to 5 years of age who are at nutritional risk (Hamner & others, 2019; Lauer & others, 2019). WIC serves approximately 7,500,000 participants in the United States. In recent research, when mothers participated in WIC programs when they were pregnant and during their children's first few years, the children showed short-term cognitive benefits and longer-term reading and math benefits (L. W. Chen & others, 2018; Martinez-Brockman & others, 2018; McCoy & others, 2018).

Overweight Children   Being overweight has become a serious health problem in childhood (Insel & Roth, 2020). Exemplifying the eating habits of young children that contribute to being overweight, a study of U.S. 2- and 3-year-olds found that French fries and other fried potatoes were the vegetable they were most likely to consume (Fox & others, 2010). A survey of 34 countries revealed that the United States had the second highest rate of childhood obesity (Janssen & others, 2005).

The Centers for Disease Control and Prevention (2019) has established categories for obesity, overweight, and at risk of being overweight. These categories are determined by body mass index (BMI), which is computed by a formula that takes into account height and weight. Children and adolescents whose BMI is at or above the 97th percentile are classified as obese; those whose BMI is at or above the 95th percentile are overweight; and those whose BMI is at or above the 85th percentile are at risk of becoming overweight.

The percentages of young children who are overweight or at risk of being overweight in the United States have increased dramatically in recent decades (Schiff, 2019). In 2009–2010, 12.1 percent of U.S. 2- to 5-year-olds were classified as obese, compared with 5 percent in 1976–1980 and 10.4 percent in 2007–2008 (Ogden & others, 2012). In 2015–2016, 13.9 percent of 2- to 5-year-olds were obese. Also, more children are overweight in middle and late childhood than in early childhood. In 2015–2016, 18.4 percent of 6- to 11-year-old U.S. children were classified as obese, an increase of one percent since 2009–2010 (Hales & others, 2017). Also, if people are overweight or obese as young children their likelihood of being overweight or obese in adolescence and adulthood increases dramatically. For example, in one U.S. study, overweight 5-year-olds were four times more likely to be obese at 14 years of age than their counterparts who began kindergarten at a normal weight (Cunningham, Kramer, & Narayan, 2014). Also, in another study, preschool children who were obese were five times more likely to be overweight or obese as adults (Ogden & others, 2014).

Consequences of Obesity   The increasing number of overweight children in recent decades is cause for great concern,

What are some trends in the eating habits and weight of young children?
Jamie Grill/Getty Images

Helping Overweight Children Lose Weight

Most parents with an overweight child want to help the child lose weight but aren't sure of the most effective ways to accomplish this goal. Since overweight children are likely to become overweight adolescents and adults, it is important for parents to help their children attain a healthy weight and maintain it. Following are some ways parents can help their overweight children lose weight (DiLeonardo, 2015; Matthiessen, 2015; Moninger, 2015):

- Work on a healthy project together and involve the child in the decision-making process. Get the child involved in an activity that helps him or her lose weight, such as purchasing pedometers for all family members and developing goals for how many steps to take each day. When children are involved in making decisions about the family's health, they may begin to take responsibility for their own health.

- Be a healthy model for your child. In many aspects of life, what people do is more influential than what they say. If parents are overweight and engaging in unhealthy behaviors such as eating unhealthy fast food and being inactive, then simply telling their overweight children to lose weight is unlikely to be effective. In a recent study of Latino families, parents who had a healthy weight were 3.7 times more likely to have a child who had a healthy weight (Coto & others, 2019).

- Engage in physical activities with children. Parents and children can engage in activities like bicycling, jogging, hiking, and swimming together. A parent might say something like "Let's take a bike ride after dinner this evening. It would be fun and could help us both get in better shape."

If their children are overweight, what are some positive strategies parents can adopt to help them lose weight?
Blend Images/Getty Images

- Give children opportunities to decide what they want to do to lose weight. Take them to the grocery store and let them select the fruits and vegetables they are willing to eat. Let them choose which sport or type of exercise they would like to do.

- Eat healthy family meals together on a regular basis. Children who eat meals with their family are less likely to be overweight.

- Reduce screen time. Children who spend large numbers of hours per day in screen time are more likely to be overweight than their counterparts who are physically active.

Brand X Pictures/PunchStock

because being overweight raises the risk for many medical and psychological problems (Song & others, 2018). Overweight children are at risk for developing pulmonary problems such as sleep apnea (which involves upper-airway obstruction), and for having hip problems (Andersen, Holm, & Homoe, 2019). Type 2 diabetes, hypertension (high blood pressure), and elevated blood cholesterol levels also are common in children who are overweight (Chung, Onuzuruike, & Magge, 2018; Larkins & others, 2019). Further, a recent Chinese study found that children and adolescents who were obese were more likely to have depression and anxiety symptoms than non-obese children and adolescents (S. Wang & others, 2019). And a recent research review concluded that obesity is linked with low self-esteem in children (Moharei & others, 2018).

Treatment of Obesity   A combination of diet, exercise, and behavior modification is often recommended to help children lose weight (Graham, Holt/Hale, & Parker, 2020; Martin & others, 2018). Intervention programs that emphasize getting parents to engage in more healthful life styles themselves, as well as to feed their children healthy foods and get them to exercise more, can produce weight reduction in overweight and obese children (Parsons, Rutkowski, & Turel, 2019; Yackobovitch-Gavan & others, 2018). Recently, the following 5-2-1-0 obesity prevention guidelines have been made for young children: 5 or more servings of fruits and vegetables, 2 hours or less of screen time, minimum of 1 hour of physical activity, and 0 sugar-sweetened beverages daily (Khalsa & others, 2017).

For more information about ways to help children lose weight, see the *Connecting Development to Life* interlude.

ADOLESCENCE

Nutrition and being overweight are also key problems among adolescents (Donatelle, 2019; Telljohann & others, 2020). National data indicated that the percentage of obese U.S. 12- to 19-year-olds increased from 11 percent in the early 1990s to nearly 21 percent in 2013–2014 (Ogden & others, 2016).

An international study of adolescents in 56 countries found fast food consumption is high in childhood and continues to increase in adolescence (Braithwaite & others, 2014). In this study, adolescents who ate fast food frequently or very frequently had higher body mass indices than adolescents in the lower frequency categories. A comparison of adolescents in 28 countries found that U.S. adolescents ate more junk food than teenagers ate in most other countries (World Health Organization, 2000). The National Youth Risk Survey has found that U.S. high school students show a long-term linear decrease in their intake of fruits and vegetables with 59.2 percent of high school students not eating vegetables one or more times in the last 7 days (Kann & others, 2018).

What are some other aspects of adolescents' lives that are linked to being overweight or obese? One study revealed that playing on a sports team was an important factor in adolescents' weight (Drake & others, 2012). In this study, among a wide range of activities (other physical activity, physical education, screen time, and diet quality, for example), team sports participation was the strongest predictor of lower risk for being overweight or obese. Another study revealed that participating in family meals during adolescence protected against the development of being overweight or obese in adulthood (Berge & others, 2015). Further, increases in screen time in adolescence are associated with adolescent overweight and obesity (Furthner & others, 2018; Zhu & others, 2019).

What types of interventions have been successful in reducing overweight in adolescents? One review indicated that a combination of calorie restriction, exercise (such as walking or biking to school and participating in a regular exercise program), reduction of sedentary activity (such as watching TV or playing video games), and behavioral therapy (such as keeping weight-loss diaries and receiving rewards for meeting goals) have been moderately effective in helping overweight adolescents lose weight (Fowler-Brown & Kahwati, 2004). Also, a recent meta-analysis concluded that supervised exercise, especially aerobic exercise, was linked to a reduction of abdominal fat in adolescents (Gonzalez-Ruis & others, 2017). And a recent study found that a combination of regular exercise and a diet plan resulted in weight loss and enhanced executive function in adolescents (Xie & others, 2017). Further, an after-school athletics program reduced the obesity risk of adolescents after one year of intervention (Glabska & others, 2019).

Anorexia Nervosa   Although most U.S. girls have been on a diet at some point, slightly less than 1 percent ever develop anorexia nervosa. **Anorexia nervosa** is an eating disorder that involves the relentless pursuit of thinness through starvation. It is a serious disorder that can lead to death (Bryant-Waugh, 2019; Haliburn, 2018). According to the *DSM-5* psychiatric classification system, individuals have anorexia nervosa when the following factors are present: (1) restricted energy intake leading to significantly low body weight; (2) presence of intense fear of gaining weight or becoming fat or persistent behavior that interferes with gaining weight; and (3) disturbance in how body weight or shape is experienced or not recognizing the seriousness of the current low weight. Obsessive thinking about weight and compulsive exercise also are linked to anorexia nervosa (Smith, Mason, & Lavender, 2018). Even when they are extremely thin, individuals with this eating disorder see themselves as too fat (Phillipou, Castle, & Rossell, 2019). They never think they are thin enough, especially in the abdomen, buttocks, and thighs. They usually weigh themselves frequently, often take their body measurements, and gaze critically at themselves in mirrors.

Anorexia nervosa typically begins in the early to middle adolescent years, often following an episode of dieting and some type of life stress (Fitzpatrick, 2012). It is about 10 times more likely to occur in females than males. When anorexia nervosa does occur in males, the symptoms and other characteristics (such as a distorted body image and family conflict) are usually similar to those reported by females who have the disorder (Ariceli & others, 2005).

Although anorexia nervosa can be present in individuals from any ethnic group, it is more common non-Latina White adolescent or young adult females who come from well-educated, middle- and upper-income families and are competitive and high-achieving (Darcy, 2012). Individuals with anorexia nervosa often set high standards, become stressed about not being able to reach the standards, and are intensely concerned about how others perceive them

Anorexia nervosa has become an increasing problem for adolescent girls and young adult women. *What are some possible causes of anorexia nervosa?*
PeopleImages/Getty Images

anorexia nervosa An eating disorder that involves the relentless pursuit of thinness through starvation.

(Calugi & Dalle Grave, 2019). Unable to meet these unrealistic expectations, they turn to something they can control—their weight. Also, a recent study revealed that cognitive inflexibility, especially in perfectionistic adolescents, was associated with anorexia nervosa (Buzzichelli & others, 2018). Offspring of mothers with anorexia nervosa are at increased risk for becoming anorexic themselves (Striegel-Moore & Bulik, 2007). Problems in family functioning are increasingly being found to be linked to anorexia nervosa in adolescent girls (Dimitropoulos & others, 2018), and family therapy is often recommended as a treatment for adolescent girls with anorexia nervosa (Ganci, Pradel, & Hughes, 2018; Wong, Goh, & Ramachandran, 2019).

Biology and culture are involved in anorexia nervosa (Ehrlich, King, & Boehm, 2019; Wierenga & others, 2018). Genes play an important role in the development of this disorder (Meyre & others, 2018; Steiger & others, 2019). Also, the physical effects of dieting may change brain functioning and neural networks and thus sustain the disordered pattern (Seidel & others, 2019). The thin fashion image in U.S. culture likely contributes to the incidence of anorexia nervosa (Cazzato & others, 2016). The media portray thin as beautiful in their choice of fashion models, whom many adolescent girls strive to emulate (Carr & Peebles, 2012). A recent study found that having an increase in Facebook friends across two years was linked to enhanced motivation to be thin (Tiggemann & Slater, 2017). And many adolescent girls who strive to be thin hang out together.

Bulimia Nervosa   Although anorexics control their eating by restricting it, most bulimics cannot. **Bulimia nervosa** is an eating disorder in which the individual consistently follows a binge-and-purge eating pattern. According to the DSM-V classification system, an individual with bulimia nervosa is characterized by: (1) eating in a specific amount of time (such as within a 2-hour time frame) an amount of food that is larger than what most people would eat in a similar period in similar circumstances, and (2) sense of a lack of control over eating during an episode (Gorrell & others, 2019). The bulimic goes on an eating binge and then purges by self-induced vomiting or use of a laxative. Although some people binge and purge occasionally and some experiment with it, a person is considered to have a serious bulimic disorder only if the episodes occur at least twice a week for three months (Castillo & Weiselberg, 2017).

As with anorexics, most bulimics are preoccupied with food, have a strong fear of becoming overweight, and are depressed or anxious (Smith, Mason, & Lavender, 2018). Also, a recent meta-analysis concluded that anorexics and bulimics engage in maladaptive perfectionism (Norris, Gleaves, and Hutchinson, 2019). In addition, one study found that bulimics have difficulty controlling their emotions (Lavender & others, 2014). Unlike anorexics, people who binge and purge typically fall within a normal weight range, a characteristic that makes bulimia more difficult to detect.

Bulimia nervosa typically begins in late adolescence or early adulthood. About 90 percent of the cases are women. It is estimated that approximately 1 to 2 percent of women develop bulimia nervosa. Many women who develop bulimia nervosa were somewhat overweight before the onset of the disorder, and the binge eating often began during an episode of dieting. Drug therapy and psychotherapy have been effective in treating anorexia nervosa and bulimia nervosa (Hoskins & others, 2019). Cognitive behavior therapy has especially been helpful in treating bulimia nervosa (Forrest & others, 2018; Wade, 2019).

Binge Eating Disorder (BED)   **Binge eating disorder (BED)** involves frequent binge eating but without compensatory behavior like the purging that characterizes bulimics (Walsh, 2019). Individuals with BED engage in recurrent episodes of eating large quantities of food, during which they feel a lack of control over eating. Because they don't purge, individuals with BED are frequently overweight (Dakanalis & others, 2018). For the first time, binge eating disorder was included by the American Psychiatric Association in the fifth edition of its classification of psychiatric disorders in 2013. As with anorexia nervosa and bulimia disorder, far more females than males develop BED.

Researchers are examining the role of biological and psychological factors in BED (Kakoschke, Aarts, & Verdero-Garcia, 2019; Mitchison & others, 2018; Stopyra & others, 2019). Genes play a role, as does dopamine, the neurotransmitter related to reward pathways in the brain (Bulik, Blake, & Austin, 2019; Palmeira & others, 2019). An fMRI study also found that the areas of the brain involved in self-regulation and impulse control, especially the prefrontal cortex, showed diminished activity in individuals with binge eating disorder (Balodis & others, 2013). Another study found that adolescents with BED were more likely to live in families with less effective family functioning, especially in the area of emotional involvement (Tetzlaff &

bulimia nervosa An eating disorder in which the individual consistently follows a binge-and-purge eating pattern.

binge eating disorder (BED) Involves frequent binge eating without compensatory behavior like the purging that characterizes bulimics.

others, 2016). In a recent national study, all three eating disorders we have discussed here—anorexia, bulimia, and binge eating disorder—were associated with a higher incidence of major depressive disorder more than any other disorder, followed by alcohol use disorder (Udo & Grilo, 2019). Cognitive behavior therapy and pharmacological treatments have been successful with BED patients (Amodeo & others, 2019; Hilbert, 2019; Quilty & others, 2019).

ADULT DEVELOPMENT AND AGING

Nutrition and eating behavior continue to play important roles in adult physical development and health. Among the topics we discuss in this section are obesity, exercising and dieting to lose weight, and links between aging, weight, and nutrition.

Obesity Obesity is a serious and pervasive health problem for many individuals (Insel & Roth, 2020; Teague, Mackenzie, & Rosenthal, 2019).

In the United States, 39.8 percent of adults 20 years and older were classified as obese in 2016 (Hales & others, 2017). This represents a 9.1 percent increase since 2000 and a 4.7 percent increase since 2012. The prevalence of obesity in middle-aged adults (40.8 percent) was higher than in younger adults (35.7 percent). No significant differences in obesity were found between adults 60 years and older (41 percent) and younger age groups. Women had higher rates of obesity than men in all three age groups, with the highest rate for women being in the middle-aged group (44.7 percent). In terms of ethnic groups, Latinos and African American adults had the highest obesity rates (47 and 46.8 percent, respectively), followed by non-Latino White adults (37.6 percent). Asian American adults had the lowest rate of obesity by far (12.7 percent). The highest rate of obesity combining gender and ethnicity occurred for African American females (54.8 percent), the lowest for Asian American men (10.1 percent).

Overweight and obesity are linked to increased risk of earlier death, hypertension, diabetes, and cardiovascular disease (Luo & others, 2018; Schiff, 2019). For individuals who are 30 percent overweight, the probability of dying in middle adulthood increases by about 40 percent. Also, in a recent large-scale study, obesity was associated with shorter longevity and increased risk of death due to cardiovascular disease compared with normal-weight individuals (Khan & others, 2018). Further, in another recent study, obese middle-aged and older adults were more likely to have chronic diseases and experience an earlier death than their normal-weight counterparts (Stenholm & others, 2017). And in a Chinese study, men and women who gained an average of 22 pounds from 20 to 45–60 years of age had an increased risk of hypertension and cholesterol, as well as elevated triglyceride levels in middle age (Zhou & others, 2018).

Overweight and obesity also are associated with mental health problems (Zhang & others, 2018). For example, in a recent research review, depression was linked to abdominal obesity in older adults (Repousi & others, 2018).

What causes obesity? Some individuals do inherit a tendency to be overweight (Kleinert & others, 2018; Russell & Russell, 2019). However, one study found that a high level of activity reduced the degree of genetic linkage for obesity in same-sex twins (Hom & others, 2015). Only 10 percent of children who do not have obese parents become obese themselves, whereas 40 percent of children who become obese have one obese parent. Further, 70 percent of children who become obese have two obese parents. Researchers also have documented that animals can be inbred to have a propensity for obesity (Mathes & others, 2010).

Environmental factors play an important role in obesity (Donatelle & Ketcham, 2020; Kimura & others, 2018). Strong evidence of the environment's influence on weight is the doubling of the rate of obesity in the United States since 1900. This dramatic increase in obesity likely is due to greater availability of food (especially food high in fat), labor-saving devices, and declining physical activity.

Sociocultural factors are involved in obesity, which is six times more prevalent among women with low incomes than among women with high incomes. Americans also have higher rates of obesity than Europeans and people in many other areas of the world. For example, in recent international comparisons of 33 countries, the average obesity rate was 23.2 percent. The United States had the highest adult obesity rate (38.2 percent), followed by Mexico (32.4 percent), and Japan the lowest rate (3.7 percent) followed by South Korea (5.3 percent) (OECD, 2017).

Losing Weight One fact that we do know about losing weight is that the most effective programs include exercise (Donatelle & Ketcham, 2020). Researchers have found that higher

How effective are diet programs?
Juice Images/Getty Images

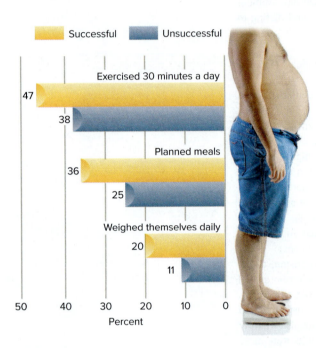

developmental **connection**

Theories

Evolutionary theory proposes explanations of development and aging. Connect to "Biological Beginnings."

levels of physical activity, especially endurance training, are linked to weight loss maintenance (Petridou, Siopi, & Mougios, 2019). Although many Americans regularly embark on a diet, few are successful in keeping weight off over the long term and many dieters risk becoming fatter (Corbin & others, 2019). However, some individuals do lose weight and maintain the loss (Primack, 2018). A research review concluded that adults who engaged in diet-plus-exercise programs lost more weight than those who relied on diet-only programs (Wu & others, 2009). And a study of approximately 2,000 U.S. adults found that exercising 30 minutes a day, planning meals, and weighing themselves daily were the main strategies used by successful dieters compared with unsuccessful dieters (Kruger, Blanck, & Gillespie, 2006) (see Figure 9).

Calorie Restriction and Longevity

Some studies have shown that calorie restriction in laboratory animals (such as rats and round-worms) can increase the animals' longevity (Someya & others, 2017). And researchers have found that chronic problems such as cardiovascular, kidney, and liver disease appear at a later age when calories are restricted (Contreras & others, 2018; Hegab & others, 2019). In addition, some recent research indicates that calorie restriction may provide neuroprotection for aging central nervous and immune systems (White & others, 2017). Another study found that calorie restriction maintained more youthful functioning in the hippocampus, which is an important brain structure for memory (Schafer & others, 2015).

No one knows for certain how calorie restriction (CR) works to increase the life span of animals. Some scientists suggest that CR might lower the level of free radicals and reduce oxidative stress in cells (Gultekin & others, 2018). Others argue that CR might trigger a state of emergency called "survival mode" in which the body eliminates all unnecessary functions to focus only on staying alive (Moatt & others, 2019; Schreiber, O'Leary, & Kennedy, 2016).

However, a 25-year longitudinal study conducted by the National Institute of Aging casts some doubt on whether a calorie-restricted diet will increase longevity (Mattison & others, 2012). In this study, monkeys that were fed 30 percent fewer calories did not live longer than a control group of monkeys. The researchers concluded that genes and diet composition are likely better predictors of longevity than calorie restriction per se. The results in the National Institute of Aging study contrast with an ongoing study at the Wisconsin National Primate Research Center, which has reported a 30 percent improved survival rate for calorie-restricted monkeys (Colman & others, 2009). Whether very low-calorie diets can stretch the human life span is not known (Le Bourg & Redman, 2018). In some instances, the animals in these studies ate 40 percent less than normal. In humans, a typical level of calorie restriction involves a 30 percent decrease, resulting in about 1,120 calories a day for the average woman and 1,540 for the average man. In conclusion, the research findings on the effects of calorie restriction in humans are mixed (Locher & others, 2016). Thus, an appropriate conclusion at this time is that further research is needed to definitively determine whether calorie restriction increases longevity, especially in humans.

Do underweight women and men live longer lives? One study revealed that women who were 20 pounds or more underweight lived longer even after controlling for smoking, hypertension, alcohol intake, and other factors (Wandell, Carlsson, & Theobald, 2009). In this study, underweight men did not live longer when various factors were controlled.

The Controversy Over Vitamins and Aging

For years, most experts on aging and health argued that a balanced diet was all that was needed for successful aging; vitamin supplements were not recommended. However, researchers recently began exploring the possibility that some vitamin supplements—mainly a group called "antioxidants" consisting of vitamin C, vitamin E, and beta-carotene—might help to slow the aging process and improve the health of older adults (Prasad, 2017; Yeung & others, 2019).

FIGURE 9

COMPARISON OF STRATEGIES USED BY SUCCESSFUL AND UNSUCCESSFUL DIETERS.

iStock.com/Ljupco

■ Successful ■ Unsuccessful

Exercised 30 minutes a day — 47, 38

Planned meals — 36, 25

Weighed themselves daily — 20, 11

Percent

Imagestate Media (John Foxx)/Imagestate

The theory is that antioxidants counteract the cell damage caused by free radicals, which are produced both by the body's own metabolism and by environmental factors such as smoking, pollution, and harmful chemicals in the diet (Jaheen & others, 2018; Jeremic & others, 2018). When free radicals cause damage (oxidation) in one cell, a chain reaction of damage follows. In this theory, antioxidants act much like a fire extinguisher, helping to neutralize free-radical activity.

What have research studies found about the role of antioxidants in health? In two studies, no link was found between antioxidant vitamin intake and mortality (Henriquez-Sanchez & others, 2016; Stepaniak & others, 2016). Additionally, research reviews have not supported the belief that antioxidant vitamin supplements can reduce the incidence of cancer and cardiovascular disease (Khodaeian & others, 2015; Paganini-Hill, Kawas, & Corrada, 2015). However, a meta-analysis of seven studies concluded that dietary intakes (not vitamin supplements) of vitamins E, C, and beta-carotene were linked to a reduced risk of Alzheimer disease (Li, Shen, & Ji, 2012). And in a recent analysis, it was concluded that antioxidant supplements do not increase the life span and even can increase the incidence of diseases (Millsav, Ribaric, & Poljsak, 2019).

Review *Connect* Reflect

 LG2 Characterize developmental changes in nutrition and eating behavior.

Review
- What are some important aspects of nutrition and eating behavior in infancy?
- What are some key nutritional problems in American children?
- How can eating behavior and disorders in adolescence be characterized?
- What are some controversies and issues involving nutrition and eating behavior in the adult years?

Connect
- What does the nature versus nurture debate suggest about children's risk of becoming obese?

Reflect *Your Own Personal Journey of Life*
- How good are you at choosing nutritious foods? Have your lifestyle and behavior in this area affected your health? Might your food choices today affect your health in the future?

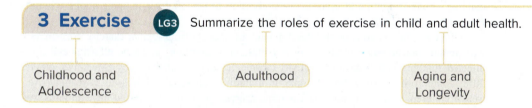

3 Exercise   **LG3**   Summarize the roles of exercise in child and adult health.

Childhood and Adolescence   Adulthood   Aging and Longevity

We have seen the important role exercise plays in losing weight. Exercise is linked with many aspects of physical and mental health. Let's explore the impact of exercise throughout the life span.

CHILDHOOD AND ADOLESCENCE

American children and adolescents are not getting enough exercise (Rink, 2020). Educators and policy makers in the United States and numerous countries around the world, including China, Finland, and Great Britain, have become very concerned about the sedentary lifestyles of many children and adolescents in their countries (Dumuid & others, 2017; Ndabi, Nevill, & Sandercock, 2019; Tomkinson & Wong, 2019).

Childhood   To optimize the development and coordination of large muscles, especially in the arms and legs, children need daily exercise (Martin & others, 2018; Teague, Mackenzie, & Rosenthal, 2019). Four expert panels from Australia, Canada, the United Kingdom, and the United States have put forth physical activity guidelines for young children that are quite similar (Pate & others 2015). The guidelines recommend that young children get 15 or more minutes of physical activity per hour over a 12-hour period, or about 3 hours per day total. These guidelines reflect an increase from earlier guidelines established in 2002.

How much physical activity should preschool children engage in per day?
RubberBall Productions/Getty Images

Also, a recent study examined children's physical activity as they made the transition from elementary to middle school (Pate & others, 2019). In this study, the following activities were associated with children's greater physical activity: parents' encouragement of physical activity, parents' support of physical activity, time children spent outdoors, children's sports participation, and number of physical activity facilities near their home.

An increasing number of studies document the importance of exercise in children's physical development (Meeks, Heit, & Page, 2020). An experimental study found that 13 weeks of aerobic training had significant benefits for insulin resistance and body fat levels of overweight/obese elementary school children, regardless of gender or ethnicity (Davis & others, 2012). A study of more than 6,000 elementary school children revealed that 55 minutes or more of moderate-to-vigorous physical activity daily was associated with a lower incidence of obesity (Nemet, 2016). Also, a recent study of 7- to 9-year-olds found that participating in organized leisure-time sports for approximately one year was linked to a decrease in cardiovascular risk (Hebert & others, 2017). And research strongly supports the positive effects of exercise on children's bone strength and even on the prevention of osteoporosis in aging adults (Gomez-Bruton & others, 2017).

Children's brain and cognitive development also benefit from regular exercise. Researchers have found that aerobic exercise improves children's attention, memory, effortful and goal-directed thinking and behavior, creativity, academic success, and literacy (Martin & others, 2018; Tomporowski, 2016). For example, in a study of physically unfit 8- to 11-year-old overweight children, a daily instructor-led aerobic exercise program that lasted eight months was effective in improving the efficiency or flexible modulation of neural circuits that support better cognitive functioning (Kraftt & others, 2014). In addition, a recent meta-analysis concluded that sustained physical activity programs were linked to improvements in children's attention, executive function, and academic achievement (de Greeff & others, 2018). Another recent meta-analysis concluded that prolonged exercise interventions with 6- to 12-year-olds that consisted of multiple exercise activities per week and lasted for more than 6 weeks were effective in improving the children's executive function in general and their inhibitory control in particular (Xue, Yang, & Huang, 2019).

Also, a recent study found that a 6-week, high-intensity exercise program with 7- to 13-year-olds improved their cognitive control and working memory (Moreau, Kirk, & Waldie, 2017). And in another study, 60 minutes of physical activity per day in preschool academic contexts improved early literacy (Kirk & Kirk, 2016).

Parents and schools strongly influence children's exercise habits (Brusseau & others, 2018; Pate & others, 2019). Growing up with parents who exercise regularly provides positive models of exercise for children. A study found that school-based physical activity was successful in improving children's fitness and lowering their levels of body fat (Kriemler & others, 2011).

Adolescence   Researchers have found that individuals tend to become less active as they reach and progress through adolescence (Kwan & others, 2012). A national study of U.S. 9- to

15-year-olds revealed that almost all 9- and 11-year-olds met the federal government's moderate to vigorous exercise recommendations per day (a minimum of 60 minutes daily), but only 31 percent of 15-year-olds met the recommendations on weekdays, and on weekends only 17 percent met the recommendations (Nader & others, 2008). The national study also found that adolescent boys were more likely than girls to engage in moderate to vigorous exercise. Figure 10 shows the average amount of exercise engaged in by U.S. boys and girls from 9 to 15 years of age on weekdays and weekends.

Ethnic differences in exercise participation rates of U.S. adolescents also occur, and these rates vary by gender. As indicated in Figure 11, in the National Youth Risk Survey, non-Latino White boys exercised the most, African American girls the least (Kann & others, 2016a).

Exercise is linked to a number of positive physical outcomes in adolescence (Janz & Baptista, 2018; Owen & others, 2018). For example, regular exercise has a positive effect on adolescents' weight status (Medrano & others, 2018). Other positive physical outcomes of exercise in adolescence are reduced triglyceride levels, lower blood pressure, and a lower incidence of type II diabetes (Rowland, 2018; Toffrey, Zakrzewski-Fruer, & Thackray, 2018). One study found that adolescents who were high in physical fitness had better connectivity between brain regions than adolescents who were low in physical fitness (Herting & others, 2014). And in another study, an exercise program of 180 minutes per week improved the sleep patterns of obese adolescents (Mendelson & others, 2016).

Exercise in adolescence also is linked to other positive outcomes, including academic, cognitive, and socioemotional development (Kemp & others, 2019; Ludyga & others, 2018). In a recent study, adolescents who exercised regularly had higher academic achievement (Owen & others, 2018). In addition, a recent research review concluded that school and community-based physical activity interventions can improve overweight and obese adolescents' executive function (higher-level thinking) (Martin & others, 2018). Also, in a recent research review, among a number of cognitive factors, memory was the factor that most often was improved by exercise in adolescence (Li & others, 2017). In terms of socioemotional development, a recent large-scale study of Dutch adolescents found that those who were physically active has fewer emotional and peer problems (Kuiper & others, 2018). Also, in another study, a high-intensity exercise program reduced depressive symptoms and improved the moods of depressed adolescents (Carter & others, 2016). And researchers recently have found that exercise reduces the symptoms of attention deficit hyperactivity disorder (ADHD) (Jeyanthi, Arumugam, & Parasher, 2019; Rassovsky & Alfassi, 2019; Vysniauske & others, 2019).

As with children, parents play an important role in influencing adolescents' exercise patterns (Baker & others, 2019; Foster & others, 2018). A research review also found that peers play an especially important role in adolescents' physical activity (Fitzgerald, Fitzgerald, & Aherne, 2012). In this review, among the peer factors that were linked to adolescents' exercise levels were peer/friend support of exercise and friendship quality and acceptance. Schools also can influence adolescents' exercise and developmental outcomes. In a recent study, a school-based exercise program of 20 minutes of exercise a day over 8 weeks improved students' working memory (Ludyga & others, 2018).

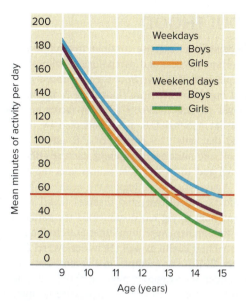

FIGURE 10

AVERAGE AMOUNT OF MODERATE TO VIGOROUS EXERCISE ENGAGED IN BY U.S. 9- TO 15-YEAR-OLDS ON WEEKDAYS AND WEEKENDS. *Note:* The federal government recommends 60 minutes of moderate to vigorous physical activity per day.

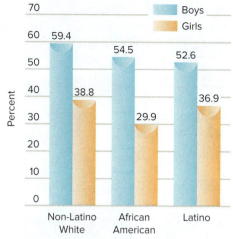

FIGURE 11

EXERCISE RATES OF U.S. HIGH SCHOOL STUDENTS: GENDER AND ETHNICITY.
Note: Data are for high school students who were physically active doing any kind of physical activity that increased their heart rate and made them breathe hard some of the time for a total of at least 60 minutes a day on five or more of the seven days preceding the survey.
Source: Kann, L., & others (2016a, June 10). Youth Risk Behavior Surveillance—United States 2015. MMWR, 65, 1–174, CDC.

In 2007, Texas became the first state to test students' physical fitness. The student shown here is performing the trunk lift. Other assessments include aerobic exercise, muscle strength, and body fat. Assessments will be done annually.
©Vernon Bryant/Dallas Morning News

ADULTHOOD

The benefits of exercise continue in adulthood. Both moderate and intense exercise produce important physical and psychological gains (Strandberg, 2019; Walker, 2019). The enjoyment and pleasure we derive from exercise added to its physical benefits make exercise one of life's most important activities (Donatelle & Ketcham 2020). The World Health Organization recognizes physical inactivity as a key factor in dying earlier (Han, Neufer, & Pilegaard, 2019). A recent national U.S. poll conducted by the Centers for Disease Control and Prevention found that only 22.9 percent of U.S. adults 18 to 64 years of age met federal guidelines for aerobic and muscle-strengthening exercise (Blackwell & Clarke, 2018). In this poll, 27.2 percent of men and 18.7 percent of women met the exercise guidelines.

Among the most important health benefits of exercise are reduced risks for obesity, cardiovascular disease, and diabetes (Insel & Roth, 2020; Kokkinos & others, 2019). Even getting hogs to jog has documented the cardiovascular benefits of exercise (see Figure 12).

Researchers have found that exercise benefits not only the physical health of adults, but their mental health as well (Belvederi Murri & others, 2019; Elbe & others, 2019; Paolucci & others, 2018). For example, in a recent study of almost 18,000 adults, engaging in both regular moderate-to-vigorous physical activity and muscle-strengthening exercise were associated with the lowest incidence of depressive symptoms (Bennie & others, 2019). And a one-year exercise intervention decreased stress symptoms in working adults (Kettunen, Vuorimaa, & Vasankari, 2015).

Although exercise designed to strengthen muscles and bones or to improve flexibility is important to fitness, many health experts stress the benefits of aerobic exercise. **Aerobic exercise** is sustained activity—jogging, swimming, or cycling, for example—that stimulates heart and lung functioning.

Many health experts recommend that adults engage in 45 minutes or more of moderate physical activity on most, or preferably all, days of the week. Most recommend trying to raise your heart rate to at least 60 percent of your maximum heart rate. However, only about one-fifth of adults achieve these recommended levels of physical activity.

AGING AND LONGEVITY

Although we may be in the evening of our lives in late adulthood, we are not meant to live out our remaining years passively. Everything we know about older adults suggests they are healthier and happier the more active they are (Strandberg, 2019; Walker, 2019). Can regular exercise lead to a healthier late adulthood and increased longevity? Let's examine several research studies on exercise and aging.

In one study, exercise literally meant a difference between life and death for middle-aged and older adults (Blair, 1990). More than 10,000 men and women were divided into categories of low fitness, medium fitness, and high fitness (Blair & others, 1989). Then they were studied over a period of eight years. As shown in Figure 13, sedentary participants (low fitness) were more than twice as likely to die during the eight-year time span of the study as those who were moderately fit and more than three times as likely to die as those who were highly fit. The positive effects of being physically fit occurred for both men and women in this study. Also, a longitudinal study found that men who exercised regularly at 72 years of age had a 30 percent higher probability of still being alive at 90 years of age than their sedentary counterparts (Yates & others, 2008). And a study of more than 11,000 women found that low cardiorespiratory fitness was a significant predictor of all-cause mortality (Farrell & others, 2010). Also, a study of joggers in Copenhagen, Denmark, revealed that engaging in light or moderate jogging on a regular basis was linked to increased longevity (Schnohr & others, 2015). Further, in a recent study, relative to individuals with low physical fitness, those who increased from low to intermediate or high fitness were at a lower risk for all-cause mortality (Brawner & others, 2017).

Gerontologists increasingly recommend strength training in addition to aerobic activity and stretching for older adults (Grgic & others, 2018; Lavin & others, 2019). The average person's lean body mass declines with age—about 6.6 pounds of lean muscle are lost each decade during the adult years. The rate of muscle loss accelerates after age 45. Resistance exercise can preserve and possibly increase muscle mass in older adults (Nordheim &

FIGURE 12

THE JOGGING HOG EXPERIMENT.
Jogging hogs reveal the dramatic effects of exercise on health. In one investigation, a group of hogs was trained to run approximately 100 miles per week (Bloor & White, 1983). Then the researchers narrowed the arteries that supplied blood to the hogs' hearts. The hearts of the jogging hogs developed extensive alternate pathways for blood supply, and 42 percent of the threatened heart tissue was salvaged compared with only 17 percent in a control group of nonjogging hogs.
Courtesy of Maxine Bloor

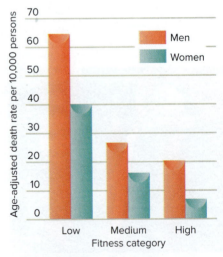

FIGURE 13

PHYSICAL FITNESS AND MORTALITY. In a study of middle-aged and older adults, being moderately fit or highly fit meant that individuals were less likely to die over a period of eight years than their less fit (sedentary) counterparts (Blair & others, 1989).

others, 2018). And a recent study of older adults found that resistance training improved their physical function, psychological well-being, and quality of life (Pedersen & others, 2017).

Exercise is an excellent way to maintain health and live longer (Fahey, Insel, & Roth, 2019; Strandberg, 2019). The current recommended level of aerobic activity for adults 60 years of age and older is 30 minutes of moderately intense activity, such as brisk walking or riding a stationary bicycle, five or more days a week, and strength training two or more days a week (Der Ananian & Prohaska, 2007).

Researchers continue to document the positive effects of exercise in older adults:

- *Exercise is linked to increased longevity.* A recent study of middle-aged adults revealed that their estimated age based on exercise stress testing was a better predictor of how long they would live than their chronological age (Harb & others, 2019). Also, a study of older adults found that total daily physical activity was linked to increased longevity across a four-year period (Buchman & others, 2012). In one analysis, energy expenditure by older adults during exercise that burns up at least 1,000 calories a week was estimated to increase life expectancy by about 30 percent, and burning up 2,000 calories a week in exercise was estimated to increase life expectancy by about 50 percent (Lee & Skerrett, 2001).

- *Exercise is related to prevention of common chronic diseases.* Exercise can reduce the risk of developing arthritis, cardiovascular disease, type 2 diabetes, osteoporosis, stroke, and breast cancer (Cisternas, Murphy, & Carlson, 2019; Mora & Valencia, 2018).

- *Exercise is associated with improved outcomes for many diseases* (Henderson & others, 2018; Long & others, 2019). When exercise is used as part of the treatment, individuals with the following disorders show improvement in symptoms: arthritis, pulmonary disease, congestive heart failure, coronary artery disease, hypertension, type 2 diabetes, obesity, and Alzheimer disease (Baptista & others, 2018; Kokkinos & others, 2019; Scott & others, 2018).

- *Exercise improves older adults' cellular functioning.* Researchers increasingly are finding that exercise improves cellular functioning in older adults (Srivastava & Veech, 2019).

- *Exercise improves immune system functioning in older adults* (Duggal & others, 2019; Minuzzi & others, 2018).

- *Exercise can optimize body composition and reduce the decline in motor skills as aging occurs.* Exercise can increase muscle mass and bone mass, improve balance and reduce falls, as well as decrease bone fragility (Fougere & Cesari, 2019; Sgro & others, 2018).

- *Exercise reduces the likelihood that older adults will develop mental health problems and can be effective as part of the treatment of mental health problems* (Ku & others, 2018; Sexton & Taylor, 2019). For example, a recent research review concluded that exercise reduces depressive symptoms in older adults (Seo & Chao, 2018).

- *Exercise is linked to improved brain and cognitive functioning in older adults.* Older adults who exercise show better brain functioning and more efficient processing of information than older adults who don't exercise (Coetsee & Terblanche, 2019; Erickson & Oberlin, 2017; Smith, Hendy, & Tempest, 2018; Tsai & Chang, 2019).

Despite the extensive documentation of exercise's power to improve older adults' health and quality of life, a national survey in 2014 found that 65- to 74-year-olds exercised less than 25- to 64-year-olds and that the older adults continued to decrease their exercise at 75 years and older (Centers for Disease Control and Prevention, 2015). Nonetheless, older adults have increased the amount of time they exercise in recent years—in 2006 slightly more than 20 percent of 65- to 74-year-olds reported engaging in regular exercise but in 2014 that figure has increased to more than 40 percent (Centers for Disease Control and Prevention, 2008, 2015).

Johnny Kelley finishes one of the many Boston Marathons he ran as an older adult. In 1991, he ran his sixteenth Boston Marathon and, in 2000, he was named "Runner of the Century" by *Runner's World* magazine. At 70 years of age, Kelley was still running 50 miles a week. At that point in his life, Kelley said, "I'm afraid to stop running. I feel so good. I want to stay alive." He lived 27 more years and died at age 97 in 2004.
Charles Krupa/AP Images

aerobic exercise Sustained activity that stimulates heart and lung functioning.

Possible explanations of older adults' reduction in exercise compared with middle-aged adults focus on such factors as chronic illnesses, life crises (such as a spouse's death) that disrupt exercise schedules, embarrassment at being around others who are in better shape (especially if they haven't exercised much earlier in life), and the "why bother?" factor (not believing that exercise will improve their lives much). But as we have seen, it is never too late to begin exercising, and older adults can significantly benefit from regular exercise (Mora & Valencia, 2018; Walker, 2019). A recent study even found that when older adults regularly walk their dog it predicts better health for them (Curl, Bibbo, & Johnson, 2017).

Review *Connect* Reflect

LG3 Summarize the roles of exercise in child and adult health.

Review

- How extensively do U.S. children and adolescents exercise?
- What roles does exercise play in adult health?
- How does exercise influence development in aging adults?

Connect

- Consider what you have learned so far about parents' potential influence on children's health. Do active parents send a different message to their children than sedentary parents do?

Reflect *Your Own Personal Journey of Life*

- Imagine that you have become middle-aged and someone asks you this question: "What would give you the greater advantage: exercising more or eating less?" What would your answer be?

4 Substance Use

 LG4 Evaluate substance use in adolescence and adulthood.

Adolescence and Emerging Adulthood

Substance Use in Older Adults

Besides exercising, another important way to preserve health is not to engage in substance abuse (Lynch, Vail-Smith, & Kotecki, 2018; Goode, 2020). For example, in one longitudinal study, individuals who did not abuse alcohol at age 50 were more likely to still be alive and healthy at 75 to 80 years of age than their counterparts who abused alcohol at age 50 (Vaillant, 2002). In the chapter titled "Biological Beginnings," we described the negative effects on the fetus and developing child that can result from substance use by the pregnant mother. Here we examine the effects of substance use on adolescents, emerging adults, and older adults.

ADOLESCENCE AND EMERGING ADULTHOOD

Adolescence is a critical time for the onset of substance abuse (Goldberg & Mitchell, 2019). Many individuals who abuse drugs begin to do so during the adolescent years. Let's explore some trends in adolescent drug use and then examine drug use in emerging adulthood.

Trends in Adolescent Drug Use   Each year since 1975, Lloyd Johnston and his colleagues at the Institute of Social Research at the University of Michigan have monitored the drug use of America's high school seniors in a wide range of public and private high schools. Since 1991, they also have surveyed drug use by eighth- and tenth-graders. In 2018, the study surveyed more than 44,500 secondary school students in 392 public and private schools (Johnston & others, 2019).

According to this study, the proportions of eighth-, tenth-, and twelfth-grade U.S. students who used any illicit drug declined in the late 1990s and the first decade of the twenty-first century (Johnston & others, 2019). The use of drugs among U.S. secondary school students declined in the 1980s but began to increase in the early 1990s (Johnston & others, 2019).

In the late 1990s and the early part of the twenty-first century, the proportion of secondary school students reporting the use of any illicit drug has been declining. The overall decline in the use of illicit drugs by adolescents during this time frame is approximately one-third for eighth-graders, one-fourth for tenth-graders, and one-eighth for twelfth-graders. The most notable declines in drug use by U.S. adolescents in the twenty-first century have occurred for LSD, cocaine, cigarettes, sedatives, tranquilizers, and Ecstasy. Marijuana is the illicit drug most widely used in the United States and Europe (Hibell & others, 2004; Johnston & others, 2019). Even with the recent decline in use, the United States still has one of the highest rates of adolescent drug use of any industrialized nation.

How extensive is alcohol use by U.S. adolescents? Sizable declines in adolescent alcohol use have occurred in recent years (Johnston & others, 2019). The percentage of U.S. eighth-graders who reported having had any alcohol to drink in the past 30 days fell from a 1996 high of 26 percent to 8.2 percent in 2018. The 30-day prevalence fell among tenth-graders from 39 percent in 2001 to 18.6 percent in 2018 and among high school seniors from 72 percent in 1980 to 30.2 percent in 2018. Binge drinking (defined in the University of Michigan surveys as having five or more drinks in a row in the last two weeks) by high school seniors declined from 41 percent in 1980 to 17.5 percent in 2018. Binge drinking by eighth- and tenth-graders also has dropped in recent years. A consistent gender difference occurs in binge drinking, with males engaging in this behavior more than females do (Johnston & others, 2019).

A special concern is adolescents who drive while they are under the influence of alcohol or other substances (White & others, 2018; Williams & others, 2018; Wilson & others, 2018). In one of the University of Michigan Monitoring the Future surveys, 30 percent of high school seniors said they had been in a vehicle with a drugged or drinking driver in the past two weeks (Johnston & others, 2008). And in a national study, one in four twelfth-graders reported that they had consumed alcohol mixed with energy drinks in the last 12 months, and this combination was linked to their unsafe driving (Martz, Patrick, & Schulenberg, 2015). There is an increasing concern about adolescents who mix alcohol and energy drinks, which is linked to a higher rate of risky driving (Wilson & others, 2018).

Cigarette smoking is decreasing among adolescents. Cigarette smoking among U.S. adolescents peaked in 1996 and 1997 and has gradually declined almost annually since then (Johnston & others, 2019). Following peak use in 1996, smoking rates for U.S. eighth-graders have fallen by 50 percent. In 2018, the percentages of twelfth-graders who said they had smoked cigarettes in the last 30 days was 7.6 percent (an 11 percent decrease from 2011), 4.2 percent (tenth grade), and 2.2 percent (eighth grade). Since the mid-1990s an increasing percentage of adolescents have reported that they perceive cigarette smoking as dangerous, that they disapprove of it, that they are less accepting of being around smokers, and that they prefer to date nonsmokers (Johnston & others, 2019).

E-cigarettes are battery-powered devices that use a heating element to produce a vapor that users inhale (Barrington-Trimis & others, 2018). In most cases the vapor contains nicotine, but the specific contents are not regulated (Gorukanti & others, 2017). In 2014, for the first time in the University of Michigan drug study, e-cigarette use was assessed (Johnston & others, 2015). E-cigarette use by U.S. adolescents in 2014 surpassed tobacco cigarette use—in the previous 30 days, 9 percent of eighth-graders, 16 percent of tenth-graders, and 17 percent of twelfth-graders reported using e-cigarettes.

However, in 2015 and 2016, e-cigarette use declined significantly at all three grade levels, but was still higher than cigarette use at all three grade levels (Johnston & others, 2017). In 2017, 11.0 percent of twelfth-graders, 8.2 percent of tenth-graders, and 3.5 percent of eighth-graders vaped nicotine (Johnston & others, 2018). These percentages continued to dramatically increase in 2018—20.9 percent of twelfth-graders, 16.1 percent of eleventh-graders, and 6.1 percent of eighth-graders (Johnston & others, 2019). Thus, adolescents currently are vaping nicotine far more than they are smoking cigarettes. Also a recent meta-analysis of longitudinal studies concluded that adolescents who use e-cigarettes are four times more likely to subsequently smoke cigarettes than adolescents who do not use e-cigarettes (Soneji & others, 2017).

The Roles of Development, Parents, Peers, and Educational Success A special concern involves adolescents who begin to use drugs early in adolescence or even in childhood (Goode, 2020). A longitudinal study of individuals from 8 to 42 years of age also

developmental connection

Biological Processes

Early maturation in adolescence is linked with an increased likelihood of substance abuse problems in adolescent girls. Connect to "Physical Development and Biological Aging."

found that early onset of drinking was linked to increased risk of heavy drinking in middle age (Pitkanen, Lyyra, & Pulkkinen, 2005). Another study revealed that the onset of alcohol use before age 11 was linked to a higher risk of alcohol dependence in early adulthood (Guttmannova & others, 2012). Also, researchers found that early onset of drinking and a quick progression to drinking to intoxication were linked to drinking problems in high school (Morean & others, 2014). And another study indicated that early- and rapid-onset trajectories of alcohol, marijuana, and substance use were associated with substance abuse in early adulthood (Nelson, Van Ryzin, & Dishion, 2015). Further, a longitudinal study found that earlier age at first use of alcohol was linked to risk of heavy alcohol use in early adulthood (Liang & Chikritzhs, 2015).

Parents play an important role in preventing adolescent drug abuse (Cruz & others, 2018; Marsiglia & others, 2019). Positive relationships with parents and others can reduce adolescents' drug use (Eun & others, 2018). One study found that low parental knowledge of adolescents' peer relations and behavior, and friends' delinquency, predicted adolescent substance use (McAdams & others, 2014). In another study, maternal and paternal knowledge of the adolescent's activities and whereabouts at age 13 were linked to lower alcohol use at age 16 for girls and boys (Lindfors & others, 2019). Researchers have found that parental monitoring is linked with a lower incidence of drug use (Wang & others, 2014). In a recent meta-analysis of parenting factors involved in adolescent alcohol use, higher levels of parental monitoring, support, and involvement were associated with a lower risk of adolescent alcohol misuse (Yap & others, 2017). A recent study also revealed that adolescent dishonesty promoted future alcohol use by reducing parental monitoring knowledge (Lushin, Jaccard, & Kaploun, 2017). Further, in a recent intervention study, Latino parents who participated in a program that emphasized the importance of parental monitoring had adolescents with a lower level of drug use than a control group of adolescents whose parents did not participate in the program (Estrada & others, 2017). In addition, a research review concluded that the more frequently adolescents ate dinner with their family, the less likely they were to have substance abuse problems (Sen, 2010). And researchers have found that authoritative parenting was linked to lower adolescent alcohol consumption (Piko & Balazs, 2012), while parent-adolescent conflict was related to higher adolescent alcohol consumption (Chaplin & others, 2012). Finally, a recent study of 14- to 15-year-olds revealed that heavy episodic drinking by parents was a risk factor for adolescent drinking, with girls being especially vulnerable to their parents' heavy episodic drinking (Homel & Warren, 2019).

Peer relations also are linked to adolescent substance use (Cambron & others, 2018; Janssen & others, 2018). One study indicated that of various risk factors the strongest predictors of adolescent substance use involved peer relations (Choukas-Bradley & Prinstein, 2016). Further, another study found that neighborhood disadvantage was linked a higher level of adolescent alcohol use two years later, mainly through a pathway that included exposure to delinquent peers (Trucco & others, 2014). And a large-scale national study of adolescents indicated that friends' use of alcohol was a stronger influence on alcohol use than parental use (Deutsch, Wood, & Slutske, 2018).

Educational success is also a strong buffer for the emergence of drug problems in adolescence. An analysis by Jerald Bachman and his colleagues (2008) revealed that early educational achievement considerably reduced the likelihood that adolescents would develop drug problems, including those involving alcohol abuse, smoking, and abuse of various illicit drugs.

Emerging Adults' Drug Use

The transition from high school to college is often a critical risk period for alcohol abuse (Hartman & others, 2019; Prince, Read, & Colder, 2019). The large majority of emerging adults recognize that drinking is common among individuals their age and is largely acceptable, even expected by their peers. They also perceive that they get some social and coping benefits from alcohol use and even occasional heavy drinking. One study revealed that only 20 percent of college students reported that they abstain from drinking alcohol (Huang & others, 2009).

In surveys of drinking, binge drinking is usually defined as having 5 or more drinks in a row in the 2 weeks prior to the survey. As shown in Figure 14, recent data from the *Monitoring the Future* study at the University of Michigan indicate that binge drinking peaked at 21 to 22 years of age, with

What kinds of problems are associated with binge drinking in college?

Sean Murphy/Photodisc/Getty Images

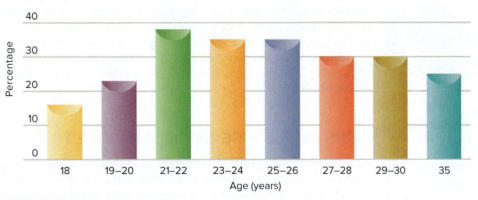

FIGURE 14

BINGE DRINKING IN THE ADOLESCENCE–EARLY ADULTHOOD TRANSITION. Note that the percentage of individuals engaging in binge drinking peaked at 21–22 years of age, remained high through the mid-twenties, then began to decline in the late twenties. Binge drinking was defined as having five or more alcoholic drinks in a row in the past two weeks.
Source: Schulenberg, J.E., & others (2017). Monitoring the Future national survey results on drug use, 1975-2016: Vol. II, college students and adults, aged 19-55. Ann Arbor, MI: Institute for Social Research, University of Michigan/NIH.

38 percent in this age group reporting that they had engaged in binge drinking at least once in the last two weeks (Schulenberg & others, 2017).

The effects of heavy drinking take a toll on college students (Wombacher & others, 2018). In a national survey of drinking patterns on 140 campuses, almost half of the binge drinkers reported problems that included missed classes, physical injuries, troubles with police, and unprotected sex (Wechsler & others, 2002). This survey also found that binge-drinking college students were eleven times more likely to drive after drinking and twice as likely to have unprotected sex as college students who did not binge drink. And a longitudinal study revealed that frequent binge drinking and marijuana use during the freshman year of college predicted delayed college graduation (White & others, 2018).

While drinking rates among college students have remained high, overall levels of drinking, including binge drinking, in this age group have declined in recent years. For example, binge drinking declined from 37.4 percent in 2012 to 32.4 percent in 2016 (Schulenberg & others, 2017).

Drinking alcohol before going out—called *pregaming*—has become common among college students (Chaney & others, 2019; Perrotte & others, 2019). One study revealed that almost two-thirds of students on one campus had pregamed at least once in a two-week period (DeJong, DeRicco, & Schneider, 2010). Drinking games, in which the goal is to become intoxicated, also have become common on college campuses (Perrotte & others, 2018; Zamboranga & others, 2018). Higher levels of alcohol use have been consistently linked to higher rates of sexual risk taking, such as engaging in casual sex without using contraceptives, as well as increased risk of being a perpetrator or victim of sexual assault (Looby & others, 2019).

Do individuals smoke cigarettes more in emerging adulthood than in adolescence? Smoking half a pack of cigarettes daily occurs more often among individuals in their twenties than among high school seniors, as many light and moderate smokers in high school transition into a pattern of heavier use after high school (Johnston & others, 2017). In 2016, the prevalence of smoking half a pack or more of cigarettes daily rose from 2 percent of 18-year-olds to 7 percent of 29- to 30-year-olds, with a slight further increase to 8 percent for individuals 35 years and older and 9 percent for those 55 years and older (Johnston & others, 2017). Overall, though, cigarette smoking has been declining significantly at all ages in the population.

However, recently, just as there has been in adolescence, there has been a dramatic increase in use of e-cigarettes among individuals in emerging and early adulthood (Cooper & others, 2018). In 2016, 8 percent of 19- to 22-year-olds used electronic vaporizers (which include e-cigarettes) in a 30-day period, then usage dropped at 23-24 years of age to

developmental **connection**
Sexuality
When emerging adults drink alcohol, they are most likely to have casual sex. Connect to "Gender and Sexuality."

Age Group	Percent	Drinks Per Occasion	Frequency
18–24	28	9	4.2
25–34	28	8	4.2
35–44	19	8	4.1
45–64	13	7	4.7
65 & over	4	5	5.5

FIGURE 15

BINGE DRINKING THROUGH THE LIFE SPAN.
Note: Percent refers to percent of individuals in a particular age group who engaged in binge drinking on at least one occasion in the past 30 days (4 or more drinks for women, 5 or more for men). Drinks per occasion reflects the intensity of the binge drinking. Frequency indicates the number of occasions in which binge drinking occurred in the past 30 days.
Source: Centers for Disease Control and Prevention, 2012, Table 1.

7 percent and further to 4–5 percent among 25- to 30-year-olds (Schulenberg & others, 2017). Research indicated that marijuana and alcohol use were risk factors for using e-cigarettes in emerging adulthood (Cohn & others, 2015). Another study found that emerging adults who used e-cigarettes were more likely to view emerging adulthood as a time of experimentation and were likely to be experiencing such role transitions as loss of a job, dating someone new, or experiencing a romantic break-up (Allen & others, 2015).

SUBSTANCE USE IN OLDER ADULTS

As indicated earlier, alcohol and substance abuse peak in emerging adulthood and then decline somewhat by the mid-twenties. Of course, alcohol and substance abuse continue to raise serious health concerns for many people in early and middle adulthood. How extensive is substance abuse in older adults? A national survey found that in 2010 the percentage of individuals who engaged in binge drinking (defined as four or more drinks for women and five or more drinks for men on one occasion in the past 30 days) declined considerably in middle and late adulthood compared with early adulthood (Centers for Disease Control and Prevention, 2012) (see Figure 15). However, the frequency of binge drinking in the past 30 days was highest in older adults (5.5 episodes).

Although there has been a decline in binge drinking in late adulthood, the Substance Abuse and Mental Health Services Administration (2005) has identified substance abuse among older adults as an "invisible epidemic" in the United States. The belief is that substance abuse often goes undetected in older adults, and there is concern about older adults who abuse not only illicit drugs but prescription drugs as well (Bien & Bien-Barkowska, 2018). Optimization of drug use, especially not overdosing, is a key factor in successful aging (Petrovic & others, 2019). The consequences of abuse—such as depression, inadequate nutrition, congestive heart failure, and frequent falls—may erroneously be attributed to other medical or psychological conditions (Hoyer & Roodin, 2009). As the number of older adults rises, substance abuse is likely to characterize an increasing number of older adults. For older adults who are taking multiple medications, the dangers of substance abuse rise. For example, when combined with tranquilizers or sedatives, alcohol use can impair breathing, produce excessive sedation, and even be fatal.

Despite the concerns about substance abuse in later adulthood, researchers have found a protective effect of moderate alcohol use in older adults (O'Keefe & others, 2014). One study of older adults revealed that those who drank moderately (compared with those who drank heavily or did not drink at all) had better physical and mental health, and increased longevity (Rozzini, Ranhoff, & Trabucchi, 2007). And a recent study revealed that moderate drinkers were more likely to be alive and not have a cognitive impairment at 85 years of age (Richard & others, 2017). The explanation of moderate drinking's benefits involves better physical and mental performance, being more open to social contacts, and being able to assert mastery over one's life.

Researchers have especially found that moderate drinking of red wine is linked to better health and increased longevity (Li, Li, & Lin, 2018; Li & others, 2019). Explanations of the benefits of red wine involve its connection to lowering stress and reducing the risk of coronary heart disease (Chen & others, 2017). Evidence is increasing that a chemical in the skin of red wine grapes—resveratrol—plays a key role in red wine's health benefits (Li, Li, & Lin, 2018; Wu & others, 2019). One study found that red wine, but not white, killed several lines of cancer cells (Wallenborg & others, 2009). Scientists are exploring how resveratrol might activate SIRT1, an enzyme that is involved in DNA repair and aging (Granchi & Minutolo, 2018; S. H. Li & others, 2019; Yoon & others, 2019).

What might explain the finding that drinking red wine in moderation is linked to better health and increased longevity?
Creatas/PictureQuest

Review *Connect* Reflect

LG4 Evaluate substance use in adolescence and adulthood.

Review

- How extensively do adolescents take drugs? What factors are linked with drug abuse by adolescents? What is the nature of substance use in college students and young adults?
- How can substance use in older adults be described?

Connect

- Research has shown that older adults fare better when they are given more responsibility and control over their lives. In what other age periods is giving individuals more responsibility and control especially important for their development? In what ways is this helpful?

Reflect *Your Own Personal Journey of Life*

- Do you know someone who has a drug problem? If so, describe the nature of the problem. Is the person willing to admit to having a problem?

---

reach your **learning goals**

Health

1 Health, Illness, and Disease

LG1 Describe developmental changes in health.

Children's Health

Adolescents' Health

Emerging and Young Adults' Health

Health and Aging

- Prevention and poverty are important factors in children's health. Children need timely immunizations. Accident prevention is a key aspect of children's health. Of special concern are children living in poverty, who often are malnourished. A major concern is the number of children under 5 years of age who die around the world and the poor health conditions for children in many countries.

- Adolescence is a critical juncture in health because many health habits—good or bad—still are being formed. Social contexts, including family, peers, and schools, influence the health of adolescents.

- Few emerging and young adults have chronic health problems. Many emerging and young adults don't stop to think about how their personal lifestyles will affect their health later in life. Emerging adults have double the mortality rate of adolescents.

- Chronic disorders increase in middle-aged adults and are common in older adults. Osteoporosis is a concern, especially among older women. Various forms of dementia, especially Alzheimer disease, are a major health problem. Another type of brain disorder is Parkinson disease. Stress increasingly is recognized as a key factor in disease, especially in its connection to the immune system. A special concern is the quality of nursing homes for older adults and the treatment of older adults in nursing homes.

2 Nutrition and Eating Behavior

 LG2 Characterize developmental changes in nutrition and eating behavior.

Infancy

Childhood

- The importance of adequate energy intake consumed in a loving and supportive environment in infancy cannot be overstated. The growing consensus is that breast feeding is better for the baby's health than bottle feeding. Nutritional supplements can improve infants' cognitive development.

- Concerns about nutrition in childhood focus on fat content in diet and obesity. Thirty percent of U.S. children are at risk for being overweight. Obesity increases a child's risk of developing many medical and psychological problems. Poor nutrition in children from low-income families is a special concern.

| Adolescence | • | Nutrition and being overweight are also key problems among adolescents. Anorexia nervosa, bulimia nervosa, and binge eating disorder can develop in adolescence; most anorexics, bulimics, and individuals with binge eating disorder are females. |

| Adult Development and Aging | • | Obesity is a major concern in adulthood, and dieting is pervasive. Calorie restriction is associated with longevity in many animal studies, but a recent longitudinal study did not find greater longevity for calorie-restricted monkeys. A balanced diet is usually recommended for older adults. Recent research reviews have found that antioxidant supplements do not reduce the risk for many diseases, such as cancer and cardiovascular disease. |

3 Exercise

 LG3 Summarize the roles of exercise in child and adult health.

| Childhood and Adolescence | • | Most children and adolescents are not getting nearly enough exercise. |

| Adulthood | • | Both moderate and intense exercise produce physical and psychological advantages such as reduced rates of heart disease and anxiety. |

| Aging and Longevity | • | Regular exercise in middle-aged and older adults can promote health and increase longevity. |

4 Substance Use

 LG4 Evaluate substance use in adolescence and adulthood.

| Adolescence and Emerging Adulthood | • | The United States has one of the highest adolescent drug use rates of any industrialized country. Alcohol and cigarette smoking are special concerns. Development, parents, peers, and educational success play important roles in preventing drug abuse in adolescents. Forty percent of U.S. college students say they drink heavily. Substance use peaks in emerging adulthood and then often decreases by the mid-twenties. |

| Substance Use in Older Adults | • | Alcohol use declines in older adults, although abuse is more difficult to detect in older adults than in younger adults. There is concern about older adults who abuse prescription drugs and illicit drugs. |

key terms

aerobic exercise	binge eating disorder (BED)	chronic disorders	osteoporosis
Alzheimer disease	bulimia nervosa	dementia	Parkinson disease
anorexia nervosa			

key people

Lloyd Johnston	Margie Lachman	Ellen Langer	Judith Rodin

chapter 5

MOTOR, SENSORY, AND PERCEPTUAL DEVELOPMENT

chapter outline

Image Source/Getty Images

preview

Think about what is required for us to find our way around our environment, to play sports, or to create art. These activities require both active perception and precisely timed motor actions. Neither innate, automatic movements nor simple sensations are enough to let us do the things we take for granted every day. How do we develop perceptual and motor abilities, and what happens to them as we age? In this chapter, we will focus first on the development of motor skills, then on sensory and perceptual development, and finally on the coupling of perceptual-motor skills.

1 Motor Development

LG1 Describe how motor skills develop.

| The Dynamic Systems View | Reflexes | Gross Motor Skills | Fine Motor Skills |

Most adults are capable of coordinated, purposive actions of considerable skill, including driving a car, playing golf, and typing accurately on a computer keyboard. Some adults have extraordinary motor skills, such as those involved in winning an Olympic pole vault competition, painting a masterpiece, or performing heart surgery. Look all you want at a newborn infant, and you will observe nothing even remotely approaching these skilled actions. How, then, do the motor behaviors of adults come about?

THE DYNAMIC SYSTEMS VIEW

Developmentalist Arnold Gesell (1934) thought his painstaking observations had revealed how people develop their motor skills. He had discovered that infants and children develop rolling, sitting, standing, and other motor skills in a fixed order and within specific time frames. These observations, said Gesell, show that motor development comes about through the unfolding of a genetic plan, or maturation.

Later studies, however, demonstrated that the sequence of developmental milestones is not as fixed as Gesell indicated and not due as much to heredity as Gesell argued (Adolph, 2018; Adolph & Hoch, 2019). In the past two decades, the study of motor development experienced a renaissance as psychologists developed new insights about *how* motor skills develop (Adolph, 2018; Adolph & Hoch, 2019). One increasingly influential perspective is dynamic systems theory, proposed by Esther Thelen (Thelen & Smith, 1998, 2006).

According to **dynamic systems theory,** infants assemble motor skills for perceiving and acting (Thelen & Smith, 2006). To develop motor skills, infants must perceive something in the environment that motivates them to act and then use their perceptions to fine-tune their movements. Motor skills represent pathways to the infant's goals (Adolph, 2018; Adolph & Hoch, 2019).

How is a motor skill developed, according to this theory? When infants are motivated to do something, they might create a new motor behavior. The new behavior is the result of many converging factors: the development of the nervous system, the body's physical properties and its possibilities for movement, the goal the child is motivated to reach, and the environmental support for the skill. For example, babies learn to walk only when maturation of the nervous system allows them to control certain leg muscles, when their legs have grown enough to support their weight, and when they want to move.

Mastering a motor skill requires the infant's active efforts to coordinate several components of the skill. Infants explore and select possible solutions to the demands of a new task; they assemble adaptive patterns by modifying their current movement patterns. The first step occurs when the infant is motivated by a new challenge—such as the desire to cross a room—and gets into the "ballpark" of the task demands by taking a couple of stumbling steps. Then the infant "tunes" these movements to make them smoother and more effective. The tuning is achieved through repeated cycles of action and perception of the consequences of that action. According to the dynamic systems view, even universal milestones, such as crawling, reaching,

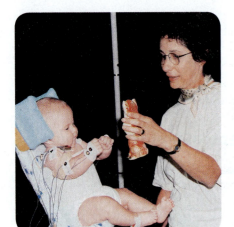

Esther Thelen is shown conducting an experiment to discover how infants learn to control their arms to reach and grasp for objects. A computer device is used to monitor the infant's arm movements and to track muscle patterns. Thelen's research is conducted from a dynamic systems perspective. *What is the nature of this perspective?*
Courtesy of Dr. David Thelen

The experiences of the first three years of life are almost entirely lost to us, and when we attempt to enter into a small child's world, we come as foreigners who have forgotten the landscape and no longer speak the native tongue.

—SELMA FRAIBERG
Developmentalist and Child Advocate, 20th Century

dynamic systems theory A theory proposed by Esther Thelen that seeks to explain how infants assemble motor skills for perceiving and acting.

and walking, are learned through this process of adaptation: Infants modulate their movement patterns to fit a new task by exploring and selecting possible configurations (Adolph, 2018; Comalli, Persand, & Adolph, 2017; Hoch, O'Grady, & Adolph, 2019).

To see how dynamic systems theory explains motor behavior, imagine that you offer a new toy to a baby named Gabriel (Thelen & others, 1993). There is no exact program that can tell Gabriel ahead of time how to move his arm and hand and fingers to grasp the toy. Gabriel must adapt to his goal—grasping the toy—and the context. From his sitting position, he must make split-second adjustments to extend his arm, holding his body steady so that his arm and torso don't plow into the toy. Muscles in his arm and shoulder contract and stretch in a host of combinations, exerting a variety of forces. He improvises a way to reach out with one arm and wrap his fingers around the toy.

Thus, according to dynamic systems theory, motor development is not a passive process in which genes dictate the unfolding of a sequence of skills over time. Rather, the infant actively puts together a skill to achieve a goal within the constraints set by the infant's body and environment (Adolph, 2018; Adolph & Hoch, 2019; Kyvelidou & Stergiou, 2019). Nature and nurture, the infant and the environment, are all working together as part of an ever-changing system (Van Hooren, Meijer, & McCrum, 2019).

Recently, Karen Adolph and Justine Hoch (2019) described four key aspects that reflect the dynamic systems theory of motor development: (1) embodied, (2) embedded, (3) enculturated, and (4) enabling.

- *Motor Development Is Embodied.* Opportunities for motor behavior involve the current status of a child's body. Changes in infants' bodies modify the nature of their motor behavior. Walking is a good example of motor behavior being embodied. Over weeks and months of walking experiences, infants improve their walking skills. Initially, they walk very slowly in halting, inconsistent ways and have poor balance. With extensive experiences, they walk faster, their steps become more consistent, and they have much better balance. Their changing body interacts with experiences and opportunities to walk as they physically grow.
- *Motor Development Is Embedded.* Environmental circumstances can facilitate or restrict possibilities for motor behavior. Motor behavior occurs in a physical environment and a changing world. Variations in the environment require infants to be flexible and adapt to these changing circumstances. As they encounter steep slopes, narrow passageways, stairs, and many other variations in their physical environment, infants have to be flexible and modify how they move.
- *Motor Development Is Enculturated.* Social and cultural contexts influence motor behavior. Caregivers play important roles in infants' motor development. Caregivers often hold infants' hands and "walk" them around a room. And infants' first steps in learning to walk are likely in a social context as they go toward a caregiver's open arms. Cultures also vary in how much caregivers engage in behavior that stimulates and encourages infants' and children's motor development.
- *Motor Development Is Enabling.* Motor development is not isolated from other aspects of development, and it contributes to infants' and children's development in other domains. Motor development allows infants and children to more autonomously explore and learn about much wider and more complex aspects of the environment. Before infants learn to crawl and walk, their exploration of the world depends on where their caregivers place them, but their expanding motor skills provide them with more independence in exploring and learning about the world that can improve their cognitive and socioemotional development.

As you read about the course of motor development, you will see how dynamic systems theory applies to some specific skills. First, though, let's examine how the story of motor development begins with reflexes.

REFLEXES

Newborn infants are not completely helpless. Among other things, they have some basic reflexes. For example, when they are submerged, they will hold their breath and contract their throat to keep water out. Reflexes allow infants to respond adaptively to their environment before they have had the opportunity to learn.

How might dynamic systems theory explain the development of learning to walk?
Vitalinka/Shutterstock

developmental **connection**

Nature and Nurture
The epigenetic view states that development is an ongoing, bidirectional interchange between heredity and the environment. Connect to "Biological Beginnings."

rooting reflex A newborn's built-in reaction that occurs when the infant's cheek is stroked or the side of the mouth is touched. In response, the infant turns its head toward the side that was touched, in an apparent effort to find something to suck.

sucking reflex A newborn's reaction of sucking an object placed in its mouth. The sucking reflex enables the infant to get nourishment before it has begun to associate a nipple with food.

Moro reflex A startle response that occurs in reaction to a sudden, intense noise or movement. When startled, the newborn arches its back, throws its head back, and flings out its arms and legs. Then the newborn rapidly closes its arms and legs to the center of the body.

grasping reflex A reflex that occurs when something touches an infant's palms. The infant responds by grasping tightly.

gross motor skills Motor skills that involve large-muscle activities, such as walking.

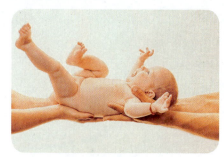

Moro reflex

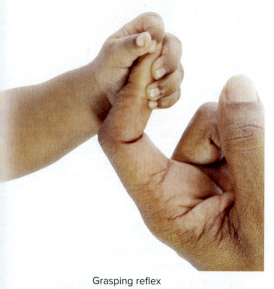

Grasping reflex

FIGURE 1

NEWBORN REFLEXES

(*Top*): Volodymyr Tverdokhlib/Shutterstock; (*bottom*): Stockbyte/PunchStock

The rooting and sucking reflexes are important examples. Both have survival value for newborn mammals, who must find a mother's breast to obtain nourishment. The **rooting reflex** occurs when an infant's cheek is stroked or the side of the mouth is touched. In response, the infant turns its head toward the side that was touched in an apparent effort to find something to suck. The **sucking reflex** occurs when newborns suck an object placed in their mouth. This reflex enables newborns to get nourishment before they have associated a nipple with food; it also serves as a self-soothing or self-regulating mechanism.

Another example is the **Moro reflex,** which occurs in response to a sudden, intense noise or movement (see Figure 1). When startled, newborns arch their back, throw back their head, and fling out their arms and legs. Then they rapidly close their arms and legs. The Moro reflex is believed to be a way of grabbing for support while falling, because it would have had survival value for our primate ancestors.

Some reflexes—coughing, sneezing, blinking, shivering, and yawning, for example—persist throughout life. They are as important for the adult as they are for the infant. Other reflexes, though, disappear several months following birth, as the infant's brain matures and voluntary control over many behaviors develops. The rooting and Moro reflexes, for example, tend to disappear when the infant is 3 to 4 months old.

The movements of some reflexes eventually become incorporated into more complex, voluntary actions. One important example is the **grasping reflex,** which occurs when something touches the infant's palms (see Figure 1). The infant responds by grasping tightly. By the end of the third month, the grasping reflex diminishes, and the infant shows a more voluntary grasp. As its motor development becomes smoother, the infant will grasp objects, carefully manipulate them, and explore their qualities.

Individual differences in reflexive behavior appear soon after birth. For example, the sucking capabilities of newborns vary considerably. Some newborns are efficient at sucking forcefully and obtaining milk; others are not as adept and get tired before they are full. Most infants take several weeks to establish a sucking style that is coordinated with the way the mother is holding the infant, the way milk is coming out of the bottle or breast, and the infant's temperament (Blass, 2008).

The old view of reflexes portrayed them as exclusively genetic, built-in mechanisms that govern the infant's movements. The new perspective on infant reflexes is that they are not automatic or completely beyond the infant's control. For example, infants can deliberately control such movements as alternating their legs to make a mobile jiggle or change their sucking rate to listen to a recording (Adolph & Robinson, 2015).

GROSS MOTOR SKILLS

Ask any parents about their baby, and sooner or later you are likely to hear about one or more advances in motor skills, such as "Cassandra just learned to crawl," "Jesse is finally sitting alone," or "Angela took her first step last week." Parents proudly announce such milestones as their children transform themselves from babies unable to lift their heads to toddlers who grab things off the grocery store shelf, chase a cat, and participate actively in the family's social life (Thelen, 2000). These milestones are examples of **gross motor skills,** skills that involve large-muscle activities such as moving one's arms and walking.

The Development of Posture   How do gross motor skills develop? As a foundation, these skills require postural control (Adolph & Hoch, 2019; Franchak, Kretch, & Adolph, 2019). For example, to track moving objects, you must be able to control your head in order to stabilize your gaze; before you can walk, you must be able to balance on one leg.

Posture is more than just holding still and straight. Posture is a dynamic process that is linked with sensory information in the skin, joints, and muscles, which tell us where we are in space; in vestibular organs in the inner ear that regulate balance and equilibrium; and in vision and hearing (Thelen & Smith, 2006).

Newborn infants cannot voluntarily control their posture. Within a few weeks, though, they can hold their head erect, and soon they can lift their head while prone. By 2 months of age, babies can sit while supported on a lap or an infant seat, but they cannot sit independently until they are 6 or 7 months of age. Standing also develops gradually during the first year of life. By about 8 to 9 months of age, infants usually learn to pull themselves up and hold onto a chair, and they often can stand alone by about 10 to 12 months of age.

What are some developmental changes in posture during infancy?
Serhiy Kobyakov/Shutterstock

Learning to Walk Locomotion and postural control are closely linked, especially in walking upright (Adolph, Hoch, & Cole, 2018).

Even young infants can make the alternating leg movements that are needed for walking. The neural pathways that control leg alternation are in place from a very early age, even at birth or before. Indeed, researchers have found that alternating leg movements occur during the fetal period and at birth (Adolph & Robinson, 2015).

If infants can produce forward stepping movements so early, why does it take them so long to learn to walk? The key skills in learning to walk appear to be stabilizing balance on one leg long enough to swing the other forward and shifting the weight without falling. This is a difficult biomechanical problem to solve, and it takes infants about a year to do it.

In learning to locomote, infants must discover what kinds of places and surfaces are safe for crawling or walking (Adolf, Hoch, & Cole, 2018). Karen Adolph (1997) investigated how experienced and inexperienced crawling and walking infants go down steep slopes (see Figure 2). Newly crawling infants, who averaged about 8 months in age, rather indiscriminately went down the steep slopes, often falling in the process (with their mothers standing next to the slope to catch them). After weeks of practice, the crawling babies became more adept at judging which slopes were too steep to crawl down and which ones they could navigate safely.

Thus, practice and learning are very important in the development of new motor skills (Adolph, 2018; Adolph & Berger, 2015). In one study, Adolph and her colleagues (2012) observed 12- to 19-month-olds during free play. Locomotor experience was extensive, with the infants averaging 2,368 steps and 17 falls per hour.

A recent study examined how infants plan and guide their locomotion in the challenging context of navigating a series of bridges varying in width (Kretch & Adolph, 2017). Infants' visual exploration (direction of their gaze) was assessed using a head-mounted eye-tracking device and their locomotor actions were captured using video. The 14-month-olds engaged in visual exploration from a distance as an initial assessment before they crossed almost every bridge. The visual information led to modifications in their gait when approaching narrow bridges, and they used haptic (touch) information at the edge of the bridges. As they gained more walking experience, their exploratory behaviors became more efficient and they became better at discerning which bridges were safe to walk across.

Might the development of walking be linked to advances in other aspects of development? Walking experience leads to being able to gain contact with objects that were previously out of reach and to initiate interaction with parents and other adults, thereby promoting language development (Adolph & Hoch, 2019; Walle & Campos, 2014). Thus, just as with advances in postural skills, walking skills can produce a cascade of changes in the infant's development.

The First Year: Motor Development Milestones and Variations Figure 3 summarizes important accomplishments in gross motor skills during the first year, culminating in the ability to walk easily. The timing of these milestones, especially the later ones, may vary by as much as two to four months, and experiences can modify the onset of these accomplishments (Hoch, O'Grady, & Adolph, 2019). For example, in the early 1990s, pediatricians began recommending that parents place their babies on their backs to sleep. Following that instruction, babies who back-sleep began crawling later, typically several weeks later than babies who sleep prone (Davis & others, 1998). Also, some infants do not follow the standard sequence of motor accomplishments (Eaton & others, 2008). For example, many American infants never crawl on their belly or on their hands and knees. They might discover an idiosyncratic form of locomotion before walking, such as rolling, or they might never locomote until they get upright (Adolph & Robinson, 2015). In Jamaica, approximately one-fourth of babies skip crawling altogether (Hopkins, 1991).

The early view that growth and motor development simply reflect the age-related output of maturation is, at best, incomplete. Rather, infants develop new skills with the guidance of their caregivers in a real-world environment of objects, surfaces, and planes (Adolph & Hoch, 2019; Hoch, O'Grady, & Adolph, 2019).

A recent study identified a number of factors that are linked to motor development in the first year of life (Flensborg-Madsen & Mortensen, 2017). Twelve developmental milestones were assessed, including grasping, rolling, sitting, and crawling; standing and walking; and overall mean of milestones. A larger size at birth (based on birth weight, birth length, or head circumference) was the aspect of pregnancy and delivery that showed the strongest link to reaching motor milestones earlier. Maternal smoking during the last trimester of prenatal development was associated with reaching the motor milestones later. Also, increases in size (weight increase,

Newly crawling infant

Experienced walker

FIGURE 2

THE ROLE OF EXPERIENCE AND LEARNING IN CRAWLING AND WALKING INFANTS' JUDGMENTS OF WHETHER TO GO DOWN A SLOPE. Karen Adolph (1997) found that locomotor experience rather than age was the primary predictor of adaptive responding on slopes of varying steepness. Newly crawling and walking infants could not judge the safety of the various slopes. With experience, they learned to avoid slopes where they would fall. When expert crawlers began to walk, they again made mistakes and fell, even though they had judged the same slope accurately when crawling. Adolph referred to this as the specificity of learning because it does not transfer across crawling and walking.
Dr. Karen Adolph, New York University

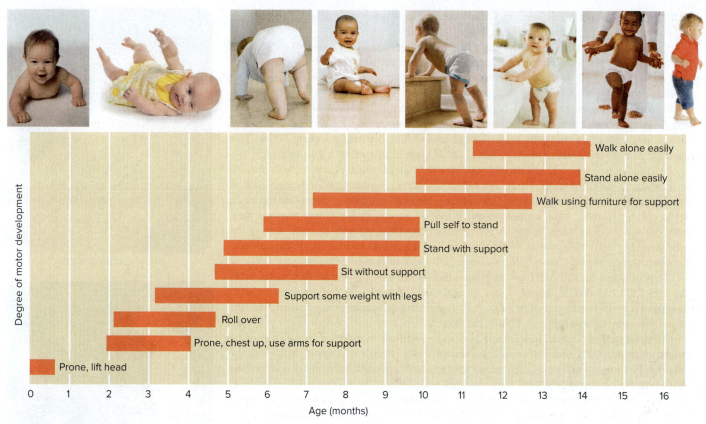

FIGURE 3

MILESTONES IN GROSS MOTOR DEVELOPMENT. The horizontal red bars indicate the range in which most infants reach various milestones in gross motor development.

(*Left to right*): Barbara Penoyar/Getty Images; Benjamin Simeneta/Shutterstock; Image Source/Alamy; Victoria Blackie/Getty Images; Cohen/Ostrow/Digital Vision/Getty Images; Fotosearch/Getty Images; Tom Grill/Corbis; amaviael/123rf

A baby is an angel whose wings decrease as his legs increase.

—FRENCH PROVERB

length increase, and head increase) in the first year were related to reaching the motor milestones earlier. Breast feeding also was linked to reaching the milestones earlier.

Development in the Second Year   The motor accomplishments of the first year bring increasing independence, allowing infants to explore their environment more extensively and to initiate interaction with others more readily. In the second year of life, toddlers become more motorically skilled and mobile (Adolph, Rachwani, & Hoch, 2018). Motor activity during the second year is vital to the child's competent development, and few restrictions, except for safety, should be placed on their adventures.

By 13 to 18 months, toddlers can pull a toy attached to a string and use their hands and legs to climb up a number of steps. By 18 to 24 months, toddlers can walk quickly or run stiffly for a short distance, balance on their feet in a squatting position while playing with objects on the floor, walk backward without losing their balance, stand and kick a ball without falling, stand and throw a ball, and jump in place.

Can parents give their babies a head start on becoming physically fit and physically talented through structured exercise classes? Most infancy experts recommend against structured exercise classes for babies. But there are other ways to guide infants' motor development. Caregivers in some cultures do handle babies vigorously, and such treatment might advance motor development, as we discuss next.

Cultural Variations in Guiding Infants' Motor Development   Mothers in developing countries tend to stimulate their infants' motor skills more than mothers in more developed countries (Hopkins, 1991). In many African, Indian, and Caribbean cultures, mothers massage and stretch their infants during daily baths (Adolph & Hoch, 2019; Adolph, Karasik, & Tamis-LeMonda, 2010). Mothers in the Gusii culture of Kenya also encourage vigorous movement in their babies.

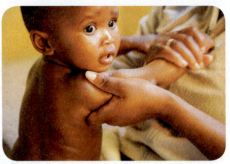

(*Left*) In the Algonquin culture in Quebec, Canada, babies are strapped to a cradle board for much of their infancy. (*Right*) In Jamaica, mothers massage and stretch their infants' arms and legs. *To what extent do cultural variations in the activity infants engage in influence the time at which they reach motor milestones?*
(*Left*): Michael Greenlar/The Image Works; (*right*): Pippa Hetherington/Earthstock/Newscom

Do these cultural variations make a difference in motor development? When caregivers provide babies with physical guidance by physically handling them in special ways (such as stroking, massaging, or stretching) or by giving them opportunities for exercise, the infants often reach motor milestones earlier than infants whose caregivers have not provided these activities (Adolph, Cole, & Vereijken, 2015; Adolph, Karasik, & Tamis-LeMonda, 2010). For example, Jamaican mothers expect their infants to sit and walk alone two to three months earlier than English mothers do (Hopkins & Westra, 1990). And in sub-Saharan Africa, traditional practices in many villages involve mothers and siblings engaging babies in exercises, such as frequent exercise for trunk and pelvic muscles (Super & Harkness, 2010).

Practices that restrain infants' movement—such as Chinese sandbags, orphanage restrictions, and failure of caregivers to encourage movement in Budapest—have been found to produce substantial delays in motor development (Adolph, Karasik, & Tamis-LeMonda, 2010). In some rural Chinese provinces, for example, babies are placed in a bag of fine sand, which acts as a diaper and is changed once a day. The baby is left alone, face up, and is visited only when being fed by the mother (Xie & Young, 1999). Some studies of swaddling show slight delays in motor development, but other studies show no delays. Cultures that swaddle infants usually do so before the infant is mobile. When the infant becomes more mobile, swaddling decreases.

To close our discussion of motor development in infancy, it is important to highlight a key theme: infants' development of a skill, such as sitting, crawling or walking, requires considerable behavioral flexibility—the ability to do what is necessary to attain life's everyday goals (Adolph & Hoch, 2019). Adaptive behavior involves an accurate solution to a current situation and challenge. The infant's movements cannot be repeated in the same way over time and in different situations because their bodies, the environments in which they behave, and the tasks they face change. Keep this theme in mind as you read about motor development in childhood next because such behavioral flexibility continues to be required for finding successful solutions to changing bodies, contexts, and tasks as children continue to develop.

Childhood The preschool child no longer has to make an effort to stay upright and to move around. As children move their legs with more confidence and carry themselves more purposefully, moving around in the environment becomes more automatic.

At 3 years of age, children enjoy simple movements, such as hopping, jumping, and running back and forth, just for the sheer delight of performing these activities. They take considerable pride in showing how they can run across a room and jump all of 6 inches. For the 3-year-old, such activity is a source of considerable pride in accomplishment.

At 4 years of age, children are still enjoying the same kinds of activities, but they have become more adventurous. They scramble over low jungle gyms as they display their athletic prowess.

What are some developmental changes in children's motor development in early childhood and middle and late childhood?
Mehmet zhan Araboga/EyeEm/Getty Images

developmental connection

Health

Exercise is linked to prevention and effective treatment of many diseases. Connect to "Health."

At 5 years of age, children are even more adventuresome than they were at 4. It is not unusual for self-assured 5-year-olds to perform hair-raising stunts on practically any climbing object. They run hard and enjoy racing with each other and their parents.

During middle and late childhood, children's motor development becomes much smoother and more coordinated than it was in early childhood. For example, only one child in a thousand can hit a tennis ball over the net at the age of 3, yet by the age of 10 or 11 most children can learn to play the sport. Running, climbing, skipping rope, swimming, bicycle riding, and skating are just a few of the many physical skills elementary school children can master. And, when mastered, these physical skills are a source of great pleasure and a sense of accomplishment. In gross motor skills involving large-muscle activity, boys usually outperform girls.

There can be long-term negative effects for children who fail to develop basic motor skills (Gorgon, 2018; Utesch & others, 2019). These children will not be as able to join in group games or participate in sports during their school years and in adulthood. In a recent study, children with a low level of motor competence had a lower motivation for sports participation and had lower global self-worth than their counterparts with a high level of motor competence (Bardid & others, 2019). Another recent study found that higher motor proficiency in preschool was linked with engaging in a higher level of physical activity in adolescence (Venetsanou & Kambas, 2017).

Organized sports are one way of encouraging children to be active and to develop their motor skills. Schools and community agencies offer programs for children that involve baseball, soccer, football, basketball, swimming, gymnastics, and other sports. For children who participate in them, these programs may play a central role in their lives.

Participation in sports can have both positive and negative consequences for children (Egger, Oberle, & Saluan, 2019; Zwinkels & others, 2018). Participation can provide exercise, opportunities to learn how to compete, enhanced self-esteem, persistence, and a setting for developing peer relations and friendships (Theokas, 2009). One study found that 8-year-old children who continued to participate in sports over the next 24 months were rated by their parents as having a higher health-related quality of life than children who did not participate in sports (Vella & others, 2014). In this study, the positive effects of sports participation were stronger for girls than boys. Further, recent research indicates that participating in sports reduces the likelihood that children will become obese (Basterfield & others, 2015; Learmonth & others, 2019). Another study revealed that children who play sports show a lower cardiovascular risk profile (Hebert & others, 2017). And in a recent study of out-of-school activities, time spent in organized sports was associated with increased positive self-identity (Lee & others, 2018).

However, sports also can bring pressure to achieve and win, physical injuries, a distraction from academic work, and unrealistic expectations for success as an athlete (Fanelli & Fanelli, 2018; von Rosen & others, 2018a, b). There is increasing concern about the occurrence of concussions in youth football and soccer (Smith & others, 2019). The *Connecting Development to Life* interlude examines the roles of parents and coaches in children's sports.

Adolescence and Adulthood Gross motor skills typically improve during adolescence. Most of us reach our peak physical performance before the age of 30, often between the ages of 19 and 26. This peak occurs both for the average young adult and for outstanding athletes. Even though athletes keep getting better than their predecessors—running faster, jumping higher, and lifting more weight—the age at which they reach their peak performance has remained virtually unchanged (Schultz & Curnow, 1988). Most swimmers and gymnasts reach their peak in their late teens. Many athletes, including track performers in sprint races (100- and 200-yard dashes), peak in their early to mid-twenties. Golfers and marathon runners tend to peak in their late twenties or even early thirties.

After an individual reaches the age of 30, most biological functions begin to decline, although the decline of specific organs can vary considerably. The decline in general biological functioning that begins at about age 30 occurs at a rate of about 0.75 to 1 percent a year. Declines often occur in cardiovascular functioning, muscle strength, bone density (especially for females), neural function, balance, and flexibility.

Older adults move more slowly than young adults, and this slowing occurs for movements with a wide range of difficulty (Davis & others, 2013) (see Figure 4). Even when they perform everyday tasks such as reaching and grasping, moving from one place to another, and continuous movement, older adults tend to move more slowly than they did when they were young

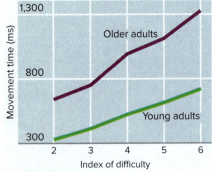

FIGURE 4

MOVEMENT AND AGING. Older adults take longer to move than young adults, and this change occurs across a range of movement difficulty (Ketcham & Stelmach, 2001).

Parents, Coaches, and Children's Sports

Most sports psychologists stress that it is important for parents to show an interest in their children's sports participation. Most children want their parents to watch them perform in sports. Many children whose parents do not come to watch them play in sporting events feel that their parents do not adequately support them. However, some children become extremely nervous when their parents watch them perform, or they get embarrassed when their parents cheer too loudly or make a fuss. If children request that their parents not watch them perform, parents should respect their children's wishes (Schreiber, 1990).

Parents should praise their children for their sports performance, and if they don't become overinvolved, they can help their children build their physical skills and guide them emotionally by discussing with them how to deal with a difficult coach, how to cope with a tough loss, and how to put in perspective a poorly played game. The following guidelines provided by the Women's Sports Foundation (2001) in its booklet *Parents' Guide to Girls' Sports* can benefit both parents and coaches of all children in sports.

What are some of the possible positive and negative aspects of children's participation in sports?
(Top): kali9/Getty Images; (bottom): BananaStock/Alamy

The Dos

- Make sports fun; the more children enjoy sports, the more they will want to play.
- Remember that it is okay for children to make mistakes; it means they are trying.
- Allow children to ask questions about the sport and discuss the sport in a calm, supportive manner.
- Show respect for the child's sports participation.
- Be positive and convince the child that he or she is making a good effort.
- Be a positive role model for the child in sports.

The Don'ts

- Yell or scream at the child.
- Condemn the child for poor play or continue to bring up failures long after they happen.
- Point out the child's errors in front of others.
- Expect the child to learn something immediately.
- Expect the child to become a pro.
- Ridicule or make fun of the child.
- Compare the child to siblings or to more talented children.
- Make sports all work and no fun.

What developmental theories offer support for the Women's Sports Foundation's assertion that parents should strive to be positive role models for their children in sports?

(Mollenkopf, 2007). Adequate mobility is an important aspect of maintaining an independent and active lifestyle in late adulthood (Patel & others, 2019; Raggi & others, 2018). Also, a recent study revealed that middle-aged and older adults who had limited mobility also had lower cognitive functioning (Demnitz & others, 2018).

Recent research connects obesity with mobility limitation in older adults (Adair, Duazo, & Borja, 2019). Also, one study found that a combined program of physical activity and weight loss helped to preserve mobility in older, obese adults in poor cardiovascular health (Rejeski & others, 2011). And another study revealed that it's not just physical exercise and weight loss that are linked to preserving older adults' motor functions; in this study, engaging in social activities protected against loss of motor abilities (Buchman & others, 2009). Further, a recent large-scale study of older adults indicated that a 554-step-per-day increase in mobility reduced physical function limitations by 5.9 percent and improved quality of life by 3.2 percent (Kabiri & others, 2018).

The risk of falling in older adults increases with age and is greater for women than for men (Francis-Coad & others, 2017; Granbom & others, 2019). Two-thirds of older adults who

Motor skills decline less in older adults who are active and biologically healthy. *What is the difference between chronological age and biological age?*
Squaredpixels/Getty Images

experience a fall are likely to fall again in the next six months. Falls are the leading cause of injury deaths among adults who are 65 years and older (National Center for Health Statistics, 2018). Each year, approximately 200,000 adults over the age of 65 (many of them women) fracture a hip in a fall. Half of these older adults die within 12 months, frequently from pneumonia. A meta-analysis concluded that exercise reduces falls in adults 60 years of age and older (Stubbs, Brefka, & Denkinger, 2015). One study revealed that participation in an exercise class once a week for three years reduced the fall risk and the number of falling incidents in older adults who were at high risk for falling (Yokoya, Demura, & Sato, 2009). Exercise also benefited frail elderly adults in another study (Danilovich, Conroy, & Hornby, 2018). In this study, high-intensity walking training reduced the older adults' frailty, increased their walking speed, and improved their balance. In another study, walking was more effective than balance training in helping older adults maintain their mobility (Okubo & others, 2016).

Decreased walking speed in older adults is associated with limited mobility, less community participation, greater cognitive decline, and increased risk of falls. A recent study of older women found that on average a reduction in walking speed occurred at about 71 years of age (Noce Kirkwood & others, 2018). A recent study also found that older adults who walked slowly were more likely to have mild cognitive impairment (Rajtar-Zembaty & others, 2019).

FINE MOTOR SKILLS

Whereas gross motor skills involve large-muscle activity, **fine motor skills** involve finely tuned movements. Buttoning a shirt, typing, or doing any task that requires finger dexterity demonstrates fine motor skills.

Infancy Infants have hardly any control over fine motor skills at birth, but newborns do have many components of what will become finely coordinated arm, hand, and finger movements. The onset of reaching and grasping marks a significant milestone in infants' increasing ability to interact with their surroundings (Wiesen, Watkins, & Needham, 2016). During the first two years of life, infants refine how they reach and grasp (Chinn & others, 2019; Keen, 2011). Initially, infants reach by moving their shoulders and elbows crudely, swinging toward an object. Later, when infants reach for an object they move their wrists, rotate their hands, and coordinate their thumb and forefinger. Infants do not have to see their own hands in order to reach for an object (Clifton & others, 1993). Cues from muscles, tendons, and joints, not sight of the limb, guide reaching by 4-month-old infants.

Infants refine their ability to grasp objects by developing two types of grasps. Initially, infants grip with the whole hand, which is called the *palmer grasp*. Later, toward the end of the first year, infants also grasp small objects with their thumb and forefinger, which is called the *pincer grip*. Their grasping system is very flexible. They vary their grip on an object depending on its size, shape, and texture, as well as the size of their own hands relative to the object's size. Infants grip small objects with their thumb and forefinger (and sometimes their middle finger too), whereas they grip large objects with all of the fingers of one hand or both hands. Research studies found that short-term training involving practice of reaching movements increased both preterm and full-term infants' reaching for and touching objects (Cunha & others, 2016; Guimaraes & Tudella, 2015).

A young girl using a pincer grip to pick up puzzle pieces.
Newstockimages/SuperStock

Perceptual-motor coupling is necessary for the infant to coordinate grasping (Keen, 2011). Which perceptual system the infant is most likely to use to coordinate grasping varies with age. Four-month-old infants rely greatly on touch to determine how they will grip an object; 8-month-olds are more likely to use vision as a guide (Newell & others, 1989). This developmental change is efficient because vision lets infants preshape their hands as they reach for an object.

Experience plays a role in reaching and grasping (Sacrey & others, 2014). In one study, providing 3-month-olds who were not yet engaging in reaching behavior with reaching

fine motor skills Motor skills that involve finely tuned movements, such as any activity that requires finger dexterity.

experiences was linked to increased object exploration and attention focusing skills at 15 months of age (Libertus, Joh, & Needham, 2016). Researchers have also found that short-term training involving practice of reaching movements increased both preterm and full-term infants' reaching for and touching objects (Cunha & others, 2016; Guimaraes & Tudella, 2015).

Amy Needham and her colleagues have used "sticky mittens" to enhance young infants' active grasping and manipulation of objects. In one study, 3-month-old infants participated in play sessions wearing "sticky mittens"—"mittens with palms that stuck to the edges of toys and allowed the infants to pick up the toys" (Needham, Barrett, & Peterman, 2002, p. 279) (see Figure 5). Infants who participated in sessions with the mittens grasped and manipulated objects earlier in their development than a control group of infants who did not receive the "mitten" experience. The experienced infants looked at the objects longer, swatted at them more during visual contact, and were more likely to mouth the objects. In one study, 5-month-old infants whose parents trained them to use the sticky mittens for 10 minutes a day over a two-week period showed advances in their reaching behavior at the end of the two weeks (Libertus & Needham, 2010).

Just as infants need to exercise their gross motor skills, they also need to exercise their fine motor skills (Wiesen, Watkins, & Needham, 2016). Especially when they can manage a pincer grip, infants delight in picking up small objects. Many develop the pincer grip and begin to crawl at about the same time, and infants at this time pick up virtually everything in sight, especially on the floor, and put the objects in their mouth. Thus, parents need to be vigilant in regularly monitoring what objects are within the infant's reach (Keen, 2005).

Rachel Keen (2011; Keen, Lee, & Adolph, 2014) emphasizes that tool use is an excellent context for studying problem solving in infants because tool use provides information about how infants plan to reach a goal. Researchers in this area have studied infants' intentional actions that range from picking up a spoon in different orientations to retrieving rakes placed inside tubes. One study explored motor origins of tool use by assessing developmental changes in banging movements in 6- to 15-month-olds (Kahrs, Jung, & Lockman, 2013). In this study, younger infants were inefficient and variable when banging an object but by 1 year of age infants showed consistent straight up-and-down hand movements that resulted in precise aiming and consistent levels of force.

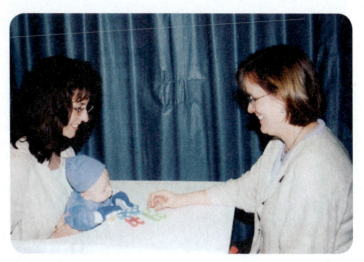

FIGURE 5

INFANTS' USE OF "STICKY MITTENS" TO EXPLORE OBJECTS. Amy Needham and her colleagues (2002) found that "sticky mittens" enhanced young infants' object exploration skills.
Courtesy of Amy Needham, Duke University

Childhood and Adolescence As children get older, their fine motor skills improve (Sveistrup & others, 2008). At 3 years of age, children have had the ability to pick up the tiniest objects between their thumb and forefinger for some time, but they are still somewhat clumsy at it. Three-year-olds can build surprisingly high block towers, each block placed with intense concentration but often not in a completely straight line. When 3-year-olds play with a form board or a simple puzzle, they are rather rough in placing the pieces. Even when they recognize the hole that a piece fits into, they are not very precise in positioning the piece. They often try to force the piece into the hole or pat it vigorously.

By 4 years of age, children's fine motor coordination has become much more precise. Sometimes 4-year-old children have trouble building high towers with blocks because, in their desire to place each of the blocks perfectly, they may upset those already stacked. By age 5, children's fine motor coordination has improved further. Hand, arm, and fingers all move together under better command of the eye. Mere towers no longer interest the 5-year-old, who now wants to build a house or a church, complete with steeple, though adults may still need to be told what each finished project is meant to be.

Increased myelination of the central nervous system is reflected in the improvement of fine motor skills during middle and late childhood. Children use their hands more adroitly as tools. Six-year-olds can hammer, paste, tie shoes, and fasten clothes. By 7 years of age, children's hands have become steadier. At this age, children prefer a pencil to a crayon for printing, and reversal of letters is less common. Printing becomes smaller. At 8 to 10 years of age, children can use their hands independently with more ease and precision; children

What are some developmental changes in children's fine motor skills?
Rollover/E+/Getty Images

can now write rather than print words. Letter size becomes smaller and more even. At 10 to 12 years of age, children begin to show manipulative skills similar to the abilities of adults. The complex, intricate, and rapid movements needed to produce fine-quality crafts or to play a difficult piece on a musical instrument can be mastered. Girls usually outperform boys in fine motor skills.

Researchers have found that children's gross and fine motor skills are associated with cognitive function (Kim & others, 2018). For example, in a study of 9-year-old children, both their gross and fine motor skills were associated with cognitive function in areas such as memory and processing speed, as well as better performance in math and reading comprehension (Geertsen & others, 2016).

Adult Development   Fine motor skills may undergo some decline in middle and late adulthood as dexterity decreases, although for most healthy individuals, fine motor skills, such as reaching and grasping, continue to be performed in functional ways (Hoogendam & others, 2014a). However, pathological conditions may result in weakness or paralysis of an individual's hands, in which case performance of fine motor skills may be impossible.

Review **Connect** Reflect

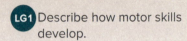 Describe how motor skills develop.

Review
- What is the dynamic systems view of motor development?
- What are reflexes? What are some reflexes of infants?
- What are gross motor skills, and how do they develop?
- What are fine motor skills? How do fine motor skills develop?

Connect
- How does the development of infants' gross motor skills differ from their development of fine motor skills?

Reflect *Your Own Personal Journey of Life*
- Imagine that you are the parent of a 7-year-old child. How would you evaluate the benefits and drawbacks of allowing your child to participate in organized competitive sports such as soccer, basketball, or tennis?

2 Sensory and Perceptual Development

LG2   Outline the course of sensory and perceptual development.

| What Are Sensation and Perception? | The Ecological View | Visual Perception | Hearing | Other Senses | Intermodal Perception | Nature/Nurture and Perceptual Development |

How do sensations and perceptions develop? Can newborn infants see? If so, what can they perceive? What about the other senses—hearing, smell, taste, touch, and pain? What are they like in the newborn, and how do they develop? How do sensation and perception change when adults become older? These are among the intriguing questions that we explore in this section.

WHAT ARE SENSATION AND PERCEPTION?

How does a newborn know that her mother's skin is soft rather than rough? How does a 5-year-old know what color his hair is? How does a 10-year-old know that a firecracker is louder than a cat's meow? Infants and children "know" these things because of information that comes through the senses. Without vision, hearing, touch, taste, smell, and other senses, we would be isolated from the world; we would live in dark silence, a tasteless, colorless, feeling-less void.

Sensation occurs when information interacts with sensory *receptors*—the eyes, ears, tongue, nostrils, and skin. The sensation of hearing occurs when waves of pulsating air are collected by the outer ear and conducted through the bones of the inner ear and the *cochlea*, where mechanical vibrations are converted into electrical impulses. Then the electrical impulses move to the *auditory nerve*, which transmits them to the brain. The sensation of vision occurs as rays of light contact the eyes and become focused on the *retina*, where light is converted into electrical impulses. Then the electrical impulses are transmitted by the *optic nerve* to the visual centers of the brain.

Perception is the interpretation of what is sensed. The air waves that contact the ears might be interpreted as noise or as musical sounds, for example. The physical energy transmitted to the retina of the eye might be interpreted as a particular color, pattern, or shape, depending on how it is perceived.

How would you use the Gibsons' ecological theory of perception and the concept of affordance to explain the role that perception is playing in this baby's activity?
Oksana Kuzmina/Shutterstock

THE ECOLOGICAL VIEW

In recent decades, much of the research on perceptual development in infancy has been guided by the ecological view of Eleanor and James J. Gibson (E. Gibson, 1969, 1989, 2001; J. Gibson, 1966, 1979). They argue that we do not have to take bits and pieces of data from sensations and build up representations of the world in our minds. Instead, our perceptual system can select from the rich information that the environment itself provides.

According to the Gibsons' **ecological view,** we directly perceive information that exists in the world around us. Perception brings us into contact with the environment in order to interact with and adapt to it (Kretch & Adolph, 2017). Perception is designed for action. Perception gives people such information as when to duck, when to turn their bodies to get through a narrow passageway, and when to put up their hands to catch something.

In the Gibsons' view, all objects and surfaces have **affordances,** which are opportunities for interaction offered by objects that fit within our capabilities to perform activities. A pot may afford you something to cook with, and it may afford a toddler something to bang. Adults immediately know when a chair is appropriate for sitting, when a surface is safe for walking, or when an object is within reach. We directly and accurately perceive these affordances by sensing information from the environment—the light or sound reflecting from the surfaces of the world—and from our own bodies through muscle receptors, joint receptors, and skin receptors (Adolph & Kretch, 2015).

An important developmental question is "What affordances can infants or children detect and use?" In one study, for example, when babies who could walk were faced with a squishy waterbed, they stopped and explored it, then chose to crawl rather than walk across it (Gibson & others, 1987). They combined perception and action to adapt to the demands of the task.

Studying infants' perception has not been an easy task. What do you think some of the research challenges might be? The *Connecting with Research* interlude describes some of the ingenious ways researchers study infants' perception.

VISUAL PERCEPTION

Some important changes in visual perception as we age can be traced to differences in how the eye itself functions over time. These changes in the eye's functioning influence, for example, how clearly we can see an object, whether we can differentiate its colors, at what distances, and in what light. But the differences between what a newborn sees and what a toddler or an adult sees go far beyond those that can be explained by changes in the eye's functioning, as we discuss in this section.

Infancy Psychologist William James (1890/1950) called the newborn's perceptual world a "blooming, buzzing confusion." More than a century later, we can safely say that he was wrong (Damon & others, 2017; Quinn, Lee, & Pascalis, 2019). Even the newborn perceives a world with some order. That world, however, is far different from the one perceived by the toddler or the adult.

Visual Acuity Just how well can infants see? At birth, the nerves and muscles and lens of the eye are still developing. As a result, newborns cannot see small things that are far away.

sensation Reaction that occurs when information interacts with sensory receptors— the eyes, ears, tongue, nostrils, and skin.

perception The interpretation of sensation.

ecological view The view proposed by the Gibsons that people directly perceive information in the world around them. Perception brings people in contact with the environment in order to interact with it and adapt to it.

affordances Opportunities for interaction offered by objects that fit within our capabilities to perform activities.

connecting with research

How Do Scientists Study the Newborn's Perception?

Scientists have developed a number of research methods and tools sophisticated enough to examine the subtle abilities of infants and to interpret their complex actions (Bendersky & Sullivan, 2007).

Visual Preference Method

Robert Fantz (1963) was a pioneer in this effort. Fantz made an important discovery that advanced the ability of researchers to investigate infants' visual perception: Infants look at different things for different lengths of time. Fantz placed infants in a "looking chamber," which had two visual displays on the ceiling above the infant's head. An experimenter viewed the infant's eyes by looking through a peephole. If the infant was fixating on one of the displays, the experimenter could see the display's reflection in the infant's eyes. This arrangement allowed the experimenter to determine how long the infant looked at each display. Fantz (1963) found that infants only 2 days old look longer at patterned stimuli, such as faces and concentric circles, than at red, white, or yellow discs. Infants 2 to 3 weeks old preferred to look at patterns—a face, a piece of printed matter, or a bull's-eye—longer than at red, yellow, or white discs (see Figure 6). Fantz's research method—studying whether infants can distinguish one stimulus from another by measuring the length of time they attend to different stimuli—is referred to as the **visual preference method.**

Habituation and Dishabituation

Another way that researchers have studied infant perception is to present a stimulus (such as a sight or a sound) a number of times. If the infant decreases its response to the stimulus after several presentations, this change indicates that the infant is no longer interested in the stimulus.

If the researcher now presents a new stimulus, the infant's response will recover—an indication that the infant can discriminate between the old and new stimulus (Snyder & Torrence, 2008).

Habituation is the name given to decreased responsiveness to a stimulus after repeated presentations of the stimulus. **Dishabituation** is the recovery of a habituated response after a change in stimulation. Newborn infants can habituate to repeated sights, sounds, smells, or touches (Rovee-Collier, 2004). Among the measures researchers use in habituation studies are sucking behavior (sucking stops when the young infant attends to a novel object), heart and respiration rates, and the length of time the infant looks at an object. Figure 7 shows the results of one study of habituation and dishabituation with newborns (Slater, Morison, & Somers, 1988).

High-Amplitude Sucking

To assess an infant's attention to sound, researchers often use a method called *high-amplitude sucking*. In this method, infants are given a nonnutritive nipple to suck, and the nipple is connected to a sound-generating system. The researcher computes a baseline high-amplitude sucking rate in a one-minute silent period. Following the baseline, presentation of a sound is made contingent on the rate of high-amplitude sucking. Initially babies suck frequently so the sound occurs often. Gradually, they lose interest in hearing the same sound so they begin to suck less often. Then the researcher changes the sound that is being presented. If the babies renew their vigorous sucking, the inference is that they have noticed the sound change and are sucking more because they want to hear the interesting new sound (Menn & Stoel-Gammon, 2009).

FIGURE 6

FANTZ'S EXPERIMENT ON INFANTS' VISUAL PERCEPTION. (*a*) Infants 2 to 3 weeks old preferred to look at some stimuli more than others. In Fantz's experiment, infants preferred to look at patterns rather than at color or brightness. For example, they looked longer at a face, a piece of printed matter, or a bull's-eye than at red, yellow, or white discs. (*b*) Fantz used a "looking chamber" to study infants' perception of stimuli.
(*Photo*): David Linton, Courtesy of the Linton Family

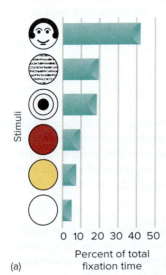

(a)

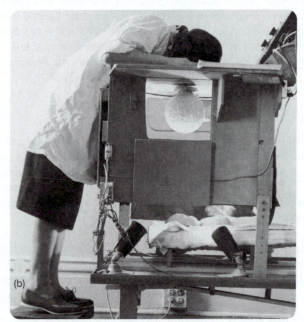

(b)

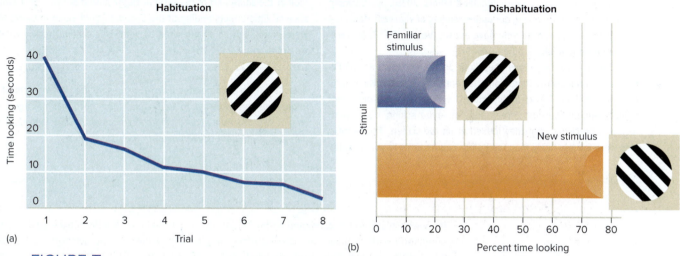

Habituation

Dishabituation

(a)

(b)

FIGURE 7

HABITUATION AND DISHABITUATION. In the first part of one study *(a)*, 7-hour-old newborns were shown a stimulus. As indicated, the newborns looked at it an average of 41 seconds when it was first presented to them (Slater, Morison, & Somers, 1988). Over seven more presentations of the stimulus, they looked at it less and less. In the second part of the study *(b)*, infants were presented with both the familiar stimulus to which they had just become habituated and a new stimulus (which was rotated 90 degrees). The newborns looked at the new stimulus three times as much as the familiar stimulus.

The Orienting Response

A technique that can be used to determine whether an infant can see or hear is the orienting response, which involves turning one's head toward a sight or sound. Another technique, tracking, measures eye movements that follow (track) a moving object; it can be used to evaluate an infant's early visual ability. A startle response can be used to determine an infant's reaction to a noise (Bendersky & Sullivan, 2007).

Equipment

Technology can facilitate the use of most methods for investigating infants' perceptual abilities. Videotape equipment allows researchers to investigate elusive behaviors. High-speed computers make it possible to perform complex data analysis in minutes. Other equipment records respiration, heart rate, body movement, visual fixation, and sucking behavior, which provide clues to what the infant is perceiving.

The most important recent advance in measuring infant perception is the development of sophisticated eye-tracking

FIGURE 8

AN INFANT WEARING EYE-TRACKING HEADGEAR. Using the ultralight, wireless, head-mounted eye-tracking equipment shown here, researchers can record where infants look while the infants freely locomote. Most studies of infant eye-tracking now use remote optics eye trackers that have a camera that is not attached to the infant's head.
Dr. Karen Adolph, New York University

equipment (van Renswoude & others, 2018). Figure 8 shows an infant wearing eye-tracking headgear in a recent study on visually guided motor behavior and social interaction.

One of the main reasons that infant perception researchers are so enthusiastic about the recent availability of sophisticated eye-tracking equipment is that looking time is among the most important measures of infant perceptual and cognitive development (Aslin, 2012). The new eye-tracking equipment allows for much greater precision than human observation in assessing various aspects of infant looking and gaze (Law & others, 2018; Stone, Smith, & Yu, 2019). Among the areas of infant perception in which eye-tracking equipment is being used are attention (Yu, Suanda, & Smith, 2019), memory (Wahl, Marinovic, & Trauble, 2019), face processing (Chhaya & others, 2017), intermodal perception (Gergely & others, 2019), language (Comishen, Bialystok, & Adler, 2019), object categorization (LaTourrette & Waxman, 2019), and

(continued)

understanding of others' needs (Koster & others, 2019). Eye-tracking equipment also is improving our understanding of atypically developing infants, such as those who have autism (Venker, 2019) or were born preterm (Imafuku & others, 2019).

One eye-tracking study shed light on the effectiveness of TV programs and DVDs that claim to educate infants (Kirkorian, Anderson, & Keen, 2012). In this study, 1-year-olds, 4-year-olds, and adults watched *Sesame Street* and the eye-tracking equipment recorded precisely what they looked at on the screen. The 1-year-olds were far less likely than their older counterparts to consistently look at the same part of the screen, suggesting that the 1-year-olds showed little understanding of the *Sesame Street* video but instead were more likely to be attracted by what was salient than by what was relevant.

Scientists have become ingenious at assessing the development of infants, discovering ways to "interview" them even though they cannot yet talk. How might researchers account for any individual differences in infant development in their studies?

The newborn's vision is estimated to be 20/240 on the well-known Snellen chart used for eye examinations, which means an object 20 feet away is only as clear to the newborn as it would be if it were 240 feet away from an adult with normal vision (20/20). By 6 months of age, though, average visual acuity is 20/40 (Aslin & Lathrop, 2008).

Faces are possibly the most important visual stimuli in children's social environment, and it is important that they extract key information from others' faces (Ichikawa & others, 2019; Palama, Maisert, & Gentaz, 2018). Infants show an interest in human faces soon after birth (Lee & others, 2013). Figure 9 shows a computer estimation of what a picture of a face looks like to an infant at different ages from a distance of about 6 inches. Infants spend more time looking at their mother's face than a stranger's face as early as 12 hours after being born (Bushnell, 2003). By 3 months of age, infants match voices to faces, distinguish between male and female faces, and discriminate between faces of their own ethnic group and those of other ethnic groups (Gaither, Pauker, & Johnson, 2012; Kelly & others, 2007, 2009; Quinn, Lee, & Pascalis, 2019).

Experience plays an important role in face processing in infancy and later in development. One aspect of this experience involves the concept of *perceptual narrowing*, in which infants are more likely to distinguish between faces to which they have been exposed than faces that they have never seen before (Kobayashi & others, 2019; Minar & Lewkowicz, 2019).

Also, as we discussed in the *Connecting with Research* interlude, young infants can perceive certain patterns. With the help of his "looking chamber," Robert Fantz (1963) found that even 2- to 3-week-old infants prefer to look at patterned displays rather than nonpatterned displays. For example, they prefer to look at a normal human face rather than one with scrambled features, and prefer to look at a bull's-eye target or black and white stripes rather than a plain circle.

visual preference method A method developed by Fantz to determine whether infants can distinguish one stimulus from another by measuring the length of time they attend to different stimuli.

habituation Decreased responsiveness to a stimulus after repeated presentations of the stimulus.

dishabituation The recovery of a habituated response after a change in stimulation.

FIGURE **9**

VISUAL ACUITY DURING THE FIRST MONTHS OF LIFE. The four photographs represent a computer estimation of what a picture of a face looks like to a 1-month-old, 2-month-old, 3-month-old, and 1-year-old (whose visual acuity approximates that of an adult).
Kevin Peterson/Photodisc/Getty Images

Color Vision The infant's color vision also improves over time (Atkinson & Braddick, 2013). By 8 weeks, and possibly as early as 4 weeks, infants can discriminate some colors (Kelly, Borchert, & Teller, 1997). By 4 months of age, they have color preferences that mirror those of adults in some cases, preferring saturated colors such as royal blue over pale blue, for example (Bornstein, 1975). A study of the reactions to blue, yellow, red, and green hues by 4- to 5-month-old infants revealed that they looked longest at reddish hues and shortest at greenish hues (Franklin & others, 2010). In part, the changes in vision described here reflect maturation. Experience, however, is also necessary for color vision to develop normally (Sugita, 2004).

Perceptual Constancy Some perceptual accomplishments are especially intriguing because they indicate that the infant's perception goes beyond the information provided by the senses (Bremner & others, 2017; Johnson, 2019a, b; Slater & others, 2011). This is the case in perceptual constancy, in which sensory stimulation is changing but perception of the physical world remains constant. If infants did not develop perceptual constancy, each time they saw an object at a different distance or in a different orientation, they would perceive it as a different object. Thus, the development of perceptual constancy allows infants to perceive their world as stable. Two types of perceptual constancy are size constancy and shape constancy.

Size constancy is the recognition that an object remains the same even though the retinal image of the object changes as you move toward or away from the object. The farther away from us an object is, the smaller its image is on our eyes. Thus, the size of an object on the retina is not sufficient to tell us its actual size. For example, you perceive a bicycle standing right in front of you as smaller than the car parked across the street, even though the bicycle casts a larger image on your eyes than the car does. When you move away from the bicycle, you do not perceive it to be shrinking even though its image on your retinas shrinks; you perceive its size as constant. But what about babies? Do they have size constancy? Researchers have found that babies as young as 3 months of age show size constancy (Bower, 1966; Day & McKenzie, 1973). However, at 3 months of age, a baby's ability is not full-blown. It continues to develop until 10 or 11 years of age (Kellman & Banks, 1998).

Shape constancy is the recognition that an object remains the same shape even though its orientation to us changes. Look around the room you are in right now. You likely see objects of varying shapes, such as tables and chairs. If you get up and walk around the room, you will see these objects from different sides and angles. Even though your retinal image of the objects changes as you walk and look, you will still perceive the objects as the same shape.

Do babies have shape constancy? As with size constancy, researchers have found that babies as young as 3 months of age have shape constancy (Bower, 1966; Day & McKenzie, 1973). Three-month-old infants, however, do not have shape constancy for irregularly shaped objects such as tilted planes (Cook & Birch, 1984).

Perception of Occluded Objects Look again at the objects surrounding you. You likely see that some objects are partly occluded (hidden) by other objects that are in front of them—possibly a desk behind a chair, some books behind a computer, or a car parked behind a tree. Do infants perceive an object as complete when it is partly occluded by an object in front of it?

In the first two months of postnatal development, infants don't perceive occluded objects as complete, but instead perceive only what is visible (Johnson, 2018, 2019b). Beginning at about 2 months of age, infants develop the ability to perceive that occluded objects are whole (Slater & others, 2011). How does perceptual completion develop? In Scott Johnson's (2004, 2011, 2018, 2019a, b) research, learning, experience, and self-directed exploration via eye movements play key roles in the development of perceptual completion in young infants.

Many of the objects in the world that are occluded appear and disappear behind closer objects, as when you are walking down the street and see cars appear and disappear behind buildings as they move or you move. Can infants predictively track briefly occluded moving objects? They develop the ability to track briefly occluded moving objects at about 3 to 5 months of age (Bertenthal, 2008). One study explored 5- to 9-month-old infants' ability to track moving objects that disappeared gradually behind an occluded partition, disappeared abruptly, or imploded (shrank quickly in size) (see Figure 10) (Bertenthal, Longo, & Kenny, 2007). In this study, the infants were more likely to accurately predict the reappearance of the moving object when it disappeared gradually than when it disappeared abruptly or imploded.

Depth Perception Might infants even perceive depth? To investigate this question, Eleanor Gibson and Richard Walk (1960) constructed a miniature cliff with a drop-off covered

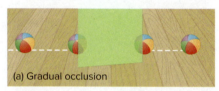

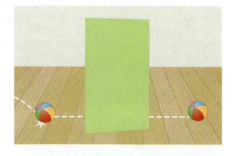
(a) Gradual occlusion

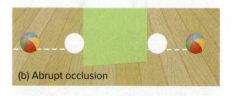
(b) Abrupt occlusion

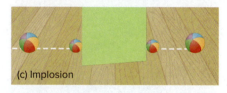
(c) Implosion

FIGURE 10

INFANTS' PREDICTIVE TRACKING OF A BRIEFLY OCCLUDED MOVING BALL

size constancy Recognition that an object remains the same even though the retinal image of the object changes as the viewer moves toward or away from the object.

shape constancy Recognition that an object remains the same even though its orientation to the viewer changes.

FIGURE 11

EXAMINING INFANTS' DEPTH PERCEPTION ON THE VISUAL CLIFF. Eleanor Gibson and Richard Walk (1960) found that most infants would not crawl out on the glass, which, according to Gibson and Walk, indicated that they had depth perception. However, critics suggest that the visual cliff may be a better indication of the infant's social referencing and fear of heights than of the infant's perception of depth.

Mark Richard/PhotoEdit

by glass. They placed infants on the edge of this visual cliff and had their mothers coax them to crawl onto the glass (see Figure 11). Most infants would not crawl out on the glass, choosing instead to remain on the shallow side, an indication that they could perceive depth. However, critics point out that the visual cliff likely is a better test of social referencing and fear of heights than of depth perception.

The 6- to 12-month-old infants in the visual cliff experiment had extensive visual experience. Do younger infants without this experience still perceive depth? Since younger infants do not crawl, this question is difficult to answer. Infants 2 to 4 months old show differences in heart rate when they are placed directly on the deep side of the visual cliff instead of on the shallow side (Campos, Langer, & Krowitz, 1970). However, these differences might mean that young infants respond to differences in some visual characteristics of the deep and shallow cliffs, with no actual knowledge of depth (Ishak, Franchak, & Adolph, 2014). Although researchers do not know exactly how early in life infants can perceive depth, we do know that infants develop the ability to use binocular cues to depth by about 3 to 4 months of age.

Childhood   Changes in children's perceptual development continue in childhood (Grimm & others, 2019; Monier, Droit-Volet, & Coull, 2019). Children become increasingly efficient at detecting the boundaries between colors (such as red and orange) at 3 to 4 years of age (Gibson, 1969). When children are about 4 or 5 years old, their eye muscles usually are developed enough that they can move their eyes efficiently across a series of letters. Many preschool children are farsighted, unable to see close up as well as they can see far away. By the time they enter the first grade, though, most children can focus their eyes and sustain their attention effectively on close-up objects.

What are the signs of vision problems in children? They include rubbing the eyes, blinking or squinting excessively, appearing irritable when playing games that require good distance vision, shutting or covering one eye, and tilting the head or thrusting it forward when looking at something. A child who shows any of these behaviors should be examined by an ophthalmologist.

After infancy, children's visual expectations about the physical world continue to develop. In one study, 2- to 4½-year-old children were given a task in which the goal was to find a ball that had been dropped through an opaque tube (Hood, 1995). As shown in Figure 12, if the ball is dropped into the tube at the top left, it will land in the box at the bottom right. However, in this task, most of the 2-year-olds, and even some of the 4-year-olds, persisted in searching in the box immediately beneath the dropping point. For them, gravity ruled and they had failed to perceive the end location of the curved tube. In two studies involving the task in Figure 12, 3-year-olds were able to overcome the gravity bias and their impulsive tendencies when they were given verbal instructions from a knowledgeable adult (Bascandziev & Harris, 2011; Joh, Jaswal, & Keen, 2011).

How do children learn to deal with situations like that in Figure 12, and how do they come to understand other laws of the physical world? These questions are addressed by studies of cognitive development, which we discuss in the chapters on "Cognitive Developmental Approaches" and "Information Processing."

FIGURE 12

VISUAL EXPECTATIONS ABOUT THE PHYSICAL WORLD. When young children see the ball dropped into the tube, many of them will search for it immediately below the dropping point.

Courtesy of Dr. Bruce Hood, University of Bristol

Adulthood   Vision changes little after childhood until the effects of aging emerge (Meng & others, 2019). Seeing, hearing, and other aspects of sensory functioning are linked with our ability to perform everyday activities (Jain & Dwarakanath, 2019; Peng & others, 2019). Researchers have found that visual decline in late adulthood is linked to (a) cognitive decline (Lee & others, 2019), and (b) having fewer social contacts and engaging in less challenging social/leisure activities (Brunes, Hansen, & Heir, 2019; Cimarolli & others, 2017). For example, in a longitudinal study of individuals 60 years and older, visual and hearing difficulties predicted cognitive difficulties in verbal fluency, processing speed, and memory 8 years later (de la Fuente & others, 2019). In this study, the most cognitive decline occurred in individuals with both visual and hearing problems. With aging, declines occur in visual acuity, color vision, and depth perception. Several diseases of the eye also may emerge in aging adults.

Visual Acuity   **Accommodation of the eye**–the eye's ability to focus and maintain an image on the retina–declines most sharply between 40 and 59 years of age. This loss of accommodation is what is commonly known as *presbyopia*. In particular, middle-aged individuals begin to have difficulty viewing close objects. The eye's blood supply also diminishes, although usually not until the fifties or sixties. The reduced blood supply may decrease the visual field's size and account for an increase in the eye's *blind spot*, the location where the retina does not register any light. And there is some evidence that the retina becomes less sensitive to low levels of illumination (Hughes, 1978). As a result, middle-aged adults begin to have difficulty reading or working in dim light. Presbyopia is correctable with bifocals, reading glasses, laser surgery, or implantation of intraocular lenses. Indeed, laser surgery and implantation of intraocular lenses have become routine procedures for correcting vision in middle-aged adults (Wallerstein & others, 2019).

In late adulthood, the decline in vision that began for most adults in early or middle adulthood becomes more pronounced (Jensen & Tubaek, 2019). Visual processing speed declines in older adults (Bezdicek & others, 2016). Night driving is especially difficult, to some extent because of diminishing sensitivity to contrasts and reduced tolerance for glare (Kimlin, Black, & Wood, 2017). *Dark adaptation* is slower–that is, older individuals take longer to recover their vision when going from a well-lighted room to semidarkness. The area of the visual field becomes smaller, an indication that the intensity of a stimulus in the peripheral area of the visual field needs to be increased if the stimulus is to be seen. Events taking place away from the center of the visual field might not be detected (Anson & others, 2017).

What are some concerns about older adults' driving based on changes in visual perception?
Rike/Getty Images

This visual decline often can be traced to a reduction in the quality or intensity of light reaching the retina. At 60 years of age, the retina receives only about one-third as much light as it did at 20 years of age (Scialfa & Kline, 2007). In extreme old age, these changes might be accompanied by degenerative changes in the retina, causing severe difficulty in seeing. Large-print books and magnifiers might be needed in such cases.

Older adults also show a decline in motion sensitivity (Conlon & others, 2017). In terms of practical applications of this decline, researchers have found that compared with younger drivers, older drivers overestimate the time needed for an approaching vehicle to reach their location (Chevalier & others, 2017). This decline in the accuracy of effortless perceptual guidance means that older adult drivers need to expend cognitive effort when driving, especially when approaching intersections.

Color Vision   Color vision also may decline with age in older adults as a result of the yellowing of the lens of the eye (Scialfa & Kline, 2007). This decline is most likely to occur in the green-blue-violet part of the color spectrum. As a result, older adults may have trouble accurately distinguishing between objects that are closely related in color, such as navy socks and black socks.

Depth Perception   As with many areas of perception, depth perception changes little after infancy until adults become older. Depth perception typically declines in late adulthood, which can make it difficult for the older adult to determine how close or far away or how high or low something is (Bian & Andersen, 2008). A decline in depth perception can make steps or street curbs difficult to manage.

Diseases of the Eye   Three diseases that can impair the vision of older adults are cataracts, glaucoma, and macular degeneration:

- **Cataracts** are a thickening of the lens of the eye that causes vision to become cloudy, opaque, and distorted (Radhakrishnan & others, 2018). By age 70, approximately 30 percent of individuals experience a partial loss of vision due to cataracts. Initially, vision impairment from cataracts can be minimized by wearing glasses; if cataracts worsen, a simple surgical procedure can remove the cloudy lens and replace it with an artificial one (Jiang & others, 2018). A recent Japanese study found that older adults (mean age: 76 years) who had cataract surgery were less likely to develop mild cognitive impairment than their counterparts who had not had the surgery (Miyata & others, 2018). Diabetes is a risk factor for the development of cataracts (Becker & others, 2018).

- **Glaucoma** damages the optic nerve because of the pressure created by a buildup of fluid in the eye (Jiang & others, 2018). Approximately 1 percent of individuals in their seventies and 10 percent of those in their nineties have glaucoma, which can be treated with eye drops. If left untreated, glaucoma can ultimately destroy a person's vision.

accommodation of the eye The eye's ability to focus and maintain an image on the retina.

cataracts A thickening of the lens of the eye that causes vision to become cloudy, opaque, and distorted.

glaucoma Damage to the optic nerve because of pressure created by a buildup of fluid in the eye.

FIGURE 13

MACULAR DEGENERATION. This simulation of the effect of macular degeneration shows how individuals with this eye disease can see their peripheral field of vision but can't clearly see what is in their central visual field.

Cordelia Molloy/Science Source

- **Macular degeneration** is a disease that causes deterioration of the macula of the retina, which corresponds to the focal center of the visual field (see Figure 13). Individuals with macular degeneration may have relatively normal peripheral vision but be unable to see clearly what is directly in front of them (Owsley & others, 2016). Macular degeneration affects 1 in 25 individuals from 66 to 74 years of age and 1 in 6 of those 75 years old and older. If the disease is detected early, it can be treated with laser surgery (Hernandez-Zimbron & others, 2018). However, macular degeneration is difficult to treat and thus a leading cause of blindness in older adults (Zhu & others, 2019). One study found that macular degeneration was linked to increased risk of falls in adults 77 years and older (Wood & others, 2011). There is increased interest in using stem-cell based therapy to treat macular degeneration (Ludwig, Freeman, & Janot, 2019).

HEARING

Can the fetus hear? What kind of changes in hearing take place in infancy? When does hearing begin to decline in adulthood?

The Fetus, Infant, and Child   During the last two months of pregnancy, as the fetus nestles in its mother's womb, it can hear sounds such as the mother's voice, music, and so on (Das & others, 2019). Two psychologists wanted to find out whether a fetus who heard Dr. Seuss' classic story *The Cat in the Hat* while still in the mother's womb would prefer hearing the story after birth (DeCasper & Spence, 1986). During the last months of pregnancy, 16 women read *The Cat in the Hat* to their fetuses. Then, shortly after the infants were born, the mothers read aloud either *The Cat in the Hat* or a story with a different rhyme and pace, *The King, the Mice and the Cheese* (which they had not read aloud during pregnancy). The infants sucked on a nipple in a different way when the mothers read the two stories, suggesting that they recognized the pattern and tone of *The Cat in the Hat* (see Figure 14). This study illustrates not only that a fetus can hear but also that it has a remarkable ability to learn even before birth. An fMRI study confirmed that the fetus can hear at 33 to 34 weeks by assessing fetal brain response to auditory stimuli (Jardri & others, 2012).

Infancy   What changes in hearing take place during infancy? They involve perception of a sound's loudness, pitch, and localization.

Immediately after birth, infants cannot hear soft sounds quite as well as adults can; a stimulus must be louder for the newborn to hear it (Trehub & others, 1991). By 3 months of age, infants' perception of sounds improves, although some aspects of loudness perception do not reach adult levels until 5 to 10 years of age (Trainor & He, 2013). Infants are also less sensitive to the pitch of a sound than adults are. *Pitch* is the frequency of a sound; a soprano voice sounds high-pitched, a bass voice low-pitched. Infants are less sensitive to low-pitched sounds and are more likely to hear high-pitched sounds (Aslin, Jusczyk, & Pisoni, 1998).

macular degeneration A vision problem in the elderly that involves deterioration of the macula of the retina.

FIGURE 14

HEARING IN THE WOMB. (*a*) Pregnant mothers read *The Cat in the Hat* to their fetuses during the last few months of pregnancy. (*b*) When they were born, the babies preferred listening to a recording of their mothers reading *The Cat in the Hat*, as evidenced by their sucking on a nipple that produced this recording, rather than another story, *The King, the Mice and the Cheese*.

(*a*): Jill Braaten/McGraw-Hill Education; (*b*): Courtesy of Dr. Melanie J. Spence

(a)

(b)

By 2 years of age, infants have considerably improved their ability to distinguish between sounds with different pitches.

Even newborns can determine the general location from which a sound is coming, but by 6 months they are more proficient at *localizing* sounds, detecting their origins. The ability to localize sounds continues to improve during the second year (Saffran, Werker, & Warner, 2006). Although young infants can process variations in sound loudness, pitch, and localization, these aspects of hearing continue to improve through the childhood years (Trainor & He, 2013).

Most children's hearing is adequate, but early hearing screening tests should be conducted during infancy, preferably in newborns (Bouillot, Vercherat, & Durand, 2019; Fowler & others, 2017). About 1 in 1,000 newborns is deaf and 6 in 1,000 have some degree of hearing loss. Hearing aids or surgery can improve hearing for many of these infants (Halpin & others, 2010).

Adolescence   Most adolescents' hearing is excellent. However, anyone who listens to loud sounds for sustained periods of time is at risk for the development of hearing problems. H.E.A.R. (Hearing Education and Awareness for Rockers) was founded by rock musicians whose hearing has been damaged by exposure to high-volume rock music. Increasingly, rock groups wear earplugs when they are playing loud music. Listening to loud music on iPods and MP3 players also can produce hearing problems. In a recent large-scale study of Korean adolescents, 17 percent had at least a slight hearing loss and this loss was associated with cumulative hours the adolescents had spent in gaming centers (Rhee & others, 2019). The adolescents' hearing loss also was related to lower academic performance (Rhee & others, 2019).

Adulthood and Aging   Few changes in hearing are believed to take place during the adult years until middle adulthood (Vaden & others, 2017). Hearing can start to decline by the age of 40. Sensitivity to high pitches usually declines first. The ability to hear low-pitched sounds does not seem to decline much in middle adulthood, however. Men usually lose their sensitivity to high-pitched sounds sooner than women do, but this sex difference might be due to men's greater exposure to noise in occupations such as mining and automobile work.

Hearing impairment usually does not become much of an impediment until late adulthood (Pacala & Yeuh, 2012). A national survey revealed that 63 percent of adults 70 years and older had a hearing loss, defined as inability to hear sounds at amplitudes below 25 dB with their better ear (Lin & others, 2011). In this study, hearing aids were used by 40 percent of those with moderate hearing loss. Fifteen percent of the population over the age of 65 is estimated to be legally deaf, usually due to degeneration of the cochlea, the primary neural receptor for hearing in the inner ear (Adams, 2009). And in a recent study of 80- to 106-year-olds, there was a substantial increase in hearing loss in the ninth and then in the tenth decades of life (Wattamwar & others, 2017).

Earlier, in discussing changes in vision, we considered research on the importance of the age of older adults in determining the degree of their visual decline. Age also is a factor in the degree of hearing decline in older adults (Hoffman & others, 2017). As indicated in Figure 15, the declines in vision and hearing are much greater in individuals 75 years and older than in individuals 65 to 74 years of age (Charness & Bosman, 1992).

What are some concerns about adolescents who listen to loud music?
George Doyle/Stockbyte/Getty Images

Perceptual System	Young-Old (65 to 74 years)	Old-Old (75 years and older)
Vision	There is a loss of acuity even with corrective lenses. Less transmission of light occurs through the retina (half as much as in young adults). Greater susceptibility to glare occurs. Color discrimination ability decreases.	There is a significant loss of visual acuity and color discrimination, and a decrease in the size of the perceived visual field. In late old age, people are at significant risk for visual dysfunction from cataracts and glaucoma.
Hearing	There is a significant loss of hearing at high frequencies and some loss at middle frequencies. These losses can be helped by a hearing aid. There is greater susceptibility to masking of what is heard by noise.	There is a significant loss at high and middle frequencies. A hearing aid is more likely to be needed than in young-old age.

FIGURE 15

VISION AND HEARING DECLINE IN THE YOUNG-OLD AND THE OLD-OLD

Older adults often don't recognize that they have a hearing problem, deny that they have one, or accept it as a part of growing old (Pacala & Yeuh, 2012). Researchers have found that older adults' hearing problems are linked to impaired activities of daily living (Mueller-Schotte & others, 2019), less time spent out of home and in leisure activities (Mikkola & others, 2016), an increase in falls (Gopinath & others, 2016), reduction in cognitive functioning (Armstrong & others, 2019), and increased loneliness (Mick & Pichora-Fuller, 2016). For example, in a recent study, hearing impairment was associated with accelerated cognitive decline in older adults (Alattar & others, 2019). Also, in another study, older adults with a hearing problem who used a hearing aid were less lonely than their hearing-impaired counterparts who did not use a hearing aid (Weinstein, Sirow, & Moser, 2016).

Two devices can be used to minimize problems created by hearing loss: (1) hearing aids that amplify sound to reduce middle-ear-based conductive hearing loss, and (2) cochlear implants that restore some hearing following neurosensory hearing loss (Willink, Reed, & Lin, 2019). In a study of 80- to 106-year-olds mentioned previously, despite the universal loss of hearing in the 647 individuals, only 59 percent of them wore hearing aids (Wattamwar & others, 2017). Researchers also are exploring the use of stem cells as an alternative to cochlear implants (Mittal & others, 2019).

What outcomes occur when older adults have dual sensory loss in vision and hearing? In a recent study of 65- to 85-year-olds, dual sensory loss in vision and hearing was linked to reduced social participation and less social support, as well as increased loneliness (Mick & others, 2018). In another recent study, this type of dual sensory loss in older adults (mean age of 82 years) involved greater functional limitations, increased loneliness, cognitive decline, and communication problems (Davidson & Gutherie, 2019). And in another recent study, older adults who had a dual sensory impairment involving vision and hearing had more depressive symptoms (Han & others, 2019).

OTHER SENSES

As we develop, we not only obtain information about the world from our eyes and our ears but also through sensory receptors in our skin, nose, and tongue.

Touch and Pain   Do newborns respond to touch (called "tactile stimulation" by scientists)? Can they feel pain? How does the perception of touch and pain change with age?

Infancy   Newborns do respond to touch. A touch to the cheek produces a turning of the head; a touch to the lips produces sucking movements.

Regular gentle tactile stimulation prenatally may have positive developmental outcomes. For example, researchers found that 3-month-olds who had regular gentle tactile stimulation as fetuses were more likely to have an easy temperament than their counterparts who had irregular gentle or no tactile stimulation as fetuses (Wang, Hua, & Xu, 2015).

Newborns can also feel pain (Britto, Jasmine, & Rao, 2017). If and when you have a son and consider whether he should be circumcised, the issue of an infant's pain perception probably will become important to you. When circumcision is performed during infancy, it usually takes place between the third and eighth days after birth. Will your young son experience pain if he is circumcised when he is 3 days old? An investigation by Megan Gunnar and her colleagues (1987) found that infant males cried intensely during circumcision. The circumcised infants also displayed amazing resiliency. Within several minutes after the surgery, they could nurse and interact in a normal manner with their mothers. And, if allowed to, the newly circumcised infants drifted into a deep sleep, which seemed to serve as a coping mechanism. Also, once researchers discovered that newborns feel pain, the practice of operating on newborns without anesthesia began to be reconsidered. Anesthesia is now used in some circumcisions (Morris & others, 2012).

A neuroimaging study revealed that the pain threshold in newborns occurs at a lower level of stimulation than for adults, confirming newborns' heightened pain sensitivity that has been found in earlier behavioral studies (Goksan & others, 2015). And in another study, kangaroo care was effective in reducing neonatal pain, especially indicated by significantly lower levels of crying when the care was instituted after the newborn's blood had been drawn by a heel stick (Seo, Lee, & Ahn, 2016).

Adulthood   There has been little research on developmental changes in touch and pain after infancy until middle and late adulthood. Changes in touch and pain are associated with aging. A national study of community-dwelling older adults revealed that 70 percent of older adults had impaired touch (Correia & others, 2016). One study found that older adults could detect touch much less in the lower extremities (ankles, knees, and so on) than in the upper extremities (wrists, shoulders, and so on) (Corso, 1977). For most older adults, though, a decline in touch sensitivity is not problematic (Hoyer & Roodin, 2009).

An estimated 60 to 75 percent of older adults report at least some persistent pain (Molton & Terrill, 2014). The most frequent pain complaints of older adults are back pain (40 percent), peripheral neuropathic pain (35 percent), and chronic joint pain (15 to 25 percent) (Denard & others, 2010). The presence of pain increases with age in older adults, and women are more likely to report having pain than are men (Tsang & others, 2008). In a recent research review, it was concluded that older adults have lower pain sensitivity but only for lower pain intensities (Lautenbacher & others, 2017). Also, a recent study found that high levels of pain were linked to memory impairment in older adults (van der Leeuw & others, 2018).

Smell   Newborns can differentiate odors (Doty & Shah, 2008). The expressions on their faces seem to indicate that they like the way vanilla and strawberry smell but do not like the way rotten eggs and fish smell (Steiner, 1979). In one investigation, 6-day-old infants who were breast fed showed a clear preference for smelling their mother's breast pad rather than a clean breast pad (MacFarlane, 1975). However, when they were 2 days old, they did not show this preference, an indication that they require several days of experience to recognize this odor.

A decline in sensitivity to odors may occur as early as the twenties, with declines continuing through each subsequent decade of life into the nineties (Margran & Boulton, 2005). Beginning in the sixties, the decrease in sensitivity to smells becomes more noticeable to most people (Hawkes, 2006). A majority of individuals 80 years of age and older experience a significant reduction in smell (Lafreniere & Mann, 2009). A decline in the sense of smell can reduce the ability to detect smoke from a fire.

The decline in the olfactory system can reduce older adults' enjoyment of food and their life satisfaction. If elderly individuals need to be encouraged to eat more, compounds that stimulate the olfactory nerve are sometimes added to food.

Taste   Sensitivity to taste is present even before birth (Doty & Shah, 2008). Human newborns learn tastes prenatally through the amniotic fluid and in breast milk after birth (Beauchamp & Mennella, 2009; Mennella, 2009). In one study, even at only 2 hours of age, babies made different facial expressions when they tasted sweet, sour, and bitter solutions (Rosenstein & Oster, 1988) (see Figure 16). At about 4 months of age, infants begin to prefer salty tastes, which as newborns they had found to be aversive (Doty & Shah, 2008).

A national study of community-dwelling older adults revealed that 74 percent had impaired taste and 22 percent had impaired smell (Correia & others, 2016). As with smell, there is less decline in taste in healthy older adults than in unhealthy older adults. However, when even relatively healthy older adults take medications, their taste sensitivity declines (Roberts & Rosenberg, 2006).

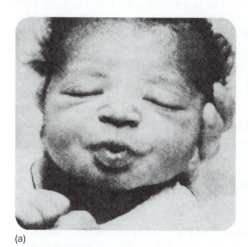
(a)

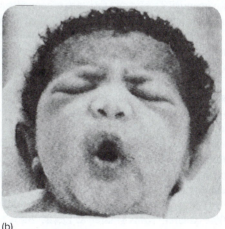
(b)

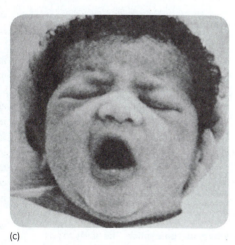
(c)

FIGURE 16

NEWBORNS' FACIAL RESPONSES TO BASIC TASTES. Facial expressions elicited by (*a*) a sweet solution, (*b*) a sour solution, and (*c*) a bitter solution.

How is intermodal perception involved in this context in which a boy is listening to headphones while working on a computer?

Özgür Donmaz/Getty Images

Many older adults prefer highly seasoned foods (sweeter, spicier, saltier) to compensate for their diminished taste and smell (Hoyer & Roodin, 2009). This preference can lead to increased eating of nonnutritious, highly seasoned "junk food."

Researchers have found that older adults show a greater decline in their sense of smell than in their taste (Schiffman, 2007). Smell, too, declines less in healthy older adults than in their less healthy counterparts.

INTERMODAL PERCEPTION

Imagine that you are playing basketball or tennis. You are experiencing many visual inputs—the ball is coming and going, other players are moving around, and so on. However, you are experiencing many auditory inputs as well: the sound of the ball bouncing or being hit, the grunts and groans of the other players, and so on. There is good correspondence between much of the visual and auditory information: When you see the ball bounce, you hear a bouncing sound; when a player stretches to hit a ball, you hear a groan. When you look at and listen to what is going on, you do not experience just the sounds or just the sights; you put all of these things together. You experience a unitary episode. This is **intermodal perception,** which involves integrating information from two or more sensory modalities, such as vision and hearing (Gergely & others, 2019). Most perception is intermodal (Bahrick, 2010; Kirkham & others, 2012).

Early, exploratory forms of intermodal perception exist even in newborns (Bahrick & Hollich, 2008). For example, newborns turn their eyes and their head toward the sound of a voice or rattle when the sound is maintained for several seconds (Clifton & others, 1981), but the newborn can localize a sound and look at an object only in a crude way (Bechtold, Bushnell, & Salapatek, 1979). These early forms of intermodal perception become sharpened with experience in the first year of life (Kirkham & others, 2012). In one study, infants as young as 3½ months old looked more at their mother when they also heard her voice and longer at their father when they also heard his voice (Spelke & Owsley, 1979). Thus, even young infants can coordinate visual-auditory information about people.

Can young infants put vision and sound together as precisely as adults do? In the first six months, infants have difficulty connecting sensory input from different modes, but in the second half of the first year they show an increased ability to make this connection mentally.

NATURE/NURTURE AND PERCEPTUAL DEVELOPMENT

Now that we have discussed many aspects of perceptual development, let's explore one of developmental psychology's key issues as it relates to perceptual development: the nature-nurture issue. There has been a long-standing interest in how strongly infants' perception is influenced by nature or nurture (Johnson, 2018, 2019a, b; Slater & others, 2011). In the field of perceptual development, nature proponents are referred to as *nativists* and those who emphasize learning and experience are called *empiricists*.

In the nativist view, the ability to perceive the world in a competent, organized way is inborn or innate. A completely nativist view of perceptual development no longer is accepted in developmental psychology.

The Gibsons argued that a key question in infant perception is what information is available in the environment and how infants learn to generate, differentiate, and discriminate the information—certainly not a nativist view. The Gibsons' ecological view also is quite different from Piaget's constructivist view. According to Piaget, much of perceptual development in infancy must await the development of a sequence of cognitive stages for infants to construct more complex perceptual tasks. Thus, in Piaget's view the ability to perceive size and shape constancy, a three-dimensional world, intermodal perception, and so on, develops later in infancy than the Gibsons envision.

The longitudinal research of Daphne Maurer and her colleagues (Lewis & Maurer, 2005, 2009; Maurer, 2016; Maurer & Lewis, 2013; Maurer & others, 1999) has focused on infants born with cataracts—a thickening of the lens of the eye that causes vision to become cloudy, opaque, and distorted and thus severely restricts infants' ability to experience their visual world. In studying infants whose cataracts were removed at different points in development, they

developmental **connection**

Theories

Piaget's theory states that children construct their understanding of the world through four stages of cognitive development. Connect to "Introduction" and "Cognitive Developmental Approaches."

intermodal perception The ability to integrate information about two or more sensory modalities, such as vision and hearing.

discovered that those whose cataracts were removed and new lenses placed in their eyes in the first several months after birth showed a normal pattern of visual development. However, the longer the delay in removing the cataracts, the more their visual development was impaired. In their research, Maurer and her colleagues (2007) have found that experiencing patterned visual input early in infancy is important for holistic and detailed face processing after infancy. Maurer's research program illustrates how deprivation and experience influence visual development, identifying an early sensitive period in which visual input is necessary for normal visual development (Maurer, 2016; Maurer & Lewis, 2013).

Today, it is clear that just as an extreme nativist position on perceptual development is unwarranted, an extreme empiricist position also is unwarranted. Much of very early perception develops from innate (nature) foundations, and the basic foundation of many perceptual abilities can be detected in newborns (Bornstein, Arterberry, & Mash, 2015). However, as infants develop, environmental experiences (nurture) refine or calibrate many perceptual functions, and they may be the driving force behind some functions (Amso & Johnson, 2010). The accumulation of experience with and knowledge about their perceptual world contributes to infants' ability to process coherent perceptions of people and things (Johnson, 2019a, b). Thus, a full portrait of perceptual development includes the influence of nature, nurture, and a developing sensitivity to information (Johnson, 2018; Maurer, 2016).

What roles do nature and nurture play in the infant's perceptual development?
lostinbids/Getty Images

Review Connect Reflect

 LG2 Outline the course of sensory and perceptual development.

Review

- What are sensation and perception?
- What is the ecological view of perception? What are some research methods used to study infant perception?
- How does vision develop?
- How does hearing develop?
- How do sensitivity to touch and pain develop? How does smell develop? How does taste develop?
- What is intermodal perception, and how does it develop?
- What roles do nature and nurture play in perceptual development?

Connect

- How might the development of vision and hearing contribute to infants' gross motor development?

Reflect *Your Own Personal Journey of Life*

- Imagine that you are the parent of a 1-year-old infant. How would you stimulate your 1-year-old's vision and hearing?

---

3 Perceptual-Motor Coupling

 LG3 Discuss the connection between perception and action.

As we come to the end of this chapter, we return to the important theme of perceptual-motor coupling. The distinction between perceiving and doing has been a time-honored tradition in psychology. However, a number of experts on perceptual and motor development question whether this distinction makes sense (Adolph & Hoch, 2019; Thelen & Smith, 2006). The main thrust of research in Esther Thelen's dynamic systems approach is to explore how people assemble motor behaviors for perceiving and acting. The main theme of the ecological approach of Eleanor and James J. Gibson is to discover how perception guides action. Action can guide perception, and perception can guide action. Only by moving one's eyes, head, hands, and arms and by moving from one location to another can an individual fully experience his or her environment and learn how to adapt to it. Perception and action are coupled.

Babies, for example, continually coordinate their movements with perceptual information to learn how to maintain balance, reach for objects in space, and move across various surfaces and terrains (Adolph & Hoch, 2019). They are motivated to move by what they perceive. Consider the sight of an attractive toy across the room. In this situation, infants must perceive the current state of their bodies and learn how to use their limbs to reach the toy. Although their

> The infant is by no means as helpless as it looks and is quite capable of some very complex and important actions.
>
> **—Herb Pick**
> *Developmental Psychologist, University of Minnesota*

Perception and action are coupled throughout the human life span.
(*Left*): Anthony Cain/Flickr/Getty Images; (*right*): Salajean/Shutterstock

movements at first are awkward and uncoordinated, babies soon learn to select patterns that are appropriate for reaching their goals.

Equally important is the other part of the perception-action coupling. That is, action educates perception (Adolph, 2018). For example, watching an object while exploring it manually helps infants to discriminate its texture, size, and hardness. Locomoting in the environment teaches babies about how objects and people look from different perspectives, or whether surfaces will support their weight. Individuals perceive in order to move and move in order to perceive. Perceptual and motor development do not occur in isolation from each other but instead are coupled.

How do infants develop new perceptual-motor couplings? Recall from our discussion earlier in this chapter that in the traditional view of Gesell, infants' perceptual-motor development is prescribed by a genetic plan to follow a fixed and sequential progression of stages in development. The genetic determination view has been replaced by the dynamic systems view that infants learn new perceptual-motor couplings by assembling skills for perceiving and acting. New perceptual-motor coupling is not passively accomplished; rather, the infant actively develops a skill to achieve a goal within the constraints set by the infant's body and the environment (Adolph & Hoch, 2019).

Driving a car illustrates the coupling of perceptual and motor skills. The decline in perceptual-motor skills in late adulthood makes driving a car difficult for many older adults (Pozzi & others, 2018). Drivers over the age of 65 are involved in more traffic accidents than middle-aged adults because of mistakes such as improper turns, not yielding the right of way, and not obeying traffic signs; their younger counterparts are more likely to have accidents because they are speeding (Lavalliere & others, 2011). Older adults can compensate for declines in perceptual-motor skills by driving shorter distances, choosing less congested routes, and driving only in daylight.

Cognitive training programs have shown some success in older adults, including improving their driving safety and making driving less difficult. In one study conducted by Karlene Ball and her colleagues (2010), training designed to enhance speed of processing produced more than a 40 percent reduction in at-fault crashes over a six-year period.

Review Connect Reflect

 LG3 Discuss the connection between perception and action.

Review
- How are perception and action coupled in development?

Connect
- If perception and action are closely linked, can parents enhance their infants' motor development or must it follow its own course?

Reflect *Your Own Personal Journey of Life*
- Describe two examples not given in the text in which perception guides action. Then describe two examples not given in the text in which action guides perception.

Motor, Sensory, and Perceptual Development

1 Motor Development   (LG1)   Describe how motor skills develop.

The Dynamic Systems View

- Thelen's dynamic systems theory seeks to explain how motor behaviors are assembled by infants for perceiving and acting. Perception and action are coupled. According to this theory, motor skills are the result of many converging factors, such as the development of the nervous system, the body's physical properties and its movement possibilities, the goal the child is motivated to reach, and environmental support for the skill.

- In the dynamic systems view, motor development involves far greater complexity than the unfolding of a genetic blueprint.

Reflexes

- Reflexes govern the newborn's movements. They include the sucking, rooting, and Moro reflexes.

Gross Motor Skills

- Gross motor skills involve large-muscle activities. Key skills developed during infancy include control of posture and walking. Gross motor skills improve dramatically during childhood.

- Peak levels of physical performance often occur between 19 and 26 years of age. In general, older adults show a slowing of movement.

Fine Motor Skills

- Fine motor skills involve finely tuned motor actions. The onset of reaching and grasping marks a significant accomplishment. Fine motor skills continue to develop during childhood and then decline somewhat with aging.

2 Sensory and Perceptual Development   (LG2)   Outline the course of sensory and perceptual development.

What Are Sensation and Perception?

- Sensation occurs when information interacts with sensory receptors. Perception is the interpretation of sensation.

The Ecological View

- Created by the Gibsons, the ecological view states that people directly perceive information that exists in the world. Perception brings people in contact with the environment so that they can interact with and adapt to it.

- Affordances provide opportunities for interaction offered by objects that fit within our capabilities to perform activities.

- Researchers have developed a number of methods to assess the infant's perception, including the visual preference method (which Fantz used to determine young infants' interest in looking at patterned over nonpatterned displays), habituation and dishabituation, and tracking.

Visual Perception

- The infant's visual acuity increases dramatically during the first year of life. Infants can distinguish some colors by 8 weeks of age and possibly by as early as 4 weeks. Young infants systematically scan human faces. By 3 months of age, infants show size and shape constancy.

- As visual perception develops, infants develop visual expectations. In Gibson and Walk's classic study, infants as young as 6 months of age had depth perception. Much of vision develops from biological foundations, but environmental experiences can contribute to the development of visual perception. During the preschool years, children become better at differentiating colors and scanning the visual world.

- After the early adult years, visual acuity declines. Eye accommodation decreases the most from 40 to 59 years of age. In older adults, the yellowing of the eye's lens reduces color differentiation, and the ability to see the periphery of a visual field declines. Significant declines in visual functioning related to glare characterize adults 75 years and older and are even more severe among those who are 85 years and older. Three diseases that can impair the vision of older adults are cataracts, glaucoma, and macular degeneration.

- The fetus can hear sounds such as the mother's voice and music during the last two months of pregnancy. Immediately after birth newborns can hear, but their sensory threshold is higher than that of adults. Developmental changes in the perception of loudness, pitch, and localization of sound occur during infancy.

- Hearing can start to decline by the age of 40, especially sensitivity to high-pitched sounds. However, hearing impairment usually doesn't become much of an impediment until late adulthood. Hearing aids can diminish hearing problems for many older adults.

- Newborns can respond to touch and feel pain. Sensitivity to pain decreases in late adulthood. Newborns can differentiate odors, and sensitivity to taste is present before birth. Smell and taste may decline in late adulthood, although in healthy individuals the decline is minimal.

- Crude, exploratory forms of intermodal perception—the ability to relate and integrate information from two or more sensory modalities—are present in newborns and become sharpened over the first year of life.

- In theorizing about perception, nature advocates are referred to as nativists and nurture proponents are called empiricists. The Gibsons' ecological view that has guided much of perceptual development research leans toward a nativist approach but still allows for developmental changes in distinctive features. Piaget's constructivist view leans toward an empiricist approach, emphasizing that many perceptual accomplishments must await the development of cognitive stages in infancy. A strong empiricist approach is unwarranted. A full account of perceptual development acknowledges the roles of nature, nurture, and the developing sensitivity to information.

3 Perceptual-Motor Coupling

 LG3 Discuss the connection between perception and action.

- Perception and action often are not isolated but rather are coupled. Action can guide perception and perception can guide action. Individuals perceive in order to move and move in order to perceive.

key **terms**

accommodation of the eye	fine motor skills	macular degeneration	size constancy
affordances	glaucoma	Moro reflex	sucking reflex
cataracts	grasping reflex	perception	visual preference method
dishabituation	gross motor skills	rooting reflex	
dynamic systems theory	habituation	sensation	
ecological view	intermodal perception	shape constancy	

key **people**

Karen Adolph	Eleanor Gibson	William James	Daphne Maurer
Karlene Ball	James J. Gibson	Scott Johnson	Esther Thelen
Robert Fantz	Megan Gunnar	Rachel Keen	Richard Walk

JGI/Jamie Grill/Getty Images

Learning is an ornament in prosperity, a refuge in adversity.

—ARISTOTLE
Greek Philosopher, 4th Century B.C.

Cognitive Processes and Development

Children thirst to know and understand. They construct their own ideas about the world around them and are remarkable for their curiosity, intelligence, and language. And it is always in season for the old to learn. In Section 3, you will read four chapters: "Cognitive Developmental Approaches," "Information Processing," "Intelligence," and "Language Development."

chapter 6

COGNITIVE DEVELOPMENTAL APPROACHES

chapter outline

preview

Cognitive developmental approaches place a special emphasis on how individuals actively construct their thinking. They also focus heavily on how thinking changes from one point in development to another. In this chapter, we will focus on the cognitive developmental approaches of Jean Piaget and Lev Vygotsky. We also will explore the possibility that adults think in a qualitatively more advanced way than adolescents do.

1 Piaget's Theory of Cognitive Development

LG1 Discuss the key processes and four stages in Piaget's theory.

| Processes of Development | Sensorimotor Stage | Preoperational Stage | Concrete Operational Stage | Formal Operational Stage |

Poet Nora Perry asks, "Who knows the thoughts of a child?" As much as anyone, Piaget knew. Through careful observations of his own three children—Laurent, Lucienne, and Jacqueline—and observations of and interviews with other children, Piaget reached groundbreaking conclusions regarding the ways children think about the world.

Piaget's theory is a general, unifying story of how biology and experience sculpt cognitive development. Piaget thought that, just as our physical bodies have structures that enable us to adapt to the world, we build mental structures that help us adapt to the world. Adaptation involves adjusting to new environmental demands. Piaget stressed that children actively construct their own cognitive worlds; information is not just poured into their minds from the environment. He sought to discover how children at different points in their development think about the world and how systematic changes in their thinking occur.

PROCESSES OF DEVELOPMENT

What processes do children use as they construct their knowledge of the world? Piaget developed several concepts to answer this question; especially important among them are schemes, assimilation, accommodation, organization, equilibrium, and equilibration.

Schemes As the infant or child seeks to construct an understanding of the world, said Piaget (1954), the developing brain creates **schemes.** These are actions or mental representations that organize knowledge. In Piaget's theory, behavioral schemes (physical activities) characterize infancy and mental schemes (cognitive activities) develop in childhood (Lamb, Bornstein, & Teti, 2002). A baby's schemes are structured by simple actions that can be performed on objects, such as sucking, looking, and grasping. Older children have schemes that include strategies and plans for solving problems. By the time we have reached adulthood, we have constructed an enormous number of diverse schemes, ranging from driving a car to balancing a budget to the concept of fairness.

Next, we will look at other important cognitive processes—assimilation, accommodation, organization, and equilibration—that individuals use throughout the life span in actively constructing their knowledge.

Assimilation and Accommodation To explain how children use and adapt their schemes, Piaget offered two concepts: assimilation and accommodation. **Assimilation** occurs when children incorporate new experiences into existing schemes.

Think about a toddler who has learned to use the word *car* to identify the family's blue car. The toddler might then see other different colors and brands of cars and call them "cars," thus assimilating these vehicles into his or her existing scheme. **Accommodation** occurs when children adjust their schemes to account for new information and experiences. For example, the child soon learns that other moving vehicles, such as motorcycles and trucks, are not cars and fine-tunes the category to exclude motorcycles and trucks, accommodating the scheme.

Jean Piaget, the famous Swiss developmental psychologist.
Bettmann/Getty Images

We are born capable of learning.

—JEAN-JACQUES ROUSSEAU
Swiss-born French Philosopher, 18th Century

schemes In Piaget's theory, actions or mental representations that organize knowledge.

assimilation Piagetian concept in which children use existing schemes to incorporate new information.

accommodation Piagetian concept of incorporating new experiences into existing schemes.

In Piaget's view, what is a scheme? What schemes might this young infant be displaying?
Maya Kovacheva Photography/Getty Images

Assimilation and accommodation operate even in very young infants. Newborns reflexively suck everything that touches their lips; they assimilate all sorts of objects into their sucking scheme. By sucking different objects, they learn about their taste, texture, shape, and so on. After several months of experience, though, they construct their understanding of the world differently. Some objects, such as fingers and the mother's breast, can be sucked, and others, such as fuzzy blankets, should not be sucked. In other words, they accommodate their sucking scheme.

Organization   To make sense of their world, said Piaget, children cognitively organize their experiences. **Organization** in Piaget's theory is the grouping of isolated behaviors and thoughts into a higher-order system. Continual refinement of this organization is an inherent part of development. A child who has only a vague idea about how to use a hammer may also have a vague idea about how to use other tools. After learning how to use each one, the child relates these uses, organizing his knowledge.

Equilibration and Stages of Development   Assimilation and accommodation always take the child to a higher ground, according to Piaget. In trying to understand the world, the child inevitably experiences cognitive conflict, or *disequilibrium*. That is, the child constantly encounters inconsistencies and counterexamples to his or her existing schemes. For example, if a child believes that pouring water from a short and wide container into a tall and narrow container changes the amount of water, then the child might be puzzled by where the "extra" water came from and whether there is actually more water to drink. The puzzle creates disequilibrium; for Piaget, an internal search for equilibrium creates motivation for change. The child assimilates and accommodates, adjusting old schemes, developing new schemes, and organizing and reorganizing the old and new schemes. Eventually, the organization is fundamentally different from the old organization; it is a new way of thinking.

In short, according to Piaget, children constantly assimilate and accommodate as they seek equilibrium. There is considerable movement between states of cognitive equilibrium and disequilibrium as assimilation and accommodation work in concert to produce cognitive change. **Equilibration** is the name Piaget gave to this mechanism by which children shift from one stage of thought to the next.

The result of these processes, according to Piaget, is that individuals go through four stages of development. A different way of understanding the world makes each stage more advanced than the previous one. Cognition is *qualitatively* different in one stage compared with another. In other words, the way children reason at one stage is different from the way they reason at another stage. Figure 1 provides a brief description of the four Piagetian stages.

SENSORIMOTOR STAGE

The **sensorimotor stage** lasts from birth to about 2 years of age. In this stage, infants construct an understanding of the world by coordinating sensory experiences (such as seeing and hearing) with physical, motoric actions—hence the term "sensorimotor." At the beginning of this stage, newborns have little more than reflexes with which to work. By the end of the sensorimotor stage, 2-year-olds can produce complex sensorimotor patterns and use primitive symbols.

organization Piagetian concept of grouping isolated behaviors and thoughts into a higher-order, more smoothly functioning cognitive system.

equilibration A mechanism that Piaget proposed to explain how children shift from one stage of thought to the next.

sensorimotor stage The first of Piaget's stages, which lasts from birth to about 2 years of age, during which infants construct an understanding of the world by coordinating sensory experiences (such as seeing and hearing) with physical, motoric actions.

Substages   Piaget divided the sensorimotor stage into six substages: (1) simple reflexes; (2) first habits and primary circular reactions; (3) secondary circular reactions; (4) coordination of secondary circular reactions; (5) tertiary circular reactions, novelty, and curiosity; and (6) internalization of schemes. Piaget argued that each substage builds on the previous one.

Simple reflexes, the first sensorimotor substage, corresponds to the first month after birth. In this substage, sensation and action are coordinated primarily through reflexive behaviors such as rooting and sucking. Soon the infant produces behaviors that resemble reflexes in the absence of the usual stimulus for the reflex. For example, a newborn will suck a nipple or bottle only when it is placed directly in the baby's mouth or touched to the lips. But soon the infant might suck when a bottle or nipple is only nearby. Even in the first month of life, the infant is initiating action and actively structuring experiences.

Primary circular reactions is the second sensorimotor substage, which develops between 1 and 4 months of age. A *primary circular reaction* is a scheme based on the attempt to reproduce

Sensorimotor Stage

The infant constructs an understanding of the world by coordinating sensory experiences with physical actions. An infant progresses from reflexive, instinctual action at birth to the beginning of symbolic thought toward the end of the stage.

Birth to 2 Years of Age

Preoperational Stage

The child begins to represent the world with words and images. These words and images reflect increased symbolic thinking and go beyond the connection of sensory information and physical action.

2 to 7 Years of Age

Concrete Operational Stage

The child can now reason logically about concrete events and classify objects into different sets.

7 to 11 Years of Age

Formal Operational Stage

The adolescent reasons in more abstract, idealistic, and logical ways.

11 Years of Age Through Adulthood

FIGURE 1

PIAGET'S FOUR STAGES OF COGNITIVE DEVELOPMENT
(*Left to right*): Stockbyte/Getty Images; Jacobs Stock Photography/BananaStock/Getty Images; Fuse/image100/Corbis; Purestock/Getty Images

an event that initially occurred by chance. For example, suppose an infant accidentally sucks his fingers when they are placed near his mouth. Later, he searches for his fingers to suck them again, but the fingers do not cooperate because the infant cannot coordinate visual and manual actions.

Habits and circular reactions are stereotyped—that is, the infant repeats them the same way each time. During this substage, the infant's own body remains the infant's center of attention. There is no outward pull by environmental events.

Secondary circular reactions is the third sensorimotor substage, which develops between 4 and 8 months of age. In this substage, the infant becomes more object oriented, moving beyond preoccupation with the self. The infant's schemes are not intentional or goal-directed, but they are repeated because of their consequences. By chance, an infant might shake a rattle. The infant repeats this action for the sake of its fascination. This is a *secondary circular reaction:* an action repeated because of its consequences. The infant also imitates some simple actions, such as the baby talk or burbling of adults, and some physical gestures. However, the baby imitates only actions that she is already able to produce.

Coordination of secondary circular reactions is Piaget's fourth sensorimotor substage, which develops between 8 and 12 months of age. To progress into this substage, the infant must coordinate vision and touch, hand and eye. Actions become more outwardly directed. Significant changes during this substage involve the coordination of schemes and intentionality. Infants readily combine and recombine previously learned schemes in a coordinated way. They might look at an object and grasp it simultaneously, or they might visually inspect a toy, such as a rattle, and finger it simultaneously, exploring it tactilely. Actions are even more outwardly directed than before. Related to this coordination is the second achievement—the presence of intentionality. For example, infants might manipulate a stick in order to bring a desired toy within reach, or they might knock over one block to reach and play with another one.

Tertiary circular reactions, novelty, and curiosity is Piaget's fifth sensorimotor substage, which develops between 12 and 18 months of age. In this substage, infants become intrigued by the many properties of objects and by the many things that they can make happen to objects.

I wish I could travel by the road that crosses the baby's mind, and out beyond all bounds; where messengers run errands for no cause between the kingdoms of kings of no history; where reason makes kites of her laws and flies them, and truth sets facts free from its fetters.

—RABINDRANATH TAGORE
Bengali Poet and Essayist, 20th Century

This 17-month-old is in Piaget's stage of tertiary circular reactions. *What might the infant do that would suggest she is in this stage?*
Tom Grill/Getty Images

object permanence The Piagetian term for one of an infant's most important accomplishments: understanding that objects continue to exist even when they cannot directly be seen, heard, or touched.

A block can be made to fall, spin, hit another object, and slide across the ground. *Tertiary circular reactions* are schemes in which the infant purposely explores new possibilities with objects, continually doing new things to them and exploring the results. Piaget says that this stage marks the starting point for human curiosity and interest in novelty.

Internalization of schemes is Piaget's sixth and final sensorimotor substage, which develops between 18 and 24 months of age. In this substage, the infant develops the ability to use primitive symbols. For Piaget, a symbol is an internalized sensory image or word that represents an event. Primitive symbols permit the infant to think about concrete events without directly acting them out or perceiving them. Moreover, symbols allow the infant to manipulate and transform the represented events in simple ways. In a favorite Piagetian example, Piaget's young daughter saw a matchbox being opened and closed. Later, she mimicked the event by opening and closing her mouth. This was an obvious expression of her image of the event. A summary of Piaget's six substages of sensorimotor development is shown in Figure 2.

Object Permanence   Imagine how chaotic and unpredictable your life would be if you could not distinguish between yourself and your world. This is what the life of a newborn must be like, according to Piaget. There is no differentiation between the self and world; objects have no separate, permanent existence.

By the end of the sensorimotor period, objects are both separate from the self and permanent. **Object permanence** is the understanding that objects continue to exist even when they cannot be seen, heard, or touched. Acquiring the sense of object permanence is one of the infant's most important accomplishments, according to Piaget.

How can anyone know whether an infant has a sense of object permanence? The principal way that object permanence is studied is by watching an infant's reaction when an interesting object disappears (see Figure 3). If infants search for the object, it is assumed that they believe it continues to exist.

Object permanence is just one of the basic concepts about the physical world developed by babies. To Piaget, children, even infants, are much like little scientists, examining the world to see how it works. How can the accuracy of this view of children's development be assessed? The *Connecting with Research* interlude describes some of the ways in which adult scientists try to discover what these "baby scientists" are finding out about the world.

Substage	Age	Description	Example
1 Simple reflexes	Birth to 1 month	Coordination of sensation and action through reflexive behaviors.	Rooting, sucking, and grasping reflexes; newborns suck reflexively when their lips are touched.
2 Primary circular reactions	1 to 4 months	A scheme based on the attempt to reproduce an event that initially occurred by chance.	Repeating a body sensation first experienced by chance (sucking thumb, for example); then infants might accommodate actions by sucking their thumb differently from how they suck on a nipple.
3 Secondary circular reactions	4 to 8 months	Infants become more object-oriented, moving beyond self-preoccupation; they repeat actions that bring interesting or pleasurable results.	An infant coos to make a person stay near; as the person starts to leave, the infant coos again.
4 Coordination of secondary circular reactions	8 to 12 months	Coordination of vision and touch—hand-eye coordination; coordination of schemes and intentionality.	Infant manipulates a stick in order to bring an attractive toy within reach.
5 Tertiary circular reactions, novelty, and curiosity	12 to 18 months	Infants become intrigued by the many properties of objects and by the many things they can make happen to objects; they experiment with new behavior.	A block can be made to fall, spin, hit another object, and slide across the ground.
6 Internalization of schemes	18 to 24 months	Infants develop the ability to use primitive symbols and form enduring mental representations.	An infant who has never thrown a temper tantrum before sees a playmate throw a tantrum; the infant retains a memory of the event, then throws one himself the next day.

FIGURE 2
PIAGET'S SIX SUBSTAGES OF SENSORIMOTOR DEVELOPMENT

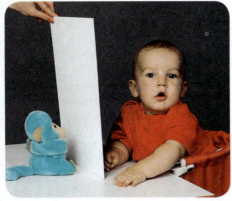

FIGURE 3

OBJECT PERMANENCE

Piaget argued that object permanence is one of infancy's landmark cognitive accomplishments. For this 5-month-old boy, "out of sight" is literally out of mind. The infant looks at the toy monkey (*left*), but when his view of the toy is blocked (*right*), he does not search for it. Several months later, he will search for the hidden toy monkey, an action reflecting the presence of object permanence.
Doug Goodman/Science Source

connecting with research

How Do Researchers Study Infants' Understanding of Object Permanence and Causality?

Two accomplishments of infants that Piaget examined were the development of object permanence and the child's understanding of causality. Let's examine two research studies that address these topics.

In both studies, Renée Baillargeon and her colleagues used a research method that involves violation of expectations. In this method, infants see an event happen as it normally would. Then the event is changed, often in a way that creates a physically impossible event. If infants look longer at the changed event, their reaction indicates they are surprised by it. In other words, this reaction is interpreted to indicate that the infant had certain expectations about the world that were violated.

In one study that focused on object permanence, researchers showed infants a toy car that moved down an inclined track, disappeared behind a screen, and then reemerged at the other end, still on the track (Baillargeon & DeVos, 1991). After this sequence was repeated several times, something different occurred: A toy mouse was placed behind the track but was hidden by the screen while the car rolled by. This was the "possible" event. Then, the researchers created an "impossible event": The toy mouse was placed on the track but was secretly removed after the screen was lowered so that the car seemed to go through the mouse. In this study, infants as young as 3½ months of age looked longer at the impossible event than at the possible event, an indication that they were surprised by it. Their surprise suggested that they remembered not only that the toy mouse still existed (object permanence) but where it was located.

Another study focused on the infant's understanding of causality (Kotovsky & Baillargeon, 1994). In this research, a cylinder rolls down a ramp and hits a toy bug at the bottom of the ramp. By 5½ and 6½ months of age, after infants have seen how far the bug will be pushed by a medium-sized cylinder, their reactions indicate that they understand that the bug will roll farther if it is hit by a large cylinder than if it is hit by a small cylinder. Thus, by the middle of the first year of life, these infants understood that the size of a moving object determines how far it will move a stationary object that it collides with.

In Baillargeon's (2008, 2014; Baillargeon & others, 2012) view, infants have a pre-adapted, innate bias called the principle of persistence that explains their assumption that objects don't change their properties—including how solid they are, their location, their color, and their form—unless some external factor intervenes (a person moves the object, for example). Shortly, we will revisit the extent to which nature and nurture are at work in the changes that take place in the infant's cognitive development.

Research discussed in this interlude and elsewhere indicates that infants develop object permanence earlier than Piaget proposed (Baillargeon, 2014, 2016; Baillargeon & others, 2011, 2012). Indeed, as you will see in the next section, a major theme of infant cognitive development today is that infants are more cognitively competent than Piaget envisioned. What methods might researchers use to arrive at this conclusion?

Evaluating Piaget's Sensorimotor Stage   Piaget opened up a new way of look-ing at infants with his view that their main task is to coordinate their sensory impressions with their motor activity. However, the infant's cognitive world is not as neatly packaged as Piaget portrayed it, and some of Piaget's explanations for the causes of change are debated. In the past several decades, sophisticated experimental techniques have been devised to study infants, and there have been a large number of research studies on infant develop-ment. Much of the new research suggests that Piaget's view of sensorimotor development needs to be modified (Adolph & Hoch, 2019; Lee & others, 2019; Van de Vondervoort & Hamlin, 2018).

The A-Not-B Error   One modification concerns Piaget's claim that certain processes are crucial in transitions from one stage to the next. The data do not always support his explanations. For example, in Piaget's theory, an important feature in the progression into substage 4, *coordination of secondary circular reactions*, is an infant's inclination to search for a hidden object in a familiar location rather than to look for the object in a new location. For example, if a toy is hidden twice, initially at location A and subsequently at location B, 8- to 12-month-old infants search initially and correctly at location A. But when the toy is subsequently hidden at location B while the infants watch, they make the mistake of continuing to search for it at location A. **A-not-B error** is the term used to describe this common mistake. Older infants are less likely to make the A-not-B error because their concept of object permanence is more complete. Researchers have found, however, that the A-not-B error does not show up consistently (MacNeill & others, 2018; Sophian, 1985). The evidence indicates that A-not-B errors are sensitive to the delay between hiding the object at B and the infant's attempt to find it (Diamond, 1985). Thus, the A-not-B error might be due to a failure in memory. And A-not-B performance may be linked to attention as well. For example, in one study, 5-month-olds' more focused attention on a separate task involving a puppet was linked to better performance on an A-not-B task that involved locating an object after it was hidden from view (Marcovitch & others, 2016). Another explanation for A-not-B error is that infants tend to repeat a previous motor behavior (Clearfield & others, 2006).

developmental **connection**

Theories

Eleanor Gibson was a pioneer in crafting the ecological view of per-ceptual development. Connect to "Motor, Sensory, and Perceptual Development."

Perceptual Development and Expectations   A number of theorists, such as Eleanor Gibson (2001) and Elizabeth Spelke (2011, 2016a, b), argue that infants' perceptual abilities are highly developed very early in life. Spelke argues that young infants interpret the world as having predictable occurrences. For example, in the chapter on "Motor, Sensory, and Perceptual Development," you read about research that demonstrated the presence of intermodal perception—the ability to coordinate information from two or more sensory modalities, such as vision and hearing—by 3½ months of age, much earlier than Piaget would have predicted (Spelke & Owsley, 1979).

Research also suggests that infants develop the ability to understand how the world works at a very early age (Jin & others, 2018; Liu & Spelke, 2017; Stavans & Baillargeon, 2018; Stavans & others, 2019). For example, what kinds of expectations do infants form? Are infants born expecting the world to obey basic physical laws, such as gravity, or if not, then when do they learn about how the world works? Experiments by Elizabeth Spelke (1991, 2000; Spelke & Hespos, 2001) have addressed these questions. She placed babies before a puppet stage and showed them a series of actions that are unexpected if you know how the physical world works—for example, one ball seemed to roll through a solid barrier, another seemed to leap between two platforms, and a third appeared to hang in midair (Spelke, 1979). Spelke measured and compared the babies' looking times for unexpected and expected actions. She concluded that by 4 months of age, even though infants do not yet have the ability to talk about objects, move around objects, manipulate objects, or even see objects with high resolution, they expect objects to be solid and continuous. However, at 4 months of age, infants do not expect an object to obey gravitational constraints (Spelke & others, 1992). Similarly, research by Renee Baillargeon (1995, 2014, 2016; Baillargeon & others, 2011, 2012) documents that infants as young as 3 to 4 months expect objects to be *substantial* (in the sense that other objects cannot move through them) and *permanent* (in the sense that objects continue to exist when they are hidden).

In sum, researchers such as Baillargeon and Spelke conclude that infants see objects as bounded, unitary, solid, and separate from their background, possibly at birth or shortly

A-not-B error   This error occurs when infants make the mistake of selecting the familiar hiding place (A) of an object rather than its new hiding place (B) as they progress into substage 4 in Piaget's sensorimotor stage.

thereafter, but definitely by 3 to 4 months of age—much earlier than Piaget envisioned. Young infants still have much to learn about objects, but the world appears both stable and orderly to them.

However, some critics argue that the Baillargeon and Spelke experiments mainly demonstrate perceptual competencies or detection of regularities in the environment (Heyes, 2014; Ruffman, 2014). The critics stress that the infants' responses in their studies reflect a very rudimentary understanding that likely differs greatly from the understanding of older children.

The Nature-Nurture Issue   In considering the big issue of whether nature or nurture plays the more important role in infant development, Elizabeth Spelke (Spelke, 2003, 2011, 2016a, b, 2017) comes down clearly on the side of nature. Spelke endorses a **core knowledge approach,** which states that infants are born with domain-specific innate knowledge systems. Among these domain-specific knowledge systems are those involving space, number sense, object permanence, and language. Strongly influenced by evolution, the core knowledge domains are theorized to be prewired to allow infants to make sense of their world (Coubart & others, 2014). After all, Spelke concludes, how could infants possibly grasp the complex world in which they live if they didn't come into the world equipped with core sets of knowledge? In this approach, the innate core knowledge domains form a foundation around which more mature cognitive functioning and learning develop. The core knowledge approach argues that Piaget greatly underestimated the cognitive abilities of infants, especially young infants (Spelke, 2017).

Recently, researchers also have explored whether preverbal infants might have a built-in innate sense of morality (Steckler & Hamlin, 2016; Van de Vondervoort & Hamlin, 2016, 2018). In this research, infants as young as 4 months of age are more likely to make visually guided reaches toward a puppet who has acted as a helper (such as helping someone get up a hill, assisting in opening a box, or giving a ball back) rather than toward a puppet who has hindered others' efforts to achieve such goals (Hamlin, 2013a, b, 2014).

In criticizing the core knowledge approach, British developmental psychologist Mark Johnson (2008) says that the infants Spelke assesses in her research already have accumulated hundreds, and in some cases even thousands, of hours of experience in grasping what the world is about, which gives considerable room for the environment's role in the development of infant cognition (Highfield, 2008). According to Johnson (2008), infants likely come into the world with "soft biases to perceive and attend to different aspects of the environment, and to learn about the world in particular ways." In line with Johnson's view, one major criticism is that nativists completely neglect the infant's social immersion in the world and instead focus only on what happens inside the infant's head apart from the environment (Nelson, 2013). And recently, the view that the emergence of morality in infancy is innate was described as problematic (Carpendale & Hammond, 2016). Instead it was argued that morality may emerge through infants' early interaction with others and later transformation through language and reflective thought.

Although debate about the cause and course of infant cognitive development continues, most developmentalists today agree that Piaget underestimated the early cognitive accomplishments of infants and that both nature and nurture are involved in infants' cognitive development (Adolph & Hoch, 2019; Bell & Broomell, 2020; Stavans & Baillargeon, 2018; Stavans & others, 2019).

Conclusions   In sum, many researchers conclude that Piaget wasn't specific enough about how infants learn about their world and that infants, especially young infants, are more competent than Piaget thought (Xie, Mallin, & Richards, 2019). As researchers have examined the specific ways that infants learn, the field of infant cognition has become very specialized. There are many researchers working on different questions, with no general theory emerging that can connect all of the different findings. Their theories often are local theories, focused on specific research questions, rather than grand theories like Piaget's (Kuhn, 1998). Among the unifying themes in the study of infant cognition are seeking to understand more precisely how developmental changes in cognition take place, to answer questions about the relative importance of nature and nurture, and to examine the brain's role in cognitive development (Aslin, 2012). Exploring connections between brain, cognition, and development is a central focus in the recently emerging field of *developmental cognitive neuroscience* (Bell & Broomell, 2020; Winkler & others, 2019).

According to contemporary researchers, what revisions in Piaget's theory of sensorimotor development need to be made?
David Kenny/Getty Images

core knowledge approach States that infants are born with domain-specific innate knowledge systems. Among these domain-specific knowledge systems are those involving space, number sense, object permanence, and language.

PREOPERATIONAL STAGE

The cognitive world of the preschool child is creative, free, and fanciful. The imaginations of preschool children work overtime, and their mental grasp of the world improves. Piaget described the preschool child's cognition as preoperational. What did he mean?

The **preoperational stage,** which lasts from approximately 2 to 7 years of age, is the second Piagetian stage. In this stage, children begin to represent the world with words, images, and drawings. They form stable concepts and begin to reason. At the same time, the young child's cognitive world is dominated by egocentrism and magical beliefs.

Because Piaget called this stage "preoperational," it might sound like an unimportant waiting period. Not so. However, the label *preoperational* emphasizes that the child does not yet perform **operations,** which are reversible mental actions that allow children to do mentally what they previously could do only physically. Mentally adding and subtracting numbers are examples of operations. *Preoperational thought* is the beginning of the ability to reconstruct in thought what has been established in behavior. It can be divided into two substages: the symbolic function substage and the intuitive thought substage.

The Symbolic Function Substage The **symbolic function substage** is the first substage of preoperational thought, occurring roughly between the ages of 2 and 4. In this substage, the young child gains the ability to mentally represent an object that is not present. This ability vastly expands the child's mental world (Callaghan & Corbit, 2015). Young children use scribble designs to represent people, houses, cars, clouds, and so on; they begin to use language and engage in pretend play. However, although young children make distinct progress during this substage, their thinking still has important limitations, two of which are egocentrism and animism.

Egocentrism is the inability to distinguish between one's own perspective and someone else's perspective. Piaget and Barbel Inhelder (1969) initially studied young children's egocentrism by devising the three mountains task (see Figure 4). The child walks around the model of the mountains and becomes familiar with what the mountains look like from different perspectives and can see that there are different objects on the mountains. The child is then seated on one side of the table on which the mountains are placed. The experimenter moves a doll to different locations around the table, at each location asking the child to select from a series of photos the one photo that most accurately reflects the view that the doll is seeing. Children in the preoperational stage often pick their own view rather than the doll's view. Preschool children frequently show the ability to take another's perspective on some tasks but not others.

Animism, another limitation of preoperational thought, is the belief that inanimate objects have lifelike qualities and are capable of action (Gelman & Opfer, 2004). A young child might show animism by saying, "That tree pushed the leaf off, and it fell down" or "The sidewalk made me mad; it made me fall down." A young child who uses animism fails to distinguish the appropriate occasions for using human and nonhuman perspectives (Opfer & Gelman, 2011).

preoperational stage The second Piagetian developmental stage, which lasts from about 2 to 7 years of age; children begin to represent the world with words, images, and drawings.

operations Reversible mental actions that allow children to do mentally what before they had done only physically.

symbolic function substage The first substage of preoperational thought, occurring roughly between the ages of 2 and 4. In this substage, the young child gains the ability to represent mentally an object that is not present.

egocentrism The inability to distinguish between one's own and someone else's perspective; an important feature of preoperational thought.

animism A facet of preoperational thought—the belief that inanimate objects have lifelike qualities and are capable of action.

Model of Mountains

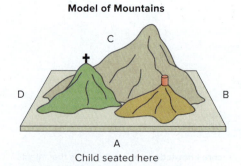

C

D   B

A
Child seated here

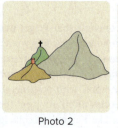

Photo 1
(View from A)

Photo 2
(View from B)

Photo 3
(View from C)

Photo 4
(View from D)

FIGURE 4

THE THREE MOUNTAINS TASK. Photo 1 shows the child's perspective from where he or she is sitting. Photos 2, 3, and 4 were taken from different perspectives. For example, Photo 2 shows what the mountains look like to a person sitting at spot B. When asked what a view of the mountains looks like from spot B, the child selects Photo 1, taken from spot A (the child's own view at the time) instead of Photo 2, the correct view.

Possibly because young children are not very concerned about reality, their drawings are fanciful and inventive. Suns are blue, skies are yellow, and cars float on clouds in their symbolic, imaginative world. One 3½-year-old looked at a scribble he had just drawn and described it as a pelican kissing a seal (see Figure 5a). The symbolism is simple but strong, like abstractions found in some modern art. Twentieth-century Spanish artist Pablo Picasso commented, "I used to draw like Raphael but it has taken me a lifetime to draw like young children." In the elementary school years, a child's drawings become more realistic, neat, and precise (see Figure 5b). Suns are yellow, skies are blue, and cars travel on roads (Winner, 1986).

The Intuitive Thought Substage

The **intuitive thought substage** is the second substage of preoperational thought, occurring between approximately 4 and 7 years of age. In this substage, children begin to use primitive reasoning and want to know the answers to all sorts of questions. Consider 4-year-old Tommy, who is at the beginning of the intuitive thought substage. Although he is starting to develop his own ideas about the world he lives in, his ideas are still simple, and he is not very good at thinking things out. He has difficulty understanding events that he knows are taking place but that he cannot see. His fantasized thoughts bear little resemblance to reality. He cannot yet answer the question "What if?" in any reliable way. For example, he has only a vague idea of what would happen if a car were to hit him. He also has difficulty negotiating traffic because he cannot do the mental calculations necessary to estimate whether an approaching car will hit him when he crosses the road.

By the age of 5, children have just about exhausted the adults around them with "why" questions. The child's questions signal the emergence of interest in reasoning and in figuring out why things are the way they are. Following are some samples of the questions children ask during the questioning period of 4 to 6 years of age (Elkind, 1976):

> *What makes you grow up?*
> *Who was the mother when everybody was a baby?*
> *Why do leaves fall?*
> *Why does the sun shine?*

Piaget called this substage *intuitive* because young children seem so sure about their knowledge and understanding yet are unaware of how they know what they know. That is, they know something but know it without the use of rational thinking.

Centration and the Limits of Preoperational Thought

One limitation of preoperational thought is **centration,** a centering of attention on one characteristic to the exclusion of all others. Centration is most clearly evidenced in young children's lack of **conservation,** the awareness that altering an object's or a substance's appearance does not change its basic properties. For example, to adults, it is obvious that a certain amount of liquid stays the same, regardless of a container's shape. But this is not at all obvious to young children. Instead, they are struck by the height of the liquid in the container; they focus on that characteristic to the exclusion of others.

The situation that Piaget devised to study conservation is his most famous task. In the conservation task, children are presented with two identical beakers, each filled to the same level with liquid (see Figure 6). They are asked if these beakers have the same amount of liquid, and they usually say yes. Then the liquid from one beaker is poured into a third beaker, which is taller and thinner than the first two. The children are then asked if the amount of liquid in the tall, thin beaker is equal to that which remains in one of the original beakers. Children who are younger than 7 or 8 years old usually say no and justify their answers in terms of the differing height or width of the beakers. Older children usually answer yes and justify their answers appropriately ("If you poured the water back, the amount would still be the same").

In Piaget's theory, failing the conservation-of-liquid task is a sign that children are at the preoperational stage of cognitive development. The failure demonstrates not only centration but also an inability to mentally reverse actions. To understand this concept, see the conservation-of-matter example shown in Figure 7. In the row labeled "matter" you'll see that preoperational children say the longer shape has more clay because they assume that "longer is more." Preoperational children cannot mentally reverse the clay-rolling process to see that the amount of clay is the same in both the shorter ball shape and the longer stick shape.

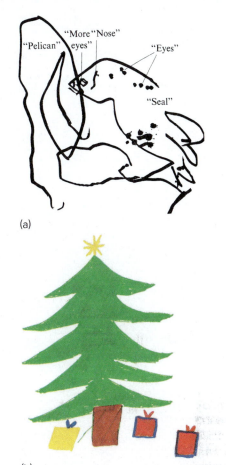

(a)

(b)

FIGURE 5

THE SYMBOLIC DRAWINGS OF YOUNG CHILDREN. (*a*) A 3½-year-old's symbolic drawing. Halfway into his drawing, the 3½-year-old artist said it was a "pelican kissing a seal." (*b*) This 11-year-old's drawing is neater and more realistic but also less inventive.

intuitive thought substage The second substage of preoperational thought, occurring between approximately 4 and 7 years of age. Children begin to use primitive reasoning and want to know the answers to all sorts of questions.

centration Focusing attention on one characteristic to the exclusion of all others.

conservation The awareness that altering the appearance of an object or a substance does not change its basic properties.

FIGURE 6

PIAGET'S CONSERVATION TASK. The beaker test is a well-known Piagetian test to determine whether a child can think operationally—that is, can mentally reverse actions and show conservation of the substance. (*a*) Two identical beakers are presented to the child. Then the experimenter pours the liquid from B into C, which is taller and thinner than A or B. (*b*) The child is asked if these beakers (A and C) have the same amount of liquid. The preoperational child says "no." When asked to point to the beaker that has more liquid, the preoperational child points to the tall, thin beaker.
Tony Freeman/PhotoEdit

In Figure 7 you can see that, in addition to failing the conservation-of-liquid task, preoperational children also fail to conserve number, matter, and length. However, children often vary in their performance on different conservation tasks. Thus, a child might be able to conserve volume but not number. An fMRI brain-imaging study of conservation of number revealed that advances in a network in the parietal and frontal lobes were linked to 9- and 10-year-olds' conservation success in comparison with non-conserving 5- and 6-year-olds (Houde & others, 2011).

Type of Conservation	Initial Presentation	Manipulation	Preoperational Child's Answer
Number	Two identical rows of objects are shown to the child, who agrees they have the same number.	One row is lengthened and the child is asked whether one row now has more objects.	Yes, the longer row.
Matter	Two identical balls of clay are shown to the child. The child agrees that they are equal.	The experimenter changes the shape of one of the balls and asks the child whether they still contain equal amounts of clay.	No, the longer one has more.
Length	Two sticks are aligned in front of the child. The child agrees that they are the same length.	The experimenter moves one stick to the right, then asks the child if they are equal in length.	No, the one on the top is longer.

FIGURE 7

SOME DIMENSIONS OF CONSERVATION: NUMBER, MATTER, AND LENGTH. *What characteristics of preoperational thought do children demonstrate when they fail these conservation tasks?*

Some developmentalists do not believe Piaget was entirely correct in his estimate of when children's conservation skills emerge. For example, Rochel Gelman (1969) showed that when the child's attention to relevant aspects of the conservation task has improved, the child is more likely to conserve. Gelman has also demonstrated that attentional training on one dimension, such as number, improves the preschool child's performance on another dimension, such as mass. Thus, Gelman noted that conservation appears earlier than Piaget thought and that attention is especially important in explaining conservation.

CONCRETE OPERATIONAL STAGE

Piaget proposed that the **concrete operational stage** lasts from approximately 7 to 11 years of age. In this stage, children can perform concrete operations, and they can reason logically as long as reasoning can be applied to specific or concrete examples. Remember that *operations* are mental actions that are reversible, and *concrete operations* are operations that are applied to real, concrete objects. When a child adds two apples together with four apples and concludes that there are now six apples, she is performing a concrete operation.

The conservation tasks described earlier indicate whether children are capable of concrete operations. Concrete operations allow the child to consider several characteristics rather than to focus on a single property of an object. In the clay example, the preoperational child is likely to focus on height or width. The concrete operational child coordinates information about both dimensions.

What other abilities are characteristic of children who have reached the concrete operational stage? One important skill is the ability to classify or divide things into different sets or subsets and to consider their interrelationships. Consider the family tree of four generations that is shown in Figure 8 (Furth & Wachs, 1975). This family tree suggests that the grandfather (A) has three children (B, C, and D), each of whom has two children (E through J), and that one of these children (J) has three children (K, L, and M). A child who comprehends the classification system can move up and down a level, across a level, and up and down and across within the system. The concrete operational child understands that person J can at the same time be father, brother, and grandson, for example.

Children who have reached the concrete operational stage are also capable of **seriation,** which is the ability to order stimuli along a quantitative dimension (such as length). To see if students can serialize, a teacher might haphazardly place eight sticks of different lengths on a table. The teacher then asks the students to order the sticks by length. Many young children end up with two or three small groups of "big" sticks or "little" sticks, rather than a correct ordering of all eight sticks. Another mistaken strategy they use is to evenly line up the tops of the sticks but ignore the bottoms. The concrete operational thinker who is capable of seriation simultaneously understands that each stick must be longer than the one that precedes it and shorter than the one that follows it.

Another aspect of reasoning about the relations between classes is **transitivity,** which is the ability to logically combine relations to reach certain conclusions. In this case, consider three sticks (A, B, and C) of differing lengths. A is the longest, B is intermediate in length, and C is the shortest. Does the child understand that, if A is longer than B and B is longer than C, then A is longer than C? In Piaget's theory, concrete operational thinkers who are capable of transitivity do; preoperational thinkers do not.

FORMAL OPERATIONAL STAGE

So far we have studied the first three of Piaget's stages of cognitive development: sensorimotor, preoperational, and concrete operational. What are the characteristics of the fourth and final stage?

The **formal operational stage,** which appears between 11 and 15 years of age, is the fourth and final Piagetian stage. In this stage, individuals move beyond concrete experiences and think in abstract and more logical ways. As part of thinking more abstractly, adolescents develop images of ideal circumstances. They might think about what an ideal parent is like and compare their parents to their ideal standards. They begin to entertain possibilities for the future and are fascinated with what they can become. In solving problems, formal operational thinkers are more systematic and use logical reasoning.

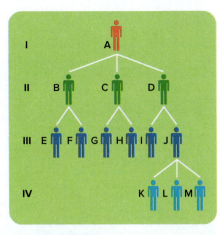

FIGURE 8

CLASSIFICATION: AN IMPORTANT ABILITY IN CONCRETE OPERATIONAL THOUGHT. A family tree of four generations (*I to IV*): The preoperational child has trouble classifying the members of the four generations; the concrete operational child can classify the members vertically, horizontally, and obliquely (up and down and across). For example, the concrete operational child understands that a family member can be a son, a brother, and a father, all at the same time.

concrete operational stage The third Piagetian stage, which lasts from approximately 7 to 11 years of age; children can perform concrete operations, and logical reasoning replaces intuitive reasoning as long as the reasoning can be applied to specific or concrete examples.

seriation The concrete operation that involves ordering stimuli along a quantitative dimension (such as length).

transitivity The ability to logically combine relations to understand certain conclusions. Piaget argued that an understanding of transitivity is characteristic of concrete operational thought.

formal operational stage The fourth and final Piagetian stage, which appears between the ages of 11 and 15; individuals move beyond concrete experiences and think in more abstract and logical ways.

Abstract, Idealistic, and Logical Thinking

The abstract quality of the adolescent's thought at the formal operational level is evident in the adolescent's verbal problem-solving ability. Whereas the concrete operational thinker needs to see the concrete elements A, B, and C to be able to make the logical inference that if A = B and B = C, then A = C, the formal operational thinker can solve this problem merely through verbal presentation.

Another indication of the abstract quality of adolescents' thought is their increased tendency to think about thought itself. One adolescent commented, "I began thinking about why I was thinking about what I was. Then I began thinking about why I was thinking about what I was thinking about what I was." If this sounds abstract, it is, and it characterizes the adolescent's enhanced focus on thought and its abstract qualities.

Accompanying the abstract nature of formal operational thought in adolescence is thought full of idealism and possibilities. Although children frequently think in concrete ways, or in terms of what is real and limited, adolescents begin to engage in extended speculation about ideal characteristics—qualities they desire in themselves and in others. Such thoughts often lead adolescents to compare themselves with others in regard to such ideal standards. And the thoughts of adolescents are often fantasy flights into future possibilities. It is not unusual for the adolescent to become impatient with these newfound ideal standards and to become perplexed over which of many ideal standards to adopt.

Might adolescents' ability to reason hypothetically and to evaluate what is ideal versus what is real lead them to engage in demonstrations such as this protest against charter schools? What other causes might be attractive to adolescents' newfound cognitive abilities of hypothetical-deductive reasoning and idealistic thinking?
Jim West/Alamy Stock Photo

As adolescents are learning to think more abstractly and idealistically, they are also learning to think more logically. Children are more likely to solve problems in a trial-and-error fashion. Adolescents begin to think more as a scientist thinks, devising plans to solve problems and systematically testing solutions. They use **hypothetical-deductive reasoning**—that is, they develop hypotheses, or best guesses, and systematically deduce (or conclude) which is the best path to follow in solving the problem.

Assimilation (incorporating new information into existing knowledge) dominates the initial development of formal operational thought, and these thinkers perceive the world subjectively and idealistically. Later in adolescence, as intellectual balance is restored, these individuals accommodate to the cognitive upheaval that has occurred (they adjust to the new information).

Some of Piaget's ideas on formal operational thought are being challenged, however (Reyna & Zayas, 2014). There is much more individual variation in formal operational thought than Piaget envisioned (Kuhn, 2009). Only about one in three young adolescents is a formal operational thinker. Many American adults never become formal operational thinkers, and neither do many adults in other cultures.

Adolescent Egocentrism

In addition to thinking more logically, abstractly, and idealistically—characteristics of Piaget's formal operational thought stage—in what other ways do adolescents change cognitively? David Elkind (1978) described how adolescent egocentrism governs the way that adolescents think about social matters. **Adolescent egocentrism** is the heightened self-consciousness of adolescents, which is reflected in their belief that others are as interested in them as they are themselves, and in their sense of personal uniqueness and invincibility. Elkind argued that adolescent egocentrism can be dissected into two types of social thinking—imaginary audience and personal fable.

The **imaginary audience** refers to the aspect of adolescent egocentrism that involves feeling that one is the center of everyone's attention and sensing that one is on stage. An adolescent boy might think that others are as aware as he is of a few hairs that are out of place. An adolescent girl walks into her classroom and thinks that all eyes are riveted on her complexion. Adolescents especially sense that they are "on stage" in early adolescence, believing they are the main actors and all others are the audience. Might the use of social media increase adolescent egocentrism? See *Connecting Development to Life* to explore this topic.

Many adolescent girls spend long hours in front of the mirror, depleting bottles of hair spray, tubes of lipstick, and jars of cosmetics. *How might this behavior be related to changes in adolescent cognitive and physical development?*
Image Source/Getty Images

Are Social Media an Amplification Tool for Adolescent Egocentrism?

Earlier generations of adolescents did not have social media to connect with large numbers of people; instead, they connected with fewer people, either in person or via telephone. Might today's teens be drawn to social media and its virtually unlimited friend base to express their imaginary audience and sense of uniqueness? A research analysis concluded that amassing a large number of friends (audience) may help to validate adolescents' perception that their life is on stage and everyone is watching them (Psychster Inc, 2010). A look at a teen's home Twitter® comments may suggest to many adults that what teens are reporting is often rather mundane and uninteresting as they update to the world at large what they are doing and having, such as: "Studying heavy. Not happy tonight." or "At Starbucks with Jesse. Lattes are great." Possibly for adolescents, though, such tweets are not trivial but rather an expression of the personal fable's sense of uniqueness (Psychster Inc, 2010).

One study of social networking sites found that the indiscriminate monologue communication from one to many, in which the

diverse interests of others are not considered, that often occurs on such sites as Facebook® may produce an egocentric tendency that undermines prosocial behavior (Chiou, Chen, & Liao, 2014). A recent meta-analysis concluded that a greater use of social networking sites was linked to a higher level of narcissism (Gnambs & Appel, 2018).

What do you think? Are social media, such as Facebook® and Twitter®, amplifying the expression of adolescents' imaginary audience, personal fable sense of uniqueness, and narcissistic tendencies?

In what ways might frequent use of social media, such as Facebook®, influence adolescents' cognitive development?
Andrey_Popov/Shutterstock

According to Elkind, the **personal fable** is the part of adolescent egocentrism that involves an adolescent's sense of personal uniqueness and invincibility. Adolescents' sense of personal uniqueness makes them believe that no one can understand how they really feel. For example, an adolescent girl thinks that her mother cannot possibly sense the hurt she feels because her boyfriend has broken up with her. As part of their effort to retain a sense of personal uniqueness, adolescents might craft stories about themselves that are filled with fantasy, immersing themselves in a world that is far removed from reality. Personal fables frequently show up in adolescent diaries.

One study of sixth- through twelfth-graders revealed that a sense of invincibility was linked to risky behaviors such as smoking cigarettes, drinking alcohol, and engaging in juvenile delinquency, whereas a sense of personal uniqueness was related to depression and suicidal thoughts (Aalsma, Lapsley, & Flannery, 2006). However, some research studies suggest that, rather than perceiving themselves to be invulnerable, many adolescents view themselves as vulnerable (Reyna & Rivers, 2008). For example, in one study, 12- to 18-year-olds were asked about their chances of dying in the next year and prior to age 20 (Fischoff & others, 2010). The adolescents greatly overestimated their chances of dying.

Some researchers have questioned the view that invulnerability is a unitary concept and argued rather that it consists of two dimensions (Duggan, Lapsley, & Norman, 2000; Lapsley & Hill, 2010):

· *Danger invulnerability,* which involves adolescents' sense of indestructibility and tendency to take on physical risks (driving recklessly at high speeds, for example)
· *Psychological invulnerability*, which captures an adolescent's felt invulnerability related to personal or psychological distress (getting one's feelings hurt, for example)

hypothetical-deductive reasoning Piaget's formal operational concept that adolescents have the cognitive ability to develop hypotheses about ways to solve problems and can systematically deduce which is the best path to follow in solving the problem.

adolescent egocentrism The heightened self-consciousness of adolescents, which is reflected in adolescents' beliefs that others are as interested in them as they are themselves, and in adolescents' sense of personal uniqueness and invincibility.

imaginary audience That aspect of adolescent egocentrism that involves feeling that one is the center of attention and sensing that one is on stage.

personal fable The part of adolescent egocentrism that involves an adolescent's sense of personal uniqueness and invincibility.

One study revealed that adolescents who scored high on a danger invulnerability scale were more likely to engage in juvenile delinquency or substance abuse, or to be depressed (Lapsley & Hill, 2010). In this study, adolescents who scored high on psychological invulnerability were less likely to be depressed, had higher self-esteem, and maintained better interpersonal relationships. In terms of psychological invulnerability, adolescents often benefit from the normal developmental challenges of exploring identity options, making new friends, asking someone to go out on a date, and learning a new skill. All of these important adolescent tasks involve risk and failure as an option but, if successful, result in enhanced self-image.

Review Connect Reflect

 LG1 Discuss the key processes and four stages in Piaget's theory.

Review
- What are the key processes in Piaget's theory of cognitive development? What are Piaget's four stages of cognitive development?
- What are the main characteristics of the sensorimotor stage?
- What are the main characteristics of the preoperational stage?
- What are the main characteristics of the concrete operational stage?
- What are the main characteristics of the formal operational stage?

Connect
- In this section, you read that by the age of 6 to 8 months infants have learned to perceive gravity and support. What aspects of physical development and perceptual/motor development occurring around this time frame might contribute to infants' exploration and understanding of these concepts?

Reflect Your Own Personal Journey of Life
- Do you consider yourself to be a formal operational thinker? Do you still sometimes feel like a concrete operational thinker? Give examples.

2 Applying and Evaluating Piaget's Theory

 LG2 Apply Piaget's theory to education and evaluate Piaget's theory.

Piaget and Education   Evaluating Piaget's Theory

What are some applications of Piaget's theory to education? What are the main contributions and criticisms of Piaget's theory?

PIAGET AND EDUCATION

Piaget was not an educator, but he provided a sound conceptual framework for viewing learning and education. Here are some ideas in Piaget's theory that can be applied to teaching children (Elkind, 1976; Heuwinkel, 1996):

1. *Take a constructivist approach.* Piaget emphasized that children learn best when they are active and seek solutions for themselves. Piaget opposed teaching methods that treat children as passive receptacles for knowledge. The educational implication of Piaget's view is that, in all subjects, students learn best by making discoveries, reflecting on them, and discussing them, rather than by blindly imitating the teacher or doing things by rote.

2. *Facilitate rather than direct learning.* Effective teachers design situations that allow students to learn by doing. These situations promote students' thinking and discovery. Teachers listen, watch, and question students, to help them gain better understanding.

3. *Consider the child's knowledge and level of thinking.* Students do not come to class with empty minds. They have concepts of space, time, quantity, and causality. These ideas

differ from the ideas of adults. Teachers need to interpret what a student is saying and respond in a way that is not too far from the student's level. Also, Piaget suggested that it is important to examine children's mistakes in thinking, not just what they get correct, to help guide them to a higher level of understanding.

4. *Promote the student's intellectual health.* When Piaget came to lecture in the United States, he was asked, "What can I do to get my child to a higher cognitive stage sooner?" He was asked this question so often here compared with other countries that he called it the American question. Piaget emphasized that children's learning should occur naturally. Children should not be pushed and pressured into achieving too much too early in their development, before they are maturationally ready. Some parents spend long hours every day holding up large flash cards with words on them to improve their baby's vocabulary. In the Piagetian view, this is not an effective way for infants to learn. It places too much emphasis on speeding up intellectual development, involves passive learning, and will not lead to positive outcomes.

What are some educational strategies that can be derived from Piaget's theory?
Fuse/Getty Images

5. *Turn the classroom into a setting of exploration and discovery.* What do actual classrooms look like when the teachers adopt Piaget's views? Several first- and second-grade math classrooms provide some good examples (Kamii, 1985, 1989). The teachers emphasize students' own exploration and discovery. The classrooms are less structured than we would expect in a typical classroom. Workbooks and predetermined assignments are not used. Rather, the teachers observe the students' interests and natural participation in activities to determine what the course of learning will be. For example, a math lesson might be constructed around counting the day's lunch money or dividing supplies among students. Often, games are prominently used in the classroom to stimulate mathematical thinking. For example, a version of dominoes teaches children about even-numbered combinations. A variation on tic-tac-toe involves replacing Xs and Os with numbers. Teachers encourage peer interaction during the lessons and games because students' different viewpoints can contribute to advances in thinking.

EVALUATING PIAGET'S THEORY

What were Piaget's main contributions? Has his theory withstood the test of time?

Piaget's Contributions   Piaget, the founder of the study of children's cognitive development, was a giant in the field of developmental psychology (Miller, 2015). Psychologists are indebted to him for devising a long list of masterful concepts of enduring power and fascination: assimilation, accommodation, object permanence, egocentrism, conservation, and others. Psychologists also owe him for instilling the current vision of children as active, constructive thinkers. And they have a debt to him for creating a theory that has generated a huge volume of research on children's cognitive development.

Piaget also was a genius when it came to observing children. His careful observations showed us inventive ways to discover how children act on and adapt to their world. Piaget pointed out some important things to look for in cognitive development, such as the shift from preoperational to concrete operational thinking. He also showed us how children need to make their experiences fit their schemes (cognitive frameworks) yet simultaneously adapt their schemes to fit their experiences. Piaget revealed that cognitive change is more likely to occur if the context is structured to allow gradual movement to the next higher level. Concepts do not emerge suddenly, full-blown, but instead develop through a series of partial accomplishments that lead to increasingly comprehensive understanding.

Criticisms of Piaget's Theory   Piaget's theory has not gone unchallenged (Miller, 2015). Questions are raised about estimates of children's competence at different developmental levels, stages, the training of children to reason at higher levels, and culture and education.

Estimates of Children's Competence   Researchers have found that some cognitive abilities emerge earlier than Piaget thought (Bell & Broomell, 2020). For example, as previously noted, some aspects of object permanence emerge earlier than he believed (Baillargeon, 2016). Even 2-year-olds are nonegocentric in some contexts. When they realize that another person does not see an object, they investigate whether the person is blindfolded or looking in a different direction. Some understanding of the conservation of number has been demonstrated as early as age 3, although Piaget did not think it emerged until age 7. Young children are not as uniformly "pre" this and "pre" that (preoperational, for example) as Piaget thought.

Other cognitive abilities also can emerge later than Piaget thought (Kuhn, 2009, 2011). Many adolescents still think in concrete operational ways or are just beginning to master formal operations. Even many adults are not formal operational thinkers. In sum, recent theoretical revisions highlight more cognitive competencies of infants and young children and more cognitive shortcomings of adolescents and adults (Dahl & others, 2018; Reyna, 2018).

Stages   Children's cognitive development is not as stage-like as Piaget envisioned (Adolph & Hoch, 2019). Because some cognitive abilities have been found to emerge earlier than Piaget thought, and others later, children do not appear to move cleanly from one stage to another. Other evidence casting doubt on the stage notion is that children often show more understanding on one task than on another similar task.

Effects of Training   Some children who are at one cognitive stage (such as preoperational) can be trained to reason at a higher cognitive stage (such as concrete operational). This discovery poses a problem for Piaget's theory. He argued that such training is only superficial and ineffective unless the child is at a maturational transition point between the stages (Gelman & Williams, 1998).

Culture and Education   Culture and education exert stronger influences on children's development than Piaget maintained (Adolph & Hoch, 2019; Feeney, Moravcik, & Nolte, 2019; Follari, 2019). For example, the age at which children acquire conservation skills is related to how much practice their culture provides in these skills. An outstanding teacher who provides instruction in the logic of math and science can promote concrete and formal operational thought.

An Alternative View   **Neo-Piagetians** argue that Piaget got some things right but that his theory needs considerable revision. They give more emphasis to how children use attention, memory, and strategies to process information (Case, 1987, 1999). They especially stress that a more accurate portrayal of children's thinking requires attention to children's strategies and other cognitive skills, such as inhibition; the speed at which children process information; the specific task involved; and the division of problems into smaller, more precise steps (Chevalier, Dauvier, & Blaye, 2018). In the chapter on "Information Processing," we further discuss these aspects of children's thought.

neo-Piagetians Developmentalists who have elaborated on Piaget's theory, emphasizing attention to children's strategies; information-processing speed; the task involved; and division of the problem into more precise, smaller steps.

An outstanding teacher and education in the logic of science and mathematics are important cultural experiences that promote the development of operational thought. *Might Piaget have underestimated the roles of culture and schooling in children's cognitive development?*
Majority World/UIG/Getty Images

Review *Connect* Reflect

 LG2 Apply Piaget's theory to education, and evaluate Piaget's theory.

Review
- How can Piaget's theory be applied to educating children?
- What are some key contributions and criticisms of Piaget's theory?

Connect
- When Piaget developed his theory, research on the development of the child's brain had not yet occurred. Based on the content in the chapter "Physical Development and Biological Aging," describe developmental changes in the brain that might serve as a foundation for the development of Piaget's stages.

Reflect *Your Own Personal Journey of Life*
- How might thinking in formal operational ways rather than concrete operational ways help students to develop better study skills?

3 Vygotsky's Theory of Cognitive Development

 LG3 Identify the main concepts in Vygotsky's theory, and compare it with Piaget's theory.

The Zone of Proximal Development	Scaffolding	Language and Thought	Teaching Strategies	Evaluating Vygotsky's Theory

Piaget's theory is a major developmental theory. Another developmental theory that focuses on children's cognition is Vygotsky's theory. Like Piaget, Lev Vygotsky emphasized that children actively construct their knowledge and understanding (Esteban-Guitart, 2019). In Piaget's theory, children develop ways of thinking and understanding by their actions and interactions with the physical world. In Vygtosky's theory, children are more often described as social creatures than in Piaget's theory (Yu & Hu, 2017). They develop their ways of thinking and understanding primarily through social interaction (Clara, 2017). Their cognitive development depends on the tools provided by society, and their minds are shaped by the cultural context in which they live (Daniels, 2017).

We briefly described Vygotsky's theory in the chapter titled "Introduction." Here we take a closer look at his ideas about how children learn and his view of the role of language in cognitive development.

THE ZONE OF PROXIMAL DEVELOPMENT

Vygotsky's belief in the importance of social influences, especially instruction, to children's cognitive development is reflected in his concept of the zone of proximal development. **Zone of proximal development (ZPD)** is Vygotsky's term for the range of tasks that are too difficult for the child to master alone but that can be learned with guidance and assistance from adults or more-skilled children. Thus, the lower limit of the ZPD is the level of skill reached by the child working independently. The upper limit is the level of additional responsibility the child can accept with the assistance of an able instructor (see Figure 9). The ZPD captures the child's cognitive skills that are in the process of maturing and can be accomplished only with the assistance of a more-skilled person (Clara, 2017). Vygotsky (1962) called these the "buds" or "flowers" of development, to distinguish them from the "fruits" of development, which the child already can accomplish independently.

What are some factors that can influence the effectiveness of the ZPD in children's learning and development? Researchers have found that the ZPD's effectiveness is enhanced by factors such as better emotion regulation, secure attachment, absence of maternal depression, and child compliance (Gauvain, 2013).

SCAFFOLDING

Closely linked to the idea of the ZPD is the concept of scaffolding. **Scaffolding** means changing the level of support. Over the course of a teaching session, a more-skilled person (a teacher or advanced peer) adjusts the amount of guidance to fit the child's current performance (Daniels, 2017). When the student is learning a new task, the skilled person may use direct instruction. As the student's competence increases, the person gives less guidance. One study found that scaffolding techniques that heightened engagement, encouraged direct exploration, and facilitated "sense-making," such as guided play, improved 4- to 5-year-old children's acquisition of geometric knowledge (Fisher & others, 2013).

Dialogue is an important tool of scaffolding in the zone of proximal development. Vygotsky viewed children as having rich but unsystematic, disorganized, and spontaneous concepts. In a dialogue, these concepts meet with the skilled helper's more systematic, logical, and rational concepts. As a result, the child's concepts become more systematic, logical, and rational. For example, a dialogue might take place between a teacher and a child when the teacher uses scaffolding to help a child understand a concept like "transportation."

zone of proximal development (ZPD) Vygotsky's term for tasks that are too difficult for children to master alone but can be mastered with guidance and assistance from adults or more-skilled children.

scaffolding In cognitive development, a term Vygotsky used to describe the changing level of support over the course of a teaching session, with the more-skilled person adjusting guidance to fit the child's current performance level.

Upper limit
Level of additional responsibility child can accept with assistance of an able instructor

Zone of proximal development (ZPD)

Lower limit
Level of problem solving reached on these tasks by child working alone

FIGURE 9

VYGOTSKY'S ZONE OF PROXIMAL DEVELOPMENT. Vygotsky's zone of proximal development has a lower limit and an upper limit. Tasks in the ZPD are too difficult for the child to perform alone. They require assistance from an adult or a more-skilled child. As children experience the verbal instruction or demonstration, they organize the information in their existing mental structures so they can eventually perform the skill or task alone.
Ariel Skelley/Blend Images LLC

Lev Vygotsky (1896–1934), shown here with his daughter, reasoned that children's cognitive development is advanced through social interaction with more-skilled individuals embedded in a sociocultural backdrop. *How is Vygotsky's theory different from Piaget's?*
Courtesy of James V. Wertsch, Washington University

LANGUAGE AND THOUGHT

The use of dialogue as a tool for scaffolding is only one example of the important role of language in a child's development. According to Vygotsky, children use speech not only for social communication but also to help them solve tasks (van der Veer & Zavershneva, 2018). Vygotsky (1962) further believed that young children use language to plan, guide, and monitor their behavior. This use of language for self-regulation is called private speech (van der Veer & Zavershneva, 2018). For Piaget, private speech is egocentric and immature—but for Vygotsky, it is an important tool of thought during the early childhood years (Lantolf, 2017).

Vygotsky said that language and thought initially develop independently of each other and then merge. He emphasized that all mental functions have external, or social, origins. Children must use language to communicate with others before they can focus inward on their own thoughts. Children also must communicate externally and use language for a long period of time before they can make the transition from external to internal speech. This transition period occurs between 3 and 7 years of age and involves talking to oneself. After a while, the self-talk becomes second nature to children, and they can act without verbalizing; at this point, children have internalized their egocentric speech in the form of *inner speech*, which becomes their thoughts (Mercer, 2008).

Vygotsky held that children who use a lot of private speech are more socially competent than those who don't (van der Veer & Zavershneva, 2018). He argued that private speech represents an early transition in becoming more socially communicative. For Vygotsky, when young children talk to themselves, they are using language to govern their behavior and guide themselves. For example, a child working on a puzzle might say to herself, "Which pieces should I put together first? I'll try those green ones first. Now I need some blue ones. No, that blue one doesn't fit there. I'll try it over here."

Researchers have found that children use private speech more often when tasks are difficult, when they have made errors, and when they are not sure how to proceed (Berk, 1994). They also have discovered that children who use private speech are more attentive and improve their performance more than children who do not use private speech (Berk & Spuhl, 1995).

TEACHING STRATEGIES

Vygotsky's theory has been embraced by many teachers and has been successfully applied to education (Clara, 2017; Esteban-Guitart, 2018; Gauvain & Perez, 2015; Holzman, 2016). Here are some ways Vygotsky's theory can be incorporated in classrooms:

1. *Use the child's ZPD in teaching.* Teaching should begin near the zone's upper limit, so that the child can reach the goal with help and move to a higher level of skill and knowledge. Offer just enough assistance. You might ask, "What can I do to help you?" or simply observe the child's intentions and attempts and provide support when needed. When the child hesitates, offer encouragement. And encourage the child to practice the skill. You may watch and appreciate the child's practice or offer support when the child forgets what to do.

2. *Use more-skilled peers as teachers.* Remember that it is not just adults who are important in helping children learn. Children also benefit from the support and guidance of more-skilled children.

3. *Monitor and encourage children's use of private speech.* Be aware of the developmental change from externally talking to oneself when solving a problem during the preschool years, to privately talking to oneself in the early elementary school years (Mercer, 2008). In the elementary school years, encourage children to internalize and self-regulate their talk to themselves.

4. *Place instruction in a meaningful context.* Educators today are moving away from abstract presentations of material, instead providing students with opportunities to experience learning in real-world settings. For example, instead of just memorizing math formulas, students work on math problems with real-world implications.

5. *Transform the classroom with Vygotskian ideas.* Tools of the Mind is an early childhood education curriculum that emphasizes children's development of self-regulation and the

cognitive foundations of literacy (Shaheen, 2014). The curriculum was created by Elena Bodrova and Deborah Leong (2007, 2015a, b) and has been implemented in more than 200 classrooms. Most of the children in the Tools of the Mind programs are at risk because of their living circumstances, which in many instances involve poverty and other difficult conditions such as being homeless and having parents with drug problems.

How can Vygotsky's ideas be applied to educating children?
IT Stock Free/Alamy Stock Photo

Tools of the Mind is grounded in Vygotsky's (1962) theory, with special attention given to cultural tools and developing self-regulation, the zone of proximal development, scaffolding, private speech, shared activity, and play as important activity. In a Tools of the Mind classroom, dramatic play has a central role. Teachers guide children in creating themes that are based on the children's interests, such as treasure hunt, store, hospital, and restaurant. Teachers also incorporate field trips, visitor presentations, videos, and books in the development of children's play. In addition, they help children develop a play plan, which increases the maturity of their play. Play plans describe what the children expect to do in the play period, including the imaginary context, roles, and props to be used. The play plans increase the quality of children's play and self-regulation.

Scaffolding writing is another important theme in the Tools of the Mind classroom. Teachers guide children in planning their own message by drawing a line to stand for each word the child says. Children then repeat the message, pointing to each line as they say the word. Then, a child writes on the lines, trying to represent each word with some letters or symbols. Figure 10 shows how the scaffolding writing process improved a 5-year-old child's writing over the course of two months. Research assessments of children's writing in Tools of the Mind classrooms revealed that children in the program have more advanced writing skills than children in other early childhood programs (Bodrova & Leong, 2007, 2015a, b) (see Figure 10). For example, they write more complex messages, use more words, spell more accurately, show better letter recognition, and have a better understanding of the concept of a sentence. The effectiveness of the Tools of the Mind approach also was examined in another study of 29 schools, 79 classrooms, and 759 students (Blair & Raver, 2014). Positive effects of the Tools of the Mind program were found for the cognitive processes of executive function

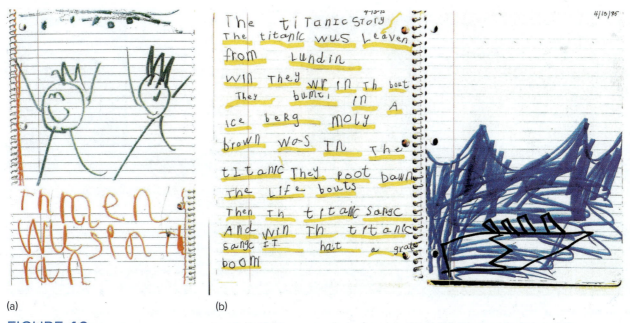

(a) (b)

FIGURE 10

WRITING PROGRESS OF A 5-YEAR-OLD BOY OVER TWO MONTHS USING THE SCAFFOLDING WRITING PROCESS IN TOOLS OF THE MIND. (a) Five-year-old Aaron's independent journal writing prior to using the scaffolded writing technique. (b) Aaron's journal after two months of using the scaffolded writing technique.

Bodrova, Elena and Leong, Deborah J. "Tools of the Mind: A Case Study of Implementing the Vygotskian Approach in American Early Childhood and Primary Classrooms," Geneva, Switzerland: International Bureau of Education, 2001, 36–38.

(improved self-regulation, for example) and attention control. Further, the Tools of the Mind program improved children's reading, vocabulary, and mathematics at the end of kindergarten and into the first grade. The most significant improvements occurred in high-poverty schools.

EVALUATING VYGOTSKY'S THEORY

Even though their theories were proposed at about the same time, most of the world learned about Vygotsky's theory later than they learned about Piaget's theory, so Vygotsky's theory has not yet been evaluated as thoroughly. Vygotsky's view of the importance of sociocultural influences on children's development fits with the current belief that it is important to evaluate the contextual factors in learning (Gauvain & Perez, 2015).

We already have considered several contrasts between Vygotsky's and Piaget's theories, such as Vygotsky's emphasis on the importance of private speech in development and Piaget's view that such speech is immature. Although both theories are constructivist, Vygotsky's is a **social constructivist approach,** which emphasizes the social contexts of learning and the construction of knowledge through social interaction (Yu & Hu, 2017).

In moving from Piaget to Vygotsky, the conceptual shift is from the individual to collaboration, social interaction, and sociocultural activity (Clara, 2017). The endpoint of cognitive development for Piaget is formal operational thought. For Vygotsky, the endpoint can differ, depending on which skills are considered to be the most important in a particular culture. For Piaget, children construct knowledge by transforming, organizing, and reorganizing previous knowledge. For Vygotsky, children construct knowledge through social interaction (Daniels, 2017). The implication of Piaget's theory for teaching is that children need support to explore their world and discover knowledge. The main implication of Vygotsky's theory for teaching is that students need many opportunities to learn with the teacher and more-skilled peers. In both Piaget's and Vygotsky's theories, teachers serve as facilitators and guides, rather than as directors and molders of learning. Figure 11 compares Vygotsky's and Piaget's theories.

Criticisms of Vygotsky's theory also have surfaced. Some critics point out that Vygotsky was not specific enough about age-related changes. Another criticism focuses on Vygotsky not adequately describing how changes in socioemotional capabilities contribute to cognitive development (Goncu & Gauvain, 2012). Yet another criticism is that he overemphasized the role

developmental **connection**

Education

Whether to follow a constructivist or direct instruction approach is a major educational issue. Connect to "Schools, Achievement, and Work."

social constructivist approach An emphasis on the social contexts of learning and construction of knowledge through social interaction. Vygotsky's theory reflects this approach.

	Vygotsky	Piaget
Sociocultural Context	Strong emphasis	Little emphasis
Constructivism	Social constructivist	Cognitive constructivist
Stages	No general stages of development proposed	Strong emphasis on stages (sensorimotor, preoperational, concrete operational, and formal operational)
Key Processes	Zone of proximal development, language, dialogue, tools of the culture	Schema, assimilation, accommodation, operations, conservation, classification
Role of Language	A major role; language plays a powerful role in shaping thought	Language has a minimal role; cognition primarily directs language
View on Education	Education plays a central role, helping children learn the tools of the culture	Education merely refines the child's cognitive skills that have already emerged
Teaching Implications	Teacher is a facilitator and guide, not a director; establish many opportunities for children to learn with the teacher and more-skilled peers	Also views teacher as a facilitator and guide, not a director; provide support for children to explore their world and discover knowledge

FIGURE 11

COMPARISON OF VYGOTSKY'S AND PIAGET'S THEORIES

(*Vygotsky*): A.R. Lauria /Dr. Michael Cole, Laboratory of Human Cognition, University of California, San Diego; (*Piaget*): Bettmann/Getty Images

of language in thinking. Also, his emphasis on collaboration and guidance has potential pitfalls. Might facilitators be too helpful in some cases, as when a parent becomes overbearing and controlling? Further, some children might become lazy and expect help when they could have done something on their own.

Review *Connect* Reflect

LG3 Identify the main concepts in Vygotsky's theory, and compare it with Piaget's theory.

Review
- What is the zone of proximal development?
- What is scaffolding?
- How did Vygotsky view language and thought?
- How can Vygotsky's theory be applied to education?
- What are some similarities and differences between Vygotsky's and Piaget's theories?

Connect
- As discussed in this section, Vygotsky's theory has been applied to education. Compare the type of education you experienced as a child with the type of education that follows Vygotsky's theory.

Reflect *Your Own Personal Journey of Life*
- Which theory—Piaget's or Vygotsky's—do you think provides a better explanation of your own development as a child? Why?

4 Cognitive Changes in Adulthood

LG4 Describe cognitive changes in adulthood.

| Piaget's View | Realistic and Pragmatic Thinking | Reflective and Relativistic Thinking | Cognition and Emotion | Is There a Fifth, Postformal Stage? | Are There Cognitive Stages in Middle and Late Adulthood? |

We have discussed the theories that Piaget and Vygotsky proposed to account for how the cognitive development of children proceeds. Neither, however, had much to say about cognitive development in adulthood. What do developmentalists know about changes in the way that adults think?

PIAGET'S VIEW

Recall that, according to Piaget, the formal operational stage of thought begins at 11 to 15 years of age. During this stage, the final one in Piaget's theory, thinking becomes more abstract, idealistic, and logical than the concrete operational thinking of 7- to 11-year-olds. Of course, young adults have more knowledge than adolescents. But, according to Piaget, adults and adolescents use the same type of reasoning. Adolescents and adults think in qualitatively the same way.

Many individuals don't reach the highest level of their formal operational thinking until adulthood. That is, though many individuals begin to plan and hypothesize about intellectual problems as adolescents, they become more systematic and sophisticated in applying these skills as young adults. Also, many adults do not think in formal operational ways (Keating, 2004).

REALISTIC AND PRAGMATIC THINKING

Some developmentalists propose that as young adults move into the world of work, their way of thinking does change. One idea is that as they face the constraints of reality that work promotes, their idealism decreases (Labouvie-Vief, 1986).

How might emerging and young adults think differently from adolescents?
Paul Bradbury/Caiaimage/Glow Images

A related change in thinking was proposed by K. Warner Schaie (1977, 2016). He concluded that it is unlikely that adults go beyond the powerful methods of scientific thinking characteristic of the formal operational stage. However, Schaie argued that adults do progress beyond adolescents in their use of intellect. For example, in early adulthood individuals often switch from acquiring knowledge to applying knowledge as they pursue success in their work.

REFLECTIVE AND RELATIVISTIC THINKING

William Perry (1970) also described changes in cognition that take place in early adulthood. He said that adolescents often view the world in terms of polarities—right/wrong, we/they, or good/bad. As youth age into adulthood, they gradually move away from this type of absolutist thinking as they become aware of the diverse opinions and multiple perspectives of others. Thus, in Perry's view, the absolutist, dualistic thinking of adolescence gives way to the reflective, relativistic thinking of adulthood. Other developmentalists also argue that reflective thinking is an important indicator of cognitive change in young adults (Mascalo & Fischer, 2010).

COGNITION AND EMOTION

Gisela Labouvie-Vief and her colleagues (Labouvie-Vief, 2009; Labouvie-Vief, Gruhn, & Studer, 2010) also argue that to understand cognitive changes in adulthood it is necessary to consider how emotional maturity might affect cognitive development. They conclude that although emerging and young adults become more aware that emotions influence their thinking, at this point thinking is often swayed too strongly by negative emotions that can produce distorted and self-serving conclusions. In their research, a subset of emerging adults who are high in empathy, flexibility, and autonomy are more likely to engage in complex, integrated cognitive-emotional thinking. Labouvie-Vief and her colleagues have found that the ability to think in this cognitively and emotionally balanced, advanced manner increases during middle adulthood. Further, they emphasize that in middle age, individuals become more inwardly reflective and less context-dependent in their thinking than they were as young adults. In the work of Labouvie-Vief and her colleagues, we see the effort to discover connections between cognitive and socioemotional development that is an increasing trend in the field of life-span development.

IS THERE A FIFTH, POSTFORMAL STAGE?

Some theorists have pieced together these descriptions of adult thinking and have proposed that young adults move into a new qualitative stage of cognitive development, postformal thought (Sinnott, 2003). **Postformal thought** is described as follows:

- *Reflective, relativistic, and contextual.* As young adults engage in solving problems, they might think deeply about many aspects of work, politics, relationships, and other areas of life (Labouvie-Vief, 1986). They find that what might be the best solution to a problem at work (with a boss or co-worker) might not be the best solution at home (with a romantic partner). Thus, postformal thought holds that the correct answer to a problem requires reflective thinking and may vary from one situation to another. Some psychologists argue that reflective thinking continues to increase and becomes more internal and

- - - - - - →

developmental **connection**

Cognitive Theory

Links between cognition and emotion are increasingly being studied. Connect to "Introduction" and "Emotional Development and Attachment."

← - - - - - - -

postformal thought Thinking that is reflective, relativistic, and contextual; provisional; realistic; and influenced by emotions.

What characterizes a possible fifth stage of cognitive development called postformal thought?
Yuri Arcurs/Alamy Stock Photo

less contextual in middle age (Labouvie-Vief, Gruhn, & Studer, 2010; Mascalo & Fischer, 2010).

- *Provisional.* Many young adults also become more skeptical about what is presented as absolute truth and seem unwilling to accept an answer as final. Thus, they come to see the search for truth as an ongoing and perhaps never-ending process.
- *Realistic.* Young adults understand that thinking can't always be abstract. In many instances, it must be realistic and pragmatic.
- *Recognized as being influenced by emotion.* Emerging and young adults are more likely than adolescents to understand that their thinking is influenced by emotions. However, too often negative emotions produce thinking that is distorted and self-serving at this point in development.

How strong is the evidence for a fifth, postformal stage of cognitive development? Researchers have found that young adults are more likely to engage in postformal thinking than adolescents are (Commons & Richards, 2003; Commons & others, 1989). But critics argue that research has yet to document that postformal thought is a qualitatively more advanced stage than formal operational thought.

ARE THERE COGNITIVE STAGES IN MIDDLE AND LATE ADULTHOOD?

Adult cognitive stages per se have not been proposed beyond the postformal fifth stage we just discussed. And for the middle and late adulthood periods of development there has been little discussion of what the contents of those stages might be like (Park & Festini, 2017; Schaie, 2016).

What are some changes in cognitive development that would provide some of the content of a stage-like description of what takes place during middle and late adulthood? Rather than qualitative stage descriptions of cognitive changes in middle and late adulthood, some gradual, quantitative cognitive changes have been proposed and studied. These include fluid and crystallized intelligence, and cognitive mechanics and cognitive pragmatics.

- *Fluid and Crystallized Intelligence.* *Fluid intelligence,* the person's ability to reason abstractly, has been theorized to decrease in middle and late adulthood (Horn & Donaldson, 1980). *Crystallized intelligence,* the individual's accumulated information and verbal skills, has been proposed to increase during middle and late adulthood.
- *Cognitive Mechanics and Cognitive Pragmatics.* *Cognitive mechanics,* linked to biological foundations and brain development, have been hypothesized to decline in middle and late adulthood. Cognitive processes that are components of cognitive mechanics include processing speed, attention, and some aspects of memory. *Cognitive pragmatics,* which are associated with experience and culture, have been proposed to increase during middle and late adulthood. Components of cognitive pragmatics include reading and writing skills, language comprehension, professional skills, and wisdom.

The overlap between fluid intelligence and cognitive mechanics, and the similarities between crystallized intelligence and cognitive pragmatics, have been recognized with the creation of the labels *fluid mechanics* and *crystallized pragmatics* (Lovden & Lindenberger, 2007).

The combination of multiple cognitive processes and abilities in an age-related manner takes on the characteristics of a stage-like description. However, as indicated earlier, at this point a stage of fluid mechanics and crystallized intelligence has not been proposed. Further discussion of these aspects of cognitive development is highlighted in the chapter on "Intelligence."

Current theory and research on changes in adult cognitive development mainly focuses on specific aspects of information processing, such as attention, memory, and thinking, but not on stages of development (Kunzmann, 2019; Nikitin & Freund, 2019; Park & Festini, 2018). In the chapter on "Information Processing" you will read about these specific cognitive processes and how they change during various stages of development.

developmental **connection**

Memory

How does memory change in middle and late adulthood? Connect to "Information Processing."

developmental **connection**

Life-Span Perspective

How might wisdom change as individuals go through the adult years? Connect to "Intelligence."

Might there be cognitive changes that describes middle-aged and/or older adults' cognitive development?
SpeedKingz/Shutterstock

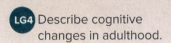

Review *Connect* Reflect

LG4 Describe cognitive changes in adulthood.

Review

- What is Piaget's view of adult cognitive development?
- Do young adults retain the idealism of the formal operational stage?
- What is Perry's view on cognitive changes from adolescence to adulthood?
- What role does emotion play in cognitive changes in emerging and early adulthood?
- What characteristics have been proposed for a fifth, postformal stage of cognitive development?
- Are there cognitive stages in middle and late adulthood?

Connect

- What does Piaget's view of adult cognitive development have in common with his views about cognitive development in adolescence?

Reflect *Your Own Personal Journey of Life*

- If you are an emerging adult (18 to 25 years of age), what do you think are the most important cognitive changes that have taken place so far in this transition period in your life between adolescence and early adulthood? If you are older, reflect on your emerging adult years and describe what cognitive changes occurred during this time.

reach your **learning goals**

Cognitive Developmental Approaches

1 Piaget's Theory of Cognitive Development

 LG1 Discuss the key processes and four stages in Piaget's theory.

Processes of Development

- In Piaget's theory, children construct their own cognitive worlds, building mental structures to adapt to their world.

- Schemes are actions or mental representations that organize knowledge. Behavioral schemes (physical activities) characterize infancy, whereas mental schemes (cognitive activities) develop in childhood.

- Adaptation involves assimilation and accommodation. Assimilation occurs when children use existing schemes to deal with new information. Accommodation happens when children adjust their schemes to account for new information and experiences. Through organization, children group isolated behaviors into a higher-order, more smoothly functioning cognitive system.

- Equilibration is a mechanism Piaget proposed to explain how children shift from one cognitive stage to the next. As children experience cognitive conflict in trying to understand the world, they seek equilibrium. The result is equilibration, which brings the child to a new stage of thought.

- According to Piaget, there are four qualitatively different stages of thought: sensorimotor, preoperational, concrete operational, and formal operational.

Sensorimotor Stage

- In sensorimotor thought, the first of Piaget's four stages, the infant organizes and coordinates sensations with physical movements. The stage lasts from birth to about 2 years of age.

- Sensorimotor thought has six substages: simple reflexes; primary circular reactions; secondary circular reactions; coordination of secondary circular reactions; tertiary circular reactions, novelty, and curiosity; and internalization of schemes.

- One key aspect of this stage is object permanence, the ability of infants to understand that objects continue to exist even though they are no longer observing them. Another aspect involves infants' understanding of cause and effect.

- In the past several decades, revisions of Piaget's view have been proposed based on research. For example, researchers have found that a stable and differentiated perceptual world is established earlier than Piaget envisioned.

Preoperational Stage

- Preoperational thought is the beginning of the ability to reconstruct at the level of thought what has been established in behavior. It involves a transition from a primitive to a more sophisticated use of symbols. In preoperational thought, the child does not yet think in an operational way.

- The symbolic function substage occurs roughly from 2 to 4 years of age and is characterized by symbolic thought, egocentrism, and animism. The intuitive thought substage stretches from about 4 to 7 years of age. It is called intuitive because children seem sure about their knowledge yet are unaware of how they know what they know.

- The preoperational child lacks conservation and asks a barrage of questions.

Concrete Operational Stage

- Concrete operational thought occurs roughly from 7 to 11 years of age. During this stage, children can perform concrete operations, think logically about concrete objects, classify things, and reason about relationships among classes of things. Concrete thought is not as abstract as formal operational thought.

Formal Operational Stage

- Formal operational thought appears between 11 and 15 years of age. Formal operational thought is more abstract, idealistic, and logical than concrete operational thought.

- Piaget argues that adolescents become capable of engaging in hypothetical-deductive reasoning. But Piaget did not give adequate attention to individual variations in adolescent thinking. Many young adolescents do not think in hypothetical-deductive ways but rather are consolidating their concrete operational thinking. In addition, adolescents develop a special kind of egocentrism that involves an imaginary audience and a personal fable about being unique and invulnerable.

2 Applying and Evaluating Piaget's Theory

 Apply Piaget's theory to education, and evaluate Piaget's theory.

Piaget and Education

- Piaget was not an educator, but his constructivist views have been applied to teaching. These applications include an emphasis on facilitating rather than directing learning, considering the child's level of knowledge, using ongoing assessment, promoting the student's intellectual health, and turning the classroom into a setting for exploration and discovery.

Evaluating Piaget's Theory

- We are indebted to Piaget for establishing the field of cognitive development. He was a genius at observing children, and he gave us a number of masterful concepts. Critics, however, question his estimates of competence at different developmental levels, his stage concept, and other ideas. Neo-Piagetians emphasize the importance of information processing.

3 Vygotsky's Theory of Cognitive Development

 Identify the main concepts in Vygotsky's theory, and compare it with Piaget's theory.

The Zone of Proximal Development

- Zone of proximal development (ZPD) is Vygotsky's term for the range of tasks that are too difficult for children to master alone but that can be learned with the guidance and assistance of more-skilled adults and peers.

Scaffolding

- Scaffolding is a teaching technique in which a more-skilled person adjusts the level of guidance to fit the child's current performance level. Dialogue is an important aspect of scaffolding.

Language and Thought

- Vygotsky argued that language plays a key role in cognition. Language and thought initially develop independently, but then children internalize their egocentric speech in the form of inner speech, which becomes their thoughts. This transition to inner speech occurs between 3 and 7 years of age. Vygotsky's view contrasts with Piaget's view that young children's self-talk is immature and egocentric.

| Teaching Strategies | • Applications of Vygotsky's ideas to education include using the child's zone of proximal development and scaffolding, using more-skilled peers as teachers, monitoring and encouraging children's use of private speech, and accurately assessing the zone of proximal development. |

• The Tools of the Mind curriculum reflects the Vygotskian approach. These practices can transform the classroom and establish a meaningful context for instruction.

| Evaluating Vygotsky's Theory | • Like Piaget, Vygotsky emphasized that children actively construct their understanding of the world. Unlike Piaget, he did not propose stages of cognitive development, and he emphasized that children construct knowledge through social interaction. In Vygotsky's theory, children depend on tools provided by the culture, which determines which skills they will develop. Some critics say that Vygotsky overemphasized the role of language in thinking. |

4 Cognitive Changes in Adulthood LG4 Describe cognitive changes in adulthood.

| Piaget's View | • Piaget said that formal operational thought, entered at 11 to 15 years of age, is the final cognitive stage, although adults are more knowledgeable than adolescents. |

| Realistic and Pragmatic Thinking | • Some experts argue that the idealism of Piaget's formal operational stage declines in young adults, being replaced by more realistic, pragmatic thinking. |

| Reflective and Relativistic Thinking | • Perry said that adolescents often engage in dualistic, absolutist thinking, whereas young adults are more likely to think reflectively and relativistically. |

| Cognition and Emotion | • Emerging and young adults become more aware that emotions influence their thinking. However, at this point in development, negative emotions often produce distorted and self-serving thinking that interferes with achieving an integrated, complex understanding of the link between cognition and emotion. Nonetheless, a subset of emotionally mature emerging and young adults achieve this understanding. |

| Is There a Fifth, Postformal Stage? | • A fifth, postformal stage that has been proposed is postformal thought, which is reflective, relativistic, and contextual; provisional; realistic; and influenced by emotions. |

| Are There Cognitive Stages in Middle and Late Adulthood? | • No cognitive stages per se have been proposed for middle and late adulthood, although the concepts of fluid mechanics and crystallized pragmatics take on stage-like characteristics. Theory and research today in adult cognitive development focuses mainly on specific aspects of information processing rather than on cognitive stages. |

key **terms**

A-not-B error
accommodation
adolescent egocentrism
animism
assimilation
centration
concrete operational stage
conservation

core knowledge approach
egocentrism
equilibration
formal operational stage
hypothetical-deductive reasoning
imaginary audience
intuitive thought substage
neo-Piagetians

object permanence
operations
organization
personal fable
postformal thought
preoperational stage
scaffolding
schemes

sensorimotor stage
seriation
social constructivist approach
symbolic function substage
transitivity
zone of proximal development (ZPD)

key **people**

Renee Baillargeon
Elena Bodrova
David Elkind
Rochel Gelman

Eleanor Gibson
Barbel Inhelder
Mark Johnson
Gisela Labouvie-Vief

Deborah Leong
William Perry
Jean Piaget
K. Warner Schaie

Elizabeth Spelke
Lev Vygotsky

INFORMATION PROCESSING

chapter outline

Westend61/Getty Images

preview

What do people notice in their environment? What do they remember? And how do they think about it? Questions like these characterize the information-processing approach. Researchers who take this approach usually do not describe individuals as being in one stage of cognitive development or another. But they do describe and analyze how the speed of processing information, attention, memory, thinking, and metacognition change over time.

1 The Information-Processing Approach

 LG1 Explain the information-processing approach and its application to development.

> The Information-Processing Approach and Its Application to Development

> Speed of Processing Information

developmental **connection**

Cognitive Theory

Piaget theorized that cognitive development occurs in four stages: sensorimotor, preoperational, concrete operational, and formal operational. Connect to "Cognitive Developmental Approaches."

developmental **connection**

Theories

In Skinner's behavioral view, it is external rewards and punishment that determine behavior, not thoughts. Connect to "Introduction."

What are some of the basic ideas of the information-processing approach? How does information processing change as individuals develop? How important is speed of processing at various points in development?

THE INFORMATION-PROCESSING APPROACH AND ITS APPLICATION TO DEVELOPMENT

The *information-processing approach* analyzes how individuals encode information, manipulate it, monitor it, and create strategies for handling it (Siegler, 2006, 2016a, b, 2017; Siegler & Braithwaite, 2017). This approach shares some characteristics with the theories of cognitive development discussed in the chapter on "Cognitive Developmental Approaches." Both those theories and the information-processing approach rejected Skinner's behavioral approach, which dominated psychology during the first half of the twentieth century. The behaviorists argued that to explain behavior it is important to examine associations between stimuli and behavior. In contrast, the information-processing approach—like the theories of Piaget and Vygotsky—focuses on how people think.

Cognitive psychologists often use the computer as an analogy to help explain the connection between cognition and the brain (Radvansky & Ashcraft, 2018). They describe the physical brain as the computer's hardware and cognition as its software. In this analogy, the sensory and perceptual systems provide an "input channel" similar to the way data are entered into the computer (see Figure 1). As input (information) comes into the mind, mental processes, or operations, act on it, just as the computer's software acts on the data. The transformed input generates information that remains in memory much in the way a computer stores what it has worked on. Finally, the information is retrieved from memory and "printed out" or "displayed" (so to speak) as an observable response.

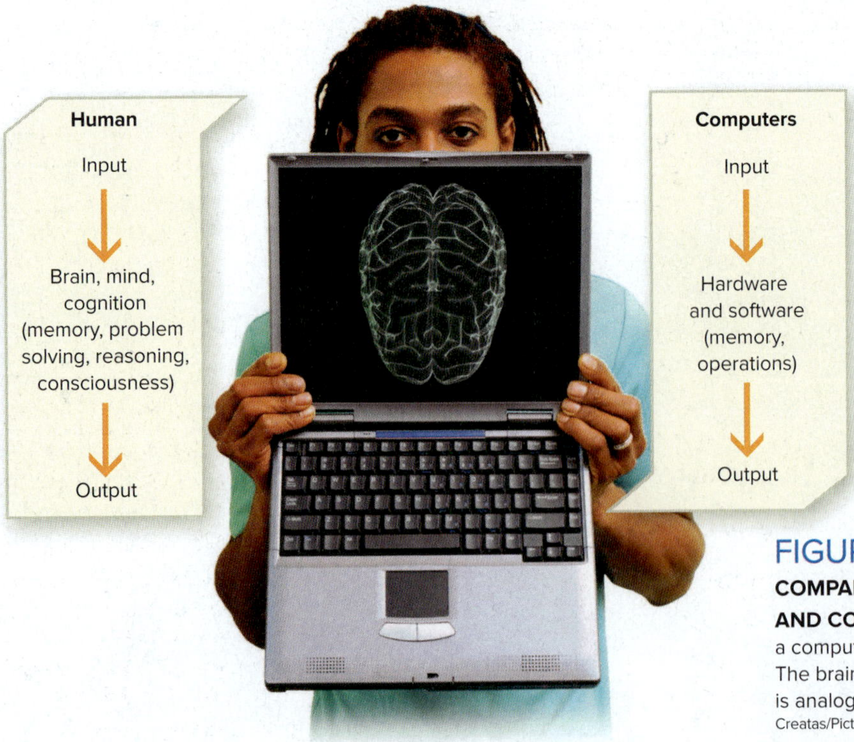

Human

Input
↓
Brain, mind, cognition (memory, problem solving, reasoning, consciousness)
↓
Output

Computers

Input
↓
Hardware and software (memory, operations)
↓
Output

FIGURE 1

COMPARING INFORMATION PROCESSING IN HUMANS AND COMPUTERS. Psychologists who study cognition often use a computer analogy to explain how humans process information. The brain is analogous to the computer's hardware, and cognition is analogous to the computer's software.
Creatas/PictureQuest

Computers provide a logical and concrete, but oversimplified, model of the mind's processing of information. Inanimate computers and human brains function quite differently in some respects. For example, most computers receive information from a human who has already coded the information and removed much of its ambiguity. In contrast, each brain cell, or neuron, can respond to ambiguous information transmitted through sensory receptors such as the eyes and ears.

Computers can do some things better than humans. For instance, computers can perform complex numerical calculations with far greater speed and accuracy than humans could ever hope to achieve. Computers can also apply and follow rules more consistently and with fewer errors than humans and can process complex mathematical patterns better than humans.

Still, the brain's extraordinary capabilities will probably not be mimicked completely by computers at any time in the near future (Sternberg, 2017). For example, although a computer can improve its ability to recognize patterns or use rules of thumb to make decisions, it does not have the means to develop new learning goals. Furthermore, the human mind is aware of itself; the computer is not. Indeed, no computer is likely to approach the richness of human consciousness.

Nonetheless, the computer's role in cognitive psychology continues to expand. An entire scientific field called **artificial intelligence (AI)** focuses on creating machines capable of performing activities that require intelligence when they are done by people (Mozer, Wiseheart, & Novikoff, 2019; Reynolds & Day, 2018; Sniecinski & Seghatchian, 2018; Yildiz, 2019). And a newly emerging field called *developmental robotics* is using robots in examining various developmental topics and issues such as motor development, perceptual development, information processing, and language development (Andries & others, 2018; Cangelosi & Scheslinger, 2015; Cochet & Guidetti, 2018; Morse & Cangelosi, 2017). The goal is to build robots that are as much like humans as possible and to learn more about humans in the process (Gordon, 2019; Vujovic & others, 2017).

Effective information processing involves attention, memory, and thinking (Nikitin & Freund, 2019). Figure 2 is a basic, simplified representation of how information processing works; it omits a great deal and does not indicate the many routes that the flow of information takes. For example, the processes may overlap and not always go in the left-to-right direction indicated in the figure. A number of different processes may be involved in the way memory functions in processing information. The purpose of the model is to get you to begin thinking in a general way about how people process information. In subsequent sections, we consider details about the way people process information and how information processing changes throughout the life span.

Robert Siegler (2006, 2016a, b, 2017) emphasizes that *mechanisms of change* play especially important roles in the advances children make in cognitive development. According to Siegler, three mechanisms work together to create changes in children's cognitive skills: encoding, automaticity, and strategy construction.

Encoding is the process by which information gets into memory (Magen & Berger-Mandelbaum, 2018). Changes in children's cognitive skills depend on increased skill at encoding relevant information and ignoring irrelevant information. For example, to a 4-year-old, an *s* in cursive writing has a shape very different from an *s* that is printed. But a 10-year-old has learned to encode the relevant fact that both are the letter *s* and to ignore the irrelevant differences in shape.

Automaticity refers to the ability to process information with little or no effort. Practice allows children to encode increasing amounts of information automatically. For example, once children have learned to read well, they do not think about each letter in a word as a letter; instead, they encode whole words. Once a task is automatic, it does not require conscious effort. As a result, as information processing becomes more automatic, we can complete tasks more quickly and handle more than one task at a time. If you did not encode words automatically but instead read this page by focusing your attention on each letter in each word, imagine how long it would take you to read it.

Strategy construction is the creation of new procedures for processing information (Graham, 2018; Harris & others, 2018). For example, children become more proficient readers when they develop the strategy of stopping periodically to take stock of what they have read so far.

I think, therefore I am.

—RENE DESCARTES
Philosopher, 17th Century

artificial intelligence (AI) Scientific field that focuses on creating machines capable of performing activities that require intelligence when they are done by people.

encoding The process by which information gets into memory.

automaticity The ability to process information with little or no effort.

The humanoid robot iCub was created by the Italian Institute of Technology to study such aspects of children's development as perception, cognition, and motor development. In this photo, the robot (the size of a 3½-year-old child) is catching a ball. This robot is being used by more than 20 laboratories worldwide and has 53 motors that move the head, arms and hands, waist, and legs. It also can see and hear, and it has the sense of proprioception (body configuration) and movement (using gyroscopes).
Marco Destefanis/Pacific Press/Sipa USA/Newscom

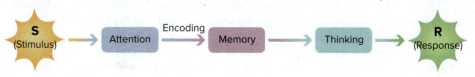

FIGURE 2

A BASIC, SIMPLIFIED MODEL OF INFORMATION PROCESSING

In addition, Siegler (2006, 2016a, b, 2017) argues that children's information processing is characterized by *self-modification*. That is, children learn to apply what they have learned in previous circumstances to adapt their responses to a new situation. Part of this self-modification draws on **metacognition,** which means "thinking about thinking or knowing about knowing" (Barenberg & Duke, 2019; Bellon, Fias, & De Smedt, 2019; Calso, Besnard, & Allain, 2019; Eddy, 2019; Flavell, 2004; Geurten, Meulemans, & Willems, 2018). One example of metacognition is what children know about the best ways to remember what they have read. Do they know that they will be better able to remember what they have read if they can relate it to their own lives in some way? Thus, in Siegler's application of information processing to development, children play an active role in their own cognitive development.

Siegler (2017) also argues that the best way to understand how children learn is to observe them while they are learning. He emphasizes the importance of using the *microgenetic method* to obtain detailed information about processing mechanisms as they are occurring from moment to moment. Siegler concludes that most research methods assess cognitive change indirectly, being more like snapshots than movies. The microgenetic method seeks to discover not just what children know but the cognitive processes involved in how they acquired the knowledge. A typical microgenetic study will be conducted across a number of trials assessed at various times over weeks or months (Miller, 2015). A number of microgenetic studies have focused on a specific aspect of academic learning, such as how children learn whole number arithmetic, fractions, and other areas of math (Braithwaite & Siegler, 2018, 2019; Siegler, 2017). Microgenetic studies also have been used to discover how children learn about a particular issue in science or master a key aspect of learning to read.

Strategies also have been the focus of a number of microgenetic investigations (Kuhn, 2013; Siegler, 2017). Using the microgenetic approach, researchers have shown that the development of effective strategies takes place gradually. This research has found considerable variability in children's use of strategies, even revealing that they may use an incorrect strategy in solving a math problem for which they had used a correct strategy several trials earlier.

SPEED OF PROCESSING INFORMATION

A limitation on processing information is the speed at which it takes place (Cui & others, 2017; Siedlecki & others, 2019; Zaremba & others, 2019). How quickly we process information often influences what we can do with that information. If you are trying to add up in your mind the cost of items you are buying at the grocery store, you need to be able to rapidly compute the sum before you have forgotten the prices of the individual items. Even in infancy, processing speed is important. For example, a longitudinal study found that 5-month-olds who were more efficient in processing information quickly had better higher-level cognitive functioning in the preschool years (Cuevas & Bell, 2014).

Researchers have devised a number of ways to assess processing speed. For example, processing speed can be measured using a reaction-time task in which individuals are asked to push a button as soon as they see a stimulus such as a light. Or individuals might be asked to match numbers with symbols on a computer screen.

Developmental Changes in Speed of Processing   There is abundant evidence that the speed with which cognitive tasks are completed improves dramatically across the childhood years (Ferrer & others, 2013). Processing speed continues to improve in early adolescence (Kuhn, 2009). For example, in one study, 10-year-olds were approximately 1.8 times slower at processing information than young adults on such tasks as reaction time, letter matching, mental rotation, and abstract matching (Hale, 1990). Twelve-year-olds were approximately 1.5 times slower than young adults, but 15-year-olds processed information on the tasks as quickly as the young adults. Also, a study of 8- to 13-year-old children revealed that processing speed increased with age and, further, that the developmental change in processing speed preceded an increase in working memory capacity (Kail, 2007). A study of 9- to 14-year-olds also revealed that faster processing speed was linked to a higher level of oral reading fluency (Jacobson & others, 2011).

Does processing speed decline in adulthood? In K. Warner Schaie's (1996, 2012) Seattle Longitudinal Study, processing speed began declining in middle adulthood. As Figure 3 shows, the slowdown in processing speed continues into late adulthood (Salthouse, 2007, 2012, 2017, 2018). The findings of a research meta-analysis were generally consistent with the graph shown in Figure 3 (Verhaeghen, 2013). The meta-analysis included data indicating that processing

strategy construction Creation of new procedures for processing information.

metacognition Cognition about cognition, or "knowing about knowing."

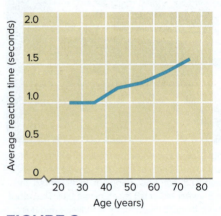

FIGURE 3

THE RELATION OF AGE TO REACTION TIME. In one study, the average reaction time began to increase in the late thirties, and this decline in processing speed accelerated in the sixties and seventies (Salthouse, 1994). The task used to assess reaction time required individuals to match numbers with symbols on a computer screen.

speed improved from childhood through adolescence (not shown in the graph). Then processing speed began to slow down in the latter part of early adulthood, as indicated in Figure 3, and continued to decline thereafter through the remainder of the life span (in other words, reaction time increased after age 35). In this analysis, age-related losses in processing speed were explained by a decline in neural connectivity or indirectly through changing levels of dopamine, or both (Verhaeghen, 2013). Also, one study revealed that age-related slowing of processing speed was linked to a breakdown of myelin in the brain (Lu & others, 2013). And in a 20-year longitudinal study of 42- to 97-year-olds, greater declines in processing speed were linked to increased mortality risk (Aichele, Rabbitt, & Ghisletta, 2015).

Recent research indicates that processing speed is an important indicator of the ability of older adults to continue to effectively drive a vehicle (Ross & others, 2016). An analysis of driving accidents revealed that approximately 50 percent of accidents in people over 50 years of age occur at intersections, compared with only about 23 percent for those under 50 years of age (Mischel, 2014). Intersections with yellow traffic lights posed difficulty for older adults, but when given advance warning 1.5 seconds before the traffic light was about to change from green to yellow, they were less likely to have an accident. Also, in a recent study of older adults with a cognitive impairment, slower processing speed was associated with unsafe driving acts that became worse with increasing age (Hotta & others, 2018).

In other research, a slowing of processing speed at baseline was linked to the emergence of dementia over the next six years (Welmer & others, 2014). Health and exercise can influence the extent to which processing speed declines (Leon & others, 2015). And one study found that 10 weeks of processing speed training improved the selective attention of older adults (O'Brien & others, 2013).

Does Processing Speed Matter?   How quickly individuals can process information through the life span is linked with their competence in many aspects of cognition (Gooch & others, 2019; Khaligh-Razavi & others, 2019; Marchman & others, 2019). For example, how quickly children can articulate a series of words affects how many words they can remember.

For some tasks in everyday life, though, speed of processing information may not be important. In addition, the strategies that people learn through experience may compensate for some decline in processing speed with age. In general, however, speed is a very important aspect of processing information (Salthouse, 2017, 2018; Tucker-Drob, Brandmaier, & Lindenberger, 2019).

Review Connect Reflect

LG1 Explain the information-processing approach and its application to development.

Review
- What is the information-processing approach, and how can it be applied to development?
- How does processing speed change developmentally?

Connect
- How are Piaget's theory and Vygotsky's theory similar to or different from the information-processing approach in explaining how individuals learn and think?

Reflect *Your Own Personal Journey of Life*
- The importance of strategies in processing information was discussed in the section you have just read. What strategies do you use to process information?

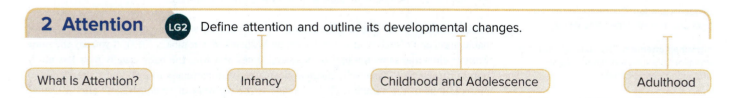

2 Attention   **LG2** Define attention and outline its developmental changes.

What Is Attention?   Infancy   Childhood and Adolescence   Adulthood

The world holds a lot of information to perceive. Right now, you are perceiving the letters and words that make up this sentence. Now look at your surroundings and focus on something other than this book. After that, curl up the toes on your right foot. In each of these circumstances, you engaged in the process of paying attention. What is attention and what effect does it have? How does it change with age?

WHAT IS ATTENTION?

Attention is the focusing of mental resources. Attention improves cognitive processing for many tasks. At any one time, though, people can pay attention to only a limited amount of information.

Individuals can allocate their attention in different ways (Posner, 2018a, b, 2019; Posner & Rothbart, 2019; Wu & Scerif, 2018). Psychologists have labeled these types of allocation as selective attention, divided attention, sustained attention, and executive attention.

This young infant's attention is riveted on the yellow toy duck that has just been placed in front of him. *What are some different types of attention?*
Sporrer/Rupp/Getty Images

- **Selective attention** is focusing on a specific aspect of experience that is relevant while ignoring others that are irrelevant. Focusing on one voice among many in a crowded room or a noisy restaurant is an example of selective attention. When you switched your attention to the toes on your right foot, you were engaging in selective attention.

- **Divided attention** involves concentrating on more than one activity at the same time. If you are listening to music or the television while you are reading this chapter, you are engaging in divided attention.

- **Sustained attention** is the ability to maintain attention to a selected stimulus for a prolonged period of time. Sustained attention, which is also called vigilance, involves being on high alert for opportunity or danger as well as paying attention for a length of time (Kamza & others, 2019; Xie, Mallin, & Richards, 2018, 2019). In a recent study, sustained attention at 10 months of age was linked to better self-regulation at 18 months of age, even when infants had insensitive mothers (Frick & others, 2018).

- **Executive attention** involves planning actions, allocating attention to goals, detecting and compensating for errors, monitoring progress on tasks, and dealing with novel or difficult circumstances.

INFANCY

How effectively can infants attend to something? Even newborns can detect a contour and fixate on it. Older infants scan patterns more thoroughly. By 4 months, infants can selectively attend to an object. One study examined 7- and 8-month-old infants' visual attention to sequences of events that varied in complexity (Kidd, Piantadosi, & Aslin, 2012). The infants tended to look away from events that were overly simple or complex, preferring instead to attend to events of intermediate complexity. As the baby gets older, the preferred level of complexity likely increases, ensuring that they are learning to process more complex information as they get older.

attention Focusing of mental resources.

selective attention Focusing on a specific aspect of experience that is relevant while ignoring others that are irrelevant.

divided attention Concentrating on more than one activity at the same time.

sustained attention The ability to maintain attention to a selected stimulus for a prolonged period of time.

executive attention Cognitive process involving planning actions, allocating attention to goals, detecting and compensating for errors, monitoring progress on tasks, and dealing with novel or difficult circumstances.

Orienting/Investigative Process Attention in the first year of life is dominated by an *orienting/investigative process* (Curtindale & others, 2019). This process involves directing attention to potentially important locations in the environment (that is, *where*) and recognizing objects and their features (such as color and form) (that is, *what*). From 3 to 9 months of age, infants can deploy their attention more flexibly and quickly.

Habituation and Dishabituation Closely linked with attention are the processes of habituation and dishabituation (de Paepe, de Williams, & Crombez, 2019). If you say the same word or show the same toy to a baby several times in a row, the baby usually pays less attention to it each time. This is *habituation*—decreased responsiveness to a stimulus after repeated presentations of the stimulus. *Dishabituation* is the recovery of responsiveness after a change in stimulation.

Infants' attention is often linked to novelty and habituation (Messinger & others, 2017; Monroy & others, 2019). When an object becomes familiar, attention becomes shorter, making infants more vulnerable to distraction.

Habituation provides a useful tool for assessing what infants can see, hear, smell, taste, and experience through touch. When infants habituate to one object, and thus it becomes familiar, they will then tend to look at an unfamiliar object, which shows they can tell the objects apart.

Knowing about habituation and dishabituation can help parents interact effectively with infants. Infants respond to changes in stimulation. Wise parents sense when an infant shows an interest and realize that they may have to repeat something many times for the infant to process information. But if the stimulation is repeated often, the infant stops responding to the parent. In parent-infant interaction, it is important for parents to do novel things and to repeat them often until the infant stops responding. The parent stops or changes behaviors when the infant redirects his or her attention (Rosenblith, 1992).

Joint Attention Another type of attention that is an important aspect of infant development is **joint attention,** which involves two or more individuals focusing on the same object or event (Suarez-Rivera, Smith, & Yu, 2019; Urqueta Alfaro & others, 2018). Joint attention requires (1) an ability to track another's behavior, such as following the other person's gaze; (2) one person directing another's attention; and (3) reciprocal interaction.

Early in infancy, joint attention usually involves a caregiver pointing or using words to direct an infant's attention. Emerging forms of joint attention may occur as early as midway through the first year, but it is not until toward the end of the first year that joint attention skills are frequently observed (Kawai & others, 2010). In a study conducted by Rechele Brooks and Andrew Meltzoff (2005), at 10 to 11 months of age infants first began engaging in "gaze following," looking where another person has just looked (see Figure 4). And by their first birthday, infants have begun to direct adults' attention to objects that capture their interest (Heimann & others, 2006). In one study, the extent to which 9-month-old infants engaged in joint attention was linked to their long-term memory (a one-week delay), possibly because joint attention enhances the relevance of attended items and improves encoding (Kopp & Lindenberger, 2012). Another study found that problems in joint attention as early as 8 months of age were linked to a child having been diagnosed with autism by 7 years of age (Veness & others, 2014). Also, another recent study that used eye-tracking equipment with 11- to 24-month-olds found that joint attention was predicted by infants' hand-eye coordination involving the connection of gaze with manual actions on objects, rather than by gaze following alone (Yu & Smith, 2017).

A mother and her infant son engaging in joint attention. *What about this photograph tells you that joint attention is occurring? Why is joint attention an important aspect of infant development?*
XiXinXing/age fotostock

Joint attention plays important roles in many aspects of infant development and considerably increases infants' ability to learn from other people (Loy, Masur, & Olson, 2018; McClure & others, 2018). Nowhere is this more apparent than in observations of interchanges between caregivers and infants as infants are learning language (Mason-Apps & others, 2018; Tomasello, 2014).

joint attention Focus by individuals on the same object or event; requires an ability to track another's behavior, one individual to direct another's attention, and reciprocal interaction.

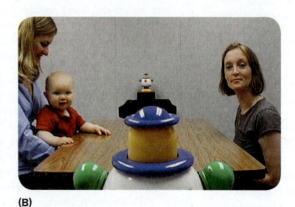

(A) **(B)**

FIGURE 4

GAZE FOLLOWING IN INFANCY. Researcher Rechele Brooks shifts her eyes from the infant to a toy in the foreground (*a*). The infant then follows her eye movement to the toy (*b*). Brooks and colleague Andrew Meltzoff (2005) found that infants begin to engage in this kind of behavior, called "gaze following," at 10 to 11 months of age. *Why might gaze following be an important accomplishment for an infant?*
Dr. Andrew Meltzoff, From: Meltzoff et al., *Science*, 2009, 325, 284–288

For example, a parent might point to a toy and say "ball." When caregivers and infants frequently engage in joint attention, infants say their first word earlier and develop a larger vocabulary (Mastin & Vogt, 2016). In a recent study, both joint attention and sustained attention at 9 months predicted vocabulary size at 12 and 15 months, but sustained attention was a stronger predictor of vocabulary size (Yu, Suanda, & Smith, 2019). Researchers also have found that joint attention is linked to better sustained attention (Yu & Smith, 2016), memory (Kopp & Lindenberger, 2011), self-regulation (Van Hecke & others, 2012), and executive function (Gueron-Sela & others, 2018).

CHILDHOOD AND ADOLESCENCE

The child's ability to pay attention improves significantly during the preschool years (Posner & others, 2018a, b; Wu & Scerif, 2018; Yan & others, 2018). Toddlers wander around, shift attention from one activity to another, and seem to spend little time focusing on any one object or event. By comparison, the preschool child might be observed watching television for a half-hour. However, one research study revealed that television watching and video game playing were both linked to attention problems in children (Swing & others, 2010).

Young children especially make advances in two aspects of attention—executive attention and sustained attention. Also, research indicates that although older children and adolescents show increases in vigilance, it is during the preschool years that individuals show the greatest increase in vigilance (Rueda & Posner, 2013).

Mary Rothbart and Maria Gartstein (2008, p. 332) described why advances in executive and sustained attention are so important in early childhood:

> The development of the . . . executive attention system supports the rapid increases in effortful control in the toddler and preschool years. Increases in attention are due, in part, to advances in comprehension and language development. As children are better able to understand their environment, this increased appreciation of their surroundings helps them to sustain attention for longer periods of time.

In at least two ways, however, the preschool child's control of attention is still deficient:

- *Salient versus relevant dimensions.* Preschool children are likely to pay attention to stimuli that stand out, or are salient, even when those stimuli are not relevant to solving a problem or performing a task. For example, if a flashy, attractive clown presents the directions for solving a problem, preschool children are likely to pay more attention to the clown than to the directions. After the age of 6 or 7, children attend more efficiently to the dimensions of the task that are relevant, such as the directions for solving a problem. This change reflects a shift to cognitive control of attention, so that children act less impulsively and reflect more.

- *Planfulness.* Although in general young children's planning improves as part of advances in executive attention, when experimenters ask children to judge whether two complex pictures are the same, preschool children tend to use a haphazard comparison strategy, not examining all of the details before making a judgment. By comparison, elementary-school-age children are more likely to systematically compare the details across the pictures, one detail at a time (Vurpillot, 1968) (see Figure 5).

In Central European countries such as Hungary, kindergarten children participate in exercises designed to improve their attention (Mills & Mills, 2000; Posner & Rothbart, 2007a, b). For example, in one eye-contact exercise, the teacher sits in the center of a circle of children, and each child is required to catch the teacher's eye before being permitted to leave the group. In other exercises created to improve attention, teachers have children participate in stop-go activities during which they have to listen for a specific signal, such as a drumbeat or an exact number of rhythmic beats, before stopping the activity.

Computer exercises also have been developed to improve children's attention (Rueda & Posner, 2013; Stevens & Bavelier, 2012). For example, one study revealed that five days of computer exercises that involved learning how to use a joystick, draw upon working memory, and resolve conflicts improved the attention of 4- to 6-year-old children (Rueda, Posner, & Rothbart, 2005). In one of the computer games, young children have to move a joystick to keep a cat on the grass and out of the mud, and in another they help a cat find a duck in a pond. Although these games are not commercially available, further information about computer exercises for improving children's attention is available at www.teach-the-brain.org/learn/attention/index.

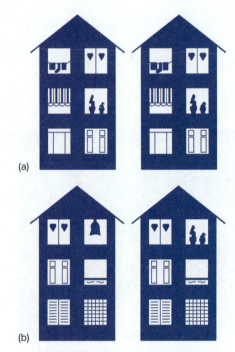

(a)

(b)

FIGURE 5

THE PLANFULNESS OF ATTENTION. In one study, children were given pairs of houses to examine, like the ones shown here (Vurpillot, 1968). For three pairs of houses, what was in the windows was identical (*a*). For the other three pairs, some of the windows had different items in them (*b*). By filming the reflection in the children's eyes, it could be determined what they were looking at, how long they looked, and the sequence of their eye movements. Children under 6 examined only a fragmentary portion of each display and made their judgments on the basis of insufficient information.

developmental connection

Brain Development

One shift in activation of the brain in middle and late childhood is from diffuse, large areas to more focused, smaller areas, which especially involves more focal activation in the prefrontal cortex. Connect to "Physical Development and Biological Aging."

How might good attentional skills benefit children's development? Preschool children's ability to control and sustain their attention is related to school readiness (Rothbart, 2011). For example, a study of more than 1,000 children revealed that their ability to sustain their attention at 54 months of age was linked to their school readiness (which included achievement and language skills) (NICHD Early Child Care Research Network, 2005b). And in another study, the ability to focus attention better at age 5 was linked to a higher level of school achievement at age 9 (Razza, Martin, & Brooks-Gunn, 2012). Attention to relevant information increases steadily during the elementary and secondary school years (Davidson, 1996). Processing of irrelevant information decreases in adolescence.

Another important aspect of attention is the ability to shift it from one activity to another as needed. For example, writing a good story requires shifting attention among the competing tasks of forming letters, composing grammar, structuring paragraphs, and conveying the story as a whole. Older children and adolescents are better than younger children at tasks that require shifting attention.

One trend involving divided attention is adolescents' multitasking, which in some cases involves not just dividing attention between two activities, but even three or more. A major factor that encourages multitasking is the availability of multiple electronic media. Many adolescents have a range of electronic media at their disposal. It is not unusual for adolescents to divide their attention by working on homework while engaging in an instant messaging conversation, surfing the Web, and listening to an iTunes playlist. And a national survey revealed that 50 percent of adolescents made and answered phone calls while driving, and 13 percent (approximately 1.7 million) wrote and/or read text messages while driving (Allstate Foundation, 2005). A recent analysis of research studies concluded that heavy media multitasking in adolescence is linked to poorer memory, increased impulsivity, and reduced volume in the brain's cerebral cortex (Uncapher & others, 2017). Further, another recent study indicated that heavy multimedia multitaskers were less likely than light multimedia multitaskers to delay gratification and more likely to endorse intuitive but wrong answers on a reflective cognitive task (Schutten, Stokes, and Arnell, 2017).

Thus, in many circumstances multitasking is not beneficial. If the key task is at all complex and challenging, such as trying to figure out how to solve a homework problem, multitasking considerably reduces attention to the key task (Myers, 2008).

Controlling attention is a key aspect of learning and thinking in adolescence and emerging adulthood (O'Halloran & others, 2018). Later in this chapter, we will further discuss some of the difficulties many adolescents encounter when faced with distractions that harm their attention.

developmental **connection**
Media/Screen Time

In a survey, when media multitasking was taken into account, 11- to 14-year-olds spent nearly 12 hours a day using media. Connect to "Peers and the Sociocultural World."

Is multitasking, which involves divided attention, beneficial or distracting?
Tim Hawley/Getty Images

ADULTHOOD

What happens to attention in adulthood? Attentional skills are often excellent in early adulthood and, of course, the discussion of divided attention and multitasking applies to many adults as well as adolescents. However, in many contexts older adults may not be able to focus on relevant information as effectively as younger adults (Gilsoul & others, 2019; Grzeschik & others, 2019; Manuel & others, 2019). Older adults have more difficulty in attention that involves various aspects of driving, distraction, selective attention, and complex vigilance tasks. Let's examine research that documents declines in older adults' attention in these areas.

Consider a study that examined the role that visual attention, involving search, selection, and switching, played in the performance of older adult drivers (Richardson & Marottoli, 2003). Thirty-five community-dwelling drivers aged 72 and older (mean age, 80) underwent an on-road driving evaluation involving parking lot maneuvers and urban, suburban, and highway driving. They were also given tests of visual attention. The worse their driving, the lower their visual attention score was. Yielding right of way and negotiating safe turns or merges were especially related to visual attention.

Might training sessions to improve older adults' attention be beneficial? One study revealed that older adults who participated in 20 one-hour video game training sessions with a commercially available program (Lumosity) showed a significant reduction in distraction and increased alertness (Mayas & others, 2014). The Lumosity program sessions focus on problem

developmental **connection**
Perception

Researchers study declines in the perceptual skills involved in older adults' driving performance. Connect to "Motor, Sensory, and Perceptual Development."

What are some developmental changes in attention in adulthood?
Digital Vision/Getty Images

solving, mental calculation, working memory, and attention. And in a recent experimental study, yoga practice that included postures, breathing, and meditation improved the attention and information processing of older adults (Gothe, Kramer, & McAuley, 2017). Another recent study found that when older adults regularly engaged in mindfulness meditation their goal-directed attention improved (Malinowski & others, 2017).

Older adults tend to be less adept at exercising selective attention—focusing on a specific aspect of experience while ignoring others—than younger adults are (Loaiza & Souza, 2019; Reuter & others, 2019; Zanto & Gazzaley, 2017). These age differences are minimal if the task involves a simple search (such as determining whether a target item is present on a computer screen) or if individuals have practiced the task (Kramer & Madden, 2008). As the demands on attention increase, however, the performance of older adults declines (Kramer & Madden, 2008). As long as two competing tasks are reasonably easy, age differences among adults are minimal or nonexistent. However, as competing tasks become more difficult, older adults divide attention less effectively than younger adults do (Maciokas & Crognale, 2003). Recent research indicates that older adults' auditory selective attention with visual distraction is especially impaired (Van Gerven & Guerreiro, 2016).

How well do older adults function on tasks that involve vigilance? On tests of simple vigilance and sustained attention, older adults usually perform as well as younger adults. For example, one study revealed that sustained attention increased in early adulthood but remained unchanged thereafter through 77 years of age (Carriere & others, 2010). However, on complex vigilance tasks, older adults' performance usually drops (Bucur & Madden, 2007).

Possibly, though, older adults' experience and wisdom might be able to offset some of their declines in vigilance. For example, consider how many young people focus intently on their smartphone rather than looking at traffic when walking across a dangerous intersection.

Review Connect Reflect

LG2 Define attention and outline its developmental changes.

Review

- What is attention? What are three ways that people allocate their attention?
- How does attention develop in infancy?
- How does attention develop in childhood and adolescence?

Connect

- Relate the characteristics of the life-span perspective to what you have learned about attention and its developmental changes.

Reflect *Your Own Personal Journey of Life*

- Imagine that you are an elementary school teacher. Devise some strategies to help your students pay attention in class.

3 Memory

LG3 Describe what memory is and how it changes through the life span.

What Is Memory? | Infancy | Childhood | Adulthood

Twentieth-century American playwright Tennessee Williams once commented that life is all memory except for that one present moment that goes by so quickly that you can hardly catch it going. But just what is memory?

WHAT IS MEMORY?

Memory is the retention of information over time. Without memory you would not be able to connect what happened to you yesterday with what is going on in your life today. Human memory is truly remarkable when you think of how much information we put into our

memory Retention of information over time.

Encoding	Storage	Retrieval
Getting information into memory	Retaining information over time	Taking information out of storage

FIGURE 6

PROCESSING INFORMATION IN MEMORY. As you read about the many aspects of memory in this chapter, think about the organization of memory in terms of these three main activities.

memories and how much we must retrieve to perform all of life's activities. However, human memory has imperfections that will be discussed shortly.

Processes of Memory Researchers study how information is initially placed in or encoded into memory, how it is retained or stored after being encoded, and how it is found or retrieved for a certain purpose later (see Figure 6). Encoding, storage, and retrieval are the basic processes required for memory. Failures can occur in any of these processes. Some part of an event might not be encoded, the mental representation of the event might not be stored, or even if the memory exists, the information may not be retrievable.

Constructing Memory Memories may be inaccurate for a number of reasons. Memory is not like a tape recorder or a camera or computer flash drive. People construct and reconstruct their memories (Schachter, 2019; St. Jacques & others, 2018; Thakral & others, 2019). According to **schema theory,** people mold memories to fit information that already exists in their minds. This process is guided by **schemas,** which are mental frameworks that organize concepts and information. Schemas influence the way people encode, make inferences about, and retrieve information. Often when we retrieve information, we fill in gaps.

We have schemas for all sorts of information. If a teacher tells your class a story about two men and two women who were involved in a train crash in France, students won't remember every detail of the story and will reconstruct the story with their own particular stamp on it. One student might reconstruct the story by saying that the people died in a plane crash, another might describe three men and three women, another might say the crash was in Germany, and so on. Such reconstruction and distortion are nowhere more apparent than in clashing testimony given by eyewitnesses at trials.

In sum, schema theory accurately predicts that people don't store and retrieve bits of data in computer-like fashion (Sekeres, Winocur, & Moscovitch, 2018). We reconstruct the past rather than take an exact photograph of it, and the mind can distort an event as it encodes and stores impressions of it (Madore, Jing, & Schacter, 2019).

INFANCY

Popular child-rearing expert Penelope Leach (1990) told parents that 6- to 8-month-old babies cannot hold a picture of their mother or father in their mind. However, child development researchers have revealed that newborns and even fetuses show a limited type of memory.

First Memories Carolyn Rovee-Collier (1987, 2007) has conducted research that demonstrates infants can remember perceptual-motor information. In a characteristic experiment, she places a baby in a crib underneath an elaborate mobile and ties one end of a ribbon to the baby's ankle and the other end to the mobile. The baby kicks and makes the mobile move (see Figure 7). Weeks later, the baby is returned to the crib, but its foot is not tied to the mobile. The baby kicks, apparently trying to make the mobile move. However, if the mobile's makeup is changed even slightly, the baby doesn't kick. If the mobile is then restored to being exactly as it was when the baby's ankle was tied to it, the baby will begin kicking again. According to Rovee-Collier, even at 2½ months the baby's memory is detailed.

developmental connection

Gender

Gender schema theory emphasizes children's gender schemas that organize the world in terms of male and female. Connect to "Gender and Sexuality."

schema theory Theory stating that people mold memories to fit information that already exists in their minds.

schemas Mental frameworks that organize concepts and information.

FIGURE 7

THE TECHNIQUE USED IN ROVEE-COLLIER'S INVESTIGATION OF INFANT MEMORY. In Rovee-Collier's experiment, operant conditioning was used to demonstrate that infants as young as 2½ months of age can retain information from the experience of being conditioned.
Courtesy of Dr. Carolyn Rovee-Collier

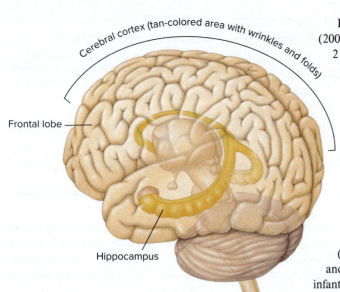

Cerebral cortex (tan-colored area with wrinkles and folds)

Frontal lobe

Hippocampus

FIGURE 8

KEY BRAIN STRUCTURES INVOLVED IN EXPLICIT MEMORY DEVELOPMENT IN INFANCY

How well can infants remember? Some researchers such as Rovee-Collier (2007; Rovee-Collier & Barr, 2010) have concluded that infants as young as 2 to 6 months of age can remember some experiences until they are 1½ to 2 years of age. However, critics such as Jean Mandler (2000), a leading expert on infant cognition, argue that the infants in Rovee-Collier's experiments are displaying only implicit memory. **Implicit memory** refers to memory without conscious recollection—memories of skills and routine procedures that are performed automatically. In contrast, **explicit memory** refers to the conscious recollection of facts and experiences.

When people think about memory, they are usually referring to explicit memory. Most researchers find that babies do not show explicit memory until the second half of the first year (Bauer & Fivush, 2014). Then explicit memory improves substantially during the second year of life (Lukowski & Bauer, 2014). In one longitudinal study, infants were assessed several times during their second year (Bauer & others, 2000). Older infants showed more accurate memory and required fewer prompts to demonstrate their memory than younger infants. Researchers have documented that 6-month-olds can remember information for 24 hours but by 20 months of age infants can remember information they encountered 12 months earlier.

In sum, most of young infants' conscious memories are fragile and short-lived, except for memory of perceptual-motor actions, which can be substantial (Mandler, 2000). Conscious memories improve across the second year of life (Bauer & Fivush, 2014).

What changes in the brain are linked to infants' memory development? From about 6 to 12 months of age, the maturation of the hippocampus and the surrounding cerebral cortex, especially the frontal lobes, makes the emergence of explicit memory possible (Mullally & Maguire, 2014; Nelson, 2013) (see Figure 8). Explicit memory continues to improve during the second year as these brain structures further mature and connections between them increase. Less is known about the areas of the brain involved in implicit memory in infancy.

Infantile Amnesia Do you remember your third birthday party? Probably not. Most adults can remember little if anything from their first three years of life (Bauer, 2019; Callaghan, Li, & Richardson, 2014). This is called infantile, or childhood, amnesia. The few reported adult memories of life at age 2 or 3 are at best very sketchy (Li, Callaghan, & Richardson, 2014).

Patricia Bauer and her colleagues (Bauer & Larkina, 2016; Larkina, Merrill, & Bauer, 2017) have been recently studying when infantile amnesia begins to occur. In one study, children's memory for events that occurred at 3 years of age was periodically assessed through age 9 (Bauer & Larkina, 2014). By 8 to 9 years of age, children's memory of events that occurred at 3 years of age began to significantly fade away. In Bauer's (2015) view, the processes that account for these developmental changes are early, gradual development of the ability to form, retain, and later retrieve memories of personally relevant past events followed by an accelerated rate of forgetting in childhood.

What causes infantile amnesia? One reason for the difficulty older children and adults have in recalling events from their infancy is the immaturity of the hippocampus and prefrontal cortex—brain regions that play key roles in memory for events (Josselyn & Frankland, 2012).

CHILDHOOD

Children's memory improves considerably after infancy (Fynes-Clinton, Marstaller, & Burianova, 2019; Ratner, Foley, & Lesnick, 2019). What are some of the significant strides in memory as children grow older? The progress includes improvements in short-term and long-term memory, as well as the use of strategies.

Short-Term and Working Memory When people talk about memory, they are usually referring to **long-term memory,** which is relatively permanent and unlimited. When you remember the types of games you enjoyed playing as a child, details of your first date, or characteristics of the life-span perspective, you are drawing on your long-term memory. But when you remember the word you just read, you are using short-term memory.

implicit memory Memory without conscious recollection—memory of skills and routine procedures that are performed automatically.

explicit memory Conscious memory of facts and experiences.

long-term memory A relatively permanent and unlimited type of memory.

short-term memory Retention of information for up to 15 to 30 seconds, without rehearsal of the information. Using rehearsal, individuals can keep the information in short-term memory longer.

Short-term memory involves retaining information for up to 30 seconds without rehearsal of the information. Using rehearsal, individuals can keep information in short-term memory longer (Yen, 2008).

Memory Span   Unlike long-term memory, short-term memory has a very limited capacity. One method of assessing that capacity is the memory-span task. You simply hear a short list of stimuli—usually digits—presented at a rapid pace (one per second, for example). Then you are asked to repeat the digits.

Research with the memory-span task suggests that short-term memory increases during childhood. For example, in one investigation, memory span increased from about two digits in 2- to 3-year-old children to about five digits in 7-year-old children. Between 7 and 12 years of age, memory span increased by only one and a half digits (Dempster, 1981) (see Figure 9). Keep in mind, though, that individuals have different memory spans.

Why does memory span change with age? Rehearsal of information is important; older children rehearse the digits more than younger children do. Speed of processing information is important, too, especially the speed with which memory items can be identified. For example, one study tested children on their speed at repeating words presented orally (Case, Kurland, & Goldberg, 1982). Speed of repetition was a powerful predictor of memory span. The children who were able to quickly repeat the presented words were also far more likely to have greater memory spans. Indeed, when the speed of repetition was controlled, the 6-year-olds' memory spans were equal to those of young adults.

Working Memory   Short-term memory is like a passive storehouse with shelves to store information until it is moved to long-term memory. Alan Baddeley (1990, 2001, 2007, 2010a, b, 2012, 2013, 2015, 2017) defines **working memory** as a kind of mental "workbench" where individuals manipulate and assemble information when they make decisions, solve problems, and comprehend written and spoken language (see Figure 10). Working memory is described as more active and powerful in modifying information than short-term memory (Baddeley, Hitch, & Allen, 2019).

Working memory develops slowly. Even by 8 years of age, children can only hold in memory half the items that adults can remember (Kharitonova, Winter, & Sheridan, 2015). Working memory is linked to many aspects of children's development (Nicolaou & others, 2018; Vernucci & others, 2019). For example, children who have better working memory are more advanced in language comprehension, math skills, problem solving, and reasoning than their counterparts with less effective working memory (Ding & others, 2019; Sanchez-Perez & others, 2018; Simms, Frausel, & Richland, 2018). In a recent study, children's verbal working memory was linked to these aspects of both first and second language learners: morphology, syntax, and grammar (Verhagen & Leseman, 2016).

Children's Long-Term Memory   In contrast with short-term and working memory, *long-term memory* is a relatively permanent type of memory that stores huge amounts of information for a long time. One aspect of long-term memory that has been extensively studied in children's development is autobiographical memory. Also, there has been considerable interest in children's memory in the courtroom when they are asked for eyewitness testimony. Keep in mind that it is important not to view memory in terms of how children add something to it but rather to underscore how children actively construct their memory (Glynn, Salmon, & Low, 2018).

Autobiographical Memory   Memory of significant events and experiences in one's life is called *autobiographical memory* (Larkina, Merrill, & Bauer, 2017). You are engaging in autobiographical memory when you answer questions such as: Who was your first-grade teacher and what was s/he like? What is the most traumatic event that happened to you as a child?

Earlier we described the phenomenon of infantile amnesia, in which individuals can't remember anything from their first three years of life, and recent research indicating that these memories especially begin to fade by 8 to 9 years of age.

During the preschool years, young children's memories increasingly take on more autobiographical characteristics (Ceci, Hritz, & Royer, 2016). In some areas, such as remembering a story, a movie, a song, or an interesting event or experience, young children have been shown to have reasonably good memories. From 3 to 5 years of age, they (1) increasingly remember events as occurring at a specific time and location, such as "on my birthday at Chuck E.

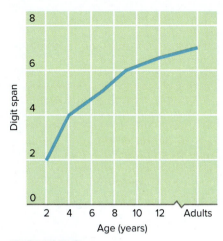

FIGURE 9

DEVELOPMENTAL CHANGES IN MEMORY SPAN. In one study, memory span increased by about three digits from 2 years to 7 years of age (Dempster, 1981). By 12 years of age, memory span had increased on average another one and a half digits.

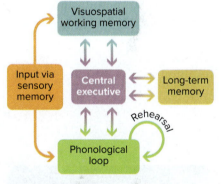

FIGURE 10

WORKING MEMORY. In Baddeley's working memory model, working memory is like a mental workbench where a great deal of information processing is carried out. Working memory consists of three main components. The phonological loop and visuospatial working memory serve as assistants, helping the central executive do its work. Input from sensory memory goes to the phonological loop, where information about speech is stored and rehearsal takes place, and visuospatial working memory, where visual and spatial information, including imagery, are stored. Working memory is a limited-capacity system, and information is stored there for only a brief time. Working memory interacts with long-term memory, using information from long-term memory in its work and transmitting information to long-term memory for longer storage.

working memory A mental "workbench" where individuals manipulate and assemble information when making decisions, solving problems, and comprehending written and spoken language.

Cheese's last year" and (2) include more elements that are rich in detail in their narratives (Bauer, 2013). In one study, children went from using four descriptive items per event at 3½ years of age to 12 such items at 6 years of age (Fivush & Haden, 1997). Although the long-term memories of preschoolers can seem to be erratic at times, they can remember a great deal of information if they are given appropriate cues and prompts. Also, a recent study of 3- to 6-year-olds found that the volume of their autobiographical memories was linked to the volume of their self-knowledge (Ross, Hutchison, & Cunningham, 2019).

As children go through middle and late childhood, and through adolescence, their autobiographical narratives broaden and become more elaborated (Bauer, 2013, 2019). Researchers have found that children develop more detailed, coherent, and evaluative autobiographical memories when their mothers reminisce with them in elaborated and evaluative ways (Fivush, 2010).

Culture influences children's autobiographical memories (de la Mata & others, 2019; Nelson, 2014). American children, especially American girls, provide autobiographical narratives that are longer, more detailed, more specific, and more personal than narratives by children from China and Korea (Bauer, 2006, 2013). The pattern is consistent with their conversations about past events, in which American mothers and their children are more elaborative and more focused on themes related to being independent while Korean mothers and their children less often engage in detailed conversations about the past. Possibly the more elaborated content of American children's narratives contributes to the earlier first memories researchers have found in American adults (Han, Leichtman, & Wang, 1998).

Eyewitness Testimony   One area in which children's long-term memory is being examined extensively relates to whether young children should be allowed to testify in court (Andrews & Lamb, 2017; Brown & Lamb, 2019). Increasingly, young children are being allowed to testify, especially if they are the only witnesses to abuse, a crime, and so forth (Pantell & others, 2019).

Several factors influence the accuracy of a young child's memory (Bruck & Ceci, 1999):

- *There are age differences in children's susceptibility to suggestion.* Preschoolers are much more susceptible to suggestion than are older children and adults (Ceci, Papierno, & Kulkofsky, 2007). For example, preschool children are more susceptible to absorbing misleading or incorrect post-event information (Ghetti & Alexander, 2004). Despite these age differences, there is still concern about the accuracy of older children's recollections of events if they are subjected to suggestive interviews (Ahern, Kowalski, & Lamb, 2018).

- *There are individual differences in susceptibility.* Some preschoolers are highly resistant to interviewers' suggestions, whereas others immediately succumb to the slightest suggestion (Andrews & Lamb, 2018). A research review concluded that suggestibility is linked to low self-concept, low support from parents, and mothers' insecure attachment in romantic relationships (Bruck & Melnyk, 2004).

- *Interviewing techniques can produce substantial distortions in children's reports about highly salient events.* Children are suggestible not just about peripheral details but also about the central aspects of an event (Malloy & others, 2012). Their false claims have been found to persist for at least three months (Ornstein, Gordon, & Larus, 1992). Nonetheless, young children are capable of recalling much that is relevant about an event (Goodman, Batterman-Faunce, & Kenney, 1992). When children do accurately recall an event, the interviewer often has a neutral tone, there is limited use of misleading questions, and there is an absence of any motivation for the child to make a false report (Bruck & Ceci, 2013). Also, a recent research review concluded that interviewer support increases children's memory accuracy (Saywitz & others, 2019).

In sum, whether a young child's eyewitness testimony is accurate or not may depend on a number of factors such as the type, number, and intensity of the suggestive techniques the child has experienced (Ahern, Van Meter, & Lamb, 2019; Andrews & Lamb, 2017). It appears that the reliability of young children's reports has as much to do with the skills and motivation of the interviewer as with any natural limitations on young children's memory (Ceci, Hritz, & Royer, 2016).

Children's long-term memory improves even more as they move into the middle and late childhood years. This advance is especially true when they use the strategies that we describe next.

What are some conclusions from research on young children's ability to provide accurate eyewitness testimony?
Buddy Norris/KRT/Newscom

Strategies   *Strategies* involve the use of mental activities to improve the processing of information (Graham, 2018, 2019; Harris & others, 2018; Graham, MacArthur, & Fitzgerald, 2019). For memory, rehearsing information and organizing are two typical strategies that older children (and adults) use to remember information more effectively. Rehearsal (repetition) works better for short-term memory. Strategies such as organization, elaborating on the information to be remembered, and making it personally relevant can make long-term memory more effective. Preschool children usually do not use strategies such as rehearsal and organization to remember (Flavell, Miller, & Miller, 2002).

Imagery   Creating mental images is another strategy for improving memory. However, using imagery to remember verbal information works better for older children than for younger children (Schneider, 2011).

Elaboration   One important strategy is **elaboration,** which involves engaging in more extensive processing of information. When individuals engage in elaboration, their memory benefits. Thinking of examples, especially those related to yourself, is an effective way to elaborate information. Thinking about personal associations with information makes the information more meaningful and helps children to remember it. For example, if the word *win* is on a list of words a child is asked to remember, the child might think of the last time she won a bicycle race.

The use of elaboration changes developmentally (Schneider, 2011). Adolescents are more likely than children to use elaboration spontaneously. Elementary school children can be taught to use elaboration strategies on a learning task, but they will be less likely than adolescents to use the strategies on other learning tasks in the future. Nonetheless, verbal elaboration can be an effective strategy even for young elementary school children.

Fuzzy Trace Theory   One theory that emphasizes the reconstructive aspects of memory provides an alternative to strategies in explaining developmental changes in children's memory. Proposed by Charles Brainerd and Valerie Reyna (1993, 2004, 2014), **fuzzy trace theory** states that memory is best understood by considering two types of memory representations: (1) verbatim memory trace and (2) gist. The verbatim memory trace consists of the precise details of the information, whereas gist refers to the central idea of the information. When gist is used, fuzzy traces are built up. Although individuals of all ages extract gist, young children tend to store and retrieve verbatim traces. At some point during the early elementary school years, children begin to use gist more and, according to the theory, its use contributes to the improved memory and reasoning of older children because fuzzy traces are more enduring and less likely to be forgotten than verbatim traces (Brainerd & Reyna, 2014).

Knowledge   An especially important influence on memory is the knowledge that individuals possess about a specific topic or skill (Ericsson & others, 2018; Varga & others, 2018). Knowledge influences what people notice and how they organize, represent, and interpret information. This skill, in turn, affects their ability to remember, reason, and solve problems (Brod & Shing, 2019).

One study found that 10- and 11-year-olds who were experienced chess players were able to remember more information about chess pieces than college students who were not chess players (Chi, 1978) (see Figure 11). In contrast, the college students were able to remember other stimuli better than the children were. Thus, the children's expertise in chess gave them

elaboration Engagement in more extensive processing of information, benefiting memory.

fuzzy trace theory States that memory is best understood by considering two types of memory representations: (1) verbatim memory trace and (2) gist.

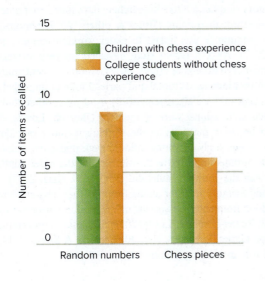

FIGURE 11
MEMORY FOR NUMBERS AND CHESS PIECES

superior memories, but only in chess. A key reason the child chess experts did better at this activity was their ability to organize (chunk) the chess pieces into meaningful subgroups based on their understanding of chess.

Teaching Strategies   So far we have described several important strategies adults can adopt when guiding children to remember information more effectively over the long term. These strategies include showing children how to organize information, how to elaborate the information, and how to develop images of the information. Another good strategy is to encourage children to understand the material that needs to be remembered rather than rotely memorizing it. Two other strategies adults can use to guide children's retention of memory were recently proposed:

- *Repeat with variation on the instructional information, and link early and often.* These are memory development research expert Patricia Bauer's (2009) recommendations to improve children's consolidation and reconsolidation of the information they are learning. Variations on a lesson theme increase the number of associations in memory storage, and linking expands the network of associations in memory storage; both strategies expand the routes for retrieving information from storage.

- *Embed memory-relevant language when instructing children.* Teachers vary considerably in how much they use memory-relevant language that encourages students to remember information. In research that involved extensive observations of a number of first-grade teachers in the classroom, Peter Ornstein and his colleagues (Ornstein, Coffman, & Grammer, 2007; Ornstein, Grammer, & Coffman, 2010; Ornstein, Haden, & Coffman, 2010; Ornstein & others, 2010) found that in the time segments observed, the teachers rarely used strategy suggestions or metacognitive (thinking about thinking) questions. In this research, when lower-achieving students were placed in classrooms in which teachers were categorized as "high-mnemonic teachers" who frequently embedded memory-relevant information in their teaching, the students' achievement increased (Ornstein, Coffman, & Grammer, 2007).

ADULTHOOD

Memory changes during the adult years, but different aspects of memory are affected differently as adults age (Cansino & others, 2019; Fraundorf & others, 2019; Park & Festini, 2018). Let's look first at working memory.

Working Memory   Working memory is an important process and resource for effective memory (Jarjat, Portrat, & Hot, 2019). Remember that working memory is like a mental "workbench" that allows us to manipulate and assemble information (Baddeley, Hitch, & Allen, 2019). Researchers have consistently found declines in working memory during late adulthood (Dai, Thomas, & Taylor, 2018; Rhodes & others, 2019). One study revealed that working memory continued to decline from 65 to 89 years of age (Elliott & others, 2011). Another study found that visually encoded working memory was linked to older adults' mobility (Kawagoe & Sekiyama, 2014).

Is plasticity part of the working memory of older adults? Researchers have found that older adults' working memory can be improved through training (Brum & others, 2019; Simon & others, 2018). In a recent study, aerobic endurance was linked to better working memory in older adults (Zettel-Watson & others, 2017). Also, a recent study revealed imagery strategy training improved older adults' working memory (Borella & others. 2017). Another recent study revealed that a cognitive training program that increased frontal and parietal lobe brain activity improved older adults' working memory (Gajewski & Falkenstein, 2018). And yet another study found that longer encoding time improved older adults' working memory (Bartsch, Loaiza, & Oberauer, 2019). Thus, there appears to be some plasticity in the working memory of older adults (Oh & others, 2018). However, a recent study of young, middle-aged, and older adults found that the working memory of all age groups improved with training, but the older adults showed less improvement with training than the younger adults did (Rhodes & Katz, 2017).

Explanations of the decline in working memory in older adults focus on their less efficient inhibition in preventing irrelevant information from entering working memory and their increased distractibility (Lopez-Higes & others, 2018; Reuter-Lorenz & Lustig, 2017). Declines in processing speed (Salthouse, 2017, 2018) and attention (Jarjat, Portrat, & Hot, 2019; Loaiza & Souza, 2019) in middle and late adulthood may play a role in working memory decline as well.

Explicit and Implicit Memory Long-term memory systems include explicit and implicit memory. Recall that *explicit memory* refers to the conscious memory of facts and experiences. Explicit memory is also sometimes called *declarative memory*. Examples of explicit memory include being at a grocery store and remembering that you want to buy something or being able to recall the plot of a movie you have seen.

Recall that *implicit memory* refers to memory of skills and routine procedures that are performed automatically. (Implicit memory is sometimes referred to as procedural memory.) Examples of implicit memory include unconsciously remembering how to drive a car, swing a golf club, or type on a computer keyboard.

Explicit Memory and Aging Explicit memory can be subdivided into episodic memory and semantic memory. **Episodic memory** is retention of information about the where and when of life's happenings. For example, what color were the walls in your bedroom when you were a child? What did you eat for breakfast this morning? What were you doing when you heard that the World Trade Center had been destroyed on 9/11/2001? Younger adults have better episodic memory than older adults have, both for real and imagined events (James, Rajah, & Duarte, 2019; Siegel & Castel, 2018; Zheng & others, 2019). One study found that episodic memory performance predicted which individuals would develop dementia 10 years prior to the clinical diagnosis of the disease (Boraxbekk & others, 2015). Further, in a recent study, a mindfulness training program was effective in improving episodic memory recall in older adults (Banducci & others, 2017).

Autobiographical memories are stored as episodic memories (Allen & others, 2018). A robust finding in autobiographical memory is called the *reminiscence bump*, in which adults remember more events from the second and third decades of their lives than from other decades (Munawar, Kuhn, & Hague, 2018; Rathbone, O'Connor, & Moulin, 2017). The "bump" is found more for positive than negative life events. One study revealed support for the reminiscence bump and indicated that these memories were more distinct and more important for identity development (Demiray, Gulgoz, & Bluck, 2009). Most studies of the reminiscence bump have focused on personal events, but a recent study found that the bump also occurs for the two most frequently mentioned high-impact public events but not less widely known ones (Tekcan & others, 2017).

Semantic memory is a person's knowledge about the world. It includes a person's fields of expertise (such as knowledge of chess, for a skilled chess player); general academic knowledge of the sort learned in school (such as knowledge of geometry); and "everyday knowledge" about meanings of words, famous individuals, important places, and common things (such as who Nelson Mandela and Mahatma Gandhi are). However, the ability to retrieve very specific information (such as names) usually declines in older adults (Hoffman & Morcom, 2018). For the most part, episodic memory declines more than semantic memory in older adults (Allen & others, 2018; Siegel & Castel, 2018).

Although older adults often take longer to retrieve semantic information, usually they can ultimately retrieve it. As shown in Figure 12, semantic memory continues to increase through the fifties, showing little decline even through the sixties (Ronnlund & others, 2005). Figure 12 also shows how the gap between semantic and episodic memory widens during middle and late adulthood. In one study, after almost five decades adults identified pictures of their high school classmates with better than 70 percent accuracy (Bahrick, Bahrick, & Wittlinger, 1975). How well do most adults remember the actual subjects they learned in high school, however? In the *Connecting with Research* interlude, we focus on another study that examined the developmental aspects of semantic memory.

Although many aspects of semantic memory are reasonably well preserved in late adulthood, a common memory problem for older adults is the *tip-of-the-tongue (TOT) phenomenon*, in which individuals can't quite retrieve familiar information but have the feeling that they should be able to retrieve it. Researchers have found that older adults are more likely to experience TOT states than younger adults (Huijbers & others, 2017). One study of older adults found that the errors in memory they most commonly reported having had in the last 24 hours were those involving tip-of-the-tongue (Ossher, Flegal, & Lustig, 2013).

episodic memory Retention of information about the where and when of life's happenings.

semantic memory A person's knowledge about the world, including fields of expertise, general academic knowledge, and "everyday knowledge" about meanings of words, names of famous individuals, important places, and common things.

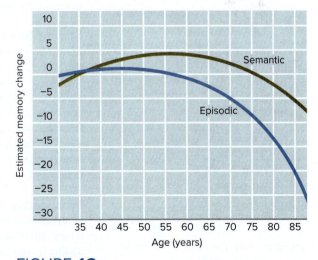

FIGURE 12

CHANGES IN EPISODIC AND SEMANTIC MEMORY IN ADULTHOOD

How Well Do Adults Remember What They Learned in High School and College Spanish?

When older adults are assessed for what they learned in high school or college, researchers find neither great durability in memory nor huge deterioration (Salthouse, 1991). In one study, non-Latino adults of various ages in the United States were studied to determine how much Spanish they remembered from classes they had taken in high school or college (Bahrick, 1984). The individuals chosen for the study had used Spanish very little since they initially learned it in high school or college. Not surprisingly, young adults who had taken Spanish classes within the last three years remembered their Spanish best. After that, the deterioration in memory was very gradual (see Figure 13). For example, older adults who had studied Spanish 50 years earlier remembered about 80 percent of what young adults did who had studied it in the last three years! The most important factor in the adults' memory of Spanish was not how long ago they had studied it but how well they initially learned it—those who got an A in Spanish 50 years earlier remembered more Spanish than those who got a C when taking Spanish only one year earlier.

What are some of the implications of the research on what adults remember from high school for improving teaching methods in U.S. schools?

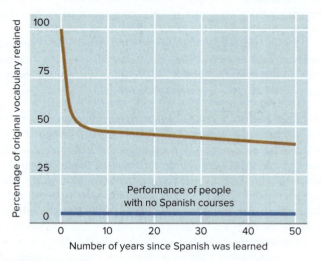

FIGURE 13

MEMORY FOR SPANISH AS A FUNCTION OF AGE SINCE SPANISH WAS LEARNED. An initial steep drop over about a three-year period in remembering the vocabulary learned in Spanish classes occurred. However, there was little drop-off in memory for Spanish vocabulary from three years after taking Spanish classes to 50 years after taking them. Even 50 years after taking Spanish classes, individuals still remembered almost 50 percent of the vocabulary they had learned.

Implicit Memory and Aging   Implicit memory is less likely than explicit memory to be adversely affected by aging (Ward, 2018). Thus, older adults are more likely to forget which items they wanted to buy at the grocery store (unless they wrote them down on a list and took it with them) than they are to forget how to drive a car. Their processing speed may be slower when driving the car, but they can remember how to do it. Further, Alzheimer disease is characterized by the early onset of explicit memory deficits, while implicit memory is not affected until later stages of the disease (Boccia, Silveri, & Guariglia, 2014).

Source Memory   **Source memory** is the ability to remember where one learned something. The contexts of source memory might be the physical setting, the emotional context, or the identity of the speaker. Failures of source memory increase with age in the adult years (Meusel & others, 2017). Such failures can be embarrassing, as when an older adult forgets who told a joke and retells it to the source. However, researchers have found that when information is more relevant to older adults, age differences in source memory are less robust (Hasher, 2003). Further, a recent study found that older adults with better source memory were characterized by healthy cardiovascular markers and psychological traits (higher achievement, less depression, for example) while lower source memory was predicted by relevant life experiences such as being retired and drinking heavily (Cansino & others, 2019).

Prospective Memory   **Prospective memory** involves remembering to do something in the future, such as remembering to take your medicine or remembering to do an errand (Monti & others, 2019; Schnitzpahn, Kvavilashvili, & Altgassen, 2019). Some researchers have found a decline in prospective memory with age (Kennedy & others, 2015; Kliegel & others, 2016). However, a number of studies show that the cause of the decline is complex and involves factors such as the nature of the task and what is being assessed (Scullin, Bugg, & McDaniel, 2012). For example, age-related deficits occur more often in time-based tasks (such as remembering to

source memory The ability to remember where something was learned.

prospective memory Remembering to do something in the future.

call someone next Friday) than in event-based tasks (remembering to tell your friend to read a particular book the next time you see her). Recent research also indicates that prospective memory is impaired in individuals with mild Alzheimer disease (Lecouvey & others, 2019).

Conclusions About Memory and Aging Most, but not all, aspects of memory decline during late adulthood. The decline occurs primarily in explicit, episodic, and working memory, not in semantic memory or implicit memory (Ward, 2018; Zheng & others, 2019). A decline in perceptual speed is associated with memory decline (Salthouse, 2017, 2018; Wilson & others, 2018). Successful aging does not mean eliminating memory decline altogether, but it does mean reducing the decline and adapting to it (Nikitin & Freund, 2019).

Older adults can use certain strategies to reduce memory decline (Hertzog & others, 2019; Karthaus, Wascher, & Getzmann, 2018). Researchers have found that strategies involving elaboration and self-referential processing are effective in improving the memory of older adults, actually helping older adults' memory more than younger adults' memory (Trelle, Henson, & Simons, 2015). And in a recent study, using compensation strategies (for example, managing appointments by routinely writing them on a calendar) was associated with higher levels of independence in everyday function in cognitively normal older adults as well as older adults with mild cognitive impairment (Tomaszewski Farias & others, 2018). Also, a recent study confirmed that when older adults engaged in higher levels of physical activity their memory improved (de Lima & others, 2019).

Prospective memory involves remembering to do something in the future. The older adult woman here is keeping track of what she plans to buy when she goes to a grocery store the next day.
imtmphoto/shutterstock

Review Connect Reflect

 LG3 Describe what memory is and how it changes through the life span.

Review
- What is memory? What are memory's processes? What is involved in constructing memory? Can new information alter memories?
- How does memory develop in infancy?
- How does memory change in childhood?
- What are some changes in memory during the adult years?

Connect
- How might the changes in the brain during late adulthood be linked to the changes in memory in older adults that were just discussed?

Reflect Your Own Personal Journey of Life
- What is your earliest memory? Why do you think this particular situation was so memorable?

---

4 Thinking   **LG4** Characterize thinking and its developmental changes.

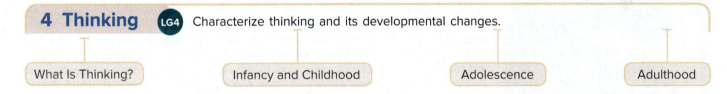

| What Is Thinking? | Infancy and Childhood | Adolescence | Adulthood |

Attention and memory are often steps toward another level of information processing—thinking. What is thinking? How does it change developmentally? What is children's scientific thinking like? Let's explore these questions.

WHAT IS THINKING?

Thinking involves manipulating and transforming information in memory. We think in order to reason, reflect, evaluate ideas, solve problems, and make decisions.

INFANCY AND CHILDHOOD

To explore thinking in infancy and childhood, we ask questions like the following: To what extent do infants form concepts and engage in categorization? What is critical thinking and how can it be encouraged in schools? What is executive function and how does it change developmentally? What is children's scientific thinking like? How do children solve problems?

thinking Manipulating and transforming information in memory, in order to reason, reflect, think critically, evaluate ideas and solve problems, and make decisions.

FIGURE 14

CATEGORIZATION IN 9- TO 11-MONTH-OLDS. These are the type of stimuli used in the study that indicated 9- to 11-month-old infants categorized birds as animals and airplanes as vehicles even though the objects were perceptually similar (Mandler & McDonough, 1993).

Infants are creating concepts and organizing their world into conceptual domains that will form the backbone of their thought throughout life.

—Jean Mandler

Contemporary Developmental Psychologist, University of California–San Diego

The author's grandson Alex at 2 years of age showing his intense, passionate interest in the category of vehicles while playing with a London taxi and a funky Malta bus.
Dr. John Santrock

concepts Cognitive groupings of similar objects, events, people, or ideas.

executive function An umbrella-like concept that encompasses a number of higher-level cognitive processes linked to the development of the brain's prefrontal cortex. Executive function involves managing one's thoughts to engage in goal-directed behavior and to exercise self-control.

Concept Formation and Categorization in Infancy

Along with attention, memory, and imitation, concepts are key aspects of infants' cognitive development (Casasola, 2018). **Concepts** are cognitive groupings of similar objects, events, people, or ideas. Without concepts, you would see each object and event as unique and you would not be able to make any generalizations.

Do infants have concepts? Yes, they do, although we do not know just how early concept formation begins (Quinn, 2015). Using habituation experiments like those described earlier in the chapter, some researchers have found that infants as young as 3 to 4 months of age can group together objects with similar appearances, such as animals (Rakison & Lawson, 2013).

Jean Mandler (2010) argues that these early categorizations are best described as *perceptual categorization*. That is, the categorizations are based on similar perceptual features of objects, such as size, color, and movement, as well as parts of objects, such as legs for animals. Mandler (2004) concludes that it is not until about 7 to 9 months of age that infants form *conceptual* categories rather than just making perceptual discriminations between different categories. In one study of 9- to 11-month-olds, infants classified birds as animals and airplanes as vehicles even though the objects were perceptually similar—airplanes and birds with their wings spread (Mandler & McDonough, 1993) (see Figure 14).

In addition to infants categorizing items on the basis of external, perceptual features such as shape, color, and parts, they also may categorize items on the basis of prototypes, or averages, that they extract from the structural regularities of items (Rakison & Lawson, 2013).

Further advances in categorization occur during the second year of life (Rakison & Lawson, 2013). Many infants' "first concepts are broad and global in nature, such as 'animal' or 'indoor thing.' Gradually, over the first two years these broad concepts become more differentiated into concepts such as 'land animal,' then 'dog,' or to 'furniture,' then 'chair'" (Mandler, 2010, p. 1).

Learning to put things into the correct categories—knowing what makes something one kind of thing rather than another kind of thing, such as what makes a bird a bird, or a fish a fish—is an important aspect of learning. As infant development researcher Alison Gopnik (2010, p. 159) pointed out, "If you can sort the world into the right categories—put things in the right boxes—then you've got a big advance on understanding the world."

Do some very young children develop an intense, passionate interest in a specific category of objects or activities? A study of 11-month-old to 6-year-old children confirmed that they do (DeLoache, Simcock, & Macari, 2007). A striking finding was the large gender difference in categories—with an extremely intense interest in particular categories stronger for boys than girls. Categorization of boys' intense interests focused on vehicles, trains, machines, dinosaurs, and balls; girls' intense interests were more likely to involve dress-ups and books/reading (see Figure 15). By the time your author's grandson Alex was 2 years old, he already had developed an intense, passionate interest in the category of vehicles. He categorized vehicles into such subcategories as cars, trucks, earthmoving equipment, and buses. In addition to common classifications of cars into police cars, jeeps, taxis, and such, and trucks into fire trucks, dump trucks, and the like, his categorical knowledge of earthmoving equipment included bulldozers and excavators, and he categorized buses into school buses, London buses, and funky Malta buses (retro buses on the island of Malta). By 2½ years of age, Alex developed an intense, passionate interest in categorizing dinosaurs.

In sum, the infant's advances in processing information—through attention, memory, and concept formation—is much richer, more gradual, and less stage-like, and occurs earlier than was envisioned by earlier theorists, such as Piaget (Bauer, 2018, 2019; Meltzoff & others, 2018, 2019). As leading infant researcher Jean Mandler (2004) concluded, "The human infant shows a remarkable degree of learning power and complexity in what is being learned and in the way it is represented" (p. 304).

Executive Function Recently, increasing interest has surrounded the development of children's **executive function**, an umbrella-like concept that encompasses a number of higher-level cognitive processes linked to the development of the brain's prefrontal cortex. Executive function involves managing one's thoughts to engage in goal-directed behavior and exercise self-control (Bervoets & others, 2018; McClelland & Cameron, 2019; McCoy, 2019). Earlier in this chapter, we described the recent interest in *executive attention*, which comes under the umbrella of executive function.

Executive Function in Children   In early childhood, executive function especially involves developmental advances in cognitive inhibition (such as inhibiting a strong tendency that is incorrect), cognitive flexibility (such as shifting attention to another item or topic), goal-setting (such as sharing a toy or mastering a skill like catching a ball), and delay of gratification (the ability to forego an immediate pleasure or reward for a more desirable one later) (Cheng & others, 2018; McClelland, Cameron, & Alonso, 2019). During early childhood, the relatively stimulus-driven toddler is transformed into a child capable of flexible, goal-directed problem solving that characterizes executive function (Zelazo & Muller, 2011).

Researcher Stephanie Carlson has conducted a number of research studies on young children's executive function. In one study, young children were read either *Planet Opposite*—a fantasy book in which everything is turned upside down—or *Fun Town*—a reality-oriented fiction book (Carlson & White, 2011). After being read one of the books, the young children completed the Less Is More Task, in which they were shown two trays of candy—one with 5 pieces, the other with 2—and told that the tray they pick will be given to the stuffed animal seated at the table. This task is difficult for 3-year-olds who tend to pick up the tray that they themselves want (and so end up losing the tray to the stuffed animal). Sixty percent of the 3-year-olds who heard the *Planet Opposite* story selected the smaller number of candies (hence keeping the five pieces of candy) compared with only 20 percent of their counterparts who heard the more straightforward story. The results indicated that learning about a topsy-turvy imaginary world likely helped the young children become more flexible in their thinking.

Walter Mischel and his colleagues (Mischel, 2014; Mischel, Cantor, & Feldman, 1996; Mischel & Moore, 1980; Mischel & others, 2011; Schlam & others, 2013; Zayas, Mischel, & Pandey, 2014) have conducted a number of studies of delay of gratification with young children. The main way they assess delay of gratification is to place a young child alone in a room with an alluring marshmallow that is within reach. The children are told that they either can ring a bell at any time and eat the marshmallow or they can wait until the experimenter returns and then get two marshmallows. For the young children who waited for the experimenter to return, what did they do to help them wait? They engaged in a number of strategies to distract their attention from the marshmallow, including singing songs, picking their noses—anything to keep from looking at the marshmallow. Mischel and his colleagues labeled these strategies "cool thoughts" (that is, doing non-marshmallow-related thoughts and activities), whereas they said the young children who looked at the marshmallow were engaging in "hot thoughts." The young children who engaged in cool thoughts were more likely to eat the marshmallow later or to wait until the experimenter returned to the room.

In longitudinal research, Mischel and his colleagues have found that the preschool children who were able to delay gratification became more academically successful, had higher SAT scores and higher grade point averages at the end of college, and coped with stress more successfully as adolescents and emerging adults (Mischel, 2014). And as adults, they made more money in their careers, were more law-abiding, were more likely to have a lower body mass index, and were happier than individuals who were unable to delay gratification as preschoolers (Mischel, 2014; Moffitt, 2012; Moffitt & others, 2011; Schlam & others, 2013). Although the ability to delay gratification in preschool was linked to academic success and coping in adolescence and

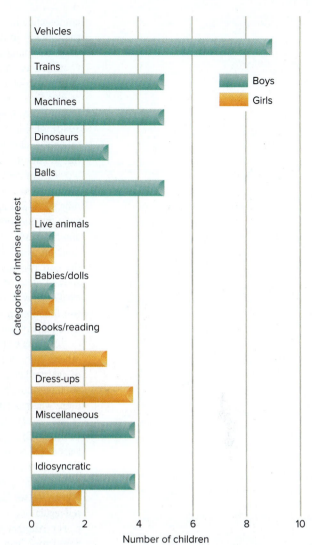

FIGURE 15

CATEGORIZATION OF BOYS' AND GIRLS' INTENSE INTERESTS

How did Walter Mischel and his colleagues study young children's delay of gratification? In their research, what later developmental outcomes were linked to the preschoolers' ability to delay gratification?
Amy Kiley Photography

competence in adulthood, Mischel (2014) emphasizes that adolescents and adults can improve their ability to delay gratification.

Are young children less likely to delay gratification in the twenty-first century than in the twentieth century? Recent research examined this question about possible cohort effects (Carlson & others, 2018). In this research, the data from the original study in the 1960s as well as data from the 1980s and 2000s were analyzed. Young children in the 2000s waited an average of 2 minutes longer than their counterparts in the 1960s and 1 minute longer than those in the 1980s. This increase in delay of gratification in recent years likely is due to increases in symbolic thought, technological advances, more widely attended early childhood education programs, and public attention to the importance of children developing higher-level skills such as self-control.

Researchers have found that advances in executive function in the preschool years are linked with academic achievement, math skills, language development, and school readiness (Duncan & others, 2018; Liu & others, 2018; Willoughby, Wylie, & Little, 2019). One study revealed that executive function skills predicted mathematical gains in kindergarten (Fuhs & others, 2014). In another study of children in low-income families in the African country of Ghana, executive function assessed at 5 years of age predicted higher subsequent literacy and math skills across the next two years (Wolf & McCoy, 2019). And a recent study found that young children who showed delayed development of executive function had a lower level of school readiness (Willoughby & others, 2017). Further, another recent study revealed that a lower level of executive function in preschool children was linked to new onset and worsening of attention deficit hyperactivity disorder and depression at 6 to 12 years of age (Hawkey & others, 2018).

Parents and teachers play important roles in the development of executive function (Bernier & others, 2015, 2017; Cheng & others, 2018). One study revealed that sensitive parenting at 3 years of age predicted fewer executive function problems at 4 years of age (Kok & others, 2014). In another study, higher levels of parental education predicted superior executive function in children, whereas harsh parenting forecast lower levels of executive function in children (Halse & others, 2019). Also, researchers have discovered that fathers' autonomy support (Meuwissen & Carlson, 2018) improved young children's executive function. Further, Ann Masten and her colleagues (Masten, 2013, 2014a, b; Masten & others, 2008; Monn & others, 2017) have found that executive function and parenting skills are linked to homeless children's success in school. Masten believes that good parenting skills are related to children's executive function. In her words, "When we see kids with good executive function, we often see adults around them that are good self-regulators. . . . Parents model, they support, and they scaffold these skills" (Masten, 2012, p. 11). Another study revealed that secure attachment to mothers during the toddler years was linked to a higher level of executive function at 5 to 6 years of age (Bernier & others, 2015). Further, a recent study indicated that teachers who conducted a six-week small group training program focusing on mindfulness and reflection improved young children's executive function more than no intervention, but a literacy training program was as effective as the mindfulness/ reflection program in improving their executive function (Zelazo & others, 2018).

How might executive function change in the middle and late childhood years and be linked to children's success in school? Adele Diamond and Kathleen Lee (2011) highlighted the following dimensions of executive function that they conclude are the most important for 4- to 11-year-old children's cognitive development and school success:

- *Self-control/inhibition.* Children need to develop self-control that will allow them to concentrate and persist on learning tasks, to inhibit their tendencies to repeat incorrect responses, and to resist the impulse to do something now that they would regret later.
- *Working memory.* Children need an effective working memory to efficiently process the masses of information they will encounter as they go through school and beyond.
- *Flexibility.* Children need to be flexible in their thinking to consider different strategies and perspectives.

Some researchers have found that executive function is a better predictor of school readiness than general IQ (Blair & Razza, 2007). A number of diverse activities have been found to increase children's executive function, such as computerized training that uses games to improve working memory (CogMed, 2013); aerobic exercise (Kvalo & others, 2017); scaffolding of self-regulation (Bodrova & Leong, 2015a, b); mindfulness training (Gallant, 2016); and some types of school curricula (the Montessori curriculum, for example) (Diamond, 2013; Diamond & Lee, 2011).

developmental **connection**

Exercise

Recent research indicates that children who are more physically fit have better thinking skills, including those involving executive function, than less physically fit children. Connect to "Health."

Executive Function in Adolescents and Emerging Adults   Cognitive development expert Deanna Kuhn (2009) discussed some important characteristics of adolescents' information processing and thinking. In her view, during the later years of childhood and continuing into adolescence, individuals approach cognitive levels that may or may not be achieved, in contrast with the largely universal cognitive levels that young children attain. By adolescence, considerable variation in cognitive functioning is present across individuals. This variability supports the argument that adolescents are producers of their own development to a greater extent than are children. Kuhn (2009) argues that the most important cognitive change in adolescence is improvement in executive control. Especially important is adolescents' and emerging adults' increasing ability to engage in cognitive control, an improvement that continues throughout adolescence and emerging adulthood (Chevalier, Dauvier, & Blaye, 2019; Romer, Reyna, & Satterthwaite, 2017).

Two categories of executive function are *cool executive function*, psychological processes involving conscious control driven by logical thinking and critical analysis; and *hot executive function*, psychological processes driven by emotion, with emotion regulation an especially important process (Kouklari, Tsermentseli, & Monks, 2019; Semenov & Zelazo, 2018). In a recent study of 12- to 17-year-olds, cool executive function increased with age, while hot executive function peaked at 14 to 15 years of age and then declined (Poon, 2018).

A very important aspect of executive function in adolescence is cognitive control. Indeed, for most purposes, executive function and cognitive control can be thought of as synonyms. Cognitive control involves exercising effective control in a number of areas, including focusing attention, reducing interfering thoughts, and being cognitively flexible (Diamond, 2013; Stewart & others, 2017). Cognitive control increases in adolescence and emerging adulthood (Chevalier, Dauvier, & Blaye, 2018; Crone & Konijn, 2018).

Think about all the times adolescents need to engage in cognitive control, such as the following situations (Galinsky, 2010):

- Making a real effort to stick with a task, avoiding interfering thoughts or environmental events, and instead doing what is most effective.
- Stopping and thinking before acting to avoid blurting out something that a minute or two later they wished they hadn't said.
- Continuing to work on something that is important but boring when there is something a lot more fun to do, inhibiting their behavior and doing the boring but important task, saying to themselves, "I have to show the self-discipline to finish this."

Controlling attention is a key aspect of cognition in adolescence and emerging adulthood (Mueller & others, 2017). Distractions that can interfere with attention in adolescence and emerging adulthood come from the external environment (other students talking while the student is trying to listen to a lecture, or the student turning on a laptop or tablet PC during a lecture and looking at a new friend request on Facebook, for example) or intrusive distractions from competing thoughts in the individual's mind. Self-oriented thoughts, such as worrying, self-doubt, and intense emotionally laden thoughts may especially interfere with focusing attention on thinking tasks (Walsh, 2011).

Another very important aspect of executive function in adolescence is *cognitive flexibility*, which involves being aware of available options and then adapting to one's situation. Before adolescents and emerging adults adapt their behavior in a situation, they must be aware that they need to change their way of thinking and be motivated to do so (Gopnik & others, 2019). Having confidence in their ability to adapt their thinking to a particular situation, an aspect of *self-efficacy*, also is important in being cognitively flexible (Bandura, 2012). In a recent study, young adolescents showed greater understanding of metaphors than children, and this understanding was linked to increased cognitive flexibility in the young adolescents (Willinger & others, 2019).

Executive Function and Aging   For the most part, executive function remains strong during early and middle adulthood and plays important roles in many aspects of people's lives. How does executive function change in late adulthood? The prefrontal cortex is one area of the brain that especially

How might information processing and thinking skills change in adolescence?
Tetra Images/Getty Images

shrinks with aging, and recent research has linked this shrinkage with a decrease in working memory and other cognitive activities in older adults (Reuter-Lorenz & Lustig, 2017). One study found that dysregulation of signaling by the neurotransmitter GABA may play a role in impaired working memory in older adults (Banuelos & others, 2014).

Executive function skills decline in older adults (Gaillardin & Baudry, 2018; Lin & others, 2017). Aspects of working memory that especially decline in older adults involve (1) updating memory representations that are relevant for the task at hand and (2) replacing old, no longer relevant information (Friedman & others, 2008). Older adults also are less effective at engaging in cognitive control than when they were younger (Turner & others, 2019; Zammit & others, 2018). For example, in terms of cognitive flexibility, older adults don't perform as well as younger adults at switching back and forth between tasks or mental sets (Chiu & others, 2018). And in terms of cognitive inhibition, older adults are less effective than younger adults at inhibiting dominant or automatic responses (Lopez-Higes & others, 2018).

Although aspects of executive function tend to decline in late adulthood, there is considerable variability in executive function among older adults. For example, some older adults have a better working memory and are more cognitively flexible than other older adults (Kayama & others, 2014). Further, there is increasing research evidence that aerobic exercise improves executive function in older adults (Eggenberger & others, 2015). For example, a recent study of older adults revealed that across a 10-year period physically active women experienced less decline in executive function (Hamer, Muniz Terrera, & Demakakos, 2018). And in another study, more physically fit older adults had greater cognitive flexibility than their less physically fit counterparts (Berryman & others, 2013). Also, in a research meta-analysis, tai chi participation was associated with better executive function in older adults (Wayne & others, 2014). Executive function increasingly is thought to be involved not only in cognitive performance but also in health, emotion regulation, adaptation to life's challenges, motivation, and social functioning (Forte & others, 2013). Research on these aspects of executive function has only recently begun. In one study, deficits in executive function but not memory predicted a higher risk of coronary heart disease and stroke three years later in older adults (Rostamian & others, 2015). And in a recent study of older adults, aerobic exercise was effective in improving their executive function (McSween & others, 2019). Further, a recent study of older adults revealed that across a 10-year period physically active women experienced less decline in executive function (Hamer, Muniz Terrera, & Demakakos, 2018).

Some critics argue that not much benefit is derived from placing various cognitive processes under the broader concept of executive function. Although we have described a number of components of executive function here—working memory, cognitive inhibition, cognitive flexibility, and so on—a consensus has not been reached on what the components are, how they are connected, and how they develop. That said, the concept of executive function is not likely to go away any time soon, and further research, especially meta-analyses, should provide a clearer picture of executive function and how it develops through the human life span (Luszcz, 2011).

Critical Thinking Executive function also involves being able to think critically. Currently, both psychologists and educators have shown considerable interest in critical thinking (Bonney & Sternberg, 2016; Halpern & Butler, 2018).

Critical thinking involves grasping the deeper meaning of ideas, keeping an open mind about different approaches and perspectives, and deciding for oneself what to believe or do. In this book, the third part of the Review *Connect* Reflect sections challenges you to think critically about a topic or an issue related to the discussion. Thinking critically includes asking not only what happened, but how and why; examining supposed "facts" to determine whether there is evidence to support them; evaluating what other people say rather than immediately accepting it as true; and asking questions and speculating beyond what is known to create new ideas and acquire new information.

In the view of critics such as Jacqueline and Martin Brooks (1993, 2001), few schools teach students to think critically. Schools spend much more time getting students to give a single correct answer than encouraging them to come up with new ideas and rethink conclusions. Too often teachers ask students to recite, define, describe, state, and list rather than to analyze, infer, connect, synthesize, criticize, create, evaluate, think, and rethink. As a result, many schools graduate students who think superficially, staying on the surface of problems rather than becoming deeply engaged in meaningful thinking.

The mind is an enchanting thing.

—Marianne Moore
American Poet, 20th Century

developmental **connection**
Education
A criticism of the No Child Left Behind legislation is that it does not give adequate attention to the development of critical thinking skills. Connect to "Schools, Achievement, and Work."

critical thinking Thinking reflectively and productively, and evaluating the evidence.

Helen Hadani, Ph.D., Developmental Psychologist, Toy Designer, and Associate Director of Research for the Center for Childhood Creativity

Helen Hadani obtained a Ph.D. in developmental psychology from Stanford University. As a graduate student at Stanford, she worked part-time for Hasbro Toys and Apple testing children's software and other computer products for young children. Her first job after graduate school was with Zowie Intertainment, which was subsequently bought by LEGO. In her work as a toy designer there, Helen conducted experiments and focus groups at different stages of a toy's development, and she also studied the age-effectiveness of each toy. In Helen's words, "Even in a toy's most primitive stage of development . . . you see children's creativity in responding to challenges, their satisfaction when a problem is solved or simply their delight in having fun" (Schlegel, 2000, p. 50).

More recently, she began working with the Bay Area Discovery Museum's Center for Childhood Creativity (CCC) in Sausalito, California, an education-focused think tank that pioneers new research, thought-leadership, and teacher training programs that advance creative thinking in all children. Helen is currently the Associate Director of Research for the CCC.

Helen Hadani has worked as both a toy designer and in a museum position that involves thinking of ways to increase children's creative thinking.
Courtesy of Helen Hadani

According to Ellen Langer (2005), *mindfulness*—being alert, mentally present, and cognitively flexible while going through life's everyday activities and tasks—is an important aspect of thinking critically. Mindful children and adults maintain an active awareness of the circumstances in their lives and are motivated to find the best solutions to challenges they confront. Mindful individuals create new ideas, are open to new information, and operate from multiple perspectives. By contrast, mindless individuals are entrapped in old ideas, engage in automatic behavior, and operate from a single perspective.

Recently, Robert Roeser and his colleagues (Roeser & Eccles, 2015; Roeser & Zelazo, 2012; Roeser & others, 2014; Zelazo & others, 2018) have emphasized that mindfulness is an important mental process that children can engage in to improve a number of cognitive and socioemotional skills, such as executive function, focused attention, emotion regulation, and empathy (Roeser & Zelazo, 2012). Some experts have proposed implementing mindfulness training in schools through practices such as using age-appropriate activities that increase children's reflection on moment-to-moment experiences and result in improved self-regulation (Zelazo & Lyons, 2012).

In a recent study, mindfulness training improved self-regulation of attention (Felver & others, 2017). In addition to mindfulness, activities such as yoga, meditation, and tai chi recently have been suggested as candidates for advancing children's cognitive and socioemotional development (Felver & others, 2017). Together these activities are being grouped under the topic of *contemplative science*, a cross-disciplinary term that involves the study of how various types of mental and physical training might enhance children's development (Roeser & Eccles, 2015; Roeser & Zelazo, 2012; Zelazo & others, 2018). For example, a training program in mindfulness and caring for others was effective in improving the cognitive control of fourth- and fifth-graders (Schonert-Reichl & others, 2015). In other research, mindfulness training has been found to improve children's attention and self-regulation (Poehlmann-Tynan & others, 2016), achievement (Schonert-Reichl & Roeser, 2016), and coping strategies in stressful situations (Dariotis & others, 2016). Also, in two recent studies, mindfulness-based intervention reduced public school teachers' stress, created a better mood in students when they were at school and at home, and was associated with better sleep (Crain, Schonert-Reichl, & Roeser, 2017; Taylor & others, 2016).

To read about one developmental psychologist who used her training in cognitive development to pursue a career in an applied area, see the *Connecting with Careers* profile.

ADOLESCENCE

Earlier, we described some important advances in executive function that take place in adolescence. Here we further discuss two other high-level thinking processes in adolescence—decision making and critical thinking.

Decision Making   Adolescence also is a time of increased decision making—deciding which friends to choose, which person to date, whether to have sex, buy a car, go to college, and so on (Duell & others, 2018; Helm, McCormick, & Reyna, 2018; Helm & Reyna, 2018; Meschkow & others, 2018; Reyna, 2019; Reyna & others, 2018; Steinberg & others, 2019). How competent are adolescents at making decisions? In some reviews, older adolescents are described as more competent than younger adolescents, who in turn are more competent than children (Keating, 2004). Compared with children, young adolescents are more likely to generate different options, examine a situation from a variety of perspectives, anticipate the consequences of decisions, and consider the credibility of sources.

However, older adolescents' (as well as adults') decision-making skills are far from perfect, and having the capacity to make competent decisions does not guarantee that such decisions will be made in everyday life, where breadth of experience often comes into play (Kuhn, 2009). Most people make better decisions when they are calm rather than emotionally aroused, and intense emotional arousal is a common state for adolescents (Crone & Konijn, 2018; Steinberg & others, 2019). Thus, the same adolescent who makes a wise decision when calm may make an unwise decision when emotionally aroused. In the heat of the moment, then, adolescents' emotions may be more likely to overwhelm their decision-making ability.

How do emotions and social contexts influence adolescents' decision making?
JodiJacobson/Getty Images

The social context plays a key role in adolescent decision making (Breiner & others, 2018; Duell & others, 2018; Sherman, Steinberg, & Chein, 2018; Steinberg & others, 2019). For example, adolescents' decisions to engage in risky behavior are more likely to occur in contexts where alcohol, drugs, and other temptations are readily available. Research reveals that the presence of peers in risk-taking situations increases the likelihood that adolescents will make risky decisions (Albert & Steinberg, 2011a, b). In one study of risk taking involving a simulated driving task, the presence of peers increased an adolescent's decision to engage in risky driving by 50 percent but had no effect on adults (Gardner & Steinberg, 2005). One possible explanation is that the presence of peers activates the brain's reward system, especially its dopamine pathways (Steinberg & others, 2019).

To better understand adolescent decision making, Valerie Reyna and her colleagues (Helm, McCormick, & Reyna, 2018; Helm & Reyna, 2018; Reyna, 2018; Reyna & others, 2011, 2015, 2018) have proposed the **fuzzy-trace theory dual-process model,** which states that decision making is influenced by two cognitive systems—"verbatim" analytical (literal and precise) and gist-based intuitional (simple, bottom-line meaning)—which operate in parallel. Basing judgments and decisions on simple gist is viewed as more beneficial than analytical thinking to adolescents' decision making. In this view, adolescents don't benefit from engaging in reflective, detailed, higher-level cognitive analysis about a decision, especially in high-risk, real-world contexts where they would get bogged down in trivial detail. In such contexts, adolescents need to rely on their awareness that some circumstances are simply so dangerous that they must be avoided at all costs (Brust-Reneck & others, 2017).

In the experiential system, in risky situations it is important for an adolescent to quickly get the *gist,* or meaning, of what is happening and glean that the situation is a dangerous context, which can cue personal values that will protect the adolescent from making a risky decision (Rahimi-Golkhandan & others, 2017; Reyna, 2019; Reyna & Zayas, 2014; Reyna & others, 2018). Further, adolescents who have a higher level of trait inhibition (self-control that helps them to manage their impulses effectively) and find themselves in risky contexts are less likely to engage in risk-taking behavior than their adolescent counterparts who have a lower level of trait inhibition (Chick & Reyna, 2012). However, some experts on adolescent cognition argue that in many cases adolescents benefit from both analytical and experiential systems (Kuhn, 2009).

fuzzy-trace theory dual-process model States that decision making is influenced by two systems—"verbatim" analytical (literal and precise) and gist-based intuition (simple bottom-line meaning)—which operate in parallel; in this model, gist-based intuition benefits adolescent decision making more than analytical thinking does.

Critical Thinking   Among the factors that provide a basis for improvement in critical thinking during adolescence are the following (Keating, 1990):

- Increased speed, automaticity, and capacity of information processing, which free cognitive resources for other purposes;
- Greater breadth of content knowledge in a variety of domains;
- Increased ability to construct new combinations of knowledge;
- A greater range and more spontaneous use of strategies and procedures for obtaining and applying knowledge, such as planning, considering the alternatives, and cognitive monitoring.

ADULTHOOD

Earlier in the chapter, we examined the changes that take place in speed of processing information, attention, memory, and executive function during adulthood. Here we continue to focus on changes in adult cognition, including some gains in thinking in middle adulthood and some of the challenges that older adults face.

Expertise   Experience as well as years of learning and effort may bring the rewards of **expertise,** or extensive, highly organized knowledge and understanding of a particular domain (Ericsson & Pool, 2016; Ericsson & others, 2018). Because it takes so long to attain, expertise shows up more often among middle-aged or older adults than among younger adults (Kim & Hasher, 2005). Individuals may be experts in areas as diverse as physics, art, or knowledge of wine.

Whatever their area of expertise, within that domain experts tend to process information differently from the way novices do (Bransford & others, 2006). Here are some of the characteristics that distinguish experts from novices:

- Experts are more likely to rely on their accumulated experience to solve problems.
- Experts often process information automatically and analyze it more efficiently when solving a problem in their domain than novices do.
- Experts have better strategies and shortcuts for solving problems in their domain than novices do.
- Experts are more creative and flexible in solving problems in their domain than novices are.

Stephen J. Hawking was a world-renowned expert in physics. Hawking authored the best-selling book *A Brief History of Time*. Hawking had a neurological disorder that prevented him from walking or talking. He communicated with the aid of a voice-equipped computer. *What distinguishes experts from novices?*
John Phillips/UK Press/Getty Images

Mindfulness   Recall that *mindfulness* involves being alert, mentally present, and cognitively flexible while going through life's everyday activities and tasks. Recently, there has been growing interest in training older adults to use techniques that promote mindfulness, particularly meditation (Fountain-Zaragoza & Prakash, 2017). Some, but not all, studies have shown that mindfulness training improves older adults' cognitive functioning (Kovach & others, 2018; Oken & others, 2018). In one study, a mindfulness-based stress reduction program involving meditation improved older adults' memory and inhibitory control (Lenze & others, 2014).

Education, Work, and Health   Education, work, and health are three important influences on the cognitive functioning of older adults (Calero, 2019; Walker, 2019). They are also three of the most important factors involved in understanding why cohort effects should be taken into account in studying the cognitive functioning of older adults. Indeed, cohort effects are very important to consider in the study of cognitive aging (Schaie, 2013, 2016). For example, one study found that older adults assessed in 2013–2014 engaged in a higher level of abstract reasoning than their counterparts who were assessed two decades earlier (Gerstorf & others, 2015). And a recent study of older adults in 10 European countries revealed improvements in memory between 2004 and 2013, with the changes being especially positive for older adults who had decreases in cardiovascular disease and increases in exercise and educational achievement (Hessel & others, 2018).

Education   Successive generations in America's twentieth century were better educated, and this trend continues in the twenty-first century (Schaie, 2013, 2016). Educational

expertise Having extensive, highly organized knowledge and understanding of a particular domain.

experiences are positively correlated with scores on intelligence tests and information-processing tasks, such as memory exercises (Steffener & others, 2014). One study found that older adults with a higher level of education had better cognitive functioning than those with less education (Rapp & others, 2013).

Not only were today's older adults more likely to go to college when they were young adults than were their parents or grandparents, but greater numbers of older adults are returning to college today to further their education than in past generations. Educational experiences are positively correlated with scores on intelligence tests and information-processing tasks, such as memory exercises (Aiken Morgan, Sims, & Whitfield, 2010). One study revealed that older adults with less education had lower cognitive abilities than those with more education (Lachman & others, 2010). However, for older adults with less education, frequently engaging in cognitive activities improved their episodic memory.

Work   Successive generations have also had work experiences that include a stronger emphasis on cognitively oriented labor. Our great-grandfathers and grandfathers were more likely to be manual laborers than were our fathers, who are more likely to be involved in cognitively oriented occupations. As the industrial society continues to be replaced by the information society, younger generations will have more experience in jobs that require considerable cognitive investment. The increased emphasis on complex information processing in jobs likely enhances an individual's intellectual abilities (Lovden, Backman, & Lindenberger, 2017; Schooler, 2007). For example, in a recent Australian study, older adults who had retired from occupations that involved higher complexity maintained their cognitive advantage over their counterparts whose occupations had involved lower complexity (Lane & others, 2017). In another study, substantive complex work was linked with higher intellectual functioning in older adults (Schooler, Mulatu, & Oates, 1999). Further, another study found that working in an occupation with a high level of mental demands was linked to higher levels of cognitive functioning before retirement and a slower rate of cognitive decline after retirement (Fisher & others, 2014). And in another recent study of older adults working in low-complexity jobs, experiencing novelty in their work (assessed through recurrent work-task changes) was linked with better processing speed and working memory (Oltmanns & others, 2017).

Health   Successive generations have also been healthier in late adulthood as better treatments for a variety of illnesses (such as hypertension) have been developed. Many of these illnesses, such as stroke, heart disease, and diabetes, have a negative impact on intellectual performance (Callisaya & others, 2019; Hagenaars & others, 2019). For example, in a recent review of older adults with type 2 diabetes, it was concluded that the disease was linked with an increase in cognitive impairment (Riederer & others, 2017). In addition, a recent study of the oldest-old Chinese revealed that early-stage chronic kidney disease was associated with cognitive decline (Bai & others, 2017). Researchers also have found age-related cognitive decline in adults with mood disorders such as depression (Farioli-Veccioli & others, 2018; Wei & others, 2019). Thus, some of the decline in intellectual performance found for older adults is likely due to health-related factors rather than to age per se (Drew & others, 2017).

A number of research studies have found that exercise is linked to improved cognitive functioning (Strandberg, 2019; Walker, 2019). Walking or any other aerobic exercise appears to get blood and oxygen pumping to the brain, which can help people think more clearly. For example, a recent study of older adults revealed that moderate to intense physical activity modified the depression-cognition connection and preserved cognitive function (Hu & others, 2019).

Dietary patterns also are linked to cognitive functioning in older adults (Perkisas & Vandewoude, 2019). For example, a recent research review concluded that multinutrient approaches using the Mediterranean diet are linked to a lower risk of cognitive impairment (Abbatecola, Russo, & Barbieri, 2018).

A final aspect of health that is related to cognitive functioning in older adults is *terminal decline*. This concept emphasizes that changes in cognitive functioning may be linked more to distance from death or cognition-related pathology than to distance from birth (Bendayan & others, 2017; Wilson & others, 2018). In one study, on average, a faster rate of cognitive decline occurred about 7.7 years prior to death and varied across individuals (Muniz-Terrera & others,

How are education, work, and health linked to cognitive functioning in older adults?
(*Top to bottom*): Silverstock/Digital VisionGetty Images; View Stock/Getty Images; Tom Grill/Getty Images

2013). Also, in a recent Swedish study, time to death was a good predictor of cognitive decline over time (Bendayan & others, 2017).

Cognitive Neuroscience and Aging   Certain regions of the brain are involved in links between aging, brain health, and cognitive functioning (Kinugawa, 2019; Nyberg & Pudas, 2019; Park & Festini, 2018). In this section, we further explore the substantial increase in interest in the brain's role in aging and cognitive functioning. The field of *developmental cognitive neuroscience* has emerged as the major discipline that studies links between development, the brain, and cognitive functioning (Benetos, 2019; Kinugawa, 2019; Park & Festini, 2018). This field especially relies on brain-imaging techniques, such as functional magnetic resonance imaging (fMRI), positron-emission tomography (PET), and DTI (diffusion tensor imaging), to reveal the areas of the brain that are activated when individuals are engaging in certain cognitive activities (Catchlove & others, 2019; Filip & others, 2019; Zavaliangos-Petropulu & others, 2019). For example, as an older adult is asked to encode and then retrieve verbal materials or images of scenes, the older adult's brain activity will be monitored by an fMRI brain scan.

Changes in the brain can influence cognitive functioning, and changes in cognitive functioning can influence the brain. For example, aging of the brain's prefrontal cortex may produce a decline in working memory. And when older adults do not regularly use their working memory, neural connections in the prefrontal lobe may atrophy. Further, cognitive interventions that activate older adults' working memory may increase these neural connections.

Although it is in its infancy as a field, the cognitive neuroscience of aging is beginning to uncover some important links between aging, the brain, and cognitive functioning (Kinugawa, 2019; Strandberg, 2019). These include the following:

- Neural circuits in specific regions of the brain's prefrontal cortex decline, and this decline is linked to poorer performance by older adults on complex reasoning tasks, working memory, and episodic memory tasks (Park & Festini, 2018; Reuter-Lorenz & Lustig, 2017) (see Figure 16).
- Older adults are more likely than younger adults to use both hemispheres of the brain to compensate for age-related declines in attention, memory, and language (Davis & others, 2012; Reuter-Lorenz & Lustig, 2017). Two neuroimaging studies revealed that better memory performance in older adults was linked to higher levels of activity in both hemispheres of the brain in processing information (Angel & others, 2011; Manenti, Cotelli, & Miniussi, 2011).
- Functioning of the hippocampus declines but to a lesser degree than the functioning of the frontal lobes in older adults (Antonenko & Floel, 2014). In K. Warner Schaie's (2013) research, individuals whose memory and executive function declined in middle age had more hippocampal atrophy in late adulthood, while those whose memory and executive function improved in middle age did not show a decline in hippocampal functioning in late adulthood.
- Patterns of neural decline with aging are more evident for retrieval than encoding (Gutchess & others, 2005).
- Compared with younger adults, older adults often show greater activity in the frontal and parietal lobes of the brain on simple tasks, but as attentional demands increase, older adults display less effective functioning in the frontal and parietal lobes of the brain that involve cognitive control (Campbell & others, 2012).
- Cortical thickness in the frontoparietal network predicts executive function in older adults (Schmidt & others, 2016).
- Younger adults have better connectivity between brain regions than older adults do (Archer & others, 2016; Damoiseaux, 2017; Madden & Parks, 2017).
- An increasing number of cognitive and fitness training studies include brain-imaging techniques such as fMRI to assess the results of such training on brain functioning (Erickson & Oberlin, 2017; Kinugawa,

developmental **connection**

Work

Cognitive ability is one of the best predictors of job performance in older adults. Connect to "Schools, Achievement, and Work."

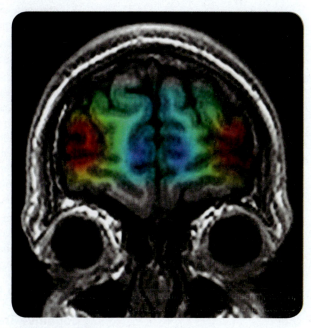

FIGURE 16

THE PREFRONTAL CORTEX. Advances in neuroimaging are allowing researchers to make significant progress in connecting changes in the brain with cognitive development. Shown here is an fMRI of the brain's prefrontal cortex. *What links have been found between the prefrontal cortex, aging, and cognitive development?*
Courtesy of Dr. Sam Gilbert, Institute of Cognitive Neuroscience, UK

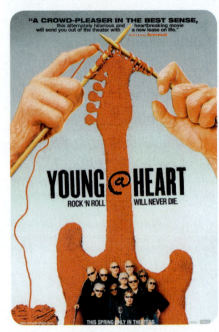

The Young@Heart chorus—whose average age is 80. Young@Heart became a hit documentary in 2008. The documentary displays the singing talents, energy, and optimism of a remarkable group of older adults, who clearly are on the "use it" side of "use it or lose it."
AF Archive/Alamy

2019; Walker, 2019). In one study, older adults who walked one hour a day three days a week for six months showed increased volume in the frontal and temporal lobes of the brain (Colcombe & others, 2006).

Denise Park and Patricia Reuter-Lorenz (2009; Reuter-Lorenz & Park, 2014) proposed a neurocognitive scaffolding view of connections between the aging brain and cognition. In this view, increased activation in the prefrontal cortex with aging reflects an adaptive brain that is compensating for the challenges of declining neural structures and function, as well as declines in various aspects of cognition, including working memory and long-term memory. Scaffolding involves the use of complementary neural circuits to protect cognitive functioning in an aging brain. Among the factors that can strengthen brain scaffolding are cognitive engagement and exercise (Kinugawa, 2019; Walker, 2019).

Use It or Lose It Changes in cognitive activity patterns might result in disuse and consequent atrophy of cognitive skills (Calero, 2019; Kinugawa, 2019; Kunzmann, 2019; Lovden, Backman, & Lindenberger, 2017). This concept is captured in the expression "use it or lose it." Mental activities that are likely to benefit the maintenance of cognitive skills in older adults include reading books, doing crossword puzzles, and attending lectures and concerts (Park & Festini, 2018). "Use it or lose it" also is a significant component of the engagement model of cognitive optimization that emphasizes how intellectual and social engagement can buffer age-related declines in intellectual development (Reuter-Lorenz & Park, 2014). The following studies support the "use it or lose it" concept and the engagement model of cognitive optimization:

- When middle-aged and older adults participated in intellectually engaging activities, it served to buffer them against cognitive decline (Hultsch & others, 1999).
- In the Baltimore Experience Corps program, an activities engagement–health promotion for older adults that involved their volunteerism in underserved urban elementary schools—improved older adults' cognitive and brain functioning (Carlson & others, 2015; Parisi & others, 2012, 2014, 2015).
- Catholic priests 65 years and older who regularly read books, did crossword puzzles, or otherwise exercised their minds were 47 percent less likely to develop Alzheimer disease than priests who rarely engaged in these activities (Wilson & others, 2002).
- Reading daily was linked to reduced mortality in men in their seventies (Jacobs & others, 2008).
- Older adults indicated how often they participated in six activities—reading, writing, doing crossword puzzles, playing card or board games, having group discussions, and playing music—on a daily basis (Hall & others, 2009). Across the five years of the study, the point at which memory loss accelerated was assessed and it was found that for each additional activity the older adult engaged in, the onset of rapid memory loss was delayed by 0.18 years. For older adults who participated in 11 activities per week compared with their counterparts who engaged in only 4 activities per week, for example, the point at which accelerated memory decline occurred was delayed by 1.29 years.
- A study of older adults over a 12-year period found that those who reduced their cognitive lifestyle activities (such as using a computer, playing bridge) subsequently showed declining cognitive functioning in verbal speed, episodic memory, and semantic memory (Small & others, 2012). The decline in cognitive functioning was linked to subsequent lower engagement in social activities.

To read further about "use it or lose it," see *Connecting Development to Life*.

Cognitive Training If older adults are losing cognitive skills, can these skills be regained through training? An increasing number of research studies indicate that they can be restored to some extent (Bonfiglio & others, 2019; Calero, 2019; Kinugawa, 2019; Lopez-Higes & others, 2018).

Consider a study of 60- to 90-year-olds which found that sustained engagement in cognitively demanding, novel activities improved the older adults' episodic memory (Park & others, 2014). To produce this result, the older adults spent an average of 16.5 hours a week for three months learning to quilt or how to use digital photography. Consider also a study of 60- to 90-year-olds in which iPad training 15 hours a week for 3 months improved their episodic

The Remarkable Helen Small

In 2010, 90-year-old Helen Small completed her master's degree at the University of Texas at Dallas (UT-Dallas). The topic of her master's degree research project was romantic relationships in late adulthood. Helen said that she only interviewed one individual who was older than she was—a 92-year-old man.

I (your author, John Santrock) first met Helen when she took my undergraduate course in life-span development in 2006. After the first test, Helen stopped showing up and I wondered what had happened to her. It turns out that she had broken her shoulder when she tripped over a curb while hurrying to class. The next semester, she took my class again and did a great job in it, even though the first several months she had to take notes with her left hand (she's right-handed) because of her lingering shoulder problem.

Helen grew up in the Great Depression and first went to college in 1938 at the University of Akron, where she only attended for one year. She got married and her marriage lasted 62 years. After her husband's death, Helen went back to college. When I interviewed her several years ago, she told me that she had promised her mother that she would finish college. Her most important advice for college students: "Finish college and be persistent. When you make a commitment, always see it through. Don't quit. Go after what you want in life."

Helen not only was a cognitively fit older adult, she also was physically fit. She regularly worked out—aerobically on a treadmill for about 30 minutes and then on six different weight machines.

What struck me most about Helen when she took my undergraduate course in life-span development was how appreciative she was of the opportunity to learn and how tenaciously she pursued studying and doing well in the course. Helen was quite popular with the younger students in the course and she was a terrific role model for them.

Helen Small with the author of your text, John Santrock, in his undergraduate course on life-span development at the University of Texas at Dallas in spring 2012. Working around her busy schedule, Helen would return each semester to talk with students in the class about cognitive aging.
Dr. John Santrock

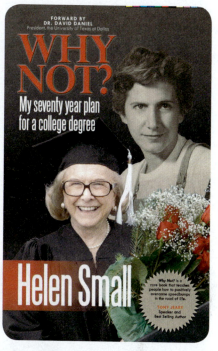

Helen Small published her first book, *Why Not? My Seventy Year Plan for a College Degree,* in 2011 at the age of 91.
Courtesy of Helen Small

After her graduation, I asked her what she planned to do during the next few years and she responded, "I've got to figure out what I'm going to do with the rest of my life." Helen came back each semester to my course in life-span development when we were discussing cognitive aging. She wowed the class and was an inspiration to all who came in contact with her.

What did Helen do to stay cognitively fit? She worked as a public ambassador both for Dr. Denise Park's Center for Vital Longevity at UT-Dallas and the Perot Science Museum. And Helen was active in delivering meals through the Meals on Wheels organization that seeks to reduce hunger and social isolation in older adults. She also wrote her first book: *Why Not? My Seventy Year Plan for a College Degree* (Small, 2011). It's a wonderful, motivating invitation to live your life fully and reach your potential no matter what your age. Following an amazing, fulfilling life, Helen Small passed away in 2017 at the age of 97.

memory and processing speed more than engaging in social or non-challenging activities (Chan & others, 2016).

Researchers are also finding that improving the physical fitness of older adults can improve their cognitive functioning (Bangsbo & others, 2019; Erickson & Oberlin, 2017; Strandberg, 2019; Walker, 2019). A review of studies revealed that aerobic fitness training for older adults improved their performance in the areas of planning, scheduling, working memory, resistance to distraction, and processing involving multiple tasks (Colcombe & Kramer, 2003). In a research review, it was concluded that Exergaming was linked to improved cognitive functioning in older adults (Ogawa, You, & Leveille, 2016). Also, in a recent study, engagement in physical activity in late adulthood was linked to decreased cognitive decline (Gow, Pattie, & Deary, 2017). And in a recent meta-analysis it was concluded that meditation, Tai Chi, and yoga interventions improved older adults' cognitive functioning (Chan & others, 2019).

Meta-examinations of four longitudinal observational studies (Long Beach Longitudinal Study; Origins of Variance in the Oldest-old [Octo-Twin] Study in Sweden; Seattle Longitudinal Study; and Victoria Longitudinal Study in Canada) of older adults' naturalistic cognitive activities found that changes in cognitive activity predicted cognitive outcomes as long as two decades later (Brown & others, 2012; Lindwall & others, 2012; Mitchell & others, 2012; Rebok & others, 2014). However, the hypothesis that engaging in cognitive activity at an earlier point in development would improve older adults' ability to later withstand cognitive decline was not supported. On a positive note, when older adults continued to increase their engagement in cognitive and physical activities, they were better able to maintain their cognitive functioning in late adulthood.

The Stanford Center for Longevity (2011) and together the Stanford Center for Longevity and the Max Planck Institute for Human Development (2014) reported information based on a consensus of leading scientists in the field of aging on the extent to which the cognitive skills of older adults can be improved. One of their concerns is the misinformation given to the public touting products that supposedly improve the functioning of the mind but for which there is no scientific evidence (Willis & Belleville, 2016). Nutritional supplements and software products have been advertised as "magic bullets" to slow the decline of mental functioning and improve the mental ability of older adults. Some of the claims are reasonable but not scientifically tested, and others are unrealistic and implausible. A research review of dietary supplements and cognitive aging linked ginkgo biloba to improvements in some aspects of attention in older adults and omega-3 polyunsaturated fatty acids to a reduced risk of age-related cognitive decline (Gorby, Brownell, & Falk, 2010). In this research review, there was no evidence of cognitive improvements in aging adults who consumed ginseng and glucose. However, an experimental study with 50- to 75-year-old females found that those who took fish oil for 26 weeks had improved executive function and beneficial effects in a number of areas of brain functioning compared with their female counterparts who took a placebo pill (Witte & others, 2014). In other studies, fish oil supplementation was linked to higher cognitive scores and less atrophy in one or more brain regions (Daiello & others, 2015) and improvements in the working memory of older adults (Boespflug & others, 2016). Overall, though, research has not provided consistent plausible evidence that most dietary supplements can facilitate major cognitive improvements in aging adults over a number of years.

To what extent can training improve the cognitive functioning of older adults?
Stewart Cohen/Pam Ostrow/Blend Images/Alamy

However, some software-based cognitive training games have been found to improve older adults' cognitive functioning (Belchior & others, 2019; Ordonez & others, 2017; Sosa & Lagana, 2019; Szelag, 2018). For example, a study of 60- to 85-year-olds found that playing a multitasking video game that simulates day-to-day driving experiences (NeuroRacer) improved cognitive control skills, such as sustained attention and working memory, after training on the video game and six months later (Anguera & others, 2013). In a recent study, computerized cognitive training slowed the decline in older adults' overall memory performance, an outcome that was linked to enhanced connectivity between the hippocampus and prefrontal cortex (Suo & others, 2016). And in another recent study, cognitive training using virtual-reality-based games with stroke patients improved their attention and memory (Gamito & others, 2017). Further, in a recent meta-analysis it was concluded that video games have small training effects on improving older adults' memory but no positive outcomes for other cognitive functions (Mansor, Chow, & Halaki, 2019). Also, it is important to consider the possibility that the training games may improve cognitive skills in a laboratory setting but not generalize to gains in the real world.

In sum, some improvements in the cognitive vitality of older adults can be accomplished through cognitive and fitness training (Farioli-Vecchioli & others, 2018; Perkisas & Vandewoude, 2019; Strandberg, 2019). However, the resulting cognitive improvements often occur only when there is a substantial amount of effortful practice over a long period of time (Hambrick, 2014). And, although sustained effortful training can improve the cognitive skills of many older adults, there is some loss in plasticity in late adulthood, especially in those who are 85 and older (Baltes, Lindenberger, & Staudinger, 2006; Gow, Pattie, & Deary, 2017).

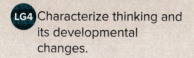

Review *Connect* Reflect

LG4 Characterize thinking and its developmental changes.

Review

- What is thinking?
- What characterizes concept formation and categorization in infancy? What is critical thinking? Do children and scientists think in the same ways? What are two important aspects of problem solving?
- What are some changes in thinking during adolescence?
- What are some changes in thinking in adulthood?

Connect

- You've learned that the nature-nurture debate examines the extent to which development is influenced by nature and by nurture. Which side of the debate would be reflected in the dual-process model that attempts to explain adolescent decision making and the "use it or lose it" view of cognitive aging?

Reflect *Your Own Personal Journey of Life*

- Choose an area in which you consider yourself at least somewhat of an expert. Compare your ability to learn in this field with the ability of a novice.

5 Metacognition

LG5 Define metacognition and summarize its developmental changes.

| What Is Metacognition? | Theory of Mind | Metacognition in Adolescence and Adulthood |

As mentioned at the beginning of this chapter, metacognition is "thinking about thinking or knowing about knowing." John Flavell (1971, 1976) pioneered theory and research on metacognition, which has developed into a major research field in the study of cognitive development. In this section, we examine the role of metacognition in performing cognitive tasks, theory of mind, children's memory abilities, and metacognition in adolescents and adults.

WHAT IS METACOGNITION?

Metacognition can take many forms. It includes thinking about and knowing when and where to use particular strategies for learning or for solving problems (Alibali, Brown, & Menendez, 2019; Fergus & Bardeen, 2019). Conceptualization of metacognition includes several dimensions of executive function, such as planning (deciding how much time to spend focusing on a task, for example), evaluation (monitoring progress toward task completion, for example), and self-regulation (modifying strategies as the task progresses, for example) (Dimmitt & McCormick, 2012).

Metacognition helps people to perform many cognitive tasks more effectively (Bellon, Fias, & De Smedt, 2019; Graham & Harris, 2019; Morris, Savani, & Fincher, 2019). A study of young children found that their metacognitive ability in the numerical domain predicted their school-based math knowledge (Vo & others, 2014). Also, a study of college students revealed that metacognition was a key factor in their ability to engage effectively in critical thinking (Magno, 2010). Another study found that metacognition played an important role in adolescents' ability to generate effective hypotheses about solving problems (Kim & Pedersen, 2010).

Metamemory, individuals' knowledge about memory, is an especially important form of metacognition. Metamemory includes general knowledge about memory, such as knowing that recognition tests (for example, multiple-choice questions) are easier than recall tests (for example, essay questions). It also encompasses knowledge about one's own memory, such as knowing whether you have studied enough for an upcoming test.

By 5 or 6 years of age, children usually know that familiar items are easier to learn than unfamiliar ones, that short lists are easier to remember than long ones, that recognition is

Cognitive developmentalist John Flavell is a pioneer in providing insights about children's thinking. Among his many contributions are establishing the field of metacognition and conducting numerous studies in this area, including metamemory and theory of mind studies.
Courtesy of Dr. John Flavell

metamemory Knowledge about memory.

easier than recall, and that forgetting becomes more likely over time (Lyon & Flavell, 1993). However, in other ways young children's metamemory is limited. They don't understand that related items are easier to remember than unrelated ones or that remembering the gist of a story is easier than remembering information verbatim (Kreutzer, Leonard, & Flavell, 1975). By fifth grade, students understand that gist recall is easier than verbatim recall.

Preschool children also have an inflated opinion of their memory abilities. For example, in one study, a majority of preschool children predicted that they would be able to recall all ten items on a list of ten items. When tested, none of the young children managed this feat (Flavell, Friedrichs, & Hoyt, 1970). As they move through the elementary school years, children give more realistic evaluations of their memory skills (Schneider, 2011).

Preschool children also have little appreciation for the importance of cues for memory, such as "It helps when you can think of an example of it." By 7 or 8 years of age, children better appreciate the importance of cueing for memory.

In general, children's understanding of their memory abilities and their skill in evaluating their performance on memory tasks are relatively poor at the beginning of the elementary school years but improve considerably by 11 to 12 years of age (Bjorklund & Rosenbaum, 2000).

THEORY OF MIND

Even young children are curious about the nature of the human mind (Bass & others, 2019; Devine & Hughes, 2018, 2019; Wellman, 2015). They have a **theory of mind,** which refers to awareness of one's own mental processes and the mental processes of others. Studies of theory of mind view the child as "a thinker who is trying to explain, predict, and understand people's thoughts, feelings, and utterances" (Harris, 2006, p. 847).

theory of mind Thoughts about how one's own mental processes work and the mental processes of others.

Developmental Changes in Children   Although whether infants have a theory of mind continues to be questioned by some (Rakoczy, 2012), the consensus is that some changes occur quite early in development, as we see next (Scott & Baillargeon, 2017). From 18 months to 3 years of age, children begin to understand three mental states:

- *Perceptions.* By 2 years of age, children recognize that another person will see what's in front of her own eyes instead of what's in front of the child's eyes (Lempers, Flavell, & Flavell, 1977), and by 3 years of age, they realize that looking leads to knowing what's inside a container (Pratt & Bryant, 1990).
- *Emotions.* The child can distinguish between positive (for example, happy) and negative (for example, sad) emotions. A child might say, "Tommy feels bad."
- *Desires.* All humans have some sort of desires. But when do children begin to recognize that someone else's desires may differ from their own? Toddlers recognize that if people want something, they will try to get it. For instance, a child might say, "I want my mommy."

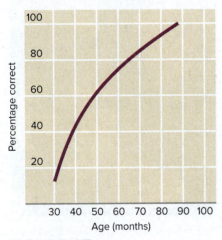

FIGURE 17

DEVELOPMENTAL CHANGES IN FALSE-BELIEF PERFORMANCE. False-belief performance—the child's understanding that a person has a false belief that contradicts reality—dramatically increases from 2½ years of age through the middle of the elementary school years. In a summary of the results of many studies, 2½-year-olds gave incorrect responses about 80 percent of the time (Wellman, Cross, & Watson, 2001). At 3 years 8 months, they were correct about 50 percent of the time and, after that, they gave increasingly correct responses.

Two- to three-year-olds understand the way that desires are related to actions and to simple emotions. For example, they understand that people will search for what they want and that if they obtain it, they are likely to feel happy, but if they don't get it they will keep searching for it and are likely to feel sad or angry (Wellman & Woolley, 1990). Children also refer to desires earlier and more frequently than they refer to cognitive states such as thinking and knowing (Bartsch & Wellman, 1995).

One of the landmark developments in understanding others' desires is recognizing that someone else may have desires that differ from one's own (Wellman, 2011, 2015). Eighteen-month-olds understand that their own food preferences may not match the preferences of others—they will give an adult the food to which she says "Yummy!" even if the food is something that the infants detest (Repacholi & Gopnik, 1997). As they get older, they can verbalize that they themselves do not like something but an adult might (Flavell & others, 1992).

Between the ages of 3 and 5, children come to understand that the mind can represent objects and events accurately or inaccurately (Tompkins & others, 2017). The realization that people can have *false beliefs*—beliefs that are not true—develops in a majority of children by the time they are 5 years old (Wellman, Cross, & Watson, 2001) (see Figure 17).

This point is often described as a pivotal one in understanding the mind—recognizing that beliefs are not just mapped directly into the mind from the surrounding world, but also that different people can have different, and sometimes incorrect, beliefs (Grosso & others, 2019; Liu & others, 2008; Tompkins, Farrar, & Montgomery, 2019). In a classic false-belief task, young children were shown a Band-Aids box and asked what was inside it (Jenkins & Astington, 1996). To the children's surprise, the box actually contained pencils. When asked what a child who had never seen the box would think was inside it, 3-year-olds typically responded, "Pencils." However, the 4- and 5-year-olds, grinning at the anticipation of the false beliefs of other children who had not seen what was inside the box, were more likely to say "Band-Aids."

In a similar task, children are told a story about Sally and Anne: Sally places a toy in a basket and then leaves the room (see Figure 18). In her absence, Anne takes the toy from the basket and places it in a box. Children are asked where Sally will look for the toy when she returns. The major finding is that 3-year-olds tend to fail false-belief tasks, saying that Sally will look in the box (even though Sally could not know that the toy had been moved to this new location). Four-year-olds and older children tend to pass the task, correctly saying that Sally will have a "false belief"—she will think the object is in the basket, even though that belief is now false. The conclusion from these studies is that children younger than 4 years old do not understand that it is possible to have a false belief.

However, there are reasons to question the focus on this one supposedly pivotal moment in the development of a theory of mind. For example, the false-belief task is a complicated one that involves a number of factors such as the characters in the story and all of their individual actions (Bloom & German, 2000). Children also have to disregard their own knowledge in making predictions about what others would think, which is difficult for young children (Birch & Bloom, 2003). Another important issue is that there is more to understanding the minds of others than this false-belief task would indicate.

One example of a limitation in 3- to 5-year-olds' understanding the mind is how they think about thinking. Preschoolers often underestimate when mental activity is likely to take place. For example, they sometimes think that a person who is sitting quietly or reading is not actually thinking very much (Flavell, Green, & Flavell, 1995). Their understanding of their own thinking is also limited. One study revealed that even 5-year-olds have difficulty reporting their thoughts (Flavell, Green, & Flavell, 1995). Children were asked to think quietly about the room in their home where they kept their toothbrushes. Shortly after this direction, many children denied they had been thinking at all and failed to mention either a toothbrush or a bathroom. In another study, when 5-year-olds were asked to try to have no thoughts at all for about 20 seconds, they reported that they were successful at doing this (Flavell, Green, & Flavell, 2000). By contrast, most of the 8-year-olds said they had engaged in mental activity during the 20 seconds and reported specific thoughts.

It is only beyond the preschool years—at approximately 5 to 7 years of age—that children have a deepening appreciation of the mind itself rather than just an understanding of mental states. For example, they begin to recognize that people's behaviors do not necessarily reflect their thoughts and feelings (Flavell, Green, & Flavell, 1993). Not until middle and late childhood do children see the mind as an active constructor of knowledge or a processing center (Flavell, Green, & Flavell, 1998) and move from understanding that beliefs can be false to realizing that the same event can be open to multiple interpretations (Carpendale & Chandler, 1996). For example, in one study, children saw an ambiguous line drawing (for example, a drawing that could be seen as either a duck or a rabbit); one puppet told the child she believed the drawing was a duck while another puppet told the child he believed the drawing was a rabbit (see Figure 19). Before the age of 7, children said that there was one right answer and that it was not okay for the two puppets to have different opinions.

Individual Differences   As in other developmental research, there are individual differences in the ages when children reach certain milestones in their theory of mind (Birch & others, 2017; Devine & Hughes, 2018). *Executive function,* which involves goal-directed behavior and self-control (as discussed earlier in the chapter), is linked to the development of a theory of mind (Carlson & others, 2018; Zelazo & others, 2018). For example, in one executive function task, children are asked to say the word *night* when they see a picture of a sun, and the word *day* when they see a picture of a moon and stars. Children who perform better at executive function tasks seem also to have a better understanding of theory of mind (Benson & Sabbagh, 2017). For example, in one study of 3- to 5-year-old children, earlier development of

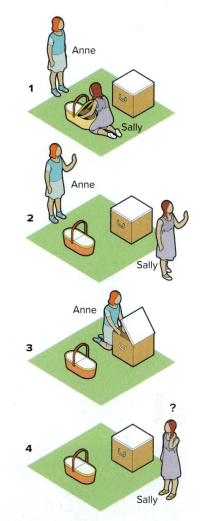

FIGURE 18

THE SALLY AND ANNE FALSE-BELIEF TASK. In the false-belief task, the skit above in which Sally has a basket and Anne has a box is shown to children. Sally places a toy in her basket and then leaves. While Sally is gone and can't watch, Anne removes the toy from Sally's basket and places it in her box. Sally then comes back and the children are asked where they think Sally will look for her toy. Children are said to "pass" the false-belief task if they understand that Sally looks in her basket first before realizing the toy isn't there.

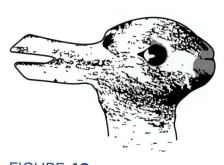

FIGURE 19

AMBIGUOUS LINE DRAWING

executive function predicted theory of mind performance, especially on false belief tasks (Doenyas, Yavuz, & Selcuk, 2018).

Among other factors that influence children's theory of mind development are advances in prefrontal cortex functioning (Powers, Chavez, & Heatherton, 2016), engagement in pretend play (Lillard & Kavanaugh, 2014), and various aspects of social interaction (Hughes & Devine, 2015). Among the social interaction factors that advance children's theory of mind are being securely attached to parents who engage children in mental state talk ("That's a good thought you have" or "Can you tell what he's thinking?") (Devine & Hughes, 2018; Laranjo & others, 2010), having older siblings and friends who engage in mental state talk (Devine & Hughes, 2018; Hughes & others, 2010), and living in a higher-socioeconomic-status family (Devine & Hughes, 2019). A recent study found that parental engagement in mind-mindedness (viewing children as mental agents by making mind-related comments to them) advanced preschool children's theory of mind (Hughes, Devine, & Wang, 2018).

Also, research indicates that children who have an advanced theory of mind are more popular with their peers and have better social skills in peer relations (Peterson & others, 2016; Slaughter & others, 2014).

Theory of Mind and Autism Another individual difference in understanding the mind involves autism (Jones & others, 2018). It is estimated that approximately 1 in 68 children have some type of autism (Christensen & others, 2016). Autism can usually be diagnosed by the age of 3 years and sometimes earlier. Children with autism show a number of behaviors different from other children their age, including deficits in theory of mind, social interaction, and communication, as well as repetitive behaviors or interests (Berenguer & others, 2018; Garon, Smith, & Bryson, 2018; von dem Hagen & Bright, 2017). A recent study found that theory of mind predicted the severity of autism in children (Hoogenhout & Malcolm-Smith, 2017).

A young boy with autism. *What are some characteristics of autistic children? What are some deficits in autistic children's theory of mind?*
©Robin Nelson/PhotoEdit

Developmental Changes in Theory of Mind in Adolescence and Adulthood Most research on theory of mind has focused on children. Recently, though, there have been efforts to chart developmental changes in theory of mind in adolescence and adulthood.

The social worlds of adolescence become more complex than in childhood, and the importance of interpersonal relationships in adolescence motivates adolescents to understand not only their own but others' minds as well (Tannes & others, 2018). Adolescents also are more likely than children to engage in *recursive thinking*, a term used to describe thinking about what other people are thinking about. With advancing cognitive skills, such as executive function, adolescents are better at understanding and predicting others' behavior than children are (Kilford, Garrett, & Blakemore, 2016). And adolescents are better than children at interpreting others' feelings and motives even when others' feelings and motives are not directly observable, although adolescents still make numerous errors in such efforts (Blakemore, 2018).

British developmental psychologist Sarah-Jayne Blakemore (2012) recently described a task that involves taking another's perspective in an ongoing communication context. The task requires constantly trying to figure out the intentions of the person you are talking with and what they want you to understand, and using their perspective to guide your behavior. In her research, the ability to consider someone else's perspective to guide ongoing decisions and behavior continues to develop well into late adolescence.

For most of adulthood, individuals retain the theory of mind accomplishments they developed in childhood and adolescence, such as those involving belief, desire, knowledge, intention, and perspective taking. An important aspect of adult life is how people employ these concepts to cope with the challenges of their social world, such as detecting when someone is lying or not or keeping up with a fast-moving conversation. But adults don't always use their theory of mind skills in everyday life. In one study, adults did not use their theory of mind skills to discredit a speaker who clearly lacked key facts about a topic (Keysar, Lin, & Barr, 2003). Further, too often adults neglect to take into account others' perspectives at all (Epley & others, 2004).

Research also indicates that theory of mind abilities decline in older adults (Hughes & others, 2019). This decline is likely related to declines in other cognitive skills, such as executive function, and changes in the brain's prefrontal cortex in older adults (Duval & others, 2011).

METACOGNITION IN ADOLESCENCE AND ADULTHOOD

Metacognition is increasingly recognized as a very important cognitive skill not only in adolescence but also in emerging adulthood. Compared with children, adolescents have an increased capacity to monitor and manage cognitive resources to effectively meet the demands of a learning task (Kuhn, 2009). This increased metacognitive ability results in improved cognitive functioning and learning. A longitudinal study revealed that from 12 to 14 years of age, young adolescents increasingly used metacognitive skills and used them more effectively in math and history classes than in other subjects (van der Stel & Veenman, 2010). For example, 14-year-olds monitored their own text comprehension more frequently and did so more effectively than their younger counterparts. Another study documented the importance of metacognitive skills, such as planning, strategizing, and monitoring, in college students' ability to think critically (Magno, 2010).

An important aspect of cognitive functioning and learning is determining how much attention will be allocated to an available resource. Evidence is accumulating that adolescents have a better understanding of how to effectively deploy their attention to different aspects of a task than children do (Kuhn, 2008, 2009). Further, adolescents have a better meta-level understanding of strategies—that is, knowing the best strategy to use and when to use it in performing a learning task.

Keep in mind, though, that there is considerable individual variation in adolescents' metacognition. Indeed, some experts argue that individual variation in metacognition becomes much more pronounced in adolescence than in childhood (Kuhn & Franklin, 2006). Thus, some adolescents are quite good at using metacognition to improve their learning, while others are far less effective.

How might metacognition change as people get older?
Rawpixel/123RF

By middle age, adults have accumulated a great deal of metacognitive knowledge. They can draw on this metacognitive knowledge to help them combat a decline in memory skills. For example, they are likely to understand that they need to have good organizational skills and reminders to help combat the decline in memory skills they face.

Older adults tend to overestimate the memory problems they experience on a daily basis. They seem to be more aware of their memory failures than younger adults and become more anxious about minor forgetfulness than younger adults do (Hoyer & Roodin, 2009). Researchers have found that in general older adults are as accurate as younger adults in monitoring the encoding and retrieval of information (Hertzog & Dixon, 2005), detecting errors when asked to proofread passages, and judging their own performance (Hargis & others, 2017). However, some aspects of monitoring information, such as source memory (discussed earlier in the chapter), decline in older adults (Isingrini, Perrotin, & Souchay, 2008).

Review Connect Reflect

LG5 Define metacognition and summarize its developmental changes.

Review
- What is metacognition? How does metamemory typically change during childhood?
- How does the child's theory of mind change during the preschool years?
- How does metacognition change in adolescence and adulthood?

Connect
- How is metacognition in children different from metacognition in adolescents?

Reflect *Your Own Personal Journey of Life*
- Take an inventory of your study skills. How might you improve your metacognitive study skills?

Information Processing

1 The Information-Processing Approach

 LG1 Explain the information-processing approach and its application to development.

The Information-Processing Approach and Its Application to Development

- The information-processing approach analyzes how individuals encode information, manipulate it, monitor it, and create strategies for handling it. Attention, memory, and thinking are involved in effective information processing. The computer has served as a model for how humans process information.

- In the information-processing approach, children's cognitive development results from their ability to overcome processing limitations by increasingly executing basic operations, expanding information-processing capacity, and acquiring new knowledge and strategies.

- According to Siegler, three important mechanisms of change in children's cognitive skills are encoding (how information gets into memory), automaticity (ability to process information with little or no effort), and strategy construction (creation of new procedures for processing information).

- Children's information processing is characterized by self-modification, and an important aspect of this self-modification involves metacognition—that is, knowing about knowing.

Speed of Processing Information

- Processing speed increases across childhood and adolescence. Processing speed slows in middle and late adulthood. However, strategies that people learn through experience can compensate to some degree for age-related decline in processing speed.

2 Attention

 LG2 Define attention and outline its developmental changes.

What Is Attention?

- Attention is the focusing of mental resources. Four ways that people can allocate their attention are selective attention (focusing on a specific aspect of experience that is relevant while ignoring others that are irrelevant); divided attention (concentrating on more than one activity at the same time); sustained attention (maintaining attention to a selected stimulus for a prolonged period of time; also referred to as vigilance); and executive attention (involving action planning, allocating attention to goals, error detection and compensation, monitoring progress on tasks, and dealing with novel or difficult tasks).

Infancy

- Even newborns can fixate visually on a contour, but as they get older they scan a pattern more thoroughly. Attention in the first year of life is dominated by the orienting/investigative process. Attention in infancy often occurs through habituation and dishabituation. Joint attention plays an important role in infant development, especially in the infant's acquisition of language.

Childhood and Adolescence

- Salient stimuli tend to capture the attention of the preschooler. After 6 or 7 years of age, there is a shift to more cognitive control of attention. Selective attention improves through childhood and adolescence. Multitasking is an example of divided attention, and it can harm adolescents' attention when they are engaging in a challenging task.

Adulthood

- Attentional skills often are excellent in early adulthood. Older adults are generally less adept than younger adults at selective and divided attention.

3 Memory

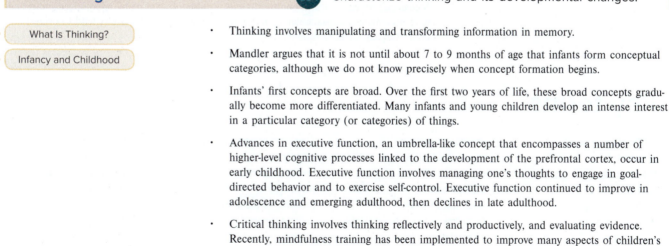

LG3 Describe what memory is and how it changes through the life span.

What Is Memory?	• Memory is the retention of information over time. Psychologists study the processes of memory: how information is initially placed or encoded into memory, how it is retained or stored, and how it is found or retrieved for a certain purpose later. People construct and reconstruct their memories. Schema theory states that people mold memories to fit the information that already exists in their minds.
Infancy	• Infants as young as 2 to 6 months of age display implicit memory, which is memory without conscious recollection, as in memory of perceptual-motor skills. However, many experts believe that explicit memory, which is the conscious memory of facts and experiences, does not emerge until the second half of the first year of life.
	• The hippocampus and frontal lobes of the brain are involved in development of memory in infancy. Older children and adults remember little if anything from the first three years of their lives.
Childhood	• One method of assessing short-term memory (the retention of information for up to 15 to 30 seconds, assuming there is no repetition of the information) is with a memory-span task, on which there are substantial developmental changes through the childhood years.
	• Working memory (a kind of "mental workbench" where individuals manipulate and assemble information when they make decisions, solve problems, and comprehend language) is linked to children's reading comprehension and problem solving.
	• Increasing interest has been shown in children's autobiographical memories, and these memories change developmentally.
	• Young children can remember a great deal of information if they are given appropriate cues and prompts. Strategies can improve children's memory, and older children are more likely to use these than younger children. Imagery and elaboration are two important strategies. Knowledge is an important influence on memory.
Adulthood	• Younger adults have better episodic memory than older adults do. Older adults have more difficulty retrieving semantic information. Working memory decreases in older adults but has some plasticity. Explicit memory is more likely to decline in older adults than is implicit memory. Source memory—remembering where one learned something—declines with age. Controversy surrounds the question of whether prospective memory, which is remembering to do something in the future, declines as adults age.

4 Thinking

LG4 Characterize thinking and its developmental changes.

What Is Thinking?	• Thinking involves manipulating and transforming information in memory.
Infancy and Childhood	• Mandler argues that it is not until about 7 to 9 months of age that infants form conceptual categories, although we do not know precisely when concept formation begins.
	• Infants' first concepts are broad. Over the first two years of life, these broad concepts gradually become more differentiated. Many infants and young children develop an intense interest in a particular category (or categories) of things.
	• Advances in executive function, an umbrella-like concept that encompasses a number of higher-level cognitive processes linked to the development of the prefrontal cortex, occur in early childhood. Executive function involves managing one's thoughts to engage in goal-directed behavior and to exercise self-control. Executive function continued to improve in adolescence and emerging adulthood, then declines in late adulthood.
	• Critical thinking involves thinking reflectively and productively, and evaluating evidence. Recently, mindfulness training has been implemented to improve many aspects of children's development, including self-control.

Adolescence

Adulthood

- Key changes in information processing occur during adolescence, including processes involved in making decisions and exercising critical thinking.

- One aspect of cognition that may improve with aging is expertise. Many aspects of executive function decline in late adulthood, but individual differences occur as well.

- In the twentieth and twenty-first centuries, successive generations of older adults have been better educated, have had work experiences that included a stronger emphasis on cognitively oriented labor, and have been healthier. These cohort effects are linked to higher cognitive functioning.

- There has been increased interest in the cognitive neuroscience of aging that focuses on links between aging, the brain, and cognitive functioning. This field especially relies on fMRI and PET scans to assess brain functioning while individuals are engaging in cognitive tasks. One of the most consistent findings in this field is a decline in the functioning of specific regions in the prefrontal cortex in older adults and links between this decline and poorer performance on tasks that involve complex reasoning, working memory, and episodic memory.

- Some improvements in the cognitive vitality of older adults can be accomplished through cognitive and fitness training. However, such benefits have not been observed in all studies.

5 Metacognition

 LG5 Define metacognition and summarize its developmental changes.

What Is Metacognition?

- Metacognition is thinking about thinking, or knowing about knowing. Metamemory is one aspect of metacognition that has been studied developmentally. By 5 to 6 years of age, children usually know that familiar items are easier to learn than unfamiliar ones and that short lists are easier to remember than long ones. By 7 to 8 years of age, children better appreciate the importance of cues for memory.

Theory of Mind

- Theory of mind is the awareness of one's own mental processes and the mental processes of others. Children begin to understand mental states involving perceptions, desires, and emotions at 2 to 3 years of age, and at 4 to 5 years of age they realize that people can have false beliefs. It is only beyond the early childhood years that children have a deepening appreciation of the mind itself rather than just understanding mental states. Autistic children have difficulty developing a theory of mind. As adolescents experience more complex social worlds, advances in their theory of mind skills occur in areas such as understanding another's intentions. For the most part, theory of mind skills remain intact during most of adulthood but decline in older adults.

Metacognition in Adolescence and Adulthood

- Adolescents have an increased capacity to monitor and manage resources to effectively meet the demands of a learning task, although there is considerable individual variation in metacognition during adolescence.

- Metacognition continues to improve in early adulthood, and many middle-aged individuals have accumulated considerable metacognitive knowledge. Older adults tend to overestimate their everyday memory problems.

key terms

artificial intelligence	executive attention	long-term memory	short-term memory
attention	executive function	memory	source memory
automaticity	expertise	metacognition	strategy construction
concepts	explicit memory	metamemory	sustained attention
critical thinking	fuzzy trace theory	prospective memory	theory of mind
divided attention	fuzzy-trace theory dual-process	schema theory	thinking
elaboration	model	schemas	working memory
encoding	implicit memory	selective attention	
episodic memory	joint attention	semantic memory	

key people

Alan Baddeley

Patricia Bauer

Charles Brainerd

Adele Diamond

John Flavell

Maria Gartstein

Deanna Kuhn

Kathleen Lee

Jean Mandler

Ann Masten

Walter Mischel

Valerie Reyna

Robert Roeser

Mary Rothbart

Carolyn Rovee-Collier

K. Warner Schaie

Robert Siegler

chapter 8

INTELLIGENCE

chapter outline

D-Keine/E+/Getty Images

preview

The concept of intelligence has generated many controversies, including debates about whether intelligence is more strongly influenced by heredity or by environment, whether there is cultural bias in intelligence testing, and whether intelligence tests are misused. We will explore these controversies, as well as the extent to which we have a single intelligence or multiple intelligences, the development of intelligence across the life span, and the extremes of intelligence and creativity.

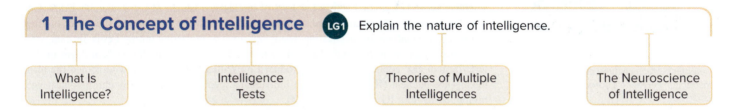

1 The Concept of Intelligence **LG1** Explain the nature of intelligence.

What Is Intelligence? Intelligence Tests Theories of Multiple Intelligences The Neuroscience of Intelligence

Intelligence is one of our most prized possessions. However, even the most intelligent people have not been able to agree on how to define and measure the concept of intelligence.

WHAT IS INTELLIGENCE?

What does the term *intelligence* mean to psychologists? Some experts describe intelligence as the ability to solve problems. Others describe it as the capacity to adapt and learn from experience. Still others argue that intelligence includes characteristics such as creativity and interpersonal skills.

The problem with intelligence is that, unlike height, weight, and age, intelligence cannot be directly measured. We can't peel back a person's scalp and see how much intelligence he or she has. We can evaluate intelligence only *indirectly* by studying and comparing the intelligent acts that people perform.

The primary components of intelligence are similar to the cognitive processes of thinking and memory that we discussed in the chapter on "Information Processing." The differences in how we described these cognitive processes in that chapter, and how we discuss intelligence, lie in the concepts of *individual differences* and assessment (Elkana & others, 2019; Kaufman, Schneider, & Kaufman, 2020). Individual differences are the stable, consistent ways in which people differ from one another (Richler & others, 2019; Sackett & others, 2017). Individual differences in intelligence generally have been measured by intelligence tests designed to tell us whether a person can reason better than others who have taken the test (Bates & Gupta, 2017; Deckert & others, 2019).

How can intelligence be defined? **Intelligence** is the ability to solve problems and to adapt and learn from experiences. But even this broad definition doesn't satisfy everyone. As you will see shortly, Robert J. Sternberg (2018a, b, c) proposes that practical know-how should be considered part of intelligence. In his view, intelligence involves weighing options carefully and acting judiciously, as well as developing strategies to improve shortcomings. Sternberg (2019a, b, c, 2020a, b, c) also recently described intelligence as the ability to adapt to, shape, and select environments. In adapting to the environment, if individuals find the environment suboptimal, they can change it to make it more suitable for their skills and desires.

Also, a definition of intelligence based on a theory such as Vygotsky's would have to include the ability to use the tools of the culture with help from more-skilled individuals. Because intelligence is such an abstract, broad concept, it is not surprising that there are so many different ways to define it.

INTELLIGENCE TESTS

What types of intelligence tests are given to children and adults? What are some contributions and criticisms of intelligence tests?

The Binet Tests   In 1904, the French Ministry of Education asked psychologist Alfred Binet to devise a method to determine which students would not profit from typical school instruction. Binet and his student Theophile Simon developed an intelligence test to fulfill this

> What a piece of work is a man! How noble in reason! How infinite in faculty! In form, in moving, how express and admirable! In action how like an angel! In apprehension how like a god!
>
> **—WILLIAM SHAKESPEARE**
> *English Playwright, 17th Century*

developmental connection

Information Processing

The information-processing approach emphasizes how individuals manipulate information, monitor it, and create strategies for handling it. Connect to "Information Processing."

developmental connection

Social Contexts

Vygotsky's theory emphasizes the social contexts of learning and constructing knowledge through social interaction. Connect to "Cognitive Developmental Approaches."

intelligence The ability to solve problems and to adapt to and learn from experiences.

Alfred Binet constructed the first intelligence test after being asked to create a measure to determine which children could benefit from instruction in France's schools and which could not.
Universal History Archive/Getty Images

request. The test consisted of 30 items ranging from the ability to touch one's nose or ear when asked to the ability to draw designs from memory and to define abstract concepts.

Binet stressed that the core of intelligence consists of complex cognitive processes such as memory, imagery, comprehension, and judgment. In addition, he noted that a developmental approach was crucial for understanding intelligence. He proposed that a child's intellectual ability increases with age. Therefore, he tested potential items and determined the age at which a typical child could answer them correctly. Thus, Binet developed the concept of **mental age (MA),** which is an individual's level of mental development relative to others. For an average child, MA scores correspond to *chronological age (CA),* which is age from birth. A bright child has an MA considerably above CA; a child with a low level of intelligence has an MA considerably below CA.

The Binet test has been revised many times to incorporate advances in the understanding of intelligence and intelligence testing. Many revisions were carried out by Lewis Terman, who developed extensive norms and provided detailed, clear instructions for each problem on the test. Terman also applied a concept introduced by William Stern (1912), who coined the term **intelligence quotient (IQ)** to refer to an individual's mental age divided by chronological age, multiplied by 100: IQ = MA/CA × 100.

If a child's mental age, as measured by the Binet test, was the same as the child's chronological age, then the child's IQ score was 100. If the measured mental age was above chronological age, then the IQ score was greater than 100. If mental age was below chronological age, the IQ score was less than 100. Although this scoring system is no longer used, the term IQ is often still used to refer to a score on a standardized intelligence test.

In 2004, the test, now called the Stanford-Binet 5 (Stanford University is where the revisions have been done), was revised to analyze an individual's responses in five content areas: fluid reasoning, knowledge, quantitative reasoning, visual-spatial reasoning, and working memory. A general composite score also is obtained. Today the test is scored by comparing the test-taker's performance with the results achieved by other people of the same age. The average score is set at 100.

The current Stanford-Binet is given to individuals from age 2 through adulthood. It includes a wide variety of items, some requiring verbal responses, and others, nonverbal responses. For example, a 6-year-old is expected to complete the verbal task of defining at least six words, such as *orange* and *envelope*, and the nonverbal task of tracing a path through a maze. An adult with average intelligence is expected to define such words as *disproportionate* and *regard*, explain a proverb, and compare the concepts of idleness and laziness.

mental age (MA) An individual's level of mental development relative to that of others.

intelligence quotient (IQ) An individual's mental age divided by chronological age, multiplied by 100; devised in 1912 by William Stern.

normal distribution A symmetrical, bell-shaped curve with a majority of the cases falling in the middle of the possible range of scores and few scores appearing toward the extremes of the range.

Over the years, the Stanford-Binet has been given to thousands of children and adults of different ages. By administering the test to large numbers of individuals selected at random from different parts of the United States, researchers have found that the scores approximate a normal distribution (see Figure 1). A **normal distribution** is a symmetrical, bell-shaped curve with a majority of the cases falling in the middle of the range of possible scores and few scores appearing toward the extremes of the range. The Stanford-Binet continues to be one of the most widely used individual tests of intelligence.

The Wechsler Scales Besides the Stanford-Binet, the other most widely used intelligence tests are the Wechsler scales (MacAllister & others, 2019). In 1939, David Wechsler introduced the first of his scales, designed for use with adults (Wechsler, 1939); the current edition is the

FIGURE 1

THE NORMAL CURVE AND STANFORD-BINET IQ SCORES. The distribution of IQ scores approximates a normal curve. Most of the population falls in the middle range of scores. Notice that extremely high and extremely low scores are very rare. Slightly more than two-thirds of the scores fall between 85 and 115. Only about 1 in 50 individuals has an IQ higher than 130, and only about 1 in 50 individuals has an IQ lower than 70.

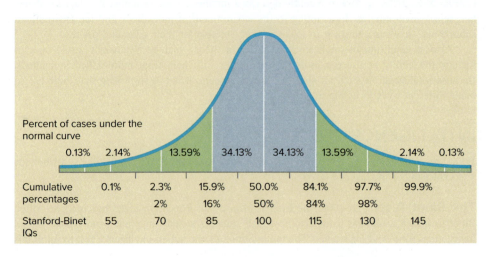

Percent of cases under the normal curve	0.13%	2.14%	13.59%	34.13%	34.13%	13.59%	2.14%	0.13%
Cumulative percentages	0.1%	2.3%	15.9%	50.0%	84.1%	97.7%	99.9%	
		2%	16%	50%	84%	98%		
Stanford-Binet IQs	55	70	85	100	115	130	145	

Wechsler Adult Intelligence Scale–Fourth Edition (WAIS-IV). The Wechsler Intelligence Scale for Children–Fifth Edition (WISC-V) is designed for children and adolescents between the ages of 6 and 16 (Wechsler, 2014). The Wechsler Preschool and Primary Scale of Intelligence–Fourth Edition (WPPSI-IV) is appropriate for children from age 2 years 6 months to 7 years 7 months.

The WISC-V now not only provides an overall IQ score but also yields five composite scores (Verbal Comprehension, Working Memory, Processing Speed, Fluid Reasoning, and Visual Spatial) (Canivez, Watkins, & Dombrowski, 2017). These scores allow the examiner to quickly see whether the individual is strong or weak in different areas of intelligence (Canivez & others, 2019). The Wechsler scales also include 16 verbal and nonverbal subscales. Three of the Wechsler subscales are shown in Figure 2.

The Use and Misuse of Intelligence Tests   Psychological tests are tools. As with all tools, their effectiveness depends on the knowledge, skill, and integrity of the user. A hammer can be used to build a beautiful kitchen cabinet or it can be used as a weapon of assault. Like a hammer, psychological tests can be used for positive purposes or they can be abused.

Intelligence tests have real-world applications as predictors of school performance, job success, and economic growth in a country (Mayer, 2020; Sackett, Shewach, & Dahlke, 2020). For example, scores on tests of general intelligence are substantially correlated with school grades and achievement test performance, both at the time of the test and years later (Brody, 2007). IQ in the sixth grade correlates about +.60 with the number of years of education the individual will eventually obtain (Jencks, 1979). Also, a recent study found that the collective IQ of a country's citizens was linked to its economic growth (Hafer, 2017).

Intelligence tests are moderately correlated with work performance (Lubinski, 2000). Individuals with higher scores on tests designed to measure general intelligence tend to get higher-paying, more prestigious jobs, and are more intrinsically satisfied with their jobs (Ganzach & Fried, 2012; Zagorsky, 2007). However, general IQ tests predict only 10 to 30 percent of the variation in job success, with the majority of job success due to motivation, education, and other factors (Sternberg, 2014). Further, the correlations between IQ and achievement decrease the longer people work at a job, presumably because as they gain more job experience they perform better (Hunt, 1995).

Thus, although there are correlations between IQ scores and academic achievement and occupational success, many other factors contribute to success in school and at work. These include the motivation to succeed, physical and mental health, and social skills (Sternberg, 2003).

The single number provided by many IQ tests can easily lead to false expectations about an individual (Rosnow & Rosenthal, 1996). Sweeping generalizations are too often made on the basis of an IQ score and can become self-fulfilling prophecies (Weinstein, 2004).

Even though they have limitations, tests of intelligence are among psychology's most widely used tools (Dale & others, 2014). To be effective, they should be used in conjunction with other information about an individual. For example, an intelligence test alone should not determine whether a child is placed in a special education or gifted class. The child's developmental history, medical background, performance in school, social competencies, and family experiences should be taken into account as well.

THEORIES OF MULTIPLE INTELLIGENCES

The use of a single score to describe how people perform on intelligence tests implies that intelligence is a general ability, a single trait. Wechsler scales provide scores for a number of intellectual skills, as well as an overall score. Do people have some general mental ability that determines how they perform on all of these tests? Or is intelligence a label for a combination of several distinct abilities? And do conventional intelligence tests measure everything that should be considered part of intelligence? Psychologists disagree about the answers to these questions.

Sternberg's Triarchic Theory   Robert J. Sternberg (1986, 2004, 2010, 2014, 2016, 2017, 2018a, b, c, 2019a, b, c, 2020a, b, c) notes that traditional IQ tests fail to measure some

Verbal Subscales

Similarities

A child must think logically and abstractly to answer a number of questions about how things might be similar.

Example: "In what way are a lion and a tiger alike?"

Comprehension

This subscale is designed to measure an individual's judgment and common sense.

Example: "What is the advantage of keeping money in a bank?"

Nonverbal Subscales

Block Design

A child must assemble a set of multicolored blocks to match designs that the examiner shows. Visual-motor coordination, perceptual organization, and the ability to visualize spatially are assessed.

Example: "Use the four blocks on the left to make the pattern on the right."

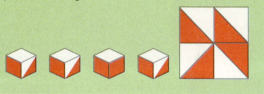

FIGURE 2

SAMPLE SUBSCALES OF THE WECHSLER INTELLIGENCE SCALE FOR CHILDREN—FIFTH EDITION (WISC-V). The Wechsler includes 16 verbal and nonverbal subscales. Three of the subscales are shown here.

Robert J. Sternberg, who developed the triarchic theory of intelligence.
Courtesy of Dr. Robert Sternberg

important dimensions of intelligence. Sternberg proposes a triarchic theory of intelligence involving three main types of intelligence: analytical, creative, and practical.

Sternberg developed the **triarchic theory of intelligence,** which states that intelligence comes in three forms: (1) *analytical intelligence,* which refers to the ability to analyze, judge, evaluate, compare, and contrast; (2) *creative intelligence,* which consists of the ability to create, design, invent, originate, and imagine; and (3) *practical intelligence,* which involves the ability to use, apply, implement, and put ideas into practice.

Sternberg (2018a, b, 2019a, 2020a) says that children with different triarchic patterns "look different" in school. Students with high analytical ability tend to be favored in conventional schooling. They often do well under direct instruction, in which the teacher lectures and gives students objective tests. They often are considered to be "smart" students who get good grades, show up in high-level tracks, do well on traditional tests of intelligence and the SAT, and later get admitted to competitive colleges.

In contrast, children who are high in creative intelligence often are not on the top rung of their class. Many teachers have specific expectations about how assignments should be done, and creatively intelligent students may not conform to those expectations. Instead of giving conformist answers, they give unique answers, for which they might get reprimanded or marked down. No teacher wants to discourage creativity, but Sternberg stresses that too often a teacher's desire to increase students' knowledge suppresses creative thinking.

Like children high in creative intelligence, children who are high in practical intelligence often do not relate well to the demands of school. However, many of these children do well outside the classroom's walls. They may have excellent social skills and good common sense. As adults, some become successful managers, entrepreneurs, or politicians in spite of having undistinguished school records.

Gardner's Theory of Multiple Intelligences According to Howard Gardner (1983, 1993, 2002, 2016), people have multiple intelligences, and IQ tests measure only a few of these. He argues that IQ tests measure verbal, math, and spatial aspects of intelligence while overlooking a number of other abilities. For evidence of the existence of multiple intelligences, Gardner uses information about the ways in which certain cognitive abilities survive particular types of brain damage. He also points to child prodigies and to some individuals with intellectual disability or autism who have an extraordinary skill in a particular domain. An example was portrayed by Dustin Hoffman in the movie *Rain Man.* Hoffman's character was autistic but had a remarkable computing ability. In one scene, he helped his brother successfully gamble in Las Vegas by keeping track of all the cards that had been played.

Gardner has proposed eight types of intelligence. They are described here, along with examples of the occupations in which they are regarded as strengths (Campbell, Campbell, & Dickinson, 2004):

Howard Gardner, working with a young child.
How many intelligences does Gardner believe there are and what are they?
Steve Hansen/The LIFE Images Collection/Getty Images

- *Verbal.* The ability to think in words and use language to express meaning (occupations: authors, journalists, speakers)
- *Mathematical.* The ability to carry out mathematical operations (occupations: scientists, engineers, accountants)
- *Spatial.* The ability to think three-dimensionally (occupations: architects, artists, sailors)
- *Bodily-kinesthetic.* The ability to manipulate objects and be physically adept (occupations: surgeons, craftspeople, dancers, athletes)
- *Musical.* A sensitivity to pitch, melody, rhythm, and tone (occupations: composers, musicians, and sensitive listeners)
- *Interpersonal.* The ability to understand and effectively interact with others (occupations: successful teachers, mental health professionals)
- *Intrapersonal.* The ability to understand oneself (occupations: theologians, psychologists)
- *Naturalist.* The ability to observe patterns in nature and understand natural and human-made systems (occupations: farmers, botanists, ecologists, landscapers)

Recently, Gardner has considered adding a ninth type of intelligence to his list of multiple intelligences—existentialist, which involves exploring and finding meaning in life, especially regarding questions about life, death, and existence.

Gardner notes that each of the eight intelligences can be destroyed by brain damage, that each involves unique cognitive skills, and that each shows up in exaggerated fashion in the gifted and in

triarchic theory of intelligence Sternberg's theory that intelligence consists of analytical intelligence, creative intelligence, and practical intelligence.

individuals with intellectual disability or autism. According to Gardner, everyone has all of these intelligences but to varying degrees. As a result, we prefer to learn and process information in different ways. People perform best when they can apply their strong intelligences to the task at hand.

Emotional Intelligence   Both Sternberg's and Gardner's theories include one or more categories related to social intelligence. In Sternberg's theory, the category is practical intelligence; in Gardner's theory, they are interpersonal intelligence and intrapersonal intelligence. Another theory that emphasizes interpersonal, intrapersonal, and practical aspects of intelligence involves **emotional intelligence,** a concept that has been popularized by Daniel Goleman (1995) in his book *Emotional Intelligence.* The concept of emotional intelligence was initially developed by Peter Salovey and John Mayer (1990), who define it as the ability to perceive and express emotion accurately and adaptively (such as taking the perspective of others), to understand emotion and emotional knowledge (such as understanding the roles that emotions play in friendship and marriage), to use feelings to facilitate thought (such as being in a positive mood, which is linked to creative thinking), and to manage emotions in oneself and others (such as being able to control one's anger).

There continues to be considerable interest in the concept of emotional intelligence (Costa & others, 2018; Evans, Hughes, & Steptoe-Warren, 2019; Gomez-Leal & others, 2018; Yip & others, 2019). One study of college students revealed that scores on both a test of general mental abilities and an assessment of emotional intelligence were linked to academic performance, although the general mental abilities test was a better predictor (Song & others, 2010). Also, one study revealed that emotional intelligence abilities were linked to academic achievement above and beyond cognitive and personality factors (Lanciano & Curci, 2014). And in a recent study of older adults, emotional intelligence was positively linked to their cognitive functioning (Saad & others, 2019).

Critics argue that emotional intelligence broadens the concept of intelligence too far to be useful and has not been adequately assessed and researched.

Do People Have One or Many Intelligences?   Figure 3 compares Sternberg's, Gardner's, and Salovey/Mayer's views of intelligence. Notice that Sternberg's view is unique in emphasizing creative intelligence and that Gardner's includes a number of types of intelligence that are not addressed by the other views. These theories of multiple intelligences have much to offer. They have stimulated us to think more broadly about what makes up people's intelligence and competence (Gardner, Kornhaber, & Chen, 2018; Sternberg, 2019a, b, 2020a, b, c), and they have motivated educators to develop programs that instruct students in different domains.

Theories of multiple intelligences have their critics (Hagmann-von Arx, Lemola, & Grob, 2018). Some argue that the research base to support these theories has not yet been developed. In particular, some critics say that Gardner's classification seems arbitrary. For example, if musical skills represent a type of intelligence, why don't we also refer to chess intelligence, prize-fighter intelligence, and so on?

A number of psychologists continue to support the concept of general intelligence (Caemmerer & others, 2018; Hagmann-von Arx, Lemola, & Grob, 2018; Holding & others, 2018). A recent study found a significant link between children's general intelligence and their self-control (Meldrum & others, 2017). Another recent study revealed that adolescents with high IQs were more likely than other adolescents to engage in a range of health-promoting behaviors such as exercise, better diet, and not smoking in middle adulthood (Wraw & others, 2018). And in a recent study, higher IQ in adolescence also was associated with having a younger subjective age 50 years later in late adulthood (Stephan & others, 2018).

One expert on intelligence, Nathan Brody (2007), argues that people who excel at one type of intellectual task are likely to excel in other intellectual tasks. Thus, individuals who do well at memorizing lists of digits are also likely to be good at solving verbal problems and spatial layout problems. This general intelligence includes abstract reasoning or thinking, the capacity to acquire knowledge, and problem-solving ability (Brody, 2000). Some experts who argue for the existence of general intelligence conclude that individuals also have specific intellectual abilities (Brody, 2007).

Advocates of the concept of general intelligence point to its success in predicting school and job success. For example, scores on tests of general intelligence are substantially correlated with school grades and achievement test performance, both at the time of the test and years later (Gregory, 2016;

emotional intelligence The ability to perceive and express emotions accurately and adaptively, to understand emotion and emotional knowledge, to use feelings to facilitate thought, and to manage emotions in oneself and others.

Gardner	Sternberg	Salovey/Mayer
Verbal Mathematical	Analytical	
Spatial Movement Musical	Creative	
Interpersonal Intrapersonal	Practical	Emotional
Naturalistic		

FIGURE 3

COMPARING STERNBERG'S, GARDNER'S, AND SALOVEY/ MAYER'S INTELLIGENCES

Sackett, Shewach, & Dahlke, 2020). For example, a research meta-analysis of 240 independent samples and more than 100,000 individuals found a correlation of +.54 between intelligence and school grades (Roth & others, 2015).

In sum, controversy still surrounds the issue of whether it is more accurate to conceptualize intelligence as a general ability, as specific abilities, or as both (Gardner, Kornhaber, & Chen, 2018). Sternberg (2019 a, b, 2020a, b) accepts that there is evidence to support the concept of general intelligence in the kinds of analytical tasks that traditional IQ tests assess, but he thinks that the range of intellectual tasks those tests measure is too narrow.

THE NEUROSCIENCE OF INTELLIGENCE

In the current era of extensive research on the brain, interest in the neurological underpinnings of intelligence has increased (Haier, 2018, 2020; Goriounova & Mansvelder, 2019; Kang & others, 2017). Among the questions about the brain's role in intelligence that are being explored are these: Is having a bigger brain linked to higher intelligence? Is intelligence located in certain brain regions? Is the speed at which the brain processes information linked to intelligence?

Are individuals with bigger brains more intelligent than those with smaller brains? Studies using MRI scans to assess total brain volume indicate a moderate correlation (about 1.3 to 1.4) between brain size and intelligence (Carey, 2007; Lerch & others, 2017; Luders & others, 2009).

Might intelligence be linked to specific regions of the brain? Early consensus was that the frontal lobes are the likely location of intelligence. Today, some experts continue to emphasize that high-level thinking skills involved in intelligence are linked to the prefrontal cortex (Santarnecchi, Rossi, & Rossi, 2015; Sternberg & Sternberg, 2017). However, other researchers have found that intelligence is distributed more widely across brain regions (Lee & others, 2012; Sepulcre & others, 2012). The most prominent finding from brain-imaging studies is that a distributed neural network involving the frontal and parietal lobes is related to higher intelligence (Colom & others, 2009, 2010; Haier, 2018, 2020; Margolis & others, 2013) (see Figure 4). In a recent study, longitudinal changes in general intelligence were linked to developmental changes that occurred in the increasing thickness and surface area of the frontal and temporal lobes of the brain (Roman & others, 2018). One study also revealed that the frontoparietal network is responsible for cognitive control and connectivity to brain regions outside the network (Cole & others, 2012). Albert Einstein's total brain size was average, but a region of his brain's parietal lobe that is very active in processing math and spatial information was 15 percent larger than average (Witelson, Kigar, & Harvey, 1999). Other brain regions that have been linked to higher intelligence (although at a lower level of significance than the frontal/parietal lobe network) include the temporal and occipital lobes, as well as the cerebellum (Luders & others, 2009).

Examining the neuroscience of intelligence has also led to study of the role that neurological speed might play in intelligence (Waiter & others, 2009). Research results have not been consistent for this possible link, although one study found that children who are gifted show faster processing speed and more accurate processing of information than children who are not gifted (Duan, Dan, & Shi, 2013).

As technological advances allow closer study of the brain's functioning in coming decades, we are likely to see more specific conclusions about the brain's role in intelligence. As this research proceeds, keep in mind that both heredity and environment likely contribute to links between the brain and intelligence, including the connections we discussed between brain size and intelligence. Also, Robert Sternberg (2014) has concluded that research on the brain's role in intelligence has been more effective in answering some questions (such as "What aspects of the brain are involved in learning a list of words?") than in answering others (such as "Why do some individuals consider shaking hands socially intelligent but others do not?").

developmental **connection**

Information Processing

Speed of processing information declines in middle adulthood and then declines further in late adulthood. Connect to "Information Processing."

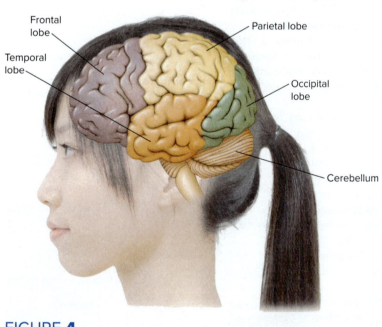

Frontal lobe

Temporal lobe

Parietal lobe

Occipital lobe

Cerebellum

FIGURE 4

INTELLIGENCE AND THE BRAIN. Researchers recently have found that a higher level of intelligence is linked to a distributed neural network in the frontal and parietal lobes. To a lesser extent than the frontal/parietal network, the temporal and occipital lobes, as well as the cerebellum, also have been found to have links to intelligence. The current consensus is that intelligence is likely to be distributed across brain regions rather than being localized in a specific region such as the frontal lobes.
Photo: Takayuki/Shutterstock

2 Controversies and Group Comparisons

LG2 Outline key controversies about differences in IQ scores.

The Influence of Heredity and Environment

Group Comparisons and Issues

We have seen that intelligence is a slippery concept with competing definitions, tests, and theories. It is not surprising, therefore, that attempts to understand the concept of intelligence are surrounded by controversy. In some cases, the controversies arise over comparisons of the intelligence of different groups, such as people from different cultural or ethnic backgrounds.

THE INFLUENCE OF HEREDITY AND ENVIRONMENT

An area of considerable debate in the study of intelligence centers on the extent to which intelligence is influenced by genetics (nature) versus the extent to which it is influenced by environment (nurture) (Sternberg, 2020d; Tan & Grigorenko, 2020). It is difficult to tease apart these influences, but psychologists keep trying to unravel them.

Genetic Influences   To what degree do our genes make us smart? Researchers have attempted to answer this question by comparing the IQ similarity of identical twins (who have the same genes) with that of fraternal twins (who do not have matching genes). Some scientists argue that there is a strong genetic component to intelligence (Hill & others, 2018; Sun & others, 2019). However, a research review found that the difference in the average correlations for identical and fraternal twins was not very high—only .15 (Grigorenko, 2000) (see Figure 5). And genetic influences may be more influential in some aspects of life than others. For example, in a recent study genes were much more strongly linked to a person's scientific achievement than to his/her artistic achievement (de Manzano & Ullen, 2018).

Have scientists been able to pinpoint specific genes that are linked to intelligence? A research review concluded that there may be more than 1,000 genes that affect intelligence, each possibly having a small influence on an individual's intelligence (Davies & others, 2011). However, researchers have not been able to identify the specific genes that contribute to intelligence (Deary, 2012; Zhao, Kong, & Qu, 2014).

Environmental Influences   Although genetic endowment influences a person's intellectual ability, the environmental experiences of children and adults do make a difference (Grigorenko & others, 2016; Must & Must, 2018; Sternberg, 2018a, b, c). In one study, researchers found that how

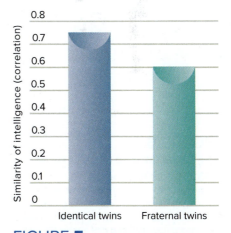

FIGURE 5

CORRELATION BETWEEN INTELLIGENCE TEST SCORES AND TWIN STATUS. The graph represents a summary of research findings that have compared the intelligence test scores of identical and fraternal twins. An approximate .15 difference has been found, with a higher correlation for identical twins (.75) and a lower correlation for fraternal twins (.60).

Students in an elementary school in South Africa. *How might schooling influence the development of children's intelligence?*
Owen Franken/Corbis/Getty Images

much parents communicated with their children during the first three years of their lives was correlated with the children's Stanford-Binet IQ scores at age 3 (Hart & Risley, 1995). The more parents communicated with their children, the higher the children's IQs were. And research by Richard Nisbett and his colleagues (2012) supported the importance of environmental influences on intelligence: A 12- to 18-point increase in IQ was found when children had been adopted from low-income families into middle- and upper-income families.

Schooling also influences intelligence (Ceci & Gilstrap, 2000; Cliffordson & Gustafsson, 2008). The biggest effects have been found when large groups of children received no formal education for an extended period, resulting in lower intelligence.

Recent research indicates that intelligence varies across countries and is linked to various environmental conditions in the countries (Flynn & Sternberg, 2020). For example, in a recent study of 22 countries (including Argentina, China, France, India, Peru, Turkey, and the United States), variations in intelligence across countries were linked to these factors: income, educational attainment, health, and socioeconomic status (Lynn, Fuerst, & Kirkegaard, 2018).

Another possible effect of education can be seen in rapidly increasing IQ test scores around the world (Flynn, 1999, 2007, 2011, 2013, 2018). IQ scores have been rising so quickly that a high percentage of people regarded as having average intelligence in the early 1900s would be considered below average in intelligence today (see Figure 6). If a representative sample of today's children took the Stanford-Binet test used in 1932, about one-fourth would be defined as very superior, a label usually accorded to less than 3 percent of the population. A meta-analysis of 53 studies since 1972 found that IQ scores have been rising about 3 points per decade since that year and that the increase in IQ scores does not seem to be diminishing (Trahan & others, 2014). This worldwide increase in intelligence test scores over a short time frame is called the *Flynn effect* after the researcher who discovered it—James Flynn (1999, 2007, 2011, 2013, 2018).

Research indicates that even the IQ scores of individuals at the highest level of intelligence are getting higher (Wai, Putallaz, & Makel, 2012). Responding to this development, some test makers have begun to include more challenging items that allow very bright individuals more room to express their ability.

Although rising intelligence test scores have been found in most countries in which cohort effects on intelligence have been assessed, a decrease in intelligence test scores has been found in Scandinavian countries (Finland, Norway, Denmark, and Norway) beginning about 1995 (Dutton & Lynn, 2013; Ronnlund & others, 2013). Explanations of the IQ decline focus on technological advances, such as television, smartphones, and social media, as well as weakening education systems. However, IQ gains continue to occur in the United States and most developing countries (Flynn & Shayer, 2018; Flynn & Sternberg, 2020). For example, in a recent study in the Sudanese capital of Khartoum in Africa, IQ scores increased by 10 points from 2004 to 2016 (Dutton & others, 2018).

Because the change in test scores has taken place in a relatively short period of time, it can't be due to heredity. Rather, it might result from environmental factors such as the exploding quantities

FIGURE 6

THE INCREASE IN IQ SCORES FROM 1932 TO 1997. As measured by the Stanford-Binet test, American children seem to be getting smarter. Scores of a group tested in 1932 fell along a bell-shaped curve with half below 100 and half above. Studies show that if children took that same test today, half would score above 120 on the 1932 scale. Very few of them would score in the "intellectually deficient" end on the left side, and about one-fourth would rank in the "very superior" range. Researchers are continuing to find support for the Flynn effect in the 21st century (Laciga & Cigler, 2017; Shenk, 2017).

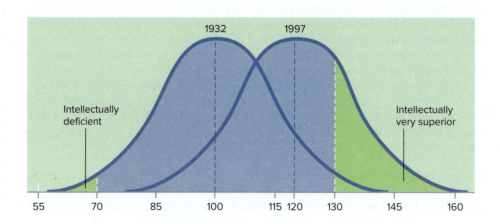

connecting with research

Can Early Intervention in the Lives of Children Growing Up in Impoverished Circumstances Improve Their Intelligence?

Each morning a young mother waited with her child for the bus that would take the child to school. The child was only 2 months old, and "school" was an experimental program at the University of North Carolina at Chapel Hill. There the child experienced a number of interventions designed to improve her intellectual development—everything from bright objects dangled in front of her eyes while she was a baby to language instruction and counting activities when she was a toddler (Wickelgren, 1999). The child's mother had an IQ of 40 and could not read signs or determine how much change she should receive from a cashier. Her grandmother had a similarly low IQ.

Today, at age 20, the child's IQ measures 80 points higher than her mother's did when the child was 2 months old. Not everyone agrees that IQ can be affected this extensively by early interventions, but it is clear that environment can make a substantial difference in a child's intelligence. As behavior geneticist Robert Plomin (1999) has said, even something that is highly heritable (like intelligence) may be malleable through interventions.

The child we just described was part of the Abecedarian Intervention program at the University of North Carolina at Chapel Hill conducted by Craig Ramey and his associates (Campbell, 2007; Campbell & others, 2012; Ramey & Campbell, 1984; Ramey & Ramey, 1998). They randomly assigned 111 young children from low-income, poorly educated families to either an intervention group, which received full-time, year-round child care along with medical and social work services, or a control group, which received medical and social benefits but no child care. The child-care program included gamelike learning activities aimed at improving language, motor, social, and cognitive skills.

The success of the program in improving IQ was evident by the time the children were 3 years of age. At that age, the experimental group showed normal IQs averaging 101, a 17-point advantage over the control group. Follow-up results suggest that the effects are long-lasting. More than a decade later, at age 15, children from the intervention group still maintained an IQ advantage of 5 points over the control-group children (97.7 to 92.6) (Campbell, 2007; Campbell & others, 2001; Ramey, Ramey, & Lanzi, 2001). They also did better on standardized tests of reading and math, and they were less likely to be held back a year in school. Also, the greatest IQ gains were made by the children whose mothers had especially low IQs—below 70. At age 15, these children showed a 10-point IQ advantage over a group of children whose mothers' IQs were below 70 but who had not experienced the child-care intervention. In one analysis of the Abecedarian intervention project, at age 30 the children who experienced the early intervention had attained more years of education but the intervention had not led to any benefits involving social adjustment or criminal activity (Campbell & others, 2012).

The Abecedarian intervention study supports other research that has found prevention/intervention to be more effective than later remediation in improving the lives of children growing up in impoverished circumstances (Phillips & Lowenstein, 2011). Thus, it is important to consider the types of environments children experience as they develop, both in the general population and in especially challenging contexts.

---

of information to which people are exposed and the much higher percentage of the population who receive education (Flynn, 2018; Flynn & Sternberg, 2020; Laciga & Cigler, 2017; Shenk, 2017).

Might increasing scores on IQ tests in a country be linked to subsequent economic benefits for that country? In a recent study of 28 countries, IQ increases in a country were associated with higher GDP (gross domestic product, a key indicator of economic prosperity) 5, 10, 15, and 20 years later (Rindermann & Becker, 2018).

Keep in mind that environmental influences are complex. Growing up with all the "advantages," for example, does not guarantee success. Children from wealthy families may have easy access to excellent schools, books, travel, and tutoring, but they may take such opportunities for granted and fail to develop the motivation to learn and achieve. In the same way, "poor" or "disadvantaged" does not automatically equal "doomed." Researchers increasingly are exploring ways to improve the early environments of children who are at risk for impoverished intelligence (Bradley, 2019; Hardy, Smeeding, & Ziliak, 2018). The emphasis is on prevention rather than remediation. Many low-income parents have difficulty providing an intellectually stimulating environment for their children (Shuey & Leventhal, 2019). Programs that educate parents to be more sensitive caregivers and better teachers, while providing support services such as quality child-care programs, can make a difference in a child's intellectual development (Bredekamp, 2020; Feeney, Moravcik, & Nolte, 2019; Follari, 2019; Morrison, 2020). In a two-year intervention study with families living in poverty, maternal scaffolding and positive home stimulation improved young children's intellectual functioning (Obradovic & others, 2016).

Can we actually measure environmental influences on intelligence? To read more, see the *Connecting with Research* interlude.

> The highest-risk children often benefit the most cognitively when they experience early interventions.
>
> —CRAIG RAMEY
> *Contemporary Psychologist, Georgetown University*

---------→
developmental connection

Nature and Nurture

The epigenetic approach emphasizes the ongoing, bidirectional interaction of heredity and environment. Connect to "Biological Beginnings."
←---------

In sum, there is a consensus among psychologists that both heredity and environment influence intelligence (Flynn & Sternberg, 2020; Tan & Grigorenko, 2020). This consensus reflects the nature-nurture issue, which was highlighted in the chapter titled "Introduction." Recall that the nature-nurture issue focuses on the extent to which development is influenced by nature (heredity) and nurture (environment). Although psychologists agree that intelligence is the product of both nature and nurture, there is still disagreement about how strongly each factor influences intelligence (Haier, 2020; Flynn & Sternberg, 2020).

GROUP COMPARISONS AND ISSUES

Group comparisons in intelligence can involve cultures and ethnic groups. We begin by discussing cross-cultural comparisons and then explore the influence of cultural bias in testing.

Cross-Cultural Comparisons   Cultures vary in the way they describe what it means to be intelligent (Sternberg, 2020d). People in Western cultures tend to view intelligence in terms of reasoning and thinking skills, whereas people in Eastern cultures see intelligence as a way for members of a community to successfully engage in social roles (Nisbett, 2003).

In a study of the Luo culture in rural Kenya, children who scored highly on a test of knowledge about medicinal herbs—a measure of practical intelligence—tended to score poorly on tests of academic intelligence (Sternberg & others, 2001). These results indicated that practical and academic intelligence can develop independently and may even conflict with each other. They also suggest that the values of a culture may influence the direction in which a child develops. In a cross-cultural context, then, intelligence depends a great deal on environment (Sternberg, 2020d).

Cultural Bias in Testing   Many of the early intelligence tests were culturally biased, favoring people who were from urban rather than rural environments, middle socioeconomic status rather than low socioeconomic status, and non-Latino White rather than African American ethnicity (Provenzo, 2002). Also, members of minority groups who do not speak English or who speak nonstandard English are at a disadvantage in trying to understand questions framed in standard English.

One potential influence on intelligence test performance is **stereotype threat**, a fear that one's behavior might confirm a negative stereotype about one's group (DeSombre & others, 2019; Williams & others, 2019). Researchers have confirmed the existence of stereotype threat (Hutter & others, 2019; Lyons & others, 2018). For example, when African Americans take an intelligence test, they may experience anxiety about confirming an old stereotype that Blacks are "intellectually inferior." Some studies support the existence of stereotype threat (Wasserberg, 2014). For example, African American students do more poorly on standardized tests if they perceive that they are being evaluated. If they think the test doesn't count, they perform as well as White students (Aronson, 2002). However, some critics argue that the extent to which stereotype threat explains the testing gap has been exaggerated (Sackett, Borneman, & Connelly, 2009).

Researchers have developed **culture-fair tests,** which are intelligence tests that are designed to avoid cultural bias. Two types of culture-fair tests have been developed. The first includes questions that are familiar to people from all socioeconomic and ethnic backgrounds. For example, a child might be asked how a bird and a dog are different, on the assumption that virtually all children are familiar with birds and dogs. The second type of culture-fair test contains no verbal questions.

Why is it so hard to create culture-fair tests? Most tests tend to reflect what the dominant culture thinks is important (Sternberg, 2020d). If tests have time limits, these will bias the test against groups not concerned with time. If languages differ, the same words might have different meanings for different language groups. Even pictures can produce bias because some cultures have less experience than others with drawings and photographs (Anastasi & Urbina, 1996). Within the same culture, different groups could have different attitudes, values, and motivation, and this could affect their performance on intelligence tests. Items that ask why buildings should be made of brick are biased against children who have little or no experience with brick houses. Questions about railroads, furnaces, seasons of the year, distances between cities, and so on can be biased against groups who have less experience than others with these contexts. Because of such difficulties, Robert Sternberg (2020d) concludes that there are no culture-fair tests, but only culture-reduced tests.

stereotype threat Anxiety regarding whether one's behavior might confirm a negative stereotype about one's group.

culture-fair tests Intelligence tests that are designed to avoid cultural bias.

Ethnic Comparisons   In the United States, children from African American and Latino families score below children from non-Latino White families on standardized intelligence tests (Yeung, 2012). On average, African American schoolchildren score 10 to 15 points lower on standardized intelligence tests than non-Latino White schoolchildren do (Brody, 2000). These are *average scores*, however. About 15 to 25 percent of African American schoolchildren score higher than half of non-Latino White schoolchildren do. The reason is that the distribution of scores for African Americans and non-Latino Whites overlap.

As African Americans have gained social, economic, and educational opportunities, the gap between African Americans and non-Latino Whites on standardized intelligence tests has begun to narrow (Ogbu & Stern, 2001). A research review concluded that the IQ gap between African Americans and non-Latino Whites has decreased considerably in recent decades (Nisbett & others, 2012). This gap especially narrows in college, where African American and non-Latino White students often experience more similar environments than during the elementary and high school years (Myerson & others, 1998). Also, when children from disadvantaged African American families are adopted into more advantaged middle-socioeconomic-status families, their scores on intelligence tests more closely resemble national averages for middle-socioeconomic-status children than for lower-socioeconomic-status children (Scarr & Weinberg, 1983). Further, a study using the Stanford Binet Intelligence Scales found no differences in overall intellectual ability between non-Latino White and African American preschool children when the children were matched on age, gender, and parental education level (Dale & others, 2014). Nonetheless, a research analysis concluded that the underrepresentation of African Americans in STEM (science, technology, engineering, and math) subjects and careers is linked to practitioners' expectations that members of this group have less innate talent for the subject matter than non-Latino Whites do (Leslie & others, 2015).

Review Connect Reflect

 LG2 Outline key controversies about differences in IQ scores.

Review

- What evidence suggests genetic influences on IQ scores?
- What evidence suggests environmental influences on IQ scores?
- What do IQ tests tell us about intelligence among people in different cultures and ethnic groups?

Connect

- Apply what you have learned about the nature-nurture debate to discuss possible gender similarities and differences in intelligence.

Reflect *Your Own Personal Journey of Life*

- Do you think your performance on standardized tests accurately reflects your intelligence?

3 The Development of Intelligence   **LG3** Discuss the development of intelligence across the life span.

| Tests of Infant Intelligence | Stability and Change in Intelligence Through Adolescence | Intelligence in Adulthood |

How can the intelligence of infants be assessed? Is intelligence stable throughout childhood? Does intelligence decline in older adults, and if so, when and by how much? These are some of the questions we will explore as we examine the development of intelligence.

TESTS OF INFANT INTELLIGENCE

The infant-testing movement grew out of the tradition of IQ testing. However, tests that assess infants are necessarily less verbal than IQ tests for older children. Tests for infants contain far more items related to perceptual-motor development. They also include measures of social

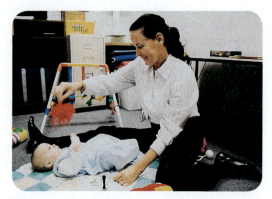

connecting with careers

Toosje Thyssen Van Beveren, Infant Assessment Specialist

Toosje Thyssen Van Beveren is a developmental psychologist at the University of Texas Medical Center in Dallas. She has a master's degree in child clinical psychology and a Ph.D. in human development. Currently, Van Beveren is involved in a 12-week program called New Connections, which is a comprehensive intervention for young children who were affected by substance abuse prenatally and for their caregivers.

In the New Connections program, Van Beveren assesses infants' developmental status and progress. She might refer the infants to a speech, physical, or occupational therapist and monitor the infants' progress during therapeutic interventions. Van Beveren trains the program staff and encourages them to use the exercises she recommends. She also discusses the child's problems with the primary caregivers, suggests activities, and assists them in enrolling infants in appropriate programs.

During her graduate work at the University of Texas at Dallas, Van Beveren was author John Santrock's teaching assistant in his undergraduate course on life-span development for four years. As a teaching assistant, she attended classes, graded exams, counseled students, and occasionally gave lectures. Each semester, Van Beveren

Toosje Thyssen Van Beveren conducts an infant assessment.
Dr. John Santrock

returns to give a lecture on prenatal development and infancy. She also teaches several courses each semester in the psychology department at UT–Dallas. In Van Beveren's words, "My days are busy and full. The work is often challenging. There are some disappointments, but mostly the work is enormously gratifying."

Bayley Scales of Infant Development Widely used scales, developed by Nancy Bayley, for assessing infant development. The current version, the Bayley-III, has five scales: cognitive, language, motor, socio-emotional, and adaptive; the first three are administered to the infant, the latter two to the caregiver.

interaction. To read about the work of one infant assessment specialist, see the *Connecting with Careers* profile.

The widely used **Bayley Scales of Infant Development** were developed by Nancy Bayley (1969) to assess infant behavior and predict later development. The current version, Bayley-III, has five scales: cognitive, language, motor, socio-emotional, and adaptive (Bayley, 2006). The first three scales are administered directly to the infant, while the latter two are questionnaires given to the caregiver. The Bayley-III also is more appropriate for use in clinical settings than the two previous editions (Gullion & others, 2019).

How should a 6-month-old perform on the Bayley cognitive scale? The 6-month-old infant should be able to vocalize pleasure and displeasure, persistently search for objects that are just outside immediate reach, and approach a mirror that is placed in front of the infant by the examiner. By 12 months of age, the infant should be able to inhibit behavior when commanded to do so, imitate words the examiner says (such as *Mama*), and respond to simple requests (such as "Take a drink").

The increasing interest in infant development has produced many new measures, especially tasks that evaluate the ways infants process information (Blankenship & others, 2019). The Fagan Test of Infant Intelligence is increasingly being used (Fagan, 1992). This test focuses on the infant's ability to process information in ways such as encoding the attributes of objects, detecting similarities and differences between objects, forming mental representations, and retrieving these representations. For example, it measures the amount of time babies look at a new object compared with the amount of time they spend looking at a familiar object.

Unlike the Bayley scales, the Fagan test is correlated with measures of intelligence in older children. In fact, evidence is accumulating that measures of habituation and dishabituation are linked to intelligence in childhood, adolescence, and even adulthood. For example, one study revealed that habituation assessed at 3 or 6 months of age was linked to

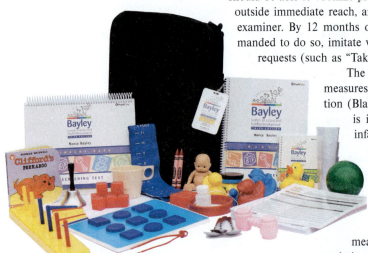

Items in the Bayley-III Scales of Infant Development.
Amy Kiley Photography

verbal skills and intelligence assessed at 32 months of age (Domsch, Lohaus, & Thomas, 2009). Another study found that selective attention to novelty at 6 to 12 months was positively correlated with intelligence at 21 years of age (Fagan, Holland, & Wheeler, 2007). And a longitudinal study revealed that scores in four information-processing domains (attention, processing speed, memory, and representational competence) assessed in infancy and early childhood were linked to general intelligence scores on the Wechsler Intelligence Scale for Children–III assessed at 11 years of age (Rose & others, 2012).

Also, a longitudinal study found that developmental milestones at 24 months of age were strongly linked to IQ at 5 to 6 years of age, but those milestones at 4, 8, and 12 months were only slightly associated with IQ at 5 to 6 years (Peyre & others, 2017). Of the four developmental milestones (language, gross motor skills, fine motor skills, and socialization), early language skills were the best predictor of IQ. Further, early language skills were linked to children who had an IQ lower than 70 (intellectual disability) (predicted from 8 months of age) and higher than 130 (gifted) (predicted from 12 months of age) at 5 to 6 years of age. And in another study, developmental milestones assessed at 3 years of age were linked to scores on the Wechsler Adult Intelligence Scale at 20 to 34 years of age, with the strongest associations occurring for the early developmental milestones of language and social interaction (Flensborg-Madsen & Mortensen, 2018).

It is important, however, not to go too far and think that connections between cognitive development in early infancy and later cognitive development are so strong that no discontinuity takes place. Significant changes in cognitive development occur after infancy.

STABILITY AND CHANGE IN INTELLIGENCE THROUGH ADOLESCENCE

A longitudinal study examined the intelligence of 200 children from 12 months (using the Bayley scales) to 4 years old (using the Stanford-Binet test) (Blaga & others, 2009). The results indicated considerable stability from late infancy through the preschool years.

An early study examined correlations between IQ test scores at a number of different ages (Honzik, MacFarlane, & Allen, 1948). There was a strong relation between IQ scores obtained at the ages of 6, 8, and 9 and IQ scores obtained at the age of 10. For example, the correlation between IQ at the age of 8 and IQ at the age of 10 was .88. The correlation between IQ at the age of 9 and IQ at the age of 10 was .90. These figures show a high degree of consistency in IQ scores obtained in these years. The correlation between IQ in the preadolescent years and IQ at the age of 18 was slightly lower but still statistically significant. For example, the correlation between IQ at the age of 10 and IQ at the age of 18 was .70. Also, in a recent study, intelligence showed considerable stability across four developmental periods: infancy, early childhood, middle and late childhood, and adolescence (Yu & others, 2018). As expected, though, when there was a greater time lapse between tests (infancy to adolescence, for example) IQ scores showed less stability than they did when testing occurred in adjacent time frames (infancy to early childhood, for example.

Much of what has been said so far about the stability of intelligence has been based on measures of groups of individuals. The stability of intelligence also can be evaluated through studies of individuals. Robert McCall and his associates (McCall, Applebaum, & Hogarty, 1973) studied 140 children between the ages of 2½ and 17. They found that the average range of IQ scores was more than 28 points. The scores of one out of three children changed by as much as 40 points.

What can we conclude about stability and changes in intelligence during childhood? Intelligence test scores can fluctuate dramatically across the childhood years, indicating that intelligence is not as stable as the original intelligence theorists envisioned. Children are adaptive beings. They have the capacity for intellectual change, but they do not become entirely new intelligent beings. In a sense, children's intelligence changes but remains connected with earlier points in development.

INTELLIGENCE IN ADULTHOOD

Does intelligence increase or decrease in adulthood? Might older adults have greater wisdom than younger adults? These are among the questions that we will explore in this section.

developmental **connection**

Life-Span Perspective

The stability-change issue is a major focus of study in the field of life-span development. Connect to "Introduction."

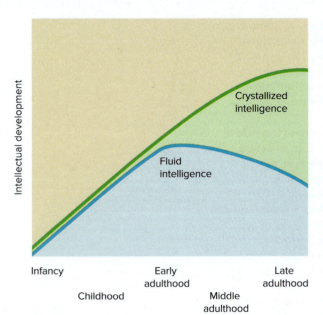

Crystallized
intelligence

Fluid
intelligence

Intellectual development

Infancy · Early adulthood · Late adulthood

Childhood · Middle adulthood

FIGURE 7

FLUID AND CRYSTALLIZED INTELLECTUAL DEVELOPMENT ACROSS THE LIFE SPAN. According to Horn, crystallized intelligence (based on cumulative learning experiences) increases throughout the life span, but fluid intelligence (reasoning effectively) steadily declines from middle adulthood onward.

crystallized intelligence An individual's accumulated information and verbal skills, which continues to increase with age.

fluid intelligence The ability to reason effectively.

Fluid and Crystallized Intelligence   John Horn emphasizes that some abilities increase throughout the life span, whereas others steadily decline from middle adulthood onward (Horn, 2007; Horn & Donaldson, 1980). Horn argues that **crystallized intelligence,** an individual's accumulated information and verbal skills, continues to increase throughout the life span. However, he notes that **fluid intelligence,** the ability to reason effectively, begins to decline in middle adulthood (see Figure 7).

Horn's data were collected in a cross-sectional manner. A *cross-sectional study* assesses individuals of different ages at the same point in time. For example, a cross-sectional study might assess the intelligence of groups of 40-, 50-, and 60-year-olds in one evaluation, such as in 1990. The average 40-year-old and the average 60-year-old were born in eras that offered different economic and educational opportunities. For example, as the 60-year-olds grew up they likely had fewer educational opportunities, which probably influenced their scores on intelligence tests. Thus, if we find differences between 40- and 60-year-olds on intelligence tests when they are assessed cross-sectionally, these differences might be due to cohort effects (attributes reflecting an individual's time of birth or generation rather than his or her age) such as educational differences rather than simply reflecting the person's age.

In contrast, in a *longitudinal study*, the same individuals are studied over a period of time. Thus, a longitudinal study of intelligence in middle adulthood might consist of giving the same intelligence test to the same individuals when they are 40, when they are 50, and when they are 60 years of age. Whether data are collected cross-sectionally or longitudinally makes a difference in what is found about intellectual decline.

In a recent study of 24- to 93-year-olds, everyday problem solving performance increased from early to middle adulthood but began to show a decline at about 50 years of age (Chen, Hertzog, & Park, 2017). In this study, fluid intelligence predicted everyday problem solving performance in young adults but with increasing age, crystallized intelligence became a better predictor. Also, in a recent large-scale study, fluid intelligence declined in individuals 65 years of age and older but not in those 45 to 60 years old (Cornelis & others, 2019).

The Seattle Longitudinal Study   K. Warner Schaie (1983, 1996, 2000, 2005, 2010, 2011, 2013, 2016) has conducted an extensive study of intellectual abilities during adulthood. Five hundred individuals initially were tested in 1956, and new waves of participants are added periodically. The main mental abilities tested in the Seattle Longitudinal Study are as follows:

- *Verbal comprehension* (ability to understand ideas expressed in words)
- *Verbal memory* (ability to encode and recall meaningful language units, such as a list of words)
- *Numeric ability* (ability to perform simple mathematical computations such as addition, subtraction, and multiplication)
- *Spatial orientation* (ability to visualize and mentally rotate stimuli in two- and three-dimensional space)
- *Inductive reasoning* (ability to recognize and understand patterns and relationships in a problem and use this understanding to solve other instances of the problem)
- *Perceptual speed* (ability to quickly and accurately make simple discriminations in visual stimuli)

As shown in Figure 8, the highest level of functioning for four of the six intellectual abilities occurred during middle adulthood (Schaie, 2013). For both women and men, performance on verbal ability, verbal memory, inductive reasoning, and spatial orientation peaked in middle age. Only two of the six abilities—numeric ability and perceptual speed—declined in middle age.

Notice in Figure 8 that the declines in functioning for most cognitive abilities began to steepen in the sixties, although the decline in verbal comprehension did not steepen until the mid-seventies. From the mid-seventies through the mid-nineties, all cognitive abilities showed considerable decline. When Schaie (1994) assessed intellectual abilities both cross-sectionally and longitudinally, he found that decline was more likely to occur in the cross-sectional than in the longitudinal assessments. For example, as shown in Figure 9, when assessed longitudinally, inductive reasoning ability increased

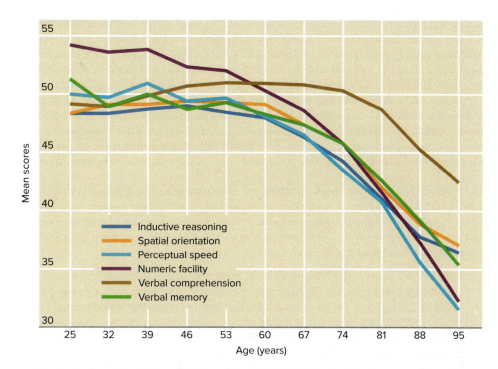

FIGURE 8

LONGITUDINAL CHANGES IN SIX INTELLECTUAL ABILITIES FROM AGE 25 TO AGE 95.

Source: Schaie, K.W. "Longitudinal Changes in Six Intellectual Abilities from Age 25 to Age 95." *Developmental Influences on Intelligence: The Seattle Longitudinal Study,* 2e, rev, 2013, 162.

until toward the end of middle adulthood and then began to show a slight decline. In contrast, when assessed cross-sectionally, inductive reasoning showed a consistent decline during middle adulthood. For the participants in the Seattle Longitudinal Study, middle age was a time of peak performance both for some aspects of crystallized intelligence (verbal comprehension) and for fluid intelligence (spatial orientation and inductive reasoning). Also recall our discussion in the "Introduction" chapter that some researchers have found that cross-sectional studies indicate more than 90 percent of cognitive decline in aging is due to a slowing of processing speed, whereas longitudinal studies reveal that 20 percent or less of cognitive decline is due to slowing of processing speed (MacDonald & others, 2003; MacDonald & Stawski, 2015, 2016; Stawski, Sliwinski, & Hofer, 2013).

Some researchers disagree with Schaie that middle adulthood is a time when the level of functioning in a number of cognitive domains is maintained or even increases (Finch, 2009). For example, Timothy Salthouse (2009, 2012, 2014, 2016) has argued that cross-sectional research on aging and cognitive functioning should not be dismissed and that this research indicates reasoning, memory, spatial visualization, and processing speed begin declining in early adulthood and show further decline in the fifties. Salthouse (2009, 2012) does agree that cognitive functioning involving accumulated knowledge, such as vocabulary and general information, does not show early age-related

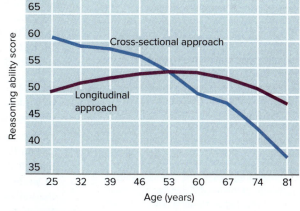

FIGURE 9

CROSS-SECTIONAL AND LONGITUDINAL COMPARISONS OF INDUCTIVE REASONING ABILITY ACROSS ADULTHOOD. In Schaie's research, the cross-sectional approach revealed declining scores with age; the longitudinal approach showed a slight rise of scores in middle adulthood and only a slight decline beginning in the early part of late adulthood.

K. Warner Schaie (*right*) is one of the leading pioneers in the field of life-span development. He is shown here with two older adults who are actively using their cognitive skills. Schaie's research represents one of the most thorough examinations of how individuals develop and change as they go through the adult years.
Courtesy of Dr. K. Warner Schaie

developmental **connection**
Culture
In Baltes' view, for older adults the benefits of evolutionary selection decrease while the need for culture increases. Connect to "Biological Beginnings."

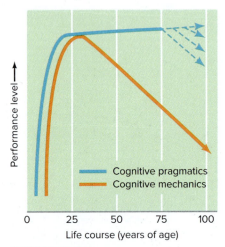

FIGURE **10**

THEORIZED AGE CHANGES IN COGNITIVE MECHANICS AND COGNITIVE PRAGMATICS. Baltes argues that cognitive mechanics declines during aging, whereas cognitive pragmatics does not, at least for many people until they become very old. Cognitive mechanics has a biological/genetic foundation; cognitive pragmatics has an experiential/cultural foundation. The broken lines from 75 to 100 years of age indicate possible individual variations in cognitive pragmatics.

cognitive mechanics The "hardware" of the mind, reflecting the neurophysiological architecture of the brain as developed through evolution. Cognitive mechanics involves the speed and accuracy of the processes involving sensory input, visual and motor memory, discrimination, comparison, and categorization.

cognitive pragmatics The culture-based "software" of the mind. Cognitive pragmatics includes reading and writing skills, language comprehension, educational qualifications, professional skills, and the self-knowledge and life skills that help us to master or cope with life.

wisdom Expert knowledge about the practical aspects of life that permits excellent judgment about important matters.

decline but rather continues to increase at least until 60 years of age. Salthouse (2009, 2012) has emphasized that a lower level of cognitive functioning in middle adulthood is likely due to age-related neurobiological decline. Salthouse (2014, 2018, 2019) has argued that a main reason for different trends in longitudinal and cross-sectional comparisons of cognitive functioning is that prior experience taking a test results in higher scores the next time the test is taken.

Schaie (2013, 2016) continues to emphasize that longitudinal studies hold the key to determining age-related changes in cognitive functioning and that middle age is the time during which many cognitive skills actually peak. In the next decade, expanding research on age-related neurobiological changes and their possible links to cognitive skills should further refine our knowledge about age-related cognitive functioning in the adult years (Kinugawa, 2019; Strandberg, 2019).

Cognitive Mechanics and Cognitive Pragmatics Paul Baltes (1993, 2000, 2003; Baltes, Lindenberger, & Staudinger, 2006) clarified the distinction between those aspects of the mind that decline with advancing age and those that remain stable or even improve. He makes a distinction between "cognitive mechanics" and "cognitive pragmatics" that extends the fluid/crystallized intelligence conceptualization described earlier:

- **Cognitive mechanics** is the "hardware" of the mind and reflects the neurophysiological architecture of the brain developed through evolution. Cognitive mechanics consists of the speed and accuracy of the processes involved in sensory input, attention, visual and motor memory, discrimination, comparison, and categorization. Because of the strong influence of biology, heredity, and health on cognitive mechanics, a decline with aging is likely.

- **Cognitive pragmatics** encompasses the culture-based "software programs" of the mind. Cognitive pragmatics includes reading and writing skills, language comprehension, educational qualifications, and professional skills, as well as self-knowledge and life skills that help us to master or cope with life. Because of the strong influence of culture on cognitive pragmatics, ongoing improvement can continue to take place. Thus, although cognitive mechanics may decline in old age, cognitive pragmatics may actually improve during this period (see Figure 10).

The distinction between cognitive mechanics and cognitive pragmatics is similar to the one between fluid (mechanics) and crystallized (pragmatics) intelligence that was described earlier. Indeed, the similarity is so strong that some experts now use the terms *fluid mechanics* and *crystallized pragmatics* to describe cognitive aging patterns (Lovden & Lindenberger, 2007).

Wisdom As you just saw, Baltes stresses that wisdom is an important aspect of cognitive pragmatics. Baltes and his colleagues (2006) define **wisdom** as expert knowledge about the practical aspects of life that permits excellent judgment about important matters. This practical knowledge involves exceptional insight about human development and life matters, good judgment, and understanding of how to cope with difficult life problems. Thus, wisdom, more than standard conceptions of intelligence, focuses on life's pragmatic concerns and human conditions (Kuntzmann, 2019; Sternberg, 2018d, 2019b; Sternberg & Glueck, 2019; Sternberg & Hagen, 2018).

In regard to wisdom, Baltes and his colleagues (Baltes & Kunzmann, 2004; Baltes, Lindenberger, & Staudinger, 2006; Baltes & Smith, 2008) have reached the following conclusions:

- High levels of wisdom are rare. Few people, including older adults, attain a high level of wisdom. That only a small percentage of adults show wisdom supports the contention that it requires experience, practice, or complex skills.

- Factors other than age are critical for wisdom to develop to a high level. For example, certain life experiences, such as being trained and working in a field concerned with difficult life problems and having wisdom-enhancing mentors, contribute to higher levels of wisdom. Also, people higher in wisdom have values that are more likely to consider the welfare of others than to focus exclusively on their own happiness.

- Personality-related factors, such as openness to experience, generativity, and creativity, are better predictors of wisdom than cognitive factors such as intelligence.

One study compared college students and older adults on a wisdom scale that had three dimensions: cognitive, reflective, and affective (Ardelt, 2010, p. 199):

- *Cognitive* scale items measured the absence of cognitive wisdom and included items on not having the ability or being unwilling to understand something thoroughly ("ignorance is bliss," for example), and tending to perceive the world as either/or instead of more complex ("People are either good or bad," for example), and being unaware of ambiguity and uncertainty in life ("There is only one right way to do anything," for example).

- *Reflective* scale items evaluated capacity and willingness to examine circumstances and issues from different perspectives ("I always try to look at all sides of a problem," for example) versus lack of self-examination and self-insight ("Things often go wrong for me through no fault of my own," for example).
- *Affective* scale items assessed positive and caring emotions ("Sometimes I feel a real compassion for everyone," for example) and the lack of those characteristics ("It's not really my problem if others are in trouble and need help," for example).

On the overall wisdom scale that included an assessment of all three dimensions combined, no differences were found between the two age groups. However, older adults with college degrees scored higher on the reflective and affective, but not the cognitive, dimensions of wisdom than the college students did.

An increasing number of research studies have focused on the developmental aspects of wisdom at different points in life (Ardelt & Jeste, 2018; Igarashi, Levenson, & Aldwin, 2018). For example, a recent study explored wisdom and meaning as important developments in emerging adulthood (Webster & others, 2018). In this study, researchers found that the search for and presence of meaning was linked to wisdom, which was assessed on the basis of five components: critical life experiences, reminiscence/reflectiveness, openness to experience, emotional regulation, and humor. Also, a recent study found that self-reflective exploratory processing of difficult life experiences (meaning-making and personal growth) was linked to a higher level of wisdom (Westrate & Gluck, 2017). Another recent study found that the personality trait of openness to experience in early adulthood predicted wisdom 60 years later (Ardelt, Gerlach, & Vaillant, 2018). Also in this study, wisdom in late adulthood could be traced back to experiences and characteristics at different points in development: a supportive childhood, adolescent competence, emotional stability in young adults, and generativity in middle adulthood. And a recent study indicated that wisdom peaked in midlife, with education especially linked to a higher level of wisdom (Ardelt, Pridgen, & Nutter-Pridgen, 2018).

Older adults might not be as quick with their thoughts or behavior as younger people, but wisdom may be an entirely different matter. This older man shares the wisdom of his experience with children at an elementary school. *How is wisdom described by life-span developmentalists?*
Michael J. Doolittle/The Image Works

Review Connect Reflect

LG3 Discuss the development of intelligence across the life span.

Review
- How is intelligence assessed during infancy?
- How much does intelligence change through childhood and adolescence?
- To what extent does intelligence change as adults age? What is wisdom, and how can it be characterized?

Connect
- In this section, you read about longitudinal and cross-sectional

studies of intelligence. What are the potential advantages and disadvantages of these research approaches?

Reflect Your Own Personal Journey of Life
- Think about your parents' and grandparents' intelligence. How might their intelligence have been influenced by cohort effects?

4 The Extremes of Intelligence and Creativity

LG4 Describe the characteristics of intellectual disability, giftedness, and creativity.

Intellectual Disability | Giftedness | Creativity

Intellectual disability and intellectual giftedness are the extremes of intelligence. Often intelligence tests are used to identify exceptional individuals. We will explore the nature of intellectual disability and giftedness, then examine how creativity differs from intelligence.

INTELLECTUAL DISABILITY

The most distinctive feature of intellectual disability (formerly called mental retardation) is inadequate intellectual functioning (Elliott & Resing, 2020; Friend, 2018). Long before formal tests were developed to assess intelligence, individuals with an intellectual disability were identified by a lack of age-appropriate skills in learning and caring for themselves. Once intelligence tests were developed, they were used to identify the degree of intellectual disability. But of two individuals with an intellectual disability who have the same low IQ, one might be married, employed, and involved in the community and the other might require constant supervision in an institution. Such differences in social competence led psychologists to include deficits in adaptive behavior in their definition of intellectual disability (Green, Landry, & Iarocci, 2016; Smith & others, 2018).

intellectual disability A condition of limited mental ability in which an individual has a low IQ, usually below 70 on a traditional test of intelligence, and has difficulty adapting to the demands of everyday life.

Intellectual disability is a condition of limited mental ability in which the individual (1) has a low IQ, usually below 70 on a traditional intelligence test; (2) has difficulty adapting to the demands of everyday life; and (3) first exhibits these characteristics by age 18. The age limit is included in the definition of intellectual disability because, for example, we don't usually think of a college student who suffers massive brain damage in a car accident, resulting in an IQ of 60, as having an "intellectual disability." The low IQ and low adaptiveness should be evident in childhood, not after normal functioning is interrupted by damage of some form. About 5 million Americans fit this definition of intellectual disability.

There are several ways to define degrees of intellectual disability (Hallahan, Kaufmann, & Pullen, 2019; Heward, Alber-Morgan, & Konrad, 2017). Most school systems use the classifications shown in Figure 11, in which IQ scores categorize intellectual disability as mild, moderate, severe, or profound.

Type of Intellectual Disability	IQ Range	Percentage of Individuals with an Intellectual Disability
Mild	55 to 70	89
Moderate	40 to 54	6
Severe	25 to 39	4
Profound	Below 25	1

FIGURE 11

CLASSIFICATION OF INTELLECTUAL DISABILITY BASED ON IQ

Note that a large majority of individuals diagnosed with an intellectual disability fit into the mild category. However, these categories are not perfect predictors of functioning. A different classification is based on the degree of support required for a person with an intellectual disability to function at the highest level. As shown in Figure 12, these categories of support are intermittent, limited, extensive, and pervasive.

Some cases of intellectual disability have an organic cause. *Organic intellectual disability* describes a genetic disorder or a lower level of intellectual functioning caused by brain damage (Mir & Kuchay, 2019). Down syndrome is one form of organic intellectual disability, and it occurs when an extra chromosome is present. Other causes of organic intellectual disability include fragile X syndrome, an abnormality in the X chromosome; prenatal malformation; metabolic disorders; and diseases that affect the brain. Most people who suffer from organic intellectual disability have IQs between 0 and 50.

When no evidence of organic brain damage can be found, cases are labeled *cultural-familial intellectual disability*. Individuals with this type of disability have IQs between 55 and 70. Psychologists suspect that this type of disability often stems from growing up in a below-average intellectual environment. Children with this type of disability can be identified in schools, where they often fail, need tangible rewards (candy rather than praise), and are highly sensitive to what others expect of them. However, as adults, they are usually not noticeable, perhaps because adult settings don't tax their cognitive skills as sorely. It may also be that their intelligence increases as they move toward adulthood.

Classification of Intellectual Disability	Level of Support Needed
Intermittent	Supports are provided "as needed." The individual may need episodic or short-term support during life-span transitions (such as job loss or acute medical crisis). Intermittent supports may be low or high intensity when provided.
Limited	Supports are intense and relatively consistent over time. They are time-limited but not intermittent, require fewer staff members, and cost less than more intense supports. These supports likely will be needed for adaptation to the changes involved in the school-to-adult period.
Extensive	Supports are characterized by regular involvement (for example, daily) in at least some setting (such as home or work) and are not time-limited (for example, extended home-living support).
Pervasive	Supports are constant, very intense, and are provided across settings. They may be of a life-sustaining nature. These supports typically involve more staff members and intrusiveness than the other support categories.

FIGURE 12

CLASSIFICATION OF INTELLECTUAL DISABILITY BASED ON LEVELS OF SUPPORT NEEDED

GIFTEDNESS

There have always been people whose abilities and accomplishments outshine those of others—the whiz kid in class, the star athlete, the natural musician. People who are **gifted** have high intelligence or superior talent of some kind. An IQ of 130 is often used as the low threshold for giftedness, although this figure is arbitrary. Programs for the gifted in most school systems select children who have intellectual superiority and academic aptitude (Elliott & Resing, 2020; Sternberg, 2018e; Sternberg & Kaufman, 2018b). They tend to overlook children who are talented in the arts or athletics or who have other special aptitudes, including their passion and sense of destiny (Sternberg & Kaufman, 2018b). Estimates vary but indicate that approximately 6 percent of U.S. students are classified as gifted (National Association for Gifted Children, 2017). This percentage is likely conservative because it focuses more on children who are gifted intellectually and academically, often failing to include those who are gifted in creative thinking or the visual and performing arts (Ford, 2012).

Until recently, giftedness and emotional distress were thought to go hand-in-hand. Virginia Woolf, Sir Isaac Newton, Vincent van Gogh, Anne Sexton, Socrates, and Sylvia Plath all had emotional problems. However, these individuals are the exception rather than the rule. In general, no connection between giftedness and mental disorder has been found. Research supports the conclusion that gifted people tend to be more mature, to have fewer emotional problems than others, and to grow up in a positive family climate (Feldhusen, 1999). One study revealed that parents and teachers identified elementary school children who are not gifted as having more emotional and behavioral risks than children who are gifted (Eklund & others, 2015). In this study, when children who are gifted did have problems, they were more likely to be internalized problems such as anxiety and depression than externalized problems such as acting out and high levels of aggression.

Characteristics of Children Who Are Gifted Aside from their abilities, do children who are gifted have distinctive characteristics? Lewis Terman (1925) conducted an extensive study of 1,500 children whose Stanford-Binet IQ scores averaged 150. Contrary to the popular myth that children who are gifted are maladjusted, Terman found that they were socially well adjusted.

developmental **connection**

Conditions, Diseases, and Disorders
Down syndrome is caused by the presence of an extra copy of chromosome 21. Connect to "Biological Beginnings."

What causes a child to develop Down syndrome? In which major classification of intellectual disability does Down syndrome fall?
George Doyle/Stockbyte/Getty Images

giftedness Having above-average intelligence (an IQ of 130 or higher) and/or superior talent for something.

Ellen Winner (1996) described three criteria that characterize gifted children, whether in art, music, or academic domains:

1. *Precocity*. Gifted children are precocious. They begin to master an area earlier than their peers. Learning in their domain is more effortless for them than for ordinary children. In most instances, these gifted children are precocious because they have an inborn high ability.

2. *Marching to their own drummer*. Gifted children learn in a qualitatively different way from ordinary children. For one thing, they need minimal help from adults to learn. In many cases, they resist explicit instruction. They also often make discoveries on their own and solve problems in unique ways.

3. *A passion to master*. Gifted children are driven to understand the domain in which they have high ability. They display an intense, obsessive interest and an ability to focus. They do not need to be pushed by their parents. They motivate themselves, says Winner.

A fourth area in which gifted children excel involves *information-processing skills*. Researchers have found that children who are gifted learn at a faster pace, process information more rapidly, are better at reasoning, use superior strategies, and monitor their understanding better than their nongifted counterparts (Ambrose & Sternberg, 2016).

Life Course of the Gifted   As a 10-year-old, Alexandra Nechita (born in 1985) was described as a child prodigy. She paints quickly and impulsively on large canvases, some as large as 5 feet by 9 feet. It is not unusual for her to complete several of these large paintings in a week's time. Her paintings sell for up to $100,000 apiece. When she was only 2 years of age, Alexandra colored in coloring books for hours. She had no interest in dolls or friends. Once she started school, she would start painting as soon as she got home. And she continues to paint as an adult—relentlessly and passionately. It is, she says, what she loves to do. Recently, Alexandra completed a degree in Fine Arts at UCLA.

A longitudinal study of individuals identified before 13 years of age as having profoundly superior math or verbal reasoning skills (top 1 in 10,000) found that they had achieved considerable success in their careers in various domains by age 38 (Kell, Lubinski, & Benbow, 2013).

Is giftedness, like Alexandra Nechita's artistic talent and the children with profoundly superior math and verbal skills just described, a product of heredity or of environment? Likely both (Duggan & Friedman, 2014; Johnson & Bouchard, 2014). Individuals who are gifted recall that they had signs of high ability in a specific area at a very young age, prior to or at the beginning of formal training (Howe & others, 1995). This suggests the importance of innate ability in giftedness. However, researchers also have found that individuals with world-class status in the arts, mathematics, science, and sports all report strong family support and years of training and practice (Bloom, 1985). Deliberate practice is an important characteristic of individuals who become experts in a specific domain. For example, in one study, the best musicians engaged in twice as much deliberate practice over their lives as the least successful ones did (Ericsson, Krampe, & Tesch-Romer, 1993).

Do gifted children become gifted and highly creative adults? In Terman's research on children with superior IQs, the children typically became experts in a well-established domain, such as medicine, law, or business. However, they did not become major creators (Winner, 2000). That is, they did not create a new domain or revolutionize an existing domain.

One reason that some gifted children do not become gifted adults is that they often have been pushed too hard by overzealous parents and teachers. As a result, they lose their intrinsic (internal) motivation (Winner, 1996, 2006). As adolescents, they may ask themselves, "Who am I doing this for?" If they are achieving in an effort to please others rather than themselves, they may not want to do it anymore. Another reason that gifted children do not become gifted adults is that the criteria for giftedness change—as an adult, an individual has to actually do something special to be labeled gifted.

Domain-Specific Giftedness   Individuals who are highly gifted are typically not gifted in many domains, and research on giftedness increasingly focuses on domain-specific developmental trajectories (Kell & Lubinski, 2014; Sternberg, 2018e; Sternberg & Kaufman, 2018b; Worrell & others, 2019). During the childhood years, the domains in which individuals are gifted usually emerge. Thus, at some point in childhood, a person who is destined to become a gifted artist or a gifted mathematician begins to show expertise in that domain. Regarding domain-specific giftedness, software genius Bill Gates (1998), the founder of Microsoft and one

Art prodigy Alexandra Nechita. *What are some characteristics of gifted children?*
Koichi Kamoshida/Hulton Archive/Getty Images

Creativity the ability to think in novel and unusual ways and to come up with unique solutions to problems.

Divergent thinking thinking that produces many answers to the same question; characteristic of creativity.

Convergent thinking thinking that produces one correct answer; characteristic of the kind of thinking required on conventional intelligence tests.

of the world's richest persons, commented that when you are good at something you may need to resist the urge to think that you will be good at everything. Gates says that because he has been so successful at software development, people expect him to be brilliant in other domains in which he is far from being a genius.

Education of Children Who Are Gifted An increasing number of experts argue that the education of gifted children in the United States requires a significant overhaul (Renzulli, 2017; Sternberg, 2018e; Sternberg & Kaufman, 2018b; Worrell & others, 2019). Consider the titles of the following books and reports: *Genius Denied: How to Stop Wasting Our Brightest Young Minds* (Davidson & Davidson, 2004) and *A Nation Deceived: How Schools Hold Back America's Brightest Students* (Colangelo, Assouline, & Gross, 2004).

Gifted children who are underchallenged can become disruptive, skip classes, and lose interest in achieving. Sometimes these children just disappear into the woodwork, becoming passive and apathetic toward school. It is extremely important for teachers to challenge children who are gifted to establish high expectations for their own performance (Sternberg, 2018e).

Some educators conclude that the inadequate education of children who are gifted has been compounded by policies established under the federal government's No Child Left Behind Act, which sought to raise the achievement level of students who were not doing well in school at the expense of enriching the education of children who were gifted (Clark, 2008). A number of experts argue that too often children who are gifted are socially isolated and underchallenged in the classroom (Karnes & Stephens, 2008). It is not unusual for them to be ostracized and labeled "nerds" or "geeks." Ellen Winner (1996, 2006) concludes that a child who is truly gifted often is the only child in the room who does not have the opportunity to learn with students of like ability.

Many eminent adults report that school was a negative experience for them, that they were bored and sometimes knew more than their teachers did (Bloom, 1985). Winner stresses that American education will benefit when standards are raised for all children. When some children are still underchallenged, she recommends that they be allowed to attend advanced classes in their domain of exceptional ability, such as allowing some especially precocious middle school students to take college classes in their area of expertise. For example, Bill Gates took college math classes and hacked a computer security system at 13; Yo-Yo Ma, a famous cellist, graduated from high school at 15 and attended Juilliard School of Music in New York City.

A final concern is that African American, Latino, and Native American children are underrepresented in gifted programs (Ford, 2012, 2014, 2015a, b; Mills, 2015). Much of the underrepresentation involves the lower test scores for these children compared with non-Latino White and Asian American children, which may be due to a number of reasons such as test bias and fewer opportunities to develop language skills such as vocabulary and comprehension (Ford, 2012, 2014, 2015a, b; Mills, 2015).

CREATIVITY

We have encountered the term "creative" on several occasions in our discussion of giftedness. What does it mean to be creative? **Creativity** is the ability to think about something in novel and unusual ways and to come up with unique, good solutions to problems.

Intelligence and creativity are not the same thing (Kaufman & Sternberg, 2019; Renzulli, 2018; Sternberg, 2018f, g; Sternberg & Kaufman, 2018a). Most creative people are quite intelligent, but the reverse is not necessarily true. Many highly intelligent people (as measured by high scores on conventional tests of intelligence) are not very creative. Many highly intelligent people are also highly productive, but their output is not necessarily novel (Sternberg, Kaufman,& Roberts, 2019).

Why don't IQ scores predict creativity? Creativity requires divergent thinking (Guilford, 1967; Runco & Acar, 2019). **Divergent thinking** produces many answers to the same question. In contrast, conventional intelligence tests require **convergent thinking.** For example, a typical question on a conventional intelligence test is "How many quarters will you get in return for 60 dimes?" There is only one correct answer to this question. In contrast, a question such as "What image comes to mind when you hear the phrase 'sitting alone in a dark room'?" has many possible answers; it calls for divergent thinking.

One study examined the divergent thinking of 1-year-olds and their parents (Hoicka & others, 2016). In this study, the creativity of the 1-year-olds was associated with the creativity

Margaret (Peg) Cagle with some of the gifted seventh- and eighth-grade math students she teaches at Lawrence Middle School in Chatsworth, California. Cagle especially advocates challenging gifted students to take intellectual risks. To encourage collaboration, she often has students work together in groups of four, and frequently tutors students during lunch hour. As 13-year-old Madeline Lewis commented, "If I don't get it one way, she'll explain it another and talk to you about it and show you until you do get it." Cagle says it is important to be passionate about teaching math and open up a world for students that shows them how beautiful learning math can be (Wong Briggs, 2007, p. 6D).
Scott Buschman

A young Bill Gates, founder of Microsoft and now one of the world's richest persons. Like many highly gifted students, Gates was not especially fond of school. He hacked a computer security system when he was 13 and as a high school student, he was allowed to take some college math classes. He dropped out of Harvard University and began developing a plan for what was to become Microsoft Corporation. *What are some ways that schools can enrich the education of such highly talented students as Gates to make it a more challenging, interesting, and meaningful experience?*
Joe McNally/Hulton ArchiveGetty Images

of their parents. How did researchers assess divergent thinking in 1-year-old children? A task called the Unusual Box Test was used, in which children play with a colorful box equipped with strings, hoops, stairs, ledges, and such, next to five novel objects. Their divergent thinking is determined by the number of different action/box combinations the children generate.

Steps in the Creative Process   The creative process has often been described as a five-step sequence:

1. *Preparation*. You become immersed in a problem or an issue that interests you and arouses your curiosity.

2. *Incubation*. You churn ideas around in your head. This is the point at which you are likely to make some unusual connections in your thinking.

3. *Insight*. You experience the "Aha!" moment when all of the pieces of the puzzle seem to fit together.

4. *Evaluation*. Now you must decide whether the idea is valuable and worth pursuing. Is the idea really novel or is it obvious?

5. *Elaboration*. This final step often covers the longest span of time and requires the hardest work. This is what the famous twentieth-century American inventor Thomas Edison was talking about when he said that creativity is 1 percent inspiration and 99 percent perspiration. Elaboration may require a great deal of perspiration.

Mihaly Csikszentmihalyi (pronounced ME-high CHICK-sent-me-high-ee) (1996) notes that this five-step sequence provides a helpful framework for thinking about how creative ideas are developed. However, he argues that creative people don't always go through the steps in a linear sequence. For example, elaboration is often interrupted by periods of incubation. Fresh insights may appear during incubation, evaluation, and elaboration. And insight might take years or only a few hours. Sometimes the creative idea consists of one deep insight. Other times it's a series of small ones.

Characteristics of Creative Thinkers   Creative thinkers tend to have the following characteristics (Perkins, 1994):

- *Flexibility and playful thinking*. Creative thinkers are flexible and play with problems, which gives rise to a paradox. Although creativity takes hard work, the work goes more smoothly if you take it lightly (Goleman, Kaufman, & Ray, 1993). When you are joking around, you are more likely to consider unusual possibilities.

- *Inner motivation*. Creative people often are motivated by the joy of creating. They tend to be less inspired by grades, money, or favorable feedback from others. Thus, creative people are motivated more internally than externally (Hennessey, 2019).

- *Willingness to risk*. Creative people make more mistakes than their less imaginative counterparts. It's not that they are less proficient but that they come up with more ideas, more possibilities (Gotlieb & others, 2019). They win some, and they lose some. For example, the twentieth-century Spanish artist Pablo Picasso created more than 20,000 paintings. Not all of them were masterpieces. Creative thinkers learn to cope with unsuccessful projects and see failure as an opportunity to learn.

- *Objective evaluation of work*. Contrary to the stereotype that creative people are eccentric and highly subjective, most creative thinkers strive to evaluate their work objectively. They may use established criteria to make this judgment or rely on the judgments of people they respect. In this manner, they can determine whether further creative thinking will improve their work.

Creativity in Schools   A special concern is that children's creative thinking appears to be declining. A study of approximately 300,000 U.S. children and adults found that creativity scores rose until 1990, but since then have been steadily declining (Kim, 2010). Among the likely causes of the creativity decline are the number of hours U.S. children spend watching TV, interacting on social media, and playing video games instead of engaging in creative activities, as well as the lack of emphasis on creative thinking skills in schools (Beghetto, 2019; Renzulli, 2017, 2018). Some countries, though, are placing increasing emphasis on stimulating creative thinking in schools. For example, historically, creative thinking has typically been discouraged in Chinese schools. However, Chinese educators are now encouraging teachers to spend more classroom time on creative activities (Plucker, 2010).

An important teaching goal is to help students become more creative (Sternberg, 2018f, g, 2019c; Sternberg & Kaufman, 2018a). Teachers need to recognize that students will show more creativity in some domains than in others (Baer, 2016). A student who shows creative thinking skills in mathematics may not exhibit these skills in art, for example.

School environments that encourage independent work, are stimulating but not distracting, and make resources readily available are likely to encourage students' creativity. There is mounting concern that the U.S. government's No Child Left Behind legislation has harmed the development of students' creative thinking by focusing attention on memorizing information to ensure high performance on standardized tests (Burke-Adams, 2007; Sternberg & Kaufman, 2018a).

Strategies for increasing children's creative thinking include the following:

- *Encourage brainstorming.* **Brainstorming** is a technique in which people are encouraged to come up with creative ideas in a group, play off each other's ideas, and say practically whatever comes to mind that seems relevant to a particular issue (Sawyer, 2019). Participants are usually told to hold off from criticizing others' ideas at least until the end of the brainstorming session.

- *Provide environments that stimulate creativity.* Some environments nourish creativity, while others inhibit it (Kaufman & Sternberg, 2019). Parents and teachers who encourage creativity often rely on children's natural curiosity. They provide exercises and activities that stimulate children to find insightful solutions to problems, rather than ask a lot of questions that require rote answers (Beghetto, 2018, 2019; Gotlieb & others, 2017). Teachers also encourage creativity by taking students on field trips to locations where creativity is valued. Science, discovery, and children's museums offer rich opportunities to stimulate creativity.

- *Don't overcontrol students.* Teresa Amabile (1993, 2018) says that telling children exactly how to do things leaves them feeling that originality is a mistake and exploration is a waste of time. If, instead of dictating which activities they should engage in, you let children select their interests and you support their inclinations, you will be less likely to destroy their natural curiosity (Hennessey, 2017, 2019).

- *Encourage internal motivation.* Excessive use of prizes, such as gold stars, money, or toys, can stifle creativity by undermining the intrinsic pleasure students derive from creative activities. Creative children's motivation is the satisfaction generated by the work itself. Competition for prizes and formal evaluations often undermine intrinsic motivation and creativity (Amabile & Hennessey, 1992; Hennessey, 2017, 2019). However, material rewards should not be eliminated altogether.

- *Build children's confidence.* To expand children's creativity, encourage them to believe in their own ability to create something innovative and worthwhile. Building children's confidence in their creative skills aligns with Bandura's (2010, 2012) concept of self-efficacy—the belief that one can master a situation and produce positive outcomes.

- *Guide children to be persistent and delay gratification.* Most highly successful creative products take years to develop. Most creative individuals work on ideas and projects for months and years without being rewarded for their efforts (Sternberg, 2017, 2018f, g).

- *Encourage children to take intellectual risks.* Creative individuals take intellectual risks and seek to discover or invent something that has never before been discovered or invented (Kaufman & Sternberg, 2019; Sternberg & Kaufman, 2018a). They risk spending extensive time on an idea or project that may not work. Creative people are not afraid of failing or getting something wrong.

developmental **connection**

Education

A number of criticisms of No Child Left Behind educational policies have been made. Connect to "Schools, Achievement, and Work."

developmental **connection**

Achievement

Intrinsic motivation involves doing something for its own sake (the activity is an end in itself). Connect to "Schools, Achievement, and Work."

developmental **connection**

Achievement

Self-efficacy is the belief that "I can"; helplessness is the belief that "I cannot." Connect to "Schools, Achievement, and Work."

brainstorming Technique in which individuals are encouraged to come up with creative ideas in a group, play off each other's ideas, and say practically whatever comes to mind that is relevant to a particular issue.

What are some good strategies for guiding children to think more creatively?
Ariel Skelley/Blend Images LLC

Living a More Creative Life

Leading expert on creativity Mihaly Csikszentmihalyi (1996) inter-viewed 90 leading figures in art, business, government, education, and science to learn how creativity works. He discovered that creative people regularly engage in challenges that absorb them. Based on his interviews with some of the most creative people in the world, he con-cluded that the first step toward a more creative life is to cultivate your curiosity and interest. Here are his recommendations for doing this:

1. *Try to be surprised by something every day.* Maybe it is something you see, hear, or read about. Become absorbed in a lecture or a book. Be open to what the world is telling you. Life is a stream of experi-ences. Swim widely and deeply in it, and your life will be richer.

2. *Try to surprise at least one person every day.* In a lot of things you do, you have to be predictable and patterned. Do something different for a change. Ask a question you normally would not ask. Invite someone to go with you to a show or a museum you have never visited.

3. *Write down each day what surprised you and how you surprised others.* Most creative people keep a diary, notes, or lab records to ensure that their experience is not forgotten. Start with a spe-cific task. Each evening, record the most surprising event that occurred that day and your most surprising action. After a few days, reread your notes and reflect on your experiences. After a few weeks, you might see a pattern emerging, one that suggests an area you can explore in greater depth.

4. *When something sparks your interest, follow it.* Usually when something captures your attention, it is short-lived—an idea, a song, a flower. Too often we are too busy to explore the idea, song, or flower further. Or we think these areas are none of our business because we are not experts about them. Yet the world is our business. We can't know which part of it is best suited to our interests until we make a serious effort to learn as much as we can about as many aspects of it as possible.

5. *Wake up in the morning with a specific goal to look forward to.* Creative people wake up eager to start the day. Why? Not neces-sarily because they are cheerful, enthusiastic types but because they know that there is something meaningful to accomplish each day, and they can't wait to get started.

6. *Take charge of your schedule.* Figure out which time of the day is your most creative time. Some of us are more creative late at

Leading creativity theorist Mihaly Csikszentmihalyi, in the setting where he gets his most creative ideas.
Courtesy of Dr. Mihaly Csiksentmihalyi

night, others early in the morning. Carve out some time for your-self during the time when your creative energy is at its best.

7. *Spend time in settings that stimulate your creativity.* In Csikszentmihalyi's (1996) research, he gave people an electronic pager and beeped them randomly at different times of the day. When he asked them how they felt, they reported the highest levels of creativity when walking, driving, or swimming. For exam-ple, one person said, "I do my most creative thinking when I'm jogging." One experimental study compared the creative thinking skills of individuals after they had experienced one of four condi-tions: sitting inside, walking on a treadmill inside, walking out-side, or being rolled outside in a wheelchair (Oppezzo & Schwartz, 2014). In this study, walking was more likely to produce the most creative thinking. Activities such as walking, jogging, and swim-ming are semiautomatic in that they take a certain amount of attention while leaving some time free to make connections among ideas. Another setting in which highly creative people report coming up with novel ideas is the half-asleep, half-awake state we are in when we are deeply relaxed or barely awake.

Can the strategies for stimulating creative thinking in children found earlier in this chapter also be used by adults? How do those strate-gies compare with those discussed here?

• *Introduce children to creative people.* Teachers can invite creative people to their classrooms and ask them to describe what helps them become creative or to demonstrate their cre-ative skills. Writers, poets, musicians, scientists, and many others can bring their props and productions to the class, turning it into a theater for stimulating students' creativity.

To find out about steps you can take to live a more creative life, see the *Connecting Development to Life* interlude.

Changes in Adulthood   At the age of 30, Thomas Edison invented the phonograph, Hans Christian Andersen wrote his first volume of fairy tales, and Mozart composed *The*

Marriage of Figaro. One early study of creativity found that individuals' most creative products were generated in their thirties and that 80 percent of the most important creative contributions were completed by age 50 (Lehman, 1960). More recently, researchers have found that creativity often peaks in the forties before declining (Simonton, 1996, 2019). However, any generalization about a link between age and creative accomplishments must be qualified by consideration of (1) the size of the decline and (2) differences across domains (Jones, Reedy, & Weinberg, 2014; McKay & Kaufman, 2014).

Even though a decline in creative contributions is often found in the fifties and later, the decline is often not great. And a study of artists from 53 to 75 years of age found no age differences in the artists' perceptions of their creativity (Reed, 2005). An impressive array of creative accomplishments have occurred in late adulthood (Tahir & Gruber, 2003). Benjamin Franklin invented the bifocal lens when he was 78 years old; Wolfgang von Goethe completed *Faust* when he was in his eighties. After a distinguished career as a physicist, Henri Chevreul switched fields in his nineties to become a pioneer in gerontological research. He published his last research paper just a year prior to his death at the age of 103!

Furthermore, the age at which creativity typically declines varies with the domain involved. In philosophy and history, for example, older adults often show as much creativity as they did when they were in their thirties and forties. In contrast, in lyric poetry, abstract mathematics, and theoretical physics, the peak of creativity is often reached in the twenties or thirties.

Researchers have found that personality traits are linked to creativity (Feist, 2019). In one study, the personality trait of openness to experience predicted creativity in the arts, while intellect predicted creativity in the sciences (Kaufman & others, 2016).

Review *Connect* Reflect

LG4 Describe the characteristics of intellectual disability, giftedness, and creativity.

Review
- What is intellectual disability, and what are its causes?
- What makes people gifted?
- What makes people creative?

Connect
- Regarding children's critical-thinking skills and problem-solving strategies, what role, if any, might these play in determining whether children become creative thinkers?

Reflect *Your Own Personal Journey of Life*
- How many of the tips in the *Connecting Development to Life* interlude, "Living a More Creative Life," do you practice? In what ways might you benefit from these suggestions, in addition to becoming more creative?

reach your **learning goals**

Intelligence

1 The Concept of Intelligence

LG1 Explain the nature of intelligence.

What Is Intelligence?

- Intelligence consists of the ability to solve problems and to adapt and learn from experiences. A key aspect of intelligence focuses on its individual variations. Traditionally, intelligence has been measured by tests designed to compare people's performance on cognitive tasks.

Intelligence Tests

- Sir Francis Galton is considered the father of mental tests. Alfred Binet developed the first intelligence test and created the concept of mental age. William Stern developed the concept of IQ for use with the Binet test. Revisions of the Binet test are called the Stanford-Binet. The test scores on the Stanford-Binet approximate a normal distribution.

Theories of Multiple Intelligences

- The Wechsler scales, created by David Wechsler, are the other main intelligence assessment tool. These tests provide an overall IQ and yield several composite scores, allowing the examiner to identify strengths and weaknesses in different areas of intelligence.

- Test scores should be only one type of information used to evaluate an individual, not the only criterion. IQ scores can produce unfortunate stereotypes and expectations.

- Sternberg's triarchic theory states that there are three main types of intelligence: analytical, creative, and practical.

- Gardner identifies eight types of intelligence: verbal skills, mathematical skills, spatial skills, bodily-kinesthetic skills, musical skills, interpersonal skills, intrapersonal skills, and naturalist skills.

- Emotional intelligence is the ability to perceive and express emotion accurately and adaptively, to understand emotion and emotional knowledge, to use feelings to facilitate thought, and to manage emotions in oneself and others.

- The multiple intelligences approaches have broadened the definition of intelligence and motivated educators to develop programs that instruct students in different domains. Critics maintain that the multiple intelligences theories include factors that really aren't part of intelligence, such as musical skills and creativity. Critics also say that not enough research has been done to support the concept of multiple intelligences.

The Neuroscience of Intelligence

- Interest in discovering links between the brain and intelligence has been stimulated by advances in brain imaging. A moderate correlation has been found between brain size and intelligence.

- Some experts emphasize that the highest level of intelligence that involves reasoning is linked to the prefrontal cortex. However, other researchers recently have found a link between a distributed neural network in the frontal and parietal lobes and intelligence. The search for a connection between neural processing speed and intelligence has produced mixed results.

2 Controversies and Group Comparisons

 LG2 Outline key controversies about differences in IQ scores.

The Influence of Heredity and Environment

- Genetic similarity might explain why identical twins show stronger correlations on intelligence tests than fraternal twins do.

- In recent decades there has been a considerable rise in intelligence test scores around the world—called the Flynn effect—and this supports the role of environment in intelligence.

- Researchers have found that the extent to which parents talk with their children in the first three years of life is correlated with the children's IQs and that being deprived of formal education lowers IQ scores. Ramey's research revealed the positive effects of educational child care on intelligence.

Group Comparisons and Issues

- Cultures vary in the way they define intelligence. Early intelligence tests favored non-Latino White, middle-socioeconomic-status, urban individuals.

- Tests may be biased against certain groups that are not familiar with a standard form of English, with the content tested, or with the testing situation. Stereotype threat may produce ethnic/cultural bias that reduces intelligence test scores.

- Tests are likely to reflect the values and experience of the dominant culture. In the United States, the average score of African American children is below the average score of non-Latino White children on standardized intelligence tests, but as African Americans have gained economic, social, and educational opportunities, the gap between these average scores has begun to narrow.

3 The Development of Intelligence   LG3 · Discuss the development of intelligence across the life span.

Tests of Infant Intelligence

- The Bayley scales are widely used to assess infant intelligence. The Fagan Test of Infant Intelligence, which assesses how effectively infants process information, is increasingly being used.

Stability and Change in Intelligence Through Adolescence

- Although intelligence is more stable across childhood and adolescence than are many other attributes, many children's and adolescents' scores on intelligence tests fluctuate considerably.

Intelligence in Adulthood

- Horn argued that crystallized intelligence continues to increase in middle adulthood, whereas fluid intelligence begins to decline. Schaie found that when assessed longitudinally, inductive reasoning is less likely to decline and more likely to improve than when assessed cross-sectionally in middle adulthood.

- The highest level of four intellectual abilities (vocabulary, verbal memory, inductive reasoning, and spatial orientation) occurs in middle adulthood.

- Baltes emphasizes a distinction between cognitive mechanics (the "hardware" of the mind, reflecting the neurophysiological architecture of the brain) and cognitive pragmatics (the culture-based "software" of the mind). Cognitive mechanics are more likely to decline in older adults than are cognitive pragmatics.

- Wisdom is expert knowledge about the practical aspects of life that permits excellent judgment about important matters. Baltes and his colleagues have found that high levels of wisdom are rare, factors other than age are critical for a high level of wisdom to develop, and personality-related factors are better predictors of wisdom than cognitive factors such as intelligence.

4 The Extremes of Intelligence and Creativity   LG4 · Describe the characteristics of intellectual disability, giftedness, and creativity.

Intellectual Disability

- Intellectual disability is a condition of limited mental ability in which the individual (1) has a low IQ, usually below 70; (2) has difficulty adapting to the demands of everyday life; and (3) has an onset of these characteristics by age 18.

- Most affected individuals have an IQ in the 55 to 70 range (mild intellectual disability). Intellectual disability can have an organic cause or a cultural/familial cause.

Giftedness

- People who are gifted have high intelligence (an IQ of 130 or higher) or some type of superior talent. Three characteristics of gifted children are precocity, marching to their own drummer, and a passion to achieve mastery in their domain.

- Giftedness is likely a consequence of both heredity and environment. A current concern is the education of children who are gifted.

Creativity

- Creativity is the ability to think about something in novel and unusual ways and come up with unique solutions to problems. Although most creative people are intelligent, individuals with high IQs are not necessarily creative. Creative people tend to be divergent thinkers, but traditional intelligence tests measure convergent thinking.

- Creativity has often been described as occurring in a five-step process: preparation, incubation, insight, evaluation, and elaboration.

- Characteristics of creative thinkers include flexibility and playful thinking, inner motivation, a willingness to take risks, and interest in objective evaluation.

- Creativity often peaks in the forties and then declines, but the decline may be slight and the peak age varies across domains. Csikszentmihalyi notes that cultivating curiosity and interest is the first step toward leading a more creative life.

key **terms**

Bayley Scales of Infant Development	creativity	giftedness	stereotype threat
brainstorming	crystallized intelligence	intellectual disability	triarchic theory of intelligence
cognitive mechanics	culture-fair tests	intelligence	wisdom
cognitive pragmatics	divergent thinking	intelligence quotient (IQ)	
convergent thinking	emotional intelligence	mental age (MA)	
	fluid intelligence	normal distribution	

key **people**

Paul Baltes	Howard Gardner	Robert Plomin	Robert J. Sternberg
Nancy Bayley	Daniel Goleman	Craig Ramey	Lewis Terman
Alfred Binet	John Horn	Peter Salovey	David Wechsler
Mihaly Csikszentmihalyi	John Mayer	K. Warner Schaie	Ellen Winner
James Flynn	Robert McCall	Theophile Simon	

LANGUAGE DEVELOPMENT

chapter outline

Giselleflissak/Getty Images

preview

In this chapter, we will tell the remarkable story of language and how it develops. The questions we will explore include these: What is language? What is the course of language development across the life span? What does biology contribute to language? How do different experiences influence language?

1 What Is Language?

 LG1 Define language and describe its rule systems.

> Defining Language

> Language's Rule Systems

Words not only affect us temporarily; they change us, they socialize us, and they unsocialize us.

—DAVID REISMAN
American Social Scientist, 20th Century

In 1799, a nude boy was observed running through the woods in France. The boy was captured when he was 11 years old. He was called the Wild Boy of Aveyron and was believed to have lived in the woods alone for six years (Lane, 1976). When found, he made no effort to communicate. He never learned to communicate effectively. A modern-day wild child named Genie was discovered in Los Angeles in 1970. Genie had been locked away in almost complete social isolation during her childhood. At age 13, Genie could not speak or stand erect. Sadly, despite intensive intervention, Genie never acquired more than a primitive form of language. Both cases—the Wild Boy of Aveyron and Genie—raise questions about the biological and environmental determinants of language, topics that we will examine later in the chapter. First, though, we need to define language.

DEFINING LANGUAGE

Language is a form of communication—whether spoken, written, or signed—that is based on a system of symbols. Language consists of the words used by a community and the rules for varying and combining them.

Think how important language is in our everyday lives. We need language to speak with others, listen to others, read, and write. Our language enables us to describe past events in detail and to plan for the future. Language lets us pass down information from one generation to the next and create a rich cultural heritage. Language learning involves comprehending a sound system (or sign system for individuals who are deaf), the world of objects, actions, and events, and how units such as words and grammar connect sound and world (Israel, 2019; Mithun, 2019).

All human languages have some common characteristics (Clark, 2017; Genetti, 2019; Ringe, 2019). These include infinite generativity and organizational rules. **Infinite generativity** is the ability to produce and comprehend an endless number of meaningful sentences using a finite set of words and rules. Rules describe the way language works. Let's explore what these rules involve.

Language allows us to communicate with others. *What are some important characteristics of language?*
FatCamera/Getty Images

LANGUAGE'S RULE SYSTEMS

When nineteenth-century American writer Ralph Waldo Emerson said, "The world was built in order and the atoms march in tune," he must have had language in mind. Language is highly ordered and organized (Clark, 2017; White, 2019). The organization involves five systems of rules: phonology, morphology, syntax, semantics, and pragmatics.

Phonology Every language is made up of basic sounds. **Phonology** is the sound system of the language, including the sounds that are used and how they may be combined

language A form of communication, whether spoken, written, or signed, that is based on a system of symbols.

infinite generativity The ability to produce and comprehend an endless number of meaningful sentences using a finite set of words and rules.

phonology The sound system of a language—includes the sounds used and how they may be combined.

(Demuth, 2019). For example, English has the initial consonant cluster *spr* as in *spring,* but no words begin with the cluster *rsp*.

Phonology provides a basis for constructing a large and expandable set of words out of two or three dozen phonemes (Swingley, 2017). A *phoneme* is the basic unit of sound in a language; it is the smallest unit of sound that affects meaning. For example, in English the sound represented by the letter *p*, as in the words *pot* and *spot*, is a phoneme. The /p/ sound is slightly different in the two words, but this variation is not distinguished in English, and therefore the /p/ sound is a single phoneme. In some languages, such as Hindi, the variations of the /p/ sound represent separate phonemes.

Morphology

Morphology refers to the units of meaning involved in word formation. A morpheme is a minimal unit of meaning; it is a word or a part of a word that cannot be broken into smaller meaningful parts (Deevy, Leonard, & Marchman, 2017; Mithun, 2019). Every word in the English language is made up of one or more morphemes. Some words consist of a single morpheme (for example, *help*), whereas others are made up of more than one morpheme (for example, *helper* has two morphemes, *help* and *er*, with the morpheme *-er* meaning "one who"—in this case "one who helps"). Thus, not all morphemes are words by themselves—for example, *pre-*, *-tion*, and *-ing* are morphemes.

Just as the rules that govern phonology describe the sound sequences that can occur in a language, the rules of morphology describe the way meaningful units (morphemes) can be combined in words (Mithun, 2019). Morphemes have many jobs in grammar, such as marking tense (for example, "she walks" versus "she walked") and number ("she walks" versus "they walk").

Syntax

Syntax involves the way words are combined to form acceptable phrases and sentences (Hendrickson & others, 2017; Indefrey, 2019; Meteyard & Vigliocco, 2019; Ringe, 2019). If someone says to you, "Bob slugged Tom" or "Bob was slugged by Tom," you know who did the slugging and who was slugged in each case because you have a syntactic understanding of these sentence structures. You also understand that the sentence "You didn't stay, did you?" is a grammatical sentence but that "You didn't stay, didn't you?" is unacceptable and ambiguous.

If you learn another language, English syntax will not get you very far. For example, in English an adjective usually precedes a noun (as in *blue sky*), whereas in Spanish the adjective usually follows the noun (*cielo azul*). Despite the differences in their syntactic structures, however, syntactic systems in all of the world's languages have some common ground (Ringe, 2019). For example, no language we know of permits sentences like the following one:

> *The mouse the cat the farmer chased killed ate the cheese.*

It appears that language users cannot process subjects and objects arranged in too complex a fashion in a sentence.

Semantics

Semantics refers to the meaning of words and sentences. Every word has a set of semantic features, which are required attributes related to meaning (Ellis & Ogden, 2017; Israel, 2019; Jefferies & Thompson, 2019). *Girl* and *woman*, for example, share many semantic features, but they differ semantically in regard to age.

Words have semantic restrictions on how they can be used in sentences (Duff, Tomblin, & Catts, 2015; MacDonald & Hsiao, 2019). The sentence *The bicycle talked the boy into buying a candy bar* is syntactically correct but semantically incorrect. The sentence violates our semantic knowledge that bicycles don't talk.

Pragmatics

A final set of language rules involves **pragmatics,** the appropriate use of language in different contexts. Pragmatics covers a lot of territory (Fay & others, 2018; Fischer, 2018; Garnham, 2019; van Berkum, 2019). When you take turns speaking in a discussion or use a question to convey a command ("Why is it so noisy in here? What is this, Grand Central Station?"), you are demonstrating knowledge of pragmatics. You also apply the pragmatics of English when you use polite language in appropriate situations (for example, when talking to your teacher) or tell stories that are interesting, jokes that are funny, and lies that are convincing. In each of these cases, you are demonstrating that you understand the rules of your culture for adjusting language to suit the context.

Pragmatic rules can be complex and differ from one culture to another (Fay & others, 2018). Consider the pragmatics of saying "thank you." Even preschoolers' use of the phrase

morphology Units of meaning involved in word formation.

syntax The ways words are combined to form acceptable phrases and sentences.

semantics The meanings of words and sentences.

pragmatics The appropriate use of language in different contexts.

Rule System	Description	Examples
Phonology	The sound system of a language. A phoneme is the smallest sound unit in a language.	The word *chat* has three phonemes or sounds: /ch/ /ă/ /t/. An example of a phonological rule in the English language is while the phoneme /r/ can follow the phonemes /t/ or /d/ in an English consonant cluster (such as *track* or *drab*), the phoneme /l/ cannot follow these letters.
Morphology	The system of meaningful units involved in word formation.	The smallest sound units that have a meaning are called morphemes, or meaning units. The word *girl* is one morpheme, or meaning unit; it cannot be broken down any further and still have meaning. When the suffix *s* is added, the word becomes *girls* and has two morphemes because the *s* changed the meaning of the word, indicating that there is more than one girl.
Syntax	The system that involves the way words are combined to form acceptable phrases and sentences.	Word order is very important in determining meaning in the English language. For example, the sentence "Sebastian pushed the bike" has a different meaning from "The bike pushed Sebastian."
Semantics	The system that involves the meaning of words and sentences.	Semantics involves knowing the meaning of individual words—that is, vocabulary. For example, semantics includes knowing the meaning of such words as *orange*, *transportation*, and *intelligent*.
Pragmatics	The system of using appropriate conversation and knowledge of how to effectively use language in context.	An example is using polite language in appropriate situations, such as being mannerly when talking with one's teacher. Taking turns in a conversation involves pragmatics.

FIGURE **1**

THE RULE SYSTEMS OF LANGUAGE

thank you varies with sex, socioeconomic status, and the age of the individual they are addressing. If you were to study the Japanese language, you would come face-to-face with countless pragmatic rules about how to say "thank you" to individuals of various social levels and with various relationships to you.

In this section, we have discussed five important rule systems involved in language. An overview of these rule systems is presented in Figure 1.

Review *Connect* Reflect

 LG1 Define language and describe its rule systems.

Review

- What is language?
- What are language's five main rule systems?

Connect

- What have you learned about thinking in childhood that might help explain why Genie and the Wild Boy of Aveyron never learned effective verbal communication skills?

Reflect *Your Own Personal Journey of Life*

- How good are your family members and friends at the pragmatics of language? Describe a situation in which an individual showed pragmatic skills and another in which a person did not.

2 How Language Develops

LG2 Describe how language develops through the life span.

Infancy | Early Childhood | Middle and Late Childhood | Adolescence | Adulthood and Aging

In the thirteenth century, Emperor Frederick II of Germany had a cruel idea. He wanted to know what language children would speak if no one talked to them. He selected several newborns and threatened their caregivers with death if they ever talked to the infants. Frederick never found out what language the children spoke because they all died. As we move forward in the twenty-first century, we are still curious about infants' development of language, although our experiments and observations are, to say the least, far more humane than the evil Frederick's.

INFANCY

Whatever language they learn, infants all over the world follow a similar path in language development. What are some key milestones in this development?

Babbling and Other Vocalizations   Long before infants speak recognizable words, they produce a number of vocalizations (Choi & others, 2019; Hirai & Kanakogi, 2019). The functions of these early vocalizations are to practice making sounds, to communicate, and to attract attention (Lee & others, 2018). Babies' sounds go through the following sequence during the first year:

- *Crying.* Babies cry even at birth. Crying can signal distress, but different types of cries signal different things.
- *Cooing.* Babies first coo at about 2 to 4 months. These gurgling sounds that are made in the back of the throat usually express pleasure during interaction with the caregiver.
- *Babbling.* In the middle of the first year, babies babble—that is, they produce strings of consonant-vowel combinations, such as *ba, ba, ba, ba* (Lee & others, 2018). In a recent study, age at babbling onset predicted when infants would say their first words (McGillion & others, 2017a). Also, in another recent study, a lack of babbling in infants was linked to a risk of having future speech and language problems (Lohmander & others, 2017). And in other research, infants' babbling has been shown to influence the behavior of their caregivers, creating social interaction that facilitates their own language development (Albert, Schwade, & Goldstein, 2019).

Gestures   Infants start using gestures, such as showing and pointing, at about 8 to 12 months of age. They may wave bye-bye, nod to mean "yes," show an empty cup to ask for more milk, and point to a dog to draw attention to it. Some early gestures are symbolic, as when an infant smacks her lips to indicate food or drink. Pointing is considered by language experts to be an important index of the social aspects of language, and it follows a specific developmental sequence: from pointing without checking on adult gaze to pointing while looking back and forth between an object and the adult (Begus & Southgate, 2012).

Lack of pointing is a significant indicator of problems in the infant's communication system (Cooperrider & Goldin-Meadow, 2018; Goldin-Meadow, 2015, 2017a, b; Lucca & Wilbourn, 2018; Novack & others, 2018). Pointing is a key aspect of the development of joint attention and an important index of the social aspects of language (Brentari & Goldin-Meadow, 2017). Failure to engage in pointing also characterizes many autistic children. In a recent study, infants at high risk for autism spectrum disorder used fewer gestures than their counterparts who were at low risk for autism spectrum disorder (Choi & others, 2019). The ability to use the pointing gesture effectively improves in the second year of life as advances in other aspects of language communication occur.

One study found that parents in families with high socioeconomic status (SES) were more likely to use gestures when communicating with their 14-month-old infants (Rowe & Goldin-Meadow, 2009). Further, the infants' use of gestures at 14 months of age in high-SES families was linked to a larger vocabulary at 54 months of age.

Why might gestures such as pointing promote further language development? Infants' gestures advance their language development since caregivers often talk to them about what they are pointing to. Also, babies' first words often are for things they have previously pointed to.

Long before infants speak recognizable words, they communicate by producing a number of vocalizations and gestures. *At approximately what ages do infants begin to produce different types of vocalizations and gestures?*
Don Hammond/Design Pics

Recognizing Language Sounds   Long before they begin to learn words, infants can make fine distinctions among the sounds of the language. In Patricia Kuhl's (1993, 2000, 2007, 2009, 2011, 2015) research, phonemes from languages all over the world are piped through a speaker for infants to hear (see Figure 2). A box with a toy bear in it is placed where the infant can see it. A string of identical syllables is played, and then the syllables are changed (for example, *ba ba ba ba,* and then *pa pa pa pa*). If the infant turns its head when the syllables change, the box lights up and the bear dances and drums, rewarding the infant for noticing the change.

FIGURE 2

FROM UNIVERSAL LINGUIST TO LANGUAGE-SPECIFIC LISTENER. In Patricia Kuhl's research laboratory, babies listen to tape-recorded voices that repeat syllables. When the sounds of the syllables change, the babies quickly learn to look at the bear. Using this technique, Kuhl has demonstrated that babies are universal linguists until about 6 months of age, but in the next six months become language-specific listeners. *Does Kuhl's research give support to the view that either "nature" or "nurture" is the source of language acquisition?*
Dr. Patricia Kuhl, Institute for Learning and Brain Sciences, University of Washington

Kuhl's research (2007, 2009, 2011, 2015) has demonstrated that from birth to about 6 months of age, infants are "citizens of the world": They recognize when sounds change most of the time, no matter what language the syllables come from. But over the next six months, infants get even better at perceiving the changes in sounds from their "own" language, the one their parents speak, and they gradually lose the ability to recognize differences that are not important in their own language. Kuhl (2015) found that the period when a baby's brain is most open to learning the sounds of a native language begins at six months for vowels and at nine months for consonants.

Also, in the second half of the first year, infants begin to segment the continuous stream of speech they encounter into words (Ota & Skarabela, 2018; Polka & others, 2017). Initially, they likely rely on statistical information such as the co-occurrence patterns of phonemes and syllables, which allows them to extract potential word forms (Lany & others, 2018; Levine & others, 2019a). For example, discovering that the sequence *br* occurs more often at the beginning of words while *nt* is more common at the end of words helps infants detect word boundaries. And as infants extract an increasing number of potential word forms from the speech stream they hear, they begin to associate these with concrete, perceptually available objects in their world (Saffran & Kirkham, 2018). For example, infants might detect that the spoken word "monkey" has a reliable statistical regularity of occurring in the visual presence of an observed monkey but not in the presence of other animals, such as bears (Pace & others, 2016). Thus, statistical learning involves extracting information from the world to learn about the environment (Sweeney & Gomez, 2019).

Richard Aslin (2017) recently emphasized that statistical learning—which involves no instruction, reinforcement, or feedback—is a powerful learning mechanism in infant development. In statistical learning, infants soak up statistical regularities in the world merely through exposure to them (Lany & others, 2018; Monroy & others, 2019; Saffran & Kirkham, 2018).

First Words Infants understand words before they can produce or speak them (Pace & others, 2016; Vihman, 2019). Between about 5 and 12 months of age, infants often indicate their first understanding of words. For many infants, the first word they understand is their own name (Bortfield & others, 2005; Golinkoff & others, 1987). The infant's first spoken word is a milestone eagerly anticipated by every parent. This event usually occurs between 10 and 15 months of age and at an average age of about 13 months. However, long before babies say their first words, they have been communicating with their parents, often by gesturing and using their own special sounds. The appearance of first words is a continuation of this communication process.

A child's first words include those that name important people (*dada*), familiar animals (*kitty*), vehicles (*car*), toys (*ball*), food (*milk*), body parts (*eye*), clothes (*hat*), household items (*clock*), and greeting terms (*bye*). Children often express various intentions with their single words, so that *cookie* might mean "That's a cookie" or "I want a cookie." Nouns are easier to learn because the majority of words in this class are more perceptually accessible than other types of words (Parish-Morris, Golinkoff, & Hirsh-Pasek, 2013). Think how the noun "car" is so much more concrete and imaginable than the verb "goes," making the word "car" much easier to acquire than the word "goes."

The first words of infants can vary across languages. The first words of English-speaking and Romance-language-speaking infants usually are nouns. However, because of the structure of the Korean language, the early words of Korean infants may be verbs (Choi & Gopnik, 1995). Indeed, the language of Korean children is often described as verb-friendly and the language of English children as noun-friendly (Waxman & others, 2013).

What characterizes the infant's early word learning?
Africa Studio/Shutterstock

On average, infants understand about 50 words by 13 months of age, but they can't say that many words until about 18 months (Menyuk, Liebergott, & Schultz, 1995). Thus, in infancy *receptive vocabulary* (words the child understands) considerably exceeds *spoken vocabulary* (words the child uses).

The infant's spoken vocabulary rapidly increases once the first word is spoken (Waxman & Goswami, 2012). The average 18-month-old can speak about 50 words, but the average 2-year-old can speak about 200 words. This rapid increase in vocabulary that begins at approximately 18 months is called the vocabulary spurt (Bloom, Lifter, & Broughton, 1985). The spurt actually involves an increase in the rate at which words are learned. That is, early on, a few words are learned every few days, later a few words are learned each day, and eventually many words are learned each day.

Does early vocabulary development predict later language development? Research studies indicate that it does (Friend & others, 2019; Rajan & others, 2019). One study found that infant vocabulary development at 16 to 24 months of age was linked to vocabulary, phonological awareness, reading accuracy, and reading comprehension five years later (Duff & others, 2015).

Like the timing of a child's first word, the timing of the vocabulary spurt varies. Figure 3 shows the range for these two language milestones in 14 children (Bloom, 1998). On average, these children said their first word at 13 months and had a vocabulary spurt at 19 months. However, the ages for the first word of individual children varied from 10 to 17 months and for their vocabulary spurt from 13 to 25 months.

Cross-linguistic differences occur in word learning (Waxman & others, 2013). Children learning Mandarin Chinese, Korean, and Japanese acquire more verbs earlier in their development than do children learning English. This cross-linguistic difference reflects the greater use of verbs in the language input to children in these Asian languages.

Children sometimes overextend or underextend the meanings of the words they use (Woodward & Markman, 1998). *Overextension* is the tendency to apply a word to objects that are inappropriate for the word's meaning by going beyond the set of referents an adult would use. For example, children at first may say "*dada*" not only for "father" but also for other men, strangers, or boys. With time, overextensions decrease and eventually disappear. *Underextension* is the tendency to apply a word too narrowly; it occurs when children fail to use a word to name a relevant event or object. For example, a child might use the word *boy* to describe a 5-year-old neighbor but not apply the word to a male infant or to a 9-year-old male.

Two-Word Utterances   By the time children are 18 to 24 months of age, they usually vocalize two-word utterances (Tomasello, 2011). To convey meaning with just two words, the child relies heavily on gesture, tone, and context. Children can communicate a wealth of meaning with a two-word utterance, as illustrated below (Slobin, 1972):

· Identification: "See doggie."
· Location: "Book there."
· Repetition: "More milk."
· Nonexistence: "All gone."
· Possession: "My candy."
· Attribution: "Big car."
· Agent-action: "Mama walk."
· Question: "Where ball?"

These examples are from children whose first language is English, German, Russian, Finnish, Turkish, or Samoan.

Notice that the two-word utterances omit many parts of speech and are remarkably succinct. In fact, in every language, a child's first combinations of words have this economical quality; they are telegraphic. **Telegraphic speech** is the use of short and precise words without grammatical markers such as articles, auxiliary verbs, and other connectives. Telegraphic speech is not limited to two words. "Mommy give ice cream" and "Mommy give Tommy ice cream" also are examples of telegraphic speech.

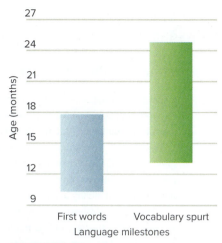

FIGURE 3

VARIATION IN LANGUAGE MILESTONES.
What are some possible explanations for variations in the timing of these milestones?

telegraphic speech   The use of short, precise words without grammatical markers such as articles, auxiliary verbs, and other connectives.

Around the world, most young children learn to speak in two-word utterances, in most cases at about 18 to 24 months of age. *What implications does this have for the biological basis of language?*
McPhoto/Age fotostock

Sharla Peltier, Speech Therapist

A speech therapist is a health professional who works with individuals who have a communication disorder. Sharla Peltier, a speech therapist in Manitoulin, Ontario, Canada, works with Native American children in the First Nations schools. She conducts screenings for speech/language and hearing problems and assesses infants as young as 6 months of age as well as school-aged children. She works closely with community health nurses to identify hearing problems.

Diagnosing problems is only about half of what Peltier does in her work. She especially enjoys treating speech/language and hearing problems. She conducts parent training sessions to help parents understand and help with their children's language problem. As part of this training, she guides parents in communicating more effectively with their children.

For more information about what speech therapists do, see the Careers in Life-Span Development appendix.

Speech therapist Sharla Peltier helps a young child improve her language and communication skills.
Courtesy of Sharla Peltier

Typical Age	Language Milestones
Birth	Crying
2 to 4 months	Cooing begins
5 months	Understands first word
6 months	Babbling begins
7 to 11 months	Change from universal linguist to language-specific listener
8 to 12 months	Uses gestures, such as showing and pointing Comprehension of words appears
13 months	First word spoken
18 months	Vocabulary spurt starts
18 to 24 months	Uses two-word utterances Rapid expansion of understanding of words

FIGURE 4

SOME LANGUAGE MILESTONES IN INFANCY. Despite great variations in the language input received by infants, around the world they follow a similar path in learning to speak.

We have discussed a number of language milestones in infancy. Figure 4 summarizes the ages at which infants typically reach these milestones.

EARLY CHILDHOOD

Toddlers move rather quickly from producing two-word utterances to creating three-, four-, and five-word combinations. Between 2 and 3 years of age, they begin the transition from saying simple sentences that express a single proposition to saying complex sentences.

As young children learn the special features of their own language, there are extensive regularities in how they acquire that specific language (Clark, 2017). For example, all children learn the prepositions *on* and *in* before other prepositions.

However, some children encounter obstacles to language development, including speech and hearing problems. To read about an individual who works with children who have speech/language problems, see the *Connecting with Careers* profile.

Understanding Phonology and Morphology   During the preschool years, most children gradually become more sensitive to the sounds of spoken words and become increasingly capable of producing all the sounds of their language (Kelly & others, 2019). By the time children are 3 years of age, they can produce all the vowel sounds and most of the consonant sounds (Stoel-Gammon & Sosa, 2010). They recognize the sounds in word combinations such as "Merry go round" before they can produce them.

By the time children move beyond two-word utterances, they demonstrate a knowledge of morphology rules (Snyder, 2016). Children begin using the plural and possessive forms of nouns (such as *dogs* and *dog's*). They put appropriate endings on verbs (such as *-s* when the subject is third-person singular and *-ed* for the past tense). They use prepositions (such as *in* and *on*), articles (such as *a* and *the*), and various forms of the verb *to be* (such as "I was going to the store"). Some of the best evidence for changes in children's use of morphological rules occurs in their overgeneralization of the rules, as when a preschool child says "foots" instead of "feet," or "goed" instead of "went."

In a classic experiment that was designed to study children's knowledge of morphological rules, such as how to make a plural, Jean Berko (1958) presented preschool children and first-grade children with cards such as the one shown in Figure 5. Children were asked to look at the card while the experimenter read aloud the words on the card. Then the children were asked to supply the missing word. This might sound easy, but Berko was interested in the children's ability to apply the appropriate morphological rule—in this case to say "wugs" with the *z* sound that indicates the plural.

What makes Berko's study impressive is that most of the words were made up for the experiment. Thus, the children could not base their responses on remembering past instances of hearing the words. That they could make the plurals or past tenses of words they had never heard before was proof that they knew the morphological rules.

Changes in Syntax and Semantics   Preschool children also learn and apply rules of syntax (Clark, 2017). They show a growing mastery of complex rules for how words should be ordered (Kyratzis, 2017; Tieu & others, 2018).

Consider *wh-* questions, such as "Where is Daddy going?" or "What is that boy doing?" To ask these questions properly, the child must know two important differences between *wh-* questions and affirmative statements (for instance, "Mommy is going to work" and "That boy is waiting on the school bus"). First, a *wh-* word must be added at the beginning of the sentence. Second, the auxiliary verb must be inverted—that is, exchanged with the subject of the sentence. Young children learn quite early where to put the *wh-* word, but they take much longer to learn the auxiliary-inversion rule. Thus, preschool children might ask, "Where Daddy is going?" and "What that girl is doing?"

Gains in semantics also characterize early childhood. Vocabulary development is dramatic (Bailey, Osipova, & Kelly, 2016). Some experts have concluded that between 18 months and 6 years of age, young children learn words at the rate of about one new word every waking hour (Gelman & Kalish, 2006)! By the time they enter first grade, it is estimated that children know about 14,000 words (Clark, 1993). However, there are individual variations in children's vocabulary, and children who enter elementary school with a small vocabulary are at risk for developing reading problems (Berninger, 2006).

Why can children learn so many new words so quickly? One possibility is **fast mapping,** which involves children's ability to make an initial connection between a word and its referent after only limited exposure to the word (Lucca & Wilbourn, 2018; Woodward, Markman, & Fitzsimmons, 1994). Researchers have found that exposure to words on multiple occasions over several days results in more successful word learning than the same number of exposures in a single day (Childers & Tomasello, 2002). Also, fast mapping allows children to learn word meanings in a deeper sense, such as understanding where the word can apply and its nuances.

What are some important aspects of how word learning optimally occurs? Following are six key principles in young children's vocabulary development (Harris, Golinkoff, & Hirsh-Pasek, 2011):

1. *Children learn the words they hear most often.* They learn the words that they encounter when interacting with parents, teachers, siblings, peers, and also from books. They especially benefit from encountering words that they do not know.

2. *Children learn words for things and events that interest them.* Parents and teachers can direct young children to experience words in contexts that interest the children; playful peer interactions are especially helpful in this regard.

3. *Children learn words best in responsive and interactive contexts rather than passive contexts.* Children who experience turn-taking opportunities, joint focusing experiences, and positive, sensitive socializing contexts with adults encounter the scaffolding necessary for optimal word learning. They learn words less effectively when they are passive learners.

4. *Children learn words best in contexts that are meaningful.* Young children learn new words more effectively when new words are encountered in integrated contexts rather than as isolated facts.

5. *Children learn words best when they access clear information about word meaning.* Children whose parents and teachers are sensitive to words the children might not understand and provide support and elaboration with hints about word meaning learn words better than those whose parents and teachers quickly state a new word and don't monitor whether children understand its meaning.

6. *Children learn words best when grammar and vocabulary are considered.* Children who experience a large number of words used in a wide variety of sentences develop a richer vocabulary and better understanding of grammar. Vocabulary learning and grammatical development are connected.

This is a wug.

Now there is another one. There are two of them. There are two _____.

FIGURE 5

STIMULI IN BERKO'S CLASSIC STUDY OF CHILDREN'S UNDERSTANDING OF MORPHOLOGICAL RULES. In Jean Berko's study, young children were presented cards such as this one with a "wug" on it. Then the children were asked to supply the missing word and say it correctly.

Children pick up words as pigeons peas.

—JOHN RAY
English Naturalist, 17th Century

fast mapping A process that helps to explain how young children learn the connection between a word and its referent so quickly.

What Characteristics of a Family Affect a Child's Language Development?

Socioeconomic status has been linked with how much parents talk to their children and with young children's vocabulary. Betty Hart and Todd Risley (1995) observed the language environments of children whose parents were professionals and children whose parents were on welfare. Compared with the professional parents, the parents on welfare talked much less to their young children, talked less about past events, and provided less elaboration. As indicated in Figure 6, the children of the professional parents had a much larger vocabulary at 36 months of age than the children whose parents were on welfare. Another study found that at 18 to 24 months of age, infants in low-SES families already had a smaller vocabulary and less efficient language processing than their infant counterparts in middle-SES families (Fernald, Marchman, & Weisleder, 2013). Further, in a recent study of English-speaking preschool children, those from lower-income families had less advanced language-processing skills than their counterparts from middle-income families, as well as syntax deficiencies and smaller vocabularies (Levine & others, 2019b).

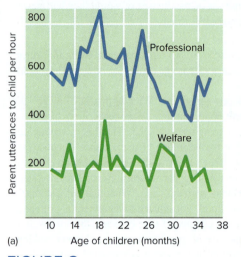
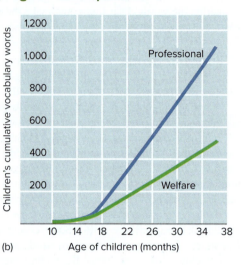

FIGURE 6

LANGUAGE INPUT IN PROFESSIONAL AND WELFARE FAMILIES AND YOUNG CHILDREN'S VOCABULARY DEVELOPMENT. (*a*) In this study (Hart & Risley, 1995), parents from professional families talked with their young children more than parents from welfare families. (*b*) All of the children learned to talk, but children from professional families developed vocabularies that were twice as large as the vocabularies of children from welfare families. Thus, by the time children go to preschool, they already have experienced considerable differences in language input in their families and developed different levels of vocabulary that are linked to their socioeconomic context. *Does this study indicate that poverty caused deficiencies in vocabulary development?*

Other research has linked how much mothers speak to their infants and the infants' vocabularies. For example, in one study by Janellen Huttenlocher and her colleagues (1991), infants whose mothers spoke more often to them had markedly higher vocabularies. By the second birthday, vocabulary differences were substantial.

However, a study of 1- to 3-year-old children living in low-income families found that the sheer amount of maternal talk was not the best predictor of a child's vocabulary growth (Pan & others, 2005). Rather, it was maternal language and literacy skills that were positively related to the children's vocabulary development. For example, when mothers used a more diverse vocabulary when talking with their children, their children's vocabulary benefited, but their children's vocabulary was not related to the total amount of time mothers spent talking to their children. Also, in one study, the conversational, communicative duet between parent and child (set up well before children began to talk) had a greater influence on language development than did the amount of language children heard (Hirsh-Pasek & others, 2015).

Children in low-income families are more likely to have less-educated parents, receive inadequate nutrition, live in low-income communities, and attend substandard schools than children in middle- and high-income families (Snow, Burns, & Griffin, 1998). However, living in a low-income family should not be used as the sole identifier in predicting whether children will have difficulties in language development, such as a low vocabulary and reading problems. If children growing up in low-income families experience effective instruction and support, they can develop effective language skills (Barbarin & Aikens, 2009).

These research studies and others (Justice & others, 2019; Law & others, 2018; NICHD Early Child Care Research Network, 2005b; Perkins, Finegood, & Swain, 2013) demonstrate the important effect that early speech input and poverty can have on the development of a child's language skills.

How might a family's socioeconomic status influence parent-child communication and vocabulary growth in children? To read about this link, see the *Connecting with Research* interlude.

Advances in Pragmatics Changes in pragmatics also characterize young children's language development (Clark, 2017; Fujiki & Brinton, 2017). A 6-year-old is simply a much better conversationalist than a 2-year-old is. What are some of the improvements in pragmatics during the preschool years?

Young children begin to engage in extended discourse. For example, they learn culturally specific rules of conversation and politeness and become sensitive to the need to adapt their speech in different settings. Their developing linguistic skills and increasing ability to take the perspective of others contribute to their generation of more competent narratives.

As children get older, they become increasingly able to talk about things that are not here (Grandma's house, for example) and not now (what happened to them yesterday or might happen tomorrow, for example). A preschool child can tell you what she wants for lunch tomorrow, something that would not have been possible at the two-word stage of language development.

Around 4 to 5 years of age, children learn to change their speech style to suit the situation. For example, even 4-year-old children speak to a 2-year-old differently from the way they speak to a same-aged peer; they use shorter sentences with the 2-year-old. They also speak to an adult differently from the way they speak to a same-aged peer, using more polite and formal language with the adult (Shatz & Gelman, 1973).

What characterizes advances in pragmatics during early childhood?
Hill Street Studios/Age fotostock

Early Literacy Concern about the ability of U.S. children to read and write has led to a careful examination of preschool and kindergarten children's experiences, with the hope that a positive orientation toward reading and writing can be developed early in life (Reutzel & Cooter, 2019; Tompkins & Rodgers, 2020). What should a literacy program for preschool children be like? The most obvious necessity is knowing a language. Children will not be able to comprehend the text they read if they don't understand the words and sentence structures. Instruction should be built on what children already know about oral language, reading, and writing (Temple & others, 2018; Vukelich & others, 2020). One study found that 60 minutes of physical activity per day in preschool academic contexts improved early literacy (Kirk & Kirk, 2016). Parents and teachers need to provide a supportive environment to help children develop literacy skills (Bredekamp, 2020; Feeney, Moravcik, & Nolte, 2019).

So far, our discussion of early literacy has focused on U.S. children. Researchers have found that the extent to which phonological awareness is linked to learning to read effectively varies across language to some degree (McBride-Chang, 2004). For example, one study of second-grade students from Beijing, Hong Kong, Korea, and the United States revealed that phonological awareness may be more important for early reading development in English and Korean than in Chinese (McBride-Chang & others, 2005). Further, rates of dyslexia (severe reading disability) differ across countries and are linked with the spelling and phonetic rules that characterize the language (McCardle & others, 2011). English is one of the more difficult languages because of its irregular spellings and pronunciations. In countries where English is spoken, the rate of dyslexia is higher than in countries where the alphabet script is more phonetically pronounced.

Books can be valuable in enhancing children's communication skills (Morrow, 2020; Reutzel & Cooter, 2019). What are some strategies for using books effectively with preschool children? Ellen Galinsky (2010) offered these recommendations:

- *Use books to initiate conversation with young children.* Ask them to put themselves in the places of the characters in the book and to imagine what the characters might be thinking or feeling.
- *Use* what *and* why *questions.* Ask young children to think about what is going to happen next in a story and then to see if it occurs.
- *Encourage children to ask questions about stories.*
- *Choose some books that play with language.* Creative books on the alphabet, including those with rhymes, often interest young children.

What are some strategies for increasing young children's literacy?
Jamie Grill/JGI/Getty Images

MIDDLE AND LATE CHILDHOOD

Upon entering school, children gain new skills that include increasing use of language to talk about things that are not physically present, knowledge of what a word is, and an ability to recognize and talk about sounds (Berko Gleason, 2003). They learn the *alphabetic principle*—the fact that the letters of the alphabet represent sounds of the language. As children develop during middle and late childhood, changes in their vocabulary and grammar continue to take place.

Vocabulary, Grammar, and Metalinguistic Awareness   During middle and late childhood, children begin to organize their mental vocabulary in new ways. When asked to say the first word that comes to mind when they hear a word, young children typically provide a word that often follows the word in a sentence. For example, when asked to respond to "dog," the young child may say "barks." In response to the word "eat," they may say "lunch." At about 7 years of age, children begin to respond with a word that is the same part of speech as the stimulus word. For example, a child may now respond to the word "dog" with "cat" or "horse." To "eat," they now might say "drink." This type of reply is evidence that children have begun to categorize their vocabulary by parts of speech (Berko Gleason, 2003).

The process of categorizing becomes easier as children increase their vocabulary (Clark, 2017). Children's vocabulary increases from an average of about 14,000 words at 6 years of age to an average of about 40,000 words by 11 years of age. Children make similar advances in grammar (Clark, 2017). During the elementary school years, children's improvement in logical reasoning and analytical skills helps them understand such constructions as the appropriate use of comparatives (*shorter, deeper*) and subjunctives ("If you were president . . ."). During the elementary school years, children become increasingly able to understand and use complex grammar, such as the following sentence: *The boy who kissed his mother wore a hat.* They also learn to use language in a more connected way, producing connected discourse.

These advances in vocabulary and grammar during the elementary school years are accompanied by the development of **metalinguistic awareness,** which is knowledge about language, such as knowing what a preposition is or being able to discuss the sounds of a language (Altman, Goldstein, & Amon-Lotem, 2018; Schiff, Nuri Ben-Shushan, & Ben-Artzi, 2017). Metalinguistic awareness allows children "to think about their language, understand what words are, and even define them" (Berko Gleason, 2009, p. 4). In one study, metalinguistic instruction improved the spelling and reading skills of children attending kindergarten (Schiff, Nuri Ben-Shushan, & Ben-Artzi, 2017). Metalinguistic awareness improves considerably during the elementary school years as defining words becomes a regular part of classroom discourse and children increase their knowledge of syntax as they study and talk about the components of sentences, such as subjects and verbs (Crain, 2012). And reading also expands metalinguistic awareness as children try to comprehend written text.

Children also make progress in understanding how to use language in culturally appropriate ways—pragmatics (Beguin, 2016). By the time they enter adolescence, most children know the rules for using language in everyday contexts—that is, what is appropriate to say and what is inappropriate to say.

developmental connection

Conditions, Diseases, and Disorders
Dyslexia is a severe impairment in the ability to read and spell. Connect to "Schools, Achievement, and Work."

metalinguistic awareness Knowledge about language.

whole-language approach A teaching approach built on the idea that reading instruction should parallel children's natural language learning and that reading materials should be whole and meaningful.

Reading   Before learning to read, children learn to use language to talk about things that are not present; they learn what a word is; and they learn how to recognize sounds and talk about them (Berko Gleason, 2003). If they develop a large vocabulary, their path to reading is eased. Children who begin elementary school with a small vocabulary are at risk of falling behind their peers in learning to read (Berko Gleason, 2003). Vocabulary development plays an important role in reading comprehension (Gunning, 2020; Vacca & others, 2018).

How did you learn to read? Debate about how children should be taught to read focuses on the whole-language approach versus the phonics approach (Dewitz & others, 2020; Reutzel & Cooter, 2019).

The **whole-language approach** stresses that reading instruction should parallel children's natural language learning. In some whole-language classes, beginning readers are taught to recognize whole words or even entire sentences, and to use the context of what they are reading to guess at the meaning of words. Reading materials that support the whole-language approach are whole and meaningful—that is, children are given material in its complete form, such as stories and poems, so that they learn to understand language's communicative function. Reading is connected with listening and writing skills. Although there are variations in whole-language programs, most share the premise that reading should be integrated with other skills and subjects, such as science and social studies, and that it should focus on real-world material. Thus, a class might read newspapers, magazines, or books, and then write about and discuss what they have read.

In contrast, the **phonics approach** emphasizes that reading instruction should teach basic rules for translating written symbols into sounds. Early phonics-centered reading instruction should involve simplified materials. Only after children have learned correspondence rules that relate spoken phonemes to the alphabet letters that are used to represent them should they be given complex reading materials such as books and poems (Bear & others, 2020; Cunningham, 2017). One study revealed that a computer-based phonics program improved first-grade students' reading skills (Savage & others, 2009).

Which approach is better? Research suggests that children can benefit from both approaches, but instruction in phonics needs to be emphasized (Reutzel & Cooter, 2019; Tompkins & Rodgers, 2020). An increasing number of experts in the field of reading now conclude that direct instruction in phonics is a key aspect of learning to read (Bear & others, 2020; Leu & Kinzer, 2017).

Beyond the phonics/whole-language issue in learning to read, becoming a good reader includes learning to read fluently (Gunning, 2020). Many beginning or poor readers do not recognize words automatically. Their processing capacity is consumed by the demands of word recognition, so they have less capacity to devote to comprehension of groupings of words as phrases or sentences. As their processing of words and passages becomes more automatic, it is said that their reading becomes more *fluent* (Dewitz & others, 2020; Little & others, 2017). Also, children's vocabulary development plays an important role in the development of their reading comprehension (Vacca & others, 2018). And metacognitive strategies, such as learning to monitor one's reading progress, getting the gist of what is being read, and summarizing, also are fundamental to becoming a good reader (Schiff, Nuri Ben-Shushan, & Ben-Artzi, 2017).

This teacher is helping a student sound out words. Researchers have found that phonics instruction is a key aspect of teaching students to read, especially beginning readers and students with weak reading skills.
Mordolff/Getty Images

Writing Children's writing emerges out of their early scribbles, which appear at around 2 to 3 years of age (Hirsh-Pasek & Golinkoff, 2007). In early childhood, children's motor skills usually develop to the point that they can begin printing letters. Most 4-year-olds can print their first names. Five-year-olds can reproduce letters and copy several short words. They gradually learn to distinguish the distinctive characteristics of letters, such as whether the lines are curved or straight, open or closed. Through the early elementary grades, many children continue to reverse letters such as *b* and *d* and *p* and *q* (Temple & others, 2018). At this age, if other aspects of the child's development are normal, letter reversals do not predict literacy problems.

As they begin to write, children often invent spellings. Usually they base these spellings on the sounds of words they hear (Spandel, 2009).

Parents and teachers should encourage children's early writing but not be overly concerned about the formation of letters or spelling. Printing errors are a natural part of the child's growth. Corrections of spelling and printing should be selective and made in positive ways that do not discourage the child's writing and spontaneity.

Like becoming a good reader, becoming a good writer takes many years and lots of practice (Graham, 2018, 2019; Gunning, 2020). Children should be given many writing opportunities (Harris & others, 2018; Tompkins, 2019). As their language and cognitive skills improve with good instruction, so will their writing skills (Morrow, 2020). For example, developing a more sophisticated understanding of syntax and grammar serves as an underpinning for better writing. So do such cognitive skills as organization and logical reasoning. During their school years, students develop increasingly sophisticated methods of organizing their ideas. In early elementary school, they narrate and describe or write short poems. In late elementary and middle school, they can combine narration with reflection and analysis in projects such as book reports.

Monitoring one's writing progress is especially important in becoming a good writer (Graham, MacArthur, & Fitzgerald, 2019; Harris & others, 2018). This includes being receptive to feedback and applying what one learns in writing one paper to making the next paper better. In one study, Self-Regulated Strategy Development (SRSD) was implemented with second-grade teachers and their students who were at risk for writing failure (Harris, Graham, & Adkins, 2015). The students were taught a general planning strategy and general writing strategies (a catchy opening, effective vocabulary, clear organization, and an effective ending). The intervention produced positive results for genre elements, story writing quality, motivation, and effort, as well as meaningful generalization to personal writing.

developmental **connection**

Information Processing
Metacognition is cognition about cognition, or knowing about knowing. Connect to "Information Processing."

phonics approach A teaching approach built on the idea that reading instruction should teach basic rules for translating written symbols into sounds.

There are increasing concerns about students' writing competence (Graham, 2018, 2019; Graham & Harris, 2020; Graham & others, 2018; Harris & Graham, 2017; Tompkins, 2019; Vukelich & others, 2020). One study revealed that 70 to 75 percent of U.S. students in grades 4 through 12 are low-achieving writers (Persky, Dane, & Jin, 2003). Two studies—one of elementary school teachers, the other of high school teachers—raise concerns about the quality of writing instruction in U.S. schools (Gilbert & Graham, 2010; Kiuhara, Graham, & Hawken, 2009). The teachers in both studies reported that their college courses had inadequately prepared them to teach writing. The fourth- through sixth-grade teachers reported that they taught writing only 15 minutes a day. The high school teachers said that their writing assignments infrequently involved analysis and interpretation, and almost 50 percent of them had not assigned any multi-paragraph writing assignments in the span of one month's time.

The metacognitive strategies involved in being a competent writer are linked with those required to be a competent reader because the writing process involves competent reading and rereading during composition and revision (Harris & others, 2017, 2018; Longa & Graham, 2020). Further, researchers have found that strategy instruction involving planning, drafting, revising, and editing improve older elementary school children's metacognitive awareness and writing competence (Graham, 2019, 2020; Graham & Harris, 2019, 2020; Graham, Rouse, & Harris, 2018).

As with reading, teachers play a critical role in students' development of writing skills (Graham, 2019; Troia, Graham, & Harris, 2017). Effective writing instruction provides guidance about planning, drafting, and revising, not only in elementary school but through the college years (Mayer, 2008). A meta-analysis (use of statistical techniques to combine the results of studies) revealed that the following interventions were the most effective in improving fourth- through twelfth-grade students' writing quality: (1) strategy instruction, (2) summarization, (3) peer assistance, and (4) setting goals (Graham & Perin, 2007).

Second-Language Learning and Bilingualism Are there sensitive periods in learning a second language? That is, if individuals want to learn a second language, how important is the age at which they begin to learn it? For many years, it was claimed that if individuals did not learn a second language prior to puberty they would never reach native-language speakers' proficiency in the second language (Johnson & Newport, 1991). However, research indicates a more complex conclusion: Sensitive periods likely vary across different language systems (Thomas & Johnson, 2008). Thus, for late language learners, such as adolescents and adults, new vocabulary is easier to learn than new sounds or new grammar (Neville, 2006). For example, children's ability to pronounce words with a native-like accent in a second language typically decreases with age, with an especially sharp drop occurring after the age of about 10 to 12. Also, adults tend to learn a second language faster than children do, but their final level of second-language attainment is not as high as children's. And the way children and adults learn a second language differs somewhat. Compared with adults, children are less sensitive to feedback, less likely to use explicit strategies, and more likely to learn a second language from large amounts of input (Thomas & Johnson, 2008).

Students in the United States are far behind their counterparts in many developed countries in learning a second language. For example, in Russia, schools have 10 grades, called *forms*, which roughly correspond to the 12 grades in American schools. Russian children begin school at age 7 and begin learning English in the third form. Because of this emphasis on teaching English, most Russian citizens under the age of 40 today are able to speak at least some English. The United States is the only technologically advanced Western nation that does not have a national foreign-language requirement at the high school level, even for students in rigorous academic programs.

Some aspects of children's ability to learn a second language are transferred more easily to the second language than others (Bialystok, 2017; Hernandez, Fernandez, & Aznar-Bese, 2019). Children who are fluent in two languages perform better than their single-language counterparts on tests of control of attention, concept formation, analytical reasoning, inhibition, cognitive flexibility, cognitive complexity, and cognitive monitoring (Bialystok, 2001, 2007, 2011, 2014, 2015, 2017). Recent research also documented that bilingual children are better at theory of mind tasks (Rubio-Fernandez, 2017). They also are more

Children in many countries learn more than one language. Shown here is author John Santrock observing a preschool in Fes, Morocco, in 2015. The young children sang songs in three different languages—Arabic, French, and English. *Do you think children in the United States should learn more than one language?*
Courtesy of Dr. John Santrock

conscious of the structure of spoken and written language and better at noticing errors of grammar and meaning, skills that benefit their reading ability (Bialystok, 1997; Kuo & Anderson, 2012). A recent study of 6- to 10-year-olds found that early bilingual exposure was a key factor in bilingual children outperforming monolingual children on phonological awareness and word learning (Jasinska & Petitto, 2018). Another recent study indicated that 3-year-old bilingual children adapted to the needs of their communication partners better than their monolingual counterparts did (Gampe, Wermelinger, & Daum, 2019).

Thus, overall, bilingualism is linked to more positive outcomes for children's language and cognitive development (Antovich & Graf Estes, 2019; Branzi, Calabria, & Costa, 2019; Comishen, Bialystok, & Adler, 2019; Singh & others, 2017; Yow & others, 2019). An especially important developmental question that many parents of infants and young children have is whether to teach them two languages simultaneously or just teach one language at a time to avoid confusion. The answer is that teaching infants and young children two languages simultaneously (as when a mother's native language is English and her husband's is Spanish) has numerous benefits and few drawbacks (Bialystok, 2014, 2015, 2017).

However, research indicates that bilingual children do have a smaller vocabulary in each language than monolingual children (Bialystok, 2011). Most children who learn two languages are not exposed to the same quantity and quality of each language. Nonetheless, bilingual children do not show delays in the rate at which they acquire language overall (Hoff, 2016). In one study, by 4 years of age children who continued to learn both Spanish and English languages had a total vocabulary growth that was greater than that of monolingual children (Hoff & others, 2014).

A different type of bilingualism occurs when immigrant children have learned only their native language at home and then must learn the main language of their new country at school. For example, in the United States, many immigrant children go from being monolingual in their home language to bilingual in that language and in English, only to end up being monolingual speakers of English. This is called *subtractive bilingualism*, and it can have negative effects on children, who often become ashamed of their home language.

A current controversy related to bilingualism involves the millions of U.S. children who come from homes in which English is not the primary language and then later at school must also learn English (Diaz-Rico, 2018, 2020; Esposito & others, 2018). What is the best way to teach these English language learners (ELLs), many of whom in the United States are from immigrant families living in poverty?

ELLs have been taught in one of two main ways: (1) instruction in English only, or (2) a *dual-language* (formerly called *bilingual*) approach that involves instruction in their home language and English (Herrell & Jordan, 2020). In a dual-language approach, instruction is given in both the ELL child's home language and English for varying amounts of time at certain grade levels. One of the arguments in favor of the dual-language approach is the research discussed earlier demonstrating that bilingual children have more advanced information-processing skills than monolingual children do (Bialystok, 2017).

If a dual-language strategy is used, too often it has been thought that immigrant children need only one or two years of this type of instruction. However, in general it takes immigrant children approximately three to five years to develop speaking proficiency and seven years to develop reading proficiency in English (Hakuta, Butler, & Witt, 2001). Also, immigrant children vary in their ability to learn English (Esposito & others, 2018). Children who come from lower socioeconomic backgrounds have more difficulty than those from higher socioeconomic backgrounds (Hakuta, 2001; Hoff & Place, 2013). Thus, especially for immigrant children from low socioeconomic backgrounds, more years of dual-language instruction may be needed than they currently are receiving.

What have researchers found regarding outcomes of ELL programs? Drawing conclusions about the effectiveness of ELL programs is difficult because of variations across programs in the number of years they are in effect, type of

A first- and second-grade bilingual English-Cantonese teacher instructs students in Chinese in Oakland, California. *What have researchers found about the effectiveness of bilingual education?*
Elizabeth Crews

Salvador Tamayo, Teacher of English Language Learners

Salvador Tamayo is an ELL fifth-grade teacher at Turner Elementary School in West Chicago. He received a National Educator Award from the Milken Family Foundation for his work in educating ELLs. Tamayo is especially adept at integrating technology into his ELL classes. He and his students have created several award-winning Web sites about the West Chicago City Museum, the local Latino community, and the history of West Chicago. His students developed an "I Want to Be an American Citizen" Web site to assist family and community members in preparing for the U.S. Citizenship Test. Tamayo also teaches an ELL class at Wheaton College.

Salvador Tamayo instructs students in his bilingual education class.
Courtesy of Salvador Tamayo

---

developmental **connection**

Cognitive Theory

According to Piaget, at 11 to 15 years of age a new stage—formal operational thought—emerges that is characterized by thought that is more abstract, idealistic, and logical. Connect to "Cognitive Developmental Approaches."

metaphor An implied comparison between two unlike things.

satire The use of irony, derision, or wit to expose folly or wickedness.

dialect A variety of language that is distinguished by its vocabulary, grammar, or pronunciation.

What are some changes in language development in adolescence?
Ian Shaw/Alamy Stock Photo

instruction, quality of schooling other than ELL instruction, teachers, children, and other factors. Further, no effective experiments have been conducted that compare bilingual education with English-only education in the United States (Snow & Kang, 2006). Some experts have concluded that the quality of instruction is more important in determining outcomes than the language in which it is delivered (Lesaux & Siegel, 2003).

Nonetheless, other experts, such as Kenji Hakuta (2001, 2005), support the combined home language and English approach because (1) children have difficulty learning a subject when it is taught in a language they do not understand; and (2) when both languages are integrated in the classroom, children learn the second language more readily and participate more actively. In support of Hakuta's view, most large-scale studies have found that the academic achievement of ELLs is higher in dual-language programs than English-only programs. To read about the work of one ELL teacher, see the *Connecting with Careers* profile.

ADOLESCENCE

Language development during adolescence includes greater sophistication in the use of words. With increasing ability to engage in abstract thinking, adolescents are much better than children at analyzing the role a word plays in a sentence.

Adolescents also develop more subtle abilities with words. They make strides in understanding **metaphor,** which is an implied comparison between unlike things. For example, individuals "draw a line in the sand" to indicate a nonnegotiable position; a political campaign is said to be a marathon, not a sprint; a person's faith is shattered. And adolescents become better able to understand and to use **satire,** which is the use of irony, derision, or wit to expose folly or wickedness. Caricatures are an example of satire. More advanced logical thinking also allows adolescents, from about 15 to 20 years of age, to understand complex literary works.

Most adolescents are also much better writers than children are. They are better at organizing ideas before they write, at distinguishing between general and specific points as they write, at stringing together sentences that make sense, and at organizing their writing into an introduction, body, and concluding remarks. Adolescents also are better than children at persuasive writing in which they have to take a position and try to convince the reader of the accuracy and strength of their position (Nippold, 2016).

Everyday speech changes during adolescence, and "part of being a successful teenager is being able to talk like one" (Berko Gleason, 2005, p. 9). Young adolescents often speak a **dialect** with their peers that is characterized by jargon and slang (Cave, 2002). A dialect is a variety of language that is distinguished by its vocabulary, grammar, or pronunciation.

For example, when meeting a friend, instead of saying hello, a young adolescent might say, "Sup?" ("What's up?"). Nicknames that are satirical and derisive ("Stilt," "Refrigerator," "Spaz") also characterize the dialect of young adolescents. Such labels might be used to show that one belongs to the group and to reduce the seriousness of a situation (Cave, 2002).

ADULTHOOD AND AGING

Most research on language development has focused on infancy and childhood. It is generally thought that for most of adulthood individuals maintain their language skills.

In the adolescent and adult years, the development of an identity, a sense of who one is, is an important life task. A distinct personal linguistic style is part of one's special identity (Berko Gleason, 2009). Further psychological goals of early adulthood that call for expanded linguistic skills include entering the world of work and establishing intimate relations with others.

Language development during the adult years varies greatly among individuals, depending on such factors as level of education and social and occupational roles. Actors, for instance, must learn not only to be heard by large audiences but also to speak the words of others using varying voices and regional dialects. Working people learn the special tones of voice and terminology associated with their own occupational language (Berko Gleason, 2005, p. 9).

The vocabulary of individuals often continues to increase throughout most of the adult years, at least until late adulthood (Schaie, 2012; Singh-Manoux & others, 2012). Many older adults "maintain or improve their knowledge of words and word meanings" (Burke & Shafto, 2004, p. 24).

In late adulthood, however, some decrements in language may appear (Payne & Federmeier, 2018; Valech & others, 2018). Among the most common language-related complaints reported by older adults is difficulty in retrieving words to use in conversation and in understanding spoken language in certain contexts (Clark-Cotton, Williams, & Goral, 2007). These often involve the *tip-of-the-tongue phenomenon*, in which individuals are confident that they can remember something but just can't quite seem to retrieve it from memory (James & others, 2018). Older adults also report that in less than ideal listening conditions they can have difficulty in understanding speech. This difficulty is most likely to occur when speech is rapid, when competing stimuli are present (a noisy room, for example), and when they can't see their conversation partner (in a telephone conversation, for example). The difficulty in understanding speech may be due to hearing loss (Benichov & others, 2012). In general, though, most language skills decline little among older adults who are healthy (Clark-Cotton & others, 2007; Thornton & Light, 2006).

Some aspects of the phonological skills of older adults differ from those of younger adults (Robert & Mathey, 2018). Older adults' speech is typically lower in volume, slower, less precisely articulated, and less fluent (more pauses, fillers, repetition, and corrections). Despite these age differences, the speech skills of most older adults are adequate for everyday communication. One study found that when retelling a story older adults were more likely than younger adults to compress discourse and less likely to improve the cohesiveness of their narratives (Saling, Laroo, & Saling, 2012).

Nonlanguage factors may be responsible for some of the declines in language skills that occur in older adults (Obler, 2009). Slower information-processing speed and a decline in working memory, especially in regard to keeping information in mind while processing, likely contribute to reduced language efficiency in older adults (Salthouse, 2013). For example, a recent study found that the lower working memory capacity of older adults compared with younger adults impaired their comprehension of sentences (Sung & others, 2017).

Language does change among individuals with Alzheimer disease (Valech & others, 2018). Word-finding/generating difficulties are one of the earliest symptoms of Alzheimer disease (Haugrud, Crossley, & Vrbancic, 2011). Individuals with Alzheimer disease especially have difficulty on tests of semantic verbal fluency, in which they have to say as many words as possible in a category (fruits or animals, for example) in a given time, typically one minute (Weakley & Schmitter-Edgecombe, 2014). Most individuals with the disease do retain much of their ability to produce well-formed sentences until the late stages of the disease. Nonetheless, they do make more grammatical errors than older adults without the disease (Huang, Meyer, & Federmeier, 2012). In a recent study, individuals with Alzheimer disease were less likely to use syntactic components in their language than those who did not have Alzheimer disease (Orimaye & others, 2017).

Recently researchers began exploring the possibility that bilingualism might delay the onset of Alzheimer disease (Antoniou & Wright, 2017; Bialystok, 2017; Borsa & others, 2018).

What are some differences in the ways older and younger adults communicate?
Tom Grill/JGI/Blend Images/Getty Images

developmental **connection**

Conditions, Diseases, and Disorders
Alzheimer disease is a progressive brain disorder characterized by a gradual deterioration of memory, reasoning, language, and eventually physical functioning. Connect to "Health."

One study found that the onset of Alzheimer disease occurred 4.5 years later in bilingual older adults (Alladi & others, 2013). Another study revealed that the onset of symptoms and first office visit for Alzheimer disease occurred several years later for bilingual than for monolingual older adults (Bialystok & others, 2014). These results led Ellen Bialystok and her colleagues (2016) to conclude that being bilingual may be one of the best ways to delay the onset of Alzheimer disease by as much as four to five years. It is not yet clear why the advantage occurs for bilingual older adults, but one explanation might be better executive function (Gasquoine, 2016). For example, a recent study found that bilingual Alzheimer patients had better neural network functioning, especially in the neural network involving executive function, than did monolingual Alzheimer patients (Perani & others, 2017).

Review *Connect* Reflect

 LG2 Describe how language develops through the life span.

Review
- What are some key milestones of language development during infancy?
- How do language skills change during early childhood?
- How does language develop in middle and late childhood?
- How does language develop in adolescence?
- How do language skills change during adulthood and aging?

Connect
- What are some aspects of metacognition that might apply to the concept of metalinguistic awareness?

Reflect *Your Own Personal Journey of Life*
- How many languages can you speak and read? If and when you have children, do you want them to learn more than one language while they are young? Explain.

---

3 Biological and Environmental Influences

 LG3 Discuss the biological and environmental contributions to language skills.

| Biological Influences | Environmental Influences | An Interactionist View of Language |

We have described how language develops, but we have not explained what makes this amazing development possible. Everyone who uses language in some way "knows" its rules and has the ability to create an infinite number of words and sentences. Where does this knowledge come from? Is it the product of biology? Or is language learned and influenced by experiences?

BIOLOGICAL INFLUENCES

Some language scholars view the remarkable similarities in how children acquire language all over the world, despite the vast variation in language input they receive, as strong evidence that language has a biological basis. What role did evolution play in the biological foundations of language?

Evolution and the Brain's Role in Language   The ability to speak and understand language requires a certain vocal apparatus as well as a nervous system with certain capabilities. The nervous system and vocal apparatus of humanity's predecessors changed over hundreds of thousands or millions of years (Pinker, 2015). With advances in the nervous system and vocal structures, *Homo sapiens* went beyond the grunting and shrieking of other animals to develop speech (Cataldo, Migliano, & Vinicius, 2018; de Boer & Verhoef, 2019; O'Grady & Smith, 2019). Although estimates vary, many experts hold that humans acquired language about 100,000 years ago, which in evolutionary time represents a very recent acquisition. Language gave humans an enormous edge over other animals and increased the chances of human survival (de Boer & Thompson, 2018).

As further support for the biological foundations of language, there is evidence that specific regions of the brain are predisposed to be used for language (Babajani-Feremi, 2017; Coulson, 2018). Two regions involved in language were first discovered in studies of

In the wild, chimps communicate through calls, gestures, and expressions, which evolutionary psychologists believe might be the roots of true language.
Andrey Gudkov/123RF

brain-damaged individuals: **Broca's area,** a region of the left frontal lobe of the brain that is involved in producing words (Maher, 2018; Zhang & others, 2017), and **Wernicke's area,** a region of the brain's left hemisphere that is involved in language comprehension (Bruckner & Kammer, 2017; Greenwald, 2018) (see Figure 7). Damage to either of these areas produces types of **aphasia,** which is a loss or impairment of language processing. Individuals with damage to Broca's area have difficulty producing words correctly, while individuals with damage to Wernicke's area have poor comprehension and often produce fluent but incomprehensible speech.

Chomsky's Language Acquisition Device (LAD)
Linguist Noam Chomsky (1957) proposed that humans are biologically prewired to learn language at a certain time and in a certain way. He said that children are born into the world with a **language acquisition device (LAD),** a biological endowment that enables the child to detect certain features and rules of language, including phonology, syntax, and semantics. Children are endowed by nature with the ability to detect the sounds of language, for example, and to follow rules such as those for forming plurals and asking questions.

Chomsky's LAD is a theoretical construct, not a physical part of the brain. Is there evidence for the existence of a LAD? Supporters of the LAD concept cite the uniformity of language milestones across languages and cultures, evidence that children create language even in the absence of well-formed input, and biological foundations of language. But, as we will see, critics argue that even if infants have something like a LAD, it cannot fully explain the process of language acquisition.

ENVIRONMENTAL INFLUENCES

Our coverage of environmental influences on language development in infancy focuses on the important role of social interaction, including child-directed speech and other caregiver strategies.

The Role of Social Interaction
Language is not learned in a social vacuum. Most children are bathed in language from a very early age, unlike the Wild Boy of Aveyron, who never learned to communicate effectively, having lived in social isolation for years. Thus, social cues play an important role in infant language learning (Ahun & others, 2018; McGillion & others, 2017b).

The linguistics problems children have to solve are always embedded in personal and interpersonal contexts.

—LOIS BLOOM
Contemporary Psychologist, Columbia University

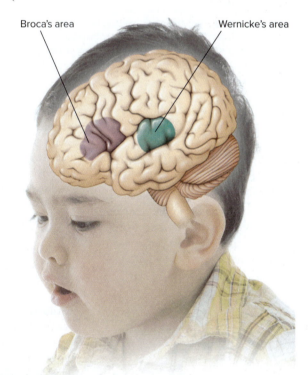

Broca's area   Wernicke's area

FIGURE 7

BROCA'S AREA AND WERNICKE'S AREA. Broca's area is located in the frontal lobe of the brain's left hemisphere, and it is involved in the control of speech. Wernicke's area is a portion of the left hemisphere's temporal lobe that is involved in understanding language. *How does the role of these areas of the brain relate to lateralization, discussed in the chapter on "Physical Development and Biological Aging"?*
Photo: Swissmacky/Shutterstock

FIGURE 8

SOCIAL INTERACTION AND BABBLING. One study focused on two groups of mothers and their 8-month-old infants (Goldstein, King, & West, 2003). One group of mothers was instructed to smile and touch their infants immediately after the babies cooed and babbled; the other group was also told to smile and touch their infants but in a random manner, unconnected to sounds the infants made. The infants whose mothers immediately responded in positive ways to their babbling subsequently made more complex, speech-like sounds, such as *da* and *gu*. The research setting for this study, which underscores how important caregivers are in the early development of language, is shown here.
Courtesy of Dr. Michael Goldstein

developmental **connection**

Screen Time

Researchers have found that infants and young children who have higher TV and DVD exposure have more difficulty with spoken language. Connect to "Peers and the Sociocultural World."

child-directed speech Language spoken in a higher pitch than normal, with simple words and sentences.

The support and involvement of caregivers and teachers greatly facilitate a child's language learning (Bredekamp, 2020; Brown & others, 2018; Gunning, 2020; Marchman & others, 2019; Tompkins & Rodgers, 2020; Weisleder & others, 2018). In one study, both full-term and preterm infants who heard more caregiver talk based on all-day recordings at 16 months of age had better language skills (receptive and expressive language, language comprehension) at 18 months of age (Adams & others, 2018). And in another study, when mothers immediately smiled and touched their 8-month-old infants after they babbled, the infants subsequently made more complex speech-like sounds than when mothers responded to their infants in a random manner (Goldstein, King, & West, 2003) (see Figure 8).

Michael Tomasello (2003, 2006, 2011, 2014) stresses that young children are intensely interested in their social world and that early in their development they can understand the intentions of other people. His emphasizes that children learn language in specific contexts. For example, when a toddler and a father are jointly focused on a book, the father might point to a picture of a bird and say, "See the birdie." In this case, even a toddler understands that the father intends to name something and knows to look in the direction of the pointing. Through this kind of joint attention, early in their development children are able to use their social skills to acquire language (Tomasello, 2014). One study revealed that joint attention at 12 and 18 months predicted language skills at 24 months of age (Mundy & others, 2007). Also, in a study involving joint attention, infants' eye-gaze behaviors during Spanish tutoring sessions at 9.5 to 10.5 months of age predicted their second-language phonetic learning at 11 months of age, indicating a strong influence of social interaction at the earliest ages of learning a second language (Conboy & others, 2015).

Thus, social cues play an important role in infant language learning (Pace & others, 2016). Joint engagement and relevant responsiveness by a social partner predict better growth in language later in development, possibly because they improve the infant's mapping process between words and the world (Tamis-LeMonda, Kurchirko, & Song, 2014).

Given that social interaction is a critical component for infants to learn language effectively, might they also be able to learn language effectively through television and videos? Researchers have found that infants and young children cannot effectively learn language (phonology or words) from television or videos (Kuhl, 2007; Zosh & others, 2017). A study of toddlers found that frequent viewing of television increased the risk of delayed language development (Lin & others, 2015). Thus, just hearing language is not enough, even when infants seemingly are fully engaged in the experience. However, one study revealed that Skype provides some improvement in child language learning over videos and TV (Roseberry, Hirsh-Pasek, & Golinkoff, 2014), and older children can use information from television in their language development.

Also, recently the American Association of Pediatrics (APA) (2016) concluded that from 15 months to 2 years of age, evidence indicates that if parents co-watch educational videos with their infant and communicate with the infant about what they are viewing, it can benefit the infant's development. This suggests that when parents treat an educational video or app like a picture book, infants can benefit from it. However, the APA still recommends no watching of videos alone when children are younger than 18 months of age.

Child-Directed Speech and Other Caregiver Strategies One intriguing component of the young child's linguistic environment is **child-directed speech** (also referred to as *parentese*), which is language spoken in a higher pitch, slower tempo, and more exaggerated intonation than normal with simple words and sentences (Broesch & Bryant, 2018; Hayashi & Mazuka, 2017; Sulpizio & others, 2018). It is hard to use child-directed speech when not in the presence of a baby. As soon as you start talking to a baby, though, you shift into child-directed speech. Much of this is automatic and something most parents are not aware they are doing. As mentioned previously, even 4-year-olds speak in simpler ways to 2-year-olds than to their 4-year-old friends. Child-directed speech serves the important functions of capturing the infant's attention, maintaining communication and social interaction between infants and caregivers, and providing infants with information about their native language by heightening differences from speech directed to adults (Golinkoff & others, 2015). In a recent study, parent coaching of 6- and 10- month-old infants that involved child-directed speech, back-and-forth interactions, and parentese speech style improved the infants' language outcomes (more advanced babbling and greater word production) at 14 months of age (Ferjan Ramirez & others, 2019).

In other research, one study found that child-directed speech in a one-to-one social context at 11 to 14 months of age was linked to greater word production at 2 years of age than standard speech and speech in a group setting (Ramirez-Esparza, Garcia-Sierra, & Kuhl, 2017). Another study of low-SES Spanish-speaking families revealed that infants who experienced more child-directed speech were better at processing words in real time and had larger vocabularies at 2 years of age (Weisleder & Fernald, 2013). And in a study involving Spanish-English bilingual children, child-directed speech at 14 months of age was linked to productive vocabulary at 24 months of age (Ramirez-Esparza, Garcia-Sierra, & Kuhl, 2017). Most research on child-directed speech has involved mothers, but a recent study in several North American urban areas and a small society on the island of Tanna in the South Pacific Ocean found that fathers in both types of contexts engaged in child-directed speech with their infants (Broesch & Bryant, 2018).

What are some good strategies for parents and teachers to use to improve infants' and young children's language development?
Roberto Westbrook/Getty Images

Adults often use strategies other than child-directed speech to enhance the child's acquisition of language, including recasting, expanding, and labeling:

- **Recasting** takes place when an adult rephrases something the child has said if the child's statement lacks the appropriate morphology or contains some other error. The adult restates the child's immature utterance in the form of a fully grammatical sentence. For example, if a 2-year-old says, "Dog bark," the adult may respond by saying, "Oh, you heard the dog barking!" The adult sentence provides an acknowledgment that the child was heard and then adds the morphology /ing/ and the article (the) that the child's utterance lacked.

- **Expanding** involves adding information to a child's incomplete utterance. For example, if a child says, "Doggie eat," the parent might reply, "Yes, the dog is eating his food out of his special dish."

- **Labeling** involves naming objects that children seem interested in. Young children are forever being asked to identify the names of objects. Roger Brown (1968) called this "the original word game." Children want to learn more than the names of objects, though; they often want information about the object as well.

Parents use these strategies naturally and in meaningful conversations. Parents do not (and should not) use any deliberate method to teach their children to talk, even for children who are slow in learning language. Children usually benefit when parents guide their children's discovery of language rather than overloading them with language; "following in" on a child's interest helps the child learn language. If children are not ready to take in some information, they are likely to let you know this (perhaps by turning away). Thus, giving the child more information is not always better.

Infants, toddlers, and young children benefit when adults read books to and with them (shared reading) (Brown & others, 2018; Sinclair & others, 2018; Thompson, 2019). In one study, reading daily to children at 14 to 24 months of age was positively related to the children's language and cognitive development at 36 months of age (Raikes & others, 2006). And in another study, Japanese mothers who used more elaborative information-seeking responses during joint picture-book reading at 20 months had children with a better productive vocabulary at 27 months (Murase, 2014). Further, a recent meta-analysis concluded that shared picture book reading was linked to children having better expressive and receptive language (Dowdall & others, 2019).

Remember, parental encouragement of language development during interactions with their children, not drill and practice, is the key. Language development is not a simple matter of imitation and reinforcement. To read further about ways that parents can facilitate children's language development, see the *Connecting Development to Life* interlude.

Our discussion of environmental influences on language development has focused mainly on parents. However, children interact with many other people who can influence their language development, including teachers and peers. A study of more than 1,800 4-year-olds focused on ways in which peers might influence children's language development (Mashburn & others, 2009). In this study, peers' expressive language abilities were positively linked with young children's receptive and expressive language development.

recasting Involves an adult's rephrasing of a child's statement that might lack the appropriate morphology or contain some other error. The adult restates the child's immature utterance in the form of a fully grammatical sentence.

expanding Adding information to the child's incomplete utterance.

labeling Naming objects that children seem interested in.

How Parents Can Facilitate Infants' and Toddlers' Language Development

Linguist Naomi Baron (1992) in *Growing Up with Language,* developmental psychologists Roberta Golinkoff and Kathy Hirsh-Pasek (1999) in *How Babies Talk,* and more recently Ellen Galinsky (2010) in *Mind in the Making,* provided ideas to help parents facilitate their infants' and toddlers' language development. A summary of their ideas follows:

- *Be an active conversational partner.* Talk to your baby from the time it is born. Initiate conversation with the baby. If the baby is in a full-day child-care program, ensure that the baby receives adequate language stimulation from adults.
- *Talk at a slowed-down pace and don't worry about how you sound to other adults when you talk to your baby.* Talking more slowly will make it easier for your baby to detect words in the sea of sounds they experience. Babies enjoy and attend to the high-pitched sound of child-directed speech.
- *Narrate your daily activities to the baby as you do them.* For example, talk about how you are putting the baby in her high chair for lunch, ask her what she would like to eat, and so on.
- *Use parent-look and parent-gesture, and name what you are looking at.* When you want your child to pay attention to something, look at it and point to it. Then name it—for example, by saying "Look, Alex, there's an airplane."
- *When you talk with infants and toddlers, be simple, concrete, and repetitive.* Don't try to talk to them in abstract, high-level ways and think you have to say something new or different all of the time. Using familiar words often will help them remember the words.
- *Play games.* Use word games like peek-a-boo and pat-a-cake to help infants learn words.
- *Remember to listen.* Since toddlers' speech is often slow and laborious, parents are often tempted to supply words and thoughts for them. Be patient and let toddlers express themselves, no matter how painstaking the process is or how great a hurry you are in.
- *Expand and elaborate language abilities and horizons with infants and toddlers.* Ask questions that encourage answers other

It is a good idea for parents to begin talking to their babies at the start. The best language teaching occurs when the talking begins before the infant becomes capable of intelligible speech. *What are some other guidelines for parents to follow in helping their infants and toddlers develop their language?*
Tetra Images/Getty Images

than "Yes" and "No." Actively repeat, expand, and recast the utterances. Your toddler might say, "Dada." You could respond by asking, "Where's Dada?" and then suggesting, "Let's go find him."
- *Adjust to your child's idiosyncrasies instead of working against them.* Many toddlers have difficulty pronouncing words and making themselves understood. Whenever possible, make toddlers feel that they are being understood.
- *Resist making normative comparisons.* Be aware of the ages at which your child reaches specific milestones (such as the first word, first 50 words), but do not measure this development rigidly against that of other children. Such comparisons can bring about unnecessary anxiety.

The first suggestion for parents of infants is to "be an active conversational partner." What did you learn earlier in this chapter about the amount of conversation mothers have with their infants? Does the amount of conversation or the mother's literacy skills and vocabulary diversity have a stronger positive effect on infants' vocabulary?

AN INTERACTIONIST VIEW OF LANGUAGE

If language acquisition depended only on biology, then Genie and the Wild Boy of Aveyron (discussed at the beginning of the chapter) should have talked without difficulty. A child's experiences influence language acquisition (Ahun & others, 2018; Morrow, 2020; Smith & others, 2019). But we have seen that language does have strong biological foundations (de Boer & Verhoef, 2019; O'Grady & Smith, 2019). No matter how much you converse with a dog, it won't learn to talk.

An interactionist view emphasizes that both biology and experience contribute to language development. This interaction of biology and experience can be seen in the variations in the acquisition of language. Children vary in their ability to acquire language, and this variation cannot be readily explained by differences in environmental input alone. However, virtually every child benefits enormously from opportunities to talk and be talked with (Marchman & others, 2019). Children whose parents and teachers provide them with a rich verbal environment show many positive outcomes (Morrison, 2020; Weisleder & others, 2018). Parents and teachers who pay attention to what children are trying to say, expand their children's utterances, read to them, and label things in the environment, are providing valuable, if unintentional, benefits (Feeney, Moravcik, & Novak, 2019; Tompkins & Rodgers, 2020).

Review Connect Reflect

 LG3 Discuss the biological and environmental contributions to language skills.

Review
- What are the biological foundations of language?
- What are the environmental aspects of language?
- How does an interactionist view describe language?

Connect
- Relate what you learned about the nature-nurture debate to understanding biological and environmental influences on the development of language skills.

Reflect *Your Own Personal Journey of Life*
- If and when you become a parent, how should you respond to your child's grammar when conversing with the child? Will you allow mistakes to continue and assume that your young child will grow out of them, or will you closely monitor your young child's grammar and correct mistakes whenever you hear them? Explain.

reach your **learning goals**

Language Development

1 What Is Language?

LG1 Define language and describe its rule systems.

Defining Language

Language's Rule Systems

- Language is a form of communication, whether spontaneous, written, or signed, that is based on a system of symbols. Language consists of all the words used by a community and the rules for varying and combining them. Infinite generativity is the ability to produce an endless number of meaningful sentences using a finite set of words and rules.

- The main rule systems of language are phonology, morphology, syntax, semantics, and pragmatics. Phonology is the sound system of a language, including the sounds used and the sound sequences that may occur in the language. Morphology refers to units of meaning in word formation. Syntax is the way words are combined to form acceptable phrases and sentences. Semantics involves the meaning of words and sentences. Pragmatics is the appropriate use of language in different contexts.

2 How Language Develops

LG2 Describe how language develops through the life span.

Infancy

- Among the milestones in infant language development are crying (birth), cooing (2 to 4 months), understanding first word (5 months), babbling (6 months), making the transition from universal linguist to language-specific listener (6 to 12 months), using gestures

(8 to 12 months), detecting word boundaries (8 months), first word spoken (13 months), vocabulary spurt (18 months), rapid expansion of understanding words (18 to 24 months), and two-word utterances (18 to 24 months).

Early Childhood

- Advances in phonology, morphology, syntax, semantics, and pragmatics continue in early childhood. The transition to complex sentences begins between 2 and 3 years and continues through the elementary school years. Fast mapping provides one explanation for how rapidly young children's vocabulary develops.

Middle and Late Childhood

- In middle and late childhood, children become more analytical and logical in their approach to words and grammar. Current debate involving how to teach children to read focuses on the whole-language approach versus the phonics approach. Researchers have found strong evidence that the phonics approach should be used in teaching children to read but that children also benefit from the whole-language approach.

- Children's writing emerges out of scribbling. Advances in children's language and cognitive development provide the underpinnings for improved writing.

- Recent research indicates a complex conclusion about whether there are sensitive periods in learning a second language. Children who are fluent in two languages have more advanced information-processing skills.

- Instruction for English language learners (ELLs) has taken one of two main forms: (1) instruction in English only, or (2) dual-language instruction in the child's home language and English. The majority of large-scale research studies have found a higher level of academic achievement when the dual-language approach is used.

Adolescence

- In adolescence, language changes include more effective use of words; improvements in the ability to understand metaphor, satire, and adult literary works; and improvements in writing.

Adulthood and Aging

- For many individuals, knowledge of words and word meanings continues unchanged or may even improve in later adulthood. However, some decline in language skills may occur in retrieving words for use in conversation, in understanding speech, in phonological skills, and in some aspects of discourse. These changes in language skills in older adults likely occur as a consequence of declines in memory or in speed of processing information, or as a result of disease.

3 Biological and Environmental Influences

 LG3 Discuss the biological and environmental contributions to language skills.

Biological Influences

- In evolution, language clearly gave humans an enormous edge over other animals and increased their chances of survival.

- A substantial portion of language processing occurs in the brain's left hemisphere, with Broca's area and Wernicke's area being important left-hemisphere locations.

- Chomsky argues that children are born with the ability to detect basic features and rules of language. In other words, they are biologically prepared to learn language with a prewired language acquisition device (LAD).

Environmental Influences

- The behaviorists' view of language development—that children acquire language as a result of reinforcement—has not been supported. Adults help children acquire language through child-directed speech, recasting, expanding, and labeling.

- Environmental influences are demonstrated by differences in the language development of children as a consequence of being exposed to different language environments in the home. Parents should talk extensively with an infant, especially about what the baby is attending to. Social cues play an important role in language learning.

An Interactionist View of Language

- The interactionist view emphasizes the contributions of both biology and experience in language development.

key terms

aphasia	infinite generativity	metaphor	satire
Broca's area	labeling	morphology	semantics
child-directed speech	language	phonics approach	syntax
dialect	language acquisition device	phonology	telegraphic speech
expanding	(LAD)	pragmatics	Wernicke's area
fast mapping	metalinguistic awareness	recasting	whole-language approach

key people

Richard Aslin	Ellen Galinsky	Kathy Hirsh-Pasek	Michael Tomasello
Naomi Baron	Roberta Golinkoff	Janellen Huttenlocher	
Jean Berko	Kenji Hakuta	Patricia Kuhl	
Noam Chomsky	Betty Hart	Todd Risley	

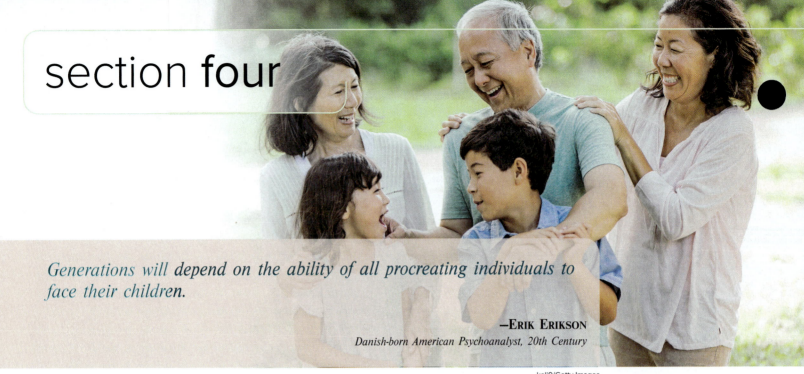

section four

> *Generations will depend on the ability of all procreating individuals to face their children.*
>
> —ERIK ERIKSON
> *Danish-born American Psychoanalyst, 20th Century*

kali9/Getty Images

Socioemotional Processes and Development

As children develop, they need "the meeting eyes of love." They split the universe into two halves: "me and not me." They juggle the need to curb their will with becoming what they can freely be. Children and youth want to fly but discover that first they have to learn to stand and walk and climb and dance. Adolescents try on one face after another, searching for a face of their own. As adults age, they seek satisfaction in their emotional lives and search for the meaning of life. This section contains four chapters: "Emotional Development and Attachment," "The Self, Identity, and Personality," "Gender and Sexuality," and "Moral Development, Values, and Religion."

chapter 10

EMOTIONAL DEVELOPMENT AND ATTACHMENT

chapter outline

Aurora Photos/Alamy Stock Photo

preview

For many years, emotion was neglected in the study of life-span development. Today, emotion is increasingly important in conceptualizations of development. For example, even as infants, individuals show different emotional styles, display varying temperaments, and begin to form emotional bonds with their caregivers. In this chapter, we study how temperament and attachment change across the life span. But first, we examine emotion itself, exploring the functions of emotions in people's lives and the development of emotion from infancy through late adulthood.

1 Exploring Emotion LG1 Discuss basic aspects of emotion.

What Are Emotions?　　　Emotion Regulation　　　Emotional Competence

Blossoms are scattered by the wind
And the wind cares nothing, but
The blossoms of the heart,
No wind can touch.

—Youshida Kenko
Buddhist Monk, 14th Century

Imagine your life without emotion. Emotion is the color and music of life, as well as the tie that binds people together. How do psychologists define and classify emotions, and why are they important to development?

WHAT ARE EMOTIONS?

For our purposes, we will define **emotion** as feeling, or affect, that occurs when a person is in a state or an interaction that is important to him or her, especially to his or her well-being. In infancy, emotions have important roles in (1) communication with others and (2) behavioral organization. Through emotions, infants communicate important aspects of their lives such as joy, sadness, interest, and fear (Taylor & Workman, 2018). In terms of behavioral organization, emotions influence children's social responses and adaptive behavior as they interact with others in their world (Denham & Bassett, 2019; Ekas, Braungart-Rieker, & Messinger, 2018).

When we think about emotions, a few dramatic feelings such as rage or glorious joy spring to mind. But emotions can be subtle as well, such as uneasiness in a new situation or the contentment a mother feels when she holds her baby. Psychologists classify the broad range of emotions in many ways, but almost all classifications designate an emotion as either positive or negative. Positive emotions include enthusiasm, joy, and love. Negative emotions include anxiety, anger, guilt, and sadness.

Emotions are influenced by biological foundations, cognitive processes, and a person's experiences (Cole & Hollenstein, 2018; Dollar & Calkins, 2019; Foroughe, 2018). Biology's importance to emotion also is apparent in the changes in a baby's emotional capacities (Martin & others, 2017). Certain regions of the brain that develop early in life (such as the brain stem, hippocampus, and amygdala) play a role in distress, excitement, and rage, and even infants display these emotions (van den Boomen, Munsters, & Kemner 2018). But, as we discuss later in the chapter, infants only gradually develop the ability to regulate their emotions, and this ability is linked to the gradual maturation of frontal regions of the cerebral cortex that can exert control over other areas of the brain (Bell, Broomell, & Patton, 2018; Bell, Ross, & Patton, 2018).

Emotion regulation also can influence whether biological and experiential factors are linked to various developmental outcomes. For example, in G × E interaction, the short version of the serotonin transporter gene (5-HTTLPR) is linked to increased risk of depression when individuals often experience stressful environments. A study of 9- to 15-year-olds who were characterized by this gene-environment combination found that they were less likely to be depressed if they were effective at emotion regulation (Ford & others, 2014).

Cognitive processes, both in immediate "in the moment" contexts and across childhood development, influence children's emotional development (Bell, Diaz, & Liu, 2019). Attention toward or away from an experience can influence children's emotional responses. For example, children who can distract themselves from a stressful encounter show a lower level of negative affect in the context and less anxiety over time (Crockenberg & Leerkes, 2006). Also, as children become older, they develop cognitive strategies for controlling their emotions and become more adept at modulating their emotional arousal (Perry & Calkins, 2018).

developmental **connection**

Brain Development

The timing of maturation of the amygdala and prefrontal cortex is linked to adolescent risk taking. Connect to "Physical Development and Biological Aging."

emotion Feeling, or affect, that occurs when a person is engaged in an interaction that is important to him or her, especially to his or her well-being.

Social relationships provide the setting for the development of a rich variety of emotions (Cole, Lougheed, & Ram, 2018; Dollar & Collins, 2019; Leerkes & Augustine, 2019; Morris & others, 2018; Perry & Calkins, 2018). When toddlers hear their parents quarreling, they often react with distress and inhibit their play. Well-functioning families make each other laugh and may develop a light mood to defuse conflicts. A study of 18- to 24-month-olds found that parents' elicitation of talk about emotions was associated with their toddlers' sharing and helping (Brownell & others, 2013). In another study of 10- to 12-year-olds, mothers of more anxious children were more likely to engage in psychologically controlling behavior intended to manipulate the children's emotional state, showed less warmth and interest in the children, and elaborated less during conversations about an emotionally negative event (Brumariu & Kerns, 2015).

Biological evolution has endowed human beings with the capacity to be *emotional*, but cultural embeddedness and relationships with others provide diversity in emotional experiences (Norona & Baker, 2017). Emotional development and coping with stress are influenced by whether caregivers have maltreated or neglected children and whether children's caregivers are depressed or not (Doyle & Cicchetti, 2018; Jackson, 2019; Thompson, 2019). When infants become stressed, they show better biological recovery from the stressors when their caregivers engage in sensitive caregiving (Sullivan & Wilson, 2018).

How do Japanese mothers handle their infants' and children's emotional development differently from non-Latina White mothers?
Lawren/Getty Images

One study documented how babies pick up on their mothers' stress (Waters, West, & Mendes, 2014). In this study, mothers were separated from their babies and asked to give a five-minute speech, with half of the mothers receiving a positive evaluation and the other half a negative evaluation. Mothers who received negative feedback reported an increase in negative emotion and cardiac stress, while those who were given positive feedback reported an increase in positive emotion. The babies quickly detected their mothers' stress, as reflected in an increased heart rate when reunited with them. And the greater the mother's stress response, the more her baby's heart rate increased.

Cultural variations characterize emotional development (Cole & Hollenstein, 2018). For example, researchers have found that East Asian infants display less frequent and less intense positive and negative emotions than non-Latino White infants (Cole & Tan, 2007). Throughout childhood, East Asian parents encourage their children to show emotional reserve rather than to be emotionally expressive (Cole, 2016). Further, Japanese parents try to prevent children from experiencing negative emotions, whereas non-Latino White mothers more frequently respond after their children become distressed and then try to help them cope (Rothbaum & Trommsdorff, 2007).

EMOTION REGULATION

Too often when people think about emotion they think about it in negative ways, such as having emotional problems. However, emotion can be adaptive and help individuals live more competent, enriching lives. In terms of emotions being adaptive, consider that infants communicate via emotion even before they understand language and their emotions are critical to their survival and thus their adaptation. As we see next, emotion regulation plays a key role in the adaptiveness of emotions, especially so they don't interfere with our daily functioning and relationships.

The ability to control one's emotions is a key dimension of development (Cole & Hollenstein, 2018; Dollar & Calkins, 2019). Emotion regulation consists of effectively managing arousal to adapt to circumstances and to reach a goal (Perry & Calkins, 2018). Arousal involves a state of alertness or activation, which can reach levels that are too high for effective functioning. Anger, for example, often requires regulation.

In infancy and early childhood, regulation of emotion gradually shifts from external sources to self-initiated, internal sources. Also, with increasing age, children tend to improve their use of cognitive strategies for regulating emotion, modulate their emotional arousal, become more adept at managing situations to minimize negative emotion, and choose effective ways to cope with stress (Bell, Diaz, & Liu, 2019).

Emotion regulation is involved in many aspects of children's and adolescents' development, and there are wide variations in children's and adolescents' ability to modulate their emotions (Cole, Ram, & English, 2019; Perry & Calkins, 2018; Dollar & Calkins, 2019). Indeed, a prominent feature of children and adolescents with problems is that they often have difficulty managing their emotions (Thompson, 2019). Ineffective emotion regulation is linked with a lower level of executive function, difficulty succeeding in school, a lower level of moral development (weak conscience and lack of internalization of rules, for example), failure to adequately cope with stress, and difficulty in peer relations (Blair, 2016, 2017; Cole, Ram, & English, 2019). Many

An emotion-coaching parent. *What are some differences in emotion-coaching and emotion-dismissing parents?*
shironosov/Getty Images

---

developmental **connection**

Emotional Intelligence

Emotional intelligence involves perceiving and expressing emotions accurately, understanding emotion and emotional knowledge, using feelings to facilitate thought, and managing emotions effectively. Connect to "Intelligence."

---

primary emotions Emotions that are present in humans and other animals, emerge early in life, and are culturally universal; examples are joy, anger, sadness, fear, and disgust.

self-conscious emotions Emotions that require consciousness and a sense of "me"; they include empathy, jealousy, embarrassment, pride, shame, and guilt, most of which first appear at some point after 18 months of age when a sense of self becomes consolidated in toddlers.

researchers consider the growth of emotion regulation in children as fundamental to the development of social competence (Thompson, 2019).

Parents can play an important role in helping young children regulate their emotions (Leerkes & Augustine, 2019). Depending on how they talk with their children about emotion, parents can be described as taking an *emotion-coaching* or an *emotion-dismissing* approach (Gottman, 2019). The distinction between these approaches is most evident in the way the parent deals with the child's negative emotions (anger, frustration, sadness, and so on). *Emotion-coaching parents* monitor their children's emotions, view their children's negative emotions as opportunities for teaching, assist them in labeling emotions, and coach them in how to deal effectively with emotions. In contrast, *emotion-dismissing parents* view their role as to deny, ignore, or change negative emotions. Researchers have observed that emotion-coaching parents interact with their children in a less rejecting manner, use more scaffolding and praise, and are more nurturant than are emotion-dismissing parents (Gottman & DeClaire, 1997). Moreover, the children of emotion-coaching parents are better at soothing themselves when they get upset, are more effective in regulating their negative affect, focus their attention better, and have fewer behavior problems than the children of emotion-dismissing parents. One study found that fathers' emotion coaching was related to children's social competence (Baker, Fenning, & Crnic, 2011). Another study revealed that having emotion-dismissing parents was linked with children's poor emotion regulation (Lunkenheimer, Shields, & Cortina, 2007). And in a recent study, mothers' emotion-dismissing parenting was linked to toddlers' lower emotional competence, while mothers' emotion-coaching parenting was associated with toddlers' higher emotional competence (Ornaghi & others, 2019).

A challenge parents face is that young children typically don't want to talk about difficult emotional topics, such as being distressed or engaging in negative behaviors. Among the strategies young children use to avoid these conversations are remaining silent, changing the topic, pushing the parent away, or running away. Young children are more likely to openly discuss difficult emotional circumstances when they are securely attached to their mothers.

EMOTIONAL COMPETENCE

In the "Intelligence" chapter, we briefly considered the concept of emotional intelligence. Here we examine a closely related concept, emotional competence, that focuses on the adaptive nature of emotional experience (Denham & Bassett, 2019). Carolyn Saarni (1999; Saarni & others, 2006) notes that becoming emotionally competent involves developing a number of skills in social contexts, including the following:

Skill	Example
· Having awareness of one's emotional states	· Being able to differentiate whether one feels sad or anxious
· Detecting others' emotions	· Understanding when another person is sad rather than afraid
· Using the vocabulary of emotion terms in socially and culturally appropriate ways	· Appropriately describing a social situation in one's culture when a person is feeling distressed
· Having empathetic and sympathetic sensitivity to others' emotional experiences	· Being sensitive to other people when they are feeling distressed
· Recognizing that inner emotional states do not have to correspond to outer expressions	· Recognizing that one can feel very angry yet manage one's emotional expression so that it appears more neutral
· Adaptively coping with negative emotions by using self-regulatory strategies that reduce the intensity or duration of such emotional states	· Reducing anger by walking away from an aversive situation and engaging in an activity that takes one's mind off the aversive situation
· Having awareness that the expression of emotions plays a major role in relationships	· Knowing that expressing anger toward a friend on a regular basis is likely to harm the friendship
· Viewing oneself overall as feeling the way one wants to feel	· Striving to cope effectively with the stress in one's life and feeling that one is successfully doing this

As children acquire these emotional competence skills in a variety of contexts, they are more likely to effectively manage their emotions, become resilient in the face of stressful circumstances, and develop more positive relationships (Cole & Hollenstein, 2018; Denham & Bassett, 2019).

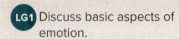

Review Connect Reflect

LG1 Discuss basic aspects of emotion.

Review

- How is emotion defined?
- What are some developmental changes in the regulation of emotion?
- What constitutes emotional competence, according to Saarni?

Connect

- How similar or different are the concepts of emotional intelligence and emotional competence?

Reflect *Your Own Personal Journey of Life*

- Think back to your childhood and adolescent years. How effective were you in regulating your emotions? Give some examples. Has your ability to regulate your emotions changed as you have grown older? Explain.

---

2 Development of Emotion

 LG2 Describe the development of emotion through the life span.

| Infancy | Early Childhood | Middle and Late Childhood | Adolescence | Adult Development and Aging |

Does an adult's emotional life differ from an adolescent's? Does a young child's emotional life differ from an infant's? Does an infant even have an emotional life? In this section, we trace the changes in emotion over the life span, looking not only at changes in emotional experience but also at the development of emotional competence.

INFANCY

What are some early developmental changes in emotions? What functions do infants' cries serve? When do infants begin to smile?

Early Emotions A leading expert on infant emotional development, Michael Lewis (2007, 2008, 2010, 2015, 2018) distinguishes between primary emotions and self-conscious emotions. **Primary emotions** are emotions that are present in humans and other animals; these emotions appear in the first six months of the human infant's development. Primary emotions include surprise, interest, joy, anger, sadness, fear, and disgust (see Figure 1 for infants' facial expressions of some of these early emotions). In Lewis' classification, **self-conscious emotions** require self-awareness that involves consciousness and a sense of "me." Self-conscious emotions include jealousy, empathy, embarrassment, pride, shame, and guilt—most of these occurring for the first time at some point after 18 months of age when a sense of self becomes consolidated in toddlers.

Researchers such as Joseph Campos (2005) and Michael Lewis (2018) debate about how early in the infant and toddler years these self-conscious emotions first appear and what their sequence is. As an indication of the controversy regarding when certain emotions first are displayed by infants, consider jealousy. Some researchers argue that jealousy does not emerge until infants are approximately 18 months old (Lewis, 2007), whereas others assert that it is displayed much earlier (Hart, 2018). Some research studies suggest that the appearance of jealousy might occur as early as 6 months of age (Hart & others, 2004). In one study, 6-month-old infants observed their mothers giving attention either to a lifelike baby doll (hugging or gently rocking it, for example) or to a book. When mothers directed their attention to the doll, the infants were more

FIGURE 1

EXPRESSION OF DIFFERENT EMOTIONS IN INFANTS
(*Joy*): Kozak_O_O/Shutterstock; (*Sadness*): Jill Braaten/McGraw Hill Companies; (*Fear*): Stanislav/Shutterstock; (*Surprise*): Photodisc Collection/EyeWire/Getty Images

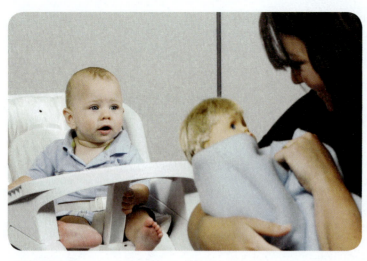

FIGURE 2

IS THIS THE EARLY EXPRESSION OF JEALOUSY? In the study by Hart and Carrington (2002), the researchers concluded that the reactions of 6-month-old infants who observed their mothers giving attention to a baby doll may indicate the early appearance of jealousy because of the negative emotions—such as anger and sadness—they displayed. However, experts on emotional development, such as Joseph Campos (2009) and Jerome Kagan (2010), argue that emotions such as jealousy don't appear during the first year. *Why do they conclude that jealousy does not occur in the first year?*
Kenny Braun/Braun Photography

What are some different types of cries?
Andy Cox/The Image Bank/Getty Images

basic cry A rhythmic pattern usually consisting of a cry, a briefer silence, a shorter inspiratory whistle that is higher pitched than the main cry, and then a brief rest before the next cry.

anger cry A cry similar to the basic cry but with more excess air forced through the vocal cords.

pain cry A sudden, initial loud cry followed by breath holding, without preliminary moaning.

likely to display negative emotions, such as anger and sadness, which may have indicated their jealousy (Hart & Carrington, 2002) (see Figure 2). Some observers have been skeptical of this interpretation, suggesting that these infants' expressions of anger and sadness simply may have reflected frustration about not being able to have the novel doll to play with. However, in one study, 9-month-old infants displayed jealousy-related behavior and EEG patterns characteristic of jealousy when their mothers gave attention to a social rival (Mize & others, 2014).

Debate about the onset of an emotion such as jealousy illustrates the complexity and difficulty of indexing early emotions. That said, some experts on infant socioemotional development, such as Jerome Kagan (2013), conclude that the structural immaturity of the infant brain makes it unlikely that emotions requiring thought—such as guilt, pride, despair, shame, empathy, and jealousy—can be experienced during the first year. Nonetheless, some leading researchers have argued that research now indicates that empathy can be expressed before the infant's first birthday (Davidov & others, 2013).

Emotional Expression and Social Relationships

Emotional expression is involved in infants' first relationships. The ability of infants to communicate emotions permits coordinated interactions with their caregivers and the beginning of an emotional bond between them (Perry & Calkins, 2018; Thompson, 2015, 2016). Not only do parents change their emotional expressions in response to infants' emotional expressions, but infants also modify their emotional expressions in response to their parents' emotional expressions. In other words, these interactions are mutually regulated (Bridgett & others, 2009). Because of this coordination, the interactions are described as reciprocal, or synchronous, when all is going well. Sensitive, responsive parents help their infants grow emotionally, whether the infants respond in distressed or happy ways (Bedford & others, 2017). One study found that a higher level of maternal positive emotionality predicted more initial infant smiling and laughter, while a higher level of parental stress predicted a lower trajectory of infant smiling and laughter (Bridgett & others, 2013). Also, a recent observational study of mother-infant interaction found that maternal sensitivity was linked to a lower level of infant fear (Gartstein, Hancock, & Iverson, 2018). Another study revealed that parents' elicitation of talk about emotion with toddlers was associated with the toddlers' sharing and helping behaviors (Brownell & others, 2013).

Cries and smiles are two emotional expressions that infants display when interacting with parents. These are babies' first forms of emotional communication.

Crying Crying is the most important mechanism newborns have for communicating with their world. The first cry verifies that the baby's lungs have filled with air. Cries also may provide information about the health of the newborn's central nervous system. A recent study found that excessive infant crying in 3-month-olds doubled the risk of behavioral, hyperactive, and mood problems at 5 to 6 years of age (Smarius & others, 2017).

Babies have at least three types of cries:

- **Basic cry.** A rhythmic pattern that usually consists of a cry, followed by a briefer silence, then a shorter inspiratory whistle that is somewhat higher in pitch than the main cry, then another brief rest before the next cry. Some infancy experts stress that hunger is one of the conditions that incite the basic cry.

- **Anger cry.** A variation of the basic cry in which more excess air is forced through the vocal cords. The anger cry has a loud, harsh sound to it, almost like shouting.

- **Pain cry.** A sudden long, initial loud cry followed by breath holding; no preliminary moaning is present. The pain cry is stimulated by a high-intensity stimulus.

Most adults can determine whether an infant's cries signify anger or pain (Zeskind, 2007). Parents can distinguish between the various cries of their own baby better than those of another baby.

Smiling Smiling is critical as a means of developing a new social skill and is a key social signal (Dau & others, 2017; Martin & Messinger, 2018). In one study, researchers found that smiling and laughter at 7 months of age were associated with self-regulation at 7 years of age (Posner & others, 2014).

Two types of smiling can be distinguished in infants:

- **Reflexive smile.** A smile that does not occur in response to external stimuli and appears during the first month after birth, usually during sleep.
- **Social smile.** A smile that occurs in response to an external stimulus, typically a face in the case of the young infant. Social smiling occurs as early as 4 to 6 weeks of age in response to a caregiver's voice (Messinger, 2008).

The infant's social smile can have a powerful impact on caregivers. Following weeks of endless demands, fatigue, and little reinforcement, their infant starts smiling at them and all of the caregivers' efforts are rewarded.

Fear One of a baby's earliest emotions is fear, which typically first appears at about 6 months of age and peaks at about 18 months. However, abused and neglected infants can show fear as early as 3 months (Campos, 2005).

The most frequent expression of an infant's fear involves **stranger anxiety,** in which an infant shows a fear and wariness of strangers (Van Hulle & others, 2017). Stranger anxiety usually emerges gradually. It first appears at about 6 months of age in the form of wary reactions. By age 9 months, the fear of strangers is often more intense, reaching a peak toward the end of the first year of life (Scher & Harel, 2008).

Not all infants show distress when they encounter a stranger. Besides individual variations, whether an infant shows stranger anxiety also depends on the social context and the characteristics of the stranger (Kagan, 2008).

Infants show less stranger anxiety when they are in familiar settings. It appears that when infants feel secure, they are less likely to show stranger anxiety.

In addition to stranger anxiety, infants experience fear of being separated from their caregivers. The result is **separation protest**—crying when the caregiver leaves. Separation protest is initially displayed by infants at approximately 7 to 8 months and peaks at about 15 months (Kagan, 2008). One study revealed that separation protest peaked at about 13 to 15 months in four different cultures (Kagan, Kearsley, & Zelazo, 1978). Although the percentage of infants who engaged in separation protest varied across cultures, the infants reached a peak of protest at about the same age—early in the second year of life.

Emotion Regulation and Coping Earlier, we discussed some general developmental changes in emotion regulation across the childhood years. Here we examine in detail how infants develop emotion regulation and coping skills.

During the first year of life, the infant gradually develops an ability to inhibit, or minimize, the intensity and duration of emotional reactions (Ekas, Braungart-Rieker, & Messinger, 2018). From early in infancy, babies put their thumbs in their mouths to soothe themselves. But at first, infants mainly depend on caregivers to help them soothe their emotions, as when a caregiver rocks an infant to sleep, sings lullabies to the infant, gently strokes the infant, and so on. In a recent study, researchers found that young infants with a negative temperament used fewer attention regulation strategies, and maternal sensitivity to infants was linked to more adaptive emotion regulation (Thomas & others, 2017). Another recent study also linked maternal sensitivity to better emotion regulation in 10-month-old infants (Frick & others, 2018).

Later in infancy, when they become aroused, infants sometimes redirect their attention or distract themselves in order to reduce their arousal. By 2 years of age, toddlers can use language to define their feeling states and the context that is upsetting them (Kopp, 2008). A toddler might say, "Feel bad. Dog scare." This type of communication may allow caregivers to help the child learn how to regulate emotion.

Contexts can influence emotion regulation (Morris & others, 2018). Infants are often affected by fatigue, hunger, time of day, the people who are around them, and where they are.

He who binds to himself a joy
Does the winged life destroy;
But he who kisses the joy as it flies
Lives in eternity's sun rise.

—WILLIAM BLAKE
English Poet, 19th Century

reflexive smile A smile that does not occur in response to external stimuli. It happens during the month after birth, usually during sleep.

social smile A smile in response to an external stimulus, which, early in development, typically is a face.

stranger anxiety An infant's fear of and wariness toward strangers; it tends to appear in the second half of the first year of life.

separation protest Reaction that occurs when infants experience a fear of being separated from a caregiver, which results in crying when the caregiver leaves.

Should a crying baby be given attention and soothed, or does this spoil the infant? Should the infant's age, the type of cry, and the circumstances be considered?
Photodisc Collection/Getty Images

Infants must learn to adapt to different contexts that require emotion regulation. Further, new demands appear as the infant becomes older and parents modify their expectations. For example, parents may take it in stride if their 6-month-old infant screams in a grocery store but may react very differently if their 2-year-old starts screaming.

To soothe or not to soothe—should a crying baby be given attention and soothed, or does this attention spoil the infant? Many years ago, behaviorist John Watson (1928) argued that parents spend too much time responding to infant crying. As a consequence, he said, parents reward crying and increase its incidence. Some researchers have found that a caregiver's quick, soothing response to crying increased crying (Gewirtz, 1977). However, infancy experts Mary Ainsworth (1979) and John Bowlby (1989) argue that a quick, comforting response to an infant's cries is an important ingredient in the development of a strong bond between the infant and caregiver. In one of Ainsworth's studies, infants whose mothers responded quickly when they cried at 3 months of age cried less later in the first year of life (Bell & Ainsworth, 1972).

Controversy continues to surround the question of whether or how parents should respond to an infant's cries. Some developmentalists argue that an infant cannot be spoiled in the first year of life, a view suggesting that parents should soothe a crying infant. Parental responsiveness should help infants develop a sense of trust and secure attachment to the caregiver. One study revealed that mothers' negative emotional reactions (anger and anxiety) to crying increased the risk of subsequent attachment insecurity (Leerkes, Parade, & Gudmundson, 2011). Another study found that problems in infant soothability at 6 months of age predicted insecure attachment at 12 months of age (Mills-Koonce, Propper, & Barnett, 2012). And one study found that mothers were more likely than fathers to use soothing techniques to reduce infant crying (Dayton & others, 2015). Further, a recent study revealed that depressed mothers rocked and touched their crying infants less than non-depressed mothers (Esposito & others, 2017). Also, recently an intervention that trained mothers to effectively use soothing techniques in the fourth week after birth resulted in infants' waking up less at night and crying less in assessments at 7, 11, and 23 weeks after birth (Ozturk Donmez & Bayik Temel, 2019).

EARLY CHILDHOOD

The young child's growing awareness of self is linked to the ability to feel an expanding range of emotions. Young children, like adults, experience many emotions during the course of a day. At times, they also try to make sense of other people's emotional reactions and to control their own emotions (Nakamichi, 2018).

Expressing Emotions   Recall from our earlier discussion that even young infants experience emotions such as joy and fear, but to experience self-conscious emotions, children must be able to refer to themselves and be aware of themselves as distinct from others (Lewis, 2018). Pride, shame, embarrassment, and guilt are examples of self-conscious emotions. Self-conscious emotions do not appear to develop until self-awareness appears in the second half of the second year of life.

During the early childhood years, emotions such as pride and guilt become more common (Lewis, 2018). They are especially influenced by parents' responses to children's behavior (Thompson, 2015). For example, a young child may experience shame when a parent says, "You should feel bad about biting your sister."

Understanding Emotions   Among the most important changes in emotional development in early childhood is an increased understanding of emotion (Denham & Bassett, 2019). During early childhood, young children increasingly understand that certain situations are likely to evoke particular emotions, facial expressions indicate specific emotions, emotions affect behavior, and emotions can be used to influence others' emotions (Cole & others, 2009). In one study, young children's emotional understanding was linked to how extensively they engaged in prosocial behavior (Ensor, Spencer, & Hughes, 2010).

Between 2 and 4 years of age, children use an increasing number of terms to describe emotions. During this time, they are also learning about the causes and consequences of feelings.

When they are 4 to 5 years of age, children show an increased ability to reflect on emotions. They also begin to understand that the same event can elicit different feelings in different people. Moreover, they show a growing awareness that they need to manage their emotions to meet social standards (Denham & Zinsser, 2015). And, by 5 years of age, most children can

A young child expressing the emotion of shame, which occurs when a child evaluates his or her actions as not living up to standards. A child experiencing shame wishes to hide or disappear. *Why is shame called a self-conscious emotion?*
James Woodson/Getty Images

accurately identify emotions that are produced by challenging circumstances and describe strategies they might call on to cope with everyday stress (Cole & others, 2009).

One program that is designed to improve young children's understanding of emotions is the Emotion-Based Prevention program (EBP) (Izard & others, 2008). This program consists of a teacher-conducted emotions course in the classroom, emotion tutoring and coaching teacher dialogues, and weekly parent messages that reinforce the lessons taught in the classroom. In the classroom, teachers ask children to label or demonstrate emotional expressions, share ideas about what causes them to feel the emotions they described, compare expressions of different emotions and their intensities, and draw pictures or act out emotion expressions for their classmates. One study found that EBP was effective in improving Head Start children's emotion knowledge and the children who participated in the program showed a decrease in negative emotional expressions and internalizing behaviors (Finion & others, 2015).

Regulating Emotions   Many researchers consider the growth of emotion regulation in children as fundamental to the development of social competence (Cole & Hollenstein, 2018; Cole, Ram, & English, 2019; Dollar & Calkins, 2019). In one study of 5- to 7-year-olds, understanding others' emotions was linked to the children's emotion regulation (Hudson & Jacques, 2014).

Emotion regulation can be conceptualized as an important component of self-regulation or of executive function (Bell, Diaz, & Liu, 2019; Perry & Calkins, 2018). Executive function is increasingly thought to be a key concept in describing the young child's higher-level cognitive functioning (McClelland & Cameron, 2019; McCoy, 2019). Cybele Raver and her colleagues (Blair, 2016, 2017; Blair & Raver, 2012, 2015, 2016; Blair, Raver, & Finegood, 2016; McCoy & Raver, 2011; Raver & others, 2011, 2012, 2013; Zhai, Raver, & Jones, 2012) are using various interventions, such as increasing caregiver emotional expressiveness, to improve young children's emotion regulation and reduce behavior problems in children growing up in poverty conditions.

Emotions play a strong role in determining the success of a child's peer relationships (Smetana & Ball, 2018). Specifically, the ability to modulate one's emotions is an important skill that benefits children in their relationships with peers. Moody and emotionally negative children are more likely to experience rejection by their peers, whereas emotionally positive children are more popular. A recent study found that young children with higher emotion regulation were more popular with their peers (Nakamichi, 2019).

MIDDLE AND LATE CHILDHOOD

During middle and late childhood, many children show marked improvement in understanding and managing their emotions (Cole & Hollenstein, 2018; Cole, Lougheed, & Ram, 2018; Morris & others, 2018). However, in some instances, such as when they experience stressful circumstances, their coping abilities may be challenged (Denham & Bassett, 2019). In a recent study, a low level of emotion regulation in childhood was especially important in predicting a higher level of externalizing problems in adolescence (Perry & others, 2017).

Developmental Changes in Emotion   Here are some important developmental changes in emotions during the middle and late childhood years (Denham, Bassett, & Wyatt, 2015; Kuebli, 1994; Perry & Calkins, 2018; Thompson, 2015):

· *Improved emotional understanding.* Children in elementary school develop an increased ability to understand complex emotions such as pride and shame. These emotions become less tied to the reactions of other people; they become more self-generated and integrated with a sense of personal responsibility. A child may feel a sense of pride about developing new reading skills or shame after hurting a friend's feelings. Also, during middle and late childhood as part of their understanding of emotions, children can engage in "mental time travel," in which they anticipate and recall the cognitive and emotional aspects of events (Hjortsvang & Lagattuta, 2017; Kramer & Lagattuta, 2018; Lagattuta, 2014a, b).

· *Marked improvements in the ability to suppress or conceal negative emotional reactions.* Children now sometimes intentionally hide their emotions. Although a boy may feel sad or angry because a friend does not want to play with him, for example, he may decide not to share those feelings with his parents.

· *The use of self-initiated strategies for redirecting feelings.* In the elementary school years, children reflect more about emotional experiences and develop strategies to cope with their emotional lives. Children can more effectively manage their emotions by cognitive means, such as using distracting thoughts. A boy may be excited about his birthday party that will take place later in the afternoon, but still be able to concentrate on his schoolwork during the day.

· *An increased tendency to take into fuller account the events leading to emotional reactions.* A fourth-grader may become aware that her sadness today is influenced by her friend's moving to another town last week.

· *Development of a capacity for genuine empathy.* Two girls see another child in distress on the playground and run to the child and ask if they can help.

Coping with Stress An important aspect of children's lives is learning how to cope with stress (Mash & Wolfe, 2019; Thompson, 2019). As children get older, they are able to more accurately appraise a stressful situation and determine how much control they have over it. Older children generate more alternatives for coping with stressful conditions and make greater use of cognitive coping strategies (Saarni & others, 2006). For example, older children are better than younger children at intentionally shifting their thoughts to a topic that is less stressful. Older children are also better at reframing, or changing their perception of a stressful situation. For example, younger children may be very disappointed that their teacher did not say hello to them when they arrived at school. Older children may reframe this type of situation and think, "She may have been busy with other things and just forgot to say hello."

By 10 years of age, most children are able to use these cognitive strategies to cope with stress (Saarni & others, 2006). However, in families that have not been supportive and are characterized by turmoil or trauma, children may be so overwhelmed by stress that they do not use such strategies (Thabet & others, 2009).

Disasters can especially harm children's development and produce adjustment problems (Masten, 2017; Masten & Kalstabakken, 2018; Masten & Palmer, 2019). Among the outcomes for children who experience disasters are acute stress reactions, depression, panic disorder, and post-traumatic stress disorder (Danielson & others, 2017; Narayan & Masten, 2019). The likelihood that a child will face these problems following a disaster depends on factors such as the nature and severity of the disaster and the type of support available to the child.

Following are descriptions of studies of how various aspects of traumatic events and disasters affect children:

· In a study of mothers and their children aged 5 years and younger who were directly exposed to the 9/11 attacks in New York City, the mothers who developed post-traumatic stress disorder (PTSD) and depression were less likely to help their children regulate their emotions and behavior than mothers who were only depressed or only had PTSD (Chemtob & others, 2010). This outcome was linked to their children having anxiety, depression, aggression, and sleep problems.

What are some effective strategies to help children cope with traumatic events such as the mass shooting at Sandy Hook Elementary School in Connecticut?
Stephanie Keith/Polaris/Newscom

· A study of the effects of the 2004 tsunami in Sri Lanka found that severe exposure to the tsunami combined with more exposure to other adversities, such as an ongoing war and family violence, was linked to poorer adjustment after the tsunami disaster (Catani & others, 2010).

· A research review revealed that children with disabilities are more likely than children without disabilities to live in poverty conditions, which increases their exposure to hazards and disasters (Peek & Stough, 2010). When a disaster occurs, children with disabilities have more difficulty escaping from the disaster.

In research on disasters and trauma, the term *dose-response effects* is often used. A widely supported finding in this research area is that the more severe the disaster or trauma (dose), the worse the adaptation and adjustment (response) following the disaster or trauma (Masten, 2017; Masten & Kalstabakken, 2018; Narayan & Masten, 2019).

Children who have developed a number of coping techniques have the best chance of adapting and functioning competently in

Melissa Jackson, Child Psychiatrist

Dr. Melissa Jackson is a child and adolescent psychiatrist in Miami, Florida. She obtained a medical degree from the University of Florida and then completed an internship and residency in psychiatry at Advocate Lutheran General Hospital in Chicago, followed by a fellowship in child and adolescent psychiatry at the University of Southern California. Among the problems and disorders that Dr. Jackson treats are post-traumatic stress disorder, ADHD, anxiety, autism, depression, and a number of behavioral issues. In addition to her psychiatric treatment of children, she founded Health for Honduras, which includes trips to Honduras to provide services to children in orphanages.

To become a child and adolescent psychiatrist like Melissa Jackson, you would need to obtain an undergraduate degree, then earn a medical degree, then spend three to four years as a resident physician in general psychiatry, and then complete a two-year fellowship in the subspecialty of child and adolescent psychiatry. An important aspect of being a psychiatrist is that psychiatrists can prescribe medication, which psychologists cannot do.

To read further about child and adolescent psychiatrists, see the Careers Appendix at the end of the "Introduction" chapter.

the face of disasters and traumas (Ungar, 2015). Following are some recommendations for helping children cope with the stress of especially devastating events (Gurwitch & others, 2001, pp. 4–11):

- *Reassure children of their safety and security.* This step may need to be taken numerous times.
- *Allow children to retell events and be patient in listening to them.*
- *Encourage children to talk about any disturbing or confusing feelings.* Tell them that these are normal feelings after a stressful event.
- *Help children make sense of what happened.* Children may misunderstand what took place. For example, young children "may blame themselves, believe things happened that did not happen, believe that terrorists are in the school, etc. Gently help children develop a realistic understanding of the event" (p. 10).
- *Protect children from re-exposure to frightening situations and reminders of the trauma.* This strategy includes limiting conversations about the event in front of the children and limiting exposure to media coverage of the event.

Child and adolescent psychiatrists are among the mental health professionals who help youth cope with stress, including traumatic experiences. To read about a child psychiatrist who treats children and adolescents, see *Connecting with Careers.*

ADOLESCENCE

Adolescence has long been described as a time of emotional turmoil (Hall, 1904). Adolescents are not constantly in a state of "storm and stress," but emotional highs and lows do increase during early adolescence (Rosenblum & Lewis, 2003; Somerville, 2018). Young adolescents can be on top of the world one moment and down in the dumps the next. In some instances, the intensity of their emotions seems out of proportion to the events that elicit them (Morris, Cui, & Steinberg, 2013). Young adolescents might sulk a lot, not knowing how to adequately express their feelings. With little or no provocation, they can blow up at their parents or siblings, a response that might reflect the defense mechanism of displacing their feelings onto another person. For some adolescents, such emotional swings can reflect serious problems.

Depression is more common in adolescence than in childhood, and it is increasing among adolescents (Dietz, Silk, & Amole, 2019). In a large-scale national study, the overall percentage of adolescents who had experienced major depressive episodes increased from 8.7 percent in 2005 to 11.3 percent in 2014 (Mojtabai, Olfson, & Han, 2016). Girls are especially vulnerable to depression in adolescence (Mash & Wolfe, 2019; Parritz, 2018). In the same national study, the percentage of adolescent girls with major depressive episodes increased from 13.1 percent in 2005 to 17.3 percent in 2014. In 2005, the percentage of adolescent boys with major depressive

developmental **connection**

Brain Development

The amygdala, where much of emotion is processed in the brain, matures by early adolescence, and the prefrontal cortex continues developing through emerging adulthood. Connect to "Physical Development and Biological Aging."

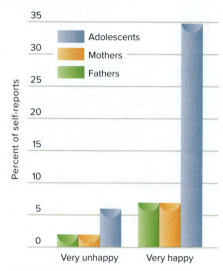

FIGURE **3**

SELF-REPORTED EXTREMES OF EMOTION BY ADOLESCENTS, MOTHERS, AND FATHERS USING THE EXPERIENCE SAMPLING METHOD. In the study by Reed Larson and Maryse Richards (1994), adolescents and their mothers and fathers were beeped at random times by researchers using the experience sampling method. The researchers found that adolescents reported more emotional extremes than their parents did.

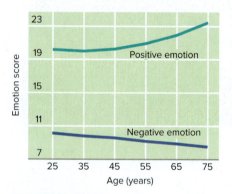

FIGURE **4**

CHANGES IN POSITIVE AND NEGATIVE EMOTION ACROSS THE ADULT YEARS. Positive and negative scores had a possible range of 6 to 30, with higher scores reflecting positive emotion and lower scores negative emotion. Positive emotion increased in middle and late adulthood, while negative emotion declined.

fight or flight Taylor's view that when men experience stress, they are more likely to become aggressive, withdraw from social contact, or drink alcohol.

tend and befriend Taylor's view that when women experience stress, they are more likely to seek social alliances with others, especially female friends.

episodes increased from 4.5 percent in 2005 to 5.7 percent in 2014. It is, however, important for adults to recognize that moodiness is a normal aspect of early adolescence and to understand that most adolescents make it through these moody times to become competent adults.

Reed Larson and Maryse Richards (1994) found that adolescents reported more extreme emotions and more fleeting emotions than their parents did. For example, adolescents were five times more likely to report being "very happy" and three times more likely to report being "very unhappy" than their parents were (see Figure 3). These findings lend support to the perception of adolescents as moody and changeable (Rosenblum & Lewis, 2003).

Emotion regulation is involved in many aspects of adolescents' development, and there are wide variations in adolescents' ability to modulate their emotions (Hollenstein & Lanteigne, 2018; Perry & Calkins, 2018). Indeed, a prominent feature of adolescents with problems is that they often have difficulty managing their emotions. Ineffective emotion regulation is linked with a lower level of executive function, difficulty succeeding in school, a lower level of moral development (weak conscience and lack of internalization of rules, for example), failure to adequately cope with stress, and difficulty in peer relations (Blair, 2017; Cole & Hollenstein, 2018).

ADULT DEVELOPMENT AND AGING

Like children, adults adapt more effectively when they are emotionally intelligent—when they are skilled at perceiving and expressing emotion, understanding emotion, using feelings to facilitate thought, and managing emotions effectively. (In the chapter on "Families, Lifestyles, and Parenting," we examine a number of aspects of relationships that involve emotions.)

Developmental changes in emotion continue through the adult years (Kunzmann & others, 2017; Mather & Ponzio, 2018). The changes often are characterized by an effort to create lifestyles that are emotionally satisfying, predictable, and manageable by making decisions about an occupation, a life partner, and other circumstances. Of course, not all individuals are successful in these efforts. A key theme of emotional development in adulthood is "the adaptive integration of emotional experience into satisfying daily life and successful relationships with others" (Thompson & Goodvin, 2007, p. 402).

Stress and Gender   Women and men differ in the way they experience and respond to stressors (Taylor, 2015, 2018). Women are more vulnerable to social stressors such as those involving romance, family, and work. For example, women experience higher levels of stress when things go wrong in romantic and marital relationships. Women also are more likely than men to become depressed when they encounter stressful life events such as a divorce or the death of a friend.

When men face stress, they are likely to respond in a **fight or flight** manner—become aggressive, withdraw from social contact, or drink alcohol. By contrast, according to Shelley Taylor (2015, 2018), when women experience stress, they are more likely to engage in a **tend and befriend** pattern, seeking social alliances with others, especially friends. Taylor argues that when women experience stress an influx of the hormone *oxytocin*, which is linked to nurturing in animals, is released.

Positive and Negative Emotions   Stereotypes suggest that older adults' emotional landscape is bleak and that most live sad, lonely lives. Researchers have found a different picture (Carstensen, 2019; Carstensen & DeLiema, 2018). One study of a very large U.S. sample examined emotions at different ages (Mroczek & Kolarz, 1998). Older adults reported experiencing more positive emotion and less negative emotion than younger adults, and positive emotion increased with age in adults at an accelerating rate (see Figure 4). In another study, emotional experiences of individuals 22 to 93 years of age were assessed in the mornings and evenings (English & Carstensen, 2014b). Older adults reported experiencing more positive emotions than younger adults at both times of the day. And in a recent study, older adults reacted with less anger about a personal memory than younger adults did (Kunzmann & others, 2017).

Overall, compared with younger adults, the feelings of older adults mellow (Carstensen, 2019). Emotional life is on a more even keel, with fewer highs and lows. It may be that although older adults have less extreme joy, they have more contentment, especially when they are connected in positive ways with friends and family. Compared with younger adults, older adults react less strongly to negative circumstances, are better at ignoring irrelevant negative information, and remember more positive than negative information (Carstensen & DeLiema, 2018). Research has also indicated that healthy older adults who age successfully show reduced responsiveness to regrets, not looking back with anger at missed opportunities in life (Brassen & others, 2012; Suri & Gross, 2012). Since opportunities to undo regrettable circumstances decrease with age, reduced connections with these situations may be a protective strategy to maintain well-being in old age. In a recent commentary, Laura Carstensen (2016) commented that when older adults focus on emotionally meaningful goals, they are more satisfied with their lives, feel better, and experience fewer negative emotions.

One study revealed that positive emotion increased and negative emotion (except for sadness) decreased from 50 years of age through the mid-eighties (Stone & others, 2010). In this study, a pronounced decline in anger occurred from the early twenties onward, and sadness was essentially unchanged from the early twenties through the mid-eighties. Another study found that aging was linked to more positive overall well-being and greater emotional stability (Carstensen & others, 2011). In this study, adults who experienced more positive than negative emotions were more likely to remain alive over a 13-year period. Other research also indicates that happier people live longer (Frey, 2011). Further, in a recent study, older men showed more engagement with highly positive contexts than did younger men (Martins & others, 2018). Also, in a recent meta-analysis of 72 studies of more than 19,000 individuals in 19 countries, it was concluded that emotional experiences are more positive in the lives of older adults than in the lives of younger adults (Laureiro-Martinez, Trujillo, & Unda, 2017), Also, in this review, it was concluded that older adults focus less on negative events in their past than younger adults do. Thus, research consistently documents that the emotional life of older adults is more positive than stereotypes suggest (Carstensen, 2019; Carstensen & DeLiema, 2018; English & Carstensen, 2014b; Paul, 2019).

Changes in the Aging Brain   How might the brain be involved in the changes that take place in older adults' emotions? Although links between the aging brain and emotion have only just begun to be studied, recent research suggests some possible connections (Fernandez & others, 2019; Malinowski & others, 2017). Reduced negative emotion in older adults may be associated with decreased physiological arousal of emotion due to aging in the amygdala and autonomic nervous system (Kaszniak & Menchola, 2012). More effective emotion regulation may be related to this reduction in subcortical activation and also to increased activation in the prefrontal cortex (Samanez-Larkin & Carstensen, 2011).

Socioemotional Selectivity Theory   One theory developed by Laura Carstensen (1991, 1998, 2006, 2009, 2011, 2014, 2015, 2019) stands out as important in thinking about developmental changes in adulthood, especially in older adults. **Socioemotional selectivity theory** states that older adults become more selective about their activities and social relationships in order to maintain social and emotional well-being. Because they place a high value on emotional satisfaction, older adults often spend more time with familiar individuals with whom they have had rewarding relationships. This theory argues that older adults deliberately withdraw from social contact with individuals peripheral to their lives while they maintain or increase contact with close friends and family members with whom they have had enjoyable relationships. This selective narrowing of social interaction maximizes positive emotional experiences and minimizes emotional risks as individuals become older. According to this theory, older adults systematically condense their social networks so that available social partners satisfy their emotional needs (Sims, Hogan, & Carstensen, 2015). Also, the fact that older adults have a decreasing number of years to live likely influences them to place more emphasis on prioritizing meaningful relationships (Moss & Wilson, 2019).

Is there research to support life-span differences in the composition of social networks? Researchers have found that the social networks of older adults are smaller than those of younger adults (Charles & Carstensen, 2010). In a study of individuals from 18 to 94 years of age, with increasing age in adulthood, they had fewer peripheral social contacts but retained close relationships with people who provided them with emotional support (English & Carstensen, 2014a).

However, in a large-scale examination of healthy living in different age groups by the Stanford Center on Longevity called the Sightlines Project, social engagement with individuals and communities appeared to be weaker than it was 15 years ago for 55- to 64-year-olds (Parker, 2016). Many of these individuals, who are about to reach retirement age, had weaker relationships with spouses, partners, family, friends, and neighbors than their counterparts of 15 years ago. The Sightlines Project (2016) offers the following recommendations to increase the social

Laura Carstensen (*right*), in a caring relationship with an older woman. Her theory of socioemotional selectivity is gaining recognition as an important perspective on aging.
Courtesy of Dr. Laura Carstensen

Recent research paints a distinctly positive picture of aging in the emotional domain.

—LAURA CARSTENSEN
Contemporary Psychologist, Stanford University

socioemotional selectivity theory The theory that older adults become more selective about their activities and social relationships in order to maintain emotional well-being.

engagement of older adults: employer wellness programs that strengthen support networks, environmental design that improves neighborhood and community life, technologies that improve personal relationships, and encouragement of volunteerism.

Socioemotional selectivity theory also focuses on the types of goals that individuals are motivated to achieve (Carstensen, 2019; Carstensen & others, 2011; Sims, Hogan, & Carstensen, 2015). According to the theory, motivation for knowledge-related goals starts relatively high in the early years of life, peaks in adolescence and early adulthood, then declines in middle and late adulthood. The trajectory for emotion-related goals is high during infancy and early childhood, declines from middle childhood through early adulthood, and increases in middle and late adulthood.

Review *Connect* Reflect

LG2 Describe the development of emotion through the life span.

Review

- How does emotion develop in infancy?
- What characterizes emotional development in early childhood?
- What changes take place in emotion during middle and late childhood?
- How does emotion change in adolescence?
- What are some key aspects of emotional development in adulthood?

Connect

- How might cognitive development and language development be linked to the development of emotion regulation and coping in young children?

Reflect *Your Own Personal Journey of Life*

- Imagine that you are the parent of an 8-month-old baby and you are having difficulty getting sufficient sleep because the baby wakes up crying in the middle of the night. How would you deal with this situation?

3 Temperament

LG3 Characterize variations in temperament and their significance.

| Describing and Classifying Temperament | Biological Foundations and Experience | Goodness of Fit and Parenting |

Do you get upset a lot? Does it take much to get you angry or to make you laugh? Even at birth, babies seem to have different emotional styles. One infant is cheerful and happy much of the time; another baby seems to cry constantly. These tendencies reflect **temperament,** which involves individual differences in behavioral styles, emotions, and characteristic ways of responding. With regard to its link to emotion, temperament refers to individual differences in how quickly the emotion is shown, how strong it is, how long it lasts, and how soon it fades away (Campos, 2009).

Another way of describing temperament is in terms of predispositions toward emotional reactivity and self-regulation (Bates & Pettit, 2015). *Reactivity* involves variations in the speed and intensity with which an individual responds to situations with positive or negative emotions. *Self-regulation* involves variations in the extent or effectiveness of an individual's control of emotions.

DESCRIBING AND CLASSIFYING TEMPERAMENT

How would you describe your temperament or the temperament of a friend? Researchers have described and classified the temperaments of individuals in different ways (Abulizi & others, 2017; Janssen & others, 2017). Here we examine three of those ways.

temperament An individual's behavioral style and characteristic way of responding.

easy child A temperament style in which the child is generally in a positive mood, quickly establishes regular routines, and adapts easily to new experiences.

Chess and Thomas' Classification Psychiatrists Alexander Chess and Stella Thomas (Chess & Thomas, 1977; Thomas & Chess, 1991) identified three basic types, or clusters, of temperament:

- An **easy child** is generally in a positive mood, quickly establishes regular routines in infancy, and adapts easily to new experiences.

- A **difficult child** reacts negatively and cries frequently, engages in irregular daily routines, and is slow to accept change.
- A **slow-to-warm-up child** has a low activity level, is somewhat negative, and displays a low intensity of mood.

In their longitudinal investigation, Chess and Thomas found that 40 percent of the children they studied could be classified as easy, 10 percent as difficult, and 15 percent as slow to warm up. Notice that 35 percent did not fit any of the three patterns. Researchers have found that these three basic clusters of temperament are moderately stable across the childhood years. One study revealed that young children with a difficult temperament showed more problems when they experienced low-quality child care and fewer problems when they experienced high-quality child care than did young children with an easy temperament (Pluess & Belsky, 2009).

What characterizes an inhibited temperament?
Jacqueline Veissid/Getty Images

Kagan's Behavioral Inhibition

Another way of classifying temperament focuses on the differences between a shy, subdued, timid child and a sociable, extraverted, bold child (Asendorph, 2008). Jerome Kagan (2002, 2008, 2010, 2013) regards shyness with strangers (peers or adults) as one feature of a broad temperament category called *inhibition to the unfamiliar*. Beginning at about 7 to 9 months, inhibited children react to many aspects of unfamiliarity with initial avoidance, distress, or subdued affect. In Kagan's research, inhibition shows some continuity from infancy through early childhood, although a substantial number of infants who are classified as inhibited become less so by 7 years of age. In one study, having an inhibited temperament at 2 to 3 years of age was related to having social phobia symptoms at 7 years of age (Lahat & others, 2014). Also, research findings indicate that infants and young children who have an inhibited temperament are at risk for developing social anxiety disorder in adolescence and adulthood (Perez-Edgar & Guyer, 2014; Rapee, 2014). In another study, if parents had a childhood history of behavioral inhibition, their children who had a high level of behavioral inhibition were at risk for developing anxiety disorders (Stumper & others, 2017).

Rothbart and Bates' Classification

New classifications of temperament continue to be forged. Mary Rothbart and John Bates (2006) argue that three broad dimensions best represent what researchers have found to characterize the structure of temperament: extraversion/surgency, negative affectivity, and effortful control (self-regulation):

- *Extraversion/surgency* includes approach, pleasure, activity, smiling, and laughter. Kagan's uninhibited children fit into this category.
- *Negative affectivity* includes "fear, frustration, sadness, and discomfort" (Rothbart, 2004, p. 495). These children are easily distressed; they may fret and cry often. Kagan's inhibited children fit this category. One study revealed that preschool children with high levels of surgency were more likely to overeat in the absence of hunger, while those with high levels of negative affectivity were more likely to have tantrums over being denied food and less likely to eat in the absence of hunger (Leung & others, 2014).
- *Effortful control* (self-regulation) includes "attentional focusing and shifting, inhibitory control, perceptual sensitivity, and low-intensity pleasure" (Rothbart, 2004, p. 495). Infants who are high on effortful control show an ability to keep their arousal from getting too high and have strategies for soothing themselves. By contrast, children low on effortful control are often unable to control their arousal; they become easily agitated and intensely emotional. One study found that young children higher in effortful control were more likely to wait longer to express anger and were more likely to use a self-regulatory strategy, distraction (Tan, Armstrong, & Cole, 2013). Another study revealed that effortful control was a strong predictor of academic success skills, including school readiness, math skills, and reading skills, in kindergarten children from low-income families (Morris & others, 2014). Also, a recent study revealed that self-regulation capacity at 4 months of age was linked to school readiness at 4 years of age (Gartstein, Putnam, & Kliewer, 2016). And in two recent studies, effortful control was linked to attention deficit hyperactivity disorder (ADHD). In the first study, a lower level of children's temperament regulation at 3 years of age predicted the presence of ADHD

difficult child A temperament style in which the child tends to react negatively and cry frequently, engages in irregular daily routines, and is slow to accept change.

slow-to-warm-up child A temperament style in which the child has a low activity level, is somewhat negative, and displays a low intensity of mood.

symptoms in the first grade (Willoughby, Gottfredson, & Stifter, 2017). In the second study, children with a lower level of effort control at 3 years of age were more likely to have ADHD symptoms at 13 years of age (Einziger & others, 2018).

The description of temperament categories so far reflects the development of normative capabilities of children, not individual differences in children. The development of these capabilities, such as effortful control, allows individual differences to emerge (Bates, 2012a, b; Bates & Pettit, 2015). For example, although maturation of the brain's prefrontal lobes must occur for any child's attention to improve and the child to achieve effortful control, some children develop effortful control while others do not. And it is these individual differences in children that are at the heart of temperament (Bates, 2012a, b; Bates & Pettit, 2015).

BIOLOGICAL FOUNDATIONS AND EXPERIENCE

How does a child acquire a certain temperament? Kagan (2002, 2008, 2010, 2013) argues that children inherit a physiology that biases them to have a particular type of temperament. However, through experience they may learn to modify their temperament to some degree (Bates & Pettit, 2015). For example, children may inherit a physiology that biases them to be fearful and inhibited, but they learn to reduce these tendencies (van Wijk & others, 2019).

Biological Influences Physiological characteristics have been linked with different temperaments (Mize & Jones, 2012). In particular, an inhibited temperament is associated with a unique physiological pattern that includes high and stable heart rate, high level of the hormone cortisol, and high activity in the right frontal lobe of the brain (Kagan, 2008). This pattern may be tied to the excitability of the amygdala, a structure of the brain that plays an important role in fear and inhibition. The temperament dimension of negative emotionality is linked to stress reactivity, which involves brain functioning (especially the hypothalamic-pituitary-adrenal (HPA) axis and its link to higher levels of cortisol) (Rothbart, 2011). And the development of effortful control is linked to advances in the brain's frontal lobes (Bates, 2012a, b).

What is heredity's role in the biological foundations of temperament? Twin and adoption studies suggest that heredity has a moderate influence on differences in temperament within a group of people (Buss & Goldsmith, 2007; van Wijk & others, 2019).

Too often the biological foundations of temperament are interpreted as meaning that temperament cannot develop or change. However, important self-regulatory dimensions of temperament such as adaptability, soothability, and persistence look very different in a 1-year-old and a 5-year-old (Easterbrooks & others, 2013). These temperament dimensions develop and change with the growth of the neurobiological foundations of self-regulation.

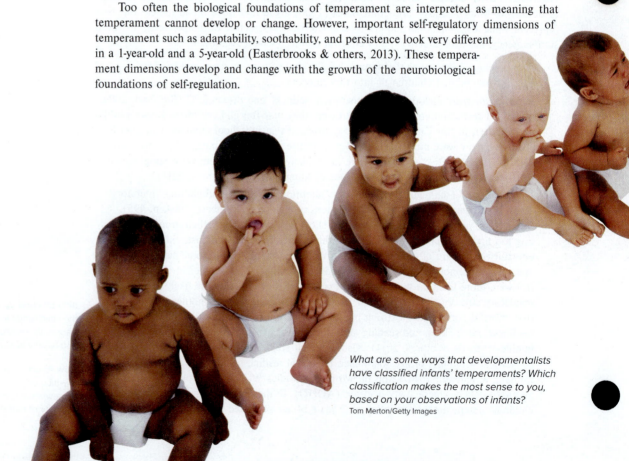

What are some ways that developmentalists have classified infants' temperaments? Which classification makes the most sense to you, based on your observations of infants?
Tom Merton/Getty Images

Gender, Culture, and Temperament   Gender may be an important factor shaping the environmental context that influences temperament (Gaias & others, 2012; Jenzer & others, 2019). Parents might react differently to an infant's temperament depending on whether the baby is a boy or a girl. For example, in one study, mothers were more responsive to the crying of irritable girls than to the crying of irritable boys (Crockenberg, 1986).

Similarly, the caregiver's reaction to an infant's temperament may depend in part on culture (Desmarais & others, 2019). For example, behavioral inhibition is more highly valued in China than in North America, and researchers have found that Chinese children are more inhibited than Canadian infants are (Chen, Fu, & Zhao, 2015). In one study, the cultural differences in temperament were linked to parents' attitudes and behaviors (Chen & others, 1998). Canadian mothers of inhibited 2-year-olds were less accepting of their infants' inhibited temperament, whereas Chinese mothers were more accepting.

An infant's temperament can vary across cultures. *What do parents need to know about a child's temperament?*
MIXA/Getty Images

Developmental Connections in Temperament   Is temperament in childhood linked with adjustment in adulthood? As described below, research has linked several of these types and

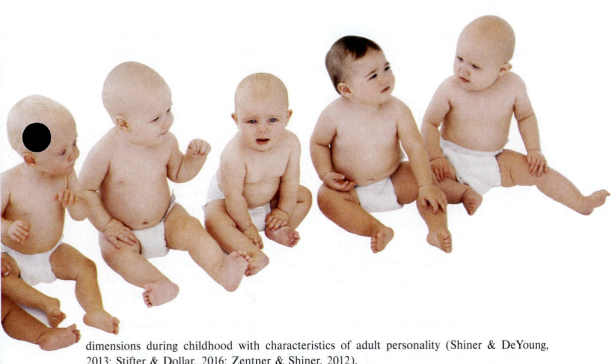

dimensions during childhood with characteristics of adult personality (Shiner & DeYoung, 2013; Stifter & Dollar, 2016; Zentner & Shiner, 2012).

- *Easy and difficult temperaments.* In one study, children who had an easy temperament at 3 to 5 years of age were likely to be well adjusted as young adults (Chess & Thomas, 1977). In contrast, many children who had a difficult temperament at 3 to 5 years of age were not well adjusted as young adults. Also, other researchers have found that boys with a difficult temperament in childhood are less likely as adults to continue their formal education, whereas girls with a difficult temperament in childhood are more likely to experience marital conflict as adults (Wachs, 2000). And a recent study revealed that a difficult temperament at 5 years of age was linked to delinquency at 15 years of age (DiLalla & DiLalla, 2018).

- *Inhibition.* Inhibition is another characteristic of temperament that has been studied extensively (Kagan, 2008, 2010, 2013). One study revealed that behavioral inhibition at 3 years of age was linked to shyness at age 7 (Volbrecht & Goldsmith, 2010). Also, research

How is temperament in childhood linked to socioemotional development in adulthood?
(*left*): Volodymyr Tverdokhlib/Shutterstock; (*right*): elenaleonova/Getty Images

indicates that individuals with an inhibited temperament in childhood are less likely as adults to be assertive or to experience social support, and more likely to delay entering a stable job track (Asendorph, 2008). Another study found that disinhibition in the toddler years was linked to career stability in middle adulthood (Blatny & others, 2015).

• *Ability to control one's emotions.* A recent study found that having an emotionally reactive temperament at 1 year of age was linked to having emotional problems at 5.5 years of age (Abulizi & others, 2017). Also, in a longitudinal study, when 3-year-old children showed good control of their emotions and were resilient in the face of stress, they were likely to continue to handle emotions effectively as adults (Block, 1993). By contrast, when 3-year-olds had low emotional control and were not very resilient, they were likely to show problems in these areas as young adults. Researchers have found that a high level of emotionality at 6 years of age is associated with depression in emerging adulthood (Bould & others, 2014).

In sum, these studies reveal some continuity between certain aspects of temperament in childhood and adjustment in early adulthood (Janssen & others, 2017; Stifter & Dollar, 2016). However, keep in mind that these connections between childhood temperament and adult adjustment are based on only a small number of studies; more research is needed to verify these linkages.

Developmental Contexts   What accounts for the continuities and discontinuities between a child's temperament and an adult's personality? Physiological and hereditary factors likely are involved in continuity (Clauss, Avery, & Blackford, 2015; DiLalla & DiLalla, 2018). Links between temperament in childhood and personality in adulthood also might vary, depending on the contexts that individuals experience (Bates & Pettit, 2015; Wachs & Bates, 2011).

In short, many aspects of a child's environment can encourage or discourage the persistence of temperament characteristics (Bates & Pettit, 2015; Gartstein, Putnam, & Kliewer, 2016; Shiner & DeYoung, 2013). For example, one study found that fathers' internalizing problems (anxiety and depression, for example) were linked to a higher level of negative affectivity in 6-month-olds (Potapova, Gartstein, & Bridgett, 2014). In another study, if parents had a childhood history of behavioral inhibition, their children who had a high level of behavioral inhibition were at risk for developing anxiety disorders (Stumper & others, 2017). Yet another study revealed that maternal negativity and child problem behavior were most strongly linked for children who were low in effortful control and living in chaotic homes (Chen, Deater-Deckard, and Bell, 2014). One useful way of thinking about temperament-environment connections involves the concept of goodness of fit, which we examine next.

developmental connection

Nature and Nurture

Twin and adoption studies have been used to sort out hereditary and environmental influences on development. Connect to "Biological Beginnings."

Parenting and the Child's Temperament

What are the implications of temperamental variations for parenting? Although answers to this question necessarily are speculative, these conclusions regarding the best parenting strategies to use in relation to children's temperament were reached by temperament experts Ann Sanson and Mary Rothbart (1995):

- *Attention to and respect for individuality.* One implication is that it is difficult to generate general prescriptions for "good" parenting. A goal might be accomplished in one way with one child and in another way with another child, depending on the child's temperament. Parents need to be sensitive and remain flexible to the infant's signals and needs.
- *Structuring the child's environment.* Crowded, noisy environments can pose greater problems for some children (such as a "difficult child") than others (such as an "easygoing" child). We might also expect that a fearful, withdrawing child would benefit from slower entry into new contexts.
- *The "difficult child" and packaged parenting programs.* Programs for parents often focus on dealing with children who have "difficult" temperaments. In some cases, "difficult child" refers to Thomas and Chess' description of a child who reacts negatively, cries frequently, engages in irregular daily routines, and is slow to accept change. In others, the concept might be used to describe a child who is irritable, displays anger frequently, does not follow directions well, or shows some other negative characteristic. Acknowledging that some children are harder than others to parent is often helpful, and advice on how to handle specific difficult characteristics can be useful. However, whether a specific characteristic is difficult depends on its fit with the environment. To label a child "difficult" has the danger of becoming a self-fulfilling prophecy. If a child is identified as "difficult," people may treat the child in a way that actually elicits "difficult" behavior.

What are some good strategies for parents to adopt when responding to their infant's temperament?
Corbis/Age fotostock

Too often, we pigeonhole children into categories without examining the context (Bates, 2012a, b; Bates & Pettit, 2015; Rothbart, 2011). Nonetheless, caregivers need to take children's temperaments into account. Research does not yet allow for many highly specific recommendations, but in general, caregivers should (1) be sensitive to the individual characteristics of the child, (2) be flexible in responding to these characteristics, and (3) avoid applying negative labels to the child.

How does the advice to "structure the child's environment" relate to what you learned about the concept of "goodness of fit"?

GOODNESS OF FIT AND PARENTING

Goodness of fit refers to the match between a child's temperament and the environmental demands the child must cope with. Some temperament characteristics pose more parenting challenges than others, at least in modern Western societies (Bates & Pettit, 2015; Parade & others, 2018; Wagers & Kiel, 2019). When children are prone to distress, as exhibited by frequent crying and irritability, their parents may eventually respond by ignoring the child's distress or trying to force the child to "behave." In one research study, though, extra support and training for mothers of distress-prone infants improved the quality of mother-infant interaction (van den Boom, 1989). Researchers also have found that decreases in infants' negative emotionality are linked to higher levels of parental sensitivity, involvement, and responsiveness (Bates & Pettit, 2015; Gartstein, Hancock, & Iverson, 2018; Parade & others, 2018). Other findings support the use of positive parenting, including high warmth and low use of harsh control, to increase children's effortful control (Bates & Pettit, 2015).

To read further about some positive strategies for parenting that take into account the child's temperament, see the *Connecting Development to Life* interlude.

goodness of fit The match between a child's temperament and the environmental demands the child must cope with.

A final comment about temperament is that recently the *differential susceptibility model* and the *biological sensitivity to context model* have been proposed and studied (Baptista & others, 2017; Belsky & Pluess, 2016; Belsky & van IJzendoorn, 2017; Jolicoeur-Martineau & others, 2019). According to these models, certain characteristics—such as a difficult temperament—that render children more vulnerable to difficulty in adverse contexts also make them more susceptible to optimal growth in very supportive conditions. Jay Belsky (2014) proposed the controversial view that intervention programs might try to target these children who are more vulnerable to difficulty in adverse conditions because of the greater cost-effectiveness involved in their being likely to flourish when given a lot of care and support. These models offer a new perspective on "negative" temperament characteristics.

Review Connect Reflect

LG3 Characterize variations in temperament and their significance.

Review
- How can temperament be described and classified?
- How is temperament influenced by biological foundations and experience?
- What is goodness of fit? What are some positive parenting strategies for dealing with a child's temperament?

Connect
- How is Chess and Thomas' classification of temperament similar to and different from Rothbart and Bates' classification?

Reflect *Your Own Personal Journey of Life*
- Consider your own temperament. We described a number of temperament categories. Which one best describes your temperament? Has your temperament changed as you have gotten older? If your temperament has changed, what factors contributed to the changes?

4 Attachment and Love

LG4 Explain attachment and its development.

Infancy and Childhood   Adolescence   Adulthood

So far, we have discussed how emotions and emotional competence change over the life span. We have also examined the role of emotional style—in effect, we have seen how emotions set the tone of our experiences in life. But emotions also write the lyrics because they are at the core of our relationships with others. Foremost among these relationships is **attachment,** a close emotional bond between two people. In this section, we focus on two types of attachment: the attachment between parents and children and the attachment between romantic partners.

INFANCY AND CHILDHOOD

Before we describe parent-child attachment in detail, we set the stage for its development by exploring the strength of social orientation among infants. We also examine infants' early development of social cognition and its important role in infants' and young children's social behavior and interaction.

Social Orientation/Cognition In Ross Thompson's (2006, 2015, 2016, 2017) view, infants are socioemotional beings who show a strong interest in the social world and are motivated to orient to it and understand it. In other words, babies are socially smarter than used to be thought (Blankenship & others, 2019; Krogh-Jerspersen & Woodward, 2016; Nolen & others, 2019). In previous chapters, we described many of the biological and cognitive foundations that contribute to the infant's development of social orientation and cognition. Using techniques such as eye-tracking, violation of expectations, and habituation that were described in earlier chapters ("Motor, Sensory, and Perceptual Development" and "Cognitive

attachment A close emotional bond between two people.

Developmental Approaches"), researchers have discovered that infants have the capacity to understand others' actions and social interactions early in their development (Krogh-Jespersen & Woodward, 2016). In this chapter we will call attention to relevant biological and cognitive factors as we explore social orientation; locomotion; intention, goal-directed behavior, and cooperation; and social referencing. Discussing biological, cognitive, and social processes together reminds us of an important aspect of development: these processes are intricately intertwined (Cole & Hollenstein, 2018; Dollar & Calkins, 2019).

A mother and her baby engage in face-to-face play. *At what age does face-to-face play usually begin, and when does it typically start decreasing in frequency?*
JGI/Tom Grill/Blend Images/Getty Images

Social Orientation   From early in their development, infants are captivated by their social world. Young infants will stare intently at faces and are attuned to the sounds of human voices, especially those of their caregivers (Quinn, Lee, & Pascalis, 2019). Later, they become adept at interpreting the meaning of facial expressions and voices (Weatherhead & White, 2017).

Face-to-face play often begins to characterize caregiver-infant interactions when the infant is about 2 to 3 months of age. The focused social interaction of face-to-face play may include vocalizations, touch, and gestures (Quinn, Lee, & Pascalis, 2019). Such play results in part from many mothers' motivation to create a positive emotional state in their infants (Parsons & others, 2017).

In part because of such positive social interchanges between caregivers and infants, by 2 to 3 months of age infants respond differently to people and objects, showing more positive emotion to people than to inanimate objects such as puppets (Legerstee, 1997). At this age, most infants expect people to react positively when the infants initiate a behavior, such as a smile or a vocalization. This finding has been discovered by use of a method called the *still-face paradigm*, in which the caregiver alternates between engaging in face-to-face interaction with the infant and remaining still and unresponsive (Busuito & others, 2019). As early as 2 to 3 months of age, infants show more withdrawal, negative emotions, and self-directed behavior when their caregivers are still and unresponsive (Adamson & Frick, 2003). The frequency of face-to-face play decreases after 7 months of age as infants become more mobile (Thompson, 2006). Infants also learn about the social world through contexts other than face-to-face play with a caregiver (Swingler & others, 2017). Even though infants as young as 6 months of age show an interest in each other, their interaction with peers increases considerably in the second half of the second year. As increasing numbers of U.S. infants experience child care outside the home, they are spending more time in social play with peers (Honig, 2019). Later in the chapter, we further discuss child care.

Locomotion   Recall from earlier in the chapter how important independence is for infants, especially in the second year of life. As infants develop the ability to crawl, walk, and run, they are able to explore and expand their social world. These newly developed self-produced locomotor skills allow the infant to independently initiate social interchanges on a more frequent basis. The development of these gross motor skills is the result of a number of factors, including the development of the nervous system, the goal the infant is motivated to reach, and environmental support for the skill (Adolph, 2018; Adolph & Hoch, 2019; Adolph, Rachwani, & Hoch, 2019).

The infant's and toddler's push for independence also is likely paced by the development of locomotor skills (Adolph, 2018). Locomotion is also important for its motivational implications. Once infants have the ability to move in goal-directed pursuits, the reward from these pursuits leads to further efforts to explore and develop skills (Adolph & Hoch, 2019).

Intention, Goal-Directed Behavior, and Cooperation   Perceiving people as engaging in intentional and goal-directed behavior is an important social cognitive accomplishment that initially occurs toward the end of the first year (Thompson, 2015). Joint attention and gaze following help the infant to understand that other people have intentions (Suarez-Rivera, Smith, & Yu, 2019). *Joint attention* occurs when the caregiver and infant focus on the same object or event. By their first birthday, infants have begun to direct the caregiver's attention to objects that capture their interest (Marsh & Legerstee, 2017).

Amanda Woodward and her colleagues (Krogh-Jerspersen, Liberman, & Woodward, 2015; Krogh-Jespersen & Woodward, 2016, 2018; Liberman, Woodward, & Kinzler, 2017; Shneidman & Woodward, 2016; Shneidman & others, 2016; Sodian & others, 2016) argue that infants' ability to understand and respond to others' meaningful intentions is a critical cognitive foundation for effectively engaging in the social world. They especially emphasize that an important aspect of this ability is the capacity to grasp social knowledge quickly in order to make an appropriate

developmental **connection**

Developmental Theories

The dynamic systems view is increasingly used to explain how infants develop. Connect to "Motor, Sensory, and Perceptual Development."

FIGURE 5

THE COOPERATION TASK. The cooperation task consisted of two handles on a box, atop which was an animated musical toy, surreptitiously activated by remote control when both handles were pulled. The handles were placed far enough apart that one child could not pull both handles. The experimenter demonstrated the task, saying, "Watch! If you pull the handles, the doggie will sing" (Brownell, Ramani, & Zerwas, 2006).

What is social referencing? What are some developmental changes in social referencing?
Dan Lepp/Getty Images

social referencing "Reading" emotional cues in others to help determine how to act in a specific situation.

social response. Although processing speed is an important contributor to social engagement, other factors are involved such as infants' motivation to interact with someone, the infant's social interactive history with the individual, the interactive partner's social membership, and culturally specific aspects of interaction (Howard & others, 2015; Krogh-Jespersen & Woodward, 2016, 2018; Liberman, Woodward, & Kinzler, 2017).

Cooperating with others also is a key aspect of effectively engaging with others in the social world. Can infants engage in cooperation with others? One study involved presenting 1- and 2-year-olds with a simple cooperative task that consisted of pulling a lever to get an attractive toy (Brownell, Ramani, & Zerwas, 2006) (see Figure 5). Any coordinated actions of the 1-year-olds appeared to be more coincidental than cooperative, whereas the 2-year-olds' behavior was characterized as more actively cooperative efforts to reach a goal. In this study, the infants also were assessed with two social understanding tasks, observation of children's behavior in a joint attention task, and the parents' perceptions of the language the children use about the self and others (Brownell, Ramani, & Zerwas, 2006). Those with more advanced social understanding were more likely to cooperate. To cooperate, the children had to connect their own intentions with the peer's intentions and put this understanding to use in interacting with the peer to reach a goal.

Social Referencing   Another important social cognitive accomplishment in infancy is developing the ability to "read" the emotions of other people (Carbajal-Valenzuela & others, 2017). **Social referencing** is the term used to describe "reading" emotional cues in others to help determine how to act in a specific situation. The development of social referencing helps infants to interpret ambiguous situations more accurately, as when they encounter a stranger and need to know whether or not to fear the person (Stenberg, 2017). By the end of the first year, a mother's facial expression—either smiling or fearful—influences whether an infant will explore an unfamiliar environment.

Infants become better at social referencing in the second year of life. At this age, they tend to "check" with their mother before they act; they look at her to see if she is happy, angry, or fearful.

Infants' Social Sophistication and Insight   In sum, researchers are discovering that infants are more socially sophisticated and insightful at younger ages than was previously envisioned (Thompson, 2006, 2015, 2016, 2017). Such sophistication and insight are reflected in infants' perceptions of others' actions as intentionally motivated and goal-directed, their motivation to share and participate in that intentionality, and their increase in emotional understanding and communication by their first birthday (Krogh-Jespesen & Woodward, 2018). These social cognitive skills could be expected to influence infants' understanding and awareness of attachment to a caregiver.

What Is Attachment?   There is no shortage of theories about why infants become attached to a caregiver. Three theorists—Freud, Erikson, and Bowlby—proposed influential views.

Freud noted that infants become attached to the person or object that provides oral satisfaction. For most infants, this is the mother, since she is most likely to feed the infant. Is feeding as important as Freud thought? A classic study by Harry Harlow (1958) reveals that the answer is no (see Figure 6).

Harlow removed infant monkeys from their mothers at birth; for six months they were reared by surrogate (substitute) "mothers." One surrogate mother was made of wire, the other of cloth. Half of the infant monkeys were fed by the wire mother, half by the cloth mother. Periodically, the amount of time the infant monkeys spent with either the wire or the cloth mother was computed. Regardless of which mother fed them, the infant monkeys spent far more time with the cloth mother. Even if the wire mother but not the cloth mother provided nourishment, the infant monkeys spent more time with the cloth mother. And when Harlow frightened the monkeys, those "raised" by the cloth mother ran to the mother and clung to it; those raised by the wire mother did not. Whether the mother provided comfort seemed to determine whether the monkeys associated the mother with security. This study clearly

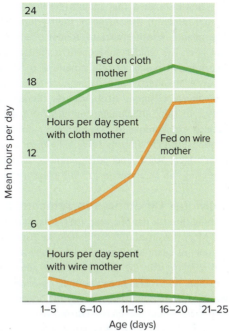

FIGURE 6

CONTACT TIME WITH WIRE AND CLOTH SURROGATE MOTHERS. *Regardless of whether the infant monkeys were fed by a wire or a cloth mother, they overwhelmingly preferred to spend contact time with the cloth mother. How do these results compare with what Freud's theory and Erikson's theory would predict about human infants?*
Martin Rogers/The Image Bank/Getty Images

demonstrated that feeding is not the crucial element in the attachment process and that contact comfort is important.

Physical comfort also plays a role in Erik Erikson's (1968) view of the infant's development. Recall Erikson's proposal that the first year of life represents the stage of trust versus mistrust. Physical comfort and sensitive care, according to Erikson (1968), are key to establishing a basic trust in infants. The infant's sense of trust, in turn, is the foundation for attachment and sets the stage for a lifelong expectation that the world will be a good and pleasant place to be.

The ethological perspective of British psychiatrist John Bowlby (1969, 1989) also stresses the importance of attachment in the first year of life and the responsiveness of the caregiver. Bowlby stresses that both infants and their primary caregivers are biologically predisposed to form attachments. He argues that the newborn is biologically equipped to elicit attachment behavior. The baby cries, clings, coos, and smiles. Later, the infant crawls, walks, and follows the mother. The immediate result is to keep the primary caregiver nearby; the long-term effect is to increase the infant's chances of survival.

Attachment does not emerge suddenly but rather develops in a series of phases, moving from a baby's general preference for human beings to a partnership with primary caregivers. Following are four such phases based on Bowlby's conceptualization of attachment (Schaffer, 1996):

- *Phase 1: From birth to 2 months.* Infants instinctively direct their attachment to human figures. Strangers, siblings, and parents are equally likely to elicit smiling or crying from the infant.
- *Phase 2: From 2 to 7 months.* Attachment becomes focused on one figure, usually the primary caregiver, as the baby gradually learns to distinguish familiar from unfamiliar people.
- *Phase 3: From 7 to 24 months.* Specific attachments develop. With increased locomotor skills, babies actively seek contact with regular caregivers such as the mother or father.
- *Phase 4: From 24 months on.* Children become aware of others' feelings, goals, and plans and begin to take these into account in forming their own actions.

Researchers' recent findings that infants are more socially sophisticated and insightful than previously envisioned suggests that some of the characteristics of Bowlby's phase 4, such as understanding the goals and intentions of the attachment figure, appear to be developing in phase 3 as attachment security is taking shape.

In Bowlby's model, what are the four phases of attachment?
Camille Tokerud/Getty Images

Strange Situation Ainsworth's observational measure of infant attachment to a caregiver that requires the infant to move through a series of introductions, separations, and reunions with the caregiver and an adult stranger in a prescribed order.

securely attached children Children who use the caregiver as a secure base from which to explore the environment.

insecure avoidant children Children who show insecurity by avoiding the mother.

insecure resistant children Children who might cling to the caregiver, then resist by fighting against the closeness, perhaps by kicking or pushing away.

insecure disorganized children Children who show insecurity by being disorganized and disoriented.

Bowlby argued that infants develop an *internal working model* of attachment: a simple mental model of the caregiver, their relationship, and the self as deserving of nurturant care. The infant's internal working model of attachment with the caregiver influences the infant's and later, the child's, subsequent responses to other people (Dozier & Bernard, 2018, 2019). The internal model of attachment also has played a pivotal role in the discovery of links between attachment and subsequent emotional understanding, conscience development, and self-concept (Psouni, 2019; Vacaru, Sterkenburg, & Schuengel, 2018; Woodhouse & others, 2019). In sum, attachment emerges from the social cognitive advances that allow infants to develop expectations for the caregiver's behavior and to determine the affective quality of their relationship (Thompson, 2017). These social cognitive advances include recognizing the caregiver's face, voice, and other features, as well as developing an internal working model of expecting the caregiver to provide pleasure in social interaction and relief from distress.

Individual Differences in Attachment Although attachment to a caregiver intensifies midway through the first year, isn't it likely that the quality of babies' attachment experiences varies? Mary Ainsworth (1979) thought so. Ainsworth created the **Strange Situation,** an observational measure of infant attachment in which the infant experiences a series of introductions, separations, and reunions with the caregiver and an adult stranger in a prescribed order. In using the Strange Situation, researchers hope that their observations will provide information about the infant's motivation to be near the caregiver and the degree to which the caregiver's presence provides the infant with security and confidence (Brown & Cox, 2019; Challacombe & others, 2017).

Based on how babies respond in the Strange Situation, they are described as being securely attached or insecurely attached (in one of three ways) to the caregiver:

- **Securely attached children** use the caregiver as a secure base from which to explore the environment. When in the presence of their caregiver, securely attached infants explore the room and examine toys that have been placed in it. When the caregiver departs, securely attached infants might protest mildly, and when the caregiver returns these infants reestablish positive interaction with her, perhaps by smiling or climbing onto her lap. Subsequently, they usually resume playing with the toys in the room.

- **Insecure avoidant children** show insecurity by avoiding the mother. In the Strange Situation, these babies engage in little interaction with the caregiver, are not distressed when she leaves the room, usually do not reestablish contact with her on her return, and may even turn their back on her. If contact is established, the infant usually leans away or looks away.

- **Insecure resistant children** often cling to the caregiver and then resist her by fighting against the closeness, perhaps by kicking or pushing away. In the Strange Situation, these babies often cling anxiously to the caregiver and don't explore the playroom. When the caregiver leaves, they often cry loudly and push away if she tries to comfort them on her return, then want to be held again.

- **Insecure disorganized children** are disorganized and disoriented. In the Strange Situation, these babies might appear dazed, confused, and fearful. To be classified as disorganized, babies must show strong patterns of avoidance and resistance or display certain specified behaviors, such as extreme fearfulness around the caregiver.

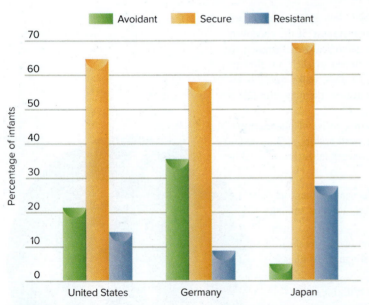

FIGURE 7

CROSS-CULTURAL COMPARISON OF ATTACHMENT. In one study, infant attachment in three countries—the United States, Germany, and Japan—was measured in the Ainsworth Strange Situation (van IJzendoorn & Kroonenberg, 1988). The dominant attachment pattern in all three countries was secure attachment. However, German infants were more avoidant and Japanese infants were less avoidant and more resistant than U.S. infants. *What are some explanations for differences in how German, Japanese, and American infants respond to the Strange Situation?*

Evaluating the Strange Situation Does the Strange Situation capture important differences among infants? As a measure of attachment, it may be culturally biased (Gernhardt, Keller, & Rubeling, 2016). For example, German and Japanese babies often show different patterns of attachment from those of American infants. As illustrated in Figure 7, German infants are more likely than U.S. infants to show an avoidant attachment pattern and Japanese infants are less likely than U.S. infants to display this pattern (van IJzendoorn & Kroonenberg, 1988). The avoidant pattern in German babies likely occurs because their caregivers encourage them to be independent (Grossmann & others, 1985). Also as shown in Figure 7, Japanese babies are more likely than American babies to be categorized as resistant. This may have more to do with the Strange Situation as a measure of attachment than with attachment insecurity itself. Japanese mothers rarely allow anyone unfamiliar with their babies to care for them. Thus, the Strange Situation might create considerably more stress for Japanese infants than for American infants, who are more accustomed to separation from their mothers (Miyake, Chen, & Campos, 1985). Even though there are cultural variations in attachment classification, the most frequent classification in every culture studied so far is secure attachment (Mooya, Sichimba, & Bakermans-Kranenburg, 2016; van IJzendoorn & Kroonenberg, 1988).

Some critics stress that behavior in the Strange Situation—like other laboratory assessments—might not indicate what infants would do in a natural environment. But researchers have found that infants' behaviors in the Strange Situation are closely related to how they behave at home in response to separation and reunion with their mothers (Pederson & Moran, 1996). Thus, many researchers stress that the Strange Situation continues to show merit as a measure of infant attachment.

Interpreting Differences in Attachment Do individual differences in attachment matter? Ainsworth notes that secure attachment in the first year of life provides an important foundation for psychological development later in life. The securely attached infant moves freely away from the mother but keeps track of where she is through periodic glances. The securely attached infant responds positively to being picked up by others and, when put back down, freely moves away to play. An insecurely attached infant, by contrast, avoids the mother or is ambivalent toward her, fears strangers, and is upset by minor, everyday separations.

If early attachment to a caregiver is important, it should influence a child's social behavior later in development. For some children, early attachments seem to foreshadow later functioning (Coyne & others, 2018; Dozier, Bernard, & Roben, 2019; Kim, Woodhouse, & Dai, 2018; Woodhouse & others, 2019). In the extensive longitudinal study conducted by Alan Sroufe and his colleagues (2005, 2016; Sroufe, Coffino, & Carlson, 2010; Sroufe & others, 2005), early secure attachment (assessed by the Strange Situation at 12 and 18 months) was linked with positive emotional health, high self-esteem, self-confidence, and socially competent interaction with peers, teachers, camp counselors, and romantic partners through adolescence. Also, a research meta-analysis concluded that secure attachment in infancy was related to social competence with peers in early childhood (Groh & others, 2014). Yet another study discovered that attachment security at 2 years of age was linked to lower rates of peer conflict at 3 years of age (Raikes & others, 2013). Further, one study revealed that infant attachment insecurity (especially insecure resistant attachment) and early childhood behavioral inhibition predicted adolescent social anxiety symptoms (Lewis-Morrarty & others, 2015). And a recent research meta-analysis concluded that secure attachment was linked to better resilience (Darling Rasmussen & others, 2019).

Few studies have assessed infants' attachment security to the mother and the father separately (Cowan & others, 2019a). However, one study revealed that infants who were insecurely attached to their mother and father ("double-insecure") at 15 months of age had more externalizing problems (out-of-control behavior, for example) during the elementary school years than their counterparts who were securely attached to at least one parent (Kochanska & Kim, 2013). Also, a recent study found that an infant's secure attachment to the father was not enough to reduce the infant's stress reactions when the mother-infant attachment was insecure (Kuo & others, 2019).

An important issue regarding attachment is whether infancy is a critical or sensitive period for development. Many, but not all, research studies reveal the power of infant attachment to predict subsequent development (Farrell & others, 2019; Hudson & others, 2016; Roisman & others, 2016; Steele & Steele, 2019; Thompson, 2015, 2016, 2017; Waters & Roisman, 2018). In one longitudinal study, attachment classification in infancy did not predict attachment classification at 18 years of age (Lewis, Feiring, & Rosenthal, 2000). In this study, the best predictor of an insecure attachment classification at 18 was the occurrence of parental divorce in the intervening years.

Consistently positive caregiving over a number of years is likely an important factor in connecting early attachment with the child's functioning later in development (Cowan & others, 2019b; O'Connor & others, 2019). Indeed, researchers have found that early secure attachment and subsequent experiences, especially maternal care and life stresses, are linked with children's later behavior and adjustment (Leerkes, Gedaly, & Su, 2016; Roisman & Cicchetti, 2017; Thompson, 2017). For example, a longitudinal study revealed that changes in attachment security/insecurity from infancy to adulthood were linked to stresses and supports in socioemotional contexts (Van Ryzin, Carlson, & Sroufe, 2011). These results suggest that attachment continuity may be a reflection of stable social contexts as much as early working models. The study just described (Van Ryzin & others, 2011) reflects an increasingly accepted view of the development of attachment and its influence on development. That is, it is important to recognize that attachment security in infancy does not always by itself produce long-term positive outcomes, but rather is linked to later outcomes through connections with the way children and adolescents subsequently experience various social contexts as they develop (O'Connor & others, 2014).

The Van Ryzin, Carlson, and Sroufe (2011) study reflects a **developmental cascade model,** which involves connections across domains over time that influence developmental pathways and outcomes (Almy & Cicchetti, 2018; Waters & Roisman, 2018). Developmental cascades can include connections between a wide range of biological, cognitive, and socioemotional processes (attachment, for example), and also can involve social contexts such as families, peers, schools, and culture. Further, links can produce positive or negative outcomes at different points in development, such as infancy, early childhood, middle and late childhood, adolescence, and adulthood (Koehn & Kerns, 2018; Waters & Roisman, 2018).

A meta-analysis supported these views just described (Pinquart, Feubner, & Ahnert, 2013). In this analysis of 127 research reports, the following conclusions were reached: (1) moderate stability of attachment security occurred from early infancy to adulthood; (2) no significant stability occurred for time intervals of more than 15 years; (3) attachment stability was greater when the time span was less than 2 years than when it was more than 5 years; and (4) securely attached children at risk were less likely to maintain attachment security, while insecurely attached children at risk were likely to continue to be insecurely attached.

Some developmentalists think that too much emphasis has been placed on the attachment bond in infancy. Jerome Kagan (2000), for example, emphasizes that infants are highly resilient and adaptive; he argues that they are evolutionarily equipped to stay on a positive developmental course, even in the face of wide variations in parenting. Kagan and others stress that genetic characteristics and temperament play more important roles in a child's social competence than the attachment theorists, such as Bowlby and Ainsworth, are willing to acknowledge (Bakermans-Kranenburg & van IJzendoorn, 2016; Kim & others, 2017; Simpson & Belsky, 2016). For example, if some infants inherit a low tolerance for stress, this, rather than an insecure attachment bond, may be responsible for an inability to get along with peers. One study found links between disorganized attachment in infancy, a specific gene, and levels of maternal responsiveness. In this study, a disorganized attachment style developed in infancy only when infants had the short version of the serotonin transporter gene—5-HTTLPR (Spangler & others, 2009). Infants were not characterized by this attachment style when they had the long version of the gene (Spangler & others, 2009). Further, this gene-environment interaction occurred only when mothers showed a low level of responsiveness toward their infants. However, some researchers have not found support for genetic influences on infant-mother attachment (Leerkes & others, 2017) or for gene-environment interactions related to infant attachment (Luijk & others, 2011; Roisman & Fraley, 2012).

Another criticism of attachment theory is that it ignores the diversity of socializing agents and contexts that exists in an infant's world. A culture's value system can influence the nature of attachment (Keller & Bard, 2017; Otto & Keller, 2018). Mothers' expectations for infants to be independent are high in northern Germany, whereas Japanese mothers are more strongly motivated to keep their infants close to them (Grossmann & others, 1985; Rothbaum & others, 2000). Not surprisingly, northern German infants tend to show less distress than Japanese infants when separated from their mothers. Also, in some cultures, infants show attachments to many people. Among the Hausa (who live in Nigeria), grandmothers and siblings provide a significant amount of care for infants (Harkness & Super, 1995). Infants in agricultural societies tend to form attachments to older siblings, who are assigned a major responsibility for younger siblings' care. In a recent study in Zambia where siblings were substantially involved in caregiving activities, infants showed strong attachments to both their mothers and their sibling caregivers (Mooya, Sichimba, & Bakermans-Kranenburg, 2017). In this study, secure attachment was the most frequent attachment classification for both mother-infant and sibling-infant relationships.

Researchers recognize the importance of competent, nurturant caregivers in an infant's development (Parke, Roisman, & Rose, 2019; Raby & others, 2019). At issue, though, is

In the Hausa culture, siblings and grandmothers provide a significant amount of care for infants. *How might these variations in care affect attachment?*
Penny Tweedie/Getty Images

developmental cascade model Involves connections across domains over time that influence developmental pathways and outcomes.

whether or not secure attachment, especially to a single caregiver, is critical (Fraley, Roisman, & Haltigan, 2013; Thompson, 2015, 2016).

Despite such criticisms, there is ample evidence that security of attachment is important to development (Coyne & others, 2018; Dozier & Bernard, 2019; Martin & others, 2019; Sroufe, 2016; Stevens & N'zi, 2018; Thompson, 2017; Woodhouse & others, 2019). Secure attachment in infancy reflects a positive parent-infant relationship and provides a foundation that supports healthy socioemotional development in the years that follow.

What is the nature of secure and insecure attachment? How are caregiving styles related to attachment classification?
George Doyle/Stockbyte/Getty Images

Caregiving Styles and Attachment Is the style of caregiving linked with the quality of the infant's attachment? Securely attached babies have caregivers who are sensitive to their signals and are consistently available to respond to their needs (Baradon & others, 2019; Coyne & others, 2018; Dozier & Bernard, 2018; Dozier, Bernard, & Roben, 2019; Groh & Haydon, 2018). These caregivers often let their babies have an active part in determining the onset and pacing of interaction in the first year of life. One study revealed that maternal sensitivity in responding was linked to infant attachment security (Finger & others, 2009). Another study found that maternal sensitivity in parenting was linked with secure attachment in infants in two different cultures: the United States and Colombia (Posada & others, 2002). Further, recent research indicates that if parents who engage in inadequate and problematic caregiving are provided with practice and feedback focused on interacting sensitively with their infants, parent-infant attachment becomes more secure (Coyne & others, 2018; Dozier, Bernard, & Roben, 2019; Slade & others, 2019; Woodhouse & others, 2019).

How do the caregivers of insecurely attached babies interact with them? Caregivers of avoidant babies tend to be unavailable or rejecting (Posada & Kaloustian, 2011). They often don't respond to their babies' signals and have little physical contact with them. When they do interact with their babies, they may behave in an angry and irritable way. Caregivers of resistant babies tend to be inconsistent; sometimes they respond to their babies' needs and sometimes they don't. In general, they tend not to be very affectionate with their babies and show little synchrony when interacting with them. Caregivers of disorganized babies often neglect or physically abuse them (Almy & Cicchetti, 2018; Roisman & Cicchetti, 2017). In some cases, these caregivers are depressed. In sum, caregivers' interactions with infants influence whether infants are securely or insecurely attached to the caregivers (Woodhouse & others, 2019).

Developmental Social Neuroscience and Attachment The emerging field of *developmental social neuroscience* examines connections between socioemotional processes, development, and the brain (Laurita, Hazan, & Spreng, 2019; Sullivan & Wilson, 2018). Attachment is one of the main areas on which theory and research on developmental social neuroscience has focused. These connections of attachment and the brain involve the neuroanatomy of the brain, neurotransmitters, and hormones.

Theory and research on the role of the brain's regions in mother-infant attachment is just emerging (Antonucci & others, 2018; Sullivan & Wilson, 2018). One theoretical view proposed that the prefrontal cortex likely has an important role in maternal attachment behavior, as do the subcortical (areas of the brain lower than the cortex) regions of the mother's amygdala (which is strongly involved in emotion) and the hypothalamus (Kim, Strathearn, & Swain, 2016). An ongoing fMRI longitudinal study is exploring the possibility that different attachment patterns can be distinguished by different patterns of brain activity (Kim & others, 2014; Kim, Strathearn, & Swain, 2016; Strathearn, 2007, 2011).

Research on the role of hormones and neurotransmitters in attachment has emphasized the importance of the neuropeptide hormone oxytocin and the neurotransmitter *dopamine* in the formation of the maternal-infant bond (Feldman, 2017; Kim, Strathearn, & Swain, 2016). *Oxytocin*, a mammalian hormone that also acts as a neurotransmitter in the brain, is released in the mother during breast feeding and by contact and warmth (Ebstein & others, 2012). Oxytocin is especially thought to be a likely candidate in the formation of infant-mother attachment (Ehrlich & others, 2016; Feldman, 2017; Polan & Hofer, 2016; Toepfer & others, 2019). A research review found strong links between levels or patterns of oxytocin production and aspects of mother-infant attachment (Galbally & others, 2011).

Although oxytocin release is stimulated by birth and lactation in mothers, might it also be released in fathers? Oxytocin is secreted in males, and one research study found that at both 6 weeks and 6 months after birth, when fathers engaged in more stimulation contact with babies, encouraged their exploration, and directed their attention to objects, the fathers'

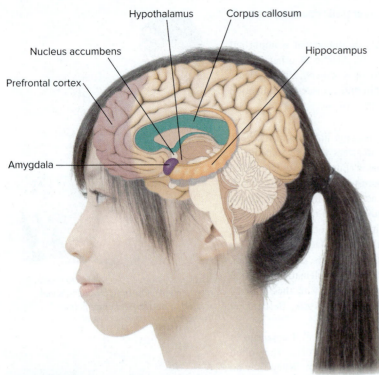

Hypothalamus   Corpus callosum

Nucleus accumbens

Hippocampus

Prefrontal cortex

Amygdala

FIGURE 8

REGIONS OF THE BRAIN PROPOSED AS LIKELY TO BE IMPORTANT IN INFANT-MOTHER ATTACHMENT. This illustration shows the brain's left hemisphere. The corpus callosum is the large bundle of axons that connect the brain's two hemispheres.
Takayuki/Shutterstock

oxytocin levels increased (Gordon & others, 2010). In this study, mothers' behaviors that increased their oxytocin levels involved more affectionate parenting, such as gazing at their babies, expressing positive affect toward them, and touching them. One study also found that fathers with lower testosterone levels engaged in more optimal parenting with their infants (Weisman, Zagoory-Sharon, & Feldman, 2014). Also in this study, when fathers were administered oxytocin, their parenting behavior improved, as evidenced in increased positive affect, social gaze, touch, and vocal synchrony when interacting with their infants.

In mothers, the experience of pleasure and reward influences the brain's dopamine circuits when mothers care for their infants and are exposed to their infants' cues, such as eye contact, smiling, and so on (Feldman, 2017; Kim, Strathearn, & Swain, 2016). These experiences and brain changes likely promote mother-infant attachment and sensitive parenting. Also, the influence of oxytocin on dopamine in the mother's nucleus accumbens (a collection of neurons in the forebrain that are involved in pleasure) likely is important in motivating the mother's approach to the baby (de Haan & Gunnar, 2009). Figure 8 shows the regions of the brain we have described that are likely to play important roles in infant-mother attachment.

In sum, it is likely that a number of brain regions, neurotransmitters, and hormones are involved in the development of infant-mother attachment (Feldman, 2017; Sullivan & Wilson, 2018). Key candidates for influencing this attachment are connections between the prefrontal cortex, amygdala, and hypothalamus; the nucleus accumbens; and the neuropeptide oxytocin and the neurotransmitter dopamine.

Mothers and Fathers as Caregivers An increasing number of U.S. fathers stay home full-time with their children (Dette-Hagenmeyer, Erzinger, & Reichle, 2016). In one survey, the number of stay-at-home dads in the United States was estimated to be 2 million in 2012 (Livingston, 2014). The 2 million figure represents a significant increase from 1.6 million in 2004 and 1.1 million in 1989. A large portion of the full-time fathers have career-focused wives who provide most of the family's income. One study revealed that the stay-at-home fathers were as satisfied with their marriage as traditional parents, although they indicated that they missed their daily life in the workplace (Rochlen & others, 2008). In this study, the stay-at-home fathers reported that they tended to be ostracized when they took their children to playgrounds and often were excluded from parent groups.

Can fathers take care of infants as competently as mothers can? Observations of fathers and their infants suggest that fathers have the ability to care for their infants as sensitively and responsively as mothers do (Parke, Roisman, & Rose, 2019). One study found that marital intimacy and partner support during prenatal development were linked to father-infant attachment following childbirth (Yu & others, 2012). Another study found that infants who showed a higher level of externalizing, disruptive problems at 1 year of age had fathers who displayed a low level of engagement with them as early as the third month of life (Ramchandani & others, 2013). In another study, researchers found that fathers with a college-level education engaged in more stimulating physical activities with their infants than less-educated fathers did and that fathers in a conflicting couple relationship participated in less caregiving and physical play with their infants (Cabrera, Hofferth, & Chae, 2011).

Consider also the Aka pygmy culture in Africa, where fathers spend as much time interacting with their infants as mothers do (Hewlett, 2000; Hewlett & MacFarlan, 2010). Remember, however, that although fathers can be active, nurturing, involved caregivers with their infants, as Aka pygmy fathers are, in many cultures men have not chosen to follow this pattern (Parkinson, 2010).

Do fathers behave differently from mothers when interacting with their infants? Maternal interactions usually center on child-care activities—feeding, changing diapers, bathing

An Aka pygmy father with his infant son. In the Aka culture, fathers were observed to be holding their infants or close to them 47 percent of the time (Hewlett, 1991).
Nick Greaves/Alamy Stock Photo

(Lamb & Lewis, 2015). Paternal interactions are more likely to include play (Parke, Roisman, & Rose, 2019), and fathers engage in more rough-and-tumble play than mothers do. They bounce infants, throw them up in the air, tickle them, and so on (Lamb, 2013). Mothers do play with infants, but their play is less physical and arousing than that of fathers. Nonetheless, mothers engage in play with their children three times as often as fathers do (Cabrera & Roggman, 2017). In a recent study of low-income families, fathers' playfulness with 2-year-olds was associated with more advanced vocabulary skills at 4 years of age, while mothers' playfulness with 2-year-olds was linked to a higher level of emotion regulation at 4 years of age (Cabrera & others, 2017).

A concern about fathers as parents involve those who have mental health problems, in which case they may not interact as effectively with their infants. For example, in a recent study, children whose fathers' behavior was more withdrawn and depressed at 3 months had a lower level of cognitive development at 24 months of age (Sethna & others, 2018). Also in this study, children whose fathers were more engaged and sensitive, as well as less controlling, at 24 months of age had a higher level of cognitive development at that age. Another study revealed that depressed fathers focused more on their own needs than on their infants' needs and that they directed more negative and critical speech toward infants (Sethna, Murray, & Ramchandani, 2012). And a recent study revealed that both fathers' and mothers' sensitivity assessed when infants were 10 to 12 months old were linked to children's cognitive development at 18 months and language development at 36 months (Malmberg & others, 2016). Other recent studies indicate that when fathers are positively engaged with their children, developmental outcomes are better (Alexander & others, 2017; Roopnarine & Yildirim, 2018).

How do most fathers and mothers interact differently with infants?
Polka Dot Images/Photolibrary

Child Care   Many U.S. children today experience multiple caregivers. Most do not have a parent staying home to care for them; instead, the children have some type of care provided by others—"child care." Many parents worry that child care might reduce their infants' emotional attachment to them, impede their infants' cognitive development, fail to teach them how to control anger, and allow them to be unduly influenced by their peers. How extensive is child care? Are the worries of these parents justified?

Parental Leave   Today far more young children are in child care than at any other time in history. About 2 million children in the United States currently receive formal, licensed child care, and uncounted millions of children are cared for by unlicensed baby-sitters.

Child-care policies around the world vary in eligibility criteria, duration of parental leaves, benefit level, and the extent to which parents take advantage of the policies (Burchinal & others, 2015; Hasbrouck & Pianta, 2016; Shivers & Fargo, 2016). Europe has led the way in creating new standards of parental leave: The European Union (EU) mandated a paid 14-week maternity leave in 1992. In most European countries today, working parents on leave receive from 70 percent of the worker's prior wage to the full wage, and paid leave averages about 16 weeks (Tolani & Brooks-Gunn, 2008). The United States currently allows workers to take up to 12 weeks of unpaid leave to care for a newborn.

Most countries restrict eligibility for maternity benefits to women employed for a minimum time prior to childbirth (Sanders & Guerra, 2016; Tolani & Brooks-Gunn, 2008), but in Denmark even unemployed mothers are eligible for extended parental leave related to childbirth. In Sweden, parents can take an 18-month job-protected parental leave with benefits that can be shared by parents and applied to full-time or part-time work.

Variations in Child Care   Because the United States does not have a policy of paid leave for child care, child care has become a major national concern (Burchinal & others, 2015; Sanders & Guerra, 2016). Many factors influence the effects of child care, including the age of the child, the type of child care, and the quality of the program.

Child-care settings in the United States vary extensively (Burchinal & others, 2015; Hasbrouck & Pianta, 2016). Child care is provided in large centers with elaborate facilities and in private homes. Some child-care centers are commercial operations; others are nonprofit centers run by churches, civic groups, and employers. Some child-care providers are professionals; others are mothers who want to earn extra money. Infants and toddlers are more likely to be found in

How are child-care policies in many European countries, such as Sweden, different from those in the United States?
Juliana Wiklund/Getty Images

Wanda Mitchell, Child-Care Director

Wanda Mitchell is the Center Director of the Hattie Daniels Day Care Center in Wilson, North Carolina. Her responsibilities include directing the operation of the center, which involves creating and maintaining an environment in which young children can learn effectively, and ensuring that the center meets state licensing requirements. Mitchell obtained her undergraduate degree from North Carolina A & T University, majoring in child development. Prior to her current position, she had been an education coordinator for Project Head Start and an instructor at Wilson Technical Community College. Describing her work, Mitchell says, "I really enjoy working in my field. This is my passion. After graduating from college, my goal was to advance in my field."

Wanda Mitchell, child-care director, works with some of the children at her center.
Courtesy of Wanda Mitchell

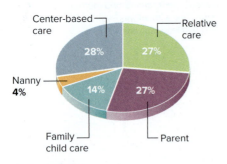

Center-based care 28%
Relative care 27%
Nanny 4%
Family child care 14%
Parent 27%

FIGURE 9

PRIMARY CARE ARRANGEMENTS IN THE UNITED STATES FOR CHILDREN UNDER 5 YEARS OF AGE WITH EMPLOYED MOTHERS

> We have all the knowledge necessary to provide absolutely first-rate child care in the United States. What is missing is the commitment and the will.
>
> —EDWARD ZIGLER
> *Contemporary Developmental Psychologist, Yale University*

family child care and informal care settings, while older children are more likely to be in child-care centers and preschool and early education programs. Figure 9 delineates primary care arrangements for children under 5 years of age with employed mothers (Clarke-Stewart & Miner, 2008).

In the United States, approximately 15 percent of children 5 years of age and younger attend more than one child-care arrangement. A study of 2- and 3-year-olds revealed that an increase in the number of child-care arrangements the children experienced was linked to an increase in behavioral problems and a decrease in prosocial behavior (Morrissey, 2009).

Child-care quality makes a difference in children's lives (Howes, 2016; Sanders & Guerra, 2016; Vu, 2016). What constitutes a high-quality child-care program for infants? In high-quality child care (Clarke-Stewart & Miner, 2008, p. 273):

> . . . caregivers encourage the children to be actively engaged in a variety of activities, have frequent, positive interactions that include smiling, touching, holding, and speaking at the child's eye level, respond properly to the child's questions or requests, and encourage children to talk about their experiences, feelings, and ideas.

High-quality child care also involves providing children with a safe environment, access to age-appropriate toys and participation in age-appropriate activities, and a low caregiver-to-child ratio that allows caregivers to spend considerable time with children on an individual basis. An Australian study revealed that higher-quality child care that included positive child-caregiver relationships at 2 to 3 years of age was linked to children's better self-regulation of attention and emotion at 4 to 5 and 6 to 7 years of age (Gialamas & others, 2014). Quality of child care matters in children's development, and according to UNICEF, the United States meets or exceeds only 3 of 10 child-care quality benchmarks. An analysis of U.S. child-care studies found that a greater quantity of child care was a strong predictor of socioemotional problems (Jacob, 2009). However, a study in Norway (a country that meets or exceeds 8 of 10 UNICEF benchmarks) revealed that the amount of time spent in child care there was not linked to children's externalizing problems (Zachrisson & others, 2013). To read about one individual who provides quality child care to individuals from impoverished backgrounds in the United States, see the *Connecting with Careers* profile.

A major, ongoing longitudinal study of U.S. child care was initiated by the National Institute of Child Health and Human Development (NICHD) in 1991. Data were collected on a diverse sample of almost 1,400 children and their families at ten locations across the United States over a period of seven years. Researchers used multiple methods (trained observers, interviews, questionnaires, and testing), and they measured many facets of children's development, including physical health, cognitive development, and socioemotional development. Following are some of the results of what is now referred to as the NICHD Study of Early

Child Care and Youth Development, or NICHD SECCYD (NICHD Early Child Care Research Network, 2001, 2002, 2003, 2004, 2005a, b, 2006, 2010).

- *Patterns of use*. Many families placed their infants in child care very soon after the child's birth, and there was considerable instability in the child-care arrangements. By 4 months of age, nearly three-fourths of the infants had entered some form of nonmaternal child care. Almost half of the infants were cared for by a relative when they first entered care; only 12 percent were enrolled in child-care centers. Low-income families were more likely than more affluent families to use child care, but infants from low-income families who were in child care averaged the same number of hours of child care as other income groups. In the preschool years, mothers who were single, those with more education, and families with higher incomes used more hours of center-based care than other families. Minority families and mothers with less education used more hours of care by relatives.

- *Quality of care*. Evaluations of quality of care were based on characteristics such as group size, child–adult ratio, physical environment, caregiver characteristics (such as formal education, specialized training, and child-care experience), and caregiver behavior (such as sensitivity to children). An alarming conclusion is that a majority of the child care in the first three years of life was of unacceptably low quality. Positive caregiving by nonparents in child-care settings was infrequent—only 12 percent of the children studied were experiencing positive nonparental child care (such as positive talk and language stimulation)! Further, infants from low-income families experienced a lower quality of child care than infants from higher-income families. When quality of caregivers' care was high, children performed better on cognitive and language tasks, were more cooperative with their mothers during play, showed more positive and skilled interaction with peers, and had fewer behavior problems. Caregiver training and good child-to-staff ratios were linked with higher cognitive and social competence when children were 54 months of age. In one study, high-quality infant-toddler child care was linked to better memory skills at the end of the preschool years (Li & others, 2013).

- In another study, higher-quality child care from birth to 4½ years of age was linked to higher cognitive-academic achievement at 15 years of age (Vandell & others, 2010). In this study, early high-quality care also was related to youth reports of less externalizing behavior (lower rates of delinquency, for example). Also, in another study, high-quality infant-toddler child care was linked to better memory skills at the end of the preschool years (Li & others, 2013).

- *Amount of child care*. In general, when children spent 30 hours or more per week in child care, their development was less than optimal (Ramey, 2005). In one study, more hours of early non-relative child care was related to higher levels of risk taking and impulsivity at 15 years of age (Vandell & others, 2010).

- *Family and parenting influences*. The influence of families and parenting was not weakened by extensive child care. Parents played a significant role in helping children to regulate their emotions. Especially important parenting influences were being sensitive to children's needs, being involved with children, and cognitively stimulating them. Indeed, parental sensitivity has been the most consistent predictor of a secure attachment, with child-care experiences being relevant in many cases only when mothers engage in insensitive parenting (Friedman, Melhuish, & Hill, 2011). An important point about the extensive NICHD research is that findings show that family factors are considerably stronger and more consistent predictors of a wide variety of child outcomes than are child-care aspects such as quality, quantity, and type.

- *Home and child-care settings*. The worst outcomes for children occur when both home and child-care settings are of poor quality. For example, one study involving the NICHD

What are some important findings from the national longitudinal study of child care conducted by the National Institute of Child Health and Human Development?
Reena Rose Sibayan/The Jersey Journal/Landov Images

SECCYD data revealed that worse socioemotional outcomes (higher levels of problem behavior, lower levels of prosocial behavior) for children occurred when they experienced both home and child-care environments that conferred risk (Watamura & others, 2011).

What are some strategies parents can follow in regard to child care? Child-care expert Kathleen McCartney (2003, p. 4) offered this advice:

- *Recognize that the quality of your parenting is a key factor in your child's development.*
- *Make decisions that will improve the likelihood you will be good parents.* "For some this will mean working full-time"—for personal fulfillment, income, or both. "For others, this will mean working part-time or not working outside the home."
- *Monitor your child's development.* "Parents should observe for themselves whether their children seem to be having behavior problems." If problems arise, parents need to talk with their child-care providers and their pediatrician about their child's behavior.
- *Take some time to find the best child care.* Observe different child-care facilities and be certain that you like what you see. "Quality child care costs money, and not all parents can afford the child care they want. However, state subsidies, and other programs like Head Start, are available for families in need."

Attachment in Middle and Late Childhood   Earlier you read about the importance of secure attachment in infancy and the role of sensitive parenting in attachment (Dozier, Bernard, & Roben, 2019; Woodhouse & others, 2019). The attachment process continues to be an important aspect of children's development in the childhood years. In middle and late childhood, attachment becomes more sophisticated, and as children's social worlds expand to include peers, teachers, and others, they typically spend less time with parents.

Kathryn Kerns and her colleagues (Brumariu, Kerns, & Seibert, 2012; Kerns & Brumariu, 2016; Kerns & Seibert, 2012; Kerns, Siener, & Brumariu, 2011; Koehn & Kerns, 2018; Siener & Kerns, 2012) have studied links between attachment to parents and various child outcomes in middle and late childhood. Secure attachment was associated with a lower level of internalized symptoms, anxiety, and depression in children (Brumariu & Kerns, 2011), as well as a higher level of children's emotion regulation and less difficulty in identifying emotions (Kerns & Brumariu, 2014).

Might certain parenting behaviors be associated with different attachment categories in children and adolescents? In recent research, a series of meta-analyses of 5- to 18-year-olds found that parents of children who were more securely attached were more responsive, provided better support of their children's autonomy, and were less punitive (Koehn & Kerns, 2018). Also in this research, parents of children who showed more avoidant attachment were less responsive and more punitive, while children with ambivalent attachment showed no association with parenting behaviors.

ADOLESCENCE

Relationships between parents and children continue to be important during the adolescent years. But the adolescent's emotions may become more involved with people outside the family, especially with romantic partners. What do psychologists know about these relationships?

Attachment to Parents   The initial interest in attachment focused on infants and their caregivers (Dozier, Bernard, & Roben, 2019; Woodhouse & others, 2019). Developmentalists have recently begun to explore the role of secure attachment and related concepts, such as connectedness to parents, during adolescence (Kobak & Kerig, 2015; Kochendorfer & Kerns, 2017; Koehn & Kerns, 2018). A recent longitudinal study revealed that secure attachment in adolescence and emerging adulthood was predicted by observations of maternal sensitivity across childhood and adolescence (Waters, Ruiz, & Roisman, 2017). And a recent study revealed that many adolescents have a fairly stable attachment style, but that attachment stability increases in adulthood (Jones & others, 2018). Adults often have more stable social environments than adolescents and have had more time to consolidate their attachment style. Also in this study, family conflict and parental separation or divorce were likely candidates to undermine attachment stability (Jones & others, 2018). In addition, a recent study revealed that adolescents who had grown up in poverty engaged in less risk-taking when they had a history of secure attachments to caregivers (Delker, Bernstein, & Laurent, 2018). Also, in another recent study, more secure attachment to parents was associated with fewer depressive symptoms in adolescents (Kerstis, Aslund, & Sonnby, 2018). In other research, Joseph Allen and his colleagues (2009) also found that adolescents who were securely attached at 14 years of age were more likely to report at age 21 that they were in an exclusive relationship, comfortable with intimacy in relationships, and attaining increased financial independence. Research indicated that the most consistent outcomes of secure attachment in adolescence are positive peer relations and emotion regulation (Allen & Miga, 2010).

Dating and Romantic Relationships   Adolescents not only have attachments to their parents but also to romantic partners (Allen & others, 2019; Bonache, Gonzalez-Mendez, & Krahe, 2017; Shulman & others, 2019). Adolescents spend considerable time either dating or thinking about dating, which has gone far beyond its original courtship function to become a form of recreation, a source of status and achievement, and a setting for learning about close relationships (Davila, Capaldi, & La Greca, 2016; Furman & Rose, 2015). One function of dating, though, continues to be mate selection.

Types of Dating and Developmental Changes   Three stages characterize the development of romantic relationships in adolescence (Connolly & McIsaac, 2009):

- *Entry into romantic attractions and affiliations at about 11 to 13 years of age.* This initial stage is triggered by puberty. From 11 to 13, adolescents become intensely interested in romance, and it dominates many conversations with same-sex friends. Developing a crush on someone is common, and the crush often is shared with a same-sex friend. Young adolescents may or may not interact with the individual who is the object of their infatuation. When dating occurs, it usually takes place in a group setting.

- *Exploring romantic relationships at approximately 14 to 16 years of age.* At this point in adolescence, two types of romantic involvement occur: casual dating and group dating. Casual dating emerges between individuals who are mutually attracted. These dating experiences are often short-lived, last a few months at best, and usually endure for only a few weeks. *Dating in groups* is common and reflects embeddedness in the peer context. A friend often acts as a third-party facilitator of a potential dating relationship by communicating their friend's romantic interest and determining whether this attraction is reciprocated.

- *Consolidating dyadic romantic bonds at about 17 to 19 years of age.* At the end of the high school years, more serious romantic relationships develop. Romantic relationships within this age group are characterized by strong emotional bonds more closely resembling those in adult romantic relationships. These bonds often are more stable and enduring than earlier bonds, typically lasting one year or more.

Two variations on these stages in the development of romantic relationships in adolescence involve early and late bloomers (Connolly & McIsaac, 2009). Early bloomers include 15 to 20 percent of 11- to 13-year-olds who say that they currently are in a romantic relationship and 35 percent who indicate that they have had some prior experience in romantic relationships. One study found that early daters had more externalized problems throughout adolescence than on-time daters and late bloomers (Connolly & others, 2013). Late bloomers comprise approximately 10 percent of 17- to 19-year-olds who say that they have had no experience with romantic relationships and another 15 percent who report that they have not engaged in any romantic relationships that lasted more than four months.

In their early exploration of romantic relationships, today's adolescents often find comfort in numbers and begin hanging out together in heterosexual groups. Sometimes they just hang out at someone's house or get organized enough to get someone to drive them to a mall or a movie. Indeed, peers and friends play an important role in adolescent romantic relationships (Kochendorfer & Kerns, 2017). One study also found that young adolescents increase their participation in mixed-gender peer groups (Connolly & others, 2004). This participation was "not explicitly focused on dating but rather brought boys and girls together in settings in which heterosocial interaction might occur but is not obligatory" (p. 201). In another study, adolescents who engaged in a higher level of intimate disclosure at age 10 reported a higher level of companionship in romantic relationships at 12 and 15 years of age (Kochendorfer & Kerns, 2017). In this study, those who reported more conflict in friendships had a lower level of companionship in romantic relationships at 15 years of age.

developmental **connection**
Sexuality
At the beginning of emerging adulthood, more than 60 percent of individuals have experienced sexual intercourse. Connect to "Gender and Sexuality."

What are dating relationships like in adolescence?
Digital Vision/Getty Images

Dating and Adjustment   Researchers have linked dating and romantic relationships with various measures of how well adjusted adolescents are (Bonache, Gonzalez-Mendez, & Krahe, 2017; Davila, Capaldi, & La Greca, 2016; Furman & Rose, 2015). For example, a study of 200 tenth-graders revealed that those with more romantic experiences reported higher levels of social acceptance, friendship competence, and romantic competence—however, having more romantic experience also was linked with a higher level of substance use, delinquency, and sexual behavior (Furman, Low, & Ho, 2009). Also, among adolescent girls but not adolescent males, having an older romantic partner was linked with an increase in depressive symptoms, largely influenced by an increase in substance use (Haydon & Halpern, 2010). Dating and romantic relationships at an early age can be especially problematic (Connolly & McIsaac, 2009). Another study found that romantic activity was linked to depression in early adolescent girls (Starr & others, 2012). Researchers also have found that early dating and "going with" someone are linked with adolescent pregnancy and problems at home and school (Florsheim, Moore, & Edgington, 2003). However, in some cases, romantic relationships in adolescence are linked with positive developmental changes. For example, in a recent study, having a supportive romantic relationship in adolescence was linked to positive outcomes for adolescents who had negative relationships with their mothers (Szwedo, Hessel, & Allen, 2017).

Sociocultural Contexts and Dating   The sociocultural context is a strong influence on adolescents' dating patterns (Cheng & others, 2012; Yoon & others, 2017). Values and religious beliefs of various cultures often dictate the age at which dating begins, how much freedom in dating is allowed, whether dates must be chaperoned by adults or parents, and the roles of males and females in dating. For example, Latino and Asian American cultures have more conservative standards regarding adolescent dating than does the Anglo-American culture.

Dating may be a source of cultural conflict for many adolescents whose families come from cultures in which dating begins at a later age with little freedom, especially for adolescent girls. One study found that Asian American adolescents were less likely to have been involved in a romantic relationship in the past 18 months than African American or Latino adolescents (Carver, Joyner, & Udry, 2003). A recent study found that mother-daughter conflict in Mexican American families was linked to an increase in adolescent daughters' romantic involvement (Tyrell & others, 2016). When immigrant adolescents choose to adopt the ways of the dominant U.S. culture (such as unchaperoned dating), they often clash with parents and extended-family members who have more traditional values.

ADULTHOOD

Attachment and romantic relationships continue to be very important aspects of close relationships in adulthood. Let's explore attachment first, then examine different types of love.

Attachment   Earlier in this chapter, we discussed the importance of attachment in infancy, childhood, and adolescence (Cowan & others, 2019a, b; Steele & Steele, 2019; Woodhouse & others, 2019). Are these earlier patterns of attachment related to adults' attachment styles?

Linking Infant Attachment to Adult Attachment   Although relationships with romantic partners differ from those with parents, romantic partners fulfill some of the same needs for adults as parents do for their children (Mikulincer & Shaver, 2019; Zayas & Hazan, 2014). Recall that *securely attached* infants are defined as those who use the caregiver as a secure base from which to explore the environment (Woodhouse & others 2019). Similarly, adults may count on their romantic partners to be a secure base to which they can return and obtain comfort and security in stressful times (Fraley, 2019; Gewirtz-Meydan & Finzi-Dottan, 2018; Mikulincer & Shaver, 2016, 2019; Simpson & Rholes, 2017).

Do adult attachment patterns with partners reflect childhood attachment patterns with parents? In a retrospective study, Cindy Hazan and Phillip Shaver (1987) revealed that young adults who were securely attached in their romantic relationships were more likely to describe their early relationship with their parents as securely attached. In a longitudinal study, infants who were securely attached at 1 year of age were securely attached 20 years later in their adult romantic relationships (Steele & others, 1998). Also, a longitudinal study revealed that securely attached infants were in more stable romantic relationships in adulthood than their insecurely attached counterparts (Salvatore & others, 2011). A longitudinal study found that insecure

How are attachment patterns in childhood linked to relationships in emerging and early adulthood?
(*left*): Ai/Getty Images; (*right*): Jade/Getty Images

avoidant attachment at 8 years of age was linked to a lower level of social initiative and pro-social behavior and a higher level of social anxiety and loneliness at 21 years of age (Fransson.& others, 2016). Further, a study of adoptees found that higher maternal sensitivity in infancy and middle and late childhood predicted more secure attachment to partners in emerging adulthood (Schoenmaker & others, 2015). However, in another longitudinal study the links between early attachment styles and later attachment styles were weakened by stressful and disruptive experiences such as the death of a parent or instability of caregiving (Lewis, Feiring, & Rosenthal, 2000).

Adult Attachment Styles   Hazan and Shaver (1987) measured attachment styles using the following brief assessment.

Read each paragraph and then place a check mark next to the one that best describes your interactions with others:

1.   I find it relatively easy to get close to others and I am comfortable depending on them and having them depend on me. I don't worry about being abandoned or about someone getting too close to me.

2.   I am somewhat uncomfortable being close to others. I find it difficult to trust them completely and to allow myself to depend on them. I get nervous when anyone gets too close to me and it bothers me when someone tries to be more intimate with me than I feel comfortable with.

3.   I find that others are reluctant to get as close as I would like. I often worry that my partner doesn't really love me or won't want to stay with me. I want to get very close to my partner, and this sometimes scares people away.

These items correspond to three attachment styles—secure attachment (option 1 in the list) and two insecure attachment styles (avoidant—option 2, and anxious—option 3):

·   **Secure attachment style.** Securely attached adults have positive views of relationships, find it easy to get close to others, and are not overly concerned with, or stressed out about, their romantic relationships. These adults tend to enjoy sexuality in the context of a committed relationship and are less likely than others to have one-night stands.

·   **Avoidant attachment style.** Avoidant individuals are hesitant about getting involved in romantic relationships and once in a relationship tend to distance themselves from their partner.

·   **Anxious attachment style.** These individuals demand closeness, are less trusting, and are more emotional, jealous, and possessive.

secure attachment style An attachment style that describes adults who have positive views of relationships, find it easy to get close to others, and are not overly concerned or stressed out about their romantic relationships.

avoidant attachment style An attachment style that describes adults who are hesitant about getting involved in romantic relationships and, once in a relationship, tend to distance themselves from their partner.

anxious attachment style An attachment style that describes adults who demand closeness, are less trusting, and are more emotional, jealous, and possessive.

What are some key dimensions of attachment in adulthood, and how are they related to relationship patterns and well-being?
Fuse/Getty Images

The majority of adults (about 60 to 80 percent) describe themselves as securely attached, and not surprisingly adults prefer having a securely attached partner (Zeifman & Hazan, 2008).

Researchers are studying links between adults' current attachment styles and many aspects of their lives (Fraley, 2019; Mikulincer & Shaver, 2016, 2019; Simpson & Karantzas, 2019). For example, securely attached adults are more satisfied with their close relationships than insecurely attached adults, and the relationships of securely attached adults are more likely to be characterized by trust, commitment, and longevity. In one study, young adults with an anxious attachment style were more likely to characterized by higher negative affect, stress, and perceived social rejection; those with an avoidant attachment style were more likely to be characterized by less desire to be with others when alone (Sheinbaum & others, 2015). In another study, secure attachment in adults was linked to fewer sleep disruptions than insecure avoidant and anxious attachment (Adams & McWilliams, 2015). A recent research review concluded that insecure attachment was linked to a higher level of social anxiety in adults (Manning & others, 2017). Further, it recently has been found that insecure anxious and insecure avoidant individuals are more likely than securely attached individuals to engage in risky health behaviors, are more susceptible to physical illness, and have poorer disease outcomes (Pietromonaco & Beck, 2018). A research meta-analysis of 94 samples of U.S. college students from 1988 to 2011 found the percentage of students with a secure attachment style decreased while the percentage of students with insecure attachment styles increased (Konrath & others, 2014). Leading experts Mario Mikulincer and Phillip Shaver (2014, 2016, 2019) have reached the following conclusions about the benefits of secure attachment:

1. Individuals who are securely attached have a well-integrated sense of self-acceptance, self-esteem, and self-efficacy.

2. They have the ability to control their emotions, are optimistic, and are resilient.

3. Facing stress and adversity, they activate cognitive representations of security, are mindful of what is happening around them, and mobilize effective coping strategies.

If you have an insecure attachment style, are you stuck with it and does it doom you to have problematic relationships? Attachment categories are somewhat stable in adulthood, but adults do have the capacity to change their attachment thinking and behavior (Mikulincer & Shaver, 2016, 2019). Although attachment insecurities are linked to relationship problems, attachment style makes only a moderate contribution to relationship functioning because other factors contribute to relationship satisfaction and success. In the chapter on "Families, Lifestyles, and Parenting," we will discuss such factors in our coverage of marital relationships.

Attachment from Early to Late Adulthood   There has been far less research on how attachment influences the lives of aging adults than on effects of attachment in children, adolescents, and young adults (Fraley, 2019; Fraley & Hudson, 2017; Homan, 2018). A research review on attachment in older adults reached the following conclusions (Van Assche & others, 2013):

1. Older adults have fewer attachment relationships than younger adults (Cicirelli, 2010).

2. With increasing age, attachment anxiety decreases (Chopik, Edelstein, & Fraley, 2013).

3. In late adulthood, attachment security is associated with psychological and physical well-being (Bodner & Cohen-Fridel, 2010).

4. Insecure attachment is linked to more perceived negative caregiver burden in caring for patients with Alzheimer disease (Karantzas, Evans, & Foddy, 2010).

A large-scale study examined attachment anxiety and avoidance in individuals from 18 to 70 years of age (Chopik, Edelstein, & Fraley, 2013). In this study, attachment anxiety was highest among adults in their mid-twenties and lowest among middle-aged and older adults. Developmental changes in avoidant attachment were not as strong as in anxious attachment, although anxious attachment was highest for middle-aged adults and lowest for young adults and older adults. And in related longitudinal data for individuals from 13 to 72 years of age, avoidant attachment declined across the life span and being in a relationship predicted lower levels of anxious and avoidant attachment across adulthood (Chopik, Edelstein, & Grimm, 2019). Further, a recent study of older adult women found that avoidant attachment was linked to higher levels of social isolation (Spence, Jacobs, & Bifulco, 2019).

Romantic Love   Think for a moment about songs and books that hit the top of the charts. Chances are, they're about love. Poets, playwrights, and musicians through the ages have lauded

What are some changes in attachment in older adults?
Purestock/SuperStock

the fiery passion of romantic love—and lamented the searing pain when it fails. **Romantic love** is also called *passionate love* or *eros;* it has strong components of sexuality and infatuation, and it often predominates in the early part of a love relationship. A meta-analysis found that males show higher avoidance and lower anxiety about romantic love than females do (Del Giudice, 2011).

Well-known love researcher Ellen Berscheid (1988) says that romantic love is what we mean when we say that we are "in love" with someone. It is romantic love, she stresses, that we need to understand if we are to learn what love is all about. According to Berscheid, sexual desire is the most important ingredient of romantic love. We discuss sexuality in more detail in the chapter on "Gender and Sexuality."

Romantic love includes a complex intermingling of emotions—fear, anger, sexual desire, joy, and jealousy, for example. Obviously, some of these emotions are a source of anguish. One study found that romantic lovers were more likely than friends to be the cause of depression (Berscheid & Fei, 1977). Another study revealed that a heightened state of romantic love in young adults was linked to stronger depression and anxiety symptoms but better sleep quality (Bajoghli & others, 2014).

Recently, romantic attraction has not only taken place in person but also over the Internet (Doucette & others, 2019; Jin, Ryu, & Mugaddam, 2019). Forty million Americans use online dating services (about 40 percent of the U.S. singles pool) (Broussard, 2015). Is looking for love online likely to work out? It didn't work out so well in 2012 for Notre Dame linebacker Manti Te'o, whose online girlfriend turned out to be a "catfish," someone who fakes an identity online. However, online dating sites claim that their sites often have positive outcomes. A poll commissioned by match.com in 2009 reported that twice as many marriages occurred between individuals who met through an online dating site as between people who met in bars, clubs, and other social settings.

In 2010, Barbara Hassan, a 47-year-old divorcee from Texas, registered with match.com and within one day had three matches, all of whom appeared to be intelligent, attractive, and well off (Marinova, 2013). Barbara's first thoughts were that they were too good to be true, and those first thoughts were right. One of her matches said he was a construction engineer from Nigeria who had designed a building for orphans. She communicated with him for several months and then he asked her to send him $2,700 so he could come to the United States. That was enough to end the connection.

Connecting online for love turned out positively for two Columbia graduate students, Michelle Przybyksi and Andy Lalinde (Steinberg, 2011). They found out they lived only a few blocks away from each other, so soon after they communicated online through Datemyschool.com, a dating site exclusively for college students, they met in person, really hit it off, applied for a marriage license 10 days later, and eventually got married.

romantic love Also called passionate love, or eros, this type of love has strong components of sexuality and infatuation, and it often predominates in the early part of a love relationship.

(*Left*) Manti Te'o; (*Right*) Michelle Przybyksi and Andy Lalinde.
(*left*): John Biever/Sports Illustrated/Getty Images; (*right*): Courtesy of Michelle and Andres Lalinde

> Love is a canvas furnished by nature and embroidered by imagination.
>
> —VOLTAIRE
> *French Essayist, 18th Century*

What are some characteristics of romantic relationships in China?
Lane Oatey/Blue Jean Images/Getty Images

What are romantic relationships like in Argentina?
Jag Images/Cultura/Getty Images

affectionate love Also called companionate love, this type of love occurs when individuals desire to have another person near and have a deep, caring affection for the person.

triangular theory of love Sternberg's theory that love includes three components or dimensions—passion, intimacy, and commitment.

However, in an editorial in *The Tower*, the student newspaper at Arcadia University in Philadelphia, Samantha Nickalls (2012) argued that online dating sites might be okay for people in their thirties and older but not for college students. She commented:

> The dating pool of our age is huge. Huge. After all, marriage is not on most people's minds when they're in college, but dating (or perhaps just hooking up) most certainly is. A college campus, in fact, is like living a dating service because the majority of people are looking for the same thing you are. As long as you put yourself out there, flirt a bit, and be friendly, chances are that people will notice.
>
> If this doesn't work for you right away, why should it really matter? As a college student, you have so many other huge things going on in your life—your career choice, your transition from kid to adult, your crazy social life. Unless you are looking to get married at age 20 (which is a whole other issue that I could debate for hours), dating shouldn't be the primary thing on your mind anyway. Besides, as the old saying goes, the best things come when you least expect them. Oftentimes, you find the best dates by accident—not by hunting them down.

Some critics argue that online romantic relationships lose the interpersonal connection, whereas others emphasize that the Internet may benefit shy or anxious individuals who find it difficult to meet potential partners in person (Holmes, Little, & Welsh, 2009). One problem with online matchmaking is that many individuals misrepresent their characteristics, such as how old they are, how attractive they are, and their occupation. Recent data indicate that men lie most about their age, height, and income; women lie most about their weight, physical build, and age (statisticbrain.com, 2017). Despite such dishonesty, researchers have found that romantic relationships initiated on the Internet are more likely than relationships established in person to last for more than two years (Bargh & McKenna, 2004). And in a large-scale study of more than 19,000 individuals, it was discovered that more than one-third of relationships that lead to marriage now begin online and that the resulting marriages are slightly less likely to break up and are characterized by slightly higher marital satisfaction than marriages that begin with contact in offline contexts (Cacioppo & others, 2013). However, one study confirmed that declaring a relationship status on Facebook was associated with both romantic love and jealousy (Orosz & others, 2015).

Developmental Changes   How do romantic relationships change in emerging adulthood? In a recent study that spanned 10 years, short-term relationships were more common as individuals moved into emerging adulthood (Lantagne & Furman, 2017). Long-term adolescent relationships were both supportive and turbulent, characterized by elevated levels of support, negative interactions, higher control, and more jealousy. In emerging adulthood, long-term relationships provided high levels of support as well as decreased levels of negative interactions, control, and jealousy.

Cross-Cultural Variations   Culture has strong influences on many aspects of human development, including romantic relationships (Luo, 2019). In collectivist countries like China and Korea, intimacy is more diffused in love because of the strong group emphasis on connections outside of a romantic love relationship. By contrast, in individualistic countries such as the United States and most European countries, intimacy is often more intensified because an individual's social network is more likely to be smaller and less group-oriented (Gao, 2016). Also, research indicates that greater passion characterizes U.S. romantic relationships compared with Chinese romantic relationships (Gao, 2001). And researchers have found that self-disclosure is more common in U.S. romantic relationships than in Japanese romantic relationships (Kito, 2005). Feelings of commitment are stronger in Chinese romantic relationships than in U.S. romantic relationships (Dion & Dion, 1993).

In an exploration of cross-cultural variations, romantic relationships were studied in four countries—Japan, Argentina, France, and Qatar (Ansari, 2015). In Japan, the marriage rate is declining so rapidly that the Japanese government is very concerned that this could lead to a considerable drop in Japan's population. In 2013, 45 percent of Japanese women 16 to 24 years of age reported that they were not interested in or despised having sexual contact. Also, the percentage of Japanese men and women who aren't involved in any romantic relationship has increased significantly in recent years.

In Argentina, romantic interest is much stronger than in Japan (Ansari, 2015). Sexual and romantic flirtation is a way of life for many Argentinians. Online dating is not nearly as frequent as in the United States, apparently because men are so forward in their romantic pursuits in person.

In France, as in Argentina, interest in passionate love is strong. However, in the three-country comparison, one aspect of French interest in romantic relationships stood out—their affinity for having extramarital affairs. In one comparison, only 47 percent of survey respondents in France stated that having an extramarital affair is morally wrong, compared with 69 percent in Japan, 72 percent in Argentina, and 84 percent in the United States (Wike, 2014). In sum, there are striking cultural variations in many aspects of romantic relationships.

In the previously mentioned exploration of romantic relationships in different countries, the Middle Eastern country of Qatar also was studied (Ansari, 2015). In Qatar, casual dating is forbidden and public displays of affection can be punished with prison time. However, with the recent advent of smartphones, social media, and the Internet, young adults in Qatar are now contacting each other about co-ed parties in hotel rooms, a private way to hang out away from the monitoring of parents, neighbors, and government officials.

Affectionate Love   Love is more than just passion (Hanley, 2020; Sternberg, 2020e, f; Youyou & others, 2017). **Affectionate love,** also called companionate love, is the type of love that occurs when individuals desire to have the other person near and have a deep, caring affection for the person.

There is a growing belief that as love matures, passion tends to give way to affection (Sternberg, 2013). One investigation interviewed 102 happily married couples in early (average age 28), middle (average age 45), and late (average age 65) adulthood to explore the nature of age and sex differences in satisfying love relationships (Reedy, Birren, & Schaie, 1981). As indicated in Figure 10, communication was more important in early adulthood, sexual intimacy was more important in early to middle adulthood, and feelings of emotional security and loyalty were more important in later-life love relationships. Young adult lovers also rated communication as more characteristic of their love than their older counterparts did. Aside from the age differences, however, there were some striking similarities in the nature of satisfying love relationships. At all ages, emotional security was ranked as the most important factor in love, followed by respect, communication, help and play behaviors, sexual intimacy, and loyalty. The findings of this research also suggested that women believe emotional security is more important in love than men do.

Sternberg's Triangular Theory of Love   Clearly, there is more to satisfying love relationships than sex (Sternberg & Sternberg, 2020). One theory of love that captures this idea has been proposed by Robert J. Sternberg (1988, 2013, 2020e, f, g). His **triangular theory of love** states that love has three main components or dimensions—passion, intimacy, and commitment (see Figure 11):

· *Passion*, as described earlier, is physical and sexual attraction to another.
· *Intimacy* is the emotional feelings of warmth, closeness, and sharing in a relationship.
· *Commitment* is each partner's cognitive appraisal of the relationship and their intent to maintain the relationship even in the face of problems.

According to Sternberg, if passion is the only ingredient (with intimacy and commitment low or absent), we are merely experiencing infatuation. This might happen in an affair or a one-night stand. But varying combinations of the dimensions of love create three qualitatively different types of love:

· A relationship marked by intimacy and commitment but low or lacking in passion is called *affectionate love,* a pattern often found among couples who have been married for many years.
· If passion and commitment are present but intimacy is not, Sternberg calls the relationship *fatuous* love, as when one person worships another from a distance.
· If passion, intimacy, and commitment are all strong, the result is *consummate love*, the fullest type of love.

Falling Out of Love   The collapse of a close relationship may feel tragic. In the long run, however, our happiness and personal development may benefit from getting over being in love and ending a close relationship.

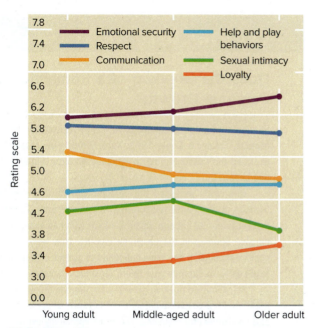

FIGURE 10

CHANGES IN SATISFYING LOVE RELATIONSHIPS ACROSS THE ADULT YEARS. In the investigation by Reedy, Birren, and Schaie (1981), emotional security was the most important factor in love at all ages. Sexual intimacy was more important in early adulthood, whereas emotional security and loyalty were more important in the love relationships of older adults. Young adult lovers also rated communication as more important in a love relationship than their older counterparts did.

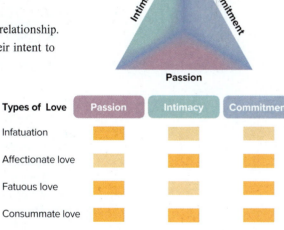

Types of Love	Passion	Intimacy	Commitment
Infatuation	Present	Absent or low	Absent or low
Affectionate love	Absent or low	Present	Present
Fatuous love	Present	Absent or low	Present
Consummate love	Present	Present	Present

Present   Absent or low

FIGURE 11

STERNBERG'S TRIANGLE OF LOVE. Sternberg identified three dimensions that shape the experience we call love: passion, intimacy, and commitment. Various combinations of the three dimensions produce particular types of love.

Does the Breakup of a Romantic Relationship Present an Opportunity for Personal Growth?

Studies of romantic breakups have mainly focused on their negative aspects (Frazier & Cook, 1993; Kato, 2005). Few researchers have explored the possibility that a romantic breakup might lead to positive changes.

One study assessed the personal growth that can follow the breakup of a romantic relationship (Tashiro & Frazier, 2003). The participants were 92 undergraduate students who had experienced a relationship breakup in the past nine months. They were asked, "What positive changes, if any, have happened as a result of your breakup that might serve to improve your future romantic relationships?" (p. 118).

Self-reported positive growth was common following a romantic breakup. Changes were categorized in terms of personal, relational, and environmental positives. The most commonly reported types of growth were personal changes, which included feeling stronger and more self-confident, more independent, and better off emotionally. Relational positive changes included gaining relational wisdom, and environmental positive changes included having better friendships because of the breakup. Figure 12 provides examples of these positive changes. Women reported more positive growth after a breakup than men did.

Of course, not all romantic relationships produce positive changes in the aftermath. In a recent large-scale study of more than 9,000 adults, experiencing a romantic breakup lowered individuals' self-esteem, but the effect disappeared one year after the breakup (Luciano & Orth, 2017).

What other aspects of romantic dissolution might be interesting to study?

FIGURE 12

EXAMPLES OF POSITIVE CHANGES IN THE AFTERMATH OF A ROMANTIC BREAKUP

Change Category	Examples of Frequently Mentioned Responses
Personal positives	1. "I am more self-confident." 2. "Through breaking up I found I could handle more on my own." 3. "I didn't always have to be the strong one, it's okay to cry or be upset without having to take care of him."
Relational positives	1. "Better communication." 2. "I learned many relationship skills that I can apply in the future (for example, the importance of saying you're sorry)." 3. "I know not to jump into a relationship too quickly."
Environmental positives	1. "I rely on my friends more. I forgot how important friends are when I was with him." 2. "Concentrate on school more: I can put so much more time and effort toward school." 3. "I believe friends' and family's opinions count—will seek them out in future relationships."

In particular, falling out of love may be wise if you are obsessed with a person who repeatedly betrays your trust; if you are involved with someone who is draining you emotionally or financially; or if you are desperately in love with someone who does not return your feelings.

Being in love when love is not returned can lead to depression, obsessive thoughts, sexual dysfunction, inability to work effectively, difficulty in making new friends, and self-condemnation (Sbarra, 2012). Thinking clearly in such relationships is often difficult because they are so colored by arousing emotions.

Some people get taken advantage of in relationships (Duck, 2011; Metts & Cupach, 2007; Sternberg, 2020f, g). For example, without either person realizing it, a relationship can evolve in a way that creates dominant and submissive roles. Detecting this pattern is an important step toward learning either to reconstruct the relationship or to end it if the problems cannot be worked out.

What other types of personal growth can follow romantic relationship breakups? To find out more about this aspect of relationships, see the *Connecting with Research* interlude.

Review *Connect* Reflect

LG4 Explain attachment and its development.

Review

- What is attachment? How does attachment develop in infancy and childhood? How are caregiving styles related to attachment? How does child care affect children's development?
- How does attachment develop in adolescence? What is the nature of dating and romantic relationships in adolescence?
- What are attachment and love like in different stages of adulthood?

Connect

- How is attachment similar or different in infancy and adolescence?

Reflect *Your Own Personal Journey of Life*

- How would you describe your attachment style? Why do you think you developed this attachment style?

reach your **learning goals**

Emotional Development and Attachment

1 Exploring Emotion

LG1 Discuss basic aspects of emotion.

What Are Emotions?

- Emotion is feeling, or affect, that expresses the pleasantness or unpleasantness of a person's state; it occurs when a person is engaged in an interaction that is important to him or her, especially to his or her well-being. Emotions can be classified as positive or negative and vary in intensity.

- Darwin described the evolutionary basis of emotions, and today psychologists note that emotions, especially facial expressions of emotions, have a biological foundation.

- Facial expressions of emotion are similar across cultures, but display rules are not culturally universal. Biological evolution endowed humans to be emotional, but culture and relationships with others provide diversity in emotional experiences.

- Children's cognitive processing, such as their attention, also influences their emotional development.

Emotion Regulation

- The ability to control one's emotions is a key dimension of development. Emotion regulation consists of effectively managing arousal to adapt and reach a goal. In infancy and early childhood, regulation of emotion gradually shifts from external sources to self-initiated, internal sources. Also with increasing age, children are likely to increase their use of cognitive strategies for regulating emotion, modulate their emotional arousal, become more adept at managing situations to minimize negative emotion, and choose effective ways to cope with stress. Emotion-coaching parents are more likely to have children who engage in effective self-regulation of their emotions than are emotion-dismissing parents.

Emotional Competence

- Saarni argues that becoming emotionally competent involves developing a number of skills such as being aware of one's emotional states, discerning others' emotions, adaptively coping with negative emotions, and understanding the role of emotions in relationships.

2 Development of Emotion

LG2 Describe the development of emotion through the life span.

Infancy

- Infants display a number of emotions early in the first six months, including sadness, surprise, interest, joy, fear, and anger—although researchers debate the onset and sequence of these emotions. Lewis distinguishes between primary emotions and self-conscious emotions.

- Crying is the most important mechanism newborns have for communicating with their world. Babies have at least three types of cries—basic, anger, and pain cries. Controversy surrounds the question of whether babies should be soothed when they cry, although increasingly experts recommend immediately responding in a caring way during the first year.

- Social smiling in response to a caregiver's voice occurs as early as 4 weeks of age. Two fears that infants develop are stranger anxiety and separation from a caregiver (which is reflected in separation protest).

Early Childhood

- Young children's range of emotions expands during early childhood as they increasingly experience self-conscious emotions such as pride, shame, and guilt. Between 2 and 4 years of age, children use an increasing number of terms to describe emotion and learn more about the causes and consequences of feelings. At 4 to 5 years of age, children show an increased ability to reflect on emotions and understand that a single event can elicit different emotions in different people. Emotion regulation is a key aspect of competent socioemotional development in childhood.

Middle and Late Childhood

- In middle and late childhood, children show a growing awareness of the need to control and manage emotions to meet social standards. Also in this age period, they show enhanced emotional understanding, markedly improve their ability to suppress or conceal negative emotions, use self-initiated strategies for redirecting feelings, have an increased tendency to take into fuller account the events that lead to emotional reactions, and develop a genuine capacity for empathy.

Adolescence

- As individuals go through early adolescence, they are less likely to report being very happy. Moodiness is a normal aspect of early adolescence. Although pubertal change is associated with an increase in negative emotions, hormonal influences are often small, and environmental experiences may contribute more to the emotions of adolescents than hormonal changes do.

Adult Development and Aging

- Older adults are better at controlling their emotions than younger adults are, and older adults experience more positive and less negative emotions than younger adults do. An important theory regarding developmental changes in emotion during adulthood, especially late adulthood, is Carstensen's socioemotional selectivity theory. Knowledge-related and emotion-related goals change across the life span; emotion-related goals become more important when individuals get older.

3 Temperament

LG3 Characterize variations in temperament and their significance.

Describing and Classifying Temperament

- Temperament is an individual's behavioral style and characteristic way of emotional responding. Developmentalists are especially interested in the temperament of infants. Chess and Thomas classified infants as (1) easy, (2) difficult, or (3) slow to warm up. Kagan argues that inhibition to the unfamiliar is an important temperament category. Rothbart and Bates' view of temperament identifies three aspects: (1) extraversion/surgency, (2) negative affectivity, and (3) effortful control (self-regulation).

Biological Foundations and Experience

- Physiological characteristics are associated with different temperaments, and a moderate influence of heredity has been found in studies of the heritability of temperament. Children inherit a physiology that biases them to have a particular type of temperament, but through experience they learn to modify their temperament style to some degree.

- Very active young children are likely to become outgoing adults. In some cases, a difficult temperament is linked to adjustment problems in early adulthood. The link between childhood temperament and adult personality depends in part on context, which helps shape the reaction to a child and thus the child's experiences. For example, the reaction to a child's temperament depends in part on the child's culture.

Goodness of Fit and Parenting

- Goodness of fit refers to the match between a child's temperament and the environmental demands the child must cope with. Goodness of fit can be an important aspect of a child's adjustment. Although research evidence is sketchy at this time, some general recommendations are that caregivers should (1) be sensitive to the individual characteristics of the child, (2) be flexible in responding to these characteristics, and (3) avoid negative labeling of the child.

4 Attachment and Love

 LG4 Explain attachment and its development.

Infancy and Childhood

- Infants show a strong interest in the social world and are motivated to understand it. Infants orient to the social world early in their development. Face-to-face play with a caregiver begins to occur at about 2 to 3 months of age. Newly developed self-produced locomotor skills significantly expand the infant's ability to initiate social interchanges and explore his or her social world more independently. Perceiving people as engaging in intentional and goal-directed behavior is an important social cognitive accomplishment that occurs toward the end of the first year. Social referencing increases in the second year of life.

- Attachment is a close emotional bond between two people. In infancy, contact comfort and trust are important in the development of attachment. Bowlby's ethological theory stresses that the caregiver and the infant are biologically predisposed to form an attachment. Attachment develops in four phases during infancy. Securely attached babies use the caregiver, usually the mother, as a secure base from which to explore the environment.

- Three types of insecure attachment are avoidant, resistant, and disorganized. Ainsworth created the Strange Situation, an observational measure of attachment. Ainsworth notes that secure attachment in the first year of life provides an important foundation for psychological development later in life. The strength of the link between early attachment and later development has varied somewhat across studies.

- Some critics argue that attachment theorists have not given adequate attention to genetics and temperament. Other critics stress that attachment theorists have not adequately taken into account the diversity of social agents and contexts.

- Cultural variations in attachment have been found, but secure attachment is the most common classification in all cultures studied to date. Caregivers of securely attached babies are sensitive to the babies' signals and are consistently available to meet their needs. Caregivers of avoidant babies tend to be unavailable or rejecting. Caregivers of resistant babies tend to be inconsistently available to their babies and usually are not very affectionate. Caregivers of disorganized babies often neglect or physically abuse their babies.

- The mother's primary role when interacting with the infant is caregiving; the father's is playful interaction. More U.S. children are in child care now than at any earlier point in history. The quality of child care in the United States is uneven, and child care remains a controversial topic. Quality child care can be achieved and seems to have few adverse effects on children. In the NICHD child-care study, infants from low-income families were more likely to receive the lowest quality of care. Also, higher quality of child care was linked with fewer child problems.

- Secure attachment continues to be important in the childhood years. Researchers have found that secure attachment to parents in middle and late childhood is linked to lower levels of internalized symptoms, anxiety, and depression.

Adolescence

- Securely attached adolescents show more competent behavior than their insecurely attached counterparts, with the most consistent outcomes involving positive peer relations and emotion regulation. Dating, or thinking about dating, becomes an important aspect of many adolescents' lives. Early dating is associated with developmental problems. Culture can exert a powerful influence on dating.

Adulthood

- Three adult attachment styles are insecure attachment, avoidant attachment, and anxious attachment. Attachment styles in early adulthood are linked with a number of relationship patterns and developmental outcomes. For example, securely attached adults often show more positive relationship patterns than insecurely attached adults. Also, adults with avoidant and anxious attachment styles tend to be more depressed and have more relationship problems than securely attached adults.

- Older adults have fewer attachment relationships than younger adults, and attachment anxiety decreases in older adults.

- Romantic love and affectionate love are two important types of love. Romantic love tends to be more important in early adulthood; affectionate love is more likely to be important in later-life love relationships. Sternberg proposed a triangular theory of love that focuses on different combinations of (1) passion, (2) intimacy, and (3) commitment. The collapse of a close relationship can be traumatic, but for some individuals it results in increased self-confidence, relational wisdom, and being better off emotionally. For most individuals, falling out of love is painful and emotionally intense.

key terms

affectionate love
anger cry
anxious attachment style
attachment
avoidant attachment style
basic cry
developmental cascade model
difficult child

easy child
emotion
fight or flight
goodness of fit
insecure avoidant children
insecure disorganized children
insecure resistant children
pain cry

primary emotions
reflexive smile
romantic love
secure attachment style
securely attached children
self-conscious emotions
separation protest
slow-to-warm-up child

social referencing
social smile
socioemotional selectivity theory
Strange Situation
stranger anxiety
temperament
tend and befriend
triangular theory of love

key people

Mary Ainsworth
John Bates
Ellen Berscheid
John Bowlby
Joseph Campos
Laura Carstensen
Alexander Chess

Erik Erikson
Harry Harlow
Cindy Hazan
Jerome Kagan
Kathryn Kerns
Reed Larson
Michael Lewis

Kathleen McCartney
Cybele Raver
Maryse Richards
Mary Rothbart
Carolyn Saarni
Phillip Shaver
Alan Sroufe

Robert J. Sternberg
Shelley Taylor
Stella Thomas
Ross Thompson
John Watson
Amanda Woodward

chapter 11

THE SELF, IDENTITY, AND PERSONALITY

chapter outline

Ariel Skelley/Getty Images

preview

Think about yourself for a few moments. Who are you? What are you like as a person? This chapter seeks to answer such questions by exploring the self, identity, and personality. We will examine these dimensions of people at different points in the life span, from infancy through late adulthood.

1 The Self LG1 Discuss the main ways the self and understanding others are conceptualized and how they develop.

Self-Understanding and Understanding Others

Self-Esteem and Self-Concept

Self-Regulation

When I say "I," I mean something absolutely unique and not to be confused with any other.

—UGO BETTI
Italian Playwright, 20th Century

Theorists and researchers who focus on the self usually argue that the self is the central aspect of the individual's personality and that the self lends an integrative dimension to our understanding of different personality characteristics (Cloninger, 2019; Crocker & Brummelman, 2019; Vater, Moritz, & Roepke, 2018). Several aspects of the self have been studied more than others. These include self-understanding, self-esteem, and self-concept. Let's now turn our attention to how these aspects of the self develop across the life span.

SELF-UNDERSTANDING AND UNDERSTANDING OTHERS

What is self-understanding? **Self-understanding** is the cognitive representation of the self, the substance of self-conceptions. For example, an 11-year-old boy understands that he is a student, a boy, a football player, a family member, a video game lover, and a rock music fan. A 13-year-old girl understands that she is a middle school student, in the midst of puberty, a girl, a soccer player, a student council member, and a movie fan. Self-understanding is based, in part, on roles and membership categories (Harter, 2012, 2013, 2016). It provides the underpinnings for the development of identity. How does self-understanding develop across the life span?

Infancy Studying the self in infancy is difficult mainly because infants cannot tell us how they experience themselves. Infants cannot verbally express their views of the self. They also cannot understand complex instructions from researchers.

A rudimentary form of self-recognition—being attentive and positive toward one's image in a mirror—appears as early as 3 months of age (Mascolo & Fischer, 2007). However, a central, more complete index of self-recognition—the ability to recognize one's physical features—does not emerge until the second year (Thompson, 2006).

One ingenious strategy to test infants' visual self-recognition is the use of a mirror technique, in which an infant's mother puts a dot of rouge on the infant's nose and then an observer watches to see how often the infant touches its nose. Next, the infant is placed in front of a mirror, and observers detect whether nose touching increases. Why does this matter? The idea is that increased nose touching indicates that the infant recognizes the self in the mirror and is trying to touch or rub off the rouge because the rouge violates the infant's view of the self. Increased touching indicates that the infant realizes that it is the self in the mirror but that something is not right since the real self does not have a dot of rouge on it.

Figure 1 displays the results of two investigations that used the mirror technique. The researchers found that before they were 1 year old, infants did not recognize themselves in the mirror (Amsterdam, 1968; Lewis & Brooks-Gunn, 1979). Signs of self-recognition began to appear among some infants when they were 15 to 18 months old. By the time they were 2 years old, most children recognized themselves in the mirror. In sum, infants begin to develop a self-understanding called self-recognition at approximately 18 months of age (Hart & Karmel, 1996).

In one study, biweekly assessments from 15 to 23 months of age were conducted (Courage, Edison, & Howe, 2004). Self-recognition gradually emerged over this time, first appearing in the form of mirror recognition, followed by use of the personal pronoun "me" and then by

self-understanding The individual's cognitive representation of the self, the substance of self-conceptions.

recognizing a photo of themselves. These aspects of self-recognition are often referred to as the first indications of toddlers' understanding of the mental state of "me"—"that they are objects in their own mental representation of the world" (Lewis, 2005, p. 363).

Late in the second year and early in the third year, toddlers show other emerging forms of self-awareness that reflect a sense of "me" (Laible & Thompson, 2007). For example, they refer to themselves by saying "Me big"; they label internal experiences such as emotions; they monitor themselves, as when a toddler says, "Do it myself"; and they say that things are theirs (Bullock & Lutkenhaus, 1990; Fasig, 2000). One study revealed that it is not until the second year that infants develop a conscious awareness of their own bodies (Brownell & others, 2009). This developmental change in body awareness marks the beginning of children's representation of their own three-dimensional body shape and appearance, providing an early step in the development of their self-image and identity (Brownell, 2009).

The development of the self in infants and toddlers does not occur in a social vacuum (Thompson, 2015). Interactions with caregivers, older siblings, and others support the development of the self in infants and toddlers. Through labeling and describing physical aspects and internal states of infants and toddlers, these persons scaffold infants' and toddlers' self-development and understanding.

Early Childhood Research studies have revealed that young children are more psychologically aware—of themselves and others—than used to be thought (Thompson, 2015). This *self-awareness* reflects young children's expanding psychological sophistication.

Self-Understanding Because children can verbally communicate, research on self-understanding in childhood is not limited to visual self-recognition, as it is during infancy (Harter, 2012, 2013, 2016). Mainly through *interviews*, researchers have probed many aspects of children's self-understanding. Here are five main characteristics of self-understanding in young children:

- *Confusion of self, mind, and body*. Young children generally confuse self, mind, and body. Most young children conceive of the self as part of the body, which usually means the head. For them, the self can be described along many material dimensions, such as size, shape, and color.
- *Concrete descriptions*. Preschool children mainly think of themselves and define themselves in concrete terms. A young child might say, "I know my ABC's," "I can count," and "I live in a big house" (Harter, 2006). Although young children mainly describe themselves in terms of concrete, observable features and action tendencies, at about 4 to 5 years of age, as they hear others use psychological trait and emotion terms, they begin to include these in their own self-descriptions (Thompson, 2006). Thus, in a self-description, a 4-year-old might say, "I'm not scared. I'm always happy."
- *Physical descriptions*. Young children also distinguish themselves from others through many physical and material attributes. Says 4-year-old Sandra, "I'm different from Jennifer because I have brown hair and she has blond hair." Says 4-year-old Ralph, "I am different from Hank because I am taller, and I am different from my sister because I have a bicycle."
- *Active descriptions*. The active dimension is a central component of the self in early childhood. For example, preschool children often describe themselves in terms of activities such as play.
- *Unrealistic positive overestimations*. Self-evaluations during early childhood are often unrealistically positive and represent an overestimation of personal attributes (Harter, 2012, 2013, 2016). A young child might say, "I know all of my ABC's" but does not; or might comment, "I'm never scared," which is not the case. These unrealistic positive overestimations of the self occur because young children (1) have difficulty differentiating between their desired and actual competence, (2) cannot yet generate an ideal self that is distinguished from a real self, and (3) rarely engage in *social comparison*—exploring how they compare with others. Young children's self-evaluations also reflect an inability to recognize that they can possess opposite attributes, such as "good" and "bad" or "nice" and "mean" (Harter, 2006).

However, as in virtually all areas of human development, there are individual variations in young children's self-conceptions. In addition, there is increasing evidence that some children are vulnerable to negative self-attributions (Thompson, 2011). For example, one study revealed that

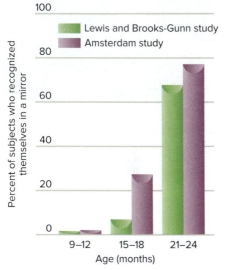

FIGURE 1

THE DEVELOPMENT OF SELF-RECOGNITION IN INFANCY. The graph shows the findings of two studies in which infants less than 1 year of age did not recognize themselves in the mirror. A slight increase in the percentage of infant self-recognition occurred around 15 to 18 months of age. By 2 years of age, a majority of children recognized themselves. *Why do researchers study whether infants recognize themselves in a mirror?*
Photo: Digital Vision/Getty Images

What characterizes young children's self-understanding?
Tatyana Aleksieva Photography/Getty Images

insecurely attached preschool children whose mothers reported a high level of parenting stress and depressive symptoms had a lower self-concept than other young children in more positive family circumstances (Goodvin & others, 2008). This research indicates that young children's generally optimistic self-ascriptions do not buffer them from adverse, stressful family conditions.

Understanding Others   Children also make advances in their understanding of others in infancy and early childhood (Landrum, Pflaum, & Mills, 2016; McDonald & Perdue, 2019). As we saw in the chapter on "Information Processing," young children's theory of mind includes understanding that other people have emotions and desires (Birch & others, 2017; Devine & Hughes, 2018). Research indicates that as early as 13 months of age, infants seem to consider another's perspective when predicting their actions (Choi & Luo, 2015).

At about 4 to 5 years, children not only start describing themselves in terms of psychological traits, but they also begin to perceive others in terms of psychological traits. Thus, a 4-year-old might say, "My teacher is nice."

An important part of children's socioemotional development is gaining an understanding that people don't always give accurate reports of their beliefs (Mills, 2013; Mills & Elashi, 2014). Researchers have found that even 4-year-olds understand that people may make statements that aren't true to obtain what they want or to avoid trouble (Lee & others, 2002). One study assessed preschool children's trust in the accuracy of an expert's comments (Landrum, Mills, & Johnston, 2013). In this study, in one condition, 5-year-olds trusted the expert's claim more than the 3-year-olds did. However, in other conditions, preschoolers tended to trust a nice non-expert more than a mean expert, indicating that young children often are more likely to believe someone who is nice to them than someone who is an expert.

Both the extensive theory of mind research and the recent research on infants' and young children's social understanding underscore that they are not as egocentric as Piaget envisioned (Birch & others, 2017; Sokol, Snjezana, & Muller, 2010; Thompson, 2012). Piaget's concept of egocentrism has become so ingrained in people's thinking about young children that too often the current research on social awareness in infancy and early childhood has been overlooked. Research increasingly shows that young children are more socially sensitive and perceptive than was previously envisioned, suggesting that parents and teachers can help them to better understand and interact in the social world by how they interact with them (Thompson, 2012, 2013). If young children are seeking to better understand various mental and emotional states (intentions, goals, feelings, desires) that they know underlie people's actions, then talking with them about these internal states can improve young children's understanding of them (Thompson, 2013).

However, there is ongoing debate about whether young children are socially sensitive or basically egocentric. Ross Thompson (2012, 2013) comes down on the side of viewing young children as socially sensitive, while Susan Harter (2012, 2013, 2016) argues that there is still evidence to support the conclusion that young children are essentially egocentric.

Young children are more psychologically aware of themselves and others than used to be thought. Some children are better than others at understanding people's feelings and desires, and to some degree, these individual differences are influenced by conversations caregivers have with young children about feelings and desires.
Don Hammond/DesignPics

Whichever side is taken in this debate, it is important to underscore that social interactions and relationships with others contribute significantly to young children's development of the self and understanding of others. In Thompson's (2013) view, "When caregivers exuberantly applaud their child's accomplishments, focus their young child's attention on the consequences of misbehavior, acknowledge shared intentions, work to repair affective mismatches, or talk with their child about emotions, they act as *relational catalysts*, fostering the child's socioemotional growth and helping to refine the child's representations of who they are (and) what other people are like . . ." (p. 113).

Middle and Late Childhood   Children's self-understanding becomes more complex during middle and late childhood (Carpendale & Lewis, 2015). And their social understanding, especially in taking the perspective of others, also increases.

Self-Understanding   Five key changes characterize the increased complexity of children's self-understanding in middle and late childhood:

· *Psychological characteristics and traits.* In middle and late childhood, especially from 8 to 11 years of age, children increasingly describe themselves in terms of psychological characteristics and traits, in contrast with the more concrete self-descriptions of younger children. Older children are more likely to describe themselves as "*popular, nice, helpful, mean, smart,* and *dumb*" (Harter, 2006, p. 526).

- *Social descriptions.* In middle and late childhood, children begin to include social aspects such as references to social groups in their self-descriptions (Harter, 2006). For example, a child might describe herself as a Girl Scout, as a Catholic, or as someone who has two close friends.

- *Social comparison.* Children's self-understanding in middle and late childhood includes increasing reference to social comparison (Harter, 2006). That is, elementary-school-age children increasingly think about what they can do in comparison with others.

- *Real self and ideal self.* In middle and late childhood, children begin to distinguish between their real and ideal selves (Harter, 2006). This change involves differentiating their actual competencies from those they aspire to have and think are the most important.

- *Realistic.* In middle and late childhood, children's self-evaluations become more realistic (Harter, 2006). This change may occur because of increased social comparison and perspective taking.

What are some changes in children's understanding of others in middle and late childhood?
Asiseeit/E+/Getty Images

Understanding Others   **Perspective taking** is especially thought to be important in determining whether children will develop prosocial or antisocial attitudes and behavior. In terms of prosocial behavior, taking another's perspective improves children's likelihood of understanding and sympathizing with others who are distressed or in need. In terms of antisocial behavior, recent research indicates that children and adolescents who do not have good perspective-taking skills are more likely to have difficulty in peer relations and to engage in more aggressive and oppositional behavior (Morosan & others, 2017; Nilsen & Bacso, 2017; O'Kearney & others, 2017).

Executive function is at work in perspective taking (Galinsky, 2010; Nilsen & Bacso, 2017). Among the executive functions called on when young children engage in perspective taking are cognitive inhibition (controlling one's own thoughts to consider the perspective of others) and cognitive flexibility (seeing situations in different ways).

In middle and late childhood, children become increasingly skeptical of some sources of information about psychological traits. A study of 6- to 9-year-olds revealed that older children were less trusting and more skeptical of others' distorted claims than were younger children (Mills & Elashi, 2014).

Adolescence   The development of self-understanding in adolescence is complex and involves a number of aspects of the self (Harter, 2012). The tendency to compare themselves with others continues to increase in the adolescent years. However, when asked whether they engage in social comparison, most adolescents deny it because they are aware that it is somewhat socially undesirable to do so.

Self-Understanding   Let's examine other ways in which the adolescent's self-understanding differs from the child's:

- *Abstract and idealistic thinking.* According to Piaget's theory of cognitive development, many adolescents begin thinking in more *abstract* and *idealistic* ways. When asked to describe themselves, adolescents are more likely than children to use abstract and idealistic labels. Consider 14-year-old Laurie's abstract description of herself: "I am a human being. I am indecisive. I don't know who I am." Also consider her idealistic description of herself: "I am a naturally sensitive person who really cares about people's feelings. I think I'm pretty good looking."

- *Self-consciousness.* Adolescents are more likely than children to be *self-conscious* and preoccupied with their self-understanding. This self-consciousness and self-preoccupation reflect adolescent egocentrism.

- *Contradictions within the self.* As adolescents begin to differentiate their concept of the self into multiple roles in different relationship contexts, they sense potential contradictions between their differentiated selves (Harter, 2006, 2012). An adolescent might use this self-description: "I'm moody *and* understanding, ugly *and* attractive, bored *and* inquisitive, caring *and* uncaring, and introverted *and* fun-loving" (Harter, 1986).

perspective taking The ability to assume another person's perspective and understand his or her thoughts and feelings.

How does self-understanding change in adolescence?
Image Source/Getty Images

Young adolescents tend to view these opposing characteristics as contradictory, which can cause internal conflict. However, older adolescents and emerging adults begin to understand that an individual can possess opposing characteristics and to integrate these opposing self-labels into their emerging identity (Harter, 2006, 2012).

- *The fluctuating self.* The adolescent's self-understanding fluctuates across situations and across time (Harter, 2006). The adolescent's self continues to be characterized by instability until the adolescent constructs a more unified theory of self, usually not until late adolescence or even early adulthood.

- *Real and ideal selves.* The adolescent's emerging ability to construct ideal selves in addition to actual ones can be perplexing and agonizing to the adolescent. In one view, an important aspect of the ideal or imagined self is the possible self—what individuals might become, what they would like to become, and what they are afraid of becoming (Markus & Kitayama, 2010, 2012; Markus & Nurius, 1986). Thus, adolescents' **possible selves** include both what adolescents hope to be and what they dread they will become (Aardema & others, 2018; Wainwright, Nee, & Vrij, 2018). The attributes of future positive selves (getting into a good college, being admired, having a successful career) can direct future positive states (Rathbone & others, 2016). The attributes of future negative selves (being unemployed, being lonely, not getting into a good college) can identify what is to be avoided. A study of adolescents in Hong Kong found that those reporting pragmatic support ("If I need to know something about the world, I can ask my parents," for example) had possible selves that were focused more on career and school, and they were more likely to think they could attain their hoped-for possible selves and avoid their feared possible selves (Zhu & others, 2014).

- *Self-integration.* In late adolescence and emerging adulthood, self-understanding becomes more integrative, with the disparate parts of the self more systematically pieced together (Harter, 2006, 2012, 2013). Older adolescents and emerging adults are more likely to detect inconsistencies in their earlier self-descriptions as they attempt to construct a general theory of self and an integrated sense of identity.

Understanding Others Of course, becoming a competent adolescent involves not only understanding oneself but also understanding others. Among the aspects of understanding others that are important in adolescent development are perceiving others' traits, understanding multiple perspectives, and monitoring their social world.

As adolescence proceeds, teenagers develop a more sophisticated understanding of others. They come to understand that other people are complex and have public and private faces (Harter, 2006, 2012).

According to Robert Selman (1980), developmental changes in perspective taking begin with the egocentric viewpoint in early childhood and end with in-depth perspective taking in adolescence.

In the chapter titled "Intelligence," you read that an important cognitive activity in metacognition is cognitive monitoring, which can also be very helpful in social situations (Roebers & Spiess, 2017). As part of their increased awareness of themselves and others, adolescents monitor their social world more extensively than they did when they were children. Adolescents engage in a number of social cognitive monitoring activities on virtually a daily basis. For example, an adolescent might think, "I would like to get to know this guy better but he is not very open. Maybe I can talk to some other students about what he is like." Another adolescent might check incoming information about a club or a clique to determine if it is consistent with her impressions of the club or clique. Yet another adolescent might question someone or paraphrase what the person has just said about her feelings to make sure that he has accurately understood them. Adolescents' ability to monitor their social world may be an important aspect of their social maturity (Flavell, 1979).

What are some important aspects of social understanding in adolescence?
SW Productions/Getty Images

possible selves What adolescents hope to become as well as what they dread they might become.

Adulthood As individuals move into the traditional college-age years and make the transition from adolescence to adulthood, they begin to engage in more self-reflection about what they want to do with their lives. The extended schooling that takes place in developed countries like the United States and Japan provides time for further self-reflection and self-understanding.

Self-Awareness   An aspect of self-understanding that becomes especially important in early adulthood is *self-awareness*—that is, the degree to which a young adult is aware of his or her psychological makeup, including strengths and weaknesses. Many individuals do not have very good awareness of their psychological makeup and skills, as well as the causes of their weaknesses (Hull, 2012). For example, how aware is the person that she or he is a good or bad listener, uses the best strategies to solve personal problems, and is assertive rather than aggressive or passive in resolving conflicts? Awareness of strengths and weaknesses in these and many other aspects of life is an important dimension of self-understanding throughout the adult years, and early adulthood is a time when individuals can benefit considerably from addressing some of their weaknesses.

Possible Selves   Another aspect of self-understanding that is important in the adult years involves possible selves (Barnett, Hernandez, & Melugin, 2019; Dark-Freudeman & West, 2016). Recall that possible selves are what individuals might become, what they would like to become, and what they are afraid of becoming (Dai & Li, 2018). Adults in their twenties mention many possible selves that they would like to become and might become. Some of these are unrealistic, such as being happy all of the time and being very rich. As individuals get older, they often describe fewer possible selves and portray them in more concrete and realistic ways. By middle age, individuals frequently describe their possible selves in terms of areas of their life in which they already have performed, such as "being good at my work" or "having a good marriage" (Cross & Markus, 1991). Also, when some individuals are middle-aged adults, their possible selves center on attaining hoped-for selves, such as acquiring material possessions, but when they become older adults, they are more concerned with maintaining what they have and preventing or avoiding health problems and dependency (Smith, 2009).

What characterizes self-awareness and possible selves in young adults?
wavebreakmedia/Shutterstock

Many individuals continue to revise their possible selves as they go through the adult years (Barnett, Hernandez, & Melugin, 2019; Croft, Schmader, & Block, 2019). This ability to revise possible selves and adapt them to find a better match between desired and achieved goals may be an important aspect of maintaining positive self-esteem and psychological well-being as individuals get older (Bengtson, Reedy, & Gordon, 1985).

Life Review   Another important aspect of self-understanding in adulthood is the *life review*. Life review is prominent in Erikson's final stage of psychosocial development, which is integrity versus despair. Life review involves looking back at one's life experiences, evaluating them, interpreting them, and often reinterpreting them. As the past marches in review, the older adult surveys it, observes it, and reflects on it. Reconsideration of previous experiences and their meaning occurs, often with revision or expanded understanding taking place. This reorganization of the past may provide a more valid picture for the individual, bringing new and significant meaning to one's life. It may also help prepare the individual for death and in the process reduce fear (Rubin, Parrish, & Miyawaki, 2019).

One aspect of life review involves identifying and reflecting on not only the positive aspects of one's life but also on regrets as part of developing a mature wisdom and self-understanding (Korte & others, 2014; Randall, 2013). The hope is that by examining not only the positive aspects of one's life but also what an individual has regretted doing, a more accurate vision of the complexity of one's life and possibly increased life satisfaction will be attained (King & Hicks, 2007).

Although thinking about regrets can be helpful as part of a life review, research indicates that it is important for older adults to not dwell on regrets, especially since opportunities to undo regrettable actions decline with age (Suri & Gross, 2012). One study revealed that an important characteristic of older adults who showed a higher level of emotion regulation and successful aging was reduced responsiveness to regrets (Brassen & others, 2012).

Some clinicians use *reminiscence therapy* with their older clients, which involves discussing past activities and experiences with another individual or group (Colombo, Balzarotti, & Greenwood, 2018; Ingersoll-Dayton & others, 2019). The therapy may include the use of photographs, familiar items, and video/audio recordings. Researchers have found that reminiscence therapy improves the mood and quality of life of older adults, including those with

> Know thyself, for once we know ourselves, we may learn how to care for ourselves, but otherwise we never shall.
>
> —SOCRATES
> *Greek Philosopher, 5th Century B.C.*

What characterizes a life review in late adulthood?
Corbis/VCG/Getty Images

dementia (Siverova & Buzgova, 2018; Yen & Lin, 2018). For example, a research review concluded that reminiscence therapy was effective in reducing depressive symptoms in older adults (Apostolo & others, 2016). Also, one study with older adults who had dementia found that reminiscence therapy reduced their depressive symptoms and improved their self-acceptance and positive relations with others (Gonzalez & others, 2015). In another study, a variation of reminiscence therapy called *instrumental* reminiscence therapy (recalling the times one coped with stressful circumstances and analyzing what it took to adapt in those contexts) improved the adaptive ability and resilience of older adults in coping with adverse situations (Meléndez & others, 2015). A recent study found that an instrumental reminiscence intervention improved the coping skills of older adults (Satorres & others, 2018). In another version of reminiscence therapy, *attachment-focused* reminiscence therapy reduced depressive symptoms, perceived stress, and emergency room visits in older African Americans (Sabir & others, 2016).

Successful aging, though, doesn't mean thinking about the past all of the time. In one study, older adults who were obsessed about the past were not as well adjusted as older adults who integrated their past and present (Wong & Watt, 1991).

SELF-ESTEEM AND SELF-CONCEPT

High self-esteem and a positive self-concept are important characteristics of children's and adults' well-being (Cloninger, 2019; Twenge & Campbell, 2020). **Self-esteem** refers to global evaluations of the self. Self-esteem is also referred to as *self-worth* or *self-image*. For example, a person may perceive that she or he is not merely a person but a *good* person. Of course, not all people have an overall positive image of themselves. **Self-concept** refers to domain-specific evaluations of the self. Individuals can make self-evaluations in many domains of their lives—academic, athletic, appearance, and so on. In sum, *self-esteem* refers to global self-evaluations, *self-concept* to domain-specific evaluations (Harter, 2006, 2012). Investigators sometimes use the terms *self-esteem* and *self-concept* interchangeably and don't always precisely define them. However, the distinction between self-esteem as global self-evaluation and self-concept as domain-specific self-evaluation should help you keep the terms straight. The foundations of self-esteem and self-concept emerge from the quality of parent-child interaction in infancy, childhood, and adolescence (Aremu, John-Akinola, & Desmennu, 2019; Ying & others, 2018). Children with high self-esteem are more likely to be securely attached to their parents and to have parents who engage in sensitive caregiving (Verschueren, 2019). In a longitudinal study, the quality of children's home environment (which involved assessment of parenting quality, cognitive stimulation, and the physical home environment) was linked to their self-esteem in early adulthood (Orth, 2017).

Issues in Self-Esteem   What are the consequences of low self-esteem? Low self-esteem has been implicated in overweight and obesity, anxiety, depression, suicide, and delinquency (Cruz-Saez & others, 2019; Gardner & Lambert, 2019; Levey & others, 2019; Moharei & others, 2018). One study revealed that youth with low self-esteem had lower life satisfaction at 30 years of age (Birkeland & others, 2012).

Is self-esteem related to school and adult job performance? There are "only modest correlations between school performance and self-esteem, and these correlations do not indicate that high self-esteem causes good performance" (Baumeister & others, 2003, p. 1). Attempts to increase students' self-esteem have not produced improvements in academic performance (Davies & Brember, 1999).

In some studies, adult job performance is linked to self-esteem, but the correlations vary greatly and the direction of the causation is not clear (Baumeister & others, 2003). Occupational success might lead to higher self-esteem, but people with high self-esteem also might be more likely to succeed than people with moderate or low self-esteem.

Is self-esteem related to happiness? Self-esteem is strongly related to happiness, and it seems likely that high self-esteem increases happiness, whereas depression lowers it (Stadelmann & others, 2017).

Is self-esteem related to physical appearance? Self-esteem is related to perceived physical appearance. For example, researchers have found that in adolescence, global self-esteem is

How is self-esteem related to school performance?
Fuse/Getty Images

self-esteem The global evaluative dimension of the self. Self-esteem is also referred to as self-worth or self-image.

self-concept Domain-specific evaluations of the self.

correlated more strongly with physical appearance than with scholastic competence, social acceptance, behavioral conduct, and athletic competence (Harter, 1999) (see Figure 2). This association between perceived physical appearance and self-esteem is not confined to adolescence but holds across the life span from early childhood through middle age (Harter, 1999, 2006).

Is low self-esteem linked to depression? A large number of studies have found that individuals with low self-esteem are more likely to report that they feel depressed than individuals with high self-esteem (Dietz, Silk, & Amole, 2019; Gardner & Lambert, 2019). One study revealed that low and decreasing self-esteem in adolescence was linked to adult depression two decades later (Steiger & others, 2014). Low self-esteem has also been implicated in suicide attempts and anorexia nervosa (Foster, Yequez & King, 2019; Pelletier-Brochu & others, 2018; Runfola & Lock, 2019).

Does self-esteem in adolescence foreshadow adjustment and competence in adulthood? A New Zealand longitudinal study assessed self-esteem at 11, 13, and 15 years of age and adjustment and competence of the same individuals when they were 26 years old (Trzesniewski & others, 2006). The results revealed that adults characterized by poorer mental and physical health, worse economic prospects, and higher levels of criminal behavior were more likely to have had low self-esteem in adolescence than their better-adjusted, more competent adult counterparts.

An important point needs to be made about much of the research on self-esteem: It is correlational rather than experimental. Correlation does not equal causation. Thus, if a correlational study finds an association between low self-esteem and depression, it could be equally likely that depression causes low self-esteem or that low self-esteem causes depression. Also, unmeasured third variables might account for an apparent correlation (for example, both depression and lower self-esteem might be jointly caused by family conflict). A longitudinal study explored whether self-esteem is a cause or consequence of social support in youth (Marshall & others, 2014). In this study, self-esteem predicted subsequent changes in social support, but social support did not predict subsequent changes in self-esteem.

Developmental Changes Self-esteem fluctuates across the life span (von Soest & others, 2018). One cross-sectional study assessed the self-esteem of a very large, diverse sample of 326,641 individuals ranging from 9 to 90 years of age (Robins & others, 2002). About two-thirds of the participants were from the United States. The individuals were asked to respond to the statement "I have high self-esteem" on a scale from 1 to 5 with 1 meaning "strongly agree" and 5 meaning "strongly disagree." This research focused on both developmental changes and gender differences. Self-esteem decreased in adolescence, increased in the twenties, leveled off in the thirties, rose in the fifties and sixties, and then dropped in the seventies and eighties (see Figure 3). In most age periods, the self-esteem of males was higher

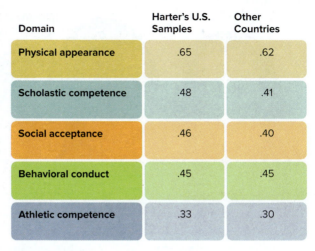

Domain	Harter's U.S. Samples	Other Countries
Physical appearance	.65	.62
Scholastic competence	.48	.41
Social acceptance	.46	.40
Behavioral conduct	.45	.45
Athletic competence	.33	.30

FIGURE 2

CORRELATIONS BETWEEN GLOBAL SELF-ESTEEM AND DOMAINS OF COMPETENCE. *Note:* The correlations shown are the average correlations computed across a number of studies. The other countries in this evaluation were England, Ireland, Australia, Canada, Germany, Italy, Greece, the Netherlands, and Japan. Correlation coefficients can range from −1.00 to +1.00. The correlations between physical appearance and global self-esteem (.65 and .62) are moderately high.

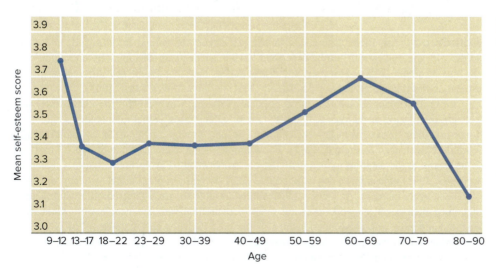

FIGURE 3

SELF-ESTEEM ACROSS THE LIFE SPAN.
One cross-sectional study found that self-esteem was high in childhood, dropped in adolescence, increased through early and middle adulthood, then dropped in the seventies and eighties (Robins & others, 2002). More than 300,000 individuals were asked the extent to which they have high self-esteem on a 5-point scale, with 5 being "Strongly Agree" and 1 being "Strongly Disagree."

Researchers have found that after 13 years of age, girls' self-esteem increases.
Ariel Skelley/Getty Images

Even when older adults have physical problems, other aspects of their lives, such as spending time with people whose company they enjoy, can help to buffer any decline in their self-esteem.
Westend61/Getty Images

than the self-esteem of females. Also, in a recent study of individuals in the second half of life, self-esteem peaked at 50 years of age and declined thereafter (von Soest & others, 2018). Let's now explore developmental changes in self-esteem in more detail.

Childhood and Adolescence   Researchers have found that the accuracy of self-evaluations increases across the elementary school years (Harter, 2006, 2012, 2016). Young children tend to provide inflated views of themselves, but by about 8 years of age most children give more realistic appraisals of their skills (Harter, 2006). For example, older elementary school children who report a positive self-image of their performance in sports indeed are the ones who are reported by peers to be good at athletics.

Adolescents in general have long been described as having low self-esteem (Robins & others, 2002). However, the majority of adolescents actually have a positive self-image. In an extensive cross-cultural study, Daniel Offer and his colleagues (1988) sampled the self-images of adolescents around the world—in the United States, Australia, Bangladesh, Hungary, Israel, Italy, Japan, Taiwan, Turkey, and West Germany. Almost three-fourths of the adolescents had a healthy self-image.

Some researchers note that gender differences in self-esteem emerge by early adolescence, and these were found in the study just described (Robins & others, 2002). Girls and boys enter first grade with roughly equivalent levels of self-esteem. Yet some research studies have shown that by the middle school years girls' self-esteem is significantly lower than boys' (American Association of University Women, 1992). For example, one study confirmed that male adolescents had higher self-esteem than female adolescents did (McLean & Breen, 2009).

However, other researchers caution that the self-esteem of girls is only slightly lower than boys' and still in the positive range (Harter, 2006, 2012, 2013, 2016; Kling & others, 1999). Researchers also have found that after age 13, girls' self-esteem increases through the remainder of adolescence and in emerging adulthood (Baldwin & Hoffman, 2002).

A current concern is that too many of today's college students grew up receiving empty praise and as a consequence have inflated self-esteem (Graham, 2005; Stipek, 2005). Too often they were given praise for performance that was mediocre or even poor. When they are in college, they may have difficulty handling competition and criticism. The title of a book, *Dumbing Down Our Kids: Why American Children Feel Good About Themselves But Can't Read, Write, or Add* (Sykes, 1995), vividly captures the theme that many U.S. children's academic problems stem from receiving unmerited praise as part of an effort to prop up their self-esteem. A similar theme—the promise of high self-esteem for students in education, especially those who are impoverished or marginalized—characterized a more recent book *Challenging the Cult of Self-Esteem in Education* (Bergeron, 2018). In a series of studies, researchers found that inflated praise, although well intended, may cause children with low self-esteem to avoid important learning experiences such as tackling challenging tasks (Brummelman & others, 2014). And one study found that narcissistic parents especially overvalue their children's talents (Brummelman & others, 2015).

Adulthood   Are there differences in the self-esteem of young, middle-aged, and older adults? In the self-esteem study described earlier, self-esteem dropped in late adulthood (Robins & others, 2002). However, some researchers have not found any differences in self-esteem across the age periods of adulthood (McGue, Hirsch, & Lykken, 1993).

Given that older adults have more physical problems, why wouldn't they have lower self-esteem than young or middle-aged adults? One possible reason is that many older adults don't interpret their "losses" as negatively, and don't become as emotionally upset, as younger adults would (Carstensen & Freund, 1994). For example, being asked to retire at age 63 may not be nearly as devastating as being fired from a job at 40. Furthermore, Laura Carstensen (1998, 2008) argues that knowledge-related goals decrease in older adults, whereas emotion-related goals increase. And many older adults are able to reach their emotion-related goals of honing their social network to spend most of their time with the people with whom they have enjoyed satisfying close relationships in the past (Scheibe & Carstensen, 2010). Finally, many older adults choose to compare themselves with other older adults rather than younger adults, which can help them maintain their positive self-image (Brandstadter, 1999).

Although older adults may derive self-esteem from earlier successes in some domains such as work and family, some aspects of their lives require continued support for self-esteem (Smith, 2009). For example, older adults' self-esteem benefits when they are told they are nice and accepted by others. One study revealed that older adults had higher self-esteem when they had a youthful identity and more positive personal experiences (Westerhof, Whitbourne, & Freeman, 2012).

Why might self-esteem decline for some older adults? Explanations include deteriorating physical health and negative societal attitudes toward older adults, although these factors were not examined in the large-scale study just described. Researchers have found that in late adulthood, being widowed, institutionalized, or physically impaired, having a low religious commitment, and experiencing a decline in health are linked to low self-esteem (Giarrusso & Bengtson, 2007). In a recent study, emotionally stable individuals' self-esteem declined the most in the second half of life (von Soest & others, 2018). In this study, not having a cohabiting partner, being unemployed, and having a disability each were associated with having a lower level of self-esteem and a steeper decline in self-esteem over a five-year period.

Strategies for Increasing Self-Esteem   What are some good strategies for increasing self-esteem? Five ways to improve self-esteem are (1) identify the causes of low self-esteem and the domains of competence important to the self; (2) provide emotional support and opportunities for social approval; (3) take responsibility for one's own self-esteem; (4) achieve goals; and (5) develop effective coping strategies.

Identifying sources of self-esteem—that is, competence in domains important to the self—is critical to improving self-esteem (Harter, 2012, 2016). Susan Harter (1990) points out that the self-esteem enhancement programs of the 1970s and 1980s, in which self-esteem itself was the target and individuals were encouraged to simply feel good about themselves, were ineffective. Rather, Harter notes that intervention must occur at the level of the *causes* of self-esteem if the individual's self-esteem is to improve significantly. Individuals have the highest self-esteem when they perform competently in domains that are important to them. Therefore, people should be encouraged to identify and value areas of competence.

Emotional support and social approval also powerfully influence self-esteem. Some children with low self-esteem come from conflicted families or conditions in which they experienced abuse or neglect—situations in which support was unavailable. In some cases, alternative sources of support can be implemented either informally through the encouragement of a teacher, a coach, or another significant adult, or more formally through programs such as Big Brothers and Big Sisters. As peer approval becomes increasingly important during adolescence, peer support is an important influence on the adolescent's self-esteem.

How can parents help children develop higher self-esteem?
Ariel Skelley/Getty Images

Developing self-confidence and believing that one has the ability to do what it takes to improve self-esteem are other good strategies. Although it is helpful to have the social support and emotional approval of others, it is also very important to take the initiative to increase one's own self-esteem.

Achievement can also improve an individual's self-esteem (Baumeister, 2013; Mruk & O'Brien, 2013). For example, self-esteem can be enhanced by the straightforward teaching of skills to individuals. People develop higher self-esteem when they know how to carry out the important tasks to accomplish goals and they realize that by carrying out these tasks they are more likely to reach their goals.

Self-esteem often increases when individuals face a problem and try to cope with it rather than avoid it (Burger, 2019; Mash & Wolfe, 2019). When coping prevails, the individual often faces problems realistically, honestly, and nondefensively. This process leads to favorable self-evaluative thoughts, which then lead to self-generated approval and higher self-esteem. The converse is true of low self-esteem. Unfavorable self-evaluations trigger denial, deception, and avoidance in an attempt to disavow that which has already been glimpsed as true. This process leads to self-generated disapproval as a form of feedback to the self about personal inadequacy.

SELF-REGULATION

Self-regulation involves the ability to control one's behavior without having to rely on others' help. Self-regulation includes the self-generation and cognitive monitoring of thoughts, feelings, and behaviors in order to reach a goal (McClelland, Cameron, & Alonso, 2019; Usher & Schunk, 2018;

self-regulation The ability to control one's behavior without having to rely on others for help.

Winne, 2018). An individual might develop better self-control in the physical, cognitive, or socio-emotional domain than in other domains.

Throughout most of the life span, individuals who engage in self-regulation are better achievers and are more satisfied with their lives than their counterparts who let external factors dominate their lives (Schunk & Greene, 2018; Turner & others, 2019). For example, researchers have found that, compared with low-achieving students, high-achieving students engage in greater self-regulation. They do this by setting more specific learning goals, using more strategies to learn and adapt, self-monitoring more, and more systematically evaluating their progress toward a goal (McClelland & others, 2017; Wigfield & others, 2015).

Infancy and Early Childhood   In the chapter on "Emotional Development and Attachment" we discussed the importance of children learning to regulate their emotions as they develop. Emotion regulation is an important aspect of the overall development of self-regulation (Cole, Ram, & English, 2019; Dollar & Calkins, 2019; Perry & Calkins, 2018). How do other aspects of self-regulation develop? Claire Kopp (1982, 1987, 2008) described a developmental process that begins early in life. Initially, beginning at about 12 to 18 months of age, infants depend completely on their caregivers for reminder signals about acceptable behaviors. At this age, infants begin to show compliance with caregivers' demands. For example, a parent might say, "No. Don't touch!" And the infant doesn't touch.

The next phase of developing self-regulation takes place at approximately 2 to 3 years of age. At this point, children begin to comply with the caregiver's expectations in the absence of external monitoring by the caregiver. Thus, most 2- to 3-year-old children are aware of where they may and may not play and which objects they may and may not touch if they are at home, on a playground, or in the homes of friends and relatives.

Nonetheless, at these young ages, there are clear limitations on self-regulation (Thompson, 2015). Given a strong stimulus, such as a ball rolling down the street or the motivation to explore an interesting place, toddlers often ignore safety and disregard exhortations. Also, only rudimentary aspects of delaying gratification are present at these early ages. For example, when 2-year-olds are confronted with an unexpected delay (such as not being able to go outside and play), they often whine and beg to engage in the activity. But there are clear signs of advances in self-initiated regulation, as when young children announce a toy cleanup without prompting from caregivers.

Preschoolers become better at self-control, learning how to resist temptation and giving themselves instructions that keep them focused (McClelland & Cameron, 2019; Thompson, 2015). Thus, toward the end of the preschool years, children might say to themselves, "No. I can't do that. I'm working," in response to a temptation to stop working and do something else, like play with an attractive toy.

Recent research confirms the importance of developing good self-control in early childhood as well as the role of parenting in the development of self-control (Cole, Ram, & English, 2019; Grolnick, Caruso, & Levitt, 2019). For example, in a recent study, low self-regulation in early childhood was linked to a higher level of externalizing problems in adolescence (Perry & others, 2018a). In further research, overcontrolling parenting at 2 years of age was related to lower emotion regulation at 5 years of age, which in turn was associated with emotional and school problems at age 10 (Perry & others, 2018b).

How does self-regulation change during childhood and adolescence?
Roy Botterell/Fuse/Getty Images

Middle/Late Childhood and Adolescence   One of the most important aspects of the self in middle and late childhood is an increased capacity for self-regulation (Schunk & Greene, 2018). This increased capacity is characterized by deliberate efforts to manage one's behavior, emotions, and thoughts that lead to increased social competence and achievement (Neuenschwander & Blair, 2017). In one study, higher levels of self-control assessed at 4 years of age were linked to improvements in the math and reading achievement of early-elementary-school children living in predominantly rural and low-income contexts (Blair & others, 2015). Also, one study revealed that children from low-income families who had a higher level of self-regulation earned better grades in school than their counterparts who had a lower level of self-regulation (Buckner, Mezzacappa, & Beardslee, 2009). Another study found that self-control increased from 4 to 10 years of age and that high self-control was linked to lower levels of deviant behavior (Vazsonyi & Huang, 2010).

Further, a longitudinal study found that a higher level of self-control in childhood was linked to a slower pace of aging (assessed with 18 biomarkers—cardiovascular and immune system, for example) at 26, 32, and 38 years of age (Belsky & others, 2017).

The increased capacity for self-regulation is linked to developmental advances in the brain's prefrontal cortex (Bell & others, 2018; Palacios-Barrios & Hanson, 2019). Increased focal activation in the prefrontal cortex is linked to improved cognitive control. Such cognitive control includes self-regulation (Blair, Raver, & Finegood, 2016). An app for iPads has been developed to help children improve their self-regulation: www.selfregulationstation.com/sr-ipad-app/.

How might self-regulation develop in adolescence? On the one hand, advances in cognitive skills (logical thinking, for example), increased introspection, and the greater independence of adolescence might lead to increased self-control. Also, advances in cognitive abilities provide adolescents with a better understanding of the importance of delaying gratification in exchange for something desirable (such as a good grade in a class) rather than seeking immediate gratification (listening to music rather than studying). On the other hand, factors such as an increased sense of invincibility (which can lead to risk taking and sensation seeking), impulsiveness, and social comparison might reduce self-control in this age group. In a recent study of more than 5,000 individuals from 10 to 30 years of age in 11 countries in Africa, Asia, Europe, and the Americas, sensation seeking increased steadily from 11 years of age through late adolescence, peaking at 19 years of age and declining through the twenties (Steinberg & others, 2019). However, in this study, self-regulation increased steadily from 11 years of age into emerging adulthood, reaching a plateau at 23 to 26 years of age.

As we indicated in the chapter on "Physical Development and Biological Aging," developmental changes in the brain are linked to self-regulation (Casey & others, 2019). Recall that the limbic system, which includes the amygdala, develops much earlier in adolescence and is associated with an increase in emotional and mood swings, as well as increases in sensation seeking and risk taking. However, the prefrontal cortex, which is at a higher level in the brain, continues to develop well into the emerging adult years and is the seat of self-regulation. Thus, during adolescence, the prefrontal cortex has not developed sufficiently to rein in the powerful emotions and passions connected with the limbic system's development.

Self-regulation is important in many aspects of adolescents' lives, including academic achievement, developing good health habits, not engaging in risky sexual behavior, and not binge drinking (Kang & You, 2018; Van Malderen & others, 2019). For example, a recent study found a reciprocal relation between school engagement and self-regulation in adolescence (Stefansson & others, 2018). Another recent study of middle school students indicated that self-control was a key factor in developing good health habits (Kang & You, 2018).

A key component of self-regulation is engaging in *effortful control*, which involves inhibiting impulses and not engaging in destructive behavior, focusing and maintaining attention despite distractions, and initiating and completing tasks that have long-term value, even if they may seem unpleasant (Kim & Kim, 2019; Qi, 2019). One study found that effortful control at 17 years of age predicted academic persistence and educational attainment at 23 to 25 years of age (Veronneau & others, 2014). In this study, effortful control was just as strong a predictor of educational attainment as were past grade point averages and parents' educational levels. And a study of Mexican American adolescents revealed that effortful control was linked to coping with stress more effectively (Taylor, Widaman, & Robins, 2017). Further, a recent study found a bidirectional pattern between effortful control and school behavioral problems in fifth- to eleventh-graders; that is, low effortful control was associated with increases in school behavioral problems, and school behavioral problems were linked to decreases in effortful control (Atherton & others, 2019). And a recent meta-analysis of children up to 18 years of age found that those who were securely attached to their parents had better effortful control (Pallini & others, 2018).

Some researchers emphasize the early development of self-regulation in childhood and adolescence as a key contributor to adult health and even longevity (Weinstein & others, 2019). For example, Nancy Eisenberg and her colleagues (2014) concluded that research indicates self-regulation fosters conscientiousness later in life, both directly and through its link to academic motivation/success and internalized compliance with norms.

Adulthood Self-control plays an important role in adult development (Dixon & Lachman, 2019; Shah, 2017). For example, higher levels of self-control are linked to better health and adjustment (Bercovitz, Ngnoumen, & Langer, 2019; Lachman, Agrigoroaei, & Hahn, 2016).

developmental **connection**

Information Processing

Cognitive control (inhibition and flexibility) increases from childhood through early adulthood. Connect to "Information Processing."

According to selective optimization with compensation theory, what characterizes successful aging?
Ariel Skelley/Blend Images/Getty Images

selective optimization with compensation theory The theory that successful aging involves three strategies: selection, optimization, and compensation.

Self-control increases in early and middle adulthood (Agrigoroaei & others, 2018). Researchers have found a decline in perceived self-control of health and cognitive functioning in older adults (Bertrand, Graham, & Lachman, 2013).

Although older adults are aware of age-related losses, most still effectively maintain a sense of self-control. Recent research indicates that self-control plays an important role in older adults' quality of life, including lower levels of depression and obesity (Bercovitz, Ngnoumen, & Langer, 2019; Zanto & Gazzaley, 2017). The negative effects of age-typical problems, such as a decline in physical and cognitive skills and an increase in illness, may be buffered by a flexible, accommodating control style (Brandstädter & Renner, 1990). Also, in a recent study, older adults who had a higher daily level of self-control perceived themselves to be younger (Bellingtier & Neupert, 2019).

Selective optimization with compensation theory states that successful aging is linked with three main factors: selection, optimization, and compensation (SOC). The theory states that individuals can produce new resources and allocate them effectively to tasks they want to master (Baltes & Smith, 2008; Nikitin & Freund, 2019).

Selection, optimization, and compensation involve the following:

· *Selection* is based on the concept that older adults have a reduced capacity and a loss of functioning, which require a reduction in performance in most life domains such as memory and physical skills.

· *Optimization* suggests that it is possible to maintain performance in some areas through continued practice and the use of new technologies. Examples might include doing crossword puzzles to maintain memory skills and exercising to optimize strength.

· *Compensation* becomes relevant when life tasks require a level of capacity beyond the current level of the older adult's performance potential. Older adults especially need to compensate in circumstances that impose high mental or physical demands, such as when thinking about and memorizing new material very rapidly, reacting quickly when driving a car, or running fast. When older adults develop an illness, the need for compensation increases.

Selective optimization with compensation theory was proposed by Paul Baltes and his colleagues (Baltes, 2003; Baltes, Lindenberger, & Staudinger, 2006). They described the life of the pianist Arthur Rubinstein (1887–1982) to illustrate their theory. When he was interviewed at 80 years of age, Rubinstein said that three factors were responsible for his ability to maintain his status as an admired concert pianist into old age. First, he mastered the weakness of old age by reducing the scope of his performances and playing fewer pieces (which reflects selection). Second, he spent more time at practice than he had spent earlier in his life (which reflects optimization). Third, he used special strategies, such as slowing down before fast segments, thus creating the illusion of faster playing (which reflects compensation).

The process of selective optimization with compensation is likely to be effective whenever people pursue successful outcomes (Alonso-Fernandez & others, 2016; Marquez-Gonzalez, Cheng, & Losada, 2019; Nitikin & Freund, 2019). In a study of individuals from 22 to 94 years of age, middle-aged and older adults, as well as individuals who were less healthy, reported higher levels of happiness on days when they used more selective optimization with compensation strategies (Teshale & Lachman, 2016).

What makes SOC attractive to researchers in aging is that it makes explicit how individuals can manage and adapt to losses (Miller, 2016; Nikitin & Freund, 2019). By using SOC, they can continue to lead satisfying lives, although in a more restricted manner. Loss is a common dimension of old age, although there are wide variations in the nature of the losses involved. Because of these individual variations, the specific form of selection, optimization, and compensation will likely vary depending on the person's life history, pattern of interests, values, health, skills, and resources. To read about some strategies for effectively engaging in selective optimization with compensation, see the *Connecting Development to Life* interlude.

In Baltes' view (Baltes & Smith, 2008), the selection of domains and life priorities is an important aspect of development. Life goals and priorities likely vary across the life course for most people. For many individuals, it is not just the sheer attainment of goals, but rather the attainment of *meaningful* goals, that makes life satisfying. In one study, younger adults were more likely to assess their well-being in terms of accomplishments and careers, whereas older adults were more likely to link well-being with good health and the ability to accept change.

connecting development to life

Strategies for Effectively Engaging in Selective Optimization with Compensation

What are some good strategies that aging adults can use to attain selective optimization with compensation? According to Paul Baltes and his colleagues (Baltes, Lindenberger, & Staudinger, 2006; Freund & Baltes, 2002), the following strategies are likely to be effective:

Selection Strategies

· Focus on the most important goal at a particular time.
· Think about what you want in life, and commit yourself to one or two major goals.
· Realize that to reach a particular goal, you may need to abandon other goals.

Optimization Strategies

· Keep working on what you have planned until you are successful.
· Persevere until you reach your goal.

· When you want to achieve something, understand that you may need to wait until the right moment arrives.

Compensation

· When things don't go the way they used to, search for other ways to achieve what you want.
· If things don't go well for you, be willing to let others help you.
· When things don't go as well as in the past, keep trying other ways until you can achieve results that are similar to what you accomplished earlier in your life.

Which of the selection, optimization, and compensation strategies have you used? Which of the strategies would you benefit from using more?

In addition, emotion-related goals become increasingly important for older adults (Carstensen, 2019; Carstensen, Smith, & Jaworski, 2015; Carstensen & others, 2011).

In one cross-sectional study, the personal life investments of 25- to 105-year-olds were assessed (Staudinger, 1996) (see Figure 4). From 25 to 34 years of age, participants said that they personally invested more time in work, friends, family, and independence, in that order. From 35 to 54 and 55 to 65 years of age, family became more important to them than friends in terms of their personal investment. Little changed in the rank ordering of persons 70 to 84 years old, but for participants 85 to 105 years old, health became the most important personal investment. Thinking about life showed up for the first time on the most important list for those who were 85 to 105 years old.

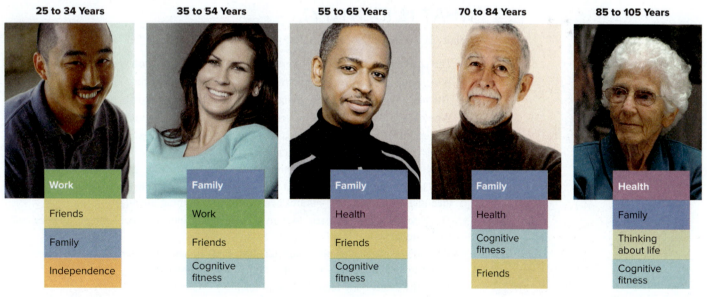

FIGURE 4

DEGREE OF PERSONAL LIFE INVESTMENT AT DIFFERENT POINTS IN LIFE. Shown here are the top four domains of personal life investment at different points in life. The highest degree of investment is listed at the top (for example, work was the highest personal investment from 25 to 34 years of age, family from 35 to 84, and health from 85 to 105).
(*left to right*): Ryan McVay/Getty Images; image100/PunchStock; Image Source/Getty Images; Fuse/Getty Images; Realistic Reflections

Review *Connect* Reflect

LG1 Discuss the main ways the self and understanding others are conceptualized and how they develop.

Review

- What is self-understanding, and how does it develop? How does understanding others develop?
- What are self-esteem and self-concept, and how do they develop? How is self-esteem related to performance, initiative, and happiness? Is there a dark side to high self-esteem? What are some ways to increase self-esteem?
- What is self-regulation, and how does it develop?

Connect

- How might the life reflection of older adults differ from the life reflection of individuals in middle adulthood?

Reflect *Your Own Personal Journey of Life*

- If a psychologist had interviewed you when you were 8 years old, 14 years old, and again today, would your self-understanding and self-esteem have been different at each of these ages?

2 Identity

LG2 Explain the key facets of identity development.

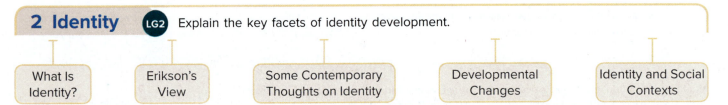

| What Is Identity? | Erikson's View | Some Contemporary Thoughts on Identity | Developmental Changes | Identity and Social Contexts |

Who am I? What am I all about? What am I going to do with my life? What is different about me? How can I make it on my own? These questions reflect the search for an identity. By far the most comprehensive and provocative theory of identity development is Erik Erikson's. In this section, we examine his views on identity and some contemporary thoughts on identity. We also discuss research on how identity develops and how social contexts influence that development.

identity versus identity confusion Erikson's fifth stage of development, which occurs during the adolescent years; adolescents are faced with finding out who they are, what they are all about, and where they are going in life.

WHAT IS IDENTITY?

Identity is a self-portrait composed of many pieces, including the following:

- The career and work path the person wants to follow (vocational/career identity)
- Whether the person is conservative, liberal, or middle-of-the-road (political identity)
- The person's spiritual beliefs (religious identity)
- Whether the person is single, married, divorced, and so on (relationship identity)
- The extent to which the person is motivated to achieve and is intellectually active (achievement, intellectual identity)
- Whether the person is heterosexual, homosexual, bisexual, or transgendered
- Which part of the world or country a person is from and how intensely the person identifies with his or her cultural heritage (cultural/ethnic identity)
- The kinds of things a person likes to do, which can include sports, music, hobbies, and so on (interests)
- The individual's personality characteristics, such as being introverted or extraverted, anxious or calm, friendly or hostile, and so on (personality)
- The individual's body image (physical identity)

When identity development has been studied, researchers mostly have looked at it in a general way rather than examining how variations in the timing and nature of identity development might vary for these different components of identity. Currently, too little research attention has been given to these and other domains of identity (Galliher, McLean, & Syed, 2017).

What are some important dimensions of identity?
Digital Vision/Getty Images

ERIKSON'S VIEW

Questions about identity surface as common, virtually universal, concerns during adolescence. Some decisions made during adolescence might seem trivial, such as whom to date, whether or not to break up, which major to study, whether to study or play, whether or not to be politically active, and so on. Over the years of adolescence, however, such decisions begin to form the core of what the individual is all about as a human being—what is called his or her identity.

It was Erik Erikson (1950, 1968) who first understood the importance of identity questions to understanding adolescent development. Identity is now believed to be a key aspect of adolescent development because of Erikson's masterful thinking and analysis. His ideas reveal rich insights into adolescents' thoughts and feelings, and reading one or more of his books is worthwhile. A good starting point is *Identity: Youth and Crisis* (1968).

According to Erikson's theory, adolescents go through a developmental stage that he called **identity versus identity confusion.** Erikson states that in this fifth of his eight stages in the life span, adolescents are faced with deciding who they are, what they are all about, and where they are going in life. These questions about identity occur throughout life, but they become especially important for adolescents. Erikson maintains that adolescents face an overwhelming number of choices. As they gradually come to realize that they will be responsible for themselves and their own lives, adolescents search for what those lives are going to be.

The search for an identity during adolescence is aided by a **psychosocial moratorium,** which is Erikson's term for the gap between childhood security and adult autonomy. During this period, society leaves adolescents relatively free of responsibilities, which allows them to try out different identities. Adolescents in effect search their culture's identity files, experimenting with different roles and personalities. They may want to pursue one career one month (lawyer, for example) and another career the next month (doctor, actor, teacher, social worker, or astronaut, for example). They may dress neatly one day, sloppily the next. This experimentation is a deliberate effort on the part of adolescents to find out where they fit into the world. Most adolescents eventually discard undesirable roles.

Youth who successfully cope with conflicting identities emerge with a new sense of self that is both refreshing and acceptable. Adolescents who do not successfully resolve this identity crisis suffer what Erikson calls identity confusion. The confusion takes one of two courses: Individuals withdraw, isolating themselves from peers and family, or they immerse themselves in the world of peers and lose their identity in the crowd.

> "Who are you?" said the caterpillar. Alice replied rather shyly, "I—I hardly know, sir, just at present—at least I know who I was when I got up this morning, but I must have changed several times since then."
>
> —LEWIS CARROLL
> *English Writer, 19th Century*

Erik Erikson.
Bettmann/Getty Images

SOME CONTEMPORARY THOUGHTS ON IDENTITY

Contemporary views of identity development suggest that it is a lengthy process, in many instances more gradual and less cataclysmic than Erikson's use of the term *crisis* implies (Syed, Juang, & Svensson, 2018; Neblett, Roth, & Syed, 2019; Vosylis, Erentaite, & Crocetti, 2018). Resolution of the identity issue during adolescence and emerging adulthood does not mean that identity will be stable through the remainder of one's life. An individual who develops a healthy identity is flexible and adaptive, open to changes in society, in relationships, and in careers. This openness ensures numerous reorganizations of identity throughout the individual's life.

Identity formation neither happens neatly nor is it usually cataclysmic (Palmeroni & others, 2019). At the bare minimum, it involves commitment to a vocational direction, an ideological stance, and a sexual orientation. Synthesizing the components of identity can be a long, drawn-out process, with many negations and affirmations of various roles. Identity development happens in bits and pieces. Decisions are not made once and for all, but must be made again and again (Kroger, 2016).

One way that researchers are examining identity changes in depth is to use a *narrative approach*. This involves asking individuals to tell their life stories and evaluate the extent to which their stories are meaningful and integrated (Sauchelli, 2018; Svensson, Berne, & Syed, 2018; Wicks, Berger, & Camic, 2019). The term *narrative identity* "refers to the stories people construct and tell about themselves to define who they are for themselves and others. Beginning in adolescence and young

psychosocial moratorium Erikson's term for the gap between childhood security and adult autonomy that adolescents experience as part of their identity exploration.

What are some contemporary thoughts about identity formation and development?
Somos/Veer/Caroline Mowry/Getty Images

adulthood, our narrative identities are the stories we live by" (McAdams, Josselson, & Lieblich, 2006, p. 4). One study using the narrative identity approach revealed that from age 11 to 18, boys increasingly engaged in thinking about the meaningfulness of their lives, especially meaning related to the self as changing (McLean, Breen, & Fournier, 2010). In other research, relationship, autonomy, and mortality events were important contributors to searching for a meaningful identity in late adolescence and emerging adulthood (McLean & Pratt, 2006; McLean & others, 2018). There also is increasing evidence that the effective management of difficult life events and circumstances contributes to the development of a meaningful identity in emerging adulthood (Pals, 2006).

In one study, researchers used both identity status and narrative approaches to examine college students' identity domains. In both approaches, the interpersonal domain was most frequently described (McLean & others, 2016). In the interpersonal domain, dating and friendships were frequently mentioned, although there was no mention of gender roles. In the narrative domain, family stories were common.

DEVELOPMENTAL CHANGES

Although questions about identity may be especially important during adolescence and emerging adulthood, identity formation neither begins nor ends during these years (Blake, 2019; Bogaerts & others, 2019; Feliciano & Rumbaut, 2019). It begins with the appearance of attachment, the development of the sense of self, and the emergence of independence in infancy; the process reaches its final phase with a life review and integration in old age. But for Erikson, it is in adolescence that identity begins to be a key dimension of individuals' lives. Why might that be so? What is important about identity development in adolescence, especially late adolescence, is that for the first time, physical development, cognitive development, and socioemotional development advance to the point at which the individual can sort through and synthesize childhood identities and identifications to construct a viable path toward adult maturity.

Identity Statuses   How do individual adolescents go about the process of forming an identity? Eriksonian researcher James Marcia (1980, 1994) analyzed Erikson's theory of identity development and concluded that it involves four statuses of identity, or ways of resolving the identity crisis: identity diffusion, identity foreclosure, identity moratorium, and identity achievement. What determines an individual's identity status? Marcia classifies individuals based on the existence or extent of their crisis or commitment (see Figure 5). **Crisis** is defined as a period of identity development during which the individual explores alternatives. Most researchers use the term *exploration* rather than *crisis*. **Commitment** is a personal investment in identity.

The four statuses of identity are as follows:

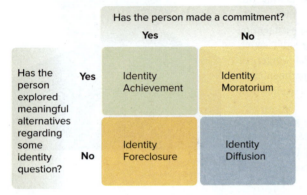

FIGURE 5

MARCIA'S FOUR STATUSES OF IDENTITY

crisis A period of identity development during which the individual is exploring alternatives.

commitment A personal investment in identity.

identity diffusion Marcia's term for the status of individuals who have not yet experienced a crisis (explored meaningful alternatives) or made any commitments.

identity foreclosure Marcia's term for the status of individuals who have made a commitment but have not experienced a crisis.

identity moratorium Marcia's term for the status of individuals who are in the midst of a crisis but whose commitments are either absent or vaguely defined.

identity achievement Marcia's term for the status of individuals who have undergone a crisis and have made a commitment.

- **Identity diffusion** is the status of individuals who have not yet experienced a crisis or made any commitments. Not only are they undecided about occupational and ideological choices, but they are also likely to show little interest in such matters.

- **Identity foreclosure** is the status of individuals who have made a commitment but have not experienced a crisis. This occurs most often when parents hand down commitments to their adolescents, usually in an authoritarian way, before adolescents have had a chance to explore different approaches, ideologies, and vocations on their own.

- **Identity moratorium** is the status of individuals who are in the midst of a crisis but whose commitments are either absent or only vaguely defined.

- **Identity achievement** is the status of individuals who have undergone a crisis and have made a commitment.

Let's explore some examples of Marcia's identity statuses. Thirteen-year-old Sarah has neither begun to explore her identity in any meaningful way nor made an identity commitment; she is *identity diffused*. Eighteen-year-old Tim's parents want him to be a medical doctor, so he is planning on majoring in premedicine in college and has not explored other options; he is *identity foreclosed*. Nineteen-year-old Sasha is not quite sure what life paths she wants to follow, but she recently went to the counseling center at her college to find out about different careers; she is in *identity moratorium* status. Twenty-one-year-old Marcelo extensively explored several career options in college, eventually getting his degree in science education, and is looking forward to his first year of teaching high school students; he is *identity achieved*. These examples focused on the career dimension of identity, but keep in mind that identity has a number of dimensions.

During early adolescence, most youth are primarily in the identity statuses of *diffusion, foreclosure*, or *moratorium*. According to Marcia (1987, 1996), at least three aspects of the young adolescent's development are important to identity formation. Young adolescents must be confident that they have parental support, must have an established sense of industry, and must be able to take a self-reflective stance toward the future.

Belgian psychologists Luc Goossens, Koen Luyckx, and their colleagues (Goossens & Luyckx, 2007; Luyckx & others, 2014, 2017, 2018) have proposed an extension of Marcia's concepts of exploration and commitment. The revisionist theorizing stresses that effective identity development involves evaluating identity commitments on a continuing basis. Some critics argue that the identity status approach does not produce enough depth in understanding identity development (Syed, Juang, & Svensson, 2018; Vosylis, Erentaite, & Crocetti, 2018). The newer *dual cycle identity model* separates out identity development into two separate processes: (1) a formation cycle that relies on exploration in breadth and identification with commitment; and (2) a maintenance cycle that involves exploration in depth as well as reconsideration of commitments (Luyckz & others, 2014, 2017).

For example, consider a first-year college student who makes a commitment to become a lawyer. Exploring this commitment in depth might include finding out as much as possible about what is involved in being a lawyer, such as educational requirements, the work conducted by lawyers in different areas, what types of college classes might be beneficial for this career, and so on. It might also include talking with several lawyers about their profession. As a result of this in-depth exploration, the college student may become more confident that being a lawyer is the career that best suits her. As she goes through the remainder of her college years, she will continue to evaluate the commitment she has made to becoming a lawyer and may change her commitment as she continues to gather new information and reflect on the life path she wants to take. In one study, planfulness was a consistent predictor of engagement in identity exploration and commitment (Luyckx & Robitschek, 2014).

Researchers have developed a consensus that the key changes in identity are most likely to take place in emerging adulthood, the period from about 18 to 25 years of age, not during adolescence (Arnett, 2016; Klimstra & others, 2018; Neblett, Roth, & Syed, 2019; McLean & others, 2018). One study found that as individuals matured from early adolescence to emerging adulthood, they increasingly engaged in in-depth exploration of their identity (Klimstra & others, 2010). Alan Waterman (1985, 1992) has found that from the years preceding high school through the last few years of college, the number of individuals who are identity achieved increases, whereas the number of individuals who are identity diffused decreases. Many young adolescents are identity diffused. College upperclassmen are more likely than high school students or college freshmen to be identity achieved.

Why might college produce some key changes in identity? Increased complexity in the reasoning skills of college students combined with a wide range of new experiences that highlight contrasts between home and college and between themselves and others stimulate them to reach a higher level of integrating various dimensions of their identity (Phinney, 2008). College contexts serve as a virtual "laboratory" for identity development through such experiences as diverse coursework and exposure to peers from diverse backgrounds. Also, one of emerging adulthood's key themes is not having many social commitments, which gives individuals considerable independence in developing a life path (Arnett, 2012, 2016; Arnett & Fischel, 2013).

A meta-analysis of 124 studies revealed that during adolescence and emerging adulthood, identity moratorium status rose steadily to age 19 and then declined; identity achievement rose across late adolescence and emerging adulthood; and foreclosure and diffusion statuses declined across the high school years but fluctuated in the late teens and emerging adulthood (Kroger, Martinussen, & Marcia, 2010). The studies also found that a large portion of individuals were not identity achieved by the time they reached their twenties.

Resolution of the identity issue during adolescence and emerging adulthood does not mean that

How does identity change in emerging adulthood?
Monkey Business Images/Shutterstock

identity will be stable through the remainder of life (Feliciano & Rumbaut, 2019; Kroger, 2016). Many individuals who develop positive identities follow what are called "MAMA" cycles; that is, their identity status changes from *moratorium* to *achievement* to *moratorium* to *achievement* (Marcia, 1994). These cycles may be repeated throughout life (Francis, Fraser, & Marcia, 1989). Marcia (2002) points out that the first identity is just that—it is not, and should not be expected to be, the final product.

Researchers have shown that identity consolidation—the process of refining and enhancing the identity choices that are made in emerging adulthood—continues well into early adulthood and possibly into the early part of middle adulthood (Feliciano & Rumbaut, 2019; Kroger, 2016). Further, as individuals move from early to middle adulthood they become more certain about their identity. For example, a longitudinal study of college women found that identity certainty increased from the thirties through the fifties (Stewart, Ostrove, & Helson, 2001).

IDENTITY AND SOCIAL CONTEXTS

Social contexts influence an adolescent's identity development (Cheon & others, 2018; Medina, Rowley, & Towson, 2019; Umana-Taylor & others, 2018; van der Does & Adem, 2019). Questions we will explore in this regard are: Do family relationships influence identity development? What roles do peers, romantic relationships, and the digital world play in identity formation? How are culture and ethnicity linked to identity development?

developmental **connection**

Attachment

Even while adolescents seek autonomy, attachment to parents is important; secure attachment in adolescence is linked to a number of positive outcomes. Connect to "Emotional Development and Attachment."

Family Processes   Parents are important figures in the adolescent's development of identity (Cooper, 2011; Crocetti & others, 2017). For example, one study found that poor communication between mothers and adolescents, as well as persistent conflicts with friends, was linked to less positive identity development (Reis & Youniss, 2004). Catherine Cooper and her colleagues (Cooper, 2011; Cooper, Behrens, & Trinh, 2009; Cooper & Grotevant, 1989) have found that a family atmosphere that promotes both individuality and connectedness is important to the adolescent's identity development:

- **Individuality** consists of two dimensions: self-assertion, which is the ability to have and communicate a point of view; and separateness, which is the use of communication patterns to express how one is different from others.
- **Connectedness** also consists of two dimensions: mutuality, which involves sensitivity to and respect for others' views; and permeability, which involves openness to others' views.

Identity and Peer/Romantic Relationships   Researchers have recently found that the capacity to explore one's identity during adolescence and emerging adulthood is linked to the quality of friendships and romantic relationships (Quimby & others, 2018; Rivas-Drake & others, 2017; Rivas-Drake & Umana-Taylor, 2017). For example, one study found that an open, active exploration of identity when adolescents are comfortable with close friends contributes to the positive quality of the friendship (Doumen & others, 2012). In another study, friends were often a safe context for exploring identity-related experiences, providing a means of testing how self-disclosing comments are viewed by others (McLean & Jennings, 2012).

In terms of links between identity and romantic relationships in adolescence and emerging adulthood, two individuals in a romantic relationship are both in the process of constructing their own identities and each person provides the other with a context for identity exploration (Pittman & others, 2011). The extent of their secure attachment with each other can influence how each partner constructs his or her own identity.

Identity Development and the Digital Environment   For today's adolescents and emerging adults, the contexts involving the digital world, especially social media platforms such as Instagram, Snapchat, and Facebook, have introduced new ways for youth to express and explore their identity (Davis & Weinstein, 2017). Adolescents and emerging adults often cast themselves as positively as they can on their digital devices—posting their most attractive photos and describing themselves in idealistic ways, along the way editing and reworking their online self-portraits to enhance them. Adolescents' and emerging adults' online world provides extensive opportunities for both expressing their identity and getting feedback about it. Of course, such feedback is not always positive, just as in their offline world. We will have much more to say about the roles of social media in adolescence and emerging adulthood in "Peers and the Sociocultural World."

individuality Characteristic consisting of two dimensions: self-assertion, the ability to have and communicate a point of view; and separateness, the use of communication patterns to express how one is different from others.

connectedness Characteristic consisting of two dimensions: mutuality, which is sensitivity to and respect for others' views; and permeability, which is openness to others' views.

Cultural and Ethnic Identity   Most research on identity development has historically been based on data obtained from adolescents and emerging adults in the United States and Canada, especially those who are non-Latino Whites (Gyberg & others, 2018; Nelson & others, 2018). Many of these individuals have grown up in cultural contexts that value individual autonomy. However, in many countries around the world, adolescents and emerging adults have grown up influenced by a collectivist emphasis on fitting in with the group and connecting with others (Polenova & others, 2018). The collectivist emphasis is especially prevalent in East Asian countries such as China. Researchers have found that self-oriented identity exploration may not be the main process through which identity achievement is attained in East Asian countries (Schwartz & others, 2012). Rather, East Asian adolescents and emerging adults may develop their identity through identification with and imitation of others in their cultural group (Bosma & Kunnen, 2001). The emphasis on interdependence in East Asian cultures includes an emphasis on adolescents and emerging adults accepting and embracing social and family roles (Berman & others, 2011). Thus, some patterns of identity development, such as the foreclosed status, may be more adaptive in East Asian countries than in North American countries (Cheng & Berman, 2012).

Identity development may take longer in some countries than in others (Azmitia, 2016). For example, research indicates that Italian youth may postpone significant identity exploration beyond adolescence and emerging adulthood, not settling on an identity until their mid- to late-twenties (Crocetti, Rabaglietti, & Sica, 2012). This delayed identity development is strongly influenced by many Italian youth living at home with their parents until 30 years of age and older.

Seth Schwartz and his colleagues (2012) pointed out that while everyone identifies with a particular "culture," many individuals in cultural majority groups take their cultural identity for granted. Thus, many adolescents and emerging adults in the cultural majority of non-Latino Whites in the United States likely don't spend much time thinking of themselves as "White American." However, for many adolescents and emerging adults who have grown up as a member of an ethnic minority group in the United States or emigrated from another country, cultural dimensions likely are an important aspect of their identity. Researchers have found that at both the high school and college level, Latino students were more likely than non-Latino White students to indicate that their cultural identity was an important dimension of their overall self-concept (Urdan, 2012).

Throughout the world, ethnic minority groups have struggled to maintain their ethnic identities while blending in with the dominant culture (Benet-Martinez & Nguyen, 2019; Erikson, 1968; Gonzalez, 2019). **Ethnic identity** is an enduring aspect of the self that includes a sense of membership in an ethnic group, along with the attitudes and feelings related to that membership (Medina, Rowley, & Towson, 2019; Polenova & others, 2018; Song, 2019; White & others, 2018). Thus, for adolescents from ethnic minority groups, the process of identity formation has an added dimension: the choice between two or more sources of identification—their own ethnic group and the mainstream, or dominant, culture (Abu-Rayya & others, 2018; Neblett, Roth, & Syed, 2019). Many adolescents resolve this choice by developing a **bicultural identity.** That is, they identify in some ways with their ethnic group and in other ways with the majority culture (Benet-Martinez & Nguyen, 2019). A study of Mexican American and Asian American college students found that they identified both with the American mainstream culture and with their culture of origin (Devos, 2006).

Time is another aspect that influences ethnic identity. The indicators of identity often differ for each succeeding generation of immigrants (Phinney, 2006; Phinney & Vedder, 2013). First-generation immigrants are likely to be secure in their identities and unlikely to change much; they may or may not develop a new identity. The degree to which they begin to feel "American" appears to be related to whether or not they learn English, develop social networks beyond their ethnic group, and become culturally competent in their new country. Second-generation immigrants are more likely to think of themselves as "American"—possibly because citizenship is granted at birth. For second-generation immigrants, ethnic identity is likely to be linked to retention of their ethnic language and social networks. In the third and later generations, the issues become more complex. Broad social factors may affect the extent to which members of this generation retain their ethnic identities. For example, media images may influence whether members of an ethnic group will continue to identify with their group and retain parts of its culture. Discrimination may force people to see themselves as cut off from the majority group and encourage them to seek the support of their own ethnic culture.

Researchers are also increasingly finding that a positive ethnic identity is related to positive outcomes for ethnic minority adolescents (Anglin & others, 2018; Umana-Taylor, 2019; Umana-Taylor & others, 2018). For example, one study found that Asian American adolescents' ethnic identity was associated with high self-esteem, positive relationships, academic

One adolescent girl, 16-year-old Michelle Chin, made these comments about ethnic identity development: "My parents do not understand that teenagers need to find out who they are, which means a lot of experimenting, a lot of mood swings, a lot of emotions and awkwardness. Like any teenager, I am facing an identity crisis. I am still trying to figure out whether I am a Chinese American or an American with Asian eyes." *What are some other aspects of developing an ethnic identity in adolescence?*
Red Chopsticks/Getty Images

ethnic identity An enduring aspect of the self that includes a sense of membership in an ethnic group, along with the attitudes and feelings related to that membership.

bicultural identity Identifying both with one's own ethnic minority group and with the majority culture.

Armando Ronquillo, High School Counselor

Armando Ronquillo is a high school counselor and admissions advisor at Pueblo High School in a low-income area of Tucson, Arizona. More than 85 percent of the students have a Latino background. Ronquillo was named the top high school counselor in the state of Arizona in 2000.

Ronquillo especially works with Latino students to guide them in developing a positive identity. He talks with them about their Latino background and what it's like to have a bicultural identity—preserving important aspects of their Latino heritage while also pursuing what is important to be successful in the contemporary culture of the United States.

Ronquillo believes that helping students stay in school and getting them to think about the lifelong opportunities provided by a college education will benefit their identity development. He also works with parents to help them understand that sending their child to college can be doable and affordable.

Armando Ronquillo counsels a Latina high school student about college.
Courtesy of Armando Ronquillo

For more information about what school counselors do, see the Careers in Life-Span Development appendix.

motivation, and lower levels of depression over time (Kiang, Witkow, & Champagne, 2013). In another study, having pride in one's ethnic group and a strong ethnic identity were linked to lower levels of substance use in adolescents (Grindal & Nieri, 2016). And in a recent study, strong ethnic group affiliation and connection served a protective function in reducing risk for psychiatric problems (Anglin & others, 2018). To read about one individual who guides Latino adolescents in developing a positive identity, see the *Connecting with Careers* profile.

Review Connect Reflect

 LG2 Explain the key facets of identity development.

Review

- What does an identity involve?
- What is Erikson's view of identity?
- What are some contemporary thoughts on identity?
- What are the four identity statuses, and how do they change developmentally?
- How do social contexts influence identity?

Connect

- Connect the concept of adolescents' "possible selves" to Erikson's view of adolescence as a time of identity versus identity confusion.

Reflect *Your Own Personal Journey of Life*

- Do you think your parents influenced your identity development? If so, how?

3 Personality   **LG3** Describe personality and its development in adulthood.

| Trait Theories and the Big Five Factors of Personality | Views on Adult Personality Development | Generativity | Stability and Change |

Earlier in the chapter, personality was defined as the enduring personal characteristics of individuals. Personality psychologists use many strategies to better understand the enduring characteristics of individuals (Cloninger, 2019; Twenge & Campbell, 2020). Some of them study the overall personality of individuals; some come up with a list of traits that best describe individuals; and others zero in on specific traits or characteristics, such as being introverted or extraverted.

In other chapters we've considered several major personality theories—psychoanalytic theories and the social cognitive theory of Albert Bandura. You might wish to review those theories at this time. Here our exploration of personality focuses on trait theory, several views of personality development in adulthood, and studies of stability and change in personality during adulthood.

TRAIT THEORIES AND THE BIG FIVE FACTORS OF PERSONALITY

Trait theories state that personality consists of broad dispositions, called traits, that tend to produce characteristic responses. In other words, people can be described in terms of the basic ways they behave, such as whether they are outgoing and friendly or whether they are dominant and assertive (Fleeson & Jayawickreme, 2019). Although trait theorists disagree about which traits make up personality, they agree that traits are the foundation of personality.

In "Emotional Development and Attachment," we described the development of temperament in infants and children. For example, we discussed Kagan's concept of inhibition to the unfamiliar, as well as Rothbart and Bates' categories of extraversion/surgency, negative affectivity, and effortful control. Many developmental psychologists use the term "temperament" when talking about personality-like categories in infancy and childhood (Janssen & others, 2017; Kagan, 2018). You might want to review the discussion of temperament in "Emotional Development and Attachment" to get a sense of the early development of personality-like categories.

Big Five Factors of Personality   One trait theory that has received considerable attention involves the **Big Five factors of personality**—the view that personality is made up of openness to experience, conscientiousness, extraversion, agreeableness, and neuroticism (see Figure 6). (Notice that if you create an acronym from these trait names, you will get the word *OCEAN*.) A number of research studies point toward these five factors as important dimensions of personality (Costa & McCrae, 1995, 2013; Costa & others, 2014; Hampson & Edmonds, 2018; Roberts & Damian, 2018; Roberts & Nickel, 2020).

Evidence for the importance of the Big Five factors indicates that they are related to such important aspects of a person's life as health, intelligence and cognitive functioning, achievement and work, and relationships (Roberts & Damian, 2018; Nye & Roberts, 2019; Strickhouser, Zell, & Krizan, 2017). The following research supports these links:

- *Openness to experience.* Individuals high in openness to experience are more likely to be tolerant of others (McCrae & Sutin, 2009); to have superior cognitive functioning, achievement, and IQ across the life span (Briley, Domiteaux, & Tucker-Drob, 2014; Sharp & others, 2010); to experience success as entrepreneurs (Zhao, Seibert, & Lumpkin, 2010); to show creative achievement in the arts (Kaufman & others, 2016); to have better health and well-being (Strickhouser, Zell, & Krizan, 2017); and to experience less negative affect to stressors (Leger & others, 2016); to eat fruits and vegetables (Conner & others, 2017). Openness to experience is associated with successful aging, and it tends to decline in advance of death in older adults (Sharp & others, 2019).
- *Conscientiousness.* Individuals high in conscientiousness often do well in a variety of life domains (Jackson & Roberts, 2016; Mike & others, 2015). For example, they are likely to

trait theories Theories emphasizing that personality consists of broad dispositions, called traits, which tend to produce characteristic responses.

Big Five factors of personality The view that personality is made up of five factors: openness to experience, conscientiousness, extraversion, agreeableness, and neuroticism.

Openness	**C**onscientiousness	**E**xtraversion	**A**greeableness	**N**euroticism (emotional stability)
• Imaginative or practical	• Organized or disorganized	• Sociable or retiring	• Softhearted or ruthless	• Calm or anxious
• Interested in variety or routine	• Careful or careless	• Fun-loving or somber	• Trusting or suspicious	• Secure or insecure
• Independent or conforming	• Disciplined or impulsive	• Affectionate or reserved	• Helpful or uncooperative	• Self-satisfied or self-pitying

FIGURE 6

THE BIG FIVE FACTORS OF PERSONALITY. Each of the broad super traits encompasses more narrow traits and characteristics. Use the acronym OCEAN to remember the Big Five personality factors (openness, conscientiousness, extraversion, agreeableness, neuroticism).

An adolescent with a high level of conscientiousness organizes his daily schedule and plans how to use his time effectively. *What are some characteristics of conscientiousness? How is it linked to adolescents' competence?*
Mint Images/Getty Images

live longer (Graham & others, 2017); to experience optimal aging, including positive affect, life satisfaction, and positive psychological well-being (Melendez & others, 2019); to have a lower risk of dementia (in African and non-Latino White older adults) (Kaup, Harmell, & Yaffe, 2019); to have better health and less stress (Gartland & others, 2014; Strickhouser, Zell, & Krizan, 2017); to engage in superior problem-focused coping (Sesker & others, 2016); to be successful in accomplishing goals (McCabe & Fleeson, 2016); to achieve higher grade point averages in college (McAbee & Oswald, 2013); and to be academically successful in medical school (Sobowale & others, 2018). They also are less likely to have an alcohol addiction (Raketic & others, 2017); to be obese (Cheng & others, 2019); to be characterized by Internet addiction (Zhou & others, 2017); or to be addicted to Instagram (Kircaburun & Griffiths, 2018); and they tend to have lower work-out burnout rates if they are nursing professionals (Perez-Fuentes & others, 2019).

- *Extraversion.* Individuals high in *extraversion* are more likely than others to be satisfied in relationships (Toy, Nai, & Lee, 2016); to show less negative affect to stressors (Leger & others, 2016); and to have a more positive sense of well-being in the future (Soto, 2015).

- *Agreeableness.* People who are high in agreeableness are likely to live longer (Graham & others, 2017) and have a lower risk of dementia (Terracciano & others, 2017); to be generous and altruistic (Caprara & others, 2010); to have more satisfying romantic relationships (Donnellan, Larsen-Rife, & Conger, 2005); to view other people positively (Wood, Harms, & Vazire, 2010); to lie less about themselves in online dating profiles (Hall & others, 2010); and to engage in more positive affect to stressors (Leger & others, 2016).

- *Neuroticism.* People high in neuroticism are likely to die at a younger age than people with lower levels of neuroticism (Graham & others, 2017); to have worse health and report having more health complaints (Strickhouser, Zell, & Krizan, 2017); to feel more negative emotion than positive emotion in daily life and to experiencing more lingering negative states (Widiger, 2009); to have worse health and report more health complaints (Carver & Connor-Smith, 2010; Strickhouser, Zell, & Krizan, 2017); to be more drug dependent (Raketic & others, 2017; Valero & others, 2014); to have coronary heart disease (Lee & others, 2014); to be characterized by higher work burnout rates if they are nursing professionals (O'Meara & South, 2019); to develop dementia (Terracciano & others, 2017); and to have a lower sense of well-being 40 years later (Gale & others, 2013).

Researchers have found that several of the Big Five factors of personality continue to change in late adulthood (Jackson & Roberts, 2016; Roberts & Damian, 2018; Roberts, Donnellan, & Hill, 2013; Roberts & Nickel, 2020). In one study, perceived social support predicted increased conscientiousness in older adults (Hill & others, 2014). And in another study, more severe depression in older adults was associated with higher levels of neuroticism and lower levels of extraversion and conscientiousness (Koorevaar & others, 2013).

Optimism Another important personality characteristic is **optimism,** which involves having a positive outlook on the future and minimizing problems (Kleiman & others, 2017). Optimism is often referred to as a style of thinking.

Somewhat surprising is that little research has been conducted on children's optimism. One study did find that from 5 to 10 years of age children increasingly understood that thinking positively improves their emotion state and that thinking negatively makes it worse (Bamford & Lagattuta, 2012). In *The Optimistic Child,* Martin Seligman (2007) described how parents, teachers, and coaches can instill optimism in children, which he argues helps to make them more resilient and less likely to develop depression.

In examining optimism in adolescents, one study found that having an optimistic style of thinking predicted a reduction in suicidal ideation for individuals who had experienced negative and potentially traumatic life events (Hirsch & others, 2009). Another study revealed that adolescents with an optimistic thinking style had a lower risk of developing depressive symptoms than their pessimistic counterparts (Patton & others, 2011).

Researchers increasingly are finding that optimism is linked to better adjustment, better health, and increased longevity (Boelen, 2015; Kolokotroni, Anagnostopoulos, & Hantzi, 2018). A recent study revealed that college students who were pessimistic had more anxious mood and stress symptoms than those who were optimistic (Lau & others, 2017). A study involving adults 50 years of age and older revealed that being optimistic and having an optimistic spouse were both associated with better health and physical functioning (Kim, Chopik, & Smith, 2014).

optimism A style of thinking that involves having a positive outlook on the future and minimizing problems.

Further, another study of married couples found that the worst health outcomes occurred when both spouses decreased in optimism across a four-year time frame (Chopik, Kim, & Smith, 2018). In another study, a higher level of optimism following an acute coronary event was linked to engaging in more physical activity and having fewer cardiac readmissions (Huffman & others, 2016). Also, in a recent study, lonely individuals who were optimistic had a lower suicide risk than their counterparts who were more pessimistic (Chang & others, 2018). A research review concluded that the positive influence of optimism on outcomes for people with chronic diseases (such as cancer, cardiovascular disease, and respiratory disease) may reflect either or both of the following factors: (a) a direct effect on the neuroendocrine system and on immune system function; and (b) an indirect effect on health outcomes as a result of protective health behaviors, adaptive coping strategies, and enhanced positive mood (Avvenuti, Baiardini, & Giardini, 2016).

Trait-Situation Interaction   The trait theories have identified a number of characteristics that are important to consider when attempting to understand an individual's personality (Fleeson & Jayawickreme, 2019; Twenge & Campbell, 2020). The trait approach also has led to advances in the assessment of personality through the development of numerous personality tests. However, some psychologists note that the trait approach gives too little attention to environmental factors and puts too much emphasis on stability (Reis & Holmes, 2019). These criticisms initially were leveled by social cognitive theorist Walter Mischel (1968). Mischel argued that personality often changes according to the situation. Thus, an individual may behave very differently at a party from the way he would behave in the library.

Today, most personality psychologists believe that personality is a product of *trait-situation interaction*. In other words, both traits and situational (context) factors must be considered to understand personality (Simpson & Winterheld, 2019; Stewart & Deaux, 2019). Also, some people are more consistent on some traits while other people are consistent on other traits.

VIEWS ON ADULT PERSONALITY DEVELOPMENT

Two important perspectives on adult development are the stage-crisis view and the life-events approach. In examining these approaches, we discuss the extent to which adults experience a midlife crisis and consider how life events influence the individual's development.

The Stage-Crisis View   Erikson's theory, which we discussed earlier, is a stage-crisis view. Here we describe the view of Daniel Levinson and examine the concept of a midlife crisis.

Levinson's Seasons of a Man's Life   In *The Seasons of a Man's Life*, clinical psychologist Daniel Levinson (1978) reported the results of extensive interviews with 40 middle-aged men. The interviews were conducted with hourly workers, business executives, academic biologists, and novelists. Levinson bolstered his conclusions with information from the biographies of famous men and the development of memorable characters in literature. Although Levinson's major focus was midlife change, he described a number of stages and transitions in the life span, as shown in Figure 7.

Levinson emphasizes that developmental tasks must be mastered at each of these stages. In early adulthood, the two major tasks are exploring the possibilities for adult living and developing a stable life structure. Levinson sees the twenties as a *novice phase* of adult development. At the end of one's teens, a transition from dependence to independence should occur. This transition is marked by the formation of a dream—an image of the kind of life the youth wants to have, especially in terms of a career and marriage. The novice phase is a time of reasonably free experimentation and of testing the dream in the real world.

From about age 28 to 33, a young man goes through a transition period in which he must face the more serious question of determining his goals. During the thirties, he usually focuses on family and career development. In the later years of this period, he enters a phase of Becoming One's Own

Era of late adulthood: 60 to 120

Late adult transition: Age 60 to 65

Culminating life structure for middle adulthood: 55 to 60

Age 50 transition: 50 to 55

Entry life structure for middle adulthood: 45 to 50

Middle adult transition: Age 40 to 45

Culminating life structure for early adulthood: 33 to 40

Age 30 transition: 28 to 33

Entry life structure for early adulthood: 22 to 28

Early adult transition: Age 17 to 22

FIGURE 7

LEVINSON'S PERIODS OF ADULT DEVELOPMENT. According to Levinson, adulthood has three main stages, which are surrounded by transition periods. Specific tasks and challenges are associated with each stage.
(top to bottom): Amos Morgan/Getty Images; Corbis/VCG/Getty Images; Nako Photography/Shutterstock

Man (or BOOM, as Levinson calls it). By age 40, he has reached a stable location in his career, has outgrown his earlier, more tenuous attempts at learning to become an adult, and now must look forward to the kind of life he will lead as a middle-aged adult.

According to Levinson, the transition to middle adulthood lasts about five years (ages 40 to 45) and requires the adult male to come to grips with four major conflicts that have existed in his life since adolescence: (1) being young versus being old, (2) being destructive versus being constructive, (3) being masculine versus being feminine, and (4) being attached to others versus being separated from them. Seventy to eighty percent of the men Levinson interviewed found the midlife transition tumultuous and psychologically painful, as many aspects of their lives came into question. According to Levinson, the success of the midlife transition rests on how effectively the individual reduces the polarities and accepts each of them as an integral part of his being.

The original Levinson data included no females. However, Levinson (1987, 1996) subsequently reported that his stages, transitions, and the crisis of middle age hold for females as well as males.

Midlife Crises   Levinson (1978) views midlife as a crisis, believing that the middle-aged adult is suspended between the past and the future, trying to cope with this gap that threatens life's continuity. George Vaillant (1977) concludes that just as adolescence is a time for detecting parental flaws and discovering the truth about childhood, the forties are a decade of reassessing and recording the truth about the adolescent and adulthood years. However, whereas Levinson sees midlife as a crisis, Vaillant notes that only a minority of adults experience a midlife crisis:

> Just as pop psychologists have reveled in the not-so-common high drama of adolescent turmoil, also the popular press, sensing good copy, have made all too much of the mid-life crisis. The term *mid-life crisis* brings to mind some variation of the renegade minister who leaves behind four children and the congregation that loved him in order to drive off in a magenta Porsche with a 25-year-old striptease artiste. As with adolescent turmoil, mid-life crises are much rarer in community samples. (Vaillant, 1977, pp. 222–223)

Vaillant's study—called the Grant Study—involved a follow-up of Harvard University men in their early thirties and in their late forties who initially had been interviewed as undergraduates. Other research has also found that midlife is not characterized by pervasive crises. For example, a longitudinal study of 2,247 individuals found few midlife crises (McCrae & Costa, 1990). The emotional well-being of these individuals did not significantly decrease during middle age (see Figure 8). In fact, some studies have documented psychological gains among middle-aged adults. For example, one study revealed that individuals from 40 to 60 years of age were less nervous and worried than those under 40. The middle-aged adults reported a growing sense of control in their work as well as increased financial security, greater environmental mastery (ability to handle daily responsibilities), and more autonomy than their younger counterparts.

Adult development experts have become virtually unanimous in their belief that midlife crises have been exaggerated (Lachman & Kranz, 2010; Pudrovska, 2009). In sum, there is a consensus that (1) the stage theories place too much emphasis on crises in development, especially midlife crises; and (2) there often is considerable individual variation in the way people experience the stages, a topic that we explore next.

Individual Variations   Stage theories especially focus on the universals of adult personality development. They try to pin down stages that all individuals go through in their adult lives. These theories do not adequately address individual variations in adult development. In an extensive study of a random sample of 500 men at midlife, it was concluded that there is extensive individual variation among men (Farrell & Rosenberg, 1981). In this view, middle-aged adults interpret, shape, alter, and give meaning to their lives (Arpanantikul, 2004). It also is important to recognize that some individuals may experience a midlife crisis in some contexts of their lives but not others (Lachman, 2004). Thus, turmoil and stress may characterize one area of a person's life (such as work) while things are going smoothly in another context (such as family).

Researchers have found that in one-third of the cases in which individuals have reported having a midlife crisis, the crisis is triggered by life events such as a job loss, financial problems, or illness (Wethington, Kessler, & Pixley, 2004). Let's further explore the role of life events in midlife development.

The Life-Events Approach   An alternative to the stage approach to adult development is the life-events approach (Marselle, Warber, & Irvine, 2019; Munro & others, 2019; Oren & others, 2017). In the early version of the life-events approach, life events were viewed as taxing

Mid-life crises are greatly exaggerated in America.

—George Vaillant
Contemporary Psychologist, Harvard University

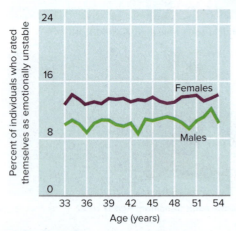

FIGURE **8**

EMOTIONAL INSTABILITY AND AGE. In one longitudinal study, the emotional instability of individuals was assessed from age 33 to age 54 (McCrae & Costa, 1990). No significant increase in emotional instability occurred during middle age.

circumstances for individuals, forcing them to change their personality (Holmes & Rahe, 1967). Events such as the death of a spouse, divorce, marriage, and so on were believed to involve varying degrees of stress, and therefore likely to influence the individual's development. One study found that stressful life events were associated with cardiovascular disease in middle-aged women (Kershaw & others, 2014). And a research meta-analysis found an association between stressful life events and autoimmune diseases such as arthritis and psoriasis (Porcelli & others, 2016).

Today's life-events approach is more sophisticated (Cui & Vaillant, 1996; Hultsch & Plemons, 1979; Patrick, Carney, & Nehrkorn, 2017). The **contemporary life-events approach** emphasizes that how life events influence the individual's development depends not only on the event but also on *mediating factors* (physical health and family supports, for example), the individual's *adaptation to the life event* (appraisal of the threat and coping strategies, for example), the *life-stage context*, and the *sociohistorical context* (see Figure 9).

Consider how the life event of divorce might affect personality. A divorce is likely to be more stressful for individuals who are in poor health and have little family support. One individual may perceive it as highly stressful (less adaptive) rather than a challenge while another may develop coping strategies to effectively deal with it (more adaptive). And a divorce may be more stressful after many years of marriage when adults are in their fifties than when they have been married only a few years and are in their twenties (an example of life-stage context). Finally, adults may be able to cope more effectively with divorce today than several decades ago because divorce has become more commonplace and accepted in today's society (an example of sociohistorical context).

Though the life-events approach is a valuable addition to understanding adult development, it has some drawbacks. One drawback is that the life-events approach places too much emphasis on change. It does not adequately recognize the stability that, at least to some degree, characterizes adult development. Another drawback is that it may not be life's major events that are the primary sources of stress, but our daily experiences (Du, Derks, & Bakker, 2018; Finegood & others, 2017; Koffer & others, 2018; Stensvehagen & others, 2019). Enduring a boring but tense job or living in poverty does not show up on scales of major life events. Yet the everyday pounding from these conditions can add up to a highly stressful life and eventually lead to illness (Sarid & others, 2018; Scott & others, 2018; Smyth & others, 2018). Greater insight into the source of life's stresses might come from focusing more on daily hassles and daily uplifts (Jacob & others, 2014). Researchers have found that young and middle-aged adults experience a greater daily frequency of stressors than older individuals do (Almeida & Horn, 2004). One study also found that stressful daily hassles were linked to increased anxiety and lower physical well-being (Falconier & others, 2015). Also, a recent study revealed that older adults engaged in more proactive coping with minor hassles in their daily lives than younger adults did, and were better able to manage these problems before they become more stressful (Neubauer, Smyth, & Sliwinski, 2019).

Different kinds of stressors affect health in different ways—life events often produce prolonged arousal, whereas daily stressors are linked to spikes in arousal (Piazza & others, 2010). Consider the effects of caring for a spouse who has Alzheimer disease. In this case, a life event (spouse diagnosed with an incurable disease) produces chronic stress for the caregiver, which also is linked to the daily stressors involved in caring for the individual.

GENERATIVITY

Erikson (1968) argues that middle-aged adults face the issue of **generativity versus stagnation,** which is the name Erikson gave to the seventh stage in his life-span theory. Generativity encompasses adults' desire to leave a legacy of themselves to the next generation (Castalanelli & others, 2019; Grossman & Gruenewald, 2017; Serrat & others, 2018). By contrast, stagnation

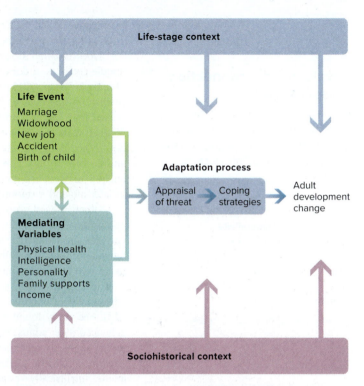

FIGURE 9

A CONTEMPORARY LIFE-EVENTS FRAMEWORK FOR INTERPRETING ADULT DEVELOPMENTAL CHANGE. According to the contemporary life-events approach, the influence of a life event depends on the event itself, on mediating variables, on the life-stage and sociohistorical context, and on the individual's appraisal of the event and coping strategies.

contemporary life-events approach The view that how a life event influences the individual's development depends not only on the event itself but also on mediating factors, the individual's adaptation to the life event, the life-stage context, and the sociohistorical context.

generativity versus stagnation The seventh stage in Erikson's life-span theory; it encompasses adults' desire to leave a legacy of themselves to the next generation.

developmental **connection**

Life-Span Perspective

Erikson's early adulthood stage is intimacy versus isolation, and his late adulthood stage is integrity versus despair. Connect to "Introduction."

Generativity

Feeling needed by people

Effort to ensure that young people get their chance to develop

Influence in my community or area of interest

A new level of productivity or effectiveness

Appreciation and awareness of older people

Having a wider perspective

Interest in things beyond my family

Identity certainty

A sense of being my own person

Excitement, turmoil, confusion about my impulses and potential (reversed)

Coming near the end of one road and not yet finding another (reversed)

Feeling my life is moving well

Searching for a sense of who I am (reversed)

Wishing I had a wider scope to my life (reversed)

Anxiety that I won't live up to opportunities (reversed)

Feeling secure and committed

FIGURE **10**

ITEMS USED TO ASSESS GENERATIVITY AND IDENTITY CERTAINTY. These items were used to assess generativity and identity certainty in the longitudinal study of Smith College women (Stewart, Ostrove, & Helson, 2001). In the assessment of identity certainty, five of the items involved reversed scoring. For example, if an individual scored high on the item "Searching for a sense of who I am," it was an indication of identity uncertainty rather than identity certainty.

(sometimes called "self-absorption") develops when individuals sense that they have done nothing for the next generation.

Does research support Erikson's theory that generativity is an important dimension of middle age? Yes, it does (Dunlop, Bannon, & McAdams, 2017; Russo-Netzer & Moran, 2018; Stewart & Deaux, 2019). In George Vaillant's (2002) longitudinal studies of aging, generativity (defined in this study as "taking care of the next generation") in middle age was more strongly related than intimacy to whether individuals would have an enduring and happy marriage at 75 to 80 years of age. One participant in Vaillant's studies said, "From twenty to thirty I learned how to get along with my wife. From thirty to forty I learned how to be a success at my job, and at forty to fifty I worried less about myself and more about the children" (p. 114). An analysis of Vaillant's data found that achieving generativity was associated with better health in later life and a smoother adjustment to aging (Landes & others, 2014).

Other research also supports Erikson's (1968) view on the importance of generativity in middle age. In one study, Carol Ryff (1984) examined the views of women and men at different ages and found that middle-aged adults especially were concerned about generativity. In a longitudinal study of Smith College women, the desire for generativity increased as the participants aged from their thirties to their fifties (Stewart, Ostrove, & Helson, 2001) (see Figure 10). And in another study, generativity was strongly linked to middle-aged adults' positive social engagement in contexts such as family life and community activities (Cox & others, 2010). Also, one study found that participating in an intergenerational civic engagement program enhanced older adults' perceptions of generativity (Gruenewald & others, 2016). Further, in a recent study, a higher level of generativity in midlife was linked to greater wisdom in late adulthood (Ardelt, Gerlach, & Vaillant, 2018). And in another recent study of middle-aged adults, intrinsically rewarding work was positively associated with feelings of generativity (Chen & others, 2019).

Middle-aged adults can develop generativity in a number of ways (Kotre, 1984). Through biological generativity, adults conceive and give birth to an infant. Through parental generativity, adults provide nurturance and guidance to children. Through work generativity, adults develop skills that are passed down to others. And through cultural generativity, adults create, renovate, or conserve some aspect of culture that ultimately survives.

STABILITY AND CHANGE

An important issue in life-span development is the extent to which individuals show stability in their development versus the extent to which they change. A number of longitudinal studies have assessed stability and change in the personalities of individuals at different points in their lives (Borghuis & others, 2017; Chopik & Kitayama, 2018; Fajkowska, 2018; Hengartner & Yamanaka-Altenstein, 2017; Roberts and Nickel, 2020; Stewart & Deaux, 2019). A common finding is that in most cases, the less time between measurements of personality characteristics, the more stability they show. Thus, if we measure a person's introversion/extraversion at the age of 20 and then again at age 30, we are likely to find more stability than if we assess the person at age 20 and then at age 40.

Costa and McCrae's Baltimore Study   Earlier we discussed the Big Five factors in personality as an important trait theory. Paul Costa and Robert McCrae (1998, 2013; McCrae & Costa, 2006) have studied the Big Five factors of approximately a thousand college-educated women and men from 20 to 96 years of age. Longitudinal data collection initially began in the 1950s to the mid-1960s on people of varying ages and is ongoing. Costa and McCrae found a great deal of stability across the adult years in the Big Five personality factors—openness to experience, conscientiousness, extraversion, agreeableness, and neuroticism.

However, more recent research indicates greater developmental changes in the Big Five personality factors in adulthood (Hill & Roberts, 2016; Roberts & Damian, 2018; Roberts, Donnellan, & Hill, 2013; Soto & others, 2011). For example, one study found that emotional stability, extraversion, openness, and agreeableness were lower in early adulthood, peaked between 40 and 60 years of age, and decreased in late adulthood, while conscientiousness showed a continuous increase from early adulthood to late adulthood (Specht, Egloff, & Schukle, 2011). Most research studies find that the greatest change occurs in early adulthood (Donnellan, Hill, & Roberts, 2015; Hill & Roberts, 2016; Lucas & Donnellan, 2011; Roberts, Walton, & Viechtbauer, 2006).

Are Personality Traits Related to Longevity?

Researchers have found that some personality traits are associated with the mortality of older adults (Mroczek, Spiro, & Griffin, 2006; Noftle & Fleeson, 2010). A research meta-analysis found that higher levels of openness to experience were linked to living longer (Ferguson & Bibby, 2012). In one study, 883 older Catholic clergy were given the NEO Five-Factor Inventory that assesses the Big Five factors of personality (Wilson & others, 2004). The clergy were followed for five years, during which 182 of the 883 clergy died. At the beginning of the study, the average age of the clergy was 75, and 69 percent of them were women. Risk of death nearly doubled in clergy who had a high score on neuroticism (90th percentile) compared with those who had a low score (10th percentile) and was halved in clergy who were very high in conscientiousness compared with those who were very low. Results for extraversion were mixed, whereas agreeableness and openness were not related to mortality. And in another study, a higher level of conscientiousness predicted greater longevity in older adults (Hill & others, 2012).

Why might a high score on neuroticism and a low score on conscientiousness lead to an earlier death? Researchers have found that older adults who are highly neurotic react more emotionally to stressful circumstances than their low-neuroticism counterparts (Mroczek, Spiro, & Griffin, 2006). Over many years, high neuroticism may elevate harmful stress hormones and produce physical damages to the cardiovascular system, thus contributing to mortality. By contrast, individuals who score high on conscientiousness engage in more healthy behaviors than those who score low (Jackson & Roberts, 2016). For example, low-conscientiousness individuals engage in more risky behaviors, such as excessive drinking and impulsive behaviors that lead to fatal accidents. It also has been proposed that they tend to have less healthy diets and are less likely to exercise regularly than highly conscientious individuals (Mroczek, Spiro, & Griffin, 2006).

An increasing number of studies are finding that conscientiousness is the Big Five factor that best predicts longevity (Jackson & Roberts, 2016; Wilson & others, 2015). A longitudinal study of more than 1,200 individuals across seven decades revealed that the Big Five personality factor of conscientiousness predicted lower mortality risk from childhood through late adulthood (Martin, Friedman, & Schwartz, 2007).

Another longitudinal study underscored the importance of the link between neuroticism and mortality in a sample of more than 1,600 aging men (Mroczek & Spiro, 2007). A high level of neuroticism and an increasing level of neuroticism were related to lower survival across an 18-year period (see Figure 11).

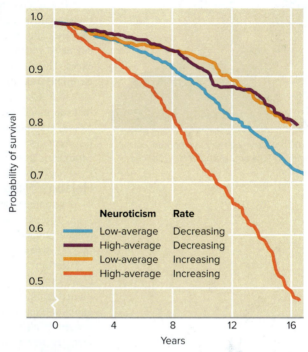

FIGURE 11

LINK BETWEEN NEUROTICISM AND SURVIVAL IN AGING MEN. *Note*: At the beginning of the study, the men were 43 to 91 years old. During the 18-year period of the study, 30 percent of the participants died, with more than 70 percent of the deaths due to cardiovascular disease and cancer.

An increasing number of researchers and theorists who study the Big Five are focusing on the role of conscientiousness in relation to health and longevity (Friedman & others, 2014; Jackson & Roberts, 2016; Raketic & others, 2017; Roberts & others, 2014; Strickhouser, Zell, & Krizan, 2017). In a longitudinal study, children's conscientiousness predicted their physical health 40 years later (Hampson & others, 2013). And a study of 66- to 102-year-olds revealed that the self-discipline component of conscientiousness was a strong predictor of living longer, with individuals who had high self-discipline showing a 34 percent increase in survival time (Costa & others, 2014).

What type of studies might researchers conduct to identify early precursors of personality traits such as conscientiousness and neuroticism in an effort to increase longevity?

Might some Big Five factors be related to how long older adults live? To find out, read the *Connecting with Research* interlude.

Berkeley Longitudinal Studies Most longitudinal studies indicate that neither extreme stability nor extreme change characterizes most people's personalities as they go through the adult years (Stewart & Deaux, 2019). One of the longest-running inquiries is the

What characterized the development of women in Ravenna Helson's Mills College Study?
Fuse/Corbis/Getty Images

series of analyses called the Berkeley Longitudinal Studies. Initially, more than 500 children and their parents were studied in the late 1920s and early 1930s. The book *Present and Past in Middle Life* (Eichorn & others, 1981) profiles these individuals as they became middle-aged.

The results from early adolescence through a portion of midlife did not support either extreme in the debate over whether personality is characterized by stability or change. Some characteristics were more stable than others, however. The most stable characteristics were the degree to which individuals were intellectually oriented, self-confident, or open to new experiences. The characteristics that changed the most included the extent to which the individuals were nurturant or hostile and whether they had good self-control.

John Clausen (1993), one of the researchers in the Berkeley Longitudinal Studies, holds that too much attention has been given to discontinuities for all members of the human species, as exemplified in the adult stage theories. Rather, he stresses that some people experience recurrent crises and change a great deal over the life course, whereas others lead more stable, continuous lives and change far less.

Helson's Mills College Studies

Another longitudinal investigation of adult personality development was conducted by Ravenna Helson and her colleagues (George, Helson, & John, 2011; Helson, 1997; Helson & Wink, 1992; Roberts, Helson, & Klohnen, 2002). They initially studied 132 women who were seniors at Mills College in California in the late 1950s. In 1981, when the women were 42 to 45 years old, they were studied again.

Helson and her colleagues distinguished three main groups among the Mills women: family-oriented (participants who had children), career-oriented (whether or not they also wanted families), and those who followed neither path (women without children who pursued only low-level work). Despite their different college profiles and their diverging life paths, the women in all three groups experienced some similar psychological changes over their adult years. However, the women in the third group changed less than those committed to career or family.

During their early forties, many of the women shared the concerns that stage theorists such as Levinson found in men: concern for young and old, introspectiveness, interest in roots, and awareness of limitations and death. However, the researchers in the Mills College Study concluded that rather than being in a midlife crisis, what the Mills women experienced was midlife *consciousness*. They also indicated that commitment to the tasks of early adulthood—whether to a career or family (or both)—helped women learn to control their impulses, develop interpersonal skills, become independent, and work hard to achieve goals. Women who did not commit themselves to one of these lifestyle patterns faced fewer challenges and did not develop as fully as the other women (Rosenfeld & Stark, 1987). In the Mills study, some women moved toward becoming "pillars of society" in their early forties to early fifties (Helson & Wink, 1992).

George Vaillant's Studies

George Vaillant (2002) has conducted three longitudinal studies of adult development and aging: (1) a sample of 268 socially advantaged Harvard graduates born about 1920 (called the "Grant Study"); (2) a sample of 456 socially disadvantaged inner-city men born about 1930; and (3) a sample of 90 middle-SES, intellectually gifted women born about 1910. These individuals have been assessed numerous times (in most cases every two years), beginning in the 1920s to 1940s and continuing today for those still living. The main assessments involve extensive interviews with the participants, their parents, and teachers.

Vaillant categorized 75- to 80-year-olds as "happy-well," "sad-sick," or "dead." He used data collected from these individuals when they were 50 years of age to predict which categories they were likely to end up in at 75 to 80 years of age. Alcohol abuse and smoking at age 50 were the best predictors of which individuals would be dead at 75 to 80 years of age. Other factors at age 50 were linked with being in the "happy-well" category at 75 to 80 years of age: getting regular exercise; avoiding being overweight; being well educated; having a stable marriage; being future-oriented; being thankful and forgiving; empathizing with others; being active with other people; and having good coping skills. Wealth and income at age 50 were not linked with being in the "happy-well" category at 75 to 80 years of age. The results for one of Vaillant's studies, the Grant Study of Harvard men, are shown in Figure 12.

Conclusions

What can we conclude about stability and change in personality development during the adult years? According to a research review by leading researchers Brent Roberts and Daniel Mroczek (2008), there is increasing evidence that personality traits

developmental **connection**

Life-Span Perspective

The extent to which development is characterized by stability and/or change is one of life-span development's key issues. Connect to "Introduction."

At age 55, actor Jack Nicholson said, "I feel exactly the same as I've always felt: a slightly reined-in voracious beast." Nicholson felt his personality had not changed much. Some others might think they have changed more. *How much does personality change and how does it stay the same through adulthood?*
Noel Vasquez/Stringer/Getty Images

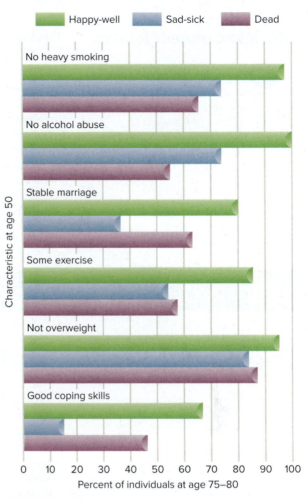

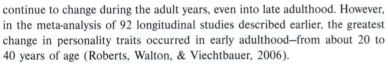

continue to change during the adult years, even into late adulthood. However, in the meta-analysis of 92 longitudinal studies described earlier, the greatest change in personality traits occurred in early adulthood—from about 20 to 40 years of age (Roberts, Walton, & Viechtbauer, 2006).

Thus, people show more stability in their personality when they reach midlife than they did when they were younger adults (Jackson & Roberts, 2016; Nye & others, 2016; Roberts & Nickel, 2020). These findings support what is called a *cumulative personality model of personality development*, which states that with time and age people become more adept at interacting with their environment in ways that promote increased stability in personality (Caspi & Roberts, 2001).

This does not mean that change is absent throughout middle and late adulthood (Ayoub & Roberts, 2018). Ample evidence shows that social contexts, new experiences, and sociohistorical changes can affect personality development, but the changes in middle and late adulthood are usually not as great as in early adulthood (Mroczek, Spiro, & Griffin, 2006). In a recent research review, the personality trait that changed the most as a result of psychotherapeutic intervention was emotional stability, followed by extraversion (Roberts & others, 2017). In this review, the personality traits of individuals with anxiety disorders changed the most and those with substance use disorders the least.

In general, changes in personality traits across adulthood also occur in a positive direction (George, 2010; Roberts & Nickel, 2020; Staudinger & Jacobs, 2010). Over time, "people become more confident, warm, responsible, and calm" (Roberts & Mroczek, 2008, p. 33). Such positive changes equate with becoming more socially mature.

In sum, recent research contradicts the old view that stability in personality begins to set in at about 30 years of age (Roberts & Damian, 2018; Roberts & Nickel, 2020). Although there are some consistent developmental changes in the personality traits of large numbers of people, at the individual level people can show unique patterns of personality traits, and these patterns often reflect life experiences related to themes of their specific developmental period (Roberts & Mroczek, 2008). For example, researchers have found that individuals who are in a stable marriage and a solid career track become more socially dominant, conscientious, and emotionally stable as they go through early adulthood (Roberts & Wood, 2006). And, for some of these individuals, there is greater change in their personality traits than for other individuals (Roberts, Donnellan, & Hill, 2013; Roberts & Nickel, 2020).

FIGURE **12**

LINKS BETWEEN CHARACTERISTICS AT AGE 50 AND HEALTH AND HAPPINESS AT AGE 75 TO 80. In a longitudinal study, the characteristics shown above at age 50 were related to whether individuals were happy-well, sad-sick, or dead at age 75 to 80 (Vaillant, 2002).

Review

- What are trait theories? What are the Big Five factors of personality?
- What are some views of adult development of personality?
- What is Erikson's view of middle-aged adults?
- What are some major longitudinal studies of adult personality development, and what implications do they have for the stability/change issue?

Connect

- This section discussed four different longitudinal studies. What are the pros and cons of using a longitudinal study to collect data?

Reflect *Your Own Personal Journey of Life*

- Think about the Big Five factors of personality for a few moments. Using the Big Five factors, describe your own personality.

reach your **learning goals**

The Self, Identity, and Personality

1 The Self

 LG1 Discuss the main ways the self and understanding others are conceptualized and how they develop.

Self-Understanding and Understanding Others

- Self-understanding is the cognitive representation of the self, the substance of self-conceptions. Developmental changes in self-understanding include the construction of the self in infancy in terms of self-recognition and transformations in self-understanding in childhood (including perspective taking).

- Self-understanding in early childhood is characterized by confusion of self, mind, and body; concrete, physical, and active descriptions; and unrealistic positive overestimations. Young children display more sophisticated self-understanding and understanding of others than was previously thought.

- Self-understanding in middle and late childhood involves an increase in the use of psychological characteristics and traits, social descriptions, and social comparison; distinction between the real and ideal self; and an increase in realistic self-evaluations. Social understanding also increases in middle and late childhood, especially in taking the perspectives of others.

- Self-definition in adolescence is more abstract and idealistic, involves more contradictions within the self, is more fluctuating, includes concern about the real self versus the ideal self, is characterized by increased self-consciousness, and is more integrative. Increases in social understanding in adolescence involve greater skepticism of others' reports of their traits, more in-depth perspective taking, and social cognitive monitoring. Developments in adults' self-understanding include expanded self-awareness, revision of possible selves, and life reviews of older adults.

Self-Esteem and Self-Concept

- Self-esteem refers to global evaluations of the self; it is also called self-worth and self-image. Self-concept consists of domain-specific evaluations of the self. Self-esteem can change over time, and low self-esteem is linked with depression.

- The accuracy of self-evaluations increases across the elementary school years. Some studies have found that self-esteem decreases in adolescence, but overall, most adolescents still have positive self-esteem. Important aspects of self-esteem include the degree to which it is linked to performance. This varies, as there are only moderate correlations with school performance and varying correlations with job performance; individuals with high self-esteem have greater initiative and this can produce positive or negative outcomes.

- Self-esteem is strongly correlated with happiness, but there is a dark side to high self-esteem in that some individuals who have high self-esteem are conceited and narcissistic. Five ways to increase self-esteem are through (1) identifying the causes of low self-esteem and the domains of competence important to the self, (2) providing emotional support and social approval, (3) taking responsibility for one's own self-esteem, (4) achieving goals, and (5) developing effective coping strategies.

Self-Regulation

- Self-regulation involves the ability to control one's behavior without having to rely on others for help. Two-year-olds may show rudimentary forms of self-regulation, but many preschoolers show increased self-regulation. Elementary-school-aged children increase their self-regulation. In adolescence, some changes may increase self-regulation, while others decrease it. Self-control increases in early and middle adulthood.

- Self-regulation may vary by domain. For example, older adults often show less self-regulation in the physical domain than younger adults do. Baltes proposed the selective optimization with compensation theory of self-regulation. Many older adults show a remarkable ability to engage in self-regulation despite encountering losses.

2 Identity

 LG2 Explain the key facets of identity development.

What Is Identity?

- Identity is a self-portrait with many pieces, including vocational/career identity, political identity, religious identity, relationship identity, sexual identity, and cultural/ethnic identity.

Erikson's View

- Identity versus identity confusion is Erikson's fifth developmental stage, which individuals experience during the adolescent years. At this time, adolescents examine who they are, what they are all about, and where they are going in life. Erikson describes the psychosocial moratorium between childhood dependence and adult independence that adolescents experience, which promotes identity exploration.

Some Contemporary Thoughts on Identity

- In the contemporary view, identity development is more gradual than Erikson's term *crisis* implies, is extraordinarily complex, neither begins nor ends with adolescence, and emphasizes multiple identities.

Developmental Changes

- According to Marcia, various combinations of crisis and commitment produce four identity statuses: identity diffused, identity foreclosed, identity moratorium, and identity achieved. A number of experts stress that the key developmental changes in identity occur in the late teens and early twenties. "MAMA" (moratorium-achievement-moratorium-achievement) cycles may continue throughout adulthood. Criticisms of Marcia's approach have been made, especially that identity exploration and commitment need to be examined more in depth and on a continuing basis.

Identity and Social Contexts

- Adolescents' identity development advances when their relationship with their parents includes both individuality and connectedness. Friendships, romantic relationships, and the digital environment influence adolescents' identity development.

- Cross-cultural variations in identity occur. Ethnic identity may present special issues for members of ethnic minority groups, and they may confront these issues for the first time in adolescence. A positive ethnic identity is increasingly linked to positive outcomes for ethnic minority adolescents.

3 Personality

LG3 Describe personality and its development in adulthood.

Trait Theories and the Big Five Factors of Personality

- Trait theories state that personality consists of broad dispositions, called traits, that tend to produce characteristic responses. One trait theory that has received considerable attention involves the Big Five factors of personality, which consist of openness to experience, conscientiousness, extraversion, agreeableness, and neuroticism. Also, optimism is linked with a number of positive developmental outcomes, including better health and living longer. Today most psychologists stress that personality is a product of trait-situation interaction.

Views on Adult Personality Development

- Two of the important adult developmental views are the stage-crisis view and the life-events approach. Levinson's and Erikson's theories are stage-crisis views. Midlife crises are not nearly as common as the stereotype suggests. What does arise is a midlife consciousness that focuses on such matters as how to adapt to aging. The life-events approach argues that life events and how people adapt to them are important in understanding adult development.

There is considerable variation in how people go through the adult stages of development and in how they experience and adapt to life events.

Generativity

- Erikson argues that middle-aged adults face a significant issue in life—generativity versus stagnation—which is the name he gave to the seventh stage in his life-span theory. Generativity encompasses adults' desire to leave a legacy of themselves to the next generation.

Stability and Change

- Four longitudinal studies that have addressed stability and change in adult development are Costa and McCrae's Baltimore Study, the Berkeley Longitudinal Studies, Helson's Mills College Study, and Vaillant's studies. The longitudinal studies have shown both stability and change in adult personality development. The cumulative personality model states that with time and age personality becomes more stable.

- Change in personality traits occurs more in early adulthood than middle and late adulthood, but a number of aspects of personality do continue to change after early adulthood. Change in personality traits across adulthood occurs in a positive direction, reflecting social maturity. At the individual level, changes in personality are often linked to life experiences related to a specific developmental period. Some people change more than others.

key **terms**

bicultural identity	ethnic identity	individuality	self-concept
Big Five factors of personality	generativity versus stagnation	optimism	self-esteem
commitment	identity achievement	perspective taking	self-regulation
connectedness	identity diffusion	possible selves	self-understanding
contemporary life-events approach	identity foreclosure	psychosocial moratorium	trait theories
	identity moratorium	selective optimization with	
crisis	identity versus identity confusion	compensation theory	

key **people**

Paul Baltes	Susan Harter	James Marcia	Ross Thompson
John Clausen	Ravenna Helson	Robert McCrae	George Vaillant
Paul Costa	Claire Kopp	Walter Mischel	Alan Waterman
Erik Erikson	Daniel Levinson	Daniel Mroczek	
Luc Goossens	Koen Luyckx	Brent Roberts	

chapter 12

GENDER AND SEXUALITY

chapter outline

① Biological, Social, and Cognitive Influences on Gender

Learning Goal 1 Explain biological, social, and cognitive influences on gender.

Biological Influences
Social Influences
Cognitive Influences

② Gender Stereotypes, Similarities, Differences, and Classification

Learning Goal 2 Discuss gender stereotypes, similarities, differences, and classification.

Gender Stereotyping
Gender Similarities and Differences
Gender-Role Classification
Going Beyond Gender as Binary

③ Gender Development Through the Life Span

Learning Goal 3 Describe the development of gender through the life span.

Childhood
Adolescence
Adulthood and Aging

④ Exploring Sexuality

Learning Goal 4 Characterize influences on sexuality, the nature of sexual orientation, and some sexual problems.

Biological and Cultural Factors
Sexual Orientation
Sexually Transmitted Infections
Forcible Sexual Behavior and Sexual Harassment

⑤ Sexuality Through the Life Span

Learning Goal 5 Summarize how sexuality develops through the life span.

Childhood
Adolescence and Emerging Adulthood
Adult Development and Aging

Tom Merton/Getty Images

preview

Human beings are involved in the existence and continuation of life. The topics of this chapter—gender and sexuality—are central aspects of human development.

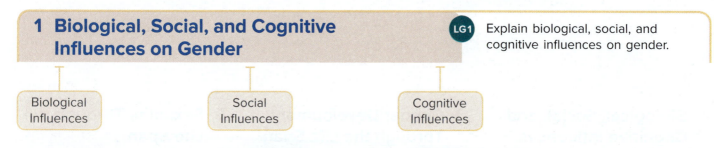

1 Biological, Social, and Cognitive Influences on Gender

LG1 Explain biological, social, and cognitive influences on gender.

- Biological Influences
- Social Influences
- Cognitive Influences

> We are born twice over; the first time for existence, the second time for life; once as human beings and later as men or as women.

—JEAN-JACQUES ROUSSEAU
French-Born Swiss Philosopher, 18th Century

gender The characteristics of people as females or males.

gender identity Involves a sense of one's own gender, including knowledge, understanding, and acceptance of being male or female.

gender role A set of expectations that prescribe how females or males should think, act, or feel.

gender-typing Acquisition of a traditional masculine or feminine role.

estrogens A class of sex hormones—an important one of which is estradiol—that primarily influences the development of female sex characteristics and helps to regulate the menstrual cycle.

androgens A class of sex hormones—an important one of which is testosterone—that primarily promotes the development of male genitals and secondary sex characteristics.

Gender refers to the characteristics of people as males and females. **Gender identity** involves a sense of one's own gender, including knowledge, understanding, and acceptance of being male or female (Brannon, 2017; Perry, 2012). **Gender roles** are sets of expectations that prescribe how females or males should think, act, and feel (Best & Puzio, 2019). During the preschool years, most children increasingly act in ways that match their culture's gender roles. **Gender-typing** refers to acquisition of a traditional masculine or feminine role. For example, fighting is more characteristic of a traditional masculine role and crying is more characteristic of a traditional feminine role (Helgeson, 2017).

One aspect of gender identity involves knowing whether you are a boy or a girl. Until recently, it was thought that this aspect of gender identity emerged at about 2½ years of age. However, a longitudinal study that explored the acquisition of gender labels in infancy and their implications for gender-typed play revealed that gender identity likely emerges before children are 2 years old (Zosuls & others, 2009). In this study, infants began using gender labels on average at 19 months of age, with girls beginning to use gender labels earlier than boys. This gender difference became present at 17 months and increased at 21 months. Use of gender labels was linked to gender-typed play, indicating that knowledge of gender categories may affect gender-typing earlier than age 2. Another study revealed that sex-typed behavior (boys playing with cars and girls with jewelry, for example) increased during the preschool years, and children who engaged in the most sex-typed behavior during the preschool years were still doing so at 8 years of age (Golombok & others, 2008).

BIOLOGICAL INFLUENCES

It was not until the 1920s that researchers confirmed the existence of human sex chromosomes, the genetic material that determines our sex. Humans normally have 46 chromosomes, arranged in pairs. A 23rd pair with two X-shaped chromosomes produces a female. A 23rd pair with an X chromosome and a Y chromosome produces a male.

Hormones   The two classes of hormones that have the most influence on gender are estrogens and androgens. Both estrogens and androgens occur in females and males, but in very different concentrations—typically based on the sex they were assigned at birth (female or male).

Estrogens primarily influence the development of female physical sex characteristics and help regulate the menstrual cycle. Estrogens are a general class of hormones. An example of an important estrogen is estradiol. In females, estrogens are produced mainly by the ovaries.

Androgens primarily promote the development of male genitals and secondary sex characteristics. One important androgen is testosterone. Androgens are produced by the adrenal glands in males and females, and by the testes in males.

During the first few weeks of gestation, female and male embryos look alike. Male sex organs start to differ from female sex organs when a gene on the Y chromosome directs a small piece of tissue in the embryo to turn into testes. Once the tissue has turned into testes, they begin to secrete testosterone. Because in females there is no Y chromosome, the tissue turns into ovaries. To explore biological influences on gender, researchers have studied individuals who are exposed to unusual levels of sex hormones early in development (Hines, 2015; Kung & others, 2018). Here are four examples of the problems that may occur as a result of such exposure (Lippa, 2005, pp. 122–124, 136–137):

- *Congenital adrenal hyperplasia (CAH).* Some girls have this condition, which is caused by a genetic defect that causes increased androgen production beginning prenatally (Deeb & others, 2019; de Jesus, Costa, & Dekemacher, 2019). Their adrenal glands enlarge, resulting in abnormally high levels of androgens. Although CAH girls are XX females, they vary in how much their genitals look like male or female genitals. Their genitals may be surgically altered to look more like those of a typical female (Iovino & others, 2019; Walia & others, 2018). Although CAH girls usually grow up to think of themselves as girls and women, they are less content with being a female and show a stronger interest in being a male than non-CAH girls (Li, Kung, & Hines, 2017). They like sports and enjoy playing with boys and boys' toys. CAH girls usually don't like typical girl activities such as playing with dolls and wearing makeup. In a recent study, CAH girls showed higher levels of aggression than non-CAH girls (Spencer & others, 2017). Also, in another recent study, CAH girls had more conduct problems, a greater likelihood of developing ADHD, and lower engagement in prosocial behavior (Kung & others, 2018).
- *Androgen-insensitive males.* Because of a genetic error, a small number of XY males don't have androgen cells in their bodies. Their bodies look female, they develop a female gender identity, and they usually are sexually attracted to males.
- *Pelvic field defect.* A small number of newborns have a disorder called pelvic field defect, which in boys involves a missing penis. These XY boys have normal amounts of testosterone prenatally but usually are castrated just after being born and raised as females. One study revealed that despite the efforts by parents to rear them as girls, most of the XY children insisted that they were boys (Reiner & Gearhart, 2004). Apparently, normal exposure to androgens prenatally had a stronger influence on their gender identity than being castrated and raised as girls.
- *Early loss of penis and sexual reassignment.* In 1966 in Manitoba, Canada, one of two identical twin boys lost his penis at the age of seven months during a botched circumcision. The twin who lost his penis was surgically reassigned to be a girl and raised as a girl. Bruce (the real name of the boy) became "Brenda." The psychologist overseeing the case reported a positive outcome of the sexual reassignment (Money, 1975), but later it became clear that "Brenda" had not adjusted well to life as a girl (Diamond & Sigmundson, 1997). As a young adult, Brenda became David and lived as a man with a wife and adopted children (Colapinto, 2000). Tragically in 2004, when David was 38 years old, he committed suicide.

Although sex hormones alone do not dictate behavior, researchers have found links between sex hormone levels and certain behaviors (Iovino & others, 2019; Li, Kung, & Hines, 2017; Pascual-Sagastizabal & others, 2019). The most established effects of testosterone on humans involve aggressive behavior and sexual behavior (Dreher & others, 2016; Nguyen, 2019). Levels of testosterone are correlated with male sexual behavior during puberty and adulthood (Grotzinger & others, 2018; Kruger & others, 2019; Nguyen & others, 2019). One study revealed that a higher fetal testosterone level measured from amniotic fluid was linked to increased male-typical play, such as increased aggression, in 6- to 10-year-old boys and girls (Auyeung & others, 2009). And in a recent study, 3-year-old boys with higher prenatal testosterone levels had shorter delay of gratification times and more attention problems (Korner & others, 2019).

The Evolutionary Psychology View Evolutionary psychology emphasizes that adaptation during the evolution of humans produced psychological differences between males and females (Antfolk, 2019; Buss, 2018; Buss & Schmidt, 2019; Euler, 2019). Evolutionary psychologists argue that primarily because of their differing roles in reproduction, males and females faced different pressures in primeval environments when the human species was

developmental **connection**

Biological Processes

The genetic difference in males and females occurs in the 23rd pair of chromosomes: the male's Y chromosome is smaller than the female's X chromosome. Connect to "Biological Beginnings."

developmental **connection**

Biological Processes

Hormones are powerful chemical substances secreted by the endocrine glands and carried through the body by the bloodstream. Connect to "Physical Development and Biological Aging."

developmental **connection**

Biological Processes

Evolutionary psychology emphasizes the importance of adaptation, reproduction, and "survival of the fittest" in shaping behavior. Connect to "Biological Beginnings."

> Sex differences are adaptations to the differing restrictions and opportunities that a society provides for its men and women.
>
> —ALICE EAGLY
>
> *Contemporary Psychologist, Northwestern University*

developmental **connection**

Social Cognitive Theory

Social cognitive theory holds that behavior, environment, and person (cognitive) factors are the key aspects of development. Connect to "Introduction."

social role theory Eagly's theory that psychological gender differences are caused by the contrasting social roles of women and men.

psychoanalytic theory of gender Theory that stems from Freud's view that preschool children develop a sexual attraction to the opposite-sex parent, then at 5 or 6 years of age renounce the attraction because of anxious feelings, subsequently identifying with the same-sex parent and unconsciously adopting the same-sex parent's characteristics.

social cognitive theory of gender The idea that children's gender development occurs through observation and imitation of gender behavior, as well as through the rewards and punishments children experience for behaviors believed to be appropriate or inappropriate for their gender.

evolving (Ellis & Del Guidice, 2019; Grebe & others, 2019; Solomon & others, 2019). In particular, because having multiple sexual liaisons improves the likelihood that males will pass on their genes, natural selection favored males who adopted short-term mating strategies. These males competed with other males to acquire more resources in order to access females. Therefore, say evolutionary psychologists, males evolved dispositions that favor violence, competition, and risk taking (Buss & Schmitt, 2019).

In contrast, according to evolutionary psychologists, females' contributions to the gene pool were improved by securing resources for their offspring, which was promoted by obtaining long-term mates who could support a family. As a consequence, natural selection favored females who devoted effort to parenting and chose mates who could provide their offspring with resources and protection. Females developed preferences for successful, ambitious men who could provide these resources (Buss, 2018; Starr & others, 2019).

Critics of evolutionary psychology argue that its hypotheses are backed by speculations about prehistory, not evidence, and that in any event people are not locked into behavior that was adaptive in the evolutionary past. Critics also claim that the evolutionary view pays little attention to cultural and individual variations in gender differences (Best & Puzio, 2019; Hyde & DeLamater, 2017).

SOCIAL INFLUENCES

Many social scientists do not locate the cause of psychological gender differences in biological dispositions. Rather, they argue that these differences are due to social experiences (Best & Puzio, 2019; Leaper & Bigler, 2018; MacPhee & Prendergast, 2019; Rose & Smith, 2018). Three theories that reflect this view have been influential.

Alice Eagly (2010, 2013, 2016, 2018) proposed **social role theory,** which states that psychological gender differences result from the contrasting roles of women and men. In most cultures around the world, women have less power and status than men do, and they control fewer resources (UNICEF, 2019). Compared with men, women perform more domestic work, spend fewer hours in paid employment, receive lower pay, and are more thinly represented in the highest levels of organizations. In Eagly's view, as women adapted to roles with less power and less status in society, they showed more cooperative, less dominant profiles than men. Thus, the social hierarchy and division of labor are important causes of gender differences in power, assertiveness, and nurture (Eagly, 2016, 2018).

The **psychoanalytic theory of gender** stems from Sigmund Freud's view that the preschool child develops a sexual attraction to the opposite-sex parent. At 5 or 6 years of age, the child renounces this attraction because of anxious feelings. Subsequently, the child identifies with the same-sex parent, unconsciously adopting the same-sex parent's characteristics. However, developmentalists do not hold that gender development proceeds as Freud proposed. Children become gender-typed much earlier than 5 or 6 years of age, and they become masculine or feminine even when the same-sex parent is not present in the family.

The social cognitive approach provides an alternative explanation of how children develop gender-typed behavior (see Figure 1). According to the **social cognitive theory of gender,** children's gender development occurs through observation and imitation, and through the rewards

Theory	Processes	Outcome
Psychoanalytic theory	Sexual attraction to opposite-sex parent at 3 to 5 years of age; anxiety about sexual attraction and subsequent identification with same-sex parent at 5 to 6 years of age	Gender behavior similar to that of same-sex parent
Social cognitive theory	Rewards and punishments of gender-appropriate and -inappropriate behavior by adults and peers; observation and imitation of models' masculine and feminine behavior	Gender behavior

FIGURE 1

PARENTS INFLUENCE THEIR CHILDREN'S GENDER DEVELOPMENT BY ACTION AND EXAMPLE

and punishments children experience for gender-appropriate and gender-inappropriate behavior (Bussey & Bandura, 1999; Leaper & Bigler, 2018).

Parents   Parents, by action and example, influence their children's and adolescents' gender development (Brannon, 2017; Helgeson, 2017). Parents often use rewards and punishments to teach their daughters to be feminine ("Karen, you are being a good girl when you play gently with your doll") and their sons to be masculine ("Keith, a boy as big as you is not supposed to cry").

Mothers and fathers often interact differently with their children and adolescents (Brown & Stone, 2018; Herbrand, 2018; Leaper & Bigler, 2018). Mothers are more involved with their children and adolescents than are fathers, although fathers increase the time they spend in parenting when they have sons, and they are less likely to become divorced when they have sons (Galambos, Berenbaum, & McHale, 2009). Mothers' interactions with their children and adolescents often center on caregiving and teaching activities, whereas fathers' interactions often involve leisure activities (Galambos, Berenbaum, & McHale, 2009). Parents frequently interact differently with sons and daughters, and these gendered interactions that begin in infancy usually continue through childhood and adolescence (Leaper, 2015). In reviewing research on this topic, Phyllis Bronstein (2006) reached these conclusions:

- *Mothers' socialization strategies.* In many cultures, mothers socialize their daughters to be more obedient and responsible than their sons. They also place more restrictions on daughters' autonomy.
- *Fathers' socialization strategies.* Fathers pay more attention to sons than to daughters, engage in more activities with sons, and put forth more effort to promote sons' intellectual development.

Thus, according to Bronstein (2006, pp. 269–270), "Despite an increased awareness in the United States and other Western cultures of the detrimental effects of gender stereotyping, many parents continue to foster behaviors and perceptions that are consonant with traditional gender role norms."

Other Adults, Media, and Peers   Children also learn about gender from observing other adults in the neighborhood and in the media (Kinsler & others, 2018; Matthes, Prieler, & Adam, 2016). As children get older, peers become increasingly important (Chen, Lee, & Chen, 2018). Peers extensively reward and punish gender behavior (Leaper & Bigler, 2018). For example, when children play in gender-stereotypical ways that are deemed culturally appropriate, they tend to be rewarded by their peers. Those who engage in activities that are considered sex-inappropriate tend to be criticized or abandoned by their peers. It is generally more accepted for girls to act like boys than for boys to act like girls; thus, use of the term *tomboy* to describe masculine girls is often thought of as less derogatory than the

What role does gender play in children's peer relations?
(*Left*): JackF/Getty Images; (*right*): Zero Creatives/Getty Images

term *sissy* to describe feminine boys (Pasterski, Golombok, & Hines, 2011). In a recent study of 9- to 10-year-olds in Great Britain, gender-nonconforming boys were most at risk for peer rejection (Braun & Davidson, 2017). In this study, gender non-conforming girls were preferred more than gender-conforming girls, with children most often citing masculine activities as the reason for this choice.

From 4 to about 12 years of age, children spend a large majority of their free play time exclusively with others of their own sex (Maccoby, 2002). What kind of socialization takes place in these same-sex play groups? In one study, researchers observed preschoolers over a period of six months (Martin & Fabes, 2001). The more time boys spent interacting with other boys, the more their activity level, rough-and-tumble play, and gender-typed choice of toys and games increased, and the less time boys spent near adults. By contrast, the more time the preschool girls spent interacting with other girls, the more their activity level and aggression decreased, and the more their girl-type play activities and time spent near adults increased. A study of preschool children (average age: 4 years) found that children selected playmates of the same sex who engaged in similar levels of gender-typed activities (Martin & others, 2013). In selecting a playmate, comparisons of gender of child and activity revealed that gender of the playmate was more important than activity. After watching elementary school children repeatedly play in same-gender groups, two researchers characterized the playground as "gender school" (Luria & Herzog, 1985). From adolescence through late adulthood, friendships also mainly consist of same-sex peers (Mehta & Strough, 2009, 2010).

Schools and Teachers   Some observers have expressed concern that schools and teachers have biases against both boys and girls (Brown & Stone, 2016). What evidence exists that the classroom setting is biased against boys? Here are some factors to consider (DeZolt & Hull, 2001):

- Compliance, following rules, and being neat and orderly are valued and reinforced in many classrooms. These are behaviors that usually characterize girls more than boys.
- A large majority of teachers are females, especially at the elementary school level. This trend may make it more difficult for boys than for girls to identify with their teachers and model their teachers' behavior. One study revealed that male teachers perceived boys more positively and saw them as more educationally competent than female teachers did (Mullola & others, 2012).
- Boys are more likely than girls to have a learning disability or ADHD and to drop out of school.
- Boys are more likely than girls to be criticized by their teachers.
- School personnel tend to stereotype boys' behavior as problematic.

What evidence is there that the classroom setting is biased against girls? Consider the views of Myra and David Sadker (2005):

- In a typical classroom, girls are more compliant and boys are more rambunctious. Boys demand more attention, and girls are more likely to quietly wait their turn. Teachers are more likely to scold and reprimand boys, as well as send boys to school authorities for disciplinary action. Educators worry that girls' tendency to be compliant and quiet comes at a cost: diminished assertiveness.
- In many classrooms, teachers spend more time watching and interacting with boys, whereas girls work and play quietly on their own. Most teachers don't intentionally favor boys by spending more time with them, yet somehow the classroom frequently ends up with this type of gendered profile.
- Boys get more instruction than girls and more help when they have trouble with a question. Teachers often give boys more time to answer a question, more hints at the correct answer, and further tries if they give the wrong answer.
- Girls and boys enter first grade with roughly equal levels of self-esteem. Yet by the middle school years, girls' self-esteem is lower than boys'.

Thus, there is evidence of gender bias against both males and females in schools. Many school personnel are not aware of their gender-biased attitudes. These attitudes are deeply entrenched in and supported by the general culture. Increasing awareness of gender bias in schools is clearly an important strategy in reducing such bias (Brown & Stone, 2016).

Might single-sex education be better for children than coeducation? The argument for single-sex education is that it eliminates distraction from the other sex and reduces sexual harassment. Single-sex public education has increased dramatically in recent years. In 2002, only 12 public schools in the United States provided single-sex education; during the 2011–2012 school year, 116 public schools were single-sex and an additional 390 provided such experiences (NASSPE, 2012).

The increase in single-sex education has especially been fueled by its inclusion in the No Child Left Behind legislation as a means of improving the educational experiences and academic achievement of low-income students of color. It appears that many of the public schools offering single-sex education have a high percentage of such youth (Klein, 2012). However, recent research reviews concluded that there have been no documented benefits of single-sex education, especially in the highest-quality studies (Goodkind, 2013; Halpern & others, 2011; Hoffnung, 2017; Pahlke, Hyde, & Allison, 2014). One review, titled "The Pseudoscience of Single-Sex Schooling," by Diane Halpern and her colleagues (2011) concluded that single-sex education is highly misguided, misconstrued, and unsupported by any valid scientific evidence. They emphasize that among the many arguments against single-sex education, the strongest is its reduction in the opportunities for boys and girls to work together in a supervised, purposeful environment.

What are some recent changes in single-sex education in the United States? What does research say about whether single-sex education is beneficial?
Jim Weber/The Commercial Appeal/Landov

There has been a special call for single-sex public education for one group of adolescents—African American boys—because of their historically poor academic achievement and high dropout rate from school (Mitchell & Stewart, 2013). In 2010, Urban Prep Academy for Young Men became the first all-male, all African American public charter school. One hundred percent of its first graduates enrolled in college, despite the school's location in a section of Chicago where poverty, gangs, and crime predominate. And continuing each year since through 2018, 100 percent of Urban Prep's graduates have gone on to college. Because so few public schools focus solely on educating African American boys, it is too early to tell whether this type of single-sex education can be effective across a wide range of participants.

COGNITIVE INFLUENCES

Observation, imitation, rewards, and punishment—these are the mechanisms by which gender develops, according to social cognitive theory. Interactions between the child and the social environment are viewed as the main keys to gender development. Some critics who adopt a cognitive approach argue that social cognitive explanations pay too little attention to the child's own mind and understanding, portraying the child as passively acquiring gender roles (Martin, Ruble, & Szkrybalo, 2002).

One influential cognitive theory is **gender schema theory,** which states that gender-typing emerges as children gradually develop gender schemas of what is gender-appropriate and gender-inappropriate in their culture (Liben & others, 2018; Martin & others, 2017). A *schema* is a cognitive structure, a network of associations that guide an individual's perceptions. A *gender schema* organizes the world in terms of female and male. Children are internally motivated to perceive the world and to act in accordance with their developing schemas. Bit by bit, children pick up what is gender-appropriate and gender-inappropriate in their culture, using this information to develop gender schemas that shape how they perceive the world and what they remember (Conry-Murray, Kim, & Turiel, 2012). Children are motivated to act in ways that conform to these gender schemas. Thus, gender schemas fuel gender-typing. How effectively do gender schemas extend to young children's judgments about occupations, for instance? For more information on this topic, see the *Connecting with Research* interlude.

In sum, cognitive factors contribute to the way children think and act as males and females (Liben, 2017; Liben & others, 2018). Through biological, social, and cognitive processes, children develop their gender attitudes and behaviors (Best & Puzio, 2019; Deeb & others, 2019; Hyde & others, 2019).

gender schema theory The theory that gender-typing emerges as children gradually develop gender schemas of what is gender-appropriate and gender-inappropriate in their culture.

connecting with research

What Are Young Children's Gender Schemas About Occupations?

In one study, researchers interviewed children 3 to 7 years old about 10 traditionally masculine occupations (airplane pilot, car mechanic) and feminine occupations (clothing designer, secretary), using questions such as these (Levy, Sadovsky, & Troseth, 2000):

· (Example of a traditionally masculine occupation item) An airplane pilot is a person who "flies airplanes for people." Who do you think would do the best job as an airplane pilot, a man or a woman?

· (Example of a traditionally feminine occupation item) A clothing designer is a person "who draws up and makes clothes for people." Who do you think would do the best job as a clothing designer, a man or a woman?

As indicated in Figure 2, the children had well-developed gender schemas, in this case reflected in stereotypes, of occupations. They "viewed men as more competent than women in masculine occupations, and rated women as more competent than men in feminine occupations" (p. 993). Also, "girls' ratings of women's competence at feminine occupations were substantially higher than their ratings of men's competence at masculine occupations. Conversely, boys' ratings of men's competence at masculine occupations were considerably greater than their ratings of women's competence at feminine occupations" (p. 1002). These findings demonstrate that children as young as 3 to 4 years of age have strong gender schemas regarding the perceived competencies of men and women in gender-typed occupations.

The researchers also asked the children to select from a list of emotions how they would feel if they grew up to have each of the 10 occupations. Girls said they would be happy with the feminine occupations and angry or disgusted with the masculine occupations. As expected, boys said they would be happy if they had the masculine occupations but angry and disgusted with the feminine occupations. However, the boys' emotions were more intense (more angry and disgusted) in desiring to avoid the feminine occupations than girls in wanting to avoid the masculine occupations. This finding supports other research that indicates gender roles often constrict boys more than girls (Matlin, 2012).

	Boy	Girl
"Masculine Occupations"		
Percentage who judged men more competent	87	70
Percentage who judged women more competent	13	30
"Feminine Occupations"		
Percentage who judged men more competent	35	8
Percentage who judged women more competent	64	92

FIGURE 2

CHILDREN'S JUDGMENTS ABOUT THE COMPETENCE OF MEN AND WOMEN IN GENDER-STEREOTYPED OCCUPATIONS.

Children in this study were at the height of gender stereotyping. Most older children, adolescents, and adults become more flexible about occupational roles (Leaper, 2013). What does our understanding of this flexibility suggest about the role of education in reducing gender-based stereotypes?

Review Connect Reflect

 LG1 Explain biological, social, and cognitive influences on gender.

Review

· What is gender? What are some components of gender?
· How does biology influence gender?
· How do cognitive factors influence gender development?

Connect

· Compare biological, social, and cognitive influences on gender.

Reflect *Your Own Personal Journey of Life*

· Which theory of gender development do you think best explains your gender development? Explain. What might an eclectic view of gender development be like? (You might want to review the discussion of an eclectic theoretical view in the "Introduction" chapter.)

| Gender Stereotyping | Gender Similarities and Differences | Gender-Role Classification | Going Beyond Gender as Binary |

To what extent do real behavioral differences exist between males and females? Are many of the reported differences just stereotypes? What are some different categories of gender classification? Is it time to go beyond the concept of gender as binary?

GENDER STEREOTYPING

Gender stereotypes are general impressions and beliefs about females and males. For example, men are powerful; women are weak. Men make good physicians; women make good nurses. Men are good with numbers; women are good with words. Women are emotional; men are not. All of these are stereotypes. They are generalizations about a group that reflect widely held beliefs. Recent research has found that gender stereotypes are, to a great extent, still present in today's world, in the lives of both children and adults (Brannon, 2017; Gustafsson-Senden & others, 2019; Ellemers, 2018). Researchers also have found that boys' gender stereotypes are more rigid than girls' (Halim, 2016).

Traditional Masculinity and Femininity A classic study in the early 1970s assessed which traits and behaviors college students believed were characteristic of females and which they believed were characteristic of males (Broverman & others, 1972). The traits associated with males were labeled *instrumental:* they included characteristics such as being independent, aggressive, and power-oriented. The traits associated with females were labeled *expressive:* they included characteristics such as being warm and sensitive.

Thus, the instrumental traits associated with males suited them for the traditional masculine role of going out into the world as the breadwinner. The expressive traits associated with females paralleled the traditional feminine role of being the sensitive, nurturing caregiver in the home. These roles and traits, however, are not just different; they also are unequal in terms of social status and power. The traditional feminine characteristics are childlike, suitable for someone who is dependent and subordinate to others. The traditional masculine characteristics suit one to deal competently with the wider world and to wield authority.

Developmental Changes in Gender Stereotyping Earlier we described how young children stereotype occupations as being "masculine" or "feminine." When do children begin to engage in gender stereotyping? In one study, gender stereotyping by children was present even in 2-year-olds but increased considerably by 4 years of age (Gelman, Taylor, & Nguyen, 2004). Another study found that 2-year-olds' knowledge of only one or the other gender categories did not predict an increase in gender stereotyping from 2 to 3 years old but their knowledge of both genders did (Zosuls, Ruble, & Tamis-LeMonda, 2014).

Gender stereotyping continues to change during middle and late childhood and adolescence (Halim, 2016). Research indicates that while gender stereotyping is often a time of gender rigidity, in middle and late childhood boys and girls become more flexible in their gender-typing (Halim, 2016). In some studies, the increase in gender flexibility characterizes girls more than boys (Halim & others, 2016). For example, a study of 3- to 10-year-old U.S. children revealed that girls and older children used a higher percentage of gender stereotypes (Miller & others, 2009). In this study, appearance stereotypes were more prevalent on the part of girls, whereas activity (sports, for example) and trait (aggressive, for example) stereotyping was more commonly engaged in by boys. During middle and late childhood, children expanded the range and extent of their gender stereotyping in areas such as occupations, sports, and school tasks. In early adolescence, gender stereotyping might increase again, a topic we will address shortly. By late adolescence, gender attitudes become more flexible.

First imagine that this is a photograph of a baby girl. *What expectations would you have for her?* Then imagine that this is a photograph of a baby boy. *What expectations would you have for him?*
Kwame Zikomo/Purestock/SuperStock

gender stereotypes General impressions and beliefs about females and males.

GENDER SIMILARITIES AND DIFFERENCES

What is the reality behind gender stereotypes? Let's examine some of the differences between the sexes, keeping the following information in mind:

- The differences are averages and do not apply to all females or all males.
- Even when gender differences occur, there often is considerable overlap between males and females.
- The differences may be due primarily to biological factors, sociocultural factors, or both.

First, we examine physical similarities and differences, and then we turn to cognitive and socioemotional similarities and differences.

Physical Similarities and Differences   We could devote pages to describing physical differences between the average man and the average woman. For example, women have about twice the body fat of men, most of it concentrated around breasts and hips. In males, fat is more likely to go to the abdomen. On average, males grow to be 10 percent taller than females. Androgens (the "male" hormones) promote the growth of long bones; estrogens (the "female" hormones) stop such growth at puberty.

Many physical differences between men and women are tied to health. From conception onward, females have a longer life expectancy than males, and females are less likely than males to develop physical or mental disorders. Females are more resistant to infection, and their blood vessels are more elastic than males'. Males have higher levels of stress hormones, which cause faster clotting and higher blood pressure.

Just how much does gender matter when it comes to brain structure and activity? Among the differences that have been discovered are the following:

- One part of the hypothalamus involved in sexual behavior tends to be larger in men than in women (Swaab & others, 2001).
- An area of the parietal lobe that functions in visuospatial skills tends to be larger in males than in females (Frederikse & others, 2000).
- The areas of the brain involved in emotional expression tend to show more metabolic activity in females than in males (Gur & others, 1995).
- Female brains are approximately 10 percent smaller than male brains (Giedd & others, 2012). However, female brains have more folds; the larger folds (called convolutions) allow more surface brain tissue within the skulls of females than males (Luders & others, 2004).

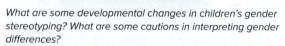

Although some gender differences in brain structure and function have been found, many of these differences are small or research results are inconsistent regarding the differences (Hyde & others, 2019). Recently, because the distributions for males and females on different brain features overlap considerably, Janet Shibley Hyde and her colleagues (2019) have concluded that in most instances it is more accurate to describe these features as a mosaic rather than as male-typical and female-typical brains. Also, when gender differences in the brain have been detected, in many cases they have not been directly linked to psychological differences (Blakemore, Berenbaum, & Liben, 2009). Also, similarities and differences in the brains of males and females may be due to biological or experiential factors (Hyde & others, 2019).

Cognitive Similarities and Differences   No gender differences occur in overall intellectual ability, but in some cognitive areas gender differences do appear (Galambos, Berenbaum, & McHale, 2009; Ganley, Vasilyeva, & Dulaney, 2014; Halpern, 2012). Some gender experts, such as Janet Shibley Hyde (2007, 2014; Hyde & others, 2019), stress that the cognitive differences between females and males have been exaggerated. For example, Hyde points out that there usually is considerable overlap in the distributions of female and male scores on visuospatial tasks (see Figure 3). However, some researchers have found that males have better visuospatial skills than females (Halpern, 2012). Despite equal participation in the

What are some developmental changes in children's gender stereotyping? What are some cautions in interpreting gender differences?
(Top): Anna.danilkova/Shutterstock; (bottom): Rebecca Nelson/Getty Images

National Geography Bee, in most years all 10 finalists have been boys (Liben, 1995). Also, a research review concluded that boys have better visuospatial skills than girls (Halpern & others, 2007). A research review found that having a stronger masculine gender role was linked to better spatial ability in males and females (Reilly & Neumann, 2013).

Are there gender differences in math ability? A very large-scale study of more than 7 million U.S. students in grades 2 through 11 revealed no differences in math scores for boys and girls (Hyde & others, 2008). And a research meta-analysis found no gender differences in math scores for adolescents (Lindberg & others, 2010). Further, in the National Assessment of Educational Progress (2017) there were virtually no gender differences in math scores at the fourth- and eighth-grade levels, with boys scoring only 2 points higher in the fourth grade and 1 point higher in the eighth grade on a 500-point scale.

Despite the similarities in math achievement scores for boys and girls, a research review concluded that girls have more negative math attitudes and that parents' and teachers' expectations for children's math competence are often gender-biased in favor of boys (Gunderson & others, 2012). And in one study, 6- to 12-year-olds reported that math is mainly for boys (Cvencek, Meltzoff, & Greenwald, 2011).

Are there gender differences in reading and writing skills? There is strong evidence that females outperform males in reading and writing. In the most recent National Assessment of Educational Progress (2017) report, girls had higher reading achievement than boys in both fourth- and eighth-grade assessments, with girls 6 points higher in the fourth grade and 10 points higher in the eighth grade. Girls also have consistently outperformed boys in writing skills in the National Assessment of Educational Progress in fourth-, eighth-, and twelfth-grade assessments.

With regard to school achievement, girls earn better grades and complete high school at a higher rate than boys (Halpern, 2012). Males are more likely than females to be assigned to special/remedial education classes. Girls are more likely than boys to be engaged with academic material, be attentive in class, put forth more academic effort, and participate more in class (DeZolt & Hull, 2001).

Keep in mind that measures of achievement in school or scores on standardized tests may reflect many factors besides cognitive ability. For example, performance in school may in part reflect attempts to conform to gender roles or differences in motivation, self-regulation, or other socioemotional characteristics (Becker & McElvany, 2018; Cole, Ram, & English, 2019). For example, a recent large-scale study of seventh-graders found that girls' perception that teachers had gendered expectations favoring boys over girls was linked to girls having more negative math beliefs and lower math achievement (McKellar & others, 2019). Also, in this study, when girls perceived that the math curriculum was personally meaningful and relevant for them, they had more positive math beliefs and higher math achievement.

Socioemotional Similarities and Differences   Are "men from Mars" and "women from Venus"? Perhaps the gender differences that most fascinate people are those regarding how males and females relate to each other as people. For just about every imaginable socio-emotional characteristic, researchers have examined whether there are differences between males and females. Here we examine just two that have been closely studied: (1) aggression and (2) emotion and its regulation.

Aggression   One of the most consistent gender differences identified is that boys are more physically aggressive than girls (Hyde, 2017). The difference occurs in all cultures and appears very early in children's development (Dayton & Malone, 2017). The difference in physical aggression is especially pronounced when children are provoked.

Although boys are consistently more physically aggressive than girls, might girls show as much or more verbal aggression, such as yelling, than boys? When verbal aggression is examined, gender differences typically disappear or aggression is even more pronounced in girls (Eagly & Steffen, 1986).

Recently, increased interest has been directed toward *relational aggression*, which involves harming someone by manipulating a relationship. Relational aggression includes such behaviors as trying to make others dislike a certain individual by spreading malicious rumors about the person (Casper & Card, 2017; Eisman & others, 2018; Padmanabhanunni & Gerhardt, 2019). Relational aggression increases in middle and late childhood

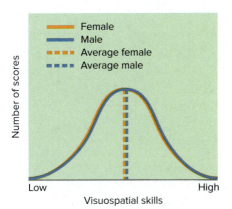

FIGURE 3

VISUOSPATIAL SKILLS OF MALES AND FEMALES. Notice that, although an average male's visuospatial skills are higher than an average female's, scores for the two sexes almost entirely overlap. Not all males have better visuospatial skills than all females—the overlap indicates that, although the average male score is higher, many females outperform most males on such tasks.

What gender differences characterize aggression?
Corbis

(Dishion & Piehler, 2009). Mixed findings have characterized research on whether girls show more relational aggression than boys, but one consistent finding is that relational aggression comprises a greater percentage of overall aggression for girls than for boys (Putallaz & others, 2007). And a research review revealed that girls engage in more relational aggression than boys in adolescence but not in childhood (Smith, Rose, & Schwartz-Mette, 2010). Further, in a longitudinal study, preschool relational aggression predicted adolescent relational aggression for girls but not for boys (Nelson & others, 2014). Also, in a recent study of adolescents, those who observed relational aggression on television were more likely to engage in relational aggression when they were texting one year later (Coyne & others, 2019).

Emotion and Emotion Regulation   Gender differences occur in some aspects of emotion (Brody, Hall, & Stokes, 2018; Connolly & others, 2019). Females express emotion more openly than males, are better than males at decoding emotion, smile more, cry more, and are happier (Gross, Frederickson, & Levenson, 1994; LaFrance, Hecht, & Paluck, 2003). Males report experiencing and expressing more anger than females do (Kring, 2000). Girls also are better at reading others' emotions and more likely to show empathy than are boys (Blakemore, Berenbaum, & Liben, 2009). A research meta-analysis found that females are better than males at recognizing nonverbal displays of emotion (Thompson & Voyer, 2014). Another meta-analysis also revealed that overall gender differences in children's emotional expression were small, with girls showing more positive emotion (sympathy, for example) and more internalized emotions (sadness and anxiety, for example) than boys (Chaplin & Aldao, 2013). In this analysis, the gender difference in positive emotions became more pronounced with age as girls more strongly expressed positive emotions than boys in middle and late childhood and in adolescence. Also, a recent study revealed that females are better than males at facial emotion perception across the life span (Olderbak & others, 2019).

An important skill is to be able to regulate and control one's emotions and behavior (Cole, Ram, & English, 2019; Denham & Bassett, 2019). Boys usually show less self-regulation than girls (Blakemore, Berenbaum, & Liben, 2009). This low self-control can translate into behavior problems (McClelland, Cameron, & Alonso, 2019).

Researchers have found that girls are more "people oriented" and boys are more "things oriented" (Galambos, Berenbaum, & McHale, 2009). In a research review, this conclusion was supported by findings that girls spend more time and energy building relationships, while boys spend more time alone, playing video games, and playing sports; that girls work at part-time jobs that are people-oriented such as waitressing and babysitting, while boys are more likely to take part-time jobs that involve manual labor and using tools; and girls are interested in careers that are more people-oriented, such as teaching and social work, while boys are more likely to be interested in object-oriented careers, such as mechanics and engineering (Perry & Pauletti, 2011). Researchers have found that adolescent girls engage in more self-disclosure (communication of intimate details about themselves) in close relationships, are better at actively listening in a conversation than are boys, and emphasize affiliation or collaboration (Hall, 2011; Leaper, 2013, 2015). Adolescent girls are especially likely to engage in self-disclosure and emotional support in friendship to a greater extent than are boys (Leaper, 2013). By contrast, boys are more likely to value self-assertion and dominance than are girls in their interactions with friends and peers (Leaper, 2013; Rose & Rudolph, 2006).

Gender Controversy   Controversy surrounds the extent of gender differences and what might cause them (Burt, Slawinski, & Klump, 2018; Hyde & others, 2019). As we saw earlier, evolutionary psychologists such as David Buss (2018) argue that gender differences are extensive and caused by the adaptive problems people have faced across their evolutionary history. Alice Eagly (2018) also concludes that gender differences are substantial but reaches a very different conclusion about their cause. She traces gender differences to social conditions that have resulted in women having less power and controlling fewer resources than men do.

By contrast, Janet Shibley Hyde (2014, 2017; Hyde & others, 2019) concludes that gender differences have been greatly exaggerated, with these comparisons being especially fueled by popular books such as John Gray's (1992) *Men Are from Mars, Women Are from Venus* and Deborah Tannen's (1990) *You Just Don't Understand*. She argues that the research indicates females and males are similar on most psychological factors. In a research review, Hyde (2005) summarized the results of 44 meta-analyses of gender differences and similarities. A *meta-analysis* is a statistical analysis that combines the results of many different studies. Gender differences in most areas—including math ability and communication—were either nonexistent

developmental **connection**

Emotion

Emotion regulation is a key aspect of children's socioemotional competence, and it changes developmentally. Connect with "Emotional Development and Attachment."

or small. Gender differences in physical aggression were moderate. The largest difference occurred on motor skills (favoring males), followed by sexuality (males masturbate more often and are more likely to endorse sex in a casual, uncommitted relationship) and physical aggression (males are more physically aggressive than females are).

Hyde's summary of meta-analyses is unlikely to quiet the controversy about gender differences and similarities, but further research should be conducted to provide a basis for more accurate judgments on this topic. Indeed, later in the chapter, after we discuss "Gender Role Classification," we will explore Hyde and her colleagues' (2019) expanded analysis of the breadth of gender similarities.

Gender in Context   In thinking about gender, it is important to consider the context of behavior (Moreau & others, 2019). Gender behavior often varies across contexts. Consider helping behavior. Males are more likely to help in contexts in which a perceived danger is present and they feel competent to help (Eagly & Crowley, 1986). For example, males are more likely than females to help a person who is stranded by the roadside with a flat tire; automobile problems are an area in which many males feel competent. In contrast, when the context involves volunteering time to help a child with a personal problem, females are more likely to help than males are, because there is little danger present and females feel more competent at nurturing. In many cultures, girls show more caregiving behavior than boys do.

Context is also relevant to gender differences in the display of emotions (Shields, 1998). Consider anger. Males are more likely to show anger toward strangers, especially other males, when they think they have been challenged. Males also are more likely than females to turn their anger into aggressive action, especially when their culture endorses such action (Tavris & Wade, 1984).

In many cultures around the world, traditional gender roles continue to guide the behavior of males and females (UNICEF, 2019). In China and Iran, for instance, it is still widely accepted for males to engage in dominant behavior and females to behave in subordinate ways. In a recent study of eighth-grade students in 36 countries, in every country girls had more egalitarian attitudes about gender roles than did boys (Dotti Sani & Quaranta, 2017). In this study, girls had more egalitarian gender attitudes in countries with higher levels of societal gender equality. In a recent study of 15- to 19-year-olds in the country of Qatar, males had more negative views of gender equality than did females (Al-Ghanim & Badahdah, 2017). Many Western cultures, such as the United States, have become more flexible about gender behavior and allow for more diversity. For example, although a girl's father might promote traditional femininity, her friends might engage in many traditionally masculine activities and her teachers might encourage her to be assertive.

In the United States, the cultural backgrounds of children and adolescents influence how boys and girls will be socialized. In one study, Latino and Latina adolescents were socialized differently as they were growing up (Raffaelli & Ontai, 2004). Latinas experienced far greater restrictions than Latinos in having curfews, interacting with members of the other sex, getting a driver's license, getting a job, and being involved in after-school activities.

In China, females and males are usually socialized to behave, feel, and think differently. The old patriarchal traditions of male supremacy have not been completely uprooted. Chinese women still make considerably less money than Chinese men do, and, in rural China (such as here in the Lixian Village of Sichuan), male supremacy still governs many women's lives.
Richard Mayer/Age fotostock

- - - - - - - - ►
developmental **connection**
Nature and Nurture
Bronfenbrenner's ecological theory emphasizes the importance of contexts; in his theory, the macrosystem includes cross-cultural comparisons. Connect to "Introduction."
◄ - - - - - - - -

GENDER-ROLE CLASSIFICATION

Not long ago, it was accepted that boys should grow up to be masculine (powerful, assertive, for example) and girls to be feminine (sensitive to others, caring, for example). In the 1970s, however, as both females and males became dissatisfied with the burdens imposed by their stereotypic roles, alternatives to femininity and masculinity were proposed. Instead of describing masculinity and femininity as a continuum in which more of one means less of the other, it was proposed that individuals could have both masculine and feminine traits.

Androgyny   The trend toward non-binary thinking about personality traits led to the development of the concept of **androgyny,** the presence of positive masculine and feminine characteristics in the same person (Bem, 1977; Spence & Helmreich, 1978). The androgynous boy might be assertive (masculine) and nurturing (feminine). The androgynous girl might be powerful (masculine) and sensitive to others' feelings (feminine). Measures have been developed to assess androgyny, such as the Bem Sex Role Inventory (Bem, 1977).

Gender experts such as Sandra Bem (1977) argue that androgynous individuals are more flexible, competent, and mentally healthy than their masculine or feminine counterparts. To some degree, though, which gender-role classification is best depends on the context

androgyny The presence of positive masculine and feminine characteristics in the same individual.

Mack Beggs, a 17-year-old high school student who is transitioning from female to male, won the Texas state wrestling championship for girls in the 110-pound weight class in 2017. The transgender wrestler is taking testosterone treatments as part of the gender transition to enhance male characteristics. Some of the wrestler's opponents have said that Mack has an unfair advantage among girls because of the testosterone treatments. Mack never lost a wrestling match during the 2016–2017 school year, going 52-0 in matches, all in the female division. *What do you think? Should Mack have been allowed to wrestle in the girls' division?*
Leslie Plaza Johnson/Icon Sportswire/Getty Images

involved. For example, in close relationships, feminine and androgynous orientations might be more desirable. One study found that girls and individuals high in femininity showed a stronger interest in caring than did boys and individuals high in masculinity (Karniol, Grosz, & Schorr, 2003). And a recent study found that androgynous boys and girls had higher self-esteem and fewer internalizing problems than masculine or feminine individuals (Pauletti & others, 2017).

However, masculine and androgynous orientations might be more desirable in traditional academic and work settings because of the achievement demands in these contexts. In a recent analysis, this emphasis on considering contexts in understanding gender identity was described in terms of *functional flexibility*. In this view, gender identity is positively linked to adjustment and one's competence involves flexibility in adapting to specific situations (Martin & others, 2017).

Transgender   Recently, considerable interest has been generated about a category of gender classification known as **transgender**, a broad term that refers to individuals who adopt a gender identity that differs from the one assigned to them at birth (Budge & Orovecz, 2018; Budge & others, 2018; Hyde & others, 2019; Sinclair-Palm, 2019). For example, an individual may have a female body but identify more strongly with being masculine than being feminine, or have a male body but identify more strongly with being feminine than masculine. A transgender identity of being born male but identifying with being a female is much more common than the reverse (Zucker, Lawrence, & Kreukels, 2016). Transgender persons also may not want to be labeled "he" or "she" but prefer a more neutral label such as "they" or "ze" (Scelfo, 2015).

Because of the nuances and complexities involved in such gender categorizations, some experts have recently argued that a better overarching umbrella term might be *trans* to identify a variety of gender identities and expressions different from the gender identity that was assigned at birth (Galupo & others, 2019; Sinclair-Palm, 2019). The variety of gender identities might include transgender, gender queer (also referred to as gender expansive, this broad gender identity category encompasses individuals who are not exclusively masculine or exclusively feminine), and gender-nonconforming (individuals whose behavior/appearance does not conform to social expectations for what is appropriate for their gender). Another recently generated term, *cisgender,* can be used to describe individuals whose gender identity and expression conform to the gender identity assigned at birth (Hyde & others, 2019).

Transgender individuals can be straight, gay, lesbian, or bisexual. A research review concluded that transgender youth have higher rates of depression, suicide attempts, and eating disorders than their cisgender peers (Connolly & others, 2016). Among the explanations for higher rates of disorders are the distress of living in the wrong body and the discrimination and misunderstanding they encounter as gender-minority individuals (Budge, Chin, & Minero, 2017).

Among youth who identify themselves as transgender persons, the majority eventually adopt a gender identity in line with the body into which they were born (Byne & others, 2012; King, 2017, 2019). Some transgender individuals seek transsexual surgery to go from a male body to a female body or vice versa, but most do not. Some choose to receive hormonal treatments, such as biological females who use testosterone to enhance their masculine characteristics, or biological males who use estrogen to increase their feminine characteristics. Yet other transgender individuals opt for another, broader strategy that involves choosing a lifestyle that challenges the traditional view of having a gender identity that fits within one of two opposing categories (King, 2017, 2019).

GOING BEYOND GENDER AS BINARY

In a number of places in our coverage of gender, we have indicated that the long-existing (for more than a century) concept of gender as having just two categories—male and female—is being challenged. In a recent analysis, leading expert, Janet Shibley Hyde and her colleagues (Hyde & others, 2019) described a number of aspects of gender where this challenge is occurring. These include the following developments: (1) neuroscience research indicates the presence of a gender mosaic rather "his or her" brains that are highly different; (2) endocrinology research reveals more hormonal similarities in males and females than had been previously

transgender A broad term that refers to individuals who adopt a gender identity that differs from the one assigned to them at birth.

envisioned; (3) recent conceptual changes in gender role classification go far beyond characterizing individuals as masculine or feminine and add a number of new gender identity categories such as trans people, transgender, cisgender, and many others; (4) developmental research indicates that the tendency to view gender as a binary category is not due only to biological factors but is also culturally determined and malleable. Further, gender categories are not mutually exclusive because an individual can identify with more than one category. Also, gender categories are fluid because an individual's gender identity can change over time. Each of the ideas described here reflects a substantial change in how gender is conceptualized and reflected in individuals' daily lives, but as we indicated earlier in the chapter there is still controversy about the extent of gender similarities and differences.

Review *Connect* Reflect

LG2 Discuss gender stereotypes, similarities, differences, and classification.

Review

- What is gender stereotyping, and how extensive is it?
- What are some physical, cognitive, and socioemotional differences between men and women?
- What are some ways that gender can be classified?
- How is the conceptualization of gender going beyond gender as binary?

Connect

- Compare cognitive and socioemotional similarities and differences based on gender. What are your conclusions?

Reflect *Your Own Personal Journey of Life*

- How do your gender behavior and thoughts stack up against the similarities and differences in gender we discussed?

3 Gender Development Through the Life Span

LG3 Describe the development of gender through the life span.

Childhood   Adolescence   Adulthood and Aging

In this section we will focus further on gender-related developmental changes in the childhood years. In addition, we will look at some changes that take place in adolescence and adulthood, including the influence of gender roles in adolescence and some of the ways in which gender roles might shift as people age.

CHILDHOOD

The amount, timing, and intensity of gender socialization differs for girls and boys (Beal, 1994). Boys receive earlier and more intense gender socialization than girls do. The social cost of deviating from the expected male role is higher for boys than is the cost for girls of deviating from the expected female role, in terms of peer rejection and parental disapproval. Imagine a girl who is wearing a toy holster, bandanna, and cowboy hat, running around in the backyard pretending to herd cattle. Now imagine a boy who is wearing a flowered hat, ropes of pearls, and lipstick, pretending to cook dinner on a toy stove. Which of these do you have a stronger reaction to—the girl's behavior or the boy's? Probably the boy's. Researchers have found that "effeminate" behavior in boys elicits more negative reactions than does "masculine" behavior in girls (Martin, 1990).

Boys might have a more difficult time learning the masculine gender role because male models are less accessible to young children and messages from adults about the male role are not always consistent. For example, most mothers and teachers would like boys to behave in masculine ways, but also to be neat, well mannered, and considerate. However, fathers and peers usually want boys to be independent and to engage in rough-and-tumble play. The mixed messages make it difficult for boys to figure out how to act.

Are gender roles more flexible for boys or for girls?
(*Top*): Andrey Bandurenko/Alamy Stock Photo; (*bottom*): Design Pics/SuperStock

Although gender roles have become more flexible in recent years, the flexibility applies more for girls than for boys (Beal, 1994). Girls can count on receiving approval if they are ambitious, competitive, and interested in sports, but relatively few adults are equally supportive of boys' being gentle, interested in fashion, and motivated to sign up for ballet classes. Instrumental traits and masculine gender roles may be evolving into a new norm for everyone.

Concern about the ways boys are being brought up has been called a "national crisis of boyhood" by William Pollack (1999) in his book *Real Boys*. Pollack says that little has been done to change what he calls the "boy code." The boy code tells boys they should not show their feelings and should act tough, says Pollack. Boys learn the boy code in many contexts—sandboxes, playgrounds, schoolrooms, camps, hangouts—and are taught the code by parents, peers, coaches, teachers, and other adults. Pollack, as well as many others, argues that boys would benefit from being socialized to express their anxieties and concerns and to better regulate their aggression.

ADOLESCENCE

Early adolescence is another transitional point that seems to be especially important in gender development. Young adolescents have to cope with the enormous changes of puberty. These changes are intensified by their expanding cognitive abilities, which make them acutely aware of how they appear to others. Relations with others change extensively as dating begins and sexuality is experienced.

As females and males undergo the physical and social changes of early adolescence, they must come to terms with new definitions of their gender roles (Pascoe, 2017). During early adolescence, individuals develop the adult, physical aspects of their sex. Some theorists and researchers have proposed that, with the onset of puberty, girls and boys experience an intensification of gender-related expectations. Puberty might signal to socializing others—parents, peers, and teachers, for example—that the adolescent is beginning to approach adulthood and therefore should begin to behave in ways that more closely resemble the stereotypical female or male adult. The **gender-intensification hypothesis** states that psychological and behavioral differences between boys and girls become greater during early adolescence because of increased pressures to conform to traditional masculine and feminine gender roles (Galambos, 2004; Hill & Lynch, 1983).

Some researchers have reported evidence of gender intensification in early adolescence (Hill & Lynch, 1983), but others have found no evidence for intensification in masculinity or femininity in young adolescents (Priess, Lindberg, & Hyde, 2009). The jury is still out on the validity of the gender-intensification hypothesis, but research has raised questions about its accuracy (Galambos, Berenbaum, & McHale, 2009).

Gender intensification may create special problems for boys. Adopting a strong masculine role in adolescence is increasingly being found to be associated with problem behaviors. Joseph Pleck (1995) argues that definitions of traditional masculinity include behaviors that do not have social approval but nonetheless validate the adolescent boy's masculinity. That is, in the male adolescent culture, male adolescents perceive that they will be thought of as more masculine if they engage in premarital sex, drink alcohol, take drugs, and participate in delinquent activities. One study revealed that both boys and girls who engaged in extreme gender-typed (hyper-gender) behaviors had lower levels of school engagement and school attachment (Ueno & McWilliams, 2010).

ADULTHOOD AND AGING

How might women's and men's development vary as they go through their adult years? How might gender be linked with aging?

Gender and Communication   Stereotypes about differences in men's and women's attitudes toward communication and about differences in how they communicate with each other have spawned countless cartoons and jokes. Are the supposed differences real?

When Deborah Tannen (1990) analyzed the talk of women and men, she found that many wives complained about their husbands by saying that "He doesn't listen to me anymore" and "He doesn't talk to me anymore." Lack of communication, although high on women's lists of reasons for divorce, is mentioned much less often by men.

gender-intensification hypothesis The view that psychological and behavioral differences between boys and girls become greater during early adolescence because of increased socialization pressures to conform to traditional gender roles.

Communication problems between men and women may come in part from differences in their preferred ways of communicating. Tannen distinguishes *rapport talk* from *report talk*. **Rapport talk** is the language of conversation; it is a way of establishing connections and negotiating relationships. **Report talk** is talk that is designed to give information; this category of communication includes public speaking. According to Tannen, women enjoy rapport talk more than report talk, and men's lack of interest in rapport talk bothers many women. In contrast, men prefer to engage in report talk. Men hold center stage through verbal performances such as telling stories and jokes. They learn to use talk as a way to get and keep attention.

How extensive are gender differences in communication? Research has yielded somewhat mixed results, although studies do reveal some gender differences (Anderson, 2006). One study of a sampling of students' e-mails found that people could accurately guess the writer's gender two-thirds of the time (Thompson & Murachver, 2001). Another study revealed that women make 63 percent of phone calls and when talking to another woman stay on the phone longer (7.2 minutes) than men do when talking with other men (4.6 minutes) (Smoreda & Licoppe, 2000). However, meta-analyses suggest that overall gender differences in communication are small in both children and adults (Hyde, 2005, 2014; Leaper & Smith, 2004).

What are some gender differences in communication?
Streetangel/Getty Images

Women's Development   Tannen's analysis of women's preference for rapport talk suggests that women place a high value on relationships and focus on nurturing their connections with others. This view echoes some ideas of Jean Baker Miller (1986), who has been an important voice in stimulating the examination of psychological issues from a female perspective. Miller argues that when researchers examine what women have been doing in life, a large part of it is active participation in the development of others. In Miller's view, women often try to interact with others in ways that will foster the other person's development along many dimensions—emotional, intellectual, and social.

Most experts stress that it is important for women not only to maintain their competency in relationships but to be self-motivated, too (Brabek & Brabek, 2006). As Harriet Lerner (1989) concludes in her book *The Dance of Intimacy*, it is important for women to bring to their relationships nothing less than a strong, assertive, independent, and authentic self. She emphasizes that competent relationships are those in which the separate "I-ness" of both persons can be appreciated and enhanced while the partners remain emotionally connected with each other.

In sum, Miller, Tannen, and other gender experts such as Carol Gilligan note that women are more relationship-oriented than men are—and that this relationship orientation should be valued more highly in our culture than it currently is. Critics of this view of gender differences in relationships contend that it is too stereotypical (Hyde & Else-Quest, 2013; Matlin, 2012). They argue that there is greater individual variation in the relationship styles of men and women than this view acknowledges.

In the field of the psychology of women, there is increased interest in women of color. To read about the work and views of one individual in this field, see the *Connecting with Careers* profile.

Men's Development   The male of the species—what is he really like? What are his concerns? According to Joseph Pleck's (1995) role-strain view, male roles are contradictory and inconsistent. Men not only experience stress when they violate men's roles, they also are harmed when they act in accord with men's roles. Here are some of the areas where men's roles can cause considerable strain (Levant, 2001):

- *Health*. Men die 8 to 10 years earlier than women do. They have higher rates of stress-related disorders, alcoholism, car accidents, and suicide. Men are more likely than women to be the victims of homicide. In sum, the male role is hazardous to men's health.

- *Male-female relationships*. Too often, the male role involves expectations that men should be dominant, powerful, and aggressive and should control women. "Real men," according to many traditional definitions of masculinity, look at women in terms of their bodies, not their minds and feelings, have little interest in rapport talk and relationships, and do not consider women equal to men in work or many other aspects of life. Thus, the traditional view of the male role encourages men to disparage women, be violent toward women, and refuse to have equal relationships with women.

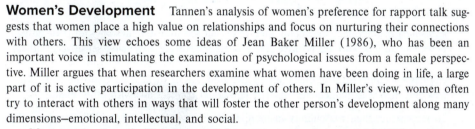

developmental **connection**

Peers

How does adult friendship differ among female friends, male friends, and cross-gender friends? Connect to "Peers and the Sociocultural World."

rapport talk   The language of conversation; a way to establish connections and negotiate relationships; preferred by women.

report talk   Language designed to convey information; a communication style preferred by men.

Cynthia de las Fuentes, College Professor and Counseling Psychologist

Cynthia de las Fuentes is a professor at Our Lady of the Lake University in San Antonio. She obtained her undergraduate degree in psychology and her doctoral degree in counseling psychology at the University of Texas at Austin. Among the courses she teaches are the psychology of women, Latino psychology, and counseling theories.

Dr. de las Fuentes is a former president of the Division of the Psychology of Women in the American

Cynthia de las Fuentes.
Dr. Cynthia de las Fuentes

Psychological Association. "'Many young women,' she says, 'take for granted that the women's movement has accomplished its goals—like equal pay for women, or reproductive rights—and don't realize that there is still work to be done.' . . . She's interested in learning about people's intersecting identities, like female and Latina, and how the two work together" (Winerman, 2005, pp. 66–67).

For more information about what college professors do, see the Careers in Life-Span Development appendix.

Tom Cruise (*left*) played Jerry Maguire in the movie *Jerry Maguire* with 6-year-old Ray, son of Jerry's love interest. The image of nurturing and nurtured males was woven throughout the movie. Jerry's relationship with Ray was a significant theme in the movie. It is through the caring relationship with Ray that Jerry makes his first genuine movement toward emotional maturity. The boy is guide to the man (Shields, 1998). Many experts on gender stress that men and boys would benefit from engaging in more nurturant behaviors.
Pictorial Press Ltd/Alamy Stock Photo

- - - - - - - - - ▶

developmental **connection**

Culture

Aging presents special challenges for ethnic minority individuals. Connect to "Peers and the Sociocultural World."

◀ - - - - - - - -

- *Male-male relationships.* Too many men have had too little interaction with their fathers, especially fathers who are positive role models. Nurturing and being sensitive to others have been considered aspects of the female role, not the male role. And the male role emphasizes competition rather than cooperation. All of these aspects of the male role have left men with inadequate positive, emotional connections with other males.

To reconstruct their masculinity in more positive ways, Ron Levant (2001) suggests that every man should (1) reexamine his beliefs about manhood, (2) separate out the valuable aspects of the male role, and (3) get rid of those parts of the masculine role that are destructive. All of these processes involve becoming more "emotionally intelligent"—that is, becoming more emotionally self-aware, managing emotions more effectively, reading emotions better (one's own emotions and those of others), and being motivated to improve close relationships.

Gender and Aging   Do our gender roles change when we become older adults? Some developmentalists maintain there is decreasing femininity in women and decreasing masculinity in men when they reach late adulthood (Gutmann, 1975). The evidence suggests that older men do become more *feminine*—nurturant, sensitive, and so on—but it appears that older women do not necessarily become more *masculine*—assertive, dominant, and so on (Turner, 1982). A longitudinal study revealed that as men entered their sixties, they endorsed more feminine items on a list of personal characteristics, which increased their classification as *androgynous* (combination of masculine and feminine traits) (Hyde, Krajnik, & Skuldt-Niederberger, 1991).

In a more recent cross-sectional study of individuals from 12 to 80 years and older, men in their seventies were more likely than adolescents and younger men to endorse androgynous traits (Strough & others, 2007). Also in this study, women in their eighties and older were less likely than younger and middle-aged women to endorse masculine and androgynous traits. And in an even more recent study, among older adult men, those who were married were more likely to endorse stereotypically masculine traits but also to have higher androgyny scores than unmarried older men (Lemaster, Delaney, & Strough, 2017). The studies of age differences just discussed here were cross-sectional in nature and may reflect cohort effects. Keep in mind that cohort effects are especially important to consider in areas such as gender roles. As sociohistorical changes take place and are assessed more frequently in life-span investigations, what were once perceived to be age effects may turn out to be cohort effects (George & Ferraro, 2016; Schaie, 2016). For example, in the study described above (Strough & others, 2007), the early-adult and middle-aged women were "baby boomers," likely influenced by the women's movement as they were growing up and developing their identity. However, the oldest-old women likely had already established their gender identity when the women's movement began, which might explain why they were less likely than younger women to endorse masculine and androgynous traits.

A possible double jeopardy also faces many older women—the burden of both ageism and sexism (Meyer & Parker, 2011). In developing countries, the poverty rate for older adult females is almost double that for older adult males.

Not only is it important to be concerned about older women's double jeopardy of ageism and sexism, but special attention also needs to be devoted to female ethnic minority older adults (Angel, Mudrazija, & Benson, 2016). Many, but not all, immigrant ethnic groups traditionally have relegated the woman's role to family maintenance. Many important decisions may be made by a woman's husband or parents, and she is often not expected to seek an independent career or enter the workforce unless the family is in dire financial need.

Some ethnic minority groups may define an older woman's role as unimportant, especially if she is unable to contribute financially. However, in some ethnic minority groups, a woman's social status improves in later life. For example, older African American women can express their own needs and have status and power in the community. Despite their positive status in the African American family and the African American culture, however, African American women over the age of 70 are the poorest population group in the United States. Three of five older African American women live alone; most of them are widowed. The low incomes of older African American women translate into less than adequate access to health care. Substantially lower incomes for African American older women are related to the kinds of jobs they have held. Frequently these jobs are not covered by Social Security or, in the case of domestic service, the incomes of these women are not reported even when reporting is legally required.

A portrayal of older African American women in cities reveals some of their survival strategies. They highly value the family as a source of mutual support and aid, adhere to the American work ethic, and view religion as a source of strength.

In sum, older African American women have faced considerable stress in their lives (Angel, Mudrazija, & Benson, 2016). In dealing with this stress, they have shown remarkable adaptiveness, resilience, responsibility, and coping skills. However, many older African American women would benefit considerably from improved support.

A special concern is the stress faced by African American elderly women. *What are some ways they cope with stress?*
Matt Gray/Getty Images

Review Connect Reflect

LG3 Describe the development of gender through the life span.

Review
- What are some developmental changes in gender during childhood?
- How does gender development change during adolescence?
- How does gender development change during adulthood?

Connect
- Relate this chapter's gender-intensification hypothesis to what you've learned about identity development in adolescence. What are your conclusions?

Reflect *Your Own Personal Journey of Life*
- How have your gender attitudes and behavior changed since childhood? Are the changes mainly age-related or do they reflect cohort effects?

4 Exploring Sexuality

LG4 Characterize influences on sexuality, the nature of sexual orientation, and some sexual problems.

| Biological and Cultural Factors | Sexual Orientation | Sexually Transmitted Infections | Forcible Sexual Behavior and Sexual Harassment |

Now that we have studied the gender aspects of being female and male, let's turn our attention to the sexual aspects. To explore sexuality, we examine biological and cultural factors, sexual orientation, sexually transmitted infections, and forcible sexual behavior and sexual harassment.

BIOLOGICAL AND CULTURAL FACTORS

We don't need sex for everyday survival the way we need food and water, but we do need it for the survival of the species. With this important role of sex in mind, let's examine some biological and cultural factors involved in sexuality.

Biological Factors   In our discussion of gender, we identified two main classes of sex hormones: estrogens (which primarily promote the development of female physical sex characteristics) and androgens (which mainly promote the development of male physical sex characteristics). The pituitary gland in the brain monitors hormone levels but is itself regulated by the hypothalamus. The pituitary gland sends out a signal to the testes or ovaries to manufacture a hormone; then the pituitary gland, through interaction with the hypothalamus, detects when the optimal level of the hormone is reached and maintains this level (Iovino & others, 2019).

As we move from lower to higher animals, the role of hormones becomes less clear, especially in females. For human males, higher androgen levels are associated with sexual motivation and orgasm frequency (Gray, McHale, & Carré, 2017; King & Regan, 2019). Nonetheless, sexual behavior is so individualized in humans that it is difficult to distinguish the effects of hormones.

Cultural Factors   Sexual motivation also is influenced by cultural factors (Carroll, 2019; Crooks & Baur, 2017). The range of sexual values across cultures is substantial (Nimbi & others, 2019). Some cultures consider sexual pleasures "weird" or "abnormal." Consider the people who live on the small island of Inis Beag off the coast of Ireland. They are some of the most sexually repressed people in the world. They know nothing about tongue kissing or hand stimulation of the penis, and they detest nudity. For both females and males, premarital sex is out of the question (Messinger, 1971).

In contrast, consider the Mangaian culture in the South Pacific. In Mangaia, young boys are taught about masturbation and are encouraged to engage in it as much as they like. At age 13, the boys undergo a ritual that initiates them into sexual manhood. First, their elders instruct them about sexual strategies, including how to help their female partner have orgasms. Then, two weeks later, the boy has intercourse with an experienced woman who helps him hold back ejaculation until she can achieve orgasm with him. By the end of adolescence, Mangaians have sex virtually every day.

As reflected in the behavior of the people in these two different cultures, our sexual motivation is influenced by **sexual scripts** (Willie & others, 2018). These are stereotyped patterns of expectations for how people should behave sexually (King & Regan, 2019; Singleton & others, 2016). Two well-known sexual scripts are the traditional religious script and the romantic script. In the **traditional religious script,** sex is acceptable only within marriage. Extramarital sex is taboo, especially for women. Sex involves reproduction and sometimes affection. In the **romantic script,** sex is synonymous with love. If we develop a relationship with someone and fall in love, it is acceptable to have sex with the person whether or not we are married.

You probably are familiar with some sex differences in sexual scripts (Kollah-Cattano & others, 2018). Females tend to link sexual intercourse with love more than males do, and males are more likely to emphasize sexual conquest. Some sexual scripts involve a double standard; for example, it is okay for male adolescents to have sex but not females, and if the female gets pregnant it's viewed as her fault for not using contraception (Tolman & Chmielewski, 2019). One study of young adult men found two main sexual scripts: (1) a traditional male "player" script, and (2) a script that emphasized mutual sexual pleasure (Morrison & others, 2014).

SEXUAL ORIENTATION

A national study of sexual behavior in the United States among adults 25 to 44 years of age found that 98 percent of the women and 97 percent of the men said that they had ever engaged in vaginal intercourse (Chandra & others, 2011). Also in this study, 89 percent of the women and 90 percent of the men reported that they had ever had oral sex with an opposite-sex partner, and 36 percent of the women and 44 percent of the men stated that they had ever had anal sex with an opposite-sex partner.

More extensive information about adult sexual patterns comes from the 1994 Sex in America survey. In this well-designed, comprehensive study of American adults' sexual

sexual scripts Stereotyped patterns of expectancies for how people should behave sexually.

traditional religious script View that sex is acceptable only within marriage; extramarital sex is taboo, especially for women; and sex means reproduction and sometimes affection.

romantic script A perspective in which sex is synonymous with love; belief that if we develop a relationship with someone and fall in love, it is acceptable to have sex with the person whether we are married or not.

patterns, Robert Michael and his colleagues (1994) interviewed more than 3,000 people from 18 to 59 years of age who were randomly selected, a sharp contrast from earlier samples that consisted of unrepresentative groups of volunteers.

Heterosexual Attitudes and Behavior   Here are some of the key findings from the 1994 Sex in America survey:

- Americans tend to fall into three categories: One-third have sex twice a week or more, one-third a few times a month, and one-third a few times a year or not at all.

- Married (and cohabiting) couples have sex more often than noncohabiting couples (see Figure 4).

- Most Americans do not engage in kinky sexual acts. When asked about their favorite sexual acts, the vast majority (96 percent) said that vaginal sex was "very" or "somewhat" appealing. Oral sex was in third place, after an activity that many have not labeled a sexual act—watching a partner undress.

- Adultery is clearly the exception rather than the rule. Nearly 75 percent of the married men and 85 percent of the married women in the survey indicated that they had never been unfaithful.

- Men think about sex far more often than women do—54 percent of the men said they thought about it every day or several times a day, whereas 67 percent of the women said they thought about it only a few times a week or a few times a month.

In sum, one of the most powerful messages in the 1994 survey was that Americans' sexual lives are more conservative than was previously believed. Although 17 percent of the men and 3 percent of the women reported having had sex with at least 21 partners, the overall impression from the survey was that sexual behavior is ruled by marriage and monogamy for most Americans.

How extensive are gender differences in sexuality? A meta-analysis revealed that men reported having slightly more sexual experiences and more permissive attitudes than women regarding most aspects of sexuality (Peterson & Hyde, 2010). For the following factors, stronger differences were found: Men said that they engaged more often in masturbation, pornography use, and casual sex, and they expressed more permissive attitudes about casual sex than their female counterparts did.

Given all the media and public attention directed toward the negative aspects of sexuality—such as adolescent pregnancy, sexually transmitted infections, rape, and so on—it is important to underscore that research strongly supports the role of sexuality in well-being (Brody, 2010; King, 2017, 2019). For example, in a Swedish study frequency of sexual intercourse was strongly linked to life satisfaction for both women and men (Brody & Costa, 2009). And in a recent study, sexual activity in adults on day 1 was linked to greater well-being the next day (Kashdan & others, 2018). Also in this study, higher reported sexual pleasure and intimacy predicted more positive affect and less negative affect the next day.

Sexual Orientation and Its Sources   Until the end of the nineteenth century, it was generally believed that people were either heterosexual or homosexual. Today, sexual orientation is viewed less as an either/or proposition than as a continuum from exclusive male-female relations to exclusive same-sex relations (Savin-Williams, 2019). Some individuals are also **bisexual,** being sexually attracted to people of both sexes. Others are **transsexual,** choosing to live full-time as a member of the desired gender and usually seeking sex reassignment surgery that involves altering their sex characteristics to match their gender identity.

Let's now further explore more aspects of such categories as bisexuality. People sometimes think that bisexuality is simply a steppingstone to same-sex sexual relationships, while others view it as a sexual orientation itself or as an indicator of sexual fluidity (King, 2019). Evidence supports the notion that bisexuality is a stable orientation that involves attraction to both sexes (King, 2019; Mock & Eibach, 2012).

Compared with men, women are more likely to change their sexual patterns and desires (Knight & Morales Hope, 2012). Women are more likely than men to have sexual experiences with same- and opposite-sex partners, even if they identify themselves strongly as being heterosexual or lesbian (King, 2019). Also, women are more likely than men to identify themselves as bisexual (Gates, 2011).

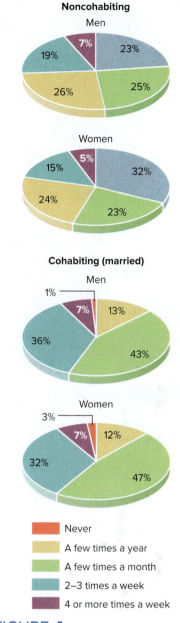

Noncohabiting

Men

Women

Cohabiting (married)

Men

Women

- Never
- A few times a year
- A few times a month
- 2–3 times a week
- 4 or more times a week

FIGURE 4

THE SEX IN AMERICA SURVEY. The percentages show noncohabiting and cohabiting (married) males' and females' responses to the question "How often have you had sex in the past year?" in a 1994 survey (Michael & others, 1994). *What was one feature of the Sex in America survey that made it superior to most surveys of sexual behavior?*

bisexuality Sexual attraction to people of both sexes.

transsexual Category that describes individuals who choose to live full-time as a member of the desired gender and usually seek to have sex reassignment surgery.

What likely determines whether a male or female has a same-sex orientation?
(*Top*): Jupiter Images; (*bottom*): Creatas Images/Jupiter Images

In the Sex in America survey, 2.7 percent of the men and 1.3 percent of the women reported having had same-sex relations in the past year (Michael & others, 1994). However, in a national survey a higher percentage (3.8 percent) of U.S. adults reported that they were gay, lesbian, bisexual, or transsexual (Gallup, 2015). And the most recent national survey of sexual orientation that included men and women from 18 to 44 years of age, almost three times as many women (17.4 percent) reported having had same-sex contact in their lifetime as men did (6.2 percent) (Copen, Chandra, & Febo-Vazquez, 2016). Feelings of attraction only toward the opposite sex were more frequent for men (92.1 percent) than for women (81 percent). Also in this study, 92.3 percent of the women and 95.1 percent of the men said they were heterosexual or straight. Further, 1.3 percent of women and 1.9 percent of men said they were homosexual, gay, or lesbian, and 5.5 percent of women and 2 percent of men reported that they were bisexual.

Why are some individuals lesbian, gay, or bisexual (LGB) and others heterosexual? Speculation about this question has been extensive. All people, regardless of their sexual orientation, have similar physiological responses during sexual arousal and seem to be aroused by the same types of tactile stimulation. Investigators typically find no differences between LGBs and heterosexuals in a wide range of attitudes, behaviors, and adjustments (Fingerhut & Peplau, 2013).

Recently, researchers have explored the possible biological basis of same-sex relations. The results of hormone studies have been inconsistent. If gay males are given male sex hormones (androgens), their sexual orientation doesn't change. Their sexual desire merely increases. A very early prenatal critical period might influence sexual orientation (Hines, 2013, 2015; Li, Kung, & Hines, 2017; Mitsui & others, 2019). In the second to fifth months after conception, exposure of the fetus to hormone levels characteristic of females might cause the individual (male or female) to become attracted to males (Ellis & Ames, 1987). If this critical-period hypothesis turns out to be correct, it would explain why clinicians have found that sexual orientation is difficult, if not impossible, to modify.

Researchers have also examined genetic influences on sexual orientation by studying twins. A Swedish study of almost 4,000 twins found that only about 35 percent of the variation in homosexual behavior in men and 19 percent in women could be explained by genetic differences (Langstrom & others, 2010). This result suggests that although genes likely play a role in sexual orientation, they are not the only factor (King, 2017, 2019).

An individual's sexual orientation is most likely determined by a combination of genetic, hormonal, cognitive, and environmental factors (Hyde & DeLamater, 2017; King, 2017, 2019). Most experts believe that no one factor alone causes sexual orientation and that the relative weight of each factor can vary from one individual to the next. That said, it has become clear that no matter whether a person is heterosexual, gay, lesbian, or bisexual, that individual cannot be talked out of his or her sexual orientation (King, 2017, 2019).

Attitudes and Behavior of Lesbians and Gays   Many gender differences that appear in heterosexual relationships also occur in same-sex relationships (Diamond, 2019; Savin-Williams, 2017, 2019). For example, lesbians have fewer sexual partners than gays, and lesbians have less permissive attitudes about casual sex outside a primary relationship than gays do (Fingerhut & Peplau, 2013).

According to psychologist Laura Brown (1989), lesbians and gays experience life as a minority in a dominant, majority culture. For lesbians and gays, developing a *bicultural identity* creates new ways of defining themselves. Brown believes that lesbians and gays adapt best when they don't define themselves in polarities, such as trying to live in an encapsulated lesbian or gay world completely divorced from the majority culture or completely accepting the dictates and biases of the majority culture. A special concern is discrimination and prejudice toward sexual minority individuals (Schrager, Goldbach, & Mamey, 2018; Shramko, Toomey, & Anhalt, 2018). One study of 15-year-olds found that sexual minority status was linked to depression mainly via peer harassment (Martin-Storey & Crosnoe, 2012).

SEXUALLY TRANSMITTED INFECTIONS

sexually transmitted infections (STIs) Diseases that are contracted primarily through sexual contact, including oral-genital contact, anal-genital contact, and vaginal intercourse.

Sexually transmitted infections (STIs) are diseases that are primarily contracted through sex—penile-vaginal intercourse as well as oral-genital and anal-genital sex. STIs affect about one of every six U.S. adults (National Center for Health Statistics, 2019). Among the most prevalent

STI	Description/cause	Incidence	Treatment
Gonorrhea	Commonly called the "drip" or "clap." Caused by the bacterium *Neisseria gonorrhoeae*. Spread by contact between infected moist membranes (genital, oral-genital, or anal-genital) of two individuals. Characterized by discharge from penis or vagina and painful urination. Can lead to infertility.	500,000 cases annually in U.S.	Penicillin, other antibiotics
Syphilis	Caused by the bacterium *Treponema pallidum*. Characterized by the appearance of a sore where syphilis entered the body. The sore can be on the external genitals, vagina, or anus. Later, a skin rash breaks out on palms of hands and bottom of feet. If not treated, can eventually lead to paralysis or even death.	100,000 cases annually in U.S.	Penicillin
Chlamydia	A common STI named for the bacterium *Chlamydia trachomatis*, an organism that spreads by sexual contact and infects the genital organs of both sexes. A special concern is that females with chlamydia may become infertile. It is recommended that adolescent and young adult females have an annual screening for this STI.	About 3 million people in U.S. annually.	Antibiotics
Genital herpes	Caused by a family of viruses with different strains. Involves an eruption of sores and blisters. Spread by sexual contact.	One of five U.S. adults	No known cure but antiviral medications can shorten outbreaks
AIDS	Caused by a virus, the human immunodeficiency virus (HIV), which destroys the body's immune system. Semen and blood are the main vehicles of transmission. Common symptoms include fevers, night sweats, weight loss, chronic fatigue, and swollen lymph nodes.	More than 300,000 cumulative cases of HIV virus in U.S. 25–34-year-olds; epidemic incidence in sub-Saharan countries	New treatments have slowed the progression from HIV to AIDS; no cure
Genital warts	Caused by the human papillomavirus, which does not always produce symptoms. Usually appear as small, hard, painless bumps in the vaginal area or around the anus. Very contagious. Certain high-risk types of this virus cause cervical cancer and other genital cancers. May recur despite treatment. A new HPV preventive vaccine, Gardasil, has been approved for girls and women 9–26 years of age.	About 5.5 million new cases annually; considered the most common STI in the U.S.	A topical drug, freezing, or surgery

FIGURE 5
SEXUALLY TRANSMITTED INFECTIONS

STIs are bacterial infections—such as gonorrhea, syphilis, and chlamydia—and STIs caused by viruses—such as AIDS (acquired immune deficiency syndrome), genital herpes, and genital warts. Figure 5 describes these sexually transmitted infections.

A concern in the United States is the recent increase in STIs (Feltman, 2018). Especially concerning are the increased rates of gonorrhea, syphilis, and chlamydia in 2016 and again in 2017 (Centers for Disease Control and Prevention, 2018). Compared with 2013, gonorrhea diagnoses increased 67 percent and syphilis cases increased 76 percent in 2017. It is especially problematic that gonorrhea is increasingly resistant to antibiotic treatments.

No single disease has had a greater impact on sexual behavior, or created more public fear in the last several decades, than infection with the human immunodeficiency virus (HIV) (Yarber & Sayed, 2019). HIV is a virus that destroys the body's immune system. Once a person is infected with HIV, the virus breaks down and overpowers the immune system, which leads to AIDS. An individual sick with AIDS has such a weakened immune system that a common cold can be life-threatening.

In 2015, 1.1 million people in the United States were living with an HIV infection (National Center for Health Statistics, 201). In 2015, male-male sexual contact continued to be the most frequent AIDS transmission category. Because of education and the development of more effective drug treatments, deaths due to HIV/AIDS have begun to decline in the United States (National Center for Health Statistics, 2018).

Globally, the number of AIDS-related deaths is decreasing, with less than 1 million people dying from the disease in 2017 (down from a peak of 1.9 million in 2004) (UNAIDS, 2018). This decrease is due to the increased availability of antiretroviral therapy. The main decrease in AIDS-related deaths is occurring in sub-Saharan Africa.

A youth group presents a play in the local marketplace in Morogoro, Tanzania. The play is designed to educate the community about HIV and AIDS.
Wendy Stone/Corbis Documentary/Getty Images

A 13-year-old boy pushes his friends around in his barrow during his break from his work as a barrow boy in a sub-Saharan Africa community. He became the breadwinner in the family because both of his parents died of AIDS.
Louise Gubb/Corbis Historical/Getty Images

What are some good strategies for protecting against HIV and other sexually transmitted infections? They include the following:

- *Knowing your own and your partner's risk status.* Anyone who has had previous sexual activity with another person might have contracted an STI without being aware of it. Spend time getting to know a prospective partner before you have sex. Use this time to inform the other person of your STI status and inquire about your partner's. Remember that many people lie about their STI status.

- *Obtaining medical examinations.* Many experts recommend that couples who want to begin a sexual relationship have a medical checkup to rule out STIs before they engage in sex. If cost is an issue, contact your campus health service or a public health clinic.

- *Having protected, not unprotected, sex.* When used correctly, latex condoms help to prevent many STIs from being transmitted. Condoms are most effective in preventing gonorrhea, syphilis, chlamydia, and HIV. They are less effective against the spread of herpes.

- *Not having sex with multiple partners.* One of the best predictors of getting an STI is having sex with multiple partners. Having more than one sex partner elevates the likelihood that you will encounter an infected partner.

FORCIBLE SEXUAL BEHAVIOR AND SEXUAL HARASSMENT

Too often, sex involves the exercise of power. Here we briefly look at three of the problems that may result: two types of rape and sexual harassment.

Rape **Rape** is forcible sexual intercourse with a person who does not give consent. Legal definitions of rape differ from state to state. For example, in some states, husbands are not prohibited from forcing their wives to have intercourse, although this has been challenged in several of those states.

Because victims may be reluctant to suffer the consequences of reporting rape, the actual number of incidents is not easily determined (Walfield, 2016). A meta-analysis found that

rape Forcible sexual intercourse, oral sex, or anal sex with a person who does not give consent. Legal definitions of rape differ from state to state.

60 percent of rape victims do not acknowledge that they have been raped, with the percentage of unacknowledged rapes especially high in college students (Wilson & Miller, 2016).

Rape occurs most often in large cities, where it has been reported that 8 of every 10,000 women 12 years and older are raped each year. Nearly 200,000 rapes are reported each year in the United States. Although most victims of rape are women, rape of men does occur (Walfield, 2019). A study of college women who had been raped revealed that only 11.5 percent of them reported the rape to authorities and of those in which the rape involved drugs and/or alcohol, only 2.7 percent of the rapes were reported (Wolitzky-Taylor & others, 2011). Men in prisons are especially vulnerable to rape, usually by heterosexual males who use rape as a means of establishing their dominance and power (Downer & Trestman, 2016).

A national study found that 7.4 percent of U.S. ninth- through twelfth-grade students reported that they had been physically forced to have intercourse against their will (Kann & others, 2018). In this study, approximately 11.3 percent of female students and 3.5 of male students reported having been forced to have sexual intercourse.

Why does rape of females occur so often in the United States? Among the causes given are that males are socialized to be sexually aggressive, to regard women as inferior beings, and to view their own pleasure as the most important objective in sexual relations (Bevens & Loughnan, 2019; Bock & Burkley, 2019; Vasquez & others, 2018). Researchers have found that male rapists share the following characteristics: aggression enhances their sense of power or masculinity; they are angry at women in general; and they want to hurt and humiliate their victims (Yarber & Sayed, 2019).

Rape is more likely to occur when one or both individuals are drinking alcohol (Brown, Horton, & Guillory, 2018). A recent study found that males and heavy drinkers are more likely to adhere to rape myths (such as women being held responsible for preventing the rape) than females or non/light drinkers (Hayes, Abbott, & Cook, 2016).

Rape is a traumatic experience for the victims and those close to them (Dworkin & others, 2018). As victims strive to get their lives back to normal, they may experience depression, posttraumatic stress disorder, fear, anxiety, increased substance use, and suicidal thoughts for months or years (Londono, 2017). Sexual dysfunctions, such as reduced sexual desire and an inability to reach orgasm, occur in 50 percent of female rape victims (Sprei & Courtois, 1988). Recovery depends on the victim's coping abilities, psychological adjustments prior to the assault, and social support (Gray, Hassija, & Steinmetz, 2017). Parents, partner, and others close to the victim can provide important support for recovery, as can mental health professionals (Ahrens & Aldana, 2012).

Date or acquaintance rape is coercive sexual activity directed at someone with whom the victim is at least casually acquainted (Angelone, Mitchell, & Smith, 2018; Gravelin, Biernat, & Bucher, 2019; Osborn & others, 2019). About two-thirds of college men admit that they fondle women against their will, and half admit to forcing sexual activity. In a recent study of 1,423 four-year universities, those with higher tuition, more liquor violations, and greater numbers of fraternity men and athletes were more likely to report rape on their campuses (Wiersma-Mosley, Jozkowski, & Martinez, 2017).

A number of colleges and universities have identified a "red zone"—a period of time early in the first year of college when women are at especially high risk for unwanted sexual experiences (Gray, Hassija, & Steinmetz, 2017). One study revealed that first-year women were at higher risk for unwanted sexual experiences, especially early in the fall term, than second-year women (Kimble & others, 2008). In an effort to reduce unwanted sexual experiences, the program "No Means No Worldwide" (https://nomeansnoworldwide.org) has been effective in reducing the incidence of sexual assault in the African countries of Kenya and Malawi (Baiocchi & others, 2017). The organization's 12-hour curriculum emphasizes interactive verbal skills, role playing, and other techniques to encourage people to speak up, prevent, or intervene in a sexual assault.

Sexual Harassment **Sexual harassment** is a manifestation of power by one person over another. It takes many forms—from inappropriate sexual remarks and physical contact (patting, brushing against one's body) to blatant propositions and sexual assaults. Millions of women experience sexual

date or acquaintance rape Coercive sexual activity directed at someone with whom the victim is at least casually acquainted.

sexual harassment Sexual persecution that can take many forms—from sexist remarks and physical contact (patting, brushing against someone's body) to blatant propositions and sexual assaults.

What are some characteristics of date or acquaintance rape?
Juanmonino/Getty Images

What characterizes the Me Too Movement?
Faye Sadou/Media Punch Inc./Alamy

harassment each year in work and educational settings (Halper & Rios, 2019; Ladika, 2018). Sexual harassment of men by women also occurs but to a far lesser extent than sexual harassment of women by men.

In a survey of 2,000 college women, 62 percent reported having experienced sexual harassment while attending college (American Association of University Women, 2006). Most of the college women said that the sexual harassment involved noncontact forms such as crude jokes, remarks, and gestures. However, almost one-third said that the sexual harassment was physical in nature.

Sexual harassment can result in serious psychological consequences for the victim. A study of almost 1,500 college women revealed that when they had been sexually harassed they reported increases in psychological distress, physical illness, and disordered eating (Huerta & others, 2006).

Eliminating such exploitation requires improvements in work and academic environments (Nielsen & others, 2017). These types of improvements help to provide equal opportunities for people to develop a career and obtain an education in a climate free of sexual harassment (Shakil, Lockwood, & Gradey, 2018; Walsh & Gates, 2018). In 2017, the Me Too Movement spread extensively, with "Me Too" (or "#MeToo") used as a hashtag on social media to show the prevalence of sexual assault and harassment of women, especially in the workplace. As a result, many women felt safe enough to openly discuss their experiences of sexual harassment after having remained silent about these experiences for years or even decades.

Review Connect Reflect

 LG4 Characterize influences on sexuality, the nature of sexual orientation, and some sexual problems.

Review

- How do biology and culture influence sexuality?
- What is the nature of heterosexual and homosexual attitudes and behavior?
- What are some common sexually transmitted infections? What are some good strategies for protecting against STIs?
- What is the nature of forcible sexual behavior and sexual harassment?

Connect

- How might our acceptance of sexual scripts be linked to ethnic identity?

Reflect *Your Own Personal Journey of Life*

- Have you ever experienced (or unwittingly committed) an act of sexual harassment?

Childhood

Adolescence and Emerging Adulthood

Adult Development and Aging

So far we have discussed a number of aspects of human sexuality. Now, let's explore sexuality at different points in development, beginning with childhood.

CHILDHOOD

Most psychologists doubt Freud's claim that preschool children have a strong sexual attraction to the parent of the other sex. But what are some aspects of sexuality in children?

A majority of children engage in some sex play, usually with friends or siblings (Lamb, White, & Plocha, 2019; Moore, 2019). Childhood sex play includes exhibiting or inspecting the genitals. Much of this sex play is likely motivated by curiosity. There does not appear to be any link between such sexual play and sexual adjustment in adolescence or adulthood.

As the elementary school years progress, sex play with others usually declines, although romantic interest in peers may be present. Curiosity about sex remains high throughout the elementary school years, and children may ask many questions about reproduction and sexuality. However, the main surge in sexual interest takes place not in childhood but in early adolescence (DeLamater, 2019).

ADOLESCENCE AND EMERGING ADULTHOOD

Adolescence is a critical juncture in the development of sexuality as pubertal changes unfold and individuals develop a sexual identity (Van de Bongardt & others, 2019). And emerging adulthood provides further opportunities for individuals to explore the sexual aspects of their lives.

Adolescence Adolescence is a time of sexual exploration and experimentation, of sexual fantasies and realities, and of incorporating sexuality into one's identity. Adolescents have an almost insatiable curiosity about sexuality. They think about whether they are sexually attractive, how to engage in sex, and what the future holds for their sexual lives. The majority of adolescents eventually manage to develop a mature sexual identity, but most experience times of vulnerability and confusion (DeLamater, 2019).

The Sexual Culture Adolescence is a bridge between the asexual child and the sexual adult (Diamond, 2019; Savin-Williams, 2019). Every society gives some attention to adolescent sexuality. In some societies, adults clamp down and protect adolescent females from males by chaperoning them. Other societies promote very early marriage. Yet others allow some sexual experimentation.

In the United States, children and adolescents learn a great deal about sex from the media (Naezer & Ringrose, 2019; Ward, Moorman, & Grower, 2019). The messages come from TV commercials, which use sex to sell just about everything, as well as from the content of TV shows. A recent study of the prime-time shows that U.S. adolescents and emerging adults watch on television found that sexual violence and abuse, casual sex, lack of contraception use, and no coverage of the consequences of risky sexual behavior were common (Kinsler & others, 2019). In another recent study of television, sexual behavior with casual

> developmental **connection**
>
> **Biological Processes**
>
> Girls enter puberty approximately two years earlier than boys, with pubertal change peaking on average at age 11½ in girls and 13½ in boys. Connect to "Physical Development and Biological Aging."

Sexual arousal emerges as a new phenomenon in adolescence, and it is important to view sexuality as a normal aspect of adolescent development.

—SHIRLEY FELDMAN
Contemporary Psychologist, Stanford University

What characterizes the sexual culture U.S. adolescents are exposed to?
Jacob Lund/Shutterstock

developmental connection

Technology

Media influences on adolescents and emerging adults include the digitally mediated social environment. Connect to "Peers and the Sociocultural World."

developmental connection

Identity

Identity can be conceptualized in terms of identity statuses: diffused, foreclosed, moratorium, and achievement. Connect to "The Self, Identity, and Personality."

acquaintances was shown almost as frequently as sexual behavior in committed relationships (Timmermans & Van den Bulck, 2018). Further, a recent study found that non-Latino White adolescents reported learning more sexual information from parents and less from the media than African American adolescents (Bleakley & others, 2018). One research review concluded that adolescents who viewed more sexual content on TV were likely to initiate sexual intercourse earlier than their peers who viewed less sexual content on TV (Brown & Strasburger, 2007).

A special concern is the recent increase in *sexting,* which involves sending sexually explicit images, videos, or text messages via electronic communication (Bianchi & others, 2019; Englander & McCoy, 2018; Handschuh, La Cross, & Smaldone, 2019). A national study of 13- to 18-year-olds found that 7 percent reported sending or showing someone sexual pictures of themselves (Ybarra & Mitchell, 2014). In this study, sharing sexual photos was linked to a wide range of sexual behaviors including oral sex and vaginal sex. In some schools, sexting occurs more frequently, as indicated in a recent study of 656 high school students at one school in which 15.8 percent of males and 13.6 percent of females reported sending and 40.5 percent of males and 30.6 percent of females reported receiving explicit sexual pictures on cell phones (Strassberg, Cann, & Velarde, 2017). And in another recent study of 13- to 21-year-old Latinos, engaging in sexting was linked to engaging in penetrative (oral, vaginal, and anal) sex (Romo & others, 2017). Further, a recent study of emerging adults found that receiving unwanted sexts and sexting under coercion were linked to higher levels of depression, anxiety, and stress, and lower self-esteem (Klettke & others, 2019).

The American Academy of Pediatrics (2010) issued a policy statement on sexuality, contraception, and the media. It pointed out that television, film, music, and the Internet are all becoming increasingly explicit, yet information about abstinence, sexual responsibility, and birth control rarely is transmitted within these media.

Developing a Sexual Identity Mastering emerging sexual feelings and forming a sense of sexual identity is a multifaceted and lengthy process (Diamond, 2019; Savin-Williams, 2019). It involves learning to manage sexual feelings (such as sexual arousal and attraction), developing new forms of intimacy, and learning the skills to regulate sexual behavior to avoid undesirable consequences. An adolescent's sexual identity is influenced by *social norms* related to sex—the extent to which adolescents perceive that their peers are having sex, using protection, and so on. These social norms have important influences on adolescents' sexual behavior. For example, one study revealed that when adolescents perceived that their peers were sexually permissive, the adolescents had a higher rate of initiating sexual intercourse and engaging in risky sexual practices (Potard, Courtois, & Rusch, 2008). An individual's sexual identity also can be linked to other developing identities, which are discussed in the chapter on "The Self, Identity, and Personality."

An adolescent's sexual identity involves activities, interests, styles of behavior, and an indication of sexual orientation (whether an individual has same-sex or other-sex attractions) (Carroll, 2019; Goldberg & Halpern, 2017). For example, some adolescents have a high anxiety level about sex, others a low level. Some adolescents are strongly aroused sexually, others less so. Some adolescents are very active sexually, others not at all. Some adolescents are sexually inactive in response to their strong religious upbringing, while others attend church regularly but their religious training does not inhibit their sexual activity.

It is commonly believed that most *sexual minority* (which can include those who are gay, lesbian, bisexual, or transsexual) individuals quietly struggle with same-sex attractions in childhood, do not engage in heterosexual dating, and gradually recognize that they are gay or lesbian in mid to late adolescence (Savin-Williams, 2017, 2019). Many youth do follow this developmental pathway, but others do not. For example, many youth have no recollection of same-sex attractions in childhood and experience a more abrupt awareness of their same-sex attraction in late adolescence. Researchers also have found that the majority of adolescents with same-sex attractions also experience some degree of other-sex attractions (Diamond, 2019). Even though some adolescents who are attracted to same-sex individuals fall in love with these individuals, others claim that their same-sex attractions are purely physical (Savin-Williams, 2016, 2017, 2019). In the timing and sequence of sexual developmental milestones, there are few individual differences between heterosexual and sexual minority adolescents except that sexual minority adolescents have to cope with their sexual identity in more stressful ways, including disclosing their sexual identity to family members (Savin-Williams, 2019).

A recent study of more than 4,500 boys and girls examined whether early childhood sex-typed behavior was linked to adolescent sexual orientation (Li, Kung, & Hines, 2017). In this study, gender-typed behavior (for example, rough-and-tumble play was a male sex-typed item and playing house was a female sex-typed item) at 3.5 and 4.75 years (but less so at 2.5 years) predicted sexual orientation at 15 years of age, with the results stronger for boy than for girls.

In sum, gay and lesbian youth have diverse patterns of initial attraction, often have bisexual attractions, and may feel physical or emotional attraction to same-sex individuals but do not always fall in love with them (Diamond, 2019; Savin-Williams, 2017, 2019). Further, the majority of sexual minority (gay, lesbian, and bisexual) adolescents have competent and successful paths of development through adolescence and become healthy and productive adults. However, in a recent large-scale study, sexual minority adolescents did engage in a higher prevalence of health-risk behaviors (greater drug use and sexual risk taking, for example) than heterosexual adolescents (Kann & others, 2016). And a recent study found that early sexual debut (first sexual intercourse before age 13) was associated with sexual risk taking, substance use, violent victimization, and suicidal thoughts/attempts in both sexual minority (in this study, gay, lesbian, or bisexual adolescents) and heterosexual youth (Lowry & others, 2017).

What are some developmental pathways of same-sex attraction in adolescence?
Steve Edreff/Shutterstock

The Timing and Frequency of Adolescent Sexual Behaviors

The timing of sexual initiation varies by country as well as by gender and other socioeconomic characteristics. In one cross-cultural study, among females, the proportion having first intercourse by age 17 ranged from 72 percent in Mali to 47 percent in the United States and 45 percent in Tanzania (Singh & others, 2000). The percentage of males who had their first intercourse by age 17 ranged from 76 percent in Jamaica to 64 percent in the United States and 63 percent in Brazil. Within the United States, male, African American, and inner-city adolescents report being the most sexually active, whereas Asian American adolescents have the most restrictive sexual timetable (Feldman, Turner, & Araujo, 1999).

What is the current profile of sexual activity of adolescents? In a U.S. national survey conducted in 2017, 57.3 percent of twelfth-graders reported having experienced sexual intercourse, compared with 30 percent of ninth-graders (Kann & others, 2018). By age 20, 77 percent of U.S. youth report having engaged in sexual intercourse (Dworkin & Santelli, 2007). Nationally, in 2017, 44.3 percent of twelfth-graders, 35.3 percent of eleventh-graders, 24.9 percent of tenth-graders, and 12.9 percent of ninth-graders reported that they were currently sexually active (Kann & others, 2018).

What trends in adolescent sexual activity have occurred in recent decades? From 1991 to 2017, decreasing percentages of adolescents reported any of the following: ever having had sexual intercourse, currently being sexually active, having had sexual intercourse before the age of 13, and having had sexual intercourse with four or more persons during their lifetime (Kann & others, 2018) (see Figure 6).

Sexual initiation varies by ethnic group in the United States (Kann & others, 2018). African Americans are likely to engage in sexual behaviors earlier than other ethnic groups, whereas Asian Americans are likely to engage in them later (Feldman, Turner, & Araujo, 1999). In a 2017 national U.S. survey of ninth- to twelfth-graders, 45.8 percent of African Americans, 37.9 percent of Latinos, and 38.6 percent of non-Latino Whites said they had experienced sexual intercourse (Kann & others, 2018). In this study, 7.5 percent of African Americans (compared with 4 percent of Latinos and 2.1 percent of non-Latino Whites) said they had their first sexual experience before 13 years of age. All of these figures reflect a significant decrease in sexual intercourse since 2011 for African American and Latino adolescents (Kann & others, 2018).

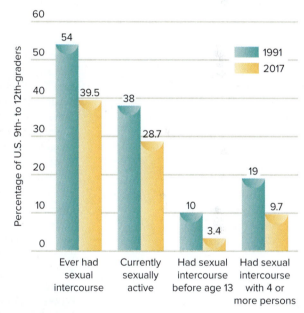

FIGURE 6

SEXUAL ACTIVITY OF U.S. ADOLESCENTS FROM 1991 TO 2017
Source: After Kann & others, 2018.

developmental connection

Culture

The high school dropout rate for Latino adolescents is higher than for any other ethnic group, except Native American adolescents. Connect to "Schools, Achievement, and Work."

What are some risks associated with early initiation of sexual intercourse?
Stockbyte/Punchstock

Recent research indicates that oral sex is now a common occurrence among U.S. adolescents (Goldstein & Halpern-Felsher, 2018). In a recent national survey of more than 7,000 15- to 24-year-olds, 58.6 percent of the females reported ever having performed oral sex and 60.4 percent said they had ever received oral sex (Holway & Hernandez, 2018). Also, in another national survey, 51 percent of U.S. 15- to 19-year-old boys and 47 percent of girls in the same age group said they had engaged in oral sex (Child Trends, 2015). Thus, more youth engage in oral sex than vaginal sex, likely because they perceive oral sex to be more acceptable and to be associated with fewer health risks.

One study also found that among female adolescents who reported having vaginal sex first, 31 percent reported having a teen pregnancy, whereas among those who initiated oral-genital sex first, only 8 percent reported having a teen pregnancy (Reese & others, 2013). Thus, how adolescents initiate their sex lives may have positive or negative consequences for their sexual health.

Sexual Risk Factors in Adolescence   Many adolescents are not emotionally prepared to handle sexual experiences, especially in early adolescence (Charlton & others, 2019; Weisman & others, 2019). Early sexual activity is linked with risky behaviors such as drug use, delinquency, and school-related problems (Cai & others, 2018; Donenberg & others, 2018; Rivera & others, 2018). In a recent study of Korean adolescent girls, early menarche was linked to earlier initiation of sexual intercourse (Kim & others, 2019). Another study confirmed that early engagement in sexual intercourse (prior to 14 years of age) is associated with high-risk sexual factors (forced sex, using drugs/alcohol at last sex, not using a condom at last sex, having multiple partners in the previous month, and becoming pregnant or causing a pregnancy), as well as experiencing dating violence (Kaplan & others, 2013). Also, a study of more than 3,000 Swedish adolescents revealed that sexual intercourse before age 14 was linked to risky behaviors such as an increased number of sexual partners, experience of oral and anal sex, negative health behaviors (smoking, drug and alcohol use), and antisocial behavior (being violent, stealing, running away from home) at 18 years of age (Kastbom & others, 2015). Further, a recent South African study found that early sexual debut predicted a lower probability of graduating from high school (Bengesai, Khan, & Dube, 2018). And in an Australian study, sex at age 15 or younger predicted higher rates of emerging adult (average age 21) pregnancy, lifetime sexual partners, and sex without using a condom (Prendergast & others, 2019). In this study, early sex also was associated with higher rates of emerging adult substance use and antisocial behavior.

Substance abuse, especially in early adolescence, is linked to sexual risk practices. For example, in a recent study, the likelihood of initiating sexual intercourse before age 13 was higher among individuals who engaged in substance abuse and had mental health problems (Okumu & others, 2019).

A number of family factors are associated with sexual risk taking. For example, one study revealed that adolescents who in the eighth grade reported greater parental knowledge of their activities and more family rules about dating were less likely to initiate sex during the eighth through tenth grades (Ethier & others, 2016). In another study, difficulties and disagreements between Latino adolescents and their parents were linked to the adolescents' early sexual initiation (Cordova & others, 2014). Another study revealed that of a number of parenting practices the factor that best predicted a lower level of risky sexual behavior by adolescents was supportive parenting (Simons & others, 2016). Also, having older sexually active siblings or pregnant/parenting teenage sisters placed adolescent girls at increased risk for pregnancy (Miller, Benson, & Galbraith, 2001). Further, in a recent study of urban, predominantly Latino and African American adolescents, talk with extended family members about sexual protection was linked to adolescents having fewer sexual partners, while talk about risks involved in sex was associated with adolescents having more sexual partners (Grossman & others, 2019).

Socioeconomic status/poverty, peer, school, and sports contexts provide further information about sexual risk taking in adolescents (Warner, 2018). The percentage of sexually active young adolescents is higher in low-income areas of inner cities (Morrison-Beedy & others, 2013). One study found that associating with more deviant peers in early adolescence was related to having more sexual partners at age 16 (Lansford & others, 2010). Further, a research review found that school connectedness was linked to positive sexuality outcomes (Markham & others, 2010). Further, one study found that adolescent females who skipped school or failed a test were more likely to frequently have sexual intercourse and less likely to use contraceptives (Hensel & Sorge, 2014). Another study found that adolescent males who play sports engage in a higher level of sexual risk taking while adolescent females who play sports engage in a lower level of sexual risk taking (Lipowski & others, 2016).

Weak self-regulation (poor ability to control one's emotions and behavior) is increasingly being implicated in sexual risk taking. For example, a longitudinal study found that weak self-regulation at 8 to 9 years of age and risk proneness (tendency to seek sensation and make poor decisions) at 12 to 13 years of age set the stage for sexual risk taking at 16 to 17 years of age (Crockett, Raffaelli, & Shen, 2006). And another study found that a high level of impulsiveness was linked to early adolescent sexual risk taking (Khurana & others, 2012).

Might adolescents' spirituality protect them from negative sexual outcomes? One study found that parents' religiosity was linked to a lower level of risky sexual behavior among adolescents, in part resulting from adolescents hanging out with peers who were less sexually permissive (Landor & others, 2011). And a recent study of African American adolescent girls indicated that those who reported that religion was of low or moderate importance to them had a much earlier sexual debut than their counterparts who said that religion was very or extremely important to them (George Dalmida & others, 2018).

Contraceptive Use   Sexual intercourse is a normal activity necessary for procreation, but if appropriate safeguards are not taken it brings the risk of unintended pregnancy and sexually transmitted infections (Carroll, 2019). Both of these risks can be reduced significantly by using certain forms of contraception, especially condoms (Apter, 2018; Fridy & others, 2018; Goldstein & Halpern-Felsher, 2018; Summit & others, 2019; Turner, 2019).

In a recent national survey of U.S. high school students, 53.8 percent reported that either they or their partner had used a contraceptive the last time they had sexual intercourse, compared with 46 percent in 1991 and 53.8 percent in 2011 (Kann & others, 2018). However, too many adolescents do not use contraceptives. In the same national survey, 13.8 percent of sexually active adolescents said they had not used any contraceptive method the last time they had sexual intercourse (Kann & others, 2018). Younger adolescents are less likely to take contraceptive precautions than are older adolescents. Researchers also have found that U.S. adolescents are less likely to use condoms than their European counterparts (Jorgensen & others, 2015).

Recently, a number of leading medical organizations and experts have recommended that adolescents use long-acting reversible contraception (LARC) (Apter, 2018; Fridy & others, 2018; Summit & others, 2019; Turner, 2019). These organizations include the Society for Adolescent Health and Medicine (2017) and the World Health Organization (2018). LARC consists of the use of intrauterine devices (IUDs) and contraceptive implants, which have a much lower failure rate and greater effectiveness in preventing unwanted pregnancy than the use of birth control pills and condoms (Diedrich, Klein, & Peipert, 2017; Society for Adolescent Health and Medicine, 2017).

One study also found that 50 percent of U.S. 15- to 19-year-old girls with unintended pregnancies ending in live births were not using any birth control method when they got pregnant, and 34 percent believed they could not get pregnant at the time (Centers for Disease Control and Prevention, 2012). Another study found that a greater age difference between sexual partners in adolescence is associated with less consistent condom use (Volpe & others, 2013).

Sexually Transmitted Infections   Earlier, we described sexually transmitted infections. Here we focus on their incidence among adolescents. Nearly half of the 20 million new STI infections in the United States occur in 15- to 24-year-olds (Kann & others, 2018). Individuals 13 to 24 years of age accounted for 21 percent of new HIV diagnoses in the United States, and 81 percent of these young people were gay or bixexual males (Kann & others, 2018).

As we discussed earlier, a special concern is the high incidence of AIDS in sub-Saharan Africa (UNICEF, 2019). Adolescent girls in many African countries are vulnerable to being infected with HIV by adult men. Far more adolescent girls than boys have AIDS in these countries, whereas in the United States adolescent males are more likely to have AIDS than their female counterparts (UNAIDS). In Kenya, 25 percent of 15- to 19-year-old girls are HIV-positive compared with 4 percent of boys.

Adolescent Pregnancy   Unintended pregnancy is another problematic outcome of sexuality in adolescence and requires major efforts to reduce its occurrence (Kahn & Halpern, 2018; Kudesia & Talib, 2019). In cross-cultural comparisons, the United States continues to have one of the highest adolescent pregnancy and childbearing rates in the industrialized world, despite a considerable decline in the 1990s (Cooksey, 2009). The U.S. adolescent

Sixteen-year-old Alberto's maternal grandmother was a heroin addict who died of cancer at 40. His father, just 17 when Alberto was born, has been in prison most of Alberto's life. His mother and stepfather are not married but have lived together for a dozen years and have four other children. Alberto's stepbrother dropped out of school when he was 17, fathered a child, and is unemployed. But Alberto, who lives in the Bronx in New York City, has different plans for his own future. He says he wants to be a dentist "like the kind of woman who fixed his teeth at Bronx-Lebanon Hospital Center clinic when he was a child" (Bernstein, 2004, p. A22). And Alberto, along with his girlfriend, Jasmine, wants to remain a virgin until he is married.
Suzanne DeChillo/The New York Times/Redux Pictures

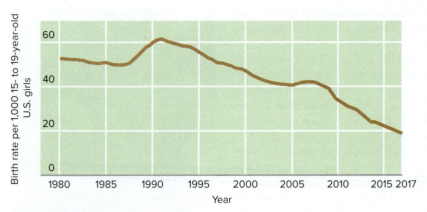

FIGURE 7

BIRTH RATES FOR U.S. 15- TO 19-YEAR-OLD GIRLS FROM 1980 TO 2017
Source: Martin, J.A., Hamilton, B.E., & Osterman, M.J. (2015, September). Births in the United States, 2014. NCHS Data Brief, 216, 1–8.

pregnancy rate is four times as high as in the Netherlands (Sedgh & others, 2015). This dramatic difference exists in spite of the fact that U.S. adolescents are no more sexually active than their counterparts in the Netherlands. In the United States, 82 percent of pregnancies to mothers 15 to 19 years of age are unintended (Koh, 2014). A cross-cultural comparison found that among 21 countries, the United States had the highest adolescent pregnancy rate among 15- to 19-year-olds and Switzerland had the lowest rate (Sedgh & others, 2015).

Despite the negative comparisons of the United States with many other developed countries, there have been some encouraging trends in U.S. adolescent pregnancy rates. In 2017, the U.S. birth rate for 15- to 19-year-olds was 18.8 births per 1,000 females, the lowest rate ever recorded, which represents a dramatic decrease from the 62 births per 1,000 females for the same age range in 1991 (Centers for Disease Control and Prevention, 2019) (see Figure 7). There also has been a substantial decrease in adolescent pregnancies across ethnic groups in recent years. Reasons for the decline include school/community health classes, increased contraceptive use, and fear of sexually transmitted infections such as AIDS.

Ethnic variations characterize adolescent pregnancy. For 15- to 19-year-old U.S. females in 2017, per 1,000 females the birth rate for Latinas was 28.9, for African Americans 27.5, for non-Latina Whites 13.2, and for Asian Americans 3.3 (Centers for Disease Control and Prevention, 2019). These figures represent substantial decreases in adolescent pregnancy rates for Latina and African American teens, especially for Latina (38 per 1,000 in 2014 and African American (35 per 1,000 in 2014) adolescent girls. However, Latina and African American girls are more likely to have a second child during adolescence than are non-Latina adolescent girls (Rosengard, 2009). And daughters of teenage mothers are at higher risk for teenage childbearing, thus perpetuating an intergenerational cycle. A study using data from the National Longitudinal Survey of Youth revealed that daughters of teenage mothers were 66 percent more likely to become teenage mothers themselves (Meade, Kershaw, & Ickovics, 2008). In this study, conditions that increased the likelihood that daughters of the teenage mothers would become pregnant included low parental monitoring and poverty.

The consequences of America's high adolescent pregnancy rate are cause for great concern (Devakumar & others, 2019; Tevendale & others, 2017; Mullick, 2019). Adolescent pregnancy creates health and developmental outcome risks for both the baby and the mother (Leftwich & Alves, 2017). Infants born to adolescent mothers are more likely to have low birth weights—a prominent factor in infant mortality—as well as neurological problems and childhood illness (Leftwich & Alves, 2017; Sawyer, Abdul-Razak, & Patton, 2019). One study assessed the reading and math achievement trajectories of children born to adolescent and nonadolescent mothers with different levels of education (Tang & others, 2016). In this study, higher levels of maternal education were linked to higher levels of academic achievement through the eighth grade. Nonetheless, the achievement of children born to adolescent mothers never reached the levels of children born to adult mothers.

Adolescent mothers also are more likely to be depressed and drop out of school than their peers (Leftwich & Alves, 2017; Siegel & Brandon, 2014). Although many adolescent mothers resume their education later in life, they generally do not catch up economically with women who bear children in their twenties. A longitudinal study revealed that these characteristics of adolescent mothers were related to their likelihood of having problems as emerging adults: a history of school problems, delinquency, hard substance use, and mental health problems (Oxford & others, 2006). Also, a study of African American urban youth found that at 32 years of age women who had been teenage mothers were more likely to be unemployed, live in poverty, depend on welfare, and not have completed college than women who became mothers during adulthood (Assini-Meytin & Green, 2015). In this study, at 32 years of age, men who had been teenage fathers were less likely to be employed than were men who had fathered children during adulthood.

A special concern is repeated adolescent pregnancy. In a recent national study, the percentage of teen births that were repeat births decreased from 21 percent in 2004 to 17 percent in 2015 (Dee & others, 2017). In a recent meta-analysis, use of effective contraception, especially

Lynn Blankinship, Family and Consumer Science Educator

Lynn Blankinship is a family and consumer science educator. She has an undergraduate degree in her specialty from the University of Arizona and has taught for more than 20 years, the last 14 at Tucson High Magnet School.

Blankinship received the Tucson Federation of Teachers Educator of the Year Award for 1999–2000 and was honored in 1999 as the Arizona Association of Family and Consumer Science Teacher of the Year.

Blankinship especially enjoys teaching life skills to adolescents. One of her favorite activities is having students care for an automated baby that imitates the needs of real babies. She says that this program has a profound impact on students because the baby must be cared for around the clock for the duration of the assignment. Blankinship also coordinates real-world work experiences and training for students in several child-care facilities in the Tucson area.

Lynn Blankinship (center) with students carrying their automated babies.
Lynn Blankinship

For more information about what family and consumer science educators do, see the Careers in Life-Span Development appendix.

LARC, and education-related factors (higher level of education and school continuation) resulted in a lower incidence of repeated teen pregnancy, while depression and a history of abortion were linked to a higher percentage of repeated teen pregnancy (Maravilla & others, 2017).

Researchers have found that adolescent mothers interact less effectively with their infants than do adult mothers. One study revealed that adolescent mothers spent more time in negative interactions and less time in play and positive interactions with their infants than did adult mothers (Riva Crugnola & others, 2014). One intervention, "My Baby and Me," that involved frequent (55), intensive home visitation coaching sessions with adolescent mothers across three years resulted in improved maternal behavior and child outcomes (Guttentag & others, 2014). And a recent study assessed the reading and math achievement trajectories of children born to adolescent and non-adolescent mothers with different levels of education (Tang & others, 2016). In this study, higher levels of maternal education were linked to growth in their children's achievement through the eighth grade. Nonetheless, the achievement of children born to the adolescent mothers never reached the levels of children born to adult mothers.

Although the consequences of America's high adolescent pregnancy rate are cause for great concern, it often is not pregnancy alone that leads to negative consequences for an adolescent mother and her offspring (Cavazos-Rehg & others, 2010a, b). Adolescent mothers are more likely to come from low-SES backgrounds (Joyner, 2009). Many adolescent mothers also were not good students before they became pregnant (Malamitsi-Puchner & Boutsikou, 2006). However, not every adolescent female who bears a child lives a life of poverty and low achievement. Thus, although adolescent pregnancy is a high-risk circumstance and adolescents who do not become pregnant generally fare better than those who do, some adolescent mothers do well in school and have positive outcomes (Schaffer & others, 2012).

All adolescents can benefit from comprehensive sexuality education, beginning prior to adolescence and continuing through adolescence (Barfield, Warner, & Kappeler, 2017; Tang & others, 2016; Mueller & others, 2017). Family and consumer science educators teach life skills, such as effective decision making, to adolescents. To read about the work of one family and consumer science educator, see the *Connecting with Careers* profile. And to learn more about ways to reduce adolescent pregnancy, see the *Connecting Development to Life* interlude.

Emerging Adulthood   At the beginning of emerging adulthood (age 18), surveys indicate that slightly more than 60 percent of individuals have experienced sexual intercourse, but by the

connecting development to life

Reducing Adolescent Pregnancy

One strategy for reducing adolescent pregnancy, called the Teen Outreach Program (TOP), focuses on engaging adolescents in volunteer community service and stimulates discussions that help adolescents appreciate the lessons they learn through volunteerism (Dryfoos & Barkin, 2006). In one study, 695 adolescents in grades 9 to 12 were randomly assigned to either a Teen Outreach group or a control group (Allen & others, 1997). They were assessed at both program entry and program exit nine months later. The rate of pregnancy was substantially lower for the Teen Outreach adolescents. These adolescents also had a lower rate of school failure and academic suspension.

Currently, a major controversy in sex education is whether schools should have an abstinence-only program or a program that emphasizes contraceptive knowledge (King & Regan, 2019). Three research reviews found that abstinence-only programs did not delay the initiation of sexual intercourse and did not reduce HIV-risk behaviors (Denford & others, 2017; Kirby, Laris, & Rolleri, 2007; Underhill, Montgomery, & Operario, 2007). The Society for Adolescent Health and Medicine (2017) recently released a policy position stating that research evidence indicates that many comprehensive sex education programs successfully delay initiation of sexual intercourse.

Some sex education programs are starting to include abstinence-plus sexuality, an approach that promotes abstinence as well as contraceptive use (Nixon & others, 2011; Realini & others, 2010).

A number of leading experts on adolescent sexuality now conclude that sex education programs that emphasize contraceptive knowledge do not increase the incidence of sexual intercourse and are more likely to reduce the risk of adolescent pregnancy and sexually transmitted infections than abstinence-only programs (Society for Adolescent Health and Medicine, 2017). What additional research might help expand the reach of such programs?

---

end of emerging adulthood (age 25), most individuals have had sexual intercourse (Lefkowitz & Gillen, 2006; Wesche & Lefkowitz, 2020). Also, the U.S. average age for a first marriage has now climbed to 29.5 years for men and 27.4 years for women, higher than at any other point in history (U.S. Census Bureau, 2018). Thus, emerging adulthood is a time frame during which most individuals are both sexually active and unmarried (Waterman & Lefkowitz, 2018).

Uncertainty characterizes many emerging adults' sexual relationships (Wesche & Lefkowitz, 2020). Consider a study of emerging adult daters and cohabitors that found nearly half reported a reconciliation (a breakup followed by a reunion) (Halpern-Meekin & others, 2013). Also, emerging adults report that on days when they have vaginal sex they have more positive affect; however, they report higher levels of negative affect or other negative consequences if they have sex with someone they are not dating (Vasilenko & Lefkowitz, 2018).

Casual sex is more common in emerging adulthood than it is during the late twenties (Wesche & Lefkowitz, 2020; Waterman & Lefkowitz, 2018; Wesche, Lefkowitz, & Vasilenko, 2018). A recent trend has involved "hooking up" to have non-relationship sex (from kissing to intercourse) (Blayney & others, 2019; Sullivan & others, 2018). One study indicated that 40 percent of 22-year-olds reported having had a recent casual sexual partner (Lyons & others, 2015). Another study also revealed that 20 percent of first-year college women on one large university campus had engaged in at least one hookup over the course of the school year (Fielder & others, 2013). In this study, impulsivity, sensation seeking, and alcohol use were among the predictors of a higher likelihood of hooking up. And in a study of more than 3,900 18- to 25-year-olds, having casual sex was negatively linked to well-being and positively related to psychological distress (Bersamin & others, 2014). Further, research indicates that when emerging adults drink alcohol (especially when they engage in binge drinking or use marijuana), they are more likely to have casual sex and less likely to discuss possible risks (Kuperberg & Padgett, 2017).

In addition to hooking up, another type of casual sex that has recently increased among emerging adults is "friends with benefits" (FWB), which involves a relationship formed by the integration of friendship and sexual intimacy without an explicit commitment characteristic of an exclusive romantic relationship (Weger, Cole, & Akbulut, 2019). A recent study found that suicidal ideation was associated with entrance into a friends with benefits relationship as well as continuation of the FWB relationship (Dube & others, 2017). Also, in a study of almost 8,000 emerging adults, males had more permissive sexual attitudes, especially regarding sexual encounters, than did females (Sprecher, Treger, & Sakaluk, 2013).

What are some characteristics of sexual patterns in emerging adulthood?
Onoky/SuperStock

ADULT DEVELOPMENT AND AGING

Earlier in our coverage of sexual orientation, we examined a number of basic ideas about heterosexual and gay/lesbian attitudes and behavior. Much of what we said there applied to young adults. Here we focus on changes in middle adulthood and late adulthood.

Middle Adulthood   What kinds of changes characterize the sexuality of women and men as they go through middle age? **Climacteric** is a term used to describe the midlife transition when fertility declines.

Menopause   **Menopause** is the time in middle age, usually during the late forties or early fifties, when a woman's menstrual periods cease (Mitchell & Woods, 2015). The average age at which U.S. women have their last period is 51 (Wise, 2006). However, there is a large variation in the age at which menopause occurs—from 39 to 59 years of age. Later menopause is linked with increased risk of breast cancer (Mishra & others, 2009).

The average age at menarche, a girl's first menstruation, has significantly decreased since the mid-nineteenth century, occurring as much as four years earlier in some countries (Susman & Dorn, 2013). Has there been a similar earlier onset in the occurrence of menopause? No, there hasn't been a corresponding change in menopause, and there is little or no correlation between the onset of menarche and the onset of menopause (Gosden, 2007). However, researchers have found that early-onset menopause is linked to a higher risk of cardiovascular disease and stroke (Kaur, Singh, & Ahula, 2012).

Perimenopause is the transitional period from normal menstrual periods to no menstrual periods at all, which often takes up to 10 years (McNamara, Batur, & DeSapri, 2015). Perimenopause occurs most often in the forties but can occur in the thirties (Raglan, Schulkin, & Micks, 2018). One study of 30- to 50-year-old women found that depressed feelings, headaches, moodiness, and heart palpitations were the perimenopausal symptoms that these women most frequently discussed with health-care providers (Lyndaker & Hulton, 2004). Lifestyle factors such as whether women are overweight, smoke, drink heavily, or exercise regularly during perimenopause influence aspects of their future health status such as whether they develop cardiovascular disease or chronic illnesses (Honour, 2018). A recent study found that the more minutes per week that women exercised during the menopausal transition, the lower their perceived stress was (Guerin & others, 2019).

In menopause, production of estrogen by the ovaries declines dramatically, and this decline produces uncomfortable symptoms in some women—"hot flashes," nausea, fatigue, and rapid heartbeat, for example (Hachul & Tufik, 2019).

Cross-cultural studies also reveal wide variations in the menopause experience (Rathnayake & others, 2018). For example, hot flashes are uncommon in Mayan women (Beyene, 1986). Asian women report fewer hot flashes than women in Western societies (Payer, 1991). In a recent study in China, Mosuo women (Mosuo is a matriarchal tribe in southern China where women have the dominant role in society, don't marry, and can take on as many lovers as they desire) had fewer negative menopausal symptoms, higher self-esteem, and better family support than Han Chinese women (the majority ethnic group in China) (Zhang & others, 2019). It is difficult to determine the extent to which these cross-cultural variations are due to genetic, dietary, reproductive, or cultural factors.

Menopause overall is not the negative experience for most women that it was once thought to be (Brown & others, 2018). Most women do not have severe physical or psychological problems related to menopause. For example, a research review concluded that there is no clear evidence that depressive disorders occur more often during menopause than at other times in a woman's reproductive life (Judd, Hickey, & Bryant, 2012).

However, the loss of fertility is an important marker for women—it means that they have to make final decisions about having children. Women in their thirties who have never had children sometimes speak about being "up against the biological clock" because they cannot postpone choices about having children much longer.

Until recently, hormone replacement therapy was often prescribed as a treatment for unpleasant side effects of menopause. *Hormone replacement therapy (HRT)* augments the declining levels of reproductive hormone production by the ovaries (Andersson, Borgquist, & Jirstrom, 2018; Lobo, 2017). HRT can consist of various forms of estrogen, usually in combination with a progestin.

climacteric The midlife transition in which fertility declines.

menopause The complete cessation of a woman's menstrual cycles, which usually occurs during the late forties or early fifties.

perimenopause The transitional period from normal menstrual periods to no menstrual periods at all, which often takes up to 10 years.

The National Institutes of Health recommends that women who have not had a hysterectomy and who are currently taking hormones consult with their doctor to determine whether they should continue the treatment. If they are taking HRT for short-term relief of menopausal symptoms, the benefits may outweigh the risks. HRT also lowers the risk of bone loss and bone fractures in post-menopausal women (de Villiers & others, 2016). Also, research indicates that if women take HRT within 10 years following menopause, it is associated with reduced risk of coronary heart disease (Langer, 2017). And research has indicated that when women start HRT in their fifties and continue its use for 5 to 30 years, there is an increase of 1.5 quality life years (Hodis & Mack, 2014). However, research indicates that hormone replacement therapy is linked to a slightly higher risk of breast cancer and the longer HRT is taken, the greater the risk of breast cancer (American Cancer Society, 2019; Breastcancer. org, 2019). The current consensus is that HRT increases the risk of breast cancer in women (Breastcancer.org, 2019).

Many middle-aged women are seeking alternatives to HRT such as regular exercise, mindfulness training, dietary supplements, herbal remedies, relaxation therapy, acupuncture, hypnosis, and nonsteroidal medications (Asghari & others, 2017; Johnson, Roberts, & Elkins, 2019; Lund & others, 2019). One study revealed that in sedentary women, aerobic training for six months decreased menopausal symptoms, especially night sweats, mood swings, and irritability (Moilanen & others, 2012). Another study found that yoga improved the quality of life of menopausal women (Reed & others, 2014). And in a recent analysis of research, it was concluded that mindfulness training is linked to improved psychological adjustment during the menopause transition (Molefi-Youri, 2019).

Hormonal Changes in Middle-Aged Men Do men go through anything like the menopause that women experience? In other words, is there a male menopause? During middle adulthood, most men do not lose their capacity to father children, although there usually is a modest decline in their sexual hormone level and activity (Kaufman & others, 2019). Men experience hormonal changes in their fifties and sixties, but nothing like the dramatic drop in estrogen that women experience. Testosterone production begins to decline about 1 percent a year during middle adulthood, and sperm count usually shows a slow decline, but men do not lose their fertility in middle age. The term *male hypogonadism* is used to describe a condition in which the body does not produce enough testosterone (Mayo Clinic, 2019). What has been referred to as "male menopause," then, may have less to do with hormonal change than with the psychological adjustment men must make when they are faced with declining physical energy and with family and work pressures.

The gradual decline in men's testosterone levels in middle age can reduce their sexual drive (Goel & others, 2009). Their erections are less full and less frequent, and men require more stimulation to achieve them. Researchers once attributed these changes to psychological factors, but increasingly they find that as many as 75 percent of the erectile dysfunctions in middle-aged men stem from physiological problems. Smoking, diabetes, hypertension, elevated cholesterol levels, depression, and lack of exercise are responsible for many erectile problems in middle-aged men (Gur & others, 2017; Rakovac Tisdall & others, 2018).

Recently, there has been a dramatic surge of interest in *testosterone replacement therapy (TRT)* (Fode & others, 2019; Larssen, Clausen, & Stahlman, 2019; Moon & Park, 2019). Recent research indicates that TRT can improve sexual functioning, muscle strength, and bone health in men with low testosterone levels (Gray, McHale, & Carré, 2017; Mayo Clinic, 2019; Rastrelli & others, 2019). A recent study indicated that TRT-related benefits in quality of life and sexual function were maintained for 36 months after initial treatment (Rosen & others, 2017). Also, recent research on TRT and cardiovascular disease is inconclusive. Some studies have revealed that testosterone replacement therapy is associated with a lower incidence of heart attack or stroke, as well as a reduction in all-cause mortality (Cheetham & others, 2017; Jones & Kelly, 2018). However, others have not reached these conclusions and some studies have shown increased rates of stroke in men taking testosterone treatments (Fode & others, 2019). Men who have prostate cancer or breast cancer should not take TRT, and men who are at risk for blood clotting (those who have atrial fibrillation, for example) also may need to avoid TRT (Osterberg, Bernie, & Ramasamy, 2014).

For many decades, it was thought that TRT increased the risk of prostate cancer, but recent research studies and reviews indicate that this is not the case, at least when TRT lasts one year or less (Debruyne & others, 2017; Yassin & others, 2017). Two studies found

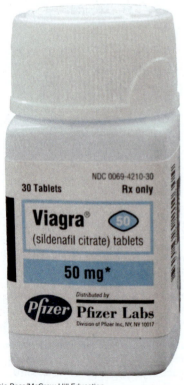

Suzie Ross/McGraw-Hill Education

that TRT improved older men's sexual function as well as their moods (Miner & others, 2013; Okada & others, 2014). Another study found that a higher testosterone level was linked to better episodic memory in middle-aged males (Panizzon & others, 2014). However, a research review concluded that the benefit-risk ratio for older adult men is uncertain (Isidori & others, 2014).

Erectile dysfunction (ED) is a common condition in aging men, affecting approximately 50 percent of men 40 to 70 years of age (Mola, 2015). Low testosterone can cause erectile dysfunction (Huang & others, 2019). Treatment for men with erectile dysfunction has focused on the drug Viagra and on similar drugs, such as Levitra and Cialis (Bennett, 2018; Gesser-Edelsburg & Hijazi, 2018; Krishnappa & others, 2019). Viagra works by allowing increased blood flow into the penis, which produces an erection. Its success rate is in the 60 to 85 percent range (Claes & others, 2010).

How frequently do middle-aged U.S. adults engage in sexual intercourse?
Kristy-Anne Glubish/Design Pics

Sexual Attitudes and Behavior   Although the ability of men and women to function sexually shows little biological decline in middle adulthood, sexual activity usually occurs on a less frequent basis than in early adulthood (Geerkens & others, 2019; Rees & others, 2018). Career interests, family matters, decreased energy levels, and routine may contribute to this decline (Avis & others, 2009).

In the Sex in America survey (described earlier in this chapter), the frequency of having sex was greatest for individuals aged 25 to 29 years old (47 percent had sex twice a week or more) and dropped off for individuals in their fifties (23 percent of 50- to 59-year-old males said they had sex twice a week or more, while only 14 percent of the females in this age group reported this frequency) (Michael & others, 1994). Note, though, that the Sex in America survey may underestimate the frequency of sexual activity of middle-aged adults because the data were collected prior to the widespread use of erectile dysfunction drugs such as Viagra. In a recent study, higher frequency of sexual activity in middle-aged and older adults was linked to better overall cognitive functioning, especially in working memory and executive function (Wright, Jenks, & Demeyere, 2019).

Living with a spouse or partner makes all the difference in whether people engage in sexual activity, especially for women over 40 years of age. In one study conducted as part of the Midlife in the United States Study (MIDUS), 95 percent of women in their forties with partners said that they had been sexually active in the last six months, compared with only 53 percent of those without partners (Brim, 1999). By their fifties, 88 percent of women living with a partner had been sexually active in the last six months, but only 37 percent of those who were neither married nor living with someone reported having had sex in the last six months.

A large-scale study of U.S. adults 40 to 80 years of age found that premature ejaculation (26 percent) and erectile difficulties (22 percent) were the most common sexual problems of older men, whereas lack of sexual interest (33 percent) and lubrication difficulties (21 percent) were the most common sexual problems of older women (Laumann & others, 2009).

A person's health in middle age is a key factor in sexual activity during this period (Field & others, 2013). A study of adults 55 years and older revealed that their level of sexual activity was associated with their physical and mental health (Bach & others, 2013). Social and relationship factors also are important in sexual functioning during middle age. For example, in a recent study of healthy middle-aged women, interpersonal aspects such as emotional support and relationship satisfaction, as well the personality traits of optimism and self-esteem, were key predictors of the quality of sexual functioning (Memone, Fiacco, & Ehlert, 2019).

What are some characteristics of sexuality in older adults? How does sexual activity change as older adults go through the late adulthood period?
Image Source/Getty Images

Late Adulthood   Too often it has been assumed that older adults do not have sexual desires (Inelmen & others, 2012). Aging does induce some changes in human sexual performance, more so in men than in women, but many older adults do have sexual desires (Estill & others, 2018; Sinkovic & Towler, 2019; Wright, Jenks, & Demeyere, 2019). Orgasm becomes less frequent in males, occurring in every second to third act of intercourse rather

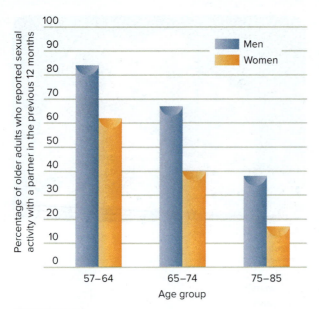

FIGURE 8

SEXUAL ACTIVITY IN OLDER ADULTS WITH A PARTNER

than every time. More direct stimulation usually is needed to produce an erection. From 65 to 80 years of age, approximately one out of four men has serious problems getting or keeping erections; for those over 80 years of age, the percentage rises to one out of two men (Butler & Lewis, 2002). Even when intercourse is impaired by infirmity, other relationship needs persist, among them closeness, sensuality, and being valued as a man or a woman (Bouman, 2008).

An interview study of more than 3,000 adults 57 to 85 years of age revealed that many older adults are sexually active as long as they are healthy (Lindau & others, 2007) (see Figure 8). Sexual activity did decline through the later years of life: 73 percent of 57- to 64-year-olds, 53 percent of 65- to 74-year-olds, and 26 percent of 75- to 85-year-olds reported that they were sexually active. Even in the sexually active oldest group (75 to 85), more than 50 percent said they still had sex at least two to three times a month. Fifty-eight percent of sexually active 65- to 74-year-olds and 31 percent of 75- to 85-year-olds said they engaged in oral sex. As with middle-aged and younger adults, older adults who did not have a partner were far less likely to be sexually active than those who had a partner. For older adults with a partner who reported not having sex, the main reason was poor health, especially the male partner's physical health. However, with recent advances in erectile dysfunction medications such as Viagra, an increasing number of older men, especially the young old, are able to have an erection (Constantinescu & others, 2017; Ozcan & others, 2017). Also, as indicated earlier, there has been a dramatic increase in testosterone replacement therapy in middle-aged adults, but the benefit-risk ratio of testosterone replacement therapy is uncertain for older males (Isidori & others, 2014).

As indicated in Figure 8, older women had a lower rate of sexual activity than did men. Indeed, a challenge for a sexually interested older woman is not having a partner. At 70 years of age, only about 35 percent of women have a partner, compared with approximately 70 percent of men of the same age. Many older women's husbands have died, and many older men are with younger women.

In other research on sexual behavior in older adults, engaging in sexual activity was linked to great enjoyment of life (Smith & others, 2019). Also, in another study, older adults were asked about their motivation for having sex (Gewirtz-Meydan & Ayalon, 2019). In this study, five main reasons for having sex were (1) to maintain their functioning; (2) to feel young again; (3) to feel attractive and desirable; (4) to go from lust to love; and (5) to change from "getting sex" to "giving sex."

At this point, we have discussed many aspects of sexuality, but we have not examined three influential factors that are explored in the chapter on "Moral Development, Values, and Religion."

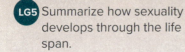

Review Connect Reflect

LG5 Summarize how sexuality develops through the life span.

Review

- What is the nature of childhood sexuality?
- How do adolescents develop a sexual identity? How does sexual behavior develop?
- What are some risk factors for sexual problems during adolescence?
- What are some patterns of behavior for emerging adults?
- How does sexuality change in middle adulthood? How does sexuality change in late adulthood?

Connect

- In this section you read that the production of estrogen by the ovaries declines dramatically in menopause. What have you learned about the role of estradiol, a type of estrogen, in puberty?

Reflect *Your Own Personal Journey of Life*

- How would you describe your sexual identity? What contributed to this identity?

Gender and Sexuality

1 Biological, Social, and Cognitive Influences on Gender

 LG1 Explain biological, social, and cognitive influences on gender.

Biological Influences

- Gender refers to the characteristics of people as males and females. Key aspects of gender include gender roles and gender-typing (the process by which children acquire the thoughts, feelings, and behaviors that are considered appropriate for their gender).

- Biological influences on gender include heredity, hormones, and evolution. A 23rd pair of chromosomes with two X-shaped chromosomes produces a female; a 23rd pair with an X and a Y chromosome produces a male. Estrogens primarily influence the development of female physical sex characteristics and help regulate the menstrual cycle. Androgens primarily promote the development of male genitals and secondary sex characteristics. To explore biological influences on gender, researchers have studied individuals who are exposed to unusual levels of sex hormones early in prenatal development. Evolutionary psychology argues that adaptation during the evolution of humans produced psychological differences between males and females.

Social Influences

- Three theories have been influential in arguing that psychological differences between the genders are due to social factors. Social role theory states that gender differences result from the contrasting roles of women and men. The psychoanalytic theory of gender stems from Freud's view that the preschool child develops a sexual attraction to the opposite-sex parent, then at 5 or 6 years of age renounces the attraction because of anxious feelings, subsequently identifies with the same-sex parent and unconsciously adopts the characteristics of the same-sex parent. The social cognitive theory of gender states that children learn about gender through observation and imitation and through reward and punishment for gender-appropriate and gender-inappropriate behavior. Parents, other adults, the media, peers, and schools and teachers influence children's gender development.

Cognitive Influences

- Gender schema theory states that gender-typing emerges as children gradually develop gender schemas of what is gender-appropriate and gender-inappropriate in their culture.

2 Gender Stereotypes, Similarities, Differences, and Classification

 LG2 Discuss gender stereotypes, similarities, differences, and classification.

Gender Stereotyping

- Gender stereotypes are general impressions and beliefs about males and females. Gender stereotypes are widespread. Gender stereotyping changes developmentally; it is present even at 2 years of age but increases considerably in early childhood. In middle and late childhood, children become more flexible in their gender attitudes, but gender stereotyping may increase again in early adolescence. By late adolescence, gender attitudes are often more flexible.

Gender Similarities and Differences

- There are a number of physical differences in males and females, small or nonexistent cognitive differences, and some socioemotional differences (males are more physically aggressive and active, but engage in less emotional self-regulation; females show a stronger interest in relationships; and females are more people-oriented, boys more object-oriented).

- Controversy surrounds how extensive gender differences are and what causes the differences. Gender in context is an important concept—gender behavior often varies across contexts, not only within a particular culture but also across cultures.

Gender-Role Classification

- Gender-role classification focuses on the degree to which individuals are masculine, feminine, or androgynous. Androgyny means having positive feminine and masculine characteristics. Recently, considerable interest has been generated about the gender category of transgender, which refers to individuals who adopt a gender identity that differs from the one assigned to them at birth. Given the complexity and variety of gender identity categories, the overarching umbrella term *trans* has been proposed.

Going Beyond Gender as Binary

- The traditional conceptualization of gender as being binary and having only two categories—male and female—is being challenged. These challenges occur in neuroscience, where human brains described more as a mosaic than as "his or her" brains; in endocrinology research that reveals more hormonal similarities in males and females than used to be thought; in the use of an increasing number of gender identity categories, including trans people, transgender, cisgender, and many more; and in developmental research that reveals the gender worlds of males and females are not only due to biological factors but are culturally influenced and malleable. Also, gender categories are not mutually exclusive and can change over time.

3 Gender Development Through the Life Span Describe the development of gender through the life span.

Childhood

- Children form many ideas about what the sexes are like from about 1½ to 3 years of age. The amount, timing, and intensity of gender socialization are different for girls and for boys. Boys receive earlier and more intense gender socialization than girls do.

Adolescence

- During early adolescence, females and males must come to terms with new definitions of their gender roles as they experience the extensive changes of puberty. There is continued controversy about whether all young adolescents experience gender intensification.

Adulthood and Aging

- Many experts argue that it is important for women to retain their relationship strengths but also to put more energy into self-development. Tannen stresses that many women prefer rapport talk and many men prefer report talk. Men have been successful at achieving career goals, but the male role involves considerable strain. There is diversity in men's experiences, just as there is in women's. Men seem to become more nurturant and sensitive when they get older, but there is mixed evidence about whether women tend to become more assertive and dominant as they get older.

4 Exploring Sexuality Characterize influences on sexuality, the nature of sexual orientation, and some sexual problems.

Biological and Cultural Factors

- The role of hormones in human sexual behavior is difficult to define. Sexual motivation is also influenced by cultural factors. Sexual scripts in cultures influence sexual behavior. In some sexual scripts, females link sexual intercourse with love more than do males, the female is blamed if she becomes pregnant, and males tend to emphasize sexual conquest.

Sexual Orientation

- An individual's sexual orientation likely is the result of a combination of genetic, hormonal, cognitive, and environmental factors. In the 1994 Sex in America survey, Americans' sexual lives were reported to be more conservative than in earlier surveys.

- Sexual orientation is generally viewed as a continuum. Regardless of sexual orientation, most people emphasize the importance of trust, affection, and shared interests in a relationship.

Sexually Transmitted Infections

- Sexually transmitted infections (STIs) are contracted primarily through sexual contact. The STI that has received the most attention in recent years is AIDS. Gonorrhea, syphilis, chlamydia, genital herpes, and HPV are among the most common STIs. Some good strategies for protecting against STIs include knowing your own and your partner's risk status; obtaining screening for STIs; avoiding unprotected sex; and not having sex with multiple partners.

Forcible Sexual Behavior and Sexual Harassment

- Rape is forcible sexual intercourse, oral sex, or anal sex with a person who does not give consent. Rape usually produces traumatic reactions in its victims. Sexual harassment occurs when one person uses his or her power over another individual in a sexual manner.

5 Sexuality Through the Life Span   **LG5** Summarize how sexuality develops through the life span.

Childhood

- A majority of children engage in some sex play, usually with siblings or friends. Their motivation is probably mainly curiosity, and there does not appear to be a link between childhood sex play and adolescent or adult sexual adjustment.

Adolescence and Emerging Adulthood

- Adolescence is a time of sexual exploration and sexual experimentation. Mastering emerging sexual feelings and forming a sense of sexual identity are two challenges of the period.

- Gay and lesbian youth have diverse patterns of initial attraction, often have bisexual attractions, and may experience same-sex emotional or physical attractions.

- National U.S. data indicate that by age 19, four out of five individuals have had sexual intercourse. A dramatic increase in oral sex has occurred in adolescence, although many adolescents are unaware of the health risks associated with oral sex.

- Risk factors for sexual problems include early sexual activity, engaging in delinquency and excessive drinking, living in a low-SES neighborhood, ineffective parenting, and having an older sibling who engages in sex.

- Contraceptive use by adolescents is increasing. About one in four sexually experienced adolescents acquires a sexually transmitted infection (STI). The adolescent pregnancy rate in the United States is high but has been decreasing in recent years.

- Emerging adults have sexual intercourse less frequently than young adults do; males have more casual sexual partners and are less selective than females in their partner choice; and by the end of emerging adulthood, most people have had sexual intercourse.

Adult Development and Aging

- Menopause usually occurs during the late forties or early fifties. Perimenopause, the transition from normal menstrual periods to no menstrual periods at all, often takes up to 10 years.

- Hormone replacement therapy (HRT) augments the declining levels of reproductive hormone production by the ovaries. HRT consists of various forms of estrogen, and usually progestin. Research has shown that HRT has benefits for many women in reducing menopausal symptoms, bone loss, bone fractures, and coronary heart disease. However, HRT is associated with increased rates of breast cancer.

- Men do not experience an inability to father children in middle age, although their testosterone level drops. In late adulthood, sexual changes do occur, more so for men than for women.

key **terms**

androgens
androgyny
bisexuality
climacteric
date or acquaintance rape
estrogens
gender
gender identity

gender-intensification hypothesis
gender role
gender schema theory
gender stereotypes
gender-typing
menopause
perimenopause
psychoanalytic theory of gender

rape
rapport talk
report talk
romantic script
sexual harassment
sexual scripts
sexually transmitted infections
    (STIs)

social cognitive theory of gender
social role theory
traditional religious script
transgender
transsexual

key **people**

Sandra Bem
Phyllis Bronstein
Laura Brown

Alice Eagly
Sigmund Freud
Janet Shibley Hyde

Harriet Lerner
Ron Levant
Robert Michael

Jean Baker Miller
Joseph Pleck
Deborah Tannen

chapter 13

MORAL DEVELOPMENT, VALUES, AND RELIGION

chapter outline

ozgurdonmaz/Getty Images

preview

Just as a person's emotional life and sexual life change with age, a person's moral life and spiritual life also develop through the life span. In this chapter we examine how moral development proceeds. We also explore how people go beyond questions of right and wrong to search for values, religion, spirituality, and meaning at different points in their lives.

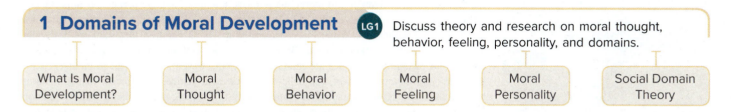

1 Domains of Moral Development

LG1 Discuss theory and research on moral thought, behavior, feeling, personality, and domains.

- What Is Moral Development?
- Moral Thought
- Moral Behavior
- Moral Feeling
- Moral Personality
- Social Domain Theory

Moral development is a topic of great concern to societies, communities, and families because it involves how we all get along. It is also one of the oldest topics of interest to those who are curious about human nature. Philosophers and theologians have talked about it and written about it for many centuries. In the twentieth century, psychologists began theorizing about and studying moral development.

WHAT IS MORAL DEVELOPMENT?

Moral development involves changes in thoughts, feelings, and behaviors regarding standards of right and wrong. Moral development has an intrapersonal dimension, which involves a person's activities when she or he is not engaged in social interaction, and an *interpersonal* dimension, which regulates social interactions and arbitrates conflict. To understand moral development, we consider five basic questions:

- First, how do individuals reason or think about moral decisions?
- Second, how do individuals actually behave in moral circumstances?
- Third, how do individuals feel about moral matters?
- Fourth, what characterizes an individual's moral personality?
- Fifth, how is the moral domain different from social conventional and personal domains?

As we consider various theories and domains in the following sections, keep in mind that thoughts, behaviors, feelings, and personality often are interrelated. For example, if the focus is on an individual's behavior, it is still important to evaluate the person's reasoning. Also, emotions can influence moral reasoning. And moral personality encompasses thoughts, behavior, and feelings.

MORAL THOUGHT

How do individuals decide what is right and wrong? Are children able to evaluate moral questions in the same way that adults can? Jean Piaget had some thoughts about these questions. So did Lawrence Kohlberg.

Piaget's Theory   Interest in how children think about moral issues was stimulated by Piaget (1932), who extensively observed and interviewed children from the ages of 4 through 12. Piaget watched children play marbles to learn how they used and thought about the game's rules. He also asked children about ethical issues—theft, lies, punishment, and justice, for example. Piaget concluded that children go through two distinct stages in how they think about morality:

- From 4 to 7 years of age, children display **heteronomous morality,** the first stage of moral development in Piaget's theory. Children who are in this stage of moral development think of justice and rules as unchangeable properties of the world, removed from the control of people.

moral development Changes in thoughts, feelings, and behaviors regarding standards of right and wrong.

heteronomous morality The first stage of moral development in Piaget's theory, occurring at 4 to 7 years of age. Justice and rules are conceived of as unchangeable properties of the world, removed from the control of people.

Piaget extensively observed and interviewed 4- to 12-year-old children as they played games to learn how they used and thought about the games' rules.
Yves de Braine/Black Star/Stock Photo

developmental **connection**

Cognitive Theory

In which of Piaget's cognitive stages is a 5-year-old heteronomous thinker likely to be? Connect to "Cognitive Developmental Approaches."

How is this child's moral thinking likely to be different about stealing a cookie depending on whether he is in Piaget's heteronomous or autonomous stage?
Fuse/Getty Images

autonomous morality The second stage of moral development in Piaget's theory, displayed by children about 10 years of age and older. At this stage, children become aware that rules and laws are created by people and that in judging an action they should consider the actor's intentions as well as the consequences.

immanent justice Belief that if a rule is broken, punishment will be meted out immediately.

- From 7 to 10 years of age, children are in a transition showing some features of the first stage of moral reasoning and some features of the second stage, autonomous morality.
- From about 10 years of age and older, children show **autonomous morality.** They become aware that rules and laws are created by people, and in judging an action, they consider the actor's intentions as well as the consequences.

Because young children are heteronomous moralists, they judge the rightness or goodness of behavior by considering its consequences, not the intentions of the actor. For example, to the heteronomous moralist, breaking twelve cups accidentally is worse than breaking one cup intentionally. As children develop into moral autonomists, intentions assume paramount importance.

The heteronomous thinker also believes that rules are unchangeable and are handed down by all-powerful authorities. When Piaget suggested to young children that they use new rules in a game of marbles, they resisted. By contrast, older children—moral autonomists—accept change and recognize that rules are merely convenient conventions, subject to change.

The heteronomous thinker also believes in **immanent justice,** the concept that if a rule is broken, punishment will be meted out immediately. The young child believes that a violation is connected automatically to its punishment. Thus, young children often look around worriedly after doing something wrong, expecting inevitable punishment. Immanent justice also implies that if something unfortunate happens to someone, the person must have transgressed earlier. Older children, who are moral autonomists, recognize that punishment occurs only if someone witnesses the wrongdoing and that, even then, punishment is not inevitable.

How do these changes in moral reasoning occur? Piaget argued that as children develop, they become more sophisticated in thinking about social matters, especially about the possibilities and conditions of cooperation. Piaget stressed that this social understanding comes about through the mutual give-and-take of peer relations. In the peer group, where others have power and status similar to the child's, plans are negotiated and coordinated, and disagreements are reasoned about and eventually settled. Parent-child relations, in which parents have the power and children do not, are less likely to advance moral reasoning, because rules are often handed down in an authoritarian way.

From Ross Thompson's perspective, young children are not as egocentric as Piaget envisioned. Thompson (2012) further elaborates on this view, arguing that recent research indicates that young children often show a non-egocentric awareness of others' goals, feelings, and desires and how such internal states are influenced by the actions of others. These ties between advances in moral understanding and theory of mind indicate that young children possess cognitive resources that allow them to be aware of others' intentions and know when someone violates a moral prohibition. One study of 3-year-olds found that they were less likely to offer assistance to an adult they had previously observed being harmful to another person (Vaish, Carpenter, & Tomasello, 2010).

However, because of limitations in their self-control skills, social understanding, and cognitive flexibility, young children's moral advancements often are inconsistent and vary across situations. They still have a long way to go before they have the capacity to develop a consistent moral character and make ethical judgments.

Kohlberg's Cognitive Developmental Theory A second major perspective on moral development was proposed by Lawrence Kohlberg (1958, 1986). Central to Kohlberg's work on moral development were interviews with individuals of different ages. In the interviews, individuals were presented with a series of stories in which characters face moral dilemmas. The following is the most cited of the Kohlberg dilemmas:

In Europe, a woman was near death from a special kind of cancer. There was one drug that the doctors thought might save her. It was a form of radium that a druggist in the same town had recently discovered. The drug was expensive to make, but the druggist was charging ten times what the drug cost him to make. He paid $200 for the radium and charged $2,000 for a small dose of the drug. The sick woman's husband, Heinz, went to everyone he knew to borrow the money, but he could only get together $1,000, which is half of what it cost. He told the druggist that his wife was dying and asked him to sell it cheaper or let him pay later. But the druggist said, "No, I discovered the drug, and I am going to make money from it." So Heinz got desperate and broke into the man's store to steal the drug for his wife. (Kohlberg, 1969, p. 379)

This story is one of eleven that Kohlberg devised to investigate the nature of moral thought. After reading the story, interviewees are asked a series of questions about the moral dilemma: Should Heinz have stolen the drug? Was stealing it right or wrong? Why? Is it a husband's duty to steal the drug for his wife if he can get it no other way? Would a good husband steal it? Did the druggist have the right to charge that much when there was no law setting a limit on the price? Why or why not?

Kohlberg's Three Levels   From the answers interviewees gave for this and other moral dilemmas, Kohlberg discovered three levels of moral development. A key concept in understanding progression through the levels is that people's morality becomes more internal or mature. That is, their judgments of whether given behaviors are morally right or wrong begin to go beyond the external or superficial reasons they gave when they were younger to encompass more complex coordination of multiple perspectives.

Lawrence Kohlberg.
Harvard University Archives, UAV 605.295.8, Box 7

- *Kohlberg's Level 1: Preconventional Reasoning.* **Preconventional reasoning** is the lowest level in Kohlberg's theory of moral development. At this level, moral reasoning is strongly influenced by external punishment or reward. For example, children and adolescents obey adults because they are afraid they will be punished. Or they decide to be obedient to get something out of it, such as a cookie. This earliest level has sometimes been described as "What's in it for me?"
- *Kohlberg's Level 2: Conventional Reasoning.* **Conventional reasoning** is the second, or intermediate, level in Kohlberg's theory of moral development. In conventional reasoning, individuals develop expectations about social roles. Individuals abide by certain standards (internal), but they are the standards of others (external), such as parents or the laws of society.
- *Kohlberg's Level 3: Postconventional Reasoning.* **Postconventional reasoning** is the highest level in Kohlberg's theory of moral development. At this level, morality involves flexible thinking and is more internalized. The individual recognizes alternative moral courses, explores the options, and then decides on a moral code. In postconventional reasoning, individuals engage in deliberate checks on their reasoning to ensure that it meets high ethical standards.

preconventional reasoning The lowest level in Kohlberg's theory of moral development. The individual's moral reasoning is controlled primarily by external rewards and punishments.

conventional reasoning The second, or intermediate, level in Kohlberg's theory of moral development. At this level, individuals abide by the standards of others such as parents or the laws of society.

postconventional reasoning The highest level in Kohlberg's theory of moral development. At this level, the individual recognizes alternative moral courses, explores the options, and then decides on a personal moral code.

Kohlberg argued that these levels occur in a sequence and are age-related: Before age 9, most children reason about moral dilemmas in a preconventional way; by early adolescence, they reason in more conventional ways. By early adulthood, a small number of individuals reason in postconventional ways. In a 20-year longitudinal investigation, the uses of level 1 decreased (Colby & others, 1983).

Any change in moral reasoning between late adolescence and early adulthood appears to be relatively gradual and is enhanced by diverse social experiences (Narváez & Hill, 2010). One study found that when 16- to 19-year-olds and 18- to 25-year-olds were asked to reason about real-life moral dilemmas (in contrast to the usual focus on hypothetical dilemmas) and their responses were coded using Kohlberg's levels, there was no significant difference in the moral reasoning of the two age groups (Walker & others, 1995). So, although someone may be capable of higher moral reasoning, in real life they may not apply it.

Influences on the Development of Moral Judgment   What factors influence movement through Kohlberg's stages? Although moral reasoning at each level presupposes a certain level of cognitive development, Kohlberg argued that maturation did not ensure advances in moral reasoning. Instead, the development of moral reasoning requires experience in dealing with moral questions and moral conflict.

Several investigators have tried to advance individuals' levels of moral development by having a model present arguments that reflect moral thinking one level above each individual's current level. This approach applies the concepts of equilibrium and conflict that Piaget used to explain cognitive development. By presenting arguments slightly beyond the person's level of moral reasoning, the researchers created a disequilibrium that motivated the person to restructure his or her moral thought. The upshot of studies using

Both Piaget and Kohlberg argued that peer relations are a critical part of the social stimulation that challenges children to advance their moral reasoning. The mutual give-and-take of peer relations provides children with role-taking opportunities that give them a sense that rules are generated democratically.
pankration/Getty Images

Carol Gilligan. *What is Gilligan's view of moral development?*
Courtesy of Dr. Carol Gilligan

this approach is that virtually any plus-level discussion, for any length of time, seems to promote more advanced moral reasoning (Walker, 1982).

Kohlberg noted that peer interaction is a critical part of the social stimulation that challenges children to change their moral reasoning. Whereas adults characteristically impose rules and regulations on children, the give-and-take among peers gives children an opportunity to take the perspective of another person and to generate rules democratically. Kohlberg stressed that in principle, encounters with any peers can produce perspective-taking opportunities that may advance a child's moral reasoning. In adolescence and emerging adulthood, diverse and intense experiences facilitate the development of moral reasoning (Rest & others, 1999).

Kohlberg's Critics   Kohlberg's theory has provoked debate, research, and criticism (Gray & Graham, 2018; Jambon & Smetana, 2020; Killen & Dahl, 2018; Lapsley, 2020; Narváez, 2018a, b, 2019, 2020; Miller, Wice, & Goyal, 2020; Smetana & Ball, 2018; Spinrad & Eisenberg, 2020). Key criticisms involve the link between moral thought and moral behavior, whether moral reasoning is conscious/deliberative or unconscious/automatic, the role of emotion, the importance of gender, as well as the roles of culture and the family in moral development.

Moral Reasoning and Moral Behavior   Kohlberg's theory has been criticized for placing too much emphasis on moral reasoning and not enough emphasis on moral behavior (Walker, 2004). Moral reasons can sometimes be used as a shelter for immoral behavior. Corrupt CEOs and politicians endorse the loftiest of moral virtues in public before their own behavior is exposed. Whatever the latest public scandal, you will probably find that the culprits displayed virtuous thoughts but engaged in immoral behavior. No one wants a nation of cheaters and thieves who can reason at the postconventional level. The cheaters and thieves may know what is right yet still do what is wrong. Heinous actions can be cloaked in a mantle of moral virtue.

Conscious/Deliberative Versus Unconscious/Automatic   Social psychologist Jonathan Haidt (2006, 2013, 2018) argues that in Kohlberg's theory, individuals spend too much time deliberating and contemplating in their reasoning before they decide on a stance. Haidt believes that moral thinking is more often an intuitive gut reaction, with deliberative moral reasoning serving as an after-the-fact justification. Thus, in his view, much of morality begins with rapid evaluative judgments of others rather than with strategic reasoning about moral circumstances (Graham & Valdesolo, 2018).

The Role of Emotion   Like Piaget, Kohlberg avoided studying emotion, understanding that it can undermine moral reasoning, which was his main focus. However, increasing evidence indicates that emotions play an important role in moral thinking (Hofmann & others, 2018; Kagan, 2018; Spinrad & Eisenberg, 2020; Valdesolo, 2018; Zaki, 2018). Later in the chapter, we will further explore the importance of emotion in moral development.

Gender and the Care Perspective   The most publicized criticism of Kohlberg's theory has come from Carol Gilligan (1982, 1992, 1996), who argues that Kohlberg's theory reflects a gender bias. According to Gilligan, Kohlberg's theory is based on a male norm that puts abstract principles above relationships and concern for others and sees the individual as standing alone and independently making moral decisions. It puts justice at the heart of morality. In contrast with Kohlberg's **justice perspective,** the **care perspective** is a moral perspective that views people in terms of their connectedness with others and emphasizes interpersonal communication, relationships with others, and concern for others. According to Gilligan, Kohlberg greatly underplayed the care perspective, perhaps because he was a male, because most of his research was with males rather than females, and because he used male responses as the primary source for his theory.

In extensive interviews with girls from 6 to 18 years of age, Gilligan and her colleagues found that girls display greater sensitivity to human relationships based on watching and listening to other people (Gilligan, 1992; Gilligan & others, 2003). However, a meta-analysis (a statistical analysis that combines the results of many different studies) casts doubt on Gilligan's claim of substantial gender differences in moral judgment (Jaffee & Hyde, 2000). And another analysis concluded that girls' moral orientations are "somewhat more likely to focus on care for others than on abstract principles of justice, but they can use both moral orientations when needed (as can boys . . .)" (Blakemore, Berenbaum, & Liben, 2009, p 132).

developmental **connection**

Gender
Janet Shibley Hyde concluded that many views and studies of gender exaggerate differences. Connect to "Gender and Sexuality."

justice perspective A moral perspective that focuses on the rights of the individual; individuals independently make moral decisions.

care perspective The moral perspective of Carol Gilligan; views people in terms of their connectedness with others and emphasizes interpersonal communication, relationships with others, and concern for others.

Culture and Moral Reasoning   Kohlberg emphasized that his stages of moral reasoning are universal, but some critics claim his theory is culturally biased (Christen, Narváez, & Gutzwiller, 2017; Gray & Graham, 2018; Miller, Wice, & Goyal, 2020). Both Kohlberg and his critics may be partially correct. One review of 45 studies in 27 cultures around the world, mostly non-European, provided support for the universality of Kohlberg's first two levels (Snarey, 1987). As Kohlberg predicted, individuals in diverse cultures developed through these first two levels in sequence. Level 3, however, has not been found in all cultures (Gibbs & others, 2007; Snarey, 1987). Furthermore, Kohlberg's scoring system does not recognize the higher-level moral reasoning of certain cultures, ignoring the possibility that moral reasoning might be more culture-specific than Kohlberg envisioned (Snarey, 1987).

One study explored links between culture, mindset, and moral judgment (Narváez & Hill, 2010). In this study, a higher level of multicultural experience was linked to open-mindedness (being cognitively flexible), a growth mindset (perceiving that one's qualities can change and improve through effort), and higher scores on moral judgment.

Darcia Narváez and Tracy Gleason (2013) have described cohort effects regarding moral reasoning. In recent years, postconventional moral reasoning has been declining in college students, not down to the middle level (conventional), but to the lowest level (personal interests) (Thoma & Bebeau, 2008). Narváez and Gleason (2013) also argue that declines in prosocial behavior have occurred in recent years and that humans, especially those living in Western cultures, are "on a fast train to demise." They emphasize that the solution to improving people's moral lives lies in better child-rearing strategies and more effective social supports for families and children. In more recent commentary, Narváez and her colleagues (Christen, Narváez, & Gutzwiller, 2017) stress that economic and technical progress are not linked to moral advances when contemporary societies are compared with earlier sustainable ones that were more in tune with community and planetary well-being.

Let's now look further at the roles of family processes in moral development.

Families and Moral Development   Kohlberg argued that family processes are essentially unimportant in children's moral development. Like Piaget, he argued that parent-child relationships usually provide children with little opportunity for give-and-take or perspective taking because of power relationships. Rather, Kohlberg said that such opportunities are more likely to be provided by children's peer relations.

Did Kohlberg underestimate the contribution of family relationships to moral development? Most developmentalists emphasize that parents play more important roles in children's moral development than Kohlberg envisioned (Laible, Padilla-Walker, & Carlo, 2020; Lapsley, 2020; Narváez, 2019, 2020). They stress that parents' responsiveness, communication, disciplinary techniques, and many other aspects of parent-child relationships influence children's moral development (Gryczkowski, Jordan, & Mercer, 2018; Lansford, 2020; Thompson, 2020). We will have more to say about this topic later in the chapter. Nonetheless, most developmentalists agree with Kohlberg and Piaget that peers play an important role in moral development.

In sum, Kohlberg's theory was a very important pioneering effort in describing and understanding the development of moral reasoning. As indicated in the criticisms of the theory, although it is still relevant in understanding the development of moral reasoning, the theory is no longer as influential as it once was. Let's now explore some additional aspects of moral development.

MORAL BEHAVIOR

What are the basic processes responsible for moral behavior? What is the nature of self-control and resistance to temptation? How do social cognitive theorists view moral development?

Basic Processes   The processes of reinforcement, punishment, and imitation have been invoked to explain how individuals learn certain responses and why their responses differ from one another's (Grusec, 2006). When individuals are reinforced for behavior that is consistent with laws and social conventions, they are likely to repeat that behavior. Also, when individuals are punished for immoral behaviors, those behaviors can be eliminated, but at the expense of sanctioning punishment by its very use and of causing emotional side effects for the individual. And when provided with models who behave morally, individuals are likely to adopt their actions. In one study, 2-year-olds watched a video of an adult engaging in prosocial behavior in response to another person's distress (Williamson, Donohue, & Tully, 2013).

developmental **connection**

Culture

Cross-cultural studies provide information about the degree to which children's development is universal, or similar, across cultures or is culture-specific. Connect to "Peers and the Sociocultural World."

Children who saw the prosocial video were more likely than children who did not see it to imitate the prosocial behavior in response to their own parents' distress.

The above comments about reinforcement, punishment, and imitation come with some important qualifiers. The effectiveness of reward and punishment depends on the consistency and timing with which they are administered. The effectiveness of modeling depends on the characteristics of the model and the cognitive skills of the observer.

Behavior is situationally dependent. Thus, individuals do not consistently display moral behavior in different situations. How consistent is moral behavior? In a classic investigation of moral behavior, one of the most extensive ever conducted, Hugh Hartshorne and Mark May (1928–1930) observed the moral responses of 11,000 children who were given the opportunity to lie, cheat, and steal in a variety of circumstances—at home, at school, at social events, and in athletics. A completely honest or a completely dishonest child was difficult to find. Situation-specific behavior was the rule. Children were more likely to cheat when their friends put pressure on them to do so and when the chance of being caught was slim. However, other analyses suggest that although moral behavior is influenced by situational determinants, some children are more likely than others to cheat, lie, and steal (Burton, 1984).

Resistance to Temptation and Self-Control   When pressures mount for individuals to cheat, lie, or steal, it is important to ask whether they have developed the ability to resist temptation and to exercise self-control (Pino-Pasternak, Valcan, & Malpique, 2019). Walter Mischel (1974) argues that self-control is strongly influenced by cognitive factors. Researchers have shown that children can instruct themselves to be more patient and, in the process, show more self-control.

Social Cognitive Theory   The role of cognitive factors in resistance to temptation and self-control illustrates ways in which cognitions mediate the link between environmental experiences and moral behavior (Grusec, 2006, 2020). The relationships between these three elements—environment, cognition, and behavior—are highlighted by social cognitive theorists. The **social cognitive theory of morality** emphasizes a distinction between an individual's moral competence (ability to perform moral behaviors) and moral performance (performing those behaviors in specific situations) (Mischel & Mischel, 1975). *Moral competencies* include what individuals are capable of doing, what they know, their skills, their awareness of moral rules and regulations, and their cognitive ability to construct behaviors. Moral competence is the outgrowth of cognitive-sensory processes. *Moral performance,* or behavior, however, is determined by motivation and the rewards and incentives to act in a specific moral way.

Albert Bandura (2002, 2015) also stresses that moral development is best understood by considering a combination of social and cognitive factors, especially those involving self-control. He proposed that in developing a moral self, individuals adopt standards of right and wrong that serve as guides and deterrents for conduct. In this self-regulatory process, people monitor their conduct and the conditions under which it occurs, judge it in relation to moral standards, and regulate their actions by the consequences they apply to themselves. They do things that provide them with satisfaction and a sense of self-worth. They refrain from behaving in ways that violate their moral standards because such conduct will bring self-condemnation. Self-sanctions keep conduct in line with internal standards. Thus, in Bandura's view, self-regulation rather than abstract reasoning is the key to positive moral development.

In his most recent book, *Moral Disengagement,* Bandura (2015) described various ways that individuals morally disengage themselves from reprehensible actions and still feel good about themselves. He especially highlights how people may use worthwhile ends to justify inhumane means. As an example, Bandura (2015) points to atrocities committed by ISIS in which religious ideology is used to justify the inhumane behavior.

MORAL FEELING

Think about a time when you did something you sensed was wrong. Did it affect you emotionally? Maybe you had a twinge of guilt. And when you gave someone a gift, you might have felt joy. What role do emotions play in moral development, and how do these emotions develop?

Psychoanalytic Theory   According to Sigmund Freud, guilt and the desire to avoid feeling guilty are the foundation of moral behavior. In Freud's theory, the *superego* is the moral branch of personality. The superego consists of two main components: the ego ideal and the conscience.

developmental connection

Social Cognitive Theory

What are the main themes of Bandura's social cognitive theory? Connect to "Introduction."

social cognitive theory of morality The theory that distinguishes between moral competence—the ability to produce moral behaviors—and moral performance—performing those behaviors in specific situations.

The **ego ideal** rewards the child by conveying a sense of pride and personal value when the child acts according to ideal standards approved by the parents. The **conscience** punishes the child for behaviors disapproved by the parents, making the child feel guilty and worthless.

How does the superego and hence guilt develop? According to Freud, children fear losing their parents' love and being punished for their unacceptable sexual attraction toward the opposite-sex parent. To reduce anxiety, avoid punishment, and maintain parental affection, children identify with the same-sex parent. Through this identification, children *internalize* the parent's standards of right and wrong, which reflect societal prohibitions, and hence develop their superego. Also, the child turns inward the hostility that was previously aimed externally at the same-sex parent. This inwardly directed hostility is then experienced self-punitively (and unconsciously) as guilt. In the psychoanalytic account of moral development, children conform to societal standards to avoid guilt. In this way, self-control replaces parental control.

Freud's claims regarding the formation of the ego ideal and conscience cannot be verified. However, researchers can examine the extent to which children feel guilty when they misbehave. Contemporary views of conscience emphasize that conscience is rooted in close relationships, constructed from advances in children's self-understanding and understanding of others, and linked to their emotions (Thompson, 2014, 2020).

Contemporary views also stress that the development of conscience goes well beyond disciplinary encounters with parents to include guilt as a motivator for cooperation and the moral influence of positive relationships between parents and children.

Recent research focuses on the role of guilt in young children's cooperation. For example, researchers have found that experiencing guilt motivates reparative behavior as early as 2 to 3 years of age and transgressors' displays of guilt motivate cooperative behavior in 4- to 5-year-olds (Vaish, 2018; Vaish Carpenter, & Tomasello, 2016).

A major interest regarding young children's conscience focuses on children's relationships with their caregivers (Kochanska & Kim, 2012, 2013). Especially important in this regard is the emergence of young children's willingness to embrace the values of their parents, an orientation that flows from a positive, close relationship (Kochanska & Aksan, 2007). For example, children who are securely attached are more likely to internalize their parents' values and rules (Kim & Kochanska, 2017; Thompson, 2014, 2015).

Empathy   Positive feelings, such as empathy, contribute to the child's moral development (Spinrad & Eisenberg, 2020; Van der Graaff & others, 2018; Zaki, 2018). **Empathy** is an affective response to another's feelings with an emotional response that is similar to the other person's feelings. To empathize is not just to sympathize; it is to put oneself in another's place emotionally.

Although empathy is an emotional state, it has a cognitive component—the ability to discern another's inner psychological states, or what we have previously discussed as *perspective taking* (Eisenberg, Spinrad, & Valiente, 2016; Spinrad & Eisenberg, 2020). Infants have the capacity for some purely empathic responses, but for effective moral action, children must learn to identify a wide range of emotional states in others and to anticipate what kinds of actions will improve another person's emotional state.

What are the milestones in children's development of empathy? According to an analysis by child developmentalist William Damon (1988), changes in empathy take place in early infancy, at 1 to 2 years of age, in early childhood, and at 10 to 12 years of age.

Global empathy is the young infant's empathic response in which clear boundaries between the feelings and needs of the self and those of another have not yet been established. For example, one 11-month-old infant fought off her own tears, sucked her thumb, and buried her head in her mother's lap after she had seen another child fall and hurt himself. Not all infants cry every time someone else is hurt, though. Many times, an infant will stare at another's pain with curiosity. Although global empathy is observed in some infants, it does not consistently characterize all infants' behavior.

When they are 1 to 2 years of age, infants may feel genuine concern for the distress of other people, but only when they reach early childhood can they respond appropriately to another person's distress. This ability depends on children's new awareness that people have different reactions to situations. By late childhood, they may begin to feel empathy for the unfortunate. To read further about Damon's description of the developmental changes in empathy from infancy through adolescence, see Figure 1.

In one study, researchers found that empathy increased from 12 to 16 years of age (Allemand, Steiger, & Fend, 2015). Also in this study, girls showed more empathy than did

What characterizes a child's conscience?
Markus Mainka/Shutterstock

ego ideal The component of the superego that rewards the child by conveying a sense of pride and personal value when the child acts according to ideal standards approved by the parents.

conscience The component of the superego that punishes the child for behaviors disapproved of by parents by making the child feel guilty and worthless.

empathy Reacting to another's feelings with an emotional response that is similar to the other's feelings.

FIGURE 1

DAMON'S DESCRIPTION OF DEVELOPMENTAL CHANGES IN EMPATHY

Age Period	Nature of Empathy
Early infancy	Characterized by global empathy, the young infant's empathic response does not distinguish between feelings and needs of self and others.
1 to 2 years of age	Undifferentiated feelings of discomfort at another's distress grow into more genuine feelings of concern, but infants cannot translate realization of others' unhappy feelings into effective action.
Early childhood	Children become aware that every person's perspective is unique and that someone else may have a different reaction to a situation. This awareness allows the child to respond more appropriately to another person's distress.
10 to 12 years of age	Children develop an emergent orientation of empathy for people who live in unfortunate circumstances—the poor, the handicapped, and the socially outcast. In adolescence, this newfound sensitivity may give a humanitarian flavor to the individual's ideological and political views.

What characterizes children's empathy and sympathy?
StockPlanets/Getty Images

boys. Further, adolescent empathy predicted a number of social competencies (adult empathy, communication skills, and relationship satisfaction, for example) two decades later. In addition, a recent study revealed that a higher degree of empathy was linked to greater civic engagement by adolescents (Metzger & others, 2018). Also, in a recent meta-analysis, it was concluded that better-quality parent-child and peer relationships were linked to higher levels of adolescents' empathy (Boele & others, 2019).

The Contemporary Perspective on the Role of Emotion in Moral Development   We have seen that classical psychoanalytic theory emphasizes the power of unconscious guilt in moral development but that other theorists, such as Damon, emphasize the role of empathy. Today, many child developmentalists believe that both positive feelings—such as empathy, sympathy, admiration, and self-esteem—and negative feelings—such as anger, outrage, shame, and guilt—contribute to children's moral development (Diaz & others, 2017; Hernandez & others, 2017; Spinrad & Eisenberg, 2020; Spinrad & Gal, 2018). When strongly experienced, these emotions influence children to act in accord with standards of right and wrong. **Sympathy** is an emotional response to another person in which the observer feels sad or concerned about the other person's well-being (Eisenberg, Spinrad, & Valiente, 2016). Feeling sympathy often motivates moral behavior (Zuffiano & others, 2018). For example, one study found that young children's sympathy predicted their willingness to share with others (Ongley & Malti, 2014).

Emotions such as empathy, shame, guilt, and anxiety over other people's violations of standards are present early in development and undergo developmental change throughout childhood and beyond (Damon, 1988). Also, connections between these emotions can occur and the connections may influence children's development. For example, in one study, participants' guilt proneness along with their empathy predicted an increase in prosocial behavior (Torstveit, Sutterlin, & Lugo, 2016).

Emotions provide a natural base for children's acquisition of moral values, motivating them to pay close attention to moral events (Carlo & others, 2018; Grusec & Davidov, 2019; Van der Graaff & others, 2018; Thompson, 2014; Zaki, 2018). However, moral emotions do not operate in a vacuum to build a child's moral awareness, and they are not sufficient in themselves to generate moral responses. They do not give the "substance" of moral regulation—the rules, values, and standards of behavior that children need to understand and act on. Moral emotions are inextricably interwoven with the cognitive and social aspects of children's development (Narváez, 2010; Spinrad & Eisenberg, 2020).

Consider a study in which 18- to 30-month-olds interacted with a parent during book reading and play with toys, contexts that provide opportunities for parental talk about emotions and mental states (Drummond & others, 2014). In an empathic helping task in which children had to observe and understand the experimenter's internal state to understand his need and help to lessen his distress (bring him a blanket as he shivered and pretended he was cold, for example), those who helped more quickly had parents who labeled emotions and mental states more frequently during joint play and who were more likely to elicit this talk during book reading.

sympathy An emotional response to another person in which the observer feels sad or concerned about the person's well-being.

moral identity The aspect of personality that is present when individuals have moral notions and commitments that are central to their lives.

MORAL PERSONALITY

So far we have examined three key dimensions of moral development: thoughts, behavior, and feelings. Recently, there has been a surge of interest in a fourth dimension: personality (Conway, 2018; Strohminger, 2018; Walker, 2016). Thoughts, behavior, and feelings can all be involved in an individual's moral personality. For many years, skepticism surrounded the idea that a set of moral characteristics or traits could be discovered that would constitute a core of moral personality. Much of this skepticism stemmed from the results of Hartshorne and May's (1928–1930) classic study, and Walter Mischel's (1968) social learning theory and research, which argued that situations trump traits when attempts are made to predict moral behavior. Mischel's (2004) subsequent research and theory and Bandura's (2012) social cognitive theory have emphasized the importance of "person" factors while still recognizing situational variation. Until recently, though, there has been little interest in studying what might constitute a moral personality. Three aspects of moral personality that have recently been emphasized are (1) moral identity, (2) moral character, and (3) moral exemplars.

Moral Identity   A central aspect of the recent interest in the role of personality in moral development focuses on **moral identity.** Individuals have a moral identity when moral notions and commitments are central to their life (Acquino & Kay, 2018; Strohminger, 2018; Walker, 2016). In this view, behaving in a manner that violates this moral commitment places the integrity of the self at risk (Lapsley & Stey, 2014). To evaluate the extent to which you have a moral identity, see Figure 2.

Darcia Narváez (2010) concluded that a mature moral individual cares about morality and being a moral person. For these individuals, moral responsibility is central to their identity. Mature moral individuals engage in moral metacognition, including moral self-monitoring and moral self-reflection. Moral self-monitoring involves monitoring one's thoughts and actions related to moral situations, and engaging in self-control when it is needed. Moral self-reflection encompasses critical evaluations of one's self-judgments and efforts to minimize bias and self-deception.

Sam Hardy and his colleagues (Hardy & others, 2013, 2014) also emphasize that identity is a way of caring about morality. Thus, when morality becomes an important aspect of your identity, you have a greater sense of obligation. If you do something immoral, you are not just violating an abstract principle (as in Kohlberg's moral reasoning theory), you are violating who you are.

Rosa Parks (*top photo*, sitting in the front of a bus after the U.S. Supreme Court ruled that segregation was illegal on her city's bus system) and Andrei Sakharov (*bottom photo*) are moral exemplars. Parks (1913–2005), an African American seamstress in Montgomery, Alabama, became famous for her quiet, revolutionary act of not giving up her bus seat to a non-Latino White man in 1955. Her heroic act is cited by many historians as the beginning of the modern civil rights movement in the United States. Across the next four decades, Parks continued to work for progress in civil rights. Sakharov (1921–1989) was a Soviet physicist who spent several decades designing nuclear weapons for the Soviet Union and came to be known as the father of the Soviet hydrogen bomb. However, later in his life he became one of the Soviet Union's most outspoken critics and worked relentlessly to promote human rights and democracy.
(*Top*): Bettmann/Getty Images; (*bottom*): Alain Nogues/Sygma/Getty Images

---

Do You Have a Moral Identity?

A moral identity questionnaire has been developed that provides a list of moral traits and asks individuals to determine the extent to which these traits characterize a person they know (Aquino & Reed, 2002). The person with these characteristics could be you or it could be someone else. For a moment, visualize the kind of person who has these characteristics. Imagine how the individual would think, feel, and act. When you have a clear image of what this person would be like, answer the questions that follow.

Moral Traits

Caring
Compassionate
Fair
Generous
Helpful
Honest
Kind

Questions

- Is being someone who has these characteristics an important part of who you are?
- Are you involved in activities that indicate to others that you have these characteristics?
- Would it make you feel good to have these characteristics?

FIGURE 2

Source: After Aquino, R., & Reed, A. (2002), The self-importance of moral identity. *Journal of Personality and Social Psychology, 83,* 1427–1428.

developmental **connection**

Identity

According to James Marcia, what are the four statuses of identity development? Connect to "The Self, Identity, and Personality."

Might moral identity change from adolescence through the adult years? In a recent study of individuals from adolescence through middle adulthood, external moral identity motivation (reflected in one's self-interest and reputation) decreased while internal moral identity motivation (characterized by concern about consequences for others, being a role model, one's self-ideals, and what an ideal relationship is) increased, suggesting that as people get older, moral motivation becomes more self-other integrated in a positive direction (Krettenauer & Victor, 2017).

What are some outcomes of having a moral identity? A study of 9,500 college students revealed that moral identity predicted all five health outcomes assessed (anxiety, depression, hazardous alcohol use, sexual risk taking, and self-esteem) (Hardy & others, 2013). Also, a study of 15- to 18-year-olds found that a higher level of moral identity could possibly reduce the incidence of moral disengagement and low self-regulation (Hardy, Bean, & Olsen, 2015).

Daniel Hart and his colleagues (Hart, 2005; Hart, Goel, & Atkins, 2017; Hart, Matsuba, & Atkins, 2014) argue that poor urban neighborhoods provide contexts that work against the formation of moral identity and commitment to moral projects. Living in high-poverty contexts often undermines moral attitudes and tolerance for divergent viewpoints. And high-poverty neighborhoods have fewer opportunities for effective engagement in the community because they lack an extensive network of organizations that support projects connected to moral goals. There are fewer opportunities for volunteering in such contexts. Hart and his colleagues advocate providing more service learning and community opportunities as a way of improving youths' moral attitudes and identity.

Moral Character   James Rest (1995) argued that moral character has not been adequately emphasized in moral development. In Rest's view, *moral character* involves having strong convictions, persisting, and overcoming distractions and obstacles. If individuals don't have moral character, they may wilt under pressure or fatigue, fail to follow through or become distracted and discouraged, and fail to behave morally. Of course, such persistence or *grit* is necessary to complete any difficult task, regardless of whether the person has moral aims in mind. Moral character presupposes that the person has set moral goals and that achieving those goals involves the commitment to act in accord with those goals (Helzer & Critcher, 2018). Rest (1995) also concluded that motivation has not been adequately emphasized in moral development. In Rest's view, *moral motivation* involves prioritizing moral values over other personal values.

Lawrence Walker (2002) has studied moral character by examining people's conceptions of moral excellence. Among the moral virtues people emphasize are "honesty, truthfulness, and trustworthiness, as well as those of care, compassion, thoughtfulness, and considerateness. Other salient traits revolve around virtues of dependability, loyalty, and conscientiousness" (Walker, 2002, p. 74). In Walker's perspective, these aspects of moral character provide a foundation for positive social relationships and optimal functioning.

Moral Exemplars   Moral exemplars are people who have lived exemplary lives. Moral exemplars have a moral personality, identity, character, and a set of virtues that reflect moral excellence and commitment (Walker, 2013, 2014, 2016; Walker, Frimer, & Dunlop, 2011). The point of studying and conducting research on moral exemplars is to be able to characterize the ideal endpoint of moral development and understand how people got there.

One study examined the personalities of exemplary young adults to determine what characterized their moral excellence (Matsuba & Walker, 2004). Forty young adults were nominated by executive directors of a variety of social organizations (such as Big Brothers, AIDS Society, and Ronald McDonald House) as moral exemplars based on their extraordinary moral commitment to these social organizations. They were compared with 40 young adults matched in age, education, and other variables who were attending a university. The moral exemplars were more advanced in moral reasoning, further along in developing an identity, and more likely to be in close relationships.

SOCIAL DOMAIN THEORY

Social domain theory states that there are different domains of social knowledge and reasoning, including moral, social conventional, and personal domains. In social domain theory, children's and adolescents' moral, social conventional, and personal knowledge and reasoning emerge from their attempts to understand and deal with different forms of social experience (Jambon & Smetana, 2018, 2020; Killen & Dahl, 2018; Turiel, 2018; Turiel & Gingo, 2017). In the view of

moral exemplars People who have a moral personality, identity, character, and set of virtues that reflect moral excellence and commitment.

social domain theory Theory that identifies different domains of social knowledge and reasoning, including moral, social conventional, and personal domains. These domains arise from children's and adolescents' attempts to understand and deal with different forms of social experience.

leading experts Judith Smetana (2013) and Eliot Turiel (2018), social domain theory emphasizes that the key aspects of morality involve judgments about welfare, justice, and rights as well as struggles that individuals face in regard to moral issues in their social lives. Social domain theory stresses that children, even very young ones, are motivated to evaluate and make sense of their social world (Smetana, Jambon, & Ball, 2014; Jambon & Smetana, 2019).

Social conventional reasoning focuses on conventional rules that have been established by social consensus in order to control behavior and maintain the social system (Jambon & Smetana, 2018, 2020). The rules themselves are arbitrary, such as raising your hand in class before speaking, using one staircase at school to go up and the other to go down, not cutting in front of someone standing in line to buy movie tickets, and stopping at a stop sign when driving. There are sanctions if we violate these conventions, although the rules can be changed by consensus. In one study, 3-year-old children were more likely to engage in conformity on a social conventional task than on moral and visual tasks (Kim & others, 2016).

In contrast, moral reasoning focuses on ethical issues and rules of morality. Unlike conventional rules, moral rules are not arbitrary. They are obligatory, widely accepted, and somewhat impersonal (Turiel, 2018). Rules pertaining to lying, cheating, stealing, and physically harming another person are moral rules because violation of these rules affronts ethical standards that exist apart from social consensus and convention. Moral judgments involve concepts of justice, whereas social conventional judgments are concepts of social organization. Violating moral rules is usually more serious than violating conventional rules.

The social conventional approach is a serious challenge to Kohlberg's approach because Kohlberg argued that social conventions are mixed in with moral concerns at the conventional level, a developmental stop-over on the road to higher moral sophistication, postconventional reasoning, where they are separated. For proponents of social conventional reasoning, social conventional reasoning is not lower than postconventional reasoning but rather something that needs to be disentangled from the moral thread (Jambon & Smetana, 2020; Killen & Smetana, 2015; Mulvey & others, 2016; Turiel, 2018).

Recently, a distinction also has been made between moral and conventional issues, which are viewed as legitimately subject to adult social regulation, and personal issues, which are more likely subject to the child's or adolescent's independent decision making and personal discretion (Killen & Dahl, 2018). Personal issues include control over one's body, privacy, and choice of friends and activities. Thus, some actions belong to a *personal* domain not governed by moral strictures or social norms.

How does social conventional reasoning differ from moral reasoning? What are some examples of social conventional reasoning?
Glow Images

social conventional reasoning Focuses on conventional rules established by social consensus and convention, as opposed to moral reasoning, which stresses ethical issues.

Review *Connect* Reflect

LG1 Discuss theory and research on moral thought, behavior, feeling, personality, and domains.

Review

- What is moral development?
- What are Piaget's and Kohlberg's theories of moral development? What are some criticisms of Kohlberg's theory? What is social conventional reasoning?
- What processes are involved in moral behavior? What is the social cognitive theory of moral development?
- How are moral feelings related to moral development?
- What characterizes moral personality?
- What is the nature of social domain theory?

Connect

- How is joint attention similar to or different from the concept of perspective taking?

Reflect *Your Own Personal Journey of Life*

- Which of the aspects of morality that we have discussed stand out for you? Which are the most interesting to you, and which ones would you like to explore further?

2 Contexts of Moral Development

LG2 Explain how parents and schools influence moral development.

Parenting

Schools

So far, we have examined the four principal domains of moral development—thoughts, behaviors, feelings, and personality. We saw that both Piaget and Kohlberg noted that peer relations exert an important influence on moral development. What other contexts play a role in moral development? In particular, what are the roles of parents and schools?

PARENTING

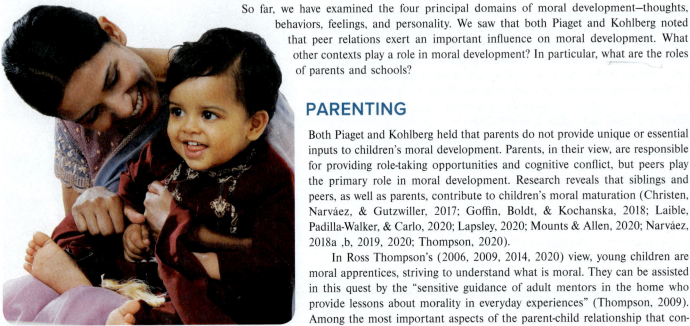

What are some aspects of relationships between parents and children that contribute to children's moral development?
Fuse/Getty Images

Both Piaget and Kohlberg held that parents do not provide unique or essential inputs to children's moral development. Parents, in their view, are responsible for providing role-taking opportunities and cognitive conflict, but peers play the primary role in moral development. Research reveals that siblings and peers, as well as parents, contribute to children's moral maturation (Christen, Narváez, & Gutzwiller, 2017; Goffin, Boldt, & Kochanska, 2018; Laible, Padilla-Walker, & Carlo, 2020; Lapsley, 2020; Mounts & Allen, 2020; Narváez, 2018a ,b, 2019, 2020; Thompson, 2020).

In Ross Thompson's (2006, 2009, 2014, 2020) view, young children are moral apprentices, striving to understand what is moral. They can be assisted in this quest by the "sensitive guidance of adult mentors in the home who provide lessons about morality in everyday experiences" (Thompson, 2009). Among the most important aspects of the parent-child relationship that contribute to children's moral development are relational quality, proactive strategies, and conversational dialogue.

Relational Quality Parent-child relationships introduce children to the mutual obligations of close relationships that involve warmth and responsibility (Laible & Thompson, 2007; Laible, Padilla-Walker, & Carlo, 2020; Laible & others, 2020; Thompson, 2009, 2014, 2020). Parents' obligations include engaging in positive caregiving and guiding children to become competent human beings. Children's obligations include responding appropriately to parents' initiatives and maintaining a positive relationship with parents.

In terms of relationship quality, secure attachment may play an important role in children's moral development (Thompson, 2020). A secure attachment can place the child on a positive path for internalizing parents' socializing goals and family values. In one study, secure attachment in infancy was linked to earlier development of conscience (Laible & Thompson, 2000). In another study, early secure attachment defused a maladaptive trajectory toward antisocial outcomes (Kochanska, Barry, & others, 2010). In yet another study, securely attached children's willing, cooperative stance was linked to positive future socialization outcomes (such as internalizing mothers' prohibitions) and a lower incidence of externalizing problems (high level of aggression, for example) (Kochanska, Woodard, & others, 2010).

Proactive Strategies An important parenting strategy is to proactively avert potential misbehavior by children before it takes place (Padilla-Walker & Son, 2020; Thompson, 2020). With younger children, being proactive means using diversion, such as distracting their attention or moving them to alternative activities. With older children, being proactive may involve talking with them about values that the parents deem important. Transmitting these values can help older children and adolescents resist temptations that inevitably emerge in contexts outside the scope of direct parental monitoring, such as peer relations and the media.

Conversational Dialogue Conversations related to moral development can benefit children, whether they occur as part of a discipline encounter or during the everyday stream of parent-child interaction (Spinrad & Eisenberg, 2020; Thompson, 2009, 2014, 2020).

------

developmental connection

Attachment

Securely attached infants use the caregiver as a secure base from which to explore the environment. Connect to "Emotional Development and Attachment."

The conversations can be planned or spontaneous and can focus on topics such as past events (for example, a child's prior misbehavior or positive moral conduct), shared future events (for example, going somewhere that may involve a temptation and will require positive moral behavior), and immediate events (for example, talking with the child about a sibling's tantrums). Even when they are not intended to teach a moral lesson or explicitly encourage better moral judgment, such conversations can contribute to children's moral development.

Along these lines, one study found that parents' talk about emotions was associated with toddlers' sharing and helping behavior (Brownell & others, 2013). In this study, children who helped and shared more quickly and frequently, especially in tasks that required complex emotional understanding, had parents who more often asked them to label and explain emotions displayed in books. Importantly, it was the parents' elicitation of emotion talk rather than parents' own production of emotion labels and explanations that was linked to toddlers' prosocial behavior. And in a recent study, maternal supportive (emotion-focused and problem-focused) reactions to young children's emotions was linked to an increase in their prosocial behavior (Eisenberg & others, 2019).

Parenting Recommendations   Nancy Eisenberg and her colleagues (Eisenberg & Spinrad, 2016; Eisenberg, Spinrad, & Morris, 2013; Eisenberg & Valiente, 2002; Spinrad & Eisenberg, 2020; Spinrad & Gal, 2018) suggest that parents who adopt the following strategies are more likely to have children who behave morally:

- Are warm and supportive, use inductive reasoning, and engage in authoritative parenting
- Are not punitive and do not use love withdrawal as a disciplinary strategy
- Provide opportunities for children to learn about others' perspectives and feelings
- Involve children in family decision making and in the process of thinking about moral decisions
- Model moral behaviors and thinking themselves, and provide opportunities for their children to do so
- Provide information about what behaviors are expected and why
- Foster an internal rather than an external sense of morality
- Help children to understand and regulate negative emotion rather than becoming overaroused

Parents who show this configuration of behaviors likely foster in their children concern and caring about others, and create a positive parent-child relationship. One study found that adolescents' moral motivation was positively linked to the quality of their relationship with their parents (Malti & Buchmann, 2010). Also, in a recent study of fifth-, tenth-, and twelfth-grade students, authoritative parents (showing a combination of warmth and control) were more likely to have children and youth who showed higher levels of prosocial behavior than parents who were moderately demanding and uninvolved (Carlo & others, 2018). Other research also has found that mothers are more likely to influence adolescents' prosocial behavior than are fathers (Carlo & others, 2011).

In addition, parenting recommendations based on Ross Thompson's (2009, 2013, 2020; Laible & Thompson, 2007; Thompson, McGinley, & Meyer, 2006) analysis of parent-child relations suggest that children's moral development is likely to benefit when there are mutual parent-child obligations involving warmth and responsibility, when parents use proactive strategies, and when parents engage children in conversational dialogue. Further, young children's prosocial behavior increases when parents elicit children's talk about emotions.

SCHOOLS

No matter how parents treat their children at home, they may feel that they have little control over a great deal of their children's moral education. Children spend extensive time away from their parents at school, and the time spent can influence children's moral development (Lapsley, Reilly, & Narváez, 2019).

The Hidden Curriculum   More than 80 years ago, educator John Dewey (1933) recognized that even when schools do not have specific programs in moral education, they provide moral education through a "hidden curriculum." The **hidden curriculum** refers to the way

> Both theory and empirical data support the conclusion that parents play an important role in children's moral development.
>
> —NANCY EISENBERG
> *Contemporary Psychologist, Arizona State University*

hidden curriculum The pervasive moral atmosphere that characterizes every school.

certain behaviors are expected and rewarded (such as waiting in turn and obeying teacher directives without question) and others are suppressed or punished (such as speaking out of turn and joking). The hidden curriculum forms part of the moral atmosphere that is a part of every school. The moral atmosphere is created by school and classroom rules, the moral orientation of teachers and school administrators, and text materials. Teachers serve as models of ethical or unethical behavior (Sanger, 2008). Classroom rules and peer relations at school transmit attitudes about cheating, lying, stealing, and consideration for others. And through its rules and regulations, the school administration infuses the school with a value system.

Recently, increased attention has been directed to the influence of classroom and school climate as part of the hidden curriculum. Darcia Narváez (2010, 2014) argues that attention should be given to the concept of "sustaining climates." In her view, a sustaining classroom climate is more than a positive learning environment and more than a caring context. Sustaining climates involve focusing on students' sense of purpose, social engagement, community connections, and ethics. In sustaining classroom and school climates, students learn skills for flourishing and reaching their potential and help others to do so as well.

Character Education   In 2018, 18 states had a legislative mandate for **character education** in schools, another 18 had legislation that encouraged character education, 7 supported character education but without legislation, and 8 had no legislation specifying character education. The classic character education approach is to model good behavior and directly teach virtue, instructing students that behaviors such as lying, stealing, and cheating are wrong, whereas honesty and obedience are right. Teachers of traditional character education programs model and directly teach moral behavior throughout school (Lapsley, Reilly, & Narváez, 2019).

As part of a traditional approach, every school should have an explicit moral code that is clearly communicated to students. According to traditional views of character education, any violations of the code should be met with sanctions. Newer approaches advocate a more democratic solution. Instruction in specified moral concepts, such as cheating, can take the form of example and definition, class discussions and role playing, or rewards for students exhibiting proper behavior. Alternatives to the traditional approach have been on the increase. For example, assisting students to develop a care perspective that involves considering others' feelings and helping others has been accepted as a relevant aspect of character education (Noddings, 2008, 2014). And recently it has been noted that purpose likely is an important aspect of character that should be emphazized in character education. In a recent study, three components of character (gratitude, compassion, and grit) were linked to character in young adolescents (Malin, Liauw, & Damon, 2017).

Lawrence Walker (2002) argues that it is important for character education to involve more than a listing of moral virtues on a classroom wall. Instead, he emphasizes that children and adolescents need to participate in critical discussions of values; they need to discuss and reflect on how to incorporate virtues into their daily lives. Walker also advocates exposing children to moral exemplars worthy of emulating and getting them to participate in community service. The character education approach reflects the moral personality domain of moral development discussed earlier in the chapter.

Values Clarification   A second approach to providing moral education is **values clarification**— that is, helping people to clarify what their lives mean and what is worth working for. Unlike character education, which tells students what their values should be, values clarification encourages students to define their own values and understand the values of others (Williams & others, 2003).

Advocates of values clarification say it is value-free. However, critics argue that its content offends community standards and that the values-clarification exercises fail to stress the right behavior.

Service Learning   **Service learning** is a form of education that promotes social responsibility and service to the community. In service learning, adolescents engage in activities such as tutoring, helping older adults, working in a hospital, assisting at a child-care center, or cleaning up a vacant lot to make a play area. An important goal of service learning is for adolescents to become less self-centered and more strongly motivated to help others (Hart, Goel, & Atkins, 2017; Hart, Matsuba, & Atkins, 2008, 2014; Hart & others, 2017). Service learning is often more effective when two conditions are met (Nucci, 2006): (1) students are given some degree of choice in the service activities in which they participate, and (2) students are provided opportunities to reflect about their participation.

character education A direct moral education program in which students are taught moral literacy to prevent them from engaging in immoral behavior.

values clarification A moral education program in which students are helped to clarify their purpose in life and decide what is worth working for. Students are encouraged to define their own values and understand others' values.

service learning A form of education that promotes social responsibility and service to the community.

Service learning takes education out into the community (Hart & van Goethem, 2017; Hart & others, 2017). Adolescent volunteers tend to be extraverted, committed to others, and have a high level of self-understanding (Eisenberg & Morris, 2004). One study revealed that adolescent girls participated more in service learning than adolescent boys did (Webster & Worrell, 2008).

Researchers have found that service learning benefits adolescents and emerging adults in a number of ways (Hart, Goel, & Atkins, 2017; Hart & van Goethem, 2017). These improvements include higher grades in school, increased goal setting, higher self-esteem, an enhanced sense of empowerment to make a difference for others, and an increased likelihood that they will serve as volunteers in the future. In one study, 74 percent of African American and 70 percent of Latino adolescents said that service-learning programs could have a "fairly or very big effect" on keeping students from dropping out of school (Bridgeland, Dilulio, & Wulsin, 2008).

An analysis revealed that 26 percent of U.S. public high schools require students to participate in service learning (Metz & Youniss, 2005). The benefits of service learning, for both the volunteer and the recipient, suggest that more adolescents should be required to participate in such programs (Enfield & Collins, 2008).

Jewel Cash, seated next to her mother, participates in a crime-watch meeting at a community center. She is an exemplar of teenage community involvement. The mayor of Boston says she is "everywhere." Jewel swayed a neighborhood group to support her proposal for a winter jobs program. Raised in one of Boston's housing projects by her mother, a single parent, Cash is a member of the Boston Student Advisory Council, mentors children, volunteers at a women's shelter, and is a member of a neighborhood crime-watch organization. (Source: Silva, 2005)
Matthew J. Lee/The Boston Globe/Getty Images

Cheating   A common moral education concern is whether students cheat and how adults should handle the cheating when it is discovered (Cheung, Wu, & Huang, 2016; Miller, 2017; Popoola & others, 2017). Academic cheating can take many forms, including plagiarism, using "cheat sheets" during an exam, copying from a neighbor during a test, purchasing papers, and falsifying lab results. A 2006 survey revealed that 60 percent of secondary school students said they had cheated on a test in school during the past year, and one-third of the students reported that they had plagiarized information from the Internet in the past year (Josephson Institute of Ethics, 2006). A study with 8- to 12-year-olds found that a majority of them cheated in a game that required them to report the accuracy of their success in the game, and older children cheated less than the younger ones (Ding & others, 2014). Also in this study, children with better working memory and inhibitory control cheated less.

Why do students cheat? Among the reasons students give for cheating are pressure to get high grades, time constraints, poor teaching, and lack of interest (Stephens, 2008). In terms of poor teaching, "students are more likely to cheat when they perceive their teacher to be incompetent, unfair, and uncaring" (Stephens, 2008, p. 140).

A long history of research also implicates the power of the situation in determining whether students cheat (Cheung, Wu, & Huang, 2016; Hartshorne & May, 1928–1930). For example, students are more likely to cheat when they are not being closely monitored during a test; when they know their peers are cheating; when they know that another student has cheated without being caught; and when student scores are made public (Anderman & Murdock, 2007; Carrell, Malmstrom, & West, 2008; Harmon, Lambrinos, & Kennedy, 2008).

Certain personality traits also are linked to cheating. One study revealed that college students who engaged in academic cheating were characterized by the personality traits of low conscientiousness and low agreeableness (Williams, Nathanson, & Paulhus, 2010).

Among the strategies for decreasing academic cheating are preventive measures such as making sure students are aware of what constitutes cheating, explaining the consequences if they do cheat, closely monitoring students' behavior while they are taking tests, and emphasizing the importance of being a moral, responsible individual who practices academic integrity. In promoting academic integrity, many colleges have instituted an honor code that emphasizes self-responsibility, fairness, trust, and scholarship (Popoola & others, 2017). However, few secondary schools have developed honor code policies. The International Center for Academic Integrity (www.academicintegrity.org/icai/home.php) has extensive materials available to help schools develop academic integrity policies.

Integrative Approaches   Darcia Narváez (2006, 2010, 2014, 2016, 2020) emphasizes an *integrative approach* to moral education that encompasses both the reflective moral thinking and commitment to justice

Why do students cheat? What are some strategies teachers can adopt to prevent cheating?
Eric Audras/PhotoAlto/Getty Images

advocated in Kohlberg's approach, and developing virtues as advocated in the character education approach. She highlights the Child Development Project as an excellent example of integrative moral education. In the Child Development Project, students are given multiple opportunities to discuss other students' experiences, which inspires empathy and perspective taking, and they participate in exercises that encourage them to reflect on their own behaviors in terms of values such as fairness and social responsibility (Battistich, 2008; Solomon, Watson, & Battistich, 2002). Adults coach students in ethical decision making and guide them in becoming more caring individuals. Students experience a caring community, not only in the classroom but also in after-school activities and through parental involvement in the program. Research evaluations of the Child Development Project indicate that it is related to an improved sense of community, increased prosocial behavior, better interpersonal understanding, and greater use of social problem solving (Battistich, 2008; Solomon & others, 1990).

Another integrative moral education program that is being implemented is called *integrative ethical education* (Narváez, 2006, 2010, 2014; Narváez & others, 2004). This program builds on the concept of expertise development within a supportive community. The goal is to turn moral novices into moral experts by educating students about four ethical skills that moral experts possess: ethical sensitivity, ethical judgment, ethical focus, and ethical action (Narváez, 2010; Narváez & Bock, 2014).

Because teachers teach values no matter what else they do, the argument is that educators should do it intentionally and holistically, especially in cultures where students are routinely exposed to non-virtuous behavior (Lapsley, Holter, & Narváez, 2013).

Review Connect Reflect

 LG2 Explain how parents and schools influence moral development.

Review
- What are some effective parenting strategies for advancing children's moral development?
- What is the hidden curriculum? What are some contemporary approaches to moral education?

Connect
- What parenting strategies might be most effective in preventing students from cheating?

Reflect *Your Own Personal Journey of Life*
- How do you think your parents influenced your moral development?

---

3 Prosocial and Antisocial Behavior

 LG3 Describe the development of prosocial and antisocial behavior.

Prosocial Behavior   Antisocial Behavior

Service learning encourages positive moral behavior. This behavior is not just moral behavior but behavior that is intended to benefit other people, and psychologists call it prosocial behavior (Carlo & others, 2018; Dirks, Dunfield, & Recchia, 2018; Streit & others, 2018). Of course, people have always engaged in antisocial behavior as well. In this section, we take a closer look at prosocial and antisocial behavior, focusing on how they develop.

PROSOCIAL BEHAVIOR

Caring about the welfare and rights of others, feeling concern and empathy for them, and acting in a way that benefits others are all components of prosocial behavior (Carlo & Conejo, 2020; Carlo & others, 2018; Spinrad & Eisenberg, 2020; Streit & others, 2018). What motivates this behavior, and how does it develop in children?

It is one of the beautiful compensations of this life that no one can sincerely try to help another without helping himself.

—CHARLES DUDLEY WARNER
American Essayist, 19th Century

Altruism and Reciprocity   The purest forms of prosocial behavior are motivated by **altruism,** an unselfish interest and voluntary effort in helping another person. Human acts of altruism are plentiful. Think of the hardworking laborer who places $5 in a Salvation Army kettle, the volunteers at homeless shelters, the person who donates a kidney so someone else can live. Altruism is found throughout the human world. It is also taught by every widely practiced religion in the world—Christianity, Judaism, Islam, Hinduism, Buddhism. The circumstances most likely to evoke altruism are empathy for an individual in need or a close relationship between the benefactor and the recipient (Batson, 1989).

altruism An unselfish interest and voluntary effort in helping another person.

The notion of *reciprocity*, which is the obligation to return a favor with a favor, pervades human interactions all over the world. Fund-raisers try to exploit the norm of reciprocity when they send free calendars or other knickknacks in the mail, hoping that you'll feel obligated to reciprocate with a donation to their cause. People feel guilty when they do not reciprocate, and they may feel angry if someone else does not reciprocate. Reciprocity or altruism may motivate many important prosocial behaviors, including sharing.

Do Infants Have Moral Awareness and Engage in Prosocial Behavior?

Recently, researchers have explored whether infants and toddlers have a moral awareness and motivation for prosocial behavior. How can moral awareness and prosocial behavior be studied in preverbal infants? Just as adults do, babies tend to look at something they find interesting or surprising. And when they are given a choice between looking at two things, babies look longer at the more pleasing thing. Based on these assumptions, several studies using the violation of expectations technique described in Renee Baillargeon's research (described in the chapter on "Cognitive Developmental Approaches") have found that characters who hinder or harm others are viewed more negatively by infants as young as 4 months of age and that they will act to punish hinderers and to reward helpers (Hamlin, 2013a, b; Hamlin & others, 2011, 2015; Steckler & Hamlin, 2016; Van de Vondervoort & Hamlin, 2016, 2018). At this point, it is wise to interpret these conclusions with caution until they have been confirmed by more research and other measures.

In one study, researchers observed the behavior of 7-month-old infants whose parents participated in an intervention in which their infants were encouraged to either release objects into a bucket or share the objects with their parents (Xu, Saether, & Sommerville, 2016). Subsequently, infants in the sharing condition shared more than infants in the bucket condition. Parental empathy influenced the amount of sharing their infants engaged in. Other research indicates that during their second year, children will offer assistance to an unfamiliar experimenter, building on their capacities for shared intentionality and awareness of others' goals and intentions (Thompson & Newton, 2013; Warneken & Tomasello, 2006). For example, maternal responsible behavior (such as teaching their children how to act in various situations) was associated with 18-month-olds' prosocial behavior (alleviating an experimenter's stress) (Schuhmacher, Collard, & Kartner, 2017).

This research indicating that older infants and toddlers possess an intuitive sense of fairness that they use in evaluating observed behavior suggests the presence of an early foundation for moral awareness that is not anticipated in Piaget's and Kohlberg's theories of moral development. However, the view that the emergence of morality in infancy is innate has been described as problematic (Carpendale & Hammond, 2016). Critics of the innate view argue that morality may emerge through infants' early interaction with others and grow with developments in language and reflective thought.

Next, we further explore sharing and fairness, focusing on the childhood and adolescent years.

Sharing and Fairness

William Damon (1988) described a developmental sequence through which sharing develops in children. Unlike the recent research just described that indicates toddlers can engage in sharing and fairness and have a moral awareness, Damon proposed that sharing during the first three years of life is done for nonempathetic reasons such as the fun of social play or simply for imitation. Then, at about 4 years of age, a combination of newly developed empathetic awareness and adult encouragement produces a sense of obligation on the part of the child to share with others. Most 4-year-olds are not selfless saints, however. Children believe they have an obligation to share but do not necessarily think they should be as generous to others as they are to themselves. Neither do their actions always support their beliefs, especially when they covet an object. What is important developmentally is that the child has developed a belief that sharing is an obligatory part of a

How does children's sharing change from the preschool to the elementary school years?
Monalyn Gracia/Getty Images

social relationship and involves a question of right and wrong. These early ideas about sharing set the stage for giant strides that children make in the years that follow.

By the start of the elementary school years, children begin to express more complicated notions of what is fair. Throughout history, varied definitions of fairness have been used as the basis for distributing goods and resolving conflicts. These definitions involve the principles of equality, merit, and benevolence—*equality* means that everyone is treated the same; *merit* means giving extra rewards for hard work, a talented performance, or other laudatory behavior; *benevolence* means giving special consideration to individuals in a disadvantaged condition.

Equality is the first of these principles used regularly by elementary school children. It is common to hear 6-year-old children use the word *fair* as synonymous with *equal* or *same*. By the mid to late elementary school years, children also believe that equality means special treatment for those who deserve it—a belief that applies the principles of merit and benevolence.

Benevolence can be evident early in life. One study found that even 5-year-olds were inclined to give more to poor than to wealthy individuals, thus indicating that their motivation to help the poor overruled their otherwise dominant inclination to share resources equally (Paulus, 2014). However, in this study 3-year-olds did not share more resources with poor than wealthy individuals. Another study revealed that 8-year-olds were more likely to donate resources to needy peers than were 4-year-olds (Ongley, Nola, & Malti, 2014).

Parental advice and prodding certainly foster standards of sharing, but the give-and-take of peer requests and arguments provides the most immediate stimulation of sharing. Parents can set examples that children carry into their interactions and communication with peers, but parents are not present during all of their children's peer exchanges. The day-to-day construction of fairness standards is done by children in collaboration and negotiation with each other. Over the course of many years and thousands of encounters, children's understanding of concepts such as equality, merit, benevolence, and compromise deepens. With this understanding comes a greater consistency and generosity in children's sharing (Damon, 1988).

How does prosocial behavior change through childhood and adolescence? Prosocial behavior occurs more often in adolescence than in childhood, although examples of caring for others and comforting someone in distress occur even during the preschool years (Eisenberg & Spinrad, 2016).

Why might prosocial behavior increase in adolescence? Cognitive changes involving advances in abstract, idealistic, and logical reasoning as well as increased empathy and emotional understanding likely are involved. With such newfound cognitive abilities, young adolescents increasingly sympathize with members of abstract groups with whom they have little experience, such as people living in poverty in other countries (Eisenberg & Spinrad, 2016). The increase in volunteer opportunities in adolescence also contributes to more frequent prosocial behavior.

Are there different types of prosocial behavior? In one study, Gustavo Carlo and his colleagues (2010, pp. 340–341) investigated this question and confirmed the presence of six types of prosocial behavior in young adolescents:

- altruism ("One of the best things about doing charity work is that it looks good.")
- public ("Helping others while I'm being watched is when I work best.")
- emotional ("I usually help others when they are very upset.")
- dire ("I tend to help people who are hurt badly.")
- anonymous ("I prefer to donate money without anyone knowing.")
- compliant ("I never wait to help others when they ask for it.")

In this study, adolescent girls reported more emotional, dire, compliant, and altruistic behavior than did boys, while boys engaged in more public prosocial behavior. Parental monitoring was positively related to emotional, dire, and compliant behavior but not the other types of behavior. Compliant, anonymous, and altruistic prosocial behavior were positively related to religiosity.

Research on prosocial behavior is often conceptualized in a global and unidimensional manner. The study by Carlo and others (2010) illustrates the important point that in thinking about and studying prosocial behavior it is important to consider its dimensions.

Two other aspects of prosocial behavior are forgiveness and gratitude. **Forgiveness** is an aspect of prosocial behavior that occurs when the injured person releases the injurer from possible behavioral retaliation (Klatt & Enright, 2009). In one investigation, individuals from

forgiveness An aspect of prosocial behavior that occurs when the injured person releases the injurer from possible behavioral retaliation.

the fourth grade through college and adulthood were asked questions about forgiveness (Enright, Santos, & Al-Mabuk, 1989). The individuals were especially swayed by peer pressure in their willingness to forgive others. A study of older adults revealed that women were more likely to forgive than men, people were more likely to forgive family members than non-family members, and forgiveness was more likely to be extended to people who were still alive than to those who were dead (Hantman & Cohen, 2010). Also, another study revealed that when adolescents encountered hurtful experiences in school settings and they disliked the transgressor, they had more hostile thoughts, feelings of anger, and avoidance/revenge tendencies than when they liked the transgressing peer (Peets, Hodges, & Salmivalli, 2013). And two recent studies found that forgiveness of others was associated with a lower risk of suicidal behavior in adolescents (Dangel, Webb, & Hirsch, 2018; Quintana-Orts & Rey, 2018).

Gratitude is a feeling of thankfulness and appreciation, especially in response to someone doing something kind or helpful (Barcaccia & others, 2017; Zeng & others, 2017). Interest in studying adolescents' gratitude or lack thereof is increasing. Consider the following recent studies:

· Young adolescent Chinese students who reported engaging in more gratitude perceived themselves to have better well-being in school (Tian & others, 2016).

· In middle school students, a higher level of gratitude was linked to a higher level of purpose (Malin, Liauw, & Damon, 2017).

· Gratitude was linked to a number of positive aspects of development in young adolescents, including satisfaction with one's family, optimism, and prosocial behavior (Froh, Yurkewicz, & Kashdan, 2009).

· Adolescents' expression of gratitude was linked to having fewer depressive symptoms (Lambert, Fincham, & Stillman, 2012).

· A longitudinal study assessed the gratitude of adolescents at 10 to 14 years of age (Bono, 2012). Four years after the initial assessment, the most grateful adolescents (top 20 percent) had a stronger sense of the meaning of life, were more satisfied with their life, were happier and more hopeful, had a lower level of negative emotions, and were less depressed than the least grateful students (bottom 20 percent).

Gender and Prosocial Behavior   Are there gender differences in prosocial behavior during childhood and adolescence? Research indicates that differences exist (Eisenberg, Spinrad, & Morris, 2013). For example, across childhood and adolescence, females engage in more prosocial behavior than males. The largest gender difference occurs for kind and considerate behavior, with a smaller difference for sharing.

Altruism and Volunteerism in Older Adults   A study of 21,000 individuals 50 to 79 years of age in 21 countries revealed that one-third give back to society, saying that they volunteer now or have volunteered in the past (HSBC Insurance, 2007). In this study, about 50 percent who volunteered reported that they did so for at least one-half day each week. Also, a national survey found that 24 percent of U.S. adults 65 years and older engaged in volunteering in 2015 (U.S. Bureau of Labor Statistics, 2016). In this survey, the highest percentage of volunteering occurred between 35 and 44 years of age (31.8 percent).

Are older adults more altruistic than younger adults? In a series of recent studies, older adults were more likely to behave in altruistic ways and to value contributions to the public good than younger adults were (Freund & Blanchard-Fields, 2014). For example, in two of the studies, older adults were more likely than younger adults to donate money to a good cause.

Volunteering is associated with a number of positive outcomes for aging adults (Carr, 2018; Guiney & Machado, 2018). Recent studies have found that when aging adults volunteer they have better health (Burr & others, 2018; Carr, Kail, & Rowe, 2018), have better cognitive functioning (Proulx, Curl, & Ermer, 2018), and are less lonely (Carr, Kail, & Rowe, 2018), Among the reasons for the positive outcomes of volunteering are its provision of constructive activities and productive roles, social integration, and enhanced meaningfulness (Tan & others, 2007).

A common perception is that older adults need to receive help rather than to give help themselves. However, might giving help as an older adult be beneficial and even be linked to longevity? In a recent study, of four indices (volunteering, informally helping others through a modest time commitment, attending religious services, and

gratitude A feeling of thankfulness and appreciation, especially in response to someone's doing something kind or helpful.

Ninety-eight-year-old volunteer Iva Broadus plays cards with 10-year-old DeAngela Williams in Dallas, Texas. Iva was recognized as the oldest volunteer in the Big Sister program in the United States. She says that the card-playing helps to keep her memory and thinking skills good and can help DeAngela's as well. *What are some other positive outcomes of volunteering as an older adult?*
Jim Mahoney/Dallas Morning News

What are some characteristics of conduct disorder?
Stockdisc/PunchStock

Comstock Images/Alamy Stock Photo

conduct disorder Age-inappropriate actions and attitudes that violate family expectations, society's norms, and the personal or property rights of others.

going to social group meetings), the strongest predictor of longevity and lower risk for cardio-vascular disease was volunteering (Han & others, 2017). Another study revealed that older adults who volunteered regularly had a lower risk of cognitive impairment (Infurna, Okun, & Grimm, 2016). And in a research meta-analysis, older adults who engaged in organizational volunteering had a lower mortality risk than those who did not (Okun, Yeung, & Brown, 2013).

ANTISOCIAL BEHAVIOR

Most children and adolescents at one time or another act out or do things that are destructive or troublesome for themselves or others. If these behaviors occur often, psychiatrists diagnose them as conduct disorders. If these behaviors result in illegal acts by juveniles, society labels them *delinquents*. Both problems are much more common in males than in females (Mash & Wolfe, 2019).

Conduct Disorder   **Conduct disorder** refers to age-inappropriate actions and attitudes that violate family expectations, society's norms, and the personal or property rights of others (Anderson, Zheng, & McMahon, 2018; Jennings, Perez, & Reingle Gonzalez, 2018). Children with conduct problems show a wide range of rule-violating behaviors, from swearing and temper tantrums to severe vandalism, theft, and assault (Mash & Wolfe, 2019; Ogundele, 2018). One study found that youth with conduct disorder characterized by its onset in childhood had more cognitive impairment (especially in executive function), psychiatric symptoms, and serious violent offenses than youth with conduct disorder characterized by the onset of antisocial behavior in adolescence (Johnson & others, 2015). And in another recent study of more than 20,000 individuals, low childhood SES, low maternal closeness, and a history of harsh discipline were associated with life course persistent conduct disorder and increased risk of substance use problems in adulthood (Moore & others, 2017).

As part of growing up, most children and youth break the rules from time to time—they fight, skip school, break curfew, steal, and so on. As many as 50 percent of the parents of 4- to 6-year-old children report that their children steal, lie, disobey, or destroy property at least some of the time (Achenbach, 1997). Most of these children show a decrease in antisocial behavior from 4 to 18 years of age, but adolescents who are referred to psychological clinics for therapy continued to show high rates of antisocial behavior (Achenbach, 1997).

It has been estimated that about 5 percent of children show serious conduct problems. These children are often described as showing an *externalizing*, or *undercontrolled*, pattern of behavior. Children who show this pattern often are impulsive, overactive, and aggressive and engage in delinquent actions (Okado & Bierman, 2015).

Conduct problems in children are best explained by a confluence of causes, or risk factors, operating over time (Mash & Wolfe, 2019). These include possible genetic inheritance of a difficult temperament, ineffective parenting, and living in a neighborhood where violence is the norm. In a study conducted in 10 urban schools serving primarily African American children from low-income backgrounds, the children were randomly assigned to either a "pre-kindergarten as usual" control condition or an intervention that consisted of a family program (13 weeks of behavioral parenting strategies) and a professional development training program for early childhood teachers (Dawson-McClure & others, 2015). For boys, but not girls, the intervention led to lower rates of conduct problems two years later.

Juvenile Delinquency   Closely linked with conduct disorder is **juvenile delinquency,** which refers to actions taken by an adolescent in breaking the law or engaging in behavior that is considered illegal. Like other categories of disorders, juvenile delinquency is a broad concept; legal infractions range from littering to murder. Because the adolescent technically becomes a juvenile delinquent only after being judged guilty of a crime by a court of law, official records do not accurately reflect the number of illegal acts that are committed by juvenile delinquents.

One issue in juvenile justice is whether an adolescent who commits a crime should be tried as an adult (Cauffman & others, 2015; Fine & others, 2017a, b). Some psychologists have proposed that individuals 12 and under should not be evaluated under adult criminal laws and that those 17 and older should be (Cauffman & others, 2015; Fine & others, 2017a, b). They also recommend that individuals 13 to 16 years of age be given some type of individualized assessment to determine whether they will be tried in a juvenile court or an adult criminal court.

Is delinquency in adolescence linked to adult outcomes? In a recent study, delinquency in adolescence was associated with a greater likelihood of being unemployed in adulthood (Carter, 2019).

Frequency   Estimates of the number of juvenile delinquents in the United States are sketchy, but FBI statistics indicate that at least 2 percent of all youth are involved in juvenile court cases. For both male and female delinquents, rates for property offenses are higher than rates for other offenses (such as offenses against persons, drug offenses, and public order offenses). Males are more likely to engage in delinquency than are females—in 2004, 72 percent of delinquency cases in the United States involved males, 28 percent females (Hockenberry & Puzzanchera, 2017). Since 2008, delinquency cases have dropped more for males than for females.

juvenile delinquency Actions taken by an adolescent in breaking the law or engaging in illegal behavior.

Developmental Changes and Pathways   As adolescents become emerging adults, do their rates of delinquency and crime change? Research indicates that rates of theft, property damage, and physical aggression decrease from 18 to 26 years of age (Schulenberg & Zarrett, 2006). The peak ages for property damage are 16 to 18 years for males and 15 to 17 years for females. However, the peak ages for violence are 18 to 19 years for males and 19 to 21 years for females (Farrington, 2004).

A distinction is made between early-onset (before age 11) and late-onset (after age 11) antisocial behavior. Early-onset antisocial behavior is associated with more negative developmental outcomes than late-onset antisocial behavior (Schulenberg & Zarrett, 2006). Early-onset antisocial behavior is more likely to persist into emerging adulthood and is associated with higher rates of mental illness and relationship problems (Roisman, Aguilar, & Egeland, 2004; Stouthamer-Loeber & others, 2004).

In the Pittsburgh Youth Study, a longitudinal study involving more than 1,500 inner-city boys, three developmental pathways to delinquency were identified (Loeber, Burke, & Pardini, 2009; Loeber & Farrington, 2001; Stouthamer-Loeber & others, 2002):

- *Authority conflict.* Youth on this pathway showed stubbornness prior to age 12, then moved on to defiance and avoidance of authority.
- *Covert.* This pathway included minor covert acts, such as lying, followed by property damage and moderately serious delinquency, then serious delinquency.
- *Overt.* This pathway included minor aggression followed by fighting and violence.

One individual whose goal is to reduce juvenile delinquency and help at-risk adolescents cope more effectively with their lives is Rodney Hammond. To read about his work, see the *Connecting with Careers* profile.

connecting with careers

Rodney Hammond, Health Psychologist

Rodney Hammond described how his college experiences influenced his choice of career: "When I started as an undergraduate at the University of Illinois Champaign-Urbana, I hadn't decided on my major. But to help finance my education, I took a part-time job in a child development research program sponsored by the psychology department. There, I observed inner-city children in settings designed to enhance their learning. I saw first-hand the contribution psychology can make, and I knew I wanted to be a psychologist" (American Psychological Association, 2003, p. 26).

After earning his undergraduate degree, Rodney Hammond went on to obtain a doctorate in school and community psychology with a focus on children's development. For a number of years, he trained clinical psychologists at Wright State University in Ohio and directed a program to reduce violence in ethnic minority youth. There, he and his associates taught at-risk youth how to use social skills to effectively manage conflict and to recognize situations that could lead to violence. Hammond became the first Director of the Division of Violence Prevention at the Centers for Disease Control and Prevention in Atlanta. He is currently Adjunct Professor of Human Development and Counseling at the University of Georgia, following his retirement from CDC.

Rodney Hammond counsels an adolescent girl about the risks of adolescence and how to cope effectively with them.
Courtesy of Dr. Rodney Hammond

What are some factors that influence whether adolescents will become delinquents?
Fertnig/Getty Images

developmental **connection**

Parenting

A neglectful parenting style is linked with lower levels of self-control in children. Connect to "Families, Lifestyles, and Parenting."

Causes of Delinquency   What causes delinquency? Many causes have been proposed, including heredity, identity problems, community influences, and family experiences. Erik Erikson (1968), for example, noted that adolescents may choose a negative identity if their development has restricted them from acceptable social roles or made them feel that they cannot measure up to the demands placed on them. Adolescents with a negative identity may find support for their delinquent image among peers, reinforcing the negative identity. For Erikson, delinquency is an attempt to establish an identity, even though it is a negative one.

Although delinquency is less exclusively a phenomenon of lower socioeconomic status today than it was in the past, some characteristics of lower-SES culture might promote delinquency (Nishina & Bellmore, 2018). A recent study of more than 10,000 children and adolescents found that family environment characterized by poverty and child maltreatment was linked to entering the juvenile justice system in adolescence (Vidal & others, 2017). The norms of many lower-SES peer groups and gangs are antisocial, or counterproductive, to the goals and norms of society at large. Getting into and staying out of trouble are prominent features of life for some adolescents in low-income neighborhoods. Adolescents from low-income backgrounds may sense that they can gain attention and status by performing antisocial actions. Furthermore, adolescents in communities with high crime rates observe many models who engage in criminal activities. Quality schooling, educational funding, and organized neighborhood activities may be lacking in these communities (Nishina & Bellmore, 2018). One study found that youth whose families had experienced repeated poverty were more than twice as likely to be delinquent at 14 and 21 years of age (Najman & others, 2010).

Certain characteristics of families are also associated with delinquency (Farrington & Hawkins, 2019; Guo, 2018; Muftic & Updegrove, 2018). Parents of delinquents are less skilled in discouraging antisocial behavior and in encouraging prosocial behavior than are parents of nondelinquents. Parental monitoring of adolescents is especially important in determining whether an adolescent becomes a delinquent (Henneberger & others, 2013). One study found that early parental monitoring in adolescence and ongoing parental support were linked to a lower incidence of criminal behavior in emerging adulthood (Johnson & others, 2011). Also, one study found that low rates of delinquency from 14 to 23 years of age were associated with an authoritative parenting style (Murphy & others, 2012). Family discord and inconsistent and inappropriate discipline are also associated with delinquency (Capaldi & Shortt, 2003).

Few studies demonstrate in an experimental design that changing parenting practices in childhood is related to a lower incidence of juvenile delinquency in adolescence. However, one study by Marion Forgatch and her colleagues (2009) randomly assigned divorced mothers with sons to an experimental group (mothers received extensive parenting training) and a control group (mothers received no parenting training) when their sons were in the first to third grades. The parenting training consisted of 14 parent group meetings that especially focused on improving parenting practices with their sons (skill encouragement, limit setting, monitoring, problem solving, and positive involvement). Best practices for emotion regulation, managing interparental conflict, and talking with children about divorce also were included in the sessions. Improved parenting practices and reduced contact with deviant peers were linked with lower rates of delinquency in the experimental group than in the control group at a nine-year follow-up assessment.

Family therapy is often effective in reducing delinquency (Amani & others, 2018; Schawo & others, 2017). A research meta-analysis found that of five program types (case management, individual treatment, youth court, restorative justice, and family treatment), family treatment was the only one that was linked to reduced recidivism for juvenile offenders (Schwalbe & others, 2012). Another research review revealed that prevention programs focused on improving the family context were more effective in reducing persistent delinquency than were individual and group-based programs (de Vries & others, 2015). Also, in one study, family therapy improved juvenile court outcomes beyond what was achieved in non-family-based treatment, especially in reducing criminal behavior and rearrests (Dakof & others, 2015).

An increasing number of studies have found that siblings can have a strong influence on delinquency (Bank, Burraston, & Snyder, 2004). In one study, high levels of hostile sibling relationships and older sibling delinquency were linked with younger sibling delinquency in both brother pairs and sister pairs (Slomkowski & others, 2001).

Having delinquent peers and friends increases the risk of becoming delinquent (Bagwell & Bukowski, 2018; Walters, 2019). In a recent study, classrooms in which higher rates of students were engaging in delinquency had an increased likelihood that other classmates would become

Does Intervention Reduce Juvenile Delinquency?

Fast Track is an intervention that attempts to lower the risk of juvenile delinquency and other problems (Conduct Problems Prevention Research Group, 2007, 2010a, b, 2011, 2015; Dodge & McCourt, 2010; Jones & others, 2010; Kassing & others, 2019; Miller & others, 2011). Schools in four areas (Durham, North Carolina; Nashville, Tennessee; Seattle, Washington; and rural central Pennsylvania) were identified as high-risk based on neighborhood crime and poverty data. Researchers screened more than 9,000 kindergarten children in the four schools and randomly assigned 891 of the highest-risk and moderate-risk children to intervention or control conditions. The average age of the children when the intervention began was 6.5 years.

The 10-year intervention consisted of behavior management training of parents, social cognitive skills training of children, reading tutoring, home visitations, mentoring, and a revised classroom curriculum that was designed to increase socioemotional competence and decrease aggression. Outcomes were assessed in the third, sixth, and ninth grades for the following behavioral problems:

- Conduct disorder (multiple instances of behaviors such as truancy, running away, fire setting, cruelty to animals, breaking and entering, and excessive fighting across a six-month period)
- Oppositional defiant disorder (an ongoing pattern of disobedient, hostile, and defiant behavior toward authority figures)
- Attention deficit hyperactivity disorder (having one or more of these characteristics over a period of time: inattention, hyperactivity, and impulsivity)
- Any externalizing disorder (presence of any of the three disorders previously described)

- Self-reported antisocial behavior (a list of 34 behaviors, such as skipping school, stealing, and attacking someone with an intent to hurt the person)

The extensive intervention was successful only for children and adolescents who were identified as the highest risk in kindergarten, and it resulted in lowering their incidence of conduct disorder, attention deficit hyperactivity disorder, any externalized disorder, and antisocial behavior. Positive outcomes for the intervention occurred as early as the third grade and continued through the ninth grade. For example, in the ninth grade the intervention reduced the likelihood that the highest-risk kindergarten children would develop conduct disorder by 75 percent, attention deficit hyperactivity disorder by 53 percent, and any externalized disorder by 43 percent.

Data have been reported through age 25 (Miller & others, 2011). Findings indicate that the comprehensive Fast Track intervention was successful in reducing youth arrest rates (Conduct Problems Prevention Research Group, 2011). Also, one study found that the intervention's impact on adolescents' antisocial behavior was linked to three social cognitive processes: reducing hostile-attribution biases, improving responses to social problems, and devaluing aggression (Dodge, Godwin, & The Conduct Problems Prevention Research Group, 2013). And in a recent study, it was found that for populations with high risk rates as little as one teacher screen taken during kindergarten or the first grade predicted whether males would have adult criminal convictions by age 25 (Kassing & others, 2019).

What might be some other strategies for intervening in the lives of high-risk children to reduce their likelihood of becoming juvenile delinquents?

---

delinquent (Kim & Fletcher, 2018). In another recent study, adolescents who engaged in delinquency were high on affiliating with deviant peers and engaging in pseudomature behavior (trying to be "cool" and more adult-like to gain higher peer status) and low on peer popularity and school achievement (Gordon Simons & others, 2018). And in a recent study of middle school adolescents, peer pressure for fighting and friends' delinquent behavior were linked to adolescents' aggression and delinquent behavior (Farrell, Thompson, & Mehari, 2017). Also, another recent study found that having a best friend who was delinquent was linked to a higher probability that adolescents themselves would become delinquent (Levey & others, 2019).

Lack of academic success is associated with delinquency (Gordon Simons & others, 2018; Mercer & others, 2016). And a number of cognitive factors such as low self-control, low intelligence, and lack of sustained attention are linked to delinquency (Muftic & Updegrove, 2018). For example, one study revealed that low self-control was linked to delinquency (Fine & others, 2016). In another recent study of female adolescents, increases in self-control were linked to decreased likelihood of police contact (Hipwell & others, 2018). Further, recent research indicates that having callous-unemotional personality traits predicts an increased risk of engaging in delinquency for adolescent males (Ray & others, 2017). Does intervening in the lives of children who show early conduct problems help reduce their delinquency risk in adolescence? See the *Connecting with Research* interlude to find out how researchers have tried to answer this question.

4 Values, Religion, Spirituality, and Meaning in Life

 LG4 Characterize the development of values, religion, spirituality, and meaning in life.

| Values | Religion and Spirituality | Meaning in Life |

James Garbarino (1999) has interviewed a number of young killers. He concludes that nobody really knows precisely why a tiny minority of youth kill, but that the cause might be a lack of a spiritual center. In many of the youth killers he interviewed, Garbarino found a spiritual or emotional emptiness that led them to seek meaning in the dark side of life. Are spirituality and religion important in your life? How much time have you spent thinking about the meaning of life? What are your values?

VALUES

Values are beliefs and attitudes about the way things should be. They involve what is important to us. We attach value to all sorts of things: politics, religion, money, sex, education, helping others, family, friends, career, recognition, self-respect, and so on. We carry with us values that influence our thoughts, feelings, and actions. To think about the values that are most important to you, see Figure 3.

One way to measure what people value is to ask them what their goals are. Over the past four decades, traditional-aged college students have shown an increased concern for personal well-being and a decreased concern for the well-being of others, especially for the disadvantaged (Stolzenberg & others, 2019). As shown in Figure 4, today's college freshmen are more strongly motivated to be well-off financially and less motivated to develop a meaningful philosophy of life than were their counterparts of 40 or even 20 years ago. In 2017, 82.5 percent of students (the highest percentage ever in this survey) viewed becoming very well-off financially as an "essential" or a "very important" objective, compared with only 42 percent in 1971.

There are, however, some signs that U.S. college students are shifting toward a stronger interest in promoting the welfare of society. In the survey just described, interest in developing a meaningful philosophy of life increased from 39 percent to 48.1 percent of U.S. freshmen from 2001 through 2017 (Stolzenberg & others, 2019) (see Figure 4). Also in this survey, the percentage of college freshmen who said the chances are very good that they will participate in volunteer or community service programs increased from 18 percent in 1990 to 36.7 percent in 2017 (Stolzenberg & others, 2019).

Our discussion of values corresponds to William Damon's (2008) view proposed in *The Path to Purpose: Helping Children Find Their Calling in Life*. Damon concluded that a major difficulty confronting today's youth is their lack of a clear sense of what they want to do with their lives—that too many youth are essentially "rudderless." Damon (2008, p. 8) found that

values Beliefs and attitudes about the way things should be.

religion An organized set of beliefs, practices, rituals, and symbols that increases an individual's connection to a sacred or transcendent other (God, higher power, or higher truth).

What Are My Values?

Look at the following list of values and think about the extent to which each value characterizes you. Place check marks next to the five values that are most important to you. Then go back over the values you selected and rank order them from 1 to 5, with 1 being the most important.

Values

____Having good friends and getting along with people
____Having a good relationship with a romantic partner
____Having self-respect
____Being well-off financially
____Having a good spiritual or religious life
____Being competent at my work
____Having the respect of others
____Making an important contribution to the world
____Being a good person
____Feeling secure
____Having peace of mind
____Being happy
____Being healthy
____Being intelligent
____Having inner peace
____Living an exciting life

The following values are most important to me:

1.
2.
3.
4.
5.

FIGURE **3**

only about 20 percent of 12- to 22-year-olds in the United States expressed "a clear vision of where they want to go, what they want to accomplish in life, and why." He argues that their goals and values too often focus on the short term, such as getting a good grade on a test this week and finding a date for a dance, rather than developing a plan for the future based on positive values. Adults can guide young people to develop more purposeful values by posing questions like these: "What's most important in your life? Why do you care about those things? . . . What does it mean to be a good person?" (Damon, 2008, p. 135).

Religion enlightens, terrifies, subdues; it gives faith, inflicts remorse, inspires resolutions, and inflames devotion.

—HENRY NEWMAN

English Churchman and Writer, 19th Century

RELIGION AND SPIRITUALITY

In Damon's (2008) view, one long-standing source for discovering purpose in life is religion. Religion and spirituality play important roles in the lives of many people around the world (Carney & Park, 2018; Krause & Pargament, 2018).

Is religion different from spirituality? Pamela King and her colleagues (King & Boyatzis, 2015; King, Carr, & Boiter, 2011) provide the following distinctions:

- **Religion** is an organized set of beliefs, practices, rituals, and symbols that increases an individual's connection to a sacred or transcendent other (God, higher power, or ultimate truth).

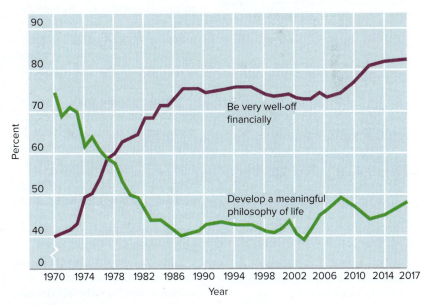

FIGURE **4**

CHANGING FRESHMAN LIFE GOALS, 1970 TO 2017. Since 1970, a significant change has occurred in the life goals of college freshmen. A far greater percentage of today's college freshmen state that an "essential" or "very important" life goal is to be very well-off financially, and far fewer state that developing a meaningful philosophy of life is an "essential" or "very important" life goal.

As an adolescent, Nina Vasan founded ACS Teens, a nationwide network of student volunteers who support the mission of the American Cancer Society. Through an online network, ACS Teens served as an incubator for social change: It trained, mobilized, mentored, and united teenagers to find creative ways to improve health in their communities and to support the ACS through advocacy, education, fundraising, and service. ACS Teens volunteers helped raise hundreds of thousands of dollars for cancer research, changed state tobacco laws, and led educational programs to prevent cancer. Nina completed her MD degree at Harvard University Medical School and currently is the director of Brainstorm: The Stanford Laboratory for Mental Health Innovation and Entrepreneurship. In 2013, she published her first book (with co-author Jennifer Przybylo), *Do Good Well*. The book reflects Nina's motivation to get others involved in leadership and to encourage them to take action in improving people's lives. *Do Good Well* became a #1 Amazon Best Seller.
Courtesy of Nina Vasan

religiousness The degree of affiliation with an organized religion, participation in prescribed rituals and practices, connection with its beliefs, and involvement in a community of believers.

spirituality Experiencing something beyond oneself in a transcendent manner and living in a way that benefits others and society.

- **Religiousness** refers to the degree of affiliation with an organized religion, participation in its prescribed rituals and practices, connection with its beliefs, and involvement in a community of believers.
- **Spirituality** involves experiencing something beyond oneself in a transcendent manner and living in a way that benefits others and society.

What developmental changes characterize the influence of religion, religiousness, and spirituality in people's lives?

Childhood, Adolescence, and Emerging Adulthood

Societies use many methods—such as Sunday schools, parochial education, and parental teaching—to ensure that people will carry on a religious tradition. In a national study, 63 percent of parents with children at home said they pray or read Scripture with their children and 60 percent reported that they send their children to religious education programs (Pew Research Center, 2008). Does this religious socialization work? In many cases it does (Paloutzian, 2000).

In general, individuals tend to adopt the religious teachings of their upbringing. For instance, individuals who are Catholics by the time they are 25 years of age, and who were raised as Catholics, likely will continue to be Catholics throughout their adult years. If a religious change or reawakening occurs, it is most likely to take place during adolescence. However, it is important to consider the quality of the parent-adolescent relationship (Ream & Savin-Williams, 2003). Adolescents who have a positive relationship with their parents or are securely attached to them are likely to adopt the religious orientation of their parents (Dudley, 1999). Adolescents who have a negative relationship with their parents or are insecurely attached to them may disaffiliate from religion or seek religion-based attachments that are missing in their family system (Streib, 1999).

Religious issues are important to many adolescents and emerging adults, but during the twenty-first century religious interest among adolescents and emerging adults has declined. In a recent national study of American college freshmen, 69.2 percent said they had attended religious services frequently or occasionally during their senior year in high school in 2017, down from 73 percent in 2010 and down from a high of 85 percent in 1997 (Stolzenberg & others, 2019).

A developmental study revealed that religiousness declined from 14 to 20 years of age in the United States (Koenig, McGue, & Iacono, 2008) (see Figure 5). In this study, religiousness was assessed with items such as frequency of prayer, frequency of discussing religious teachings, frequency of deciding moral actions for religious reasons, and the overall importance of religion in everyday life. As indicated in Figure 5, more change in religiousness occurred from 14 to 18 years of age than from 20 to 25 years of age. Also, attending religious services was highest at 14 years of age, declined from 14 to 18 years of age, and increased at 20 years of age. More change occurred in attending religious services than in religiousness. Another study found that across the first three semesters of college, students were less likely to attend religious services or engage in religious activities (Stoppa & Lefkowitz, 2010).

Analysis of the World Values Survey of 18- to 24-year-olds revealed that emerging adults in less developed countries were more likely to be religious than their counterparts in more developed countries (Lippman & Keith, 2006). For example, emerging adults' reports of religion being very important in their lives ranged from a low of 0 in Japan to 93 percent in Nigeria, and belief in God ranged from a low of 40 percent in Sweden to a high of 100 percent in Pakistan.

Religion and Cognitive Development Adolescence and emerging adulthood can be especially important junctures in religious development (King & Boyatzis, 2015). Even if children have been indoctrinated into a religion by their parents, because of advances in their cognitive development adolescents and emerging adults may question what their own religious beliefs truly are.

Many of the cognitive changes thought to influence religious development involve Piaget's cognitive developmental stages. More so than in childhood, adolescents think abstractly, idealistically, and logically. The increase in abstract thinking lets adolescents consider various religious and spiritual concepts. For example, an adolescent might ask how a loving God can possibly exist given the extensive suffering of many people in the world (Good & Willoughby, 2008). Adolescents' increasingly idealistic thinking provides a foundation for thinking about whether religion provides the best route to a better, more ideal world. And adolescents' increased capacity for logical reasoning gives them the ability to develop hypotheses and systematically sort through different answers to spiritual questions (Good & Willoughby, 2008).

Religion and Identity Development During adolescence and especially during emerging adulthood, identity development becomes a central focus (Erikson, 1968; Neblett, Roth, & Syed, 2019). Adolescents and emerging adults look for answers to questions like these: "Who am I? What am I all about as a person? What kind of life do I want to lead?" As part of their search for identity, adolescents and emerging adults begin to grapple in more sophisticated, logical ways with such questions as "Why am I on this planet? Is there really a God or higher spiritual being, or have I just been believing what my parents and the church imprinted in my mind? What really are my religious views?" An analysis of the link between identity and spirituality concluded that adolescence and adulthood can serve as gateways to a spiritual identity that "transcends, but not necessarily excludes, the assigned religious identity in childhood" (Templeton & Eccles, 2006, p. 261).

A study of Latino, African American, Asian, and non-Latino White adolescents revealed that their religious identity remained stable across high school grades but that religious participation declined (Lopez, Huynh, & Fuligni, 2011). In this study, Latino and Asian adolescents had the highest levels of religious identity, while Latino adolescents had the highest level of religious participation.

Religion and Sexuality in Adolescence and Emerging Adulthood One area of religion's influence on adolescent and emerging adult development involves sexual activity. Although variability and change in church teachings make it difficult to generalize about religious doctrines, most churches discourage premarital sex. Thus, the degree of adolescent and emerging adult participation in religious organizations may be more important than affiliation with a specific religion as a determinant of premarital sexual attitudes and behavior. Adolescents and emerging adults who frequently attend religious services are likely to hear messages about abstaining from sex until marriage. Involvement of adolescents and emerging adults in religious organizations also enhances the probability that they will become friends with adolescents who hold restrictive attitudes toward premarital sex. One study revealed that adolescents with high religiosity were less likely to have had sexual intercourse (Gold & others, 2010). And in a recent study of African American adolescent girls, those who reported that religion was of low or moderate importance to them had a younger sexual debut than their counterparts who indicated that religion was extremely important to them (George Dalmida & others, 2018).

The Positive Role of Religion in Adolescents' Lives Researchers have found that various aspects of religion are linked with positive outcomes for adolescents (King, Topalian, & Vidourek, 2019; Longo, Bray, & Kim-Spoon, 2017; Talib & Abdollahi, 2017). One study revealed that parents' religiousness during youths' adolescence was positively related to youths' own religiousness during adolescence (Spilman & others, 2013). Another study found that when youth attend religious services with their parents, this activity increases the positive influence of parenting on their psychological well-being (Petts, 2014). Religion plays a role in adolescents' health and has an influence on whether they engage in problem behaviors. A meta-analysis found that spirituality/religiosity was positively related to well-being, self-esteem, and three of the Big Five factors of personality (conscientiousness, agreeableness, openness) (Yonker, Schnabelrauch, & DeHaan, 2012). In this meta-analysis, spirituality/religion was negatively associated with risk behavior and depression. Also, in a national random sample of more than 2,000 11- to 18-year-olds, those who had a stronger interest in religion were less likely to smoke, drink alcohol, use marijuana, be truant from school, engage in delinquent activities, and be depressed than their low-religiosity counterparts (Sinha, Cnaan, & Gelles, 2007). Further, a recent study revealed that high school students who reported turning to spiritual beliefs when they were experiencing problems were less likely to engage in substance use (Debman & others, 2018). And across three countries (England, Scotland, and Canada), adolescents who reported having a higher level of spirituality were more likely to have positive health outcomes (Brooks & others, 2018). Also, a recent Slovakian study of adolescents found that spirituality but not religiosity was linked to better self-related health, fewer health complaints, and higher life satisfaction (Dankulincova Veselska & others, 2019).

Many religious adolescents also adopt their religion's message about caring and concern for people (Lerner & others, 2013; Saroglou, 2013). For example, in one survey religious youth were almost three times as likely to engage in community service as nonreligious youth (Youniss, McLellan, & Yates, 1999).

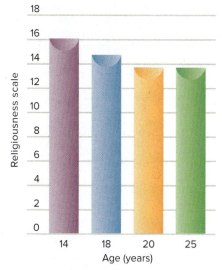

FIGURE 5

DEVELOPMENTAL CHANGES IN RELIGIOUSNESS FROM 14 TO 25 YEARS OF AGE.

Note: The religiousness scale ranged from 0 to 32, with higher scores indicating stronger religiousness.

developmental **connection**

Identity

In addition to religious/spiritual identity, what are some other identity components? Connect to "The Self, Identity, and Personality."

How does religious thinking change in adolescence? How is religion linked to adolescents' health?
Christopher Futcher/Getty Images

Many children and adolescents show an interest in religion, and many religious institutions created by adults (such as this Muslim school in Malaysia) are designed to introduce young people to religious benefits and ensure that they will carry on a religious tradition.
Lano Lan/Shutterstock

Adulthood and Aging   What roles do religion and spirituality play in the lives of adults? Is religion related to adults' health? Is there a point in adult development at which understanding of the meaning of life increases? How do religious beliefs affect the lives of older adults?

Religion and Spirituality in Adulthood   How religious are Americans? A national poll of more than 35,000 U.S. adults found that 92 percent said they believe in God, 75 percent reported that they pray at least weekly and 58 percent said they pray every day, 56 percent said that religion is very important, and 39 percent indicated that they attend religious services at least weekly (Pew Research Center, 2008). However, in a later national poll, those who said that "religion is very important" had dropped to 50 percent (Pew Research Center, 2015). And growing percentage of people in the United States consider themselves spiritual but not religious. In a 2017 national poll, 27 percent said they are spiritual but not religious, up 8 percentage points in five years (Lipka & Gecewicz, 2017). This trend is broad-based, occurring among males and females, different ages and educational levels, and different ethnic groups.

Gender and ethnic differences characterize religious interest and participation. Females have consistently shown a stronger interest in religion than males have (Idler, 2006). In a national U.S. study, 60 percent of women and 47 percent of men said that religion was very important in their lives (Pew Research Center, 2016). Compared with men, women participate more in both organized and personal forms of religion, are more likely to believe in a higher power or presence, and are more likely to feel that religion is an important dimension of their lives. Regarding ethnicity, African Americans and Latinos show higher rates of religious participation than do non-Latino White Americans (Idler, 2006).

In thinking about religion and adult development, it is important to consider individual differences. Religion is a powerful influence in some adults' lives, whereas it plays little or no role in others' lives (Myers, 2000). Further, the influence of religion in people's lives may change as they develop. In John Clausen's (1993) longitudinal investigation, some individuals who had been strongly religious in their early-adult years became less so in middle age, while others became more religious in middle age.

Religion and Health   How might religion be linked to physical health? Some cults and religious sects encourage behaviors that are damaging to health, such as ignoring sound medical advice. For individuals in the religious mainstream, researchers increasingly are finding that religion is positively linked to health (Dilmaghani, 2018; Krause, 2019; Park & Cho, 2017). In one study, spiritual well-being predicted which heart failure patients

What roles do religion and spirituality play in adults' lives?
a katz/Shutterstock

would still be alive five years later (Park & others, 2016). In another study, adults who did volunteer work had lower resting pulse rates, and their resting pulse rates improved if they were more deeply committed to religion (Krause, Ironson, & Hill, 2017). Also, another study found that older adults who had a higher level of religious identification were less likely to be depressed (Ysseldyk, Haslam, & Haslam, 2013). In addition, a number of studies have found a positive association between religious participation and longevity (Oman & Thoresen, 2006). For example, one study revealed that religious attendance was linked to increased longevity (Kim, Smith, & Kang, 2015).

Why might religion be linked to physical health?
Blend Images-Hill Street Studios/Getty Images

Why might religion promote physical health? There are several possible answers (Hill & Butter, 1995):

- *Lifestyle issues.* For example, religious individuals have lower rates of drug use than their nonreligious counterparts (Gartner, Larson, & Allen, 1991).
- *Social networks.* Well-connected individuals have fewer health problems (Benjamins & Finlayson, 2007). Religious groups, meetings, and activities provide social connectedness for individuals.
- *Coping with stress.* Religion offers a source of comfort and support when individuals are confronted with stressful events (Carney & Park, 2018; Krause, 2019; Krause & Pargament, 2018). One study revealed that highly religious individuals were less likely than their moderately religious, somewhat religious, and nonreligious counterparts to be psychologically distressed (Park, 2013).

Religious and spiritual counselors often advise people about mental health and coping (Damari & others, 2018; Sajadi & others, 2018). To read about the work of one religious counselor, see the *Connecting with Careers* profile. In the *Connecting Development to Life* interlude we further explore links between religion and coping.

Religion in Older Adults In many societies around the world, older adults are the spiritual leaders in their churches and communities. For example, in the Catholic Church, more popes have been elected during their eighties than in any other 10-year period of the human life span.

The religious patterns of older adults have increasingly been studied (Krause & Pargament, 2018). A longitudinal study found that religious service attendance was stable in middle adulthood, increased in late adulthood, then declined later in the older adult years (Hayward & Krause, 2013a). Also, a research review concluded that individuals with a stronger spiritual/religious orientation were more likely to live longer (Lucchetti, Lucchetti, & Koenig, 2011). Also, in a recent study of older adults, those who regularly attended religious services lived longer than their counterparts who did not attend these services (Idler & others, 2017).

In one study of individuals from their early thirties through their early seventies, a significant increase in spirituality occurred between late middle adulthood (mid-fifties/early sixties)

connecting with careers

Gabriel Dy-Liacco, Professor and Pastoral Counselor

Gabriel Dy-Liacco is a professor in religious and pastoral counseling at Regent University in the Virginia Beach, Virginia, area. He obtained his Ph.D. in pastoral counseling from Loyola College in Maryland and also has experience as a psychotherapist in mental health settings such as a substance-abuse program, military family center, psychiatric clinic, and community mental health center. Earlier in his career he was a pastoral counselor at the Pastoral Counseling and Consultation Centers of Greater Washington, DC, and taught at Loyola University in Maryland. As a pastoral counselor, he works with adolescents and adults to help them address the aspects of their lives that they show the most concern about—psychological, spiritual, or the interface of both. Having lived in Peru, Japan, and the Philippines, he brings considerable multicultural experience to teaching and counseling settings.

connecting development to life

Religion and Coping

Is religion linked to individuals' ability to cope with stress? Some psychologists have categorized prayer and religious commitment as defensive coping strategies, arguing that they are less effective in helping individuals cope than are life-skill, problem-solving strategies. However, religious coping often benefits individuals during times of high stress (Carney & Park, 2018; Krause, 2019; Krause & Pargament, 2018). For example, one study found that coping styles that relied on collaboration with others and turning to religious groups were more strongly related to improved psychological adjustment than a self-directed coping style (Ross & others, 2009). And in a study of veterans with combat exposure, negative religious coping was associated with higher posttraumatic stress disorder (PTSD symptoms), while positive religious/spiritual coping was linked to higher perceived posttraumatic growth (PPTG) symptoms (Park & others, 2016).

A recent interest in linking religion and coping focuses on **meaning-making coping,** which involves drawing on beliefs, values, and goals to change the meaning of a stressful situation, especially in times of high levels of stress such as when a loved one dies. In Crystal Park's (2005, 2007, 2010, 2013) view, individuals who are religious experience more disruption of their beliefs, values, and goals immediately after the death of a loved one than do individuals who are not religious. Initially, religion is linked with more depressed feelings about a loved one's death. Over time, however, as religious individuals

How is religion linked to the ability to cope with stress?
Image Source/Alamy Stock Photo

search for meaning in their loss, they often become less depressed and show better adjustment. Thus, religion can serve as a meaning system through which bereaved individuals are able to reframe their loss and even find avenues of personal growth (George & Park, 2017).

In sum, various dimensions of religiousness can help some individuals cope more effectively with challenges that arise (Krause, 2019; Krause & Pargament, 2018). Religious beliefs can shape a person's psychological perception of pain or disability. Religious cognitions can play an important role in maintaining hope and stimulating motivation toward recovery. Because of its effectiveness in reducing distress, religious coping can help prevent denial of the problem and thus facilitate early recognition and more appropriate health-seeking behavior. Religion also can forestall the development of anxiety and depression by promoting communal or social interaction (Pandya, 2018). Houses of religious worship are a readily available, acceptable, and inexpensive source of support for many individuals, especially the elderly. The socialization provided by religious organizations can help prevent isolation and loneliness (Peteet, Zaben, & Koenig, 2019).

How would you explain successful coping strategies in those who are not religious? How is religion linked to the ability to cope with stress? What characterizes the search for meaning in life?

---

and late adulthood (late sixties/mid-seventies) (Wink & Dillon, 2002) (see Figure 6). The spirituality of women increased more than that of men. In this study, spirituality in late adulthood was linked with religiosity in early adulthood (thirties). This finding supports the idea that early religious involvement predisposes individuals to engage in further spiritual development. And one survey found that 77 percent of 30- to 49-year-olds and 84 percent of 50- to 64-year-olds reported having a religious affiliation (compared with 67 percent of 18- to 29-year-olds and 90 percent of adults 90 years of age and older) (Pew Research Center, 2012).

Individuals over 65 years of age are more likely than younger people to say that religious faith is the most significant influence in their lives, that they try to put religious faith into practice, and that they attend religious services (Gallup & Bezilla, 1992). A study of more than 500 African Americans 55 to 105 years of age revealed that they had a strong identification with religious institutions and high levels of attendance and participation in religious activities (Williams, Keigher, & Williams, 2012).

Is religion related to a sense of well-being and life satisfaction in old age? In one study, older adults' self-esteem was highest when they had a strong religious commitment and lowest when they had little religious commitment (Krause, 1995). In another study, older adults who

meaning-making coping Drawing on beliefs, values, and goals to change the meaning of a stressful situation, especially in times of high levels of stress such as when a loved one dies.

derived a sense of meaning in life from religion had higher levels of life satisfaction, self-esteem, and optimism (Krause, 2003). Also, in one study, older adults who reported having a higher level of spirituality had more resilience in the face of stressful and difficult circumstances (Vahia & others, 2011). And in another study, dementia caregivers who had a higher level of religiosity/spirituality had fewer depressive symptoms their counterparts who had a lower level of religiosity/spirituality (Yoon & others, 2016).

Religion can meet some important psychological needs in older adults, helping them to face impending death, to find and maintain a sense of meaningfulness in life, and to accept the inevitable losses of old age (Krause, 2019; Park & Cho, 2017). Socially, the religious community can serve many functions for older adults, such as providing social activities, social support, and the opportunity to assume teaching and leadership roles. One study revealed that over a period of seven years, older adults who attended church regularly increased the amount of emotional support they gave and received but decreased the amount of tangible support they gave and received (Hayward & Krause, 2013b). And in another study of 57- to 85-year-olds, religious attendance was linked to a lower incidence of physiological problems and negative outcomes of health events such as spousal death (Das & Nairn, 2016).

MEANING IN LIFE

Austrian psychiatrist Viktor Frankl's mother, father, brother, and wife died in the concentration camps and gas chambers in Auschwitz, Poland. Frankl survived the concentration camp and went on to write about meaning in life. In his book, *Man's Search for Meaning*, Frankl (1984) emphasized each person's uniqueness and the finiteness of life. He believed that examining the finiteness of our existence and the certainty of death adds meaning to life. If life were not finite, said Frankl, we could spend our life doing just about whatever we pleased because time would continue forever.

Frankl said that the three most distinct human qualities are spirituality, freedom, and responsibility. Spirituality, in his view, does not have a religious underpinning. Rather, it refers to a human being's uniqueness—of spirit, philosophy, and mind. Frankl proposed that people need to ask themselves such questions as why they exist, what they want from life, and what their life means.

It is in middle adulthood that individuals begin to be faced with death more often, especially the deaths of parents and other older relatives. Also faced with fewer years ahead of them than behind them, many individuals in middle age begin to ask and evaluate the questions that Frankl proposed. And, as we indicated in the discussion of religion and coping, meaning-making coping is especially helpful in times of chronic stress and loss.

Researchers are increasingly studying the factors involved in a person's exploration of meaning in life and striving to determine whether developing a sense of meaning in life is linked to positive developmental outcomes. Many individuals state that religion played an important role in increasing their exploration of meaning in life (Krause, 2008, 2009). Studies also suggest that individuals who have found a sense of meaning in life are more physically healthy and happier, and experience less depression, than their counterparts who report that they have not discovered meaning in life (Debats, 1990; Krause, 2009).

Having a sense of meaning in life can lead to clearer guidelines for living one's life and enhanced motivation to take care of oneself and reach goals (Ju, 2017; Zhang, 2019). A higher level of meaning in life also is linked to a higher level of psychological well-being and physical health (Park, 2012a, b).

Roy Baumeister and Kathleen Vohs (2002, pp. 610–611) argue that the quest for a meaningful life can be understood in terms of four main needs for meaning that guide how people try to make sense of their lives:

- *Need for purpose.* "Present events draw meaning from their connection with future events." Purposes can be divided into (1) goals and (2) fulfillments. Life can be oriented toward a future anticipated state, such as living happily ever after or being in love.

- *Need for values.* This "can lend a sense of goodness or positive characterization of life and justify certain courses of action. Values enable people to decide whether certain acts are right or wrong." Frankl's (1984) view of meaning in life emphasized value as the main form of meaning that people need.

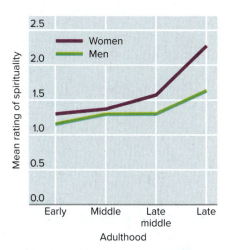

FIGURE 6

LEVEL OF SPIRITUALITY IN FOUR ADULT AGE PERIODS. In a longitudinal study, the spirituality of individuals in four different adult age periods—early (thirties), middle (forties), late middle (mid-fifties/early sixties), and late (late sixties/early seventies) adulthood—was assessed (Wink & Dillon, 2002). Based on responses to open-ended questions in interviews, the spirituality of the individuals was coded on a 5-point scale, with 5 being the highest level of spirituality and 1 the lowest.

What characterizes the search for meaning in life?
Eric Audras/Getty Images

- *Need for a sense of efficacy.* This involves the "belief that one can make a difference. A life that had purposes and values but no efficacy would be tragic. The person might know what is desirable but could not do anything with that knowledge." With a sense of efficacy, people believe that they can control their environment, which has positive physical and mental health benefits (Bandura, 2012).
- *Need for self-worth.* Most individuals want to be good, worthy persons. Self-worth can be pursued individually, such as finding out that one is very good at doing something, or collectively, as when people gain self-esteem from belonging to a group or category of people.

Review Connect Reflect

LG4 Characterize the development of values, religion, spirituality, and meaning in life.

Review
- What are values? How are the values of U.S. college students changing?
- How do individuals experience religion and spirituality at different points in the life span?
- How do people seek meaning in life?

Connect
- How might the search for meaning in life connect with what you have

learned about developmental personality changes in adults, especially in middle age?

Reflect *Your Own Personal Journey of Life*
- What characterizes your quest for a meaningful life?

---

reach your learning goals

Moral Development, Values, and Religion

1 Domains of Moral Development

 LG1 Discuss theory and research on moral thought, behavior, feeling, personality, and domains.

What Is Moral Development?

Moral Thought

- Moral development involves changes in thoughts, feelings, and behaviors regarding right and wrong. Moral development has intrapersonal and interpersonal dimensions.

- Piaget distinguished between the heteronomous morality of younger children and the autonomous morality of older children.

- Kohlberg developed an influential theory of moral reasoning. He documented three levels in the development of moral reasoning—preconventional, conventional, and postconventional. Research subsequently documented that these levels were not only related to age but also to diverse social experiences. Influences on the development of moral reasoning include cognitive maturation, cognitive conflict, peer relations, and perspective taking.

- Criticisms of Kohlberg's theory have been made, especially by Gilligan, who advocates a stronger care perspective. Other criticisms focus on the inadequacy of moral reasoning to predict moral behavior, the intuitiveness of moral thought, the role of emotion, and cultural and family influences.

Moral Behavior

- The processes of reinforcement, punishment, and imitation have been used to explain the acquisition of moral behavior, but they provide only a partial explanation. Situational variability is stressed by behaviorists. Cognitions can play a role in resistance to temptation and self-control. A social cognitive theory of morality emphasizes a distinction between moral competence and moral performance.

| Moral Feeling | • In Freud's theory, the superego is the moral branch of personality. The superego consists of the ego ideal and the conscience. According to Freud, guilt is the foundation of children's moral behavior. Empathy is an important aspect of moral feelings, and it changes developmentally. In the contemporary perspective, both positive and negative feelings contribute to moral development. |

| Moral Personality | • Recently, there has been a surge of interest in studying moral personality. This interest has focused on moral identity, moral character, and moral exemplars. |

• People who have a moral identity value moral notions and commitments to such an extent that behaving in a manner that violates this moral commitment would place the integrity of the self at risk.

• Moral character involves having the strength of your convictions, and persisting and overcoming distractions and obstacles. Moral character also means having certain virtues, such as honesty, truthfulness, loyalty, and compassion.

• Moral exemplars' identity, character, and virtues reflect moral commitment and excellence.

| Social Domain Theory | • Social domain theory states that there are different domains of social knowledge and reasoning, including moral, social conventional, and personal domains. |

2 Contexts of Moral Development Explain how parents and schools influence moral development.

| Parenting | • Warmth and responsibility in mutual obligations of parent-child relationships provide important foundations for the child's positive moral growth. Moral development can be advanced by these parenting strategies: being warm and supportive rather than punitive; providing opportunities to learn about others' perspectives and feelings; involving children in family decision making; modeling moral behaviors; averting misbehavior before it takes place; and engaging in conversational dialogue related to moral development. |

| Schools | • The hidden curriculum, initially described by Dewey, is the distinctive moral atmosphere that is present in each school. Contemporary approaches to moral education include character education, values clarification, service learning, and integrative ethical education. Cheating is a moral education concern and can take many forms. Various situational aspects influence whether students will cheat. |

3 Prosocial and Antisocial Behavior Describe the development of prosocial and antisocial behavior.

| Prosocial Behavior | • Altruism, which is an unselfish interest and voluntary effort in helping another person, and reciprocity often motivate prosocial behaviors (behaviors intended to help others) such as sharing. |

• Recent research has focused on whether infants and toddlers have moral awareness and can engage in prosocial behavior. Damon described a sequence by which children develop their understanding of fairness and begin to share with others more consistently. Peers play a key role in this development.

• Altruism is linked to having a longer life. Volunteering is associated with higher life satisfaction, less depression and anxiety, better physical health, and more positive affect and less negative affect.

| Antisocial Behavior | • Conduct disorder involves age-inappropriate actions and attitudes that violate family expectations, society's norms, and the personal or property rights of others. The disorder is more common in boys than in girls. |

• Juvenile delinquency refers to actions taken by an adolescent in breaking the law or engaging in illegal behavior. In the Pittsburgh Youth Study, pathways to delinquency included conflict with authority, minor covert acts followed by property damage and more serious acts, and overt acts of minor aggression followed by fighting and violence. Associating with peers and friends who are delinquents, low parental monitoring, ineffective discipline, having an older sibling who is a delinquent, living in an urban, high-crime area, having low self-control, and having low intelligence are also linked with delinquency.

4 Values, Religion, Spirituality, and Meaning in Life

 LG4 Characterize the development of values, religion, spirituality, and meaning in life.

Values

- Values are beliefs and attitudes about the way people think things should be. Over the last four decades, traditional-age college students have shown an increased interest in personal well-being and a decreased interest in the welfare of others.

Religion and Spirituality

- Distinctions have been made between the concepts of religion, religiousness, and spirituality. Many children, adolescents, and emerging adults show an interest in religion, and religious institutions strive to introduce them to religious beliefs.

- Cognitive changes in adolescence—such as increases in abstract, idealistic, and logical thinking—increase the likelihood that adolescents will seek a better understanding of religion and spirituality. As part of their search for identity, many adolescents and emerging adults begin to grapple with more complex aspects of religion. A downturn in religious interest among college students has occurred. When adolescents have a positive relationship with parents or are securely attached to them, they often adopt their parents' religious beliefs. Various aspects of religion are linked with positive outcomes in adolescent development.

- Religion is an important dimension of many American adults' lives as well as the lives of people around the world. Females tend to have a stronger interest in religion than males do. Although some people in certain religious sects try to avoid using medical treatment, individuals in the religious mainstream generally enjoy a positive or neutral link between religion and physical health. Religious interest often increases in late adulthood.

Meaning in Life

- Frankl argued that people need to face the finiteness of their life in order to understand life's meaning. Faced with the death of older relatives and less time to live themselves, middle-aged adults increasingly examine life's meaning.

- Baumeister described four main needs that guide how people try to make sense of their lives: (1) need for purpose, (2) need for values, (3) need for a sense of efficacy, and (4) need for self-worth.

key terms

altruism	empathy	meaning-making coping	service learning
autonomous morality	forgiveness	moral development	social cognitive theory of morality
care perspective	gratitude	moral exemplars	social conventional reasoning
character education	heteronomous morality	moral identity	social domain theory
conduct disorder	hidden curriculum	postconventional reasoning	spirituality
conscience	immanent justice	preconventional reasoning	sympathy
conventional reasoning	justice perspective	religion	values
ego ideal	juvenile delinquency	religiousness	values clarification

key people

Albert Bandura	Viktor Frankl	Lawrence Kohlberg	Judith Smetana
Roy Baumeister	Sigmund Freud	Mark May	Ross Thompson
Gustavo Carlo	James Garbarino	Walter Mischel	Eliot Turiel
William Damon	Carol Gilligan	Darcia Narváez	Lawrence Walker
John Dewey	Jonathan Haidt	Crystal Park	
Nancy Eisenberg	Sam Hardy	Jean Piaget	
Marion Forgatch	Hugh Hartshorne	James Rest	

section five

It is not enough for parents to understand children. They must also accord children the privilege of understanding them.

—MILTON SAPERSTEIN
American Psychiatrist and Writer, 20th Century

ImageDJ/age fotostock

Social Contexts of Development

As children develop, their small world widens and they discover new contexts and people. As they grow through childhood, their parents still cradle their lives, but their lives also are shaped by successive choirs of peers and friends. Parents can give adolescents both roots and wings. When some adults become parents, they recognize for the first time how much effort their parents put into rearing them. In recent decades, increasing numbers of adults have chosen to get married later or not at all. As people age, they come to sense that the generations of living things pass in a short while, and, like runners, they pass on the torch of life. This section contains three chapters: "Families, Lifestyles, and Parenting," "Peers and the Sociocultural World," and "Schools, Achievement, and Work."

chapter 14

FAMILIES, LIFESTYLES, AND PARENTING

chapter outline

(1) Family Processes

Learning Goal 1 Describe some important family processes.

Reciprocal Socialization
Family as a System
Sociocultural and Historical Influences

(2) The Diversity of Adult Lifestyles

Learning Goal 2 Discuss the diversity of adult lifestyles and how they influence people's lives.

Single Adults
Cohabiting Adults
Married Adults
Divorced Adults
Remarried Adults
Gay and Lesbian Adults

(3) Parenting

Learning Goal 3 Characterize parenting and how it affects children's development.

Parental Roles
Parenting Styles and Discipline
Parent-Adolescent and Parent-Emerging Adult Relationships
Working Parents
Children in Divorced Families
Stepfamilies
Gay and Lesbian Parents
Adoptive Parents and Adopted Children

(4) Other Family Relationships

Learning Goal 4 Explain other aspects of family relationships.

Sibling Relationships and Birth Order
Grandparenting and Great-Grandparenting
Intergenerational Relationships

Ariel Skelley/Blend Images LLC

preview

Love and attachment are two important aspects of family life. Beyond these emotional ties, what else goes on in families that influences development? And how do the choices that adults make about family life affect their development and the development of their children? These are some of the questions that we will consider in this chapter.

1 Family Processes Describe some important family processes.

- Reciprocal Socialization
- Family as a System
- Sociocultural and Historical Influences

As we examine the family and other social contexts of development, consider Urie Bronfenbrenner's (1986, 2004; Bronfenbrenner & Morris, 2006) ecological theory, which we discussed in the "Introduction" chapter. Bronfenbrenner analyzes the social contexts of development in terms of five environmental systems:

- The *microsystem*, or the setting in which the individual lives, such as a family, the world of peers, schools, work, and so on
- The *mesosystem*, which consists of links between microsystems, such as the connection between family processes and peer relations
- The *exosystem*, which consists of influences from another setting (such as parents' work) that the individual does not experience directly
- The *macrosystem*, or the culture in which the individual lives, such as an ethnic group or a nation
- The *chronosystem*, or sociohistorical circumstances, such as the increased numbers of working mothers, divorced parents, stepparent families, gay and lesbian parents, and multiethnic families in the United States in the last 30 to 40 years

RECIPROCAL SOCIALIZATION

Socialization between parents and children is not a one-way process. Parents do socialize children, but socialization in families is reciprocal (D'Angelo & others, 2019; Klein & others, 2018). **Reciprocal socialization** is socialization that is bidirectional; children socialize parents just as parents socialize children. These reciprocal interchanges and mutual influence processes are sometimes referred to as *transactional* (Dora & Baydar, 2019; Nelemans & others, 2019).

For example, the interaction of mothers and their infants is sometimes symbolized as a dance in which successive actions of the partners are closely coordinated (Provenzi & others, 2018). This coordinated dance can assume the form of synchrony—that is, each person's behavior depends on the partner's previous behavior. Or the interaction can be reciprocal in a precise sense, in which the actions of the partners can be matched, as when one partner imitates the other or when there is mutual smiling. An important example of early synchronized interaction is mutual gaze or eye contact. In one study, synchrony in parent-child relationships was positively related to children's social competence (Harrist, 1993). Also, in a recent study, inadequate dyadic synchrony was found in the preterm infant-mother relationship when compared with more positive dyadic synchrony in the full term infant-mother relationship (Spairani & others, 2018). The types of behaviors involved in reciprocal socialization in infancy are temporally connected, mutually contingent behaviors such as one partner imitating the sound of another or the mother responding with a vocalization to the baby's arm movements.

Children socialize parents just as parents socialize children.
Fuse/Getty Images

reciprocal socialization Socialization that is bidirectional in that children socialize parents just as parents socialize children.

How does the game of peek-a-boo reflect the concept of scaffolding?
MIA Studio/Shutterstock

Another example of synchronization occurs in *scaffolding*, which means adjusting the level of guidance to fit the child's performance (Clegg & Legare, 2017). The parent responds to the child's behavior with scaffolding, which in turn affects the child's behavior. For example, in the game of peek-a-boo, parents initially cover their babies, then remove the covering, and finally register "surprise" at the babies' reappearance. As infants become more skilled at peek-a-boo, they gradually do some of the covering and uncovering. Parents try to time their actions in such a way that the infant takes turns with the parent. In addition to peek-a-boo, other caregiver games such as pat-a-cake and "so-big" exemplify scaffolding and turn-taking sequences.

Scaffolding can be used to support children's efforts at any age (Graneist & Habermas, 2019; Norona & Baker, 2017). A recent study found that when adults used explicit scaffolding (encouragement and praise) with 13- and 14-month-old toddlers, the children were twice as likely to engage in helping behavior as were their counterparts who did not receive the scaffolding (Dahl & others, 2017). And a study of disadvantaged families revealed that an intervention designed to enhance maternal scaffolding with infants was linked to improved cognitive skills when the children were 4 years old (Obradovic & others, 2016).

Increasingly, genetic and epigenetic factors are being studied to discover not only parental influences on children but also children's influence on parents (Jylhava & others, 2019; Szutorisz & Hurd, 2018). Recall that the *epigenetic view* emphasizes that development is the result of an ongoing, bidirectional interchange between heredity and the environment (Ecker & Beck, 2019; Hein & others, 2019). For example, harsh, hostile parenting is associated with children's negative behavior, such as defiance and oppositional behavior (Thompson & others, 2017). This likely reflects bidirectional influences rather than a unidirectional parenting effect. That is, the parents' harsh, hostile parenting and the children's defiant, oppositional behavior may mutually influence each other. In this bidirectional influence, the parents' and children's behavior may have genetic linkages as well as experiential connections.

FAMILY AS A SYSTEM

As a social system, the family can be thought of as a constellation of subsystems defined in terms of generation, gender, and role (Kerig, 2019). Divisions of labor among family members define particular subunits, and attachments define others. Each family member participates in several subsystems—some dyadic (involving two people) and some polyadic (involving more than two people) (McHale & Sirotkin, 2019; Solomon-Moore & others, 2018). The father and child represent one dyadic subsystem, the mother and father another; the mother-father-child represent one polyadic subsystem, the mother and two siblings another.

These subsystems interact with and influence each other (Schwartz & Scott, 2018). Thus, as Figure 1 illustrates, the marital relationship, parenting, and infant/child behavior can have both direct and indirect effects on each other (Belsky, 1981). The link between marital relationships and parenting has recently received increased attention (Dubow & others, 2017; Gao & others, 2019). The most consistent findings are that compared with unhappily married parents, happily married parents are more sensitive, responsive, warm, and affectionate toward their children (Grych, 2002).

Researchers have found that promoting marital satisfaction often leads to good parenting. The marital relationship is an important support for parenting (Bergman & Cummings, 2018). When parents report more intimacy and better communication in their marriage, they are more affectionate with their children (Grych, 2002). Thus, marriage-enhancement programs may end up improving parenting and helping children (Ahluwalia, Anand, & Suman, 2018). Programs that focus on parenting skills might also benefit from including attention to the participants' marriages.

Thus, a positive family climate for children and adolescents involves not only effective parenting but also a positive relationship between parents, whether they are married or divorced (Davies, Martin, & Cummings, 2018; Ganong, Coleman, & Sanner, 2019). A recent study revealed that improvement in couples' relationship coping decreased their coparenting conflict (Zemp & others, 2017). A longitudinal study found that a positive family climate (based on positive interaction between spouses and between parents and their seventh-grade children) was linked to the degree of positive engagement the children showed toward their own spouses almost 20 years later in early adulthood (Ackerman & others, 2013).

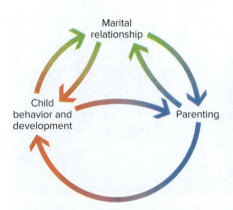

FIGURE 1

INTERACTION BETWEEN CHILDREN AND THEIR PARENTS: DIRECT AND INDIRECT EFFECTS

SOCIOCULTURAL AND HISTORICAL INFLUENCES

Family development does not occur in a social vacuum. Important sociocultural and historical influences affect family processes, which reflect Bronfenbrenner's concepts of the macrosystem and chronosystem (Bronfenbrenner & Morris, 2006). Both great upheavals such as war, famine, or mass immigration and subtle transitions in ways of life may stimulate changes in families (Masten & Kalstabakken, 2018; Masten & Palmer, 2019). One example is the effect on U.S. families of the Great Depression of the 1930s. During its height, the Depression produced economic deprivation, adult discontent, and dissatisfaction with living conditions. It also increased marital conflict, inconsistent child rearing, and unhealthy lifestyles—heavy drinking, demoralized attitudes, and health problems—especially in fathers (Elder, 1980).

A major change in families during the last several decades has been the dramatic increase in the immigration of Latino and Asian families into the United States (Ng & Wang, 2019; Halgunseth, 2019). These families often experience stressors uncommon to or less prominent among long-time residents, such as language barriers, dislocations and separations from support networks, the dual struggle to preserve identity and to acculturate, and changes in socioeconomic status (Bornstein & Cote, 2019). We discuss ethnic variations in families more extensively in the chapter on "Peers and the Sociocultural World."

Subtle changes in a culture have significant influences on the family (Muir & others, 2019; Suárez-Orozco & Suárez-Orozco, 2018). Such changes include the increased longevity of older adults; movement from rural communities to urban and suburban areas; widespread use of television, computers, and the Internet; and a general dissatisfaction and restlessness (Barr, 2019; Fernandez-Ballesteros & others, 2019; Smith & Anderson, 2018).

Early in the twentieth century, middle-aged and older adults were often closely linked to the family (Mead, 1978). Today, older parents may have lost some of their socializing role in the family as many of their children moved considerable distances away. However, as we see later in the chapter, in the twenty-first century an increasing number of grandparents are raising their grandchildren.

In the twentieth century, many families moved from farms and small towns to urban and suburban settings (Mead, 1978). In the small towns and farms, individuals were surrounded by lifelong neighbors, relatives, and friends. Today, neighborhood and extended-family support systems are not nearly as prevalent. Families now move all over the country, often uprooting children from a school and peer group they have known for a considerable length of time. And it is not unusual for this type of move to occur every several years, as one or both parents are transferred from job to job.

Further, an increasing number of children are growing up in transnational families, who move back and forth between countries, such as between the United States and Mexico or between the United States and China (Acedera & Yeoh, 2019; Santos & others, 2019). In some cases, these children are left behind in their home country or in other cases they are sent back to be raised by grandparents during their early childhood years. Such children might benefit from economic remittances but suffer emotionally from prolonged separation from their parents.

Media use and screen time also play a major role in the changing family (Barr, 2019; Hale & others, 2018). Many children who watch television, use computers, or view videos on mobile devices such as iPhones, find that parents are too busy working to share this experience with them (Maloy & others, 2016). Children increasingly experience a world in which their parents are not participants. Instead of interacting in neighborhood peer groups, children come home after school and watch television or log on to a computer (Padmapriya & others, 2019). Recent research with adolescents indicated that light use of digital media (less than 1 hour a day) was associated with much higher psychological well-being than heavy use of digital media (5+ hours a day) (Twenge & Campbell, 2019). Among the historical changes related to computers, consider the dramatic increase in young people's participation on Internet social networking sites (Negriff, 2019; Smith & Anderson, 2018). For example, in a recent study, social media use of more than 2 hours per day was linked to lower academic achievement in both middle and high school (Sampasa-Kanyinga, Chaput, & Hamilton, 2019).

Another change in families has been an increase in general dissatisfaction and restlessness (Mead, 1978). The result of such restlessness and the tendency to divorce and remarry has been a hodgepodge of family structures, with far greater numbers of divorced and remarried families than ever before. Later in the chapter, we will discuss in greater detail these aspects of the changing social world of the child and the family.

developmental connection

Family

Many families who have immigrated into the United States in recent decades, such as Mexican Americans and Asian Americans, come from collectivist cultures in which family obligations are strong. Connect to "Peers and the Sociocultural World."

developmental connection

Screen Time

Recent research indicates that children's and adolescents' media use/screen time have increased dramatically in the last decade. Connect to "Peers and the Sociocultural World."

Two important changes in families are the increased mobility of families and the increase in media use. *What are some other changes?*
(*Top*): kali9/E+/Getty Images; (*bottom*): JGI/Jamie Grill/Getty Images

Review *Connect* Reflect

LG1 Describe some important family processes.

Review

- What characterizes reciprocal socialization?
- How does the family function as a system?
- How do sociocultural and historical circumstances influence families?

Connect

- Compare mothers' and fathers' socialization strategies with this section's description of reciprocal socialization.

Reflect *Your Own Personal Journey of Life*

- Reflect for several moments on your own family as you were growing up, and give some examples of the family processes discussed in this section as you experienced them in your own family.

2 The Diversity of Adult Lifestyles

LG2 Discuss the diversity of adult lifestyles and how they influence people's lives.

Single Adults | Cohabiting Adults | Married Adults | Divorced Adults | Remarried Adults | Gay and Lesbian Adults

A striking social change in recent decades has been the decreased stigma attached to individuals who do not maintain what were long considered conventional families. Adults today choose among many lifestyles and form many types of families (Schwartz & Scott, 2018; Weinraub & Kaufman, 2019). They may live alone, cohabit, marry, divorce, or live with someone of the same sex (McConnachie & others, 2019).

In his book *The Marriage-Go-Round*, sociologist Andrew Cherlin (2009) concluded that the United States has more marriages and remarriages, more divorces, and more short-term cohabiting (living together) relationships than most countries. Combined, these lifestyles create more turnover and movement in and out of relationships in the United States than in virtually any other country. For example, in a recent cross-national comparison of the United States and seven European countries, the United States was most likely to be characterized by a high degree of union instability in marriage and cohabitation (Musick & Michelmore, 2018). Let's explore these varying relationship lifestyles.

SINGLE ADULTS

Recent decades have seen a dramatic rise in the percentage of single adults (Klinenberg, 2012, 2013). In 2009 for the first time in history the proportion of U.S. individuals 25 to 34 years of age who had never been married (46 percent) exceeded those who were married (45 percent) (U.S. Census Bureau, 2013). In 2017, 44.9 percent of U.S. adults 18 years of age and older had never been married (U.S. Census Bureau, 2018). In the 18-to-29-year age bracket, the percentage of individuals who have never been married increased from 48 percent in 2005 to 64 percent in 2014 (Gallup Poll, 2015). The increasing number of single adults is the result of rising rates of cohabitation and a trend toward postponing marriage. However, the United States actually has a lower percentage of single adults than many other countries such as Great Britain, Germany, and Japan. Moreover, the fastest growth in individuals adopting a single adult lifestyle is occurring in rapidly developing countries such as China, India, and Brazil (Klinenberg, 2012, 2013).

Even when singles enjoy their lifestyles and are highly competent individuals, they often are stereotyped (Schwartz & Scott, 2018). Stereotypes associated with being single range from the "swinging single" to the "desperately lonely, suicidal" single. Of course, most single adults are somewhere between these extremes.

Common challenges faced by single adults may include forming intimate relationships with other adults, confronting loneliness, and finding a niche in a society that is marriage-oriented. Bella DePaulo (2006, 2011) argues that society has a widespread bias against unmarried adults that is seen in everything from missed perks in jobs to deep social and financial prejudices.

Advantages of being single include having time to make decisions about one's life course, time to develop personal resources to meet goals, freedom to make autonomous decisions and pursue one's own schedule and interests, opportunities to explore new places and try out new things, and privacy. Compared with married adults, single adults are more likely to spend time with friends and neighbors, go out to restaurants, and attend art classes and lectures (Klinenberg, 2012, 2013). Once adults reach the age of 30, they may face increasing pressure to settle down and get married. This is when many single adults make a conscious decision to marry or to remain single.

A nationally representative U.S. survey of more than 5,000 single adults 21 years of age and older who were not in a committed relationship revealed that men are more interested in love, marriage, and children than their counterparts were in earlier generations (Match.com, 2011). In this study, today's women desire more independence in their relationships than their mothers did. Across every age group, more women than men reported wanting to pursue their own interests, have personal space, have their own bank account, have regular nights out with girlfriends, and take vacations on their own. In a second nationally representative survey, many single adults reported that they were looking for love but not marriage (Match.com, 2012). In this survey, 39 percent of the single adults were uncertain about whether they wanted to get married, 34 percent said they did want to marry, and 27 percent said they didn't want to get married.

In a recent national survey, millennials were far more likely than older generations to seek romance and commitment (Match.com, 2017). In this recent survey, 40 percent of actively dating single adults have dated someone they met online, while only 24 percent met through a friend. Also in this study, millennials were 48 percent more likely than older generations to have sex before the first date. This "fast sex, slow love" trend may indicate that millennials want to know as much about someone as possible before committing to a serious relationship (Fisher, 2017). Also in the recent survey, among single men 18 and older, 95 percent favor women initiating the first kiss and also asking for the man's phone number, but only 29 percent of single women actually initiate the first kiss and only 13 percent ask for the man's phone number (Match.com, 2017).

Approximately 8 percent of all individuals in the United States who reach the age of 65 have never been married. Contrary to the popular stereotype, older adults who have never been married seem to have the least difficulty coping with loneliness in old age. Many of them discovered long ago how to live autonomously and how to become self-reliant.

COHABITING ADULTS

Cohabitation refers to living together in a sexual relationship without being married. Cohabitation has undergone considerable changes in recent years (Kamp Dush & others, 2019; Lamidi, Manning, & Brown, 2019; Sassler, Michelmore, & Qian, 2018). For example, there has been a dramatic increase in the number of cohabiting U.S. couples (Konstam, 2019; Stepler, 2017). In a recent national poll, the number of cohabiting adults increased 29 percent from 2007 to 2016, reaching a total of 18 million adults in a cohabiting relationship (U.S. Census Bureau, 2016). In 2018, 15 percent of U.S. adults 25 to 34 and 9 percent who were 18 to 24 years old were cohabiting (U.S. Census Bureau, 2019). Cohabitation rates are even higher in some countries—in Sweden, for example, cohabitation before marriage is virtually universal (Stokes & Raley, 2009).

Some couples view their cohabitation not as a precursor to marriage but as an ongoing lifestyle (Rose-Greenland & Smock, 2013). These couples do not want the official aspects of marriage. In the United States, cohabiting arrangements tend to be short-lived, with one-third lasting less than a year (Hyde & DeLamater, 2017). Fewer than 1 out of 10 last five years. Of course, it is easier to dissolve a cohabitation relationship than to divorce.

One study revealed that young adults' main reasons for cohabiting are to spend time together, share expenses, and evaluate compatibility (Huang & others, 2011). In this study, gender differences emerged regarding drawbacks in cohabiting: men were more concerned about their loss of freedom while women were more concerned about delays in getting married.

Couples who cohabit face certain problems (Kamp Dush & others, 2019). Disapproval by parents and other family members can place emotional strain on the cohabiting couple. Some cohabiting couples have difficulty purchasing property jointly. Legal rights regarding the dissolution of the relationship are less certain than in a divorce. Researchers have found that following the transition from dating to cohabitation, relationships are characterized by more commitment, lower satisfaction, more negative communication, and more physical aggression

cohabitation Living together in a sexual relationship without being married.

What are some potential advantages and disadvantages of cohabitation?
Chris Ryan/OJO Images/Getty Images

than when dating (noncohabiting) (Rhoades, Stanley, & Markman, 2012). Other recent research confirms that cohabitation is a risk factor for intimate partner violence in emerging adults (Manning, Longmore, & Gordano, 2018). Also, in a recent study, cohabiting individuals were more likely to have their first sexual relationship prior to age 18 and to have cohabited two or more times in the past than both married and unmarried non-cohabiting individuals, and they were more likely than married men and women to have had an unintended birth (Nugent & Daugherty, 2018). And a recent study revealed that cohabitation was associated with increased marijuana use among women but not men (Hoffman, 2018).

Researchers also have discovered that cohabiting individuals are not as mentally healthy as their counterparts in committed marital relationships (Braithwaite & Holt-Lunstad, 2017; Fincham & May, 2017). In a recent study of long-term cohabitation (more than three years) in emerging adulthood, emotional distress was higher in long-term cohabitation than during time spent single, with men especially driving the effect (Memitz, 2019). However, heavy drinking was more common during time spent being single than in long-term cohabitation.

Cohabitation and Marital Stability/Happiness   If a couple chooses to live together before they marry, does cohabiting help or harm their chances of later having a stable and happy marriage? The majority of studies have found lower rates of marital satisfaction and higher rates of divorce in couples who lived together before getting married (Blumberg, Vahratian, & Blumberg, 2014; Rose-Greenland & Smock, 2013). However, research indicates that the link between marital cohabitation and marital instability in first marriages has weakened in recent cohorts (Copen, Daniels, & Mosher, 2013; Smock & Gupta, 2013). Further, in a recent large-scale study, women who cohabited within the first year of a sexual relationship were less likely to get married than women who waited more than one year before cohabiting (Sassler, Michelmore, & Qian, 2018).

What might explain the finding that cohabiting is linked with divorce more than not cohabiting? The most frequently given explanation is that the less traditional lifestyle of cohabitation may attract less conventional individuals who are not strong believers in marriage in the first place. An alternative explanation is that the experience of cohabiting changes people's attitudes and habits in ways that increase their likelihood of divorce.

Research has provided clarification of cohabitation outcomes. One meta-analysis found that the link between cohabitation and marital instability did not hold up when only cohabitation with the eventual marital partner was examined, indicating that these cohabitors may attach more long-term positive meaning to living together (Jose, O'Leary, & Moyer, 2010). Another study also revealed that for first marriages, cohabiting with the spouse without first being engaged was linked to more negative interaction and a higher probability of divorce than cohabiting after engagement (Stanley & others, 2010). In contrast, premarital cohabitation prior to a second marriage placed couples at risk for divorce regardless of whether they were engaged. One study also found that the marriages of couples who were cohabiting but not engaged were less likely to survive to the 10- to 15-year mark than the marriages of their counterparts who were engaged when they cohabited (Copen, Daniels, & Mosher, 2013). Also, one analysis indicated that cohabiting does not have a negative effect on marriage if the couple did not have any previous live-in lovers and did not have children prior to the marriage (Cherlin, 2009). And another study concluded that the risk of marital dissolution between cohabitors and those who married without previously cohabiting was much smaller when they cohabited in their mid-twenties and later (Kuperberg, 2014).

Cohabiting Older Adults   An increasing number of individuals 50 years of age and older cohabit. Cohabitation levels more than doubled for middle aged and older adult men from 1990 (1.5 percent) to 2015 (3.8 percent) and also increased for middle-aged and older adult women in the same time frame from less than 1 percent to 2.6 percent (Brown & Wright, 2017). These percentages are expected to continue to increase in the next decade.

In many cases, cohabiting among older couples is more for companionship than for love. In other cases—for example, when one partner faces the potential for expensive long-term care—a couple may decide to maintain their assets separately and thus not marry. One study found that older adults who cohabited had a more positive, stable relationship than younger adults who cohabited, although older adults who cohabited were less likely to make plans to marry their partner (King & Scott, 2005). In one study, cohabiting older adults were less likely to receive partner care than married older adults (Noel-Miller, 2011).

MARRIED ADULTS

Until about 1930, stable marriage was widely accepted as a hallmark of adult development. Almost a century later, however, personal fulfillment both inside and outside marriage has emerged as a goal that competes with marital stability. The changing norm of male-female equality in marriage and increasingly high expectations regarding what a successful marriage should look like have produced marital relationships that are more fragile and intense than marriages earlier in the twentieth century (Schwartz & Scott, 2018).

Marital Trends   In 2016, 50 percent of individuals 18 and older in the United States were married, down from 72 percent in 1960 (Parker & Stepler, 2017). Also, in 2018, the U.S. average age for a first marriage had climbed to 29.8 years for men and 27.8 years for women, higher than at any other point in history (U.S. Census Bureau, 2019). In 1960, the average age for a first marriage in the United States was 23 years for men and 20 years for women. Also, a higher percentage of U.S. adults never marry—in 2014, a record percentage (23 percent of men, 17 percent of women) of adults age 25 and older had never married. In addition, the increased cohabitation rate in the United States has contributed to the lower percentage of adults who are married. Although marriage rates are declining, however, the United States is still a marrying society, with 78.5 percent of U.S. adults 25 years and older in 2016 having been married at some point in their lives.

The age at which individuals get married is increasing, not just in the United States but also in many countries around the world. Also, in recent analyses, age at first marriage in most developed countries is later than it is in the United States (OECD, 2016). For example, in a comparison of 39 developed countries, average age at first marriage now is older in Sweden (34 for females and 36 for males) than the other 38 countries. Earliest average age at first marriage in these developed countries is occurring in Turkey (25 for females and 27 for males). In most of the countries, individuals are getting married later than their counterparts in the United States and in most countries marriage is occurring later than in previous decades.

Although marriage rates are declining and the average age for a first marriage is going up, research with emerging and young adults indicates that they view marriage as a very important life pursuit. Indeed, in one study young adults predicted that marriage would be more important in their life than parenting, careers, or leisure activities (Willoughby, Hall, & Goff, 2015). In a recent book, *The Marriage Paradox* (Willoughby & James, 2017), the authors concluded that the importance of marriage to emerging and young adults may be what is encouraging them to first build a better career and financial foundation to increase the likelihood that their marriage will be successful later. From this perspective, emerging and young adults may not be abandoning marriage because they don't like it or are uninterested in it, but rather postponing it because they want to position themselves in the best possible way for developing a healthy marital relationship.

One study explored what U.S. never-married men and women are looking for in a potential spouse (Wang, 2014). Following are the percentages who reported that various factors would be very important for them:

Factor	Men	Women
Similar ideas about having and raising children	62	70
A steady job	46	78
At least as much education	26	28
Same racial or ethnic background	7	10

Thus, in this study, never-married men said that the most important factor for a potential spouse was similar ideas about having and raising children, but never-married women placed greater importance on having a partner with a steady job.

How happy are people who do marry? As indicated in Figure 2, the percentage of married individuals in the United States who said their marriages were "very happy" declined from the 1970s through the early 1990s, increased around the turn of the century, but has begun to decline again (Popenoe, 2009). Notice in Figure 2 that married men consistently report being happier than married women.

The Benefits of a Good Marriage   Are there any benefits to having a good marriage? There are several (Lavner & Bradbury, 2019; Schwartz & Scott, 2018). Individuals who are happily married live longer, healthier lives than either divorced individuals or those who are unhappily

> When two people are under the influence of the most violent, most insane, most delusive, and most transient of passions, they are required to swear that they will remain in that excited, abnormal, and exhausting condition continuously until death do them part.
>
> —GEORGE BERNARD SHAW
> *Irish Playwright, 20th Century*

FIGURE 2

PERCENTAGE OF MARRIED PERSONS AGE 18 AND OLDER WITH "VERY HAPPY" MARRIAGES

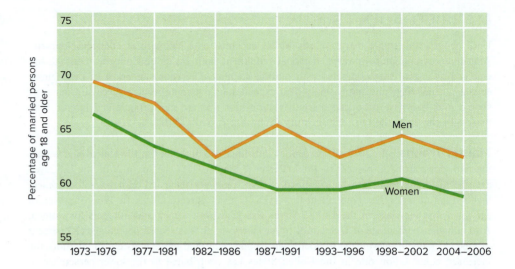

married (Robles, 2014; Williams, Sawyer, & Wahlstrom, 2017). In a research review, it was concluded that the experience of divorce or separation confers risk for poor health outcomes, including a 23 percent higher mortality rate (Sbarra, 2015). A survey of U.S. adults age 50 and older also revealed that being married for a lower proportion of adult life was linked to an increased likelihood of dying at an earlier age (Henretta, 2010). Further, an unhappy marriage can shorten a person's life by an average of four years (Gove, Style, & Hughes, 1990). And a recent research review of individuals who were married, divorced, widowed, and single found that married individuals had the best cardiovascular profile and single men the worst (Manfredini & others, 2017).

Social Contexts   Contexts within a culture and across cultures are powerful influences on marriage (John & others, 2017; McLoyd, Hardaway, & Jocson, 2019). A U.S. study found that although poor communication was rated as a relatively severe problem regardless of household income, it was rated as most severe in high-income households (Karney, Garvin, & Thomas, 2003) (see Figure 3). By contrast, drugs and infidelity were rated as more severe problems in low-income households than in middle- or high-income households.

Many aspects of marriage vary across cultures. For example, as part of China's efforts to control population growth, a 1981 law set the minimum age for marriage at 22 years for males and 20 for females. Further, in many parts of the world, such as India, arranged marriages are common.

The traits that people look for in a marriage partner vary around the world. In one large-scale study of 9,474 adults from 37 cultures on six continents and five islands, people varied most regarding how much they valued chastity—desiring a marital partner with no previous experience in sexual intercourse (Buss & others, 1990). Chastity was the most important characteristic in selecting a marital partner in China, India, Indonesia, Iran, Taiwan, and the Palestinian Arab culture. Adults from Ireland and Japan placed moderate importance on chastity. In contrast, adults in Sweden, Finland, Norway, the Netherlands, and Germany generally said that chastity was not important in selecting a marital partner.

Domesticity is also valued in some cultures and not in others. In the same study, adults from the Zulu culture in South Africa, Estonia, and Colombia placed a high value on housekeeping skills in their marital preference. By contrast, adults in the United States, Canada, and all Western European countries except Spain said that housekeeping skill was not an important trait in selecting their partner.

Religion plays an important role in marital preferences in many cultures (Lazar, 2017). For example, Islam stresses the honor of the male and the purity of the female. It also emphasizes the woman's role in childbearing, child rearing, educating children, and instilling the Islamic faith in children.

International comparisons of marriage also reveal that individuals in Scandinavian countries marry later than Americans, whereas their counterparts in many African, Asian, Latin American, and Eastern European countries marry younger (Waite, 2009). In Denmark, for example, almost 80 percent of the

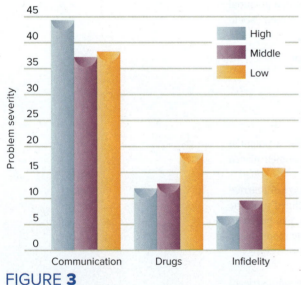

FIGURE 3

SEVERITY OF SPECIFIC RELATIONSHIP PROBLEMS IN LOW-, MIDDLE-, AND HIGH-INCOME HOUSEHOLDS

472   CHAPTER 14   Families, Lifestyles, and Parenting

(a)

(b)

(c)

(a) In Scandinavian countries, cohabitation is popular; only a small percentage of 20- to 24-year-olds are married. (b) Islam stresses male honor and female purity. (c) Japanese young adults live at home with their parents longer before marrying than young adults in most other countries.
(a): Johner Images /Getty Images; (b): Image Source/Getty Images; (c): BloomImage/Getty Images

women and 90 percent of the men aged 20 to 24 have never been married. In Hungary, less than 40 percent of the women and 70 percent of the men aged 20 to 24 have never been married. In Scandinavian countries, cohabitation is popular among young adults; however, most Scandinavians eventually marry (Popenoe, 2008). In Sweden, on average, women delay marriage until they are 31, men until they are 33. Some countries, such as Hungary, encourage early marriage and child-bearing to offset declines in the population. Like Scandinavian countries, Japan has a high proportion of unmarried young people. However, rather than cohabiting as the Scandinavians do, unmarried Japanese young adults tend to live with their parents before marrying.

What Makes Marriages Work   John Gottman (1994; Gottman & Gottman, 2009; Gottman & Silver, 1999; Gottman & others, 1998) has been studying married couples' lives since the early 1970s. He uses many methods to analyze what makes marriages work. Gottman interviews couples about the history of their marriage, their philosophy about marriage, and how they view their parents' marriages. He videotapes spouses talking with each other about how their day went and evaluates what they say about the good and bad times of their marriages. Gottman also uses physiological measures to track their heart rate, blood flow, blood pressure, and immune functioning moment by moment. He checks back with the couples every year to see how their marriage is faring. Gottman's research represents the most extensive assessment of marital relationships available. Currently he and his colleagues are following 700 couples in seven studies.

In his research, Gottman has identified the following factors as important predictors of success in marriage:

- *Establishing love maps.* Individuals in successful marriages have personal insights and detailed maps of each other's life and world. They aren't psychological strangers. In good marriages, partners are willing to share their feelings with each other. They use these "love maps" to express not only their understanding of each other but also their fondness and admiration.

- *Nurturing fondness and admiration.* In successful marriages, partners sing each other's praises. More than 90 percent of the time, when couples put a positive spin on their marriage's history, their marriage is likely to have a positive future.

- *Turning toward each other instead of away.* In good marriages, spouses are adept at turning toward each other regularly. They see each other as friends. This friendship doesn't keep arguments from occurring, but it can prevent differences from overwhelming the relationship. In these good marriages, spouses respect each other and appreciate each other's points of view despite disagreements.

- *Letting your partner influence you.* Bad marriages often involve one spouse who is unwilling to share power with the other. Although power-mongering is more common in husbands, some wives also show this trait. A willingness to share power and to respect the other person's point of view is a prerequisite to compromising. In one study, researchers found that equality in decision making was one of the main factors that predicted positive marriage quality (Amato & others, 2007).

Unlike most approaches to helping couples, mine is based on knowing what makes marriages succeed rather than fail.

–JOHN GOTTMAN
Contemporary Psychologist, University of Washington

John Gottman has conducted extensive research on what makes marriages work.
Courtesy of The Gottman Institute, www.gottman.com

- *Overcoming gridlock.* One partner wants the other to attend church, but the other is an atheist. One partner is a homebody, but the other wants to go out and socialize a lot. Such problems often produce gridlock. Gottman stresses that the key to ending gridlock is not to solve the problem but to move from gridlock to dialogue and to be patient.
- *Creating shared meaning.* The easier it is for partners to speak candidly and respectfully with each other, the more likely it is that they will create shared meaning in their marriage. This also includes sharing goals with one's spouse and working together to achieve each other's goals.

What makes marriages work? What are the benefits of having a good marriage?
Image Source Pink/Alamy Stock Photo

In a provocative book titled *Marriage: A History*, Stephanie Coontz (2005) concluded that marriages in America today are fragile not because Americans have become self-centered and career-minded but because expectations for marriage have become unrealistically high compared with those of previous generations. However, she states that many marriages today are better than those of the past, citing the increase in marriages that are equitable, loving, intimate, and protective of children. To make a marriage work, she emphasizes (as does Gottman) that partners need to develop a deep friendship, show respect for each other, and embrace commitment.

Premarital Education   Premarital education occurs in a group and focuses on relationship advice. Might premarital education improve the quality of a marriage and possibly reduce the chances that the marriage will end in divorce? Researchers have found that it can (Hawkins, 2018; Markman, Halford, & Hawkins, 2019; Simpson, Leonhardt, & Hawkins, 2018). For example, a survey of more than 3,000 adults revealed that premarital education was linked to a higher level of marital satisfaction and commitment to a spouse, a lower level of destructive marital conflict, and a 31 percent lower likelihood of divorce (Stanley & others, 2006). The premarital education programs in the study ranged from several hours to 20 hours, with a median of 8 hours. It is recommended that premarital education begin approximately six months to a year before the wedding. One study revealed that participating in premarital education predicted a higher quality of marriage (Rhoades & Stanley, 2014).

Low-income couples are especially unlikely to engage in relationship interventions despite being at greater risk for relationship dissolution (Seccombe, 2018). One study of recently married low-income couples revealed that those who received premarital education were more likely to seek therapy to improve their relationship when the marriage became distressed than those who did not receive this education (Williamson & others, 2018).

A recent analysis and review examined research on contemporary trends that influence the next generation's ability to form and sustain a positive marriage (Clyde, Hawkins, & Willoughby, 2019). In light of these trends, the authors of the research review offered four proposals to improve the effectiveness of premarital education. Figure 4 describes these trends and proposals.

Marriage in Middle and Late Adulthood   What is marriage like for middle-aged adults? How does marriage change in late adulthood?

Middle Adulthood   Some marriages that were difficult and rocky during early adulthood improve during middle adulthood (Seccombe, 2018). Although the partners may have lived through a great deal of turmoil, they eventually discover a deep and solid foundation on which to anchor their relationship. In middle adulthood, the partners may have fewer financial worries, less housework and chores, and more time to spend with each other. Partners who engage in mutual activities usually view their marriage more positively. Also, one study found that middle-aged married individuals had a lower likelihood of work-related health limitations (Lo, Cheng, & Simpson, 2016). And another study of middle-aged adults revealed that positive marital quality was linked to better health for both spouses (Choi, Yorgason, & Johnson, 2016).

In midlife, most individuals who are married voice considerable satisfaction with being married. In one large-scale study of individuals in middle adulthood, 72 percent of those who were married said their marriage was either "excellent" or "very good" (Brim, 1999). Possibly by middle age, many of the worst marriages already have dissolved. Also, in a 13-year longitudinal study, married couples who were 40 to 50 years old and had been married for at least 15 years were periodically observed while they engaged in 15-minute unrehearsed conversations

Trend	Proposal
Individualism and Commitment Ambivalence	Premarital education needs to guide couples in transitioning from "me" to "we" and developing a strong commitment to their marriage.
Meaning of and Attitudes about Marriage	Premarital education should help individuals clarify for themselves and with their partner the meaning of marriage and their attitudes about it.
Premarital Relationship History and Experiences	Premarital education needs to focus on the complexities and challenges of marriage that many couples will experience as a result of considerable premarital experience, cohabitation, and premarital childbearing.
Effects of Media	Premarital education should help couples explore the effects of media use on marital attitudes and behavior.

FIGURE 4

TRENDS AND PROPOSALS FOR IMPROVING PREMARITAL EDUCATION IN THE NEXT GENERATION

Source: After Clyde, Hawkins, and Willoughby (2019).

about an area of disagreement in their marriage (Verstaen & others, 2019). For both husbands and wives, negative emotional behavior (primarily belligerence, defensiveness, fear/tension, and whining) decreased and positive emotional behavior (primarily humor, enthusiasm, and validation) increased with age.

Might relationship skills in emerging adulthood predict marital adjustment in middle age? A longitudinal study revealed that individuals with higher levels of emotional intimacy skills in their early twenties were more likely to have well-adjusted marriages in middle age than their counterparts with lower levels of intimacy skills in their twenties (Boden, Fischer, & Niehuis, 2010).

Late Adulthood In 2016, 57.8 percent of U.S. adults over 65 years of age were married (U.S. Census Bureau, 2017). Older men were far more likely to be married than older women. In 2016, 24 percent of U.S. adults over 65 years of age were widowed (U.S. Census Bureau, 2017). There were more than four times as many widows as widowers.

Individuals who are in a marriage or a partnership in late adulthood are usually happier, are less distressed, and live longer than those who are single (Blieszner, 2018; Roberto & Weaver, 2019). One study found that older adults were more satisfied with their marriages than were young and middle-aged adults (Bookwala & Jacobs, 2004). Indeed, the majority of older adults evaluate their marriages as happy or very happy (Huyck, 1995). In a study of octogenarians, marital satisfaction helped to protect their happiness from being affected by daily fluctuations in perceived health (Waldinger & Schulz, 2010). Also, a longitudinal study of adults 75 years of age and older revealed that individuals who were married were less likely to die during a seven-year time span (Rasulo, Christensen, & Tomassini, 2005). Another study found that older adult men reported higher marital satisfaction than did older adult women (Boerner & others, 2014).

In further research, compared with other sources of social support, spousal support was more strongly linked to an important biomarker of cellular aging, telomere length (Barger & Cribbet, 2016). For both married and cohabiting couples, negative relationship quality predicted a higher level of blood pressure when both members of the couple reported having negative relationship quality (Birditt, Newton, & others, 2016).

In late adulthood, married individuals are more likely to find themselves having to care for a sick partner with a limiting health condition (Blieszner & Ogletree, 2018; Choi, 2019). The stress of caring for a spouse who has a chronic disease can place demands on intimacy (Polenick & DePasquale, 2019).

Grow old along with me!
The best is yet to be,
The last of life,
For which the first was made.

—ROBERT BROWNING
English Poet, 19th Century

What are some adaptations that many married older adults need to make?
Purestock/SuperStock

DIVORCED ADULTS

During the mid-twentieth century divorce reached epidemic proportions in the United States. However, the divorce rate declined in recent decades, peaking at 5.1 divorces per 1,000 people in 1981 and then declining to 3.2 divorces per 1,000 people in 2016 (U.S. Census Bureau, 2017). The 2016 divorce rate of 3.2 compares with a marriage rate of 6.9 per 1,000 people in 2016.

Although the divorce rate has dropped, the United States still has one of the highest divorce rates in the world. In a recent comparison of 39 developed countries, Russia had the highest divorce rate by far (4.6 divorces per 1,000 people), Chile the lowest (0.2 divorces per 1,000 people) (OECD, 2016). In the United States, nearly half of first marriages will break up within 20 years (Copen, Daniels, & Mosher, 2013).

Individuals in some groups have a higher incidence of divorce than others do (Amato, 2010). Youthful marriage, low educational level, low income, not having a religious affiliation, having parents who are divorced, and having a baby before marriage are factors that are associated with increased rates of divorce (Hoelter, 2009). And characteristics of one's partner that increase the likelihood of divorce include alcoholism, psychological problems, domestic violence, infidelity, and inadequate division of household labor (Affleck, Carmichael, & Whitley, 2018; Hoelter, 2009).

Certain personality traits also have been found to predict divorce. In a study that focused on the Big Five personality factors, low levels of agreeableness and conscientiousness, as well as high levels of neuroticism and openness to experience, were linked to daily experiences that over time negatively impacted relationship quality and eventually led to a marital breakup (Solomon & Jackson, 2014).

Earlier, we indicated that researchers have not been able to pin down a specific age that is the best time to marry in order to reduce the likelihood of divorce. However, if a divorce is going to occur, it usually takes place early in a marriage; most occur in the fifth to tenth years of marriage (National Center for Health Statistics, 2000) (see Figure 5). For example, one study found that divorce peaked in Finland at approximately 5 to 7 years after a marriage, and then the rate of divorce gradually declined (Kulu, 2014). This timing may reflect an effort by partners in troubled marriages to stay in the marriage and try to work things out. If after several years these efforts have not improved the relationship, they may then seek a divorce.

What causes people to get divorced? A recent study in Great Britain found no differences in the causes of breakdowns in marriage and cohabitation (Gravningen & others, 2017). In this study, the following percentages cited these reasons: "grew apart" (men: 39 percent, women: 36 percent); "arguments" (men: 27 percent, women: 30 percent); "unfaithfulness/adultery" (men: 18 percent, women: 24 percent); "lack of respect, appreciation" (men: 17 percent, women: 25 percent); and "domestic violence" (men: 4 percent, women: 16 percent).

Even those adults who initiated their divorce go through challenges after a marriage dissolves (Tamers & others, 2014). Both divorced women and divorced men complain of loneliness, diminished self-esteem, anxiety about the unknowns in their lives, and difficulty forming satisfactory new intimate relationships.

The stress of separation and divorce places both men and women at risk for psychological and physical difficulties (Sbarra & Borelli, 2018). Separated and divorced women and men have higher rates of psychiatric disorders, admission to psychiatric hospitals, clinical depression, alcoholism, and psychosomatic problems such as sleep disorders than do married adults (Braver & Lamb, 2013; Breslau & others, 2011; Keyes, Hatzenbuehler, & Hasin, 2011). In a recent study, individuals who were divorced had a higher risk of alcohol use disorder (Kendler & others, 2017). In another recent study of life-course partnership history, remaining unpartnered (experiencing divorce, never being married, or never cohabiting) was linked to heavy drinking and smoking in middle-aged men and women (Keenan & others, 2017). Also, a research review concluded that both divorced men and women are more likely to commit suicide than their married counterparts (Yip & others, 2015). And in one study, both divorced men and women had a higher risk for heart attack than those who were married, but the risk for this cardiovascular disease was higher for divorced women than for divorced men (Dupre & others, 2015).

There are gender differences in the process and outcomes of divorce (Braver & Lamb, 2013). Women are more likely to sense that something is

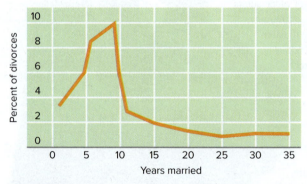

FIGURE 5

THE DIVORCE RATE IN RELATION TO NUMBER OF YEARS MARRIED. Shown here is the percentage of divorces as a function of how long couples have been married. Notice that most divorces occur in the early years of marriage, peaking in the fifth to tenth years of marriage.

wrong with the marriage and are more likely to seek a divorce than are men. Women also show better emotional adjustment and are more likely to perceive divorce as offering a "second chance" to increase their happiness, improve their social lives, and seek better work opportunities. However, divorce typically has a more negative economic impact on women that it does on men.

Coping with Divorce   Psychologically, one of the most common characteristics of divorced adults is difficulty trusting someone else in a romantic relationship. Following a divorce, though, people's lives can take diverse turns (Tashiro, Frazier, & Berman, 2006). Strategies to produce positive outcomes for divorced adults include the following (Hetherington & Kelly, 2002):

- Think of divorce as a chance to grow personally and to develop more positive relationships.
- Make decisions carefully. The consequences of your decisions regarding work, lovers, and children may last a lifetime.
- Focus more on the future than the past. Think about what is most important to help you go forward in your life, and then set some challenging goals and plan how to reach them.
- Use your strengths and resources to cope with difficulties.
- Don't expect to be successful and happy in everything you do. "The road to a more satisfying life is bumpy and will have many detours" (p. 109).
- Remember that "you are never trapped by one pathway. Most of those who were categorized as defeated immediately after divorce gradually moved on to a better life, but moving onward usually requires some effort" (p. 109).

What are some strategies for coping with divorce?
Image Source/Getty Images

Divorced Middle-Aged Adults   What trends characterize divorce in U.S. middle-aged adults? In a recent analysis that compared divorce rates for different age groups in 1990 to 2015, the divorce rate decreased for young adults but increased for middle-aged and older adults (Stepler, 2017):

25 to 39 years	40 to 49 years	50+ years
−21 percent	+14 percent	+109 percent

This recent increase in divorce among middle-aged adults has led to divorce in middle adulthood being labeled "gray divorce" when it occurs after 50 years of age (Crowley, 2019; Lin & others, 2018).

What accounts for this increase in divorce among middle-aged and older adults? One explanation is the changing view of women, who initiate approximately 60 percent of the divorces after 40 years of age. Compared with earlier decades, divorce has less stigma for women today and they are more likely to leave an unhappy marriage. Also compared with earlier decades, more women are employed and are less dependent on their husband's income. Another explanation involves the increase in remarriages, in which the divorce rate is 2½ times as high as it is for those in first marriages.

A survey by AARP (2004) of more than 1 million 40- to 79-year-olds who were divorced at least once in their forties, fifties, or sixties found that staying married because of their children was by far the main reason many people took so long to become divorced. Despite the worry and stress involved in going through the divorce process, three out of four of the divorcees said they had made the right decision to dissolve their marriage and reported a positive outlook on life. Sixty-six percent of the divorced women said they had initiated the divorce, compared with only 41 percent of the divorced men. The divorced women were much more afraid of having financial problems (44 percent) than the divorced men were (11 percent). Following are the main reasons these middle-aged and older adults cited for their divorce:

Main Causes of Divorce for Women

- Verbal, physical, or emotional abuse (23 percent)
- Alcohol or drug abuse (18 percent)
- Cheating (17 percent)

What are some characteristics of divorce in middle-aged adults?
Denkou Images/Alamy Stock Photo

Main Causes of Divorce for Men

· No obvious problems; just fell out of love (17 percent)
· Cheating (14 percent)
· Different values, lifestyles (14 percent)

In recent research on the antecedents of "gray divorce," factors traditionally associated with divorce in young adults also were reflected in the divorce of adults 50 years and older (Crowley, 2019; Lin & others, 2018). Divorce was more likely to occur for older adults when they had been married fewer years, their marriage was of lower quality (less marital satisfaction, for example), they did not own a home, and they had financial problems. Factors that were not linked to divorce in these older adults were the onset of an empty nest, the wife's or husband's retirement, and whether the wife or husband had a chronic health condition. Also, as with younger adults, middle-aged adults who are divorced have more physical and mental health problems than those who are married. In a recent Korean study of middle-aged adults, those who were divorced were more likely to smoke, binge drink, get inadequate sleep, and be more depressed than their married counterparts (Kim, Lee, & Park, 2018).

Divorce in Older Adults   An increasing number of older adults are divorced (Lin & others, 2018). In 1980, 3 percent of women 65 years and older were divorced, but that rate had increased to 13 percent by 2015. Similarly, in 1980 4 percent of men 65 and older were divorced, but that rate had increased to 11 percent by 2015 (U.S. Census Bureau, 2016). Many of these individuals were divorced or separated before they entered late adulthood.

There are social, financial, and physical consequences of divorce for older adults (Suitor, Gilligan, & Pillemer, 2016). Divorce can weaken kinship ties when it occurs in later life, especially in the case of older men. Divorced older women are less likely to have adequate financial resources than married older women and older adults who are divorced have more health problems than those who are not (Bennett, 2006). Further, a recent study of older adults in Great Britain (average age: 63) found that those were divorced were more likely to die earlier and have lower life satisfaction than their married counterparts (Bourassa, Ruiz, & Sbarra, 2019).

In further research, many of the same factors traditionally associated with divorce in younger adults were also likely to occur in older adults (Lin & others, 2018). The longer older adults had been married, the more likely they were to have better marital quality, own a home, and be wealthy, and the less likely they were to become divorced. Another recent study found that partnered older adults were more likely to receive relatively high Social Security benefits and less likely to live in poverty (Lin, Brown, & Hammersmith, 2017).

REMARRIED ADULTS

Data indicate that the remarriage rate in the United States has declined, going from 50 of every 1,000 divorced or widowed Americans in 1990 to 29 of every 1,000 in 2011 (U.S. Census Bureau, 2013). One reason for the decline is the dramatic increase in cohabitation in recent years. Men are more likely to get remarried than women; in 2013, the remarriage rate was almost twice as high for men as women (40 per 1,000 for men and 21 per 1,000 for women in that year) (Livingston, 2017). Thus, men are either more eager or more able to find new spouses than are women.

Adults who remarry usually do so rather quickly, with approximately 50 percent remarrying within three years after they initially divorce (Sweeney, 2009, 2010). Men remarry sooner than women. Men with higher incomes are more likely to remarry than their counterparts with lower incomes. Remarriage occurs sooner for partners who initiate a divorce (especially in the first several years after divorce and for older women) than for those who do not initiate it (Sweeney, 2009, 2010). And some remarried individuals are more adult-focused, responding more to the concerns of their partner, while others are more child-focused, responding more to the concerns of their children (Anderson & Greene, 2011).

Adjustment   Evidence on the benefits of remarriage is mixed. Remarried families are more likely to be unstable than first marriages, with divorce more likely to occur—especially in the first several years of the remarried family—than in first marriages (Waite, 2009). While approximately 50 percent of first marriages end in divorce within 20 years, that figure rises to 67 percent for second marriages and 73 percent for third marriages (Banschick & Tabatsky, 2011).

developmental **connection**

Widows

Women who are 65 years of age and older are far more likely to be widowed than to be divorced. Connect to "Death, Dying, and Grieving."

Adults who remarry have lower levels of mental health (higher rates of depression, for example) than adults in first marriages, but remarriage often improves the financial status of remarried adults, especially women (Waite, 2009). Researchers also have found that remarried adults' marital relationships tend to be more egalitarian and more likely to be characterized by shared decision making than first marriages (Waite, 2009).

Nonetheless, remarried adults often find it difficult to stay remarried. While the divorce rate in first marriages has declined, the divorce rate of remarriages continues to increase (DeLongis & Zwicker, 2017). Why? For one thing, many remarry not for love but for financial reasons, for help in rearing children, and to reduce loneliness. They also might carry into the stepfamily negative patterns that produced failure in an earlier marriage. Remarried couples also experience more stress in rearing children than parents in never-divorced families (Ganong & Coleman, 2018). And one study found that remarried adults had less frequent sex than those in their first marriage (Stroope, McFarland, & Uecker, 2015).

Among the strategies that can help remarried couples cope with the stress of living in a stepfamily are these (Visher & Visher, 1989):

- *Have realistic expectations.* Allow time for loving relationships to develop, and look at the complexity of the stepfamily as a challenge to overcome.
- *Develop new positive relationships within the family.* Create new traditions and ways of dealing with difficult circumstances. Allocation of time is especially important because so many people are involved. The remarried couple needs to allot some time for each person to spend alone.

Remarriage and Aging Rising divorce rates, increased longevity, and better health have led to an increase in remarriage by older adults (Papernow, 2018). What happens when an older adult wants to remarry or does remarry? Researchers have found that some older adults perceive negative social pressure about their decision to remarry. These negative sanctions range from raised eyebrows to rejection by adult children. However, the majority of adult children support the decision of their older adult parents to remarry. Researchers have found that remarried parents and stepparents provide less financial and emotional support to adult stepchildren than do parents in first marriages (Ganong & Coleman, 2018).

GAY AND LESBIAN ADULTS

Until recently, the legal context of marriage created barriers to breaking up that did not exist for same-sex partners. However, the legalization of same-sex marriage in all 50 states in 2015 extended this context to same-sex partners (Diamond, 2017; Holley, 2017). In many additional ways, researchers have found that gay and lesbian relationships are similar—in their satisfactions, loves, joys, and conflicts—to heterosexual relationships (Balsam, Rostosky, & Riggle, 2017). For example, like heterosexual couples, gay and lesbian couples need to find a balance of romantic love, affection, autonomy, and equality that is acceptable to both partners (Baker & Halford, 2019; Fingerhut & Peplau, 2013). And like heterosexual couples, many gay and lesbian couples are creating families that include children (Farr & Goldberg, 2018; Patterson, 2019; Sumontha, Farr, & Patterson, 2018).

Lesbian couples especially place a high priority on equality in their relationships. One study revealed that over the course of ten years of cohabitation, partners in gay and lesbian relationships showed a higher average level of relationship quality than heterosexual couples did (Kurdek, 2008). Also, another survey found that a greater percentage of same-sex, dual-earner couples than different-sex couples said they share laundry (44 versus 31 percent), household repairs (33 versus 15 percent), and routine (74 versus 38 percent) and sick (62 versus 32 percent) child care responsibilities (Matos, 2015).

There are a number of misconceptions about gay and lesbian couples (Farr, 2017; Simon & others, 2018). Contrary to stereotypes, one partner is masculine and the other feminine in only a small percentage of gay and lesbian couples. Only a small segment of the gay population has a large number of sexual partners, and this is uncommon among lesbians. Furthermore, researchers have found that gay and lesbian couples prefer long-term, committed relationships (Fingerhut & Peplau, 2013). About half of committed gay couples do have an open relationship that allows the possibility of sex (but not affectionate love) outside of the relationship. Lesbian couples usually do not have this type of relationship.

What are some characteristics of lesbian and gay relationships?
(Top): 2009 JupiterImages Corporation;
(bottom): Wavebreakmedia/Shutterstock

A special concern is the stigma, prejudice, and discrimination that lesbian, gay, and bisexual individuals experience because of widespread social devaluation of same-sex relationships (Holley, 2017; Stewart, Frost, & LeBlanc, 2019). However, one study indicated that many individuals in these relationships saw stigma as bringing them closer together and strengthening their relationship (Frost, 2011).

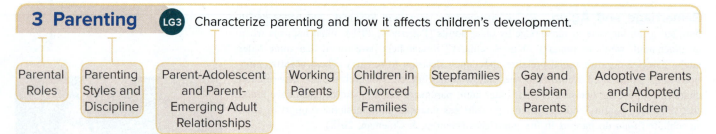

Review **Connect** Reflect

 LG2 Discuss the diversity of adult lifestyles and how they influence people's lives.

Review
- What characterizes single adults?
- What are the lives of cohabiting adults like?
- What are some key aspects of the lives of married adults?
- How does divorce affect adults?
- What are the lives of remarried adults like?
- What characterizes the lifestyles of gay and lesbian adults?

Connect
- What have you learned about the sexual attitudes and behaviors of lesbians and gays?

Reflect *Your Own Personal Journey of Life*
- Which type of lifestyle are you living today? What do you think are its advantages and disadvantages? If you could have a different lifestyle, which one would it be? Why?

3 Parenting   **LG3**   Characterize parenting and how it affects children's development.

Parental Roles	Parenting Styles and Discipline	Parent-Adolescent and Parent-Emerging Adult Relationships	Working Parents	Children in Divorced Families	Stepfamilies	Gay and Lesbian Parents	Adoptive Parents and Adopted Children

Just as there are diverse lifestyles that adults can adopt, so are there diverse styles of parenting and diverse types of parents. Before we examine these diverse styles and types, let's explore the roles of parents.

PARENTAL ROLES

Many adults plan when to become parents and consider how parenting will fit with their economic situation. For others, the discovery that they are about to become parents is a startling surprise. In either event, the prospective parents may have mixed emotions and romantic illusions about having a child (Carl, 2012). The needs and expectations of parents have stimulated many myths about parenting.

Some recent media accounts have portrayed many parents as unhappy, feeling little joy in caring for their children. However, researchers have found that parents are more satisfied with their lives than are nonparents, feel relatively better on a daily basis than do nonparents, and have more positive feelings related to caring for their children than from other daily activities (Nelson & others, 2013). Also, a research review concluded that parents are unhappy when they experience more negative emotions, financial problems, sleep problems, and troubled marriages (Nelson, Kushlev, & Lyubomirsky, 2014). In this review, it was concluded that parents are happy when they experience meaning in life, satisfaction of basic needs, more positive emotions than negative ones, and positive social roles.

Currently, there is a tendency for couples to have fewer children. The number of one-child families is increasing. Is there a best time to have children? What are some of the restrictions individuals face when they become parents? These are some of the questions we now consider.

Timing of Parenthood   Like the age when individuals first marry, the age at which individuals begin to have children has been increasing (Ryan & Padilla, 2019; Schwartz & Scott, 2018). Births occurred more frequently among women in their thirties than among women in their twenties in 2016 for the first time ever, although the average age overall was 27 (Centers for Disease Control and Prevention, 2017). Also, a national poll of 40- to 50-year-old U.S. women found that those with a master's degree or higher first became mothers at 30; in comparison, the average age of first-time mothers with a high school diploma was just 24 (Pew Research Center, 2015a).

As birth control has become common practice, many individuals consciously choose when they will have children and how many children they will rear. The number of one-child families is increasing, for example, and U.S. women overall are having fewer children or not having children at all. What are some of the advantages of having children early or late? Some of the advantages of having children early (in the twenties) are these: (1) the parents are likely to have more physical energy—for example, they can cope better with such matters as getting up in the middle of the night with infants and waiting up until adolescents come home at night; (2) the mother is likely to have fewer medical problems with pregnancy and childbirth; and (3) the parents may be less likely to build up expectations for their children, as do many couples who have waited many years to have children.

What characterizes the transition to parenting?
Chris Ryan/OJO Images/Getty Images

There are also advantages to having children later (in the thirties): (1) the parents have had more time to consider their goals in life, such as what they want from their family and career roles; (2) the parents are more mature and are able to benefit from their experiences to engage in more competent parenting; and (3) the parents are better established in their careers and have more income for child-rearing expenses.

The Transition to Parenting Whether people become parents through pregnancy, adoption, or stepparenting, they face disequilibrium and must adapt (Carlson & VanOrman, 2017; Perry-Jenkins & Schoppe-Sullivan, 2019; Ryan & Padilla, 2019). In a longitudinal investigation of couples from late pregnancy until 3½ years after the baby was born, most couples enjoyed more positive marital relations before the baby was born than after (Cowan & Cowan, 2000, 2009). Still, almost one-third showed an increase in marital satisfaction. Some couples said that the baby had both brought them closer together and moved them farther apart; being parents enhanced their sense of themselves and gave them a new, more stable identity as a couple. Babies opened men up to a concern with intimate relationships, and the demands of juggling work and family roles stimulated women to manage family tasks more efficiently and pay attention to their own personal growth. One study revealed that when new mothers had low marital satisfaction it often was linked to reductions in quality time spent with husbands and perceptions of unequal sharing of housework (Dew & Wilcox, 2011).

The Bringing Baby Home project is a workshop for new parents that helps couples strengthen their relationship, understand and become acquainted with their baby, resolve conflict, and develop parenting skills (Gottman, Gottman, & Shapiro, 2009). Evaluations of the project revealed that participants were better able to work together as parents, fathers were more involved with their baby and sensitive to the baby's behavior, mothers had a lower incidence of postpartum depression symptoms, and their babies showed better overall development than the babies of participants in a control group (Gottman, 2012; Shapiro & Gottman, 2005). More recent research involving the Bringing Home Baby Project found that fathers who participated in the program felt more appreciated by their wives and that mothers also were more satisfied with the division of labor when fathers were more involved in parenting (Shapiro, Gottman, & Fink, 2019).

Other studies have explored the transition to parenthood (Kuersten-Hogan, 2017; Olsavsky & others, 2019; Ryan & Padilla, 2019). One study indicated that women and less avoidantly attached new parents adapted to the introduction of child care tasks better than most men, especially men who were avoidantly attached (Fillo & others, 2015). In another study, mothers experienced unmet expectations in the transition to parenting, with fathers doing less than their partners had anticipated (Biehle & Mickelson, 2012). Also, in a study of dual-earner couples, a gender division of labor accompanied the transition to parenthood (Yavorksy, Dush, & Schoppe-Sullivan, 2015). In this study, a gender gap was not present prior to the transition to parenthood, but after a child was born, women did more than 2 hours of additional work per day, compared with an additional 40 minutes for men. And in another study, in comparison with married fathers, cohabiting fathers' personal dedication and relationship confidence decreased and their feelings of constraint increased across the transition to parenting (Kamp Dush & others, 2014).

Parents as Managers of Children's Lives Parents can play important roles as managers of children's opportunities, as monitors of their lives, and as social initiators and arrangers (Kelly, Becker, & Spirito, 2017; Soenens, Vansteenkiste, & Beyers, 2019).

Method	12 Months	24 Months
Spank with hand	14	45
Slap infant's hand	21	31
Yell in anger	36	81
Threaten	19	63
Withdraw privileges	18	52
Time-out	12	60
Reason	85	100
Divert attention	100	100
Negotiate	50	90
Ignore	64	90

FIGURE 6

PARENTS' METHODS FOR MANAGING AND CORRECTING INFANTS' UNDESIRABLE BEHAVIOR.
Shown here are the percentages of parents who had used various corrective methods by the time the infants were 12 and 24 months old.
Source: Based on data presented in Table 1 in Vittrup, Holden, & Buck (2006).

An important developmental task of childhood and adolescence is to learn how to make competent decisions in an increasingly independent manner. To help children and adolescents reach their full potential, an important parental role is to be an effective manager—one who finds information, makes contacts, helps structure choices, and provides guidance. Parents who fulfill this important managerial role help children and adolescents to avoid pitfalls and to work their way through the myriad choices and decisions they face.

Managing and Guiding Infants' Behavior In addition to sensitive parenting involving warmth and caring that can result in infants being securely attached to their parents, other important aspects of parenting infants involve managing and guiding their behavior in an attempt to reduce or eliminate undesirable behaviors (Holden, Vittrup, & Rosen, 2011). This management process includes (1) being proactive and childproofing the environment so infants won't encounter potentially dangerous objects or situations, and (2) engaging in corrective methods when infants engage in undesirable behaviors, such as excessive fussing and crying, throwing objects, and so on.

One study assessed discipline and corrective methods that parents had used by the time their infants were 12 and 24 months old (Vittrup, Holden, & Buck, 2006) (see Figure 6). Notice in Figure 6 that the main method parents used by the time infants were 12 months old was diverting the infants' attention, followed by reasoning, ignoring, and negotiating. Also note in Figure 6 that more than one-third of parents had yelled at their infant, about one-fifth had slapped the infant's hands or threatened the infant, and approximately one-sixth had spanked the infant by their first birthday.

As infants move into the second year of life and become more mobile and capable of exploring a wider range of environments, parental management of the toddler's behavior often includes increased corrective feedback and discipline (Holden, Vittrup, & Rosen, 2011). As indicated in Figure 6, in the study just described, yelling increased from 36 percent at 1 year of age to 81 percent by 2 years of age, slapping the infant's hands increased from 21 percent at 1 year to 31 percent by age 2, and spanking increased from 14 percent at age 1 to 45 percent by age 2 (Vittrup, Holden, & Buck, 2006).

A special concern is that such corrective discipline tactics not become abusive. Too often what starts out as mild to moderately intense discipline on the part of parents can move into highly intense anger. Later in this chapter, you will read more extensively about the use of punishment with children and child maltreatment.

Parents as Regulators of Children's Activities Parents can serve as regulators of opportunities for their children's activities (Collins & Madsen, 2019; Tilton-Weaver & others, 2013). From infancy through adolescence, mothers are more likely than fathers to have a managerial role in guiding and managing the activities in which children participate. In infancy, this might involve taking a child to a doctor and arranging for child care; in early childhood, it might involve a decision about which preschool the child should attend and contacting other parents who have young children whom their child can play with; in middle and late childhood, it might include directing the child to take a bath, to match their clothes and wear clean clothes, and to put away toys; in adolescence, it could involve participating in a parent-teacher conference and subsequently managing the adolescent's homework activity. Researchers have found that family-management practices are related to students' grades and self-responsibility (Lowe & Dotterer, 2013).

Parental Monitoring and Adolescents' Information Management A key aspect of the managerial role of parenting is effective monitoring, which is especially important as children move into the adolescent years (Bendezu & others, 2018; Clements-Nolle & others, 2019; Rusby & others, 2018). Monitoring includes supervising adolescents' choice of social settings, activities, and friends as well as their academic efforts. In a recent study of fifth- to eighth-graders, a higher level of parental monitoring was associated with students' earning higher grades (Top, Liew, & Luo, 2017).

In one study, low parental monitoring was a key factor in predicting a developmental trajectory of delinquency and substance use in adolescence (Wang & others, 2014). A recent study revealed that better parental monitoring was linked to lower marijuana use by adolescents (Haas & others, 2018), and in another recent study, lower parental monitoring was associated

Janis Keyser, Parent Educator

Janis Keyser is a parent educator who also teaches in the Department of Early Childhood Education at Cabrillo College in California. In addition to teaching college classes and conducting parenting workshops, she has coauthored a book with Laura Davis (Davis & Keyser, 1997) titled *Becoming the Parent You Want to Be: A Sourcebook of Strategies for the First Five Years.*

Keyser coauthors a nationally syndicated parenting column, "Growing Up, Growing Together." She is the mother of three, stepmother of five, grandmother of twelve, and great-grandmother of six.

Janis Keyser (*right*) conducts a parenting workshop.
Courtesy of Janis Keyser

with earlier initiation of alcohol use, binge drinking, and marijuana use in 13- to 14-year-olds (Rusby & others, 2018).

Recent research indicated that a higher level of general parental monitoring of adolescents' spending habits, friends, and whereabouts was linked to adolescents having healthier weight status, better dietary habits, more physical exercise, and less screen time (Kim & others, 2019). Further, research indicated that higher parental monitoring reduced negative peer influence on adolescents' risk taking (Wang & others, 2016). And a research meta-analysis revealed that a higher level of parental monitoring and rule enforcement were linked to later initiation of sexual intercourse and increased use of condoms by adolescents (Dittus & others, 2015). Further, a recent study revealed that two types of parental media monitoring (active monitoring and connective co-use (engaging in media with the intent to connect with adolescents) were linked to lower media use by adolescents (Padilla-Walker & others, 2018). Also, a recent study of young adolescents found that they got more sleep if their parents engaged in closer monitoring of their waking activities (Gunn & others, 2019).

What characterizes adolescents' management of their parents' access to information?
Ryan McVay/Getty Images

A current interest involving parental monitoring focuses on adolescents' management of their parents' access to information, especially disclosing or concealing details about their activities (Campione-Barr & Smetana, 2019; Hawk, 2017; Rote & Smetana, 2016, 2018). When parents engage in positive parenting practices, adolescents are more likely to disclose information. For example, disclosure increases when parents ask adolescents questions and when adolescents' relationship with parents is characterized by a high level of trust, acceptance, and quality (Smetana, Robinson, & Rote, 2015). Researchers have found that adolescents' disclosure to parents about their whereabouts, activities, and friends is linked to positive adolescent adjustment (Laird & Marrero, 2010). Also, recent research indicated that adolescents who engaged in problem behavior were more secretive and disclosed less information to parents (Darling & Tilton-Weaver, 2019).

To read about one individual who helps parents become more effective in managing their children's lives, see the *Connecting with Careers* profile.

PARENTING STYLES AND DISCIPLINE

A few years ago, there was considerable interest in Mozart CDs that were marketed with the promise that playing them would enrich infants' and young children's brains. Some of the parents who bought them probably thought, "I don't have enough time to spend with my children so I'll just play these CDs and then they won't need me as much." Similarly, one-minute bedtime stories have been marketed for parents to read to their children (Walsh, 2000). There are one-minute bedtime bear books, puppy books, and so on. Parents who buy them know it is a good idea to read to their children, but they don't want to spend a lot of time doing it. Behind the popularity of these products is an unfortunate theme that suggests that parenting can be done quickly, with little or no inconvenience (Sroufe, 2000).

What is wrong with these quick-fix parenting strategies? Good parenting takes time and effort (Lindsay, 2018; Thompson & Baumrind, 2019). You can't do it in a minute here and a minute there. You can't do it with CDs or DVDs.

One survey of American parents found that approximately half of fathers and one-fourth of mothers reported feeling that they were not spending enough time with their children (Pew Research Center, 2013). Nonetheless, in this survey, both mothers and fathers were spending more time with their children than the previous generation of parents did.

Of course, it's not just the quantity of time parents spend with children that is important for children's development—the quality of the parenting is clearly important (Grolnick, Caruso, & Levitt, 2019; Laible, Carlo, & Padilla-Walker, 2020). To further understand variations in parenting, let's consider the styles parents use when they interact with their children, how they discipline their children, and how they engage in coparenting.

Baumrind's Parenting Styles   Diana Baumrind (1971, 2012) argues that parents should be neither punitive nor aloof. Rather, they should develop rules for their children and be affectionate with them. She has described four types of parenting styles:

- **Authoritarian parenting** is a restrictive, punitive style in which parents exhort the child to follow their directions and respect their work and effort. The authoritarian parent places firm limits and controls on the child and allows little verbal exchange. For example, an authoritarian parent might say, "You will do it my way or else." Authoritarian parents also might spank the child frequently, enforce rules rigidly but not explain them, and show rage toward the child. Children of authoritarian parents are often unhappy, fearful, and anxious about comparing themselves with others, fail to initiate activity, and have weak communication skills. Sons of authoritarian parents may behave aggressively (Hart & others, 2003). Also, a national study of U.S. adolescents revealed that adolescents whose parents engaged in authoritarian parenting were more likely to have depressive symptoms than their counterparts who experienced authoritative parenting, the parenting style we discuss next (King, Vidourek & Merianos, 2016). Further, a recent study of young children found that an authoritarian parenting style, as well as pressuring the child to eat, were linked to increased risk for being overweight or obese in the children (Melis Yavuz & Selcuk, 2018). In addition, a recent study revealed that authoritarian parenting style was associated with being a bully perpetrator (Krisnana & others, 2019). And in another recent study, authoritarian parenting was associated with all types of child maltreatment (Lo & others, 2019).

- **Authoritative parenting** encourages children to be independent but still places limits and controls on their actions. Extensive verbal give-and-take is allowed, and parents are warm and nurturant toward the child. An authoritative parent might put his arm around the child in a comforting way and say, "You know you should not have done that. Let's talk about how you can handle the situation better next time." Authoritative parents show pleasure and support in response to children's constructive behavior. They also expect mature, independent, and age-appropriate behavior by children. Children whose parents are authoritative are often cheerful, self-controlled, self-reliant, and achievement-oriented; they tend to maintain friendly relations with peers, cooperate with adults, and cope well with stress. A recent study of Mexican American families revealed that authoritative parents were more likely to have adolescents who engaged in higher levels of prosocial behavior than parents using the other styles described here (Carlo & others, 2018). Also, in a recent research review, authoritative parenting was the most effective parenting style in predicting which children and adolescents would be less likely to be overweight or obese later in their development (Sokol, Qin, & Poti, 2017). Further, in a recent study, authoritative parenting was associated with a lower risk of all types of child maltreatment (Lo & others, 2019).

- **Neglectful parenting** is a style in which the parent is very uninvolved in the child's life. Children whose parents are neglectful develop the sense that other aspects of the parents' lives are more important than they are. These children tend to be socially incompetent. Many have poor self-control and don't handle independence well. They frequently

authoritarian parenting A restrictive, punitive style in which parents exhort the child to follow their directions and to respect their work and effort. Firm limits are placed on the child, and little verbal exchange is allowed.

authoritative parenting A style that encourages children to be independent but still places limits and controls on children's actions; extensive verbal give-and-take is allowed, and parents are warm and nurturant toward the child.

neglectful parenting A style in which the parent is very uninvolved in the child's life.

have low self-esteem, are immature, and may be alienated from their family. In adolescence, they may show patterns of truancy and delinquency.

· **Indulgent parenting** is a style in which parents are highly involved with their children but place few demands or controls on them. Such parents let their children do what they want. The result is that the children never learn to control their own behavior and always expect to get their way. Some parents deliberately rear their children in this way because they believe the combination of warm involvement and few restraints will produce a creative, confident child. However, children whose parents are indulgent rarely learn respect for others and tend to have difficulty controlling their behavior. They might be domineering, egocentric, and noncompliant, and have difficulties in peer relations.

These four classifications of parenting involve combinations of acceptance and responsiveness on the one hand and demand and control on the other (Maccoby & Martin, 1983). How these dimensions combine to produce authoritarian, authoritative, neglectful, and indulgent parenting is shown in Figure 7.

Parenting Styles in Context   Do the benefits of authoritative parenting transcend the boundaries of ethnicity, socioeconomic status, and household composition? Although some exceptions have been found, evidence linking authoritative parenting with competence on the part of the child occurs in research across a wide range of ethnic groups, social strata, cultures, and family structures (Garcia, Lopez-Fernandez, & Serra, 2019; Morris, Cui, & Steinberg, 2012).

Other research with ethnic groups suggests that some aspects of the authoritarian style may be associated with positive child outcomes. Elements of the authoritarian style may take on different meanings and have different effects depending on the context (Pinquart & Kauser, 2018). For example, Asian American parents often continue aspects of traditional Asian child-rearing practices that have sometimes been described as authoritarian. The parents exert considerable control over their children's lives. However, Ruth Chao (2005, 2007; Chao & Otsuki-Clutter, 2011; Chao & Tseng, 2002) argues that the style of parenting used by many Asian American parents is distinct from the domineering control of the authoritarian style. Instead, Chao argues that the control reflects concern and involvement in their children's lives and is best conceptualized as a type of training. The high academic achievement of Asian American children may be a consequence of their "training" parents (Stevenson & Zusho, 2002). In other research involving Chinese American adolescents and their parents, parental control was endorsed, as were the Confucian parental goals of perseverance, hard work in school, obedience, and sensitivity to parents' wishes (Russell, Crockett, & Chao, 2010).

Further Thoughts on Parenting Styles   Several caveats about parenting styles are in order. First, the parenting styles do not capture the important themes of reciprocal socialization and synchrony. Keep in mind that children socialize parents, just as parents socialize children (Cox & others, 2018; D'Angelo & others, 2019). Second, many parents use a combination of techniques rather than a single technique, although one technique may be dominant. Although consistent parenting is usually recommended, the wise parent may sense the importance of being more permissive in certain situations, more authoritarian in some circumstances, and more authoritative in others. Moreover, parenting styles often are talked about as if both parents have the same style, but this is not always the case. Also, some critics argue that the concept of parenting style is too broad and that more research needs to be conducted to "unpack" parenting styles by studying the influence of various components of the styles (Maccoby, 2007). For example, is parental monitoring more important than warmth in predicting child and adolescent outcomes? Further, much of the parenting style research has involved mothers, not fathers. In many families, mothers will use one style, fathers another style. Especially in traditional cultures, fathers often have an authoritarian style and mothers a more permissive, indulgent style. It has often been said that it is beneficial for parents to engage in similar parenting style; however, if fathers are authoritarian and aren't willing to change, children benefit when mothers use an authoritative style.

	Accepting, responsive	Rejecting, unresponsive
Demanding, controlling	Authoritative	Authoritarian
Undemanding, uncontrolling	Indulgent	Neglectful

FIGURE 7

CLASSIFICATION OF PARENTING STYLES. The four types of parenting styles (authoritative, authoritarian, indulgent, and neglectful) involve the dimensions of acceptance and responsiveness, on the one hand, and demand and control on the other. For example, authoritative parenting involves being both accepting/responsive and demanding/controlling.
Steve Debenport/Getty Images

According to Ruth Chao, what type of parenting style do many Asian American parents use?
Tanya Constantine/Getty Images

indulgent parenting A style in which parents are very involved with their children but place few demands or controls on them.

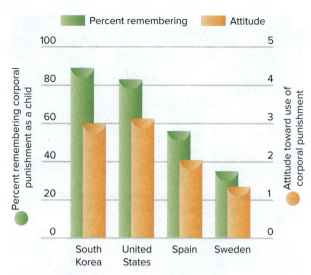

Percent remembering   Attitude

FIGURE 8

CORPORAL PUNISHMENT IN DIFFERENT COUNTRIES. A 5-point scale was used to assess attitudes toward corporal punishment, with scores closer to 1 indicating an attitude against its use and scores closer to 5 suggesting an attitude favoring its use. *Why are studies of corporal punishment correlational studies, and how does that affect their usefulness?*

Punishment   Use of corporal (physical) punishment is legal in every state in the United States. A national survey of U.S. parents with 3- and 4-year-old children found that 26 percent of parents reported spanking their children frequently, and 67 percent reported yelling at their children frequently (Regalado & others, 2004). A study of more than 11,000 U.S. parents indicated that 80 percent of the parents reported spanking their children by the time they reached kindergarten (Gershoff & others, 2012). Another recent research review concluded that there is widespread approval of corporal punishment by U.S. parents (Chiocca, 2017). A cross-cultural comparison found that individuals in the United States were among those with the most favorable attitudes toward corporal punishment and were most likely to remember it being used by their parents (see Figure 8) (Curran & others, 2001). Physical punishment is illegal in 41 countries, mainly to provide children with protection from abuse and exploitation (Committee on the Rights of the Child, 2014). Also, in a recent study, interviews with college students indicated that daughters were less likely than sons to be physically punished by both parents (Mehlhasen-Hassoen, 2019).

What are some reasons for avoiding spanking or similar punishments? They include the following:

- When adults punish a child by yelling, screaming, or spanking, they are presenting children with out-of-control models for handling stressful situations. Children may imitate this behavior.

- Punishment can instill fear, rage, or avoidance. For example, spanking the child may cause the child to avoid being near the parent and to fear the parent.

- Punishment tells children what not to do rather than what to do. Children should be given constructive feedback, such as "Why don't you try this?"

- Parents might unintentionally become so angry when they are punishing the child that they become abusive.

Most child psychologists recommend handling misbehavior by reasoning with the child, especially explaining the consequences of the child's actions for others. *Time out*, in which the child is removed from a setting that offers positive reinforcement, can also be effective. For example, when the child has misbehaved, a parent might forbid TV viewing for a specified time. Debate about the effects of punishment on children's development continues (Afifi & others, 2017a, b; Ferguson, 2013; Gershoff, Lee, & Durrant, 2017; Gershoff & others, 2018; Grusec & others, 2013; Holden & others, 2017; Lansford, 2019a, 2020). Several longitudinal studies also have found that physical punishment of young children is associated with higher levels of aggression later in childhood and adolescence (Berlin & others, 2009; Gershoff & others, 2012; Lansford & others, 2014; Taylor & others, 2010; Thompson & others, 2017). And in one longitudinal study, harsh physical punishment in childhood was linked to a higher incidence of intimate partner violence in adulthood (Afifi & others, 2017b).

However, a meta-analysis that focused on longitudinal studies revealed that the negative outcomes of punishment on children's internalizing and externalizing problems were minimal (Ferguson, 2013). Also, a research review of 26 studies concluded that only severe or predominant use of spanking, not mild spanking, compared unfavorably with alternative discipline practices (Larzelere & Kuhn, 2005). Nonetheless, in a research meta-analysis, physical punishment that was not abusive was still linked to detrimental child outcomes (Gershoff & Grogan-Kaylor, 2016).

In addition to considering whether physical punishment is mild or out-of-control, another factor in evaluating effects on children's development involves cultural contexts. Researchers have found that physical punishment has less harmful effects in countries where corporal punishment is considered normal, but in all countries studied, corporal punishment was linked to increased child aggression and anxiety (Lansford & others, 2005, 2012).

Thus, in the view of some experts, it is still difficult to determine whether the effects of physical punishment are harmful to children's development, although such a view might be distasteful to some individuals (Ferguson, 2013; Grusec & others, 2013). Also, as with other research on parenting, research on punishment is correlational in nature, making it difficult to discover causal factors. Also, consider the concept of reciprocal socialization discussed at the beginning of

How do most child psychologists recommend handling a child's misbehavior?
Zoey/Image Source/Alamy Stock Photo

Are Marital Conflict, Individual Hostility, and the Use of Physical Punishment Linked?

A longitudinal study assessed couples across the transition to parenting to investigate possible links between marital conflict, individual adult hostility, and the use of physical punishment with young children (Kanoy & others, 2003). Before the birth of the first child, the level of marital conflict was observed in a marital problem-solving discussion; answers to questionnaires regarding individual characteristics were also obtained. Thus, these characteristics of the couples were not influenced by characteristics of the child. When the children were 2 and 5 years old, the couples were interviewed about the frequency and intensity of their physical punishment of the children. At both ages, the parents' level of marital conflict was again observed in a marital problem-solving discussion.

The researchers found that both hostility and marital conflict were linked with the use of physical punishment. Individuals with high rates of hostility on the prenatal measures used more frequent and more severe physical punishment with their children. The same was evident for marital conflict—when marital conflict was high, both mothers and fathers were more likely to use physical punishment in disciplining their young children.

If parents who have a greater likelihood of using physical punishment can be identified in prenatal classes, these families could be encouraged to use other forms of discipline before they develop a pattern of physically punishing their children. How might counselors help prevent this pattern from developing? How do most child psychologists recommend handling a child's misbehavior?

---

this chapter, which emphasizes bidirectional child and parent influences (Lansford & others, 2018). Researchers have found links between children's early behavioral problems and parents' greater use of physical punishment over time (Laible, Thompson, & Froimson, 2015; Sheehan & Watson, 2008). Nonetheless, a large majority of leading experts on parenting conclude that physical punishment has harmful effects on children and should not be used (Afifi & others, 2017a, b; Gershoff, Lee, & Durrant, 2017; Gershoff & others, 2018; Holden & others, 2017).

In a research review, Elizabeth Gershoff (2013) concluded that the defenders of spanking have not produced any evidence that spanking produces positive outcomes for children, while negative outcomes of spanking have been replicated in many studies. Also, it is clear that when physical punishment involves abuse, it can be very harmful to children's development, as discussed later in this chapter (Almy & Cicchetti, 2018; Cicchetti, 2018).

Considering the family as a system (as discussed earlier in this chapter), what connections might be found between marital relationships and parenting practices? To read about a family systems study involving marital conflict and the use of physical punishment, see the *Connecting with Research* interlude.

Coparenting The relationship between marital conflict and the use of punishment highlights the importance of **coparenting,** which is the support that parents provide one another in jointly raising a child. Poor coordination between parents, undermining of the other parent, lack of cooperation and warmth, and disconnection by one parent are conditions that place children at risk for problems (Bertoni & others, 2018; Le & others, 2019; McHale, Negrini, & Sirotkin, 2019; McHale & Sirotkin, 2019). For example, one study revealed that coparenting influenced young children's effortful control above and beyond maternal and paternal parenting by themselves (Karreman & others, 2008). Another study found that greater father involvement in young children's play was linked to an increase in supportive coparenting (Jia & Schoppe-Sullivan, 2011). And a more recent study found that parents' joint involvement predicted that adolescents would engage in fewer risky behaviors (Riina & McHale, 2014). In this study, there was a bidirectional influence: adolescents' engagement in a lower level of risk behaviors predicted higher levels of joint parental involvement. Further, a recent study revealed that coparenting involving couple supportiveness, especially when their children were 3 to 5 years of age, was linked to reduced levels of externalizing problems 8 to 10 years later (Parkes, Green, & Mitchell, 2019). Also, in another study, unmarried African American parents who were instructed in coparenting techniques during the prenatal period and also one month after the baby was born showed improvements in rapport, communication, and problem-solving skills when the baby was 3 months old (McHale, Salman-Engin, & Coovert, 2015).

What characterizes coparenting?
Hero/Corbis/Glow Images

coparenting The support that parents provide one another in jointly raising a child.

Darla Botkin, Marriage and Family Therapist

Darla Botkin is a marriage and family therapist who teaches, conducts research, and engages in marriage and family therapy. She is on the faculty of the University of Kentucky. Botkin obtained a bachelor's degree in elementary education with a concentration in special education and went on to receive a master's degree in early childhood education. She spent the next six years working with children and their families in a variety of settings, including child care, elementary school, and Head Start. These experiences led Botkin to recognize the interdependence of the developmental settings that children and their parents experience (such as home, school, and work). She returned to graduate school and obtained a Ph.D. in family studies from the University of Tennessee. She then became a faculty member in the Family Studies program at the University of Kentucky. Completing further coursework and clinical training in marriage and family therapy, she became certified as a marriage and family therapist.

Botkin's current interests include working with young children in family therapy, understanding gender and ethnic issues in family therapy, and exploring the role of spirituality in family wellness.

Darla Botkin (*left*) conducts a family therapy session.
Courtesy of Dr. Darla Botkin

For more information about what marriage and family therapists do, see the Careers in Life-Span Development appendix.

Eight-year-old Donnique Hein lovingly holds her younger sister, 6-month-old Maria Paschel, after a meal at Laura's Home, a crisis shelter run by the City Mission in Cleveland, Ohio.
Joshua Gunter/The Plain Dealer/Landov Images

child abuse The term used most often by the public and many professionals to refer to both abuse and neglect.

child maltreatment The term increasingly used by developmentalists in referring not only to abuse and neglect but also to diverse conditions.

physical abuse Infliction of physical injury by punching, beating, kicking, biting, burning, shaking, or otherwise harming a child.

Parents who do not spend enough time with their children or who have problems in child rearing can benefit from counseling and therapy. To read about the work of marriage and family therapist Darla Botkin, see the *Connecting with Careers* profile.

Child Maltreatment   Unfortunately, punishment sometimes leads to the abuse of infants and children (Doyle & Cicchetti, 2018; Sturge-Apple & others, 2019). In 2017, approximately 674,000 U.S. children were found to be victims of child abuse at least once during that year (U.S. Department of Health and Human Services, 2017). In 2017, 1,720 U.S. children died of child maltreatment. Ninety-one percent of abused children were harmed by one or both parents. Laws in many states now require physicians and teachers to report suspected cases of child abuse, yet many cases go unreported, especially those involving battered infants.

Whereas the public and many professionals use the term **child abuse** to refer to both abuse and neglect, developmentalists increasingly use the term **child maltreatment** (Almy & Cicchetti, 2018; Whitaker & Rogers-Brown, 2019). This term does not have quite the emotional impact of the term *abuse* and acknowledges that maltreatment includes diverse conditions.

Types of Child Maltreatment   The four main types of child maltreatment are physical abuse, child neglect, sexual abuse, and emotional abuse (National Clearinghouse on Child Abuse and Neglect, 2019):

- **Physical abuse** is characterized by the infliction of physical injury as a result of punching, beating, kicking, biting, burning, shaking, or otherwise harming a child. The parent or other person may not have intended to hurt the child; the injury may have resulted from excessive physical punishment (Lakhdir & others, 2019; Smith & others, 2018). In 2017, 18.3 percent of maltreated children were physically abused (U.S. Department of Health and Human Services, 2017).

- **Child neglect** is characterized by failure to provide for the child's basic needs (Clemens & others, 2018). Child neglect is extensive—in 2017, 74.9 percent of maltreated children were neglected (U.S. Department of Health and Human Services, 2017). Neglect can be physical (abandonment, for example), educational (allowing chronic truancy, for example), or emotional (marked inattention to the child's needs, for example) (Read & others, 2018). Child neglect is by far the most common form of child maltreatment. In every country where relevant data have been collected, neglect occurs up to three times as often as abuse. A recent research review of risk factors for engaging in child neglect found that most risks involved parent factors, including a history of antisocial behavior/criminal offending, having mental/physical problems, and experiencing abuse in their own childhood (Mulder & others, 2018).

- **Sexual abuse** includes fondling a child's genitals, intercourse, incest, rape, sodomy, exhibitionism, and commercial exploitation through prostitution or the production of pornographic materials (Ingrassia, 2018; Knack & others, 2019). Unlike physical abuse, many cases of sexual abuse produce no outward physical signs that abuse has taken place. In 2017, 8.6 percent of maltreated children in the United States were sexually abused (U.S. Department of Health and Human Services, 2017).

- **Emotional abuse** (psychological/verbal abuse/mental injury) includes acts or omissions by parents or other caregivers that have caused, or could cause, serious behavioral, cognitive, or emotional problems (Ross, Kaminski, & Herrington, 2019; Zeanah & Humphreys, 2018).

Although any of these forms of child maltreatment may be found separately, they often occur in combination. Emotional abuse is almost always present when other forms are identified.

The Context of Abuse

No single factor causes child maltreatment (Cicchetti, 2018). A combination of factors, including the culture, neighborhood, family, and development, likely contribute to child maltreatment.

The extensive violence that takes place in American culture is reflected in the occurrence of violence in the family (Leppakoski, Flinck, & Paavilainen, 2015). A regular diet of violence appears on television screens, and parents often resort to power assertion as a disciplinary technique. In China, where physical punishment is rarely used to discipline children, the incidence of child abuse is reportedly very low.

The family itself is obviously a key part of the context of abuse (McCarroll & others, 2017; Whitaker & Rogers-Brown, 2019). Among the family and family-associated characteristics that may contribute to child maltreatment are parenting stress, substance abuse, social isolation, single parenting, and socioeconomic difficulties (especially poverty) (Doyle & Cicchetti, 2018). The interactions of all family members should be considered, regardless of who performs the violent acts against the child. For example, even though the father may be the one who physically abuses the child, contributions by the mother, the child, and siblings also should be evaluated.

Were parents who abuse children abused by their own parents? A 30-year longitudinal study found that offspring of parents who had engaged in child maltreatment and neglect are at risk for engaging in child neglect and sexual maltreatment themselves (Widom, Czaja, & DuMont, 2015). It is estimated that about one-third of parents who were abused when they were young abuse their own children (Cicchetti & Toth, 2016). Thus, some, but not a majority, of parents who were maltreated in childhood are locked into an intergenerational transmission of child maltreatment.

Developmental Consequences of Abuse

Among the consequences of child maltreatment are poor emotion regulation, attachment problems, problems in peer relations, difficulty in adapting to school, and other psychological problems such as depression, delinquency, and substance abuse during childhood and adolescence (Bell & others, 2018; Cicchetti & Handley, 2019; DePasquale, Handley, & Cicchetti, 2019). For example, a recent study also found that physical abuse was linked to lower levels of cognitive development and school engagement in children (Font & Cage, 2018). As shown in Figure 9, maltreated young children in foster care were more likely to show abnormal stress hormone levels than middle-SES young children living with their birth family (Gunnar & Fisher, 2006). In this study, the abnormal stress hormone levels were mainly present in the foster children who experienced neglect, best described as "institutional neglect" (Fisher, 2005). Adolescents who experienced abuse or neglect as children are more likely than adolescents who were not maltreated as children to engage in violent

child neglect Failure to provide for a child's basic needs, including physical, educational, or emotional needs.

sexual abuse Fondling a child's genitals, intercourse, incest, rape, sodomy, exhibitionism, and commercial exploitation through prostitution or the production of pornographic materials.

emotional abuse Acts or omissions by parents or other caregivers that have caused, or could cause, serious behavioral, cognitive, or emotional problems.

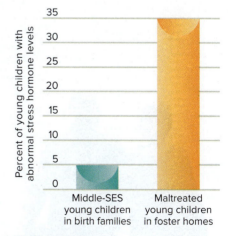

FIGURE 9

ABNORMAL STRESS HORMONE LEVELS IN YOUNG CHILDREN IN DIFFERENT TYPES OF REARING CONDITIONS

romantic relationships, suicide attempts, delinquency, sexual risk taking, and substance abuse (Miller & others, 2013). For example, a recent study found that experiencing maltreatment or parental divorce in childhood was linked to midlife suicidal ideation (Stansfield & others, 2017).

Later, during the adult years, individuals who were maltreated as children are more likely to experience physical, emotional, and sexual problems (Brown & others, 2018; Gekker & others, 2019). As adults, maltreated children are also at higher risk for violent behavior toward other adults—especially dating partners and marital partners—as well as for substance abuse, anxiety, and depression (Miller-Perrin, Perrin, & Kocur, 2009). Also, in a longitudinal study, experiencing early abuse and neglect in the first five years of life were linked to having more interpersonal problems and lower academic achievement from childhood through their thirties (Raby & others, 2019). Further, a 30-year longitudinal study found that middle-aged adults who had experienced child maltreatment had increased risk for diabetes, lung disease, malnutrition, and vision problems (Widom & others, 2012). And adults who were maltreated as children often have difficulty establishing and maintaining healthy intimate relationships (Dozier, Stovall-McClough, & Albus, 2009). An important research agenda is to discover how to prevent child maltreatment or intervene in children's lives when they have been maltreated (Almy & Cicchetti, 2018). In one study of maltreating mothers and their 1-year-olds, two treatments were effective in reducing child maltreatment: (1) home visitation that emphasized improved parenting, coping with stress, and increased support for the mother; and (2) parent-infant psychotherapy that focused on improving maternal-infant attachment (Cicchetti, Toth, & Rogosch, 2005).

PARENT–ADOLESCENT AND PARENT–EMERGING ADULT RELATIONSHIPS

Even the best parents may find their relationship with their child strained during adolescence, yet attachment to parents is an important aspect of adolescent development. As individuals become emerging adults, their relationship with their parents changes. Earlier in the chapter, we discussed the important strategy of parental monitoring in adolescence. Here we explore other aspects of parent-adolescent relationships.

Parent-Adolescent Relationships   Important aspects of parent-adolescent relationships include autonomy/attachment and conflict (Soenens, Vansteenkiste, & Beyers, 2019). First, we explore the young adolescent's push for autonomy.

Autonomy and Attachment   The young adolescent's push for autonomy and responsibility puzzles and angers many parents. Parents see their teenager slipping from their grasp. They may have an urge to assert stronger control as the adolescent seeks autonomy and responsibility. Heated emotional exchanges may ensue, with either side calling names, making threats, and doing whatever seems necessary to gain control. Most parents anticipate that their teenager will have some difficulty adjusting to the changes that adolescence brings, but few parents can imagine and predict just how strong will be an adolescent's desire to spend time with peers or how much adolescents will want to show that it is they—not their parents—who are responsible for their successes and failures.

The ability to attain autonomy and gain control over one's behavior in adolescence is acquired through appropriate adult reactions to the adolescent's desire for control (Li & Hein, 2019; McElhaney & Allen, 2012). At the onset of adolescence, the average individual does not have the knowledge to make mature decisions in all areas of life. As the adolescent pushes for autonomy, the wise adult relinquishes control in those areas in which the adolescent can make reasonable decisions but continues to guide the adolescent to make reasonable decisions in areas where the adolescent's knowledge is more limited. Gradually, adolescents acquire the ability to make mature decisions on their own. In one study, young adolescents' perception that their parents promoted more psychological autonomy and less psychological control predicted fewer depressive symptoms two years later (Sher-Censor, Parke, & Coltrane, 2010). A recent study also found that from 16 to 20 years of age, adolescents perceived that they had increasing independence and improved relationships with their parents (Hadiwijaya & others, 2017).

Expectations about the appropriate timing of adolescent autonomy often vary across cultures, parents, and adolescents (McElhaney & Allen, 2012). For example, expectations for early autonomy on the part of adolescents are more prevalent in non-Latino Whites, single parents, and adolescents themselves than they are in Asian Americans or Latinos, married parents, and

What strategies can parents use to guide adolescents in effectively handling their increased motivation for autonomy?
Hero Images/Getty Images

parents themselves (Feldman & Rosenthal, 1999). Nonetheless, although Latino cultures may place a stronger emphasis on parental authority and restrict adolescent autonomy, one study revealed that regardless of where they were born, Mexican-origin adolescent girls living in the United States expected autonomy at an earlier age than their mothers preferred (Bamaca-Colbert & others, 2012). Another study of Mexican immigrant mothers and their U.S.-raised 13- to 14-year-old daughters explored future autonomy expectations when the daughters reach 15 years of age (Romo, Mireles-Rios, & Lopez-Tello, 2014). In this study, the daughters hoped for less strict rules regarding social activities while mothers reported that they still expected to exert control, although they were willing to allow more autonomy in personal matters such as physical appearance and to allow the daughter to group date.

Gender differences characterize autonomy-granting in adolescence, with boys being given more independence than girls are allowed to have. In one study, this was especially true in those U.S. families with a traditional gender-role orientation (Bumpus, Crouter, & McHale, 2001). Even while adolescents seek autonomy, parent-child attachment remains important (Gorrese & Ruggieri, 2012). Mothers maintain closer emotional ties with adolescents, especially daughters, than fathers do (Collins & Steinberg, 2006).

One of the most widely discussed aspects of socioemotional development in infancy is secure attachment to caregivers (Woodhouse & others, 2019). In the past several decades, researchers have explored whether secure attachment also might be an important element in adolescents' relationships with their parents (Arriaga & others, 2018; Hocking & others, 2018). A recent study revealed that many adolescents have a fairly stable attachment style but that attachment stability increases in adulthood (Jones & others, 2018). Adults often have more stable social environments than adolescents and have had more time to consolidate their attachment style. This study also indicated that family conflict and parental separation/divorce were likely candidates to undermine attachment stability.

In other research, Joseph Allen and his colleagues (2009) found that adolescents who were securely attached at age 14 were more likely to report at age 21 that they were in an exclusive relationship, comfortable with intimacy in relationships, and moving toward financial independence. In addition, a recent study revealed that when they had grown up in poverty, adolescents engaged in less risk-taking when they had a history of secure attachments to care-givers (Delker, Bernstein, & Laurent, 2018). Also, in another recent study, more secure attachment to the mother and to the father was associated with fewer depressive symptoms in adolescents (Kerstis, Aslund, & Sonnby, 2018). Further, in a recent study of Latino families, a higher level of secure attachment with mothers was associated with less heavy drug use by adolescents (Gattamorta & others, 2017). And a research analysis concluded that the most consistent outcomes of secure attachment in adolescence involve positive peer relations and development of the adolescent's capacity for emotion regulation (Allen & Miga, 2010).

Parent-Adolescent Conflict   Although attachment to parents may remain strong during adolescence, the connectedness is not always smooth. Early adolescence is a time when conflict with parents escalates (Martin & others, 2019; Moed & others, 2015). Much of the conflict involves the everyday issues of family life, such as keeping a bedroom clean, dressing neatly, getting home by a certain time, and not talking incessantly on the phone. The conflicts rarely involve major dilemmas such as drugs and delinquency.

The increased conflict in early adolescence may be due to a number of factors: the biological changes of puberty, cognitive changes involving increased idealism and logical reasoning, social changes focused on independence and identity, maturational changes in parents, and expectations that are violated by parents and adolescents (Collins & Steinberg, 2006). Adolescents compare their parents with an ideal standard and then criticize their flaws. Many parents see their adolescent changing from a compliant child to someone who is noncompliant, oppositional, and resistant to paren-tal standards. Also, early-maturing adolescents experience more conflict with their parents than do adolescents who mature late or on time (Collins & Steinberg, 2006).

Conflict with parents increases in early adolescence. *What is the nature of this conflict in a majority of American families?*
Wavebreak Media/age fotostock

It is not unusual to hear parents of young adolescents ask, "Is it ever going to get better?" Things usually do get better as adolescents move from early to late adolescence. Conflict with parents often escalates during early adolescence, remains somewhat stable during the high school years, and then lessens as the adolescent reaches 17 to 20 years of age. For example, in a recent study of Chinese American families, parent-adolescent conflict increased in early

Old Model		New Model
Autonomy, detachment from parents; parent and peer worlds are isolated Intense, stressful conflict throughout adolescence; parent-adolescent relationships are filled with storm and stress on virtually a daily basis		Attachment and autonomy; parents are important support systems and attachment figures; adolescent-parent and adolescent-peer worlds have some important connections Moderate parent-adolescent conflict is common and can serve a positive developmental function; conflict greater in early adolescence

FIGURE 10

OLD AND NEW MODELS OF PARENT-ADOLESCENT RELATIONSHIPS

Martin Barraud/Caia Image/Glow Images

adolescence, peaked at about 16 years of age, and then decreased through late adolescence and emerging adulthood (Juang & others, 2018). Also, parent-adolescent relationships become more positive if adolescents go away to college than if they live at home while attending college (Sullivan & Sullivan, 1980).

The everyday conflicts that characterize parent-adolescent relationships may serve a positive function. These minor disputes and negotiations facilitate the adolescent's transition from being dependent on parents to becoming an autonomous individual. For example, in one study, adolescents who expressed disagreement with their parents explored identity development more actively than did adolescents who did not express disagreement with their parents (Cooper & others, 1982). One way for parents to cope with the adolescent's push for independence and identity is to recognize that adolescence is a decade-long transitional period in the journey to adulthood, rather than an overnight accomplishment. Recognizing that conflict and negotiation can serve a positive developmental function can further tone down parental hostility. Understanding parent-adolescent conflict, though, is not easy (Riesch & others, 2003). A high degree of intense conflict characterizes some parent-adolescent relationships and if prolonged is associated with a number of adolescent problems, such as running away from home, juvenile delinquency, dropping out of school, adolescent pregnancy, and substance abuse (Skinner & McHale, 2016). For example, one study found that a higher level of parent-adolescent conflict was associated with higher levels of adolescent anxiety, depression, and aggression, and lower levels of self-esteem (Smokowski & others, 2016). And in another recent study of Latino families, parent-adolescent conflict was linked to adolescents' higher level of aggressive behavior (Smokowski & others, 2017).

In sum, the old model of parent-adolescent relationships suggested that parent-adolescent conflict is intense and stressful throughout adolescence. The new model emphasizes that most parent-adolescent conflict is moderate rather than intense and that the moderate conflict can serve a positive function. Figure 10 summarizes the old and new models of parent-adolescent relationships, which include changes in thinking about attachment and autonomy.

Still, a high degree of conflict characterizes some parent-adolescent relationships. According to one estimate, parents and adolescents engage in prolonged, intense, repeated, unhealthy conflict in about one in five families (Montemayor, 1982). In other words, 4 to 5 million American families encounter serious, highly stressful parent-adolescent conflict. And this prolonged, intense conflict is associated with a number of adolescent problems—movement out of the home, juvenile delinquency, school dropout, pregnancy and early marriage, membership in religious cults, and drug abuse (Delgado & others, 2019).

When families emigrate to another country, adolescents typically acculturate more quickly to the norms and values of their new country than do their parents (Nair & others, 2018; Nguyen & others, 2018). This likely occurs because of immigrant adolescents' exposure in school to the language and culture of the host country. The norms and values immigrant adolescents experience are especially likely to diverge from those of their parents in areas such as autonomy and romantic relationships. Such divergences are likely to increase parent-adolescent conflict in immigrant families. Andrew Fuligni (2012) argues that these conflicts aren't always expressed openly but are often present in underlying, internal feelings. For example, immigrant adolescents may feel that their parents want them to give up their personal interests for the sake of the family, and the adolescents think this is unfair. Such acculturation-based conflict focuses on issues related to core cultural values and is likely to occur in immigrant families, such as Latino and

Asian American families, who come to the United States to live (Juang & Umana-Taylor, 2012). In a study of Chinese American families, parent-adolescent conflict was linked to a sense of alienation between parents and adolescents, which in turn was related to more depressive symptoms, delinquent behavior, and lower academic achievement (Hou, Kim, & Wang, 2016).

Conclusions   We have seen that parents play very important roles in adolescent development. Although adolescents are moving toward independence, they still need to stay connected with families. Competent adolescent development is most likely when adolescents have parents who show them warmth and mutual respect, demonstrate sustained interest in their lives, recognize and adapt to their cognitive and socioemotional development, communicate expectations for high standards of conduct and achievement, and display constructive ways of dealing with problems and conflict (Small, 1990). These ideas coincide with Diana Baumrind's (1971, 1991, 2012) authoritative parenting style.

Emerging Adults' Relationships with Their Parents   For the most part, emerging adults' relationships with their parents improve when they leave home. They often grow closer psychologically to their parents and share more with them than they did before they left home (Arnett, 2007, 2015a, b; Padilla-Walker, Memmott-Elison, & Nelson, 2017; Padilla-Walker & Nelson, 2019). However, challenges in the parent–emerging adult relationship involve the emerging adult's possessing adult status in many areas while still depending on parents in some manner (Fingerman, Cheng, & others, 2012). Many emerging adults can make their own decisions about where to live, whether to stay in college, which lifestyle to adopt, whether to get married, and so on (Padilla-Walker & Nelson, 2017). At the same time, parents often provide support for their emerging adult children even after they leave home. This might be accomplished through loans and monetary gifts for education or purchase of a car, financial contributions to living arrangements, and emotional support.

In successful emerging adulthood, individuals separate from their parents without cutting off ties completely or fleeing to some substitute emotional refuge. Complete cutoff from parents rarely solves emotional problems. Emerging adulthood is a time for young people to sort out emotionally what they will take along from the family of origin, what they will leave behind, and what they will create.

The vast majority of studies of parenting have focused on outcomes for children and adolescents and have involved mothers rather than fathers. One study revealed that parents act as "scaffolding" and "safety nets" to support their children's successful transition through emerging adulthood (Swartz & others, 2011). Also, in a recent study, evidence for the continued importance of parenting was found in the fourth year of college as low parental permissiveness was associated with reduced rates of risky drinking even as their offspring turned 21 (Mallett & others, 2019).

Are parents in some countries more involved with college students than are parents in other countries? A recent cross-cultural study found that college students across four countries (the United States, Germany, Hong Kong, and Korea) experienced frequent contact with and support from their parents (Fingerman & others, 2016). In this study, Asian students were given more frequent support than U.S. or German students but were less satisfied with the support.

Now that we have explored many aspects of parenting at different points in development—childhood, adolescence, and emerging adulthood—we turn our attention to parent-child relationships in different types of families—working parents, children in divorced families, stepfamilies, gay and lesbian parents, and adoptive parents and adopted children.

According to one adolescent girl, Stacey Christensen, age 16: "I am lucky enough to have open communication with my parents. Whenever I am in need or just need to talk, my parents are there for me. My advice to parents is to let your teens grow at their own pace, be open with them so that you can be there for them. We need guidance; our parents need to help but not be too overwhelming."
Stockbyte/Getty Images

What are some strategies that can benefit the relationship between emerging adults and their parents?
Comstock Images/Getty Images

WORKING PARENTS

More than one of every two U.S. mothers with a child under the age of 5 is in the labor force; more than two of every three with a child from 6 to 17 years of age work outside the home. Maternal employment is a part of modern life, but its effects continue to be debated.

In a recent national survey, working mothers (60 percent) were more likely than fathers (52 percent) to report that balancing work and family is difficult (Livingston & Bialik, 2018). Also in this survey, slightly more than half (54 percent) indicate that mothers do more than fathers when children's schedules and activities are involved. In another recent national survey, nearly one-fourth (24 percent) of working parents said that their children have asked them to work less, and a similar percentage (23 percent) report that work is negatively impacting their relationship with their children (Career Builder, 2018).

How does work affect parenting?
imagewerks/Getty Images

Most research on parental work has focused on young children and the mother's employment (Han, Hetzner, & Brooks-Gunn, 2019). However, the effects of parental work involve the father as well as the mother when matters such as work schedules, work-family stress, and unemployment are considered (O'Brien & others, 2014). Research indicates that the nature of parents' work matters more to children than whether one parent works outside the home (Clarke-Stewart & Parke, 2014). And one study of almost 3,000 adolescents found a negative association between the father's, but not the mother's, unemployment and the adolescents' health (Bacikova-Sleskova, Benka, & Orosova, 2014). Also, a study of dual-earner couples found that work-family enrichment experiences had positive outcomes on parenting quality, which in turn was linked to positive child outcomes; by contrast, work-family conflict experiences were associated with poorer parenting quality, which in turn was related to negative child outcomes (Vieria & others, 2016). And a recent study found that mothers' and fathers' work-family conflict was linked to lower self-control in 4-year-old children (Ferreira & others, 2018).

Work can have positive and negative effects on parenting. Ann Crouter (2006) described how parents bring their experiences at work into their homes. She concluded that parents who have poor working conditions, such as long hours, overtime work, stressful work, and lack of autonomy on the job, are likely to be more irritable at home and to engage in less effective parenting than their counterparts who have better working conditions at their jobs. A consistent finding is that children (especially girls) of working mothers engage in less gender stereotyping and have more egalitarian views of gender (Goldberg & Lucas-Thompson, 2008). Also, one study revealed that mothers' positive mood after work was linked with adolescents' reports of more positive affect, better sleep quality, and longer sleep duration (Lawson & others, 2014). Further, this study indicated that mothers with more positive work experiences had adolescents who reported less negative affect and fewer physical health problems.

CHILDREN IN DIVORCED FAMILIES

It is estimated that 40 percent of children born to married parents in the United States will experience their parents' divorce (Hetherington & Stanley-Hagan, 2002). Let's examine some important questions about children in divorced families:

- *Are children better adjusted in intact, never-divorced families than in divorced families?* Most researchers agree that children from divorced families show poorer adjustment than their counterparts in nondivorced families (Amato & Anthony, 2014; Ganong, Coleman, & Sanner, 2019; Hetherington, 2006; Kravdal & Grundy, 2019; Lansford, 2013, 2019b; Sbarra, Bourassa, & Manvelian, 2019; Wallerstein, 2008; Weinraub & Kaufman, 2019). See Figure 11. Those who have experienced multiple divorces are at greater risk. Children in divorced families are more likely than children in nondivorced families to have academic problems, to show externalizing problems (such as acting out and delinquency) and internalizing problems (such as anxiety and depression), to be less socially responsible, to have less competent intimate relationships, to drop out of school, to become sexually active at an earlier age, to take drugs, to associate with antisocial peers, to have low self-esteem, and to be less securely attached as young adults (Lansford, 2009, 2013, 2019b). In a recent study, both parental divorce and child maltreatment were linked to midlife suicidal ideation (Stansfield & others, 2017). One study revealed that adolescent girls with divorced parents were especially vulnerable to developing symptoms of depression (Oldehinkel & others, 2008). Also, a recent meta-analysis found that when their parents had been divorced, adults were more likely to have depression (Sands, Thompson, & Gaysina, 2017). Nonetheless, keep in mind that a majority of children in divorced families do not have significant adjustment problems (Ahrons, 2007).

However, one study concluded that experiencing a parental divorce during childhood was linked to increased rates of cohabiting/marital partnerships and negative partner relationships from 16 to 30 years of age (Fergusson, McLeod, & Horwood, 2014). An important point is that the outcomes just described for the life event of childhood divorce were explained by a variety of other factors and social contexts—parental history of illicit drug use, experience of childhood sexual abuse, lower-SES status at the child's birth, and parental history of criminality.

Note that marital conflict may have negative consequences for children in the context of marriage or divorce (Davies, Martin, & Cummings, 2018; Gao & others, 2019). A longitudinal

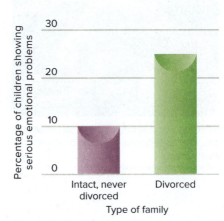

FIGURE 11

DIVORCE AND CHILDREN'S EMOTIONAL PROBLEMS. In Hetherington's research, 25 percent of children from divorced families showed serious emotional problems compared with only 10 percent of children from intact, never-divorced families. However, keep in mind that a substantial majority (75 percent) of the children from divorced families did not show serious emotional problems.

study revealed that conflict in nondivorced families was associated with emotional problems in children (Amato, 2006). Indeed, many of the problems that children from divorced homes experience begin during the predivorce period, a time when parents are often in active conflict with each other. Thus, when children from divorced homes show problems, the problems may be due not only to the divorce but also to the months or years of marital conflict that led to it.

E. Mark Cummings and his colleagues (Cummings & others, 2017; Davies, Martin, & Cummings, 2018) have proposed *emotional security theory*, which has its roots in attachment theory and states that children appraise marital conflict in terms of their sense of security and safety in the family. These researchers make a distinction between marital conflict that is negative for children (such as hostile emotional displays and destructive conflict tactics) and marital conflict that can be positive for children (such as marital disagreement that involves a calm discussion of each person's perspective and working together to reach a solution).

What concerns are involved in whether parents should stay together for the sake of the children or become divorced?
Image Source/Getty Images

- *Should parents stay together for the sake of the children?* Whether parents should stay in an unhappy or conflicted marriage for the sake of their children is one of the most commonly asked questions about divorce (Hetherington, 2006; Morrison, Fife, & Hertlein, 2017). If the stresses and disruptions in family relationships associated with an unhappy, conflictual marriage that erode the well-being of children are reduced by the move to a divorced, single-parent family, divorce can be advantageous. However, if the diminished resources and increased risks associated with divorce also are accompanied by inept parenting and sustained or increased conflict, not only between the divorced couple but also among the parents, children, and siblings, the best choice for the children would be that an unhappy marriage be retained (Hetherington & Stanley-Hagan, 2002). It is difficult to determine how these "ifs" will play out when parents either remain together in an acrimonious marriage or become divorced.

- *How much do family processes matter in divorced families?* In divorced families, family processes matter a great deal (Ganong, Coleman, & Sanner, 2019; Hetherington, 2006; Lansford, 2019b). When the divorced parents have a harmonious relationship and use authoritative parenting, the adjustment of adolescents is improved (Hetherington, 2006). When the divorced parents can agree on child-rearing strategies and can maintain a cordial relationship with each other, frequent visits by the noncustodial parent usually benefit the child (Fabricius & others, 2010). Following a divorce, father involvement with children drops off more than mother involvement, especially for fathers of girls. In one study, children were more likely to have behavior problems if their post-divorce home environment was less supportive and stimulating, their mother was less sensitive and more depressed, and if their household income was lower (Weaver & Schofield, 2015). Also, a study involving divorced families revealed that an intervention focused on improving the mother-child relationship was linked to improvements in relationship quality that increased children's coping skills over the short term (6 months) and long term (6 years) (Velez & others, 2011). Further, a study of non-residential fathers in divorced families indicated that high father-child involvement and low interparental conflict were linked to positive child outcomes (Flam & others, 2016). Also, a research review concluded that coparenting (mutual parental support, cooperation, and agreement) following divorce was positively related to child outcomes such as lower anxiety and depression, as well as higher self-esteem and academic performance (Lamela & Figueiredo, 2016).

- *What factors influence an individual child's vulnerability to suffering negative consequences as a result of living in a divorced family?* Among the factors involved in the child's risk and vulnerability are the child's adjustment prior to the divorce, as well as the child's personality and temperament, and the custody situation (Hetherington, 2006). Children whose parents later divorce show poorer adjustment before the breakup (Amato & Booth, 1996). Children who are socially mature and responsible, who show few behavioral problems, and who have an easy temperament are better able to cope with their parents' divorce. Children with a difficult temperament often have problems coping with their parents' divorce (Hetherington, 2006). In one study, higher levels of predivorce maternal sensitivity and child IQ served as protective factors in reducing child problems

Communicating with Children About Divorce

Ellen Galinsky and Judy David (1988) developed a number of guidelines for communicating with children about divorce:

- *Explain the separation.* As soon as daily activities in the home make it obvious that one parent is leaving, tell the children. If possible, both parents should be present when children are told about the separation to come. The reasons for the separation are very difficult for young children to understand. No matter what parents tell children, children can find reasons to argue against the separation. It is extremely important for parents to let the children know who will take care of them and to describe the specific arrangements for seeing the other parent.

- *Explain that the separation is not the child's fault.* Young children often believe their parents' separation or divorce is their own fault. Therefore, it is important to tell children that they are not the cause of the separation. Parents need to repeat this point a number of times.

- *Explain that it may take time to feel better.* Tell young children that it's normal not to feel good about what is happening and that many other children feel this way when their parents become separated. It is also okay for divorced parents to share some of their emotions with children by saying something like "I'm having a hard time since the separation just like you, but I know it's going to get better after a while." Such statements are best kept brief and should not criticize the other parent.

- *Keep the door open for further discussion.* Tell your children to come to you any time they want to talk about the separation. It is healthy for children to express their pent-up emotions in discussions with their parents and to learn that the parents are willing to listen to their feelings and fears.

- *Provide as much continuity as possible.* The less children's worlds are disrupted by the separation, the easier their transition to a single-parent family will be. This guideline means maintaining the rules already in place as much as possible. Children need parents who care enough not only to give them warmth and nurturance but also to set reasonable limits.

- *Provide support for your children and yourself.* After a divorce or separation, parents are as important to children as they were before the divorce or separation. Divorced parents need to provide children with as much support as possible. Parents function best when other people are available to give them support as adults and as parents. Divorced parents can find people who provide practical help and with whom they can talk about their problems.

How well do these strategies complement E. Mavis Hetherington's six strategies for divorced adults, discussed earlier in this chapter?

after the divorce (Weaver & Schofield, 2015). Joint custody works best for children when the parents can get along with each other (Steinbach, 2019).

- ***What role does socioeconomic status play in the lives of children in divorced families?*** Custodial mothers experience the loss of about one-fourth to one-half of their predivorce income, in comparison with a loss of only one-tenth by custodial fathers (Emery, 1999). This income loss for divorced mothers is accompanied by increased workloads, high rates of job instability, and residential moves to less desirable neighborhoods with inferior schools (Braver & Lamb, 2013). One study found that children from families with higher incomes before the separation/divorce had fewer internalizing problems (Weaver & Schofield, 2015).

In sum, many factors affect how divorce influences a child's development (Lansford, 2013, 2019b). To read about some strategies for helping children cope with the divorce of their parents, see the *Connecting Development to Life* interlude.

STEPFAMILIES

Not only are parents divorcing more, they are also getting remarried more (Bray, 2019; Ganong & Coleman, 2018; Ganong, Coleman, & Sanner, 2019; Jensen, 2019; Papernow, 2018b). The number of remarriages involving children has grown steadily in recent years. About half of all children whose parents divorce will have a stepparent within four years of parental separation. However, divorces occur at a much higher rate in remarriages than in first marriages (DeLongis & Zwicker, 2017).

In some cases, the stepfamily may have been preceded by the death of the spouse. However, by far the largest number of stepfamilies are preceded by divorce rather than death.

Three common types of stepfamily structure are (1) stepfather, (2) stepmother, and (3) blended or complex. In stepfather families, the mother typically had custody of the children and remarried, introducing a stepfather into her children's lives. In stepmother families, the father usually had custody and remarried, introducing a step-mother into his children's lives. In a blended or complex stepfamily, both parents bring children from previous marriages to live in the newly formed stepfamily.

In E. Mavis Hetherington's (2006) most recent longitudinal analyses, children and adolescents who had been in a simple step-family (stepfather or stepmother) for a number of years were adjusting better than in the early years of the remarried family and were functioning well in comparison with children and adolescents in conflictual nondivorced families and children and adolescents in complex (blended) stepfamilies. More than 75 percent of the adolescents in long-established simple stepfamilies described their relationships with their stepparents as "close" or "very close." Hetherington (2006) concluded that in long-established simple stepfamilies, adolescents seem eventually to benefit from the presence of a stepparent and the resources provided by the stepparent.

Children often have better relationships with their custodial parents (mothers in stepfather families, fathers in stepmother families) than with stepparents (Santrock, Sitterle, & Warshak, 1988). Nonetheless, recent research indicated that stepfather' affinity-seeking (developing a friendly relationship with his stepchild) was linked to less conflict with stepchildren, a better couple relationship, and closer stepfamily ties (Ganong & others, 2019). Also, children in simple stepfamilies (stepmother, stepfather) often show better adjustment than their counterparts in complex (blended) stepfamilies (Anderson & others, 1999; Hetherington & Kelly, 2002).

How does living in a stepfamily influence a child's development?
Todd Wright/Blend Images/Getty Images

As in divorced families, children in stepfamilies show more adjustment problems than children in nondivorced families (Hetherington & Kelly, 2002). The adjustment problems are similar to those found among children of divorced parents—academic problems and lower self-esteem, for example (Anderson & others, 1999). However, it is important to recognize that a majority of children in stepfamilies do not have problems. As mentioned earlier, in one study 25 percent of children from stepfamilies showed adjustment problems compared with 10 percent in intact, never-divorced families (Hetherington & Kelly, 2002). Adolescence is an especially difficult time in stepfamilies (Anderson & others, 1999). This difficulty may occur because becoming part of a stepfamily exacerbates normal adolescent concerns about identity, sexuality, and autonomy. In recent research, a positive relationship between adolescents and their stepfather was associated with a higher level of physical health and a lower level of mental health problems in adolescents (Jensen & Harris, 2017; Jensen & others, 2018).

GAY AND LESBIAN PARENTS

Increasingly, gay and lesbian couples are creating families that include children (Farr & Goldberg, 2018; Goldberg & Sweeney, 2019; McConnachie & others, 2019; Sumontha, Farr, & Patterson, 2017; Patterson, 2019). Data indicate that approximately 20 percent of same-sex couples in the United States are raising children under the age of 18 (Gates, 2013).

An important aspect of gay and lesbian families with children is the sexual identity of parents at the time of a child's birth or adoption (Goldberg & Sweeney, 2019; Patterson, 2013, 2014, 2019). The largest group of children with gay and lesbian parents are likely those who were born in the context of heterosexual relationships, with one or both parents only later identifying themselves as gay or lesbian. Gay and lesbian parents may be single or they may have same-gender partners. In addition, gays and lesbians are increasingly choosing parenthood through donor insemination or adoption. Researchers have found that the children created through new reproductive technologies—such as in vitro fertilization—are as well-adjusted as their counterparts conceived by natural means (Golombok, 2011a, b; Golombok & Tasker, 2010).

Earlier in the chapter, we describe the positive outcomes of coparenting for children. One study compared the incidence of coparenting in adoptive heterosexual, lesbian, and gay couples with preschool-aged children (Farr & Patterson, 2013). Both self-reports and observations found that lesbian and gay couples shared child care more than heterosexual couples did, with lesbian couples being the most supportive and gay couples the least supportive. Further, another study revealed more positive parenting in adoptive gay father families and fewer child externalizing problems in these families than in heterosexual families (Golombok & others, 2014).

Another issue focuses on custody arrangements for adolescents. Many gays and lesbians have lost custody of their adolescents to heterosexual spouses following divorce. For this reason, many gay fathers and lesbian mothers are noncustodial parents.

Researchers have found few differences between children growing up with gay fathers and lesbian mothers and children growing up with heterosexual parents (Farr & Goldberg, 2018; Goldberg & Sweeney, 2019; Patterson, 2014, 2019). For example, children growing up in gay or lesbian families are just as popular with their peers, and there are no differences between the adjustment and mental health of children living in these families and children living in heterosexual families (Hyde & DeLamater, 2017). For example, in a recent study, the adjustment of school-aged children adopted during infancy by gay, lesbian, and heterosexual parents showed no differences (Farr, 2017). Rather, children's behavior patterns and family functioning were predicted by earlier child adjustment issues and parental stress. In another study of lesbian and gay adoptive parents, 98 percent of the adoptive parents reported that their children had adjusted well to school (Farr, Oakley, & Ollen, 2017). Also, the overwhelming majority of children growing up in a gay or lesbian family have a heterosexual orientation (Golombok & Tasker, 2010).

ADOPTIVE PARENTS AND ADOPTED CHILDREN

Another variation in the type of family in which children live involves adoption, the social and legal process by which a parent-child relationship is established between persons unrelated at birth. As we see next, an increase in diversity has characterized the adoption of children in the United States in recent years.

The Increased Diversity of Adopted Children and Adoptive Parents   A number of changes have characterized adopted children and adoptive parents in the last three to four decades (Brodzinsky & Pinderhughes, 2002; Compton, 2016; Farr & Grotevant, 2019; Pinderhughes & Brodzinsky, 2019). In the first half of the twentieth century, most U.S. adopted children were healthy, non-Latino White infants who were adopted at birth or soon after; however, in recent decades as abortion became legal and contraception increased, fewer of these infants became available for adoption. Increasingly, U.S. couples have adopted a much wider diversity of children—from other countries, from other ethnic groups, children with physical and/or mental problems, and children who had been neglected or abused (Zill, 2017).

An increasing number of Hollywood celebrities are adopting children from developing countries. Actress Angelina Jolie (*above*) with her adopted children, carrying adopted daughter Zahara with adopted sons Maddox and Pax alongside them.
Jackson Lee/Tom Meinelt/Newscom

Changes also have characterized adoptive parents in the last three to four decades (Brodzinsky & Pinderhughes, 2002). In the first half of the twentieth century, most adoptive parents were people from non-Latino White middle or upper socioeconomic status backgrounds who were married and did not have any type of disability. However, in recent decades, increased diversity has characterized adoptive parents. Many adoption agencies today have no income requirements for adoptive parents and now allow adults from a wide range of backgrounds to adopt children, including single adults, gay and lesbian adults, and older adults (Farr, 2017; Farr & others, 2016; McConnachie & others, 2019). Further, many adoptions involve other family members (such as aunts, uncles, or grandparents); currently, 30 percent of U.S. adoptive placements are with relatives (Ledesma, 2012). And slightly more than 50 percent of U.S. adoptions occur through the foster care system; in 2014, almost 110,000 children in the U.S. foster care system were waiting for someone to adopt them. Three pathways to adoption are (1) domestic adoption from the public welfare system, (2) domestic infant adoption through private agencies and intermediaries, and (3) international adoption (Grotevant & McDermott, 2014). In the next decade, the mix of U.S. adoptions is likely to include fewer domestic infant and international adoptions and more adoptions via the child welfare system (Grotevant & McDermott, 2014).

The changes in adoption practice over the last several decades make it difficult to generalize about the average adopted child or average adoptive parent (Woolgar & Scott, 2013). As we see next, though, some researchers have provided useful comparisons between adopted children and nonadopted children and their families.

Developmental Outcomes for Adopted and Nonadopted Children   How do adopted children fare after they are adopted? A research review concluded that adopted children are at higher risk for externalizing (aggression and conduct problems, for example), internalizing (anxiety and depression, for example), and attention problems (ADHD, for example) (Grotevant & McDermott, 2014). In another recent research review of internationally adopted adolescents, although a majority were well adjusted, adoptees had a higher level of mental health problems than their non-adopted counterparts (Askeland & others, 2017). Nevertheless, the majority of adopted children and adolescents (including those adopted at older ages, transracially, and across national borders) adjust effectively, and their parents report considerable satisfaction with their decision to adopt (Brodzinsky & Pinderhughes, 2002; Castle & others, 2010).

An ongoing issue in adopting children is whether there should be any connection with children's biological parents (Farr, 2017; Farr & Grotevant, 2019). Open adoption involves sharing identifying information and having contact with the biological parents, versus closed adoption, which consists of not having such sharing and contact. Most adoption agencies today offer adoptive parents the opportunity to have either an open or a closed adoption. A longitudinal study found that when their adopted children reached adulthood, adoptive parents described open adoption positively and saw it as serving the child's best interests (Siegel, 2013). Another longitudinal study found that birth mothers, adoptive parents, and birth children who had contact were more satisfied with their arrangements than those who did not have contact (Grotevant & others, 2013). Also, in this study, contact was linked to more optimal adjustment for adolescents and emerging adults (Grotevant & others, 2013). Further, birth mothers who were more satisfied with their contact arrangements had less unresolved grief 12 to 20 years after placement.

Parenting Adopted Children Many of the keys to effectively parenting adopted children are no different from those for effectively parenting biological children: be supportive and caring; be involved and monitor the child's behavior and whereabouts; be a good communicator; and help the child learn to develop self-control. However, parents of adopted children face some unique circumstances. They need to recognize the differences involved in adoptive family life, communicate about these differences, show respect for the birth family, and support the child's search for self and identity.

Because many children begin to ask where they came from when they are about 4 to 6 years old, this is a natural time for parents to begin talking in simple ways to children about their adoption status (Warshak, 2017). Some parents (although not as many as in the past) decide not to tell their children about the adoption. This secrecy may create psychological risks for the child if he or she later finds out about the adoption.

What are some strategies for parenting adopted children at different points in their development?
Photodisc/Getty Images

Review Connect Reflect

(LG3) Characterize parenting and how it affects children's development.

Review
- What are some parental roles?
- What are four main parenting styles? Which parenting style is most often linked with children's social competence? Is physical punishment a wise choice by parents? Does coparenting have positive effects on children? What is the nature of child maltreatment?
- How can parent–adolescent relationships and parent–emerging adult relationships be described?
- What are the effects of working parents on children's development?
- How does divorce affect children's development?
- What influence does growing up in a stepfamily have on children's development?
- What characterizes gay and lesbian parenting?
- How do the lives of adoptive parents and adopted children differ from the lives of nonadoptive parents and nonadopted children?

Connect
- How does what you learned about working parents in this chapter connect with the discussion of child care in the chapter on "Emotional Development"?

Reflect *Your Own Personal Journey of Life*
- What characterized your relationship with your parents during middle school and high school? Has your relationship with your parents changed since then? Does it involve less conflict? What do you think are the most important aspects of parenting adolescents competently?

4 Other Family Relationships Explain other aspects of family relationships.

| Sibling Relationships and Birth Order | Grandparenting and Great-Grandparenting | Intergenerational Relationships |

As important as child-parent relationships are to children's development, other family relationships are also important. Here we briefly examine sibling relationships, grandparenting and great-grandparenting, and intergenerational relationships.

SIBLING RELATIONSHIPS AND BIRTH ORDER

What are sibling relationships like? How extensively does birth order influence behavior?

Sibling Relationships   Approximately 80 percent of American children have one or more siblings—that is, sisters and brothers (Dunn, 2007, 2015; Fouts & Bader, 2017). If you grew up with siblings, you probably have a rich memory of aggressive, hostile interchanges. Siblings in the presence of each other when they are 2 to 4 years of age, on average, have a conflict once every 10 minutes, and then the conflicts decrease somewhat from 5 to 7 years of age (Kramer, 2006). What do parents do when they encounter siblings having a verbal or physical confrontation? One study revealed that they do one of three things: (1) intervene and try to help them resolve the conflict, (2) admonish or threaten them, or (3) do nothing at all (Kramer & Perozynski, 1999). Of interest is that in families with two siblings 2 to 5 years of age, the most frequent parental reaction is to do nothing at all. A research review concluded that sibling relationships in adolescence are more egalitarian and not as close or as intense as sibling relationships during childhood (East, 2009). Indeed, beginning in adolescence, sibling companionship begins to decline in many cultures as boys and girls become increasingly involved in the world beyond their family (McHale, Updegraff, & Whiteman, 2013).

Negative aspects of sibling relationships, such as high conflict, are linked to negative outcomes for children and adolescents (Dunn, 2015; Kramer & others, 2019; Fouts & Bader, 2017). The negative outcomes can develop not only through conflict but also through direct modeling of a sibling's behavior, as when a younger sibling has an older sibling who has poor study habits and engages in delinquent behavior. By contrast, close and supportive sibling relationships can buffer the negative effects of stressful circumstances in children's and adolescents' lives (Kramer & others, 2019).

Laurie Kramer (2006), who conducted a number of research studies on siblings, says that not intervening and letting sibling conflict escalate is not a good strategy. She developed a program titled "More Fun with Sisters and Brothers," which teaches 4- to 8-year-old siblings social skills for carrying out positive interactions (Kramer & Radey, 1997). Among the social skills taught in the program are how to appropriately initiate play, how to accept and refuse invitations to play, how to take another's perspective, how to deal with angry feelings, and how to manage conflict.

However, conflict is only one of the many dimensions of sibling relations (Dunn, 2015; Feinberg & others, 2013; Fouts & Bader, 2017; McHale, Updegraff, & Whiteman, 2013). Sibling relationships include helping, sharing, teaching, fighting, and playing, and siblings can act as emotional supports, rivals, and communication partners. One study found that adolescent siblings spent an average of 10 hours a week together, with an average of 12 percent of that time spent in constructive pursuits (creative activities such as art, music, and hobbies; sports; religious activities; and games) and 25 percent in nonconstructive activities (watching TV and hanging out) (Tucker, McHale, & Crouter, 2003).

Judy Dunn (2007, 2015), a leading expert on sibling relationships, described three important characteristics of sibling relationships:

- *Emotional quality of the relationship.* Intense positive and negative emotions are often expressed by siblings toward each other. Many children and adolescents have mixed feelings toward their siblings.

What characterizes children's sibling relationships?
(*all*): RubberBall Productions/Getty Images

- *Familiarity and intimacy of the relationship.* Siblings typically know each other very well, and this intimacy suggests that they can either provide support or tease and undermine each other, depending on the situation.
- *Variation of the relationship.* Some siblings describe their relationships more positively than others. Thus, there is considerable variation in sibling relationships. We've indicated that many siblings have mixed feelings about each other, but some children and adolescents mainly describe their sibling in warm, affectionate ways, whereas others primarily talk about how irritating and mean a sibling is.

Do parents usually favor one sibling over others—and if so, does it make a difference in an adolescent's development? One study of 384 adolescent sibling pairs revealed that 65 percent of their mothers and 70 percent of their fathers showed favoritism toward one sibling (Shebloski, Conger, & Widaman, 2005). When favoritism of one sibling occurred, it was linked to lower self-esteem and sadness in the less-favored sibling. Indeed, equality and fairness are major concerns in siblings' relationships with each other and how they are treated by their parents (Aldercotte, White, & Hughes, 2016; Campione-Barr, Greer, & Kruse, 2013).

What role might sibling conflict play in adolescent development? High levels of sibling conflict and low levels of sibling warmth can be detrimental to adolescent development (Tanskanen & others, 2017). A meta-analysis found that less sibling conflict and higher sibling warmth were associated with fewer internalizing and externalizing problems (Buist, Dekovic, & Prinzie, 2013).

In some instances, siblings may be stronger socializing influences on the child than parents are (Cicirelli, 1994). Someone close in age to the child—such as a sibling—may be able to understand the child's problems and communicate more effectively than parents can. In dealing with peers, coping with difficult teachers, and discussing taboo subjects such as sex, siblings may have more influence than parents.

Is sibling interaction the same around the world? In industrialized societies such as the United States, parents tend to delegate responsibility for younger siblings to older siblings primarily to give the parents freedom to pursue other activities. However, in nonindustrialized countries such as Kenya, the older sibling's role as a caregiver to younger siblings has much more importance. In industrialized countries, the older sibling's caregiving role is often discretionary; in nonindustrialized countries, it is more obligatory (Cicirelli, 1994).

Birth Order   Whether a child has older or younger siblings has been linked to development of certain personality characteristics. For example, one review concluded that "firstborns are the most intelligent, achieving, and conscientious, while later-borns are the most rebellious, liberal, and agreeable" (Paulhus, 2008, p. 210). Compared with later-born children, firstborn children have also been described as more adult-oriented, helpful, conforming, and self-controlled. However, when such birth-order differences are reported, they often are small.

What might account for even small differences related to birth order? Proposed explanations usually point to variations in interactions with parents and siblings associated with being in a specific position in the family (Feinberg, McHale, & Whiteman, 2019). This is especially true in the case of the firstborn child (Teti, 2001). The oldest child is the only one who does not have to share parental love and affection with other siblings—until another sibling comes along. An infant requires more attention than an older child; thus the firstborn sibling receives less attention after the newborn arrives. Does this result in conflict between parents and the firstborn? In one research study, mothers became more negative, coercive, and restraining and played less with the firstborn following the birth of a second child (Dunn & Kendrick, 1982).

What is the only child like? The popular conception is that the only child is a "spoiled brat" with undesirable characteristics such as dependency, lack of self-control, and self-centered behavior. But researchers present a more positive portrayal of the only child. Only children often are achievement-oriented and display a desirable personality, especially in comparison with later-borns and children from large families (Falbo & Poston, 1993).

So far, our discussion suggests that birth order might be a strong predictor of behavior. However, an increasing number of family researchers stress that when all of the factors that influence behavior are considered, birth order by itself shows limited ability to predict behavior. In a recent large-scale study, a birth order effect occurred for intelligence, with first borns having slightly higher intelligence; however, there were no birth order effects for life

A one-child policy has been in place for a number of decades in China. However, in 2016, the Chinese government began allowing two children per family without a financial penalty. *In general, though, what have researchers found the only child to be like?*
Image Source/Getty Images

satisfaction, internal/external control, trust, risk taking, patience, and impulsivity (Rohrer, Egloff, & Schmukle, 2017).

Think about some of the other important factors in children's lives beyond birth order that influence their behavior. They include heredity, models of competency or incompetency that parents present to children on a daily basis, peer influences, school influences, socioeconomic factors, sociohistorical factors, and cultural variations. When someone says firstborns are always like this but last-borns are always like that, the person is making overly simplistic statements that do not adequately take into account the complexity of influences on a child's development.

Sibling Relationships in Adulthood   Sibling relationships persist over the entire life span for most adults (Bedford, 2009). Eighty-five percent of today's adults have at least one living sibling. Sibling relationships in adulthood may be extremely close, apathetic, or highly rivalrous, but the majority of sibling relationships in adulthood have been found to be close (Cicirelli, 2009). Those siblings who are psychologically close to each other in adulthood tended to be that way in childhood. It is rare for sibling closeness to develop for the first time in adulthood (Dunn, 1984). One study revealed that adult siblings often provide practical and emotional support to each other (Voorpostel & Blieszner, 2008).

GRANDPARENTING AND GREAT-GRANDPARENTING

The increase in longevity is influencing the nature of grandparenting (Dolbin-MacNab, 2019; Huo & Fingerman, 2018; Smith & Wild, 2019). In 1900 only 4 percent of 10-year-old children had four living grandparents, but in 2000 that figure had risen to more than 40 percent. And in 1990 only about 20 percent of adults 30 years of age had living grandparents, a figure that was projected to increase to 80 percent in 2020 (Hagestad & Uhlenberg, 2007). Further increases in longevity are likely to support this trend in the future, although the current trend of delaying childbearing is likely to undermine it (Szinovacz, 2009).

How might U.S. grandparents compare with their counterparts in other countries? In a recent cross-cultural comparison, U.S. grandparents were characterized by higher parental efficacy, more role satisfaction, better well-being, and more attachment than Chinese grandparents, who were characterized by better resilience and more authoritative parenting (Wang & others, 2019).

Most research on grandparents has focused on grandchildren as children or adolescents. A recent study focused on grandparents and adult grandchildren (Huo & others, 2018). In this study, grandparents' affective connections with their adult grandchildren involved frequent listening, emotional support, and companionship. Also in this study, grandparents provided more frequent emotional support to their adult grandchildren when parents were having life problems and more frequent financial support when parents were unemployed.

Grandparent Roles   Grandparents play important roles in the lives of many grandchildren (Huo & Fingerman, 2018; Smith & Wild, 2019). Many adults become grandparents for the first time during middle age. Researchers have consistently found that grandmothers have more contact with grandchildren than do grandfathers (Watson, Randolph, & Lyons, 2005). Perhaps women tend to define their role as grandmothers as part of their responsibility for maintaining ties between family members across generations. Men may have fewer expectations about the grandfather role and see it as more voluntary.

Three prominent meanings are attached to being a grandparent (Neugarten & Weinstein, 1964). For some older adults, being a grandparent is a source of biological reward and continuity. For others, being a grandparent is a source of emotional self-fulfillment, generating feelings of companionship and satisfaction that may have been missing in earlier adult-child relationships. And for yet others, being a grandparent is a remote role.

The Changing Profile of Grandparents   In 2014, 10 percent (7.4 million) of children in the United States lived with at least one grandparent, a dramatic increase since 1981 when 4.7 million children were living with at least one grandparent (U.S. Census Bureau, 2015). Divorce, adolescent pregnancies, and drug use by parents are the main reasons that grandparents are thrust back into the "parenting" role they thought they had shed (Amorim, 2019).

What is the changing profile of grandparents in the United States?
Dex Images/Getty Images

The generations of living things pass in a short time, and like runners hand on the torch of life.

—LUCRETIUS
Roman Poet, 1st Century B.C.

empty nest syndrome View that a decline in marital satisfaction occurs when children leave home; however, research indicates that for most parents there is an upswing in marital satisfaction when children are launched into an adult life.

One study revealed that grandparent involvement was linked with better adjustment when it occurred in single-parent and stepparent families than in two-parent biological families (Attar-Schwartz & others, 2009).

Grandparents who are full-time caregivers for grandchildren are at elevated risk for health problems, depression, and stress (Silverstein, 2009). A review concluded that grandparents raising grandchildren are especially at risk for developing depression (Hadfield, 2014).

Caring for grandchildren is linked with these problems in part because full-time grandparent caregivers are often characterized by low-income minority status, and by not being married (Minkler & Fuller-Thompson, 2005). Grandparents who are part-time caregivers are less likely to have the negative health profiles that full-time grandparent caregivers have. In a study of part-time grandparent caregivers, few negative effects on grandparents were found (Hughes & others, 2007).

As divorce and remarriage have become more common, a special concern of grandparents is visitation privileges with their grandchildren (Huo & Fingerman, 2018). In the last 10 to 15 years, more states have passed laws giving grandparents the right to petition a court for visitation privileges with their grandchildren, even if a parent objects. Whether such forced visitation rights for grandparents are in the child's best interest is still being debated.

Great-Grandparenting Because of increased longevity, more grandparents today than in the past are also great-grandparents. At the turn of the previous century, the three-generation family was common, but now the four-generation family is common. One contribution of great-grandparents is to transmit family history by telling their children, grandchildren, and great-grandchildren where the family came from, what their members achieved, what they endured, and how their lives changed over the years (Harris, 2002).

There has been little research on great-grandparenting. One study examined the relationship between young adults and their grandparents and great-grandparents (Roberto & Skoglund, 1996). The young adults interacted with and participated in more activities with their grandparents than with their great-grandparents. They also perceived their grandparents to have a more defined role and to be more influential in their lives than great-grandparents.

At the beginning of the twentieth century, the three-generation family was common, but now the four-generation family is common as well. Thus, an increasing number of grandparents are also great-grandparents. The four-generation family shown here is the Jordans—author John Santrock's mother-in-law, daughter, granddaughter, and wife.
Courtesy of Dr. John Santrock

INTERGENERATIONAL RELATIONSHIPS

Family is important to most people (Sechrist & Fingerman, 2018). When 21,000 adults aged 40 to 79 in 21 countries were asked, "When you think of who you are, you think mainly of . . .", 63 percent said "family," 9 percent said "religion," and 8 percent said "work" (HSBC Insurance, 2007). In this study, in all 21 countries, middle-aged and older adults expressed a strong feeling of responsibility between generations in their family, with the strongest intergenerational ties indicated in Saudi Arabia, India, and Turkey. More than 80 percent of the middle-aged and older adults reported that adults have a duty to care for their parents (and parents-in-law) in time of need later in life.

The Empty Nest and Its Refilling An important event in a family is the launching of a child into adult life. Parents face new adjustments as a result of the child's absence. Students usually think that their parents suffer from their absence. In fact, parents who live vicariously through their children might experience the **empty nest syndrome,** which includes a decline in marital satisfaction after children leave the home. For most parents, however, marital satisfaction does not decline after children have left home. Rather, for most parents marital satisfaction increases during the years after child rearing (Fingerman & Baker, 2006). With their children gone, marital partners have time to pursue careers and other interests and more time for each other. One study revealed that the transition to an empty nest increased marital satisfaction and this increase was linked to an increase in the quality of time—but not the quantity of time—spent with partners (Gorchoff, John, & Helson, 2008).

In today's uncertain economic climate, the refilling of the empty nest is becoming a common occurrence as adult children return to live at home after several years of college, after graduating from college, or to save money after taking a full-time job (Fingerman, Cheng, & others, 2012). Young

Middle-aged and older adults around the world show a strong sense of family responsibility. A study of middle-aged and older adults in 21 countries revealed that the strongest intergenerational ties were in Saudi Arabia.
Reza/National Geographic/Getty Images

What are some strategies that can help parents and their young adult children get along better?
Fuse/Getty Images

adults also may move back in with their parents after an unsuccessful career or a divorce. And some individuals don't leave home at all until their middle to late twenties because they cannot financially support themselves. Numerous labels have been applied to these young adults who return to their parents' homes to live, including "boomerang kids" and "B2B" (or Back-to-Bedroom) (Furman, 2005).

The middle generation has always provided support for the younger generation, even after the nest is bare. Through loans and monetary gifts for education, and through emotional support, the middle generation has helped the younger generation. Adult children appreciate the financial and emotional support their parents provide them at a time when they often feel considerable stress about their career, work, and lifestyle. And parents feel good that they can provide this support.

However, as with most family living arrangements, there are both pluses and minuses when adult children live with their parents (Fingerman & others, 2016). One of the most common complaints voiced by both adult children and their parents is a loss of privacy. The adult children complain that their parents restrict their independence, cramp their sex lives, reduce their music listening, and treat them as children rather than adults. Parents often complain that their quiet home has become noisy, that they stay up late worrying about when their adult children will come home, that meals are difficult to plan because of conflicting schedules, that their relationship as a married or partnered couple has been invaded, and that they have to shoulder too much responsibility for their adult children. In sum, when adult children return home to live, the changes in family life require considerable adaptation on the part of parents and their adult children.

When adult children ask to return home to live, parents and their adult children should agree on the conditions and expectations beforehand. For example, they might discuss and agree on whether young adults will pay rent, wash their own clothes, cook their own meals, do any household chores, pay their phone bills, come and go as they please, be sexually active or drink alcohol at home, and so on. If these conditions aren't negotiated at the beginning, conflict often results because the expectations of parents and young adult children will likely be violated.

Research indicates that today's parents and their emerging adult/young adult children have more contact with each other than did earlier generations, with the connections especially strengthening during the first decade of the twenty-first century (Fingerman, Pillemer, & others, 2012). Keeping in touch has become easier with advances in technology, and today's emerging and young adults frequently text their parents and become friends with their parents on Facebook. Recent research indicates that today's emerging adults and young adults appreciate their parents' emotional and financial support. Nonetheless, there is concern when this parental support becomes too intense, in which case it can restrict emerging and young adults' development of autonomy (Fingerman, Pillemer, & others, 2012). The term "helicopter parents" has been applied to this type of support (Weitkamp & Seiffge-Krenke, 2019). In a recent study, high levels of parental control and helicopter parenting were detrimental to emerging adults' vocational identity development and perceived competence in transitioning to adulthood (Lindell, Campione-Barr, & Killoren, 2017). And in another recent study, helicopter parenting was related to more negative emotional functioning, less competent decision making, and lower grades/poorer adjustment in college-age adults (Luebbe & others, 2018).

Recently, a new term that characterizes a number of parents today is "lawn mower parent"—a parent who goes to great lengths to prevent their child from experiencing adversity, stress, or failure. By "mowing down" obstacles and potential negative experiences for their children, these parents are not allowing their children to learn how to cope with such experiences themselves. When their children have to face these struggles on their own as they leave home and go to college or enter a career, they are less likely to handle the pressure and challenges as well as they would have if their parents had provided them more space to make decisions and learn how to cope on their own.

As discussed in the next section, a considerable degree of ambivalence characterizes intergenerational relationships in many families, with middle-aged adults playing a key role in connecting generations.

The Midlife Generation Adults in midlife play important roles in the lives of the young and the old (Birditt & others, 2019; Fingerman & others, 2019; Huo & others, 2018, 2019). Middle-aged adults share their experience and transmit values to the younger generation. They may be launching children and experiencing the empty nest, adjusting to having grown children return home, or becoming grandparents. They also may be giving or receiving financial assistance, caring for a widowed or sick parent, or adapting to being the oldest generation after both parents have died.

Middle-aged adults have been described as the "sandwich," "squeezed," or "overload" generation because of the responsibilities they have for their adolescent and young adult children on the one hand and their aging parents on the other (Etaugh & Bridges, 2010). However, Karen Fingerman and her colleagues (Fingerman, Zarit, & Birditt, 2019; Fingerman & others, 2019; Sechrist & Fingerman, 2018) offer an alternative view, concluding that in the United States, a "sandwich" generation, in which the middle generation cares for both grown children and aging parents simultaneously, occurs less often than a "pivot" generation, in which the middle generation alternates attention between the demands of grown children and aging parents.

Many middle-aged adults experience considerable stress when their parents become very ill and die (Bangerter & others, 2017; Fingerman, Zarit, and Birditt, 2019; Huo & others, 2018; Zarit & others, 2019). One survey found that when adults enter midlife, 41 percent have both parents alive, but that 77 percent leave midlife with no parents alive (Bumpass & Aquilino, 1994). By middle age, more than 40 percent of adult children (most of them daughters) provide care for aging parents or parents-in-law (Blieszner & Roberto, 2012). However, researchers have found that middle-aged parents are more likely to provide support to their grown children than to their parents (Fingerman & others, 2011). In this research, when middle-aged adults have a parent with a disability, their support for that parent increases (Huo & others, 2019). The support might involve locating a nursing home and monitoring its quality, procuring medical services, arranging public service assistance, and handling finances. In some cases, adult children provide direct assistance with daily living, including such activities as eating, bathing, and dressing. Even less severely impaired older adults may need help with shopping, housework, transportation, home maintenance, and bill paying.

In most cases researchers have found that relationships between aging parents and their children are characterized by ambivalence (Fingerman, Zarit, & Birditt, 2019; Fingerman & others, 2019; Sechrist & Fingerman, 2018). Perceptions include love, reciprocal help, and shared values on the positive side and isolation, family conflicts and problems, abuse, neglect, and caregiver stress on the negative side. One study found that middle-aged adults positively supported family responsibility to emerging adult children but were more ambivalent about providing care for aging parents, viewing it as both a joy and a burden (Igarashi & others, 2013). With each new generation, personality characteristics, attitudes, and values are replicated or changed (Sechrist & Fingerman, 2018). As older family members die, their biological, intellectual, emotional, and personal legacies are carried on in the next generation. Their children become the oldest generation and their grandchildren the second generation. As adult children become middle-aged, they often develop more positive perceptions of their parents (Field, 1999). Both similarity and dissimilarity across generations are found. For example, similarity between parents and an adult child is most noticeable in religion and politics, least in gender roles, lifestyle, and work orientation.

Gender Gender differences also characterize intergenerational relationships (Pei, Cong, & Wu, 2019). Women have an especially important role in maintaining family relationships across generations. Women's relationships across generations are typically closer than other family bonds (Merrill, 2009). In one study, mothers and their daughters had much closer relationships during their adult years than mothers and sons, fathers and daughters, and fathers and sons (Rossi, 1989). Also in this study, married men were more involved with their wives' kin than with their own. And maternal grandmothers and maternal aunts were cited twice as often as their counterparts on the paternal side of the family as the most important or loved relative.

What is the nature of intergenerational relationships?
Steve Casimiro/The Image Bank/Getty Images

reach your **learning goals**

Families, Lifestyles, and Parenting

1 Family Processes

 LG1 Describe some important family processes.

- Reciprocal Socialization
- Family as a System
- Sociocultural and Historical Influences

- Reciprocal socialization is socialization that is bidirectional; children socialize parents just as parents socialize children. Synchrony and scaffolding are two important types of reciprocal socialization.

- The family system consists of subsystems defined by generation, gender, and role. These subsystems interact with each other and can have direct and indirect effects on each other.

- Sociocultural and historical contexts influence families, reflecting Bronfenbrenner's concepts of macrosystem and chronosystem. Both great upheavals such as war and subtle transitions in ways of life may influence families. A major change in families in the last several decades has been the extensive immigration of Latino and Asian families into the United States.

2 The Diversity of Adult Lifestyles

LG2 Discuss the diversity of adult lifestyles and how they influence people's lives.

- Single Adults
- Cohabiting Adults
- Married Adults

- Being single has become an increasingly prominent lifestyle. There are advantages and disadvantages to being single, autonomy being one of the advantages. Intimacy, loneliness, and finding a positive identity in a marriage-oriented society are concerns of single adults. Approximately 8 percent of 65-year-old adults have never been married. Many of them cope effectively with loneliness in old age.

- Cohabitation is an increasingly prevalent lifestyle for many adults that offers some advantages as well as problems. Cohabitation does not lead to greater marital happiness but rather to no differences or to differences suggesting that it is not good for a marriage. An increasing number of older adults cohabit, in many cases more for companionship than for love.

- Even though adults are remaining single longer and the divorce rate is high, Americans still show a strong predilection for marriage. The age at which individuals marry, expectations about what the marriage will be like, and the developmental course of marriage vary not only over time within a culture but also across cultures.

- John Gottman has conducted extensive research on what makes marriages work. In his research, the following factors are among the most important for having a good marriage:

establishing love maps, nurturing fondness and admiration, turning toward each other instead of away, letting your partner influence you, overcoming gridlock, and creating shared meaning.

- Premarital education is associated with positive relationship outcomes. The benefits of marriage include better physical and mental health and a longer life. A majority of middle-aged adults who are married say their marriage is very good or excellent. The time from retirement until death is sometimes called the final stage in the marital process. Married older adults are often happier than single older adults.

Divorced Adults

- The U.S. divorce rate increased dramatically in the twentieth century but began to decline in the 1980s. Divorce is complex and emotional. In the first year following divorce, a disequilibrium in the divorced adult's behavior occurs, but by several years after the divorce, more stability has been achieved. The divorced displaced homemaker may encounter excessive stress; however, men do not go through a divorce unscathed. There are social, financial, and physical consequences of divorce for older adults.

Remarried Adults

- Divorced adults remarry on average within four years of their divorce. Stepfamilies are complex and adjustment is difficult. Only about one-third of stepfamily couples stay remarried. Rising divorce rates, increased longevity, and better health have led to an increase in remarriage by older adults.

Gay and Lesbian Adults

- One of the most striking findings about gay and lesbian couples is how similar they are to heterosexual couples—for example, gay and lesbian couples prefer committed, long-term relationships and work to find a balance of romantic love, affection, and autonomy. There are many misconceptions about gay and lesbian adults.

3 Parenting

LG3 Characterize parenting and how it affects children's development.

Parental Roles

- Currently, there is a trend toward having fewer children and choosing when to have children. The transition to parenting involves a great deal of adaptation for many people. A key aspect of being a competent parent is effectively managing children's lives and understanding adolescents' information management.

Parenting Styles and Discipline

- Authoritarian, authoritative, neglectful, and indulgent are four main parenting styles. Authoritative parenting is the style most often associated with children's social competence. Physical punishment is widely used by U.S. parents, but there are a number of reasons why it is not a good choice.

- Coparenting can have positive effects on children's development if it is accompanied by parental warmth and cooperation.

- The four main types of child maltreatment are physical abuse, child neglect, sexual abuse, and emotional abuse. An understanding of child abuse requires information about cultural, familial, and community influences. Child maltreatment places the child at risk for a number of developmental problems.

Parent–Adolescent and Parent–Emerging Adult Relationships

- Adolescents seek to be independent, but secure attachment to parents is a positive influence on development. Conflict with parents often increases in adolescence but usually is moderate rather than severe. An increasing number of emerging adults are returning home to live with their parents, often for economic reasons. Both emerging adults and their parents need to adapt when emerging adults return home to live.

Working Parents

- In general, having both parents employed full-time outside the home has not been shown to have negative effects on children. However, the nature of parents' work can affect the quality of their parenting.

Children in Divorced Families

- Overall, divorce is linked with adjustment problems in children, but not for all children. Whether parents should stay together for the sake of the children is a difficult question to answer. Family processes, such as harmony between parents, quality of parenting, and support systems, matter in the development of children of divorced parents. So does socioeconomic status.

Stepfamilies

- Children in stepparent families have more problems than their counterparts in nondivorced families. Adolescence is an especially difficult time for remarriage of parents to occur. Restabilization takes longer in stepfamilies than in divorced families.

Gay and Lesbian Parents	• Researchers have found few differences between children growing up with gay or lesbian parents and children growing up with heterosexual parents.
Adoptive Parents and Adopted Children	• Although adopted children and adolescents have more problems than their nonadopted counterparts, the vast majority of adopted children adapt effectively. When adoption occurs very early in development, the outcomes for the child are improved. Because of the dramatic changes that have occurred in adoption in recent decades, it is difficult to generalize about characteristics of the average adopted child or average adoptive family.

4 Other Family Relationships

 LG4 Explain other aspects of family relationships.

Sibling Relationships and Birth Order	• Siblings interact with each other in positive and negative ways. Birth order is related in certain ways to child characteristics, but some critics argue that birth order is not a good predictor of behavior. Sibling relationships persist over the entire life span for most adults.
Grandparenting and Great-Grandparenting	• There are different grandparent roles and styles. Grandmothers spend more time with grandchildren than grandfathers do, and the grandmother role involves greater expectations for maintaining ties across generations than the grandfather role. The profile of grandparents is changing because of factors such as divorce and remarriage. An increasing number of U.S. grandchildren live with their grandparents. Because of increased longevity, more grandparents today are also great-grandparents. One contribution of great-grandparents is their knowledge of family history.
Intergenerational Relationships	• For most families, there is an upswing in marital satisfaction when children are launched into adulthood. Family members usually maintain contact across generations. Mothers and daughters have the closest relationships. The middle-aged generation plays an important role in linking generations. In many families, ambivalence characterizes intergenerational relationships.

key terms

authoritarian parenting	child neglect	empty nest syndrome	reciprocal socialization
authoritative parenting	cohabitation	indulgent parenting	sexual abuse
child abuse	coparenting	neglectful parenting	
child maltreatment	emotional abuse	physical abuse	

key people

Joseph Allen	Ann Crouter	Karen Fingerman	E. Mavis Hetherington
Diana Baumrind	E. Mark Cummings	John Gottman	Laurie Kramer

chapter 15

PEERS AND THE SOCIOCULTURAL WORLD

chapter outline

① Peer Relations in Childhood and Adolescence

Learning Goal 1 Discuss peer relations in childhood and adolescence.

Exploring Peer Relations
Peer Statuses
Bullying
Gender and Peer Relations
Adolescent Peer Relations

② Friendship

Learning Goal 2 Explain the role of friendship through the life span.

Functions of Friendship
Friendship During Childhood

Friendship During Adolescence and Emerging Adulthood
Adult Friendship

③ Play and Leisure

Learning Goal 3 Describe the developmental aspects of play and leisure.

Childhood
Adolescence
Adulthood

④ Aging and the Social World

Learning Goal 4 Summarize the social aspects of aging.

Social Theories of Aging
Stereotyping of Older Adults

Social Support and Social Integration
Successful Aging

⑤ Sociocultural Influences

Learning Goal 5 Evaluate sociocultural influences on development.

Culture
Socioeconomic Status and Poverty
Ethnicity

Aldo Murillo/Getty Images

preview

The social worlds outside the family play important roles in life-span development. As we go through life, we interact with a convoy of people through peer relations, friendships, cliques, and support systems in many different cultural worlds.

1 Peer Relations in Childhood and Adolescence

LG1 Discuss peer relations in childhood and adolescence.

- Exploring Peer Relations
- Peer Statuses
- Bullying
- Gender and Peer Relations
- Adolescent Peer Relations

As children grow older, peer relations consume increasing amounts of their time. In some cases these relations are positive influences, in others negative.

EXPLORING PEER RELATIONS

Some important questions involving peer relations are the following: What are the functions of a child's peer group? How are peer relations and adult-child relations linked? What are some developmental changes in peer relations during childhood? What role does social cognition play in peer relations? How is emotion regulation involved in peer relations?

Functions of Peer Groups Peers are individuals of about the same age or maturity level. Peer groups provide a source of information and comparison about the world outside the family. Children receive feedback about their abilities from their peer group. They evaluate what they can do in terms of whether it is better than, as good as, or worse than what other children do. It is hard to make such comparisons at home because siblings are usually older or younger.

Researchers have found that children's peer relations can have long-term consequences (Prinstein & others, 2018). For example, one study indicated that low peer status in childhood (low acceptance/likeability) was linked to increased probability of being unemployed and having mental health problems in adulthood (Almquist & Brannstrom, 2014).

Both Jean Piaget (1932) and Harry Stack Sullivan (1953) stressed that children learn reciprocity through interaction with their peers. Children explore the meanings of fairness and justice by working through disagreements with peers. They also learn to be keen observers of peers' interests and perspectives in order to smoothly integrate themselves into ongoing peer activities. Susceptibility to peer influences can have positive or negative consequences (Bukowski, Laursen, & Rubin, 2018; Rubin & Barstead, 2018). For example, in one study, children who associated with peers who engaged in prosocial behavior at age 9 had a higher level of self-control at age 10, and those who associated with peers who engaged in deviant behavior at age 9 had a lower level of self-control at age 10 (Meldrum & Hay, 2012). And a recent study that examined parent and peer influences on adolescents' smoking revealed that peers had a more powerful influence than parents did (Scalici & Schulz, 2017).

Being rejected or overlooked by peers leads some children to feel lonely or hostile. Further, rejection and neglect by peers are related to an individual's subsequent mental health difficulties and criminal problems. Withdrawn children who are rejected by peers or victimized and lonely are at risk for depression (Rubin & Barstead, 2018). Children who are aggressive with their peers are at risk for developing a number of problems, including conduct problems, delinquency, and dropping out of school (Vitaro, Boivin, & Poulin, 2018). Peers can also undermine parental values and control (Masten, 2005).

Keep in mind that the influences of peer experiences vary according to the type of peer experience, developmental status, and outcome (such as achievement, delinquency, depression,

What are some functions of a peer group?
Monkey Business Images/Shutterstock

peers Individuals who share the same age or maturity level.

and so on) (Bukowski, Laursen, & Rubin, 2018; Coplan & others, 2018). "Peers" and "peer group" are global concepts. For example, "peer group" might refer to acquaintances, members of a clique, neighborhood associates, a friendship network, or an activity group (Brown, 1999).

Adult-Child and Peer Relations   Parents may influence their children's peer relations in many ways, both direct and indirect (Booth-Laforce & Groh, 2018; Ladd & Kochenderfer-Ladd, 2019). Parents affect their children's peer relations through their interactions with their children, how they manage their children's lives, and the opportunities they provide to their children.

Basic lifestyle decisions by parents—their choices of neighborhoods, churches, schools, and their own friends—largely determine the pool from which their children select possible friends. These choices in turn affect which children their children meet, their purpose in interacting, and eventually which children become their friends.

Children and adolescents live in a connected world with parents and peers, not one in which parents and peers are disconnected from each other (Wang & others, 2016). For example, one study found that when mothers coached their preschool daughters about the negative aspects of peer conflicts involving relational aggression (harming someone by manipulating a relationship), the daughters engaged in lower rates of relational aggression (Werner & others, 2014). And in a recent study, mothers with a permissive parenting style had adolescents who were negatively attached to their peers (Llorca, Richaud, & Malonda, 2017).

Do these findings indicate that children's peer relations always are wedded to parent-child relationships? Although parent-child relationships influence children's subsequent peer relations, children also learn other modes of relating through their relationships with peers. For example, rough-and-tumble play occurs mainly with other children, not in parent-child interaction. In times of stress, children more often turn to parents than to peers for support. Parent-child relationships teach children how to relate to authority figures. With their peers, children are likely to interact on a much more equal basis and to learn a mode of relating based on mutual influence.

Peer Contexts   Peer interaction is influenced by contexts that can include the type of peer the individual interacts with—such as an acquaintance, a crowd, a clique, a friend, or a romantic partner—and the situation or location where they interact—such as a school, neighborhood, community center, dance, religious setting, sporting event, and so on, as well as the culture in which the individual lives (Brown & Larson, 2009). As they interact with peers in these various contexts, individuals are likely to encounter different messages and different opportunities to engage in adaptive or maladaptive behavior that can influence their development (Prinstein & others, 2018).

Individual Difference Factors   Individual differences among peers also are important considerations in understanding peer relations (van Aken & Asendorpf, 2018). Among the wide range of individual differences that can affect peer relations are personality traits such as how shy or outgoing an individual is. For example, a very shy individual is more likely than a gregarious individual to be neglected by peers and to feel anxious about introducing himself or herself to new peers. One individual difference factor that has been found to impair peer relations is the trait of negative emotionality, which involves a relatively low threshold

developmental **connection**
Attachment
Securely attached infants use the caregiver as a secure base from which to explore their environment. Connect to "Emotional Development and Attachment."

How are parent-child and peer relationships connected?
(*Top*): Monkeybusinessimages/iStockphoto/Getty Images;
(*bottom*): Kali9/Getty Images

What are some examples of how social contexts and individual difference factors influence adolescents' peer relations?
MM Productions/Corbis

for experiencing anger, fear, anxiety, and irritation. For example, one study revealed that adolescents characterized by negative emotionality tended to engage in negative interpersonal behavior when interacting with a friend or a romantic partner (Hatton & others, 2008).

Developmental Changes in Childhood   Around the age of 3, children already prefer to spend time with same-sex rather than opposite-sex playmates, and this preference increases in early childhood. During these same years, the frequency of peer interaction, both positive and negative, picks up considerably (Hartup, 1983). Although aggressive interaction and rough-and-tumble play increase during this period of development, there is a decreasing proportion of aggressive exchanges compared with friendly exchanges. Many preschool children spend considerable time in peer interaction just playing, conversing with peers, trying out roles, and negotiating rules (Rubin, Bukowski, & Bowker, 2015). In early childhood, children distinguish between friends and nonfriends (Howes, 2009). For most young children, a friend is someone to play with. Young preschool children are more likely than older children to have friends of different gender and ethnicity (Howes, 2009).

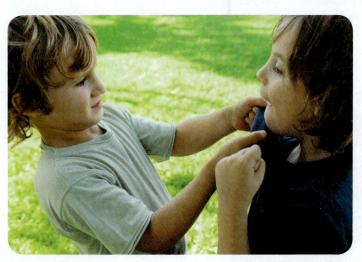

What are some developmental changes in peer relations during childhood?
Hero Images/Getty Images

As children enter the elementary school years, reciprocity becomes especially important in peer interchanges. Children play games together, interact in groups, and cultivate friendships. Until about 12 years of age, their preference for same-sex groups increases. The amount of time children spend in peer interaction also rises during middle and late childhood and adolescence. Researchers estimate that the percentage of time spent in social interaction with peers increases from approximately 10 percent at 2 years of age to more than 30 percent in middle and late childhood (Rubin, Bukowski, & Bowker, 2015). Other changes in peer relations as children move through middle and late childhood involve peer group expansion and peer interaction that is less closely supervised by adults (Rubin, Bukowski, & Bowker, 2015).

developmental **connection**

Social Cognition

Social cognition refers to the processes involved in understanding the world around us, especially how we think and reason about others. Connect to "The Self, Identity, and Personality."

Social Cognition   A boy accidentally trips and knocks another boy's soft drink out of his hand. That boy misinterprets the encounter as hostile, which leads him to retaliate aggressively against the boy who tripped. Through repeated encounters of this kind, the aggressive boy's classmates come to perceive him as habitually acting in inappropriate ways.

This example demonstrates the importance of *social cognition*—thoughts about social matters, such as the aggressive boy's interpretation of an encounter as hostile and his classmates' perception of his behavior as inappropriate (Fiske, 2018; Greifneder, Bless, & Fielder, 2018). Children's social cognition about their peers becomes increasingly important for understanding peer relationships in middle and late childhood. Of special interest are the ways in which children process information about peer relations and their social knowledge (Dodge, 2011a, b).

Kenneth Dodge (1983, 2011a, b) argues that children go through six steps in processing information about their social world. They selectively attend to social cues, attribute intent, generate goals, access behavioral scripts from memory, make decisions, and enact behavior. Dodge has found that aggressive boys are more likely to perceive another child's actions as hostile when the child's intention is ambiguous. And, when aggressive boys search for cues to determine a peer's intention, they respond more rapidly, less efficiently, and less reflectively than do nonaggressive boys. These are among the social cognitive factors believed to be involved in children's and adolescents' conflicts.

Social knowledge also is involved in children's ability to get along with peers (Fiske, 2018). They need to know what goals to pursue in poorly defined or ambiguous situations, how to initiate and maintain a social bond, and what scripts to follow to get other children to be their friends. For example, as part of the script for getting friends, it helps to know that making positive comments to the peer will make the peer like the child more.

What are some aspects of social cognition that are involved in getting along with peers?
Odilon Dimier/PhotoAlto/Getty Images

Regulation of Emotion and Peer Relations   Emotions play a strong role in determining whether a child's peer relationships are successful (Cole, Ram, & English, 2019; Liu & others, 2019). Moody and emotionally negative children are often rejected by their peers, whereas emotionally positive children are often popular (Martinez & others, 2015). The ability to engage in self-regulation and modulate one's emotions is an important skill that benefits children in their relationships with peers (Schunk & Greene, 2018).

PEER STATUSES

Which children are likely to be popular with their peers and which ones tend to be disliked? Developmentalists address these and similar questions by examining sociometric status, a term that describes the extent to which children are liked or disliked by their peer group (Cillessen & Bukowski, 2018; Ettekal & Ladd, 2019). Sociometric status is typically assessed by asking children to rate how much they like or dislike each of their classmates. Or it may be assessed by asking children to nominate the children they like the most and those they like the least.

Developmentalists have distinguished five peer statuses (Wentzel & Asher, 1995):

· **Popular children** are frequently nominated as a best friend and are rarely disliked by their peers.

· **Average children** receive an average number of both positive and negative nominations from their peers.

· **Neglected children** are infrequently nominated as a best friend but are not disliked by their peers.

· **Rejected children** are infrequently nominated as someone's best friend and are actively disliked by their peers.

What are some statuses that children have with their peers?
BananaStock

· **Controversial children** are frequently nominated both as someone's best friend and as being disliked.

Popular children have a number of social skills that contribute to their being well liked (Ferguson & Ryan, 2019; McDonald & Asher, 2018). Researchers have found that popular children give out reinforcements, listen carefully, maintain open lines of communication with peers, are happy, control their negative emotions, show enthusiasm and concern for others, and are self-confident without being conceited (Rubin, Bukowski, & Bowker,, 2015). one study, the popularity of adolescents with their peers was associated with their dating popularity (Houser, Mayeux, & Cross, 2014). Neglected children engage in low rates of interaction with their peers and are often described as shy by peers. The goal of many training programs for neglected children is to help them learn how to attract attention from their peers in positive ways and to hold that attention by asking questions, by listening in a warm and friendly way, and by saying things about themselves that relate to the peers' interests. They also are taught to enter groups more effectively.

Rejected children often have more serious adjustment problems than those who are neglected. One study revealed a link between peer rejection and depression in adolescence (Platt, Kadosh, & Lau, 2013). The combination of being rejected by peers and being aggressive especially forecasts problems (Hymel & others, 2011). Peer rejection is consistently linked to the development and maintenance of conduct problems and antisocial behavior (Kornienko, Ha, & Dishion, 2019; Prinstein & others, 2018). In one study of young adolescents, peer rejection predicted increases in aggressive and rule-breaking behavior (Janssens & others, 2017). And in another recent study of adolescents, peer rejection increased the likelihood that victims and bullies would engage in nonsuicidal self-injury, such as cutting, burning, or hitting oneself (Esposito, Bacchini, & Affuso, 2019).

John Coie (2004, pp. 252–253) gave three reasons why aggressive peer-rejected boys have problems in social relationships:

· First, the rejected, aggressive boys are more impulsive and have problems sustaining attention. As a result, they are more likely to be disruptive of ongoing activities in the classroom and in focused group play.

> Peer rejection contributes to subsequent problems of adaptation, including antisocial behavior.
>
> **—JOHN COIE**
> *Contemporary Developmental Psychologist, Duke University*

popular children Children who are frequently nominated as a best friend and are rarely disliked by their peers.

average children Children who receive an average number of both positive and negative nominations from their peers.

neglected children Children who are infrequently nominated as a best friend but are not disliked by their peers.

rejected children Children who are infrequently nominated as a best friend and are actively disliked by their peers.

controversial children Children who are frequently nominated both as someone's best friend and as being disliked.

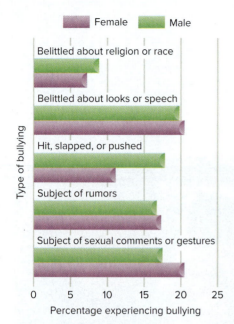

Female **Male**

Type of bullying

- Belittled about religion or race
- Belittled about looks or speech
- Hit, slapped, or pushed
- Subject of rumors
- Subject of sexual comments or gestures

0   5   10   15   20   25
Percentage experiencing bullying

FIGURE 1

BULLYING BEHAVIORS AMONG U.S. YOUTH. This graph shows the types of bullying most often experienced by U.S. youth. The percentages reflect the extent to which bullied students said that they had experienced a particular type of bullying. In terms of gender, note that when they were bullied, boys were more likely to be hit, slapped, or pushed than girls were.

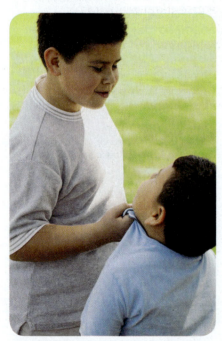

Who is likely to be bullied? What are some outcomes of bullying?
Don Hammond/Design Pics Inc./Alamy Stock Photo

- Second, rejected, aggressive boys are more emotionally reactive. They are aroused to anger more easily and probably have more difficulty calming down once aroused. Because of this they are more prone to become angry at peers and attack them verbally and physically.
- Third, rejected children have fewer social skills in making friends and maintaining positive relationships with peers.

Not all rejected children are aggressive (Rubin, Bukowski, & Bowker, 2015). Although aggression and its related characteristics of impulsiveness and disruptiveness underlie rejection about half the time, approximately 10 to 20 percent of rejected children are shy.

How can rejected children be trained to interact more effectively with their peers? Rejected children may be taught to more accurately assess whether the intentions of their peers are negative (Fontaine & others, 2010). They may be asked to engage in role playing or to discuss hypothetical situations involving negative encounters with peers, such as when a peer cuts into a line ahead of them. In some programs, children are shown videotapes of appropriate peer interaction and asked to draw lessons from what they have seen (Ladd, Buhs, & Troop, 2004).

BULLYING

Significant numbers of students are victimized by bullies (Mutiso & others, 2019; Tas & others, 2019). In a national survey of more than 15,000 students in grades 6 through 10, nearly one of every three students said that they had experienced occasional or frequent involvement as a victim or perpetrator in bullying (Nansel & others, 2001). In this study, bullying was defined as verbal or physical behavior intended to disturb someone less powerful (see Figure 1). Boys are more likely to be bullies than girls, but gender differences regarding victims of bullying are less clear (Salmivalli & Peets, 2018).

Who is likely to be bullied? In the study just described, boys and younger middle school students were most likely to be affected (Nansel & others, 2001). Children who said they were bullied reported more loneliness and difficulty in making friends, while those who did the bullying were more likely to have low grades and to smoke and drink alcohol.

Researchers have found that anxious, socially withdrawn, and aggressive children are often the victims of bullying (Chu & others, 2019; Coplan & others, 2018). Anxious and socially withdrawn children may be victimized because they are nonthreatening and unlikely to retaliate if bullied, whereas aggressive children may be the targets of bullying because their behavior is irritating to bullies (Rubin & others, 2018). The social context of the peer group also plays an important role in bullying (Troop-Gordon, 2017). Recent research indicates that 70 to 80 percent of victims and their bullies are in the same school classroom (Salmivalli & Peets, 2018). Classmates are often aware of bullying incidents and likely to witness bullying. In many cases, bullies torment victims to gain higher status in the peer group and bullies need others to witness their power displays. Many bullies are not rejected by the peer group.

What are the outcomes of bullying? Researchers have found that children who are bullied are more likely to experience depression, engage in suicidal ideation, attempt suicide, engage in antisocial behavior, and have weight problems than their counterparts who have not been the victims of bullying (Eastman & others, 2018; Naveed & others, 2019). One study indicated that peer victimization during the elementary school years was a leading predictor of internalizing problems (depression, for example) in adolescence (Schwartz & others, 2015). Also, in a recent study of 12- to 15-year-olds in 48 countries worldwide, being a victim of bullying was a risk factor in 47 of the 48 countries (Koyanagi & others, 2019).

And meta-analyses have concluded that engaging in bullying during middle school is linked to an increased likelihood of antisocial and criminal behavior later in adolescence and adulthood (Kim & others, 2011). Also, a longitudinal study found that children who were bullied at 6 years of age were more likely to have excessive weight gain when they were 12 to 13 years of age (Sutin & others, 2016). In addition, a recent study of 10- to 14-year-olds indicated that being a victim of a bully often led to a cascading effect of bullying perpetration that eventually produced disordered eating behavior (Lee & Vaillancourt, 2019). Further, one research analysis concluded that bullying can have long-term negative effects, including difficulty in forming lasting relationships and problems in the workplace (Wolke & Lereya, 2015). In addition, another recent study revealed that being a victim of bullying in childhood was linked to increased use of mental health services by the victims five decades later (Evans-Lacko & others, 2017).

An increasing concern is peer bullying and harassment on the Internet (called *cyberbullying*) (Holfeld & Mishna, 2018; Moyano & others, 2019; Myers & Cowie, 2019). One study involving third- to sixth-graders revealed that engaging in cyber aggression was related to loneliness, lower self-esteem, fewer mutual friendships, and lower peer popularity (Schoffstall & Cohen, 2011). Further, research indicates that cyberbullying was more strongly associated with suicidal ideation that traditional bullying (van Geel, Vedder, & Tanilon, 2014). Also, a meta-analysis concluded that being the victim of cyberbullying was linked to stress and suicidal ideation (Kowalski & others, 2014). And another research meta-analysis revealed that cyberbullying occurred twice as much as traditional bullying and that those who engaged in cyberbullying were likely to also have engaged in traditional bullying (Modecki & others, 2014). In addition, a recent study revealed that adolescents who were bullied both in a direct way and through cyberbullying had more behavioral problems and lower self-esteem than adolescents who were only bullied in one of these two ways (Wolke, Lee, & Guy, 2017). Also, a recent study found that the most common behavioral reactions to cyberbullying were informing a friend, counterattacking, and ignoring the cyber incident (Heiman, Olenik-Shemesh, & Frank, 2019). In this study, victims of cyberbullying were less likely than nonvictims to use problem-focused coping strategies and more likely to use emotion-focused coping strategies. Information about preventing cyberbullying can be found at www.stopcyberbullying.org/

What leads some children to become bullies and others to fall victim to bullying? To read further about bullying, see the *Connecting with Research* interlude.

connecting with research

How Are Perspective Taking and Moral Motivation Linked to Bullying?

Researchers have become increasingly interested in links between moral factors and bullying behavior (Killer & others, 2019). One study explored the roles that perspective taking and moral motivation play in the lives of bullies, bully-victims, victims, and prosocial children (Gasser & Keller, 2009):

- Bullies are highly aggressive toward other children but are not victims of bullying.
- Bully-victims not only are highly aggressive toward other children but also are the recipients of other children's bullying.
- Victims are passive, non-aggressive respondents to bullying.
- Prosocial children engage in positive behaviors such as sharing, helping, comforting, and empathizing.

Teacher and peer ratings in 34 classrooms of 7- and 8-year-old students were used to classify 212 boys and girls into the aforementioned four categories. On a five-point scale (from never to several times a week), teachers rated (1) how often the child bullied others and (2) how often the child was bullied. The ratings focused on three types of bullying and being victimized: physical, verbal, and excluding others. On a four-point scale (from not applicable to very clearly applicable), teachers also rated children's prosocial behavior on three items: "willingly shares with others," "comforts others if necessary," and "empathizes with others." Peer ratings assessed children's nominations of which children in the classroom acted as bullies, were victimized by bullies, and engaged in prosocial behavior. Combining the teacher and peer ratings after eliminating those that did not agree on which children were bullies, victims, or prosocial children, the final sample consisted of 49 bullies, 80 bully-victims, 33 victims, and 50 prosocial children.

Children's perspective-taking skills were assessed using theory of mind tasks, and moral motivation was examined by interviewing children about aspects of right and wrong in stories about children's transgressions. In one theory of mind task, children were tested to see whether they understood that people may have false beliefs about another individual. In another theory of mind task, children were assessed to determine whether they understood that people sometimes hide their emotions by showing emotions that differ from what they really feel. A moral interview also was conducted in which children were told four moral transgression stories (with content about being unwilling to share with a classmate, stealing candy from a classmate, hiding a victim's shoes, and verbally bullying a victim) and then asked to judge whether the acts were right or wrong and how the participants in the stories likely felt.

The results of the study indicated that only bully-victims—but not bullies—were deficient in perspective taking. Further analysis revealed that both aggressive groups of children—bullies and bully-victims—had a deficiency in moral motivation. The analyses were consistent with a portrait of bullies as socially competent and knowledgeable in terms of perspective-taking skills and ability to interact effectively with peers. However, bullies use this social knowledge for their own manipulative purposes. The analysis also confirmed the picture of the bully as being morally insensitive. Another study also found that bullying was linked to moral disengagement (Obermann, 2011).

How can researchers ensure that results that might help prevent bullying are properly applied in school settings (and not, for instance, used to label potential bullies or segregate potential victims)?

Extensive interest is being directed to preventing and treating bullying and victimization (Acosta & others, 2019; Cunningham & others, 2019; Nickerson & others, 2019; Tiiri & others, 2019). A research review revealed mixed results for school-based intervention (Vreeman & Carroll, 2007). School-based interventions vary greatly, ranging from involving the whole school in an anti-bullying campaign to providing individualized social skills training (Strohmeier & Noam, 2012). One of the most promising bullying intervention programs has been created by Dan Olweus (2003, 2013). This program focuses on 6- to 15-year-olds with the goal of decreasing opportunities and rewards for bullying. School staff are instructed in ways to improve peer relations and make schools safer. When properly implemented, the program reduces bullying by 30 to 70 percent (Olweus, 2003). A research review concluded that interventions focused on the whole school, such as Olweus', are more effective than interventions involving classroom curricula or social skills training (Cantone & others, 2015). Also, a teacher intervention in elementary and secondary schools to decrease bullying that focused on increasing bullies' empathy and condemning their behavior was effective in increasing the bullies' intent to stop being a bully (Garandeau & others, 2016). In this study, blaming the bully had no effect.

GENDER AND PEER RELATIONS

We know that boys are far more likely to be involved in bullying than girls are. Indeed, there is increasing evidence that gender plays an important role in peer relations, as we saw in the chapter on "Gender and Sexuality" (Chen, Lee, & Chen, 2018; Felton & others, 2019; Rose & Smith, 2018). Gender influences the composition of children's groups, their size, and the interaction within groups (Maccoby, 2002):

- *Gender composition.* Around the age of 3, children already prefer to spend time with same-sex playmates. From 4 to 12 years of age, this preference for playing in same-sex groups increases (see Figure 2).
- *Group size.* From about 5 years of age onward, boys tend to associate in larger clusters than girls do. Girls are more likely than boys to play in groups of two or three.
- *Interaction in same-sex groups.* Boys are more likely to participate in organized group games than girls are. They also are more likely to engage in rough-and-tumble play, competition, conflict, ego displays, risk taking, and dominance seeking. By contrast, girls are more likely to engage in "collaborative discourse."

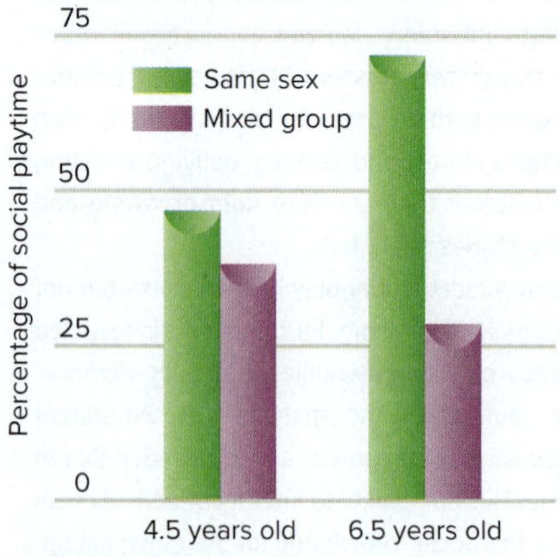

FIGURE 2

DEVELOPMENTAL CHANGES IN PERCENTAGE OF TIME SPENT IN SAME-SEX AND MIXED-GROUP SETTINGS. Observations of children show that they are more likely to play in same-sex than mixed-sex groups. This tendency increases between 4 and 6 years of age.

ADOLESCENT PEER RELATIONS

Peers play powerful roles in the lives of adolescents (Juvonen, 2018; Hennenberger, Gest, & Zadzora, 2019; Thompson, Mehari, & Farrell, 2019; Yearwood & others, 2019). And just as there are gender differences in peer relations in childhood, adolescent peer relations are influenced by gender (Rose and Smith, 2018). A meta-analysis concluded that adolescent girls show stronger peer attachment, especially related to trust and communication, than do adolescent boys (Gorrese & Ruggieri, 2012).

Children usually socialize in informal collections of friends or neighborhood acquaintances, while adolescents are often members of formal and heterogeneous groups. Such groups often include adolescents who may not be friends or neighborhood acquaintances. Adolescent groups are also more likely than childhood groups to include both boys and girls.

Do these and other peer groups matter? Yes, they do. Researchers have found that the standards of peer groups and the influence of crowds and cliques become increasingly important during adolescence (Brown & others, 2008). And as we see next, the contexts in which adolescents engage in peer relations has changed in recent years.

Peer Contexts Nowhere have the changing influences on peer relations been more evident in recent years than the increased connections adolescents make with peers and friends through networked technologies (Glover & Fritsch, 2018; Nesi & Prinstein, 2020; Yau & Reich, 2019).

Compared with earlier decades when the vast majority of adolescent contacts with peers and friends were made in person, today adolescents also spend considerable time using social media to connect with peers and friends (Nesi & Prinstein, 2019). Text messaging has become the main way adolescents connect with friends, surpassing even face-to-face contact (Lenhart, 2015a, b).

A recent analysis described five ways in which social media transform adolescent peer relationships (Nesi, Choukas-Bradley, & Prinstein, 2018):

1. *Changing the frequency or immediacy of experiences* (potential for immediate, frequent social support, reassurance, negative feedback, and co-rumination)

2. *Amplifying experiences and demands* (heightened feedback seeking and expectations for relationship maintenance and access)

3. *Altering the qualitative aspects of interactions* (less rich social support, increased comfort in interactions)

4. *Facilitating new opportunities for compensatory behaviors* (possible exclusive online relationships and communication with geographically distant friends)

5. *Creating completely novel behaviors* (new opportunities to publicize "top friends" and relationships

Later in this chapter we will further discuss adolescents' use of social media.

How might social media influence peer relationships?
Peathegee Inc/Blend Images LLC

Peer Pressure Young adolescents conform more closely to peer standards than children do (Prinstein & Giletta, 2016). Around the eighth and ninth grades, conformity to peers—especially to their antisocial standards—peaks (Brechwald & Prinstein, 2011). At this point, adolescents are most likely to go along with a peer to steal hubcaps off a car, draw graffiti on a wall, or steal cosmetics from a store counter. One study found that U.S. adolescents are more likely than Japanese adolescents to put pressure on their peers to resist parental influence (Rothbaum & others, 2000). Adolescents are more likely to conform to their peers when they are uncertain about their social identity and when they are in the presence of someone they perceive to have higher status than they do (Prinstein & Giletta, 2016). Also, one study found that boys were more likely to be influenced by peer pressure involving sexual behavior than were girls (Widman & others, 2016).

What characterizes peer pressure in adolescence? What characterizes adolescent cliques? How are they different from crowds?
Christin Rose/Getty Images

Cliques and Crowds Cliques and crowds assume more important roles in the lives of adolescents than in the lives of children (Zarbatany & others, 2019). **Cliques** are small groups that range from 2 to about 12 individuals and average about 5 or 6 individuals. The clique members are usually of the same sex and about the same age.

Cliques can form because adolescents engage in similar activities, such as being in a club or on a sports team. Some cliques also form because of friendship. Several adolescents may form a clique because they have spent time with each other, share mutual interests, and enjoy each other's company. Not necessarily friends, they often develop a friendship if they stay in the clique. What do adolescents do in cliques? They share ideas and hang out together. Often they develop an in-group identity in which they believe that their clique is better than other cliques.

Crowds are larger than cliques and less personal. Adolescents are usually members of a crowd based on reputation, and they may or may not spend much time together. Many crowds are defined by the activities adolescents engage in (such as "jocks" who are good at sports, "brains" who excel in academics, or "druggies" who take drugs). One study indicated that adolescents who identify with some crowds ("populars," for example) have fewer externalizing problem behaviors than their counterparts who identify with other crowds ("metal heads," for example) (Doornwaard & others, 2012). In this study, some crowds had a higher level of internalizing problems ("nonconformists," for example) than others ("jocks," for example).

cliques Small groups that range from 2 to 12 individuals and average about 5 or 6 individuals. Clique members usually are of the same age and same sex and often engage in similar activities, such as belonging to a club or participating in a sport.

crowds A crowd is a larger group than a clique. Adolescents usually are members of a crowd based on reputation and may not spend much time together. Many crowds are defined by the activities in which adolescents engage.

Review *Connect* Reflect

LG1 Discuss peer relations in childhood and adolescence.

Review

- What are peers, and what are the functions of peer groups? What are Piaget's and Sullivan's views on peers? How are the worlds of parents and peers distinct but coordinated? What is the developmental course of peer relations in childhood? How is social cognition involved in peer relations? What role does emotion regulation play in peer relations?
- Describe five types of peer statuses.
- What is the nature of bullying?
- How is gender involved in children's peer relations?
- How do adolescent peer groups differ from childhood peer groups? What are peer pressure and conformity like in adolescence? How are cliques and crowds involved in adolescent development? What are some cultural variations in adolescent peer relations?

Connect

- Most developmentalists agree that peers play an important role in the development of moral reasoning. Of the five peer status groups you learned about in this section of the chapter, in which one(s) do you think children would have the least opportunity to fully develop their moral reasoning capacities and why?

Reflect *Your Own Personal Journey of Life*

- Think back to your childhood and adolescent years. Which peer status would you use to describe yourself? How influential do you think your peer status was on your development?

---

2 Friendship

LG2 Explain the role of friendship through the life span.

| Functions of Friendship | Friendship During Childhood | Friendship During Adolescence and Emerging Adulthood | Adult Friendship |

The world of peers is one of varying acquaintances; each day we interact with some people we barely know and with others we know well. It is to the latter type—friends—that we now turn.

FUNCTIONS OF FRIENDSHIP

Why are friendships important? They serve the following functions (Gottman & Parker, 1987):

- *Companionship.* Friendship provides a familiar partner and playmate, someone who is willing to spend time with us and join in collaborative activities.
- *Stimulation.* Friendship provides interesting information, excitement, and amusement.
- *Ego support.* Friendship provides the expectation of support, encouragement, and feedback, which helps us maintain an impression of ourselves as competent, attractive, and worthwhile individuals.
- *Social comparison.* Friendship provides information about where we stand vis-à-vis others and how we are doing.
- *Affection and intimacy.* Friendship provides a warm, close, trusting relationship with another individual. **Intimacy in friendships** is characterized by self-disclosure and the sharing of private thoughts. Research reveals that intimate friendships may not appear until early adolescence (Berndt & Perry, 1990).

FRIENDSHIP DURING CHILDHOOD

Children's friendships are typically characterized by similarity (referred to as homophily, the tendency to associate with similar others) (Neal, Neal, & Cappella, 2014). Similarity is a central aspect of friendship that may or may not be beneficial (Prinstein & Giletta, 2016).

intimacy in friendship Self-disclosure and the sharing of private thoughts.

Throughout childhood, friends are more similar than dissimilar in terms of age, sex, ethnicity, and many other factors. Friends often have similar attitudes toward school, similar educational aspirations, and closely aligned achievement orientations.

Although having friends can be a developmental advantage, all friendships are not alike (Bagwell & Bukowski, 2018). People differ in the company they keep—that is, who their friends are. Developmental advantages occur when children have friends who are socially skilled, supportive, and oriented toward academic achievement (Ryan & Shin, 2018). However, it is not developmentally advantageous to have coercive, conflict-ridden, and poor-quality friendships (Clayton & others, 2019; Zhang & others, 2018). One study found that students who engaged in aggressive-disruptive behavior in the classroom were more likely to have aggressive friends (Powers & Bierman, 2013). To read about strategies for helping children develop friendships, see the *Connecting Development to Life* interlude.

What characterizes children's friendships?
Image Source/Alamy Stock Photo

FRIENDSHIP DURING ADOLESCENCE AND EMERGING ADULTHOOD

How are adolescent friendships different from childhood friendships? What characterizes friendship in emerging adulthood?

Adolescence   For most children, being popular with their peers is a strong motivator. The focus of their peer relations is on being liked by classmates and being included in games or lunchroom conversations. Beginning in early adolescence, however, teenagers typically prefer to have a smaller number of friendships that are more intense and intimate than those of young children.

Harry Stack Sullivan (1953) has been the most influential theorist in the study of adolescent friendships. Sullivan argued that friends are also important in shaping the development of children and adolescents. Everyone, said Sullivan, has basic social needs, such as the need for secure attachment, playful companionship, social acceptance, intimacy, and sexual relations. Whether or not these needs are fulfilled largely determines our emotional well-being. For example, if the need for playful companionship goes unmet, then we become bored and depressed; if the need for social acceptance is not met, we suffer a diminished sense of self-worth.

connecting development to life

Effective and Ineffective Strategies for Making Friends

Here are some strategies that adults can recommend to children and adolescents for making friends (Wentzel, 1997):

- *Initiate interaction.* Learn about a friend: Ask for his or her name, age, favorite activities. Use these prosocial overtures: Introduce yourself, start a conversation, and invite him or her to do things.
- *Be nice.* Show kindness, be considerate, and compliment the other person.
- *Engage in prosocial behavior.* Be honest and trustworthy: Tell the truth, keep promises. Be generous, share, and be cooperative.
- *Show respect for yourself and others.* Have good manners, be polite and courteous, and listen to what others have to say. Have a positive attitude and personality.
- *Provide social support.* Show you care.

And here are some ineffective strategies for making friends that adults can advise children and adolescents to avoid (Wentzel, 1997):

- *Be psychologically aggressive.* Show disrespect and have bad manners. Use others, be uncooperative, don't share, ignore others, gossip, and spread rumors.
- *Present yourself negatively.* Be self-centered, snobby, conceited, and jealous; show off, care only about yourself. Be mean, have a bad attitude, be angry, throw temper tantrums, and start trouble.
- *Behave antisocially.* Be physically aggressive, yell at others, pick on them, make fun of them, be dishonest, tell secrets, and break promises.

These suggestions were developed for adults to use in guiding children. Do you think there is any period of the life span in which they would not be appropriate? Are some more effective in some periods of the life span than in others? If so, which ones and why?

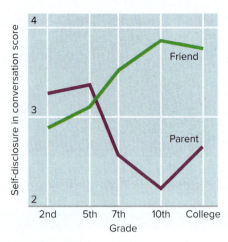

FIGURE 3

DEVELOPMENTAL CHANGES IN SELF-DISCLOSING CONVERSATIONS. Self-disclosing conversations with friends increase dramatically in adolescence while self-disclosure with parents declines in an equally dramatic fashion. However, self-disclosing conversations with parents begin to pick up somewhat during the college years. In this study, self-disclosure was measured using a five-point rating scale completed by the children and youth, with a higher score representing greater self-disclosure. The data shown represent the means for each age group.

A man's growth is seen in the successive choirs of his friends.

—RALPH WALDO EMERSON

American Author and Poet, 19th Century

developmental connection

Gender

Deborah Tannen emphasizes gender differences in report talk and rapport talk. Connect to "Gender and Sexuality."

During adolescence, said Sullivan, friends become increasingly important in meeting social needs. In particular, Sullivan argued that the need for intimacy intensifies during early adolescence, motivating teenagers to develop close friendships. If adolescents fail to forge such close friendships, they often feel lonely and inadequate.

Many of Sullivan's ideas have withstood the test of time. For example, adolescents report disclosing intimate and personal information to their friends more often than younger children do (Buhrmester, 1998) (see Figure 3). Adolescents also say they depend more on friends than on parents to satisfy their needs for companionship, reassurance of worth, and intimacy. The ups and downs of experiences with friends shape adolescents' well-being (Bagwell & Bukowski, 2018; Laursen, 2018).

Are the friendships of adolescent girls more intimate than the friendships of adolescent boys? Girls' friendships in adolescence are more likely to focus on intimacy; boys' friendships tend to emphasize power and excitement (Rose & Smith, 2018). Boys may discourage one another from openly disclosing their problems because self-disclosure is not considered masculine (Maccoby, 1998).

A study of third- through ninth-graders, though, revealed that one aspect of girls' social support in friendship may have costs as well as benefits (Rose, Carlson, & Waller, 2007). In the study, girls' co-rumination (as reflected in excessively discussing problems) predicted not only an increase in positive friendship quality but also an increase in further co-rumination as well as an increase in depressive and anxiety symptoms. One implication of the research is that some girls who are vulnerable to developing internalized problems may go undetected because they have supportive friendships.

The study just described indicates that the characteristics of an adolescent's friends can influence whether the friends have a positive or negative influence on the adolescent (Felton & others, 2019; Wentzel & Munecks, 2016). Positive relationships with friends in adolescence are associated with a host of positive outcomes, including lower rates of delinquency, substance abuse, risky sexual behavior, and bullying victimization, and a higher level of academic achievement and exercise (Ryan & Shin, 2018). Not having a close relationship with a best friend, having less contact with friends, having friends who are depressed, and experiencing peer rejection all increase depressive tendencies in adolescents (Prinstein & others, 2018; Rubin & others, 2018). Researchers have found that interacting with delinquent peers and friends greatly increases the risk of becoming delinquent (Deutsch & others, 2012; Walters, 2019). One study found that adolescents adapted their smoking and drinking behavior to match that of their best friends (Wang & others, 2016). Another recent study of adolescent girls revealed that friends' dieting predicted whether an adolescent girl would engage in dieting or extreme dieting (Balantekin, Birch, & Savage, 2018).

Although most adolescents develop friendships with individuals who are close to their own age, some adolescents become best friends with younger or older individuals. Do older friends encourage adolescents to engage in delinquent behavior or early sexual behavior? Adolescents who interact with older youth do engage in these behaviors more frequently, but it is not known whether the older youth guide younger adolescents toward deviant behavior or whether the younger adolescents were already prone to deviant behavior before they developed the friendship with the older youth (Billy, Rodgers, & Udry, 1984). A study also revealed that over time from the sixth through tenth grades girls were more likely to have older male friends, which places some girls on a developmental trajectory for engaging in problem behavior (Poulin & Pedersen, 2007).

Emerging Adulthood   Many aspects of friendship are the same in emerging adulthood as they were in adolescence. One difference was found, however, in a longitudinal study (Collins & van Dulmen, 2006). Close relationships—between friends, family members, and romantic partners—were more integrated and similar in emerging adulthood than they were in adolescence. Also in this study, the number of friendships declined from the end of adolescence through emerging adulthood.

Another research study indicated that best friendships often decline in satisfaction and commitment in the first year of college (Oswald & Clark, 2003). In this study, maintaining communication with high school friends and keeping the same best friends across the transition to college lessened the decline.

ADULT FRIENDSHIP

As in childhood and adolescence, adult friends tend to be similar in a number of ways. Among the similarities in friendship during the adult years are occupational status, ethnicity, age, marital status, income, education, gender, and religion (Rawlins, 2009).

How is adult friendship different among female friends, male friends, and cross-gender friends?
(*Left to right*): Stockbyte/Punchstock; Loreanto/Shutterstock; Ingram Publishing/age fotostock

Gender Differences   As in the childhood and adolescent years, there are gender differences in adult friendships. Women have more close friends than men do, and their friendships are more intimate (Wood, 2011, 2012). When adult female friends get together, they often talk, whereas adult male friends are more likely to engage in activities, especially outdoors. Thus, the adult male pattern of friendship often involves keeping one's distance while sharing useful information. When women talk with their friends, they expect to be able to express their feelings, reveal their weaknesses, and discuss their problems. They anticipate that their friends will listen at length and be sympathetic. In contrast, men are less likely to talk about their weaknesses with their friends, and they want practical solutions to their problems rather than sympathy (Tannen, 1990). Also, adult male friendships are more competitive than those of women (Sharkey, 1993). For example, male friends disagree with each other more. Keep in mind, however, that these differences in same-sex adult friendship tend to be small (Sabini, 1995).

What about female-male friendship? Cross-gender friendships are more common among adults than among elementary school children, but not as common as same-gender friendships (Wood, 2011, 2012). Cross-gender friendships can provide both opportunities and problems (Trinh & Choukas-Bradley, 2018). The opportunities involve learning more about common feelings and interests and shared characteristics, as well as acquiring knowledge and understanding of beliefs and activities that historically have been typical of the other gender.

Problems can arise in cross-gender friendships because of different expectations. For example, a woman might expect sympathy from a male friend but might receive a directive solution rather than a shoulder to cry on (Tannen, 1990). Another problem that can plague adult cross-gender friendship is unclear sexual boundaries, which can produce tension and confusion (Swain, 1992).

Friendship in Late Adulthood   In early adulthood, friendship networks expand as new social connections are made away from home. In late adulthood, new friendships are less likely to be forged, although some adults do seek out new friendships, especially following the death of a spouse (Blieszner, & Ogletree, 2017, 2018).

Aging expert Laura Carstensen and her colleagues (1998, 2009; Sims, Hogan, & Carstensen, 2015) concluded that people choose close friends over new friends as they grow older. And as long as they have several close people in their network, they seem content, says Carstensen. Supporting Carstensen's view, researchers found that in comparison with younger adults, older adults said they tended to experience less intense positive emotions with new friends and equal levels of positive emotions with established friends (Charles & Piazza, 2007) (see Figure 4). Also, in a recent study, compared with younger adults, older adults reported fewer problems with friends, fewer negative friendship qualities, less frequent contact with friends, and more positive friendship qualities with a specific friend (Schlosnagle & Strough, 2017).

And in other research, older adults 75 years of age and older who maintained close ties with friends were less likely to die across a seven-year age span (Rasulo, Christensen, & Tomassini, 2005). The findings were stronger for women than for men.

What are some characteristics of older adults' friendships?
kali9/Getty Images

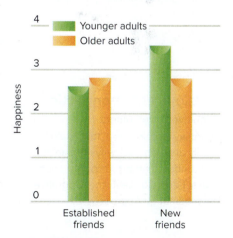

FIGURE 4

HAPPINESS OF YOUNGER ADULTS AND OLDER ADULTS WITH NEW AND ESTABLISHED FRIENDS. *Note:* The happiness scale ranged from 0 to 6, with participants rating how intensely they experienced happiness (0 = not at all, 6 = extremely intense). Older adults' mean age was 71; younger adults' mean age was 23.

Review Connect Reflect

LG2 Explain the role of friendship through the life span.

Review
- What are five functions of friendship?
- What is the developmental significance of friendship during childhood?
- How can adolescents' friendships be characterized? What is Sullivan's view on friendship? What are friendships in emerging adulthood like?
- How do adults' friendships vary based on gender and age?

Connect
- Connect this section's discussion of friendship in late adulthood with what you've learned about health and aging.

Reflect *Your Own Personal Journey of Life*
- What characterizes your relationships with friends at this point in your life? How are your friendships different from what they were like when you were younger?

3 Play and Leisure

 LG3 Describe the developmental aspects of play and leisure.

Childhood   Adolescence   Adulthood

Peers and friends often engage in play and enjoy leisure activities together. Let's explore the developmental aspects of play and leisure.

CHILDHOOD

An extensive amount of peer interaction during childhood involves play; however, social play is but one type of play. **Play** is a pleasurable activity that is engaged in for its own sake.

Play's Functions Play is an important aspect of children's development (Taggart, Eisen, & Lillard, 2018; Yogman & others, 2019). Theorists have focused on different aspects of play and highlighted a long list of functions.

According to Freud and Erikson, play helps the child master anxieties and reduce conflicts (Demanachick, 2015). Because tensions are relieved in play, the child can cope more effectively with life's problems. Play permits the child to work off excess physical energy and release pent-up tensions. Therapists use **play therapy** both to allow the child to release frustrations and to analyze the child's conflicts and ways of coping with them. Children may feel less threatened and be more likely to express their true feelings in the context of play (Clark, 2016).

Piaget (1962) maintained that play advances children's cognitive development. At the same time, he said that children's cognitive development constrains the way they play. Play permits children to practice their competencies and skills in a relaxed, pleasurable way (Hirsh-Pasek & Golinkoff, 2014). Piaget thought that cognitive structures need to be exercised, and play provides the perfect setting for this exercise (DeLisi, 2015). For example, children who have just learned to add or multiply begin to play with numbers in different ways as they perfect these operations, laughing as they do so.

Vygotsky (1962) also considered play to be an excellent setting for cognitive development. He was especially interested in the symbolic and make-believe aspects of play, as when a child substitutes a stick for a horse and rides the stick as if it were a horse (Bodrova & Leong, 2015). For young children, the imaginary situation is real. Parents should encourage such imaginary play, because it advances the child's cognitive development, especially creative thought. Both Piaget and Vygotsky described play as the work of the child.

Daniel Berlyne (1960) described play as exciting and pleasurable in itself because it satisfies our exploratory drive. This drive involves curiosity and a desire for information about something new or unusual. Play is a means whereby children can safely explore and seek out new information. Play encourages exploratory behavior by offering children the possibilities of novelty, complexity, uncertainty, surprise, and incongruity.

> You are troubled at seeing him spend his early years in doing nothing. What! Is it nothing to be happy? Is it nothing to skip, to play, to run about all day long? Never in his life will he be so busy as now.
>
> —JEAN-JACQUES ROUSSEAU
> *Swiss-born French Philosopher, 18th Century*

developmental **connection**

Cognitive Development

Vygotsky emphasized that children mainly develop their ways of thinking and understanding through social interaction. Connect to "Cognitive Developmental Approaches."

play A pleasurable activity that is engaged in for its own sake.

play therapy Therapy that lets children work off frustrations while therapists analyze their conflicts and coping methods.

More recently, play has been described as an important context for the development of language and communication skills (Taggart, Eisen, & Lillard, 2018; Toub & others, 2018). Language and communication skills may be enhanced through discussions and negotiations regarding roles and rules in play as young children practice various words and phrases. These types of social interactions during play can benefit young children's literacy skills. Play is a central focus of the child-centered kindergarten and is thought to be an essential aspect of early childhood education (Feeney, Moravcik, & Nolte, 2019; Follari, 2019).

An increasing concern is that the large number of hours children spend with electronic media, such as television and computers, takes time away from play (Lissak, 2018). A recent study of 2- to 5-year-olds found that television/DVD/video viewing was negatively linked to young children's social skills while outdoor play was positively associated with their social skills (Hinkley & others, 2018). Thus, an important agenda for parents is to include ample time for play in their children's lives.

Types of Play   The contemporary perspective on types of play emphasizes both cognitive and social aspects of play (Akhutina & Romanova, 2017; Yogman & others, 2019). Among the most widely studied types of children's play today are sensorimotor and practice play, pretense/symbolic play, social play, constructive play, and games.

Sensorimotor and Practice Play   **Sensorimotor play** is behavior by infants to derive pleasure from exercising their sensorimotor schemes. The development of sensorimotor play follows Piaget's description of sensorimotor thought. Infants initially engage in exploratory and playful visual and motor transactions in the second quarter of the first year of life. By the end of the third quarter, infants begin to select novel objects for exploration and play, especially responsive objects such as toys that make noise or bounce. At 12 months of age, infants enjoy making things work and exploring cause and effect.

Practice play involves repetition of behavior when new skills are being learned or when physical or mental mastery and coordination of skills are required for games or sports. Sensorimotor play, which often involves practice play, is primarily confined to infancy, whereas practice play can be engaged in throughout life. During the preschool years, children frequently engage in practice play. Although practice play declines in the elementary school years, practice play activities such as running, jumping, sliding, twirling, and throwing balls or other objects are frequently observed on the playgrounds at elementary schools.

Pretense/Symbolic Play   **Pretense/symbolic play** occurs when the child transforms aspects of the physical environment into symbols. Between 9 and 30 months of age, children increase their use of objects in symbolic play. They learn to transform objects—substituting them for other objects and acting toward them as if they were those other objects (Taggart, Eisen, & Lillard, 2018). For example, a preschool child treats a table as if it were a car and says, "I'm fixing the car," as he grabs a leg of the table.

Many experts on play consider the preschool years the "golden age" of symbolic/pretense play that is dramatic or sociodramatic in nature. This type of make-believe play often appears at about 18 months of age and reaches a peak at 4 to 5 years of age, then gradually declines.

Some child psychologists conclude that pretense/symbolic play is an important aspect of young children's development and often reflects advances in their cognitive development, especially as an indication of symbolic understanding (Taggart, Eisen, & Lillard, 2018). For example, Catherine Garvey (2000) and Angeline Lillard (2015) emphasize that hidden in young children's pretend play narratives are capacities for role-taking, balancing of social roles, metacognition (thinking about thinking), testing of the reality-pretense distinction, and numerous non-egocentric capacities that reveal the remarkable cognitive skills of young children.

Social Play   **Social play** is play that involves interaction with peers. Social play increases dramatically during the preschool years (Solovieva & Quintanar, 2017). Social play includes varied interchanges such as turn taking, conversations about numerous topics, social games and routines, and physical play (Sumaroka & Bornstein, 2008). Social play often involves a high degree of pleasure on the part of the participants (Sumaroka & Bornstein, 2008).

Constructive Play   **Constructive play** combines sensorimotor/practice play with symbolic representation. Constructive play occurs when children engage in the self-regulated creation of a product or a solution. Constructive play increases in the preschool years as symbolic play increases and sensorimotor play decreases. In the preschool years, some practice play is

A preschool "superhero" at play.
Michelle D. Milliman/Shutterstock

developmental **connection**

Education

The child-centered kindergarten emphasizes the education of the whole child and the importance of play in young children's development. Connect to "Schools, Achievement, and Work."

sensorimotor play Behavior in which infants derive pleasure from exercising their sensorimotor schemes.

practice play Play that involves repetition of behavior when new skills are being learned or when mastery and coordination of skills are required for games or sports.

pretense/symbolic play Play that occurs when a child transforms aspects of the physical environment into symbols.

social play Play that involves interaction with peers.

constructive play Combination of sensorimotor/practice play with symbolic representation.

What are some different types of play?
Fotostorm/Getty Images

replaced by constructive play. For example, instead of moving their fingers around and around in finger paint (practice play), children are more likely to draw the outline of a house or a person in the paint (constructive play). Constructive play is also a frequent form of play in the elementary school years, both within and outside the classroom.

Games   **Games** are activities that are engaged in for pleasure and have rules. Often they involve competition. Preschool children may begin to participate in social games that involve simple rules of reciprocity and turn taking. However, games take on a much stronger role in the lives of elementary school children.

In sum, play ranges from an infant's simple exercise of a new sensorimotor skill to a preschool child's riding a tricycle to an older child's participation in organized games. Note that children's play can involve a combination of the play categories we have discussed. For example, social play can be sensorimotor (rough-and-tumble), symbolic, or constructive.

Trends in Play   Kathy Hirsh-Pasek, Roberta Golinkoff, and Dorothy Singer (Hirsh-Pasek & others, 2009; Singer, Golinkoff, & Hirsh-Pasek, 2006) are concerned about the limited amount of time that young children engage in free play, reporting that it has declined considerably in recent decades. They especially are worried about young children's playtime being restricted at home and school so they can spend more time on academic subjects. They also point out that many schools have eliminated recess. And it is not just the decline in free play time that bothers them. They underscore that learning in playful contexts captivates children's minds in ways that enhance their cognitive and socioemotional development. In fact, Singer, Golinkoff, and Hirsh-Pasek's (2006) first book on play was titled: *Play = Learning.* Among the cognitive benefits of play they described are these skills: creative, abstract thinking; imagination; attention, concentration, and persistence; problem-solving; social cognition, empathy, and perspective taking; language; and mastering new concepts. Among the socioemotional experiences and development they believe play promotes are enjoyment, relaxation, and self-expression; cooperation, sharing, and turn-taking; anxiety reduction; and self-confidence. With so many positive cognitive and socioemotional outcomes of play, clearly it is important that we find more time for play in young children's lives (Toub & others, 2018; Yogman & others, 2019).

ADOLESCENCE

Leisure refers to the pleasant times when individuals are free to pursue activities and interests of their own choosing—hobbies, sports, or reading, for example. How much leisure time do U.S. adolescents have compared with adolescents in other countries? How do U.S. adolescents use their leisure time?

Figure 5 indicates that U.S. adolescents spend more time in leisure activities than do adolescents in other industrialized countries (Larson & Verma, 1999). About 40 to 50 percent of U.S. adolescents' waking hours (not counting summer vacation) is spent in leisure activities, compared with 25 to 35 percent in East Asia and 35 to 45 percent in Europe. Whether this additional leisure time is a liability or an asset for U.S. adolescents, of course, depends on how they use it.

games Activities that are engaged in for pleasure and include rules.

leisure The pleasant times when individuals are free to pursue activities and interests of their own choosing.

Activity	Nonindustrial, Unschooled Populations	Postindustrial, Schooled Populations		
		United States	Europe	East Asia
TV viewing	Insufficient data	1.5 to 2.5 hours	1.5 to 2.5 hours	1.5 to 2.5 hours
Talking	Insufficient data	2 to 3 hours	Insufficient data	45 to 60 minutes
Sports	Insufficient data	30 to 60 minutes	20 to 80 minutes	0 to 20 minutes
Structured voluntary activities	Insufficient data	10 to 20 minutes	10 to 20 minutes	0 to 10 minutes
Total free time	4 to 7 hours	6.5 to 8.0 hours	5.5 to 7.5 hours	4.0 to 5.5 hours

Note: The estimates in the table are averaged across a 7-day week, including weekdays and weekends. The data for nonindustrial, unschooled populations come primarily from rural peasant populations in developing countries.

FIGURE 5

AVERAGE DAILY LEISURE TIME OF ADOLESCENTS IN DIFFERENT REGIONS OF THE WORLD

The largest amounts of U.S. adolescents' free time are spent engaging in screen-based activities, hanging out, and engaging in unstructured leisure activities, often with friends. U.S. and European adolescents spend more time in voluntary structured activities—such as sports, hobbies, and organizations—than East Asian adolescents do.

According to Reed Larson and his colleagues (Larson, 2001; Larson, Orson, & Bowers, 2017; Larson, Walker, & McGovern, 2018), in terms of optimal development U.S. adolescents may have too much unstructured time because when they are allowed to choose what to do with their time, they typically engage in unchallenging leisure activities such as hanging out and watching TV. Although relaxation and social interaction are important aspects of adolescence, it seems unlikely that spending large numbers of hours per week in unchallenging activities fosters development. Structured voluntary activities may hold more promise for adolescent development than unstructured time, especially if adults give responsibility to adolescents, challenge them, and provide competent guidance in these activities (Larson, McGovern & Orson, 2018).

developmental **connection**

Culture

In the research of Harold Stevenson and his colleagues, the longer students were in school, the wider the gap was between Asian and U.S. students in math achievement. Connect to "Schools, Achievement, and Work."

How do U.S. adolescents spend their time differently from European and East Asian adolescents?
Allan Shoemake/Getty Images

ADULTHOOD

Sigmund Freud said that the two things adults need to do well to adapt to society's demands are to work and to love. To his list we add "to play." In our fast-paced society, it is all too easy to get caught up in the frenzied, hectic pace of our achievement-oriented work world and ignore leisure and play. *Imagine your life as a middle-aged adult. What would be the ideal mix of work and leisure? What leisure activities do you want to enjoy as a middle-aged adult?*
wundervisuals/Getty Images

As adults, not only must we learn how to work well, but we also need to learn how to relax and enjoy leisure (Finkel, Andel, & Pedersen, 2018; Hagnas & others, 2018). In an analysis of what U.S. adults regret the most, not engaging in more leisure was one of the top six regrets (Roese & Summerville, 2005).

Leisure can be an especially important aspect of middle adulthood (Mannell, 2000). By middle adulthood, more money is available to many individuals, and there may be more free time and paid vacations. In short, midlife changes may produce expanded opportunities for leisure. For many individuals, middle adulthood is the first time in their lives when they have the opportunity to diversify their interests.

In one study, 12,338 men 35 to 57 years of age were assessed each year for five years regarding whether they took vacations or not (Gump & Matthews, 2000). Then the researchers examined the medical and death records over nine years for men who lived for at least a year after the last vacation survey. Compared with those who never took vacations, men who went on annual vacations were 21 percent less likely to die over the nine years and 32 percent less likely to die of coronary heart disease. The qualities that lead men to avoid taking a vacation tend to promote heart disease, such as not trusting anyone to fill in while they are gone or fearing that they will get behind in their work and someone will replace them. These are behaviors that sometimes have been described as part of the Type A behavioral pattern.

Recent research further indicates the importance of leisure in cognitive and health outcomes (Lahti, Lahelma, & Rahkonen, 2017; Werneck & others, 2019). One study found that engaging in higher complexity of work before retirement was associated with less cognitive decline during retirement (Andel, Finkel, & Pedersen, 2016). Also, a Danish longitudinal study of 20- to 93-year-olds found that those who engaged in a light level of leisure-time physical activity lived 2.8 years longer, those who engaged in a moderate level of leisure-time physical activity lived 4.5 years longer, and those who engaged in high level of leisure-time physical activity lived 5.5 years longer (Schnohr & others, 2017). One study revealed that middle-aged adults who engaged in active leisure-time pursuits had a higher-level cognitive performance in late adulthood (Ihle & others, 2015). In another study, individuals who engaged in a greater amount of sedentary screen-based leisure-time activity (TV, video games, computer use) had shorter telomere length (telomeres cover the end of chromosomes and as people age their telomeres become shorter and this shorter telomere length is linked to earlier mortality) (Loprinzi, 2015). And another study revealed that middle-aged individuals who engaged in high levels of leisure-time physical activity were less likely to have Alzheimer disease 28 years later (Tolppanen & others, 2015). Further, a recent study of more than 300,000 individuals from 50 to 71 years of age found that those who engaged in the most leisure-time physical activity were at lowest risk for all-cause, cardiovascular-disease-related, and cancer-related mortality (Saint-Maurice & others, 2019).

Adults at midlife need to begin preparing psychologically for retirement. Participating in constructive and fulfilling leisure activities in middle adulthood is an important part of this preparation (Kelly, 1996). If adults develop leisure activities that they can continue into retirement, the transition from work to retirement can be less stressful.

Review Connect Reflect

LG3 Describe the developmental aspects of play and leisure.

Review

- What are the functions of play? What are the different types of play?
- What is leisure? How do adolescents use their discretionary time?
- What are some key aspects of leisure in adulthood?

Connect

- How might friendship and moral development interact during adolescence?

Reflect *Your Own Personal Journey of Life*

- Do you think your life as a child and now as an adult is too structured and leaves too little time for play? Did you have too much unstructured time as an adolescent? Explain.

| Social Theories of Aging | Stereotyping of Older Adults | Social Support and Social Integration | Successful Aging |

What happens to our social world when we get older? Does it shrink? Do we become more selective and spend more time with our closest friends? How do social experiences influence the aging process? In this section we'll explore some theories of aging that give social experiences an important role.

SOCIAL THEORIES OF AGING

Socioemotional selectivity theory states that older adults become more selective about their social networks and often seek greater emotional quality in relationships with friends and family. One explanation for prioritizing meaningful relationships when getting older is the increasingly limited time left in life (Moss & Wilson, 2017). Researchers have found extensive support for socioemotional selectivity theory (Carstensen, 2019; Carstensen & DeLiema, 2018). Let's consider two other social theories of aging.

Disengagement theory states that to cope effectively, older adults should gradually withdraw from society. This theory was proposed half a century ago (Cumming & Henry, 1961). In this view, older adults develop increasing self-preoccupation, lessen emotional ties with others, and show decreasing interest in society's affairs. By following these strategies of disengagement, it was thought that older adults would enjoy enhanced life satisfaction. This theory generated a storm of protest and met with a quick death. We present it because of its historical relevance. Although not formally proposed until 1961, it summarized the prevailing beliefs about older adults in the first half of the twentieth century.

Activity theory states that the more active and involved older adults are, the more satisfied they will be with their lives. Thus, activity theory is the exact opposite of disengagement theory. Researchers have found strong support for activity theory, beginning in the 1960s and continuing into the twenty-first century (Antonucci & Webster, 2019; Duggal & others, 2019; Strandberg, 2019; Walker, 2019). One longitudinal study found that a greater overall activity level (which included social activities such as visiting relatives or friends, solitary activities such as hobbies, and productive activities such as volunteer work and gardening) at the beginning of the study was related to greater happiness, better physical and cognitive functioning, and reduced mortality six years later (Menec, 2003). Another study found that older adults who increased their leisure-time activity were three times more likely to have a slower progression to having a functional disability (Chen & others, 2016). And a recent study indicated that an activity-based lifestyle was linked to lower levels of depression in older adults (Juang & others, 2018). In sum, when older adults are active, energetic, and productive, they age more successfully and are happier than if they disengage from society (Walker, 2019).

STEREOTYPING OF OLDER ADULTS

Social participation by older adults is often discouraged by **ageism,** which is prejudice against others because of their age, especially prejudice against older adults (Avalon, 2019; Gendron & others, 2019; Lytle, Levy, & Meeks, 2019; Wilson, Errasti-Ibarrondo, & Low, 2019). Older adults are often perceived as incapable of thinking clearly, learning new things, enjoying sex, contributing to the community, or holding responsible jobs (Senger, 2019). Because of their age, older adults might not be hired for new jobs or might be eased out of old ones; they might be shunned socially; and they might be edged out of their family life.

Ageism is widespread (Castle, 2019; O'Connor & Kelson, 2018; Shippee & others, 2019). One study found that men were more likely to negatively stereotype older adults than were women (Rupp, Vodanovich, & Crede, 2005). Research indicates that the most frequent form

developmental **connection**
Social Contexts
Socioemotional selectivity theory also focuses on the types of goals individuals are motivated to achieve as they go through the adult years. Connect to "Emotional Development and Attachment."

This photographer is 105-year-old Li Yuzhen, who still works in a photo studio in Lianhua, China. *How does this centenarian's behavior contradict negative stereotyping of older adults?*
Imagine China/Newscom

disengagement theory The theory that, to cope effectively, older adults should gradually withdraw from society; this theory is not supported by research.

activity theory The theory that the more active and involved older adults are, the more likely they are to be satisfied with their lives.

ageism Prejudice against people because of their age, especially prejudice against older adults.

of ageism is disrespect for older adults, followed by assumptions about ailments or frailty caused by age (Palmore, 2004). Also, a recent study conducted in 29 European countries examined age discrimination by individuals 15 to 115 years of age (Bratt & others, 2018). In this study, younger individuals showed more age discrimination toward older adults than did older individuals.

SOCIAL SUPPORT AND SOCIAL INTEGRATION

Social support and social integration play important roles in the physical and mental health of older adults (Smith & others, 2018). In the *social convoy* model of social relations, individuals go through life embedded in a personal network of individuals to whom they give, and from whom they receive, social support (Antonucci & Webster, 2019; Antonucci & others, 2016). Social support can help individuals of all ages cope more effectively with life's challenges.

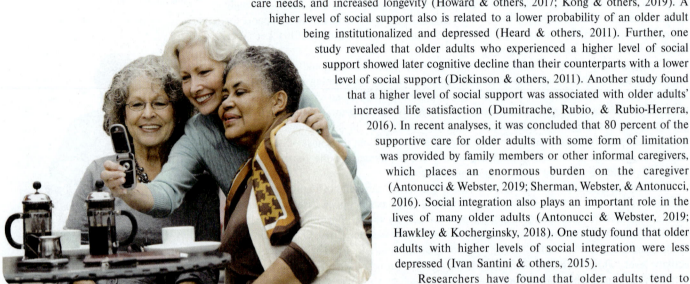

For older adults, social support is related to their physical and mental health as well as their life satisfaction (Antonucci & Webster, 2019; Kim & Lee, 2019; Suanet & others, 2019). It is linked with a reduction in symptoms of disease, with the ability to meet one's own health-care needs, and increased longevity (Howard & others, 2017; Kong & others, 2019). A higher level of social support also is related to a lower probability of an older adult being institutionalized and depressed (Heard & others, 2011). Further, one study revealed that older adults who experienced a higher level of social support showed later cognitive decline than their counterparts with a lower level of social support (Dickinson & others, 2011). Another study found that a higher level of social support was associated with older adults' increased life satisfaction (Dumitrache, Rubio, & Rubio-Herrera, 2016). In recent analyses, it was concluded that 80 percent of the supportive care for older adults with some form of limitation was provided by family members or other informal caregivers, which places an enormous burden on the caregiver (Antonucci & Webster, 2019; Sherman, Webster, & Antonucci, 2016). Social integration also plays an important role in the lives of many older adults (Antonucci & Webster, 2019; Hawkley & Kocherginsky, 2018). One study found that older adults with higher levels of social integration were less depressed (Ivan Santini & others, 2015).

What characterizes social integration in the lives of older adults?
Yellow Dog Productions/Getty Images

Researchers have found that older adults tend to report being less lonely than younger adults and less lonely than would be expected based on their circumstances (Schnittker, 2007). Their reports of feeling less lonely than younger adults likely reflect their more selective social networks and greater acceptance of loneliness in their lives (Antonucci & Webster, 2019). In one study, the most consistent factor that predicted loneliness in older adults at 70, 78, and 85 years of age was not being married (Stessman & others, 2014). In other research with 60- to 80-year-olds, the partner's death was a stronger indicator of loneliness for men than for women (Nicolaisen & Thorsen, 2014). And in a recent study, 18 percent of older adults stated they were often or frequently lonely (Due, Sandholdt, & Waldorff, 2017). In this study, the most important predictors of feeling lonely were anxiety and depressive symptoms, living alone, and low social participation.

SUCCESSFUL AGING

On a number of occasions, we have called attention to the positive aspects of aging. In fact, examining the positive aspects of aging is an important trend in life-span development and is likely to benefit future generations of older adults (Fernandez-Ballesteros, 2019; Robine, 2019).

There are many robust, healthy older adults. With a proper diet, an active lifestyle, mental stimulation and flexibility, positive coping skills, good social relationships and support, and the absence of disease, many abilities can be maintained or in some cases even improved as we get older (Caprara & Mendoza-Ruvalcaba, 2019; Marquez-Gonzalez, Cheng, & Losada, 2019). Even when individuals develop a disease, improvements in medical technology mean that increasing numbers of older adults can continue to lead active, constructive lives. A Canadian study found that the predicted self-rated probability of aging successfully was 41 percent for those 65 to 74, 33 percent for those 75 to 84, and 22 percent for those 85 years of age and older (Meng & D'Arcy, 2014). In this study, being younger, married, a regular drinker, healthy, and satisfied with life were associated with successful aging. Presence of disease was linked to a significant decline in successful aging. Having selective positive family and friendship relationships is associated with successful aging (Carstensen, 2015, 2016, 2019). And in a recent study, the following four factors characterized successful aging: proactive engagement, wellness resources, positive spirit, and valued relationships (Lee, Kahana, & Kahana, 2017).

Being active is especially important to successful aging (Walker, 2019). Older adults who exercise regularly, attend meetings, participate in religious activities, and go on trips are more satisfied with their lives than their counterparts who disengage from society (Strandberg, 2019). Older adults who engage in challenging cognitive activities are more likely to retain their cognitive skills for a longer period of time (Kinugawa, 2019; Kunzmann, 2019). Older adults who are emotionally selective, optimize their choices, and compensate effectively for losses increase their chances of aging successfully (Nikitin & Freund, 2019; Paul, 2019). And a very important agenda for researchers is to continually improve our understanding of how people can live longer, healthier, more productive and satisfying lives.

Laura Carstensen (2015, 2016, 2019) has described the challenges and opportunities involved in the dramatic increase in life expectancy that has been occurring and continues to occur. In her view, the remarkable increase in the number of people living to an old age has occurred in such a short time that science, technology, and behavioral adaptations have not kept pace. She proposes that the challenge is to change a world constructed mainly for young people to a world that is more compatible and supportive for the increasing number of people living to 100 and older.

In further commentary, Carstensen (2015, p. 70) remarked that achieving this transformation would be no small feat:

> . . . parks, transportation systems, staircases, and even hospitals presume that the users have both strength and stamina; suburbs across the country are built for two parents and their young children, not single people, multiple generations or elderly people who are not able to drive. Our education system serves the needs of young children and young adults and offers little more than recreation for experienced people.
>
> Indeed, the very conception of work as a full-time endeavor ending in the early sixties is ill suited for long lives. Arguably the most troubling is that we fret about ways the older people lack the qualities of younger people rather than exploit a growing new resource right before our eyes: citizens who have deep expertise, emotional balance, and the motivation to make a difference.

Eighty-eight-year-old Warren Buffett, one of the world's richest individuals, continues to have a very active, successful life. He has donated more than $30 billion to several foundations, with the bulk of the money given to the Bill and Melinda Gates Foundation, which plans to use it to reduce poverty, improve education, and solve health problems.
Nati Harnik/AP Images

Review Connect Reflect

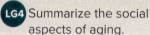 LG4 Summarize the social aspects of aging.

Review

- What are three social theories of aging?
- How extensively are older adults stereotyped?
- What roles do social support and social integration play in the development of older adults?
- What are some important aspects of successful aging?

Connect

- Connect the research on intergenerational relationships with this section's discussion of successful aging.

Reflect Your Own Personal Journey of Life

- Consider your parents, grandparents, and possibly even great-grandparents who are still alive. How have their social lives changed as they have aged?

Culture

Socioeconomic Status and Poverty

Ethnicity

Cartesia/Getty Images

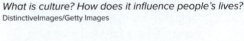

What is culture? How does it influence people's lives?
DistinctiveImages/Getty Images

culture The behavior, patterns, beliefs, and all other products of a group of people that are passed on from generation to generation.

cross-cultural studies Studies that compare aspects of two or more cultures to provide information about the degree to which development is similar or universal across the cultures, or is instead culture-specific.

Personal relations with friends and other peers form only part of the social world outside the family that influences development. As we have seen throughout this book, development is also influenced by the sociocultural context. Here we take a closer look at three aspects of that context: culture, socioeconomic status, and ethnicity.

CULTURE

Culture refers to the behavior, patterns, beliefs, and all other products of a group of people that are passed on from generation to generation. It results from the interaction between people and their environment over many years (Cai & others, 2018; Gardiner, 2019). **Cross-cultural studies** compare aspects of two or more cultures, providing information about the degree to which development is similar, or universal, across cultures, or is instead culture-specific (Bond, 2019; Duell & others, 2018; Matsumoto & Hwang, 2019).

One study revealed that from the beginning of seventh grade through the end of eighth grade, U.S. adolescents valued academics less and their motivational behavior also decreased (Wang & Pomerantz, 2009). By contrast, the value placed on academics by Chinese adolescents did not change across this time frame and their motivational behavior was sustained. In the chapter on "Schools, Achievement, and Work," we discuss in greater detail the higher math and science achievement of Asian children in comparison with U.S. children.

The concept of culture is broad; it includes many components and can be analyzed in many ways (Allik & Realo, 2019; Miller, Wice, & Goyal, 2019). Cross-cultural expert Richard Brislin (1993) described a number of characteristics of culture:

- Culture is made up of ideals, values, and assumptions about life that guide people's behavior.
- Culture consists of those aspects of the environment that people make.
- Culture is transmitted from generation to generation, with responsibility for the transmission resting on the shoulders of parents, teachers, and community leaders.
- When their cultural values are violated or their cultural expectations are ignored, people react emotionally.
- It is not unusual for people to accept a cultural value at one point in their lives and reject it at another point. For example, rebellious adolescents and young adults might accept a culture's values and expectations after having children of their own.

Classical research by American psychologist Donald Campbell and his colleagues (Brewer & Campbell, 1976; Campbell & LeVine, 1968) revealed that people in all cultures tend to do the following things:

- think that what happens in their culture is "natural" and "correct" and that what happens in other cultures is "unnatural" and "incorrect";
- perceive their cultural customs as universally valid—that is, conclude that "what is good for us is good for everyone";
- behave in ways that favor their cultural group; and
- feel hostile toward other cultural groups.

In other words, people in all cultures tend to display **ethnocentrism,** the tendency to consider one's own group superior to others.

The Relevance of Culture for the Study of Life-Span Development   Global interdependence is an inescapable reality (Cai, Huang, & Jing, 2019; UNICEF, 2019).

Children, adolescents, and adults are not just citizens of one country; they are citizens of the world—a world that, through advances in transportation and technology, has become increasingly connected. By better understanding cultures around the world, we may be able to interact more effectively with each other and make this planet a more hospitable, peaceful place (Smith & others, 2019).

Individualism and Collectivism What cultural differences are significant in life-span development? One finding in cross-cultural research is that cultures around the world tend to take two very different orientations to life and social relations (Feinberg & others, 2019; Heu, van Zomeren, & Hansen, 2019; Yamaguchi & Sawaumi, 2019). That is, cultures tend to emphasize either individualism or collectivism:

· **Individualism** involves giving priority to personal goals rather than to group goals; it emphasizes values that serve the self, such as feeling good, obtaining personal distinction through achievement, and preserving independence.
· **Collectivism** emphasizes values that serve the group by subordinating personal goals to preserve group integrity, supporting interdependence of the members, and promoting harmonious relationships.

Figure 6 summarizes some of the main characteristics of individualistic and collectivistic cultures. Many Western cultures, such as those of the United States, Canada, Great Britain, and the Netherlands, are described as individualistic; many Eastern cultures, such as those of China, Japan, India, and Thailand, are described as collectivistic (Mackinnon & others, 2017). However, a study conducted from 1970 to 2008 found that although China continued to be characterized by collectivistic values, the frequency of words used in China to index individualistic values had increased (Zeng & Greenfield, 2015).

Many of the assumptions about contemporary ideas in fields like life-span development were developed in individualistic cultures (Triandis, 1994, 2001, 2007). Consider the flurry of self-terms in psychology that have an individualistic focus: *self-actualization, self-awareness, self-efficacy, self-reinforcement, self-criticism, self-serving, selfishness,* and *self-doubt* (Lonner, 1988).

Self-conceptions are related to culture. In one study, American and Chinese college students completed 20 sentences beginning with "I am" (Trafimow, Triandis, & Goto, 1991). As indicated in Figure 7, the American college students were much more likely than the Chinese students to describe themselves with personal traits ("I am assertive," for example), than to identify themselves by their group affiliations ("I am a member of the math club," for example). However, researchers found that from 1990 to 2007, Chinese 18- to 65-year-olds increasingly included more individualistic characteristics in their descriptions of what constitutes happiness and well-being (Steele & Lynch, 2013). Likewise, a recent research review concluded that individualism is rising in Japan (Ogihara, 2017). These increases in individualism in Japan include stronger individualistic values and standards in the workplace and schools, parents giving more individualistic names to their children, and more frequent appearance of words such as "individual" and "uniqueness" in the media.

Some social scientists note that many problems in Western cultures are intensified by the Western cultural emphasis on individualism. The rates of suicide, drug abuse, crime, teenage pregnancy, divorce, child abuse, and mental disorders are higher in individualistic cultures than in collectivistic ones. A study across 62 countries found that reported student aggressive behavior for fourth- and eighth-graders was higher in individualistic countries than in collectivistic cultures (Bergmuller, 2013).

Individualistic	Collectivistic
Focuses on individual.	Focuses on groups.
Self is determined by personal traits independent of groups; self is stable across contexts.	Self is defined by in-group terms; self can change with context.
Private self is more important.	Public self is most important.
Personal achievement, competition, power are important.	Achievement is for the benefit of the in-group; cooperation is stressed.
Cognitive dissonance is frequent.	Cognitive dissonance is infrequent.
Emotions (such as anger) are self-focused.	Emotions (such as anger) are often relationship based.
People who are the most liked are self-assured.	People who are the most liked are modest, self-effacing.
Values: pleasure, achievement, competition, freedom.	Values: security, obedience, in-group harmony, personalized relationships.
Many casual relationships.	Few, close relationships.
Save own face.	Save own and other's face.
Independent behaviors: swimming, sleeping alone in room, privacy.	Interdependent behaviors: co-bathing, co-sleeping.
Relatively rare mother-child physical contact.	Frequent mother-child physical contact (such as hugging, holding).

FIGURE 6
CHARACTERISTICS OF INDIVIDUALISTIC AND COLLECTIVISTIC CULTURES

ethnocentrism The tendency to consider one's own group superior to other groups.

individualism Giving priority to personal goals rather than to group goals; emphasizing values that serve the self, such as feeling good, obtaining personal distinction through achievement, and preserving independence.

collectivism Emphasizing values that serve the group by subordinating personal goals to preserve group integrity, supporting interdependence of members, and promoting harmonious relationships.

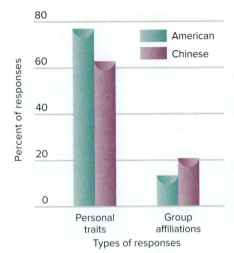

FIGURE **7**

AMERICAN AND CHINESE SELF-CONCEPTIONS. College students from the United States and China completed 20 "I am" sentences. Both groups filled in personal traits more than group affiliations. However, the Chinese students filled in the blanks with group affiliations more often than the U.S. students did.

Critics of the concept of individualistic and collectivistic cultures argue that these terms are too broad and simplistic, especially with globalization increasing (Sugimura & Mizokami, 2012). Regardless of their cultural background, people need both a positive sense of self and connectedness to others to develop fully as human beings. Carolyn Tamis-LeMonda and her colleagues (2008) emphasize that in many families, children are not reared in environments that uniformly endorse either individualistic or collectivistic values, thoughts, and actions. Rather, in many families, children are "expected to be quiet, assertive, respectful, curious, humble, self-assured, independent, dependent, affectionate, or reserved depending on the situation, people present, children's age, and social-political and economic circles." Nonetheless, a number of studies continue to find differences between individualistic and collectivistic cultures in a number of areas (Huppert & others, 2019; Xiang & others, 2019; Zabihzadeh & others, 2019).

Media/Screen Time If the amount of time spent in an activity is any indication of its importance, there is no doubt that media viewing and screen time play important roles in children's and adolescents' lives (Lever-Duffy & McDonald, 2018; Roblyer & Hughes, 2019; Smaldino & others, 2019). Few developments in society in the second half of the twentieth century had a greater impact on children than television. Television continues to have a strong influence on children's development, but children's use of other media and information/communication devices has led to the use of the term *screen time*, which encompasses the total amount of time individuals spend watching television or DVDs, playing video games, and using computers or mobile media such as smartphones (Lissak, 2018; Vandendriessche & others, 2019).

Among the concerns about children having so much screen time are decreasing time spent in play, less time interacting with peers, decreased physical activity, increased risk of being overweight or obese, poor sleep habits, and higher rates of aggression (Li & others, 2017; Xu & others, 2016). Further, a study of Canadian youth found that duration of screen time was linked to depression and anxiety (Maras & others, 2015). Also, in a recent study of preschool children, compared with children with less than 30 minutes of screen time a day, those with two hours or more a day were much more likely to have inattention problems (including a higher risk of developing ADHD symptoms) and externalizing problems (Tamana & others, 2019). Further, a recent study revealed that less screen time was associated with adolescents having a better quality of life (Yan & others, 2017). And screen time involving mobile phone use has especially increased in adolescents and adults. A recent study found that nighttime mobile phone use and poor sleep behavior increased from 13 to 16 years of age (Vernon, Modecki, & Barber, 2018). In this study, increased nighttime mobile phone use was linked to increased externalizing problems, as well as decreased self-esteem and coping.

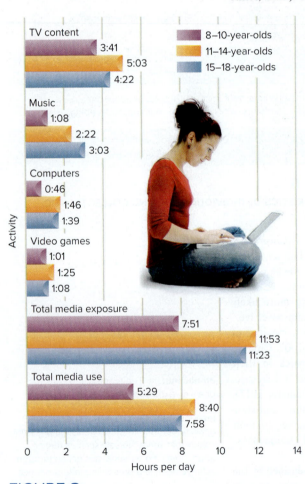

FIGURE **8**

DEVELOPMENTAL CHANGES IN THE AMOUNT OF TIME U.S. 8- TO 18-YEAR-OLDS SPEND WITH DIFFERENT TYPES OF MEDIA

Sidneybernstein/iStockphoto.com

To better understand various aspects of U.S. children's and adolescents' media use/screen time, the Kaiser Family Foundation funded national surveys in 1999, 2004, and 2009. The 2009 survey included more than 2,000 8- to 18-year-olds and documented that children's and adolescents' media use had increased dramatically in recent years (Rideout, Foehr, & Roberts, 2010). Today's youth live in a world in which they are encapsulated by media. In this survey, in 2009, 8- to 11-year-olds used media 5 hours and 29 minutes a day, but 11- to 14-year-olds used media an average of 8 hours and 40 minutes a day and 15- to 18-year-olds an average of 7 hours and 58 minutes a day (see Figure 8). Thus, daily media use jumps by more than 3 hours in early adolescence. The largest increases in media use in early adolescence are for TV viewing and video gaming. TV use by youth increasingly has involved watching TV on the Internet, an iPod/MP3 player, or on a cell phone. As indicated in Figure 8, time spent listening to music and using computers also increases considerably among 11- to 14-year-old adolescents. Based on the 2009 survey, adding up the daily media use figures to obtain weekly media use leads to the staggering levels of more than 60 hours a week of media use by 11- to 14-year-olds and almost 56 hours a week by 15- to 18-year-olds.

A major trend in the use of technology is the dramatic increase in media multitasking (Courage & others, 2015). In the 2009 survey conducted by the Kaiser Family Foundation, when the amount of time spent multitasking was included in computing media use, 11- to 14-year-olds spent nearly 12 hours a day (as compared with almost 9 hours a day when multitasking was not included) exposed to media (Rideout, Foehr, & Roberts, 2010). In this survey, 39 percent of seventh- to twelfth-graders said "most of the time" they use two or more media concurrently, such as surfing the Web while listening to music. In some cases, media multitasking—such as text messaging, listening to an iPod, and updating a YouTube site—is engaged in at the same time as doing homework. It is hard to imagine that this allows a student to do homework efficiently.

In a more recent 2015 survey, 51 percent of adolescents reported that they "often" or "sometimes" watch TV or use social media (50 percent) while doing homework and even more say the same thing about texting (60 percent) and listening to music (76 percent) (Common Sense Media, 2015). Almost two-thirds of adolescents indicate that they don't think watching TV (63 percent), texting (64 percent), or using social media (55 percent) while doing homework makes any difference in the quality of their work.

What are some outcomes when adolescents frequently engage in media multitasking? In a research review, a higher level of media multitasking was linked to lower levels of school achievement, executive function, and growth mindset in adolescents (Cain & others, 2016). Further, in a recent study of 11- to 18-year-olds in Spain, media multitasking during homework was linked to lower executive function, a lower level of working memory, and worse academic performance in language and math (Martin-Perina, Vinas Poch, & Malo Cerrato, 2019). In another study, heavy media multitaskers were more likely to be depressed and have social anxiety than their counterparts who engaged in media multitasking less heavily (Becker, Alzahabi, & Hopwood, 2013). In addition, a recent study found that media multitasking was linked to a higher risk for obesity and increased responsiveness to rewarding food stimuli (Lopez, Heatherton, & Wagner, 2019). And a research review concluded that at a general level, using digital technologies (surfing the Internet, texting someone) while engaging in a learning task (reading, listening to a lecture) distracts learners and impairs performance on many tasks (Courage & others, 2015).

Mobile media, such as smartphones, are mainly driving the increased media use by adolescents. For example, in 2004, 39 percent owned a cell phone, a figure that jumped to 66 percent in 2009, then to 87 percent in 2016 and is continuing to increase (eMarketer.com, 2017; Rideout, Foehr, & Roberts, 2010).

Television   Many children spend more time watching television than they spend interacting with their parents. Although it is only one of the many mass media that affect children's behavior, television may be the most influential. The persuasive capabilities of television are staggering. The 20,000 hours of television watched by the time the average American adolescent graduates from high school are greater than the number of hours spent in the classroom.

Television can have positive or negative effects on children's and adolescents' development. Television can have a positive influence by presenting motivating educational programs, increasing children's and adolescents' information about the world beyond their immediate environment, and providing models of prosocial behavior (Wilson, 2008).

Some types of TV shows are linked to positive outcomes for children. For example, a recent meta-analysis found that children's exposure to prosocial media is linked to higher levels of prosocial behavior and empathetic concern (Coyne & others, 2018). And a meta-analysis of studies in 14 countries found positive outcomes for watching the TV show *Sesame Street* in three areas: cognitive, learning about the world, and social reasoning and attitudes toward outgroups (Mares & Pan, 2013). However, television can have a negative influence on children and adolescents by making them passive learners, distracting them from doing homework, teaching them stereotypes, providing them with violent models of aggression, and presenting them with unrealistic views of the world (Matos, Ferreira, & Haase, 2012). Further, researchers have found that a high level of TV viewing is linked to a greater incidence of obesity in children and adolescents. For example, a recent study of 2- to 6-year-olds indicated that increased TV viewing time on weekends was associated with a higher risk of being overweight or obese (Kondolot & others, 2017).

The extent to which children and adolescents are exposed to violence and aggression on television raises special concerns (Al-Ali & others, 2018; Khurana & others, 2019). In a study of children, greater exposure to TV violence, video game violence, and music video violence was independently associated with a higher level of physical aggression (Coker & others, 2015).

Video Games   Violent video games, especially those that are highly realistic, also raise concerns about their effects on children and adolescents (Coyne & others, 2018). In a recent research review, it was concluded that the majority of correlational and experimental studies

indicate that children and adolescents who extensively play violent electronic games are more aggressive and engage in less prosocial behavior than their counterparts who spend less time playing the games or do not play them at all (Anderson & others, 2018). Also, the American Psychological Association Task Force recently concluded that exposure to violent video games increases aggressive behavior and decreases empathy (Calvert & others, 2017). Further, one study revealed that video game consumption was linked to rape myth acceptance (shifting blame for sexual assault from the perpetrator to the victim) through connections with interpersonal aggression and hostile sexism (Fox & Potocki, 2016). Many recently developed video games have increased their sexualized portrayal of females to appeal to a male audience.

Are there any positive outcomes when adolescents play video games? Researchers found that middle-school students who played prosocial video games subsequently behaved in more prosocial ways (Gentile & others, 2009). Research also indicates that playing video games can improve adoles-

How might playing violent video games be related to adolescent aggression?
Godong/Alamy Stock Photo

cents' visuospatial skills (Schmidt & Vandewater, 2008). One study found that playing action video games improved attentional control (Chisholm & Kingstone, 2015). Further, researchers have found that video games requiring exercise are linked to weight loss in overweight adolescents (Bond, Richards, & Calvert, 2013; Calvert, 2015). For example, a recent study of African American and Latino 10- to 15-year-olds living in a high-poverty neighborhood improved their physical fitness by playing Wii Fit games for 6 weeks (Flynn & others, 2018). The weight loss in the competitive condition also was linked to improved executive function in this study.

Media/Screen Time, Learning, and Children's Development   The effects of media/screen time on children depend on how old children are and the type of media involved (Calvert, 2015). A research review reached the following conclusions about media/screen viewing by infants and young children (Kirkorian, Wartella, & Anderson, 2008):

- *Infancy.* Learning from media is difficult for infants and toddlers, and they learn much more easily from direct experiences with people.

- *Early childhood.* At about 3 years of age, children can learn from media with educational material if the media use effective strategies such as repeating concepts a number of times, use images and sounds that get young children's attention, and use children's rather than adults' voices. However, the vast majority of media that young children experience is geared toward entertainment rather than education.

The American Academy of Pediatrics (2001) recommends that children under 2 years of age not watch television because doing so is likely to reduce direct interactions with parents. One study found that the more hours of TV viewed per day by 1- and 3-year-olds, the more likely they were to have attention problems at 7 years of age (Christakis & others, 2004), and another study also revealed that daily TV exposure at 18 months was linked to increased inattention/hyperactivity at 30 months of age (Cheng & others, 2010). A study of 2- to 48-month-olds indicated that each hour of audible TV was linked to a reduction in child vocalizations (Christakis & others, 2009), and another study revealed that 8- to 16-month-olds who viewed baby DVDs/videos had poor language development (Zimmerman, Christakis, & Meltzoff, 2007).

What have researchers found about infants who watch TV and videos?
Deyan Georgiev/Alamy Stock Photo

A study revealed that 12 percent of 2- to 4-year-old U.S. children use computers every day and 22 percent of 5- to 8-year-olds use computers daily (Common Sense Media, 2011). A recommendation stated that for children 2 to 4 years of age, screen time should be limited to no more than 1 hour per day (Tremblay & others, 2012). Many children spend more time with various screen media than they do interacting with their parents and peers.

Higher levels of parental monitoring of children's media use have been linked to a number of positive outcomes (more sleep, better school performance, less aggressive behavior, and more prosocial behavior) (Barr, 2019; Gentile & others, 2014). Further, a recent study indicated that parental monitoring of media violence exposure was linked to less aggressive behavior in adolescents (Khurana & others, 2018). Another study found that parents' reduction of their own screen time was associated with decreased child screen time (Xu, Wen, & Rissel, 2015).

How much screen time is recommended for young children?
Luca Cappelli/Getty Images

The more time that children and adolescents spend watching TV, the lower their school achievement (Comstock & Scharrer, 2006). For example, a research review concluded that higher levels of screen time (mostly involving TV viewing) were associated with lower levels of cognitive development in early childhood (Carson & others, 2015). In a recent study of adolescents, increased screen time was associated with lower academic achievement in English and math (Hunter, Leatherdale, & Carson, 2018). Another recent study of adolescents confirmed that lower screen time was linked to higher math achievement (Poulain & others, 2018).

Children also benefit when parents are knowledgeable about the best digital applications (apps) for children. In one survey, 72 percent of the best apps for sale in Apple's App Store were in the toddler/preschool category! Leading expert Kathy Hirsh-Pasek and her colleagues (2015) offer the following recommendations on the best types of educational apps parents can purchase for their young children:

- *Active Involvement.* It is important that the app require thinking, reflection, and manipulation of information requiring "minds on" activity rather than just physical tapping and swiping.

- *Engagement.* Children learn the content better when it requires focused attention and is embedded in an app-based story. However, if the app includes distracting side games and noise, children's learning is often harmed.

- *Meaningfulness.* Children's learning benefits when the app is meaningfully linked to past knowledge/experience or if it is personally relevant and purposeful for the children.

- *Social Interaction.* Children's learning also is aided when the app encourages quality social interaction with others, as when the app motivates them to discuss its content with parents or teachers.

Technology and Digitally Mediated Communication   Culture involves change, and nowhere is that change greater than in the technological revolution individuals are experiencing with increased use of computers and the Internet (Lever-Duffy & McDonald, 2018; Smaldino & others, 2019). Society still relies on some basic nontechnological competencies— for example, good communication skills, positive attitudes, and the ability to solve problems and to think deeply and creatively. But how people pursue these competencies is changing in new ways and at a speed that few people had to cope with in previous eras. For youth to be adequately prepared for tomorrow's jobs, technology needs to become an integral part of their lives (Roblyer & Hughes, 2019).

The digitally mediated social environment of youth includes e-mail, instant messaging, social networking sites such as Facebook, chat rooms, videosharing and photosharing, multiplayer online computer games, and virtual worlds. Most of these digitally mediated social interactions began on computers but more recently have also shifted to smartphones.

A national survey revealed dramatic increases in adolescents' use of social media and text messaging (Lenhart, 2015a). Ninety-two percent of U.S. 13- to 17-year-olds reported using social networking sites daily. Twenty-four percent of the adolescents said they go online almost constantly. Much of this increase in going online has been fueled by smartphones and mobile devices. Also, in a recent national survey, 78 percent of 18- to 24-year-olds reported that they use Snapchat, 71 percent said they use Instagram, 68 percent said they use Facebook, and almost half (45 percent) indicated they use Twitter (Smith & Anderson, 2018). And in this recent survey, a whopping 94 percent in this age group said they use YouTube. A recent study indicated that a higher level of social media use was associated with a higher level of heavy drinking by adolescents (Brunborg, Andreas, & Kvaavik, 2017).

What characterizes the online social environment of adolescents?
Anne Ackermann/Digital Vision/Alamy Stock Photo

Text messaging has now become the main way that adolescents connect with their friends, surpassing face-to-face contact, e-mail, instant messaging, and voice calling (Lenhart, 2015a). A survey of 12- to 17-year-olds found that they send an average of 55 text messages per day (Lenhart, 2015b). A special concern is *sexting,* which involves sending sexually explicit images, videos, or sexually explicit text messages via electronic communication. However, voice mail is the primary way that most adolescents prefer to connect with parents.

Concerns have emerged about children's and adolescents' access to information on the Internet, which has been largely unregulated. Youth can access adult sexual material, instructions for making bombs, and other information that is inappropriate for them. Clearly, parents need to monitor and regulate adolescents' use of the Internet.

The Internet and Aging Adults The Internet plays an increasingly important role in providing access to information and communication for adults as well as youth (Arcury & others, 2019; Gavett & others, 2017; Gillain & others, 2019). In 2016, 67 percent of U.S. adults age 65 and older used the Internet, up from 59 percent in 2013 and 14 percent in 2000 (Anderson, 2017). In the general U.S. population, 90 percent are Internet users. Younger seniors use the Internet more (82 percent of 65- to 69-year-olds compared with 44 percent of people age 80 and older). Increasing numbers of older adults use e-mail and smartphones to communicate, especially with friends and relatives (Gillain & others, 2019). In 2016, approximately 40 percent of U.S. adults age 65 and older were smartphone users, up 24 percent from 2013 (Anderson, 2017). In this survey, 59 percent of 65- to 69-year-olds but only 17 percent of those 80 and over used smartphones. The researchers also found that lower-SES older adults use smartphones and the Internet much less than middle- and upper-SES older adults do.

Older adults also are using social media more than in the past. In 2016, 34 percent of U.S. adults age 65 and older reported using social networking sites like Facebook and Twitter, 7 percent more than in 2013 (Anderson, 2017).

Are older adults keeping up with changes in technology?
Sami Sarkis/Getty Images

How is Internet use linked to various aspects of older adults' lives? A longitudinal study revealed that Internet use by older adults reduced their likelihood of being depressed by one-third (Cotten & others, 2014). And in a recent study of older adults, having an iPad strengthened their family ties and brought a greater sense of overall connection to society (Delello & McWhorter, 2017). In a recent Hong Kong study, adults 75 and older who used smartphones and the Internet to connect with family, friends, and neighbors had a higher level of psychological well-being than their counterparts who did not use this technology (Fang & others, 2018). Also, as with children and younger adults, cautions about verifying the accuracy of information—especially on topics involving health care—on the Internet should always be kept in mind.

Although computers, smartphones, and the Internet are now playing more important roles in the lives of people of all ages, people continue to watch extensive amounts of television, especially in late adulthood. In a 2016 Nielsen survey, adults age 65 and older watched television an average of 51 hours, 32 minutes per week (Recode, 2016). That 51+ hours per week is far more than the averages for other age groups—25 to 34 years (23 hrs, 26 min), 35 to 49 years (32 hrs, 07 min), and 50 to 64 years (44 hrs, 6 min). The staggering number of hours older adults watch television each week raises concerns about how such lengthy sedentary behavior might interfere with participating in physical exercise and social activities, which are linked to healthy development.

Aging and Culture Culture plays an important role in aging (McCall & Borjesson, 2017; Yeo & Yoshikawa, 2019). What promotes a good old age in most cultures? What factors are associated with whether older adults are accorded a position of high status in a culture? Seven factors are most likely to predict high status for the elderly in a culture (Sangree, 1989):

- Older persons have valuable knowledge.
- Older persons control key family/community resources.
- Older persons are permitted to engage in useful and valued functions as long as possible.
- There is role continuity throughout the life span.
- Age-related role changes involve greater responsibility, authority, and advisory capacity.
- The extended family is a common family arrangement in the culture, and the older person is integrated into the extended family.

In general, respect for older adults is greater in collectivistic cultures (such as China and Japan) than in individualistic cultures (such as the United States). However, some researchers are finding that this collectivistic/individualistic difference in respect accorded to older adults is not as strong as it used to be and that in some cases older adults in individualistic cultures receive considerable respect (Antonucci, Vandewater, & Lansford, 2000).

SOCIOECONOMIC STATUS AND POVERTY

Analyzing cultures represents just one way to understand the social context of life-span development. Another approach focuses on inequalities present in every society (Nieto & Bode, 2018). That is, how do people in a particular society differ in their access to economic, social, and psychological resources, and how do these differences affect their development through life?

What Is Socioeconomic Status? **Socioeconomic status (SES)** refers to a grouping of people with similar occupational, educational, and economic characteristics. Generally, members of a society (1) hold occupations that vary in prestige, with some individuals having more access than others to higher-status occupations; (2) attain different levels of education, with some individuals having more access than others to better education; (3) possess different economic resources; and (4) have different degrees of power to influence a community. These differences go together. That is, people with prestigious occupations tend also to have higher levels of educational attainment, more economic resources, and greater power. These differences in the ability to control resources and to participate in society's rewards produce unequal opportunities for people (Watson, 2018).

Cultures differ in the amount of prestige they give to older adults. In Navajo culture, older adults are especially treated with respect because of their wisdom and extensive life experiences. *What are some other factors that are linked with respect for older adults in a culture?*
meunierd/Shutterstock

The number of different socioeconomic statuses depends on the community's size and complexity. In most investigators' descriptions of socioeconomic status, two broad categories—low-SES and middle-SES—are used, although as many as five categories are delineated. Sometimes low-SES is described as low-income, working-class, or blue-collar; sometimes middle-SES is described as middle-income, managerial, or white-collar. Examples of low-SES occupations are factory worker and maintenance worker. Examples of middle-SES occupations include managerial and professional careers (doctor, lawyer, teacher, accountant, and so on).

Socioeconomic Variations in Neighborhoods and Families A parent's SES is likely linked to the neighborhoods in which children live and the schools they attend (Kelleher, Reece, & Sandel, 2018; McLoyd, Hardaway, & Jocson, 2019). Such variations in neighborhood settings can influence children's adjustment (Green & others, 2018; Magnuson & Duncan, 2019).

Neighborhood crime and isolation have been linked with low self-esteem and psychological distress in children (Ruiz, McMahon, & Jason, 2018). Further, schools in low-income neighborhoods have fewer resources than schools in higher-income neighborhoods, and they are likely to have more students with lower achievement test scores, low rates of graduation, and smaller percentages of graduates going on to college (American Psychological Association, 2019).

socioeconomic status (SES) A grouping of people with similar occupational, educational, and economic characteristics.

In the United States and most other Western cultures, differences have been found in child rearing among different SES groups (Hoff, Laursen, & Tardif, 2002, p. 246):

- Lower-SES parents (1) "are more concerned that their children conform to society's expectations," (2) "create a home atmosphere in which it is clear that parents have authority over children," (3) use physical punishment more in disciplining their children, and (4) are more directive and less conversational with their children.

- Higher-SES parents (1) "are more concerned with developing children's initiative and ability to delay gratification," (2) "create a home atmosphere in which children are more nearly equal participants and in which rules are discussed as opposed to being laid down" in an authoritarian manner, (3) are less likely to use physical punishment, and (4) are less directive and more conversational with their children.

What characterizes socioeconomic variations in neighborhoods?
zodebala/Getty Images

Consequences of SES for Children and Adolescents Children and adolescents from low-SES backgrounds are at risk for experiencing low achievement and emotional problems, as well as lower occupational attainment in adulthood (Coley & others, 2018; Rosen & others, 2018; Tian & others, 2019; Xuan & others, 2019). Problems such as smoking, depression, and juvenile delinquency, as well as medical conditions, are more prevalent among low-SES adolescents than among economically advantaged adolescents (Holmes & others, 2019; Simon & others, 2017). For example, a recent study found that of 13 risk factors, low SES was most likely to be associated with smoking initiation in fifth-graders (Wellman & others, 2018). Also, in a recent Chinese study, adolescents in low-income families had higher than average rates of depressive symptoms (Zhou, Fan, & Yin, 2017). Further, in a U.S. longitudinal study, low SES in adolescence was linked to having a higher level of depressive symptoms at age 54 for females (Pino & others, 2018). And in this study, low-SES females who completed college were less likely to have depressive symptoms at age 54 than low-SES females who did not complete college. In another longitudinal study, low SES in adolescence was a risk factor for having cardiovascular disease 30 years later (Doom & others, 2017). In this study, the following factors were found to be involved in the pathway to cardiovascular disease for low-SES individuals: health-compromising behaviors, financial stress, inadequate medical care, and lower educational attainment. In addition, a longitudinal study indicated that lower SES in childhood was associated with lower cognitive function and more cognitive decline in middle and late adulthood (Liu & Lachman, 2019). Also, a recent Australian study revealed that children and adolescents from lower-SES backgrounds were less likely achieve a healthy physical fitness level than their higher-SES counterparts (Peralta & others, 2019).

Nevertheless, a sizable portion of children from low-SES backgrounds are competent and perform well in school; some perform better than many middle-SES and higher-SES students. When students from low-SES backgrounds earn high grades, it is not unusual to find a parent or parents making special sacrifices to provide the conditions that contribute to academic success.

So far we have focused on the challenges faced by many adolescents from low-income families. However, Suniya Luthar and her colleagues (Ansary, McMahon, & Luthar, 2012, 2017; Luthar, 2006; Luthar, Crossman, & Small, 2015) found that adolescents from affluent families also face challenges. In her research, adolescents from affluent families are vulnerable to high rates of substance abuse. Also, in the affluent families she has studied, males tend to have more adjustment difficulties than females, with affluent female adolescents being more likely to attain superior levels of academic success.

Further, in a recent study of more than 13,000 high school students, those attending schools with more affluent classmates were more likely to use drugs, become intoxicated, and engage in property crime, while those attending poorer schools had more depressive and anxiety symptoms, and also engaged in more violent behavior (Coley & others, 2018).

Poverty When sixth-graders in a poverty-stricken area of St. Louis were asked to describe a perfect day, one boy said he would erase the world, then he would sit and think. Asked if he wouldn't rather go outside and play, the boy responded, "Are you kidding, out there?" (Children's Defense Fund, 1992). The world is a dangerous and unwelcoming place for too many of America's children, especially those who live in poverty (Children's Defense Fund, 2019). Some children are resilient and cope with the challenges of poverty without any major setbacks, but too many struggle unsuccessfully (Liu, Kia-Keating, & Nylund-Gibson, 2018; Magnuson & Duncan, 2019). Each child of poverty who reaches adulthood unhealthy, unskilled, or alienated keeps our nation from being as competent and productive as it could be.

Poverty Rates Children who grow up in poverty represent a special concern (Coley & others, 2018). In 2017, 17.5 percent (down from 21.1 percent in 2014) of U.S. children under 18 years of age were living in families with incomes below the poverty line, with African American (33 percent) and Latino families (26 percent) with children having especially high rates of poverty (U.S. Census Bureau, 2018). In 2017, 11 percent of non-Latino White children were living in poverty. The U.S. figure of 17.4 percent of children and adolescents living in poverty is much higher than figures from other industrialized nations. For example, Canada has a child poverty rate of 9 percent and Sweden has a rate of 2 percent.

Compared with non-Latino White children and adolescents, ethnic minority children and adolescents are more likely to experience persistent poverty over many years and to live in isolated, poor neighborhoods where social supports are minimal and threats to positive development abundant (Jarrett, 1995) (see Figure 9).

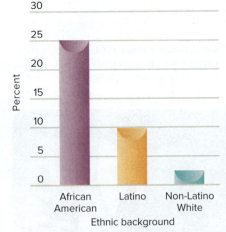

FIGURE 9

PERCENTAGES OF YOUTH UNDER 18 WHO ARE LIVING IN DISTRESSED NEIGHBORHOODS. *Note:* a distressed neighborhood is defined by high levels (at least one standard deviation above the norm) of (1) poverty; (2) female-headed families: (3) high school dropouts; (4) unemployment; and (5) reliance on public assistance programs.

Poverty also is demarcated along educational lines. In 2014, among adults 25 years and older living in poverty in the United States, 29 percent had no high school diploma, 14 percent had a high school diploma but no college, 10 percent had some college but no degree, and only 5 percent had a bachelor's degree or higher (DeNavas-Walt & Proctor, 2015).

Psychological Ramifications of Poverty   Poor children are often exposed to unhealthful living conditions, inadequate housing and homelessness, less effective schools, environmental toxins, and violence (Allen & Goldman-Mellor, 2018; Magnuson & Duncan, 2019). What are the psychological ramifications of living in poverty? First, the poor are often powerless. At work, they rarely are the decision makers; rules are handed down to them. Second, the poor are often vulnerable to disaster. They are not likely to be given notice before they are laid off from work, and they usually do not have financial resources to fall back on when problems arise. Third, their alternatives are restricted. Only a limited number of jobs are open to them. Even when alternatives are available, the poor might not know about them or be prepared to make a wise decision because of inadequate education and inability to read well. Fourth, being poor means having less prestige.

One research review concluded that compared with their economically more advantaged counterparts, poor children experience widespread environmental inequities (Evans, 2004). For example, one study found that a higher percentage of children in poor families than in middle-income families were exposed to family turmoil, separation from a parent, violence, crowding, excessive noise, and poor housing (Evans & English, 2002).

Persistent and long-standing poverty can have especially damaging effects on children (Chaudry & others, 2017; Magnuson & Duncan, 2019; Green & others, 2018). One study revealed that the more years children spent in poverty, the higher were their physiological indices of stress (Evans & Kim, 2007). Persistent economic hardship as well as very early poverty are linked to lower cognitive functioning in children at 5 years of age (Schoon & others, 2012). Another study revealed that poverty-related adversity in family and school contexts in early childhood was linked to less effective executive functioning in second and third grades (Cybele Raver & others, 2013). Also, researchers have found that youth living in neighborhoods where poverty increased from when they were 11 until they were 19 years of age experienced high levels of *allostatic load*, which involves a wearing down of the body's physiological systems due to stressors (Brody & others, 2014). However, for youth who received high levels of emotional support, allostatic load did not increase across this time frame when poverty increased.

(*Top*) Children playing in Nueva Era, a low-income area on the outskirts of Nuevo Laredo, Mexico. (*Bottom*) Children who live in an impoverished section of the South Bronx in New York City. *How does poverty affect the development of children like these?*
(*Top*) Paul S. Howell/Liaison/Getty Images; (*bottom*) Andy Levin/Science Source

Feminization of Poverty   The term **feminization of poverty** refers to the fact that far more women than men live in poverty. A special concern is the high percentage of children and adolescents growing up in mother-headed households in poverty (McLoyd, Hardaway, & Jocson, 2019; Weinraub & Kaufman, 2019). In 2017, 35.6 percent of single-mother families (down from 39.6 percent in 2013) lived in poverty, more than four times the poverty rate for married-couple families (8 percent) (U.S. Census Bureau, 2018).

Because poor, single mothers are more distressed than their middle-SES counterparts are, they tend to show lower levels of support, nurturance, and involvement with their children. Among the reasons for the high poverty rate of single mothers are women's lower pay, infrequent awarding of alimony payments, and poorly enforced child support by fathers.

Families and Poverty   One study documented the important links among economic well-being, parenting behavior, and social adjustment (Mistry & others, 2002). Lower levels of economic well-being and elevated perceptions of economic pressure were linked with parenting behavior. Distressed parents reported feeling less effective and capable in disciplining their children and were observed to be less affectionate in parent-child interactions. In turn, less optimal parenting predicted lower teacher ratings of children's social behavior and higher ratings of behavior problems.

Benefits provided to low-income parents may have positive outcomes for children (Dawson-McClure, Calzada, & Brotman, 2017; Magnuson & Duncan, 2019). As described in the "Introduction" chapter, the Minnesota Family Investment Program (MFIP) was primarily designed to improve the lives of adults—specifically, to move adults off the welfare rolls and into paid employment. A key element of the program was its guarantee that adults who participated in the program would receive more money if they worked than if they did not. When the adults' income rose, how did it affect their children? A study of the effects of MFIP found that increases in the incomes of working poor parents were linked with benefits for their

feminization of poverty The fact that far more women than men live in poverty. Women's lower income, divorce, infrequent awarding of alimony, and poorly enforced child support by fathers—which usually leave women with less money than they and their children need to adequately function—are the likely causes.

developmental connection

Environment

Reducing the poverty level and improving the lives of children living in poverty are important goals of U.S. social policy. Connect to "Introduction."

What are some characteristics of older U.S. adults living in poverty conditions?
JerryPDX/Getty Images

Consider the flowers of a garden: though differing in kind, color, form, and shape, yet, inasmuch as they are refreshed by the waters of one spring, revived by the breath of one wind, invigorated by the rays of one sun, this diversity increases their charm and adds to their beauty. . . . How unpleasing to the eye if all the flowers and plants, the leaves and blossoms, the fruits, the branches, and the trees of that garden were all the same shape and color! Diversity of hues, form, and shape enriches and adorns the garden and heightens its effect.

—Abdu'l Baha
Persian Baha'i Religious Leader, 19th/20th Century

children (Gennetian & Miller, 2002). The children's achievement in school improved and their behavior problems decreased.

Also as described in the "Introduction" chapter, a trend in antipoverty programs is to conduct two-generation interventions (Aspen Institute, 2019). This involves providing services for children and adolescents (such as educational child care, preschool education, or after-school programs for youth) as well as services for parents (such as adult education, literacy training, and job skills training).

Schools and school programs are the focus of some poverty interventions (Dragoset & others, 2017). In an intervention with first-generation immigrant children attending high-poverty schools, the City Connects program was successful in improving children's math and reading achievement at the end of elementary school (Dearing & others, 2016). The program is directed by a full-time school counselor or social worker in each school. Annual reviews of children's needs are conducted during the first several months of each school year. Then site coordinators and teachers collaborate to develop a student support plan that might include an after-school program, tutoring, mentoring, or family counseling. For children identified as having intense needs (about 8 to 10 percent), a wider team of professionals becomes involved, possibly including school psychologists, principals, nurses, and/or community agency staff, to create additional supports.

Another study assessed the effects of the Positive Action program in 14 urban, low-income Chicago schools across 6 years from grades 3 to 8 (Lewis & others, 2013). The Positive Action program is a K–12 curriculum that focuses on self-concept, self-control and responsibility, physical and mental health, honesty, getting along with others, and continually striving for self-improvement. The program includes teacher, counselor, family, and community training and activities to improve school-wide atmosphere. In comparison with control group schools that did not participate in the Positive Action program, students in the program engaged in a lower rate of violence-related behavior and received fewer disciplinary referrals and suspensions from school.

SES, Poverty, and Aging   Another group of special concern consists of older adults who are poor (Lin, Brown, & Hammersmith, 2017; Saito & others, 2019; Willink & others, 2019). Researchers have found that poverty in late adulthood is linked to an increase in physical and mental health problems (Lubetkin & Jia, 2017). Poverty also is linked to lower levels of physical and cognitive fitness in older adults (Basta & others, 2008). One study found that processing speed was slower in older adults living in poverty (Zhang & others, 2015). Another study revealed that low SES increases the risk of earlier death in older adults (Krueger & Chang, 2008).

Census data suggest that the overall number of older people living in poverty has declined since the 1960s, but in 2017, 9.2 percent of older adults in the United States still were living in poverty (U.S. Census Bureau, 2018). In 2017, U.S. women 65 years and older (10.6 percent) were much more likely to live in poverty than their male counterparts (7.6 percent) (U.S. Census Bureau, 2018). There is a special concern about poverty among older women, especially those who are divorced and never-married, and considerable discussion about the role of Social Security in providing a broad economic safety net for them (Mutchler, Li, & Xu, 2019).

ETHNICITY

As our discussion of poverty and aging indicated, differences in SES often overlap with ethnic differences. The United States is a showcase for these differences because it has been a great magnet for people from many ethnic groups. Cultural heritages from every continent have connected and mixed here (Banks, 2019; Bennett, 2019). Native Americans, European Americans, African Americans, Latinos, Chinese Americans, and other groups have retained parts of their culture of origin, lost other parts, and seen some elements transformed as they became part of the mainstream culture.

A special point needs to be made as we explore various aspects of ethnicity. For too long, the prevailing perspective on ethnic differences was deficit-based and assumed that children and adolescents in ethnic minority groups were inherently challenged and overwhelmed by stressors, especially in the case of immigrant ethnic minority adolescents (Bornstein & Cote, 2019; Perez-Brena & others, 2018). Countering this perspective is research indicating that ethnic minority adolescents, including those who are immigrants, fare better than expected (Perreira & others, 2019). Adolescents in immigrant families often assume higher levels of responsibility than non-immigrant adolescents and help their parents adapt to their new society (Anguiano, 2018; Halgunseth, 2019).

Immigration   Relatively high rates of minority immigration have contributed to growth in the proportion of ethnic minorities in the U.S. population. In 2016, 51 percent of children 18 years and younger were non-Latino White; by 2060, this figure is projected to decrease to 36 percent (U.S. Census Bureau, 2018). The ethnic minority U.S. population age 18 and younger is predicted to outnumber its non-Latino White counterpart in 2020. In 2016, among individuals age 18 and younger in the United States, 25 percent were Latino, 14 percent were African American, and 5 percent were Asian American. Increases in the proportion of ethnic minorities are expected to continue throughout the twenty-first century. Today the United States is more ethnically diverse than ever before (Banks, 2019). Ninety-three languages are spoken in Los Angeles alone.

Immigrants often experience special stressors (Ng & Wang, 2019; Kim & others, 2018; White & others, 2019). These include language barriers, separation from support networks, changes in SES, health problems, and the challenges of preserving ethnic identity while adapting to the majority culture (Hill & others, 2019; Hou & Kim, 2018; Simha, 2019). In a recent study comparing Asian, Latino, and non-Latino White immigrant adolescents, immigrant Asian adolescents had the highest level of depression and the lowest self-esteem, and they were the most likely to report experiencing discrimination (Lo & others, 2017).

Latino immigrants in the Rio Grande Valley, Texas. *What are some characteristics of the families who have recently immigrated to the United States?*
Allison Wright/Corbis/Getty Images

Parents and children in immigrant families may be at different stages of *acculturation*, the process of adapting to the majority culture. The result may be conflict over cultural values (Sam, 2018). One study examined values in immigrant (Vietnamese, Armenian, and Mexican) and nonimmigrant families (African American and European American) (Phinney, 1996). In all groups, parents endorsed family obligations more than adolescents did, and the differences between generations generally increased with time spent in the United States.

Ethnicity and Families   Families within different ethnic groups in the United States differ in their size, structure, composition, reliance on kinship networks, and levels of income and education (Bennett, 2019; Halgunseth, 2019; Ng & Wang, 2019). Large and extended families are more common among minority groups than among the non-Latino White majority. For example, 19 percent of Latino families have three or more children, compared with 14 percent of African American and 10 percent of non-Latino White families. African American and Latino children interact more with their grandparents, aunts, uncles, cousins, and more distant relatives than do non-Latino White children.

Single-parent families are more common among African Americans and Latinos than among non-Latino White Americans (U.S. Census Bureau, 2018). In comparison with two-parent households, single parents often have more limited resources of time, money, and energy (Weinraub & Kaufman, 2019). Ethnic minority parents also tend to be less educated and are more likely to live in low-income circumstances than are their non-Latino White counterparts (McLoyd, Hardaway, & Jocson, 2019). Still, many impoverished ethnic minority families manage to find ways to raise competent children (Magnuson & Duncan, 2019).

Recently immigrated families have had to face special problems. Many individuals in immigrant families are dealing with the problem of being undocumented. Living in an undocumented family can affect children's developmental outcomes through parents being unwilling to sign up for services for which they may be eligible, unfavorable conditions linked to low-wage work and lack of benefits, increased stress, discrimination, and a lack of cognitive stimulation in the home (Amuedo-Durantes & Arenas-Arroyo, 2019; Calzada & others, 2018). In a recent study, immigrant children who were once separated from their parents had a lower level of literacy and a higher level of psychological problems than those who migrated with parents (Lu, He, & Brooks-Gunn, 2019). Also in this study, a protracted period of separation and prior undocumented status of parents further increased the children's disadvantages.

What characterizes families in different ethnic groups in the United States?
Jack Hollingsworth/Getty Images

Poverty contributes to the stressful life experiences of many ethnic minority children (Magnuson & Duncan, 2019). But even when they are not poor, economic advantage does not enable ethnic minority children to escape entirely the prejudice and discrimination directed at them (Barajas & others, 2019; McDermott, Umana-Taylor, & Zeiders, 2019). Although middle-SES ethnic minority children have more resources available to counter the destructive influences of prejudice and discrimination, they still cannot completely avoid the pervasive influence of negative stereotypes about ethnic minority groups.

Vonnie McLoyd (1990) concluded that ethnic minority children experience a disproportionate share of the adverse effects of poverty and unemployment in the United States today. Thus, many ethnic minority children experience a double disadvantage: (1) prejudice and discrimination because of their ethnic minority status, and (2) the stressful effects of poverty. Some aspects of home life can help protect ethnic minority children from injustice. The community and the family can filter out destructive racist messages, and parents can present alternative frames of reference to offset those presented by the majority. The extended family also can serve as an important buffer to stress.

Research indicates that many members of families that have recently immigrated to the United States adopt a bicultural orientation, selecting characteristics of the U.S. culture that help them to survive and advance, while still retaining aspects of their culture of origin (Tikhonova & others, 2019; Younis & Hassan, 2019). Immigration also involves cultural brokering, which has increasingly occurred in the United States as children and adolescents serve as mediators (cultural and linguistic) for their immigrant parents (Anguiano, 2018; Sim & others, 2019). Further, a study of Asian American adolescents found that a bicultural orientation of both adolescents and their parents enhanced the adolescents' academic achievement (Kim & others, 2015).

However, while many ethnic/immigrant families adopt a bicultural orientation, parenting in many ethnic minority families also focuses on issues associated with promoting children's ethnic pride, knowledge of their ethnic group, and awareness of discrimination (Umana-Taylor, 2018).

Many of the families that have immigrated into the United States in recent decades, such as Mexican Americans and Asian Americans, come from collectivistic cultures in which duty to one's family is an important value. Family obligations may include assisting parents in their occupations and contributing to the family's welfare. In a recent study, a higher level of family obligation was linked to Latino adolescents' higher academic achievement (Anguiano, 2018).

In adopting characteristics of the U.S. culture, Latino families are increasingly embracing the importance of education (Toyokawa & Toyokawa, 2019). Although their school dropout rates have remained higher than those of other ethnic groups, they declined considerably in the last decade (National Center for Education Statistics, 2018). Ross Parke and his colleagues (2011) have found that Latino families are retaining a strong commitment to family when they immigrate to the United States despite facing challenges advancing economically. For example, divorce rates for Latino families are lower than for non-Latino White families of similar socioeconomic status.

However, there are variations in immigrant Latino families' experiences and the degree to which their children and adolescents change as they are exposed to American culture (Halgunseth, 2019). One study found that following their immigration, Mexican American adolescents spent less time with their family and identified less with family values (Updegraff & others, 2012). However, in this study, teens with stronger family values in early adolescence were less likely to engage in risky behavior in late adolescence.

Of course, individual families vary, and how successfully ethnic minority families deal with stress depends on many factors (Bornstein & Cote, 2019; Kim & others, 2018; Perez-Brena & others, 2018). Whether the parents are native-born or immigrants, how long the family has been in the United States, its socioeconomic status, and its national origin all make a difference. The characteristics of the family's social context also influence its adaptability. What are the attitudes toward the family's ethnic group within their neighborhood or city? Can the family's children attend good schools? Are there community groups that welcome people from the family's ethnic group? Do members of the family's ethnic group form community groups of their own?

Ethnicity and Aging   Of special concern are ethnic minority older adults, especially African Americans and Latinos, who are overrepresented in poverty statistics (U.S. Census Bureau, 2018). Comparative information about African Americans, Latinos, and non-Latino Whites indicates a possible double jeopardy for elderly ethnic minority individuals. They face problems related to both ageism and racism (Allen, 2016). They are likely to have a history of less education, longer periods of unemployment, worse housing conditions, poorer health, higher levels of stress, and shorter life expectancies than their non-Latino White counterparts

(Lin & Kelley-Moore, 2017). Also, non-Latino White men and women with 16 years or more of schooling have a life expectancy that is 14 years higher than that of African Americans with fewer than 12 years of education (Antonucci & others, 2016).

Despite the stress and discrimination older ethnic minority individuals face, many of these older adults have developed coping mechanisms that have allowed them to survive in the dominant non-Latino White world. Extension of family networks helps older minority group individuals cope with having only the bare essentials of living and gives them a sense of being loved (Antonucci & Webster, 2019). Churches in African American and Latino communities provide avenues for meaningful social participation, feelings of power, and a sense of internal satisfaction (Hill & others, 2006). And residential concentrations of ethnic minority groups give their older members a sense of belonging. Thus, it is important to consider individual variations in the lives of aging minorities. To read about one individual who is providing help for aging minorities, see the *Connecting with Careers* profile.

Review Connect Reflect

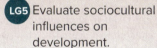 **LG5** Evaluate sociocultural influences on development.

Review
- How can culture, cross-cultural comparisons, and individualism/collectivism be defined? What are some outcomes of the increase in media use? How is culture related to development?
- What is socioeconomic status? How are socioeconomic status and poverty linked to development?
- What is ethnicity? How is ethnicity involved in development? What aspects of ethnicity are important to recognize?

Connect
- Compare what you learned in this section about the digitally mediated world of children and adolescents with the chapter's earlier discussion of the importance of play. What are your conclusions?

Reflect Your Own Personal Journey of Life
- No matter how well intentioned people are, their life circumstances likely have given them some prejudices. If they don't have prejudices toward people with different cultural and ethnic backgrounds, other kinds of people may bring out prejudices in them. For example, prejudices can be developed about people who have certain religious or political convictions, people who are unattractive or too attractive, people with a disability, and people who live in a nearby town. As a parent or teacher, how would you attempt to reduce children's prejudices?

Peers and the Sociocultural World

1 Peer Relations in Childhood and Adolescence

 LG1 Discuss peer relations in childhood and adolescence.

Exploring Peer Relations

- Peers are individuals who share the same age or maturity level. Peers provide a means of social comparison and a source of information about the world outside the family.

- Good peer relations may be necessary for normal social development. The inability to "plug in" to a social network is associated with a number of problems. Peer relations can be both positive and negative. Piaget and Sullivan stressed that peer relations provide the context for learning the reciprocal aspects of relationships.

- Healthy family relations usually promote healthy peer relations. Parents can model or coach their children in ways of relating to peers. Parents' choices of neighborhoods, churches, schools, and their own friends influence the pool from which their children might select possible friends. Rough-and-tumble play occurs mainly in peer relations rather than in parent-child relations. In times of stress, children usually turn to parents rather than peers. Peer relations have a more equal basis than parent-child relations.

- Contexts and individual differences influence peer relations. The frequency of peer interaction, both positive and negative, increases in the preschool years. Children spend even more time with peers during the elementary and secondary school years.

- Social information-processing skills and social knowledge are important dimensions of social cognition in peer relations. Emotion regulation plays an important role in determining whether a child's peer relationships are successful.

Peer Statuses

- Popular children are frequently nominated as a best friend and are rarely disliked by their peers. Average children receive an average number of both positive and negative nominations from their peers. Neglected children are infrequently nominated as a best friend but are not disliked by their peers. Rejected children are infrequently nominated as a best friend and are actively disliked by their peers. Controversial children are frequently nominated both as a best friend and as being disliked by peers.

Bullying

- Significant numbers of students are bullied, and bullying can result in short-term and long-term negative effects for the victim. Anxious, withdrawn children and aggressive children often are victims of bullying, and boys are far more likely to be involved in bullying than girls are.

Gender and Peer Relations

- Gender is linked to peer relations in several ways. From 4 to 12 years of age, preference for playing in same-sex groups increases. Boys' groups are larger than girls', and boys participate in more organized games than girls do. Boys are more likely to engage in rough-and-tumble play, competition, ego displays, risk taking, and dominance, whereas girls are more likely to engage in collaborative discourse. Peers play more important roles in adolescents' lives in some cultures than in others, with some countries restricting adolescents' access to peers, especially for girls.

Adolescent Peer Relations

- Childhood groups are less formal and less heterogeneous than adolescent groups; childhood groups are also more likely to have same-sex participants. The pressure to conform to peers is strong during adolescence, especially during the eighth and ninth grades.

- Cliques and crowds assume more importance in the lives of adolescents than in the lives of children. Membership in certain crowds—especially jocks and populars—is associated with increased self-esteem. Independents also show high self-esteem.

2 Friendship

LG2 Explain the role of friendship through the life span.

Functions of Friendship

Friendship During Childhood

Friendship During Adolescence and Emerging Adulthood

Adult Friendship

- The functions of friendship include companionship, stimulation, ego support, social comparison, and intimacy/affection.

- Throughout childhood and adolescence, friends are generally similar—in terms of age, sex, ethnicity, and many other factors. Although having friends is usually a developmental advantage, the quality of friendships varies and having a coercive, conflict-ridden friendship can be harmful.

- Sullivan argued that there is a dramatic increase in the psychological importance of intimacy among close friends in adolescence. He believed friendships were important sources of support for adolescents, and research findings generally support his view.

- The friendships of adolescent girls are more intimate than those of adolescent boys. Adolescents who become friends with older individuals engage in more deviant behaviors than their counterparts with same-age friends.

- Many aspects of friendship are the same in emerging adulthood as in adolescence, although the transition to college can bring changes in friendship.

- Friendships play an important role in adult development, especially in providing emotional support. Female, male, and female-male friendships often have different characteristics. Regardless of age, friendship is an important aspect of relationships. In old age, there often is more change in male than in female friendships.

3 Play and Leisure

LG3 Describe the developmental aspects of play and leisure.

Childhood

Adolescence

Adulthood

- The functions of play include affiliation with peers, tension release, advances in cognitive development, and exploration. The contemporary perspective emphasizes both social and cognitive aspects of play. The most widely studied types of play include sensorimotor and practice play, pretense/symbolic play, social play, constructive play, and games.

- Leisure refers to the pleasant times when individuals are free to pursue activities and interests of their own choosing—hobbies, sports, or reading, for example. U.S. adolescents have more discretionary time than do adolescents in other industrialized countries, but they often fill this time with unchallenging activities such as hanging out and watching television. U.S. adolescents spend more time in voluntary structured activities—such as hobbies, sports, and organizations—than do East Asian adolescents. Some scholars argue that U.S. adolescents have too much unstructured discretionary time that should be replaced with more challenging activities.

- As adults, we not only need to learn to work well, but we also need to learn to enjoy leisure. Midlife may be an especially important time for leisure because of expanded free time, because of the availability of more money to many individuals, and because of the need for psychological preparation for an active retirement.

4 Aging and the Social World

LG4 Summarize the social aspects of aging.

Social Theories of Aging

Stereotyping of Older Adults

Social Support and Social Integration

Successful Aging

- Disengagement theory, in which older adults supposedly benefit from gradually withdrawing from society, has not held up, but socioemotional selectivity theory and activity theory are viable theories of aging.

- There is extensive stereotyping of older adults, and ageism is a common occurrence.

- Social support is an important aspect of helping people cope with stress. Older adults usually have less integrated social networks and engage in less social activity than their younger counterparts, although these findings may be influenced by cohort effects.

- Increasingly, the positive aspects of aging are being studied. Factors that are linked with successful aging include an active lifestyle, positive coping skills, good social relationships and support, and self-efficacy.

5 Sociocultural Influences

 LG5 Evaluate sociocultural influences on development.

Culture

- Culture refers to the behavior, patterns, beliefs, and all other products of a group of people that are passed on from generation to generation. Cross-cultural comparisons involve the comparison of one culture with one or more other cultures to gain information about the degree to which aspects are universal or culture-specific. One way that the influence of culture has been studied is to characterize cultures as individualistic (giving priority to personal rather than group goals) or collectivistic (emphasizing values that serve the group).

- There is substantial concern about the extensive increase in media/screen time by U.S. children and adolescents. Many experts argue that exposure to television violence is linked to increased aggression. Heavy TV watching is linked to lower school achievement. Children and youth also spend substantial amounts of time on the Internet. Large numbers of adolescents and college students engage in social networking on Facebook. Although older adults are less likely to have a computer and to use the Internet than younger adults, they are the fastest-growing age segment of Internet users.

- Respect for the aged may vary across cultures. Factors that predict high status for older adults across cultures range from the perception that they have valuable knowledge to the belief that they serve useful functions.

Socioeconomic Status and Poverty

- Socioeconomic status (SES) is the grouping of people with similar occupational, educational, and economic characteristics. The neighborhoods and families of children have SES characteristics that are related to children's development.

- Parents from low-SES families are more concerned that their children conform to society's expectations, have an authoritarian parenting style, use physical punishment more in disciplining their children, and are more directive and less conversational with their children than higher-SES parents.

- Poverty is defined by economic hardship. The subculture of the poor is often characterized not only by economic hardship but also by social and psychological difficulties. Persistent, long-lasting poverty especially has adverse effects on children's development. Older adults who live in poverty are a special concern.

Ethnicity

- Ethnicity is based on cultural heritage, nationality characteristics, race, religion, and language. Immigration brings a number of challenges as people adapt to their new culture. Although not all ethnic minority families are poor, poverty contributes to the stress of many ethnic minority families and between ethnic minority groups and the non-Latino White majority. African American and Latino children are more likely than non-Latino White children to live in single-parent families, to have larger families, and to maintain extended family connections. A special concern involves ethnicity and aging.

key **terms**

activity theory	cross-cultural studies	individualism	popular children
ageism	crowds	intimacy in friendship	practice play
average children	culture	leisure	pretense/symbolic play
cliques	disengagement theory	neglected children	rejected children
collectivism	ethnocentrism	peers	sensorimotor play
constructive play	feminization of poverty	play	social play
controversial children	games	play therapy	socioeconomic status (SES)

key **people**

Daniel Berlyne	Kenneth Dodge	Reed Larson	Vonnie McLoyd
Richard Brislin	Catherine Garvey	Angeline Lillard	Ross Parke
Donald Campbell	Kathy Hirsh-Pasek	Suniya Luthar	Harry Stack Sullivan
John Coie			

SCHOOLS, ACHIEVEMENT, AND WORK

chapter outline

Yuri_Arcurs/Getty Images

preview

This chapter is about becoming educated, achieving, and working. We will begin by exploring the importance of schools in development and then examine many aspects of a topic that is closely linked to success in school and life—achievement. The final section of the chapter focuses on key aspects of career development, the role of work across the life span, and retirement as a help or a hindrance to our development.

1 Schools · LG1 · Describe the role of schools in development.

| Contemporary Approaches to Student Learning and Assessment | Schools and Developmental Status | Educating Children with Disabilities | Socioeconomic Status and Ethnicity in Schools |

developmental connection

Cognitive Theory

Piaget's and Vygotsky's theories can be applied to children's education. Connect to "Cognitive Developmental Approaches."

We discuss many aspects of schools throughout this book, but especially in the chapters on cognitive processes and development. These chapters cover topics such as the applications of Piaget's and Vygotsky's theories to education, strategies for encouraging children's critical thinking in schools, applications of Gardner's and Sternberg's theories of intelligence to education, and bilingual education. Among the topics related to schools that we explore in this chapter are contemporary approaches to student learning, education for individuals at different developmental levels, educating children with disabilities, and the impact of socioeconomic status and ethnicity in schools.

CONTEMPORARY APPROACHES TO STUDENT LEARNING AND ASSESSMENT

Because there are so many approaches to education, controversy swirls about the best way to teach children (Morrison, 2020; Powell, 2019). There also is considerable interest in finding the best way to hold schools and teachers accountable for whether children are learning (Brookhart & Nitko, 2019; McMillan, 2018).

Constructivist and Direct Instruction Approaches

The **constructivist approach** is learner centered, and it emphasizes the importance of individuals actively constructing their knowledge and understanding with guidance from the teacher. In the constructivist view, teachers should not attempt to simply pour information into children's minds. Rather, children should be encouraged to explore their world, discover knowledge, reflect, and think critically, with careful monitoring and meaningful guidance from the teacher (Bredekamp, 2020; Burden & Byrd, 2019). Constructivists believe that for too long in American education children have been required to sit still, be passive learners, and rotely memorize irrelevant as well as relevant information (Johnson & others, 2018; Brookhart & Nitko, 2019). Today, constructivism may include an emphasis on collaboration—children working with each other in their efforts to know and understand (Joyce, Weil, & Calhoun, 2018; Parkay, 2020).

By contrast, the **direct instruction approach** is structured and teacher centered. It is characterized by teacher direction and control, high teacher expectations for students' progress, maximum time spent by students on academic tasks, and efforts by the teacher to keep negative affect to a minimum. An important goal in the direct instruction approach is maximizing student learning time (Burden & Byrd, 2020; Van de Walle, Karp, & Bay-Williams, 2019).

Advocates of the constructivist approach argue that the direct instruction approach turns children into passive learners and does not adequately challenge them to think in critical and creative ways (Sadker & Zittleman, 2018). The direct instruction enthusiasts say that the

Is this classroom more likely constructivist or direct instruction? Explain.
Elizabeth Crews

constructivist approach A learner-centered approach that emphasizes the individual's active, cognitive construction of knowledge and understanding with guidance from the teacher.

direct instruction approach A teacher-centered approach characterized by teacher direction and control, high expectations for students' progress, and maximum time spent on academic tasks.

constructivist approaches do not give enough attention to the content of a discipline, such as history or science. They also believe that the constructivist approaches are too relativistic and vague.

Some experts in educational psychology believe that many effective teachers use both a constructivist and a direct instruction approach rather than using either approach exclusively (Parkay, 2020). Further, some circumstances may require a constructivist approach, others a direction instruction approach. For example, experts increasingly recommend an explicit, intellectually engaging direct instruction approach when teaching students with a reading or a writing disability (Temple & others, 2018).

Accountability   Since the 1990s, the U.S. public and governments at every level have demanded increased accountability from schools. One result has been the spread of state-mandated tests to measure just what students have or have not learned (Brookhart & Nitko, 2019; McMillan, 2018). Many states have identified objectives for students in their state and created tests to measure whether students are meeting those objectives. This approach became national policy in 2002 when the No Child Left Behind (NCLB) legislation was signed into law.

Advocates argue that statewide standardized testing will have a number of positive effects. These include improved student performance; more time teaching the subjects that are tested; high expectations for all students; identification of poorly performing schools, teachers, and administrators; and improved confidence in schools as test scores rise.

Critics argue that the NCLB legislation is doing more harm than good (Sadker & Zittleman, 2018). One criticism stresses that using a single test as the sole indicator of students' progress and competence presents a very narrow view of students' skills (Bland & Gareis, 2018). This criticism is similar to the one leveled at IQ tests. To assess student progress and achievement, many psychologists and educators emphasize that a number of measures should be used, including tests, quizzes, projects, portfolios, classroom observations, and so on. Also, the tests used as part of NCLB don't measure creativity, motivation, persistence, flexible thinking, or social skills (Flitcroft & Woods, 2018; Ladd, 2017). Critics point out that teachers end up spending far too much class time "teaching to the test" by drilling students and having them memorize isolated facts at the expense of teaching that focuses on thinking skills, which students need for success in life (Brookhart & Nitko, 2019). Also, some individuals are concerned that No Child Left Behind educational policy overlooks the needs of students who are gifted because of its primary focus on raising the achievement level of students who are not doing well (Ballou & Springer, 2017).

Consider also the following: Each state is allowed to establish different criteria for what constitutes passing or failing grades on tests designated for NCLB inclusion. An analysis of NCLB data indicated that almost every fourth-grade student in Mississippi knows how to read but only half of Massachusetts' students do (Birman & others, 2007). Clearly, Mississippi's standards for passing the reading test are far below those of Massachusetts. Like Mississippi, many states have taken the safe route by choosing a low passing score. Thus, while one of NCLB's goals was to raise standards for achievement in U.S. schools, apparently allowing states to set their own standards has instead lowered achievement standards in many schools.

Most educators support high expectations and high standards of excellence for students and teachers. At issue, however, is whether the tests and procedures mandated by NCLB are the best means of achieving these high standards (McMillan, 2018).

In 2009, the Common Core State Standards Initiative was endorsed by the National Governors Association in an effort to implement more rigorous state guidelines for educating students. The Common Core Standards specify what students should know and the skills they should develop at each grade level in various content areas (Common Core State Standards Initiative, 2014). A large majority of states have agreed to implement the Standards, yet the initiative has generated considerable controversy. Some critics argue that the Common Core Standards are simply a further effort by the federal government to control education and that they emphasize a "one size fits all" approach that pays little attention to individual variations in students (Cizek, 2019). Supporters say that the Standards provide much-needed detailed guidelines and important milestones for students to achieve (McMillen, Graves-Demario, & Kieliszek, 2018).

What are some criticisms of the NCLB legislation? What is the Common Core State Standards Initiative? What is the Every Student Succeeds Act?
Ocean/Comstock Images/Corbis

Every Student Succeeds Act (ESSA)   The most recent initiative in U.S. education is the *Every Student Succeeds Act (ESSA)*, which was passed

child-centered kindergarten Education that involves the whole child by considering both the child's physical, cognitive, and socioemotional development and the child's needs, interests, and learning styles.

Montessori approach An educational philosophy in which children are given considerable freedom and spontaneity in choosing activities and are allowed to move from one activity to another as they desire.

into law in December 2015 and was supposed to be fully implemented in the 2017–2018 school year. However, in 2019 implementation was still occurring and ESSA continues to be a work in progress (Klein, 2019). ESSA gives states much more flexibility in implementing the law than was the case for NCLB (Ujifusa, 2019). The law replaces *No Child Left Behind*, in the process modifying but not completely eliminating standardized testing. ESSA retains annual testing for reading and writing success in grades 3 to 8, then once more in high school. The new law also allows states to scale back the role that tests play in holding schools accountable for student achievement. And schools must use at least one nonacademic factor—such as student engagement—when tracking schools' success.

Other aspects of the new law include still requiring states and districts to improve their lowest-performing schools and to ensure that they improve their work with historically underperforming students, such as English-language learners, ethnic minority students, and students with a disability. Also, states and districts are required to put in place challenging academic standards, although they can opt out of state standards involving Common Core.

SCHOOLS AND DEVELOPMENTAL STATUS

Let's now explore how schools work for students at different developmental levels. We will begin with early childhood education.

Early Childhood Education   How do early education programs treat children, and how do the children fare? Our exploration of early childhood education focuses on variations in programs, education for children who are disadvantaged, and some controversies in early childhood education.

Variations in Early Childhood Education   There are many variations in the way young children are educated (Feeney, Moravcik, & Nolte, 2019; Morrison, 2020). The foundation of early childhood education is the child-centered kindergarten.

What are some characteristics of the child-centered kindergarten?
Image100/PunchStock

Nurturing is a key aspect of the **child-centered kindergarten,** which emphasizes the education of the whole child and concern for his or her physical, cognitive, and socioemotional development (Bredekamp, 2020; Follari, 2019). Instruction is organized around children's needs, interests, and learning styles. Emphasis is on the process of learning, rather than what is learned. The child-centered kindergarten honors three principles: (1) each child follows a unique developmental pattern; (2) young children learn best through firsthand experiences with people and materials; and (3) play is extremely important in the child's total development. *Experimenting, exploring, discovering, trying out, restructuring, speaking,* and *listening* are frequent activities in excellent kindergarten programs. Such programs are closely attuned to the developmental status of 4- and 5-year-old children.

Montessori schools are patterned on the educational philosophy of Maria Montessori (1870–1952), an Italian physician-turned-educator who at the beginning of the twentieth century crafted a revolutionary approach to young children's education. The **Montessori approach** is a philosophy of education in which children are given considerable freedom and spontaneity in

(Left) Larry Page and Sergey Brin, founders of the highly successful Internet search engine Google, said that their early years at Montessori schools were a major factor in their success (International Montessori Council, 2006). During an interview with Barbara Walters, they said they learned how to be self-directed and self-starters at Montessori (ABC News, 2005). They commented that Montessori experiences encouraged them to think for themselves and allowed them the freedom to develop their own interests. *(Right)* Another leading American business executive, Amazon CEO Jeff Bezos, became the world's richest person in 2018 and recently provided $2 billion to fund a new network of preschools in underserved communities that he says will be Montessori inspired (Guernsey, 2019).
(Left) James Leynse/Corbis Historical/Getty Images; *(right)* Leigh Vogel/Getty Images

choosing activities. They are allowed to move from one activity to another as they desire. The teacher acts as a facilitator rather than a director (Hiles, 2018). The teacher shows the child how to perform intellectual activities, demonstrates interesting ways to explore curriculum materials, and offers help when the child requests it (Jor'dan, 2018; Lillard, 2017). "By encouraging children to make decisions from an early age, Montessori programs seek to develop self-regulated problem solvers who can make choices and manage their time effectively" (Hyson, Copple, & Jones, 2006, p. 14). The number of Montessori schools in the United States has expanded dramatically in recent years, from one school in 1959 to 355 schools in 1970 to approximately 4,500 in 2016, with estimates of Montessori schools worldwide at approximately 20,000 in 2016 (North American Montessori Teachers' Association, 2016).

What are some important aspects of developmentally appropriate practice?
Ariel Skelley/Blend Images/Getty Images

Some developmental psychologists favor the Montessori approach, but others believe that it neglects children's socioemotional development. For example, although the Montessori approach fosters independence and the development of cognitive skills, it deemphasizes verbal interaction between the teacher and child and between peers. Montessori's critics also argue that it restricts imaginative play and that its heavy reliance on self-corrective materials may not adequately allow for creativity and for a variety of learning styles.

Many educators and psychologists conclude that preschoolers and young elementary school children learn best through active, hands-on teaching methods such as games and dramatic play. They know that children develop at varying rates and that schools need to allow for these individual differences (Follari, 2019; Morrison, 2020). They also argue that schools should focus on supporting children's socioemotional development as well as their cognitive development. Educators refer to this type of schooling as **developmentally appropriate practice (DAP),** which is based on knowledge of the typical development of children within a particular age span (age appropriateness), as well as on the uniqueness of the individual child (individual appropriateness). DAP emphasizes the importance of creating settings that reflect children's interests and capabilities while encouraging them to be active learners (Bredekamp, 2020). Desired outcomes for DAP include thinking critically, working cooperatively, solving problems, developing self-regulatory skills, and enjoying learning. The emphasis in DAP is on the process of learning rather than on its content.

Do developmentally appropriate educational practices support young children's development? Some researchers have found that young children in developmentally appropriate classrooms are likely to feel less stress, be more motivated, be more socially skilled, have better work habits, be more creative, have better language skills, and demonstrate better math skills than children in developmentally inappropriate classrooms (Hart & others, 2003). Recent changes in the concept have given more attention to how strongly academic skills should be emphasized and how they should be taught.

Education for Young Children Who Are Disadvantaged For many years, U.S. children from low-income families did not receive any education before they entered the first grade. Often when they began first grade they were already several steps behind their classmates in readiness to learn. In the summer of 1965, the federal government began an effort to break the cycle of poverty and substandard education for young children through **Project Head Start.** Head Start is a compensatory program designed to give children from low-income families the opportunity to acquire skills and experiences that are important for success in school (Morrison, 2020). More than half a century after the program was founded, Head Start continues to be the largest federally funded program for U.S. children, with almost 1 million children enrolled in it annually.

Early Head Start was established in 1995 to serve children from birth to age 3. In 2007, half of all new funds appropriated for Head Start programs were used for the expansion of Early Head Start. Researchers have found these programs to have positive effects (Burgette & others, 2017).

Head Start programs are not all created equal. It has been estimated that 40 percent of the 1,400 Head Start programs are of questionable quality (Zigler & Styfco, 1994). More attention needs to be given to developing consistently high-quality Head Start programs (Paschall & Mastergeorge, 2018). One person who is strongly motivated to make Head Start a valuable learning experience for young children from disadvantaged backgrounds is Yolanda Garcia. To read about her work, see the *Connecting with Careers* profile.

Mixed results have been found for Head Start (Miller, Farkas, & Duncan, 2016; Lee, 2019). One study found that one year of Head Start was linked to higher performance in early

developmentally appropriate practice (DAP) Education that focuses on the typical developmental patterns of children (age appropriateness) and the uniqueness of each child (individual appropriateness). Such practice contrasts with developmentally inappropriate practice, which has an academic, direct instruction approach focused largely on abstract paper-and-pencil activities, seatwork, and rote/drill practice activities.

Project Head Start Compensatory prekindergarten education designed to provide children from low-income families the opportunity to acquire skills and experiences important for school success.

Yolanda Garcia, Director of Children's Services, Head Start

Yolanda Garcia has been the director of the Children's Services Department of the Santa Clara, California, County Office of Education since 1980. As director, she is responsible for managing child development programs for 2,500 3- to 5-year-old children in 127 classrooms. Her training includes two master's degrees: one in public policy and child welfare from the University of Chicago and another in educational administration from San Jose State University.

Garcia has served on many national advisory committees that have resulted in improvements in the staffing of Head Start programs. Most notably, she served on the Head Start Quality Committee that recommended the development of Early Head Start and revised performance standards for Head Start programs. Garcia currently is a member of the American Academy of Sciences Committee on the Integration of Science and Early Childhood Education.

Yolanda Garcia, Director of Children's Services/Head Start, works with a Head Start child in Santa Clara, California.
Courtesy of Yolanda Garcia

math, early reading, and receptive vocabulary (Miller & others, 2014). In another study, the best results occurred for Head Start children who had low initial cognitive ability, whose parents had low levels of education, and who attended Head Start more than 20 hours a week (Lee & others, 2014). And two recent studies found that improved parenting engagement and skills were linked to the success of children in Head Start programs (Ansari & Gershoff, 2016; Roggman & others, 2016). Nonetheless, too often early gains occur through Head Start and then evaporate in elementary school (Jenkins & others, 2018).

One-fourth of Head Start children have mothers who also participated in Head Start. In a multigenerational study, a positive influence on cognitive and socioemotional development (assessed in the third grade) occurred for Head Start children whose mothers had also attended Head Start programs (in comparison with Head Start children whose mothers had not attended Head Start) (Chor, 2018). This result likely occurred because of improved family resources and home learning environments.

One high-quality early childhood education program (although not a Head Start program) was the Perry Preschool Project in Ypsilanti, Michigan, a two-year preschool program conducted from 1962 to 1967 that included weekly home visits from program personnel. In analyses of the long-term effects of the program, adults who had participated in the Perry Preschool Project were compared with a control group of adults from the same background who had not received the enriched early childhood education (Schweinhart & others, 2005; Weikert, 1993). Those who had been in the Perry Preschool Project had fewer teen pregnancies and better high school graduation rates, and at age 40 they were more likely to be in the workforce, own a home, have a savings account, and have fewer arrests.

Also, in an early childhood intervention designed to improve developmental outcomes and enhance the quality of Head Start programs in high-violence, high-crime areas of Chicago, initial assessments at the end of preschool indicated that the children involved in the intervention showed fewer behavior problems and had gains in executive function and academic achievement (Raver & others, 2008). In a recent analysis, 10 to 11 years after the intervention was finished, the children had long-term positive effects for executive function and grades but there was no evidence of long-term effects on behavioral problems (Watts & others, 2018).

Controversy Over Curriculum   A current controversy in early childhood education involves what the curriculum for early childhood education should be (Bredekamp, 2020; Follari, 2019). On one side are those who advocate a child-centered, constructivist approach much like that emphasized by the National Association for the Education of Young Children (NAEYC), along the lines of developmentally appropriate practice. On the other side are those who advocate an academic, direct-instruction approach.

In practice, many high-quality early childhood education programs encompass both academic and constructivist approaches. Many education experts such as Lilian Katz (1999), however, worry about academic approaches that place too much pressure on young children to achieve and don't provide opportunities to actively construct knowledge. Competent early childhood programs should focus on both cognitive development and socioemotional development, not exclusively on cognitive development (Feeney, Moravcik, & Nolte, 2019).

Elementary School   For many children, entering the first grade signals a change from being a "home-child" to being a "school-child"—a situation in which they experience new roles and obligations. Children take up the new role of being a student, interact, develop new relationships, adopt new reference groups, and develop new standards by which to judge themselves (Collins & Madsen, 2019). School provides children with a rich source of new ideas to shape their sense of self.

Too often, however, early schooling proceeds mainly on the basis of negative feedback. For example, children's self-esteem in the later years of elementary school is lower than it is in the earlier years, and older children rate themselves as less smart, less good, and less hardworking than do younger ones (Eccles, 2003).

What is the curriculum controversy in early childhood education?
Ronnie Kaufman/Corbis/Getty Images

Educating Adolescents   How do students experience the transition from elementary to middle or junior high school? What are the characteristics of effective schools for adolescents?

The Transition to Middle or Junior High School   The transition to middle school or junior high school can be stressful. Why? The transition takes place at a time when many changes—in the individual, in the family, and in school—are occurring simultaneously (Crosnoe & Ressler, 2019; Madjar, Cohen, & Shoval, 2018). These changes include puberty and related concerns about body image; the emergence of at least some aspects of formal operational thought, including accompanying changes in social cognition; increased responsibility and decreased dependency on parents; change to a larger, more impersonal school structure; change from one teacher to many teachers and from a small, homogeneous set of peers to a larger, more heterogeneous set of peers; and an increased focus on achievement and performance and their assessment. Also, when students make the transition to middle or junior high school, they experience the **top-dog phenomenon,** moving from being the oldest, biggest, and most powerful students in elementary school to being the youngest, smallest, and least powerful students in middle or junior high school. A recent study in Spain discovered that middle school students had a lower level of self-concept in a number of areas (academic, social, family, and physical) than elementary school students did (Onetti, Fernandez-Garcia, & Castillo-Rodriguez, 2019). Further, a recent study found that teacher warmth was higher in the last four years of elementary school and then dropped in the middle school years (Hughes & Cao, 2018). The drop in teacher warmth was associated with lower student math scores.

top-dog phenomenon The circumstance of moving from the top position in elementary school to the youngest, smallest, and least powerful position in middle or junior high school.

There can also be positive aspects to the transition to middle or junior high school. Students are more likely to feel grown up, have more subjects from which to select, have more opportunities to spend time with peers and locate compatible friends, and enjoy increased independence from direct parental monitoring. They also may be more challenged intellectually by academic work.

Effective Schools for Young Adolescents   Educators and psychologists worry that junior high and middle schools have become watered-down versions of high schools, mimicking their curricular and extracurricular schedules. Critics argue that these schools should offer activities that reflect a wide range of individual differences in biological and psychological development among young adolescents (Wigfield, Rosenzweig, & Eccles, 2017). The Carnegie Foundation (1989) issued an extremely negative evaluation of U.S. middle schools. It concluded that most young adolescents attended massive, impersonal schools, learned from irrelevant curricula, trusted few adults in school, and lacked access to health care and counseling. It recommended that the nation develop smaller "communities" or "houses" to lessen the impersonal nature of large middle schools; have lower student-to-counselor ratios (10 to 1 instead of several hundred to 1); involve parents and

The transition from elementary to middle or junior high school occurs at the same time as a number of other developmental changes. *What are some of these other developmental changes?*
Creatas Images/Punchstock

community leaders in schools; develop new curricula; have teachers team teach in more flexibly designed curriculum blocks that integrate several disciplines; boost students' health and fitness with more in-school physical education programs; and help students who need public health care to get it. Three decades later, many of the Carnegie Foundation's recommendations have not been implemented, and middle schools throughout the nation continue to need a major redesign if they are to be effective in educating adolescents (Voight & Hanson, 2017).

High School   Just as there are concerns about U.S. middle school education, so are there concerns about U.S. high school education (Bill and Melinda Gates Foundation, 2011, 2017). A recent analysis indicated that only 25 percent of U.S. high school graduates have the academic skills to succeed in college (Bill & Melinda Gates Foundation, 2017). Not only are many high school graduates poorly prepared for college, they also are poorly prepared for the demands of the modern, high-performance workplace (Bill & Melinda Gates Foundation, 2019).

Critics stress that many high schools foster passivity and that schools should create a variety of pathways for students to achieve an identity. Many students graduate from high school with inadequate reading, writing, and mathematical skills; of these, many go on to college and must enroll in remediation classes there. Other students drop out of high school and do not have skills that would allow them to obtain decent jobs, much less to be informed citizens.

The transition to high school can have problems, just as the transition to middle school can. These problems may include the following (Benner, Boyle, & Bakhtiari, 2017; Wigfield, Rosenzweig, & Eccles, 2017): high schools are often even larger, more bureaucratic, and more impersonal than middle schools are; there isn't much opportunity for students and teachers to get to know each other, which can lead to distrust; and teachers too infrequently make content relevant to students' interests. Such experiences likely undermine the motivation of students.

Robert Crosnoe's (2011) book, *Fitting In, Standing Out,* highlighted another major problem with U.S. high schools: How the negative social aspects of adolescents' lives undermine their academic achievement. In his view, adolescents become immersed in complex peer group cultures that demand conformity. High school is supposed to be about getting an education but in reality for many youth it is as much about navigating the social worlds of peer relations that may or may not value education and academic achievement. The adolescents who fail to fit in, especially those who are obese or gay, become stigmatized. Crosnoe recommends increased school counseling services, expanded extracurricular activities, and improved parental monitoring to reduce such problems (Crosnoe & Benner, 2015; Crosnoe, Pivnick, & Benner, 2019).

Adolescents in U.S. schools usually have a wide array of extracurricular activities they can participate in beyond their academic courses. These activities include such diverse activities as sports, academic clubs, band, drama, and math clubs. Researchers have found that participation in extracurricular activities is linked to higher grades, greater school engagement and motivation, less likelihood of dropping out of school, improved probability of going to college, higher self-esteem, and lower rates of depression, delinquency, and substance abuse (Denault & Guay, 2017). One study also revealed that the more adolescents participated in organized out-of-school activities, the more likely they were to be characterized by positive outcomes—educational attainment, civic engagement, and psychological flourishing—in emerging adulthood (Mahoney & Vest, 2012). And another study revealed that immigrant adolescents who participated in extracurricular activities improved their academic achievement and increased their school engagement (Camacho & Fuligni, 2015). Adolescents benefit from engaging in a variety of extracurricular activities more than from focusing on a single extracurricular activity. In a longitudinal study, both breadth and intensity of extracurricular activity involvement in the tenth grade were associated with higher educational attainment 8 years after high school (Haghighat & Knifsend, 2019).

In the first two decades of the twenty-first century, U.S. high school dropout rates declined (National Center for Education Statistics, 2018). In the 1940s, more than half of U.S. 16- to 24-year-olds had dropped out of school; by 1990, this rate had dropped to 12 percent, and by 2000 it was 10.9 percent. In 2016, the dropout rate had decreased further to 6.1 percent. The lowest dropout rate in 2016 occurred for Asian American adolescents (1 percent), followed by non-Latino White adolescents (5.2 percent), African American adolescents (6.2 percent), and Latino adolescents (8.6 percent) (National Center for Education Statistics, 2018). The dropout rates have dropped considerably since 2000 when the dropout rate for non-Latino Whites was 6.9, for African Americans 13.1 percent, and for Latinos 27.8 percent.

Gender differences have characterized U.S. dropout rates for many decades, but they have been narrowing in recent years. In 2016, the dropout rate for males was 7.1 percent and for females it was 5.1 percent, compared with 12.0 and 9.9 respectively in 2000 (National Center for Education Statistics, 2018).

The average U.S. high school dropout rates just described mask some very high dropout rates in low-income areas of inner cities. For example, in cities such as Detroit, Cleveland, and Chicago, dropout rates are above 50 percent. Also, the percentages cited earlier are for 16- to 24-year-olds. When dropout rates are calculated in terms of students who do not graduate from high school within four years, the percentage is much higher than the figures described earlier. Thus, in considering high school dropout rates, it is important to examine students' ages at graduation, the number of years it takes for them to complete high school, and various contexts including ethnicity, gender, and school location.

Students drop out of school for many reasons (Bill & Melinda Gates Foundation, 2019). In one study, almost 50 percent of the dropouts cited school-related reasons for leaving school, such as not liking school or being expelled or suspended (Rumberger, 1995). Twenty percent of the dropouts (but 40 percent of the Latino students) cited economic reasons for leaving school. One-third of the female students dropped out for personal reasons, such as pregnancy or marriage. One study revealed that when children's parents were involved in their school in middle and late childhood and when parents and adolescents had good relationships in early adolescence, a positive trajectory toward academic success was the likely outcome (Englund, Egeland, & Collins, 2008). By contrast, those who had poor relationships with their parents were more likely to drop out of high school even if they were doing well academically and behaviorally.

An important educational goal is to increase the high school graduation rate of Native youth. An excellent strategy to accomplish this goal is high-quality early childhood educational programs such as this one at St. Bonaventure Indian School on the Navajo Nation in Thoreau, New Mexico.
Jim West/Alamy Stock Photo

The Bill and Melinda Gates Foundation (2017) funds efforts to reduce the dropout rate in schools where dropout rates are high. One strategy that is being emphasized in programs sponsored by the Gates Foundation is keeping students who are at risk for dropping out of school with the same teachers through their high school years. The hope is that the teachers will get to know these students much better, that their relationship with the students will improve, and that they will be able to monitor and guide the students toward graduating from high school. Recent initiatives by the Gates Foundation (2017, 2019) involve creating a new generation of courseware that adapts to students' learning needs and blending face-to-face instruction with digital tools that help students to learn independently.

"I Have a Dream" (IHAD) is an innovative, comprehensive, long-term dropout prevention program administered by the National "I Have a Dream" Foundation in New York. Since the National IHAD Foundation was established in 1986, it has grown to comprise more than 180 projects in 64 cities and 27 states serving more than 15,000 children ("I Have a Dream" Foundation, 2019). Local IHAD projects around the country "adopt" entire grades (usually the third or fourth) from public elementary schools, or corresponding age cohorts from public housing developments. These children—"Dreamers"—are then provided with a program of academic, social, cultural, and recreational activities throughout their elementary, middle school, and high school years. When participants complete high school, IHAD provides the tuition assistance necessary for them to attend a state or local college or vocational school.

The IHAD program was created in 1981, when philanthropist Eugene Lang made an impromptu offer of college tuition to a class of graduating sixth-graders at P.S. 121 in East Harlem. Evaluations of IHAD programs have found dramatic improvements in grades, test scores, and school attendance, as well as reduced rates of behavioral problems of Dreamers. In one analysis of the I Have a Dream program in Houston, 91 percent of the participants received passing grades in reading/English, 83 percent said they liked school, 98 percent said getting good grades is important to them, 100 percent said they plan to graduate from high school, and 94 percent reported that they plan to go to college ("I Have a Dream" Foundation, 2015).

These adolescents are participating in the "I Have a Dream" (IHAD) Program, a comprehensive, long-term dropout prevention program that has been very successful. *What are some other strategies for reducing high school dropout rates?*
Courtesy of "I Have a Dream" Foundation of Boulder County (www.ihadboulder.org)

College and Adult Education Having a college degree is a strong asset. College graduates can enter careers that will earn them considerably more money in their lifetimes than those who do not go to college, and income differences between college graduates and high school graduates continue to grow (*Occupational Outlook Handbook, 2018–2019*). Recent media

The transition from high school to college often involves positive as well as negative features. In college, students are likely to feel grown up, be able to spend more time with peers, have more opportunities to explore different lifestyles and values, and enjoy greater freedom from parental monitoring. However, college involves a larger, more impersonal school structure and an increased focus on achievement and its assessment. *What was your transition to college like?*
Stockbyte/PunchStock

accounts have highlighted the dramatically rising costs of a college education and somewhat bleak job prospects for recent college graduates, raising questions about whether a college education is worth the expense. Recent data indicate that in the United States a college graduate will make approximately 1 million dollars more on average in lifetime income than a high school graduate will earn (Georgetown University Center on Education, 2016). This means that on average a college graduate will earn $17,000 more per year than a high school graduate. College graduates also are much less likely to become unemployed during their lifetime than are high school graduates. Individuals with a college education also live two years longer on average than their counterparts who only graduate from high school.

Transition to College   What is the transition to college like? Are adults seeking more education than in the past?

Just as the transition from elementary school to middle or junior high school involves change and possible stress, so does the transition from high school to college. The two transitions have many parallels. Going from being a senior in high school to being a freshman in college replays the top-dog phenomenon of transferring from the oldest and most powerful group of students to the youngest and least powerful group of students that occurred earlier as adolescence began. For many students, the transition from high school to college involves movement to a larger, more impersonal school structure; interaction with peers from more diverse geographical and sometimes more diverse ethnic backgrounds; and increased focus on achievement and its assessment. And like the transition from elementary to middle or junior high school, the transition from high school to college can involve positive features. Students are more likely to feel grown up, have more subjects from which to select, have more time to spend with peers, have more opportunities to explore different lifestyles and values, enjoy greater independence from parental monitoring, and be challenged intellectually by academic work (Santrock & Halonen, 2013).

Today's college students experience more stress and are more depressed than those of the past, according to a national study of more than 300,000 freshmen at more than 500 colleges and universities (Stolzenberg & others, 2019). In 2017, 38.7 percent (up from 16 percent in 1985 and 27 percent in 2009) said they frequently "felt overwhelmed with what I have to do." In 2017, female students (51 percent) were more than twice as likely as their male counterparts (23 percent) to say that they felt overwhelmed with all they had to do. And college freshmen in 2017 indicated that they felt more depressed than their counterparts from the 1980s had indicated. The pressure to succeed in college, get a great job, and make lots of money were pervasive concerns of these students.

What makes college students happy? One study of 222 undergraduates compared the upper 10 percent of college students who were very happy with average and very unhappy college students (Diener & Seligman, 2002). The very happy college students were highly social, more extraverted, and had stronger romantic and social relationships than the less happy college students, who spent more time alone (see Figure 1).

Adult Education   An increasing number of adults older than the traditional college age go to school. Adult education refers to all forms of schooling and learning in which adults participate. Adult education includes literacy training, community development, university credit programs, on-the-job training, and continuing professional education. Institutions that offer education to adults include colleges, libraries, museums, government agencies, businesses, and churches.

In 1985, individuals over the age of 25 represented 45 percent of the enrollment in credit courses in the United States. In the second decade of the twenty-first century, that figure is over 50 percent. A large and expanding number of college students are adults who pursue education and advanced degrees on a part-time basis. The increase in adult education is a result of increased leisure time for some individuals and the need to update information and skills for others. Some older adults simply take educational courses because they enjoy learning and want to keep their minds active.

Women represent the majority of adult learners—almost 60 percent. In the 35-and-over age group, women constitute an even greater percentage of the enrollment in adult education—almost 70 percent. Some of these women devoted their early adult lives to parenting and decided to go back to school to enter a new career.

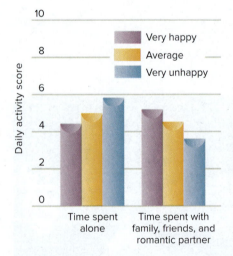

FIGURE 1

DAILY ACTIVITY SELF-RATINGS AND COLLEGE STUDENTS' HAPPINESS. In this study of undergraduates, the daily activity scores reflect mean times with 0 representing no time and 8 indicating 8 hours per day (Diener & Seligman, 2002). Students were classified as very happy, average, or very unhappy based on their self-ratings.

Going back to a classroom after being away from school for a long time can be stressful. However, returning students should realize that they bring a wealth of experience to college and should feel good about the contributions they can make.

EDUCATING CHILDREN WITH DISABILITIES

So far we have discussed schools as they are experienced by the majority of U.S. students. Of all children in the United States, 12.9 percent from 3 to 21 years of age received special education or related services in 2015–2016, an increase of 3 percent since 1980–1981 (National Center for Education Statistics, 2017). Figure 2 shows the five largest groups of students with a disability who were served by federal programs during the 2015–2016 school year (National Center for Education Statistics, 2017). As indicated in Figure 2, students with a learning disability were by far the largest group of students with a disability to be given special education, followed by children with speech or language impairments, intellectual disability, and emotional disturbance. Note that the U.S. Department of Education includes both students with a learning disability and students with ADHD in the category of learning disability.

Many immigrants to the United States, such as this Spanish-speaking woman enrolled in an English class, take adult education classes. *What are some trends in adult education?*
Newscom

Learning Disabilities   The U.S. government defines whether a child should be classified as having a learning disability in the following way: A child with a **learning disability** has difficulty in learning that involves understanding or using spoken or written language, and the difficulty can appear in listening, thinking, reading, writing, and spelling (Friend, 2018; Turnbull & others, 2020). A learning disability also may involve difficulty in doing mathematics (Stein & others, 2018). To be classified as a learning disability, the learning problem is not primarily the result of visual, hearing, or motor disabilities; intellectual disability; emotional disorders; or due to environmental, cultural, or economic disadvantage.

About three times as many boys as girls are classified as having a learning disability. Among the explanations for this gender difference are a greater biological vulnerability among boys and *referral bias.* That is, boys are more likely than girls to be referred by teachers for treatment because of troublesome behavior.

Approximately 80 percent of children with a learning disability have a reading problem (Shaywitz, Gruen, & Shaywitz, 2007). Three types of learning disabilities are dyslexia, dysgraphia, and dyscalculia:

- **Dyslexia** is a category reserved for individuals with a severe impairment in their ability to read and spell (Kershner, 2019; Nergard-Nilssen & Eklund, 2018).

- **Dysgraphia** is a learning disability that involves difficulty in handwriting (Johnson, Ross, & Kiran, 2019). Children with dysgraphia may write very slowly, their writing products may be virtually illegible, and they may make numerous spelling errors because of their inability to match up sounds and letters.

- **Dyscalculia,** also known as developmental arithmetic disorder, is a learning disability that involves difficulty in math computation (Moreau & others, 2019; Stein & others, 2018).

The precise causes of learning disabilities have not yet been determined (Hallahan, Kauffman, & Pullen, 2019). To reveal any regions of the brain that might be involved in learning disabilities, researchers use brain-imaging techniques such as magnetic resonance imaging (Ramus & others, 2018) (see Figure 3). This research indicates that it is unlikely that learning disabilities reside in a single, specific brain location. More likely, learning disabilities are due to problems with integrating information from multiple brain regions or subtle difficulties in brain structures and functions.

Interventions with children who have a learning disability often focus on improving reading ability (Turnbull & others, 2020). Intensive instruction in reading over a period of time by a competent teacher can help many children (Temple & others, 2018).

Disability	Percentage of All Children in Public Schools
Learning disabilities	4.6
Speech and language impairments	2.7
Autism	1.2
Intellectual disability	0.8
Emotional disturbance	0.7

FIGURE 2

U.S. CHILDREN WITH A DISABILITY WHO RECEIVE SPECIAL EDUCATION SERVICES. Figures are for the 2015–2016 school year and represent the five categories with the highest numbers and percentages of children. Both learning disability and attention deficit hyperactivity disorder are combined in the learning disabilities category (National Center for Education Statistics, 2017).

learning disabilities Disabilities in which children experience difficulty in learning that involves understanding or using spoken or written language; the difficulty can appear in listening, thinking, reading, writing, and spelling. A learning disability also may involve difficulty in doing mathematics. To be classified as a learning disability, the learning problem is not primarily the result of visual, hearing, or motor disabilities; intellectual disability; emotional disorders; or environmental, cultural, or economic disadvantage.

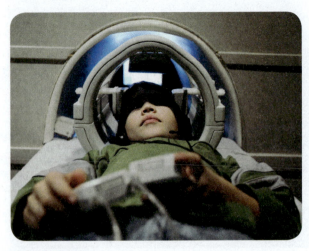

FIGURE 3

BRAIN SCANS AND LEARNING DISABILITIES. An increasing number of studies are using MRI brain scans to examine the brain pathways involved in learning disabilities. Shown here is 9-year-old Patrick Price, who has dyslexia. Patrick is going through an MRI scanner disguised by drapes to look like a child-friendly castle. Inside the scanner, children must lie virtually motionless as words and symbols flash on a screen, and they are asked to identify them by clicking different buttons.
Manuel Balce Ceneta/AP Images

Many children with ADHD show impulsive behavior, such as this boy reaching to pull a girl's hair. *How would you handle this situation if you were a teacher and this were to happen in your classroom?*
Nicole Hill/Rubberball/Getty Images

dyslexia A learning disability that involves a severe impairment in the ability to read and spell.

dysgraphia A learning disability that involves difficulty in handwriting.

dyscalculia Also known as developmental arithmetic disorder, this term refers to a learning disability that involves difficulty in math computation.

attention deficit hyperactivity disorder (ADHD) A disability in which children consistently show one or more of the following characteristics: (1) inattention, (2) hyperactivity, and (3) impulsivity.

Attention Deficit Hyperactivity Disorder (ADHD) Attention deficit hyperactivity disorder (ADHD) is a disability in which children consistently show one or more of the following characteristics over a period of time: (1) inattention, (2) hyperactivity, and (3) impulsivity. Children who are inattentive have so much difficulty focusing on any one thing that they may get bored with a task after only a few minutes—or even seconds. Children who are hyperactive show high levels of physical activity, seeming to be almost constantly in motion. Children who are impulsive have difficulty curbing their reactions; they do not do a good job of thinking before they act. Depending on the characteristics that children with ADHD display, they can be diagnosed as (1) ADHD with predominantly inattention, (2) ADHD with predominantly hyperactivity/impulsivity, or (3) ADHD with both inattention and hyperactivity/impulsivity.

The number of children diagnosed and treated for ADHD has increased substantially in recent decades. The Centers for Disease Control and Prevention (2016) estimates that ADHD has continued to increase in 4- to 17-year-old children, going from 8 percent in 2003 to 9.5 percent in 2007 and to 11 percent in 2016. According to the Centers for Disease Control and Prevention, 13.2 percent of U.S. boys and 5.6 percent of U.S. girls have ever been diagnosed with ADHD. The disorder is diagnosed as much as four to nine times as often in boys as in girls. There is controversy, however, about the increased diagnosis of ADHD (Hallahan, Kauffman, & Pullen, 2019). Some experts attribute the increase mainly to heightened awareness of the disorder; others are concerned that many children are being incorrectly diagnosed.

One study examined the possible misdiagnosis of ADHD (Bruchmiller, Margraf, & Schneider, 2012). In this study, child psychologists, psychiatrists, and social workers were given vignettes of children with ADHD (some vignettes matched the diagnostic criteria for the disorder, while others did not). Whether each child was male or female varied. The researchers assessed whether the mental health professionals gave a diagnosis of ADHD to the child described in the vignette. The professionals overdiagnosed ADHD almost 20 percent of the time, and regardless of the symptoms described, boys were twice as likely as girls to be given a diagnosis of ADHD.

Definitive causes of ADHD have not been found (Mash & Wolfe, 2019). However, a number of causes have been proposed. Some children likely inherit a tendency to develop ADHD from their parents (Hess & others, 2018; van Dongen & others, 2019). Other children likely develop ADHD because of damage to their brain during prenatal or postnatal development (Hinshaw, 2018; Wang & others, 2019). Among early possible contributors to ADHD are maternal exposure to cigarettes and alcohol during prenatal development, as well as a high level of maternal stress during prenatal development and low birth weight (Scheinost & others, 2017; Sourander & others, 2019; Tole & others, 2019).

As with learning disabilities, the development of brain-imaging techniques is leading to a better understanding of ADHD (Shephard & others, 2019; Sun & others, 2018). One study revealed that peak thickness of the cerebral cortex occurred three years later (10.5 years) in children with ADHD than in children without ADHD (peak at 7.5 years) (Shaw & others, 2007). The delay was more prominent in the prefrontal regions of the brain that are especially important in attention and planning (see Figure 4). Another study also found delayed development in the brain's frontal lobes among children with ADHD, which likely was due to delayed or decreased myelination (Nagel & others, 2011). Researchers also are exploring the roles that various neurotransmitters, such as serotonin and dopamine, might play in ADHD (Hou & others, 2018).

The delays in brain development just described are in areas linked to executive function. An increasing focus of research on children with ADHD is their difficulty on tasks involving executive function, such as behavioral inhibition when necessary, use of working memory, and effective planning (Yasumura & others, 2019; Krieger & Amador-Campos, 2018; Munroe & others, 2019). Researchers also have found deficits in theory of mind in children with ADHD (Maoz & others, 2017). Children diagnosed with ADHD have an increased risk of school dropout, adolescent pregnancy, substance use problems, and antisocial behavior (Machado & others, 2019; van der Burg & others, 2019). Also, a recent research review concluded that

ADHD in childhood was linked to these long-term outcomes: failure to complete high school, other mental and substance use disorders, criminal activity, and unemployment (Erskine & others, 2016). Further, a recent study found that childhood ADHD was associated with long-term underachievement in math and reading (Voigt & others, 2017). Another recent study revealed that individuals with ADHD were more likely to become parents at 12 to 16 years of age (Ostergaard & others, 2017).

Experts previously thought that most children "grow out" of ADHD. However, evidence suggests otherwise (Drake, Riccio, & Hale, 2019; Pinzone & others, 2019). As many as 70 percent of adolescents (Sibley & others, 2012) and 66 percent of adults (Buitelaar, Karr, & Asherton, 2010) who were diagnosed as children continue to experience ADHD symptoms.

Stimulant medication such as Ritalin or Adderall (which has fewer side effects than Ritalin) is effective in improving the attention of many children with ADHD, but it usually does not improve their attention to the same level as children who do not have ADHD (Luo & Levin, 2017). A recent research review also concluded that stimulant medications are effective in treating ADHD during the short term but that longer-term benefits of stimulant medications are not clear (Rajeh & others, 2017). A meta-analysis concluded that behavior management treatments are effective in reducing the effects of ADHD (Fabiano & others, 2009). Researchers have often found that a combination of medication (such as Ritalin) and behavior management improves the behavior of children with ADHD better than medication alone or behavior management alone, although not in all cases (Centers for Disease Control and Prevention, 2016).

The sheer number of ADHD diagnoses has prompted speculation that psychiatrists, parents, and teachers are labeling normal childhood behavior as psychopathology (Mash & Wolfe, 2019). One reason for concern about overdiagnosing ADHD is that the form of treatment in well over 80 percent of cases is psychoactive drugs, including stimulants such as Ritalin and Adderall (Garfield & others, 2012). Further, there is increasing concern that children who are given stimulant drugs such as Ritalin or Adderall are at risk for developing substance abuse problems, although research results on this concern so far have been mixed (McCabe & others, 2017; van der Burg & others, 2019).

In addition to stimulant drug treatment and behavior management, recently three other strategies for treating ADHD have been explored—neurofeedback, mindfulness training, and exercise:

- Researchers are exploring the possibility that neurofeedback might improve the attention of children with ADHD (Bijlenga & others, 2019; Cueli & others, 2019; Goode & others, 2019). Neurofeedback trains individuals to become more aware of their physiological responses so that they can attain better control over their brain's prefrontal cortex, where executive control primarily occurs. Individuals with ADHD have higher levels of electroencephalogram (EEG) abnormalities, such as lower beta waves that involve attention and memory, and lower sensorimotor rhythms (which involve control of movements). Neurofeedback produces audiovisual profiles of brain waves so that individuals can learn how to achieve normal EEG functioning (Riesco-Matias & others, 2019). In one study, 7- to 14-year-olds with ADHD were randomly assigned either to take Ritalin or to undergo 40 sessions of a neurofeedback treatment (Meisel & others, 2013). Both groups showed a lower level of ADHD symptoms six months after the treatment, but only the neurofeedback group performed better academically. And a recent meta-analysis found that neurofeedback had medium effects on improving children's attention and reducing their hyperactivity/impulsivity for at least 6 months after treatment (Van Doren & others, 2019).

- Mindfulness training also recently has been given to children, adolescents, and adults with ADHD (Lo & others, 2019; Siebelink & others, 2019). A recent meta-analysis concluded that mindfulness training significantly improved the attention of children with ADHD (Cairncross & Miller, 2019).

- Exercise also is being investigated as a possible treatment for children with ADHD (Pan & others, 2019). A research meta-analysis concluded that physical exercise is effective in reducing cognitive symptoms of ADHD in individuals 3 to 25 years of age (Tan, Pooley, & Speelman, 2016). Also, a second meta-analysis concluded that short-term aerobic exercise is effective in reducing symptoms such as inattention, hyperactivity, and impulsivity (Cerillo-Urbina & others, 2015). Further, a more recent meta-analysis indicated that exercise is associated with better executive function in children with ADHD

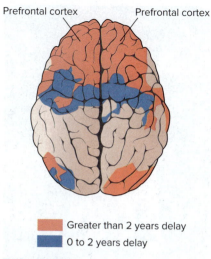

Prefrontal cortex   Prefrontal cortex

■ Greater than 2 years delay
■ 0 to 2 years delay

FIGURE 4

REGIONS OF THE BRAIN IN WHICH CHILDREN WITH ADHD HAD A DELAYED PEAK IN THE THICKNESS OF THE CEREBRAL CORTEX.

Note: The greatest delays occurred in the prefrontal cortex.

developmental **connection**

Cognitive Processes

Mindfulness training is being used to improve students' executive function. Connect to "Information Processing."

What characterizes autism spectrum disorders?
Rob Crandall/Alamy Stock Photo

developmental **connection**

Conditions, Diseases, and Disorders
Autistic children have difficulty in developing a theory of mind, especially in understanding others' beliefs and emotions. Connect to "Information Processing."

autism spectrum disorders (ASDs) Also called pervasive developmental disorders, these range from the severe disorder labeled autistic disorder to the milder disorder called Asperger syndrome. Children with these disorders are characterized by problems in social interaction, verbal and nonverbal communication, and repetitive behaviors.

autistic disorder A severe autism spectrum disorder that has its onset in the first three years of life and includes deficiencies in social relationships; abnormalities in communication; and restricted, repetitive, and stereotyped patterns of behavior.

asperger syndrome A relatively mild autism spectrum disorder in which the child has relatively good verbal language skills, milder nonverbal language problems, and a restricted range of interests and relationships.

(Vysniauske & others, 2019). And a research review recently concluded that physical exercise was effective in improving the attention of children with ADHD (Jeyanthi, Arumugam, & Parasher, 2019).

Despite the encouraging recent studies of using neurofeedback, mindfulness training, and exercise to improve the attention of children with ADHD, it still remains to be determined whether these non-drug therapies are as effective as stimulant drugs or whether they benefit children as add-ons to stimulant drugs to provide a combination treatment (Den Heijer & others, 2017; Riesco-Matias & others, 2019).

Autism Spectrum Disorders   **Autism spectrum disorders (ASDs),** also called pervasive developmental disorders, range from the more severe disorder called *autistic disorder* to the milder disorder called *Asperger syndrome.* Autism spectrum disorders are characterized by problems in social interaction, problems in verbal and nonverbal communication, and repetitive behaviors (McCauley, Mundy, & Solomon, 2019; Watkins & others, 2019). A recent study also found that a lower level of working memory was the executive function most strongly associated with autism spectrum disorders (Ziermans & others, 2017). Children with these disorders may also show atypical responses to sensory experiences (National Institute of Mental Health, 2019). Intellectual disability is present in some children with autism; others show average or above-average intelligence (Volkmar & others, 2014). Autism spectrum disorders can often be detected in children as young as 1 to 3 years of age.

In 2013, the American Psychiatric Association proposed that in the new DSM-5 psychiatric classification of disorders, autistic disorder, Asperger syndrome, and several other autistic variations ought to be consolidated in the overarching category of autism spectrum disorder (Autism Research Institute, 2015). Distinctions will be made in terms of the severity of problems based on amount of support needed due to challenges involving social communication, restricted interests, and repetitive behaviors. Critics of this proposal argue that the umbrella category proposed for autism spectrum disorder masks the heterogeneity that characterizes the subgroups of autism (Lai & others, 2013).

Recent estimates of autism spectrum disorders indicate that they are increasing in occurrence or are increasingly being detected and labeled (Hall, 2018). Autism was once thought to affect only 1 in 2,500 individuals. However, in 2008 it was estimated that 1 in 88 children had autism (Centers for Disease Control & Prevention, 2012). And in a more recent survey, the estimated proportion of 8-year-old children with autism spectrum disorders had increased to 1 in 68 (Christensen & others, 2016). In the most recent survey, autism spectrum disorders were identified five times more often in boys than in girls (National Center for Education Statistics, 2017). Also, in two recent surveys, only a minority of parents reported that their child's autism spectrum disorder had been identified prior to 3 years of age, and one-third to one-half of the cases were identified after 6 years of age (Sheldrick, Maye, & Carter, 2017). However, researchers are conducting studies that seek to identify earlier determinants of autism spectrum disorder (Dan, 2018).

Autistic disorder is a severe developmental autism spectrum disorder that has its onset in the first three years of life and includes deficiencies in social relationships; abnormalities in communication; and restricted, repetitive, and stereotyped patterns of behavior. **Asperger syndrome** is a relatively mild autism spectrum disorder in which the child has relatively good verbal language skills, milder nonverbal language problems, and a restricted range of interests and relationships (Randall & others, 2018; Saisanen & others, 2019). Children with Asperger syndrome often engage in obsessive, repetitive routines and preoccupations with a particular subject. For example, a child may be obsessed with baseball scores or specific videos on YouTube.

What causes autism spectrum disorders? The current consensus is that autism is a brain dysfunction characterized by abnormalities in brain structure and neurotransmitters (Edgar & others, 2019; Fernandez, Mollinedo-Gajate, & Penagarikano, 2018). Recent interest has focused on brain networks and a lack of connectivity between brain regions as a key factor in autism (Aghdam, Sharifi, & Pedram, 2019; Hong & others, 2019; Nunes & others, 2019).

Genetic factors also are likely to play a role in the development of autism spectrum disorders (Almandil & others, 2019; Carter, 2019). In a recent review, it was concluded that approximately 800 genes are linked to autism (Gabrielli, Manzardo, & Butler, 2019). One study revealed that mutations—missing or duplicated pieces of DNA on chromosome 16—can raise a child's risk of developing autism 100-fold (Weiss & others, 2008). There is no evidence that family socialization causes autism.

Carissa Barnes, Special Education Teacher

Carissa Barnes is a lead special education resource teacher in the Montgomery County Public Schools in Maryland. She has undergraduate and master's degrees in special education from the University of Maryland—College Park. When Carissa was in middle school, she participated in service learning that involved volunteering at a child care center where too often families were turned away when they either did not have enough money or their child's needs were too severe. Such experiences motivated her to pursue a career in educating children with special needs. Marissa says that every day in her

work she is gratified to see students with special needs overcome their limitations and learn effectively (Office of Special Education and Rehabilitative Services Blog, 2018).

Special education teachers work with students who have a wide range of disabilities. They adapt educational content and materials in subjects such as reading, writing and math to make them accessible to special education students. A bachelor's degree and state-issued certification in special education is required in public schools and the bachelor's degree also is required in private schools but not the certification. The job outlook for special education teachers is good, with a predicted 8 percent growth in special education jobs predicted through 2028 (Occupational Outlook Handbook, 2018–2019).

Children with autism benefit from a well-structured classroom, individualized instruction, and small-group instruction. Behavior modification techniques are sometimes effective in helping autistic children learn (Alberto & Troutman, 2017; Wheeler & Richey, 2019).

Educational Issues   Until the 1970s most U.S. public schools either refused enrollment to children with disabilities or inadequately served them. This changed in 1975 when Public Law 94-142, the Education for All Handicapped Children Act, required that all students with disabilities be given a free, appropriate public education. In 1990, Public Law 94-142 was recast as the Individuals with Disabilities Education Act (IDEA). IDEA was amended in 1997 and then reauthorized in 2004 and renamed the Individuals with Disabilities Education Improvement Act.

IDEA spells out broad mandates for services to children with disabilities of all kinds (Cook & Richardson-Gibbs, 2018). These services include evaluation and eligibility determination, appropriate education and an individualized education plan (IEP), and education in the least restrictive environment (LRE) (Turnbull & others, 2020).

IDEA mandates free, appropriate education for all children. *What services does IDEA mandate for children with disabilities?*
E.D. Torial/Alamy Stock Photo

An **individualized education plan (IEP)** is a written statement that spells out a program that is specifically tailored for a student with a disability. The **least restrictive environment (LRE)** is a setting that is as similar as possible to the one in which children who do not have a disability are educated. This provision of the IDEA has given a legal basis to efforts to educate children with a disability in the regular classroom. The term **inclusion** describes educating a child with special educational needs full-time in the regular classroom (Hallahan, Kauffman, & Pullen, 2019; Mastropieri & Scruggs, 2018). Recent analysis indicated that in 2016 the percentage of time students with disabilities spend in the regular classroom reached its highest level (61 percent) since it had been assessed (National Center for Education Statistics, 2017). To read about the career of a special education teacher, see *Connecting with Careers.*

Many legal changes regarding children with disabilities have been extremely positive (Friend & Bursuck, 2019; Turnbull & others, 2020). Compared with several decades ago, far more children today are receiving competent, specialized services. For many children, inclusion in the regular classroom, with modifications or supplemental services, is appropriate. However, some leading experts on special education argue that some children with disabilities may not benefit from inclusion in the regular classroom (Hallahan, Kauffman, & Pullen, 2019). James Kauffman and his colleagues, for example, advocate a more individualized approach that does not necessarily involve full inclusion but allows options such as special education outside the regular classroom with trained professionals and adapted curricula (Kauffman, McGee, & Brigham, 2004). They go on to say, "We sell students with disabilities short when we pretend that they are not different from typical students. We make the same error when we pretend that

individualized education plan (IEP) A written statement that spells out a program tailored to a child with a disability. The plan should be (1) related to the child's learning capacity, (2) specially constructed to meet the child's individual needs and not merely a copy of what is offered to other children, and (3) designed to provide educational benefits.

least restrictive environment (LRE) A setting that is as similar as possible to the one in which children without a disability are educated.

inclusion Education of a child with special educational needs full-time in the regular classroom.

they must not be expected to put forth extra effort if they are to learn to do some things—or learn to do something in a different way" (p. 620). Like general education, special education should challenge students with disabilities to become all they can be.

SOCIOECONOMIC STATUS AND ETHNICITY IN SCHOOLS

Children from low-income, ethnic minority backgrounds have more difficulties in school than do their middle-socioeconomic-status, non-Latino White counterparts (Magnuson & Duncan, 2019). Why? Critics argue that schools have not done a good job of educating low-income, ethnic minority students to overcome the barriers to their achievement (Banks, 2019).

The Education of Students from Low-Income Backgrounds   Many children in poverty face problems that present barriers to their learning (McLoyd, Hardaway, & Jocson, 2019). They might have parents who don't set high educational standards for them, who are incapable of reading to them, or who don't have enough money to pay for educational materials and experiences, such as books and trips to zoos and museums. They might be malnourished or live in areas where crime and violence are a way of life. One study revealed that neighborhood disadvantage (involving characteristics such as low neighborhood income and high unemployment) was linked to less consistent, less stimulating, and more punitive parenting, and ultimately to negative child outcomes such as behavioral problems and low verbal ability (Kohen & others, 2008). Another study revealed that the longer children experienced poverty, the more detrimental the poverty was to their cognitive development (Najman & others, 2009).

Compared with schools in higher-income areas, schools in low-income areas are more likely to have higher percentages of students with low achievement test scores, lower graduation rates, and smaller percentages of students going to college; they are more likely to have young teachers with less experience, larger proportions of non-credentialed or unqualified teachers, and substitute teachers regularly filling in to teach; they are more likely to encourage rote learning; and they are less likely to provide adequate support for English-language learners (Crosnoe & Benner, 2015). Too few schools in low-income neighborhoods provide students with environments that are conducive to learning (Bennett, 2019). Many of the schools' buildings and classrooms are old and crumbling. In sum, far too many schools in low-income neighborhoods provide students with environments that are not conducive to effective learning (Kelleher, Reece, & Sandel, 2018).

Schools and school programs are the focus of some poverty interventions (Abrahamse, Jonkman, & Harting, 2018). In a longitudinal study, implementation of the Child-Parent Center Program in high-poverty neighborhoods in Chicago that provided school-based educational enrichment and comprehensive family services from 3 to 9 years of age was linked to higher rates of postsecondary degree completion, including more years of education, an associate's degree or higher, and master's degree (Reynolds, Ou, & Temple, 2018).

An important effort to improve the education of children growing up in low-income conditions is Teach for America (2019), a nonprofit organization that recruits and selects college graduates from universities to serve as teachers. The selected members commit to teaching for two years in a public school in a low-income community. Since its inception in 1990, more than 42,000 individuals have taught more than 50,000 students for Teach for America. These teachers can be, but don't have to be, education majors. In the summer before beginning to teach, they attend an intensive training program. To read about one individual who became a Teach for America instructor, see the *Connecting with Careers* interlude.

Ethnicity in Schools   More than one-third of all African American and almost one-third of all Latino students attend schools in the 47 largest city school districts in the United States, compared with only 5 percent of all White and 22 percent of all Asian American students. Many of these inner-city schools are still segregated, are grossly underfunded, and do not provide adequate opportunities for children to learn effectively. Thus, the effects of socioeconomic status·(SES) and the effects of ethnicity are often intertwined (Banks, 2019).

In *The Shame of the Nation*, Jonathan Kozol (2005) criticized the inadequate quality and lack of resources in many U.S. schools, especially those in the poverty areas of inner cities that have high concentrations of ethnic minority children. Kozol praises teachers like Angela Lively who keeps a box of shoes in her Indianapolis classroom for students in need.
Michael Conroy/AP Images

Ahou Vaziri, Teach for America Instructor

Ahou Vaziri was a top student in author John Santrock's educational psychology course at the University of Texas at Dallas where she majored in Psychology and Child Development. The following year she served as a teaching intern for the educational psychology course, then submitted an application to join Teach for America and was accepted. Ahou was assigned to work in a low-income area of Tulsa, Oklahoma, where she taught English to seventh- and eighth-graders. In her words, "The years I spent in the classroom for Teach for America were among the most rewarding experiences I have had thus far in my career. I was able to go home every night after work knowing that I truly made a difference in the lives of my students."

After her two-year teaching experience with Teach for America, Ahou continued to work for the organization in their recruitment of college students to become Teach for America instructors. Subsequently, she moved into a role that involved developing curricula for Teach for America. Recently she earned a graduate degree

Ahou Vaziri with her students in the Teach for America program. *What is Teach for America?*
Courtesy of Ahou Vaziri

in counseling from Southern Methodist University, and she is continuing her work in improving children's lives.

The school experiences of students from different ethnic groups vary considerably (Bennett, 2019). African American and Latino students are much less likely than non-Latino White or Asian American students to be enrolled in academic, college preparatory programs and are much more likely to be enrolled in remedial and special education programs. Asian American students are far more likely than other ethnic minority groups to take advanced math and science courses in high school. African American students are twice as likely as Latinos, Native Americans, or Whites to be suspended from school.

However, it is very important to note that diversity characterizes every ethnic group (Banks, 2019). For example, the higher percentage of Asian American students in advanced classes is mainly true for students with Chinese, Taiwanese, Japanese, Korean, and East Indian cultural backgrounds, but students with Hmong and Vietnamese cultural backgrounds have had less academic success.

Following are some strategies for improving relationships among ethnically diverse students:

- *Turn the class into a jigsaw classroom.* When Elliot Aronson was a professor at the University of Texas at Austin, the school system contacted him for ideas on how to reduce the increasing racial tension in classrooms. Aronson (1986) developed the concept of a "jigsaw classroom," in which students from different cultural backgrounds are placed in a cooperative group in which they have to construct different parts of a project to reach a common goal. Aronson used the term *jigsaw* because he saw that the technique resembled a group of students cooperating to put different pieces together to complete a jigsaw puzzle. How might this process work? Team sports, drama productions, and musical performances are examples of contexts in which students cooperate to reach a common goal.

- *Encourage students to have positive personal contact with diverse other students.* Contact alone does not do the job of improving relationships with diverse others. For example, busing ethnic minority students to predominantly non-Latino White schools, or vice versa, has not reduced prejudice or improved interethnic relations (Minuchin & Shapiro, 1983). What matters is what happens after children get to school. Especially beneficial in improving interethnic relations is

What are some features of a jigsaw classroom?
Ken Karp/McGraw-Hill Education

extrinsic motivation Doing something to obtain something else (the activity is a means to an end).

intrinsic motivation Doing something for its own sake; involves factors such as self-determination and opportunities to make choices.

sharing one's worries, successes, failures, coping strategies, interests, and other personal information with people of other ethnicities. When this sharing happens, people tend to look at others as individuals rather than as members of a homogeneous group.

- *Encourage students to engage in perspective taking.* Exercises and activities that help students see others' perspectives can improve interethnic relations. These help students "step into the shoes" of peers who are culturally different and to discover what it feels like to be treated in fair or unfair ways.
- *Reduce bias.* Teachers can reduce bias by displaying images of children from diverse ethnic and cultural groups, selecting play materials and classroom activities that encourage cultural understanding, helping students resist stereotyping, and working with parents.
- *View the school and community as a team.* James Comer (2004, 2006, 2010) emphasizes that a community, team approach is the best way to educate children. Three important aspects of the Comer Project for Change are (1) a governance and management team that develops a comprehensive school plan, assessment strategy, and staff development plan; (2) a mental health or school support team; and (3) a parents' program. Comer says that the entire school community should have a cooperative rather than an adversarial attitude. The Comer program is currently operating in more than 600 schools in 26 states.

Review **Connect** Reflect

LG1 Describe the role of schools in development.

Review
- What are some contemporary approaches to student learning?
- How do schools change as children develop?
- What are learning disabilities, ADHD, and autism spectrum disorders? What is involved in educating children with disabilities?
- What roles do socioeconomic status and ethnicity play in schools?

Connect
- What did you learn in this section about educating children that might connect with what you've learned about socioeconomic status and ethnicity?

Reflect *Your Own Personal Journey of Life*
- What was your middle or junior high school like? How did it measure up to the Carnegie Foundation's recommendations?

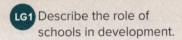

2 Achievement

LG2 Explain the key aspects of achievement.

| Extrinsic and Intrinsic Motivation | Mastery Motivation and Mindset | Self-Efficacy | Goal Setting, Planning, and Self-Monitoring | Grit | Expectations | Ethnicity and Culture |

In any classroom, whoever the teacher is and whatever approach is used, some children achieve more than others. Why? Among the reasons for variations in achievement are characteristics of the child and sociocultural contexts related to motivation (Schunk & Greene, 2018; Yeager, Dahl, & Dweck, 2018).

EXTRINSIC AND INTRINSIC MOTIVATION

The behavioral perspective emphasizes the importance of extrinsic motivation. **Extrinsic motivation** involves doing something to obtain something else (the activity is a means to an end). Extrinsic motivation is often influenced by external incentives such as rewards and punishments (Thomas & Guillich, 2019). For example, a student may study for a test in order to obtain a good grade.

Whereas the behavioral perspective emphasizes extrinsic motivation in achievement, the cognitive perspective stresses the importance of intrinsic motivation (Reitz, 2019). **Intrinsic motivation** involves the internal motivation to do something for its own sake (the activity is an end in itself). For example, a student may study hard for a test because he or she enjoys the content of the course.

Life is a gift . . . Accept it.

Life is a puzzle . . . Solve it.

Life is an adventure . . . Dare it.

Life is an opportunity . . . Take it.

Life is a mystery . . . Unfold it.

Life is a mission . . . Fulfill it.

Life is a struggle . . . Face it.

Life is a goal . . . Achieve it.

—AUTHOR UNKNOWN

Let's first consider the intrinsic motivation of self-determination and personal choice. Next, we'll identify some developmental changes in intrinsic and extrinsic motivation as students move up the educational ladder. Finally, we will draw some conclusions about intrinsic and extrinsic motivation.

Self-Determination and Choice   One view of intrinsic motivation emphasizes that students want to believe that they are doing something because of their own will, not because of external success or rewards (Ryan & Deci, 2016, 2019; Ryan & Moller, 2017; Zimmer-Gembeck & others, 2019). Students' internal motivation and intrinsic interest in school tasks increase when they have opportunities to make choices and take responsibility for their learning (Sevil & others, 2019). A recent meta-analysis concluded that self-determination plays a central role in human motivation (Howard, Gagne, & Bureau, 2017). In this view, students' internal motivation and intrinsic interest in school tasks increase when they have opportunities to make choices and take responsibility for their learning (Anderson, Sanchez, & McMahon, 2019; Harackiewicz & Knogler, 2017; Ryan & Deci, 2019; Ryan, Soenens, & Vansteenkiste, 2019). And researchers have found that that a number of contextual factors, such as autonomy support, instructor approachability, involvement opportunities, and course material relevance, are linked to situational interest and in turn may support individual interest (Linnenbrink-Garcia & others, 2018). The architects of self-determination theory, Richard Ryan and Edward Deci (2016, 2019), refer to parents and teachers who create circumstances for students to engage in self-determination as *autonomy-supportive parents and teachers*. A recent Chinese study revealed that a higher level of autonomy-supportive parenting was related to adolescents' adaptive school adjustment, while a higher level of parental psychological control was linked to their maladaptive school adjustment (Xiang, Liu, & Bai, 2017).

Developmental Shifts in Intrinsic and Extrinsic Motivation   Many psychologists and educators stress that it is important for children to develop intrinsic motivation as they grow older. However, as students move from the early elementary school years to the high school years, intrinsic motivation tends to decline (Harter, 1996). In one study, the biggest drop in intrinsic motivation and the largest increase in extrinsic motivation occurred between the sixth and seventh grades (Harter, 1981).

Jacquelynne Eccles and her colleagues (Eccles & Roeser, 2015; Wigfield, Rosenzweig, & Eccles, 2017) have identified some specific changes in the school context that help to explain the decline in intrinsic motivation. Middle schools and junior high schools are more impersonal, more formal, more evaluative, and more competitive than elementary schools. Students compare themselves more with other students because they are increasingly graded in terms of their relative performance on assignments and standardized tests.

Conclusions about Intrinsic and Extrinsic Motivation   An overwhelming conclusion of motivation research is that teachers should encourage students to become intrinsically motivated (Ryan & Deci, 2019; Winne, 2018). Similarly, teachers should create learning environments that promote students' cognitive engagement and self-responsibility for learning (Usher & Schunk, 2018). That said, the real world includes both intrinsic and extrinsic motivation, and too often intrinsic and extrinsic motivation have been pitted against each other as polar opposites. In many aspects of students' lives, both intrinsic and extrinsic motivation are at work (Schunk & Greene, 2018). Further, intrinsic and extrinsic motivation can operate simultaneously. Thus, a student may work hard in a course because she enjoys the content and likes learning about it (intrinsic) and because she wants to earn a good grade (extrinsic). Keep in mind, though, that many educational psychologists suggest that extrinsic motivation by itself is not a good strategy.

MASTERY MOTIVATION AND MINDSET

The increasingly competitive, impersonal atmosphere of middle schools obviously does not discourage all students. To some, these characteristics represent a challenge. How students typically respond to challenges has a lot to do with how much they achieve (Wigfield, Rosenzweig, & Eccles, 2017). Becoming cognitively engaged and self-motivated to improve are characteristics of individuals with mastery motivation. These individuals also have a growth mindset—a belief that they can produce positive outcomes if they put forth sufficient effort.

Meredith MacGregor, pictured here as a senior at Fairview High School in Boulder, Colorado, is an aspiring scientist and was one of Colorado's top high school long-distance runners. She maintained a 4.0 grade point average, participated in a number of school organizations, and cofounded the AfriAid Club. She was named a USA Today High School Academic All-Star and was awarded the Intel Foundation Young Scientist Award (Wong Briggs, 2007). *What are some factors that were likely involved in Meredith's motivation to achieve?*
Kevin Moloney

FIGURE 5

BEHAVIORS THAT SUGGEST A HELPLESS ORIENTATION

Keep the growth mindset in your thoughts. Then, when you bump up against obstacles, you can turn to it . . . showing you a path into the future.

—Carol Dweck

Contemporary Psychologist, Stanford University

mastery orientation A perspective in which one is task-oriented—concerned with learning strategies and the process of achievement rather than the outcome.

helpless orientation An orientation in which one seems trapped by the experience of difficulty and attributes one's difficulty to a lack of ability.

performance orientation An orientation in which one focuses on winning, rather than on achievement outcome; happiness is thought to result from winning.

mindset The cognitive view individuals develop for themselves that perceives their potential either as fixed or as capable of growth.

Mastery Motivation Carol Dweck and her colleagues (Dweck, 2012, 2013; Dweck & Elliott, 1983; Dweck & Molden, 2017; Dweck & Yeager, 2019) have found that individuals respond in two distinct ways to difficult or challenging circumstances. People who display a **mastery orientation** are task-oriented—they concentrate on learning strategies and implementing the process of achievement rather than focusing on their ability or the outcome. By contrast, those with a **helpless orientation** seem trapped by the experience of difficulty, and they attribute their difficulty to lack of ability. They frequently say such things as "I'm not very good at this," even though they might earlier have demonstrated their ability through many successes. And, once they view their behavior as failure, they often feel anxious, and their performance worsens even further. Figure 5 describes some behaviors that might reflect helplessness (Stipek, 2002).

In contrast, mastery-oriented individuals often instruct themselves to pay attention, to think carefully, and to remember strategies that have worked for them in previous situations. They frequently report feeling challenged and excited by difficult tasks, rather than being threatened by them (Dweck, 2012).

Another issue in motivation involves whether to adopt a mastery or a performance orientation. Individuals with a **performance orientation** are focused on winning, rather than on an achievement outcome, and believe that happiness results from winning. Does this focus mean that mastery-oriented individuals do not like to win and that performance-oriented individuals are not motivated to experience the self-efficacy that comes from being able to take credit for one's accomplishments? No. A matter of emphasis or degree is involved, though. For mastery-oriented individuals, winning isn't everything; for performance-oriented individuals, skill development and self-efficacy take a backseat to winning.

The U.S. government's No Child Left Behind Act (NCLB) emphasizes testing and accountability. Although NCLB may motivate some teachers and students to work harder, motivation experts worry that it encourages a performance rather than a mastery motivation orientation on the part of students (Schunk, 2016).

A final point needs to be made about mastery and performance goals: They are not always mutually exclusive. Students can be both mastery- and performance-oriented, and researchers have found that mastery goals combined with performance goals often benefit students' success (Schunk, 2016).

Mindset Carol Dweck's (2006, 2007, 2012, 2015, 2016) most recent analysis of motivation for achievement stresses the importance of developing a **mindset,** which she defines as the cognitive view individuals develop for themselves. She concludes that individuals have one of two mindsets: (1) a *fixed mindset*, in which they believe that their qualities are carved in stone and cannot change; or (2) a *growth mindset*, in which they believe their qualities can change and improve through their effort. A fixed mindset is similar to a helpless orientation; a growth mindset is much like having mastery motivation.

In *Mindset*, Dweck (2006) argued that individuals' mindsets influence whether they will be optimistic or pessimistic, shape their goals and how hard they will strive to reach those goals, and affect many aspects of their lives, including achievement and success in school and sports. Dweck says that mindsets begin to be shaped as children and adolescents interact with parents, teachers, and coaches, who themselves have either a fixed mindset or a growth mindset.

In recent research by Dweck and her colleagues, students from lower-income families were less likely to have a growth mindset than their counterparts from wealthier families (Claro, Paunesku, & Dweck, 2016). However, the achievement of students from lower-income families who did have a growth mindset was more likely to be protected from the negative effects of poverty.

Also, Dweck and her colleagues (Blackwell, Trzesniewski, & Dweck, 2007; Dweck, 2015, 2016) recently incorporated information about the brain's plasticity into their effort to improve students' motivation to achieve and succeed. In one study, they assigned two groups of students to eight sessions of either (1) study skills instruction or (2) study skills instruction plus information about the importance of developing a growth mindset (called *incremental theory* in the research) (Blackwell, Trzesniewski, & Dweck, 2007). One of the exercises in the growth mindset group was titled "You Can Grow Your Brain," and it emphasized that the brain is like a muscle that can change and grow as it gets exercise and develops new connections. Students were informed that the more you challenge your brain to learn, the more your brain cells grow. Both groups had a pattern of declining math scores prior to the intervention. Following the intervention, math scores of the group who had received only the study skills instruction continued to decline, but the group that received the combination of study skills instruction plus the growth mindset emphasis reversed the downward trend and improved their math achievement. And in another study conducted by Dweck and her colleagues (Paunesku & others, 2015), underachieving high school students read online modules about how the brain changes when people learn and study hard. Following the online exposure about the brain and learning, the underachieving students improved their grade point averages.

In other work, Dweck has created a computer-based workshop, "Brainology," to teach students that their intelligence can change (Blackwell & Dweck, 2008). Students experience six modules about how the brain works and how the students can make their brain improve. After the program was tested in 20 New York City schools, students strongly endorsed the value of the computer-based brain modules. Said one student, "I will try harder because I know that the more you try the more your brain knows" (Dweck & Master, 2009, p. 137).

A screen from Carol Dweck's Brainology program, which is designed to cultivate children's growth mindset.
Courtesy of Dr. Carol S. Dweck

Dweck and her colleagues also recently have found that a growth mindset can prevent negative stereotypes from undermining achievement. For example, women who believe that math ability can be learned are protected from negative gender stereotyping about math (Good, Rattan, & Dweck, 2012). Also, in recent research, having a growth mindset helped to protect women's and minorities' outlook when they chose to confront expressions of bias toward them (Rattan & Dweck, 2018).

SELF-EFFICACY

Albert Bandura's (1997, 2001, 2009, 2010, 2012, 2015) social cognitive theory stresses that a critical factor in whether or not students achieve is **self-efficacy,** the belief that one can master a situation and produce favorable outcomes. Self-efficacy is the belief that "I can"; helplessness is the belief that "I cannot." Students with high self-efficacy endorse statements such as "I know that I will be able to learn the material in this class" and "I expect to be able to do well at this activity."

Dale Schunk (2016) has applied the concept of self-efficacy to many aspects of students' achievement. In his view, self-efficacy influences a student's choice of activities. Students with low self-efficacy for learning may avoid many learning tasks, especially those that are challenging. By contrast, those with high self-efficacy eagerly work at learning tasks (Zimmerman, Schunk, & DiBenedetto, 2017). High-self-efficacy students are more likely than low-self-efficacy students to expend effort and persist longer at a learning task.

Children's and adolescents' development is influenced by their parents' self-efficacy. One study revealed a number of positive developmental outcomes, including more daily opportunities for optimal functioning, better peer relations, and fewer problems, for children and adolescents whose parents had high self-efficacy (Steca & others, 2011).

developmental **connection**
Cognitive Theory
Social cognitive theory holds that behavior, environment, and person/cognitive factors are the key influences on development. Connect to "Introduction."

They can because they think they can.

—VIRGIL
Roman Poet, 1st Century B.C.

GOAL SETTING, PLANNING, AND SELF-MONITORING

Setting goals, planning how to reach those goals, and engaging in self-regulation and monitoring of progress toward goals are important aspects of achievement (Schunk & Greene, 2018; Winne, 2018). Self-efficacy and achievement improve when individuals set goals that are specific, proximal, and challenging (Schunk, 2016). A nonspecific, fuzzy goal is "I want to be successful." A more concrete, specific goal is "I want to make the honor roll by the end of the semester."

Students can set both long-term (distal) and short-term (proximal) goals. It is okay for individuals to set some long-term goals, such as "I want to graduate from high school" or "I want to go to college," but they also need to create short-term goals, which are steps along the way. "Getting an A on the next math test" is an example of a short-term, proximal goal. So is "Doing all of my homework by 4 p.m. Sunday."

self-efficacy The belief that one can master a situation and produce favorable outcomes.

An adolescent works with her daily planner. *How are goals, planning, and self-regulation involved in adolescent achievement?*
Stephen Coburn/Shutterstock

Another good strategy is to set challenging goals (Fisher & others, 2018). A challenging goal is a commitment to self-improvement. Strong interest and involvement in activities are sparked by challenges. Goals that are easy to reach generate little interest or effort. However, goals should be optimally matched to the individual's skill level. If goals are unrealistically high, the result will be repeated failures that lower the individual's self-efficacy.

It is not enough just to set goals. In order to achieve, it also is important to plan how to reach those goals. Being a good planner means managing time effectively, setting priorities, and being organized.

Individuals should not only plan their next week's activities but also monitor how well they are sticking to their plan. Once engaged in a task, they need to monitor their progress, judge how well they are doing on the task, and evaluate the outcomes to regulate what they do in the future (Wigfield, Rosenzweig, & Eccles, 2017). High-achieving children are often self-regulatory learners (Zimmerman, Schunk, & DiBenedetto, 2017). For example, high-achieving children monitor their learning and systematically evaluate their progress toward a goal more than low-achieving students do. Encouraging children to monitor their learning conveys the message that they are responsible for their own behavior and that learning requires their active, dedicated participation.

In addition to planning and self-regulation/monitoring, delaying gratification is an important aspect of reaching goals—especially long-term goals (Mischel, 2014). Delay of gratification involves postponing immediate rewards in order to attain larger, more valuable rewards at a later time. While adolescents may prefer to hang out with friends today rather than working on a project that is due for a class assignment later in the week, their decision not to delay gratification can have negative consequences for their academic achievement.

GRIT

Recently, as part of the continuing effort to study key aspects of achievement, there has been interest in the concept of **grit**, a quality that involves passion and persistence in achieving long-term goals. Research has shown that grit is linked to academic engagement and success, including students' grade point averages (Clark & Malecki, 2019; Eskreis-Winkler & others, 2014; Muenks, Yang, & Wigfield, 2018; Steinmayr, Weidinger, & Wigfield, 2018). In a recent study, the persistence aspect of grit in eighth-graders was linked to their school achievement and engagement in ninth grade (Tang & others, 2019). Recent research also indicates that life purpose commitment (Hill & others, 2016), mindfulness (Raphiphatthana, Jose, & Slamon, 2018), and goal commitment (Tang & others, 2019) are antecedents of grit.

EXPECTATIONS

Expectations play important roles in children's and adolescents' achievement (Wigfield, Rosenzweig, & Eccles, 2017). These expectations involve not only the expectations of children and adolescents themselves but also the expectations of parents, teachers, and other adults.

How hard students will work can depend on how much they expect to accomplish. If they expect to succeed, they are more likely to work hard to reach a goal than if they expect to fail. Jacquelynne Eccles (2007) defined expectations for students' success as beliefs about how well they will do on upcoming tasks, in either the immediate or long-term future. Three aspects of ability beliefs, according to Eccles, are students' beliefs about how good they are at a particular activity, how good they are in comparison with other individuals, and how good they are in relation to their performance in other activities.

How hard students work also depends on the value they place on the goal (Wigfield, Rosenzweig, & Eccles, 2017). Indeed, the combination of expectancy and value has been the focus of a number of efforts to better understand students' achievement motivation. In Eccles' (2007) model, students' expectancies and values are assumed to directly influence their performance, persistence, and task choice.

Researchers have found that parents' expectations are linked with children's and adolescents' academic achievement (Burchinal & others, 2002). One longitudinal study revealed that children whose mothers had higher academic expectations for them in the first grade were more likely to reach a higher level of educational attainment in emerging adulthood (age 23) than children whose mothers had lower expectations for them in the first grade (Englund & others, 2004).

developmental **connection**

Information Processing

Using the classic marshmallow test, researchers found that young children's delay of gratification is linked to higher levels of achievement as well as positive physical and mental health outcomes in adolescence and adulthood. Connect to "Information Processing."

grit Involves passion and persistence in achieving long-term goals.

Too often parents attempt to protect children's and adolescents' self-esteem by setting low standards (Graham, 2005; Stipek, 2005). In reality, it is more beneficial to set standards that challenge them and to expect the highest level of performance that they are capable of achieving.

Teachers' expectations also are important influences on children's achievement. In an observational study of twelve classrooms, teachers with high expectations spent more time providing a framework for students' learning, asked higher-level questions, and were more effective in managing students' behavior than teachers with average or low expectations (Rubie-Davies, 2007). In another study, pre-service elementary school teachers had lower expectations for girls' than boys' math achievement (Mizala, Martinez, & Martinez, 2015).

ETHNICITY AND CULTURE

How do ethnicity and culture influence children's achievement? Of course, diversity exists within every group in terms of achievement. But Americans have been especially concerned about two questions related to ethnicity and culture. First, does their ethnicity deter ethnic minority children from high achievement in school? And second, is there something about American culture that accounts for the poor performance of U.S. children in math and science?

A student and a teacher at Langston Hughes Elementary School in Chicago, a school whose teachers have high expectations for students. *How do teachers' expectations influence students' achievement?*
Ralf-Finn Hestoft/Corbis Historical/Getty Images

Ethnicity   Analyzing the effects of ethnicity in the United States is complicated by the fact that a disproportionate number of ethnic minorities have low socioeconomic status. Disentangling the effects of SES and ethnicity can be difficult, and many investigations overlook the socioeconomic status of ethnic minority students. In many instances, when ethnicity and socioeconomic status are investigated, socioeconomic status predicts achievement better than ethnicity does. Students from middle- and upper-income families fare better than their counterparts from low-income backgrounds in a host of achievement situations—for example, expectations for success, achievement aspirations, recognition of the importance of effort, and school achievement (Magnuson & Duncan, 2019; Spencer & others, 2017; Xuan & others, 2019). A longitudinal study revealed that African American children or children from low-income families benefited more than children from higher-income families when they did homework more frequently, had Internet access at home, and had a community library card (Xia, 2010). And a recent research review found that increases in family income for children in poverty were associated with increased achievement in middle school as well as greater educational attainment in adolescence and emerging adulthood (Duncan, Magnuson, & Votruba-Drzal, 2017).

Sandra Graham (1986, 1990) has conducted a number of studies that reveal stronger differences in achievement connected with socioeconomic status than with ethnicity. She is struck by how consistently middle-income African American students, like their non-Latino White middle-income counterparts, have high achievement expectations and understand that failure is usually due to a lack of effort. An especially important factor in the lower achievement of students from low-income families regardless of their ethnic background is lack of adequate resources to support students' learning, such as an up-to-date computer in the home or even any computer at all (Schunk, 2016).

Cross-Cultural Comparisons   International assessments indicate that students in the United States have not fared well compared with their peers in many other countries in terms of math and science performance (Desilver, 2017). In rankings of the performance of 15-year-olds on the Programme for International Student Assessment (PISA) conducted in 2015, the United States placed 38th out of 71 countries in math and 24th in science (PISA, 2015). In an assessment of fourth- and eighth-grade students carried out as part of the Trends in International Mathematics and Science Study (TIMSS), U.S. students fared somewhat better, placing eleventh out of 48 countries in fourth-grade math and eighth in fourth-grade science (TIMSS, 2015). Also in the TIMSS study, U.S. eighth-graders placed eighth in math and eighth in science among the 37 countries studied. The top five spots in the international assessments mainly go to East Asian countries, especially Singapore, China, and Japan. The only two non-Asian countries to crack the top five in recent years for math and science are Finland and Estonia.

Despite the recent gains made by U.S. elementary school students, it is disconcerting to note that U.S. students' performance on assessments of reading, math, and science decline in comparison with students in other countries as they go from elementary school to high school. Also, U.S. students' achievement scores in math and science continue to be far below those of students in many East Asian countries.

developmental **connection**

Culture

Ethnicity refers to characteristics rooted in cultural heritage, including nationality, race, religion, and language. Connect to "Introduction" and "Peers and the Sociocultural World."

Asian grade schools intersperse studying with frequent periods of activities. This approach helps children maintain their attention and likely makes learning more enjoyable. Shown here are Japanese fourth-graders making wearable masks. *What are some differences in the way children in many Asian countries are taught compared with children in the United States?*
Eiji Miyazawa/Stock Photo/Black Star

Harold Stevenson's (1995, 2000; Stevenson, Hofer, & Randel, 1999; Stevenson & others, 1990) research has explored possible reasons for the poor performance of American students. Stevenson and his colleagues have completed five cross-cultural comparisons of students in the United States, China, Taiwan, and Japan. In these studies, Asian students consistently outperform American students. And, the longer the students are in school, the wider the gap becomes between Asian and American students—the lowest difference is in the first grade, the highest in the eleventh grade (the highest grade studied).

To learn more about the reasons for these large cross-cultural differences, Stevenson and his colleagues spent thousands of hours observing in classrooms as well as interviewing and surveying teachers, students, and parents. They found that the Asian teachers spent more of their time teaching math than did the American teachers. For example, more than one-fourth of total classroom time in the first grade was spent on math instruction in Japan, compared with only one-tenth of the time in the U.S. first-grade classrooms. Also, the Asian students were in school an average of 240 days a year, compared with 178 days in the United States.

In addition to the substantially greater time spent on math instruction in the Asian schools than the American schools, differences were found between the Asian and American parents. The American parents had much lower expectations for their children's education and achievement than did the Asian parents. Also, the American parents were more likely to believe that their children's math achievement was due to innate ability; the Asian parents were more likely to say that their children's math achievement was the consequence of effort and training (see Figure 6). The Asian students were more likely to do math homework than were the American students, and the Asian parents were far more likely to help their children with their math homework than were the American parents (Chen & Stevenson, 1989).

In one study, researchers looked for factors that might account for the superior academic performance of Asian American children (Hsin & Xie, 2014). In this study, the Asian American advantage was mainly due to children exerting greater academic effort and not to advantages in tested cognitive abilities or sociodemographic factors.

Eva Pomerantz (2014) offers the following recommendations for parents of children and adolescents regarding motivation to do well in school:

- *Keep in mind that ability is not fixed and can change.* Although it is difficult and takes a lot of patience, understand that children's and adolescents' abilities can improve.
- *Be involved.* One of the most important things parents can do is to become involved in their children's and adolescents' academic life and talk often with them about what they are learning.
- *Support autonomy and self-initiative.* An important aspect of children's and adolescents' motivation to do well in school is whether they are made to feel that they are responsible for their learning and must be self-motivated.
- *Be positive.* Too often schoolwork and homework can be frustrating for children and adolescents. Interact with them in positive ways and let them know that life is often tough but that you are confident that they can do well and overcome difficulties.
- *Understand that each child and adolescent is different.* Get to know your child or adolescent—don't let them be a psychological stranger to you. Be sensitive to their unique characteristics and know that sometimes you need to adapt to such idiosyncrasies.

In the *Connecting with Research* interlude, you can read further about efforts to discover why parenting practices are likely to be an important aspect of the lower achievement of U.S. children compared with East Asian children, as well as potential implications for other aspects of children's development.

FIGURE 6

MOTHERS' BELIEFS ABOUT THE FACTORS RESPONSIBLE FOR CHILDREN'S MATH ACHIEVEMENT IN THREE COUNTRIES. In one study, mothers in Japan and Taiwan were more likely to believe that their children's math achievement was due to effort rather than innate ability, whereas U.S. mothers were more likely to believe their children's math achievement was due to innate ability (Stevenson, Lee, & Stigler, 1986). If parents believe that their children's math achievement is due to innate ability and their children are not doing well in math, the implication is that they are less likely to think their children will benefit from putting forth more effort.

Parenting and Children's Achievement: My Child Is My Report Card, Tiger Moms, and Tiger Babies Strike Back

There is rising concern that U.S. children are not reaching their full potential, which ultimately will hinder the success of the United States in competing with other countries (Ng & others, 2019; Pomerantz & Grolnick, 2017). Eva Pomerantz is interested in determining how parents can maximize their children's motivation and achievement in school while also maintaining positive emotional adjustment. To this end, Pomerantz and her colleagues are conducting research with children and their parents not only in the United States but also in China, where children often attain higher levels of achievement than their U.S. counterparts (Pomerantz & Grolnick, 2017; Qu & Pomerantz, 2015).

As indicated earlier regarding Harold Stevenson's research, East Asian parents spend considerably more time helping their children with homework than do U.S. parents (Chen & Stevenson, 1989). Pomerantz's research indicates that East Asian parental involvement in children's learning is present as early as the preschool years and continues during the elementary school years (Ng, Pomerantz, & Deng, 2014). In East Asia, children's learning is considered to be a far greater responsibility of parents than in the United States (Ng, Pomerantz, & Lam, 2013). In one study, a decline in U.S. young adolescents' but not Chinese young adolescents' sense of responsibility to parents occurred (Qu & Pomerantz, 2015). The U.S. adolescents' decline in sense of responsibility to parents was linked to the lower value they placed on school and their lower engagement in school as they went from the beginning of the seventh grade to the end of eighth grade (Qu & Pomerantz, 2015).

Pomerantz and her colleagues also are conducting research on the role of parental control in children's achievement. In a study in which the title of the resulting article included the phrase "My Child Is My Report Card," Chinese mothers exerted more control (especially psychological control) over their children than did U.S. mothers (Ng, Pomerantz, & Deng, 2014). Also in this study, Chinese mothers' sense of self-worth was more contingent on their children's achievement than was the case for U.S. mothers.

Pomerantz's research reflects the term "training parents," a variation of authoritarian parenting in which many Asian parents train their children to achieve high levels of academic success. In 2011, Amy Chua's book, *Battle Hymn of the Tiger Mom,* sparked considerable interest in the role of parenting in children's achievement. Chua uses the term *Tiger Mom* to mean a mother who engages in strict disciplinary practices. In another book, *Tiger Babies Strike Back*, Kim Wong Keltner (2013) argues that the Tiger Mom parenting style can be so demanding and confining that being an Asian American child is like being in an "emotional jail." She says that the Tiger Mom authoritarian style does provide some advantages for children, such as emphasizing the value of going for what you want and not taking

Qing Zhou, who has conducted research on authoritarian parenting of immigrant children, with her children. *What are the results of her research?*
Courtesy of Qing Zhou

no for an answer, but that too often the outcome is not worth the emotional costs that accompany it.

Research on Chinese-American immigrant families with first- and second-grade children has found that the children with authoritarian (highly controlling) parents are more aggressive, are more depressed, have a higher anxiety level, and show poorer social skills than children whose parents engage in non-authoritarian styles of child-rearing (Zhou & others, 2012). Qing Zhou (2013), lead author on the study just described and the director of the University of California's Culture and Family Laboratory, is conducting workshops to teach Chinese mothers positive parenting strategies such as using listening skills, praising their children for good behavior, and spending more time with their children in fun activities. Also, in a study conducted recently in China, young adolescents with authoritative parents showed better adjustment than their counterparts with authoritarian parents (Zhang & others, 2017).

In sum, while an authoritarian, psychologically controlling style of parenting may be associated with higher levels of achievement, especially in Asian children, there are concerns that this parenting style also may produce more emotional difficulties in children (Pomerantz & Grolnick, 2017).

What do you think are the best parenting strategies overall for rearing children to reach high levels of achievement and to be emotionally healthy?

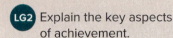

Review

- What are intrinsic motivation and extrinsic motivation? How are they related to achievement?
- How are mastery, helpless, and performance orientations linked with achievement?
- What is self-efficacy, and how is it related to achievement?
- Why are goal setting, planning, and self-monitoring important in achievement?
- What is grit? How is it linked to achievement outcomes?
- How are expectations involved in an individual's achievement motivation?
- How do cultural, ethnic, and socioeconomic variations influence achievement?

Connect

- One of Carol Dweck's exercises in the growth-mindset group was titled "You Can Grow Your Brain." Can you actually grow your brain? What physical changes, if any, are still occurring in the brain in middle and late childhood and in adolescence?

Reflect *Your Own Personal Journey of Life*

- Think about several of your own past schoolmates who showed low motivation in school. Why do you think they behaved that way? What teaching strategies might have helped them?

3 Careers, Work, and Retirement

LG3 Discuss career development, work, and retirement.

Career Development | Work | Retirement

The quality of schooling children experience and the achievement orientation they develop provide the foundation for career success and the type of work they pursue when they become adults. Choosing a career, developing in a career, working, and coping with retirement—these are important themes in adulthood.

CAREER DEVELOPMENT

When you were a child, what were your thoughts about a career? How did your thinking about careers change as you became an adolescent? What are your thoughts now?

Developmental Changes Many children have idealistic fantasies about what they want to be when they grow up. For example, many young children want to be superheroes, sports stars, or movie stars. In the high school years, they often have begun to think about careers in a somewhat less idealistic way. In their late teens and early twenties, their career decision making has usually turned more serious as they explore different career possibilities and zero in on the career they want to enter. In college, this focus often means choosing a major or specialization that is designed to lead to work in a specific field. By their early and mid-twenties, many individuals have completed their education or training and entered a full-time occupation. From the mid-twenties through the remainder of early adulthood, individuals often seek to establish their emerging career in a particular field. They may work hard to move up the career ladder and improve their financial standing.

Phyllis Moen (2009a) described the *career mystique*—ingrained cultural beliefs that engaging in hard work for long hours through adulthood will automatically lead to status, security, and happiness. That is, many individuals have an idealized concept of a career path toward achieving the American dream by upward mobility through occupational ladders. However, the lockstep career mystique has never been a reality for many individuals, especially ethnic minority individuals, women, and poorly educated adults. Further, the career mystique has increasingly become a myth for many individuals in middle-income occupations as global outsourcing

of jobs and changes in the U.S. economy during the 2007–2009 recession have meant reduced job security for millions of Americans.

Monitoring the Occupational Outlook and the Job Outlook for College Graduates As you explore the type of work you are likely to enjoy and in which you can succeed, it is important to become knowledgeable about different fields and companies. Occupations may have many job openings one year but few in another year as economic conditions change. Thus, it is critical to keep up with the occupational outlook in various fields. An excellent resource for doing this is the U.S. government's *Occupational Outlook Handbook*, which is revised every two years.

According to the 2018–2019 edition of the *Occupational Outlook Handbook,* solar power installers, wind turbine service technicians, home health aides, physician assistants, nurse practitioners, statisticians, physical therapist assistants, and software developers are the job categories that are projected to grow most rapidly through 2026. Projected job growth varies widely by educational requirements. Jobs that require a college degree are expected to grow the fastest. Most of the highest-paying occupations require a college degree.

The job outlook in 2018 for college graduates in the United States is the best it has been in a decade, with 80 percent of employers indicating that they were planning to hire college graduates in 2018—up from 74 percent in 2017 and 58 percent in 2008 (careerbuilder.com). Also, in 2018, nearly half of employers expressed intentions to increase the starting salaries they would offer to recent college graduates.

To read about the work of one individual who advises college students about careers, see the *Connecting with Careers* profile.

WORK

Work is one of the most important activities in people's lives. Our developmental coverage of work begins with adolescence and concludes with late adulthood.

Work in Adolescence One of the greatest changes in adolescents' lives in recent years has been the increased number of adolescents who work part-time and still attend school on a

What are some advantages and disadvantages of part-time work during adolescence?
Corey Lowenstein/MCT/Landov Images

regular basis. Our discussion of adolescents and work focuses on the sociohistorical context of adolescent work and the advantages and disadvantages of part-time work at this stage of life.

Even though education keeps many of today's youth from holding full-time jobs, it has not prevented them from working part-time while going to school. In 1940, only 1 of 25 tenth-grade males attended school and simultaneously worked part-time. In the 1970s, the number had increased to 1 in 4. Today, it is estimated that 80 to 90 percent of adolescents are employed at some point during high school (Staff, Messersmith, & Schulenberg, 2009). As adolescents go from the eighth to the twelfth grade, their likelihood of working and the average number of hours they work during the school year increase. In the eighth through tenth grades, the majority of students don't work in paid employment during the school year, but in the twelfth grade only one-fourth don't engage in paid employment during the school year. Almost 10 percent of employed twelfth-graders work more than 30 hours per week during the school year (Staff, Messersmith, & Schulenberg, 2009).

Overall, the weight of the evidence suggests that spending large amounts of time in paid labor produces limited developmental benefits for youth, and for some it is associated with risky behavior and costs to physical health (Larson, Wilson, & Rickman, 2009). For example, one research study found that it was not just working that affected adolescents' grades—more important was how many hours they worked per week (Greenberger & Steinberg, 1986). Tenth-graders who worked more than 14 hours a week suffered a drop in grades. Eleventh-graders worked up to 20 hours a week before their grades dropped. When adolescents spend more than 20 hours per week working, there is little time to study for tests and to complete homework assignments. In addition, working adolescents felt less involved in school, were absent more, and said that they did not enjoy school as much as their nonworking counterparts did. Adolescents who worked long hours also were more frequent users of alcohol and marijuana. Also, another study found that high school students with paid part-time jobs were more likely to drink alcohol, binge drink, and use marijuana (Leeman & others, 2014).

Some youth, though, are engaged in challenging work activities, receive constructive supervision from adults, and experience favorable working conditions (Staff, Messersmith, & Schulenberg, 2009). For example, work may benefit adolescents in low-income, urban contexts by providing them with economic benefits and adult monitoring. These factors may increase school engagement and decrease delinquency.

Work in Emerging Adulthood The work patterns of emerging adults have changed over the last 100 years (Hamilton & Hamilton, 2009). As an increasing number of emerging adults have participated in higher education, many leave home and begin their careers at later ages. Changing economic conditions have made the job market more competitive for emerging adults and increased the demand for more highly skilled workers (Gauthier & Furstenberg, 2005).

A diversity of school and work patterns characterizes emerging adults (Borges & others, 2008; Hamilton & Hamilton, 2009). Some emerging adults are attending college full-time; others are working full-time. Some emerging adults work full-time immediately after high school, others after they graduate from college. Many emerging adults who attend college drop out and enter the workforce before they complete their degree; some of these individuals return to college later. Some emerging adults are attending two-year colleges, others four-year colleges; and some are working part-time while going to college but others are not.

The nature of the transition from school to work in emerging adulthood is strongly influenced by the individual's level of education (Swanson, 2013). The MacArthur Foundation Research Network on Emerging Adults concluded that for emerging adults who don't go to college, the problem is not being unable to find any job at all but being unable to get a good job.

These emerging adults are college graduates who have started their own business. Emerging adults follow a diversity of work and educational pathways. *What are some of these variations in education and work that characterize emerging adults?*
Paul Bradbury/Caiaimage/Glow Images

Working During College

The percentage of full-time U.S. college students who also held jobs increased from 34 percent in 1970 to 47 percent in 2008, then declined to 43 percent in 2015 (down from a peak of 52 percent in 2000) (National Center for Education Statistics, 2017). In 2015, 78 percent of part-time U.S. college students were employed, up from 74 percent in 2011 but down slightly from 81 percent in 2008.

Working can pay for college tuition or help offset some of the costs, but working also can restrict students' opportunities to learn. For those who identified themselves primarily as students, one national study found that as the number of hours worked per week increased, their grades suffered (National Center for Education Statistics, 2002) (see Figure 7). Thus, college students need to carefully consider whether the number of hours they work is having a negative impact on their college success.

Of course, jobs also can contribute to a student's education. More than 1,000 colleges in the United States offer *cooperative (co-op) programs,* which are paid apprenticeships in specific fields. (You may not be permitted to participate in a co-op program until your junior year.) Other useful opportunities for working while going to college include internships and part-time or summer jobs relevant to your field of study. In a national survey of employers, almost 60 percent said their entry-level college hires had co-op or internship experience (Collins, 1996). Participating in these work experiences can be a key factor in landing the job you want when you graduate.

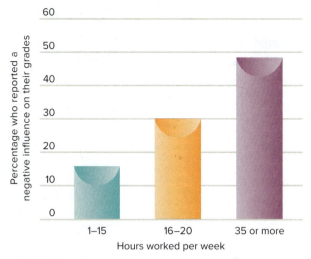

FIGURE 7

THE RELATION BETWEEN HOURS WORKED PER WEEK IN COLLEGE AND GRADES. Among students working to pay for school expenses, 16 percent of those working 1 to 15 hours per week reported that working negatively influenced their grades (National Center for Education Statistics, 2002). Thirty percent of college students who worked 16 to 20 hours a week said the same, as did 48 percent who worked 35 hours or more per week.

As unpaid internships become more common, some students complain that they are merely a way for organizations to obtain free labor. How can student interns ensure that they have a rewarding experience in spite of not being paid?

The Research Network also stated that community colleges are an underutilized resource for connecting high schools and employers. A special concern is the large number of students who begin their college education in a community college but drop out before getting a degree (Horn & Nevill, 2006).

What about work during college? To read about the pluses and minuses of working during college, see the *Connecting Development to Life* interlude.

Work in Adulthood   Both Sigmund Freud and the Russian Count Leo Tolstoy described love and work as the two most important things that adults need to do well. We discussed love in the chapter on "Emotional Development." Let's now explore work in the adult years.

The Work Landscape   Do you work to live or live to work? Most adults spend about one-third of their lives at work. In one survey, U.S. individuals 18 years of age and older who were employed full-time worked an average of 47 hours per week, almost a full workday longer than the standard 9 to 5, five days a week schedule (Saad, 2014). In this survey, half of all individuals working full-time reported that they work more than 40 hours a week and nearly 40 percent said they work 50 hours a week or more. Only 8 percent indicated that they worked less than 40 hours per week.

Work defines people in fundamental ways (Chalofsky & Cavallaro, 2019; Yeoman & others, 2019). It is an important influence on their financial standing, housing, the way they spend their time, where they live, their friendships, and their health. Some people define their identity through their work (Hardy, 2019). Work also creates a structure and rhythm to life that is

What are some characteristics of work settings linked with employees' stress?
Creativa Images/Shutterstock

often missed when individuals do not work for an extended period. When they are unable to work, many individuals experience emotional distress and low self-esteem.

A trend in the U.S. workforce is the disappearing long-term career for an increasing number of adults, especially men in private-sector jobs. Among the reasons for the disappearance of many long-term jobs is the dramatic increase in technology and companies' use of cheaper labor in other countries.

An important consideration regarding work is how stressful it is (Lee & Jang, 2019; Takahashi, 2019). One study revealed that stressors at work were linked to arterial hypertension in employees (Lamy & others, 2014). Another recent study indicated that increases in job strain increased workers' insomnia, while decreases in job strain reduced their insomnia (Halonen & others, 2017).

Unemployment   Unemployment produces stress regardless of whether the job loss is temporary, cyclical, or permanent (Frasquilho & others, 2016). In 2018, there was very positive news about the U.S. unemployment rate with the rate dropping to its lowest point in almost 50 years. However, problems with banks and the economic recession toward the end of the first decade of the twenty-first century led to very high unemployment rates, especially in the United States.

Researchers have found that unemployment is related to increased rates of physical problems (such as hypertension, heart attack, and stroke), mental problems (such as depression and anxiety), substance abuse, and marital difficulties (Yoo & others, 2016). In one study, unemployment was associated with higher rates of tobacco and illicit drug use, as well as heavy alcohol use (Compton & others, 2014). And in a recent study, depression following job loss predicted increased risk of continued unemployment (Stolove, Galatzer-Levy, & Bonanno, 2017).

Stress related to unemployment comes not only from a loss of income and the resulting financial hardships but also from decreased self-esteem (Alvaro & others, 2019; Howe & others, 2012; Zechmann & Paul, 2019). Individuals who cope best with unemployment have financial resources to rely on, often savings or the earnings of other family members. The support of understanding, adaptable family members also helps individuals to cope with unemployment. Job counseling and self-help groups can provide practical advice on job searching, résumé writing, and interviewing skills, and also can lend emotional support (van Hooft, 2014). A recent study found that following a period of unemployment, recovery of a sense of well-being upon reemployment was fast and enduring even when individuals took less favorable employment upon returning to work (Zhou & others, 2019).

Might unemployment be linked to certain characteristics in childhood? Longitudinal data revealed that low self-control in childhood was linked to the emergence and persistence of unemployment from 21 to 50 years of age (Daly & others, 2015). Further, a recent study found that heavy drinking from 16 to 30 years of age was linked to higher rates of unemployment in middle age (Berg & others, 2018).

Dual-Career Couples   Dual-career couples may have special problems finding a balance between work and family life (Carlson, Thompson, & Kacmar, 2019; Gronlund & Oun, 2018). If both partners are working outside the home, who cleans up the house or calls the repairman or takes care of the other endless details involved in maintaining a home? If the couple has children, who is responsible for making sure that the children get to school or to piano practice, and who writes the notes to approve field trips or attends parent-teacher conferences or schedules dental appointments?

Although single-earner married families still make up a sizable minority of families, the number of two-earner couples has increased considerably in recent decades. A recent projection indicates that women's share of the U.S. labor force will increase through 2026 (*Occupational Outlook Handbook,* 2018–2019). As more U.S. women work outside the home, the division of responsibility for work and family has changed in three ways: (1) U.S. men are taking increased responsibility for maintaining the home; (2) U.S. women are taking increased responsibility for breadwinning; and (3) U.S. men are showing greater interest in their families and parenting.

Many jobs have been designed for single earners, usually male breadwinners, without taking account of family responsibilities and the realities of people's lives. Consequently, many dual-earner couples engage in a range of adaptive strategies to coordinate their work and manage the family side of the work-family equation (Flood & Genadek, 2016). Researchers have found that even though couples may strive for gender equality in dual-earner families, gender inequalities persist (Cunningham, 2009). For example, women still do not earn as much as men in the same jobs, and this inequity perpetuates gender divisions in how much time each partner spends in paid work, homemaking, and caring for children. Thus, dual-earner career decisions often are made in favor of men's greater earning power, and women end up spending more time than men in homemaking and caring for children (Moen, 2009b). One study indicated that women reported more family interference from work than did men (Allen & Finkelstein, 2014). Another study found that partner coping, having a positive attitude toward multiple roles, using planning and management skills, and not having to cut back on professional responsibilities were linked to better relationships between dual earners (Matias & Fontaine, 2015).

As more women have worked outside the home, how has the division of responsibility for work and family changed?
Image Source/Getty Images

Careers and Work in Middle Adulthood   The role of work—whether a person works in a full-time career, in a part-time job, as a volunteer, or as a homemaker—is central during middle age. Middle-aged adults may reach their peak in position and earnings but also be saddled with financial burdens from rent or mortgage, child care, medical bills, home repairs, college tuition, or bills from nursing homes for care of an elderly parent.

In the United States, approximately 80 percent of individuals 40 to 59 years of age are employed. In the 51-to-59 age group, slightly less than 25 percent do not work. More than half of this age group say that a health condition or an impairment limits the type of paid work that they do (Sterns & Huyck, 2001). Also, one study found that difficulty managing different job demands was associated with poor health in middle-aged adults (Nabe-Nielsen & others, 2014).

However, leading Finnish researcher Clas-Hakan Nygard (2013) concludes from his longitudinal research that the ability to work effectively peaks during middle age because of increased motivation, work experience, employer loyalty, and better strategic thinking. Nygard also has found that the quality of work done by employees in middle age is linked to how much their work is appreciated and how well they get along with their immediate supervisors. And Nygard and his colleagues discovered that work ability in middle age was linked to mortality and disability 28 years later (von Bonsdorff & others, 2011, 2012).

Do middle-aged workers perform their work as competently as younger adults? Age-related declines occur in some occupations, such as air traffic controllers and professional athletes, but for most jobs, no differences have been found in the work performance of young adults and middle-aged adults (Salthouse, 2012).

The progression of career trajectories in middle age is diverse, with some individuals having stable careers, whereas others move in and out of the labor force, experiencing layoffs and unemployment (Lachman, 2004). Middle-aged adults also may experience age-related discrimination in some job situations. Finding a job in midlife may be difficult because technological advances may render the midlife worker's skills outdated.

Some midlife career changes are the consequence of losing one's job; others are self-motivated (Moen & Spencer, 2006). Among the work issues that some people face in midlife are recognizing limitations in career progress, deciding whether to change jobs or careers, considering whether to rebalance family and work, and planning for retirement (Brand, 2014).

Economic downturns in the United States have forced some middle-aged individuals into premature retirement because of job loss and fear of not being able to reenter the work force (Cahill, Giandrea, & Quinn, 2015). Such premature retirement also may result in accumulating insufficient financial resources to cover an increasingly long retirement period (de Wind & others, 2014).

A final point to make about career development in middle adulthood is that cognitive factors earlier in development are linked to occupational attainment in middle age. In one study, task persistence at 13 years of age was related to occupational success in middle age (Andersson & Bergman, 2011).

Work in Late Adulthood   In 2000, 23 percent of U.S. 65- to 69-year-olds were in the work force; in 2017, this percentage had jumped to 32 percent (Mislinksi, 2018). For 70- to 74-year-olds in 2000, 13 percent were in the workforce, but this percentage had increased to 19 percent in 2017. The increase in the percentage of older U.S. workers has occurred more for women than men. For example, the labor force participation for 75-and-over women has risen 87 percent since 2000, while participation in the work force for 75-and-over men has increased 45 percent (Mislinski, 2017). These increases likely are mainly driven by the need to have adequate money to meet living expenses in old age (Cahill, Giandrea, & Quinn, 2016). The U.S. Labor Department projects that by 2020 35 percent of 65- to 74-year-old men and 28 percent of 65- to 74-year-old women will be in the work force (Hayutin, Beals, & Borges, 2013). A recent study found the following were among the most important motives and preconditions involved when older adults worked beyond retirement age: financial, health, knowledge, and purpose in life (Sewdas & others, 2017).

Cognitive ability is one of the best predictors of job performance in older adults (Lovden, Backman, & Lindenberger, 2017). And older workers have lower rates of absenteeism, fewer accidents, and increased job satisfaction compared with their younger counterparts (Warr, 1994). Thus the older worker can be of considerable value to a company, above and beyond the older worker's cognitive competence. Changes in federal law now allow individuals over the age of 65 to continue working. Also, remember that substantively complex work is linked with a higher level of intellectual functioning (Schooler, 2007). Further, a recent study found that working in an occupation with a high level of mental demands was linked to higher levels of cognitive functioning before retirement and a slower rate of cognitive decline after retirement (Fisher & others, 2014). In sum, a cognitively stimulating work context promotes successful aging (Fisher & others, 2017).

Several recent studies also have found that older adults who work have better physical profiles than those who retire. For example, one study found that physical functioning declined faster in retirement than in full-time work for employees 65 years of age and older, with the difference not explained by absence of chronic diseases and lifestyle risks (Stenholm & others, 2014). Another study revealed that retirement increased the risk of having a heart attack in older adults (Olesen & others, 2014). And in another recent study of older adults, those who continued to work in paid jobs had better physical and cognitive functioning than retirees (Tan & others, 2017).

RETIREMENT

How is retirement in the United States similar to and different from retirement in other countries? What factors predict whether individuals will adapt well to retirement?

Retirement in the United States and Other Countries What are some life paths that retired individuals follow? Do many people return to the workforce at some point after they have retired? What is retirement like in other countries?

The option to retire is a twentieth-century phenomenon in the United States. It exists largely thanks to the implementation in 1935 of the Social Security system, which gives benefits to older workers when they retire. In 2017, in the United States, the average age of retirement for men was 64 and for women 62 (Anspach, 2017). The average number of years spent in retirement by Americans is 18. A recent study found that baby boomers expect to work longer than their predecessors in prior generations (Dong & others, 2017).

In the past, when most people reached an accepted retirement age—usually at some point during their sixties—retirement meant a one-way exit from full-time work to full-time leisure. Increasingly, individuals are delaying retirement and moving into and out of work as the traditional lock-step process of going from full-time work to full-time retirement occurs less often (Cahill & others, 2019). Currently, there is no single dominant pattern to retirement but rather a diverse mix of pathways involving occupational identities, finances, health, and expectations and perceptions of retirement (Kojola & Moen, 2016). Leading expert Phyllis Moen (2007) described how today, when people reach their sixties, the life path they follow is less clear than in the past:

- Some don't retire—they continue in their career jobs.
- Some retire from their career work and then take up a new and different job.
- Some retire from career jobs but do volunteer work.
- Some retire from a postretirement job and go on to yet another job.
- Some move in and out of the workforce, so they never really have a "career" job from which they retire.
- Some who are in poor health move to a disability status and eventually into retirement.
- Some who are laid off define it as "retirement."

At age 92, Russell "Bob" Harrell (*right*) continued to put in 12-hour days at Sieco Consulting Engineers in Columbus, Indiana. A highway and bridge engineer, he designed and planned roads. James Rice (age 48), a vice president of client services at Sieco, said that Bob wanted to learn something new every day and that he had learned many life lessons from being around him. Harrell said he was not planning to retire. *What are some variations in work and retirement in older adults?*
Greg Sailor

Increasingly, both spouses are in the workforce and both expect to retire. Historically retirement has been a male transition, but today more and more couples are planning two retirements—his and hers (Lee, 2017).

Economic downturns, high unemployment rates, and potential changes in Social Security and health insurance coverage for retired individuals in the United States have made it difficult for many workers to set aside enough money for retirement. A 2017 survey indicated that only 18 percent of American workers felt very confident that they would have enough money to have a comfortable retirement (Greenwald, Copeland, & VanDerhei, 2017). However, 60 percent said they felt somewhat or very confident they would have enough money for a comfortable retirement. In this recent survey, 30 percent of American workers reported that preparing for retirement made them feel mentally or emotionally distressed. In regard to retirement income, the two main worries of individuals as they approach retirement are: (1) drawing retirement income from savings, and (2) paying for health care expenses (Yakoboski, 2011).

Just as the life path after individuals reach retirement age may be varied, so are their reasons for working. For example, some older adults who reach retirement age work for financial reasons, others to stay busy, and yet others "to give back" (Moen, 2007).

In the cross-national study of retirees, to what extent did Japanese retirees miss the work and the money in comparison with U.S. retirees?
Ronnie Kaufman/Blend Images LLC

Work and Retirement Around the World   One analysis concluded that France has the youngest average retirement age—60 for men and 61 for women (OECD, 2017). In this analysis, South Korea had the oldest average retirement age—72 for men and 73 for women. A large-scale study of 21,000 individuals aged 40 to 79 examined patterns of work and retirement in 21 countries (HSBC Insurance, 2007). On average, 33 percent of individuals in their sixties and 11 percent in their seventies were still in some kind of paid employment. In this study, 19 percent of those in their seventies in the United States were still working. A substantial percentage of individuals expect to continue working as long as possible before retiring (HSBC Insurance, 2007).

In the study of work and retirement in 21 countries, Japanese retirees missed the work slightly more than they expected and the money considerably less than they expected (HSBC Insurance, 2007). U.S. retirees missed both the work and the money slightly less than they expected. German retirees were the least likely to miss the work, Turkish and Chinese retirees the most likely to miss it. Regarding money, Japanese and Chinese retirees were the least likely to miss it, Turkish retirees the most likely to miss it.

Early retirement policies were introduced by many companies in the 1970s and 1980s with an intent to make room for younger workers. A recent research review found that workplace organizational pressures, financial security, and poor physical and mental health were antecedents of early retirement (Topa, Depolo, & Alcover, 2018). However, in the 21-country study, there was some indication that an increasing number of adults are beginning to reject the early retirement option as they hear about people who retired and then regretted it. In the 21-country study, on average only 12 percent of individuals in their forties and fifties expected to take early retirement, whereas 16 percent in their sixties and seventies had taken early retirement. Only in Germany, South Korea, and Hong Kong did a higher percentage of individuals expect earlier retirement than in the past.

What are some keys to adjusting effectively in retirement?
Bronwyn Kidd/Photodisc/Getty Images

Adjustment to Retirement   Older adults who adjust best to retirement are healthy, have adequate incomes, are active, are better educated, have an extended social network including both friends and family, and usually were satisfied with their lives before they retired (Ilmakunnas & Ilmakunnas, 2018; Miller, 2018). Older adults with inadequate incomes and poor health, and those who must adjust to other stress that occurs at the same time as retirement, such as the death of a spouse, have the most difficult time adjusting to retirement (Biro & Elek, 2018; Mossburg, 2018). One study also found that individuals who had difficulty adjusting to retirement had a strong attachment to work, including full-time jobs and a long work history, lack of control over the transition to retirement, and low self-efficacy (van Solinge & Henkens, 2005).

Planning and then successfully carrying out the plan is an important aspect of adjusting well in retirement (Greenwald, Copeland, & VanDerhei, 2017). A special concern in retirement planning involves the fact that women are likely to live longer than men and more likely to live alone (less likely to remarry and more likely to be widowed) (Moen, 2007).

Review *Connect* Reflect

 LG3 Discuss career development, work, and retirement.

Review
- What is involved in developing a career?
- What are some key aspects of work?
- What characterizes retirement?

Connect
- U.S. adolescents spend more time in unstructured leisure activities than East Asian adolescents do. How might establishing challenging lifelong leisure activities in adolescence benefit an individual at retirement age?

Reflect *Your Own Personal Journey of Life*
- At what age would you like to retire? Or would you prefer to continue working as long as you are healthy? At what age did your father and/or mother retire, if they are no longer working? How well did they adjust to retirement?

reach your **learning goals**

Schools, Achievement, and Work

1 Schools

LG1 Describe the role of schools in development.

Contemporary Approaches to Student Learning and Assessment

- Contemporary approaches to student learning include the direct instruction approach and the constructivist approach. Today, many effective teachers use both a constructivist approach and a direct instruction approach.

- Increased concern by the public and government in the United States has produced extensive state-mandated testing, which has both strengths and weaknesses and is controversial. The most visible example of the increased state-mandated testing is the No Child Left Behind federal legislation.

Schools and Developmental Status

- The child-centered kindergarten emphasizes the education of the whole child, with special attention to individual variation, the process of learning, and the importance of play in development. The Montessori approach allows children to choose from a range of activities while teachers serve as facilitators.

- Developmentally appropriate practice focuses on the typical patterns of children (age appropriateness) and the uniqueness of each child (individual appropriateness). Such practice contrasts with developmentally inappropriate practice, which ignores the concrete, hands-on approach to learning.

- The U.S. government has tried to break the poverty cycle with programs such as Head Start. Model programs have been shown to have positive effects on children who live in poverty.

- Controversy surrounds early childhood education curricula. On the one side are the child-centered, constructivist advocates; on the other are those who advocate a direct instruction, academic approach. A special concern is that early elementary school education proceeds too much on the basis of providing negative feedback to children.

- The transition from elementary school to middle or junior high school can be stressful. Successful schools for young adolescents focus on individual differences, show a deep concern for what is known about early adolescence, and emphasize social as well as cognitive development.

Educating Children with Disabilities

- There are concerns about high school dropout rates and the need to improve the high school experience. The transition to college can involve a number of positive and negative experiences.

- An estimated 12.9 percent of U.S. children enrolled in public schools receive special education or related services. Slightly more than a third of students with disabilities are classified as having a learning disability. In the federal government classification, this category includes attention deficit hyperactivity disorder, or ADHD.

- Children with learning disabilities have difficulty in learning that involves understanding or using spoken or written language, and the difficulty can appear in listening, thinking, reading, writing, and spelling. A learning disability also may involve difficulty in doing mathematics. To be classified as a learning disability, the learning problem is not primarily the result of visual, hearing, or motor disabilities; intellectual disability; emotional disorders; or environmental, cultural, or economic disadvantage.

- Dyslexia is a category of learning disabilities that involves a severe impairment in the ability to read and spell.

- Attention deficit hyperactivity disorder (ADHD) is a disability in which individuals consistently show problems in one or more of these areas: (1) inattention, (2) hyperactivity, and (3) impulsivity. ADHD has been increasingly diagnosed in recent years.

- Autism is a severe disorder with an onset in the first three years of life, and it involves abnormalities in social relationships and communication. It also is characterized by repetitive behaviors. The current consensus is that autism involves an organic brain dysfunction. Autism spectrum disorders (ASD) range from the classical, severe form of autism to a milder condition known as Asperger syndrome.

- In 1975, Public Law 94-142, the Education for All Handicapped Children Act, required that all children with disabilities be given a free, appropriate public education. This law was renamed the Individuals with Disabilities Education Act (IDEA) in 1990 and updated in 2004. IDEA includes requirements that children with disabilities receive an individualized education plan (IEP), which is a written plan that spells out a program tailored to the child, and that they be educated in the least restrictive environment (LRE), which is a setting that is as similar as possible to the one in which children without disabilities are educated. Today's trend is toward inclusion, although some aspects of inclusion have recently been criticized.

Socioeconomic Status and Ethnicity in Schools

- Children living in poverty face problems at home and at school that present barriers to learning. The school experiences of children from different ethnic groups vary considerably. A number of strategies can be adopted to improve relationships with diverse others.

2 Achievement

LG2 Explain the key aspects of achievement.

Extrinsic and Intrinsic Motivation

- Extrinsic motivation involves doing something to obtain something else (a means to an end). Intrinsic motivation involves the internal motivation to do something for its own sake (an end in itself). Overall, most experts recommend that teachers create a classroom climate in which students are intrinsically motivated to learn.

- One view of intrinsic motivation emphasizes its self-determining characteristics. Giving students some choice and providing opportunities for personal responsibility increase intrinsic motivation. When rewards are used, they should convey information about task mastery rather than external control.

- Researchers have found that as students move from the early elementary school years to high school, their intrinsic motivation declines, especially during the middle school years. Intrinsic motivation is typically favored by educational psychologists, although in many aspects of achievement, both intrinsic and extrinsic factors are at work.

Mastery Motivation and Mindset

- A mastery orientation is preferred over helpless or performance orientations in achievement situations. Mindset is the cognitive view, either fixed or growth, that individuals develop for themselves. Dweck argues that a key aspect of optimal development is guiding children and adolescents to develop a growth mindset.

Self-Efficacy	• Self-efficacy is the belief that one can master a situation and produce positive outcomes. Bandura stresses that self-efficacy is a critical factor that determines whether students will achieve. Schunk argues that self-efficacy influences a student's choice of tasks, with low-efficacy students avoiding many learning tasks.
Goal Setting, Planning, and Self-Monitoring	• Setting specific, proximal (short-term), and challenging goals benefits students' self-efficacy and achievement. Being a good planner means managing time effectively, setting priorities, and being organized. Self-monitoring is a key aspect of self-regulation that benefits student learning.
Grit	• Grit involves passion and persistence in achieving long-term goals. Grit is linked to academic engagement and success, including students' grade point averages.
Expectations	• Students' expectations for success and the value they place on what they want to achieve influence their motivation. The combination of expectancy and value has been the focus of a number of efforts to understand students' achievement motivation. Individuals benefit when their parents, teachers, and other adults have high expectations for their achievement.
Ethnicity and Culture	• In most investigations, socioeconomic status predicts achievement better than ethnicity. U.S. children do more poorly on math and science achievement tests than children in Asian countries such as China, Taiwan, and Japan.

3 Careers, Work, and Retirement Discuss career development, work, and retirement.

Career Development	• Many young children have idealistic fantasies about a career. In the late teens and early twenties, their career thinking has usually become more serious. By their early to mid-twenties, many individuals have started in a career. In the remainder of early adulthood, they seek to establish their career and start moving up the career ladder.
	• Service-producing industries will account for the most jobs in America in the next decade. Jobs that require a college education will be the fastest-growing and highest-paying.
Work	• Work defines people in fundamental ways and is a key aspect of their identity. Most individuals spend about one-third of their adult lives at work. People often become stressed if they are unable to work, but work also can produce stress, as when there is a heavy workload and time pressure.
	• Working part-time during adolescence can have advantages or disadvantages, although working too many hours harms students' grades. Working during college can have negative outcomes when students work long hours, or positive outcomes when students participate in co-op programs, internships, or part-time or summer work relevant to their field of study. The work patterns of emerging adults have changed over the last 100 years, and diverse school and work patterns now characterize emerging adults.
	• The nature of the transition from school to work is strongly influenced by the individual's educational level. Many emerging adults change jobs, which can involve searching or floundering. Unemployment produces stress regardless of whether the job loss is temporary, cyclical, or permanent.
	• The increasing number of women who work in careers outside the home has led to new work-related issues. There has been a considerable increase in the time men spend in household work and child care.
	• For many people, midlife is a time of reflection, assessment, and evaluation of their current work and what they plan to do in the future. Midlife job or career changes can be self-motivated or forced on individuals.
	• Some individuals continue a life of strong work productivity throughout late adulthood. An increasing number of older U.S. men and women are working, and since the mid-1990s there has been a substantial rise in the percentage of older adults who work full-time and a considerable decrease in the percentage of older adults who work part-time.
Retirement	• A retirement option for older workers is a late-twentieth-century phenomenon in the United States. The United States has extended the mandatory retirement age upward, and efforts have been made to reduce age discrimination in work-related circumstances.

- The pathways individuals follow when they reach retirement age today are less clear than in the past. Individuals adjust to retirement more smoothly if they are healthy, have adequate incomes, are active, are better educated, have an extended social network of friends and family, and are satisfied with their lives before they retire.

key terms

Asperger syndrome
attention deficit hyperactivity
    disorder (ADHD)
autism spectrum disorders
    (ASDs)
autistic disorder
child-centered kindergarten
constructivist approach

developmentally appropriate
    practice (DAP)
direct instruction approach
dyscalculia
dysgraphia
dyslexia
extrinsic motivation
grit

helpless orientation
inclusion
individualized education plan
    (IEP)
intrinsic motivation
learning disabilities
least restrictive environment
    (LRE)

mastery orientation
mindset
Montessori approach
performance orientation
Project Head Start
self-efficacy
top-dog phenomenon

key people

Elliot Aronson
Albert Bandura
James Comer
Robert Crosnoe

Carol Dweck
Jacquelynne Eccles
Sandra Graham
James Kauffman

Phyllis Moen
Maria Montessori
Clas-Hakan Nygard
Eva Pomerantz

Dale Schunk
Harold Stevenson

section six

Years following years steal something every day: At last they steal us from ourselves away.

—**ALEXANDER POPE**
English Poet, 18th Century

Endings

Our life ultimately ends—when we approach life's grave sustained and soothed with unfaltering trust or rave at the close of day; when at last years steal us from ourselves, and when we are linked to our children's children's children by an invisible cable that runs from age to age. This final section contains one chapter: "Death, Dying, and Grieving."

chapter 17

DEATH, DYING, AND GRIEVING

chapter outline

Fuse/Getty Images

preview

In this final chapter, we will explore many aspects of death and dying. Among the questions that we will ask are these: What characterizes the death system and its cultural and historical contexts? How can death be defined? What are some links between development and death? How do people face their own death? How do individuals cope with the death of someone they love?

1 The Death System and Cultural Contexts

 LG1 Describe the death system and its cultural and historical contexts.

The Death System and Its Cultural Variations

Changing Historical Circumstances

Every culture has a death system, and variations in this death system occur across cultures. Also, when, where, and how people die have changed historically in the United States.

THE DEATH SYSTEM AND ITS CULTURAL VARIATIONS

Robert Kastenbaum (2004, 2009, 2012) emphasizes that a number of components compose the *death system* in any culture. These components include the following:

- *People.* Because death is inevitable, everyone is involved with death at some point, both their own death and the deaths of others. Some individuals have a more systematic role with death, such as those who work in the funeral industry or belong to the clergy, as well as people who work in life-threatening contexts, such as firefighters and the police.
- *Places or contexts.* These include hospitals, funeral homes, cemeteries, hospices, battlefields, and memorials (such as the Vietnam Veterans Memorial Wall in Washington, D.C.).
- *Times.* Death involves times or occasions—such as Memorial Day in the United States and the Day of the Dead in Mexico—which are set aside to honor those who have died. Also, anniversaries of disasters such as D-Day in World War II, 9/11/2001, and Hurricane Sandy in 2012, as well as the 2004 tsunami in Southeast Asia that took approximately 100,000 lives, are times when those who died are remembered in special ways such as ceremonies.
- *Objects.* Many objects in a culture are associated with death, including caskets and various colored objects such as clothes, armbands, and hearses. In the United States black is associated with death, but in China white is linked to death.
- *Symbols.* Symbols such as a skull and crossbones, as well as last rites in the Catholic religion and various religious ceremonies, are connected to death.

Kastenbaum (2004, 2007, 2009, 2012) also argues that the death system serves certain functions in a culture. These functions include *issuing warnings and predictions* (by such providers as weather-forecasting services and the media, laboratories that analyze test results, and doctors that communicate with patients and their families); *preventing death* (by people such as firefighters, the police, physicians, and researchers who work to improve safety and find cures for diseases); *caring for the dying* (by various health professionals such as physicians and nurses, as well as places where dying individuals are cared for, such as hospitals or hospices); *disposing of the dead* (removal of the body, embalming or cremation, and so on); *social consolidation after death* (coping and adapting by family members and friends of the deceased, who often need support and counseling); *making sense of the death* (how people in the society try to understand death); and *killing* (when, how, and for what reasons people in the culture can be killed, such as criminals, and whether the death penalty should be given

Shown here is some of the damage caused by Hurricane Michael in Mexico Beach, Florida, in October, 2018, that claimed more than 30 lives. *How might people from different cultural backgrounds view and deal with the death caused by the hurricane?*
Scott Olson/Getty Images

to some individuals). Figure 1 describes the functions of the death system in the context of Hurricane Katrina in 2005 (Kastenbaum, 2007, 2009).

Cultural variations characterize death and dying (Pereira Gray & others, 2018; Smid & others, 2018). To live a full life and to die with glory were the prevailing goals of the ancient Greeks. Individuals are more conscious of death in times of war, famine, and plague. Whereas Americans are conditioned from early in life to live as though they were immortal, in much of the world this fiction cannot be maintained. Death crowds the streets of Calcutta in daily overdisplay, as it does the scrubby villages of Africa's Sahel. Children live with the ultimate toll of malnutrition and disease, mothers lose as many babies as survive into adulthood, and it is rare that a family remains intact for many years. Even in peasant areas where life is better, and health and maturity may be reasonable expectations, the presence of dying people in the house, the large attendance at funerals, and the daily contact with aging adults prepare the young for death and provide them with guidelines on how to die. By contrast, in the United States it is not uncommon to reach adulthood without having talked about death or experienced the death of someone close.

Most societies throughout history have had philosophical or religious beliefs about death, and most societies have a ritual that deals with death (Ahluwalia & Mohabir, 2019; Tseng & others, 2018). Death may be seen as a punishment for one's sins, an act of atonement, or a judgment of a just God. For some, death means loneliness; for others, death is a quest for happiness. For still others, death represents redemption, a relief from the trials and tribulations of the earthly world. Some embrace death and welcome it; others abhor and fear it. For those who welcome it, death may be seen as the fitting end to a fulfilled life. From this perspective, how we depart from life is influenced by how we have lived.

In most societies, death is not viewed as the end of existence—although the biological body has died, the spiritual body is believed to live on (Sheppard & others, 2018). This religious perspective is favored by most Americans as well. Cultural variations in attitudes toward death include belief in reincarnation, which is an important aspect of the Hindu and Buddhist religions (Chandradasa & Champika, 2018). In the Gond culture of India, death is believed to be caused by magic and demons. The members of the Gond culture react angrily to death. In the Tanala culture of Madagascar, death is believed to be caused by natural forces. The members of the Tanala culture show a much more peaceful reaction to death than their counterparts in the Gond culture. Figure 2 shows a ritual associated with death in South Korea.

In many ways, we in the United States are death avoiders and death deniers (Gold, 2011). This denial can take many forms:

- The tendency of the funeral industry to gloss over death and fashion lifelike qualities in the dead
- The adoption of euphemistic language for death—for example, exiting, passing on, never say die, and good for life, which implies forever
- The persistent search for a fountain of youth
- The rejection and isolation of the aged, who may remind us of death
- The adoption of the concept of a pleasant and rewarding afterlife, suggesting that we are immortal
- The medical community's emphasis on prolonging biological life rather than on diminishing human suffering

Death System Function	Hurricane Katrina
Warnings and predictions	Long-standing recognition of vulnerability; clear advance warning of impending disaster.
Preventing death	The hurricane itself could not be prevented; loss of life, social disorganization, and massive property destruction could have been sharply reduced by better advance planning and emergency response.
Caring for the dying	Medical care was interrupted and undermined by damage to hospitals and communications.
Disposing of the dead	Recovering bodies was delayed, and there were major problems in identifying bodies.
Social consolidation after death	Community cohesiveness and support were negatively impacted by evacuation, scattering of family members, and limited response by overwhelmed human service agencies.
Making sense of death	There was intense criticism of government agencies, whose alleged failures contributed to death and destruction.
Killing	The media reported spikes in lethal violence after the hurricane, but those reports were later found to be inaccurate.

FIGURE 1
HURRICANE KATRINA AND DEATH SYSTEM FUNCTIONS

FIGURE 2
A RITUAL ASSOCIATED WITH DEATH. Family memorial day at the national cemetery in Seoul, South Korea.
Ahn Young-joon/AP Images

CHANGING HISTORICAL CIRCUMSTANCES

developmental connection

Life Expectancy

The upper boundary of the human life span is 122 years of age (based on the oldest age documented). Connect to "Introduction."

One historical change involves the age group that death most often strikes. Two hundred years ago, nearly half of all children died before the age of 10, and one parent died before children grew up. Today, death occurs most often among older adults. Life expectancy has increased from 47 years for a person born in 1900 to 79 years for someone born today (U.S. Census Bureau, 2018). In 1900, most people died at home, cared for by their family. As our population has aged and become more mobile, a larger number of older adults die apart from their families. In the United States today, more than 80 percent of all deaths occur in institutions or hospitals. The care of a dying older person has shifted away from the family and minimized our exposure to death and its painful surroundings.

Review Connect Reflect

LG1 Describe the death system and its cultural and historical contexts.

Review

- What characterizes the death system in a culture? What are some cultural variations in the death system?
- What are some changing sociohistorical circumstances regarding death?

Connect

- You just read about how changes in life expectancy over time have

affected the experience of death. What did you learn about life expectancy and life span from other chapters?

Reflect *Your Own Personal Journey of Life*

- How extensively have death and dying been discussed in your family? Explain.

2 Defining Death and Life/Death Issues

LG2 Evaluate issues in determining death and decisions regarding death.

Issues in Determining Death

Decisions Regarding Life, Death, and Health Care

Is there one point in the process of dying that is the point at which death takes place, or is death a more gradual process? What are some decisions individuals can make about life, death, and health care?

ISSUES IN DETERMINING DEATH

Twenty-five years ago, determining whether someone was dead was simpler than it is today. The end of certain biological functions—such as breathing and blood pressure, and the rigidity of the body (rigor mortis)—were considered to be clear signs of death. In the past several decades, defining death has become more complex (Ganapathy, 2018).

Brain death is a neurological definition of death which states that a person is brain dead when all electrical activity of the brain has ceased for a specified period of time. A flat EEG (electroencephalogram) recording for a specified period of time is one criterion of brain death. The higher portions of the brain often die sooner than the lower portions. Because the brain's lower portions monitor heartbeat and respiration, individuals whose higher brain areas have died may continue breathing and have a heartbeat. The definition of brain death currently followed by most physicians includes the irreversible death of both the higher cortical functions and the lower brain stem functions (Rizvi, Batchala, & Mukherjee, 2018).

Some medical experts argue that the criteria for death should include only higher cortical functioning. If the cortical death definition were adopted, then physicians could claim a person is dead who has no cortical functioning, even though the lower brain stem

brain death A neurological definition of death—an individual is dead when all electrical activity of the brain has ceased for a specified period of time.

is functioning. Supporters of the cortical death policy argue that the functions we associate with being human, such as intelligence and personality, are located in the higher cortical part of the brain. They believe that when these functions are lost, the "human being" is no longer alive.

DECISIONS REGARDING LIFE, DEATH, AND HEALTH CARE

In cases of catastrophic illness or accidents, patients might not be able to respond adequately to participate in decisions about their medical care. To prepare for this situation, some individuals make choices earlier.

Advance Care Planning *Advance care planning* refers to the process of patients thinking about and communicating their preferences about end-of-life care (Sulmasy, 2018). For many patients in a coma, it is not clear what their wishes regarding termination of treatment might be if they still were conscious. One study found that advance care planning decreased life-sustaining treatment, increased hospice use, and decreased hospital use (Brinkman-Stoppelenburg, Rietjens, & van der Heide, 2014). And a recent study revealed that completion of an advance directive was associated with a lower probability of receiving life-sustaining treatments (Yen & others, 2018). Recognizing that some terminally ill patients might prefer to die rather than linger in a painful or vegetative state, the organization "Choice in Dying" created the *living will*, a legal document that reflects the patient's advance care planning.

Physicians' concerns over malpractice suits and the efforts of people who support the living will concept have produced natural death legislation (Coats, Asakura, & Matthews, 2019). Laws in all 50 states now accept an *advance directive*, such as a living will. An advance directive states such preferences as whether life-sustaining procedures should or should not be used to prolong the life of an individual when death is imminent (Cattagni Kleiner & others, 2019; Myers & others, 2018). An advance directive must be signed while the individual still is able to think clearly. A study of end-of-life planning revealed that only 15 percent of patients 18 years of age and older had a living will (Clements, 2009). In the same study, almost 90 percent of the patients reported that it was important to discuss health care wishes with their family, but only 60 percent of them had done so. Also, a research review concluded that physicians have a positive attitude toward advance directives (Coleman, 2013).

Recently, Physician Orders for Life-Sustaining Treatment (POLST), a document that is more specific than previous advance directives, was created (Hickman & others, 2019; Lammers & others, 2018). POLST translates treatment preferences into medical orders such as those involving cardiopulmonary resuscitation, extent of treatment, and artificial nutrition via a tube (Mayoral & others, 2018; Torke & others, 2019).

Euthanasia **Euthanasia** ("easy death") is the act of painlessly ending the lives of individuals who are suffering from an incurable disease or severe disability (Nicolini & others, 2019; Preston, 2018). Sometimes euthanasia is called "mercy killing." Distinctions are made between two types of euthanasia: passive and active. **Passive euthanasia** occurs when a person is allowed to die by withholding available treatment, such as withdrawing a life-sustaining device. For example, this might involve turning off a respirator or a heart-lung machine. **Active euthanasia** occurs when death is deliberately induced, as when a physician or a third party ends the patient's life by administering a lethal dose of a drug.

Technological advances in life-support devices raise the issue of quality of life (Jouffre & others, 2018). Nowhere was this more apparent than in the highly publicized case of Terri Schiavo, who suffered severe brain damage related to cardiac arrest and a lack of oxygen to the brain. She went into a coma and spent 15 years in a vegetative state. Across the 15 years, whether passive euthanasia should be implemented, or whether she should be kept in the vegetative state with the hope that her condition might change for the

euthanasia The act of painlessly ending the lives of persons who are suffering from incurable diseases or severe disabilities; sometimes called "mercy killing."

passive euthanasia The withholding of available treatments, such as life-sustaining devices, and allowing the person to die.

active euthanasia Death induced deliberately, as when a physician or a third party ends the patient's life by administering a lethal dose of a drug.

Terri Schiavo (right) with her mother in an undated photo. *What issues does the Terri Schiavo case raise?*
Stringer/Getty Images

Dr. Jack Kevorkian assisted a number of people in Michigan to end their lives through active euthanasia. *Where do you stand on the use of active euthanasia?*
Jeff Kowalsky/ZumaPress/Newscom

better, was debated between family members and eventually at a number of levels in the judicial system. At one point toward the end of her life in early spring 2005, a judge ordered her feeding tube be removed. However, subsequent appeals led to its reinsertion twice. The feeding tube was removed a third and final time on March 18, 2005, and she died 13 days later. Withholding the life-support system allowed Terri Schiavo to die from passive euthanasia.

Should individuals like Terri Schiavo be kept alive in a vegetative state? The trend is toward acceptance of passive euthanasia in the case of terminally ill patients (Hurst & Mauron, 2017; McClelland & Goligher, 2019). However, one study revealed that family members were reluctant to have their relatives disconnected from a ventilator but rather wanted an escalation of treatment for them (Sviri & others, 2009). In this study, most of the individuals said that in similar circumstances they would not want to be chronically ventilated or resuscitated.

The most widely publicized cases of active euthanasia involve "assisted suicide." **Assisted suicide** occurs when a physician supplies the information and/or the means of committing suicide (such as giving the patient a prescription for a lethal dose of sleeping pills) but requires the patient to self-administer the lethal medication and to determine when and where to do this. Thus, assisted suicide differs from active euthanasia, in which a physician causes the death of an individual through a direct action in response to a request by the person (Borasioi, Jox, & Gamondi, 2019; Hosie, 2018; Roest, Trappenburg, & Leget, 2019). The most widely publicized assisted suicides were carried out by Jack Kevorkian, a Michigan physician, who assisted a number of terminally ill patients in ending their lives. After a series of trials, Kevorkian was convicted in the state of Michigan of second-degree murder and served eight years in prison for his actions. In 2007, he was released from prison at age 79 for good behavior and he promised not to participate in any further assisted suicides. Kevorkian died at the age of 83.

Assisted suicide is now legal in Belgium, Canada, Finland, Luxembourg, the Netherlands, and Switzerland. The United States government has no official policy on assisted suicide and leaves the decision up to each of the states. Currently, six states allow assisted suicide—California, Oregon, Washington, Montana, New Mexico, and Vermont, as well as Washington DC. A research review revealed that the percentage of physician-assisted deaths ranged from 0.1 to 0.2 percent in the United States and Luxembourg to 1.8 to 2.9 percent in the Netherlands (Steck & others, 2013). In this review, the percentage of assisted suicide cases reported to authorities has increased in recent years and the individuals who die through assisted suicide are most likely to be males from 60 to 75 years of age.

To what extent do people in the United States think euthanasia and assisted suicide should be legal? A Gallup poll found that 69 percent of U.S. adults said euthanasia should be legal, 51 percent said they would consider ending their own lives if faced with a terminal illness, and 50 percent reported that physician-assisted suicide is morally acceptable (Swift, 2016).

Why are euthanasia and assisted suicide so controversial? Those in favor of euthanasia and assisted suicide argue that death should be calm and dignified, not full of agony, pain, and prolonged suffering. Those against euthanasia and assisted suicide stress that it is a criminal act of murder in most states in the United States and in most countries. Many religious individuals, especially Christians, say that taking a life for any reason is against God's will and is an act of murder.

Needed: Better Care for Dying Individuals   Too often, death in America is lonely, prolonged, and painful. Scientific advances sometimes have made dying harder by delaying the inevitable. Also, even though painkillers are available, too many people experience severe pain during the last days and months of life (Buiting & de Graas, 2018; Merchant & others, 2019). A study found that 61 percent of dying patients were in pain in the last year of life and that nearly one-third had symptoms of depression and confusion prior to death (Singer & others, 2015). Many health-care professionals have not been trained to provide adequate end-of-life care or to understand its importance.

Care providers are increasingly interested in helping individuals experience a "good death" (Cain & McCleskey, 2019; Thiamwong & Pungchompoo, 2018). One view is that a good death involves physical comfort, support from loved ones, acceptance, and appropriate medical care (Krishnan, 2017). For some individuals, a good death involves accepting one's impending death and not feeling like a burden to others (Carr & Luth, 2016). In a research review, the three

assisted suicide Involves a physician supplying the information and/or the means of committing suicide but requires the patient to self-administer the lethal medication and to determine when and where to do this.

most frequent themes described in articles on a good death involved (1) preference for dying process (94 percent of reports); (2) pain-free status (81 percent); and (3) emotional well-being (64 percent) (Meier & others, 2016).

Recent criticisms of the "good death" concept emphasize that death itself has shifted from being an event at a single point in time to being a process that takes place over years and even decades (Pollock & Seymour, 2018; Smith & Periyakoli, 2018). Thus, say the critics, we need to move away from the concept of a "good death" as a specific event for an individual person to a larger vision of a world that not only meets the needs of individuals at their moment of death but also focuses on making their lives better during the last years and decades of their lives.

Hospice is a program committed to making the end of life as free from pain, anxiety, and depression as possible (Tatterton, Summers, & Brennan, 2019). Traditionally, a hospital's goals have been to cure illness and prolong life; by contrast, hospice care emphasizes **palliative care,** which involves reducing pain and suffering and helping individuals die with dignity (Devik, Enmarker, & Hellzen, 2019; Hassankhani & others, 2019). However, U.S. hospitals have rapidly expanded their provision of palliative care in recent years. One study found that more than 85 percent of mid- to large-size U.S. hospitals had a palliative care team (Morrison, 2013). Hospice-care professionals work together to treat the dying person's symptoms, make the individual as comfortable as possible, show interest in the person and the person's family, and help everyone involved cope with death (Amador & others, 2019; Stiel & others, 2018).

A majority of hospice care today is provided in patients' homes. In some cases, home-based care is provided by community-based health-care professionals or volunteers; in other cases, home-based care is provided by home health-care agencies or Visiting Nurse Associations (Abrahamson, Davila, & Hountz, 2019; Johnson & others, 2019). There is a rapidly growing need for competent home health aides in hospice and palliative care (Franzosa, Tsui, & Baron, 2018; Landes & Wang, 2019). Also, some hospice care is provided in free-standing, full-service hospice facilities and in hospice units in hospitals. To read about the work of a home hospice nurse, see *Connecting with Careers*.

What characterizes hospice care?
Comstock Images/PictureQuest

hospice A program committed to making the end of life as free from pain, anxiety, and depression as possible. The goals of hospice contrast with those of a hospital, which are to cure disease and prolong life.

palliative care Emphasized in hospice care; involves reducing pain and suffering and helping individuals die with dignity.

connecting with careers

Kathy McLaughlin, Home Hospice Nurse

Kathy McLaughlin is a home hospice nurse in Alexandria, Virginia. She provides care for individuals with terminal cancer, Alzheimer disease, and other diseases. There currently is a shortage of home hospice nurses in the United States.

Kathy says that she has seen too many people dying in pain, away from home, hooked up to needless machines. In her work as a home hospice nurse, she comments, "I know I'm making a difference. I just feel privileged to get the chance to meet this person who is not going to be around much longer. I want to enjoy the moment with this person. And I want them to enjoy the moment. They have great stories. They are better than novels" (McLaughlin, 2003, p. 1).

Hospice nurses like Kathy McLaughlin care for terminally ill patients and seek to make their remaining days of life as pain-free and comfortable as possible. They typically spend several hours a day in the terminally ill patient's home, serving not just as a medical caregiver but also as an emotional caregiver. Hospice nurses usually coordinate the patient's care through an advising physician.

A hospice nurse must be a registered nurse (RN) who is also certified as a hospice worker. The educational requirement is an

Kathy McLaughlin with her hospice patient, Mary Monteiro.
Courtesy of the Family of Mary Monteiro

undergraduate degree in nursing; some hospice nurses also have graduate degrees in nursing. A certified hospice nurse must have a current license as an RN, acquire a minimum of two years of experience as an RN in hospice-nursing settings, and pass an exam administered by the National Board for the Certification of Hospice Nurses.

Review *Connect* Reflect

LG2 Evaluate issues in determining death and decisions regarding death.

Review

- What are some issues regarding the determination of death?
- What are some decisions to be made regarding life, death, and health care?

Connect

- In this section you learned that hospices try to provide adequate pain management for dying patients.

What did you learn about older adults in the chapter on "Motor, Sensory, and Perceptual Development" that might help them deal with pain better than younger adults?

Reflect *Your Own Personal Journey of Life*

- Have you signed an advance directive (living will)? Why or why not?

3 A Developmental Perspective on Death

LG3 Discuss death and attitudes about it at different points in development.

| Causes of Death | Attitudes Toward Death at Different Points in the Life Span | Suicide |

Today in the United States, the deaths of older adults account for approximately two-thirds of the 2 million deaths that occur each year. Thus, what we know about death, dying, and grieving mainly is based on information about older adults. Youthful death is far less common. When, where, and how people die have changed historically in the United States (DeSpelder & Strickland, 2020).

CAUSES OF DEATH

Death can occur at any point in the human life span. Death can occur during prenatal development through miscarriages or stillborn births. Death can also occur during the birth process or in the first few days after birth, which usually happens because of a birth defect or because infants have not developed adequately to sustain life outside the uterus. *Sudden infant death syndrome* (SIDS), in which infants stop breathing (usually during the night) and die without apparent cause (Newberry, 2019), is the leading cause of infant death in the United States, with the risk highest at 2 to 4 months of age (NICHD, 2019).

In childhood, death occurs most often because of accidents or illness. Accidental death in childhood can be the consequence of an event such as an automobile accident, drowning, poisoning, fire, or a fall from a high place. Major illnesses that cause death in children are heart disease, cancer, and birth defects.

Compared with childhood, death in adolescence is more likely to occur because of motor vehicle accidents, suicide, and homicide. Many motor vehicle accidents that cause death in adolescence are alcohol-related. We will examine suicide in greater depth shortly.

Older adults are more likely to die from chronic diseases, such as heart disease and cancer, whereas younger adults are more likely to die from accidents. Older adults' diseases often incapacitate before they kill, which produces a course of dying that slowly leads to death. Of course, many young and middle-aged adults die of illnesses such as heart disease and cancer.

developmental **connection**

Conditions, Diseases, and Disorders

Nearly 3,000 deaths of infants each year in the United States are attributed to SIDS. Connect to "Physical Development and Biological Aging."

ATTITUDES TOWARD DEATH AT DIFFERENT POINTS IN THE LIFE SPAN

The ages of children and adults influence the way they experience and think about death (Yang & Park, 2017). As children grow, they gradually develop a more mature approach to death. A mature, adult-like conception of death includes an understanding that death is final and irreversible, that death represents the end of life, and that all living things die.

Childhood Researchers have found that children's conception of death changes as they develop, but that even young children have begun to develop fairly sophisticated views of death, ones that are more cognitively advanced than previously thought (Rosengren, Gutierrez, & Schein, 2014a, b) For example, a recent study found that as early as 4 to 5 years of age, many young children understand the irreversibility of death and that it involves the cessation of mental and physical functioning (Panagiotaki & others, 2018). At some point in middle and late childhood, many children develop realistic and accurate perceptions of death, such as increasingly viewing its cause as biological in nature (Panagiotaki & others, 2018).

Children's views of death and their experiences with death vary with the contexts and cultures in which they grow up. As indicated earlier in this chapter, U.S. children are not exposed to death nearly as much as children in some cultures. In one study, higher-SES non-Latino White parents were more likely to shield their children from death, whereas immigrant Mexican American parents thought it was important for their children to learn about death and talk about it (Gutierrez, Rosengren, & Miller, 2014).

Three- to nine-year-old children with their mother visiting their father's grave in Kenya. *What are some developmental changes in children's conceptions of death?*
Per-Anders Pettersson/Getty Images

The death of a parent is especially difficult for children (Fearnley & Boland, 2019; Weber & others, 2019). When a child's parent dies, the child's school performance and peer relationships often suffer. For some children, as well as adults, a parent's death can be devastating and result in a hypersensitivity about death, including a fear of losing others who are close to the individual. In some cases, loss of a sibling can result in similar negative outcomes. However, a number of factors, such as the quality of the relationship and type of the death (whether due to an accident, long-standing illness, suicide, or murder, for example), can influence a child's response following the death of a person close to him or her.

Most psychologists stress that honesty is the best strategy in discussing death with children. Treating the concept as unmentionable is thought to be an inappropriate strategy, yet most of us have grown up in a society in which death is rarely discussed.

In addition to honesty, what other strategies can be adopted in discussing death with children? The best response to the child's query about death might depend on the child's maturity level (Sheehan & others, 2019). For example, a preschool child requires a less elaborate explanation than an older child. Death can be explained to preschool children in simple physical and biological terms. Actually, what young children need more than elaborate explanations of death is reassurance that they are loved and will not be abandoned. Regardless of children's ages, adults should be sensitive and sympathetic, encouraging them to express their feelings and ideas.

Also, support programs for parentally bereaved children and their caregivers can be beneficial. In a recent research review, it was concluded that relatively brief interventions can prevent bereaved children from developing severe problems such as traumatic grief and mental disorders (Bergman, Axberg, & Hanson, 2017). One of the most successful programs is the Family Bereavement Program, a 12-session program designed to promote effective parenting and teach coping skills following the death of a parent or caregiver. In a recent experimental study, children and adolescents who participated in the program showed better adjustment up to six years following the program (Sandler & others, 2017). And in another recent study, the Family Bereavement Program resulted in fewer mental health problems and less service use by bereaved young adults and their parents compared with a control group who did not participate in the program (Sandler & others, 2018).

Adolescence Adolescents develop more abstract conceptions of death than children do. For example, adolescents describe death in terms of darkness, light, transition, or nothingness (Wenestam & Wass, 1987). They also develop religious and philosophical views about the nature of death and whether there is life after death.

developmental connection

Cognitive Development

In Piaget's theory, adolescents think more abstractly, idealistically, and logically than do children. Connect to "Cognitive Developmental Approaches."

What are children's and adolescents' attitudes about death? What are some good strategies for helping children and adolescents understand death?
Cavan Images/Getty Images

How might older adults' attitudes about death differ from those of younger adults?
Ruslan Guzov/Shutterstock

Adulthood There is no evidence that a special orientation toward death develops in early adulthood. An increase in consciousness about death accompanies individuals' awareness that they are aging, which usually intensifies in middle adulthood. In our discussion of middle adulthood, we described midlife as a period when adults begin to think more about how much time is left in their lives. Researchers have found that middle-aged adults actually fear death more than do young adults or older adults (Kalish & Reynolds, 1976). Older adults, though, think about death more and talk about it more in conversation with others than do middle-aged and young adults. They also have more direct experience with death as their friends and relatives become ill and die (Hayslip & Hansson, 2003). Older adults are forced to examine the meanings of life and death more frequently than are younger adults. One study of young adults and middle-aged adults found that women had more difficulty than men in adjusting to the death of a parent and also that women had a more intense grief response to a parent's death (Hayslip, Pruett, & Caballero, 2015).

Younger adults who are dying are more likely to feel cheated than are older adults who are dying (Kalish, 1987). Younger adults are more likely to think they have not had the opportunity to do what they want to do with their lives. Younger adults perceive they are losing what they might achieve; older adults perceive they are losing what they have attained.

In older adults, one's own death may take on an appropriateness it lacked in earlier years. Some of the increased thinking and conversing about death, and an increased sense of integrity developed through a positive life review, may help older adults accept death. Older adults are less likely to have unfinished business than are younger adults. They usually do not have children who need to be guided to maturity, their spouses are more likely to be dead, and they are less likely to have work-related projects that require completion. Lacking such anticipations, death may be less emotionally painful to them. Even among older adults, however, attitudes toward death vary (Chen & others, 2017).

SUICIDE

What are some of the factors that place people at increased risk for suicide? They include serious physical illnesses, mental disorders, feelings of hopelessness, social isolation, failure in school and work, loss of loved ones, serious financial difficulties, drug use, and a prior suicide attempt.

There are cultural differences in suicide (Keller & others, 2019; Snowdon & others, 2018). Recent cross-cultural comparisons of suicide rates for all ages of individuals found the highest suicide rate took place in the eastern European country of Lithuania, followed by South Korea, and the lowest rate occurred in South Africa (OECD, 2017). Recent cross-cultural comparisons of 15- to 19-year-olds indicated that the highest suicide rates occurred in New Zealand, followed by Iceland, and that the lowest rates occurred in Greece and Israel (OECD, 2017).

Adolescence Suicidal behavior is rare in childhood but escalates in adolescence and then increases further in emerging adulthood (Park & others, 2006). Suicide is the third leading cause of death among 10- to 19-year-olds today in the United States (U.S. Census Bureau, 2019). After increasing to high levels in the 1990s, suicide rates in adolescents have declined in recent years. Emerging adults have triple the suicide rate of adolescents (Park & others, 2006).

Although a suicide threat should always be taken seriously, far more adolescents contemplate or attempt it unsuccessfully than actually commit it (Lee & Ham, 2018). As indicated in Figure 3, in the last two decades there has been a considerable decline in the percentage of adolescents who think seriously about committing suicide, although from 2009 to 2017 this percentage increased from 14 to 17.2 percent (Kann & others, 2018). In this national study conducted in 2017, 7.4 percent of U.S. students in grades 9 through 12 attempted suicide one or more times in the

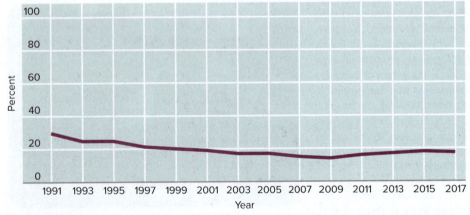

FIGURE **3**

PERCENTAGE OF U.S. NINTH- TO TWELFTH-GRADE STUDENTS WHO SERIOUSLY CONSIDERED ATTEMPTING SUICIDE IN THE PREVIOUS MONTH FROM 1991 TO 2017

past 12 months and 2.4 percent engaged in suicide attempts that required medical attention (Kann & others, 2018). Approximately 4,600 U.S. adolescents commit suicide each year.

The suicidal behavior of adolescents varies not only by gender but also by ethnicity (Molina & Farley, 2019). In 2017, 9.3 percent of U.S. female adolescents attempted suicide, compared with 5.1 percent of their male counterparts (Kann & others, 2018). When we consider both gender and ethnicity, the highest attempted suicide rate for adolescents was among African American females (12.5 percent) and the lowest was among non-Latino White males (4.6 percent). However, other surveys that include Native American adolescents indicate that they have the highest attempted and completed suicide rate (Goldston & others, 2008). A major risk factor for their high suicide rate involves alcohol abuse.

Just as genetic factors are associated with depression, they also are associated with suicide (Jokinen & others, 2018; Zai & others, 2019). The closer a person's genetic relationship to someone who has committed suicide, the more likely that person is to also commit suicide.

Distal, or early-life, experiences often are involved in suicide attempts as well (Jimenez-Trevino & others, 2019; King & others, 2018). The adolescent may have a long-standing history of family instability and unhappiness. Just as a lack of affection and emotional support, high control, and pressure for achievement by parents during childhood are related to adolescent depression, such combinations of family experiences also are likely to show up as distal factors in adolescents' suicide attempts. In two recent studies, maltreatment during the childhood years was linked with suicide attempts in adulthood (Park, 2017; Turner & others, 2017). Also, a recent study confirmed that childhood sexual abuse is linked to later suicide attempts (Ng & others, 2018).

What is the psychological profile of the suicidal adolescent? Suicidal adolescents often have depressive symptoms. Although not all depressed adolescents are suicidal, depression is the most frequently cited factor associated with adolescent suicide (Thompson & Swartout, 2018). In a recent study, the most significant factor in a first suicide attempt during adolescence was major depressive episode, while for children it was child maltreatment (Peyre & others, 2017). A sense of hopelessness, low self-esteem, and high self-blame also are associated with adolescent suicide (Chang, 2017). In a recent study, a sense of hopelessness predicted an increase in suicidal ideation in depressed adolescents (Wolfe & others, 2019).

Family and peer relationships also are linked to suicide attempts (Gould & others, 2019; King & others, 2018). One study found that family discord and negative relationships with parents were associated with increased suicide attempts by depressed adolescents (Consoli & others, 2013). Further, as discussed in the chapter on socioemotional development in middle and late childhood, being victimized by bullying is associated with suicide-related thoughts and behavior (John & others, 2018). In a recent cross-cultural study of more than 130,000 12- to 15-year-olds, in 47 of 48 countries being a victim of bullying was associated with a higher probability of attempting suicide (Kovanagi & others, 2019). And a recent meta-analysis revealed that adolescents who had been victims of cyberbullying were 2½ times more likely to attempt suicide and 2 times more likely to have suicidal thoughts than non-victims (John & others, 2018).

Recent and current stressful circumstances, such as getting poor grades in school or experiencing the breakup of a romantic relationship, may trigger suicide attempts (Liu & others, 2019; Stewart & others, 2019). In one study, a higher level of school connectedness was associated with decreased suicidal ideation in female and male adolescents, and with decreased suicide attempts in female adolescents (Langille & others, 2015).

In some instances, suicides in adolescence occur in clusters. That is, when one adolescent commits suicide, other adolescents who find out about it also commit suicide. Such "copycat" suicides raise the issue of whether or not suicides should be reported in the media; a news report might plant the idea of committing suicide in other adolescents' minds.

Adulthood and Aging   Suicide is increasing among U.S. adults. The number of deaths from suicide now surpasses the number of deaths from automobile crashes (Centers for Disease Control and Prevention, 2015).

In 2015, in the United States the highest suicide rate per 100,000 population was 19.6 for 45- to 64-year-olds, with the second highest rate (19.4) occurring for those 85 years of age and older (Centers for Disease Control and Prevention, 2015). In 2015, younger age groups had lower suicide rates than middle-aged and older adults. In 2015, 20- to 34-year-olds had a suicide rate of 15.5 per 100,000 (Centers for Disease Control and Prevention, 2015). From 2000 to 2015, the greatest percentage increase in suicide occurred in the 45- to 64-year-old age group (from 13.5 to 19.4).

developmental **connection**

Peer Relationships

Bullying victimization is associated with suicide-related thoughts and behavior. Connect to "Peers and the Sociocultural World."

What to do	**What not to do**
1. Ask direct, straightforward questions in a calm manner: "Are you thinking about hurting yourself?"	1. Do not ignore the warning signs.
2. Assess the seriousness of the suicidal intent by asking questions about feelings, important relationships, who else the person has talked with, and the amount of thought given to the means to be used. If a gun, pills, a rope, or other means have been obtained and a precise plan has been developed, clearly the situation is dangerous. Stay with the person until help arrives.	2. Do not refuse to talk about suicide if a person approaches you about it.
	3. Do not react with humor, disapproval, or repulsion.
	4. Do not give false reassurances by saying such things as "Everything is going to be OK." Also do not give out simple answers or platitudes, such as "You have everything to be thankful for."
3. Be a good listener and be very supportive without being falsely reassuring.	5. Do not abandon the individual after the crisis has passed or after professional help has commenced.
4. Try to persuade the person to obtain professional help and assist him or her in getting this help.	

FIGURE 4

WHAT TO DO AND WHAT NOT TO DO WHEN SOMEONE IS LIKELY TO ATTEMPT SUICIDE

Females are three times more likely to attempt suicide than are males, but males are four times more likely than females to commit suicide (Centers for Disease Control and Prevention, 2015). Older non-Latino White men are more likely to commit suicide than any other group (Centers for Disease Control and Prevention, 2015). One study found that African Americans are less likely to commit suicide than non-Latino Whites, but African Americans commit suicide at a younger age (median age of 34 years compared with 44 years for non-Latino Whites) (Garlow, Purselle, & Heninger, 2005). For all adult age groups (as for adolescents), males are more likely to commit suicide than are females (Centers for Disease Control and Prevention, 2015). The older adult most likely to commit suicide is a male who lives alone, has lost his spouse, and is experiencing failing health (Heisel, 2006). One study revealed that perceiving oneself as burdensome also may be a contributing factor in suicide attempts by older adults (Corna & others, 2010). A recent study further explored the influencing and protective factors involving suicidal ideation in older adults (Huang & others, 2017). In this study, the triggers for suicidal ideation included physical discomfort, loss of respect and/or support from family, impulsive emotions due to conflicts with others, and painful memories. Psychological factors contributing to suicidal ideation included feelings of loneliness, sense of helplessness, and low self-worth. Protective factors that were linked to lower levels of suicidal ideation included a supportive network of family and friends, emotional control, and comfort from religion.

It is important to know what to do and what not to do when someone is likely to attempt suicide. Figure 4 provides some valuable guidance.

Review **Connect** Reflect

 LG3 Discuss death and attitudes about it at different points in development.

Review

- What are some developmental changes in the cause of death?
- What are some attitudes about death at different points in development?
- Why do people commit suicide? What are some links of suicide to development?

Connect

- In this section you learned that children 3 to 5 years of age often believe the dead can be brought back to life spontaneously, by magic or by giving them food or medical treatment. During which of Piaget's stages of development is a child's cognitive world dominated by egocentrism and magical beliefs?

Reflect *Your Own Personal Journey of Life*

- What is your current attitude about death? Has it changed since you were an adolescent? If so, how?

4 Facing One's Own Death

LG4 Explain the psychological aspects involved in facing one's own death and the contexts in which people die.

Kübler-Ross' Stages of Dying

Perceived Control and Denial

The Contexts in Which People Die

Knowledge of death's inevitability permits us to establish priorities and structure our time accordingly. As we age, these priorities and structurings change in recognition of diminishing future time. Values concerning the most important uses of time also change. For example, when asked how they would spend six remaining months of life, younger adults described such activities as traveling and accomplishing things they previously had not done; older adults described more inner-focused activities—contemplation and meditation, for example (Kalish & Reynolds, 1976).

Most dying individuals want an opportunity to make some decisions regarding their own life and death (Kastenbaum, 2012). Some individuals want to complete unfinished business; they want time to resolve problems and conflicts and to put their affairs in order.

> Man is the only animal that finds his own existence a problem he has to solve and from which he cannot escape. In the same sense man is the only animal who knows he must die.
>
> —ERICH FROMM
> *American Psychotherapist, 20th Century*

KÜBLER-ROSS' STAGES OF DYING

We are all born to die, and our lives are in a way preparation for that finality. Dealing with one's own death usually only takes front and center in a person's life when they are nearing death, but we live with that awareness throughout our lives. However, as indicated earlier in this chapter, people (especially in the United States) often tend to deny death by trying to avoid the topic altogether.

Might there be a sequence of stages we go through as we face death? Elisabeth Kübler-Ross (1969) divided the behavior and thinking of dying persons into five stages: denial and isolation, anger, bargaining, depression, and acceptance.

Denial and isolation is Kübler-Ross' first stage of dying, in which the person denies that death is really going to take place. The person may say, "No, it can't be me. It's not possible." This is a common reaction to terminal illness. However, denial is usually only a temporary defense. It is eventually replaced with increased awareness when the person is confronted with such matters as financial considerations, unfinished business, and worry about the welfare of surviving family members.

Anger is Kübler-Ross' second stage of dying, in which the dying person recognizes that denial can no longer be maintained. Denial often gives way to anger, resentment, rage, and envy. The dying person's question is "Why me?" At this point, the person becomes increasingly difficult to care for as anger may become displaced and projected onto physicians, nurses, family members, and even God. The realization of loss is great, and those who symbolize life, energy, and competent functioning are especially salient targets of the dying person's resentment and jealousy.

Bargaining is Kübler-Ross' third stage of dying, in which the person develops the hope that death can somehow be postponed or delayed. Some persons enter into bargaining or negotiation—often with God—as they try to delay their death. Psychologically, the person is saying, "Yes, me, but . . ." In exchange for a few more days, weeks, or months of life, the person promises to lead a reformed life dedicated to God or to the service of others.

Depression is Kübler-Ross' fourth stage of dying, in which the dying person perceives the certainty of his or her death. At this point, a period of depression or preparatory grief may appear. The dying person may become silent, refuse visitors, and spend much of the time crying or grieving. This behavior is normal and is an effort to disconnect the self from love objects. Attempts to cheer up the dying person at this stage should be discouraged, says Kübler-Ross, because the dying person has a need to contemplate impending death.

Acceptance is Kübler-Ross' fifth stage of dying, in which the person develops a sense of peace, an acceptance of one's fate, and—in many cases—a desire to be left alone. In this stage, feelings and physical pain may be virtually absent. Kübler-Ross describes this fifth stage as the

denial and isolation Kübler-Ross' first stage of dying, in which the dying person denies that she or he is really going to die.

anger Kübler-Ross' second stage of dying, in which the dying person's denial gives way to anger, resentment, rage, and envy.

bargaining Kübler-Ross' third stage of dying, in which the dying person develops the hope that death can somehow be postponed.

depression Kübler-Ross' fourth stage of dying, in which the dying person perceives the certainty of her or his death. A period of depression or preparatory grief may appear.

acceptance Kübler-Ross' fifth stage of dying, in which the dying person develops a sense of peace, an acceptance of her or his fate, and, in many cases, a desire to be left alone.

Denial and isolation

Anger

Bargaining

Depression

Acceptance

FIGURE 5

KÜBLER-ROSS' STAGES OF DYING. According to Elisabeth Kübler-Ross, we go through five stages of dying: denial and isolation, anger, bargaining, depression, and acceptance. *Does everyone go through these stages, or go through them in the same order? Explain.*
skynesher/Getty Images

---

developmental connection

Religion

Religion can fulfill some important psychological needs in older adults, helping them face impending death and accept the inevitable losses of old age. Connect to "Moral Development, Values, and Religion."

---

end of the dying struggle, the final resting stage before death. A summary of Kübler-Ross' dying stages is presented in Figure 5.

What is the current evaluation of Kübler-Ross' theory about the stages of dying? According to Robert Kastenbaum (2009, 2012), there are some problems with Kübler-Ross' approach:

- The existence of the five-stage sequence has not been demonstrated by either Kübler-Ross or independent research.
- The stage interpretation neglected the patients' situations, including relationship support, specific effects of illness, family obligations, and institutional climate in which they were interviewed.

Despite these limitations, Kübler-Ross' pioneering efforts were important in calling attention to those who are attempting to cope with life-threatening illnesses. She did much to encourage attention to the quality of life for dying persons and their families.

Because of the criticisms of Kübler-Ross' stages, some psychologists prefer to describe them not as stages but as potential reactions to dying. At any one moment, a number of emotions may wax and wane. Hope, disbelief, bewilderment, anger, and acceptance may come and go as individuals try to make sense of what is happening to them.

In facing their own death, some individuals struggle until the end, desperately trying to hang on to their lives. Acceptance of death never comes for them. Some psychologists note that the harder individuals fight to avoid the inevitable death they face and the more they deny it, the more difficulty they will have in dying peacefully and in a dignified way; other psychologists argue that not confronting death until the end may be adaptive for some individuals (Lifton, 1977).

The extent to which people have found meaning and purpose in their lives is linked with how they approach death. In a recent research review of interventions with heart failure patients, half of the studies involving interventions that emphasized meaning-making coping found significant improvements in patients' quality of life, compared with fewer than one-third of studies involving interventions that did not focus on meaning-making coping (self-care or medical adherence, for example) (Sacco, Leahey, & Park, 2019). Also, in a study of 160 individuals with less than three months to live revealed that those who had found purpose and meaning in their lives felt the least despair in the final weeks, whereas dying individuals who saw no reason for living were the most distressed and wanted to hasten death (McClain, Rosenfeld, & Breitbart, 2003). In this and other studies, spirituality helped to buffer dying individuals from severe depression (Smith, McCullough, & Poll, 2003).

Do individuals become more spiritually oriented as they get closer to death? A study of more than 100 patients with advanced congestive heart failure who were studied at two times six months apart found that as the patients perceived they were closer to death, they became more focused on spiritual matters (Park, 2008).

PERCEIVED CONTROL AND DENIAL

Perceived control may work as an adaptive strategy for some older adults who face death. When individuals are led to believe they can influence and control events—such as prolonging their lives—they may become more alert and cheerful. Giving nursing home residents options for control can improve their attitudes and increase their longevity (Rodin & Langer, 1977).

Denial also may be a fruitful way for some individuals to approach death. It can be adaptive or maladaptive (Cottrell & Duggleby, 2016). Denial can be used to avoid the destructive impact of shock by delaying the necessity of dealing with one's death. Denial can insulate the individual from having to cope with intense feelings of anger and hurt—however, if denial keeps us from having a life-saving operation, it clearly is maladaptive. Denial is neither good nor bad; its adaptive qualities need to be evaluated on an individual basis.

THE CONTEXTS IN WHICH PEOPLE DIE

For dying individuals, the context in which they die is important. More than 50 percent of Americans die in hospitals, and nearly 20 percent die in nursing homes. Some people spend their final days in isolation and fear. An increasing number of people choose to die in the humane atmosphere of hospice care (Fridman & others, 2018). A Canadian study revealed that 71 percent preferred to be at home if they were near death, 15 percent preferred a hospice/palliative care facility, 7 percent a hospital, and only 2 percent a nursing home (Wilson & others, 2013).

Hospitals offer several important advantages to the dying individual--for example, professional staff members are readily available, and the medical technology present may prolong life. But a hospital may not be the best place for many people to die. Most individuals would prefer to die in their home (Bannon & others, 2018). However, even though most individuals say they would rather die at home, many feel that they will be a burden at home, that their home has limited space, and that dying at home may alter relationships. Individuals who are facing death also worry about the competency and availability of emergency medical treatment if they remain at home.

Review Connect Reflect

LG4 Explain the psychological aspects involved in facing one's own death and the contexts in which people die.

Review

- What are Kübler-Ross' five stages of dying? What conclusions can be reached about them?
- What roles do perceived control and denial play in facing one's own death?
- What are the contexts in which people die?

Connect

- In this section you learned that the extent to which people have found meaning and purpose in their lives is linked with the way they approach death. In the chapter on "Moral Development, Values, and Religion," what did Roy Baumeister and Kathleen Vohs say are the four main needs for meaning that guide how people try to make sense of their lives?

Reflect Your Own Personal Journey of Life

- How do you think you will psychologically handle facing your own death?

---

5 Coping with the Death of Someone Else

LG5 Identify ways to cope with the death of another person.

| Communicating with a Dying Person | Grieving | Making Sense of the World | Losing a Life Partner | Forms of Mourning |

Loss can come in many forms in our lives—divorce, a pet's death, loss of a job—but no loss is greater than that which comes through the death of someone we love and care for: a parent, child, sibling, spouse, relative, or friend. In the ratings of life's stresses that require the most adjustment, death of a spouse is given the highest number. How should we communicate with a dying individual? How do we cope with the death of someone we love?

COMMUNICATING WITH A DYING PERSON

Most psychologists stress that it is best for dying individuals to know that they are dying and that significant others know they are dying so they can interact and communicate with each other on the basis of this mutual knowledge. What are some of the advantages of this open awareness for the dying individual? First, dying individuals can close their lives in accord

Communicating with a Dying Person

Effective strategies for communicating with a dying person include these:

1. Establish your presence, be at the same eye level; don't be afraid to touch the dying person—dying individuals are often starved for human touch.
2. Eliminate distraction—for example, ask whether it is okay to turn off the TV. Realize that excessive small talk can be a distraction.
3. Dying individuals who are very frail often have little energy. If the dying person you are visiting is very frail, you may not want to visit for very long.
4. Don't insist that the dying person feel acceptance about death if he or she wants to deny the reality of the situation; on the other hand, don't insist on denial if the dying individual indicates acceptance.
5. Allow the dying person to express guilt or anger; encourage the expression of feelings.
6. Don't be afraid to ask the person what the expected outcome for the illness is. Discuss alternatives and unfinished business.
7. Sometimes dying individuals don't have access to other people. Ask the dying person whether there is anyone he or she would like to see whom you can contact.
8. Encourage the dying individual to reminisce, especially if you have memories in common.

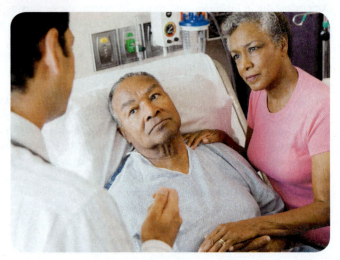

What are some good strategies for communicating with a dying person?
Stockbroker/Photolibrary

9. Talk with the individual when she or he wishes to talk. If this is impossible, make a later appointment and keep it.
10. Express your regard for the dying individual. Don't be afraid to express love, and don't be afraid to say good-bye.

How would you adjust these strategies if the dying person were very young or very old?

Everyone can master grief but he who has it.

—WILLIAM SHAKESPEARE
English Playwright, 17th Century

grief The emotional numbness, disbelief, separation anxiety, despair, sadness, and loneliness that accompany the loss of someone we love.

with their own ideas about proper dying. Second, they may be able to complete some plans and projects, can make arrangements for survivors, and can participate in decisions about a funeral and burial. Third, dying individuals have the opportunity to reminisce, to converse with others who have been important in their life, and to end life conscious of what life has been like. And fourth, dying individuals have more understanding of what is happening within their bodies and what the medical staff is doing to them (Kalish, 1981). In the *Connecting Development to Life* interlude, you can read further about effective communication strategies with a dying person.

GRIEVING

Grief is a complex emotional state that is an evolving process with multiple dimensions. Our exploration of grief focuses on dimensions of grieving and how coping may vary with the type of death.

Dimensions of Grieving Grief is the emotional numbness, disbelief, separation anxiety, despair, sadness, and loneliness that accompany the loss of someone we love. Grief is not a simple emotional state but rather a complex, evolving process with multiple dimensions (Bonanno & Malgaroli, 2019; Bui & Okereke, 2018). An important dimension of grief is pining for the lost person. Pining or yearning reflects an intermittent, recurrent wish or need to recover the lost person. Another important dimension of grief is separation anxiety, which not only includes pining and preoccupation with thoughts of the deceased person but also focuses on places and things associated with the deceased, as well as crying or sighing. Grief may also involve despair and sadness, which include a sense of hopelessness and defeat, depressive symptoms, apathy, loss of meaning for activities that used to involve the person who is gone, and growing desolation (Schwartz, Howell, & Jamison, 2018). In a recent study, meaning was negatively associated with depression but positively associated with grief in suicide survivors (Scharer & Hibberd, 2019).

These feelings occur repeatedly shortly after a loss. As time passes, pining and protest over the loss tend to diminish, although episodes of depression and apathy may remain or increase. The sense of separation anxiety and loss may continue to the end of one's life, but most of us emerge from grief's tears, turning our attention once again to productive tasks and regaining a more positive view of life (Lichtenberg, 2017).

The grieving process is more like a roller-coaster ride than an orderly progression of stages with clear-cut time frames. The ups and downs of grief often involve rapidly changing emotions, meeting the challenges of learning new skills, detecting personal weaknesses and limitations, creating new patterns of behavior, and forming new friendships and relationships. For most individuals, grief becomes more manageable over time, with fewer abrupt highs and lows. But many grieving spouses report that even though time has brought some healing, they have never gotten over their loss. They have just learned to live with it. An estimated 80 to 90 percent of survivors experience normal or uncomplicated grief reactions that include sadness and even disbelief or considerable anguish. By six months after their loss, they accept it as a reality, are more optimistic about the future, and function competently in their everyday lives. However, six months after their loss, approximately 7 to 10 percent of bereaved individuals have difficulty moving on with their life, feel numb or detached, believe their life is empty without the deceased, and feel that the future has no meaning (Maccalum & Bryant, 2013; Shear, Ghesquiere, & Glickman, 2013). This type of grief, which involves enduring despair that remains unresolved over an extended period of time, has been labeled **complicated grief or prolonged grief disorder** (Comtesse & Rosner, 2019; Ghesquiere & others, 2019; Maciejewski & Prigerson, 2017; Tsai & others, 2018). Complicated grief usually has negative consequences for physical and mental health (Maccallum & Bryant, 2019; Trevino & others, 2018). In a recent meta-analysis, 9.8 percent of adult bereavement cases were classified as characterized by prolonged grief disorder (Lundorff & others, 2017). In this study, the older a person was, the greater his or her risk of experiencing prolonged grief disorder.

A person who loses someone on whom he or she was emotionally dependent is often at greatest risk for developing prolonged grief (Rodriguez Villar & others, 2012). Also, a recent 7-year longitudinal study of older adults found that those experiencing prolonged grief had greater cognitive decline than their counterparts with normal grief (Perez & others, 2018). Further, another recent study revealed that individuals with complicated grief had a higher level of the personality trait neuroticism (Goetter & others, 2019). And recent research indicated that cognitive-behavioral therapy reduced prolonged grief symptoms (Bartl & others, 2018; Lichtenthal & others, 2019).

Complicated grief or prolonged grief disorder has been considered for possible inclusion in DSM-V, the psychiatric classification system for mental health disorders (Bonanno & Malgaroli, 2019; Bryant, 2012, 2013). Although it ended up not being included as a psychiatric disorder, it was described in an appendix (American Psychiatric Association, 2013). The argument for not including complicated grief or prolonged grief as a psychiatric disorder was based on concerns that normal grieving would be turned into a medical condition.

Another type of grief is **disenfranchised grief,** which describes an individual's grief over a deceased person that is a socially ambiguous loss and can't be openly mourned or supported (Patlamazoglou, Simmonds, & Snell, 2018). Examples of disenfranchised grief include a relationship that isn't socially recognized such as an ex-spouse, a hidden loss such as an abortion, and circumstances of the death that are stigmatized such as death because of AIDS. Disenfranchised grief may intensify an individual's grief because it cannot be publicly acknowledged (Garcini & others, 2019). This type of grief may be hidden or repressed for many years, only to be reawakened by later deaths.

What are some different types of grief?
Cohen/Ostrow/Digital Vision

complicated grief or prolonged grief disorder Grief that involves enduring despair and remains unresolved over an extended period of time.

disenfranchised grief Grief involving a deceased person that is a socially ambiguous loss that can't be openly mourned or supported.

Dual-Process Model of Coping with Bereavement The **dual-process model** of coping with bereavement consists of two main dimensions: (1) loss-oriented stressors and (2) restoration-oriented stressors (Stroebe, Schut, & Boerner, 2017). Loss-oriented stressors focus on the deceased individual and can include grief work and both positive and negative reappraisal of the loss. A positive reappraisal of the loss might include acknowledging that death brought relief at the end of suffering, whereas a negative reappraisal might involve yearning for the loved one and ruminating about the death. Restoration-oriented stressors involve the secondary stressors that emerge as indirect outcomes of bereavement (Mulligan & Karel, 2018). They can include a changing identity (such as from "wife" to "widow") and mastering skills (such as dealing with finances). Restoration rebuilds "shattered assumptions about the world and one's own place in it" (Stroebe, Schut, & Boerner, 2017).

In the dual-process model, effectively coping with bereavement often involves an oscillation between coping with loss and coping with restoration. Earlier models often emphasized a sequence of coping with loss through such strategies as grief work as an initial phase, followed by restoration efforts. However, in the dual-process model, coping with loss and engaging in restoration can take place concurrently. According to this model, the person coping with death might be involved in grief group therapy while settling the affairs of the loved one. Oscillation might occur in the short term during a specific day as well as across weeks, months, and even years. Although loss and restoration coping can occur concurrently, over time there often is an initial emphasis on coping with loss followed by greater emphasis on restoration.

Recently, a variation of the dual-process model has been developed for families (Stroebe & Schut, 2017; Stroebe, Schut, & Boerner, 2017). The original model focused mainly on the bereaved individual but many people do not grieve in isolation; most do so with immediate family members and relatives who also are bereaved by the loss. This recent extension of the dual-process model also focuses on such matters as reduced finances, legal consequences, and changed family relationships that that have to be dealt with, and seeks to integrate intrapersonal and interpersonal coping.

The dual-process model has been used as a conceptual framework in a number of studies involving grief and bereavement (Lundberg & others, 2018; Ross & others, 2019). In one recent study, parents who were coping with the death of their infant oscillated among various coping strategies (Currie & others, 2019). In a recent study focusing on spousal bereavement, individuals who engaged mainly in restoration-oriented coping were better adjusted both early and later in the bereavement process than those who engaged mainly in loss-oriented coping (Lundorff & others, 2019).

Coping and Type of Death The impact of death on surviving individuals is strongly influenced by the circumstances under which the death occurs (Lovgren & others, 2019). Deaths that are sudden, untimely, violent, or traumatic are likely to have more intense and prolonged effects on surviving individuals and make the coping process more difficult for them (Pitman & others, 2018). Such deaths often are accompanied by post-traumatic stress disorder (PTSD) symptoms, such as intrusive thoughts, flashbacks, nightmares, sleep disturbance, and problems in concentrating (Cullen, 2018). The death of a child can be especially devastating and extremely difficult for parents (Fu & others, 2019; Wang & others, 2019).

In sum, people grieve in a variety of ways. Thus, there is no ideal way to grieve. There are many different ways to feel about a deceased person and no set series of stages that the bereaved must pass through to become well adjusted. What is needed is an understanding that healthy coping with the death of a loved one involves growth, flexibility, and appropriateness within a cultural context.

MAKING SENSE OF THE WORLD

One beneficial aspect of grieving is that it stimulates many individuals to try to make sense of their world (Bottomley & others, 2019; Breen & others, 2018; Wojtkowiak, Vanherf, & Schuhmann, 2019). A common occurrence is to go over again and again all

developmental **connection**

Stress and Coping

Meaning-making coping includes drawing on beliefs, values, and goals to change the meaning of a stressful situation, especially in times of chronic stress such as when a loved one dies. Connect to "Moral Development, Values, and Religion."

dual-process model A model of coping with bereavement that emphasizes oscillation between loss-oriented stressors and restoration-oriented stressors.

of the events that led up to the death. In the days and weeks after the death, the closest family members share experiences with each other, sometimes reminiscing about family experiences.

In trying to make sense of a person's death, each individual may offer a piece of death's puzzle. "When I saw him last Saturday, he looked as though he were rallying," says one family member. "Do you think it might have had something to do with his sister's illness?" remarks another. "I doubt it, but I heard from an aide that he fell going to the bathroom that morning," comments yet another. "That explains the bruise on his elbow," says the first individual. "No wonder he told me that he was angry because he could not seem to do anything right," chimes in a fourth family member. So it goes in the attempt to understand why someone who was rallying on Saturday was dead on Wednesday.

When a death is caused by an accident or a disaster, the effort to make sense of it is pursued more vigorously (Park, 2016). As added pieces of news come trickling in, they are integrated into the puzzle. The bereaved want to put the death into a perspective that they can understand—divine intervention, a curse from a neighboring tribe, a logical sequence of cause and effect, or whatever it may be.

LOSING A LIFE PARTNER

In 2017, 33 percent of women 65 years and older were widowed, compared with only 11 percent of their male counterparts (Administration on Aging, 2018). Those left behind after the death of an intimate partner often suffer profound grief and may also endure financial loss, loneliness, increased physical illness, and psychological disorders, including depression (Chen, Chow, & Tang, 2019; Einio & Martikainen, 2019; Holm, Berland, & Severinsson, 2019). In a recent cross-cultural study in the United States, England, Europe, Korea, and China, depression peaked in the first year of widowhood for men and women (Jadhav & Weir, 2018). In this study, women recovered to levels similar to married individuals in all countries, but widowed men continued to have high levels of depression 6 to 10 years post-bereavement everywhere except in Europe. A recent meta-analysis of mental disorders in widows found that depressive disorders were the most prevalent conditions, followed by anxiety disorders (Blanner Kristiansen & others, 2019). In another recent study of the mental health of widows and widowers, widows were more likely to use positive reframing, active distraction, help-seeking, and turning to God for strength, while widowers were more likely to use avoidant strategies and seek connection with their late spouse (Carr, 2019). In another study, becoming widowed was associated with a 48 percent increase in risk of mortality (Sullivan & Fenelon, 2014). If their spouse's death was unexpected, the mortality risk for the surviving spouse is higher for men but not for women.

Becoming widowed is likely to be especially difficult for individuals who have been happily married for a number of decades. In such circumstances, losing their spouse, who may also have been their best friend and the person with whom they lived a deeply connected life, can be an extremely emotional event that is difficult to cope with.

Surviving spouses seek to cope with the loss of their spouse in various ways (King, Carr, & Taylor, 2019; Yopp & others, 2019). In one study, widowed individuals were likely to intensify their religious and spiritual beliefs following the death of a spouse, and this increase was linked with a lower level of grief (Brown & others, 2004). And one study revealed that widowed persons who did not expect to be reunited with their loved ones in the afterlife reported more depression, anger, and intrusive thoughts at 6 and 18 months after their loss (Carr & Sharp, 2014).

Many widows are lonely and benefit considerably from social support (Zhou & Hearst, 2016). The poorer and less educated they are, the lonelier they tend to be. The bereaved are also at increased risk for many health problems (Daoulah & others, 2017;

These restaurant workers, who lost their jobs on 9/11/01, made a bittersweet return by establishing a New York restaurant to call their own. Colors, named for the many nationalities and ethnic groups among its owners, is believed to be the city's first cooperative restaurant. World-famous restaurant Windows on the World was destroyed and 73 workers killed when the Twin Towers were destroyed by terrorists. The former Windows survivors at the new venture split 60 percent of the profits between themselves and donate the rest to a fund to open other cooperative restaurants.
Thomas Hinton/Splash News/Newscom

developmental **connection**

Community

For older adults, social support is linked with a reduction in the symptoms of disease and mortality. Connect to "Peers and the Sociocultural World."

connecting with research

How Is Widowhood Related to Women's Physical and Mental Health?

A three-year longitudinal study of more than 130,000 women 50 to 79 years of age in the United States, as part of the Women's Health Initiative, examined the relation of widowhood to physical and mental health, health behaviors, and health outcomes (Wilcox & others, 2003). Women were categorized as (1) remaining married, (2) transitioning from married to widowed, (3) remaining widowed, and (4) transitioning from widowed to married. Widows were further subdivided into the recently widowed (widowed for less than one year) and longer-term widowed (widowed for more than one year).

The measures used to assess the older women's health were:

- *Physical health.* Blood pressure was assessed after five minutes of quiet rest using the average of two readings with 30 seconds between the readings. Hypertension was defined as a reading higher than 140/90. Body mass index (BMI) was calculated and used to determine whether a woman was obese. A health survey assessed physical function and health status.
- *Mental health.* Depressive symptoms were assessed by a six-item depression scale, with participants rating the frequency of their depressed thoughts during the past week. The participants' self-reports of antidepressant medicine use were also obtained. Information about social functioning and mental health was based on participants' responses on the Social Functioning Scale (Ware, Kosinski, & Dewey, 2000).
- *Health behaviors.* Dietary behaviors were assessed with a modified version of the National Cancer Institute Health Habits and

History Questionnaire. Participants also were asked if they smoked tobacco and, if so, how much. To assess physical activity, participants were asked how often they walked outside the home each week and the extent to which they engaged in strenuous or moderate exercise. To assess health care use, they were asked whether they had visited their doctor in the past year.

- *Health outcomes.* Cardiovascular disease and cancer occurrences were assessed annually and any overnight hospitalizations were noted.

At the beginning of the three-year study, married women reported better physical and mental health, and better health in general, than widowed women. Women who remained married over the three-year period of the study showed stability in mental health, recent widows experienced marked impairments in mental health, and longer-term widows showed stability or slight improvements in mental health. Both groups of widows (recent and longer term) reported more unintentional weight loss across the three years.

These findings underscore the resilience of older women and their capacity to reestablish connections but point to the need for services that strengthen social support for those who have difficulty during the transition from marriage to widowhood. How might the study's specific findings be applied to designing new or improved social services for widowed women?

Jadhav & Weir, 2018). How might you expect widowhood to affect a woman's physical and mental health, for instance? In the *Connecting with Research* interlude, researchers explore this link.

Optimal adjustment after a death depends on various factors. Women do better than men largely because, in our society, women are responsible for the emotional life of a couple, whereas men usually manage the finances and material goods (Fry, 2001). Thus, women have better networks of friends, closer relationships with relatives, and experience in taking care of themselves psychologically (Antonucci & Webster, 2019). Older widows do better than younger widows, perhaps because the death of a partner is more expected for older women. For their part, widowers usually have more money than widows do, and they are far more likely to remarry.

One study found that psychological and religious factors—such as personal meaning, optimism, the importance of religion, and access to religious support—were related to the psychological well-being of older adults following the loss of a spouse (Fry, 2001). Other studies have indicated that religiosity and coping skills are related to well-being following the loss of a spouse in late adulthood (Whitbourne & Meeks, 2011). Also, in recent research, when widows engaged in volunteering to help others, it reduced their loneliness (Carr & others, 2018).

A widow with the photo of her husband who was recently killed in Afghanistan. *What are some factors that are related to the adjustment of a widow after the death of her husband?*
Peter Power/Toronto Star/Getty Images

For either widows or widowers, social support helps them adjust to the death of a spouse (Antonucci & Webster, 2019). The Widow-to-Widow program, begun in the 1960s, provides support for newly widowed women. Volunteer widows reach out to other widows, introducing them to others who may have similar problems, leading group discussions, and organizing social activities. The program has been adopted by the AARP and disseminated throughout the United States as the Widowed Persons Service. The model has since been adopted by numerous community organizations to provide support for those going through a difficult transition.

FORMS OF MOURNING

One decision facing the bereaved is what to do with the body. In 2017, 51.6 percent of deaths in the United States were followed by cremation—a significant increase from a cremation rate of 14 percent in 1985 and 27 percent in 2000 (Cremation Association of North America, 2018). Cremation is more popular in the Pacific region of the United States, less popular in the South. Cremation also is more popular in Canada than in the United States and most popular of all in Japan and many other Asian countries. In Canada, 70.5 percent of deaths were followed by cremation. In the United States, the trend is away from public funerals and displaying the dead body in an open casket and toward private funerals followed by a memorial ceremony (Callahan, 2009).

The funeral industry has been the source of controversy in recent years. Funeral directors and their supporters argue that the funeral provides a form of closure to the relationship with the deceased, especially when there is an open casket. Their critics claim that funeral directors are just trying to make money and that embalming is grotesque. One way to avoid being exploited during bereavement is to purchase funeral arrangements in advance.

In some cultures, a ceremonial meal is held after a death; in others, a black armband is worn for one year following a death. The family and the community have important roles in mourning in some cultures. Two of those cultures are the Amish and traditional Judaism (Worthington, 1989).

The Amish are a conservative group with approximately 80,000 members in the United States, Ontario, and several small settlements in South and Central America. The Amish live in a family-oriented society in which family and community support is essential for survival. Today, they live at the same unhurried pace as did their ancestors, using horses instead of cars and facing death with the same steadfast faith as their forebears. At the time of death, close neighbors assume the responsibility of notifying others of the death. The Amish community handles virtually all aspects of the funeral.

The funeral service is held in a barn in warmer months and in a house during colder months. Calm acceptance of death, influenced by a deep religious faith, is an integral part of the Amish culture. Following the funeral, a high level of support is given to the bereaved family for at least a year. Visits to the family, special scrapbooks and handmade items for the family, new work projects started for the widow, and quilting days that combine fellowship and productivity are among the supports given to the bereaved family. A profound example of the Amish culture's religious faith and acceptance of death occurred after Charles Roberts shot and killed five Amish schoolgirls and then apparently took his own life in October 2006 in the small town of Nickel Mines in Bart Township, Pennsylvania. Soon after the murders and suicide, members of the Amish community visited the widow of the murderer and offered their support and forgiveness.

The family and community also have specific and important roles in mourning in traditional Judaism. The program of

A funeral in the United States.
Mike Kemp/Getty Images

A crowd gathered at a cremation ceremony in Bali, Indonesia, balancing decorative containers on their heads.
Agung Parameswara/ZumaPress/Newscom

A funeral procession of horse-drawn buggies on their way to the burial of five young Amish girls who were murdered in October 2006. A remarkable aspect of their mourning involved the outpouring of support and forgiveness they gave to the widow of the murderer.
Glenn Fawcett/Baltimore Sun/MCT/Getty Images

Meeting in a Jewish graveyard.
Gil Cohen Magen/Reuters/Landov Images

mourning is divided into graduated time periods, each with its appropriate practices. The observance of these practices is required of the spouse and the immediate blood relatives of the deceased. The first period is *aninut,* the period between death and burial—which must take place within one day. The next two periods make up *avelut,* or mourning proper. The first of these is *shivah,* a period of seven days, which commences with the burial. It is followed by *sheloshim,* the 30-day period following the burial, including shivah. At the end of sheloshim, the mourning process is considered over for all but one's parents. For parents, mourning continues for 11 months, although observances are minimal.

The seven-day period of the shivah is especially important in traditional Judaism. The mourners, sitting together as a group for an extended period, have an opportunity to project their feelings to the group as a whole. Visits from others during shivah may help the mourner deal with feelings of guilt. After shivah, the mourner is encouraged to resume normal social interaction. In fact, it is customary for the mourners to walk together a short distance as a symbol of their return to society. In its entirety, the elaborate mourning system of traditional Judaism is designed to promote personal growth and to reintegrate bereaved individuals into the community.

Some Final Comments   We have arrived at the end of *A Topical Approach to Life-Span Development.* I hope this edition and course have been a window to the life span of the human species and a window to your own personal journey in life.

Our study of the human life span has been long and complex. You have read about many physical, cognitive, and socioemotional changes that take place from conception through death. This is a good time to reflect on what you have learned. Which theories, studies, and ideas were especially interesting to you? What did you learn about your own development?

I wish you all the best in the remaining years of your journey though the human life span.

John W. Santrock

Review Connect Reflect

 LG5 Identify ways to cope with the death of another person.

Review

- What are some strategies for communicating with a dying person?
- What is the nature of grieving?
- How is making sense of the world a beneficial outcome of grieving?
- What are some characteristics and outcomes of losing a life partner?
- What are some forms of mourning? What is the nature of the funeral?

Connect

- In this section you learned that one advantage of knowing you are dying is that you have the opportunity to reminisce. Which of Erikson's stages of development involves reflecting on the past and either piecing together a positive life review or concluding that one's life has not been well spent?

Reflect *Your Own Personal Journey of Life*

- What are considered appropriate forms of mourning in the culture in which you live?

Death, Dying, and Grieving

1 The Death System and Cultural Contexts

 Describe the death system and its cultural and historical contexts.

The Death System and Its Cultural Variations

- In Kastenbaum's view, every culture has a death system that involves people, places, times, objects, and symbols. He also argues that the death system serves certain functions in a culture that include issuing warnings and predictions, preventing death, caring for the dying, disposing of the dead, attaining social consolidation after the death, making sense of the death, and killing.

- Most societies throughout history have had philosophical or religious beliefs about death, and most societies have rituals that deal with death. Most cultures do not view death as the end of existence—spiritual life is thought to continue. The United States has been described as more of a death-denying and death-avoiding culture than most cultures.

Changing Historical Circumstances

- When, where, and why people die have changed historically. Today, death occurs most often among older adults. More than 80 percent of all deaths in the United States now occur in a hospital or other institution; our exposure to death in the family has been minimized.

2 Defining Death and Life/Death Issues

 Evaluate issues in determining death and decisions regarding death.

Issues in Determining Death

- Twenty-five years ago, determining whether someone was dead was simpler than it is today. Brain death is a neurological definition of death which states that a person is brain dead when all electrical activity of the brain has ceased for a specified period of time. Medical experts debate whether this definition should include both the higher and lower brain functions or just the higher cortical functions. Most physicians use the cessation of brain function (both higher and lower) as a standard for determining death.

Decisions Regarding Life, Death, and Health Care

- Decisions regarding life, death, and health care can involve advance care planning, euthanasia, and hospice care.

- Advance care planning can involve living wills and advance directives. Physician Orders for Life-Sustaining Treatment (POLST) is a more detailed and specific document than previous advance directives.

- Euthanasia is the act of painlessly ending the life of a person who is suffering from an incurable disease or disability. Distinctions are made between active and passive euthanasia.

- Hospice care emphasizes reducing pain and suffering rather than prolonging life.

3 A Developmental Perspective on Death

 Discuss death and attitudes about it at different points in development.

Causes of Death

- Although death is more likely to occur in late adulthood, it can come at any point in development. In children and younger adults, accidents are the most frequent cause of death. In older adults, death is most often caused by chronic diseases.

Attitudes Toward Death at Different Points in the Life Span

- Infants do not have a concept of death. Preschool children also have little or no concept of death. Preschool children sometimes blame themselves for a person's death.

- During the elementary school years, children develop a more realistic orientation toward death. Most psychologists stress that honesty is the best strategy for helping children cope with death.

- Death may be glossed over in adolescence. Adolescents have more abstract, philosophical views of death than children do. There is no evidence that a special orientation toward death emerges in early adulthood.

- Middle adulthood is a time when adults show a heightened consciousness about death and death anxiety.

- The deaths of some persons, especially children and younger adults, are often perceived to be more tragic than those of others, such as very old adults, who have had an opportunity to live a long life.

- Older adults often show less death anxiety than middle-aged adults, but older adults experience and converse about death more. Attitudes about death may vary considerably among adults of any age.

Suicide

- Among the factors that place people at risk for suicide are serious physical illnesses, feelings of hopelessness, social isolation, failure in school and work, loss of loved ones, serious financial difficulties, and depression.

- Suicide behavior is rare in childhood but escalates in adolescence. Both earlier and later experiences can influence suicide. U.S. suicide rates remain rather stable in early and middle adulthood, then increase in late adulthood.

4 Facing One's Own Death

 Explain the psychological aspects involved in facing one's own death and the contexts in which people die.

Kübler-Ross' Stages of Dying

- Kübler-Ross proposed five stages of dying: denial and isolation, anger, bargaining, depression, and acceptance. Not all individuals go through the same sequence. Critics emphasize that many individuals don't go through the stages in the order Kübler-Ross proposed.

Perceived Control and Denial

- Perceived control and denial may work together as an adaptive orientation for the dying individual. Denial can be adaptive or maladaptive, depending on the circumstances.

The Contexts in Which People Die

- Most deaths in the United States occur in hospitals; this has advantages and disadvantages. Most individuals say they would rather die at home, but they worry that they will be a burden and they are concerned about the availability of medical care.

5 Coping with the Death of Someone Else

 Identify ways to cope with the death of another person.

Communicating with a Dying Person

- Most psychologists recommend communicating openly with the dying. Communication should not dwell on pathology or preparation for death but should emphasize the dying person's strengths.

Grieving

- Grief is the emotional numbness, disbelief, separation anxiety, despair, sadness, and loneliness that accompany the loss of someone we love. Grief is multidimensional and in some cases may last for years.

- Complicated grief or prolonged grief disorder involves enduring despair that remains unresolved over an extended period of time.

- In the dual-process model of coping with bereavement, oscillation occurs between two dimensions: loss-oriented stressors and restoration-oriented stressors.

- Grief and coping vary with the type of death. There are cultural variations in grieving.

Making Sense of the World

- The grieving process may stimulate individuals to strive to make sense out of their world; each individual may contribute a piece to death's puzzle.

Losing a Life Partner

Forms of Mourning

- Usually the most difficult loss is the death of a spouse. The bereaved are at risk for many health problems, although there are variations in the distress experienced by a surviving spouse. Social support benefits widows and widowers.

- Forms of mourning vary across cultures. In 2015, almost 49 percent of corpses were cremated. An important aspect of mourning in many cultures is the funeral. In recent years, the funeral industry has been the focus of controversy. In some cultures, a ceremonial meal is held after a death.

key **terms**

acceptance	brain death	disenfranchised grief	palliative care
active euthanasia	complicated grief or	dual-process model	passive euthanasia
anger	prolonged grief disorder	euthanasia	
assisted suicide	denial and isolation	grief	
bargaining	depression	hospice	

key **people**

Robert Kastenbaum   Elisabeth Kübler-Ross

glossary

A

A-not-B error   This error occurs when infants make the mistake of selecting the familiar hiding place (A) of an object rather than its new hiding place (B) as they progress into substage 4 in Piaget's sensorimotor stage.

acceptance   Kübler-Ross' fifth stage of dying, in which the dying person develops a sense of peace, an acceptance of her or his fate, and, in many cases, a desire to be left alone.

accommodation   Piagetian concept of incorporating new experiences into existing schemes.

accommodation of the eye   The eye's ability to focus and maintain an image on the retina.

active euthanasia   Death induced deliberately, as when a physician or a third party ends the patient's life by administering a lethal dose of a drug.

active (niche-picking) genotype-environment correlations   Correlations that exist when children seek out environments they find compatible and stimulating.

activity theory   The theory that the more active and involved older adults are, the more likely they are to be satisfied with their lives.

adolescent egocentrism   The heightened self-consciousness of adolescents, which is reflected in adolescents' beliefs that others are as interested in them as they are themselves, and in adolescents' sense of personal uniqueness and invincibility.

adoption study   A study in which investigators seek to discover whether, in behavior and psychological characteristics, adopted children are more like their adoptive parents, who provided a home environment, or more like their biological parents, who contributed their heredity. Another form of the adoption study compares adoptive and biological siblings.

aerobic exercise   Sustained activity that stimulates heart and lung functioning.

affectionate love   Also called companionate love, this type of love occurs when individuals desire to have another person near and have a deep, caring affection for the person.

affordances   Opportunities for interaction offered by objects that fit within our capabilities to perform activities.

ageism   Prejudice against people because of their age, especially prejudice against older adults.

altruism   An unselfish interest and voluntary effort in helping another person.

Alzheimer disease   A progressive, irreversible brain disorder characterized by a gradual deterioration of memory, reasoning, language, and eventually, physical function.

amygdala   A part of the brain's limbic system that is the seat of emotions such as anger.

androgens   A class of sex hormones—an important one of which is testosterone—that primarily promotes the development of male genitals and secondary sex characteristics.

androgyny   The presence of positive masculine and feminine characteristics in the same individual.

anger   Kübler-Ross' second stage of dying, in which the dying person's denial gives way to anger, resentment, rage, and envy.

anger cry   A cry similar to the basic cry but with more excess air forced through the vocal cords.

animism   A facet of preoperational thought—the belief that inanimate objects have lifelike qualities and are capable of action.

anorexia nervosa   An eating disorder that involves the relentless pursuit of thinness through starvation.

anxious attachment style   An attachment style that describes adults who demand closeness, are less trusting, and are more emotional, jealous, and possessive.

Apgar Scale   A widely used method to assess the health of newborns at one and five minutes after birth; it evaluates an infant's heart rate, respiratory effort, muscle tone, body color, and reflex irritability.

aphasia   A loss or impairment of language processing resulting from damage to Broca's area or Wernicke's area.

artificial intelligence (AI)   Scientific field that focuses on creating machines capable of performing activities that require intelligence when they are done by people.

Asperger syndrome   A relatively mild autism spectrum disorder in which the child has relatively good verbal language skills, milder nonverbal language problems, and a restricted range of interests and relationships.

assimilation   Piagetian concept in which children use existing schemes to incorporate new information.

assisted suicide   Involves a physician supplying the information and/or the means of committing suicide but requires the patient to self-administer the lethal medication and to determine when and where to do this.

attachment   A close emotional bond between two people.

attention   Focusing of mental resources.

attention deficit hyperactivity disorder (ADHD)   A disability in which children consistently show one or more of the following characteristics: (1) inattention, (2) hyperactivity, and (3) impulsivity.

authoritarian parenting   A restrictive, punitive style in which parents exhort the child to follow their directions and to respect their work and effort. Firm limits are placed on the child, and little verbal exchange is allowed.

authoritative parenting   A style that encourages children to be independent but still places limits and controls on children's actions; extensive verbal give-and-take is allowed, and parents are warm and nurturant toward the child.

autism spectrum disorders (ASDs)   Also called pervasive developmental disorders, these range from the severe disorder labeled autistic disorder to the milder disorder called Asperger syndrome. Children with these disorders are characterized by problems in social interaction, verbal and nonverbal communication, and repetitive behaviors.

autistic disorder   A severe autism spectrum disorder that has its onset in the first three years of life and includes deficiencies in social relationships; abnormalities in communication; and restricted, repetitive, and stereotyped patterns of behavior.

automaticity   The ability to process information with little or no effort.

autonomous morality   The second stage of moral development in Piaget's theory, displayed by children about 10 years of age and older. At this stage, children become aware that rules and laws are created by people and that in judging an action they should consider the actor's intentions as well as the consequences.

average children   Children who receive an average number of both positive and negative nominations from their peers.

avoidant attachment style   An attachment style that describes adults who are hesitant about getting involved in romantic relationships and, once in a relationship, tend to distance themselves from their partner.

B

bargaining   Kübler-Ross' third stage of dying, in which the dying person develops the hope that death can somehow be postponed.

basic cry   A rhythmic pattern usually consisting of a cry, a briefer silence, a shorter inspiratory whistle that is higher pitched than the main cry, and then a brief rest before the next cry.

Bayley Scales of Infant Development   Widely used scales, developed by Nancy Bayley, for assessing infant development. The current version, the Bayley-III, has five scales: cognitive, language, motor, socio-emotional, and adaptive; the first three are administered to the infant, the latter two to the caregiver.

behavior genetics   The field that seeks to discover the influence of heredity and environment on individual differences in human traits and development.

bicultural identity   Identifying both with one's own ethnic minority group and with the majority culture.

Big Five factors of personality The view that personality is made up of five factors: openness to experience, conscientiousness, extraversion, agreeableness, and neuroticism.

binge eating disorder (BED) Involves frequent binge eating without compensatory behavior like the purging that characterizes bulimics.

biological processes Processes that produce changes in an individual's physical nature.

bisexuality Sexual attraction to people of both sexes.

bonding The formation of a close connection, especially a physical bond between parents and their newborn in the period shortly after birth.

brain death A neurological definition of death—an individual is dead when all electrical activity of the brain has ceased for a specified period of time.

brainstorming Technique in which individuals are encouraged to come up with creative ideas in a group, play off each other's ideas, and say practically whatever comes to mind that is relevant to a particular issue.

Broca's area An area of the brain's left frontal lobe that is involved in producing words.

Bronfenbrenner's ecological theory Bronfenbrenner's environmental systems theory that focuses on five environmental systems: microsystem, mesosystem, exosystem, macrosystem, and chronosystem.

bulimia nervosa An eating disorder in which the individual consistently follows a binge-and-purge eating pattern.

C

care perspective The moral perspective of Carol Gilligan; views people in terms of their connectedness with others and emphasizes interpersonal communication, relationships with others, and concern for others.

case study An in-depth look at a single individual.

cataracts A thickening of the lens of the eye that causes vision to become cloudy, opaque, and distorted.

cellular clock theory Leonard Hayflick's theory that the number of times human cells can divide is about 75 to 80. As we age, our cells become less able to divide.

centration Focusing attention on one characteristic to the exclusion of all others.

cephalocaudal pattern The sequence in which the fastest growth occurs at the top of the body—the head—with physical growth in size, weight, and feature differentiation gradually working from top to bottom.

character education A direct moral education program in which students are taught moral literacy to prevent them from engaging in immoral behavior.

child abuse The term used most often by the public and many professionals to refer to both abuse and neglect.

child maltreatment The term increasingly used by developmentalists in referring not only to abuse and neglect but also to diverse conditions.

child neglect Failure to provide for a child's basic needs, including physical, educational, or emotional needs.

child-centered kindergarten Education that involves the whole child by considering both the child's physical, cognitive, and socioemotional development and the child's needs, interests, and learning styles.

child-directed speech Language spoken in a higher pitch than normal, with simple words and sentences.

chromosomes Threadlike structures made up of deoxyribonucleic acid, or DNA.

chronic disorders Disorders characterized by slow onset and long duration.

climacteric The midlife transition during which fertility declines.

cliques Small groups that range from 2 to 12 individuals and average about 5 or 6 individuals. Clique members usually are of the same age and same sex and often engage in similar activities, such as belonging to a club or participating in a sport.

cognitive mechanics The "hardware" of the mind, reflecting the neurophysiological architecture of the brain as developed through evolution. Cognitive mechanics involves the speed and accuracy of the processes involving sensory input, visual and motor memory, discrimination, comparison, and categorization.

cognitive pragmatics The culture-based "software" of the mind. Cognitive pragmatics includes reading and writing skills, language comprehension, educational qualifications, professional skills, and the self-knowledge and life skills that help us to master or cope with life.

cognitive processes Processes that involve changes in an individual's thought, intelligence, and language.

cohabitation Living together in a sexual relationship without being married.

cohort effects Characteristics attributable to a person's time of birth, era, or generation but not to actual age.

collectivism Emphasizing values that serve the group by subordinating personal goals to preserve group integrity, supporting interdependence of members, and promoting harmonious relationships.

commitment A personal investment in identity.

complicated grief or prolonged grief disorder Grief that involves enduring despair and remains unresolved over an extended period of time.

concepts Cognitive groupings of similar objects, events, people, or ideas.

concrete operational stage The third Piagetian stage, which lasts from approximately 7 to 11 years of age; children can perform concrete operations, and logical reasoning replaces intuitive reasoning as long as the reasoning can be applied to specific or concrete examples.

conduct disorder Age-inappropriate actions and attitudes that violate family expectations, society's norms, and the personal or property rights of others.

connectedness Characteristic consisting of two dimensions: mutuality, which is sensitivity to and respect for others' views; and permeability, which is openness to others' views.

conscience The component of the superego that punishes the child for behaviors disapproved of by parents by making the child feel guilty and worthless.

conservation The awareness that altering the appearance of an object or a substance does not change its basic properties.

constructive play Combination of sensorimotor/practice play with symbolic representation.

constructivist approach A learner-centered approach that emphasizes the individual's active, cognitive construction of knowledge and understanding with guidance from the teacher.

contemporary life-events approach The view that how a life event influences the individual's development depends not only on the event itself but also on mediating factors, the individual's adaptation to the life event, the life-stage context, and the sociohistorical context.

continuity-discontinuity issue Debate that focuses on the extent to which development involves gradual, cumulative change (continuity) or distinct stages (discontinuity).

controversial children Children who are frequently nominated both as someone's best friend and as being disliked.

conventional reasoning The second, or intermediate, level in Kohlberg's theory of moral development. At this level, individuals abide by the standards of others such as parents or the laws of society.

convergent thinking Thinking that produces one correct answer; characteristic of the kind of thinking required on conventional intelligence tests.

coparenting The support that parents provide one another in jointly raising a child.

core knowledge approach States that infants are born with domain-specific innate knowledge systems. Among these domain-specific knowledge systems are those involving space, number sense, object permanence, and language.

corpus callosum A large bundle of axon fibers that connects the brain's left and right hemispheres.

correlation coefficient A number based on a statistical analysis that is used to describe the degree of association between two variables.

correlational research A type of research that strives to describe the strength of the relationship between two or more events or characteristics.

creativity The ability to think in novel and unusual ways and to come up with unique solutions to problems.

crisis A period of identity development during which the individual is exploring alternatives.

critical thinking Thinking reflectively and productively, and evaluating the evidence.

cross-cultural studies Comparisons of one culture with one or more other cultures. These provide information about the degree to which development is similar, or universal, across cultures, and the degree to which it is culture-specific.

cross-sectional approach   A research strategy in which individuals of different ages are compared at one time.

crowds   A crowd is a larger group than a clique. Adolescents usually are members of a crowd based on reputation and may not spend much time together. Many crowds are defined by the activities in which adolescents engage.

crystallized intelligence   An individual's accumulated information and verbal skills, which continues to increase with age.

culture   The behavior, patterns, beliefs, and all other products of a group of people that are passed on from generation to generation.

culture-fair tests   Intelligence tests that are designed to avoid cultural bias.

D

date or acquaintance rape   Coercive sexual activity directed at someone with whom the victim is at least casually acquainted.

dementia   A global term for any neurological disorder in which the primary symptom is deterioration of mental functioning.

denial and isolation   Kübler-Ross' first stage of dying, in which the dying person denies that she or he is really going to die.

depression   Kübler-Ross' fourth stage of dying, in which the dying person perceives the certainty of her or his death. A period of depression or preparatory grief may appear.

descriptive research   A type of research that aims to observe and record behavior.

development   The pattern of movement or change that begins at conception and continues through the human life span.

developmental cascade model   Involves connections across domains over time that influence developmental pathways and outcomes.

developmentally appropriate practice (DAP)   Education that focuses on the typical developmental patterns of children (age appropriateness) and the uniqueness of each child (individual appropriateness). Such practice contrasts with developmentally inappropriate practice, which has an academic, direct instruction approach focused largely on abstract paper-and-pencil activities, seatwork, and rote/drill practice activities.

dialect   A variety of language that is distinguished by its vocabulary, grammar, or pronunciation.

difficult child   A temperament style in which the child tends to react negatively and cry frequently, engages in irregular daily routines, and is slow to accept change.

direct instruction approach   A teacher-centered approach characterized by teacher direction and control, high expectations for students' progress, and maximum time spent on academic tasks.

disenfranchised grief   Grief involving a deceased person that is a socially ambiguous loss that can't be openly mourned or supported.

disengagement theory   The theory that, to cope effectively, older adults should gradually withdraw from society; this theory is not supported by research.

dishabituation   The recovery of a habituated response after a change in stimulation.

divergent thinking   Thinking that produces many answers to the same question; characteristic of creativity.

divided attention   Concentrating on more than one activity at the same time.

DNA   A complex molecule that has a double helix shape and contains genetic information.

doula   A caregiver who provides continuous physical, emotional, and educational support for the mother before, during, and after childbirth.

Down syndrome   A chromosomally transmitted form of intellectual disability caused by the presence of an extra copy of chromosome 21.

dual-process model   A model of coping with bereavement that emphasizes oscillation between loss-oriented stressors and restoration-oriented stressors.

dynamic systems theory   A theory proposed by Esther Thelen that seeks to explain how infants assemble motor skills for perceiving and acting.

dyscalculia   Also known as developmental arithmetic disorder, this term refers to a learning disability that involves difficulty in math computation.

dysgraphia   A learning disability that involves difficulty in handwriting.

dyslexia   A learning disability that involves a severe impairment in the ability to read and spell.

E

easy child   A temperament style in which the child is generally in a positive mood, quickly establishes regular routines, and adapts easily to new experiences.

eclectic theoretical orientation   An orientation that does not follow any one theoretical approach but rather selects from each theory whatever is considered best in it.

ecological view   The view proposed by the Gibsons that people directly perceive information in the world around them. Perception brings people in contact with the environment in order to interact with it and adapt to it.

ego ideal   The component of the superego that rewards the child by conveying a sense of pride and personal value when the child acts according to ideal standards approved by the parents.

egocentrism   The inability to distinguish between one's own and someone else's perspective; an important feature of preoperational thought.

elaboration   Engagement in more extensive processing of information, benefiting memory.

embryonic period   The period of prenatal development that occurs from two to eight weeks after conception. During the embryonic period, the rate of cell differentiation intensifies, support systems for the cells form, and organs appear.

emerging adulthood   The developmental time frame occurring from approximately 18 to 25 years of age; this transitional period between adolescence and adulthood is characterized by experimentation and exploration.

emotion   Feeling, or affect, that occurs when a person is engaged in an interaction that is important to him or her, especially to his or her well-being.

emotional abuse   Acts or omissions by parents or other caregivers that have caused, or could cause, serious behavioral, cognitive, or emotional problems.

emotional intelligence   The ability to perceive and express emotions accurately and adaptively, to understand emotion and emotional knowledge, to use feelings to facilitate thought, and to manage emotions in oneself and others.

empathy   Reacting to another's feelings with an emotional response that is similar to the other's feelings.

empty nest syndrome   View that a decline in marital satisfaction occurs when children leave home; however, research indicates that for most parents there is an upswing in marital satisfaction when children are launched into an adult life.

encoding   The process by which information gets into memory.

epigenetic view   Perspective emphasizing that development is the result of an ongoing, bidirectional interchange between heredity and environment.

episodic memory   Retention of information about the where and when of life's happenings.

equilibration   A mechanism that Piaget proposed to explain how children shift from one stage of thought to the next.

Erikson's theory   Theory that proposes eight stages of human development. Each stage consists of a unique developmental task that confronts individuals with a crisis that must be resolved.

estradiol   A hormone associated in girls with breast, uterine, and skeletal development.

estrogens   A class of sex hormones—an important one of which is estradiol—that primarily influences the development of female sex characteristics and helps to regulate the menstrual cycle.

ethnic gloss   Use of an ethnic label such as African American or Latino in a superficial way that portrays an ethnic group as being more homogeneous than it really is.

ethnic identity   An enduring aspect of the self that includes a sense of membership in an ethnic group, along with the attitudes and feelings related to that membership.

ethnicity   Categorization of an individual based on cultural heritage, nationality characteristics, race, religion, and language.

ethnocentrism   The tendency to consider one's own group superior to other groups.

ethology   Theory stressing that behavior is strongly influenced by biology, is tied to evolution, and is characterized by critical or sensitive periods.

euthanasia The act of painlessly ending the lives of persons who are suffering from incurable diseases or severe disabilities; sometimes called "mercy killing."

evocative genotype-environment correlations Correlations that exist when the child's characteristics elicit certain types of environments.

evolutionary psychology A branch of psychology that emphasizes the importance of adaptation, reproduction, and "survival of the fittest" in shaping behavior.

executive attention Cognitive process involving planning actions, allocating attention to goals, detecting and compensating for errors, monitoring progress on tasks, and dealing with novel or difficult circumstances.

executive function An umbrella-like concept that encompasses a number of higher-level cognitive processes linked to the development of the brain's prefrontal cortex. Executive function involves managing one's thoughts to engage in goal-directed behavior and to exercise self-control.

expanding Adding information to the child's incomplete utterance.

experiment Carefully regulated procedure in which one or more factors believed to influence the behavior being studied are manipulated while all other factors are held constant.

expertise Having extensive, highly organized knowledge and understanding of a particular domain.

explicit memory Conscious memory of facts and experiences.

extrinsic motivation Doing something to obtain something else (the activity is a means to an end).

F

fast mapping A process that helps to explain how young children learn the connection between a word and its referent so quickly.

feminization of poverty The fact that far more women than men live in poverty. Women's lower income, divorce, infrequent awarding of alimony, and poorly enforced child support by fathers—which usually leave women with less money than they and their children need to adequately function—are the likely causes.

fertilization A stage in reproduction when an egg and a sperm fuse to create a single cell, called a zygote.

fetal alcohol spectrum disorders (FASD) A cluster of abnormalities that may appear in the offspring of mothers who drink alcohol heavily during pregnancy.

fetal period The prenatal period of development that begins two months after conception and lasts for seven months, on average.

fight or flight Taylor's view that when men experience stress, they are more likely to become aggressive, withdraw from social contact, or drink alcohol.

fine motor skills Motor skills that involve finely tuned movements, such as any activity that requires finger dexterity.

fluid intelligence The ability to reason effectively.

forgiveness An aspect of prosocial behavior that occurs when the injured person releases the injurer from possible behavioral retaliation.

formal operational stage The fourth and final Piagetian stage, which appears between the ages of 11 and 15; individuals move beyond concrete experiences and think in more abstract and logical ways.

fragile X syndrome (FXS) A chromosomal disorder involving an abnormality in the X chromosome, which becomes constricted and often breaks.

free-radical theory A microbiological theory of aging stating that people age because when their cells metabolize energy, they generate waste that includes unstable oxygen molecules, known as free radicals, that damage DNA and other structures.

fuzzy trace theory States that memory is best understood by considering two types of memory representations: (1) verbatim memory trace and (2) gist.

fuzzy-trace theory dual-process model States that decision making is influenced by two systems—"verbatim" analytical (literal and precise) and gist-based intuition (simple bottom-line meaning)—which operate in parallel; in this model, gist-based intuition benefits adolescent decision making more than analytical thinking does.

G

games Activities that are engaged in for pleasure and include rules.

gender The characteristics of people as females or males.

gender identity Involves a sense of one's own gender, including knowledge, understanding, and acceptance of being male or female.

gender-intensification hypothesis The view that psychological and behavioral differences between boys and girls become greater during early adolescence because of increased socialization pressures to conform to traditional gender roles.

gender role A set of expectations that prescribe how females or males should think, act, or feel.

gender schema theory The theory that gender-typing emerges as children gradually develop gender schemas of what is gender-appropriate and gender-inappropriate in their culture.

gender stereotypes General impressions and beliefs about females and males.

gender-typing Acquisition of a traditional masculine or feminine role.

gene × environment (G × E) interaction The interaction of a specific measured variation in the DNA and a specific measured aspect of the environment.

generativity versus stagnation The seventh stage in Erikson's life-span theory; it encompasses adults' desire to leave a legacy of themselves to the next generation.

genes Units of hereditary information composed of DNA. Genes help cells to reproduce themselves and assemble proteins that direct body processes.

genotype All of a person's actual genetic material.

germinal period The period of prenatal development that takes place during the first two weeks after conception; it includes the creation of the zygote, continued cell division, and the attachment of the zygote to the wall of the uterus.

giftedness Having above-average intelligence (an IQ of 130 or higher) and/or superior talent for something.

glaucoma Damage to the optic nerve because of pressure created by a buildup of fluid in the eye.

gonadotropins Hormones that stimulate the testes or ovaries.

gonads The sex glands, which are the testes in males and the ovaries in females.

goodness of fit The match between a child's temperament and the environmental demands the child must cope with.

grasping reflex A reflex that occurs when something touches an infant's palms. The infant responds by grasping tightly.

gratitude A feeling of thankfulness and appreciation, especially in response to someone's doing something kind or helpful.

grief The emotional numbness, disbelief, separation anxiety, despair, sadness, and loneliness that accompany the loss of someone we love.

grit Involves passion and persistence in achieving long-term goals.

gross motor skills Motor skills that involve large-muscle activities, such as walking.

H

habituation Decreased responsiveness to a stimulus after repeated presentations of the stimulus.

helpless orientation An orientation in which one seems trapped by the experience of difficulty and attributes one's difficulty to a lack of ability.

heteronomous morality The first stage of moral development in Piaget's theory, occurring at 4 to 7 years of age. Justice and rules are conceived of as unchangeable properties of the world, removed from the control of people.

hidden curriculum The pervasive moral atmosphere that characterizes every school.

hormonal stress theory The theory that aging in the body's hormonal system can lower resistance to stress and increase the likelihood of disease.

hormones Powerful chemical substances secreted by the endocrine glands and carried through the body by the bloodstream.

hospice A program committed to making the end of life as free from pain, anxiety, and depression as possible. The goals of hospice contrast with those of a hospital, which are to cure disease and prolong life.

hypothalamus A structure in the brain that is involved with eating and sexual behavior.

hypotheses Specific assumptions and predictions that can be tested to determine their accuracy.

hypothetical-deductive reasoning Piaget's formal operational concept that adolescents have the cognitive ability to develop hypotheses about ways to solve problems and can systematically deduce which is the best path to follow in solving the problem.

I

identity achievement   Marcia's term for the status of individuals who have undergone a crisis and have made a commitment.

identity diffusion   Marcia's term for the status of individuals who have not yet experienced a crisis (explored meaningful alternatives) or made any commitments.

identity foreclosure   Marcia's term for the status of individuals who have made a commitment but have not experienced a crisis.

identity moratorium   Marcia's term for the status of individuals who are in the midst of a crisis but whose commitments are either absent or vaguely defined.

identity versus identity confusion   Erikson's fifth stage of development, which occurs during the adolescent years; adolescents are faced with finding out who they are, what they are all about, and where they are going in life.

imaginary audience   That aspect of adolescent egocentrism that involves feeling that one is the center of attention and sensing that one is on stage.

immanent justice   Belief that if a rule is broken, punishment will be meted out immediately.

implicit memory   Memory without conscious recollection–memory of skills and routine procedures that are performed automatically.

inclusion   Education of a child with special educational needs full-time in the regular classroom.

individualism   Giving priority to personal goals rather than to group goals; emphasizing values that serve the self, such as feeling good, obtaining personal distinction through achievement, and preserving independence.

individuality   Characteristic consisting of two dimensions: self-assertion, the ability to have and communicate a point of view; and separateness, the use of communication patterns to express how one is different from others.

individualized education plan (IEP)   A written statement that spells out a program tailored to a child with a disability. The plan should be (1) related to the child's learning capacity, (2) specially constructed to meet the child's individual needs and not merely a copy of what is offered to other children, and (3) designed to provide educational benefits.

indulgent parenting   A style in which parents are very involved with their children but place few demands or controls on them.

infinite generativity   The ability to produce and comprehend an endless number of meaningful sentences using a finite set of words and rules.

information-processing theory   Theory emphasizing that individuals manipulate information, monitor it, and strategize about it. Central to this theory are the processes of memory and thinking.

insecure avoidant children   Children who show insecurity by avoiding the mother.

insecure disorganized children   Children who show insecurity by being disorganized and disoriented.

insecure resistant children   Children who might cling to the caregiver, then resist by fighting against the closeness, perhaps by kicking or pushing away.

intellectual disability   A condition of limited mental ability in which an individual has a low IQ, usually below 70 on a traditional test of intelligence, and has difficulty adapting to the demands of everyday life.

intelligence quotient (IQ)   An individual's mental age divided by chronological age, multiplied by 100; devised in 1912 by William Stern.

intelligence   The ability to solve problems and to adapt to and learn from experiences.

intermodal perception   The ability to integrate information about two or more sensory modalities, such as vision and hearing.

intimacy in friendship   Self-disclosure and the sharing of private thoughts.

intrinsic motivation   Doing something for its own sake; involves factors such as self-determination and opportunities to make choices.

intuitive thought substage   The second substage of preoperational thought, occurring between approximately 4 and 7 years of age. Children begin to use primitive reasoning and want to know the answers to all sorts of questions.

J

joint attention   Focus by individuals on the same object or event; requires an ability to track another's behavior, one individual to direct another's attention, and reciprocal interaction.

justice perspective   A moral perspective that focuses on the rights of the individual; individuals independently make moral decisions.

juvenile delinquency   Actions taken by an adolescent in breaking the law or engaging in illegal behavior.

K

kangaroo care   A way of holding a preterm infant so that there is skin-to-skin contact.

Klinefelter syndrome   A chromosomal disorder in which males have an extra X chromosome, making them XXY instead of XY.

L

labeling   Naming objects that children seem interested in.

laboratory   A controlled setting from which many of the complex factors of the "real world" have been removed.

language   A form of communication, whether spoken, written, or signed, that is based on a system of symbols.

language acquisition device (LAD) Chomsky's term that describes a biological endowment that enables the child to detect certain features and rules of language, including phonology, syntax, and semantics.

lateralization   Specialization of function in one hemisphere or the other of the cerebral cortex.

learning disabilities   Disabilities in which children experience difficulty in learning that involves understanding or using spoken or written language; the difficulty can appear in listening, thinking, reading, writing, and spelling. A learning disability also may involve difficulty in doing mathematics. To be classified as a learning disability, the learning problem is not primarily the result of visual, hearing, or motor disabilities; intellectual disability; emotional disorders; or environmental, cultural, or economic disadvantage.

least restrictive environment (LRE)   A setting that is as similar as possible to the one in which children without a disability are educated.

leisure   The pleasant times when individuals are free to pursue activities and interests of their own choosing.

life span   The upper boundary of life, which is the maximum number of years an individual can live. The maximum life span of humans is about 120 years of age.

life-span perspective   View of development as being lifelong, multidimensional, multidirectional, plastic, multidisciplinary, and contextual; involving growth, maintenance, and regulation of loss; and constructed through biological, sociocultural, and individual factors working together.

limbic system   The region of the brain where emotions and rewards are experienced.

long-term memory   A relatively permanent and unlimited type of memory.

longitudinal approach   A research strategy in which the same individuals are studied over a period of time, usually several years or more.

low birth weight infants   Infants who weigh less than 5½ pounds at birth.

M

macular degeneration   A vision problem in the elderly that involves deterioration of the macula of the retina.

mastery orientation   A perspective in which one is task-oriented—concerned with learning strategies and the process of achievement rather than the outcome.

meaning-making coping   Drawing on beliefs, values, and goals to change the meaning of a stressful situation, especially in times of high levels of stress such as when a loved one dies.

meiosis   A specialized form of cell division that occurs to form eggs and sperm (or gametes).

memory   Retention of information over time.

menarche   A girl's first menstrual period.

menopause   The complete cessation of a woman's menstrual cycles, which usually occurs during the late forties or early fifties.

mental age (MA)   An individual's level of mental development relative to that of others.

metacognition   Cognition about cognition, or "knowing about knowing."

metalinguistic awareness   Knowledge about language.

metamemory   Knowledge about memory.

metaphor   An implied comparison between two unlike things.

mindset   The cognitive view individuals develop for themselves that perceives their potential either as fixed or as capable of growth.

mitochondrial theory   The theory that aging is caused by the decay of the mitochondria, which are tiny cellular bodies that supply energy for cell function, growth, and repair.

mitosis   Cellular reproduction in which the cell's nucleus duplicates itself; two new cells are formed, each containing the same DNA as the original cell, arranged in the same 23 pairs of chromosomes.

Montessori approach   An educational philosophy in which children are given considerable freedom and spontaneity in choosing activities and are allowed to move from one activity to another as they desire.

moral development   Changes in thoughts, feelings, and behaviors regarding standards of right and wrong.

moral exemplars   People who have a moral personality, identity, character, and set of virtues that reflect moral excellence and commitment.

moral identity   The aspect of personality that is present when individuals have moral notions and commitments that are central to their lives.

Moro reflex   A startle response that occurs in reaction to a sudden, intense noise or movement. When startled, the newborn arches its back, throws its head back, and flings out its arms and legs. Then the newborn rapidly closes its arms and legs to the center of the body.

morphology   Units of meaning involved in word formation.

mTOR pathway   A cellular pathway that involves the regulation of growth and metabolism and has been proposed as a key aspect of longevity

myelination   The process of encasing axons with a myelin sheath, thereby improving the speed and efficiency of information processing.

N

natural childbirth   A childbirth method that attempts to reduce the mother's pain by decreasing her fear through education about childbirth stages and relaxation techniques during delivery.

naturalistic observation   Observing behavior in real-world settings.

nature-nurture issue   Debate about whether development is primarily influenced by nature or nurture. Nature refers to an organism's biological inheritance, nurture to its environmental experiences. The "nature proponents" claim biological inheritance is the more important influence on development; the "nurture proponents" claim that environmental experiences are more important.

neglected children   Children who are infrequently nominated as a best friend but are not disliked by their peers.

neglectful parenting   A style in which the parent is very uninvolved in the child's life.

neo-Piagetians   Developmentalists who have elaborated on Piaget's theory, emphasizing attention to children's strategies; information-processing speed; the task involved; and division of the problem into more precise, smaller steps.

neuroconstructivist view   Developmental perspective in which biological processes and environmental conditions influence the brain's development; the brain has plasticity and is context dependent; and cognitive development is closely linked with brain development.

neurogenesis   The generation of new neurons.

neurons   Nerve cells that handle information processing at the cellular level.

nonnormative life events   Unusual occurrences that have a major impact on an individual's life.

normal distribution   A symmetrical, bell-shaped curve with a majority of the cases falling in the middle of the possible range of scores and few scores appearing toward the extremes of the range.

normative age-graded influences   Influences that are similar for individuals in a particular age group.

normative history-graded influences   Influences that are common to people of a particular generation because of historical circumstances.

O

object permanence   The Piagetian term for one of an infant's most important accomplishments: understanding that objects continue to exist even when they cannot directly be seen, heard, or touched.

operations   Reversible mental actions that allow children to do mentally what before they had done only physically.

optimism   A style of thinking that involves having a positive outlook on the future and minimizing problems.

organization   Piagetian concept of grouping isolated behaviors and thoughts into a higher-order, more smoothly functioning cognitive system.

organogenesis   Process of organ formation that takes place during the first two months of prenatal development.

osteoporosis   A disorder that involves an extensive loss of bone tissue and is the main reason many older adults walk with a marked stoop. Women are especially vulnerable to osteoporosis.

P

pain cry   A sudden, initial loud cry followed by breath holding, without preliminary moaning.

palliative care   Emphasized in hospice care; involves reducing pain and suffering and helping individuals die with dignity.

Parkinson disease   A chronic, progressive disease characterized by muscle tremors, slowing of movement, and partial facial paralysis.

passive euthanasia   The withholding of available treatments, such as life-sustaining devices, and allowing the person to die.

passive genotype-environment correlations   Correlations that exist when the biological parents, who are genetically related to the child, provide a rearing environment for the child.

peers   Individuals who share the same age or maturity level.

perception   The interpretation of sensation.

performance orientation   An orientation in which one focuses on winning, rather than on achievement outcome; happiness is thought to result from winning.

perimenopause   The transitional period from normal menstrual periods to no menstrual periods at all, which often takes up to 10 years.

personal fable   The part of adolescent egocentrism that involves an adolescent's sense of personal uniqueness and invincibility.

perspective taking   The ability to assume another person's perspective and understand his or her thoughts and feelings.

phenotype   Observable and measurable characteristics of an individual, such as height, hair color, and intelligence.

phenylketonuria (PKU)   A genetic disorder in which an individual cannot properly metabolize phenylalanine, an amino acid; PKU is now easily detected—but, if left untreated, results in intellectual disability and hyperactivity.

phonics approach   A teaching approach built on the idea that reading instruction should teach basic rules for translating written symbols into sounds.

phonology   The sound system of a language—includes the sounds used and how they may be combined.

physical abuse   Infliction of physical injury by punching, beating, kicking, biting, burning, shaking, or otherwise harming a child.

Piaget's theory   Theory stating that children actively construct their understanding of the world and go through four stages of cognitive development.

pituitary gland   An important endocrine gland that controls growth and regulates the activity of other glands.

play   A pleasurable activity that is engaged in for its own sake.

play therapy   Therapy that lets children work off frustrations while therapists analyze their conflicts and coping methods.

popular children   Children who are frequently nominated as a best friend and are rarely disliked by their peers.

possible selves   What adolescents hope to become as well as what they dread they might become.

postconventional reasoning   The highest level in Kohlberg's theory of moral development. At this level, the individual recognizes alternative moral courses, explores the options, and then decides on a personal moral code.

postformal thought   Thinking that is reflective, relativistic, and contextual; provisional; realistic; and influenced by emotions.

postpartum depression   A major depressive episode that typically occurs about four weeks after delivery; women with this condition have such strong feelings of sadness, anxiety, or despair that they have trouble coping with daily tasks during the postpartum period.

postpartum period   The period after childbirth when the mother adjusts, both physically and psychologically, to the process of childbirth. This period lasts for about six weeks or until her body has completed its adjustment and returned to a near prepregnant state.

practice play   Play that involves repetition of behavior when new skills are being learned or when mastery and coordination of skills are required for games or sports.

pragmatics   The appropriate use of language in different contexts.

preconventional reasoning   The lowest level in Kohlberg's theory of moral development. The individual's moral reasoning is controlled primarily by external rewards and punishments.

prefrontal cortex   The highest level of the frontal lobes that is involved in reasoning, decision making, and self-control.

preoperational stage   The second Piagetian developmental stage, which lasts from about 2 to 7 years of age; children begin to represent the world with words, images, and drawings.

prepared childbirth   Developed by French obstetrician Ferdinand Lamaze, a childbirth strategy similar to natural childbirth but one that teaches a special breathing technique to control pushing in the final stages of labor and provides details about anatomy and physiology.

pretense/symbolic play   Play that occurs when a child transforms aspects of the physical environment into symbols.

preterm infants   Infants born three weeks or more before the pregnancy has reached its full term.

primary emotions   Emotions that are present in humans and other animals, emerge early in life, and are culturally universal; examples are joy, anger, sadness, fear, and disgust.

Project Head Start   Compensatory prekindergarten education designed to provide children from low-income families the opportunity to acquire skills and experiences important for school success.

prospective memory   Remembering to do something in the future.

proximodistal pattern   The sequence in which growth starts at the center of the body and moves toward the extremities.

psychoanalytic theories   Theories that describe development as primarily unconscious and heavily colored by emotion. Behavior is merely a surface characteristic, and the symbolic workings of the mind must be analyzed to understand behavior. Early experiences with parents are emphasized.

psychoanalytic theory of gender   Theory that stems from Freud's view that preschool children develop a sexual attraction to the opposite-sex parent, then at 5 or 6 years of age renounce the attraction because of anxious feelings, subsequently identifying with the same-sex parent and unconsciously adopting the same-sex parent's characteristics.

psychosocial moratorium   Erikson's term for the gap between childhood security and adult autonomy that adolescents experience as part of their identity exploration.

puberty   A brain-neuroendocrine process occurring primarily in early adolescence that provides stimulation for the rapid physical changes that occur in this period of development.

R

rape   Forcible sexual intercourse, oral sex, or anal sex with a person who does not give consent. Legal definitions of rape differ from state to state.

rapport talk   The language of conversation; a way to establish connections and negotiate relationships; preferred by women.

recasting   Involves an adult's rephrasing of a child's statement that might lack the appropriate morphology or contain some other error. The adult restates the child's immature utterance in the form of a fully grammatical sentence.

reciprocal socialization   Socialization that is bidirectional in that children socialize parents just as parents socialize children.

reflexive smile   A smile that does not occur in response to external stimuli. It happens during the month after birth, usually during sleep.

rejected children   Children who are infrequently nominated as a best friend and are actively disliked by their peers.

religion   An organized set of beliefs, practices, rituals, and symbols that increases an individual's connection to a sacred or transcendent other (God, higher power, or higher truth).

religiousness   The degree of affiliation with an organized religion, participation in prescribed rituals and practices, connection with its beliefs, and involvement in a community of believers.

report talk   Language designed to convey information; a communication style preferred by men.

romantic love   Also called passionate love, or eros, this type of love has strong components of sexuality and infatuation, and it often predominates in the early part of a love relationship.

romantic script   A perspective in which sex is synonymous with love; belief that if we develop a relationship with someone and fall in love, it is acceptable to have sex with the person whether we are married or not.

rooting reflex   A newborn's built-in reaction that occurs when the infant's cheek is stroked or the side of the mouth is touched. In response, the infant turns its head toward the side that was touched, in an apparent effort to find something to suck.

S

satire   The use of irony, derision, or wit to expose folly or wickedness.

scaffolding   In cognitive development, a term Vygotsky used to describe the changing level of support over the course of a teaching session, with the more-skilled person adjusting guidance to fit the child's current performance level.

schema theory   Theory stating that people mold memories to fit information that already exists in their minds.

schemas   Mental frameworks that organize concepts and information.

schemes   In Piaget's theory, actions or mental representations that organize knowledge.

secure attachment style   An attachment style that describes adults who have positive views of relationships, find it easy to get close to others, and are not overly concerned or stressed out about their romantic relationships.

securely attached children   Children who use the caregiver as a secure base from which to explore the environment.

selective attention   Focusing on a specific aspect of experience that is relevant while ignoring others that are irrelevant.

selective optimization with compensation theory   The theory that successful aging involves three strategies: selection, optimization, and compensation.

self-concept   Domain-specific evaluations of the self.

self-conscious emotions   Emotions that require consciousness and a sense of "me"; they include empathy, jealousy, embarrassment, pride, shame, and guilt, most of which first appear at some point after 18 months of age when a sense of self becomes consolidated in toddlers.

self-efficacy   The belief that one can master a situation and produce favorable outcomes.

self-esteem   The global evaluative dimension of the self. Self-esteem is also referred to as self-worth or self-image.

self-regulation   The ability to control one's behavior without having to rely on others for help.

self-understanding   The individual's cognitive representation of the self, the substance of self-conceptions.

semantic memory   A person's knowledge about the world, including fields of expertise, general academic knowledge, and "everyday knowledge" about meanings of words, names of famous individuals, important places, and common things.

semantics   The meanings of words and sentences.

sensation   Reaction that occurs when information interacts with sensory receptors—the eyes, ears, tongue, nostrils, and skin.

sensorimotor play   Behavior in which infants derive pleasure from exercising their sensorimotor schemes.

sensorimotor stage   The first of Piaget's stages, which lasts from birth to about 2 years of age, during which infants construct an understanding of the world by coordinating sensory experiences (such as seeing and hearing) with physical, motoric actions.

separation protest   Reaction that occurs when infants experience a fear of being separated from a caregiver, which results in crying when the caregiver leaves.

seriation   The concrete operation that involves ordering stimuli along a quantitative dimension (such as length).

service learning   A form of education that promotes social responsibility and service to the community.

sexual abuse   Fondling a child's genitals, intercourse, incest, rape, sodomy, exhibitionism, and commercial exploitation through prostitution or the production of pornographic materials.

sexual harassment   Sexual persecution that can take many forms—from sexist remarks and physical contact (patting, brushing against someone's body) to blatant propositions and sexual assaults.

sexual scripts   Stereotyped patterns of expectancies for how people should behave sexually.

sexually transmitted infections (STIs)   Diseases that are contracted primarily through sexual contact, including oral-genital contact, anal-genital contact, and vaginal intercourse.

shape constancy   Recognition that an object remains the same even though its orientation to the viewer changes.

short-term memory   Retention of information for up to 15 to 30 seconds, without rehearsal of the information. Using rehearsal, individuals can keep the information in short-term memory longer.

sickle-cell anemia   A genetic disorder that affects the red blood cells and occurs most often in African Americans.

sirtuins   A family of proteins that have been proposed as having important influences on longevity, mitochondrial functioning in energy, calorie restriction benefits, stress resistance, and cardiovascular functioning.

size constancy   Recognition that an object remains the same even though the retinal image of the object changes as the viewer moves toward or away from the object.

slow-to-warm-up child   A temperament style in which the child has a low activity level, is somewhat negative, and displays a low intensity of mood.

small for date infants   Infants whose birth weights are below normal when the length of pregnancy is considered; also called small for gestational age infants. Small for date infants may be preterm or full-term.

social cognitive theory   Theoretical view that behavior, environment, and cognition are the key factors in development.

social cognitive theory of gender   The idea that children's gender development occurs through observation and imitation of gender behavior, as well as through the rewards and punishments children experience for behaviors believed to be appropriate or inappropriate for their gender.

social cognitive theory of morality   The theory that distinguishes between moral competence—the ability to produce moral behaviors—and moral performance—performing those behaviors in specific situations.

social constructivist approach   An emphasis on the social contexts of learning and construction of knowledge through social interaction. Vygotsky's theory reflects this approach.

social conventional reasoning   Focuses on conventional rules established by social consensus and convention, as opposed to moral reasoning, which stresses ethical issues.

social domain theory   Theory that identifies different domains of social knowledge and reasoning, including moral, social conventional, and personal domains. These domains arise from children's and adolescents' attempts to understand and deal with different forms of social experience.

social play   Play that involves interaction with peers.

social policy   A government's course of action designed to promote the welfare of its citizens.

social referencing   "Reading" emotional cues in others to help determine how to act in a specific situation.

social role theory   Eagly's theory that psychological gender differences are caused by the contrasting social roles of women and men.

social smile   A smile in response to an external stimulus, which, early in development, typically is a face.

socioeconomic status (SES)   Classification of a person's position in society based on occupational, educational, and economic characteristics.

socioemotional processes   Processes that involve changes in an individual's relationships with other people, emotions, and personality.

socioemotional selectivity theory   The theory that older adults become more selective about their activities and social relationships in order to maintain emotional well-being.

source memory   The ability to remember where something was learned.

spirituality   Experiencing something beyond oneself in a transcendent manner and living in a way that benefits others and society.

stability-change issue   Debate as to whether and to what degree we become older renditions of our earlier selves (stability) or whether we develop into someone different from who we were at an earlier point in development (change).

standardized test   A test with uniform procedures for administration and scoring. Many standardized tests allow a person's performance to be compared with the performance of other individuals.

stereotype threat   Anxiety regarding whether one's behavior might confirm a negative stereotype about one's group.

Strange Situation   Ainsworth's observational measure of infant attachment to a caregiver that requires the infant to move through a series of introductions, separations, and reunions with the caregiver and an adult stranger in a prescribed order.

stranger anxiety   An infant's fear of and wariness toward strangers; it tends to appear in the second half of the first year of life.

strategy construction   Creation of new procedures for processing information.

sucking reflex   A newborn's reaction of sucking an object placed in its mouth. The sucking reflex enables the infant to get nourishment before it has begun to associate a nipple with food.

sudden infant death syndrome (SIDS)   Condition in which an infant stops breathing, usually during the night, and suddenly dies without an apparent cause.

sustained attention   The ability to maintain attention to a selected stimulus for a prolonged period of time.

symbolic function substage   The first substage of preoperational thought, occurring roughly between the ages of 2 and 4. In this substage, the young child gains the ability to represent mentally an object that is not present.

sympathy   An emotional response to another person in which the observer feels sad or concerned about the person's well-being.

syntax   The ways words are combined to form acceptable phrases and sentences.

T

telegraphic speech   The use of short, precise words without grammatical markers such as articles, auxiliary verbs, and other connectives.

temperament   An individual's behavioral style and characteristic way of responding.

tend and befriend   Taylor's view that when women experience stress, they are more likely to seek social alliances with others, especially female friends.

teratogen   Any agent that can potentially cause a birth defect or negatively alter cognitive and behavioral outcomes.

testosterone   A hormone associated in boys with the development of the genitals, increased height, and voice changes.

theory   An interrelated, coherent set of ideas that helps to explain phenomena and make predictions.

theory of mind   Thoughts about how one's own mental processes work and the mental processes of others.

thinking   Manipulating and transforming information in memory, in order to reason, reflect, think critically, evaluate ideas and solve problems, and make decisions.

top-dog phenomenon   The circumstance of moving from the top position in elementary school to the youngest, smallest, and least powerful position in middle or junior high school.

traditional religious script   View that sex is acceptable only within marriage; extramarital sex is taboo, especially for women; and sex means reproduction and sometimes affection.

trait theories   Theories emphasizing that personality consists of broad dispositions, called traits, which tend to produce characteristic responses.

transgender   A broad term that refers to individuals who adopt a gender identity that differs from the one assigned to them at birth.

transitivity   The ability to logically combine relations to understand certain conclusions. Piaget argued that an understanding of transitivity is characteristic of concrete operational thought.

transsexual Category that describes individuals who choose to live full-time as a member of the desired gender and usually seek to have sex reassignment surgery.

triangular theory of love Sternberg's theory that love includes three components or dimensions—passion, intimacy, and commitment.

triarchic theory of intelligence Sternberg's theory that intelligence consists of analytical intelligence, creative intelligence, and practical intelligence.

Turner syndrome A chromosomal disorder in females in which either an X chromosome is missing, making the person XO instead of XX, or part of one X chromosome is deleted.

twin study A study in which the behavioral similarity of identical twins is compared with the behavioral similarity of fraternal twins.

V

values Beliefs and attitudes about the way things should be.

values clarification A moral education program in which students are helped to clarify their purpose in life and decide what is worth working for. Students are encouraged to define their own values and understand others' values.

visual preference method A method developed by Fantz to determine whether infants can distinguish one stimulus from another by measuring the length of time they attend to different stimuli.

Vygotsky's theory Sociocultural cognitive theory that emphasizes how culture and social interaction guide cognitive development.

W

Wernicke's area An area of the brain's left hemisphere that is involved in language comprehension.

whole-language approach A teaching approach built on the idea that reading instruction should parallel children's natural language learning and that reading materials should be whole and meaningful.

wisdom Expert knowledge about the practical aspects of life that permits excellent judgment about important matters.

working memory A mental "workbench" where individuals manipulate and assemble information when making decisions, solving problems, and comprehending written and spoken language.

X

XYY syndrome A chromosomal disorder in which males have an extra Y chromosome.

Z

zone of proximal development (ZPD) Vygotsky's term for tasks that are too difficult for children to master alone but can be mastered with guidance and assistance from adults or more-skilled children.

zygote A single cell formed through fertilization.

references

A

AAA Foundation (2016, December 6). *Missing 1-2 hours of sleep doubles crash risk.* Washington, DC: AAA Foundation.

Aalsma, M., Lapsley, D.K., & Flannery, D. (2006). Narcissism, personal fables, and adolescent adjustment. *Psychology in the Schools, 43,* 481-491.

Aardema, F., & others (2018). The role of feared possible selves in obsessive-compulsive and related disorders: A comparative analysis of a core cognitive self-construct in clinical samples. *Clinical Psychology and Psychotherapy, 25,* e19-e29.

AARP (2004). *The divorce experience: A study of divorce at midlife and beyond.* Washington, DC: Author.

Abbatecola, A.M., Russo, M., & Barbieri, M. (2018). Dietary patterns and cognition in older persons. *Current Opinion in Clinical Nutrition and Metabolic Care, 21,* 10-13.

Abbott, A. (2003). Restless nights, listless days. *Nature, 425,* 896-898.

ABC News (2005, December 12). Larry Page and Sergey Brin. Retrieved June 24, 2006, from www.Montessori.org/enews/barbaraWalters.html

Aben, B., & others (2019, in press). Context-dependent modulation of cognitive control involves different temporal profiles of fronto-parietal activity. *NeuroImage.*

Abrahamse, M.E., Jonkman, C.S., & Harting, J. (2018). A school-based interdisciplinary approach to promote health and academic achievement among children in a deprived neighborhood: Study protocol for a mixed-methods evaluation. *BMC Public Health, 18,* 465.

Abrahamson, K., Davila, H., & Hountz, D. (2019, in press). Involving nursing assistants in nursing home QI. *American Journal of Nursing.*

Abulizi, X., & others (2017). Temperament in infancy and behavioral and emotional problems at age 5.5: The EDEN mother-child cohort. *PLoS One, 12*(2), 0171971.

Abu-Rayya, H.M., & others (2018). Comparative associations between achieved bicultural identity, achieved ego identity, and achieved religious identity and adaptation among Australian adolescent Muslims. *Psychological Reports, 12,* 324-333.

Accornero, V.H., & others (2007). Impact of prenatal cocaine exposure on attention and response inhibition as assessed by continuous performance tests. *Journal of Developmental and Behavioral Pediatrics, 28,* 195-205.

Acedera, K.A., & Yeoh, B.S. (2019). 'Making time': Long-distance marriages and the temporalities of the transnational family. *Current Sociology, 67,* 250-272.

Achenbach, T.M. (1997). What is normal? What is abnormal? Developmental perspectives on behavioral and emotional problems. In S.S. Luthar, J.A. Burack, D. Cicchetti, & J.R. Weisz (Eds.), *Developmental psychopathology: Perspectives on adjustment, risk, and disorder.* New York: Cambridge University Press.

Ackerman, J.P., Riggins, T., & Black, M.M. (2010). A review of the effects of prenatal cocaine exposure among school-aged children. *Pediatrics, 125,* 554-565.

Ackerman, R.A., & others (2013). The interpersonal legacy of a positive family climate in adolescence. *Psychological Science, 24,* 243-250.

Acosta, J., & others (2019, in press). Evaluation of a whole-school change intervention: Findings from a two-year cluster-randomized trial of restorative practices intervention. *Journal of Youth and Adolescence.*

Adair, L.S., Duazo, P., & Borja, J.B. (2019, in press). How overweight and obesity relate to the development of functional limitations among Filipino women. *Geriatrics.*

Adams, G.C., & McWilliams, L.A. (2015). Relationships between adult attachment style ratings and sleep disturbances in a nationally representative sample. *Journal of Psychosomatic Research, 79,* 37-42.

Adams, J.C. (2009). Immunocytochemical traits of type IV fibrocytes and their possible relation to cochlear function and pathology. *Journal of the Association for Research in Otolaryngology, 10,* 369-382.

Adams, K.A., & others (2018). Caregiver talk and medical risk as predictors of language outcomes in full term and preterm toddlers. *Child Development, 89,* 1674-1690.

Adamson, L., & Frick, J. (2003). The still face: A history of a shared experimental paradigm. *Infancy, 4,* 451-473.

Administration on Aging (2018). *A profile of older Americans: 2017.* Washington, DC: U.S. Department of Health and Human Services.

Adolescent Sleep Working Group, AAP (2014). School start times for adolescents. *Pediatrics, 134,* 642-649.

Adolph, K.E. (1997). Learning in the development of infant locomotion. *Monographs of the Society for Research in Child Development, 62*(3, Serial No. 251).

Adolph, K.E. (2018). Motor development. In M.H. Bornstein (Ed.), *SAGE encyclopedia of lifespan human development.* Thousand Oaks, CA: Sage.

Adolph, K.E., & Berger, S.E. (2015). Physical and motor development. In M.H. Bornstein & M.E. Lamb (Eds.), *Developmental science* (7th ed.). New York: Psychology Press.

Adolph, K.E., Cole, W.G., & Vereijken, B. (2015). Intra-individual variability in the development of motor skills in childhood. In M. Diehl, K. Hooker, & M.J. Sliwinski (Eds.), *Handbook of intraindividual variability across the life span.* New York: Routledge.

Adolph, K.E., & Hoch, J.E. (2019). Motor development: Embodied, embedded, enculturated, and enabling. *Annual Review of Psychology* (Vol. 70). Palo Alto, CA: Annual Reviews.

Adolph, K.E., Hoch, J.E., & Cole, W.G. (2018). Development of walking: 15 suggestions. *Trends in Cognitive Science, 22,* 699-711.

Adolph, K.E., Karasik, L.B., & Tamis-LeMonda, C.S. (2010). Moving between cultures: Cross-cultural research on motor development. In M. Bornstein & L.R. Cote (Eds.), *Handbook of cross-cultural developmental science, Vol. 1: Domains of development across cultures.* Clifton, NJ: Psychology Press.

Adolph, K.E., & Kretch, K.S. (2015). Gibson's theory of perceptual learning. In J.D. Wright (Ed.), *International encyclopedia of the social and behavioral sciences* (2nd ed.). New York: Elsevier.

Adolph, K.E., Rachwani, J., & Hock, J.E. (2019, in press). Motor and physical development: Locomotion. *Neuroscience and Biobehavioral Psychology.*

Adolph, K.E., & Robinson, S.R. (2015). Motor development. In R.M. Lerner (Ed.), *Handbook of child psychology and developmental science* (7th ed.). New York: Wiley.

Adolph, K.E., & others (2012). How do you learn to walk? Thousands of steps and dozens of falls per day. *Psychological Science, 23*(11), 1387-1394.

Affleck, W., Carmichael, V., & Whitley, R. (2018). Men's mental health: Social determinants and its implications for services. *Canadian Journal of Psychiatry, 63,* 581-589.

Afifi, T.O., & others (2017a). Spanking and adult mental health impairment: The case for the designation of spanking as an adverse childhood experience. *Child Abuse and Neglect, 11,* 24-31.

Afifi, T.O., & others (2017b). The relationships between harsh physical punishment and child maltreatment in childhood and intimate partner violence in adulthood. *BMC Public Health, 17*(1), 493.

Afsharnia, E., Pakgohar, M., Haghani, H., Sarani, A., & Khosravi, S. (2019, in press). The severity of hypogonadism symptoms and its risk factors among male employees of Tehran University of Medical Sciences. *Aging Male.*

Agency for Healthcare Research and Quality (2007). *Evidence report/Technology assessment number 153: Breastfeeding and maternal and infant health outcomes in developed countries.* Rockville, MD: U.S. Department of Health and Human Services.

Aghdam, M.A., Sharifi, A., & Pedram, M.M. (2019, in press). Diagnosis of autism spectrum disorders in young children based on resting-state functional magnetic resonance imaging data using convolutional neural networks. *Journal of Digital Imaging.*

Agostini, A., & others (2017). An experimental study of adolescent sleep restriction during a simulated school week: Changes in phase, sleep staging, performance, and sleepiness. *Journal of Sleep Research, 26.* 227-235.

Agricola, E., & others (2016). Investigating paternal preconception risk factors for adverse pregnancy outcomes in a population of Internet users. *Reproductive Health, 13,* 37.

Agrigoroaei, S., & others (2019). Cognition at midlife: Antecedents and consequences. In C.D. Ryff & R.F. Krueger (Eds.), *Oxford handbook of integrated health science.* New York: Oxford University Press.

Ahern, E., Kowalski, M., & Lamb, M.E. (2018). A case study perspective: The experiences of young persons testifying to child sexual exploitation in British Criminal Court. *Journal of Child Sexual Abuse, 28,* 321-334.

Ahern, E., Van Meter, F., & Lamb, M.E. (2019, in press). A macro-coding perspective: Interviewer support and child comfort in investigative interviews with young alleged victims of sexual abuse. *Children and Youth Services Review.*

Ahlfors, S.P., & Mody, M. (2019). Overview of MEG. *Organic Research Methods, 22*, 95–115.

Ahluwalia, H., Anand, T., & Suman, L.N. (2018). Marital and family therapy. *Indian Journal of Psychiatry, 60*(Suppl. 4), S501–S505.

Ahluwalia, M.K., & Mohabir, R.K. (2019). Turning to Waheguru: Religious and cultural coping mechanism of bereaved Sikhs. *Omega, 78*, 302–313.

Ahmadi, M., Golalipour, M., & Samaei, N.M. (2019, in press). Mitochondrial common deletion in blood: New insight into the effects of age and body mass index. *Current Aging Science.*

Ahrens, C.E., & Aldana, E. (2012). The ties that bind: Understanding the impact of sexual assault disclosure on survivors' relationships with friends, family, and partners. *Journal of Trauma & Dissociation, 13*, 226–243.

Ahrons, C.R. (2007). Family ties after divorce: Long-term implications for children. *Family Process, 46*, 53–65.

Ahun, M.N., Aboud, F.E., Aryeetey, R., Colecraft, E., & Marquis, G.S. (2018). Child development in rural Ghana: Associations between cognitive/language milestones and indicators of nutrition and stimulation of children under two years of age. *Canadian Journal of Public Health, 108*, e578–e585.

Aichele, S., Rabbitt, P., & Ghisletta, P. (2015). Life span decrements in fluid intelligence and processing speed predict mortality risk. *Psychology and Aging, 30*, 598–612.

Aiken Morgan, A., Sims, R.C., & Whitfield, K.E. (2010). Cardiovascular health and education as sources of individual variability in cognitive aging among African Americans. *Journal of Aging and Health, 22*(4), 477–503.

Ainsworth, M.D.S. (1979). Infant-mother attachment. *American Psychologist, 34*, 932–937.

Akers, K.G., & others (2018). Regulatory influence of sleep and epigenetics on adult hippocampal neurogenesis and cognitive and emotional function. *Stem Cells, 36*, 969–976.

Akhter, R., & Bekris, L.M. (2019, in press). Potential role of miRNA-140 in Alzheimer's disease. *Aging.*

Akhutina, T., & Romanova, A. (2017). Games as a tool for facilitating cognitive development. In T. Bruce & others (Eds.), *Routledge international handbook of early childhood play.* New York: Routledge.

Akinsola, E.F., & Petersen, A.C. (2018). Adolescent development and capacity building. In J.E. Lansford & P. Banati (Eds.), *Handbook of adolescent development research and its impact on global policy.* New York: Oxford University Press.

Aksgaede, L., & others (2013). 47, XXY Klinefelter syndrome: Clinical characteristics and age-specific recommendations for medical management. *American Journal of Medical Genetics C: Seminars in Medical Genetics, 163*, 55–63.

Al-Ali, N.M., & others (2018). Parents' knowledge and beliefs about the impact of exposure to media violence on children's aggression. *Issues in Mental Health Nursing, 39*, 592–599.

Alattar, A.A., & others (2019, in press). Hearing impairment and cognitive decline in older, community-dwelling adults. *Journals of Gerontology A: Biological Sciences and Medical Sciences.*

Albert, D., & Steinberg, L. (2011a). Judgment and decision making in adolescence. *Journal of Research on Adolescence, 21*, 211–224.

Albert, D., & Steinberg, L. (2011b). Peer influences on adolescent risk behavior. In M. Bardo, D. Fishbein, & R. Milich (Eds.), *Inhibitory control and drug abuse prevention: From research to translation.* New York: Springer.

Albert, R.R., Schwade, J.A., & Goldstein, M.H. (2019, in press). The social functions of babbling: Acoustic and contextual characteristics that facilitate maternal responsiveness. *Developmental Science.*

Alberto, P.A., & Troutman, A.C. (2017). *Applied behavior analysis for teachers* (9th ed.). Upper Saddle River, NJ: Pearson.

Aldercotte, A., White, N., & Hughes, C. (2016). Sibling and peer relationships in early childhood. In L. Balter & C.S. Tamis-Lemonda (Eds.), *Child psychology* (3rd ed.). New York: Routledge.

Alegret, M., & others (2014). Cognitive, genetic, and brain perfusion factors associated with four-year incidence of Alzheimer's disease from mild cognitive impairment. *Journal of Alzheimer's Disease, 41*, 739–748.

Alexander, C.P., & others (2017). Fathers make a difference: Positive relationships with mother and baby in relation to infant colic. *Child Care, Health, and Development, 43*, 687–696.

Alexopoulos, G.S., & Kelly, R.E. (2017). Late-life depression: Translating neurobiological hypotheses into novel treatments. In R. Cabeza, L. Nyberg, & D.C. Park (Eds.), *Cognitive neuroscience of aging* (2nd ed.). New York: Oxford University Press.

Alfredsson, J., & others (2018). Sex differences in management and outcomes of patients with type 2 diabetes and cardiovascular disease: A report from TECOS. *Diabetes, Obesity, and Metabolism, 20*, 2379–2388.

Al-Ghanim, K.A. & Badahdah, A.M. (2017). Gender roles in the Arab world: Development and psychometric properties of the Arab Adolescents Gender Roles Attitude Scale. *Sex Roles, 77*, 169–177

Alibali, M.W., Brown, S.A., & Menendez, D. (2019). Understanding strategy change: Contextual, individual, and metacognitive factors. *Advances in Child Development and Behavior, 56*, 227–256.

Alladi, S., & others (2013). Bilingualism delays age of onset of dementia, independent of education and immigration status. *Neurology, 81*, 1938–1944.

Allemand, M., Steiger, A.E., & Fend, H.A. (2015). Empathy development in adolescence predicts social competencies in adulthood. *Journal of Personality, 83*, 229–241.

Allen, A.P., & others (2018). Autobiographical memory, the aging brain, and mechanisms of psychological interventions. *Aging Research Reviews, 42*, 100–111.

Allen, J.O. (2016). Ageism as a risk factor for chronic disease. *Gerontologist, 56*, 610–614.

Allen, J.P., Forster, M., Neiberger, A., & Unger, J.B. (2015). Characteristics of emerging adulthood and e-cigarette use: Findings from a pilot study. *Addictive Behaviors, 50*, 40–44.

Allen, J.P., & Miga, E.M. (2010). Attachment in adolescence: A move to the next level of emotion regulation. *Journal of Social and Personal Relationships, 27*, 181–190.

Allen, J.P., Philliber, S., Herring, S., & Kuperminc, G.P. (1997). Preventing teen pregnancy and academic failure: Experimental evaluation of a developmentally-based approach. *Child Development, 68*, 729–742.

Allen, J.P., & others (2009, April). *Portrait of the secure teen as an adult.* Paper presented at the meeting of the Society for Research in Child Development, Denver.

Allen, J.P., & others (2019, in press). Adolescent peer relationship qualities as predictors of long-term romantic life satisfaction. *Child Development.*

Allen, K., & Goldman-Mellor, S. (2018). Neighborhood characteristics and adolescent suicidal behavior: Evidence from a population-based study. *Suicide and Life-Threatening Behavior, 48*, 677–689.

Allen, K.D., & others (2018). Physical therapy vs internet-based exercise training for patients with knee osteoarthritis: Results of a randomized controlled trial. *Osteoarthritis and Cartilage, 26*, 383–396.

Allen, M., & others (2017). Metacognitive ability correlates with hippocampal and prefrontal microstructure. *NeuroImage, 149*, 415–423.

Allen, T.D., & Finkelstein, L.M. (2014). Work-family conflict among members of full-time dual-earner couples: An examination of family life stage, gender, and age. *Journal of Occupational Health Psychology, 19*, 376–384.

Allik, J., & Realo, A. (2019). Culture and personality. In D. Matsumoto & H.C. Hwang (Eds.), *Handbook of cross-cultural psychology* (2nd ed.). New York: Oxford University Press.

Allstate Foundation (2005). *Chronic: A report on the state of teen driving.* Northbrook, IL: Author.

Alm, B., Wennergren, G., Mollborg, P., & Lagercrantz, H. (2016). Breastfeeding and dummy use have a protective effect on sudden infant death syndrome. *Acta Pediatrica, 105*, 31–38.

Almandil, N.B., & others (2019, in press). Environmental and genetic factors in autism spectrum disorders: Special emphasis on data from Arabic studies. *International Journal of Environmental Research and Public Health.*

Almeida, D.M., & Horn, M.C. (2004). Is daily life more stressful during middle adulthood? In C.D. Ryff & R.C. Kessler (Eds.), *A portrait of midlife in the United States.* Chicago: University of Chicago Press.

Almeida, M.J. (2018). *Approved drugs for Alzheimer's disease.* Retrieved March 1, 2018, from https://alzheimersnewstoday.com/alzheimers-disease-treatment/approved-drugs/

Almeida, N.D., & others (2016). Risk of miscarriage in women receiving antidepressants in early pregnancy, correcting for induced abortions. *Epidemiology, 27*, 538–546.

Almeida-Filho, D.G., Queiroz, C.M., & Ribeiro, S. (2018). Memory corticalization triggered by REM sleep: Mechanisms of cellular and systems consolidation. *Cellular and Molecular Life Sciences, 75*, 3715–3740.

Almquist, Y.B., & Brannstrom, L. (2014). Childhood peer status and the clustering of social, economic, and health-related circumstances in adulthood. *Social Science & Medicine, 105*, 67–75.

Almy, B., & Cicchetti, D. (2018). Developmental cascades. In M.H. Bornstein (Ed.), *SAGE encyclopedia of lifespan human development.* Thousand Oaks, CA: Sage.

Alonso-Fernandez, M., & others (2016). Acceptance and commitment therapy and selective optimization with compensation for institutionalized older people with chronic pain. *Pain Medicine, 17*, 264–277.

Altman, C., Goldstein, T., & Amon-Lotem, S. (2018). Vocabulary, metalinguistic awareness, and language dominance among bilingual preschool children. *Frontiers in Psychology, 9,* 1953.

Alvaro, J.L., & others (2019). Unemployment, self-esteem, and depression: Differences between men and women. *Spanish Journal of Psychology, 22,* E1.

Alzheimer's Association (2018). *Alzheimer's disease facts and figures.* Chicago: Author.

Alzheimer's Association (2019). *Help & support.* Chicago: Author.

Amabile, T.M. (1993). (Commentary). In D. Goleman, P. Kaufman, & M. Ray (Eds.), *The creative spirit.* New York: Plume.

Amabile, T.M. (2018). Creativity and the labor of love. In R.J. Sternberg & J.C. Kaufman (Eds.), *The nature of human creativity.* New York: Cambridge University Press.

Amabile, T.M., & Hennessey, B.A. (1992). The motivation for creativity in children. In A.K. Boggiano & T.S. Pittman (Eds.), *Achievement and motivation.* New York: Cambridge University Press.

Amador, S., & others (2019). A systematic review and critical appraisal of quality indicators to assess optimal palliative care for older people with dementia. *Palliative Medicine, 33,* 415–429.

Amani, B., & others (2018). Families and the juvenile justice system: Considerations for family-based interventions. *Family and Community Health, 41,* 55–63.

Amare, A.T., & others (2019, in press). Bivariate genome-wide association analyses of the broad depression phenotype combined with major depressive disorder, bipolar disorder or schizophrenia reveal eight novel genetic loci for depression. *Molecular Psychiatry.*

Amato, P.R. (2006). Marital discord, divorce, and children's well-being: Results from a 20-year longitudinal study of two generations. In A. Clarke-Stewart & J. Dunn (Eds.), *Families count.* New York: Cambridge University Press.

Amato, P.R. (2010). Research on divorce: Continuing trends and new developments. *Journal of Marriage and the Family, 72*(3), 650–666.

Amato, P.R., & Anthony, C.J. (2014). Estimating the effects of parental divorce and death with fixed effects models. *Journal of Marriage and the Family, 76,* 370–386.

Amato, P.R., & Booth, A. (1996). A prospective study of divorce and parent-child relationships. *Journal of Marriage and the Family, 58,* 356–365.

Amato, P.R., Booth, A., Johnson, D.R., & Rogers, S.J. (2007). *Alone together: How marriage in America is changing.* Cambridge, MA: Harvard University Press.

Ambrose, D., & Sternberg, R.J. (2016). *Giftedness and talent in the 21st century.* Rotterdam, The Netherlands: Sense Publishers.

American Academy of Pediatrics (2001). Committee on Public Education: Children, adolescents, and television. *Pediatrics, 107,* 423–426.

American Academy of Pediatrics (2010). Policy statement—sexuality, contraception, and the media. *Pediatrics, 126,* 576–582.

American Academy of Pediatrics (2016). *American Association of Pediatrics announces new recommendations for children's media use.* Elk Grove Village, IL: AAP.

American Academy of Pediatrics Section on Breastfeeding (2012). Breastfeeding and the use of human milk. *Pediatrics, 129,* e827–e841.

American Association of University Women (1992). *How schools shortchange girls: A study of major findings on girls and education.* Washington, DC: Author.

American Association of University Women (2006). *Drawing the line: Sexual harassment on campus.* Washington, DC: Author.

American Cancer Society (2018). *Menopausal hormone therapy and cancer risk.* Retrieved February 22, 2018, from www.cancer.org

American Psychiatric Association (2013). *Diagnostic and statistical manual of mental disorders,* 5th ed. (DSM-V). Washington, DC: Author.

American Psychological Association (2003). *Psychology: Scientific problem solvers.* Washington, DC: Author.

American Psychological Association (2019). *Education and socioeconomic status.* Retrieved April 19, 2019, from www.apa.org/pi/ses/resources/publications/education

American Society for Reproductive Medicine & others (2019). Prepregnancy counseling: Committee opinion No. 762. *Fertility and Sterility, 111,* 32–42.

Amodeo, G., & others (2019, in press). Pharmacotherapeutic strategies for treating binge eating disorder. Evidence from clinical trials and implications for clinical practice. *Expert Opinion on Pharmacotherapy.*

Amole, M.C., Cvranowksi, J.M., Wright, A.G., & Swartz, H.A. (2017). Depression impacts the physiological responsiveness of mother-daughter dyads during interaction. *Depression and Anxiety, 34,* 118–126.

Amorim, M. (2019). Are grandparents a blessing or a burden? Multigenerational coresidence and child-related spending. *Social Science Research, 80,* 132–144.

Amso, D., & Johnson, S.P. (2010). Building object knowledge from perceptual input. In B. Hood & L. Santos (Eds.), *The origins of object knowledge.* New York: Oxford University Press.

Amsterdam, B.K. (1968). *Mirror behavior in children under two years of age.* Unpublished doctoral dissertation, University of North Carolina, Chapel Hill.

Amuedo-Durantes, C., & Arenas-Arroyo, E. (2019). Immigration enforcement and children's living arrangements. *Journal of Policy Analysis and Management, 38,* 11–40.

An, R., & others (2019). Dietary habits and cognitive impairment risk among oldest-old Chinese. *Journals of Gerontology B: Psychological Sciences and Social Sciences, 74,* 474–483.

Anastasi, A., & Urbina, S. (1996). *Psychological testing* (7th ed.). Upper Saddle River, NJ: Prentice-Hall.

Andel, R., Finkel, D., & Pedersen, N.L. (2016). Effects of preretirement work complexity and postretirement leisure activity on cognitive aging. *Journals of Gerontology B: Psychological Sciences and Social Sciences, 71,* 849–856.

Anderman, E.M., & Murdock, T.B. (Eds.). (2007). *Psychology of academic cheating.* San Diego: Academic Press.

Andersen, I.G., Holm, J.C., & Homoe, P. (2019, in press). Obstructive sleep apnea in children and adolescents with and without obesity. *European Archives of Otorhinolaryngology.*

Andersen, S.L., Sebastiani, P., Dworkis, D.A., Feldman, L., & Perls, T.T. (2012). Health span approximates life span among many supercentenarians: Compression of morbidity at the approximate limit of life span. *Journals of Gerontology A: Biological Sciences and Medical Sciences, 67,* 395–405.

Anderson, A.J., Sanchez, B., & McMahon, S.D. (2019). Natural mentoring, academic motivation, and values toward education among Latinx adolescents. *American Journal of Community Psychology, 63,* 99–109.

Anderson, C.A., & others (2018). Screen violence and youth behavior. *Pediatrics, 140*(Suppl. 2), S142–S147.

Anderson, D.G., & others (2019). Emerging differences between Huntington's disease-like 2 and Huntington's disease: A comparison using MRI brain volumetry. *NeuroImage Clinics, 21,* 101666.

Anderson, E.R., & Greene, S.M. (2011). "My child and I are a package deal": Balancing adult and child concerns in repartnering after divorce. *Journal of Family Psychology, 25,* 741–750.

Anderson, E.R., Greene, S.M., Hetherington, E.M., & Clingempeel, W.G. (1999). The dynamics of parental remarriage. In E.M. Hetherington (Ed.), *Coping with divorce, single parenting, and remarriage.* Mahwah, NJ: Erlbaum.

Anderson, M.A. (2017, May 17). *Technology use among seniors.* Washington, DC: Pew Research Center.

Anderson, P.A. (2006). The evolution of biological sex differences in communication. In K. Dindia & D.J. Canary (Eds.), *Sex differences and similarities in communication.* Mahwah, NJ: Erlbaum.

Anderson, S.E., Gooze, R.A., Lemeshow, S., & Whitaker, R.C. (2012). Quality of early maternal-child relationship and risk of adolescent obesity. *Pediatrics, 129,* 132–140.

Anderson, S.L., Zheng, Y., & McMahon, R.J. (2018). Do callous-unemotional traits and conduct disorder symptoms predict the onset and development of adolescent substance use? *Child Psychiatry and Human Development., 49,* 688–698.

Anderson, S.L., & others (2019). Reduced prevalence and incidence of cognitive impairment among centenarian offspring. *Journals of Gerontology A: Biological Sciences and Medical Sciences, 74,* 108–113.

Anderson-Hall, U.K., & others (2019, in press). Maternal obesity and gestational diabetes mellitus affect body composition through infancy: The PONCH study. *Pediatric Research.*

Andersson, G., Borgquist, S., & Jirstrom, K. (2018). Hormonal factors and pancreatic cancer risk in women: The Malmo Diet and Cancer Study. *International Journal of Cancer, 143,* 152–162.

Andersson, H., & Bergman, L.R. (2011). The role of task persistence in young adolescence for successful educational and occupational attainment in middle adulthood. *Developmental Psychology, 47,* 950–960.

Andescavage, N.N., & others (2017). Complex trajectories of brain development in the healthy human fetus. *Cerebral Cortex, 27,* 5274–5283.

Andrew, N., & Meeks, S. (2018). Fulfilled preferences, perceived control, life satisfaction, and loneliness in elderly long-term care residents. *Aging and Mental Health, 22,* 183–189.

Andrews, S.J., & Lamb, M.E. (2017). The structural linguistic complexity of lawyers' questions and children's responses in Scottish criminal courts. *Child Abuse and Neglect, 65,* 182–193.

Andries, M., & others (2018). Affordance equivalences in robotics: A formalism. *Frontiers in Neurobiology, 12,* 26.

Angel, J.L., Mudrazija, S., & Benson, R. (2016). Racial and ethnic inequalities in health. In L.K. George & K.F. Ferraro (Eds.), *Handbook of aging and the social sciences* (8th ed.). New York: Elsevier.

Angel, L., Fay, S., Bouazzaoui, B., & Isingrini, M. (2011). Two hemispheres for better memory in old age: Role of executive functioning. *Journal of Cognitive Neuroscience, 23,* 3767-3777.

Angelone, D.J., Mitchell, D., & Smith, D. (2018). The influence of gender ideology, victim resistance, and spiking a drink on acquaintance rape attributions. *Journal of Interpersonal Violence, 33,* 3186-3210.

Anglin, D.M., & others (2018). Ethnic identity, racial discrimination, and attenuated psychotic symptoms in an urban population of emerging adults. *Early Intervention in Psychiatry, 12,* 380-390.

Anguera, J.A., & others (2013). Video game training enhances cognitive control in older adults. *Nature, 501,* 97-101.

Anguiano, R.M. (2018). Language brokering among Latino immigrant families: Moderating variables and youth outcomes. *Journal of Youth and Adolescence, 47,* 222-242.

Ansari, A. (2015). *Modern romance.* New York: Penguin.

Ansari, A., & Gershoff, E. (2016). Parent involvement in Head Start and children's development: Indirect effects through parenting. *Journal of Marriage and the Family, 78,* 562-579.

Ansary, N.S., McMahon, T.J., & Luthar, S.S. (2012). Socioeconomic context and emotional-behavioral achievement links: Concurrent and prospective associations among low- and high-income youth. *Journal of Research on Adolescence, 22,* 14-30.

Ansary, N.S., McMahon, T.J., & Luthar, S.S. (2017). Trajectories of emotional-behavioral difficulty and academic competence: A 6-year, person-centered prospective study of affluent suburban adolescents. *Development and Psychopathology, 29,* 215-234.

Anson, E., Thompson, E., Odle, B.L., Jeka, J., Walls, Z.F., & Panus, P.C. (2018). Influences of age, obesity, and adverse drug effects on balance and mobility testing scores in ambulatory older adults. *Journal of Geriatric Physical Therapy, 41,* 218-229.

Anson, E., & others (2017). Loss of peripheral sensory function explains much of the increase in postural sway in healthy older adults. *Frontiers in Aging Neuroscience, 9,* 202.

Anspach, D. (2017). *Average retirement age in the United States.* Retrieved March 30, 2017, from www. thebalance.com

Antfolk, J. (2019, in press). Age limits. *Evolutionary Psychology.*

Antonenko, D., & Floel, A. (2014). Healthy aging by staying selectively connected: A mini-review. *Gerontology, 60*(1), 3-9.

Antoniou, M., & Wright, S.M. (2017). Uncovering the mechanisms responsible for why language learning may promote healthy cognitive aging. *Frontiers in Psychology, 8,* 2217.

Antonucci, L.A., & others (2018). Attachment style: The neurobiological substrate, interaction with genetics, and role in neurodevelopmental disorder risk pathways. *Neuroscience and Biobehavioral Reviews, 95,* 515-527.

Antonucci, T.C., Vandewater, E.A., & Lansford, J.E. (2000). Adulthood and aging: Social processes and development. In A. Kazdin (Ed.), *Encyclopedia of psychology.* New York: American Psychological Association and Oxford University Press.

Antonucci, T.C., & Webster, N.J. (2019). Involvement with life and social networks: A pathway to successful aging. In R. Fernandez-Ballesteros, A. Benetos, &

J-M. Robine (Eds.), *Cambridge handbook of successful aging.* New York: Cambridge University Press.

Antonucci, T.C., & others (2016). Society and the individual at the dawn of the twenty-first century. In K.W. Schaie & S.L. Willis (Eds.), *Handbook of the psychology of aging* (8th ed.). New York: Elsevier.

Antovich, D.M., & Graf Estes, K. (2019, in press). Learning across languages: Bilingual experience supports dual language statistical word segmentation. *Developmental Science.*

Aoki, K., Sakuma, M., & Endo, N. (2018). The impact of exercise and vitamin D supplementation on physical function in community-dwelling elderly individuals: A randomized trial. *Journal of Orthopedic Sciences, 23,* 682-687.

Apostolo, J., & others (2016). The effectiveness of nonpharmacological interventions in older adults with depressive disorders: A systematic review. *JBI Database of Systematic Reviews and Implementation Reports, 13,* 220-278.

Apter, D. (2018). Contraception options: Aspects unique to adolescent and young adult. *Best Practices and Research: Clinical Obstetrics and Gynecology, 48,* 115-127.

Aquino, K., & Kay, A. (2018). A social cognitive model of moral identity. In K. Gray & J. Graham (Eds.), *Atlas of moral psychology.* New York: Guilford.

Aquino, K., & Reed, A. (2002). The self-importance of moral identity. *Journal of Personality and Social Psychology, 83,* 1423-1440.

Arabi, A.M.E., & others (2018). Perinatal outcomes following Helping Babies Breathe training and regular peer-peer skills practice among village midwives in Sudan. *Archives of Disease in Childhood, 103,* 24-27.

Archer, J.A., Lee, A., Qui, A., & Chen, S.H. (2016). A comprehensive analysis of connectivity and aging over the adult lifespan. *Brain Connectivity, 6,* 169-185.

Arcury, T.A., & others (2019, in press). Older adult Internet use and eHealth literacy. *Journal of Applied Gerontology.*

Ardelt, M. (2010). Are older adults wiser than college students? A comparison of two age cohorts. *Journal of Adult Development, 17,* 193-207.

Ardelt, M., Gerlach, K.R., & Vaillant, G.E. (2018). Early and midlife predictors of wisdom and subjective well-being in old age. *Journals of Gerontology B: Psychological Sciences and Social Sciences, 73,* 1514-1525.

Ardelt, M., & Jeste, D.V. (2018). Wisdom and hard times: The ameliorating effect of wisdom on the negative association between adverse life events and well-being. *Journals of Gerontology B: Psychological Sciences and Social Sciences, 73,* 1374-1383.

Ardelt, M., Pridgen, S., & Nutter-Pridgen, K.L. (2018). The relation between age and three-dimensional wisdom: Variations by wisdom dimensions and education. *Journals of Gerontology B: Psychological Sciences and Social Sciences, 73,* 1339-1349.

Aremu, T.A., John-Akinola, Y.O., & Desmennu, A.T. (2019). Relationship between parenting styles and adolescents' self-esteem. *International Quarterly of Community Health Education, 39,* 91-99.

Ariceli, G., Castro, J., Cesena, J., & Toro, J. (2005). Anorexia nervosa in male adolescents: Body image, eating attitudes, and psychological traits. *Journal of Adolescent Health, 36,* 221-226.

Armstrong, N.M., & others (2019, in press). Temporal sequence of hearing impairment and cognition in the

Baltimore Longitudinal Study of Aging. *Journals of Gerontology A: Biological Sciences and Medical Sciences.*

Arnett, J.J. (2006). Emerging adulthood: Understanding the new way of coming of age. In J.J. Arnett & J.L. Tanner (Eds.), *Emerging adults in America.* Washington, DC: American Psychological Association.

Arnett, J.J. (2007). Socialization in emerging adulthood. In J.E. Grusec & P.D. Hastings (Eds.), *Handbook of socialization.* New York: Guilford.

Arnett, J.J. (Ed.) (2012). *Adolescent psychology around the world.* New York: Psychology Press.

Arnett, J.J. (2014). *Getting to 30: A parent's guide to the 20-something years.* New York: Workman.

Arnett, J.J. (2015a). *Emerging adulthood* (2nd ed.). New York: Oxford University Press.

Arnett, J.J. (2015b). Socialization in emerging adulthood. In J.E. Grusec & P.D. Hastings (Eds.), *Handbook of socialization* (2nd ed.). New York: Guilford.

Arnett, J.J. (2016). Identity development from adolescence to emerging adulthood: What we know and (especially) don't know. In K.C. McLean & M. Syed (Eds.), *The Oxford handbook of identity development.* New York: Oxford University Press.

Arnett, J.J. (2016a). Does emerging adulthood theory apply across social classes? National data on a persistent question. *Emerging Adulthood, 4,* 227-235.

Arnett, J.J. (2016b). Emerging adulthood and social class: Rejoinder to Furstenberg, Silva, and du Bois-Reymond. *Emerging Adulthood, 4,* 244-247.

Arnett, J.J., & Fischel, E. (2013). *When will my grown-up kid grow up?* New York: Workman.

Arns, M., & Vollebreght, M.A. (2019, in press). Editorial: Time to wake up: Appreciating the role of sleep in ADHD. *Journal of the American Academy of Child and Adolescent Psychiatry.*

Aron, A., Coups, E.J., & Aron, E.N. (2019). *Statistics for psychology, brief course* (6th ed.). Upper Saddle River, NJ: Pearson.

Aronson, E. (1986, August). *Teaching students things they think they already know about: The case of prejudice and desegregation.* Paper presented at the meeting of the American Psychological Association, Washington, DC.

Aronson, J. (2002). Stereotype threat: Contending and coping with unnerving expectations. *Improving academic achievement.* San Diego: Academic Press.

Arpanantikul, M. (2004). Midlife experiences of Thai women. *Journal of Advanced Nursing, 47,* 49-56.

Arriaga, X.B., & others (2018). Revising working models across time: Relationship situations that enhance attachment security. *Personality and Social Psychology Review, 22,* 71-96.

Ary, D., & others (2019). *Introduction to research in education* (10th ed.). Boston: Cengage.

Asendorpf, J.B. (2008). Shyness. In M.M. Haith & J.B. Benson (Eds.), *Encyclopedia of infant and early childhood development.* Oxford, UK: Elsevier.

Asghari, M., & others (2017). Effect of aerobic exercise and nutrition education on quality of life and early menopause symptoms: A randomized controlled trial. *Women and Health, 57,* 173-188.

Askeland, K.G., & others (2017). Mental health in internationally adopted adolescents: A meta-analysis. *Journal of the American Academy of Child and Adolescent Psychiatry, 56,* 202-213.

Aslin, R. (2017). Statistical learning: A powerful mechanism that operates by mere exposure. *Wiley Interdisciplinary Reviews: Cognitive Science, 8,* 1-2.

Aslin, R.N. (2012). Infant eyes: A window on cognitive development. *Infancy, 17,* 126-140.

Aslin, R.N., Jusczyk, P.W., & Pisoni, D.B. (1998). Speech and auditory processing during infancy: Constraints on and precursors to language. In W. Damon (Ed.), *Handbook of child psychology* (5th ed., Vol. 2). New York: Wiley.

Aslin, R.N., & Lathrop, A.L. (2008). Visual perception. In M.M. Haith & J.B. Benson (Eds.), *Encyclopedia of infant and early childhood development.* Oxford, UK: Elsevier.

Aspen Institute (2013). *Two generations, one future.* Washington, DC: Aspen Institute.

Aspen Institute (2019). *Making tomorrow better together.* Washington, DC: Aspen Institute.

Assini-Meytin, L.C., & Green, K.M. (2015). Long-term consequences of adolescent parenthood among African-American youth: A propensity score matching approach. *Journal of Adolescent Health, 56,* 529-535.

Atherton, O.E., & others (2019, in press). The codevelopment of effortful control and school behavioral problems. *Journal of Personality and Social Psychology.*

Atkins, J.L., & others (2019, in press). Impact of low cardiovascular risk profiles on geriatric outcomes: Evidence from 421,000 participants in two cohorts. *Journals of Gerontology A: Biological Sciences and Medical Sciences.*

Atkinson, J., & Braddick, O. (2013). Visual development. In P.D. Zelazo (Ed.), *Oxford handbook of developmental psychology.* New York: Oxford University Press.

Attar-Schwartz, S., Tan, J.P., Buchanan, A., Flouri, E., & Griggs, J. (2009). Grandparenting and adolescent adjustment in two-parent biological, lone-parent, and step-families. *Journal of Family Psychology, 23*(1), 67-75.

Aubuchon-Endsley, N., & others (2019, in press). Maternal pre-pregnancy obesity and gestational weight gain influence neonatal neurobehavior. *Maternal and Child Nutrition.* doi:10.1111/mcn.12317

Autism Research Institute (2015). *DSM-V and autism.* New York: Autism Research Institute.

Auyeung, B., & others (2009). Fetal testosterone predicts sexually differentiated childhood behavior in girls and boys. *Psychological Science, 20,* 144-148.

Avalon, L. (2019, in press). Are older adults perceived as a threat to society? Exploring age-based threats in 29 nations. *Journals of Gerontology B: Psychological Sciences and Social Sciences.*

Avis, N.E., & others (2009). Longitudinal changes in sexual functioning as women transition through menopause: Results from the Study of Women's Health Across the Nation. *Menopause, 16,* 425-426.

Avvenuti, G., Baiardini, I., & Giardini, A. (2016). Optimism's explicative role for chronic diseases. *Frontiers in Psychology, 7,* 295.

Ayoub, M., & Roberts, B.W. (2018). Environmental conditions and the development of personality. In V. Hill & T.K. Shackelford (Eds.), *Encyclopedia of Personality and Individual Differences.* New York: Springer.

Azar, S., & Wong, T.E. (2017). Sickle cell disease: A brief update. *Medical Clinics of North America, 101,* 375-393.

Azmitia, M. (2016). Reflections on the cultural lenses of identity development. In K.C. McLean & M. Syed (Eds.), *Oxford handbook of identity development.* New York: Oxford University Press.

B

Babajani-Feremi, A. (2017). Neural mechanism underlying comprehension of narrative speech and its heritability: Study in a large population. *Brain Topography, 30,* 592-609.

Bacchi, M., & others (2018). Aquatic activities during pregnancy prevent excessive maternal weight gain and preserve birthweight. *American Journal of Health Promotion, 32,* 729-735.

Bach, L.E., Mortimer, J.A., Vandeweerd, C., & Corvin, J. (2013). The association of physical and mental health with sexual activity in older adults in a retirement community. *Journal of Sexual Medicine, 10*(11), 2671-2678.

Bachman, J.G., & others (2008). *The education-drug use connection.* Clifton, NJ: Psychology Press.

Bachmann, N., & others (2019, in press). Novel deletion in 11p15.5 imprinting center region 1 in a patient with Beckwith-Wiedemann syndrome provides insight into distal enhancer regulation and tumorigenesis. *Pediatric Blood & Cancer.*

Bacikova-Sleskova, M., Benka, J., & Orosova, O. (2014). Parental employment status and adolescents' health: The role of financial situation, parent-adolescent relationship, and adolescents' resilience. *Psychology and Health, 30,* 400-422.

Bacon, J.L., & Tomich, P. (2017). *Obstetrics and gynecology.* New York: Elsevier.

Baddeley, A.D. (1990). *Human memory: Theory and practice.* Boston: Allyn & Bacon.

Baddeley, A.D. (2001). *Is working memory still working?* Paper presented at the meeting of the American Psychological Association, San Francisco.

Baddeley, A.D. (2007). *Working memory, thought and action.* New York: Oxford University Press.

Baddeley, A.D. (2010a). Long-term and working memory: How do they interact? In L. Backman & L. Nyberg (Eds.), *Memory, aging, and the brain.* New York: Psychology Press.

Baddeley, A.D. (2010b). Working memory. *Current Biology, 20,* 136-140.

Baddeley, A.D. (2012). Prefatory. *Annual Review of Psychology* (Vol. 63). Palo Alto, CA: Annual Reviews.

Baddeley, A.D. (2013). On applying cognitive psychology. *British Journal of Psychology, 104,* 443-456.

Baddeley, A.D. (2015). Origins of the multicomponent working memory model. In M. Eysenck & D. Groome (Eds.), *Cognitive psychology: Revisiting the classic studies.* Thousand Oaks, CA: Sage.

Baddeley, A.D. (2017). *Working memories.* New York: Routledge.

Baddeley, A.D., Hitch, G.J., & Allen, R.J. (2019, in press). From short-term store to multicomponent working memory: The role of the modal model. *Memory and Cognition.*

Baer, J. (2016). Creativity doesn't develop in a vacuum. *New Directions in Child and Adolescent Development, 151,* 9-20.

Baer, R.J., & others (2019). Risk of preterm and early term birth by maternal drug use. *Journal of Perinatology, 39,* 286-294.

Bagwell, C.L., & Bukowki, W.M. (2018). Friendship in childhood and adolescence. In W. M. Bukowski & others (Eds.), *Handbook of peer interactions, relationships, and groups* (2nd ed.). New York: Guilford.

Bahrick, H.P. (1984). Semantic memory content in permastore: Fifty years of memory for Spanish learned in school. *Journal of Experimental Psychology: General, 113,* 1-35.

Bahrick, H.P., Bahrick, P.O., & Wittlinger, R.P. (1975). Fifty years of memory for names and faces: A cross-sectional approach. *Journal of Experimental Psychology: General, 104,* 54-75.

Bahrick, L.E. (2010). Intermodal perception and selective attention to intersensory redundancy: Implications for social development and autism. In J.G. Bremner & T.D. Wachs (Eds.), *Wiley-Blackwell handbook of infant development* (2nd ed.). New York: Wiley.

Bahrick, L.E., & Hollich, G. (2008). Intermodal perception. In M.M. Haith & J.B. Benson (Eds.), *Encyclopedia of infant and early childhood development.* Oxford, UK: Elsevier.

Bai, K., & others (2017). Kidney function and cognitive decline in an oldest-old Chinese population. *Clinical Interventions in Aging, 12,* 1049-1054.

Bailey, A.L., Osipova, A., & Kelly, K.R. (2016). Language development. In L. Corno & E.M. Anderman (Eds.), *Handbook of educational psychology* (3rd ed.). New York: Routledge.

Baillargeon, R. (1995). The object concept revisited: New directions in the investigation of infants' physical knowledge. In C.E. Granrud (Ed.), *Visual perception and cognition in infancy.* Hillsdale, NJ: Erlbaum.

Baillargeon, R. (2008). Innate ideas revisited: For a principle of persistence in infants' physical reasoning. *Perspectives on Psychological Science, 3,* 2-13.

Baillargeon, R. (2014). Cognitive development in infancy. *Annual Review of Psychology* (Vol. 65). Palo Alto, CA: Annual Reviews.

Baillargeon, R. (2016). Cognitive development in infancy. *Annual Review of Psychology* (Vol. 67). Palo Alto, CA: Annual Reviews.

Baillargeon, R., & DeVos, J. (1991). Object permanence in young children: Further evidence. *Child Development, 62,* 1227-1246.

Baillargeon, R., Li, J., Gertner, Y., & Wu, D. (2011). How do infants reason about physical events? In U. Goswami (Ed.), *Wiley-Blackwell handbook of childhood cognitive development* (2nd ed.). New York: Wiley.

Baillargeon, R., & others (2012). Object individuation and physical reasoning in infancy: An integrative account. *Language, Learning, and Development, 8,* 4-46.

Baiocchi, M., & others (2017). A behavior-based intervention that prevents sexual assault: The results of matched-pairs, cluster-randomized study in Nairobi, Kenya. *Prevention Science, 18,* 818-827.

Bajoghli, H., & others (2014). "I love you more than I can stand!"—romantic love, symptoms of depression and anxiety, and sleep complaints are related among young adults. *International Journal of Psychiatry and Clinical Practice, 18,* 169-174.

Bakeman, R., & Brown, J.V. (1980). Early interaction: Consequences for social and mental development at three years. *Child Development, 51,* 437-447.

Baker, J.K., Fenning, R.M., & Crnic, K.A. (2011). Emotion socialization by mothers and fathers: Coherence among behaviors and associations with parent attitudes and children's competence. *Social Development, 20,* 412–430.

Baker, K.M., & others (2019, in press). Adolescent weight and health behaviors and their associations with individual, social, and parental factors. *Journal of Physical Activity and Health.*

Baker, N.A., & Halford, W.K. (2019, in press). Assessment of couple relationships standards in same-sex attracted adults. *Family Process.*

Bakermans-Kranenburg, M.J., & van IJzendoorn, M.H. (2016). Attachment, parenting, and genetics. In J. Cassidy & P.R. Shaver (Eds.), *Handbook of parenting* (3rd ed.). New York: Guilford.

Balantekin, K.N., Birch, L.L., & Savage, J.S. (2018). Family, friend, and media factors are associated with patterns of weight-control behavior among adolescent girls. *Eating and Weight Disorders, 23,* 215–223.

Baldwin, S.A., & Hoffman, J.P. (2002). The dynamics of self-esteem: A growth-curve analysis. *Journal of Youth and Adolescence, 31,* 101–113.

Ball, K., Edwards, J.D., Ross, L.A., & McGwin, G. (2010). Effects of cognitive training interventions with older adults: A randomized controlled trial. *Journal of the American Geriatrics Society, 55,* 1–10.

Ballou, D., & Springer, M.G. (2017). Has NCLB encouraged educational triage? Accountability and the distribution of achievement gains. *Education Finance and Policy, 12,* 77–106.

Balodis, I.M., & others (2013). Divergent neural substrates of inhibitory control in binge eating disorder relative to other manifestations of obesity. *Obesity, 21*(2), 367–377.

Balsam, K.F., Rostosky, S.S., & Riggle, E.D. (2017). Breaking up is hard to do: Women's experience of dissolving their same-sex relationship. *Journal of Lesbian Studies, 21,* 30–46.

Baltes, P.B. (1987). Theoretical propositions of life-span developmental psychology: On the dynamics between growth and decline. *Developmental Psychology, 23,* 611–626.

Baltes, P.B. (1993). The aging mind: Potentials and limits. *Gerontologist, 33,* 580–594.

Baltes, P.B. (2000). Life-span developmental theory. In A. Kazdin (Ed.), *Encyclopedia of psychology.* New York: Oxford University Press.

Baltes, P.B. (2003). On the incomplete architecture of human ontogeny: Selection, optimization, and compensation as foundation of developmental theory. In U.M. Staudinger & U. Lindenberger (Eds.), *Understanding human development.* Boston: Kluwer.

Baltes, P.B., & Kunzmann, U. (2004). The two faces of wisdom: Wisdom as a general theory of knowledge and judgment about excellence in mind and virtue vs. wisdom as everyday realization in people and products. *Human Development, 47,* 290–299.

Baltes, P.B., & Lindenberger, U. (1997). Emergence of a powerful connection between sensory and cognitive functions across the adult life span: A new window to the study of cognitive aging? *Psychology and Aging, 12,* 12–21.

Baltes, P.B., Lindenberger, U., & Staudinger, U. (2006). Life span theory in developmental psychology. In W. Damon & R. Lerner (Eds.), *Handbook of child psychology* (6th ed.). New York: Wiley.

Baltes, P.B., Reuter Lorenz, P., & Rosler, F. (Eds.) (2012). *Life development and the brain: The perspective of biocultural co-constructivism.* New York: Cambridge University Press.

Baltes, P.B., & Smith, J. (2003). New frontiers in the future of aging: From successful aging of the young to the dilemmas of the fourth age. *Gerontology, 49,* 123–135.

Baltes, P.B., & Smith, J. (2008). The fascination of wisdom: Its nature, ontogeny, and function. *Perspectives on Psychological Science, 3,* 56–64.

Bamaca-Colbert, M.Y., Umana-Taylor, A.J., Espinosa-Hernandez, G., & Brown, A.M. (2012). Behavioral autonomy and expectations among Mexican-origin mother-daughter dyads: An examination of within-group variability. *Journal of Adolescence, 35,* 691–700.

Bamford, C., & Lagattuta, K.H. (2012). Looking on the bright side: Children's knowledge about the benefits of positive versus negative thinking. *Child Development, 83,* 667–682.

Banducci, S.E., & others (2017). Active experiencing training improves episodic memory recall in older adults. *Frontiers in Aging Neuroscience, 9,* 133.

Bandura, A. (1997). *Self-efficacy.* New York: W.H. Freeman.

Bandura, A. (1998, August). *Swimming against the mainstream: Accentuating the positive aspects of humanity.* Paper presented at the meeting of the American Psychological Association, San Francisco.

Bandura, A. (2001). Social cognitive theory. *Annual Review of Psychology* (Vol. 52). Palo Alto, CA: Annual Reviews.

Bandura, A. (2002). Selective moral disengagement in the exercise of moral agency. *Journal of Moral Education, 31,* 101–119.

Bandura, A. (2009). Social and policy impact of social cognitive theory. In M. Mark, S. Donaldson, & B. Campbell (Eds.), *Social psychology and program/policy evaluation.* New York: Guilford.

Bandura, A. (2010a). Self-efficacy. In D. Matsumoto (Ed.), *Cambridge dictionary of psychology.* New York: Cambridge University Press.

Bandura, A. (2010b). Self-reinforcement. In D. Matsumoto (Ed.), *Cambridge dictionary of psychology.* New York: Cambridge University Press.

Bandura, A. (2012). Social cognitive theory. *Annual Review of Clinical Psychology* (Vol. 8). Palo Alto, CA: Annual Reviews.

Bandura, A. (2015). *Moral disengagement.* New York: Worth.

Bandura, A. (2018). Toward a psychology of human agency: Pathways and reflections. *Perspectives on Psychological Science, 13,* 130–136.

Bangerter, L.R., & others (2017). Everyday support to aging parents: Links to middle-aged children's diurnal cortisol and daily mood. *The Gerontologist, 58,* 654–662.

Bangsbo, J., & others (2019, in press). Copenhagen consensus statement 2019: Physical activity and aging. *British Journal of Sports Medicine.*

Bank, L., Burraston, B., & Snyder, J. (2004). Sibling conflict and ineffective parenting as predictors of adolescent boys' antisocial behavior and peer difficulties: Additive and interactive effects. *Journal of Research on Adolescence, 14,* 99–125.

Banks, J.A. (2019). *Multicultural education* (6th ed.). Upper Saddle River, NJ: Pearson.

Bannon, F., & others (2018). Insights into the factors associated with achieving the preference of home death in terminal cancer: A national population-based study. *Palliative and Supportive Care, 16,* 749–755.

Banschick, M.R., & Tabatsky, D. (2011). *The intelligent divorce: Taking care of yourself.* New York: Intelligent Book Press.

Banuelos, C., & others (2014). Prefrontal cortical GABAergic dysfunction contributes to age-related working memory impairment. *Journal of Neuroscience, 34,* 3457–3466.

Baptista, J., & others (2017). Serotonin transporter polymorphism moderates the effects of caregiver intrusiveness on ADHD symptoms among institutionalized preschoolers. *European Child and Adolescent Psychiatry, 26,* 303–313.

Baptista, L.C., Machado-Rodrigues, A.M., & Martins, R.A. (2018). Back to basics with active lifestyles: Exercise is more effective than metformin to reduce cardiovascular risk in older adults with type 2 diabetes. *Biology of Sport, 35,* 363–372.

Baradon, T., & others (2019). New beginnings: A time-limited group intervention for high-risk infants and mothers. In H. Steele & M. Steele (Eds.), *Handbook of attachment-based interventions.* New York: Guilford.

Barajas, C.B., & others (2019, in press). Coping, discrimination, and physical health conditions among predominantly poor, urban African Americans: Implications for community-level health services. *Journal of Community Health.*

Barakat, R., & others (2017). Influence of land and water exercise in pregnancy on outcomes: A cross-sectional study. *Medicine & Science in Sports and Exercise, 49,* 1397–1403.

Barbarin, O., & Aikens, N. (2009). Supporting parental practices in the language and literacy development of young children. In O. Barbarin & H. Wasik (Eds.), *Handbook of child development and education.* New York: Guilford.

Barboza, J. (2019, in press). Pharmaceutical strategies for smoking cessation during pregnancy. *Expert Opinion in Pharmacotherapy.*

Barcaccia, B., & others (2017). Bullying and the detrimental role of un-forgiveness in adolescents' well-being. *Psicothema, 29,* 217–222.

Bardid, F., & others (2019, in press). Configurations of actual and perceived motor competence among children: Associations with motivation for sports and global self-worth. *Human Movement Science.*

Barenberg, J., & Duke, S. (2019). Testing and metacognition: Retrieval practice effects on metacognitive monitoring in learning from text. *Memory, 27,* 269–279.

Barfield, W.D., Warner, L., & Kappeler, E. (2017). Why we need evidence-based, community-wide prevention of teen pregnancy. *Journal of Adolescent Health, 60*(Suppl. 3), S3–S6.

Barger, M.K. (2019, in press). Current resources for evidence-based practice, March/April 2019. *Journal of Midwifery and Women's Health.*

Barger, S.D., & Cribbet, M.R. (2016). Social support sources matter: Increased cellular aging among adults with unsupportive spouses. *Biological Psychiatry, 115,* 43–49.

Bargh, J.A., & McKenna, K.Y.A. (2004). The Internet and social life. *Annual Review of Psychology* (Vol. 55). Palo Alto, CA: Annual Reviews.

Barnett, M.D., Hernandez, J., & Melugin, P.R. (2019, in press). Influence of future possible selves on outcome expectancies, intended behavior, and academic performance. *Psychological Reports.*

Baron, N.S. (1992). *Growing up with language.* Reading, MA: Addison-Wesley.

Barooah, A., & others (2019). Immediate aftermath of a client's death: The experience of home health aides. *Home Health Care Services Quarterly, 38,* 14–28.

Barr, R. (2019). Parenting in the digital age. In M.H. Bornstein (Ed.), *Handbook of parenting* (3rd ed.). New York: Routledge.

Barrington-Trimis, J.L., & others (2018). Type of e-cigarette device used by adolescents and young adults: Findings from a pooled analysis of 8 studies of 2,166 vapors. *Nicotine and Tobacco Research, 183,* 43–50.

Barry, C., & Overland, G. (2019). *Responding to global poverty.* New York: Cambridge University Press.

Bartick, M.C., & others (2017). Disparities in breastfeeding: Impact of maternal and child health outcomes and costs. *Journal of Pediatrics, 181,* 49–55.

Bartick, M.C., & others (2019, in press). Suboptimal breastfeeding in the United States: Maternal and pediatric health outcomes and costs. *Maternal and Child Nutrition.*

Bartl, H., & others (2018). Does prolonged grief treatment foster posttraumatic growth? Secondary results from a treatment study with long-term follow-up and mediation analysis. *Psychology and Psychotherapy, 91,* 27–41.

Bartolomeo, P., & Seidel Malkinson, T. (2019). Hemispheric lateralization of attention processes in the human brain. *Current Opinion in Psychology, 29,* 90–96.

Bartsch, K., & Wellman, H.M. (1995). *Children talk about the mind.* New York: Oxford University Press.

Bartsch, L.M., Loaiza, V.M., & Oberauer, K. (2019). Does limited working memory capacity underlie age differences in associative long-term memory? *Psychology and Aging, 34,* 268–281.

Bascandziev, I., & Harris, P.L. (2011). The role of testimony in young children's solution of a gravity-driven invisible displacement task. *Cognitive Development, 25,* 233–246.

Bass, L., & others (2019). Children's developing theory of mind and pedagogical evidence selection. *Developmental Psychology, 55,* 286–302.

Basta, N.E., Matthews, F.E., Chatfield, M.D., Byrnes, C., & MRC-FFAS (2008). Community-level socio-economic status and cognitive and functional impairment in the older population. *European Journal of Public Health, 18,* 48–54.

Basterfield, L., & others (2015). Longitudinal associations between sports participation, body composition, and physical activity from childhood to adolescence. *Journal of Science and Medicine in Sport, 18*(2), 178–182.

Bates, J.E. (2012a). Behavioral regulation as a product of temperament and environment. In S.L. Olson & A.J. Sameroff (Eds.), *Biopsychosocial regulatory processes in the development of childhood behavioral problems.* New York: Cambridge University Press.

Bates, J.E. (2012b). Temperament as a tool in promoting early childhood development. In S.L. Odom, E.P. Pungello, & N. Gardner-Neblett (Eds.), *Infants, toddlers, and families in poverty.* New York: Guilford.

Bates, J.E., & Pettit, G.S. (2015). Temperament, parenting, and social development. In J.E. Grusec &

P.D. Hastings (Eds.), *Handbook of socialization* (2nd ed.). New York: Guilford.

Bates, T.C., & Gupta, S. (2017). Smart groups of smart people: Evidence for IQ as the origin of collective intelligence in the performance of human groups. *Intelligence, 60,* 46–56.

Batson, C.D. (1989). Personal values, moral principles, and the three-path model of prosocial motivation. In N. Eisenberg & J. Reykowski (Eds.), *Social and moral values.* Hillsdale, NJ: Erlbaum.

Battistich, V.A. (2008). The Child Development Project: Creating caring school communities. In L. Nucci & D. Narváez (Eds.), *Handbook of moral and character education.* Clifton, NJ: Psychology Press.

Bauer, K.W., & others (2019, in press). Maternal executive function and the family food environment. *Appetite.*

Bauer, P.J. (2006). Event memory. In W. Damon & R. Lerner (Eds.), *Handbook of child psychology* (6th ed.). New York: Wiley.

Bauer, P.J. (2009). Neurodevelopmental changes in infancy and beyond: Implications for learning and memory. In O.A. Barbarin & B.H. Wasik (Eds.), *Handbook of child development and early education.* New York: Oxford University Press.

Bauer, P.J. (2013). Memory. In P.D. Zelazo (Ed.), *Oxford handbook of developmental psychology.* New York: Oxford University Press.

Bauer, P.J. (2015). A complementary processes account of the development of childhood amnesia and a personal past. *Psychological Review, 122,* 204–231.

Bauer, P.J. (2018). Memory development. In J. Rubenstein & P. Rakic (Eds.). *Neural circuit development and function in the healthy and diseased brain* (2nd ed.). New York: Elsevier.

Bauer, P.J. (2019, in press). Memory development. *Comprehensive Developmental Neuroscience.*

Bauer, P.J., & Fivush, R. (Eds.) (2014). *Wiley-Blackwell handbook of children's memory.* New York: Wiley.

Bauer, P.J., & Larkina, M. (2014). The onset of childhood amnesia in childhood: A prospective investigation of the course and determinants of forgetting of early-life events. *Memory, 22,* 907–924.

Bauer, P.J., & Larkina, M. (2016). Predicting and remembering and forgetting of autobiographical memories in children and adults: A prospective study. *Memory, 24,* 1345–1368.

Bauer, P.J., Wenner, J.A., Dropik, P.L., & Wewerka, S.S. (2000). Parameters of remembering and forgetting in the transition from infancy to early childhood. *Monographs of the Society for Research in Child Development, 65*(4, Serial No. 263).

Baumeister, R.F. (2013). Self-esteem. In E. Anderson (Ed.), *Psychology of classroom learning: An encyclopedia.* Detroit: Macmillan.

Baumeister, R.F., Campbell, J.D., Krueger, J.I., & Vohs, K.D. (2003). Does high self-esteem cause better performance, interpersonal success, happiness, or healthier lifestyles? *Psychological Science in the Public Interest, 4*(1), 1–44.

Baumeister, R.F., & Vohs, K.D. (2002). The pursuit of meaningfulness in life. In C.R. Snyder & S.J. Lopez (Eds.), *Handbook of positive psychology.* New York: Oxford University Press.

Baumrind, D. (1971). Current patterns of parental authority. *Developmental Psychology Monographs, 4*(I, Pt. 2).

Baumrind, D. (1991). Effective parenting during the early adolescent transition. In P.A. Cowan & E.M. Hetherington (Eds.), *Advances in family research* (Vol. 2). Hillsdale, NJ: Erlbaum.

Baumrind, D. (2012). Authoritative parenting revisited: History and current status. In R. Larzelere, A.S. Morris, & A.W. Harrist (Eds.), *Authoritative parenting.* Washington, DC: American Psychological Association.

Baye, K., Tariku, A., & Mouquet-Rivier, C. (2019, in press). Caregiver-infant's feeding behaviors are associated with energy intake of 9-11 month-old infants in rural Ethiopia. *Maternal and Child Nutrition.*

Bayley, N. (1969). *Manual for the Bayley Scales of Infant Development.* New York: Psychological Corporation.

Bayley, N. (2006). *Bayley Scales of Infant and Toddler Development* (3rd ed.). San Antonio: Pearson Assessment.

Baysinger, C.L. (2010). Imaging during pregnancy. *Anesthesia and Analgesia, 110,* 863–867.

Beal, C.R. (1994). *Boys and girls: The development of gender roles.* New York: McGraw-Hill.

Beal, M.A., Yauk, C.L., & Marchetti, F. (2017). From sperm to offspring: Assessing the heritable genetic consequences of paternal smoking and potential public health impacts. *Mutation, 773,* 26–50.

Bear, D.R., & others (2020). *Words their way* (7th ed.). Upper Saddle River, NJ: Pearson.

Beauchamp, G., & Mennella, J.A. (2009). Early flavor learning and its impact on later feeding behavior. *Journal of Pediatric Gastroenterology and Nutrition, 48*(Suppl. 1), S25–S30.

Bechtold, A.G., Bushnell, E.W., & Salapatek, P. (1979, April). *Infants' visual localization of visual and auditory targets.* Paper presented at the meeting of the Society for Research in Child Development, San Francisco.

Becker, C., & others (2018). Cataract in patients with diabetes mellitus—Incidence rates in the UK and risk factors. *Eye, 32,* 1028–1035.

Becker, M., & McElvany, N. (2018). The interplay of gender and social background: A longitudinal study of interaction effects in reading attitudes and behavior. *British Journal of Educational Psychology, 88,* 529–549.

Becker, M.W., Alzahabi, R., & Hopwood, C.J. (2013). Media multitasking is associated with symptoms of depression and social anxiety. *Cyberpsychology, Behavior, and Social Networking, 16,* 132–135.

Becker, S.P., & others (2018a). Sleep problems and suicidal behaviors in college students. *Journal of Psychiatric Research, 99,* 122–128.

Becker, S.P., & others (2018b). Sleep in a large, multi-university sample of college students: Sleep problem prevalence, sex differences, and mental health correlates. *Sleep Health, 4,* 174–181.

Becker, S.P., & others (2019, in press). Shortened sleep duration causes sleepiness, inattention, and oppositionality in adolescents with ADHD: Findings from a crossover sleep restriction/extension study. *JAACAP.*

Bedford, R., & others (2017). The role of infants' mother-directed gaze, maternal sensitivity, and emotion regulation in childhood. *European Child and Adolescent Psychiatry, 26,* 947–956.

Bedford, V.H. (2009). Sibling relationships: Adulthood. In D. Carr (Eds.), *Encyclopedia of the life course and human development.* Boston: Gale Cengage.

Beeghly, M., & others (2006). Prenatal cocaine exposure and children's language functioning at 6 and 9.5 years: Moderating effects of child age, birthweight, and gender. *Journal of Pediatric Psychology, 31,* 98–115.

Beghetto, R.A. (2018). Do we choose our scholarly paths or do they choose us? My reflections on exploring the nature of creativity in educational settings. In R.J. Sternberg & J.C. Kaufman (Eds.), *The nature of human creativity.* New York: Cambridge University Press.

Beghetto, R.A. (2019). Creativity in classrooms. In J.C. Kaufman & R.J. Sternberg (Eds.), *Cambridge handbook of creativity* (2nd ed.). New York: Cambridge University Press.

Beguin, M. (2016). Object pragmatics and language development. *Integrative Psychological and Behavioral Science, 50,* 603–620.

Begus, K., & Southgate, V. (2012). Infant pointing serves an interrogative function. *Developmental Science, 15*(5), 611–617.

Belal, S., & others (2018). Identification of memory reactivation during sleep by EEG classification. *NeuroImage, 176,* 203–214.

Belchior, P., & others (2019, in press). Computer and videogame interventions for older adults' cognitive and everyday functioning. *Games for Health Journal.*

Belk, C., & Maier, V.B. (2019). *Biology* (6th ed.). Upper Saddle River, NJ: Pearson.

Bell, M.A., & Broomell, A.P.R. (2020, in press). Development of inhibitory control from infancy to early childhood. In O. Houde & G. Borst (Eds.), *Cambridge handbook of cognitive development.* New York: Cambridge University Press.

Bell, M.A. (2015). Bringing the field of infant cognition and perception toward a biopsychosocial perspective. In S.D. Calkins (Ed.), *Handbook of infant development.* New York: Guilford.

Bell, M.A., Broomell, A.P.R., & Patton, L.K. (2018). Emotion regulation. In M.H. Bornstein (Ed.), *SAGE encyclopedia of lifespan human development.* Thousand Oaks, CA: Sage.

Bell, M.A., Diaz, A., & Liu, R. (2019). Cognition-emotion interactions. In V. LoBe & others (Eds.), *Handbook of emotional development.* New York: Springer.

Bell, M.A., Kraybill, J.H., & Diaz, A. (2014). Reactivity, regulation, and remembering: Associations between temperament and memory. In P.J. Bauer & R. Fivush (Eds.), *Handbook on the development of children's memory.* New York: Wiley.

Bell, M.A., Ross, A.P., & Patton, L.K. (2018). Emotion regulation. In M.H. Bornstein (Ed.), *SAGE encyclopedia of lifespan human development.* Thousand Oaks, CA: Sage.

Bell, M.A., & others (2018). Brain development. In M.H. Bornstein (Ed.), *SAGE encyclopedia of lifespan human development.* Thousand Oaks, CA: Sage.

Bell, M.F., & others (2018). School readiness and maltreated children: Associations of timing, type, and chronicity of maltreatment. *Child Abuse and Neglect, 76,* 426–439.

Bell, S.M., & Ainsworth, M.D.S. (1972). Infant crying and maternal responsiveness. *Child Development, 43,* 1171–1190.

Bellingtier, J.A., & Neupert, S.D. (2019, in press). Feeling young and in control: Daily control beliefs are associated with younger subjective ages. *Journals of Gerontology B: Psychological Sciences and Social Sciences.*

Bellon, E., Fias, W., & De Smedt, B. (2019). More than number sense: The additional role of executive functions and metacognition in arithmetic. *Journal of Experimental Child Psychology, 182,* 38–60.

Belsky, D.W., & others (2017). Impact of early personal-history characteristics on the pace of aging: Implications for clinical trials of therapies to slow aging and extend healthspan. *Aging Cell, 16,* 644–651.

Belsky, J. (1981). Early human experience: A family perspective. *Developmental Psychology, 17,* 3–23.

Belsky, J. (2014, November 28). The downside of resilience. *New York Times.* Retrieved September 10, 2016, from www.nytimes.com/2014/11/30/opinion/sunday/the-downside-of-resilience

Belsky, J., & Pluess, M. (2016). Differential susceptibility to context: Implications for developmental psychopathology. In D. Cicchetti (Ed.), *Developmental psychopathology* (3rd ed.). New York: Wiley.

Belsky, J., & van IJzendoorn, M.H. (2017). What works for whom? Genetic moderation of intervention efficacy. *Development and Psychopathology, 15,* 125–130.

Belvederi Murri, M., & others (2019). Physical exercise in major depression: Reducing the mortality gap while improving clinical outcomes. *Frontiers in Psychology, 9,* 762.

Bem, S.I. (1977). On the utility of alternative procedures for assessing psychological androgyny. *Journal of Consulting and Clinical Psychology, 45,* 196–205.

Bendayan, R., & others (2017). Decline in memory, visuospatial ability, and crystalized cognitive abilities in older adults: Normative aging or terminal decline? *Journal of Aging Research, 2017,* 6210105.

Bendersky, M., & Sullivan, M.W. (2007). Basic methods in infant research. In A. Slater & M. Lewis (Eds.), *Introduction to infant development* (2nd ed.). New York: Oxford University Press.

Bendezu, J.J., & others (2018). Longitudinal relations among parental monitoring strategies, knowledge, and adolescent delinquency in a racially diverse at-risk sample. *Journal of Clinical Child and Adolescent Psychology, 47*(Suppl. 1), S21–S34.

Benet-Martinez, V., & Nguyen, A.D. (2019). Multicultural identity and experiences: Cultural, social, and personality processes. In K. Deaux & M. Snyder (Eds), *Oxford handbook of personality and social psychology.* New York: Oxford University Press.

Benetos, A. (2019). The biomedical bases of successful aging. In R. Fernandez-Ballesteros, A. Benetos, & J-M. Robine (Eds.), *Cambridge handbook of successful aging.* New York: Cambridge University Press.

Benetos, A., & others (2019). Arterial stiffness and blood pressure during the aging process. In R. Fernandez-Ballesteros, A. Benetos, & J-M. Robine (Eds.), *Cambridge handbook of successful aging.* New York: Cambridge University Press.

Bengesai, A.V., Khan, H.T.A., & Dube, R. (2018). Effect of early sexual debut on high completion in South Africa. *Journal of Biological Science, 50,* 124–143.

Bengtson, V.L., Reedy, M.N., & Gordon, C. (1985). Aging and self-conceptions: Personality processes and social contexts. In J.E. Birren & K.W. Schaie (Eds.), *Handbook of the psychology of aging.* New York: Van Nostrand Reinhold.

Benichov, J., Cox, L.C., Tun, P.A., & Wingfield, A. (2012). Word recognition within a linguistic context: Effects of age, hearing acuity, verbal ability, and cognitive function. *Ear and Hearing, 33,* 250–256.

Benjamins, M.R., & Finlayson, M. (2007). Using religious services to improve health: Findings from a sample of middle-aged and older adults with multiple sclerosis. *Journal of Aging and Health, 19,* 537–553.

Benner, B., & Bakhtiari, F. (2017). Understanding students' transition to high school: Demographic variation and the role of supportive relationships. *Journal of Youth and Adolescence, 46,* 2129–2142.

Bennett, C. (2019). *Comprehensive multicultural education* (9th ed.). Upper Saddle River, NJ: Pearson.

Bennett, J.M., Fagundes, C.P., & Kiecolt-Glaser, J.K. (2016). The chronic stress of caregiving accelerates the natural aging of the immune system. In A.C. Phillips, J.M. Lord, & J.A. Bosch (Eds.), *Immunosenescence: Psychological and behavioral determinants.* New York: Springer.

Bennett, K.M. (2006). Does marital status and marital status change predict physical health in older adults? *Psychological Medicine, 36,* 1313–1320.

Bennett, N. (2018). Sexual dysfunction: Behavioral, medical, and surgical treatment. *Medical Clinics of North America, 102,* 349–360.

Bennie, J.A., & others (2019, in press). Associations between aerobic and muscle-strengthening exercise with depressive symptom severity among 17,839 U.S. adults. *Preventive Medicine.*

Benowitz-Fredericks, C.A., Garcia, K., Massey, M., Vassagar, B., & Borzekowski, D.L. (2012). Body image, eating disorders, and the relationship to adolescent media use. *Pediatric Clinics of North America, 59,* 693–704.

Benson, J.E., & Sabbagh, M.A. (2017). Executive functioning helps children think about and learn from others' mental states. In M.J. Hoskyn & others (Eds.), *Executive functions in children's everyday lives.* New York: Oxford University Press.

Bera, A., & others (2014). Effects of kangaroo care on growth and development of low birthweight babies up to 12 months of age: A controlled clinical trial. *Acta Pediatrica, 103,* 643–650.

Bercovitz, K.E., Ngnoumen, C., & Langer, E.J. (2019). Personal control and successful aging. In R. Fernandez-Ballesteros, A. Benetos, & J-M. Robine (Eds.), *Cambridge handbook of successful aging.* New York: Cambridge University Press.

Berenguer, C., & others (2018). Contribution of theory of mind, executive functioning, and pragmatics to socialization behaviors of children with high-functioning autism. *Journal of Autism and Developmental Disorders, 48,* 430–441.

Berg, N., & others (2018). Associations between unemployment and heavy episodic drinking from adolescence to midlife in Sweden and Finland. *European Journal of Public Health, 28,* 258–263.

Berge, J.M., & others (2015). The protective role of family meals for youth obesity: 10-year longitudinal associations. *Journal of Pediatrics, 166,* 296–301.

Bergeron, K.E. (2018). *Challenging the cult of self-esteem in education.* New York: Routledge.

Berglund, A., & others (2019). Changes in cohort composition of Turner syndrome and severe non-diagnosis of Klinefelter, 47, XXX, and 47, XYY syndrome: A nationwide cohort study. *Orphanet Journal of Rare Diseases, 14*(1), 16.

Bergman, A.S., Axberg, U., & Hanson, E. (2017). When a parent dies—a systematic review of the effects of support programs for parentally bereaved children and their caregivers. *BMC Palliative Care, 16,* 39.

Bergman, M., & Cummings, E.M. (2018). Innovations in research on conflict, families, and children. *Family Court Review, 56,* 207-208.

Bergmuller, S. (2013). The relationship between cultural individualism-collectivism and student aggression across 62 countries. *Aggressive Behavior, 39,* 182-200.

Berk, L.E. (1994). Why children talk to themselves. *Scientific American, 271*(5), 78-83.

Berk, L.E., & Spuhl, S.T. (1995). Maternal interaction, private speech, and task performance in preschool children. *Early Childhood Research Quarterly, 10,* 145-169.

Berko, J. (1958). The child's learning of English morphology. *Word, 14,* 150-177.

Berko Gleason, J. (2003). Unpublished review of J.W. Santrock's *Life-span development,* 9th ed. (New York: McGraw-Hill).

Berko Gleason, J. (2005). The development of language: An overview. In J. Berko Gleason & N.B. Ratner (Eds.), *The development of language* (6th ed.). Boston: Allyn & Bacon.

Berko Gleason, J. (2009). The development of language: An overview. In J. Berko Gleason & N.B. Ratner (Eds.), *The development of language* (7th ed.). Boston: Allyn & Bacon.

Berlin, L.J., & others (2009). Correlates and consequences of spanking and verbal punishment for low-income White, African-American, and Mexican American toddlers. *Child Development, 80,* 1403-1420.

Berlyne, D.E. (1960). *Conflict, arousal, and curiosity.* New York: McGraw-Hill.

Berman, S.L., You, Y., Schwartz, S., Teo, G., & Mochizuki, K. (2011). Identity exploration, commitment, and distress: A cross-national investigation in China, Taiwan, Japan, and the United States. *Child Youth Care Forum, 40,* 65-75.

Berndt, T.J., & Perry, T.B. (1990). Distinctive features and effects of early adolescent friendships. In R. Montemayor (Ed.), *Advances in adolescent research.* Greenwich, CT: JAI Press.

Bernier, A., Beauchamp, M.H., Carlson, S.M., & Lalonde, G. (2015). A secure base from which to regulate: Attachment security in toddlerhood is a predictor of executive functioning at school entry. *Developmental Psychology, 51,* 1177-1189.

Bernier, A., Calkins, S.D., & Bell, M.A. (2016). Longitudinal associations between the quality of maternal parenting behavior and brain development across infancy. *Child Development, 87,* 1159-1174.

Bernier, A., & others (2013). Sleep and cognition in preschool years: Specific links to executive functioning. *Child Development, 84*(5), 1542-1553.

Bernier, A., & others (2017). Parenting and young children's executive function development. In M.J. Hoskyn & others (Eds.), *Executive function in children's everyday lives.* New York: Oxford University Press.

Berninger, V.W. (2006). Learning disabilities. In W. Damon & R. Lerner (Eds.), *Handbook of child psychology* (6th ed.). New York: Wiley.

Bernstein, N. (2004, March 7). Young love, new caution. *The New York Times,* p. A22.

Berryman, N., & others (2013). Executive function, physical fitness, and mobility in well-functioning older adults. *Experimental Gerontology, 48,* 1402-1409.

Bersamin, M.M., & others (2014). Risky business: Is there an association between casual sex and mental health among emerging adults? *Journal of Sex Research, 51,* 43-51.

Berscheid, E. (1988). Some comments on love's anatomy: Or, whatever happened to old-fashioned lust? In R.J. Sternberg (Ed.), *Anatomy of love.* New Haven, CT: Yale University Press.

Berscheid, E., & Fei, J. (1977). Sexual jealousy and romantic love. In G. Clinton & G. Smith (Eds.), *Sexual jealousy.* Englewood Cliffs, NJ: Prentice-Hall.

Bertenthal, B.I. (2008). Perception and action. In M.M. Haith & J.B. Benson (Eds.), *Encyclopedia of infant and early childhood development.* Oxford, UK: Elsevier.

Bertenthal, B.I., Longo, M.R., & Kenny, S. (2007). Phenomenal permanence and the development of predictive tracking in infancy. *Child Development, 78,* 350-363.

Bertoni, A., & others (2018). The associations for separated parents in Italy: Their role for parents' well-being and coparenting. *Health & Social Care in the Community, 26,* e571-e577.

Bertrand, R., Graham, E.K., & Lachman, M.E. (2013). Personality development in adulthood and old age. In I.B. Weiner & others (Eds.), *Handbook of psychology* (2nd ed., Vol. 6). New York: Wiley.

Bervoets, J., & others (2018). Enhancing executive functions among Dutch elementary school children using the Train Your Mind program: Protocol for a cluster randomized trial. *JMIR Research Protocols, 7*(6), e144.

Best, D.L., & Puzio, A.R. (2019). Gender and culture. In D. Matsumoto & H.C. Hwang (Eds.), *Handbook of culture and psychology* (2nd ed.). New York: Oxford University Press.

Betts, K.S., Williams, G.M., Najman, J.M., & Alati, R. (2014). Maternal depressive, anxious, and stress symptoms during pregnancy predict internalizing problems in adolescence. *Depression and Anxiety, 31,* 9-18.

Bevens, C.L., & Loughnan, S. (2019, in press). Insights into men's sexual aggression toward women: Dehumanization and objectification. *Sex Roles.*

Bewersdorf, J.P., & others (2019, in press). Epigenetic therapy combinations in acute myeloid leukemia: What are the options? *Therapeutic Advances in Hematology.*

Beyene, Y. (1986). Cultural significance and physiological manifestations of menopause: A biocultural analysis. *Culture, Medicine and Psychiatry, 10,* 47-71.

Bezdicek, O., & others (2016). Toward the processing speed theory of activities of daily living in healthy aging: Normative data of the Functional Activities Questionnaire. *Aging: Clinical and Experimental Research, 28,* 239-247.

Bhattacharya, I., & others (2019). Testosterone augments FSH signaling by upregulating the expression and activity of FSH-receptor in pubertal primate sertoli cells. *Molecular and Cellular Endocrinology, 482,* 70-80.

Bialystok, E. (1997). Effects of bilingualism and biliteracy on children's emerging concepts of print. *Developmental Psychology, 33,* 429-440.

Bialystok, E. (2001). *Bilingualism in development: Language, literacy, and cognition.* New York: Cambridge University Press.

Bialystok, E. (2007). Acquisition of literacy in preschool children: A framework for research. *Language Learning, 57,* 45-77.

Bialystok, E. (2011). *Becoming bilingual: Emergence of cognitive outcomes of bilingualism in immersion education.* Paper presented at the meeting of the Society for Research in Child Development, Montreal.

Bialystok, E. (2014). Language experience changes language and cognitive ability: Implications for social policy. In B. Spolsky, O. Inbar-Lourie, & M. Tannenbaum (Eds.), *Challenges for language education and policy.* New York: Routledge.

Bialystok, E. (2015). The impact of bilingualism on cognition. In R. Scott & S. Kosslyn (Eds.), *Emerging trends in the social and behavioral sciences.* New York: Wiley.

Bialystok, E. (2017). The bilingual adaptation: How minds accommodate experience. *Psychological Bulletin, 143,* 233-262.

Bialystok, E., Craik, F.I., Binns, M.A., Ossher, L., & Freedman, M. (2014). Effects of bilingualism on the age of onset and progression of MCI and AD: Evidence from executive function tests. *Neuropsychology, 28,* 290-304.

Bialystok, E., & others (2016). Aging in two languages: Implications for public health. *Aging Research Reviews, 27,* 56-60.

Bian, Z., & Andersen, G.J. (2008). Aging and the perceptual organization of 3-D scenes. *Psychology and Aging, 23,* 342-352.

Bianchi, D., & others (2019, in press). A bad romance: Sexting motivations and teen dating violence. *Journal of Interpersonal Violence.*

Bianchi, D.W. (2019, in press). Turner syndrome: New insights from prenatal genomics and transcriptomics. *American Journal of Medical Genetics C: Seminars in Medical Genetics.*

Bick, J., & Nelson, C.A. (2016). Early adverse experiences and the developing brain. *Neuropsychopharmacology, 41,* 177-196.

Bick, J., & Nelson, C.A. (2017). Early experience and brain development. *Wiley Interdisciplinary Review of Cognitive Science, 8,* 1-2.

Bick, J., & others (2019). Early parenting intervention and adverse family environments affect neural function in middle childhood. *Biological Psychiatry, 85,* 326-335.

Biehle, S.N., & Mickelson, K.D. (2012). First-time parents' expectations about the division of childcare and play. *Journal of Family Psychology, 26,* 36-45.

Bien, B., & Bien-Barkowska, K. (2018). Prescribing or deprescribing in older persons: What are the real-life concerns in geriatric practice? *Policy Archives of Internal Medicine, 128,* 200-208.

Bihagi, S.W. (2019, in press). Early life exposure to lead (Pb) and changes in DNA methylation: Relevance to Alzheimer's disease. *Research on Environmental Health.*

Bijlenga, D., & others (2019). The role of the circadian system in the etiology and pathophysiology of ADHD: Time to redefine ADHD? *Attention Deficit and Hyperactivity Disorders, 11,* 5-19.

Bill and Melinda Gates Foundation (2011). *College-ready education.* Retrieved August 21, 2011, from www.gatesfoundation.org/college-ready-education/Pages/default.aspx

Bill and Melinda Gates Foundation (2017). *K-12 education.* Retrieved March 28, 2017, from www.gatesfoundation.org/What-We-Do/US-Programs/K-12-Education

Bill and Melinda Gates Foundation (2019). *All lives have equal value.* Retrieved May 4, 2019, from www.gatesfoundation.org

Billeci, L., & others (2018). Heart rate variability during a joint attention task in toddlers with autism spectrum disorders. *Frontiers in Physiology, 9,* 467.

Billy, J.O.G., Rodgers, J.L., & Udry, J.R. (1984). Adolescent sexual behavior and friendship choice. *Social Forces, 62,* 653-678.

Birch, S.A., & Bloom, P. (2003). Children are cursed: An asymmetric bias in mental state attribution. *Psychological Science, 14,* 283-286.

Birch, S.A., & others (2017). Perspectives on perspective taking: How children think about the minds of others. *Advances in Child Development and Behavior, 52,* 185-226.

Birditt, K.S., Newton, N.J., Cranford, J.A., & Ryan, L.H. (2016). Stress and negative relationship quality among older couples: Implications for blood pressure. *Journals of Gerontology B: Psychological Sciences and Social Sciences, 71,* 775-785.

Birditt, K.S., & others (2019, in press). Conflict strategies in the parent-adult child tie: Generation differences and implications for well-being. *Journals of Gerontology B: Psychological Sciences and Social Sciences.*

Birkeland, M.S., Melkevick, O., Holsen, I., & Wold, B. (2012). Trajectories of global self-esteem development during adolescence. *Journal of Adolescence, 35,* 43-54.

Birman, B.F., & others (2007). *State and local implementation of the "No Child Left Behind Act." Volume II–Teacher quality under "NCLB": Interim report.* Jessup, MD: U.S. Department of Education.

Birnbaum, J.H., & others (2018). Oxidative stress and altered mitochondrial protein expression in the absence of amyloid-*B* and tau pathology in iPAC-derived neurons from sporadic Alzheimer's disease patients. *Stem Cell Research, 27,* 121-130.

Biro, A., & Elek, P. (2018). How does retirement affect healthcare expenditures? Evidence from a change in the retirement age. *Health Economics, 27,* 802-818.

Birren, J.E. (2002). Unpublished review of J.W. Santrock's *Life-span development,* 9th ed. (New York: McGraw-Hill).

Bjorklund, D.F. (2018). A metatheory for cognitive development (or "Piaget is dead" revisited). *Child Development, 89,* 2288-2302.

Bjorklund, D.F., & Pellegrini, A.D. (2002). *The origins of human nature.* New York: Oxford University Press.

Bjorklund, D.F., & Rosenbaum, K. (2000). Middle childhood: Cognitive development. In A. Kazdin (Ed.), *Encyclopedia of psychology.* New York: Oxford University Press.

Black, J.J., & Rofey, D.L. (2018). An overview of common psychiatric problems among adolescent and young adult females: Focus on mood and anxiety. *Best Practices in Research and Clinical Obstetrics and Gynecology, 48,* 165-173.

Black, M.M., & Hurley, K.M. (2017). Responsive feeding: Strategies to promote healthy mealtime interactions. *Nestle Nutrition Institute Workshop Series, 87,* 153-165.

Black, M.M., & others (2017). Early childhood development coming of age: Science through the life course. *The Lancet, 389,* P77-P90.

Blackwell, D.L., & Clarke, T.C. (2018, June 28). State variation in meeting the 2008 federal guidelines for both aerobic and muscle-strengthening activities through leisure-time physical activity among adults aged 18-64: United States 2010-2015. *National Health Statistics Reports, 112,* 1-21.

Blackwell, L.S., & Dweck, C.S. (2008). *The motivational impact of a computer-based program that teaches how the brain changes with learning.* Unpublished manuscript, Department of Psychology, Stanford University, Palo Alto, CA.

Blackwell, L.S., Trzesniewski, K.H., & Dweck, C.S. (2007). Implicit theories of intelligence predict achievement across an adolescent transition: A longitudinal study and an intervention. *Child Development, 78,* 246-263.

Blaga, O.M., & others (2009). Structure and continuity of intellectual development in early childhood. *Intelligence, 37,* 106-113.

Blair, C. (2016). The development of executive functions and self-regulation: A bidirectional psychobiological model. In K.D. Vohs & R. Baumeister (Eds.), *Handbook of self-regulation* (3rd ed.). New York: Guilford.

Blair, C. (2017). Educating executive function. *Wiley Interdisciplinary Reviews: Cognitive Science, 8, 1-2.*

Blair, C., & Raver, C.C. (2012). Child development in the context of poverty: Experiential canalization of brain and behavior. *American Psychologist, 67,* 309-318.

Blair, C., & Raver, C.C. (2014). Closing the achievement gap through modification and neuroendocrine function: Results from a cluster randomized controlled trial of an innovative approach for the education of children in kindergarten. *PLoS One, 9*(11), e112393.

Blair, C., & Raver, C.C. (2015). School readiness and self-regulation: A developmental psychobiological approach. *Annual Review of Psychology* (Vol. 66). Palo Alto, CA: Annual Reviews.

Blair, C., & Raver, C.C. (2016). Poverty, stress, and brain development: New directions for prevention and intervention. *Academic Pediatrics, 16*(Suppl. 3), S30-S36.

Blair, C., Raver, C.C., & Finegood, E.D. (2016). Self-regulation and developmental psychopathology: Experiential canalization of brain and behavior. In D. Cicchetti (Ed.), *Developmental psychopathology* (3rd ed.). New York: Wiley.

Blair, C., & Razza, R.P. (2007). Relating effortful control, executive functioning, and false belief understanding to emerging math and literacy ability in kindergarten. *Child Development, 78,* 647-663.

Blair, C., & others (2015). Multiple aspects of self-regulation uniquely predict mathematics but not letter-word knowledge in the early elementary grades. *Developmental Psychology, 5,* 459-472.

Blair, S.N. (1990, January). Personal communication. Aerobics Institute, Dallas.

Blair, S.N., & others (1989). Physical fitness and all-cause mortality: A prospective study of healthy men and women. *Journal of the American Medical Association, 262,* 2395-2401.

Blake, J.S., Munoz, K.D., & Volpe, S. (2019). *Nutrition* (4th ed.). Upper Saddle River, NJ: Pearson.

Blake, M.K. (2019). Self and group racial/ethnic identification among emerging adults. *Emerging Adulthood, 7,* 138-149.

Blakemore, J.E.O., Berenbaum, S.A., & Liben, L.S. (2009). *Gender development.* Clifton, NJ: Psychology Press.

Blakemore, S-J. (2012, June 5). *The adolescent brain.* Retrieved March 9, 2019, from www.edge.org/conversation/sarah_jayne_blakemore-the-adolescent-brain

Blakemore, S-J. (2018). *Inventing ourselves: The secret life of the teenage brain.* London: Public Affairs.

Bland, L.M., & Gareis, C.R. (2018). Performance assessments: A review of definitions, quality characteristics, and outcomes associated with their use in K-12 schools. *Teacher Educators' Journal, 11,* 52-69.

Blankenburg, H., Pramstaller, P.P., & Domingues, F.S. (2018). A network-based meta-analysis for characterizing the genetic landscape of aging. *Biogerontology, 19,* 81-94.

Blankenship, T.L., Broomell, A.P.R., & Bell, M.A. (2019, in press). Semantic future thinking and executive functions at age 4: The moderating role of frontal activation. *Developmental Psychobiology.*

Blankenship, T.L., & others (2019, in press). Attention and executive functioning in infancy: Links to childhood executive function and reading achievement. *Developmental Science.*

Blanner Kristiansen, C., & others (2019). Prevalence of common mental disorders in widowhood: A systematic review and meta-analysis. *Journal of Affective Disorders, 245,* 1016-1023.

Blass, E. (2008). Suckling. In M.M. Haith & J.B. Benson (Eds.), *Encyclopedia of infant and early childhood development.* Oxford, UK: Elsevier.

Blatny, M., Millova, K., Jelinek, M., & Osecka, T. (2015). Personality predictors of successful development: Toddler temperament and adolescent personality traits predict well-being and career stability in middle adulthood. *PLoS One, 10*(94), e0126032.

Blayney, J.A., & others (2019, in press). Examining the influence of gender and sexual motivation in college hookups. *Journal of American College Health.*

Bleakley, A., & others (2018). How patterns of learning about sexual information among adolescents are related to sexual behaviors. *Perspectives on Sexual and Reproductive Health, 50,* 15-23.

Bleker, L.S., & others (2019). Exploring the effect of antenatal depression treatment on children's epigenetic profiles: Findings from a pilot randomized controlled trial. *Clinical Epigenetics, 11*(1), 18.

Blieszner, R.A. (2018). Family life cycle. In M.H. Bornstein (Ed.), *SAGE encyclopedia of lifespan human development.* Thousand Oaks, CA: Sage.

Blieszner, R.A., & Ogletree, A.M. (2017). We get a little help from our friends. *Generations, 41,* 55-62.

Blieszner, R.A., & Ogletree, A.M. (2018). Relationships in middle and late adulthood. In A.L. Vangelisti & D. Perlman (Eds.), *Cambridge handbook of personal relationships* (2nd ed.). New York; Cambridge University Press.

Blieszner, R.A., & Roberto, K.A. (2012). Intergenerational relationships and aging. In S.K. Whitbourne & M. Sliwinski (Eds.), *Wiley-Blackwell handbook of adult development and aging.* New York: Wiley-Blackwell.

Block, J. (1993). Studying personality the long way. In D. Funder, R.D. Parke, C. Tomlinson-Keasey, & K. Widaman (Ed.), *Studying lives through time.* Washington, DC: American Psychological Association.

Bloom, B. (1985). *Developing talent in young people.* New York: Ballantine.

Bloom, L. (1998). Language acquisition in its developmental context. In W. Damon (Ed.), *Handbook of child psychology* (5th ed., Vol. 2). New York: Wiley.

Bloom, L., Lifter, K., & Broughton, J. (1985). The convergence of early cognition and language in the second year of life: Problems in conceptualization and measurement. In M. Barrett (Ed.), *Single word speech*. London: Wiley.

Bloom, P., & German, T.P. (2000). Two reasons to abandon the false belief task as a test of theory of mind. *Cognition, 77*, B25–B31.

Blumberg, S.J., Vahratian, A., & Blumberg, J.H. (2014). Marriage, cohabitation, and men's use of preventive health services. *NCHS Data Brief, 154*, 1–8.

Blumel, J.E., Lavin, P., Vellejo, M.S., & Sarra, S. (2014). Menopause or climacteric, just a semantic discussion or has it clinical implications? *Climacteric, 17*, 235–241.

Boccia, M., Silveri, M.C., & Guariglia, C. (2014). Visuo-perceptive priming in Alzheimer's disease: Evidence for a multi-componential implicit memory system. *Journal of Alzheimer's Disease, 40*, 455–463.

Bock, J., & Burkley, M. (2019). On the prowl: Examining the impact of men-as-predators and women-as-prey metaphors on attitudes that perpetuate sexual violence. *Sex Roles, 5-6*, 262–276.

Boden, J.S., Fischer, J.L., & Niehuis, S. (2010). Predicting marital adjustment from young adults' initial levels of and changes in emotional intimacy over time: A 25-year longitudinal study. *Journal of Adult Development, 17*, 121–134.

Bodner, E., & Cohen-Fridel, S. (2010). Relations between attachment styles, ageism, and quality of life in late life. *International Psychogeriatrics, 22*, 1353–1361.

Bodrova, E., & Leong, D.J. (2007). *Tools of the mind* (2nd ed.). Geneva, Switzerland: International Bureau of Education, UNESCO.

Bodrova, E., & Leong, D.J. (2015a). Standing 'A head taller than himself': Vygotskian and post-Vygotskian views on children's play. In J.E. Johnson & others (Eds.), *Handbook of the study of play*. Blue Ridge Summit, PA: Rowman & Littlefield.

Bodrova, E., & Leong, D.J. (2015b). Vygotskian and post-Vygotskian views of children's play. *American Journal of Play, 7*, 371–388.

Boele, S., & others (2019, in press). Linking parent-child and peer relationship quality to empathy in adolescence: A multi-level meta-analysis. *Journal of Youth and Adolescence*.

Boelen, P.A. (2015). Optimism in prolonged grief and depression following loss: A three-wave longitudinal study. *Psychiatry Research, 227*, 313–317.

Boerner, K., Jopp, J.S., Carr, D., Sosinsky, L., & Kim, S.K. (2014). "His" and "her" marriage? The role of positive and negative characteristics in global marital satisfaction among older adults. *Journals of Gerontology B: Psychological Sciences and Social Sciences, 69*, 579–589.

Boespflug, E.L., & others (2016). Fish oil supplementation increases event-related posterior cingulate activation in older adults with subjective memory impairment. *Journal of Nutritional Health and Aging, 20*, 161–169.

Bogaerts, A., & others (2019, in press). Identity structure and processes in adolescence: Examining the directionality of between- and within-person associations. *Journal of Youth and Adolescence*.

Bojorquez, G.R., & Fry-Bowers, E.K. (2019, in press). Beyond eligibility: Access to federal public benefit programs for immigrant families in the United States. *Journal of Pediatric Health Care*.

Bombard, J.M., & others (2018). Vital signs: Trends and disparities in infant safe sleep practices—United States, 2009-2015. *MMWR Morbidity and Mortality Weekly Report, 67*(1), 39–46.

Bonache, H., Gonzalez-Mendez, R., & Krahe, B. (2017). Romantic attachment, conflict resolution styles, and teen dating violence victimization. *Journal of Youth and Adolescence, 46*, 1905–1917.

Bonanno, G.A., & Malgaroli, M. (2019, in press). Trajectories of grief: Comparing symptoms from the DSM-5 and ICD-11 diagnoses. *Depression and Anxiety*.

Bond, B.J., Richards, M.N., & Calvert, S.L. (2013). Media and pediatric obesity. In D. Lemish (Ed.), *The handbook of children and the media*. New York: Routledge.

Bond, M.H. (2019). Traveling from the past into the future of cross-cultural psychology: A personal scientific journey. In D. Matsumoto & H.C. Hwang (Eds.), *Handbook of cross-cultural psychology* (2nd ed.). New York: Oxford University Press.

Bonfiglio, T., Vergassola, M., Olivero, G., & Pittaluga, A. (2019, in press). Environmental training and synaptic functions in young and old brain: A presynaptic perspective. *Current Medicinal Chemistry*. doi:10.2174/0929867325666180228170450

Bonney, C.R., & Sternberg, R.J. (2016). Learning to think critically. In R.E. Mayer & P.A. Alexander (Eds.), *Handbook of learning and instruction* (2nd ed.). New York: Routledge.

Bono, G. (2012, August 5). *Searching for the developmental role of gratitude: A 4-year longitudinal analysis*. Paper presented at the American Psychological Association, Orlando.

Bonzano. S., & De Marchis, S. (2017). Detecting neuronal differentiation markers in newborn cells of the adult brain. *Methods in Molecular Biology, 1560*, 163–177.

Bookwala, J., & Jacobs, J. (2004). Age, marital processes, and depressed affect. *The Gerontologist, 44*, 328–338.

Booth-Laforce, C., & Groh, A.M. (2018). Parent-child attachment and peer relations. In W.M. Bukowski & others (Eds.), *Handbook of peer interaction, relationships, and groups*. New York: Guilford.

Borasio, G.D., Jox, R.J., & Gamondi, C. (2019). Regulation of assisted suicide limits the number of assisted deaths. *Lancet, 393*, 982–983.

Boraxbekk, C.J., & others (2015). Free recall episodic memory performance predicts dementia ten years prior to clinical diagnosis: Findings from the Betula Longitudinal Study. *Dementia and Geriatric Cognitive Disorders Extra, 5*, 191–202.

Borella, E., & others (2017). Training working memory in older adults: Is there an advantage of using strategies? *Psychology and Aging, 32*, 178–191.

Borges, N.J., McNally, C.J., Maguire, C.P., Werth, J.L., & Britton, P.J. (2008). Work, health, diversity, and social justice: Expanding and extending the discussion. *The Counseling Psychologist, 36*, 127–131.

Borghuis, J., & others (2017). Big Five personality stability, change, and codevelopment across adolescence and early adulthood. *Journal of Personality and Social Psychology, 113*, 641–657.

Bornstein, M.H. (1975). Qualities of color vision in infancy. *Journal of Experimental Child Psychology, 19*, 401–409.

Bornstein, M.H. (Ed.) (2019). *Handbook of parenting* (3rd Ed.). New York: Routledge.

Bornstein, M.H., Arterberry, M.E., & Mash, C. (2015). Perceptual development. In M.H. Bornstein & M.E. Lamb (Eds.), *Developmental psychology: An advanced textbook* (7th ed.). New York: Psychology Press.

Bornstein, M.H., & Cote, L.R. (2019). Immigrant parenting. In M.H. Bornstein (Ed.), *Handbook of parenting* (3rd ed.). New York: Routledge.

Bornstein, M.H., & Lansford, J.E. (2019). Culture and family functioning. In *APA handbook of contemporary family psychology*. Washington, DC: APA Books.

Borrelli, A., & others (2018). Role of gut microbiota and oxidative stress in the progression of non-alcoholic fatty liver disease to hepatocarcinoma: Current and innovative therapeutic approaches. *Redox Biology, 15*, 467–479.

Borsa, V.M., & others (2018). Bilingualism and healthy aging: Aging effects and neural maintenance. *Neuropsychologia, 111*, 51–61.

Borsani, E., & others (2019, in press). Correlation between human nervous system development and acquisition of fetal skills: An overview. *Brain Development*.

Bortfield, H., & others (2005). Mommy and me: Familiar names help launch babies into speech-stream segmentation. *Psychological Science, 16*, 298–304.

Boschen, K.E., Keller, S.M., Roth, T.L., & Klintsova, A.Y. (2018). Epigenetic mechanisms in alcohol- and adversity-induced developmental origins of neurobehavioral functioning. *Neurotoxicology, 66*, 63–79.

Bosma, H.A., & Kunnen, E.S. (2001). Determinants and mechanisms in ego identity development: A review and synthesis. *Developmental Review, 21*, 39–66.

Bottomley, J.S., & others (2019). Distinguishing the meaning making processes of survivors of suicide loss: An expansion of the meaning of loss codebook. *Death Studies, 43*, 92–102.

Bouillot, L., Vercherat, M., & Durand, C. (2019). Implementing universal hearing screening in the French Rhone-Alps region. State of affairs in 2016 and the 1st half of 2017. *International Journal of Pediatric Otorhinolaryngology, 117*, 30–36.

Boukhris, T., Sheehy, O., Mottron, L., & Berard, A. (2016). Antidepressant use during pregnancy and the risk of autism spectrum disorder in children. *JAMA Pediatrics, 170*, 117–124.

Bould, H., & others (2014). Association between early temperament and depression at 18 years. *Depression and Anxiety, 31*, 729–736.

Boulton, E., & others (2019, in press). Implementing behavior change theory and techniques to increase physical activity and prevent functional decline among adults aged 61-70: The PreventIT Project. *Progress in Cardiovascular Diseases*.

Bouman, W.P. (2008). Sexuality in later life. In R. Jacoby, C. Oppenheimer, T. Dening, & A. Thomas (Eds.), *Oxford textbook of old age psychiatry*. New York: Oxford University Press.

Bourassa, K.J., Ruiz, J.M., & Sbarra, D.A. (2019, in press). Smoking and physical activity explain the increased mortality risk following marital separation and divorce: Evidence from the English Longitudinal Study of Aging. *Annals of Behavioral Medicine*.

Bovbjerg, M.L., Cheyney, M., & Everson, C. (2016). Maternal and newborn outcomes following waterbirth:

The Midwives Alliance of North America Statistics Project, 2004 to 2009 cohort. *Journal of Midwifery and Women's Health, 61,* 11-20.

Bower, T.G.R. (1966). Slant perception and shape constancy in infants, *Science, 151,* 832-834.

Bowlby, J. (1969). *Attachment and loss* (Vol. 1). London: Hogarth Press.

Bowlby, J. (1989). *Secure and insecure attachment.* New York: Basic Books.

Boyes, M.E., & others (2019). Mental health in South African adolescents living with HIV: Correlates of internalizing and externalizing symptoms. *AIDS Care, 31,* 95-104.

Boyle, J., & Cropley, M. (2004). Children's sleep: Problems and solutions. *Journal of Family Health Care, 14,* 61-63.

Bozek, K., & others (2017). Lipidome determinants of maximal lifespan in animals. *Scientific Reports, 7(1),* 5.

Brabek, M.M., & Brabek, K.M. (2006). Women and relationships. In J. Worell & C.D. Goodheart (Eds.), *Handbook of girls' and women's psychological health.* New York: Oxford University Press.

Braccio, S., Sharland, M., & Ladhani, S.N. (2016). Prevention and treatment of mother-to-child syphilis. *Current Opinion on Infectious Diseases, 29,* 268-274.

Bradford, N.J., & Syed, M. (2019, in press). Transnormativity and transgender identity development: A master narrative approach. *Sex Roles.*

Bradley, R.H. (2019, in press). Environment and parenting. In M.H. Bornstein (Ed.), *Handbook of parenting* (3rd ed., Vol. 2). New York: Routledge.

Brainerd, C.J., & Reyna, V.F. (1993). Domains of fuzzy-trace theory. In M.L. Howe & R. Pasnak (Eds.), *Emerging themes in cognitive development.* New York: Springer.

Brainerd, C.J., & Reyna, V.F. (2004). Fuzzy-trace theory and memory development. *Developmental Review, 24,* 396-439.

Brainerd, C.J., & Reyna, V.F. (2014). Dual processes in memory development: Fuzzy-trace theory. In P. Bauer & R. Fivush (Eds.), *Wiley-Blackwell handbook of children's memory.* New York: Wiley.

Braithwaite, D.W., & Siegler, R.S. (2018a). Developmental changes in whole number bias. *Developmental Science.* doi:10.1111/desc.12541

Braithwaite, D.W., & Siegler, R.S. (2018b). Children learn spurious associations in their math textbooks: Examples from fraction arithmetic. *Journal of Experimental Psychology: Learning, Memory, and Cognition, 44,* 1765-1777.

Braithwaite, D.W., & Siegler, R.S. (2019, in press). Developmental changes in whole number bias. *Developmental Science.*

Braithwaite, I., & others (2014). Fast-food consumption and body mass index in children and adolescents: An international cross-sectional study. *BMJ Open, 4(12),* e005813.

Braithwaite, S., & Holt-Lunstad, J. (2017). Romantic relationships and mental health. *Current Opinion in Psychology, 13,* 120-125.

Brand, J. (2014). Social consequences of job loss and unemployment. *Annual Review of Sociology* (Vol. 40). Palo Alto, CA: Annual Reviews.

Brandstädter, J. (1999). Sources of resilience in the aging self: Toward integrated perspectives. In T.M. Hess & F. Blanchard-Fields (Eds.), *Social cognition and aging.* San Diego: Academic Press.

Brandstädter, J., & Renner, G. (1990). Tenacious goal pursuit and flexible goal adjustment: Explication and age-related analysis of assimilative and accommodative strategies of coping. *Psychology and Aging, 5,* 58-67.

Brannon, L. (2017). *Gender.* New York: Routledge.

Bransford, J., & others (2006). Learning theories in education. In P.A. Alexander & P.H. Winne (Eds.), *Handbook of educational psychology* (2nd ed.). Mahwah, NJ: Erlbaum.

Branzi, F.M., Calabria, M., & Costa, A. (2019). Cross-linguistic/bilingual language production. In S-A. Rueschemeyer & M. Gareth Gaskell (Eds.), *Oxford handbook of psycholinguistics* (2nd ed.). New York: Oxford University Press.

Brassen, S., Gamer, M., Peters, J., Gluth, S., & Buchel, C. (2012). Don't look back in anger! Responsiveness to missed chances in successful and nonsuccessful aging. *Science, 336,* 612-614.

Bratt, C., & others (2018). Perceived age discrimination across age in Europe: From an aging society to a society for all ages. *Developmental Psychology, 54,* 167-180.

Braun, S.S., & Davidson, A.J. (2017). Gender (non) conformity in middle childhood: A mixed methods approach to understanding gender-typed behavior, friendship, and peer preference. *Sex Roles, 77,* 16-29.

Braver, S.L., & Lamb, M.E. (2013). Marital dissolution. In G.W. Peterson & K.R. Bush (Eds.), *Handbook of marriage and the family* (3rd ed.). New York: Springer.

Brawner, C.A., & others (2017). Change in maximal exercise capacity is associated with survival in men and women. *Mayo Clinic Proceedings, 92,* 383-390.

Bray, J.H. (2019). Remarriage and stepfamilies. In B.H. Friese (Ed.), *APA handbook of contemporary family psychology.* Washington, DC: APA Books.

Breastcancer.org (2018). Using HRT (hormone replacement therapy). Retrieved February 20, 2018, from www.breastcancer.org/risk/factors/hrt

Brechwald, W.A., & Prinstein, M.J. (2011). Beyond homophily: A decade of advances in understanding peer influence processes. *Journal of Research on Adolescence, 21,* 166-179.

Bredekamp, S. (2020). *Effective practices in early childhood education* (4th ed.). Upper Saddle River, NJ: Pearson.

Breen, L.J., & others (2018). Differences in meanings made according to prolonged grief symptomatology. *Death Studies, 42,* 69-78.

Breiner, K., & others (2018). Combined effects of peer presence, social cues, and rewards on cognitive control in adolescence. *Developmental Psychobiology, 60,* 292-302.

Bremner, J.G., & others (2017). Limits of object persistence: Young infants perceive continuity of vertical and horizontal trajectories but not 45-degre oblique trajectories. *Infancy, 44,* 240-248.

Brent, R.L. (2009). Saving lives and changing family histories: Appropriate counseling of pregnant women and men and women of reproductive age concerning the risk of diagnostic radiation exposure during and before pregnancy. *American Journal of Obstetrics and Gynecology, 200,* 4-24.

Brent, R.L. (2011). The pulmonologist's role in caring for pregnant women with regard to the reproductive risks of diagnostic radiological studies or radiation therapy. *Clinics in Chest Medicine, 32(1),* 33-42.

Brentari, D., & Goldin-Meadow, S. (2017). Language emergence. *Annual Review of Linguistics, 3,* 363-388.

Breslau, J., & others (2011). A multinational study of mental disorders, marriage, and divorce. *Acta Psychiatrica Scandinavica, 124,* 1474-1486.

Breveglieri, G., & others (2019, in press). Non-invasive prenatal testing using fetal DNA. *Molecular Design and Analysis.*

Brewer, M.B., & Campbell, D.T. (1976). *Ethnocentrism and intergroup attitudes.* New York: Wiley.

Brewster, G.S., Riegel, B., & Gehrman, P.R. (2018). Insomnia in the older adult. *Sleep Medicine Clinics, 13,* 13-19.

Bridgeland, J.M., Dilulio, J.J., & Wulsin, S.C. (2008). *Engaged for success.* Washington, DC: Civic Enterprises.

Bridgett, D.J., Laake, L.M., Gartstein, M.A., & Dorn, D. (2013). Development of infant positive emotionality: The contribution of maternal characteristics and effects on subsequent parenting. *Infant and Child Development, 22(4),* 362-382.

Bridgett, D.J., & others (2009). Maternal and contextual influences and the effect of temperament development during infancy on parenting in toddlerhood. *Infant Behavior and Development, 32,* 103-116.

Briley, D.A., Domiteaux, M., & Tucker-Drob, E.M. (2014). Achievement-relevant personality: Relations with the Big Five and validation of an efficient instrument. *Learning and Individual Differences, 32,* 26-39.

Brim, O. (1999). *The MacArthur Foundation study of midlife development.* Vero Beach, FL: MacArthur Foundation.

Brimdyr, K., & Caldwell, K. (2018). A plausible causal relationship between the increased use of fentanyl as an obstetric analgesic and the current opioid epidemic in the US. *Medical Hypotheses, 119,* 540-557.

Brinkman, J.E., & Sharma, S. (2018, January 8). *Physiology, sleep.* Treasure Island, FL: SatPearls Publishing.

Brinkman-Stoppelenburg, A., Rietjens, J.A., & van der Heide, A. (2014). The effects of advance care planning on end-of-life care: A systematic review. *Palliative Medicine, 28,* 1000-1025.

Brinskma, D.M., & others (2017). Age-dependent role of pre- and perinatal factors in interaction with genes on ADHD symptoms across adolescence. *Journal of Psychiatric Research, 90,* 110-117.

Brislin, R. (1993). *Understanding culture's influence on behavior.* Fort Worth, TX: Harcourt Brace.

Brito, N.H., & others (2019, in press). Beyond the Bayley: Neurocognitive assessments of development during infancy and toddlerhood. *Developmental Neuropsychology.*

Britto, C., Jasmine, P.N., & Rao, S. (2017). Assessment of neonatal pain during heel prick: Lancet versus needle—A randomized controlled study. *Journal of Tropical Pediatrics, 63,* 346-351.

Brod, G., & Shing, Y.L. (2019, in press). A boon and a bane: Comparing the effects of prior knowledge on memory across the lifespan. *Developmental Psychology.*

Brody, G.H., Lei, M.K., Chen, E., & Miller, G.E. (2014). Neighborhood poverty and allostatic load in African American youth. *Pediatrics, 134,* e1362-e1368.

Brody, G.H., & others (2017). Protective prevention effects on the association of poverty with brain development. *JAMA Pediatrics, 17,* 46–52.

Brody, L.R., Hall, J.A., & Stokes, L.R. (2018). Gender and emotion: Theory, findings, and content. In L.F. Barrett & others (Eds.), *Handbook of emotion* (4th ed.). New York: Guilford.

Brody, N. (2000). Intelligence. In A. Kazdin (Ed.), *Encyclopedia of psychology.* New York: Oxford University Press.

Brody, N. (2007). Does education influence intelligence? In P.C. Kyllonen, R.D. Roberts, & L. Stankov (Eds.), *Extending intelligence.* Mahwah, NJ: Erlbaum.

Brody, S. (2010). The relative health benefits of different sexual activities. *Journal of Sexual Medicine, 7,* 1336–1361.

Brody, S., & Costa, R.M. (2009). Satisfaction (sexual, life, relationship, and mental health) is associated directly with penile-vaginal intercourse, but inversely related to other sexual behavior frequencies. *Journal of Sexual Medicine, 6,* 1947–1954.

Brodzinsky, D.M., & Pinderhughes, E. (2002). Parenting and child development in adoptive families. In M.H. Bornstein (Ed.), *Handbook of parenting* (Vol. 1). Mahwah, NJ: Erlbaum.

Broesch, T., & Bryant, G.A. (2018). Fathers' infant-directed speech in a small-scale society. *Child Development, 89,* e29–e41.

Bronfenbrenner, U. (1986). Ecology of the family as a context for human development: Research perspectives. *Developmental Psychology, 22,* 723–742.

Bronfenbrenner, U. (2004). *Making human beings human.* Thousand Oaks, CA: Sage.

Bronfenbrenner, U., & Morris, P. (1998). The ecology of developmental processes. In W. Damon (Ed.), *Handbook of child psychology* (5th ed., Vol. 1). New York: Wiley.

Bronfenbrenner, U., & Morris, P. (2006). The ecology of developmental processes. In W. Damon & R. Lerner (Eds.), *Handbook of child psychology* (6th ed.). New York: Wiley.

Bronstein, P. (2006). The family environment: Where gender role socialization begins. In J. Worell & C.D. Goodheart (Eds.), *Handbook of girls' and women's psychological health.* New York: Oxford University Press.

Brookhart, S.M., & Nitko, A.J. (2019). *Educational assessment of students* (8th ed.). Upper Saddle River, NJ: Pearson.

Brooks, F., & others (2018). Spirituality as a protective health asset for young people: An international comparative analysis from three countries. *International Journal of Public Health, 63,* 387–395.

Brooks, J.G., & Brooks, M.G. (1993). *The case for constructivist classrooms.* Alexandria, VA: Association for Supervision and Curriculum.

Brooks, J.G., & Brooks, M.G. (2001). *The case for constructivist classrooms* (2nd ed.). Upper Saddle River, NJ: Erlbaum.

Brooks, R., & Meltzoff, A.N. (2005). The development of gaze in relation to language. *Developmental Science, 8,* 535–543.

Brooks, R.C., & Garratt, M.G. (2017). Life history evolution, reproduction, and the origins of sex-dependent aging and longevity. *Annals of the New York Academy of Sciences, 1389,* 92–107.

Brooks-Gunn, J., & Warren, M.F. (1989). The psychological significance of secondary sexual characteristics in 9- to 11-year-old girls. *Child Development, 59,* 161–169.

Broussard, M. (2015). *Dating stats you should know.* Retrieved June 18, 2015, from www.match.com/magazine/article/4671/

Broverman, I., Vogel, S., Broverman, D., Clarkson, F., & Rosenkranz, P. (1972). Sex-role stereotypes: A current appraisal. *Journal of Social Issues, 28,* 59–78.

Brown, A.L., Horton, J., & Guillory, A. (2018). The impact of victim alcohol consumption and perpetrator use of force on perceptions in an acquaintance rape vignette. *Violence and Victims, 33,* 40–52.

Brown, B.B. (1999). Measuring the peer environment of American adolescents. In S.L. Friedman & T.D. Wachs (Eds.), *Measuring environment across the life span.* Washington, DC: American Psychological Association.

Brown, B.B., Bakken, J.P., Ameringer, S.W., & Mahon, S.D. (2008). A comprehensive conceptualization of the peer influence process in adolescence. In M.J. Prinstein & K.A. Dodge (Eds.), *Understanding peer influence in children and adolescents.* New York: Guilford.

Brown, B.B., & Larson, J. (2009). Peer relationships in adolescence. In R.M. Lerner & L. Steinberg (Eds.), *Handbook of adolescent psychology* (3rd ed.). New York: Wiley.

Brown, C.L., & others (2012). Social activity and cognitive functioning over time: A coordinated analysis of four longitudinal studies. *Journal of Aging Research,* 493598.

Brown, C.S., & Stone, E.A. (2016). Gender stereotypes and discrimination: How sexism impacts development. *Advances in Child Development and Behavior, 50,* 105–133.

Brown, C.S., & Stone, E.A. (2018). Environmental and social contributions to children's gender-typed toy play: The role of family, peers, and the media. In E.S. Weisgram & L.M. Dinella (Eds.), *Gender typing of children's play.* Washington, DC: APA Books.

Brown, D., & Lamb, M.E. (2018, in press). Forks in the road, routes chosen, and journeys that beckon: A selective review of scholarship on children's testimony. *Applied Cognitive Psychology.*

Brown, G.L., & Cox, M.J. (2019, in press). Pleasure in parenting and father-child attachment security. *Attachment and Human Development.*

Brown, H.L., & Graves, C.R. (2013). Smoking and marijuana in pregnancy. *Clinical Obstetrics and Gynecology, 56,* 107–113.

Brown, J.D., & Strasburger, V.C. (2007). From Calvin Klein to Paris Hilton and MySpace: Adolescents, sex, and the media. *Adolescent Medicine: State of the Art Reviews, 18,* 484–507.

Brown, L., & others (2018). It's not as bad as you think: Menopausal representations are more positive in postmenopausal women. *Journal of Psychosomatic Obstetrics and Gynecology, 39,* 81–88.

Brown, L.S. (1989). New voices, new visions: Toward a lesbian/gay paradigm for psychology. *Psychology of Women Quarterly, 13,* 445–458.

Brown, M.I., & others (2018). Promoting language and social communication development in babies through an early storybook reading intervention. *International Journal of Speech-Language Pathology, 20,* 337–349.

Brown, M.T., & Wolf, D.A. (2018). Estimating the prevalence of serious mental illness and dementia diagnoses among Medicare beneficiaries in the Health and Retirement Study. *Research on Aging, 40,* 668–686.

Brown, Q.L., & others (2016). Trends in marijuana use among pregnant and non-pregnant reproductive-aged women 2002–2014. *Journal of the American Medical Association, 317,* 207–209.

Brown, R. (1968). *Words and things.* Glencoe, IL: Free Press.

Brown, R.C., & others (2018). The impact of child maltreatment on non-suicidal self-injury: Data from a representative sample of the general population. *BMC Psychiatry, 18*(1), 181.

Brown, S.L., Nesse, R.M., House, J.S., & Utz, R.L. (2004). Religion and emotional compensation: Results from a prospective study of widowhood. *Personality and Social Psychology Bulletin, 30,* 1165–1174.

Brown, S.L., & Wright, M.W. (2017). Marriage, cohabitation, and divorce in later life. *Innovations in Aging, 1*(2).

Brownell, C. (2009). *Brownell–Early social development lab.* Retrieved November 9, 2009, from www.pitt.edu/~toddlers/ESDL/brownell.html

Brownell, C.A., Nichols, S., Svetlova, M., Zerwas, S., & Ramani, G. (2009). The head bone's connected to the neck bone: When do toddlers represent their own body topography? *Child Development, 81*(3), 797–810.

Brownell, C.A., Ramani, G.B., & Zerwas, S. (2006). Becoming a social partner with peers: Cooperation and social understanding in one- and two-year-olds. *Child Development, 77,* 803–821.

Brownell, C.A., Svetlova, M., Anderson, R., Nichols, S.R., & Drummond, J. (2013). Socialization of early prosocial behavior: Parents' talk about emotions is associated with sharing and helping in toddlers. *Infancy, 18,* 91–119.

Brownstein, C.A., & others (2018). Genetics of sudden infant death syndrome. In J.R. Duncan & R.W. Byard (Eds.), *SIDS sudden infant and early childhood death.* Adelaide, Australia: University of Adelaide Press.

Bruchmiller, K., Margraf, J., & Schneider, S. (2012). Is ADHD diagnosed in accord with diagnostic criteria? Overdiagnosis and influence of client gender on diagnosis. *Journal of Consulting and Clinical Psychology, 80,* 128–138.

Bruck, M., & Ceci, S.J. (1999). The suggestibility of children's memory. *Annual Review of Psychology, 50,* 419–439.

Bruck, M., & Ceci, S.J. (2013). Expert testimony in a child sex abuse case: Translating memory development research. *Memory, 21,* 556–565.

Bruck, M., & Melnyk, L. (2004). Individual difference in children's suggestibility: A review and a synthesis. *Applied Cognitive Psychology, 18,* 947–996.

Bruckner, S., & Kammer, T. (2017). Both anodal and cathodal transcranial direct current stimulation improves semantic processing. *Neuroscience, 343,* 269–275.

Brum, P.S., & others (2019, in press). Verbal working memory training in older adults: An investigation of dose response. *Aging and Mental Health.*

Brumariu, L.E., & Kerns, K.A. (2011). Parent-child attachment in early and middle childhood. In P.K. Smith & C.H. Hart (Eds.), *Wiley-Blackwell handbook of social development* (2nd ed.). New York: Wiley.

Brumariu, L.E., & Kerns, K.A. (2015). Mother-child emotion communication and childhood anxiety symptoms. *Cognition and Emotion, 29,* 416–431.

Brumariu, L.E., Kerns, K.A., & Seibert, A.C. (2012). Mother-child attachment, emotion regulation, and anxiety symptoms in middle childhood. *Personal Relationships, 19*(3), 569–585.

Brummelman, J.E., Thomaes, S., Orobio de Castro, B., Overbeek, G., & Bushman, B.J. (2014). "That's not just beautiful—that's incredibly beautiful!": The adverse impact of inflated praise on children with low self-esteem. *Psychological Science, 25*, 728–735.

Brummelman, J.E., & others (2015). My child is God's gift to humanity: Development and validation of the Parental Overvaluation Scale (POS). *Journal of Personality and Social Psychology, 108*, 665–679.

Brunborg, G.S., Andreas, J.B., & Kvaavik, E. (2017). Social media use and episodic heavy drinking among adolescents. *Psychological Reports, 120*, 475–490.

Brunes, A., Hansen, M., & Heir, T. (2019). Loneliness among adults with visual impairment: Prevalence, associated factors, and relationship to life satisfaction. *Health Quality and Life Outcomes, 17*(1), 24.

Brunet, A., & Rando, T.A. (2017). Interaction between epigenetic and metabolism in aging stem cells. *Current Opinion in Cell Biology, 45*, 1–7.

Brusseau, T.A., & others (2018). Trends in physical activity, health-related fitness, and gross motor skills in children during a two-year comprehensive school physical activity program. *Journal of Science and Medicine in Sport, 21*, 828–832.

Brust-Reneck, P.G., Reyna, V.F., Wilhelms, E.A., & Lazar, A.N. (2017). A fuzzy-trace theory of judgment and decision-making in healthcare: Explanations, predictions, and applications. In M.A. Diefenbach & others (Eds.), *Handbook of health and decision science.* New York: Springer.

Bryant, R.A. (2012). Grief as a psychiatric disorder. *British Journal of Psychiatry, 201*, 9–10.

Bryant, R.A. (2013). Is pathological grief lasting more than 12 months grief or depression? *Current Opinion in Psychiatry, 26*, 41–46.

Bryant Ludden, A., & Wolfson, A.R. (2010). Understanding adolescent caffeine use: Connecting use patterns with expectancies, reasons, and sleep. *Health Education and Behavior, 37*, 330–337.

Bryant-Waugh, R. (2019). Feeding and eating disorders in children. *Psychiatric Clinics of North America, 42*, 157–167.

Buchman, A.S., Yu, L., Boyle, P.A., Shah, R.C., & Bennett, D.A. (2012). Total daily physical activity and longevity in old age. *Archives of Internal Medicine, 172*, 444–446.

Buchman, A.S., & others (2009). Association between late-life social activity and motor decline in older adults. *Archives of Internal Medicine, 169*, 1139–1146.

Buckner, J.C., Mezzacappa, E., & Beardslee, W.R. (2009). Self-regulation and its relations to adaptive functioning in low-income youths. *American Journal of Orthopsychiatry, 79*, 19–30.

Bucur, B., & Madden, D.J. (2007). Information processing/cognition. In J.E. Birren (Ed.), *Encyclopedia of gerontology* (2nd ed.). San Diego: Academic Press.

Budge, S.L., Chin, M.Y., & Minero, L.P. (2017). Trans individuals' facilitative coping: An analysis of internal and external processes. *Journal of Counseling Psychology, 64*, 12–25.

Budge, S.L., & Orovecz, J.J. (2018). Gender fluidity. In K. Nadal (Ed.), *SAGE encyclopedia of psychology and gender.* Thousand Oaks, CA: Sage.

Budge, S.L., & others (2018). Trans individuals' facilitative coping: An analysis of internal and external processes. *Journal of Counseling Psychology, 64*, 12–25.

Buhrmester, D. (1998). Need fulfillment, interpersonal competence, and the developmental contexts of early adolescent friendship. In W.M. Bukowski & A.F. Newcomb (Eds.), *The company they keep: Friendship in childhood and adolescence.* New York: Cambridge University Press.

Bui, E., & Okereke, O. (2018). From bereavement to grief to cognitive decline: A call for novel treatment and prevention approaches. *American Journal of Geriatric Psychiatry, 26*, 481–482.

Buist, K.L., Dekovic, M., & Prinzie, P. (2013). Sibling relationship quality and psychopathology of children and adolescents: A meta-analysis. *Clinical Psychology Review, 33*, 97–106.

Buitelaar, J., Karr, C., & Asherton, P. (2010). *ADHD in adulthood.* New York: Cambridge University Press.

Buiting, H.M., & de Graas, T. (2018). Possible underestimation of the provision of palliative care. *JAMA Oncology, 4*, 885–886.

Bukowski, W.M., Laursen, B., & Rubin, K. (2018). Peer relations. In M.H. Bornstein (Ed.), *SAGE encyclopedia of lifespan human development.* Thousand Oaks, CA: Sage.

Bulik, C.M., Blake, L., & Austin, J. (2019). Genetics of eating disorders: What the clinician needs to know. *Psychiatric Clinics of North America, 42*, 59–73.

Bullock, M., & Lutkenhaus, P. (1990). Who am I? Self-understanding in toddlers. *Merrill-Palmer Quarterly, 36*, 217–238.

Bumpass, L., & Aquilino, W. (1994). *A social map of midlife: Family and work over the middle life course.* Center for Demography and Ecology, University of Wisconsin, Madison, WI.

Bumpus, M.F., Crouter, A.C., & McHale, S.M. (2001). Parental autonomy granting during adolescence: Exploring gender differences in context. *Developmental Psychology, 37*, 163–173.

Burani, K., & others (2019, in press). Longitudinal increases in reward-related neural activity in early adolescence: Evidence from event-related potentials (ERPs). *Developmental Cognitive Neuroscience.*

Burchinal, M., Magnuson, K., Powell, D., & Hong, S.S. (2015). Early child care and education. In R.M. Lerner (Ed.), *Handbook of child psychology and developmental science* (7th ed.). New York: Wiley.

Burchinal, M.R., Peisner-Feinberg, E., Pianta, R., & Howes, C. (2002). Development of academic skills from preschool through second grade: Family and classroom predictors of developmental trajectories. *Journal of School Psychology, 40*(5), 415–436.

Burden, P.R., & Byrd, D.M. (2019). *Methods for effective teaching* (8th ed.). Upper Saddle River, NJ: Pearson.

Burden, P.R., & Byrd, D.M. (2020). *Foundations of teaching education: A practical perspective.* Upper Saddle River, NJ: Pearson.

Burger, J.M. (2019). *Personality* (10th ed.). Boston: Cengage.

Burgette, J.M., & others (2017). Impact of Early Head Start in North Carolina on dental care use among children younger than 3 years. *American Journal of Public Health, 107*, 614–620.

Burke, D.M., & Shafto, M.A. (2004). Aging and language production. *Current Directions in Psychological Science, 13*, 21–24.

Burke-Adams, A. (2007). The benefits of equalizing standards and creativity: Discovering a balance in instruction. *Gifted Child Quarterly, 30*, 58–63.

Burnett, A.C., & others (2019, in press). Trends in executive functioning in extremely preterm children across 3 birth eras. *Pediatrics.*

Burnette, C.B., Kwitowski, M.A., & Mazzeo, S.E. (2017). "I don't need people to tell me I'm pretty on social media": A qualitative study of social media and body image in early adolescent girls. *Body Image, 23*, 114–125.

Burr, J.A., & others (2018). Health benefits associated with three helping behaviors: Evidence for incident cardiovascular disease. *Journals of Gerontology B: Psychological Sciences and Social Sciences, 73*, 492–500.

Burrello, J., & others (2017). Is there a role for genomics in the management of hypertension? *International Journal of Molecular Science, 18*, 6.

Burt, S.A., Slawinski, B.L., & Klump, K.L. (2018). Are there sex differences in the etiology of youth antisocial behavior? *Journal of Abnormal Psychology, 127*, 66–78.

Burton, R.V. (1984). A paradox in theories and research in moral development. In W.M. Kurtines & J.L. Gewirtz (Eds.), *Morality, moral behavior, and moral development.* New York: Wiley.

Bushnell, I.W.R. (2003). Newborn face recognition. In O. Pascalis & A. Slater (Eds.), *The development of face processing in infancy and early childhood.* New York: NOVA Science.

Buss, D.M. (2008). *Evolutionary psychology* (3rd ed.). Boston: Allyn & Bacon.

Buss, D.M. (2012). *Evolutionary psychology* (4th ed.). Boston: Allyn & Bacon.

Buss, D.M. (2015). *Evolutionary psychology* (5th ed.). Upper Saddle River, NJ: Pearson.

Buss, D.M. (2018). Sexual and emotional infidelity: Evolved gender differences in jealousy prove robust and reliable. *Perspectives on Psychological Science, 13*, 155–160.

Buss, D.M., & Schmitt, D.P. (2019). Mate preferences and their behavioral manifestations. *Annual Review of Psychology* (Vol. 70). Palo Alto, CA: Annual Reviews.

Buss, D.M., & others (1990). International preferences in selecting mates: A study of 37 cultures. *Journal of Cross-Cultural Psychology, 21*, 5–47.

Buss, K.A., & Goldsmith, H.H. (2007). Biobehavioral approaches to early socioemotional development. In C.A. Brownell & C.B. Kopp (Eds.), *Socioemotional development in the toddler years.* New York: Guilford.

Bussey, K., & Bandura, A. (1999). Social cognitive theory of gender development and differentiation. *Psychological Review, 106*, 676–713.

Bussu, G., & others (2018). Prediction of autism at 3 years from behavioral and developmental measures in high-risk infants: A longitudinal cross-domain classifier analysis. *Journal of Autism and Developmental Disorders, 48*, 2418–2433.

Busuito, A., & others (2019, in press). In sync: Physiological correlates of behavioral synchrony in infants and mothers. *Developmental Psychology.*

Butler, R.N., & Lewis, M. (2002). *The new love and sex after 60.* New York: Ballantine.

Butterfield, D.A. (2018). Perspectives on oxidative stress in Alzheimer's disease and predictions of future research emphases. *Journal of Alzheimer's Disease, 64*(Suppl. 1), S469–S479.

Buzzichelli, S., & others (2018). Perfectionism and cognitive rigidity in anorexia nervosa: Is there an association? *European Eating Disorder Review, 26,* 360–366.

Byne, W., & others (2012). Report of the American Psychiatric Association Task Force on the treatment of gender identity disorder. *Archives of Sexual Behavior, 41,* 759–796.

Byrne, L., & Drake, A.J. (2019, in press). Pediatrician's guide to epigenetics. *Archives of Disease in Childhood.*

C

Caballero, B. (2019). Humans against obesity: Who will win? *Advances in Nutrition, 10*(Suppl. 1), S4–S9.

Cabeza, R. (2002). Hemispheric asymmetry reduction in older adults: The HAROLD model. *Psychology and Aging, 17,* 85–100.

Cabeza, R., & Dennis, N.A. (2013). Frontal lobes and aging: Deterioration and compensation. In D.T. Stuss & R.T. Knight (Eds.), *Principles of frontal lobe function* (2nd ed.). New York: Oxford University Press.

Cabrera, N.J., Hofferth, S.L., & Chae, S. (2011). Patterns and predictors of father-infant engagement across race/ethnic groups. *Early Childhood Research Quarterly, 26,* 365–375.

Cabrera, N.J., & Roggman, L. (2017). Father play: Is it special? *Infant Mental Health Journal, 38,* 706–708.

Cabrera, N.J., & others (2017). The magic of play: Low-income mothers' and fathers' playfulness and children's emotion regulation and vocabulary skills. *Infant Mental Health Journal, 38,* 757–771.

Cacioppo, J.T., Cacioppo, S., Gonzaga, G.C., Ogburn, E.L., & VanderWheele, T.J. (2013). Marital satisfaction and break-ups differ across on-line and off-line meeting venues. *Proceedings of the National Academy of Sciences, 110*(25), 10135–10140.

Caemmerer, J.M., & others (2018). Effects of cognitive abilities on child and youth academic achievement: Evidence from WISC-V and WIAT-III. *Intelligence, 68,* 6–20.

Cahill, K.E., Giandrea, M.D., & Quinn, J.F. (2015). Retirement patterns and the macroeconomy, 1992–2010: The prevalence and determinants of bridge jobs, retirement, and reentry among three recent cohorts of older Americans. *Gerontologist, 55,* 384–403.

Cahill, K.E., Giandrea, M.D., & Quinn, J.F. (2016). Evolving patterns of work and retirement. In L.K. George & K.F. Ferraro (Eds.), *Handbook of aging and the social sciences* (8th ed.). New York: Elsevier.

Cahill, M., & others (2019, in press). The transition to retirement experiences of academics in "higher education": a meta-ethnography. *Gerontologist.*

Cai, H., Huang, Z., & Jing, Y. (2019). Living in a changing world: The change of culture and psychology. In D. Matsumoto & H.C. Hwang (Eds.), *Handbook of cross-cultural psychology* (2nd ed.). New York: Oxford University Press.

Cai, H., & others (2018). Increasing need for uniqueness in contemporary China: Empirical evidence. *Frontiers in Psychology, 9,* 554.

Cai, T., & others (2018). The school contextual effect of sexual debut on sexual risk-taking: A joint parameter approach. *Journal of School Health, 88,* 200–207.

Cain, C.L., & McCleskey, S. (2019, in press). Expanded definitions of the 'good death'? Race, ethnicity, and medical aid in dying. *Sociology of Health and Illness.*

Cain, M.S., Leonard, J.A., Gabriel, J.D., & Finn, A.S. (2016). Media multitasking in adolescence. *Psychonomic Bulletin and Review, 23,* 1932–1941.

Caino, S., & others (2010). Short-term growth in head circumference and its relationship with supine length in healthy infants. *Annals of Human Biology, 37,* 108–116.

Cairncross, M., & Miller, C.J. (2019, in press). The effectiveness of mindfulness-based therapies for ADHD: A meta-analytic review. *Journal of Attention Disorders.*

Calamaro, C.J., Mason, T.B., & Ratcliffe, S.J. (2009). Adolescents living the 24/7 lifestyle: Effects of caffeine and technology on sleep duration and daytime functioning. *Pediatrics, 123,* e1005–e1010.

Calero, M.D. (2019). Effects of environmental enrichment and training across the life span in cognition. In R. Fernandez-Ballesteros, A. Benetos, & J-M. Robine (Eds.), *Cambridge handbook of successful aging.* New York; Cambridge University Press.

Callaghan, B.L., Li, S., & Richardson, R. (2014). The elusive engram: What can infantile amnesia tell us about memory? *Trends in Neuroscience, 37,* 47–53.

Callaghan, T., & Corbit, J. (2015). The development of symbolic representation. In R.M. Lerner (Ed.), *Handbook of child psychology and developmental science* (7th ed.). New York: Wiley.

Callahan, D. (2009). Death, mourning, and medical practice. *Perspectives in Biological Medicine, 52,* 103–115.

Callisaya, M.L., Beare, R., Moran, C., Phan, T., Wang, W., & Srikanth, V.K. (2019). Type 2 diabetes mellitus, brain atrophy, and cognitive decline in older people: A longitudinal study. *Diabetologia, 62,* 448–458.

Calso, C., Besnard, J., & Allain, P. (2019). Frontal lobe functions in normal aging: Metacognition, autonomy, and quality of life. *Experimental Aging Research, 45,* 10–27.

Calugi, S., & Dalle Grave, R. (2019, in press). Body image concern and treatment outcomes in adolescents with anorexia nervosa. *International Journal of Eating Disorders.*

Calvert, S.L. (2015). Children and digital media. In R.M. Lerner (Ed.), *Handbook of child psychology and developmental science* (7th ed.). New York: Wiley.

Calvert, S.L., & others (2017). The American Psychological Association Task Force assessment of violent video games: Science in the service of public interest. *American Psychologist, 72,* 126–143.

Calvo-Garcia, M.A. (2016). Guidelines for scanning twins and triplets with US and MRI. *Pediatric Radiology, 46,* 156–166.

Calzada, E.J., & others (2018). Mental health issues in Latino populations. In A.D. Martinez & S.D. Rhodes (Ed.), *New and emerging issues in Latina/o families.* New York: Springer.

Camacho, D.E., & Fuligni, A.J. (2015). Extracurricular participation among adolescents from immigrant families. *Journal of Youth and Adolescence, 44,* 1251–1262.

Cambron, C., & others (2018). Neighborhood, family, and peer factors associated with early adolescent smoking and alcohol use. *Journal of Youth and Adolescence, 47,* 369–382.

Campbell, D.T., & LeVine, K.A. (1968). Ethnocentrism and intergroup relations. In R. Abelson & others (Eds.), *Theories and cognitive consistency: A sourcebook.* Chicago: Rand-McNally.

Campbell, F.A. (2007). The malleability of the cognitive development of children of low-income African-American families: Intellectual test performance over twenty-one years. In P.C. Kyllonen, R.D. Roberts, & L. Stankov (Eds.), *Extending intelligence.* Mahwah, NJ: Erlbaum.

Campbell, F.A., Pungello, E.P., Miller-Johnson, S., Burchinal, M., & Ramey, C.T. (2001). The development of cognitive and academic abilities: Growth curves from an early childhood educational experiment. *Developmental Psychology, 37,* 231–243.

Campbell, F.A., & others (2012). Adult outcomes as a function of an early childhood educational program: An Abecedarian Project follow-up. *Developmental Psychology, 48,* 1033–1043.

Campbell, L., Campbell, B., & Dickinson, D. (2004). *Teaching and learning through multiple intelligences* (3rd ed.). Boston: Allyn & Bacon.

Campione-Barr, N., Greer, K.B., & Kruse, A. (2013). Differential associations between domains of sibling conflict and adolescent emotional adjustment. *Child Development, 84*(3), 938–954.

Campione-Barr, N., & Smetana, J.G. (2019). Families with adolescents. In B.H. Friese (Ed.), *APA handbook of contemporary family psychology.* Washington, DC: APA Books.

Campos, J.J. (2005). Unpublished review of J.W. Santrock's *Life-span development,* 11th ed. (New York: McGraw-Hill).

Campos, J.J. (2009). Unpublished review of J.W. Santrock's *Life-span development,* 13th ed. (New York: McGraw-Hill).

Campos, J.J., Langer, A., & Krowitz, A. (1970). Cardiac responses on the visual cliff in prelocomotor human infants. *Science, 170,* 196–197.

Candow, D.G., & Chilibeck, P.D. (2005). Differences in size, strength, and power of upper and lower body muscle groups in young and older men. *Journals of Gerontology A: Biological Sciences and Medical Sciences, 60,* 148A–156A.

Cangelosi, A., & Schlesinger, M. (2015). *Developmental robotics: From babies to robots.* Cambridge, MA: MIT Press.

Canivez, G.L., Watkins, M.W., & Dombrowski, S.C. (2017). Structural validity of the Wechsler Intelligence Scale for Children–Fifth Edition: Confirmatory factor analysis with the 16 primary and secondary subtests. *Psychological Assessment, 29,* 458–472.

Canivez, G.L., & others (2019, in press). Construct validity of the WISC-V in clinical cases: Exploratory and confirmatory factor analyses of the 10 primary subtests. *Assessment.*

Cansino, S., & others (2019). Predictors of source memory success and failure in older adults. *Frontiers in Aging Neuroscience, 11,* 17.

Cantone, E., & others (2015). Interventions on bullying and cyberbullying in schools: A systematic review. *Clinical Practice and Epidemiology in Mental Health, 11*(Suppl. 1), S58–S76.

Capaldi, D.M., & Shortt, J.W. (2003). Understanding conduct problems in adolescence from a lifespan perspective. In G.R. Adams & M.D. Berzonsky (Eds.), *Blackwell handbook of adolescence.* Malden, MA: Blackwell.

Caprara, G.V., & others (2010). The contributions of agreeableness and self-efficacy beliefs to prosociality. *European Journal of Personality, 24,* 36–55.

Caprara, M.G., & Mendoza-Ruvalcaba, N. (2019). Promoting successful aging: A psychosocial perspective. In R. Fernandez-Ballesteros, A. Benetos, & J-M. Robine (Eds.), *Cambridge handbook of successful aging.* New York: Cambridge University Press.

Carbajal-Valenzuela, C.C., & others (2017). Development of emotional face processing in premature and full-term infants. *Clinical EEG and Neuroscience, 48,* 88–95.

Career Builder (2018). *Working parents.* Chicago: Career Builder.

Carey, D.P. (2007). Is bigger really better? The search for brain size and intelligence in the twenty-first century. In S. Della Sala (Ed.), *Tall tales about the mind and brain: Separating fact from fiction.* Oxford, UK: Oxford University Press.

Carl, J.D. (2012). *Short introduction to the U.S. Census.* Upper Saddle River, NJ: Pearson.

Carlin, R.E., & Moon, R.Y. (2017). Risk factors, protective factors, and current recommendations to reduce sudden infant death syndrome: A review. *JAMA Pediatrics, 17,* 175–180.

Carlo, G., & Conejo, L.D. (2020, in press). Traditional and culture-specific parenting of prosociality in U.S. Latino/as. In D.J. Laible & others (Eds.), *Oxford handbook of parenting and moral development.* New York: Oxford University Press.

Carlo, G., Knight, G.P., McGinley, M., Zamboanga, B.L., & Jarvis, L.H. (2010). The multidimensionality of prosocial behaviors and evidence of measurement equivalence in Mexican American and European American early adolescents. *Journal of Research on Adolescence, 20,* 334–358.

Carlo, G., Mestre, M.V., Samper, P., Tur, A., & Armenta, B.E. (2011). The longitudinal relations among dimensions of parenting styles, sympathy, prosocial moral reasoning, and prosocial behaviors. *International Journal of Behavioral Development, 35,* 116–124.

Carlo, G., & others (2018). Longitudinal relations among parenting styles, prosocial behaviors, and academic outcomes in U.S. Mexican adolescents. *Child Development, 89,* 577–592.

Carlson, D.S., Thompson, M.J., & Kacmar, K.M. (2019). Double crossed: The spillover effects of work demands on work outcomes throughout the family. *Journal of Applied Psychology, 104,* 214–228.

Carlson, M.C., & others (2015). Impact of the Baltimore Experience Corps trial on cortical and hippocampal volumes. *Alzheimer's and Dementia, 11,* 1340–1348.

Carlson, M.J, & VanOrman, A.G. (2017). Trajectories of relationship supportiveness after childbirth: Does marriage matter? *Social Science Research, 66,* 102–117.

Carlson, S.M., & White, R. (2011). Unpublished research. Institute of Child Development, University of Minnesota, Minneapolis.

Carlson, S.M., & others (2018). Cohort effects in children's delay of gratification. *Developmental Psychology, 54,* 1395–1407.

Carlsson, A.C., & others (2016). Physical activity, obesity, and risk of cardiovascular disease in midde-aged men during a median of 30 years of follow-up. *European Journal of Preventive Cardiology, 23,* 359–365.

Carmona, S., Hardy, J., & Guerreiro, R. (2018). The genetic landscape of Alzheimer's disease. *Handbook of Clinical Neurology, 148,* 395–408.

Carnegie Foundation (1989). *Turning points: Preparing youth for the 21st century.* New York: Author.

Carney, L.M., & Park, C. (2018). Cancer survivors' understanding of the cause and cure of their illness: Religious and secular appraisals. *Psycho-Oncology, 27,* 1553–1558.

Carpendale, J.I., & Chandler, M.J. (1996). On the distinction between false belief understanding and subscribing to an interpretive theory of mind. *Child Development, 67,* 1686–1706.

Carpendale, J.I., & Hammond, S.I. (2016). The development of moral sense and moral thinking. *Current Opinion in Pediatrics, 28,* 743–747.

Carpendale, J.I., & Lewis, C. (2015). The development of social understanding. In R.M. Lerner (Ed.), *Handbook of child psychology and developmental science* (7th ed.). New York: Wiley.

Carr, D. (2018). Volunteering among older adults: Life course correlates and consequences. *Journals of Gerontology B: Psychological Sciences and Social Sciences, 73,* 479–481.

Carr, D. (2019). Mental health of older widows and widowers: Which coping strategies are most protective? *Aging and Mental Health.*

Carr, D., Kail, B.L., & Rowe, J.W. (2018). The relation of volunteering and subsequent changes in physical disability in older adults. *Journals of Gerontology B: Psychological Sciences and Social Sciences, 73,* 511–521.

Carr, D., & Luth, E. (2016). End-of-life planning and health care. In L.K. George & K.F. Ferraro (Eds.), *Handbook of aging and the social sciences* (8th ed.). New York: Elsevier.

Carr, D., & Sharp, S. (2014). Do afterlife beliefs affect psychological adjustment to late-life spousal loss? *Journals of Gerontology B: Psychological Sciences and Social Sciences, 69,* 103–112.

Carr, D., & others (2018). Does becoming a volunteer attenuate loneliness among recently widowed older adults? *Journals of Gerontology B: Psychological Sciences and Social Sciences, 73,* 501–510.

Carr, R., & Peebles, R. (2012). Developmental considerations of media exposure risk for eating disorders. In J. Lock (Ed.), *Oxford handbook of child and adolescent eating disorders: Developmental perspectives.* New York: Oxford University Press.

Carrell, S.E., Malmstrom, F.V., & West, J.E. (2008). Peer effects in academic cheating. *Journal of Human Resources, 43,* 173–207.

Carriere, J.S., Cheyne, J.A., Solman, G.J., & Smilek, D. (2010). Age trends for failures in sustained attention. *Psychology and Aging, 25*(3), 569–574.

Carroll, J.L. (2019). *Sexuality now* (6th ed.). Boston: Cengage.

Carskadon, M.A. (Ed.). (2002). *Adolescent sleep patterns.* New York: Cambridge University Press.

Carskadon, M.A. (2004). Sleep difficulties in young people. *Archives of Pediatric and Adolescent Health, 158,* 597–598.

Carskadon, M.A. (2005). Sleep and circadian rhythms in children and adolescents: Relevance for athletic performance of young people. *Clinical Sports Medicine, 24,* 319–328.

Carskadon, M.A. (2006, April). *Adolescent sleep: The perfect storm.* Paper presented at the meeting of the Society for Research on Adolescence, San Francisco.

Carskadon, M.A. (2011a). Sleep in adolescents: The perfect storm. *Pediatric Clinics of North America, 58,* 637–647.

Carskadon, M.A. (2011b). Sleep's effects on cognition and learning in adolescence. *Progress in Brain Research, 190,* 137–143.

Carskadon, M.A., & Tarokh, L. (2014). Developmental changes in sleep biology and potential effects on adolescent behavior and caffeine use. *Nutrition Review, 72*(Suppl. 1), S60–S64.

Carson, V., & others (2015). Systematic review of sedentary behavior and cognitive development in early childhood. *Preventive Medicine, 78,* 15–22.

Carstensen, L.L. (1991). Selectivity theory: Social activity in life-span context. *Annual Review of Gerontology and Geriatrics, 11,* 195–217.

Carstensen, L.L. (1998). A life-span approach to social motivation. In J. Heckhausen & C. Dweck (Eds.), *Motivation and self-regulation across the life span.* New York: Cambridge University Press.

Carstensen, L.L. (2006). The influence of a sense of time on human development. *Science, 312,* 1913–1915.

Carstensen, L.L. (2008, May). *Long life in the 21st century.* Paper presented at the meeting of the Association for Psychological Science, Chicago.

Carstensen, L.L. (2009). *A long bright future.* New York: Random House.

Carstensen, L.L. (2011). *A long bright future: Happiness, health, and financial health in an age of increased longevity.* New York: Public Affairs.

Carstensen, L.L. (2014). Our aging population may just save us all. In P. Irving (Ed.), *The upside of aging.* New York: Wiley.

Carstensen, L.L. (2015, February). The new age of much older age. *Time, 185*(6), 68–70.

Carstensen, L.L. (2016, February). The new age of aging. *Time, 186*(2), 22–29.

Carstensen, L.L. (2016, December 26). Commentary in Wisniewski, M. "Finding reasons to be cheerful gets easier." *Chicago Tribune.* Retrieved March 4, 2017, from www.chicagotribune.com/news/columnists/ct-joy-aging-wisniewski-column-201612216-story.html

Carstensen, L.L. (2019). Integrating cognitive and emotion paradigms to address the paradox of aging. *Cognition and Emotion, 33,* 119–125.

Carstensen, L.L., & DeLiema, M. (2018). The positivity effect: A negativity bias in youth fades with age. *Current Opinion in Behavioral Sciences, 19,* 7–12.

Carstensen, L.L., & Freund, A.M. (1994). Commentary: The resilience of the aging self. *Developmental Review, 14,* 81–92.

Carstensen, L.L., Smith, K., & Jaworski, D. (2015). Selectivity as an emotion regulation strategy: Lessons from older adults. *Current Opinion in Psychology, 3,* 80–84.

Carstensen, L.L., & others (2011). Emotional experience improves with age: Evidence based on over 10 years of sampling. *Psychology and Aging, 26,* 21–33.

Carter, A. (2019). The consequences of adolescent delinquent behavior for adult employee outcomes. *Journal of Youth and Adolescence, 48,* 17–29.

Carter, C.J. (2019). Autism genes and the leukocyte transcriptome in autistic toddlers relate to pathogen interactomes, infection, and the immune system. A role for excess neurotrophic sAPPa and reduced antimicrobial AB. *Neurochemistry International, 126,* 36–58.

Carter, T., Morres, I., Repper, J., & Callaghan, P. (2016). Exercise for adolescents with depression: Valued aspects and perceived change. *Journal of Psychiatric and Mental Health Nursing, 23,* 37–44.

Cartwright, R., Agargun, M.Y., Kirkby, J., & Friedman, J.K. (2006). Relation of dreams to waking concerns. *Psychiatry Research, 141,* 261–270.

Carver, C.S., & Connor-Smith, J. (2010). Personality and coping. *Annual Review of Psychology* (Vol. 61). Palo Alto, CA: Annual Reviews.

Carver, K., Joyner, K., & Udry, J.R. (2003). National estimates of adolescent romantic relationships. In P. Florsheim (Eds.), *Adolescent romantic relationships and sexual behavior.* Mahwah, NJ: Erlbaum.

Casabona, G., & others (2019). Six years of experience using an advanced algorithm for botulinum toxin application. *Journal of Cosmetic Dermatology, 18,* 21–35.

Casasola, M. (2018). Above and beyond objects: The development of infants' spatial concepts. *Advances in Child Development and Behavior, 54,* 87–121.

Case, R. (1987). Neo-Piagetian theory: Retrospect and prospect. *International Journal of Psychology, 22,* 773–791.

Case, R. (1999). Conceptual development in the child and the field: A personal view of the Piagetian legacy. In E.K. Skolnick, K. Nelson, S.A. Gelman, & P.H. Miller (Eds.), *Conceptual development.* Mahwah, NJ: Erlbaum.

Case, R., Kurland, D.M., & Goldberg, J. (1982). Operational efficiency and the growth of short-term memory span. *Journal of Experimental Child Psychology, 33,* 386–404.

Casey, B.J., & others (2019, in press). Development of the emotional brain. *Neuroscience Letters.*

Casper, D.M., & Card, N.A. (2017). Overt and relational victimization: A meta-analytic review of their overlap and associations with social-psychological adjustment. *Child Development, 88,* 466–483.

Caspi, A., & Roberts, B.W. (2001). Personality development across the life course: The argument for change and continuity. *Psychological Inquiry, 12,* 49–66.

Caspi, A., & others (2003). Influence of life stress on depression: Moderation by a polymorphism in the 5-HTT gene. *Science, 301,* 386–389.

Cassidy, J. (2016). The nature of the child's ties. In J. Cassidy & P.R. Shaver (Eds.), *Handbook of attachment* (3rd ed.). New York: Guilford.

Castalanelli, N., & others (2019, in press). Higher cardiorespiratory fitness is associated with better verbal generativity in community dwelling older adults. *Journal of Aging and Physical Activity.*

Castillo, M., & Weiselberg, E. (2017). Bulimia nervosa/purging disorder. *Current Problems in Pediatric and Adolescent Health Care, 47,* 85–94.

Castillo-Morales, A., & others (2019). Postmitotic cell longevity-associated genes: A transcriptional signature of postmitotic maintenance in neural tissues. *Neurobiology of Aging, 74,* 147–160.

Castle, J., & others (2010). Parents' evaluation of adoption success: A follow-up study of intercountry and domestic adoptions. *American Journal of Orthopsychiatry, 79,* 522–531.

Castle, S.C. (2019). Despite active public health campaigns, death from falls increased 30% in the past decade: Is ageism part of the barrier to self-awareness? *Clinics in Geriatric Medicine, 35,* 147–159.

Cataldo, D.M., Migliano, A.B., & Vinicius, L. (2018). Speech, stone tool-making, and the evolution of language. *PLoS One, 13*(1), e019071.

Catani, C., & others (2010). Tsunami, war, and cumulative risk in the lives of Sri Lankan school children. *Child Development, 81,* 1176–1191.

Catchlove, S.J., & others (2019, in press). Regional cerebrovascular reactivity and cognitive performance in healthy aging. *Journal of Experimental Neuroscience.*

Cattagni Kleiner, A., & others (2019). Advance care planning dispositions: The relationship between knowledge and perception. *BMC Geriatrics, 19*(1), 118.

Cauffman, E., Shulman, E., Bechtold, J., & Steinberg, L. (2015). Children and the law. In R.M. Lerner (Ed.), *Handbook of child psychology and developmental science* (7th ed.). New York: Wiley.

Cavanagh, S.E. (2009). Puberty. In D. Carr (Ed.), *Encyclopedia of the life course and human development.* Boston: Gale Cengage.

Cavazos-Rehg, P.A., & others (2010a). Number of sexual partners and associations with initiation and intensity of substance abuse. *AIDS Behavior, 15*(4), 869–874.

Cavazos-Rehg, P.A., & others (2010b). Understanding adolescent parenthood from a multisystemic perspective. *Journal of Adolescent Health, 46,* 525–531.

Cave, R.K. (2002, August). *Early adolescent language: A content analysis of child development and educational psychology textbooks.* Unpublished doctoral dissertation, University of Nevada, Reno.

Cazzato, V., & others (2016). The effects of body exposure on self-body image and esthetic appreciation in anorexia nervosa. *Experimental Brain Research, 234,* 695–709.

Ceci, S.J., & Gilstrap, L.L. (2000). Determinants of intelligence: Schooling and intelligence. In A. Kazdin (Ed.), *Encyclopedia of psychology.* New York: Oxford University Press.

Ceci, S.J., Hritz, A., & Royer, C.E. (2016). Understanding suggestibility. In W. O'Donohue & M. Fanetti (Eds.), *A guide to evidence-based practice.* New York: Springer.

Ceci, S.J., Papierno, P.B., & Kulkofsky, S. (2007). Representational constraints on children's suggestibility. *Psychological Science, 18,* 503–509.

Center for Health Statistics (2018). *Health: United States.* Atlanta: Centers for Disease Control and Prevention.

Centers for Disease Control and Prevention (2008). *National Health Interview Study.* Atlanta: Author.

Centers for Disease Control and Prevention (2012). *By the numbers full year 2011: Health measures from the National Health Interview Study, January–December 2011.* Atlanta: Author.

Centers for Disease Control and Prevention (2012). *CDC estimates 1 in 88 children in the United States has been identified as having an autism spectrum disorder.* CDC Division of News & Electronic Media. Retrieved from http://www.cdc.gov/media/releases/2012/p0329_autism_disorder.html

Centers for Disease Control and Prevention (2012). Prepregnancy contraceptive use among teens with unintended pregnancies resulting in live births—Pregnancy Risk Assessment Monitoring System (PRAMS), 2004–2008. *MMWR Morbidity and Mortality Weekly Report, 61*(2), 25–29.

Centers for Disease Control and Prevention (2015). *National Health Interview Survey, 2014.* Atlanta: Author.

Centers for Disease Control and Prevention (2015). *Suicide.* Atlanta: Author.

Centers for Disease Control and Prevention (2016). *ADHD.* Retrieved January 12, 2016, from www.cdc.gov/ncbddd/adhd/data.html

Centers for Disease Control and Prevention (2016). *Adolescent pregnancy.* Atlanta, GA: U.S. Department of Health and Human Services.

Centers for Disease Control and Prevention (2016). *Breastfeeding.* Atlanta: Author.

Centers for Disease Control and Prevention (2017). *Births, marriages, divorces, and deaths.* Atlanta: Author.

Centers for Disease Control and Prevention (2018). *High blood pressure facts.* Atlanta: Author.

Centers for Disease Control and Prevention (2018). *Sexually transmitted disease surveillance.* Atlanta: U.S. Department of Heath and Human Services.

Centers for Disease Control and Prevention (2019). *Obesity.* Atlanta: Author.

Centers for Disease Control and Prevention (2019, January 10). *Reproductive health: Teen pregnancy.* Retrieved March 29, 2019, from www.cdc.gov/teenpregnancy/

Central Intelligence Agency (2015). *The world factbook: Life expectancy at birth.* Washington, DC: CIA.

Cercignani, M., & others (2017). Characterizing axonal myelination within the healthy population: A tract-by-tract mapping of effects of age and gender on the fiber-g ratio. *Neurobiology of Aging, 49,* 109–118.

Cerillo-Urbina, A.J., & others (2015). The effects of physical exercise in children with attention deficit hyperactivity disorder: A systematic review and meta-analysis of randomized controlled trials. *Child Care, Health, and Development, 41,* 779–788.

Challacombe, F.L., & others (2017). A pilot randomized controlled trial of time-intensive cognitive-behavior therapy for postpartum obsessive-compulsive disorder: Effects on maternal symptoms, mother-infant interactions, and attachment. *Psychological Medicine, 47,* 1478–1488.

Chalofsky, N., & Cavallaro, E. (2019). To have lived well: Well-being and meaningful work. In R. Yeoman & others (Eds.), *Oxford handbook of meaningful work.* New York: Oxford University Press.

Chan, J.S.Y., & others (2019, in press). Effects of meditation and mind-body exercises on older adults' cognitive performance: A meta-analysis. *Gerontologist.*

Chan, M.Y., Haber, S., Drew, L.M., & Park, D.C. (2016). Training older adults to use tablet computers: Does it enhance cognitive function? *Gerontologist, 56,* 475–484.

Chandra, A., Mosher, W.D., Copen, C., & Sionean, C. (2011, March 3). Sexual behavior, sexual attraction, and sexual identity in the United States: Data from the 2006–2008 National Survey of Family Growth. *National Health Statistics Reports, 36,* 1–28.

Chandradasa, M., & Champika, L. (2018). Reincarnation type presentations of children with high-functioning autism in Sri Lanka. *Explore, 14,* 230–233.

Chaney, B.H., & others (2019, in press). Pregaming: A field-based investigation of alcohol quantities consumed prior to visiting a bar and restaurant district. *Substance Use and Misuse.*

Chang, A.C.Y., & Blau, H.M. (2018). Short telomeres—a hallmark of heritable cardiomyopathies. *Differentiation, 100,* 31–36.

Chang, E.C. (2017). Hope and hopelessness as predictors of suicide ideation in Hungarian college students. *Death Studies, 41,* 455-460.

Chang, E.C., & others (2018). Does optimism weaken the negative effects of being lonely on suicide risk? *Death Studies, 42,* 63-68.

Chang, H.Y., & others (2014). Prenatal maternal depression is associated with low birth weight through shorter gestational age in term infants in Korea. *Early Human Development, 90,* 15-20.

Chao, R.K. (2005, April). *The importance of* Guan *in describing control of immigrant Chinese.* Paper presented at the meeting of the Society for Research in Child Development, Atlanta.

Chao, R.K. (2007, March). *Research with Asian Americans: Looking back and moving forward.* Paper presented at the meeting of the Society for Research in Child Development, Boston.

Chao, R.K., & Otsuki-Clutter, M. (2011). Racial and ethnic differences: Sociocultural and contextual explanations. *Journal of Research on Adolescence, 21,* 47-60.

Chao, R.K., & Tseng, V. (2002). Parenting of Asians. In M.H. Bornstein (Ed.), *Handbook of parenting* (2nd ed., Vol. 4). Mahwah, NJ: Erlbaum.

Chaplin, J.E., & others (2012). Improvements in behavior and self-esteem following growth hormone treatment in short prepubertal children. *Hormone Research in Pediatrics, 75*(4), 291-303.

Chaplin, T.M., & Aldao, A. (2013). Gender differences in emotion expression in children: A meta-analytic review. *Psychological Bulletin, 139,* 735-765.

Chapman, S.N., & others (2019, in press). Limits to fitness benefits of prolonged post-reproductive lifespan in women. *Current Biology.*

Charles, S.T., & Carstensen, L.L. (2010). *Social and emotional aging.* In S. Fiske & S. Taylor (Eds.), *Annual Review of Psychology* (Vol. 61). Palo Alto, CA: Annual Reviews.

Charles, S.T., & Piazza, J.R. (2007). Memories of social interactions: Age differences in emotional intensity. *Psychology and Aging, 22,* 300-309.

Charlton, B.M., & others (2019, in press). Teen pregnancy risk factors among young women of diverse sexual orientations. *Pediatrics.*

Charness, N., & Bosman, E.A. (1992). Human factors and aging. In F.I.M. Craik & T.A. Salthouse (Eds.), *The handbook of aging and cognition.* Hillsdale, NJ: Erlbaum.

Charpak, N., & others (2019, in press). Twenty-year follow-up of kangaroo mother care versus traditional care. *Pediatrics.*

Chasnoff, I.J. (2017). Medical marijuana laws and pregnancy: Implications for public health policy. *American Journal of Obstetrics and Gynecology, 16,* 27-30.

Chatterton, Z., & others (2017). In utero exposure to maternal smoking is associated with DNA methylations and reduced neuronal content in the developing fetal brain. *Epigenetics Chromatin, 10,* 4.

Chaudry, A., & others (2017). *Cradle to kindergarten: A new plan to combat inequality.* New York: Russell Sage Foundation.

Chavarria, M.C., & others (2014). Puberty in the corpus callosum. *Neuroscience, 265,* 1-8.

Cheetham, T.C., & others (2017). Association of testosterone replacement with cardiovascular outcomes among men with androgen deficiency. *JAMA Internal Medicine, 177,* 491-499.

Cheetham-Blake, T.J., & others (2019, in press). Resilience characteristics and prior life stress determine anticipatory response to acute social stress in children aged 7-11 years. *British Journal of Health Psychology.*

Chemtob, C.M., & others (2010). Impact of maternal posttraumatic stress disorder and depression following exposure to the September 11 attacks on preschool children's behavior. *Child Development, 81,* 1129-1141.

Chen, A.C., & others (2017). Resveratrol relieves Angiostrongylus cantonensis-induced meningoencephalitis by activating sirtuin-1. *Acta Tropica, 173,* 76-84.

Chen, C., Chow, A.Y.M., & Tang, S. (2019, in press). Trajectories of depressive symptoms in Chinese elderly during widowhood: A secondary analysis. *Aging and Mental Health.*

Chen, C., & Stevenson, H.W. (1989). Homework: A cross-cultural examination. *Child Development, 60*(3), 551-561.

Chen, F.R., Rothman, E.F., & Jaffee, S.R. (2019, in press). Early puberty, friendship, group characteristics, and dating abuse in U.S. girls. *Pediatrics.*

Chen, G., & others (2017). An association study revealed substantial effects of dominance, epistasis, and substance dependence co-morbidity on alcohol dependence symptom account. *Addiction Biology, 22,* 1475-1485.

Chen, H., & others (2019, in press). Two novel genetic variants in the STK38L and RAB27A genes are associated with glioma susceptibility. *International Journal of Cancer.*

Chen, J., & others (2019). Wanting to be remembered: Intrinsically rewarding work and generativity in early midlife. *Canadian Review of Sociology, 56,* 30-46.

Chen, L.W., & others (2016). Maternal caffeine intake during pregnancy and risk of pregnancy loss: A categorical and dose-response meta-analysis of prospective studies. *Public Health Nutrition, 19,* 1233-1244.

Chen, L.W., & others (2018). Measuring the cost and value of quality improvement initiatives for local health departments. *Journal of Public Health Management and Practice, 24,* 164-171.

Chen, N., Deater-Deckard, K., & Bell, M.A. (2014). The role of temperament by family interactions in child maladjustment. *Journal of Abnormal Child Psychology, 42,* 1251-1262.

Chen, P.J., & others (2017). Effects of prenatal yoga on women's stress and immune function across pregnancy: A randomized controlled trial. *Complementary Therapies in Medicine, 31,* 109-117.

Chen, Q., & others (2017). Attitudes of older Chinese patients toward death and dying. *Journal of Palliative Medicine, 20,* 1389-1394.

Chen, W., & others (2018). ApoE4 may be a promising target for treatment of coronary heart disease and Alzheimer's disease. *Current Drug Targets, 19,* 1038-1044.

Chen, X., Fu, R., & Zhao, S. (2015). Culture and socialization. In J.E. Grusec & P.D. Hastings (Eds.), *Handbook of socialization* (2nd ed.). New York: Guilford.

Chen, X., Lee, J., & Chen, L. (2018). Culture and peer relationships. In W.M. Bukowski & others (Eds.), *Handbook of peer interactions, relationships, and groups* (2nd ed.). New York: Guilford.

Chen, X., & others (1998). Childrearing attitudes and behavioral inhibition in Chinese and Canadian toddlers: A cross-cultural study. *Developmental Psychology, 34,* 677-686.

Chen, X.I., Hertzog, C., & Park, D.C. (2017). Cognitive predictors of everyday problem solving across the lifespan. *Gerontology, 63,* 372-384.

Chen, Y., & others (2019). The transitions between dynamic micro-states reveal age-related functional network reorganization. *Frontiers in Physiology, 9,* 1852.

Chen, Y.H., & others (2019). Magnetoencephalography and the infant brain. *NeuroImage, 189,* 445-458.

Chen, Y.M., & others (2016). Trajectories of older adults' leisure time activity and functional disability: A 12-year follow-up. *International Journal of Behavioral Medicine, 23,* 697-706.

Cheng, H., & others (2019, in press). Biomedical, psychological, environmental, and behavioral factors associated with adult obesity in a nationally representative sample. *Journal of Public Health.*

Cheng, H.M., & others (2017). Vascular aging and hypertension: Implications for the clinical application of central blood pressure. *International Journal of Cardiology, 230,* 209-213.

Cheng, M., & Berman, S.L. (2012). Globalization and identity development: A Chinese perspective. *New Directions in Child and Adolescent Development, 138,* 103-121.

Cheng, M.H., Lee, S.J., Wang, P.H., & Fuh, J.L. (2007). Does menopausal transition affect the quality of life? A longitudinal study of middle-aged women in Kinmen. *Menopause, 14,* 885-890.

Cheng, N., & others (2018). Quality of maternal parenting of 9-month-old infants predicts executive function performance at 2 and 3 years of age. *Frontiers in Psychology, 8,* 2293.

Cheng, S., & others (2010). Early television exposure and children's behavioral and social outcomes at age 30 months. *Journal of Epidemiology, 20*(Suppl. 2), S482-S489.

Cheng, Y., Lou, C., Gao, E., Emerson, M.R., & Zabin, L.S. (2012). The relationship between contact and unmarried adolescents' and young adults' traditional beliefs in three East Asian cities: A cross-cultural analysis. *Journal of Adolescent Health, 50*(Suppl. 3), S4-S11.

Cheon, Y.M., & others (2018). The development of ethnic/racial self-labeling: Individual differences in context. *Journal of Youth and Adolescence, 47,* 2261-2278.

Cheong, J.L.Y., & Miller, S.P. (2018). Imaging the neonatal brain in the 21st century: Why, when, and how? *Archives of Disease in Childhood: Fetal and Neonatal Edition, 103,* F4-F5.

Cherlin, A.J. (2009). *The marriage-go-round.* New York: Random House.

Chess, S., & Thomas, A. (1977). Temperamental individuality from childhood to adolescence. *Journal of Child Psychiatry, 16,* 218-226.

Cheung, H.Y., Wu, J., & Huang, Y. (2016). Why do Chinese students cheat? Initial findings based on the self-reports of high school students in China. *Australian Educational Researcher, 43,* 245-271.

Chevalier, A., & others (2017). Predictors of older drivers' involvement in rapid deceleration events. *Accident Analysis and Prevention, 98,* 312-319.

Chevalier, N., Dauvier, B., & Blaye, A. (2018). Adverse childhood experiences and early initiation of marijuana and alcohol use: The potential moderating effects of internal assets. *Substance Use and Misuse, 53,* 1624-1632.

Chevalier, N., Dauvier, B., & Blaye, A. (2018). From prioritizing objects to prioritizing cues: A developmental shift for cognitive control. *Developmental Science, 21(2),* e12534.

Chhaya, R., & others (2018). The feasibility of an automated eye-tracking-modified Fagan test of memory for human faces in young Ugandan HIV-exposed children. *Child Neuropsychology, 24,* 656–701.

Chi, M.T. (1978). Knowledge structures and memory development. In R.S. Siegler (Ed.), *Children's thinking: What develops?* Hillsdale, NJ: Erlbaum.

Chick, C.F., & Reyna, V.F. (2012). A fuzzy trace theory of adolescent risk taking: Beyond self-control and sensation seeking. In V.F. Reyna & others (Eds.), *The adolescent brain.* Washington, DC: American Psychological Association.

Child Trends (2015, November). *Oral sex behaviors among teens.* Washington, DC: Child Trends.

Childers, J.B., & Tomasello, M. (2002). Two-year-olds learn novel nouns, verbs, and conventional actions from massed or distributed exposures. *Developmental Psychology, 38,* 967–978.

Children's Defense Fund (2019). *A shameful state: Child poverty crisis continues in states across our nation.* Washington, DC: Author.

ChildStats.gov (2018). *POP3 Race and Hispanic origin composition.* Washington, DC: Author.

Chinn, L.K., & others (2019). Development of infant reaching strategies to tactile targets on the face. *Frontiers in Psychology, 10,* 9.

Chiocca, E.M. (2017). American parents' attitudes and beliefs about corporal punishment: An integrative literature review. *Journal of Pediatric Health Care, 31,* 372–383.

Chiou, W.B., Chen, S.W., & Liao, D.C. (2014). Does Facebook promote self-interest? Enactment of indiscriminate one-to-many communication on online social networking sites decreases prosocial behavior. *Cyberpsychology, Behavior, and Social Networking, 17,* 68–73.

Chisholm, J.D., & Kingstone, A. (2015). Action video games and improved attentional control: Disentangling selection- and response-based processes. *Psychonomic Bulletin & Review, 22,* 1430–1436.

Chiu, H.L., & others (2018). Effectiveness of executive function training on mental set shifting, working memory, and inhibition in healthy older adults: A double-blind randomized controlled trial. *Journal of Advanced Nursing, 74,* 1099–1113.

Chiu, M., Wesson, V., & Sadavoy, J. (2014). Improving caregiver competence, stress coping, and well-being in informal dementia caregivers. *World Journal of Psychiatry, 3(3),* 65–73.

Cho, J., Martin, P., Poon, L.W., & the Georgia Centenarian Study (2015). Successful aging and subjective well-being among the oldest-old adults. *Gerontologist, 55,* 132–143.

Cho, J., & others (2019, in press). Caregiving centenarians: Cross-national comparison in caregiver burden between the United States and Japan. *Aging and Mental Health.*

Choi, B., & others (2019, in press). Gesture development, caregiver responsiveness, and language, and diagnostic outcomes in infants at high and low risk for autism. *Journal of Autism and Developmental Disorders.*

Choi, H. (2019, in press). Giving or receiving spouse care and marital satisfaction among older Korean individuals. *Social Science Medicine.*

Choi, H., Yorgason, J.B., & Johnson, D.R. (2016). Marital quality and health in middle and later adulthood: Dyadic associations. *Journals of Gerontology B: Psychological Sciences and Social Sciences, 7,* 154–164.

Choi, S., & Gopnik, A. (1995). Early acquisition of verbs in Korean: A cross-linguistic study. *Journal of Child Language, 22,* 497–529.

Choi, Y.J., & Luo, Y. (2015). 13-month-olds' understanding of social interaction. *Psychological Science, 26,* 274–283.

Chomsky, N. (1957). *Syntactic structures.* The Hague: Mouton.

Chopik, W.J., Edelstein, R.S., & Fraley, R.C. (2013). From the cradle to the grave: Age differences in attachment from early adulthood to old age. *Journal of Personality, 81(2),* 171–183.

Chopik, W.J., Edelstein, R.S., & Grimm, K.J. (2019). Longitudinal changes in attachment orientation over a 59-year period. *Journal of Personality and Social Psychology, 116,* 598–611.

Chopik, W.J., Kim, E.S., & Smith, J. (2018). An examination of dyadic changes in optimism and physical health over time. *Health Psychology, 37,* 42–50.

Chopik, W.J., & Kitayama, S. (2018). Personality change across the life span: Insights from a cross-cultural, longitudinal study. *Journal of Personality, 86,* 508–521.

Chor, E. (2018). Multigenerational Head Start participation: An unexpected marker of progress. *Child Development, 89,* 264–279.

Choudhary, M., & others (2016). To study the effect of kangaroo mother care on pain response in preterm neonates and to determine the behavioral and physiological responses to painful stimuli in preterm neonates: A study from western Rajasthan. *Journal of Maternal-Fetal and Neonatal Medicine, 29,* 826–831.

Choukas-Bradley, S., & Prinstein, M.J. (2016). Peer relationships and the development of psychopathology. In M. Lewis & D. Rudolph (Eds.), *Handbook of developmental psychopathology* (3rd ed.). New York: Springer.

Christakis, D.A., Zimmerman, F.J., DiGiuseppe, D.L., & McCarty, C.A. (2004). Early television exposure and subsequent attentional problems in children. *Pediatrics, 113,* 708–713.

Christakis, D.A., & others (2009). Audible television and decreased adult words, infant vocalizations, and conversational turns. *Archives of Pediatric & Adolescent Medicine, 163,* 554–558.

Christen, M., Narváez, D., & Gutzwiller, E. (2017). Comparing and integrating biological and cultural moral progress. *Ethical Theory and Moral Practice, 20,* 53–73.

Christensen, D.L., & others (2016). *Prevalence and characteristics of autism spectrum disorder among children aged 8 years–Autism and Developmental Disabilities Monitoring Network, 11 sites, United States 2012.* Atlanta: Centers for Disease Control and Prevention.

Christensen, L.B., Johnson, R.B., & Turner, L.A. (2020). *Research methods, design, and analysis* (13th ed., loose leaf). Upper Saddle River, NJ: Pearson.

Chu, X.W., & others (2019). Does bullying victimization really influence adolescents' psychosocial problems? A three-wave longitudinal study in China. *Journal of Affective Disorders, 246,* 603–610.

Chung, S.T., Onuzuruike, A.U., & Magge, S.N. (2018). Cardiometabolic risk in obese children. *Annals of the New York Academy of Sciences, 141,* 166–183.

Cicchetti, D. (2018). A multilevel developmental approach to the prevention of psychopathology in children and adolescents. In J.N. Butcher & others (Eds.), *APA handbook of psychopathology.* Washington, DC: American Psychological Association.

Cicchetti, D., & Handley, E.D. (2019, in press). Child maltreatment and the development of substance use and disorder. *Neurobiology of Stress.*

Cicchetti, D., & Toth, S.L. (2016). Child maltreatment and developmental psychopathology: A multi-level perspective. In D. Cicchetti (Ed.), *Developmental psychopathology* (3rd ed.). New York: Wiley.

Cicchetti, D., Toth, S.L., & Rogosch, F.A. (2005). *A prevention program for child maltreatment.* Unpublished manuscript, University of Rochester, Rochester, NY.

Cicek, D., & others (2018). Clinical follow-up data and the rate of development of precocious and rapidly progressive puberty in patients with premature thelarche. *Journal of Pediatric Endocrinology and Metabolism, 31,* 305–312.

Cicirelli, V.G. (1994). Sibling relationships in cross-cultural perspective. *Journal of Marriage and Family, 56,* 7–20.

Cicirelli, V.G. (2009). Sibling relationships, later life. In D. Carr (Eds.), *Encyclopedia of the life course and human development.* Boston: Gale Cengage.

Cicirelli, V.G. (2010). Attachment relationships in old age. *Journal of Social and Personal Relationships, 27,* 191–199.

Cillessen, A.H.N., & Bukowski, W.M. (2018). Sociometric perspectives. In W.M. Bukowski & others (Eds.), *Handbook of peer interactions, relationships, and groups* (2nd ed.). New York: Guilford.

Cimarolli, V.R., & others (2017). A population study of correlates of social participation in older adults with age-related vision loss. *Clinical Rehabilitation, 31,* 115–125.

Cisternas, M.G., Murphy, L.B., & Carlson, S.A. (2019). Walking and the 2-year risk of functional decline: An observational study of U.S. adults with arthritis. *Preventive Medicine, 119,* 100–107.

Citkovitz, C., Schnyer, R.N., & Hoskins, I.A. (2011). Acupuncture during labour: Data are more promising than a recent review suggests. *British Journal of Obstetrics and Gynecology, 118,* 101.

Cizek, G.J. (2019). Common Core-ruption: The gulf between large-scale and classroom assessment. *Education Week, 38(29),* 24.

Claes, H.I., & others (2010). Understanding the effects of sildenafil treatment on erection maintenance and erection hardness. *Journal of Sexual Medicine, 7,* 2184–2191.

Clara, M. (2017). How instruction influences conceptual development: Vygotsky's theory revisited. *Educational Psychologist, 52,* 50–62.

Clark, B. (2008). *Growing up gifted* (7th ed.). Upper Saddle River, NJ: Prentice Hall.

Clark, B.C. (2019). Neuromuscular changes with aging and sarcopenia. *Journal of Frailty and Aging, 8,* 7–9.

Clark, C.D. (2016). *Play and well-being.* New York: Routledge.

Clark, E.V. (1993). *The lexicon in acquisition.* New York: Cambridge University Press.

Clark, E.V. (2017). *Language in children.* New York: Psychology Press.

Clark, K.N., & Malecki, C.K. (2019). Academic Grit Scale: Psychometric properties and associations with achievement and life satisfaction. *Journal of School Psychology, 72,* 49-66.

Clark-Cotton, M.R., Williams, R.K., & Goral, M. (2007). Language and communication in aging. In J.E. Birren (Ed.), *Encyclopedia of gerontology* (2nd ed.). San Diego: Academic Press.

Clarke-Stewart, A.K., & Miner, J.L. (2008). Child and day care, effects of. In M.M. Haith & J.B. Benson (Eds.), *Encyclopedia of infant and early childhood development.* Oxford, UK: Elsevier.

Clarke-Stewart, A.K., & Parke, R.D. (2014). *Social development* (2nd ed.). New York: Wiley.

Claro, S., Paunesku, D., & Dweck, C.S. (2016). Growth mindset tempers the effect of poverty on academic achievement. *Proceedings of the National Academy of Sciences USA, 113,* 8664-8868.

Clausen, J.A. (1993). *American lives.* New York: Free Press.

Clauss, J.A., Avery, S.N., & Blackford, J.U. (2015). The nature of individual differences in inhibited temperament and risk for psychiatric disease: A review and meta-analysis. *Progress in Neurobiology, 127-128,* 23-45.

Clayton, M.G., & others (2019, in press). Determinants of excessive reassurance-seeking: Adolescents' internalized distress, friendship conflict, and behavioral inhibition as prospective predictors. *Journal of Clinical Child and Adolescent Psychology.*

Cleal, K., Norris, K., & Baird, D. (2019, in press). Telomere length dynamics and the evolution of cancer genome architecture. *International Journal of Molecular Sciences.*

Clearfield, M.W., Diedrich, F.J., Smith, L.B., & Thelen, E. (2006). Young infants reach correctly in A-not-B tasks: On the development of stability and perseveration. *Infant Behavior and Development, 29,* 435-444.

Clegg, J.M., & Legare, C.H. (2017). Parents scaffold flexible imitation during early childhood. *Journal of Experimental Child Psychology, 153,* 1-14.

Clemens, V., & others (2018). Association of child maltreatment subtypes and long-term physical health in a German representative sample. *European Journal of Psychotraumatology.*

Clemens-Cope, L., & others (2019). Pregnant women with opioid use disorder and their infants in three state Medicaid programs in 2013-2016. *Drug and Alcohol Dependence, 195,* 156-163.

Clements, J.M. (2009). Patient perceptions on the use of advance directives and life-prolonging technology. *American Journal of Hospice and Palliative Care, 26,* 270-276.

Clements-Nolle, K., & others (2019). Youth assets and alcohol-related problems among male and female youth: Results from a longitudinal cohort study. *Preventive Medicine, 123,* 192-196.

Cliffordson, C., & Gustafsson, J-E. (2008). Effects of age and schooling on intellectual performance: Estimates obtained from analysis of continuous variation in age and length of schooling. *Intelligence, 36,* 143-152.

Clifton, R.K., Morrongiello, B.A., Kulig, J.W., & Dowd, J.M. (1981). Developmental changes in auditory localization in infancy. In R.N. Aslin, J.R. Alberts, & M.R. Petersen (Eds.), *Development of perception* (Vol. 1). Orlando, FL: Academic Press.

Clifton, R.K., Muir, D.W., Ashmead, D.H., & Clarkson, M.G. (1993). Is visually guided reaching in early infancy a myth? *Child Development, 64,* 1099-1110.

Cloninger, S. (2019). *Theories of personality* (7th ed.). Upper Saddle River, NJ: Pearson.

Clyde, T.L., Hawkins, A.J., and Willoughby, B.J. (2019, in press). Revising premarital relationship interventions for the next generation. *Journal of Marital and Family Therapy.*

Coats, H., Asakura, Y., & Matthews, E.E. (2019). Implementing advance care planning: Barriers and facilitators. *Oncology Nursing Forum, 46,* 271-274.

Cochet, H., & Guidetti, M. (2018). Contribution of developmental psychology to the study of social interactions: Some factors in play, joint attention, and joint action and implications for robotics. *Frontiers in Psychology, 9,* 1992.

Coetsee, C., & Terblanche, E. (2019, in press). The effect of three different exercise training modalities on cognitive and physical function in a healthy older population. *European Review of Aging and Physical Activity.*

CogMed (2013). *CogMed: Working memory is the engine of learning.* Upper Saddle River, NJ: Pearson.

Cohn, A., & others (2015). The association between alcohol, marijuana use, and new and emerging tobacco products in a young adult population. *Addictive Behaviors, 48,* 79-88.

Coie, J.D. (2004). The impact of negative social experiences on the development of antisocial behavior. In J.B. Kupersmidt & K.A. Dodge (Eds.), *Children's peer relations: From development to intervention.* Washington, DC: American Psychological Association.

Coker, T.R., & others (2015). Media violence exposure and physical aggression in fifth-grade children. *Academic Pediatrics, 15,* 82-88.

Colangelo, N.C., Assouline, S.G., & Gross, M.U.M. (2004). *A nation deceived: How schools hold back America's brightest students.* The Templeton National Report on Acceleration. Retrieved March 6, 2005, from http://nationdeceived.org/

Colapinto, J. (2000). *As nature made him.* New York: Simon & Schuster.

Colby, A., Kohlberg, L., Gibbs, J., & Lieberman, M. (1983). A longitudinal study of moral judgment. *Monographs of the Society for Research in Child Development, 48*(21, Serial No. 201).

Colcombe, S.J., & Kramer, A.F. (2003). Fitness effects on the cognitive function of older adults: A meta-analytic study. *Psychological Science, 14,* 125-130.

Colcombe, S.J., & others (2006). Aerobic exercise training increases brain volume in aging humans. *Journals of Gerontology: Medical Sciences, 61A,* 1166-1170.

Cole, M.A., & others (2018). Extracellular matrix regulation of fibroblast function: Redefining our perspective on skin aging. *Journal of Cell Communication and Signaling, 12,* 35-43.

Cole, M.W., Yarkoni, T., Repovs, G., Anticevic, A., & Braver, T.S. (2012). Global connectivity of prefrontal cortex predicts cognitive control and intelligence. *Journal of Neuroscience, 32,* 8988-8999.

Cole, P.M. (2016). Emotion and the development of psychopathology. In D. Cicchetti (Ed.), *Developmental psychopathology* (3rd ed.). New York: Wiley.

Cole, P.M., Dennis, T.A., Smith-Simon, K.E., & Cohen, L.H. (2009). Preschoolers' emotion regulation strategy understanding: Relations with emotion socialization and child self-regulation. *Social Development, 18*(2), 324-352.

Cole, P.M., & Hollenstein, T. (Eds.) (2018). *Emotion regulation.* New York: Routleldge.

Cole, P.M., Lougheed, J.P., & Ram, N. (2018). The development of emotion regulation in early childhood. In P.M. Cole & T. Hollenstein (Eds.), *Emotion regulation.* New York: Routledge.

Cole, P.M., Ram, N., & English, M.S. (2019, in press). Toward a unifying model of self-regulation: A developmental approach. *Child Development Perspectives.*

Cole, P.M., & Tan, P.Z. (2007). Emotion socialization from a cultural perspective. In J.E. Grusec & P.D. Hastings (Eds.), *Handbook of socialization.* New York: Guilford.

Coleman, A.M. (2013). Physicians' attitudes toward advance directives: A literature review of variables impacting on physicians' attitude toward advance directives. *American Journal of Hospice and Palliative Care, 30,* 696-706.

Coleman, P.D. (1986, August). *Regulation of dendritic extent: Human aging brain and Alzheimer's disease.* Paper presented at the meeting of the American Psychological Association, Washington, DC.

Coleman-Phox, K., Odouli, R., & Li, D-K. (2008). Use of a fan during sleep and the risk of sudden infant death syndrome. *Archives of Pediatric and Adolescent Medicine, 162,* 963-968.

Coley, R.L., & others (2018). Locating economic risks for adolescent mental and behavioral health: Poverty and affluence in families, neighborhoods, and schools. *Child Development, 89,* 360-369.

Collins, M. (1996, Winter). The job outlook for '96 grads. *Journal of Career Planning,* 51-54.

Collins, W.A., & Madsen, S.D. (2019). Parenting during middle and late childhood. In M.H. Bornstein (Ed.), *Handbook of parenting* (3rd ed.). New York: Routledge.

Collins, W.A., & Steinberg, L. (2006). Adolescent development in interpersonal context. In W. Damon & R. Lerner (Eds.), *Handbook of child psychology* (6th ed.). New York: Wiley.

Collins, W.A., & van Dulmen, M. (2006). The significance of middle childhood peer competence for work and relationships in early adulthood. In A.C. Huston & M.N. Ripke (Eds.), *Developmental contexts in middle childhood.* New York: Cambridge University Press.

Colman, R.J., & others (2009). Caloric restriction delays disease onset and mortality in rhesus monkeys. *Science, 325,* 201-204.

Colom, R., Karama, S., Jung, R.E., & Haier, R.J. (2010). Human intelligence and brain networks. *Dialogues in Clinical Neuroscience, 12,* 489-501.

Colom, R., & others (2009). Gray matter correlates of fluid, crystallized, and spatial intelligence. *Intelligence, 37,* 124-135.

Colombo, B., Balzarotti, S., & Greenwood, A. (2019, in press). Using a reminiscence-based approach to investigate the cognitive reserve in a healthy aging population. *Clinical Gerontology.*

Comalli, D.M., Persand, D., & Adolph, K.E. (2017). Motor decisions are not black and white: Selecting actions in the "gray zone." *Experimental Brain Research. 235.* 1793-1807.

Comer, J. (2004). *Leave no child behind.* New Haven, CT: Yale University Press.

Comer, J. (2006). Child development: The under-weighted aspect of intelligence. In P.C. Kyllonen,

R.D. Roberts, & L. Stankov (Eds.), *Extending intelligence.* Mahwah, NJ: Erlbaum.

Comer, J. (2010). Comer School Development Program. In J. Meece & J. Eccles (Eds.), *Handbook of research on schools, schooling, and human development.* New York: Routledge.

Comishen, K.J., Bialystok, E., & Adler, S.A. (2019, in press). The impact of bilingual environments on selective attention in infancy. *Developmental Science.*

Committee on the Rights of the Child (2014). *The Convention on the Rights of the Child and its treaty body—the Committee on the Rights of the Child.* Retrieved April 14, 2015, from http://endcorporalpunishment.org/pages/hrlaw/crc_session.html

Common Core State Standards Initiative (2014). *Common Core.* Retrieved June 1, 2014, from www.corestandards.org/

Common Sense Media (2011). *Zero to eight: Children's media use in America.* Retrieved June 21, 2012, from www.commonsensemedia.org/research.

Common Sense Media (2015). *The Common Sense Media census: Media use by tweens and teens.* New York: Common Sense.

Commoner, B. (2002). Unraveling the DNA myth: The spurious foundation of genetic engineering. *Harper's Magazine, 304,* 39-47.

Commons, M.L., & Richards, F.A. (2003). Four postformal stages. In J. Demick & C. Andreoletti (Eds.), *Handbook of adult development.* New York: Kluwer.

Commons, M.L., Sinnott, J.D., Richards, F.A., & Armon, C. (1989). *Adult development, Vol. 1: Comparisons and applications of developmental models.* New York: Praeger.

Compton, R.J. (2016). *Adoption beyond borders.* New York: Oxford University Press.

Compton, W.M., Gfoerer, J., Conway, I.P., & Finger, M.S. (2014). Unemployment and substance outcomes in the United States 2002-2010. *Drug and Alcohol Dependence, 142,* 350-353.

Comstock, G., & Scharrer, E. (2006). Media and popular culture. In W. Damon & R. Lerner (Eds.), *Handbook of child psychology* (6th ed.). New York: Wiley.

Comtesse, H., & Rosner, R. (2019). Prolonged grief disorder among asylum seekers in Germany: The influence of losses and residence status. *European Journal of Psychotraumatology, 10*(1), 1591330.

Conboy, B.T., Brooks, R., Meltzoff, A.N., & Kuhl, P.K. (2015). Social interaction in infants' learning of second-language phonetics: An exploration of brain-behavior relations. *Developmental Neuropsychology, 40,* 216-229.

Conde-Agudelo, A., & Diaz-Rossello, J.L. (2014). Kangaroo mother care to reduce morbidity and mortality in low birthweight infants. *Cochrane Database of Systematic Reviews, 4,* CD002771.

Conduct Problems Prevention Research Group (2007). The Fast Track randomized controlled trial to prevent externalizing psychiatric disorders: Findings from grades 3 to 9. *Journal of the American Academy of Child and Adolescent Psychiatry, 46,* 1250-1262.

Conduct Problems Prevention Research Group (2010a). The difficulty of maintaining positive intervention effects: A look at disruptive behavior, deviant peer relations, and social skills during the middle school years. *Journal of Early Adolescence, 30,* 593-624.

Conduct Problems Prevention Research Group (2010b). Fast Track intervention effects on youth arrests and delinquency. *Journal of Experimental Criminology, 6,* 131-157.

Conduct Problems Prevention Research Group (2011). The effects of Fast Track preventive intervention on the development of conduct disorder across childhood. *Child Development, 82,* 331-345.

Conduct Problems Prevention Research Group (2015). Impact of early intervention on psychopathology, crime, and well-being at age 25. *American Journal of Psychiatry, 71,* 59-70.

Conlon, E.G., & others (2017). The impact of older age and sex on motion discrimination. *Experimental Aging Research, 43,* 55-79.

Conner, T.S., & others (2017). The role of personality traits in young adult fruit and vegetable consumption. *Frontiers in Psychology, 8,* 119.

Connolly, H.L., & others (2019). Sex differences in emotion recognition: Evidence for a small overall female superiority on facial disgust. *Emotion, 19,* 455-464.

Connolly, J., Craig, W., Goldberg, A., & Pepler, D. (2004). Mixed-gender groups, dating, and romantic relationships in early adolescence. *Journal of Research on Adolescence, 14,* 185-207.

Connolly, J.A., & McIsaac, C. (2009). Romantic relationships in adolescence. In R.M. Lerner & L. Steinberg (Eds.), *Handbook of adolescent psychology* (3rd ed.). New York: Wiley.

Connolly, J.A., Nguyen, H.N., Pepler, D., Craig, W., & Jiang, D. (2013). Developmental trajectories of romantic stages and associations with problem behaviors during adolescence. *Journal of Adolescence, 36*(6), 1013-1024.

Connolly, M.D., & others (2016). The mental health of transgender youth: Advances in understanding. *Journal of Adolescent Health, 59,* 489-495.

Conover, K., & Romero, S. (2018). Drowning prevention in pediatrics. *Pediatric Annals, 47*(3), e112-e117.

Conry-Murray, C., Kim, J.M., & Turiel, E. (2012, April). *U.S. and Korean children's judgments of gender norm violations.* Paper presented at the Gender Development Research conference, San Francisco.

Consoli, A., & others (2013). Suicidal behaviors in depressed adolescents: Role of perceived relationships in the family. *Child and Adolescent Psychiatry and Mental Health, 7*(1), 8.

Constantinescu, M., & others (2017). Treatment with sildenafil and donepezil improves angiogenesis in experimentally induced critical limb ischemia. *Biomedical Research International, 2017,* 9532381.

Contreras, N.A., & others (2018). Calorie restriction induces reversible lymphopenia and lymphoid organ atrophy due to cell redistribution. *Geroscience, 40,* 279-291.

Conway, P. (2018). The core of morality is the moral self. In K. Gray & J. Graham (Eds.), *Atlas of moral psychology.* New York: Guilford.

Cook, M., & Birch, R. (1984). Infant perception of the shapes of tilted plane forms. *Infant Behavior and Development, 7,* 389-402.

Cook, R.E., & Richardson-Gibbs, A.M. (Eds.) (2018). *Strategies for including children with special needs in early childhood settings* (2nd ed.). Boston: Cengage.

Cooksey, E.C. (2009). Sexual activity, adolescent. In D. Carr (Ed.), *Encyclopedia of the life course and human development.* Boston: Gale Cengage.

Coontz, S. (2005). *Marriage: A history.* New York: Penguin.

Cooper, C.R. (2011). *Bridging multiple worlds.* New York: Oxford University Press.

Cooper, C.R., & Grotevant, H.D. (1989, April). *Individuality and connectedness in the family and adolescent's self and relational competence.* Paper presented at the meeting of the Society for Research in Child Development, Kansas City.

Cooper, C.R., Behrens, R., & Trinh, N. (2009). Identity development. In R.A. Shweder & others (Eds.), *The Chicago companion to the child.* Chicago: University of Chicago Press.

Cooper, C.R., Grotevant, H.D., Moore, M.S., & Condon, S.M. (1982, August). *Family support and conflict: Both foster adolescent identity and role taking.* Paper presented at the meeting of the American Psychological Association, Washington, DC.

Cooper, M., & others (2018). A longitudinal study of risk perceptions and e-cigarette initiation among college students: Interactions with smoking status. *Drug and Alcohol Dependence, 186,* 257-263.

Cooper, M., Warland, J., & McCutcheon, H. (2018). Australian midwives' views and experiences of practice and politics related to water immersion for labor and birth: A web based survey. *Women and Birth, 31,* 184-193.

Cooper, S., & others (2019). Attitudes to E-cigarettes and cessation support for pregnant women from English Stop Smoking Services: A mixed methods study. *International Journal of Environmental Research and Public Health, 16,* 110.

Cooperrider, K., & Goldin-Meadow, S. (2018). Gesture, language, and cognition. In B. Dancygier (Ed.), *Cambridge handbook of cognitive linguistics.* New York: Cambridge University Press.

Copen, C.E., Chandra, A., & Febo-Vazquez, I. (2016). Sexual behavior, sexual attraction, and sexual orientation among adults aged 18-44 in the United States: Data from the 2011-2013 National Survey of Family Growth. *National Health Statistics Report, 88,* 1-14.

Copen, C.E., Daniels, C.E., & Mosher, W.D. (2013, April 4). First premarital cohabitation in the United States: 2006-2010 National Survey of Family Growth. *National Health Statistics Reports, 64,* 1-16.

Coplan, R.J., & others (2018). Peer-based interventions for behaviorally inhibited, socially withdrawn, and socially anxious children. In W.M. Bukowski & others (Eds.), *Handbook of peer interaction, relationships, and groups.* New York: Guilford.

Corbin, C., & others (2019). *Concepts of fitness and wellness* (12th ed.). New York: McGraw-Hill.

Cordier, S. (2008). Evidence for a role of paternal exposure in developmental toxicity. *Basic and Clinical Pharmacology and Toxicology, 102,* 176-181.

Cordova, D., Huang, S., Lally, M., Estrada, Y., & Prado, G. (2014). Do parent-adolescent discrepancies in family functioning increase the risk of Hispanic adolescent HIV risk behaviors? *Family Process, 53,* 348-363.

Corna, D.R., Cukrowicz, K.C., Linton, K., & Prabhu, F. (2010). The mediating effect of perceived burdensomeness on the relation between depressive symptoms and suicide ideation in a community sample of older adults. *Aging and Mental Health, 50,* 785-797.

Cornelis, M.C., & others (2019). Age and cognitive decline in the UK Biobank. *PLoS One, 14*(3), e0213948.

Correia, C., & others (2016). Global sensory impairment in older adults in the United States. *Journal of the American Geriatrics Society, 64,* 306–313.

Corso, J.F. (1977). Auditory perception and communication. In J.E. Birren & K.W. Schaie (Eds.), *Handbook of the psychology of aging* (2nd ed.). New York: Van Nostrand Reinhold.

Costa, P.T., & McCrae, R.R. (1995). Solid ground on the wetlands of personality: A reply to Black. *Psychological Bulletin, 117,* 216–220.

Costa, P.T., & McCrae, R.R. (1998). Personality assessment. In H.S. Friedman (Ed.), *Encyclopedia of mental health* (Vol. 3). San Diego: Academic Press.

Costa, P.T., & McCrae, R.R. (2013). A theoretical context for adult temperament. In T.D. Wachs & others (Eds.), *Temperament in context.* New York: Psychology Press.

Costa, P.T., & others (2014). Personality facets and all-causes mortality among Medicare patients aged 66 to 102 years: A follow-up study of Weiss and Costa (2005). *Psychosomatic Medicine, 76,* 370–378.

Costa, S., & others (2018). The intergenerational transmission of trait emotional intelligence: The mediating role of parental autonomy support and psychological control. *Journal of Adolescence, 68,* 105–116.

Coto, J., & others (2019, in press). Parents as role models: Associations between parents and young children's weight, dietary intake, and physical activity in a minority sample. *Maternal and Child Health Journal.*

Cotten, S.R., Ford, G., Ford, S., & Hale, T.M. (2014). Internet use and depression among retired older adults in the United States: A longitudinal analysis. *Journals of Gerontology B: Psychological Sciences and Social Sciences, 69,* 763–771.

Cottrell, L., & Duggleby, W. (2016). The "good death": An integrative literature review. *Palliative and Supportive Care, 14,* 686–712.

Coubart, A., & others (2014). Dissociation between small and larger numerosities in newborn infants. *Developmental Science, 17,* 11–22.

Coulson, S. (2018). Language and the brain. In B. Dancygier (Ed.), *Cambridge handbook of cognitive linguistics.* New York: Cambridge University Press.

Council of Economic Advisors (2000). *Teens and their parents in the 21st century: An examination of trends in teen behavior and the role of parent involvement.* Washington, DC: Author.

Courage, M.L., Bakhtiar, A., Fitzpatrick, C., Kenny, S., & Brandeau, K. (2015). Growing up multitasking: The costs and benefits for cognitive development. *Developmental Review, 35,* 5–41.

Courage, M.L., Edison, S.C., & Howe, M.L. (2004). Variability in the early development of visual self-recognition. *Infant Behavior and Development, 27,* 509–532.

Cowan, P., & Cowan, C. (2000). *When partners become parents: The big life change for couples.* Mahwah, NJ: Erlbaum.

Cowan, P.A., & Cowan, C.P. (2009). How working with couples fosters children's development: From prevention science to public policy. In M.S. Schultz, M.K. Pruett, P.K. Kerig, & R.D. Parke (Eds.), *Feathering the nest: Couple relationships, couples interventions, and children's development.* Washington, DC: American Psychological Association.

Cowan, P.A., & others (2019a). Supporting father involvement: A father-inclusive couples group approach to parenting interventions. In H. Steele & M. Steele (Eds.), *Handbook of attachment interventions.* New York: Guilford.

Cowan, P.A., & others (2019b, in press). Fathers' and mothers' attachment styles, couple conflict, parenting quality, and children's behavior problems: An intervention test of mediation. *Attachment and Human Development.*

Cox, K.S., Wilt, J., Olson, B., & McAdams, D.P. (2010). Generativity, the Big Five, and psychosocial adaptation in midlife adults. *Journal of Personality, 78,* 1185–1208.

Cox, M.J., & others (2018). Bidirectional relationships between alcohol-specific parental socialization behaviors and adolescent alcohol misuse. *Substance Use and Abuse, 53,* 1645–1656.

Coyne, J., & others (2018). The circle of security. In C.H. Zeanah (Ed.), *Handbook of infant mental health* (4th ed.). New York: Guilford.

Coyne, S.M., Padilla-Walker, L.M., & Holmgren, H.G. (2018). A six-year longitudinal study of texting trajectories during adolescence. *Child Development, 89,* 58–65.

Coyne, S.M., & others (2018). Violent video games, externalizing behavior, and prosocial behavior: A five-year longitudinal study during adolescence. *Developmental Psychology, 54,* 1868–1880.

Coyne, S.M., & others (2019, in press). "We're not gonna be friends anymore": Associations between viewing relational aggression on television and relational aggression in text messaging during adolescence. *Aggressive Behavior.*

Crain, S. (2012). Sentence scope. In E.L. Bavin (Ed.), *Cambridge handbook of child language.* New York: Cambridge University Press.

Crain, T.L., Schonert-Reichl, K.A., & Roeser, R.W. (2017). Cultivating teacher mindfulness: Effects of a randomized controlled trial on work, home, and sleep outcomes. *Journal of Occupational Health Psychology, 22,* 138–152.

Crane, J.D., Macneil, L.G., & Tarnopolsky, M.A. (2013). Long-term aerobic exercise is associated with greater muscle strength throughout the life span. *Journals of Gerontology A: Biological Sciences and Medical Sciences, 68*(6), 631–638.

Cremation Association of North America (2018). *Statistics about cremation trends.* Retrieved October 15, 2018, from http://www.cremationassociation.org/?page=industrystatistics

Crocetti, E., Rabaglietti, E., & Sica, L.S. (2012). Personal identity in Italy. *New Directions in Child and Adolescent Development, 138,* 87–102.

Crocetti, E., & others (2017). Identity processes and parent-child and sibling relationships in adolescence: A five-wave multi-informant longitudinal study. *Child Development, 88,* 210–228.

Crockenberg, S.B. (1986). Are temperamental differences in babies associated with predictable differences in caregiving? In J.V. Lerner & R.M. Lerner (Eds.), *Temperament and social interaction during infancy and childhood.* San Francisco: Jossey-Bass.

Crockenberg, S.B., & Leerkes, E.M. (2006). Infant and maternal behaviors moderate reactivity to novelty to predict anxious behavior at 2.5 years. *Development and Psychopathology, 18,* 17–24.

Crocker, J., & Brummelman, E. (2019). The self: Dynamics of persons and situations. In K. Deaux & M. Snyder (Eds.), *Oxford handbook of personality and social psychology.* New York: Oxford University Press.

Crockett, L.J., Raffaelli, M., & Shen, Y-L. (2006). Linking self-regulation and risk proneness to risky sexual behavior: Pathways through peer pressure and early substance use. *Journal of Research on Adolescence, 16,* 503–525.

Croft, A., Schmader, T., & Block, K. (2019, in press). Life in the balance: Are women's possible selves constrained by men's domestic involvement? *Personality and Social Psychology Bulletin.*

Crone, E. (2017). *The adolescent brain.* New York: Routledge.

Crone, E.A., & Konijn, E.A. (2018). Media use and brain development during adolescence. *Nature Communications, 9*(1), 588.

Crooks, R.L., & Baur, K. (2017). *Our sexuality* (13th ed.). Boston: Cengage.

Crosnoe, R. (2011). *Fitting in, standing out.* New York: Cambridge University Press.

Crosnoe, R., & Benner, A.D. (2015). Children at school. In R.M. Lerner (Ed.), *Handbook of child psychology and developmental science* (7th ed.). New York: Wiley.

Crosnoe, R., Pivnick, L., & Benner, A. (2019, in press). The social contexts of high schools. In B. Schneider (Ed.), *Handbook of the sociology of education in the 21st century.* New York: Springer.

Crosnoe, R., & Ressler, R.W. (2019). Parenting the child in school. In M.H. Bornstein (Ed.), *Handbook of parenting* (3rd ed.). New York: Routledge.

Cross, S., & Markus, H. (1991). Possible selves across the lifespan. *Human Development, 34,* 230–255.

Crouter, A.C. (2006). Mothers and fathers at work. In A. Clarke-Stewart & J. Dunn (Eds.), *Families count.* New York: Cambridge University Press.

Crowley, J.E. (2019). Gray divorce: Explaining midlife marital splits. *Journal of Women and Aging, 31,* 49–72.

Crowley, K., Callahan, M.A., Tenenbaum, H.R., & Allen, E. (2001). Parents explain more to boys than to girls during shared scientific thinking. *Psychological Science, 12,* 258–261.

Crume, T. (2019). Tobacco use during pregnancy. *Clinical Obstetrics and Gynecology, 62,* 128–141.

Cruz, R.A., & others (2018). Mexican-origin youth substance use trajectories: Associations with cultural and family factors. *Developmental Psychology, 54,* 111–126.

Cruz-Saez, S., & others (2019, in press). The effect of body satisfaction on disordered eating: The mediating role of self-esteem and negative affect in male and female adolescents. *Journal of Health Psychology.*

Csikszentmihalyi, M. (1996). *Creativity.* New York: HarperCollins.

Cueli, M., & others (2019, in press). Differential efficacy of neurofeedback in children with ADHD presentations. *Journal of Clinical Medicine.*

Cuevas, K., & Bell, K.A. (2014). Infant attention and early childhood executive function. *Child Development, 85*(2), 397–404.

Cuevas-Sierra, A., & others (2019). Diet, gut microbiota, and obesity: Links with host genetics and epigenetics and potential applications. *Advances in Nutrition, 10*(Suppl. 1), S17–S30.

Cui, J., & others (2017). Examining the relationship between rapid automatized naming and arithmetic fluency in Chinese kindergarten children. *Journal of Experimental Child Psychology, 154,* 146-153.

Cui, R., & others (2019, in press). RNN-based longitudinal analysis of diagnosis of Alzheimer's disease. *Computational Medical Imaging and Graphics.*

Cui, X., & Vaillant, G.E. (1996). Antecedents and consequents of negative life events in adulthood: A longitudinal study. *American Journal of Psychiatry, 153,* 123-126.

Cullen, K.R. (2018). Persistent impairment: Life after losing a parent. *American Journal of Psychiatry, 175,* 820-821.

Cumming, E., & Henry, W. (1961). *Growing old.* New York: Basic Books.

Cummings, E.M., & others (2017). Emotional insecurity about the community: A dynamic, within-person mediator of child adjustment in contexts of political violence. *Development and Psychopathology, 29,* 27-36.

Cunha, A.B., & others (2016). Effect of short-term training on reaching behavior in infants: A randomized controlled trial. *Journal of Motor Behavior, 48,* 132-142.

Cunningham, C.E., & others (2019, in press). What antibullying program designs motivate student intervention in grades 5 to 8? *Journal of Clinical Child and Adolescent Psychology.*

Cunningham, M. (2009). Housework. In D. Carr (Ed.), *Encyclopedia of the life course and human development.* Boston: Gale Cengage.

Cunningham, P.M. (2017). *Phonics they use* (7th ed.). Upper Saddle River, NJ: Pearson.

Cunningham, S.A., Kramer, M.R., & Narayan, K.M. (2014). Incidence of childhood obesity in the United States. *New England Journal of Medicine, 370,* 403-411.

Cunningham, S.D., & others (2019). Group prenatal care reduces risk of preterm birth and low birth weight: A matched cohort study. *Journal of Women's Health, 28,* 17-22.

Curl, A.L., Bibbo, J., & Johnson, R.A. (2017). Dog walking, the human-animal bond, and older adults' physical health. *Gerontologist, 57,* 930-939.

Curran, K., DuCette, J., Eisenstein, J., & Hyman, I.A. (2001, August). *Statistical analysis of the cross-cultural data: The third year.* Paper presented at the meeting of the American Psychological Association, San Francisco.

Currie, E.R., & others (2019). Life after loss: Parent bereavement and coping experiences after infant death in the neonatal intensive care unit. *Death Studies, 43,* 333-342.

Curtindale, L.M., & others (2019). Effects of multimodal synchrony on infant attention and heart rate during events with social and nonsocial stimuli. *Journal of Experimental Child Psychology, 178,* 283-294.

Cvencek, D., Meltzoff, A.N., & Greenwald, A.G. (2011). Math-gender stereotypes in elementary school children. *Child Development, 82,* 766-779.

Cybele Raver, C., McCoy, D.C., Lowenstein, A.E., & Pess, R. (2013). Predicting individual differences in low-income children's executive control from early to middle childhood. *Developmental Science, 16,* 394-408.

D

D'Angelo, C.M., & others (2019, in press). Coping, attributions, and health functioning among adolescents with chronic illness and their parents: Reciprocal relations over time. *Journal of Clinical Psychology in Medical Settings.*

D'Aversa, E., & others (2019, in press). Non-invasive fetal sex diagnosis in plasma of early weeks pregnants using droplet digital PCR. *Molecular Medicine.*

da Rosa, G., & others (2014). Examination of important life experiences of the oldest-old: Cross-cultural comparisons of U.S. and Japanese centenarians. *Journal of Cross-Cultural Gerontology, 29,* 109-130.

da Silva, C.C., & others (2017). Dissociation between dopaminergic response and motor behavior following intrastriatal, but not intravenous, transplant of bone marrow mononuclear stem cells in a mouse model of Parkinson's disease. *Behavioral Brain Research, 324,* 30-40.

Dahl, A., & others (2017). Explicit scaffolding increases simple helping in younger infants. *Developmental Psychology, 53,* 407-416.

Dahl, R.E. (2004). Adolescent brain development: A period of vulnerabilities and opportunities. *Annals of the New York Academy of Sciences, 1021,* 1-22.

Dahl, R.E., & others (2018). Importance of investing in adolescence from a developmental science perspective. *Nature, 554,* 441-450.

Dahm, C.C., & others (2019, in press). Adolescent diet quality and cardiovascular disease risk factors and incident cardiovascular disease in middle-aged women. *Journal of the American Heart Association.*

Dai, H., & Li, C. (2018). How experiencing and anticipating temporal landmarks influence motivation. *Current Opinion in Psychology, 26,* 44-48.

Dai, R., Thomas, A.K., & Taylor, H.A. (2018). Age-related differences in the use of spatial and categorical relationships in a visuo-spatial working memory task. *Memory and Cognition, 46,* 809-825.

Dai, X.J., & others (2018). Plasticity and susceptibility of brain morphometry alterations to insufficient sleep. *Frontiers in Psychiatry, 9,* 266.

Daiello, L.A., & others (2015). Association of fish oil supplement use with preservation of brain volume and cognitive function. *Alzheimer's and Dementia, 11,* 226-235.

Dakanalis, A., & others (2018). Classifying binge eating-disordered adolescents based on severity levels. *Journal of Adolescence, 62,* 47-54.

Dakof, G.A., & others (2015). A randomized clinical trial of family therapy in juvenile drug court. *Journal of Family Psychology, 29,* 232-241.

Dale, B., & others (2014). Utility of the Stanford-Binet Intelligence Scales, 5th ed., with ethnically diverse preschoolers. *Psychology in the Schools, 51,* 581-590.

Dale, W., & others (2018). Cognitive function and its risk factors among older U.S. adults living at home. *Alzheimer Disease and Associated Disorders, 32.* 207-213.

Daly, M., Delaney, L., Egan, M., & Baumeister, R.F. (2015). Childhood self-control and unemployment through the life span: Evidence from two British cohort studies. *Psychological Science, 26,* 709-723.

Damari, B., & others (2018). Developing a training course for spiritual counselors in health care: Evidence from Iran. *Indian Journal of Palliative Care, 24,* 145-149.

Damoiseaux, J.S. (2017). Effects of aging on functional and structural brain connectivity. *NeuroImage, 160,* 32-40.

Damon, F., & others (2017). Preference for facial averageness: Evidence for a common mechanism in human and macaque infants. *Scientific Reports, 7,* 46303.

Damon, W. (1988). *The moral child.* New York: Free Press.

Damon, W. (2008). *The path to purpose.* New York: Free Press.

Dan, B. (2018). Very early diagnosis of autism spectrum disorder. *Developmental Medicine and Child Neurology, 60*(1), 1066.

Dangel, T.J., Webb, J.R., & Hirsch, J.K. (2018). Forgiveness and suicidal behavior: Cynicism and psychache as serial mediators. *Journal of Psychology, 152,* 77-95.

Daniels, H. (Ed.) (2017). *Introduction to Vygotsky* (3rd ed.). New York: Routledge.

Danielson, C.K., & others (2017). Clinical decision-making following disasters: Efficient identification of PTSD risk in adolescents. *Journal of Abnormal Child Psychology, 48,* 117-128.

Danilovich, M., Conroy, D., & Hornby, T.G. (2018). Feasibility and impact of high intensity walking training in frail older adults. *Journal of Aging and Physical Activity, 25,* 533-538.

Dankulincova Veselska, Z., & others (2019, in press). Spirituality but not religiosity is associated with better health and higher life satisfaction among adolescents. *International Journal of Environmental Research and Public Health.*

Danner, D., Snowdon, D., & Friesen, W. (2001). Positive emotions in early life and longevity: Findings from the Nun Study. *Journal of Personality and Social Psychology, 80*(5), 804-813.

Daoulah, A., & others (2017). Widowhood and severity of coronary artery disease: A multicenter study. *Coronary Artery Disease, 28,* 98-103.

Darby-Stewart, A., & Strickland, C. (2019). Group prenatal care to reduce preterm labor and improve outcomes. *American Family Physician, 99,* 141-142.

Darcy, E. (2012). Gender issues in child and adolescent eating disorders. In J. Lock (Ed.), *Oxford handbook of child and adolescent eating disorders: Developmental perspectives.* New York: Oxford University Press.

Dariotis, J.K., & others (2016). A qualitative evaluation of student learning and skills use in a school-based mindfulness and yoga program. *Mindfulness, 7,* 76-89.

Dark-Freudeman, A., & West, R.L. (2016). Possible selves and self-regulatory beliefs: Exploring the relationship between health selves, health efficacy, and psychological well-being. *International Journal of Aging and Human Development, 82,* 139-165.

Darling, N., & Tilton-Weaver, L. (2019). All in the family: Within-family differences in parental monitoring and adolescent information management. *Developmental Psychology, 55,* 390-402.

Darling Rasmussen, P., & others (2019, in press). Attachment as a core feature of resilience: A systematic review and meta-analysis. *Psychological Reports.*

Darwin, C. (1859). *On the origin of species.* London: John Murray.

Das, A., & Nairn, S. (2016). Religious attendance and physiological problems in late life. *Journals of Gerontology B: Psychological Sciences and Social Sciences, 71,* 291-308.

Das, R., & others (2019, in press). Ultrasound assessment of fetal hearing response to vibroacoustic stimulation. *Journal of Maternal-Fetal and Neonatal Medicine.*

Dathe, K., & Schaefer, C. (2018). Drug safety and pregnancy: The German Embryotox Institute. *European Journal of Clinical Pharmacology, 74,* 171-179.

Dau, A.L., & others (2017). Postpartum depressive symptoms and maternal sensitivity: An exploration of possible social media-based measures. *Archives of Women's Mental Health, 20,* 221-224.

Davanzo, R., & others (2013). Intermittent kangaroo mother care: A NICU protocol. *Journal of Human Lactation, 29*(3), 332-338.

Davidov, M., Zhan-Waxler, C., Roth-Hanania, C., & Knafo, A. (2013). Concern for others in the first year of life: Theory, evidence, and avenues of research. *Child Development Perspectives, 7,* 126-131.

Davidson, D. (1996). The effects of decision characteristics on children's selective search of predecisional information. *Acta Psychologica, 92,* 263-281.

Davidson, J., & Davidson, B. (2004). *Genius denied: How to stop wasting our brightest young minds.* New York: Simon & Schuster.

Davidson, J.G.S., & Gutherie, D.M. (2019). Older adults with a combination of vision and hearing impairment experience higher rates of cognitive impairment, functional dependence, and worse outcomes across a set of quality indicators. *Journal of Aging and Health, 31,* 85-108.

Davies, G., & others (2011). Genome-wide association studies establish that human intelligence is highly heritable and polygenic. *Molecular Psychiatry, 16,* 996-1005.

Davies, J., & Brember, I. (1999). Reading and mathematics attainments and self-esteem in years 2 and 6: An eight-year cross-sectional study. *Educational Studies, 25,* 145-157.

Davies, P.T., Martin, M.J., & Cummings, E.M. (2018). Interparental conflict and children's social problems: Insecurity and friendship affiliation as cascading mediators. *Developmental Psychology, 54,* 83-97.

Davies, R., Davis, D., Pearce, M., & Wong, N. (2015). The effect of waterbirth on neonatal mortality and morbidity: A systematic review and meta-analysis. *JBI Database of Systematic Reviews and Implementation Reports, 13,* 180-231.

Davila, J., Capaldi, D.M., & La Greca, A.M. (2016). Adolescent/young adult romantic relationships and psychopathology. In D. Cicchetti (Ed.), *Developmental psychopathology* (3rd ed.). New York: Wiley.

Davis, B.E., Moon, R.Y., Sachs, M.C., & Ottolini, M.C. (1998). Effects of sleep position on infant motor development. *Pediatrics, 102,* 1135-1140.

Davis, C.L., & others (2012). Exercise dose and diabetes risk in overweight and obese children: A randomized controlled trial. *Journal of the American Medical Association, 308,* 1103-1112.

Davis, K., & Weinstein, E. (2017). Identity development in the digital age: An Eriksonian perspective. In M.F. Wright (Ed.), *Identity, sexuality, and relationships in the digital age.* Hershey, PA: IGI Global.

Davis, L., & Keyser, J. (1997). *Becoming the parent you want to be: A sourcebook of strategies for the first five years.* New York: Broadway Books.

Davis, M.C., Burke, H.M., Zautra, A.J., & Stark, S. (2013). Arthritis and musculoskeletal conditions. In I.B. Weiner & others (Eds.), *Handbook of psychology* (2nd ed., Vol. 9). New York: Wiley.

Davis, S.W., Kragel, J.E., Madden, D.J., & Cabeza, R. (2012). The architecture of cross-hemispheric communication in the aging brain: Linking behavior to functional structural connectivity. *Cerebral Cortex, 22,* 232-242.

Dawson-McClure, S., Calzada, E.J., & Brotman, L.M. (2017). Engaging parents in preventive interventions for young children: Working with cultural diversity within low-income, urban neighborhoods. *Prevention Science, 18,* 660-670.

Dawson-McClure, S., & others (2015). A population-level approach to promoting healthy child development and school success in low-income, urban neighborhoods: Impact of parenting and child conduct problems. *Prevention Science, 16,* 279-290.

Day, N.L., Goldschmidt, L., & Thomas, C.A. (2006). Prenatal marijuana exposure contributes to the prediction of marijuana use at age 14. *Addiction, 101,* 1313-1322.

Day, R.H., & McKenzie, B.E. (1973). Perceptual shape constancy in early infancy. *Perception, 2,* 315-320.

Dayton, C.J., & Malone, J.C. (2017). Development and socialization of physical aggression in very young boys. *Infant Mental Health, 38,* 150-165.

Dayton, C.J., Walsh, T.B., Oh, W., & Volling, B. (2015). Hush now baby: Mothers' and fathers' strategies for soothing their infants and associated parenting outcomes. *Journal of Pediatric Health Care, 29,* 145-155.

de Boer, B., & Thompson, B. (2018). Biology-culture co-evolution in finite populations. *Scientific Reports, 8*(1), 1209.

de Boer, B., & Verhoef, T. (2019). Evolution of speech. In S-A. Rueschemeyer & M. Gareth Gaskell (Eds.), *Oxford handbook of psycholinguistics* (2nd ed.). New York: Oxford University Press.

De Genna, N.M., Goldschmidt, L., Day, N.L., & Cornelius, M.D. (2016). Prenatal and postnatal maternal trajectories of cigarette use predict adolescent cigarette use. *Nicotine and Tobacco Research, 18,* 988-992.

De Giovanni, N., & Marchetti, D. (2012). Cocaine and its metabolites in the placenta: A systematic review of the literature. *Reproductive Toxicology, 33*(1), 1-14.

de Greeff, J.W., & others (2018). Effects of physical activity on executive functions, attention, and academic performance in preadolescent children: A meta-analysis. *Journal of Science and Medicine in Sport, 21,* 501-507.

de Gregorio, C. (2018). Physical training and cardiac rehabilitation in heart failure patients. *Advances in Experimental Medicine and Biology, 1067,* 161-181.

de Guzman, N.S., & Nishina, A. (2014). A longitudinal study of body dissatisfaction and pubertal timing in an ethnically diverse adolescent sample. *Body Image, 11,* 68-71.

de Haan, M. (2015). Neuroscientific methods with children. In R.M. Lerner (Ed.), *Handbook of child psychology and developmental science* (7th ed.). New York: Wiley.

de Haan, M., & Gunnar, M.R. (Eds.). (2009). *Handbook of developmental social neuroscience.* New York: Guilford.

de Haan, M., & Johnson, M.H. (2016). Typical and atypical human functional brain development. In D. Cicchetti (Ed.), *Developmental psychopathology* (3rd ed.). New York: Wiley.

de Jesus, L.E., Costa, E.C., & Dekemacher, S. (2019, in press). Gender dysphoria and XX congenital adrenal hyperplasia: How frequent is it? Is male-sex rearing a good idea? *Journal of Pediatric Surgery.*

de Klerk, C.C.J.M., Hamilton, A.F.C., & Southgate, V. (2018). Eye contact modulates facial mimicry in 4-month-old infants: An EMG and fNIRS study. *Cortex, 106,* 93-103.

de la Fuente, J., & others (2019, in press). Longitudinal associations of sensory and cognitive functioning: A structural equation modeling approach. *Journals of Gerontology B: Psychological Sciences and Social Sciences.*

de la Fuente, M. (2019). Biopsychosocial bridge: The psychoneuroimmune system in successful aging. In R. Fernandez-Ballesteros, A. Benetos, & J-M. Robine (Eds.), *Cambridge handbook of successful aging.* New York: Cambridge University Press.

de la Mata, M.L., & others (2019). The relationship between social factors and autobiographical memories from childhood: The role of formal schooling. *Memory, 27,* 103-114.

de Lima, D.B., & others (2019, in press). Episodic memory boosting in older adults: Exploring the association of encoding strategies and physical activity. *Aging and Mental Health.*

de Magalhaes, J.P., & Tacutu, R. (2016). Integrative genomics and aging. In M.R. Kaeberlein & G.M. Martin (Eds.), *Handbook of the biology of aging* (8th ed.). New York: Elsevier.

de Manzano, O., & Ullen, F. (2018). Genetic and environmental influences on the phenotypic associations between intelligence, personality, and creative achievement in the arts and sciences. *Intelligence, 69,* 123-133.

de Medeiros, T.S., & others (2017). Caffeine intake during pregnancy in different intrauterine environments and its association with infant anthropometric measurements at 3 and 6 months of age. *Maternal and Child Health Journal, 21,* 1297-1307.

de Paepe, A., de Williams, A.C., & Crombez, G. (2019, in press). Habituation to pain: A motivational-ethological perspective. *Pain.*

de Villiers, T.J. (2018). Should women be screened for osteoporosis at midlife? *Climacteric, 21,* 239-242.

de Villiers, T.J., & others (2016). Revised global consensus statement on menopausal hormone therapy. *Climacteric, 19,* 313-315.

De Vitis, M., Berardinelli, F., & Sgura, A. (2019, in press). Telomere length maintenance in cancer: At the crossroads between telomerase and alternative lengthening of telomeres (ALT). *International Journal of Molecular Sciences.*

de Vries, S.L., Hoeve, M., Assink, M., Stams, G.J., & Asscher, J.J. (2015). Practitioner review: Effective ingredients of prevention programs for youth at risk of persistent juvenile delinquency—recommendations for clinical practice. *Journal of Child Psychology and Psychiatry, 56,* 108-121.

de Wind, A.W., & others (2014). Health, job characteristics, skills, and social and financial factors in relation to early retirement—results from a longitudinal study in the Netherlands. *Scandinavian Journal of Work, Environment, and Health, 40,* 186-194.

Dearing, E., & others (2016). Can community and school-based supports improve the achievement of first-generation immigrant children attending high-poverty schools? *Child Development, 87,* 883-897.

Deary, I. (2012). Intelligence. *Annual Review of Psychology* (Vol. 63). Palo Alto, CA: Annual Reviews.

Deaton, A. (2008). Income, health, and well-being around the world: Evidence from the Gallup World Poll. *Journal of Economic Perspectives, 22,* 53-72.

Debats, D.L. (1990). The Life Regard Index: Reliability and validity. *Psychological Reports, 67,* 27-34.

Debman, K.J., & others (2018). The moderating role of spirituality in the association between stress and substance use among adolescents: Differences by gender. *Journal of Youth and Adolescence, 47,* 818-828.

Debruyne, F.M., & others (2017). Testosterone treatment is not associated with increased risk of prostate cancer or worsening of lower urinary tract symptoms: Prostate health outcomes in the Registry of Hypogonadism in Men. *BJU International, 119,* 216-224.

DeCasper, A.J., & Spence, M.J. (1986). Prenatal maternal speech influences newborns' perception of speech sounds. *Infant Behavior and Development, 9,* 133-150.

Deckert, M., & others (2019, in press). Metaphor processing in middle childhood and at the transition to early adolescence: The role of chronological age, mental age, and verbal intelligence. *Journal of Child Language.*

Dee, D.L., & others (2017). Trends in repeat births and use of postpartum contraception among teens–United States, 2004-2015. *MMWR Monthly Mortality Weekly Reports, 66,* 422-426.

Deeb, A., & others (2019). Sex assignment practice in disorders of sexual differentiation: Survey results from pediatric endocrinologists in the Arab region. *Journal of Pediatric Endocrinology and Metabolism, 32,* 75-82.

Deevy, P., Leonard, L.B., & Marchman, V.A. (2017). Sensitivity to morphosyntactic information in 3-year-old children with typical language development: A feasibility study. *Journal of Speech, Language, and Hearing Research, 60,* 668-674.

Degrelle, S.A., & Fournier, T. (2018). Fetal-sex determination of human placental tissues. *Placenta, 61,* 103-105.

DeJong, W., DeRicco, B., & Schneider, S.K. (2010). Pregaming: An exploratory study of strategic drinking by college students in Pennsylvania. *Journal of American College Health, 58,* 307-316.

Del Campo, M., & Jones, K.L. (2017). A review of the physical features of the fetal alcohol syndrome disorders. *European Journal of Medical Genetics, 60,* 55-64.

Del Giudice, M. (2011). Sex differences in romantic attachment: A meta-analysis. *Personality and Social Psychology Bulletin, 37,* 193-214.

Del Rio-Bermudez, C., & Blumberg, M.S. (2018). Active sleep promotes functional connectivity in developing sensorimotor networks. *Bioessays, 40*(4), e1700234.

DeLamater, J. (2019). The diversity of adolescent male sexuality. In S. Lamb & J. Gilbert (Eds.), *Cambridge handbook of sexual development.* New York: Cambridge University Press.

Delello, J.A., & McWhorter, R.R. (2017). Reducing the digital divide: Connecting older adults to iPad technology. *Journal of Applied Gerontology, 36,* 3-28.

Delgado, M.Y., & others (2019, in press). Discrimination, parent-adolescent conflict, and peer intimacy: Examining risk and resilience in Mexican-origin youths' adjustment trajectories. *Child Development.*

DeLisi, R. (2015). Piaget's sympathetic but unromantic account of children's play. In J.E. Johnson & others (Eds.), *Handbook of the study of play.* Blue Ridge Summit, PA: Rowman & Littlefield.

Delker, B.C., Bernstein, R.E., & Laurent, H.K. (2018). Out of harm's way: Secure versus insecure-disorganized attachment predicts less adolescent risk taking related to childhood poverty. *Development and Psychopathology, 30,* 283-296.

DeLoache, J.S., Simcock, G., & Macari, S. (2007). Planes, trains, automobiles–and tea-sets: Extremely intense interests in very young children. *Developmental Psychology, 43,* 1579-1586.

DeLongis, A., & Zwicker, A. (2017). Marital satisfaction and divorce in couples in stepfamilies. *Current Opinion in Psychology, 13,* 158-161.

Demanachick, S.P. (2015). The interpretation of play: Psychoanalysis and beyond. In J.E. Johnson & others (Eds.), *Handbook of the study of play.* Blue Ridge Summit, PA: Rowman & Littlefield.

Demiray, B., Gulgoz, S., & Bluck, S. (2009). Examining the life story account of the reminiscence bump: Why we remember more from early adulthood. *Memory, 17,* 708-723.

Demnitz, N., & others (2018). Cognition and mobility show a global association in middle- and late-adulthood: Analyses from the Canadian Longitudinal Study of Aging. *Gait and Posture, 64,* 238-243.

Dempster, F.N. (1981). Memory span: Sources of individual and developmental differences. *Psychological Bulletin, 80,* 63-100.

Demuth, K. (2019). Development of prosodic pragmatics. In S-A. Rueschemeyer & M. Gareth Gaskell (Eds.), *Oxford handbook of psycholinguistics* (2nd ed.). New York: Oxford University Press.

Den Heijer, A.E., & others (2017). Sweat it out? The effects of physical exercise on cognition and behavior in children and adults with ADHD: A systematic literature review. *Journal of Neural Transmission, 124*(Suppl. 1), S3-S26.

Denard, P.J., & others (2010). Back pain, neurogenic symptoms, and physical function in relation to spondylolisthesis among elderly men. *Spine Journal, 10,* 865-887.

Denault, A.S., & Guay, F. (2017). Motivation toward extracurricular activities and motivation at school: A test of the generalization effect hypothesis. *Journal of Adolescence, 54,* 94-103.

DeNavas-Walt, C., & Proctor, B.D. (2015). *Income and poverty in the United States, 2014.* Washington, DC: U.S. Census Bureau.

Denford, S., & others (2017). A comprehensive review of reviews of school-based interventions to improve sexual health. *Health Psychology Review, 11,* 33-52.

Deng, Y., & others (2018). Timing of spermarche and menarche among urban students in Guangzhou, China: Trends from 2005 to 2012 and association with obesity. *Scientific Reports, 8*(1), 263.

Denham, S.A., & Bassett, H.H. (2019). Implications of preschoolers' emotional competence in the classroom. In K. Keefer & others (Eds.), *Handbook of emotional intelligence in education.* New York: Springer.

Denham, S.A., Bassett, H.H., & Wyatt, T. (2015). The socialization of emotional competence. In J.E. Grusec & P.D. Hastings (Eds.), *Handbook of socialization* (2nd ed.). New York: Guilford.

Denham, S.A., & Zinsser, K.M. (2015). Promoting social and emotional learning in early childhood. In T.P. Gullotta & M. Bloom (Eds.), *Encyclopedia of primary prevention and health promotion* (2nd ed.). New York: Academic/Plenum Publishers.

Denmark, F.L., Russo, N.F., Frieze, I.H., & Eschuzur, J. (1988). Guidelines for avoiding sexism in psychological research: A report of the ad hoc committee on nonsexist research. *American Psychologist, 43,* 582-585.

Dennis, M., & others (2014). Functional plasticity in childhood brain disorders: When, what, how, and whom to assess. *Neuropsychology Review, 24*(4), 389-408.

Deoni, S.C., & others (2016). White matter maturation profiles through early childhood predict general cognitive ability. *Brain Structure and Function, 22,* 1189-1203.

DePasquale, C.E., Handley, E.D., & Cicchetti, D. (2019, in press). Investigating multilevel pathways of developmental consequences of maltreatment. *Development and Psychopathology.*

DePaulo, B. (2006). *Singled out.* New York: St. Martin's Press.

DePaulo, B. (2011). Living single: Lightening up those dark, dopey myths. In W.R. Cupach & B.H. Spitzberg (Eds.), *The dark side of close relationships.* New York: Routledge.

Der Ananian, C., & Prohaska, T.R. (2007). Exercise and physical activity. In J.E. Birren (Ed.), *Encyclopedia of gerontology* (2nd ed.). San Diego: Academic Press.

DeSesso, M. (2019). The arrogance of teratology: A brief chronology of attitudes throughout history. *Birth Defects Research, 111,* 123-141.

Desilver, D. (2017). *U.S. students' academic achievement still lags that of their peers in many other countries.* Washington, DC: Pew Research Center.

Desmarais, E., & others (2019). Cross-cultural differences in temperament: Comparing paternal ratings of U.S. and Dutch infants. *European Journal of Developmental Psychology, 16,* 137-151.

Desombre, C., & others (2019, in press). The distinct effect of multiple sources of stereotype threat. *Journal of Social Psychology.*

DeSpelder, L.A., & Strickland, A.L. (2020). *The last dance* (11th ed.). New York: McGraw-Hill.

Dette-Hagenmeyer, D.E., Erzinger, A.G., & Reichle, B. (Eds.) (2016). *Fathers in families.* New York: Psychology Press.

Dettori, E., & Gupta, G.R. (2018). Gender and the SDGs: Collective impact for change. In J.E. Lansford & P. Banati (Eds.), *Handbook of adolescent development research and its impact on global policy.* New York: Oxford University Press.

Deutsch, A.R., Crockett, L.J., Wolf, J.M., & Russell, S.T. (2012). Parent and peer pathways to adolescent delinquency: Variations by ethnicity and neighborhood context. *Journal of Youth and Adolescence, 41,* 1078-1094.

Deutsch, A.R., Wood, P.K., & Slutske, W.S. (2018). Developmental etiologies of alcohol use and their relations to parent and peer influences over adolescence and young adulthood: A genetically informed approach. *Alcoholism: Clinical and Experimental Research, 41,* 2151-2162.

Devakumar, D., & others (2019). *Oxford textbook of global health of women, newborns, children, and adolescents.* New York: Oxford University Press.

Devik, S.A., Enmarker, I., & Hellzen, O. (2019, in press). Nurses' experiences of compassion when giving palliative care at home. *Nursing Ethics.*

Devine, R.T., & Hughes, C. (2018). Family correlates of false belief understanding in early childhood: A meta-analysis. *Child Development, 89,* 971-987.

Devine, R.T., & Hughes, C. (2019, in press). Let's talk: Parents' mental talk (not mind-mindedness or mindreading capacity) predicts children's false belief understanding. *Child Development.*

Devore, E.E., Grodstein, F., & Schemhammer, E.S. (2016). Sleep duration in relation to cognitive function among older adults: A systematic review of observational studies. *Neuroepidemiology, 46,* 57–78.

Devos, T. (2006). Implicit bicultural identity among Mexican American and Asian American college students. *Cultural Diversity and Ethnic Minority Psychology, 12,* 381–402.

Dew, J., & Wilcox, W.B. (2011). "If momma ain't happy": Explaining declines in marital satisfaction among new mothers. *Journal of Marriage and the Family, 73,* 1–12.

Dewey, J. (1933). *How we think.* Lexington, MA: D.C. Heath.

Dewitz, P.F., & others (2020). *Teaching reading in the 21st century* (6th ed.). Upper Saddle River, NJ: Pearson.

DeZolt, D.M., & Hull, S.H. (2001). Classroom and school climate. In J. Worell (Ed.), *Encyclopedia of women and gender.* San Diego: Academic Press.

Di Domenico, F., & others (2018). mTOR in Down syndrome: Role in A*B* and tau neuropathology and transition to Alzheimer disease-like dementia. *Free Radical Biology and Medicine. 114,* 94–101.

Di Florio, A., & others (2014). Mood disorders and parity—a clue to the etiology of the postpartum trigger. *Journal of Affective Disorders, 152,* 334–349.

Diamond, A. (2013). Executive functions. *Annual Review of Psychology* (Vol. 64). Palo Alto, CA: Annual Reviews.

Diamond, A., Barnett, W.S., Thomas, J., & Munro, S. (2007). Preschool program improves cognitive control. *Science, 318,* 1387–1388.

Diamond, A., & Lee, K. (2011). Interventions shown to aid executive function development in children 4 to 12 years old. *Science, 333,* 959–964.

Diamond, A.D. (1985). Development of the ability to use recall to guide action as indicated by infants' performance on AB. *Child Development, 56,* 868–883.

Diamond, L.M. (2017). Three critical questions for future research on lesbian families. *Journal of Lesbian Studies, 21,* 106–119.

Diamond, L.M. (2019). The dynamic expression of sexual-minority and gender-minority experience during childhood and adolescence. In S. Lamb & J. Gilbert (Eds.), *Cambridge handbook of sexual development.* New York: Cambridge University Press.

Diamond, M., & Sigmundson, H.K. (1997). Sex reassignment at birth: Long-term review and clinical implications. *Archives of Pediatric and Adolescent Medicine, 151,* 295–304.

Diaz, A., & others (2017). Relations of positive and negative expressivity and effortful control in kindergarteners' student-teacher relationship, academic engagement, and externalizing problems at school. *Journal of Research in Personality, 67,* 3–14.

Diaz-Rico, L.T. (2018). *Crosscultural, language, and academic development handbook: A complete K-12 reference guide* (6th ed.). Upper Saddle River, NJ: Pearson.

Diaz-Rico, L.T. (2020). *A course for teaching English learners* (3rd ed.). Upper Saddle River, NJ: Pearson.

Dickinson, W.J., & others (2011). Change in stress and social support as predictors of cognitive decline in older adults with and without depression. *International Journal of Geriatric Psychiatry, 26,* 1267–1274.

Diedrich, J.T., Klein, D.A., & Peipert, J.F. (2017). Long-acting reversible contraception in adolescents: A systematic review and meta-analysis. *American Journal of Obstetrics and Gynecology, 364,* e1–e12.

Diego, M.A., Field, T., & Hernandez-Reif, M. (2008). Temperature increases in preterm infants during massage therapy. *Infant Behavior and Development, 31,* 149–152.

Diego, M.A., Field, T., & Hernandez-Reif, M. (2014). Preterm infant weight gain is increased by massage therapy and exercise via different underlying mechanisms. *Early Human Development, 90,* 137–140.

Diekelmann, S. (2014). Sleep for cognitive enhancement. *Frontiers in Systems Neuroscience, 8,* 46.

Diener, E. (2019). *Subjective well-being.* Retrieved January 30, 2019, from labspsychologyllinois. edu/~ediener/SWLS.html

Diener, E., & Seligman, M.E.P. (2002). Very happy people. *Psychological Science, 13,* 81–84.

Dietz, L.J., Silk, J., & Amole, M. (2019). Depressive disorders. In T.H. Ollendick & others (Eds.), *Oxford handbook of clinical child and adolescent psychology.* New York: Oxford University Press.

DiLalla, L.F., & DiLalla, D.L. (2018). Gene-environment correlations affecting children's early rule-breaking and aggressive play behaviors. *Twin Research and Human Genetics, 21,* 285–288.

DiLeonardo, M.J. (2015). *Talking about weight with your child.* Retrieved February 25, 2015, from www.webmd. com/parenting/raising-fit-kids/weight/talk-child-...

Dilmaghani, M. (2018). Importance of religion or spirituality and mental health in Canada. *Journal of Religion and Health, 57,* 120–135.

Dimitropoulos, G., & others (2018). Open trial of family-based treatment of anorexia nervosa for transition age of youth. *Journal of the Canadian Academy of Child and Adolescent Psychiatry, 27,* 50–61.

Dimmitt, C., & McCormick, C.B. (2012). Metacognition in education. In K.R. Harris, S. Graham, & T. Urdan (Eds.), *Handbook of educational psychology.* Washington, DC: American Psychological Association.

Dimock, M. (2019, January 17). *Defining generations: Where millennials end and generation Z begins.* Washington, DC: Pew Research Center.

Ding, X.P., & others (2014). Elementary school children's cheating behavior and its cognitive correlates. *Journal of Experimental Child Psychology, 121,* 85–95.

Ding, Y., & others (2018). Evaluation of basal sex hormone levels for activation of the hypothalamic-pituitary-gonadal axis. *Journal of Pediatric Endocrinology and Metabolism, 31,* 323–329.

Ding, Y., & others (2019). Effects of working memory, strategy use, and single-step mental addition on multi-step mental addition in Chinese elementary students. *Frontiers in Psychology, 10,* 148.

Dion, K.L., & Dion, K.K. (1993). Individualistic and collectivistic perspectives on gender and the cultural context of love and intimacy. *Journal of Social Issues, 49,* 53–69.

Dirks, M.A., Dunfield, K.A., & Recchia, H.E. (2018). Prosocial behavior with peers: Intentions, outcomes, and interpersonal adjustment. In W.M. Bukowski & others (Eds.), *Handbook of peer interactions, relationships, and groups* (2nd ed.). New York: Guilford.

Dishion, T.J., & Piehler, T.F. (2009). Deviant by design: Peer contagion in development, interventions, and schools. In K.H. Rubin, W.M. Bukowski, & B. Laursen (Eds.), *Handbook of peer interactions, relationships, and groups.* New York: Guilford.

Dittus, P.J., & others (2015). Parental monitoring and its associations with adolescent sexual risk behavior: A meta-analysis. *Pediatrics, 136,* e1587–e1599.

Divo, M.J., & others (2018). Chronic obstructive pulmonary disease (COPD) as a disease of early aging: Evidence from the EpiChron cohort. *PLoS One, 13* (2), e0193143.

Dixon, R.A., & Lachman, M.E. (2019). Risk and protective factors in cognitive aging: Advances in the assessment, prevention, and promotion of alternative pathways. In E.G. Samanez-Larkin (Ed.), *The aging brain.* Washington, DC: American Psychological Association.

Dodge, K.A. (1983). Behavioral antecedents of peer social status. *Child Development, 54,* 1386–1399.

Dodge, K.A. (2011a). Context matters in child and family policy. *Child Development, 82,* 433–442.

Dodge, K.A. (2011b). Social information processing models of aggressive behavior. In M. Mikulincer & P.R. Shaver (Eds.), *Understanding and reducing aggression, violence, and their consequences.* Washington, DC: American Psychological Association.

Dodge, K.A., Godwin, J., & The Conduct Problems Prevention Research Group (2013). Social-information-processing patterns mediate the impact of preventive intervention on adolescent antisocial behavior. *Psychological Science, 24,* 456–465.

Dodge, K.A., & McCourt, S.N. (2010). Translating models of antisocial behavioral development into efficacious intervention policy to prevent adolescent violence. *Developmental Psychobiology, 52*(3), 277–285.

Doenyas, C., Yavuz, H.M., Selcuk, B. (2018). Not just a sum of its parts: How tasks of theory of mind scale relate to executive function across time. *Journal of Experimental Child Psychology, 166,* 485–501.

Dolbin-MacNab, M.L. (2019). Grandparenthood. In B.H. Friese (Ed.), *APA handbook of contemporary family psychology.* Washington, DC: APA Books.

Dollar, J., & Calkins, S.D. (2019). Developmental psychology. In T. Ollendick & others (Eds.), *Oxford handbook of clinical child and adolescent psychology.* New York: Oxford University Press.

Domsch, H., Lohaus, A., & Thomas, H. (2009). Influence of information processing and disengagement on infants' looking behavior. *Infant and Child Development, 19,* 161–174.

Donatelle, R.J. (2019a). *Health* (13th ed.). Upper Saddle River, NJ: Pearson.

Donatelle, R.J. (2019b). *My health* (3rd ed.). Upper Saddle River, NJ: Pearson.

Donatelle, R.J., & Ketcham, P. (2020). *Access to health* (16th ed.). Upper Saddle River, NJ: Pearson.

Donegan, S., & others (2010). Two food-assisted maternal and child health nutrition programs helped mitigate the impact of economic hardship on child stunting in Haiti. *Journal of Nutrition, 140,* 1139–1145.

Donenberg, G., & others (2018). Sexual risk among African American girls seeking psychiatric care: A social-personal framework. *Journal of Consulting and Clinical Psychology, 86,* 24–38.

Dong, X.S., & others (2017). Baby boomers in the United States: Factors associated with working longer and delaying retirement. *American Journal of Industrial Medicine, 60,* 315–328.

Donnellan, M.B., Hill, P.L., & Roberts, B.W. (2015). Personality development across the life span: Current findings and future directions. In L. Cooper & M. Mikulincer (Eds.), *Handbook of personality and social psychology.* Washington, DC: American Psychological Association.

Donnellan, M.B., Larsen-Rife, D., & Conger, R.D. (2005). Personality, family history, and competence in early adult romantic relationships. *Journal of Personality and Social Psychology, 88,* 562–576.

Dooley, J., Bass, N., & McCabe, R. (2018). How do doctors deliver a diagnosis of dementia in memory clinics? *British Journal of Psychiatry, 212,* 239–245.

Doom, J.R., & others (2017). Pathways between childhood/adolescent adversity, adolescent socioeconomic status, and long-term cardiovascular disease risk in young adulthood. *Social Science & Medicine, 188,* 166–175.

Doornwaard, S.M., Branje, S., Meeus, W.H.J., & ter Bogt, T.F.M. (2012). Development of adolescents' peer crowd identification in relation to changes in problem behaviors. *Developmental Psychology, 48,* 1366–1380.

Dora, B., & Baydar, N. (2019, in press). Transactional associations of maternal depressive symptoms with child externalizing behaviors are small after age 3. *Development and Psychopathology.*

Dorffner, G., Vitr, M., & Anderer, P. (2015). The effects of aging on sleep architecture in healthy subjects. *Advances in Experimental Medicine and Biology, 821,* 93–100.

Dotti Sani, G.M., & Quaranta, M. (2017). The best is yet to come? Attitudes toward gender roles among adolescents in 36 countries. *Sex Roles, 77,* 30–45.

Doty, R.L., & Shah, M. (2008). Taste and smell. In M.M. Haith & J.B. Benson (Eds.), *Encyclopedia of infant and early childhood development.* Oxford, UK: Elsevier.

Doucette, H., & others (2019, in press). Perpetration of electronic impulsiveness among adolescent females: Associations with in-person dating violence. *Journal of Interpersonal Violence.*

Doumen, S., & others (2012). Identity and perceived peer relationship quality in emerging adulthood: The mediating role of attachment-related emotions. *Journal of Adolescence, 35,* 1417–1425.

Dowdall, N., & others (2019, in press). Shared picture book reading interventions for child language development: A systematic review and meta-analysis. *Child Development.*

Downer, A.V., & Trestman, R.L. (2016). The prison rape elimination act and correctional psychiatrists. *Journal of the American Academy of Psychiatry and the Law, 44,* 9–13.

Doyle, C., & Cicchetti, D. (2018). Child maltreatment. In M.H. Bornstein (Ed.), *SAGE encyclopedia of lifespan human development.* Thousand Oaks, CA; Sage.

Dozier, M., & Bernard, K. (2018). Attachment and biobehavioral catch-up. In C.H. Zeanah (Ed.), *Handbook of infant mental health* (4th ed.). New York: Guilford.

Dozier, M., & Bernard, K. (2019). *Coaching parents of vulnerable infants.* New York: Guilford.

Dozier, M., Bernard, K., & Roben, C.K.P. (2019). Attachment and biobehavioral catch-up. In H. Steele,

& M. Steele (Eds.), *Handbook of attachment-based interventions.* New York: Guilford.

Dozier, M., Stovall-McClough, K.C., & Albus, K.E. (2009). Attachment and psychopathology in adulthood. In J. Cassidy & P.R. Shaver (Eds.), *Handbook of attachment* (2nd ed.). New York: Guilford.

Dragoset, L., & others (2017). School improvement grants: Implementation and effectiveness. NCEE 2017-4013. *ERIC,* ED572215.

Drake, K.M., & others (2012). Influence of sports, physical education, and active commuting to school on adolescent weight status. *Pediatrics, 130,* e296–e304.

Drake, M.B., Riccio, C.A., & Hale, N.S. (2019, in press). Assessment of adult ADHD with college students. *Journal of Attention Disorders.*

Drake, S.A., & others (2019, in press). A descriptive and geospatial analysis of environmental factors attributing to sudden unexpected infant death. *American Journal of Forensic Medicine and Pathology.*

Dreher, J.C., & others (2016). Testosterone causes both prosocial and antisocial status-enhancing behaviors in human males. *Proceedings of the National Academy of Sciences USA, 113,* 11633–11638.

Drew, D.A., & others (2017). Cognitive decline and its risk factors in prevalent hemodialysis patients. *American Journal of Kidney Diseases, 69,* 780–787.

Drewelies, J., & others (2018). Age variations in cohort differences in the United States: Older adults report fewer constraints nowadays than those 18 years ago, but mastery beliefs are diminished among younger adults. *Developmental Psychology, 54,* 1408–1425.

Dron, J.S., & Hegele, R.A. (2019, in press). The evolution of genetic-based risk scores for lipids and cardiovascular disease. *Current Opinion in Lipidology.*

Drummond, J., Paul, E.F., Waugh, W.E., Hammong, S.I., & Brownell, C.A. (2014). Here, there, and everywhere: Emotion and mental state talk in different social contexts predicts empathic helping in toddlers. *Frontiers in Psychology, 5,* 361.

Dryfoos, J.G., & Barkin, C. (2006). *Adolescence: Growing up in America today.* New York: Oxford University Press.

Du, D., Derks, D., & Bakker, A.B. (2018). Daily spillover from family to work: A test of the work-home resources model. *Journal of Occupational Health Psychology, 23,* 237–247.

Duan, X., Dan, Z., & Shi, J. (2014). The speed of information processing of 9- to 13-year-old intellectually gifted children. *Psychology Reports, 112,* 20–32.

Dubal, D.B., & Rogine, C. (2017). Apolipoprotein E4 and risk factors for Alzheimer disease—let's talk about sex. *JAMA Neurology, 74,* 1167–1168.

Dube, S., & others (2017). Psychological well-being as a predictor of casual sex relationships and experiences among adolescents: A short-term prospective study. *Archives of Sexual Behavior, 46,* 807–818.

Dubol, M., & others (2018). Dopamine transporter and reward anticipation in a dimensional perspective: A multimodal brain imaging study. *Neuropsychopharmacology, 43,* 820–827.

Dubow, E.F., & others (2017). Conducting longitudinal, process-oriented research with conflict-affected youth: Solving the inevitable challenges. *Development and Psychopathology, 29,* 85–92.

Duck, S. (2011). *Rethinking relationships.* Thousand Oaks, CA: Sage.

Dudley, R.L. (1999). Youth religious commitment over time: Longitudinal study of retention. *Review of Religious Research, 41,* 110–121.

Due, T.D., Sandholdt, H., & Waldorff, F.B. (2017). Social relations and loneliness among older patients consulting a general practitioner. *Danish Medical Journal, 64,* 3.

Duell, N., & others (2018). Age patterns in risk taking across the world. *Journal of Youth and Adolescence, 47,* 1052–1072.

Duff, D., Tomblin, J.B., & Catts, H. (2015). The influence of reading on vocabulary growth: A case for a Matthew effect. *Journal of Speech, Language, and Hearing Research, 58,* 853–864.

Duff, F.J., Reen, G., Plunkett, K., & Nation, K. (2015). Do infant vocabulary skills predict school-age language and literacy outcomes? *Journal of Child Psychology and Psychiatry, 56,* 848–856.

Duggal, N.A., & others (2019, in press). Major features of immunosenescence, including reduced thymic output, are ameliorated by high levels of physical activity in adulthood. *Aging Cell.*

Duggan, K.A., & Friedman, H.S. (2014). Lifetime biopsychosocial trajectories of the Terman gifted children: Health, well-being, and longevity. In D.K. Simonton (Ed.), *Wiley-Blackwell handbook of genius.* New York: Oxford University Press.

Duggan, P.M., Lapsley, D.K., & Norman, K. (2000, April). *Adolescent invulnerability and personal uniqueness: Scale development and initial contact validation.* Paper presented at the biennial meeting of the Society for Research in Child Development, Chicago.

Duke, S.A., Balzer, B.W., & Steinbeck, K.S. (2014). Testosterone and its effects on human male adolescent mood and behavior: A systematic review. *Journal of Adolescent Health, 55,* 315–322.

Dumas, A.A., & Desroches, S. (2019, in press). Women's use of social media; What is the evidence about their impact on weight management and body image? *Current Obesity Reports.*

Dumitrache, C.G., Rubio, L., & Rubio-Herrera, R. (2016). Perceived health status and life satisfaction in old age, and the moderating role of social support. *Aging and Mental Health, 8,* 1–7.

Dumuid, D., & others (2017). Health-related quality of life and lifestyle behavior clusters in school-aged children from 12 countries. *Journal of Pediatrics, 183,* 178–183.

Duncan, G.J., Magnuson, K., & Votruba-Drzal, E. (2017). Moving beyond correlations in assessing the consequences of poverty. *Annual Review of Psychology* (Vol. 68). Palo Alto, CA: Annual Reviews.

Duncan, J.R., & Byard, R.W. (2019). Sudden infant death syndrome: An overview. In J.R. Duncan & R.W. Byarad (Ed.), *SIDS sudden infant and early childhood death.* Adelaide, Australia: University of Adelaide Press.

Duncan, R.J., & others (2018). Combining a kindergarten readiness summer program with a self-regulation intervention improves school readiness. *Early Childhood Research Quarterly, 42,* 291–300.

Dunlop, W.L., Bannon, B.L., & McAdams, D.P. (2017). Studying the motivated agent through time: Personal goal development during the adult life span. *Journal of Personality, 85,* 207–219.

Dunn, J. (1984). Sibling studies and the developmental impact of critical incidents. In P.B. Baltes & O.G. Brim

(Eds.), *Life-span development and behavior* (Vol. 6). Orlando, FL: Academic Press.

Dunn, J. (2007). Siblings and socialization. In J.E. Grusec & P.D. Hastings (Eds.), *Handbook of socialization*. New York: Guilford.

Dunn, J. (2015). Siblings. In J.E. Grusec & P.D. Hastings (Eds.), *Handbook of socialization* (2nd ed.). New York: Guilford.

Dunn, J., & Kendrick, C. (1982). *Siblings*. Cambridge, MA: Harvard University Press.

Dunster, G.P., & others (2019, in press). Sleepmore in Seattle: Later school start times are associated with more sleep and better performance in high school students. *Science Advances.*

Dupre, M.E., George, L.K., Liu, G., & Peterson, E.D. (2015). Association between divorce and risks for acute myocardial infarction. *Circulation: Cardiovascular Quality and Outcomes, 8,* 244-251.

Durston, S., & others (2006). A shift from diffuse to focal cortical activity with development. *Developmental Science, 9,* 1-8.

Dutton, E., & Lynn, R. (2013). A negative Flynn effect in Finland, 1997-2009. *Intelligence, 41,* 817-820.

Dutton, E., & others (2018). A Flynn effect in Khartoum, the Sudanese capital, 2004-2016. *Intelligence, 68,* 82-86.

Dutton, H., & others (2018). Obesity in pregnancy: Optimizing outcomes for mom and baby. *Medical Clinics of North America, 102,* 87-106.

Duval, C., Piolino, P., Bejanin, A., Eustache, F., & Desgranges, B. (2011). Age effects on different components of theory of mind. *Consciousness and Cognition, 20,* 627-642.

Dweck, C.S. (2006). *Mindset*. New York: Random House.

Dweck, C.S. (2007). Boosting achievement with messages that motivate. *Education Canada, 47,* 6-10.

Dweck, C.S. (2012). Mindsets and human nature: Promoting change in the Middle East, the school yard, the racial divide, and willpower. *American Psychologist, 67,* 614-622.

Dweck, C.S. (2013). Social development. In P. Zelazo (Ed.), *Oxford handbook of developmental psychology*. New York: Oxford University Press.

Dweck, C.S. (2015, September 23). Carol Dweck revisits the 'growth mindset'. *Education Week, 35*(5), 24-26.

Dweck, C.S. (2016, March 11). *Growth mindset revisited*. Invited presentation at Leaders to Learn From. Washington, DC: Education Week.

Dweck, C.S., & Elliott, E. (1983). Achievement motivation. In P. Mussen (Ed.), *Handbook of child psychology* (4th ed., Vol. 4). New York: Wiley.

Dweck, C.S., & Master, A. (2009). Self-theories and motivation: Students' beliefs about intelligence. In K.R. Wentzel & A. Wigfield (Eds.), *Handbook of motivation at school*. New York: Routledge.

Dweck, C.S., & Molden, D.C. (2017). Mindsets: Their impact on competence motivation and acquisition. In A.J. Elliot, C.S. Dweck, & D.S. Yeager (Eds.), *Handbook of competence and motivation* (2nd ed.). New York: Guilford.

Dweck, C.S., & Yeager, D.S. (2019, in press). Mindsets: A view from two eras. *Perspectives on Psychological Science.*

Dworkin, E.R., & others (2018). Social support predicts reductions in PTSD symptoms when substances are not used to cope: A longitudinal study of sexual assault survivors. *Journal of Affective Disorders, 229,* 135-140.

Dworkin, S.L., & Santelli, J. (2007). Do abstinence-plus interventions reduce sexual risk behavior among youth? *PloS Medicine, 4,* 1437-1439.

E

Eagly, A.H. (2010). Gender roles. In J. Levine & M. Hogg (Eds.), *Encyclopedia of group process and intergroup relations*. Thousand Oaks, CA: Sage.

Eagly, A.H. (2013). Science and politics: A reconsideration. In M.K. Ryan & N.R. Branscombe (Eds.), *SAGE handbook of gender and psychology.* Thousand Oaks, CA: Sage.

Eagly, A.H. (2016). Has the psychology of women stopped playing handmaiden to social values? *Feminism & Psychology, 26,* 282-291.

Eagly, A.H. (2018). Making a difference: Feminist scholarship. In C.B. Gravis & J.W. White (Eds.), *Handbook of the psychology of women*. Washington, DC: APA Books.

Eagly, A.H., & Crowley, M. (1986). Gender and helping behavior: A meta-analytic review of the social psychological literature. *Psychological Bulletin, 100,* 283-308.

Eagly, A.H., & Steffen, V.J. (1986). Gender and aggressive behavior: A meta-analytic review of the social psychological literature. *Psychological Bulletin, 100,* 309-330.

East, P. (2009). Adolescent relationships with siblings. In R.M. Lerner & L. Steinberg (Eds.), *Handbook of adolescent psychology* (3rd ed.). New York: Wiley.

Easterbrooks, M.A., Bartlett, J.D., Beeghly, M., & Thompson, R.A. (2013). Social and emotional development in infancy. In I.B. Weiner & others (Eds.), *Handbook of psychology* (2nd ed., Vol. 6). New York: Wiley.

Eastman, M., & others (2018). Profiles of internalizing and externalizing symptoms associated with bullying victimization. *Journal of Adolescence, 65,* 101-110.

Eaton, D.K., & others (2008). Youth risk behavior surveillance—United States, 2007. *MMWR, 57,* 1-131.

Ebstein, R.P., Knafo, A., Mankuta, D., Chew, S.H., & Lai, P.S. (2012). The contributions of oxytocin and vasopressin pathway genes to human behavior. *Hormones and Behavior, 61,* 359-379.

Eccles, J. (2003). Education: Junior and high school. In G. Adams & M. Berzonsky (Eds.), *Blackwell handbook of adolescence*. Malden, MA: Blackwell.

Eccles, J.S. (2007). Families, schools, and developing achievement-related motivations and engagement. In J.E. Grusec & P.D. Hastings (Eds.), *Handbook of socialization.* New York: Guilford.

Eccles, J.S., & Roeser, R.W. (2015). School and community influences on human development. In M.H. Bornstein & M.E. Lamb (Eds.), *Developmental science* (7th ed.). New York: Psychology Press.

Ecker, S., & Beck, S. (2019). The epigenetic clock: A molecular crystal ball for human aging? *Aging, 11,* 833-835.

Eckler, P., Kalyango, Y., & Paasch, E. (2017). Facebook use and negative body image among U.S. college women. *Women and Health, 57,* 249-267.

Eddy, S.L. (2019, in press). Recent research in science teaching and learning. *CBE Life Sciences Education.*

Edgar, J.C., & others (2019, in press). Abnormal maturation of the resting-state peak alpha frequency in children with autism spectrum disorder. *Human Brain Mapping.*

Ednick, M., & others (2010). Sleep-related respiratory abnormalities and arousal pattern in achondroplasia during early infancy. *Journal of Pediatrics, 155,* 510-515.

Eggenberger, P., & others (2015). Does multicomponent physical exercise with simultaneous cognitive training boost cognitive performance in older adults? A 6-month randomized controlled trial with a 1-year follow-up. *Clinical Interventions in Aging, 10,* 1335-1349.

Egger, A.C., Oberle, L.M., & Saluan, P. (2019). The effects of endurance sports on children and youth. *Sports Medicine and Arthroscopy Review, 27,* 35-39.

Ehninger, D., Neff, F., & Xie, K. (2014). Longevity, aging, and rapamycin. *Cellular and Molecular Life Sciences, 71,* 4325-4346.

Ehrlich, K.B., Miller, G.E., Jones, J.D., & Cassidy, J. (2016). Attachment and psychoneuroimmunology. In J. Cassidy & P.R. Shaver (Eds.), *Handbook of attachment* (3rd ed.). New York: Guilford.

Ehrlich, S., King, J.A., & Boehm, L. (2019). Editorial: Connecting the nodes of altered brain network organization in eating disorders. *Journal of the American Academy of Child and Adolescent Psychiatry, 58,* 156-158.

Eichorn, D.H., Clausen, J.A., Haan, N., Honzik, M.P., & Mussen, P.H. (Eds.). (1981). *Present and past in middle life*. New York: Academic Press.

Ein-Dor, T., Verbeke, W.J.M.I., Mokry, M., & Vrlicka, P. (2018). Epigenetic modification of the oxytocin and glucocorticoid receptor genes is linked to attachment avoidance in young adults. *Attachment and Human Development, 20,* 439-454.

Einio, E., & Martikainen, P. (2019). Risk of hospitalization for cancer, musculoskeletal disorders, injuries, and poisonings surrounding widowhood. *American Journal of Epidemiology, 188,* 110-118.

Einziger, T., & others (2018). Predicting ADHD symptoms in adolescence from early childhood temperament traits. *Journal of Abnormal Child Psychology, 46,* 265-276.

Eisenberg, N., Duckworth, A., Spinrad, L., & Valiente, C. (2014). Conscientiousness and healthy aging. *Developmental Psychology, 50,* 1331-1349.

Eisenberg, N., & Morris, A.S. (2004). Moral cognitions and prosocial responding in adolescence. In R. Lerner & L. Steinberg (Eds.), *Handbook of adolescent psychology* (2nd ed.). New York: Wiley.

Eisenberg, N., & Spinrad, T.L. (2016). Multidimensionality of prosocial behavior: Rethinking the conceptualization and development of prosocial behavior. In L. Padilla-Walker & G. Carlo (Eds.), *Prosocial behavior*. New York: Oxford University Press.

Eisenberg, N., Spinrad, T.L., & Morris, A.S. (2013). Prosocial development. In P.D. Zelazo (Ed.), *Oxford handbook of developmental psychology*. New York: Oxford University Press.

Eisenberg, N., Spinrad, T.L., & Valiente, C. (2016). Emotion-related self-regulation and children's social, psychological, and academic functioning. In. L. Balter & C.S. Tamis-LeMonda (Eds.), *Child psychology: A contemporary handbook* (3rd ed.). New York: Psychology Press.

Eisenberg, N., & Valiente, C. (2002). Parenting and children's prosocial and moral development.

In M.H. Bornstein (Ed.), *Handbook of parenting* (2nd ed.). Mahwah, NJ: Erlbaum.

Eisenberg, N., & others (2019, in press). Relations of inhibition and emotion-related parenting to young children's prosocial and vicariously induced distress behavior. *Child Development.*

Eisman, A.B., Stoddard, S.A., Bauermeister, J.A., Caldwell, C.H., & Zimmerman, M.A. (2018). Organized activity participation and relational aggression: The role of positive youth development. *Violence and Victims, 33,* 91-108.

Ekas, N.A., Braungart-Rieker, J.M., & Messinger, D.S. (2018). The development of infant emotion regulation: Time is of the essence. In P.M. Cole & T. Hollenstein (Eds.), *Emotion regulation.* New York: Routledge.

Eklund, K., Tanner, N., Stoll, K., & Anway, L. (2015). Identifying emotional and behavioral risk among gifted and nongifted children: A multi-gate, multi-informant approach. *School Psychology Quarterly, 30,* 197-211.

Elbe, A-M., & others (2019). Is regular physical activity a key to mental health? Commentary. *Journal of Sport and Health Science, 8,* 6-7.

Elder, D. (2015). Reducing the risk of sudden infant death syndrome—a steady gain but still room for improvement. *New Zealand Medical Journal, 128,* 13-14.

Elder, G.H. (1980). Adolescence in historical perspective. In J. Adelson (Ed.), *Handbook of adolescent psychology.* New York: Wiley.

Eliasieh, K., Liets, L.C., & Chalupa, L.M. (2007). Cellular reorganization in the human retina during normal aging. *Investigative Ophthalmology and Visual Science, 48,* 2824-2830.

Elkana, O., & others (2019, in press). WAIS Information Subtest as an indicator of crystallized cognitive abilities and brain reserve among highly educated older adults: A three-year longitudinal study. *Applied Neuropsychology: Adult.*

Elkind, D. (1976). *Child development and education: A Piagetian perspective.* New York: Oxford University Press.

Elkind, D. (1978). Understanding the young adolescent. *Adolescence, 13,* 127-134.

Ellemers, N. (2018). Gender stereotypes. *Annual Review of Psychology* (Vol. 69). Palo Alto, CA: Annual Reviews.

Elliott, E.M., & others (2011). Working memory in the oldest-old: Evidence from output serial position curves. *Memory and Cognition, 10,* 20-27.

Elliott, J.G., & Resing, W.C. (2020, in press). Extremes of intelligence. In R.J. Sternberg (Ed.), *Human intelligence.* New York: Cambridge University Press.

Ellis, B.J., & Del Giudice, M. (2019). Developmental adaptation to stress: An evolutionary perspective. *Annual Review of Psychology* (Vol. 70). Palo Alto, CA: Annual Reviews.

Ellis, L., & Ames, M.A. (1987). Neurohormonal functioning and sexual orientation. *Psychological Bulletin, 101,* 233-258.

Ellis, N.C., & Ogden, D.C. (2017). Thinking about multiword constructions: Usage-based approaches to acquisition and processing. *Topics in Cognitive Science, 9,* 604-620.

El-Sheikh, M. (2013). *Auburn University Child Sleep, Health, and Development Center.* Auburn, AL: Auburn University.

Eltonsy, S., Martin, B., Ferreira, E., & Blais, L. (2016). Systematic procedure for the classification of proven and potential teratogens for use in research. *Birth Defects Research A: Clinical and Molecular Teratology, 106,* 285-297.

eMarketer.com (2017). *Teens' ownership of smartphones has surged.* Retrieved April 2, 2017, from www. emarketer.com/Article/Teens-Ownership-of-Smartphones-Has-Surged/1014161

Emberson, L.L., & others (2017a). Using fNIRS to examine occipital and temporal responses to stimulus repetition in young infants: Evidence of selective frontal cortex involvement. *Developmental Cognitive Neuroscience, 23,* 26-38.

Emberson, L.L., & others (2017b). Deficits in top-down sensory prediction in infants at risk due to premature birth. *Current Biology, 27,* 431-436.

Emberson, L.L., & others (2019, in press). Expectation affects neural repetition suppression in infancy. *Developmental Cognitive Neuroscience.*

Emery, R.E. (1999). *Renegotiating family relationships* (2nd ed.). New York: Guilford.

Endendijk, J.J., & others (2018). Mothers' neural responses to infant faces are associated with activation of the maternal care system and observed intrusiveness with their own child. *Cognive, Affective, and Behavioral Neuroscience, 18,* 609-621.

Enfield, A., & Collins, D. (2008). The relationships of service-learning, social justice, multicultural competence, and civic engagement. *Journal of College Student Development, 49,* 95-109.

Engels, A.C., & others (2016). Sonographic detection of central nervous system in the first trimester of pregnancy. *Prenatal Diagnosis, 36,* 266-273.

Englander, E., & McCoy, M. (2018). Sexting—prevalence, age, sex, and outcomes. *JAMA Pediatrics, 172,* 317-318.

English, T., & Carstensen, L.L. (2014). Will interventions targeting conscientiousness improve aging outcomes? *Developmental Psychology, 50,* 1478-1481.

English, T., & Carstensen, L.L. (2014a). Emotional experience in the mornings and the evenings: Consideration of age differences in specific emotions by time of day. *Frontiers in Psychology, 5,* 185.

English, T., & Carstensen, L.L. (2014b). Selective narrowing of social networks across adulthood is associated with improved emotional experience in life. *International Journal of Behavioral Development, 38,* 195-202.

Englund, M.M., Egeland, B., & Collins, W.A. (2008). Exceptions to high school dropout predictions in a low-income sample: Do adults make a difference? *Journal of Social Issues, 64,* 77-93.

Englund, M.M., Luckner, A.E., Whaley, G.J.L., & Egeland, B. (2004). Children's achievement in early elementary school: Longitudinal effects of parental involvement, expectations, and quality of assistance. *Journal of Educational Psychology, 96,* 723-730.

Enright, R.D., Santos, M.J., & Al-Mabuk, R. (1989). The adolescent as forgiver. *Journal of Adolescence, 12,* 95-110.

Ensembl Human (2008). *Explore the Homo sapiens genome.* Retrieved April 14, 2008, from www.ensembl. org/Homo_sapiens/index.html.

Ensor, R., Spencer, D., & Hughes, C. (2010). "You feel sad?" Emotion understanding mediates effects of verbal ability and mother-child mutuality on prosocial behaviors: Findings from 2 to 4 years. *Social Development, 20*(1), 93-110.

Epley, N., & others (2004). Perspective taking as egocentric anchoring and adjustment. *Journal of Personality and Social Psychology, 87,* 327-339.

Epperson, A.E., & others (2019, in press). Gender and ethnic/racial differences in adolescent intentions and willingness to smoke cigarettes: Evaluation of a structural equation model. *Journal of Health Psychology.*

Erickson, K.I., & Oberlin, L.E. (2017). Effects of exercise on cognition, brain structure, and brain function in older adults. In R. Cabeza, L. Nyberg, & D.C. Park (Eds.), *Cognitive neuroscience of aging* (2nd ed.). New York: Oxford University Press.

Erickson, K.I., & others (2011). Exercise training increases the size of the hippocampus and improves memory. *Proceedings of the National Academy of Sciences U.S.A., 108,* 3017-3022.

Ericsson, K.A., Krampe, R., & Tesch-Romer, C. (1993). The role of deliberate practice in the acquisition of expert performance. *Psychological Review, 100,* 363-406.

Ericsson, K.A., & Pool, R. (2016). *Peak: Secrets from the new science of expertise.* New York: Houghton Mifflin Harcourt.

Ericsson, K.A., & others (Eds.) (2018). *Cambridge handbook of expertise and expert performance* (2nd ed.). New York: Cambridge University Press.

Erikson, E.H. (1950). *Childhood and society.* New York: Norton.

Erikson, E.H. (1968). *Identity: Youth and crisis.* New York: Norton.

Erskine, H.E., & others (2016). Long-term outcomes of attention-deficit/hyperactivity disorder and conduct disorder: A systematic review and meta-analysis. *Journal of the American Academy of Child and Adolescent Psychiatry, 55,* 841-850.

Eskreis-Winkler, L., & others (2014). The grit effect: Predicting retention in the military, the workplace, school, and marriage. *Frontiers in Psychology, 5,* 00036.

Esposito, A.G., & others (2018). Bilingual education. In M.H. Bornstein (Ed.), *SAGE encyclopedia of lifespan human development.* Thousand Oaks, CA: Sage.

Esposito, C., Bacchini, D., & Affuso, G. (2019, in press). Adolescent non-suicidal self-injury and its relationship with school bullying and peer rejection. *Psychiatry Research.*

Esposito, G., & others (2017). Response to infant cry in clinically depressed and non-depressed mothers. *PLoS One, 12*(1), e0169066.

Esteban-Guitart, M. (2018). The biosocial foundation of the early Vygotsky: Educational psychology before the zone of proximal development. *History of Psychology, 21,* 384-401.

Estill, A., & others (2018). The effects of subjective age and aging attitudes on mid- to late-life sexuality. *Journal of Sex Research, 55,* 146-151.

Estrada, Y., & others (2017). Parent-centered prevention of risky behaviors among Hispanic youths in Florida. *American Journal of Public Health, 107,* 607-613.

Etaugh, C., & Bridges, J.S. (2010). *Women's lives* (2nd ed.). Boston: Allyn & Bacon.

Ethier, K.A., Harper, C.R., Hoo, E., & Ditts, P.J. (2016). The longitudinal impact of perceptions of parental monitoring on adolescent initiation of sexual activity. *Journal of Adolescent Health, 59,* 570-576.

Ettekal, I., & Ladd, G.W. (2019, in press). Development of aggressive-victims from childhood through adolescence:

Associations with emotion dysregulation, withdrawn behaviors, moral disengagement, peer rejection, and friendships. *Development and Psychopathology.*

Euler, H.A. (2019, in press). Gender differences in attachment from an evolutionary perspective: What is good for the goose may not be good for the gander. *Attachment and Human Development.*

Eun, J.D., & others (2018). Parenting style and mental disorders in a nationally representative sample of U.S. adolescents. *Social Psychiatry and Psychiatric Epidemiology, 53,* 11-20.

Evans, B.C., & others (2019, in press). Impulsivity and affect reactivity prospectively predict disordered eating attitudes in adolescents: A 6-year longitudinal study. *European Child and Adolescent Psychiatry.*

Evans, G.W. (2004). The environment of childhood poverty. *American Psychologist, 59,* 77-92.

Evans, G.W., & English, G.W. (2002). The environment of poverty. *Child Development, 73,* 1238-1248.

Evans, G.W., & Kim, P. (2007). Childhood poverty and health: Cumulative risk exposure and stress dysregulation. *Psychological Science, 18,* 953-957.

Evans, T.R., Hughes, D.J., & Steptoe-Warren, G. (2019, in press). A conceptual replication of emotional intelligence as a second-stratum factor of intelligence. *Emotion.*

Evans-Lacko, S., & others (2017). Childhood bullying victimization is associated with the use of mental health services over five decades: A longitudinal nationally representative study. *Psychological Medicine, 47,* 127-135.

F

Fabi, R. (2019). Why physicians should advocate for undocumented immigrants' unimpeded access to prenatal care. *AMA Journal of Ethics, 21,* E93-E99.

Fabiano, G.A., & others (2009). A meta-analysis of behavioral treatments for attention deficit/hyperactivity disorder. *Clinical Psychology Review, 29*(2), 129-140.

Fabricius, W.V., Braver, S.L., Diaz, P., & Schenck, C. (2010). Custody and parenting time: Links to family relationships and well-being after divorce. In M.E. Lamb (Ed.), *The role of the father in child development* (5th ed.). New York: Wiley.

Fagan, J.F. (1992). Intelligence: A theoretical viewpoint. *Current Directions in Psychological Science, 1,* 82-86.

Fagan, J.F., Holland, C.R., & Wheeler, K. (2007). The prediction, from infancy, of adult IQ and achievement. *Intelligence, 35,* 225-231.

Fagundes, C.P., Gillie, B.L., Derry, H.M., Bennett, J.M., & Kiecolt-Glaser, J.K. (2016). Resilience and immune function in older adults. In G.C. Smith and B. Hayslip (Eds.), *Annual Review of Gerontology and Geriatrics.* New York: Springer.

Fahey, T., Insel, P., & Roth, W. (2019). *Fit and well* (13th ed.). New York: McGraw-Hill.

Fajemiroye, J.O., & others (2018). Aging-induced biological changes and cardiovascular diseases. *Biomedical Research International, 2018,* 7156435.

Fajkowska, M. (2018). Personality traits: Hierarchically organized systems. *Journal of Personality, 86,* 36-54.

Falandry, C. (2019). The connection between cellular senescence and age-related diseases. In R. Fernandez-Ballesteros, A. Benetos, & J-M. Robine (Eds.),

Cambridge handbook of successful aging. New York: Cambridge University Press.

Falbe, J., & others (2015). Sleep duration, restfulness, and screens in the sleep environment. *Pediatrics, 135,* e367-e375.

Falbo, T., & Poston, D.L. (1993). The academic personality and physical outcomes of only children in China. *Child Development, 64,* 18-35.

Falconier, M.K., & others (2015). Stress from daily hassles in couples: Its effects on intradyadic relationship satisfaction and physical and psychological well-being. *Journal of Marital and Family Therapy, 41,* 221-235.

Falsetti, L., & others (2018). Interactions between atrial fibrillation, cardiovascular risk factors, and ApoE genotype in promoting cognitive decline in patients with Alzheimer's disease: A prospective cohort study. *Journal of Alzheimer's Disease, 62,* 713-725.

Fanelli, G.C., & Fanelli, D.G. (2018). Multiple ligament knee injuries. *Journal of Knee Surgery, 31,* 399-409.

Fang, Y., Tang, S., & Li, X. (2019, in press). Sirtuins in metabolic and epigenetic regulation of stem cells. *Trends in Endocrinology and Metabolism.*

Fang, Y., & others (2018). Information and communicative technology use enhances psychological well-being of older adults: The roles of age, social connectedness, and frailty status. *Aging and Mental Health, 22,* 1516-1524.

Fantz, R.L. (1963). Pattern vision in newborn infants. *Science, 140,* 286-297.

Farioli-Vecchioli, S., & others (2018). The role of physical exercise and omega-3 acids in depressive illness in the elderly. *Current Neuropharmacology, 16,* 308-326.

Farr, R.H. (2017). Does parental sexual orientation matter? A longitudinal follow-up of adoptive families with a school-age child. *Developmental Psychology, 53,* 252-264.

Farr, R.H., Crain, E.E., Oakley, M.K., Cashen, K.K., & Garber, K.J. (2016). Microaggression, feelings of difference, and resilience among adoptive children with sexual minority parents. *Journal of Youth and Adolescence, 45,* 85-104.

Farr, R.H., & Goldberg, A.E. (2018). Sexual orientation, gender identity, and adoption law. *Family Court Review, 56,* 374-383.

Farr, R.H., & Grotevant, H.G. (2019). Adoption. In B. Fiese (Ed.), *APA handbook of contemporary family psychology.* Washington, DC: American Psychological Association.

Farr, R.H., Oakley, M.K., & Ollen, E.W. (2017). School experiences of young children and their lesbian and gay adoptive parents. *Psychology of Sexual Orientation and Gender Diversity, 3,* 442-447.

Farr, R.H., & Patterson, C.J. (2013). Coparenting among lesbian, gay, and heterosexual couples: Associations with adopted children's outcomes. *Child Development, 84,* 226-240.

Farrell, A.D., Thompson, E.L., & Mehari, K.R. (2017). Dimensions of peer influences and their relationship to adolescents' aggression, other problem behaviors, and prosocial behavior. *Journal of Youth and Adolescence, 46,* 1351-1369.

Farrell, A.K., & others (2019). Early maternal sensitivity, attachment security in young adulthood, and cardiovascular risk at midlife. *Attachment and Human Development, 29,* 70-86.

Farrell, M.P., & Rosenberg, S.D. (1981). *Men at mid-life.* Boston: Auburn House.

Farrell, S.W., Fitzgerald, S.J., McAuley, P., & Barlow, C.E. (2010). Cardiorespiratory fitness, adiposity, and all-cause mortality in women. *Medicine and Science in Sports Exercise, 42*(11), 2006-2012.

Farrington, D. (2004). Conduct disorder, aggression, and delinquency. In R. Lerner & L. Steinberg (Eds.), *Handbook of adolescent psychology.* New York: Wiley.

Farrington, D., & Hawkins, J.D. (2019, in press). The need for long-term follow-ups of delinquency prevention experiments. *JAMA Network Open.*

Fasbender, K., Wiebe, A., & Bates, T.C. (2019, in press). Physical and cultural inheritance enhance agency, but what are the origins of this concern to establish a legacy? A nationally-representative twin study of Erikson's concept of generativity. *Behavior Genetics.*

Fasig, L. (2000). Toddlers' understanding of ownership: Implications for self-concept development. *Social Development, 9,* 370-382.

Fathollahi, A., & others (2019, in press). Epigenetics in osteoarthritis: Novel spotlight. *Journal of Cellular Physiology.*

Faucher, M.A. (2018). Updates from the literature, September/October 2017. *Journal of Midwifery and Women's Health, 63,* 1-4.

Fay, N., & others (2018). Universal principles of human communication: Preliminary evidence from a cross-cultural communication game. *Cognitive Science, 42.* doi:10.1111/cogs.12664

Faye, P.M., & others (2016). Kangaroo care for low birth weight infants at Albert-Royer National Children Hospital Center of Dakar. *Archives of Pediatrics, 23,* 268-274.

Fazio, L.K., DeWolf, M., & Siegler, R.S. (2016). Strategy use and strategy choice in fraction magnitude comparison. *Journal of Experimental Psychology: Learning, Memory, and Cognition, 42,* 1-16.

Fearnley, R., & Boland, J.W. (2019, in press). Parental life-limiting illness: What do we tell the children? *Healthcare.*

Federal Drug Administration (2018a). *Oxytocin.* Washington, DC: Author.

Feeney, S., Moravcik, E., & Nolte, S. (2019). *Who am I in the lives of children?* (11th ed.). Upper Saddle River, NJ: Pearson.

Feinberg, L., & Campbell, L.G. (2019). Shorter sleep durations in adolescents reduce power density in a wide range of waking electroencephalogram frequencies. *PLoS One, 14*(1), e0210649.

Feinberg, M., & others (2019). A world of blame to go around: Cross-cultural determinants of responsibility and punishment judgments. *Personality and Social Psychology Bulletin. 45,* 634-651.

Feinberg, M.E., McHale, S.M., & Whiteman, S.D. (2019). Parenting singles. In M.H. Bornstein (Ed.), *Handbook of parenting* (3rd ed.). New York: Routledge.

Feinberg, M.E., Sakuma, K-L., Hostetler, M., & McHale, S.M. (2013). Enhancing sibling relationships to prevent adolescent problem behaviors: Theory, design, and feasibility. *Siblings Are Special: Evaluation and Program Planning, 36*(1), 97-106.

Feist, G.J. (2019). The function of personality in creativity: Updates on the creative personality. In J.C. Kaufman & R.J. Sternberg (Eds.), *Cambridge handbook of creativity* (2nd ed.). New York: Cambridge University Press.

Feldhusen, J. (1999). Giftedness and creativity. In M.A. Runco & S.R. Pritzker (Eds.), *Encyclopedia of creativity.* San Diego: Academic Press.

Feldkamp, M.L., & others (2017). Etiology and clinical presentation of birth defects: Population based study. *BMJ, 357,* j2249.

Feldman, R. (2017). The neurobiology of human attachments. *Trends in Cognitive Science, 21,* 80–89.

Feldman, S.S., & Rosenthal, D.A. (1999). *Factors influencing parents' and adolescents' evaluations of parents as sex communicators.* Unpublished manuscript, Stanford Center on Adolescence, Stanford University.

Feldman, S.S., Turner, R., & Araujo, K. (1999). Interpersonal context as an influence on sexual timetables of youths: Gender and ethnic effects. *Journal of Research on Adolescence, 9,* 25–52.

Feldman-Winter, L., & others (2018). Weight gain in the first week of life predicts overweight at 2 years: A prospective cohort study. *Maternal and Child Nutrition, 14.*

Feliciano, C., & Rumbaut, R.G. (2019). The evolution of ethnic identity from adolescence to middle adulthood: The case of the immigrant second generation. *Emerging Adulthood, 7,* 85–96.

Feltman, R. (2018). Sexually transmitted diseases are at an all-time high (again). But why? Retrieved September 5, 2018, from www.popsci.com/sexually-transmitted-disease-increase

Felton, J.W., & others (2019). Talking together, thinking alone: Relations among co-rumination, peer relationships, and rumination. *Journal of Youth and Adolescence, 48,* 731–743.

Feltosa, C.M. (2018). Determination of parameters of oxidative stress in vitro models of neurodegenerative diseases—A review. *Current Clinical Pharmacology, 13,* 100–109.

Felver, J.C., & others (2017). Contemplative intervention reduces physical interventions in residential psychiatric treatment. *Prevention Science, 18,* 164–173.

Fergus, T.A., & Bardeen, J.R. (2019). The metacognitions questionnaire–30. *Assessment, 26,* 223–234.

Ferguson, C.J. (2013). Spanking, corporal punishment, and negative long-term outcomes: A meta-analytic review of longitudinal studies. *Clinical Psychology Review, 33,* 196–208.

Ferguson, E., & Bibby, P.A. (2012). Openness to experience and all-cause mortality: A meta-analysis and *r* (equivalent) from risk ratios and odd ratios. *British Journal of Health Psychology, 17,* 85–102.

Ferguson, S.M., & Ryan, A.M. (2019). It's lonely at the top: Adolescent students' perceived popularity and self-perceived social contentment. *Journal of Youth and Adolescence, 48,* 341–358.

Fergusson, D.M., Horwood, L.J., & Shannon, F.T. (1987). Breastfeeding and subsequent social adjustment in 6- to 8-year-old children. *Journal of Child Psychology and Psychiatry, 28,* 378–386.

Fergusson, D.M., McLeod, G.F., & Horwood, L.J. (2014). Parental separation/divorce in childhood and partnership outcomes at age 30. *Journal of Child Psychology and Psychiatry, 55,* 352–360.

Ferjan Ramirez, N., & others (2019, in press). Parent coaching at 6 and 10 months improves language outcomes at 14 months: A randomized controlled trial. *Developmental Science.*

Fernald, A., Marchman, V.A., & Weisleder, A. (2013). SES differences in language processing skill and vocabulary are evident at 18 months. *Developmental Science, 16,* 234–248.

Fernandez, C., & others (2019). Age-related decline in emotional perspective-taking: Its effect on the late positive potential. *Cognitive and Affective Behavioral Neuroscience, 19,* 109–122.

Fernandez, M., Mollinedo-Gajate, I., & Penagarikano, O. (2018). Neural circuits for social cognition: Implications for autism. *Neuroscience, 370,* 148–162.

Fernandez-Ballesteros, R. (2019). The concept of successful aging and related terms. In R. Fernandez-Ballesteros, A. Benetos, & J-M. Robine (Eds.), *Cambridge handbook of successful aging.* New York: Cambridge University Press.

Fernandez-Ballesteros, R., Benetos, A., & Robine, J-M. (Eds.) (2019). *Cambridge handbook of successful aging.* New York: Cambridge University Press.

Ferrarelli, F., & others (2019, in press). An increase in sleep slow waves predicts better working memory performance in healthy individuals. *NeuroImage.*

Ferrazzi, G., & others (2018). An efficient sequence for fetal brain imaging at 3T with enhanced T1 contrast and motion robustness. *Magnetic Resonance Medicine, 80,* 137–146.

Ferreira, T., & others (2018). Trajectories of parental engagement in early childhood among dual-earner families: Effects on child self-control. *Developmental Psychology, 54,* 731–743.

Ferrer, E., & others (2013). White matter maturation supports the development of reasoning ability through its influence on processing speed. *Developmental Science, 16,* 941–951.

Field, D. (1999). A cross-cultural perspective on continuity and change in social relations in old age: Introduction to a special issue. *International Journal of Aging and Human Development, 48,* 257–262.

Field, N., & others (2013). Associations between health and sexual lifestyles in Britain: Findings from the third National Survey of Sexual Attitudes and Lifestyles (Natsal-3). *Lancet, 382,* 1830–1844.

Field, T.M. (2001). Massage therapy facilitates weight gain in preterm infants. *Current Directions in Psychological Science, 10,* 51–55.

Field, T.M. (2007). *The amazing infant.* Malden, MA: Blackwell.

Field, T.M. (2010). Postpartum depression effects on early interactions, parenting, and safety practices: A review. *Infant Behavior and Development, 33,* 1–6.

Field, T.M. (2016). Massage therapy research review. *Complementary Therapies in Clinical Practice, 24,* 19–31.

Field, T.M. (2017). Preterm newborn pain research review. *Infant Behavior and Development, 49,* 141–150.

Field, T.M., Diego, M., & Hernandez-Reif, M. (2008). Prematurity and potential predictors. *International Journal of Neuroscience, 118,* 277–289.

Field, T.M., Diego, M., & Hernandez-Reif, M. (2011). Preterm infant massage therapy research: A review. *Infant Behavior and Development, 34,* 383–389.

Field, T.M., & others (1986). Tactile/kinesthetic stimulation effects on preterm neonates. *Pediatrics, 77,* 654–658.

Fielder, R.L., Walsh, J.L., Carey, K.B., & Carey, M.P. (2013). Predictors of sexual hookups: A theory-based, prospective study of first-year college women. *Archives of Sexual Behavior, 42,* 1425–1441.

Fiese, B. (Ed.) (2019). *APA handbook of contemporary family psychology.* Washington, DC: American Psychological Association.

Filip, P., & others (2019, in press). Neural scaffolding as the foundation for stable performance of aging cerebellum. *Cerebellum.*

Fillo, J., Simpson, J.A., Rholes, W.S., & Kohn, J.L. (2015). Dads doing diapers: Individual and relational outcomes associated with the division of childcare across the transition to parenthood. *Journal of Personality and Social Psychology, 108,* 298–316.

Finch, C.E. (2009). The neurobiology of middle-age has arrived. *Neurobiology of Aging, 30.*

Finch, C.E. (2011). Inflammation and aging. In E. Masoro & S. Austad (Eds.), *Handbook of the biology of aging* (7th ed.). New York: Elsevier.

Finch, K.H., & others (2017). Lateralization of ERPs to speech and handedness in the early development of autism spectrum disorder. *Journal of Neurodevelopmental Disorders.* doi:10.1186/s11689-017-9185-x

Fincham, F.D., & May, R.W. (2017). Infidelity in romantic relationships. *Current Opinion in Psychology, 13,* 70–74.

Fine, A., & others (2016). Self-control assessments and their implications for predicting adolescent offending. *Journal of Youth and Adolescence, 45,* 701–712.

Fine, A., & others (2017a). And justice for all: Determinants and effects of probation officers' processing decisions regarding first-time juvenile offenders. *Psychology, Public Policy, and the Law, 23,* 105–117.

Fine, A., & others (2017b). Is the effect of justice system attitudes on recidivism stable after youths' first arrests? Race and legal socialization among first-time offenders. *Law and Human Behavior, 46,* 1488–1502.

Finegood, E.D., & others (2017). Parenting in poverty: Attention bias and anxiety interact to predict parents' perceptions of daily parenting hassles. *Journal of Family Psychology, 31,* 51–60.

Finger, B., Hans, S.L., Bernstein, V.J., & Cox, S.M. (2009). Parent relationship quality and infant-mother attachment. *Attachment and Human Development, 11,* 285–306.

Fingerhut, A.W., & Peplau, L.A. (2013). Same-sex romantic relationships. In C.J. Patterson & A.R. D'Augelli (Eds.), *Handbook of psychology and sexual orientation.* New York: Oxford University Press.

Fingerman, K.L., & Baker, B. (2006). Socioemotional aspects of aging. In J. Wilmouth & K. Ferraro (Eds.), *Perspectives in gerontology* (3rd ed.). New York: Springer.

Fingerman, K.L., Cheng, Y-P., Wesselmann, E.D., Zarit, S., Furstenberg, F., & Birditt, K.S. (2012). Helicopter parents and landing pad kids: Intense parental support of grown children. *Journal of Marriage and the Family, 74*(4), 880–896.

Fingerman, K.L., Pillemer, K.A., Silverstein, M., & Suitor, J.J. (2012). The Baby Boomers' intergenerational relationships. *Gerontologist, 52,* 199–209.

Fingerman, K.L., Zarit, S.H., & Birditt, K.S. (2019). Parent-child relationships in adulthood and old age. In M.H. Bornstein (Ed.), *Handbook of parenting* (3rd ed.). New York: Routledge.

Fingerman, K.L., & others (2011). Who gets what and why: Help middle-aged adults provide to parents and grown children. *Journals of Gerontology B: Psychological Sciences and Social Sciences, 66,* 87–98.

Fingerman, K.L., & others (2016). Coresident and noncoresident emerging adults' daily experiences with parents. *Emerging Adulthood, 5,* 337-350.

Fingerman, K.L., & others (2019, in press). A family affair: Family typologies of life problems and midlife well-being. *Gerontologist.*

Finion, K.J., & others (2015). Emotion-based preventive intervention: Effectively promoting emotion knowledge and adaptive behavior among at-risk preschoolers. *Development and Psychopathology, 27,* 1353-1365.

Finkel, D., Andel, R., & Pedersen, N.L. (2018). Gender differences in longitudinal trajectories of change in physical, social, and cognitive/sedentary leisure activities. *Journals of Gerontology B: Psychological Sciences and Social Sciences, 73,* 1491-1500.

Fischer, K. (2018). Cognitive linguistics and pragmatics. In B. Dancyier (Ed.), *Cambridge handbook of cognitive linguistics.* New York: Cambridge University Press.

Fischhoff, B., Bruine de Bruin, W., Parker, A.M., Millstein, S.G., & Halpern-Felsher, B.L. (2010). Adolescents' perceived risk of dying. *Journal of Adolescent Health, 46,* 265-269.

Fisher, G.G., & others (2014). Mental work demands, retirement, and longitudinal trajectories of cognitive functioning. *Journal of Occupational Health Psychology, 19,* 231-242.

Fisher, G.G., & others (2017). Cognitive functioning, aging, and work: A review and recommendations for research and practice. *Journal of Occupational Health Psychology, 22,* 314-336.

Fisher, H. (2017). Commentary in *Match.com Singles in America 2017.* Retrieved August 17, 2017, from www. singlesinamerica.com

Fisher, J.H., & others (2018). Using goal achievement training in juvenile justice settings to improve substance use services for youth on community supervision. *Health and Justice, 6*(1), 10.

Fisher, K.R., Hirsh-Pasek, K., Newcombe, N., & Golinkoff, R.M. (2013). Taking shape: Supporting preschoolers' acquisition of geometric knowledge through guided play. *Child Development, 84,* 1872-1878.

Fisher, P.A. (2005, April). *Translational research on underlying mechanisms of risk among foster children: Implications for prevention science.* Paper presented at the meeting of the Society for Research in Child Development, Washington, DC.

Fiske, S. (2018). *Social cognition.* New York: Psychology Press.

Fisker, A.B., & Thysen, S.M. (2018). Implementation and assessment of vaccination programs: The importance of vaccination sequence for overall health outcomes. *Human Vaccines and Immunotherapeutics, 14,* 2900-2903.

Fitzgerald, A., Fitzgerald, N., & Aherne, C. (2012). Do peers matter? A review of peer and/or friends' influence on physical activity among American adolescents. *Journal of Adolescence, 35,* 941-958.

Fitzpatrick, K.K. (2012). Developmental considerations when treating anorexia nervosa in adolescents and young adults. In J. Lock (Ed.), *Oxford handbook of child and adolescent eating disorders: Developmental perspectives.* New York: Oxford University Press.

Fivush, R. (2010). The development of autobiographical memory. *Annual Review of Psychology* (Vol. 62). Palo Alto, CA: Annual Reviews.

Fivush, R., & Haden, C.A. (1997). Narrating and representing experience: Preschoolers' developing autobiographical accounts. In P. van den Broek, P.J. Bauer, & T. Bourg (Eds.), *Developmental spans in event representations and comprehension: Bridging fictional and actual events.* Mahwah, NJ: Erlbaum.

Fjell, A.M., & Walhovd, K.B. (2010). Structural brain changes in aging: Courses, causes, and consequences. *Reviews in the Neurosciences, 21,* 187-122.

Flam, K.K., Sanlder, I., Wolchik, S., & Tein, J.Y. (2016). Non-residential father-child involvement, interparental conflict, and mental health of children following divorce: A person-focused approach. *Journal of Youth and Adolescence, 45,* 581-593.

Flavell, J.H. (1971). First discussant's comments: What is memory development the development of? *Human Development, 14,* 272-278.

Flavell, J.H. (1976). Metacognitive aspects of problem solving. In L.B. Resnick (Ed.), *The nature of intelligence.* Englewood Cliffs, NJ: Prentice Hall.

Flavell, J.H. (1979). Metacognition and cognitive monitoring. A new area of psychological inquiry. *American Psychologist, 34,* 906-911.

Flavell, J.H. (2004). Theory-of-mind development. *Merrill-Palmer Quarterly, 50,* 274-290.

Flavell, J.H., Friedrichs, A., & Hoyt, J. (1970). Developmental changes in memorization processes. *Cognitive Psychology, 1,* 324-340.

Flavell, J.H., Green, F.L., & Flavell, E.R. (1993). Children's understanding of the stream of consciousness. *Child Development, 64,* 95-120.

Flavell, J.H., Green, F.L., & Flavell, E.R. (1995). The development of children's knowledge about intentional focus. *Developmental Psychology, 31,* 706-712.

Flavell, J.H., Green, F.L., & Flavell, E.R. (1998). The mind has a mind of its own: Developing knowledge about mental uncontrollability. *Cognitive Development, 13,* 127-138.

Flavell, J.H., Green, F.L., & Flavell, E.R. (2000). Development of children's awareness of their own thoughts. *Journal of Cognition and Development, 1,* 97-112.

Flavell, J.H., Miller, P.H., & Miller, S. (2002). *Cognitive development* (4th ed.). Upper Saddle River, NJ: Prentice Hall.

Flavell, J.H., Mumme, D., Green, F., and Flavell, E. (1992). Young children's understanding of different types of beliefs. *Child Development, 63,* 960-977.

Fleeson, W., & Jayawickreme, E. (2019). Perspectives on the person: Rapid growth and opportunities for integration. In K. Deaux & M. Snyder (Eds.), *Oxford handbook of personality and social psychology.* New York: Oxford University Press.

Flensborg-Madsen, T., & Mortensen, E.L. (2018). Associations of early developmental milestones with adult intelligence. *Child Development, 54,* 1434-1444.

Fletcher, S., & others (2019, in press). Tracking of toddler fruit and vegetable preferences to intake and adiposity later in childhood. *Maternal and Child Nutrition.*

Flicek, P., & others (2013). Ensembl 2013. *Nucleic Acids Research, 41,* D48-D55.

Flint, M.S., Baum, A., Chambers, W.H., & Jenkins, F.J. (2007). Induction of DNA damage, alteration of DNA repair, and transcriptional activation by stress hormones. *Psychoneuroendocrinology, 32,* 470-479.

Flitcroft, D., & Woods, K. (2018). What does research tell us about student motivation for test performance? *Pastoral Care in Education, 36,* 112-125.

Flood, S.M., & Genadek, K.R. (2016). Time for each other: Work and family constraints among couples. *Journal of Marriage and the Family, 78,* 142-164.

Florsheim, P., Moore, D., & Edgington, C. (2003). Romantic relationships among pregnant and parenting adolescents. In P. Florsheim (Ed.), *Adolescent romantic relations and sexual behavior.* Mahwah, NJ: Erlbaum.

Flynn, J.R. (1999). Searching for justice: The discovery of IQ gains over time. *American Psychologist, 54,* 5-20.

Flynn, J.R. (2007). The history of the American mind in the 20th century: A scenario to explain gains over time and a case for the irrelevance of *g.* In P.C. Kyllonen, R.D. Roberts, & L. Stankov (Eds.), *Extending intelligence.* Mahwah, NJ: Erlbaum.

Flynn, J.R. (2011). Secular changes in intelligence. In R.J. Sternberg & S.B. Kaufman (Eds.), *Cambridge handbook of intelligence.* New York: Cambridge University Press.

Flynn, J.R. (2013). *Are we getting smarter?* New York: Cambridge University Press.

Flynn, J.R. (2018). Reflections about intelligence over 40 years. *Intelligence, 70,* 73-83.

Flynn, J.R., & Shayer, M. (2018). IQ decline and Piaget: Does the rot start at the top? *Intelligence, 66,* 112-121.

Flynn, J.R., & Sternberg, R.J. (2020, in press). Environment and intelligence. In R.J. Sternberg (Ed.), *Human intelligence.* New York: Cambridge University Press.

Flynn, R.M., & others (2018). The influence of active gaming on cardiorespiratory fitness in Black and Hispanic youth. *Journal of School Health, 88,* 768-777.

Fode, M., & others (2019, in press). Late-onset hypogonadism and testosterone therapy—a summary of guidelines from the American Urological Association and the European Association of Urology. *European Urology Focus.*

Foley, P.B. (2019, in press). Dopamine in psychiatry: A historical perspective. *Journal of Neural Transmission.*

Follari, L. (2019). *Foundations and best practices in early childhood education* (4th ed.). Upper Saddle River, NJ: Pearson.

Fong, J.H., & Feng, J. (2018). Comparing the loss of functional independence of older adults in the U.S. and China. *Archives of Gerontology and Geriatrics, 74,* 123-127.

Fonseca-Machado Mde, O., & others (2015). Depressive disorder in Latin women: Does intimate partner violence matter? *Journal of Clinical Nursing, 24,* 1289-1299.

Font, S.A., & Cage, J. (2018). Dimensions of physical punishment and their associations with children's cognitive performance and school adjustment. *Child Abuse and Neglect, 75,* 29-40.

Fontaine, R.G., & others (2010). Does response evaluation and decision (RED) mediate the relation between hostile attributional style and antisocial behavior in adolescence? *Journal of Abnormal Child Psychology, 38,* 615-626.

Fontenot, K., Semega, J., & Kollar, M. (2018, September 18). *Income and poverty in the United States: 2017.* Washington, DC: U.S. Census Bureau.

Forbes, J.M., & Thorburn, D.R. (2018). Mitochondrial dysfunction in diabetic kidney disease. *Nature Reviews: Nephrology, 14,* 291-312.

Ford, B.Q., & others (2014). Emotion regulation moderates the risk associated with the 5-HTT gene and stress in children. *Emotion, 14,* 930–939.

Ford, D.Y. (2012). Gifted and talented education: History, issues, and recommendations. In K.R. Harris, S. Graham, & T. Urdan (Eds.), *APA handbook of educational psychology.* Washington, DC: American Psychological Association.

Ford, D.Y. (2014). Why education must be multicultural: Addressing a few misperceptions with counterarguments. *Gifted Child Today, 37,* 59–62.

Ford, D.Y. (2015a). Multicultural issues: Recruiting and retaining Black and Hispanic students in gifted education: Equality versus equity in schools. *Gifted Child Today, 38,* 187–191.

Ford, D.Y. (2015b). Culturally responsive gifted classrooms for culturally different students: A focus on invitational learning. *Gifted Child Today, 38,* 67–69.

Forgatch, M.S., Patterson, G.R., Degarmo, D.S., & Beldavs, Z.G. (2009). Testing the Oregon delinquency model with 9-year follow-up of the Oregon Divorce Study. *Development and Psychopathology, 21,* 637–660.

Foroughe, M. (Ed.) (2018). *Emotion focused family therapy with children and caregivers.* New York: Routledge.

Forrest, L.N., & others (2018). Core psychopathology in anorexia nervosa and bulimia nervosa: A network analysis. *International Journal of Eating Disorders, 51,* 668–679.

Forte, R., & others (2013). Executive function moderates the role of muscular fitness in determining functional mobility in older adults. *Aging: Clinical and Experimental Research, 25,* 291–298.

Foster, C., & others (2018). Physical activity and family-based obesity treatment: A review of expert recommendations on physical activity in youth. *Clinical Obesity, 8,* 68–79.

Foster, C.E., Yequez, C.E., & King, C.A. (2019). Youth with suicidal thoughts. In T. Ollendick & others (Eds.), *Oxford handbook of clinical child and adolescent psychology.* New York: Oxford University Press.

Fougere, B., & Cesari, M. (2019). Prevention of frailty. In R. Fernandez-Ballesteros, A. Benetos, & J-M. Robine (Eds.), *Cambridge handbook of successful aging.* New York: Cambridge University Press.

Fountain-Zaragoza, S., & Prakash, R.S. (2017). Mindfulness training for healthy aging: Impact of attention, well-being, and inflammation. *Frontiers in Aging Neuroscience, 9,* 11.

Fouts, H.N., & Bader, L.R. (2017). Transitions in siblinghood: Integrating developments, cultural, and evolutionary perspectives. In D. Narváez & others (Eds.), *Contexts for young child flourishing.* New York: Oxford University Press.

Fowler, K.B., & others (2017). A targeted approach for congenital cytomegalovirus screening within newborn hearing screening. *Pediatrics, 139.* doi:10.1542/peds.2016-2128

Fowler-Brown, A., & Kahwati, L.C. (2004). Prevention and treatment of overweight in children and adolescents. *American Family Physician, 69,* 2591–2598.

Fox, J., & Potocki, B. (2016). Lifetime video game consumption, interpersonal aggression, hostile sexism, and rape myth acceptance: A cultivation perspective. *Journal of Interpersonal Violence, 31,* 1912–1931.

Fox, M.K., & others (2010). Food consumption patterns of young preschoolers: Are they starting off on the right path? *Journal of the American Dietetic Association, 110*(Suppl. 12), S52–S59.

Fraley, R.C. (2019). Attachment in adulthood: Recent developments, emerging debates, and future directions. *Annual Review of Psychology* (Vol. 70). Palo Alto, CA: Annual Reviews.

Fraley, R.C., & Hudson, N.W. (2017). The development of attachment styles. In J. Specht (Ed.), *Personality development across the lifespan.* New York: Academic Press.

Fraley, R.C., Roisman, G.I., & Haltigan, J.D. (2013). The legacy of early experiences in development: Formalizing alternative models of how early experiences are carried forward over time. *Developmental Psychology, 49*(1), 109–126.

Franchak, J.M., Kretch, K.S., & Adolph, K.E. (2019, in press). See and be seen: Infant-caregiver social looking during free mobile play. *Developmental Science.*

Francis, J., Fraser, G., & Marcia, J.E. (1989). *Cognitive and experimental factors in moratorium-achievement (MAMA) cycles.* Unpublished manuscript. Department of Psychology, Simon Fraser University, Burnaby, British Columbia.

Francis-Coad, J., & others (2017). The effects of complex falls prevention interventions on falls in residential aged care settings: A systematic review protocol. *JBI Database of Systematic Reviews and Implementation Reports, 15,* 236–244.

Franco, P., & others (2019, in press). Early polysomnographic characteristics associated with neurocognitive development at 36 months of age. *Sleep Medicine.*

Frankl, V. (1984). *Man's search for meaning.* New York: Basic Books.

Franklin, A., Vevis, L., Ling, Y., & Hurlbert, A. (2010). Biological components of color preference in infancy. *Developmental Science, 13,* 346–354.

Fransson, M., & others (2016). Is middle childhood attachment related to social functioning in young adulthood? *Scandinavian Journal of Psychology, 57,* 108–116.

Franzmeier, N., & others (2019, in press). Functional connectivity associated with tau levels in aging, Alzheimer's, and small vessel disease. *Brain.*

Franzosa, E., Tsui, E.K., & Baron, S. (2018). Home health aides' perceptions of quality care: Goals, challenges, and implications for a rapidly changing industry. *New Solutions, 27,* 629–647.

Frasquilho, D., & others (2016). Distress and unemployment: The related economic and noneconomic factors in a sample of unemployed adults. *International Journal of Public Health, 61,* 821–828.

Fraundorf, S.H., & others (2019). Aging and recognition memory: A meta-analysis. *Psychological Bulletin, 145,* 339–371.

Frazier, P.A., & Cook, S.W. (1993). Correlates of distress following heterosexual relationship dissolution. *Journal of Social and Personal Relationships, 10,* 55–67.

Freberg, L.A. (2019). *Discovering behavioral neuroscience* (4th ed.). Boston: Cengage.

Frederikse, M., & others (2000). Sex differences in inferior lobule volume in schizophrenia. *American Journal of Psychiatry, 157,* 422–427.

Freeman, S., & others (2020). *Biological science* (7th ed.). Upper Saddle River, NJ: Pearson.

Freud, S. (1917). *A general introduction to psychoanalysis.* New York: Washington Square Press.

Freund, A.M., & Baltes, P.B. (2002). Life-management strategies of selection, optimization, and compensation: Measurement by self-report and construct validity. *Journal of Personality and Social Psychology, 82,* 642–662.

Freund, A.M., & Blanchard-Fields, F. (2014). Age-related differences in altruism across adulthood: Making personal financial gain versus contributing to the public good. *Developmental Psychology, 50,* 1125–1136.

Frey, B.S. (2011). Happy people live longer. *Science, 331,* 542–543.

Frick, M.A., & others (2018). The role of sustained attention, maternal sensitivity, and infant temperament in the development of early self-regulation. *British Journal of Psychology, 109,* 277–298.

Fridman, I., & others (2018). Information framing reduces initial negative attitudes in cancer patients' decisions about hospice care. *Journal of Pain and Symptom Management, 55,* 1540–1545.

Fridy, R.L., & others (2018). Pediatricians' knowledge and practices related to long-acting reversible contraceptives for adolescent girls. *Journal of Pediatric and Adolescent Gynecology, 31,* 394–399.

Friedman, D., Nessler, D., Johnson, R., Ritter, W., & Bersick, M. (2008). Age-related changes in executive function: An event-related potential (ERP) investigation of task-switching. *Aging, Neuropsychology, and Cognition, 15,* 95–128.

Friedman, H.S., & others (2014). A new life-span approach to conscientiousness and health: Combining the pieces of the causal puzzle. *Developmental Psychology, 50,* 1377–1389.

Friedman, J. (2013). Twin separation. Retrieved February 14, 2013, from http://christinabaglivitinglof.com/twin-pregnancy/six-twin-experts-tell-all/

Friedman, S.L., Melhuish, E., & Hill, C. (2011). Childcare research at the dawn of a new millennium: Update. In J.G. Bremner & T.D. Wachs (Eds.), *Wiley-Blackwell handbook of infant development* (2nd ed.). New York: Wiley.

Friend, M. (2018). *Special education* (5th ed.). Upper Saddle River, NJ: Pearson.

Friend, M., & Bursuck, W.D. (2019). *Including students with special needs* (8th ed.). Upper Saddle River, NJ: Pearson.

Friend, M., & others (2019). Language status at age 3: Group and individual prediction from vocabulary comprehension in the second year. *Developmental Psychology, 55,* 9–22.

Froh, J.J., Yurkewicz, C., & Kashdan, T.B. (2009). Gratitude and subjective well-being in early adolescence: Examining gender differences. *Journal of Adolescence, 32,* 633–650.

Frost, D.M. (2011). Stigma and intimacy in same-sex relationships: A narrative approach. *Journal of Family Psychology, 25,* 1–10.

Fry, P.S. (2001). The unique contribution of key existential factors to the prediction of psychological well-being of older adults following spousal loss. *The Gerontologist, 41,* 69–81.

Fry, R., & Parker, K. (2018, November 15). *Early benchmarks show 'post-millennials' on track to be most diverse, best-educated generation yet.* Washington, DC: Pew Research Center.

Fu, F., & others (2019, in press). Mothers' grief experiences of losing their only child in the 2008

Sichuan earthquake: A qualitative longitudinal study. *Omega.*

Fuhrmann, D., & others (2019, in press). The neurocognitive correlates of academic diligence in adolescent girls. *Cognitive Neuroscience.*

Fuhs, M.W., Nesbitt, K.T., Farran, D.C., & Dong, N. (2014). Longitudinal associations between executive functioning and academic skills across content areas. *Developmental Psychology, 50,* 1698-1709.

Fujiki, M., & Brinton, B. (2017). Pragmatics and social communication in child language disorders. In R. Schwartz (Ed.), *Handbook of child language disorders* (2nd ed.). New York: Routledge.

Fuligni, A.J. (2012). Gaps, conflicts, and arguments between adolescents and their parents. *New Directions for Child and Adolescent Development, 135,* 105-110.

Fulop, T., & others (2019). From inflamm-aging to immunosenescence. In R. Fernandez-Ballesteros, A. Benetos, & J-M. Robine (Eds.), *Cambridge handbook of successful aging.* New York: Cambridge University Press.

Fumagalli, M., & others (2018). From early stress to 12-month development in very preterm infants: Preliminary findings on epigenetic mechanisms and brain growth. *PLoS One, 13*(1), e0190602.

Funk, C.M., & others (2016). Local slow waves in superficial layers of primary cortical areas during REM sleep. *Current Biology, 26,* 396-403.

Furman, E. (2005). *Boomerang nation.* New York: Fireside.

Furman, L. (2019, in press). Kangaroo care 20 years later: Connecting infants and families. *Pediatrics.*

Furman, W., Low, S., & Ho, M. (2009). Romantic experience and psychosocial adjustment in middle adolescence. *Journal of Clinical Child and Adolescent Psychology, 38,* 1-16.

Furman, W., & Rose, A.J. (2015). Friendships, romantic relationships, and other dyadic peer relationships in childhood and adolescence: A unified relational perspective. In R.M. Lerner (Ed.), *Handbook of child psychology and developmental science* (7th ed.). New York: Wiley.

Furth, H.G., & Wachs, H. (1975). *Thinking goes to school.* New York: Oxford University Press.

Furthner, D., & others (2018). Education, school type, and screen time were associated with overweight and obesity in 2,930 adolescents. *Acta Pediatrica, 107,* 517-522.

Fynes-Clinton, S., Marstaller, L., & Burianova, H. (2019). Differentiation of functional networks during long-term memory retrieval in children and adolescents. *NeuroImage, 19,* 93-103.

G

Gabrielli, A.P., Manzardo, A.M., & Butler, M.G. (2019, in press). GeneAnalytics pathways and profiling of shared autism and cancer genes. *International Journal of Molecular Sciences.*

Gaias, L.M., & others (2012). Cross-cultural temperamental differences in infants, children, and adults in the United States of America and Finland, *53,* 119-128.

Gaillard, A., & others (2014). Predictors of postpartum depression: Prospective study of 264 women followed during pregnancy and postpartum. *Psychiatry Research, 215,* 341-346.

Gaillardin, F., & Baudry, S. (2018). Influence on working memory and executive function on stair ascent and descent in young and older adults. *Experimental Gerontology, 106,* 74-79.

Gaine, M.E., Chatterjee, S., & Abel, T. (2019). Sleep deprivation and the genome. *Frontiers in Neural Circuits, 12,* 14.

Gainotti, G. (2019, in press). A historical review of investigations on laterality of emotions in the human brain. *Journal of the History of the Neurosciences.*

Gaither, S.E., Pauker, K., & Johnson, S.P. (2012). Biracial and monoracial infant own-race face perception: An eye tracking study. *Developmental Science, 15*(6), 775-782.

Gajewski, P.D., & Falkenstein, M. (2018). ERP and behavioral effects of physical and cognitive training on working memory in aging: A randomized controlled study. *Neural Plasticity, 2018,* 3454835.

Galambos, N.L. (2004). Gender and gender role development in adolescence. In R. Lerner & L. Steinberg (Eds.), *Handbook of adolescence.* New York: Wiley.

Galambos, N.L., Berenbaum, S.A., & McHale, S.M. (2009). Gender development in adolescence. In R.M. Lerner & L. Steinberg (Eds.), *Handbook of adolescent psychology.* New York: Wiley.

Galambos, N.L., Howard, A.L., & Maggs, J.L. (2011). Rise and fall of sleep quality with student experiences across the first year of the university. *Journal of Research on Adolescence, 21,* 342-349.

Galbally, M., Lewis, A.J., IJzendoorn, M., & Permezel, M. (2011). The role of oxytocin in mother-infant relations: A systematic review of human studies. *Harvard Review of Psychiatry, 19,* 1-14.

Gale, C.R., Booth, T., Mottus, R., Kuh, D., & Deary, J.J. (2013). Neuroticism and extraversion in youth predict mental wellbeing and life satisfaction 40 years later. *Journal of Research in Personality, 47,* 687-697.

Galinsky, E. (2010). *Mind in the making.* New York: HarperCollins.

Galinsky, E., & David, J. (1988). *The preschool years: Family strategies that work—from experts and parents.* New York: Times Books.

Galland, B.C., Taylor, B.J., Edler, D.E., & Herbison, P. (2012). Normal sleep patterns in infants and children: A systematic review of observational studies. *Sleep Medicine Review, 16,* 213-222.

Gallant, S.N. (2016). Mindfulness meditation practice and executive functioning: Breaking down the benefit. *Consciousness and Cognition, 40,* 116-130.

Galliher, R.V., McLean, K.C., & Syed, M. (2017). An integrated model for studying identity content in context. *Developmental Psychology, 53,* 2011-2022.

Gallo, R.B.S., & others (2018). Sequential application of non-pharmacological interventions reduces the severity of labor pain, delays use of pharmacological analgesia, and improves some obstetrics outcomes: A randomized trial. *Journal of Physiotherapy, 64,* 33-40.

Galloway, J.C., & Thelen, E. (2004). Feet first: Object exploration in young infants. *Infant Behavior & Development, 27,* 107-112.

Gallup (2015, May 21). *Americans greatly overstate percent gay, lesbian in U.S.* Washington, DC: Gallup.

Gallup (2015). *Fewer young people say I do—to any relationship.* Princeton, NJ: Gallup.

Gallup, G.W., & Bezilla, R. (1992). *The religious life of young Americans.* Princeton, NJ: Gallup Institute.

Galupo, P., & others (2019, in press). "Like a constantly flowing river": Gender identity flexibility among non-binary transgender individuals. In J.D. Sinnott (Ed.), *Identity flexibility during adulthood.* New York: Springer.

Gamito, P., & others (2017). Cognitive training on stroke patients via virtual reality-based serious games. *Disability and Rehabilitation, 39,* 385-388.

Gampe, A., Wemelinger, S., & Daum, M.M. (2019). Bilingual children adapt to the needs of their communication partners, monolinguals do not. *Child Development, 90,* 98-107.

Ganapathy, K. (2018). Brain death revisited. *Neurology India, 66,* 308-315.

Ganci, M., Pradel, M., & Hughes, E.K. (2018). Feasibility of a parent education and skills workshop for improving response to family-based treatment of adolescent anorexia nervosa. *International Journal of Eating Disorders, 51,* 358-362.

Ganea, N., & others (2018). Development of adaptive communication skills in infants of blind parents. *Developmental Psychology, 54,* 2265-2273.

Gangisetty, O., Cabrera, M.A., & Murugan, S. (2018). Impact of epigenetics in aging and age related neurodegenerative diseases. *Frontiers in Bioscience, 23,* 1445-1464.

Ganley, C.M., Vasilyeva, M., & Dulaney, A. (2014). Spatial ability mediates the gender difference in middle school students' science performance. *Child Development, 85,* 1419-1432.

Ganong, L., & Coleman, M. (2018). Studying stepfamilies: Four eras of scholarship. *Family Process, 57,* 7-24.

Ganong, L., Coleman, M., & Sanner, C. (2019). Divorced and remarried parenting. In M.H. Bornstein (Ed.), *Handbook of parenting* (3rd ed.). New York: Routledge.

Ganong, L., & others (2019, in press). Stepfathers' affinity-seeking with stepchildren, stepfather-stepchild relationship quality, marital quality, and stepfamily cohesion among stepfathers and mothers. *Journal of Family Psychology.*

Ganzach, Y., & Fried, I. (2012). The role of intelligence in the formation of well-being: From job rewards to job satisfaction. *Intelligence, 40,* 333-342.

Gao, C., & others (2019, in press). The neural sources of N170: Understanding timing of activation in face-selective areas. *Psychophysiology.*

Gao, G. (2001). Intimacy, passion, and commitment in Chinese and U.S. American romantic relationships. *International Journal of Intercultural Relations, 25,* 329-342.

Gao, G. (2016), Cross-cultural romantic relationships. *Oxford research encyclopedia on romantic relationships.* New York: Oxford University Press.

Gao, M.M., & others (2019). Marital conflict behaviors and parenting: Dyadic links over time. *Family Relations, 68,* 135-149.

Garandeau, C.F., Vartio, A., Poskiparta, E., & Salmivalli, C. (2016). School bullies' intention to change behavior following teacher interventions: Effects of empathy arousal, condemning of bullying, and blaming the perpetrator. *Prevention Science, 17,* 1034-1043.

Garbarino, J. (1999). *Lost boys: Why our sons turn violent and how we can save them.* New York: Free Press.

Garbarino, J., Governale, A., & Kostelny, K. (2019). Parenting and public policy. In M.H. Bornstein (Ed.), *Handbook of parenting.* New York: Routledge.

Garcia, O.F., Lopez-Fernandez, O., & Serra, E. (2019, in press). Raising Spanish children with an antisocial tendency: Do we know what the optimal parenting style is? *Journal of Interpersonal Violence.*

Garcini, L.M., & others (2019, in press). Miles over mind: Transnational death and its association with psychological distress among undocumented Mexican immigrants. *Death Studies.*

Gardiner, H.W. (2019). Culture, context, and development. In D. Matsumoto & H.C. Hwang (Eds.), *Handbook of cross-cultural psychology* (2nd ed.). New York: Oxford University Press.

Gardner, A.A., & Lambert, C.A. (2019). Examining the interplay of self-esteem, trait-emotional intelligence, and age with depression across adolescence. *Journal of Adolescence, 71,* 162–166.

Gardner, B., & others (2017). Specifying the content of home-based health behavior change interventions for older people with frailty or at risk of frailty: An exploratory systematic review. *BMJ Open, 7*(2), e014127.

Gardner, H. (1983). *Frames of mind.* New York: Basic Books.

Gardner, H. (1993). *Multiple intelligences.* New York: Basic Books.

Gardner, H. (2002). The pursuit of excellence through education. In M. Ferrari (Ed.), *Learning from extraordinary minds.* Mahwah, NJ: Erlbaum.

Gardner, H. (2016). *Multiple intelligences: Prelude, theory, and aftermath.* In R.J. Sternberg, S.T. Fiske, & J. Foss (Eds.), *Scientists making a difference.* New York: Cambridge University Press.

Gardner, H., Kornhaber, W., & Chen, J-Q. (2018). The theory of multiple intelligences: Psychological and educational perspectives. In R.J. Sternberg (Ed.), *The nature of human intelligence.* New York: Cambridge University Press.

Gardner, M., Brooks-Gunn, J., & Chase-Lansdale, P.L. (2016). The two-generation approach to building human capital: Past, present, and future. In E. Votruba-Drzal & E. Dearing (Eds.), *Handbook of early childhood development programs, practices, and policies.* New York: Wiley.

Gardner, M., & Steinberg, L. (2005). Peer influence on risk taking, risk preference, and risky decision making in adolescence and adulthood. *Developmental Psychology, 41,* 625–635.

Gardosi, J., & others (2013). Maternal and fetal risk factors for stillbirth: Population-based study. *British Medical Journal, 346,* f108.

Gareri, P., & others (2017). The Citicholinage study: Citicoline plus cholinesterase inhibitors in aged patients affected with Alzheimer's disease study. *Journal of Alzheimer's Disease, 56,* 557–565.

Garfield, C.F., & others (2012). Trends in attention deficit hyperactivity disorder ambulatory diagnosis and medical treatment in the United States, 2000–2010. *Academic Pediatrics, 12,* 110–116.

Gariepy, G., Janssen, I., Sentenac, M., & Elgar, F.J. (2017). School start time and sleep in Canadian adolescents. *Journal of Sleep Research, 26,* 195–201.

Garlow, S.J., Purselle, D., & Heninger, M. (2005). Ethnic differences in patterns of suicide across the life cycle. *American Journal of Psychiatry, 162,* 319–323.

Garnham, A. (2019). Pragmatics and inference. In S-A. Rueschemeyer & M. Gareth Gaskell (Eds.), *Oxford handbook of psycholinguistics* (2nd ed.). New York: Oxford University Press.

Garon, N., Smith, I.M., & Bryson, S.E. (2018). Early executive dysfunction in ASD: Simple versus complex skills. *Autism Research, 11,* 318–330.

Garthe, A., Roeder, I., & Kempermann, G. (2016). Mice in an enriched environment learn more flexibly because of adult hippocampal neurogenesis. *Hippocampus, 26,* 261–271.

Gartland, N., O'Connor, D.B., Lawton, R., & Ferguson, R. (2014). Investigating the effects of conscientiousness on daily stress, affect, and physical symptom processes: A daily diary study. *British Journal of Health Psychology, 19,* 311–328.

Gartner, J., Larson, D.B., & Allen, G.D. (1991). Religious commitment and mental health: A review of the empirical literature. *Journal of Psychology and Theology, 19,* 6–25.

Gartsein, M.A., Hancock, G.R., & Iverson, S.L. (2018). Positive affectivity and fear trajectories in infancy: Contributions of mother-child interaction factors. *Child Development, 89,* 1519–1534.

Gartstein, M.A., Putnam, S., & Kliewer, R. (2016). Do infant temperament characteristics predict core academic abilities in preschool-aged children? *Learning and Individual Differences, 45,* 299–306.

Garvey, C. (2000). *Play* (expanded ed.). Cambridge, MA: Harvard University Press.

Gasquoine, P.G. (2016). Effects of bilingualism on vocabulary, executive functions, age of dementia onset, and regional brain structure. *Neuropsychology, 30,* 988–997.

Gasquoine, P.G. (2018). Effects of physical activity on delayed memory measures in randomized controlled trials with nonclinical older, mild cognitive impairment, and dementia participants. *Journal of Clinical and Experimental Neuropsychology, 40,* 874–886.

Gasser, L., & Keller, M. (2009). Are the competent morally good? Perspective taking and moral motivation of children involved in bullying. *Social Development, 18*(4), 798–816.

Gates, G.J. (2011). *How many people are lesbian, gay, bisexual, and transgender?* Los Angeles: Williams Institute, School of Law.

Gates, G.J. (2013, February). *LGBT parenting in the United States.* Los Angeles: The Williams Institute, UCLA.

Gates, W. (1998, July 20). Charity begins when I'm ready (interview). *Fortune Magazine.*

Gattamorta, K.A., & others (2017). Psychiatric symptoms, parental attachment, and reasons for use as correlates of heavy substance use among treatment-seeking Hispanic adolescents. *Substance Use and Misuse, 52,* 392–400.

Gatzke-Kopp, L.M., & others (2019, in press). Magnitude and chronicity of environmental smoke exposure across infancy and early childhood in a sample of low-income children. *Nicotine and Tobacco Research.*

Gauthier, A.H., & Furstenberg, F.F. (2005). Historical trends in the patterns of time use among young adults in developed countries. In R.A. Setterson, F.F. Furstenberg, & R.G. Rumbaut (Eds.), *On the frontier of adulthood: Theories, research, and social policy.* Chicago: University of Chicago Press.

Gauvain, M. (2013). Sociocultural contexts of development. In P.D. Zelazo (Ed.), *Oxford handbook of developmental psychology.* New York: Oxford University Press.

Gauvain, M. (2016). Peer contributions to cognitive development. In K. Wentzel & G.B. Ramani (Eds.), *Handbook of social influences in school contexts.* New York: Routledge.

Gauvain, M., & Perez, S. (2015). Cognitive development in the context of culture. In R.M. Lerner (Ed.), *Handbook of child psychology and developmental science* (7th ed.). New York: Wiley.

Gavett, B.E., & others (2017). Phishing suspiciousness in older and younger adults: The role of executive functioning. *PLoS One, 12*(2), e0171620.

Geerkens, M.J.M., & others (2019, in press). Sexual dysfunction and bother due to erectile dysfunction in the healthy elderly male population: Prevalence from a systematic review. *European Urology Focus.*

Geertsen, S.S., & others (2016). Motor skills and exercise capacity are associated with objective measures of cognitive functions and academic performance in preadolescent children. *PLoS One, 11*(8), e0161960.

Gekker, M., & others (2019, in press). Early scars are forever: Childhood abuse in patients with adult-onset PTSD is associated with increased prevalence and severity of psychiatric comorbidity. *Psychiatry Research.*

Gekle, M. (2017). Kidney and aging—A narrative review. *Experimental Gerontology, 87*(Pt. B), 153–155.

Gelman, R. (1969). Conservation acquisition: A problem of learning to attend to relevant attributes. *Journal of Experimental Child Psychology, 7,* 67–87.

Gelman, R., & Williams, E.M. (1998). Enabling constraints for cognitive development and learning. In W. Damon (Ed.), *Handbook of child psychology* (5th ed., Vol. 4). New York: Wiley.

Gelman, S.A., & Kalish, C.W. (2006). Conceptual development. In W. Damon & R. Lerner (Eds.), *Handbook of child psychology* (6th ed.). New York: Wiley.

Gelman, S.A., & Opfer, J.E. (2004). Development of the animate-inanimate distinction. In U. Goswami (Ed.), *Blackwell handbook of childhood cognitive development.* Malden, MA: Blackwell.

Gelman, S.A., Taylor, M.G., & Nguyen, S.P. (2004). Mother-child conversations about gender. *Monographs of the Society for Research in Child Development, 69*(1, Serial No. 275).

Genc, S., & others (2018). Age, sex, and puberty related development of the corpus callosum: A multi-technique diffusion MRI study. *Brain Structure and Function, 223,* 2753–2765.

Gendron, T., & others (2019, in press). Development of the relational ageism scale: Confirmatory test on survey data. *International Journal of Aging and Development.*

Genetti, C. (Ed.) (2019). *How languages work* (2nd ed.). New York: Cambridge University Press.

Gennetian, L.A., & Miller, C. (2002). Children and welfare reform: A view from an experimental welfare reform program in Minnesota. *Child Development, 73,* 601–620.

Gentile, D.A., & others (2009). The effects of prosocial video games on prosocial behaviors: International evidence from correlational, longitudinal, and experimental studies. *Personality and Social Psychology Bulletin, 35,* 752–763.

Gentile, D.A., & others (2014). Protective effects of parental monitoring of children's media use: A prospective study. *JAMA Pediatrics, 168,* 479–484.

Gentner, M.B., & Leppert, M.L.O. (2019, in press). Environmental influences on health and development: Nutrition, substance exposure, and adverse childhood experiences. *Developmental Medicine and Child Neurology.*

Geoba (2019). *The world: Life expectancy.* Retrieved February 20, 2019, from www.geoba.se

George Dalmida, S., & others (2018). Sexual risk behaviors of African American adolescent females: The role of cognitive and religious factors. *Journal of Transcultural Nursing, 29,* 74–83.

George, L., & Park, C.L. (2017). Does spirituality confer meaning in life among heart failure patients and cancer survivors? *Psychology of Religion and Spirituality, 9,* 131–137.

George, L.G., Helson, R., & John, O.P. (2011). The "CEO" of women's work lives: How Big Five conscientiousness, extraversion, and openness predict 50 years of work experiences in a changing sociocultural context. *Journal of Personality and Social Psychology, 101,* 812–830.

George, L.K. (2010). Still happy after all these years: Research frontiers on subjective well-being in later life. *Journals of Gerontology B: Psychological Sciences and Social Sciences, 65B,* 331–339.

George, L.K., & Ferraro, K.F. (2016). Aging and the social sciences: Progress and prospects. In L.K. George & K.F. Ferraro (Eds.), *Handbook of aging and the social sciences* (8th ed.). New York: Elsevier.

Georgetown University Center on Education (2016). *Georgetown University Center on Education and the Workforce report.* Washington, DC: Georgetown University.

Gergely, A., & others (2019, in press). Auditory-visual matching of conspecifics and non-conspecifics by dogs and human infants. *Animals.*

Gernhardt, A., Keller, H., & Rubeling, H. (2016). Children's family drawings as expressions of attachment representations across cultures: Possibilities and limitations. *Child Development, 87,* 1069–1078.

Gershoff, E.T. (2013). Spanking and development: We know enough now to stop hitting our children. *Child Development Perspectives, 7,* 133–137.

Gershoff, E.T., & Grogan-Kaylor, A. (2016). Spanking and child outcomes: Old controversies and new meta-analyses. *Journal of Family Psychology, 30,* 453–469.

Gershoff, E.T., Lansford, J.E., Sexton, H.R., Davis-Kean, P., & Sameroff, A. (2012). Longitudinal links between spanking and children's externalizing behaviors in a national sample of White, Black, Hispanic, and Asian American families. *Child Development, 83,* 838–843.

Gershoff, E.T., Lee, S.J., & Durrant, J.E. (2017). Promising intervention strategies for reducing parents' use of physical punishment. *Child Abuse and Neglect, 71,* 9–23.

Gershoff, E.T., & others (2018). The strength of the causal evidence against physical punishment of children and its implications for parents, psychologists, and policymakers. *American Psychologist, 73,* 628–638.

Gerstorf, D., & others (2015). Secular changes in late-life cognition and well-being: Towards a long bright future with a short brisk ending. *Psychology and Aging, 30,* 301–310.

Gesell, A. (1934). *An atlas of infant behavior.* New Haven, CT: Yale University Press.

Gesser-Edelsburg, A., & Hijazi, R. (2018). The magic pill: The branding of impotence and the positioning of Viagra as its solution through edutainment. *Journal of Health Communication, 23,* 281–290.

Geurten, M., Meulemans, T., & Willems, S. (2018). A closer look at children's metacognitive skills: The case of the distinctiveness heuristic. *Journal of Experimental Child Psychology, 172,* 130–148.

Gewirtz, J. (1977). Maternal responding and the conditioning of infant crying: Directions of influence within the attachment-acquisition process. In B.C. Etzel, J.M. LeBlanc, & D.M. Baer (Eds.), *New developments in behavioral research.* Hillsdale, NJ: Erlbaum.

Gewirtz-Meydan, A., & Ayalon, L. (2019, in press). Why do older adults have sex? Approach and avoidance sexual motives among older women and men. *Journal of Sexual Research.*

Gewirtz-Meydan, A., & Finzi-Dottan. R. (2018). Sexual satisfaction among couples: The role of attachment orientation and sexual motives. *Journal of Sex Research, 55,* 178–190.

Ghesquiere, A., & others (2019, in press). Investigating associations between pain and complicated grief symptoms in Japanese older adults. *Aging and Mental Health.*

Ghetti, S., & Alexander, K.W. (2004). "If it happened, I would remember it": Strategic use of event memorability in the rejection of false autobiographical events. *Child Development, 75,* 542–561.

Gialamas, A., & others (2014). Quality of childcare influences children's attentiveness and emotional regulation at school entry. *Journal of Pediatrics, 165,* 813–819.

Giannakakos, A.R., Vladescu, J.C., & Simon, R. (2018). Teaching installation and use of child passenger restraints. *Journal of Applied Behavior Analysis, 51,* 915–923.

Giarrusso, R., & Bengtson, V.L. (2007). Self-esteem. In J.E. Birren (Ed.), *Encyclopedia of gerontology* (2nd ed.). San Diego: Academic Press.

Gibbs, J.C., Basinger, K.S., Grime, R.L., & Snarey, J.R. (2007). Moral judgment across cultures: Revisiting Kohlberg's universality claims. *Developmental Review, 27,* 443–500.

Gibson, E.J. (1969). *Principles of perceptual learning and development.* New York: Appleton-Century-Crofts.

Gibson, E.J. (1989). Exploratory behavior in the development of perceiving, acting, and the acquiring of knowledge. *Annual Review of Psychology* (Vol. 39). Palo Alto, CA: Annual Reviews.

Gibson, E.J. (2001). *Perceiving the affordances.* Mahwah, NJ: Erlbaum.

Gibson, E.J., & Walk, R.D. (1960). The "visual cliff." *Scientific American, 202,* 64–71.

Gibson, E.J., & others (1987). Detection of the traversability of surfaces by crawling and walking infants. *Journal of Experimental Psychology: Human Perception and Performance, 13,* 533–544.

Gibson, J.J. (1966). *The senses considered as perceptual systems.* Boston: Houghton Mifflin.

Gibson, J.J. (1979). *The ecological approach to visual perception.* Boston: Houghton Mifflin.

Giedd, J.N. (2007, September 27). Commentary in S. Jayson, "Teens driven to distraction." *USA Today,* pp. D1–2.

Giedd, J.N., & others (2012). Automatic magnetic resonance imaging of the developing child and adolescent brain. In V.F. Reyna & others (Eds.), *The adolescent brain.* Washington, DC: American Psychological Association.

Gilbert, G., & Graham, S. (2010). Teaching writing to students in grades 4–6: A national survey. *Elementary School Journal, 110,* 494–518.

Gillain, D., & others (2019). Gerontechnologies and successful aging. In R. Fernandez-Ballesteros, A. Benetos, & J-M. Robine (Eds.), *Cambridge handbook of successful aging.* New York: Cambridge University Press.

Gillen-O'Neel, C., Huynh, V.W., & Fuligni, A.J. (2013). To study or to sleep? The academic costs of extra studying at the expense of sleep. *Child Development, 84*(1), 133–142.

Gilligan, C. (1982). *In a different voice.* Cambridge, MA: Harvard University Press.

Gilligan, C. (1992, May). *Joining the resistance: Girls' development in adolescence.* Paper presented at the symposium on development and vulnerability in close relationships, Montreal.

Gilligan, C. (1996). The centrality of relationships in psychological development: A puzzle, some evidence, and a theory. In G.G. Noam & K.W. Fischer (Eds.), *Development and vulnerability in close relationships.* Hillsdale, NJ: Erlbaum.

Gilligan, C., Spencer, R., Weinberg, M.K., & Bertsch, T. (2003). On the listening guide: A voice-centered relational model. In P.M. Carnic & J.E. Rhodes (Eds.), *Qualitative research in psychology.* Washington, DC: American Psychological Association.

Gilsoul, J., & others (2019). Do attentional capacities and processing speed mediate the effect of age on executive functioning? *Neuropsychology, Development, and Cognition B: Aging, Neuropsychology, and Cognition, 26,* 282–317.

Gimovsky, A.C., & others (2019, in press). Genetic abnormalities seen on CVS in early pregnancy failure. *Journal of Maternal-Fetal and Neonatal Medicine.*

Glabska, D., & others (2019, in press). The National After-School Athletics Program participation as a tool to reduce the risk of obesity in adolescents after one year of intervention: A nationwide study. *International Journal of Environmental Research and Public Health.*

Glaser, R., & Kiecolt-Glaser, J.K. (2005). Stress-induced immune dysfunction: Implications for health. *Nature Review: Immunology, 5,* 243–251.

Gliga, T., & others (2018). Early visual foraging in relationship to familial risk for autism and hyperactivity/inattention. *Journal of Attention Disorders, 22,* 839–847.

Glover, J., & Fritsch, S.L. (2018). #KidsAnxiety and social media; A review. *Child and Adolescent Psychiatry Clnics of North America, 27,* 171–182.

Glynn, R., Salmon, K., & Low, J. (2018). It's in the details: The role of selective discussion in forgetting of children's autobiographical memories. *Journal of Experimental Child Psychology, 167,* 117–127.

Gnambs, T., & Appel, M. (2018). Narcissism and social networking behavior: A meta-analysis. *Journal of Personality, 86,* 200–212.

Gobinath, A.R., & others (2018). Voluntary running influences the efficacy of fluoxetine in a model of postpartum depression. *Neuropharmacology, 128,* 106–128.

Goel, A., Sinha, R.J., Delela, D., Sankhwar, S., & Singh, V. (2009). Andropause in Indian men: A preliminary cross-sectional study. *Urology Journal, 6,* 40–46.

Goetter, E., & others (2019). The five-factor model in bereaved adults with and without complicated grief. *Death Studies, 43,* 204–209.

Goffin, K.C., Boldt, L.J., & Kochanska, G. (2018). A secure base from which to cooperate: Security, child and parent willing stance, and adaptive and maladaptive outcomes in two longitudinal studies. *Journal of Abnormal Child Psychology, 46,* 1061–1075.

Gogtay, N., & Thompson, P.M. (2010). Mapping gray matter development: Implications for typical development and vulnerability to psychopathology. *Brain and Cognition, 72,* 6–15.

Goksan, S., & others (2015). fMRI reveals neural activity overlap between adult and infant pain. *eLife, 4,* e06356.

Gold, D. (2011). Death and dying. In R.H. Binstock & L.K. George (Eds.), *Handbook of aging and the social sciences* (7th ed.). New York: Elsevier.

Gold, M.A., & others (2010). Associations between religiosity and sexual and contraceptive behaviors. *Journal of Pediatric and Adolescent Gynecology, 23,* 290–297.

Goldberg, A.E., & Romero, A. (Eds.) (2019, in press). *LGBTQ divorce and relationship dissolution.* New York: Oxford University Press.

Goldberg, A.E., & Sweeney, K.K. (2019). LGBTQ parent families. In B.H. Friese (Ed.), *APA handbook of contemporary family psychology.* Washington, DC: APA Books.

Goldberg, R., & Mitchell, P. (2019). *Drugs across the spectrum* (8th ed.). Boston: Cengage.

Goldberg, S.K., & Halpern, C.T. (2017). Sexual initiation patterns of U.S. sexual minority youth: A latent class analysis. *Perspectives on Sex and Reproductive Health, 49,* 55–67.

Goldberg, W.A., & Lucas-Thompson, R. (2008). Effects of maternal and paternal employment. In M.M. Haith & J.B. Benson (Eds.), *Encyclopedia of infant and early childhood development.* Oxford, UK: Elsevier.

Goldin-Meadow, S. (2015). Nonverbal communication: The hand's role in talking and thinking. In R.M. Lerner (Ed.), *Handbook of child psychology and developmental science* (7th ed.). New York: Wiley.

Goldin-Meadow, S. (2017a). Using our hands to change our minds. *Cognitive Science, 8,* 1–2.

Goldin-Meadow, S. (2017b). What the hands can tell us about language emergence. *Psychonomic Bulletin & Review, 24,* 213–218.

Goldschmidt, L., Richardson, G.A., Willford, J., & Day, N.L. (2008). Prenatal marijuana exposure and intelligence test performance at age 6. *Journal of the American Academy of Child and Adolescent Psychiatry, 47*(3), 254–263.

Goldstein, D.S., & others (2018). Cerebrospinal fluid biomarkers of central dopamine deficiency predict Parkinson's disease. *Parkinsonism and Related Disorders, 50,* 108–112.

Goldstein, E.B. (2019). *Cognitive psychology* (5th ed.). Boston: Cengage.

Goldstein, M.H., King, A.P., & West, M.J. (2003). Social interaction shapes babbling: Testing parallels between birdsong and speech. *Proceedings of the National Academy of Sciences, 100,* 8030–8035.

Goldstein, R., & Halpern-Felsher, B. (2018). Adolescent oral sex and condom use: How much should we worry

and what can we do? *Journal of Adolescent Health, 62,* 363–364.

Goldston, D.B., & others (2008). Cultural considerations in adolescent suicide prevention and psychosocial treatment. *American Psychologist, 63,* 14–31.

Goleman, D. (1995). *Emotional intelligence.* New York: Basic Books.

Goleman, D., Kaufman, P., & Ray, M. (1993). *The creative spirit.* New York: Plume.

Golinkoff, R.M., Can, D.D., Soderstrom, M., & Hirsh-Pasek, K. (2015). (Baby) talk to me: The social context of infant-directed speech and its effect on early language acquisition. *Current Directions in Psychological Science, 24,* 339–344.

Golinkoff, R.M., & Hirsh-Pasek, K. (1999). *How babies talk.* New York: Dutton/Penguin Press.

Golinkoff, R.M., Hirsh-Pasek, K., Gordon, L., & Cauley, K. (1987). The eyes have it: Lexical and word order comprehension in a new context. *Journal of Child Language, 14,* 23–45.

Golombok, S. (2011a). Children in new family forms. In R. Gross (Ed.), *Psychology* (6th ed.). London: Hodder.

Golombok, S. (2011b). Why I study lesbian families. In S. Ellis, V. Clarke, E. Peel, & D. Riggs (Eds.), *LGBTQ psychologies.* New York: Cambridge University Press.

Golombok, S., & Tasker, F. (2010). Gay fathers. In M.E. Lamb (Ed.), *The role of the father in child development* (5th ed.). New York: Wiley.

Golombok, S., & others (2008). Development trajectories of sex-typed behavior in boys and girls: A longitudinal general population study of children aged 2.5–8 years. *Child Development, 79,* 1583–1593.

Golombok, S., & others (2014). Adoptive gay father families: Parent-child relationships and children's psychological adjustment. *Child Development, 85,* 456–468.

Gomez, S.Z., & others (2019, in press). The impact of immunosuppressive drugs on human placental explants. *Reproductive Science.*

Gomez-Bruton, A., & others (2017). Plyometric exercise and bone health in children and adolescents: A systematic review. *World Journal of Pediatrics, 13,* 112–121.

Gomez-Leal, R., & others (2018). The relationship between three models of emotional intelligence and psychopathy: A systematic review. *Frontiers in Psychiatry, 9,* 307.

Goncu, A., & Gauvain, M. (2012). Sociocultural approaches in educational psychology. In K.H. Harris, S. Graham, & T. Urdan (Eds.), *APA educational psychology handbook.* Washington, DC: American Psychological Association.

Gong, N.J., & others (2019, in press). Imaging beta amyloid aggregation and iron accumulation in Alzheimer's disease using quantitative susceptibility mapping MRI. *NeuroImage.*

Gonzales-Ruis, K., & others (2017). The effects of exercise on abdominal fat and liver enzymes in pediatric obesity: A systematic review and meta-analysis. *Child Obesity, 13,* 272–282.

Gonzalez, E. (2019). Ethnoracial attitudes and identity-salient experiences among indigenous Mexican adolescents and emerging adults. *Emerging Adulthood, 7,* 128–137.

Gonzalez, J., & others (2015). Reminiscence and dementia: A therapeutic intervention. *International Psychogeriatrics, 27,* 1731–1737.

Gooch, D., & others (2019, in press). Does inattention and hyperactivity moderate the relation between speed of processing and language skills? *Child Development.*

Good, C., Rattan, A., & Dweck, C.S. (2012). Why do women opt out? Sense of belonging and women's representation in mathematics. *Journal of Personality and Social Psychology, 102,* 700–717.

Good, M., & Willoughby, T. (2008). Adolescence as a sensitive period for spiritual development. *Child Development Perspectives, 2,* 32–37.

Goode, A.P., & others (2019, in press). Nonpharmacologic treatments for attention-deficit/hyperactivity disorder: A systematic review. *Pediatrics.*

Goode, E. (2020). *Drugs in American society* (10th ed.). New York: McGraw-Hill.

Goodkind, S. (2013). Single-sex public education for low-income youth of color: A critical theoretical review. *Sex Roles, 69,* 393–402.

Goodman, G.S., Batterman-Faunce, J.M., & Kenney, R. (1992). Optimizing children's testimony: Research and social policy issues concerning allegations of child sexual abuse. In D. Cicchetti & S. Toth (Eds.), *Child abuse, child development and social policy.* Norwood, NJ: Ablex.

Goodman, S. (2019, January 14). *How many people live to be 100 across the globe?* Retrieved February 20, 2019, from www.thecentenarian.co.uk

Goodvin, R., Meyer, S., Thompson, R.A., & Hayes, R. (2008). Self-understanding in early childhood: Associations with child attachment security and maternal negative affect. *Attachment and Human Development, 10,* 433–450.

Goossens, L., & Luyckx, K. (2007). Identity development in college students: Variable-centered and person-centered analysis. In M. Watzlawik & A. Born (Eds.), *Capturing identity.* Lanham, MD: University of America Press.

Gopinath, B., McMahon, C.M., Burlutsky, G., Mitchell, P. (2016). Hearing and vision impairment and the 5-year incidence of falls in older adults. *Age and Aging, 45,* 409–414.

Gopnik, A. (2010). Commentary in E. Galinsky (2010), *Mind in the making.* New York: Harper Collins.

Gopnik, A., & others (2019, in press). Changes in cognitive flexibility and hypothesis search across human life history from childhood to adolescence to adulthood. *Proceedings of the National Academy of Sciences U.S.A.*

Gorby, H.E., Brownell, A.M., & Falk, M.C. (2010). Do specific dietary constituents and supplements affect mental energy? Review of the evidence. *Nutrition Reviews, 68,* 697–718.

Gorchoff, S.M., John, O.P., & Helson, R. (2008). Contextualizing change in marital satisfaction during middle age: An 18-year longitudinal study. *Psychological Science, 19,* 1194–1200.

Gordon, I., Zagoory-Sharon, O., Leckman, J.F., & Feldman, R. (2010). Oxytocin and the development of parenting in humans. *Biological Psychiatry, 68,* 377–382.

Gordon, J.S. (2019, in press). Building moral robots: Ethical pitfalls and challenges. *Science and Engineering Ethics.*

Gordon Simons, L., & others (2018). The cost of being cool: How adolescents' pseudomature behavior maps onto adult adjustment. *Journal of Youth and Adolescence, 47,* 1007–1021.

Gorenjak, V., Akbar, S., Stathopoulou, M.G., & Visvikis-Siest, S. (2018). The future of telomere length in personalized medicine. *Frontiers in Bioscience, 23,* 1628–1654.

Gorgon, E.J.R. (2018). Caregiver-provided physical therapy home programs for children with motor delay: A scoping review. *Physical Therapy, 98,* 481–493.

Goriounova, N.A., & Mansvelder, H.D. (2019). Genes, cells, and brain areas of intelligence. *Frontiers in Human Neuroscience, 13,* 44.

Gorrell, S., & others (2019, in press). A test of the DSM-5 severity specifier for bulimia nervosa in adolescents: Can we anticipate clinical treatment outcomes? *International Journal of Eating Disorders.*

Gorrese, A., & Ruggieri, R. (2012). Peer attachment: A meta-analytic review of gender and age differences and associations with parent attachment. *Journal of Youth and Adolescence, 41,* 650–672.

Gorukanti, A., Delucchi, K., Ling, P., Fisher-Travis, R., & Halpern-Felsher, B. (2017). Adolescents' attitudes towards e-cigarette ingredients, safety, addictive properties, social norms, and regulation. *Preventive Medicine, 94,* 65–71.

Gosden, R.G. (2007). Menopause. In J.E. Birren (Ed.), *Encyclopedia of gerontology* (2nd ed.). San Diego: Academic Press.

Gothe, N.P., Kramer, A.F., & McAuley, E. (2017). Hatha yoga practice improves attention and processing speed in older adults: Results from an 8-week randomized control trial. *Journal of Alternative and Complimentary Medicine, 23,* 35–40.

Gotlieb, R., Jahner, E., Immordino-Yang, M.H., & Kaufman, S.B. (2017). How social-emotional imagination facilitates deep learning and creativity in the classroom. In R.A. Beghetto & J.C. Kaufman (Eds.), *Nurturing creativity in the classroom.* New York: Cambridge University Press.

Gotlieb, R.J., & others (2019). Imagination is the seed of creativity. In J.C. Kaufman & R.J. Sternberg (Eds.), *Cambridge handbook of creativity* (2nd ed.). New York: Cambridge University Press.

Gottlieb, G. (2007). Probabilistic epigenesis. *Developmental Science, 10,* 1–11.

Gottman, J.M. (1994). *Why marriages succeed or fail.* New York: Simon & Schuster.

Gottman, J.M. (2012). *Research on parenting.* Retrieved September 15, 2012, from www.gottman.com/parenting/research

Gottman, J.M. (2019). *Research on parenting.* Retrieved March 22, 2019, from www.gottman.com/parenting/research

Gottman, J.M., Coan, J., Carrere, S., & Swanson, C. (1998). Predicting marital happiness and stability from newlywed interactions. *Journal of Marriage and the Family, 60,* 5–22.

Gottman, J.M., & DeClaire, J. (1997). *The heart of parenting: Raising an emotionally intelligent child.* New York: Simon & Schuster.

Gottman, J.M., & Gottman, J.S. (2009). Gottman method of couple therapy. In A.S. Gurman (Ed.), *Clinical handbook of couple therapy* (4th ed.). New York: Guilford.

Gottman, J.M., Gottman, J.S., & Shapiro, A. (2009). A new couples approach to interventions for the transition to parenthood. In M.S. Schultz, M.K. Pruett, P.K. Kerig, & R.D. Parke (Eds.), *Feathering the nest: Couple relationships, couples interventions, and*

children's development. Washington, DC: American Psychological Association.

Gottman, J.M., & Parker, J.G. (Eds.). (1987). *Conversations of friends.* New York: Cambridge University Press.

Gottman, J.M., & Silver, N. (1999). *The seven principles for making marriages work.* New York: Crown.

Gouin, K., & others (2011). Effects of cocaine use during pregnancy on low birthweight and preterm birth: Systematic review and metaanalyses. *American Journal of Obstetrics and Gynecology, 201,* e1–e12.

Gould, M.S., & others (2019, in press). Exposure to suicide in high schools: Impact on serious suicidal ideation/behavior, depression, maladaptive coping strategies, and attitudes toward help-seeking. *International Journal of Environmental Research and Public Health.*

Gove, W.R., Style, C.B., & Hughes, M. (1990). The effect of marriage on the well-being of adults: A theoretical analysis. *Journal of Health and Social Behavior, 24,* 122–131.

Gow, A.J., Pattie, A., & Deary, I.J. (2017). Lifecourse activity participation from early, mid, and later adulthood as determinants of cognitive aging: The Lothian birth cohort 1921. *Journals of Gerontology B: Psychological Sciences and Social Sciences, 72,* 25–37.

Gradisar, M., Gardner, G., & Dohnt, H. (2011). Recent worldwide sleep patterns and problems during adolescence: A review and meta-analysis of age, region, and sleep. *Sleep Medicine, 12,* 110–118.

Graham, E.K., & others (2017). Personality and mortality risk: An integrative data analysis of 15 international longitudinal studies. *Journal of Research on Personality, 70,* 174–186.

Graham, G., Holt/Hale, A., & Parker, M. (2020). *Children moving* (10th ed.). New York: McGraw-Hill.

Graham, J., & Valdesolo, P. (2018). Morality. In K. Deaux & M. Snyder (Eds.), *Oxford handbook of personality and social psychology* (2nd ed.). New York: Oxford University Press.

Graham, S. (1986, August). *Can attribution theory tell us something about motivation in Blacks?* Paper presented at the meeting of the American Psychological Association, Washington, DC.

Graham, S. (1990). Motivation in Afro-Americans. In G.L. Berry & J.K. Asamen (Eds.), *Black students: Psychosocial issues and academic achievement.* Newbury Park, CA: Sage.

Graham, S. (2005, February 16). Commentary in *USA Today,* p. 2D.

Graham, S. (2018). Writing research and practice. In D. Lapp & D. Fisher (Eds.), *Handbook of research on teaching the English language.* New York: Routledge.

Graham, S. (2019, in press). Changing how writing is taught. In T. Pigott & others (Eds.), *Review of research in education.* Washington, DC: AERA.

Graham, S. (2020, in press). Writers in a community model: 15 recommendations for future research using writing to promote science learning. In V. Prain & B. Hand (Eds.), *Future research in science education.* New York: Springer.

Graham, S., & Harris, K.R. (2019). Designing an effective writing program. In S. Graham, C. MacArthur & M. Herbert (Eds.), *Best practices in writing instruction* (3rd ed.). New York: Guilford.

Graham, S., & Harris, K.R. (2020, in press). Writing and students with learning disabilities. In A. Martin &

others (Eds.), *Handbook of educational psychology and students with special needs.* New York: Routledge.

Graham, S., MacArthur, C., & Fitzgerald, J. (2019). *Best practices in writing instruction* (3rd ed.). New York: Guilford.

Graham, S., & Perin, D. (2007). A meta-analysis of writing instruction for adolescent students. *Journal of Educational Psychology, 99,* 445–476.

Graham, S., Rouse, A., & Harris, K.R. (2018). Scientifically supported writing practices. In A. O'Donnell (Ed.), *Oxford handbook of educational psychology.* New York: Oxford University Press.

Graham, S., & others (2018). Self-regulation and writing. In D. Schunk & J. Greene (Eds.), *Handbook of self-regulation of learning and performance* (2nd ed.). New York: Routledge.

Granbom, M., & others (2019). Preventing falls among older fallers: Study protocol for a two-phase pilot study of the multicomponent LIVE LIFE program. *Trials, 20*(1), 2.

Granchi, C., & Minutolo, F. (2018). Activators of Sirtuin-1 and their involvement in cardioprotection. *Current Medicinal Chemistry, 25,* 4432–4456.

Graneist, A., & Habermas, T. (2019, in press). Beyond the text given: Studying the scaffolding of narrative emotion regulation as a contribution to Bruner and Feldman's cultural cognitive developmental psychology. *Integrated Psychology and Behavioral Science.*

Gravelin, C.R., Biernat, M., & Bucher, C.E. (2019). Blaming the victim of acquaintance rape: Individual, situational, and sociocultural factors. *Frontiers in Psychology, 9,* 2422.

Gravetter, F.J., & Forzano, L.B. (2019). *Research methods for the behavioral sciences* (6th ed.). Boston: Cengage.

Gravningen, K., & others (2017). Reported reasons for breakdown of marriage and cohabitation in Britain: Findings from the third National Survey of Sexual Attitudes and Lifestyles (Natsal-3). *PLoS One, 12*(3), e0174129.

Gray, J. (1992), *Men are from Mars, women are from Venus.* New York: Harper Collins.

Gray, K., & Graham, J. (2018). *The atlas of moral psychology.* New York: Guilford.

Gray, M.J., Hassija, C.M., & Steinmetz, S.E. (2017). *Sexual assault prevention on college campuses.* New York: Routledge.

Gray, P.B., McHale, T.S., & Carré, J.M. (2017). A review of human male field studies of hormones and behavioral reproductive effort. *Hormones and Behavior, 91,* 52–67.

Graziano, A., & Raulin, M. (2020). *Research methods* (9th ed., loose leaf). Upper Saddle River, NJ: Pearson.

Grebe, N.M., & others (2019). Pair-bonding, fatherhood, and the role of testosterone: A meta-analytic review. *Neuroscience and Biobehavioral Reviews, 98,* 221–233.

Green, C.G., Landry, O., & Iarocci, G. (2016). Developments in the developmental approach to intellectual disability. In D. Cicchetti (Ed.), *Developmental psychopathology* (3rd ed.). New York: Wiley.

Green, M.J., & others (2018). Timing of poverty in childhood and adolescent health: Evidence from the US and UK. *Social Science and Medicine, 197,* 136–143.

Greenberger, E., & Steinberg, L. (1986). *When teenagers work: The psychological and social costs of adolescent employment.* New York: Basic Books.

Greenwald, L., Copeland, C., & VanDerhei, J. (2017, March 21). *The 2017 retirement confidence survey.* Retrieved March 27, 2017, from www.ebri.org

Greenwald, M.L. (2018). Wernicke's aphasia: Auditory processing and comprehension. In A.M. Raymer & L.J. Gonzalez Rothi (Eds.), *Oxford handbook of aphasia and language disorders.* New York: Oxford University Press.

Greer, F.R., Sicherer, S.H., Burks, A.W., & The Committee on Nutrition and Section on Allergy and Immunology (2008). Effects of early nutritional interventions on the development of atopic disease in infants and children: The role of maternal dietary restriction, breast feeding, timing of introduction of complementary foods and hydrolyzed formulas. *Pediatrics, 121,* 183-191.

Gregory, R.J. (2016). *Psychological testing* (8th ed.). Boston: Cengage.

Greifneder, R., Bless, H., & Fielder, R. (2018). *Social cognition.* New York: Psychology Press.

Grgic, J., & others (2018). Effect of resistance training frequency on gains in muscular strength; A systematic review and meta-analysis. *Sports Medicine, 48,* 1207-1220.

Griffiths, P.D., & others (2018). Should we perform in utero MRI on a fetus at increased risk of a brain abnormality if ultrasonography is normal or shows non-specific findings? *Clinical Radiology, 73,* 123-134.

Grigorenko, E. (2000). Heritability and intelligence. In R.J. Sternberg (Ed.), *Handbook of intelligence.* New York: Cambridge University Press.

Grigorenko, E.L., & others (2016). The trilogy of G × E. Genes, environments, and their interactions: Conceptualizations, operationalization, and application. In D. Cicchetti (Ed.), *Developmental psychopathology* (3rd ed.). New York: Wiley.

Grimm, R., & others (2019). Children probably store short rather than frequent or predictable chunks: Quantitative evidence from a corpus study. *Frontiers in Psychology, 10,* 80.

Grindal, M., & Nieri, T. (2016). The relationship between ethnic-racial socialization and adolescent substance abuse: An examination of social learning as a causal mechanism. *Journal of Ethnicity in Substance Abuse, 15,* 3-24.

Groh, A.M., & Haydon, K.C. (2018). Mothers' neural and behavioral responses to their infants' distress cues: The role of secure base script knowledge. *Psychological Science, 29,* 242-253.

Groh, A.M., & others (2014). The significance of attachment security for children's social competence with peers: A meta-analytic study. *Attachment and Human Development, 16,* 103-136.

Grolnick, W.S., Caruso, A., & Levitt, M. (2019). Parenting and children's self-regulation. In M.H. Bornstein (Ed.), *Handbook of parenting* (3rd ed.). New York: Routledge.

Gronlund, A., & Oun, I. (2018). The gender-job satisfaction paradox and the dual-earner society: Are women (still) making work-family trade-offs? *Work, 59,* 535-545.

Gross, J.J., Frederickson, B.L., & Levenson, R.W. (1994). The psychology of crying. *Psychophysiology, 31,* 460-468.

Grossman, J.M., & others (2019, in press). Extended-family talk about sex and teen sexual behavior. *International Journal of Environmental Research and Public Health.*

Grossman, M.R., & Gruenewald, T.L. (2017). Caregiving and perceived generativity: A positive and protective aspect of providing care? *Clinical Gerontology, 40,* 435-447.

Grossmann, K., Grossmann, K.E., Spangler, G., Suess, G., & Unzner, L. (1985). Maternal sensitivity and newborns' orientation responses as related to quality of attachment in northern Germany. In I. Bretherton & E. Waters (Eds.), Growing points of attachment theory and research. *Monographs of the Society for Research in Child Development, 50*(1-2, Serial No. 209).

Grosso, S.S., & others (2019). 33-month-old children succeed in false belief task with reduced processing demands: A replication of Setoh et al. (2016). *Infant Behavior and Development, 54,* 151-155.

Grotevant, H., & McDermott, J.M. (2014). Adoption: Biological and social processes related to adoption. *Annual Review of Psychology* (Vol. 65). Palo Alto, CA: Annual Reviews.

Grotevant, H.D., McRoy, R.G., Wrobel, G.M., & Ayers-Lopez, S. (2013). Contact between adoptive and birth families: Perspectives from the Minnesota/Texas Adoption Research Project. *Child Development Perspectives, 7,* 193-198.

Grotzinger, A.D., & others (2018). Hair and salivary testosterone, hair cortisol, and externalizing behaviors in adolescence. *Psychological Science, 29,* 688-699.

Gruber, K.J., Cupito, S.H., & Dobson, C.F. (2013). Impact of doulas on healthy birth outcomes. *Journal of Perinatal Education, 22,* 49-58.

Gruenewald, T.L., & others (2016). The Baltimore Experience Corps trial: Enhancing generativity via intergenerational activity engagement in later life. *Journals of Gerontology B: Psychological Sciences and Social Sciences, 71,* 661-670.

Grunblatt, E., & others (2018). Combining genetic and epigenetic parameters of the serotonin transporter gene in obsessive-compulsive disorder. *Journal of Psychiatric Research, 96,* 209-217.

Grusec, J.E. (2006). Development of moral behavior and a conscience from a socialization perspective. In M. Killen & J.G. Smetana (Eds.), *Handbook of moral development.* Mahwah, NJ: Erlbaum.

Grusec, J.E. (2020, in press). Domains of socialization: Implications for parenting and the development of children's moral behavior and cognitions. In D.J. Laible & others (Eds.), *Oxford handbook of parenting and moral development.* New York: Oxford University Press.

Grusec, J.E., & Davidov, M. (2019). Parent socialization and children's values. In M.H. Bornstein (Ed.), *Handbook of parenting* (3rd ed., Vol. 3). New York: Routledge.

Grusec, J.E., Chaparro, M.P., Johnston, M., & Sherman, A. (2013). Social development and social relationships in middle childhood. In I.B. Weiner & others, *Handbook of psychology* (2nd ed., Vol. 6). New York: Wiley.

Grych, J.H. (2002). Marital relationships and parenting. In M.H. Bornstein (Ed.), *Handbook of parenting.* Mahwah, NJ: Erlbaum.

Gryczkowski, M., Jordan, S.S., & Mercer, S.H. (2018). Moderators of the relations between mothers' and fathers' parenting practices and children's prosocial behavior. *Child Psychiatry and Human Development, 49,* 409-419.

Grzeschik, R., & others (2019). The contribution of visual attention and declining verbal memory abilities to age-related rote learning deficits. *Cognition, 187,* 50-61.

Guerin, E., & others (2019, in press). Physical activity and perceptions of stress during the menopause transition: A longitudinal study. *Journal of Health Psychology.*

Guernsey, L. (2019, March 10). Will Jeff Bezos' billions for Montessori-inspired schools help early childhood education? *Pacific Standard.* Retrieved April 27, 2019, from https://psmag.com/education

Gueron-Sela, N., & others (2018). Maternal depressive symptoms, mother-child interactions, and children's executive function. *Developmental Psychology, 54,* 71-82.

Guest, F.L. (2019). Early detection and treatment of patients with Alzheimer's disease: Future perspectives. *Advances in Experimental Medicine and Biology.*

Guilford, J.P. (1967). *The structure of intellect.* New York: McGraw-Hill.

Guimaraes, E.L., & Tudella, E. (2015). Immediate effect of training at the onset of reaching in preterm infants: Randomized clinical trial. *Journal of Motor Behavior, 47,* 535-549.

Guiney, H., & Machado, L. (2018). Volunteering in the community: Potential benefits for cognitive aging. *Journals of Gerontology B: Psychological Sciences and Social Sciences, 73,* 399-408.

Gulick, D., & Gamsby, J.J. (2018). Racing the clock: The role of circadian rhythmicity in addiction across the lifespan. *Pharmacology and Therapeutics, 188,* 124-139.

Gullion, L., & others (2019, in press). The impact of early neuroimaging and developmental assessment in a preterm infant diagnosed with cerebral palsy. *Case Reports in Pediatrics.*

Gultekin, F., Naziroglu, M., Savas, H. B., & Cig, B. (2018). Calorie restriction protects against apoptosis, mitochondrial oxidative stress, and increased calcium signaling through inhibition of TRPV1 channel in the hippocampus and dorsal root ganglion of rats. *Metabolic Brain Disease 33,* 1761-1774.

Gump, B., & Matthews, K. (2000, March). *Annual vacations, health, and death.* Paper presented at the meeting of the American Psychosomatic Society, Savannah, GA.

Gunderson, E.A., Ramirez, G., Beilock, S.L., & Levine, S.C. (2012). The role of parents and teachers in the development of gender-related attitudes. *Sex Roles, 66,* 153-166.

Gunes, C., Avila, A.I., & Rudolph, K.L. (2018). Telomeres in cancer. *Differentiation, 99,* 41-50.

Gunn, H.E., & others (2019). Young adolescent sleep is associated with parental monitoring. *Sleep Health, 5,* 58-63.

Gunn, J.K., & others (2016). Prenatal exposure to cannabis and maternal and child health outcomes: A systematic review and meta-analysis. *BMJ Open, 6*(4), e009986.

Gunnar, M.R., & Fisher, P.A. (2006). Bringing basic research on early experience and stress neurobiology to bear on preventive interventions for neglected and maltreated children. *Development and Psychopathology, 18,* 651-677.

Gunnar, M.R., Malone, S., & Fisch, R.O. (1987). The psychobiology of stress and coping in the human neonate: Studies of the adrenocortical activity in response to stress in the first week of life. In T. Field, P. McCabe, & N. Schneiderman (Eds.), *Stress and coping.* Hillsdale, NJ: Erlbaum.

Gunning, T.G. (2020). *Creating literacy for all students* (10th ed.). Upper Saddle River, NJ: Pearson.

Guo, S. (2018). A model of religious involvement, family processes, self-control, and juvenile delinquency in two-parent families. *Journal of Adolescence, 63,* 175–190.

Gur, O., & others (2017). The comparison of the effects of nebivolol and metoprolol on erectile dysfunction in the cases with coronary artery bypass surgery. *Annals of Thoracic and Cardiovascular Surgery, 23,* 91–95.

Gur, R.C., & others (1995). Sex differences in regional cerebral glucose metabolism during a resting state. *Science, 267,* 528–531.

Gurwitch, R.H., Silovksy, J.F., Schultz, S., Kees, M., & Burlingame, S. (2001). *Reactions and guidelines for children following trauma/disaster.* Norman, OK: Department of Pediatrics, University of Oklahoma Health Sciences Center.

Gustafsson Senden, M., & others (2019). The (not so) changing man: Dynamic gender stereotypes in Sweden. *Frontiers in Psychology, 10,* 37.

Gutchess, A. (2019). *Cognitive and social neuroscience of aging.* New York: Cambridge University Press.

Gutchess, A.H., & others (2005). Aging and the neural correlates of successful picture encoding: Frontal activations compensate for decreased medial-temporal activity. *Journal of Cognitive Neuroscience, 17,* 84–96.

Gutierrez, I.T., Rosengren, K.S., & Miller, P. (2014). Mexican American immigration in the Centerville region: Teachers, children, and parents. In K.S. Rosengren & others (Eds.), Children's understanding of death: Toward a contextualized and integrated account. *Monographs of the Society for Research on Child Development, 79* (1), 97–112.

Gutmann, D.L. (1975). Parenthood: A key to the comparative study of the life cycle. In N. Datan & L. Ginsberg (Eds.), *Life-span developmental psychology: Normative life crises.* New York: Academic Press.

Guttentag, C.L., & others (2014). "My Baby & Me": Effects of an early, comprehensive parenting intervention on at-risk mothers and their children. *Developmental Psychology, 50,* 1482–1496.

Guttmannova, K., & others (2012). Examining explanatory mechanisms of the effects of early alcohol use on young adult alcohol competence. *Journal of Studies of Alcohol and Drugs, 73,* 379–390.

Guyer, A.E., Perez-Edgar, K., & Crone, E.A. (2018). Opportunities for neurodevelopmental plasticity from infancy through early adulthood. *Child Development, 89,* 687–697.

Guyon-Harris, K.L., Humphreys, K.L., Degnan, K., Fox, N.A., Nelson, C.A., & Zeanah, C.H. (2019). A prospective longitudinal study of reactive attachment disorder following early institutional care: Considering variable- and person-centered approaches. *Attachment and Human Development, 21,* 95–110.

Gyberg, F., & others (2018). "Another kind of Swede." *Emerging Adulthood, 6,* 17–31.

H

Haas, A.L., & others (2018). Perceived access and parental monitoring as moderators of impulsivity and marijuana use among adolescents. *Journal of Primary Prevention, 39,* 155–169.

Hachul, H., & Tufik, S. (2019, in press). Hot flashes: Treating the mind, body, and soul. *Menopause.*

Hadfield, J.C. (2014). The health of grandparents raising grandchildren: A literature review. *Journal of Gerontological Nursing, 40,* 32–42.

Hadiwijaya, H., & others (2017). On the development of harmony, turbulence, and independence in parent-adolescent relationships: A five-wave longitudinal study. *Journal of Youth and Adolescence, 46,* 1772–1788.

Hafer, R.W. (2017). New estimates on the relationship between IQ, economic growth, and welfare. *Intelligence, 61,* 92–101.

Hagenaars, S.P., & others (2019, in press). Polygenic risk for coronary artery disease is associated with cognitive ability in older adults. *International Journal of Epidemiology.*

Hagestad, G.O., & Uhlenberg, P. (2007). The impact of demographic changes on relations between the age groups and generations: A comparative perspective. In K.W. Schaie & P. Uhlenberg (Eds.), *Demographic changes and the well-being of older persons.* New York: Springer.

Haghighat, M.D., & Knifsend, C.A. (2019). The longitudinal influence of 10th grade extracurricular activity involvement: Implications for 12th grade academic practices and future educational attainment. *Journal of Youth and Adolescence, 48,* 609–618.

Hagmann-von Arx, P., Lemola, S., & Grob, A. (2018). Does IQ = IQ? Comparability of intelligence test scores in typically developing children. *Assessment, 25,* 691–701.

Hagnas, M.J., & others (2018). High leisure-time physical activity is associated with reduced risk of sudden cardiac death among men with low cardiorespiratory fitness. *Canadian Journal of Cardiology, 34,* 288–294.

Haidt, J. (2006). *The happiness hypothesis.* New York: Basic Books.

Haidt, J. (2013). *The righteous mind.* New York: Random House.

Haidt, J. (2018). *Three stories about capitalism.* New York: Pantheon.

Haier, R.J. (2018). A view from the brain. In R.J. Sternberg (Ed.), *The nature of human intelligence.* New York: Cambridge University Press.

Haier, R.J. (2020, in press). Biological approaches to intelligence. In R.J. Sternberg (Ed.), *Human intelligence.* New York: Cambridge University Press.

Hair, N.L., Hanson, J.L., Wolfe, B.L., & Pollack, S.D. (2015). Association of poverty, brain development, and academic achievement. *JAMA Pediatrics, 169,* 822–829.

Hakuta, K. (2001, April 5). *Key policy milestones and directions in the education of English language learners.* Paper prepared for the Rockefeller Foundation Symposium, Leveraging change: An emerging framework for educational equity. Washington, DC.

Hakuta, K. (2005, April). *Bilingualism at the intersection of research and public policy.* Paper presented at the meeting of the Society for Research in Child Development, Atlanta.

Hakuta, K., Butler, Y.G., & Witt, D. (2001). *How long does it take English learners to attain proficiency?* Berkeley, CA: The University of California Linguistic Minority Research Institute Policy Report 2000-1.

Hale, L., & others (2018). Youth screen media habits and sleep: Sleep-friendly screen behavior recommendations for clinicians, educators, and parents.

Child and Adolescent Psychiatric Clinics of North America 27, 229–245.

Hale, S. (1990). A global developmental trend in cognitive processing speed. *Child Development, 61,* 653–663.

Hales, C.M., & others (2017, October). Prevalence of obesity among adults and youth: United States, 2015–2016. *NCHS Data Brief,* No. 288, pp. 1–8.

Hales, D. (2019). *An invitation to health* (18th ed.). Boston: Cengage.

Halgunseth, L.C. (2019). Latino and Latin American parenting. In M.H. Bornstein (Ed.), *Handbook of parenting* (3rd ed.). New York: Routledge.

Haliburn, J. (2018). Anorexia nervosa is a body-image disorder. *Australian New Zealand Journal of Psychiatry, 52,* 491–492.

Halim, M.L. (2016). Pink princesses and strong superheroes: Gender rigidity in early childhood. *Child Development Perspectives, 10,* 155–160.

Halim, M.L., & others (2016). Children's dynamic gender identities: Cognition, context, and culture. In B. Balter & C.S. Tamis-LeMonda (Eds.), *Child psychology* (3rd ed.). New York: Routledge.

Hall, C.B., & others (2009). Cognitive activities delay onset of memory decline in persons who develop dementia. *Neurology, 73,* 356–361.

Hall, D.A., & Berry-Kravis, E. (2018). Fragile X syndrome and fragile X-associated tremor ataxia syndrome. *Handbook of Clinical Neurology, 147,* 377–391.

Hall, G.S. (1904). *Adolescence* (Vols. 1 & 2). Englewood Cliffs, NJ: Prentice Hall.

Hall, J.A. (2011). Sex differences in friendship expectations: A meta-analysis. *Journal of Social and Personal Relationships, 28,* 723–747.

Hall, J.A., Park, N., Song, H., & Cody, M.J. (2010). Strategic misrepresentation in online dating: The effects of gender, self-monitoring, and personality traits. *Journal of Social and Personal Relationships, 27,* 117–135.

Hall, L.J. (2018). *Autism spectrum disorders* (3rd ed.). Upper Saddle River, NJ: Pearson.

Hallahan, D.P., Kauffman, J.M., & Pullen, P.C. (2019). *Exceptional learners* (14th ed.). Upper Saddle River, NJ: Pearson.

Halonen, J.I., & others (2017). Change in job strain as a predictor of insomnia symptoms: Analyzing observational data as a non-randomized pseudo-trial. *Sleep, 40,* 1.

Halper, L.R., & Rios, K. (2019). Feeling powerful but incompetent: Fear of negative evaluation predicts men's sexual harassment of subordinates. *Sex Roles, 80,* 247–261.

Halpern, D.F. (2012). *Sex differences in cognitive abilities* (2nd ed.). New York: Psychology Press.

Halpern, D.F., & Butler, H.A. (2018). Is critical thinking a better model of intelligence? In R.J. Sternberg (Ed.), *The nature of intelligence.* New York: Cambridge University Press.

Halpern, D.F., & others (2007). The science of sex differences in science and mathematics. *Psychological Science in the Public Interest, 8,* 1–51.

Halpern, D.F., & others (2011). The pseudoscience of single-sex schooling. *Science, 333,* 1706–1717.

Halpern-Meekin, S., Manning, W., Giordano, P.C., & Longmore, M.A. (2013). Relationship churning in emerging adulthood: On/off relationships and sex with an ex. *Journal of Adolescent Research, 28,* 166–188.

Halpin, K.S., Smith, K.Y., Widen, J.E., & Chertoff, M.E. (2010). Effects of universal newborn hearing screening on an early intervention program for children with hearing loss, birth to 3 yr of age. *Journal of the American Academy of Audiology, 21,* 169-175.

Halse, M., & others (2019, in press). Parental predictors of children's executive functioning from ages 6 to 10. *British Journal of Developmental Psychology.*

Hambrick, D.Z. (2014, December 2). Brain training doesn't necessarily make you smarter: Scientists doubt claims from brain training companies. *Scientific American,* pp. 1-8.

Hamer, M., Muniz Terrera, G., & Demakakos, P. (2018). Physical activity and trajectories of cognitive function: English Longitudinal Study of Aging. *Journal of Epidemiology and Community Health, 72,* 477-483.

Hamilton, J.L., & others (2014). Pubertal timing and vulnerabilities to depression in early adolescence: Differential pathways to depressive symptoms by sex. *Journal of Adolescence, 37,* 165-174.

Hamilton, S.F., & Hamilton, M.A. (2009). The transition to adulthood: Challenges of poverty and structural lag. In R.M. Lerner & L. Steinberg (Eds.), *Handbook of adolescent psychology* (3rd ed.). New York: Wiley.

Hamlin, J.K. (2013a). Failed attempts to help and harm: Intention versus outcome in preverbal infants' social evaluations. *Cognition, 128,* 451-474.

Hamlin, J.K. (2013b). Moral judgment and action in preverbal infants and toddlers: Evidence for an innate moral core. *Current Directions in Psychological Science, 22,* 186-193.

Hamlin, J.K. (2014). The origins of human morality: Complex socio-moral evaluations by preverbal infants. In J. Decety & Y. Christen (Eds.), *New frontiers in social neuroscience.* New York: Springer.

Hamlin, J.K., Wynn, K., Bloom, P., & Mahajan, N. (2011). How infants and toddlers react to antisocial others. *Proceedings of the National Academy of Sciences, 108,* 19931-19936.

Hamlin, J.K., & others (2015). The mentalistic basis of core social cognition: Experiments in preverbal infants and a computational model. *Developmental Science, 16,* 209-226.

Hamner, H.C., & others (2019, in press). Food and beverage intake from 12 to 23 months by WIC status. *Pediatrics.*

Hampson, D.R., Hooper, A.W.M., & Nilbori, Y. (2019, in press). The application of adeno-associated viral vector gene therapy to the treatment of Fragile X syndrome. *Brain Sciences.*

Hampson, S.E., & Edmonds, G.W. (2018). A new twist on old questions: A life span approach to the trait concept. *Journal of Personality, 86,* 97-108.

Hampson, S.E., & others (2013). Childhood conscientiousness relates to objectively measured adult physical health four decades later. *Health Psychology, 32,* 925-938.

Han, J., Neufer, D., & Pilegaard, H. (2019, in press). Exercise physiology: Future opportunities and challenges. *Pflugers Archiv—European Journal of Physiology.*

Han, J.H., & others (2019, in press). Effects of self-reported hearing or vision impairment on depressive symptoms: A population-based longitudinal study. *Epidemiology and Psychiatric Sciences.*

Han, J.J., Leichtman, M.D., & Wang, Q. (1998). Autobiographical memory in Korean, Chinese, and American children. *Developmental Psychology, 34,* 701-713.

Han, S.H., & others (2017). Social activities, incident cardiovascular disease, and mortality: Health behaviors mediation. *Journal of Aging and Health, 29,* 268-288.

Han, W.J., Hetzner, & Brooks-Gunn (2019). Employment and parenting. In M.H. Bornstein (Ed.), *Handbook of parenting* (3rd ed.). New York: Routledge.

Hanc, T., & others (2018). Perinatal risk factors and ADHD in children and adolescents: A hierarchical structure of disorder predictors. *Journal of Attention Disorders, 22,* 855-863.

Handelsman, D.J., Hirschberg, A.L., & Bermon, S. (2018). Circulating testosterone as the hormonal basis of sex differences in athletic performance. *Endocrine Reviews, 39,* 803-829.

Handschuh, C., La Cross, A., & Smaldone, A. (2019). Is sexting associated with sexual behaviors during adolescence? A systematic literature review and meta-analysis. *Journal of Midwifery and Women's Health, 64,* 88-97.

Hanley, C.J., Burianova, H., & Tommerdahl, M. (2019, in press). Towards establishing age-related cortical plasticity on the basis of somatosensation. *Neuroscience.*

Hanley, R. (Ed.) (2020, in press). *Love: A history.* New York: Oxford University Press.

Hantman, S., & Cohen, O. (2010). Forgiveness in late life. *Journal of Gerontological Social Work, 53,* 613-630.

Hao, S., & others (2019). Prediction of Alzheimer's disease—associated genes by integration of GWAS summary data and expression data. *Frontiers in Genetics, 9,* 653.

Harackiewicz, J.M., & Knogler, M. (2017). Interest: Theory and application. In A.J. Elliot, C.S. Dweck, & D.S. Yeager (Eds.), *Handbook of competence and motivation* (2nd ed.). New York: Guilford.

Harb, S.C., & others (2019, in press). Estimated age based on exercise stress testing performance outperforms chronological age in predicting mortality. *European Journal of Preventive Cardiology.*

Hardy, B., Smeeding, T., & Ziliak, J.P. (2018). The changing safety net for low-income parents and their children: Structural or cyclical changes in income support policy. *Demography, 55,* 189-221.

Hardy, N. (2019). Identity and meaningful and meaningless work. In R. Yeoman & others (Eds.) (2019). *Oxford handbook of meaningful work.* New York: Oxford University Press.

Hardy, S.A., Bean, D.S., & Olsen, J.A. (2015). Moral identity and adolescent prosocial and antisocial behaviors: Interactions with moral disengagement and self-regulation. *Journal of Youth and Adolescence, 44,* 1542-1544.

Hardy, S.A., & others (2013). The roles of identity formation and moral identity in college student mental health, health-risk behaviors, and psychological well-being. *Journal of Clinical Psychology, 69,* 364-382.

Hardy, S.A., & others (2014). Moral identity as moral ideal self: Links to adolescent outcomes. *Developmental Psychology, 50,* 45-57.

Hargis, M.B., & others (2017). Metacognition and proofreading: The roles of aging, motivation, and interest. *Neuropsychology, Development, and Cognition, Section B: Aging, Neuropsychology, and Cognition, 24,* 216-226.

Harkness, S., & Super, E.M. (1995). Culture and parenting. In M.H. Bornstein (Ed.), *Handbook of parenting* (Vol. 3). Hillsdale, NJ: Erlbaum.

Harlow, H.F. (1958). The nature of love. *American Psychologist, 13,* 673-685.

Harmon, O.R., Lambrinos, J., & Kennedy, P. (2008). Are online exams an invitation to cheat? *Journal of Economic Education, 39,* 116-125.

Harris, G. (2002). *Grandparenting: How to meet its responsibilities.* Los Angeles: The Americas Group.

Harris, J., Golinkoff, R.M., & Hirsh-Pasek, K. (2011). Lessons from the crib for the classroom: How children really learn vocabulary. In S.B. Neuman & D.K. Dickinson (Eds.), *Handbook of early literacy research* (Vol. 3). New York: Guilford.

Harris, K.R., & Graham, S. (2017). Self-regulated strategy development: Theoretical bases, critical instructional elements, and future research. In R. Fidalgo, K.R. Harris, & M. Braaksma (Eds.), *Design principles for teaching effective writing.* Leiden, Netherlands: Brill.

Harris, K.R., Graham, S., & Adkins, M. (2015). Practice-based professional development and self-regulated strategy development for tier 2, at-risk writers in second grade. *Contemporary Educational Psychology, 40,* 5-16.

Harris, K.R., & others (2017). Self-regulated strategy development in writing: A classroom example of developing executive function and future directions. In L. Meltzer (Eds.), *Executive functioning in education* (2nd ed.). New York: Guilford.

Harris, K.R., & others (2018). Self-regulated strategy development in writing. In C. Bazerman & others (Eds.), *The lifespan development of writing.* Urbana, IL: National Council of English.

Harris, P.L. (2006). Social cognition. In W. Damon & R. Lerner (Eds.), *Handbook of child psychology* (6th ed.). New York: Wiley.

Harrist, A.W. (1993, March). *Family interaction styles as predictors of children's competence: The role of synchrony and nonsynchrony.* Paper presented at the biennial meeting of the Society for Research in Child Development, New Orleans.

Hart, B., & Risley, T.R. (1995). *Meaningful differences in the everyday experience of young Americans.* Baltimore: Paul H. Brookes.

Hart, C.H., Yang, C., Charlesworth, R., & Burts, D.C. (2003, April). *Early childhood teachers' curriculum beliefs, classroom practices, and children's outcomes: What are the connections?* Paper presented at the biennial meeting of the Society for Research in Child Development, Tampa, FL.

Hart, D. (2005). The development of moral identity. In G. Carlo & C.P. Edwards (Eds.), *Nebraska Symposium on Motivation* (Vol. 51). Lincoln, NE: University of Nebraska Press.

Hart, D., Goel, N., & Atkins, R. (2017). Prosocial tendencies, antisocial behavior, and moral development in childhood. In A. Slater & G. Bremner (Eds.), *Introduction to developmental psychology* (3rd ed.). New York: Wiley.

Hart, D., & Karmel, M.P. (1996). Self-awareness and self-knowledge in humans, great apes, and monkeys. In A. Russon, K. Bard, & S. Parker (Eds.), *Reaching into thought.* New York: Cambridge University Press.

Hart, D., Matsuba, M.K., & Atkins, R. (2008). The moral and civic effects of learning to serve. In L. Nucci &

D. Narváez (Eds.), *Handbook of moral and character education*. Clifton, NJ: Psychology Press.

Hart, D., Matsuba, M.K., & Atkins, R. (2014). The moral and civic effects of learning to serve. In L. Nucci, T. Krettenauer, & D. Narváez (Eds.), *Handbook of moral and character education* (2nd ed.). New York: Routledge.

Hart, D., & van Goethem, A. (2017). The role of civic and political participation in successful early adulthood. In L. Padilla-Walker & L. Nelson (Eds.), *Flourishing in emerging adulthood*. New York: Oxford University Press.

Hart, D., & others (2017). Morality and mental health. In C. Markey (Ed.), *Encyclopedia of mental health*. New York: Elsevier.

Hart, S. (2018). Jealousy and attachment: Adaptations to threat posed by the birth of a sibling. *Evolutionary Behavioral Sciences, 12,* 263-275.

Hart, S., & Carrington, H. (2002). Jealousy in 6-month-old infants. *Infancy, 3,* 395-402.

Hart, S., Carrington, H., Tronick, E.Z., & Carroll, S.R. (2004). When infants lose exclusive maternal attention: Is it jealousy? *Infancy, 6,* 57-78.

Harter, S. (1981). A new self-report scale of intrinsic versus extrinsic orientation in the classroom: Motivational and informational components. *Development Psychology, 17,* 300-312.

Harter, S. (1990). Processes underlying adolescent self-concept formation. In R. Montemayor, G.R. Adams, & T.P. Gullotta (Eds.), *From childhood to adolescence: A transitional period?* Newbury Park, CA: Sage.

Harter, S. (1996). Teacher and classmate influences on scholastic motivation, self-esteem, and level of voice in adolescents. In J. Juvonen & K.R. Wentzel (Eds.), *Social motivation*. New York: Cambridge University Press.

Harter, S. (1999). *The construction of the self*. New York: Guilford.

Harter, S. (2006). The self. In W. Damon & R. Lerner (Eds.), *Handbook of child psychology* (6th ed.). New York: Wiley.

Harter, S. (2012). *The construction of the self* (2nd ed.). New York: Wiley.

Harter, S. (2013). The development of self-esteem. In M.H. Kernis (Ed.), *Self-esteem issues and answers*. New York: Psychology Press.

Harter, S. (2016). I-self and me-self processes affecting developmental psychopathology and mental health. In D. Cicchetti (Ed.), *Developmental psychopathology* (3rd ed.). New York: Wiley.

Hartescu, I., Morgan, K., & Stevinson, C.D. (2016). Sleep quality and recommended levels of physical activity in older adults. *Journal of Aging and Physical Activity, 24,* 201-206.

Hartman, J.D., & others (2019, in press). Indirect and moderated effects of parent-child communication on drinking outcomes in the transition to college. *Addictive Behaviors.*

Hartshorne, H., & May, M.S. (1928-1930). *Moral studies in the nature of character. Studies in deceit* (Vol. 1); *Studies in self-control* (Vol. 2); *Studies in the organization of character* (Vol. 3). New York: Macmillan.

Hartup, W.W. (1983). The peer system. In P.H. Mussen (Ed.), *Handbook of child psychology* (4th ed., Vol. 4). New York: Wiley.

Hasbrouck, S.L., & Pianta, R. (2016). Understanding child care quality and implications for dual language learners. In K.E. Sanders & A.W. Guerra (Eds.), *The culture of child care*. New York: Oxford University Press.

Hasher, L. (2003, February 28). Commentary in "The wisdom of the wizened," *Science, 299,* 1300-1302.

Hasher, L., Chung, C., May, C.P., & Foong, N. (2001). Age, time of testing, and proactive interference. *Canadian Journal of Experimental Psychology, 56,* 200-207.

Hassankhani, H., & others (2019, in press). Palliative care models for cancer patients: Learning for planning in nursing (Review). *Journal of Cancer Education.*

Hatoun, J., & others (2018). Tobacco control laws and pediatric asthma. *Pediatrics, 141*(Suppl. 1), S130-S136.

Hatton, H., & others (2008). Family and individual difference predictors of trait aspects of negative interpersonal behaviors during emerging adulthood. *Journal of Family Psychology, 22,* 448-455.

Haugrud, N., Crossley, M., & Vrbancic, M. (2011). Clustering and switching strategies during verbal fluency performance differentiate Alzheimer's disease and healthy aging. *Journal of the International Alzheimer's Society, 17,* 1153-1157.

Haverbusch, V.C.E., & others (2019, in press). An examination of the factors contributing to the expansion of subspecialty genetic counseling. *Journal of Genetic Counseling.*

Hawk, S.T. (2017). Chinese adolescents' reports of covert parental monitoring: Comparisons with overt monitoring and links with information management. *Journal of Adolescence, 55,* 24-35.

Hawkes, C. (2006). Olfaction in neurodegenerative disorder. *Advances in Otorhinolaryngology, 63,* 133-151.

Hawkey, E.J., & others (2018). Preschool executive function predicts childhood resting-state functional connectivity and attention-deficit/hyperactivity disorder and depression. *Biological Psychatry. Cognitive Neuroscience and Neuroimaging, 3,* 927-936.

Hawkins, A.J. (2018). Shifting the relationship education field to prioritize youth relationship education. *Journal of Couple and Relationship Therapy, 17,* 165-180.

Hawkley, L.C., & Kocherginsky, M. (2018). Transitions in loneliness among older adults: A 5-year follow-up in the National Social Life, Health, and Aging Project. *Research on Aging, 40,* 365-387.

Hay, W.W., & others (2017). *Current diagnosis and treatment pediatrics* (23rd ed.). New York: McGraw-Hill.

Hayashi, A., & Mazuka, R. (2017). Emergence of Japanese infants' prosodic preferences in infant-directed vocabulary. *Developmental Psychology, 53,* 28-37.

Haydon, A., & Halpern, G.T. (2010). Older romantic partners and depressive symptoms during adolescence. *Journal of Youth and Adolescence, 39,* 1240-1251.

Hayes, R.M., Abbott, R.L., & Cook, S. (2016). It's her fault: Student acceptance of rape myths on two college campuses. *Violence Against Women, 22,* 1540-1555.

Hayflick, L. (1977). The cellular basis for biological aging. In C.E. Finch & L. Hayflick (Eds.), *Handbook of the biology of aging*. New York: Van Nostrand.

Haynes, R.L. (2018). Biomarkers of sudden infant death syndrome (SIDS) risk and SIDS death. In J.R. Duncan & R.W. Byard (Eds.), *SIDS sudden infant and early childhood death*. Adelaide, Australia: University of Adelaide Press.

Hayslip, B., & Hansson, R. (2003). Death awareness and adjustment across the life span. In C.D. Bryant (Ed.), *Handbook of death and dying*. Thousand Oaks, CA: Sage.

Hayslip, B., Pruett, J.H., & Cabellero, D.M. (2015). The "how" and "when" of parental loss in adulthood: Effects on grief and adjustment. *Omega, 71,* 3-18.

Hayutin, A., Beals, M., & Borges, E. (2013). *The aging labor force*. Palo Alto, CA: Stanford Center on Longevity.

Hayward, R.D., & Krause, N. (2013a). Changes in church-based social support relationships during older adulthood. *Journals of Gerontology B: Psychological Sciences and Social Sciences, 68,* 85-96.

Hayward, R.D., & Krause, N. (2013b). Patterns of change in religious service attendance across the life course: Evidence from a 34-year longitudinal study. *Social Science Research, 42,* 1480-1489.

Hazan, C., & Shaver, P.R. (1987). Romantic love conceptualized as an attachment process. *Journal of Personality and Social Psychology, 52,* 522-524.

Heard, E., & others (2011). Mediating effects of social support on the relationship among perceived stress, depression, and hypertension in African Americans. *Journal of the National Medical Association, 103,* 116-122.

Hebert, J.J., & others (2017). The prospective association of organized sports participation with cardiovascular disease risk in children (the CHAMPS Study-DK). *Mayo Clinic Proceedings, 92,* 57-65.

Hedberg-Oldfors, C., & others (2019, in press). Cardiomyopathy with lethal arrhythmias associated with inactivation of KLHL24. *Human Molecular Genetics.*

Hegab, A.E., & others (2019). Calorie restriction enhances adult mouse lung stem cells function and reverses several aging-induced changes. *Journal of Tissue Engineering and Regenerative Medicine, 13,* 295-308.

Heiman, T., Olenik-Shemesh, D., & Frank, G. (2019). Patterns of coping with cyberbullying: Emotional, behavioral, and strategic coping reactions among middle school students. *Violence and Victimization, 34,* 28-45.

Heimann, M., & others (2006). Exploring the relation between memory, gestural communication, and the emergence of language in infancy: A longitudinal study. *Infant and Child Development, 75,* 233-249.

Hein, S., & others (2019, in press). Negative parenting modulates the association between mother's DNA methylation profiles and adult offspring depression. *Developmental Psychobiology.*

Heinrich, J. (2017). Modulation of allergy risk by breast feeding. *Current Opinion in Clinical Nutrition and Metabolic Care, 20,* 217-221.

Heisel, M.J. (2006). Suicide and its prevention in older adults. *Canadian Journal of Psychiatry, 51,* 143-154.

Helgeson, V.S. (2017). *The psychology of gender* (5th ed.). New York: Routledge.

Helgesson, G., & others (2018). Ethical aspects of diagnosis and interventions for children with fetal alcohol spectrum disorder (FASD) and their families. *BMC Medical Ethics, 19*(1), 1.

Helm, R.K., McCormick, M., & Reyna, V.F. (2018). Expert decision-making: A fuzzy-trace theory perspective. In L.J. Ball & A. Thompson (Eds.), *International handbook of thinking and reasoning*. New York: Routledge.

Helm, R.K., & Reyna, V.F. (2018). Cognitive and neurobiological aspects of risk. In M. Raue & others (Eds.), *Psychological aspects of risk and risk analysis.* New York: Springer.

Helmuth, L. (2003). The wisdom of the wizened. *Science, 299,* 1300-1302.

Helson, R. (1997, August). *Personality change: When is it adult development?* Paper presented at the meeting of the American Psychological Association, Chicago.

Helson, R., & Wink, P. (1992). Personality change in women from the early 40s to early 50s. *Psychology and Aging, 7,* 46-55.

Helzer, E.G., & Critcher, C.R. (2018). What do we evaluate when we evaluate moral character? In K. Gray & J. Graham (Eds.), *Atlas of moral psychology.* New York: Guilford.

Hendricks-Munoz, K.D., & others (2013). Maternal and neonatal nurse perceived value of kangaroo mother care and maternal care partnership in the Neonatal Intensive Care Unit. *American Journal of Perinatology 30*(10), 875-880.

Hendrickson, K., & others (2017). Assessing a continuum of lexical-semantic knowledge in the second year of life: A multimodal approach. *Journal of Experimental Child Psychology, 158,* 95-111.

Hengartner, M.P., & Yamanaka-Altenstein, M. (2017). Personality, psychopathology, and psychotherapy. *Frontiers in Psychology, 8,* 9.

Henneberger, A.K., Durkee, M.I., Truong, N., Atkins, A., & Tolan, P.H. (2013). The longitudinal relationship between peer violence and popularity and delinquency in adolescent boys: Examining effects by family functioning. *Journal of Youth and Adolescence, 42,* 1651-1660.

Hennenberger, A.K., Gest, S.D., & Zadzora, K.M. (2019). Preventing adolescent substance use: A content analysis of peer processes targeted within universal school-based programs. *Journal of Primary Prevention, 40,* 213-230.

Hennessey, B. (2017). Intrinsic motivation and creativity: Have we come full circle? In R.A. Beghetto & J.C. Kaufman (Eds.), *Nurturing creativity in the classroom* (2nd ed.). New York: Cambridge University Press.

Hennessey, B. (2019). Motivation and creativity. In J.C. Kaufman & R.J. Sternberg (Eds.), *Cambridge handbook of creativity* (2nd ed.). New York: Cambridge U. Press.

Hennessy, G. (2018). Marijuana and pregnancy. *American Journal of Addiction, 27,* 44-45.

Henretta, J.C. (2010). Lifetime marital history and mortality after age 50. *Journal of Aging and Health, 22*(8), 1198-1212.

Henriquez-Sanchez, P., & others (2016). Dietary total antioxidant capacity and mortality in the PREDIMED study. *European Journal of Nutrition, 55,* 227-236.

Hensel, D.J., & Sorge, B.H. (2014). Adolescent women's daily academic behaviors, sexual behaviors, and sexually related emotions. *Journal of Adolescent Health, 55,* 845-847.

Herbrand, C. (2018). Ideals, negotiations, and gender roles in gay and lesbian co-parenting arrangements. *Anthropology and Medicine, 25,* 311-328.

Heredia-Pi, I.B., & others (2018). The Mexican experience adapting CenteringPregnancy: Lessons learned in a publicly funded health care system serving vulnerable women. *Journal of Midwifery and Women's Health, 63,* 602-610.

Herman-Giddens, M.E., & others (2012). Secondary sex characteristics in boys: Data from the pediatric research in office settings network. *Pediatrics, 130,* e1058-e1068.

Hernandez, A.E., Fernandez, E.M., & Aznar-Bese, N. (2019). Bilingual sentence processing. In S.A. Rueschemeyer & M. Gereth Gaskell (Eds), *Oxford handbook of psycholinguistics* (2nd ed.). New York: Oxford University Press.

Hernandez, M.M., & others (2017). Observed emotions as predictors of kindergarteners' social relationships. *Social Development, 26,* 21-39.

Hernandez-Reif, M., Diego, M., & Field, T. (2007). Preterm infants show reduced stress behaviors and activity after 5 days of massage therapy. *Infant Behavior and Development, 30,* 557-561.

Hernandez-Zimbron, L.F., & others (2018) Age-related macular degeneration: New paradigms for treatment and management of AMD. *Oxidative Medicine and Cell Longevity.* doi:10.1155/2018/8374647

Heron, M. (2013, December 20). Deaths: Leading causes for 2010. *National Vital Statistics Reports, 62*(6), 1-96.

Heron, M. (2016). Deaths: Leading causes for 2013. *National Vital Statistics Reports, 65*(2), 1-95.

Herrell, A.L., & Jordan, M. (2020). *50 strategies for teaching English Language Learners* (6th ed.). Upper Saddle River, NJ: Pearson.

Hershner, S.D., & Chervin, R.D. (2015). Causes and consequences of sleepiness among college students. *Nature and Science of Sleep, 6,* 73-84.

Hershner, S.D., & O'Brien, L.M. (2018). The impact of a randomized sleep education intervention for college students. *Journal of Clinical Sleep Medicine, 14,* 337-347.

Herting, M.M., Colby, J.B., Sowell, E.R., & Nagel, B.J. (2014). White matter connectivity and aerobic fitness in male adolescents. *Developmental Cognitive Neuroscience, 7,* 65-75.

Hertzog, C., & Dixon, R.A. (2005). Metacognition in midlife. In S.L. Willis & M. Martin (Eds.), *Middle adulthood: A lifespan perspective.* Thousand Oaks, CA: Sage.

Hertzog, C., & others (2019, in press). Behaviors and strategies supporting everyday memory in older adults. *Gerontology.*

Hess, J.L., & others (2018). Why is there selective cortical vulnerability in ADHD? Clues from postmortem brain gene expression data. *Molecular Psychiatry, 23,* 1787-1793.

Hess, T.M., Auman, C., Colcombe, S.J., & Rahhal, T.A. (2003). The impact of stereotype threat on age differences in memory performance. *Journals of Gerontology B: Psychological Sciences and Social Sciences, 58,* P3-P11.

Hessel, P., & others (2018). Trends and determinants of the Flynn effect in cognitive functioning among older individuals in 10 European countries. *Journal of Epidemiology and Community Health, 72,* 383-389.

Hetherington, E., & others (2018). Vulnerable women's perceptions of individual versus group prenatal care: Results of a cross-sectional survey. *Maternal and Child Health Journal, 22,* 1632-1638.

Hetherington, E.M. (1993). An overview of the Virginia Longitudinal Study of Divorce and Remarriage with a focus on early adolescence. *Journal of Family Psychology, 7,* 39-56.

Hetherington, E.M. (2006). The influence of conflict, marital problem solving, and parenting on children's adjustment in nondivorced, divorced, and remarried families. In A. Clarke-Stewart & J. Dunn (Eds.), *Families count.* New York: Cambridge University Press.

Hetherington, E.M., & Kelly, J. (2002). *For better or for worse: Divorce reconsidered.* New York: Norton.

Hetherington, E.M., & Stanley-Hagan, M. (2002). Parenting in divorced and remarried families. In M.H. Bornstein (Ed.), *Handbook of parenting* (2nd ed.). Mahwah, NJ: Erlbaum.

Heu, L., van Zomeren, M., & Hansen, N. (2019). Lonely alone or together? A cultural-psychological examination of individualism-collectivism and loneliness in five European countries. *Personality and Social Psychology Bulletin, 45,* 780-793.

Heuwinkel, M.K. (1996). New ways of learning: Five new ways of teaching. *Childhood Education, 72,* 27-31.

Heward, W.L., Alber-Morgan, S., & Konrad, M. (2017). *Exceptional children* (11th ed.). Upper Saddle River, NJ: Pearson.

Hewlett, B.S. (1991). *Intimate fathers.* Ann Arbor, MI: University of Michigan Press.

Hewlett, B.S. (2000). Culture, history and sex: Anthropological perspectives on father involvement. *Marriage and Family Review, 29,* 324-340.

Hewlett, B.S., & MacFarlan, S.J. (2010). Fathers' roles in hunter-gatherer and other small-scale cultures. In M.E. Lamb (Ed.), *The role of the father in child development* (5th ed.). New York: Wiley.

Heyes, C. (2014). Rich interpretations of infant behavior are popular, but are they valid? A reply to Scott and Baillargeon. *Developmental Science, 17,* 665-666.

Hibell, B., Andersson, B., Bjarnasson, T., & others (2004). *The ESPAD report 2003: Alcohol and other drug use among students in 35 European countries.* The Swedish Council for Information on Alcohol and Other Drugs (CAN) and Council of Europe Pompidou Group.

Hickman, S.E., & others (2019, in press). A tool to assess patient and surrogate knowledge about the POLST (Physician Orders for Life-Sustaining Treatment) program. *Journal of Pain and Symptom Management.*

Highfield, R. (2008, April 30). *Harvard's baby brain research lab.* Retrieved January 24, 2009, from www.telegraph.co.uk/scienceandtechnology/science/sciencenews/3341166/Harvard

Hilbert, A. (2019). Binge eating disorder. *Psychiatric Clinics of North America, 42,* 33-43.

Hiles, E. (2018). Parents' reasons for sending their children to Montessori school. *Journal of Montessori Research, 4,* 1-13.

Hill, D.J., & others (2019, in press). Depressive symptoms in Latina mothers in an emerging immigrant community. *Cultural Diversity and Ethnic Minority Psychology.*

Hill, J.P., & Lynch, M.E. (1983). The intensification of gender-related role expectations during early adolescence. In J. Brooks-Gunn & A.C. Petersen (Eds.), *Girls at puberty: Biological and psychosocial perspectives.* New York: Plenum Press.

Hill, L.G. (2019, in press). Expanding our horizons: Risk, protection, and intervention in emerging adulthood. *Prevention Science.*

Hill, P.C., & Butter, E.M. (1995). The role of religion in promoting physical health. *Journal of Psychology and Christianity, 14,* 141-155.

Hill, P.L., Burrow, A.L., & Bronk, A.C. (2016). Persevering with positivity and purpose: An examination of purpose commitment and positive affect as predictors of grit. *Journal of Happiness Studies, 17*, 257-269.

Hill, P.L., & Roberts, B.W. (2016). Personality and health: Reviewing recent research and setting a directive for the future. In K.W. Schaie & S.L. Willis (Eds.), *Handbook of the psychology of aging* (8th ed.). New York: Elsevier.

Hill, P.L., Turiano, N.A., Mroczek, D.K., & Roberts, B.W. (2012). Examining concurrent and longitudinal relations between personality traits and social well-being in adulthood. *Social Psychological and Personality Science, 3*(6), 698-705.

Hill, P.L., & others (2014). Perceived social support predicts increased conscientiousness during older adulthood. *Journals of Gerontology B: Psychological Sciences and Social Sciences.*

Hill, T.D., Burdette, A.M., Angel, J.L., & Angel, R.J. (2006). Religious attendance and cognitive functioning among older Mexican Americans. *Journals of Gerontology B: Psychological Sciences and Social Sciences, 61*, P31-P39.

Hill, W.D., & others (2019). A combined analysis of genetically correlated traits identifies 187 loci and a role for neurogenesis and myelination in intelligence. *Molecular Psychiatry, 24*, 169-181.

Hines, M. (2013). Sex and sex differences. In P.D. Zelazo (Ed.), *Oxford handbook of developmental psychology.* New York: Oxford University Press.

Hines, M. (2015). Gendered development. In R.M. Lerner (Ed.), *Handbook of child psychology and developmental science* (7th ed.). New York: Wiley.

Hinkley, T., & others (2018). Cross sectional associations of screen time and outdoor play with social skills in preschool children. *PLoS One, 13*(4), 0193700.

Hinnant, J.B., & others (2019). Rewarding safe choices in peer contexts: Adolescent brain activity during decision making. *Biological Psychiatry, 142*, 45-53.

Hinshaw, H.P. (2018). Attention deficit hyperactivity disorder (ADHD): Controversy, developmental mechanisms, and multiple levels of analysis. *Annual Review of Clinical Psychology, 14*. 291-316.

Hipwell, A.E., & others (2018). Police contacts, arrests, and decreasing self-control and personal responsibility among female adolescents. *Journal of Child Psychology and Psychiatry, 50*, 1252-1260.

Hirai, M., & Kanakogi, Y. (2019, in press). Communicative hand-waving gestures facilitate object learning in preverbal infants. *Developmental Science.*

Hirsch, J.K., Wolford, K., Lalonde, S.M., Brunk, L., & Parker-Morris, A. (2009). Optimistic explanatory style as a moderator of the association between negative life events and suicide ideation. *Crisis, 30*, 48-53.

Hirsh-Pasek, K., & Golinkoff, R.M. (2007). *Celebrate the scribble.* Bethlehem, PA: Crayola Beginnings Press.

Hirsh-Pasek, K., & Golinkoff, R.M. (2014). Early language and literacy: Six principles. In S. Gilford (Ed.), *Head Start teacher's guide.* New York: Teacher's College Press.

Hirsh-Pasek, K., Golinkoff, R.M., Singer, D., & Berk, L. (2009). *A mandate for playful learning in preschool: Presenting the evidence.* New York: Oxford University Press.

Hirsh-Pasek, K., & others (2015a). The contribution of early communication quality to low-income children's language success. *Psychological Science, 26*, 1071-1083.

Hirsh-Pasek, K., & others (2015b). Putting education in "educational" apps: Lessons from the science of learning. *Psychological Science in the Public Interest, 16*, 3-34.

Hjortsvang, K., & Lagattuta, K.H. (2017). Emotional development. In A.E. Wenzel (Ed.), *SAGE encyclopedia of abnormal and clinical psychology.* Thousand Oaks, CA: Sage.

Hoch, J.E., O'Grady, S., & Adolph, K.E. (2019, in press). It's the journey, not the destination: Locomotor exploration in infants. *Developmental Science.*

Hockenberry, M.J., Wilson, D., & Rodgers, C.C. (2017). *Wong's essentials of pediatric nursing* (10th ed.). Maryland Heights, MO: Mosby.

Hockenberry, M.J., Wilson, D., & Rodgers, C.C. (2019). *Wong's essentials of pediatric nursing* (11th ed.). Maryland Heights, MO: Mosby.

Hockenberry, S., & Puzzanchera, C. (2017, April). *Juvenile court statistics 2014.* Washington, DC: National Center for Juvenile Justice.

Hocking, E.C., & others (2018). Adult attachment and drinking context as predictors of alcohol problems and relationship satisfaction in college students. *American Journal of Drug and Alcohol Abuse, 44*, 339-347.

Hodis, H.N., & Mack, W.J. (2014). Hormone replacement therapy and the association with coronary heart disease and overall mortality: Clinical application of the timing hypothesis. *Journal of Steroid Biochemistry and Molecular Biology, 142*, 68-75.

Hoefnagels, M. (2019). *Biology: Essentials* (3rd ed.). New York: McGraw-Hill.

Hoelter, L. (2009). Divorce and separation. In D. Carr (Ed.), *Encyclopedia of the life course and human development.* Boston: Gale Cengage.

Hoff, E. (2016). Language development. In M.H. Bornstein & M.E. Lamb (Eds.), *Developmental science* (7th ed.). New York: Psychology Press.

Hoff, E., Laursen, B., & Tardif, T. (2002). Socioeconomic status and parenting. In M.H. Bornstein (Ed.), *Handbook of parenting* (2nd ed.). Mahwah, NJ: Erlbaum.

Hoff, E., & Place, S. (2013). Bilingual language learners. In S.L. Odom, E. Pungello, & N. Gardner-Neblett (Eds.), *Re-visioning the beginning: Developmental and health science contributions to infant/toddler programs for children and families living in poverty.* New York: Guilford.

Hoff, E., & others (2014). Expressive vocabulary development in children from bilingual homes: A longitudinal study from two to four years. *Early Childhood Research Quarterly, 29*, 433-444.

Hoffman, H.J., & others (2017). Declining prevalence of hearing loss in U.S. adults aged 20 to 65. *JAMA Otolaryngology—Head and Neck Surgery, 143*, 274-285.

Hoffman, J.P. (2018). Cohabitation, marijuana use, and heavy alcohol use in young adulthood. *Substance Use and Abuse, 3*, 2394-2404.

Hoffman, P., & Morcom, A.M. (2018). Age-related changes in the neural networks supporting semantic cognition: A meta-analysis of 47 functional neuroimaging studies. *Neuroscience and Biobehavioral Reviews, 84*, 134-150.

Hoffman, S., & Warschburger, P. (2017). Weight, shape, and muscularity concerns in male and female adolescents: Predictors of change and influences on eating disorders. *International Journal of Eating Disorders, 50*, 139-147.

Hoffman, S., & Warschburger, P. (2018). Patterns of body image concerns in adolescence and early adulthood: A latent profile analysis. *Eating Behavior, 29*, 28-34.

Hoffnung, M. (2017). Separate is never equal: The repackaging of single-sex education. *Sex Roles, 76*, 135-136.

Hofmann, W., Brandt, M.J., Wisneski, D.C., Rockenbach, B., & Skitka, L.J. (2018). Moral punishment in everyday life. *Personality and Social Psychology Bulletin, 44*, 1697-1711.

Hohls, J.K., & others (2019). Association of generalized anxiety symptoms and panic with health care costs in older age—results from the ESTHER cohort study. *Journal of Affective Disorders, 245*, 978-986.

Hoicka, E., & others (2016). One-year-olds think creatively, just like their parents. *Child Development, 87*, 1099-1105.

Holden, G.W., Vittrup, B., & Rosen, L.H. (2011). Families, parenting, and discipline. In M.K. Underwood & L.H. Rosen (Eds.), *Social development.* New York: Guilford.

Holden, G.W., & others (2017). The emergence of "positive parenting" as a new paradigm: Theory, processes, and evidence. In D. Narváez & others (Eds.), *Contexts for young child flourishing.* New York: Oxford University Press.

Holding, P., & others (2018). Can we measure cognitive constructs consistently within and across cultures? Evidence from a test battery in Bangladesh, Ghana, & Tanzania. *Applied Neuropsychology: Child, 7, 1-13.*

Holfeld, B., & Mishna, F. (2018). Longitudinal associations in youth involvement as victimized, bullying, or witnessing bullying. *Cyberpsychology, Behavior, and Social Networking, 21*, 234-239.

Hollams, E.M., de Klerk, N.H., Holt, P.G., & Sly, P.D. (2014). Persistent effects of maternal smoking during pregnancy on lung function and asthma in adolescents. *American Journal of Respiratory and Critical Care Medicine, 189*, 401-407.

Hollenstein, T., & Lanteigne, D.M. (2018). Emotion regulation dynamics in adolescence. In P.M. Cole & T. Hollenstein (Eds.), *Emotion regulation.* New York: Routledge.

Holler-Wallscheid, M.S., & others (2017). Bilateral recruitment of prefrontal cortex in working memory is associated with task demand but not with age. *Proceedings of the National Academy of Sciences U.S.A., 114*, E830-E839.

Holley, S.R. (2017). Perspectives on contemporary lesbian relationships. *Journal of Lesbian Studies, 21*, 1-6.

Holm, A.L., Berland, A.K., & Severinsson, E. (2019). Factors that influence the health of older widows and widowers—A systematic review of quantitative research. *Nursing Open, 26*, 591-611.

Holmes, C., & others (2019). Structural home environment effects on developmental trajectories of self-control and adolescent risk taking. *Journal of Youth and Adolescence, 48*, 43-55.

Holmes, R.M., Little, K.C., & Welsh, D. (2009). Dating and romantic relationships, adulthood. In D. Carr (Ed.), *Encyclopedia of the life course and human development.* Boston: Gale Cengage.

Holmes, T.H., & Rahe, R.H. (1967). The social readjustment rating scale. *Journal of Psychosomatic Research, 11*, 213-218.

Holsen, I., Carlson Jones, D., & Skogbrott Birkeland, M. (2012). Body image satisfaction among Norwegian adolescents and young adults: A longitudinal study of interpersonal relationships and BMI. *Body Image, 9,* 201-208.

Holway, G.V., & Hernandez, S.M. (2018). Oral sex and condom use in a US national sample of adolescents and young adults. *Journal of Adolescent Health, 62,* 402-410.

Holzman, L. (2017). *Vygotsky at work and play* (2nd Ed.). New York: Routledge.

Hom, E.E., Turkheimer, E., Strachan, E., & Duncan, G.E. (2015). Behavioral and environmental modification of the genetic influence on body mass index: A twin study. *Behavior Genetics, 45,* 409-426.

Homan, K.J. (2018). Secure attachment and eudaimonic well-being in late adulthood: The moderating role of self-compassion. *Aging and Mental Health, 22,* 363-370.

Homel, J., & Warren, D. (2019, in press). The relationship between parent drinking and adolescent drinking: Differences for mothers and fathers and boys and girls. *Substance Use and Abuse.*

Hong, S.J., & others (2019, in press). Atypical functional connectome hierarchy in autism. *Nature Communications.*

Hong, X., & others (2015). Normal aging selectivity diminishes alpha lateralization in visual spatial attention. *NeuroImage, 106,* 353-363.

Honig, A.S. (2019). Choosing childcare for young children. In M.H. Bornstein (Ed.), *Handbook of parenting* (3rd ed.) (Vol.5). New York: Routledge.

Honour, J.W. (2018). Biochemistry and menopause. *Annals of Clinical Biochemistry, 55,* 18-33.

Honzik, M.P., MacFarlane, I.W., & Allen, L. (1948). The stability of mental test performance between two and eighteen years. *Journal of Experimental Education, 17,* 309-324.

Hood, B.M. (1995). Gravity rules for 2- to 4-year-olds? *Cognitive Development, 10,* 577-598.

Hoogendam, Y.Y., & others (2014a). Older age relates to worsening of fine motor skills: A population-based study of middle-aged and elderly persons. *Frontiers in Aging Neuroscience, 6,* 259.

Hoogenhout, M., & Malcolm-Smith, S. (2017). Theory of mind predicts severity level in autism. *Autism, 21,* 242-252.

Hopkins, B. (1991). Facilitating early motor development: An intercultural study of West Indian mothers and their infants living in Britain. In J.K. Nugent, B.M. Lester, & T.B. Brazelton (Eds.), *The cultural context of infancy, Vol. 2: Multicultural and interdisciplinary approaches to parent-infant relations.* New York: Ablex.

Hopkins, B., & Westra, T. (1990). Motor development, maternal expectations, and the role of handling. *Infant Behavior and Development, 13,* 117-122.

Horn, J. (2007). Spearman's g, expertise, and the nature of human cognitive capacity. In P.C. Kyllonen, R.D. Roberts, & L. Stankov (Eds.), *Extending intelligence.* Mahwah, NJ: Erlbaum.

Horn, J.L., & Donaldson, G. (1980). Cognitive development II: Adulthood development of human abilities. In O.G. Brim & J. Kagan (Eds.), *Constancy and change in human development.* Cambridge, MA: Harvard University Press.

Horn, L., & Nevill, S. (2006). *Profile of undergraduates in U.S. postsecondary education institutions: 2003-2004, with a special analysis of community college students* (NCES 2006-184). Washington, DC: National Center for Education Statistics.

Horne, R.S., Franco, P., Adamson, T.M., Groswasser, J., & Kahn, A. (2002). Effects of body position on sleep and arousal characteristics in infants. *Early Human Development, 69,* 25-33.

Horne, R.S.C. (2018). Cardiovascular autonomic dysfunction in sudden infant death syndrome. *Clinical Automatic Research, 28,* 535-543.

Hosie, A., (2018). Medical assistance in dying—unanswered questions. *JAMA Internal Medicine, 178,* 156.

Hoskins, J.L., & others (2019, in press). Patients' experiences of brief cognitive behavioral therapy for eating disorders: A qualitative investigation. *International Journal of Eating Disorders.*

Hotta, R., & others (2018). Cognitive function and unsafe driving acts during on-road test among community-dwelling older adults with cognitive impairments. *Geriatrics and Gerontology International, 18,* 847-852.

Hou, Y., & Kim, S.Y. (2018). Acculturation-related stressors and individual adjustment in Asian American families. In S.S. Chuang & C. Costigan (Eds.), *An international approach to parenting and parent-child families in immigrant families.* New York: Routledge.

Hou, Y., Kim, S.Y., & Wang, Y. (2016). Parental acculturative stressors and adolescent adjustment through interparental and parent-child relationships in Chinese American families. *Journal of Youth and Adolescence, 45,* 1466-1481.

Hou, Y.W., & others (2018). Association of serotonin receptors with attention deficit hyperactivity disorder: A systematic review and meta-analysis. *Current Medical Science, 38,* 538-551.

Houde, O., & others (2011). Functional magnetic resonance imaging study of Piaget's conservation-of-number task in preschool and school-age children: A neo-Piagetian approach. *Journal of Experimental Child Psychology, 110*(3), 332-346.

Houser, J.J., Mayeux, L., & Cross, C. (2014). Peer status and aggression as predictors of dating popularity in adolescence. *Journal of Youth and Adolescence, 44,* 683-695.

Howard, J.L., Gagne, M., & Bureau, J.S. (2017). Testing a continuum structure of self-determined motivation: A meta-analysis. *Psychological Bulletin, 143,* 1346-1377.

Howard, L.H., Henderson, A.M.E., Carrazza, C., & Woodward, A.L. (2015). Infants' and young children's imitation of linguistic in-group and out-group informants. *Child Development, 86,* 259-275.

Howard, S., & others (2017). Perceived social support predicts lower cardiovascular reactivity to stress in older adults. *Biological Psychology, 125,* 70-75.

Howard, S.R., & others (2018). Contributions of function-altering variants in genes implicated in pubertal timing and body mass for self-limited delayed puberty. *Journal of Clinical Endocrinology and Metabolism, 103,* 649-659.

Howe, G.W., Homberger, A.P., Weihs, K., Moreno, F., & Neiderhiser, J.M. (2012). Higher-order structure in the trajectories of depression and anxiety following sudden involuntary unemployment. *Journal of Abnormal Psychology, 121,* 325-338.

Howe, M.J.A., Davidson, J.W., Moore, D.G., & Sloboda, J.A. (1995). Are there early childhood signs of musical ability? *Psychology of Music, 23,* 162-176.

Howell, D.C. (2017). *Fundamental statistics for the behavioral sciences* (9th ed.). Boston: Cengage.

Howes, C. (2009). Friendship in early childhood. In K.H. Rubin, W.M. Bukowski, & B. Laursen (Eds.), *Handbook of peer interactions, relationships, and groups.* New York: Guilford.

Howes, C. (2016). Children and child care: A theory of relationships within cultural communities. In K. Sanders & A.W. Guerra (Eds.), *The culture of child care.* New York: Oxford University Press.

Hoyer, W.J. (2015). Brain aging: Behavioral, cognitive, and personality consequences. In J.D. Wright (Ed.), *International encyclopedia of the social and behavioral sciences* (2nd ed.). New York; Elsevier.

Hoyer, W.J., & Roodin, P.A. (2009). *Adult development and aging* (6th ed.). New York: McGraw-Hill.

Hoyt, L.T., & others (2018a). Girls' sleep trajectories across the pubertal transition: Emerging racial/ethnic differences. *Journal of Adolescent Health, 62,* 496-503.

Hoyt, L.T., & others (2018b). Adolescent sleep barriers: Profiles within a diverse sample of urban youth. *Journal of Youth and Adolescence, 47,* 2169-2180.

HSBC Insurance (2007). *The future of retirement: The new age—global report.* London: HSBC.

Hsin, A., & Xie, Y. (2014). Explaining Asian Americans' academic advantage over whites. *Proceedings of the National Academy of Sciences U.S.A., 111*(23), 8416-8421.

Hsueh, A.J., & He, J. (2018). Gonadotropins and their receptors: Co-evolution, genetic variants, receptor imaging, and functional antagonists. *Biological Reproduction, 99,* 3-12.

Hu, L., & others (2019). Physical activity modifies the association between depression and cognitive function in older adults. *Journal of Affective Disorders, 246,* 800-805.

Hu, X., & others (2019). Cognitive aging trajectories and mortality of Chinese oldest-old. *Archives of Gerontology and Geriatrics, 82,* 81-87.

Hu, Z., & others (2019, in press). Maternal metabolic factors during pregnancy predict early childhood growth trajectories and obesity risk: The CANDLE study. *International Journal of Obesity.*

Hua, L., & others (2016). Four-locus gene interaction between IL13, IL4, FCER1B, and ADRB2 for asthma in Chinese Han children. *Pediatric Pulmonology, 51,* 364-371.

Huang, C.H., & others (2019). Change in quality of life and potentially associated factors in patients receiving home-based primary care: A prospective cohort study. *BMC Geriatrics, 19*(1), 21.

Huang, H.W., Meyer, A.M., & Federmeier, K.D. (2012). A "concrete view" of aging: Event-related potentials reveal age-related changes in basic integrated processes in language. *Neuropsychologia, 50,* 26-35.

Huang, J.H., DeJong, W., Towvim, L.G., & Schneider, S.K. (2009). Sociodemographic and psychobehavioral characteristics of U.S. college students who abstain from alcohol. *Journal of American College Health, 57,* 395-410.

Huang, L., & others (2019, in press). Maternal smoking and attention-deficit/hyperactivity disorder in offspring: A meta-analysis. *Pediatrics.*

Huang, L.B., & others (2017). Influencing and protective factors of suicide ideation among older adults. *International Journal of Mental Health Nursing, 26,* 191-199.

Huang, P.M., Smock, P.J., Manning, W.D., & Bergstrom-Lynch, C.A. (2011). He says, she says: Gender and cohabitation. *Journal of Family Issues, 32,* 876–905.

Huang, Y.P., & others (2019). Free testosterone correlated with erectile dysfunction severity among young men with normal total testosterone. *International Journal of Impotence, 31,* 132–138.

Hudson, A., & Jacques, S. (2014). Put on a happy face! Inhibitory control and socioemotional knowledge predict emotion regulation in 5- to 7-year-olds. *Journal of Experimental Child Psychology, 123,* 36–52.

Hudson, N.W., Fraley, R.C., Chopik, W.J., & Heffernan, M.E. (2016). Not all attachment relationships change alike: Normative cross-sectional age trajectories in attachment to romantic partners, friends, and parents across the lifespan. *Journal of Research in Personality, 59,* 44–55.

Huerta, M., Cortina, L.M., Pang, J.S., Torges, C.M., & Magley, V.J. (2006). Sex and power in the academy: Modeling sexual harassment in the lives of college women. *Personality and Social Psychology Bulletin, 32,* 616–628.

Huffman, J.C., & others (2016). Effects of optimism and gratitude on physical activity, biomarkers, and readmissions after an acute coronary syndrome: The Gratitude Research in Acute Coronary Events Study. *Circulation: Cardiovascular Quality and Outcomes, 9,* 55–63.

Hughes, C., & Devine, R.T. (2015). Individual differences in theory of mind: A social perspective. In R.M. Lerner (Ed.), *Handbook of child psychology and developmental science* (7th ed.). New York: Wiley.

Hughes, C., Devine, R.T., & Wang, Z. (2018). Does parental mind-mindedness account for cross-cultural differences in preschoolers' theory of mind? *Child Development, 89,* 1296–1310.

Hughes, C., Marks, A., Ensor, R., & Lecce, S. (2010). A longitudinal study of conflict and inner state talk in children's conversations with mothers and younger siblings. *Social Development, 19,* 822–837.

Hughes, C., & others (2019). Age differences in specific neural connections within the default mode network underlie theory of mind. *NeuroImage, 191,* 269–277.

Hughes, J.N., & Cao, Q. (2018).Trajectories of teacher-student warmth and conflict at the transition to middle school: Effects on academic engagement and achievement. *Journal of School Psychology, 67,* 148–162.

Hughes, M.E., Waite, L.J., LaPierre, T.A., & Luo, Y. (2007). All in the family: The impact of caring for grandchildren on grandparents' health. *Journals of Gerontology B: Psychological Sciences and Social Sciences, 62*(2), S108–S119.

Hughes, P.C. (1978). In J.L. Fozard & S.J. Popkin, Optimizing adult development: Ends and means of an applied psychology of aging. *American Psychologist, 33,* 975–989.

Huhdanpaa, H., & others (2018). Sleep and psychiatric symptoms in young child psychiatric outpatients. *Clinical Child Psychology and Psychiatry, 23,* 77–95.

Hui, L. (2019). Noninvasive approaches to prenatal diagnosis: Historical perspective and future directions. *Methods in Molecular Biology.*

Huijbers, W., & others (2017). Age-related increases in tip-of-the-tongue are distinct from decreases in remembering names: A functional MRI study. *Cerebral Cortex, 27,* 4339–4349.

Hull, J. (2012). A self-awareness model of the causes and effects of alcohol consumption. In K. Vohs & R.F. Baumeister (Eds.), *Self and identity.* Thousand Oaks, CA: Sage.

Hultsch, D.F., Hertzog, C., Small, B.J., & Dixon, R.A. (1999). Use it or lose it: Engaged lifestyle as a buffer of cognitive decline in aging? *Psychology and Aging, 14,* 245–263.

Hultsch, D.F., & Plemons, J.K. (1979). Life events and life-span development. In P.B. Baltes & O.G. Brim (Eds.), *Life-span development and behavior.* New York: Academic Press.

Hunt, E. (1995). *Will we be smart enough? A cognitive analysis of the coming work force.* New York: Russell Sage.

Hunter, S., Leatherdale, S.T., & Carson, V. (2018). The 3-year longitudinal impact of sedentary behavior on the academic achievement of secondary school students. *Journal of School Health, 88,* 660–668.

Huo, M., & Fingerman, K.L. (2018). Grandparents. In M.H. Bornstein (Ed.), *SAGE encyclopedia of lifespan human development.* Thousand Oaks, CA: Sage.

Huo, M., & others (2018). Aging parents' disabilities and daily support exchanges with adult children. *Gerontologist, 58,* 872–882.

Huo, M., & others (2018). Support grandparents give to their adult grandchildren. *Journals of Gerontology B: Psychological Sciences and Social Sciences, 73,* 1006–1015.

Huo, M., & others (2019). Aging parents' daily support exchanges with adult children suffering problems. *Journals of Gerontology B: Psychological Sciences and Social Sciences, 74,* 449–459.

Huppert, E., & others (2019). The development of children's preferences for equality and equity across 13 individualistic and collectivist cultures. *Developmental Science, 22*(2), e12729.

Hurst, S.A., & Mauron, A. (2017). Assisted suicide in Switzerland: Clarifying the liberties and claims. *Bioethics, 31,* 199–208.

Hurt, H., Brodsky, N.L., Roth, H., Malmud, F., & Giannetta, J.M. (2005). School performance of children with gestational cocaine exposure. *Neurotoxicology and Teratology, 27,* 203–211.

Huttenlocher, J., Haight, W., Bruk, A., Seltzer, M., & Lyons, T. (1991). Early vocabulary growth: Relation to language input and gender. *Developmental Psychology, 27,* 236–248.

Huttenlocher, P.R., & Dabholkar, A.S. (1997). Regional differences in synaptogenesis in human cerebral cortex. *Journal of Comparative Neurology, 37*(2), 167–178.

Hutter, R.R.C., & others (2019, in press). Women's stereotype threat-based performance motivation and prepotent inhibitory ability. *British Journal of Social Psychology.*

Huyck, M.H. (1995). Marriage and close relationships of the marital kind. In R. Blieszner & V.H. Bedford (Eds.), *Handbook of aging and the family.* Westport, CT: Greenwood Press.

Hyde, J.S. (2005). The gender similarities hypothesis. *American Psychologist, 60,* 581–592.

Hyde, J.S. (2007). *Half the human experience* (7th ed.). Boston: Houghton Mifflin.

Hyde, J.S. (2014). Gender similarities and differences. *Annual Review of Psychology* (Vol. 65). Palo Alto, CA: Annual Reviews.

Hyde, J.S. (2017). Gender similarities. In C.B. Travis & J.W. White (Eds.), *APA handbook of the psychology of women.* Washington, DC: American Psychological Association.

Hyde, J.S., & DeLamater, J.D. (2017). *Understanding human sexuality* (13th ed.). New York: McGraw-Hill.

Hyde, J.S., & Else-Quest, N. (2013). *Half the human experience* (8th ed.). Boston: Cengage.

Hyde, J.S., Krajnik, M., & Skuldt-Niederberger, K. (1991). Androgyny across the life span: A replication and longitudinal follow-up. *Developmental Psychology, 27,* 516–519.

Hyde, J.S., Lindberg, S.M., Linn, M.C., Ellis, A.B., & Williams, C.C. (2008). Gender similarities characterize math performance. *Science, 321,* 494–495.

Hyde, J.S., & others (2019). The future of sex and gender in psychology: Five challenges to the gender binary. *American Psychology, 74,* 171–193.

Hyde, Z., & others (2012). Prevalence and predictors of sexual problems in men aged 75–95 years: A population-based study. *Journal of Sexual Medicine, 9,* 442–453.

Hymel, S., Closson, L.M., Caravita, C.S., & Vaillancourt, T. (2011). Social status among peers: From sociometric attraction to peer acceptance to perceived popularity. In P.K. Smith & C.H. Hart (Eds.), *Wiley-Blackwell handbook of childhood social development* (2nd ed.). New York: Wiley.

Hysing, M., & others (2015). Sleep and school attendance in adolescence: Results from a large population-based study. *Scandinavian Journal of Public Health, 43,* 2–9.

Hysing, M., & others (2016). Sleep and academic performance in later adolescence: Results from a large population-based study. *Journal of Sleep Research, 25,* 318–324.

Hyson, M.C., Copple, C., & Jones, J. (2006). Early childhood development and education. In W. Damon & R. Lerner (Eds.), *Handbook of child psychology* (6th ed.). New York: Wiley.

I

Iacono, D., & Feltis, G.C. (2019). Impact of Apolipoprotein E gene polymorphism during normal and pathological conditions of the brain across the lifespan. *Aging, 11*(2), 787–816.

Ichikawa, H., & others (2019). A longitudinal study of infant view-invariant face processing during the first 3–8 months of life. *NeuroImage, 186,* 817–824.

Idler, E. (2006). Religion and aging. In R.H. Binstock & L.K. George (Eds.), *Handbook of aging and the social sciences* (6th ed.). San Diego: Academic Press.

Idler, E., & others (2017). Religion, a social determinant of mortality? A 10-year follow-up of the Health and Retirement Study. *PLoS One, 12*(12), e0189134.

Igarashi, H., Hooker, K., Coehlo, D.P., & Maoogian, M.M. (2013). "My nest is full": Intergenerational relationships at midlife. *Journal of Aging Studies, 27,* 102–112.

Igarashi, H., Levenson, M.R., & Aldwin, C.M. (2018). The development of wisdom: A social ecological approach. *Journals of Gerontology B: Psychological Sciences and Social Sciences, 73,* 1350–1358.

"I Have a Dream" Foundation (2015). *Research on "I Have a Dream."* Retrieved from www.ihad.org

"I Have a Dream" Foundation (2019). *About us.* Retrieved January 25, 2017, from www.ihad.org

Ihle, A., & others (2015). The association of leisure activities in middle adulthood with cognitive performance in old age: The moderating role of educational level. *Gerontology, 61*, 543–550.

Ilmakunnas, P., & Ilmakunnas, S. (2018). Health and retirement age: Comparison of expectations and actual retirement. *Scandinavian Journal of Public Health, 46* (Suppl. 19), S18–S31.

Imafuku, M., & others (2019). Audiovisual speech perception and language acquisition in preterm infants: A longitudinal study. *Early Human Development, 128*, 93–100.

Indefrey, P. (2019). The relationship between semantic production and comprehension. In S-A. Rueschemeyer & M. Gareth Gaskell (Eds.), *Oxford handbook of psycholinguistics* (2nd ed.). New York: Oxford University Press.

Inderkum, A.P., & Tarokh, L. (2019, in press). High heritability of adolescent sleep-wake behavior on free, but not school days: A long-term twin study. *Sleep.*

Inelmen, E.M., & others (2012). The importance of sexual health in the elderly: Breaking down barriers and taboos. *Aging: Clinical and Experimental Research, 24*(Suppl. 3), S31–S34.

Infurna, F.J., Okun, M.A., & Grimm, K.J. (2016). Volunteering is associated with lower risk in cognitive impairment. *Journal of the American Geriatrics Society, 64*, 2263–2269.

Ingersoll-Dayton, B., & others (2019, in press). A systematic review of dyadic approaches to reminiscence and life review among older adults. *Aging and Mental Health.*

Ingrassia, A. (2018). The independent inquiry into child sexual abuse in the UK: Reflecting on the mental health needs of victims and survivors. *British Journal of Psychiatry, 213*, 571–573.

Insel, P., & Roth, W. (2020). *Core concepts in health* (16th ed.). New York: McGraw-Hill.

International Montessori Council (2006). Larry Page and Sergey Brin, founders of Google.com, credit their Montessori education for much of their success on prime-time television. Retrieved June 24, 2006, from http://www.Montessori.org/enews/Barbara_walters.html

Iovino, M., & others (2019, in press). Neuroendocrine mechanisms involved in sexual and emotional behavior. *Endocrine, Metabolic, and Immune Disorders Drug Targets.*

Ip, S., Chung, M., Raman, G., Trikalinos, T.A., & Lau, J. (2009). A summary of the Agency for Healthcare Research and Quality's evidence report on breastfeeding in developed countries. *Breastfeeding Medicine, 4*(Suppl. 1), S17–S30.

Irwin, C.E. (2010). Young adults are worse off than adolescents. *Journal of Adolescent Health, 46*, 405–406.

Isaev, N.K., Stelmashook, E.V., & Genrikhs, E.E. (2019). Neurogenesis and brain aging. *Reviews in the Neurosciences.*

Ishak, S., Franchak, J.M., & Adolph, K.E. (2014). Fear of height in infants. *Current Directions in Psychological Science, 23*, 60–66.

Ishtiak-Ahmed, K., & others (2018). Social relations at work and incident dementia: 29-years' follow-up of the Copenhagen Male Study. *Journal of Occupational and Environmental Medicine, 60*, 12–18.

Isidori, A.M., & others (2014). A critical analysis of the role of testosterone in erectile function: From pathophysiology to treatment—a systematic analysis. *European Urology, 65*(1), 99–112.

Isingrini, M., Perrotin, A., & Souchay, C. (2008). Aging, metamemory regulation, and executive functioning. *Progress in Brain Research, 169*, 377–392.

Ismail, K., & others (2016). Compression of morbidity is observed across cohorts with exceptional longevity. *Journal of the American Geriatrics Society, 64*, 1583–1591.

Israel, M. (2019). Semantics. In C. Genetti (Ed.), *How languages work* (2nd ed.). New York: Cambridge University Press.

Ivan Santini, Z., Koyanagi, A., Tyrovolas, S., & Haro, J.M. (2015). The association of relationship quality and social networks with depression, anxiety, and suicidal ideation among older married adults: Findings from a cross-sectional analysis of The Irish Longitudinal Study on Aging (TILDA). *Journal of Affective Disorders, 179*, 134–141.

Iwata, S., & others (2012). Qualitative brain MRI at term and cognitive outcomes at 9 years after very preterm birth. *Pediatrics, 129*, e1138–1147.

Izard, C.E., & others (2008). Accelerating the development of emotional competence in Head Start children: Effects on adaptive and maladaptive behavior. *Development and Psychopathology, 20*, 369–397.

J

Jabeen, H., & others (2018). Investigating the scavenging of reactive oxygen species by antioxidants via theoretical and experimental methods. *Journal of Photochemistry and Photobiology B, 180*, 268–275.

Jackson, J.J., & Roberts, B.W. (2016). Conscientiousness. In T.A. Widiger (Ed.), *Oxford handbook of the five factor model.* New York: Oxford University Press.

Jackson, Y. (2019). Child maltreatment. In T.H. Ollendick & others (Eds.), *Oxford handbook of clinical child and adolescent psychology.* New York: Oxford University Press.

Jacob, J.I. (2009). The socioemotional effects of non-maternal childcare on children in the USA: Critical review of recent studies. *Early Child Development and Care, 179*, 559–570.

Jacob, R., & others (2014). Daily hassles' role in health seeking behavior among low-income populations. *American Journal of Health Behavior, 38*, 297–306.

Jacobs, J.M., Hammerman-Rozenberg, R., Cohen, A., & Stressman, J. (2008). Reading daily predicts reduced mortality among men from a cohort of community-dwelling 70-year-olds. *Journals of Gerontology B: Psychological Sciences and Social Sciences, 63*, S73–S80.

Jacobson, L.A., & others (2011). Working memory influences processing speed and reading fluency in ADHD. *Child Neuropsychology, 17*(3), 209–224.

Jadhav, A., & Weir, D. (2018). Widowhood and depression in a cross-national perspective: Evidence from the United States, Europe, Korea, and China. *Journals of Gerontology B: Psychological Sciences and Social Sciences, 73*, e143–e153.

Jadhav, K.S., & Boutrel, B. (2019, in press). Prefrontal cortex development and emergence of self-regulatory competence: The two cardinal features of adolescence disrupted in context of alcohol abuse. *European Journal of Neuroscience.*

Jaekel, J., & others (2019). Head growth and intelligence from birth to adulthood in very preterm

and term born individuals. *Journal of the International Neuropsychology Association, 25*, 48–56.

Jaffee, S., & Hyde, J.S. (2000). Gender differences in moral orientation: A meta-analysis. *Psychological Bulletin, 126*, 703–726.

Jain, C., & Dwarakanath, V.M. (2019, in press). Influence of subcortical auditory processing and cognitive measures on cocktail party listening in younger and older adults. *International Journal of Audiology.*

Jain, S. & others (2019, in press). Adult neurogenesis in the mouse dendate gyrus protects the hippocampus from neuronal injury following severe seizures. *Hippocampus.*

Jambon, M., & Smetana, J.G. (2018). Individual differences in prototypical moral and conventional judgments and children's proactive and reactive aggression. *Child Development, 89*, 1343–1359.

Jambon, M., & Smetana, J.G. (2019, in press). Self-reported moral emotions and physical and relational aggression in early childhood: A social domain approach. *Child Development.*

Jambon, M., & Smetana, J.G. (2020, in press). Socialization of moral judgments and reasoning. In D.J. Laible & others (Eds.), *Oxford handbook of parenting and moral development.* New York: Oxford University Press.

James, J.E., Kristijansson, A.L., & Sigfusdottir, I.D. (2011). Adolescence substance use, sleep, and academic achievement: Evidence of harm due to caffeine. *Journal of Adolescence, 34*, 665–673.

James, L.E., & others (2018). Tip of the tongue states increase under evaluative observation. *Journal of Psycholinguistic Research, 47*, 169–178.

James, S., & others (2018). Links between childhood exposure to violent contexts and risky adolescent health behaviors. *Journal of Adolescent Health, 63*, 94–101.

James, T., Rajah, M.N., & Duarte, A. (2019, in press). Multielement episodic encoding in young and older adults. *Journal of Cognitive Neuroscience.*

James, W. (1890/1950). *The principles of psychology.* New York: Dover.

Jan, J.E., & others (2010). Long-term sleep disturbances in children: A cause of neuronal loss. *European Journal of Pediatric Neurology, 14*, 380–390.

Jang, S., & others (2017). Measurement invariance of the Satisfaction with Life Scale across 26 countries. *Journal of Cross-Cultural Psychology, 48*, 560–576.

Janssen, I., & others (2005). Comparison of overweight and obesity prevalence in school-aged youth from 34 countries and their relationships with physical activity and dietary patterns. *Obesity Reviews, 6*, 123–132.

Janssen, J.A., & others (2017). Childhood temperament predictors of adolescent physical activity. *BMC Public Health, 17*(1), 8.

Janssen, T., & others (2018). Developmental relations between alcohol expectancies and social norms in predicting alcohol onset. *Developmental Psychology, 54*, 281–292.

Janssens, A., & others (2017). Adolescent externalizing behavior, psychological control, and rejection: Transactional links and dopaminergic moderation. *British Journal of Developmental Psychology, 35*, 420–438.

Janz, K.F., & Baptista, F. (2018). Bone strength and exercise during youth—the year that was 2017. *Pediatric Exercise Science, 30*, 28–31.

Jardri, R., & others (2012). Assessing fetal response to maternal speech using a noninvasive functional brain imaging technique. *International Journal of Developmental Neuroscience, 30,* 159–161.

Jaremka, L.M., Derry, H., & Kiecolt-Glaser, J.K. (2016). Psychoneuroimmunology of interpersonal relationships: Both the presence/absence of social ties and relationship quality matter. In D.I. Mostofksy (Ed.), *Handbook of Behavioral Medicine.* New York: Wiley.

Jarjat, G., Portrat, S., & Hot, P. (2019, in press). Aging influences the efficiency of attentional maintenance in verbal working memory. *Journals of Gerontology B: Psychological Sciences and Social Sciences.*

Jarrett, R.L. (1995). Growing up poor: The family experiences of socially mobile youth in low-income African-American neighborhoods. *Journal of Adolescent Research, 10,* 111–135.

Jaruratanasirikul, S., & others (2017). A population-based study of Down syndrome in Southern Thailand. *World Journal of Pediatrics, 13,* 63–69.

Jasinska, K.K., & Petitto, L-A. (2018). Age of bilingual exposure is related to the contribution of phonological and semantic knowledge to successful reading development. *Child Development, 89,* 310–331.

Jefferies, E., & Thompson, H. (2019).Varieties of semantic deficit: Single word comprehension. In S.A. Rueschemeyer & M. Gareth-Gaskell (Eds.), *Oxford handbook of psycholinguistics* (2nd ed.). New York: Oxford University Press.

Jencks, C. (1979). *Who gets ahead? The determinants of economic success in America.* New York: Basic Books.

Jenkins, J.M., & Astington, J.W. (1996). Cognitive factors and family structure associated with theory of mind development in young children. *Developmental Psychology, 32,* 70–78.

Jenkins, J.M., & others (2018). Do high quality kindergarten and first-grade classrooms mitigate preschool fadeout? *Journal of Research on Educational Effectiveness, 11,* 339–374.

Jennifer, R.E. (2018). *International handbook of positive aging.* New York: Routledge.

Jennings, W.G., Perez, N.M., & Reingle Gonzalez, J.M. (2018). Conduct disorders and neighborhood effects. *Annual Review of Clinical Psychology, 14,* 317–341.

Jensen, H., & Tubaek, G. (2019, in press). Elderly people need an eye examination before entering nursing homes. *Danish Medical Journal.*

Jensen, T.M. (2019, in press). Stepfamily processes and youth adjustment: The role of perceived neighborhood collective efficacy. *Journal of Research on Adolescence.*

Jensen, T.M., & Harris, K.M. (2017). A longitudinal study of stepfamily relationship quality and adolescent physical health. *Journal of Adolescent Health, 61,* 486–492.

Jensen, T.M., & others (2018). Stepfamily relationship quality and children's internalizing and externalizing problems. *Family Process, 57,* 477–495.

Jenzer, T., & others (2019, in press). Coping trajectories in emerging adulthood: The influence of temperament and gender. *Journal of Personality.*

Jeong, Y., & others (2018). Placental transfer of persistent organic pollutants and feasibility using the placenta as a non-invasive biomonitoring matrix. *Science of the Total Environment, 612,* 1498–1505.

Jeremic, S., & others (2018). Selected anthraquinones as potential free radical scavengers and P-glycoprotein inhibitors. *Organic and Biomedical Chemistry, 16,* 1890–1902.

Jeuring, H.W., & others (2019, in press). The tide has turned: Incidence of depression declined in community living young-old adults over one decade. *Epidemiology and Psychiatric Sciences.*

Jeyanthi, S., Arumugam, N., & Parasher, R.K. (2019, in press). Effect of physical exercises on attention, motor skill, and physical fitness in children with attention deficit hyperactivity disorder: A systematic review. *Attention Deficit and Hyperactivity Disorders.*

Ji, B.T., & others (1997). Paternal cigarette smoking and the risk of childhood cancer among offspring of nonsmoking mothers. *Journal of the National Cancer Institute, 89,* 238–244.

Ji, N., & others (2019). Aerobic exercise promotes the expression of ERCC1 to prolong lifespan: A new possible mechanism. *Medical Hypotheses, 122,* 22–25.

Jia, G., Hill, M.A., & Sowers, J.A. (2018). Diabetic cardiomyopathy: An update of mechanisms contributing to this clinical entity. *Circulation Research, 122,* 624–638.

Jia, R., & Schoppe-Sullivan, S.J. (2011). Relations between coparenting and father involvement in families with preschool-age children. *Developmental Psychology, 47,* 106–118.

Jiang, N., & others (2018). Meta-analysis of the efficacy and safety of combined surgery in the management of eyes with coexisting cataract and open angle glaucoma. *International Journal of Ophthalmology, 11,* 279–286.

Jiang, Y., Granja, M.R., & Koball, H. (2017). *Basic facts about low-income children.* New York: National Center for Children in Poverty, Columbia University.

Jimenez-Trevino, L., & others (2019). 5-HTTLPR-brain-derived neurotrophic factor (BDNF) gene interactions and early adverse life events effect on impulsivity in suicide attempters. *World Journal of Biological Psychiatry, 20,* 137–149.

Jin, I., & others (2018). Young infants expect an unfamiliar adult to comfort a crying baby: Evidence from a standard violation-of-expectation task and a novel infant-triggered video task. *Cognitive Psychology, 102,* 1–20.

Jin, M.M., & others (2019). A critical role of autophagy in regulating microglia polarization in neurodegeneration. *Frontiers in Aging Neuroscience, 10,* 378.

Jin, S.V., Ryu, E., & Mugaddam, A. (2019, in press). Romance 2.0 on Instagram: "What type of girlfriend would you date?" *Evolutionary Psychology.*

Jo, J., & Lee, Y.J. (2018). Effectiveness of acupuncture in women with polycystic ovarian syndrome undergoing in vitro fertilization or intracytoplasmic sperm injection: A systematic review and meta-analysis. *Acupuncture in Medicine, 35,* 162–170.

Joh, A.S., Jaswal, V.K., & Keen, R. (2011). Imagining a way out of the gravity bias: Preschoolers can visualize the solution to a spatial problem. *Child Development, 82,* 744–750.

John, A., & others (2018). Self-harm, suicidal behaviors, and cyberbullying in children and young people: Systematic review. *Journal of Medical Internet Research, 20,* e129.

John, N.A., & others (2017). Understanding the meaning of marital relationship quality among couples in peri-urban Ethiopia. *Culture, Health, and Sexuality, 19,* 267–278.

Johnson, A., Roberts, L., & Elkins, G. (2019, in press). Complementary and alternative medicine for menopause. *Journal of Evidence-Based Integrative Medicine.*

Johnson, G., & Losos, J. (2020). *Essentials of the living world* (6th ed.). New York: McGraw-Hill.

Johnson, J.A., & others (2018). *Foundations of American education* (17th ed.). Upper Saddle River, NJ: Pearson.

Johnson, J.P., Ross, K., & Kiran, S. (2019). Multi-step treatment for acquired alexia and agraphia (Part 1): Efficacy, generalization, and identification of beneficial treatment steps. *Neuropsychological Rehabilitation, 29,* 534–564.

Johnson, J.S., & Newport, E.L. (1991). Critical period effects on universal properties of language: The status of subjacency in the acquisition of a second language. *Cognition, 39,* 215–258.

Johnson, L., Giordano, P.C., Manning, W.D., & Longmore, M.A. (2011). Parent-child relations and offending during young adulthood. *Journal of Youth and Adolescence, 40*(7), 786–799.

Johnson, M. (2008, April 30). Commentary in R. Highfield, *Harvard's baby brain research lab.* Retrieved January 24, 2008, from www.telegraph.co.uk/scienceandtechnology/science/sciencenews/3341166/Harvards-baby-brain-research-labl.html

Johnson, M.H., Gliga, T., Jones, E., & Charman, T. (2015). Annual research review: Infant development, autism, and ADHD—early pathways to emerging disorders. *Journal of Child Psychology and Psychiatry, 56,* 228–247.

Johnson, M.H., Grossmann, T., & Cohen-Kadosh, K. (2009). Mapping functional brain development: Building a social brain through interactive specialization. *Developmental Psychology, 45,* 151–159.

Johnson, M.H., Jones, E., & Gliga, T. (2015). Brain adaptation and alternative developmental trajectories. *Development and Psychopathology, 27,* 425–442.

Johnson, M.H., Senju, A., & Tomalski, P. (2015). The two-process theory of face processing: Modifications based on two decades of data from infants and adults. *Neuroscience and Biobehavioral Reviews, 50,* 169–179.

Johnson, R., & others (2019, in press). Developing a health interview tool for Medicaid home and community-based services clients and home care aides through a community-engaged approach. *Home Health Care Services Quarterly.*

Johnson, S.P. (2004). Development of perceptual completion in infancy. *Psychological Science, 15,* 769–775.

Johnson, S.P. (2011). A constructivist view of object perception in infancy. In L.M. Oakes & others (Eds.), *Infant perception and cognition.* New York: Oxford University Press.

Johnson, S.P. (2018). Perception. In M.H. Bornstein (Ed.), *SAGE encyclopedia lifespan human development.* Thousand Oaks, CA: Sage.

Johnson, S.P. (2019a, in press). Object perception. In O. Braddick (Ed.), *Oxford research encyclopedia of psychology.* New York: Oxford University Press.

Johnson, S.P. (2019b, in press). Mechanisms of statistical learning in infancy. In I.B., Childers & others (Eds.), *Learning language and concepts from multiple examples in infancy and childhood.* New York: Springer.

Johnson, V.A., & others (2015). Childhood- versus adolescent-onset antisocial youth with conduct disorder: Psychiatric illness, neuropsychological and psychosocial function. *PLoS One, 10*(4), e0121627.

Johnson, W., & Bouchard, T.J. (2014). Genetics of intellectual and personality traits associated with creative genius: Could geniuses be cosmobian dragon kings? In D.K. Simonton (Ed.), *Wiley-Blackwell handbook of genius.* New York: Wiley.

Johnston, L.D., & others (2015). *Monitoring the Future, 1975-2014.* Ann Arbor, MI: Institute of Social Research, University of Michigan.

Johnston, L.D., & others (2017). *Monitoring the Future, 2016: College students and adults ages 19-55* (Vol. 2). Ann Arbor, MI: Institute of Social Research, University of Michigan.

Johnston, L.D., & others (2018). *Monitoring the Future: National survey results on drug use, 1975-2017.* Ann Arbor, MI: Institute for Social Research, University of Michigan.

Johnston, L.D., & others (2019). *Monitoring the Future: National survey results on drug use, 1975-2018.* Ann Arbor, MI: Institute for Social Research, University of Michigan.

Johnston, L.D., O'Malley, P.M., Bachman, J.G., & Schulenberg, J.E. (2008). *Monitoring the Future national survey results on drug use, 1975-2007, Volume 1: Secondary school students* (NIH Publication No. 08-6418A). Bethesda, MD: National Institute on Drug Abuse.

Johnston, S.B., Riis, J.L., & Noble, K.G. (2016). State of the art review: Poverty and the developing brain. *Pediatrics, 137*(4).

Jokinen, J., & others (2018). Epigenetic changes in the CRH gene are related to severity of suicide attempt and a general psychogeriatric risk score in adolescents. *EBioMedicine, 27,* 123-133.

Jolicoeur-Martineau, A., & others (2019, in press). Distinguishing differential susceptibility, diathesis-stress, and vantage sensitivity: Beyond the single gene and environment model. *Development and Psychopathology.*

Joling, K.J., & others (2018). Quality indicators for community care for older people: A systematic review. *PLoS One, 13*(1), e0190298.

Jones, B.F., Reedy, E.J., & Weinberg, B.A. (2014). Age and scientific genius. In D.K. Simonton (Ed.), *Wiley-Blackwell handbook of genius.* New York: Wiley.

Jones, C.R.G., & others (2018). The association between theory of mind, executive function, and the symptoms of autism spectrum disorder. *Autism Research, 11,* 95-109.

Jones, D., & others (2010). The impact of the Fast Track prevention trial on health services utilization by youth at risk for conduct problems. *Pediatrics, 125,* 130-136.

Jones, J.D., & others (2018). Stability of attachment style in adolescence: An empirical test of alternative developmental processes. *Child Development, 89,* 871-880.

Jones, M.C. (1965). Psychological correlates of somatic development. *Child Development, 36,* 899-911.

Jones, T.H., & Kelly, D.M. (2018). Randomized controlled trials—mechanistic studies of testosterone and the cardiovascular system. *Asian Journal of Andrology, 20,* 120-130.

Jor'dan, J.R. (2018). Predominately Black institutions and public Montessori schools: Reclaiming the "genius"

in African American children. *Multicultural Learning and Teaching, 13,* 1.

Jorgensen, M.J., & others (2015). Sexual behavior among young Danes aged 15-29 years: A cross-sectional study of core indicators. *Sexually Transmitted Infections, 91,* 171-177.

Jose, A., O'Leary, K.D., & Moyer, A. (2010). Does premarital cohabitation predict subsequent marital stability and marital quality? A meta-analysis. *Journal of Marriage and the Family, 72,* 105-116.

Josephson Institute of Ethics (2006). *2006 Josephson Institute report card on the ethics of American youth. Part one—integrity.* Los Angeles: Josephson Institute.

Joshanloo, M., & Jovanovic, V. (2019, in press). Similarities and differences in predictors of life satisfaction across age groups: A 150-country study. *Journal of Health Psychology.*

Josselyn, S.A., & Frankland, P.W. (2012). Infantile amnesia: A neurogenic hypothesis. *Learning and Memory, 19,* 423-433.

Jouffre, S., & others (2018). Personalizing patients' advance directives decreases the willingness of intensive care unit residents to stop treatment: A randomized study. *Journal of Palliative Medicine, 21,* 1157-1160.

Joyce, B.R., Weil, M., & Calhoun, E. (2018). *Models of teaching* (9th ed.). Upper Saddle River, NJ: Pearson.

Joyner, K. (2009). Transition to parenthood. In D. Carr (Ed.), *Encyclopedia of the life course and human development.* Boston: Gale Cengage.

Ju, H. (2017). The relationship between physical activity, meaning in life, and subjective vitality in community-dwelling older adults. *Archives of Gerontology and Geriatrics, 73,* 120-124.

Juang, C., & others (2018). Understanding the mechanisms of change in a lifestyle intervention for older adults. *Gerontologist. 58,* 353-361.

Juang, L.P., & Umana-Taylor, A.J. (2012). Family conflict among Chinese- and Mexican-origin adolescents and their parents in the U.S.: An introduction. *New Directions in Child and Adolescent Development, 135,* 1-12.

Juang, L.P., & others (2018). Time-varying associations of parent-adolescent cultural conflict and youth adjustment among Chinese American families. *Developmental Psychology, 54,* 938-949.

Judd, F.K., Hickey, M., & Bryant, C. (2012). Depression and midlife: Are we overpathologising the menopause? *Journal of Affective Disorders, 136,* 199-211.

Justice, L.M., & others (2019, in press). Conditions of poverty, parent-child interactions, and toddlers' early language skills in low-income families. *Maternal and Child Health Journal.*

Juvonen, J. (2018). The potential of schools to facilitate and constrain peer relationships. In W.M. Bukowski & others (Eds.), *Handbook of peer interactions, relationships, and groups* (2nd ed.). New York: Guilford.

Jylhava, J., & others (2019, in press). Longitudinal changes in the genetic and environmental influences on the epigenetic clocks across old age: Evidence from two twin cohorts. *EBioMedicine.*

K

Kabiri, M., & others (2018). Long-term health and economic value of improved mobility among older adults in the United States. *Value in Health, 21,* 792-798.

Kader, F., Ghai, M., & Maharaj, L. (2018). The effects of DNA methylation on human psychology. *Behavioral Brain Research, 346,* 47-65.

Kaewpradub, N., & others (2017). Association among Internet usage, body image, and eating behaviors among secondary school students. *Shanghai Archives of Psychiatry, 29,* 208-217.

Kagan, J. (2000). Temperament. In A. Kazdin (Ed.), *Encyclopedia of psychology.* New York: Oxford University Press.

Kagan, J. (2002). Behavioral inhibition as a temperamental category. In R.J. Davidson, K.R. Scherer, & H.H. Goldsmith (Eds.), *Handbook of affective sciences.* New York: Oxford University Press.

Kagan, J. (2008). Fear and wariness. In M.M. Haith & J.B. Benson (Eds.), *Encyclopedia of infant and early childhood development.* Oxford, UK: Elsevier.

Kagan, J. (2010). Emotions and temperament. In M.H. Bornstein (Ed.), *Handbook of cultural developmental science.* New York: Psychology Press.

Kagan, J. (2013). Temperamental contributions to inhibited and uninhibited profiles. In P.D. Zelazo (Ed.), *Oxford handbook of developmental psychology.* New York: Oxford University Press.

Kagan, J. (2018a). Perspectives on two temperamental biases. *Philosophical transactions of the Royal Society of London, Series B: Biological Sciences, 373,* 1744.

Kagan, J. (2018b). Three unresolved issues in human morality. *Perspectives on Psychological Science, 13.* 346-358.

Kagan, J., Kearsley, R.B., & Zelazo, P.R. (1978). *Infancy: Its place in human development.* Cambridge, MA: Harvard University Press.

Kagan, S.H. (2008). Faculty profile, University of Pennsylvania School of Nursing. Retrieved January 5, 2008, from www.nursing.upenn.edu/faculty/profile.asp

Kahn, N.F., & Halpern, C.T. (2018). Associations between patterns of sexual initiation, sexual partnering, and sexual health outcomes from adolescence to early adulthood *Archives of Sexual Behavior, 47,* 1791-1810.

Kahrs, B.A., Jung, W.P., & Lockman, J.J. (2013). Motor origins of tool use. *Child Development, 84*(3), 810-816.

Kail, R.V. (2007). Longitudinal evidence that increases in processing speed and working memory enhance children's reasoning. *Psychological Science, 18,* 312-313.

Kakoschke, N., Aarts, E., & Verdero-Garcia, A. (2019). The cognitive drivers of compulsive eating behavior. *Frontiers in Behavioral Neuroscience, 12,* 338.

Kalashnikova, M., Goswami, U., & Burnham, D. (2019, in press). Mothers speak differently to infants at-risk for dyslexia. *Developmental Science.*

Kalish, R.A. (1981). *Death, grief, and caring relationships.* Monterey, CA: Brooks/Cole.

Kalish, R.A. (1987). Death. In G.L. Maddox (Ed.), *Encyclopedia of aging.* New York: Springer.

Kalish, R.A., & Reynolds, D.K. (1976). *An overview of death and ethnicity.* Farmingdale, NY: Baywood.

Kamal, M.A., & others (2017). Inhibition of butyrylcholinesterase with fluorobenzylcymserine, an experimental Alzheimer's drug candidate: Validation of enzoinformatics results by classical and innovative enzyme kinetic analyses. *CNS & Neurological Disorders Drug Targets, 16,* 820-827.

Kamii, C. (1985). *Young children reinvent arithmetic: Implications of Piaget's theory.* New York: Teachers College Press.

Kamii, C. (1989). *Young children continue to reinvent arithmetic.* New York: Teachers College Press.

Kamp Dush, C.M., Rhoades, G.K., Sandberg, S.E., & Schoppe-Sullivan, S. (2014). Commitment across the transition to parenthood among married and cohabiting couples. *Couple and Family Psychology, 3,* 126–136.

Kamp Dush, C.M., & others (2019). Cohabitation and single mothering in the United States: A review and call for psychological research. In B.H. Friese (Ed.), *APA handbook of contemporary family psychology.* Washington, DC: APA Books.

Kamza, A., & others (2019). Can sustained attention adapt to prior cognitive effort? An evidence from experimental study. *Acta Psychologica, 192,* 181–193.

Kancherla, V., & Oakley, G.P. (2018). Total prevention of folic acid-preventable spina bifida and anencephaly would reduce child mortality in India: Implications in achieving 3.2 of the sustainable development goals. *Birth Defects Research, 110,* 421–428.

Kancherla, V., & others (2019). Teratology society position statement on surveillance and prevalence estimation of neural tube defects. *Birth Defects Research, 111,* 5–8.

Kang, N.G., & You, M.A. (2018). Association of perceived stress and self-control with health-promoting behaviors in adolescents: A cross-sectional study. *Medicine, 97*(34), e11880.

Kang, X., & others (2017). Post-mortem whole-body magnetic resonance imaging of human fetuses: A comparison of 3-T vs. 1.5-T MR imaging with classical autopsy. *European Radiology, 27,* 3542–3553.

Kann, L., & others (2016, August 12). Sexual identity, sex of sexual contacts, and health-related behaviors among students in grades 9-12–United States and selected sites, 2015. *MMWR Surveillance Summary, 65*(9), 1–202.

Kann, L., & others (2016a, June 10). Youth Risk Behavior Surveillance–United States, 2015. *MMWR, 65,* 1–174.

Kann, L., & others (2018, June 15). Youth Risk Behavior Surveillance–United States, 2017. *MMWR, 67,* 1–479.

Kanoy, K., Ulku-Steiner, B., Cox, M., & Burchinal, M. (2003). Marital relationship and individual psychological characteristics that predict physical punishment of children. *Journal of Family Psychology, 17,* 20–28.

Kantoch, A., & others (2018). Treatment of cardiovascular diseases among elderly residents of long-term care facilities. *Journal of the American Medical Directors Association, 19,* 428–432.

Kaplan, D.L., Jones, E.J., Olson, E.C., & Yunzal-Butler, C.B. (2013). Early age of first sex and health risk in an urban adolescent population. *Journal of School Health, 83,* 350–356.

Kaplan, R.M., & Saccuzzo, D.P. (2018). *Psychological testing* (9th ed.). Boston: Cengage.

Karantzas, G.C., Evans, L., & Foddy, M. (2010). The role of attachment in current and future parent caregiving. *Journals of Gerontology B: Psychological Sciences and Social Sciences, 65,* 573–580.

Karlamangla, A.S., & others (2013). Biological correlates of adult cognition: Midlife in the United States (MIDUS). *Neurobiology of Aging, 35*(2), 387–394.

Karlamangla, A.S., & others (2017). Evidence for cognitive aging in midlife women: Study of women's health across the nation. *PLoS One, 12*(1), e169008.

Karnes, F.A., & Stephens, K.R. (2008). *Achieving excellence: Educating the gifted and talented.* Upper Saddle River, NJ: Prentice Hall.

Karney, B.R., Garvin, C.W., & Thomas, M.S. (2003). *Family Formation in Florida 2003 baseline survey of attitudes, beliefs, and demographics relating to marriage and family formation.* Gainesville, FL: The University of Florida. Retrieved from http://www.phhp.ufl.edu/~usringe/FMP/Publications/REPORT.pdf

Karniol, R., Grosz, E., & Schorr, I. (2003). Caring, gender-role orientation, and volunteering. *Sex Roles, 49,* 11–19.

Karreman, A., van Tuiji, C., van Aken, M.A.G., & Dekovic, M. (2008). Parenting, coparenting, and effortful control in preschoolers. *Journal of Family Psychology, 22,* 30–40.

Karthaus, M., Wascher, E., & Getzmann, S. (2018). Proactive vs. reactive car driving: EEG evidence for different driving strategies for older drivers. *PLoS One, 13*(1), e0191500.

Kashdan, T.B., & others (2018). Sexuality leads to boosts in mood and meaning in life with no evidence for the reverse direction: A daily diary investigation. *Emotion, 18,* 563–576.

Kassing, F., & others (2019). Using early childhood behavior problems to predict adult convictions. *Journal of Abnormal Child Psychology, 47,* 765–778.

Kastbom, A.A., Sydsjo, G., Bladh, M., Priee, G., & Svedin, C.G. (2015). Sexual debut before the age of 14 leads to poorer psychosocial health and risky behavior later in life. *Acta Pediatrica, 104,* 91–100.

Kastenbaum, R.J. (2004). *Death, society, and human experience* (8th ed.). Boston: Allyn & Bacon.

Kastenbaum, R.J. (2007). *Death, society, and human experience* (9th ed.). Boston: Allyn & Bacon.

Kastenbaum, R.J. (2009). *Death, society, and human experience* (10th ed.). Boston: Allyn & Bacon.

Kastenbaum, R.J. (2012). *Death, society, and human experience* (11th ed.). Upper Saddle River, NJ: Pearson.

Kaszniak, A.W., & Menchola, M. (2012). Behavioral neuroscience of emotion in aging. *Current Topics in Behavioral Neuroscience, 10,* 51–56.

Kato, T. (2005). The relationship between coping with stress due to romantic break-ups and mental health. *Japanese Journal of Social Psychology, 20,* 171–180.

Katz, L. (1999). Curriculum disputes in early childhood education. *ERIC Clearinghouse on Elementary and Early Childhood Education,* Document EDO-PS-99-13.

Kauffman, J.M., McGee, K., & Brigham, M. (2004). Enabling or disabling? Observations on changes in special education. *Phi Delta Kappan, 85,* 613–620.

Kaufman, A.S., Schneider, W.J., & Kaufman, J.C. (2020, in press). Psychometric approaches to intelligence. In R.J. Sternberg (Ed.), *Human intelligence.* New York: Cambridge University Press.

Kaufman, A.S., & Sternberg, R.J. (Eds.) (2019). *Cambridge handbook of creativity* (2nd ed.). New York: Cambridge University Press.

Kaufman, J.M., & others (2019, in press). Aging and the male reproductive system. *Endocrine Reviews.*

Kaufman, S.B., & others (2016). Openness to experience and intellect differentially predict creative achievement in the arts and sciences. *Journal of Personality, 84,* 248–258.

Kaup, A.R., Harmell, A.L., & Yaffe, K. (2019). Conscientiousness is associated with lower risk of dementia among Black and White older adults. *Neuroepidemiology, 52,* 86–92.

Kaur, M., Singh, H., & Ahula, G.K. (2012). Cardiac performance in relation to age of onset of menopause. *Journal of the Indian Medical Association, 109,* 234–237.

Kawagoe, T., & Sekiyama, K. (2014). Visually encoded working memory is closely associated with mobility in older adults. *Experimental Brain Research, 232,* 2035–2043.

Kawai, M., & others (2010). Developmental trends in mother-infant interaction from 4 months to 42 months: Using an observation technique. *Journal of Epidemiology, 20*(Suppl. 2), S427–S434.

Kawakita, T., & others (2016). Adverse maternal and neonatal outcomes in adolescent pregnancy. *Journal of Pediatric and Adolescent Gynecology, 29,* 130–136.

Kayama, H., & others (2014). Effects of a Kinect-based exercise game on improving executive cognitive performance in community-dwelling elderly: Case control study. *Journal of Medical Internet Research, 16,* e61.

Kayle, J.A., & others (2019, in press). Baby-friendly community initiative–from national guidelines to implementation: A multisectoral platform for improving infant and young child feeding practices and integrated health services. *Maternal and Child Nutrition.*

Keage, H.A., & others (2012). What sleep characteristics predict cognitive decline in the elderly? *Sleep Medicine, 13,* 886–892.

Keating, D.P. (1990). Adolescent thinking. In S.S. Feldman & G.R. Elliott (Eds.), *At the threshold: The developing adolescent.* Cambridge, MA: Harvard University Press.

Keating, D.P. (2004). Cognitive and brain development. In R. Lerner & L. Steinberg (Eds.), *Handbook of adolescent psychology* (2nd ed.). New York: Wiley.

Keen, R. (2005). Unpublished review of J.W. Santrock, *A topical approach to life-span development,* 3rd ed. (New York: McGraw-Hill).

Keen, R. (2011). The development of problem solving in young children: A critical cognitive skill. *Annual Review of Psychology* (Vol. 63). Palo Alto, CA: Annual Reviews.

Keen, R., Lee, M-H., & Adolph, K.E. (2014). Planning and action: A developmental progression for tool use. *Ecological Psychology, 26,* 98–108.

Keenan, K., & others (2017). Life-course partnership history and midlife health behaviors in a population-based birth cohort. *Journal of Epidemiology and Community Health, 71,* 232–238.

Kell, H.J., & Lubinski, D. (2014). The study of mathematically precocious youth at maturity: Insights into elements of genius. In D.K. Simonton (Ed.), *Wiley-Blackwell handbook of genius.* New York: Wiley.

Kell, H.J., Lubinski, D., & Benbow, C.P. (2013). Who rises to the top? Early indicators. *Psychological Science, 24,* 648–659.

Kelleher, K., Reece, J., & Sandel, M. (2019, in press). The Healthy Neighborhood, Healthy Families Initiative. *Pediatrics.*

Keller, H., & Bard, K.A. (Eds.) (2017). *The cultural nature of attachment.* Cambridge, MA: MIT Press.

Keller, S., & others (2019, in press). A look at culture and stigma of suicide: Textual analysis of community theatre performances. *International Journal of Environmental Research and Public Health.*

Kellman, P.J., & Banks, M.S. (1998). Infant visual perception. In W. Damon (Ed.), *Handbook of child psychology* (5th ed., Vol. 2). New York: Wiley.

Kelly, C., & others (2019). The effectiveness of a classroom-based phonological awareness program for 4-5-year-olds. *International Journal of Speech-Language Pathology, 21,* 101-113.

Kelly, D.J., & others (2007). Cross-race preferences for same-race face extend beyond the African versus Caucasian contrast in 3-month-old infants. *Infancy, 11,* 87-95.

Kelly, D.J., & others (2009). Development of the other-race effect in infancy: Evidence towards universality? *Journal of Experimental Child Psychology, 104,* 105-114.

Kelly, J.P., Borchert, J., & Teller, D.Y. (1997). The development of chromatic and achromatic sensitivity in infancy as tested with the sweep VEP. *Vision Research, 37,* 2057-2072.

Kelly, J.R. (1996). Leisure. In J.E. Birren (Ed.), *Encyclopedia of gerontology* (Vol. 2). San Diego: Academic Press.

Kelly, L.M., Becker, S.J., & Spirito, A. (2017). Parental monitoring protects against the effects of parent and adolescent depressed mood on adolescent drinking. *Addictive Behaviors, 75,* 7-11.

Kelly, Y., & others (2013). Light drinking versus abstinence in pregnancy—behavioral and cognitive outcomes in 7-year-old children: A longitudinal cohort study. *BJOG, 120,* 1340-1347.

Keltner, K.W. (2013). *Tiger babies strike back.* New York: William Morrow.

Kemp, B.J., & others (2019, in press). Longitudinal changes in domains of physical activity during childhood and adolescence: A systematic review. *Journal of Science and Medicine in Sport.*

Kempermann, G. (2019, in press). Environmental enrichment, new neurons, and the neurobiology of individuality. *Nature Reviews. Neuroscience.*

Kempermann, G., van Praag, H., & Gage, F.H. (2000). Activity-dependent regulation of neuronal plasticity and self repair. *Progress in Brain Research 127,* 35-48.

Kendler, K.S., & others (2017). Divorce and the onset of alcohol use disorder: A Swedish population-based longitudinal cohort and co-relative study. *American Journal of Psychiatry, 174,* 45-58.

Kennedy, K.M., & others (2015). Lifespan age trajectory differences in functional brain activation under conditions of low and high processing demands. *NeuroImage, 104,* 31-34.

Kennell, J.H. (2006). Randomized controlled trial of skin-to-skin contact from birth versus conventional incubator for physiological stabilization in 1200 g to 2199 g newborns. *Acta Paediatrica, 95,* 15-16.

Kennell, J.H., & McGrath, S.K. (1999). Commentary: Practical and humanistic lessons from the third world for perinatal caregivers everywhere. *Birth, 26,* 9-10.

Kenney, E.L., & Gortmaker, S.L. (2017). United States adolescents' television, computer, videogame, smartphone, and tablet use: Associations with sugary drinks, sleep, physical activity, and obesity. *Journal of Pediatrics, 182,* 144-149.

Kenyon, C. (2010). A pathway that links reproductive status to lifespan in *Caenorhabditis elegans. Annals of the New York Academy of Sciences, 1204,* 156-162.

Kerig, P.K. (2019). Parenting and family systems. In M.H. Bornstein (Ed.), *Handbook of parenting* (3rd ed.). New York: Routledge.

Kerns, K.A., & Brumariu, L.E. (2014). Is insecure attachment a risk factor for the development of anxiety in childhood or adolescence? *Child Development Perspectives, 8,* 12-17.

Kerns, K.A., & Brumariu, L.E. (2016). Attachment in middle childhood. In J. Cassidy & P. Shaver (Eds.), *Handbook of attachment* (3rd ed.). New York: Guilford.

Kerns, K.A., & Seibert, A.C. (2012). Finding your way through the thicket: Promising approaches to assessing attachment in middle childhood. In E. Waters, B. Vaughn, & H. Waters (Eds.), *Measuring attachment.* New York: Guilford.

Kerns, K.A., Siener, S., & Brumariu, L.E. (2011). Mother-child relationships, family context, and child characteristics as predictors of anxiety symptoms in middle childhood. *Development and Psychopathology, 23,* 593-604.

Kershaw, K.N., & others (2014). Associations of stressful life events and social strain with incident cardiovascular disease in the Women's Health Initiative. *Journal of the American Heart Association, 3*(3), e000687.

Kershner, J.R. (2019). Neurobiological systems in dyslexia. *Trends in Neuroscience and Education, 14,* 11-24.

Kerstis, B., Aslund, C., & Sonnby, K. (2018). More secure attachment to the father and the mother is associated with fewer depressive symptoms in adolescence. *Uppsala Journal of Medical Sciences, 123,* 62-67.

Kerstis, B., & others (2016). Association between parental depressive symptoms and impaired bonding with the infant. *Archives of Women's Mental Health, 19,* 87-94.

Kesaniemi, J., & others (2019). Exposure to environmental radionuclides associates with tissue-specific impacts on telomerase expression and telomere length. *Scientific Reports, 9*(1), 850.

Ketcham, C.J., & Stelmach, G.E. (2001). Age-related declines in motor control. In J.E. Birren & K.W. Schaie (Eds.), *Handbook of the psychology of aging* (5th ed.). San Diego: Academic Press.

Kettunen, O., Vuorimaa, T., & Vasankari, T. (2015). A 12-month exercise intervention decreased stress symptoms and increased mental resources among working adults—results perceived after a 12-month follow-up. *International Journal of Occupational Medicine and Environmental Health, 28,* 157-168.

Keunen, K., Counsell, S.J., & Benders, M.J. (2017). The emergence of functional architecture during early brain development. *NeuroImage, 160,* 2-14.

Keyes, K.M., Hatzenbuehler, M.L., & Hasin, D.S. (2011). Stressful life experiences, alcohol consumption, and alcohol use disorders: The epidemiological evidence for four main types of stressors. *Psychopharmacology, 218*(1), 1-17.

Keyes, K.M., Maslowsky, J., Hamilton, A., & Schulenberg, J. (2015). The great sleep recession: Changes in sleep duration among U.S. adolescents, 1991-2012. *Pediatrics, 135.*

Keysar, B., Lin, S., & Barr, D.J. (2003). Limits on theory of mind use in adults. *Cognition, 89,* 25-41.

Khairullah, A., & others (2014). Testosterone trajectories and reference ranges in a large longitudinal sample of adolescent males. *PLoS One, 9*(9), e108838.

Khaligh-Razavi, S.M., & others (2019). Integrated cognitive assessment: Speed and accuracy of visual processing as a reliable proxy to cognitive performance. *Scientific Reports, 9*(1), 1102.

Khalsa, A.S., & others (2017). Attainment of '5-2-1-0' obesity recommendations in preschool-aged children. *Preventive Medicine Reports, 8,* 79-87.

Khan, S.S., & others (2018). Association of body mass index with lifetime risk of cardiovascular disease and compression of morbidity. *JAMA Cardiology, 3,* 280-287.

Kharitonova, M., Winter, W., & Sheridan, M.A. (2015). As working memory grows: A developmental account of neural bases of working memory capacity in 5- to 8-year-old children and adults. *Journal of Cognitive Neuroscience, 27,* 1775-1788.

Khodaeian, M., & others (2015). Effects of vitamins C and E on insulin resistance in diabetes: A meta-analysis study. *European Journal of Clinical Investigation, 45,* 1161-1174.

Khoury, J.E., & Milligan, K. (2019, in press). Comparing executive functioning in children and adolescents with fetal alcohol spectrum disorders and ADHD: A meta-analysis. *Journal of Attention Disorders.*

Khurana, A., & others (2012). Early adolescent sexual debut: The mediating role of working memory ability, sensation seeking, and impulsivity. *Developmental Psychology, 48*(5), 1416-1428.

Khurana, A., & others (2019). Media violence exposure and aggression in adolescents: A risk and resilience perspective. *Aggressive Behavior, 45,* 70-81.

Kiang, L., Witkow, M.R., & Champagne, M.C. (2013). Normative changes in ethnic and American identities and links with adjustment among Asian American adolescents. *Developmental Psychology, 49,* 1713-1722.

Kidd, C., Piantadosi, S.T., & Aslin, R.N. (2012). The Goldilocks effect: Human infants allocate attention to visual sequences that are neither too simple nor too complex. *PLoS One, 7*(5), e36399.

Kiecolt-Glaser, J.K. (2018). Marriage, divorce, and the immune system. *American Psychologist, 73,* 1098-1108.

Kiecolt-Glaser, J.K., & Wilson, S.J. (2017). Caregiver vulnerability and brain structural markers: Compounding risk. *American Journal of Geriatric Psychiatry, 25,* 592-594.

Kiecolt-Glaser, J.K., Wilson, S.J., & Madison, A. (2019, in press). Marriage and gut (microbiome) feelings: Tracing novel dyadic pathways to accelerated aging. *Psychosomatic Medicine.*

Kiecolt-Glaser, J.K., & others (2003). Chronic stress and age-related increases in the proinflammatory cytokine IL-6. *Proceedings of the National Academy of Science USA, 100,* 9090-9095.

Kilford, E.J., Garrett, E., & Blakemore, S.J. (2016). The development of social cognition in adolescence: An integrated perspective. *Neuroscience and Biobehavioral Reviews, 70,* 106-120.

Kilic, S., & others (2012). Environmental tobacco smoke exposure during intrauterine period promotes granulosa cell apoptosis: A prospective, randomized study. *Journal of Maternal-Fetal and Neonatal Medicine, 25,* 1904-1908.

Killen, M., & Dahl, A. (2018). Moral judgment: Reflective, interactive, spontaneous, challenging, and always evolving. In K. Gray & J. Graham (Eds.), *The atlas of moral psychology.* New York: Guilford.

Killen, M., & Smetana, J.G. (2015). Morality: Origins and development. In R.M. Lerner (Ed.), *Handbook of child psychology and developmental science* (7th ed.). New York: Wiley.

Killer, B., & others (2019, in press). A meta-analysis of the relationship between moral disengagement and bullying roles in youth. *Aggressive Behavior.*

Kim, A., Lee, J.A., & Park, H.S. (2018). Health behaviors and illness according to marital status in middle-aged Koreans. *Journal of Public Health, 40,* e99-e106.

Kim, B.R., & others (2017). Trajectories of mothers' emotional availability: Relations with infant temperament in predicting attachment security. *Attachment and Human Development, 19,* 38-57.

Kim, D.J., & others (2019). Childhood poverty and the organization of the structural brain connectome. *NeuroImage, 184,* 409-416.

Kim, E.B., Chen, C., Smetana, J.G., & Greenberger, E. (2016). Does children's moral compass waver under social behavior? Using the conformity paradigm to test preschoolers' moral and social-conventional judgments. *Journal of Experimental Child Psychology, 150,* 241-251.

Kim, E.S., Chopik, W.J., & Smith, J. (2014). Are people healthier if their partners are more optimistic? The dyadic effect of optimism on health among older adults. *Journal of Psychosomatic Research, 76,* 447-453.

Kim, H. (2019). To prevent child maltreatment, home visiting programs are one part of a complete response. *American Journal of Public Health, 109,* 653-655.

Kim, H., & others (2018). Developmental relations among motor and cognitive processes and mathematics skills. *Child Development, 89,* 476-494.

Kim, H.J., & Pedersen, S. (2010). Young adolescents' metacognition and domain knowledge as predictors of hypothesis-development performance in a computer-supported context. *Educational Psychology, 30,* 565-582.

Kim, J., & Fletcher, J.M. (2018). The influence of classmates on adolescent criminal activities in the United States. *Deviant Behavior, 39,* 275-292.

Kim, J., & Kim, H.K. (2019). Intergenerational transmission of effortful control in families with school-age children in Korea. *Journal of Family Psychology, 33,* 88-97.

Kim, J., Smith, T.W., & Kang, J.H. (2015). Religious affiliation, religious service attendance, and mortality. *Journal of Religion and Health, 54,* 2052-2072.

Kim, J.I., & others (2019, in press). Interaction of DRD4 methylation and phthalate metabolites affects continuous performance test performance in ADHD. *Journal of Attention Disorders.*

Kim, K.H. (2010, July 10). Interview. *Newsweek,* 42-48.

Kim, K.W., & others (2019). Associations of parental general monitoring with adolescent weight-related behaviors and weight status. *Obesity, 27,* 280-287.

Kim, M., Woodhouse, S.S., & Dai, C. (2018). Learning to provide children with a secure base and safe haven: The Circle of Security-Parenting (COS-P) group intervention. *Journal of Clinical Psychology, 74,* 1319-1332.

Kim, M.J., Catalano, R.F., Haggerty, K.P., & Abbott, R.D. (2011). Bullying at elementary school and problem behavior in young adulthood: A study of bullying, violence, and substance use from age 11 to age 21. *Criminal Behavior and Mental Health, 21,* 136-144.

Kim, P., Strathearn, L., & Swain, J.E. (2016). The maternal brain and its plasticity in humans. *Hormones and Behavior, 77,* 113-123.

Kim, S., & Hasher, L. (2005). The attraction effect in decision making: Superior performance by older adults. *Quarterly Journal of Experimental Psychology, 58A,* 120-133.

Kim, S., & Kochanska, G. (2017). Relational antecedents and social implications of the emotion of empathy: Evidence from three studies. *Emotion, 17,* 981-992.

Kim, S., & others (2014). Oxytocin and postpartum depression: Delivering on what's known and what's not. *Brain Research, 1580,* 219-232.

Kim, S.H., & others (2019, in press). Early menarche and risk-taking behavior in Korean adolescent students. *Asia Pacific-Psychiatry.*

Kim, S.T., Wang, Y., Chen, Q., Shen, Y., & Hou, Y. (2015). Parent-child acculturation profiles as predictors of Chinese American adolescents' academic trajectories. *Journal of Youth and Adolescence, 44,* 1263-1274.

Kim, S.Y., & others (2018). Culture's influence on stressors, parental socialization, and developmental processes in the mental health of children of immigrants. *Annual Review of Clinical Psychology* (Vol. 14). Palo Alto, CA: Annual Reviews.

Kim, S.Y., & others (2018). Lack of sleep is associated with Internet use for leisure. *PLoS One, 13*(1), e191713.

Kim, Y.B., & Lee, S.H. (2019, in press). Social support network types and depressive symptoms among community-dwelling older adults in South Korea. *Asia Pacific Journal of Public Health.*

Kimble, M., Neacsiu, A.D., Flack, W.F., & Horner, J. (2008). Risk of unwanted sex for college women: Evidence for a red zone. *Journal of American College Health, 57,* 331-338.

Kim-Fuchs, C., & others (2014). Chronic stress accelerates pancreatic cancer growth and invasion: A critical role for beta-adrenergic signaling in the pancreatic microenvironment. *Brain, Behavior, and Immunity, 40,* 40-47.

Kimlin, J.A., Black, A.A., & Wood, J.M. (2017). Nighttime driving in older adults: Effects of glare and association with mesopic visual function. *Investigative Ophthalmology and Visual Science, 58,* 2796-2803.

Kimura, Y., & others (2018). Development of a new diet-induced obesity (DIO) model using Wistar lean rats. *Experimental Animals, 67,* 155-161.

King, B.M., Carr, D.C., & Taylor, M.G. (2019, in press). Depressive symptoms and the buffering effect of resilience on widowhood by gender. *Gerontologist.*

King, B.M., & Regan, M. (2019). *Human sexuality today* (9th ed.). Upper Saddle River, NJ: Pearson.

King, J.D., & others (2018). The interpersonal-psychological theory of suicide in adolescents: A preliminary report of changes following treatment. *Suicide and Life-Threatening Behavior, 48,* 294-304.

King, K.A., Topalian, A., & Vidourek, R.A. (2019, in press). Religiosity and adolescent major depressive episodes among 12-17-year-olds. *Journal of Religion and Health.*

King, K.A., Vidourek, R.A., & Merianos, A.L. (2016). Authoritarian parenting and youth depression: Results from a national study. *Journal of Prevention and Intervention in the Community, 44,* 130-139.

King, L.A. (2017). *The science of psychology: An appreciative view* (4th ed.). New York: McGraw-Hill.

King, L.A. (2019). *Experience psychology* (4th ed.). New York: McGraw-Hill.

King, L.A., & Hicks, J.A. (2007). Whatever happened to "What might have been?" Regrets, happiness, and maturity. *American Psychologist, 62,* 625-636.

King, P.E., & Boyatzis, C.J. (2015). The nature and functions of religious and spiritual development in childhood and adolescence. In R.M. Lerner (Ed.), *Handbook of child psychology and developmental science* (7th ed.). New York: Oxford University Press.

King, P.E., Carr, A., & Boiter, C. (2011). Spirituality, religiosity, and youth thriving. In R.M. Lerner, J.V. Lerner, & J.B. Benson (Eds.), *Advances in child development and behavior: Positive youth development.* New York: Elsevier.

King, V., & Scott, M.E. (2005). A comparison of cohabiting relationships among older and younger adults. *Journal of Marriage and the Family, 67,* 271-285.

Kingdon, D., Cardoso, C., & McGrath, J.J. (2016). Research review: Executive function deficits in fetal alcohol spectrum disorders and attention-deficit/hyperactivity disorder—a meta-analysis. *Journal of Child Psychology and Psychiatry, 57,* 116-131.

Kingsbury, A.M., Plotnikova, M., & Najman, J.M. (2018). Commonly occurring adverse birth outcomes and maternal depression: A longitudinal study. *Public Health, 155,* 43-54.

Kins, E., & Beyers, W. (2010). Failure to launch, failure to achieve criteria for adulthood. *Journal of Adolescent Research, 25,* 206-217.

Kinsler, J.J., & others (2019, in press). A content analysis of how sexual behavior and reproductive health are being portrayed on primetime television shows being watched by teens and young adults. *Health Communication.*

Kinugawa, K. (2019). Plasticity of the brain and cognition in older adults. In R. Fernandez-Ballesteros, A. Benetos, & J-M. Robine (Eds.), *Cambridge handbook of successful aging.* New York: Cambridge University Press.

Kirby, D.B., Laris, B.A., & Rolleri, L.A. (2007). Sex and HIV education programs: Their impact on sexual behavior of young people throughout the world. *Journal of Adolescent Health, 40,* 206-217.

Kircaburun, K., & Griffiths, M.D. (2018). Instagram addiction and the Big Five of personality: The mediating role of self-liking. *Journal of Behavioral Addictions, 7,* 158-170.

Kirk, S.M., & Kirk, E.P. (2016). Sixty minutes of physical activity per day included within preschool academic lessons improves early literacy. *Journal of School Health, 86,* 155-163.

Kirkham, N.Z., Wagner, J.B., Swan, K.A., & Johnson, S.P. (2012). Sound support: Intermodal information facilitates infants' perception of an occluded trajectory. *Infant Behavior and Development, 35,* 174-178.

Kirkland, J.B., & Meyer-Ficca, M.L. (2018). Niacin. *Advances in Food and Nutrition Research, 83,* 83-149.

Kirkorian, H.L., Anderson, D.R., & Keen, R. (2012). Age differences in online processing of video: An eye movement study. *Child Development, 83,* 497-507.

Kirkorian, H.L., Wartella, E.A., & Anderson, D.A. (2008). Media and young children's learning. *Future of Children, 18*(1), 39-61.

Kito, M. (2005). Self-disclosure in romantic relationships and friendships among American and Japanese college students. *Journal of Social Psychology, 145,* 127-140.

Kiuhara, S.A., Graham, S., & Hawken, L.S. (2009). Teaching writing to high school students: A national survey. *Journal of Educational Psychology, 101,* 136-160.

Klahr, A.M., & Burt, S.A. (2014). Elucidating the etiology of individual differences in parenting:

A meta-analysis of behavioral genetic research. *Psychological Bulletin, 140,* 544–586.

Klatt, J., & Enright, R. (2009). Investigating the place of forgiveness within the positive youth development paradigm. *Journal of Moral Education, 38,* 35–52.

Klaus, M., & Kennell, H.H. (1976). *Maternal-infant bonding.* St. Louis: Mosby.

Kleiman, E.M., & others (2017). Optimism and well-being: A prospective multi-method and multi-dimensional examination of optimism as a resilience factor following the occurrence of stressful life events. *Cognition and Emotion, 31,* 269–283.

Klein, A.C. (2019). Q & A: Answering your ESSA questions. *Education Week, 38*(27), 20–21.

Klein, M.R., & others (2018). Bidirectional relations between temperament and parenting predicting preschool-age children's adjustment. *Journal of Clinical Child and Adolescent Psychology, 47*(Suppl. 1), S113–S126.

Klein, S. (2012). *State of public school segregation in the United States, 2007–2010.* Washington, DC: Feminist Majority Foundation.

Kleinert, M., & others (2018). Animal models in obesity and diabetes mellitus. *Nature Reviews. Endocrinology, 14,* 140–162.

Kleinman, C., & Reizer, A. (2018). Negative caregiving representations and postpartum depression: The mediating roles of parenting efficacy and relationship satisfaction. *Health for Women International, 39,* 79–84.

Klettke, B., & others (2019, in press). Sexting and psychological distress: The role of unwanted and coerced sexts. *Cyberpsychology, Behavior, and Social Networking.*

Kliegel, M., & others (2016). Prospective memory in older adults: Where we are now and what is next. *Gerontology, 62,* 459–466.

Klimstra, T.A., Hale, W.W., Raaijmakers, Q.A., Branje, S.J.T., & Meeus, W.H. (2010). Identity formation in adolescence: Change or stability? *Journal of Youth and Adolescence, 39,* 150–162.

Klimstra, T.A., & others (2018). Personality development and adjustment in college: A multifaceted, cross-national view. *Journal of Personality and Social Psychology, 115,* 338–361.

Klinenberg, E. (2012, February 4). Sunday Review: One's a crowd. *The New York Times,* Retrieved from http://www.nytimes.com/2012/02/05/opinion/sunday/living-alone-means-being-social.html?pagewanted5 all&_r50

Klinenberg, E. (2013). *Going solo: The extraordinary rise and surprising appeal of living alone.* New York: Penguin.

Kling, K.C., Hyde, J.S., Showers, C.J., & Buswell, B.N. (1999). Gender differences in self-esteem: A meta-analysis. *Psychological Bulletin, 125,* 470–500.

Klug, W.S., & others (2020). *Essentials of genetics* (10th ed.). Upper Saddle River, NJ: Pearson.

Knack, N., & others (2019, in press). Primary and secondary prevention of child sexual abuse. *International Review of Psychiatry.*

Knight, L.F., & Morales Hope, D.A. (2012). Correlates of same-sex attractions and behaviors among self-identified heterosexual university students. *Archives of Sexual Behavior, 41,* 1199–1208.

Kobak, R.R., & Kerig, P.K. (2015). Introduction to the special issue: Attachment-based treatments for adolescents. *Attachment and Human Development, 17,* 111–118.

Kobayashi, M., & others (2019, in press). Perceptual narrowing towards adult faces is a cross-cultural phenomenon in infancy: A behavioral and near-infrared spectroscopy study with Japanese infants. *Developmental Science.*

Kobayashi, S., & others (2017). Assessment and support during early labor for improving birth outcomes. *Cochrane Database of Systematic Reviews, 4,* CD011516.

Koch, S., & others (2019, in press). Effects of male postpartum depression on father-infant interactions: The mediating role of face processing. *Infant Mental Health Journal.*

Kochanska, G., & Aksan, N. (2007). Conscience in childhood: Past, present, and future. *Merrill-Palmer Quarterly, 50,* 299–310.

Kochanska, G., Barry, R.A., Stellern, S.A., & O'Bleness, J.J. (2010). Early attachment organization moderates the parent-child mutually coercive pathway to children's antisocial conduct. *Child Development, 80,* 1288–1300.

Kochanska, G., & Kim, S. (2012). Toward a new understanding of the legacy of early attachments for future antisocial trajectories: Evidence from two longitudinal studies. *Development and Psychopathology, 24*(3), 783–806.

Kochanska, G., & Kim, S. (2013). Early attachment organization with both parents and future behavior problems: From infancy to middle childhood. *Child Development, 84*(1), 283–296.

Kochanska, G., & others (2010). Positive socialization mechanisms in secure and insecure parent-child dyads: Two longitudinal studies. *Journal of Child Psychology and Psychiatry, 51,* 998–1009.

Kochendorfer, L.B., & Kerns, K.A. (2017). Perceptions of parent-child attachment relationships and friendship qualities: Predictors of romantic relationship involvement and quality in adolescence. *Journal of Youth and Adolescence, 46,* 1009–1021.

Koehn, A., & Kerns, K.A. (2018). Parent-child attachment: Meta-analysis of associations with parenting behaviors in middle childhood and adolescence. *Attachment and Human Development, 20,* 378–405.

Koenig, L.B., McGue, M., & Iacono, W.G. (2008). Stability and change in religiousness during emerging adulthood. *Developmental Psychology, 44,* 523–543.

Koenig, S.N., Lincoln, J., & Garg, V. (2019, in press). Genetic basis of aortic valvular disease. *Current Opinion in Cardiology.*

Koffer, R., & others (2019). The role of general and daily control beliefs for affective stressor-reactivity across adulthood and old age. *Journals of Gerontology B: Psychological Sciences and Social Sciences, 74,* 242–253.

Koh, H. (2014). The Teen Pregnancy Prevention Program: An evidence-based public health program model. *Journal of Adolescent Health, 54*(Suppl. 1), S1–S2.

Kohen, D.E., Leventhal, T., Dahinten, V.S., & McIntosh, C.N. (2008). Neighborhood disadvantage: Pathways of effects for young children. *Child Development, 79,* 156–169.

Kohlberg, L. (1958). *The development of modes of moral thinking and choice in the years 10 to 16.* Unpublished doctoral dissertation, University of Chicago.

Kohlberg, L. (1969). Stage and sequence: The cognitive-developmental approach to socialization. In D.A. Goslin (Ed.), *Handbook of socialization theory and research.* Chicago: Rand McNally.

Kohlberg, L. (1986). A current statement on some theoretical issues. In S. Modgil & C. Modgil (Eds.), *Lawrence Kohlberg.* Philadelphia: Falmer.

Kojola, E., & Moen, P. (2016). No more lock-step retirement: Boomers' shifting meanings of work and retirement. *Journal of Aging Studies, 36,* 59–70.

Kok, R., & others (2014). Parenting, corpus callosum, and executive function in preschool children. *Child Neuropsychology, 20,* 583–606.

Kok, R., & others (2015). Normal variation in early parental sensitivity predicts child structural brain development. *Journal of the American Academy of Child and Adolescent Psychiatry, 54,* 824–831.

Kokkinos, P., & others (2019, in press). Cardiorespiratory fitness, body mass index, and heart failure. *European Journal of Heart Failure.*

Kolesnik, A., & others (2019). Increased cortical reactivity to repeated tones at 8 months in infants with later ASD. *Translational Psychiatry, 9*(1), 46.

Kollath-Cattano, C.L., Mann, E.S., Zegbe, E.M., & Thrasher, J.F. (2018). Sexual scripts in contemporary Mexican cinema: A quantitative content analysis. *Sexuality and Culture, 22,* 90–105.

Koller, S.H., Santana, J.P., & Raffaelli, M. (2018). Poverty, risk, and resilience: The case of street-involved youth. In J.E. Lansford & P. Banati (Eds.), *Handbook of adolescent development research and its impact on global policy.* New York: Oxford University Press.

Kolokotroni, P., Anagnostopoulos, F., & Hantzi, A. (2018). The role of optimism, social constraints, coping, and cognitive processing in psychosocial adjustment among breast cancer survivors. *Journal of Clinical Psychology in Medical Settings, 25,* 452–462.

Kondolot, M., & others (2017). Risk factors for overweight and obesity in children 2–6 years. *Journal of Pediatric Endocrinology and Metabolism, 30,* 499–505.

Kong, A., & others (2012). Rate of *de novo* mutations and the importance of father's age to disease risk. *Nature, 488,* 471–475.

Kong, L.N., & others (2019). Relationships among social support, coping strategy, and depressive symptoms in older adults with diabetes. *Journal of Gerontological Nursing, 45,* 40–46.

Konrath, S.H., Chopik, W.J., Hsing, C.K., & O'Brien, E. (2014). Changes in adult attachment styles in American college students over time: A meta-analysis. *Personality and Social Psychology Bulletin, 18,* 326–348.

Konstam, V. (2019). *Romantic lives of emerging adults.* New York: Oxford University Press.

Kontis, V., & others (2017). Future life expectancy in 35 industrialized countries: Projections with a Bayesian model ensemble. *Lancet, 389*(10076), 1323–1335.

Koo, Y.J., & others (2012). Pregnancy outcomes according to increasing maternal age. *Taiwan Journal of Obstetrics and Gynecology, 51,* 60–65.

Koorevaar, A.M., & others (2013). Big Five personality factors and depression diagnosis, severity, and age of onset in older adults. *Journal of Affective Disorders, 151,* 178–185.

Kopp, C.B. (1982). The antecedents of self-regulation. *Developmental Psychology, 18,* 199–214.

Kopp, C.B. (1987). The growth of self-regulation: Caregivers and children. In N. Eisenberg (Ed.), *Contemporary topics in developmental psychology.* New York: Wiley.

Kopp, C.B. (2008). Self-regulatory processes. In M.M. Haith & J.B. Benson (Eds.), *Encyclopedia of infant and early childhood development*. Oxford, UK: Elsevier.

Kopp, F., & Lindenberger, U. (2012). Effects of joint attention on long-term memory in 9-month-old infants: An event-related potentials study. *Developmental Science, 15,* 540-556.

Koren, G., & Ornoy, A. (2018). The role of the placenta in drug transport and fetal drug exposure. *Expert Review of Clinical Pharmacology, 11,* 373-385.

Korja, R., & others (2017). The relations between maternal prenatal anxiety or stress and the child's early negative reactivity or self-regulation: A systematic review. *Child Psychiatry and Human Development, 48,* 851-869.

Korner, L.M., & others (2019). Prenatal testosterone exposure is associated with delay of gratification and attention problems/overactive behavior in 3-year-old boys. *Psychoneuroimmunology, 104,* 49-54.

Kornienko, O., Ha, T., & Dishion, T.J. (2019, in press). Dynamic pathways between rejection and antisocial behavior in peer networks: Update and test of confluence model. *Development and Psychopathology*.

Korte, J., Dorssaert, C.H., Westerhof, G.J., & Bohlmeijer, E.T. (2014). Life review in groups? An explorative analysis of social processes that facilitate or hinder the effectiveness of life review. *Aging and Mental Health, 18,* 376-384.

Koster, M., & others (2019, in press). From understanding others' needs to prosocial action: Motor and social abilities promote infants' helping. *Developmental Science*.

Kotovsky, L., & Baillargeon, R. (1994). Calibration-based reasoning about collision events in 11-month-old infants. *Cognition, 51,* 107-129.

Kotre, J. (1984). *Outliving the self: Generativity and the interpretation of lives*. Baltimore: Johns Hopkins University Press.

Kouklari, E.C., Tsermentseli, S., & Monks, C.P. (2019, in press). Developmental trends of hot and cool executive function in school-aged children with and without autism spectrum disorder: Links with theory of mind. *Development and Psychopathology*.

Kovach, C.R., & others (2018). Feasibility and pilot testing of a mindfulness intervention for frail older adults and individuals with dementia. *Research in Gerontological Nursing, 11,* 137-150.

Kovanagi, A., & others (2019, in press). Bullying victimization and suicide attempt among adolescents aged 1-15 years from 48 countries. *Journal of the American Academy of Child and Adolescent Psychiatry*.

Kowalski, R.M., Giumetti, G.W., Schroeder, A.N., & Lattanner, M.R. (2014). Bullying in the digital age: A critical review and meta-analysis of cyberbullying research on youth. *Psychological Bulletin, 140,* 1073-1137.

Koyanagi, A., & others (2019, in press). Bullying victimization and suicide attempt among adolescents aged 12-15 years from 48 countries. *Journal of the American Academy of Child and Adolescent Psychiatry*.

Koyanagi, L., & others (2019). Memory consolidation during sleep and adult hippocampal neurogenesis. *Neural Regeneration Research, 14,* 20-23.

Kozhimanni, K.B., & Hardeman, R.R. (2016). Coverage for doula services: How state Medicaid programs can address concerns about maternity care costs and quality. *Birth, 43,* 97-99.

Kozol, J. (2005). *The shame of the nation*. New York: Crown.

Kraen, M., & others (2017). Ethnocardiographic consequences of smoking status in middle-aged subjects. *Echocardiography, 34,* 14-19.

Kraftt, C.E., & others (2014). An eight-month randomized controlled exercise trial alters brain activation during cognitive tasks in overweight children. *Obesity, 22,* 232-242.

Kraig, E., & others (2018). A randomized control trial to establish the feasibility and safety of rapamycin treatment in an older human cohort: Immunological, physical performance and cognitive effects. *Experimental Gerontology, 105,* 53-69.

Kramer, A.F., & Madden, D.J. (2008). Attention. In F.I.M. Craik & T.A. Salthouse (Eds.), *Handbook of aging and cognition* (3rd ed.). Mahwah, NJ: Erlbaum.

Kramer, H.J., & Lagattuta, K.H. (2018). Affective forecasting. In M.H. Bornstein (Ed.), *SAGE encyclopedia of lifespan human development*. Thousand Oaks, CA: Sage.

Kramer, L. (2006, July 10). Commentary in "How your siblings make you who you are" by J. Kluger. *Time,* 46-55.

Kramer, L., & Perozynski, L. (1999). Parental beliefs about managing sibling conflict. *Developmental Psychology, 35,* 489-499.

Kramer, L., & Radey, C. (1997). Improving sibling relationships among young children: A social skills training model. *Family Relations, 46,* 237-246.

Kramer, L., & others (2019). Siblings. In B.H. Friese (Ed.), *APA handbook of contemporary family psychology*. Washington, DC: APA Books.

Krause, N. (1995). Religiosity and self-esteem among older adults. *Journals of Gerontology B: Psychological Science, 50,* P236-P246.

Krause, N. (2003). Religious meaning and subjective well-being in late life. *Journals of Gerontology B: Psychological Science and Social Science, 58,* S160-S170.

Krause, N. (2008). The social foundations of religious meaning in life. *Research on Aging, 30*(4), 395-427.

Krause, N. (2009). Deriving a sense of meaning in late life. In V.L. Bengtson, D. Gans, N.M. Putney, & M. Silverstein (Eds.), *Handbook of theories of aging*. New York: Springer.

Krause, N. (2019). Assessing the relationships among stress, God-mediated control, and psychological distress/well-being: Does the level of education matter? *Journal of Social Psychology, 159,* 2-14.

Krause, N., Ironson, G., & Hill, P.C. (2017). Volunteer work, religious commitment, and resting pulse rates. *Journal of Religion and Health, 56,* 591-603.

Krause, N., & Pargament, K.I. (2018). Reading the Bible, stressful life events, and hope: Assessing an overlooked coping resource. *Journal of Religion and Health, 57,* 1428-1439.

Kravdal, O., & Grundy, E. (2019). Children's age at parental divorce and depression in early and mid-adulthood. *Population Studies, 73,* 37-56.

Kretch, K.S., & Adolph, K.E. (2017). The organization of exploratory behaviors in infant locomotor planning. *Developmental Science,* e12421.

Krettenauer, T., & Victor, R. (2017). Why be moral? Moral identity motivation and age. *Developmental Psychology, 53,* 1589-1596.

Kreutzer, M.A., Leonard, C., & Flavell, J.H. (1975). An interview study of children's knowledge about memory. *Monographs of the Society for Research in Child Development, 40*(1, Serial No. 159).

Krieger, V., & Amador-Campos, J.A. (2018). Assessment of executive function in ADHD adolescents: Contribution of performance tests and rating scales. *Child Neuropsychology, 24,* 1063-1087.

Kriemler, S., & others (2011). Effect of school-based interventions on activity and fitness in children and adolescents: A review of reviews and systematic update. *British Journal of Sports Medicine, 45,* 923-930.

Kring, A.M. (2000). Gender and anger. In A.H. Fischer (Ed.), *Gender and emotion*. New York: Cambridge University Press.

Krishnan, P. (2017). Concept analysis of good death in long term care residents. *International Journal of Palliative Nursing, 23,* 29-34.

Krishnan, S., & others (2018). Deep brain stimulation for movement disorders. *Neurology India, 66*(Suppl.), S90-S101.

Krishnappa, P., & others (2019). Sildenafil/Viagra in the treatment of premature ejaculation. *International Journal of Impotence Research 31,* 65-70.

Krisnana, I., & others (2019, in press). Adolescent characteristics and parenting style as the determinant of bullying in Indonesia: A cross-sectional study. *International Journal of Adolescent Medicine and Health*.

Kroger, J. (2016). Identity development through adulthood: The move toward "wholeness." In K.C. McLean & M. Syed (Eds.), *Oxford handbook of identity development*. New York: Oxford University Press.

Kroger, J., Martinussen, M., & Marcia, J.E. (2010). Identity change during adolescence and young adulthood: A meta-analysis. *Journal of Adolescence, 33,* 683-698.

Krogh-Jespersen, S., Liberman, Z., & Woodward, A.L. (2015). Think fast! The relationship between goal prediction speed and social competence in infants. *Developmental Science, 18,* 815-823.

Krogh-Jespersen, S., & Woodward, A.L. (2016). Infant origins of social cognition. In L. Balter & C. Tamis-LeMonda (Eds.), *Child psychology* (3rd ed.). New York: Psychology Press.

Krogh-Jespersen, S., & Woodward, A.L. (2018). Reaching the goal: Active experience facilitates 8-month-old infants' prospective analysis of goal-based actions. *Journal of Experimental Psychology, 171,* 31-45.

Krueger, P.M., & Chang, V.W. (2008). Being poor and coping with stress: Health behaviors and the risk of death. *American Journal of Public Health, 98,* 889-896.

Kruger, J., Blanck, H.M., & Gillespie, C. (2006). Dietary and physical activity behaviors among adults successful at weight loss management. *International Journal of Behavioral Nutrition and Physical Activity, 3,* 17.

Kruger, T.H.C., & others (2019). Child sexual offenders show prenatal and epigenetic alterations of the androgen system. *Translational Psychiatry, 9*(1), 28.

Krzepota, J., Sadowska, D., & Biernat, E. (2019, in press). Relationships between physical activity and quality of life in pregnant women in the second and third trimester. *International Journal of Environmental Research and Public Health*.

Ku, P.W., & others (2018). Prospective relationship between objectively measured light physical activity and depressive symptoms in later life. *International Journal of Geriatric Psychiatry, 3,* 58-65.

Kübler-Ross, E. (1969). *On death and dying*. New York: Macmillan.

Kudesia, R., & Talib, H.J. (2019). Fertility counseling for adolescents. *Pediatric Annals, 48,* e86-e91.

Kuebli, J. (1994, March). Young children's understanding of everyday emotions. *Young Children*, 36–48.

Kuersten-Hogan, R. (2017). Bridging the gap across the transition to coparenthood: Triadic interactions and coparenting representations from pregnancy through 12 months postpartum. *Frontiers in Psychology, 8,* 475.

Kuhl, P.K. (1993). Infant speech perception: A window on psycholinguistic development. *International Journal of Psycholinguistics., 9,* 33–56.

Kuhl, P.K. (2000). A new view of language acquisition. *Proceedings of the National Academy of Sciences, 97*(22), 11850–11857.

Kuhl, P.K. (2007). Is speech learning "gated" by the social brain? *Developmental Science, 10,* 110–120.

Kuhl, P.K. (2009). Linking infant speech perception to language acquisition: Phonetic learning predicts language growth. In J. Colombo, P. McCardle, & L. Freund (Eds.), *Infant pathways to language.* New York: Psychology Press.

Kuhl, P.K. (2011). Social mechanisms in early language acquisition: Understanding integrated brain systems and supporting language. In J. Decety & J. Cacioppo (Eds.), *Handbook of social neuroscience.* New York: Oxford University Press.

Kuhl, P.K. (2015). Baby talk. *Scientific American, 313,* 64–69.

Kuhn, D. (1998). Afterword to Volume 2: Cognition, perception, and language. In W. Damon (Ed.), *Handbook of child psychology* (5th ed., Vol. 2). New York: Wiley.

Kuhn, D. (2008). Formal operations from a twenty-first-century perspective. *Human Development, 51,* 48–55.

Kuhn, D. (2009). Adolescent thinking. In R.M. Lerner & L. Steinberg (Eds.), *Handbook of adolescent psychology* (3rd ed.). New York: Wiley.

Kuhn, D. (2011). What is scientific thinking and how does it develop? In U. Goswami (Ed.), *Wiley-Blackwell handbook of childhood cognitive development* (2nd ed.). New York: Wiley-Blackwell.

Kuhn, D. (2013). Reasoning. In P.D. Zelazo (Ed.), *Oxford handbook of developmental psychology.* New York: Oxford University Press.

Kuhn, D., & Franklin, S. (2006). The second decade: What develops (and how)? In W. Damon & R. Lerner (Eds.), *Handbook of child psychology* (6th ed.). New York: Wiley.

Kuiper, J., Broer, J., & van der Wouden, J.C. (2018). Association between physical exercise and psychosocial problems in 96,617 Dutch adolescents in secondary education: A cross-sectional study. *European Journal of Public Health, 28,* 468–473.

Kulmala, J., & others (2013). Perceived stress symptoms in midlife predict disability in old age: A 28-year prospective study. *Journals of Gerontology A: Biological Sciences and Medical Sciences, 68,* 984–991.

Kulu, H. (2014). Marriage duration and divorce: The seven-year itch or a lifelong itch? *Demography, 51,* 881–893.

Kumar, K., & others (2018). Recent advances in the neurobiology and neuropharmacology of Alzheimer's disease. *Biomedicine and Pharmacology, 98,* 297–307.

Kumar, S.V., Oliffe, J.L., & Kelly, M.T. (2018). Promoting postpartum mental health in fathers: Recommendations for nurse practitioners. *American Journal of Men's Health, 12,* 221–228.

Kung, K.T.E., & others (2018). Emotional and behavioral adjustment in 4- to 11-year-old boys and girls with classic congenital adrenal hyperplasia and unaffected siblings. *Psychoneuroendocrinology, 97,* 104–110.

Kunzmann, U. (2019). Wisdom: The royal road to personality growth. In R. Fernandez-Ballesteros, A. Benetos, & J-M. Robine (Eds.), *Cambridge handbook of successful aging.* New York: Cambridge University Press.

Kunzmann, U., & others (2017). Speaking about feelings: Further evidence for multidirectional age differences in anger and sadness. *Psychology and Aging, 32,* 93–103.

Kunzweiler, C. (2007). Twin individuality. *Fresh Ink: Essays from Boston College's First-Year Writing Seminar, 9*(1), 2–3.

Kuo, L.J., & Anderson, R.C. (2012). Effects of early bilingualism on learning phonological regularities in a new language. *Journal of Experimental Child Psychology, 111,* 455–467.

Kuo, P.X., & others (2019, in press). Is one secure attachment enough? Infant cortisol reactivity and the security of infant-mother and infant-father attachments at the end of the first year. *Attachment and Human Development.*

Kupari, M., Talola, N., Luukkaala, T., & Tihtonen, K. (2016). Does an increased cesarean section rate improve neonatal outcome in term pregnancies? *Archives of Gynecology and Obstetrics, 294,* 41–46.

Kuperberg, A. (2014). Age at coresidence, premarital cohabitation, and marriage dissolution: 1985–2009. *Journal of Marriage and Family, 76,* 352–369.

Kuperberg, A., & Padgett, J.E. (2017). Partner meeting contexts and risky behavior in college students' other-sex and same-sex hookups. *Journal of Sex Research, 54,* 55–72.

Kurdek, L.A. (2008). Change in relationship quality for partners from lesbian, gay male, and heterosexual couples. *Journal of Family Psychology, 22,* 701–711.

Kurita, N. (2019). Association of the Great East Japan earthquake and the Daiichi nuclear disaster in Fukushima City, Japan, with birth rates. *JAMA Network Open, 2*(1), e187455.

Kuznetsov, I.A., & Kuznetsov, A.V. (2018). How the formation of amyloid plaques and neurofibrillary tangles may be related: A mathematical modeling study. *Proceedings. Mathematical, Physical, and Engineering Sciences, 474,* 20170777.

Kvalo, S.E., & others (2017). Does increased physical activity in school affect children's executive function and aerobic fitness? *Scandinavian Journal of Medicine and Science in Sports, 27,* 1833–1841.

Kwan, M.Y., Cairney, J., Faulkner, G.E., & Pullenayegum, E.E. (2012). Physical activity and other health-risk behaviors during the transition into early adulthood: A longitudinal cohort study. *American Journal of Preventive Medicine, 42,* 14–20.

Kwon, D., & others (2019, in press). Regional growth trajectories of cortical myelination in adolescents and young adults: Longitudinal validation and functional correlates. *Brain Imaging and Behavior.*

Kymre, I.G. (2014). NICU nurses' ambivalent attitudes in skin-to-skin care practice. *International Journal of Qualitative Studies on Health and Well-Being, 9,* 23297.

Kyratzis, A. (2017). Children's co-construction of sentence and discourse in early childhood: Implications for development. In N. Budwig & others (Eds.), *New perspectives on human development.* New York: Cambridge University Press.

Kyvelidou, A., & Stergiou, N. (2019, in press). Visual and somatosensory contributions to infant sitting postural control. *Somatosensory and Motor Research.*

L

Laborte-Lemoyne, E., Currier, D., & Ellenberg, D. (2017). Exercise during pregnancy enhances cerebral maturation in the newborn: A randomized controlled trial. *Journal of Clinical and Experimental Neuropsychology, 39,* 347–354.

Labouvie-Vief, G. (1986, August). *Modes of knowing and life-span cognition.* Paper presented at the meeting of the American Psychological Association, Washington, DC.

Labouvie-Vief, G. (2009). Cognition and equilibrium regulation in development and aging. In V. Bengtson & others (Eds.), *Handbook of theories of aging.* New York: Springer.

Labouvie-Vief, G., Gruhn, D., & Studer, J. (2010). Dynamic integration of emotion and cognition: Equilibrium regulation in development and aging. In M.E. Lamb, A. Freund, & R.M. Lerner (Eds.), *Handbook of life-span development* (Vol. 2). New York: Wiley.

Lacaze-Masmonteil, T., & O'Flaherty, P. (2018). Managing infants born to mothers who have used opioids during pregnancy. *Pediatrics and Child Health, 23,* 220–226.

Lachman, M., & Kranz, E. (2010). The midlife crisis. In I. Wiener & E. Craighead (Eds.), *The Corsini encyclopedia of psychology* (4th ed.). New York: Wiley.

Lachman, M.E. (2004). Development in midlife. *Annual Review of Psychology* (Vol. 55). Palo Alto, CA: Annual Reviews.

Lachman, M.E., Agrigoroaei, S., & Hahn, E.A. (2016). Making sense of control: Change and consequences. In R. Scott & S. Kosslyn (Eds.), *Emerging trends in the social and behavioral sciences.* New York: Wiley.

Lachman, M.E., Agrigoroaei, S., Murphy, C., & Tun, P.A. (2010). Frequent cognitive activity compensates for education difference in episodic memory. *American Journal of Geriatric Psychiatry, 18,* 4–10.

Lachman, M.E., Neupert, S., & Agrigoroaei, S. (2011). The relevance of control beliefs for health and aging. In K.W. Schaie & S.L. Willis (Eds.), *Handbook of the psychology of aging* (7th ed.). New York: Elsevier.

Laciga, J., & Cigler, H. (2017). The Flynn effect in the Czech Republic. *Intelligence, 61,* 7–10.

Lacosta, J., & others (2019, in press). A positive association between a polymorphism in the HTR2B gene and cocaine-crack in a French Afro-Caribbean population. *World Journal of Psychiatry.*

Ladd, G., Buhs, E., & Troop, W. (2004). School adjustment and social skills training. In P.K. Smith & C.H. Hart (Eds.), *Wiley-Blackwell handbook of childhood social development.* Malden, MA: Blackwell.

Ladd, G.W., & Kochenderfer-Ladd, B. (2019). Parents and children's peer relationships. In M.H. Bornstein (Ed.), *Handbook of parenting* (3rd ed.). New York: Routledge.

Ladd, H.C. (2017). No Child Left Behind: A deeply flawed federal policy. *Journal of Policy Analysis and Management, 36,* 461–469.

Ladika, S. (2018). Sexual harassment: Health care, it is #YouToo. *Managed Care, 27,* 14–17.

Ladouceur, C.D., & others (2019). Neural systems underlying reward cue processing in early adolescence: The role of puberty and puberty hormones. *Psychoneuroendocrinology, 102,* 281-291.

LaFrance, M., Hecht, M.A., & Paluck, E.L. (2003). The contingent smile: A meta-analysis of sex differences in smiling. *Psychological Bulletin, 129,* 305-334.

Lafreniere, D., & Mann, N. (2009). Anosmia: Loss of smell in the elderly. *Otolaryngologic Clinics of North America, 42,* 123-131.

Lagattuta, K.H. (2014a). *Children and emotion. New insights into developmental affective science.* Basel, Switzerland: Karger.

Lagattuta, K.H. (2014b). Linking past, present, and future: Children's ability to connect mental states and emotions across time. *Child Development Perspectives, 8,* 90-95.

Lahat, A., & others (2014). Early behavioral inhibition and increased error monitoring predict later social phobia symptoms in childhood. *Journal of the American Academy of Child and Adolescent Psychiatry, 53,* 447-455.

Lahti, J., Lahelma, E., & Rahkonen, O. (2017). Changes in leisure-time physical activity and subsequent common mental disorders among aging employees. *European Journal of Public Health, 27,* 765-767.

Lahtinen, A., & others (2019). A distinctive DNA methylation pattern in insufficient sleep. *Scientific Reports, 9*(1), 1193.

Lai, M-C., Lombardo, M.V., Chakrabarti, B., & Baron-Cohen, S. (2013). Subgrouping the autism "spectrum": Reflections on DSM-5. *PLoS Biology, 11*(4), e1001544.

Laible, D.J., Carlo, G., & Padilla-Walker, L.M. (Eds.) (2020, in press). *Oxford handbook of parenting and moral development.* New York: Oxford University Press.

Laible, D.J., & Thompson, R.A. (2000). Mother-child discourse, attachment security, shared positive affect, and early conscience development. *Child Development, 71,* 1424-1440.

Laible, D.J., & Thompson, R.A. (2007). Early socialization: A relationship perspective. In J.E. Grusec & P.D. Hastings (Eds.), *Handbook of socialization.* New York: Guilford.

Laible, D.J., Thompson, R.A., & Froimson, J. (2015). Early socialization: The influence of close relationships. In J.E. Grusec & P.D. Hastings (Eds.), *Handbook of socialization* (2nd ed.). New York: Guilford.

Laible, D.J., & others (2020, in press). The socialization of children's moral understanding in the context of everyday discourse. In D.J. Laible & others (Eds.), *Oxford handbook of parenting and moral development.* New York: Oxford University Press.

Laird, R.D., & Marrero, M.D. (2010). Information management and behavior problems: Is concealing misbehavior necessarily a sign of trouble? *Journal of Adolescence, 33,* 297-308.

Laisk, T., & others (2019, in press). Demographic and evolutionary trends in ovarian functioning and aging. *Human Reproduction Update.*

Lakhdir, M.P.A., & others (2019, in press). Physical maltreatment and its associated factors among adolescents in Karachi, Pakistan. *Journal of Interpersonal Violence.*

Lakoski, S., & others (2013, June 2). *Exercise lowers cancer risk in middle-aged men.* Paper presented at the American Society of Clinical Oncology meeting, Chicago, IL.

Lamb, M.E. (1994). Infant care practices and the application of knowledge. In C.B. Fisher & R.M. Lerner (Eds.), *Applied developmental psychology.* New York: McGraw-Hill.

Lamb, M.E. (2013). Commentary: Early experience, neurobiology, plasticity, vulnerability, and resilience. In D. Narváez & others (Eds.), *Evolution, early experience, and human development.* New York: Oxford University Press.

Lamb, M.E., Bornstein, M.H., & Teti, D.M. (2002). *Development in infancy* (4th ed.). Mahwah, NJ: Erlbaum.

Lamb, M.E., & Lewis, C. (2015). The role of parent-child relationships in child development. In M.H. Bornstein & M.E. Lamb (Eds.), *Developmental science* (7th ed.). New York: Psychology Press.

Lamb, S., White, L., & Plocha, A. (2019). Are children sexual? Who, what, where, when, and how? In S. Lamb & J. Gilbert (Eds.), *Cambridge handbook of sexual development.* New York: Cambridge University Press.

Lambert, N.M., Fincham, F.D., & Stillman, T.F. (2012). Gratitude and depressive symptoms: The role of positive reframing and positive emotion. *Cognition and Emotion, 26,* 615-633.

Lamela, D., & Figueiredo, B. (2016). Coparenting after marital dissolution and children's mental health: A systematic review. *Journal de Pediatria (Rio), 92,* 331-342.

Lamidi, E.O., Manning, W.D., & Brown, S.L. (2019). Change in the stability of first premarital cohabitation among women in the United States, 1983-2013. *Demography, 56,* 427-450.

Lamm, C., & others (2018). Impact of early institutionalization on attention mechanisms underlying the inhibition of planned action. *Neuropsychologia, 117,* 339-346.

Lammers, A.J., Zive, D.M., Tole, S.W., & Fromme, E.K. (2018). The oncology specialist's role in POLST completion. *American Journal of Hospice and Palliative Care, 35,* 297-303.

Lamont, R.A., Nelis, S.M., Quinn, C., & Clare, L. (2017). Social support and attitudes to aging in later life. *International Journal of Aging and Human Development, 84,* 109-125.

Lampl, M. (1993). Evidence of saltatory growth in infancy. *American Journal of Human Biology, 5,* 641-652.

Lampl, M. (2018). Summary on a systems perspective on growth. *Nestle Nutrition Workshop Series, 89,* 55-61.

Lampl, M., & Johnson, M.L. (2011). Infant growth in length follows prolonged sleep and increased naps. *Sleep, 34,* 641-650.

Lamy, S., & others (2014). Psychological and organizational work factors and incidence of arterial hypertension among female healthcare workers: Results of the Organisation des Soins et Sante des Soignants cohort. *Journal of Hypertension, 32,* 1229-1236.

Lanciano, T., & Curci, A. (2014). Incremental validity of emotional intelligence ability in predicting academic achievement. *American Journal of Psychology, 127,* 447-461.

Landes, S.D., Ardelt, M., Vaillant, G.E., & Waldinger, R.J. (2014). Childhood diversity, midlife generativity, and later life well-being. *Journals of Gerontology B: Psychological Sciences and Social Sciences, 69,* 942-952.

Landes, S.D., & Wang, S.S. (2019, in press). Racial-ethnic differences in turnover intent among home health aides. *Journal of Applied Gerontology.*

Landi, F., & others (2018). Sarcopenia: An overview on current definitions, diagnosis, and treatment. *Current Protein and Peptide Science, 19,* 633-638.

Landor, A., Simons, L.G., Simons, R.L., Brody, G.H., & Gibbons, F.X. (2011). The role of religiosity in the relationship between parents, peers, and adolescent risky sexual behavior. *Journal of Youth and Adolescence, 40*(3), 296-309.

Landrum, A.R., Mills, C.M., & Johnston, A.M. (2013). When do children trust the expert? Benevolence information influences children's trust more than expertise. *Developmental Science, 16,* 622-638.

Landrum, A.R., Pflaum, A., & Mills, C.M. (2016). Inducing knowledgeability from niceness: Children use social features for making epistemic inferences. *Journal of Cognition and Development, 17,* 699-717.

Lane, A.P., & others (2017). Is occupational complexity associated with cognitive performance or decline? Results from the Australia Longitudinal Study of Aging. *Gerontology, 63,* 550-559.

Lane, H. (1976). *The wild boy of Aveyron.* Cambridge, MA: Harvard University Press.

Langer, E.J. (2005). *On becoming an artist.* New York: Ballantine.

Langer, R.D. (2017). The evidence base for HRT: What can we believe? *Climacteric, 20,* 91-98.

Langille, D.B., Asbridge, M., Cragg, A., & Rasic, D. (2015). Associations of school connectedness with adolescent suicidality: Gender differences and the role of risk of depression. *Canadian Journal of Psychiatry, 60,* 258-267.

Langstrom, N., Rahman, Q., Carlstrom, E., & Lichtenstein, P. (2010). Genetic and environmental effects on same-sex behavior: A population study of twins in Sweden. *Archives of Sexual Behavior, 39,* 75-80.

Lanning, R.K., & others (2019). Doulas in the operating room: An innovative approach to supporting skin-to-skin care during Cesarean birth. *Journal of Midwifery and Women's Health, 64,* 112-117.

Lansford, J.E. (2009). Parental divorce and children's adjustment. *Perspectives on Psychological Science, 4,* 140-152.

Lansford, J.E. (2013). Single- and two-parent families. In J. Hattie & E. Anderman (Eds.), *International handbook of student achievement.* New York: Routledge.

Lansford, J.E. (2019a). Parenting and child discipline. In M.H. Bornstein (Ed.), *Handbook of parenting* (3rd ed.). New York: Routledge.

Lansford, J.E. (2019b). Single- and two-parent families. In J. Hattie & E. Anderman (Eds.), *International handbook of student achievement.* New York: Routledge.

Lansford, J.E. (2020, in press). Parental discipline practices associated with preventing children's aggressive and immoral behavior. In D.J. Laible & others (Eds.), *Oxford handbook of parenting and moral development.* New York: Oxford University Press.

Lansford, J.E., & Banati, P. (2018). Conclusions: Adolescent development research and its impact on global policy. In J.E. Lansford & P. Banati (Eds.), *Handbook of adolescent development and its impact on global policy.* New York: Oxford University Press.

Lansford, J.E., Malone, P.S., Dodge, K.A., Petti, G.S., & Bates, J.E. (2010). Developmental cascades of peer rejection, social information processing biases, and aggression during middle school. *Development and Psychopathology, 22,* 593–602.

Lansford, J.E., Wager, L.B., Bates, J.E., Pettit, G.S., & Dodge, K.A. (2012). Forms of spanking and children's externalizing problems. *Family Relations, 61*(2), 224–236.

Lansford, J.E., & others (2005). Cultural normativeness as a moderator of the link between physical discipline and children's adjustment: A comparison of China, India, Italy, Kenya, Philippines, and Thailand. *Child Development, 76,* 1234–1246.

Lansford, J.E., & others (2014). Corporal punishment, maternal warmth, and child adjustment: A longitudinal study in eight countries. *Journal of Clinical Child and Adolescent Psychology, 43,* 670–685.

Lansford, J.E., & others (2018). Bidirectional relations between parenting and behavior problems from age 8 to 13 in nine countries. *Journal of Research on Adolescence, 28,* 571–590.

Lantagne, A., & Furman, W. (2017). Romantic relationship development: The interplay of age and relationship length. *Developmental Psychology, 53,* 1738–1749.

Lantolf, J. (2017). Materialist dialectics in Vygotsky's methodological approach: Implications for second language education research. In C. Ratner & D. Silva (Eds.), *Vygotsky and Marx.* New York: Routledge.

Lany, J., Shoaib, A., Thompson, A., & Estes, K.G. (2018). Infant statistical-learning ability is related to real-time language processing. *Journal of Child Language, 45,* 368–391.

Lapsley, D. (2020). Moral formation of the family: A research agenda in time future. In D. Laible, G. Carlo, & L. Padilla-Walker (Eds.), *Oxford handbook of parenting and moral development.* New York: Oxford University Press.

Lapsley, D.K., & Hill, P.L. (2010). Subjective invulnerability, optimism bias, and adjustment in emerging adulthood. *Journal of Youth and Adolescence, 39,* 847–857.

Lapsley, D., Holter, A., & Narváez, D. (2013). Teaching for character: Three strategies for teacher education. In M. Sanger & R. Osgulthorpe (Ed.), *The moral work of teaching.* New York: Teachers College Press.

Lapsley, D., Reilly, T., & Narváez, D. (2019, in press). Children's moral development. In L.J. Arnett (Ed.), *Oxford handbook of moral development.* New York: Oxford University Press.

Lapsley, D., & Stey, P.C. (2014). Moral self-identity as the aim of education. In L. Nucci, T. Krettenauer, & D. Narváez (Eds.), *Handbook of moral and character education* (2nd ed.). New York: Routledge.

Laranjo, J., Bernier, A., Meins, E., & Carlson, S.M. (2010). Early manifestations of theory of mind: The roles of maternal mind-mindedness and infant security of attachment. *Infancy, 15,* 300–323.

Larkina, M., Merrill, N.A., & Bauer, P.J. (2017). Developmental changes in consistency of autobiographical memories: Adolescents' and young adults' repeated recall of recent and distant events. *Memory, 25,* 1036–1051.

Larkins, N.G., & others (2019, in press). The population-based prevalence of hypertension and correlates of blood pressure among Australian children. *Pediatric Nephrology.*

Larson, R., & Richards, M.H. (1994). *Divergent realities.* New York: Basic Books.

Larson, R., & Verma, S. (1999). How children and adolescents spend time around the world: Work, play, and developmental opportunities. *Psychological Bulletin, 125,* 701–736.

Larson, R.W. (2001). How U.S. children spend time: What it does (and doesn't) tell us about their development. *Current Directions in Psychological Science, 10,* 160–164.

Larson, R.W., McGovern, G., & Orson, C. (2018). How adolescents develop self-motivation in complex learning environments: Processes and practices in afterschool programs. In A. Renninger & S. Hidi (Eds.), *Cambridge handbook of motivation and learning.* New York: Cambridge University Press.

Larson, R.W., Orson, C., & Bowers, J. (2017). Positive youth development: How intrinsic motivation amplifies social-emotional learning. In M. Warren & S. Donaldson (Eds.), *Scientific advances in positive psychology.* Santa Barbara, CA: Praeger.

Larson, R.W., Walker, K.C., & McGovern, G. (2018). Youth programs as contexts for development of moral agency. In L.A. Jensen (Ed.), *Handbook of moral development: An interdisciplinary perspective.* New York: Oxford University Press.

Larson, R.W., Wilson, S., & Rickman, A. (2009). Globalization, societal change, and adolescence across the world. In R.M. Lerner & L. Steinberg (Eds.), *Handbook of adolescent psychology* (3rd ed.). New York: Wiley.

Larssen, E., Clausen, S., & Stahlman, S. (2019). Testosterone replacement therapy use among active component service men, 2017. *MSMR, 26*(3), 26–31.

Larzelere, R.E., & Kuhn, B.R. (2005). Comparing child outcomes of physical punishment and alternative disciplinary tactics: A meta-analysis. *Clinical Child and Family Psychology Review, 8,* 1–37.

LaTourrette, A., & Waxman, S.R. (2019, in press). Defining the role of language in infants' object categorization with eye-tracking paradigms. *Journal of Visualized Experiments.*

Lau, E.Y., & others (2017). Sleep and optimism: A longitudinal study of bidirectional causal relationship and its mediating and moderating variables in a Chinese student sample. *Chronobiology International, 34,* 360–372.

Lauer, E.A., & others (2019, in press). Identifying barriers and supports to breastfeeding in the workplace experienced by mothers in the New Hampshire supplemental nutrition program for women, infants, and children utilizing the total worker health framework. *International Journal of Environmental Research and Public Health.*

Laumann, E.O., Glasser, D.B., Never, R.C., & Moreira, E.D. (2009). A population-based survey of sexual activity, sexual problems, and associated help-seeking behavior patterns in mature adults in the United States of America. *International Journal of Impotence Research, 21,* 171–178.

Laureiro-Martinez, D., Trujillo, C.A., & Unda, J. (2017). Time perspective and age: A review of age associated differences. *Frontiers in Psychology, 8,* 101.

Laurita, A.C., Hazan, C., & Spreng, R.N. (2019, in press). An attachment theoretical perspective for the neural representation of close others. *Social Cognitive and Affective Neuroscience.*

Laursen, B. (2018). Peer influence. In W.M. Bukowski & others (Eds.). *Handbook of peer interactions, relationships, and groups* (2nd ed.). New York: Guilford.

Lautenbacher, S., & others (2017). Age changes in pain perception: A systematic-review and meta-analysis of age effects on pain and tolerance thresholds. *Neuroscience and Biobehavioral Reviews.*

Lavalliere, M., & others (2011). Changing lanes in a simulator: Effects of aging on the control of the vehicle and visual inspection of mirrors and the blind spot. *Traffic Injury Prevention, 12,* 191–200.

Lavender, J.M., & others (2014). Dimensions of emotion dysregulation in bulimia nervosa. *European Eating Disorders Review, 22,* 212–216.

Lavezzi, A.M. (2019, in press). Toxic effect of cigarette smoke on brainstem nicotinic receptor expression: Primary cause of sudden unexplained perinatal infant death. *Toxics.*

Lavin, K.M., & others (2019). The importance of resistance exercise training to combat neuromuscular aging. *Physiology, 34,* 112–122.

Lavner, J.A., & Bradbury, T.N. (2019). Marriage and committed partnerships. In B.H. Friese (Ed.), *APA handbook of contemporary family psychology.* Washington, DC: APA Books.

Law, B.H.Y., & others (2018). Analysis of neonatal resuscitation using eye tracking: A pilot study. *Archives of Disease in Childhood: Fetal and Neonatal Edition, 103,* F82–F84.

Law, J., & others (2018). Early home activities and oral language skills in middle childhood: A quantile analysis. *Child Development, 89,* 295–309.

Lawson, K.M., & others (2014). Daily positive spillover and crossover from mothers' work to youth health. *Journal of Family Psychology, 28,* 897–907.

Lazar, A. (2017). Moderating effects of religiousness and marriage duration on the relation between sexual and marital satisfaction among Jewish women. *Archives of Sexual Behavior, 46,* 513–523.

Le Bourg, E., & Redman, L.M. (2018). Do-it-yourself calorie-restriction: The risk of simplistically translating findings in animal models to humans. *Bioessays, 40,* e1800111.

Le Page, A., & others (2018). Role of the peripheral innate immune system in the development of Alzheimer's disease. *Experimental Gerontology, 107,* 59–66.

Le, Y., & others (2019). Cross-day influences between couple closeness and coparenting support among new parents. *Journal of Family Psychology, 33,* 360–369.

Leach, P. (1990). *Your baby and child: From birth to age five.* New York: Knopf.

Leaper, C. (2013). Gender development during childhood. In P.D. Zelazo (Ed.), *Oxford handbook of developmental psychology.* New York: Oxford University Press.

Leaper, C. (2015). Gender development from a social-cognitive perspective. In R.M. Lerner (Ed.), *Handbook of child psychology and developmental science* (7th ed.). New York: Wiley.

Leaper, C., & Bigler, R.S. (2018). Societal causes and consequences of gender typing on children's toys. In E.S. Weisgram & L.M. Dinella (Eds.), *Gender typing of children's play.* Washington, DC: APA Books.

Leaper, C., & Smith, T.E. (2004). A meta-analytic review of gender variations in children's language use: Talkativeness, affiliative speech, and assertive speech. *Developmental Psychology, 40,* 993–1027.

Learmonth, Y.C., & others (2019, in press). Physical education and leisure-time sport reduce overweight and obesity: A number needed to treat analysis. *International Journal of Obesity.*

Lebel, C., & Deoni, S. (2018). The development of brain white matter microstructure. *NeuroImage, 182,* 207–218.

Lebenbaum, M., & others (2018). Development and validation of a population based risk algorithm for obesity: The Obesity Population Risk Tool (OPoRT). *PLoS One, 13*(1), e0191169.

Lecouvey, G., & others (2019). An impairment of prospective memory in mild Alzheimer's disease: A ride in a virtual town. *Frontiers in Psychology, 10,* 241.

Ledesma, K. (2012). A place to call home. *Adoptive Families.* Retrieved August 8, 2012, from www.adoptivefamilies.com/articles.php?aid=2129

Lee, A. (2017). Late career job loss and retirement behavior of couples. *Research on Aging, 39,* 7–28.

Lee, A., & others (2019, in press). BOADICEA: A comprehensive breast cancer risk prediction model incorporating genetic and nongenetic risk factors. *Genetics in Medicine.*

Lee, C.C., & others (2018). Babbling development as seen in canonical babbling ratios: A naturalistic evaluation of all-day recordings. *Infant Behavior and Development, 50,* 140–153.

Lee, C.T., Tsai, M.C., Lin, C.Y., & Strong, C. (2017). Longitudinal effects of self-report pubertal timing and menarchal age on adolescent psychological and behavioral outcomes in female youths from Northern Taiwan. *Pediatrics and Neonatology, 58,* 313–320.

Lee, D.K., & others (2019, in press). The cost of simplifying complex developmental phenomena. *Developmental Science.*

Lee, E., & Jang., I. (2019, in press). Nurses' fatigue, job stress, organizational culture, and turnover intention: A culture-work-health model. *Western Journal of Nursing.*

Lee, G., & Ham, O.K. (2018). Behavioral and psychosocial factors associated with suicidal ideation among adolescents. *Nursing and Health Education, 20,* 394–401.

Lee, G., & others (2019). Predicting Alzheimer's disease progression using multi-modal deep learning approach. *Scientific Reports, 9*(1), 1952.

Lee, H.B., & others (2014). Five-factor model personality traits as predictors of incident coronary heart disease in the community: A 10.5-year cohort study based on the Baltimore epidemiological catchment area follow-up study. *Psychosomatics, 55,* 352–361.

Lee, I.M., & Skerrett, P.J. (2001). Physical activity and all-cause mortality: What is the dose-response relation? *Medical Science and Sports Exercise, 33*(Suppl. 6), S459–S471.

Lee, J.E., Kahana, B., & Kahana, E. (2017). Successful aging from the viewpoint of older adults: Development of a brief Successful Aging Inventory (SAI). *Gerontology, 63,* 359–371.

Lee, J.H., & others (2019). Neonatal outcomes of very low birth weight infants in Korean Neonatal Network from 2013 to 2016. *Journal of Korean Medical Science, 34*(5), e40.

Lee, K. (2019). Impact of Head Start quality on children's developmental outcomes. *Social Work in Public Health, 27,* 1–12.

Lee, K., Cameron, C.A., Doucette, J., & Talwar, V. (2002). Phantoms and fabrications: Young children's detection of implausible lies. *Child Development, 73,* 1688–1702.

Lee, K., Martin, P., & Poon, L.W. (2017). Predictors of caregiving burden: Impact of subjective health, negative affect, and loneliness of octogenarians and centenarians. *Aging and Mental Health, 21,* 1214–1221.

Lee, K., Quinn, P.C., Pascalis, O., & Slater, A. (2013). Development of face processing ability in childhood. In P.D. Zelazo (Ed.), *Oxford handbook of developmental psychology.* Oxford, UK: Oxford University Press.

Lee, K., & others (2018). Effects of life events, social supports, and personality on mental status in later life. *International Journal of Aging and Human Development, 86,* 111–130.

Lee, K.S., & Vaillancort, T. (2019, in press). Longitudinal associations among bullying by peers, disordered eating behavior, and symptoms of depression during adolescence. *JAMA Psychiatry.*

Lee, K.T.H., & others (2018). Out-of-school time and behaviors during adolescence. *Journal of Research on Adolescence, 28,* 284–293.

Lee, K.Y., & others (2011). Effects of combined radiofrequency radiation exposure on the cell cycle and its regulatory proteins. *Bioelectromagnetics, 32,* 169–178.

Lee, M.J., & others (2019, in press). Memory and confusion complaints in visually impaired older adults: An understudied aspect of well-being. *Gerontology and Geriatric Medicine.*

Lee, R., Zhai, F., Brooks-Gunn, J., Han, W.J., & Waldfogel, J. (2014). Head Start participation and school readiness: Evidence from the Early Childhood Longitudinal Study-Birth Cohort. *Developmental Psychology, 50,* 202–215.

Lee, S.H., & others (2019). Sirtuin signaling in cellular senescence and aging. *BMB Reports, 52,* 24–34.

Lee, T-W., Wu, Y-T., Yu, Y., Wu, H-C., & Chen, T-J. (2012). A smarter brain is associated with stronger neural interaction in healthy young females: A resting EEG coherence study. *Intelligence, 40,* 38–48.

Leeman, R.F., & others (2014). Impulsivity, sensation-seeking, and part-time job status in relation to substance use and gambling in adolescents. *Journal of Adolescent Health, 54,* 460–466.

Leerkes, E.M., & Augustine, M.E. (2019). Parenting and emotions. In M.H. Bornstein (Ed.)., *Handbook of parenting* (3rd ed.) (Vol. 3). New York: Routledge.

Leerkes, E.M., Gedaly, L., & Su, J. (2016). Parental sensitivity and infant attachment. In L. Balter & C.S. Tamis-LeMonda (Eds.), *Child psychology* (3rd ed.). New York: Psychology Press.

Leerkes, E.M., Parade, S.H., & Gudmundson, J.A. (2011). Mothers' emotional reactions to crying pose risk for subsequent attachment insecurity. *Journal of Family Psychology, 25,* 635–643.

Leerkes, E.M., & others (2017). Further evidence of the limited role of candidate genes in relation to mother-infant attachment. *Attachment and Human Development, 19,* 76–105.

Lefkowitz, E.S., & Gillen, M.M. (2006). "Sex is just a normal part of life": Sexuality in emerging adulthood. In J.J. Arnett & J.L. Tanner (Eds.), *Emerging adults in America.* Washington, DC: American Psychological Association.

Leftwich, H., & Alves, M.V. (2017). Adolescent pregnancy. *Pediatric Clinics of North America, 64,* 381–388.

Leger, D., Beck, F., Richard, J.B., & Godeau, E. (2012). Total sleep time severely drops in adolescence. *PLoS One, 7*(10), e45204.

Leger, K.A., & others (2016). Personality and stressor-related affect. *Journal of Personality and Social Psychology, 111,* 917–928.

Legerstee, M. (1997). Contingency effects of people and objects on subsequent cognitive functioning in 3-month-old infants. *Social Development, 6,* 307–321.

Lehman, H.C. (1960). The age decrement in outstanding scientific creativity. *American Psychologist, 15,* 128–134.

Lemaster, P., Delaney, R., & Strough, J.N. (2017). Crossover, degendering, or . . . ? A multidimensional approach to lifespan gender development. *Sex Roles, 76,* 669–681.

Lempers, J.D., Flavell, E.R., & Flavell, J.H. (1977). The development in very young children of tacit knowledge concerning visual perception. *Genetic Psychology Monographs, 95,* 3–53.

Lenhart, A. (2015a, April 9). *Teens, social media, and technology: Overview 2015.* Washington, DC: Pew Research Center.

Lenhart, A. (2015b, August 6). *Teens, technology, and friendship.* Washington, DC: Pew Research Center,

Lenoir, C.P., Mallet, E., & Calenda, E. (2000). Siblings of sudden infant death syndrome and near miss in about 30 families: Is there a genetic link? *Medical Hypotheses, 54,* 408–411.

Lenze, E.J., & others (2014). Mindfulness-based stress reduction for older adults with worry symptoms and co-occurring cognitive dysfunction. *International Journal of Geriatric Psychiatry, 29,* 991–1000.

Leon, M.E., & others (2015). European code against cancer (4th ed.). *Cancer Epidemiology, 10,* S18777–187382.

Leonard, B.E. (2018). Inflammation and depression: A causal or coincidental link to the pathophysiology? *Acta Neuropsychiatrica, 30,* 1–16.

Lepore, S.J., & others (2018). Kids Safe and Smokefree (KiSS) multilevel intervention to reduce child tobacco smoke exposure: Long-term results of a randomized controlled trial. *International Journal of Environmental Research and Public Health, 15,* 1239.

Leppakoski, T.H., Flinck, A., & Paavilainen, E. (2015). Greater commitment to the domestic violence training is required. *Journal of Interprofessional Care, 29*(3), 281–283.

Leppanen, J.M., & others (2018). Early development of attention to threat-related facial expressions. *PLoS One, 13* (5), e0197424.

Lerch, J.P., & others (2017). Studying neuroanatomy using MRI. *Nature Neuroscience, 20,* 314–326.

Lerner, H.G. (1989). *The dance of intimacy.* New York: Harper & Row.

Lerner, J.V., & others (2013). Positive youth development: Processes, philosophies, and programs. In I.B. Weiner & others (Eds.), *Handbook of psychology* (2nd ed., Vol. 6). New York: Wiley.

Lerner, R.M., Boyd, M., & Du, D. (2008). Adolescent development. In I.B. Weiner & C.B. Craighead (Eds.), *Encyclopedia of psychology* (4th ed.). Hoboken, NJ: Wiley.

Lerner, R.M., & others (2018). Studying positive youth development in different nations: Theoretical and methodological issues. In J.E. Lansford & P. Banati (Eds.), *Handbook of adolescent development*

research and its impact on global policy. New York: Oxford University Press.

Lesaux, N.K., & Siegel, L.S. (2003). The development of reading in children who speak English as a second language. *Developmental Psychology, 39,* 1005-1019.

Leslie, S.J., Cimpian, A., Meyer, M., & Freeland, E. (2015). Expectations of brilliance underlie gender distributions across academic disciplines. *Science, 347,* 262-265.

Lester, B.M., & others (2002). The maternal lifestyle study: Effects of substance exposure during pregnancy on neurodevelopmental outcome in 1-month-old infants. *Pediatrics, 110,* 1182-1192.

Leu, D.J., & Kinzer, C.K. (2017). *Phonics, phonemic awareness, and word analysis for teachers* (10th ed.). Upper Saddle River, NJ: Pearson.

Leung, C.Y., & others (2014). Surgency and negative affectivity, but not effortful control, are uniquely associated with obesogenic eating behaviors among low-income preschoolers. *Appetite, 78,* 139-146.

Levant, R.F. (2001). Men and masculinity. In J. Worell (Ed.), *Encyclopedia of women and gender.* San Diego: Academic Press.

Levelt, W.J.M. (1989). *Speaking: From intention to articulation.* Cambridge, MA: MIT Press.

Lever-Duffy, J., & McDonald, J. (2018). *Teaching and learning with technology* (6th ed.). Upper Saddle River, NJ: Pearson.

Levey, D.F., & others (2019). Genetic associations with suicide attempt severity and genetic overlap with major depression. *Translational Psychiatry, 9*(1), 22.

Levey, E.K.V., & others (2019, in press). The longitudinal role of self-concept clarity and best friend delinquency in adolescent delinquency behavior. *Journal of Youth and Adolescence.*

Levine, D., & others (2019a, in press). Finding events in a continuous world: A developmental account. *Developmental Psychology.*

Levine, D., & others (2019b, in press). Evaluating socioeconomic gaps in preschoolers' vocabulary, syntax, and language process skills with the Quick Interactive Language Screener (QUILS). *Early Childhood Research Quarterly.*

Levine, T.P., & others (2008). Effects of prenatal cocaine exposure on special education in school-aged children. *Pediatrics, 122,* e83-e91.

Levinson, D.J. (1978). *The seasons of a man's life.* New York: Knopf.

Levinson, D.J. (1987, August). *The seasons of a woman's life.* Paper presented at the meeting of the American Psychological Association, New York.

Levinson, D.J. (1996). *Seasons of a woman's life.* New York: Knopf.

Levy, B., & Stosic, M. (2019). Traditional prenatal diagnosis: Past to present. *Methods in Molecular Biology, 1885,* 3-22.

Levy, G.D., Sadovsky, A.L., & Troseth, G.L. (2000). Aspects of young children's perceptions of gender-typed occupations. *Sex Roles, 42,* 993-1006.

Lewiecki, E.M., Binkley, N., & Biiezikian, J.P. (2019, in press). Treated osteoporosis is still osteoporosis. *Journal of Bone and Mineral Research.*

Lewis, B.A., & others (2018). The effect of sleep pattern changes on postpartum depressive symptoms. *BMC Women's Health, 18*(1), 12.

Lewis, K.M., & others (2013). Problem behavior and urban, low-income youth: A randomized controlled trial of positive action in Chicago. *American Journal of Preventive Medicine, 44,* 622-630.

Lewis, L., & others (2018a). The perceptions and experiences of women who achieved and did not achieve waterbirth. *BMC Pregnancy and Childbirth, 18*(1), 23.

Lewis, L., & others (2018b). Obstetric and neonatal outcomes for women intending to use immersion in water for labor and birth in Western Australia (2015-2016): A retrospective audit of clinical outcomes. *Australian and New Zealand Journal of Obstetrics and Gynecology, 58,* 539-547.

Lewis, M. (2005). Selfhood. In B. Hopkins (Ed.), *The Cambridge encyclopedia of child development.* Cambridge, UK: Cambridge University Press.

Lewis, M. (2007). Early emotional development. In A. Slater & M. Lewis (Eds.), *Introduction to infant development.* Malden, MA: Blackwell.

Lewis, M. (2008). The emergence of human emotions. In M. Lewis, J.M. Haviland Jones, & L. Feldman Barrett (Eds.), *Handbook of emotions* (3rd ed.). New York: Guilford.

Lewis, M. (2010). The emergence of consciousness and its role in human development. In W.F. Overton & R.M. Lerner (Eds.), *Handbook of life-span development.* New York: Wiley.

Lewis, M. (2015). Emotional development and consciousness. In R.M. Lerner (Ed.), *Handbook of child psychology and developmental science* (7th ed.). New York: Wiley.

Lewis, M. (2018). The emergence of human emotions. In L.F. Barrett & others (Eds.), *Handbook of emotion* (4th ed.). New York: Guilford.

Lewis, M., & Brooks-Gunn, J. (1979). *Social cognition and the acquisition of the self.* New York: Plenum.

Lewis, M., Feiring, C., & Rosenthal, S. (2000). Attachment over time. *Child Development, 71,* 707-720.

Lewis, T.L., & Maurer, D. (2005). Multiple sensitive periods in human visual development: Evidence from visually deprived children. *Developmental Psychobiology, 46,* 163-183.

Lewis, T.L., & Maurer, D. (2009). Effects of early pattern deprivation on visual development. *Optometry and Vision Science, 86,* 640-646.

Lewis-Morrarty, E., & others (2015). Infant attachment security and early childhood behavioral inhibition interact to predict adolescent social anxiety symptoms. *Child Development, 86,* 598-613.

Li, C.P., & others (2019). A novel fluorescence assay for resveratrol determination in red wine based on competitive host-guest recognition. *Food Chemistry, 283,* 191-198.

Li, F.J., Shen, L., & Ji, H.F. (2012). Dietary intakes of vitamin E, vitamin C, and b-carotene, and risk of Alzheimer's disease: A meta-analysis. *Journal of Alzheimer's Disease, 31*(2), 253-258.

Li, G., Kung, K.T., & Hines, M. (2017). Childhood gender-typed behavioral and adolescent sexual orientation: A longitudinal population-based study. *Developmental Psychology, 53,* 764-777.

Li, J., & others (2018). Physical activity in relation to sleep among community-dwelling older adults in China. *Journal of Aging and Physical Activity, 26,* 647-654.

Li, J., Vitiello, M.V., & Gooneratne, N.S. (2018). Sleep in normal aging. *Sleep Medicine Reviews, 13,* 1-11.

Li, J.S.Z., & Denchi, E.L. (2018). How stem cells keep telomeres in check. *Differentiation, 100,* 21-25.

Li, J.W., & others (2017). The effect of acute and chronic exercise on cognitive function and academic performance in adolescents: A systematic review. *Journal of Science and Medicine in Sport, 20,* 841-848.

Li, M., & others (2017a). Parental expectations and child screen and academic sedentary behaviors in China. *American Journal of Preventive Medicine, 52,* 680-689.

Li, M., & others (2017b). Robust and rapid algorithms facilitate large-scale whole genome sequencing downstream analysis in an integrative framework. *Nucleic Acids Research, 45,* e75.

Li, M., & others (2019). What do DNA methylation studies tell us about depression? A systematic review. *Translational Psychiatry, 9*(1), 68.

Li, N., & Hein, S. (2019). Parenting, autonomy in learning, and development during adolescence in China. *New Directions in Child and Adolescent Development, 163,* 67-80.

Li, S., Callaghan, B.L., & Richardson, R. (2014). Infantile amnesia: Forgotten but not gone. *Learning and Memory, 21,* 135-139.

Li, T., & others (2019). The associations between left-hand digit ration (2D:4D) and puberty characteristics in Chinese girls. *Early Human Development, 130,* 22-26.

Li, W., Farkas, G., Duncan, G.J., Burchinal, M.R., & Vandell, D.L. (2013). Timing of high-quality child care and cognitive, language, and preacademic development. *Developmental Psychology, 49*(8), 1440-1451.

Li, Y.R., Li, S., & Lin, C.C. (2018). Effect of resveratrol and pterostilbene on aging and longevity. *Biofactors, 44,* 69-82.

Li, Z., & others (2013). Maternal severe life events and risk of neural tube defects among rural Chinese. *Birth Defects Research A: Clinical and Molecular Teratology, 97,* 109-114.

Liang, W., & Chikritzhs, T. (2015). Age at first use of alcohol predicts the risk of heavy alcohol use in early adulthood: A longitudinal study in the United States. *International Journal on Drug Policy, 26,* 131-134.

Liben, L.S. (1995). Psychology meets geography: Exploring the gender gap on the national geography bee. *Psychological Science Agenda, 8,* 8-9.

Liben, L.S. (2017). Gender development: A constructivist-ecological perspective. In N. Budwig, E. Turiel, & P.D. Zelazo (Eds.), *New perspectives on human development.* New York: Cambridge University Press.

Liben, L.S., & others (2018). Cognitive consequences of gendered toy play. In E.S. Weisgram & L.M. Dinella (Eds.), *Gender typing of children's play.* Washington, DC: APA Books.

Liberman, Z., Woodward, A.L., & Kinzler, K.D. (2017). The origins of social categorization. *Trends in Cognitive Science, 21,* 556-568.

Libertus, K., Joh, A.S., & Needham, A.W. (2016). Motor training at 6 months affects exploration 12 months later. *Developmental Science, 19,* 1058-1066.

Libertus, K., & Needham, A. (2010). Teach to reach: The effects of active vs. passive reaching experiences on action and perception. *Vision Research, 50,* 2750-2757.

Lichtenberg, P.A. (2017). Grief and healing in young and middle age: A widower's journey. *Gerontologist, 57,* 96-102.

Lichtenthal, W.G., & others (2019). An open trial of meaning-centered grief therapy: Rationale and preliminary evaluation. *Palliative Support and Care, 17,* 2-12.

Lifton, R.J. (1977). The sense of immortality: On death and the continuity of life. In H. Feifel (Ed.), *New meanings of death*. New York: McGraw-Hill.

Lillard, A. (2015). The development of play. In R.M. Lerner (Ed.), *Handbook of child psychology and developmental science* (7th ed.). New York: Wiley.

Lillard, A.S. (2017). *Montessori* (3rd ed.). New York: Oxford University Press.

Lillard, A.S., & Kavanaugh, R.D. (2014). The contribution of symbolic skills to the development of explicit theory of mind. *Child Development, 85,* 1535-1551.

Lim, S.H., & others (2018). Enhanced skin pigmentation of anti-wrinkle peptides via molecular modification. *Scientific Reports, 8*(1), 1596.

Limousin, P., & Foltynie, T. (2019, in press). Long-term outcomes of deep brain stimulation in Parkinson disease. *Nature Reviews: Neurology.*

Lin, F.R., Thorpe, R., Gordon-Salant, S., & Ferrucci, L. (2011). Hearing loss prevalence and risk factors among older adults in the United States. *Journals of Gerontology A: Biological Sciences and Medical Sciences, 66A*(5), 582-590.

Lin, F.V., & others (2017). Identification of successful cognitive aging in the Alzheimer's Disease Neuroimaging Initiative Study. *Journal of Alzheimer's Disease, 59,* 101-111.

Lin, I.F., Brown, S.L., & Hammersmith, A.M. (2017). Marital biography, social security receipt, and poverty. *Research on Aging, 39,* 86-110.

Lin, J., & Kelley-Moore, J. (2017). Intraindividual variability in late-life functional limitations among White, Black, and Hispanic older adults. *Research on Aging, 39,* 549-572.

Lin, L.F., & others (2018). Antecedents of gray divorce: A life course perspective. *Journals of Gerontology B: Psychological Sciences and Social Sciences, 73,* 1022-1031.

Lin, L.Y., & others (2015). Effects of television exposure on developmental skills of young children. *Infant Behavior and Development, 38,* 20-26.

Lindahl-Jacobsen, R., & Christensen, K. (2019). Gene-lifestyle interactions in longevity. In R. Fernandez-Ballesteros, A. Benetos, & J-M. Robine (Eds.), *Cambridge handbook of successful aging*. New York: Cambridge University Press.

Lindau, S.T., & others (2007). A study of sexuality and health among older adults in the United States. *New England Journal of Medicine, 357,* 762-774.

Lindberg, S.M., Hyde, S.S., Petersen, J.L., & Lin, M.C. (2010). New trends in gender and mathematics performance: A meta-analysis. *Psychological Bulletin, 136,* 1123-1135.

Lindell, A.K., Campione-Barr, N., & Killoren, S.E. (2017). Implications of parent-child relationships for emerging adults' feelings about adulthood. *Journal of Family Psychology, 31,* 810-820.

Lindfors, P., & others (2019). Do maternal knowledge and paternal knowledge of children's whereabouts buffer differently against alcohol use? A longitudinal study among Finnish boys and girls. *Drug and Alcohol Dependency, 194,* 351-357.

Lindsay, A.C., Wasserman, M., Muñoz, M.A., Wallington, S.F., & Greaney, M.L. (2018). Examining influences of parenting styles and practices on physical activity and sedentary behaviors in Latino children in the United States: Integrative review. *JMR Public Health and Surveillance, 4*(1), e14.

Lindwall, M., & others (2012). Dynamic associations of change in physical activity and change in cognitive function: Coordinated analyses across four studies with up to 21 years of longitudinal data. *Journal of Aging Research, 493598.*

Linnenbrink-Garcia, L., & others (2018). Multiple pathways to success: An examination of integrative motivational profiles among upper elementary and college students. *Journal of Educational Psychology, 110,* 1026-1048.

Lipka, M., & Gecewicz, C. (2017, September 6). *More Americans now say they're spiritual but not religious.* Washington, DC: Pew Research Center.

Lipowski, M., Lipowska, M., Jochimek, M., & Krokosz, D. (2016). Resilience as a factor protecting youths from risky behavior: Moderating effects of gender and sport. *European Journal of Sport Science, 16,* 246-255.

Lippa, R.A. (2005). *Gender, nature, and nurture* (2nd ed.). Mahwah, NJ: Erlbaum.

Lippman, L.A., & Keith, J.D. (2006). The demographics of spirituality among youth: International perspectives. In E. Roehlkepartain, P.E. King, L. Wagener, & P.L. Benson (Eds.), *The handbook of spirituality in childhood and adolescence*. Thousand Oaks, CA: Sage.

Lissak, G. (2018). Adverse physiological and psychological effects of screen time on children and adolescents: Literature review and case study. *Environmental Research, 164,* 149-157.

Little, C.W., & others (2017). Exploring the co-development of reading fluency and reading comprehension: A twin study. *Child Development, 88,* 934-945.

Liu, B.P., & others (2019). Stressful life events, insomnia, and suicidality in a large sample of Chinese adolescents. *Journal of Affective Disorders, 249,* 404-409.

Liu, D., Wellman, H.M., Tardif, T., & Sabbagh, M.A. (2008). Theory of mind development in Chinese children: A meta-analysis of false-belief understanding across cultures and languages. *Developmental Psychology, 44,* 523-531.

Liu, H., & others (2017). Aging of cerebral white matter. *Aging Research Reviews, 34,* 64-76.

Liu, J., & others (2019, in press). Evaluating links among shyness, peer relations, and internalizing problems in Chinese young adolescents. *Journal of Research on Adolescence.*

Liu, K., & others (2012). Advanced reproductive age and fertility. *International Journal of Gynecology and Obstetrics, 117*(1), 95-102.

Liu, P.Z., & Nusslock, R. (2018). Exercise-mediated neurogenesis in the hippocampus vis BDNF. *Frontiers in Neuroscience, 12,* 52.

Liu, Q., & Tan, Y.Q. (2019, in press). Advances in the identification of susceptibility gene defects of hereditary colorectal cancer. *Journal of Cancer.*

Liu, R., & others (2018). Executive function mediates the association between toddler negative affectivity and early academic achievement. *Early Education and Development, 29,* 641-654.

Liu, S., & Spelke, E.S. (2017). Six-month-old infants expect agents to minimize the cost of their actions. *Cognition, 160,* 35-42.

Liu, S.R., Kia-Keating, M., & Nylund-Gibson, K. (2018). Patterns of adversity and pathways to health among White, Black, and Latino youth. *Child Abuse and Neglect, 86,* 89-99.

Liu, X., & Liu, L. (2005). Sleep habits and insomnia in a sample of elderly persons in China. *Sleep, 28,* 1579-1587.

Liu, Y., & Lachman, M.E. (2019, in press). Socio-economic status and parenting style in childhood: Long-term effects on cognitive function in middle and later adulthood. *Journals of Gerontology B: Psychological Sciences and Social Sciences.*

Liu, Y., & others (2018). The unique role of executive function skills in predicting Hong Kong kindergarteners' reading comprehension. *British Journal of Educational Psychology, 88,* 628-644.

Liu, Z., & others (2018). Disability prior to death among the oldest-old in China. *Journals of Gerontology A: Biological Sciences and Medical Sciences, 73,* 1701-1707.

Livingston, G. (2014, June 5). *Growing number of dads home with the kids*. Washington, DC: Pew Research Center.

Livingston, G. (2017). *5 facts on love and marriage in America*. Washington, DC: Pew Research Center.

Livingston, G., & Bialik, K. (2018, May 10). *7 facts about U.S. moms*. Washington, DC: Pew Research Center.

Llorca, A., Richaud, C.M., & Malonda, E. (2017). Parenting, peer relationships, academic self-efficacy, and academic achievement: Direct and mediating effects. *Frontiers in Psychology, 8,* 2120.

Lo, C.C., Cheng, T.C., & Simpson, G.M. (2016). Marital status and work-related health limitation: A longitudinal study of young adult and middle-aged Americans. *International Journal of Public Health, 61,* 91-100.

Lo, C.C., & others (2017). Racial/ethnic differences in emotional health: A longitudinal study of immigrants' adolescent children. *Community Mental Health Journal, 53,* 92-101.

Lo, C.K.M., & others (2019, in press). Prevalence of child maltreatment and its association with parenting style: A population study in Hong Kong. *International Journal of Environmental Research and Public Health.*

Lo, H.H.M., & others (2019, in press). The effects of family-based mindfulness intervention for ADHD symptomology in young children and their parents: A randomized controlled trial. *Journal of Attention Disorders.*

Lo, J.C., & others (2016). Self-reported sleep duration and cognitive performance in older adults: A systematic review and meta-analysis. *Sleep Medicine, 17,* 87-98.

Loaiza, V.M., & Souza, A.S. (2019). An age-related deficit in preserving the benefits of attention in working memory. *Psychology and Aging, 34,* 282-293.

Lobo, R.A. (2017). Hormone-replacement therapy: Current thinking. *Nature Reviews. Endocrinology, 13,* 220-231.

Locher, J.L., & others (2016). Caloric restriction in overweight older adults: Do benefits exceed potential risks? *Experimental Gerontology, 86,* 4-13.

Lock, M. (1998). Menopause: Lessons from anthropology. *Psychosomatic Medicine, 60,* 410-419.

Lockhart, P.A., & others (2017). The relationship of fertility, lifestyle, and longevity among women. *Journals of Gerontology A: Biological Sciences and Medical Sciences, 72,* 754-759.

Locquet, M., & others (2018). Bone health assessment in older people with or without muscle health impairment. *Osteoporosis International, 29,* 1057-1067.

Loeber, R., Burke, J., & Pardini, D. (2009). The etiology and development of antisocial and delinquent behavior.

Annual Review of Psychology (Vol. 60). Palo Alto, CA: Annual Reviews.

Loeber, R., & Farrington, D.P. (Eds.). (2001). *Child delinquents: Development, intervention and service needs.* Thousand Oaks, CA: Sage.

Lohmander, A., & others (2017). Observation method identifies that a lack of canonical babbling can indicate future speech and language problems. *Acta Pediatrica, 106,* 935-943.

Lomanowska, A.M., & others (2017). Parenting begets parenting: A neurobiological perspective on early adversity and the transmission of parenting styles across generations. *Neuroscience, 342,* 120-139.

Londono, P. (2017). *Human rights and violence against women.* New York: Oxford University Press.

Long, L., & others (2019). Exercise-based cardiac rehabilitation for adults with heart failure. *Cochrane Database of Systematic Reviews, 2019, 1:* CD003331.

Longa, A., & Graham, S. (2020, in press). Effective practices for teaching writing in the United States. In S. Sharma & S. Salend (Eds.), *Encyclopedia of inclusive and special education.* New York: Oxford University Press.

Longo, G.S., Bray, B.C., & Kim-Spoon, J. (2017). Profiles of adolescent religiousness using latent profile analysis: Implications for psychopathology. *British Journal of Developmental Psychology, 35,* 91-105.

Lonner, W.J. (1988). *The introductory psychology text and cross-cultural psychology: A survey of cross-cultural psychologists.* Bellingham: Western Washington University, Center for Cross-Cultural Research.

Looby, A., & others (2019, in press). Alcohol-related protective behavioral strategies as a mediator of the relationship between drinking motives and risky sexual behaviors. *Addictive Behaviors.*

Lopez, A.B., Huynh, V.W., & Fuligni, A.J. (2011). A longitudinal study of religious identity and participation during adolescence. *Child Development, 82,* 1297-1309.

Lopez, R.B., Heatherton, T.E., & Wagner, D.D. (2019, in press). Media multitasking is associated with higher risk for obesity and increased responsiveness to rewarding food stimuli. *Brain Imaging and Behavior.*

Lopez-Higes, R., & others (2018). Efficacy of cognitive training in older adults with and without subjective cognitive decline is associated with inhibition efficiency and working memory span, not cognitive reserve. *Frontiers in Aging Neuroscience, 10,* 23.

Loprinzi, P.D. (2015). Dose-response association of moderate-to-vigorous physical activity with cardiovascular biomarkers and all-cause mortality: Considerations of individual sports, exercise, and recreational physical activities. *Preventive Medicine, 81,* 73-77.

Lorenz, K.Z. (1965). *Evolution and the modification of behavior.* Chicago: University of Chicago Press.

Lorgen-Ritchie, M., & others (2019). Imprinting methylation in SNRPN and MEST1 in adult blood predicts cognitive ability. *PLoS One, 14*(2), e0211799.

Lovden, M., & Lindenberger, U. (2007). Intelligence. In J.E. Birren (Ed.), *Encyclopedia of gerontology* (2nd ed.). San Diego: Academic Press.

Lovden, M., Backman, L., & Lindenberger, U. (2017). The link of intellectual engagement to cognition and brain aging. In R. Cabeza, L. Nyberg, & D.C. Park (Eds.), *Cognitive neuroscience and aging* (2nd ed.). New York: Oxford University Press.

Lovgren, M., & others (2019, in press). Spirituality and religious coping are related to cancer-bereaved siblings' long-term grief. *Palliative and Supportive Care.*

Lowe, K., & Dotterer, A.M. (2013). Parental monitoring, parental warmth, and minority youths' academic outcomes: Exploring the integrative model of parenting. *Journal of Youth and Adolescence, 42,* 1413-1475.

Lowenstein, A., Katz, R., & Tur-Sinai, A. (2019). Intergenerational family relationships and successful aging. In R. Fernandez-Ballesteros, A. Benetos, & J-M. Robine (Eds.), *Cambridge handbook of successful aging.* New York: Cambridge University Press.

Lowry, R., & others (2017). Early sexual debut and associated risk behaviors among sexual minority youth. *American Journal of Preventive Medicine, 52,* 379-384.

Loy, M., Masur, E.F., & Olson, J. (2018). Developmental changes in infants' and mothers' pathways to achieving joint attention episodes. *Infant Behavior and Development, 50,* 264-273.

Lu, P.H., & others (2011). Age-related slowing in cognitive processing speed is associated with myelin integrity in a very healthy elderly sample. *Journal of Clinical and Experimental Neuropsychology, 33,* 1059-1068.

Lu, X., & others (2013). Prevalence of hypertension in overweight and obese children from a large school-based population in Shanghai, China. *BMC Public Health, 13,* 24.

Lu, Y., He, Q., & Brooks-Gunn, J. (2019, in press). Diverse experience of immigrant children: How do separation and reunification shape their development? *Child Development.*

Lubetkin, E.I., & Jia, H. (2017). Burden of disease associated with lower levels of income among U.S. adults aged 65 and older. *BMJ Open, 7*(1), e013720.

Lubinski, D. (2000). Measures of intelligence: Intelligence tests. In A. Kazdin (Ed.), *Encyclopedia of psychology.* New York: Oxford University Press.

Lucas, R.E., & Donnellan, M.B. (2011). Personality development across the life span: Longitudinal analyses with a national sample in Germany. *Journal of Personality and Social Psychology, 101,* 847-861.

Lucca, K., & Wilbourn, M.P. (2018). Communicating to learn: Infants' pointing gestures result in optimal learning. *Child Development, 89,* 941-960.

Lucchetti, G., Lucchetti, A.L., & Koenig, H.G. (2011). Impact of spirituality/religiosity on mortality: Comparison with other health interventions. *Explore, 7,* 234-238.

Luciano, E.C., & Orth, U. (2017). Transitions in romantic relationships and development of self-esteem. *Journal of Personality and Social Psychology, 112,* 307-328.

Luders, E., Narr, K.L., Thompson, P.M., & Toga, A.W. (2009). Neuroanatomical correlates of intelligence. *Intelligence, 37,* 156-163.

Luders, E., & others (2004). Gender difference in cortical complexity. *Nature Neuroscience, 7,* 799-800.

Ludwig, P.E., Freeman, S.C., & Janot, A.C. (2019). Novel stem cell and gene therapy in diabetic retionopathy, age related macular degeneration, and retinitis pigmentosa. *International Journal of Retina Vitreous, 5,* 7.

Ludyga, S., Gerber, M., Kamijo, K., Brand, S., & Puhse, U. (2018). The effects of a school-based exercise program on neurophysiological indices of working memory operations in adolescents. *Journal of Science and Medicine in Sport, 21,* 833-838.

Luebbe, A.M., & others (2018). Dimensionality of helicopter parenting and relations to emotional, decision-making, and academic functioning in emerging adults. *Assessment, 25,* 841-857.

Luijk, M.P., & others (2011). Dopaminergic, serotonergic, and oxytonergic candidate genes associated with infant attachment security and disorganization? In search of main and interaction effects. *Journal of Child Psychology and Psychiatry, 52,* 1295-1307.

Lukowski, A.F., & Bauer, P.J. (2014). Long-term memory in infancy and early childhood. In P.J. Bauer & R. Fivush (Eds.), *Wiley-Blackwell handbook of children's memory.* New York: Wiley.

Lumsden, M.A., & Sassarini, J. (2019, in press). The evolution of human menopause. *Climacteric.*

Lund, H.G., Reider, B.D., Whiting, A.B., & Prichard, J.R. (2010). Sleep patterns and predictors of disturbed sleep in a large population of college students. *Journal of Adolescent Health, 46,* 124-136.

Lund, K.S., & others (2019). Efficacy of a standardized acupuncture approach for women with bothersome menopausal symptoms: A pragmatic randomized study in primary care (the ACOM study). *BMJ Open, 9*(1), e023637.

Lundberg, T., & others (2018). Bereavement stressors and psychological well-being of young adults following the loss of a parent—a cross-sectional survey. *European Journal of Oncology Nursing, 35,* 33-38.

Lundorff, M., & others (2017). Prevalence of prolonged grief disorder in adult bereavement: A systematic review and meta-analysis. *Journal of Affective Disorders, 212,* 138-149.

Lundorff, M., & others (2019). How do loss- and restoration-oriented coping change across time? A prospective study on adjustment following spousal bereavement. *Anxiety, Stress, and Coping, 32,* 270-285.

Lunghi, M., & others (2019, in press). The neural correlates of orienting to walking direction in 6-month-old infants: An ERP study. *Developmental Science.*

Lunkenheimer, E.S., Shields, A.M., & Cortina, K.S. (2007). Parental emotion coaching and dismissing in family interaction. *Social Development, 16,* 232-248.

Luo, H., & others (2018). Obesity and the onset of depressive symptoms among middle-aged and older adults in China: Evidence from CHARLS. *BMC Public Health, 18*(1), 909.

Luo, S.X., & Levin, F.R. (2017). Towards precision addiction treatment: New findings in co-morbid substance use and attention-deficit hyperactivity disorder. *Current Psychiatry Reports, 19*(3), 14.

Luo, X. (2019, in press). Gender and dating violence perpetration and victimization: A comparison of American and Chinese college students. *Journal of Interpersonal Violence.*

Luo, Y., Zhang, Z., & Gu, D. (2015). Education and mortality among older adults in China. *Social Science and Medicine, 137,* 134-142.

Luria, A., & Herzog, E. (1985, April). *Gender segregation across and within settings.* Paper presented at the biennial meeting of the Society for Research in Child Development, Toronto.

Lurie, D.L. (2019, in press). An integrative approach to neuroinflammation in psychiatric disorders and neuropathic pain. *Journal of Experimental Neuroscience.*

Lushin, V., Jaccard, J., & Kaploun, V. (2017). Parental monitoring, adolescent dishonesty, and underage drinking: A nationally representative study. *Journal of Adolescence, 57,* 99-107.

Luszcz, M. (2011). Executive functioning and cognitive aging. In K.W. Schaie & S.L. Willis (Eds.), *Handbook of the psychology of aging* (7th ed.). New York: Elsevier.

Luthar, S.S. (2006). Resilience in development: A synthesis of research across five decades. In D. Cicchetti & D.J. Cohen (Eds.), *Developmental psychopathology: Vol. 3. Risk, disorder, and adaptation* (2nd ed.). Hoboken, NJ: Wiley.

Luthar, S.S., Crossman, E.J., & Small, P.J. (2015). Resilience in the face of adversities. In R.M. Lerner (Ed.), *Handbook of child psychology and developmental science* (7th ed.). New York: Wiley.

Luyckx, K., & Robitschek, C. (2014). Personal growth initiative and identity formation in adolescence through young adulthood: Mediating processes on the pathway to well-being. *Journal of Adolescence, 37,* 973-981.

Luyckx, K., Teppers, E., Klimstra, T.A., & Rassart, J. (2014). Identity processes and personality traits and types in adolescence: Directionality of effects and developmental trajectories. *Developmental Psychology, 50,* 2144-2153.

Luyckx, K., & others (2017). Identity processes and intrinsic and extrinsic goal pursuits: Directionality of effects in college students. *Journal of Youth and Adolescence, 46,* 1758-1771.

Luyckx, K., & others (2018). Illness identity in young adults with refractory epilepsy. *Epilepsy and Behavior, 80,* 48-55.

Luyster, F.S., & others (2012). Sleep: A health imperative. *Sleep, 35,* 727-734.

Luzzatto, L., & Makani, J. (2019). Hydroxyurea—an essential medicine for sickle cell disease in Africa. *New England Journal of Medicine, 380*(2), 187-189.

Lynch, A., Vail-Smith, K., & Kotecki, J. (2018). *Choosing health* (3rd ed.). Upper Saddle River, NJ: Pearson.

Lyndaker, C., & Hulton, L. (2004). The influence of age on symptoms of perimenopause. *Journal of Obstetric, Gynecological, and Neonatal Nursing, 33,* 340-347.

Lynn, R., Fuerst, J., & Kirkegaard, E.O.W. (2018). Regional differences in intelligence in 22 countries and their economic, social, and demographic correlates: A review. *Intelligence, 69,* 24-36.

Lyon, T.D., & Flavell, J.H. (1993). Young children's understanding of forgetting over time. *Child Development, 64,* 789-800.

Lyons, D.M., & others (2010). Stress coping stimulates hippocampal neurogenesis in adult monkeys. *Proceedings of the National Academy of Sciences U.S.A., 107,* 14823-14827.

Lyons, E.M., & others (2018). Stereotype threat effects on learning from a cognitively demanding math lesson. *Cognitive Science, 42,* 678-690.

Lyons, H., Manning, W.D., Longmore, M.A., & Giordano, P.C. (2015). Gender and casual sexual activity from adolescence to emerging adulthood: Social and life course correlates. *Journal of Sex Research, 52,* 543-557.

Lytle, A., Levy, S.R., & Meeks, S. (2019, in press). Reducing ageism: Education about aging and extended contact with older adults. *Gerontologist.*

M

Maag, J.W. (2018). *Behavior management from theoretical implications* (3rd ed.). Boston: Cengage.

Maatta, S., & others (2019, in press). Maturation changes the excitability and effective connectivity of the frontal lobe: A developmental TMS-EEG study. *Human Brain Mapping.*

MacAllister, W.S., & others (2019, in press). The WISC-V in children and adolescents with epilepsy. *Child Neuropsychology.*

Maccallum, F., & Bryant, R.A. (2013). A cognitive attachment model of prolonged grief: Integrating attachments, memory, and identity. *Clinical Psychology Review, 33,* 713-727.

Maccallum, F., & Bryant, R.A. (2019, in press). A network approach to understanding quality of life impairments in prolonged grief disorder. *Journal of Traumatic Stress.*

Maccoby, E.E. (1998). *The two sexes: Growing up apart, coming together.* Cambridge, MA: Harvard University Press.

Maccoby, E.E. (2002). Gender and group process: A developmental perspective. *Current Directions in Psychological Science, 11,* 54-57.

Maccoby, E.E. (2007). Historical overview of socialization theory and research. In J.E. Grusec & P.D. Hastings (Eds.), *Handbook of socialization.* New York: Guilford.

Maccoby, E.E., & Martin, J.A. (1983). Socialization in the context of the family: Parent-child interaction. In P.H. Mussen (Ed.), *Handbook of child psychology* (4th ed., Vol. 4). New York: Wiley.

MacDonald, M.C., & Hsiao, Y. (2019). Sentence comprehension. In S-A. Rueschemeyer & M. Gareth Gaskell (Eds.), *Oxford handbook of psycholinguistics* (2nd ed.). New York: Oxford University Press.

MacDonald, S.W.S., Hultch, D., Strauss, E., & Dixon, R. (2003). Age-related slowing of digit symbol substitution revisited: What do longitudinal age changes reflect? *Journals of Gerontology B: Psychological Sciences and Social Sciences, 58B,* P187-P184.

MacDonald, S.W.S., & Stawski, R.S. (2015). Intraindividual variability—an indicator of vulnerability or resilience in adult development and aging? In M. Diehl, I. Hooker, & M. Sliwinski (Eds.), *Handbook of intraindividual variability across the life span.* New York: Routledge.

MacDonald, S.W.S., & Stawski, R.S. (2016). Methodological perspectives for the psychology of aging in a lifespan context. In K.W. Schaie & S.L. Willis (Eds.), *Handbook of the psychology of aging* (8th ed.). New York: Elsevier.

MacFarlane, J.A. (1975). Olfaction in the development of social preferences in the human neonate. In *Parent-infant interaction.* Ciba Foundation Symposium No. 33. Amsterdam: Elsevier.

MacGregor, S., & others (2018). Genome-wide association study of intraocular pressure uncovers new pathways for glaucoma. *Nature Genetics, 50,* 1067-1071.

Machado, A., & others (2019, in press). ADHD among offenders: Prevalence and relationship with psychopathic traits. *Journal of Attention Disorders.*

Machielse, A. (2015). The heterogeneity of socially isolated older adults: A social isolation typology. *Journal of Gerontological Social Work, 58,* 338-356.

Maciejewski, P.K., & Prigerson, H.G. (2017). Prolonged, but not complicated, grief is a mental disorder. *British Journal of Psychology, 211,* 189-191.

Maciokas, J.B., & Crognale, M.A. (2003). Cognitive and attentional changes with age: Evidence from attentional blink deficits. *Experimental/Aging Research, 29,* 137-153.

Mackinnon, S.P., & others (2017). Cross-cultural comparisons of drinking motives in 10 countries: Data from the DRINC project. *Drug and Alcohol Review, 36,* 721-730.

MacMillan Uribe, A.L., Woelky, K.R., & Olson, B.H. (2019, in press). Exploring family-medicine providers' perspectives on group care visits for maternal and infant nutrition education. *Journal of Nutrition Education and Behavior.*

MacNeill, L., & others (2018). Trajectories of infants' biobehavioral development: Timing and rate of A-not-B performance gains and EEG maturation. *Child Development, 89,* 711-724.

MacPhee, D., & Prendergast, S. (2019). Room for improvement: Girls' and boys' home environments are still gendered. *Sex Roles, 80*(5-6), 332-346.

Madden, D.J., & Parks, E.L. (2017). Age differences in structural connectivity: DTI and WMHs. In R. Cabeza, L. Nyberg, & D.C. Park (Eds.), *Cognitive neuroscience and aging* (2nd ed.). New York: Oxford University Press.

Madden, D.J., & others (1999). Aging and recognition memory: Changes in regional cerebral blood flow associated with components of reaction time distributions. *Journal of Cognitive Neuroscience, 11,* 511-520.

Mader, S., & Windelspecht, M. (2020). *Inquiry into life* (16th ed.). New York: McGraw-Hill.

Madjar, N., Cohen, V., & Shoval, G. (2018). Longitudinal analysis of the trajectories of academic and social motivation across the transition from elementary to middle school. *Educational Psychology, 38,* 221-247.

Madore, K.P., Jing, H.G., & Schacter, D.L. (2019, in press). Selective effects of specificity induction is on episodic details: Evidence for an event construction account. *Memory.*

Madrasi, K., & others (2018). Regulatory perspectives in pharmacometric models of osteoporosis. *Journal of Clinical Pharmacology, 58,* 572-585.

Magen, H., & Berger-Mandelbaum, A. (2018). Encoding strategies in self-initiated visual working memory. *Memory and Cognition, 46,* 1093-1108.

Magno, C. (2010). The role of metacognitive skills in developing critical thinking. *Metacognition and Learning, 5,* 137-156.

Magnuson, K.A., & Duncan, G.J. (2019). Parents in poverty. In M.H. Bornstein (Ed.), *Handbook of parenting* (3rd ed.). New York: Routledge.

Magro-Malosso, E.R., & others (2017). Exercise during pregnancy and risk of gestational hypertensive disorders: A systematic review and meta-analysis. *Acta Obstetricia and Gynecologica Scandinavica, 96,* 263-273.

Maher, L.M. (2018). Broca's aphasia and grammatical processing. In A.M. Rayner & L.J. Gonzalez Rothi (Eds.), *Oxford handbook of aphasia and language disorders.* New York: Oxford University Press.

Mahoney, J.L., & Vest, A.E. (2012). The overscheduling hypothesis revisited: Intensity of organized activity participation during adolescence and young adult outcomes. *Journal of Research on Adolescence, 22,* 409-418.

Maid, S., & Power, J.H.T. (2018). Oxidative stress and decreased mitochondrial superoxide dismutase 2 and peroxiredoxin 1 and 4 based mechanism of concurrent activation of AMPK and mTOR in Alzheimer's disease. *Current Alzheimer Research, 15,* 764-776.

Maier, J.G., & others (2019, in press). Sleep orchestrates indices of local plasticity and global network stability in the human cortex. *Sleep.*

Majeed, A., & others (2019, in press). Can ultrasound in early gestation improve visualization of fetal cardiac structures in obese pregnant women? *Journal of Ultrasound Medicine.*

Malamitsi-Puchner, A., & Boutsikou, T. (2006). Adolescent pregnancy and perinatal outcome. *Pediatric Endocrinology Review, 3*(Suppl. 1), 170-171.

Malek-Ahmadi, M., & others (2016). Longer self-reported sleep duration is associated with decreased performance on the Montreal cognitive assessment in older adults. *Aging: Clinical and Experimental Research, 28,* 333-337.

Malin, H., Liauw, I., & Damon, W. (2017). Purpose and character development in early adolescence. *Journal of Youth and Adolescence, 46,* 1200-1215.

Malinowski, P., & others (2017). Mindful aging: The effects of regular brief mindfulness practice on electrophysiological markers of cognitive and affective processing in older adults. *Mindfulness, 8,* 78-84.

Mallett, K.A., & others (2019). An examination of parental permissiveness of alcohol use and monitoring, and their association with emerging adult drinking outcomes across college. *Alcoholism: Clinical and Experimental Research, 43,* 758-766.

Malloy, L.C., La Rooy, D.J., Lamb, M.A., & Katz, C. (2012). Developmentally sensitive interviewing for legal purposes. In M.E. Lamb, D.J. La Rooy, L.C. Malloy, & C. Katz (Eds.), *Children's testimony* (2nd ed.). New York: Wiley.

Malmberg, L.E., & others (2016). The influence of mothers' and fathers' sensitivity in the first year of life on children's cognitive outcomes at 18 and 36 months. *Child Care, Health, and Development, 42,* 1-7.

Malnou, E.C., Umlauf, D., Mouysset, M., & Cavaillé, J. (2019). Imprinted microRNA gene clusters in the evolution, development, and functions of mammalian placenta. *Frontiers in Genetics, 9,* 706.

Maloy, R.W., & others (2016). *Transforming learning with new technologies* (3rd ed.). Upper Saddle River, NJ: Pearson.

Malti, T., & Buchmann, M. (2010). Socialization and individual antecedents of adolescents' and young adults' moral motivation. *Journal of Youth and Adolescence, 39,* 138-149.

Mandler, J.M. (2000). Unpublished review of J.W. Santrock's *Life-span Development,* 8th ed. (New York: McGraw-Hill).

Mandler, J.M. (2004). *The functions of mind.* New York: Oxford University Press.

Mandler, J.M. (2010). *Jean Mandler.* Retrieved May 26, 2010, from http://www.cogsci.ucsd.edu/~jean/

Mandler, J.M., & McDonough, L. (1993). Concept formation in infancy. *Cognitive Development, 8,* 291-318.

Manenti, R., Cotelli, M., & Miniussi, C. (2011). Successful physiological aging and episodic memory: A brain stimulation study. *Behavioral Brain Research, 216*(1), 153-158.

Manfredini, R., & others (2017). Marital status, cardiovascular diseases, and cardiovascular risk factors:

A review of the evidence. *Journal of Women's Health, 26,* 624-632.

Manganaro, L., & others (2018). Highlights on MRI of the fetal body. *La Radiologia Medica, 123,* 271-285.

Mannell, R.C. (2000). Older adults, leisure, and wellness. *Journal of Leisurability, 26,* 3-10.

Manning, L.A., & Peifer, M. (2019, in press). Getting into shape: Tissue tension drives oriented cell divisions during organogenesis. *EMBO Journal.*

Manning, R.P., & others (2017). A systematic review of adult attachment and social anxiety. *Journal of Affective Disorders, 211,* 44-59.

Manning, W.D., Longmore, M.A., & Gordano, P.C. (2018). Cohabitation and intimate partner violence during emerging adulthood: High constraints and low commitment. *Journal of Family Issues, 39,* 1030-1055.

Mansor, N.S., Chow, C.M., & Halaki, M. (2019, in press). Cognitive effects of videogames in older adults and their moderators: A systematic review with meta-analysis and meta-regression. *Aging and Mental Health.*

Manuck, S.B., & McCaffery, J.M. (2014). Gene-environment interaction. *Annual Review of Psychology* (Vol. 65). Palo Alto, CA: Annual Reviews.

Manuel, A.L., & others (2019, in press). Sustained attention failures on a 3-min reaction time task is a sensitive marker of dementia. *Journal of Neurology.*

Maoz, H., Gvirts, H. Z., Sheffer, M., & Bloch, Y. (2017). Theory of mind and empathy in children with ADHD. *Journal of Attention Disorders.* doi:10.1177/1087054717710766

Maras, D., & others (2015). Screen time is associated with depression and anxiety in Canadian youth. *Preventive Medicine, 73,* 133-138.

Maravilla, J.C., & others (2017). Factors influencing repeated adolescent pregnancy: A review and meta-analysis. *American Journal of Obstetrics and Gynecology, 2017,* 529-545.

Marcdante, K., & Kliegman, R.M. (2018). *Nelson essentials of pediatrics* (8th ed.). New York: Elsevier.

March of Dimes (2018). *Premature birth report card.* White Plains, NY: Author.

Marchman, V.A., & others (2019a). Caregiver talk to young Spanish-English bilinguals: Comparing direct observation and parent report measures of dual-language exposure. *Developmental Science.*

Marchman, V.A., & others (2019b). Predictors of early vocabulary growth in children born preterm and full term: A study of processing speed and medical complications. *Child Neuropsychology.*

Marcia, J.E. (1980). Ego identity development. In J. Adelson (Ed.), *Handbook of adolescent psychology.* New York: Wiley.

Marcia, J.E. (1987). The identity status approach to the study of ego identity development. In T. Honess & K. Yardley (Eds.), *Self and identity: Perspectives across the lifespan.* London: Routledge & Kegan Paul.

Marcia, J.E. (1994). The empirical study of ego identity. In H.A. Bosma, T.L.G. Graafsma, H.D. Grotevant, & D.J. De Levita (Eds.), *Identity and development.* Newbury Park, CA: Sage.

Marcia, J.E. (1996). Unpublished review of J.W. Santrock's *Adolescence,* 7th ed., for Brown & Benchmark, Dubuque, Iowa.

Marcia, J.E. (2002). Identity and psychosocial development in adulthood. *Identity, 2,* 7-28.

Marcovitch, S., Clearfield, M.W., Swinger, M., Calkins, S.D., & Bell, M.A. (2016). Attentional predictors of

5-month-olds' performance on a looking A-not-B task. *Infant and Child Development, 25,* 233-246.

Mares, I., & others (2018). Revealing the neural time-course of direct gaze processing via spatial frequency manipulation of faces. *Biological Psychology, 135,* 76-83.

Mares, M-L., & Pan, Z. (2013). Effects of *Sesame Street*: A meta-analysis of children's learning in 15 countries. *Journal of Applied Developmental Psychology, 34,* 140-151.

Margolis, A., & others (2013). Using IQ discrepancy scores to examine neural correlates of specific cognitive abilities. *Journal of Neuroscience, 33,* 14135-14145.

Margran, T.H., & Boulton, M. (2005). Sensory impairment. In M.L. Johnson (Ed.), *The Cambridge handbook of age and aging.* New York: Cambridge University Press.

Marinova, P. (2013, February 12). The upside of online dating: There's always a funny story to tell. *CNN Living.* Retrieved February 27, 2013, from www.cnn.com/2012/02/11/living/online-dating-irpt

Marioni, R.E., & others (2018). Meta-analysis of epigenome association studies of cognitive abilities. *Molecular Psychiatry, 23,* 2133-2144.

Mark, K.S., & others (2015). Knowledge, attitudes, and practice of electronic cigarette use among pregnant women. *Journal of Addiction Medicine, 9,* 266-272.

Markham, C.M., & others (2010). Neighborhood poverty, aspirations and expectations, and initiation of sex. *Journal of Adolescent Health, 47,* 399-406.

Markman, H.J., Halford, W.K., & Hawkins, A.J. (2019). Couple and relationship education. In B.H. Fiese (Ed.), *APA handbook of contemporary family psychology.* Washington, DC: APA Books.

Markus, H.R., & Kitayama, S. (2010). Cultures and selves: A cycle of multiple constitution. *Perspectives on Psychological Science, 5,* 420-430.

Markus, H.R., & Kitayama, S. (2012). Culture and the self. In K. Vohs & R.F. Baumeister (Eds.), *Self and identity.* Thousand Oaks, CA: Sage.

Markus, H.R., & Nurius, P. (1986). Possible selves. *American Psychologist, 41,* 954-969.

Marquez-Gonzalez, M., Cheng, S-K., & Losada, A. (2019). Coping mechanisms through successful aging. In R. Fernandez-Ballesteros, A. Benetos, & J-M. Robine (Eds.), *Cambridge handbook of successful aging.* New York: Cambridge University Press.

Marselle, M.R., Warber, S.L., & Irvine, K.N. (2019). Growing resilience through interaction with nature: Can group walks buffer the effects of stressful life events on mental health? *International Journal of Environmental Research and Public Health, 16,* 986.

Marsh, H.L., & Legerstee, M. (2017). Awareness of goal-directed behavior during infancy and early childhood, in human- and non-human primates. *Infant Behavior and Development, 48,* 30-37.

Marshall, J., & others (2019). Family-centered perinatal services for children with Down Syndrome and their families in Florida. *Journal of Obstetric, Gynecologic, and Neonatal Nursing, 48,* 78-89.

Marshall, K.A., & Hale, D. (2018). Elder abuse. *Home Healthcare Now, 36,* 51-52.

Marshall, N.A., & others (2018). Socioeconomic disadvantage and altered corticostriatal circuitry in urban youth. *Human Brain Mapping, 39,* 1982-1994.

Marshall, S.L., Parker, P.D., Ciarrochi, J., & Heaven, P.C.L. (2014). Is self-esteem a cause or consequence of social support? A 4-year longitudinal study. *Child Development, 85,* 1275-1291.

Marsiglia, F.F., & others (2019, in press). The role of culture of origin on the effectiveness of parents-involved intervention to prevent substance use among Latino middle school youth: Results from a cluster randomized controlled trial. *Prevention Science.*

Martin, A., & others (2018). Physical activity, diet, and other behavioral interventions for improving cognition and school achievement in children and adolescents with obesity or overweight. *Cochrane Database of Systematic Reviews, 1,* CD009728.

Martin, C.L. (1990). Attitudes and expectations about children with nontraditional and traditional gender roles. *Sex Roles, 22,* 151-165.

Martin, C.L., & Fabes, R.A. (2001). The stability and consequences of young children's same-sex peer interactions. *Developmental Psychology, 37,* 431-446.

Martin, C.L., Ruble, D.N., & Szkrybalo, J. (2002). Cognitive theories of early gender development. *Psychological Bulletin, 128,* 903-933.

Martin, C.L., & others (2013). The role of sex of peers and gender-typed activities in young children's peer affiliative networks: A longitudinal analysis of selection and influence. *Child Development, 84*(3), 921-937.

Martin, C.L., & others (2017). Reviving androgyny: A modern day perspective on flexibility of gender identity and behavior. *Sex Roles, 76,* 592-603.

Martin, J., & others (2019, in press). Maternal sensitivity in the first 3½ years of life predicts electrophysiological responding to and cognitive appraisals of infant crying at midlife. *Developmental Psychology.*

Martin, J.A., & others (2017). Births: Final data for 2015. *National Vital Statistics Reports, 66*(1).

Martin, K.B., & Messinger, D.B. (2018). Smile. In M.H. Bornstein (Ed.), *SAGE encyclopedia of lifespan human development.* Thousand Oaks, CA: Sage.

Martin, L.R., Friedman, H.S., & Schwartz, J.E. (2007). Personality and mortality risk across the lifespan: The importance of conscientiousness as a biopsychosocial attribute. *Health Psychology, 26,* 428-436.

Martin, M.J., & others (2017). The mediating role of cortisol reactivity and executive functioning difficulties in the pathways between childhood histories of emotional insecurity and adolescent school problems. *Development and Psychopathology, 29,* 1483-1498.

Martin, M.J., & others (2019, in press). Attachment behavior and hostility as explanatory factors linking parent-adolescent conflict and adolescent adjustment. *Journal of Family Psychology.*

Martin, M.M., & others (2016). Cocaine-induced neurodevelopmental deficits and underlying mechanisms. *Birth Defects Research C: Embryo Today, 108,* 147-173.

Martin-Perina, M.M., Vinas Poch, F., & Malo Cerrato, S. (2019). Media multitasking impact in homework, executive function, and academic performance in Spanish students. *Psicothema, 31,* 81-87.

Martin-Storey, A., & Crosnoe, R. (2012). Sexual minority status, peer harassment, and adolescent depression. *Journal of Adolescence, 35,* 1001-1011.

Martinez, Y.A., Schneider, B.H., Zambrana, A., Batista, G.S., & Soca, Z.S. (2015). Does comorbid anger exacerbate the rejection of children with depression by their school peers? *Child Psychiatry and Human Development, 46,* 493-500.

Martinez-Brockman, J.L., & others (2018). Impact of Lactation Advice through Texting Can Help (LATCH) trial on time to first contact and exclusive breastfeeding among WIC participants. *Journal of Nutrition Education and Behavior, 50,* 33-42.

Martins, B., Sheepes, G., Gross, J.J., & Mather, M. (2018). Age differences in emotion regulation choice: Older adults use distraction less than young adults in high-intensity positive contexts. *Journals of Gerontology B: Psychological Sciences and Social Sciences, 73,* 603-611.

Martz, M.E., Patrick, M.E., & Schulenberg, J.E. (2015). Alcohol mixed with energy drink use among U.S. 12th grade students: Prevalence, correlates, and associations with safe driving. *Journal of Adolescent Health, 56,* 557-563.

Mascolo, M.F., & Fischer, K.W. (2007). The co-development of self and socio-moral emotions during the toddler years. In C.A. Brownell & C.B. Kopp (Eds.), *Transitions in early development.* New York: Guilford.

Mascolo, M.F., & Fischer, K.W. (2010). The dynamic development of thinking, feeling, and acting over the life span. In W.F. Overton & R.M. Lerner (Eds.), *Handbook of life-span development* (Vol. 1). New York: Wiley.

Mash, E.J., & Wolfe, D.A. (2019). *Abnormal child psychology* (7th ed.). Boston: Cengage.

Mashburn, A.J., Justice, L.M., Downer, J.T., & Pianta, R.C. (2009). Peer effects on children's language achievement during pre-kindergarten. *Child Development, 80,* 686-702.

Mason-Apps, E., & others (2018). Longitudinal predictors of early language in infants with Down syndrome: A preliminary study. *Research in Developmental Disabilities, 81,* 37-51.

Masoodi, N. (2013). Review: Cholinesterase inhibitors do not reduce progression to dementia from mild cognitive impairment. *Annals of Internal Medicine, 158,* JC2-JC3.

Masten, A.S. (2001). Ordinary magic: Resilience processes in development. *American Psychologist, 56*(3), 227-238.

Masten, A.S. (2005). Peer relationships and psychopathology in developmental perspective: Reflections on progress and promise. *Journal of Clinical Child and Adolescent Psychology, 34,* 87-92.

Masten, A.S. (2006). Developmental psychopathology: Pathways to the future. *International Journal of Behavioral Development, 31,* 46-53.

Masten, A.S. (2009). Ordinary Magic: Lessons from research on resilience in human development. *Education Canada, 49*(3), 28-32.

Masten, A.S. (2011). Resilience in children threatened by extreme adversity: Frameworks for research, practice, and translational synergy. *Development and Psychopathology, 23,* 141-153.

Masten, A.S. (2012). Faculty profile: Ann Masten. *The Institute of Child Development further developments.* Minneapolis: School of Education.

Masten, A.S. (2013). Risk and resilience in development. In P.D. Zelazo (Ed.), *Oxford handbook of developmental psychology.* New York: Oxford University Press.

Masten, A.S. (2014a). *Ordinary magic.* New York: Guilford.

Masten, A.S. (2014b). Global perspectives on resilience in children and youth. *Child Development, 85,* 6-20.

Masten, A.S. (2015). Pathways to integrated resilience science. *Psychological Inquiry, 27,* 187-196.

Masten, A.S. (2017). Building a transformational science on children and youth affected by political violence and armed conflict: A commentary. *Development and Psychopathology, 29,* 79-84.

Masten, A.S. (2019, in press). Resilience from a developmental systems perspective. *World Psychiatry.*

Masten, A.S., & Kalstabakken, A.W. (2018). Developmental perspectives on psychopathology in children and adolescents. In J. Butcher (Ed.), *APA handbook of psychopathology.* Washington, DC: American Psychological Association.

Masten, A.S., & Palmer, A. (2019). Parenting to promote resilience in children. In M.H. Bornstein (Ed.), *Handbook of parenting* (3rd ed., Vol. 5). New York: Routledge.

Mastin, J.D., & Vogt, P. (2016). Infant engagement and early vocabulary development: a naturalistic observation study of Mozambican infants from 1;1 to 2;1. *Journal of Child Language, 43,* 235-264.

Mastorakos, T., & Scott, K.L. (2019). Attention biases and social-emotional development in preschool-aged children who have been exposed to domestic violence. *Child Abuse and Neglect, 89,* 78-86.

Mastropieri, M.A., & Scruggs, T.E. (2018). *Inclusive classroom* (6th ed.). Upper Saddle River, NJ: Pearson.

Match.com (2011). *The Match.com Single in America Study.* Retrieved February 7, 2011, from http://blog.match.com/singles-study

Match.com (2012). *Singles in America 2012.* Retrieved June 10, 2012, from http://blog.match.com/singles-in-america

Match.com (2017). *Singles in America 2017.* Retrieved August 16, 2017, from www.singlesinamerica.com

Mateos, R.M., & others (2018). Excess hydrocortisone hampers placental nutrient uptake disrupting cellular mechanism. *Biomedical Research International, 2018,* 5106174.

Mather, M., & Ponzio, A. (2018). Emotion and aging. In. L.F. Barrett & others (Eds.), *Handbook of emotion* (4th ed.). New York: Guilford.

Mathes, W.F., & others (2010). Dopaminergic dysregulation in mice selectively bred for excessive exercise or obesity. *Behavioral Brain Research, 210,* 155-163.

Matias, M., & Fontaine, M. (2015). Coping with work and family: How do dual-earners interact? *Scandinavian Journal of Psychology, 56,* 212-222.

Matlin, M.W. (2012). The *psychology of women* (7th ed.). Belmont, CA: Wadsworth.

Matlow, J.N., Jubetsky, A., Alesksa, K., Berger, H., & Koren, G. (2013). The transfer of ethyl glucuronide across the dually perfused human placenta. *Placenta, 34,* 369-373.

Matos, A.P., Ferreira, J.A., & Haase, R.F. (2012). Television and aggression: A test of a mediated model with a sample of Portuguese students. *Journal of Social Psychology, 152,* 75-91.

Matos, K. (2015). *Modern families: Same- and different-sex couples negotiating at home.* New York: Families and Work Institute.

Matsuba, M.K., & Walker, L.J. (2004). Extraordinary moral commitment: Young adults involved in social organizations. *Journal of Personality, 72,* 413-436.

Matsumoto, D., & Hwang, H.C. (Eds.). (2019). *Handbook of culture and psychology* (2nd ed.). New York: Oxford University Press.

Matthes, J., Prieler, M., & Adam, K. (2016). Gender-role portrayals in television advertising across the globe. *Sex Roles, 75,* 314-327.

Matthiessen, C. (2015). *Overweight children: Tips for parents.* Retrieved February 25, 2015, from www.webmd.com/parenting/raising-fit-kids/mood/talking-kids . . .

Mattison, J.A., & others (2012). Impact of caloric restriction on health and survival in rhesus monkeys from the NIA study. *Nature, 489,* 318-321.

Maurer, D. (2016). How the baby learns to see: Donald O. Hebb Award lecture, Canadian Society for Brain, Behavior, and Cognitive Science, Ottawa, June 2015. *Canadian Journal of Experimental Psychology, 70,* 195-200.

Maurer, D., & Lewis, T.L. (2013). Sensitive periods in visual development. In P.D. Zelazo (Ed.), *Oxford handbook of developmental psychology.* New York: Oxford University Press.

Maurer, D., Lewis, T.L., Brent, H.P., & Levin, A.V. (1999). Rapid improvement in the acuity of infants after visual input. *Science, 286,* 108-110.

Maurer, D., Mondloch, C.J., & Leis, T.L. (2007). Effects of early visual deprivation on perceptual and cognitive development. In C. von Hofsten & K. Rosander (Eds.), *Progress in Brain Research, 164,* 87-104.

Mayas, J., Parmentier, F.B., Andres, P., & Ballesteros, S. (2014). Plasticity of attentional functions in older adults after non-action video game training: A randomized controlled trial. *PloS One, 9*(3), e92269.

Mayer, R.E. (2008). *Curriculum and instruction* (2nd ed.). Upper Saddle River, NJ: Prentice Hall.

Mayer, R.E. (2020, in press). Intelligence, education, and society. In R.J. Sternberg (Ed.), *Human intelligence.* New York: Cambridge University Press.

Mayo Clinic (2019). *Male hypogonadism.* Rochester, MN: Mayo Clinic.

Mayo, J.A., & others (2019, in press). Parental age and stillbirth: A population-based cohort study of nearly 10 million California deliveries from 1991 to 2011. *Annals of Epidemiology.*

Mayoral, V.F.S., & others (2018). Cross-cultural adaptation of the Physician Orders for Life-Sustaining Treatment form to Brazil. *Journal of Palliative Medicine, 21,* 815-819.

McAbee, S.T., & Oswald, F.L. (2013). The criterion-related validity of personality measures for predicting GPA: A meta-analytic validity comparison. *Psychological Assessment, 25,* 532-544.

McAdams, D.P., Josselson, R., & Lieblich, A. (Eds.). (2006). *Identity and story: Creating self in narrative.* Washington, DC: American Psychological Association Press.

McAdams, T.A., & others (2014). Co-occurrence of antisocial behavior and substance use: Testing for sex differences in the impact of older male friends, low parental knowledge, and friends' delinquency. *Journal of Adolescence, 37,* 247-256.

McBride, D.L. (2013). Like girls, boys are entering puberty earlier, new research finds. *Journal of Pediatric Nursing, 28*(2), 189-190.

McBride, K.L., & others (2019, in press). Phenylalanine and tyrosine measurements across gestation by tandem mass spectrometer on dried blood spot cards from normal pregnant women. *Genetics in Medicine.*

McBride-Chang, C. (2004). *Children's literacy development* (Texts in Developmental Psychology Series). London: Edward Arnold/Oxford Press.

McBride-Chang, C., & others (2005). Changing models across cultures: Associations of phonological and morphological awareness to reading in Beijing, Hong Kong, Korea, and America. *Journal of Experimental Child Psychology, 92,* 140-160.

McCabe, K.O., & Fleeson, W. (2016). Are traits useful? Explaining trait manifestations as tools in the pursuit of goals. *Journal of Personality and Social Psychology, 110,* 287-301.

McCabe, S.E., & others (2017). Adolescents' prescription stimulant use and adult functional outcomes: A national prospective study. *Journal of the Academy of Child and Adolescent Psychiatry, 56,* 226-233.

McCall, M.E., & Borjesson, U. (2017). Integration or specialization? Similarities and differences between Sweden and the United States in gerontology education and training. *Gerontology and Geriatrics Education, 38,* 47-60.

McCall, R.B., Applebaum, M.I., & Hogarty, P.S. (1973). Developmental changes in mental performance. *Monographs of the Society for Research in Child Development, 38* (Serial No. 150).

McCardle, P., Miller, B., Lee, J.R., & Tzeng, O.J. (2011). *Dyslexia across languages.* Baltimore: Paul H. Brookes.

McCarroll, J.E., & others (2017). Characteristics, classification, and prevention of child maltreatment fatalities. *Military Medicine, 182,* e1551-e1557.

McCartney, K. (2003, July 16). Interview with Kathleen McCartney in A. Bucuvalas, "Child care and behavior," *HGSE News,* 1-4. Cambridge, MA: Harvard Graduate School of Education.

McCauley, J.B., Mundy, P., & Solomon, M. (2019). Parenting and autism spectrum disorder. In M.H. Bornstein (Ed.), *Handbook of parenting* (3rd ed.). New York: Routledge.

McClain, C.S., Rosenfeld, B., & Breitbart, W.S. (2003). *The influence of spirituality on end-of-life despair in cancer patients close to death.* Paper presented at the meeting of the American Psychosomatic Society, Phoenix.

McClelland, M.M., & Cameron, C.E. (2019, in press). Developing together: The role of executive function and motor skills in children's early academic lives. *Early Childhood Research Quarterly.*

McClelland, M.M., Cameron, C.E., & Alonso, J. (2019). The development of self-regulation in young children. In D. Whitebread (Ed.), *Handbook of developmental psychology and early childhood education.* Thousand Oaks, CA: Sage.

McClelland, M.M., & others (2017). Self-regulation. In N. Halfon & others (Eds.), *Handbook of life course health development.* New York: Springer.

McClelland, W., & Goligher, E.C. (2019). Withholding or withdrawing life support versus physician-assisted death: A distinction with a difference? *Current Opinion in Anesthesiology, 32,* 184-189.

McClure, E.R., & others (2018). Look at that! Video chat and joint visual attention development among infants and toddlers. *Child Development, 89,* 27-36.

McConnachie, A.L., & others (2019, in press). Father-child attachment in adoptive gay father families. *Attachment and Human Development.*

McCoy, D.C. (2019). Measuring young children's executive function and self-regulation in classrooms and other real-world settings. *Clinical Child and Family Psychology Review, 22,* 63-74.

McCoy, D.C., & Raver, C.C. (2011). Caregiver emotional expressiveness, child emotion regulation, and child behavior problems among Head Start families. *Social Development, 20*(4), 741-761.

McCoy, M.B., & others (2018). Associations between peer counseling and breastfeeding initiation and duration: An analysis of Minnesota participants in the Special Supplemental Nutrition Program for Women, Infants, and Children (WIC). *Maternal and Child Health Journal, 22,* 71-81.

McCrae, R.R., & Costa, P.T. (1990). *Personality in adulthood.* New York: Guilford.

McCrae, R.R., & Costa, P.T. (2006). Cross-cultural perspectives on adult personality trait development. In D.K. Mroczek & T.D. Little (Eds.), *Handbook of personality development.* Mahwah, NJ: Erlbaum.

McCrae, R.R., & Sutin, A.R. (2009). Openness to experience. In M.R. Leary & R.H. Hoyle (Eds.), *Handbook of individual differences in social behavior.* New York: Guilford.

McCullogh, S. (2016). *Highest C-section rates by country.* Retrieved April 26, 2017, from www.bellybelly.com

McDermott, E.R., Umana-Taylor, A.J., & Zeiders, K.H. (2019, in press). Profiles of coping with ethnic-racial discrimination and Latina/o adolescents' adjustment. *Journal of Youth and Adolescence.*

McDonagh, M.S., Holmes, R., & Hsu, F. (2019, in press). Pharmacologic treatments for sleep disorders in children: A systematic review. *Journal of Child Neurology.*

McDonald, K.L., & Asher, S.R. (2018). Peer acceptance, peer rejection, and popularity: Social cognitive and behavioral perspectives. In W.M. Bukowski & others (Eds.), *Handbook of peer interactions, relationships, and groups* (2nd ed.). New York: Guilford.

McDonald, N.M., & Perdue, K.L. (2018). The infant brain in the social world: Moving toward interactive social neuroscience with functional near-infrared spectroscopy. *Neuroscience and Biobehavioral Reviews, 87,* 38-49.

McDougall, S., & others (2019, in press). Myelination of axons corresponds with faster transmission speed in the prefrontal cortex of developing male rats. *eNeuro.*

McDowell, J.J. (2019). On the current state of the evolutionary theory of behavior dynamics. *Journal of the Experimental Analysis of Behavior, 111,* 130-145.

McDowell, M., Cain, M.A., & Brumley, J. (2019). Excessive gestational weight gain. *Journal of Midwifery and Women's Health, 64,* 46-54.

McElhaney, K.B., & Allen, J.P. (2012). Sociocultural perspectives on adolescent autonomy. In P.K. Kreig, M.S. Schulz, & S.T. Hauser (Eds.), *Adolescence and beyond.* New York: Oxford University Press.

McGarry, J., Kim, H., Sheng, X., Egger, M., & Baksh, L. (2009). Postpartum depression and help-seeking behavior. *Journal of Midwifery and Women's Health, 54,* 50-56.

McGillion, M., Pine, J.M., Herbert, J.S., & Matthews, D. (2017b). A randomized controlled trial to test the effect of promoting caregiver contingent talk on language development in infants from diverse socioeconomic status backgrounds. *Journal of Child Psychology and Psychiatry, 58,* 1122-1131.

McGillion, M., & others (2017a). What paves the way to conventional language? The predictive value of babble, pointing, and socioeconomic status. *Child Development, 88,* 156-166.

McGue, M., Hirsch, B., & Lykken, D.T. (1993). Age and the self-perception of ability: A twin analysis. *Psychology and Aging, 8,* 72–80.

McHale, J.P., Negrini, L., & Sirotkin, Y. (2019). Coparenting. In B.H. Friese (Ed.), *APA handbook of contemporary family psychology.* Washington, DC: APA Books.

McHale, J.P., Salman-Engin, S., & Coovert, M.D. (2015). Improvements in unmarried African American parents' rapport, communication, and problem-solving following a prenatal coparenting intervention. *Family Process, 54,* 619–629.

McHale, J.P., & Sirotkin, Y. (2019). Coparenting in diverse family systems. In M.H. Bornstein (Ed.), *Handbook of parenting* (3rd ed.). New York: Routledge.

McHale, S.M., Updegraff, K.A., & Whiteman, S.D. (2013). Sibling relationships. In G.W. Peterson & K.R. Bush (Eds.), *Handbook of marriage and family* (3rd ed.). New York: Springer.

McKay, A.S., & Kaufman, J.C. (2014). Literary geniuses: Their life, work, and death. In D.K. Simonton (Ed.), *Wiley-Blackwell handbook of genius.* New York: Wiley.

McKellar, S.E., & others (2019, in press). Threats and supports to female students' math beliefs and achievement. *Journal of Research on Adolescence.*

McLaughlin, C.N., & Broihier, H.T. (2018). Keeping neurons young and foxy: FoxOs promote neuronal plasticity. *Trends in Genetics, 34,* 65–78.

McLaughlin, K. (2003, December 30). Commentary in K. Painter, "Nurse dispenses dignity for dying." *USA Today,* pp. D1–D2.

McLean, K.C., & Breen, A.V. (2009). Processes and content of narrative identity development in adolescence: Gender and well-being. *Developmental Psychology, 45,* 702–710.

McLean, K.C., Breen, A.V., & Fournier, M.A. (2010). Constructing the self in early, middle, and late adolescent boys: Narrative identity, individuation, and well-being. *Journal of Research on Adolescence, 20,* 166–187.

McLean, K.C., & Jennings, L.E. (2012). Teens telling tall tales: How maternal and peer audiences support narrative identity development. *Journal of Adolescence, 35,* 1455–1469.

McLean, K.C., & Pratt, M.W. (2006). Life's little (and big) lessons: Identity statuses and meaning-making in the turning point narratives of emerging adults. *Developmental Psychology, 42,* 714–722.

McLean, K.C., Syed, M., Yoder, A., & Greenhoot, A. (2016). The role of domain content in understanding identity development processes. *Journal of Research on Adolescence, 26,* 60–75.

McLean, K.C., & others (2018). Identity development in cultural context: The role of deviating from master narratives. *Journal of Personality, 86,* 631–651.

McLeish, J., & Redshaw, M. (2018). A qualitative study of volunteer doulas working alongside midwives at births in England: Mothers' and doulas' experiences. *Midwivery, 56,* 53–60.

McLoyd, V.C. (1990). The impact of economic hardship on Black families and children: Psychological distress, parenting, and socioemotional development. *Child Development, 61,* 311–346.

McLoyd, V.C., Hardaway, C., & Jocson, R.M. (2019). African American parenting. In M.H. Bornstein (Ed.), *Handbook of parenting* (3rd ed.). New York: Routledge.

McMahon, M., & Stryjewski, G. (2011). *Pediatrics.* New York: Elsevier.

McManus, B.M., & others (2019). Timing and intensity of early intervention service use and outcomes among a safety-net population of children. *JAMA Network Open, 2*(1), e187529.

McMillan, J.H. (2018). *Classroom assessment* (7th ed.). Upper Saddle River, NJ: Pearson.

McMillen, C.M., Graves-Demario, A., & Kieliszek, D. (2018). Tackling literacy: A collaborative approach to developing materials for assessing science literacy skills in content classrooms through a STEM perspective. *Language and Literacy Spectrum, 28,* 2.

McNamara, M., Batur, P., & DeSapri, K.T. (2015). In the clinic: Perimenopause. *Annals in Internal Medicine, 162,* 1–15.

McQuire, C., & others (2019, in press). The causal web of fetal alcohol spectrum disorders: A review and causal diagram. *European Child and Adolescent Psychiatry.*

McSweeen, M.P., & others (2019). The immediate effects of acute aerobic exercise on cognition in healthy older adults: A systematic review. *Sports Medicine, 49,* 67–82.

Mead, M. (1978, Dec. 30–Jan. 5). The American family: An endangered species. *TV Guide,* 21–24.

Meade, C.S., Kershaw, T.S., & Ickovics, J.R. (2008). The intergenerational cycle of teenage motherhood: An ecological approach. *Health Psychology, 27,* 419–429.

Medford, E., & others (2018). Treatment adherence and psychological wellbeing in maternal caregivers of children with phenylketonuria (PKU). *JMD Reports, 39,* 107–116.

Medina, A.C., Rowley, S.J., & Towson, S.J. (2019). Race matters for Black Canadians: The intersection of acculturation and racial identity in emerging adulthood. *Emerging Adulthood, 7,* 97–108.

Medrano, M., & others (2018). Evidence-based exercise recommendations to reduce hepatic fat content in youth—A systematic review and meta-analysis. *Progress in Cardiovascular Disease, 61,* 222–231.

Meeks, L., Heit, P., & Page, R. (2020). *Comprehensive school health education* (9th ed.). New York: McGraw-Hill.

Mehlhausen-Hassoen, D. (2019, in press). Gender-specific differences in corporal punishment and children's perceptions of their mothers' and fathers' parenting. *Journal of Interpersonal Violence.*

Mehta, C.M., & Strough, J. (2009). Sex segregation in friendships and normative contexts across the life span. *Development Review, 29,* 201–220.

Mehta, C.M., & Strough, J. (2010). Gender segregation and gender-typing in adolescence. *Sex Roles, 63,* 251–263.

Mei, F., & others (2019, in press). Analysis of HBV x gene quasispecies characteristics by next generation sequencing and cloning-based sequencing and its association with hepatocellular carcinoma progression. *Journal of Medical Virology.*

Meier, E.A., & others (2016). Defining a good death (successful dying): Literature review and a call for research and public dialogue. *American Journal of Geriatric Psychiatry, 24,* 261–271.

Meisel, V., Servera, M., Garcia-Banda, G., Cardo, E., & Moreno, I. (2013). Neurofeedback and standard pharmacological intervention in ADHD: A randomized controlled trial with six-month follow-up. *Biological Psychology, 94,* 12–21.

Meldrum, R.C., & Hay, C. (2012). Do peers matter in the development of self-control? Evidence from a longitudinal study of youth. *Journal of Youth and Adolescence, 41,* 691–703.

Meldrum, R.C., & others (2017). Reassessing the relationship between general intelligence and self-control in childhood. *Intelligence, 60,* 1–9.

Meléndez, J.C., Fortuna, F.B., Sales, A., & Mayordomo, T. (2015). The effects of instrumental reminiscence on resilience and coping in elderly. *Archives of Gerontology and Geriatrics, 60,* 294–298.

Melendez, J.C., & others (2019). Big Five and psychological and subjective well-being in Colombian older adults. *Archives of Gerontology and Geriatrics, 82,* 88–93.

Melis Yavuz, H., & Selcuk, B. (2018). Predictors of obesity and overweight in preschoolers: The role of parenting styles and feeding practices. *Appetite, 120,* 491–499.

Meltzoff, A.N., & others (2018). Infant brain responses to felt and observed touch of hands and feet: An MEG study. *Developmental Science, 21*(5), e13030.

Meltzoff, A.N., & others (2019). Eliciting imitation in early infancy. *Developmental Science, 22*(2), e12738.

Memitz, S.A. (2019, in press). The mental health implications of emerging adult long-term cohabitation. *Emerging Adulthood.*

Memone, L., Fiacco, S., & Ehlert, U. (2019). Psychobiological factors in sexual functioning in aging women—Findings from the Women 40+ Healthy Aging Study. *Frontiers in Psychology, 10,* 546.

Mendelson, M., & others (2016). Sleep quality, sleep duration, and physical activity in obese adolescents: Effects of exercise training. *Pediatric Obesity, 11,* 26–32.

Mendle, J., Ryan, R.M., & McKone, K.M.P. (2019, in press).Age at menarche, depression, and antisocial behavior in adulthood. *Pediatrics.*

Mendoza Laiz, N., & others (2018). Potential benefits of a cognitive training program in mild cognitive impairment (MCI). *Restorative Neurology and Neuroscience, 36,* 207–213.

Mendoza-Denton, R., & Worrell, F. (2019). Culture, race, ethnicity, and personality. In D. Cohen & S. Kitayama (Eds.). *Handbook of cultural psychology.* New York: Guilford.

Mendoza-Nunez, V.M., & de la Luz Martinez-Maldonado, M. (2019). Promoting successful aging in the community. In R. Fernandez-Ballesteros, A. Benetos, & J-M. Robine (Eds.), *Cambridge handbook of successful aging.* New York: Cambridge University Press.

Menec, V.H. (2003). The relation between everyday activities and successful aging: A 6-year longitudinal study. *Journals of Gerontology B: Psychological Sciences and Social Sciences, 58,* 574–582.

Meng, Q., & others (2019). Age-related changes in local and global visual perception. *Journal of Vision, 19*(1), 10.

Meng, X., & D'Arcy, C. (2014). Successful aging in Canada: Prevalence and predictors from a population-based sample of older adults. *Gerontology, 60,* 65–72.

Menn, L., & Stoel-Gammon, C. (2009). Phonological development: Learning sounds and sound patterns. In J. Berko Gleason (Ed.), *The development of language* (7th ed.). Boston: Allyn & Bacon.

Mennella, J.A. (2009). Taste and smell. In R.A. Shweder & others (Eds.), *The child: An encyclopedic companion.* Chicago: University of Chicago Press.

Menon, R., & others (2011). Cigarette smoking induces oxidative stress and atopsis in normal fetal membranes. *Placenta, 32,* 317–322.

Menyuk, P., Liebergott, J., & Schultz, M. (1995). *Early language development in full-term and premature infants.* Hillsdale, NJ: Erlbaum.

Mercer, N. (2008). Talk and the development of reasoning and understanding. *Human Development, 51,* 90–100.

Mercer, N., & others (2016). Childhood predictors and adult life success of adolescent delinquency abstainers. *Journal of Abnormal Child Psychology, 44,* 613–624.

Merchant, S.J., & others (2019, in press). Palliative care and symptom burden in the last year of life: A population-based study of patients with gastrointestinal cancer. *Annals of Surgical Oncology.*

Meredith, N.V. (1978). Research between 1960 and 1970 on the standing height of young children in different parts of the world. In H.W. Reece & L.P. Lipsitt (Eds.), *Advances in child development and behavior* (Vol. 12). New York: Academic Press.

Merrill, D.M. (2009). Parent-child relationships: Later-life. In D. Carr (Ed.), *Encyclopedia of the life course and human development.* Boston: Gale Cengage.

Mervak, B.M., & others (2019, in press). MRI in pregnancy: Indications and practical considerations. *Journal of Magnetic Resonance Imaging.*

Meschkow, A.M., & others (2018). Risk taking. In M.H. Bornstein (Ed.), *SAGE encyclopedia of lifespan human development.* Thousand Oaks, CA: Sage.

Messerlian, C., & Basso, O. (2018). Cohort studies in the context of obstetric and gynecologic research: A methodological overview. *Acta Obstetricia et Gynecologica Scandinavica, 97,* 371–379.

Messiah, S.E., Miller, T.L., Lipshultz, S.E., & Bandstra, E.S. (2011). Potential latent effects of prenatal cocaine exposure on growth and the risk of cardiovascular and metabolic disease in childhood. *Progress in Pediatric Cardiology, 31,* 59–65.

Messier, S.P., & others (2018). Intentional weight loss for overweight and obese knee osteoarthritis patients: Is more better? *Arthritis Care and Research, 70,* 1569–1575.

Messinger, D. (2008). Smiling. In M.M. Haith & J.B. Benson (Eds.), *Encyclopedia of infant and early childhood development.* Oxford, UK: Elsevier.

Messinger, D.S., & others (2017). Temporal dependency and the structure of early looking. *PLoS One, 12,* e0169458.

Messinger, J.C. (1971). Sex and repression in an Irish folk community. In D.S. Marshall & R.C. Suggs (Eds.), *Human sexual behavior: Variations in the ethnic spectrum.* New York: Basic Books.

Meteyard, L., Vigliocco, G. (2019). Lexico-semantics. In S.A. Rueschemeyer & M. Gareth Gaskell (Eds.), *Oxford handbook of psycholinguistics* (2nd ed.). New York: Oxford University Press.

Metts, S., & Cupach, W.R. (2007). Responses to relational transgressions. In M. Tafoya & B.H. Spitzberg (Eds.), *The dark side of interpersonal communication.* Mahwah, NJ: Erlbaum.

Metz, E.C., & Youniss, J. (2005). Longitudinal gains in civic development through school-based required service. *Political Psychology, 26,* 413–437.

Metzger, A., & others (2018). The intersection of emotional and sociocognitive competencies with civic engagement in middle childhood and adolescence. *Journal of Youth and Adolescence, 47,* 1663–1683.

Meusel, L.A., & others (2017). Brain-behavior relationships in source memory: Effects of age and memory ability. *Cortex, 91,* 221–233.

Meuwissen, A.S., & Carlson, S.M. (2018). The role of father parenting in children's school readiness: A longitudinal follow-up. *Journal of Family Psychology, 32,* 588–599.

Meyer, M.H., & Parker, W.M. (2011). Gender, aging, and social policy. In R.H. Binstock & L.K. George (Eds.), *Handbook of aging and the social sciences* (7th ed.). New York: Elsevier.

Meyre, D., & others (2018). An evolutionary genetic perspective of eating disorders. *Neuroendocrinology, 106,* 292–306.

Mi, S.J., & others (2019, in press). Association of sleep patterns with metabolic syndrome indices, body composition, and energy intake in children and adolescents. *Pediatric Obesity.*

Michael, R.T., Gagnon, J.H., Laumann, E.O., & Kolate, G. (1994). *Sex in America.* Boston: Little Brown.

Mick, P., & Pichora-Fuller, M.K. (2016). Is hearing loss associated with poorer health in older adults who might benefit from hearing screening? *Ear and Hearing, 37,* e194–e201.

Mick, P., & others (2018). Associations between sensory loss and social networks, participation, support, and loneliness: Analysis of the Canadian Longitudinal Study of Aging. *Canadian Family Physician, 64,* e33–e41.

Mike, A., Harris, K., Roberts, B.W., & Jackson, J.J. (2015). Conscientiousness: Lower-order structure, life course consequences, and development. In J. Wright (Ed.), *International encyclopedia of social and behavioral sciences* (2nd ed.). New York: Elsevier.

Mikkola, T.M., & others (2016). Self-reported hearing is associated with time spent out-of-home and withdrawal from leisure activities in older community-dwelling adults. *Aging: Clinical and Experimental Research, 28,* 297–302.

Mikulincer, M., & Shaver, P.R. (2014). The role of attachment security in adolescent and adult close relationships. In J.A. Simpson & L. Campbell (Eds.), *Oxford handbook of close relationships.* New York: Oxford University Press.

Mikulincer, M., & Shaver, P.R. (2016). *Attachment in adulthood* (2nd ed.). New York: Guilford.

Mikulincer, M., & Shaver, P.R. (2019). Attachment theory expanded: A behavioral systems approach to personality. In K. Deaux & M. Snyder (Eds.), *Oxford handbook of personality and social psychology.* New York: Oxford University Press.

Miller, A.B., Esposito-Smythers, C., Weismoore, J.T., & Renshaw, K.D. (2013). The relation between child maltreatment and adolescent suicidal behavior: A systematic review and critical examination of the literature. *Clinical Child and Family Psychology Review, 16*(2), 146–172.

Miller, B., Baptist, J., & Johannes, E. (2018). Health needs and challenges of rural adolescents. *Rural Remote Health, 18*(3), 4325.

Miller, B.C., Benson, B., & Galbraith, K.A. (2001). Family relationships and adolescent pregnancy risk: A research synthesis. *Developmental Review, 21,* 1–38.

Miller, C.B. (2017). *The character gap.* New York: Oxford University Press.

Miller, C.F., Lurye, L.E., Zosuls, K.M., & Ruble, D.N. (2009). Accessibility of gender stereotype domains: Developmental and gender differences in children. *Sex Roles, 60,* 870–881.

Miller, E.B., Farkas, G., & Duncan, G.J. (2016). Does Head Start differentially benefit children with risk by the program's service model? *Early Child Research Quarterly, 34,* 1–12.

Miller, E.B., Farkas, G., Vandell, D.L., & Duncan, G.J. (2014). Do the effects of Head Start vary by parental preacademic stimulation? *Child Development, 85*(4), 1385–1400.

Miller, J.B. (1986). *Toward a new psychology of women* (2nd ed.). Boston: Beacon Press.

Miller, J.G., Wice, M., & Goyal, N. (2019). Culture and moral development. In D. Matsumoto & H.C. Hwang (Eds.), *Handbook of cross-cultural psychology* (2nd ed.). New York: Oxford University Press.

Miller, J.G., Wice, M., & Goyal, N. (2020, in press). Culture, parenting practices, and moral development. In D.J. Laible & others (Eds.), *Oxford handbook of moral development.* New York: Oxford University Press.

Miller, M.S. (2018). Save for retirement. *Annals of Emergency Medicine 71,* 252.

Miller, P.H. (2015). *Theories of developmental psychology* (6th ed.). New York: Worth.

Miller, R., Wankerl, M., Stalder, T., Kirschbaum, C., & Alexander, N. (2013). The serotonin transporter gene-linked polymorphic region (5-HTTLPR) and cortisol stress reactivity: A meta-analysis. *Molecular Psychiatry, 18,* 1018–1024.

Miller, S., Malone, P., Dodge, K.A., & The Conduct Problems Prevention Research Group (2011). Developmental trajectories of boys' and girls' delinquency: Sex differences and links to later adolescent outcomes. *Journal of Abnormal Child Psychology, 38*(7), 1021–1032.

Miller, S.M. (2016). Connecting East and West by a developmental theory for older adults: Application of Baltes' selection, optimization, and compensation model. *Applied Nursing Research, 29,* 113–115.

Miller, W.R. (2019, in press). Self-management behaviors of children with spina bifida. *Journal of Neuroscience Nursing.*

Miller-Perrin, C.L., Perrin, R.D., & Kocur, J.L. (2009). Parental, physical, and psychological aggression: Psychological symptoms in young adults. *Child Abuse and Neglect, 33,* 1–11.

Mills, C.M. (2013). Knowing when to doubt: Developing a critical stance when learning from others. *Developmental Psychology, 114,* 63–76.

Mills, C.M., & Elashi, F.B. (2014). Children's skepticism: Developmental and individual differences in children's ability to detect and explain distorted claims. *Journal of Experimental Psychology, 124,* 1–17.

Mills, D., & Mills, C. (2000). *Hungarian kindergarten curriculum translation.* London: Mills Production.

Mills, M.T. (2015). Narrative performance of gifted African American school-aged children from low-income backgrounds. *American Journal of Speech-Language Pathology, 24,* 36–46.

Millsav, L., Ribaric, S., & Poljsak, B. (2019, in press). Antioxidant vitamins and aging. *Sub-cellular Biochemistry.*

Mills-Koonce, W.R., Propper, C.B., & Barnett, M. (2012). Poor infant soothability and later insecure-ambivalent attachment: Developmental change in phenotypic markers of risk or two measures of the same construct? *Infant Behavior and Development, 35,* 215–235.

Milne, E., & others (2012). Parental prenatal smoking and risk of childhood acute lymphoblastic leukemia. *American Journal of Epidemiology, 175,* 43–53.

Min, Z., Gao, J., & Yu, Y. (2019). The roles of mitochondrial SIRT4 in cellular metabolism. *Frontiers in Endocrinology, 9,* 783.

Minar, N.J., & Lewkowicz, D.J. (2019, in press). Overcoming the other-race effect in infancy with multisensory redundancy: 10-12-month-olds discriminate dynamic other-race faces producing speech. *Developmental Science.*

Miner, B., & Kryger, M.H. (2017). Sleep in the aging population. *Sleep Medicine Clinics, 12,* 31–38.

Miner, M.M., Bhattacharya, R.K., Blick, G., Kushner, H., & Khera, M. (2013). 12-month observation of testosterone replacement effectiveness in a general population of men. *Postgraduate Medicine, 125,* 8–18.

Minkler, M., & Fuller-Thompson, E. (2005). African American grandparents raising grandchildren: A national study using the Census 2000 American Community Survey. *Journals of Gerontology B: Psychological Sciences and Social Sciences, 60,* S82–S92.

Minnes, S., & others (2010). The effects of prenatal cocaine exposure on problem behavior in children 4–10 years. *Neurotoxicology and Teratology, 32,* 443–451.

Minnes, S., & others (2016). Executive function in children with prenatal cocaine exposure (12–15 years). *Neurotoxicology and Teratology, 57,* 79–86.

Minnesota Family Investment Program (2009). *Longitudinal study of early MFIP recipients.* Retrieved January 12, 2009, from www.dhs.state.mn.us/main/

Minsart, A.F., Buekens, P., De Spiegelaere, M., & Englert, Y. (2013). Neonatal outcomes in obese mothers: A population-based analysis. *BMC Pregnancy and Childbirth, 13,* 36.

Minuchin, P.O., & Shapiro, E.K. (1983). The school as a context for social development. In P.H. Mussen (Ed.), *Handbook of child psychology* (4th ed., Vol. 4). New York: Wiley.

Minuzzi, L.G., & others (2018). Effects of lifelong training on senescence and mobilization of T lymphocytes in response to acute exercise. *Exercise Immunology Review, 24,* 72–84.

Mir, Y.R., & Kuchay, R.A.H. (2019, in press). Advances in identification of genes involved in autosomal recessive intellectual disability: A brief review. *Journal of Medical Genetics.*

Mireku, M.O., & others (2019). Night-time screen-based media device use and adolescents' sleep and health-related quality of life. *Environmental Intervention, 124,* 66–78.

Mischel, W. (1968). *Personality and assessment.* New York: Wiley.

Mischel, W. (1974). Process in delay of gratification. In L. Berkowitz (Ed.), *Advances in experimental social psychology* (Vol. 7). New York: Academic Press.

Mischel, W. (2004). Toward an integrative science of the person. *Annual Review of Psychology* (Vol. 55). Palo Alto, CA: Annual Reviews.

Mischel, W. (2014). *The marshmallow test: Mastering self-control.* New York: Little Brown.

Mischel, W., Cantor, N., & Feldman, S. (1996). Principles of self-regulation: The nature of will power and self-control. In E.T. Higgins & A.W. Kruglanski (Eds.), *Social psychology.* New York: Guilford.

Mischel, W., & Mischel, H. (1975, April). *A cognitive social-learning analysis of moral development.* Paper presented at the meeting of the Society for Research in Child Development, Denver.

Mischel, W., & Moore, B.S. (1980). The role of ideation in voluntary delay for symbolically presented rewards. *Cognitive Therapy and Research, 4,* 211–221.

Mischel, W., & others (2011). 'Willpower' over the life span: Decomposing self-regulation. *Social Cognitive and Affective Neuroscience, 6,* 252–256.

Mishra, G.D., Cooper, R., Tom, S.E., & Kuh, D. (2009). Early life circumstances and their impact on menarche and menopause. *Women's Health, 5,* 175–190.

Mislinski, J. (2017). *Demographic trends for the 50-and-older work force.* Retrieved April 13, 2017, from https://www.advisorperspectives.com/dshort/updates/2017/04/11/demographic-trends-for-the-50-and-older-work-force

Mislinski, J. (2018). *Demographic trends for the 50-and-older work force.* Retrieved March 2, 2018, from https://seekingalpha.com/article/4136795-demographic-trends-50-older-workforce

Mistry, R.S., Vandewater, E.A., Huston, A.C., & McLoyd, V.C. (2002). Economic well-being and children's social adjustment: The role of family process in an ethnically diverse low-income sample. *Child Development, 3,* 935–951.

Mitchell, A.B., & Stewart, J.B. (2013). The efficacy of all-male academies: Insights from critical race theory (CRT). *Sex Roles, 69,* 382–392.

Mitchell, E.A., & Krous, H.F. (2015). Sudden unexpected death in infancy: A historical perspective. *Journal of Pediatric and Child Health, 51,* 108–112.

Mitchell, E.S., & Woods, N.F. (2015). Hot flush severity during the menopausal transition and early postmenopause: Beyond hormones. *Climacteric, 18,* 536–544.

Mitchell, M.B., & others (2012). Cognitively stimulating activities: Effects on cognition across four studies with up to 21 years of longitudinal data. *Journal of Aging Research, 461592.*

Mitchison, D., & others (2018). Indicators of clinical significance among women in the community with binge-eating disorder symptoms: Delineating the roles of binge frequency, body mass index, and overvaluation. *International Journal of Eating Disorders, 51,* 165–169.

Mithun, M. (2019). Morphology: What's in a word? In C. Genetti (Ed.), *How languages work* (2nd ed.). New York: Cambridge University Press.

Mitsui, T., & others (2019). Effects of prenatal sex hormones on behavioral sexual dimorphism. *Pediatric International, 61,* 140–146.

Mittal, R., & others (2019, in press). Effect of bone marrow-derived mesenchymal stem cells on cochlear function in an experimental rat model. *Anatomical Record.*

Miyake, K., Chen, S., & Campos, J. (1985). Infants' temperament, mothers' mode of interaction and attachment in Japan: An interim report. In I. Bretherton & F. Waters (Eds.), Growing points of attachment theory and research, *Monographs of the Society for Research in Child Development, 50*(1–2, Serial No. 109), 276–297.

Miyata, K., & others (2018). Effects of cataract surgery on cognitive function in elderly: Results of Fujiwara-kyo Eye Study. *PLoS One, 13*(2), e0192677.

Miyazaki, Y., Song, J.W., & Takahashi, E. (2016). Asymmetry of radial and symmetry of tangential neuronal migration pathways in developing human fetal brains. *Frontiers in Neuroanatomy, 10,* 2.

Mizala, A., Martinez, F., & Martinez, S. (2015). Pre-service elementary school teachers' expectations about student performance: How their beliefs are affected by their mathematics anxiety and student's gender. *Teaching and Teacher Education, 50,* 70–78.

Mize, K.D., & Jones, N.A. (2012). Infant physiological and behavioral responses to loss of maternal attention to a social-rival. *International Journal of Psychophysiology, 83,* 16–23.

Mize, K.D., Pineda, M., Blau, A.K., Marsh, K., & Jones, N.A. (2014). Infant physiological and behavioral responses to a jealousy-provoking condition. *Infancy, 19,* 338–348.

Moatt, J.P., & others (2019, in press). Reconciling nutritional geometry with classical dietary restriction: Effects of nutrient intake, not calories, on survival and reproduction. *Aging Cell.*

Mock, S.E., & Eibach, R.P. (2012). Stability and change in sexual orientation identity over a 10-year period in adulthood. *Archives of Sexual Behavior, 41,* 641–648.

Modecki, K.L., & others (2014). Bullying prevalence across contexts: A meta-analysis measuring cyber and traditional bullying. *Journal of Adolescent Health, 55,* 602–611.

Moed, A., & others (2015). Parent-adolescent conflict as sequences of reciprocal negative emotion: Links with conflict resolution and adolescents' behavior problems. *Journal of Youth and Adolescence, 44,* 1607–1622.

Moehrlen, T., & others (2018). Trauma mechanisms and injury patterns in pediatric burn patients. *Burns, 44,* 326–334.

Moen, P. (2007). Unpublished review of J.W. Santrock's *Life-span development,* 12th ed. (New York: McGraw-Hill).

Moen, P. (2009a). Careers. In D. Carr (Ed.), *Encyclopedia of the life course and human development.* Boston: Gale Cengage.

Moen, P. (2009b). Dual-career couples. In D. Carr (Ed.), *Encyclopedia of the life course and human development.* Boston: Gale Cengage.

Moen, P., & Spencer, D. (2006). Converging divergences in age, gender, health, and well-being. In R.H. Binstock & L.K. George (Eds.), *Handbook of aging and the social sciences* (6th ed.). San Diego: Academic Press.

Moerdler, S., & Manwani, D. (2018). New insights into the pathophysiology and development of novel therapies for sickle cell disease. *Hematology: The Education Program of the American Society of Hematology, 2018*(1), 493–506.

Moffitt, T.E. (2012). *Childhood self-control predicts adult health, wealth, and crime.* Paper presented at the Symposium on Symptom Improvement in Well-Being, Copenhagen.

Moffitt, T.E., & others (2011). A gradient of childhood self-control predicts health, wealth, and public safety. *Proceedings of the National Academy of Sciences U.S.A., 108,* 2693-2698.

Mogliski, J.K., & others (2019, in press). Jealousy, consent, and comparison within monogamous and consensually non-monogamous romantic relationships. *Archives of Sexual Behavior.*

Mohamed, N.V., & others (2019, in press). One step into the future: New iPSC tools to advance research in Parkinson's disease and neurological disorders. *Journal of Parkinson's Disease.*

Moharaei, F., & others (2018). Evaluating of psychiatric behavior in obese children and adolescents. *Iranian Journal of Child Neurology, 12,* 26-36.

Moilanen, J.M., & others (2012). Effect of aerobic training on menopausal symptoms—a randomized controlled trial. *Menopause, 19,* 691-696.

Mojtabai, R., Olfson, M., & Han, B. (2016). National trends in the prevalence and treatment of depression in adolescents and young adults. *Pediatrics, 138*(6), 1878.

Mok, Y., & others (2019, in press). American Heart Association's life's simple 7 at middle age and prognosis after myocardial infarction in later life. *Journal of the American Heart Association.*

Mola, J.R. (2015). Erectile dysfunction in the older adult male. *Urological Nursing, 35,* 87-93.

Molefi-Youri, W. (2019, in press). Is there a role for mindfulness-based interventions (here defined as MBCT and MBSR) in facilitating optimal psychological adjustment in the menopause? *Post Reproductive Health.*

Molgora, S., & others (2019, in press). Dyadic coping and marital adjustment during pregnancy: A cross-sectional study of Italian couples expecting their first child. *International Journal of Psychology.*

Molina, D.K., & Farley, N.J. (2019, in press). A 25-year review of pediatric suicides: Distinguishing features and risk factors. *American Journal of Forensic Medicine and Pathology.*

Moline, H.R., & Smith, J.F. (2016). The continuing threat of syphilis in pregnancy. *Current Opinion in Obstetrics and Gynecology, 28,* 101-104.

Mollart, L., & others (2019). Midwives' personal use of complementary and alternative medicine (CAM) influences their recommendations to women experiencing a post-date pregnancy. *Women and Birth, 34,* 235-239.

Mollenkopf, H. (2007). Mobility and flexibility. In J.E. Birren (Ed.), *Encyclopedia of gerontology* (2nd ed.). San Diego: Academic Press.

Molton, I.R., & Terrill, A.L. (2014). Overview of persistent pain in older adults. *American Psychologist, 69,* 197-207.

Monahan, K., Guyer, A., Sil, J., Fitzwater, T., & Steinberg, L. (2016). Integration of developmental neuroscience and contextual approaches to the study of adolescent psychopathology. In D. Cicchetti (Ed.), *Handbook of developmental psychology* (3rd ed.). New York: Wiley.

Money, J. (1975). Ablatio penis: Normal male infant sex-reassigned as a girl. *Archives of Sexual Behavior, 4,* 65-71.

Monier, F., Droit-Volet, S., & Coull, J.T. (2019, in press). The beneficial effect of synchronized action on motor and perceptual timing in children. *Developmental Science.*

Moninger, J. (2015). *How to talk with your child about losing weight.* Retrieved February 25, 2015, from http://www.parents.com/kids/teens/weight-loss/how-to-talk-to-your-child-about-losing-weight/

Monn, A.R., & others (2017). Executive function and parenting in the context of homelessness. *Journal of Family Psychology, 31,* 61-70.

Monroy, C., & others (2019). Visual habituation in deaf and hearing infants. *PLoS One, 14*(2), e0209265.

Monroy, C.D., Meyer, M., Schroer, L., Gerson, S.A., & Hunnius, S. (2019). The infant motor system predicts actions based on visual statistical learning. *NeuroImage, 185,* 947-954.

Montemayor, R. (1982). The relationship between parent-adolescent conflict and the amount of time adolescents spend with parents, peers, and alone. *Child Development, 53,* 1512-1519.

Monti, C., & others (2019, in press). Prospective memories and working memories: Shared resources or distinct mechanisms? *Applied Neuropsychology: Adult.*

Moon, D.G., & Park, H.J. (2019, in press). The ideal goal of testosterone replacement therapy: Maintaining testosterone levels of managing symptoms? *Journal of Clinical Medicine.*

Moon, R.Y., & Hauck, F.R. (2018). Risk factors and theories. In J.R. Duncan & R.W. Byard (Eds.), *SIDS sudden death infant and early childhood death.* Adelaide, Australia: University of Adelaide Press.

Moon, R.Y., & others (2017). Health messaging and African-American infant sleep location: A randomized controlled trial. *Journal of Community Health, 42,* 1-9.

Mooney-Leber, S.M., & Brummelte, S. (2017). Neonatal pain and reduced maternal care: Early-life stressors interacting to impact brain and behavioral development. *Neuroscience, 342,* 21-36.

Moore, A. (2019). Toward a central theory of childhood sexuality: A relational approach. In S. Lamb & J. Gilbert (Eds.), *Cambridge handbook of sexual development.* New York: Cambridge University Press.

Moore, A.A., & others (2017). Life course persistent and adolescence limited conduct disorder in a nationally representative U.S. sample: Prevalence, predictors, and outcomes. *Social Psychiatry and Psychiatric Epidemiology, 88,* 1057-1062.

Moore, D. (2001). *The dependent gene.* New York: W.H. Freeman.

Moore, D. (2013). Behavioral genetics, genetics, and epigenetics. In P.D. Zelazo (Ed.), *Handbook of developmental psychology.* New York: Oxford University Press.

Moore, D. (2015). *The developing genome.* New York: Oxford University Press.

Moore, D.S. (2017). Behavioral epigenetics. *Wiley Interdisciplinary Reviews. Systems Biology and Medicine, 9,* 1.

Moore, M. (2012). Behavioral sleep problems in children and adolescents. *Journal of Clinical Psychology in Medical Settings, 19,* 77-83.

Moore, S.R., Harden, K.P., & Mendle, J. (2014). Pubertal timing and adolescent sexual behavior in girls. *Developmental Psychology, 50*(6), 1734-1745.

Mooya, H., Sichimba, F., & Bakermans-Kranenburg, M. (2016). Infant-mother and infant-sibling attachment in Zambia. *Attachment and Human Development, 18,* 618-635.

Mora, J.C., & Valencia, W.M. (2018). Exercise and older adults. *Clinics in Geriatric Medicine, 34,* 145-152.

Morbelli, S., & Baucknecht, M. (2018). Amyloid PET imaging: Standardization and integration with other Alzheimer's disease biomarkers. *Methods in Molecular Biology, 1750,* 203-212.

Morean, M.E., & others (2014). First drink to first drunk: Age of onset and delay to intoxication are associated with adolescent alcohol use and binge drinking. *Alcoholism: Clinical and Experimental Research, 38,* 2615-2621.

Moreau, C., & others (2019, in press). Measuring gender norms about relationships in early adolescence: Results from the global early adolescent study. *SSM–Population Health.*

Moreau, D., Kirk, L.J., & Waldie, K.E. (2017). High-intensity training enhances executive function in children in a randomized, placebo-controlled trial. *Elife, 22,* 6.

Moreau, D., & others (2019). Volumetric and surface characteristics of gray matter in adult dyslexia and dyscalculia. *Neuropsychologia, 127,* 204-210.

Mori, E., & others (2019, in press). Fatigue, depression, maternal confidence, and maternal satisfaction during the first month postpartum: A comparison of Japanese mothers by age and parity. *International Journal of Nursing Practice.*

Morin, A.J.S., & others (2017). Adolescents' body image trajectories: A further test of the self-equilibrium hypothesis. *Developmental Psychology, 53,* 1501-1521.

Morosan, L., & others (2017). Emotion recognition and perspective taking: A comparison between typical and incarcerated male adolescents. *PLoS One, 12*(1), e0170646.

Morris, A., Cui, L., & Steinberg, L. (2012). Parenting research and themes: What we have learned and where to go next. In R.E. Larzelere, A.S. Morris, & A.W. Harrist (Eds.), *Authoritative parenting.* Washington, DC: American Psychological Association.

Morris, A., Cui, L., & Steinberg, L. (2013). Arrested development: The effects of incarceration on the development of psychosocial maturity. *Development and Psychopathology, 24*(3), 1073-1090.

Morris, A.S., & others (2014). Effortful control, behavior problems, and peer relations: What predicts academic adjustment in kindergartners from low-income families? *Early Education and Development, 24,* 813-828.

Morris, B.J., & others (2012). A 'snip' in time: What is the best age to circumcise? *BMC Pediatrics, 12,* 20.

Morris, M.W., Savani, K., & Fincher, K. (2019). Metacognition fosters cultural learning: Evidence from individual differences and situational prompts. *Journal of Personality and Social Psychology, 116,* 46-68.

Morris, S., & others (2018). Emotion regulation dynamics during parent-child interactions: Implications for research and practice. In P.M. Cole & T. Hollenstein (Eds.), *Emotion regulation.* New York: Routledge.

Morrison, D.M., & others (2014). "He enjoys giving her pleasure": Diversity and complexity in young men's sexual scripts. *Archives of Sexual Behavior, 44,* 655-688.

Morrison, G.S. (2018). *Early childhood education today* (14th ed.). Upper Saddle River, NJ: Pearson.

Morrison, G.S. (2020). *Fundamentals of early childhood education* (9th ed.). Upper Saddle River, NJ: Pearson.

Morrison, R.S. (2013). Models of palliative care delivery in the United States. *Current Opinion in Supportive and Palliative Care, 7,* 201–206.

Morrison, S.C., Fife, T., & Hertlein, K.M. (2017). Mechanisms behind prolonged effects of parental divorce: A phenomenological study. *Journal of Divorce and Remarriage, 58,* 54–63.

Morrison-Beedy, D., & others (2013). Reducing sexual risk behavior in adolescent girls: Results from a randomized trial. *Journal of Adolescent Health, 52,* 314–322.

Morrissey, T.W. (2009). Multiple child-care arrangements and young children's behavioral outcomes. *Child Development, 80,* 59–76.

Morrow, L.M. (2020). *Literacy development in the early years* (9th ed.). Upper Saddle River, NJ: Pearson.

Morse, A.F., & Cangelosi, A. (2017). Why are there developmental stages in language learning? A developmental robotics model of language development. *Cognitive Science, 41*(Suppl. 1), S32–S51.

Moss, S.A., & Wilson, S.G. (2018). Why are older people often so responsible and considerate even when their future seems limited? A systematic review. *International Journal of Aging and Human Development, 86,* 82–108.

Mossburg, S.E. (2018). Baby boomer retirement: Are you up to the challenge? *Nursing Management, 49,* 13–14.

Motti-Stefanidi, F., & Coll, C.G. (2018). We have come a long way baby: "Explaining positive adaptation of immigrant youth across cultures". *Journal of Adolescence, 62,* 218–221.

Mounts, N.S., & Allen, C. (2020, in press). Parenting styles and practices: Traditional approaches and their application to multiple types of moral behavior. In D.J. Laible & others (Eds.), *Oxford handbook of parenting and moral development.* New York: Oxford University Press.

Moura, J., & others (2019). Immune aging in diabetes and its implications in wound healing. *Clinical Immunology, 200,* 43–54.

Moyano, N., & others (2019). Children's social integration and low perception of negative relationships as protectors against bullying and cyberbullying. *Frontiers in Psychology, 10,* 643.

Mozer, M.C., Wiseheart, M., & Novikoff, T.P. (2019, in press). Artificial intelligence to support human instruction. *Proceedings of the National Academy of Sciences U.S.A.*

Mparmpakas, D., & others (2013). Immune system function, stress, exercise, and nutrition profile can affect pregnancy outcome: Lessons from a Mediterranean cohort. *Experimental and Therapeutic Medicine, 5,* 411–418.

Mroczek, D.K., & Kolarz, C.M. (1998). The effect of age on positive and negative affect: A developmental perspective on happiness. *Journal of Personality and Social Psychology, 75,* 1333–1349.

Mroczek, D.K., & Spiro, A. (2007). Personality change influences mortality in older men. *Psychological Science, 18,* 371–376.

Mroczek, D.K., Spiro, A., & Griffin, P.W. (2006). Personality and aging. In J.E. Birren & K.W. Schaie (Eds.), *Handbook of the psychology of aging* (6th ed.). San Diego: Academic Press.

Mroczek, D.K., & others (2015). Emotional reactivity and mortality: Longitudinal findings from the VA Normative Aging Study. *Journals of Gerontology B: Psychological Sciences and Social Sciences, 70(3),* 398–406.

Mrowka, R. (2017). Arterial hypertension. *Acta Physiologica, 219,* 697–699.

Mruk, C.J., & O'Brien, E.J. (2013). Changing self-esteem through competence and worthiness training: A positive therapy. In V. Zeigler-Hill (Ed.), *Self-esteem.* New York: Psychology Press.

Mucke, M., & others (2018). Moderate-to-vigorous physical activity, executive functions, and prefrontal brain oxygenation in children: A functional near-infrared spectroscopy study. *Journal of Sports Sciences, 36,* 630–636.

Mueller, S.C., & others (2017). Evidence for the triadic model of adolescent brain development: Cognitive load and task-relevance of emotion differentially affect adolescents and adults. *Developmental Cognitive Neuroscience, 26,* 91–100.

Mueller, T., & others (2017). Teen pregnancy prevention: Implementation of a multicomponent, community-wide approach. *Journal of Adolescent Health, 60*(Suppl. 3), S9–S17.

Mueller-Schotte, S. & others (2019, in press). Trajectories of limitations in instrumental activities of daily living in frail older adults with vision, hearing, or dual sensory loss. *Journals of Gerontology A: Biological Sciences and Medical Sciences.*

Muenks, K., Yang, J.S., & Wigfield, A. (2018). Associations between grit, motivation, and achievement in high school students. *Motivation Science, 4,* 158–176.

Muftic, L.R., & Updegrove, A.H. (2018). The mediating effect of self-control on parenting and delinquency: A gendered approach with a multinational sample. *International Journal of Offender Therapy and Comparative Criminology, 62,* 3058–3076.

Muir, N.M., & others (2019). Indigenous parenting. In M.H. Bornstein (Ed.), *Handbook of parenting* (3rd ed.). New York: Routledge.

Mukherjee, R.A.S. (2019). Diagnosis and management of fetal alcohol spectrum disorder. *Current Opinion in Psychiatry, 32,* 92–96.

Mulder, T.M., & others (2018). Risk factors for child neglect: A meta-analytic review. *Child Abuse and Neglect, 77,* 198–210.

Mullally, S.L., & Maguire, E.A. (2014). Learning to remember: The early ontogeny of episodic memory. *Developmental Cognitive Neuroscience, 9,* 12–29.

Mullick, S. (2019). Adolescent sexual and reproductive health. In D. Devakumar & others (Eds.), *Oxford textbook of global health of women, infants, children, and adolescents.* New York: Oxford University Press.

Mulligan, E.A., & Karel, M.J. (2018). Development of a bereavement group in a geriatric mental health clinic for veterans. *Clinical Gerontology, 41,* 445–457.

Mullola, S., & others (2012). Gender differences in teachers' perceptions of students' temperament, educational competence, and teachability. *British Journal of Educational Psychology, 82*(2), 185–206.

Mulvey, K.L., Hitti, A., Smetana, J.G., & Killen, M. (2016). Morality, context, and development. In L. Balter & C.S. Tamis-LeMonda (Eds.), *Child psychology: A contemporary handbook* (3rd ed.). New York: Psychology Press.

Munawar, K., Kuhn, S.K., & Hague, S. (2018). Understanding the reminiscence bump: A systematic review. *PLoS One, 13*(12), e0208595.

Mundy, P., & others (2007). Individual differences and the development of joint attention in infancy. *Child Development, 78,* 938–954.

Muniz-Terrera, G., & others (2013). Investigating terminal decline: Results from a UK population-based study of aging. *Psychology and Aging, 28,* 377–385.

Munro, C.A., & others (2019, in press). Stressful life events and cognitive decline: Sex differences in the Baltimore Epidemiologic Catchment Area Follow-Up Study. *International Journal of Geriatric Psychiatry.*

Munroe, B.A., & others (2019, in press). Physiological substrates of executive functioning: A systematic review of the literature. *Attention Deficit and Hyperactivity Disorders.*

Murase, T. (2014). Japanese mothers' utterances about agents and actions during joint picture-book reading. *Frontiers in Psychology, 5,* 357.

Murdock, K.K., Horissian, M., & Crichlow-Ball, C. (2017). Emerging adults' text message use and sleep characteristics: A multimethod, naturalistic study. *Behavioral Sleep Medicine, 15,* 228–241.

Murphy, D.A., Brecht, M.L., Huang, D., & Herbeck, D.M. (2012). Trajectories of delinquency from age 14 to 23 in the National Longitudinal Survey of Youth sample. *International Journal of Adolescence and Youth, 17,* 47–62.

Murray, A.L., & others (2019, in press). The intergenerational effects of intimate partner violence in pregnancy: Mediating pathways and implications for prevention. *Trauma, Violence, and Abuse.*

Murray, P.G., Dattani, M.T., & Clayton, P.E. (2016). Controversies in the diagnosis and management of growth hormone deficiency in childhood and adolescence. *Archives of Disease in Childhood, 101,* 96–100.

Musick, K., & Michelmore, K. (2018). Cross-national comparisons of union stability in cohabiting and married families with children. *Demography, 55,* 1389–1421.

Mussen, P.H., Honzik, M., & Eichorn, D. (1982). Early adult antecedents of life satisfaction at age 70. *Journal of Gerontology, 37,* 316–322.

Must, O., & Must, A. (2018). Speed and the Flynn effect. *Intelligence, 68,* 37–47.

Mutchler, J.E., Li, Y., & Xu, P. (2019). How strong is the Social Security safety net? Using the elder index to assess gaps in economic security. *Journal of Aging and Social Policy, 31,* 123–137.

Mutiso, V.N., & others (2019, in press). Relationship between bullying, substance use, psychiatric disorders, and social problems in a sample of Kenyan secondary schools. *Prevention Science.*

Myers, C.A., & Cowie, H. (2019, in press). Cyberbullying across the lifespan of education: Issues and interventions from school to university. *International Journal of Environmental Research and Public Health.*

Myers, D.G. (2000). *The American paradox.* New Haven, CT: Yale University Press.

Myers, D.G. (2008, June 2). Commentary in S. Begley & Interlandi, The dumbest generation? Don't be dumb. Retrieved July 22, 2008, from www.newsweek.com/id/13856/

Myers, D.G. (2010). *Psychology* (9th ed.). New York: Worth.

Myers, J., & others (2018). Provider tools for advance care planning and goals of care discussion: A systematic review. *American Journal of Hospice and Palliative Care, 35,* 1123–1132.

Myerson, J., Rank, M.R., Raines, F.Q., & Schnitzler, M.A. (1998). Race and general cognitive ability: The myth of diminishing returns in education. *Psychological Science, 9,* 139–142.

N

Nabe-Nielsen, K., & others (2014). Demand-specific work ability, poor health, and working conditions in middle-aged full-time employees. *Applied Ergonomics, 45,* 1174–1180.

Nader, P.R., Bradley, R.H., Houts, R.M., McRitchie, S.L., & O'Brian, M. (2008). Moderate-to-vigorous physical activity from 9 to 15 years. *Journal of the American Medical Association, 300,* 295–305.

Naezer, M., & Ringrose, J. (2019). Adventure, intimacy, identity, and knowledge: Exploring how social media are shaping and transforming youth sexuality. In S. Lamb & J. Gilbert (Eds.), *Cambridge handbook of sexual development.* New York: Cambridge University Press.

Nagel, B.J., & others (2011). Altered white matter microstructure in children with attention-deficit/hyperactivity disorder. *Journal of the American Academy of Child and Adolescent Psychiatry, 50,* 283–292.

Nair, R.L., Roche, K.M., & White, R.M.B. (2018). Acculturation gap distress among Latino youth: Prospective links to family processes and youth depressive symptoms, alcohol use, and academic performance. *Journal of Youth and Adolescence, 47,* 105–120.

Najman, J.M., & others (2009). The impact of episodic and chronic poverty on child cognitive development. *Journal of Pediatrics, 154,* 284–289.

Najman, J.M., & others (2010). Timing and chronicity of family poverty and development of unhealthy behaviors in children: A longitudinal study. *Journal of Adolescent Health, 46,* 538–544.

Nakagawa, T., & others (2019, in press). Subjective well-being in centenarians: A comparison of Japan and the United States. *Aging and Mental Health.*

Nakamichi, K. (2019, in press). Differences in young children's peer preference by inhibitory control and emotion regulation. *Psychological Reports.*

Nansel, T.R., & others (2001). Bullying behaviors among U.S. youth. *Journal of the American Medical Association, 285,* 2094–2100.

Narayan, A.J., & Masten, A.S. (2019, in press). Resilience in the context of violence and trauma: Promotive and protective processes of positive caregiving. In. J. Osofsky & B.M. Groves (Eds.), *Violence and trauma in the lives of children.* Santa Barbara, CA: Praeger.

Narváez, D. (2006). Integrative moral education. In M. Killen & J. Smetana (Ed.), *Handbook of moral development.* Mahwah, NJ: Erlbaum.

Narváez, D. (2010). Building a sustaining classroom climate for purposeful ethical citizenship. In T. Lovat, R. Toomey, & N. Clement (Eds.), *International research handbook of values education and student well-being.* New York: Springer.

Narváez, D. (2014). *The neurobiology and development of human morality.* New York: Norton.

Narváez, D. (2016). *Embodied morality.* New York: Palgrave-McMillan.

Narváez, D. (2018a). Ethogenesis: Evolution, early experience, and moral becoming. In J. Graham &

K. Gray (Eds.), *The atlas of moral psychology.* New York: Guilford Press.

Narváez, D. (2018b). Evolution, childrearing, and compassionate morality. In P. Gilbert (Ed.), *Compassion.* New York: London.

Narváez, D. (2019). Moral development and moral values: Evolutionary and neurobiological influences. In D.P. McAdams & others (Eds.), *Handbook of personality.* New York: Guilford.

Narváez, D. (2020). Evolution and the parenting ecology of moral development. In D. Laible, L. Padilla-Walker, & G. Carlo (Ed.), *Handbook of parenting and moral development.* New York: Oxford University Press.

Narváez, D., & Bock, T. (2014). Developing ethical expertise and moral personalities. In L. Nucci & D. Narváez (Eds.), *Handbook of moral and character education* (2nd ed.). New York: Routledge.

Narváez, D., Bock, T., Endicott, L., & Lies, J. (2004). Minnesota's Community Voices and Character Education Project. *Journal of Research in Character Education, 2,* 89–112.

Narváez, D., & Gleason, T.R. (2013). Developmental optimism. In D. Narváez & others, *Evolution, early experience, and human development.* New York: Oxford University Press.

Narváez, D., & Hill, P.L. (2010). The relation of multicultural experiences to moral judgment and mindsets. *Journal of Diversity in Higher Education, 3,* 43–55.

Nascimento, B.S., & Little, A.C. (2019, in press). Mate retention strategies, self-esteem, mate value, and facial attractiveness disparity in Brazil and in the UK. *Journal of Sex and Marital Therapy.*

Nascimento, D.D.C., & others (2018). The impact of sarcopenic obesity on inflammation, lean body mass, and muscle strength in elderly women. *International Journal of General Medicine, 11,* 443–449.

Nash, J.M. (1997, February 3). Fertile minds. *Time,* 50–54.

National Assessment of Educational Progress (2017). *Mathematics and Reading 4th and 8th grade.* Washington, DC: National Center for Education Statistics.

National Association for Gifted Children (2017). *Frequently asked questions about gifted children.* Washington, DC: Author.

National Association for Single Sex Public Education (NASSPE) (2012). *Single-sex schools/schools with single-sex classrooms/what's the difference.* Retrieved from www.singlesexschools.org/schools-schools.com

National Center for Education Statistics (2002). *Work during college.* Washington, DC: U.S. Department of Education.

National Center for Education Statistics (2017). *The condition of education 2017.* Washington, DC: U.S. Office of Education.

National Center for Education Statistics (2018). *School dropouts.* Washington, DC: Author.

National Center for Health Statistics (2000). *Health United States, 1999.* Atlanta: Centers for Disease Control and Prevention.

National Center for Health Statistics (2018a). *Accidents and deaths.* Atlanta: Centers for Disease Control and Prevention.

National Center for Health Statistics (2018b). *Obesity.* Atlanta: Centers for Disease Control and Prevention.

National Center for Health Statistics (2019). *Sexually transmitted diseases.* Atlanta: Centers for Disease Control and Prevention.

National Clearinghouse on Child Abuse and Neglect (2019). *What is child abuse and neglect?* Washington, DC: U.S. Department of Health and Human Services.

National Institute of Drug Abuse (2018). *Treating opioid use disorder during pregnancy.* Washington, DC: Author.

National Institute of Mental Health (2019). *Autism spectrum disorders.* Retrieved from www.nimh.nih.gov/health/topics/autism-spectrum-disorders-asd/index.shtml

National Sleep Foundation (2007). *Sleep in America poll 2007.* Washington, DC: Author.

National Sleep Foundation (2019). *Children's sleep habits.* Retrieved February 20, 2019, from http://www.sleepfoundation.org

Naveed, S., & others (2019). Association of bullying experiences with depressive symptoms and psychosocial functioning among school going children and adolescents. *BMC Research Notes, 12*(1), 198.

Nazarian, A., Yashin, A.I., & Kulminski, A.M. (2019). Genome-wide analysis of genetic predisposition to Alzheimer's disease and related sex disparities. *Alzheimer's Research and Therapy, 11*(1), 5.

Ncube, C.N., & Mueller, B.A. (2017). Daughters of mothers who smoke: A population-based cohort study of maternal prenatal tobacco use and subsequent prenatal smoking in offspring. *Pediatric and Perinatal Epidemiology, 31,* 14–20.

Ndabi, J., Nevill, A.M., & Sandercock, G.R.H. (2019). Cross-cultural comparisons of aerobic and muscular fitness in Tanzanian and English youth: An allometric approach. *PLoS One, 14*(2), e0211414.

Neal, J.W., Neal, Z.P., & Cappella, E. (2014). I know who my friends are, but do you? Predictors of self-reported and peer-inferred relationships. *Child Development, 85,* 1366–1372.

Neblett, E.W., Roth, W.D., & Syed, M. (2019). Ethnic and racial identity development from an interdisciplinary perspective: Introduction to the special issue. *Emerging Adulthood, 7,* 1–12.

Needham, A., Barrett, T., & Peterman, K. (2002). A pick-me-up for infants' exploratory skills: Early simulated experiences reaching for object using "sticky mittens" enhances young infants' object exploration skills. *Infant Behavior and Development, 25,* 279–295.

Negriff, S. (2019, in press). Depressive symptoms predict characteristics of online social networks. *Journal of Adolescent Health.*

Neikrug, A.B., & Ancoli-Israel, S. (2010). Sleep disorders in the older adult: A mini-review. *Gerontology, 56,* 181–189.

Neiterman, E., & Fox, B. (2017). Controlling the unruly maternal body: Losing and gaining control over the body during pregnancy and the postpartum period. *Social Science & Medicine, 174,* 142–148.

Nelemans, S.A., & others (2019, in press). Transactional links between social anxiety symptoms and parenting across adolescence: Between- and within-person associations. *Child Development.*

Nelson, C. (2006). Unpublished review of J.W. Santrock's *Topical approach to life-span development,* 4th ed. (New York: McGraw-Hill).

Nelson, C.A. (2003). Neural development and lifelong plasticity. In R.M. Lerner, R. Jacobs, & D. Wertlieb (Eds.), *Handbook of applied developmental science* (Vol. 1). Thousand Oaks, CA: Sage.

Nelson, C.A. (2007). A developmental cognitive neuroscience approach to the study of atypical development: A model system involving infants of diabetic mothers. In D. Coch, G. Dawson, & K.W. Fischer (Eds.), *Human behavior, learning, and the developing brain.* New York: Guilford.

Nelson, C.A. (2013). Brain development and behavior. In A.M. Rudolph, C. Rudolph, L. First, G. Lister, & A.A. Gershon (Eds.), *Rudolph's pediatrics* (22nd ed.). New York: McGraw-Hill.

Nelson, C.A., Fox, N.A., & Zeanah, C.H. (2014). *Romania's abandoned children.* Cambridge, MA: Harvard University Press.

Nelson, D.A., & others (2014). Parenting, relational aggression, and borderline personality features: Associations over time in a Russian longitudinal sample. *Development and Psychopathology, 26,* 773-787.

Nelson, K. (2014). Sociocultural theories of memory development. In P. Bauer & R. Fivush (Eds.), *Wiley handbook of the development of children's memory.* New York: Wiley.

Nelson, S.C., & others (2018). Identity and the body: Trajectories of body esteem from adolescence to emerging adulthood. *Developmental Psychology, 54,* 1159-1171.

Nelson, S.E., Van Ryzin, M.J., & Dishion, T.J. (2015). Alcohol, marijuana, and tobacco use trajectories from age 12 to 24 years: Demographic correlates and young adult substance use problems. *Development and Psychopathology, 27,* 253-277.

Nelson, S.K., Kushlev, K., English, T., Dunn, E.W., & Lyubomirsky, S. (2013). In defense of parenthood: Children associated with more joy than misery. *Psychological Science, 24,* 3-10.

Nelson, S.K., Kushlev, K., & Lyubomirsky, S. (2014). The pains and pleasures of parenting: When, why, and how is parenthood associated with more or less well-being? *Psychological Bulletin, 140,* 846-895.

Nemet, D. (2016). Childhood obesity, physical activity, and exercise. *Pediatric Exercise Science, 28,* 48-51.

Nene, R.V., & others (2018). Cdc73 suppresses genome instability by mediating telomere homeostasis. *PLoS One, 14*(1), e1007170.

Neophytou, A.M., & others (2018). Secondhand smoke exposure and asthma outcomes among African American and Latino children with asthma. *Thorax, 73,* 1041-1048.

Nergard-Nilssen, T., & Eklund, K. (2018). Evaluation of the psychometric properties of the Norwegian screening test for dyslexia. *Dyslexia, 24,* 250-262.

Nesi, J., Choukas-Bradley, S., & Prinstein, M.J. (2018). Transformation of adolescent peer relations in the social media context: Part 2—Application to peer group processes and future directions of research. *Clinical Child and Family Psychology Review, 21,* 295-319.

Nesi, J., & Prinstein, M.J. (2020, in press). In search of likes: Longitudinal associations between adolescents' digital status seeking and health-seeking behaviors. *Journal of Clinical Child and Adolescent Psychology.*

Neubauer, A.B., Smyth, J.M., & Sliwinski, M.J. (2019, in press). Age differences in proactive coping with minor hassles in daily life. *Journals of Gerontology B: Psychological Sciences and Social Sciences.*

Neuenschwander, R., & Blair, C. (2017). Zooming in on children's behavior during delay of gratification: Disentangling impulsigenic and volitional processes underlying self-regulation. *Journal of Experimental Child Psychology, 154,* 46-63.

Neugarten, B.L., & Weinstein, K.K. (1964). The changing American grandparent. *Journal of Marriage and the Family, 26,* 199-204.

Neuman, W.L. (2020). *Social science research methods* (8th ed.). Upper Saddle River, NJ: Pearson.

Nevarez, M.D., & others (2010). Associations of early life risk factors with infant sleep duration. *Academic Pediatrics, 10,* 187-193.

Neville, H.J. (2006). Different profiles of plasticity within human cognition. In Y. Munakata & M.H. Johnson (Eds.), *Attention and Performance XXI: Processes of change in brain and cognitive development.* Oxford, UK: Oxford University Press.

Newberry, J.A. (2019). Creating a safe sleep environment for the infant: What the pediatric nurse needs to know. *Journal of Pediatric Nursing, 44,* 119-122.

Newell, K., Scully, D.M., McDonald, P.V., & Baillargeon, R. (1989). Task constraints and infant grip configurations. *Developmental Psychobiology, 22,* 817-832.

Newton, E.R., & May, L. (2019, in press). Adaptation of maternal-fetal physiology to exercise in pregnancy: The basis of guidelines for physical activity in pregnancy. *Clinical and Medical Insights: Women's Health.*

Ng, F., & Wang, Q. (2019). Asian American parenting. In M.H. Bornstein (Ed.), *Handbook of parenting* (3rd ed.). New York: Routledge.

Ng, F.F., Pomerantz, E.M., & Deng, C. (2014). Why are Chinese parents more psychologically controlling than American parents? "My child is my report card." *Child Development, 85,* 355-369.

Ng, F.F., Pomerantz, E.M., & Lam, S. (2013). Mothers' beliefs about children's learning in Hong Kong and the United States: Implications for mothers' child-based self-worth. *International Journal of Behavioral Development, 37,* 387-394.

Ng, F.F., & others (2019, in press). The role of mothers' child-based worth in their affective responses to children's performance. *Child Development.*

Ng, M., & others (2017). Environmental factors associated with autism spectrum disorder: A scoping review for the years 2003-2013. *Health Promotion and Chronic Disease Prevention in Canada, 37,* 1-23.

Ng, Q.X., & others (2018). Early life sexual abuse is associated with increased suicide attempts: An update meta-analysis. *Journal of Psychiatric Research, 99,* 129-141.

Ng, Q.X., & others (2019). A meta-analysis of the effectiveness of yoga-based interventions for maternal depression during pregnancy. *Complementary Therapies in Clinical Practice, 34,* 8-12.

Nguyen, D.J., & others (2018). Prospective relations between parent-adolescent acculturation conflict and mental health symptoms among Vietnamese American adolescents. *Cultural Diversity and Ethnic Minority Psychology, 24,* 151-161.

Nguyen, T.V. (2019, in press). Developmental effects of androgens on the human brain. *Journal of Neuroendocrinology.*

NICHD (2019). *SIDS.* Retrieved January 6, 2019, from https://www.nichd.nih.gov/health/topics/sids/Pages/default.aspx

NICHD Early Child Care Research Network (2001). Nonmaternal care and family factors in early development: An overview of the NICHD study of early child care. *Journal of Applied Developmental Psychology, 22,* 457-492.

NICHD Early Child Care Research Network (2002). Structure → Process → Outcome: Direct and indirect effects of child care quality on young children's development. *Psychological Science, 13,* 199-206.

NICHD Early Child Care Research Network (2003). Does amount of time spent in child care predict socioemotional adjustment during the transition to kindergarten? *Child Development, 74,* 976-1005.

NICHD Early Child Care Research Network (2004). Type of child care and children's development at 54 months. *Early Childhood Research Quarterly, 19,* 203-230.

NICHD Early Child Care Research Network (2005a). *Child care and development.* New York: Guilford.

NICHD Early Child Care Research Network (2005b). Duration and developmental timing of poverty and children's cognitive and social development from birth through third grade. *Child Development, 76,* 795-810.

NICHD Early Child Care Research Network (2006). Infant-mother attachment classification: Risk and protection in relation to changing maternal caregiving quality. *Developmental Psychology, 42,* 38-58.

NICHD Early Child Care Research Network (2010). Testing a series of causal propositions relating time spent in child care to children's externalizing behavior. *Developmental Psychology, 46*(1), 1-17.

Nickalls, S. (2012, March 9). Why college students shouldn't online date. *The Tower.* Philadelphia: Arcadia University. Retrieved February 27, 2013, from http://tower.arcadia.edu/?p=754

Nickerson, A.B., & others (2019). Social emotional learning (SEL) practices in schools: Effects on perceptions of bullying victimization. *Journal of School Psychology, 73,* 74-88.

Nicolaisen, M., & Thorsen, K. (2014). Loneliness among men and women—a five-year follow-up study. *Aging and Mental Health, 18,* 194-206.

Nicolaou, E., & others (2018). Changes in verbal and visuospatial working memory from grade 1 to grade 3 in primary school: Population longitudinal study. *Child: Care, Health, and Development, 44,* 392-400.

Nicolini, M.E., & others (2019, in press). Euthanasia and assisted suicide of persons with psychiatric disorders: The challenge of personality disorders. *Psychological Medicine.*

Nicoteri, J.A., & Miskovsky, M.J. (2014). Revisiting the freshman "15": Assessing body mass index in the first college year and beyond. *Journal of the American Association of Nurse Practitioners, 126,* 220-224.

Nielsen, M.K., & others (2017). Predictors of complicated grief and depression in bereaved caregivers: A nationwide prospective cohort study. *Journal of Pain and Symptom Management, 53,* 540-550.

Nieto, S., & Bode, P. (2018). *Affirming diversity* (7th ed.). Upper Saddle River, NJ: Pearson.

Nikitin, J., & Freund, A.M. (2019). The adaptation process of aging. In R. Fernandez-Ballesteros, A. Benetos, & J-M. Robine (Eds.), *Cambridge handbook of successful aging.* New York: Cambridge University Press.

Nikmat, A.W., Al-Mashoor, S.H., & Hashim, N.A. (2015). Quality of life in people with cognitive impairment: Nursing homes versus home care. *International Psychogeriatrics, 27*(5), 815-824.

Nilsen, E.S., & Bacso, S.A. (2017). Cognitive and behavioral predictors of adolescents' communicative perspective-taking and social relationships. *Journal of Adolescence, 56,* 52-63.

Nimbi, F.M., & others (2019, in press). Male sexual desire: An overview of biological, psychological, sexual, relational, and cultural factors influencing desire. *Sexual Medicine Reviews.*

Nippold, M.A. (2016). *Later language development: School-age children, adolescents, and young adults* (4th ed.). Austin, TX: Pro-Ed.

Nisbett, R. (2003). *The geography of thought.* New York: Free Press.

Nisbett, R.E., & others (2012). Intelligence: New findings and theoretical developments. *American Psychologist, 67,* 130-159.

Nishigori, H., & others (2019, in press). The prevalence and risk factors for postpartum depression symptoms of fathers at one and 6 months postpartum: Birth cohort study of an adjunct study of the Japan Environment & Children's Study. *Journal of Maternal-Fetal and Neonatal Medicine.*

Nishina, A., & Bellmore, A. (2018). Inequality and neighborhood effects on peer relations. In W.M. Bukowski & others (Eds.), *Handbook of peer interactions, relationships, and groups* (2nd ed.). New York: Guilford.

Nixon, S.A., Rubincam, C., Casale, M., & Flicker, S. (2011). Is 80% a passing grade? Meanings attached to condom use in an abstinence-plus HIV prevention programme in South Africa. *AIDS Care, 23,* 213-220.

Noce Kirkwood, R., & others (2018). The slowing down phenomenon: What is the age of major gait velocity decline? *Maturitas, 115,* 31-36.

Noddings, N. (2008). Caring and moral education. In L. Nucci & D. Narváez (Eds.), *Handbook of moral and character education.* Clifton, NJ: Psychology Press.

Noddings, N. (2014). Caring and moral education. In L. Nucci, T. Krettenauer, & D. Narváez (Eds.), *Handbook of moral and character education* (2nd ed.). New York: Routledge.

Noel-Miller, C.M. (2011). Partner caregiving in older cohabiting couples. *Journals of Gerontology B: Psychological Sciences and Social Sciences, 66B,* 341-353.

Noftle, E.E., & Fleeson, W. (2010). Age differences in Big Five factor behavior averages and variabilities across the adult life span: Moving beyond retrospective, global summary accounts of personality. *Psychology and Aging, 25,* 95-107.

Nolen, M.M.P.G., & others (2019). Empathic distress and concern predict aggression in toddlerhood: The moderating role of sex. *Infant Behavior and Development, 54,* 57-65.

Noll, J.G., & others (2017). Childhood sexual abuse and early timing of puberty. *Journal of Adolescent Health, 60,* 65-71.

Nordheim, K.L., & others (2018). Inflammation relates to resistance training-induced hypertrophy in elderly patients. *Medicine and Science in Sports and Exercise, 49,* 1079-1085.

Norman-McKay, L.P. (2019). *Microbiology.* Upper Saddle River, NJ: Pearson.

Norona, A.N., & Baker, B.L. (2017). The effects of early positive parenting and developmental delay status on child emotion dysregulation. *Journal of Intellectual Disability Research, 61,* 130-143.

Norris, S.C., Gleaves, D.H., & Hutchinson, A.D. (2019, in press). Anorexia nervosa and perfectionism: A meta-analysis. *International Journal of Eating Disorders.*

North American Montessori Teachers' Association (2016). *Montessori schools.* Retrieved January 6, 2016, from www.montessori-namta.org

Nottelmann, E.D., & others (1987). Gonadal and adrenal hormone correlates of adjustment in early adolescence. In R.M. Lerner & T.T. Foch (Eds.), *Biological-psychological interactions in early adolescence.* Hillsdale, NJ: Erlbaum.

Novack, M.A., & others (2018). Gesture's role in reflecting and fostering conceptual change. In T. Amin & O. Levini (Eds.), *Converging and complementary perspectives on conceptual change.* New York: Routledge.

Novak, C.M., & Graham, E.M. (2019, in press). Obstetric management, tests, and technologies that impact childhood development. *Developmental Medicine and Child Neurology.*

Nowson, C.A., & others (2018). The impact of dietary factors on indices of chronic disease in older people: A systematic review. *Journal of Nutrition, Health, and Aging, 22,* 282-296.

Nucci, L. (2006). Education for moral development. In M. Killen & J. Smetana (Eds.), *Handbook of moral development.* Mahwah, NJ: Erlbaum.

Nugent, C.N., & Daugherty, J. (2018, May). A demographic, attitudinal, and behavioral profile of cohabiting adults in the United States, 2011-2015. *National Health Statistics Reports, 111,* 1-11.

Nunes, A.S., & others (2019). Idiosyncratic organization of cortical networks in autism spectrum disorder. *NeuroImage, 190,* 182-190.

Nyberg, L., & Pudas, S. (2019). Successful memory aging. *Annual Review of Psychology* (Vol. 71). Palo Alto, CA: Annual Reviews.

Nye, C.D., & Roberts, B.W. (2019, in press). A neo-socioanalytic model of personality development. In B. Baltes (Ed.), *Work over the lifespan.* New York: Elsevier.

Nye, C.D., & others (2016). Personality trait differences between young and middle-aged adults: Measurement artifacts or actual trends? *Journal of Personality, 84,* 473-492.

Nygard, C-H. (2013). *The ability to work peaks in middle age.* Interview. Retrieved September 15, 2013, from http://researchandstudy.uta.fi/2013/09/12/the-ability-to-work-peaks-in-middle-age/

Nystrom, P., & others (2018). Enhanced pupillary light reflex in infancy is associated with autism diagnosis in toddlerhood. *Nature Communications, 9*(1), 1678.

O

O'Brien, J.L., & others (2013). Cognitive training and selective attention in the aging brain: An electrophysiological study. *Clinical Neurophysiology, 124,* 2198-2208.

O'Brien, M., & others (2014). Women's work and child care: Perspectives and prospects. In E.T. Gershoff, R.S. Mistry, & D.A. Crosby (Eds.), *Societal contexts of child development.* New York: Oxford University Press.

O'Connor, D., & Kelson, E. (2018). Boomer matters: Responding to emotional health needs in an aging society. *Journal of Gerontological Social Work, 61,* 61-77.

O'Connor, E.E., Scott, M.A., McCormick, M.P., & Weinberg, S.L. (2014). Early mother-child attachment and behavior problems in middle childhood: The role of the subsequent caregiving environment. *Attachment and Human Development, 17,* 590-612.

O'Connor, M.J., & others (2019, in press). Suicide risk in adolescents with fetal alcohol spectrum disorders. *Birth Defects Research.*

O'Connor, T.G., & others (2019, in press). Early caregiving predicts attachment representations in adolescence: Findings from two longitudinal studies. *Journal of Child Psychology and Psychiatry.*

O'Dell, C. (2013). *Centenarians' secrets. What you can learn from people who've lived 100-plus years.* Retrieved February 20, 2013, from www.caring.com/articles/centenarians-secrets

O'Halloran, L., & others (2018). Neural circuitry underlying sustained attention in healthy adolescents and in ADHD symptomatology. *NeuroImage, 160,* 395-406.

O'Hara, M.W., & Engeldinger, J. (2018). Treatment of postpartum depression: Recommendations for the clinician. *Clinical Obstetrics and Gynecology, 61,* 604-614.

O'Hara, M.W., & McCabe, F. (2013). Postpartum depression: Current status and future directions. *Annual Review of Clinical Psychology.* Palo Alto, CA: Annual Reviews.

O'Kearney, R., & others (2017). Emotional abilities in children with oppositional defiant disorder (ODD): Impairment of perspective-taking and understanding mixed emotions are associated with high callous-unemotional traits. *Child Psychiatry and Human Development, 48,* 346-357.

O'Keefe, J.H., Bhatti, S.K., Baiwa, A., Dinicolantonio, J.J., & Lavie, C.J. (2014). Alcohol and cardiovascular health: The dose does make the poison . . . or the remedy. *Mayo Clinic Proceedings, 89,* 382-393.

O'Keeffe, L.M., Greene, R.A., & Kearney, P.M. (2014). The effect of moderate gestational alcohol consumption during pregnancy on speech and language outcomes in children: A systematic review. *Systematic Reviews, 3,* 1.

O'Malley, E.G., & others (2018). Folate and vitamin B12 levels in early pregnancy and maternal obesity. *European Journal of Obstetrics, Gynecology, and Reproductive Biology, 231,* 80-84.

O'Meara, M.S., & South, S.C. (2019, in press). Big Five personality domains and relationship satisfaction: Direct effects and correlated change over time. *Journal of Personality.*

Obermann, M.L. (2011). Moral disengagement in self-reported and peer-nominated school bullying. *Aggressive Behavior, 37,* 133-144.

Obler, L.K. (2009). Developments in the adult years. In J. Berko Gleason & N.B. Ratner (Eds.), *The development of language* (7th ed.). Boston: Allyn & Bacon.

Obradovic, J., Yousafzai, A.K., Finch, J.E., & Rasheed, M.A. (2016). Maternal scaffolding and home stimulation: Key mediators of early intervention effects on children's cognitive development. *Developmental Psychology, 52,* 1409-1421.

Occupational Outlook Handbook (2018-2019). Washington, DC: U.S. Department of Labor, Bureau of Labor Statistics.

OECD (2014). Life satisfaction. *Society at a glance 2014: OECD social indicators.* Paris: Author.

OECD (2016). *Marriage and divorce rates.* Paris: Author.

OECD (2017). *Obesity update 2017.* Paris: Author.

OECD (2017). *Pensions at a glance 2017.* Paris: Author.

OECD (2017). *Teenage suicide.* Paris: Author.

Offer, D., Ostrove, E., Howard, K.I., & Atkinson, R. (1988). *The teenage world: Adolescents' self-image in ten countries.* New York: Plenum Press.

Office of Special Education and Rehabilitative Services Blog (2018). *Teachers change lives.* Retrieved October 18, 2018, from https://sites.ed.gov/osers/tag/why-i-teach/

Ogawa, E.F., You, T., & Leveille, S.G. (2016). Potential benefits of exergaming for cognition and dual-task function in older adults: A systematic review. *Journal of Aging and Physical Activity, 24,* 332–336.

Ogbu, J., & Stern, P. (2001). Caste status and intellectual development. In R.J. Sternberg & E.L. Grigorenko (Eds.), *Environmental effects on cognitive abilities.* Mahwah, NJ: Erlbaum.

Ogden, C.L., & others (2016). Trends in obesity prevalence among children and adolescents in the United States, 1988–1994 through 2013–2014. *Journal of the American Medical Association, 315,* 2292–2299.

Ogden, C.L., Carroll, M.D., Kit, B.K., & Flegal, K.M. (2012, January). Prevalence of obesity in the United States, 2009–2010. *NCHS Data Brief,* 1–9.

Ogden, C.L., Carroll, M.D., Kit, B.K., & Flegal, K.M. (2014). Prevalence of childhood obesity in the United States, 2011–2012. *Journal of the American Medical Association, 311,* 806–814.

Ogihara, Y. (2017). Temporal changes in individualism and their ramifications in Japan: Rising individualism and conflicts with persisting collectivism. *Frontiers in Psychology, 8,* 695.

O-Grady, C., & Smith, K. (2019). Models of language evolution. In S-A. Rueschemyer & M. Gareth Gaskell (Eds.), *Oxford handbook of psycholinguistics* (2nd ed.). New York: Oxford University Press.

Ogundele, M.O. (2018). Behavioral and emotional disorders in childhood: A brief overview for pediatricians. *World Journal of Clinical Psychology, 7*(1), 9–26.

Oh, S., & others (2017). Prevalence and correlates of alcohol and tobacco use among pregnant women in the United States: Evidence from the NSDUH 205-2014. *Preventive Medicine, 97,* 93–99.

Oh, S.J., & others (2018). Effects of smartphone-based memory training for older adults with subjective memory complaints: A randomized controlled trial. *Aging and Mental Health, 22,* 526–534.

Okada, H.C., Alleyne, B., Varghai, K., Kinder, K., & Guyuron, B. (2013). Facial changes caused by smoking: A comparison between smoking and non-smoking identical twins. *Plastic and Reconstructive Surgery, 132*(5), 1085–1092.

Okada, K., & others (2014). Comprehensive evaluation of androgen replacement therapy in aging Japanese men with late-onset hypogonadism. *Aging Male, 17,* 72–75.

Okado, Y., & Bierman, K.L. (2015). Differential risk for late adolescent conduct problems and mood dysregulation among children with early externalizing behavior problems. *Journal of Abnormal Child Psychology, 43,* 735–747.

Oken, B.S., & others (2018). Predictors of improvements in mental health from mindfulness meditation in stressed older adults. *Alternative Therapies in Health and Medicine, 24,* 48–55.

Okubo, Y., & others (2016). Walking can be more effective than balance in fall prevention among community-dwelling older adults. *Geriatrics and Gerontology International, 16,* 118–125.

Okumu, M., & others (2019, in press). Psychosocial syndemics and sexual risk practices among U.S. adolescents: Findings from the 2017 U.S. Youth Behavioral Survey. *International Journal of Behavioral Medicine.*

Okun, M.A., Yeung, E.W., & Brown, S. (2013). Volunteering by older adults and risk of mortality: A meta-analysis. *Psychology and Aging, 28,* 564–577.

Oldehinkel, A.J., Ormel, J., Veenstra, R., De Winter, A., & Verhulst, F.C. (2008). Parental divorce and offspring depressive symptoms: Dutch developmental trends during early adolescence. *Journal of Marriage and the Family, 70,* 284–293.

Olderbak, S., & others (2019, in press). Sex differences in facial emotion perception ability across the lifespan. *Cognition and Emotion.*

Olesen, K., Rugulies, R., Rod, N.H., & Bonde, J.P. (2014). Does retirement reduce the risk of myocardial infarction? A prospective registry linkage study of 617,511 Danish workers. *International Journal of Epidemiology, 43,* 160–167.

Olsavsky, A.L., & others (2019, in press). New fathers' perceptions of dyadic adjustment: The roles of maternal gatekeeping and coparenting closeness. *Family Process.*

Olshansky, S.J., & others (2012). Differences in life expectancy due to race and educational differences are widening, and many may not catch up. *Health Affairs, 31,* 1803–1813.

Oltmanns, J., & others (2017). Don't lose your brain at work—the role of recurrent novelty at work in cognitive and brain aging. *Frontiers in Psychology, 8,* 117.

Olweus, D. (2003). Prevalence estimation of school bullying with the Olweus bully/victim questionnaire. *Aggressive Behavior, 29*(3), 239–269.

Olweus, D. (2013). School bullying: Development and some important changes. *Annual Review of Clinical Psychology* (Vol. 9). Palo Alto, CA: Annual Reviews.

Oman, D., & Thoresen, C.E. (2006). Do religion and spirituality influence health? In R.F. Paloutzian & C.L. Park (Eds.), *Handbook of the psychology of religion and spirituality.* New York: Guilford.

Onders, B., & others (2019, in press). Pediatric injuries related to window blinds, shades, and cords. *Pediatrics.*

Onen, S.H., & Onen, F. (2018). Chronic medical conditions and sleep in the older adult. *Sleep Medicine Clinics, 13,* 71–79.

Onetti, W., Fernández-Garcia, J.C., & Castillo-Rodríguez, A. (2019). Transition to middle school: Self-concept changes. *PLoS One, 14*(2), e0212640.

Ongley, S.F., & Malti, T. (2014). The role of moral emotions in the development of children's sharing behavior. *Developmental Psychology, 50,* 1148–1159.

Ongley, S.F., Nola, M., & Malti, T. (2014). Children's giving: Moral reasoning and moral emotions in the development of donation behaviors. *Frontiers in Psychology, 5,* 456.

Onojighofia Tobore, T. (2019, in press). On the etiopathogenesis and pathophysiology of Alzheimer's disease: A comprehensive theoretical view. *Journal of Alzheimer's Disease.*

Opfer, J.E., & Gelman, S.A. (2011). Development of the animate-inanimate distinction. In U. Goswami (Ed.), *Wiley-Blackwell handbook of childhood cognitive development* (2nd ed.). New York: Wiley.

Oppezzo, M., & Schwartz, D.L. (2014). Give your ideas some legs: The positive effect of walking on creative thinking. *Journal of Experimental Psychology: Learning, Memory, and Cognition, 40,* 1142–1152.

Orbeta, R.L., Overpeck, M.D., Ramamcharran, D., Kogan, M.D., & Ledsky, R. (2006). High caffeine intake in adolescents: Associations with difficulty sleeping and feeling tired in the morning. *Adolescent Health, 38,* 451–453.

Ordonez, T.N., & others (2017). Activity station: Effects on global cognition of mature adults and healthy elderly program using electronic games. *Dementia and Neuropsychology, 11,* 186–197.

Oreland, L., & others (2018). Personality as an intermediate phenotype for genetic dissection of alcohol use disorder. *Journal of Neural Transmission, 725,* 107–130.

Oren, E., & others (2017). Self-reported stressful life events during adolescence and subsequent asthma: A longitudinal study. *Journal of Allergy and Clinical Immunology: In Practice, 5,* 427–434.

Orimaye, S.O., & others (2017). Predicting probable Alzheimer's disease using linguistic deficits and biomarkers. *BMC Bioinformatics, 18*(1), 34.

Ornaghi, V., & others (2019, in press). The contribution of emotion knowledge, language ability, and maternal emotion socialization style to explaining toddlers' emotion regulation. *Social Development.*

Ornstein, P.A., Coffman, J.L., & Grammer, J.K. (2007, April). *Teachers' memory-relevant conversations and children's memory performance.* Paper presented at the biennial meeting of the Society for Research in Child Development, Boston.

Ornstein, P.A., Coffman, J.L., Grammer, J.K., San Souci, P.P., & McCall, L.E. (2010). Linking the classroom context and the development of children's memory skills. In J. Meece & J. Eccles (Eds.), *The handbook of research on schools, schooling, and human development.* New York: Routledge.

Ornstein, P.A., Gordon, B.N., & Larus, D. (1992). Children's memory for a personally experienced event: Implications for testimony. *Applied Cognition and Psychology, 6,* 49–60.

Ornstein, P.A., Grammer, J., & Coffman, J. (2010). Teacher's "mnemonic style" and the development of skilled memory. In H.S. Waters & W. Schneider (Eds.), *Metacognition, strategy use, and instruction.* New York: Guilford.

Ornstein, P.A., Haden, C.A., & Coffman, J.L. (2010). Learning to remember: Mothers and teachers talking with children. In N.L. Stein & S. Raudenbush (Eds.), *Development science goes to school.* New York: Taylor & Francis.

Orosz, G., & others (2015). Elevated romantic love and jealousy if relationship is declared on Facebook. *Frontiers in Psychology, 6,* 214.

Orth, U. (2017). The family environment in early childhood has a long-term effect on self-esteem: A longitudinal study from birth to age 27 years. *Journal of Personality and Social Psychology, 110,* 133–149.

Orzabal, M.R., & others (2019, in press). Chronic exposure to e-cig aerosols during early development causes vascular dysfunction and offspring growth deficits. *Translational Research*.

Osborn, K., Davis, J.P., Button, S., & Foster, J. (2019, in press). Juror decision making in acquaintance and marital rape: The influence of clothing, alcohol, and preexisting stereotypical attitudes. *Journal of Interpersonal Violence*.

Ossher, L., Flegal, K.E., & Lustig, C. (2013). Everyday memory errors in older adults. *Neuropsychology, Development, and Cognition, B: Aging, Neuroscience, and Cognition, 20*, 220-242.

Ostan, R., & others (2016). Gender, aging, and longevity in humans: An update of an intriguing/neglected scenario paving the way to gender-specific medicine. *Clinical Science, 130*, 1711-1725.

Osterberg, E.C., Bernie, A.M., & Ramasamy, R. (2014). Risk of replacement testosterone therapy in men. *Indian Journal of Urology, 30*, 2-7.

Ostergaard, S.D., & others (2017). Teenage parenthood and birth rates for individuals with and without attention-deficit/hyperactivity disorder: A nationwide cohort study. *Journal of the American Academy of Child and Adolescent Psychiatry, 56*, 578-584.

Ostfeld, B.M., & others (2019, in press). Prematurity and sudden unexpected infant deaths in the United States. *Pediatrics*.

Ostlund, S.B. (2019, in press). The push and pull of dopamine in cue-reward learning. *Learning and Behavior*.

Oswald, D.L., & Clark, E.M. (2003). Best friends forever? High school best friendships and the transition to college. *Personal Relationships, 10*, 187-196.

Ota, M., & Skarabela, B. (2018). Reduplication facilitates early word segmentation. *Journal of Child Language, 45*, 204-218.

Otto, H., & Keller, H. (Eds) (2018). *Different faces of attachment*. New York: Cambridge University Press.

Owen, K.B., & others (2018). Regular physical activity and educational outcomes in youth: A longitudinal study. *Journal of Adolescent Health, 62*, 334-340.

Owens, J.A., Belon, K., & Moss, P. (2010). Impact of delaying school start time on adolescent sleep, mood, and behavior. *Archives of Pediatric and Adolescent Medicine, 164*, 608-614.

Owsley, C., & others (2016). Comparison of visual function in older eyes in the earliest stages of age-related macular degeneration to those in normal macular health. *Current Eye Research, 41*, 266-272.

Oxford, M.L., Gilchrist, L.D., Gillmore, M.R., & Lohr, M.J. (2006). Predicting variation in the life course of adolescent mothers as they enter adulthood. *Journal of Adolescent Health, 39*, 20-36.

Ozcan, L., & others (2017). Effects of taking tadalafil 5 mg once daily on erectile function and total testosterone levels in patients with metabolic syndrome. *Andrologia, 49*.

Ozturk Donmez, R., & Bayik Temel, A. (2019, in press). Effect of soothing techniques on infants' self-regulation behaviors (sleeping, crying, feeding): A randomized controlled study. *Japanese Journal of Nursing Science*.

P

Pacala, J.T., & Yeuh, B. (2012). Hearing defects in the older patient: "I didn't notice anything." *Journal of the American Medical Association, 307*, 1185-1194.

Pace, A., Levine, D.F., Morini, G., Hirsh-Pasek, K., & Golinkoff, R.M. (2016). Language acquisition: From words to world and back again. In L. Balter & C.S. Tamis-LeMonda (Eds.), *Child psychology: A contemporary handbook* (3rd ed.). New York: Psychology Press.

Padilla-Walker, L.M., Memmott-Elison, M., & Nelson, L. (2017). Positive relationships as an indicator of flourishing during emerging adulthood. In L.M. Padilla-Walker & L. Nelson (Eds.), *Flourishing in emerging adulthood*. New York: Oxford University Press.

Padilla-Walker, L.M., & Nelson, L.J. (Eds.) (2017). *Flourishing in emerging adulthood*. New York: Oxford University Press.

Padilla-Walker, L.M., & Nelson, L.J. (2019). *Parenting in emerging adulthood*. In M.H. Bornstein (Ed.), *Handbook of parenting* (3rd ed.). New York: Routledge.

Padilla-Walker, L.M., & Son, D. (2020, in press). Proactive parenting and moral development. In D.J. Laible & others (Eds.), *Oxford handbook of parenting and moral development*. New York: Oxford University Press.

Padilla-Walker, L.M., & others (2018). The protective role of parental media monitoring style from early to late adolescence. *Journal of Youth and Adolescence, 47*, 445-459.

Padmanabhanunni, A., & Gerhardt, M. (2019, in press). Normative beliefs as predictors of physical, non-physical, and relational aggression among South African adolescents. *Journal of Child and Adolescent Mental Health*.

Padmapriya, N., & others (2019, in press). Sex-specific longitudinal associations of screen viewing time in children at 2-3 years with adiposity at 3-5 years. *International Journal of Obesity*.

Pagani, L.S., Levesque-Seck, F., Archambault, I., & Janosz, M. (2017). Prospective longitudinal associations between household smoke exposure in early childhood and antisocial behavior at age 12. *Indoor Air, 27*, 622-630.

Paganini-Hill, A., Kawas, C.H., & Corrada, M.M. (2015). Antioxidant vitamin intake and mortality: The Leisure World Cohort Study. *American Journal of Epidemiology, 181*, 120-126.

Pahlke, E., Hyde, J.S., & Allison, C.M. (2014). The effects of single-sex compared with coeducational schooling on students' performance and attitudes: A meta-analysis. *Psychological Bulletin, 140*, 1042-1072.

Pakhomov, S.V., & Hemmy, L.S. (2014). A computational linguistic measure of clustering behavior on semantic verbal fluency task predicts risk of future dementia in the Nun Study. *Cortex, 55*, 97-106.

Palacios-Barrios, E.E., & Hanson, J.L. (2019). Poverty and self-regulation: Connecting psychosocial processes, neurobiology, and the risk for psychopathology. *Comprehensive Psychology, 90*, 52-64.

Palama, A., Maisert, J., & Gentaz, E. (2018). Are 6-month-old human infants able to transfer emotional information (happy or angry) voices to faces? An eye-tracking study. *PLoS One, 13*, e0194579.

Pallini, S., & others (2018). The relation of attachment security status to effortful self-regulation: A meta-analysis. *Psychological Bulletin, 144*, 501-531.

Palmeira, L., & others (2019). Association study of variants in genes FTO, SLC6A4, DRD2, BDNF, and GHRL with binge eating disorder (BED) in Portuguese women. *Psychiatry Research, 273*, 309-311.

Palmer, C.A., Oosterhoff, B., Bower, J.L., Kaplow, J.B., & Alfano, C.A. (2018). Associations among adolescent sleep problems, emotion regulation, and affective disorders: Findings from a nationally representative sample. *Journal of Psychiatric Research, 96*, 1-8.

Palmeroni, N., & others (2019, in press). Identity stress throughout adolescence and emerging adulthood: Age trends and associations with exploration and commitment processes. *Emerging Adulthood*.

Palmore, E.B. (2004). Research note: Ageism in Canada and the United States. *Journal of Cross Cultural Gerontology, 19*, 41-46.

Paloutzian, R.F. (2000). *Invitation to the psychology of religion* (3rd ed.). Needham Heights, MA: Allyn & Bacon.

Pals, J.L. (2006). Constructing the "springboard effect": Causal connections, self-making, and growth within the life story. In D.P. McAdams, R. Josselson, & A. Lieblich (Eds.), *Identity and story*. Washington, DC: American Psychological Association.

Pan, B.A., Rowe, M.L., Singer, J.D., & Snow, C.E. (2005). Maternal correlates of growth in toddler vocabulary production in low-income families. *Child Development, 76*, 763-782.

Pan, C.Y., & others (2019). Effects of physical exercise intervention on motor skills and executive functions with ADHD: A pilot study. *Journal of Attention Disorders, 23*, 384-397.

Pan, Z., & Chang, C. (2012). Gender and the regulation of longevity: Implications for autoimmunity. *Autoimmunity Reviews, 11*, A393-A403.

Panagiotaki, G., & others (2018). Children's and adults' understanding of death: Cognitive, parental, and experiential influences. *Journal of Experimental Child Psychology, 166*, 96-115.

Pandya, S.P. (2018). Spiritual counseling program for children with anxiety disorders: A multi-city experiment. *Journal of Pastoral Care and Counseling, 72*, 45-57.

Panel, M., Ghaleh, B., & Morin, D. (2019, in press). Mitochondria and aging: A role for the mitochondrial transition pore? *Aging Cell*.

Panizzon, M.S., & others (2014). Interaction of APOE genotype and testosterone on episodic memory in middle-aged men. *Neurobiology of Aging, 35*, e1-e8.

Pantell, R.H., & others (2019, in press). The child witness in the courtroom. *Pediatrics*.

Paolucci, E.M., & others (2018). Exercise reduces depression and inflammation but intensity matters. *Biological Psychology, 133*, 79-84.

Papastavrou, E., Charlalambous, A., Tsangari, H., & Karayiannis, G. (2012). The burdensome and depressive experience of caring: What cancer, schizophrenia, and Alzheimer's disease caregivers have in common. *Cancer Nursing, 35*, 187-194.

Papernow, P.L. (2018). Recoupling in mid-life and beyond: From love at last to not so fast. *Family Process, 57*, 52-69.

Parade, S.H., & others (2018). Family context moderates the association of maternal postpartum depression and stability of infant attachment. *Child Development, 89*, 2118-2135.

Parashar, S., & others (2018). DNA methylation signatures of breast cancer in peripheral T-cells. *BMC Cancer, 18*(1), 574.

Parish-Morris, J., Golinkoff, R.M., & Hirsh-Pasek, K. (2013). From coo to code: A brief story of language development. In P.D. Zelazo (Ed.), *Oxford handbook of developmental psychology*. New York: Oxford University Press.

Parisi, J.M., & others (2012). The role of education and intellectual activity on cognition. *Journal of Aging Research, 2012,* 416132.

Parisi, J.M., & others (2014). The association between lifestyles and later-life depression. *Activities, Adaptation, and Aging, 38,* 1–10.

Parisi, J.M., & others (2015). Increases in lifestyle activity as a result of Experience Corps participation. *Journal of Urban Health, 92,* 55–66.

Park, C.D., & Festini, S. (2018). Cognitive health. In M.H. Bornstein (Ed.), *SAGE encyclopedia of lifespan human development*. Thousand Oaks, CA: Sage.

Park, C.L. (2005). Religion as a meaning-making system. *Psychology of Religion Newsletter, 30*(2), 1–9.

Park, C.L. (2007). Religiousness/spirituality and health: A meaning systems perspective. *Journal of Behavioral Medicine, 30,* 319–328.

Park, C.L. (2008). Estimated longevity and changes in spirituality in the context of advanced congestive heart failure. *Palliative and Supportive Care, 6,* 1–9.

Park, C.L. (2010). Making sense out of the meaning literature: An integrative review of meaning making and its effect on adjustment to stressful life events. *Psychological Bulletin, 136,* 257–301.

Park, C.L. (2012a). Meaning making in cancer survivorship. In P.T.P. Wong (Ed.), *Handbook of meaning* (2nd ed.). Mahwah, NJ: Sage.

Park, C.L. (2012b). Meaning, spirituality, and growth: Protective and resilience factors in health and illness. In A.S. Baum, T.A. Revenson, & J.E. Singer (Eds.), *Handbook of health psychology* (2nd ed.). New York: Sage.

Park, C.L. (2013). Religion and meaning. In R.F. Paloutzian & C.L. Park (Eds.), *Handbook of the psychology of religion* (2nd ed.). New York: Guilford.

Park, C.L. (2016). Meaning making in the context of disasters. *Journal of Clinical Psychology, 72,* 1234–1246.

Park, C.L., & Cho, D. (2017). Spiritual well-being and spiritual distress predict adjustment in adolescent and young adult cancer survivors. *Psycho-Oncology, 26,* 1293–1300.

Park, C.L., & others (2016). Positive and negative religious/spiritual coping and combat exposure as predictors of posttraumatic stress and perceived growth in Iraq and Afghanistan veterans. *Psychology of Religion and Spirituality, 9.* doi:10.1037/rel0000086

Park, C.L., & others (2016). Spirituality predicts five-year mortality risk in heart failure patients. *Health Psychology, 35,* 203–210.

Park, D.C., & Festini, S. (2018). Cognitive health. In M.H. Bornstein (Ed.), *SAGE encyclopedia of lifespan human development*. Thousand Oaks, CA: Sage.

Park, D.C., & Reuter-Lorenz, P. (2009). The adaptive brain: Aging and neurocognitive scaffolding. *Annual Review of Psychology* (Vol. 60). Palo Alto, CA: Annual Reviews.

Park, D.C., & others (2014). The impact of sustained engagement on cognitive function in older adults: The Synapse Project. *Psychological Science, 25,* 103–112.

Park, J.H., & others (2017). Trends in overall mortality, and timing and cause of death among

extremely preterm infants near the limit of viability. *PLoS One, 12*(1), e0170220.

Park, J.S., & others (2018). Variants of cancer susceptibility genes in Korean BRCA1/2 mutation-negative patients with high risk for hereditary breast cancer. *BMC Cancer, 18*(1), 83.

Park, M., & others (2018). Maternal depression trajectories from pregnancy to 3 years postpartum are associated with children's behavior and executive functions at 3 and 6 years. *Archives of Women's Mental Health, 21,* 353–363.

Park, M.J., Brindis, C.D., Chang, F., & Irwin, C.E. (2008). A midcourse review of the Healthy People 2010: 21 critical health objectives for adolescents and young adults. *Journal of Adolescent Health, 42,* 329–334.

Park, M.J., Mulye, T.P., Adams, S.H., Brindis, C.D., & Irwin, C.E. (2006). The health status of young adults in the United States. *Journal of Adolescent Health, 39,* 305–317.

Park, S., Mori, R., & Shimokawa, I. (2013). Do sirtuins promote mammalian longevity? A critical review on its relevance to the longevity effect induced by calorie restriction. *Molecules and Cells, 35,* 474–480.

Park, S.H., & others (2013). Sarcopenic obesity as an independent risk factor of hypertension. *Journal of the American Society of Hypertension, 7*(6), 420–425.

Park, Y.M. (2017). Relationship between child maltreatment, suicidality, and bipolarity: A retrospective study. *Psychiatry Investigation, 14,* 136–140.

Parkay, F.W. (2020). *Becoming a teacher* (11th ed.). Upper Saddle River, NJ: Pearson.

Parke, R.D., & Buriel, R. (2006). Socialization in the family: Ethnic and ecological perspectives. In W. Damon & R. Lerner (Eds.), *Handbook of child psychology* (6th ed.). New York: Wiley.

Parke, R.D., Coltrane, S., & Schofield, T. (2011). The bicultural advantage. In J. Marsh, R. Mendoza-Denton, & J.A. Smith (Eds.), *Are we born racist?* Boston: Beacon Press.

Parke, R.D., & Elder, G.H. (2020). *Children in changing worlds*. New York: Cambridge University Press.

Parke, R.D., Roisman, G.I., & Rose, A.J. (2019, in press). *Social development* (3rd ed.). New York: Wiley.

Parker, C.B. (2016, February 11, 2016). Stanford project suggests longer, healthier lives possible. *Stanford Report,* 1–4.

Parker, K., & Stepler, R. (2017, September 14). *As U.S. marriage rate hovers at 50%, education gap in marital status widens.* Washington, DC: Pew Research Center.

Parkes, A., Green, M., & Mitchell, K. (2019). Coparenting and parenting pathways from the couple relationship to children's behavior problems. *Journal of Family Psychology, 33,* 215–225.

Parkinson, P. (2010). Changing policies regarding separated fathers in Australia. In M.E. Lamb (Ed.), *The role of the father in child development* (5th ed.). New York: Wiley.

Parmar, M. (2019, in press). Towards stem cell based therapies for Parkinson's disease. *Development.*

Parritz, R.H. (2018). *Disorders of childhood* (3rd ed.). Boston: Cengage.

Parsons, C.E., & others (2017). Interpreting infant emotional expressions: Parenthood has differential

effects on men and women. *Quarterly Journal of Experimental Psychology 70,* 554–564.

Parsons, K., Rutkowski, E.M., & Turel, O. (2019, in press). Health behavior knowledge among Hispanic California islanders: Evaluation of a parental educational intervention. *Journal for Specialists in Pediatric Nursing.*

Pascal, A., & others (2018). Neurodevelopmental outcome in very preterm and very-low-birthweight infants born over the past decade: A meta-analytic review. *Developmental Medicine and Child Neurology, 60,* 342–355.

Paschall, K.W., & Mastergeorge, A.M. (2018). A longitudinal, person-centered analysis of Head Start mothers' parenting. *Infant Mental Health, 39,* 70–84.

Pascoe, C.J. (2017). Making masculinity: Adolescence, identity, and high school. In L. Saraswati & others (Eds.), *Introduction to women's, gender, and sexuality studies*. New York: Oxford University Press.

Pascual-Sagastizabal, E., & others (2019). Testosterone and cortisol modulate the effects of empathy and aggression in children. *Psychoneuroendocrinology, 103,* 118–124.

Pasterski, V., Golombok, S., & Hines, M. (2011). Sex differences in social behavior. In P.K. Smith & C.H. Hart (Eds.), *Wiley-Blackwell handbook of childhood social development* (2nd ed.). New York: Wiley.

Pate, R.R., & others (2015). Prevalence of compliance with a new physical activity guideline for preschool-aged children. *Childhood Obesity, 11,* 45–70.

Pate, R.R., & others (2019). Change in children's physical activity: Predictors in the transition from elementary to middle school. *American Journal of Preventive Medicine, 56*(3), e65–e73.

Patel, K.V., & others (2019). Symptom burden among community-dwelling older adults in the United States. *Journal of the American Geriatrics Society, 67,* 223–231.

Patel, N., & others (2017). Role of second-hand smoke (SH)-induced proteostasis/autophagy impairment in pediatric lung diseases. *Molecular and Cellular Pediatrics, 4*(1), 3.

Patel, R., & others (2018). Prostate cancer susceptibility and growth linked to Y chromosome genes. *Frontiers in Bioscience, 10,* 423–436.

Paterson, K.L., & Gates, L. (2019). Clinical assessment and management of foot and ankle osteoarthritis: A review of current evidence and focus on pharmacological treatment. *Drugs and Aging, 36,* 203–211.

Patlamazoglou, L., Simmonds, J.G., & Snell, T.L. (2018). Same-sex partner bereavement. *Omega, 78,* 178–196.

Patrick, J.H., Carney, A.K., & Nehrkorn, A.M. (2017). Aging in the context of life events. *International Journal of Aging and Human Development, 84,* 209–212.

Patterson, C.J. (2013). Family lives of gay and lesbian adults. In G.W. Peterson & K.R. Bush (Eds.), *Handbook of marriage and the family* (3rd ed.). New York: Springer.

Patterson, C.J. (2014). Sexual minority youth and youth with sexual minority parents. In G.B. Melton, A. Ben-Arieh, J. Cashmore, G.S. Goodman, & N.K. Worley (Eds.), *SAGE handbook of child research*. Thousand Oaks, CA: Sage.

Patterson, C.J. (2019). Lesbian and gay parenthood. In M.H. Bornstein (Ed.), *Handbook of parenting* (3rd ed.). New York: Routledge.

Patterson, G.D., & others (2018). Recurrent acute chest syndrome in pediatric sickle cell disease: Clinical features and risk factors. *Journal of Pediatric Hematology/Oncology, 40,* 51–55.

Patton, G.C., & others (2011). A prospective study of the effects of optimism on adolescent health risks. *Pediatrics, 127,* 308–316.

Paul, C. (2019). Emotions and successful aging. In R. Fernandez-Ballesteros, A. Benetos, & J-M. Robine (Eds.), *Cambridge handbook of successful aging.* New York: Cambridge University Press.

Paul, S., & Corwin, E.J. (2019, in press). Identifying clusters from multidimensional symptom trajectories in postpartum women. *Research in Nursing and Health.*

Pauletti, R.E., & others (2017). Psychological androgyny and children's mental health: A new look with new measures. *Sex Roles, 76,* 705–718.

Paulhus, D.L. (2008). Birth order. In M.M. Haith & J.B. Benson (Eds.), *Encyclopedia of infant and early childhood development.* Oxford, UK: Elsevier.

Paulson, J.F., Bazemore, S.D., Goodman, J.H., & Leiferman, J.A. (2016). The course and interrelationship of maternal and paternal perinatal depression. *Archives of Women's Mental Health, 19,* 655–663.

Paulson, J.L., & Miller-Graff, L. (2019). Prenatal sleep quality and mental health symptoms across the perinatal period: A longitudinal study of high-risk women. *Journal of Psychosomatic Research, 116,* 31–36.

Paulus, M. (2014). The early origins of human charity: Developmental changes in preschoolers' sharing with poor and wealthy individuals. *Frontiers in Psychology, 5,* 344.

Paunesku, D., & others (2015). Mind-set interventions are a scalable treatment for academic under-achievement. *Psychological Science, 26,* 784–793.

Paus, T., & others (2008). Morphological properties of the action–observation cortical network in adolescents with low and high resistance to peer influence. *Social Neuroscience, 3,* 303–316.

Pawluski, J.L., Lonstein, J.S., & Fleming, A.S. (2017). The neurobiology of postpartum period anxiety and depression. *Trends in Neuroscience, 40,* 106–120.

Payer, L. (1991). The menopause in various cultures. In H. Burger & M. Boulet (Eds.), *A portrait of menopause.* Park Ridge, NJ: Parthenon.

Payne, B.R., & Federmeier, K.D. (2018). Contextual constraints on lexico-semantic processing in aging: Evidence from single-word event-related brain potentials. *Brain Research, 1687,* 117–128.

Pazmandi, J., & others (2019). Early-onset inflammatory bowel disease as a model disease to identify key regulators of immune homeostasis mechanisms. *Immunology Reviews, 287,* 162–185.

Pedersen, C.B., McGrath, J., Mortensen, P.B., & Pedersen, L. (2014). The importance of the father's age to schizophrenia risk. *Molecular Psychiatry, 19,* 530–531.

Pedersen, M.T., & others (2017). Effect of team sports and resistance training on physical function, quality of life, and motivation in older adults. *Scandinavian Journal of Medicine and Science in Sports, 27,* 852–864.

Pederson, D.R., & Moran, G. (1996). Expressions of the attachment relationship outside of the Strange Situation. *Child Development, 67,* 915–927.

Pedrinolla, A., Schena, F., & Venturelli, M. (2018). Resilience to Alzheimer's disease: The role of physical activity. *Current Alzheimer Research, 14,* 546–553.

Peek, L., & Stough, L.M. (2010). Children with disabilities in the context of disaster: A social vulnerability perspective. *Child Development, 81,* 1260–1270.

Peets, K., Hodges, E.V., & Salmivalli, C. (2013). Forgiveness and its determinants depending on the interpersonal context of hurt. *Journal of Experimental Child Psychology, 114,* 131–145.

Pei, G., & others (2019). Investigation of multi-trait associations using pathway-based analysis of GWAS summary statistics. *BMC Genomics, 20*(Suppl. 1), 79.

Pei, Y., Cong, Z., & Wu, B. (2019, in press). The impact of living alone and intergenerational support on depressive symptoms among older Mexican Americans: Does gender matter? *International Journal of Aging and Human Development.*

Pelletier Brochu, J., & others (2018). Adolescents' perceptions of the quality of interpersonal relationships and eating disorder symptom severity: The mediating role of low self-esteem and negative mood. *Eating Disorders, 26,* 388–406.

Pelton, S.I., & Leibovitz, E. (2009). Recent advances in otitis media. *Pediatric and Infectious Disease Journal, 28*(Suppl. 10), S133–S137.

Penazzi, L., Bakota, L., & Brandt, R. (2016). Microtubule dynamics in neuronal development, plasticity, and neurodegeneration. *International Review of Cell and Molecular Biology, 321,* 89–169.

Peng, K., & others (2019). Incidence, risk factors, and economic burden of fall-related injuries in older Chinese people: A systematic review. *Injury Prevention, 25,* 4–12.

Peralta, L.R., & others (2019, in press). Influence of school-level socioeconomic status on children's physical activity, fitness, and fundamental movement skills. *Journal of School Health.*

Perani, D., & others (2017). The impact of bilingualism on brain reserve and metabolic connectivity in Alzheimer's disease. *Proceedings of the National Academy of Sciences USA, 114,* 1690–1695.

Pereira Gray, D.J., & others (2018). Continuity of care with doctors—a matter of life or death? A systematic review of continuity of care and mortality. *BMJ Open, 8*(6), e021161.

Perez, H.C.S., & others (2018). Prolonged grief and cognitive decline: A prospective population-based study in middle-aged and older persons. *American Journal of Geriatric Psychiatry, 26,* 451–460.

Perez-Brena, N.J., & others (2018). Contributions of the integrative model for the study of developmental competencies in minority children: What have we learned about adaptive culture? *American Psychologist, 73,* 713–726.

Perez-Edgar, K.E., & Guyer, A.E. (2014). Behavioral inhibition: Temperament or prodrome? *Current Behavioral Neuroscience Reports, 1,* 182–190.

Perez-Escamilla, R., & Engmann, C. (2019, in press). Integrating nutrition services into health care systems platforms: Where are we and where do we go from here? *Maternal and Child Nutrition.*

Perez-Escamilla, R., & Moran, V.H. (2017). The role of nutrition in integrated early child development in the 21st century: Contribution from the Maternal and Child Nutrition journal. *Maternal and Child Nutrition, 13,* 3–6.

Perez-Fuentes, M.D.C., & others (2019). Burnout and engagement: Personality profiles in nursing professionals. *Journal of Clinical Medicine, 8,* 3.

Perkins, D. (1994, September). Creativity by design. *Educational Leadership, 51,* 18–25.

Perkins, S.C., Finegood, E.D., & Swain, J.E. (2013). Poverty and language development: Roles of parenting and stress. *Innovations in Clinical Neuroscience, 10,* 10–19.

Perkisas, S., & Vandewoude, M. (2019). Nutrition and cognition. In R. Fernandez-Ballesteros, A. Benetos, & J-M. Robine (Eds.), *Cambridge handbook of successful aging.* New York: Cambridge University Press.

Perlman, L. (2008, July 22). Am I an I or We? *Twins,* 1–2.

Perlman, L. (2013). Twin psychological development. Retrieved February 14, 2013, from http://christinabaglivitinglof.com/twin-pregnancy/six-twin-experts-tell-all/

Perls, T.T. (2007). Centenarians. In J.E. Birren (Ed.), *Encyclopedia of gerontology* (2nd ed.). San Diego: Academic Press.

Perreira, K.M., & Pedroza, J.M. (2019). Policies of exclusion: Implications for the health of immigrants and their children. *Annual Review of Public Health.* Palo Alto, CA: Annual Reviews.

Perreira, K.M., & others (2019). Stress and resilience: Key correlates of mental health and substance use in the Hispanic Community Health Study of Latino Youth. *Journal of Immigrant and Minority Health, 21,* 4–13.

Perrotte, J.K., & others (2019, in press). Pregaming among Latina/o emerging adults: Do acculturation and gender matter? *Journal of Ethnicity in Substance Abuse.*

Perry, D.G. (2012, April). *The intrapsychics of gender.* Paper presented at the Gender Development Research conference, San Francisco.

Perry, D.G., & Pauletti, R.E. (2011). Gender and adolescent development. *Journal of Research in Adolescence, 21,* 61–74.

Perry, N.B., & Calkins, S.D. (2018). Emotion regulation across childhood. In P.M. Cole & T. Hollenstein (Eds.), *Emotion regulation.* New York: Routledge.

Perry, N.B., Calkins, S.D., Dollar, J.M., Keane, S.P., & Shanahan, L. (2018a). Self-regulation as a predictor of patterns of change in externalizing behaviors from infancy to adolescence. *Development and Psychopathology, 30,* 497–510.

Perry, N.B., Dollar, J.M., Calkins, S.D., Keane, S.P., & Shanahan, L. (2018b). Childhood self-regulation as a mechanism through which early overcontrolling parenting is associated with adjustment in preadolescence. *Developmental Psychology, 54,* 1542–1554.

Perry, S.E., & others (2018). *Maternal child nursing care* (6th ed.). New York: Elsevier.

Perry, W.G. (1970). *Forms of intellectual and ethical development in the college years.* New York: Holt, Rinehart & Winston.

Perry-Jenkins, M., & Schoppe-Sullivan, S. (2019). The transition to parenthood in social context. In B.H. Friese (Ed.), *APA handbook of contemporary family psychology.* Washington, DC: APA Books.

Persky, H.R., Dane, M.C., & Jin, Y. (2003). *The nation's report card: Writing 2002.* U.S. Department of Education.

Peskin, H. (1967). Pubertal onset ego functioning. *Journal of Abnormal Psychology, 72,* 1-15.

Peteet, J.R., Zaben, F.A., & Koenig, H.G. (2019). Integrating spirituality into the care of older adults. *International Psychogeriatrics, 31,* 31-38.

Petersen, I.T., & others (2012). Interaction between serotonin transporter polymorphism (5-HTTLPR) and stressful life events in adolescents' trajectories of anxious/depressed symptoms. *Developmental Psychology, 48*(5), 1463-1475.

Peterson, C.C., & others (2016). Peer social skills and theory of mind in children with autism, deafness, or typical development. *Developmental Psychology, 52,* 46-57.

Peterson, J.L., & Hyde, J.S. (2010). A meta-analytic review of research on gender differences in sexuality, 1973-2007. *Psychological Bulletin, 136,* 21-38.

Petrangelo, A., & others (2019, in press). Cannabis abuse or dependence during pregnancy: A population-based cohort study on 12 million births. *Journal of Obstetrics and Gynecology Canada.*

Petridou, A., Siopi, A., & Mougios, V. (2019). Exercise in the management of obesity. *Metabolism, 92,* 163-169.

Petrie, J.R., Guzik, T.J., & Touyz, R.M. (2018). Diabetes, hypertension, and cardiovascular disease: Clinical insights and vascular mechanisms. *Canadian Journal of Cardiology, 34,* 575-584.

Petrovic, M., & others (2019). Optimization of drug use in older people: A key factor for successful aging. In R. Fernandez-Ballesteros, A. Benetos, & J-M. Robine (Eds.), *Cambridge handbook of successful aging.* New York: Cambridge University Press.

Petts, R.J. (2014). Family, religious attendance, and trajectories of psychological well-being among youth. *Journal of Family Psychology, 28,* 759-768.

Pew Research Center (2008). *Pew Forum on Religion and Public Life: U.S. Religious Landscape Survey.* Washington, DC: Author.

Pew Research Center (2010). *Millennials: Confident, connected, open to change.* Washington, DC: Pew Research Center.

Pew Research Center (2012). *Religion and Public Life Project.* Washington, DC: Pew Research.

Pew Research Center (2013). *Social and demographic trends.* Washington, DC: Pew Research Center.

Pew Research Center (2015). *U.S. public becoming less religious.* Washington, DC: Pew Research.

Pew Research Center (2015a). *For most highly educated women, motherhood doesn't start until the 30s.* Washington, DC: Pew Research Center.

Pew Research Center (2016). *The gender gap in religion around the world.* Washington, DC: Pew Research.

Peyre, H., & others (2017). Contributing factors and mental health outcomes of first suicide attempt during childhood and adolescence: Results from a nationally representative study. *Journal of Clinical Psychiatry, 78,* e622-e630.

Peyre, H., & others (2017). Do developmental milestones at 4, 8, 12, and 24 months predict IQ at 5-6 years old? Results of the EDEN mother-child cohort. *European Journal of Paediatric Neurology, 21,* 272-279.

Pfeifer, C.M. (2019, in press). Maternal-fetal medicine specialists should manage patients requiring fetal MRI of the central nervous system. *AJNR. American Journal of Neuroradiology.*

Phillipou, A., Castle, D.J., & Rossell, S.L. (2019). Direct comparisons of anorexia nervosa and body dysmorphic disorder: A systematic review. *Psychiatry Research, 274,* 129-137.

Phillips, D.A., & Lowenstein, A.E. (2011). Early care, education, and child development. *Annual Review of Psychology* (Vol. 62). Palo Alto, CA: Annual Reviews.

Phinney, J.S. (1996). When we talk about American ethnic groups, what do we mean? *American Psychologist, 51,* 918-927.

Phinney, J.S. (2006, April). *Acculturation and adaptation of immigrant adolescents in thirteen countries.* Paper presented at the meeting of the Society for Research on Adolescence, San Francisco.

Phinney, J.S. (2008). Bridging identities and disciplines: Advances and challenges in understanding multiple identities. *New Directions for Child and Adolescent Development, 120,* 97-109.

Phinney, J.S., & Vedder, P. (2013). Family relationship values of adolescents and parents: Intergenerational discrepancies and adaptation. In J.W. Berry & others (Eds.), *Immigrant youth in cultural transition.* New York: Psychology Press.

Phull, A.R., & others (2018). Oxidative stress, consequences, and ROS mediated cellular signaling in rheumatoid arthritis. *Chemico-Biological Interactions, 281,* 121-136.

Pi, Y.L., & others (2019). Motor skill learning includes brain network plasticity: A diffusion-tensor imaging study. *PLoS One, 14*(2), e0210015.

Piaget, J. (1932). *The moral judgment of the child.* New York: Harcourt Brace Jovanovich.

Piaget, J. (1954). *The construction of reality in the child.* New York: Basic Books.

Piaget, J. (1962). *Play, dreams, and imitation in childhood.* New York: Norton.

Piaget, J., & Inhelder, B. (1969). *The child's conception of space* (F.J. Langdon & J.L. Lunger, Trans.). New York: W.W. Norton.

Piazza, J.R., Almeida, D.M., Dmitrieva, N.O., & Klein, L.C. (2010). Frontiers in the use of biomarkers of health in research on stress and aging. *Journals of Gerontology B: Psychological Sciences and Social Sciences, 65B,* 513-525.

Piazza, J.R., Stawski, R.S., & Sheffler, J.L. (2019, in press). Age, daily stress processes, and allostatic load: A longitudinal study. *Journal of Aging and Health.*

Piazza, J.R., & others (2013). Affective reactivity to daily stressors and long-term risk of reporting a chronic physical health condition. *Annals of Behavioral Medicine, 45,* 110-120.

Pietromonaco, P.R., & Beck, L.A. (2018). Adult attachment and physical health. *Current Opinion in Psychology, 25,* 115-120.

Pignolo, R.J. (2019). Exceptional human longevity. *Mayo Clinic Proceedings, 94,* 110-124.

Pijl, M.K.J., & others (2019). Temperament as an early risk marker for autism spectrum disorders? A longitudinal study of high-risk and low-risk infants. *Journal of Autism and Developmental Disorders, 49,* 1825-1836.

Piko, B.F., & Balazs, M.A. (2012). Authoritative parenting style and adolescent smoking and drinking. *Addictive Behaviors, 37,* 353-356.

Pinderhughes, E.E., & Brodzinsky, D.M. (2019). Parenting in adoptive families. In M.H. Bornstein (Ed.), *Handbook of parenting* (3rd ed.). New York: Routledge.

Ping, H., & Hagopian, W. (2006). Environmental factors in the development of type 1 diabetes. *Reviews in Endocrine and Metabolic Disorders, 7,* 149-162.

Pinheiro, M.B., & others (2018). Genetic and environmental influences to low back pain and symptoms of depression and anxiety: A population-based twin study. *Journal of Psychosomatic Research, 105,* 92-98.

Pinker, S. (2015). *Language, cognition, and human nature.* New York: Oxford University Press.

Pino, E.C., & others (2018). Adolescent socioeconomic status and depressive symptoms in later life: Evidence from structural equation models. *Journal of Affective Disorders, 225,* 702-708.

Pino-Pasternak, D., Valcan, D., & Malpique, A. (2019, in press). Development of self-regulation in young children. In D. Whitebread & others (Eds.), *SAGE handbook of developmental psychology and early childhood education.* Thousand Oaks, CA: Sage.

Pinquart, M., Feubner, C., & Ahnert, L. (2013). Meta-analytic evidence for stability of attachments from infancy to early adulthood. *Attachment and Human Development, 15,* 189-218.

Pinquart, M., & Kauser, R. (2018). Do the association of parenting styles with behavior problems and academic achievement vary by culture? Results from a meta-analysis. *Cultural Diversity and Ethnic Minority Psychology, 24,* 75-100.

Pinsker, J.E. (2012). Turner syndrome: Updating the paradigm of clinical care. *Journal of Clinical Endocrinology and Metabolism, 97*(6), E994-E1003.

Pinto Pereira, S.M., van Veldhoven, K., Li, L., & Power, C. (2016). Combined early and adult life risk factor associations for mid-life obesity in a prospective birth cohort: Assessing potential public health impact. *BMJ Open, 6*(4), e011044.

Pinzone, V., & others (2019). Temperament correlates in adult ADHD: A systematic review. *Journal of Affective Disorders, 252,* 394-403.

PISA (2015). *PISA 2015: Results in focus.* Paris: OECD.

Pisch, M., Wiesemann, F., & Karmiloff-Smith, A. (2019). Infant wake after sleep onset serves as a marker for different trajectories in cognitive development. *Journal of Child Psychology and Psychiatry, 60,* 189-198.

Pitkanen, T., Lyyra, A.L., & Pulkkinen, L. (2005). Age of onset of drinking and the use of alcohol in adulthood: A follow-up study from age 8-42 for females and males. *Addiction, 100,* 652-661.

Pitman, A.L., & others (2018). The stigma associated with bereavement by suicide and other sudden deaths: A qualitative interview study. *Social Science and Medicine, 198,* 121-129.

Pittman, J.F., Keiley, M.H., Kerpelman, J.L., & Vaughn, B.E. (2011). Attachment, identity, and intimacy: Parallels between Bowlby's and Erikson's paradigms. *Journal of Family Theory and Review, 3,* 32-46.

Platt, B., Kadosh, K.C., & Lau, J.Y. (2013). The role of peer rejection in adolescent depression. *Depression and Anxiety, 30,* 809-821.

Pleck, J.H. (1995). The gender-role strain paradigm. In R.F. Levant & W.S. Pollack (Eds.), *A new psychology of men.* New York: Basic Books.

Plomin, R. (1999). Genetics and general cognitive ability. *Nature, 402*(Suppl.), C25-C29.

Plucker, J. (2010, July 10). Interview. In P. Bronson & A. Merryman, The creativity crisis. *Newsweek*, 42–48.

Pluess, M., & Belsky, J. (2009). Differential susceptibility to rearing experience: The case of childcare. *Journal of Child Psychology and Psychiatry, 50*, 396–404.

Podrebarac, S.K., & others (2017). Antenatal exposure to antidepressants is associated with altered brain development in very preterm-born neonates. *Neuroscience, 342*, 252–262.

Poehlmann-Tynan, J., & others (2016). A pilot study of contemplative practices with economically disadvantaged preschoolers: Children's empathic and self-regulatory behaviors. *Mindfulness, 7*, 46.

Pohlabein, H., & others (2017). Further evidence for the role of pregnancy-induced hypertension and other early life influences in the development of ADHD: Results from the IDEFICS study. *European Child and Adolescent Psychiatry. 26*, 957–967.

Polan, H.J., & Hofer, M.A. (2016). Psychobiological origins of infant attachment and its role in development. In J. Cassidy & P.R. Shaver (Eds.), *Handbook of attachment* (3rd ed.). New York: Guilford.

Polenick, C.A., & DePasquale, N. (2019, in press). Predictors of secondary role strains among spousal caregivers of older adults with functional disability. *Gerontologist.*

Polenova, E., & others (2018). Emerging between two worlds. *Emerging Adulthood, 6*, 53–65.

Polka, L., & others (2017). Segmenting words from fluent speech during infancy—challenges and opportunities in a bilingual context. *Developmental Science, 20*, e12419. doi:10.1111/desc.12419

Pollack, W. (1999). *Real boys*. New York: Owl Books.

Pollock, K., & Seymour, J. (2018). Reappraising 'the good death' for populations in the age of aging. *Age and Aging, 47*, 328–330.

Pomerantz, E.M. (2014). *Six principles to motivate your child to do well in school*. Retrieved November 20, 2014, from http://i-parents.illinois.edu/research/pomerantz.html

Pomerantz, E.M., & Grolnick, W.S. (2017). The role of parenting in children's motivation and competence: What underlies facilitative parenting? In A.S. Elliot, C.S. Dweck, and D.S. Yeager (Eds.), *Handbook of competence and motivation* (2nd ed.). New York: Guilford.

Pomerantz, H., & others (2017). Pubertal timing and internalizing psychopathology: The role of relational aggression. *Journal of Child and Family Studies, 26*, 416–423.

Poon, K. (2018). Hot and cool executive functions in adolescence: Development and contributions to important developmental outcomes. *Frontiers in Psychology, 8*, 2311.

Poon, L.W., & others (2010). Understanding centenarians' psychosocial dynamics and their contributions to health and quality of life. *Current Gerontology and Geriatrics Research*. doi:10.1155/2010/680657

Poon, L.W., & others (2012). Understanding dementia prevalence among centenarians. *Journals of Gerontology A: Biological Sciences and Medical Sciences, 67*, 358–365.

Popadin, K., & others (2019, in press). Slightly deleterious genomic variants and transcriptome perturbations in Down syndrome embryonic selection. *Genome Research.*

Popenoe, D. (2008). *Cohabitation, marriage, and child wellbeing: A cross-national perspective*. Piscataway, NJ: The National Marriage Project, Rutgers University.

Popenoe, D. (2009). *The state of our unions 2008. Updates of social indicators: Tables and charts*. Piscataway, NJ: The National Marriage Project.

Popoola, I., & others (2017). How does ethics institutionalization reduce academic cheating? *Journal of Education for Business, 92*, 29–35.

Popova, N.K., & Naumenko, V.S. (2019, in press). Neuronal and behavioral plasticity: The role of serotonin and BDNF systems tandem. *Expert Opinion on Therapeutic Targets.*

Porcelli, B., & others (2016). Association between stressful life events and autoimmune diseases: A systematic review and meta-analysis of retrospective case-control studies. *Autoimmunity Reviews, 15*, 325–334.

Posada, G., & Kaloustian, G. (2011). Parent-infant interaction. In J.G. Bremner & T.D. Wachs (Eds.), *Wiley-Blackwell handbook of infant development* (2nd ed.). New York: Wiley.

Posada, G., & others (2002). Maternal caregiving and infant security in two cultures. *Developmental Psychology, 38*, 67–78.

Posner, M.I. (2018a). Current landscape and historical context. In K. Nobre & S. Kastner (Eds.), *Oxford handbook of attention*. New York: Oxford University Press.

Posner, M.I. (2018b). Developing attention and self-regulation in childhood. In K. Nobre & S. Kastner (Eds.), *Oxford handbook of attention*. New York: Oxford University Press.

Posner, M.I. (2019, in press). Rehabilitating the brain through meditation and electrical stimulation. *Cortex.*

Posner, M.I., & Rothbart, M.K. (2007a). *Educating the human brain*. Washington, DC: American Psychological Association.

Posner, M.I., & Rothbart, M.K. (2007b). Research on attention networks as a model for the integration of psychological sciences. *Annual Review of Psychology, 58*, 1–23.

Posner, M.I., & Rothbart, M.K. (2019, in press). Temperament and brain networks of attention. *Philosophical Transactions of the Royal Society of London. Series B: Biological Sciences.*

Posner, M.I., Rothbart, M.K., Sheese, B.E., & Voelker, P. (2014). Developing attention: Behavioral and brain mechanisms. *Advances in Neuroscience, 2014*, 405094.

Potapova, N.V., Gartstein, M.A., & Bridgett, D.J. (2014). Paternal influences on infant temperament: Effects of father internalizing problems, parent-related stress, and temperament. *Infant Behavior and Development, 37*, 105–110.

Potard, C., Courtois, R., & Rusch, E. (2008). The influence of peers on risky behavior during adolescence. *European Journal of Contraception and Reproductive Health Care, 13*, 264–270.

Poulain, T., Peschel, T., Vogel, M., Jurkulat, A., & Kiess, W. (2018). Cross-sectional and longitudinal associations of screen time and physical activity with school performance at different types of secondary school. *BMC Public Health, 18*(1), 563.

Poulakis, K., & others (2018). Heterogeneous patterns of brain atrophy in Alzheimer's disease, *65*, 95–108.

Poulin, F., & Pedersen, S. (2007). Developmental changes in gender composition of friendship networks in adolescent girls and boys. *Developmental Psychology, 43*, 1484–1496.

Powell, S.D. (2019). *Your introduction to education* (4th ed.). Upper Saddle River, NJ: Pearson.

Powers, C.J., & Bierman, K.L. (2013). The multifaceted impact of peer relations on aggressive-disruptive behavior in early elementary school. *Developmental Psychology, 49*, 1174–1186.

Powers, K.E., Chavez, R.S., & Heatherton, T.F. (2016). Individual differences in response of dorsomedial prefrontal cortex predict daily social behavior. *Social Cognitive and Affective Neuroscience, 11*, 121–126.

Pozzi, C., & others (2018). Why older people stop to drive? A cohort study of older patients admitted to a rehabilitation setting. *Aging: Clinical and Experimental Research, 30*, 543–546.

Pradhan, R., & others (2017). Longevity and healthy aging genes FOXO3A and SIRT3: Serum protein marker and new road map to burst oxidative stress in Withania somnifera. *Experimental Gerontology, 95*, 9–15.

Prasad, K.N. (2017). Oxidative stress, pro-inflammatory cytokines, and antioxidants regulate expression levels of microRNAs in Parkinson's disease. *Current Aging Research, 10*, 177–184.

Pratt, C., & Bryant, P.E. (1990). Young children understand that looking leads to knowing (so long as they are looking in a single barrel). *Child Development, 61*, 973–982.

Prendergast, L.E., & others (2019). Outcomes of early adolescent sexual behavior in Australia: Longitudinal findings in young adulthood. *Journal of Adolescent Health, 64*, 516–522.

Prenoveau, J.M., & others (2017). Maternal postnatal depression and anxiety and their association with child emotional negativity and behavior problems at two years. *Developmental Psychology, 53*, 50–62.

Preston, J.D., Reynolds, L.J., & Pearson, K.J. (2018). Developmental origins of health span and life span: A mini-review. *Gerontology, 64*, 237–245.

Preston, R. (2018). Death on demand? An analysis of physician-administered euthanasia in the Netherlands. *British Medical Bulletin, 125*, 145–155.

Price, D.J., & others (2018). *Building brains* (2nd ed.). New York: Wiley.

Priess, H.A., Lindberg, S.M., & Hyde, J.S. (2009). Adolescent gender-role identity and mental health: Gender intensification revisited. *Child Development, 80*, 1531–1544.

Primack, C. (2018). A review and critique of published real-world weight management program studies. *Postgraduate Medicine, 130*, 548–560.

Prince, M.A., Read, J.P., & Colder, C.R. (2019, in press). Trajectories of college alcohol involvement and their associations with later alcohol disorder symptoms. *Prevention Science.*

Prinstein, M.J., & Giletta, M. (2016). Peer relations and developmental psychopathology. In D. Cicchetti (Ed.), *Developmental psychopathology* (3rd ed.). New York: Wiley.

Prinstein, M.J., & others (2018). Peer status and psychopathology. In W.M. Bukowski & others (Eds.), *Handbook of peer interaction, relationships, and groups* (2nd ed.). New York: Guilford.

Proulx, C.M., Curl, A.L., & Ermer, A.E. (2018). Longitudinal associations between formal volunteering and cognitive functioning. *Journals of Gerontology B: Psychological Sciences and Social Sciences, 73,* 522–531.

Provenzi, L., & others (2018). Disentangling the dyadic dance: Theoretical, methodological, and outcomes systematic review of mother-infant dyadic processes. *Frontiers in Psychology, 9,* 348.

Provenzo, E.F. (2002). *Teaching, learning, and schooling in American culture: A critical perspective.* Boston: Allyn & Bacon.

Psouni, E. (2019, in press). The influence of attachment representations and co-parents' scripted knowledge of attachment on fathers' and mothers' caregiving representations. *Attachment and Human Development.*

Psychster Inc (2010). *Psychology of social media.* Retrieved February 21, 2013, from www.psychster.com.

Pudrovska, T. (2009). Midlife crises and transitions. In D. Carr (Ed.), *Encyclopedia of the life course and human development.* Boston: Gale Cengage.

Puodziuviene, E., & others (2018). A five-year retrospective study of the epidemiological characteristics and visual outcomes of pediatric ocular trauma. *BMC Ophthalmology, 18*(1), 10.

Putallaz, M., & others (2007). Overt and relational aggression and victimization: Multiple perspectives within the school setting. *Journal of School Psychology, 45,* 523–547.

Q

Qi, W. (2019, in press). Parental conflict and problematic Internet use in Chinese adolescents: Testing a moderated mediation model of adolescents' effortful control and emotion dysregulation. *Journal of Interpersonal Violence.*

Qiu, R., & others (2017). Greater intake of fruits and vegetables is associated with greater bone density and lower osteoporosis risk in middle-aged and elderly adults. *PLoS One, 12*(1), e168906.

Qu, Y., & Pomerantz, E.M. (2015). Divergent school trajectories in early adolescence in the United States and China: An examination of underlying mechanisms. *Journal of Youth and Adolescence, 44,* 2095–2109.

Quereshi, I.A., & Mehler, M.F. (2018). Epigenetic mechanisms underlying nervous system diseases. *Handbook of Clinical Neurology, 147,* 43–58.

Quilty, L.C., & others (2019). A randomized comparison of long acting methylphenidate and cognitive behavioral therapy in the treatment of binge eating disorder. *Psychiatry Research, 273,* 467–474.

Quimby, D., & others (2018). Positive peer association among Black American youth and the roles of ethnic identity and gender. *Journal of Research on Adolescence, 28,* 711–730.

Quindry, J.C., & others (2019, in press). Benefits and risks of high-intensity interval training in patients with coronary artery disease. *American Journal of Cardiology.*

Quinn, P.C. (2015). What do infants know about cats, dogs, and people? Development of a "like-people" representation for nonhuman animals. In L. Esposito & others (Eds.), *Social neuroscience of human-animal interaction.* New York: Elsevier.

Quinn, P.C., Lee, K., & Pascalis, O. (2019). Face processing in infancy and beyond: The case of social categories. *Annual Review of Psychology* (Vol. 70). Palo Alto, CA: Annual Reviews.

Quintana-Orts, C., & Rey, L. (2018). Forgiveness, depression, and suicidal behavior in adolescents: Gender differences in this relationship. *Journal of Genetic Psychology, 179,* 85–89.

R

Raajashri, R., & others (2018). Maternal perceptions and factors affecting kangaroo mother care continuum at home: A descriptive study. *Journal of Maternal-Fetal and Neonatal Medicine, 31,* 666–669.

Rabinovici, G.D. (2019). Late-onset Alzheimer disease. *Continuum, 25,* 14–33.

Raby, K.L., & others (2019, in press). The legacy of early abuse and neglect: Social and academic competence from childhood to adulthood. *Child Development.*

Radhakrishnan, D., & Goyal, V. (2018). Parkinson's disease: A review. *Neurology India, 66*(Suppl.), S26–S35.

Radhakrishnan, S., & others (2018). Laser peripheral iridotomy in primary angle closure: A report by the American Academy of Ophthalmology. *Ophthalmology, 125,* 1110–1120.

Radvansky, G.A., & Ashcraft, M.H. (2018). *Cognition* (7th ed.). Upper Saddle River, NJ: Pearson.

Raemaekers, M., & others (2018). Knowing left from right: Asymmetric functional connectivity during resting state. *Brain Structure and Function, 223,* 1909–1922.

Raffaelli, M., & Ontai, L.L. (2004). Gender socialization in Latino/a families: Results from two retrospective studies. *Sex Roles, 50,* 287–299.

Raggi, A., & others (2018). Determinants of mobility in populations of older adults: Results from a cross-sectional study in Finland, Poland, and Spain. *Maturitas, 115,* 84–91.

Raglan, G.B., Schulkin, J., & Micks, E. (2019, in press). Depression during perimenopause: The role of the obstetrician-gynecologist. *Archives of Women's Mental Health.*

Rahilly-Tierney, C.R., Spiro, A., Vokonas, P., & Gaziano, J.M. (2011). *American Journal of Cardiology, 107,* 1173–1177.

Rahimi-Golkhandan, S., & others (2017). A fuzzy trace theory of risk and time preferences in decision making: Integrating cognition and motivation. In J.R. Stevens (Ed.), *Impulsivity: How risk and time influence decision making.* New York: Springer.

Raikes, H., & others (2006). Mother-child bookreading in low-income families: Correlates and outcomes during the first three years of life. *Child Development, 77,* 924–953.

Raikes, H.A., Virmani, E.A., Thompson, R.A., & Hatton, H. (2013). Declines in peer conflict from preschool through first grade: Influences from early attachment and social information processing. *Attachment and Human Development, 15,* 65–82.

Rajan, V., & others (2019, in press). Novel word learning at 21 months predicts receptive vocabulary outcomes in later childhood. *Journal of Child Language.*

Rajeh, A., & others (2017). Interventions in ADHD: A comparative review of stimulant medication and behavioral therapies. *Asian Journal of Psychiatry, 25,* 131–135.

Rajeshwari, R., & others (2019, in press). New multitarget hybrids bearing tacrine and phenylbenzothiazole motifs as potential drug candidates for Alzheimer's disease. *Molecules.*

Rajtar-Zembaty, A., & others (2019, in press). Slow gait as a motor marker of mild cognitive impairment? The relationships between functional mobility and mild cognitive impairment. *Neuropsychology, Development, and Cognition: Section B, Aging, Neuropsychology, and Cognition.*

Raketic, D., & others (2017). Five-factor model personality profiles: The differences between alcohol and opiate addiction among females. *Psychiatria Danubina, 29,* 74–80.

Rakison, D.H., & Lawson, C.A. (2013). Categorization. In P.D. Zelazo (Ed.), *Oxford handbook of developmental psychology.* New York: Oxford University Press.

Rakoczy, H. (2012). Do infants have a theory of mind? *British Journal of Developmental Psychology, 30,* 59–74.

Rakoczy, H., & others (2018). Theory of mind and wisdom: The development of different forms of perspective-taking in late adulthood. *British Journal of Psychology, 109,* 8–24.

Rakovac Tisdall, A., & others (2018). Erectile dysfunction: They don't talk, we don't ask. *Diabetic Medicine, 35,* 667–668.

Ramanoel, S., & others (2018). Gray matter volume and cognitive performance during normal aging. A voxel-based morphometry study. *Frontiers in Aging Neuroscience, 10,* 235.

Ramaswami, G., & Geschwind, D.H. (2018). Genetics of autism spectrum disorder. *Handbook of Clinical Neurology, 147,* 321–329.

Ramchandani, P.G., & others (2013). Do early father-infant interactions predict the onset of externalizing behaviors in young children? Findings from a longitudinal cohort study. *Journal of Child Psychology and Psychiatry, 54,* 56–64.

Ramey, C.T., & Campbell, F.A. (1984). Preventive education for high-risk children: Cognitive consequences of the Carolina Abecedarian Project. *American Journal of Mental Deficiency, 88,* 515–523.

Ramey, C.T., & Ramey, S.L. (1998). Early prevention and early experience. *American Psychologist, 53,* 109–120.

Ramey, C.T., Ramey, S.L., & Lanzi, R.G. (2001). Intelligence and experience. In R.J. Sternberg & E.L. Grigorenko (Eds.), *Environmental effects on cognitive development.* Mahwah, NJ: Erlbaum.

Ramey, S.L. (2005). Human developmental science serving children and families: Contributions of the NICHD study of early child care. In NICHD Early Child Care Network (Eds.), *Child care and development.* New York: Guilford.

Ramirez-Esparza, N., Garcia-Sierra, A., & Kuhl, P.K. (2017). The impact of early social interactions on later language development in Spanish-English bilingual infants. *Child Development, 88,* 1216–1234.

Ramos, A.M., & others (2019, in press). Did I inherit my moral compass? Examining socialization and evocative mechanisms for virtuous character development. *Behavior Genetics.*

Ramus, F., & others (2018). Neuroanatomy of developmental dyslexia: Pitfalls and promises. *Neuroscience and Biobehavioral Reviews, 84,* 434–452.

Rana, B.K., & others (2018). Association of sleep quality on memory-related executive functions in middle age. *Journal of the International Neuropsychology Society, 24,* 67-76.

Randall, M., & others (2018). Diagnostic tests for autism spectrum disorder (ASD) in preschool children. *Cochrane Database of Systematic Reviews, 7,* CD009044.

Randall, W.L. (2013). The importance of being ironic: Narrative openness and personal resilience in later life. *Gerontologist, 53*(1), 9-16.

Rapee, R.M. (2014). Preschool environment and temperament as predictors of social and nonsocial anxiety disorders in middle adolescence. *Journal of the American Academy of Child and Adolescent Psychiatry, 53,* 320-328.

Raphiphatthana, B., Jose, P., & Slamon, K. (2018). Does dispositional mindfulness predict the development of grit? *Journal of Individual Differences, 29,* 76-87.

Rapp, S.R., & others (2013). Educational attainment, MRI changes, and cognitive function in older postmenopausal women from the Women's Health Initiative Memory Study. *International Journal of Psychiatry in Medicine, 46,* 121-143.

Rassovsky, Y., & Alfassi, T. (2019). Attention improves during physical exercise in individuals with ADHD. *Frontiers in Psychology, 9,* 27474.

Rastrelli, G., & others (2019, in press). Testosterone replacement therapy for sexual symptoms. *Sexual Medicine Reviews.*

Rasulo, D., Christensen, K., & Tomassini, C. (2005). The influence of social relations on mortality in later life: A study on elderly Danish twins. *The Gerontologist, 45,* 601-608.

Rathbone, C.J., O'Connor, A.R., & Moulin, C.J. (2017). The tracks of my years: Personal significance contributes to the reminiscence bump. *Memory and Cognition, 45,* 137-150.

Rathbone, C.J., & others (2016). Imagining the future: A cross-cultural perspective on possible selves. *Consciousness and Cognition, 42,* 113-124.

Rathnayake, N., & others (2018). Cross cultural adaptation and analysis of psychometric properties of Sinhala version of Menopause Rating Scale. *Health and Quality of Life Outcomes, 16*(1), 161.

Rathunde, K., & Csikszentmihalyi, M. (2006). The developing person: An experiential perspective. In W. Damon & R. Lerner (Eds.), *Handbook of child psychology* (6th ed.). New York: Wiley.

Ratner, H.H., Foley, M.A., & Lesnick, C.S. (2019, in press). Kindergarten children's event memory: The role of action prediction in remembering. *Cognitive Processing.*

Rattan, A., & Dweck, C.S. (2018). What happens after prejudice is confronted in the workplace? How mindsets affect minorities' and women's outlook on future social relations. *Journal of Applied Psychology, 103,* 676-687.

Raver, C.C., & others (2008). Improving preschool classroom processes: Preliminary findings from a randomized trial implemented in Head Start settings. *Early Childhood Research Quarterly, 23,* 10-26.

Raver, C.C., & others (2011). CSRP's impact on low-income preschoolers' preacademic skills: Self-regulation as a mediating mechanism. *Child Development, 82,* 362-378.

Raver, C.C., & others (2012). Testing models of children's self-regulation within educational contexts: Implications for measurement. *Advances in Child Development and Behavior, 42,* 245-270.

Raver, C.C., & others (2013). Predicting individual differences in low-income children's executive control from early to middle childhood. *Developmental Science, 16*(3), 394-408.

Rawlins, W.K. (2009). *The compass of friendship.* Thousand Oaks, CA: Sage.

Ray, J., & others (2017). Callous-unemotional traits predict self-reported offending in adolescent boys: The mediating role of delinquent peers and the moderating role of parenting practices. *Developmental Psychology, 53,* 319-328.

Razaz, N., & others (2016). Five-minute Apgar score as a marker for developmental vulnerability at 5 years of age. *Archives of Disease in Childhood: Fetal and Neonatal Edition, 101,* F114-F120.

Razza, R.A., Martin, A., & Brooks-Gunn, J. (2012). The implications of early attentional regulation for school success among low-income children. *Journal of Applied Developmental Psychology, 33,* 311-319.

Read, J., Harper, D., Tucker, I., & Kennedy, A. (2018). How do mental health services respond when child abuse or neglect become known? A literature review. *International Journal of Mental Health Nursing, 27,* 1606-1617.

Realini, J.P., Buzi, R.S., Smith, P.B., & Martinez, M. (2010). Evaluation of "big decisions": An abstinence-plus sexuality. *Journal of Sex and Marital Therapy, 36,* 313-326.

Ream, G.L., & Savin-Williams, R. (2003). Religious development in adolescence. In G. Adams & M. Berzonsky (Eds.), *Blackwell handbook of adolescence.* Malden, MA: Blackwell.

Rebok, G.W., & others (2014). Ten-year effects of the ACTIVE Cognitive Training for Independent and Vital Elderly cognitive training trial on cognition and everyday functioning in older adults. *Journal of the American Geriatrics Society, 62,* 16-24.

Recode (2016, June 27). *You are still watching a staggering amount of TV every day.* Retrieved March 6, 2018, from https://www.recode.net/2016/6/27/12041028/tv-hours-per-week-nielsen

Reed, I.C. (2005). Creativity: Self-perceptions over time. *International Journal of Aging & Development, 60,* 1-18.

Reed, S.D., & others (2014). Menopausal quality of life: RCT of yoga, exercise, and omega-3 supplements. *American Journal of Obstetrics and Gynecology, 210*(3), 244.e1-e11.

Reedy, M.N., Birren, J.E., & Schaie, K.W. (1981). Age and sex differences in satisfying relationships across the adult life span. *Human Development, 24,* 52-66.

Rees, M., & others (2018). Joint position paper—"Aging and sexual health" by the European Board & College of Obstetrics and Gynecology (EBCOG) and the European Menopause and Andropause Society (EMAS). *European Journal of Obstetrics & Gynecology, and Reproductive Biology, 220,* 132-134.

Rees, M., & others (2019, in press). Menopause: Women should not suffer in silence. *Maturitas.*

Reese, B.M., Haydon, A.A., Herring, A.H., & Halpern, C.T. (2013). The association between sequences of sexual initiation and the likelihood of teenage pregnancy. *Journal of Adolescent Health, 52,* 228-233.

Regalado, M., Sareen, H., Inkelas, M., Wissow, L.S., & Halfon, N. (2004). Parents' discipline of young children: Results from the National Survey of Early Childhood Health. *Pediatrics, 113,* 1952-1958.

Regev, R.H., & others (2003). Excess mortality and morbidity among small-for-gestational-age premature infants: A population-based study. *Journal of Pediatrics, 143,* 186-191.

Reid, P.T., & Zalk, S.R. (2001). Academic environments: Gender and ethnicity in U.S. higher education. In J. Worell (Ed.), *Encyclopedia of women and gender.* San Diego: Academic Press.

Reilly, D., & Neumann, D.L. (2013). Gender-role differences in spatial ability: A meta-analytic review. *Sex Roles, 68,* 521-535.

Reiner, W.G., & Gearhart, J.P. (2004). Discordant sexual identity in some genetic males with cloacal exstrophy assigned to female sex at birth. *New England Journal of Medicine, 350,* 333-341.

Reis, H.T., & Holmes, G. (2019). Perspectives on the situation. In K. Deaux & M. Snyder (Eds.), *Oxford handbook of personality and social psychology.* New York: Oxford University Press.

Reis, O., & Youniss, J. (2004). Patterns of identity change and development in relationships with mothers and friends. *Journal of Adolescent Research, 19,* 31-44.

Reitz, R. (2019). Creating a culture of intrinsic motivation. *Family Practice Management, 26*(2), 36.

Rejeski, W.J., & others (2011). Translating weight loss and physical activity programs into the community to preserve mobility in older, obese adults in poor cardiovascular health. *Archives of Internal Medicine, 171*(10), 880-886.

Rejeski, W.J., & others (2017). Community weight loss to combat obesity and disability in at-risk older adults. *Journals of Gerontology A: Biological Sciences and Medical Sciences, 72,* 1547-1553.

Renzulli, J. (2017). Developing creativity across all areas of the curriculum. In R.A. Beghetto & J.C. Kaufman (Eds.), *Nurturing creativity in the classroom* (2nd ed.). New York: Cambridge University Press.

Renzulli, J. (2018). The malleability of creativity: A career in helping students discover and nurture their creativity. In R.J. Sternberg & J.C. Kaufman (Eds.), *The nature of human creativity.* New York: Cambridge University Press.

Repacholi, B.M., & Gopnik, A. (1997). Early reasoning about desires: Evidence from 14- and 18-month-olds. *Developmental Psychology, 33,* 12-21.

Repousi, N., & others (2018). Depression and metabolic syndrome in the older population: A review of the evidence. *Journal of Affective Disorders, 237,* 58-64.

Rescorla, L.A., & others (2019, in press). Effects of society and culture on parents' ratings of children's mental health problems in 45 societies. *European Child and Adolescent Psychiatry.*

Rest, J.R. (1995). *Concerns for the social-psychological development of youth and educational strategies: Report for the Kaufmann Foundation.* Minneapolis: University of Minnesota, Department of Educational Psychology.

Rest, J.R., & others (1999). *Postconventional moral thinking: A neo-Kohlbergian approach.* Mahwah, NJ: Erlbaum.

Reuter, E.M., & others (2019). A non-linear relationship between selective attention and associated ERP markers across the lifespan. *Frontiers in Psychology, 10,* 30.

Reuter-Lorenz, P., & Lustig, C. (2017). Working memory and executive functions in the aging brain. In R. Cabeza, L. Nyberg, & D.C. Park (Eds.), *Cognitive neuroscience and aging* (2nd ed.). New York: Oxford University Press.

Reuter-Lorenz, P.A., & Park, D.C. (2014). How does it STAC up? Revisiting the scaffolding theory of aging and cognition. *Neuropsychology Review, 24,* 355-370.

Reuter-Lorenz, P.A., & others (2000). Age difference in the frontal lateralization of verbal and spatial working memory revealed by PET. *Journal of Cognitive Neuroscience, 12,* 174-187.

Reutzel, D.R., & Cooter, R.B. (2019). *Teaching children to read* (8th ed.). Upper Saddle River, NJ: Pearson.

Revelas, M., & others (2018). Review and meta-analysis of genetic polymorphisms associated with exceptional human longevity. *Mechanisms of Aging and Development, 175,* 24-34.

Reyna, V.F. (2018). Neurobiological models of risky decision-making and adolescent substance use. *Current Addiction Reports, 5,* 128-133.

Reyna, V.F., & Rivers, S.E. (2008). Current theories of risk and rational decision making. *Developmental Review, 28,* 1-11.

Reyna, V.F., Wilhelms, E.A., McCormick, M.J., & Weldon, R.B. (2015). Development of risky decision making: Fuzzy-trace theory and neurobiological perspectives. *Child Development Perspectives, 9,* 122-127.

Reyna, V.F., & Zayas, V. (Eds). (2014). *The neuroscience of risky decision making.* Washington, DC: American Psychological Association.

Reyna, V.F., & others (2011). Neurobiological and memory models of risky decision making in adolescents versus young adults. *Journal of Experimental Psychology: Learning, Memory, and Cognition, 37,* 1125-1142.

Reyna, V.F., & others (2018). Brain activation covaries with reported criminal behaviors when making risky choices. *Journal of Experimental Psychology: General, 147,* 1094-1109.

Reynolds, A.J., Ou, S.R., & Temple, J.A. (2018). A multicomponent, preschool to third grade preventive intervention and educational attainment at 35 years of age. *JAMA Pediatrics, 172,* 247-256.

Reynolds, G.D., & Richards, J.E. (2019, in press). Infant visual attention and stimulus repetition effects on object recognition. *Child Development.*

Reynolds, R.J., & Day, S.M. (2018). The growing role of machine learning and artificial intelligence in developmental medicine. *Developmental Medicine and Child Neurology, 60,* 858-859.

Rhee, J., & others (2019). Hearing loss in Korean adolescents: The prevalence thereof and its association with leisure noise exposure. *PLoS One 14*(1), e0209254.

Rhoades, G.K., & Stanley, S.M. (2014). *Before "I do": What do premarital experiences have to do with marital quality among today's young adults?* Charlottesville, VA: The National Marriage Project at the University of Virginia.

Rhoades, G.K., Stanley, S.M., & Markman, H.J. (2012). The impact of transition to cohabitation on relationship functioning: Cross-sectional and longitudinal findings. *Journal of Family Psychology, 26,* 348-358.

Rhodes, R.E., & Katz, B. (2017). Working memory plasticity and aging. *Psychology and Aging, 32,* 51-59.

Rhodes, S., & others (2019, in press). Storage and processing in working memory: Assessing dual-task performance and task prioritization across the adult lifespan. *Journal of Experimental Psychology: General.*

Ribeiro, O., & Araujo, L. (2019). Defining 'success' in exceptional longevity. In R. Fernandez-Ballesteros, A. Benetos, & J-M. Robine (Eds.), *Cambridge handbook of successful aging.* New York: Cambridge University Press.

Richard, E.L., & others (2017). Alcohol intake and cognitively healthy longevity in community-dwelling adults: The Rancho Bernardo study. *Journal of Alzheimer's Disease, 59,* 803-814.

Richards, J.E. (2009). Attention to the brain in infancy. In S. Johnson (Ed.), *Neuroconstructivism: The new science of cognitive development.* New York: Oxford University Press.

Richards, J.E. (2010). Infant attention, arousal, and the brain. In L.M. Oakes, C.H. Cashon, M. Casasola, & D.H. Rakison (Eds.), *Infant perception and cognition.* New York: Oxford University Press.

Richards, J.E. (2013). Cortical sources of ERP in the prosaccade and antisaccade task using realistic source models. *Frontiers in Systems Neuroscience, 7,* 27.

Richards, J.E., Boswell, C., Stevens, M., & Vendemia, J.M. (2015). Evaluating methods for constructing average high-density electrode positions. *Brain Topography, 28,* 70-86.

Richards, J.E., Reynolds, G.D., & Courage, M.I. (2010). The neural bases of infant attention. *Current Directions in Psychological Science, 19,* 41-46.

Richardson, E.D., & Marottoli, R.A. (2003). Visual attention and driving behaviors among community-living older persons. *Journals of Gerontology A: Biological Sciences and Medical Sciences, 58,* M832-M836.

Richardson, G.A., Goldschmidt, L., Leech, S., & Williford, J. (2011). Prenatal cocaine exposure: Effects on mother- and teacher-rated behavior problems and growth in school-aged children. *Neurotoxicology and Teratology, 33,* 69-77.

Richardson, G.A., Goldschmidt, L., & Williford, J. (2008). The effects of prenatal cocaine use on infant development. *Neurotoxicology and Teratology, 30,* 96-106.

Richardson, G.A., & others (2019). Prenatal cocaine exposure: Direct and indirect associations with 21-year-old offspring substance use and behavior problems. *Drug and Alcohol Dependence, 195,* 121-131.

Richardson, M.A., & others (2016). Psychological distress among school-aged children with and without intrauterine cocaine exposure: Perinatal versus contextual effects. *Journal of Abnormal Child Psychology, 44,* 547-560.

Richler, J.J., & others (2019). Individual differences in object recognition. *Psychological Review, 126,* 226-251.

Rideout, V.J., Foehr, U.G., & Roberts, D.F. (2010). *Generation M: Media in the lives of 8- to 18-year-olds.* Menlo Park, CA: Kaiser Family Foundation.

Riederer, P., & others (2017). The diabetic brain and cognition. *Journal of Neural Transmission, 124,* 1431-1454.

Riekkola, J., & others (2019, in press). Healthcare professionals' perspective on how to promote older couples' participation in everyday life when using respite care. *Scandinavian Journal of Caring Science.*

Riesch, S.K., & others (2003). Conflict and conflict resolution: Parent and young teen perceptions. *Journal of Pediatric Health Care, 17,* 22-31.

Riesco-Matias, P., & others (2019, in press). What do meta-analyses have to say about the efficacy of neurofeedback applied to children with ADHD? Review of previous meta-analyses and a new meta-analysis. *Journal of Attention Disorders.*

Riina, E.M., & McHale, S.M. (2014). Bidirectional influences between dimensions of coparenting and adolescent adjustment. *Journal of Youth and Adolescence, 43,* 257-269.

Rijnders, M., & others (2019, in press). Women-centered care: Implementation of CenteringPregnancy in the Netherlands. *Birth.*

Rindermann, H., & Becker, D. (2018). Flynn-effect and economic growth: Do national increases in intelligence lead to increases in GDP? *Intelligence, 69,* 87-93.

Ringe, D. (2019). *An introduction to grammar for language learners.* New York: Cambridge University Press.

Rink, J. (2020). *Teaching physical education for learning* (8th ed.). New York: McGraw-Hill.

Rios, A.C., & Clevers, H. (2018). Imaging organoids: A bright future ahead. *Nature Methods, 15,* 24-26.

Riva Crugnola, C., Ierardi, E., Gazzotti, S., & Albizzati, A. (2014). Motherhood in adolescent mothers: Maternal attachment, mother-infant styles of interaction, and emotion regulation at three months. *Infant Behavior and Development, 37,* 44-56.

Rivas-Drake, D., & Umana-Taylor, A. (2017). Ethnic-racial identity and friendships in adolescence. *Child Development, 88,* 725-742.

Rivas-Drake, D., & others (2017). Ethnic-racial identity and friendships in early adolescence. *Child Development, 88,* 710-724.

Rivera, P.M., & others (2018). Linking patterns of substance use with sexual risk-taking among female adolescents with and without histories of maltreatment. *Journal of Adolescent Health, 62,* 556-562.

Riveros-McKay, F., & others (2019). Genetic architecture of human thinness compared to severe obesity. *PLoS Genetics, 15*(1), e1007603.

Rizvi, T., Batchala, P., & Mukherjee, S. (2018). Brain death: Diagnosis and imaging techniques. *Seminars in Ultrasound, CT, and MR, 39,* 515-529.

Robert, C., & Mathey, S. (2018). The oral and written side of word production in young and older adults: Generation of lexical neighbors. *Neuropsychology, Development, and Cognition B: Aging, Neuropsychology, and Cognition, 25,* 231-243.

Roberto, K.A., & Skoglund, R.R. (1996). Interactions with grandparents and great-grandparents: A comparison of activities, influences, and relationships. *International Journal of Aging and Human Development, 43,* 107-117.

Roberto, K.A., & Weaver, R.H. (2019). Late-life families. In B.H. Friese (Ed.), *APA handbook of contemporary family psychology.* Washington, DC: APA Books.

Roberts, B.W., & Damian, R.I. (2018). The principles of personality trait development and their relation to psychopathology. In D. Lynam & D. Samuel (Eds.), *Using personality research to inform the personality disorders.* New York: Oxford University Press.

Roberts, B.W., Donnellan, M.B., & Hill, P.L. (2013). Personality trait development in adulthood: Findings and implications. In I.B. Weiner & others (Eds.), *Handbook of psychology* (2nd ed., Vol. 5). New York: Wiley.

Roberts, B.W., Helson, R., & Klohnen, E.C. (2002). Personality development and growth in women across 30 years: Three perspectives. *Journal of Personality, 70*, 79–102.

Roberts, B.W., & Mroczek, D. (2008). Personality trait change in adulthood. *Current Directions in Psychological Science, 17*, 31–35.

Roberts, B.W., & Nickel, L.B. (2020, in press). Personality development across the life course: A neo-socioanalytic perspective. In O.P. John & R.W. Robins (Eds.), *Handbook of personality theory and research.* New York: Guilford.

Roberts, B.W., Walton, K.E., & Viechtbauer, W. (2006). Pattern of mean-level change in personality traits across the life course: A meta-analysis of longitudinal studies. *Psychological Bulletin, 132*, 1–25.

Roberts, B.W., & Wood, D. (2006). Personality development in the context of the Neo-Socioanalytic Model of personality. In D. Mroczek & T. Little (Eds.), *Handbook of personality development.* Mahwah, NJ: Erlbaum.

Roberts, B.W., & others (2014). What is conscientiousness and how can it be assessed? *Developmental Psychology, 50*, 1315–1330.

Roberts, B.W., & others (2017). A systematic review of personality trait change through intervention. *Psychological Bulletin, 143*, 117–141.

Roberts, D.F., & Foehr, U.G. (2008). Trends in media use. *Future of Children, 18*(1), 11–37.

Roberts, S.B., & Rosenberg, I. (2006). Nutrition and aging: Changes in the regulation of energy metabolism with aging. *Physiology Review, 86*, 651–667.

Robine, J-M. (2019). Successful aging and the longevity revolution. In R. Fernandez-Ballesteros, A. Benetos, & J-M. Robine (Eds), *Cambridge handbook of successful aging.* New York: Cambridge University Press.

Robins, R.W., Trzesniewski, K.H., Tracey, J.L., Potter, J., & Gosling, S.D. (2002). Age differences in self-esteem from age 9 to 90. *Psychology and Aging, 17*, 423–434.

Robinson, A.T., & others (2017). Short-term regular aerobic exercise reduces oxidative stress produced by acute in the adipose microvasculature. *American Journal of Physiology: Heart and Circulatory Physiology, 312*, H896–H906.

Robinson, C.L., & others (2019). Advisory Committee on Immunization Practices recommended immunization schedule for children and adolescents aged 18 years or younger—United States, 2019. *MMWR Morbidity and Mortality Weekly Report, 68*(5), 112–114.

Robles, T.F. (2014). Marital quality and health: Implications for marriage in the 21st century. *Current Directions in Psychological Science, 23*, 427–432.

Robyler, M.D., & Hughes, J.E. (2019). *Integrating technology into teaching* (8th ed.). Upper Saddle River, NJ: Pearson.

Rocca, M.S., & others (2016). The Klinefelter syndrome is associated with high recurrence of copy number variations on the X chromosome with a potential role in the clinical phenotype. *Andrology, 4*, 328–334.

Rochlen, A.B., McKelley, R.A., Suizzo, M-A., & Scaringi, V. (2008). Predictors of relationship satisfaction, psychological well-being, and life-satisfaction among stay-at-home fathers. *Psychology of Men and Masculinity, 9*, 17–28.

Roda, A.R., Montoliu-Gaya, L., & Villegas, S. (2019, in press). The role of apolipoprotein E isoforms in Alzheimer disease. *Journal of Alzheimer's Disease.*

Rode, S.S., Chang, P., Fisch, R.O., & Sroufe, L.A. (1981). Attachment patterns of infants separated at birth. *Developmental Psychology, 17*, 188–191.

Rodgers, C. (2013). Why kangaroo care should be standard for all newborns. *Journal of Midwifery and Women's Health, 58*, 249–252.

Rodin, J., & Langer, E.J. (1977). Long-term effects of a control-relevant intervention with the institutionalized aged. *Journal of Personality and Social Psychology, 35*, 397–402.

Rodriguez Villar, S., & others (2012). Prolonged grief disorder in the next of kin of adult patients who die during or after admission to intensive care. *Chest, 141*, 1635–1636.

Rodrique, K.M., & Kennedy, K.M. (2011). The cognitive consequences of structural changes to the aging brain. In K.W. Schaie & S.L. Willis (Eds.), *Handbook of the psychology of aging* (7th ed.). New York: Elsevier.

Roebers, C.M., & Spiess, M. (2017). The development of metacognitive monitoring and control in second graders: A short-term longitudinal study. *Journal of Cognition and Development, 18*, 110–128.

Roese, N.J., & Summerville, A. (2005). What we regret most . . . and why. *Personality and Social Psychology Bulletin, 31*, 1273–1285.

Roeser, R.W., & Eccles. J.S. (2015). Mindfulness and compassion in human development: Introduction to the special section. *Developmental Psychology, 51*, 1–6.

Roeser, R.W., & Zelazo, P.D. (2012). Contemplative science, education and child development. *Child Development Perspectives, 6*, 143–145.

Roeser, R.W., & others (2014). Contemplative education. In L. Nucci & others (Eds.), *Handbook of moral and character education.* New York: Routledge.

Roest, B., Trappenburg, M., & Leget, C. (2019). The involvement of the family in the Dutch practice of euthanasia and physician assisted suicide: A systematic mixed studies review. *BMC Medical Ethnics, 20*(1), 23.

Rogers, E.E., & Hintz, S.R. (2016). Early neurodevelopmental outcomes of extremely preterm infants. *Seminars in Perinatology, 40*, 497–509.

Roggman, L.A., & others (2016). Home visit quality variations in two Early Head Start programs in relation to parenting and child vocabulary outcomes. *Infant Mental Health Journal, 37*, 193–207.

Rognum, I.J., & others (2014). Serotonin metabolites in the cerebrospinal fluid in sudden infant death syndrome. *Journal of Neuropathology and Experimental Neurology, 73*, 115–122.

Rohrer, J.M., Egloff, B., & Schmukle, S.C. (2017). Probing birth-order effects on narrow traits using specification-curve analysis. *Psychological Science, 28*, 1821–1832.

Roisman, G.l., Aguilar, B., & Egeland, B. (2004). Antisocial behavior in the transition to adulthood: The independent and interactive roles of developmental history and emerging development tasks. *Development and Psychopathology, 16*, 857–872.

Roisman, G.I., & Cicchetti, D. (2017). Attachment in the context of atypical caregiving: Harnessing insights from developmental psychopathology. *Development and Psychopathology, 29*, 331–335.

Roisman, G.I., & Fraley, R.C. (2012). A behavior-genetic study of the legacy of early caregiving experiences: Academic skills, social competence, and externalizing behavior in kindergarten. *Child Development, 83*, 728–742.

Roisman, G.I., & others (2016). Strategic considerations in the search for transactional processes. *Development and Psychopathology, 28*, 791–800.

Rolfes, S.R., Pinna, K., & Whitney, E. (2018). *Understanding normal and clinical nutrition* (11th ed.). Boston: Cengage.

Rolland, B., & others (2016). Pharmacotherapy for alcohol dependence: The 2015 recommendations of the French Alcohol Society, issued in partnership with the European Federation of Addiction Societies. *CNS Neuroscience and Therapeutics, 22*, 25–37.

Rolland, Y., & others (2011). Treatment strategies for sarcopenia and frailty. *Medical Clinics of North America, 95*, 427–438.

Roman, F.J., & others (2018). Brain-intelligence relationships across childhood and adolescence: A latent-variable approach. *Intelligence, 68*, 21–29.

Romer, D., Reyna, V.F., & Satterthwaite, T.D. (2017). Beyond stereotypes of adolescent risk taking: Placing the adolescent brain in developmental context. *Developmental Cognitive Neuroscience, 26*, 19–34.

Romo, D.L., & others (2017). Social media use and its association with sexual risk and parental monitoring among a primarily Hispanic adolescent population. *Journal of Pediatric and Adolescent Gynecology, 30*, 466–473.

Romo, L.F., Mireles-Rios, R., & Lopez-Tello, G. (2014). Latina mothers' and daughters' expectations for autonomy at age 15 (La Quinceañera). *Journal of Adolescent Research, 29*(2), 279–294.

Ronnlund, M., Nyberg, L., Buckman, L., & Nilsson, L.-G. (2005). Stability, growth, and decline in adult life span development of declarative memory: Cross-sectional and longitudinal data from a population-based study. *Psychology and Aging, 20*, 3–18.

Ronnlund, M., & others (2013). Secular trends in cognitive test performance: Swedish conscript data, 1970-1993. *Intelligence, 41*, 19–24.

Roopanarine, J.L., & Vildirim, E.D. (2018). *Fathering in cultural contexts.* New York: Routledge.

Rose, A.J., Carlson, W., & Waller, E.M. (2007). Prospective associations of co-rumination with friendship and emotional adjustment: Considering the socioemotional trade-offs of co-rumination. *Developmental Psychology, 43*, 1019–1031.

Rose, A.J., & Rudolph, K.D. (2006). A review of sex differences in peer relationship processes: Potential tradeoffs for the emotional and behavioral development of girls and boys. *Psychological Bulletin, 132*, 98–131.

Rose, A.J., & Smith, R.L. (2018). Gender and peer relationships. In W.M. Bukowski & others (Eds.), *Handbook of peer interaction, relationships, and groups.* New York: Guilford.

Rose, A.J., & others (2012). How girls and boys expect disclosure about problems will make them feel: Implications for friendship. *Child Development, 83*, 844–863.

Roseberry, S., Hirsh-Pasek, K., & Golinkoff, R. (2014). Skype me! Socially contingent interactions help toddlers learn language. *Child Development, 85,* 956–970.

Rose-Clarke, K., & others (2019). Peer-facilitated community-based interventions for adolescent health in low- and middle-income countries: A systematic review. *PLoS One, 14*(1), e-210468.

Rose-Greenland, F., & Smock, P.J. (2013). Living together unmarried: What do we know about cohabiting families? In G.W. Peterson & K.R. Bush (Eds.), *Handbook of marriage and the family* (3rd ed.). New York: Springer.

Rosen, L., & others (2018). Protecting children from tobacco smoke exposure: A pilot study of Project Zero exposure. *Pediatrics, 141*(Suppl. 1), S107–S117.

Rosen, M.L., & others (2018). Socioeconomic disparities in academic achievement: A multi-modal investigation of neural mechanisms in children and adolescents. *NeuroImage, 173,* 298–310.

Rosen, R.C., & others (2017). Quality of life and sexual function benefits of long-term testosterone treatment: Longitudinal results from the registry of hypogonadism in men (RHYME). *Journal of Sexual Medicine, 14,* 1104–1115.

Rosenblith, J.F. (1992). *In the beginning* (2nd ed.). Newbury Park, CA: Sage.

Rosenblum, G.D., & Lewis, M. (2003). Emotional development in adolescence. In G. Adams & M. Berzonsky (Eds.), *Blackwell handbook of adolescence.* Malden, MA: Blackwell.

Rosenfeld, A., & Stark, E. (1987, May). The prime of our lives. *Psychology Today,* pp. 62–72.

Rosengard, C. (2009). Confronting the intendedness of adolescent rapid repeat pregnancy. *Journal of Adolescent Health, 44,* 5–6.

Rosengren, K.S., Gutierrez, I.T., & Schein, S.S. (2014a). Cognitive dimensions of death in context. In K.S. Rosengren & others (Eds.), Children's understanding of death: Toward a contextualized and integrative account. *Monographs of the Society for Research in Child Development, 79*(1), 62–82.

Rosengren, K.S., Gutierrez, I.T., & Schein, S.S. (2014b). Cognitive models of death. In K.S. Rosengren & others (Eds.), Children's understanding of death: Toward a contextualized and integrative account. *Monographs of the Society for Research in Child Development, 79*(1), 83–96.

Rosenson, R.S., Hegele, R.A., & Koenig, W. (2019). Cholesterol-lowering agents. *Circulation Research, 124,* 364–385.

Rosenstein, D., & Oster, H. (1988). Differential facial responses to four basic tastes in newborns. *Child Development, 59,* 1555–1568.

Rosnow, R.L., & Rosenthal, R. (1996). *Beginning behavioral research* (2nd ed.). Upper Saddle River, NJ: Prentice Hall.

Ross, J., Hutchison, J., & Cunningham, S.J. (2019, in press). The me in memory: The role of the self in autobiographical memory development. *Child Development.*

Ross, J.L., Lee, P.A., Gut, R., & Gemak, J. (2015). Attaining genetic height potential: Analysis of height outcomes from the ANSWER program in children treated with growth hormone over 5 years. *Growth Hormone & IGF Research, 25,* 286–293.

Ross, K., Handal, P.J., Clark, E.M., & Vander Wal, J.S. (2009). The relationship between religion and religious coping: Religious coping as a moderator between coping and adjustment. *Journal of Religion and Health, 48,* 454–467.

Ross, L.A., & others (2016). The transfer of cognitive speed of processing training to older adults' driving mobility across 5 years. *Journals of Gerontology B: Psychological Sciences and Social Sciences, 71,* 87–97.

Ross, N.D., Kaminski, P.L., & Herrington, R. (2019). From childhood emotional maltreatment to depressive symptoms in adulthood: The roles of self-compassion and shame. *Child Abuse and Neglect, 92,* 32–42.

Ross, V., & others (2019, in press). Parents' experiences of suicide-bereavement: A qualitative study at 6 and 12 months after loss. *International Journal of Environmental Research and Public Health.*

Rossi, A.S. (1989). A life-course approach to gender, aging, and intergenerational relations. In K.W. Schaie & C. Schooler (Eds.), *Social structure and aging.* Hillsdale, NJ: Erlbaum.

Rossi, S., & others (2005). Age-related functional changes of prefrontal cortex in long-term memory: A repetitive transcranial magnetic stimulation study. *Journal of Neuroscience, 24,* 7939–7944.

Rostamian, S., & others (2015). Executive function, but not memory, associates with incident coronary heart disease and stroke. *Neurology, 85,* 783–789.

Rostamzadeh, D., & others (2019, in press). mTOR signaling pathway as a master regulator of memory CD8+ T-cells, Th17, and NK cells development and their functional properties. *Journal of Cellular Physiology.*

Rote, W.M., & Smetana, J.G. (2016). Beliefs about parents' right to know: Domain distinctions and associations with change in concealment. *Journal of Research on Adolescence, 26,* 334–344.

Rote, W.M., & Smetana, J.G. (2018). Within-family dyadic patterns of parental monitoring and adolescent information management. *Developmental Psychology, 54,* 2302–2315.

Rotenberg, J., & others (2018). Home-based primary care: Beyond extension of the independence at home demonstration. *Journal of the American Geriatrics Society, 66,* 812–817.

Roth, B., & others (2015). Intelligence and school grades: A meta-analysis. *Intelligence, 53,* 118–137.

Rothbart, M.K. (2004). Temperament and the pursuit of an integrated developmental psychology. *Merrill-Palmer Quarterly, 50,* 492–505.

Rothbart, M.K. (2011). *Becoming who we are.* New York: Guilford.

Rothbart, M.K., & Bates, J.E. (2006). Temperament. In W. Damon & R. Lerner (Eds.), *Handbook of child psychology* (6th ed.). New York: Wiley.

Rothbart, M.K., & Gartstein, M.A. (2008). Temperament. In M.M. Haith & J.B. Benson (Eds.), *Encyclopedia of infant and early childhood development.* Oxford, UK: Elsevier.

Rothbaum, F., Poll, M., Azuma, H., Miyake, K., & Weisz, J. (2000). The development of close relationships in Japan and the United States: Paths of symbiotic harmony and generative tension. *Child Development, 71,* 1121–1142.

Rothbaum, F., & Trommsdorff, G. (2007). Do roots and wings complement or oppose one another? The socialization of relatedness and autonomy in cultural context. In J.E. Grusec & P.D. Hastings (Eds.), *Handbook of socialization.* New York: Guilford.

Roushandeh, A.M., Kuwahara, Y., & Roudkenar, M.H. (2019, in press). Mitochondrial transplantation as a potential and novel master key for treatment of various incurable diseases. *Cytotechnology.*

Rovee-Collier, C. (1987). Learning and memory in children. In J.D. Osofsky (Ed.), *Handbook of infant development* (2nd ed.). New York: Wiley.

Rovee-Collier, C. (2004). Infant learning and memory. In U. Goswami (Ed.), *Blackwell handbook of childhood cognitive development.* Malden, MA: Blackwell.

Rovee-Collier, C. (2007). The development of infant memory. In N. Cowan & M. Courage (Eds.), *The development of memory in childhood.* Philadelphia: Psychology Press.

Rovee-Collier, C., & Barr, R. (2010). Infant learning and memory. In J.G. Bremner & T.D. Wachs (Ed.), *Wiley-Blackwell handbook of infant development* (2nd ed.). New York: Wiley.

Rowe, M.L., & Goldin-Meadow, S. (2009). Differences in early gesture explain SES disparities in child vocabulary size at school entry. *Science, 323,* 951–953.

Rowland, T. (2018). Cardiovascular physiology and diseases in youth—the year that was 2017. *Pediatric Exercise Science, 30,* 32–34.

Royner, P., & others (2018). Induction of the LH surge in premenarchal girls confirms early maturation of the hypothalamic-pituitary-ovarian axis. *Reproductive Sciences, 25,* 33–38.

Rozzini, R., Ranhoff, A., & Trabucchi, M. (2007). Alcoholic beverage and long-term mortality in elderly people living at home. *Journals of Gerontology A: Biological Sciences and Medical Science, 62A,* M1313–M1314.

Rubie-Davies, C.M. (2007). Classroom interactions: Exploring the practices of high- and low-expectation teachers. *British Journal of Educational Psychology, 77,* 289–306.

Rubin, A., Parrish, D.E., & Miyawaki, C.E. (2019). Benchmarks for evaluating life review and reminiscence therapy in alleviating depression among older adults. *Social Work, 64,* 61–72.

Rubin, K.H., & Barstead, M. (2018). Social withdrawal and solitude. In M.H. Bornstein (Ed.), *SAGE encyclopedia of lifespan human development.* Thousand Oaks, CA: Sage.

Rubin, K.H., Bukowski, W.M., & Bowker, J. (2015). Children in peer groups. In R.E. Lerner (Ed.), *Handbook of child psychology and developmental science* (7th ed.). New York: Wiley.

Rubin, K.H., & others (2018). Avoiding and withdrawing from the peer group. In W.M. Bukowski & others (Eds.), *Handbook of peer interaction, relationships, and groups.* New York: Guilford.

Rubio-Fernandez, P. (2017). Why are bilinguals better than monolinguals at false-belief tasks? *Psychonomic Bulletin and Review, 24,* 987–998.

Rubio-Ruiz, M.E., & others (2019, in press). Mechanisms underlying syndrome-related sarcopenia and possible therapeutic measures. *International Journal of Molecular Science.*

Rudolph, K.D., Troop-Gordon, W., Lambert, S.F., & Natsuaki, M.N. (2014). Long-term consequences of pubertal timing for youth depression: Identifying personal and contextual pathways of risk. *Development and Psychopathology, 26,* 1423–1444.

Rueda, M.R., & Posner, M.I. (2013). Development of attentional networks. In P.D. Zelazo (Ed.), *Oxford handbook of developmental psychology.* New York: Oxford University Press.

Rueda, M.R., Posner, M.I., & Rothbart, M.K. (2005). The development of executive attention: Contributions to the emergence of self-regulation. *Developmental Neuropsychology, 28,* 573–594.

Ruffman, T. (2014). To belief or not belief: Children's theory of mind. *Developmental Review, 34,* 265–293.

Ruisch, I.H., & others (2018). Maternal substance use during pregnancy and offspring conduct problems: A meta-analysis. *Neuroscience and Biobehavioral Reviews, 84,* 325–336.

Ruiter, M., & others (2012, June 11). *Short sleep predicts stroke symptoms in persons of normal weight.* Paper presented at the annual meeting of the Associated Professional Sleep Societies (APSS), Boston.

Ruiz, L.D., & Scherr, R.E. (2018). Risk of energy drink consumption to adolescent health. *American Journal of Lifestyle Medicine, 13,* 22–25.

Ruiz, L.D., McMahon, S.D., & Jason, L.A. (2018). The role of neighborhood context and school climate in school-level academic achievement. *American Journal of Community Psychology, 61,* 296–309.

Rumberger, R.W. (1995). Dropping out of middle school: A multilevel analysis of students and schools. *American Education Research Journal, 3,* 583–625.

Runco, M.A., & Acar, S. (2019). Divergent thinking. In J.C. Kaufman & R.J. Sternberg (Eds.), *Cambridge handbook of creativity* (2nd ed.). New York; Cambridge University Press.

Runfola, C., & Lock, J. (2019). Feeding and eating disorders. In T. H. Ollendick & others (Eds.), *Oxford handbook of child and adolescent psychology.* New York: Oxford University Press.

Rupp, D.E., Vodanovich, S.J., & Crede, M. (2005). The multidimensional nature of ageism: Construct validity and group differences. *Journal of Social Psychology, 145,* 335–362.

Rusby, J.C., & others (2018). Influence of parent-youth relationship, parental monitoring, and parent substance use on adolescent substance use onset. *Journal of Family Psychology, 32,* 310–320.

Russell, C.G., & Russell, A. (2019, in press). A biopsychosocial approach to processes and pathways in the development of overweight and obesity in childhood: Insights from developmental theory and research. *Obesity Reviews.*

Russell, S.T., Crockett, L.J., & Chao, R.K. (2010). *Asian American parenting and parent-adolescent relationships.* New York: Springer.

Russo-Netzer, P., & Moran, G. (2018). Positive growth from adversity and beyond: Insights gained from cross-examination of clinical and non-clinical samples. *American Journal of Orthopsychiatry, 88,* 59–68.

Ryan, A.M., & Shin, H. (2018). Peers, academics, and teachers. In W.M. Bukowski & others (Eds.), *Handbook of peer interactions, relationships, and groups* (2nd ed.). New York: Guilford.

Ryan, R.M., & Deci, E.L. (2016). Facilitating and hindering motivation, learning, and well-being in schools: Research and observations from self-determination theory. In K.R. Wentzel & D.B. Miele (Eds.), *Handbook of motivation at school* (2nd ed.). New York: Routledge.

Ryan, R.M., & Deci, E.L. (2019, May, 22). *Self-determination theory.* Plenary talk at the International Self-Determination Theory conference, Amsterdam.

Ryan, R.M., & Moller, A.C. (2017). Competence as central, but not sufficient, for high-quality motivation: A self-determination theory perspective. In A.J. Elliott, C.S. Dweck, & D.S. Yeager (Eds.), *Handbook of competence and motivation* (2nd ed.). New York: Guilford.

Ryan, R.M., & Padilla, C.M. (2019). Transition to parenting. In M.H. Bornstein (Ed.), *Handbook of parenting* (3rd ed.). New York: Routledge.

Ryan, R.M., Soenens, B., & Vansteenkiste, M. (2019). Reflections on self-determination theory as an organizing framework for personality psychology: Interfaces, integrations, issues, and unfinished business. *Journal of Personality, 87,* 115–145.

Ryff, C.D. (1984). Personality development from the inside: The subjective experience of change in adulthood and aging. In P.B. Baltes & O.G. Brim (Eds.), *Life-span development and behavior.* New York: Academic Press.

Ryskina, K.L., Lam, C., & Jung, H.Y. (2019, in press). Association between clinician specialization in nursing home care and nursing home clinical quality scores. *Journal of the American Medical Directors Association.*

S

Saab, A.S., & Nave, K.A. (2017). Myelin dynamics: Protecting and shaping neurons. *Current Opinion in Neurobiology, 47,* 104–112.

Saad, L. (2014). The "40-hour" workweek is actually longer—by seven hours. Washington, DC: Gallup.

Saad, O., & others (2019, in press). The right kind of smart: Emotional intelligence's relationship to cognitive status in community-dwelling older adults. *International Psychogeriatrics.*

Saarni, C. (1999). *The development of emotional competence.* New York: Guilford.

Saarni, C., Campos, J., Camras, L.A., & Witherington, D. (2006). Emotional development. In W. Damon & R. Lerner (Eds.), *Handbook of child psychology* (6th ed.). New York: Wiley.

Sabini, J. (1995). *Social psychology* (2nd ed.). New York: Norton.

Sabir, M., Henderson, C.R., Kang, S.Y., & Pillemer, K. (2016). Attachment-focused integrative reminiscence with older African Americans: A randomized controlled intervention study. *Aging and Mental Health, 20,* 517–528.

Sacco, S.J., Leahey, T.M., & Park, C.L. (2019). Meaning-making and quality of life in heart failure interventions: A systematic review. *Quality of Life Research, 28,* 557–565.

Sackett, P.R., Borneman, M.J., & Connelly, B.S. (2009). Responses to issues raised about validity, bias, and fairness in high-stakes testing. *American Psychologist, 64,* 285–287.

Sackett, P.R., Shewach, O.R., & Dahlke, J.A. (2020, in press). The predictive value of intelligence. In R.J. Sternberg (Ed.), *Human intelligence.* New York: Cambridge University Press.

Sackett, P.R., & others (2017). Individual differences and their measurement: A review of 100 years of research. *Journal of Applied Psychology. 102,* 254–273.

Sacrey, L.A., Germani, T., Bryson, S.E., & Zwaigenbaum, L. (2014). Reaching and grasping in autism spectrum disorder: A review of recent literature. *Frontiers in Neurology, 5,* 6.

Sadeh, A. (2008). Sleep. In M.M. Haith & J.B. Benson (Eds.), *Encyclopedia of infant and early childhood development.* Oxford, UK: Elsevier.

Sadeh, A., & others (2015). Infant sleep predicts attention regulation and behavior problems at 3–4 years of age. *Developmental Neuropsychology, 40,* 122–137.

Sadker, D.M., & Zittleman, K. (2018). *Teachers, schools, and society: A brief introduction to education* (5th ed.). New York: McGraw-Hill.

Sadker, M.P., & Sadker, D.M. (2005). *Teachers, schools, and society* (7th ed.). New York: McGraw-Hill.

Safa, M.D., & others (2019, in press). U.S. Mexican-origin adolescents' bicultural competence and mental health in context. *Cultural Diversity and Ethnic Minority Psychology.*

Saffran, J.R., & Kirkham, N.Z. (2018). Infant statistical learning. *Annual Review of Psychology* (Vol. 69). Palo Alto, CA: Annual Reviews.

Saffran, J.R., Werker, J.F., & Werner, L.A. (2006). The infant's auditory world: Hearing, speech, and the beginnings of language. In R.M. Lerner & W. Damon (Eds.), *Handbook of child psychology* (6th ed.). New York: Wiley.

Saint Onge, J.M. (2009). Mortality. In D. Carr (Ed.), *Encyclopedia of the life course and human development.* Boston: Gale Cengage.

Saint-Maurice, P.F., & others (2019). Association of leisure-time physical activity across the adult life course with all-cause and cause-specific mortality. *JAMA Network Open, 2*(3), e190355.

Saisanen, L., & others (2019, in press). Functional and structural symmetry in primary motor cortex in Asperger syndrome: A navigated TMS and imaging study. *Brain Topography.*

Saito, M., & others (2019, in press). Relative deprivation, poverty, and mortality in Japanese older adults: A six-year follow-up of the JAGES Cohort Survey. *International Journal of Environmental Research and Public Health.*

Sajadi, M., & others (2018). Effect of spiritual counseling on spiritual well-being in Iranian women with cancer: A randomized clinical trial. *Complementary Therapies in Clinical Practice, 30,* 79–84.

Salama, R.H., & others (2013). Clinical and biochemical effects of environmental tobacco smoking on pregnancy outcome. *Indian Journal of Clinical Biochemistry, 28,* 368–373.

Saling, L.L., Laroo, N., & Saling, M.M. (2012). When more is less: Failure to compress discourse with re-telling in normal aging. *Acta Psychologica, 139,* 220–224.

Salmivalli, C., & Peets, K. (2018). Bullying and victimization. In W.M. Bukowski & others (Eds.), *Handbook of peer interactions, relationships, and groups* (2nd ed.). New York: Guilford.

Salomone, E., & others (2018). Adaptive behavior and cognitive skills: Stability and change from 7 months to 7 years in siblings at high familial risk of autism spectrum disorder. *Journal of Autism and Developmental Disorders, 48,* 2901–2911.

Salovey, P., & Mayer, J.D. (1990). Emotional intelligence. *Imagination, Cognition, and Personality, 9,* 185–211.

Salthouse, T.A. (1991). *Theoretical perspectives on cognitive aging.* Hillsdale, NJ: Erlbaum.

Salthouse, T.A. (1994). The nature of influence of speed on adult age differences in cognition. *Developmental Psychology, 30,* 240–259.

Salthouse, T.A. (2007). Reaction time. In J.E. Birren (Ed.), *Encyclopedia of gerontology* (2nd ed.). San Diego: Academic Press.

Salthouse, T.A. (2009). When does age-related cognitive decline begin? *Neurobiology of Aging, 30,* 507–514.

Salthouse, T.A. (2012). Consequences of age-related cognitive decline. *Annual Review of Psychology* (Vol. 63). Palo Alto, CA: Annual Reviews.

Salthouse, T.A. (2013). Executive functioning. In D.C. Park & N. Schwartz (Eds.), *Cognitive aging* (2nd ed.). New York: Psychology Press.

Salthouse, T.A. (2014). Why are there different age relations in cross-sectional and longitudinal comparisons of cognitive functioning? *Current Directions in Psychological Science, 23,* 252–256.

Salthouse, T.A. (2016). Aging cognition unconfounded by prior test experiences. *Journals of Gerontology B: Psychological Sciences and Social Sciences, 71,* 49–58.

Salthouse, T.A. (2017). Neural correlates of age-related slowing. In R. Cabeza, L. Nyberg, & D.C. Park (Eds.), *Cognitive neuroscience of aging* (2nd ed.). New York: Oxford University Press.

Salthouse, T.A. (2018). Why is cognitive change more negative with increased age? *Neuropsychology, 32,* 110–120.

Salthouse, T.A. (2019, in press). Comparable consistency, coherence, and commonality of measures of cognitive functioning across adulthood. *Assessment.*

Salvatore, J.E., Kuo, S.I., Steele, R.D., Simpson, J.A., & Collins, W.A. (2011). Recovering from conflict in romantic relationships: A developmental perspective. *Psychological Science, 22,* 376–383.

Salvatore, J.E., & others (2018). Genetics, the rearing environment, and the intergenerational transmission of divorce: A Swedish National Adoption Study. *Psychological Science 29,* 370–378.

Salzberg, S.L., & others (2018). Open questions: How many genes do we have? *BMC Biology, 816,* 94.

Salzwedel, A.P., & others (2016). Thalamocortical functional connectivity and behavioral disruptions in neonates with prenatal cocaine exposure. *Neurotoxicology and Teratology, 56,* 16–25.

Sam, D.L. (2018). Understanding positive immigrant youth adaptation in the context of multiculturalism. *Journal of Adolescence, 62,* 222–225.

Samanez-Larkin, G.R., & Carstensen, L. L. (2011). Socioemotional functioning and the aging brain. In J. Decety & J.T. Cacioppo (Eds.), *Handbook of social neuroscience.* New York: Oxford University Press.

Sampassa-Kanyinga, H., Chaput, J.P., & Hamilton, H.A. (2019). Social media use, school connectedness, and academic performance among adolescents. *Journal of Primary Prevention, 40,* 189–211.

Sampath, A., Maduro, G., & Schillinger, J.A. (2019, in press). Infant deaths due to herpes simplex virus, congenital syphilis, and HIV in New York City. *Pediatrics.*

Sanchez-Perez, N., & others (2018). Computer-based training in math and working memory improves cognitive skills and academic achievement in primary school children: Behavioral results. *Frontiers in Psychology, 8,* 2327.

Sanders, K.E., & Guerra, A.W. (Eds.) (2016). *The culture of child care.* New York: Oxford University Press.

Sandler, I., & others (2017). *Evidence-based programs: Family Bereavement Program.* Retrieved September 9, 2017, from https://reachinstitute.asu.edu/programs/family-bereavement

Sandler, L., & others (2018). Three perspectives on mental health problems of young adults and their parents at a 15-year follow-up of the family bereavement program. *Journal of Consulting and Clinical Psychology, 88,* 845–855.

Sands, A., Thompson, E.J., & Gaysina, D. (2017). Long-term influences of parental divorce on offspring affective disorders: A systematic review and meta-analysis. *Journal of Affective Disorders, 218,* 105–114.

Sanger, M.N. (2008). What we need to prepare teachers for the moral nature of their work. *Journal of Curriculum Studies, 40,* 169–185.

Sangree, W.H. (1989). Age and power: Life-course trajectories and age structuring of power relations in East and West Africa. In D.I. Kertzer & K.W. Schaie (Eds.), *Age structuring in comparative perspective.* Hillsdale, NJ: Erlbaum.

Sanson, A., & Rothbart, M.K. (1995). Child temperament and parenting. In M.H. Bornstein (Ed.), *Handbook of parenting* (Vol. 4). Hillsdale, NJ: Erlbaum.

Santacreu, M., Rodriguez, A., & Molina, M.A. (2019). Behavioral health. In R. Fernandez-Ballesteros, A. Benetos, & J-M. Robine (Eds.), *Cambridge handbook of successful aging.* New York: Cambridge University Press.

Santarnecchi, E., Rossi, S., & Rossi, A. (2015). The smarter, the stronger: Intelligence level correlates with brain resilience to systematic insults. *Cortex, 64,* 293–309.

Santos, J.R.F., & others (2019, in press). Validatioin of a prototype tau Thr231 phosphorylation in CSF ELISA as a potential biomarker for Alzheimer's disease. *Journal of Neural Transmission.*

Santos, L.M., & others (2016). Prevention of neural tube defects by fortification of flour with folic acid: A population-based retrospective study in Brazil. *Bulletin of the World Health Organization, 94,* 22–29.

Santos, M.G., & others (2019, in press). The health literacy of U.S. immigrant adolescents: A neglected research priority in a changing world. *International Journal of Environmental Research and Public Health.*

Santrock, J.W., & Halonen, J.A. (2013). *Your guide to college success* (7th ed.). Belmont, CA: Wadsworth.

Santrock, J.W., Sitterle, K.A., & Warshak, R.A. (1988). Parent-child relationship in stepfather families. In P. Bronstein & C.P. Cowan (Eds.), *Fatherhood today: Men's changing roles in the family.* New York: Wiley.

Sarid, O., & others (2018). Daily hassles score associates with the somatic and psychological health of patients with Crohn's disease. *Journal of Clinical Psychology, 74,* 969–988.

Sarman, I. (2018). Review shows that early fetal alcohol exposure may cause adverse effects even when the mother consumes low levels. *Acta Pediatrica, 107,* 938–941.

Saroglou, V. (2013). Religion, spirituality, and altruism. In K.I. Pargament, J. Exline, & J. Jones (Eds.), *Handbook of psychology, religion, and spirituality.* Washington, DC: American Psychological Association.

Sarquella-Brugada, G., & others (2016). Sudden infant death syndrome caused by cardiac arrhythmias: Only a matter of genes encoding ion channels? *International Journal of Legal Medicine, 130,* 415–420.

Sassler, S., Michelmore, K., & Qian, Z. (2018). Transitions from sexual relationships into cohabitation and beyond. *Demography, 55,* 511–524.

Satorres, E., & others (2018). Effectiveness of instrumental reminiscence intervention on improving coping in healthy older adults. *Stress and Health, 34,* 227–234.

Saucheilli, A. (2018). Life-extending enhancements in the narrative approach to personal identity. *Journal of Medical Ethics, 44,* 219–225.

Saul, J.S., & Rodgers, R.F. (2018). Adolescent eating disorder risk and the online world. *Child and Adolescent Psychiatric Clinics of North America, 27,* 221–228.

Savage, R.S., Abrami, P., Hipps, G., & Dealut, L. (2009). A randomized controlled trial study of the ABRACADABRA reading intervention program in grade 1. *Journal of Educational Psychology, 101,* 590–604.

Savin-Williams, R.C. (2016). *Becoming who I am: Young men on being gay.* Cambridge, MA: Harvard University Press.

Savin-Williams, R.C. (2017). *Mostly straight, sexually fluid.* Cambridge, MA: Harvard University Press.

Savin-Williams, R.C. (2019, in press). Developmental trajectories and milestones of sexual-minority youth. In J. Gilbert & S. Lamb (Eds.), *Cambridge handbook of sexuality.* New York: Cambridge University Press.

Savvidou, M., & Jauniaux, E. (2019). Prenatal spina bifida: What has changed in diagnosis and management. *BJOG, 126*(3), 329.

Sawyer, R.K. (2019). Individual and group creativity. In J.C. Kaufman & R.J. Sternberg (Eds.), *Cambridge handbook of creativity* (2nd ed.). New York: Cambridge University Press.

Sawyer, S., Abdul-Razak, S., & Patton, G. (2019). Introduction to adolescent health. In D. Devakumar & others (Eds.), *Oxford handbook of global health of women, newborns, children, and adolescents.* New York: Oxford University Press.

Saxena, M., Srivastava, N., & Banerjee, M. (2018). Cytokine gene variants as predictors of type 2 diabetes. *Current Diabetes Review, 14,* 307–319.

Saywitz, K.J., & others (2019). Effects of interviewer support on children's memory and suggestibility: Systematic review and meta-analyses of experimental research. *Trauma, Violence, and Abuse, 20,* 22–39.

Sbarra, D.A. (2012). Marital dissolution and physical health outcomes: A review of mechanisms. In L. Campbell, J. LaGuardia, J.M. Olson, & M.P. Zanna (Eds.), *The science of the couple. The Ontario Symposium* (Vol. 12). New York: Psychology Press.

Sbarra, D.A. (2015). Divorce and health: Current trends and future directions. *Psychosomatic Medicine, 77,* 227–236.

Sbarra, D.A., & Borelli, J.L. (2018). Attachment reorganization following divorce: Normative processes and individual differences. *Current Opinion in Psychology, 25,* 71–75.

Sbarra, D.A., Bourassa, K.J., & Manvelian, A. (2019). Marital separation and divorce: Correlates and consequences. In B.H. Friese (Ed.), *APA handbook of contemporary family psychology.* Washington, DC: APA Books.

Scalici, F., & Schulz, P.J. (2017). Parents' and peers' normative influence on adolescents' smoking: Results from a Swiss-Italian sample of middle school students. *Substance Abuse Treatment, Prevention, and Policy, 12*(1), 5.

Scarabino, D., & others (2017). Common variants of human TERT and TERC genes and susceptibility to sporadic Alzheimer's disease. *Experimental Gerontology, 88,* 19–24.

Scarr, S. (1993). Biological and cultural diversity: The legacy of Darwin for development. *Child Development, 64,* 1333–1353.

Scarr, S., & Weinberg, R.A. (1983). The Minnesota adoption studies: Genetic differences and malleability. *Child Development, 54,* 182–259.

Scelfo, J. (2015, February 3). A university recognizes a third gender: neutral. *New York Times.* Retrieved December 20, 2016, from www.newyorktimes.com/2015/02/08/education/edlife/a-university-re...

Schachter, D.L. (2019). Implicit memory, constructive memory, and imagining the future: A career perspective. *Perspectives on Psychological Science, 14,* 256–272.

Schafer, M.J., & others (2015). Calorie restriction suppresses age-dependent hippocampal transcriptional signatures. *PLoS One, 10*(7), e0133923.

Schaffer, H.R. (1996). *Social development.* Cambridge, MA: Blackwell.

Schaffer, M.A., Goodhue, A., Stennes, K., & Lanigan, C. (2012). Evaluation of a public health nurse visiting program for pregnant and parenting teens. *Public Health Nursing, 29,* 218–231.

Schaie, K.W. (1977). Toward a stage theory of adult cognitive development. *Aging and Human Development, 8,* 129–138.

Schaie, K.W. (1983). Consistency and changes in cognitive functioning of the young-old and old-old. In M. Bergner, U. Lehr, E. Lang, & R. Schmidt-Scherzer (Eds.), *Aging in the eighties and beyond.* New York: Springer.

Schaie, K.W. (1994). The life course of adult intellectual abilities. *American Psychologist, 49,* 304–313.

Schaie, K.W. (1996). *Intellectual development in adulthood: The Seattle Longitudinal Study.* New York: Cambridge University Press.

Schaie, K.W. (2000). The impact of longitudinal studies on understanding development from young adulthood to old age. *International Journal of Behavioral Development, 24,* 257–266.

Schaie, K.W. (2005). *Developmental influences on adult intelligence: The Seattle Longitudinal Study.* New York: Oxford University Press.

Schaie, K.W. (2010). Adult intellectual abilities. *Corsini encyclopedia of psychology.* New York: Wiley.

Schaie, K.W. (2011). Historical influences on aging and behavior. In K.W. Schaie & S.L. Willis (Eds.), *Handbook of the psychology of aging* (7th ed.). New York: Elsevier.

Schaie, K.W. (2012). *Developmental influences on adult intelligence: The Seattle Longitudinal Study* (2nd ed.). New York: Oxford University Press.

Schaie, K.W. (2013). *The Seattle Longitudinal Study: Developmental influences on adult intellectual development* (2nd ed.). New York: Oxford University Press.

Schaie, K.W. (2016). Theoretical perspectives for the psychology of aging in a lifespan context. In K.W. Schaie & S.L. Willis (Eds.), *Handbook of the psychology of aging* (8th ed.). New York: Elsevier.

Scharer, J.L., & Hibberd, R. (2019, in press). Meaning differentiates depression and grief among suicide survivors. *Death Studies.*

Schawo, S., & others (2017). The search for relevant outcome measures for cost-utility analysis of systematic family interventions in adolescents with substance use disorder and delinquent behavior: A systematic literature review. *Health and Quality of Life Outcomes, 15*(1), 179.

Scheibe, S., & Carstensen, L.L. (2010). Emotional aging: Recent and future trends. *Journals of Gerontology B: Psychological Sciences, 65,* 135–144.

Scheinost, D., & others (2017). Does prenatal stress alter the development connectome? *Pediatric Research, 81,* 214–226.

Schenk, A., & others (2019). Acute exercise increases the expression of KIR2DS4 by promoter demethylation in NK cells. *International Journal of Sports Medicine, 40,* 62–70.

Scher, A., & Harel, J. (2008). Separation and stranger anxiety. In M.M. Haith & J.B. Benson (Eds.), *Encyclopedia of infant and early childhood development.* Oxford, UK: Elsevier.

Schiff, R., Nuri Ben-Shushan, Y., & Ben-Artzi, E. (2017). Metacognitive strategies: A foundation for early word spelling and reading in kindergarteners with SLI. *Journal of Learning Disabilities, 50,* 143–157.

Schiff, W. (2019). *Nutrition for healthy living* (5th ed.). New York: McGraw-Hill.

Schiffman, S.S. (2007). Smell and taste. In J.E. Birren (Ed.,), *Encyclopedia of gerontology* (2nd ed.), San Diego: Academic Press.

Schlam, T.R., Wilson, N.L., Shoda, Y., Mischel, W., & Ayduk, O. (2013). Preschoolers' delay of gratification predicts their body mass 30 years later. *Journal of Pediatrics, 162*(1), 90–93.

Schlegel, M. (2000). All work and play. *Monitor on Psychology, 31*(11), 50–51.

Schlosnagle, L., & Strough, J. (2017). Understanding adult age differences in the frequency of problems with friends. *International Journal of Aging and Human Development, 84,* 159–179.

Schmidt, E.L., Burge, W., Visscher, K.M., & Ross, L.A. (2016). Cortical thickness in frontoparietal and cingulo-opercular networks predicts executive function performance in older adults. *Neuropsychology, 30,* 322–331.

Schmidt, M.E., & Vandewater, E.A. (2008). Media and attention, cognition, and school achievement. *Future of Children, 18*(1), 64–85.

Schneider, A.L.C., & Ornstein, P.A. (2019, in press). Determinants of memory development in childhood and adolescence. *International Journal of Psychology.*

Schneider, A.L.C., & others (2019, in press). Neural correlates of domain-specific cognitive decline: The ARIC-NCS study. *Neurology.*

Schneider, W. (2011). Memory development in childhood. In U. Goswami (Ed.), *Wiley-Blackwell handbook of childhood cognitive development.* New York: Wiley.

Schnittker, J. (2007). Look (closely) at all the lonely people: Age and social psychology of school support. *Journal of Aging and Health, 19,* 659–682.

Schnitzspahn, K.M., Kvavilashvili, L., & Altgassen, M. (2019, in press). Redefining the pattern of age-prospective memory-paradox: New insights on age effects in lab-based, naturalistic, and self-assigned tasks. *Psychological Research.*

Schnohr, P., & others (2015). Dose of jogging and long-term mortality: The Copenhagen Heart Study. *Journal of the American College of Cardiology, 65,* 411–419.

Schnohr, P., & others (2017). Impact of persistence and non-persistence in leisure time physical activity on coronary heart disease and all-cause mortality: The Copenhagen City Heart Study. *European Journal of Cardiology, 24,* 1615–1623.

Schoenmaker, C., & others (2015). From maternal sensitivity in infancy to adult attachment representations: A longitudinal adoption study with secure base scripts. *Attachment and Human Development, 17,* 241–256.

Schoffstall, C.L., & Cohen, R. (2011). Cyber aggression: The relation between online offenders and offline social competence. *Social Development, 20*(3), 587–604.

Schonert-Reichl, K.A., & Roeser, R.W. (Eds.) (2016). *Mindfulness in education.* New York: Springer.

Schonert-Reichl, K.A., & others (2015). Enhancing cognitive and socio-emotional development through a simple-to-administer mindfulness-based school program for elementary school children: A randomized controlled trial. *Developmental Psychology, 51,* 52–56.

Schooler, C. (2007). Use it—and keep it longer, probably: A reply to Salthouse (2006). *Perspectives on Psychological Science, 2,* 24–29.

Schooler, C., Mulatu, S., & Oates, G. (1999). The continuing effects of substantively complex work on the intellectual functioning of older workers. *Psychology and Aging, 14,* 483–506.

Schoon, I., Jones, E., Cheng, H., & Maughan, B. (2012). Family hardship, family instability, and cognitive development. *Journal of Epidemiology and Community Health, 66*(8), 716–722.

Schork, A.J., & others (2019, in press). A genome-wide association study of shared risk across psychiatric disorders implicates gene regulation during fetal neurodevelopment. *Nature Neuroscience.*

Schrager, S.M., Goldbach, J.T., & Mamey, M.R. (2018). Development of the Sexual Minority Adolescent Stress Inventory. *Frontiers in Psychology, 9,* 319.

Schreiber, K.H., O'Leary, M., & Kennedy, B.K. (2016). The mTOR pathway and aging. In M. Kaeberlein & G.M. Martin (Eds.), *Handbook of the psychology of aging* (8th ed.). New York: Elsevier.

Schreiber, L.R. (1990). *The parents' guide to kids' sports.* Boston: Little, Brown.

Schreuders, E., Klapwijk, E.T., Will, G.-J., & Guroglu, B. (2018). Friend versus foe: Neural correlates of prosocial decisions for liked and disliked peers. *Cognitive, Affective, and Behavioral Neuroscience, 18,* 127–142.

Schuhmacher, N., Collard, J., & Kartner, J. (2017). The differential role of parenting, peers, and temperament in explaining interindividual differences in 18-months-olds' comforting and helping. *Infant Behavior and Development, 46,* 124–134.

Schulenberg, J.E., Sameroff, A.J., & Cicchetti, D. (2004). The transition to adulthood as a critical juncture in the course of psychopathology and mental health. *Development and Psychopathology, 16,* 799–806.

Schulenberg, J.E., & Zarrett, N.R. (2006). Mental health during emerging adulthood: Continuities and discontinuities in course, content, and meaning. In J.J. Arnett & J. Tanner (Eds.), *Advances in emerging adulthood.* Washington, DC: American Psychological Association.

Schulenberg, J.E., & others (2017). *Monitoring the Future national survey results on drug use, 1975-2016: Vol. II, college students and adults, aged 19-55.* Ann Arbor, MI: Institute for Social Research, University of Michigan.

Schultz, M.L., Kostic, M., & Kharasch, S. (2018). A case of toxic breast-feeding? *Pediatric Emergency Care, 35,* e9-e10.

Schultz, R., & Curnow, C. (1988). Peak performance and age among super athletes: Track and field, swimming, baseball, and golf. *Journal of Gerontology, 43,* P113-P120.

Schunk, D.H. (2016). *Learning theories: An educational perspective* (7th ed.). Upper Saddle River, NJ: Prentice Hall.

Schunk, D.H., & Greene, J.A. (Eds.) (2018). *Handbook of self-regulation of learning and performance* (2nd ed.). New York: Routledge.

Schurz, H., & others (2019a). A sex-stratified genome-wide association study of tuberculosis using a multi-ethnic genotyping array. *Frontiers in Genetics, 9,* 678.

Schurz, H., & others (2019b). The X chromosome and sex-specific effects in infectious disease susceptibility. *Human Genomics, 13*(1), 2.

Schutten, D., Stokes, K.A., & Arnell, K.M. (2017). I want to media multitask and I want to do it now: Individual differences in media multitasking predict delay of gratification and system-1 thinking. *Cognitive Research: Principles and Implications, 2*(1), 8.

Schwalbe, C.S., Gearing, R.E., MacKenzie, M.J., Brewer, K.B., & Ibrahim, R. (2012). A meta-analysis of experimental studies of diversion programs for juvenile offenders. *Clinical Psychology Review, 32,* 26-33.

Schwartz, D., & others (2015). Peer victimization during middle childhood as a lead indicator of internalizing problems and diagnostic outcomes in late adolescence. *Journal of Clinical Child and Adolescent Psychology, 44,* 393-404.

Schwartz, J.A., Wright, E.M., & Valgardson, B.A. (2019). Adverse childhood experiences and deleterious outcomes in adulthood: A consideration of the simultaneous role of genetic and environmental influences in two independent samples from the United States. *Child Abuse and Neglect, 88,* 420-431.

Schwartz, L.E., Howell, K.H., & Jamison, L.E. (2018). Effect of time since loss on grief, resilience, and depression among bereaved emerging adults. *Death Studies, 43,* 537-547.

Schwartz, M.A., & Scott, B.M. (2018). *Marriage and family* (8th ed.). Upper Saddle River, NJ: Pearson.

Schwartz, S.J., & Petrova, M. (2019, in press). Prevention science in emerging adulthood: A field is coming of age. *Prevention Science.*

Schwartz, S.J., Zamboanga, B.L., Meca, A., & Ritchie, R.A. (2012). Identity around the world: An overview. *New Directions in Child and Adolescent Development, 138,* 1-14.

Schweinhart, L.J., & others (2005). *Lifetime effects: The High/Scope Perry Preschool Study through age 40.* Ypsilanti, MI: High/Scope Press.

Scialfa, C.T., & Kline, D.W. (2007). Vision. In J.E. Birren (Ed.), *Encyclopedia of gerontology* (2nd ed.). San Diego: Academic Press.

Scott, D., & others (2018). Associations of components of sarcopenic obesity with bone health and balance in older adults. *Archives of Gerontology and Geriatrics, 75,* 125-131.

Scott, R.M., & Baillargeon, R. (2017). Early false-belief understanding. *Trends in Cognitive Science, 21,* 237-249.

Scott, S.B., & others (2018). Perceived neighborhood characteristics predict severity and emotional response to daily stressors. *Social Science and Medicine, 200,* 262-270.

Scourfield, J., Van den Bree, M., Martin, N., & McGuffin, P. (2004). Conduct problems in children and adolescents: A twin study. *Archives of General Psychiatry, 61,* 489-496.

Scullin, M.K., Bugg, J.M., & McDaniel, M.A. (2012). Whoops, I did it again: Commission errors in prospective memory. *Psychology of Aging, 27,* 46-53.

Sebastiani, P., & Perls, T.T. (2012). The genetics of extreme longevity: Lessons from the New England Centenarian study. *Frontiers in Genetics, 30*(3), 277.

Seccombe, K. (2018). *Exploring marriages and families* (3rd ed.). Upper Saddle River, NJ: Pearson.

Sechrist, J., & Fingerman, K.L. (2018). Intergenerational relationships. In M.H. Bornstein (Ed.), *SAGE encyclopedia of lifespan human development.* Thousand Oaks, CA: Sage.

Sedgh, G., & others (2015). Adolescent pregnancy, birth, and abortion rates across countries: Levels and recent trends. *Journal of Adolescent Health, 56,* 223-230.

Segerberg, O. (1982). *Living to be 100: 200 who did and how they did it.* New York: Charles Scribner's Sons.

Seidel, M., & others (2019, in press). Abnormal spontaneous regional brain activity in young patients with anorexia nervosa. *Journal of the American Academy of Child and Adolescent Psychiatry.*

Seiffert, D.J., & others (2019, in press). Beyond medical actionability: Public perceptions of important actions in response to hypothetical genetic testing results. *Journal of Genetic Counseling.*

Sekeres, M.J., Winocur, G., & Moscovitch, M. (2018). The hippocampus and related neocortical structures in memory transformation. *Neuroscience Letters, 680,* 39-53.

Seligman, M.E.P. (2007). *The optimistic child.* New York: Mariner.

Selkie, E. (2019, in press). When age-based guidance is not enough: The problem of early puberty. *Pediatrics.*

Selman, R.L. (1980). *The growth of interpersonal understanding.* New York: Academic Press.

Semenov, A.D., & Zelazo, P.D. (2018). The development of hot and cool executive function: A foundation for learning in the preschool years. In L. Melzer (Ed.), *Executive function in education.* New York: Guilford.

Sen, B. (2010). The relationship between frequency of family dinner and adolescent problem behaviors after adjusting for other characteristics. *Journal of Adolescence, 33,* 187-196.

Senger, E. (2019). Ageism in medicine: A pressing problem. *CMAJ, 191*(2), E55-E56.

Sengpiel, V., & others (2013). Maternal caffeine intake during pregnancy is associated with birth weight but not gestational length: Results from a large prospective observational cohort study. *BMC Medicine, 11,* 42.

Senin-Calderon, C., & others (2017). Body image and adolescence: A behavioral impairment model. *Psychiatry Research, 248,* 121-126.

Senthelal, S., & Thomas, M.A. (2018). Arthritis. *StatPearls.* Treasure Island, FL: StatPearls Publishing.

Seo, J.Y., & Chao, Y.Y. (2018). Effects of exercise interventions on depressive symptoms among community-dwelling older adults in the United States: A systematic review. *Journal of Gerontological Nursing, 44,* 31-38.

Seo, Y.S., Lee, J., & Ahn, H.Y. (2016). Effects of kangaroo care on neonatal pain in South Korea. *Journal of Tropical Pediatrics, 62,* 246-249.

Sepulcre, J., & others (2012). Stepwise connectivity of the model cerebral cortex reveals the multimodal organization of the human brain. *Journal of Neuroscience, 32,* 10649-10661.

Serrano-Pozo, A., & Growdon, J.H. (2019). Is Alzheimer's disease risk modifiable? *Journal of Alzheimer's Disease, 67,* 795-819.

Serrat, R., & others (2018, in press). On the quality of adjustment to retirement: The longitudinal role of personality traits and generativity. *Journal of Personality.*

Sesker, A.A., Suilleabhain, P.O., Howard, S., & Hughes, B.M. (2016). Conscientiousness and mindfulness in midlife coping: An assessment based on MIDUS II. *Personality and Mental Health, 10,* 28-42.

Sethna, V., Murray, L., & Ramchandani, P.G. (2012). Depressed fathers' speech to their 3-month-old infants: A study of cognitive and mentalizing features in paternal speech. *Psychological Medicine, 42*(11), 2361-2371.

Sethna, V., & others (2018). Father-child interactions at 3 months and 24 months: Contributions to children's cognitive development at 24 months. *Infant Mental Health Journal, 229,* 364-370.

Sevil, J., & others (2019, in press). Which school community agents influence adolescents' motivational outcomes and physical activity? Are more autonomy-supportive relationships necessarily better? *International Journal of Environmental Research and Public Health.*

Sewdas, R., & others (2017). Why older workers work beyond the retirement age: A qualitative study. *BMC Public Health, 17*(1), 672.

Sexton, B.P., & Taylor, N.F. (2019, in press). To sit or not to sit? A systematic review and meta-analysis of seated exercise for older adults. *Australian Journal of Aging.*

Sgro, P., & others (2018). Physical exercise, nutrition, and hormones: Three pillars to fight sarcopenia. *Aging Male, 16,* 1-14.

Shah, A.A., & others (2018). Meeting the mental health needs of Hurricane Harvey evacuees. *American Journal of Psychiatry, 175,* 13-14.

Shah, J.Y. (Ed.) (2017). *Self-control.* New York: Routledge.

Shaheen, S. (2014). How child's play impacts executive function-related behaviors. *Applied Neuropsychology: Child, 3,* 182-187.

Shahoei, R., & others (2017). The effect of perineal massage during the second stage of birth on nulliparous women perineal: A randomization clinical trial. *Electronic Physician, 9,* 5588-5595.

Shakil, S., Lockwood, M., & Grady, D. (2018). Persistence of sexual harassment and gender bias in medicine across generations—Us Too. *JAMA Internal Medicine, 178,* 324-325.

Shallie, P.D., & Naicker, T. (2019). The placenta as a window to the brain: A review on the role of placental markers in prenatal programming of neurodevelopment. *International Journal of Neuroscience, 73,* 41-49.

Shan, Z.Y., Liu, J.Z., Sahgal, V., Wang, B., & Yue, G.H. (2005). Selective atrophy of left hemisphere and frontal lobe of the brain in older men. *Journals of Gerontology A: Biological Sciences and Medical Sciences, 60,* A165-A174.

Shankaran, S., & others (2010). Prenatal cocaine exposure and BMI and blood pressure at 9 years of age. *Journal of Hypertension, 28,* 1166-1175.

Shapiro, A.F., & Gottman, J.M. (2005). Effects on marriage of a psycho-education intervention with couples undergoing the transition to parenthood: Evaluation at 1-year post intervention. *Journal of Family Communication, 5,* 1-24.

Shapiro, A.F., Gottman, J.M., & Fink, B.C. (2019, in press). Father's involvement when bringing baby home: Efficacy testing of a couple-focused transition to parenthood intervention for promoting father involvement. *Psychological Reports.*

Sharkey, W. (1993). Who embarrasses whom? Relational and sex differences in the use of intentional embarrassment. In P.J. Kalbfleisch (Ed.), *Interpersonal communication.* Mahwah, NJ: Erlbaum.

Sharma, R., Murki, S., & Oleti, T.P. (2018). Study comparing "kangaroo ward care" with "intermediate intensive care" for improving growth outcome and cost effectiveness: Randomized control trial. *Journal of Maternal-Fetal and Neonatal Medicine, 31,* 2986-2993.

Sharony, R., & others (2018). The impact of third-trimester genetic counseling. *Archives of Gynecology and Obstetrics, 297,* 659-665.

Sharp, E.S., Reynolds, C.A., Pedersen, N.L., & Gatz, M. (2010). Cognitive engagement and cognitive aging: Is openness protective? *Psychology and Aging, 25,* 60-73.

Sharp. E.S., & others (2019). Openness declines in advance of death in late adulthood. *Psychology and Aging, 34,* 124-138.

Shatz, M., & Gelman, R. (1973). The development of communication skills: Modifications in the speech of young children as a function of the listener. *Monographs of the Society for Research in Child Development, 38*(Serial No. 152).

Shaw, P., & others (2007). Attention-deficit/hyperactivity disorder is characterized by a delay in cortical maturation. *Proceedings of the National Academy of Sciences, 104*(49), 19649-19654.

Shay, J.W., & Wright, W.E. (2019, in press). Telomeres and telomerase: Three decades of progress. *Nature Reviews: Genetics.*

Shaywitz, S.E., Gruen, J.R., & Shaywitz, B.A. (2007). Management of dyslexia, its rationale, and underlying neurobiology. *Pediatric Clinics of North America, 54,* 609-623.

Shear, M.K., Ghesquiere, A., & Glickman, K. (2013). Bereavement and complicated grief. *Current Psychiatric Reports, 15*(11), 406.

Shebloski, B., Conger, K.J., & Widaman, K.F. (2005). Reciprocal links among differential parenting, perceived partiality, and self-worth: A three-wave longitudinal study. *Journal of Family Psychology, 19,* 633-642.

Sheehan, D.K., & others (2019). Telling adolescents that a parent has died. *Journal of Hospice and Pediatric Nursing, 21,* 152-159.

Sheehan, M.J., & Watson, M.W. (2008). Reciprocal influences between maternal discipline and techniques and aggression in children and adolescents. *Aggressive Behavior, 34,* 245-255.

Sheinbaum, T., & others (2015). Attachment style predicts affect, cognitive appraisals, and social functioning in daily life. *Frontiers in Psychology, 6,* 296.

Sheinkopf, S.J., & others (2019). Developmental trajectories of autonomic functioning in autism from birth to early childhood. *Biological Psychology, 142,* 13-18.

Sheldrick, R.C., Maye, M.P., & Carter, A.S. (2017). Age at first identification of autism spectrum disorder: An analysis of two U.S. surveys. *Journal of the American Academy of Child and Adolescent Psychiatry, 56,* 313-320.

Shenk, D. (2017). What is the Flynn effect, and how does it change our understanding of IQ? *Wiley Interdisciplinary Reviews: Cognitive Science, 8,* 1-2.

Shenoda, B.B. (2017). An overview of the mechanisms of abnormal GABAergic interneuronal cortical migration associated with prenatal ethanol exposure. *Neurochemical Research, 42,* 1279-1287.

Shephard, E., & others (2019). Oscillatory neural networks underlying resting-state, attentional control, and social cognition task conditions in children with ASD, ADHD and ASD+ADHD. *Cortex, 117,* 96-110.

Sheppard, V.B., & others (2018). Spirituality in African-American breast cancer patients: Implications for clinical and psychosocial care. *Journal of Religion and Health, 57,* 1918-1930.

Sher-Censor, E., Parke, R.D., & Coltrane, S. (2010). Parents' promotion of psychological autonomy, psychological control, and Mexican-American adolescents' adjustment. *Journal of Youth and Adolescence, 40*(5), 620-632.

Sheridan, M.A., & others (2018). Early deprivation disruption of association learning is a developmental pathway to depression and social problems. *Nature Communications, 9*(1), 2216.

Sherman, C.W., Webster, N.J., & Antonucci, T.C. (2016). Dementia caregiving in the context of late life remarriage: Support networks, relationship quality, and well-being. In K.W. Schaie & S.L. Willis (Eds.), *Handbook of the psychology of aging* (8th ed.). New York: Elsevier.

Sherman, L., Steinberg, L., & Chein, J. (2018). Connecting brain responsivity and real-world risk taking: Strengths and weaknesses of current methodological approaches. *Developmental Cognitive Neuroscience, 33,* 27-41.

Sherwood, C.C., & others (2011). Aging of the cerebral cortex differs between humans and chimpanzees. *Proceedings of the National Academy of Sciences U.S.A., 108,* 13029-13034.

Shi, C., & others (2017). Cdk5-Foxo3 axis: Initially neuroprotective, eventually neurodegenerative in Alzheimer's disease. *Journal of Cell Science, 129,* 1815-1830.

Shields, S.A. (1998, August). *What Jerry Maguire can tell us about gender and emotion.* Paper presented at the meeting of the International Society for Research on Emotions, Würzburg, Germany.

Shiner, R.L., & DeYoung, C.G. (2013). The structure of temperament and personality: A developmental approach. In P.D. Zelazo (Ed.), *Oxford handbook of developmental psychology.* New York: Oxford University Press.

Shippee, T.P., & others (2019). Long-term effects of age discrimination on mental health: The role of perceived financial strain. *Journals of Gerontology B: Psychological Sciences and Social Sciences, 74,* 664-674.

Shivarama Shetty, M., & Sajikumar, S. (2017). 'Tagging' along memories in aging: Synaptic tagging and capture mechanisms in the aged hippocampus. *Aging Research Reviews, 55,* 22-35.

Shivers, E., & Fargo, F. (2016). Where the children are: Exploring quality, community, and support for family, friend, and neighbor care. In K.E. Sanders & A.W. Guerra (Eds.), *The culture of child care.* New York: Oxford University Press.

Shlyakhto, E. (2018). Gendered innovations in the study of cardiovascular diseases. *Advances in Experimental and Medical Biology, 1065,* 655-675.

Shneidman, L., & Woodward, A.L. (2016). Are child-directed interactions the cradle of social learning? *Psychological Bulletin, 142,* 1-17.

Shneidman, O., Gweon, H., Schultz, L., & Woodward, A.L. (2016). Learning from others and spontaneous exploration: A cross-cultural investigation. *Child Development, 87,* 1221-1232.

Shohayeb, B., & others (2018). Factors that influence adult neurogenesis as potential therapy. *Translational Neurodegeneration 7,* 4.

Shors, T.J. (2009). Saving new brain cells. *Scientific American, 300,* 46-52.

Short, M.A., Gradisar, M., Lack, L.C., Wright, H.R., & Dohnt, H. (2012). The sleep patterns and well-being of Australian adolescents. *Journal of Adolescence, 36*(1), 103-110.

Shramko, M., Toomey, R.B., & Anhalt, K. (2018). Profiles of minority stressors and identity centrality among sexual minority Latinx youth. *American Journal of Orthopsychiatry, 88,* 471-482.

Shuey, E.A., & Leventhal, T. (2019). Neighborhoods and parenting. In M.H. Bornstein (Ed.), *Handbook of parenting* (3rd ed.) (Vol. 2). New York: Routledge.

Shulman, S., & others (2019, in press). Adolescents' sexual encounters with either romantic or casual partners and the quality of their romantic relationships four years later. *Journal of Sex Research.*

Sibley, M.H., & others (2012). Diagnosing ADHD in adolescence. *Journal of Consulting and Clinical Psychology, 80,* 139-150.

Sidtis, J.J., & others (2018). Switching language modes: Complementary brain patterns for formulaic and propositional language. *Brain Connectivity, 8,* 189-198.

Siebelink, N.M., & others (2019, in press). Genetic and environmental etiologies of associations between dispositional mindfulness and ADHD traits: A population-based twin study. *European Child and Adolescent Psychiatry.*

Siedlecki, K.L., & others (2019, in press). Examining processing speed as a a predictor of subjective well-being across age and time in the German Aging Survey. *Neuropsychology, Development, and Cognition. Section B: Aging and Cognition.*

Siegel, A.L.M., & Castel, A.D. (2018). Memory for important item-location association in younger and older adults. *Psychology and Aging, 33,* 30-45.

Siegel, D.H. (2013). Open adoption: Adoptive parents' reactions two decades later. *Social Work, 58,* 43-52.

Siegel, R.S., & Brandon, A.R. (2014). Adolescents, pregnancy, and mental health. *Journal of Pediatric and Adolescent Gynecology, 27,* 138-150.

Siegler, R.S. (2006). Microgenetic analysis of learning. In W. Damon & R. Lerner (Eds.), *Handbook of child psychology* (6th ed.). New York: Wiley.

Siegler, R.S. (2013). How do people become experts? In J. Staszewski (Ed.), *Experience and skill acquisition.* New York: Taylor & Francis.

Siegler, R.S. (2016a). Continuity and change in the field of cognitive development and in the perspective of one cognitive developmentalist. *Child Development Perspectives, 10,* 128-133.

Siegler, R.S. (2016b). How does change occur? In R. Sternberg, S. Fiske, & D. Foss (Eds.), *Scientists make a difference: One hundred eminent behavioral and brain scientists talk about their most important contributions.* Cambridge, UK: Cambridge University Press.

Siegler, R.S. (2017). Foreword: Build it and they will come. In D.G. Geary & others (Eds.), *Acquisition of complex arithmetic skills and higher order mathematics concepts.* New York: Academic Press.

Siegler, R.S., & Braithwaite, D.W. (2017). Numerical development. *Annual Review of Psychology* (Vol. 68). Palo Alto, CA: Annual Reviews.

Siener, S., & Kerns, K.A. (2012). Emotion regulation and depressive symptoms in preadolescence. *Child Psychiatry and Human Development, 43,* 414-430.

Sievert, L.L., & Obermeyer, C.M. (2012). Symptom clusters at midlife: A four-country comparison of checklist and qualitative responses. *Menopause, 19,* 133-144.

Sightlines Project (2016). *Seeing our way to living long, living well in 21st century America.* Palo Alto, CA: Stanford University.

Silva, C. (2005, October 31). When teen dynamo talks, city listens. *Boston Globe,* pp. 81-84.

Silva, R., & others (2019). Atrial fibrillation and risk of dementia: Epidemiology, mechanisms, and effect of anticoagulation. *Frontiers in Neuroscience, 13,* 18.

Silverman, M.E., & others (2017). The risk factors for postpartum depression: A population-based study. *Depression and Anxiety, 34,* 178-187.

Silverstein, M. (2009). Caregiving. In D. Carr (Ed.), *Encyclopedia of the life course and human development.* Boston: Gale Cengage.

Sim, L., & others (2019). Parenting and centrality: The role of life meaning as a mediator for parenting and language broker role identity. *Journal of Youth and Adolescence, 48,* 510-526.

Simha, S. (2019). The impact of family separation on immigrant and refugee families. *North Carolina Medical Journal, 80,* 95-96.

Simms, N.K., Frausel, R.R., & Richland, E.E. (2018). Working memory predicts children's analogical reasoning. *Journal of Experimental Child Psychology, 166,* 160-177.

Simon, E.J. (2020). *Biology* (3rd ed.). Upper Saddle River, NJ: Pearson.

Simon, K.A., & others (2018). Envisioning future parenthood among bisexual, lesbian, and heterosexual women. *Psychology of Sexual Orientation and Gender Diversity, 5,* 253-259.

Simon, S.S., & others (2018). Is computerized working memory training effective in healthy older adults? Evidence from a multi-site, randomized controlled trial. *Journal of Alzheimer's Disease, 65,* 1-19.

Simons, L.G., & others (2016). Mechanisms that link parenting practices to adolescents' risky sexual behavior: A test of six competing theories. *Journal of Youth and Adolescence, 45,* 255-270.

Simonton, D.C. (2019). Creativity's role in society. In J.C. Kaufman & R.J. Sternberg (Eds.), *Cambridge handbook of creativity* (2nd ed.). New York: Cambridge University Press.

Simonton, D.K. (1996). Creativity. In J.E. Birren (Ed.), *Encyclopedia of aging.* San Diego: Academic Press.

Simpson, D.M., Leonhardt, N.D., & Hawkins, A.J. (2018). Learning about love: A meta-analytic of individually-oriented relationship education programs for adolescents and emerging adults. *Journal of Youth and Adolescence, 47,* 477-489.

Simpson, J.A., & Belsky, J. (2016). Attachment theory within a modern evolutionary framework. In J. Cassidy & P. Shaver (Eds.), *Handbook of attachment theory and research* (3rd ed.). New York: Guilford.

Simpson, J.A., & Karantzas, G.C. (2019). Editorial overview: Attachment in adulthood: A dynamic field with a rich past and a bright future. *Current Opinion in Psychology, 25,* 177-181.

Simpson, J.A., & Rholes, W.S. (2017). Adult attachment, stress, and romantic relationships. *Current Opinion in Psychology, 13,* 19-24.

Simpson, J.S., & Winterheld, H.A. (2019). Person-by-situation: Perspectives on close relationships. In K. Deaux & M. Snyder (Eds.), *Oxford handbook of personality and social psychology.* New York: Oxford University Press.

Sims, T., Hogan, C., & Carstensen, L.L. (2015). Selectivity as an emotion regulation strategy. Lessons from older adults. *Current Opinion in Psychology, 3,* 80-84.

Sin, N.L., Sloan, R.P., McKinley, P.S., & Almeida, D.M. (2016). Linking daily stress processes and laboratory-based heart rate variability in a national sample of midlife and older adults. *Psychosomatic Medicine, 78,* 573-582.

Sinclair, E.M. & others (2018). Home literacy environment and shared reading in the newborn period. *Journal of Developmental and Behavioral Pediatrics, 39,* 66-71.

Sinclair-Palm, J. (2019). Conceptualizing sexuality in research about trans youth. In S. Lamb & J. Gilbert (Eds.), *Cambridge handbook of sexual development.* New York: Cambridge University Press.

Singer, A.E., & others (2015). Symptom trends in the last year of life from 1998 to 2010: A cohort study. *Annals of Internal Medicine, 162,* 175-183.

Singer, D., Golinkoff, R.M., & Hirsh-Pasek, K. (Eds.) (2006). *Play = learning: How play motivates and enhances children's cognitive and social-emotional growth.* New York: Oxford University Press.

Singer, M., & Anderson, A.C. (2019). Revolutionizing cancer immunology: The power of next-generation sequencing technologies. *Cancer Immunology Research, 7,* 168-173.

Singer, M.A. (2016). The origins of aging: Evidence that aging is an adaptive phenotype. *Current Aging Science, 9,* 95-115.

Singh, L., & others (2017). Novel word learning in bilingual and monolingual infants: Evidence for a bilingual advantage. *Child Development, 89,* e183-e196.

Singh, P.B., Shioma, V.V., & Belyakin, S.N. (2019, in press). Maternal regulation of chromosomal imprinting in animals. *Chromosoma.*

Singh, S., Wulf, D., Samara, R., & Cuca, Y.P. (2000). Gender differences in the timing of first intercourse: Data from 14 countries. *International Family Planning Perspectives, 26,* 21-28, 43.

Singh-Manoux, A., & others (2012). Timing and onset of cognitive decline: Results from Whitehall II prospective cohort study. *BMJ, 344,* d7622.

Singleton, R., Schroffel, H., Findlay, T., & Winskell, K. (2016). Cultural scripts surrounding young people's sexual and romantic relationships in the Western Highlands of Guatemala. *Culture, Health, and Sex, 18,* 1039-1053.

Sinha, J.W., Cnaan, R.A., & Gelles, R.J. (2007). Adolescent risk behaviors and religion: Findings from a national study. *Journal of Adolescence, 30,* 231-249.

Sinkovic, M., & Towler, L. (2019, in press). Sexual aging: A systematic review of qualitative research on the sexuality and sexual health of older adults. *Quality Health Research.*

Sinnott, J.D. (2003). Postformal thought and adult development: Living in balance. In J. Demick & C. Andreoletti (Eds.), *Handbook of adult development.* New York: Kluwer.

Sirsch, U., Dreher, E., Mayr, E., & Willinger, U. (2009). What does it take to be an adult in Austria? Views of adulthood in Austrian adolescents, emerging adults, and adults. *Journal of Adolescent Research, 24,* 275-292.

Siverova, J., & Buzgova, R. (2018). The effect of reminiscence therapy on quality of life attitudes to aging and depressive symptoms in institutionalized elderly adults with cognitive impairment: A quasi-experimental study. *International Journal of Mental Health Nursing, 27,* 1430-1438.

Skaper, S.D., & others (2017). Synaptic plasticity, dementia, and Alzheimer disease. *CNS & Neurological Disorders Drug Targets, 16,* 220-233.

Skinner, B.F. (1938). *The behavior of organisms: An experimental analysis.* New York: Appleton-Century-Crofts.

Skinner, O.D., & McHale, S.M. (2016). Parent-adolescent conflict in African American families. *Journal of Youth and Adolescence, 45,* 2080-2093.

Skrzypek, H., & Hui, L. (2017). Noninvasive prenatal testing for fetal aneuploidy and single gene disorders. *Best Practices and Research. Clinical Obstetrics and Gynecology, 42,* 26-38.

Skuse, D., Printzlau, F., & Wolstencroft, J. (2018). Sex chromosome aneuploidies. *Handbook of Clinical Neurology, 147,* 355-376.

Slade, A., & others (2019). Minding the baby: Complex trauma and attachment-based home intervention. In H. Steele & M. Steele (Eds.), *Handbook of attachment-based interventions.* New York: Guilford.

Slater, A., Morison, V., & Somers, M. (1988). Orientation discrimination and cortical function in the human newborn. *Perception, 17,* 597-602.

Slater, A.M., Bremner, J.G., Johnson, S.P., & Hayes, R. (2011). The role of perceptual processes in infant addition/subtraction events. In L.M. Oakes, C.H. Cashon, M. Casasola, & D.H. Rakison (Eds.), *Early perceptual and cognitive development*. New York: Oxford University Press.

Slaughter, V., & others (2014). Meta-analysis of theory of mind and peer popularity in the preschool and early school years. *Child Development, 86*, 1159–1174.

Slobin, D. (1972, July). Children and language: They learn the same way around the world. *Psychology Today*, pp. 71–76.

Slomkowski, C., Rende, R., Conger, K.J., Simons, R.L., & Conger, R.D. (2001). Sisters, brothers, and delinquency: Social influence during early and middle adolescence. *Child Development, 72*, 271–283.

Smaldino, S.E., & others (2019). *Instructional technology and media for learning* (12th ed.). Upper Saddle River, NJ: Pearson.

Small, B.J., Rawson, K.S., Eisel, S., & McEvoy, C.L. (2012). Memory and aging. In S.K. Whitbourne & M. Sliwinski (Eds.), *Wiley-Blackwell handbook of adulthood and aging*. New York: Wiley.

Small, H. (2011). *Why not? My seventy year plan for a college degree*. Franklin, TN: Carpenter's Son Publishing.

Small, S.A. (1990). *Preventive programs that support families with adolescents*. Washington, DC: Carnegie Council on Adolescent Development.

Smarius, L.J., & others (2017). Excessive infant crying doubles the risk of mood and behavioral problems at age 5: Evidence for mediation by maternal characteristics. *European Child and Adolescent Psychiatry, 26*, 293–302.

Smetana, J.G. (2013). Moral development: The social domain theory view. In P.D. Zelazo (Ed.), *Oxford handbook of developmental psychology*. New York: Oxford University Press.

Smetana, J.G., & Ball, C.L. (2018). Young children's moral judgments: justifications, and emotion attributions in peer relationship contexts. *Child Development, 89*, 2245–2263.

Smetana, J.G., Jambon, M., & Ball, C. (2014). The social domain approach to children's moral and social judgments. In M. Killen & J.G. Smetana (Eds.), *Handbook of moral development* (2nd ed.). New York: Psychology Press.

Smetana, J.G., Robinson, J., & Rote, W.M. (2015). Socialization in adolescence. In J.E. Grusec & P.D. Hastings (Eds.), *Handbook of socialization* (2nd ed.). New York: Guilford.

Smid, G.E., & others (2018). Toward cultural assessment of grief and grief-related psychopathology. *Psychiatric Services, 69*, 1050–1052.

Smith, A., & Anderson, M. (2018). *Social media use in 2018*. Washington, DC: Pew Research Center.

Smith, A.E., Hendy, A.M., & Tempest, G.D. (2018). The importance of understanding the underlying physiology of exercise when designing interventions for brain health. *Journal of Physiology, 596*, 1131–1132.

Smith, A.K., & Periyakoli, V.S. (2018). Should we bury "The good death"? *Journal of the American Geriatrics Society, 66*, 856–858.

Smith, A.R., & others (2019). A cross-brain regions study of ANK1 DNA methylation in different neurodegenerative diseases. *Neurobiology of Aging, 74*, 70–76.

Smith, D.D., & others (2018). *Introduction to contemporary special education* (2nd ed.). Upper Saddle River, NJ: Pearson.

Smith, E.B., & others (2019). Pediatric traumatic brain injury and associated topics: An overview of abusive head trauma, nonaccidental trauma, and sports concussions. *Anesthesiology Clinics, 37*, 119–134.

Smith, E.B., & others (2019, in press). Positive aging views in the general population predict better long-term cognition for elders in eight countries. *Journal of Aging and Health*.

Smith, E.R., & others (2017). Barriers and enablers of health system adoption of kangaroo care: A systematic review of caregiver perspectives. *BMC Pediatrics, 17*(1), 35.

Smith, J. (2009). Self. In D. Carr (Ed.), *Encyclopedia of the life course and human development*. Boston: Gale Cengage.

Smith, J., & others (2019). Associations between early maternal behaviors and child language at 36 months in a cohort experiencing adversity. *International Journal of Language and Communication Disorders*.

Smith, K.E., Mason, T.B., & Lavender, J.M. (2018). Rumination and eating disorder psychopathology: A meta-analysis. *Clinical Psychology Review, 61*, 9–23.

Smith, K.Z., & others (2018). Child maltreatment and physical victimization: Does heavy drinking mediate the relationship? *Child Maltreatment, 23*, 234–243.

Smith, L., & others (2019). Sexual activity is associated with greater enjoyment in life in older adults. *Sexual Medicine, 7*(1), 11–18.

Smith, L.E., & Howard, K.S. (2008). Continuity of paternal social support and depressive symptoms among new mothers. *Journal of Family Psychology, 22*, 763–773.

Smith, P.K., & Wild, L.G. (2019). Grandparenting. In M.H. Bornstein (Ed.), *Handbook of parenting* (3rd ed.). New York: Routledge.

Smith, R.A., & Davis, S.F. (2016). *The psychologist as detective* (7th ed.). Upper Saddle River, NJ: Prentice Hall.

Smith, R.L., Rose, A.J., & Schwartz-Mette, R.A. (2010). Relational and overt aggression in childhood and adolescence: Clarifying mean-level gender differences and associations with peer acceptance. *Social Development, 19*, 243–269.

Smith, S.G., & others (2018). Social isolation, health literacy, and mortality risk: Findings from the English Longitudinal Study of Aging. *Health Psychology, 37*, 160–169.

Smith, T.B., McCullough, M.E., & Poll, J. (2003). Religiousness and depression: Evidence for a main effect and the moderating influences of stressful life events. *Psychological Bulletin, 129*, 614–636.

Smithson, L., & others (2019, in press). Shorter sleep duration is associated with reduced cognitive development at two years of age. *Sleep Medicine*.

Smock, P.J., & Gupta, S. (2013). Cohabitation in contemporary North America. In A. Booth, A.C. Crouter, & N.S. Landale (Eds.), *Just living together*. New York: Psychology Press.

Smokowski, P.R., Guo, S., Cotter, K.L., Evans, C.B., & Rose, R.A. (2016). Multi-level risk factors and developmental assets associated with aggressive behavior in disadvantaged adolescents. *Aggressive Behavior, 42*, 222–238.

Smokowski, P.R., & others (2017). Family dynamics and aggressive behavior in Latino adolescents. *Cultural Diversity and Ethnic Minority Psychology, 23*, 81–90.

Smoreda, Z., & Licoppe, C. (2000). Gender-specific use of the domestic telephone. *Social Psychology Quarterly, 63*, 238–252.

Smyth, J.M., & others (2018). Everyday stress response targets in the science of behavior change. *Behavior Research and Therapy, 101*, 20–29.

Snarey, J. (1987, June). A question of morality. *Psychology Today*, pp. 6–8.

Sneve, M.H., & others (2019, in press). High-expanding regions of the primate cortical brain evolution support supramodal cognitive flexibility. *Cerebral Cortex*.

Sniecinski, I., & Seghatchian, J. (2018). Artificial intelligence: A joint narrative on potential use in pediatric stem and immune cell therapies and regenerative medicine. *Transfusion and Apheresis Science, 57*, 422–424.

Snow, C.E., Burns, M.S., & Griffin, P. (1998). *Preventing reading difficulties in young children*. Washington, DC: National Academies Press.

Snow, C.E., & Kang, J.Y. (2006). Becoming bilingual, biliterate, and bicultural. In W. Damon & R. Lerner (Eds.), *Handbook of child psychology* (6th ed.). New York: Wiley.

Snowdon, D.A. (1997). Aging and Alzheimer's disease: Lessons from the nun study. *Gerontologist, 37*, 150–156.

Snowdon, D.A. (2002). *Aging with grace: What the Nun Study teaches us about leading longer, healthier, and more meaningful lives*. New York: Bantam.

Snowdon, D.A. (2003). Healthy aging and dementia: Findings from the Nun Study. *Annals of Internal Medicine, 139*, 450–454.

Snowdon, J., & others (2018). A longitudinal comparison of age patterns and rates of suicide in Hong Kong, Taiwan, and Japan and two Western countries. *Asian Journal of Psychiatry, 31*, 15–20.

Snyder, J.S. (2019, in press). Recalibrating the relevance of adult neurogenesis. *Trends in Neuroscience*.

Snyder, K.A., & Torrence, C.M. (2008). Habituation and novelty. In M.M. Haith & J.B. Benson (Eds.), *Encyclopedia of infant and early childhood development*. Oxford, UK: Elsevier.

Snyder, W. (2016). Compound word formation. In J. Lidz, W. Snyder, & J. Pater (Eds.), *Oxford handbook of developmental linguistics*. New York: Oxford University Press.

Sobowale, K., & others (2018). Personality traits are associated with academic achievement in medical school: A nationally representative study. *Academic Psychiatry, 42*, 338–345.

Society for Adolescent Health and Medicine (2017). Improving knowledge about, access to, and utilization of long-acting reversible contraception among adolescents and young adults. *Journal of Adolescent Health, 60*, 472–474.

Sodian, B., & others (2016). Understanding of goals, beliefs, and desires predicts morally relevant theory of mind: A longitudinal investigation. *Child Development, 87*, 1221–1232.

Soenens, B., Vansteenkiste, M., & Beyers, W. (2019). Parenting adolescents. In M.H. Bornstein (Ed.), *Handbook of parenting* (3rd ed.). New York: Routledge.

Sokol, B.W., Snjezana, H., & Muller, U. (2010). Social understanding and self-regulation: From perspective-taking to theory of mind. In B. Sokol, U. Muller, J. Carpendale, A. Young, & G. Iarocci (Eds.), *Self- and social cognition.* New York: Oxford University Press.

Sokol, R.L., Qin, B., & Poti, J.M. (2017). Parenting styles and body mass index: A systematic review of prospective studies among children. *Obesity Reviews, 18,* 281-292.

Solomon, B.C., & Jackson, J.J. (2014). Why do personality traits predict divorce? Multiple pathways through satisfaction. *Journal of Personality and Social Psychology, 106,* 978-996.

Solomon, D., Watson, P., & Battistich, V.A. (2002). Teaching and school effects on moral/prosocial development. In V. Richardson (Ed.), *Handbook for research on teaching.* Washington, DC: American Educational Research Association.

Solomon, D., Watson, P., Schapes, E., Battistich, V., & Solomon, J. (1990). Cooperative learning as part of a comprehensive program designed to promote prosocial development. In S. Sharan (Ed.), *Cooperative learning.* New York: Praeger.

Solomon, E., & others (2019). *Biology* (11th ed.). Boston: Cengage.

Solomon-Moore, E., & others (2018). Roles of mothers and fathers in supporting child physical activity: A cross-sectional mixed-methods study. *BMJ Open, 8*(1), e019732.

Soloski, K.L., Kale Monk, J., & Durtschi, J.A. (2016). Trajectories of early binge drinking: A function of family cohesion and peer use. *Journal of Marital and Family Therapy, 42,* 76-90.

Solovieva, Y., & Quintanar, L. (2017). Play with social roles as a method for psychological development in young children. In T. Bruce & others (Eds.), *Routledge international handbook of early childhood play.* New York: Routledge.

Somerville, L.H. (2018). Emotional development in adolescence. In L.F. Barrett & others (Eds.), *Handbook of emotion* (4th ed.). New York: Guilford.

Someya, S., & others (2017). Effects of calorie restriction on the lifespan and healthspan of POLG mitochondrial mutator mice. *PLoS One, 12*(2), e0171159.

Sommer, T.E., Sabol, T.J., Chase-Lansdale, P.L., & Brooks-Gunn, J. (2016). Two-generation education programs for parents and children. In S. Jones & N. Lesaux (Eds.), *The leading edge of early childhood education.* Cambridge, MA: Harvard Education Press.

Son, J.M., & Lee, C. (2019). Mitochondria: Multifaceted regulators of aging. *BMB Reports, 52,* 13-23.

Soneji, S., & others (2017). E-cigarette use and subsequent cigarette smoking among adolescents and young adults: A systematic review and meta-analysis. *JAMA Pediatrics, 171,* 788-797.

Song, L.J., & others (2010). The differential effects of general mental ability and emotional intelligence on academic performance and social interactions. *Intelligence, 38,* 137-143.

Song, M. (2019). Learning from your children: Multiracial parents' identifications and reflections on their own racial socialization. *Emerging Adulthood, 7,* 119-127.

Song, P., & others (2018). Prevalence and correlates of metabolic syndrome in Chinese children: The China Health and Nutrition Survey. *Nutrients, 9,* 79.

Song, Y., & others (2018, in press). T-cell immunoglobulin and ITIMdomain contributes to CD8+ T-cell immunosenescence. *Aging Cell.*

Sophian, C. (1985). Perseveration and infants' search: A comparison of two- and three-location tasks. *Developmental Psychology, 21,* 187-194.

Sosa, G.W., & Lagana, L. (2019). The effects of video game training on the cognitive functioning of older adults: A community-based randomized controlled trial. *Archives of Gerontology and Geriatrics, 80,* 20-30.

Soto, C.J. (2015). Is happiness good for your personality? Concurrent and prospective relations of the Big Five with subjective well-being. *Journal of Personality, 83,* 45-55.

Soto, C.J., John, O.P., Gosling, S.D., & Potter, J. (2011). Age differences in personality traits from 10 to 65: Big Five domains and facets in a large cross-sectional sample. *Journal of Personality and Social Psychology, 100,* 333-348.

Sourander, A., & others (2019, in press). Prenatal cotinine levels and ADHD among offspring. *Pediatrics.*

Sousa, S.S., Amaro Jr., E., Crego, A., Goncalves, O.F., & Sampaio, A. (2018, in press). Developmental trajectory of the prefrontal cortex: A systematic review of diffusion tensor imaging studies. *Brain Imaging and Behavior, 12,* 1197-1210.

Spairani, S., & others (2018). The mother-child relationship during the first months of life: Preliminary considerations in preterm as compared with term mother-infant dyads. *American Journal of Perinatology, 35,* 578-582.

Spandel, V. (2009). *Creating young writers* (3rd ed.). Boston: Allyn & Bacon.

Spangler, G., Johann, M., Ronai, Z., & Zimmermann, P. (2009). Genetic and environmental influence on attachment disorganization. *Journal of Child Psychology and Psychiatry, 50,* 952-961.

Specht, J., Egloff, B., & Schukle, S.C. (2011). Stability and change of personality across the life course: The impact of age and major life events on mean-level and rank-order stability of the Big Five. *Journal of Personality and Social Psychology, 101,* 862-882.

Spelke, E.S. (1979). Perceiving bimodally specified events in infancy. *Developmental Psychology, 5,* 626-636.

Spelke, E.S. (1991). Physical knowledge in infancy. Reflections on Piaget's theory. In S. Carey & R. Gelman (Eds.), *The epigenesis of mind: Essays on biology and cognition.* Hillsdale, NJ: Erlbaum.

Spelke, E.S. (2000). Core knowledge. *American Psychologist, 55,* 1233-1243.

Spelke, E.S. (2003). Developing knowledge of space: Core systems and new combinations. In S.M. Kosslyn & A. Galaburda (Eds.), *Languages of the brain.* Cambridge, MA: Harvard University Press.

Spelke, E.S. (2011). Natural number and natural geometry. In E. Brannon & S. Dehaene (Eds.), *Space, time, and number in the brain.* New York: Oxford University Press.

Spelke, E.S. (2016a). Core knowledge and conceptual change: A perspective on social cognition. In D. Barner & A.S. Baron (Eds.), *Core knowledge and conceptual change.* New York: Oxford University Press.

Spelke, E.S. (2016b). Cognitive abilities of infants. In R.J. Sternberg, S.T. Fiske, & J. Foss (Eds.), *Scientists making a difference.* New York: Cambridge University Press.

Spelke, E.S. (2017). Core knowledge. Language and number. *Language learning and development, 132,* 147-170.

Spelke, E.S., Breinlinger, K., Macomber, J., & Jacobson, K. (1992). Origins of knowledge. *Psychological Review, 99,* 605-632.

Spelke, E.S., & Hespos. S.J. (2001). Continuity, competence, and the object concept. In E. Dupoux (Ed.), *Language, brain, and behavior.* Cambridge, MA: Bradford/MIT Press.

Spelke, E.S., & Owsley, C.J. (1979). Intermodal exploration and knowledge in infancy. *Infant Behavior and Development, 2,* 13-28.

Spence, A.P. (1989). *Biology of human aging.* Englewood Cliffs, NJ: Prentice Hall.

Spence, J.T., & Helmreich, R. (1978). *Masculinity and femininity: Their psychological dimensions.* Austin: University of Texas Press.

Spence, R., Jacobs, C., & Bifulco, A. (2019, in press). Attachment style, loneliness, and depression in older women. *Aging and Mental Health.*

Spencer, D., & others (2017). Prenatal androgen exposure and children's aggressive behavior and activity level. *Hormones and Behavior, 96,* 156-165.

Spencer, S., & others (2017). Contribution of spoken language and socio-economic background to adolescents' educational achievement at age 16 years. *International Journal of Language and Communication Disorders, 52,* 184-196.

Sperling, R. (2017). Disambiguating preclinical Alzheimer's disease from cognitive aging. In R. Cabeza, L. Nyberg, & D.C. Park (Eds.), *Cognitive neuroscience of aging* (2nd ed.). New York: Oxford University Press.

Spilman, S.K., Neppl, T.K., Donnellan, M.B., Schofield, T.J., & Conger, R.D. (2013). Incorporating religiosity into a developmental model of positive family functioning across generations. *Developmental Psychology, 49*(4), 762-774.

Spinrad, T.L., & Eisenberg, N. (2020, in press). Socialization of moral emotions and behavior. In D.J. Laible & others (Eds.), *Oxford handbook of parenting and moral development.* New York: Oxford University Press.

Spinrad, T.L., & Gal, D.E. (2018). Fostering prosocial behavior and empathy in young children. *Current Opinion in Psychology, 20,* 40-44.

Sprecher, S., Treger, S., & Sakaluk, J.K. (2013). Premarital sexual standards and sociosexuality: Gender, ethnicity, and cohort differences. *Archives of Sexual Behavior, 42,* 1395-1405.

Sprei, J.E., & Courtois, C.A. (1988). The treatment of women's sexual dysfunctions arising from sexual assault. In R.A. Brown & J.R. Fields (Eds.), *Treatment of sexual problems in individual and group therapy.* Great Neck, NY: PMA.

Spruyt, K., & others (2019). Mind-wandering, or the allocation of attentional resources, is sleep-driven across childhood. *Scientific Reports, 9*(1), 1269.

Squarzoni, P., & others (2018). Reduced grey matter volume of the thalamus and hippocampal region in elderly healthy adults with no impact of APOE 4: A longitudinal voxel-based morphometry study. *Journal of Alzheimer's Disease, 62,* 757-771.

Srivastava, S., & Veech, R.L. (2019). Brown and brite: The fat soldiers in the anti-obesity fight. *Frontiers in Physiology, 10,* 38.

Sroufe, L.A. (2000, Spring). The inside scoop on child development: Interview. *Cutting through the hype*. Minneapolis: College of Education and Human Development, University of Minnesota.

Sroufe, L.A. (2016). The place of attachment in development. In J. Cassidy & P.R. Shaver (Eds.), *Handbook of attachment* (3rd ed.). New York: Guilford.

Sroufe, L.A., Coffino, B., & Carlson, E.A. (2010). Conceptualizing the role of early experience: Lessons from the Minnesota longitudinal study. *Developmental Review, 30,* 36-51.

Sroufe, L.A., Egeland, B., Carlson, E., & Collins, W.A. (2005). The place of early attachment in developmental context. In K.E. Grossman, K. Grossman, & E. Waters (Eds.), *The power of attachment research.* New York: Guilford.

St. Jacques, P.L., & others (2018). Remembering and imagining alternative versions of the personal past. *Neuropsychologia, 110,* 170-179.

Stadelmann, S., & others (2017). Self-esteem in 8-14-year-old children with psychiatric disorders: Disorder- and gender-specific effects. *Child Psychiatry and Human Development, 48,* 40-52.

Staff, J., Messersmith, E.E., & Schulenberg, J.E. (2009). Adolescents and the world of work. In R.M. Lerner & L. Steinberg (Eds.), *Handbook of adolescent psychology* (3rd ed.). New York: Wiley.

Stafford, A.C., Alswayan, M.S., & Tenni, P.C. (2010). Inappropriate prescribing in older residents of Australian care homes. *Journal of Clinical Pharmacy and Therapeutics, 36,* 33-44.

Stamou, G., Garcia-Palacios, A., & Botella, C. (2018). Cognitive-behavioral therapy and interpersonal psychotherapy for the treatment of post-natal depression: A narrative review. *BMC Psychology, 6*(1), 28.

Stancil, S.L., & others (2019, in press). Contraceptive provision to adolescent females prescribed teratogenic medicines. *Pediatrics.*

Stanford Center for Longevity (2011). *Experts' consensus on brain health.* Retrieved April 30, 2011, from http://longevity.stanford.edu/my mind/cognitiveagingstatement

Stanford Center for Longevity and Max Planck Institute for Human Development (2014). *A consensus on the brain training industry from the scientific community.* Retrieved September 16, 2015, from http://longevity3.stanford.edu.blog/2014/10/15

Stanley, S.M., Amato, P.R., Johnson, C.A., & Markman, H.J. (2006). Premarital education, marital quality, and marital stability: Findings from a large, household survey. *Journal of Family Psychology, 20,* 117-126.

Stanley, S.M., Rhoades, G.K., Amato, P.R., Markman, H.J., & Johnson, C.A. (2010). The timing of cohabitation and engagement: Impact on first and second marriages. *Journal of Marriage and the Family, 72,* 906-918.

Stanovich, K.E. (2019). *How to think straight about psychology* (11th ed.). Upper Saddle River, NJ: Pearson.

Stansfield, S.A., & others (2017). Childhood adversity and midlife suicidal ideation. *Psychological Medicine, 47,* 327-340.

Starr, C., & others (2019). *Biology* (15th ed.). Boston: Cengage.

Starr, L.R., & others (2012). Love hurts (in more ways than one): Specificity of psychological symptoms as predictors and consequences of romantic activity among early adolescent girls. *Journal of Clinical Psychology, 68,* 403-420.

statisticbrain (2017). *Online dating statistics.* Retrieved November 4, 2017, from www.statisticbrain.com/online-dating-statistics

Staudinger, U.M. (1996). Psychologische produktivitat and delbstenfaltung im alter. In M.M. Baltes & L. Montada (Eds.), *Produktives leben im alter.* Frankfurt: Campus.

Staudinger, U.M., & Jacobs, C.B. (2010). Life-span perspectives on positive personality development in adulthood and old age. In R.M. Lerner, W.F. Overton, A.M. Freund, & M.E. Lamb (Eds.), *Handbook of life-span development.* New York: Wiley.

Stavans, M., & Baillargeon, R. (2018). Four-month-old infants individuate and track simple tools following functional demonstrations. *Developmental Science, 21,* e12500.

Stavans, M., & others (2019). Catastrophic individuation failures in infancy: A new model and predictions. *Psychological Review, 126,* 196-225.

Stawski, R.S., Sliwinski, M.J., & Hofer, S.M. (2013). Between-person and within-person associations among processing speed, attention switching, and working memory in younger and older adults. *Experimental Aging Research, 39,* 194-214.

Steca, P., Bassi, M., Caprara, G.V., & Fave, A.D. (2011). Parents' self-efficacy beliefs and their children's psychosocial adaptation during adolescence. *Journal of Youth and Adolescence, 40*(3), 320-331.

Steck, N., & others (2013). Euthanasia and assisted suicide in selected European countries and U.S. states: Systematic literature review. *Medical Care, 51,* 938-944.

Steckler, C.M., & Hamlin, J.K. (2016). Theories of moral development. In H. Miller (Ed.), *Encyclopedia of theory in psychology.* Thousand Oaks, CA: Sage.

Steele, H., & Steele, J. (Eds.) (2019). *Handbook of attachment-based interventions.* New York: Guilford.

Steele, J., Waters, E., Crowell, J., & Treboux, D. (1998, June). *Self-report measures of attachment: Secure bonds to other attachment measures and attachment theory.* Paper presented at the meeting of the International Society for the Study of Personal Relationships, Saratoga Springs, NY.

Steele, L.G., & Lynch, S.M. (2013). The pursuit of happiness in China: Individualism, collectivism, and subjective well-being during China's economic and social transformation. *Social Indicators Research, 114*(2).

Steffener, J., Barulli, D., Habeck, C., & Stern, Y. (2014). Neuroimaging explanations of age-related differences in task performance. *Frontiers in Aging Neuroscience, 6,* 46.

Steiger, A.E., Allemand, M., Robins, R.W., & Fend, H.A. (2014). Low and decreasing self-esteem during adolescence predict adult depression two decades later. *Journal of Personality and Social Psychology, 106,* 325-338.

Steiger, H., & others (2019, in press). A longitudinal, epigenome-wide study of DNA methylation in anorexia nervosa: Results in actively ill, partially weight-restored, long-term remitted, and non-eating-disordered women. *Journal of Psychiatry and Neuroscience.*

Stein, M., & others (2018). *Direct instruction mathematics* (5th ed.). Upper Saddle River, NJ: Pearson.

Steinbach, A. (2019, in press). Children's and parents' well-being in joint physical custody: A literature review. *Family Process.*

Steinberg, L., & others (2018). Around the world, adolescence is a time of heightened sensation seeking and immature self-regulation. *Developmental Science, 21.* doi:10.1111/desc.12532

Steinberg, S. (2011, June 11). New dating site helps college students find love. *CNN Living.* Retrieved February 27, 2013, from www.cnn.com/2011/LIVING/06/22date.my.school/index.html

Steiner, J.E. (1979). Human facial expression in response to taste and smell stimulation. In H. Reese & L. Lipsitt (Eds.), *Advances in child development and behavior* (Vol. 13). New York: Academic Press.

Steinmayr, R., Weidinger,A.F., & Wigfield, A. (2018). Does students' grit predict their school achievement above and beyond their personality, motivation, and engagement? *Contemporary Educational Psychology, 53,* 106-122.

Stenberg, G. (2017). Does contingency in adults' responding influence 12-month-old infants' social referencing? *Infant Behavior and Development, 46,* 67-79.

Stenholm, S., & others (2014). Age-related trajectories of physical functioning in work and retirement: The role of sociodemographic factors, lifestyles, and disease. *Journal of Epidemiology and Community Health, 68,* 503-509.

Stenholm, S., & others (2017). Body mass indicator as a predictor of healthy and disease-free life expectancy between ages 50 and 75: A multicohort study. *International Journal of Obesity, 41,* 769-775.

Stensvehagen, M.T., & others (2019, in press). How women experience and cope with daily hassles after sexual abuse—a retrospective qualitative study. *Scandinavian Journal of Caring Science.*

Stepaniak, U., & others (2016). Antioxidant vitamin intake and mortality in three Central and Eastern European urban populations: The HAPIEE study. *European Journal of Nutrition, 55,* 547-560.

Stephan, Y., & others (2018). Higher IQ in adolescence is related to a younger subjective age in later life: Findings from the Wisconsin Longitudinal Study. *Intelligence, 69,* 195-199.

Stephens, F.B., & Tsintzas, K. (2018). Metabolic and molecular changes associated with the increased skeletal muscle insulin action 24-48 h after exercise in young and old humans. *Biochemical Society Transactions, 467,* 111-118.

Stephens, J.M. (2008). Cheating. In N.J. Salkind (Ed.), *Encyclopedia of educational psychology.* Thousand Oaks, CA: Sage.

Stepler, R. (2017). *Led by baby boomers, divorce rates climb for America's 50+ population.* Washington, DC: Pew Research Center.

Steptoe, A., Deaton, A., & Stone, A.A. (2015). Subjective well being, health, and aging. *Lancet, 385,* 640-648.

Steptoe, A., & others (2017). The longitudinal relationship between cortisol responses to mental stress and leukocyte telomere attrition. *Journal of Clinical Endocrinology and Metabolism, 102,* 962-969.

Steric, M., & others (2015). The outcome and course of pregnancies complicated with fetal neural tube defects. *Clinical and Experimental Obstetrics and Gynecology, 42,* 57-61.

Stern, W. (1912). The psychological methods of testing intelligence. *Educational Psychology Monographs* (No. 13).

Sternberg, R.J. (1986). *Intelligence applied.* San Diego. Harcourt Brace Jovanovich.

Sternberg, R.J. (1988). *The triangle of love.* New York: Basic Books.

Sternberg, R.J. (2003). Contemporary theories of intelligence. In I.B. Weiner (Ed.), *Handbook of psychology* (Vol. 7). New York: Wiley.

Sternberg, R.J. (2004). Individual differences in cognitive development. In U. Goswami (Ed.), *Blackwell handbook of childhood cognitive development.* Malden, MA: Blackwell.

Sternberg, R.J. (2010). Componential models of creativity. In M. Runco & S. Spritzker (Eds.), *Encyclopedia of creativity.* New York: Elsevier.

Sternberg, R.J. (2013). Searching for love. *The psychologist, 26*(Part 2), 98-101.

Sternberg, R.J. (2014). Teaching about the nature of intelligence. *Intelligence, 42,* 176-179.

Sternberg, R.J. (2016). What does it mean to be intelligent? In R.J. Sternberg & others (Eds.), *Scientists making a difference.* New York: Cambridge University Press.

Sternberg, R.J. (2017). Intelligence and competence in theory and practice. In A.J. Elliot & C.S. Dweck (Eds.), *Handbook of competence and motivation* (2nd ed.). New York: Guilford.

Sternberg, R.J. (2018a). Successful theory in theory, research, and practice. In R.J. Sternberg (Ed.), *The nature of intelligence.* New York: Cambridge University Press.

Sternberg, R.J. (2018b). The triangle of intelligence. In R.J. Sternberg & J.C. Kaufman (Eds.), *The nature of human creativity.* New York: Cambridge University Press.

Sternberg, R.J. (2018c). Triarchic theory of intelligence. In B. Frey (Eds.), *SAGE encyclopedia of educational research, measurement, and evaluation.* Thousand Oaks, CA: Sage.

Sternberg, R.J. (2018d). Wisdom. In S.J. Lopez (Ed.), *Encyclopedia of positive psychology* (2nd ed.). New York: Wiley.

Sternberg, R.J. (2018e). 21 ideas: A 42-year search to understand the nature of giftedness. *Roeper Review, 40,* 7-20.

Sternberg, R.J. (2018f). The psychology of creativity. In S. Nalbantian & P.M. Matthews (Eds.), *Secrets of creativity.* New York: Oxford University Press.

Sternberg, R.J. (2018g). The triangle of creativity. In R.J. Sternberg & J.C. Kaufman (Eds.), *The nature of human creativity.* New York: Cambridge University Press.

Sternberg, R.J. (2019a). Intelligence. In R.J. Sternberg & W.E. Pickren (Eds.), *Cambridge handbook of the intellectual history of psychology.* New York: Cambridge University Press.

Sternberg, R.J. (2019b). Race to Samarra: The critical importance of wisdom. In R.J. Sternberg & J. Gluck (Eds.), *Cambridge handbook of wisdom.* New York: Cambridge University Press.

Sternberg, R.J. (2019c). Enhancing people's creativity. In J.C. Kaufman, & R.J. Sternberg (Eds.),

Cambridge handbook of creativity (2nd ed.). New York: Cambridge University Press.

Sternberg, R.J. (2020a, in press). What is intelligence and what are the big questions about it? In R.J. Sternberg (Ed.), *Human intelligence.* New York: Cambridge University Press.

Sternberg, R.J. (2020b, in press). Approaches to understanding intelligence. In R.J. Sternberg (Ed.), *Human intelligence.* New York: Cambridge University Press.

Sternberg, R.J. (2020c, in press). Early history of theory and research on intelligence. In R.J. Sternberg (Ed.), *Human intelligence.* New York: Cambridge University Press.

Sternberg, R.J. (2020d, in press). Cultural approaches to intelligence. In R.J. Sternberg (Ed.), *Human intelligence.* New York: Cambridge University Press.

Sternberg, R.J. (2020e, in press). Reflections on love. In R. Hanley (Ed.), *Love: A history.* New York: Oxford University Press.

Sternberg, R.J. (2020f, in press). The ups and downs of love—what makes love go well, or badly? In A. Kostic & D. Chadee (Eds.), *Current research in positive psychology.* London, UK: Palgrave-Macmillan.

Sternberg, R.J. (2020g, in press). When love goes awry (Part 1): Applications of the duplex theory of love and its development to relationships gone bad. In R.J. Sternberg & K. Sternberg (Eds.), *The new psychology of love* (2nd ed.). New York: Cambridge University Press.

Sternberg, R.J., & Glueck, J. (Eds.) (2019). *Cambridge handbook of wisdom.* New York: Cambridge University Press.

Sternberg, R.J., & Hagen, E. (2018). Wisdom. In M.H. Bornstein (Ed), *SAGE encyclopedia of lifespan human development.* Thousand Oaks, CA: Sage.

Sternberg, R.J., & Kaufman, J.C. (2018a). *The nature of human creativity.* New York: Cambridge University Press.

Sternberg, R.J., & Kaufman, J.C. (2018b). Theories and conceptions of giftedness. In S. Pfeiffer (Ed.), *Handbook of giftedness in children* (2nd ed.). New York: Springer.

Sternberg, R.J., Kaufman, J.C., & Roberts, A.M. (2019). The relation of creativity to intelligence and wisdom. In J.C. Kaufman & R.J. Sternberg (Eds.), *Cambridge handbook of creativity* (2nd ed.). New York: Cambridge University Press.

Sternberg, R.J., & Sternberg, K. (2017). *Cognitive psychology* (7th ed.). Boston: Cengage.

Sternberg, R.J., & Sternberg, K. (Eds.) (2020, in press). *The new psychology of love* (2nd ed.). New York: Cambridge University Press.

Sternberg, R.J., & others (2001). The relationship between academic and practical intelligence: A case study in Kenya. *Intelligence, 29,* 401-418.

Sterns, H.L., & Huyck, H. (2001). The role of work in midlife. In M.E. Lachman (Ed.), *Handbook of midlife development.* New York: John Wiley.

Stessman, J., & others (2014). Loneliness, health, and longevity. *Journals of Gerontology B: Psychological Sciences and Social Sciences, 69,* 744-750.

Stevens, C., & Bavelier, D. (2012). The role of selective attention on academic foundations: A cognitive neuroscience perspective. *Developmental Cognitive Neuroscience, 15*(Suppl. 1), S30-S48.

Stevens, M., & N'zi, A. (2018). Parent-child interaction therapy. In C.H. Zeanah (Ed.), *Handbook of infant mental health* (4th ed.). New York; Guilford.

Stevenson, H.W. (1995). Mathematics achievement of American students: First in the world by the year 2000? In C.A. Nelson (Ed.), *Basic and applied perspectives on learning, cognition, and development.* Minneapolis: University of Minnesota Press.

Stevenson, H.W. (2000). Middle childhood: Education and schooling. In A. Kazdin (Ed.), *Encyclopedia of psychology.* Washington, DC, & New York: American Psychological Association and Oxford University Press.

Stevenson, H.W., & others (1990). Contexts of achievement. *Monographs of the Society for Research in Child Development, 55*(Serial No. 221).

Stevenson, H.W., & Zusho, A. (2002). Adolescence in China and Japan: Adapting to a changing environment. In B.B. Brown, R.W. Larson, & T.S. Saraswathi (Eds.), *The world's youth.* New York: Cambridge University Press.

Stevenson, H.W., Hofer, B.K., & Randel, B. (1999). *Middle childhood: Education and schooling.* Unpublished manuscript, Department of Psychology, University of Michigan, Ann Arbor.

Stevenson, H.W., Lee, S., & Stigler, J.W. (1986). Mathematics achievement of Chinese, Japanese, and American children. *Science, 231,* 693-699.

Stewart, A.J., & Deaux, K. (2019). Personality and social contexts as sources of change and continuity across the life span. In K. Deaux & M. Snyder (Eds.), *Oxford handbook of personality and social psychology.* New York: Oxford University Press.

Stewart, A.J., Ostrove, J.M., & Helson, R. (2001). Middle aging in women: Patterns of personality change from the 30s to the 50s. *Journal of Adult Development, 8,* 23-37.

Stewart, D.E., & Vigod, S.N. (2019). Postpartum depression: Pathophysiology, treatment, and emerging therapeutics. *Annual Review of Medicine, 70,* 183-196.

Stewart, J.G., & others (2017). Cognitive control deficits differentiate adolescent suicide ideators from attempters. *Journal of Clinical Psychology, 78,* e614-e621.

Stewart, J.G., & others (2019, in press). Life stress and suicide in adolescents. *Journal of Abnormal Child Psychology.*

Stewart, S.F., Frost, D.M., & LeBlanc, A.J. (2019). Understanding how emerging same-sex couples make meaning of minority stress: A narrative approach. *Journal of Family Psychology, 33,* 183-193.

Stiel, S., & others (2018). Palliative sedation in Germany: Factors and treatment practices associated with different sedation rate estimates in palliative and hospice care services. *BMC Palliative Care, 17*(1), 48.

Stifter, C., & Dollar, J. (2016). Temperament and developmental psychopathology. In D. Cicchetti (Ed.), *Developmental psychology* (3rd ed.). New York: Wiley.

Stipek, D.J. (2002). *Motivation to learn* (4th ed.). Boston: Allyn & Bacon.

Stipek, D.J. (2005, February 16). Commentary in *USA Today,* p. 1D.

Stoel-Gammon, C., & Sosa, A.V. (2010). Phonological development. In E. Hoff & M. Shatz (Eds.), *Blackwell handbook of language development* (2nd ed.). New York: Wiley.

Stokes, C.E., & Raley, R.K. (2009). Cohabitation. In D. Carr (Ed.), *Encyclopedia of the life course and human development.* Boston: Gale Cengage.

Stolove, C.A., Galatzer-Levy, I.R., & Bonanno, G.A. (2017). Emergence of depression following job loss prospectively predicts lower rates of reemployment. *Psychiatry Research, 253,* 79-83.

Stolzenberg, E.B., & others (2019). *The American freshman: National norms fall 2017.* Los Angeles: Higher Education Research Insitute, UCLA.

Stone, A.A., Schwartz, J.E., Broderick, J.E., & Deaton, A. (2010). A snapshot of the age distribution of psychological well-being in the United States. *Proceedings of the National Academy of Sciences USA, 107,* 9985-9990.

Stone, L.K., Smith, L.B., & Yu, C. (2019, in press). Self-generated variability in object images predicts vocabulary growth. *Developmental Science.*

Stoppa, T.M., & Lefkowitz, E.S. (2010). Longitudinal changes in religiosity among emerging adult college students. *Journal of Research on Adolescence, 20,* 23-38.

Stopyra, M.A., & others (2019). Altered functional connectivity in binge eating disorder and bulimia nervosa: A resting-state MRI study. *Brain and Behavior, 9*(2), e-01207.

Stouthamer-Loeber, M., Loeber, R., Wei, E., Farrington, D.P., & Wikstrom, P.H. (2002). Risk and promotive effects in the explanation of persistent serious delinquency in boys. *Journal of Consulting and Clinical Psychology, 70,* 111-123.

Stouthamer-Loeber, M., Wei, E., Loeber, R., & Masten, A. (2004). Desistance from serious delinquency in the transition to adulthood. *Development and Psychopathology, 16,* 897-918.

Strandberg, T.E. (2019). Preventive effects of physical activity in older people. In R. Fernandez-Ballesteros, A. Benetos, & J-M. Robine (Eds.), *Cambridge handbook of successful aging.* New York: Cambridge University Press.

Strassberg. D.S., Cann, D., & Velarde, V. (2017). Sexting by high school students. *Archives of Sexual Behavior, 46,* 1667-1672.

Strathearn, L. (2007). Exploring the neurobiology of attachment. In L.C. Mayes, P. Fonagy, & M. Target (Eds.), *Developmental science and psychoanalysis.* London: Karnac Press.

Strathearn, L. (2011). Maternal neglect: Oxytocin, dopamine, and the neurobiology of attachment. *Journal of Neuroendocrinology, 23,* 1054-1065.

Streib, H. (1999). Off-road religion? A narrative approach to fundamentalist and occult orientations of adolescents. *Journal of Adolescence, 22,* 255-267.

Streit, C., & others (2018). Family relationships and prosocial behavior in U.S. Mexican youth: The mediating effect of cultural processes. *Journal of Family Issues, 39,* 1056-1064.

Strickhouser, J.E., Zell, E., & Krizan, Z. (2017). Does personality predict health and well-being? A metasynthesis. *Health Psychology, 36,* 797-810.

Striegel-Moore, R.H., & Bulik, C.M. (2007). Risk factors for eating disorders. *American Psychologist, 62,* 181-198.

Stroebe, M., & Schut, H. (2017). The dual process model of coping with bereavement—rationale and description. In M. Barkam & others (Eds.), *Clinical Psychology II–Treatments and interventions.* Thousand Oaks, CA: Sage.

Stroebe, M., Schut, H., & Boerner, K. (2017). Models of coping with bereavement—an updated overview. *Journal of Studies in Psychology, 38,* 582-607.

Strohmeier, D., & Noam, G.G. (2012). Bullying in schools: What is the problem and how can educators solve it? *New Directions in Youth Development, 133,* 7-13.

Strohminger, N. (2018). Identity is essentially moral. In K. Gray & J. Graham (Eds.), *Atlas of moral psychology.* New York: Guilford.

Stroope, S., McFarland, M.J., & Uecker, J.E. (2015). Marital characteristics and the sexual relationships of U.S. older adults: An analysis of national social life, health, and aging project data. *Archives of Sexual Behavior, 44,* 233-247.

Strough, J., Leszczynski, J.P., Neely, T.L., Flinn, J.A., & Margrett, J. (2007). From adolescence to later adulthood: Femininity, masculinity and androgyny in six age groups. *Sex Roles, 57,* 385-396.

Stubbs, B., Brefka, S., & Denkinger, M.D. (2015). What works to prevent falls in community-dwelling older adults? An umbrella review of meta-analyses of randomized controlled trials. *Physical Therapy, 95,* 1095-1110.

Stuebe, A.M., & Schwartz, E.G. (2010). The risks and benefits of infant feeding practices for women and their children. *Journal of Perinatology, 30,* 155-162.

Stumper, A., & others (2017). Parents' behavioral inhibition moderates association between preschoolers' BI with risk for age 9 anxiety disorders. *Journal of Affective Disorders, 210,* 35-42.

Sturge-Apple, M.L., & others (2019). Parental maltreatment. In M.H. Bornstein (Ed.), *Handbook of parenting* (3rd ed.). New York: Routledge.

Suanet, B., & others (2019, in press). The social support-health link unraveled: Pathways linking social support to functional capacity in later life. *Journal of Aging and Health.*

Suárez-Orozco, C., & Suárez-Orozco, M. (2018). The experience of Latino/a immigrant origin adolescents in the U.S. In J. Bhabha & others (Eds.), *Research handbook on migration and childhood.* Cheltenham, UK: Elgar Publishing.

Suarez-Rivera, C., Smith, L.B., & Yu, C. (2019). Multimodal parent behaviors within joint attention support sustained attention in infants. *Developmental Psychology, 55,* 96-109.

Substance Abuse and Mental Health Services Administration (2005). Substance use tables [online database]. Retrieved November 15, 2005, from http://www.icpsr.umich.edu/

Sugimura, K., & Mizokami, S. (2012). Personal identity in Japan. *New Directions in Child and Adolescent Development, 138,* 123-143.

Sugita, Y. (2004). Experience in early infancy is indispensable for color perception. *Current Biology, 14,* 1267-1271.

Sugiura, M. (2016). Functional neuroimaging of normal aging: Declining brain, adapting brain. *Aging Research Reviews, 30,* 61-72.

Suitor, J.J., Gilligan, M., & Pillemer, K. (2016). Stability, change, and complexity in later life families. In L.K. George & G.E. Ferraro (Eds.), *Handbook of aging and the social sciences* (8th ed.). New York: Elsevier.

Sullivan, A.R., & Fenelon, A. (2014). Patterns of widowhood mortality. *Journals of Gerontology B: Psychological Sciences and Social Sciences, 69B,* 53-62.

Sullivan, H.S. (1953). *The interpersonal theory of psychiatry.* New York: W.W. Norton.

Sullivan, K., & Sullivan, A. (1980). Adolescent-parent separation. *Developmental Psychology, 16,* 93-99.

Sullivan, R., & Wilson, D. (2018). Neurobiology of infant attachment. *Annual Review of Psychology* (Vol. 69). Palo Alto, CA: Annual Reviews.

Sullivan, S.P., & others (2018). "It was supposed to be a one time thing": Experiences of romantic and sexual relationship typologies among young gay, bisexual, and other men who have sex with men. *Archives of Sexual Behavior, 47,* 1221-1230.

Sulmasy, D.P. (2018). Italy's new advance directive law: When in Rome. *JAMA Internal Medicine, 178,* 607-608.

Sulovari, A., & Li, D. (2019, in press). VI power: Simulation-based tool for estimating power of viral integration detection via high-throughput sequencing. *Geonomics.*

Sulpizio, S., & others (2018). Discriminating between mothers' infant- and adult-directed speech: Cross-linguistic generalizability from Japanese to Italian and German. *Neuroscience Research, 133,* 21-27.

Sumaroka, M., & Bornstein, M.H. (2008). Play. In M.M. Haith & J.B. Benson (Eds.), *Encyclopedia of infant and early childhood development.* Oxford, UK: Elsevier.

Summit, A.K., & others (2019). Integration of onsite long-acting reversible contraception services into school-based health centers. *Journal of School Health, 89,* 226-231.

Sumontha, J., Farr, R.H., & Patterson, C.J. (2017). Children's gender development: Associations with parental sexual orientation, division of labor, and gender ideology. *Psychology of Sexual Orientation and Gender Diversity, 4,* 438-445.

Sun, H., & others (2018). Psychoradiologic utility of MR imaging for diagnosis of attention deficit hyperactivity disorder: A radiomics analysis. *Radiology, 287,* 20-30.

Sun, R., & others (2019, in press). Identification of novel loci associated with infant cognitive ability. *Molecular Psychiatry.*

Sundstrom Poromaa, I., & others (2017). Sex differences in depression during pregnancy and the postpartum period. *Journal of Neuroscience Research, 95,* 719-730.

Sung, J.E., & others (2017). Effects of age, working memory, and word order on passive-sentence comprehension: Evidence from a verb-final language. *International Psychogeriatrics, 29,* 939-948.

Suo, C., & others (2016). Therapeutically relevant structural and functional mechanisms triggered by physical and cognitive exercise. *Molecular Psychiatry, 21,* 1633-1642.

Super, C.M., & Harkness, S. (2010). Culture in infancy. In J.G. Bremner & T.D. Wachs (Eds.), *Wiley-Blackwell handbook of infant development* (2nd ed.). New York: Wiley.

Suri, G., & Gross, J.J. (2012). Emotion regulation and successful aging. *Trends in Cognitive Science, 16,* 409-410.

Susman, E.J., & Dorn, L.D. (2013). Puberty: Its role in development. In I.B. Weiner & others (Eds.), *Handbook of psychology* (2nd ed., Vol. 6). New York: Wiley.

Sutin, A.R., Robinson, E., Daly, M., & Terracciano, A. (2016). Parent-reported bullying and child weight gain between 6 and 15. *Child Obesity, 12,* 482-487.

Sveistrup, H., Schneiberg, S., McKinley, P.A., McGadyen, B.J., & Levin, M.F. (2008). Head, arm and trunk coordination during reaching in children. *Experimental Brain Research, 188,* 237-247.

Svensson, Y., Berne, J., & Syed, M. (2018). A narrative approach to the role of others in ethnic identity formation. *Cultural Diversity and Ethnic Minority Psychology, 24,* 187-195.

Sviri, S., & others (2009). Contraindications in end-of-life decisions for self and others, expressed by relatives of chronically ventilated persons. *Journal of Critical Care, 24,* 293-301.

Swaab, D.F., Chung, W.C., Kruijver, F.P., Hofman, M.A., & Ishunina, T.A. (2001). Structural and functional sex differences in the human hypothalamus. *Hormones and Behavior, 40,* 93-98.

Swain, S.O. (1992). Men's friendships with women. In P.M. Nardi (Ed.), *Gender in intimate relationships.* Belmont, CA: Wadsworth.

Swanson, J.L. (2013). Traditional and emerging career development theory and the psychology of working. In D.L. Blustein (Ed.), *Oxford handbook of the psychology of working.* New York: Oxford University Press.

Swartz, T.T., Kim, M., Uno, M., Mortimer, J., & O'Brien, K.B. (2011). Safety nets and scaffolds: Parental support in the transition to adulthood. *Journal of Marriage and the Family, 73,* 414-429.

Sweeeney, L., & Gomez, R.L.(2019). Statistical learning. In S-A. Rueschemeyer & M. Gareth Gaskell (Eds.), *Oxford handbook of psycholinguistics* (2nd ed.). New York: Oxford University Press.

Sweeney, M.D., & others (2019). Vascular dysfunction—the disregarded partner of Alzheimer's disease. *Alzheimer's and Dementia, 15,* 158-167.

Sweeney, M.M. (2009). Remarriage. In D. Carr (Ed.), *Encyclopedia of the life course and human development.* Boston: Gale Cengage.

Sweeney, M.M. (2010). Remarriage and stepfamilies: Strategic sites for family scholarship in the 21st century. *Journal of Marriage and the Family, 72*(3), 667-684.

Swift, A. (2016, June 24). *Euthanasia still acceptable to a majority in the U.S.* Washington, DC: Gallup.

Swing, E.L., Gentile, D.A., Anderson, C.A., & Walsh, D.A. (2010). Television and video game exposure and the development of attention problems. *Pediatrics, 126,* 214-221.

Swingler, M.M., & others (2017). Maternal behavior predicts infant neurophysiological and behavioral attention processes in the first year. *Developmental Psychology, 53,* 13-37.

Swingley, D. (2017). The infant's developmental path in phonological acquisition. *British Journal of Psychology, 108,* 28-30.

Syed, M., Juang, L.P., & Svensson, Y. (2018). Toward a new understanding of ethnic-racial settings for ethnic-racial identity development. *Journal of Research on Adolescence, 28,* 262-276.

Sykes, C.J. (1995). *Dumbing down our kids: Why America's children feel good about themselves but can't read, write, or add.* New York: St. Martin's Press.

Szekanecz, Z., & others (2019). Common mechanisms and holistic care in atherosclerosis and osteoporosis. *Arthritis Research and Therapy, 21*(1), 15.

Szelag, E. (2018). Commentary: Effects of video game training on measures of selective attention and working memory in older adults: Results from a randomized controlled trial. *Frontiers of Aging and Neuroscience, 9,* 442.

Szinovacz, M.E. (2009). Grandparenthood. In D. Carr (Ed.), *Encyclopedia of the life course and human development.* Boston: Gale Cengage.

Szutorisz, H., & Hurd, Y.L. (2018). High times for cannabis: Epigenetic imprint and its legacy on brain and behavior. *Neuroscience and Biobehavioral Reviews, 85,* 93-101.

Szwedo, D.E., Hessel, E.T., & Allen, J.P. (2017). Supportive romantic relationships as predictors of resilience against early adolescent maternal negativity. *Journal of Youth and Adolescence, 46,* 454-465.

T

Taggart, J., Eisen, S., & Lillard, A.S. (2018). Pretense. In M.H. Bornstein (Ed.), *SAGE encyclopedia of lifespan human development.* Thousand Oaks, CA: Sage.

Tahir, L., & Gruber, H.E. (2003). Developmental trajectories and creative work in late life. In J. Demick & C. Andreoletti (Eds.), *Handbook of adult development.* New York: Kluwer.

Taige, N.M., & others (2007). Antenatal maternal stress and long-term effects on child neurodevelopment: How and why? *Journal of Child Psychology and Psychiatry, 48,* 245-261.

Takahashi, M. (2019, in press). Sociomedical problems of overwork-related deaths and disorders in Japan. *Journal of Occupational Health.*

Takei, Y. (2019, in press). Age-dependent decline in neurogenesis of the hippocampus and extracellular nucleotides. *Human Cell.*

Taler, S.J. (2009). Hypertensions in women. *Current Hypertensions Reports, 11,* 23-28.

Talib, M.A., & Abdollahi, A. (2017). Spirituality moderates hopelessness, depression, and suicidal behavior among Malaysian adolescents. *Journal of Religion and Health, 56,* 784-795.

Tamai, K., & others (2018). Fetal ultrasonographic findings including cerebral hyperchogenicity in a patient with non-lethal form of Raine syndrome. *American Journal of Medical Genetics A, 176,* 682-686.

Tamana, S.K., & others (2019). Screen-time is associated with inattention problems in preschoolers: Results from the CHILD birth cohort study. *PLoS, 14*(4), e0213995.

Tamers, S.L., & others (2014). The impact of stressful life events on excessive alcohol consumption in the French population: Findings from the GAZEL cohort study. *PLoS One, 9*(1), e87653.

Tamis-LeMonda, C.S., Kuchirko, Y., & Song, L. (2014). Why is infant language learning facilitated by parental responsiveness? *Current Directions in Psychological Science, 23,* 121-126.

Tamis-LeMonda, C.S., & others (2008). Parents' goals for children: The dynamic coexistence of individualism and collectivism in cultures and individuals. *Social Development, 17,* 183-209.

Tan, B.W., Pooley, J.A., & Speelman, C.P. (2016). A meta-analytic review of the efficacy of physical exercise interventions on cognition in individuals with autism spectrum disorder and ADHD. *Journal of Autism and Developmental Disorders, 46,* 3126-3143.

Tan, E.J., Xue, Q.L., Li, T., Carlson, M.C., & Fried, L.P. (2007). Volunteering: A physical activity intervention for older adults—The Experience Corps program in Baltimore. *Journal of Urban Health, 83,* 954-969.

Tan, M., & Grigorenko, E.L. (2020, in press). Genetics/genomics and intelligence. In R.J. Sternberg (Ed.), *Human intelligence.* New York: Cambridge University Press.

Tan, M.E., & others (2017). Employment status among the Singapore elderly and its correlates. *Psychogeriatrics, 17,* 155-163.

Tan, P.Z., Armstrong, L.M., & Cole, P.M. (2013). Relations between temperament and anger regulation over early childhood. *Social Development, 22,* 755-772.

Tan, X.L., & others (2019, in press). Factors associated with physical activity engagement among adults with rheumatoid arthritis: A cross-sectional study. *Musculoskeletal Care.*

Tang, S., Davis-Kean, P.E., Chen, M., & Sexton, H.R. (2016). Adolescent pregnancy's intergenerational effects: Does an adolescent mother's education have consequences for children's achievement? *Journal of Research on Adolescence, 26,* 180-193.

Tang, X., Wang, M.T., Guo, J., & Salmela-Aro, K. (2019, in press). Building grit: The longitudinal pathways between mindset, commitment, grit, and academic outcomes. *Journal of Youth and Adolescence.*

Tannen, D. (1990). *You just don't understand: Women and men in conversation.* New York: Ballantine.

Tannes, C.K., & others (2018). Social perspective taking is associated with self-reported prosocial behavior and regional cortical thickness across adolescence. *Developmental Psychology, 54,* 1745-1757.

Tanskanen, A.O., & others (2017). Sibling conflicts in full- and half-sibling households in the U.K. *Journal of Biosocial Science, 49,* 31-47.

Tas, D., & others (2019, in press). The effects of parental and peer factors on psychiatric symptoms in adolescents with obesity. *Eating and Weight Disorders.*

Tashiro, T., & Frazier, P. (2003). "I'll never be in a relationship like that again": Personal growth following romantic relationship breakups. *Personal Relationships, 10,* 113-128.

Tashiro, T., Frazier, P., & Berman, M. (2006). Stress-related growth following divorce and relationship dissolution. In M.A. Fine & J.H. Harvey (Eds.), *Handbook of divorce and relationship dissolution.* Mahwah, NJ: Erlbaum.

Tatterton, M.J., Summers, R., & Brennan, C.Y. (2019). A qualitative descriptive analysis of nurses' perceptions of hospice care for deceased children following organ donation in hospice cool rooms. *International Journal of Palliative Nursing, 25,* 166-175.

Tavris, C., & Wade, C. (1984). *The longest war: Sex differences in perspective* (2nd ed.). San Diego: Harcourt Brace Jovanovich.

Taylor, C., & others (2016). Examining ways that a mindfulness-based intervention reduces stress in public school teachers: A mixed-methods study. *Mindfulness, 7,* 115-129.

Taylor, C.A., Manganello, J.A., Lee, S.J., & Rice, J.C. (2010). Mothers' spanking of 3-year-old children and subsequent risk of children's aggressive behavior. *Pediatrics, 125,* e1057-e1065.

Taylor, H., & others (2016). Neonatal outcomes of waterbirth: A systematic review and meta-analysis. *Archives of Disease in Childhood: Fetal and Neonatal Edition, 101,* F357-F365.

Taylor, S., & Workman, L. (2018). *The psychology of human social development.* New York: Routledge.

Taylor, S.E. (2015). *Health psychology* (9th ed.). New York: McGraw-Hill.

Taylor, S.E. (2018). *Health psychology* (10th ed.). New York: McGraw-Hill.

Taylor, Z.E., Widaman, K.F., & Robins, R.W. (2018). Longitudinal relations of economic hardship and effortful control to active coping in Latino youth. *Journal of Research on Adolescence, 28*, 396-411.

Taylor, K., & others (2019). Prioritizing putative influential genes in cardiovascular disease susceptibility by applying tissue-specific Mendelian randomization. *Genome Medicine, 11*(1), 6.

Teach for America (2019). *Teach for America.* Retrieved from www.teachforamerica.org

Teague, M., Mackenzie, S., & Rosenthal, D. (2018). *Your health today* (7th ed.). New York: McGraw-Hill.

Tee, L.M., Kan, E.Y., Cheung, J.C., & Leung, W.C. (2016). Magnetic resonance imaging of the fetal brain. *Hong Kong Medical Journal, 6*, 328466.

Tegin, G., & others (2018). E-cigarette toxicity? *Southern Medical Journal, 111*, 35-38.

Tekcan, A.I., & others (2017). Life-span retrieval of public events: Reminiscence bump for high-impact events, recency for others. *Memory and Cognition, 45*, 1095-1112.

Telljohann, S., & others (2020). *Health education: Elementary and middle school applications* (9th ed.). New York: McGraw-Hill.

Temple, C.A., & others (2018). *All children read: Teaching for literacy* (5th ed.). Upper Saddle River, NJ: Pearson.

Templeton, J.L., & Eccles, J.S. (2006). The relation between spiritual development and identity processes. In E. Roehlkepartain, P.E. King, L. Wagener, & P.L. Benson (Eds.), *The handbook of spirituality in childhood and adolescence.* Thousand Oaks, CA: Sage.

Terman, L. (1925). *Genetic studies of genius. Vol. 1: Mental and physical traits of a thousand gifted children.* Stanford, CA: Stanford University Press.

Terracciano, A., & others (2017). Personality traits and risk of cognitive impairment and dementia. *Journal of Psychiatric Research, 89*, 22-27.

Terry, D.F., Nolan, V.G., Andersen, S.L., Perls, T.T., & Cawthon, R. (2008). Association of longer telomeres with better health in centenarians. *Journals of Gerontology A: Biological Sciences and Medical Sciences, 63*, 809-812.

Teshale, S.M., & Lachman, M.E. (2016). Managing daily happiness: The relationship between selection, optimization, and compensation strategies and well-being in adulthood. *Psychology and Aging, 31*, 687-692.

Teti, D. (2001). Retrospect and prospect in the psychological study of sibling relationships. In J.P. McHale & W.S. Grolnick (Eds.), *Retrospect and prospect in the psychological study of families.* Mahwah, NJ: Erlbaum.

Tetzlaff, A., Schmidt, R., Brauhardt, A., & Hilbert, A. (2016). Family functioning in adolescents with binge-eating disorder. *European Eating Disorders Review, 24*, 430-433.

Tevendale, H.D., & others (2017). Practical approaches to evaluating progress and outcomes in community-wide teen pregnancy prevention initiatives. *Journal of Adolescent Health, 60*(Suppl. 3), S63-S68.

Thabet, A.A., Ibraheem, A.N., Shivram, R., Winter, E.A., & Vostanis, P. (2009). Parenting support and PTSD in children of a war zone. *International Journal of Social Psychiatry, 55*, 225-227.

Thakral, P.P., & others (2019, in press). Adaptive constructive processes: An episodic specificity induction impacts false recall in the Deese-Roediger-McDermott paradigm. *Journal of Experimental Psychology: General.*

Thanh, N.X., & Jonsson, E. (2016). Life expectancy of people with fetal alcohol syndrome. *Journal of Population Therapeutics and Clinical Pharmacology, 23*, e53-e59.

Thelen, E. (2000). Perception and motor development. In A. Kazdin (Ed.), *Encyclopedia of psychology.* Washington, DC, & New York: American Psychological Association and Oxford University Press.

Thelen, E., & Smith, L.B. (1998). Dynamic systems theory. In W. Damon & R. Lerner (Eds.), *Handbook of child psychology* (5th ed., Vol. 1.). New York: Wiley.

Thelen, E., & Smith, L.B. (2006). Dynamic development of action and thought. In W. Damon & R. Lerner (Eds.), *Handbook of child psychology* (6th ed.). New York: Wiley.

Thelen, E., & others (1993). The transition to reaching: Mapping intention and intrinsic dynamics. *Child Development, 64*, 1058-1098.

Theokas, C. (2009). Youth sports participation—A view of the issues: Introduction to the special section. *Developmental Psychology, 45*, 303-306.

Thiamwong, L., & Pungchompoo, W. (2018). Embedding palliative care into healthy aging: A narrative case study from Thailand. *Journal of Hospice and Palliative Nursing, 20*, 416-420.

Thoma, S.J., & Bebeau, M. (2008). *Moral judgment competency is declining over time: Evidence from 20 years of defining issues test data.* Paper presented at the meeting of the American Educational Research Association, New York, NY.

Thomas, A., & Chess, S. (1991). Temperament in adolescence and its functional significance. In R.M. Lerner, A.C. Petersen, & J. Brooks-Gunn (Eds.), *Encyclopedia of adolescence* (Vol. 2). New York: Garland.

Thomas, A., & Guillich, A. (2019, in press). Childhood practice and play as determinants of adolescent intrinsic and extrinsic motivation among elite young athletes. *European Journal of Sport Science.*

Thomas, J.C., & others (2017). Developmental origins of infant emotion regulation: Mediation by temperamental negativity and moderation by maternal sensitivity. *Developmental Psychology, 53*, 611-628.

Thomas, K.A., & Spieker, S. (2016). Sleep, depression, and fatigue in late postpartum. *MCN: American Journal of Maternal and Child Nursing, 41*, 104-109.

Thomas, M.S.C., & Johnson, M.H. (2008). New advances in understanding sensitive periods in brain development. *Current Directions in Psychological Science, 17*, 1-5.

Thompson, A.E., & Voyer, D. (2014). Sex differences in the ability to recognize non-verbal displays of emotion: A meta-analysis. *Cognition and Emotion, 28*, 1164-1195.

Thompson, E.L., Mehari, K.R., & Farrell, A.D. (2019, in press). Deviant peer factors during early adolescence: Cause or consequence of physical aggression. *Child Development.*

Thompson, M.P., & Swartout, K. (2018). Epidemiology of suicide attempts among youth transitioning to adulthood. *Journal of Youth and Adolescence, 47*, 807-817.

Thompson, R., & Murachver, T. (2001). Predicting gender from electronic discourse. *British Journal of Social Psychology, 40*, 193-201.

Thompson, R., & others (2017). Is the use of physical discipline associated with aggressive behaviors in children? *Academic Pediatrics, 17*, 34-44.

Thompson, R.A. (2006). The development of the person. In W. Damon & R. Lerner (Eds.), *Handbook of child psychology* (6th ed.). New York: Wiley.

Thompson, R.A. (2009). Early foundations: Conscience and the development of moral character. In D. Narváez & D. Lapsley (Eds.), *Personality, identity, and character.* New York: Cambridge University Press.

Thompson, R.A. (2011). The emotionate child. In D. Cicchetti & G.I. Roisman (Eds.), The origins and organization of adaptation and maladaptation. *Minnesota Symposium on Child Psychology* (Vol. 36). New York: Wiley.

Thompson, R.A. (2012). Whither the preoperational child? Toward a life-span moral development theory. *Perspectives on Child Development, 6*, 423-429.

Thompson, R.A. (2013). Attachment and its development: Precis and prospect. In P. Zelazo (Ed.), *Oxford handbook of developmental psychology.* New York: Oxford University Press.

Thompson, R.A. (2014). Conscience development in early childhood. In M. Killen & J.G. Smetana (Eds.), *Handbook of moral development* (2nd ed.). New York: Psychology Press.

Thompson, R.A. (2015). Relationships, regulation, and development. In R.M. Lerner (Ed.), *Handbook of child psychology and developmental science* (7th ed.). New York: Wiley.

Thompson, R.A. (2016). Early attachment and later development: New questions. In J. Cassidy & P.R. Shaver (Eds.), *Handbook of attachment* (3rd ed.). New York: Guilford.

Thompson, R.A. (2017). Twenty-first century attachment theory. In H. Keller & K.A. Bard (Eds.), *The cultural nature of attachment.* Cambridge, MA: MIT Press.

Thompson, R.A. (2019). Emotion dysregulation and early social relationships. In T.P. Beauchaine & S.E. Crowell (Eds.), *Oxford handbook of emotion dysregulation.* New York: Oxford University Press.

Thompson, R.A. (2019, in press). On what is read, shared, and felt: Parent-child conversation about stories. *Attachment and Human Development.*

Thompson, R.A. (2020, in press). Early moral development and attachment theory. In D.J. Laible & others (Eds.), *Oxford handbook of parenting and moral development.* New York: Oxford University Press.

Thompson, R.A., & Baumrind, D. (2019). The ethics of parenting. In M.H. Bornstein (Ed.), *Handbook of parenting* (3rd ed.). New York: Routledge.

Thompson, R.A., & Goodvin, R. (2007). Taming the tempest in the teapot: Emotion regulation in toddlers. In C.A. Brownell & C.B. Kopp (Eds.), *Socioemotional development in toddlers.* New York: Guilford.

Thompson, R.A., & Newton, E.K. (2013). Baby altruists? Examining the complexity of prosocial motivation in young children. *Infancy, 18*, 120-133.

Thompson, R.A., McGinley, M., & Meyer, S. (2006). Understanding values in relationships. In M. Killen & J.G. Smetana (Eds.), *Handbook of moral development.* Mahwah, NJ: Erlbaum.

Thompson, S., & others (2019). The effect of exercise on blood pressure in chronic kidney disease: A systematic review and meta-analysis of randomized controlled trials. *PLoS One, 14*(2), e0211032.

Thornton, R., & Light, L.L. (2006). Language comprehension and production in normal aging. In J.E. Birren & K.W. Schaie (Eds.), *Handbook of the psychology of aging* (6th ed.). San Diego: Academic Press.

Tian, J., & others (2019). Socioeconomic position over the life course from childhood and smoking status in mid-adulthood: Results from a 25-year follow-up study. *BMC Public Health, 19*(1), 169.

Tian, L., Pi, L., Huebner, E.S., & Du, M. (2016). Gratitude and adolescents' subjective well-being in school: The multiple mediating roles of basic psychological needs satisfaction at school. *Frontiers in Psychology, 7,* 1409.

Tian, S., & Xu, Y. (2016). Association of sarcopenic obesity with the risk of all-cause mortality: A meta-analysis of prospective cohort studies. *Geriatrics and Gerontology International, 16,* 155–166.

Tieu, L., & others (2018). Children's comprehension of plural predicate conjunction. *Journal of Child Language, 45,* 242–259.

Tiggemann, M., & Slater, A. (2017). Facebook and body image concern in adolescent girls: A prospective study. *International Journal of Eating Disorders, 50,* 80–83.

Tiiri, E., & others (2019, in press). Did bullying victimization decrease after nationwide school-based anti-bullying program? A time-trend study. *Journal of the American Academy of Child and Adolescent Psychiatry.*

Tikhonova, A.A., & others (2019, in press). Bicultural identity harmony and American identity are associated with positive mental health in U.S. racial and ethnic minority adolescents. *Cultural Diversity and Ethnic Minority Psychology.*

Tikotzky, L., & Shaashua, L. (2012). Infant sleep and early parental sleep-related cognitions predict sleep in pre-school children. *Sleep Medicine, 13,* 185–192.

Tilton-Weaver, L.C., Burk, W.J., Kerr, M., & Stattin, H. (2013). Can parental monitoring and peer management reduce the selection or influence of delinquent peers? Testing the question using a dynamic social network approach. *Developmental Psychology, 49,* 2057–2070.

Timmermans, E., & Van den Bulck, J. (2018). Casual sexual scripts on the screen: A quantitative content analysis. *Archives of Sexual Behavior, 47,* 1482–1496.

TIMSS (Trends in International Mathematics and Science Study) (2015). *TIMSS 2015 and TIMSS advanced 2015 international results.* Chestnut Hill, MA: TIMSS.

Toepfer, P., & others (2019, in press). A role of oxytocin receptor gene brain tissue expression quantitative trait locus rs237895 in the intergenerational transmission of the effects of maternal childhood maltreatment. *Journal of the American Academy of Child and Adolescent Psychiatry.*

Toffrey, K., Zakrzewski-Fruer, J.K., & Thackray, A.E. (2018). Metabolism and exercise during youth—the

year that was 2017. *Pediatric Exercise Science, 30,* 38–41.

Tolani, N., & Brooks-Gunn, J. (2008). Family support, international trends. In M.M. Haith & J.B. Benson (Eds.), *Encyclopedia of infant and early childhood development.* Oxford, UK: Elsevier.

Tole, F., & others (2019, in press). The role of pre-, peri-, and postnatal risk factors in bipolar disorder and adult ADHD. *Journal of Neural Transmission.*

Tolman, D.L., & Chmielewski, J.F. (2019). From tightrope to minefield: How the sexual double standard "lives" in adolescent girls' and young women's lives. In S. Lamb & J. Gilbert (Eds.), *Cambridge handbook of sexual development.* New York: Cambridge University Press.

Tolppanen, A.M., & others (2015). Leisure-time physical activity from mid- to late life, body mass index, and risk of dementia. *Alzheimer's and Dementia, 11,* 434–443.

Tomasello, M. (2003). *Constructing a language: A usage-based theory of language acquisition.* Cambridge, MA: Harvard University Press.

Tomasello, M. (2006). Acquiring linguistic constructions. In W. Damon & R. Lerner (Eds.), *Handbook of child psychology* (6th ed.). New York: Wiley.

Tomasello, M. (2011). Language development. In U. Goswami (Ed.), *Wiley-Blackwell handbook of childhood cognitive development* (2nd ed.). New York: Wiley.

Tomasello, M. (2014). *A natural history of human thinking.* Cambridge, MA: Harvard University Press.

Tomaszewski Farias, S., & others (2018). Compensation strategies in older adults: Association with cognition and everyday function. *American Journal of Alzheimer's Disease and other Dementias, 33,* 184–191.

Tomkinson, G.R., & Wong, S.H.S. (2019). Special issue: Global matrix 3.0—An introduction to the report cards on the physical activity of children and youth from five Asian countries and regions. *ScienceDirect, 17*(1), 1–2.

Tompkins, G.E. (2019). *Teaching writing* (7th ed.). Upper Saddle River, NJ: Pearson.

Tompkins, G.E., & Rodgers, E. (2020). *Literacy in the early grades* (5th ed.). Upper Saddle River, NJ: Pearson.

Tompkins, V., Farrar, M.J., & Montgomery, D.E. (2019). Speaking your mind: Language and narrative in young children's theory of mind development. *Advances in Child Behavior and Development, 56,* 109–140.

Tompkins, V., & others (2017). Child language and parent discipline mediate the relation between family income and false belief understanding. *Journal of Experimental Psychology, 158,* 1–18.

Tomporowski, P.D. (2016). Exercise and cognition. *Pediatric Exercise Science, 28,* 23–27.

Tonnsen, B., Richards, J.E., & Roberts, J.E. (2018, in press). Heart-rate-defined sustained attention in infants at risk for autism. *Journal of Neurodevelopmental Disorders.*

Tononi, G., & Cirelli, C. (2019, in press). Sleep and synaptic down-selection. *European Journal of Neuroscience.*

Top, N., Liew, J., & Luo, W. (2017). Family and school influences on youths' behavioral and academic outcomes: Cross-level interactions between parental

monitoring and character development curriculum. *Journal of Genetic Psychology, 178,* 108–118.

Topa, G., Depolo, M., & Alcover, C.M. (2018). Early retirement: A meta-analysis of its antecedent and subsequent correlates. *Frontiers in Psychology, 8,* 2157.

Topiwala, A., & others (2019). Predicting cognitive resilience from midlife lifestyle and multi-modal MRI: A 30-year prospective cohort study. *PLoS One, 14*(2), e0211273.

Torke, A.M., & others (2019). POLST facilitation in complex care management: A feasibility study. *American Journal of Hospice and Palliative Care, 36,* 5–12.

Toro, C.A., Aylwin, C.F., & Lomniczi, A. (2019, in press). Hypothalamic epigenetics driving female puberty. *Journal of Neuroendocrinology.*

Torstveit, L., Sutterlin, S., & Lugo, R.G. (2016). Empathy, guilt proneness, and gender: Relative contributions to prosocial behavior. *European Journal of Psychology, 12,* 260–275.

Tortora, G.J., & others (2019). *Microbiology* (13th ed.). Upper Saddle River, NJ: Pearson.

Toub, T., & others (2018). The language of play: Developing preschool vocabulary through play following shared book-reading. *Early Childhood Research Quarterly, 45,* 1–17.

Toupance, S., & Benetos, A. (2019). Telomere dynamics and aging related diseases. In R. Fernandez-Ballesteros, A. Benetos, & J-M. Robine (Eds.), *Cambridge handbook of successful aging.* New York: Cambridge University Press.

Toy, W., Nai, Z.L., & Lee, H.W. (2016). Extraversion and agreeableness: Divergent routes to daily satisfaction with social relationships. *Journal of Personality, 84,* 121–134.

Toyokawa, N., & Toyokawa, T. (2019). Interaction of familism and socioeconomic status on academic outcomes of adolescent children of Latino immigrant families. *Journal of Adolescence, 71,* 138–149.

Toyoshima, A., & others (2018). The relationship between vision impairment and well-being among centenarians: Findings from the Georgia Centenarian Study. *International Journal of Geriatric Psychiatry, 33,* 414–422.

Trafimow, D., Triandis, H.C., & Goto, S.G. (1991). Some tests of the distinction between the prime and collective self. *Journal of Personality and Social Psychology, 60,* 649–655.

Trager, T.D., & others (2019, in press). The genetic changes of Wilms tumor. *Nature Reviews. Necrology.*

Trahan, L.H., Stuebing, K.K., Fletcher, J.M., & Hiscock, M. (2014). The Flynn effect: A meta-analysis. *Psychological Bulletin, 140,* 1332–1360.

Trainor, L.J., & He, C. (2013). Auditory and musical development. In P.D. Zelazo (Ed.), *Oxford handbook of developmental psychology.* New York: Oxford University Press.

Traynor, J.M., & others (2019, in press). Eye tracking effort expenditure and autonomic arousal to social and circumscribed interest stimuli in autism spectrum disorder. *Journal of Autism and Developmental Disorders.*

Trehub, S.E., Schneider, B.A., Thorpe, L.A., & Judge, P. (1991). Observational measure of auditory sensitivity in early infancy. *Developmental Psychology, 27,* 40–49.

Trelle, A.N., Henson, R.N., & Simons, J.S. (2015). Identifying age-invariant and age-limited mechanisms for enhanced memory performance: Insights from self-referential processing in younger and older adults. *Psychology and Aging, 30,* 324–333.

Tremblay, M.S., & others (2012). Canadian sedentary behavior guidelines for the early years (0–4 years). *Applied Physiology, Nutrition, and Metabolism, 37,* 370–380.

Trevino, K.M., & others (2018). Bereavement challenges and their relationship to physical and psychological adjustment to loss. *Journal of Palliative Medicine, 21,* 479–488.

Triandis, H.C. (1994). *Culture and social behavior.* New York: McGraw-Hill.

Triandis, H.C. (2001). Individualism and collectivism. In D. Matsumoto (Eds.), *The handbook of culture and psychology.* New York: Oxford University Press.

Triandis, H.C. (2007). Culture and psychology: A history of their relationship. In S. Kitayama & D. Cohen (Eds.), *Handbook of cultural psychology.* New York: Guilford.

Trimble, J.E. (1988, August). *The enculturation of contemporary psychology.* Paper presented at the meeting of the American Psychological Association, New Orleans.

Trinh, S.L., & Choukas-Bradley, S. (2018). "No messages needed—just pats on the back": Exploring young men's reports of male and female friends' sexual communications. *Psychology of Men and Masculinity, 19,* 430–438.

Troia, G., Graham, S., & Harris, K.R. (2017). Writing and students with language and learning disabilities. In J.M. Kauffman & others (Eds.), *Handbook of special education* (2nd ed.). New York: Routledge.

Troop-Gordon, W. (2017). Peer victimization in adolescence: The nature, progression, and consequences of being bullied within a developmental context. *Journal of Adolescence, 55,* 116–128.

Trucco, E.M., & others (2014). Early adolescent alcohol use in context: How neighborhoods, parents, and peers impact youth. *Development and Psychopathology, 26,* 425–436.

Trujillo, P., & others (2019). Dopamine effects on frontal cortical blood flow and motor inhibition in Parkinson's disease. *Cortex, 115,* 99–111.

Trzesniewski, K.H., & others (2006). Low self-esteem during adolescence predicts poor health, criminal behavior, and limited economic prospects during adulthood. *Developmental Psychology, 42,* 381–390.

Tsai, H.J., & Chang, F.K. (2019). Associations of exercise, nutritional status, and smoking with cognitive decline among older adults in Taiwan: Results from a longitudinal population-based study. *Archives of Gerontology and Geriatrics, 82,* 133–138.

Tsai, W., Kuo, S.C., Wen, F.H., Prigerson, H.G., & Tang, S.T. (2018). Prolonged grief disorder and depression are distinct for caregivers across their first bereavement year. *Psychooncology, 27,* 1027–1034.

Tsang, A., & others (2008). Common persistent pain conditions in developed and developing countries: Gender and age differences and comorbidity with depression-anxiety disorders. *Journal of Pain, 9,* 883–891.

Tsang, T.W., & others (2016). Prenatal alcohol exposure, FASD, and child behavior: A meta-analysis. *Pediatrics, 137,* e20152542.

Tseng, Y.F., & others (2018). The meaning of rituals after a stillbirth: A qualitative study of mothers with a stillborn baby. *Journal of Clinical Nursing, 27,* 1134–1142.

Tso, W., & others (2016). Sleep duration and school readiness of Chinese preschool children. *Journal of Pediatrics, 169,* 266–271.

Tso, W., & others (2019, in press). Early sleep deprivation and attention deficit/hyperactivity disorder. *Pediatric Research.*

Tubay, A.T., & others (2019, in press). The effects of group prenatal care on infant birthweight and maternal well-being: A randomized controlled trial. *Military Medicine.*

Tucker, C.J., McHale, S.M., & Crouter, A.C. (2003). Conflict resolution: Links with adolescents' family relationships and individual well-being. *Journal of Family Issues, 24,* 715–726.

Tucker-Drob, E.M., Brandmaier, A.M., & Lindenberger, U. (2019). Coupled cognitive changes in adulthood: A meta-analysis. *Psychological Bulletin, 145,* 273–301.

Turiel, E. (2018). Reasoning at the root of morality. In K. Gray & J. Graham (Eds.), *Atlas of moral psychology.* New York: Guilford.

Turiel, E., & Gingo, M. (2017). Development in the moral domain: Coordination and the need to consider other domains of social reasoning. In N. Budwig, E. Turiel, & P.D. Zelazo (Eds.), *New perspectives on human development.* New York: Cambridge University Press.

Turnbull, A., & others (2020). *Exceptional lives* (9th ed.). Upper Saddle River, NJ: Pearson.

Turner, B.F. (1982). Sex-related differences in aging. In B.B. Wolman (Ed.), *Handbook of developmental psychology.* Englewood Cliffs, NJ: Prentice Hall.

Turner, G.R., & others (2019). Goal-oriented attention self-regulation (GOALS) training in older adults. *Aging and Mental Health, 6,* 1–10.

Turner, J.H. (2019, in press). Long-acting reversible contraceptives: Addressing adolescents' barriers. *Nurse Practitioner.*

Turner, S., Taillieu, T., Cheung, K., & Afifi, T.O. (2017). The relationship between childhood sexual abuse and mental health outcomes among males: Results from a nationally representative United States sample. *Child Abuse and Neglect, 66,* 64–72.

Tweed, E.J., & others (2016). Five-minute Apgar scores and educational outcomes: Retrospective cohort study of 751,369 children. *Archives of Disease in Child, Fetal, and Neonatal Medicine, 101,* F121–F126.

Twenge, J., & Campbell, K. (2020). *Personality psychology* (2nd ed.). Upper Saddle River, NJ: Pearson.

Twenge, J.M., & Campbell, W.K. (2019, in press). Media use is linked to lower psychological well-being: Evidence from three datasets. *Psychiatric Quarterly.*

Twenge, J.M., Hisler, G.C., & Krizan, Z. (2019, in press). Associations between screen time and sleep duration are primarily driven by portable electronic devices: Evidence from a population-based study of U.S. children 0–17. *Sleep Medicine.*

Tyas, S.L., & others (2007). Transitions to mild cognitive impairments, dementia, and death: Findings from the Nun Study. *American Journal of Epidemiology, 165,* 1231–1238.

Tyrell, F.A., & others (2016). Family influences on Mexican American adolescents' romantic relationships: Moderation by gender and culture. *Journal of Research on Adolescence, 26,* 142–158.

U

U.S. Bureau of Labor Statistics (2016). *Volunteering in the United States: 2015.* Washington, DC: Author.

U.S. Census Bureau (2011). *People.* Washington, DC: U.S. Department of Labor.

U.S. Census Bureau (2013). *Marriages, births, and deaths.* Washington, DC: U.S. Department of Labor.

U.S. Census Bureau (2015). *Marriages.* Washington, DC: U.S. Department of Labor.

U.S. Census Bureau (2016). *People.* Washington, DC: Author.

U.S. Census Bureau (2017). *Families and living arrangements: 2016.* Washington, DC: Author.

U.S. Census Bureau (2018). *Births, deaths, marriages, divorces.* Washington, DC: Author.

U.S. Census Bureau (2018). *Death statistics.* Washington, DC: Author.

U.S. Census Bureau (2018). *Marriages.* Washington, DC: U.S. Department of Labor.

U.S. Census Bureau (2018). *People.* Washington, DC: Author.

U.S. Census Bureau (2018). *Unmarried and single Americans.* Washington, DC: Author.

U.S. Census Bureau (2019). *Death statistics.* Washington, DC: Author.

U.S. Census Bureau (2019). *Families and living arrangements.* Washington, DD: Author.

U.S. Department of Energy (2001). *The human genome project.* Washington, DC: U.S. Department of Energy.

U.S. Department of Health and Human Services (2015, May). *Health United States 2014.* Washington, DC: Author.

U.S. Department of Health and Human Services (2017). *Child maltreatment 2017.* Washington, DC: Author.

U.S. Department of Health and Human Services (2017). *Health, United States 2014.* Washington, DC: Author.

U.S. Department of Health and Human Services (2019). *Folic acid.* Washington, DC: Author.

Uchida, S., & Kagitani, F. (2019, in press). Neural mechanisms involved in the noxious physical stress-induced inhibition of ovarian estradiol secretion. *Anatomical Record.*

Uchino, B.N., & others (2012). Social relationships and health: Is feeling positive, negative, or both (ambivalent) about your social ties related to telomeres? *Health Psychology, 31*(6), 789–796.

Udo, T., & Grilo, C.M. (2019). Psychiatric and medical correlates of DSM-5 eating disorders in a nationally representative sample of adults in the United States. *International Journal of Eating Disorders, 52,* 42–50.

Ueno, K., & McWilliams, S. (2010). Gender-typed behaviors and school adjustment. *Sex Roles, 63,* 580–591.

Ujifusa, A. (2019). Hitting the elusive target of school accountability. *Education Week, 38*(27), 8–9.

Ulfsdottir, H., Saltvedt, S., & Georgsson, S. (2018). Waterbirth in Sweden—a comparative study. *Acta Obstetricia et Gynecologica Scandinavica, 97,* 341–348.

Ullah, M., & Sun, Z. (2019, in press). Klotho deficiency accelerates stem cells aging by impairing telomerase activity. *Journals of Gerontology A: Biological Sciences and Medical Sciences.*

Umana-Taylor, A. (2018). Intervening in cultural development: The case of ethnic-racial identity. *Development and Psychopathology, 30,* 1907–1922.

Umana-Taylor, A., & others (2018). A universal intervention program increases ethnic-racial identity exploration and resolution to predict adolescent psychosocial functioning one year later. *Journal of Youth and Adolescence, 47,* 1–15.

UNAIDS (2018). *UNAIDS data 2018.* Geneva, Switzerland: Author.

Unalmis Erdogan, S., Yanikkerem, E., & Goker, A. (2017). Effects of low back massage on perceived birth pain and satisfaction. *Complementary Therapies in Clinical Practice, 28,* 169–175.

Uncapher, M.R., & others (2017). Media multitasking and cognitive, psychological, neural, and learning differences. *Pediatrics, 140*(Suppl. 2), S62–S66.

Underhill, K., Montgomery, P., & Operario, D. (2007). Sexual abstinence programs to prevent HIV infection in high-income countries. *British Medical Journal, 335,* 248.

Ungar, M. (2015). Practitioner review: Diagnosing childhood resilience—a systematic approach to the diagnosis of adaptation in adverse social and physical ecologies. *Journal of Child Psychology and Psychiatry, 56,* 4–17.

UNICEF (2007). *The state of the world's children, 2007.* Geneva, Switzerland: Author.

UNICEF (2018). *The state of the world's children, 2018.* Geneva, Switzerland: Author.

UNICEF (2019). *The state of the world's children, 2019.* Geneva, Switzerland: Author.

United Health Foundation (2018). *America's Health Rankings.* Retrieved February 8, 2019, from www.AmericasHealth Rankings.com

United Nations (2017). *World population aging 2017.* New York: United Nations.

Updegraff, K.A., Umana-Taylor, A.J., McHale, S.M., Wheeler, L.A., & Perez-Brena, J. (2012). Mexican-origin youths' cultural orientations and adjustment: Changes from early to late adolescence. *Child Development, 83,* 1655–1671.

Urdan, T. (2012). Factors affecting the motivation and achievement of immigrant students. In K.R. Harris, S. Graham, & T. Urdan (Eds.), *APA educational psychology handbook.* Washington, DC: American Psychological Association.

Urqueta Alfaro, A., Morash, V.S., Lei, D., & Orel-Bixler, D. (2018). Joint engagement in infants and its relationship to their visual impairment measurements. *Infant Behavior and Development, 50,* 311–323.

Urry, L.A., & others (2020). *Campbell biology in focus* (3rd ed.). Upper Saddle River, NJ: Pearson.

Usher, E.L., & Schunk, D.H. (2018). Social cognitive perspective of self-regulation. In D.H. Schunk & J.A. Greene (Eds.), *Handbook of self-regulation of learning and performance* (2nd ed.). New York: Routledge.

Utesch, T., & others (2019, in press). The relationship between motor competence and physical fitness from early childhood to early adulthood: A meta-analysis. *Sports Medicine.*

Uwaezuoke, S.N., Eneh, C.I., & Ndu, I.K. (2019, in press). Relationship between exclusive breastfeeding and lower risk of childhood obesity: A narrative review of published evidence. *Clinical Medicine Insights. Pediatrics.*

V

Vacaru, V.S., Sterkenburg, P.S., & Schuengel, C. (2018). Self-concept in institutionalized children with disturbed attachment: The mediating role of exploratory behaviors. *Child: Care, Health, and Development, 44,* 476–484.

Vacca, J.A., & others (2018). *Reading and learning to read* (10th ed.). Boston: Allyn & Bacon.

Vaden, K.L., & others (2017). Longitudinal changes in audiometric phenotypes of age-related hearing loss. *Journal of the Association for Research in Otolaryngology, 18,* 371–385.

Vahia, I.V., & others (2011). Correlates of spirituality in older women. *Aging and Mental Health, 15*(1), 97–102.

Vaillant, G.E. (1977). *Adaptation to life.* Boston: Little Brown.

Vaillant, G.E. (2002). *Aging well.* Boston: Little Brown.

Vaish, A. (2018). The prosocial functions of early emotions: The case of guilt. *Current Opinion in Psychology, 20,* 25–29.

Vaish, A., Carpenter, M., & Tomasello, M. (2010). Young children selectively avoid helping people with harmful intentions. *Child Development, 81,* 1661–1669.

Vaish, A., Carpenter, M., & Tomasello, M. (2016). The early emergence of guilt-motivated prosocial behavior. *Child Development, 87,* 1772–1782.

Valdesolo, P. (2018). Getting emotions right in moral psychology. In K. Gray & J. Graham (Eds.), *Atlas of moral psychology.* New York: Guilford.

Valech, N., & others (2018). Executive and language subjective cognitive decline complaints discriminate preclinical Alzheimer's disease from normal aging. *Journal of Alzheimer's Disease, 61,* 689–703.

Valentin, M., & others (2018). Acid folic and pregnancy: A mandatory supplementation. *Annals of Endocrinology, 79,* 91–94.

Valero, S., & others (2014). Neuroticism and impulsivity: Their hierarchical organization in the personality characterization of drug-dependent patients from a decision tree learning perspective. *Comprehensive Psychiatry, 55,* 1227–1233.

Valimaki, T.H., & others (2016). Impact of Alzheimer's disease on the family caregiver's long-term quality of life: Results from the ALSOVA follow-up study. *Quality of Life Research, 25,* 687–697.

van Aken, M.A.G., & Asendorpf, J.B. (2018). Personality and peer relationships. In W.M. Bukowski & others (Eds.), *Handbook of peer interactions, relationships, and groups* (2nd ed.). New York: Guilford.

Van Assche, L., & others (2013). Attachment in old age: Theoretical assumptions, empirical findings, and implications for clinical practice. *Clinical Psychology Review, 33*(1), 67–81.

Van Berkum, J.A. (2019). Language comprehension, emotion, and sociality: Aren't we missing something? In S-A. Rueschemeyer & J. Gareth Gaskell (Eds.), *Oxford handbook of psycholinguistics* (2nd ed.). New York: Oxford University Press.

Van Beveren, T.T. (2011, March). Personal conversation. Richardson, TX: Department of Psychology, University of Texas at Dallas.

van de Bongardt, D., & others (2019). *Romantic relationships and sexuality in adolescence and young adulthood.* New York: Routledge.

Van de Vondervoort, J., & Hamlin, J.K. (2016). Evidence for intuitive morality: Preverbal infants make sociomoral evaluations. *Child Development Perspectives, 10,* 143–148.

Van de Vondervoort, J., & Hamlin, J.K. (2018). The infantile roots of sociomoral evaluations. In K. Gray & J. Graham (Eds.), *The atlas of moral psychology.* New York: Guilford.

Van de Walle, J.A., Karp, K.S., & Bay-Williams, J.M. (2019). *Elementary and secondary mathematics* (10th ed.). Upper Saddle River, NJ: Pearson.

van den Boom, D.C. (1989). Neonatal irritability and the development of attachment. In G.A. Kohnstamm, J.E. Bates, & M.K. Rothbart (Eds.), *Temperament in childhood.* New York: Wiley.

van den Boomen, C., Munsters, N.M., & Kemner, C. (2019). Emotion processing in the infant brain: The importance of local information. *Neuropsychologia, 126,* 62–68.

van den Heuvel, M.I., & others (2018). Hubs in the human fetal brain network. *Developmental Cognitive Neuroscience, 30,* 108–115.

van der Burg, D., & others (2019, in press). Diagnosis and treatment of patients with comorbid substance use disorder and adult attention-deficit and hyperactivity disorder: A review of recent publications. *Current Opinion in Psychology.*

van der Does, T., & Adem, M. (2019). Gendered paths in ethnic identity exploration between adolescence and emerging adulthood. *Emerging Adulthood, 7,* 109–118.

Van der Graaff, J., & others (2018). Prosocial behavior in adolescence: Gender differences in development and its links with empathy. *Journal of Youth and Adolescence, 47,* 1086–1099.

van der Leeuw, G., & others (2018). The effect of pain on major cognitive impairment in older adults. *Journal of Pain, 19,* 1435–1444.

Van der Merwe, C., & others (2019). Concordance of genetic variation that increases risk for anxiety disorders and posttraumatic stress disorders and that influences their underlying neurocircuitry. *Journal of Affective Disorders, 245,* 885–896.

van der Stel, M., & Veenman, M.V.J. (2010). Development of metacognitive skillfulness: A longitudinal study. *Learning and Individual Differences, 20,* 220–224.

van der Veer, R., & Zavershneva, E. (2018). The final chapter of Vygotsky's Thinking and Speech: A reader's guide. *Journal of the History of the Behavioral Sciences, 54,* 101–110.

van Deurzen, L., & Vanhoutte, B. (2019, in press). A longitudinal study of allostatic load in later life: The role of sex, birth cohorts, and risk accumulation. *Research on Aging.*

van Dongen, J., & others (2019, in press). Epigenome-wide association study of attention-deficit/hyperactivity disorder symptoms in adults. *Biological Psychiatry.*

Van Doren, J., & others (2019). Sustained effects of neurofeedback in ADHD: A systematic review and meta-analysis. *European Child and Adolescent Development, 28,* 293–305.

Van Elderen, S.S., & others (2016). Brain volume as an integrated marker for the risk of death in a community-based sample: Age gene/environment susceptibility-Reykjavik study. *Journals of Gerontology A: Biological Sciences and Medical Sciences, 71,* 131–137.

van Geel, M., Vedder, P., & Tanilon, J. (2014). Relationship between peer victimization, cyberbullying, and suicide in children and adolescents: A meta-analysis. *JAMA Pediatrics, 168,* 435–442.

Van Gerven, P.W., & Guerreiro, M.J. (2016). Selective attention and sensory modality in aging: Curses and blessings. *Frontiers in Human Neuroscience, 10,* 147.

Van Hecke, V., & others (2012). Infant responding to joint attention, executive processes, and self-regulation in preschool children. *Infant Development and Behavior, 35,* 303–311.

van Hooft, E.A. (2014). Motivating and hindering factors during the reemployment process: The added value of employment counselors' assessment. *Journal of Occupational Health Psychology, 19,* 1–17.

Van Hooren, B., Meijer, K., & McCrum, C. (2019). Attractive gait training: Applying dynamical systems theory to the improvement of locomotor performance across the lifespan. *Frontiers in Physiology, 9,* 1934.

Van Hulle, C.A., & others (2017). Infant stranger fear trajectories predict anxious behaviors and diurnal cortisol rhythm during childhood. *Development and Psychopathology, 29,* 1119–1130.

van IJzendoorn, M.H., & Kroonenberg, P.M. (1988). Cross-cultural patterns of attachment: A meta-analysis of the Strange Situation. *Child Development, 59,* 147–156.

Van Malderen, E., & others (2019, in press). The interplay of self-regulation and affectivity in binge eating among adolescents. *European Child and Adolescent Psychiatry.*

van Renswoude, D.R., & others (2018). Gazepath: An eye-tracking analysis tool that accounts for individual differences and data quality. *Behavior Research Methods, 50,* 834–852.

Van Ryzin, M.J., Carlson, E.A., & Sroufe, L.A. (2011). Attachment discontinuity in a high-risk sample. *Attachment and Human Development, 13,* 381–401.

Van Ryzin, M.J., Johnson, A.B., Leve, L.D., & Kim, H.K. (2011). The number of sexual partners and health-risking sexual behavior: Prediction from high school entry to high school exit. *Archives of Sexual Behavior, 40*(5), 939–949.

Van Solinge, H., & Henkens, K. (2005). Couples' adjustment to retirement: A multi-actor panel study. *Journals of Gerontology B: Psychological Sciences and Social Sciences, 60,* S11–S20.

van Tilborg, E., & others (2018). Origin and dynamics of oligodendrocytes in the developing brain: Implications for perinatal white matter injury. *Glia, 66,* 221–238.

van Wijk, I.C., & others (2019). Behavioral genetics of temperament from frontal asymmetry in early childhood. *Journal of Experimental Child Psychology, 179,* 348–361.

Vandell, D.L., & others (2010). Do effects of early childcare extend to age 15 years? From the NICHD Study of Early Child Care and Youth Development. *Child Development, 81,* 737–756.

Vandendriessche, A., & others (2019, in press). Does sleep mediate the association between school pressure, physical activity, screen time, and psychological symptoms in early adolescents? A 12-country study. *International Journal of Environmental Research and Public Health.*

Vara-Garcia, C., & others (2019, in press). Stress and blood pressure in dementia caregivers: The moderator role of mindfulness. *Clinical Gerontology.*

Varahra, A., & others (2018). Exercise to improve functional outcomes in persons with osteoporosis: A systematic review and meta-analysis. *Osteoporosis International, 29,* 265–286.

Varga, N.L., & others (2018). Knowledge. In M.H. Bornstein (Ed.), *SAGE encyclopedia of lifespan human development.* Thousand Oaks, CA: Sage.

Varner, F.A., & others (2018). Racial discrimination experiences of African American youth adjustment: The role of parenting profiles based on racial socialization and involved-vigilant parenting. *Cultural Diversity and Ethnic Minority Psychology, 24,* 173–186.

Varner, M.W., & others (2014). Association between stillbirth and illicit drug use and smoking during pregnancy. *Obstetrics and Gynecology, 123,* 113–125.

Vasilenko, S.A., & Lefkowitz, E.S. (2018). Sexual behavior and daily affect in emerging adulthood. *Emerging Adulthood, 6,* 191–199.

Vasquez, E.A., & others (2018). The object of my aggression: Sexual objectification increases physical aggression against women. *Aggressive Behavior, 44,* 5–17.

Vasung, L., & others (2019, in press). Exploring early human brain development with structural and physiological neuroimaging. *NeuroImage.*

Vater, A., Moritz, S., & Roepke, S. (2018). Does a narcissism epidemic exist in modern western societies? Comparing narcissism and self-esteem in East and West Germany. *PLoS One, 13*(1), e0188287.

Vaughn, B.E., & others (2015). Sleep as a support for social competence, peer relations, and cognitive functioning in preschool children. *Behavioral Sleep Medicine, 13,* 92–106.

Vaughn, C.P., & others (2019, in press). AGS report on engagement related to the NIH Inclusion Across the Lifespan Policy. *Journal of the American Geriatrics Association.*

Vazsonyi, A.T., & Huang, L. (2010). Where self-control comes from: On the development of self-control and its relationship to deviance over time. *Developmental Psychology, 46,* 245–257.

Velez, C.E., Wolchik, S.A., Tein, J.Y., & Sandler, I. (2011). Protecting children from the consequences of divorce: A longitudinal study of the effects of parenting on children's coping responses. *Child Development, 82,* 244–257.

Vella, S.A., Cliff, D.P., Magee, C.A., & Okely, A.D. (2014). Sports participation and parent-reported health-related quality of life in children: Longitudinal associations. *Journal of Pediatrics, 164,* 1469–1474.

Veness, C., Prior, M., Eadie, P., Bavin, E., & Reilly, S. (2014). Predicting autism diagnosis by 7 years of age using parent report of infant social communication skills. *Journal of Pediatrics and Child Health, 50,* 693–700.

Venetsanou, F., & Kambas, A. (2017). Can motor proficiency in preschool age affect physical activity in adolescence? *Pediatric Exercise Science, 49,* 254–259.

Venker, C.E. (2019). Cross-situational and ostensive word learning in children with and without autism spectrum disorder. *Cognition, 183,* 181–191.

Venneri, A., & others (2019, in press). Beyond episodic memory: Semantic processing as independent predictor of hippocampal/perirhinal volume in aging and mild cognitive impairment due to Alzheimer's disease. *Neuropsychology.*

Venners, S.A., & others (2004). Paternal smoking and pregnancy loss: A prospective study using a biomarker of pregnancy. *American Journal of Epidemiology, 159,* 993–1001.

Vereczkei, A., & others (2019). Association of purinergic receptor P2RX7 gene polymorphisms with depression symptoms. *Progress in Neuro-psychopharmacology and Biological Psychiatry, 92,* 207–216.

Verhaeghen, P. (2013). *The elements of cognitive aging: Meta-analyses of age-related differences in processing speed and their consequences.* New York: Oxford University Press.

Verhagen, J., & Leseman, P. (2016). How do verbal short-term memory and working memory relate to the acquisition of vocabulary and grammar? A comparison between first and second language learners. *Journal of Experimental Child Psychology, 141,* 65–82.

Verhoef, E., & others (2019). Disentangling polygenic associations between attention-deficit/hyperactivity disorder, educational attainment, literacy, and language. *Translational Psychiatry, 9,* 35.

Vernon, L., Modecki, K.L., & Barber, B.L. (2018). Mobile phones in the bedroom: Trajectories of sleep habits and subsequent adolescent psychological development. *Child Development, 89,* 66–77.

Vernucci, S., & others (2019, in press). Working memory training in children: A review of basic methodological criteria. *Psychological Reports.*

Veronneau, M.H., Racer, K.H., Fosco, G.M., & Dishion, T.J. (2014). The contribution of adolescent effortful control to early adult educational attainment. *Journal of Educational Psychology, 106,* 730–743.

Verschueren, K. (2019, in press). Attachment, self-esteem, and socio-emotional adjustment: There is more than just the mother. *Attachment and Human Development.*

Verstaen, A., & others (2019, in press). Age-related changes in emotional behavior: Evidence from a 13-year longitudinal study of long-term married couples. *Emotion.*

Vidal, S., & others (2017). Maltreatment, family environment, and social risk factors: Determinants of the child welfare to juvenile justice transition among maltreated children and adolescents. *Child Abuse and Neglect, 63,* 7–18.

Vieira, S.A., & others (2019, in press). Exclusive breast-feeding and sociodemographic characteristics are associated with dietary patterns in children aged 4–7 years. *Public Health Nutrition.*

Vieria, J.M., & others (2016). Parents' work-family experiences and children's problem behaviors: The mediating role of parent-child relationship. *Journal of Family Psychology, 30,* 419–430.

Vihman, M.M. (2019). First word learning. In S-A. Rueschemeyer & M. Gareth Gaskell (Eds.), *Oxford handbook of psycholinguistics* (2nd ed.). New York: Oxford University Press.

Vijayakumar, N., & others (2018). Structural brain development: A review of methodological approaches and best practices. *Developmental Cognitive Neuroscience, 33,* 129–148.

Villegas, R., & others (2008). Duration of breast-feeding and the incidence of type 2 diabetes mellitus in the Shanghai Women's Health Study. *Diabetologia, 51*, 258–266.

Villemagne, V.L., & others (2018). Imaging tau and amyloid-*B* proteinopathies in Alzheimer disease and other conditions. *Nature Reviews: Neurology, 14*, 225–236.

Vina, J. (2019, in press). The free radical theory of frailty: Mechanisms and opportunities for interventions to promote successful aging. *Free Radical Biology and Medicine.*

Vinke, E.J., Ikram, M.A., & Vernooij, M.W. (2019). Brain aging: More of the same? *Aging, 11*, 849–850.

Virta, J.J., & others (2013). Midlife cardiovascular risk factors and late cognitive development. *European Journal of Epidemiology, 28*, 405–416.

Visher, E., & Visher, J. (1989). Parenting coalitions after remarriage: Dynamics and therapeutic guidelines. *Family Relations, 38*, 65–70.

Vitaro, F., Boivin, M., & Poulin, F. (2018). The interface of aggression and peer relations in childhood and adolescence. In W.M. Bukowski & others (Eds.), *Handbook of peer interactions, relationships, and groups* (2nd ed.). New York: Guilford.

Vittrup, B., Holden, G.W., & Buck, M. (2006). Attitudes predict the use of physical punishment: A prospective study of the emergence of disciplinary practices. *Pediatrics, 117*, 2055–2064.

Vo, V.A., Li, R., Kornell, N., Pouget, A., & Cantlon, J.F. (2014). Young children bet on their numerical skills: Metacognition in the numerical domain. *Psychological Science, 25*, 1712–1721.

Voight, A., & Hanson, T. (2017). How are middle school climate and academic performance related across schools and over time? REL 2017-212. *ERIC,* ED572366.

Voigt, R.G., & others (2017). Academic achievement in adults with a history of attention-deficit/hyperactivity disorder: A population-based prospective study. *Journal of Developmental and Behavioral Pediatrics, 38*, 1–11.

Volbrecht, M.M., & Goldsmith, H.H. (2010). Early temperamental and family predictors of shyness and anxiety. *Developmental Psychology, 46*, 1192–1205.

Volkmar, F.R., Riechow, B., Westphal, A., & Mandell, D.S. (2014). Autism and autism spectrum diagnostic concepts. In F.R. Volkmar & others (Eds.), *Handbook of autism and pervasive developmental disorders.* New York: Wiley.

Volkow, N.D., Compton, W.M., & Wargo, E.M. (2017). The risks of marijuana use during pregnancy. *Journal of the American Medical Association, 317*, 129–130.

Volpe, E.M., & others (2013). What's age got to do with it? Partner age difference, power, intimate partner violence, and sexual risk in urban adolescents. *Journal of Interpersonal Violence, 28*, 2068–2087.

von Bonsdorff, M.B., & others (2011). Work ability in midlife as a predictor of mortality and disability in later life: A 28-year prospective follow-up study. *Canadian Medical Association Journal, 183*, E235–E242.

von Bonsdorff, M.B., & others (2012). Work ability as a determinant of old age disability severity: Evidence from the 28-year Finnish longitudinal study on municipal employees. *Aging: Clinical and Experimental Research, 24*, 354–360.

von dem Hagen, E.A., & Bright, N. (2017). High autistic trait individuals do not modulate gaze behavior in response to social presence but look away more when actively engaged in an interaction. *Autism Research, 10*, 359–368.

Von Rosen, P., & others (2018a). Young, talented, and injured: Injury perceptions, experiences, and consequences in adolescent elite athletes. *European Journal of Sport Science, 18*, 731–740.

Von Rosen, P., & others (2018b). High injury burden in elite adolescent athletes: A 52-week prospective study. *Journal of Athletic Training, 53*, 262–270.

Von Soest, T., & others (2018). Self-esteem across the second half of life: The role of socioeconomic status, physical health, social relationships, and personality factors. *Journal of Personality and Social Psychology, 114*, 945–958.

Voorpostel, M., & Blieszner, R. (2008). Intergenerational solidarity and support between adult siblings. *Journal of Marriage and the Family, 70*, 157–167.

Vorona, R.D., & others (2014). Adolescent crash rates and school start times in two central Virginia counties, 2009–2011: A follow-up study to a southeastern Virginia study, 2007–2008. *Journal of Clinical Sleep Medicine, 10*, 1169–1177.

Vosylis, R., Erentaite, R., & Crocetti, E. (2018). Global versus domain-specific identity processes. *Emerging Adulthood, 6*, 32–41.

Votavova, H., & others (2012). Deregulation of gene expression induced by environmental tobacco smoke exposure in pregnancy. *Nicotine and Tobacco Research, 14*(9), 1073–1082.

Vreeman, R.C., & Carroll, A.E. (2007). A systematic review of school-based interventions to prevent bullying. *Archives of Pediatric and Adolescent Medicine, 161*, 78–88.

Vu, J.A. (2016). The fourth 'R': Relationships, shifting from risk to resilience. In K.E. Sanders & A.W. Guerra (Eds.), *The culture of child care.* New York: Oxford University Press.

Vujovic, V., & others (2017). Evolutionary developmental robotics: Improving morphology and control of physical robots. *Artificial Life, 23*, 169–185.

Vukelich, C., & others (2020). *Helping children learn language and literacy* (5th ed.). Upper Saddle River, NJ: Pearson.

Vuksanovic, V., & others (2019, in press). Cortical thickness and surface area networks in healthy aging, Alzheimer's disease, and behavioral variant front-temporal dementia. *International Journal of Neural Systems.*

Vurpillot, E. (1968). The development of scanning strategies and their relation to visual differentiation. *Journal of Experimental Child Psychology, 6*, 632–650.

Vygotsky, L.S. (1962). *Thought and language.* Cambridge, MA: MIT Press.

Vysniauske, R., Verburgh, L., Oosterlaan, J., & Molendijk, M.L. (2019, in press). The effects of physical exercise on functional outcomes in the treatment of ADHD. *Journal of Attention Disorders.*

W

Wachs, T.D. (2000). *Necessary but not sufficient.* Washington, DC: American Psychological Association.

Wachs, T.D., & Bates, J.E. (2011). Temperament. In J.G. Bremner & T.D. Wachs (Eds.), *Wiley-Blackwell handbook of infant development* (2nd ed.). New York: Wiley.

Wade, M., & others (2019). Long-term effects of institutional rearing, foster care, and brain activity on memory and executive functioning. *PNAS, 116*, 1803–1813.

Wade, T.D. (2019). Recent research on bulimia nervosa. *Psychiatric Clinics of North America, 42*, 21–32.

Wagers, K.B., & Kiel, E.J. (2019,in press). The influence of parenting and temperament on empathy development in toddlers. *Journal of Family Psychology.*

Wagner, D.A. (2018). *Human development and international development.* New York: Routledge.

Wahl, H-W., & Gitlin, L.N. (2019). Linking the socio-physical environment to successful aging: From basic research to intervention to implementation science considerations. In R. Fernandez-Ballesteros, A. Benetos, & J-M. Robine (Eds.), *Cambridge handbook of successful aging.* New York: Cambridge University Press.

Wahl, S., Marinovic, V., & Trauble, B. (2019, in press). Gaze cues of isolated eyes facilitate the encoding and further processing of objects in 4-month-old infants. *Developmental Cognitive Neuroscience.*

Wai, J., Putallaz, M., & Makel, M.C. (2012). Studying intellectual outliers: Are there sex differences and are the smart getting smarter? *Current Directions in Psychological Science, 21*, 382–390.

Wainwright, L., Nee, C., & Vrij, A. (2018). "I don't know how, but I'll figure it out somehow": Future possible selves and aspiration in "at-risk" adolescents. *International Journal of Offender Therapy and Comparative Criminology, 62*, 504–523.

Waite, L.J. (2009). Marriage. In D. Carr (Ed.), *Encyclopedia of the life course and human development.* Boston: Gale Cengage.

Waiter, G.D., & others (2009). Exploring possible neural mechanisms of intelligence differences using processing speed and working memory tasks. *Intelligence, 37*, 199–206.

Waldenstrom, U., & others (2014). Adverse pregnancy outcomes related to advanced maternal age compared with smoking and being overweight. *Obstetrics and Gynecology, 123*, 104–112.

Waldinger, R.J., & Schulz, M.C. (2010). What's love got to do with it? Social functioning, perceived health, and daily happiness in married octogenarians. *Psychology and Aging, 25*, 422–431.

Walfield, S.M. (2016). When a cleared rape is not cleared: A multilevel study of arrest and exceptional clearance. *Journal of Interpersonal Violence, 31*, 1767–1792.

Walfield, S.M. (2019, in press). "Men cannot be raped": Correlates of male rape myth acceptance. *Journal of Interpersonal Violence.*

Walia, R., & others (2018). Disorders of sex development: A study of 194 cases. *Endocrine Connections, 7*, 364–371.

Walker, A. (2019). The promise of active aging. In R. Fernandez-Ballesteros, A. Benetos, & J-M. Robine (Eds.), *Cambridge handbook of successful aging.* New York: Cambridge University Press.

Walker, L.J. (1982). The sequentiality of Kohlberg's stages of moral development. *Child Development, 53*, 1130–1136.

Walker, L.J. (2002). Moral exemplarity. In W. Damon (Ed.), *Bringing in a new era of character education.* Stanford, CA: Hoover Press.

Walker, L.J. (2004). Progress and prospects in the psychology of moral development. *Merrill-Palmer Quarterly, 50,* 546–557.

Walker, L.J. (2013). Exemplars' moral behavior is self-regarding. *New Directions in Child and Adolescent Development, 142,* 27–40.

Walker, L.J. (2014). Moral personality, motivation, and identity. In M. Killen & J.G. Smetana (Eds.), *Handbook of moral development* (2nd ed.). New York: Psychology Press.

Walker, L.J. (2016). The moral character of heroes. In. S.T. Allison & others (Eds.), *Handbook of heroism and heroic leadership.* New York: Elsevier.

Walker, L.J., Frimer, J.A., & Dunlop, W.L. (2011). Varieties of moral personality: Beyond the banality of heroism. *Journal of Personality, 78*(3), 907–942.

Walker, L.J., & others (1995). Reasoning about morality and real-life moral problems. In M. Killen & D. Hart (Eds.), *Morality in everyday life.* New York: Cambridge University Press.

Walle, E.A., & Campos, J.J. (2014). Infant language development is related to the acquisition of walking. *Developmental Psychology, 50,* 336–348.

Wallenborg, K., & others (2009). Red wine triggers cell death and thiroredoxin reductase inhibition: Effects beyond resveratrol and SIRT 1. *Experimental Cell Research, 315*(8), 1360–1371.

Wallerstein, A., & others (2019). Primary topography-guided LASIK: Refractive, visual, and subjective quality of vision outcomes for astigmatism >2.00 diopters. *Journal of Refractive Surgery, 35,* 78–86.

Wallerstein, J.S. (2008). Divorce. In M.M. Haith & J.B. Benson (Eds.), *Encyclopedia of infant and early childhood development.* Oxford, UK: Elsevier.

Walsh, B.T. (2019). Diagnostic categories for eating disorders: Current status and what lies ahead. *Psychiatric Clinics of North America, 42,* 1–10.

Walsh, L.A. (2000, Spring). The inside scoop on child development: Interview. *Cutting through the hype.* Minneapolis: College of Education and Human Development, University of Minnesota.

Walsh, M.N., & Gates, C.C. (2018). Zero tolerance for sexual harassment in cardiology. *Journal of the American College of Cardiology, 71,* 1176–1177.

Walsh, R. (2011). Lifestyle and mental health. *American Psychologist, 66,* 79–92.

Walters, G.D. (2019, in press). Peer influence or projection bias? Predicting respondent delinquency with perceptual measures of peer delinquency in 22 samples. *Journal of Adolescence.*

Wandell, P.E., Carlsson, A.C., & Theobald, H. (2009). The association between BMI value and long-term mortality. *International Journal of Obesity, 33,* 577–582.

Wang, B., & others (2014). The impact of youth, family, peer, and neighborhood risk factors on developmental trajectories of risk involvement from early through middle adolescence. *Social Science Medicine, 106,* 43–52.

Wang, B., & others (2016). The influence of sensation-seeking and parental and peer influences in early adolescence on risk involvement through middle adolescence: A structural equation modeling analysis. *Youth and Society, 48,* 220–241.

Wang, C.D., & others (2019, in press). Grandparents as the primary care providers for their grandchildren: A cross-cultural comparison of Chinese and U.S. samples. *International Journal of Aging and Human Development.*

Wang, D.X., & others (2019). A candidate-gene approach identifies novel associations between common variants in/near syndromic obesity genes and body-mass index in pediatric and adult European populations. *Diabetes, 68,* 724–732.

Wang, H., Lee, J.H., & Tian, Y. (2019). Critical genes in white adipose tissue based on gene expression profile following exercise. *International Journal of Sports Medicine, 40,* 57–61.

Wang, H., Lin, S.L., Leung, G.M., & Schooling, C.M. (2016). Age at onset of puberty and adolescent depression: "Children of 1997" birth cohort.

Wang, J., & others (2018). Association between body mass index and all-cause mortality among oldest old Chinese. *Journal of Nutrition, Health, and Aging, 22,* 262–268.

Wang, J., & others (2019, in press). Breastfeeding and respiratory tract infections during the first 2 years of life. *ERJ Open Research.*

Wang, Q., & Pomerantz, E.M. (2009). The motivational landscape of early adolescence in the United States and China: A longitudinal study. *Child Development, 80,* 1272–1287.

Wang, S., & others (2019, in press). Brain functional organization with language lateralization. *Cerebral Cortex.*

Wang, S., & others (2019, in press). The prevalence of depression and anxiety symptoms among overweight/obese and non-overweight/non-obese children/adolescents in China: A systematic review and meta-analysis. *International Journal of Environmental Research and Public Health.*

Wang, S.C., & others (2019, in press). The experience of parents living with a child with cancer at the end of life. *European Journal of Cancer Care.*

Wang, W. (2014). *Record shares of Americans have never been married.* Washington, DC: Pew Research Center.

Wang, X., Hu, S., & Liu, L. (2017). Phosphorylation and acetylation modifications of FOXO3a: Independently or synergistically? *Oncology Letters, 13,* 2867–2872.

Wang, Y., & others (2019). Prenatal tobacco exposure modulated the association of genetic variants with diagnosed ADHD and its symptom domain in children: A community based case-control study. *Scientific Reports, 9*(1), 4274.

Wang, Z.W., Hua, J., & Xu, Y.H. (2015). The relationship between gentle tactile stimulation on the fetus and its temperament 3 months after birth. *Behavioral Neuroscience, 2015,* 371906.

Ward, E.V. (2018). Reduced recognition and priming in older relative to young adults for incidental and intentional information. *Consciousness and Cognition, 57,* 62–73.

Ward, L.M., Moorman, J., & Grower, P. (2019). Entertainment media's role in the sexual socialization of Western youth: A review of research from 2000–2017. In S. Lamb & J. Gilbert (Eds.), *Cambridge handbook of sexual development.* New York: Cambridge University Press.

Ware, J.E., Kosinski, M., & Dewey, J.E. (2000). *How to score Version 2 of the SF-36 Health Survey.* Boston: Quality Metric.

Wariki, W.M., & others (2013). Risk factors associated with outcomes of very low birthweight infants in four Asian countries. *Journal of Pediatrics and Child Health, 49,* E23–E27.

Warneken, F., & Tomasello, M. (2006). Altruistic helping in human infants and young chimpanzees. *Science, 311,* 1301–1303.

Warner, T.D. (2018). Adolescent sexual risk taking: The distribution of youth behaviors and perceived peer attitudes across neighborhood contexts. *Journal of Adolescent Health, 62,* 226–233.

Warr, P. (1994). Age and employment. In M. Dunnette, L. Hough, & H. Triandis (Eds.), *Handbook of industrial and organizational psychology* (Vol. 4). Palo Alto, CA: Consulting Psychologists Press.

Warren, S.F., & others (2017). The longitudinal effects of parenting on adaptive behavior in children with Fragile X syndrome. *Journal of Autism and Developmental Disorders, 47,* 768–784.

Warshak, R.A. (2017, March). Personal communication. Department of Psychology, University of Texas at Dallas, Richardson.

Wasserberg, M.J. (2014). Stereotype threat effects on African American children in an urban elementary school. *Journal of Experimental Education, 82,* 502–517.

Wataganara, T., & others (2016). Fetal magnetic resonance imaging and ultrasound. *Journal of Perinatal Medicine, 44,* 533–542.

Watamura, S.E., Phillips, D.A., Morrissey, D.A., McCartney, T.W., & Bub, K. (2011). Double jeopardy: Poorer social-emotional outcomes for children in the NICHD SECCYD who experience home and child-care environments that convey risk. *Child Development, 82,* 48–65.

Waterman, A.S. (1985). Identity in the context of adolescent psychology. In A.S. Waterman (Ed.), *Identity in adolescence: Processes and contents.* San Francisco: Jossey-Bass.

Waterman, A.S. (1992). Identity as an aspect of optimal psychological functioning. In G.R. Adams, T.P. Gulotta, & R. Montemayor (Eds.), *Adolescent identity formation.* Newbury Park, CA: Sage.

Waterman, E.A., & Lefkowtiz, E.S. (2018). Sexuality across the lifespan. In M.H. Bornstein (Ed.), *SAGE encyclopedia of lifespan human development.* Thousand Oaks, CA: Sage.

Waters, S.F., West, T.V., & Mendes, W.B. (2014). Stress contagion: Physiological covariation between mothers and infants. *Psychological Science, 25,* 934–942.

Waters, T.E., & Roisman, G.I. (2018). The secure base script concept: An overview. *Current Opinion in Psychology, 25,* 162–166.

Waters, T.E., Ruiz, S.K., & Roisman, G.I. (2017). Origins of secure base script knowledge and the developmental construction of attachment representations. *Child Development, 88,* 198–209.

Watkins, L., & others (2019). An interest-based intervention package to increase peer social interaction in young children with autism spectrum disorder. *Journal of Applied Behavior Analysis, 52,* 132–149.

Watson, J.A., Randolph, S.M., & Lyons, J.L. (2005). African-American grandmothers as health educators in the family. *International Journal of Aging and Human Development, 60,* 343–356.

Watson, J.B. (1928). *Psychological care of infant and child.* New York: Norton.

Watson, V. (2018). *Transformative schooling.* New York: Routledge.

Wattamwar, K., & others (2017). Increases in the rate of age-related hearing loss in the older old. *JAMA Otolaryngology—Head and Neck Surgery, 143,* 41-45.

Watts, T.W., & others (2018). The Chicago School Readiness Project: Examining long-term impacts of an early childhood intervention. *PLoS One, 13*(7), e0200144.

Waxman, S., & Goswami, U. (2012). Acquiring language: Learning the spoken and written word. In S. Pauen & M. Bornstein (Eds.), *Early child development and later outcome.* New York: Cambridge University Press.

Waxman, S., & others (2013). Are nouns learned before verbs? Infants provide insight into a longstanding debate. *Child Development Perspectives, 7,* 155-159.

Wayne, P.M., & others (2014). Effect of tai chi on cognitive performance in older adults: Systematic review and meta-analysis. *Journal of the American Geriatrics Society, 62,* 25-39.

Weakley, A., & Schmitter-Edgecombe, M. (2014). Analysis of verbal fluency ability in Alzheimer's disease: The role of clustering, switching, and semantic proximities. *Archives of Clinical Neuropsychology, 29,* 256-268.

Weatherhead, D., & White, K.S. (2017). Read my lips: Visual speech influences word processing by infants. *Cognition, 160,* 103-109.

Weaver. J.M., & Schofield, T.J. (2015). Mediation and moderation of divorce effects on children's behavior problems. *Journal of Family Psychology, 29,* 39-48.

Webb, M.S., Passmore, D., Cline, G., & Maguire, D. (2014). Ethical issues related to caring for low birth weight infants. *Nursing Ethics, 21,* 731-741.

Weber, M., & others (2019). Communication in families with minor children following the loss of a parent to cancer. *European Journal of Oncology Nursing, 39,* 41-46.

Webster, J.D., & others (2018). Wisdom and meaning in emerging adulthood. *Emerging Adulthood, 6,* 118-136.

Webster, N.S., & Worrell, F.C. (2008). Academically-talented adolescents' attitudes toward service in the community. *Gifted Child Quarterly, 52,* 170-179.

Wechsler, D. (1939). *The measurement of adult intelligence.* Baltimore: Williams & Wilkins.

Wechsler, D. (2014). *Wechsler Intelligence Scale for Children* (5th ed.). Upper Saddle River, NJ: Pearson.

Wechsler, H., & others (2002). Trends in college binge drinking during a period of increased prevention efforts: Findings from four Harvard School of Public Health college alcohol study surveys, 1993-2001. *Journal of American College Health, 50,* 203-217.

Weech-Maldonado, R., & others (2019, in press). Nursing home quality and financial performance: Is there a business case for quality? *Inquiry.*

Weger, H.W., Cole, M., & Akbulut, V. (2019). Relationship maintenance across platonic and non-platonic cross-sex friendships in emerging adults. *Journal of Social Psychology, 159,* 15-29.

Wei, J., & others (2019). Late-life depression and cognitive function among older adults in the U.S.: The National Health and Nutrition Examination Survey, 2011-2014. *Journal of Psychiatric Research 111,* 30-35.

Wei, W., & Ji, S. (2018). Cellular senescence: Molecular mechanisms and pathogenicity. *Journal of Cellular Physiology, 233,* 9121-9135.

Weikert, D.P. (1993). *Long-term positive effects in the Perry Preschool Head Start Program.* Unpublished data. High/Scope Foundation, Ypsilanti, MI.

Weinraub, M., & Kaufman, R. (2019). Single parenthood. In M.H. Bornstein (Ed.), *Handbook of parenting* (3rd ed.). New York: Routledge.

Weinraub, M., & others (2012). Patterns of developmental change in infants' nighttime sleep awakenings from 6 through 36 months of age. *Developmental Psychology, 148,* 1511-1528.

Weinstein, B.E., Sirow, L.W., & Moser, S. (2016). Relating hearing aid use to social and emotional loneliness in older adults. *American Journal of Audiology, 25,* 54-61.

Weinstein, N., & others (2019). Autonomous orientation predicts longevity: New findings from the Nun Study. *Journal of Personality, 87,* 181-193.

Weinstein, R.S. (2004). *Reaching higher: The power of expectations in schooling.* Cambridge, MA: Harvard University Press.

Weisleder, A., & Fernald, A. (2013). Talking to children matters: Early language experience strengthens processing and builds vocabulary. *Psychological Science, 24,* 2143-2152.

Weisleder, A., & others (2018). Reading aloud and child development: A cluster-randomized trial in Brazil. *Pediatrics, 141.* doi:10.1542/peds.2017-0723

Weisman, J., & others (2019, in press). Adolescent sexual behavior and emergency department use. *Pediatric Emergency Care.*

Weisman, O., Zagoory-Sharon, O., & Feldman, R. (2014). Oxytocin administration, salivary testosterone, and father-infant social behavior. *Progress in Neuro-Psychopharmacology and Biological Psychiatry, 49,* 47-52.

Weiss, L.A., & others (2008). Association between microdeletion and microduplication at 16p 11.2 and autism. *New England Journal of Medicine, 358,* 667-675.

Weitkamp, K., & Seiffge-Krenke, I. (2019). The association between parental rearing dimensions and adolescent psychopathology: A cross-cultural study. *Journal of Youth and Adolescence, 48,* 469-483.

Wellman, H.M. (2011). Developing a theory of mind. In U. Goswami (Ed.), *The Blackwell handbook of childhood cognitive development* (2nd ed.). New York: Wiley.

Wellman, H.M. (2015). *Making minds.* New York: Oxford University Press.

Wellman, H.M., Cross, D., & Watson, J. (2001). Meta-analysis of theory-of-mind development: The truth about false belief. *Child Development, 72,* 655-684.

Wellman, H.M., & Woolley, J.D. (1990). From simple desires to ordinary beliefs: The early development of everyday psychology. *Cognition, 35,* 245-275.

Wellman, R.J., & others (2018). Socioeconomic status is associated with the prevalence and co-occurrence of risk factors for cigarette smoking initiation during adolescence. *International Journal of Public Health, 63,* 125-136.

Welmer, A.K., Rizzuto, D., Qiu, C., Caracciolo, B., & Laukka, E.J. (2014). Walking speed, processing speed, and dementia: A population-based longitudinal study. *Journals of Gerontology A: Biological Sciences and Medical Sciences, 69,* 1503-1510.

Wen, S.W., & Wong, C.H.Y. (2019). Aging- and vascular-related pathologies. *Microcirculation, 26*(2), e12463.

Wenestam, C.G., & Wass, H. (1987). Swedish and U.S. children's thinking about death: A qualitative study and cross-cultural comparison. *Death Studies, 11,* 99-121.

Wenger, N.S., & others (2003). The quality of medical care provided to vulnerable community-dwelling older patients. *Annals of Internal Medicine, 139,* 740-747.

Wennergren, G., & others (2015). Updated Swedish advice on reducing the risk of sudden infant death syndrome. *Acta Pediatrica, 104,* 444-448.

Wentzel, K. (1997). Student motivation in middle school: The role of perceived pedagogical caring. *Journal of Educational Psychology, 89,* 411-419.

Wentzel, K.R., & Asher, S.R. (1995). The academic lives of neglected, rejected, popular, and controversial children. *Child Development, 66,* 754-763.

Wentzel, K.R., & Munecks, K. (2016). Peer influence on students' motivation, academic achievement, and social behavior. In K.R. Wentzel & G. Ramani (Eds.), *Handbook of social influences in school contexts.* New York: Routledge.

Werneck, A.O., & others (2019). Leisure time physical activity reduces the association between TV-viewing and depressive symptoms: A large study among 59,401 Brazilian adults. *Journal of Affective Disorders, 252,* 310-314.

Werner, N.E., & others (2014). Maternal social coaching quality interrupts the development of relational aggression during early childhood. *Social Development, 23,* 470-486.

Wesche, R., & Lefkowitz, E.S. (2020, in press). Normative sexual development and milestones. In S. Hupp & J. Jewell (Eds.), *Encyclopedia of child and adolescent development.* New York: Wiley-Blackwell.

Wesche, R., Lefkowitz, E.S., & Vasilenko, S.A. (2018). Latent classes of sexual behaviors: Prevalence, predictors, and consequences. *Sexuality Research and Social Policy, 14,* 100-111.

Westerhof, G.J., Whitbourne, S.K., & Freeman, G.P. (2012). The aging self in cultural context: The relation of conceptions of aging to identity processes and self-esteem in the United States and the Netherlands. *Journals of Gerontology B: Psychological Sciences and Social Sciences, 67,* 52-60.

Westrate, N.M., & Gluck, J. (2017). Hard-earned wisdom: Exploratory processing of difficult life experience is positively associated with wisdom. *Developmental Psychology, 53,* 800-814.

Wethington, E., Kessler, R., & Pixley, J. (2004). Turning points in adulthood. In G. Brim, C.D. Ryff, & R. Kessler (Eds.), *How healthy we are: A national study of well-being in midlife.* Chicago: University of Chicago Press.

Wheaton, A.G., & others (2018). Short sleep duration among middle school and high school students— . United States, 2015. *MMWR Morbidity and Mortality Weekly Reports, 67*(3), 85-90.

Wheeler, J.J., & Richey, D.D. (2019). *Behavior management* (4th ed.). Upper Saddle River, NJ: Pearson.

Whitaker, D.J., & Rogers-Brown, J.S. (2019). Child maltreatment and the family. In B.H. Friese (Ed.), *APA handbook of contemporary family psychology*. Washington, DC: APA Books.

White, C.L., & others (2018). Advancing care for family caregivers of persons with dementia through caregiver and community partnerships. *Research Involvement and Engagement, 4*, 1.

White, E.R., & others (2018). Freshman year alcohol and marijuana use prospectively predict time to college graduation and subsequent adult roles and independence. *Journal of American College Health, 65*, 413-422.

White, L. (2019). Segmentation of speech. In S-A Rueschemeyer & M. Gareth Gaskell (Eds.), *Oxford handbook of psycholinguistics* (2nd ed.). New York: Oxford University Press.

White, L.R., & others (2016). Neuropathic comorbidity and cognitive impairment in the Nun and Honolulu-Asia Aging Studies. *Neurology, 66*, 1000-1008.

White, M.J., & others (2017). Calorie restriction attenuates terminal differentiation of immune cells. *Frontiers in Neuroscience, 7*, 667.

White, R.M., & others (2018). Ethnic socialization in neighborhood contexts: Implications for ethnic attitude and identity development among Mexican-origin adolescents. *Child Development, 89*, 1004-1021.

White, R.M.B., & others (2019). U.S. Mexican parents' use of harsh parenting in the context of neighborhood danger. *Journal of Family Psychology, 33*, 77-87.

Wickelgren, I. (1999). Nurture helps to mold able minds. *Science, 283*, 1832-1834.

Wicks, S., Berger, Z., & Camic, P.M. (2019). It's how I am... it's what I am... it's a part of who I am: A narrative of the impact of adolescent-onset chronic illness on identity formation in young people. *Clinical Child Psychology and Psychiatry, 24*, 40-52.

Widiger, T.A. (2009). Neuroticism. In M.R. Leary & R.H. Hoyle (Eds.), *Handbook of individual differences in social behavior*. New York: Guilford.

Widman, L., Choukas-Bradley, S., Helms, S.W., & Prinstein, M.J. (2016). Adolescent susceptibility to peer influence in sexual situations. *Journal of Adolescent Health, 58*, 323-329.

Widom, C.S., Czaja, S.J., Bentley, T., & Johnson, M.S. (2012). A prospective investigation of physical health outcomes in abused and neglected children: New findings from a 30-year follow-up. *American Journal of Public Health, 102*(6), 1135-1144.

Widom, C.S., Czaja, S.J., & DuMont, K.A. (2015). Intergenerational transmission of child abuse and neglect: Real or detection bias? *Science, 347*, 1480-1485.

Wierenga, C.E., & others (2018). The acceptability, feasibility, and possible benefits of a neurobiologically-informed 5-day multifamily treatment for adults with anorexia nervosa. *International Journal of Eating Disorders, 51*, 863-869.

Wiersma-Mosley, J.D., Jozkowski, K.N., & Martinez, T. (2017). An empirical investigation of campus demographics and reported rapes. *Journal of American College Health, 65*, 482-491.

Wiesen, S.E., Watkins, R.M., & Needham, A.W. (2016). Active motor training has long-term effects on infants' object exploration. *Frontiers in Psychology, 7*, 599.

Wigfield, A., Rosenzweig, E.Q., & Eccles, J.S. (2017). Achievement values, interactions, interventions, and future directions. In A.J. Elliott, C.S. Dweck, & D.S. Yeager (Eds.), *Handbook of competence and motivation* (2nd ed.). New York: Guilford.

Wigfield, A., & others (2015). Development of achievement motivation and engagement. In R.M. Lerner (Ed.), *Handbook of child psychology and developmental science* (7th ed.). New York: Wiley.

Wike, R. (2014, January 14). French more accepting of infidelity than people in other countries. *Pew Research Center*.

Wilcox, S., & others (2003). The effects of widowhood on physical and mental health, health behaviors, and health outcomes: The women's health initiative. *Health Psychology, 22*, 513-522.

Willcox, D.C., Scapagnini, G., & Willcox, B.J. (2014). Healthy aging diets other than Mediterranean: A focus on the Okinawan diet. *Mechanisms of Aging and Development, 136-137*, 148-162.

Willey, J., Sandman, K., & Wood, D. (2020). *Prescott's microbiology* (11th ed.). New York: McGraw-Hill.

Williams, B.K., Sawyer, S.C., & Wahlstrom, C.M. (2017). *Marriage, families, and intimate relationships* (4th ed.). Upper Saddle River, NJ: Pearson.

Williams, D.D., Yancher, S.C., Jensen, L.C., & Lewis, C. (2003). Character education in a public high school: A multi-year inquiry into unified studies. *Journal of Moral Education, 32*, 3-33.

Williams, D.P., & others (2019, in press). Stereotype threat, trait perseveration, and vagal activity: Evidence for mechanisms underpinning health disparities in Black Americans. *Ethnicity and Health*.

Williams, G.L., Keigher, S., & Williams, A.V. (2012). Spiritual well-being among older African Americans in a midwestern city. *Journal of Religion and Health, 51*(2), 355-370.

Williams, K.M., Nathanson, C., & Paulhus, D.L. (2010). Identifying and profiling academic cheaters: Their personality, cognitive ability, and motivation. *Journal of Experimental Psychology: Applied, 16*, 293-307.

Williams, M.E. (1995). *The American Geriatric Society's complete guide to aging and health*. New York: Harmony Books.

Williams, R.D., & others (2018). High-risk driving behaviors among 12th grade students: Differences between alcohol-only and alcohol mixed with energy drink users. *Substance Use and Misuse, 53*, 137-142.

Williamson, H.C., & others (2018). Premarital education and later relationship help-seeking. *Journal of Family Psychology, 32*, 276-281.

Williamson, R.A., Donohue, M.R., & Tully, E.C. (2013). Learning how to help others: Two-year-olds' social learning of a prosocial act. *Journal of Experimental Child Psychology, 114*, 543-550.

Willie, T.C., & others (2018). "Think like a man": How sexual cultural scripting and masculinity influence changes in men's use of intimate partner violence. *American Journal of Community Psychology, 61*, 240-250.

Willinger, U., & others (2019, in press). Developmental steps in metaphorical language abilities: The influence of age, gender, cognitive flexibility, information processing speed, and analogical reasoning. *Language and Speech*.

Willink, A., & others (2019, in press). Are older Americans getting the long-term services and supports they need? *Issue Brief*.

Willink, A., Reed, N.S., & Lin, F.R. (2019, in press). Cost-benefit analysis of hearing care services: What is it worth to Medicare? *Journal of the American Geriatrics Society*.

Willis, S.L., & Belleville, S. (2016). Cognitive training in later adulthood. In K.W. Schaie & S.L. Willis (Eds.), *Handbook of the psychology of aging* (8th ed.). New York: Elsevier.

Willoughby, B.J., Hall, S.S., & Goff, S. (2015). Marriage matters but how much? Marital centrality among young adults. *Journal of Psychology, 149*, 796-817.

Willoughby, B.J., & James, S.L. (2017). *The marriage paradox*. New York: Oxford University Press.

Willoughby, M.T., Gottfredson, N.C., & Stifter, C.A. (2017). Observed temperament from ages 6 to 36 months predicts parent- and teacher-reported attention deficit/hyperactivity disorder symptoms in first grade. *Development and Psychopathology, 29*, 107-120.

Willoughby, M.T., Wylie, A.C., & Little, M.H. (2019, in press). Testing longitudinal associations between executive function and academic achievement. *Developmental Psychology*.

Willoughby, M.T., & others (2017). Developmental delays in executive function from 3 to 5 years of age predict kindergarten academic readiness. *Journal of Learning Disabilities, 50*, 359-372.

Wilson, B.J. (2008). Media and children's aggression, fear, and altruism. *Future of Children, 18*(1), 87-118.

Wilson, D.M., Cohen, J., Deliens, L., Hewitt, J.A., & Houttekier, D. (2013). The preferred place of last days: Results of a representative population-based survey. *Journal of Palliative Medicine, 16*(5), 502-508.

Wilson, D.M., Errasti-Ibarrondo, B., & Low, G. (2019). Where are we now in relation to determining the prevalence of ageism in this era of escalating population aging? *Aging Research and Reviews, 51*, 78-84.

Wilson, L.C., & Miller, K.E. (2016). Meta-analysis of the prevalence of unacknowledged rape. *Trauma, Violence, and Abuse, 17*, 149-159.

Wilson, M.N., & others (2018). Driving under the influence behaviors among high school students who mix alcohol with energy drinks. *Preventive Medicine, 111*, 402-409.

Wilson, R.S., Mendes de Leon, C.F., Bienas, J.L., Evans, D.A., & Bennett, D.A. (2004). Personality and mortality in old age. *Journals of Gerontology B: Psychological Sciences and Social Sciences, 59*, 110B-116B.

Wilson, R.S., & others (2002). Participation in cognitively stimulating activities and risk of incident Alzheimer disease. *Journal of the American Medical Association, 287*, 742-748.

Wilson, R.S., & others (2015). Conscientiousness, dementia related pathology, and trajectories of cognitive aging. *Psychology and Aging, 30*, 74-82.

Wilson, R.S., & others (2018). Terminal decline of episodic memory and perceptual speed in a biracial population. *Neuropsychology, Development, and Cognition B: Aging, Neuropsychology, and Cognition, 25*, 378-389.

Wilson, S.H., & others (2018). Labor analgesia onset with dural puncture epidural versus traditional epidural using a 26-gauge Whitacre needle and 0.125% bupivacaine bolus: A randomized clinical trial. *Anesthesia and Analgesia, 126*, 545-551.

Wilson, S.J., & others (2019, in press). When distress becomes somatic: Dementia family caregivers' distress and genetic vulnerability to pain and sleep problems. *Gerontologist.*

Winerman, L. (2005, January). Leading the way. *Monitor on Psychology, 36*(1), 64–67.

Wink, P., & Dillon, M. (2002). Spiritual development across the adult life course: Findings from a longitudinal study. *Journal of Adult Development, 9*, 79–94.

Winkler, M., Mueller, J.L., Friederici, A.D., & Mäniel, C. (2019, in press). Infant cognition includes the potentially human-unique ability to encode embedding. *Scientific Advances.*

Winne, P.H. (2018). Cognition and metacognition within self-regulated learning. In D.H. Schunk & J.A. Greene (Eds.), *Handbook of self-regulation of learning and performance* (2nd ed.). New York: Cambridge University Press.

Winne, P.H. (2018). Cognition and metacognition within self-regulated learning. In D.A. Schunk & J.A. Greene (Eds.), *Handbook of self-regulation of learning and performance* (2nd ed.). New York: Routledge.

Winner, E. (1986, August). Where pelicans kiss seals. *Psychology Today,* pp. 24–35.

Winner, E. (1996). *Gifted children: Myths and realities.* New York: Basic Books.

Winner, E. (2000). The origins and ends of giftedness. *American Psychologist, 55,* 159–169.

Winner, E. (2006). Development in the arts: Drawing and music. In W. Damon & R. Lerner (Eds.), *Handbook of child psychology* (6th ed.). New York: Wiley.

Wise, P.M. (2006). Aging of the female reproductive system. In E.J. Masor & S.N. Austad (Eds.), *Handbook of the biology of aging* (6th ed.). New York: Elsevier.

Witelson, S.F., Kigar, D.L., & Harvey, T. (1999). The exceptional brain of Albert Einstein. *The Lancet, 353,* 2149–2153.

Withers, M., Kharazmi, N., & Lim, E. (2018). Traditional beliefs and practices in pregnancy, childbirth, and postpartum: A review of the evidence from Asian countries. *Midwifery, 56,* 158–170.

Witkin, H.A., & others (1976). Criminality in XYY and XXY men. *Science, 193,* 547–555.

Witt, W.P., & others (2014). Maternal stressful life events prior to conception and the impact on infant birth weight in the United States. *American Journal of Public Health, 104*(Suppl. 1), S81–S89.

Witte, A.V., & others (2014). Long-chain omega-3 fatty acids improve brain function and structure in older adults. *Cerebral Cortex, 24,* 3059–3068.

Wojtkowiak, J., Vanherf, N.C., & Schuhmann, C.M. (2019). Grief in a biography of losses: Meaning-making in hard drug users' grief narratives on drug-related deaths. *Death Studies, 43,* 122–132.

Wolf, S., & McCoy, D.C. (2019, in press). The role of executive function and social-emotional skills in the development of literacy and numeracy during preschool: A cross-lagged longitudinal survey. *Developmental Science.*

Wolfe, K.L., & others (2019). Hopelessness as a predictor of suicide ideation in depressed male and female adolescent youth. *Suicide and Life-Threatening Behavior, 49*(1), 253–263.

Wolff, J.L., Mulcahy, J., Huang, J., Roth, D.L., Covinsky, K., & Kasper, J.D. (2018). Family caregivers of older adults, 1999–2015: Trends in characteristics, circumstances, and role-related appraisal. *Gerontologist, 58,* 1021–1032.

Wolitzky-Taylor, K.B., & others (2011). Reporting rape in a national sample of college women. *American Journal of College Health, 59,* 582–587.

Wolke, D., Lee, K., & Guy, A. (2017). Cyberbullying: A storm in a teacup? *European Child and Adolescent Psychiatry, 26,* 899–908.

Wolke, D., & Lereya, S.T. (2015). Long-term effects of bullying. *Archives of Disease in Childhood, 100,* 879–885.

Wombacher, K., & others (2018). "It just kind of happens": College students' rationalizations for blackout drinking. *Health Communication, 34,* 1–10.

Women's Sports Foundation (2001). *The 10 commandments for parents and coaches in youth sports.* Eisenhower Park, NY: Author.

Wong Briggs, T. (2007, October 18). An early start for learning. *USA Today,* p. 6D.

Wong, A.P., & others (2014). Estimating volume of the pituitary gland from T1-weighted magnetic-resonance images: Effects of age, puberty, testosterone, and estradiol. *NeuroImage, 94,* 216–221.

Wong, L., Goh, L.G., & Ramachandran, R. (2019, in press). Family-based therapy for anorexia nervosa: Results from a 7-year longitudinal Singapore study. *Eating and Weight Disorders.*

Wong, P.T.P., & Watt, L.M. (1991). What types of reminiscence are associated with successful aging? *Psychology and Aging, 6,* 272–279.

Wood, D., Harms, P., & Vazire, S. (2010). Perceiver effects as projective tests: What your perceptions of others say about you. *Journal of Personality and Social Psychology, 99,* 174–190.

Wood, J., & others (2011). Risk of falls, injurious falls, and other injuries resulting from visual impairment among older adults with age-related macular degeneration. *Investigative Ophthalmology & Visual Science, 52*(8), 5088–5092.

Wood, J.T. (2011). *Communication mosaics* (6th ed.). Boston: Cengage.

Wood, J.T. (2012). *Communication in our lives* (6th ed.). Boston: Cengage.

Woodhouse, S.S., & others (2019). The Circle of Security intervention. In H. Steele & M. Steele (Eds.), *Handbook of attachment-based interventions.* New York: Guilford.

Woodward, A.L., & Markman, E.M. (1998). Early word learning. In D. Kuhn & R.S. Siegler (Eds.), *Handbook of child psychology* (5th ed., Vol. 2). New York: Wiley.

Woodward, A.L., Markman, E.M., & Fitzsimmons, C. (1994). Rapid word learning in 13- and 18-month-olds. *Developmental Psychology, 30,* 553–556.

Woolgar, M., & Scott, S. (2013). The negative consequences of over-diagnosing attachment disorders in adopted children: The importance of comprehensive formulations. *Clinical Child Psychology and Psychiatry, 19,* 355–366.

World Health Organization (2000, February 2). *Adolescent health behavior in 28 countries.* Geneva, Switzerland: World Health Organization.

World Health Organization (2018). *Adolescent pregnancy: Fact sheet.* Geneva, Switzerland: World Health Organization.

Worrell, F.C., & others (2019). Gifted students. *Annual Review of Psychology* (Vol. 71). Palo Alto, CA: Annual Reviews.

Worthington, E.L. (1989). Religious faith across the life span: Implications for counseling and research. *Counseling Psychologist, 17,* 555–612.

Wraw, C., & others (2018). Intelligence in youth and health behaviors in middle age. *Intelligence, 69,* 71–86.

Wright, H., Jenks, R.A., & Demeyere, N. (2019). Frequent sexual activity predicts specific cognitive abilities in older adults. *Journals of Gerontology B: Psychological Sciences & Social Sciences, 74,* 47–51.

Wu, C-S., Jew, C.P., & Lu, H-C. (2011). Lasting impacts of prenatal cannabis exposure and the role of endogenous cannabinoids in the developing brain. *Future Neurology, 6,* 459–480.

Wu, M., & others (2019). Resveratrol alleviates chemotherapy-induced oogonial stem cell apoptosis and ovarian aging in mice. *Aging, 11,* 1030–1044.

Wu, R., & Scerif, G. (2018). Attention. In M.H. Bornstein (Ed.), *SAGE encyclopedia of lifespan human development.* Thousand Oaks, CA: Sage.

Wu, T., Gao, X., Chen, M., & van Dam, R.M. (2009). Long-term effectiveness of diet-plus-exercise interventions vs. diet-only interventions for weight loss: A meta-analysis. *Obesity Reviews, 10,* 313–323.

Wu, T.D., & others (2019). In-home secondhand smoke exposure among urban children with asthma: Contrasting homes with and without residential smokers. *Journal of Public Health Management and Practice, 25*(2), E7–E16.

Wu, Y., & others (2019). Adverse maternal and neonatal outcomes among singleton pregnancies in women of very advanced maternal age: A retrospective cohort study. *BMC Pregnancy and Childbirth, 19*(1), 3.

X

Xaverius, P., & others (2016). Risk factors associated with very low birth weight in a large urban area, stratified by adequacy of prenatal care. *Maternal and Child Health Journal, 20,* 623–629.

Xi, S., & others (2017). Effects of health education combining diet and exercise supervision in Chinese women with perimenopausal symptoms: A randomized controlled trial. *Climacteric, 13,* 561–569.

Xia, N. (2010). *Family factors and student outcomes.* Unpublished doctoral dissertation, RAND Corporation, Pardee RAND Graduate School, Pittsburgh.

Xiang, P., & others (2019). Individualist-collectivist differences in climate change inaction: The role of perceived intractability. *Frontiers in Psychology, 10,* 187.

Xiang, S., Liu, Y., & Bai, L. (2017). Parenting styles and adolescents' school adjustment: Investigating the mediating role of achievement goals within the 2 × 2 framework. *Frontiers in Psychology, 8,* 1809.

Xiao, J., & others (2018). Sarcopenic obesity and health outcomes in patients seeking weight loss treatment. *Clinical Nutrition ESPEN, 23,* 79–83.

Xiao, Q., Wu, M., & Zeng, T. (2019, in press). Social support networks in Chinese older adults: Health outcomes and health related behaviors: A path analysis. *Aging and Mental Health.*

Xiao, S.X., & others (2019). Will they listen to me? An examination of in-group gender bias in children's communication beliefs. *Sex Roles, 3-4,* 172–185.

Xie, C., & others (2017). Exercise and dietary program-induced weight reduction is associated with cognitive function in obese adolescents: A longitudinal study. *PeerJ, 5,* e3286.

Xie, Q., & Young, M.E. (1999). Integrated child development in rural China. *Education: The World Bank.* Washington, DC: The World Bank.

Xie, W., Mallin, B.M., & Richards, J.E. (2018). Development of infant sustained attention and its relation to EEG oscillations: An EEG and cortical course analysis study. *Developmental Science, 21*(3), e12562.

Xie, W., Mallin, B.M., & Richards, J.E. (2019). Development of brain functional connectivity and its relation to infant sustained attention in the first year of life. *Developmental Science, 22*(1), e12703.

Xie, W., & Richards, J.E. (2016). Effects of interstimulus intervals on behavioral, heart rate, and event-related potential indices of infant engagement and sustained attention. *Psychophysiology, 53,* 1128–1142.

Xie, W., & Richards, J.E. (2017). The relation between infant covert orienting, sustained attention, and brain activity. *Brain Topography, 30,* 198–219.

Xie, W., & others (2019, in press). Neural correlates of facial emotion processing in infancy. *Developmental Science.*

Xu, A., & others (2019, in press). Microtubule regulators act in the nervous system to modulate fat metabolism and longevity through DAF-16 in *C. elegans. Aging Cell.*

Xu, G., Zheng, H., & Li, J.Y. (2019, in press). Next-generation whole exome sequencing of glioblastoma with a primitive neuronal component. *Brain Tumor Pathology.*

Xu, H., Wen, L.M., Hardy, L.L., & Rissel, C. (2016). Associations of outdoor play and screen time with nocturnal sleep duration and pattern among young children. *Acta Pediatrica, 105,* 297–303.

Xu, H., Wen, L.M., & Rissel, C. (2015). Associations of parental influences with physical activity and screen time among young children: A systematic review. *Journal of Obesity, 2015,* 546925.

Xu, J. (2016). Mortality among centenarians in the United States, 2000–2014. *NCHS Data Brief, 233,* 1–8.

Xu, J., Saether, L., & Sommerville, J. (2016). Experience facilitates the emergence of sharing behavior among 7.5-month-old infants. *Developmental Psychology, 52,* 1732–1743.

Xu, P., & others (2019, in press). Intergenerational financial exchange and cognitive impairment among older adults in China. *Aging and Mental Health.*

Xuan, X., & others (2019). Relationship among school socioeconomic status, teacher-student relationship, and middle school students' academic achievement in China: Using the multilevel mediation model. *PLoS One, 14*(3), e0213783

Xue, Y., Yang, Y., & Huang, T. (2019, in press). Effects of chronic exercise interventions on executive function among children and adolescents: A systematic review with meta-analysis. *British Journal of Sports Medicine.*

Y

Yackobovitch-Gavan, M., & others (2018). Intervention for childhood obesity based on parents only or parents and child compared with follow-up alone. *Pediatric Obesity, 13,* 647–655.

Yakoboski, P.J. (2011). Worries and plans as individuals approach retirement. *Benefits Quarterly, 27,* 34–37.

Yamaguchi, S., & Sawaumi, T. (2019). Control orientations in East and West. In D. Matsumoto & H.C. Hwang (Eds.), *Handbook of cross-cultural psychology* (2nd ed.). New York: Oxford University Press.

Yamaoka, Y., Fujiwara, T., & Tamiya, N. (2016). Association between maternal postpartum depression and unintentional injury among 4-month-old infants in Japan. *Maternal and Child Health Journal, 20,* 326–336.

Yan, C., & others (2018). Developmental trajectories of attention in typically developing Chinese children: A four-wave longitudinal study. *Developmental Neuropsychology, 43,* 479–496.

Yan, H., & others (2017). Associations among screen time and unhealthy behaviors, academic performance, and well-being in Chinese-American adolescents. *International Journal of Environmental Research and Public Health, 14,* 6.

Yang, J.R., & Chen, X. (2019). Dosage sensitivity of X-linked genes in human embryonic single cells. *BMC Genomics, 20*(1), 42.

Yang, S., & Park, S. (2017). A sociocultural approach to children's perceptions of death and loss. *Omega, 76,* 53–77.

Yang, Y. (2008). Social inequalities in happiness in the United States, 1972–2004: An age-period-cohort analysis. *American Sociological Review, 73,* 204–226.

Yap, M.B., & others (2017). Modifiable parenting factors associated with adolescent alcohol misuse: A systematic review and meta-analysis of longitudinal studies. *Addiction, 112,* 1142–1162.

Yarber, W., & Sayed, B. (2019). *Human sexuality* (10th ed.). New York: McGraw-Hill.

Yassin, A.A., & others (2017). Is there a protective role of testosterone against high-grade prostate cancer? Incidence and severity of prostate cancer in 553 patients who underwent prostate biopsy: A prospective data register. *Aging Male, 20,* 125–133.

Yasukochi, Y., & others (2018). Identification of three genetic variants as novel susceptibility loci for body mass index in a Japanese population. *Physiological Genomics, 50,* 179–189.

Yasumura, A., & others (2019, in press). Age-related differences in frontal lobe function in children with ADHD. *Brain Development.*

Yates, L.B., Djuousse, L., Kurth, T., Buring, J.E., & Gaziano, J.M. (2008). Exceptional longevity in men: Modifiable factors associated with survival and function to age 90 years. *Archives of Internal Medicine, 168,* 284–290.

Yau, J.C., & Reich, S.M. (2019, in press). "It's just a lot of work": Adolescents' self-presentation norms and practices on Facebook and Instagram. *Journal of Research on Adolescence.*

Yavorsky, J.E., Dush, C.M., & Schoppe-Sullivan, S.J. (2015). The production of inequality: The gender division of labor across the transition to parenthood. *Journal of Marriage and the Family, 77,* 662–679.

Yazigi, A., & others (2017). Fetal and neonatal abnormalities due to congenital rubella syndrome: A review of the literature. *Journal of Maternal-Fetal and Neonatal Medicine, 30,* 274–278.

Ybarra, M.L., & Mitchell, K.J. (2014). "Sexting" and its relation to sexual activity and sexual risk behavior in a national survey of adolescents. *Journal of Adolescent Health, 55,* 757–764.

Ye, Y., Yang, Z., & Lei, J. (2019, in press). Stochastic telomere shortening and the route to limitless replicative potential. *Journal of Computational Biology.*

Yeager, D.S., Dahl, R., & Dweck, C.S. (2018). Why programs to influence adolescent behavior often fail but could succeed. *Perspectives on Psychological Science, 13,* 101–122.

Yearwood, K., & others (2019). When do peers matter? The moderating role of peer support in the relationship between environmental adversity, complex trauma, and adolescent psychopathology in socially disadvantaged adolescents. *Journal of Adolescence, 72,* 14–22.

Yen, H.Y., & Lin, L.J. (2018). A systematic review of reminiscence therapy for older adults in Taiwan. *Journal of Nursing Research, 26,* 138–150.

Yen, S.C. (2008). Short-term memory. In N.J. Salkind (Ed.), *Encyclopedia of educational psychology.* Thousand Oaks, CA: Sage.

Yen, Y.F., & others (2018). Association of advance directives completion with the utilization of life-sustaining treatments during end-of-life care in older patients. *Journal of Pain and Symptom Management, 55,* 265–271.

Yeo, G., & Yoshikawa, T. (2019, in press). To the future of ethnogeriatric research and publication. *Journal of the American Geriatrics Society.*

Yeo, S.C., & others (2019, in press). Associations of sleep duration on school nights with self-rated health, overweight, and depression symptoms in adolescents: Problems and possible solutions. *Sleep Medicine.*

Yeoman, R., & others (Eds.) (2019). *Oxford handbook of meaningful work.* New York: Oxford University Press.

Yeung, A.W.K., & others (2019, in press). Antioxidants: Scientific literature landscape analysis. *Oxidative Stress and Cellular Longevity.*

Yeung, W.J. (2012). Explaining the black-white achievement gap: An international stratification and developmental perspective. In K.R. Harris, S. Graham, & T. Urdan (Eds.), *APA handbook of educational psychology.* Washington, DC: American Psychological Association.

Yildiz, T. (2019, in press). Human-computer interaction problem in learning: Could the key be hidden somewhere between social interaction and development of tools? *Integrative Psychological and Behavioral Science.*

Ying, L., & others (2018). Parent-child communication and self-esteem mediate the relationship between interparental conflict and children's depressive symptoms. *Child Care and Health Development, 44,* 908–915.

Yip, D.K., & others (2018). A network approach to exploring the functional basis of gene-gene epistatic interactions in disease susceptibility. *Bioinformatics, 34,* 1741–1749.

Yip, J.A., Stein, D.H., Cote, S., & Carney, D.R. (2019, in press). Follow your gut? Emotional intelligence moderates the association between physiologically measured somatic markers and risk-taking. *Emotion.*

Yip, P.S., & others (2015). The roles of culture and gender in the relationship between divorce and suicide risk: A meta-analysis. *Social Science and Medicine, 138,* 87–94.

Yogman, M., & others (2019, in press). The power of play: A pediatric role in enhancing skills in young children. *Pediatrics.*

Yokoya, T., Demura, S., & Sato, S. (2009). Three-year follow-up of the fall risk and physical function characteristics of the elderly participating in a community exercise class. *Journal of Physiological Anthropology, 28,* 55–62.

Yonker, J.E., Schnabelrauch, C.A., & DeHaan, L.G. (2012). The relationship between spirituality and religiosity on psychological outcomes in adolescents and emerging adults: A meta-analytic review. *Journal of Adolescence, 35,* 299–314.

Yoo, J., Kim, Y., Cho, E.R., & Jee, S.H. (2017). Biological age as a useful index to predict seventeen-year survival and mortality in Koreans. *BMC Geriatrics, 17*(1), 7.

Yoo, K.B., & others (2016). Association between employment status change and depression in Korean adults. *BMJ Open, 6*(3), e008570.

Yoon, D.S., & others (2019, in press). MPK-1/ERK is required for the full activity of resveratrol in extended lifespan and reproduction. *Aging Cell.*

Yoon, E., & others (2017). East Asian adolescents' ethnic identity development and cultural integration: A qualitative investigation. *Journal of Counseling Psychology, 64,* 65–79.

Yoon, K.H., & others (2016). The moderating effect of religiosity on caregiving burden and depressive symptoms in caregivers of patients with dementia. *Aging and Mental Health, 23,* 1–7.

Yopp, J.M., & others (2019, in press). Psychological and parental functioning of widowed fathers: The first two years. *Journal of Family Psychology.*

Young, K.T. (1990). American conceptions of infant development from 1955 to 1984: What the experts are telling parents. *Child Development, 61,* 17–28.

Younis, T., & Hassan, G. (2019, in press). Second-generation Western Muslims: A qualitative analysis of multiple social identities. *Transcultural Psychiatry.*

Youniss, J., McLellan, J.A., & Yates, M. (1999). Religion, community service, and identity in American youth. *Journal of Adolescence, 22,* 243–253.

Yousefi, M., & others (2013). Relationships between age of puberty onset and height at age 18 years in girls and boys. *World Journal of Pediatrics, 9,* 230–238.

Youyou, W., & others (2017). Birds of a feather do flock together. *Psychological Science, 28,* 276–284.

Yow, W.Q., & others (2019, in press). A bilingual advantage in 54-month-olds' use of referential cues in fast mapping. *Developmental Science.*

Ysseldyk, R., Haslam, S.A., & Haslam, C. (2013). Abide with me: Religious group identification among older adults promotes health and well-being by maintaining multiple group memberships. *Aging and Mental Health, 17,* 869–879.

Yu, C., & Smith, L.B. (2016). The social origins of sustained attention in one-year-old humans. *Current Biology, 26,* 1235–1240.

Yu, C., & Smith, L.B. (2017). Hand-eye coordination predicts joint attention. *Child Development, 88,* 2060–2078.

Yu, C., Suanda, S.H., & Smith, L.B. (2019, in press). Infant sustained attention but not joint attention to objects at 9 months predicts vocabulary at 12 and 15 months. *Developmental Science.*

Yu, C.Y., & others (2012). Prenatal predictors for father-infant attachment after childbirth. *Journal of Clinical Nursing, 21*(11–12), 1577–1583.

Yu, H., & others (2018). Stability of intelligence from infancy through adolescence: Autoregressive latent variable model. *Intelligence, 69,* 8–15.

Yu, S., & Hu, G. (2017). Can higher-proficiency L2 learners benefit from working with lower-proficiency partners in peer feedback? *Teaching in Higher Education, 22,* 178–192.

Yu, T., & others (2018). Impact of stressful life events on patients with chronic obstructive pulmonary disease. *Respiration, 95,* 73–79.

Z

Zabihzadeh, A., & others (2019, in press). Cultural differences in conceptual representation of "privacy": A comparison between Iran and the United States. *Journal of Social Psychology.*

Zachrisson, H.D., Lekhal, R., Dearing, E., & Toppelberg, C.O. (2013). Little evidence that time in child care causes externalizing problems during early childhood in Norway. *Child Development. 84,* 1152–1170.

Zaghlool, S.B., & others (2018). Deep molecular phenotypes link complex disorders and physiological insult to CpG methylation. *Human Molecular Genetics, 27,* 1106–1121.

Zagorsky, J.L. (2007). Do you have to be smart to be rich? The impact of IQ on wealth, income, and financial distress. *Intelligence, 35,* 489–501.

Zai, C.C., & others (2019). An examination of genes, stress, and suicidal behavior in two First Nation communities: The role of the brain-derived neurotropic factor gene. *Psychiatry Research, 275,* 247–252.

Zaki, J. (2018). Empathy is a moral force. In K. Gray & J. Graham (Eds.), *Atlas of moral psychology.* New York: Guilford.

Zalli, A., & others (2015). Shorter telomeres with high telomerase activity are associated with raised allostatic load and impoverished psychosocial resources. *Proceedings of the National Academy of Sciences U.S.A., 111,* 4519–4524.

Zamboranga, B.L., & others (2016). Drinking game participation among high school and incoming college students: A narrative review. *Journal of Addictions Nursing, 27,* 24–31.

Zammit, A.R., & others (2018). Identification of heterogeneous cognitive subgroups in community-dwelling older adults: A latent class analysis of the Einstein Aging Study. *Journal of the International Neuropsychology Society, 24,* 511–523.

Zamora-Sarabia, A.L., & others (2019, in press). Child health and the possibilities for childcare in a context of poverty and food insecurity: The narratives of parents attending a self-managed foodbank in Spain. *Health and Social Care in the Community.*

Zandona, M.R., & others (2017). Validation of obesity susceptibility loci identified by genome-wide association studies in early childhood in South Brazilian children. *Pediatric Obesity, 12,* 85–92.

Zannas, A.S., & others (2012). Stressful life events, perceived stress, and 12-month course of geriatric depression: Direct effects and moderation by the 5-HTTLPR and COMT Val158Met polymorphisms. *Stress, 15*(4), 425–434.

Zanolie, K., & Crone, E.A. (2018). Development of cognitive control across childhood and adolescence. In J. Wixsted (Ed.), *The Stevens' handbook of experimental psychology and cognitive neuroscience* (5th ed.). New York: Wiley.

Zanto, P.T., & Gazzaley, A. (2017). Cognitive control and the aging brain. In T. Egner (Ed.), *Wiley handbook of cognitive control.* New York: Wiley.

Zarbatany, L., & others (2019). The moderating role of clique hierarchical organization on resource control by central clique members. *Journal of Youth and Adolescence, 48,* 359–371.

Zaremba, D., & others (2019, in press). The effects of processing speed on memory impairment in patients with major depressive disorder. *Progress in Neuro-Psychopharmacology and Biological Psychiatry.*

Zarit, S.H., & others (2019). Family support and caregiving in middle and late life. In B.H. Friese (Ed.), *APA handbook of contemporary family psychology.* Washington, DC: APA Books.

Zavaliangos-Petropulu, A., & others (2019). Diffusion MRI indices and their relation to cognitive impairment in brain aging: The updated multi-protocol approach in ADN13. *Frontiers in Neuroinformatics, 13,* 2.

Zayas, V., & Hazan, C. (2014) (Eds.). *Bases of adult attachment.* New York: Springer.

Zayas, V., Mischel, W., & Pandey, G. (2014). Mind and brain in delay of gratification. In V.F. Reyna & V. Zayas (Eds.), *The neuroscience of risky decision making.* Washington, DC: American Psychological Association.

Zeanah, C.H., & Humphreys, K.L. (2018). Child abuse and neglect. *Journal of the American Academy of Child and Adolescent Psychiatry, 57,* 637–644.

Zechmann, A., & Paul, K.I. (2019, in press). Why do individuals suffer during unemployment? Analyzing the role of deprived psychological needs in a six-wave longitudinal study. *Journal of Occupational Health Psychology.*

Zeiders, K.A., & others (2019, in press). Latina/o youths' discrimination experiences in the U.S. Southwest: Estimates from three studies. *Applied Developmental Science.*

Zeifman, D., & Hazan, C. (2008). Pair bonds as attachments: Reevaluating the evidence. In J. Cassidy & P.R. Shaver (Eds.), *Handbook of attachment* (2nd ed.). New York: Guilford.

Zelazo, P.D. (2013). Developmental psychology: A new synthesis. In P.D. Zelazo (Ed.), *Oxford handbook of developmental psychology.* New York: Oxford University Press.

Zelazo, P.D., & Lyons, K.E. (2012). The potential benefits of mindfulness training in early childhood: A developmental social cognitive neuroscience perspective. *Child Development Perspectives, 6,* 154–160.

Zelazo, P.D., & Muller, U. (2011). Executive function in typical and atypical development. In U. Goswami (Ed.), *Wiley-Blackwell handbook of childhood cognitive development.* New York: Wiley.

Zelazo, P.D., & others (2018). Mindfulness plus reflection training: Effects on executive function in early childhood. *Frontiers in Psychology, 9,* 208.

Zemp, M., & others (2017). Improvement in couples' dyadic coping decreases coparenting conflict. *Journal of Child and Family Studies, 31,* 347–357.

Zeng, R., & Greenfield, P.M. (2015). Cultural evolution over the last 40 years in China: Using the Google Ngram viewer to study implications of social and political change for cultural values. *International Journal of Psychology, 50,* 47–55.

Zeng, Y., & Shen, K. (2010). Resilience significantly contributes to exceptional longevity. *Current Gerontology and Geriatrics Research.* doi:10.1155/2010/525693

Zeng, Y., & others (2016). Interaction between the FOXO1A-209 genotype and tea drinking is significantly associated with reduced mortality at advanced ages. *Rejuvenation Research, 19,* 195–203.

Zeng, Y., & others (2017). The psychometric properties of the 5-item gratitude questionnaire in Chinese adolescents. *Journal of Psychiatric and Mental Health Nursing, 24,* 203–210.

Zentner, M., & Shiner, R.L. (Eds.) (2012). Fifty years of progress in temperament research: A synthesis of major themes, findings, challenges, and a look forward. In M. Zentner & R. Shiner (Eds.), *Handbook of temperament.* New York: Guilford.

Zeskind, P.S. (2007). Impact of the cry of the infant at risk on psychosocial development. In R.E. Tremblay, R. de V. Peters, M. Boivin, & R.G. Barr (Eds.), *Encyclopedia on early childhood development.* Montreal: Centre of Excellence for Early Childhood Development. Retrieved November 24, 2008, from www.child-encyclopedia.com/en-ca/list-of-topics.html

Zettel-Watson, L., & others (2017). Aging well: Processing speed inhibition and working memory related to balance and aerobic endurance. *Geriatrics and Gerontology International, 17,* 108–115.

Zhai, F., Raver, C.C., & Jones, S. (2012). Quality of subsequent schools and impacts of early interventions: Evidence from a randomized controlled trial in Head Start settings. *Children and Youth Services Review, 34*(5), 946–954.

Zhan, Y., & Hagg, S. (2019, in press). Telomere length and cardiovascular disease risk. *Current Opinion in Cardiology.*

Zhang, D., & others (2017). Is maternal smoking during pregnancy associated with an increased risk of congenital heart defects among offspring? A systematic review and meta-analysis of observational studies. *Journal of Maternal-Fetal and Neonatal Medicine, 30,* 645–657.

Zhang, D.F., & others (2019, in press). Genetic analysis of Alzheimer's disease in China: Achievements and perspectives. *ACS Chemical Neuroscience.*

Zhang, F., & Roeyers, H. (2019). Exploring brain functions in autism spectrum disorder: A systematic review of functional near-infrared spectroscopy (fNIRS) studies. *International Journal of Psychophysiology, 137,* 41–53.

Zhang, J., & others (2019). Prenatal diagnosis of Tay-Sachs disease. *Methods in Molecular Biology, 1885,* 233–250.

Zhang, M., & others (2015). Cognitive function in older adults according to current socioeconomic status. *Neuropsychology, Development, and Cognition B: Aging, Neuropsychology, and Cognition, 22,* 534–543.

Zhang, S., & others (2018). Intra- and inter-individual differences in adolescent depressive mood: The role of relationships with parents and friends. *Journal of Abnormal Child Psychology, 46,* 811–824.

Zhang, W., & others (2017). Reconsidering parenting in Chinese culture: Subtypes, stability, and change of maternal parenting style during early adolescence. *Journal of Youth and Adolescence, 46,* 1117–1136.

Zhang, X.C., & others (2018). Do health-related factors predict major depression? A longitudinal epidemiologic study. *Clinical Psychology and Psychotherapy, 25,* 378–387.

Zhang, Y., & others (2017). Cross-cultural consistency and diversity in intrinsic functional organization of Broca's region. *NeuroImage, 150,* 177–190.

Zhang, Y., & others (2019). A cross-cultural comparison of climacteric symptoms, health-seeking behavior, and attitudes toward menopause among Mosuo women and Han Chinese women in Yunnan, China. *Transcultural Psychiatry, 56,* 287–301.

Zhang, Z. (2019, in press). Outdoor group activity, depression, and subjective well-being among retirees of China: The mediating role of meaning in life. *Journal of Health Psychology.*

Zhao, H., Seibert, S.E., & Lumpkin, G.T. (2010). The relationship of personality to entrepreneurial intentions and performance: A meta-analytic review. *Journal of Management, 36,* 381–404.

Zhao, M., Kong, L., & Qu, H. (2014). A systems biology approach to identify intelligence quotient score-related genomic regions, and pathways relevant to potential therapeutic targets. *Scientific Reports, 4,* 4176.

Zheng, Z., & others (2019). Episodic reconstruction contributes to high-confidence false recognition memories in older adults: Evidence from event-related potentials. *Brain and Cognition, 132,* 13–21.

Zhi, L., & others (2019, in press). Loss of PINK1 causes age-dependent decrease in dopamine release and mitochondrial dysfunction. *Neurobiology of Aging.*

Zhong, B.L., & others (2017). Loneliness and cognitive function in older adults: Findings from the Chinese Longitudinal Healthy Longevity Study. *Journals of Gerontology B: Psychological Sciences and Social Sciences, 72,* 120–128.

Zhou, J., & Hearst, N. (2016). Health-related quality of life among elders in rural China: The effect of widowhood. *Quality of Life Research, 25,* 3087–3095.

Zhou, Q. (2013). Commentary in S. Smith, Children of "tiger parents" develop more aggression and depression, research shows. Retrieved July 20, 2013, from http://www.cbsnews.com/news/children-of-tiger-parents-develop-more-aggression-and-depression-research-shows/

Zhou, Q., Fan, L., & Yin, Z. (2017). Association between family socioeconomic status and depressive symptoms among Chinese adolescents: Evidence from a national household survey. *Psychiatry Research, 259,* 81–88.

Zhou, Q., & others (2012). Asset and protective factors for Asian American children's mental health adjustment. *Child Development Perspectives, 6,* 312–319.

Zhou, Y., & others (2017). Big Five personality and adolescent Internet addiction: The mediating role of coping style. *Addictive Behaviors, 64,* 42–48.

Zhou, Y., & others (2018). Weight changes since age 20 and cardiovascular risk factors in a middle-aged Chinese population. *Journal of Public Health, 40,* 253–261.

Zhou, Y., & others (2019, in press). The restorative effect of work after unemployment: An intraindividual analysis of subjective well-being recovery through reemployment. *Journal of Applied Psychology.*

Zhou, Z., Wang, P., & Fang, Y. (2018). Social engagement and its change are associated with dementia risk among Chinese older adults: A longitudinal study. *Scientific Reports, 8,* 1551.

Zhou, Z., & others (2018). The C-terminal tails of endogenous GluA1 and GluA2 differentially contribute to hippocampal synaptic plasticity and learning. *Nature Neuroscience.*

Zhu, Q.B., Bao, A.M., & Swaab, D. (2019, in press). Activation of the brain to postpone dementia: A concept originating from postmortem brain studies. *Neuroscience Bulletin.*

Zhu, S., Tse, S., Cheung, S.H., & Oyserman, D. (2014). Will I get there? Effects of parental support on children's possible selves. *British Journal of Educational Psychology, 84,* 435–453.

Zhu, Z., & others (2018). Causal associations between risk factors and common diseases inferred from GWAS summary data. *Nature Communications, 9*(1), 224.

Zhu, Z., & others (2019). Physical activity, screen viewing time, and overweight/obesity among Chinese children and adolescents: An update from the 2017 physical activity and fitness in China—The Youth Study. *BMC Public Health, 19*(1), 197.

Zhu, Z., & others (2019, in press). Association of age-related macular degeneration with risk of all-cause and specific-cause mortality in the National Health and Nutrition Examination Survey, 2005 to 2008. *JAMA Ophthalmology.*

Ziermans, T., & others (2017). Formal thought disorder and executive functioning in children and adolescents with autism spectrum disorder: Old leads and new avenues. *Journal of Autism and Developmental Disorders, 47,* 1756–1768.

Zigler, E.F., & Styfco, S.J. (1994). Head Start: Criticisms in a constructive context. *American Psychologist, 49,* 127–132.

Zill, N. (2017). *The changing face of adoption in the United States.* Charlottesville, VA: Institute for Family Studies.

Zimmer-Gembeck, M.J., & others (2019, in press). Self-determination theory and food-related parenting: The parent socioemotional context of feeding questionnaire. *Journal of Family Psychology.*

Zimmerman, B.J., Schunk, D.H., & DiBenedetto, M.K. (2017). Role of self-efficacy and related beliefs in self-regulation of learning and performance. In A.J. Elliott, C.S. Dweck, & D.S. Yeager (Eds.). *Handbook of competence and motivation* (2nd ed.). New York: Guilford.

Zimmerman, C.A., & others (2019). Stress dynamically regulates co-expression networks of glucocorticoid receptor-dependent MDD and SCZ risk genes. *Translational Psychiatry, 9*(1), 41.

Zimmerman, F.J., Christakis, D.A., & Meltzoff, A.N. (2007). Association between media viewing and language development in children under age 2 years. *Journal of Pediatrics, 151,* 364–368.

Zosh, J., & others (2017). Putting the education back in education apps: How content and context interact to promote learning. In R. Barr & D. Linebarger (Eds.), *Media exposure during infancy and early childhood.* New York: Springer.

Zosuls, K.M., Ruble, D.N., & Tamis-LeMonda, C.S. (2014). Self-socialization of gender in African American, Dominican immigrant, and Mexican immigrant children. *Child Development, 85,* 2202–2217.

Zosuls, K.M., & others (2009). The acquisition of gender labels in infancy: Implications for gender-typed play. *Developmental Psychology, 45,* 688–701.

Zou, K., Ding, G., & Huang, H. (2019, in press). Advances in research into gamete and embryo-fetal origins of adult diseases. *Science China: Life Sciences.*

Zucker, K.J., Lawrence, A.A., & Kreukels, B.P. (2016). Gender dysphoria in adults. *Annual Review of Clinical Psychology* (Vol. 12). Palo Alto, CA: Annual Reviews.

Zuffiano, A., & others (2018). The codevelopment of sympathy and overt aggression from middle childhood to adolescence. *Developmental Psychology, 54,* 98–110.

Zwinkels, M., & others (2018). Effects of a school-based sports program on physical fitness, physical activity, and cardiometabolic health in youth with physical disabilities: Data from the Sport-2-Stay-Fit Study. *Frontiers in Pediatrics, 6,* 75.

name index

Brito, N. H., 100
Britto, C., 178
Brod, G., 227
Brody, G. H., 103, 539
Brody, L., 398
Brody, N., 257, 259, 265
Brody, S., 407
Brodzinsky, D., 498, 499
Broesch, T., 302, 303
Broihier, H., 53, 98
Bronfenbrenner, U., 26, 27, 465, 467
Bronstein, P., 391
Brookhart, S., 548, 549
Brooks, F., 455
Brooks, J., 236
Brooks, M., 236
Brooks, R., 120
Brooks-Gunn, J., 11, 92, 221, 337, 354, 494, 541
Broomell, A., 100, 193, 202, 310
Brotman, L., 539
Broughton, J., 289
Broussard, M., 345
Broverman, I., 395
Brown, A., 411
Brown, B., 511
Brown, B. B., 511, 516
Brown, C., 391, 392
Brown, C. L., 244
Brown, D., 226
Brown, G., 332
Brown, H., 69
Brown, J., 80, 414
Brown, L., 302, 421, 490
Brown, L. S., 408
Brown, M., 131
Brown, Q. L., 70
Brown, R., 303
Brown, S., 245, 448, 469, 470, 478, 540
Brown, S. L., 603
Brownell, A., 244
Brownell, C., 330
Brownell, C. A., 311, 314, 355, 441
Brownstein, C. A., 112
Bruchmiller, K., 558
Bruck, M., 226
Bruckner, S., 301
Brum, P. S., 228
Brumariu, L., 311, 340
Brumley, J., 71
Brummelman, E., 354
Brummelman, J. E., 362
Brummelte, S., 80
Brunborg, G., 535
Brunes, A., 174
Brunet, A., 121
Brusseau, T. A., 147
Brust-Reneck, P. G., 238
Bryant, C., 421
Bryant, G., 302, 303
Bryant, P., 246
Bryant, R., 601
Bryant, R. A., 601
Bryant Ludden, A., 114
Bryant-Waugh, R., 141
Bryson, S., 248
Bucher, C., 411
Buchanan, A. S., 149, 165
Buchmann, M., 441
Buck, M., 482
Buckner, J., 364
Bucur, B., 222
Budge, S., 8, 400
Bugg, J., 230
Buhrmester, D., 520

Buhs, E., 514
Bui, E., 600
Buist, K., 501
Buitelaar, J., 559
Buiting, H., 590
Bukowki, W., 450, 520
Bukowski, W., 510–514
Bulik, C., 142
Bullock, M., 355
Bumpass, L., 505
Bumpus, M., 491
Burani, K., 105
Burchinal, M., 337
Burchinal, M. R., 568
Burden, P., 548
Bureau, J., 565
Burger, J. M., 363
Burgette, J. M., 551
Burianova, H., 98, 224
Buriel, R., 37
Burke, D., 299
Burke, J., 449
Burke-Adams, A., 277
Burkley, M., 411
Burnett, A. C., 79
Burnette, C., 93
Burnham, D., 61
Burns, M., 292
Burr, J. A., 447
Burraston, B., 450
Burrello, J., 51
Bursuck, W., 561
Burt, S., 59, 398
Burton, R. V., 434
Bushnell, E., 180
Bushnell, I. W. R., 172
Buss, D., 18, 26, 47, 389, 390
Buss, D. M., 398, 472
Buss, K., 324
Bussey, K., 391
Bussu, G., 100
Busuito, A., 329
Butler, H., 236
Butler, M., 560
Butler, R., 424
Butler, Y., 297
Butter, E., 457
Butterfield, D. A., 132
Buzgova, R., 359
Buzzichelli, S., 142
Byard, R., 111
Byne, W., 400
Byrd, D., 548
Byrne, L., 60

Caballero, B., 52
Cabellero, D., 594
Cabeza, R., 109
Cabrera, M., 132
Cabrera, N., 336, 337
Cacioppo, J. T., 346
Caemmerer, J. M., 259
Cage, J., 489
Cahill, K., 577, 578
Cai, H., 416, 530
Cain, C., 590
Cain, M., 71
Cain, M. S., 533
Caino, S., 88
Cairncross, M., 559
Calabria, M., 297
Calamaro, C., 114
Caldwell, K., 71
Calenda, E., 112
Calero, M. D., 5, 49, 61, 239, 242

Calhoun, E., 548
Calkins, S., 100, 310, 311, 314, 317, 320, 329, 364
Callaghan, B., 224
Callaghan, T., 194
Callahan, D., 605
Callisaya, M. L., 240
Calso, C., 216
Calugi, S., 93, 142
Calvert, S., 534
Calvert, S. L., 534
Calvo-Garcia, M. A., 66
Calzada, E., 539
Calzada, E. J., 541
Camacho, D., 554
Cambron, C., 152
Cameron, C., 233, 317, 363, 364, 398
Camic, P., 369
Campbell, B., 258
Campbell, D., 530
Campbell, F., 263
Campbell, F. A., 101, 241
Campbell, L., 31, 258
Campbell, W., 360, 374, 377, 467
Campione-Barr, N., 483, 501, 504
Campos, J., 161, 174, 333
Campos, J. J., 313, 315, 322
Candow, D., 94
Cangelosi, A., 215
Canivez, G., 257
Cann, D., 414
Cansino, S., 228, 230
Cantone, E., 516
Cantor, N., 233
Cao, Q., 553
Capaldi, D., 341, 342, 450
Cappella, E., 518
Caprara, G. V., 376
Caprara, M., 529
Carbajal-Valenzuela, C. C., 330
Card, N., 397
Cardoso, C., 69
Carey, D. P., 260
Carl, J. D., 480
Carlin, R., 112
Carlo, G., 433, 436, 440, 441, 444, 446, 484
Carlson, D., 576
Carlson, E., 333, 334
Carlson, M., 481
Carlson, M. C., 242
Carlson, S., 149, 233, 234
Carlson, S. M., 234, 247
Carlson, W., 520
Carlson Jones, D., 93
Carlsson, A., 144
Carlsson, A. C., 95
Carmichael, V., 476
Carmona, S., 132
Carney, A., 379
Carney, L., 453, 457, 458
Carpendale, J., 193, 247, 356, 445
Carpenter, M., 430, 435
Carr, A., 453
Carr, D., 447, 590, 603, 604
Carr, R., 142
Carré, J., 406, 422
Carrell, S., 443
Carriere, J. S., 222
Carrington, H., 314
Carroll, A., 516
Carroll, J. L., 406, 414, 417
Carskadon, M., 114

Carskadon, M. A., 114
Carson, V., 535
Carstensen, L., 15, 320–322, 362, 367, 521, 527
Carstensen, L. L., 4, 5, 321, 529
Carter, A., 448, 560
Carter, C. J., 560
Carter, T., 147
Cartwright, R., 111
Caruso, A., 364, 484
Carver, C., 376
Carver, K., 342
Casabona, G., 94
Casasola, M., 232
Case, R., 202, 225
Casey, B. J., 104–106, 365
Casper, D., 397
Caspi, A., 60, 383
Cassidy, J., 19
Castalanelli, N., 379
Castel, A., 229
Castillo, M., 142
Castillo-Morales, A., 53
Castillo-Rodriguez, A., 553
Castle, D., 141
Castle, J., 499
Castle, S. C., 527
Cataldo, D., 300
Catani, C., 318
Catchlove, S. J., 241
Cattagni Kleiner, A., 589
Catts, H., 285
Cauffman, E., 448
Cavallaro, E., 575
Cavanagh, S. E., 93
Cavazos-Rehg, P. A., 419
Cave, R. K., 298, 299
Cazzato, V., 142
Ceci, S., 225, 226, 262
Cercignani, M., 107
Cerillo-Urbina, A. J., 559
Cesari, M., 96, 130, 149
Chae, S., 336
Challacombe, F. L., 332
Chalofsky, N., 575
Chalupa, L., 109
Champagne, M., 374
Champika, L., 587
Chan, J. S. Y., 244
Chan, M. Y., 243
Chandler, M., 193, 247, 445
Chandra, A., 406, 408
Chandradasa, M., 587
Chaney, B. H., 153
Chang, A., 121
Chang, C., 117
Chang, E. C., 377, 595
Chang, F., 149
Chang, H. Y., 72
Chang, V., 540
Chao, R., 485
Chao, Y., 149
Chaplin, J. E., 152
Chaplin, T., 398
Chapman, S. N., 119
Chaput, J., 467
Charles, S., 321, 521
Charlton, B. M., 416
Charness, N., 177
Charpak, N., 80
Chase-Lansdale, P., 11
Chasnoff, I. J., 70
Chatterjee, S., 52
Chatterton, Z., 52
Chaudry, A., 539
Chavarria, M. C., 104
Chavez, R., 248

Cheetham, T. C., 422
Cheetham-Blake, T. J., 31
Chein, J., 104, 105, 238
Chemtob, C. M., 318
Chen, C., 570, 571, 603
Chen, F., 93
Chen, G., 55, 154
Chen, H., 51
Chen, J., 380
Chen, L., 391, 516
Chen, L. W., 68, 139, 527
Chen, N., 326
Chen, P. J., 74
Chen, Q., 594
Chen, S., 199, 333
Chen, W., 132
Chen, X., 54, 268, 325, 391, 516
Chen, Y., 107
Chen, Y. H., 100
Cheng, H., 376
Cheng, H. M., 97
Cheng, M., 373
Cheng, M. H., 96
Cheng, N., 233, 234
Cheng, S., 534
Cheng, T., 474
Cheng, Y., 342
Cheng, Y-P., 493, 503
Cheon, Y. M., 372
Cherlin, A. J., 468
Chervin, R., 115
Chess, S., 322, 325
Cheung, H., 443
Chevalier, A., 175
Chevalier, N., 24, 202, 235
Cheyney, M., 77
Chhaya, R., 31, 171
Chi, M. T., 227
Chick, C., 238
Chikritzhs, T., 152
Childers, J., 291
Chilibeck, P., 94
Chin, M., 400
Chinn, L. K., 166
Chiocca, E. M., 486
Chiou, W., 199
Chisholm, J., 534
Chiu, M., 134
Chmielewski, J., 406
Cho, D., 456, 459
Cho, J., 118
Choi, B., 287
Choi, H., 474, 475
Choi, S., 288
Choi, Y., 356
Chomsky, N., 301
Chopik, W., 344, 376, 377
Chor, E., 552
Choudhary, M., 80
Choukas-Bradley, S., 152, 517, 521
Chow, A., 603
Chow, C., 244
Christakis, D., 534
Christakis, D. A., 534
Christen, M., 433, 440
Christensen, D. L., 248, 560
Christensen, K., 6, 19, 60, 98, 132, 475, 521
Christensen, L., 32
Chu, X. W., 514
Chung, S., 140
Cicchetti, D., 19, 33, 61, 311, 334, 335, 487–490
Cicek, D., 92
Cicirelli, V. G., 344, 501, 502

Gordon, B., 226
Gordon, C., 359
Gordon, I., 336
Gordon, J. S., 215
Gordon Simons, L., 451
Gorenjak, V., 121
Gorgon, E. J. R., 164
Goriounova, N., 260
Gorrell, S., 142
Gorrese, A., 491, 516
Gortmaker, S., 114
Gorukanti, A., 151
Goswami, U., 61, 289
Gothe, N., 222
Gotlieb, R., 277
Gotlieb, R. J., 276
Goto, S., 531
Gottfredson, N., 324
Gottlieb, G., 52, 60
Gottman, J., 312, 473, 481, 518
Gottman, J. M., 312
Gouin, K., 70
Gould, M. S., 595
Gove, W., 472
Governale, A., 9
Gow, A., 244
Goyal, N., 432, 433, 530
Goyal, V., 134
Gradisar, M., 113
Grady, D., 412
Grady, S., 159, 161
Graf Estes, K., 297
Graham, E., 67, 366
Graham, E. K., 376
Graham, G., 129, 140
Graham, J., 432, 433
Graham, S., 215, 226, 245, 295, 296, 362, 569
Grammer, J., 228
Granbom, M., 165
Granchi, C., 154
Graneist, A., 466
Granja, M., 10
Gravelin, C., 411
Graves, C., 69
Graves-Demario, A., 549
Gravetter, F., 28, 31, 32
Gravningen, K., 476
Gray, J., 398
Gray, K., 432, 433
Gray, M., 411
Gray, P., 406, 422
Graziano, A., 28, 32
Grebe, N. M., 390
Green, C., 272
Green, F., 247
Green, K., 418
Green, M., 487
Green, M. J., 537, 539
Greenberger, E., 574
Greene, J., 364, 513, 564, 565, 567
Greene, S., 478
Greenfield, P., 531
Greenwald, A., 397
Greenwald, L., 579, 580
Greenwald, M. L., 301
Greenwood, A., 359
Greer, F. R., 137
Greer, K., 501
Gregory, R. J., 259
Greifneder, R., 512
Grgic, J., 148
Griffin, P., 292, 381, 383
Griffiths, M., 376
Griffiths, P. D., 66
Grigorenko, E., 261, 264

Grilo, C., 143
Grimm, K., 344, 448
Grimm, R., 174
Grindal, M., 374
Grob, A., 259
Grodstein, F., 115
Grogan-Kaylor, A., 486
Groh, A., 335, 511
Groh, A. M., 333
Grolnick, W., 364, 484, 571
Gronlund, A., 576
Gross, J., 321, 359, 398
Gross, M., 275
Grossman, J. M., 416
Grossman, M., 379
Grossmann, K., 333, 334
Grossmann, T., 104
Grosso, S. S., 247
Grosz, E., 400
Grotevant, H., 372, 498, 499
Grotzinger, A. D., 389
Growdon, J., 131, 132
Grower, P., 413
Gruber, H., 279
Gruber, K., 75
Gruen, J., 557
Gruenewald, T., 379
Gruenewald, T. L., 380
Gruhn, D., 208, 209
Grunblatt, E., 60
Grundy, E., 494
Grusec, J., 436
Grusec, J. E., 433, 434, 486
Grych, J. H., 466
Gryczkowski, M., 433
Grzeschik, R., 221
Gu, D., 119
Guariglia, C., 230
Guay, F., 554
Gudmundson, J., 316
Guerin, E., 421
Gueron-Sela, N., 220
Guerra, A., 337, 338
Guerreiro, M., 222
Guerreiro, R., 132
Guest, F. L., 131
Guidetti, M., 215
Guilford, J. P., 275
Guillich, A., 564
Guillory, A., 411
Guimaraes, E., 166, 167
Guiney, H., 447
Gulgoz, S., 229
Gulick, D., 105
Gullion, L., 266
Gultekin, F., 144
Gump, B., 526
Gunderson, E. A., 397
Gunes, C., 121
Gunn, H. E., 483
Gunn, J. K., 70
Gunnar, M., 336, 489
Gunnar, M. R., 178
Gunning, T. G., 294, 295, 302
Guo, S., 450
Gupta, G., 8
Gupta, S., 255, 470
Gur, O., 422
Gur, R. C., 396
Gurwitch, R. H., 319
Gustafsson, J- E., 262
Gustafsson Senden, M., 395
Gutchess, D., 13
Gutchess, A. H., 241
Gutherie, D., 178
Gutierrez, I., 593
Gutmann, D. L., 404

Guttentag, C. L., 419
Guttmannova, K., 152
Gutzwiller, E., 433, 440
Guy, A., 515
Guyer, A., 103, 323
Guyon-Harris, K. L., 100
Guzik, T., 95
Gyberg, F., 373

Ha, T., 513
Haas, A. L., 482
Haase, R., 533
Habermas, T., 466
Hachul, H., 421
Haden, C., 226, 228
Hadfield, J. C., 503
Hadiwijaya, H., 490
Hafer, R. W., 257
Hagen, E., 5, 271
Hagenaars, S. P., 240
Hagestad, G., 502
Hagg, S., 121
Haghighat, M., 554
Hagnas, M. J., 526
Hagopian, W., 137
Hague, S., 229
Hahn, E., 135, 365
Haidt, J., 432
Haier, R. J., 260, 264
Hair, N. L., 103
Hakuta, K., 297, 298
Halaki, M., 244
Hale, A., 129, 140
Hale, D., 135
Hale, L., 467
Hale, N., 559
Hale, S., 216
Hales, C. M., 139, 143
Hales, D., 129
Halford, W., 474, 479
Halgunseth, L. C., 467, 541, 542
Haliburn, J., 141
Halim, M. L., 395
Hall, C. B., 242
Hall, D., 56
Hall, G. S., 319
Hall, J., 398
Hall, J. A., 376, 398
Hall, L. J., 560
Hall, S., 471
Hallahan, D., 8, 272, 557, 558, 561
Halonen, J., 556
Halonen, J. I., 576
Halper, L., 412
Halpern, C., 414, 417
Halpern, D., 236
Halpern, D. F., 393, 396, 397
Halpern, G., 342
Halpern-Felsher, B., 416, 417
Halpern-Meekin, S., 420
Halpin, K. S., 177
Halse, M., 234
Haltigan, J., 335
Ham, O., 594
Hambrick, D. Z., 244
Hamer, M., 236
Hamilton, A., 100
Hamilton, H., 467
Hamilton, J. L., 93
Hamilton, M., 574
Hamilton, S., 574
Hamlin, J., 192, 193, 445
Hammersmith, A., 478, 540
Hamner, H. C., 139
Hampson, D., 54, 56

Hampson, S., 375
Hampson, S. E., 381
Han, B., 319
Han, J., 148, 226
Han, J. H., 178
Han, S. H., 448
Han, W., 494
Hanc, T., 78
Hancock, G., 314, 327
Handelsman, D., 92
Handley, E., 489
Handschuh, C., 414
Hanley, C., 98
Hanley, R., 347
Hansen, M., 174
Hansen, N., 531
Hanson, E., 593
Hanson, J., 365
Hanson, T., 554
Hansson, R., 594
Hantman, S., 447
Hantzi, A., 376
Hao, S., 51
Hara, M., 82, 83
Harackiewicz, J., 565
Harb, S. C., 149
Hardaway, C., 472, 537, 539, 541, 562
Hardeman, R., 76
Harden, K., 93
Hardy, B., 263
Hardy, J., 132
Hardy, N., 575
Hardy, S., 438
Hardy, S. A., 437, 438
Harel, J., 315
Hargis, M. B., 249
Harkness, S., 163, 334
Harlow, H. F., 330
Harmell, A., 376
Harmon, O., 443
Harms, P., 376
Harris, G., 503
Harris, J., 291
Harris, K., 245, 295, 296, 497
Harris, K. R., 215, 226, 295
Harris, P., 174
Harris, P. L., 246
Harrist, A. W., 465
Hart, B., 262, 292
Hart, C. H., 484, 551
Hart, D., 354, 438, 442, 443
Hart, S., 313, 314
Harter, S., 354–358, 360–363, 565
Hartescu, I., 116
Harting, J., 562
Hartman, J. D., 152
Hartshorne, H., 434, 437, 443
Hartup, W. W., 512
Harvey, T., 260
Hasbrouck, S., 337
Hasher, L., 16, 230, 239
Hashim, N., 136
Hasin, D., 476
Haslam, C., 457
Haslam, S., 457
Hassan, G., 542
Hassankhani, H., 591
Hassija, C., 411
Hatoun, J., 127
Hatton, H., 512
Hatzenbuehler, M., 476
Hauck, F., 112
Haugrud, N., 299
Haverbusch, V. C. E., 56, 57
Hawk, S. T., 483

Hawken, L., 296
Hawkes, C., 179
Hawkey, E. J., 234
Hawkins, A., 474
Hawkins, J., 450
Hawkley, L., 528
Hay, C., 510
Hay, W. W., 90
Hayashi, A., 302
Haydon, A., 342
Haydon, K., 335
Hayes, R., 411
Hayflick, L., 121
Haynes, R. L., 112
Hayslip, B., 594
Hayutin, A., 578
Hayward, R., 457, 459
Hazan, C., 335, 342–344
He, C., 176, 177
He, J., 91
He, Q., 541
Heard, E., 528
Hearst, N., 603
Heatherton, T., 248, 533
Hebert, J. J., 146, 164
Hecht, M., 398
Hedberg-Oldfors, C., 51
Hegab, A. E., 144
Hegele, R., 55, 95
Heiman, T., 515
Heimann, M., 219
Hein, S., 8, 61, 119, 466, 490
Heinrich, J., 137
Heir, T., 174
Heisel, M. J., 596
Helgeson, V. S., 35, 388, 391
Helgesson, G., 69
Hellzen, O., 591
Helm, R., 238
Helmreich, R., 399
Helmuth, L., 16
Helson, R., 372, 380, 382, 503
Helzer, E., 438
Hemmy, L., 108
Hendricks-Munoz, K. D., 80
Hendrickson, K., 285
Hendy, A., 149
Hengartner, M., 380
Heninger, M., 596
Henkens, K., 580
Henneberger, A. K., 450
Hennenberger, A., 516
Hennessey, B., 276, 277
Hennessy, G., 70
Henretta, J. C., 472
Henriquez-Sanchez, P., 145
Henry, W., 527
Hensel, D., 417
Henson, R., 231
Herbrand, C., 391
Heredia-Pi, I. B., 73
Herman-Giddens, M. E., 92
Hernandez, A., 296
Hernandez, J., 359
Hernandez, M. M., 436
Hernandez, S., 416
Hernandez-Reif, M., 81
Hernandez-Zimbron, L. F., 176
Heron, M., 111, 130
Herrell, A., 297
Herrington, R., 489
Hershner, S., 115
Herting, M. M., 147
Hertlein, K., 495
Hertzog, C., 231, 249, 268
Herzog, E., 392

Menon, R., 63
Menyuk, P., 289
Mercer, N., 204, 451
Mercer, S., 433
Merchant, S. J., 590
Meredith, N. V., 90
Merianos, A., 484
Merrill, D. M., 505
Merrill, N., 224, 225
Mervak, B. M., 66
Meschkow, A. M., 238
Messerlian, C., 33
Messersmith, E., 574
Messiah, S. E., 70
Messier, S. P., 130
Messinger, D., 310, 315
Messinger, D. S., 218, 315
Messinger, J. C., 406
Meteyard, L., 285
Metts, S., 348
Metz, E., 443
Metzger, A., 436
Meulemans, T., 216
Meusel, L. A., 230
Meuwissen, A., 234
Meyer, A., 299
Meyer, M., 405
Meyer, S., 441
Meyer-Ficca, M., 119
Meyre, D., 142
Mezzacappa, E., 364
Mi, S. J., 112
Michael, R. T., 407, 408, 423
Michelmore, K., 468–470
Mick, P., 178
Mickelson, K., 481
Micks, E., 421
Miga, E., 341, 491
Migliano, A., 300
Mike, A., 375
Mikkola, T. M., 178
Mikulincer, M., 342, 344
Miller, A. B., 490
Miller, B., 129, 416
Miller, C., 11, 540, 559
Miller, C. B., 443
Miller, C. F., 395
Miller, E., 551
Miller, E. B., 552
Miller, J., 432, 433, 530
Miller, J. B., 403
Miller, K., 411
Miller, M. S., 579
Miller, P., 227, 593
Miller, P. H., 22, 24, 201, 216
Miller, R., 61
Miller, S., 66, 227, 451
Miller, S. M., 366
Miller, W. R., 65
Miller-Graff, L., 82
Miller-Perrin, C., 490
Milligan, K., 69
Mills, C., 220, 356, 357
Mills, C. M., 275
Mills, D., 220
Millsav, L., 145
Mills-Koonce, W., 316
Milne, E., 73
Min, Z., 122
Minar, N., 172
Miner, B., 115, 116
Miner, J., 338
Miner, M. M., 423
Minero, L., 400
Miniussi, C., 241
Minkler, M., 503
Minnes, S., 70

Minsart, A. F., 71
Minuchin, P., 563
Minutolo, F., 154
Minuzzi, L. G., 149
Mir, Y., 273
Mireku, M. O., 113
Mireles-Rios, R., 491
Mischel, H., 434
Mischel, W., 24, 217, 233, 234,
   377, 434, 437, 568
Mishna, F., 515
Mishra, G. D., 421
Miskovsky, M., 130
Mislinski, J., 577, 578
Mistry, R. S., 539
Mitchell, A., 393
Mitchell, D., 411
Mitchell, E., 112, 421
Mitchell, K., 414, 487
Mitchell, M. B., 244
Mitchell, P., 150
Mitchison, D., 142
Mithun, M., 284, 285
Mitsui, T., 408
Mittal, R., 178
Miyake, K., 333
Miyata, K., 175
Miyawaki, C., 359
Miyazaki, Y., 65
Mizala, A., 569
Mize, K., 324
Mize, K. D., 314
Mizokami, S., 532
Moatt, J. P., 144
Mock, S., 407
Modecki, K., 532
Modecki, K. L., 515
Mody, M., 100
Moed, A., 491
Moehrlen, T., 127
Moen, P., 572, 577–580
Moerdler, S., 56
Moffitt, T. E., 233
Mogliski, J. K., 47
Mohabir, R., 587
Mohamed, N. V., 135
Moharaei, F., 140, 360
Moilanen, J. M., 422
Mojtabai, R., 319
Mok, Y., 95
Mola, J. R., 423
Molden, D., 566
Molefi-Youri, W., 422
Molgora, S., 73
Molina, D., 595
Molina, M., 94, 122
Moline, H., 71
Mollart, L., 77
Mollenkopf, H., 165
Moller, A., 565
Mollinedo-Gajate, I., 560
Molton, I., 179
Monahan, K., 101, 105
Money, J., 389
Monier, F., 174
Moninger, J., 140
Monks, C., 235
Monn, A. R., 234
Monroy, C. D., 218, 288
Montemayor, R., 492
Montgomery, J., 247
Montgomery, P., 420
Monti, C., 230
Montoliu-Gaya, L., 132
Moon, D., 422
Moon, R., 112
Moon, R. Y., 112

Mooney-Leber, S., 80
Moore, A., 413
Moore, A. A., 448
Moore, B., 233
Moore, D., 51, 61, 342
Moore, D. S., 52
Moore, M., 112
Moore, S., 93
Moorman, J., 413
Mooya, H., 333, 334
Mora, J., 149, 150
Morales Hope, D., 407
Moran, G., 333, 380
Moran, V., 137
Moravcik, E., 202, 263, 293,
   305, 523, 550, 553
Morbelli, S., 132
Morcom, A., 229
Morean, M. E., 152
Moreau, C., 399
Moreau, D., 147, 557
Morgan, K., 116
Mori, E., 82
Mori, R., 122
Morin, A. J. S., 93
Morin, D., 121
Morison, V., 170, 171
Moritz, S., 354
Morosan, L., 357
Morris, A., 319, 441, 443, 447, 485
Morris, A. S., 323
Morris, B. J., 178
Morris, M., 245
Morris, P., 26, 27, 465, 467
Morris, S., 311, 315, 317
Morrison, D. M., 406
Morrison, G. S., 8, 263, 305,
   548, 550, 551
Morrison, R. S., 591
Morrison, S., 495
Morrison-Beedy, D., 416
Morrissey, T. W., 338
Morrow, L. M., 293, 295, 304
Morse, A., 215
Mortensen, E., 161, 267
Moscovitch, M., 223
Moser, S., 178
Mosher, W., 470, 476
Moss, P., 114
Moss, S., 5, 321, 527
Mossburg, S. E., 579
Mougios, V., 144
Moulin, C., 229
Mounts, N., 440
Mouquet-Rivier, C., 137
Moura, J., 122
Moyano, N., 515
Moyer, A., 470
Mozer, M., 215
Mparmpakas, D., 72
Mroczek, D., 320, 381–383
Mroczek, D. K., 135
Mrowka, R., 95
Mruk, C., 363
Mucke, M., 98
Mudrazija, S., 405
Mueller, B., 69
Mueller, S. C., 235
Mueller, T., 419
Mueller-Schotte, S., 178
Muenks, K., 568
Muftic, L., 450, 451
Mugaddam, A., 345
Muir, N. M., 467
Mukherjee, R. A. S., 69
Mukherjee, S., 588
Mulatu, S., 240

Mulder, T. M., 489
Mullally, S., 224
Muller, U., 233, 356
Mullick, S., 418
Mulligan, E., 602
Mullola, S., 392
Mulvey, K. L., 439
Munawar, K., 229
Mundy, P., 302, 560
Munecks, K., 520
Muniz Terrera, G., 236
Muniz-Terrera, G., 240
Munoz, K., 137, 138
Munro, C. A., 378
Munroe, B. A., 558
Munsters, N., 310
Murachver, T., 403
Murase, T., 303
Murdock, K., 115
Murdock, T., 443
Murki, S., 80
Murphy, D. A., 450
Murphy, L., 149
Murray, A. L., 72
Murray, L., 337
Murray, P., 90
Murugan, S., 132
Musick, K., 468
Mussen, P., 130
Must, A., 261
Must, O., 261
Mutchler, J., 540
Mutiso, V. N., 514
Myers, C., 79
Myers, D. G., 62, 221, 456
Myers, J., 589
Myerson, J., 265

Nabe-Nielsen, K., 577
Nader, P. R., 147
Naezer, M., 413
Nagel, B. J., 558
Nai, Z., 376
Naicker, T., 72
Nair, R., 6
Nair, R. L., 492
Nairn, S., 459
Najman, J., 72
Najman, J. M., 450, 562
Nakagawa, T., 118
Nakamichi, K., 316, 317
Nansel, T. R., 514
Narayan, A., 318
Narayan, K., 139
Narváez, D., 431–433, 436, 437,
   440–444
Nascimento, B., 8
Nascimento, D. D. C., 95
Nash, J. M., 103
Nathanson, C., 443
Naumenko, V., 103
Nave, K., 99
Naveed, S., 514
Nazarian, A., 55
Ncube, C., 69
Ndabi, J., 146
Ndu, I., 137
Neal, J., 518
Neal, Z., 518
Neblett, E., 369, 371, 373, 455
Nee, C., 358
Needham, A., 166, 167
Neel, C., 113
Neff, F., 122
Negriff, S., 467
Negrini, L., 487

Nehrkorn, A., 379
Neikrug, A., 115
Neiterman, E., 82
Nelemans, S. A., 465
Nelson, C., 100, 102
Nelson, C. A., 100, 105, 107,
   224, 226
Nelson, D. A., 398
Nelson, L., 14, 493
Nelson, S., 152, 480
Nelson, S. K., 480
Nemet, D., 146
Nene, R. V., 121
Neophytou, A. M., 127
Nergard-Nilssen, T., 557
Nesi, J., 516, 517
Neubauer, A., 379
Neuenschwander, R., 364
Neufer, D., 148
Neugarten, B., 502
Neuman, W. L., 29, 31, 35
Neumann, D., 397
Neupert, S., 135, 366
Nevill, A., 146
Nevill, S., 575
Neville, H. J., 296
Newberry, J. A., 111, 592
Newell, K., 166
Newport, E., 296
Newton, E., 74, 445
Newton, N., 475
Ng, F., 467, 541, 571
Ng, F. F., 571
Ng, M., 79
Ng, Q. X., 72, 595
Ngnoumen, C., 17, 365, 366
Nguyen, A., 373
Nguyen, D. J., 492
Nguyen, S., 395
Nguyen, T. V., 90, 389
Nickalls, S., 346
Nickel, L., 375, 376, 380, 383
Nickerson, A. B., 516
Nicolaisen, M., 528
Nicolaou, E., 225
Nicolini, M. E., 589
Nicoteri, J., 130
Niehuis, S., 475
Nielsen, M. K., 412
Nieri, T., 374
Nieto, S., 8, 36, 537
Nikitin, J., 22, 209, 215, 231,
   366, 529
Nikmat, A., 136
Nilbori, Y., 54, 56
Nilsen, E., 357
Nimbi, F. M., 406
Nippold, M. A., 298
Nisbett, R., 264
Nisbett, R. E., 262, 265
Nishigori, H., 83
Nishina, A., 93, 450
Nitko, A., 548, 549
Nixon, S. A., 420
Noam, G., 516
Noble, K., 104
Noce Kirkwood, R., 166
Noddings, N., 442
Noel-Miller, C. M., 470
Noftle, E., 381
Nola, M., 446
Nolen, M. M. P. G., 328
Noll, J. G., 92
Nolte, S., 202, 263, 293, 305,
   523, 550, 553
Nordheim, K. L., 148
Norman, K., 199

Norman-McKay, L. P., 50, 53
Norona, A., 311, 466
Norris, K., 121
Norris, S., 142
Nottelmann, E. D., 92
Novack, M. A., 287
Novak, C., 67
Novikoff, T., 215
Nowson, C. A., 97, 130
Nucci, L., 442
Nugent, C., 470
Nunes, A. S., 560
Nuri Ben-Shushan, Y., 294, 295
Nurius, P., 358
Nusslock, R., 109
Nutter-Pridgen, K., 271
Nyberg, L., 241
Nye, C., 375
Nye, C. D., 383
Nygard, C- H., 577
Nylund-Gibson, K., 538
Nystrom, P., 100
N'zi, A., 335

Oakley, G., 72
Oakley, M., 498
Oates, G., 240
Oberauer, K., 228
Oberle, L., 164
Oberlin, L., 149, 241, 243
Obermann, M. L., 515
Obermeyer, C., 96
Obler, L. K., 299
Obradovic, J., 263, 466
O'Brien, J. L., 217
O'Brien, M., 494
O'Connor, E. E., 334
O'Dell, C., 119
Odouli, R., 112
Offer, D., 362
Ogawa, E., 243
Ogbu, J., 265
Ogden, C. L., 139, 140
Ogden, D., 285
Ogihara, Y., 531
Ogletree, A., 475, 521
Ogundele, M. O., 448
Oh, S., 69
Oh, S. J., 228
O'Halloran, L., 221
Okada, H. C., 94
Okada, K., 423
Okado, Y., 448
O'Keefe, J. H., 154
O'Keeffe, L. M., 69
Oken, B. S., 239
Okereke, O., 600
Okubo, Y., 166
Okumu, M., 416
Okun, M., 448
Oldehinkel, A. J., 494
Olderbak, S., 398
Olenik-Shemesh, D., 515
Olesen, K., 578
Oleti, T., 80
Olfson, M., 319
Oliffe, J., 83
Ollen, E., 498
Olsavsky, A. L., 481
Olsen, J., 438
Olshansky, S. J., 117
Olson, B., 137
Olson, J., 219
Oltmanns, J., 240
Olweus, D., 516
O'Malley, E. G., 65

Oman, D., 457
Onders, B., 127
Onen, F., 115
Onen, S., 115
Onetti, W., 553
Ongley, S., 436, 446
Onojighofia Tobore, T., 132
Ontai, L., 399
Onuzuruike, A., 140
Operario, D., 420
Opfer, J., 194
Oppezzo, M., 278
Orbeta, R. L., 114
Ordonez, T. N., 244
Oreland, L., 54
Oren, E., 378
Orimaye, S. O., 299
Ornaghi, V., 312
Ornoy, A., 63, 71
Ornstein, P., 103, 226, 228
Orosova, O., 494
Orosz, G., 346
Orovecz, J., 8, 400
Orson, C., 525
Orth, U., 348, 360
Orzabal, M. R., 70
Osborn, K., 411
Osipova, A., 291
Ossher, L., 229
Ostan, R., 117
Oster, H., 179
Osterberg, E., 422
Ostergaard, S. D., 559
Ostfeld, B. M., 69
Ostlund, S. B., 99
Ostrove, J., 372, 380
Oswald, D., 520
Oswald, F., 376
Ota, M., 288
Otsuki-Clutter, M., 485
Otto, H., 334
Ou, S., 562
Oun, I., 576
Overland, G., 10
Owen, K. B., 147
Owens, J., 114
Owsley, C., 176, 180, 192
Oxford, M. L., 418
Ozcan, L., 424
Ozturk Donmez, R., 316

Paasch, E., 93
Paavilainen, E., 48
Pacala, J., 177, 178
Pace, A., 288, 302
Padgett, J., 420
Padilla, C., 480, 481
Padilla-Walker, L., 14, 433, 440, 484, 493
Padilla-Walker, L. M., 483
Padmanabhanunni, A., 397
Padmapriya, N., 467
Pagani, L. S., 127
Paganini-Hill, A., 145
Page, R., 128, 146
Pahlke, E., 393
Pakhomov, S., 108
Palacios-Barrios, E., 365
Palama, A., 172
Pallini, S., 365
Palmeira, L., 142
Palmer, A., 10, 318, 467
Palmer, C. A., 113
Palmeroni, N., 369
Palmore, E. B., 528
Paloutzian, R. F., 454

Pals, J. L., 370
Paluck, E., 398
Pan, B. A., 292
Pan, C. Y., 559
Pan, Z., 117, 533
Panagiotaki, G., 593
Pandey, G., 233
Panel, M., 121
Panizzon, M. S., 423
Pantell, R. H., 226
Paolucci, E. M., 148
Papastavrou, E., 133
Papernow, P. L., 479, 496
Papierno, P., 226
Parade, S., 316
Parade, S. H., 327
Parashar, S., 52
Parasher, R., 147, 560
Pardini, D., 449
Pargament, K., 453, 457, 458
Parish-Morris, J., 288
Parisi, J. M., 242
Park, C., 453, 456–459, 598
Park, C. L., 457–459, 598, 603
Park, D., 3, 5, 15, 30, 31, 107, 132, 209, 228, 241, 242, 268
Park, H., 422, 478
Park, J. H., 78
Park, J. S., 107, 119
Park, M., 72
Park, M. J., 129, 594
Park, S., 122, 592
Park, S. H., 95
Park, Y. M., 595
Parkay, F. W., 548, 549
Parke, R., 8, 11, 18, 37, 334, 336, 337, 490, 494
Parke, R. D., 542
Parker, C. B., 321
Parker, J., 518
Parker, K., 35, 471
Parker, W., 405
Parkes, A., 487
Parkinson, P., 336
Parks, E., 241
Parmar, M., 135
Parrish, D., 359
Parritz, R. H., 319
Parsons, C. E., 329
Parsons, K., 140
Pascal, A., 79
Pascalis, O., 169, 172, 329
Paschall, K., 551
Pascoe, C. J., 402
Pascual-Sagastizabal, E., 389
Pasterski, V., 392
Pate, R. R., 146, 147
Patel, K. V., 165
Patel, N., 69
Patel, R., 53, 119
Paterson, K., 130
Patlamazoglou, L., 601
Patrick, J., 379
Patrick, M., 151
Patterson, C., 479, 497
Patterson, C. J., 498
Patterson, G. D., 56
Pattie, A., 244
Patton, G. C., 376
Patton, L., 100, 310
Pauker, K., 172
Paul, C., 16, 321, 529
Paul, K., 576
Paul, S., 82
Pauletti, R., 398
Pauletti, R. E., 400
Paulhus, D., 443

Paulhus, D. L., 501
Paulson, J., 82
Paulson, J. F., 83
Paulus, M., 446
Paunesku, D., 566, 567
Paus, T., 106
Pawluski, J., 82
Payer, L., 96, 421
Payne, B., 299
Pazmandi, J., 55
Pearson, K., 71
Pedersen, C. B., 73
Pedersen, M. T., 149
Pedersen, N., 526
Pedersen, S., 245, 520
Pederson, D., 333
Pedram, M., 560
Pedrinolla, A., 132
Pedroza, J., 8
Peebles, R., 142
Peek, L., 318
Peets, K., 447, 514
Pei, G., 51
Pei, Y., 505
Peifer, M., 63
Peipert, J., 417
Pellegrini, A., 48
Pelletier Brochu, J., 361
Pelton, S., 137
Penagarikano, O., 560
Penazzi, L., 106
Peng, K., 174
Peplau, L., 408, 479
Peralta, L. R., 538
Perani, D., 300
Perdue, K., 101, 356
Pereira Gray, D. J., 587
Perez, H. C. S., 601
Perez, N., 448
Perez, S., 204, 206
Perez-Brena, N. J., 540, 542
Perez-Edgar, K., 103, 323
Perez-Escamilla, R., 137, 138
Perez-Fuentes, M. D. C., 376
Perin, D., 296
Periyakoli, V., 591
Perkins, D., 276
Perkins, S., 292
Perkisas, S., 240, 244
Perlman, L., 59
Perls, T., 118
Perls, T. T., 117
Perozynski, L., 500
Perreira, K., 8
Perreira, K. M., 540
Perrin, R., 490
Perrotin, A., 249
Perrotte, J. K., 153
Perry, B., 398
Perry, D. G., 388
Perry, N., 310, 311, 314, 317, 320, 364
Perry, N. B., 364
Perry, S. E., 90
Perry, T., 518
Perry, W. G., 208
Perry-Jenkins, M., 481
Persand, D., 159
Persky, H., 296
Peskin, H., 93
Peteet, J., 458
Peterman, K., 167
Petersen, A., 9, 128
Petersen, I. T., 61
Peterson, C. C., 248
Peterson, J., 407
Petitto, L- A., 297

Petrangelo, A., 70
Petridou, J., 82
Petrie, J., 95
Petrova, M., 14
Petrovic, M., 154
Pettit, G., 322, 324, 326, 327
Petts, R. J., 455
Peyre, H., 267, 595
Pfeifer, C. M., 66
Pflaum, A., 356
Phillipou, A., 141
Phillips, D., 263
Phinney, J., 373
Phinney, J. S., 371, 541
Phull, A. R., 121
Pi, Y. L., 98
Piaget, J., 22, 187, 194, 429, 510, 522
Pianta, R., 337
Piantadosi, S., 218
Piazza, J., 122, 521
Piazza, J. R., 135, 379
Pichora-Fuller, M., 178
Piehler, T., 398
Pietromonaco, P., 344
Pignolo, R. J., 53
Pijl, M. K. J., 100
Piko, B., 152
Pilegaard, H., 148
Pillemer, K., 478, 504
Pinderhughes, E., 498, 499
Ping, H., 137
Pinheiro, M. B., 58
Pinker, S., 300
Pinna, K., 137, 138
Pino, E. C., 538
Pino-Pasternak, D., 434
Pinquart, M., 334, 485
Pinsker, J. E., 56
Pinto Pereira, S. M., 71
Pinzone, V., 559
Pisch, M., 112
Pisoni, D., 176
Pitkanen, T., 152
Pittman, J. F., 372
Pivnick, L., 554
Pixley, J., 378
Place, S., 297
Platt, B., 513
Pleck, J. H., 402, 403
Plemons, J., 379
Plocha, A., 413
Plomin, R., 263
Plotnikova, M., 72
Plucker, J., 277
Pluess, M., 323, 328
Podrebarac, S. K., 72
Poehlmann-Tynan, J., 237
Pohlabein, H., 69
Polan, H., 335
Polenick, C., 475
Polenova, E., 373
Poljsak, B., 145
Polka, L., 288
Poll, J., 598
Pollack, W., 402
Pollock, K., 591
Pomerantz, E., 530, 571
Pomerantz, E. M., 570
Pomerantz, J., 93
Ponzio, A., 320
Pool, R., 239
Pooley, J., 559
Poon, K., 235
Poon, L., 118
Poon, L. W., 118
Popadin, K., 55

Simmonds, J., 601
Simms, N., 225
Simon, E. J., 50
Simon, K. A., 479
Simon, R., 127
Simon, S. S., 228
Simons, J., 231
Simons, L. G., 416
Simonton, D. K., 279
Simpson, D., 474
Simpson, G., 474
Simpson, J., 334, 342, 344, 377
Sims, R., 240
Sims, T., 321, 322, 521
Sin, N. L., 135
Sinclair, E. M., 303
Sinclair-Palm, J., 400
Singer, A. E., 590
Singer, D., 524
Singer, M., 51
Singer, M. A., 120
Singh, H., 421
Singh, L., 297
Singh, P., 54
Singh, S., 415
Singh-Manoux, A., 299
Singleton, R., 406
Sinha, J., 455
Sinkovic, M., 423
Sinnott, J. D., 208
Siopi, A., 144
Sirotkin, Y., 466, 487
Sirow, L., 178
Sirsch, U., 15
Sitterle, K., 497
Siverova, J., 359
Skaper, S. D., 106
Skarabela, B., 288
Skerrett, P., 149
Skinner, B. F., 24
Skinner, O., 492
Skogbrott Birkeland, M., 93
Skoglund, R., 503
Skrzypek, H., 67
Skuldt-Niederberger, K., 404
Skuse, D., 56
Slade, A., 335
Slamon, K., 568
Slater, A., 93, 142, 170, 171
Slater, A. M., 173, 180
Slaughter, V., 248
Slawinski, B., 398
Sliwinski, M., 269, 379
Slobin, D., 289
Slomkowski, C., 450
Slutske, W., 152
Smaldino, S. E., 532, 535
Smaldone, A., 414
Small, B. J., 242
Small, H., 243
Small, P., 538
Small, S. A., 493
Smarius, L. J., 314
Smeeding, T., 263
Smetana, J., 317, 432, 438, 439, 483
Smid, G. E., 587
Smith, A., 6, 149, 467, 535, 591
Smith, A. R., 132
Smith, D., 411
Smith, D. D., 272
Smith, E. B., 164, 531
Smith, E. R., 80
Smith, I., 248
Smith, J., 15, 71, 271, 304, 359, 363, 366, 376, 377

Smith, K., 141, 142, 367
Smith, K. Z., 488
Smith, L., 83, 158, 160, 171, 181, 219, 220, 329, 424
Smith, P., 502
Smith, R., 20, 390, 398, 516, 520
Smith, S. G., 528
Smith, T., 403, 457, 598
Smithson, L., 112
Smock, P., 469, 470
Smokowski, P. R., 492
Smoreda, Z., 403
Smyth, J., 379
Smyth, J. M., 379
Snarey, J., 433
Snell, T., 601
Sneve, M. H., 48
Sniecinski, I., 215
Snjezana, H., 356
Snow, C., 292, 298
Snowdon, D., 108
Snowdon, D. A., 108
Snowdon, J., 594
Snyder, J., 450
Snyder, J. S., 107
Snyder, K., 170
Snyder, W., 290
Sobowale, K., 376
Sodian, B., 329
Soenens, B., 481, 490, 565
Sokol, B., 356
Sokol, R., 484
Solomon, B., 476
Solomon, D., 444
Solomon, E., 390
Solomon, M., 560
Solomon-Moore, E., 466
Soloski, K., 129
Solovieva, Y., 523
Somers, M., 170, 171
Somerville, L. H., 319
Someya, S., 144
Sommer, T. E., 11
Sommerville, J., 445
Son, D., 440
Son, J., 121
Soneji, S., 151
Song, J., 65
Song, L., 302
Song, L. J., 259
Song, M., 373
Song, P., 140
Song, Y., 122
Sonnby, K., 341, 491
Sophian, C., 192
Sorge, B., 417
Sosa, A., 290
Sosa, G., 244
Soto, C. J., 376, 380
Souchay, C., 249
Sourander, A., 558
Sousa, S. S., 101
South, S., 376
Southgate, V., 100, 287
Souza, A., 222, 228
Spairani, S., 465
Spandel, V., 295
Spangler, G., 334
Specht, J., 380
Speelman, C., 559
Spelke, E., 180, 192
Spelke, E. S., 192, 193
Spence, A. P., 106
Spence, J., 399
Spence, M., 176
Spence, R., 344

Spencer, D., 316, 577
Spencer, S., 389, 569
Sperling, R., 108
Spieker, S., 82
Spiess, M., 358
Spilman, S. K., 455
Spinrad, T., 432, 435, 436, 440, 441, 444, 446, 447
Spirito, A., 481
Spiro, A., 381, 383
Sprecher, S., 420
Sprei, J., 411
Spreng, R., 335
Springer, M., 549
Spruyt, K., 110
Spuhl, S., 204
Squarzoni, P., 106
Srivastava, N., 55
Srivastava, S., 149
Sroufe, L., 333, 334
Sroufe, L. A., 335, 484
St. Jacques, P. L., 223
Stadelmann, S., 360
Staff, J., 574
Stafford, A., 135
Stahlman, S., 422
Stamou, G., 83
Stancil, S. L., 68
Stanley, S., 470, 474
Stanley, S. M., 470, 474
Stanley-Hagan, M., 494, 495
Stanovich, K. E., 28
Stansfield, S. A., 490, 494
Stark, E., 382
Starr, C., 390
Starr, L. R., 342
Staudinger, U., 5, 244, 270, 271, 366, 383
Staudinger, U. M., 367
Stavans, M., 192, 193
Stawski, R., 33, 122, 269
Steca, P., 567
Steck, N., 590
Steckler, C., 193, 445
Steele, H., 333, 342
Steele, J., 333, 342
Steele, L., 531
Steffen, V., 397
Steffener, J., 240
Steiger, A. E., 361
Steiger, H., 142
Stein, M., 557
Steinbach, A., 496
Steinbeck, K., 92
Steinberg, L., 104, 105, 238, 319, 365, 485, 491, 574
Steinberg, S., 345
Steiner, J. E., 179
Steinmayr, R., 568
Steinmetz, S., 411
Stelmashook, E., 109
Stenberg, G., 330
Stenholm, S., 143, 578
Stensvehagen, M. T., 379
Stepaniak, U., 145
Stephan, Y., 259
Stephens, F., 52
Stephens, J. M., 443
Stepler, R., 469, 471, 477
Steptoe, A., 16, 122
Steptoe-Warren, G., 259
Stergiou, N., 159
Steric, M., 65
Sterkenburg, P., 332
Stern, P., 265
Stern, W., 256
Sternberg, K., 260, 347

Sternberg, R., 5, 236, 260, 262–264, 271, 273–275, 277, 347
Sternberg, R. J., 215, 255, 257–261, 347, 348
Sterns, H., 577
Stessman, J., 528
Stevens, C., 220
Stevens, M., 335
Stevenson, H., 485, 570, 571
Stevinson, C., 116
Stewart, A., 372, 377, 380, 381
Stewart, D., 83
Stewart, J., 393
Stewart, J. G., 235, 595
Stewart, S., 480
Stey, P., 437
Stiel, S., 591
Stifter, C., 324–326
Stigler, J., 570
Stillman, T., 447
Stipek, D. J., 362, 566, 569
Stoel-Gammon, C., 170, 290
Stokes, C., 469
Stokes, K., 221
Stokes, L., 398
Stolove, C., 576
Stolzenberg, E. B., 452, 454, 556
Stone, A., 16
Stone, A. A., 15, 321
Stone, E., 391, 392
Stone, L., 171
Stoppa, T., 454
Stopyra, M. A., 142
Stough, L., 318
Stouthamer-Loeber, M., 449
Stovall-McClough, K., 490
Strandberg, T. E., 5, 148, 149, 240, 241, 243, 244, 270, 527, 529
Strasburger, V., 414
Strathearn, L., 335, 336
Streib, H., 454
Streit, C., 444
Strickhouser, J., 375, 376, 381
Strickland, A., 592
Strickland, C., 74
Striegel-Moore, R., 142
Stroebe, M., 602
Strohmeier, D., 516
Strohminger, N., 437
Stroope, S., 479
Strough, J., 392, 404, 521
Stryjewski, G., 89
Stubbs, B., 166
Studer, J., 208, 209
Stuebe, A., 138
Stumper, A., 323, 326
Sturge-Apple, M. L., 488
Styfco, S., 551
Style, C., 472
Su, J., 334
Suanda, S., 171, 220
Suanet, B., 528
Suárez-Orozco, C., 467
Suárez-Orozco, M., 467
Suarez-Rivera, C., 219, 329
Sugimura, K., 532
Sugita, Y., 173
Sugiura, M., 109
Suitor, J., 478
Sullivan, A., 492, 603
Sullivan, H. S., 510, 519
Sullivan, K., 492
Sullivan, M., 170, 171

Sullivan, R., 13, 100, 311, 335, 336
Sullivan, S. P., 420
Sulovari, A., 51
Sulpizio, S., 302
Suman, L., 466
Sumaroka, M., 523
Summers, R., 591
Summerville, A., 526
Summit, A. K., 417
Sumontha, J., 479, 497
Sun, H., 558
Sun, R., 261
Sun, Z., 121
Sundstrom Poromaa, I., 83
Sung, J. E., 299
Suo, C., 244
Super, C., 163
Super, E., 334
Suri, G., 321, 359
Susman, E., 91–93, 421
Sutin, A., 375
Sutin, A. R., 514
Sutterlin, S., 436
Sveistrup, H., 167
Svensson, Y., 37, 369, 371
Sviri, S., 590
Swaab, D., 107
Swaab, D. F., 396
Swain, J., 292, 335, 336
Swain, S. O., 521
Swanson, J. L., 574
Swartout, K., 595
Swartz, T. T., 493
Sweeeney, L., 288
Sweeney, K., 497, 498
Sweeney, M. D., 132
Sweeney, M. M., 478
Swift, A., 590
Swing, E. L., 220
Swingler, M. M., 329
Swingley, D., 285
Syed, M., 8, 37, 368, 369, 371, 373, 455
Sykes, C. J., 362
Szekanecz, Z., 130
Szelag, E., 244
Szinovacz, M. E., 502
Szkrybalo, J., 393
Szutorisz, H., 60, 466
Szwedo, D., 342

Tabatsky, D., 478
Tacutu, R., 122
Taggart, J., 522, 523
Tahir, L., 279
Taige, N. M., 72
Takahashi, E., 65
Takahashi, M., 576
Takei, Y., 109
Taler, S. J., 95
Talib, H., 417
Talib, M., 455
Tamai, K., 66
Tamana, S. K., 532
Tamers, S. L., 476
Tamis-LeMonda, C., 162, 163, 302, 395
Tamis-LeMonda, C. S., 532
Tamiya, N., 83
Tan, B., 559
Tan, E. J., 447
Tan, M., 261, 264
Tan, M. E., 578
Tan, P., 311, 323
Tan, X. L., 130

Tan, Y., 53
Tang, S., 122, 418, 419, 603
Tang, X., 568
Tanilon, J., 515
Tannen, D., 398, 402, 521
Tanner, J. M., 90
Tannes, C. K., 248
Tanskanen, A. O., 501
Tardif, T., 537
Tariku, A., 137
Tarnopolsky, M., 96
Tarokh, L., 58, 114
Tas, D., 514
Tashiro, T., 348, 477
Tasker, F., 497, 498
Tatterton, M., 591
Tavris, C., 399
Taylor, C., 237
Taylor, C. A., 486
Taylor, H., 76, 77, 228
Taylor, K., 51, 53
Taylor, M., 395, 603
Taylor, N., 149
Taylor, S., 310
Taylor, S. E., 320
Taylor, Z., 365
Teague, M., 7, 143, 146
Tee, L. M., 66
Tegin, G., 70
Tekcan, A. I., 229
Teller, D., 173
Telljohann, S., 7, 127, 140
Tempest, G., 149
Temple, C. A., 293, 295,
   549, 557
Temple, J., 562
Templeton, J., 455
Tenni, P., 135
Terblanche, E., 149
Terman, L., 273
Terracciano, A., 376
Terrill, A., 179
Terry, D. F., 121
Tesch-Romer, C., 274
Teshale, S., 366
Teti, D., 187, 501
Tetzlaff, A., 143
Tevendale, H. D., 418
Thabet, A. A., 318
Thackray, A., 147
Thakral, P. P., 223
Thanh, N., 69
Thelen, E., 88, 158–160, 181
Theobald, H., 144
Theokas, C., 164
Thiamwong, L., 590
Thoma, S., 433
Thomas, A., 228, 322, 325, 564
Thomas, C., 70
Thomas, H., 267
Thomas, J. C., 315
Thomas, K., 82
Thomas, M., 130, 296, 472
Thompson, A., 398
Thompson, B., 300
Thompson, E., 451, 494, 516
Thompson, H., 285
Thompson, M., 576, 595
Thompson, P., 101, 103
Thompson, R., 320, 355,
   403, 441, 445, 466, 484,
   486, 487
Thompson, R. A., 303, 311, 312,
   314, 316–318, 328–330,
   332–335, 354, 356, 364,
   430, 433, 435, 436, 440
Thompson, S., 97

Thorburn, D., 121
Thoresen, C., 457
Thornton, R., 299
Thorsen, K., 528
Thysen, S., 127
Tian, J., 538
Tian, L., 447
Tian, S., 95
Tian, Y., 52
Tieu, L., 291
Tiggemann, M., 93, 142
Tiiri, E., 516
Tikhonova, A. A., 542
Tikotzky, L., 110
Tilton-Weaver, L., 483
Tilton-Weaver, L. C., 482
Timmermans, E., 414
Toepfer, P., 335
Toffrey, K., 147
Tolani, N., 337
Tole, F., 558
Tolman, D., 406
Tolppanen, A. M., 526
Tomalski, P., 100
Tomasello, M., 219, 289, 291,
   302, 430, 435, 445
Tomassini, C., 475, 521
Tomaszewski Farias, S., 231
Tomblin, J., 285
Tomich, P., 76
Tomkinson, G., 146
Tommerdahl, M., 98
Tompkins, G., 293, 295,
   302, 305
Tompkins, G. E., 295, 296
Tompkins, V., 246, 247
Tomporowski, P. D., 146
Tonnsen, B., 100
Tononi, G., 110
Toomey, R., 408
Top, N., 482
Topa, G., 579
Topalian, A., 455
Topiwala, A., 98
Torke, A. M., 589
Torrence, C., 170
Torstveit, L., 436
Tortora, G. J., 50, 53
Toth, S., 489, 490
Toub, T., 523, 524
Toupance, S., 26, 31, 119, 121
Touyz, R., 95
Towler, L., 423
Towson, S., 372, 373
Toy, W., 376
Toyokawa, N., 542
Toyokawa, T., 542
Toyoshima, A., 118
Trabucchi, M., 154
Trafimow, D., 531
Trager, T. D., 54
Trahan, L. H., 262
Trainor, L., 176, 177
Trappenburg, M., 590
Trauble, B., 171
Traynor, J. M., 31
Treger, S., 420
Trehub, S. E., 176
Trelle, A., 231
Tremblay, M. S., 535
Trestman, R., 411
Trevino, K. M., 601
Triandis, H., 531
Triandis, H. C., 531
Trimble, J. E., 36
Trinh, N., 372
Trinh, S., 521

Troia, G., 296
Trommsdorff, G., 311
Troop, W., 514
Troop-Gordon, W., 514
Troseth, G., 394
Troutman, A., 561
Trucco, E. M., 152
Trujillo, C., 321
Trujillo, P., 134
Trzesniewski, K., 566
Trzesniewski, K. H., 361
Tsai, H., 149
Tsai, W., 601
Tsang, A., 179
Tsang, T. W., 69
Tseng, V., 485
Tseng, Y. F., 587
Tsintzas, K., 52
Tso, W., 112
Tsui, E., 136, 591
Tubaek, G., 175
Tubay, A. T., 74
Tucker, C., 500
Tucker-Drob, E., 217, 375
Tudella, E., 166, 167
Tufik, S., 421
Tully, E., 433
Turel, O., 140
Turiel, E., 393, 438, 439
Turnbull, A., 557, 561
Turner, B. F., 404
Turner, G. R., 236, 364
Turner, J. H., 417
Turner, L., 32
Turner, R., 415
Turner, S., 595
Tur-Sinai, A., 6
Tweed, E. J., 78
Twenge, J., 114, 360, 374,
   377, 467
Tyas, S. L., 108
Tyrell, F. A., 342

Uchida, S., 91
Uchino, B. N., 121
Udo, T., 143
Udry, J., 342, 520
Uecker, J., 479
Ueno, K., 402
Uhlenberg, P., 502
Ujifusa, A., 550
Ulfsdottir, H., 77
Ullah, M., 121
Ullen, F., 261
Umana-Taylor, A., 8, 372, 373,
   493, 542
Unalmis Erdogan, S., 77
Uncapher, M. R., 221
Unda, J., 321
Underhill, K., 420
Ungar, M., 319
Updegraff, K., 500
Updegraff, K. A., 542
Updegrove, A., 450, 451
Urbina, S., 264
Urdan, T., 373
Urqueta Alfaro, A., 219
Urry, L. A., 48
Usher, E., 363, 565
Utesch, T., 164
Uwaezuoke, S., 137

Vacaru, V., 332
Vacca, J. A., 294, 295
Vaden, K. L., 177

Vahia, I. V., 459
Vahratian, A., 470
Vaillancort, T., 514
Vaillant, G., 271, 379, 380
Vaillant, G. E., 150, 378,
   380, 382
Vail-Smith, K., 150
Vaish, A., 430, 435
Valcan, D., 434
Valdesolo, P., 432
Valech, N., 299
Valencia, W., 149, 150
Valentin, M., 65
Valero, S., 376
Valgardson, B., 60
Valiente, C., 435, 436, 441
Valimaki, T. H., 134
van Aken, M., 511
Van Assche, L., 344
Van Berkum, J. A., 285
Van Beveren, T. T., 77
van de Bongardt, D., 413
Vandell, D. L., 339
van den Boom, D. C., 327
van den Boomen, C., 310
Van den Bulck, J., 414
Vandendriessche, A., 532
van den Heuvel, M. I., 65
van der Burg, D., 558, 559
van der Does, T., 372
Van der Graaff, J., 435, 436
VanDerhei, J., 579, 580
van der Heide, A., 589
van der Leeuw, G., 179
Van der Merwe, C., 51
van der Stel, M., 249
van der Veer, R., 204
van Deurzen, L., 122
Van de Vondervoort, J., 192,
   193, 445
Van de Walle, J., 548
Vandewater, E., 534, 537
Vandewoude, M., 240, 244
van Dongen, J., 558
Van Doren, J., 559
van Dulmen, M., 520
Van Elderen, S. S., 106
van Geel, M., 515
Van Gerven, P., 222
van Goethem, A., 443
Van Hecke, V., 220
van Hooft, E. A., 576
Van Hooren, B., 159
Vanhoutte, B., 122
Van Hulle, C. A., 315
van IJzendoorn, M., 328
   333, 334
Van Malderen, E., 365
Van Meter, F., 226
VanOrman, A., 481
van Praag, H., 107
van Renswoude, D. R., 31, 171
Van Ryzin, M., 152, 334
Van Solinge, H., 580
Vansteenkiste, M., 481, 490, 565
van Tilborg, E., 99
van Wijk, I. C., 324
van Zomeren, M., 531
Vara-Garcia, C., 97
Varahra, A., 131
Varga, N. L., 227
Varner, F. A., 8
Varner, M. W., 70
Vasankari, T., 148
Vasilenko, S., 420
Vasilyeva, M., 396

Vasquez, E. A., 411
Vasung, L., 65, 100
Vater, A., 354
Vaughn, B. E., 112
Vaughn, C. P., 10
Vazire, S., 376
Vazsonyi, A., 364
Vedder, P., 373, 515
Veech, R., 149
Veenman, M., 249
Velarde, V., 414
Velez, C. E., 495
Vella, S. A., 164
Veness, C., 219
Venetsanou, F., 164
Venker, C. E., 172
Venneri, A., 132
Venners, S. A., 73
Venturelli, M., 132
Vercherat, M., 177
Verdero-Garcia, A., 142
Vereczkei, A., 51
Vereijken, B., 163
Verhaeghen, P., 216, 217
Verhagen, J., 225
Verhoef, E., 51
Verhoef, T., 300, 304
Verma, S., 524
Vernon, L., 532
Vernooij, M., 98
Vernucci, S., 225
Veronneau, M. H., 365
Verschueren, K., 360
Verstaen, A., 475
Vest, A., 554
Victor, R., 438
Vidal, S., 450
Vidourek, R., 455, 484
Viechtbauer, W., 380, 383
Vieira, S. A., 137
Vieria, J. M., 494
Vigliocco, G., 285
Vigod, S., 83
Vihman, M. M., 288
Vijayakumar, N., 104
Vildirim, E., 337
Villegas, R., 137
Villegas, S., 132
Villemagne, V. L., 132
Vina, J., 121
Vinas Poch, F., 533
Vinicius, L., 300
Vinke, E., 98
Virta, J. J., 95
Visher, E., 479
Visher, J., 479
Vitaro, F., 129, 510
Vitiello, M., 116
Vitr, M., 115
Vittrup, B., 482
Vladescu, J., 127
Vo, V. A., 245
Vodanovich, S., 527
Vogt, P., 220
Vohs, K., 459
Voight, A., 554
Voigt, R. G., 559
Volbrecht, M., 325
Volkmar, F. R., 560
Volkow, N., 70
Vollebreght, M., 112
Volpe, E. M., 417
Volpe, S., 137, 138
von Arx, P., 259
von Bonsdorff, M. B., 577
von dem Hagen, E., 248
Von Rosen, P., 164

Yeung, A. W. K., 132, 145
Yeung, E., 448
Yeung, W. J., 265
Yildiz, T., 215
Yin, Z., 538
Ying, L., 360
Yip, D. K., 55
Yip, J. A., 259
Yip, P. S., 476
Yogman, M., 522–524
Yokoya, T., 166
Yonker, J., 455
Yoo, J., 17
Yoo, K. B., 576
Yoon, D. S., 154
Yoon, E., 342
Yoon, K. H., 459
Yopp, J. M., 603
Yorgason, J., 474
Yoshikawa, T., 536
You, M., 365
You, T., 243
Young, K. T., 138
Young, M., 163
Younis, T., 542
Youniss, J., 372, 443, 455

Yousefi, M., 92
Youyou, W., 347
Yow, W. Q., 297
Ysseldyk, R., 457
Yu, C., 171, 219, 220, 329
Yu, C. Y., 336
Yu, H., 267
Yu, S., 203, 206
Yu, T., 135
Yu, Y., 122
Yurkewicz, C., 447

Zaben, F., 458
Zabihzadeh, A., 532
Zachrisson, H. D., 338
Zadzora, K., 516
Zaghlool, S. B., 52
Zagoory-Sharon, O., 336
Zagorsky, J. L., 257
Zai, C. C., 595
Zaki, J., 435, 436
Zakrzewski-Fruer, J., 147
Zalk, S., 36
Zalli, A., 121
Zamboranga, B. L., 153

Zammit, A. R., 5, 236
Zamora-Sarabia, A. L., 128
Zandona, M. R., 31
Zanolie, K., 104, 105
Zanto, P. T., 222, 366
Zarbatany, L., 517
Zaremba, D., 216
Zarit, S., 505
Zarrett, N., 449
Zavaliangos-Petropulu, A., 241
Zavershneva, E., 204
Zayas, V., 198, 233, 238, 342
Zeanah, C., 100, 102, 489
Zechmann, A., 576
Zeiders, K., 542
Zeiders, K. A., 8
Zeifman, D., 344
Zelazo, P., 233, 235, 237, 315
Zelazo, P. D., 98, 234, 247
Zell, E., 375, 376, 381
Zemp, M., 466
Zeng, R., 531
Zeng, T., 118
Zeng, Y., 118, 119, 447
Zentner, M., 325
Zerwas, S., 330

Zeskind, P. S., 315
Zettel-Watson, L., 228
Zhai, F., 317
Zhan, Y., 121
Zhang, D., 69
Zhang, D. F., 51
Zhang, F., 100
Zhang, J., 56
Zhang, M., 540
Zhang, S., 519
Zhang, W., 571
Zhang, X. C., 143
Zhang, Y., 301, 421
Zhang, Z., 119, 459
Zhao, H., 375
Zhao, M., 261
Zhao, S., 325
Zheng, H., 51
Zheng, Y., 448
Zheng, Z., 229, 231
Zhi, L., 121
Zhong, B. L., 119
Zhou, J., 603
Zhou, Q., 538, 571
Zhou, Y., 99, 143, 376, 576
Zhou, Z., 118

Zhu, Q., 107
Zhu, S., 358
Zhu, Z., 65, 141, 176
Ziermans, T., 560
Zigler, E., 551
Ziliak, J., 263
Zill, N., 498
Zimmer-Gembeck, M. J., 565
Zimmerman, B., 567, 568
Zimmerman, C. A., 52
Zimmerman, F., 534
Zinsser, K., 316
Zittleman, K., 548, 549
Zosh, J., 302
Zosuls, K., 395
Zosuls, K. M., 388
Zou, K., 63
Zucker, K., 9, 400
Zuffiano, A., 436
Zusho, A., 485
Zwicker, A., 479, 496
Zwinkels, M., 164

subject index